RUSSIA
48

FINLAND
18

EST. 53
LAT. 53
LITH. 53
BELARUS 52
POLAND
47

UKRAINE
52

ROM.
45

GREECE
45

TURKEY
62

CYPRUS
62

SYR.
62

IRAQ
66

IRAN
66

KUWAIT 58

LIBYA
110

EGYPT
110

SAUDI
ARABIA
58

BAH.
58

QATAR
58

U.A.E.
58

OMAN
58

YEMEN
58

CHAD
110

SUDAN
110

ERITREA 110

DJIB.
110

ETHIOPIA
110

C. AFR. REP.
110

UGANDA
114

KENYA
114

SOMALIA
115

DEM. REP.
OF
CONGO
114

RWA.
114

BUR.
114

TANZANIA
114

MAL.
114

ANGOLA
114

ZAMBIA
114

NAMIBIA
118

ZIMBABWE
119

BOTSWANA
119

MOZAMBIQUE
119

SWAZILAND 119

LESOTHO
119

SOUTH
AFRICA
119

SEYCHELLES
119

MADAGASCAR
119

MAURITIUS
RÉUNION 119

KAZAKHSTAN
48

UZBEKISTAN
48

TURKMENISTAN
48

KYRGYZSTAN
48

TAJIKISTAN
48

AFGHAN.
68

PAKISTAN
68

NEPAL
68

BH.

INDIA
68

BANG.
68

SRI
LANKA
68

MONGOLIA
77

CHINA
77

BURMA
72

LAOS

THAILAND
72

CAMB.
72

VIETNAM
72

MALAYSIA
85

SING.
72

BRUNEI

INDONESIA
85

N. KOREA
80

S. KOREA
80

JAPAN
81

TAIWAN
77

HONG KONG
78

PHILIPPINES
82

GUAM
86

PACIFIC OCEAN
Page 87

ASIA
Page 54

PAPUA
NEW
GUINEA
84

SOLOMON IS.
86

VANUATU
87

FIJI
86

SAMOA
86

NEW
CALEDONIA
86

NORTHERN
TERRITORY
93

QUEENSLAND
95

WESTERN
AUSTRALIA
92

SOUTH
AUSTRALIA
94

NEW SOUTH WALES
96

VICTORIA
96

TASMANIA
99

NEW
ZEALAND
100

AUSTRALIA
Page 88

FINLAND
18

NORWAY
18

SWEDEN
18

UNITED KINGDOM
10

SCOTLAND
15

DENMARK 21

IRELAND 17

ENGLAND
13

WALES

ESTONIA
53

LATVIA
53

LITHUANIA
53

RUSSIA
48

BELARUS
52

RUSSIA

GERMANY
22

POLAND
47

UKRAINE
52

BELG.
LUX.

CZECH
REP. 41

SLVK.
41

FRANCE
28

SWITZ. 39

AUST.
41

HUN. 41

SLO.

MOLDOVA 52

ROMANIA
45

ITALY

MON.

CRO.

BOS.

YUGO.
45

BULGARIA
45

ALB.
45

MAC.
45

GEORGIA
52

ARMENIA 52

AZERBAIJAN
52

AND.

34

PORTUGAL
32

SPAIN
33

MEDITERRANEAN
36

GREECE
45

TURKEY
62

IRAN
66

TUNISIA
106

MALTA
34

CYPRUS
62

SYRIA
62

IRAQ
66

MOROCCO
106

ALGERIA
106

LIBYA
110

EGYPT
110

LEBANON 62

ISRAEL
65

JORDAN
65

SAUDI ARABIA 58

WORLD ATLAS

WORLD

ATLAS

Hammond Publications Advisory Board

ENTIRE CONTENTS © COPYRIGHT MCMXCIX
BY HAMMOND INCORPORATED

PRINTED IN THE UNITED STATES OF AMERICA

ISBN 1-56251-282-X

Contents

GAZETTEER-INDEX OF THE WORLD I   GLOSSARY OF ABBREVIATIONS VI

Part I—Terrain Maps of Land Forms and Ocean Floors

Contents IX   Index VII

Part II—Modern Maps and Indexes

World Index 325

Welcome to the *AAA World Atlas*, a comprehensive compilation of the most up-to-date maps and indexes available. It is fitting that AAA should publish a world atlas at this time, as we continue to expand our services internationally through global partnerships.

With the ever-changing pace of our world, it can be difficult to stay on top of the constant fluctuation of political boundaries. However, AAA wants to make sure that consumers have the most up-to-date information available. Therefore, the printing of this atlas was carefully scheduled to ensure that any recent developments in the world's political climate are accurately illustrated. All revisions reflect new nations and boundaries as well as shifting political divisions within each country. Ongoing research and worldwide correspondence have generated the most current geographic and demographic information possible for this atlas.

The *AAA World Atlas* is sensibly organized to make the access of knowledge easy and effective. All information regarding a specific country is presented as a single unit, with supplementary maps and specific data following each basic reference map. Also provided within each unit are detailed indexes, population information, the capital, and the highest geographic point. Adjacent locator maps show the subject's relation to the rest of the world, and a topographic map gives a three-dimensional representation of the area. An economic map and a flag of each independent nation or state are also included.

A complete A-to-Z index of all place names and physical features shown on the maps and insets is furnished in the back of the atlas. The alphabetical order, irregular spellings, and alternate names presented in the index enable readers to find information quickly and accurately.

The *AAA World Map* will become an indispensable reference guide for families, students, executives, travelers, or anyone with a thirst for knowledge about today's ever-changing world. An itinerant adventure awaits those who journey through the pages of this atlas. Let your first steps be among many as you enjoy this geographic treasure.

Alan B. Borne
Managing Director, Publishing

Introduction to the Maps and Indexes

The following notes have been added to aid the reader in making the best use of this atlas. Though the reader may be familiar with maps and map indexes, the publisher believes that a quick review of the material below will add to his enjoyment of this reference work.

Arrangement—The Plan of the Atlas. The atlas has been designed with maximum convenience for the user as its objective. Part I of the atlas is devoted to the physical world—terrain maps of land forms and the sea floor. Part II contains the general political reference maps, area by area. All geographically related information pertaining to a country or region appears on adjacent pages, eliminating the task of searching throughout the entire volume for data on a given area. Thus, the reader will find, conveniently assembled, political, topographic, economic and special maps of a political area or region, accompanied by detailed map indexes, statistical data, and illustrations of the national flags of the area.

The sequence of country units in this American-designed atlas is international in arrangement. Units on the world as a whole are followed by a section on the polar regions which, in turn, is followed by pages devoted to Europe and its countries. Every continent map is accompanied by special population distribution, climatic and vegetation maps of that continent. Following the maps of the European continent and its countries, the geographic sequence plan proceeds as follows: Asia, the Pacific and Australia, Africa, South America, North America, and ends with detailed coverage on the United States.

Political Maps—The Primary Reference Tool. The most detailed maps in each country unit are the *political maps.* It is our feeling that the reader is likely to refer to these maps more often than to any other in the book when confronted by such questions as—Where? How big? What is it near? Answering these common queries is the function of the political maps. Each political map stresses *political* phenomena—countries, internal political divisions, boundaries, cities and towns. The major political unit or units, shown on the map, are banded in distinctive colors for easy identification and delineation. First-order political subdivisions (states, provinces, counties on the state maps) are shown, scale permitting.

The reader is advised to make use of the *legend* appearing under the title on each political map. Map *symbols,* the special "language" of maps, are explained in the legend. Each variety of dot, circle, star or interrupted line has a special meaning which should be clearly understood by the user so that he may interpret the map data correctly.

Each country has been portrayed at a *scale* commensurate with its political, areal, economic or tourist importance. In certain cases, a whole map unit may be devoted to a single nation if that nation is considered to be of prime interest to most atlas users. In other cases, several nations will be shown on a single map if, as separate entities, they are of lesser relative importance. Areas of dense settlement and important significance within a country have been enlarged and portrayed in inset maps inserted on the margins of the main map. The scale of each map is indicated as a fractional representation (1:1,000,000). The reader is advised to refer to the linear or "bar" scale appearing on each map or map inset in order to determine the distance between points.

The *projection* system used for each map is noted near the title of the map. Map projections are the special graphic systems used by cartographers to render the curved three-dimensional surface of the globe on a flat surface. Optimum map projections determined by the attributes of the area have been used by the publishers for each map in the atlas.

A word here as to the choice of place names on the maps. Throughout the atlas names appear, with a few exceptions, in their local official spellings. However, conventional Anglicized spellings are used for major geographical divisions and for towns and topographic features for which English forms exist; i.e., "Spain" instead of "España" or "Munich" instead of "München." Names of this type are normally followed by the local official spelling in parentheses. As an aid to the user the indexes are cross-referenced for all current and most former spellings of such names.

Names of cities and towns in the United States follow the forms listed in the *Post Office Directory* of the United States Postal Service. Domestic physical names follow the decisions of the Board on Geographic Names, U.S. Department of the Interior, and of various state geographic name boards. It is the belief of the publishers that the boundaries shown in a general reference atlas should reflect current geographic and political realities. This policy has been followed consistently in the atlas. The presentation of *de facto* boundaries in cases of territorial dispute between various nations does not imply the political endorsement of such boundaries by the publisher, but simply the honest representation of boundaries as they exist at the time of the printing of the atlas maps.

Indexes—Pinpointing a Location. Each political map is accompanied by a comprehensive index of the place names appearing on the map. if you are unfamiliar with the location of a particular geographical place and wish to find its position within the confines of the subject area of the map, consult the map index as your first step. The name of the feature sought will be found in its proper alphabetical sequence with a key reference letter-number combination corresponding to its location on the map. After noting the key reference letter-number combination for the place name, turn to the map. The place name will be found within the square formed by the two lines of latitude and the two lines of longitude which enclose the coordinates—i.e., the marginal letters and numbers. The diagram below illustrates the system of indexing.

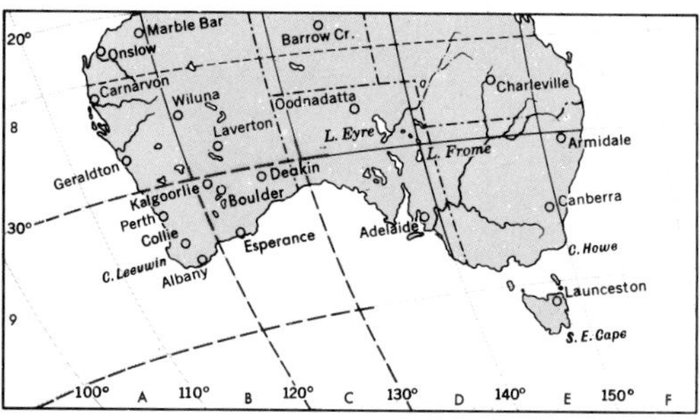

In the case of maps consisting entirely of insets, the place name is found near the intersection point of the imaginary lines connecting the coordinates at right angles. See below.

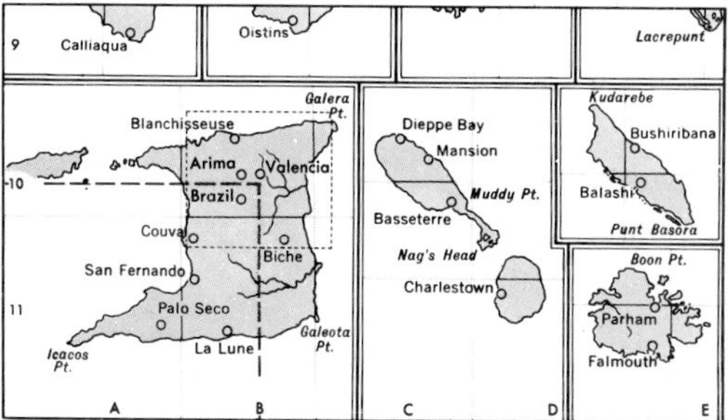

Where space on the map has not permitted giving the complete form of the place name, the complete form is shown in the index. Where a place is known by more than one name or by various spellings of the same name, the different forms have been included in the index. Physical features are listed under their proper names and not according to their generic terms; that is to say, Rio Negro will be found under Negro and not under Rio Negro. On the other hand, Rio Grande will be found under Rio Grande. Accompanying most index entries for cities and towns, and for other political units, are *population figures* for the particular entries. The large number of population figures in the atlas makes this work one of the most comprehensive statistical sources available to the public today. The population figures have been taken from the latest official censuses and estimates of the various nations.

Population and area figures for countries and major political units are listed in bold type *fact lists* on the margins of the index. In addition, the capital, largest city, highest point, monetary unit, principal languages and the prevailing religions of the country concerned are also listed, The Gazetteer-Index of the World on the following pages provides a quick reference index for countries and other important areas. Though population and area figures for each major unit are also found in the map section, the Gazetteer-Index provides a conveniently arranged statistical comparison contained in five pages.

Relief Maps. Accompanying each political map is a relief map of the area. The purpose of the relief map is to illustrate the surface configuration (TOPOGRAPHY) of the region. A shading technique in color simulates the relative ruggedness of the terrain — plains, plateaus, valleys, hills and mountains. Graded colors, ranging from greens for lowlands, yellows for intermediate elevations to brown in the highlands, indicate the height above sea level of each part of the land. A vertical scale at the margin of the map shows the approximate height in meters and feet represented by each color.

Economic Maps—Agriculture, Industry and Resources. One of the most interesting features that will be found in each country unit is the economic map. From this map one can determine the basic activities of a nation as expressed through its economy. A perusal of the map yields a full understanding of the area's economic geography and natural resources.

The agricultural economy is manifested in two ways: color bands and commodity names. The color bands express broad categories of dominant land use, such as cereal belts, forest lands, livestock range lands or nonagricultural wastes. The red commodity names, on the other hand, pinpoint the areas of production of *specific* crops, i.e., wheat, cotton, sugar beets, etc.

Major mineral occurrences are denoted by standard letter symbols appearing in blue. The relative size of the letter symbols signifies the relative importance of the deposit.

The manufacturing sector of the economy is presented by means of diagonal line patterns expressing the various *industrial* areas of consequence within a country.

The fishing industry is represented by names of commercial fish species appearing offshore in blue letters. Major waterpower sites are designated by blue symbols.

The publishers have tried to make this work the most comprehensive and useful atlas available, and it is hoped that it will prove a valuable reference work. Any constructive suggestions from the reader will be welcomed.

Sources and Acknowledgements

A multitude of sources goes into the making of a large-scale reference work such as this. To list them all would take many pages and would consume space better devoted to the maps and reference materials themselves. However, certain general sources were very useful in preparing this work and are listed below.

STATISTICAL OFFICE OF THE UNITED NATIONS.
Demographic Yearbook. New York. Issued annually.

STATISTICAL OFFICE OF THE UNITED NATIONS.
Statistical Yearbook. New York. Issued annually.

THE GEOGRAPHER, U.S. DEPARTMENT OF STATE.
International Boundary Study papers. Washington. Various dates.

THE GEOGRAPHER, U.S. DEPARTMENT OF STATE.
Geographic Notes. Washington. Various dates.

UNITED STATES BOARD ON GEOGRAPHIC NAMES.
Decisions on Geographic Names in the United States. Washington. Various dates.

UNITED STATES BOARD ON GEOGRAPHIC NAMES.
Official Standard Names Gazetteers. Washington. Various dates.

CANADIAN PERMANENT COMMITTEE ON GEOGRAPHICAL NAMES.
Gazetteer of Canada series. Ottawa. Various dates.

UNITED STATES POSTAL SERVICE.
National Five Digit ZIP Code and Post Office Directory. Washington. Issued annually.

UNITED STATES POSTAL SERVICE.
Postal Bulletin. Washington. Issued weekly.

UNITED STATES DEPARTMENT OF THE INTERIOR, BUREAU OF MINES.
Minerals Yearbook. 4 vols. Washington. Various dates.

UNITED STATES GEOLOGICAL SURVEY.
Elevations and distances in the United States. Reston, Va. 1990.

CARTACTUAL.
Cartactual — Topical Map Service. Budapest. Issues bi-monthly.

AMERICAN GEOGRAPHICAL SOCIETY.
Focus. New York. Issued ten times a year.

THE AMERICAN UNIVERSITY.
Foreign Area Studies. Washington. Various dates.

CENTRAL INTELLIGENCE AGENCY.
General reference maps. Washington. Various dates.

A sample list of sources used for specific countries follows:

Afghanistan
CENTRAL STATISTICS OFFICE.
Preliminary Results of the First Afghan Population Census 1979. Kabul.

Albania
DREJTORIA E STATISTIKES.
1979 Census. Tiranë.

Argentina
INSTITUTO NACIONAL DE ESTADISTICA Y CENSOS.
Censo Nacional de Población y Vivienda 1980. Buenos Aires.

Australia
AUSTRALIAN BUREAU OF STATISTICS.
Census of Population and Housing 1986. Canberra.

Brazil
FUNDACAO INSTITUTO BRASILEIRO DE GEOGRAFIA E ESTATISTICA.
IX Recenseamento Geral do Brasil 1980. Rio de Janeiro.

Canada
STATISTICS CANADA.
1986 Census of Canada. Ottawa.

Cuba
COMITE ESTATAL DE ESTADISTICAS.
Censo de Población y Viviendas 1981. Havana.

Hungary
HUNGARIAN CENTRAL STATISTICAL OFFICE.
1990 Census. Budapest.

Indonesia
BIRO PUSAT STATISTIK.
Sensus Penduduk 1980. Jakarta.

Kuwait
CENTRAL OFFICE OF STATISTICS.
1985 Census. Al Kuwait.

New Zealand
DEPARTMENT OF STATISTICS.
New Zealand Census of Population and Dwellings 1986. Wellington.

Panama
DIRECCION DE ESTADISTICA Y CENSO.
Censos Nacionales de 1990. Panamá.

Papua New Guinea
BUREAU OF STATISTICS.
National Population Census 1980. Port Moresby.

Philippines
NATIONAL CENSUS AND STATISTICS OFFICE.
1980 Census of Population. Manila.

Saint Lucia
CENSUS OFFICE.
1980 Population Census. Castries.

Singapore
DEPARTMENT OF STATISTICS.
Census of Population 1980. Singapore.

Russia
CENTRAL STATISTICAL ADMINISTRATION.
1989 Census. Moscow.

United States
BUREAU OF THE CENSUS.
1990 Census of Population. Washington.

Vanuatu
CENSUS OFFICE.
1979 Population Census. Port Vila.

Zambia
CENTRAL STATISTICAL OFFICE.
1980 Census of Population and Housing. Lusaka.

Gazetteer-Index of the World

This alphabetical list of continents, countries, states, possessions and other major geographical areas provides a quick reference to their area in square miles and square kilometers, population, capital or chief town, map page number and an alpha-numeric index reference. The index reference indicates the square on the respective page in which the name may be found. The population figures used in each case are the latest reliable figures obtainable. The government listings are based primarily on the nomenclature contained in the World Factbook published by the CIA of the United States Government. Those governments currently unsettled or in transition are indicated with a † symbol.

Country	Square Miles	Area Square Kilometers	Population	Capital or Chief Town	Page and Index Ref.	Government or Ownership
*Afghanistan	250,775	649,507	16,450,000	Kabul	68/A 2	authoritarian†
Africa	11,707,000	30,321,130	648,000,000	....	102/....	
Alabama, U.S.	51,705	133,916	4,040,587	Montgomery	195/....	state of the U.S.
Alaska, U.S.	591,004	1,530,700	550,043	Juneau	196/....	state of the U.S.
*Albania	11,100	28,749	3,335,000	Tiranë	45/E 5	emerging democracy†
Alberta, Canada	255,285	661,185	2,545,553	Edmonton	182/....	province of Canada
*Algeria	919,591	2,381,740	26,022,000	Algiers	106/D 3	republic
American Samoa	77	199	46,773	Pago Pago	87/J 7; 86/....	unincorporated, unorganized territory of the U.S.
*Andorra	188	487	53,000	Andorra la Vella	33/G 1	parliamentary democracy
*Angola	481,351	1,246,700	8,668,000	Luanda	114/C 6	Marxist people's republic†
Anguilla, U.K.	35	91	7,000	The Valley	156/F 3	dependent territory of the U.K.
Antarctica	5,500,000	14,245,000	....	....	5/....	
*Antigua and Barbuda	171	443	64,000	St. John's	161/E11; 156/G 3	parliamentary democracy
*Argentina	1,072,070	2,776,661	32,664,000	Buenos Aires	143/....	republic
Arizona, U.S.	114,000	295,260	3,665,228	Phoenix	198/....	state of the U.S.
Arkansas, U.S.	53,187	137,754	2,350,725	Little Rock	202/....	state of the U.S.
*Armenia	11,506	29,800	3,283,000	Yerevan	52/F 6	republic
Aruba, Netherlands	75	193	64,000	Oranjestad	161/E 9	autonomous member of the Netherlands realm
Ascension Island, St. Helena	34	88	719	Georgetown	102/A 5	part of St. Helena
Ashmore & Cartier Islands, Australia	61	159	....	(Canberra, Austr.)	88/C 2	territory of Australia
Asia	17,128,500	44,362,815	3,176,000,000	....	54/....	
*Australia	2,966,136	7,682,300	17,288,000	Canberra	88/....	federal parliamentary state
Australian Capital Territory	927	2,400	221,609	Canberra	96/E 4	territory of Australia
*Austria	32,375	83,851	7,666,000	Vienna	40/B 3	federal republic
*Azerbaijan	33,436	86,600	7,029,000	Baku	52/G 6	republic
Azores, Portugal	902	2,335	275,900	Ponta Delgada	32/....	autonomous region of Portugal
*Bahamas	5,382	13,939	252,000	Nassau	156/C 1	independent commmonwealth
*Bahrain	240	622	537,000	Manama	58/F 4	traditional monarchy
Baker Island, U.S.	1	2.6	....	....	87/J 5	unincorporated territory of the U.S.
Balearic Islands, Spain	1,936	5,014	655,909	Palma	33/H 3	autonomous community of Spain
*Bangladesh	55,126	142,776	116,601,000	Dhaka	68/G 4	republic
*Barbados	166	430	255,000	Bridgetown	161/B 8	parliamentary democracy
*Belarus	80,154	207,600	10,200,000	Minsk	52/C 4	republic
*Belgium	11,781	30,513	9,922,000	Brussels	27/E 7	constitutional monarchy
*Belize	8,867	22,966	228,000	Belmopan	154/C 2	parliamentary democracy
*Benin	43,483	112,620	4,832,000	Porto-Novo	106/E 6	democratic reform†
Bermuda, U.K.	21	54	58,000	Hamilton	156/H 3	dependent territory of the U.K.
*Bhutan	18,147	47,000	1,598,000	Thimphu	68/G 3	monarchy
*Bolivia	424,163	1,098,582	7,157,000	La Paz; Sucre	136/.....	republic
Bonaire, Neth. Antilles	112	291	8,087	Kralendijk	161/E 9	part of Netherland Antilles
*Bosnia & Herzegovina	19,940	51,129	4,124,256	Sarajevo	45/C 3	emerging democracy†
*Botswana	224,764	582,139	1,258,000	Gaborone	119/C 4	parliamentary republic
Bouvet Island, Norway	22	57	....	....	5/D 1	territory of Norway
*Brazil	3,284,426	8,506,663	155,356,000	Brasília	132/.....	federal republic
British Columbia, Canada	366,253	948,596	3,282,061	Victoria	184/....	province of Canada
British Indian Ocean Terr., U.K.	29	75	2,000	(London, U.K.)	54/L10	dependent territory of the U.K.
British Virgin Islands	59	153	12,000	Road Town	157/H 1	dependent territory of the U.K.
*Brunei	2,226	5,765	398,000	Bandar Seri Begawan	85/E 4	constitutional sultanate
*Bulgaria	42,823	110,912	8,911,000	Sofia	45/F 4	democratic reform†
*Burkina Faso	105,869	274,200	9,360,000	Ouagadougou	106/D 6	parliamentary
*Burma (Myanmar)	261,789	678,034	42,112,000	Rangoon	72/B 2	military
*Burundi	10,747	27,835	5,831,000	Bujumbura	114/E 4	republic
California, U.S.	158,706	411,049	29,760,021	Sacramento	204/.....	state of the U.S.
*Cambodia	69,898	181,036	7,146,000	Phnom Penh	72/E 4	constitutional monarchy†
*Cameroon	183,568	475,441	11,390,000	Yaoundé	114/B 2	one-party republic
*Canada	3,851,787	9,976,139	27,296,859	Ottawa	162/.....	confederation with parliamentary democracy
Canary Islands, Spain	2,808	7,273	1,367,646	Las Palmas; Santa Cruz	32/B 4	autonomous community of Spain
*Cape Verde	1,557	4,033	387,000	Praia	106/B 8	republic
Cayman Islands, U.K.	100	259	27,000	Georgetown	156/B 3	dependent territory of the U.K.
Celebes, Indonesia	72,986	189,034	7,732,383	Ujung Pandang	85/G 6	part of Indonesia
*Central African Republic	242,000	626,780	2,952,000	Bangui	114/C 2	republic
Central America	197,480	511,475	28,296,000	....	154/.....	
*Chad	495,752	1,283,998	5,122,000	N'Djamena	111/C 4	republic
Channel Islands, U.K.	75	194	133,000	St. Helier; St. Peter Port	13/E 8	part of the United Kingdom
*Chile	292,257	756,946	13,287,000	Santiago	138/.....	republic
*China, People's Rep. of	3,691,000	9,559,690	1,151,487,000	Beijing	77/.....	communist party-led state
China, Republic of (Taiwan)	13,971	36,185	20,659,000	Taipei	77/K 7	multiparty democratic
Christmas Island, Australia	52	135	3,184	Flying Fish Cove	54/M11	territory of Australia
Clipperton Island, France	2	5.2	....	....	146/H 8	possession of France
Cocos (Keeling) Islands, Australia	5.4	14	555	West Island	54/N11	territory of Australia

*Member of the United Nations

Gazetteer-Index of the World

Country	Square Miles	Area Square Kilometers	Population	Capital or Chief Town	Page and Index Ref.	Government or Ownership
*Colombia	439,513	1,138,339	33,778,000	Bogotá	126/.....	republic
Colorado, U.S.	104,091	269,596	3,294,394	Denver	208/.....	state of the U.S.
*Comoros	719	1,862	477,000	Moroni	119/G 2	republic
*Congo, Dem. Rep. of the	905,063	2,344,113	37,832,000	Kinshasa	114/D 4	republic
*Congo, Rep. of the	132,046	342,000	2,309,000	Brazzaville	114/B 4	republic
Connecticut, U.S.	5,018	12,997	3,287,116	Hartford	210/.....	state of the U.S.
Cook Islands, New Zealand	91	236	18,000	Avarua	87/K 7	self-governing in free association with New Zealand
Coral Sea Islands, Australia	8.5	22	....	....	88/J 3	territory of Australia
Corsica, France	3,352	8,682	249,737	Ajaccio; Bastia	28/B 6	part of France
*Costa Rica	19,575	50,700	3,111,000	San José	154/E 5	democratic republic
Côte d'Ivoire, see Ivory Coast						
*Croatia	22,050	56,538	4,601,469	Zagreb	45/B 3	parliamentary democracy
*Cuba	44,206	114,494	10,732,000	Havana	158/.....	communist state
Curaçao, Neth. Antilles	178	462	145,430	Willemstad	161/G 7	part of Netherlands Antilles
*Cyprus	3,473	8,995	709,000	Nicosia	62/E 5	republic
*Czech Republic	30,449	78,863	10,291,927	Prague	41/C 2	parliamentary democracy
Delaware, U.S.	2,044	5,294	666,168	Dover	245/R 3	state of the U.S.
*Denmark	16,629	43,069	5,133,000	Copenhagen	21/.....	constitutional monarchy
District of Columbia, U.S.	69	179	606,900	Washington	244/F 5	district of the United States
*Djibouti	8,880	23,000	346,000	Djibouti	111/H 5	republic
*Dominica	290	751	86,000	Roseau	161/E 7	parliamentary democracy
*Dominican Republic	18,704	48,443	7,385,000	Santo Domingo	158/D 6	republic
*Ecuador	109,483	283,561	10,752,000	Quito	128/C 3	republic
*Egypt	386,659	1,001,447	54,452,000	Cairo	110/E 2	republic
*El Salvador	8,260	21,393	5,419,000	San Salvador	154/C 4	republic
England, U.K.	50,516	130,836	46,220,955	London	13/.....	part of the United Kingdom
*Equatorial Guinea	10,831	28,052	379,000	Malabo	114/A 3	republic
*Eritrea	45,410	117,600	2,614,700	Asmara	110/G 4	transitional government†
*Estonia	17,413	45,100	1,573,000	Tallinn	53/.....	republic
*Ethiopia	426,366	1,104,300	50,576,300	Addis Ababa	110/G5.	federal republic
Europe	4,057,000	10,507,630	689,000,000	....	7/.....	
Falkland Islands & Dependencies, U.K.	6,198	16,053	1,813	Stanley	120/E 8; 143/D 7	dependent territory of the U.K.
Faroe Islands, Denmark	540	1,399	48,000	Tórshavn	21/B 2	self-governing overseas administrative division of Denmark
*Fiji	7,055	18,272	764,000	Suva	87/H 8; 86/.....	republic
*Finland	130,128	337,032	4,991,000	Helsinki	18/O 6	republic
Florida, U.S.	58,664	151,940	12,937,926	Tallahassee	212/.....	state of the U.S.
*France	210,038	543,998	58,073,553	Paris	28/.....	republic
French Guiana	35,135	91,000	114,678	Cayenne	131/E 3	overseas department of France
French Polynesia	1,544	4,000	195,000	Papeete	87/L 8	overseas territory of France
*Gabon	103,346	267,666	1,080,000	Libreville	114/B 4	republic
*Gambia	4,127	10,689	875,000	Banjul	106/A 6	republic
Gaza Strip	139	360	642,000	Gaza	65/A 4	occupied by Israel
*Georgia	26,911	69,700	5,449,000	Tbilisi	52/F 6	republic
Georgia, U.S.	58,910	152,577	6,478,216	Atlanta	217/.....	state of the U.S.
*Germany	137,753	356,780	79,548,000	Berlin	22/.....	republic
*Ghana	92,099	238,536	15,617,000	Accra	106/D 7	constitutional democracy
Gibraltar, U.K.	2.28	5.91	30,000	Gibraltar	33/D 4	dependent territory of the U.K.
*Great Britain & Northern Ireland (United Kingdom)	94,399	244,493	57,236,000	London	10/.....	see United Kingdom
*Greece	50,944	131,945	10,043,000	Athens	45/F 6	presidential parliamentary republic
Greenland, Denmark	840,000	2,175,600	57,000	Nuuk (Godthåb)	4/B12	self-governing overseas administrative division of Denmark
*Grenada	133	344	84,000	St. George's	161/D 9; 156/G 4	parliamentary democracy
Guadeloupe & Dependencies, France	687	1,779	386,987	Basse-Terre	161/A 5; 156/F 4	overseas department of France
Guam, U.S.	209	541	133,152	Agaña	87/E 4; 86/.....	organized, unincorporated territory of the U.S.
*Guatemala	42,042	108,889	9,266,000	Guatemala	154/B 3	republic
*Guinea	94,925	245,856	7,456,000	Conakry	106/B 6	republic
*Guinea-Bissau	13,948	36,125	1,024,000	Bissau	106/A 6	republic
*Guyana	83,000	214,970	750,000	Georgetown	131/B 3	republic
*Haiti	10,694	27,697	6,287,000	Port-au-Prince	158/C 5	republic
Hawaii, U.S.	6,471	16,760	1,108,229	Honolulu	218/.....	state of the U.S.
Heard & McDonald Islands, Australia	113	293	....	....	2/N 8	territory of Australia
Holland, see Netherlands						
*Honduras	43,277	112,087	4,949,000	Tegucigalpa	154/D 3	republic
Hong Kong	403	1,044	5,856,000	Victoria	77/H 7; 78/.....	special administrative region of China
Howland Island, U.S.	1	2.6	....	....	87/J 5	unincorporated territory of the U.S.
*Hungary	35,919	93,030	10,558,000	Budapest	41/D 3	republic
*Iceland	39,768	103,000	260,000	Reykjavík	21/B 1	republic
Idaho, U.S.	83,564	216,431	1,006,749	Boise	220/.....	state of the U.S.
Illinois, U.S.	56,345	145,934	11,430,602	Springfield	222/.....	state of the U.S.
*India	1,269,339	3,287,588	869,515,000	New Delhi	68/D 4	federal republic
Indiana, U.S.	36,185	93,719	5,544,159	Indianapolis	227/.....	state of the U.S.
*Indonesia	788,430	2,042,034	193,560,000	Jakarta	85/D 7	republic
Iowa, U.S.	56,275	145,752	2,776,755	Des Moines	229/.....	state of the U.S.

Gazetteer-Index of the World

Country	Area Square Miles	Area Square Kilometers	Population	Capital or Chief Town	Page and Index Ref.	Government or Ownership
*Iran	636,293	1,648,000	59,051,000	Tehran	66/F 4	theocratic republic
*Iraq	172,476	446,713	19,525,000	Baghdad	66/C 4	republic
*Ireland	27,136	70,282	3,489,000	Dublin	17/.....	republic
Ireland, Northern, U.K.	5,452	14,121	1,543,000	Belfast	17/F 2	part of the United Kingdom
Isle of Man, U.K.	227	588	64,000	Douglas	13/C 3	part of the United Kingdom
*Israel	7,847	20,324	4,558,000	Jerusalem	65/B 4	republic
*Italy	116,303	301,225	57,772,000	Rome	34/.....	republic
*Ivory Coast (Côte d'Ivoire)	124,504	322,465	12,978,000	Yamoussoukro	106/C 7	republic
*Jamaica	4,411	11,424	2,489,000	Kingston	158/.....	parliamentary democracy
Jan Mayen, Norway	144	373	....	....	6/D 1	territory of Norway
*Japan	145,730	377,441	124,017,000	Tokyo	81/.....	constitutional monarchy
Jarvis Island, U.S.	1	2.6	....	....	87/K 6	unincorporated territory of the U.S.
Java, Indonesia	48,842	126,500	73,712,411	Jakarta	85/J 2	part of Indonesia
Johnston Atoll, U.S.	0.91	2.4	327	....	87/K 4	unincorporated territory of the U.S.
*Jordan	35,000	90,650	3,413,000	Amman	65/D 3	constitutional monarchy
Kansas, U.S.	82,277	213,097	2,477,574	Topeka	232/.....	state of the U.S.
*Kazakhstan	1,048,300	2,715,100	16,538,000	Aqmola	48/G 5	republic
Kentucky, U.S.	40,409	104,659	3,685,296	Frankfort	237/.....	state of the U.S.
*Kenya	224,960	582,646	25,242,000	Nairobi	115/G 3	republic
Kermadec Islands, New Zealand	13	33	5	....	87/J 9	part of New Zealand
Kingman Reef, U.S.	0.1	0.26	....	....	87/K 5	unincorporated territory of the U.S.
Kiribati	291	754	78,000	Tarawa	87/J 6	republic
*Korea, North	46,540	120,539	21,815,000	P'yŏngyang	80/D 3	communist
*Korea, South	38,175	98,873	43,134,000	Seoul	80/D 5	republic
*Kuwait	6,532	16,918	2,204,000	Al Kuwait	58/E 4	constitutional monarchy
*Kyrgyzstan	76,641	198,500	4,291,000	Bishkek	48/H 5	republic
*Laos	91,428	236,800	4,113,000	Vientiane	72/D 3	communist
*Latvia	24,595	63,700	2,681,000	Riga	53/.....	republic
*Lebanon	4,015	10,399	3,385,000	Beirut	62/F 6	republic
*Lesotho	11,720	30,355	1,801,000	Maseru	119/D 5	constitutional monarchy
*Liberia	43,000	111,370	2,730,000	Monrovia	106/C 7	republic
*Libya	679,358	1,759,537	4,353,000	Tripoli	110/B 2	socialist people's (masses) state
*Liechtenstein	61	158	28,000	Vaduz	39/J 2	hereditary constitutional monarchy
*Lithuania	25,174	65,200	3,690,000	Vilnius	53/.....	republic
Louisiana, U.S.	47,752	123,678	4,219,973	Baton Rouge	238/.....	state of the U.S.
*Luxembourg	999	2,587	388,000	Luxembourg	27/J 9	constitutional monarchy
Macau, Portugal	6	16	446,000	Macau	77/H 7	overseas territory of Portugal
*Macedonia	9,889	25,713	1,909,136	Skopje	45/E 5	emerging democracy
*Madagascar	226,657	587,041	12,185,000	Antananarivo	119/H 3	republic
Madeira Islands, Portugal	307	796	262,800	Funchal	32/A 2	autonomous region of Portugal
Maine, U.S.	33,265	86,156	1,227,928	Augusta	243/.....	state of the U.S.
*Malawi	45,747	118,485	9,438,000	Lilongwe	114/F 6	multiparty democracy
Malaya, Malaysia	50,806	131,588	11,138,227	Kuala Lumpur	72/D 6	part of Malaysia
*Malaysia	128,308	332,318	17,982,000	Kuala Lumpur	72/D 6; 85/E 4	constitutional monarchy
*Maldives	115	298	226,000	Male	54/L 9	republic
*Mali	464,873	1,204,021	8,339,000	Bamako	106/C 6	republic
*Malta	122	316	356,000	Valletta	34/E 7	parliamentary democracy
Manitoba, Canada	250,999	650,087	1,091,942	Winnipeg	179/.....	province of Canada
Marquesas Islands, French Polynesia	492	1,274	5,419	Atuona	87/N 6	part of French Polynesia
*Marshall Islands	70	181	54,000	Majuro	87/G 4	constitutional; free association with the U.S.
Martinique, France	425	1,101	359,572	Fort-de-France	161/D 5	overseas department of France
Maryland, U.S.	10,460	27,091	4,781,468	Annapolis	245/.....	state of the U.S.
Massachusetts, U.S.	8,284	21,456	6,016,425	Boston	249/.....	state of the U.S.
*Mauritania	419,229	1,085,803	1,996,000	Nouakchott	106/B 5	republic
*Mauritius	790	2,046	1,081,000	Port Louis	119/G 5	parliamentary democracy
Mayotte, France	144	373	75,000	Mamoutzou	119/G 2	territorial collectivity of France
*Mexico	761,601	1,972,546	90,007,000	Mexico City	150/.....	federal republic
Michigan, U.S.	58,527	151,585	9,295,297	Lansing	250/.....	state of the U.S.
*Micronesia, Federated States of	....	....	120,347	Palikir	87/E 5	constitutional; free association with the U.S.
Midway Islands, U.S.	1.9	4.9	453	....	87/J 3	unincorporated territory of the U.S.
Minnesota, U.S.	84,402	218,601	4,375,099	St. Paul	255/.....	state of the U.S.
Mississippi, U.S.	47,689	123,515	2,573,216	Jackson	256/.....	state of the U.S.
Missouri, U.S.	69,697	180,515	5,117,073	Jefferson City	261/.....	state of the U.S.
*Moldova	13,012	33,700	4,341,000	Chişinău	52/C 5	republic
*Monaco	368 acres	149 hectares	30,000	....	28/G 6	constitutional monarchy
*Mongolia	606,163	1,569,962	2,247,000	Ulaanbaatar	77/E 2	republic
Montana, U.S.	147,046	380,849	799,065	Helena	262/.....	state of the U.S.
Montserrat, U.K.	40	104	13,000	Plymouth	157/G 3	dependent territory of the U.K.
*Morocco	172,414	446,550	26,182,000	Rabat	106/C 2	constitutional monarchy
*Mozambique	303,769	786,762	15,113,000	Maputo	119/E 4	republic
Myanmar, see Burma						
*Namibia	317,827	823,172	1,521,000	Windhoek	118/B 3	republic
Nauru	7.7	20	10,000	Yaren (district)	87/G 6	republic
Navassa Island, U.S.	2	5	....	....	156/C 3	unincorporated territory of the U.S.
Nebraska, U.S.	77,355	200,349	1,578,385	Lincoln	264/.....	state of the U.S.
*Nepal	54,663	141,577	19,612,000	Kathmandu	68/E 3	parliamentary democracy
*Netherlands	15,892	41,160	15,022,000	The Hague; Amsterdam	27/F 5	constitutional monarchy
Netherlands Antilles	320	817	184,000	Willemstad	156/E 4	autonomous member of the Netherlands realm
Nevada, U.S.	110,561	286,353	1,201,833	Carson City	266/.....	state of the U.S.

Gazetteer-Index of the World

Country	Square Miles	Area Square Kilometers	Population	Capital or Chief Town	Page and Index Ref.	Government or Ownership
New Brunswick, Canada	28,354	73,437	723,900	Fredericton	170/.....	province of Canada
New Caledonia & Dependencies, France	7,335	18,998	172,000	Nouméa	87/G 8	overseas territory of France
Newfoundland, Canada	156,184	404,517	568,474	St. John's	166/.....	province of Canada
New Hampshire, U.S.	9,279	24,033	1,109,252	Concord	268/.....	state of the U.S.
New Jersey, U.S.	7,787	20,168	7,730,188	Trenton	273/.....	state of the U.S.
New Mexico, U.S.	121,593	314,926	1,515,069	Santa Fe	274/.....	state of the U.S.
New South Wales, Australia	309,498	801,600	5,401,881	Sydney	96/B 2	state of Australia
New York, U.S.	49,108	127,190	17,990,455	Albany	276/.....	state of the U.S.
*New Zealand	103,736	268,676	3,309,000	Wellington	100/.....	parliamentary democracy
*Nicaragua	45,698	118,358	3,752,000	Managua	154/D 4	republic
*Niger	489,189	1,267,000	8,154,000	Niamey	106/F 5	republic
*Nigeria	357,000	924,630	122,471,000	Abuja	106/F 6	military
Niue, New Zealand	100	259	3,578	Alofi	87/K 7	self-governing territory in free association with New Zealand
Norfolk Island, Australia	13.4	34.6	2,175	Kingston	88/L 5	territory of Australia
North America	9,363,000	24,250,170	427,000,000	....	146/.....	
North Carolina, U.S.	52,669	136,413	6,628,637	Raleigh	281/.....	state of the U.S.
North Dakota, U.S.	70,702	183,118	638,800	Bismarck	282/.....	state of the U.S.
Northern Ireland, U.K.	5,452	14,121	1,543,000	Belfast	17/F 2	part of the United Kingdom
Northern Marianas, U.S.	184	477	43,345	Saipan	87/E 4	commonwealth associated with the U.S.
Northern Territory, Australia	519,768	1,346,200	154,848	Darwin	93/.....	territory of Australia
*North Korea	46,540	120,539	21,815,000	P'yŏngyang	80/D 3	communist state
Northwest Territories, Canada	1,304,896	3,379,683	57,649	Yellowknife	187/G 3	territory of Canada
*Norway	125,053	323,887	4,273,000	Oslo	18/F 7	constitutional monarchy
Nova Scotia, Canada	21,425	55,491	899,942	Halifax	168/.....	province of Canada
Oceania	3,292,000	8,526,280	23,000,000	....	87/.....	
Ohio, U.S.	41,330	107,045	10,847,115	Columbus	284/.....	state of the U.S.
Oklahoma, U.S.	69,956	181,186	3,145,585	Oklahoma City	288/.....	state of the U.S.
*Oman	120,000	310,800	1,534,000	Muscat	58/G 6	absolute monarchy
Ontario, Canada	412,580	1,068,582	10,084,885	Toronto	175,177/	province of Canada
Oregon, U.S.	97,073	251,419	2,842,321	Salem	291/.....	state of the U.S.
Orkney Islands, Scotland	376	974	17,675	Kirkwall	15/E 1	part of the United Kingdom
*Pakistan	310,403	803,944	117,490,000	Islamabad	68/B 3	federal republic
*Palau	188	487	15,122	Koror	86/D 5	constitutional; free association with the U.S.
Palmyra Atoll, U.S.	12	31	....	....	87/K 5	unincorporated territory of the U.S.
*Panama	29,761	77,082	2,476,000	Panamá	154/G 6	constitutional republic
*Papua New Guinea	183,540	475,369	3,913,000	Port Moresby	85/B 7; 87/E 6	parliamentary democracy
Paracel Islands, China	....	....			85/E 2	occupied by China; claimed by Taiwan and Vietnam
*Paraguay	157,047	406,752	4,799,000	Asunción	144/.....	republic
Pennsylvania, U.S.	45,308	117,348	11,881,643	Harrisburg	294/.....	state of the U.S.
*Peru	496,222	1,285,215	22,362,000	Lima	128/.....	republic
*Philippines	115,707	299,681	65,759,000	Manila	82/.....	republic
Pitcairn Islands, U.K.	18	47	54	Adamstown	87/O 8	dependent territory of the U.K.
*Poland	120,725	312,678	37,800,000	Warsaw	47/.....	democratic
*Portugal	35,549	92,072	10,388,000	Lisbon	32/B 3	parliamentary democracy
Prince Edward Island, Canada	2,184	5,657	129,765	Charlottetown	168/E 2	province of Canada
Puerto Rico, U.S.	3,515	9,104	3,522,037	San Juan	161/.....	commonwealth associated with the U.S.
*Qatar	4,247	11,000	518,000	Doha	58/F 4	traditional monarchy
Québec, Canada	594,857	1,540,680	6,895,963	Québec	172,174/	province of Canada
Queensland, Australia	666,872	1,727,200	2,587,315	Brisbane	95/.....	state of Australia
Réunion, France	969	2,510	597,823	St-Denis	119/F 5	overseas department of France
Rhode Island, U.S.	1,212	3,139	1,003,464	Providence	249/H 5	state of the U.S.
*Romania	91,699	237,500	23,397,000	Bucharest	45/F 3	republic
*Russia	6,592,812	17,075,400	147,386,000	Moscow	48/D 4	federation
*Rwanda	10,169	26,337	7,903,000	Kigali	114/E 4	republic
Sabah, Malaysia	29,300	75,887	1,002,608	Kota Kinabalu	85/F 4	state of Malaysia
Saint Helena & Dependencies, U.K.	162	420	7,000	Jamestown	102/B 6	dependent territory of the U.K.
*Saint Kitts and Nevis	104	269	40,000	Basseterre	156/F 3; 161/C11	constitutional monarchy
*Saint Lucia	238	616	153,000	Castries	161/G 6	parliamentary democracy
Saint Pierre & Miquelon, France	93.5	242	6,392	Saint-Pierre	166/C 4	territorial collectivity of France
*Saint Vincent & the Grenadines	150	388	114,000	Kingstown	161/A 8; 157/G 4	constitutional monarchy
Sakhalin, Russia	29,500	76,405	655,000	Yuzhno-Sakhalinsk	48/P 4	part of Russia
*Samoa	1,133	2,934	204,000	Apia	87/J 7	constitutional monarchy
*San Marino	23.4	60.6	23,000	San Marino	34/D 3	republic
*São Tomé and Príncipe	372	963	128,000	São Tomé	106/F 8	republic
Sarawak, Malaysia	48,202	124,843	1,294,753	Kuching	85/E 5	state of Malaysia
Sardinia, Italy	9,301	24,090	1,450,483	Cagliari	34/B 4	region of Italy
Saskatchewan, Canada	251,699	651,900	988,928	Regina	181/.....	province of Canada
*Saudi Arabia	829,995	2,149,687	17,870,000	Riyadh	58/D 4	monarchy
Scotland, U.K.	30,414	78,772	5,117,146	Edinburgh	15/.....	part of the United Kingdom
*Senegal	75,954	196,720	7,953,000	Dakar	106/A 5	republic
*Seychelles	145	375	69,000	Victoria	119/H 5	republic
Shetland Islands, Scotland	552	1,430	18,494	Lerwick	15/G 2	part of the United Kingdom
Siam, see Thailand						
Sicily, Italy	9,926	25,708	4,628,918	Palermo	34/D 6	region of Italy
*Sierra Leone	27,925	72,325	4,275,000	Freetown	106/B 7	constitutional democracy
*Singapore	226	585	2,756,000	Singapore	72/F 6	republic
*Slovakia	18,924	49,014	4,991,168	Bratislava	41/E 2	parliamentary democracy
*Slovenia	7,898	20,251	1,891,864	Ljubljana	45/A 3	emerging democracy

Gazetteer-Index of the World

Country	Square Miles	Area Square Kilometers	Population	Capital or Chief Town	Page and Index Ref.	Government or Ownership
Society Islands, French Polynesia	677	1,753	117,703	Papeete	87/L 7	part of French Polynesia
*Solomon Islands	11,500	29,785	386,000	Honiara	87/G 6; 86/.....	parliamentary democracy
*Somalia	246,200	637,658	6,709,000	Mogadishu	115/H 3	no functioning government
*South Africa	455,318	1,179,274	40,601,000	Cape Town; Pretoria	118/C 5	republic
South America	6,875,000	17,806,250	297,000,000	....	120/.....	
South Australia, Australia	379,922	984,000	1,345,945	Adelaide	94/.....	state of Australia
South Carolina, U.S.	31,113	80,583	3,486,703	Columbia	296/.....	state of the U.S.
South Dakota, U.S.	77,116	199,730	696,004	Pierre	298/.....	state of the U.S.
*South Korea	38,175	98,873	43,134,000	Seoul	80/D 5	republic
*Spain	194,881	504,742	39,385,000	Madrid	33/.....	parliamentary monarchy
Spratly Islands	....	....	....	....	85/E 4	in dispute; claims by China, Malaysia, Philippines, Taiwan, Vietnam
*Sri Lanka	25,332	65,610	17,424,000	Colombo	68/E 7	republic
*Sudan	967,494	2,505,809	27,220,000	Khartoum	110/E 4	transitional†
Sumatra, Indonesia	164,000	424,760	19,360,400	Medan	84/B 5	see Indonesia
*Suriname	55,144	142,823	402,000	Paramaribo	131/C 3	republic
Svalbard, Norway	23,957	62,049	3,431	Longyearbyen	18/C 2	territory of Norway
*Swaziland	6,705	17,366	859,000	Mbabane	119/E 5	monarchy
*Sweden	173,665	449,792	8,564,000	Stockholm	18/J 8	constitutional monarchy
Switzerland	15,943	41,292	6,784,000	Bern	39/.....	federal republic
*Syria	71,498	185,180	12,966,000	Damascus	62/G 5	military republic
Tahiti, French Polynesia	402	1,041	95,604	Papeete	87/L 7	see French Polynesia
Taiwan	13,971	36,185	16,609,961	Taipei	77/K 7	multiparty democratic
*Tajikistan	55,251	143,100	5,112,000	Dushanbe	48/G 6	republic
*Tanzania	363,708	942,003	26,869,000	Dar es Salaam	114/F 5	republic
Tasmania, Australia	26,178	67,800	436,353	Hobart	99/.....	state of Australia
Tennessee, U.S.	42,144	109,153	4,877,185	Nashville	237/.....	state of the U.S.
Texas, U.S.	266,807	691,030	16,986,510	Austin	303/.....	state of the U.S.
*Thailand	198,455	513,998	56,814,000	Bangkok	72/D 3	constitutional monarchy
Tibet, China	463,320	1,200,000	1,790,000	Lhasa	76/C 5	part of China
*Togo	21,622	56,000	3,811,000	Lomé	106/E 3	republic†
Tokelau, New Zealand	3.9	10	1,575	Fakaofo	87/J 6	territory of New Zealand
Tonga	270	699	105,000	Nuku'alofa	87/J 8	hereditary constitutional monarchy
*Trinidad and Tobago	1,980	5,128	1,285,000	Port-of-Spain	157/G 5; 161/A10	parliamentary democracy
Tristan da Cunha, St. Helena	38	98	251	Edinburgh	2/J 7	see St. Helena
Tuamotu Archipelago, French Polynesia	341	883	9,052	Apataki	87/M 7	see French Polynesia
*Tunisia	63,378	164,149	8,276,000	Tunis	106/F 1	republic
*Turkey	300,946	779,450	58,581,000	Ankara	62/D 3	republican parliamentary democracy
*Turkmenistan	188,455	488,100	3,534,000	Ashgabat	48/F 6	republic
Turks and Caicos Islands, U.K.	166	430	10,000	Cockburn Town, Grand Turk	156/D 2	dependent territory of the U.K.
Tuvalu	9.78	25.33	10,000	Funafuti	87/H 6	democracy
*Uganda	91,076	235,887	18,690,000	Kampala	114/F 3	republic
*Ukraine	233,089	603,700	51,704,000	Kiev	52/D 5	republic
*United Arab Emirates	32,278	83,600	2,390,000	Abu Dhabi	58/F 5	federation of sheikdoms
*United Kingdom	94,399	244,493	57,515,000	London	10/.....	constitutional monarchy
*United States	3,623,420	9,384,658	252,502,000	Washington, D.C.	188/.....	federal republic
*Uruguay	72,172	186,925	3,121,000	Montevideo	145/.....	republic
Utah, U.S.	84,899	219,888	1,722,850	Salt Lake City	304/.....	state of the U.S.
*Uzbekistan	173,591	449,600	19,906,000	Tashkent	48/G 5	republic
*Vanuatu	5,700	14,763	170,000	Port-Vila	87/G 7	republic
Vatican City	108.7 acres	44 hectares	1,000	....	34/B 6	sacerdotal (priest-related) monarchy
*Venezuela	352,143	912,050	20,189,000	Caracas	124/.....	republic
Vermont, U.S.	9,614	24,900	562,758	Montpelier	268/.....	state of the U.S.
Victoria, Australia	87,876	227,600	4,019,478	Melbourne	96/B 5	state of Australia
*Vietnam	128,405	332,569	67,568,000	Hanoi	72/E 3	communist state
Virginia, U.S.	40,767	105,587	6,187,358	Richmond	307/.....	state of the U.S.
Virgin Islands, British	59	153	12,000	Road Town	157/H 1	dependent territory of the U.K.
Virgin Islands, U.S.	132	342	101,809	Charlotte Amalie	161/A 4	organized, unincorporated territory of the U.S.
Wake Island, U.S.	2.5	6.5	302	Wake Islet	87/G 4	unincorporated territory of the U.S.
Wales, U.K.	8,017	20,764	2,790,462	Cardiff	13/D 5	part of the United Kingdom
Wallis and Futuna, France	106	275	17,000	Mata Utu	87/J 7	overseas territory of France
Washington, U.S.	68,139	176,480	4,866,692	Olympia	310/.....	state of the U.S.
West Bank	2,100	5,439	1,105,000	....	65/C 3	occupied by Israel
Western Australia, Australia	975,096	2,525,500	1,406,929	Perth	92/.....	state of Australia
Western Sahara	102,703	266,000	197,000	....	106/B 3	occupied by Morocco
West Virginia, U.S.	24,231	62,758	1,793,477	Charleston	312/.....	state of the U.S.
Wisconsin, U.S.	56,153	145,436	4,891,769	Madison	317/.....	state of the U.S.
World (land)	57,970,000	150,142,300	5,292,000,000	....	1,2/.....	
Wyoming, U.S.	97,809	253,325	453,588	Cheyenne	319/.....	state of the U.S.
*Yemen	188,321	487,752	10,063,000	Sanaa	58/D 7	republic
*Yugoslavia	38,989	102,173	11,371,275	Belgrade	45/C 3	republic
Yukon Territory, Canada	207,075	536,324	27,797	Whitehorse	186/E 3	territory of Canada
*Zambia	290,586	752,618	8,446,000	Lusaka	114/E 7	republic
*Zimbabwe	150,803	390,580	10,720,000	Harare	119/D 3	parliamentary democracy

V

Glossary of Abbreviations

A

A.A.F. — Army Air Field
Acad. — Academy
A.C.T. — Australian Capital Territory
adm. — administration; administrative
A.F.B. — Air Force Base
Afgh., Afghan. — Afghanistan
Afr. — Africa
Ala. — Alabama
Alb. — Albania
Alg. — Algeria
Alta. — Alberta
Amer. — American
Amer. Samoa — American Samoa
And. — Andorra
Ant., Antarc. — Antarctica
Ant. & Bar. — Antigua and Barbuda
Ar. — Arabia
arch. — archipelago
Arg. — Argentina
Ariz. — Arizona
Ark. — Arkansas
Arm. — Armenia
Aust. — Austria
Aust. Cap. Terr. — Australian Capital Territory
Austr., Austral. — Australian, Australia
aut. — autonomous
Aut. Obl. — Autonomous Oblast
Aut. Rep. — Autonomous Republic
Azer. — Azerbaijan

B

B. — Bay
Bah. — Bahamas
Barb. — Barbados
Battlef. — Battlefield
Bch. — Beach
Bel. — Belarus
Belg. — Belgium
Berm. — Bermuda
Bol. — Bolivia
Bos. — Bosnia & Hercegovina
Bots. — Botswana
Br. — Branch
Br. — British
Braz. — Brazil
Br. Col. — British Columbia
Br. Ind. Oc. Terr. — British Indian Ocean Territory
Bulg. — Bulgaria

C

C. — Cape
Calif. — California
Can. — Canada
can. — canal
cap. — capital
Cent. Afr. Rep. — Central African Republic
Cent. Amer. — Central America
C.G. Sta. — Coast Guard Station
C.H. — Court House
chan. — channel
Chan. Is. — Channel Islands
Chem. Ctr. — Chemical Center
co. — county
Col. — Colombia
Colo. — Colorado
comm. — commlssary
Conn. — Connecticut
cont. — continent
cord. — cordillera (mountain range)
C. Rica — Costa Rica
Cro. — Croatia
C.S. — County Seat
C. Verde — Cape Verde
Czech. — Czech Republic

D

D.C. — District of Columbia
Del. — Delaware
Dem. — Democratic
Den. — Denmark
depr. — depression
dept. — department
des. — desert
dist., dist's — district, districts
div. — division
Dom. Rep. — Dominican Republic

E

E. — East
Ec., Ecua. — Ecuador
elec. div. — electoral division
El Salv. — El Salvador
Eng. — England

Equat. Guinea, Eq. Guin. — Equatorial Guinea
Erit. — Eritrea
escarp. — escarpment
est. — estuary
Est. — Estonia
Eth. — Ethiopia

F

Falk. Is. — Falkland Islands
Fin. — Finland
Fk., Fks. — Fork, Forks
Fla. — Florida
for. — forest
Fr. — France, French
Fr. Gui. — French Guiana
Fr. Poly. — French Polynesia
Ft. — Fort

G

G. — Gulf
Ga. — Georgia (state)
Game Res. — Game Reserve
Geo. — Georgia (nation)
Ger. — Germany
geys. — geyser
Gibr. — Gibraltar
glac. — glacier
gov. — governorate
Gr. — Group
Greenl. — Greenland
Gren. — Grenada
Gt. Brit. — Great Britain
Guad. — Guadeloupe
Guat. — Guatemala
Guinea-Biss. — Guinea-Bissau
Guy. — Guyana

H

har., harb., hbr. — harbor
hd. — head
highl. — highland, highlands
Hist. — Historic, Historical
Hond. — Honduras
Hts. — Heights
Hung. — Hungary

I

I., isl. — island, isle
I.C. — independent city
Ice., Icel. — Iceland
Ida. — Idaho
Ill. — Illinois
Ind. — Indiana
ind. city — independent city
Indon. — Indonesia
Ind. Res. — Indian Reservation
int. div. — internal division
inten. — intendency
Int'l — International
Ire. — Ireland
Is., isls. — islands
Isr. — Israel
isth. — isthmus
Iv. Coast — Ivory Coast

J

Jam. — Jamaica
Jct. — Junction

K

Kans. — Kansas
Kaz., Kazakh. — Kazakhstan
Ky. — Kentucky
Kyr. — Kyrgyzstan

L

L. — Lake, Loch, Lough
La. — Louisiana
Lab. — Laboratory
lag. — lagoon
Lat. — Latvia
ld. — land
Leb. — Lebanon
Les. — Lesotho
Liecht. — Liechtenstein
Lith. — Lithuania
Lux. — Luxembourg

M

Mac. — Macedonia
Mad., Madag. — Madagascar
Man. — Manitoba
Mart. — Martinique
Mass. — Massachusetts
Maur. — Mauritania
Md. — Maryland
met. area — metropolitan area

Mex. — Mexico
Mich. — Michigan
Minn. — Minnesota
Miss. — Mississippi
Mo. — Missouri
Mold. — Moldova
Mon. — Monument
Mong. — Mongolia
Mont. — Montana
Mor. — Morocco
Moz., Mozamb. — Mozambique
mt. — mount
mtn. — mountain

N

N., No. — North
N. Amer. — North America
Nam., Namib. — Namibia
N.A.S. — Naval Air Station
Nat'l — National
Nat'l Cem. — National Cemetery
Nat'l Mem. Park — National Memorial Park
Nat'l Mil. Park — National Military Park
Nat'l Pkwy. — National Parkway
Nav. Base — Naval Base
Nav. Sta. — Naval Station
N.B., N. Br. — New Brunswick
N.C. — North Carolina
N. Dak. — North Dakota
Nebr. — Nebraska
Neth. — Netherlands
Neth. Ant. — Netherlands Antilles
Nev. — Nevada
New Bruns. — New Brunswick
New Cal., New Caled. — New Caledonia
Newf. — Newfoundland
New Hebr. — New Hebrides
N.H. — New Hampshire
Nic. — Nicaragua
N. Ire. — Northern Ireland
N.J. — New Jersey
N. Mex. — New Mexico
Nor. — Norway, Norwegian
North. — Northern
North. Terr., No. Terr. — Northern Territory (Australia)
N.S. — Nova Scotia
N.S.W., N.S. Wales — New South Wales
N.W.T., N.W. Terrs. — Northwest Territories (Canada)
N.Y. — New York
N.Z., N. Zealand — New Zealand

O

Obl. — Oblast
Okla. — Oklahoma
Okr. — Okrug
Ont. — Ontario
Ord. Depot — Ordnance Depot
Oreg. — Oregon

P

Pa. — Pennsylvania
Pak. — Pakistan
Pan. — Panama
Papua N.G. — Papua New Guinea
Par. — Paraguay
par. — parish
passg. — passage
P.E.I. — Prince Edward Island
pen. — peninsula
Phil., Phil. Is. — Philippines
Pk. — Park
pk. — peak
plat. — plateau
P.N.G. — Papua New Guinea
Pol. — Poland
Port. — Portugal, Portuguese
Pr. Edward I. — Prince Edward Island
pref. — prefecture
P. Rico — Puerto Rico
prom. — promontory
prov. — province, provincial
pt. — point

Q

Que. — Québec
Queens. — Queensland

R

R. — River

ra. — range
Rec., Recr. — Recreation, Recreational
reg. — region
Rep. — Republic
res. — reservoir
Res. — Reservation, Reserve
R.I. — Rhode Island
riv. — river
Rom. — Romania

S

S. — South
sa. — sierra, serra
S. Afr., S. Africa — South Africa
salt dep. — salt deposit
salt des. — salt desert
S. Amer. — South America
São T. & Pr. — São Tomé and Príncipe
Sask. — Saskatchewan
Saudi Ar. — Saudi Arabia
S. Aust., S. Austral. — South Australia
S.C. — South Carolina
Scot. — Scotland
Sd. — Sound
S. Dak. — South Dakota
Sen. — Senegal
Seych. — Seychelles
Sing. — Singapore
S. Leone — Sierra Leone
Slvk. — Slovakia
Slvn. — Slovenia
S. Marino — San Marino
Sol. Is. — Solomon Islands
Sp. — Spanish
Spr., Sprs. — Spring, Springs
St., Ste. — Saint, Sainte
Sta. — Station
St. P. & M. — Saint Pierre and Miquelon
St. Vin. & Grens. — St. Vincent & The Grenadines
str., strs. — strait, straits
Sur. — Suriname
Swaz. — Swaziland
Switz. — Swltzerland

T

Taj. — Tajikistan
Tanz. — Tanzania
Tas. — Tasmania
Tenn. — Tennessee
terr., terrs. — territory, territories
Tex. — Texas
Thai. — Thailand
trad. — traditional
Trin. & Tob. — Trinidad and Tobago
Tun. — Tunisia
Turk. — Turkmenistan
twp. — township

U

U.A.E. — United Arab Emirates
U.K. — United Kingdom
Ukr. — Ukraine
urb. area — urban area
Urug. — Uruguay
U.S. — United States
Uzb. — Uzbekistan

V

Va. — Virginia
Ven., Venez. — Venezuela
V.I. (U.K.) — Virgin Islands (U.K.)
V.I. (U.S.) — Virgin Islands (U.S.)
Vic. — Victoria
Viet. — Vietnam
Vill. — Village
vol. — volcano
Vt. — Vermont

W

W. — West, Western
Wash. — Washington
W. Aust., W. Austral. — Western Australia
W. Indies — West Indies
Wis. — Wisconsin
W. Va. — West Virginia
Wyo. — Wyoming

Y

Yugo. — Yugoslavia
Yukon — Yukon Territory

Z

Zim. — Zimbabwe

Index to Terrain Maps

on pages X through XXXII

This index contains only names of land and ocean physical features. Names of towns, internal divisions and countries are not included. The entry name is followed by a letter-number combination which refers to the area on the map in which the name will be found. The number following the map reference for the entry refers, not to the page on which the entry will be found, but to the map plate number.

Index Continued

HAMMOND®

THE PHYSICAL WORLD

Terrain Maps of Land Forms and Ocean Floors

PHYSICAL WORLD

CONTENTS

THE WORLD ____ X-XI
EUROPE ____ XII
WESTERN EUROPE ____ XIII
ASIA ____ XIV
SOUTHWEST ASIA ____ XV
SOUTHERN ASIA ____ XVI
EAST ASIA ____ XVII
SOUTHEAST ASIA ____ XVIII
AUSTRALIA AND NEW ZEALAND ____ XIX
PACIFIC OCEAN ____ XX-XXI
AFRICA ____ XXII
NORTHERN AFRICA ____ XXIII
SOUTHERN AFRICA ____ XXIV
SOUTH AMERICA ____ XXV
NORTHERN SOUTH AMERICA ____ XXVI
SOUTHERN SOUTH AMERICA ____ XXVII
NORTH AMERICA ____ XXVIII
CANADA ____ XXIX
UNITED STATES ____ XXX-XXXI
MIDDLE AMERICA ____ XXXII

RELIEF MODELS BY ERNST G. HOFMANN, ASSISTED BY RAFAEL MARTINEZ

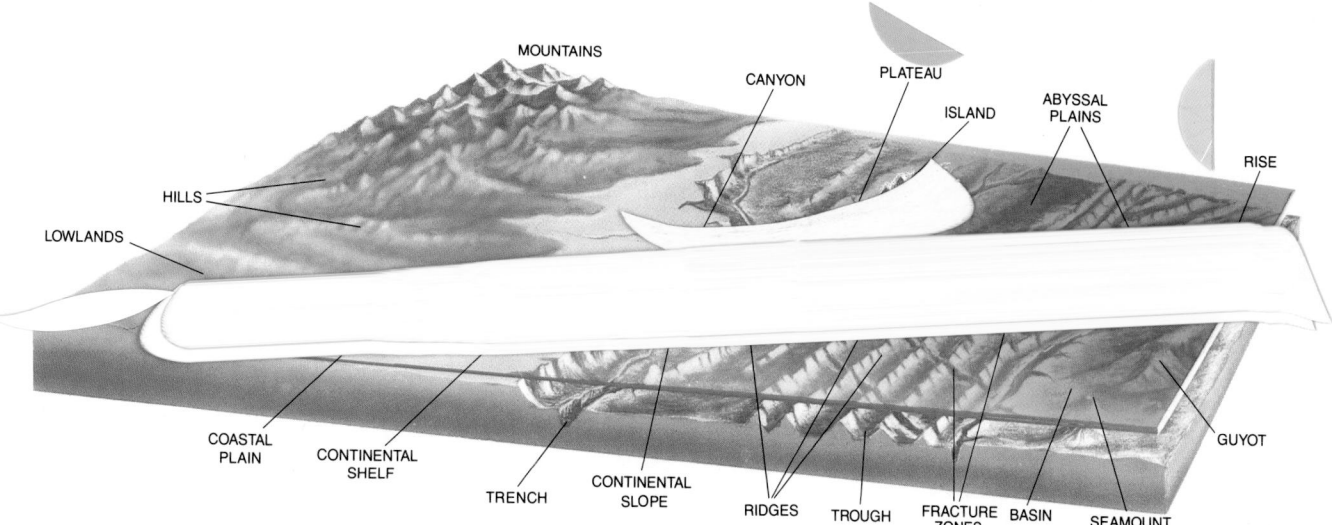

The oblique view diagram above is designed to provide a detailed view of the ocean floor as if seen through the depth of the sea. Graduating blue tones are used to contrast ocean floor depths: from light blue to represent shallow continental shelves to dark blues in the greater depths. Land relief is shown in conventional hypsometric tints.

In this dramatic collection of topographic maps of continents, oceans and major regions of the world, Hammond introduces a revolutionary new technique in cartography.

While most maps depicting terrain are created from painted artwork that is then photographed, Hammond now premiers the use of a remarkable sculptured model mapping technique created by one of our master cartographers.

The process begins with the sculpting of large scale three-dimensional models. Once physical details have been etched on the models and refinements completed, relief work is checked for accurate elevation based on a vertical scale exaggerated for visual effect.

Finished models are airbrushed and painted, then photographed using a single northwesterly light source to achieve a striking three-dimensional effect. The result is the dynamic presentation of mountain ranges and peaks on land, and canyons, trenches and seamounts on the ocean floor. Never before have maps conveyed such rich beauty while providing a realistic representation of the world as we know it.

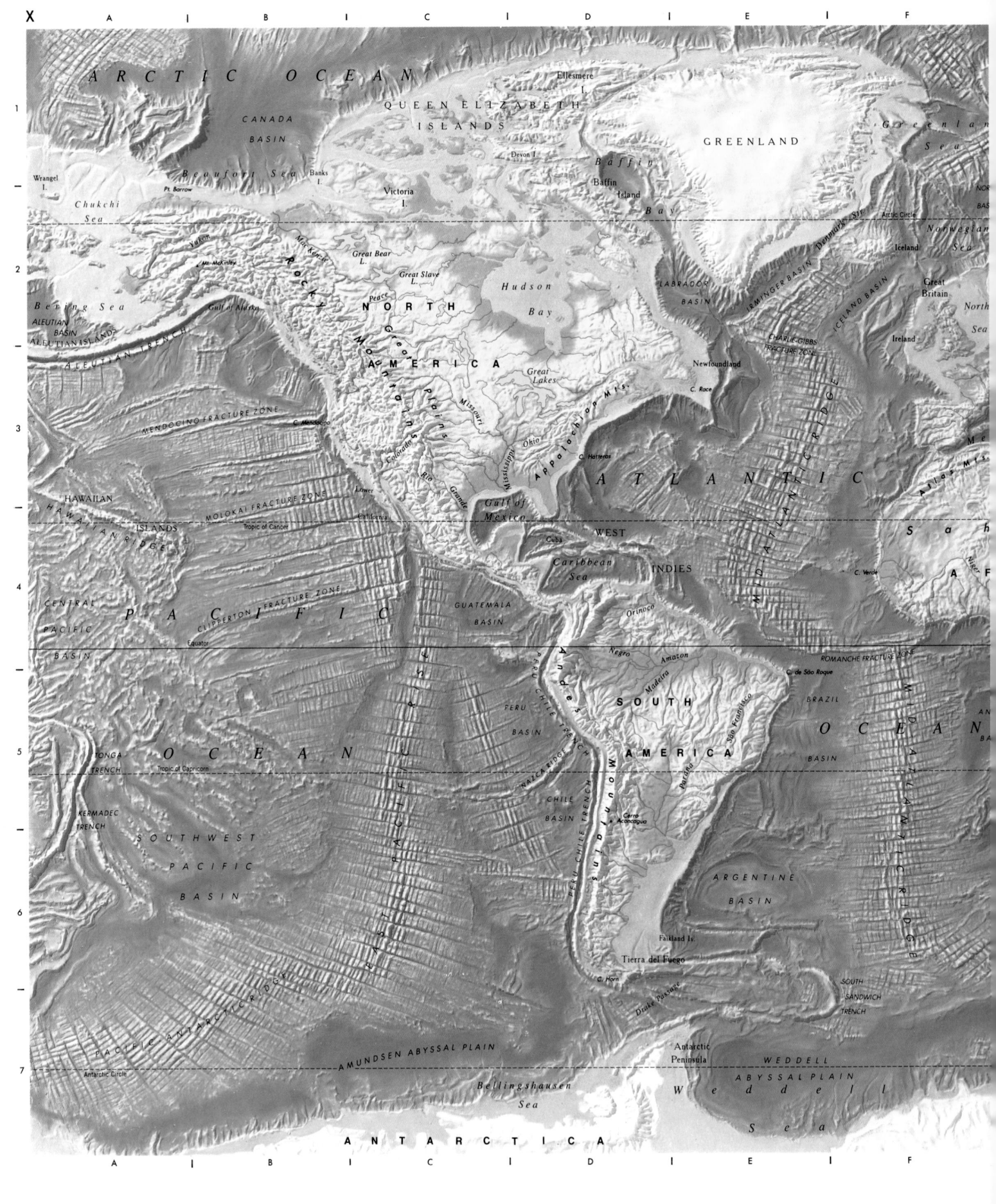

ARCTIC   OCEAN

FRANZ JOSEF LAND   SEVERNAYA
                          ZEMLYA

SVALBARD   NEW SIBERIAN IS.

        Novaya
        Zemlya   Laptev
Nordkapp   Kara   Sea   Wrangel
    Barents   Sea   I.
    Sea   —

                                    S i b e r i a

Kölen   2
        L.
        Ladoga   Yenisey   Lena
Baltic Sea   Ob   Aldan
                                    Angara
                        Irtysh   Kamchatka   Bering Sea
E U R O P E   A S I A   L. Baykal   Pen.   ALEUTIAN
        Dnieper   Volga   Sea   BASIN
Rhine   of   ALEUTIAN ISLANDS
Danube   Black Sea   Caspian Sea   Okhotsk
                    Aral   Amur   Sakhalin   ALEUTIAN TRENCH
diterranean Sea   Sea   L.   Gobi   3
                        Balkhash   NORTHWEST
                                                    Sea of   KURIL-KAMCHATKA TRENCH
                    Kunlun   Honshu Japan   PACIFIC
                    Euphrates   East   JAPAN   BASIN
R I C A   Nile   Himalaya   China   TRENCH
            Red Sea   Mt. Everest   Chang   Huang Sea
                        Ganges   PACIFIC
    Arabian   Taiwan   Tropic of Cancer
    Sea   MARIANA
    ARABIAN   Bay of   Mekong   PHILIPPINE MARIANA IS.
    BASIN   Bengal   Luzon   BASIN TRENCH   MARSHALL IS. CENTRAL
            C. Comorin   South   Challenger   PACIFIC
    CARLSBERG   China   Deep   BASIN
    RIDGE   Ceylon   Sea   Mindanao
SOMALI   CEYLON   CAROLINE IS.   MELANESIAN   Equator
    CENTRAL   PLAIN   Borneo   New Guinea BASIN
Victoria   O C E A N   4
Congo   Kilimanjaro   BASIN   Sumatra   Java   Celebes
        INDIAN   JAVA TRENCH
GOLA   Zambezi   RIDGE   N D I A N   Coral
                    Madagascar   Sea   Fiji Is.
SIN   —

        NINETYEAST RIDGE   O C E A N   AUSTRALIA   Tropic of Capricorn
WALVIS RIDGE   BROKEN   North Cape 5
    Orange   PLATEAU
CAPE   C. of Good Hope   SOUTHWEST INDIAN RIDGE C. Leeuwin   Tasman   North I.
BASIN   SOUTHEAST INDIAN RIDGE   S. AUSTRALIA BASIN Sea
AGULHAS RIDGE   Great Barrier Reef   South I.
                                                              Tasmania
                    KERGUELEN   6
                    PLATEAU   SOUTHEAST INDIAN RIDGE

    ENDERBY ABYSSAL PLAIN   AUSTRALIAN-ANTARCTIC BASIN

                                                              Antarctic Circle   7
        Amery
        Ice Shelf   C. Adare
A N T A R C T I C A   Ross Sea
                © Copyright 1987 by HAMMOND INCORPORATED, Maplewood, N.J.

LEGEND FOR TERRAIN MAPS

International Boundaries   —·—   Mountain Peaks   ▴
State and Provincial Boundaries   —··—   National Capitals   ⊛
Other Boundaries   ----   Other Capitals   ⊙
Boundaries Along Rivers   ⌇   Canals

World | **Plate 1**

Plate 2 | Europe

GREENLAND (Den.)
DENMARK STRAIT
IRMINGER BASIN
REYKJANES RIDGE
KOLBEINSEY RIDGE
JAN MAYEN RIDGE
AEGIR RIDGE
NORWEGIAN BASIN
VORING PLATEAU
ICELAND
Reykjavík
Arctic Circle
ICELAND BASIN
ICELAND-FAEROE RISE
ROCKALL PLATEAU
ROCKALL BANK
ROCKALL TROUGH
PORCUPINE BANK
PORCUPINE ABYSSAL PLAIN
BISCAY ABYSSAL PLAIN
IBERIAN ABYSSAL PLAIN
ATLANTIC OCEAN
NORWEGIAN SEA
BARENTS SEA
Novaya Zemlya
Kolguyev I.
Cheshskaya Bay
Nordkapp
Hammerfest
Murmansk
Kola Pen.
WHITE SEA
Archangel
Northern Dvina
Vesterålen
Lofoten
Vestfjord
Kiruna
Oulu
FINLAND
Gulf of Bothnia
NORWAY
SWEDEN
Trondheim
Glittertind 8,110 ft. (2472 m.)
Bergen
Oslo
Sundsvall
Tampere
Helsinki
Lake Ladoga
Lake Onega
St. Petersburg
Gulf of Finland
Tallinn
ESTONIA
Hiiumaa
Saaremaa
Stockholm
Vänern
Göteborg
Gotland
Skagerrak
Kattegat
Lindesnes
Shetland Is.
Orkney Is.
Faroe Is.
Hebrides
Ben Nevis 4,406 ft. (1343 m.)
Aberdeen
Glasgow
UNITED KINGDOM
Great Britain
NORTH SEA
DENMARK
Copenhagen
BALTIC SEA
Bornholm
Rügen
Riga
LATVIA
LITHUANIA
Vilnius
Minsk
BELARUS
RUSSIA
Gdańsk
IRELAND
Dublin
IRISH SEA
Liverpool
Birmingham
London
St. George's Chan.
CELTIC SHELF
Land's End
English Channel
Channel Is. (U.K.)
Frisian Is.
NETHERLANDS
Amsterdam
Hamburg
Elbe
Berlin
GERMANY
POLAND
Vistula
Łódź
Oder
BELGIUM
Brussels
Cologne
Bonn
LUX.
Leipzig
Prague
CZECH REP.
Le Havre
Seine
Paris
Loire
Nantes
FRANCE
Bay of Biscay
Bordeaux
Dordogne
Garonne
Lyon
Rhône
Stuttgart
Munich
SWITZ.
Bern
Mt. Blanc 15,771 ft. (4807 m.)
Milan
Turin
Vienna
AUSTRIA
Graz
Brno
SLOVAKIA
Cracow
Budapest
HUNGARY
Cluj-Napoca
Carpathian Mts.
Lviv
Bug
Kiev
Dnieper
Khar'kov
UKRAINE
Donetsk
Odessa
Dnestr
MOLDOVA
Prut
ROMANIA
Bucharest
Danube
SLOV.
Zagreb
CROATIA
Sava
BOS. & HERZ.
Belgrade
YUGOSLAVIA
Balkan Mts.
Sofia
BULGARIA
Skopje
MAC.
Tirane
ALBANIA
GREECE
Thessaloniki
Dardanelles
AEGEAN SEA
Athens
Crete
Istanbul
Bosporus
Sea of Marmara
Izmir
Ankara
TURKEY
Moscow
RUSSIA
Nizhniy Novgorod
Volga
Kazan'
Kuybyshev Res.
Samara
Perm'
Kama
Yekaterinburg
Chelyabinsk
Ural Mountains
Narodnaya 6,214 ft. (1894 m.)
Pechora
Ob'
Irtysh
Ishim
Tobol
Ural
KAZAKHSTAN
ARAL SEA
UZBEK.
TURKMENISTAN
Volgograd
Don
Tsimlyansk Res.
Astrakhan'
CASPIAN SEA
SEA OF AZOV
Crimea
Krasnodar
BLACK SEA
Caucasus
El'brus 18,510 ft. (5642 m.)
GEORGIA
Tbilisi
ARMENIA
AZERBAIJAN
Baku
Araks
Ararat 16,946 ft. (5165 m.)
L. Urmia
L. Van
Tehran
IRAN
Tigris
Euphrates
IRAQ
Baghdad
SYRIA
LEBANON
Beirut
Damascus
CYPRUS
Nicosia
Rhodes
PORTUGAL
Porto
Lisbon
C. de São Vicente
SPAIN
Madrid
Douro
Tagus
Guadiana
Ebro
Bilbao
Zaragoza
Valencia
Pyrenees
ANDORRA
Barcelona
Gulf of Lions
Marseille
MONACO
Cádiz
Málaga
GIBRALTAR (U.K.)
Str. of Gibraltar
Tangier
Rabat
Casablanca
MOROCCO
Oran
Algiers
ALGERIA
Balearic Is.
Majorca
Minorca
Ibiza
ALGERIAN PLAIN
Corsica
Sardinia
C. Teulada
Tunis
TUNISIA
AFRICA
MEDITERRANEAN SEA
ITALY
Apennines
Venice
SAN MARINO
ADRIATIC SEA
VATICAN CITY
Rome
Naples
TYRRHENIAN SEA
TYRRHENIAN BASIN
Palermo
Sicily
Etna 11,053 ft. (3369 m.)
C. Passero
MALTA
Valletta
IONIAN SEA
IONIAN BASIN
C. Tainaron
© Copyright by HAMMOND INCORPORATED, Maplewood, N.J.
0 100 200 300 400 500 MILES
0 100 200 300 400 500 KILOMETERS

© Copyright by HAMMOND INCORPORATED, Maplewood, N.J.

Plate 4 | **Asia**

© Copyright by HAMMOND INCORPORATED, Maplewood, N.J.

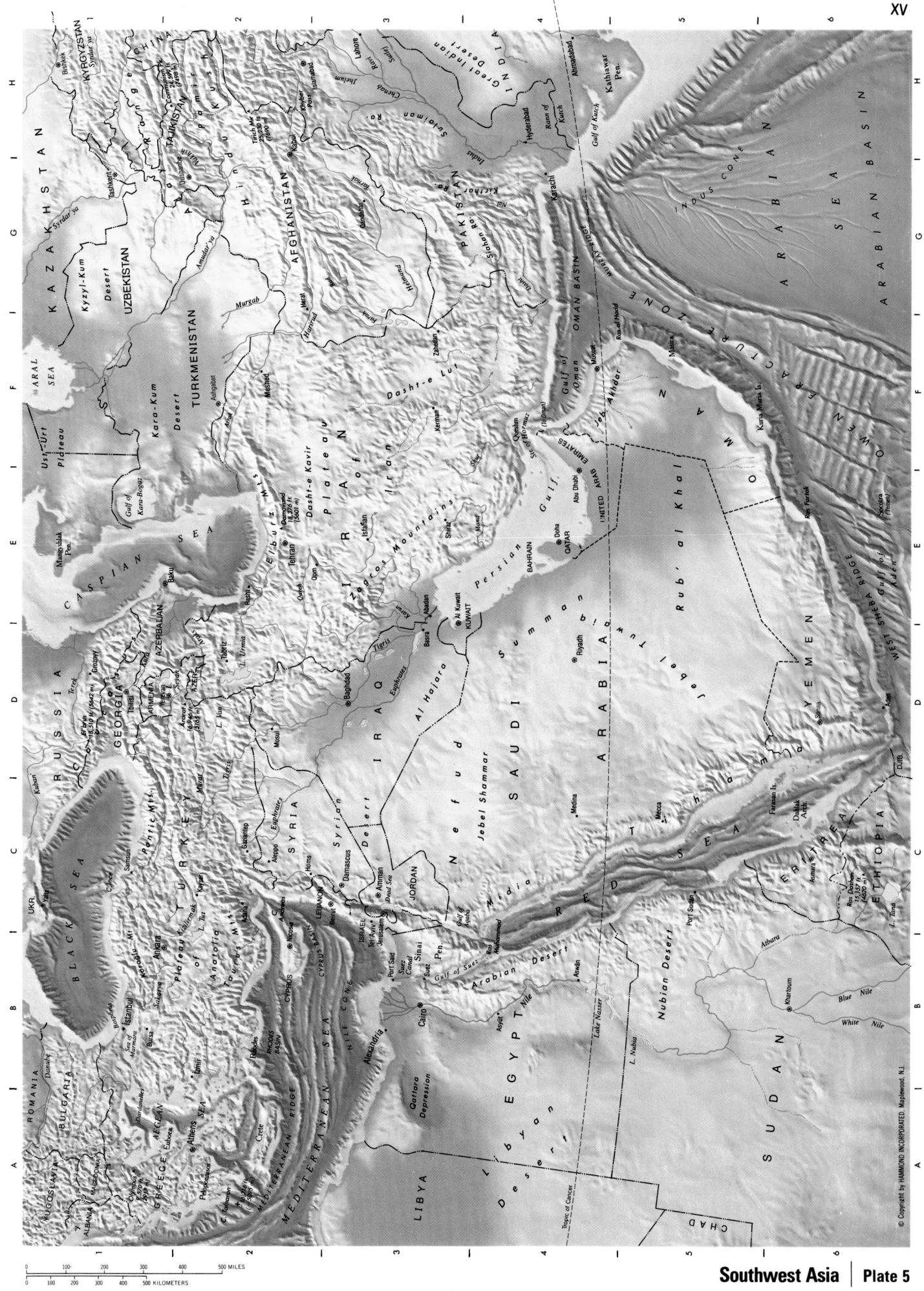

Southwest Asia | Plate 5

0   100   200   300   400   500 MILES

0 100 200 300 400 500 KILOMETERS

KAZAKHSTAN

KYRGYZSTAN
Bishkek ⊛
Syrdar'ya

CHINA

UZBEKISTAN
Tashkent ⊛
Kyzyl-Kum
Desert

Amudar'ya

TAJIKISTAN
Kara Range
Hindu Kush
Communism Pk.
24,590 ft. (7495 m)

Khyber
Pass

Great Indian
Desert

Lahore

Jhelum
Chenab
Sutlej
Ravi

Ahmadabad ⊛

Kathiawar
Pen.

Gulf of
Kutch

ARAL
SEA

Ust-Urt
Plateau

Mangyshlak
Pen.

Gulf of
Kara-Bogaz

Kara-Kum
Desert

TURKMENISTAN
Ashgabat ⊛

Murgab

Herat

Harirud

AFGHANISTAN
Kabul ⊛

Tirich Mir
25,230 ft. (7690 m)

Kunduz

Helmand

Kandahar

Quetta

PAKISTAN

Sulaiman Ra.

Indus

Kirthar Ra.

Sijahn Ra.

Karachi ⊛

Rann of
Kutch

Hyderabad ⊛

ARABIAN
SEA

INDUS CONE

ARABIAN
BASIN

OWEN
FRACTURE
ZONE

CASPIAN
SEA

Baku ⊛

Rasht

Elburz Mts.
Tehran ⊛

IRAN

Dasht-e Kavir

Dasht-e Lut

Plateau of Iran

Demovand
18,376 ft. (5601 m)

Mashed ⊛

Ahvaz

Zahedan ⊛

Kerman ⊛

Qeshm I.
(Tidman)

MURRAY RIDGE

OMAN BASIN

Gulf of Oman

Str. of Hormuz

Muscat ⊛

Ras al Hadd

Matrah

Kuria Muria Is.

OMAN

Jeb. Akhdar

Ras Fartak

Socotra
(Yemen)

Gulf of Aden

WEST SHEBA RIDGE

RUSSIA

Kuban

Terek

Mt. Elbrus
18,510 ft. (5642 m)

GEORGIA
Tbilisi ⊛

Kura

ARMENIA
Yerevan ⊛

Ararat
16,946 ft.
(5165 m)

AZERBAIJAN

AZER.

L. Van

L. Urmia

Tabriz ⊛

Qom

Isfahan ⊛

Shiraz ⊛

Mand

Persian
Gulf

BAHRAIN
Doha ⊛
QATAR

Abu Dhabi ⊛
UNITED ARAB
EMIRATES

Summan

Tuwaiq

Rub' al Khali

YEMEN

Sanaa ⊛

Aden ⊛

DJIB.

Tigris

Mosul

Euphrates

Baghdad ⊛

IRAQ

Kirkuk

Al Kuwait ⊛
KUWAIT

Basra

Abadan

Al Hajara

Riyadh ⊛

SAUDI ARABIA

Jebel Shammar

Nefud

Medina ⊛

Mecca ⊛

RED
SEA

Farasan Is.

Dahlak
Arch.

Ras Dashan
15,157 ft.
(4620 m)

Asmara ⊛

ERITREA

ETHIOPIA

L. Tana

Blue Nile

Khartoum ⊛

White Nile

Atbara

Nubian
Desert

SUDAN

UKR.

BLACK SEA

Yalta

Pontic Mts.

Samsun

Sinop

TURKEY
Ankara ⊛

Kizilirmak

Kayseri

Adana

Plateau of Anatolia

Taurus Mts.

Gaziantep

Aleppo ⊛

SYRIA

Homs
Damascus ⊛

Syrian
Desert

LEBANON
Beirut ⊛

ISRAEL
Tel-Aviv ⊛
Jerusalem ⊛

Amman ⊛
JORDAN

Dead Sea

Gulf of
Aqaba

Sinai
Pen.

Ras
Muhammad

Midian

Port Sudan ⊛

Arabian Desert

ROMANIA

BULGARIA

Danube

Istanbul ⊛

Bosporus

Sea of Marmara

Bursa

Dardanelles

Izmir ⊛

MEDITERRANEAN RIDGE

NILE CONE

CYPRUS
BASIN

CYPRUS

Nicosia ⊛

RHODES BASIN

Rhodes

Crete

AEGEAN SEA

Euboea

GREECE
Athens ⊛

C. Matapan

C. Krio

YUGOSLAVIA

MACEDONIA
ALBANIA

C. Tainaron

Peloponnesus

MEDITERRANEAN
SEA

Port Said

Suez Canal

Suez

Gulf of Suez

Alexandria ⊛

Cairo ⊛

Qattara
Depression

LIBYA

EGYPT

Nile

Asyut

Aswan ⊛

Lake Nasser

L. Nubia

Libyan Desert

Tropic of Cancer

CHAD

XVI

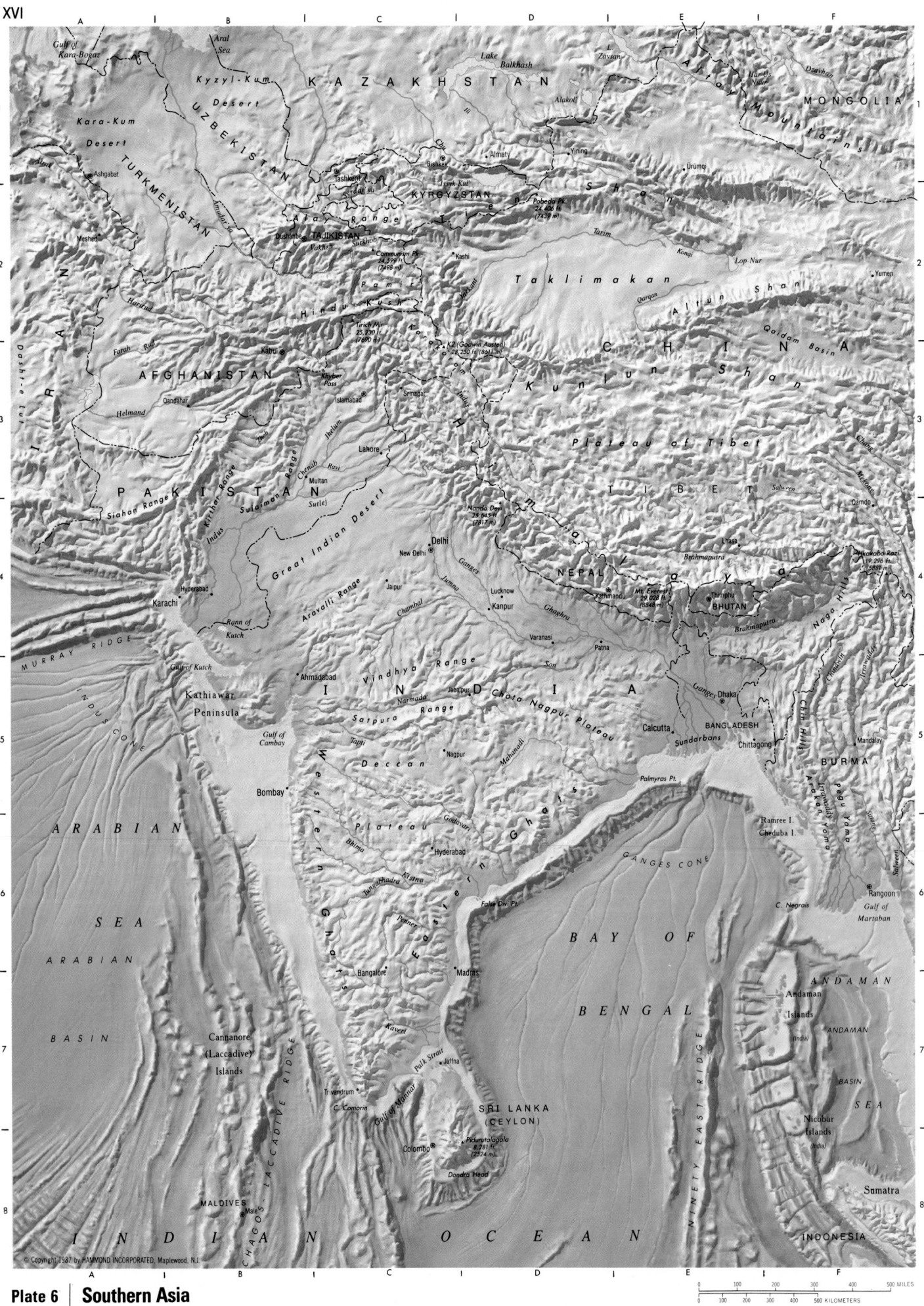

© Copyright 1987 by HAMMOND INCORPORATED, Maplewood, N.J.

Plate 6 | Southern Asia

0   100   200   300   400   500 MILES
0 100 200 300 400 500 KILOMETERS

East Asia | Plate 7

RUSSIA
KAZAKHSTAN
Semipalatinsk
Lake Balkhash
Zaysan
Alakol
Almaty
Bishkek
Issyk Kul
KYRGYZSTAN
Communism Peak 24,599 ft. (7498m.)
Pobeda Peak 24,406 ft. (7439m.)
Yining
Urumqi
Kashi
Pamir
TAJIKISTAN
PAK.
K2 (Godwin Austen) 28,250 ft. (8611m.)
Srinagar
Tian Shan
Tarim
Taklimakan
Lop Nur
Qarqan
Altun Shan
Kunlun Shan
Qaidam Basin
Qinghai Hu
Plateau of Tibet
TIBET
Himalaya
Lhasa
NEPAL
Kathmandu
Mt. Everest 29,028 ft. (8848m.)
Thimphu
BHUTAN
Brahmaputra
INDIA
Delhi
New Delhi
Kanpur
Patna
Ganges
Jumna
Jabalpur
Eastern Ghats
BANGLADESH
Dhaka
Calcutta
Chittagong
GANGES CONE
BAY OF BENGAL
C. Negrais
Rangoon
ANDAMAN SEA
Andaman Is. (India)
BURMA
Shan Plateau
Mandalay
Irrawaddy
Hkakabo Razi 19,296 ft. (5881m.)
Qamdo
Salween
Mekong
Chang
Yalong
Gongga Shan 24,790 ft. (7556m.)
Chengdu
Chongqing
Kunming
Guiyang
Nanning
Hanoi
Haiphong
Gulf of Tonkin
Hainan
Leizhou Bandao
LAOS
Vientiane
Korat Plateau
THAILAND
Bangkok
CAMBODIA
VIETNAM
DaNang
Irkutsk
Lake Baykal
Chita
Hovsgol Nuur
Uvs Nuur
Altay Mountains
Selenge
Orhon
Ulaanbaatar
MONGOLIA
Kerulen
Gobi
Hulun Nur
Da Hinggan Ling
Yumen
Lanzhou
Huang
Ordos
Baotou
CHINA
Xi'an
Wei
Taiyuan
Beijing
Tianjin
Jinan
Zhengzhou
Xuzhou
Hongze Hu
Huai
Nanjing
Shanghai
Wuhan
Han
Nanchang
Poyang Hu
Changsha
Fuzhou
Xiamen
Guangzhou
HONG KONG
Macau (Port.)
Blagoveshchensk
Amur
Khabarovsk
Qiqihar
Harbin
Changchun
Vladivostok
Shenyang
Anshan
NORTH KOREA
P'yongyang
Korea Bay
Dalian
Bo Hai
Seoul
SOUTH KOREA
Shandong Bandao
Qingdao
YELLOW SEA
Pusan
Korea Strait
Cheju
EAST CHINA SEA
Sakhalin
KURIL BASIN
La Perouse Str.
Hokkaido
Sapporo
JAPAN BASIN
SEA OF JAPAN
Honshu
Tokyo
Fuji 12,389 ft. (3776m.)
Nagoya
Osaka
Shikoku
Fukuoka
Kyushu
JAPAN TRENCH
PACIFIC OCEAN
Ryukyu Islands
Okinawa
RYUKYU TRENCH
Taipei
TAIWAN
Taiwan (Formosa)
Taiwan Strait
CONTINENTAL SHELF
SOUTH CHINA SEA
SOUTH CHINA BASIN
Babuyan Is.
C. Engaño
Luzon
PHILIPPINES
Manila
C. Bolinao
PHILIPPINE BASIN
PHILIPPINE SEA
KYUSHU-PALAU RIDGE
© Copyright 1987 by HAMMOND INCORPORATED, Maplewood, N.J.
0 100 200 300 400 500 600 MILES
0 100 200 300 400 500 600 KILOMETERS

Plate 8 | Southeast Asia

© Copyright 1987 by HAMMOND INCORPORATED Maplewood, N.J.

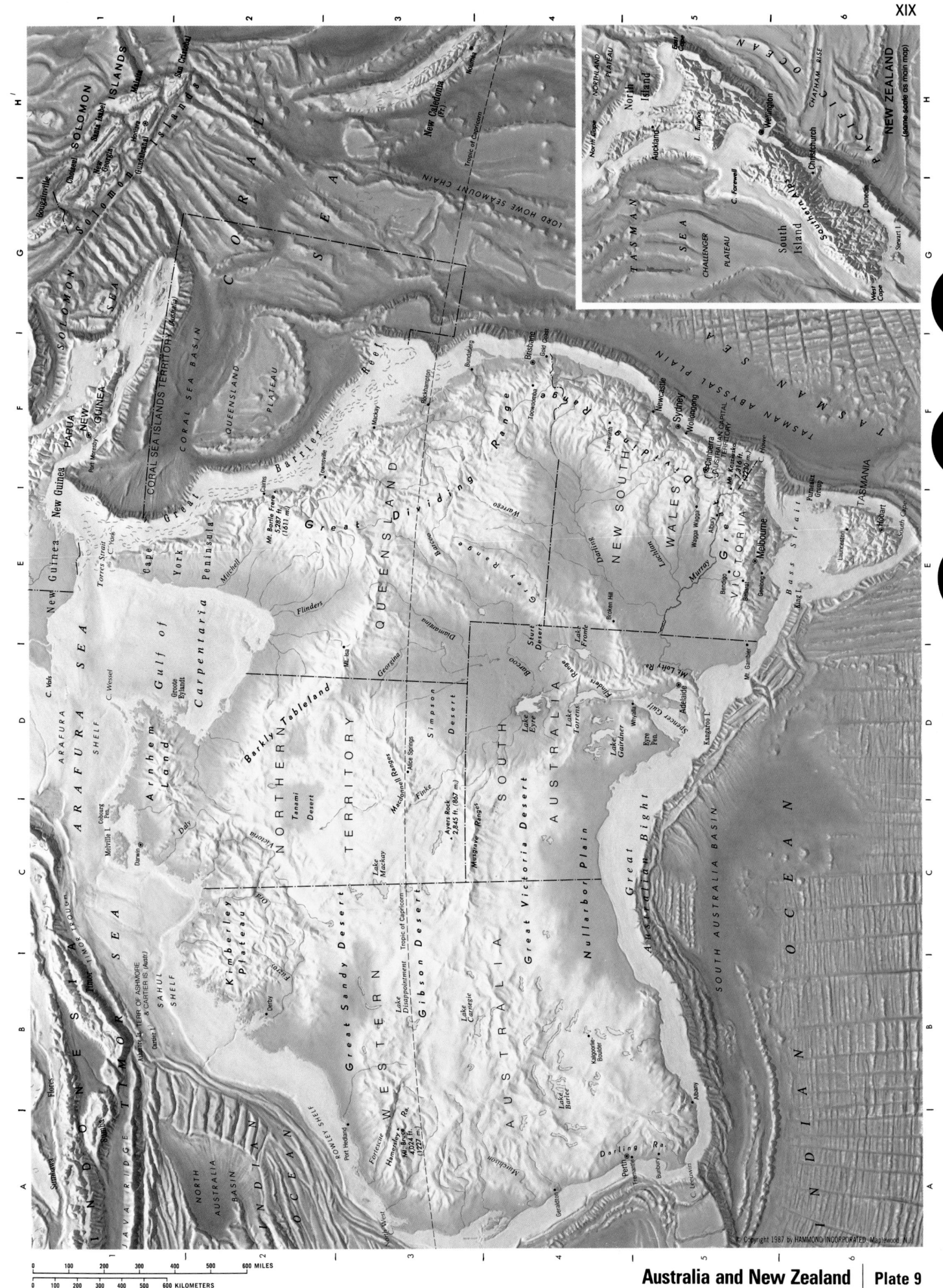

Australia and New Zealand | Plate 9

NEW ZEALAND
(same scale as main map)

SOLOMON ISLANDS

INDONESIA

PAPUA NEW GUINEA

New Guinea

ARAFURA SEA

TIMOR SEA

CORAL SEA

TASMAN SEA

New Caledonia (Fr.)

Gulf of Carpentaria

Cape York Peninsula

Arnhem Land

NORTHERN TERRITORY

QUEENSLAND

WESTERN AUSTRALIA

Kimberley Plateau

Great Sandy Desert

Gibson Desert

Great Victoria Desert

Tanami Desert

Simpson Desert

SOUTH AUSTRALIA

Nullarbor Plain

Great Australian Bight

Great Dividing Range

NEW SOUTH WALES

VICTORIA

TASMANIA

INDIAN OCEAN

PACIFIC OCEAN

Ayers Rock 2,845 ft. (867 m.)

Alice Springs

Darwin

Perth

Adelaide

Melbourne

Sydney

Canberra

Brisbane

Barkly Tableland

Tropic of Capricorn

North Island

South Island

Southern Alps

Wellington

Auckland

Christchurch

Dunedin

© Copyright 1987 by HAMMOND INCORPORATED, Maplewood, N.J.

0 100 200 300 400 500 600 MILES

0 100 200 300 400 500 600 KILOMETERS

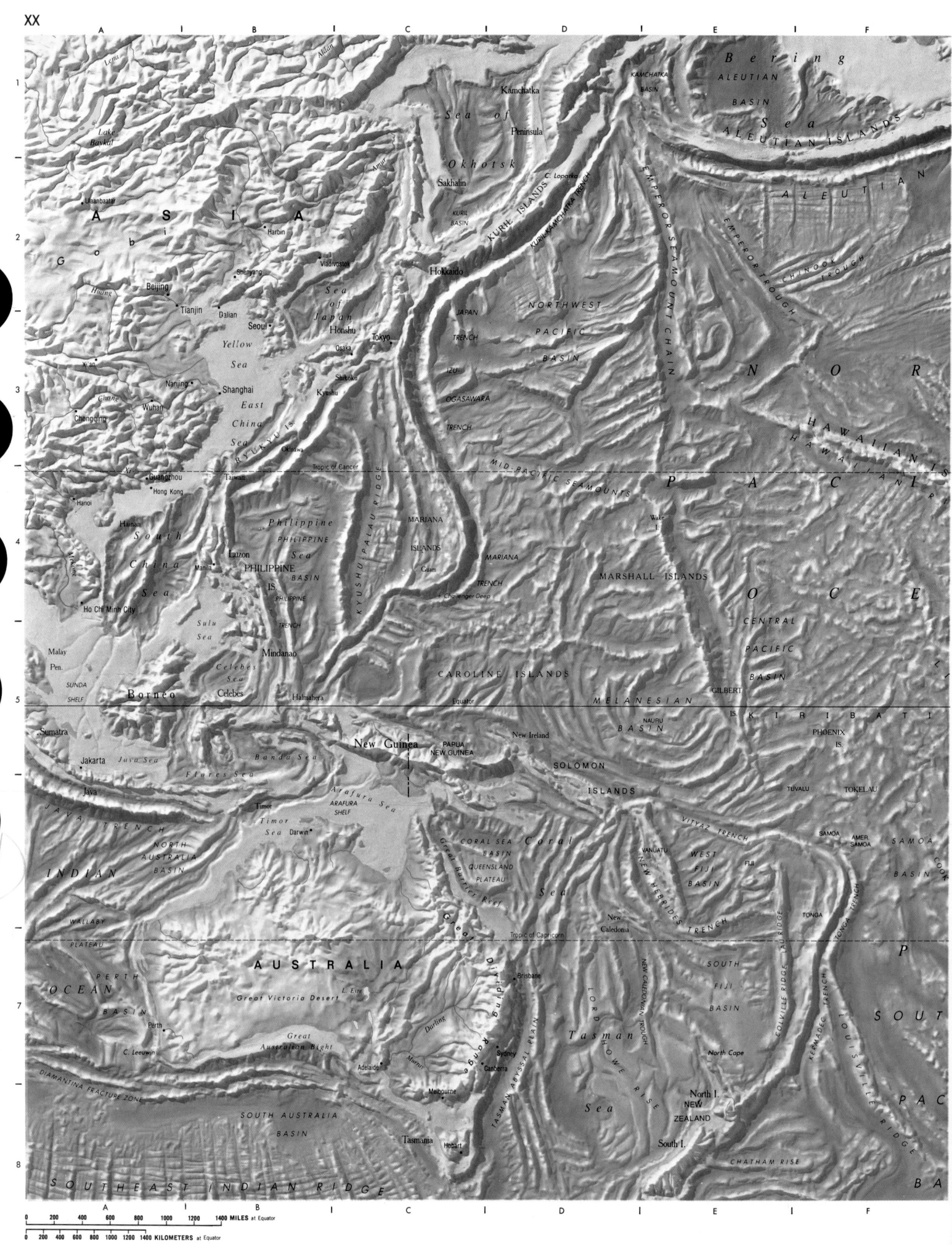

A   A   B   B   C   C   D   D   E   E   F   F

Lena

Aldan

Bering

1

ALEUTIAN

BASIN

KAMCHATKA

Lake Baykal

Sea of

Kamchatka

Sea

ALEUTIAN ISLANDS

Okhotsk

Peninsula

A   S   I   A

ALEUTIAN

• Ulaanbaatar

Sakhalin

C. Lopatka

G   o   b   i

KURIL-KAMCHATKA TRENCH

CHINOOK

EMPEROR SEAMOUNT CHAIN

EMPEROR TROUGH

TROUGH

2

• Harbin

KURIL

BASIN

Huang

• Beijing

• Shenyang

Vladivostok •

Hokkaido

NORTHWEST

N O R

• Tianjin

Dalian •

Sea of

JAPAN

PACIFIC

Seoul •

Japan

TRENCH

• Xi'an

Yellow

Honshu

Osaka

BASIN

Sea

Tokyo

Chang

Nanjing •

• Shanghai

Shikoke

IZU

3

Chongqing •

• Wuhan

East

Kyushu

HAWAIIAN IS.

China

OGASAWARA

HAWAIIAN RI

RYUKYU IS.

Sea

TRENCH

Xi •

• Guangzhou

Okinawa

Tropic of Cancer

MID-PACIFIC SEAMOUNTS

P   A   C

• Hanoi

Taiwan

Hong Kong •

MARIANA

Philippine

KYUSHU PALAU RIDGE

Wake

Hainan

PHILIPPINE

ISLANDS

I.

4

South

Sea

• Manila

China

Luzon

MARIANA

MARSHALL ISLANDS

O   C   E

PHILIPPINE

Mekong

IS.

Guam

• Ho Chi Minh City

Sea

PHILIPPINE

BASIN

TRENCH

CENTRAL

+ Challenger Deep

Sulu

TRENCH

Mindanao •

PACIFIC

Sea

Malay

GILBERT

BASIN

Pen.

Celebes

SUNDA

Sea

Halmahera

CAROLINE ISLANDS

5

SHELF

Borneo

Celebes •

Equator

MELANESIAN

IS.

K I R I B A T I

NAURU

• Sumatra

BASIN

PHOENIX

• Jakarta

Java Sea

Banda Sea

New Ireland

IS.

New Guinea

PAPUA

Flores Sea

NEW GUINEA

SOLOMON

• Java

Arafura Sea

ISLANDS

TUVALU

TOKELAU

JAVA

ARAFURA

VITYAZ TRENCH

Timor •

SHELF

TRENCH

Timor

Darwin •

SAMOA

AMER

SAMOA

Sea

CORAL SEA

SAMOA

NORTH

BASIN

VANUATU

WEST

AUSTRALIA

QUEENSLAND

FIJI

Coral

FIJI •

BASIN

INDIAN

BASIN

PLATEAU

NEW HEBRIDES TRENCH

COOK

Sea

TONGA

BASIN

WALLABY

Great Barrier Reef

New

PLATEAU

Caledonia

Tropic of Capricorn

SOUTH

OCEAN

AUSTRALIA

FIJI

P

Brisbane •

Dividing

BASIN

PERTH

Great Victoria Desert

LORD

Tasman

SOUT

7

BASIN

L. Eyre

NEW CALEDONIAN TROUGH

HOWE

COLVILLE RIDGE

KERMADEC TRENCH

LOUISVILLE RIDGE

• Perth

Darling

Great

Range

Sea

RISE

North Cape

C. Leeuwin

Australian Bight

Sydney •

PAC

Adelaide •

Murray

Canberra •

North I.

Melbourne •

NEW

ZEALAND

DIAMANTINA FRACTURE ZONE

Tasman Abyssal Plain

South I.

SOUTH AUSTRALIA

Tasmania

Hobart •

BASIN

CHATHAM RISE

8

BA

S O U T H E A S T   I N D I A N   R I D G E

| 0 | 200 | 400 | 600 | 800 | 1000 | 1200 | 1400 MILES at Equator |

| 0 | 200 | 400 | 600 | 800 | 1000 | 1200 | 1400 KILOMETERS at Equator |

A   B   I   C   D   I   E   F

G H I H I J I K I L I M

Gulf of Alaska

Alaska
Pen.
Kodiak I.

Juneau

Coast Mountains

Fraser

Vancouver
Vancouver
Seattle
Columbia
Snake

ROCKY Mountains

Edmonton
Calgary

S. Saskatchewan

Regina

Missouri

Winnipeg

Coast Ranges

C. Mendocino

San Francisco

Salt Lake City

Colorado

Los Angeles
San Diego

Lower

California

Phoenix

HUDSON Bay

Churchill

Nelson

NORTH

Lake
Winnipeg

Minneapolis

Thunder Bay

Great
Lakes

St. Lawrence

Ottawa
Montréal
Toronto
Boston

Detroit
New York

AMERICA

Chicago

Denver
St. Louis
Washington

Platte

Missouri
Ohio

Appalachian Mts.

C. Hatteras

Dallas

Arkansas

Red

Tennessee

Atlanta

ATLANTIC

Mississippi

Houston
New Orleans

C. Canaveral

OCEAN

Monterrey

Gulf of
Mexico

Miami

Rio Grande

TRENCH

MENDOCINO FRACTURE ZONE

T H E

MURRAY FRACTURE ZONE

MOLOKAI FRACTURE ZONE

Tropic of Cancer

C. San
Lucas

Havana

Cuba

WEST

INDIES

P A C I F I C

RIDGE

LANDS

Hawaii

CLARION FRACTURE ZONE

CLIPPERTON FRACTURE ZONE

A N

Mexico City

Acapulco

MIDDLE AMERICA TRENCH

Caribbean Sea

GUATEMALA

BASIN

COLÓN RIDGE

Panamá

PANAMA
BASIN

Magdalena

Orinoco

Bogotá

Vaupés

NEW ISLANDS

GALÁPAGOS FRACTURE ZONE

Equator

GALÁPAGOS
ISLANDS

Guayaquil

Amazon

SOUTH

PENRHYN
BASIN

MARQUESAS FRACTURE ZONE

MARQUESAS
Is.

TIKIT

SOUTH

TUAMOTU ARCH

BASIN

SOCIETY
ISLANDS

Tahiti

EAST

BAUER
BASIN

MENDANA FRACTURE ZONE

PACIFIC RISE

PERU
BASIN

Pta.
Aguja

Lima

L. Titicaca

Andes

Marañón

AMERICA

Ucayali

Purus

PERU-CHILE TRENCH

AUSTRALIS

Pitcairn
I.

Easter I.

Tropic of Capricorn

SALA Y GOMEZ RIDGE

ROGGEVEEN
BASIN

CHALLENGER
FRACTURE ZONE

CHILE RISE

NAZCA RIDGE

CHILE
BASIN

Santiago

PERU-CHILE TRENCH

Mountains

HWEST

OCEAN

I. de Chiloé

Solado

IFIC

SIN

© Copyright 1987 by HAMMOND INCORPORATED, Maplewood, N.J.

G H I H I J I K I L I M

Pacific Ocean | Plate 10

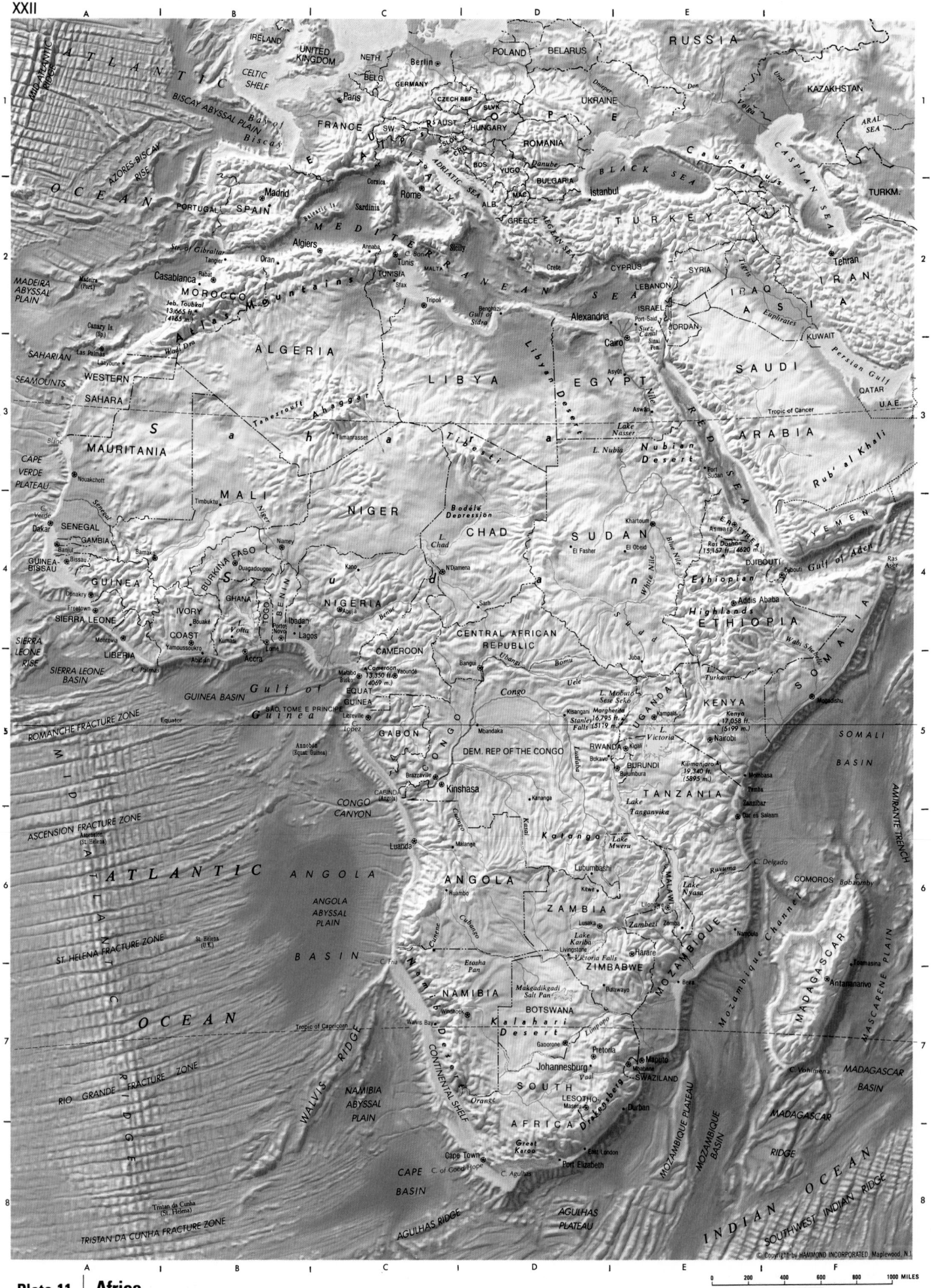

Plate 11 | Africa

© Copyright by HAMMOND INCORPORATED, Maplewood, N.J.

| 0 | 200 | 400 | 600 | 800 | 1000 MILES |

| 0 | 200 | 400 | 600 | 800 | 1000 KILOMETERS |

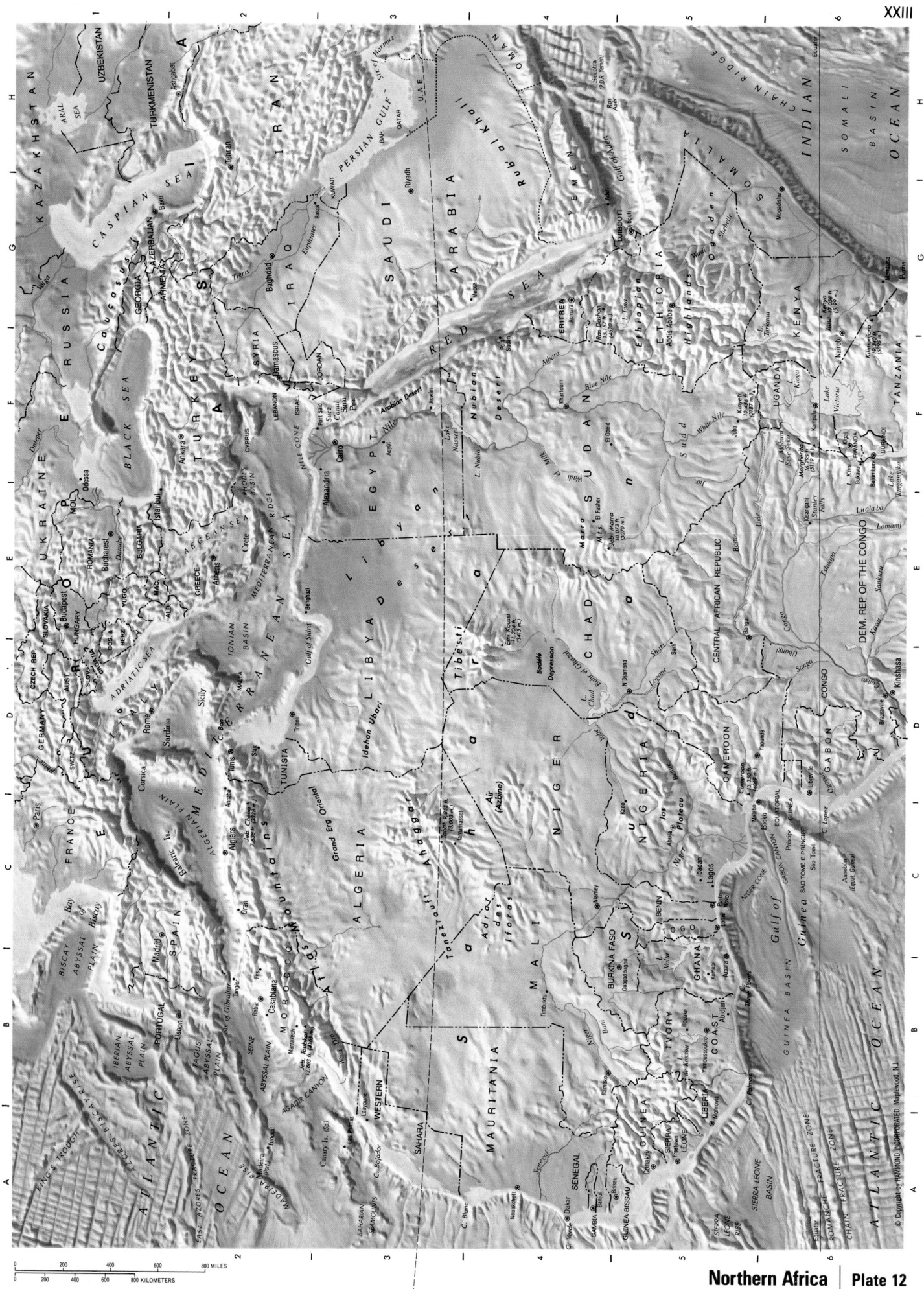

Northern Africa | Plate 12

0   200   400   600   800 MILES
0   200   400   600   800 KILOMETERS

© Copyright by HAMMOND INCORPORATED, Maplewood, N.J.

AREA 4,057,000 sq. mi.
(10,507,630 sq. km.)
POPULATION 689,000,000
LARGEST CITY Paris
HIGHEST POINT El'brus 18,510 ft.
(5,642 m.)
LOWEST POINT Caspian Sea -92 ft.
(-28 m.)

Population Distribution

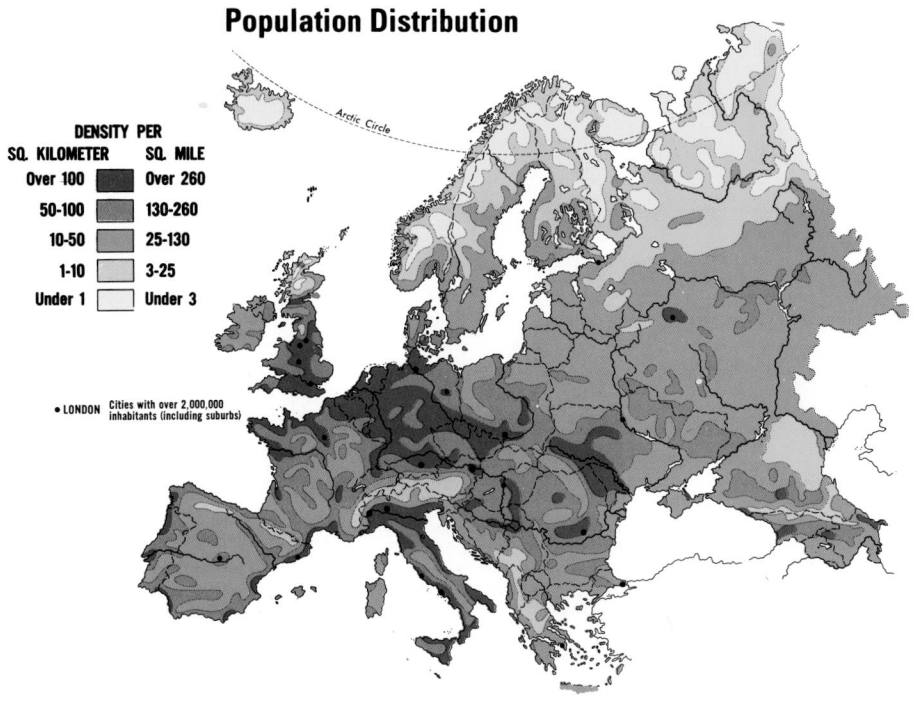

DENSITY PER	
SQ. KILOMETER	SQ. MILE
Over 100	Over 260
50-100	130-260
10-50	25-130
1-10	3-25
Under 1	Under 3

● LONDON Cities with over 2,000,000 inhabitants (including suburbs)

Vegetation

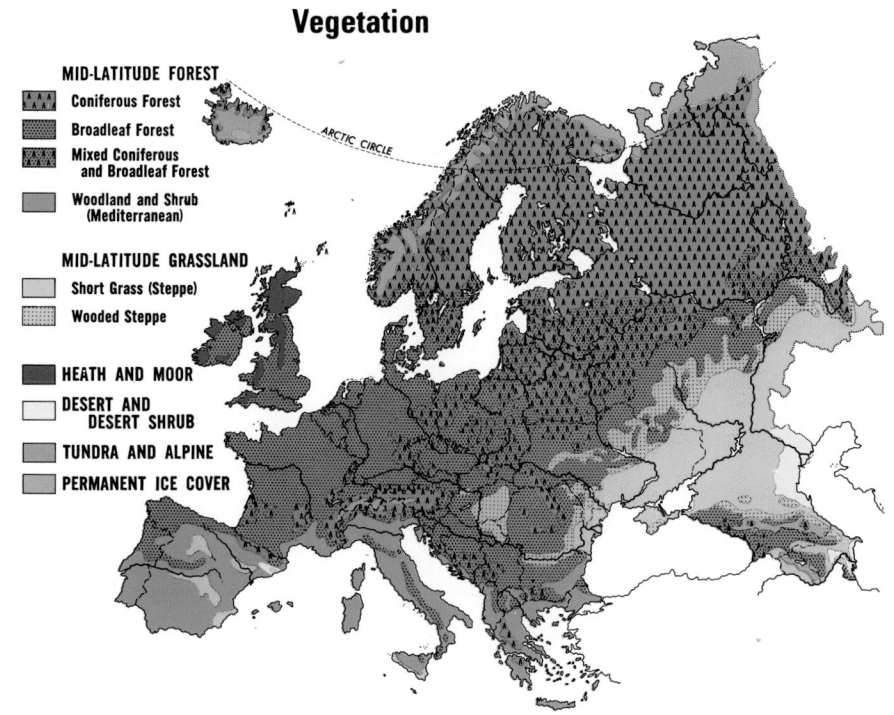

MID-LATITUDE FOREST
- Coniferous Forest
- Broadleaf Forest
- Mixed Coniferous and Broadleaf Forest
- Woodland and Shrub (Mediterranean)

MID-LATITUDE GRASSLAND
- Short Grass (Steppe)
- Wooded Steppe

HEATH AND MOOR

DESERT AND DESERT SHRUB

TUNDRA AND ALPINE

PERMANENT ICE COVER

© Copyright HAMMOND INCORPORATED, Maplewood, N.J.

Vegetation/Relief

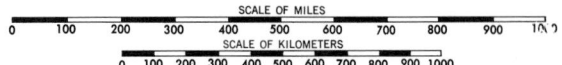

SCALE OF MILES
0   100   200   300   400   500   600   700   800   900   1000

SCALE OF KILOMETERS
0   100   200   300   400   500   600   700   800   900   1000

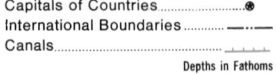

Capitals of Countries ....⊛
International Boundaries .... —··—··—
Canals .... ··········

Depths in Fathoms

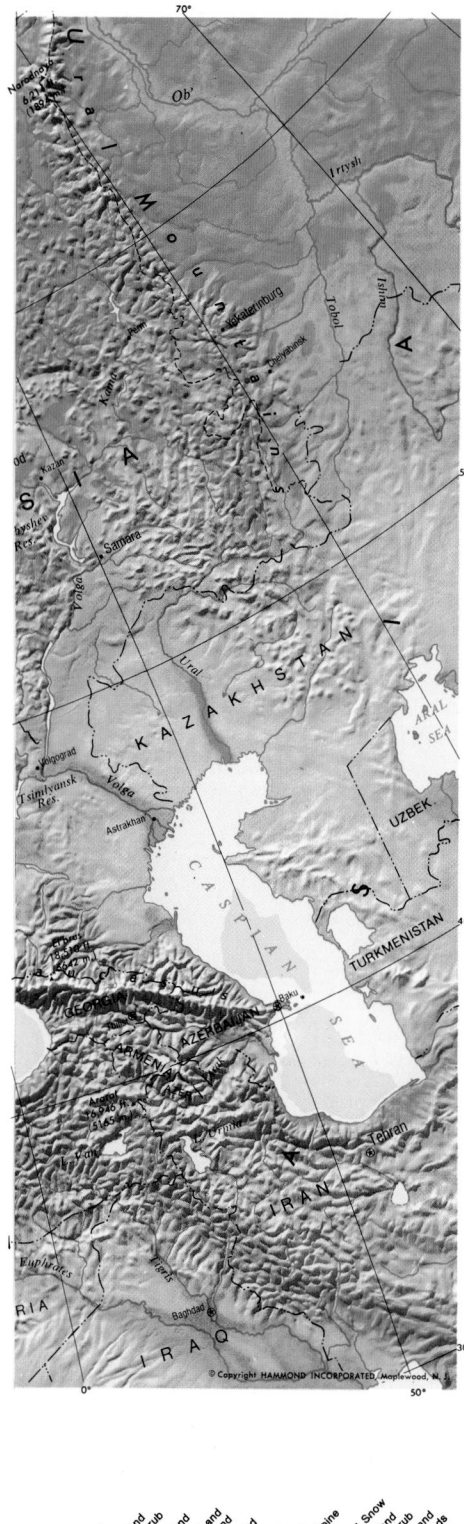

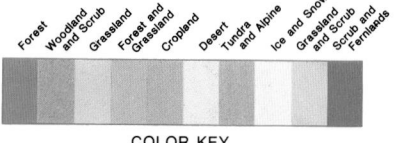

COLOR KEY

Rainfall

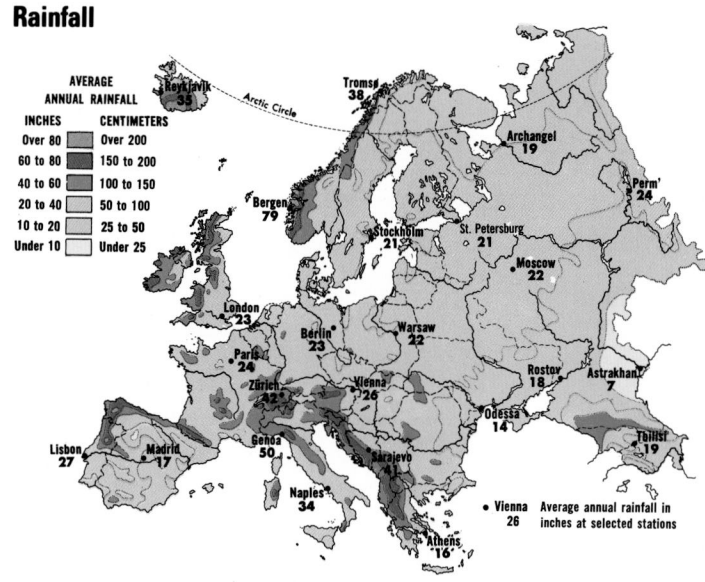

AVERAGE
ANNUAL RAINFALL

INCHES	CENTIMETERS
Over 80	Over 200
60 to 80	150 to 200
40 to 60	100 to 150
20 to 40	50 to 100
10 to 20	25 to 50
Under 10	Under 25

• Vienna   Average annual rainfall in
   26   inches at selected stations

Average January Temperature

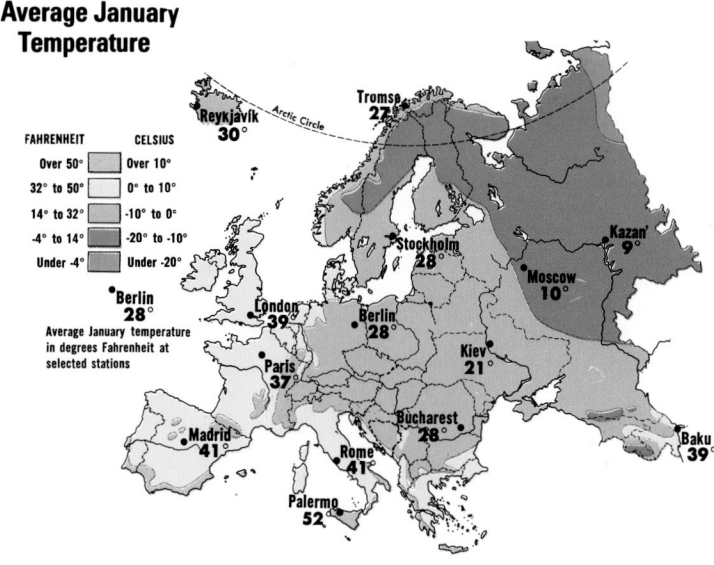

FAHRENHEIT	CELSIUS
Over 50°	Over 10°
32° to 50°	0° to 10°
14° to 32°	-10° to 0°
-4° to 14°	-20° to -10°
Under -4°	Under -20°

Berlin   Average January temperature
28°   in degrees Fahrenheit at
          selected stations

Average July Temperature

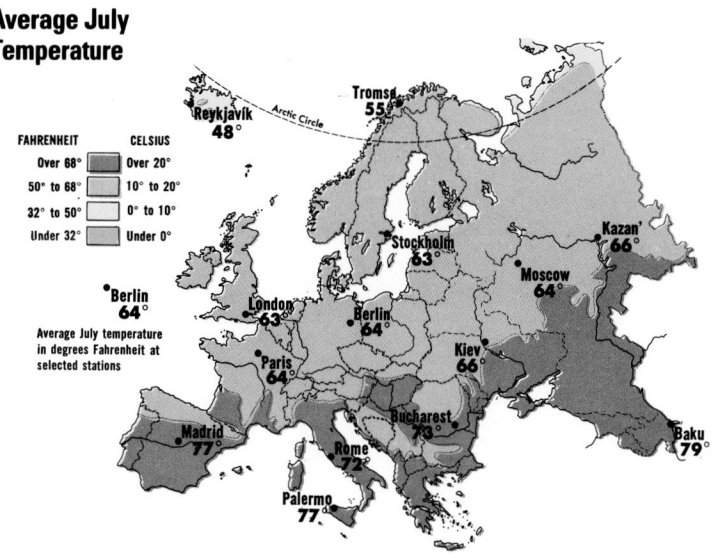

FAHRENHEIT	CELSIUS
Over 68°	Over 20°
50° to 68°	10° to 20°
32° to 50°	0° to 10°
Under 32°	Under 0°

Berlin   Average July temperature
64°   in degrees Fahrenheit at
          selected stations

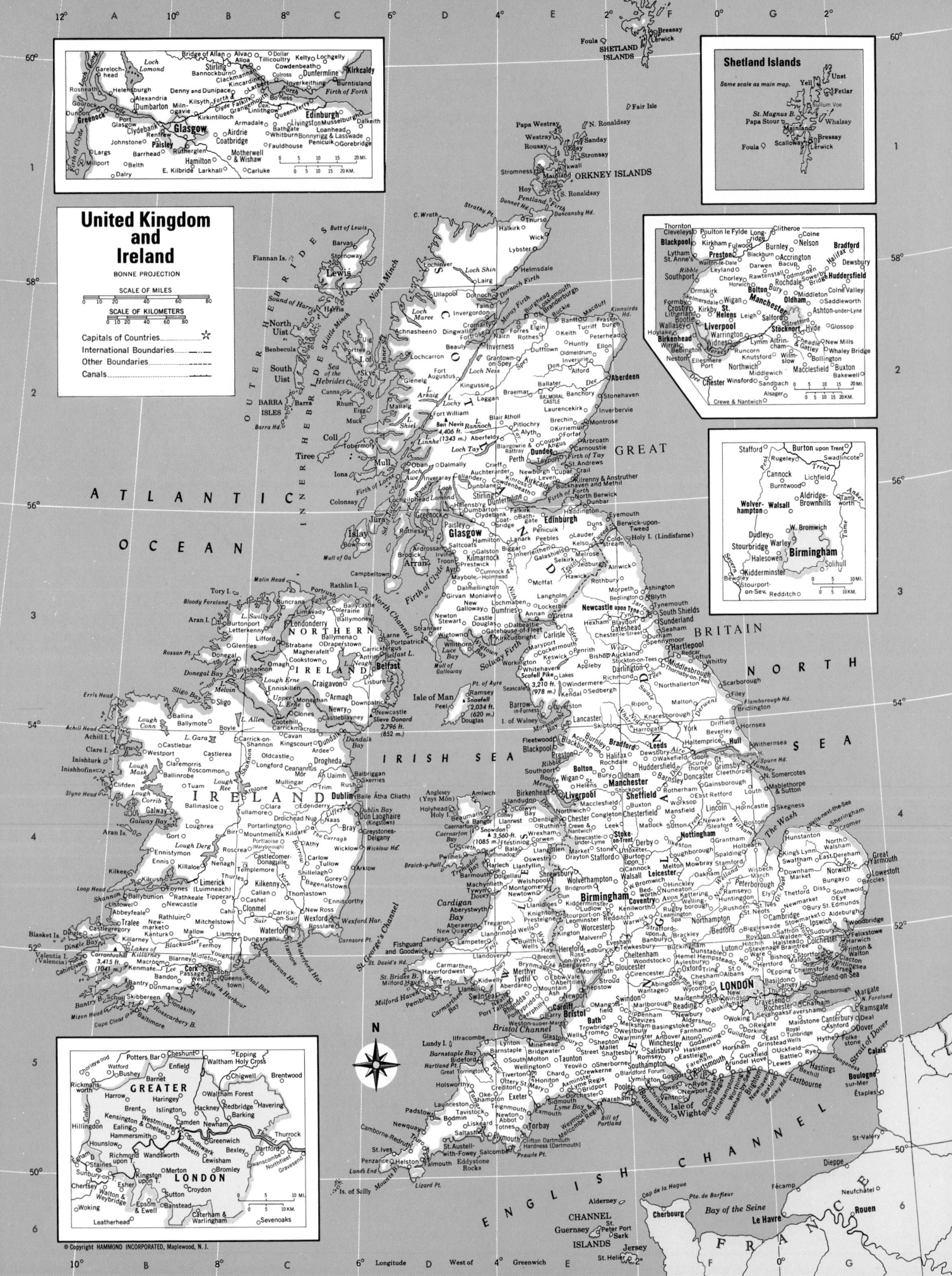

United Kingdom and Ireland

BONNE PROJECTION

SCALE OF MILES

SCALE OF KILOMETERS

Capitals of Countries............★
International Boundaries.......— · —
Other Boundaries..............— · · —
Canals

Shetland Islands

Same scale as main map.

© Copyright HAMMOND INCORPORATED, Maplewood, N.J.

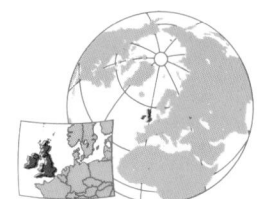

UNITED KINGDOM

AREA 94,399 sq. mi. (244,493 sq. km.)
POPULATION 57,236,000
CAPITAL London
LARGEST CITY London
HIGHEST POINT Ben Nevis 4,406 ft. (1,343 m.)
MONETARY UNIT pound sterling
MAJOR LANGUAGES English, Gaelic, Welsh
MAJOR RELIGIONS Protestantism, Roman Catholicism

IRELAND

AREA 27,136 sq. mi. (70,282 sq. km.)
POPULATION 3,540,643
CAPITAL Dublin
LARGEST CITY Dublin
HIGHEST POINT Carrantuohill 3,415 ft. (1,041 m.)
MONETARY UNIT Irish pound
MAJOR LANGUAGES English, Gaelic (Irish)
MAJOR RELIGION Roman Catholicism

ENGLAND
(map on page 13)

COUNTIES

Avon 900,947 ....E6
Bedfordshire 502,164 ....G5
Berkshire 670,859 ....F6
Buckinghamshire 562,221 ....G6
Cambridgeshire 569,893 ....G5
Cheshire 921,623 ....E4
Cleveland 565,845 ....F3
Cornwall 418,631 ....C7
Cumbria 471,696 ....D3
Derbyshire 901,831 ....F4
Devon 930,112 ....D7
Dorset 578,993 ....E7
Durham 598,881 ....F3
East Sussex 641,016 ....H6
Essex 1,416,890 ....H6
Gloucestershire 493,166 ....E5
Hampshire 1,442,598 ....F6
Hereford and Worcester 624,393 ....E5
Hertfordshire 950,760 ....G6
Humberside 843,282 ....G4
Isle of Wight 114,879 ....F7
Isles of Scilly A7
Kent 1,448,393 ....H6
Lancashire 1,362,801 ....E4
Leicestershire 835,647 ....F5
Lincolnshire 542,944 ....G4
London 6,608,598 ....H8
Manchester 2,575,407 ....H2

Merseyside 1,503,120 ....G2
Norfolk 685,232 ....H5
North Yorkshire 653,456 ....F3
Northamptonshire 524,967 ....G5
Northumberland 295,451 ....E2
Nottinghamshire 976,748 ....F4
Oxfordshire 507,230 ....F6
Shropshire 370,355 ....E5
Somerset 417,457 ....E6
South Yorkshire 1,292,029 ....F4
Staffordshire 1,005,641 ....E5
Suffolk 590,133 ....H5
Surrey 992,489 ....G6
Tyne and Wear 1,135,492 ....H3
Warwickshire 469,801 ....F5
West Midlands 2,628,491 ....F5
West Sussex 650,124 ....G7
West Yorkshire 2,021,707 ....J1
Wiltshire 512,635 ....E6
Yorkshire, North 653,456 ....F3
Yorkshire, South 1,292,029 ....F4
Yorkshire, West 2,021,707 ....J1

CITIES and TOWNS

Abingdon 29,130 ....F6
Accrington 36,459 ....H1
Adwickle Street 10,293 ....K2
Aldershot 53,665 ....G8
Aldridge 17,549 ....E5
Alfreton 21,284 ....F4
Alsager 12,944 ....E4
Alton 14,163 ....G6
Altrincham 39,528 ....H2

Amersham⊙ 21,326 ....G7
Andover 30,632 ....F6
Arnold 37,721 ....F4
Ashford 45,198 ....H6
Ashington 27,786 ....F2
Ashton-under-Lyne 43,605 ....H2
Aylesbury 51,999 ....G7
Aylesford 21,017 ....J8
Bacup 14,082 ....H1
Banbury 37,463 ....F5
Banstead 35,360 ....H8
Barking 149,132 ....H8
Barnet 289,277 ....H7
Barnoldswick 10,125 ....H1
Barnsley 76,783 ....J2
Barnstaple 24,490 ....D6
Barrow-in-Furness 50,174 ....D3
Basildon 94,800 ....J8
Basingstoke 73,027 ....F6
Bath 84,283 ....E6
Batley 45,582 ....J1
Beaconsfield 13,397 ....G8
Bebington 62,618 ....G2
Beccles 10,677 ....J5
Bedford 75,632 ....G5
Bedlington 15,074 ....F2
Bedworth 29,192 ....F5
Beeston and
  Stapleford 64,785 ....F5
Benfleet 50,783 ....J8
Bentley with Arksey 34,273 ....F4
Berkhamsted 16,874 ....G7
Berwick-upon-Tweed 12,772 ....F2
Beverley 19,368 ....G4

Bexhill 34,625 ....H7
Bexley 213,215 ....H8
Bicester 15,946 ....F6
Biddulph 16,697 ....H2
Bideford 13,826 ....C6
Biggleswade 10,905 ....G5
Birkenhead 99,075 ....G2
Birmingham 1,013,995 ....F5
Bishop Auckland 23,560 ....E3
Bishop's Stortford 22,535 ....H6
Blackburn 109,564 ....H1
Blackpool 146,297 ....G1
Blaydon 16,719 ....H3
Blyth 35,101 ....F2
Bodmin 11,992 ....C7
Bognor Regis 50,323 ....G7
Boldon 11,639 ....J3
Bolsover 11,497 ....J2
Bolton 143,960 ....H2
Bootle 70,860 ....G2
Boston 33,908 ....G5
Bournemouth 142,829 ....F7
Bracknell 52,257 ....G8
Bradford 293,336 ....J1
Braintree 30,975 ....H6
Brent 251,238 ....H8
Brentford 51,212 ....J8
Bridgnorth 10,332 ....E5
Bridgwater 30,782 ....D6
Bridlington 28,426 ....G3
Bridport 10,615 ....E7
Brighouse 32,597 ....J1
Brighton 134,581 ....G7
Bristol 413,861 ....E6

Broadstairs 21,551 ....J6
Bromley 280,525 ....H8
Bromsgrove 24,576 ....E5
Brownhills 18,200 ....E5
Buckingham 6,439 ....G6
Burgess Hill 23,577 ....G7
Burnham-on-Sea 17,022 ....D6
Burnley 76,365 ....H1
Burntwood 28,938 ....F5
Burton upon Trent 59,040 ....F5
Bury 61,785 ....H2
Bury Saint Edmunds 30,563 ....H5
Bushey 15,759 ....H7
Buxton 19,502 ....J2
Calne 10,235 ....F6
Camborne-Redruth 34,262 ....B7
Cambridge 87,111 ....G5
Camden 161,098 ....H8
Cannock 54,503 ....E5
Canterbury 34,546 ....H6
Canvey Island 35,243 ....J8
Carlisle 72,206 ....D3
Carlton 46,053 ....F5
Carterton 10,876 ....F6
Caterham and Warlingham
  30,331 ....H8
Charlton Kings 10,786 ....F6
Chatham 65,835 ....J8
Cheadle 10,470 ....E5
Cheadle and Gatley 59,478 ....H2
Chelmsford 91,109 ....J7
Cheltenham 87,188 ....E6
Chertsey 10,195 ....G8
Chesham 20,883 ....G7
Cheshunt 49,616 ....H7
Chester 80,154 ....G2
Chester-le-Street 34,776 ....J3
Chesterfield 73,352 ....J2
Chichester 26,050 ....G7
Chippenham 21,325 ....E6
Chorley 33,465 ....G2
Christchurch 32,854 ....F7
Cirencester 13,491 ....E6
Clacton 39,618 ....J6
Cleethorpes 33,238 ....H4
Clevedon 17,875 ....D6
Clitheroe 13,671 ....H1
Coalville 28,831 ....F5
Colchester 87,476 ....H6
Colne 19,094 ....H1
Congleton 23,482 ....H2
Consett 22,409 ....H3
Corby 48,704 ....G5
Corsham 11,259 ....E6
Coventry 318,718 ....F5
Cowes 16,134 ....F7
Cranleigh 10,334 ....G6
Crawley 80,113 ....G6
Crewe 59,097 ....E4
Crosby 54,103 ....G2
Crowborough 17,008 ....H6
Croydon 298,794 ....H8
Darlington 85,519 ....F3
Dartford 62,032 ....J8
Darton 13,743 ....J2
Darwen 30,883 ....H1
Daventry 16,096 ....F5
Deal 26,311 ....J6
Dearne 13,391 ....K2
Denton 37,784 ....H2
Derby 218,026 ....F5
Devizes 12,430 ....F6
Dewsbury 49,612 ....J1
Didcot⊙ 15,147 ....F6
Doncaster 74,727 ....F4
Dorchester 13,734 ....E7
Dorking 14,602 ....G8
Dover 33,461 ....J6
Droitwich 18,025 ....E5
Dronfield 22,641 ....F4
Dudley 186,513 ....E5
Dunstable 48,436 ....G6
Durham 38,105 ....J3
Ealing 278,677 ....H8
East Dereham 11,798 ....H5
East Grinstead 23,867 ....G6
East Retford 19,308 ....G4
Eastbourne 86,715 ....H7
Eastleigh 58,585 ....F7
Egham 21,810 ....G8
Ellesmere Port 65,829 ....G2

Enfield 257,154 ....H7
Epping 10,148 ....H7
Epsom and Ewell 65,830 ....G8
Esher 46,688 ....H8
Eston⊙ 37,694 ....F3
Eton G8
Evesham 15,069 ....F5
Exeter 88,235 ....D7
Exmouth 28,037 ....D7
Fareham 55,563 ....F7
Farnborough 48,063 ....G8
Farnham 34,541 ....G8
Farnworth 25,591 ....H2
Faversham 15,914 ....J6
Felixstowe 24,207 ....J6
Felling 36,377 ....J3
Fleet 27,406 ....G8
Fleetwood 27,899 ....D4
Folkestone 42,949 ....J6
Formby 26,852 ....G2
Frinton and Walton 12,689 ....J6
Frome 19,678 ....E6
Gainsborough 20,326 ....G4
Gateshead 91,421 ....J3
Gillingham 92,531 ....J8
Glastonbury 6,751 ....E6
Glossop 29,923 ....J2
Gloucester 106,526 ....E6
Godalming 18,758 ....G8
Golborne 20,633 ....G2
Goole 19,394 ....G4
Gosport 69,664 ....F7
Grantham 30,700 ....G5
Gravesend 53,450 ....J8
Great Grimsby 91,532 ....G4
Great Harwood 10,968 ....H1
Great Malvern
  (Malvern) 30,153 ....E5
Great Yarmouth 54,777 ....J5
Greenwich 211,013 ....H8
Guildford 61,509 ....G8
Guisborough 19,242 ....F3
Hackney 179,529 ....H8

Hailsham 16,367 ....H7
Hale 16,362 ....H2
Halesowen 57,533 ....E5
Halifax 76,675 ....J1
Hammersmith 144,616 ....H8
Haringey 202,650 ....H8
Harlow 79,150 ....H7
Harrogate 63,637 ....J1
Harrow 195,292 ....G8
Hartlepool 91,749 ....F3
Harwich 17,245 ....J6
Haslemere 10,544 ....G8
Haslingden 14,347 ....H1
Hastings 74,979 ....H7
Hatfield 33,174 ....H7
Havant 50,098 ....G7
Haverhill 16,970 ....H5
Havering 238,335 ....J8
Haxby 11,415 ....F3
Hazel Grove and Bramhall
  40,819 ....H2
Heanor 21,863 ....F4
Hebburn 20,098 ....J3
Hemel Hempstead 80,110 ....G7
Henley-on-Thames 10,910 ....G8
Hereford 48,277 ....E5
Hertford 21,350 ....H7
Hetton 14,529 ....J3
Heywood 29,639 ....H2
High Wycombe 69,575 ....G8
Hillingdon 226,659 ....G8
Hinckley 55,510 ....F5
Hitchin 33,480 ....G6
Hoddesdon 37,960 ....H7
Holmfirth 21,138 ....J2
Horley 17,700 ....H8
Horsham 38,356 ....G6
Horwich 16,758 ....G2
Houghton-le-Spring 35,337 ....J3
Hounslow 198,938 ....G8
Hove 65,587 ....G7
Hoylake 31,609 ....G2
Hoyland Nether 15,845 ....J2
Hucknall 27,463 ....F4

(continued on following page)

UNITED KINGDOM

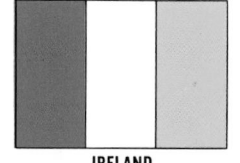

IRELAND

ENGLAND

AREA 50,516 sq. mi. (130,836 sq. km.)
POPULATION 46,220,955
CAPITAL London
LARGEST CITY London
HIGHEST POINT Scafell Pike 3,210 ft. (978 m.)

WALES

AREA 8,017 sq. mi. (20,764 sq. km.)
POPULATION 2,749,640
CAPITAL Cardiff
LARGEST CITY Cardiff
HIGHEST POINT Snowdon 3,560 ft. (1,085 m.)

SCOTLAND

AREA 30,414 sq. mi. (78,772 sq. km.)
POPULATION 5,130,735
CAPITAL Edinburgh
LARGEST CITY Glasgow
HIGHEST POINT Ben Nevis 4,406 ft. (1,343 m.)

NORTHERN IRELAND

AREA 5,452 sq. mi. (14,121 sq. km.)
POPULATION 1,543,000
CAPITAL Belfast
LARGEST CITY Belfast
HIGHEST POINT Slieve Donard 2,796 ft. (852 m.)

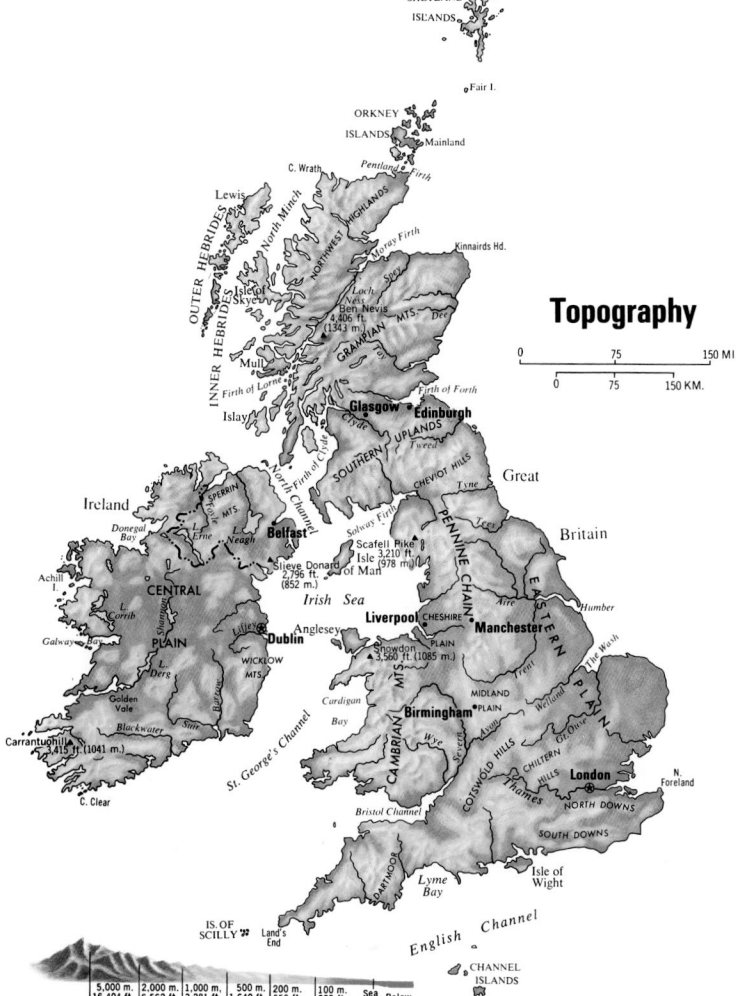

Topography

0   75   150 MI.
0   75   150 KM.

5,000 m. 2,000 m. 1,000 m. 500 m. 200 m. 100 m. Sea
16,404 ft. 6,562 ft. 3,281 ft. 1,640 ft. 656 ft. 328 ft. Level Below

Huddersfield 147,825 J2
Hugh Town⊙ A8
Hull 322,144 G4
Huntingdon 14,395 G5
Huyton-with-Roby 62,011 G2
Hyde 30,461 H2
Hythe 13,118 H6
Ilkeston 34,683 F5
Immingham⊙ 11,480 G4
Ipswich 129,661 J5
Islington 157,522 H8
Jarrow 31,345 J3
Kempston 15,454 G5
Kendal 23,710 E3
Kenilworth 18,782 F5
Kensington and Chelsea 125,892 G8
Kettering 44,758 G5
Kidderminster 50,385 E5
Kidsgrove 27,999 E4
King's Lynn 37,323 H5
Kingston upon Thames 130,829 H8
Kingswood 54,736 E6
Kirkby 52,825 G2
Knaresborough 12,910 F4
Knutsford 13,628 H2
Lambeth 244,143 H8
Lancaster 43,902 E3
Leamington Spa 56,552 F5
Leatherhead 42,399 G8
Leeds 451,841 J1
Leek 18,495 H2
Leicester 324,394 F5
Leigh 42,627 H2
Letchworth 31,146 G6
Lewes 14,499 H7
Lewisham 230,488 H8
Leyland 36,694 G1
Lichfield 25,408 F5
Lincoln 79,980 G4
Litherland 21,989 G2
Littlehampton 46,028 G7
Liverpool 538,809 G2
London (cap.) 7,566,620 H8
Long Eaton 42,285 F5
Longbenton 36,780 J3
Loughborough 44,895 F5
Louth 13,019 H4
Lowestoft 59,430 J5
Luton 163,209 G6
Lymington 11,614 F7
Lymm 10,036 H2
Lytham Saint Anne's 39,559 G1
Macclesfield 47,525 H2
Maidenhead 59,809 G8
Maidstone 86,067 J8
Maldon 14,638 H6
Malvern 30,153 E5
Manchester 448,604 H2
Mangotsfield 28,664 E6
Mansfield 71,325 K2
Mansfield Woodhouse 17,564 F4
March 14,155 H5
Margate 53,137 J6
Market Harborough 15,852 G5
Marlow 18,584 G8
Matlock 13,706 J2
Melksham 13,248 E6
Melton Mowbray 23,379 G5
Merton 165,102 H8
Middlesbrough 158,516 F3
Middleton 51,373 H2
Milton Keynes 93,305 G5
Morpeth 14,301 F2
Nantwich 11,867 E4
Nelson 30,449 H1
Neston 14,902 G2
New Romney 6,559 J7
Newark 33,143 G4
Newbury 31,488 F6
Newcastle upon Tyne 199,064 H3
Newcastle-under-Lyme 73,208 E4
Newham 209,128 H8
Newhaven 10,697 H7
Newmarket 15,861 H5
Newport, Isle of Wight 19,758 F7
Newport, Shropshire 10,339 E5
Newport Pagnell 10,733 G5
Newquay 13,905 B7
Newton Abbot 20,567 D7
Newton-le-Willows 19,466 H2
Northallerton 13,566 F3
Northampton 154,172 F5
Northfleet 21,400 J8
Northwich 32,664 H2
Norton-Radstock 17,668 E6
Norwich 169,814 J5
Nottingham 273,300 F5
Nuneaton 60,337 F5
Oadby 18,331 F5
Oldham 107,095 H2
Ormskirk 22,308 G2
Oswaldtwistle 11,188 H1
Oswestry 13,200 E5
Oxford 113,847 F6
Padiham 13,856 H1
Penrith 12,086 E3
Penzance 18,501 B7
Peterborough 113,404 G5
Peterlee⊙ 31,405 J3
Petersfield 10,078 F6
Plymouth 238,583 C7
Ponteland 10,215 H3
Poole 122,815 E7
Portishead 13,684 E6
Portslade 17,831 G7
Portsmouth 174,218 F7
Potters Bar 22,610 H7
Poulton-le-Fylde 18,477 G1
Preston 166,675 G1
Prestwich 31,854 H2
Prudhoe 11,140 H3
Radcliffe 27,664 H2
Ramsbottom 16,334 H2
Ramsgate 36,678 J6
Rawtenstall 21,247 H1
Rayleigh 28,574 J8
Reading 194,727 G8
Redbridge 226,977 H8
Redcar⊙ 35,373 F3
Redditch 61,639 E5
Reigate 48,241 H8
Richmond upon Thames 157,304 H8
Rickmansworth 15,960 G8
Ringwood 10,941 F7
Ripley 17,548 F4
Ripon 13,036 F3
Rochdale 97,292 H2
Rochester 23,840 J8
Romney (New Romney) 6,559 J7
Romsey 14,818 F6
Rotherham 122,374 K2
Royal Leamington Spa 56,552 F5
Royal Tunbridge Wells 57,699 H6
Royston 12,904 G5
Rugby 59,039 F5
Rugeley 23,751 E5
Runcorn 63,995 G2
Rushden 22,394 G5
Ryde 19,384 F7
Ryton 15,138 H3
Saffron Walden 11,879 H5
Saint Albans 76,709 H7
Saint Austell 20,267 C7
Saint Helens 114,397 G2
Saint Ives, Cambridgeshire 13,431 G5
Saint Ives, Cornwall 9,439 B7
Saint Neots 12,468 G5
Sale 57,872 H2
Salford 96,525 H2
Salisbury 36,890 F6
Saltash 12,486 C7
Sandbach 13,734 H2
Sandhurst 13,539 G8
Sandown-Shanklin 15,252 F7
Scarborough 36,665 G3
Scunthorpe 79,043 G4
Seaford 16,367 H7
Seaham 21,807 J3
Selby 12,224 F4
Sevenoaks 24,493 J8
Sheffield 470,685 J2
Shepshed 10,479 F5
Shildon 11,583 F3
Shoreham 20,562 G7
Shrewsbury 57,731 E5
Sidmouth 10,808 D7
Sittingbourne 35,893 H6
Skegness 12,645 H4
Skelmersdale 42,611 G2
Skipton 13,009 H1
Slough 106,341 G8
Solihull 93,940 F5
South Shields 86,488 J3
Southampton 211,321 F7
Southend-on-Sea 155,720 H6
Southport 88,596 G1
Southwark 209,735 H8
Southwick 11,364 G7
Sowerby Bridge 11,280 H1
Spalding 18,182 G5
Spennymoor 18,563 F3
Stafford 60,915 E5
Staines 51,949 G8
Stamford 16,127 G5
Standish 11,504 G2
Stanley 20,058 H3
Staveley 24,457 K2
Stevenage 74,757 G6
Stockport 135,489 H2
Stocksbridge 13,394 J2
Stockton-on-Tees 86,699 F3
Stoke-on-Trent 272,446 E4
Stone 12,119 E5
Stourbridge 55,136 E5
Stourport-on-Severn 17,880 E5
Stowmarket 10,913 J5
Stratford-upon-Avon 20,941 F5
Stretford 47,522 H2
Stroud 37,791 E6
Sudbury 17,723 H5
Sunbury 28,240 G8
Sunderland 195,064 J3
Sutton 165,323 H8
Sutton in Ashfield 39,536 K2
Swadlincote 33,667 F5
Swindon 127,348 F6
Tadley 13,668 F6
Tamworth 63,260 F5
Taunton 47,793 D6
Teignmouth 11,995 D7
Telford⊙ 28,645 E5
Tewkesbury 9,454 E6
Thatcham 14,940 F6
Thetford 19,529 H5
Thornaby⊙ 26,319 F3
Thornbury 11,948 E6
Thorne⊙ 16,662 F4
Thornton Cleveleys 26,697 G1
Tiverton 14,745 D7
Todmorden 11,936 H1
Tonbridge 34,407 H8
Torbay 93,995 D7
Tower Hamlets 139,996 H8
Tring 10,610 G7
Trowbridge 27,299 E6
Truro 17,852 B7
Tynemouth 17,877 J3
Uckfield 10,749 H7
Ulverston 11,976 D3
Urmston 43,706 H2
Uttoxeter 10,008 E5
Wakefield 74,764 J2
Wallasey 62,465 G2
Wallsend 44,542 J3
Walsall 177,923 E5
Waltham Forest 214,595 H8
Waltham Holy Cross 16,498 H7
Walton and Weybridge 50,031 G8
Wandsworth 252,240 H8
Ware 15,344 H7
Warminster 14,826 E6
Warrington 81,366 G2
Warsop 10,294 F4
Warwick 21,701 F5
Washington 48,856 J3
Waterloo 57,296 G7
Watford 109,503 H7
Wellingborough 38,598 G5
Wellington 8,980 D7
Welwyn 40,665 H7
West Bridgford 27,463 F5
West Bromwich 153,725 F5
Westminster 163,892 H8
Weston-super-Mare 60,821 D6
Weymouth 38,384 E7
Whickham 17,882 J3
Whitby 12,982 G3
Whitehaven 27,512 D3
Whitley Bay 36,040 J3
Widnes 55,973 G2
Wigan 88,725 G2
Wigston 32,373 F5
Wilmslow 28,827 H2
Wilton 4,002 F6
Wimborne Minster 14,193 E7
Winchester 34,127 F6
Windermere 6,835 E3
Windsor 30,832 G8
Winsford 26,548 G2
Wisbech 22,932 H5
Witham 21,875 H6
Witney 14,215 F6
Woking 92,667 G8
Wokingham 30,344 G8
Wolverhampton 263,501 E5
Wombwell 17,143 K2
Worcester 75,466 E5
Workington 25,978 D3
Worksop 34,551 F4
Worsbrough 10,821 J2
Worthing 90,687 G7
Yateley⊙ 14,121 G8
Yeovil 36,114 E7
York 123,126 F4

OTHER FEATURES

Aire (riv.) F4
Avon (riv.) F5
Barnstaple (bay) C6
Beachy (head) H7
Blackwater (riv.) H6
Bristol (chan.) C6
Cheviot (hills) E2
Chiltern (hills) G6
Cleveland (hills) F3
Colne (riv.) G8
Cotswold (hills) E6
Cross Fell (mt.) E3
Cumbrian (mts.) D3
Dart (riv.) D7
Dartmoor National Park C7
Dee (riv.) D4
Derwent (riv.) G3
Derwent (riv.) H3
Don (riv.) F4
Dove (riv.) J2
Dover (strait) J7
Dungeness (prom.) J7
Eddyston (rocks) C7
Eden (riv.) E3
English (chan.) D8
Esk (riv.) D2
Exe (riv.) D7
Exmoor National Park D6
Fens, The (reg.) G5
Flamborough (head) G3
Foulness Island (pen.) J6
Great Ouse (riv.) H5
Hartland (pt.) C6
Holderness (pen.) G4
Holy (isl.) F2
Humber (riv.) G4
Irish (sea) B4
Kennet (riv.) F6
Lake District National Park D3
Land's End (prom.) B7
Lea (riv.) G6
Lincoln Wolds (hills) G4
Lindisfarne (Holy) (isl.) F2
Lizard (pt.) B8
Lundy (isl.) C6
Lyme (bay) D7
Medway (riv.) H6
Mendip (hills) E6
Mersey (riv.) G2
Morecambe (bay) D3
Mounts (bay) B7
Naze, The (prom.) J6
Nene (riv.) H5
New (for.) F7
North (sea) J4
North Downs (hills) G6
North Foreland (prom.) J6
Northumberland National Park E2
North York Moors National Park G3
Ouse (riv.) G6
Ouse (riv.) G4
Peak District National Park F4
Peak, The (mt.) J2
Pennine Chain (range) E3
Portland, Bill of (pt.) E7
Purbeck, Isle of (pen.) F7
Ribble (riv.) E4
Saint Bees (head) D3
Saint Mary's (isl.) A8
Scafell Pike (mt.) D3
Scilly (isls.) A7
Severn (riv.) E6
Sheppey (isl.) J6
Sherwood (for.) F4
Solent (chan.) F7
Solway (firth) D3
South Downs (hills) G7
South Foreland (prom.) J6
Spithead (chan.) F7
Stonehenge (ruin) F6
Stour (riv.) H6
Stour (riv.) E7
Stour (riv.) J6
Swale (riv.) F3
Tees (riv.) F3
Thames (riv.) H6
Tintagel (head) C7
Trent (riv.) G4
Tweed (riv.) E2
Tyne (riv.) F3
Ure (riv.) F3
Walney, Isle of (isl.) D3
Wash, The (bay) H5
Weald, The (reg.) H6
Wear (riv.) F3
Welland (riv.) G5
Wey (riv.) G6
Wharfe (riv.) E3
Wight (isl.) 114,879 F7
Wirral (pen.) G2
Wolds, The (hills) G4
Wye (riv.) D5
Yare (riv.) J5
Yorkshire Dales National Park E3

CHANNEL ISLANDS

CITIES and TOWNS

Saint Helier (cap.), Jersey⊙ 27,549 E8
Saint Peter Port (cap.), Guernsey⊙ 16,085 E8
Saint Sampson's⊙ 7,475 E8

OTHER FEATURES

Alderney (isl.) 2,130 E8
Guernsey (isl.) 55,421 E8
Herm (isl.) 59 E8
Jersey (isl.) 82,809 E8
Sark (isl.) 560 E8

ISLE of MAN

CITIES and TOWNS

Castletown 2,788 C3
Douglas (cap.) 19,897 C3
Laxey 1,242 C3
Onchan 6,395 C3
Peel 3,295 C3
Port Erin 2,356 C3
Port Saint Mary 1,525 C3
Ramsey 5,372 C3

OTHER FEATURES

Ayre (pt.) C3
Calf of Man (isl.) C3
Langness (prom.) C3
Snaefell (mt.) C3

WALES

COUNTIES

Clwyd 385,581 D4
Dyfed 323,040 C6
Gwent 436,500 D6
Gwynedd 222,291 C4
Mid Glamorgan 533,770 D6
Powys 108,121 D5
South Glamorgan 376,718 A7
West Glamorgan 363,619 D6

CITIES and TOWNS

Abercarn 16,811 B6
Aberdare 31,617 A6
Abergavenny 13,880 B6
Abergele 12,264 D4
Abertillery and Brynmawr 28,239 B6
Aberystwyth 10,290 C5
Ammanford 10,735 C6
Bangor 12,244 C4
Barry 44,443 B7
Bethesda 3,558 D4
Brecknock (Brecon) 7,166 D6
Bridgend 31,008 A7
Brynmawr and Abertillery 28,239 B6
Buckley 16,693 G2
Caernarfon 9,271 C4
Caerphilly 28,681 B6
Caldicot 12,310 E6
Cardiff (cap.) 262,313 B7
Cardigan 3,815 C5
Carmarthen 13,860 C6
Chepstow 9,039 E6
Colwyn Bay 27,002 D4
Connah's Quay 14,785 G2
Cwmbran 44,592 B6
Denbigh 7,710 D4
Ebbw Vale 21,048 B6
Ffestiniog 4,507 D5
Flint 11,411 G2
Gelligaer 16,812 A6
Gwersyllt 13,374 E4
Harlech⊙ 1,292 C5
Haverfordwest 13,572 B6
Hawarden⊙ 22,361 G2
Holyhead 12,569 C4
Holywell 11,101 G2
Llandeilo 1,598 C6
Llandovery 1,676 D5
Llandrindod Wells 4,232 D5
Llandudno 13,202 D4
Llanelli 45,336 C6
Llanfairfechan 3,173 D4
Llangollen 2,546 D5
Llanidloes 2,392 D5
Llantrisant⊙ 8,317 A7
Llantwit Major 13,375 A7
Maesteg 21,821 D6
Menai Bridge 2,942 C4
Merthyr Tydfil 38,893 A6
Milford Haven 13,883 B6
Mold 8,487 G2
Monmouth 7,379 E6
Montgomery D5
Mountain Ash 23,520 A6
Narberth C6
Neath 48,687 D6
Nefyn⊙ 2,086 C5
Newport 115,896 B6
Newtown 8,906 D5
Neyland 3,095 B6
Ogmore 7,092 A6
Pembroke 8,235 C6
Penarth 22,467 B7
Pontypool 36,064 B6
Pontypridd 29,465 A6
Port Talbot 40,078 D6
Porthcawl 15,162 D6
Prestatyn 16,246 D4
Pwllheli 3,978 C5
Rhondda 70,980 A6
Rhosllanerchrugog 11,080 D4
Rhyl 23,130 D4
Risca 16,627 B6
Ruthin 4,417 D4
Saint David's⊙ 1,428 B6
Swansea 172,433 C6
Tenby 5,226 C6
Tredegar 16,188 B6
Welshpool 4,869 D5
Wrexham 39,929 E4
Ystradgynlais 10,406 D6

OTHER FEATURES

Anglesey (isl.) C4
Bardsey (isl.) C5
Brecon Beacons National Park D6
Bristol (chan.) C6
Caldy (isl.) C6
Cambrian (mts.) D5
Cardigan (bay) C5
Carmarthen (bay) C6
Conwy (bay) C4
Dee (riv.) D4
Gower (pen.) C6
Great Ormes (head) C4
Holy (isl.) C4
Irish (sea) B4
Lleyn (pen.) C5
Menai (strait) C4
Milford Haven (inlet) B6
Pembrokeshire Coast National Park C6
Radnor (for.) D5
Saint Brides (bay) B6
Saint George's (chan.) B5
Severn (riv.) E6
Snowdon (mt.) C4
Snowdonia National Park C4
Taff (riv.) B7
Teifi (riv.) C5
Towy (riv.) D6
Tremadoc (prom.) C5
Usk (riv.) B6
Wye (riv.) D5
Ynys Môn (Anglesey) (isl.) C4

⊙ Population of parish.

SCOTLAND

(map on page 15)

REGIONS

Borders 99,784 E5
Central 273,391 D4
Dumfries and Galloway 145,139 E5
Fife 327,362 E4
Grampian 471,942 F3
Highland 200,150 D3
Lothian 738,372 E5
Orkney (islands area) 19,056 E1
Shetland (islands area) 27,277 F2
Strathclyde 2,404,532 C4
Tayside 391,846 E4
Western Isles (islands area) 31,884 A3

CITIES and TOWNS

Aberchirder 1,021 F3
Aberdeen 190,465 F3
Aberfeldy 1,613 E4
Aberfoyle 793 D4
Abernethy 776 E4
Aboyne 1,529 F3
Achiltibuie⊙ 1,564 C3
Achnasheen⊙ 1,078 C3
Airdrie 45,747 C2
Alexandria 26,329 A1
Alford 764 F3
Alloa 26,428 C1
Alness 6,289 D3
Altnaharra⊙ 1,227 D2
Alva 4,874 C1
Alyth 2,289 E4
Annan 8,314 E6
Annbank Station 3,223 D5
Arbroath 24,119 F4
Ardrishaig 1,325 C4
Ardrossan 11,421 D5
Armadale 9,527 C2
Auchinleck 4,463 D5
Auchterarder 2,904 E4
Auchtermuchty 1,646 E4
Aviemore 1,224 E3
Ayr 49,522 D5
Baillieston 7,671 B2
Balerno 3,576 D2
Balfron 1,127 B1
Ballantrae 262 C5
Ballater 1,218 F3
Ballingry 7,021 D1
Balloch 1,484 B1
Banchory 4,890 F3
Banff 3,938 F3
Bankhead 1,492 F3
Bannockburn 5,889 C1
Barrhead 18,418 B2
Bathgate 14,477 C2
Bearsden 27,183 B2
Beauly 1,148 D3
Beith 5,742 D5
Bellsbank 2,482 D5
Bellshill 39,676 C2
Berriedale⊙ 1,927 E2
Bieldside 1,137 F3
Biggar 1,938 E5
Bishopbriggs 23,501 B2
Bishopton 5,283 B2
Blackburn 5,785 C2
Blair Atholl 437 D4
Blairgowrie and Rattray 7,184 E4
Blantyre 19,948 B2
Bo'ness 14,641 C1
Boddam 1,367 G3
Bonhill 4,385 B1
Bonnybridge 5,701 C1
Bonnyrigg and Lasswade 14,399 D2
Brechin 7,692 F4
Bridge of Allan 4,694 C1
Bridge of Don 4,086 F3
Bridge of Weir 4,724 A2
Brightons 3,106 C1
Brora 1,736 E2
Broxburn 12,032 D1
Buckhaven and Methil 18,265 F4
Buckie 7,839 E3
Bucksburn 6,567 F3
Burghead 1,380 E3
Burntisland 5,865 D1
Callander 2,520 D4
Cambuslang 14,607 B2
Campbeltown 6,098 C5
Caol 3,719 C4
Cardenden 5,898 D1
Carluke 11,674 E5
Carnoustie 9,225 F4
Carnwath 1,374 E5
Carron 2,626 C1
Castle Douglas 3,521 E6
Catrine 2,790 D5
Cawdor 111 E3
Chirnside 1,263 F5
Chryston 11,067 C2
Clackmannan 3,258 C1
Clarkston 8,404 B2
Clydebank 51,854 B2
Coalburn 1,241 E5
Coatbridge 50,957 C2
Cockenzie and Port Seton 3,760 D1
Coldstream 1,645 F5
Comrie 1,477 E4
Cononbridge 2 187 D3
Corpach 1,296 C4
Coupar Angus 2,186 E4
Cove and Kilcreggan 1,220 A1
Cove Bay 2,840 F3
Cowdenbeath 12,272 D1
Cowie 2,513 C1
Crail 1,181 F4
Creetown 769 D6
Crieff 5,477 E4
Crimond 1,002 G3
Cromarty 492 E3
Cruden Bay 1,453 G3
Cullen 1,414 F3
Culross 504 C1
Cults 3,336 F3
Cumbernauld 47,901 C1
Cumnock and Holmhead 9,650 D5
Cupar 6,637 E4
Currie 6,764 D2
Dailly 1,098 D5
Dalbeattie 3,917 E6
Dalkeith 11,255 D2
Dalmellington 1,425 D5
Dalry 5,856 D5
Dalrymple 1,237 D5
Darvel 3,461 D5
Denny and Dunipace 23,158 C1
Dervaig⊙ 1,081 B4
Dingwall 4,842 D3
Dollar 2,486 E4
Dornoch 880 D3
Douglas 1,727 E5
Doune 1,046 D4
Drongan 3,129 D5
Dufftown 1,643 E3
Dumbarton 23,430 B1
Dumfries 32,100 E5
Dunbar 6,035 F4
Dunblane 6,855 E4
Dundee 174,345 F4
Dundonald 2,669 D5
Dunfermline 52,227 D1
Dunoon 9,369 A2
Duns 2,253 F5
Duntocher 3,532 B2
Dyce 7,039 F3
Eaglesham 3,166 D5
Earlston 1,610 F5
East Calder 5,112 D2
East Kilbride 70,676 B2
East Linton 1,206 F5
Eastriggs 1,845 E5
East Wemyss 1,782 D1
Edinburgh (cap.) 420,169 D1
Elderslie 5,204 B2
Elgin 18,908 E3
Ellon 6,319 F3
Errol 762 E4
Eyemouth 3,398 F5
Fairlie 1,326 D5
Falkirk 36,880 C1
Falkland 998 E4
Fallin 2,663 C1
Fauldhouse 5,036 C2
Findhorn 664 E3
Findochty 1,019 E3
Fochabers 1,483 E3
Forfar 12,770 F4
Forres 8,354 E3
Forth 2,890 C2
Fortrose 1,332 D3
Fort William 11,061 C4
Fraserburgh 12,512 G3
Gairloch 125 C3
Galashiels 12,244 F5
Galston 5,311 D5
Garelochhead 2,072 A1
Gatehouse-of-Fleet 835 D6
Giffnock 33,634 B2
Girvan 7,795 D5
Glamis 190 F4
Glasgow 765,030 B2
Glenbarr⊙ 691 C5
Glencoe 195 C4
Glenelg⊙ 1,468 C3
Glenrothes 32,971 E4
Golspie 1,491 E3
Gorebridge 6,036 D2
Gourock 11,203 A1
Grangemouth 21,599 C1
Grantown-on-Spey 2,034 E3
Greenock 59,016 A2
Gretna 2,811 E5
Gullane 2,232 F4
Haddington 8,139 F5
Halkirk 679 E2
Hamilton 51,718 C2
Harthill 4,161 C2
Hawick 16,364 F5
Heathhall 1,365 E5
Helensburgh 16,621 A1
Helmsdale 727 E2
Hillside 1,233 F4
Hillswick⊙ 696 G2
Hopeman 1,398 E3
Huntly 3,952 F3
Hurlford 4,294 D5
Inchnadamph⊙ 833 D2
Innerleithen 2,468 E5
Insch 1,256 F3
Inveraray 473 C4
Inverbervie 1,799 F4
Invercassley⊙ 1,067 D3
Invergordon 4,067 D3
Invergowrie 1,389 E4
Inverie⊙ 1,468 C3
Inverkeithing 5,770 D1
Inverness 40,010 D3
Inverurie 7,680 F3
Irvine 32,968 D5
Jedburgh 4,069 F5
John O'Groats 195 E2
Johnstone 42,669 B2
Keith 4,407 F3
Kelso 5,648 F5
Kelty 5,623 D1
Kemnay 3,034 F3
Kilbarchan 2,669 A2
Kilbirnie 8,710 A2
Kilchoan⊙ 764 B4
Kildonan⊙ 1,105 E2
Killearn 1,771 B1
Kilmacolm 3,676 A2
Kilmarnock 52,083 D5
Kilmaurs 2,738 D5
Kilrenny and Anstruther 2,951 F4
Kilsyth 10,538 B1
Kilwinning 16,266 D5
Kinbrace⊙ 1,105 E2
Kincardine 3,166 C1
Kinghorn 2,698 D1
Kingussie 1,229 D3
Kinlochewe⊙ 1,794 C3
Kinlochleven 1,047 D4
Kinloss 2,813 E3
Kinross 3,496 E4
Kintore 1,644 F3
Kirkcaldy 46,522 D1
Kirkconnel 2,656 E5
Kirkcudbright 3,427 E6
Kirkintilloch 33,148 B2
Kirkmuirhill 3,624 E5
Kirkwall 5,995 E2
Kirriemuir 5,326 E4
Kyle of Lochalsh 687 C3
Kylestrome⊙ 745 D2
Ladybank 1,355 E4
Lairg 572 D2
Lanark 9,806 E5
Langholm 2,615 E5
Larbert 4,922 C1
Largs 9,905 A2
Larkhall 16,216 E5
Lauder 639 F5
Laurencekirk 1,329 F4
Lennoxtown 4,829 B1
Lerwick 7,561 G2
Leslie 3,551 E4
Lesmahagow 3,408 E5
Letham 804 F4
Leuchars 2,244 F4
Leven 8,624 F4
Lhanbryde 1,811 E3
Limekilns 1,444 D1
Linlithgow 9,582 C1
Linwood 10,510 B2
Livingston 38,954 C2
Loanhead 6,159 D2
Lochailort⊙ 673 C4
Locharbriggs 4,230 E5
Lochgelly 7,334 D1
Lochgilphead 2,461 C4
Lochinver 283 C3
Lochmaben 1,713 E5
Lochore 2,994 D1
Lochwinnoch 2,273 A2
Lockerbie 3,561 E5

(continued)

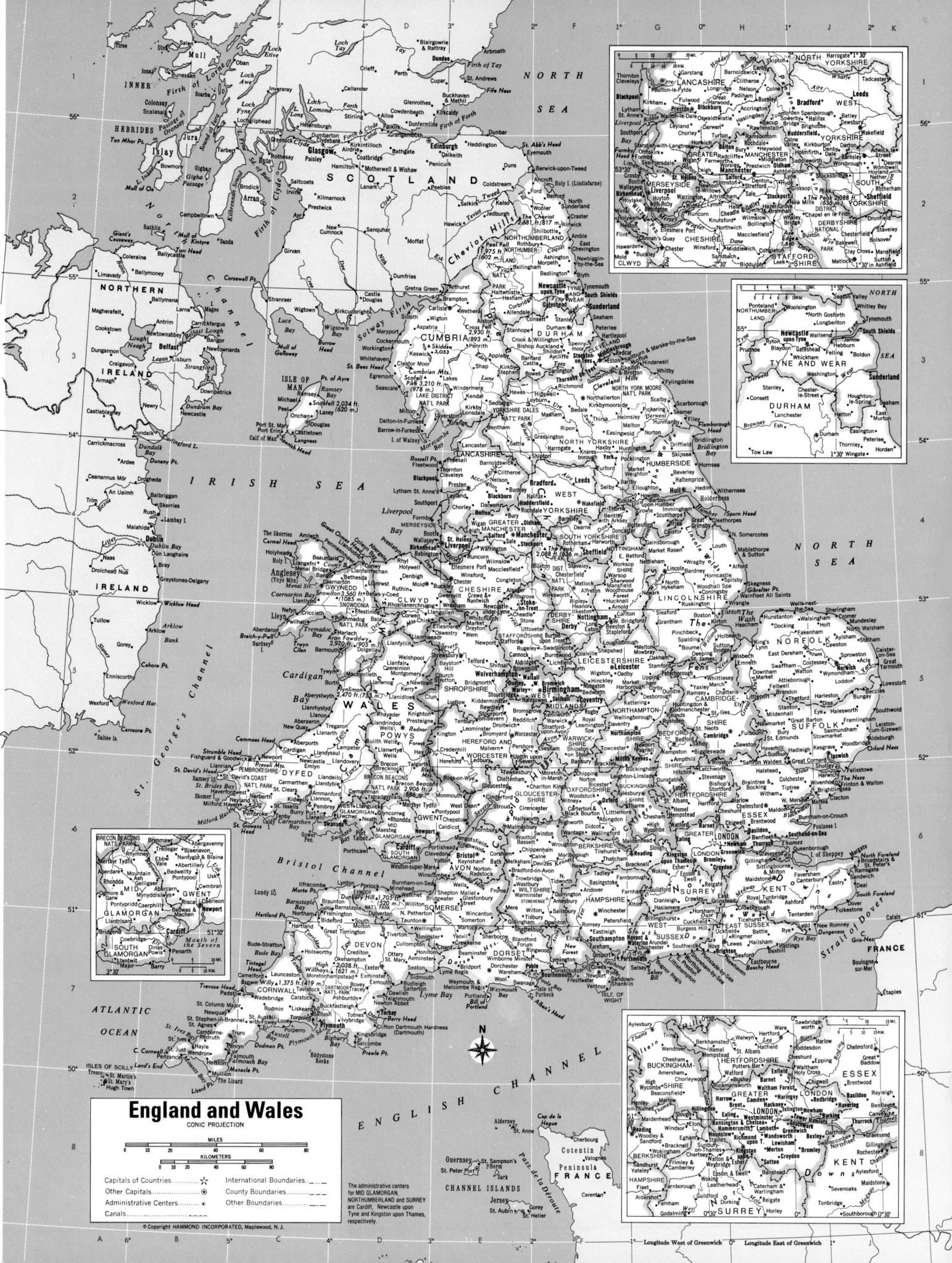

England and Wales

CONIC PROJECTION

MILES

KILOMETERS

Capitals of Countries.......... ☆
Other Capitals.......... ●
Administrative Centers.......... ⊛
Canals..........

International Boundaries..........
County Boundaries..........
Other Boundaries..........

The administrative centers for MID GLAMORGAN, NORTHUMBERLAND and SURREY are Cardiff, Newcastle upon Tyne and Kingston upon Thames, respectively.

® Copyright HAMMOND INCORPORATED, Maplewood, N.J.

14 United Kingdom and Ireland

(continued)

Lossiemouth and Branderburgh 6,847 E3
Macduff 3,887 F3
Mallaig 903 C4
Markinch 2,078 E4
Mauchline 3,663 D5
Maud 634 F3
Maybole 4,798 D5
Mayfield 1,333 D2
Melrose 2,345 F5
Melvaig⊙ 1,794 C3
Millport 1,472 A2
Milnathort 1,118 E4
Milngavie 12,067 B1
Mintlaw 2,299 F3
Moffat 2,051 E5
Monifieth 7,100 F4
Montrose 12,325 F4
Motherwell 30,676 C2
Muir of Ord 1,714 D3
Muirkirk 2,356 E5
Musselburgh 19,081 D2
Nairn 7,705 E3
Neilston 4,678 B2
Newarthill 7,003 C2
Newburgh 2,002 E4
Newcastleton 903 F5
New Cumnock 4,484 D5
New Galloway 337 D5
Newmains 6,847 C2
Newmilns and Greenholm 3,339 D5
New Pitsligo 1,125 F3
Newport-on-Tay 3,652 F4
New Scone 4,173 E4
Newtongrange 4,555 D2
Newton Mearns 15,543 B2
Newton Stewart 3,246 D6
Newtown Saint Boswells 1,095 F5
North Berwick 5,162 F4
Oakley 4,157 C1
Oban 8,111 C4
Old Kilpatrick 3,256 B2
Oldmeldrum 1,356 F3
Paisley 84,954 B2
Patna 2,490 D5
Peebles 6,692 E5
Penicuik 17,607 D2
Perth 43,010 E4
Peterculter 3,226 F3
Peterhead 17,085 G3
Pitlochry 12,621 E4
Pitmedden 1,103 F3
Pittenweem 1,544 F4
Poolewe⊙ 1,794 C3
Port Appin⊙ 2,172 C4
Port Askaig⊙ 1,795 B5
Port Bannatyne 1,414 A2
Port Ellen 1,020 B5
Port Glasgow 22,580 A2
Portknockie 1,239 F3
Portree 1,505 B3
Portsoy 1,784 F3
Prestonpans 7,621 D1
Prestwick 13,599 D5
Queensferry 7,540 D1
Renfrew 21,458 B2
Renton 3,443 A1
Rhu 1,540 A1
Rigside 1,066 E5
Rosehearty 1,243 F3
Rosneath 1,439 A1
Rothes 1,425 E3
Rothesay 5,455 A2
Rutherglen 24,091 B2
Saint Andrews 11,369 F4
Saint Monance 1,244 F4
Saline 1,192 C1
Saltcoats 12,834 D5
Sandbank 1,435 A1
Sanquhar 2,082 D5
Sauchie 6,082 C1
Selkirk 5,437 F5
Shotts 9,427 C2
Skelmorlie 1,689 A2
Slamannan 1,578 C2
Stanley 1,170 E4
Stenhousemuir 19,771 C1
Stevenston 11,337 D5
Stewarton 6,330 D5
Stirling 38,842 C1
Stonehaven 7,922 F4
Stonehouse 5,308 D5
Stornoway 8,638 B2
Stranraer 10,873 C6
Strathaven 6,152 D5
Stromeferry⊙ 1,724 C3
Stromness 1,832 E2
Sullam Voe G2
Tain 3,486 D3
Tarbert 1,403 C5
Tarbolton 2,012 D5
Tayport 3,029 F4
Thornhill, Central 443 D4
Thornhill, Dumfries and Galloway 1,473 E5
Thurso 8,896 E2
Tillicoultry 6,161 C1
Tobermory 652 B4
Tolob⊙ 2,033 G2
Tranent 8,079 F5
Troon 14,233 D5
Tullibody 6,082 C1
Turriff 3,683 F3
Tweedsmuir⊙ 105 E5
Tyndrum⊙ 1,153 D4
Uddingston 10,678 B2
Uig, Highland 103 B3
Uig, Western Isles⊙ 1,948 A2
Ullapool 1,146 C3
Uphall 3,035 C1
Viewpark 15,343 C2
Walkerburn 842 F5
Wemyss Bay 1,322 A2
West Calder 2,281 C2
West Kilbride 4,241 D5
West Linton 705 D2
Whitburn 12,610 C2
Whitehills 875 F3
Whithorn 990 D6
Wick 7,900 E2
Wigtown 1,015 D6
Winchburgh 2,398 D1
Wishaw 37,783 C2

OTHER FEATURES

A'Chralaig (mt.) C3
Annan (riv.) E5
Appin (dist.) 2,006 C4
Ardgour (dist.) 315 C4
Ardnamurchan (pt.) B4
Ardnamurchan (pen.) 764 B4
Argyll (dist.) 4,940 C4
Arisaig (sound) C4
Arkaig, Loch (lake) C4
Arran (isl.) 3,564 C5
Askival (mt.) B4
Assynt (dist.) 833 C2
Athol (dist.) 1,082 D4
Atlantic Ocean B2
Awe, Loch (lake) C4
Ayr (riv.) D5
Badenoch (dist.) 2,717 D4
Baleshare (isl.) 64 A3
Balmoral Castle (site) E3
Barra (head) A4
Barra (isl.) 1,005 A4
Barra Isles (isls.) 1,092 A4
Beauly (riv.) D3
Beinn a Ghlo (mt.) E4
Beinn Bheigeir (mt.) B5
Beinn Dearg (mt.) D3
Beinn Dhorain (mt.) E2
Beinn Eighe (mt.) C3
Ben Alder (mt.) D4
Ben Barvas (mt.) B2
Benbecula (isl.) 1,355 A3
Ben Cruachan (mt.) C4
Ben Hope (mt.) D2
Ben Kilbreck (mt.) D2
Ben Lawers (mt.) D4
Ben Lomond (mt.) D4
Ben Macdhui (mt.) E3
Ben Mhor (mt.) A3
Ben More (mt.) D4
Ben More Assynt (mt.) D2
Ben Nevis (mt.) D4
Bernera (isl.) 276 B2
Berneray (isl.) 131 A3
Berneray (isl.) 6 A4
Bidean nam Bian (mt.) D4
Black Isle (pen.) 7,209 D3
Blackwater (res.) D4
Bracadale, Loch (inlet) B3
Braemar (dist.) 7,624 E3
Bran (riv.) D3
Breadalbane (dist.) 3,649 D4
Bressay (isl.) 248 G2
Broad (bay) B2
Broad Law (mt.) E5
Broom, Loch (inlet) C3
Brough Ness (prom.) F2
Buchan (dist.) 40,089 F3
Buchan Ness (prom.) G3
Burray (isl.) 209 F2
Burrow (head) D6
Bute (isl.) 8,423 C5
Butt of Lewis (prom.) B2
Cairn Gorm (mt.) E3
Cairngorm (mts.) E3
Cairnsmore (mt.) D5
Caledonian (canal) D3
Canna (isl.) 22 B3
Carn Eige (mt.) C3
Carrick (dist.) 21,425 D5
Carron (riv.) C1
Cheviot (hills) F5
Cheviot, The (mt.) F5
Clisham (mt.) B3
Clyde (firth) D5
Clyde (riv.) D5
Coll (isl.) 144 B4
Colonsay (isl.) 137 B4
Corserine (mt.) D5
Corsewall (pt.) C5
Cowal (dist.) 15,548 C4
Cromarty (firth) D3
Cuillin (hills) B3
Cuillin (sound) B3
Dee (riv.) F3
Dennis (head) F1
Deveron (riv.) F3
Don (riv.) F3
Doon (riv.) D5
Dornoch (firth) D3
Duirinish (dist.) 1,085 B3
Duncansby (head) F2
Dunnet (head) E2
Dunnet (bay) E2
Earn (riv.) E4
Earn, Loch (lake) D4
East Loch Tarbert (inlet) B3
Eday (isl.) 179 F1
Eddrachillis (bay) C2
Eigg (isl.) 69 B4
Eishort, Loch (inlet) B3
Enard (bay) C2
Eriboll, Loch (inlet) D2
Ericht, Loch (lake) D4
Eriskay (isl.) 219 A3
Erisort, Loch (inlet) B2
Esk (riv.) F5
Etive, Loch (inlet) C4
Ewe, Loch (inlet) C3
Eye (pen.) 850 B2
Eynhallow (sound) E1
Eynort, Loch (inlet) A3
Fair Isle (isl.) 65 F3
Fannich, Loch (lake) D3
Fetlar (isl.) 88 G2
Fife Ness (prom.) F4
Findhorn (riv.) E3
Fionn Loch (lake) C3
Flannan (isls.) 3 A2
Fleet, Loch (inlet) D3
Formartine (dist.) 10,768 F3
Forth (firth) F4
Forth (riv.) B1
Forth and Clyde (canal) B2
Foula (isl.) 33 F2
Fyne, Loch (inlet) C5
Gairloch, Loch (inlet) C3
Gallan (head) A2
Galloway (dist.) 54,972 D5
Galloway, Mull of (prom.) D6
Garioch (dist.) 6,863 F3
Garry, Loch (lake) D3
Gigha (isl.) 174 C5
Glen More (dist.) 55,035 D3
Goat Fell (mt.) C5
Grampian (mts.) D4
Great Cumbrae (isl.) 1,296 A2
Green Lowther (mt.) E5
Greenstone (pt.) C3
Gruinard (bay) C3
Harris (dist.) 2,175 B3
Heads of Ayr (cape) D5
Hebrides (sea) B3
Hebrides, Inner (isls.) 14,881 B4
Hebrides, Outer (isls.) 29,615 A3
Helmsdale (riv.) E2
Herma Ness (prom.) G2
Hope, Loch (lake) D2
Hourn, Loch (inlet) C3
Hoy (isl.) 419 E2
Indaal, Loch (inlet) B5
Inner (sound) C3
Inner Hebrides (isls.) 14,881 B4
Iona (isl.) 145 B4
Islay (isl.) 3,816 B5
Jura (isl.) 210 C5
Katrine, Loch (lake) D4
Kerrera (isl.) 27 C4
Kilbrannan (sound) C5
Kinnairds (head) G3
Kintyre (pen.) 10,077 C5
Kintyre, Mull of (prom.) C5
Knapdale (dist.) 4,082 C5
Kyle of Tongue (inlet) D2
Ladder (hills) E3
Lammermuir (hills) F5
Langavat (lake) B2
Laxford, Loch (inlet) C2
Lennox (hills) B1
Leven (lake) E4
Leven, Loch (inlet) D4
Lewis (dist.) 20,047 B2
Lewis, Butt of (prom.) B2
Liddel Water (riv.) F5
Linnhe, Loch (inlet) C4
Lismore (isl.) 166 C4
Little Minch (sound) B3
Lochaber (dist.) 13,813 D4
Lochnagar (mt.) E4
Lochy, Loch (lake) D3
Lomond, Loch (lake) D4
Long, Loch (inlet) D4
Lorne (dist.) 12,162 C4
Lorne (firth) C4
Loyal, Loch (lake) D2
Loyne, Loch (lake) C3
Luce (bay) D6
Luing (isl.) 151 C4
Machers, The (pen.) 6,192 D6
Maddy, Loch (inlet) A3
Mainland (isl.) 12,747 E1
Mainland (isl.) 12,944 G2
Mar (dist.) 23,931 F3
Maree, Loch (lake) C3
May, Isle of (isl.) 10 F4
Merrick (mt.) D5
Minginish (dist.) 772 B3
Mingulay (isl.) A4
Moidart (dist.) 155 C4
Monach (isls.) A3
Monadhliath (mts.) D3
Monar, Loch (lake) C3
Moorfoot (hills) E5
Morar, Loch (lake) C4
Moray (firth) E3
Morven (mt.) E2
Morven (dist.) 398 C4
Muck (isl.) 24 B4
Muckle Flugga (isl.) 3 G2
Mull (isl.) 2,024 C4
Mull (head) F2
Mullardoch, Loch (lake) C3
Mull of Galloway (prom.) D6
Mull of Kintyre (prom.) C5
Mull of Oa (prom.) B5
Nairn (riv.) D3
Naver (riv.) D2
Ness (riv.) D3
Ness, Loch (lake) D3
Nevis, Loch (inlet) C3
Nith (riv.) E5
North (chan.) C5
North (sea) G4
North (sound) F1
North Esk (riv.) F4
North Minch (sound) B3
North Ronaldsay (isl.) 134 F1
North Uist (isl.) 1,469 A3
Noss (head) F2
Noup (head) E1
Oa, Mull of (prom.) B5
Ochil (hills) E4
Oich (riv.) D3
Oich, Loch (lake) D3
Orkney (isls.) 17,675 F1
Oronsay (isl.) 2 B4
Outer Hebrides (isls.) 29,615 A3
Oykel (riv.) D3
Pabbay (isl.) 4 A3
Papa Stour (isl.) 24 F2
Papa Westray (isl.) 106 F1
Paps of Jura (mt.) C5
Park (dist.) 210 B2
Peel Fell (mt.) F5
Pentland (firth) E2
Pentland (hills) D2
Quoich, Loch (lake) C3
Raasay (isl.) 163 C3
Rannoch (dist.) 1,177 D4
Rannoch, Loch (lake) D4
Renish (pt.) B3
Resort, Loch (inlet) A2
Rhinns (pt.) B5
Rhinns, The (pen.) 8,295 C6
Rhum (sound) B4
Riddon, Loch (inlet) C5
Roag, Loch (inlet) B2
Rona (isl.) 3 B3
Ronay (isl.) A3
Rora (head) E2
Ross of Mull (pen.) 585 B4
Rousay (isl.) 181 E1
Rudha Hunish (cape) B3
Rum (sound) B4
Rum (isl.) 40 B3
Ryan, Loch (inlet) C5
Saint Abbs (head) F5
Saint Kilda (isl.) 65 A2
Saint Magnus (bay) F2
Sanday (isl.) 592 F1
Sandray (isl.) A4
Scalpay (isl.) 483 B3
Scalpay (isl.) 5 C3
Scapa Flow (chan.) E2
Scarba (isl.) C4
Scarp (isl.) 12 A2
Scridain, Loch (inlet) B4
Seaforth, Loch (inlet) B3
Seil (isl.) 326 C4
Sgurr Alasdair (mt.) B3
Sgurr Mor (mt.) C3
Sgurr na Ciche (mt.) C3
Sgurr na Lapaich (mt.) C3
Shapinsay (isl.) 346 F1
Shetland (isls.) 18,494 G2
Shiant (isls.) B3
Shiel, Loch (lake) C4
Shin, Loch (lake) D2
Sidlaw (hills) E4
Sinclair's (bay) E2
Skye, Isle of (isl.) 7,183 B3
Sleat (dist.) 449 C3
Sleat (pt.) B4
Sleat (sound) C3
Small Isles (isls.) 171 B4
Snizort, Loch (inlet) B3
Soay (isl.) 5 B3
Solway (firth) E6
South Esk (riv.) F4
South Ronaldsay (isl.) 776 F2
South Uist (isl.) 2,281 A3
Spean (riv.) D4
Spey (riv.) E3
Staffa (isl.) B4
Start (pt.) F1
Stoer (pt.) C2
Storr, The (mt.) B3
Strathbogie (dist.) 7,959 F3
Strathmore (valley) E4
Strathspey (dist.) 6,668 E3
Striven Loch (inlet) A2
Stroma (isl.) 8 E2
Stronsay (isl.) 436 F1
Sumburgh (head) G2
Summer Isles (isls.) C2
Sunart Loch (inlet) C4
Taransay (isl.) 5 A3
Tarbat Ness (prom.) E3
Tarbert, East Loch (inlet) B3
Tarbert, Loch (inlet) B5
Tarbert, West Loch (inlet) A3
Tarbert, West Loch (inlet) C5
Tay (firth) F4
Tay (riv.) E4
Tay, Loch (lake) D4
Teith (riv.) D4
Teviot (riv.) F5
Thurso (riv.) E2
Tiree (isl.) 875 B4
Tiumpan (head) B2
Toe (head) A3
Tolsta (head) B2
Tor Ness (prom.) E2
Torridon, Loch (inlet) C3
Trossachs, The (valley) D4
Trotternish (dist.) 1,948 B3
Troup (head) F3
Tummel (lake) E4
Tweed (riv.) F5
Tyne (riv.) F5
Ulva (isl.) 23 B4
Unst (isl.) 1,124 G2
Vaternish (pt.) B3
Vaternish (dist.) 162 B3
Vatersay (isl.) 77 A4
Watten, Loch (lake) E2
West Loch Tarbert (inlet) C5
West Loch Tarbert (inlet) A3
Westray (isl.) 735 E1
Whalsay (isl.) 870 G2
White Coomb (mt.) E5
Wiay (isl.) A3
Wigtown (bay) D6
Wrath (cape) C2
Yarrow (riv.) E5
Yell (isl.) 1,143 G2
Yell (sound) G2

⊙ Population of parish.

Agriculture, Industry and Resources

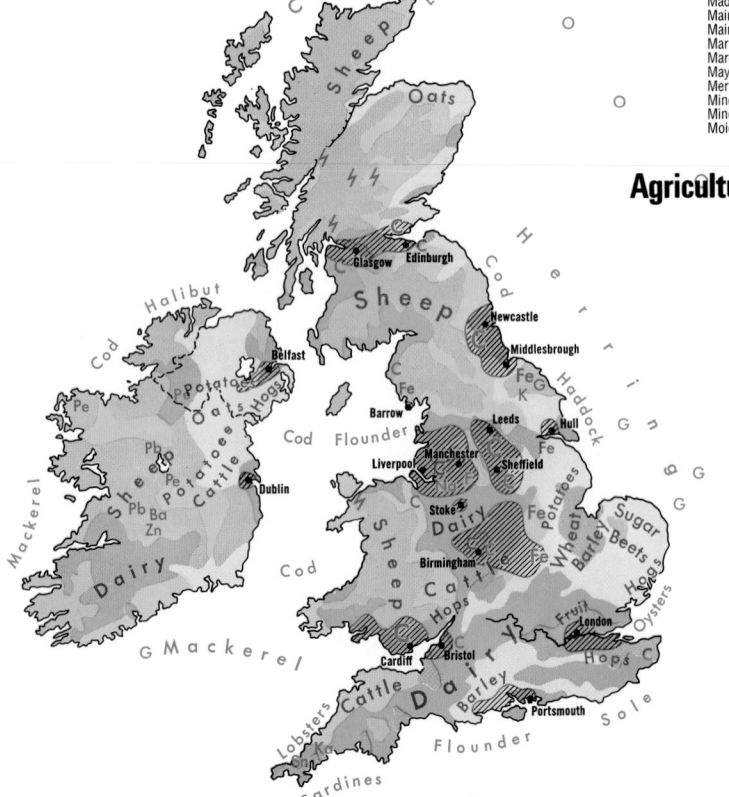

DOMINANT LAND USE

Cereals (chiefly oats, barley)
Truck Farming, Horticulture
Dairy, Mixed Farming
Livestock, Mixed Farming
Pasture Livestock

MAJOR MINERAL OCCURRENCES

Ba Barite
C Coal
F Fluorspar
Fe Iron Ore
G Natural Gas
K Potash
Ka Kaolin (china clay)
Na Salt
O Petroleum
Pb Lead
Pe Peat
Sn Tin
Zn Zinc

Water Power
Major Industrial Areas

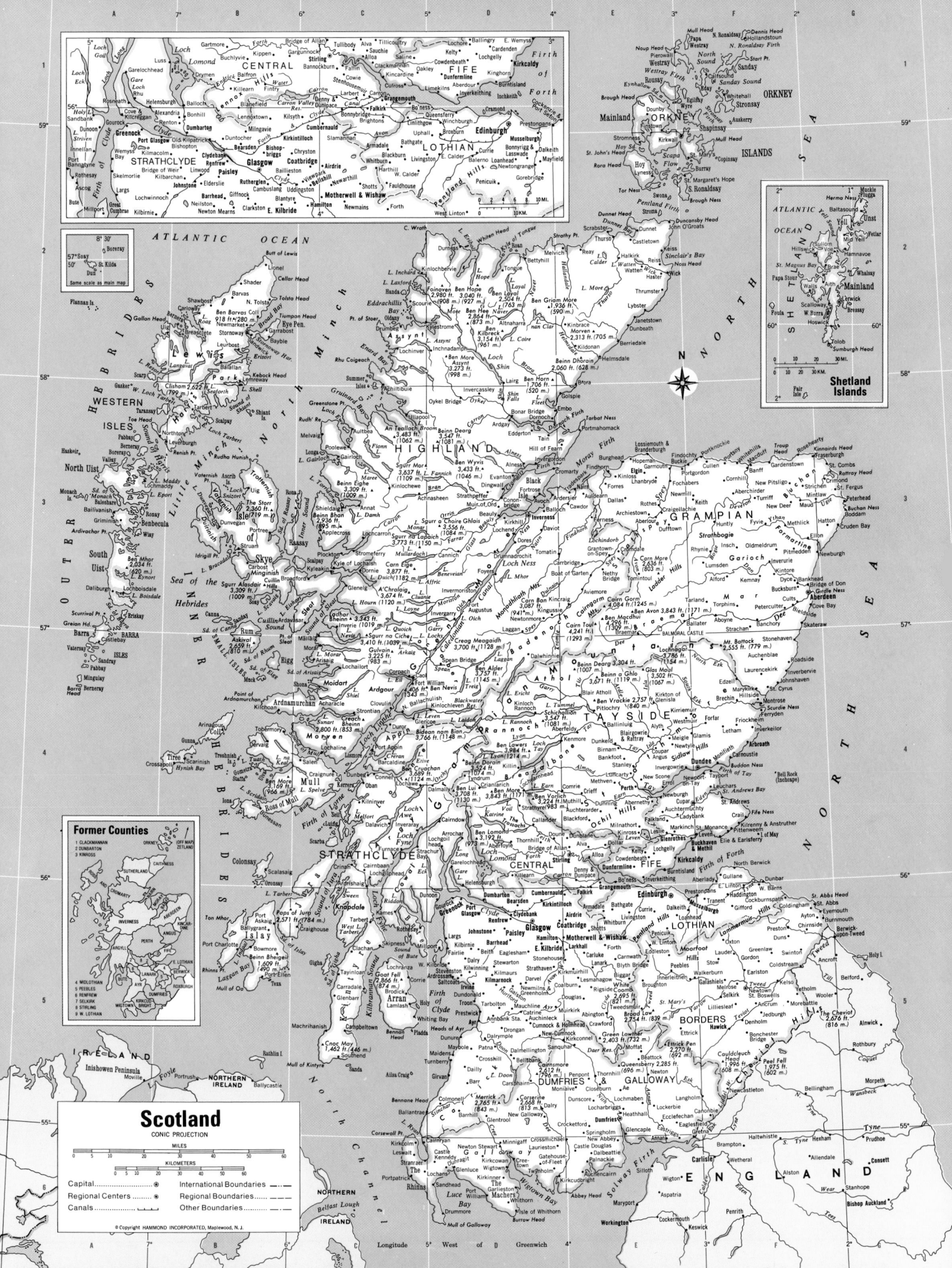

Scotland

CONIC PROJECTION

MILES

KILOMETERS

Capital .... ⊛
Regional Centers .... ⊛
Canals ....

International Boundaries ....
Regional Boundaries ....
Other Boundaries ....

© Copyright HAMMOND INCORPORATED, Maplewood, N.J.

Former Counties

1 CLACKMANNAN
2 DUNBARTON
3 KINROSS
4 MIDLOTHIAN
5 PEEBLES
6 RENFREW
7 SELKIRK
8 STIRLING
9 W. LOTHIAN

Shetland Islands

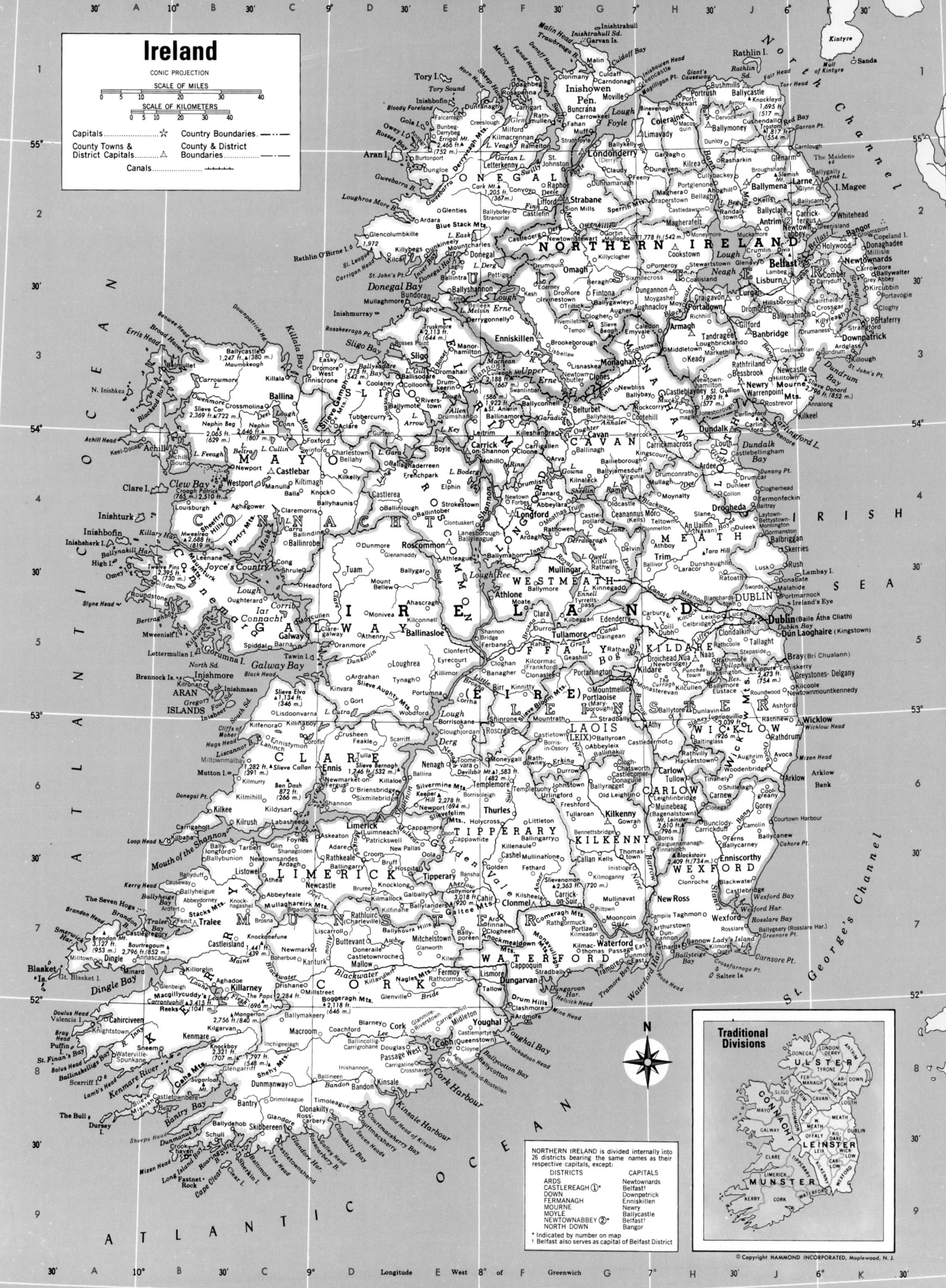

Ireland

CONIC PROJECTION

SCALE OF MILES

SCALE OF KILOMETERS

Capitals.....................☆ Country Boundaries.—·—·—
County Towns & County & District
District Capitals.........△ Boundaries.................
Canals.....................

Traditional Divisions

NORTHERN IRELAND is divided internally into
26 districts bearing the same names as their
respective capitals, except:

DISTRICTS	CAPITALS
ARDS	Newtownards
CASTLEREAGH ① *	Belfast
DOWN	Downpatrick
FERMANAGH	Enniskillen
MOURNE	Newry
MOYLE	Ballycastle
NEWTOWNABBEY ② *	Belfast †
NORTH DOWN	Bangor

* Indicated by number on map
† Belfast also serves as capital of Belfast District

© Copyright HAMMOND INCORPORATED, Maplewood, N.J.

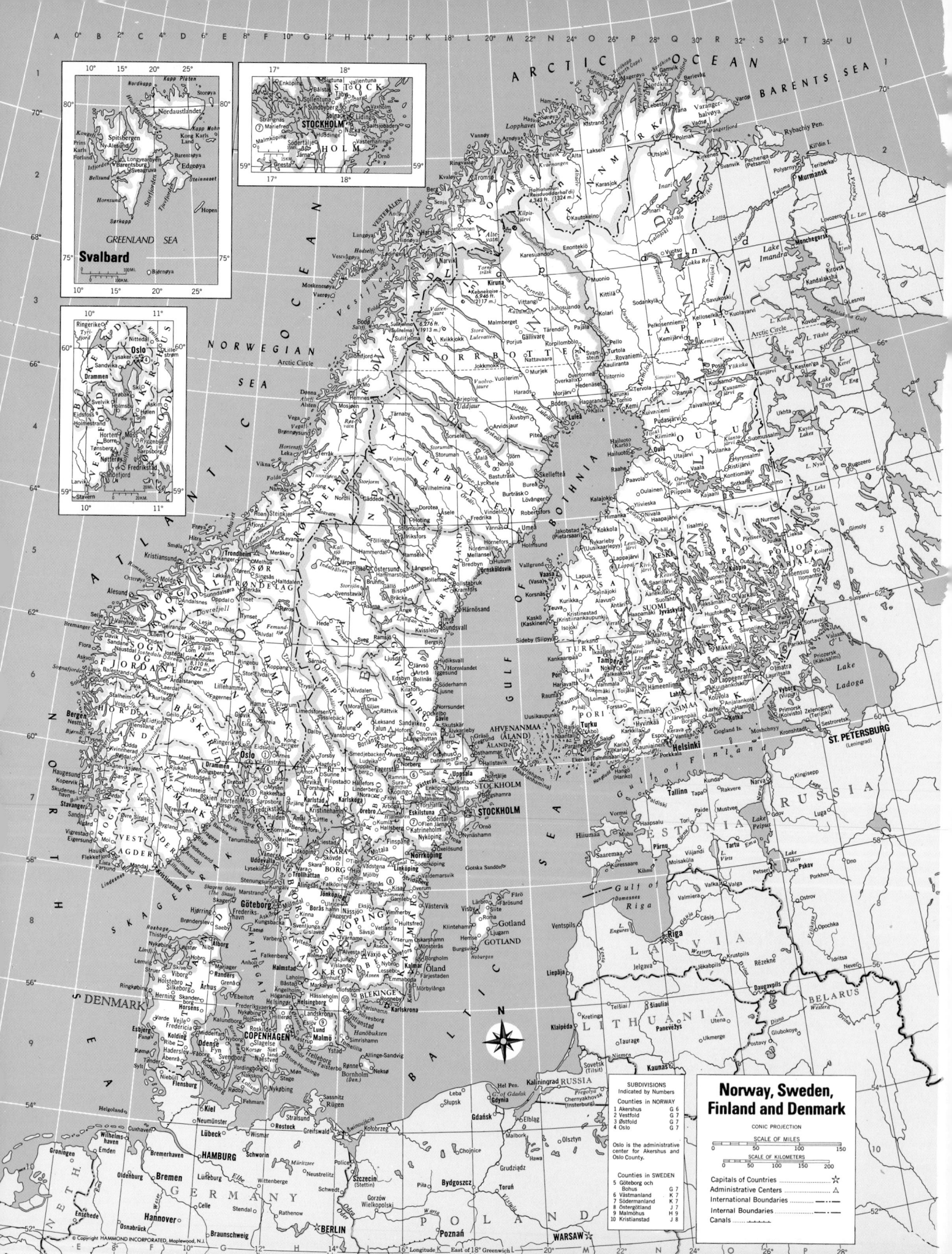

Norway, Sweden, Finland and Denmark

CONIC PROJECTION

Svalbard

GREENLAND SEA

ARCTIC OCEAN

BARENTS SEA

NORWEGIAN SEA

ATLANTIC OCEAN

GULF OF BOTHNIA

BALTIC SEA

Gulf of Finland

Gulf of Riga

SUBDIVISIONS
Indicated by Numbers

Counties in NORWAY
1 Akershus .... G 6
2 Vestfold .... G 7
3 Østfold .... G 7
4 Oslo .... G 7

Oslo is the administrative
center for Akershus and
Oslo County.

Counties in SWEDEN
5 Göteborg och
  Bohus .... G 8
6 Västmanland .... K 7
7 Södermanland .... K 7
8 Östergötland .... J 7
9 Malmöhus .... H 9
10 Kristianstad .... J 8

SCALE OF MILES
0   50   100   150

SCALE OF KILOMETERS
0   50   100   150   200

Capitals of Countries .... ☆
Administrative Centers .... △
International Boundaries .... ———
Internal Boundaries .... —·—·—
Canals .... ········

© Copyright HAMMOND INCORPORATED, Maplewood, N.J.

AREA 125,053 sq. mi.
(323,887 sq. km.)
POPULATION 4,242,000
CAPITAL Oslo
LARGEST CITY Oslo
HIGHEST POINT Glittertinden
8,110 ft. (2,472 m.)
MONETARY UNIT krone
MAJOR LANGUAGE Norwegian
MAJOR RELIGION Protestantism

AREA 173,665 sq. mi.
(449,792 sq. km.)
POPULATION 8,541,000
CAPITAL Stockholm
LARGEST CITY Stockholm
HIGHEST POINT Kebnekaise 6,946 ft.
(2,117 m.)
MONETARY UNIT krona
MAJOR LANGUAGE Swedish
MAJOR RELIGION Protestantism

AREA 130,128 sq. mi.
(337,032 sq. km.)
POPULATION 4,973,000
CAPITAL Helsinki
LARGEST CITY Helsinki
HIGHEST POINT Haltiatunturi
4,343 ft. (1,324 m.)
MONETARY UNIT markka
MAJOR LANGUAGES Finnish, Swedish
MAJOR RELIGION Protestantism

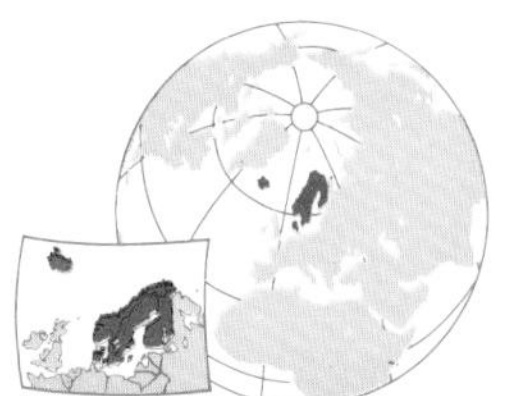

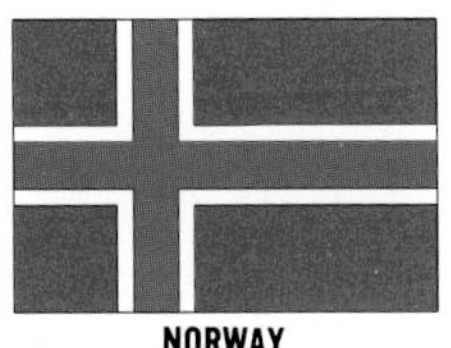

NORWAY

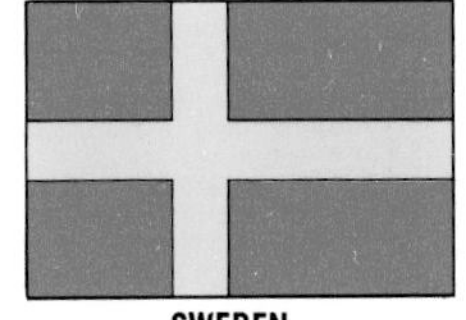

SWEDEN

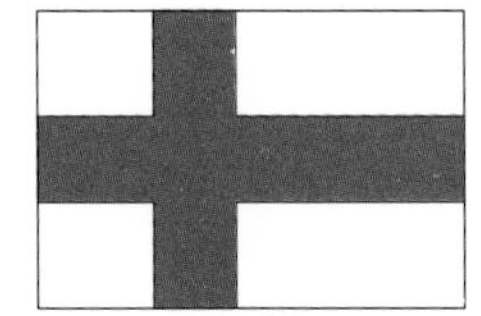

FINLAND

FINLAND

PROVINCES

Ahvenanmaa 23,591	L6
Åland (Ahvenanmaa) 23,591	L6
Häme 677,750	O5
Keski-Suomi 247,693	O5
Kuopio 256,036	P5
Kymi 340,665	Q6
Lappi 200,943	P3
Mikkeli 239,029	P6
Oulu 432,141	O4
Pohjois-Karjala 177,567	Q5
Turku ja Pori 713,050	N6
Uusimaa 1,187,851	O6
Vaasa 444,348	N5

CITIES and TOWNS

Abo (Turku) 161,398	N6
Alavus 10,701	N5
Äänekoski 11,447	O5
Anjalamkoski 19,703	P6
Borga 19,513	O6
Espoo 156,778	O6
Forssa 20,074	N6
Haapajärvi 8,454	O5
Hämeenlinna 42,382	O6
Hamina 10,313	P6
Hangö 12,071	N7
Hanko (Hangö) 12,071	N7
Harjavalta 8,955	M6
Heinola 16,112	P6
Helsinki (cap.) 485,795	O6
Hyvinkää 38,742	O6
Iisalmi 23,612	P5
Ikaalinen 8,184	N6
Imatra 35,085	Q5
Jakobstad 20,458	N5
Jämsä 12,498	O6
Järvenpää 27,220	O6
Joensuu 46,850	R5
Jyväskylä 65,282	O5
Kajaani 36,020	P4
Kankaanpää 13,652	M6
Karis (Karjaa)	N6
Karkkila 8,355	N6
Kauniainen 7,746	O6
Kemi 26,421	O4
Kemijärvi 12,762	P3
Kerava 26,207	O6
Kokemäki 9,741	N6
Kokkola 34,489	N5
Kotka 58,956	P6
Kouvola 31,829	P6
Kristiinankaupunki (Kristinestad) 9,081	N5
Kristinestad 9,081	N5
Kuopio 78,124	Q5
Kurikka 11,512	M5
Kuusankoski 22,089	P6
Lahti 94,447	O6
Lappeenranta 54,102	P6
Lapua 14,644	N5
Lieksa 18,588	R5
Loimaa 7,053	N6
Lovisa 8,697	P6
Maarianhamina (Mariehamn) 9,829	M7
Mänttä 8,092	O6
Mariehamn 9,829	M7
Mikkeli 31,636	P6
Naantali 10,246	M6
Nokia 24,325	N6
Nurmes 11,419	Q5
Nykarleby 7,768	N5
Oulainen 8,225	O4
Oulu 97,297	O4
Outokumpu 9,678	Q5
Parainen 11,618	N6
Parkano 8,692	N6
Pieksämäki 14,372	P5
Pietarsaari (Jakobstad) 20,458	N5
Pori 78,376	M6
Pudasjärvi 11,453	P4
Raahe 18,932	O4

OTHER FEATURES

Åland (isls.)	L6
Baltic (sea)	K9
Bothnia (gulf)	M5
Finland (gulf)	P7
Hailuoto (isl.)	O4
Haltiatunturi (mt.)	M2
Haukivesi (lake)	Q5
Iijoki (riv.)	P4
Inari (lake)	P2
Ivalojoki (riv.)	P2
Kallavesi (lake)	P5
Karlö (Hailuoto) (isl.)	O4
Keitele (lake)	O5
Kemijärvi (lake)	P3
Kemijoki (riv.)	O3
Lapland (reg.)	N3
Lappajärvi (lake)	O5
Lapuanjoki (riv.)	N5
Lokka (reg.)	Q3
Muojärvi (lake)	R4
Muonio (riv.)	M2
Näsijärvi (lake)	O6
Orihvesi (lake)	Q5
Oulujärvi (lake)	P4
Oulujoki (riv.)	O4
Ounasjoki (riv.)	O3
Päijänne (lake)	O6
Pielinen (lake)	Q5
Porkkala (pen.)	O7
Puruvesi (lake)	Q6
Saimaa (lake)	Q6
Tana (riv.)	P2
Tornionjoki (riv.)	O3
Ylikitka (lake)	Q3

NORWAY

COUNTIES

Akershus 399,797	G6
Aust-Agder 95,475	E7
Buskerud 221,384	F6
Finnmark 74,690	O2
Hedmark 186,305	G6
Hordaland 402,343	E6
Møre og Romsdal 237,489	E5
Nordland 241,048	J3
Nord-Trøndelag 126,648	H4
Oppland 181,620	F6
Oslo (city) 449,220	D3
Østfold 235,813	G7
Rogaland 326,611	D7
Sogn og Fjordane 105,466	E6
Sør-Trøndelag 247,354	G5
Telemark 162,595	F7
Troms 146,595	L2
Vest-Agder 141,284	E7
Vestfold 192,934	G7

CITIES and TOWNS

Ålesund 40,868	D5
Ålgård 2,322	D7
Alta 5,582	N2
Åndalsnes 2,574	F5
Årdalstangen 2,360	F6
Arendal 11,701	F7
Årnes 2,267	G6
Askim 8,413	E4
Bamble† 7,031	F7
Bergen 213,434	D6
Bodø 31,077	J2
Borge† 3,294	H2
Brate 2,107	C4
Brønnøysund 3,130	G4
Drammen 50,777	C4
Drøbak 4,538	D4
Eidsvoll 2,906	G6
Eigersund 11,379	D7
Elverum 7,391	G6
Farsund 8,908	E7
Flekkefjord 8,750	E7
Flora 8,822	D6
Fredrikstad 29,024	D4
Gjøvik 25,963	G6
Grimstad 13,091	F7
Halden 27,087	G7
Hamar 16,418	F6
Hammerfest 7,610	N1
Harstad 21,125	K2
Hauge 2,079	E7
Haugesund 27,386	D7
Holmestrand 8,246	C4
Honningsvag 3,780	O1
Horten 13,746	D4
Kirkenes 4,466	Q2
Kongsberg 19,854	F7
Kongsvinger 16,146	H6
Kopervik 4,221	D7
Kornsjø† 6,079	C4
Kragerø 5,249	F7
Kristiansand 59,488	E8
Kristiansund 18,847	E5
Kvinnherad† 2,898	C4
Larvik 9,097	C4
Lenvik† 11,098	L2
Levanger 5,066	G5
Lillehammer 21,248	F6
Lillesand 3,028	F7
Lillestrøm† 11,550	E3
Lodingen 1,840	J2
Longyearbyen	D2
Lysaker† 81,612	D3
Mandal 11,579	E7
Meråker† 2,907	G5
Mo 21,033	J3
Molde 20,334	E5
Mosjøen 9,341	H4
Moss 25,786	D4
Mysen 3,760	D4
Namsos 11,452	G4
Narvik 19,582	K2
Nesttun† 11,519	D6
Nittedal† 8,889	D3
Notodden 12,970	F7
Nøtterøy 11,944	D4
Odda 7,401	E6
Oppdal 2,173	F5
Orkanger 3,685	F5
Oslo (cap.) 462,732	D3
Oslo* 645,413	D3
Porsgrunn 31,709	G7
Rakkestad 2,392	D4
Ringerike 30,156	C3
Risør 6,560	F7
Rjukan 5,334	F7
Røros 3,041	G5
Sætermoen 2,114	L2
Sandefjord 33,350	C4
Sandnes 34,330	D7
Sandvika† 34,337	C3
Sarpsborg 12,889	D4
Seljet 3,386	D5
Ski 9,081	D4
Skien 47,105	F7
Skudeneshavn 2,206	D7
Stavanger 86,639	D7
Stavern 2,604	D4
Steinkjer 20,553	G4
Stor-Elvdal† 2,993	G6
Sunndalsøra 5,114	E5
Svelvik 2,256	D4
Svolvaer 3,942	J2
Tana 1,893	Q1
Tønsberg 9,964	D4
Tromsø 43,830	L2
Trondheim 134,910	F5
Tvedestrand 1,689	F7
Ullensvang† 2,326	E6
Vadsø 6,019	Q1
Vanylven 1,966	E5
Vardø 3,875	R1
Vik 1,019	E6
Volda 3,511	E5
Voss 5,944	E6

OTHER FEATURES

Andøya (isl.)	J2
Barentsøya (isl.)	D2
Bjørnøya (isl.)	D3
Boknafjord (fjord)	D7
Dovrefjell (hills)	F5
Edgeøya (isl.)	E2
Femundsjø (lake)	G5
Folda (fjord)	G4
Folda (fjord)	J3
Frohavet (bay)	F5
Frøya (isl.)	F5
Glittertinden (mt.)	F6
Greenland (sea)	C3
Hadselfjorden (fjord)	J2
Haltiatunturi (mt.)	M2
Hardangerfjord (fjord)	D7
Hardangervidda (plat.)	E6
Hinlopenstreten (strait)	C1
Hornøya (isl.)	K2
Hitra (isl.)	F5
Hortensfjord (fjord)	G4
Isfjorden (fjord)	C2
Kjølen (mts.)	K3
Kvaenangen (fjord)	N2
Kvaløy (isl.)	K2
Kvaløya (isl.)	O1
Laksefjorden (fjord)	P1
Langøya (isl.)	J2
Lapland (reg.)	K2
Lindesnes (cape)	E8
Lofoten (isls.)	H2
Lopphavet (bay)	M1
Magerøya (isl.)	P1
Moskenesøya (isl.)	H3
Namsen (riv.)	H4
Nordaustlandet (isl.)	D1
Nordfjord (fjord)	E6
Nordkapp (fjord)	C1
North Cape (Nordkapp) (cape)	P1
Norwegian (sea)	F3
Ofotfjorden (fjord)	K2
Oslofjord (fjord)	D4
Otra (riv.)	E7
Pasvikelv (riv.)	Q2
Porsangen (fjord)	O1
Prins Karls Forland (isl.)	B2
Rana (riv.)	H3
Rauma (riv.)	F5
Ringvassøy (isl.)	L2
Romsdalsfjorden (fjord)	E5
Saltfjorden (fjord)	J3
Seiland (isl.)	N1
Senja (isl.)	K2
Skagerrak (strait)	F8
Sognafjorden (fjord)	D6
Sørkapp (pt.)	C2
Sørøya (isl.)	N1
Spitsbergen (isl.)	C2
Steinneset (cape)	E2
Storfjorden (fjord)	D2
Sulitjelma (mt.)	J3
Svalbard (isls.)	C3
Tana (riv.)	P1
Tanafjord (fjord)	Q1
Trondheimsfjorden (fjord)	G5
Tyrifjord (lake)	C3
Vannøy (isl.)	L1
Varangerfjord (fjord)	Q2
Varangerhalvøya (pen.)	Q1
Vegafjorden (fjord)	G4
Vesterålen (isl.)	J2
Vestfjord (fjord)	H3
Vestvågøya (isl.)	H3
Vikna (isls.)	G4

(continued on following page)

Horn

Fontur

Nordkapp (North Cape)

Varangerfjord

Faxaflói

VATNA-JÖKULL

VESTER-ÁLEN

Inari

Reykjavík

Hekla 4,891 ft. (1491 m.)

Hvannadals-hnukur 6,946 ft. (2117 m.)

Iceland

LOFOTEN

Haltiatunturi 4,343 ft. (1324 m.)

Tana

Ivalo

Vestfjord

Kebnekaise 6,946 ft. (2117 m.)

Muonio

Torne

Ounas

Ylikitka

Nordfjord

Trondheims Fjorden

Uddjaur

Ångerman

Ume

Lule

Skellefte

Kemi

Ii

Oulu

Oulujärvi

Storsjön

Indals

GULF OF BOTHNIA

Sognefjorden

Glittertinden 8,110 ft. (2472 m.)

Ljusnan

Dal

Klar

Bergen

Hardanger fjord

Oslo

Mjøsa

Glåma

ÅLAND IS.

Kumo

Kymi

Saimaa

Helsinki

Lindesnes

Otta

Lågen

Vänern

Stockholm

Göteborg

Gotland

Topography

Skagerrak

Kattegat

Göta Canal

Vättern

Öland

Yding Skovhoj 568 ft. (173 m.)

FYR

Sjaelland

Copenhagen

Lolland

Bornholm

Below Sea Level	100 m. 328 ft.	200 m. 656 ft.	500 m. 1,640 ft.	1,000 m. 3,281 ft.	2,000 m. 6,562 ft.	5,000 m. 16,404 ft.

0   100   200 MI.

0   100   200 KM.

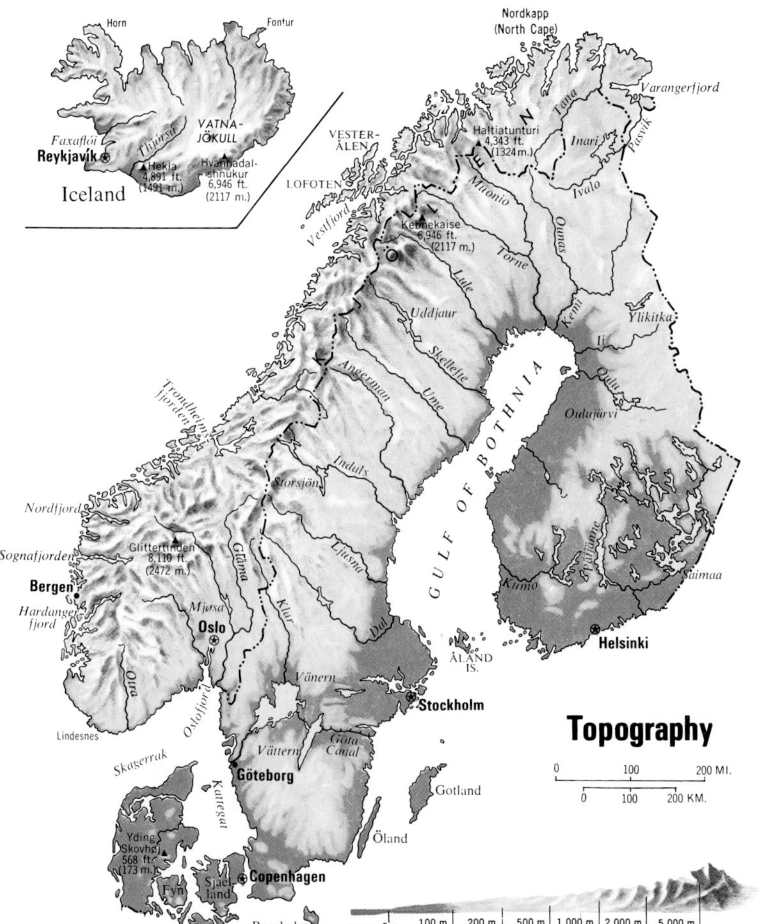

Agriculture, Industry and Resources

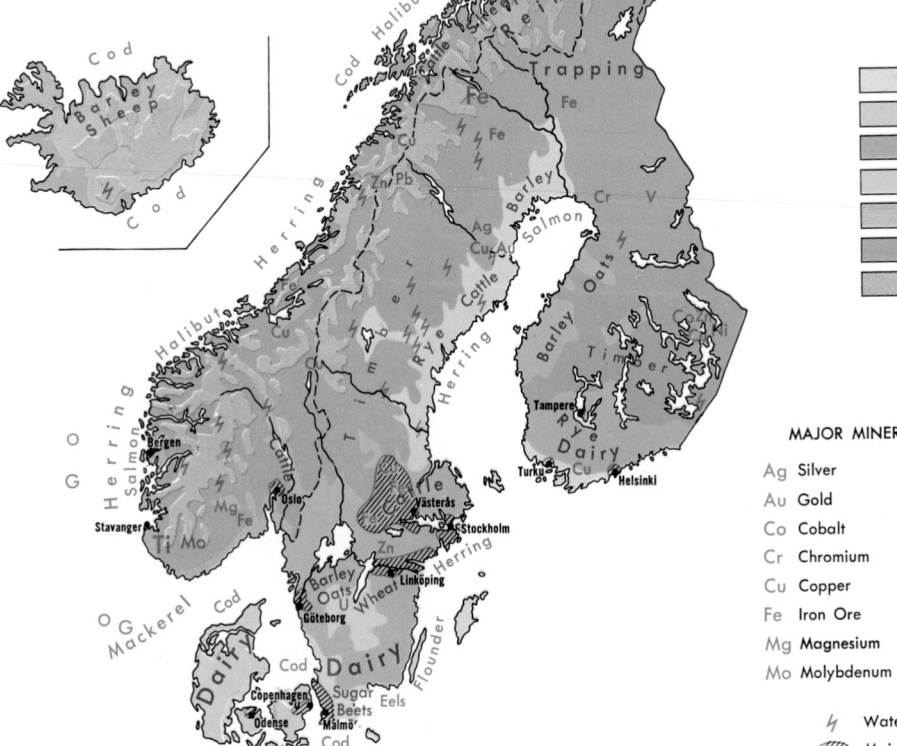

DOMINANT LAND USE

- Cash Cereals, Dairy
- Dairy, Cattle, Hogs
- Dairy, General Farming
- General Farming (chiefly cereals)
- Nomadic Sheep Herding
- Forests, Limited Mixed Farming
- Nonagricultural Land

MAJOR MINERAL OCCURRENCES

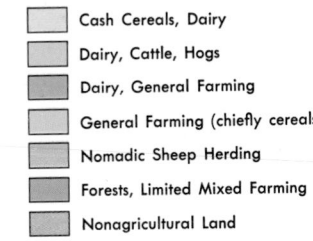

Ag	Silver	Ni	Nickel
Au	Gold	O	Petroleum
Co	Cobalt	Pb	Lead
Cr	Chromium	Ti	Titanium
Cu	Copper	U	Uranium
Fe	Iron Ore	V	Vanadium
Mg	Magnesium	Zn	Zinc
Mo	Molybdenum		

⚡ Water Power

▨ Major Industrial Areas

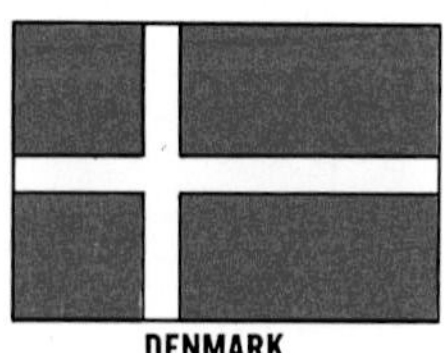

DENMARK

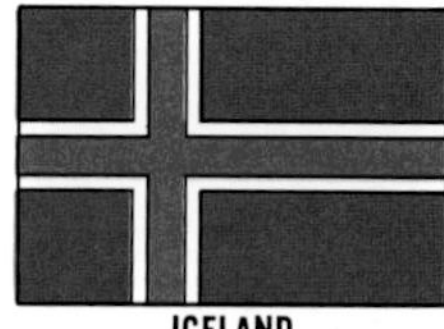

ICELAND

DENMARK
AREA 16,629 sq. mi. (43,069 sq. km.)
POPULATION 5,135,000
CAPITAL Copenhagen
LARGEST CITY Copenhagen
HIGHEST POINT Yding Skovhøj
 568 ft. (173 m.)
MONETARY UNIT krone
MAJOR LANGUAGE Danish
MAJOR RELIGION Protestantism

ICELAND
AREA 39,768 sq. mi. (103,000 sq. km.)
POPULATION 250,000
CAPITAL Reykjavík
LARGEST CITY Reykjavík
HIGHEST POINT Hvannadalshnúkur
 6,952 ft. (2,119 m.)
MONETARY UNIT króna
MAJOR LANGUAGE Icelandic
MAJOR RELIGION Protestantism

Denmark and Iceland

CONIC PROJECTION

SCALE OF MILES

SCALE OF KILOMETERS

Capitals of Countries _____ ★
Capitals of Counties (amter) ___ △
International Boundaries _____
Internal Boundaries _____

Denmark is divided into fourteen Counties plus Copenhagen and Frederiksberg communes.

© Copyright HAMMOND INCORPORATED, Maplewood, N.J.

Germany
CONIC PROJECTION
SCALE OF MILES
0 20 40 60 80
SCALE OF KILOMETERS
0 20 40 60 80
Capitals of Countries
State Capitals
International Boundaries
State Boundaries
Canals
Scale 1:3,040,000
Longitude East 10° of Greenwich
DENMARK
BALTIC SEA
NORTH SEA
NORTH FRISIAN ISLANDS
EAST FRISIAN ISLANDS
WEST FRISIAN ISLANDS
SCHLESWIG-HOLSTEIN
MECKLENBURG
WESTERN POMERANIA
LOWER SAXONY
SAXONY-ANHALT
BRANDENBURG
BERLIN
NORTH RHINE-WESTPHALIA
HESSE
THURINGIA
SAXONY
RHINELAND-PALATINATE
SAARLAND
BADEN-WÜRTTEMBERG
BAVARIA
NETHERLANDS
BELGIUM
LUXEMBOURG
FRANCE
SWITZERLAND
AUSTRIA
CZECH REPUBLIC
POLAND
HAMBURG
BREMEN
Kiel
Schwerin
Hannover
Magdeburg
Potsdam
Düsseldorf
Wiesbaden
Mainz
Erfurt
Dresden
Saarbrücken
Stuttgart
MUNICH
Cologne
Frankfurt
Leipzig
Nürnberg
Berlin
© Copyright HAMMOND INCORPORATED, Maplewood, N. J.

AREA 137,753 sq. mi. (356,780 sq. km.)
POPULATION 78,890,000
CAPITAL Berlin
LARGEST CITY Berlin
HIGHEST POINT Zugspitze 9,718 ft. (2,962 m.)
MONETARY UNIT Deutsche mark
MAJOR LANGUAGE German
MAJOR RELIGIONS Protestantism, Roman
Catholicism

GERMANY

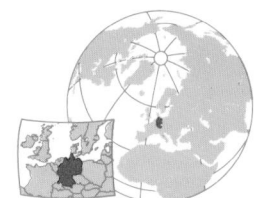

Topography

Scale 0 50 100 MI. / 0 50 100 KM.

Below Sea Level | 100 m. 328 ft. | 200 m. 656 ft. | 500 m. 1,640 ft. | 1,000 m. 3,281 ft. | 2,000 m. 6,562 ft. | 5,000 m. 16,404 ft.

Zugspitze 9,718 ft. (2962 m.)

GERMANY

STATES

Baden-Württemberg
9,432,709 ....C4
Bavaria 11,049,263 ....D4
Berlin 3,304,561 ....E4
Brandenberg* E2
Bremen 661,992 ....C2
Hamburg 1,603,070 ....D2
Hesse 5,568,892 ....C3
Lower Saxony 7,184,943 ....C2
Mecklenburg-Western
Pomerania* E2
North Rhine-Westphalia
16,874,059 ....B3
Rhineland-Palatinate
3,653,155 ....B4
Saarland 1,054,142 ....E3
Saxony* E3
Saxony-Anhalt* D3
Schleswig-Holstein
2,564,565 ....C1
Thuringia* D3

*East German States
15,611,488 ....D-E 2-3

CITIES and TOWNS

Aachen 233,255 ....B3
Aalen 62,812 ....D4
Ahaus 30,180 ....B2
Ahlen 52,836 ....B3
Ahrensburg 27,174 ....D2
Alfeld 21,986 ....C3
Alsdorf 46,328 ....B3
Alsfeld 16,686 ....C3
Altena 23,301 ....B3
Altenburg 53,602 ....E3
Amberg 42,246 ....D4
Andernach 27,171 ....B3
Anklam 19,946 ....E2
Annaberg-Buchholz 26,002...E3
Ansbach 36,912 ....D4
Apolda 28,230 ....D3
Arnsberg 73,912 ....C3
Arnstadt 30,207 ....D3
Aschaffenburg 62,048 ......C4
Aschersleben 34,166 ....D3
Aue 27,935 ....E3
Auerbach 22,324 ....E3
Augsburg 247,731 ....D4
Aurich 36,063 ....B2
Backnang 30,583 ....C4
Bad Berleburg 20,080 ......C3
Bad Driburg 16,866 ....C3
Bad Dürkheim 16,670 ....C4
Baden-Baden 50,761 ....C4
Bad Harzburg 23,079 ....D3
Bad Hersfeld 28,214 ....C3
Bad Homburg vor der Höhe
51,035 ....C3
Bad Honnef 21,812 ....B3
Bad Kissingen 20,237 ......D3
Bad Kreuznach 39,400 ......B4
Bad Langensalza 17,027 ....D3
Bad Mergentheim 19,801 ....C4
Bad Münstereifel 15,232 ...B3
Bad Nauheim 27,561 ....C3
Bad Neuenahr-Ahrweiler
24,610 ....B3
Bad Oldesloe 20,473 ....D2
Bad Pyrmont 20,437 ....C3
Bad Reichenhall 16,365 ....E5
Bad Salzuflen 50,875 ......C2
Bad Salzungen 21,387 ......C3
Bad Schwartau 19,960 ......D2
Bad Vilbel 24,567 ....C3
Bad Zwischenahn 23,348 ....C2
Balingen 30,615 ....C4
Bamberg 69,809 ....D4
Barsinghausen 37,792 ......C2
Bautzen 52,354 ....F3
Bayreuth 70,933 ....D4
Berchtesgaden 7,644 ....E5
Bergen 16,713 ....E1
Bergisch Gladbach 101,983 .B3
Berleburg
(Bad Berleburg) 20,080 ..C3

Berlin (cap.) 3,304,561 ....E4
Bernau bei Berlin 19,919 ...E2
Bernburg 40,834 ....D3
Biberach an der Riss 28,319 .C4
Bielefeld 311,946 ....C2
Bietigheim-Bissingen 37,573 .C4
Bingen 23,141 ....B4
Bitburg 10,758 ....B4
Bitterfeld 20,869 ....E3
Blankenburg am Harz 19,279 .D3
Böblingen 43,400 ....C4
Bocholt 67,565 ....B3
Bochum 389,087 ....B3
Bonn 282,190 ....B3
Borghorst 17,238 ....B2
Borken 34,710 ....B3
Borna 24,397 ....E3
Bornheim 34,536 ....B3
Bottrop 116,363 ....B3
Brake 16,069 ....C2
Bramsche 24,653 ....C2
Brandenburg 94,755 ....D2
Braunschweig 253,794 ......D2
Bremen 535,058 ....C2
Bremerhaven 126,934 ....C2
Bremervörde 17,629 ....C2
Bretten 23,894 ....C4
Brilon 24,341 ....C3
Bruchsal 36,831 ....C4
Brühl 40,710 ....B3
Buchholz in der Nordheide
30,523 ....C2
Bückeburg 19,758 ....C2
Büdingen 17,013 ....C3
Bühl 23,470 ....C4
Bünde 39,103 ....C2
Büren 17,720 ....C3
Burg bei Magdeburg 28,359 .D2
Burghausen 16,761 ....E4
Burgsteinfurt 31,367 ......B2
Butzbach 21,095 ....C3
Buxtehude 31,132 ....C2
Castrop-Rauxel 77,660 .....B3
Celle 71,050 ....D2
Cham 16,641 ....E4
Chemnitz 313,799 ....E3
Clausthal-Zellerfeld 16,069 .D3
Cloppenburg 22,536 ....B2
Coburg 43,233 ....D3
Coesfeld 31,979 ....B3
Cologne 937,482 ....B3
Coswig 27,590 ....E3
Cottbus 126,592 ....F3
Crailsheim 26,618 ....D4
Crimmitschau 24,440 ....E3
Cuxhaven 55,249 ....C2
Dachau 34,183 ....D4
Darmstadt 136,067 ....C4
Deggendorf 28,680 ....E4
Delitzsch 27,636 ....E3
Delmenhorst 72,901 ....C2
Demmin 16,992 ....E2
Dessau 103,538 ....D3
Detmold 66,809 ....C3
Dillenburg 23,672 ....C3
Dillingen 21,358 ....D4
Döbeln 27,706 ....E3
Donaueschingen 18,296 .....C5
Donauwörth 17,420 ....D4
Dorsten 75,518 ....B3
Dortmund 587,328 ....B3
Dresden 519,810 ....E3
Duderstadt 22,265 ....D3
Duisburg 527,447 ....B3
Dülmen 39,344 ....B3
Düren 83,120 ....B3
Düsseldorf 569,641 ....B3
Eberswalde-Finow 54,566 ...E2
Eckernförde 22,197 ....C1
Ehingen 22,886 ....C4
Eilenburg 21,931 ....E3
Einbeck 25,813 ....C3
Eisenach 49,534 ....D3
Eisenhüttenstadt 51,729 ...F2
Eisleben 26,484 ....D3
Ellwangen 21,857 ....D4
Elmshorn 42,784 ....C2
Emden 49,803 ....B2
Emmendingen 22,959 ....B4
Emmerich 27,906 ....B3
Emsdetten 31,063 ....B2
Erfurt 217,134 ....D3

Erkelenz 36,525 ....B3
Erlangen 100,583 ....D4
Eschwege 21,527 ....C3
Eschweiler 53,516 ....B3
Espelkamp 23,868 ....C2
Essen 620,594 ....B3
Esslingen am Neckar 90,537 .C4
Ettlingen 37,269 ....C4
Euskirchen 47,756 ....B3
Eutin 16,567 ....D1
Falkensee 23,024 ....E3
Fellbach 39,612 ....C4
Finsterwalde 23,857 ....E3
Flensburg 85,830 ....C1
Forchheim 28,784 ....D4
Forst 26,501 ....F3
Frankenberg-Eder 16,283 ...C3
Frankenthal 45,408 ....C4
Frankfurt am Main 625,258 .C3
Frankfurt an der Oder 86,441 .F2
Frechen 42,516 ....B3
Freiberg 50,415 ....E3
Freiburg im Breisgau
183,979 ....B5
Freising 35,201 ....D4
Freital 43,092 ....E3
Freudenstadt 21,355 ....C4
Friedberg 24,279 ....C3
Friedrichshafen 52,295 ....C5
Fulda 54,320 ....C3
Fürstenfeldbruck 30,313 ...D4
Fürstenwalde 35,282 ....F2
Fürth 98,832 ....D4
Füssen 13,173 ....D5
Gaggenau 28,182 ....C4
Garbsen 59,225 ....C2
Garmisch-Partenkirchen
25,908 ....D5
Geesthacht 25,054 ....D2
Geislingen an der Steige
26,176 ....C4
Geldern 28,465 ....B3
Gelnhausen 18,866 ....C3
Gelsenkirchen 287,255 .....B3
Genthin 17,347 ....D2
Georgsmarienhütte 30,880 ..B2
Gera 132,319 ....E3
Geretsried 21,081 ....D5
Gifhorn 35,697 ....D2
Glauchau 28,309 ....E3
Goch 29,592 ....B3
Göppingen 52,873 ....C4
Görlitz 78,856 ....F3
Goslar 45,614 ....D3
Gotha 57,423 ....D3
Göttingen 118,873 ....D3
Greifswald 67,298 ....E1
Greiz 34,858 ....E3
Greven 29,671 ....B2
Grevenbroich 59,204 ....B3
Griesheim 20,531 ....C4
Grimma 17,812 ....E3
Gronau 39,397 ....B2
Guben 34,605 ....F3
Gummersbach 49,017 ....B3
Günzburg 18,303 ....D4
Güstrow 38,971 ....D2
Gütersloh 83,407 ....C3
Haar 16,553 ....D4
Hagen 210,640 ....B3
Halberstadt 47,017 ....D3
Haldensleben 20,369 ....D2
Halle 236,148 ....D3
Halle-Neustadt 93,477 .....D3
Haltern 33,093 ....B3
Hamburg 1,603,070 ....D2
Hameln 57,642 ....C2
Hamm 173,611 ....B3
Hanau 84,300 ....C3
Hannover 498,495 ....C2
Hassloch 18,646 ....C4
Heide 19,909 ....C1
Heidelberg 131,429 ....C4
Heidenau 19,133 ....E3
Heidenheim an der Brenz
48,497 ....D4
Heilbronn 112,279 ....C4
Helmstedt 26,554 ....D2
Hennef 30,516 ....B3
Hennigsdorf bei Berlin
26,574 ....E3
Herborn 20,409 ....C3

Herford 61,700 ....C2
Herne 174,664 ....B3
Hettstedt 21,861 ....D3
Hildesheim 103,512 ....D2
Hof 50,938 ....D3
Holzminden 20,877 ....C3
Homburg 41,888 ....B4
Höxter 31,925 ....C3
Hoyerswerda 69,113 ....F3
Hückelhoven 33,841 ....B3
Hürth 49,094 ....B3
Husum 20,649 ....C1
Ibbenbüren 43,424 ....B2
Idar-Oberstein 33,227 .....B4
Ilmenau 29,338 ....D3
Ingolstadt 97,702 ....D4
Iserlohn 93,337 ....B3
Itzehoe 32,342 ....C2
Jena 107,610 ....D3
Jülich 30,496 ....B3
Kaiserslautern 96,990 .....B4
Kamenz 18,323 ....F3
Karlsruhe 265,100 ....C4
Kassel 189,156 ....C3
Kaufbeuren 39,192 ....D5
Kehl 28,902 ....B4
Kempten 60,052 ....D5
Kevelaer 22,633 ....B3
Kiel 240,675 ....D1
Kirchheim unter Teck 34,534 .C4
Kitzingen 19,085 ....C4
Koblenz 107,286 ....B3
Köln (Cologne) 937,482 ....B3
Königs Wusterhausen 19,085 .E2
Königswinter 34,136 ......B3
Konstanz 72,862 ....C5
Köpenick 118,059 ....F4
Korbach 21,406 ....C3
Kornwestheim 28,519 ....C4
Köthen 34,617 ....E3
Krefeld 235,423 ....B3
Kreuztal 29,716 ....C3
Kronach 18,246 ....D3
Kulmbach 27,116 ....D3
Lage 32,612 ....C3
Lahnstein 17,972 ....B3
Lahr 33,369 ....B4
Lampertheim 30,263 ....C4
Landau in der Pfalz 36,297 .C4
Landsberg am Lech 19,808 ..D4
Landshut 57,194 ....D4
Langen 31,206 ....C4
Langenhagen 46,298 ....C2
Lauchhammer 24,391 ....E3
Lauenburg an der Elbe
10,786 ....D2
Lauf an der Pegnitz
22,593 ....D4
Leer 31,292 ....B2
Lehrte 39,600 ....D2
Leipzig 550,641 ....E3
Lemgo 38,351 ....C2
Lengerich 20,235 ....B2
Leverkusen 157,358 ....B3
Lichtenberg 95,426 ....F4
Lichtenfels 20,252 ....D3
Limburg an der Lahn 29,196 .C3
Limbach-Oberfrohna 22,059 .E3

Lindau 23,699 ....C5
Lingen 47,837 ....B2
Lippstadt 60,396 ....C3
Löbau 18,492 ....F3
Löhne 36,882 ....C2
Lörrach 41,087 ....B5
Lübbenau 20,815 ....E3
Lübeck 210,681 ....D2
Luckenwalde 26,761 ....E2
Lüdenscheid 76,118 ....B3
Ludwigsburg 79,342 ....C4
Ludwigshafen am Rhein
158,478 ....C4
Lüneburg 60,053 ....D2
Lünen 85,584 ....B3
Magdeburg 288,975 ....D2
Mainz 174,828 ....C4
Mannheim 300,468 ....C4
Marburg 70,905 ....C3
Marktredwitz 18,605 ....E4
Marl 89,601 ....B3
Mayen 18,427 ....B3
Mechernich 21,986 ....B3
Meerane 21,879 ....E3
Meiningen 25,823 ....D3
Meissen 37,757 ....E3
Melle 40,490 ....C2
Memmingen 37,942 ....D4
Meppen 29,900 ....B2
Merseburg 46,188 ....D3
Merzig 29,312 ....B4
Meschede 30,853 ....C3
Metzingen 19,895 ....C4
Minden 75,169 ....C2
Mittenwald 7,998 ....D5
Mittweida 18,469 ....E3
Mönchengladbach 252,910 ...B3
Mosbach 23,897 ....C4
Mülhausen 43,046 ....D3

Mülheim an der Ruhr
175,454 ....B3
München (Munich)
1,211,617 ....D4
Münchberg 19,312 ....D4
Munich 1,211,617 ....D4
Münster 248,919 ....B3
Nagold 20,405 ....C4
Naumburg 32,100 ....D3
Neckarsulm 21,765 ....C4
Neubrandenburg 87,235 .....E2
Neuburg an der Donau
24,502 ....D4
Neu-Isenburg 34,896 ....C3
Neumarkt in der Oberpfalz
33,603 ....D4
Neumünster 79,574 ....C1
Neunkirchen 50,784 ....B4
Neuruppin 26,934 ....E2
Neuss 143,976 ....B3
Neustadt an der Weinstrasse
50,453 ....B4
Neustadt bei Coburg 16,211 .D3
Neustrelitz 27,300 ....E2
Neu-Ulm 45,116 ....D4
Neuwied 60,665 ....B3
Nienburg 29,545 ....C2
Norden 23,655 ....B2
Nordenham 28,393 ....C2
Norderstedt 66,747 ....D2
Nordhausen 47,681 ....D3
Nordhorn 48,556 ....B2
Nördlingen 18,278 ....D4
Northeim 30,349 ....C3
Nuremberg 480,078 ....D4
Nürnberg (Nuremberg)
480,078 ....D4
Nürtingen 36,807 ....C4
Oberammergau 4,980 ....D5
Oberhausen 221,017 ....B3

Oberursel 39,105 ....C3
Offenbach am Main 112,450 .C3
Offenburg 51,730 ....B4
Oldenburg 140,785 ....C2
Oranienburg 28,667 ....E2
Oschatz 19,100 ....E3
Oschersleben 16,976 ......D2
Osnabrück 154,594 ....C2
Osterholz-Scharmbeck
24,205 ....C2
Osterode am Harz 26,631 ...D3
Paderborn 114,148 ....C3
Pankow 62,847 ....F4
Papenburg 29,237 ....B2
Parchim 23,454 ....D2
Passau 49,137 ....E4
Peenemünde E1
Peine 45,522 ....D2
Pfaffenhofen an der Ilm
18,335 ....D4
Pforzheim 108,887 ....C4
Pinneberg 36,583 ....C2
Pirmasens 47,102 ....B4
Pirna 46,991 ....E3
Plauen 77,514 ....E3
Plettenberg 28,113 ....C3
Pössneck 17,895 ....D3
Potsdam 141,231 ....E2
Prenzlau 23,642 ....E2
Quedlinburg 29,168 ....D3
Radeberg 15,702 ....E3
Radebeul 33,757 ....E3
Radolfzell 25,712 ....C5
Rastatt 40,909 ....C4
Rastede 18,191 ....C2
Rathenow 31,302 ....E2
Ratingen 89,880 ....B3
Ravensburg 44,146 ....C5
Recklinghausen 121,666 ...B3
Regensburg 119,078 ....E4

(continued on following page)

24 Germany

(continued)

Germany Before World War I 1871-1914

Germany Between Wars 1919-1937

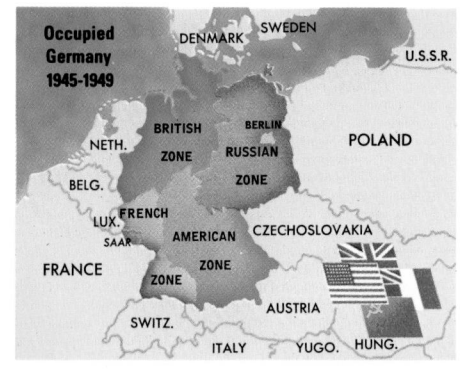

Occupied Germany 1945-1949

Reichenbach 24,749 .....E3	Schwalmstadt 17,371 ...C3
Remagen 14,375 .....B3	Schwandorf im Bayern
Remscheid 120,979 .....B3	25,874 .....E4
Rendsburg 30,752 .....C1	Schwedt 51,753 .....F2
Reutlingen 100,400 .....C4	Schweinfurt 52,818 .....D3
Rheda-Wiedenbrück 36,990 ..C3	Schwelm 29,564 .....B3
Rheine 69,324 .....B2	Schwerin 128,328 .....D2
Rheinfelden 27,711 .....B5	Schwetzingen 18,029 .....C4
Ribnitz-Damgarten 17,512 ...E1	Seesen 21,604 .....D3
Riesa 49,108 .....E3	Selb 19,275 .....D3
Rietberg 23,058 .....C3	Senftenberg 32,428 .....F3
Rinteln 26,120 .....C2	Siegburg 34,402 .....B3
Rosenheim 54,304 .....D5	Siegen 106,160 .....C3
Rotenburg 18,392 .....C2	Sigmaringen 15,270 .....C4
Roth bei Nürnberg 20,288 ...D4	Sindelfingen 57,524 .....C4
Rothenburg ob der Tauber	Singen 42,605 .....C5
11,071 .....D4	Soest 40,775 .....C3
Rottenburg am Neckar	Solingen 160,824 .....B3
33,907 .....C4	Soltau 19,115 .....C2
Rottweil 23,080 .....C4	Sömmerda 23,398 .....D3
Rudolstadt 32,264 .....D3	Sondershausen 24,178 .....D3
Rüsselsheim 58,426 .....C4	Sonneberg 28,512 .....D3
Saalfeld 33,453 .....D3	Sonthofen 20,037 .....D5
Saarbrücken 188,467 .....B4	Spandau E3
Saarlouis 37,662 .....B4	Speyer 45,089 .....C4
Salzgitter 111,674 .....D2	Spremberg 24,815 .....F3
Salzwedel 23,163 .....D2	Springe 29,209 .....C2
Sangerhausen 33,604 .....D3	Stade 41,223 .....C2
Sankt Ingbert 40,527 .....B4	Stadthagen 22,218 .....C2
Sankt Wendel 26,649 .....B4	Starnberg 19,845 .....D4
Saulgau 14,864 .....C5	Stassfurt 27,372 .....D3
Schleswig 26,648 .....C1	Stendal 47,880 .....D2
Schmalkalden 17,409 .....D3	Stolberg 56,182 .....B3
Schneeberg 22,105 .....E3	Stralsund 75,857 .....E1
Schönebeck 45,155 .....D2	Straubing 40,612 .....E4
Schramberg 18,208 .....C4	Strausberg 27,527 .....F2
Schwabach 34,217 .....D4	Stuttgart 562,658 .....C4
Schwäbisch Gmünd 57,861 ..C4	Suhl 55,295 .....D3
Schwäbisch Hall 31,375 .....C4	Sulzbach 19,753 .....B4
	Sulzbach-Rosenberg 18,134 ..D4

Telgte 16,834 .....B3	Weilheim im Oberbayern
Tempelhof F4	17,602 .....D5
Thale 16,605 .....D3	Weimar 63,910 .....D3
Torgau 22,749 .....E3	Weingarten 21,522 .....C5
Traunstein 17,145 .....E5	Weinheim 41,876 .....C4
Treptow 58,938 .....F4	Weissenburg im Bayern
Treuchtlingen 12,314 .....D4	17,318 .....D4
Triberg im Schwarzwald	Weissenfels 38,763 .....E3
5,697 .....C4	Weissensee 31,858 .....F3
Trier 95,692 .....B4	Weisswasser 36,472 .....F3
Troisdorf 62,011 .....B3	Werdau 19,451 .....E3
Tübingen 76,046 .....C4	Wernigerode 36,499 .....D3
Tuttlingen 31,752 .....C5	Wertheim 20,457 .....C4
Übach-Palenberg 23,005 .....B3	Wesel 57,986 .....B3
Überlingen 18,043 .....C5	Westerstede 18,184 .....B2
Ueckermünde 12,304 .....F1	Wiehl 21,897 .....C3
Uelzen 34,891 .....D2	Wiesbaden 254,209 .....C3
Uetersen 17,218 .....C2	Wiesmoor 10,827 .....B2
Ulm 106,508 .....C4	Wilhelmshaven 89,892 .....B2
Varel 23,718 .....C2	Winsen 26,139 .....D2
Vechta 22,759 .....C2	Wismar 58,066 .....D2
Verden 23,770 .....C2	Witten 103,637 .....B3
Viersen 76,163 .....B3	Wittenberg 53,670 .....E3
Villingen-Schwenningen	Wittenberge 30,389 .....D2
76,258 .....C4	Wolfen 43,606 .....E3
Völklingen 42,916 .....B4	Wolfenbüttel 50,960 .....D2
Waldheim 10,316 .....E3	Wolfsburg 125,831 .....D2
Waldkirch 18,893 .....B4	Worms 74,809 .....C4
Waldkraiburg 23,177 .....E4	Wunstorf 37,115 .....C2
Waldshut-Tiengen 21,372 .....C5	Wuppertal 371,283 .....B3
Walsrode 22,232 .....C2	Würzburg 125,589 .....C4
Waltershausen 14,127 .....D3	Wurzen 19,330 .....E3
Wangen im Allgäu 23,822 .....C5	Xanten 16,097 .....B3
Warburg 21,802 .....C3	Zeitz 42,985 .....E3
Waren 24,318 .....E2	Zerbst 18,717 .....E3
Warendorf 33,891 .....B3	Zeulenroda 14,409 .....D3
Wedel 30,158 .....C2	Zirndorf 21,608 .....D4
Weida 10,602 .....D3	Zittau 39,305 .....F3
Weiden in der Oberpfalz	Zweibrücken 33,377 .....B4
41,539 .....D4	Zwickau 120,923 .....E3

OTHER FEATURES

Aller (riv.) C2	Havel (riv.) E2
Allgäu (reg.) D5	Hegau (reg.) C5
Altmark (reg.) D2	Helgoland (bay) C1
Ammersee (lake) D4	Helgoland (isl.) B1
Amrum (isl.) C1	Hunsrück (mts.) B4
Arkona (cape) E1	Iller (riv.) D4
Baltic (sea) E1	Ilmenau (riv.) D2
Bavarian (forest) E4	Inn (riv.) E4
Bavarian Alps (range) D5	Isar (riv.) E4
Bayerischer Wald Nat'l Park ...E4	Jade (bay) C2
Black (forest) C4	Juist (isl.) B2
Black Elster (riv.) E3	Kaiserstuhl (mt.) B4
Bodensee (Constance) (lake) ..C5	Kiel (bay) D1
Bohemian (forest) E4	Kiel (Nord-Ostsee) (canal) C1
Borkum (isl.) B2	Königssee (lake) E5
Breisgau (reg.) B5	Lahn (riv.) C3
Brocken (mt.) D3	Lech (riv.) D4
Chiemsee (lake) E5	Leine (riv.) C2
Constance (lake) C5	Lippe (riv.) C3
Danube (riv.) C4	Lüneburger Heide (dist.) D2
Donau (Danube) (riv.) C4	Lusatia (reg.) F3
East Friesland (reg.) B2	Main (riv.) C4
Eder (riv.) C3	Mecklenburg (bay) D1
Elbe (riv.) D2	Mosel (riv.) B3
Elde (riv.) D2	Mulde (riv.) E3
Ems (riv.) B2	Müritzsee (lake) E2
Erzgebirge (mts.) E3	Naab (riv.) E4
Fehmarn (isl.) D1	Neckar (riv.) C4
Feldberg (mt.) C5	Neisse (riv.) F3
Fichtelberg (mt.) E3	Nord-Ostsee (canal) C1
Fichtelgebirge (range) D3	Nordstrand (isl.) C1
Föhr (isl.) C1	North (sea) B2
Franconian Jura (range) D4	North Friesland (reg.) C1
Frisian, East (isls.) B2	Odenwald (forest) C4
Frisian, North (isls.) B1	Oder-Haff (lag.) F2
Fulda (riv.) C3	Our (riv.) B3
Grosser Arber (mt.) E4	Peene (riv.) E2
Harz (mts.) D3	

Pellworm (isl.) C1	
Plauersee (lake) E2	
Pomeranian (bay) F1	
Regnitz (riv.) D4	
Rhine (riv.) B3	
Rhön (mts.) D3	
Rügen (isl.) E1	
Ruhr (riv.) B3	
Saale (riv.) D3	
Saar (riv.) B4	
Salzach (riv.) E5	
Sauer (riv.) B4	
Sauerland (reg.) B3	
Schwarzwald (Black) (forest) ..C4	
Schwerinsee (lake) D2	
Spessart (range) C4	
Spiekeroog (isl.) B2	
Spree (riv.) F3	
Spreewald (forest) F3	
Starnbergersee (lake) D5	
Swabian Jura (range) C4	
Sylt (isl.) C1	
Taunus (range) C3	
Tegernsee (lake) D5	
Teutoburger Wald (forest) C3	
Thüringer Wald (forest) D3	
Unstrut (riv.) D3	
Usedom (isl.) F1	
Vechte (riv.) B2	
Vogelsberg (mts.) C3	
Walchensee (lake) D5	
Wasserkuppe (mt.) C3	
Watzmann (mt.) E5	
Werra (riv.) D3	
Weser (riv.) C2	
Westerwald (forest) B3	
White Elster (riv.) E3	
Würmsee (Starnbergersee)	
(lake) D5	
Zugspitze (mt.) D5	

Agriculture, Industry and Resources

DOMINANT LAND USE

- Wheat, Sugar Beets
- Cereals (chiefly rye, oats, barley)
- Potatoes, Rye
- Dairy, Livestock
- Mixed Cereals, Dairy
- Truck Farming
- Grapes, Fruit
- Forests

MAJOR MINERAL OCCURRENCES

Ag	Silver	K	Potash
Ba	Barite	Lg	Lignite
C	Coal	Na	Salt
Cu	Copper	O	Petroleum
Fe	Iron Ore	Pb	Lead
G	Natural Gas	U	Uranium
Gr	Graphite	Zn	Zinc

⚡ Water Power
▨ Major Industrial Areas

AREA 15,892 sq. mi. (41,160 sq. km.)
POPULATION 14,906,000
CAPITALS The Hague, Amsterdam
LARGEST CITY Amsterdam
HIGHEST POINT Vaalserberg 1,056 ft. (322 m.)
MONETARY UNIT guilder (florin)
MAJOR LANGUAGE Dutch
MAJOR RELIGIONS Protestantism, Roman
Catholicism

AREA 11,781 sq. mi. (30,513 sq. km.)
POPULATION 9,883,000
CAPITAL Brussels
LARGEST CITY Brussels (greater)
HIGHEST POINT Botrange 2,277 ft.
(694 m.)
MONETARY UNIT Belgian franc
MAJOR LANGUAGES French (Walloon),
Flemish
MAJOR RELIGION Roman Catholicism

AREA 999 sq. mi. (2,587 sq. km.)
POPULATION 378,000
CAPITAL Luxembourg
LARGEST CITY Luxembourg
HIGHEST POINT Ardennes Plateau
1,825 ft. (556 m.)
MONETARY UNIT Luxembourg franc
MAJOR LANGUAGES Luxembourgeois
(Letzeburgisch), French, German
MAJOR RELIGION Roman Catholicism

NETHERLANDS

BELGIUM

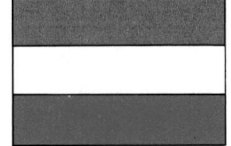

LUXEMBOURG

BELGIUM

PROVINCES

Antwerp 1,569,876 ....F6
Brabant 2,221,222 ....F7
East Flanders 1,331,192 ...D7
Hainaut 1,301,477 ....D7
Liège 999,413 ....H7
Limburg 716,888 ....G7
Luxembourg 221,926 ....G9
Namur 407,400 ....F8
West Flanders 1,079,253 ..B7

CITIES and TOWNS

Aalst 78,938 ....D7
Aalter 15,554 ....C6
Aarlen (Arlon) 22,279 ......H9
Aarschot 25,168 ....F7
Alken 9,563 ....G7
Amay 12,725 ....G7
Andenne 22,341 ....G8
Anderlecht 94,764 ....B9

Anderlues 11,700 ....E8
Ans 26,016 ....H7
Antoing 7,970 ....C7
Antwerp 185,897 ....E6
Antwerp* 918,144 ....E6
Antwerpen (Antwerp)
185,897 ....E6
Ardooie 9,458 ....C7
Arendonk 10,561 ....G6
Arlon 22,279 ....H9
Asse 26,425 ....F7
Assenede 13,353 ....D6
Aubange 14,696 ....H9
Audenarde (Oudenaarde)
26,615 ....D7
Auderghem 30,435 ....C9
Aywaille 8,194 ....H8
Baarle-Hertog 2,111 ....F6
Balen 18,162 ....G6
Bastenaken (Bastogne)
11,386 ....H9
Bastogne 11,386 ....H9
Beauraing 7,641 ....F8
Beernem 13,526 ....C6

Beloeil 13,553 ....D7
Berchem 45,423 ....F6
Berchem-Sainte-Agathe
18,719 ....B9
Bergen (Mons) 94,417 .....E8
Beringen 34,254 ....G6
Bertrix 7,244 ....G9
Beveren 40,857 ....E6
Bilzen 25,683 ....G7
Binche 33,651 ....E8
Blankenberge 14,832 ......C6
Bocholt 10,142 ....H6
Boom 14,827 ....E6
Borgerhout 43,521 ....E6
Borgworm
(Waremme) 11,907 ......G7
Bourg-Léopold
(Leopoldsburg) 9,593 ...G6
Boussu 21,558 ....E8
Braine-l'Alleud 30,028 .....E7
Braine-le-Comte 16,475 ...D7
Brecht 16,391 ....F6
Bredene 10,538 ....B6
Bree 13,345 ....H6

Bruges 118,020 ....C6
Brugge (Bruges) 118,020 ..C6
Brussels (cap.)* 997,293 ...C9
Bruxelles (Brussels)
(cap.)* 997,293 ....C9
Charleroi 222,343 ....E8
Charleroi* 443,832 ....E8
Châtelet 38,506 ....F8
Chimay 9,273 ....E8
Ciney 13,330 ....G8
Comines 18,034 ....B7
Courcelles 29,757 ....E8
Courtrai (Kortrijk) 75,917 ..C7
Couvin 12,909 ....F8
Damme 9,881 ....C6
De Haan 8,655 ....C6
Deinze 24,871 ....C7
Denderleeuw 16,497 ....E7
Dendermonde 22,119 ......E6
De Panne 9,507 ....B6
Dessel 8,074 ....G6
Destelbergen 15,741 ....D6
Deurne 77,635 ....E6
Diest 20,491 ....F7

Diksmuide 15,347 ....B6
Dilbeek 35,050 ....B9
Dilsen 15,910 ....H6
Dinant 12,105 ....G8
Dison 14,225 ....H7
Dixmude (Diksmuide) 15,347 ..B6
Doornik (Tournai) 67,906 ..C7
Dour 17,737 ....D8
Duffel 14,684 ....F6
Durbuy 7,729 ....H8
Ecaussinnes 9,739 ....E7
Edingen (Enghien) 10,095 ..D7
Eeklo 19,637 ....D6
Eghezée 10,683 ....F7
Eigenbrakel
(Braine-l'Alleud) 30,028 ..E7
Ekeren 30,294 ....E6
Enghien 10,095 ....D7
Erquelinnes 10,029 ....E8
Esneux 11,559 ....H7
Essen 12,505 ....F6
Estampuis 9,601 ....C7
Etterbeek 44,218 ....B9
Eupen 16,847 ....J7

Evere 30,520 ....C9
Evergem 28,974 ....D6
Farciennes 12,205 ....E8
Flémalle 28,217 ....G7
Fleurus 22,574 ....E8
Florennes 10,537 ....F8
Forest 50,607 ....B9
Fosses-La-Ville 7,678 ......F8
Frameries 21,470 ....D8
Frasnes-lez Anvaing 10,751 ..D7
Furnes (Veurne) 11,253 ...B6
Ganshoren 21,445 ....B9
Geel 31,463 ....F6
Geldenaken (Jodoigne) 8,983 ..F7
Gembloux-sur-Orneau 17,636 ..F7
Genk 61,502 ....H7
Gent (Ghent) 239,256 ......D6
Geraardsbergen 17,533 ...D7
Gerpinnes 10,808 ....F8
Ghent 239,256 ....D6
Ghent* 485,565 ....D6
Gistel 9,531 ....B6
Grammont
(Geraardsbergen) 17,533 ..D7
Grez-Doiceau 8,795 ....F7
Grimbergen 32,038 ....F7
Haacht 11,285 ....F7
Hal (Halle) 15,293 ....E7
Halen 7,865 ....G7
Halle 15,293 ....E7
Hamme 22,790 ....E6
Hamont-Achel 11,939 .....H6
Hannuit (Hannut) 11,527 ..G7
Hannut 11,527 ....G7
Harelbeke 25,214 ....C7
Hasselt 64,613 ....G7
Heist-op-den-Berg 34,617 ..F6
Hensies 6,806 ....D8
Herentals 23,797 ....F6
Herselt 11,340 ....F6
Herstal 38,592 ....H7
Herve 14,276 ....H7
Heuvelland 8,540 ....B7
Hoboken 34,563 ....E6
Hoei (Huy) 17,331 ....G8
Hoeselt 8,497 ....G7
Hoogstraten 14,368 ....F6
Huy 17,331 ....G8
Ichtegem 12,259 ....B6
Ieper 34,425 ....B7
Ingelmunster 10,434 ......C7
Ixelles 75,723 ....C9
Izegem 26,410 ....C7
Jabbeke 10,629 ....C6
Jemappes 18,632 ....D8
Jemeppe-sur-Sambre 17,120 ..F8
Jette 40,109 ....B9
Jodoigne 8,983 ....F7
Kalmthout 14,960 ....F6
Kapellen 14,536 ....E6
Kasterlee 14,612 ....F6
Kinrooi 10,138 ....H6
Knokke-Heist 28,868 ......C6
Koekelare 7,606 ....B6
Koekelberg 16,643 ....B9
Koksijde 13,679 ....B6
Kontich 17,878 ....E6
Kortemark 12,580 ....C6
Kortrijk 75,917 ....C7
Kraainem 11,780 ....C9
La Louvière 77,326 ....E8
Lanaken 20,272 ....H7
Landen 14,081 ....G7
Langemark-Poelkapelle 7,097 ..B7
Lasne 10,919 ....F7
Lede 17,249 ....D7
Lens 3,726 ....D7
Leopoldsburg 9,593 ....G6
Le Roeulx 7,754 ....E8
Lessen (Lessines) 16,553 ..D7
Lessines 16,553 ....D7
Leuven 85,076 ....F7
Leuze-en-Hainaut 12,863 ..D7
Libramont-Chevigny 7,859 ..G9
Lichtervelde 7,459 ....C6
Liedekerke 11,609 ....E7
Liège 214,119 ....H7
Liège* 605,123 ....H7

Lier 31,261 ....F6
Lierre (Lier) 31,261 ....F6
Limbourg 5,350 ....J7
Limburg (Limbourg) 5,350 ..J7
Linter 6,568 ....G7
Lochristi 16,125 ....D6
Lokeren 33,369 ....D6
Lommel 25,412 ....G6
Louvain (Leuven) 85,076 ..F7
Luik (Liège) 214,119 ....H7
Lummen 11,793 ....G7
Maaseik 20,056 ....H6
Maasmechelen 33,618 ....H7
Machelen 11,273 ....C9
Maldegem 42,694 ....C6
Malines (Mechelen) 77,269 ..F6
Malmédy 10,036 ....J8
Marche-en-Famenne 14,115 ..G8
Mechelen 77,269 ....F6
Meerhout 8,613 ....G6
Meise 15,170 ....E7
Menen 33,542 ....C7
Menin (Menen) 33,542 ....C7
Merchtem 12,972 ....E7
Merelbeke 19,773 ....D7
Merksem 41,600 ....E6
Merksplas 6,136 ....F6
Mettet 9,958 ....F8
Meulebeke 10,471 ....C7
Middelkerke 14,168 ....B6
Moeskroen
(Mouscron) 54,590 ....C7
Mol 29,798 ....G6
Molenbeek-Saint-Jean
70,850 ....B9
Mons 94,417 ....E8
Montigny-le-Tilleul 9,726 ..E8
Moorslede 10,974 ....B7
Mortsel 26,746 ....E6
Mouscron 54,590 ....C7
Namen (Namur) 102,321 ..F8
Namur 102,321 ....F8
Nazareth 9,248 ....D7
Neerpelt 12,779 ....G6
Neufchâteau 6,039 ....G9
Nevele 10,471 ....D6
Nieuport (Nieuwpoort) 8,195 ..B6
Nieuwpoort 8,195 ....B6
Nijvel (Nivelles) 21,580 ...E7
Ninove 33,393 ....D7
Nivelles 21,580 ....E7
Oostende (Ostend) 68,915 ..B6
Oostkamp 19,747 ....C6
Opwijk 11,451 ....E7
Ostend 68,915 ....B6
Oudenaarde 26,615 ....D7
Oudenburg 8,138 ....C6
Oud-Turnhout 10,733 ......F6
Oupeye 22,453 ....H7
Overijse 21,428 ....C9
Overpelt 11,233 ....G6
Peer 12,099 ....G6
Péruwelz 16,664 ....D8
Philippeville 6,916 ....F8
Poelkapelle-Langemark 7,097 ..B7
Pont-à-Celles 15,444 ......E8
Poperinge 19,886 ....B7
Profondeville 8,724 ....F8
Putte 14,017 ....F6
Quaregnon 20,071 ....D8
Quévy 7,391 ....D8
Quiévrain 6,945 ....D8
Raeren 8,046 ....J7
Ravels 10,328 ....G6
Rebecq 8,891 ....E7
Renaix (Ronse) 25,056 ....D7
Retie 8,359 ....G6
Rochefort 4,357 ....G8
Roeselare 51,984 ....C7
Ronse (Renaix) 25,056 ....D7
Roulers (Roeselare) 51,984 ..C7
Saint-Gilles 46,076 ....B9
Saint-Josse-ten-Noode
20,381 ....C9
Saint-Nicolas 25,755 ....D6
Saint-Trond
(Sint-Truiden) 36,374 ...G7
Saint-Vith (Sankt Vith) 8,434 ..J8
(continued on following page)

Agriculture, Industry and Resources

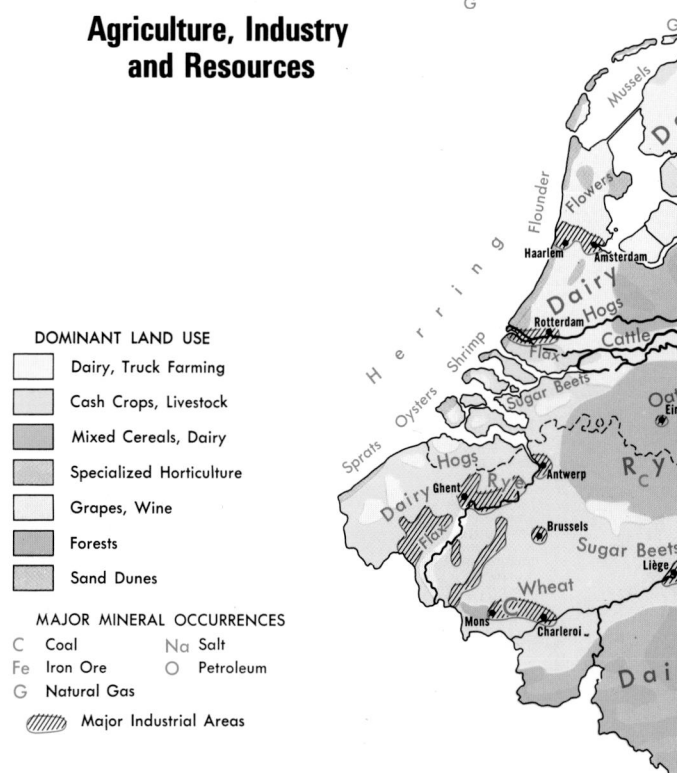

DOMINANT LAND USE

- Dairy, Truck Farming
- Cash Crops, Livestock
- Mixed Cereals, Dairy
- Specialized Horticulture
- Grapes, Wine
- Forests
- Sand Dunes

MAJOR MINERAL OCCURRENCES

C Coal
Fe Iron Ore
G Natural Gas
Na Salt
O Petroleum

Major Industrial Areas

Sankt Vith 8,434 .... J8
Schaerbeek 106,754 .... C9
Schoten 31,128 .... F6
Seraing 64,543 .... G7
's-Gravenbrakel (Braine-le-Comte) 16,475 .... D7
Sint-Laureins 6,620 .... D6
Sint-Niklaas 67,992 .... E6
Sint-Pieters-Leeuw 27,968 .... B9
Sint-Truiden 36,374 .... G7
Soignies 23,352 .... D7
Spa 9,619 .... H8
Sprimont 9,660 .... H8
Staden 11,135 .... B7
Steenokkerzeel 9,638 .... C9
Stekene 14,125 .... E6
Tamise (Temse) 23,525 .... E6
Temse 23,525 .... E6
Termonde (Dendermonde) 22,119 .... E6
Tessenderlo 13,800 .... G6
Theux 9,167 .... H8
Thuin 13,757 .... E8
Tielt 19,103 .... C7
Tielt-Winge 8,237 .... F7
Tienen 32,620 .... F7
Tirlemont 32,620 .... F7
Tongeren 29,603 .... G7
Tongres (Tongeren) 29,603 .... G7
Torhout 17,165 .... C6
Tournai 67,906 .... C7
Tubeke (Tubize) 19,827 .... E7
Tubize 19,827 .... E7
Turnhout 37,453 .... F6
Uccle 76,004 .... B9
Ukkel (Uccle) 76,004 .... B9
Verviers 55,371 .... H7
Veurne 11,253 .... B6
Vielsalm 6,731 .... H8
Vilvoorde 33,264 .... F7
Vilvorde (Vilvoorde) 33,264 .... F7
Viroinval 5,589 .... F8
Virton 10,490 .... H9
Visé 16,469 .... H7
Vorst (Forest) 50,607 .... B9
Waarschoot 7,574 .... D6
Wachtebeke 6,951 .... D6
Waimes (Weismes) 5,713 .... J8
Walcourt 14,866 .... F8
Waregem 32,810 .... C7
Waremme 11,907 .... G7
Waterloo 24,755 .... E7
Watermael-Boitsfort 24,880 .... C9
Watermael-Bosvoorde (Watermael-Boitsfort) 24,880 .... C9
Waver (Wavre) 25,153 .... F7
Wavre 25,153 .... F7
Wemmel 13,547 .... B9
Wervik 18,086 .... B7
Westerlo 19,459 .... F6
Wetteren 23,460 .... D7
Wezembeek-Oppem 12,006 .... D9
Wezet (Visé) 16,469 .... H7
Willebroek 22,265 .... E6
Wilrijk 42,328 .... E6
Wingene 12,188 .... C6
Woluwe-Saint-Lambert 48,801 .... C9
Woluwe-Saint-Pierre 40,686 .... C9
Ypres (Ieper) 34,425 .... B7
Yvoir 6,527 .... F8
Zaventem 25,393 .... C9
Zedelgem 19,198 .... C6
Zele 19,631 .... E6
Zelzate 12,934 .... D6
Zemst 17,167 .... E7
Zinnik (Soignies) 23,352 .... D7
Zonhoven 15,965 .... G6
Zottegem 25,109 .... D7

OTHER FEATURES

Albert (canal) F6
Ardennes (forest) F9
Botrange (mt.) J8
Dender (riv.) D7
Deûle (riv.) B7
Dyle (riv.) F7
Hohe Venn (plat.) H8
Lys (riv.) B7
Mark (riv.) F6
Meuse (riv.) F8
Nethe (riv.) F6
North (sea) D4
Ourthe (riv.) G8
Rupel (riv.) F7
Sambre (riv.) D8
Schelde (Scheldt) (riv.) C7
Scheldt (riv.) C7
Semois (riv.) G9
Senne (riv.) E7
Vaalserberg (mt.) J7
Vesdre (riv.) H7
Yser (riv.) B7

LUXEMBOURG

CITIES and TOWNS

Bascharage 4,870 .... H9
Diekirch† 5,470 .... J9
Differdange 15,940 .... H9
Dudelange† 14,070 .... J1
Echternach† 4,290 .... J9
Esch-sur-Alzette† 23,800 .... H9
Ettelbruck† 6,600 .... J9
Grevenmacher† 2,940 .... J9
Hesperange 9,470 .... J9
Luxembourg (cap.) 75,540 .... J9
Mamer 6,090 .... H9
Mersch 5,560 .... J9
Mertert 3,000 .... J9
Pétange 11,800 .... H9
Remich 2,430 .... J9
Troisvierges 1,890 .... J9
Vianden† 1,510 .... J9
Wasserbillig 2,097 .... J9
Wiltz 3,850 .... H9

OTHER FEATURES

Alzette (riv.) J9
Clerf (riv.) J8
Mosel (riv.) J9
Our (riv.) J9
Sauer (riv.) J9

NETHERLANDS

PROVINCES

Drenthe 439,066 .... K3
Flevoland 202,678 .... G4
Friesland 599,190 .... H2
Gelderland 1,794,678 .... H4
Groningen 555,200 .... K2
Limburg 1,099,622 .... H6
North Brabant 2,172,604 .... F5
North Holland 2,365,160 .... F3
Overijssel 1,014,949 .... J4
South Holland 3,200,408 .... E5
Utrecht 1,004,632 .... G4
Zeeland 355,585 .... D6

CITIES and TOWNS

Aalsmeer 21,984 .... F4
Aalten 18,202 .... K5
Alkmaar 88,571 .... F3
Almelo 62,008 .... K4
Almere 63,785 .... G4
Alphen aan de Rijn 59,586 .... F4
Amersfoort 96,072 .... G4
Amstelveen 69,505 .... B5
Amsterdam (cap.) 694,680 .... B4
Apeldoorn 147,270 .... H4
Appingedam 12,668 .... K2
Arnhem 128,946 .... H4
Assen 49,398 .... K3
Asten 14,965 .... H6
Axel 12,219 .... D6
Baarn 24,897 .... G4
Barneveld 41,649 .... H4
Beilen 14,057 .... K3
Bemmel 15,842 .... H5
Bergen 14,075 .... F3
Bergen op Zoom 46,842 .... E5
Berkel 15,690 .... F5
Beverwijk 35,126 .... F4
Bloemendaal 8,977 .... E4
Bodegraven 17,720 .... F4
Bolsward 9,799 .... H2
Borculo 10,057 .... J4
Borger 12,730 .... K3
Borne 21,261 .... K4
Boskoop 14,524 .... F4
Boxmeer 14,363 .... H5
Boxtel 24,951 .... G5
Breda 121,362 .... F5
Brielle 14,973 .... E5
Brummen 20,802 .... J4
Brunssum 29,799 .... J7
Bussum 31,988 .... G4
Capelle 57,423 .... F5
Castricum 22,433 .... F3
Coevorden 14,344 .... K3
Culemborg 21,116 .... G5
De Bilt 31,729 .... G4
Delft 88,135 .... E4
Delfzijl 23,472 .... K2
Denekamp 12,206 .... L4
Den Helder 62,094 .... F3
Deurne 29,308 .... H6
Deventer 66,398 .... J4
Didam 16,036 .... J5
Diemen 18,083 .... C5
Dinxperlo 8,133 .... K5
Dirksland 7,341 .... E5
Doesburg 10,578 .... J4
Doetinchem 41,260 .... J5
Dongen 21,124 .... F5
Doorn 10,419 .... G4
Dordrecht 108,519 .... F5
Driebergen 18,294 .... G4
Dronten 24,281 .... H3
Druten 14,630 .... H5
Echt 16,927 .... H6
Edam-Volendam 24,572 .... G4
Ede 92,293 .... H4
Egmond aan Zee 11,163 .... E3
Eindhoven 190,736 .... G6
Elst 17,654 .... H5
Emmen 92,422 .... K3
Enkhuizen 15,939 .... G3
Enschede 145,223 .... K4
Epe 33,872 .... H4
Ermelo 25,644 .... H4
Etten-Leur 32,010 .... F5
Flushing 44,022 .... C6
Geertruidenberg 6,645 .... F5
Geldermalsen 22,017 .... G5
Geldrop 25,817 .... H6
Geleen 33,756 .... H7
Gemert 17,613 .... H5
Gendringen 20,186 .... J5
Genemuiden 7,545 .... H3
Gennep 16,264 .... H5
Giessendam 16,722 .... F5
Gilze 22,577 .... F5
Goes 31,815 .... D6
Goirle 18,852 .... G5
Goor 11,804 .... K4
Gorinchem 28,222 .... G5
Gouda 63,232 .... F4
Gramsbergen 6,080 .... K3
Grave 10,447 .... H5
Groenlo 8,895 .... K4
Groesbeek 18,221 .... H5
Groningen 167,788 .... K2
Haaksbergen 22 690 .... K4
Haarlem 149,198 .... F4
Haarlemmermeer (Hoofddorp) 93,427 .... F4
Hague, The (cap.) 443,845 .... E4
Hardenberg 32,065 .... J3
Harderwijk 34,600 .... H4
Hardinxveld-Giessendam 16,722 .... G5
Harlingen 15,727 .... G2
Hasselt 6,871 .... J3
Hattem 11,571 .... H4
Heemskerk 32,910 .... F3
Heemstede 26,308 .... F4
Heerde 18,171 .... H4
Heerenveen 37,700 .... H3
Heerhugowaard 35,522 .... F3
Heerlen 94,149 .... J7
Heesch 11,309 .... G5
Heiloo 20,467 .... F3
Hellendoorn 34,287 .... J4
Hellevoetsluis 34,276 .... E5
Helmond 66,791 .... H6
Hengelo 76,175 .... J4
's Hertogenbosch 90,584 .... G5
Heusden 5,761 .... G5
Hillegom 20,001 .... F4
Hilvarenbeek 9,975 .... G6
Hilversum 84,983 .... G4
Hoek van Holland (Hook of Holland) D4
Hoofddorp (Haarlemmermeer) 93,427 .... F4
Hoogeveen 45,601 .... J3
Hoogezand-Sappemeer 34,618 .... K2
Hook of Holland D4
Hoorn 56,474 .... G3
Horst 17,614 .... H6
Huissen 15,544 .... H5
Huizen 20,501 .... G4
Hulst 18,575 .... E6
IJsselstein 19,516 .... F4
Kampen 32,769 .... H3
Katwijk aan Zee 39,441 .... E4
Kerkrade 52,994 .... J7
Kesteren 9,389 .... G5
Krimpen aan den IJssel 27,638 .... F5
Landsmeer 9,121 .... C4
Laren 11,643 .... G4
Leek 17,743 .... J2
Leerdam 19,015 .... G5
Leeuwarden 85,296 .... H2
Leiden 109,254 .... E4
Lelystad 58,125 .... H3
Lisse 20,826 .... F4
Lith 6,115 .... G5
Lochem 18,295 .... J4
Loon op Zand 21,372 .... G5
Losser 22,526 .... L4
Maarssen 37,629 .... F4
Maasbree 11,752 .... H6
Maassluis 33,155 .... E5
Maastricht 116,380 .... H7
Margraten 13,365 .... H7
Medemblik 6,876 .... G3
Meerssen 20,462 .... H7
Meppel 23,492 .... J3
Middelburg 39,462 .... C6
Middelharnis 15,480 .... E5
Millingen aan den Rijn 5,287 .... J5
Monnickendam 9,953 .... C4
Montfoort 12,397 .... G4
Muiden 6,772 .... G4
Muntendam 5,022 .... K2
Naaldwijk 27,683 .... E4
Naarden 16,101 .... G4
Neede 10,982 .... K4
Nieuwegein 58,316 .... G4
Nieuwkoop 10,723 .... F4
Nijkerk 25,613 .... H4
Nijmegen 145,405 .... H5
Noordwijk 24,996 .... E4
Norg 6,595 .... J2
Nunspeet 24,573 .... H4
Odoorn 12,225 .... K3
Oisterwijk 18,177 .... G5
Oldenzaal 29,680 .... K4
Olst 9,039 .... J4
Ommen 17,957 .... J3
Oostburg 18,145 .... C6
Oosterhout 48,157 .... F5
Oostzaan 7,292 .... C4
Oss 50,987 .... H5
Oud-Beijerland 20,385 .... E5
Oude-Pekela 8,028 .... K2
Oudenbosch 12,576 .... E5
Oudewater 9,410 .... F4
Purmerend 56,233 .... F4
Putten 20,898 .... H4
Raalte 26,883 .... J4
Renkum 33,841 .... H5
Reusel 7,813 .... G6
Rheden 46,088 .... J4
Rhenen 16,613 .... H5
Ridderkerk 46,163 .... F5
Rijnsburg 13,412 .... F4
Rijssen 23,927 .... J4
Rijswijk 48,189 .... E4
Roden 18,331 .... J2
Roermond 38,486 .... J6
Roosendaal 59,237 .... F5
Rotterdam 576,232 .... E5
Ruurlo 7,418 .... J4
Sappemeer-Hoogezand 34,618 .... K2
Schagen 16,759 .... F3
Schiedam 69,438 .... E5
Schijndel 21,397 .... G5
Schoonebeek 7,740 .... K3
Schoonhoven 11,231 .... F5
's Gravendeel 8,424 .... E5
's Gravenhage (The Hague) (cap.) 443,845 .... E4
's Gravenzande 18,453 .... E4
Simpelveld 11,882 .... J7
Sittard 44,894 .... H6
Sliedrecht 22,833 .... F5
Slochteren 13,958 .... K2
Sloten H3
Sluis 2,882 .... C6
Smilde 9,212 .... K3
Sneek 29,408 .... H2
Soest 41,598 .... G4
Stadskanaal 33,047 .... L3
Staphorst 13,580 .... J3
Staveren G3
Steenbergen 13,826 .... E5
Steenwijk 20,907 .... J3
Stiens H2
Tegelen 18,991 .... J6
Ter Apel L3
Termunten 4,378 .... K2
Terneuzen 35,043 .... D6
The Hague (cap.) 443,845 .... E4
Tholen 19,019 .... E5
Tiel 31,394 .... G5
Tilburg 155,110 .... G5
Twello J4
Uden 35,057 .... H5
Uithoorn 22,205 .... F4
Uithuizen K2
Ulrum 3,657 .... J2
Urk 12,728 .... H3
Utrecht 230,634 .... G4
Vaals 10,639 .... H7
Valkenswaard 29,811 .... H6
Veendam 28,234 .... K2
Veenendaal 47,258 .... G4
Veere 4,836 .... D5
Veghel 25,701 .... H5
Veldhoven 38,644 .... G6
Velsen 57,608 .... F4
Venlo 63,607 .... J6
Venraij 34,172 .... H6
Vianen 18,704 .... G5
Vlaardingen 74,480 .... E5
Vlagtwedde 16,181 .... L3
Vlijmen 15,655 .... G5
Vlissingen (Flushing) 44,022 .... C6
Volendam-Edam 24,572 .... G4
Voorburg 40,455 .... E4
Voorst 23,678 .... J4
Vorden 8,282 .... J4
Vriezenveen 18,601 .... K4
Vught 23,718 .... G5
Waalre 15,126 .... G6
Waalwijk 28,674 .... F5
Wageningen 32,370 .... H5
Warmenhuizen 4,765 .... F3
Weert 40,068 .... H6
Weesp 18,362 .... C5
Westkapelle 2,666 .... C5
Wierden 22,200 .... K4
Wijhe 7,155 .... J4
Wijk bij Duurstede 15,401 .... G5
Willemstad 3,357 .... F5
Winschoten 19,680 .... L2
Winsum 6,583 .... K2
Winterswijk 28,024 .... K5
Woensdrecht 10,077 .... E6
Woerden 34,166 .... F4
Wolvega J3
Workum G3
Zaandam (Zaanstad) 129,653 .... B4
Zaltbommel 9,534 .... G5
Zandvoort 15,428 .... E4
Zeewolde 5,930 .... G4
Zeist 59,431 .... G4
Zevenaar 26,848 .... J5
Zevenbergen 15,562 .... E5
Zierikzee 9,804 .... D5
Zundert 13,385 .... F6
Zutphen 31,144 .... J4
Zwartsluis 4,465 .... H3
Zwijndrecht 41,357 .... E5
Zwolle 92,517 .... J3

OTHER FEATURES

Alkmaardermeer (lake) F3
Ameland (isl.) H2
Beulaker Wijde (lake) H3
Borndiep (chan.) H2
De Fluessen (lake) G3
De Honte (bay) D6
De Peel (reg.) H6
De Twente (reg.) K4
De Zaan (riv.) B4
Dollard (bay) L2
Dommel (riv.) H6
Duiveland (isl.) D5
Eems (riv.) K2
Eijerlandsche Gat (strait) F2
Flevoland Polders G4
Frisian, West (isls.) G2
Goeree (isl.) D5
Grevelingen (strait) E5
Griend (isl.) G2
Groninger Wad (sound) J2
Groote IJ Polder B4
Haarlemmermeer Polder B5
Haringvliet (strait) E5
Het IJ (est.) C4
Hoek van Holland (cape) D5
Houtrak Polder A4
Hunse (riv.) K3
IJmeer (bay) C4
IJssel (riv.) J4
IJsselmeer (lake) G3
Lauwers (chan.) J1
Lauwers Zee (bay) J2
Lek (riv.) F5
Lower Rhine (riv.) H5
Maas (riv.) G5
Marken (isl.) G4
Markerwaard Polder G3
Marsdiep (chan.) F3
North (sea) E3
North Beveland (isl.) D5
North East Polder H3
North Holland (canal) C4
North Sea (canal) F4
Old Rhine (riv.) E4
Oostzaan Polder B4
Orange (canal) K3
Overflakkee (isl.) E5
Rhine (riv.) J5
Roer (riv.) J6
Scheldt, Eastern (est.) D5
Scheldt, Western (De Honte) (bay) D6
Schiermonnikoog (isl.) J1
Schouwen (isl.) D5
Slotermeer (lake) H3
Sneekermeer (lake) H2
South Beveland (isl.) D6
Terschelling (isl.) G2
Texel (isl.) F2
Tjeukemeer (lake) H3
Vaalserberg (mt.) J7
Vecht (riv.) F4
Vechte (riv.) J3
Veersche Meer (lake) D5
Veluwe (reg.) H4
Vlieland (isl.) F2
Vliestroom (strait) G2
Voorne (isl.) D5
Waal (riv.) G5
Waddenzee (sound) G2
Walcheren (isl.) C5
West Frisian (isls.) F2
Wester Eems (chan.) K1
Western Scheldt (De Honte) (bay) D6
Wieringermeer Polder G3
Wilhelmina (canal) G6
Willems (canal) G5

* City and suburbs.
† Population of urban area.

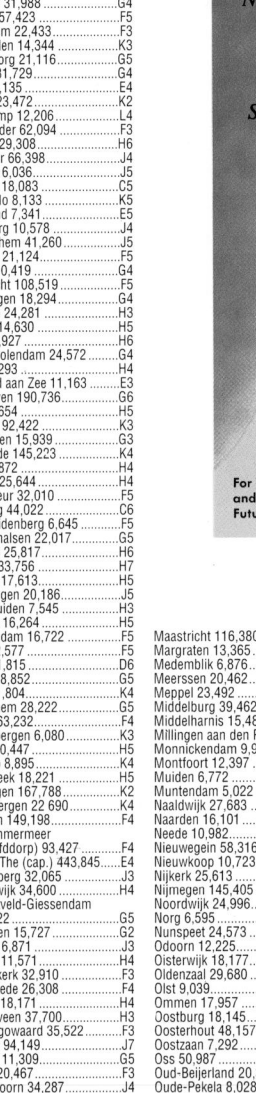

Land from the Sea

Reclaimed Land and Dates of Completion
Future Polders
□ =10 Square Miles

For centuries the Dutch have been renowned for the drainage of marshes and the construction of polders, i.e., arable land reclaimed from the sea. Future projects will convert much of the present IJsselmeer to agricultural land.

Topography

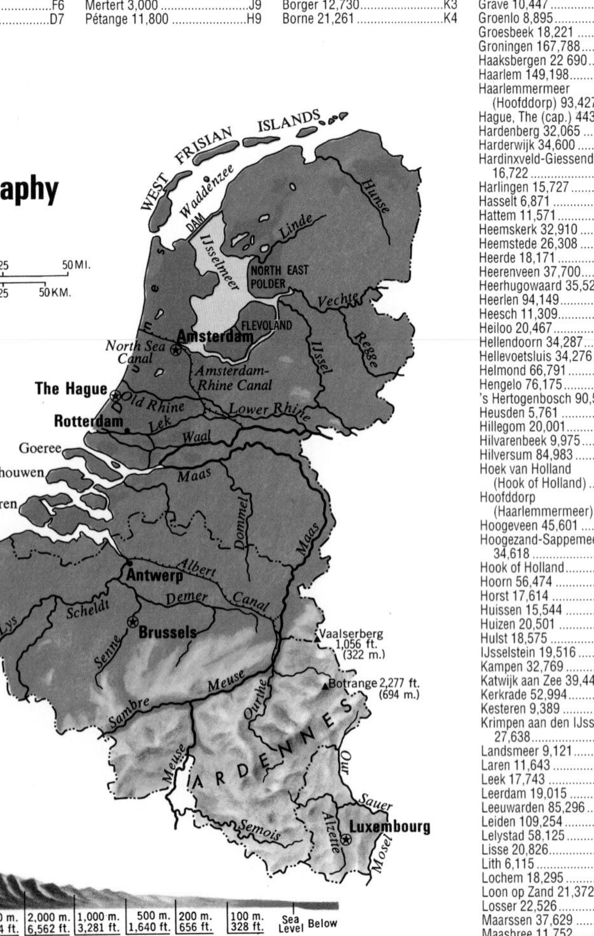
WEST FRISIAN ISLANDS
Waddenzee
DAM
IJsselmeer
NORTH EAST POLDER
FLEVOLAND
North Sea Canal
Amsterdam
Amsterdam-Rhine Canal
The Hague
Old Rhine
Rotterdam
Lek
Lower Rhine
Waal
Goeree
Schouwen
Walcheren
Maas
Antwerp
Albert
Canal
Demer
Scheldt
Lys
Yser
Brussels
Senne
Sambre
Meuse
Ourthe
Vaalserberg 1,056 ft. (322 m.)
Botrange 2,277 ft. (694 m.)
ARDENNES
Semois
Alzette
Sauer
Our
Mosel
Luxembourg
0 25 50 MI.
0 25 50 KM.

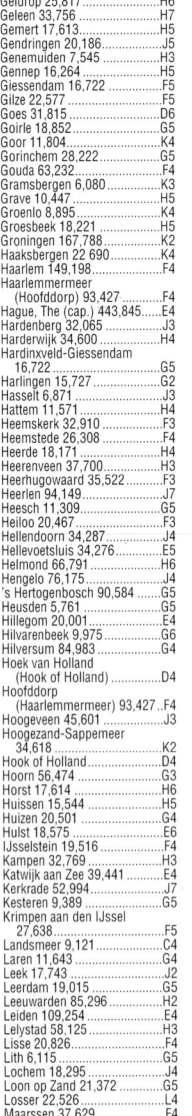

Netherlands, Belgium and Luxembourg

CONIC PROJECTION

SCALE OF MILES

0 5 10 20 30 40

SCALE OF KILOMETRES

0 5 10 20 30 40 50

Capitals of Countries _____ ☆
Provincial Capitals _____ △
International Boundaries _____
Provincial Boundaries _____
Canals _____

© Copyright HAMMOND INCORPORATED, Maplewood, N.J.

© Copyright HAMMOND INCORPORATED, Maplewood, N.J.

France
CONIC PROJECTION
SCALE OF MILES
0 20 40 60 80 100
SCALE OF KILOMETERS
0 20 40 60 80 100
Capitals of Countries
Capitals of Departments
International Boundaries
Department Boundaries
Canals
Paris and Environs
VAL-D'OISE
Épinay-sur-Seine
Le Blanc-Mesnil
Argenteuil
Sartrouville
St-Denis
Aulnay-sous-Bois
Colombes
Gennevilliers
La Courneuve
Drancy
SEINE-ST-DENIS
Asnières-sur-Seine
St-Ouen
Bobigny
Nanterre
Courbevoie
Aubervilliers
Pantin
Levallois-Perret
Noisy-le-Sec
Gagny
Puteaux
Neuilly
Bagnolet
Villemomble
Chelles
Rueil-Malmaison
Suresnes
Montreuil
Boulogne-Billancourt
PARIS
Vincennes
St-Cloud
St-Mandé
Fontenay-sous-Bois
Le Chesnay
HAUTS-DE-SEINE
Charenton-le-Pont
Champigny-sur-Marne
Sèvres
Issy-les-Moulineaux
Malakoff
Meudon
Montrouge
Ivry-sur-Seine
Maisons-Alfort
St-Maur-des-Fossés
Versailles
Clamart
Châtillon
Gentilly
Villejuif
Vitry
Créteil
VAL-DE-MARNE
Sceaux
Choisy-le-Roi
ESSONNE
Bièvres
Antony
Orly
Corsica
Same Scale as Main Map
C. Corse
Rogliano
Bastia
L'Île-Rousse
HAUTE-CORSE
Calvi
Calenzana
Cervione
Mt. Cinto 8,892 ft. (2710 m.)
Corte
Aléria
Bastelica
Ghisonaccia
Ajaccio
Mt. L'Incudine 7,008 ft. (2136 m.)
G. d'Ajaccio
CORSE-DU-SUD
Sartène
Porto-Vecchio
Bonifacio
Str. of Bonifacio
MEDITERRANEAN SEA
UNITED KINGDOM
ENGLAND
LONDON
NORTH SEA
NETHERLANDS
Amsterdam
The Hague
Rotterdam
BELGIUM
Brussels
LUXEMBOURG
Luxembourg
GERMANY
SWITZERLAND
Bern
ITALY
Turin
ANDORRA
SPAIN
BARCELONA
ENGLISH CHANNEL (La Manche)
Strait of Dover (Pas de Calais)
CHANNEL ISLANDS
BAY OF BISCAY
Gulf of Lions
MEDITERRANEAN SEA
Gulf of St-Malo
PARIS
Lille
Amiens
Rouen
Le Havre
Caen
Cherbourg
Reims
Metz
Strasbourg
Nancy
Orléans
Tours
Le Mans
Rennes
Brest
Nantes
Angers
Dijon
Besançon
Lyon
St-Étienne
Grenoble
Clermont-Ferrand
Limoges
Poitiers
Bordeaux
Toulouse
Montpellier
Nîmes
Marseille
Toulon
Nice
Cannes
MONACO
Avignon
Perpignan
Pau
Bayonne
Biarritz
NORD
PAS-DE-CALAIS
SOMME
AISNE
ARDENNES
SEINE-MARITIME
OISE
CALVADOS
MANCHE
EURE
ORNE
YVELINES
ESSONNE
SEINE-ET-MARNE
MARNE
MEUSE
MOSELLE
BAS-RHIN
HAUT-RHIN
VOSGES
MEURTHE-ET-MOSELLE
HAUTE-MARNE
AUBE
YONNE
CÔTE-D'OR
HAUTE-SAÔNE
DOUBS
JURA
FINISTÈRE
CÔTES-DU-NORD
MORBIHAN
ILLE-ET-VILAINE
MAYENNE
SARTHE
EURE-ET-LOIR
LOIRET
LOIR-ET-CHER
INDRE-ET-LOIRE
MAINE-ET-LOIRE
LOIRE-ATLANTIQUE
VENDÉE
DEUX-SÈVRES
VIENNE
INDRE
CHER
NIÈVRE
SAÔNE-ET-LOIRE
ALLIER
CREUSE
HAUTE-VIENNE
CHARENTE
CHARENTE-MARITIME
CORRÈZE
PUY-DE-DÔME
LOIRE
RHÔNE
AIN
HAUTE-SAVOIE
SAVOIE
ISÈRE
DRÔME
ARDÈCHE
HAUTE-LOIRE
CANTAL
LOZÈRE
DORDOGNE
GIRONDE
LOT
LOT-ET-GARONNE
LANDES
GERS
TARN-ET-GARONNE
TARN
AVEYRON
GARD
HÉRAULT
HAUTE-GARONNE
PYRÉNÉES-ATLANTIQUES
HAUTES-PYRÉNÉES
ARIÈGE
AUDE
PYRÉNÉES-ORIENTALES
BOUCHES-DU-RHÔNE
VAUCLUSE
VAR
ALPES-DE-HAUTE-PROVENCE
HAUTES-ALPES
ALPES-MARITIMES
Mt. Blanc 15,771 ft. (4807 m.)
Puy-de-Dôme 4,806 ft. (1465 m.)
Plomb du Cantal 6,096 ft. (1858 m.)
Mt. Mézenc 5,755 ft. (1754 m.)
Les Écrins 13,461 ft. (4103 m.)
Vignemale 10,820 ft. (3298 m.)
Pico de Aneto 11,168 ft. (3404 m.)
Mte. Perdido 11,007 ft. (3355 m.)
Monts Dore
Massif Central
Jura Mts.
Lake Geneva
Loire
Seine
Garonne
Rhône
N
Longitude 2° West of Greenwich
0° Longitude
East of 2° Greenwich
© Copyright HAMMOND INCORPORATED, Maplewood, N. J.

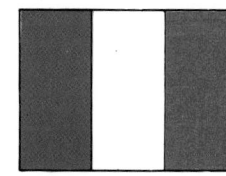

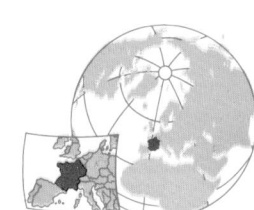

DEPARTMENTS

Ain 418,516........... F 4
Aisne 533,970........ E 3
Allier 369,580......... E 4
Alpes-de-Haute-
Provence 119,068.....G 5
Alpes-Maritimes
881,198........... G 6
Ardèche 267,970......F 5
Ardennes 302,338......E 3
Ariège 135,725........ D 6
Aube 289,300......... E 3
Aude 280,686......... E 6
Aveyron 278,654....... E 5
Bas-Rhin 915,676......G 3
Belfort 131,999........ G 4
Bouches-du-Rhône
1,724,199......... F 6
Calvados 589,559..... C 3
Cantal 162,838....... E 5
Charente 340,770..... D 5
Charente-Maritime
513,220..........C 5
Cher 320,174.........E 4
Corrèze 241,448...... D 5
Corse du Sud
108,604...........B 6
Côte-d'Or 473,548......F 4
Côtes-du-Nord
538,869...........B 3
Creuse 139,968....... D 5
Deux-Sèvres
342,812...........C 4
Dordogne 377,356..... D 5
Doubs 477,163....... G 4
Drôme 389,781........ F 5
Essonne 988,000......E 3
Eure 462,323......... D 3
Eure-et-Loir 362,813... D 3
Finistère 828,364...... A 3
Gard 530,478......... F 6
Gers 174,154......... D 6
Gironde 1,127,546..... C 5
Haute-Corse
131,574...........B 6
Haute-Garonne
824,501...........D 6
Haute-Loire 205,895.... E 5
Haute-Marne
210,670........... F 3
Hautes-Alpes
105,070........... G 5
Haute-Saône
231,962........... G 4
Haute-Savoie
494,505........... G 5
Hautes-Pyrénées
227,922...........D 6
Haute-Vienne
355,737...........D 5
Haut-Rhin 650,372..... G 4
Hauts-de-Seine
1,387,039......... A 2
Hérault 706,499....... E 6
Ille-et-Vilaine
749,764...........C 3
Indre 243,191........ D 4
Indre-et-Loire
506,097...........D 4
Isère 936,771........ F 5
Jura 242,925......... F 4
Landes 297,424....... C 5

Loire 739,521.........F 5
Loire-Atlantique
995,498...........C 4
Loiret 535,669........ E 4
Loir-et-Cher 296,220... D 4
Lot 154,533.......... D 5
Lot-et-Garonne
298,522...........D 5
Lozère 74,294........ E 5
Maine-et-Loire
675,321...........C 4
Manche 465,948...... C 3
Marne 543,627....... F 3
Mayenne 271,784..... C 3
Meurthe-et-Moselle
716,846........... G 3
Meuse 200,101....... F 3
Morbihan 590,889..... B 4
Moselle 1,007,189.... G 3
Nièvre 239,635....... E 4
Nord 2,520,526...... E 2
Oise 661,781........ E 2
Orne 295,472........ C 3
Paris 2,188,918...... B 2
Pas-de-Calais
1,412,413......... E 2
Puy-de-Dôme
594,365...........E 5
Pyrénées-Atlantiques
555,696...........C 6
Pyrénées-Orientales
334,557...........E 6
Rhône 1,445,208..... F 5
Saône-et-Loire
571,852...........F 4
Sarthe 504,768...... D 3
Savoie 323,675...... G 5
Seine-et-Marne
887,112...........E 3
Seine-Maritime
1,324,301......... D 3
Seine-Saint-Denis
1,324,301......... C 1
Somme 544,570...... E 3
Tarn 339,345........ E 6
Tarn-et-Garonne
190,485...........D 5
Val-de-Marne
1,193,655......... C 1
Val-d'Oise 920,598.... E 3
Var 708,331......... G 6
Vaucluse 427,343..... F 6
Vendée 483,027...... C 4
Vienne 371,428...... D 4
Vosges 395,769...... G 3
Yonne 311,019....... E 4
Yvelines 1,196,111.... B 2

CITIES and TOWNS

Aigues-Mortes 4,106... F 6
Aix-en-Provence
100,221...........F 6
Aix-les-Bains 22,331... G 5
Ajaccio 48,324....... B 7
Alençon 30,952...... D 3
Amboise 10,823...... D 4
Amiens 130,302...... E 3
Angers 135,293...... C 4
Angoulême 45,495.... D 5
Annecy 49,753....... G 5
Antibes 62,427....... G 6
Argenteuil 94,826..... A 1

Arles 37,554..........F 6
Armentières 22,849.... E 2
Arras 41,376......... E 2
Asnières-sur-Seine
71,058............A 1
Aubervilliers 67,684.... B 1
Aubusson 5,326...... E 4
Aulnay-sous-Bois
75,543............B 1
Aurignac 772........ D 6
Avignon 75,178...... F 6
Ax-les-Thermes
1,283.............D 6
Bagnolet 32,556..... B 2
Barbizon 478........ E 3
Barcelonnette 2,674... G 5
Barfleur 617......... C 3
Bastia 43,502....... B 6
Bayeux 14,568...... C 3
Bayonne 40,088..... C 6
Beaucaire 10,622.... F 6
Beaune 19,110...... F 4
Beauvais 51,542..... E 3
Belfort 51,034...... G 4
Bergerac 24,604.... D 5
Besançon 112,023... G 4
Bessèges 4,352..... F 5
Béziers 74,114...... E 6
Biarritz 26,579...... C 6
Blois 46,925....... D 4
Bobigny 42,630..... B 1
Bonifacio 1,727..... B 7
Bordeaux 201,965... C 5
Boulogne-Billancourt
102,582...........A 2
Boulogne-sur-Mer
47,482............D 2
Bourg-en-Bresse
37,582............F 4
Bourges 74,622..... E 4
Brest 154,110...... A 3
Brignoles 8,529..... G 6
Brive-la-Gaillarde
50,898............D 5
Bruay-en-Artois
22,502............E 2
Caen 112,332...... C 3
Calais 76,206...... D 2
Caluire-et-Cuire
41,864............F 5
Cambrai 35,070..... E 2
Cannes 71,888..... G 6
Carcassonne
38,379............E 6
Castres 39,216..... E 6
Chalons-sur-Marne
49,941............F 3

AREA 210,038 sq. mi. (543,998 sq. km.)
POPULATION 56,160,000
CAPITAL Paris
LARGEST CITY Paris
HIGHEST POINT Mont Blanc 15,771 ft. (4,807 m.)
MONETARY UNIT franc
MAJOR LANGUAGE French
MAJOR RELIGION Roman Catholicism

Topography

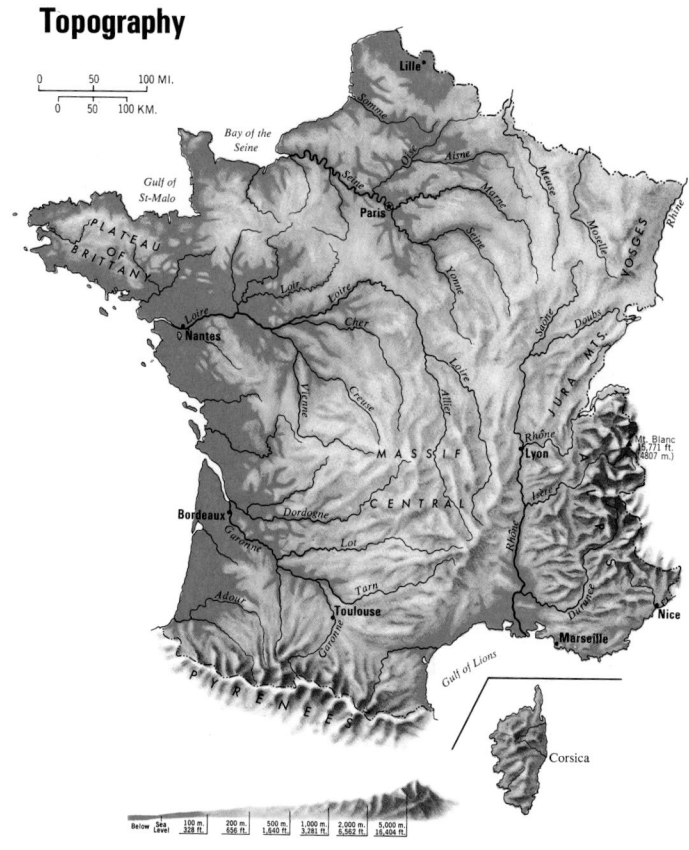

Historic Provinces

A resident of the city of Caen thinks of himself as a Norman rather than as a citizen of the modern department of Calvados. In spite of the passing of nearly two centuries, the historic provinces which existed before 1790 command the local patriotism of most Frenchmen.

Chalon-sur-Saône
53,893............F 4
Chambéry 49,465..... F 5
Chambord 159....... D 4
Chamonix-Mont-Blanc
7,406.............G 5
Champigny-sur-Marne
76,039............C 2
Chantilly 10,065...... E 3
Charleville-Mézières
7,814.............F 3
Chartres 36,706..... D 3
Châteaudun 15,905... D 3
Châteauneuf-sur-Loire
5,630.............E 4
Châteauroux 51,744.. D 4
Château-Thierry
14,427............E 3
Chatou 28,435...... A 1
Cherbourg 28,324.... C 3
Chinon 6,030...... D 4
Choisy-le-Roi 35,443.. B 2
Cholet 51,620...... C 4
Clamart 48,210..... A 2
Clermont-Ferrand
145,901...........E 5
Clichy 46,830...... B 1
Cluny 4,133....... F 4
Cognac 20,247..... C 5
Colmar 61,560..... G 3
Colombes 78,485.... A 1
Compiègne 39,909... E 3
Courbevoie 59,821... A 1
Creil 34,332...... E 3
Créteil 71,559..... B 2
Deauville 4,682.... C 3
Dieppe 35,659..... D 3
Digne 12,540..... G 5
Dijon 139,188..... F 4
Dinard 9,562..... B 3
Domrémy-la-Pucelle
162...............F 3
Douai 41,576..... E 2
Drancy 60,122.... B 1
Dunkirk 71,756.... E 2

Ernée 5,253.........C 3
Évreux 45,215...... D 3
Falaise 8,424...... C 3
Fécamp 21,212..... D 3
Foix 9,212........ D 6
Fontainebleau
14,687............E 3
Fontenay-sous-Bois
52,397............C 2
Gex 4,776........ G 4
Grasse 24,257..... G 6
Grenoble 156,437... F 5
Guise 6,179....... E 3
Harfleur 9,470..... D 3
Hazebrouck 19,266.. E 2
Hendaye 10,492.... C 6
Héricourt 9,239..... G 4
Honfleur 8,125..... D 3
Issy-les-Moulineaux
45,702............A 2
Istres 21,286...... F 6
Ivry-sur-Seine
55,682............B 2
La Baule-Escoublac
13,151............B 4
La Courneuve
33,525............B 1
Langres 9,718..... F 4
Lapalisse 3,173.... E 4
La Rochelle 74,728... C 4
La Roche-sur-Yon
42,026............C 4
Laval 53,582..... C 3
Le Bourget 11,020... B 1
Le Creusot 32,013... F 4
Le Havre 198,700... C 3
Le Mans 145,976... C 3
Le Puy 22,806.... F 5
Le Tréport 6,330... D 2
Levallois-Perret
51,289............B 1
Lille 167,791...... E 2
Limoges 137,809... D 5
Lisieux 24,454.... D 3
Lorient 62,207.... B 4

Lourdes 17,252.......C 6
Lunéville 21,200.... G 3
Lyon 410,455...... F 5
Mâcon 36,517..... F 4
Maisons-Alfort
51,041............B 2
Maisons-Laffitte
22,565............A 1
Mantes-la-Jolie
43,551............D 3
Marmande 14,264... C 5
Marseille 868,435... F 6
Maubeuge 35,424... F 2
Mayenne 12,156.... C 3
Meaux 44,386..... E 3
Melun 34,379..... E 3
Mende 10,520.... E 5
Menton 22,234.... G 6
Metz 113,236..... G 3
Meudon 29,356.... A 2
Montauban 36,122.. D 5
Montbéliard 31,174.. G 4
Montceau-les-Mines
26,877............F 4
Mont-de-Marsan
25,896............C 6
Mont-Dore 2,091... E 5
Montfort 4,029..... C 3
Montluçon 49,737... E 4
Montmédy 1,880... F 3
Montpellier 190,423.. E 6
Montreuil 96,441... B 2
Mont-Saint-Michel
65................C 3
Mulhouse 111,742.. G 4
Nancy 95,654..... G 3
Nanterre 88,567... A 1
Nantes 237,789... C 4
Narbonne 38,222.. E 6
Nemours 11,624... E 3
Neufchâtel-en-Bray
5,452.............D 3
Neuilly-sur-Seine
64,093............A 1
Nice 331,165..... G 6

Nîmes 120,515........F 6
Niort 56,256...... C 4
Nogent-le-Rotrou
11,963............D 3
Noisy-le-Sec 36,821.. B 1
Nontron 3,407..... D 5
Noyon 13,949..... E 3
Nyons 5,219..... F 5
Orléans 81,615.... D 3
Orly 23,729...... B 2
Oyonnax 22,516... F 4
Paris (cap.)
2,165,892......... B 2
Paris *10,073,059.... B 2
Pau 82,186...... C 6
Périgueux 32,632... D 5
Perpignan 107,812.. E 6
Pessac 49,019.... C 5
Poitiers 76,793.... D 4
Pontoise 27,885... E 3
Port-Vendres 4,871.. E 6
Privas 9,253..... F 5
Quimper 52,335... A 4
Rambouillet 21,136... D 3
Redon 9,071..... C 4
Reims 176,419.... E 3
Rennes 190,861... C 3
Roanne 48,574.... E 4
Rochefort 25,392.. C 4
Roubaix 101,488... E 2
Rouen 100,696... D 3
Rueil-Malmaison
63,310............A 2
Saint-Brieuc 48,259.. B 3
Saint-Cloud 28,561... A 2
Saint-Denis 90,686... B 1
Saint-Dizier 34,074.. F 3
Sainte-Mère-Église
1,205.............C 3
Saint-Étienne
193,938...........F 5
Saint-Germain-en-Laye
36,585............D 3
Saint-Jean-d'Angély
9,268.............C 4

(continued on following page)

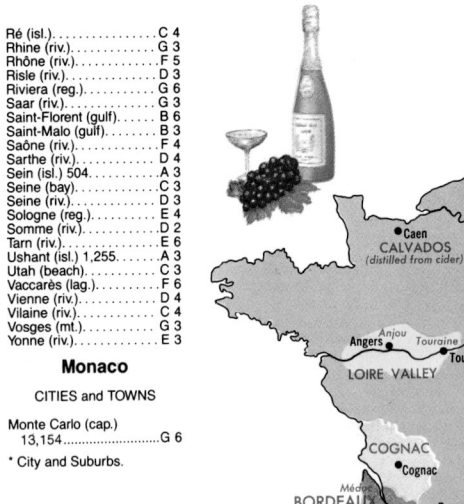

Wine Regions

Climate, soil and variety of grape planted determine the quality of wine. Long, hot and fairly dry summers with cool, humid nights constitute an ideal climate. The nature of the soil is such a determining influence that identical grapes planted in Bordeaux, Burgundy and Champagne, will yield wines of widely different types.

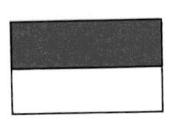

MONACO

368 acres
(149 hectares)
27,063

Agriculture, Industry and Resources

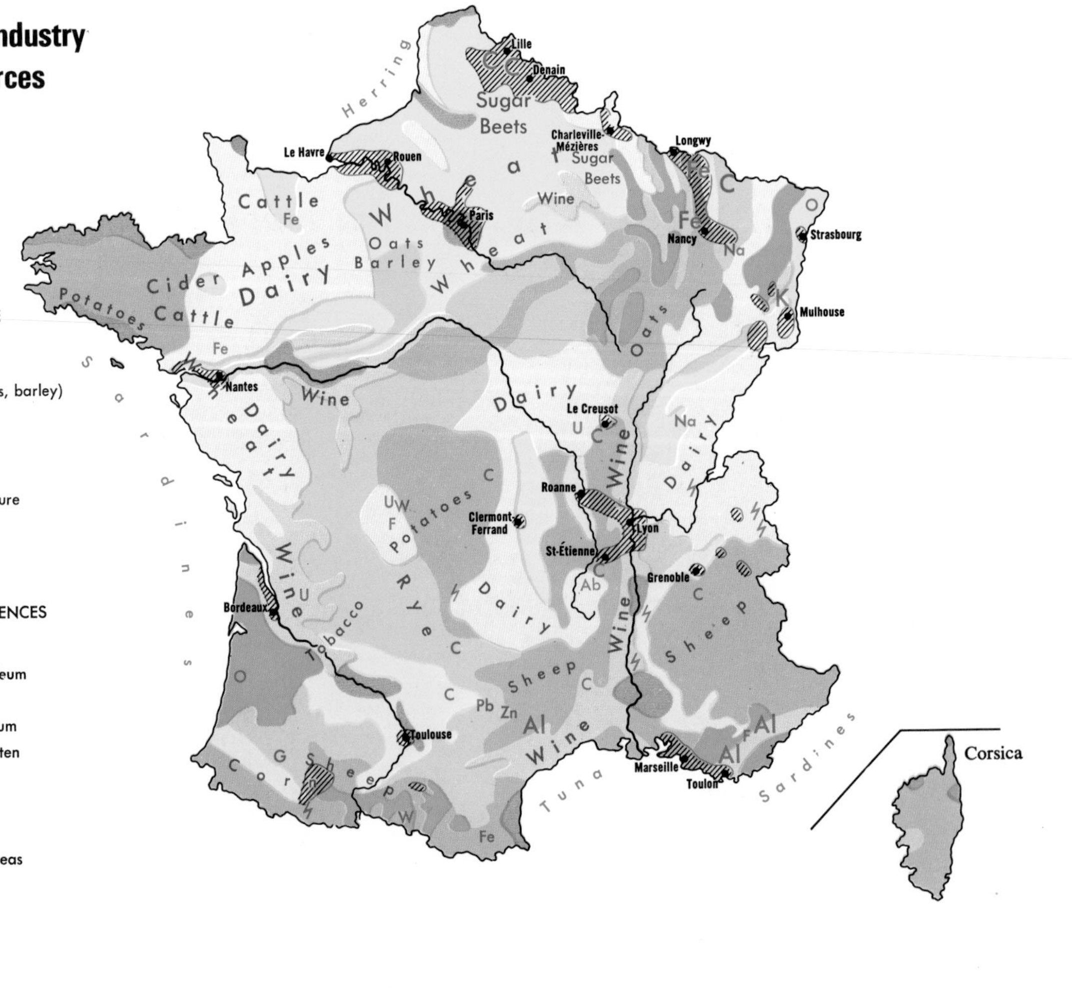

DOMINANT LAND USE

- Cereals (chiefly wheat)
- Cereals (chiefly rye, oats, barley)
- Dairy
- Pasture Livestock
- Truck Farming, Horticulture
- Grapes, Wine
- Forests

MAJOR MINERAL OCCURRENCES

Ab	Asbestos	Na	Salt
Al	Bauxite	O	Petroleum
C	Coal	Pb	Lead
F	Fluorspar	U	Uranium
Fe	Iron Ore	W	Tungsten
G	Natural Gas	Zn	Zinc
K	Potash		

⚡ Water Power

▨ Major Industrial Areas

Corsica

ANDORRA

SPAIN

PORTUGAL

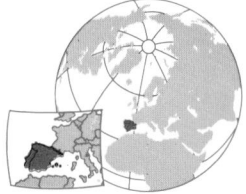

(continued on following page)

Agriculture, Industry and Resources

DOMINANT LAND USE

- Cereals (chiefly wheat)
- Livestock (chiefly sheep goats)
- Mixed Cereals, Livestock
- Olives, Fruit
- Grapes, Fruit, Nuts, Mixed Cereals
- Forests
- Nonagricultural Land

MAJOR MINERAL OCCURRENCES

Ag	Silver	Na	Salt
C	Coal	O	Petroleum
Cu	Copper	Pb	Lead
Fe	Iron Ore	Py	Pyrites
G	Natural Gas	Sb	Antimony
Hg	Mercury	Sn	Tin
K	Potash	U	Uranium
Lg	Lignite	W	Tungsten
Mg	Magnesium	Zn	Zinc

⚡ Water Power

▨ Major Industrial Areas

(continued on following page)

Oliva 16,717 ... F3
Oliva de la Frontera 8,560 ... C3
Olivenza 7,616 ... C3
Olot 18,062 ... H1
Olvera 9,825 ... D4
Onda 13,012 ... F3
Onteniente 23,685 ... F3
Orense 63,542 ... C1
Orihuela 17,610 ... F3
Osuna 17,384 ... D4
Oviedo 130,021 ... D1
Padul 6,377 ... E4
Palafrugell 10,421 ... H2
Palamós 7,679 ... H2
Palencia 58,327 ... D2
Palma 191,416 ... H3
Palma del Río 15,075 ... D4
Pamplona 142,686 ... F1
Pego 8,861 ... F3
Peñaranda de Bracamonte 6,094 ... D2
Peñarroya-Pueblonuevo 15,649 ... D3
Pinos-Puente 7,634 ... E4
Plasencia 26,897 ... C2
Pola de Lena 5,760 ... C1
Pollensa 7,625 ... H3
Ponferrada 22,838 ... C1
Pontevedra 27,118 ... B1
Porcuna 8,169 ... D4
Portugalete 45,589 ... E1
Posadas 7,245 ... D4
Pozoblanco 13,280 ... D3
Pozuelo de Alarcón 14,041 ... D4
Priego de Córdoba 12,676 ... D4
Puente-Genil 22,888 ... D4
Puertollano 50,609 ... D3
Puerto Real 13,993 ... C4
Puigcerdá 4,418 ... G1
Quesada 6,965 ... E4
Quintana de la Serena 5,171 ... D3
Quintanar de la Orden 7,764 ... E3
Reinosa 10,863 ... D1
Requena 9,836 ... F3
Reus 47,240 ... G2
Ripoll 9,283 ... H1
Ronda 22,094 ... D4
Roquetes 5,617 ... G2
Roses 5,448 ... H1
Rota 20,021 ... C4
Rute 8,294 ... D4
Sabadell 148,223 ... H2
Sagunto 17,052 ... F3
Salamanca 125,132 ... C2
Sallent 7,118 ... H2
Salobreña 5,961 ... E4
Salt 5,572 ... H2
San Clemente 6,016 ... E3
San Fernando 59,309 ... C4
San Lorenzo de El Escorial 8,098 ... D2
San Roque 8,224 ... D4
San Sebastián 159,557 ... E1
Santa Cruz de la Palma 10,393 ... F4
Santa Cruz de Mudela 6,354 ... E3

Santa Cruz de Tenerife 74,910 ... F4
Santa Eugenia de Ribeira 5,946 ... B1
Santa Fé 8,990 ... E4
Santander 130,019 ... D1
Santiago 51,620 ... B1
Santo Domingo de la Calzada 5,638 ... E1
Santoña 9,546 ... E1
San Vicente de Alcántara 7,006 ... C3
Sanlúcar de Barrameda 29,483 ... C4
Saragossa 449,319 ... F2
Saragossa‡ 500,000 ... F2
Segorbe 6,962 ... F3
Segovia 41,880 ... D2
Seville 511,447 ... D4
Seville‡ 560,000 ... D4
Sitges 8,906 ... G2
Socuéllamos 12,610 ... E3
Sóller 6,470 ... H3
Solsona 5,346 ... G1
Sonseca 6,594 ... D3
Soria 24,744 ... E2
Sotrondio 5,914 ... D1
Sueca 20,019 ... F3
Tabernes de Valldigna 13,962 ... F3
Tafalla 8,858 ... E1
Talavera de la Reina 39,889 ... D2
Tarancón 8,238 ... E3
Tarazona 11,067 ... E2
Tarazona de la Mancha 5,952 ... F3
Tarifa 9,201 ... D4
Tarragona 53,548 ... G2
Tárrega 9,036 ... G2
Tauste 6,832 ... F2
Telde 13,257 ... C3
Terrassa 134,481 ... H1
Teruel 20,614 ... F2
Tobarra 5,887 ... E4
Toledo 43,905 ... D3
Tolosa 15,164 ... E1
Tomelloso 26,041 ... E3
Tordesillas 5,815 ... D2
Toro 8,455 ... D2
Torredonjimeno 12,507 ... D4
Torrejón de Ardoz 21,081 ... G4
Torrelavega 19,933 ... D1
Torremolinos 20,484 ... D4
Torrente 38,397 ... F3
Torrevieja 9,431 ... F4
Torrijos 6,362 ... D3
Torrox 5,583 ... E4
Tortosa 20,030 ... G2
Totana 12,714 ... F4
Trigueros 6,280 ... C4
Trujillo 9,024 ... D3
Tudela 20,942 ... F1
Úbeda 28,306 ... E3
Ubrique 13,166 ... D4
Utiel 9,168 ... F3
Utrera 28,287 ... C4
Valdemoro 6,263 ... E2
Valdepeñas 24,018 ... E3

Valencia 626,675 ... F3
Valencia‡ 700,000 ... F3
Valencia de Alcántara 5,963 ... C3
Valladolid 227,511 ... D2
Vall de Uxó 23,976 ... F3
Vallecas ... G2
Valls 14,189 ... G2
Valverde del Camino 10,566 ... C4
Vejer de la Frontera 6,184 ... C4
Vélez-Málaga 20,794 ... D4
Vergara 11,541 ... E1
Vic 23,449 ... H1
Vigo 114,526 ... B1
Vilafranca del Penedés 16,875 ... G2
Vilanova i la Geltrú 35,714 ... G2
Villacañas 9,883 ... E3
Villacarrillo 9,452 ... E3
Villafranca de los Barros 12,610 ... C3
Villagarcía 6,601 ... B1
Villajoyosa 12,573 ... F3
Villanueva de Córdoba 11,270 ... D3
Villanueva del Arzobispo 8,076 ... E3
Villanueva de la Serena 16,687 ... D3
Villanueva de los Infantes 8,154 ... E3
Villarreal de los Infantes 29,482 ... G3
Villarrobledo 19,698 ... E3
Villaverde ... G4
Villena 23,483 ... F3
Vinaroz 13,727 ... G2
Vitoria 124,791 ... E1
Yecla 19,352 ... F3
Zafra 11,583 ... C3
Zalamea de la Serena 6,017 ... D3
Zamora 48,791 ... D2
Zaragoza (Saragossa) 449,319 ... F2

OTHER FEATURES

Adaja (riv.) ... D2
Agueda (riv.) ... C2
Alagón (riv.) ... C2
Alarcón (res.) ... E3
Alborán (isl.) ... E5
Alcántara (res.) ... C3
Alcudia (bay) ... H3
Almendra (res.) ... C2
Almería (gulf) ... E4
Almanzora (riv.) ... F4
Aneto (peak) ... G1
Aragón (riv.) ... F1
Ardila (riv.) ... C3
Arga (riv.) ... E1
Arosa, Ria de (est.) ... B1
Balearic (Baleares) (isls.) ... H3
Biscay (bay) ... D1
Cabrera (isl.) ... H3
Cádiz (gulf) ... C4
Calaburras (pt.) ... D4

Canary (isls.) ... F4
Cantabrian (range) ... C1
Cijara (res.) ... D3
Cinca (riv.) ... F1
Columbretes (isls.) ... G3
Cope (cape) ... F4
Costa Brava (reg.) ... H2
Costa de Sola (Costa del Sol) (reg.) ... D4
Costa Verde (reg.) ... C1
Creus (cape) ... H1
Cuenca, Sierra de (range) ... F3
Demanda, Sierra de la (range) ... E1
Duero (Douro) (riv.) ... D2
Dragonera (isl.) ... H3
Duratón (riv.) ... D2
Ebro (riv.) ... G2
Eresma (riv.) ... D2
Esla (riv.) ... D2
Estaca de Bares (pt.) ... C1
Estats (peak) ... G1
Finisterre (cape) ... B1
Formentera (isl.) ... G3
Formentor (cape) ... H3
Fuerteventura (isl.) ... G5
Gata (cape) ... F4
Gata, Sierra de (mts.) ... C2
Genil (riv.) ... D4
Gibraltar (str.) ... D5
Gomera (isl.) ... F5
Graciosa (isl.) ... F5
Gran Canaria (isl.) ... F5
Gredos, Sierra de (range) ... D2
Guadalimar (riv.) ... E3
Guadalquivir (riv.) ... C4
Guadarrama, Sierra de (range) ... E2
Guadiana (riv.) ... C4
Gúdar, Sierra de (range) ... F2
Henares (riv.) ... E2
Hierro (isl.) ... F5
Huelva (riv.) ... C4
Ibiza (isl.) ... G3
Jalón (riv.) ... E2
Jarama (riv.) ... E2
Júcar (riv.) ... E3
Lanzarote (isl.) ... G4
La Palma (isl.) ... F4
Llobregat (riv.) ... G2
Mallorca (Majorca) (isl.) ... H3
Mar Menor (lag.) ... F4
Menorca (Minorca) (isl.) ... H3
Mequinenza (res.) ... F2
Miño (riv.) ... B1
Moncayo (mt.) ... F2
Moncayo, Sierra de (range) ... F2
Morena, Sierra (range) ... D3
Mulhacén (mt.) ... E4
Nao (cape) ... G3
Navia (riv.) ... C1
Nevada, Sierra (mts.) ... E4
Odiel (riv.) ... C4
Órbigo (riv.) ... D1
Ortegal (cape) ... B1
Palma (bay) ... H3
Palos (cape) ... F4
Peñalara (mt.) ... E2

Peñas (cape) ... D1
Perdido (mt.) ... F1
Prior (cape) ... B1
Pyrenees (range) ... F1
Ricobayo (res.) ... D2
Rosas (gulf) ... H1
Sacratif (gulf) ... E4
Salinas (cape) ... H3
San Jorge (gulf) ... G2
San Pedro, Sierra de (range) ... C3
Segre (riv.) ... G1
Segura (riv.) ... F4
Sil (riv.) ... C1
Tagomago (isl.) ... G3
Tagus (riv.) ... D3
Tajo (Tagus) (riv.) ... C3
Teide, Pico de (peak) ... F5
Teleno (mt.) ... C1
Tenerife (isl.) ... B4
Ter (riv.) ... H1
Toledo (mts.) ... D3
Tortosa (cape) ... G2

Trafalgar (cape) ... C4
Turia (riv.) ... F3
Ulla (riv.) ... B1
Valdecañas (res.) ... D3
Valencia (gulf) ... G3

PORTUGAL

DISTRICTS

Aveiro 545,230 ... B2
Azores 275,900 ... B4
Beja 204,440 ... C3
Braga 609,415 ... B2
Bragança 180,395 ... C2
Castelo Branco 254,355 ... C3
Coimbra 399,380 ... B2
Évora 178,475 ... C3
Faro 268,040 ... B4
Guarda 210,720 ... C2
Leiria 376,940 ... B3
Lisbon 1,568,020 ... A1

Madeira 262,800 ... A2
Oporto (Porto) 1,309,560 ... B2
Portalegre 145,545 ... C3
Porto 1,309,560 ... B2
Santarém 427,995 ... B3
Setúbal 469,555 ... B3
Viana do Castelo 250,510 ... B2
Vila Real 265,605 ... C2
Viseu 410,795 ... C2

CITIES and TOWNS

Abrantes 11,775 ... B3
Águeda 9,343 ... B2
Alcácer do Sal 13,187 ... B3
Almada 38,990 ... A1
Almeirim 8,780 ... B3
Alportel 7,632 ... C4
Amadora 65,870 ... A1
Amora 10,330 ... A1
Angra do Heroísmo 13,795 ... B4
Aveiro 19,905 ... B2

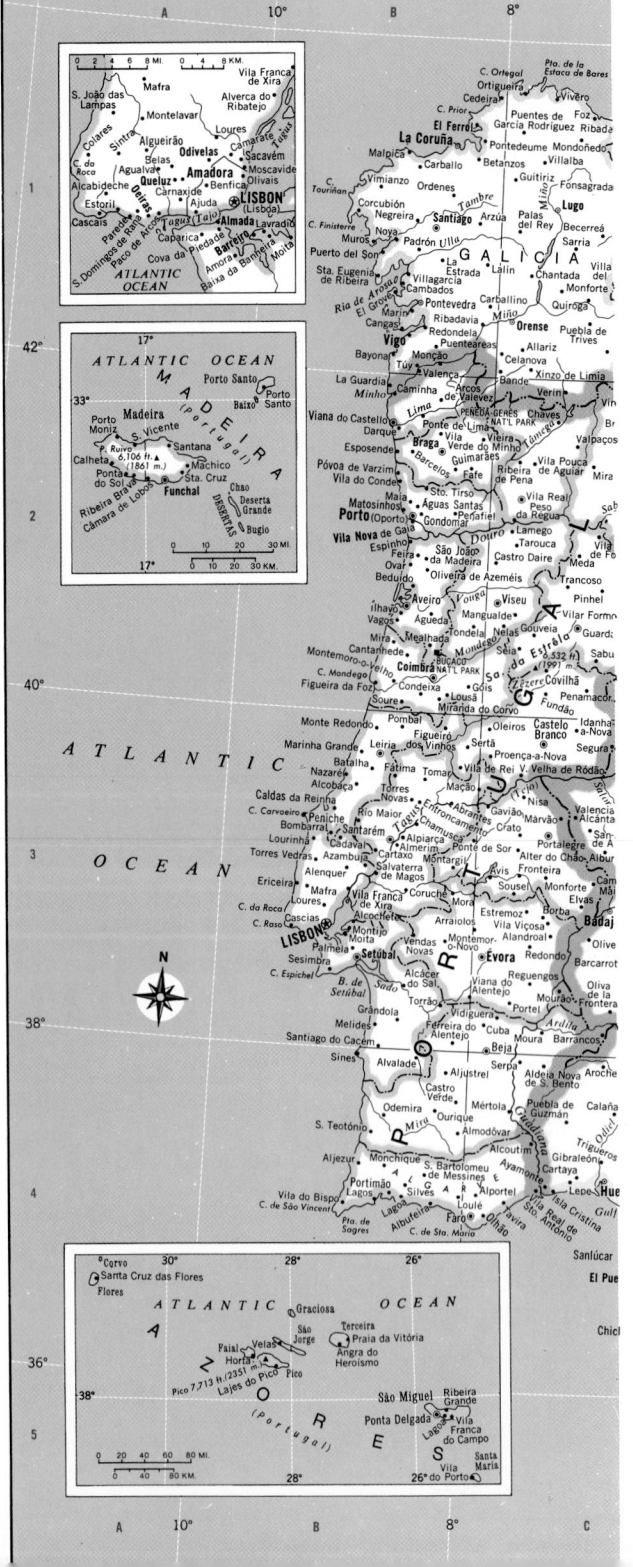

Topography

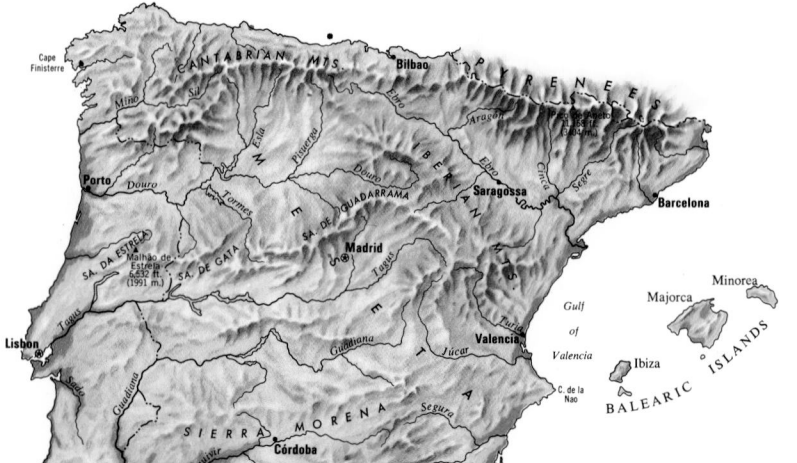

0   50   100 MI.

0   50   100 KM.

Below Sea Level | 100 m. 328 ft. | 200 m. 656 ft. | 500 m. 1,640 ft. | 1,000 m. 3,281 ft. | 2,000 m. 6,562 ft. | 5,000 m. 16,404 ft.

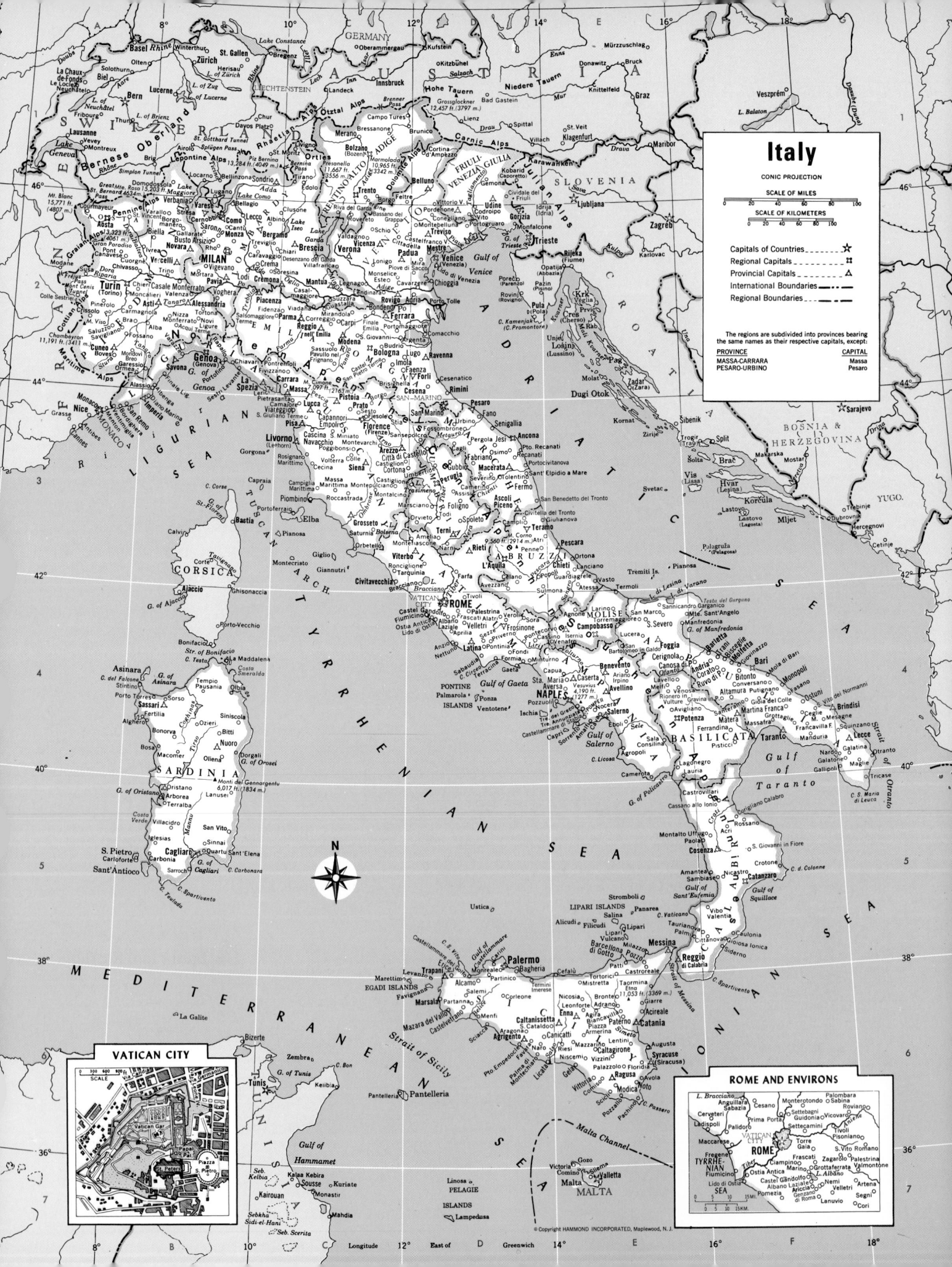

Italy
CONIC PROJECTION
SCALE OF MILES
0 20 40 60 80 100
SCALE OF KILOMETERS
0 20 40 60 80 100
Capitals of Countries
Regional Capitals
Provincial Capitals
International Boundaries
Regional Boundaries
The regions are subdivided into provinces bearing the same names as their respective capitals, except:
PROVINCE
CAPITAL
MASSA-CARRARA
Massa
PESARO-URBINO
Pesaro
VATICAN CITY
ROME AND ENVIRONS
SWITZERLAND
AUSTRIA
GERMANY
SLOVENIA
CROATIA
BOSNIA & HERZEGOVINA
YUGO.
TUNISIA
LIGURIAN SEA
TYRRHENIAN SEA
ADRIATIC SEA
IONIAN SEA
MEDITERRANEAN SEA
Gulf of Taranto
Gulf of Venice
Strait of Sicily
Strait of Otranto
Strait of Messina
Malta Channel
CORSICA
SARDINIA
SICILY
MALTA
LIPARI ISLANDS
EGADI ISLANDS
PONTINE ISLANDS
PELAGIE ISLANDS
ROME
MILAN
NAPLES
Turin
Genoa
Venice (Venezia)
Florence (Firenze)
Bologna
Palermo
Bari
Trieste
Cagliari
Ancona
Catanzaro
Potenza
Campobasso
L'Aquila
Perugia
Trento
Aosta
SAN MARINO
VATICAN CITY
© Copyright HAMMOND INCORPORATED, Maplewood, N. J.
Longitude 12° East of D Greenwich 14°

VATICAN CITY

AREA 108.7 acres (44 hectares)
POPULATION 1,000

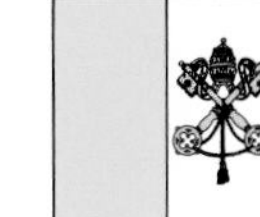

SAN MARINO

AREA 23.4 sq. mi. (60.6 sq. km.)
POPULATION 23,000

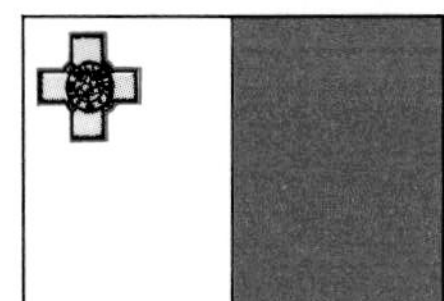

MALTA

AREA 122 sq. mi. (316 sq. km.)
POPULATION 353,000
CAPITAL Valletta
LARGEST CITY Sliema
HIGHEST POINT 787 ft. (240 m.)
MONETARY UNIT Maltese lira
MAJOR LANGUAGES Maltese, English
MAJOR RELIGION Roman Catholicism

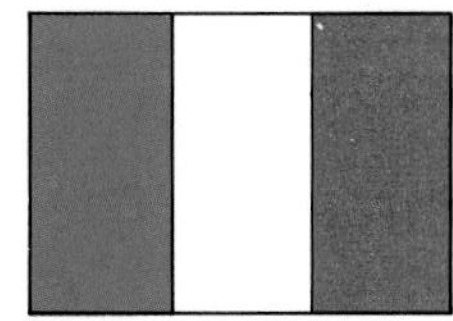

ITALY

AREA 116,303 sq. mi. (301,225 sq. km.)
POPULATION 57,574,000
CAPITAL Rome
LARGEST CITY Rome
HIGHEST POINT Dufourspitze (Mte. Rosa) 15,203 ft. (4,634 m.)
MONETARY UNIT lira
MAJOR LANGUAGE Italian
MAJOR RELIGION Roman Catholicism

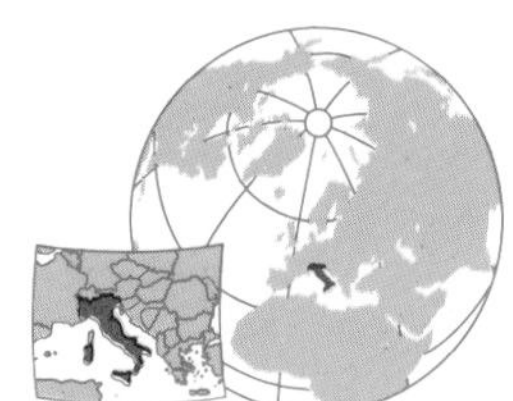

ITALY

REGIONS

Abruzzi 1,217,791 ... D3
Aosta 112,353 ... A2
Apulia (Puglia) 3,871,617 ... F4
Basilicata 610,186 ... F4
Calabria 2,061,182 ... F5
Campania 5,463,134 ... E4
Emilia-Romagna 3,957,513 ... C2
Friuli-Venezia Giulia 1,233,984 ... D1
Latium (Lazio) 5,001,684 ... D3
Liguria 1,807,893 ... B2
Lombardy 8,891,652 ... B2
Marche 1,412,404 ... D3
Molise 328,371 ... E4
Piedmont 4,479,031 ... A2
Sardinia 1,594,175 ... B4
Sicily 4,906,878 ... D6
Trentino-Alto Adige 873,413 ... C1
Tuscany 3,581,051 ... C3
Umbria 807,552 ... D3
Veneto 4,345,047 ... C2

PROVINCES

Agrigento 466,495 ... D6
Alessandria 466,102 ... B2
Ancona 433,417 ... D3
Arezzo 313,157 ... C3
Ascoli Piceno 352,567 ... D3
Asti 215,382 ... B2
Avellino 434,021 ... E4
Bari 1,464,627 ... F4
Belluno 220,335 ... D1
Benevento 289,143 ... E4
Bergamo 896,117 ... B2
Bologna 930,284 ... C2
Bolzano-Bozen 430,568 ... C1
Brescia 1,017,093 ... C2
Brindisi 391,064 ... G4
Cagliari 730,473 ... B5
Caltanissetta 285,829 ... D6
Campobasso 235,847 ... E4
Caserta 755,628 ... E4
Catania 1,005,577 ... E6
Catanzaro 744,834 ... F5
Chieti 370,534 ... E3
Como 755,979 ... B2
Cosenza 743,255 ... F5
Cremona 332,236 ... B2
Cuneo 548,452 ... A2
Enna 190,939 ... E6
Ferrara 381,118 ... C2
Florence 1,202,013 ... C3
Foggia 681,595 ... E4
Forlì 599,420 ... D2
Frosinone 460,395 ... D4
Genoa 1,045,109 ... B2
Gorizia 144,726 ... D2
Grosseto 220,905 ... C3
Imperia 223,738 ... B3
Isernia 92,524 ... E4
L'Aquila 291,742 ... D3
La Spezia 241,371 ... B2
Latina 434,086 ... D4
Lecce 762,017 ... G4
Livorno (Leghorn) 346,657 ... C3
Lucca 385,876 ... C3
Macerata 292,932 ... D3
Mantua 377,158 ... C2
Massa-Carrara 203,530 ... C2
Matera 203,570 ... F4
Messina 669,323 ... E5
Milan 4,018,108 ... B2
Modena 596,025 ... C2
Naples 2,970,563 ... E4
Novara 507,367 ... B2
Nuoro 274,817 ... B4
Padua 809,667 ... C2
Palermo 1,198,575 ... D5
Parma 400,192 ... C2
Pavia 512,895 ... B2
Perugia 580,988 ... D3
Pesaro e Urbino 333,488 ... D3
Pescara 286,240 ... E3
Piacenza 278,424 ... B2
Pisa 388,800 ... C3
Pistoia 264,995 ... C3
Pordenone 275,888 ... D2
Potenza 406,616 ... E4
Ragusa 274,583 ... E6
Ravenna 358,654 ... D2
Reggio di Calabria 573,093 ... E5
Reggio nell'Emilia 413,396 ... C2
Rieti 142,794 ... D3
Rome 3,695,961 ... F6
Rovigo 253,508 ... C2
Salerno 1,013,779 ... E4
Sassari 433,842 ... B4
Savona 297,675 ... B2
Siena 255,118 ... C3
Sondrio 174,009 ... B1
Syracuse 394,692 ... E6
Taranto 572,314 ... F4
Teramo 269,275 ... D3
Terni 807,552 ... D3
Trapani 420,865 ... D5
Trento 442,845 ... C1
Treviso 720,580 ... D2
Trieste 283,641 ... D2
Turin 2,345,771 ... A2
Udine 529,729 ... D1
Varese 788,057 ... B2
Venice 838,794 ... D2
Vercelli 395,957 ... B2
Verona 775,745 ... C2
Vicenza 726,418 ... C2
Viterbo 268,448 ... C3

CITIES and TOWNS

Acireale 46,711 ... E6
Acqui Terme 20,951 ... B2
Adrano 32,865 ... E6
Agrigento 38,681 ... D6
Alba 25,853 ... B2
Albano Laziale 27,796 ... F7
Alcamo 41,626 ... D6
Alessandria 79,552 ... B2
Alghero 32,519 ... B4
Altamura 50,539 ... F4
Amalfi 4,423 ... E4
Ancona 97,118 ... D3
Andria 84,070 ... F4
Anzio 25,932 ... D4
Aosta 36,649 ... A2
Aprilia 31,604 ... D4
Arezzo 74,477 ... C3
Ascoli Piceno 44,411 ... D3
Assisi 4,683 ... D3
Asti 65,483 ... B2
Augusta 37,162 ... E6
Avellino 50,894 ... E4
Aversa 55,788 ... E4
Avezzano 30,227 ... D3
Avola 30,360 ... E6
Bagheria 39,869 ... D5
Barcellona Pozzo di Gotto 33,404 ... E5
Bari 369,444 ... F4
Barletta 82,290 ... F4
Bassano del Grappa 33,724 ... C2
Belluno 28,468 ... D1
Benevento 51,831 ... E4
Bergamo 121,389 ... B2
Biancavilla 20,047 ... E6
Biella 52,587 ... B2
Bisceglie 46,209 ... F4
Bitonto 46,538 ... F4
Bologna 454,897 ... C2
Bolzano (Bolzen) 103,241 ... C1
Borgomanero 18,701 ... B2
Bra 21,304 ... A2
Brescia 202,539 ... C2
Brindisi 84,887 ... G4
Bronte 17,477 ... E6
Busto Arsizio 79,321 ... B2
Cagliari 219,423 ... B5
Caltagirone 32,860 ... E6
Caltanissetta 57,704 ... D6
Camaiore 24,284 ... C3
Campobasso 41,687 ... E4
Canicatti 31,726 ... D6
Canosa di Puglia 30,555 ... E4
Cantù 35,644 ... B2
Capannori 39,717 ... C3
Carbonia 25,140 ... B5
Carmagnola 19,581 ... A2
Carpi 49,370 ... C2
Carrara 61,709 ... C2
Casale Monferrato 37,157 ... B2
Cascina-Navacchio 32,570 ... C3
Caserta 59,185 ... E4
Cassino 22,406 ... D4
Castel Gandolfo 6,176 ... F7
Castelfranco Veneto 20,196 ... D2
Castellammare di Stabia 70,507 ... E4
Castelvetrano 29,503 ... D6
Castrovillari 18,648 ... F5
Catania 379,754 ... E6
Catanzaro 96,930 ... F5
Cava de'Tirreni 47,007 ... E4
Cecina 22,264 ... C3
Ceglie Messapico 17,915 ... F4
Cerignola 48,105 ... E4
Cesena 72,145 ... D2
Cesenatico 15,634 ... D2
Chiavari 29,171 ... B2
Chieri 28,296 ... A2
Chieti 49,267 ... E3
Chioggia 46,728 ... D2
Chivasso 22,230 ... A2
Ciampino 31,981 ... F7
Città di Castello 21,492 ... C3
Civitavecchia 46,465 ... C3
Comiso 25,469 ... E6
Como 94,167 ... B2
Conegliano 32,406 ... D2
Conversano 18,518 ... F4
Corato 41,078 ... F4
Cosenza 101,144 ... F5
Crema 33,901 ... B2
Cremona 74,341 ... B2
Crotone 51,204 ... F5
Cuneo 47,836 ... A2
Desenzano del Garda 17,296 ... C2
Domodossola 19,825 ... A1
Eboli 24,152 ... E4
Empoli 34,066 ... C3
Enna 26,760 ... E6
Fabriano 21,155 ... D3
Faenza 40,635 ... D2
Fano 42,440 ... D3
Fasano 22,918 ... F4
Favara 30,031 ... D6
Fermo 17,603 ... D3
Ferrara 117,590 ... C2
Fidenza 19,482 ... B2
Fiesole 3,711 ... C3
Firenze (Florence) 442,721 ... C3
Fiumicino 21,167 ... F7
Florence 442,721 ... C3
Floridia 17,790 ... E6
Foggia 150,480 ... E4
Foligno 41,696 ... D3
Fondi 19,580 ... D4
Forlì 91,366 ... D2
Formia 29,147 ... D4
Fossano 17,116 ... A2
Francavilla Fontana 31,371 ... F4
Frascati 18,356 ... F7
Frosinone 42,626 ... D4
Gaeta 23,190 ... D4
Galatina 22,611 ... G4
Gallarate 47,259 ... B2
Gela 74,077 ... E6
Genoa 755,389 ... B2
Genova (Genoa) 787,011 ... B2
Giarre 23,377 ... E6
Gioia del Colle 23,868 ... F4
Giovinazzo 18,832 ... F4
Giulianova 20,189 ... E3
Gorizia 40,679 ... D2
Gravina in Puglia 35,891 ... F4
Grosseto 55,569 ... C3
Grottaglie 27,140 ... F4
Iglesias 26,313 ... B5
Imola 47,365 ... C2
Imperia 39,151 ... B3
Isernia 16,919 ... E4
Ivrea 26,446 ... B2
Jesi 37,075 ... D3
L'Aquila 40,467 ... D3
La Spezia 110,632 ... B2
Lanciano 25,828 ... E3
Latina 64,529 ... D4
Lecce 80,127 ... G4
Lecco 51,160 ... B2
Leghorn (Livorno) 171,811 ... C3
Legnago 23,232 ... C2
Lentini 30,950 ... E6
Leonforte 15,745 ... E6
Licata 40,309 ... D6
Lido di Ostia 85,043 ... F7
Lido di Venezia 20,863 ... D2
Livorno 171,811 ... C3
Lodi 41,338 ... B2
Lucca 84,836 ... C3
Lucera 31,252 ... E4
Lugo 21,593 ... D2
Macerata 34,409 ... D3
Manduria 28,112 ... F4
Manfredonia 52,162 ... F4
Mantua 52,477 ... C2
Marino 30,261 ... F7
Marsala 76,843 ... D6
Martina Franca 34,911 ... F4
Massa 60,810 ... C2
Massafra 26,172 ... F4
Matera 48,226 ... F4
Mazara del Vallo 42,320 ... D6
Merano 31,854 ... C1
Mesagne 29,770 ... G4
Messina 240,121 ... E5
Mestre 197,952 ... D2
Milan 1,601,797 ... B2
Milazzo 29,868 ... E5
Minturno 15,795 ... D4
Mira Taglio 26,031 ... D2
Modena 164,529 ... C2
Modica 34,488 ... E6
Mola di Bari 25,744 ... F4
Molfetta 64,738 ... F4
Moncalieri 59,344 ... A2
Monfalcone 29,960 ... D2
Monopoli 33,928 ... F4
Monreale 18,168 ... D5
Monte Sant'Angelo 16,491 ... F4
Montebelluna 19,708 ... D2
Monterotondo 25,383 ... F6
Montevarchi 17,110 ... C3
Monza 122,541 ... B2
Naples 1,210,365 ... E4
Nardò 27,384 ... F4
Nettuno 27,929 ... D4
Nicastro-Sambiase 49,325 ... F5
Niscemi 25,677 ... E6
Nocera Inferiore 43,879 ... E4
Noto 20,609 ... E6
Novara 94,477 ... B2
Novi Ligure 28,756 ... B2
Nuoro 35,491 ... B4
Olbia 26,702 ... B4
Oristano 23,938 ... B5
Orvieto 7,509 ... D3
Ostia Antica 3,939 ... F7
Ostuni 27,948 ... F4
Otranto 4,334 ... G4
Pachino 20,631 ... E6
Padua 228,333 ... C2
Palermo 698,481 ... D5
Palma di Montechiaro 23,918 ... D6
Palmi 16,394 ... E5
Pantelleria 3,454 ... C6
Parma 160,374 ... C2
Partinico 27,479 ... D6
Paterno 42,916 ... E6
Pavia 82,629 ... B2
Perugia 103,542 ... D3
Pesaro 78,550 ... D3
Pescara 131,016 ... E3
Piacenza 103,584 ... B2
Piazza Armerina 20,119 ... E6
Pietrasanta 20,404 ... B3
Pinerolo 33,176 ... A2
Piombino 35,312 ... C3
Pisa 95,015 ... C3
Pistoia 78,105 ... C3
Poggibonsi 22,644 ... C3
Pomezia 19,453 ... F7
Pordenone 51,270 ... D2
Porto Empedocle 16,126 ... D6
Porto Torres 20,233 ... B4
Portocivitanova 28,155 ... D3
Portoferraio 8,108 ... C3
Portofino 615 ... B2
Potenza 55,175 ... E4
Pozzuoli 61,856 ... D4
Prato 156,894 ... C3
Putignano 22,361 ... F4
Quartu Sant'Elena 40,506 ... B5
Ragusa 60,871 ... E6
Rapallo 26,457 ... B2
Ravenna 87,582 ... D2
Reggio di Calabria 159,416 ... E5
Reggio nell'Emilia 107,484 ... C2
Rho 50,373 ... B2
Rieti 33,614 ... D3
Rimini 111,991 ... D2
Rome (cap.) 2,605,441 ... F6
Rovereto 31,286 ... C2
Rovigo 41,050 ... C2
Ruvo di Puglia 23,510 ... F4
Salerno 150,252 ... E4
Saluzzo 13,078 ... A2
San Benedetto del Tronto 43,189 ... E3
San Cataldo 20,694 ... D6
San Giovanni in Fiore 19,391 ... F5
Sannicandro Garganico 18,652 ... E4
San Remo 59,872 ... A3
San Severo 53,948 ... E4
Santa Maria Capua Vetere 32,129 ... E4
Santeramo in Colle 21,154 ... F4
San Vito dei Normanni 18,366 ... F4
Saronno 36,732 ... B2
Sassari 104,334 ... B4
Sassuolo 37,515 ... C2
Savona 65,040 ... B2
Schio 30,738 ... C2
Sciacca 35,063 ... D6
Scicli 18,419 ... E6
Senigallia 27,474 ... D3
Sesto Fiorentino 43,307 ... C3
Sestri Levante 19,672 ... B2
Siena 54,982 ... C3
Siracusa (Syracuse) 109,038 ... E6
Sondrio 19,955 ... B1
Sora 20,380 ... D4
Sorrento 15,747 ... E4
Spoleto 21,625 ... D3
Stresa 4,290 ... B2
Sulmona 21,504 ... D3
Syracuse 109,038 ... E6
Taranto 231,441 ... F4
Teramo 35,142 ... D3
Termini Imerese 24,252 ... D6

(continued on following page)

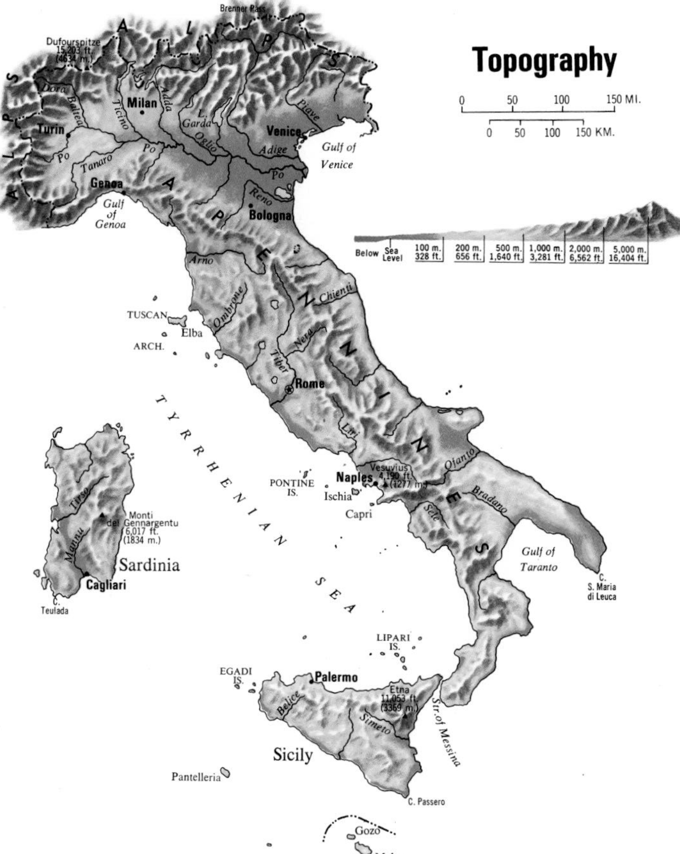

Topography
0 50 100 150 MI.
0 50 100 150 KM.
Below Sea Level
100 m. 328 ft.
200 m. 656 ft.
500 m. 1,640 ft.
1,000 m. 3,281 ft.
2,000 m. 6,562 ft.
5,000 m. 16,404 ft.
Brenner Pass
Dufourspitze
Milan
Turin
Po
Tanaro
Genoa
Gulf of Genoa
Venice
Gulf of Venice
Adige
Piave
Garda
Ticino
Reno
Bologna
Arno
Tiber
Rome
TUSCAN ARCH.
Elba
Naples
Vesuvius
Ischia
Capri
PONTINE IS.
T Y R R H E N I A N S E A
Sardinia
Cagliari
Monti del Gennargentu 6,017 ft. (1834 m.)
C. Teulada
Gulf of Taranto
C. S. Maria di Leuca
LIPARI IS.
EGADI IS.
Palermo
Etna
Str. of Messina
Sicily
C. Passero
Pantelleria
Gozo
Malta
Lampedusa

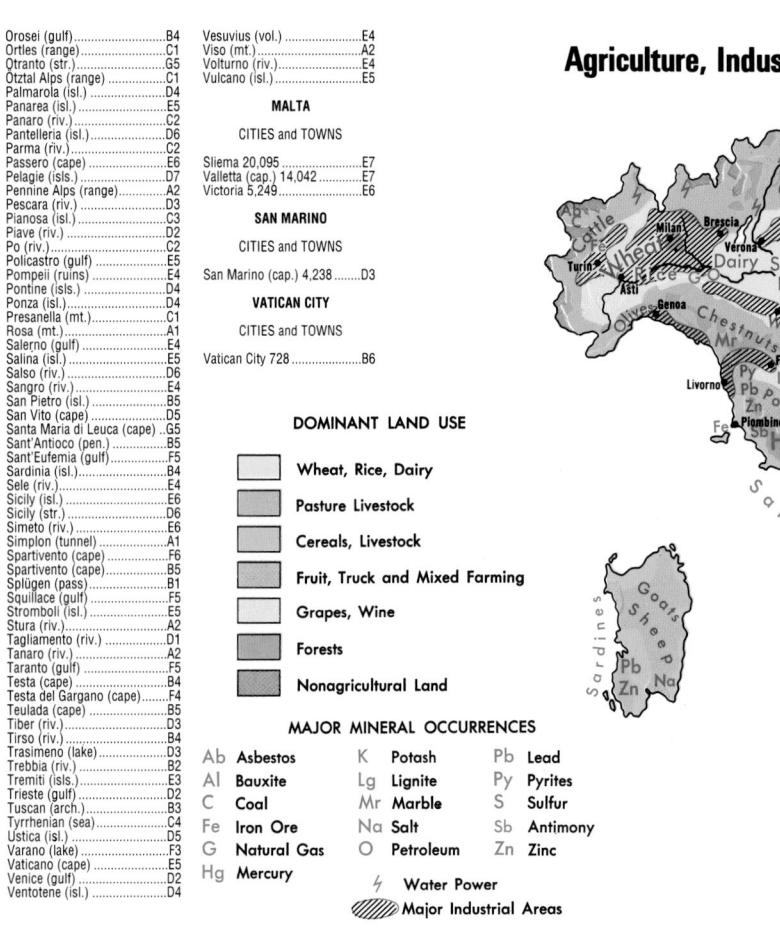

Agriculture, Industry and Resources

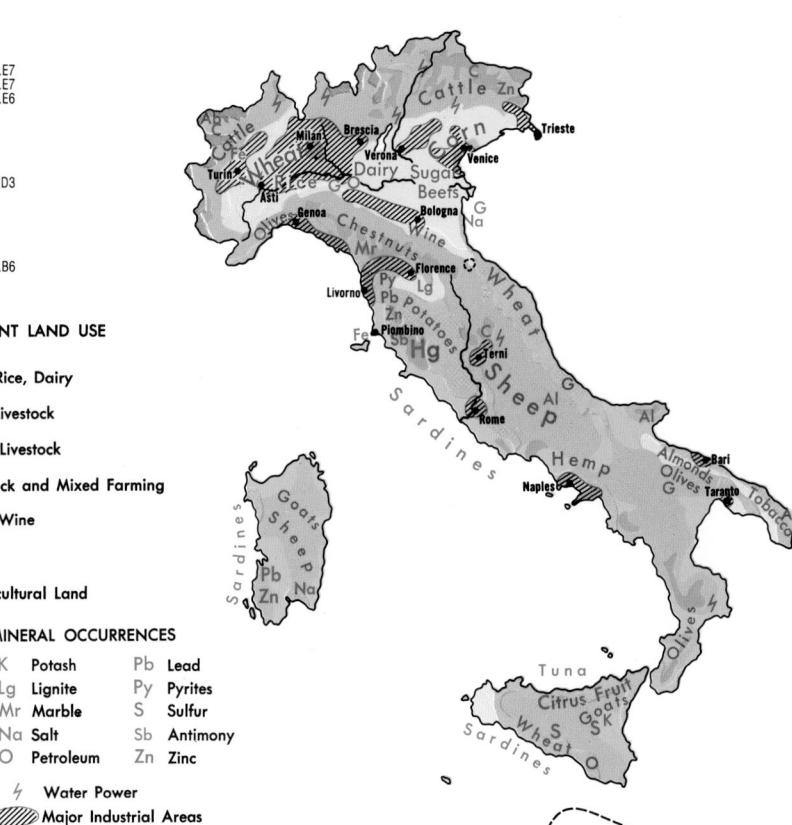

DOMINANT LAND USE

- Wheat, Rice, Dairy
- Pasture Livestock
- Cereals, Livestock
- Fruit, Truck and Mixed Farming
- Grapes, Wine
- Forests
- Nonagricultural Land

MAJOR MINERAL OCCURRENCES

Ab Asbestos	K Potash	Pb Lead
Al Bauxite	Lg Lignite	Py Pyrites
C Coal	Mr Marble	S Sulfur
Fe Iron Ore	Na Salt	Sb Antimony
G Natural Gas	O Petroleum	Zn Zinc
Hg Mercury		

⚡ Water Power

▨ Major Industrial Areas

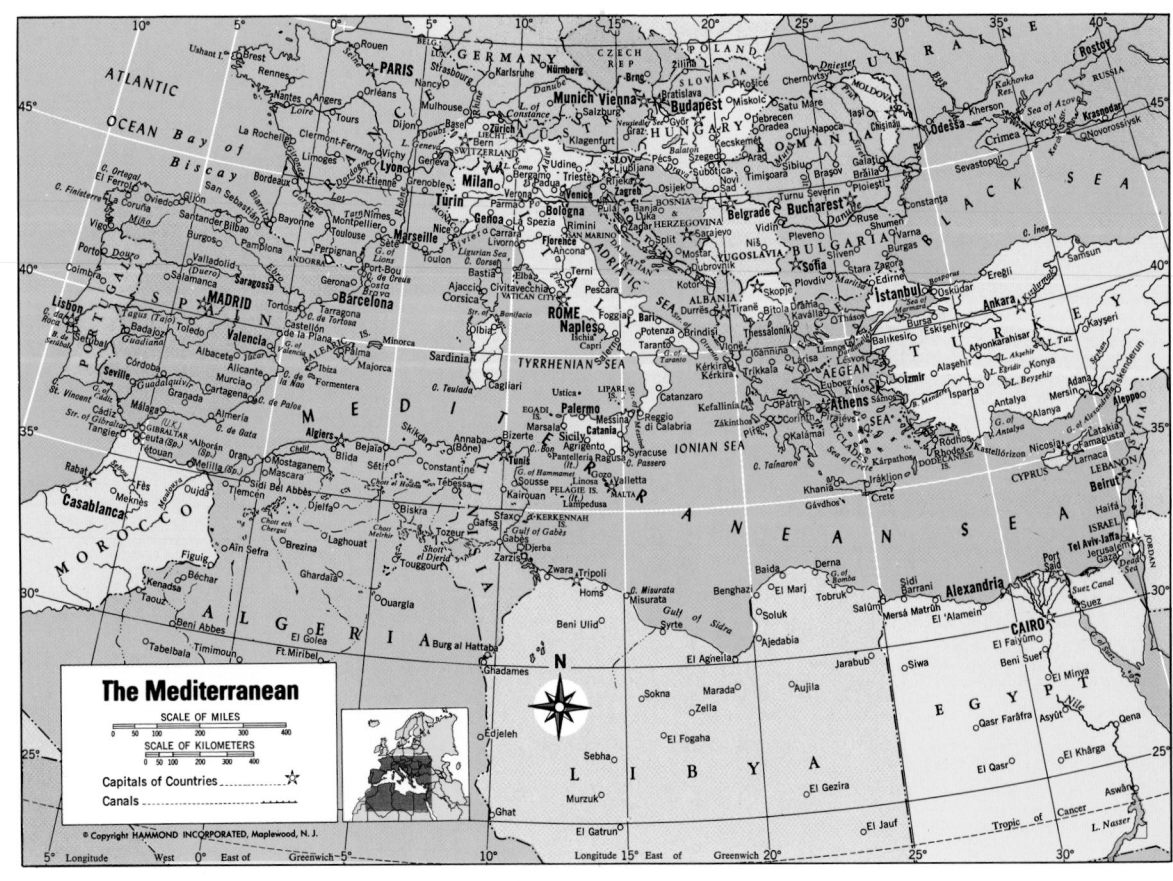

The Mediterranean

SCALE OF MILES
0 50 100 200 300 400

SCALE OF KILOMETERS
0 50 100 200 300 400

Capitals of Countries .... ☆

Canals ....

© Copyright HAMMOND INCORPORATED, Maplewood, N.J.

SWITZERLAND

AREA 15,943 sq. mi. (41,292 sq. km.)
POPULATION 6,647,000
CAPITAL Bern
LARGEST CITY Zürich
HIGHEST POINT Dufourspitze
(Mte. Rosa) 15,203 ft. (4,634 m.)
MONETARY UNIT Swiss franc
MAJOR LANGUAGES German, French,
Italian, Romansch
MAJOR RELIGIONS Protestantism,
Roman Catholicism

LIECHTENSTEIN

AREA 61 sq. mi. (158 sq. km.)
POPULATION 28,000
CAPITAL Vaduz
LARGEST CITY Vaduz
HIGHEST POINT Grauspitze 8,527 ft.
(2,599 m.)
MONETARY UNIT Swiss franc
MAJOR LANGUAGE German
MAJOR RELIGION Roman Catholicism

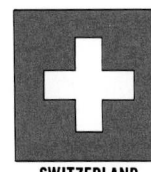

SWITZERLAND

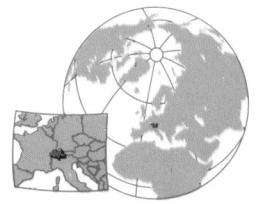

LIECHTENSTEIN

Languages

German
French
Italian
Romansch

Switzerland is a multilingual nation with four
official languages. 70% of the people speak
German, 19% French, 10% Italian and 1% Romansch.

SWITZERLAND

CANTONS

Aargau 453,442 ....F2
Appenzell, Ausser Rhoden
47,611 ....H2
Appenzell, Inner Rhoden
12,844 ....H2
Baselland 219,822 ....E2
Baselstadt 203,915 ....E1
Bern 912,022 ....D2
Fribourg 185,246 ....D3
Geneva (Genève) 349,040....B4
Glarus 36,718 ....H3
Graubünden (Grisons)
164,641 ....H3
Jura 64,986 ....D2
Lucerne (Luzern) 296,159.....F2
Luzern 296,159 ....F2
Neuchâtel 158,368 ....C3
Nidwalden 28,617 ....F3
Obwalden 25,865 ....F3
Sankt Gallen 391,995 ....H2
Schaffhausen 69,413 ....G1
Schwyz 97,354 ....G2
Soleure (Solothurn) 218,102 ..E2
Solothurn 218,102 ....E2
Thurgau 183,795 ....H1
Ticino 265,899 ....G4
Uri 33,883 ....G3
Valais 218,707 ....D4
Vaud 528,747 ....B3

Zug 75,930 ....G2
Zürich 1,122,839 ....G2

CITIES and TOWNS

Aadorf 3,257 ....G2
Aarau 15,788 ....F2
Aarberg 3,212 ....D2
Aarburg 5,354 ....E2
Adelboden 3,276 ....E3
Adliswil 16,418 ....F2
Affoltern am Albis 8,064 ....F2
Aigle 6,233 ....C4
Allschwil 17,952 ....D1
Alpnach 3,556 ....F3
Altdorf 8,230 ....G3
Altstätten 9,260 ....J2
Amriswil 8,790 ....H1
Appenzell 4,781 ....H2
Arbedo-Castione 3,058 ....G4
Arbon 11,333 ....H1
Arosa 2,782 ....J3
Arth 7,795 ....F2
Ascona 4,722 ....G4
Au 5,434 ....J2
Avenches 2,177 ....D3
Baar 15,196 ....F2
Bad Ragaz 3,721 ....H2
Baden 13,870 ....F2
Balerna 3,455 ....G5
Balsthal 5,090 ....E2
Bäretswil 3,145 ....G2
Basel 182,143 ....E1

Basel 364,813 ....E1
Bassecourt 2,942 ....D2
Bauma 3,010 ....G2
Bellinzona 16,743 ....H4
Belp 7,578 ....D3
Bern (cap.) 145,254 ....D3
Bettlach 3,851 ....D2
Bex 4,843 ....D4
Biasca 5,447 ....H4
Biberist 7,519 ....D2
Biel 53,793 ....D2
Binningen 14,195 ....D1
Bischofszell 3,390 ....H1
Bolligen 32,312 ....E3
Boudry 4,488 ....C3
Breitenbach 2,518 ....E2
Bremgarten 4,815 ....F2
Brienz 2,759 ....F3
Brig 9,608 ....F4
Brittnau 2,822 ....E2
Brugg 8,911 ....F2
Bubikon 3,601 ....G2
Buchs 9,066 ....H2
Bülach 12,292 ....G1
Bulle 7,595 ....D3
Buochs 3,742 ....F3
Büren an der Aare 2,761 ....D2
Burgdorf 15,379 ....E2
Bürglen 3,456 ....G3
Bussigny-près-Lausanne
4,909 ....B3
Bütschwil 3,423 ....H2
Carouge 13,100 ....B4
Castagnola 4,430 ....G4
Cham 9,275 ....F2
Château-d'Oex 2,872 ....D4
Châtel-Saint-Denis 3,141 ....C3
Chêne-Bougeries 9,068 ....B4
Chiasso 8,583 ....G5
Chur 32,037 ....J3
Collombey-Muraz 2,982 ....C4
Collonge-Bellerive 4,531 ....B4
Conthey 4,828 ....D4
Courrendlin 2,435 ....D2
Couvet 2,627 ....C3
Davos 10,468 ....J3
Degersheim 3,269 ....H2
Delémont 11,682 ....D2
Derendingen 4,675 ....E2
Dielsdorf 3,767 ....F1
Diepoldsau 3,562 ....J2
Diessenhofen 2,535 ....G1
Dietikon 21,765 ....F2
Disentis-Mustér 2,320 ....G3
Domat-Ems 6,266 ....H3
Dornach 5,442 ....E2
Döttingen 3,264 ....F1
Dübendorf 20,683 ....G2
Düdingen 5,572 ....D3
Dürnten 4,927 ....G2
Ebnat-Kappel 4,950 ....H2
Echallens 2,163 ....C3
Ecublens 7,615 ....B3
Effretikon 14,788 ....G2
Egg 6,074 ....G2
Eggiwil 2,323 ....E3
Egnach 3,397 ....H1
Einsiedeln 9,629 ....G2
Elgg 3,041 ....G2
Emmen 22,392 ....F2
Engelberg 2,963 ....F3
Ennenda 2,512 ....H2
Entlebuch 3,238 ....F3
Erstfeld 4,158 ....G3
Eschenbach 3,661 ....G2
Escholzmatt 3,033 ....E3
Estavayer-le-Lac 3,662 ....C3
Feuerthalen 2,920 ....G1
Flawil 8,575 ....H2
Fleurier 3,573 ....C3
Flims 2,136 ....H3
Flums 4,228 ....H2
Frauenfeld 18,607 ....G1
Freienbach 9,912 ....G2
Fribourg 37,400 ....D3
Frick 3,116 ....E1
Frutigen 5,779 ....E3
Fully 3,926 ....D4
Gais 2,388 ....H2
Gelterkinden 4,954 ....E2

(continued on following page)

Agriculture, Industry and Resources

DOMINANT LAND USE

Cereals, Dairy

Pasture Livestock

General Farming, Livestock

Fruit, Truck, Mixed Farming

Forests

Nonagricultural Land

⚡ Water Power
▨ Major Industrial Areas

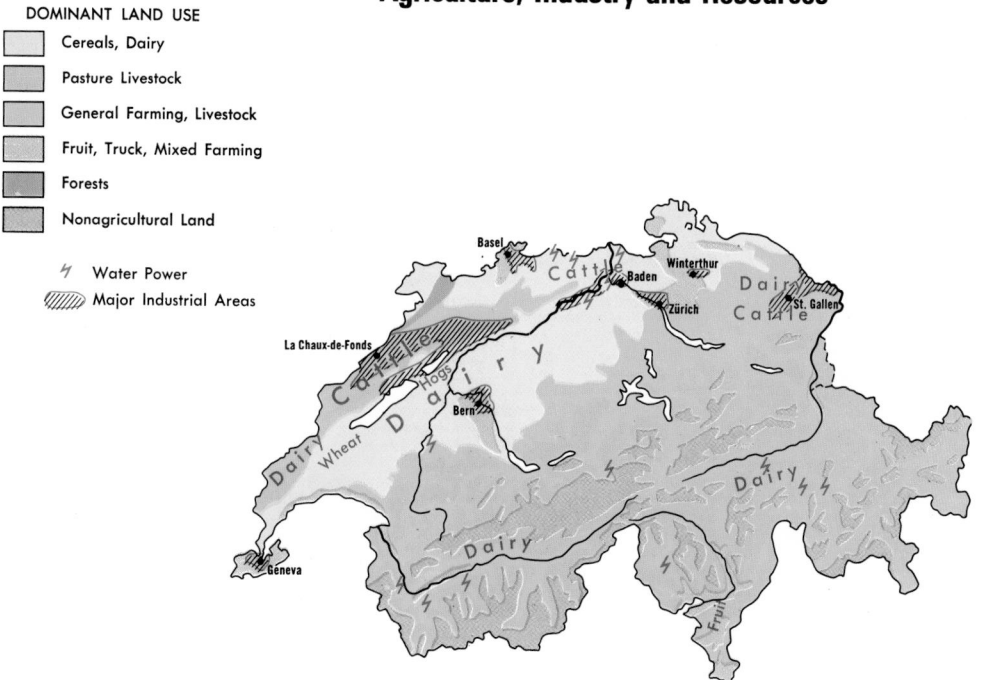

Switzerland and Liechtenstein

(continued)

Topography

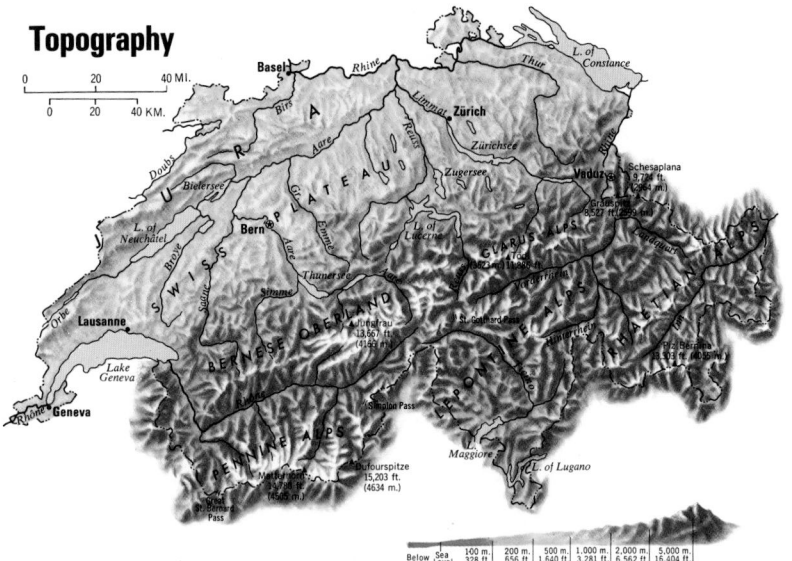

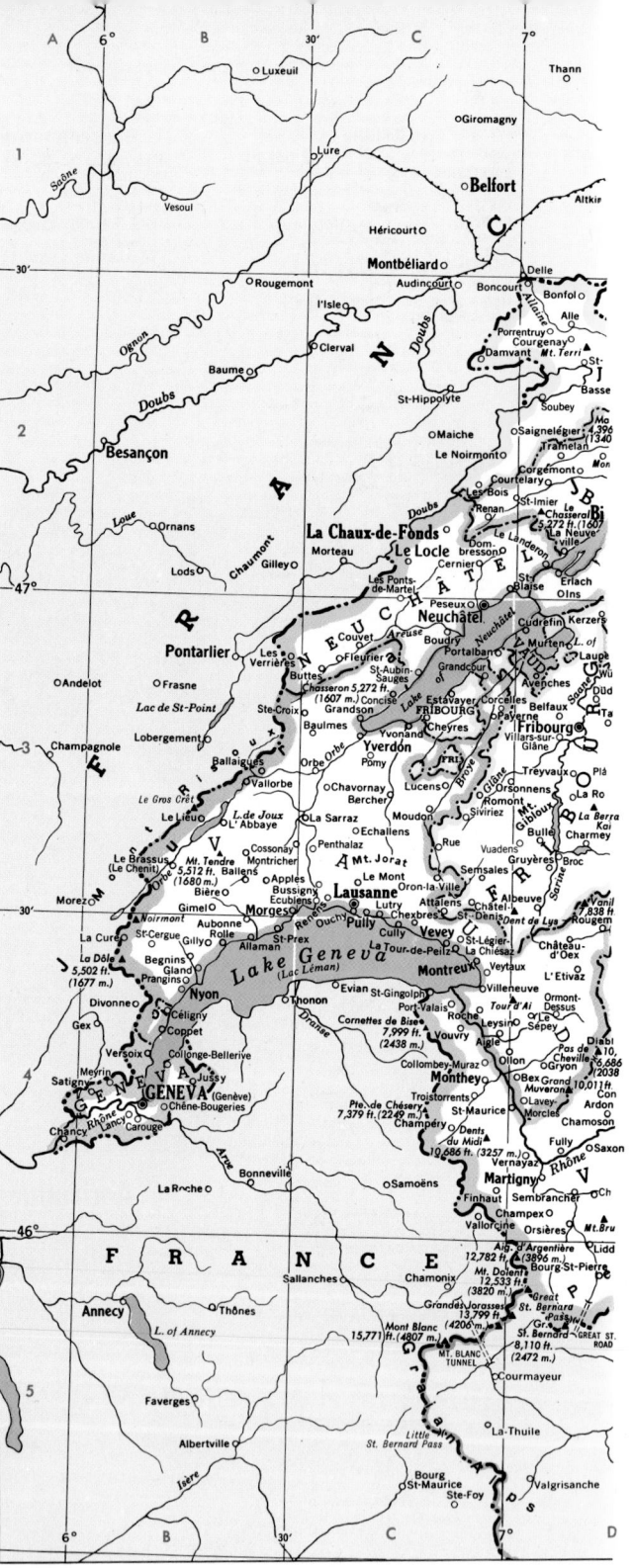

Geneva (Genève) 156,505.......B4
Giswil 2,595.......F3
Giubiasco 6,585.......H4
Gland 4,906.......B4
Glarus 5,969.......H2
Glattfelden 2,753.......F1
Glis 3,389.......E4
Gordola 2,956.......G4
Gossau 14,584.......H2
Grabs 4,844.......H2
Grenchen 16,800.......D2
Grindelwald 3,555.......E3
Grosswangen 2,235.......F2
Gstaad.......D4
Heiden 3,620.......H2
Heimberg 4,107.......E3
Hergiswil 4,254.......F3
Herisau 14,160.......H2
Herzogenbuchsee 5,107.......E2
Hilterfingen 3,600.......E3
Hinwil 7,554.......G2
Hochdorf 6,034.......F2
Horgen 16,577.......G2
Huttwil 4,612.......E2
Igis 5,392.......J3
Ingenbohl 6,232.......G2
Ins 2,608.......D2
Interlaken 4,852.......E3
Jegenstorf 3,541.......D2
Jona 12,156.......G2
Kaltbrunn 2,735.......H2
Kerns 4,200.......F3
Kerzers 2,658.......D3
Kirchberg, Bern 3,966.......E2
Kirchberg, St. Gallen 6,398.....G2
Klingnau 2,433.......F1
Klosters-Serneus 3,487.......J3
Kloten 15,845.......G2
Kölliken 3,080.......F2
Köniz 33,441.......D3
Konolfingen 4,360.......E3
Kreuzlingen 16,101.......H1
Kriens 21,097.......F2
Küsnacht 12,766.......G2
Küssnacht am Rigi 8,091.......F2
Küttigen 4,356.......F2
La Chaux-de-Fonds 37,234.....C2
Lachen 5,352.......G2
Lancy 23,527.......B4
La Neuveville 3,519.......D2
Langenthal 13,408.......E2
Langnau am Albis 6,694.......G2
Langnau in Emmental 8,821...E3
La Tour-de-Peilz 9,411.......C4
Laufen 4,444.......D2
Laupen 2,261.......D3
Lauperswil 2,482.......E3
Lausanne 127,349.......C3
Lauterbrunnen 3,077.......E3
Le Brassus 4,359.......B3
Le Châble 4,541.......D4
Le Chenit (Le Brassus) 4,359 .B3
Le Landeron 3,287.......C2
Le Locle 12,039.......C2
Le Mont-sur-Lausanne 3,664 .C3
Lengnau 4,317.......D2
Lenk 2,089.......D4
Lens 2,412.......D4
Lenzburg 7,585.......F2
Leuk 2,983.......E4
Leukerbad 1,070.......E4
Liestal 12,158.......E2
Liestal-Sissach 40,800.......E2
Littau 14,996.......F2
Locarno 14,103.......G4
Lucerne 63,278.......F2
Lugano 27,815.......G4
Lutry 5,884.......C3
Lützelflüh 3,770.......E3
Luzern (Lucerne) 63,278.......F2
Lyss 8,723.......D2
Malters 4,900.......F2
Männedorf 7,833.......G2
Martigny 11,309.......C4
Meilen 10,430.......G2
Meiringen 4,072.......F3
Mellingen 3,285.......F2
Mels 6,235.......H2
Mendrisio 6,590.......G5
Menzingen 3,564.......G2
Menznau 2,248.......E2
Meyrin 18,808.......B4
Minusio 5,602.......G4
Möhlin 6,360.......E1
Mollis 2,621.......H2
Monthey 11,285.......C4
Montreux 19,685.......C4
Morges 13,057.......B3
Moudon 3,805.......C3
Moutier 7,959.......D2
Mümliswil-Ramiswil 2,386.......E2
Münchenbuchsee 8,395.......E2
Münsingen 9,340.......E3
Muotathal 2,896.......G3
Muri 5,399.......F2
Muri bei Bern 12,285.......E3
Murten 4,558.......D3
Muttenz 16,911.......E1
Näfels 3,766.......H2
Naters 6,662.......E4
Nendaz 4,372.......D4
Netstal 2,642.......H2
Neuchâtel 34,428.......C3
Neuenegg 3,727.......D3
Neuhausen am Rheinfall 10,662.......G1
Niederbipp 3,165.......E2
Niederurnen 3,438.......G2
Nyon 12,842.......B4
Oberägeri 3,563.......G2
Oberburg 2,869.......E2
Oberdiessbach 2,319.......E3
Oberriet 6,222.......J2
Obersiggenthal 7,442.......F1
Oberuzwil 4,616.......H2
Oensingen 3,543.......E2
Oftringen 9,006.......E2
Ollon 4,429.......D4
Olten 18,991.......E2
Opfikon 11,444.......G2
Orbe 3,985.......C3
Orsières 2,357.......D4
Paradiso 3,261.......G5
Payerne 6,713.......C3
Peseux 5,212.......C3
Pfäffikon 8,306.......G2
Pfaffnau 2,453.......E2
Pieterlen 3,127.......D2
Porrentruy 7,039.......C2
Poschiavo 3,294.......J4
Prangins 2,028.......B4
Pratteln 15,751.......E1
Pully 14,988.......C4
Rafz 2,325.......G1
Rapperswil 7,826.......G2
Regensdorf 12,300.......F2
Reichenbach im Kandertal 2,948.......E3
Reiden 3,363.......F2
Reinach in Aargau 5,696.......F2
Reinach in Baselland 17,813...E2
Renens 16,977.......C3
Rheineck 3,037.......J2
Rheinfelden 9,456.......E1
Richterswil 8,672.......G2
Riehen 20,611.......E1
Riggisberg 2,196.......D3
Roggwil 3,333.......E2
Rolle 3,409.......B4
Romanshorn 7,893.......H1
Romont 3,495.......C3
Rorschach 9,878.......H2
Rothrist 6,015.......E2
Rüti, Zürich 9,331.......G2
Rumlang 5,055.......G2
Ruswil 4,870.......F2
Saanen 5,522.......D4
Sachseln 3,406.......F3
Saint-Blaise 2,788.......D2
Sainte-Croix 4,543.......B3
Saint-Imier 5,430.......D2
Saint-Légier-La Chiésaz 2,787 C4
Saint-Maurice 3,458.......C4
Saint Moritz 5,900.......J3
Saint Niklaus 2,036.......E4
Saint-Prex 2,937.......B4
Samedan 2,553.......J3
Sankt Gallen 75,847.......H2
Sankt Margrethen 4,935.......J2
Sargans 4,267.......H2
Sarnen 7,372.......F3
Savièse 4,097.......D4
Saxon 2,394.......D4
Schänis 2,426.......H2
Schaffhausen 34,250.......G1
Schattdorf 4,516.......G3
Schiers 2,253.......J3
Schlieren 12,891.......F2
Schönenwerd 4,746.......E2
Schübelbach 4,720.......G2
Schüpfheim 3,537.......F3
Schwanden 2,519.......H2
Schwyz 12,100.......G2
Sempach 2,237.......F2
Seon 3,826.......F2
Seuzach 4,659.......G1
Sevelen 2,839.......H2
Sierre 13,050.......D4
Signau 2,606.......E3
Sigriswil 3,536.......E3
Silenen 2,115.......G3
Simplon 328.......F4
Sins 2,625.......F2
Sion 22,877.......D4
Sirnach 4,170.......G2
Sissach 4,564.......E2
Solothurn (Soleure) 15,778....E2
Spiez 9,800.......E3
Stäfa 10,558.......G2
Stans 5,681.......F3
Steckborn 3,232.......G1
Steffisburg 12,539.......E3
Stein am Rhein 2,507.......G1
Suhr 7,366.......F2
Sumiswald 5,070.......E2
Sursee 7,645.......F2
Tafers 2,263.......D3
Tavannes 3,336.......D2
Teufen 5,027.......H2
Thal 4,725.......J2
Thalwil 15,412.......G2
Thayngen 3,751.......G1
Therwil 7,311.......E1
Thun 36,891.......E3
Thunstetten 2,567.......E2
Thusis 2,525.......H3
Tramelan 4,733.......D2
Turbenthal 2,975.......G2
Uetendorf 4,538.......E3
Unterägeri 5,371.......G2
Unterkulm 2,558.......F2
Unterseen 4,568.......E3
Uster 23,702.......G2
Utzenstorf 3,141.......E2
Uznach 4,269.......H2
Uzwil 9,614.......H2
Vallorbe 3,375.......B3
Vechigen 4,036.......E3
Versoix 7,483.......B4
Vevey 16,139.......C4
Vevey-Montreux 60,558.......C4
Villars-sur-Glâne 5,788.......D3
Villeneuve 3,573.......C4
Visp 6,383.......E4
Wädenswil 18,485.......G2
Wängi 2,909.......G1
Wahlern 5,104.......D3
Wald 7,447.......G2
Waldkirch 2,622.......H2
Walenstadt 3,605.......H2
Wallisellen 10,887.......G2
Wartau 3,692.......H2
Wattwil 7,874.......H2
Weinfelden 8,793.......H1
Wettingen 18,377.......F2
Wetzikon 15,859.......G2
Wil 16,245.......H2
Willisau 2,639.......F2
Windisch 7,598.......F1
Winterthur 86,758.......G1
Wohlen 12,024.......F2
Wohlen 15,746.......F2
Wohlen bei Bern 7,666.......D3
Wolhusen 3,670.......F2
Worb 11,080.......E3
Wünnewil 3,774.......D3
Yverdon 20,802.......C3
Zell 4,138.......G2
Zermatt 3,548.......E4
Zofingen 8,643.......E2
Zollikofen 8,717.......D3
Zollikon 12,134.......G2
Zug 21,609.......G2
Zürich 369,522.......F2
Zurzach 3,068.......F1
Zweisimmen 2,852.......D3

OTHER FEATURES

Aa (riv.).......F3
Aare (riv.).......E3
Ägerisee (lake).......G2
Aiguille d'Argentière (mt.).......C5
Albristhorn (mt.).......D4
Aletschhorn (mt.).......F4
Allaine (riv.).......D2
Areuse (riv.).......C3
Aroser Rothorn (mt.).......J3
Ault (peak).......H3
Baldeggersee (lake).......F2
Balmhorn (mt.).......E4
Bärenhorn (mt.).......H3
Basodino (peak).......G4
Bernese Oberland (reg.).......E3
Bernina (mts.).......J4
Bernina (pass).......K4
Bernina (peak).......J4
Bernina (riv.).......J4
Beverin (peak).......H3
Bielersee (lake).......D2
Bietschhorn (mt.).......E4
Birs (riv.).......D2
Blas (peak).......G3
Blinnenhorn (mt.).......F4
Blümlisalp (mt.).......E3
Bodensee (Constance) (lake)..H1
Borgne (riv.).......D4
Breithor (mt.).......E5
Breithorn (mt.).......E4
Brienzer Rothorn (mt.).......F3
Brienzersee (lake).......F3
Broye (riv.).......C3
Brule (mt.).......D4
Buchegg (mts.).......D2
Buin (peak).......K3
Bürkelkopf (mt.).......K3
Bütschelegg (mt.).......D3
Calancasca (riv.).......H4
Campo Tencia (peak).......G4
Ceneri (mt.).......G4
Chasseron (mt.).......C3
Chésery, Pointe de (mt.).......C4
Cheville (pass).......D4
Churfirsten (mt.).......H2
Clariden (mt.).......G3
Collon (mt.).......D5
Constance (Bodensee) (lake)..H1
Cornettes de Bise (mts.).......C4
Dammastock (mt.).......F3
Davos (valley).......J3
Dent Blanche (mt.).......E4
Dent de Lys (mt.).......D4
Dent de Ruth (mt.).......D3
Dent d'Hérens (mt.).......E5
Dents du Midi (mt.).......C4
Diablerets (mt.).......D4

Doldenhorn (mt.).......E4
Dolent (mt.).......C5
Dom (mt.).......E4
Doubs (riv.).......C2
Drance (riv.).......D4
Dufourspitze (mt.).......E5
Emmental (riv.).......E3
Engadine (valley).......K3
Err (peak).......J3
Finsteraarhorn (mt.).......F3
Finstermünz (pass).......K3
Fletschhorn (mt.).......F4
Fluchthorn (mt.).......K3
Flüela (pass).......J3
Fluhberg (mt.).......G2
Fort (mt.).......D4
Frienisberg (mt.).......D2
Furka (pass).......F3
Gelgia (riv.).......J3
Generoso (mt.).......H5
Geneva (lake).......C4
Giacomo (pass).......G4
Gibloux (mt.).......D3
Glâne (riv.).......C3
Glärnisch (mt.).......H2
Glarus Alps (mts.).......H3
Glatt (riv.).......G2
Goms (valley).......F4
Grand Combin (mt.).......D5
Grand Muveran (mt.).......D4
Grande Dixence (dam).......D4
Grauehörner (mts.).......H3
Great Saint Bernard (mt.).......D5
Great Saint Bernard (pass).....D5
Great Saint Bernard (tunnel)...D5
Greifensee (lake).......G2
Greina (pass).......G3
Gridone (mt.).......G4
Grimsel (pass).......F3
Gross Emme (riv.).......E2
Gross Litzner (mt.).......K3
Hallwilersee (lake).......F2
Hausstock (mt.).......H3
Helsenhorn (mt.).......F4
Hinterrhein (riv.).......H3
Hochwang (mt.).......J3
Hohenstollen (mt.).......F3
Honegg (mt.).......E3
Hörnli (mt.).......G2
Ilfis (riv.).......E3
Inn (riv.).......K3
Joch (pass).......F3
Jorat (mt.).......C3
Joux (lake).......B3
Jungfrau (mt.).......E3
Jura (mts.).......B3
Kaiseregg (mt.).......D3
Kesch (peak).......J3
Kisten (pass).......H3
Klausen (pass).......G3
Kleine Emme (riv.).......F3
La Berra (mt.).......D3
La Dôle (mt.).......B4
Landquart (riv.).......J3
Le Chasseral (mt.).......D2
Le Gros Crêt (mt.).......B3

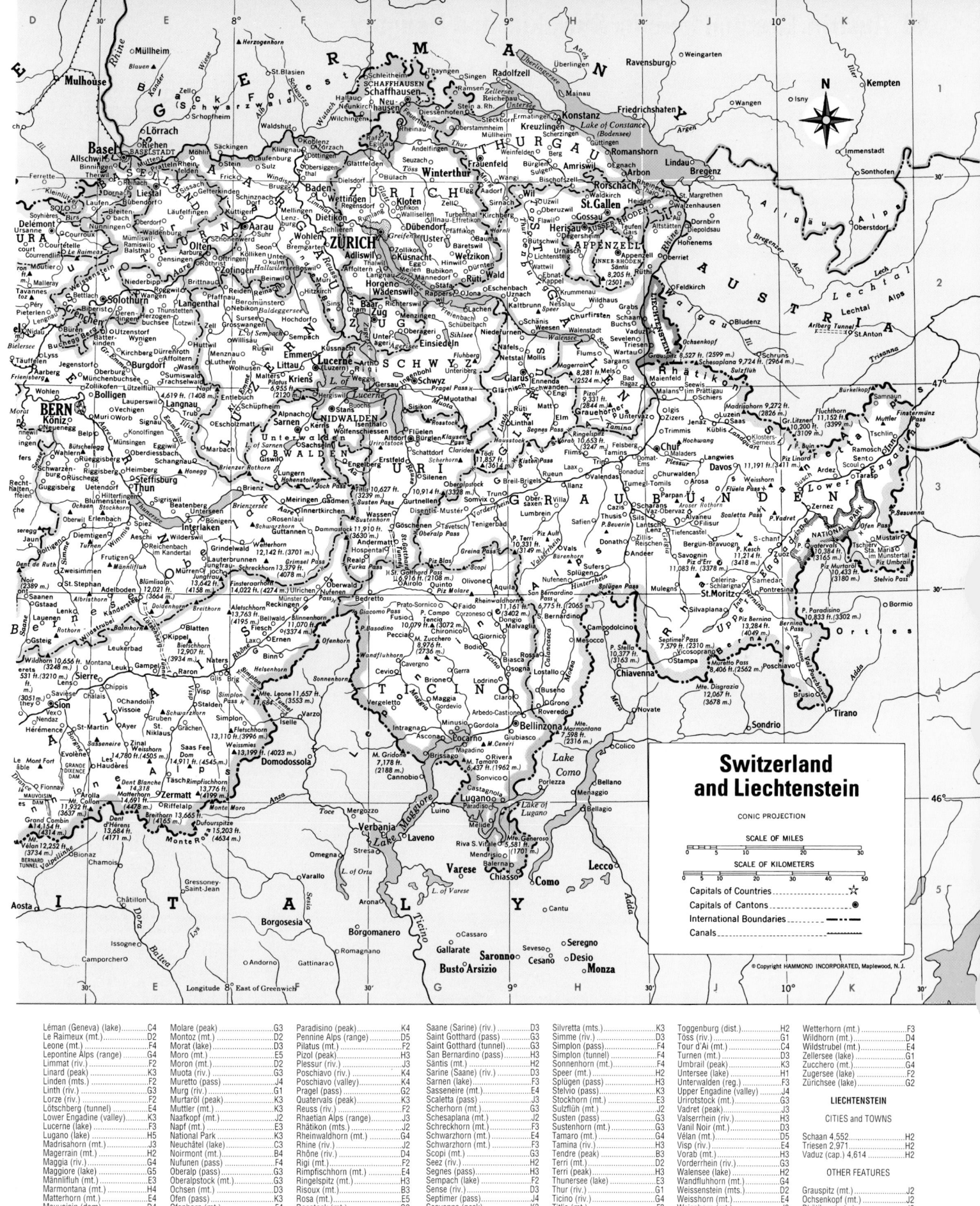

Switzerland and Liechtenstein

CONIC PROJECTION

SCALE OF MILES

0 5 10 20 30

SCALE OF KILOMETERS

0 5 10 20 30 40 50

Capitals of Countries........................☆
Capitals of Cantons..........................◉
International Boundaries.........─ ∙∙ ─ ∙∙ ─
Canals...

© Copyright HAMMOND INCORPORATED, Maplewood, N.J.

40 Austria, Czech Republic, Slovakia and Hungary

Czech Republic

Czech Republic

Czech Republic

Záparočeský

Region	Value	Grid

Česká Kamenice 7,272 ....C1
Česká Lípa 24,924 ....C1
Česká Třebová 17,136 ....D2
Čáslav 9,950 ....C2

Topography

Topography

0   50   100 MI.
0   50   100 KM.

5,000 m. / 2,000 m. / 1,000 m. / 500 m. / 200 m. / 100 m. / Sea Level / Below
16,404 ft. / 6,562 ft. / 3,281 ft. / 1,640 ft. / 656 ft. / 328 ft.

© Copyri

AUSTRIA
AREA 32,375 sq. mi. (83,851 sq. km.)
POPULATION 7,666,000
CAPITAL Vienna
LARGEST CITY Vienna
HIGHEST POINT Grossglockner
  12,457 ft. (3,797 m.)
MONETARY UNIT schilling
MAJOR LANGUAGE German
MAJOR RELIGION Roman Catholicism

CZECH REPUBLIC
AREA 30,449 sq. mi. (78,863 sq. km.)
POPULATION 10,291,927
CAPITAL Prague
LARGEST CITY Prague
HIGHEST POINT Sněžka 5,256 ft.
  (1,602 m.)
MONETARY UNIT Czech koruna
MAJOR LANGUAGE Czech
MAJOR RELIGIONS Roman Catholicism,
  Protestantism

HUNGARY
AREA 35,919 sq. mi. (93,030 sq. km.)
POPULATION 10,558,000
CAPITAL Budapest
LARGEST CITY Budapest
HIGHEST POINT Kékes 3,330 ft.
  (1,015 m.)
MONETARY UNIT forint
MAJOR LANGUAGE Hungarian
MAJOR RELIGIONS Roman
  Catholicism, Protestantism

SLOVAKIA
AREA 18,924 sq. mi. (49,014 sq. km.)
POPULATION 4,991,168
CAPITAL Bratislava
LARGEST CITY Bratislava
HIGHEST POINT Gerlachovky Štít 8,707 ft.
  (2,654 m.)
MONETARY UNIT Slovak koruna
MAJOR LANGUAGE Slovak
MAJOR RELIGIONS Roman Catholicism,
  Protestantism

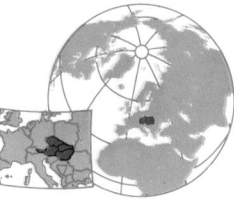

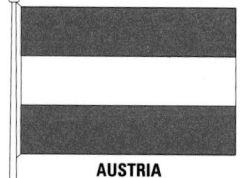

AUSTRIA

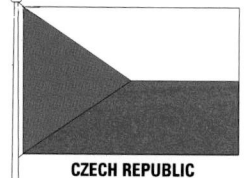

CZECH REPUBLIC

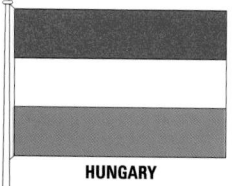

HUNGARY

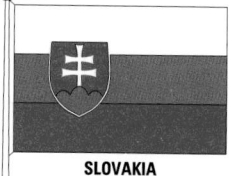

SLOVAKIA

Austria, Czech Republic Slovakia and Hungary

CONIC PROJECTION

SCALE OF MILES
0 10 20   40   60   80

SCALE OF KILOMETERS
0 10 20   40   60   80

Capitals of Countries..........☆   International Boundaries..........
Administrative Centers..........△   Internal Boundaries..........
                                     Canals..........

Fulnek 8,214 D2
Havířov 89,920 E2
Havlíčkuv Brod 24,550 C2
Hlinsko 10,635 C2
Hlučín 22,581 E2
Hodonín 25,485 D2
Holešov 13,323 D2
Hořice v Podkrkonoší 9,251 C1
Hradec Králové 95,588 C1
Hranice 18,099 D2
Hronov 9,609 D1
Humpolec 10,042 C2
Ivančice 9,746 D2
Jablonec nad Nisou 42,179 C1
Jablunkov 15,962 E2
Jaroměř 11,562 C1
Jeseník 14,314 D1
Jičín 16,440 C1
Jihlava 51,144 C2
Jindřichuv Hradec 20,096 C2
Jiřkov 11,980 B1
Kadaň 18,420 B1
Karlovy Vary 60,950 B1
Karviná 78,334 E2
Kladno 71,141 B1
Klatovy 21,782 B2
Kojetín 8,881 D2
Kolín 30,921 C1
Kralupy nad Vltavou 17,528 C1
Kraslice 7,371 B1
Krnov 25,678 D1
Kroměříž 25,887 D2
Krupka 9,336 B1
Kutná Hora 20,927 C2
Kyjov 12,632 D2
Lanškroun 10,620 D2
Liberec 97,474 C1
Lidice C1
Lipník nad Bečvou 9,961 D2
Litoměřice 23,835 C1
Litomyšl 10,079 D2

Prague (Praha) (cap.) 1,182,186 C1
Přelouč 8,561 C1
Přerov 50,265 D2
Příbor 12,711 E2
Příbram 37,854 C2
Prostějov 49,599 D2
Rakovník 16,233 B1
Říčany u Prahy 10,703 C2
Rokycany 15,041 B2
Roudnice nad Labem 13,956 C1
Rožnov pod Radhoštěm 15,468 E2
Rumburk 10,255 C1
Rychnov nad Kněžnou 8,955 D1
Rýmařov 9,927 D2
Sedlčany 7,453 C2
Semily 8,464 C1
Slaný 14,705 C1
Slavkov 6,316 D2
Soběslav 8,406 C2
Sokolov 28,523 B1
Staré Město 6,293 D2
Šternberk 16,342 D2
Strakonice 22,611 B2
Stříbro 8,169 B2
Studénka 12,497 E2
Šumperk 31,873 D2
Sušice 11,400 B2
Svitavy 19,075 D2
Tábor 31,867 C2
Tachov 12,798 B2
Teplice 53,964 B1
Tišnov 12,179 D2
Třebíč 30,246 C2
Třeboň 8,878 C2
Třinec 44,739 E2
Trutnov 27,648 C1
Turnov 13,906 C1
Ústí nad Labem 87,909 C1

Jihlava (riv.) D2
Jizera (riv.) C1
Krušné Hory (Erzgebirge) (mts.) B1
Labe (riv.) C1
Lipno (res.) C2
Lužnice (riv.) C2
Moldau (Vltava) (riv.) C2
Morava (riv.) D2
Mže (riv.) B2
Oder (Odra) (riv.) D2
Ohře (riv.) B1
Ondava (riv.) F2
Orlice (riv.) D1
Orlická (res.) C2
Otava (riv.) B2
Radbuza (riv.) B2
Sázava (riv.) C2
Sudeten (mts.) C1
Svitava (riv.) D2
Svratka (riv.) D2
Úhlava (riv.) B2
Vltava (riv.) C2

HUNGARY

COUNTIES

Bács-Kiskun 553,000 E3
Baranya 434,000 E4
Békés 416,000 F3
Borsod-Abaúj-Zemplén 779,000 F2
Budapest (city) 2,104,000 E3
Csongrád 457,000 F3
Fejér 426,000 E3
Győr-Sopron 426,000 D3
Hajdú-Bihar 549,000 F3
Heves 338,000 F3
Komárom 320,000 E3
Nógrád 229,000 E3
Pest 988,000 E3

Csorna 13,000 D3
Dabas 13,075 E3
Debrecen 217,000 F3
Derecske 9,579 F3
Dévaványa 11,208 F3
Dombóvár 21,000 E3
Dorog 13,000 E3
Dunaföldvár 10,318 E3
Dunaharaszti 15,788 E3
Dunakeszi 29,000 E3
Dunaújváros 62,000 E3
Edelény 12,000 F2
Eger 67,000 F3
Egyek 7,956 F3
Endrőd 8,136 F3
Enying 7,518 E3
Érd 44,904 E3
Esztergom 30,476 E3
Fegyvernek 8,421 F3
Fehérgyarmat 9,000 G3
Füzesgyarmat 7,097 F3
Gödöllő 30,000 E3
Gyöngyös 36,000 E3
Gyoma 10,392 F3
Győr 131,000 D3
Gyula 36,000 F3
Hadházteglás 13,626 F3
Hajdúböszormény 31,000 F3
Hajdúdorog 10,118 F3
Hajdúnánás 18,000 F3
Hajdúsámson 7,492 F3
Hajdúszoboszló 24,000 F3
Hatvan 25,000 E3
Heves 11,000 F3
Hódmezővásárhely 54,000 F3
Izsák 7,686 E3
Jánoshalma 12,534 E3
Jászapáti 10,424 F3
Jászárokszállás 10,139 E3
Jászberény 30,000 E3
Jászladány 7,823 F3
Kalocsa 20,000 E3

Mezőtúr 21,000 F3
Mindszent 8,730 F3
Miskolc 210,000 F2
Mohács 21,000 E4
Monor 16,838 E3
Mór 12,066 E3
Mosonmagyaróvár 30,000 D3
Nádudvar 9,447 F3
Nagyatád 15,000 D3
Nagyecsed 8,225 G3
Nagykálló 11,282 F3
Nagykanizsa 55,000 D3
Nagykáta 11,922 E3
Nagykőrös 27,000 E3
Nagyszénás 7,124 F3
Nyíradony 7,146 F3
Nyírbátor 14,000 G3
Nyíregyháza 119,000 F3
Orosháza 36,000 F3
Oroszlány 22,000 E3
Ózd 45,000 F2
Paks 26,000 E3
Pápa 35,000 D3
Pásztó 12,000 E3
Pécs 182,000 E3
Pilis 9,055 E3
Pilisvörösvár 10,217 E3
Polgár 9,429 F3
Püspökladány 16,000 F3
Putnok 7,103 F2
Ráckeve 7,534 E3
Rákospalota 60,983 E3
Sajószentpéter 13,992 F2
Salgótarján 49,000 E2
Sárbogárd 13,000 E3
Sarkad 11,937 F3
Sárospatak 15,000 F2
Sárvár 16,000 D3
Sátoraljaújhely 20,000 F2
Siklós 11,000 E4
Siófok 24,000 E3
Soltvadkert 7,934 E3

OTHER FEATURES

Bakony (mts.) D3
Balaton (lake) D3
Berettyó (riv.) F3
Börzsöny (mts.) E3
Bükk (mts.) F2
Csepelsziget (isl.) E3
Danube (riv.) E3
Dráva (riv.) D3
Duna (Danube) (riv.) E3
Fertő tó (Neusiedler See) (lake) D3
Great Alföld (plain) F3
Hernád (riv.) F2
Ipoly (riv.) E2
Kapos (riv.) D3
Kékes (mt.) E3
Korishegy (mt.) D3
Körös (riv.) F3
Little Alföld (plain) D3
Maros (riv.) F3
Mátra (mts.) E3
Mecsek (mts.) D3
Mura (riv.) D3
Rába (riv.) D3
Sajó (riv.) F2
Sárviz csatorna (canal) E3
Sebes Körös (riv.) F3
Sió csatorna (canal) E3
Szentendreisziget (isl.) E3
Tarna (riv.) F3
Tisza (riv.) F3
Zagyva (riv.) E3
Zala (riv.) D3

SLOVAKIA

REGIONS

Bratislava (city) 380,259 D2
Středoslovenský

Liptovský Mikuláš 24,520 E2
Lučenec 26,399 E2
Malacky 15,218 D2
Martin 56,208 E2
Michalovce 29,765 F2
Modra 7,679 D2
Myjava 11,668 D2
Nitra 76,663 E2
Nová Baňa 8,321 E2
Nové Město nad Váhom 18,170 D2
Nové Zámky 34,147 D3
Partizánske 23,266 E2
Pezinok 17,116 D2
Piešťany 30,487 D2
Poprad 38,077 F2
Považská Bystrica 30,444 E2
Prešov 71,500 F2
Prievidza 40,813 E2
Púchov 17,554 E2
Revúca 11,881 F2
Rimavská Sobota 19,699 F2
Rožňava 18,039 F2
Ružomberok 26,396 E2
Sabinov 7,008 F2
Šafárikovo 7,021 F2
Šahy 8,034 E2
Šal'a 19,167 D2
Samorín 9,677 D2
Senec 10,772 D2
Senica 15,515 D2
Sereď 16,071 D2
Skalica 13,833 D2
Snina 13,347 G2
Spišská Nová Ves 31,917 F2
Stropkov 7,405 F2
Štúrovo 12,807 E3
Šurany 11,320 E2
Svidník 7,538 F2
Topol'čany 31,340 E2
Trebišov 14,961 F2
Trenčín 47,887 E2

Agriculture, Industry and Resources

DOMINANT LAND USE

Cereals (chiefly wheat, corn)
Other Cereals, Livestock, Dairy
General Farming, Livestock
General Farming, Truck Farming
Pasture Livestock
Grapes, Wine
Forests
Nonagricultural Land

MAJOR MINERAL OCCURRENCES

Ag Silver
Al Bauxite
C Coal
Cu Copper
Fe Iron Ore
G Natural Gas
Gr Graphite
Hg Mercury
Lg Lignite
Mg Magnesium
Mn Manganese
Na Salt
O Petroleum
Pb Lead
Sb Antimony
U Uranium
W Tungsten
Zn Zinc

Water Power
Major Industrial Areas

Litovel 12,454 D2
Litvínov 22,624 B1
Louny 20,436 B1
Lovosice 11,456 C1
Lysá nad Labem 9,113 C1
Mariánské Lázně 17,932 B2
Mělník 18,941 C1
Mikulov 8,472 D2
Milevsko 8,852 C2
Mimoň 7,437 C1
Mladá Boleslav 45,896 C1
Mnichovo Hradiště 7,340 C1
Mohelnice 9,405 D2
Moravská Třebová 11,543 D2
Moravské Budějovice 8,943 C2
Most 60,119 B1
Náchod 19,892 D1
Nejdek 9,768 B1
Nové Město na Moravě 11,330 D2
Nový Bohumín 16,700 E2
Nový Bor 10,493 C1
Nový Bydžov 9,317 C1
Nový Jičín 31,506 D2
Nymburk 14,033 C1
Odry 10,032 D2
Olomouc 102,112 D2
Opava 59,384 D2
Orlová 31,190 E2
Ostrava 322,073 E2
Ostrov 19,618 B1
Pardubice 91,855 C1
Písek 28,104 C2
Plzeň 170,701 B2
Poděbrady 13,782 C1
Pohořelice 5,125 D2
Polička 8,972 D2
Prachatice 10,354 B2

Ustí nad Orlicí 15,945 D2
Uherské Hradiště 36,756 D2
Uherský Brod 17,459 D2
Uničov 12,507 D2
Valašské Meziříčí 26,531 D2
Varnsdorf 16,356 C1
Velké Meziříčí 14,073 D2
Veselí nad Moravou 12,464 D2
Vimperk 7,257 B2
Vítkov 7,543 D2
Vlašim 13,284 C2
Vodňany 6,989 C2
Vrbno pod Pradědem 6,912 D1
Vrchlabí 12,419 C1
Vsetín 29,927 D2
Vyškov 18,330 D2
Vysoké Mýto 10,887 D2
Zábřeh 15,184 D2
Žatec 19,529 B1
Žďár nad Sázavou 25,015 C2
Zlín 83,983 D2
Znojmo 39,271 D2

OTHER FEATURES

Bečva (riv.) E2
Berounka (riv.) C2
Bohemian (for.) B2
Bohemian-Moravian Heights (hills) C2
Chrudimka (riv.) C2
Cidlina (riv.) C1
Danube (riv.) C2
Dyje (riv.) D2
Erzgebirge (mts.) B1
Jablunka (pass) E2
Jeseníky (mts.) D1

Somogy 349,000 D3
Szabolcs-Szatmár 570,000 G3
Szolnok 428,000 F3
Tolna 263,000 E3
Vas 277,000 D3
Veszprém 387,000 D3
Zala 311,000 D3

CITIES and TOWNS

Abádszalók 6,386 F3
Abaújszántó 4,209 F2
Abony 15,624 E3
Ács 8,423 E3
Ajka 34,000 D3
Albertirsa 11,252 E3
Alsózsolca 5,045 F2
Bácsalmás 8,000 E3
Baja 41,000 E3
Balassagyarmat 20,000 E2
Balatonfüred 15,000 D3
Balkány 7,667 F3
Balmazújváros 17,371 F3
Barcs 12,000 D4
Bátaszék 7,274 E3
Battonya 9,324 F3
Békés 22,000 F3
Békéscsaba 71,000 F3
Berettyóújfalu 18,000 F3
Bicske 13,000 E3
Bonyhád 15,000 E3
Budafok 40,623 E3
Budakeszi 10,429 E3
Budaörs 22,000 E3
Budapest (cap.) 2,104,000 E3
Cegléd 40,000 E3
Celldömölk 12,000 D3
Csepel 71,693 E3
Csongrád 21,000 F3

Kaposvár 74,000 D3
Kapuvár 11,000 D3
Karcag 25,000 F3
Kazincbarcika 39,000 F2
Kecel 10,493 E3
Kecskemét 105,000 E3
Keszthely 23,000 D3
Kisbér 8,000 D3
Kiskőrös 15,000 E3
Kiskunfélegyháza 35,000 E3
Kiskunhalas 32,000 E3
Kiskunmajsa 14,439 E3
Kispest 65,106 E3
Kistelek 8,544 E3
Kisújszállás 13,000 F3
Kisvárda 17,828 G2
Komádi 8,765 F3
Komárom 19,955 E3
Komló 30,301 E3
Kondoros 7,319 F3
Körmend 12,000 D3
Kőszeg 14,000 D3
Kunhegyes 10,116 F3
Kunmadaras 7,343 F3
Kunszentmárton 12,000 F3
Kunszentmiklós 7,952 E3
Lajosmizse 12,872 E3
Leninváros 19,000 F3
Lenti 9,000 D3
Létavértes 9,106 F3
Lőrinci 10,679 E3
Makó 29,000 F3
Marcali 13,000 D3
Mátészalka 20,000 G3
Mélykút 7,640 E3
Mezőberény 12,702 F3
Mezőhegyes 8,631 F3
Mezőkovácsháza 7,000 F3
Mezőkövesd 18,000 F3

Sopron 57,000 D3
Szabadszállás 8,223 E3
Szarvas 19,000 F3
Százhalombatta 18,000 E3
Szeged 188,000 F3
Szeghalom 10,000 F3
Székesfehérvár 113,000 E3
Szekszárd 39,000 E3
Szentendre 20,000 E3
Szentes 35,000 F3
Szentgotthárd 8,000 D3
Szerencs 10,000 F2
Szigetvár 13,000 D3
Szolnok 81,000 F3
Szombathely 87,000 D3
Tamási 10,000 E3
Tapolca 18,000 D3
Tata 26,000 E3
Tatabánya 76,000 E3
Tiszaföldvár 12,560 F3
Tiszafüred 14,000 F3
Tiszakécske 10,497 F3
Tiszavasvári 14,000 F3
Tolna 8,997 E3
Törökszentmiklós 24,000 F3
Tótkomlós 8,803 F3
Tura 8,235 E3
Túrkeve 11,000 F3
Újfehértó 14,412 F3
Újpest 80,384 E3
Vác 36,000 E3
Várpalota 28,000 E3
Vásárosnamény 9,000 G2
Vecsés 19,193 E3
Veszprém 66,000 D3
Vészto 9,815 F3
Zalaegerszeg 63,000 D3
Zalaszentgrót 8,000 D3
Zirc 11,000 D3

1,524,766 E2
Východoslovenský 1,402,252 F2
Západoslovenský 1,683,891 D2

CITIES and TOWNS

Bánovce nad Bebravou 15,342 E2
Banská Bystrica 66,412 E2
Banská Štiavnica 9,180 E2
Bardejov 23,741 F2
Bratislava (cap.) 380,259 D2
Brezno 17,872 E2
Bytča 11,789 E2
Čadca 19,319 E2
Čalovo 8,063 D3
Detva 14,261 E2
Dolný Kubín 13,971 E2
Dubnica nad Váhom 15,580 E2
Dunajská Streda 18,715 D3
Fil'akovo 10,497 E2
Galanta 15,477 D2
Handlová 17,777 E2
Hlohovec 21,148 D2
Holíč 8,741 D2
Hriňová 8,485 E2
Humenné 27,285 F2
Hurbanovo 7,613 E3
Kežmarok 17,570 F2
Kolárovo 11,295 D3
Komárno 32,520 D3
Košice 202,368 F2
Kremnica 7,168 E2
Krupina 7,337 E2
Kysucké Nové Mesto 14,083 E2
Levice 26,132 E2
Levoča 11,025 F2
Liptovský Hrádok 9,197 E2

Trnava 64,062 D2
Turzovka 6,962 E2
Vel'ké Kapušany 8,459 G2
Vráble 7,586 E2
Vranov nad Teplou 18,423 F2
Žiar nad Hronom 19,098 E2
Žilina 83,016 E2
Zlaté Moravce 14,119 E2
Zvolen 36,538 E2

OTHER FEATURES

Beskids, East (mts.) F2
Beskids, West (mts.) E2
Dudvá (riv.) D2
Dukla (pass) F2
Dunajec (riv.) F2
Gerlachovka (mt.) F2
Hornád (riv.) F2
Hron (riv.) E2
Ipel' (riv.) E2
Laborec (riv.) F2
Latorica (riv.) F2
Nitra (riv.) E2
Orava (riv.) E2
Poprad (riv.) F2
Slaná (riv.) F2
Slovenské Rudohorie (mts.) E2
Tatra, High (riv.) F2
Topl'a (riv.) F2
Torysa (riv.) F2
Už (riv.) G2
Váh (riv.) D2
White Carpathians (mts.) E2

†Population of Austrian cities are communes.

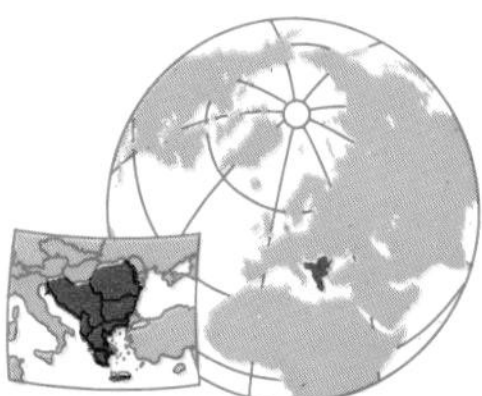

ALBANIA

AREA 11,100 sq. mi. (28,749 sq. km.)
POPULATION 3,199,000
CAPITAL Tiranë
LARGEST CITY Tiranë
HIGHEST POINT Korab 9,026 ft. (2,751 m.)
MONETARY UNIT lek
MAJOR LANGUAGE Albanian
MAJOR RELIGIONS Islam, Eastern Orthodoxy, Roman Catholicism

BOSNIA AND HERZEGOVINA

AREA 19,940 sq. mi. (51,129 sq. km.)
POPULATION 4,124,256
CAPITAL Sarajevo
LARGEST CITY Sarajevo
HIGHEST POINT Pločna 7,310 ft. (2,228 m.)
MONETARY UNIT Yugoslav dinar
MAJOR LANGUAGE Serbo-Croatian
MAJOR RELIGIONS Islam, Roman Catholicism, Eastern Orthodoxy,

BULGARIA

AREA 42,823 sq. mi. (110,912 sq. km.)
POPULATION 8,981,000
CAPITAL Sofia
LARGEST CITY Sofia
HIGHEST POINT Musala 9,597 ft. (2,925 m.)
MONETARY UNIT lev
MAJOR LANGUAGE Bulgarian
MAJOR RELIGION Eastern Orthodoxy

CROATIA

AREA 22,050 sq. mi. (56,538 sq. km.)
POPULATION 4,601,469
CAPITAL Zagreb
LARGEST CITY Zagreb
HIGHEST POINT Mali Rajinac 5,574 ft. (1,699 m.)
MONETARY UNIT Croatian dinar
MAJOR LANGUAGE Serbo-Croatian
MAJOR RELIGIONS Roman Catholicism, Eastern Orthodoxy

GREECE

AREA 50,944 sq. mi. (131,945 sq. km.)
POPULATION 9,983,000
CAPITAL Athens
LARGEST CITY Athens
HIGHEST POINT Olympus 9,570 ft. (2,917 m.)
MONETARY UNIT drachma
MAJOR LANGUAGE Greek
MAJOR RELIGION Eastern (Greek) Orthodoxy

MACEDONIA

AREA 9,889 sq. mi. (25,713 sq. km.)
POPULATION 1,909,136
CAPITAL Skopje
LARGEST CITY Skopje
HIGHEST POINT Solunska Glava 8,333 ft. (2,540 m.)
MONETARY UNIT denar
MAJOR LANGUAGES Macedonian, Serbo-Croatian, Albanian
MAJOR RELIGIONS Eastern Orthodoxy, Islam, Roman Catholicism

ROMANIA

AREA 91,699 sq. mi. (237,500 sq. km.)
POPULATION 23,249,000
CAPITAL Bucharest
LARGEST CITY Bucharest
HIGHEST POINT Molodoveanul 8,343 ft. (2,543 m.)
MONETARY UNIT leu
MAJOR LANGUAGES Romanian, Hungarian
MAJOR RELIGION Eastern Orthodoxy

SLOVENIA

AREA 7,898 sq. mi. (20,251 sq. km.)
POPULATION 1,891,864
CAPITAL Ljubljana
LARGEST CITY Ljubljana
HIGHEST POINT Triglav 9,393 ft. (2,863 m.)
MONETARY UNIT tolar
MAJOR LANGUAGES Slovenian, Serbo-Croatian
MAJOR RELIGIONS Roman Catholicism, Eastern Orthodoxy

YUGOSLAVIA

AREA 38,989 sq. mi. (102,173 sq. km.)
POPULATION 11,371,275
CAPITAL Belgrade
LARGEST CITY Belgrade
HIGHEST POINT Daravica 8,714 ft. (2,656 m.)
MONETARY UNIT Yugoslav dinar
MAJOR LANGUAGES Serbo-Croatian, Slovenian, Montenegrin, Albanian
MAJOR RELIGIONS Eastern Orthodoxy, Roman Catholicism

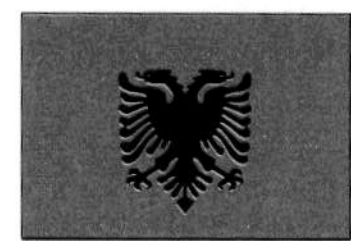
ALBANIA

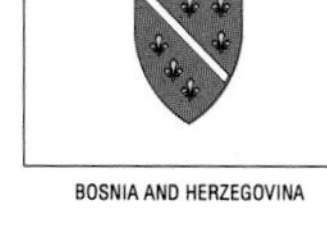
BOSNIA AND HERZEGOVINA

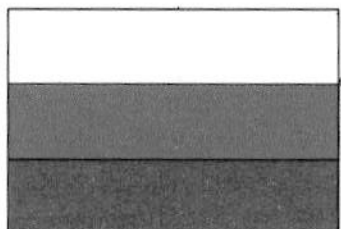
BULGARIA

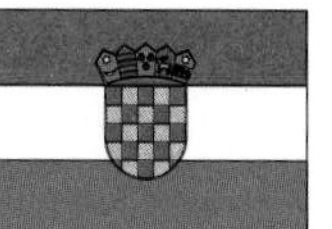
CROATIA

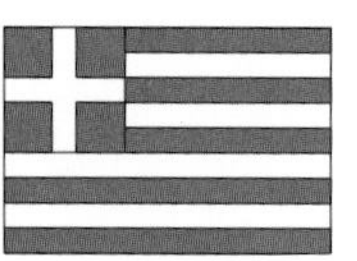
GREECE

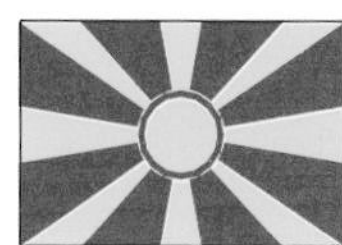
MACEDONIA

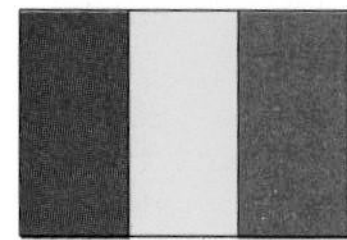
ROMANIA

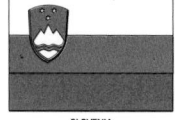

SLOVENIA

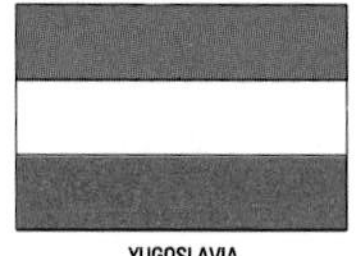
YUGOSLAVIA

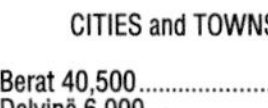

Agriculture, Industry and Resources

DOMINANT LAND USE

- Cereals (chiefly wheat, corn)
- Mixed Farming, Horticulture
- Pasture Livestock
- Tobacco, Cotton
- Grapes, Wine
- Forests
- Nonagricultural Land

MAJOR MINERAL OCCURRENCES

Ab	Asbestos	Mg	Magnesium
Ag	Silver	Mn	Manganese
Al	Bauxite	Mr	Marble
C	Coal	Na	Salt
Cr	Chromium	Ni	Nickel
Cu	Copper	O	Petroleum
Fe	Iron Ore	Pb	Lead
G	Natural Gas	Sb	Antimony
Hg	Mercury	U	Uranium
Lg	Lignite	Zn	Zinc

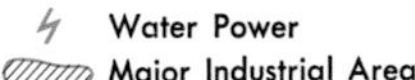
Water Power
Major Industrial Areas

ALBANIA

CITIES and TOWNS

Berat 40,500 ... D5
Delvinë 6,000 ... D6
Durrës (Durazzo) 78,700 ... D5
Elbasan 78,300 ... E5
Fier 40,300 ... D5
Gjirokastër 23,800 ... E5
Kavajë 24,200 ... D5
Korçë 61,500 ... E5
Krujë 9,600 ... D5
Kuçovë (Stalin) 20,600 ... D5
Kukës 9,500 ... E4
Lezhë 6,900 ... D5
Lushnjë 26,900 ... D5
Peshkopi 7,600 ... E5
Pogradec 13,100 ... E5
Sarandë 10,800 ... E6
Shijak 6,200 ... D5
Shkodër 76,300 ... D4
Stalin 20,600 ... D5
Tiranë (Tirana) (cap.) 225,700 ... E5
Vlorë 67,700 ... D5

OTHER FEATURES

Adriatic (sea) ... B4
Drin (riv.) ... E4
Korab (mt.) ... E4
Ohrid (lake) ... E5
Otranto (str.) ... D5
Prespa (lake) ... E5
Sazan (isl.) ... D5
Scutari (lake) ... D4
Vijosë (riv.) ... D5

BOSNIA and HERZEGOVINA

CITIES and TOWNS

Banja Luka 183,618 ... C3
Bihać 65,544 ... B3
Bijeljina 92,808 ... D3
Bileca 13,199 ... D4
Bosanska Dubica 30,867 ... C3
Bosanska Gradiška 58,095 ... C3
Bosanska Krupa 55,229 ... C3
Bosanski Brod 32,286 ... D3
Bosanski Novi 42,142 ... C3
Bosanski Petrovac 16,095 ... C3
Bosanski Šamac 32,320 ... D3
Brčko 82,768 ... D3
Bugojno 39,969 ... C3
Čapljina 26,032 ... C4
Cazin 57,110 ... B3
Derventa 57,010 ... C3
Doboj 99,548 ... C3
Drvar 17,983 ... C3
Donji Vakuf 22,606 ... C3
Foča 44,661 ... D4
Gacko 10,729 ... D4
Glamoč 14,120 ... C3
Gornji Vakuf 22,432 ... C4
Gračanica 54,311 ... D3
Gradačac 54,281 ... D3
Jajce 41,197 ... C3
Kladanj 15,641 ... D3
Ključ 40,008 ... C3
Konjic 43,677 ... C4
Livno 40,438 ... C4
Ljubinje 4,516 ... D4
Ljubuški 27,603 ... C4
Maglaj 42,160 ... D3
Modriča 34,541 ... D3
Mostar 110,377 ... C4
Nevesinje 16,326 ... D4
Prijedor 108,868 ... C3
Prozor 19,108 ... C4
Rogatica 23,578 ... D4
Sanski Most 62,467 ... C3
Sarajevo (cap.) 448,500 ... D4
Srebrenica 36,292 ... D3
Stolac 18,910 ... C4
Teslić 60,434 ... C3
Travnik 64,100 ... C3
Trebinje 30,372 ... D4
Tuzla 121,717 ... D3
Vareš 22,822 ... D3
Višegrad 23,201 ... D4
Visoko 40,901 ... D4
Vlasenica 30,498 ... D3
Zenica 132,733 ... C3
Žepče 19,754 ... D3
Zvornik 73,845 ... D3

OTHER FEATURES

Adriatic (sea) ... B4
Bosna (riv.) ... D3
Dinaric Alps (mts.) ... B3
Drina (riv.) ... D3
Neretva (riv.) ... D4
Tara (riv.) ... D4
Una (riv.) ... C3
Vrbas (riv.) ... C3

BULGARIA

CITIES and TOWNS

Asenovgrad 47,159 ... G5
Aytos 23,124 ... H4
Balchik 12,764 ... J4
Bansko 10,025 ... F5
Berkovitsa 16,340 ... F4
Blagoevgrad 65,481 ... F5
Botevgrad 22,659 ... F4
Burgas 182,856 ... H4
Byala 11,017 ... G4
Byala Slatina 16,034 ... F4
Chirpan 20,440 ... G4
Dimitrovgrad 54,056 ... G4
Dobrich (Tolbukhin) 109,170 ... H4
Dryanovo 10,306 ... G4
Elkhovo 13,655 ... H4
Gabrovo 81,629 ... G4
Gorna Oryakhovitsa 40,895 ... G4
Gotse Delchev 19,836 ... F5
Grudovo 10,736 ... H4
Ikhtiman 13,001 ... F4
Isperikh 11,235 ... H4
Karlovo 28,403 ... G4
Karnobat 22,536 ... H4
Kavarna 12,024 ... J4
Kazanlŭk 61,396 ... G4
Kharmanli 21,050 ... G5
Khaskovo 87,847 ... G5
Kubrat 10,758 ... H4
Kŭrdzhali 55,201 ... G5
Kyustendil 53,498 ... F4
Lom 32,307 ... F4
Lovech 48,992 ... G4
Lukovit 10,645 ... G4
Mikhaylovgrad 51,714 ... F4
Momchilgrad 10,189 ... G5
Nesebŭr 8,130 ... H4
Nova Zagora 25,327 ... H4
Novi Pazar 16,314 ... H4
Omurtag 9,505 ... H4
Oryakhovo 14,012 ... F4
Panagyurishte 22,034 ... G4
Pazardzhik 77,603 ... G4
Pernik 94,460 ... F4
Peshtera 18,763 ... G4
Petrich 26,451 ... F5
Pirdop 8,248 ... G4
Pleven 129,863 ... G4
Plovdiv 343,064 ... G4
Pomorie 13,507 ... H4
Popovo 21,236 ... H4
Provadiya 15,762 ... H4
Radomir 16,733 ... F4
Razgrad 49,582 ... H4
Razlog 14,010 ... F5
Rositsa 185,485 ... H4
Ruse 185,485 ... H4
Samokov 27,485 ... F4
Sandanski 24,629 ... F5
Sevlievo 26,560 ... G4
Shumen 100,125 ... H4
Silistra 53,537 ... H3
Sliven 9,037 ... H4
Smolyan 31,456 ... G5
Sofia (cap.) 1,121,763 ... F4
Stanke Dimitrov 41,897 ... F4
Stara Zagora 151,163 ... G4
Svilengrad 17,472 ... H5
Svishtov 30,555 ... G4
Teteven 12,784 ... G4
Tolbukhin 109,170 ... H4
Troyan 26,179 ... G4
Tŭrgovishte 46,043 ... H4
Tutrakan 12,153 ... H4
Varna 302,816 ... H4
Veliko Tŭrnovo 69,173 ... G4
Vidin 62,541 ... F4
Vratsa 75,180 ... F4
Yambol 90,019 ... H4
Zlatograd 8,780 ... G5

OTHER FEATURES

Arda (riv.) ... G5
Balkan (mts.) ... G4
Black (sea) ... J4
Danube (riv.) ... H4
Dunav (Danube) (riv.) ... H4
Emine (cape) ... J4
Iskŭr (riv.) ... G4
Kaliakra (cape) ... J4
Maritsa (riv.) ... G4
Mesta (riv.) ... F5
Midzhur (mt.) ... F4
Musala (mt.) ... F4
Osŭm (riv.) ... G4
Rhodope (mts.) ... G5
Rujen (mt.) ... F4
Struma (riv.) ... F5
Timok (riv.) ... F3
Tundzha (riv.) ... G4
Vit (riv.) ... G4

CROATIA

CITIES and TOWNS

Beli Manastir 53,409 ... D3
Biograd 15,865 ... B4
Bjelovar 66,553 ... C3
Čakovec 116,825 ... C2
Daruvar 31,424 ... C3
Djakovo 52,349 ... D3
Dubrovnik 66,131 ... D4
Fiume (Rijeka) 193,044 ... B3
Gospić 31,263 ... B3
Gračac 11,863 ... B3
Karlovac 78,363 ... B3
Knin 43,731 ... C3
Koprivnica 61,166 ... C2
Kostajnica 15,548 ... C3
Križevci 41,316 ... C2
Krk 13,334 ... B3
Kutina 38,597 ... C3
Makarska 17,819 ... C4
Našice 38,938 ... D3
Nova Gradiška 61,267 ... C3
Novska 24,530 ... C3
Ogulin 31,076 ... B3
Omiš 24,082 ... C4
Opatija 29,274 ... B3
Osijek 158,790 ... D3
Pag 7,076 ... B3
Petrinja 33,570 ... C3
Ploče (Kardeljevo) 11,328 ... C4
Pola (Pula) 77,278 ... A3

(continued on following page)

(continued)

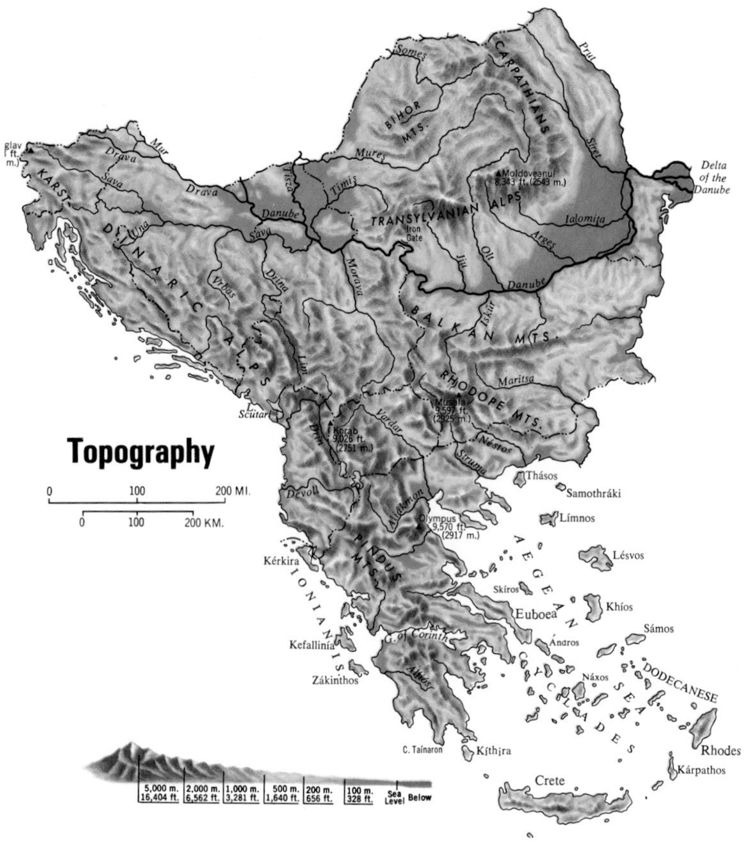

Poreč 19,946 A3
Pula 77,278 A3
Rab 8,877 B3
Ragusa (Dubrovnik) 66,131 C4
Rijeka 193,044 B3
Rovinj 18,277 A3
Samobor 43,855 B3
Senj 9,582 B3
Šibenik 80,148 C4
Sinj 59,298 C4
Sisak 84,756 C3
Slavonska Požega 71,286 C3
Slavonski Brod 106,400 D3
Split 235,922 C4
Trogir 19,856 C4
Varaždin 90,729 C2
Vinkovci 95,245 D3
Virovitica 47,417 C3
Vukovar 81,203 D3
Zadar 116,174 B3
Zagreb (cap.) 681,173 C3
Zara (Zadar) 116,174 B3

OTHER FEATURES

Adriatic (sea) B4
Brač (isl.) C4
Cazma (riv.) C3
Cres (isl.) B3
Dalmatia (reg.) C4
Danube (riv.) E3
Dinaric Alps (mts.) B3
Drava (riv.) C3
Dugi Otok (isl.) B3
Hvar (isl.) C4
Istria (pen.) A3
Kamenjak (cape) A3
Korčula (isl.) C4
Kornat (isl.) B4
Krk (isl.) B3
Kupa (riv.) B3
Kvarner (gulf) B3
Lastovo (Lagosta) (isl.) C4
Lošinj (isl.) B3
Mljet (isl.) C4
Pag (isl.) B3
Palagruža (Pelagosa) (isl.) C4
Rab (isl.) B3
Sava (riv.) D3
Slavonia (reg.) C3
Šolta (isl.) C4
Una (riv.) C3
Vis (isl.) C4
Žirje (isl.) B4

GREECE

REGIONS

Aegean Islands 417,813 G6
Athens, Greater 3,027,331 F7
Áyion Óros (aut. dist.) 1,732 G5
Central Greece and Euboea 1,099,841 F6
Crete 502,165 G8
Epirus 324,541 E6
Ionian Islands 182,651 D6
Macedonia 2,121,953 F5
Pelopónnisos 1,012,528 F7
Thessaly 695,654 F6
Thrace 345,220 G5

CITIES and TOWNS

Agrínion 34,328 E6
Aíyion 20,824 F6
Alexandroúpolis 34,535 G5
Amaliás 14,698 E7
Árgos 20,702 F7
Árta 18,283 E6
Atalándi 5,456 F6
Athens (cap.) 885,737 F7
Áyios Nikólaos 8,130 G8
Candia (Iráklion) 101,634 G8
Canea (Khaniá) 40,564 G8
Corinth 22,658 F7
Dhidhimótikhon 8,374 H5
Dráma 36,109 G5
Édhessa 16,054 F5
Ermoúpolis 13,876 G7
Flórina 12,562 E5
Grevená 7,433 E5
Ierápetra 8,575 G8
Ioánnina 44,829 E6
Iráklion 101,634 G8
Itháki 2 037 E6
Kalámai 41,911 F7
Kálimnos 10,118 H7
Kardhítsa 27,291 E6
Kastoría 17,133 E5
Kateríni 38,016 F5
Kavála 56,375 G5
Kérkira 33,561 D6
Khalkís 44,867 F6
Khaniá 40,564 G8
Khíos 24,070 G6
Kiáton 7,392 F6
Kilkís 11,148 F5
Komotiní 34,051 G5
Koropí 11,214 G7
Kos 11,851 H7
Kozáni 30,994 F5
Lamía 41,667 F6
Lárisa 102,048 F6
Lávrion 8,921 G7
Levádhia 16,864 F6
Marathón 2,052 G6
Mégara 17,719 F6
Mesolóngion 10,164 E6
Mitilíni 24,115 H6
Náousa 19,383 F5
Návpaktos 9,012 F6
Návplion 10,609 F7
Náxos 3,735 G7
Orestías 12,685 H5
Pátrai 141,529 E6
Piraiévs (Piraeus) 196,389 F7
Pírgos 21,958 E7
Préveza 12,662 E6
Psakhná 5,320 F6
Ptolemaís 22,109 E5
Réthimnon 17,736 G8
Rhodes (Ródhos) 40,392 J7
Salamís 20,437 F6
Salonika (Thessaloníki) 406,413 F5
Sámos 5,575 H7
Samothráki 941 G5
Sérrai 45,213 F5
Sparta 11,911 F7
Thásos 2,300 G5
Thessaloníki 406,413 F5
Thívai 18,712 F6
Tirnávos 10,965 F6
Tríkkala 40,857 E6
Trípolis 21,311 F7
Vérria 37,087 F5
Vólos 71,378 F6
Vónitsani 3,627 E6
Xánthi 31,541 G5
Yiannitsá 21,082 F5
Zante (Zákinthos) 9,764 E7

OTHER FEATURES

Aegean (sea) G6
Akrí (cape) E7
Aktí (pen.) G5
Amorgós (isl.) G7
Anáfi (isl.) G7
Andikíthira (isl.) F8
Ándros (isl.) G7
Árda (riv.) G5
Argolís (gulf) F7
Astipálaia (isl.) H7
Áthos (mt.) G5
Áyios Evstrátios (isl.) G6
Áyios Yeóryios (cape) G5
Cephalonia (Kefallinía) (isl.) E6
Corfu (Kérkira) (isl.) D6
Corinth (gulf) F6
Crete (isl.) G8
Crete (sea) G8
Cyclades (isls.) G7
Día (isl.) G8
Dodecanese (isls.) H8
Euboea (Évvoia) (isl.) G6
Évros (riv.) H5
Gávdhos (isl.) F8
Ídhi (mt.) G8
Ikaría (isl.) G7
Ionian (sea) D7
Íos (isl.) G7
Itháki (Ithaca) (isl.) E6
Kafirévs (cape) G6
Kálimnos (isl.) H7
Kárpathos (isl.) H8
Kásos (isl.) H8
Kassándra (pen.) F6
Kéa (isl.) G7
Kefallinía (isl.) E6
Kérkira (isl.) D6
Khálki (isl.) H7
Khaniá (gulf) G8
Khíos (isl.) G6
Kímilos (isl.) G7
Kiparissía (gulf) E7
Kíthira (isl.) F7
Kíthnos (isl.) G7
Kos (isl.) H7
Kriós (cape) F8
Kríti (Crete) (isl.) G8
Lakonía (gulf) F7
Léros (isl.) H7
Lésvos (isl.) G6
Levítha (isl.) H7
Levkás (isl.) E6
Límnos (isl.) G6
Maléa (cape) F7
Matapan (Taínaron) (cape) F7
Merabéllou (gulf) H8
Mesará (gulf) G8
Messíni (gulf) E7
Míkonos (isl.) G7
Mílos (isl.) G7
Mirtóön (sea) F7
Náxos (isl.) G7
Néstos (riv.) G5
Nísiros (isl.) H7
Northern Sporades (isls.) F6
Olympia (isls.) E7
Olympus (mt.) F5
Parnassus (mt.) F6
Páros (isl.) G7
Pátmos (isl.) H7
Paxoí (isl.) D6
Pindus (mts.) E6
Pinió (riv.) E6
Prespa (lake) E5
Psará (isl.) G6
Psevdhókavos (cape) G6
Rhodes (isl.) H7
Rhodope (mts.) G5
Salonika (Thermaic) (gulf) F6
Sámos (isl.) H7
Samothráki (isl.) G5
Saría (isl.) H8
Saronic (gulf) F7
Sérifos (isl.) G7
Sídheros (cape) H8
Sífnos (isl.) G7
Sími (isl.) H7
Síros (isl.) G7
Sithoniá (pen.) F5
Skíros (isl.) G6
Spátha (cape) F8
Strimón (gulf) G5
Strofádhes (isls.) E7
Taínaron (cape) F7
Thásos (isls.) G5
Thermaic (gulf) F5
Thíra (isl.) G7
Tílos (isl.) H7
Tínos (isl.) G7
Toronaic (gulf) F5
Vardar (riv.) E5
Vólvi (lake) F5
Voïviïs (lake) F6
Voúxa (cape) F8
Zákinthos (Zante) (isl.) E7

MACEDONIA

CITIES and TOWNS

Berovo 20,226 F5
Bitola 137,835 E5
Debar 22,506 E5
Gevgelija 32,023 F5
Gostivar 101,188 E5
Kavadarci 39,738 F5
Kičevo 51,452 E5
Kočani 47,976 F5
Kumanovo 126,368 E4
Ohrid 64,316 E5
Prilep 99,941 E5
Radoviš 28,574 F5
Skopje (cap.) 506,547 E5
Štip 46,651 F5
Struga 54,489 E5
Strumica 87,446 F5
Tetovo 162,414 E5
Titov Veles 64,901 E5

OTHER FEATURES

Korab (mt.) E5
Ohrid (lake) E5
Prespa (lake) E5
Rujen (mt.) F4
Vardar (riv.) E5

ROMANIA

CITIES and TOWNS

Aiud 27,600 F2
Alba Iulia 53,000 F2
Alexandria 43,700 G3
Anina 11,300 E3
Arad 182,000 E2
Babadag 9,000 J3
Bacău 156,200 H2
Baia Mare 123,300 F2
Băileşti 21,500 F3
Balş 17,300 G3
Beiuş 10,100 F2
Bicaz 9,300 G2
Bîrlad 63,800 H2
Bistrita 59,800 G2
Blaj 22,200 F2
Borşa 25,287 F2
Botoşani 84,900 H2
Brad 18,600 F2
Brăila 219,200 H3
Braşov 320,200 G3
Bucharest (Bucureşti) (cap.) 1,929,400 G3
Buhuşi 20,300 H2
Buzău 116,300 H3
Buziaş 8,700 E3
Calafat 17,100 F3
Călăraşi 58,000 H3
Caracal 33,600 G3
Caransebeş 28,800 F3
Carei 25,500 F2
Cernavodă 15,000 J3
Chişineu Criş 9,600 E2
Cîmpia Turzii 25,300 F2
Cîmpina 35,300 G3
Cîmpulung 37,400 G3
Cîmpulung Moldovenesc 20,500 G2
Cisnădie 21,100 G3
Cluj-Napoca 289,800 F2
Comăneşti 18,500 H2
Constanta 293,900 J3
Corabia 20,300 G4
Costeşti 10,900 G3
Craiova 239,700 F3
Curtea de Argeş 26,900 G3
Darabani 11,500 H1
Dej 36,500 F2
Deva 73,300 F3
Dorohoi 25,700 H2
Drăgăneşti Olt 11,800 G3
Drăgăşani 17,300 G3
Drobeta-Turnu Severin 86,600 F3
Făgăraş 37,200 G3
Fălticeni 24,000 H2
Feteşti 29,600 H3
Focşani 70,700 H3
Găeşti 14,000 G3
Galati 268,000 H3
Gheorghe Gheorghiu-Dej 46,100 H2
Gheorghieni 21,800 G2
Gherla 20,700 F2
Giurgiu 57,000 G4
Hateg 10,200 F3
Hîrlău 8,900 H2
Hîrşova 9,000 J3
Huedin 8,700 F2
Hunedoara 85,700 F3
Huşi 26,000 J2
Iaşi 279,800 H2
Ineu 10,800 E2
Jimbolia 14,600 E3
Lipova 12,900 E2
Luduş 16,000 G2
Lugoj 50,000 E3
Lupeni 29,100 F3
Mangalia 31,100 J4
Medgidia 45,300 J3
Mediaş 69,000 G2
Miercurea Ciuc 40,400 G2
Mizil 15,200 H3
Moineşti 21,200 H2
Moldova Nouă 17,800 E3
Moreni 18,900 G3
Ocna Mureş 16,200 G2
Odorheiu Secuiesc 36,200 G2
Oltenita 26,800 H3
Oradea 192,600 E2
Orăştie 19,900 F3
Oravita 114,300 E3
Orşova 115,800 F3
Panciu 77,900 H3
Paşcani 229,500 H2
Petrila 25,900 F3
Petroşeni 45,600 F3
Piatra Neamt 93,300 H2
Piteşti 143,600 G3
Ploieşti 219,900 H3
Pucioasa 14,100 G3
Rădăuti 26,000 G2
Reghin 33,600 G2
Reşita 96,800 E3
Rîmnicu Sărat 32,400 H3
Rîmnicu Vîlcea 78,900 G3
Roman 62,700 H2
Roşiori de Vede 31,700 G3
Săcele 33,900 G3
Salonta 20,400 E2
Satu Mare 115,600 F2
Sebeş 29,500 F3
Segarcea 8,700 F3
Sfîntu Gheorghe 57,900 G3
Sibiu 164,200 G3
Sighetu Marmaţiei 40,500 F2
Sighişoara 33,000 G2
Şimleul Silvaniei 15,100 F2
Sinaia 14,700 G3
Sînnicolaul Mare 13,600 E2
Slatina 62,800 G3
Slobozia 39,400 H3
Sovata 11,200 G2
Strehaia 11,800 F3
Suceava 76,500 H2
Tăşnad 10,400 F2
Techirghiol 11,800 J3
Tecuci 40,300 H3
Timişoara 288,200 E3
Tîrgovişte 77,500 G3
Tîrgu Jiu 75,200 F3
Tîrgu Mureş 141,300 G2
Tîrgu Neamt 16,600 H2
Tîrgu Ocna 12,800 H2
Tîrgu Secuiesc 19,800 H2
Tîrnăveni 27,900 G2
Toplita 15,200 G2
Tulcea 73,600 J3
Turdă 58,700 F2
Turnu Măgurele 33,000 G4
Urlata 11,200 H3
Urziceni 14,300 H3
Vaslui 50,100 H2
Vatra Dornei 17,800 G2
Videle 11,500 G3
Vişeul de Sus 20,800 G2
Zalău 43,300 F2
Zărneşti 25,000 G3
Zimnicea 16,400 G4

OTHER FEATURES

Argeş (riv.) G3
Bîrlad (riv.) H2
Black (sea) J4
Brăila (marshes) H3
Buzău (riv.) H3
Carpathian (mts.) G2
Crişul Alb (riv.) F2
Crişul Repede (riv.) F2
Danube (delta) J3
Danube (riv.) H4
Ialomiţa (marshes) J3
Ialomiţa (riv.) H3
Jijia (riv.) H2
Jiu (riv.) F3
Moldoveanul (mt.) G3
Mureş (riv.) F2
Olt (riv.) G3
Peleaga (mt.) F3
Pietrosul (mt.) G2
Prut (riv.) J2
Siret (riv.) H2
Someş (riv.) F2
Timiş (riv.) E3
Tîrnava Mare (riv.) G2
Transylvanian Alps (mts.) G3

SLOVENIA

CITIES and TOWNS

Bled 4,710 A2
Brežice 25,238 C3
Celje 63,877 B2
Jesenice 31,094 A2
Kočevje 18,139 B3
Koper 41,843 A3
Kranj 66,879 B2
Krško 27,774 B3
Ljubljana (cap.) 305,211 B3
Maribor 185,699 B2
Murska Sobota 64,299 C2
Nova Gorizia 56,758 A3
Novo Mesto 55,584 B3
Piran 15,235 A3
Postojna 19,892 B3
Ptuj 67,754 B2
Ravne na Koroškem 25,907 B2
Škofja Loka 35,276 B2
Trbovlje 18,786 B2
Tržič 14,014 B2
Velenje 38,041 B2

OTHER FEATURES

Adriatic (sea) B4
Drava (riv.) C3
Kupa (riv.) B3
Mur (riv.) B2
Triglav (mt.) A2

YUGOSLAVIA

INTERNAL DIVISIONS

Kosovo (aut. reg.) 1,240,919 E4
Montenegro (rep.) 527,207 D4
Serbia (rep.) 8,401,673 E3
Vojvodina (aut. prov.) 1,953,980 D3

CITIES and TOWNS

Aleksinac 67,286 E4
Apatin 33,843 D3
Arendjelovac 46,803 E3
Bačka Topola 41,889 D3
Bar 32,535 D4
Bečej 44,243 E3
Bela Crkva 25,690 E3
Belgrade (cap.) 1,470,073 E3
Beograde (Belgrade) (cap.) 1,470,073 E3
Bijelo Polje 55,634 D4
Bor 56,486 E3
Čačak 110,676 E4
Caribrod (Dimitrovgrad) 15,158 F4
Cetinje 20,213 D4
Ćuprija 38,841 E4
Dimitrovgrad 15,158 F4
Djakovica 92,203 E4
Gnjilane 84,085 E4
Gornji Milanovac 50,651 E3
Herceg Novi 23,258 D4
Ivangrad 49,772 D4
Kanjiža 32,709 D2
Kikinda 69,854 E3
Knjaževac 48,789 F4
Kosovska Mitrovica 105,353 E4
Kotor 20,455 D4
Kragujevac 164,823 E3
Kraljevo 121,622 E4
Kruševac 132,972 E4
Leskovac 159,001 E4
Loznica 84,180 D3
Negotin 63,973 F3
Nikšic 72,299 D4
Niš 230,711 E4
Novi Pazar 74,000 E4
Novi Sad 257,685 D3
Pančevo 123,791 E3
Paraćin 64,718 E4
Peć 111,071 E4
Pirot 69,653 F4
Plav 19,560 D4
Pljevlja 43,316 D4
Podgorica 132,290 D4
Požarevac 81,123 E3
Preševo 33,948 E4
Priboj 35,200 D4
Prijedor 108,868 C3
Prijepolje 46,902 D4
Priština 210,040 E4
Prizren 134,526 E4
Prokuplje 56,256 E4
Ruma 55,083 D3
Šabac 119,668 D3
Senta 30,519 D3
Šid 37,459 D3
Sjenica 35,570 E4
Smederevo 107,366 E3
Smederevska Palanka 60,945 E3
Sombor 99,168 D3
Sremska Mitrovica 65,129 D3
Subotica 154,611 D2
Surdulica 27,029 F4
Svetozarevo 76,460 E4
Svilajnac 34,888 E3
Titovo Užice 77,049 D4
Trstenik 53,695 E4
Ub 36,259 E3
Ulcinj 21,575 D5
Uroševac 113,680 E4
Valjevo 95,449 D3
Velika Plana 52,619 E3
Veliki Bečkerek (Zrenjanin) 139,000 E3
Vranje 82,527 E4
Vrbas 45,755 D3
Vršac 61,005 E3
Vučitrn 65,512 E4
Zaječar 76,681 F4
Zrenjanin 139,000 E3

OTHER FEATURES

Adriatic (sea) B4
Bobotov Kuk (mt.) D4
Danube (riv.) E3
Drina (riv.) D3
Ibar (riv.) E4
Lim (riv.) D4
Midzhur (mt.) F4
Morava (riv.) E3
Sava (riv.) D3
Scutari (lake) D4
Timok (riv.) F3
Tisa (riv.) E3

The Balkan States

CONIC PROJECTION

SCALE OF MILES

0 25 50 75 100 125 150 175

SCALE OF KILOMETERS

0 25 50 75 100 125 150 175

Capitals of Countries _ _ _ _ _ _ _ ☆
Administrative Centers _ _ _ _ _ _ △
International Boundaries _ _ _ _ _ _
Major Internal Boundaries _ _ _ _ _ _
Minor Internal Boundaries _ _ _ _ _ _
Canals _ _ _ _ _ _ _ _

BULGARIA and GREECE are divided into regions and departments, respectively. Because of the scale no attempt has been made to delimit and name these subdivisions; their administrative centers have, however, been designated.

The larger divisions named in Greece are well-known geographical regions, without administrative function.

ROMANIA consists of thirty-nine counties and three cities of regional status, Bucharest, Constanţa and Petroşeni. Scale does not permit delimiting these counties.

ALBANIA is divided into twenty-seven districts. Scale does not permit the delimitation of these divisions.

© Copyright HAMMOND INCORPORATED, Maplewood, N. J.

Topography

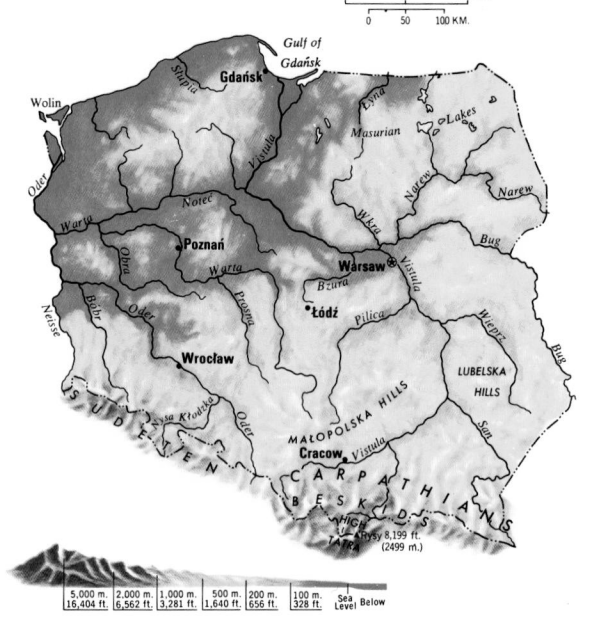

MAJOR MINERAL OCCURRENCES

Ag Silver
C Coal
Cu Copper
Fe Iron Ore
G Natural Gas
K Potash
Lg Lignite

Na Salt
Ni Nickel
O Petroleum
Pb Lead
S Sulfur
Zn Zinc

⚡ Water Power
▨ Major Industrial Areas

DOMINANT LAND USE

▢ Cereals (chiefly wheat)

▢ Rye, Oats, Barley, Potatoes

▢ General Farming, Livestock

▢ Forests

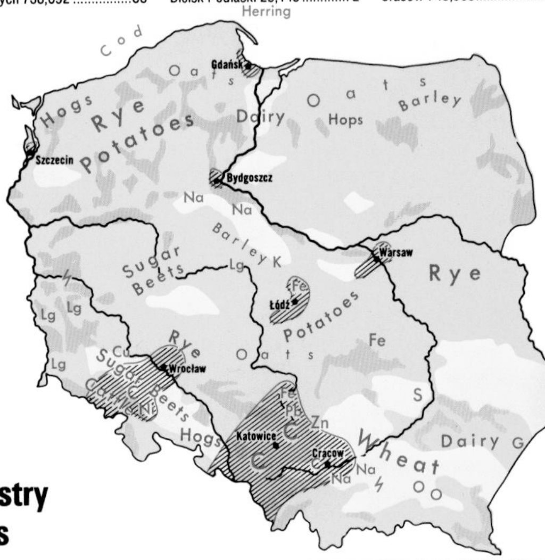

PROVINCES

Biała Podlaska 304,028 ......F3
Białystok 687,806 ....F2
Bielsko 895,357 ....D4
Bydgoszcz 1,104,048 ....C2
Chełm 245,484 ....F3
Ciechanów 425,608 ....E2
Cracow (Kraków) 1,223,137 ...E3
Cracow (city) 651,300 ....E3
Częstochowa 773,365 ....D3
Elbląg 475,862 ....D1
Gdańsk 1,417,801 ....D1
Gorzów 497,342 ....B2
Jelenia Góra 514,947 ....B3
Kalisz 706,514 ....D3
Katowice 3,953,769 ....D3
Kielce 1,123,691 ....E3
Konin 465,928 ....D2
Koszalin 502,750 ....C1
Krosno 491,471 ....E4
Legnica 510,000 ....C3
Leszno 383,315 ....C3
Łódź 777,800 ....D3

Łódź (city) 1,139,379 ....D3
Łomża 344,518 ....F2
Lublin 1,010,641 ....F3
Nowy Sącz 690,737 ....E4
Olsztyn 746,185 ....E2
Opole 1,010,416 ....C3
Ostrołęka 393,427 ....E2
Piła 475,953 ....C2
Piotrków 638,948 ....D3
Płock 512,626 ....D2
Poznań 1,323,368 ....C2
Przemyśl 404,200 ....F4
Radom 745,374 ....E3
Rzeszów 716,317 ....F4
Siedlce 648,111 ....E2
Sieradz 408,082 ....D3
Skierniewice 416,690 ....D3
Słupsk 410,049 ....C1
Suwałki 467,048 ....F1
Szczecin 964,298 ....B2
Tarnobrzeg 594,255 ....E3
Tarnów 664,953 ....E4
Toruń 656,421 ....D2
Wałbrzych 738,092 ....C3

Warsaw 2,415,950 ....E2
Warsaw (city) 1,377,100 .....E2
Włocławek 427,418 ....D2
Wrocław 1,122,806 ....C3
Zamość 488,193 ....F3
Zielona Góra 655,146 ....B3

CITIES and TOWNS

Aleksandrów Łódzki 19,711 ...D3
Allenstein (Olsztyn) 160,956 ..E2
Andrychów 22,387 ....D4
Augustów 28,307 ....F2
Auschwitz (Oświęcim)
45,402 ....D3
Bartoszyce 25,195 ....E1
Będzin 76,883 ....B3
Bełchatów 55,632 ....D3
Beuthen (Bytom) 229,991 .....A3
Biała Podlaska 52,119 ....F3
Białogard 23,973 ....C1
Białystok 267,670 ....F2
Bielawa 34,224 ....C3
Bielsk Podlaski 26,145 ......F2

Bielsko-Biała 181,072 ....D4
Biłgoraj 25,542 ....F3
Bochnia 28,846 ....E4
Bogatynia 18,616 ....B3
Boguszów-Gorce 19,452 ....B3
Bolesławiec 43,076 ....B3
Braniewo 17,594 ....D1
Breslau (Wrocław) 640,557 ...C3
Brieg (Brzeg) 38,504 ....C3
Brodnica 26,056 ....D2
Brzeg 38,504 ....C3
Busko Zdrój 17,675 ....E3
Bydgoszcz 380,426 ....C2
Bytom 229,991 ....A3
Bytów 16,720 ....C1
Chełm 64,683 ....F3
Chełmno 21,506 ....D2
Chodzież 19,831 ....C2
Chojnice 37,733 ....C2
Chorzów 131,850 ....B4
Chrzanów 42,195 ....B4
Ciechanów 43,068 ....E2
Cieszyn 36,682 ....D4
Cracow 745,568 ....E3

Agriculture, Industry and Resources

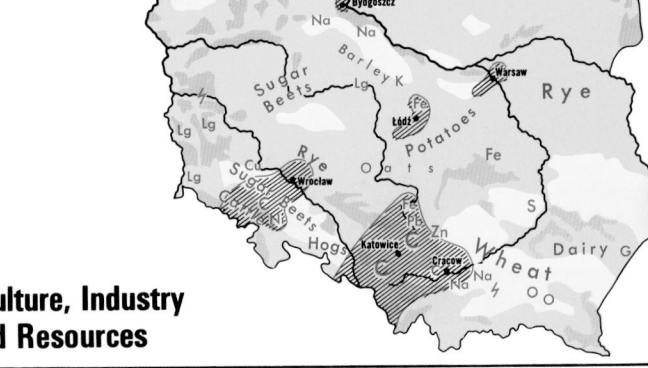

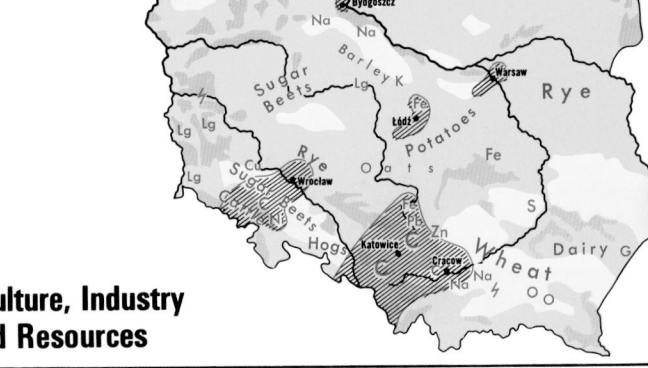

Former Republics of Yugoslavia

CONIC PROJECTION

MILES
0 — 25 — 50 — 75 — 100

KILOMETERS
0 — 25 — 50 — 75 — 100

Capitals
◉ National
★ Federal Republics
⊙ Autonomous Provinces

Boundaries

Canals

© Copyright HAMMOND INCORPORATED, Maplewood, N.J.

Longitude 18° East of Greenwich

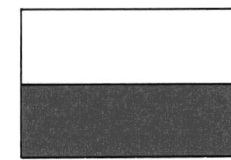

AREA 120,725 sq. mi. (312,678 sq. km.)
POPULATION 37,931,000
CAPITAL Warsaw
LARGEST CITY Warsaw
HIGHEST POINT Rysy 8,199 ft.
  (2,499 m.)
MONETARY UNIT zloty
MAJOR LANGUAGE Polish
MAJOR RELIGION Roman Catholicism

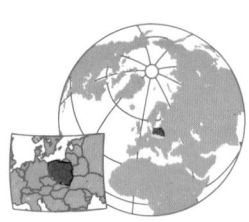

Poland
CONIC PROJECTION

SCALE OF MILES
0   10   20   40   60   80

SCALE OF KILOMETERS
0   10 20   40   60   80

Capitals of Countries ....★
Other Capitals ....⊛
International Boundaries ....
Internal Boundaries ....
Canals ....

Poland is divided into 49 provinces (bearing the same name as their capitals) and the autonomous cities of Warsaw, Łódź and Cracow.

© Copyright HAMMOND INCORPORATED, Maplewood, N.J.

48 Russia and Neighboring Countries

ARMENIA

AZERBAIJAN

BELARUS

GEORGIA

KAZAKHSTAN

KYRGYZSTAN

MOLDOVA

RUSSIA

TAJIKISTAN

TURKMENISTAN

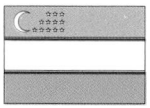
UKRAINE

UZBEKISTAN

ARMENIA
AREA 11,506 sq. mi. (29,800 sq. km.)
POPULATION 3,283,000
CAPITAL Yerevan
LARGEST CITY Yerevan
HIGHEST POINT Alagez 13,435 ft. (4,095 m.)
MAJOR LANGUAGES Armenian, Azerbaijani, Kurdish, Russian
MAJOR RELIGIONS Eastern (Armenian Apostolic) Orthodoxy, Islam

AZERBAIJAN
AREA 33,436 sq. mi. (86,680 sq. km.)
POPULATION 7,029,000
CAPITAL Baku
LARGEST CITY Baku
HIGHEST POINT Bazardyuzyu 14,653 ft. (4,466 m.)
MAJOR LANGUAGES Azerbaijani, Russian, Armenian
MAJOR RELIGIONS Islam, Eastern (Russian) Orthodoxy

BELARUS (BELORUSSIA)
AREA 80,154 sq. mi. (207,600 sq. km.)
POPULATION 10,200,000
CAPITAL Minsk
LARGEST CITY Minsk
HIGHEST POINT Dzerzhinskaya 1,135 ft. (346 m.)
MAJOR LANGUAGES Belorussian, Russian, Polish, Ukrainian, Yiddish
MAJOR RELIGIONS Eastern (Russian) Orthodoxy, Roman Catholicism, Judaism

GEORGIA
AREA 26,911 sq. mi. (69,700 sq. km.)
POPULATION 5,449,000
CAPITAL Tbilisi
LARGEST CITY Tbilisi
HIGHEST POINT Kazbek 16,558 ft. (5,047 m.)
MAJOR LANGUAGES Georgian, Armenian, Russian, Azerbaijani, Abkhazian, Ossetian
MAJOR RELIGIONS Eastern (Georgian) Orthodoxy, Islam

KAZAKHSTAN
AREA 1,048,300 sq. mi. (2,715,100 sq. km.)
POPULATION 16,538,000
CAPITAL Aqmola
LARGEST CITY Almaty
HIGHEST POINT Khan-Tengri 22,951 ft. (6,995 m.)
MAJOR LANGUAGES Kazakh, Russian, German, Ukrainian, Uzbek, Tatar
MAJOR RELIGIONS Islam, Eastern (Russian) Orthodoxy

KYRGYZSTAN (KIRGIZIA)
AREA 76,641 sq. mi. (198,500 sq. km.)
POPULATION 4,291,000
CAPITAL Bishkek (Frunze)
LARGEST CITY Bishkek (Frunze)
HIGHEST POINT Pobeda Peak 24,406 ft. (7,439 m.)
MAJOR LANGUAGES Kirgiz, Russian, Uzbek, Ukrainian, German, Tatar
MAJOR RELIGIONS Islam, Eastern (Russian) Orthodoxy

MOLDOVA
AREA 13,012 sq. mi. (33,700 sq. km.)
POPULATION 4,341,000
CAPITAL Chişinău
LARGEST CITY Chişinău
HIGHEST POINT 1,408 ft. (429 m.)
MAJOR LANGUAGES Moldavian (Romanian), Ukrainian, Russian, Gagauzi, Yiddish
MAJOR RELIGIONS Eastern (Romanian) Orthodoxy, Judaism

RUSSIA
AREA 6,592,812 sq. mi. (17,075,400 sq. km.)
POPULATION 147,386,000
CAPITAL Moscow
LARGEST CITY Moscow
HIGHEST POINT El'brus 18,510 ft. (5,642 m.)
MONETARY UNIT ruble
MAJOR LANGUAGES Russian, Tatar, Ukrainian, Chuvash, Bashkir, Belorussian, Mordvinian, German, Kazakh, Yiddish, Chechen, Udmurt, Ossetian, Buryat, Yakut, Ingush, Tuvan
MAJOR RELIGIONS Eastern (Russian) Orthodoxy, Roman Catholicism, Islam, Judaism, Lamaism, Buddhism, Animism

TAJIKISTAN
AREA 55,251 sq. mi. (143,100 sq. km.)
POPULATION 5,112,000
CAPITAL Dushanbe
LARGEST CITY Dushanbe
HIGHEST POINT Communism Peak 24,590 ft. (7,495 m.)
MAJOR LANGUAGES Tajik, Uzbek, Russian, Tatar, Kirgiz
MAJOR RELIGIONS Islam, Eastern (Russian) Orthodoxy

TURKMENISTAN
AREA 188,455 sq. mi. (488,100 sq. km.)
POPULATION 3,534,000
CAPITAL Ashgabat
LARGEST CITY Ashgabat
HIGHEST POINT Rize 9,653 ft. (2,942 m.)
MAJOR LANGUAGES Turkmenian, Russian, Uzbek, Kazakh, Tatar
MAJOR RELIGIONS Islam, Eastern (Russian) Orthodoxy

UKRAINE
AREA 233,089 sq. mi. (603,700 sq. km.)
POPULATION 51,704,000
CAPITAL Kiev
LARGEST CITY Kiev
HIGHEST POINT Goverla 6,762 ft. (2,061 m.)
MAJOR LANGUAGES Ukrainian, Russian, Yiddish, Belorussian, Moldavian (Romanian), Polish, Tatar
MAJOR RELIGIONS Eastern (Ukrainian) Orthodoxy, Roman (Ukrainian Uniate) Catholicism, Judaism

UZBEKISTAN
AREA 173,591 sq. mi. (449,600 sq. km.)
POPULATION 19,906,000
CAPITAL Tashkent
LARGEST CITY Tashkent
HIGHEST POINT Khodzha-Pir'yakh 14,515 ft. (4,424 m.)
MAJOR LANGUAGES Uzbek, Russian, Tajik, Kazakh, Tatar, Karakalpak, Kirgiz, Ukrainian, Turkmenian
MAJOR RELIGIONS Islam, Eastern (Russian) Orthodoxy

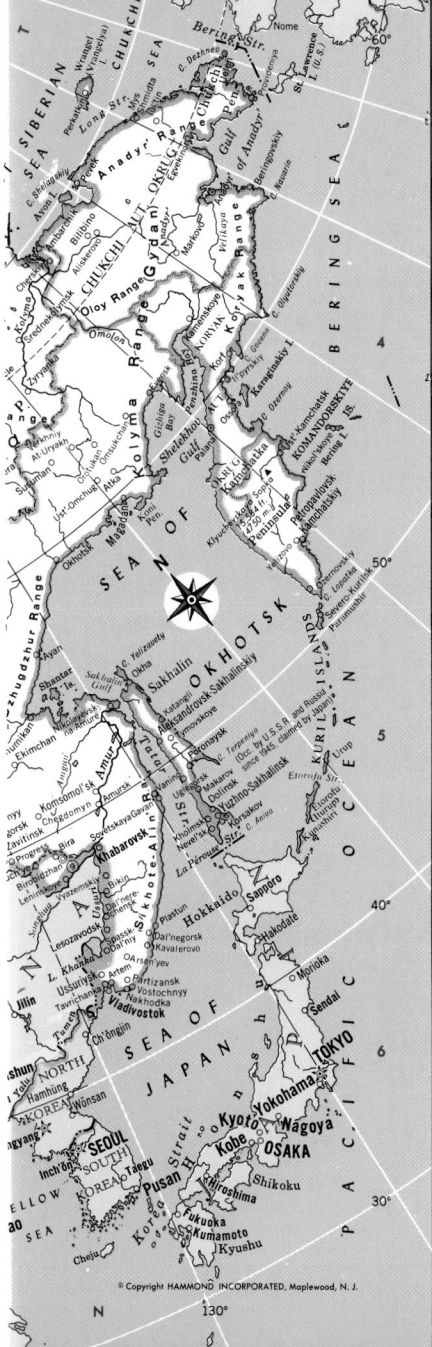

© Copyright HAMMOND INCORPORATED, Maplewood, N.J.

Topography

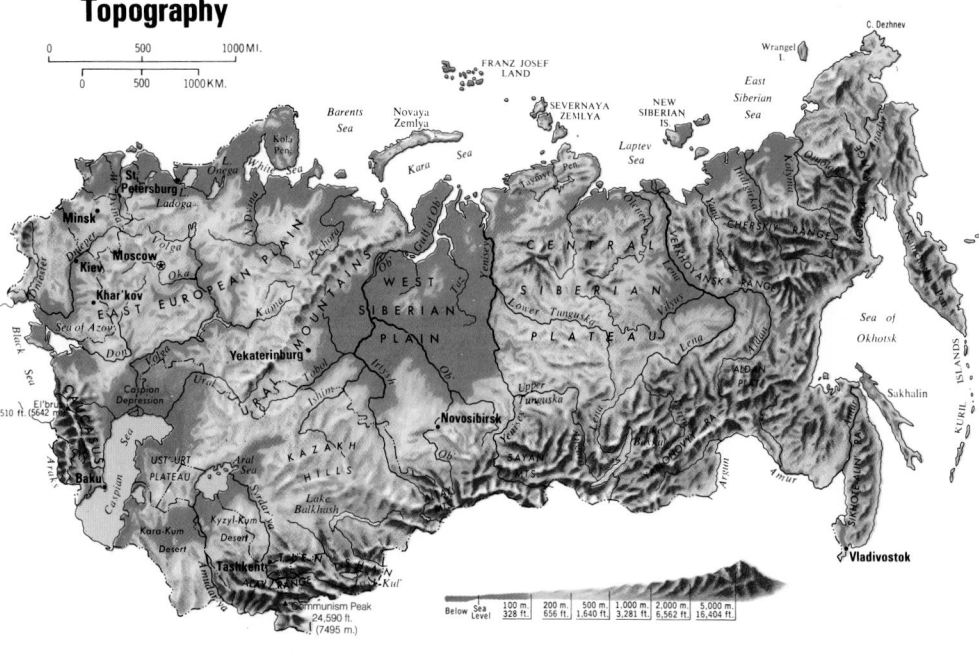

(continued)

Agriculture, Industry and Resources
(Eastern Europe)

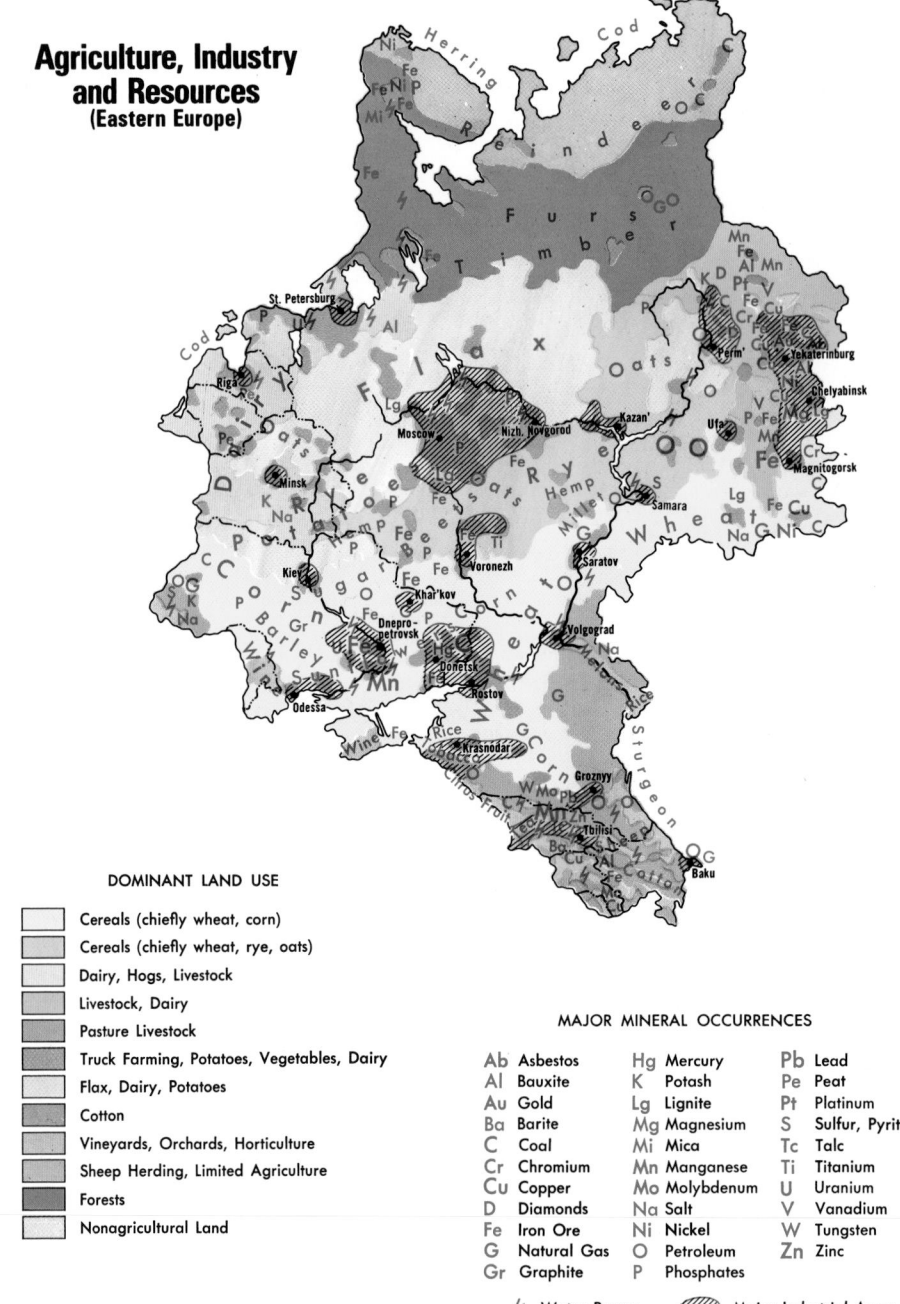

DOMINANT LAND USE

- Cereals (chiefly wheat, corn)
- Cereals (chiefly wheat, rye, oats)
- Dairy, Hogs, Livestock
- Livestock, Dairy
- Pasture Livestock
- Truck Farming, Potatoes, Vegetables, Dairy
- Flax, Dairy, Potatoes
- Cotton
- Vineyards, Orchards, Horticulture
- Sheep Herding, Limited Agriculture
- Forests
- Nonagricultural Land

MAJOR MINERAL OCCURRENCES

Ab	Asbestos	Hg	Mercury	Pb	Lead
Al	Bauxite	K	Potash	Pe	Peat
Au	Gold	Lg	Lignite	Pt	Platinum
Ba	Barite	Mg	Magnesium	S	Sulfur, Pyrites
C	Coal	Mi	Mica	Tc	Talc
Cr	Chromium	Mn	Manganese	Ti	Titanium
Cu	Copper	Mo	Molybdenum	U	Uranium
D	Diamonds	Na	Salt	V	Vanadium
Fe	Iron Ore	Ni	Nickel	W	Tungsten
G	Natural Gas	O	Petroleum	Zn	Zinc
Gr	Graphite	P	Phosphates		

⚡ Water Power   ▨ Major Industrial Areas

Agriculture, Industry and Resources
(Northern Asia)

DOMINANT LAND USE

- Cereals (chiefly wheat, corn)
- Livestock, Dairy
- Truck Farming, Potatoes, Vegetables, Dairy
- Cotton
- Sheep Herding, Limited Agriculture
- Forests
- Nonagricultural Land

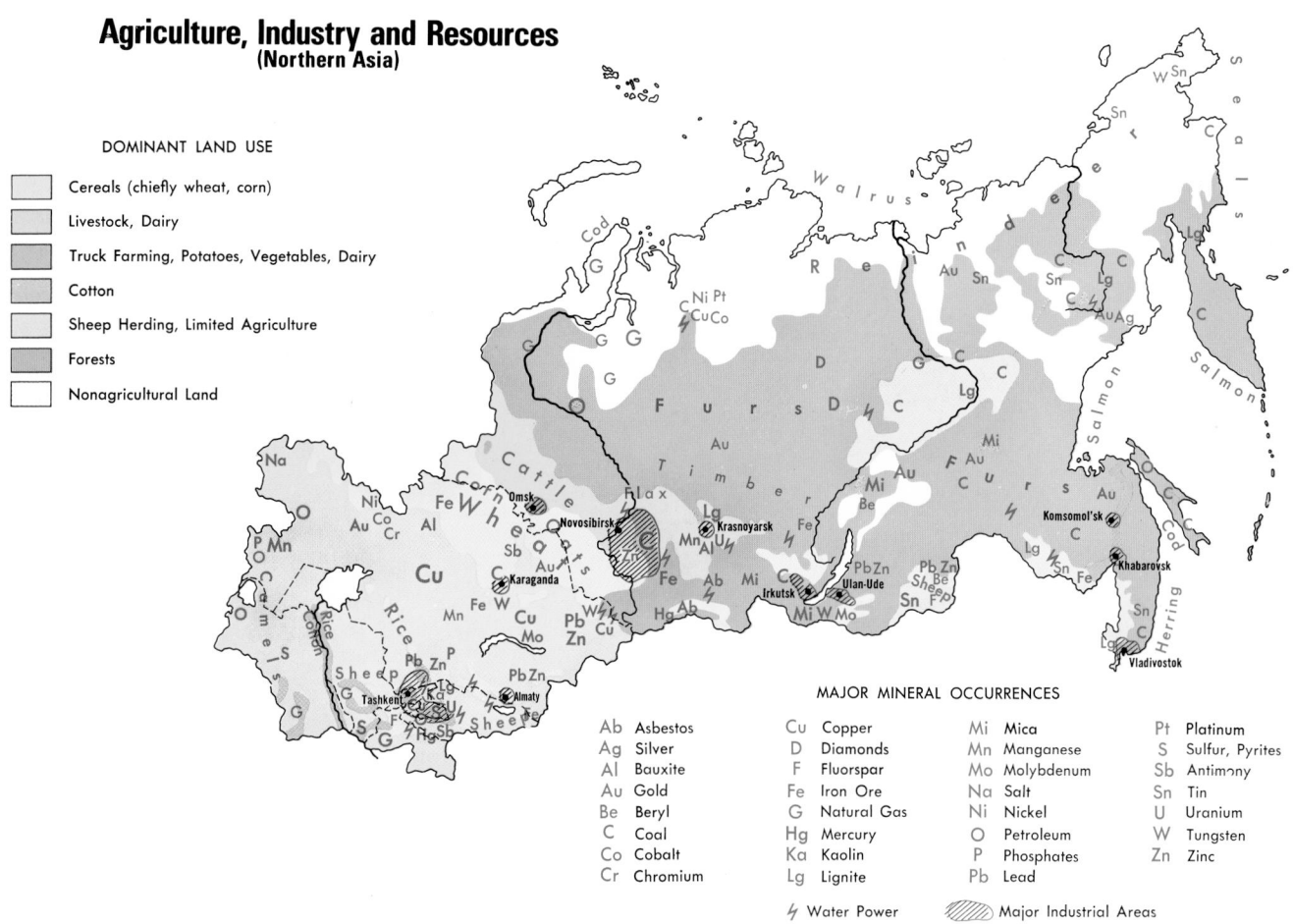

MAJOR MINERAL OCCURRENCES

Ab	Asbestos	Cu	Copper	Mi	Mica	Pt	Platinum
Ag	Silver	D	Diamonds	Mn	Manganese	S	Sulfur, Pyrites
Al	Bauxite	F	Fluorspar	Mo	Molybdenum	Sb	Antimony
Au	Gold	Fe	Iron Ore	Na	Salt	Sn	Tin
Be	Beryl	G	Natural Gas	Ni	Nickel	U	Uranium
C	Coal	Hg	Mercury	O	Petroleum	W	Tungsten
Co	Cobalt	Ka	Kaolin	P	Phosphates	Zn	Zinc
Cr	Chromium	Lg	Lignite	Pb	Lead		

⚡ Water Power   ▨ Major Industrial Areas

Russia and Neighboring Countries
European Part
CONIC PROJECTION
SCALE OF MILES
0 50 100 300
SCALE OF KILOMETERS
0 50 100 200 300
National Capitals
Administrative Centers
International boundaries
Aut. Rep. Oblast, Kray boundaries
Autonomous Oblast boundaries
Autonomous Okrug boundaries
© Copyright HAMMOND INCORPORATED, Maplewood, N. J.
ARCTIC OCEAN
BARENTS SEA
KARA SEA
PECHORA SEA
WHITE SEA
BALTIC SEA
BLACK SEA
CASPIAN SEA
Sea of Azov
GULF OF BOTHNIA
GULF OF OB'
KAZAKHSTAN
TURKEY
ROMANIA
BULGARIA
IRAN
SWEDEN
FINLAND
POLAND
LAPLAND
Administrative Divisions bear same names as their respective Capitals or Centers, except:
Abkhaz Aut. Rep. Sukhumi F6
Adygey Aut. Oblast Maykop F6
Adzhar Aut. Rep. Batumi F6
Bashkir Aut. Rep. Ufa J4
Chechen-Ingush Aut. Rep. Groznyy G6
Chuvash Aut. Rep. Cheboksary G3
Crimean Oblast Simferopol' D6
Dagestan Aut. Rep. Makhachkala G6
Kabardin-Balkar Aut. Rep. Nal'chik F6
Kalmuck Aut. Rep. Elista F5
Karachay-Cherkess Aut. Obl. Cherkessk F6
Karelian Aut. Rep. Petrozavodsk D2
Komi Aut. Rep. Syktyvkar H2
Komi-Permyak Aut. Okrug Kudymkar H3
Mari Aut. Rep. Yoshkar-Ola G3
Mordvinian Aut. Rep. Saransk G4
Nagorno-Karabakh Aut. Obl. Stepanakert G7
Nenets Aut. Okrug Nar'yan-Mar H1
North Ossetian Aut. Rep. Vladikavkaz F6
South Ossetian Aut. Obl. Tskhinvali F6
Tatar Aut. Rep. Kazan G3
Trans-Carpathian Oblast Uzhgorod B5
Udmurt Aut. Rep. Izhevsk H3
Volyn Oblast Lutsk C4

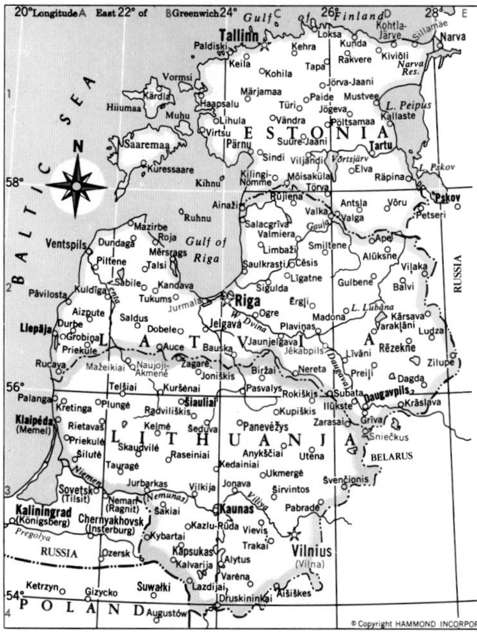

ESTONIA
LATVIA
LITHUANIA

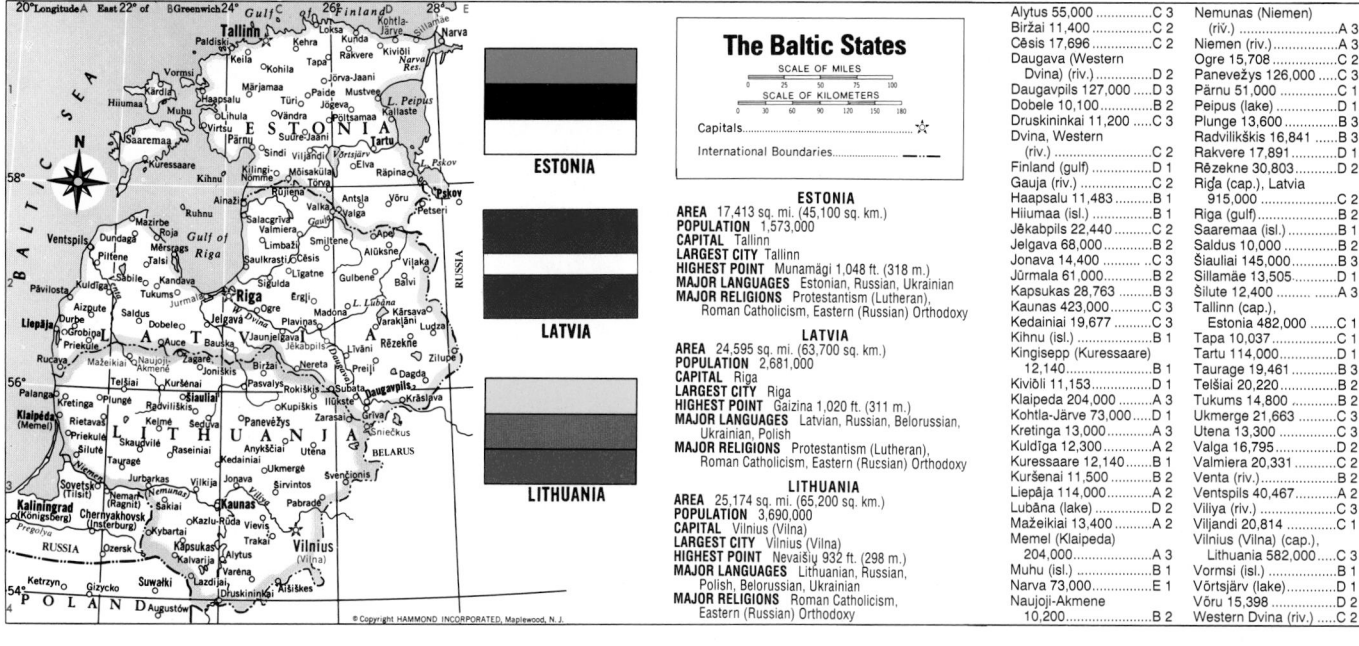

The Baltic States

SCALE OF MILES: 0 25 50 75 100
SCALE OF KILOMETERS: 0 30 60 90 120 150 180
Capitals .... ☆
International Boundaries .... —·—

ESTONIA

AREA 17,413 sq. mi. (45,100 sq. km.)
POPULATION 1,573,000
CAPITAL Tallinn
LARGEST CITY Tallinn
HIGHEST POINT Munamägi 1,048 ft. (318 m.)
MAJOR LANGUAGES Estonian, Russian, Ukrainian
MAJOR RELIGIONS Protestantism (Lutheran), Roman Catholicism, Eastern (Russian) Orthodoxy

LATVIA

AREA 24,595 sq. mi. (63,700 sq. km.)
POPULATION 2,681,000
CAPITAL Riga
LARGEST CITY Riga
HIGHEST POINT Gaizina 1,020 ft. (311 m.)
MAJOR LANGUAGES Latvian, Russian, Belorussian, Ukrainian, Polish
MAJOR RELIGIONS Protestantism (Lutheran), Roman Catholicism, Eastern (Russian) Orthodoxy

LITHUANIA

AREA 25,174 sq. mi. (65,200 sq. km.)
POPULATION 3,690,000
CAPITAL Vilnius (Vilna)
LARGEST CITY Vilnius (Vilna)
HIGHEST POINT Nevaišių 932 ft. (298 m.)
MAJOR LANGUAGES Lithuanian, Russian, Polish, Belorussian, Ukrainian
MAJOR RELIGIONS Roman Catholicism, Eastern (Russian) Orthodoxy

Alytus 55,000 .... C 3
Biržai 11,400 .... C 2
Cēsis 17,696 .... C 2
Daugava (Western Dvina) (riv.) .... D 2
Daugavpils 127,000 .... D 3
Dobele 10,100 .... B 2
Druskininkai 11,200 .... C 3
Dvina, Western (riv.) .... C 2
Finland (gulf) .... D 1
Gauja (riv.) .... C 2
Haapsalu 11,483 .... B 1
Hiiumaa (isl.) .... B 1
Jēkabpils 22,440 .... C 2
Jelgava 68,000 .... B 2
Jonava 14,400 .... C 3
Jūrmala 61,000 .... B 2
Kapsukas 28,763 .... B 3
Kaunas 423,000 .... C 3
Kedainiai 19,677 .... C 3
Kihnu (isl.) .... B 1
Kingisepp (Kuressaare) 12,140 .... B 1
Kiviõli 11,153 .... D 1
Klaipeda 204,000 .... A 3
Kohtla-Järve 73,000 .... D 1
Kretinga 13,000 .... A 3
Kuldīga 12,300 .... A 2
Kuressaare 12,140 .... B 1
Kuršenai 11,500 .... B 2
Liepāja 114,000 .... A 2
Lubāna (lake) .... D 2
Mažeikiai 13,400 .... A 2
Memel (Klaipeda) 204,000 .... A 3
Muhu (isl.) .... B 1
Narva 73,000 .... E 1
Naujoji-Akmene 10,200 .... B 2
Nemunas (Niemen) (riv.) .... A 3
Niemen (riv.) .... A 3
Ogre 15,708 .... C 2
Panevežys 126,000 .... C 3
Pärnu 51,000 .... C 1
Peipus (lake) .... D 1
Plunge 13,600 .... B 3
Radvilikškis 16,841 .... B 3
Rakvere 17,891 .... D 1
Rēzekne 30,803 .... D 2
Riga (cap.), Latvia 915,000 .... C 2
Riga (gulf) .... B 2
Saaremaa (isl.) .... B 1
Saldus 10,000 .... B 2
Šiauliai 145,000 .... B 3
Sillamäe 13,505 .... D 1
Šilute 12,400 .... A 3
Tallinn (cap.), Estonia 482,000 .... C 1
Tapa 10,037 .... C 1
Tartu 114,000 .... D 1
Taurage 19,461 .... B 3
Telšiai 20,220 .... B 2
Tukums 14,800 .... B 2
Ukmerge 21,663 .... C 3
Utena 13,300 .... C 3
Valga 16,795 .... D 2
Valmiera 20,331 .... C 2
Venta (riv.) .... B 2
Ventspils 40,467 .... A 2
Viliya (riv.) .... C 3
Viljandi 20,814 .... C 1
Vilnius (Vilna) (cap.), Lithuania 582,000 .... C 3
Vormsi (isl.) .... B 1
Võrtsjärv (lake) .... D 1
Võru 15,398 .... D 2
Western Dvina (riv.) .... C 2

ARMENIA

CITIES and TOWNS

Kirovakan 162,000 .... F6
Kumayri 120,000 .... F6
Leninakan (Kumayri) 120,000 .... F6
Yerevan (cap.) 1,199,000 .... F6

OTHER FEATURES

Alagez (mt.) F6
Araks (riv.) G7
Caucasus (mts.) F6
Kapydzhik (mt.) G7
Sevan (lake) G6

AZERBAIJAN

INTERNAL DIVISIONS

Nagorno-Karabakh Aut. Obl. 188,000 .... G7
Nakhichevan' Aut. Rep. 295,000 .... F7

CITIES and TOWNS

Baku (cap.) 1,150,000 .... H6
Gyandzhe 278,000 .... G6
Kirovabad (Gyandzhe) 278,000 .... G6
Mingechaur 60,000 .... G6
Nakhichevan' 33,279 .... G7
Stepanakert 30,293 .... G7
Sumgait 231,000 .... G6

OTHER FEATURES

Apsheron (pen.) H6
Araks (riv.) G7
Caspian (sea) G6
Caucasus (mts.) F6
Kura (riv.) G6

BELARUS (BELORUSSIA)

CITIES and TOWNS

Baranovichi 159,000 .... C4
Bobruysk 223,000 .... C4
Borisov 144,000 .... C4
Brest 258,000 .... B4
Gomel' 500,000 .... D4
Grodno 270,000 .... B4
Lida 73,000 .... C4
Minsk (cap.) 1,589,000 .... C4
Mogilev 356,000 .... C4
Molodechno 82,000 .... C4
Mozyr' 101,000 .... C4
Orsha 123,000 .... D4
Pinsk 119,000 .... C4
Polotsk 71,000 .... C3
Rechitsa 67,000 .... C4
Soligorsk 82,000 .... C4
Vitebsk 350,000 .... C3

OTHER FEATURES

Berezina (riv.) C4
Bug (riv.) B4
Dnieper (riv.) D5
Dvina, Western (riv.) C3
Goryn' (riv.) C4
Niemen (riv.) B4
Pripet (marshes) C4
Pripyat' (riv.) C4
Western Dvina (riv.) C3

GEORGIA

INTERNAL DIVISIONS

Abkhaz Aut. Rep. 537,000 .... F6
Adzhar Aut. Rep. 393,000 .... F6
South Ossetian Aut. Obl. 99,000 .... F6

CITIES and TOWNS

Batumi 136,000 .... F6
Gori 60,000 .... F6
Kutaisi 235,000 .... F6
Makaradzhe (Ozurgeti) 21,679 .... F6
Ozurgeti 21,679 .... F6
Poti 45,979 .... F6
Rustavi 159,000 .... G6
Sukhumi 121,000 .... F6
Tbilisi (cap.) 1,260,000 .... F6
Tiflis (Tbilisi) 1,260,000 .... F6
Tskhinvali 30,311 .... F6

OTHER FEATURES

Black (sea) D6
Caucasus (mts.) F6

MOLDOVA (MOLDAVIA)

CITIES and TOWNS

Bel'tsy 159,000 .... C5
Bendery 130,000 .... C5
Kishinev (cap.) 665,000 .... C5
Tighina (Bendery) 130,000 .... C5
Tiraspol' 182,000 .... D5

OTHER FEATURES

Black (sea) D6
Dniester (riv.) C5
Prut (riv.) C5

RUSSIA

INTERNAL DIVISIONS

Adygey Aut. Obl. 432,000 .... F6
Bashkir Aut. Rep. 3,952,000 .... J4
Chechen-Ingush Aut. Rep. 1,277,000 .... G6
Chuvash Aut. Rep. 1,336,000 .... G3
Dagestan Aut. Rep. 1,792,000 .... G6
Kabardin-Balkar Aut. Rep. 760,000 .... F6
Kalmuck Aut. Rep. 322,000 .... F5
Karachay-Cherkess Aut. Obl. 418,000 .... F6
Karelian Aut. Rep. 792,000 .... D2
Komi Aut. Rep. 1,263,000 .... H2
Komi-Permyak Aut. Okr. 159,000 .... H3
Mari Aut. Rep. 750,000 .... G3
Mordvinian Aut. Rep. 964,000 .... G4
Nenets Aut. Okr. 55,000 .... H1
North Ossetian Aut. Rep. 634,000 .... F6
Tatar Aut. Rep. 3,640,000 .... G3
Udmurt Aut. Rep. 1,609,000 .... H3

CITIES and TOWNS

Akhtubinsk 51,000 .... G5
Al'met'yevsk 129,000 .... H3
Archangel (Arkhangel'sk) 416,000 .... F2
Armavir 161,000 .... F5
Arzamas 109,000 .... F3
Astrakhan' 509,000 .... G5
Azov 79,000 .... E5
Balakovo 198,000 .... G4
Balashov 97,000 .... F4
Bataysk 95,000 .... E5
Belgorod 300,000 .... E4
Berezniki 201,000 .... J3
Borisoglebsk 63,000 .... F4
Borovichi 63,000 .... D3
Bryansk 452,000 .... D4
Bugul'ma 85,000 .... H4
Buzuluk 76,000 .... H4
Chapayevsk 86,000 .... G4
Chaykovskiy 76,000 .... H3
Cheboksary 420,000 .... G3
Cherepovets 310,000 .... E3
Cherkessk 113,000 .... F6
Chistopol' 65,000 .... H3
Derbent 78,000 .... G6
Dimitrovgrad 124,000 .... G4
Dzerzhinsk 285,000 .... F3
Elektrostal' 153,000 .... E3
Elista 80,000 .... F5
Engel's 182,000 .... G4
Gatchina 78,000 .... D3
Glazov 104,000 .... H3
Groznyy 401,000 .... G6
Gubkin 70,000 .... E4
Gukovo 71,000 .... F5
Gus'-Khrustal'nyy 74,000 .... F3
Ishimbay 63,000 .... J4
Ivanovo 481,000 .... E3
Izhevsk 635,000 .... H3
Kaliningrad, Kaliningrad 401,000 .... B4
Kaliningrad, Moscow Oblast 160,000 .... E3
Kaluga 312,000 .... E4
Kamensk-Shakhtinskiy 75,000 .... F5
Kamyshin 122,000 .... F4
Kazan' 1,094,000 .... G3
Khasavyurt 72,000 .... G6
Kimry 60,000 .... E3
Kineshma 105,000 .... F3
Kirov 441,000 .... G3
Kirovo-Chepetsk 83,000 .... H3
Kislovodsk 114,000 .... F6
Klintsy 71,000 .... D4
Kolomna 162,000 .... E4
Kolpino 142,000 .... D3
Königsberg (Kaliningrad) 410,000 .... B4
Kostroma 278,000 .... F3
Kotlas 66,000 .... G2
Kovrov 160,000 .... F3
Krasnodar 620,000 .... E6
Kropotkin 73,000 .... F5
Kungur 82,000 .... J3
Kursk 424,000 .... E4
Kuznetsk 97,000 .... G4
Leningrad (St. Petersburg) 4,456,000 .... C3
Lipetsk 450,000 .... E4
Lys'va 76,000 .... J3
Lyubertsy 165,000 .... E3
Makhachkala 315,000 .... G6
Maykop 149,000 .... F6
Michurinsk 109,000 .... F4
Mineral'nye Vody 72,000 .... F6
Moscow (Moskva) (cap.) 8,769,000 .... E3
Murmansk 468,000 .... D1
Murom 124,000 .... F3
Mytishchi 154,000 .... E3
Naberezhnye Chelny 501,000 .... H3
Nal'chik 235,000 .... F6
Neftekamsk 107,000 .... H3
Nevinnomyssk 121,000 .... F6
Nizhnekamsk 191,000 .... H3
Nizhniy Novgorod (Gor'kiy) 1,438,000 .... F3
Novgorod 229,000 .... D3
Novocherkassk 187,000 .... F5
Novokuybyshevsk 113,000 .... G4
Novomoskovsk 146,000 .... E4
Novorossiysk 186,000 .... E6
Novoshakhtinsk 106,000 .... E5
Novotroitsk 106,000 .... J4
Obninsk 100,000 .... E3
Oktyabr'skiy 105,000 .... H4
Ordzhonikidze (Vladikavkaz) 300,000 .... F6
Orekhovo-Zuyevo 137,000 .... D3
Orel 337,000 .... E4
Orenburg 547,000 .... J4
Orsk 271,000 .... J4
Penza 483,000 .... G4
Perm' (Molotov) 1,091,000 .... J3
Petrozavodsk 270,000 .... D2
Podol'sk 210,000 .... E3
Pskov 204,000 .... C3
Pyatigorsk 129,000 .... F6
Rostov 1,020,000 .... F5
Ryazan' 515,000 .... E4
Rybinsk 252,000 .... E3
Rzhev 70,000 .... D3
St. Petersburg 4,456,000 .... C3
Salavat 150,000 .... H4
Samara (Kuybyshev) 1,257,000 .... H4
Saransk 312,000 .... G4
Sarapul 111,000 .... H3
Saratov 905,000 .... G4
Sergiyev Posad 115,000 .... E3
Serpukhov 144,000 .... E4
Sevastopol' 356,000 .... D6
Severodvinsk 249,000 .... E2
Shakhty 224,000 .... F5
Shchekino 70,000 .... E4
Shuya 72,000 .... F3
Simbirsk 625,000 .... G4
Smolensk 341,000 .... D4
Sochi 337,000 .... E6
Solikamsk 110,000 .... J3
Stalingrad (Volgograd) 999,000 .... F5
Staryy Oskol 174,000 .... E4
Stavropol' 318,000 .... F5
Sterlitamak 248,000 .... J4
Stupino 72,000 .... E4
Syktyvkar 233,000 .... H2
Syzran' 174,000 .... G4
Taganrog 291,000 .... E5
Tambov 305,000 .... F4
Togliatti (Tol'yatti) 630,000 .... G4
Tula 540,000 .... E4
Tver' (Kalinin) 451,000 .... E3
Ufa 1,083,000 .... J4
Ukhta 111,000 .... H2
Ul'yanovsk (Simbirsk) 625,000 .... G4
Velikiye Luki 114,000 .... D3
Viipuri (Vyborg) 79,000 .... C2
Vladikavkaz 300,000 .... F6
Vladimir 350,000 .... F3
Volgodonsk 176,000 .... F5
Volgograd 999,000 .... F5
Vologda 283,000 .... F3
Volzhskiy 269,000 .... G5
Vorkuta 116,000 .... K1
Voronezh 887,000 .... E4
Voskresensk 79,000 .... E3
Votkinsk 103,000 .... H3
Vyborg 79,000 .... C2
Vyshniy Volochek 71,000 .... D3
Yaroslavl' 633,000 .... E3
Yelets 120,000 .... E4
Yessentuki 82,000 .... F6
Yeysk 75,000 .... E5
Yoshkar-Ola 242,000 .... G3
Zagorsk (Sergiyev Posad) 115,000 .... E3
Zelenodol'sk 88,000 .... G3
Zheleznodorozhnyy 76,000 .... H2
Zheleznogorsk 74,000 .... E4

OTHER FEATURES

Azov (sea) E5
Baltic (sea) B3
Barents (sea) E1
Baydarata (bay) L1
Belaya (riv.) H3
Beloye (lake) E2
Black (sea) D6
Bolvanskiy Nos (cape) K1
Caspian (sea) G6
Caucasus (mts.) F6
Central Ural (mts.) J2
Cheshskaya (bay) G1
Chir (riv.) F5
Denezhkin Kamen' (mt.) J2
Desna (riv.) D4
Dnieper (riv.) D5
Dolgiy (isl.) J1
Don (riv.) F5
Dvina (bay) E2
Dvina (riv.) F2
Dykhtau (mt.) F6
El'brus (mt.) F6
Finland (gulf) C3
Ilek (riv.) J4
Il'men' (lake) D3
Imandra (lake) D1
Izhma (riv.) H2
Kama (res.) J3
Kama (riv.) H2
Kandalaksha (gulf) D1
Kanin (pen.) G1
Kanin Nos (cape) F1
Kara (sea) K1
Karskiye Vorota (str.) J1
Kazbek (mt.) F6
Khoper (riv.) F4
Kil'din (isl.) D1
Kinel' (riv.) H4
Kola (pen.) E1
Kolguyev (isl.) G1
Kolva (riv.) J1
Kuban' (riv.) E5
Kubeno (lake) E3
Kuma (riv.) G5
Kuybyshev (res.) G4
Kuyto (lake) D2
Lacha (lake) E2
Ladoga (lake) D2
Lapland (reg.) D1
Lovat' (riv.) D3
Mansel'ka (mts.) C1
Manych-Gudilo (lake) F5
Matveyev (isl.) J1
Medveditsa (riv.) F4
Mezen' (bay) F1
Mezen' (riv.) G1
Mezhdusharskiy (isl.) H1
Moksha (riv.) F4
Moskva (riv.) E3
Msta (riv.) D3
Narodnaya (mt.) J1
Northern Dvina (riv.) F2
North Ural (mts.) K1
Novaya Zemlya (isls.) H1
Oka (riv.) F4
Onega (bay) E2
Onega (lake) E2
Onega (riv.) E2
Payyer (mt.) K1
Pechora (bay) H1
Pechora (riv.) H1
Pechora (sea) H1
Peipus (lake) C3
Pinega (riv.) G2
Ponoy (riv.) E1
Russkiy Zavorot (cape) H1
Rybachiy (pen.) D1
Rybinsk (res.) E3
Samara (riv.) H4
Seg (lake) D2
Solovetskiye (isls.) E1
South Ural (mts.) J4
Suda (riv.) E3
Sukhona (riv.) F2
Sura (riv.) G4
Svir' (riv.) D2
Sysola (riv.) H2
Tel'pos-Iz (mt.) K2
Timan (ridge) G1
Top (lake) D1
Tsil'ma (riv.) H1
Tsimlyansk (res.) F5
Tuloma (riv.) D1
Ufa (riv.) J3
Unzha (riv.) F3
Ural (mts.) J2
Ural (riv.) J4
Usa (riv.) K1
Vaga (riv.) F2
Valday (hills) D3
Vashka (riv.) G2
Vaygach (isl.) K1
Velikaya (riv.) C3
Vetluga (riv.) G3
Vishera (riv.) J2
Vodl (lake) E2
Volga (riv.) G5
Volga-Don (canal) F5
Volgograd (res.) G5
Volkhov (riv.) D3
Vorona (riv.) F4
Vorskla (riv.) E4
Vozhe (lake) F2
Vyatka (riv.) H3
Vychegda (riv.) G2
Vyg (lake) E2
Vym' (riv.) H2
Western Dvina (riv.) C3
White (sea) E1
Yamantau (mt.) J4
Yug (riv.) G2
Yugorskiy (pen.) K1

UKRAINE

INTERNAL DIVISIONS

Crimean Oblast 2,456,000 .... D6
Trans-Carpathian Obl. 1,252,000 .... B5
Volyn Oblast 1,062,000 .... C4

CITIES and TOWNS

Aleksandriya 103,000 .... D5
Balaklava D6
Belaya Tserkov' 197,000 .... C5
Belgorod-Dnestrovskiy 51,000 .... D5
Berdichev 85,000 .... C5
Berdyansk 132,000 .... E5
Cherkassy 290,000 .... D5
Chernigov 296,000 .... D4
Chernovtsy 257,000 .... C5
Dneprodzerzhinsk 282,000 .... D5
Dnepropetrovsk 1,179,000 .... D5
Donetsk 1,110,000 .... E5
Drogobych 73,000 .... B5
Feodosiya 81,000 .... D5
Gorlovka 337,000 .... E5
Ivano-Frankovsk 214,000 .... B5
Izmail 87,000 .... C5
Kadiyevka (Stakhanov) 112,000 .... E5
Kalush 64,000 .... B5
Kamenets-Podol'skiy 102,000 .... C5
Kerch' 174,000 .... E5
Khar'kov 1,611,000 .... E5
Kherson 355,000 .... D5
Khmel'nitskiy 237,000 .... C5
Kiev (cap.) 2,587,000 .... D4
Kirovograd 269,000 .... D5
Lugansk 497,000 .... E5
Lutsk 198,000 .... B4
Lviv (L'vov) (Lwów) 790,000 .... B5
Makeyevka 430,000 .... E5
Mariupol' 517,000 .... E5
Melitopol' 174,000 .... D5
Mukachevo 82,000 .... B5
Nikolayev 503,000 .... D5
Nikopol' 158,000 .... D5
Odessa 1,115,000 .... D5
Osipenko (Berdyansk) 132,000 .... E5
Pavlograd 131,000 .... E5
Pervomaysk 76,000 .... D5
Poltava 315,000 .... D5
Priluki 70,000 .... D4
Rovno 228,000 .... C4
Rubezhnoye 68,000 .... E5
Sevastopol' 356,000 .... D6
Severodonetsk 131,000 .... E5
Shostka 82,000 .... D4
Simferopol' 344,000 .... D6
Slavyansk 135,000 .... E5
Smela 70,000 .... D5
Stakhanov 112,000 .... E5
Sumy 291,000 .... E4
Ternopol' 205,000 .... C5
Uman' 85,000 .... D5
Uzhgorod 117,000 .... B5
Vinnitsa 374,000 .... C5
Voroshilovgrad (Lugansk) 497,000 .... E5
Yalta 85,000 .... D6
Yenakiyevo 121,000 .... E5
Yevpatoriya 108,000 .... D5
Zaporozh'ye 884,000 .... E5
Zhitomir 292,000 .... C4

OTHER FEATURES

Azov (sea) E5
Berezina (riv.) C4
Black (sea) D6
Bug (riv.) B4
Crimea (pen.) D5
Desna (riv.) D4
Dnieper (riv.) D5
Dniester (riv.) C5
Donets (riv.) E5
Goryn' (riv.) C4
Kakhovka (res.) D5
Kiev (res.) C4
Pripet (marshes) C4
Pripyat' (riv.) C4
Prut (riv.) C5
Psel (riv.) D4
Seym (riv.) D4
Vorskla (riv.) E4

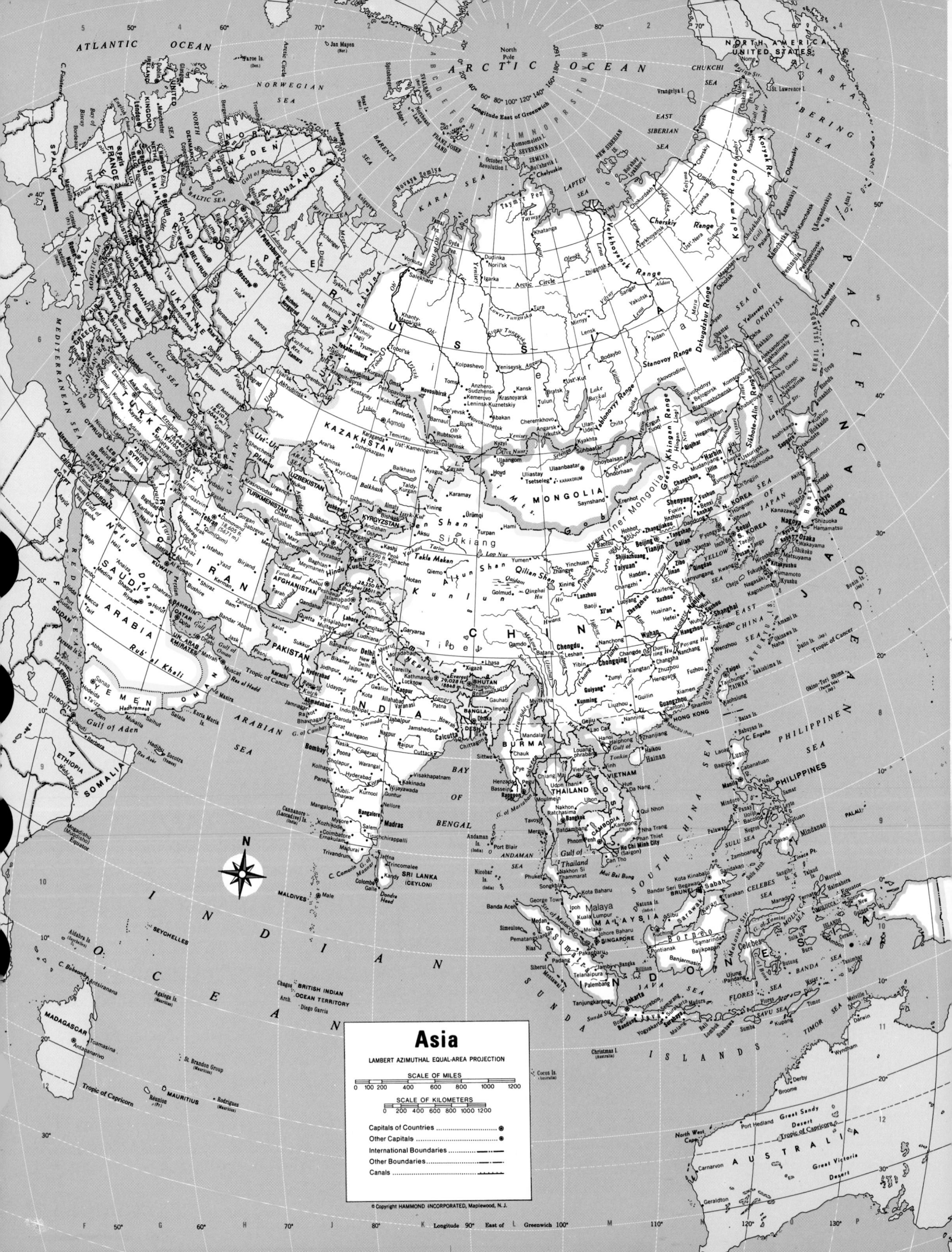

Asia

LAMBERT AZIMUTHAL EQUAL-AREA PROJECTION

SCALE OF MILES
0 100 200   400   600   800   1000   1200

SCALE OF KILOMETERS
0   200 400 600 800 1000 1200

Capitals of Countries .... ⊛
Other Capitals .... ⊙
International Boundaries ....
Other Boundaries...................
Canals ....

© Copyright HAMMOND INCORPORATED, Maplewood, N.J.

Population Distribution

AREA 17,128,500 sq. mi.
(44,362,815 sq. km.)
POPULATION 3,176,000,000
LARGEST CITY Tokyo
HIGHEST POINT Mt. Everest 29,028 ft.
(8,848 m.)
LOWEST POINT Dead Sea -1,296 ft.
(-395 m.)

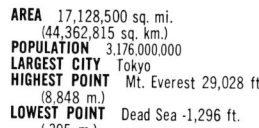

Vegetation

DENSITY PER

SQ. KILOMETER	SQ. MILE
Over 100	Over 260
50-100	130-260
10-50	25-130
1-10	3-25
Under 1	Under 3

• Cities with over 3,000,000
inhabitants (including suburbs)

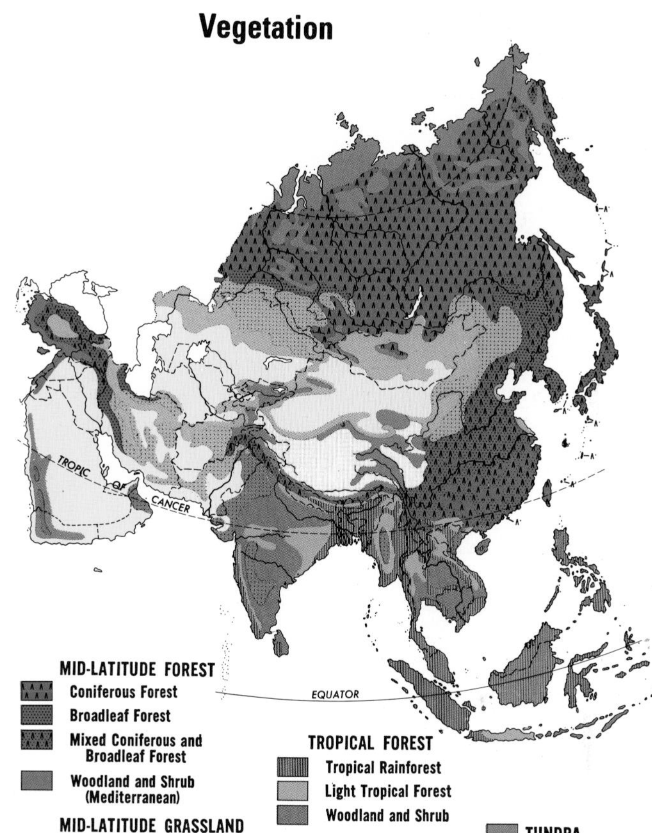

MID-LATITUDE FOREST
Coniferous Forest
Broadleaf Forest
Mixed Coniferous and Broadleaf Forest
Woodland and Shrub (Mediterranean)

MID-LATITUDE GRASSLAND
Short Grass (Steppe)
Wooded Steppe

DESERT AND DESERT SHRUB

TROPICAL FOREST
Tropical Rainforest
Light Tropical Forest
Woodland and Shrub

TROPICAL GRASSLAND
Grass and Shrub (Savanna)
Wooded Savanna

TUNDRA AND ALPINE

UNCLASSIFIED HIGHLANDS

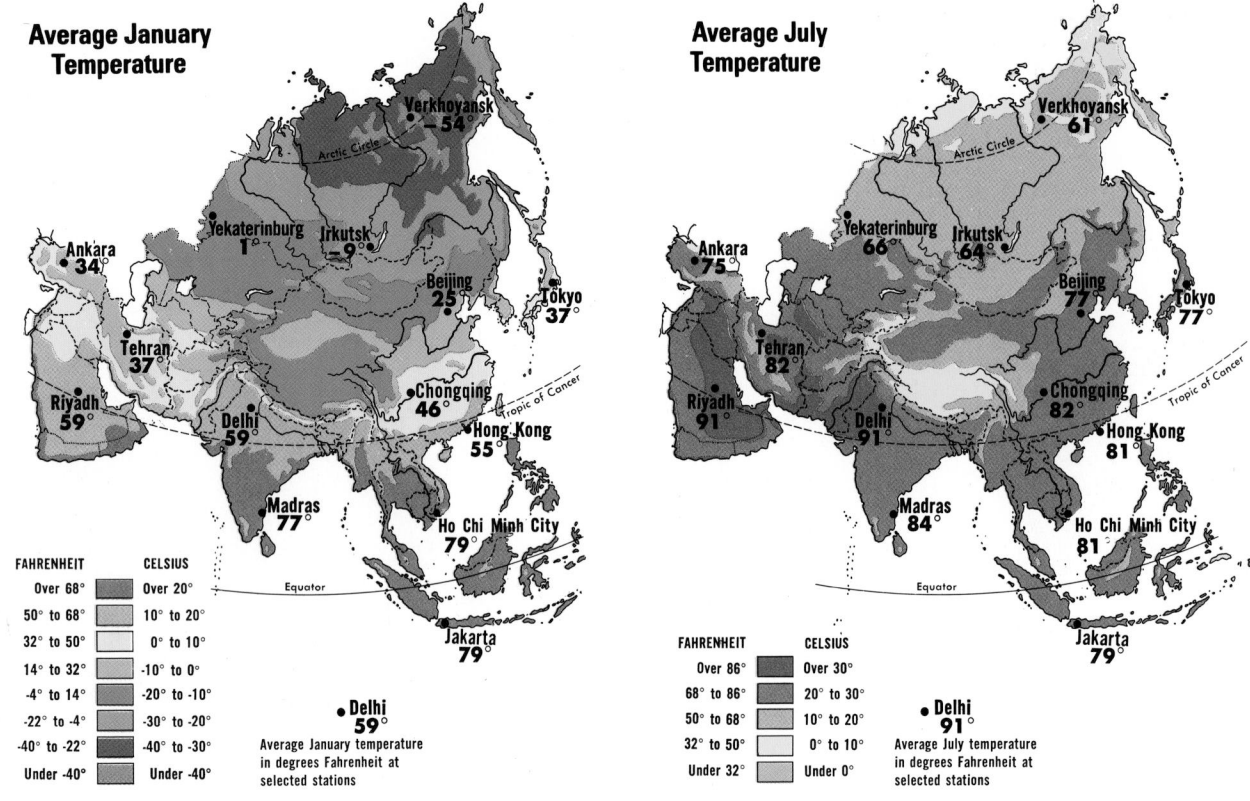

Average January Temperature

Verkhoyansk −54°
Yekaterinburg 1°
Irkutsk −9°
Ankara 34°
Beijing 25°
Tokyo 37°
Tehran 37°
Chongqing 46°
Riyadh 59°
Delhi 59°
Hong Kong 55°
Madras 77°
Ho Chi Minh City 79°
Jakarta 79°

Arctic Circle
Tropic of Cancer
Equator

FAHRENHEIT	CELSIUS
Over 68°	Over 20°
50° to 68°	10° to 20°
32° to 50°	0° to 10°
14° to 32°	-10° to 0°
-4° to 14°	-20° to -10°
-22° to -4°	-30° to -20°
-40° to -22°	-40° to -30°
Under -40°	Under -40°

• Delhi 59°
Average January temperature in degrees Fahrenheit at selected stations

Average July Temperature

Verkhoyansk 61°
Yekaterinburg 66°
Irkutsk 64°
Ankara 75°
Beijing 77°
Tokyo 77°
Tehran 82°
Chongqing 82°
Riyadh 91°
Delhi 91°
Hong Kong 81°
Madras 84°
Ho Chi Minh City 81°
Jakarta 79°

Arctic Circle
Tropic of Cancer
Equator

FAHRENHEIT	CELSIUS
Over 86°	Over 30°
68° to 86°	20° to 30°
50° to 68°	10° to 20°
32° to 50°	0° to 10°
Under 32°	Under 0°

• Delhi 91°
Average July temperature in degrees Fahrenheit at selected stations

Rainfall

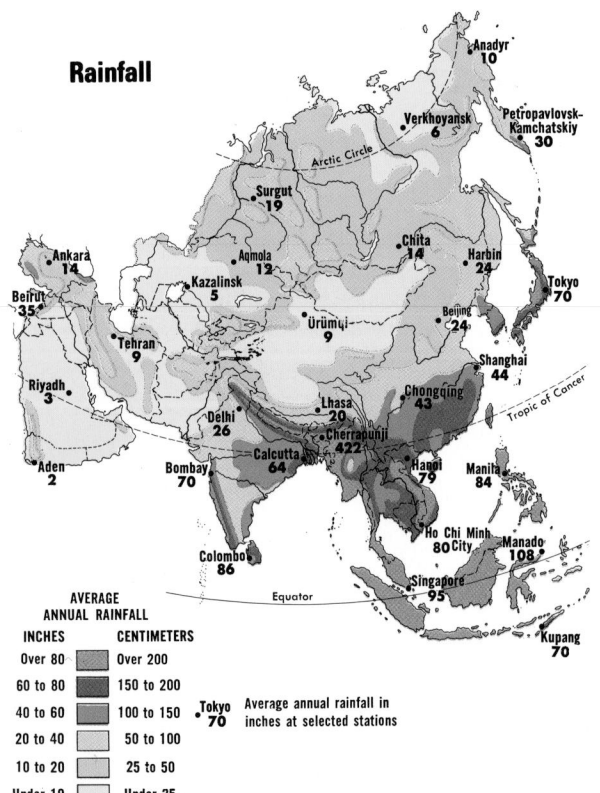

Anadyr 10
Verkhoyansk 6
Petropavlovsk-Kamchatskiy 30
Surgut 19
Ankara 14
Aqmola 12
Chita 14
Harbin 24
Beirut 35
Kazalinsk 5
Tokyo 70
Tehran 9
Ürümqi 9
Beijing 24
Riyadh 3
Shanghai 44
Lhasa 20
Chongqing 43
Delhi 26
Cherrapunji 422
Tropic of Cancer
Aden 2
Calcutta 64
Hanoi 79
Manila 84
Bombay 70
Ho Chi Minh City 80
Manado 108
Colombo 86
Singapore 95
Equator
Kupang 70

Arctic Circle

AVERAGE ANNUAL RAINFALL

INCHES	CENTIMETERS
Over 80	Over 200
60 to 80	150 to 200
40 to 60	100 to 150
20 to 40	50 to 100
10 to 20	25 to 50
Under 10	Under 25

• Tokyo 70
Average annual rainfall in inches at selected stations

Vegetation/Relief

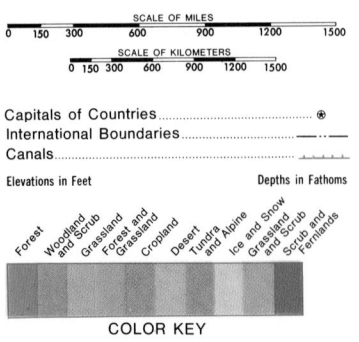

SCALE OF MILES
0 150 300   600   900   1200   1500

SCALE OF KILOMETERS
0 150 300   600   900   1200   1500

Capitals of Countries .... ⊛
International Boundaries ....
Canals ....

Elevations in Feet   Depths in Fathoms

Forest
Woodland and Scrub
Grassland
Forest and Grassland
Cropland
Desert
Tundra and Alpine
Ice and Snow
Grassland and Scrub
Scrub and Fernlands

COLOR KEY

North Pole
ARCTIC OCEAN
ATLANTIC OCEAN
NORWEGIAN SEA
NORTH SEA
BARENTS SEA
KARA SEA
LAPTEV SEA
EAST SIBERIAN SEA
BERING SEA
Bering Str.
C. Dezhnev
Alaska
UNITED STATES
Aleutian Islands
ICELAND
GREENLAND
Svalbard (Nor.)
Franz Josef Ld.
Severnaya Zemlya
Novaya Zemlya
New Siberian Is.
Chelyuskin
Nordkapp
Arctic Circle
IRELAND
UNITED KINGDOM
London
Bay of Biscay
English Chan.
PORTUGAL
FRANCE
Paris
Berlin
Rome
NORWAY
SWEDEN
FINLAND
BALTIC SEA
POLAND
BELARUS
UKRAINE
Danube
EUROPE
MEDITERRANEAN SEA
BLACK SEA
CASPIAN SEA
ARAL SEA
Moscow
Volga
Ural
Ural Mountains
Ob'
Yenisey
Lena
Angara
RUSSIA
Siberia
Chelyabinsk
Omsk
Novosibirsk
Krasnoyarsk
Yakutsk
Lake Baykal
Yablonovyy Ra.
Kamchatka Peninsula
SEA OF OKHOTSK
Sakhalin
Kuril Is.
PACIFIC OCEAN
KAZAKHSTAN
L. Balkhash
Karaganda
Almaty
UZBEKISTAN
TURKMENISTAN
KYRGYZSTAN
Tashkent
Tarim
Taklimakan
MONGOLIA
Ulaanbaatar
Gobi
Great Khingan Ra.
Harbin
Shenyang
Beijing
Tianjin
Dalian
N. KOREA
S. KOREA
Seoul
SEA OF JAPAN
JAPAN
Hokkaido
Honshu
Tokyo
Nagoya
Osaka
Shikoku
Kyushu
YELLOW SEA
EAST CHINA SEA
Shanghai
Nanjing
Wuhan
Chengdu
Chongqing
Lanzhou
Xi'an
CHINA
Tibet
Ryukyu Is.
Taipei
Taiwan
Tropic of Cancer
Guangzhou
HONG KONG
Hainan
TURKEY
CYPRUS
LEBANON
SYRIA
ISRAEL
JORDAN
IRAQ
Baghdad
Euphrates
IRAN
Tehran
KUWAIT
SAUDI ARABIA
Riyadh
BAHRAIN
QATAR
U.A.E.
OMAN
Muscat
Gulf of Oman
Rub' al Khali
YEMEN
Aden
Gulf of Aden
Cairo
EGYPT
Nile
RED SEA
SUDAN
ERITREA
ETHIOPIA
SOMALIA
Ras Aser
Socotra
AFGHANISTAN
Kabul
Hindu Kush
PAKISTAN
Islamabad
Lahore
Karachi
Indus
INDIA
Delhi
New Delhi
Kanpur
Ganges
Ahmadabad
Narbada
Bombay
Godavari
Hyderabad
Krishna
Western Ghats
Madras
Bangalore
Calcutta
Dhaka
BANGLADESH
Brahmaputra
C. Comorin
SRI LANKA (CEYLON)
Colombo
Dondra Head
MALDIVES
ARABIAN SEA
BAY OF BENGAL
Andaman Is.
ANDAMAN SEA
Nicobar Is.
BURMA
Rangoon
THAILAND
Bangkok
CAMBODIA
VIETNAM
Hanoi
Ho Chi Minh City
Gulf of Siam
SOUTH CHINA SEA
PHILIPPINES
Luzon
C. Engaño
Manila
Palawan
Mindanao
SULU SEA
CELEBES SEA
Celebes
BANDA SEA
MALAYSIA
Kuala Lumpur
SINGAPORE
BRUNEI
Borneo
Sumatra
Jakarta
Java
Surabaya
JAVA SEA
FLORES SEA
Timor
TIMOR SEA
INDONESIA
Sunda Islands
New Guinea
Equator
SEYCHELLES
COMOROS
BRITISH INDIAN OCEAN TERR.
INDIAN OCEAN
MADAGASCAR
Réunion (Fr.)
MAURITIUS
Tropic of Capricorn
AUSTRALIA
Longitude 70° East of Greenwich

SAUDI ARABIA

KUWAIT

YEMEN

BAHRAIN

QATAR

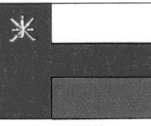
OMAN

AFGHANISTAN

CITIES and TOWNS

Andkhvoy 13,137................H2
Aybak 33,016.....................J2
Baghlan 75,130..................J2
Bamian 7,355.....................J3
Chaghcharan 2,974............J3

Charikar 25,093.................J2
Farah 18,797......................H3
Feyzabad 10,142...............K2
Gardez 11,415...................J3
Ghazni 30,425...................J3
Ghurian 12,404..................H3
Herat 163,960....................H3
Jalalabad 56,384...............K3
Kabul (cap.) 905,108..........J3

Kalat (Qalat) 5,946............J3
Kandahar (Qandahar)
     178,409.......................J3
Khanabad 26,803..............J2
Kholm 28,078....................J2
Khowst...............................H3
Kuhestan...........................H3
Landay..............................H3
Lashkar Gah 26,646..........H3

Mazar-e Sharif 122,567......J2
Meymaneh 54,954.............H2
Pol-e Khomri 31,101...........J2
Qalat 5,946.......................J3
Qal'eh-ye Now 5,340.........H3
Qandahar 178,409............J3
Qonduz 107,191................J2
Sar-i Pol 15,699.................H2
Sheberghan 54,870...........H2

Taloqan 46,202.................J2
Zaranj 6,477.....................H3

OTHER FEATURES

Farah Rud (riv.)..................H3
Gowd-e Zerreh (depr.).......H4
Harirud (riv.)......................H3
Helmand (riv.)...................J3

Hindu Kush (mts.)..............J2
Kabul (riv.)........................K3
Konar (riv.)........................K2
Lurah (riv.).........................J3
Margow, Dasht-e (des.)......H3
Murghab (riv.)....................H2
Namaksar (salt lake).........H3
Nurestan (reg.)..................K2
Paropamisus (mts.)............H3

Qonduz (riv.).....................J2
Rigestan (reg.)..................H3
Vakhan (reg.).....................K2

BAHRAIN

CITIES and TOWNS

Manama (cap.) 88,785.......F4

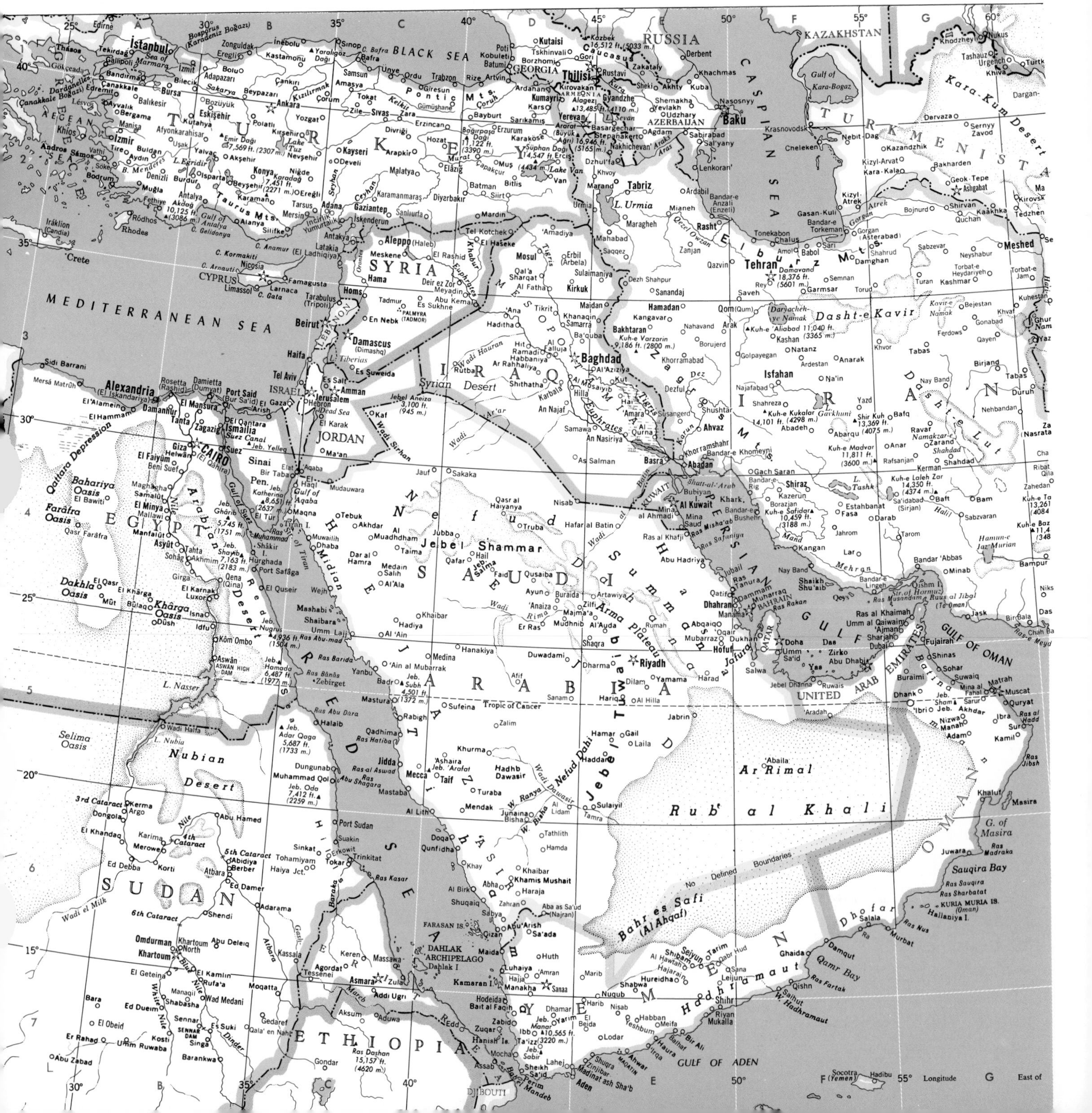

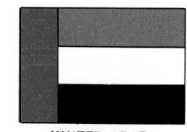

UNITED ARAB EMIRATES

Muharraq 37,732 ....F4

GAZA STRIP

CITIES and TOWNS

Gaza*
  118,272 ....B3

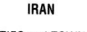

IRAN
CITIES and TOWNS

Abadan 296,081 ....E3
Abadeh 16,000 ....F3
Abarqu 8,000 ....F3
Ahvaz 329,006 ....E3
Amol 68,782 ....F2

Anarak 2,038 ....F3
Arak 114,507 ....E3
Ardabil 147,404 ....E2
Ardestan 5,868 ....F3
Asterabad (Gorgan) 88,348...F2
Babol 67,790 ....F2
Bafq 5,000 ....G3
Baft 6,000 ....G4
Bakhtaran 290,861 ....E3

Bam 22,000 ....G4
Bandar 'Abbas 89,103 ....G4
Bandar-e Anzali (Enzeli)
  55,978 ....E2
Bandar-e Bushehr 57,681 ....F4
Bandar-e Khomeyni 6,000....E3
Bandar-e Lengeh 4,920 ....F4
Bandar-e Rig 1,889 ....F4
Bandar-e Torkeman 13,000...F2

Bejestan 3,823 ....G3
Birjand 25,854 ....G3
Bojnurd 31,248 ....G2
Borazjan 20,000 ....F4
Borujerd 100,103 ....E3
Chalus 15,000 ....F2
Damghan 13,000 ....F2
Darab 13,000 ....G4
Dezful 110,287 ....E3

(continued on following page)

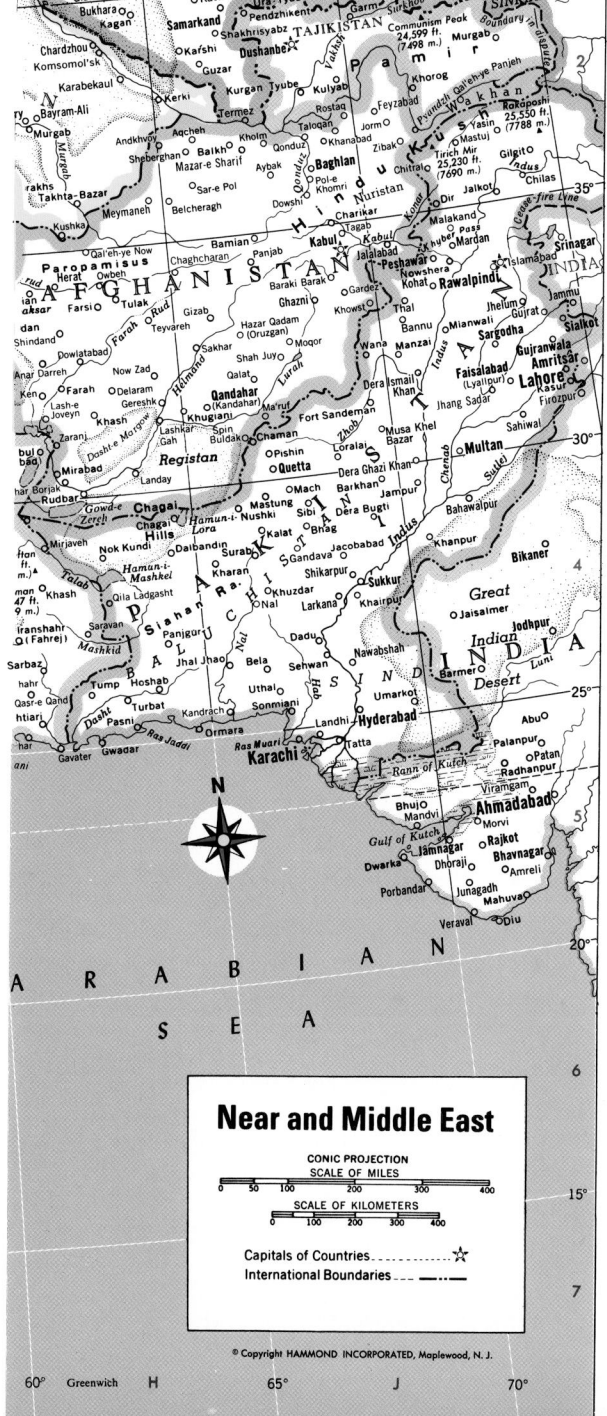

SAUDI ARABIA

AREA	829,995 sq. mi.
	(2,149,687 sq. km.)
POPULATION	14,435,000
CAPITAL	Riyadh
MONETARY UNIT	Saudi riyal
MAJOR LANGUAGE	Arabic
MAJOR RELIGION	Islam

YEMEN

AREA	188,321 sq. mi. (487,792 sq. km.)
POPULATION	10,183,000
CAPITAL	Sanaa
MONETARY UNIT	Yemeni rial
MAJOR LANGUAGE	Arabic
MAJOR RELIGION	Islam

QATAR

AREA	4,247 sq. mi. (11,000 sq. km.)
POPULATION	422,000
CAPITAL	Doha
MONETARY UNIT	Qatari riyal
MAJOR LANGUAGE	Arabic
MAJOR RELIGION	Islam

KUWAIT

AREA	6,532 sq. mi. (16,918 sq. km.)
POPULATION	2,048,000
CAPITAL	Al Kuwait
MONETARY UNIT	Kuwaiti dinar
MAJOR LANGUAGE	Arabic
MAJOR RELIGION	Islam

BAHRAIN

AREA	240 sq. mi. (622 sq. km.)
POPULATION	489,000
CAPITAL	Manama
MONETARY UNIT	Bahraini dinar
MAJOR LANGUAGE	Arabic
MAJOR RELIGION	Islam

OMAN

AREA	120,000 sq. mi. (310,800 sq. km.)
POPULATION	2,000,000
CAPITAL	Muscat
MONETARY UNIT	Omani rial
MAJOR LANGUAGE	Arabic
MAJOR RELIGION	Islam

UNITED ARAB EMIRATES

AREA	32,278 sq. mi. (83,600 sq. km.)
POPULATION	1,206,000
CAPITAL	Abu Dhabi
MONETARY UNIT	dirham
MAJOR LANGUAGE	Arabic
MAJOR RELIGION	Islam

Topography

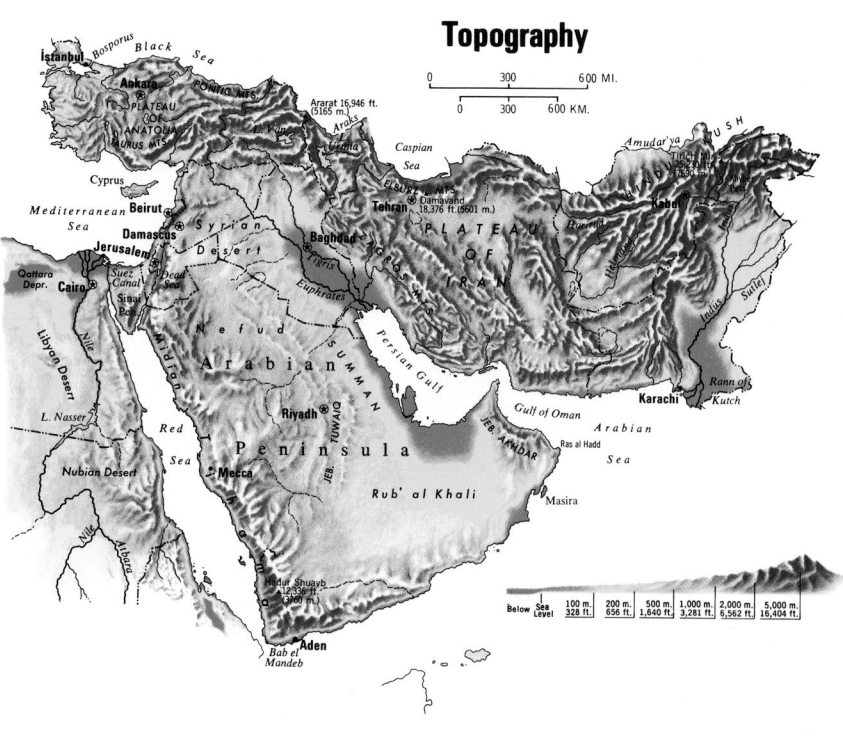

Near and Middle East

CONIC PROJECTION
SCALE OF MILES
0 50 100   200   300   400

SCALE OF KILOMETERS
0   100   200   300   400

Capitals of Countries .... ☆
International Boundaries ---------

© Copyright HAMMOND INCORPORATED, Maplewood, N.J.

(continued)

Dezh Shahpur 1,384 ....E2
Enzeli 55,978 ....E2
Estahbanat 18,187 ....F4
Fahrej (Iranshahr) 5,000....H4
Fasa 19,000....F4
Ferdows 11,000....G3
Garmsar 4,723....F2
Golpayegan 20,515....F3
Gonabad 8,000....G3
Gorgan 88,348....F2
Hamadan 155,846....E3
Iranshahr 5,000....H4
Isfahan 671,825....F3
Jahrom 38,236....F4
Jask 1,078....G4
Kangan 2,682....F4
Kangavar 9,414....E3
Kashan 84,545....F3
Kashmar 17,000....G2
Kazerun 51,309....F4
Kerman 140,309....G3
Khash 7,439....H4
Khorramabad 104,928....E3
Khorramshahr 146,709....E3
Khvaf 5,000....G3
Khvor 2,912....G3
Khvoy 70,040....E2
Lar 22,000....F4
Mahabad 28,610....E2
Maragheh 60,820....E2
Marand 24,000....E2
Meshed 670,180....H2
Mianeh 28,447....E2
Minab 4,228....G4
Mirjaveh 11,000....H4
Nahavand 24,000....E3
Na'in 5,925....F3
Najafabad 76,236....F3
Nasratabad (Zabol) 20,000....H3
Natanz 4,370....F3
Nehbandan 2,130....G3
Neyshabur 59,101....G2
Nikshahr 1,879....H4
Qasr-e Qand 1,879....H4
Qayen 6,000....G3
Qazvin 138,527....E2
Qom 246,831....F3
Quchan 29,133....G2
Qum (Qom) 246,831....F3
Rafsanjan 21,000....G3
Rasht 187,203....E2
Ravar 5,074....G3
Rey 102,825....F2
Reza'iyeh (Urmia) 163,991....D2
Sabzevar 69,174....G2
Sabzvaran 7,000....G4
Sa'idabad 20,000....G4
Sanandaj 95,834....E2
Saqqez 17,000....E2
Saravan 4,012....H4
Sari 70,936....F2
Saveh 17,565....F2
Semnan 31,058....F2
Shahdad 2,777....G3
Shahreza 34,220....F3
Shahrud 30,767....G2
Shiraz 416,408....F4
Shirvan 11,000....G2
Shushtar 24,000....E3
Sirjan (Sa'idabad) 20,000....G4
Susangerd 21,000....E3
Tabas 10,000....G3
Tabriz 598,576....E2
Tehran (cap.) 4,496,159....F2
Tonekabon 12,000....F2
Torbat-e Heydariyeh 30,106....G2
Torbat-e Jam 13,000....H2
Torud 721....F2
Urmia 163,991....D2
Yazd 135,978....F3
Zabol 20,000....H3
Zahedan 92,628....H4
Zanjan 99,967....E2
Zarand 5,000....G3

OTHER FEATURES

'Aliabad, Kuh-e (mt.)....F3
Aras (riv.)....E2
Bazman, Kuh-e (mt.)....H4
Damavand (mt.)....F2
Dez (riv.)....E3
Elburz (mts.)....F2
Euphrates (riv.)....E3
Gavkhuni (lake)....F3
Gorgan (riv.)....F2
Halil (riv.)....G4
Hormuz (str.)....G4
Jaz Murian, Hamun-e (marsh)....G4
Karun (riv.)....E3
Kavir, Dasht-e (salt des.)....G3
Kavir-e Namak (salt des.)....G3
Khark (isl.)....F4
Kukalar, Kuh-e (mt.)....F3
Laleh Zar, Kuh-e (mt.)....G4
Lut, Dasht-e (salt des.)....G3
Madvar, Kuh-e (mt.)....F3
Maidani, Ras (cape)....G4
Mand Rud (riv.)....F4
Mashkid (riv.)....H4
Mehran (riv.)....F4
Namak, Daryacheh-ye (salt lake)....F3
Namakzar-e Shahdad (salt lake)....G3
Oman (gulf)....G5
Persian (gulf)....F4
Qeshm (isl.)....G4
Qeys (isl.)....F4
Qezel Owzan (riv.)....E2
Safidar, Kuh-e (mt.)....F4
Shaikh Shu'aib (isl.)....F4
Shatt-al-'Arab (riv.)....E4
Shir Kuh (mt.)....F3
Taftan, Kuh-e (mt.)....H4
Talab (riv.)....H4
Tashk (lake)....F4
Tigris (riv.)....E3
Urmia (lake)....E2
Varzarin, Kuh-e (mt.)....E3
Zagros (mts.)....E3

IRAQ

CITIES and TOWNS

Al 'Aziziya 7,450....E3
Al Falluja 38,072....D3
Al Fatha 15,329....D2
Al Musaiyib 15,955....D3
Al Qurna 5,638....E3
'Amara 64,847....E3
'Ana 15,729....D3
An Najaf 128,096....D3
An Nasiriya 60,405....E3
Arbela (Erbil) 90,320....D2
Ar Rahhaliya 1,579....D3
As Salman 1,789....E3
Baghdad (cap.) 502,503....E3
Baghdad* 1,745,328....E3
Baq'uba 34,575....D3
Basra 313,327....E3
Erbil 90,320....D2
Habbaniya 14,405....D3
Haditha 6,870....D3
Hai 16,988....E3
Hilla 84,717....D3
Hit 9,131....D3
Karbal'a 83,301....D3
Khanaqin 23,522....D3
Kirkuk 167,413....D2
Kirkuk* 176,794....D2
Kut 42,116....E3
Mosul 315,157....D2
Qal'a Sharqat 2,434....D2
Ramadi 28,723....D3
Rutba 5,091....D3
Samarra 24,746....D3
Samawa 33,473....D3
Shithatha 2,326....D3
Sulaimaniya 86,822....E2
Tikrit 9,921....D3

OTHER FEATURES

'Ar'ar, Wadi (dry riv.)....D3
'Aneiza, Jebel (mt.)....C3
Batin, Wadi al (dry riv.)....E4
Euphrates (riv.)....E3
Hauran, Wadi (dry riv.)....D3
Mesopotamia (reg.)....D3
Persian (gulf)....F4
Shatt-al-'Arab (riv.)....E4
Syrian (El Hamad)(des.)....D3
Tigris (riv.)....E3

KUWAIT

CITIES and TOWNS

Al Kuwait (cap.) 181,774....E4
Mina al Ahmadi....E4
Mina Sa'ud....E4

OTHER FEATURES

Bubiyan (isl.)....E4
Persian (gulf)....F4

OMAN

CITIES and TOWNS

'Ibri....G5
Matrah 15,000....G5
Muscat (cap.) 7,500....G5
Quryat....G5
Raysut (Risut)....F6
Salala 4,000....F6
Sohar....G5
Suwaiq....G5

OTHER FEATURES

Akhdar, Jebel (range)....G5
Batina (reg.)....G5
Dhofar (reg.)....F6
Hadd, Ras al (cape)....G5
Hallaniya (isl.)....G6
Hormuz (str.)....G4
Jibsh, Ras (cape)....G5
Kuria Muria (isls.)....G6
Madraka, Ras (cape)....G6
Masira (gulf)....G6
Masira (isl.)....G5
Musandam, Ras (cape)....G4
Nus, Ras (cape)....G6
Oman (gulf)....G5
Oman (reg.)....G5
Ruus al Jibal (dist.)....G4
Sauqira (bay)....G6
Sauqira, Ras (cape)....G6
Sham, Jebel (mt.)....G5
Sharbatat, Ras (cape)....G6

QATAR

CITIES and TOWNS

Doha (cap.) 150,000....F4
Dukhan....F4
Umm Sa'id....F5

OTHER FEATURES

Persian (gulf)....F4
Rakan, Ras (cape)....F4

SAUDI ARABIA

CITIES and TOWNS

Aba as Sa'ud 47,501....D6
Abha 30,150....D6
Abu 'Arish....D6
Abu Hadriya....E4
'Ain al Mubarrak....C5
Al 'Ain....E4
Al Birk....D6
Al Hilla....E5
Al Lidam....D5
Al Muadhdham....C4
'Anaiza....D4
Artawiya....E4
Ayun....D4
Badr....C5
Bisha....D5
Buraida 69,940....D4
Dammam 127,844....F4
Dhaba....C4
Dhahran....E4
Dilam....E5
El Haql....C4
Er Ras....D4
Hadiya....C4
Hafar al Batin....E4
Hail 40,502....D4
Hofuf 101,271....E4
Jauf....C4
Jidda 561,104....C5
Jizan (Qizan) 32,812....D6
Jubail....E4
Jubba....D4
Kaf....C3
Khaibar, Hejaz....C4
Khamis Mushait 49,581....D6
Mastaba....C5
Mastura....C5
Mecca 366,801....C5
Medina 198,186....D5
Mubarraz 54,325....E4
Najran (Aba as Sa'ud) 47,501....D6
Nisab....D4
'Oqair....E4
Qadhima....C5
Qatif....E4
Qizan 32,812....D6
Ra's al Khafji....E4
Ras Tanura....F4
Riyadh (cap.) 666,840....E5
Rumah....E4
Sakaka....D4
Shaqra....E4
Sufeina....D5
Taif 204,857....D5
Tebuk (Tabuk) 74,825....C4
Turaba....D5
Umm Lajj....C4
Wejh....C4
Yenbo....C5
Zahran....D6
Zalim....D5

OTHER FEATURES

Abu-Mad, Ras (cape)....C5
'Aneiza, Jebel (mt.)....C3
Aqaba (gulf)....C4
Arafat, Jebel (mt.)....D5
'Ar'ar, Wadi (dry riv.)....D3
Arma (plat.)....E4
'Asir (reg.)....D6
Aswad, Ras al (cape)....C5
Bab el Mandeb (str.)....D7
Bahr es Safi (des.)....E6
Barida, Ras (cape)....C5
Batin, Wadi al (dry riv.)....E4
Bisha, Wadi (dry riv.)....D5
Dahana (des.)....E4
Dawasir, Hadhb (range)....D5
Dawasir, Wadi (dry riv.)....D5
Farasan (isls.)....D6
Hatiba, Ras (cape)....C5
Hejaz (reg.)....C4
Jafura (des.)....F5
Mashabi (isl.)....C4
Midian (dist.)....C4
Misha'ab, Ras (cape)....E4
Nefud (des.)....D4
Nefud Dahi (des.)....D5
Nejd (reg.)....D4
Persian (gulf)....F4
Ranya, Wadi (dry riv.)....D5
Red (sea)....C5
Rima, Wadi (dry riv.)....D4
Rimal, Ar (des.)....F5
Rub al Khali (des.)....F5
Safaniya, Ras (cape)....E4
Salma, Jebel (mts.)....D4
Shaibara (isl.)....C4
Shammar, Jebel (plat.)....D4
Sirhan, Wadi (dry riv.)....C3
Subh, Jebel (mt.)....C5
Summan (plat.)....E4
Tihama (reg.)....C5
Tiran (isl.)....C4
Tiran (str.)....C4
Tuwaiq, Jebel (range)....E5

UNITED ARAB EMIRATES

CITIES and TOWNS

Abu Dhabi (cap.) 347,000....F5
'Ajman....G4
Buraimi....G5
Dubai....F4
Fujairah....G4
Jebel Dhanna....F5
Ras al Khaimah....G4
Ruwais....F5
Sharjah....F4
Umm al Qaiwain....G4

OTHER FEATURES

Das (isl.)....F4
Oman (gulf)....G5
Yas (isl.)....F5
Zirko (isl.)....F5

WEST BANK

CITIES and TOWNS

Hebron 38,309....C3

OTHER FEATURES

Dead (sea)....C3

YEMEN

CITIES and TOWNS

Aden 240,370....E7
Al Hawtah....E6
'Amran....D6
Bait al Faqih....D7
Balhaf....E7
Bir 'Ali....E7
Damqut....F6
Dhamar 19,467....D7
El Beida 5,975....E7
Hadibu....F7
Hajja 5,814....D6
Hodeida 80,314....D7
Hureidha....E6
Ibb 19,066....D7
Lodar....E7
Luhaiya....D6
Madinat ash Sha'b....E7
Marib 292....E6
Meifa....E7
Mocha....D7
Mukalla 45,000....E7
Nisab....E7
Qabr Hud....E6
Qishn....F6
Riyan....E7
Sa'ada 4,252....D6
Saihut....F6
Sanaa (cap.) 134,588....D6
Sana....F6
Seiyun 20,000....E6
Shabwa....E6
Sheikh Sa'id....D7
Shibam....E6
Shihr....E7
Shuqra....E7
Ta'izz 78,642....D7
Tarim....E6
Yarim....D7
Yeshbum....E7
Zabid....D7

OTHER FEATURES

Bab el Mandeb (str.)....D7
Fartak, Ras (cape)....F6
Hadhramaut (dist.)....E7
Hadhramaut, Wadi (dry riv.)....F7
Hanish (isls.)....D7
Jebel Manar (mt.)....D7
Jebel Sabir (mt.)....D7
Kamaran (isl.)....D6
Manar, Jebel (mt.)....D7
Mandeb, Bab el (str.)....D7
Maqatin (ruins)....E7
Perim (isl.)....D7
Qamr (bay)....F6
Ras Fartak (cape)....F6
Red (sea)....C5
Sabir, Jebel (mt.)....D7
Socotra (isl.)....F7
Tihama (reg.)....C5
Wadi Hadhramaut (dry riv.)....F7
Zuqar (isl.)....D7

† Population of commune.

* City and suburbs.

Agriculture, Industry and Resources

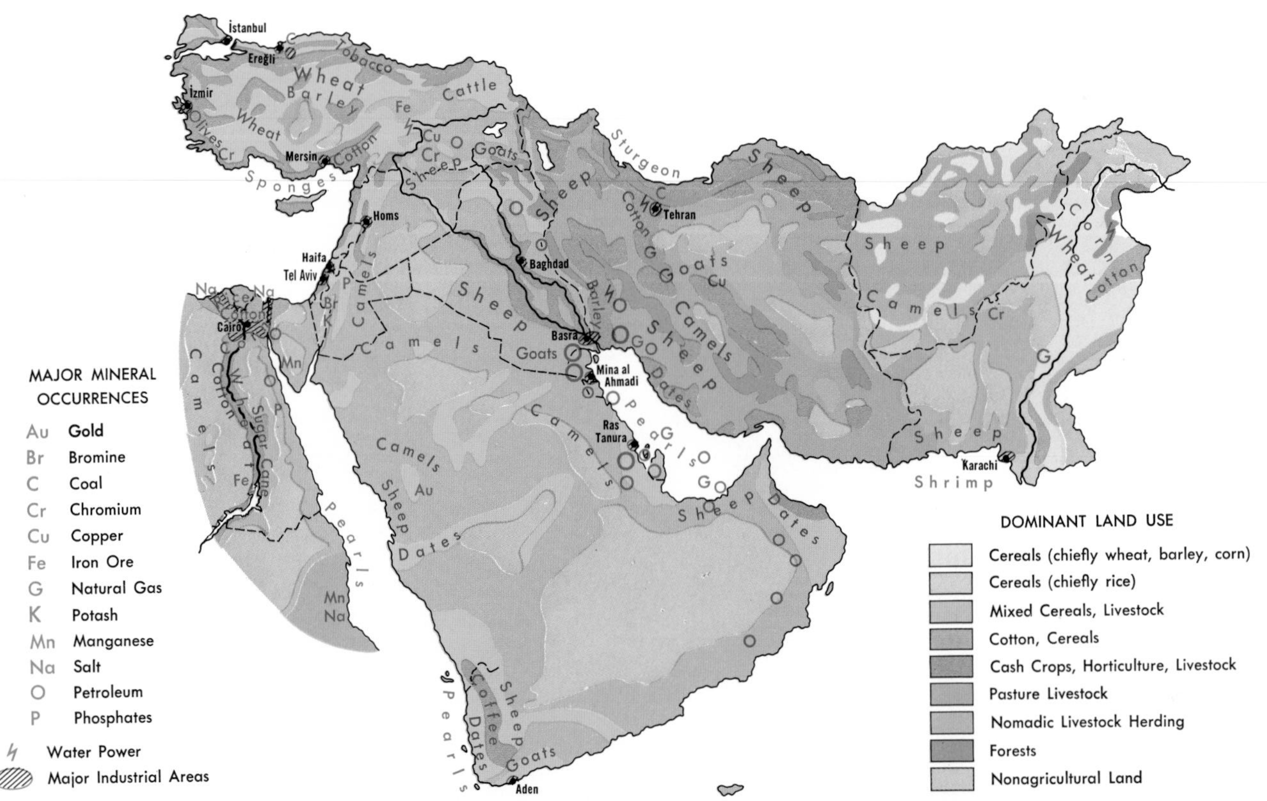

İstanbul
Ereğli
Tobacco
Wheat
Barley
Cattle
Fe
İzmir
Olives
Wheat
Cr
Mersin
Cotton
Cu
Goats
Sponges
Sheep
Sturgeon
Tehran
Homs
Haifa
Tel Aviv
Baghdad
Cotton
Goats
Camels
Barley
Sheep
Cu
Cairo
Cotton
Na
Mn
Basra
Goats
Camels
Sheep
Mina al Ahmadi
Dates
Pearls
Ras Tanura
Camels
Au
Sugar Cane
Wheat
Dates
Sheep
Fe
Pearls
Mn
Na
Coffee
Goats
Aden
Sheep
Camels
Cr
Wheat
Corn
Cotton
Karachi
Shrimp
MAJOR MINERAL OCCURRENCES
Au Gold
Br Bromine
C Coal
Cr Chromium
Cu Copper
Fe Iron Ore
G Natural Gas
K Potash
Mn Manganese
Na Salt
O Petroleum
P Phosphates
Water Power
Major Industrial Areas
DOMINANT LAND USE
Cereals (chiefly wheat, barley, corn)
Cereals (chiefly rice)
Mixed Cereals, Livestock
Cotton, Cereals
Cash Crops, Horticulture, Livestock
Pasture Livestock
Nomadic Livestock Herding
Forests
Nonagricultural Land

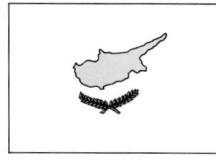
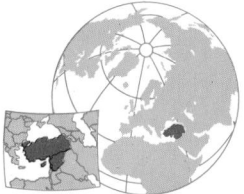

TURKEY **SYRIA** **LEBANON** **CYPRUS**

TURKEY
AREA 300,946 sq. mi.
(779,450 sq. km.)
POPULATION 56,741,000
CAPITAL Ankara
LARGEST CITY Istanbul
HIGHEST POINT Ararat 16,946 ft.
(5,165 m.)
MONETARY UNIT Turkish lira
MAJOR LANGUAGE Turkish
MAJOR RELIGION Islam

SYRIA
AREA 71,498 sq. mi. (185,180 sq. km.)
POPULATION 11,719,000
CAPITAL Damascus
LARGEST CITY Damascus
HIGHEST POINT Hermon 9,232 ft.
(2,814 m.)
MONETARY UNIT Syrian pound
MAJOR LANGUAGES Arabic, French,
Kurdish, Armenian
MAJOR RELIGIONS Islam, Christianity

LEBANON
AREA 4,015 sq. mi. (10,399 sq. km.)
POPULATION 2,897,000
CAPITAL Beirut
LARGEST CITY Beirut
HIGHEST POINT Qurnet es Sauda
10,131 ft. (3,088 m.)
MONETARY UNIT Lebanese pound
MAJOR LANGUAGES Arabic, French
MAJOR RELIGIONS Christianity, Islam

CYPRUS
AREA 3,473 sq. mi. (8,995 sq. km.)
POPULATION 699,000
CAPITAL Nicosia
LARGEST CITY Nicosia
HIGHEST POINT Troödos 6,406 ft. (1,953 m.)
MONETARY UNIT Cypriot pound
MAJOR LANGUAGES Greek, Turkish, English
MAJOR RELIGIONS Eastern (Greek) Orthodoxy,

CYPRUS

CITIES and TOWNS

Famagusta 38,960 ....F5
Kyrenia 3,892 ....E5
Kythrea 3,400 ....E5
Lapithos 3,600 ....E5
Larnaca 19,608 ....E5
Lefka 3,650 ....E5
Limassol 79,641 ....E5
Morphou 9,040 ....E5
Nicosia (cap.) 115,718 ....E5
Paphos 8,984 ....E5
Polis 2,200 ....E5
Rizokarpasso 3,600 ....E5
Yialousa 2,750 ....E5

OTHER FEATURES

Andreas (cape) F5
Arnauti (cape) E5
Famagusta (bay) E5
Gata (cape) E5
Greco (cape) E5
Klides (isls.) F5
Kormakiti (cape) E5
Larnaca (bay) E5
Morphou (bay) E5
Pomos (cape) E5
Troodos (mt.) E5

LEBANON

CITIES and TOWNS

'Aleih 18,630 ....F6
Amyun 7,926 ....F5
Ba'albek 15,560 ....G5
Beirut (cap.) 474,870 ....F6
Beirut* 938,940 ....F6
Merj 'Uyun 9,318 ....F6
Rasheiya 6,731 ....F6
Saida 32,200 ....F6

Sidon (Saida) 32,200 ....F6
Sur 16,483 ....F6
Tarabulus 127,611 ....F5
Tripoli (Tarabulus) 127,611 ..F5
Tyre (Sur) 16,483 ....F6
Zahle 53,121 ....F6
Zegharta 18,210 ....G5

OTHER FEATURES

Lebanon (mts.) F6
Leontes (Litani) (riv.) F6
Litani (riv.) F6
Sauda, Qurnet es (mt.) G5

SYRIA

PROVINCES

Aleppo 1,316,872 ....G4
Damascus 1,457,934 ....G6
Deir ez Zor 292,780 ....H5
Der'a 230,481 ....G6
El Quneitra 16,490 ....F6
Es Suweida 139,650 ....G6
Hama 514,748 ....G5
Haseke 468,506 ....J4
Homs 546,176 ....G5
Idlib 383,695 ....G4
Latakia 389,552 ....G5
Rashid 243,736 ....H5
Tartus 302,065 ....G5

CITIES and TOWNS

Abu Kemal 6,907 ....J5
'Ain el 'Arab 4,529 ....H4
Aleppo 639,428 ....G4
Azaz 13,923 ....G4
Baniyas 8,537 ....G5
Damascus (cap.) 836,668 ..G6
Damascus* 923,253 ....G6
Deir ez Zor 66,164 ....H5
Der'a 27,651 ....G6

Dimashq (Damascus)
(cap.) 836,668 ....G6
Duma 30,050 ....G6
El Bab 27,366 ....G4
El Haseke 32,746 ....J4
El Ladhiqa (Latakia) 125,716 F5
El Qaryatein G5
El Quneitra 17,752 ....F6
El Rashid 37,151 ....H5
En Nebk 16,334 ....G5
Es Suweida 29,524 ....G6
Et Tell el Abyad H4
Haffe 4,656 ....G5
Haleb (Aleppo) 639,428 ....G4
Hama 137,421 ....G5
Harim 6,837 ....G4
Homs 215,423 ....G5
Idlib 34,515 ....G5
Izra 3,226 ....G6
Jeble 15,715 ....F5
Jerablus 8,610 ....G4
Jisr esh Shughur 13,131 ...G5
Khan Sheikhun G5
Latakia 125,716 ....F5
Masyaf 7,058 ....G5
Membij 13,796 ....G4
Meskene H5
Meyadin 12,515 ....J5
Qal'at es Salihiye J5
Qamishliye 31,448 ....J4
Quteife 4,993 ....G6
Raqqa (El Rashid) 37,151 ..H5
Safita 9,650 ....G5
Selemiya 21,677 ....G5
Tadmur 10,670 ....H5
Tartus 29,842 ....F5
Telkalakh 6,242 ....F5
Zebdani 10,010 ....G6

OTHER FEATURES

Abdul 'Aziz, Jebel (mts.) ...J4
'Amrit (ruins) F5
Arwad (Ruad) (isl.) F5

'Asi (Orontes) (riv.) G5
Bahrat Assad (lake) H4
Druz, Jebel ed (mts.) G6
El Furat (riv.) H4
Euphrates (El Furat) (riv.) ..H4
Hermon (mt.) F6
Khabur (riv.) J5
Orontes (riv.) G5
Palmyra (Tadmor) (ruins) ..H5
Tigris (riv.) K4

TURKEY

PROVINCES

Adana 1,485,743 ....F4
Adiyaman 367,595 ....H4
Afyonkarahisar 597,516 ....D3
Ağri 368,009 ....K3
Amasya 341,287 ....F2
Ankara 2,854,689 ....E3
Antalya 748,706 ....D4
Artvin 228,997 ....J2
Aydin 652,488 ....B4
Balikesir 853,177 ....B3
Bilecik 147,001 ....D2
Bingöl 228,702 ....J3
Bitlis 257,908 ....J3
Bolu 471,751 ....D2
Burdur 235,009 ....D4
Bursa 1,148,492 ....C2
Çanakkale 338,091 ....B2
Çankiri 258,436 ....E2
Çorum 571,831 ....F2
Denizli 603,338 ....C4
Diyarbakir 778,150 ....H4
Edirne 363,286 ....B2
Elâziğ 440,808 ....H3
Erzincan 282,022 ....H3
Erzurum 801,809 ....J3
Eskişehir 543,802 ....D3
Gaziantep 808,697 ....G4
Giresun 480,083 ....H2
Gümüşhane 275,191 ....H2

Hakkâri 155,463 ....K4
Hatay 856,271 ....G4
İçel 842,817 ....F4
Isparta 301,166 ....D4
İstanbul 3,264,393 ....C2
İzmir 1,976,763 ....B3
Kahramanmaraş 738,032 ..G4
Kars 700,238 ....K2
Kastamonu 450,946 ....E2
Kayseri 778,383 ....F3
Kırklareli 283,408 ....B2
Kırşehir 240,497 ....F3
Kocaeli 596,899 ....C2
Konya 1,562,139 ....E4
Kütahya 497,089 ....C3
Malatya 669,962 ....H3
Manisa 941,941 ....B3
Mardin 564,967 ....J4
Muğla 438,145 ....C4
Muş 302,406 ....J3
Nevşehir 256,933 ....F3
Niğde 512,071 ....F4
Ordu 713,535 ....G2
Rize 361,258 ....J2
Sakaryá 548,747 ....D2
Samsun 1,008,113 ....F2
Siirt 445,483 ....J4
Sinop 276,242 ....F2
Sivas 750,144 ....G3
Tekirdağ 360,742 ....B2
Tokat 624,508 ....G2
Trabzon 731,045 ....H2
Tunceli 157,974 ....H3
Urfa 602,736 ....H4
Uşak 247,224 ....C3
Van 468,646 ....K3
Yozgat 504,433 ....F3
Zonguldak 972,856 ....D2

CITIES and TOWNS

Adalia (Antalya) 176,446 ...D4
Adana 842,845 ....F4
Adapazari 131,400 ....D2

Adilcevaz 10,342 ....K3
Adiyaman 116,986 ....H4
Afşin 20,084 ....G3
Afyonkarahisar 597,516 ....D3
Ahlat 10,422 ....K3
Akçaabat 13,384 ....H2
Akçadağ 8,015 ....G3
Akçakale 11,184 ....H4
Akdağmadeni 10,192 ....F3
Akhisar 61,491 ....B3
Aksaray 62,927 ....F3
Akşehir 40,312 ....D3
Akseki 6,815 ....D4
Akyazi 14,795 ....D2
Alaca 15,649 ....F2
Alanya 22,190 ....D4
Alaşehir 25,611 ....C3
Alexandretta
(İskenderun) 120,985 .....G4
Alibeyköyü 33,387 ....D6
Altındağ 608,689 ....E2
Altınova 6,980 ....B3
Alucra 8,795 ....H2
Amasya 48,010 ....F2
Anamur 23,025 ....E4
Andırın 6,045 ....G4
Ankara (cap.) 2,203,729 ...E3
Antakya 99,551 ....G4
Antalya 176,446 ....D4
Antioch (Antakya) 99,551 ..G4
Arapkir 8,816 ....H3
Ardahan 14,912 ....K2
Ardeşen 9,582 ....J2
Arhavi 6,801 ....J2
Artvin 14,203 ....J2
Aşkale 12,045 ....J3
Avanos 8,927 ....F3
Ayancık 8,287 ....F1
Aybasti 13,517 ....G2
Aydın 37,696 ....B4

Aydıncık 19,371 ....E4
Ayvalık 19,371 ....B3
Babaeski 18,145 ....B2
Bafra 50,213 ....F2
Bahçe 12,366 ....G4
Bakırköy 234,226 ....D6
Balıkesir 124,122 ....B3
Banaz 8,356 ....C3
Bandırma 53,497 ....B2
Bartin 20,728 ....E2
Başkale 9,770 ....K3
Batman 86,172 ....J4
Bayat 5,366 ....F2
Bayburt 22,578 ....J2
Bayındır 12,440 ....B3
Bayramiç 7,842 ....B3
Besni 15,833 ....G4
Beşiktaş 188,117 ....D6
Beykoz 94,101 ....D5
Beyoğlu 223,360 ....D6
Beypazari 16,971 ....D2
Beyşehir 15,845 ....D4
Biga 16,359 ....B2
Bigadiç 8,955 ....C3
Bilecik 15,108 ....C2
Bingöl (Çapakçur) 27,904 ..J3
Birecik 20,412 ....H4
Bismil 19,059 ....J4
Bitlis 27,114 ....J3
Bodrum 32,517 ....B4
Boğazliyan 10,827 ....F3
Bolu 38,400 ....D2
Bolvadin 30,599 ....D3
Bor 45,480 ....F4
Bornova 60,397 ....B3
Boyabat 14,397 ....F2
Bozdoğan 7,682 ....C4
Bozova 5,510 ....H4
Bozüyük 18,052 ....C3
Bucak 18,852 ....D4
Bulancak 16,089 ....H2
Bulanık 9,140 ....K3
Buldan 10,939 ....C3

(continued on following page)

Agriculture, Industry and Resources

DOMINANT LAND USE

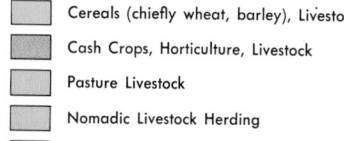

☐ Cereals (chiefly wheat, barley), Livestock
☐ Cash Crops, Horticulture, Livestock
☐ Pasture Livestock
☐ Nomadic Livestock Herding
☐ Forests
☐ Nonagricultural Land

MAJOR MINERAL OCCURRENCES

Ab Asbestos
Al Bauxite
C Coal
Cr Chromium
Cu Copper
Fe Iron Ore
Hg Mercury
Mg Magnesium

Na Salt
O Petroleum
P Phosphates
Pb Lead
Py Pyrites
Sb Antimony
Zn Zinc

 Water Power
Major Industrial Areas

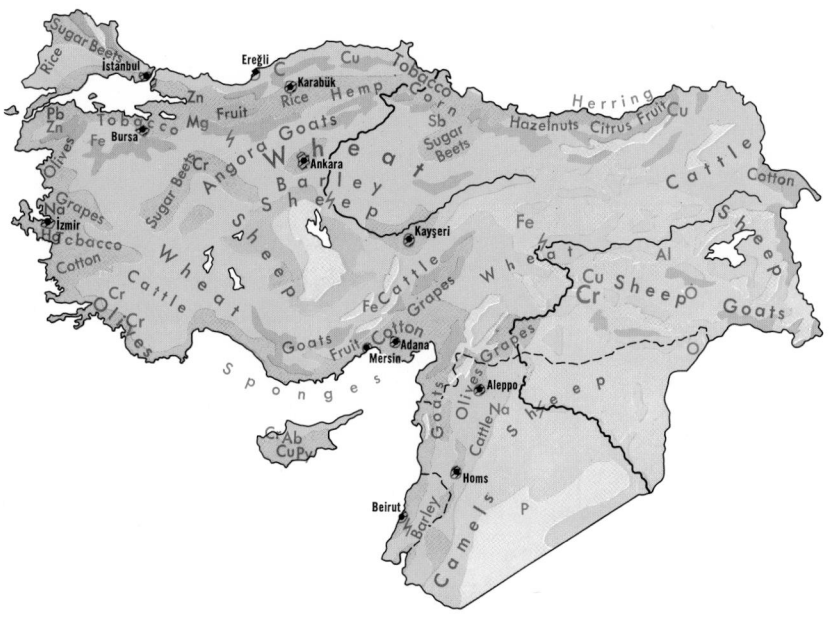

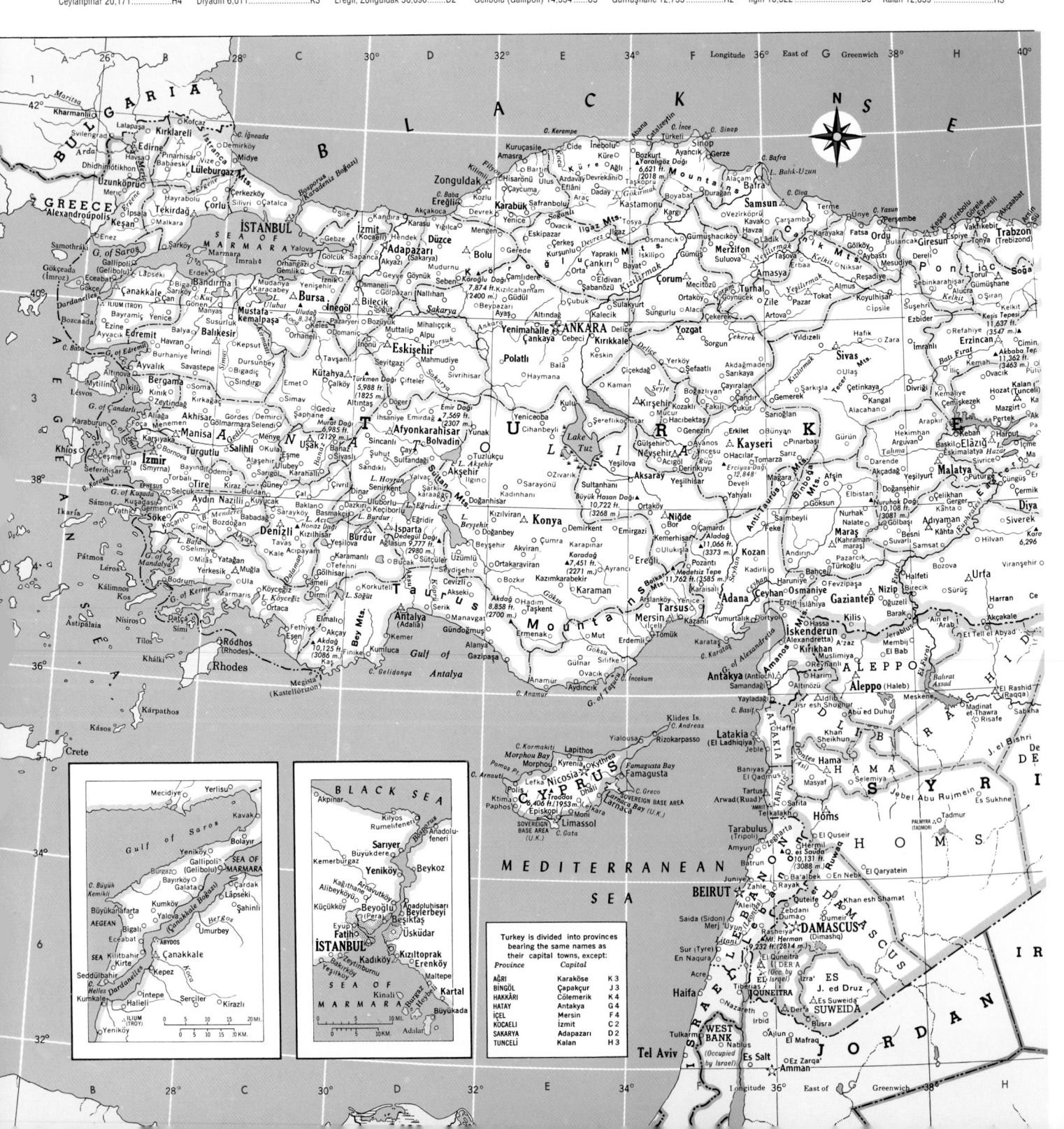

Turkey is divided into provinces bearing the same names as their capital towns, except:

Province	Capital	
AĞRI	Karaköse	K 3
BİNGÖL	Çapakçur	J 3
HAKKÂRİ	Çölemerik	K 4
HATAY	Antakya	G 4
İÇEL	Mersin	F 4
KOCAELİ	İzmit	C 2
SAKARYA	Adapazarı	D 2
TUNCELİ	Kalan	H 3

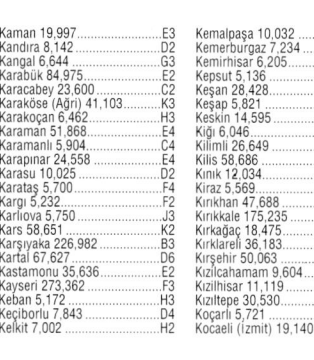

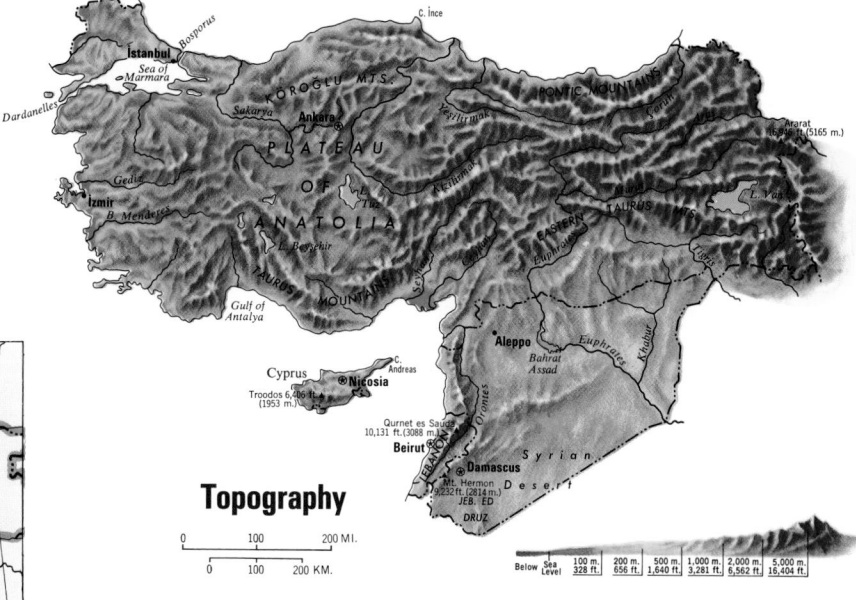

Topography

| Below Sea Level | 100 m. 328 ft. | 200 m. 656 ft. | 500 m. 1,640 ft. | 1,000 m. 3,281 ft. | 2,000 m. 6,562 ft. | 5,000 m. 16,404 ft. |

0 100 200 MI.
0 100 200 KM.

Turkey, Syria, Lebanon and Cyprus

© Copyright HAMMOND INCORPORATED, Maplewood, N.J.

SCALE OF MILES
0 25 50 75 100 125 150

SCALE OF KILOMETERS
0 25 50 75 100 125 150

Capitals of Countries ....★   Capitals of Provinces ....△

Provincial Boundaries _____

*City and suburbs

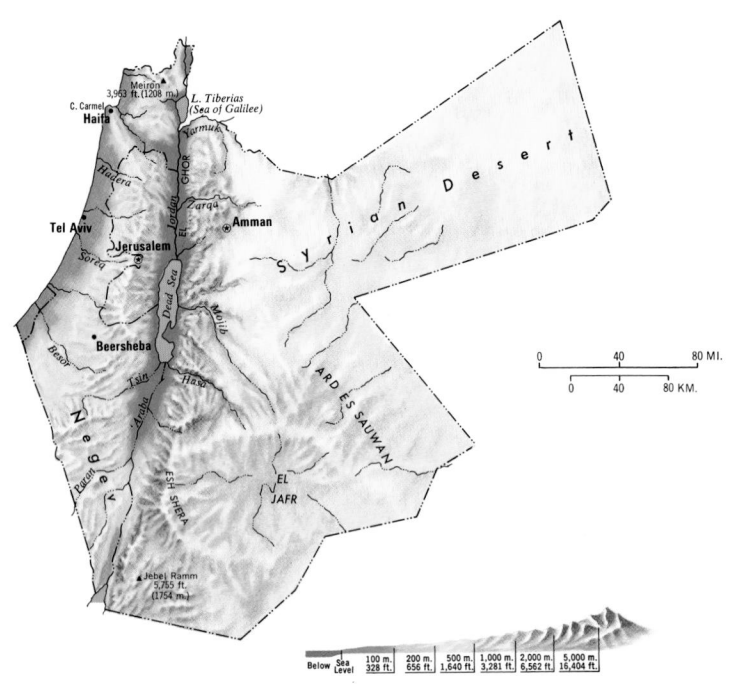

Archaeological Sites in Palestine

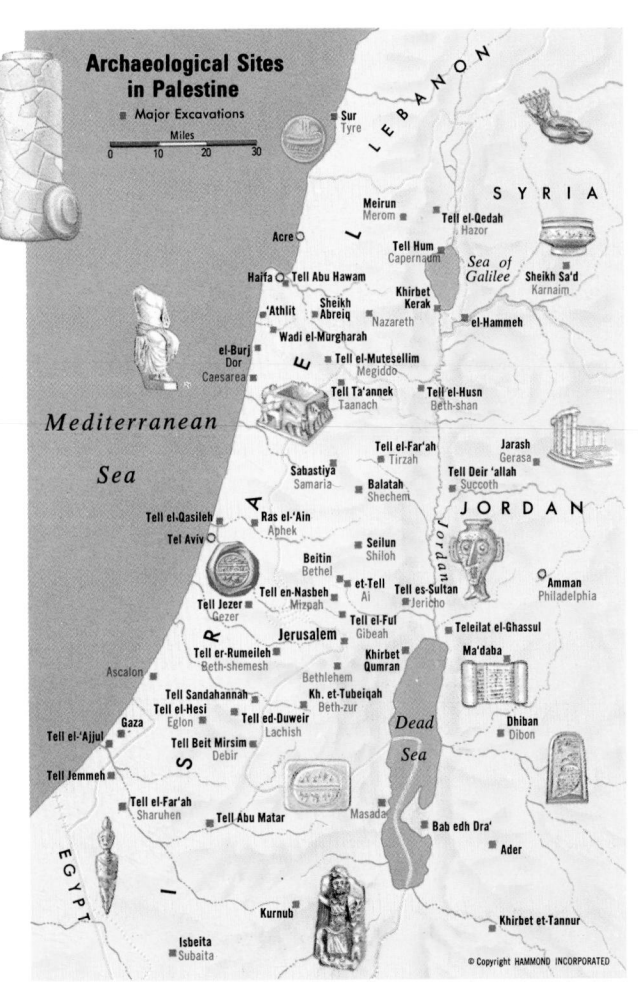

Agriculture, Industry and Resources

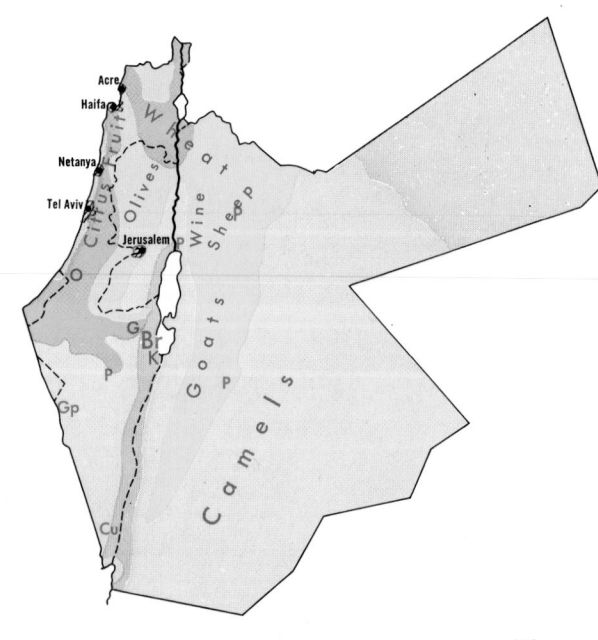

DOMINANT LAND USE

- Cereals, Livestock
- Cash Crops, Horticulture
- Nomadic Livestock Herding
- Nonagricultural Land

MAJOR MINERAL OCCURRENCES

Br Bromine
Cu Copper
G Natural Gas
Gp Gypsum

K Potash
O Petroleum
P Phosphates

Major Industrial Areas

ISRAEL

JORDAN

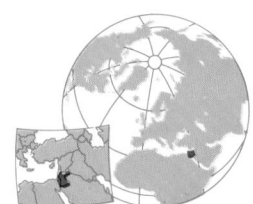

ISRAEL

AREA 7,847 sq. mi. (20,324 sq. km.)
POPULATION 4,625,000
CAPITAL Jerusalem
LARGEST CITY Tel Aviv
HIGHEST POINT Meiran 3,963 ft.
(1,208 m.)
MONETARY UNIT shekel
MAJOR LANGUAGES Hebrew, Arabic
MAJOR RELIGIONS Judaism, Islam,
Christianity

JORDAN

AREA 35,000 sq. mi.
(90,650 sq. km.)
POPULATION 2,779,000
CAPITAL Amman
LARGEST CITY Amman
HIGHEST POINT Jeb. Ramm 5,755 ft.
(1,754 m.)
MONETARY UNIT Jordanian dinar
MAJOR LANGUAGE Arabic
MAJOR RELIGION Islam

GAZA STRIP

CITIES and TOWNS

'Abasan 1,481 ....A5
Bani Suheila 7,561 ....A5
Beit Hanun 4,756 ....A4
Deir el Balah 10,854 ....A5
Deir el Balah* 18,118 ....A5
Gaza 87,793 ....A5
Gaza* 118,272 ....A5
Jabaliya 10,508 ....A4
Jabaliya* 43,604 ....A4
Khan Yunis 29,522 ....A5
Khan Yunis* 52,997 ....A5
Rafah 10,812 ....A5
Rafah* 49,812 ....A5

WEST BANK

CITIES and TOWNS

'Ajja 1,322 ....C3
'Anabta 3,426 ....C3
Anin 914 ....C2
'Anza 807 ....C3
'Aqqaba 1,127 ....C3
'Aqraba 2,501 ....C3
Ariha (Jericho) 5,312 ....C4
'Arraba 4,231 ....C3
'Arura 849 ....C3
'Attil 3,808 ....C3
Beit Fajjar 2,474 ....C4
Beit Hanina 1,177 ....C4
Beit Jala 6,041 ....C4
Beit Lahm
   (Bethlehem) 14,439 ....C4
Beit Sahur 5,380 ....C4
Bethlehem 14,439 ....C4
Biddu 1,259 ....C4
Birqin 2,036 ....C3
Bir Zeit 2,311 ....C3
Burqa 2,477 ....C3
Deir Ballut 1,058 ....C3
Deir Sharaf 973 ....C3
Dhahiriya 4,875 ....C4
Dura 4,954 ....C4
El Bira 9,674 ....C4
El Bira* 13,037 ....C4
El Khalil (Hebron) 38,309 .....C4
Er Rihiya 679 ....C5
Ez Zababida 1,474 ....C3
Halhul 6,041 ....C4
Hebron 38,309 ....C4
Idna 3,713 ....B4
Jaba 2,817 ....C3
Jalama 784 ....C3
Jalbun 914 ....C3
Jenin 8,346 ....C3
Jenin* 13,365 ....C3
Jericho 5,312 ....C4
Jericho* 6,931 ....C4
Jifna 655 ....C4
Kharas 1,364 ....C4
Nablus (Nablus) 41,799 ....C3
Nahhalin 1,109 ....C4
Ni'lin 1,227 ....C3
Qabalan 1,970 ....C3
Qabatiya 6,005 ....C3
Qaffin 2,480 ....C3
Qalqiliya 8,926 ....C4
Qibya 926 ....C4
Rafidiya 1,123 ....C3
Ramallah 12,134 ....C4
Rammun 1,198 ....C4
Rantis 897 ....C3
Salfit 3,201 ....C3
Samu 3,784 ....C5
Shu'fat 10,255 ....C3
Shuweika 2,332 ....C3
Silat Dhahr 2,104 ....C3
Sinjil 1,823 ....C3
Siris 1,285 ....C3
Tammun 2,952 ....C3
Tarqumiya 2,412 ....C4
Tubas 5,262 ....C3
Tulkarm 10,255 ....C3
Tulkarm* 15,275 ....C3
Tur 12,200 ....C4
Ya'bad 4,857 ....C3
Yamun 4,384 ....C3
Yatta 7,281 ....C5

OTHER FEATURES

Ebal (mt.) C3
Golan Heights (reg.) D1
Judaea (reg.) C4
Khirbet Qumran (site) C4
Mashash, Wadi (riv.) C4
Samaria (reg.) C3
Tell 'Asur (mt.) C4
West Bank (reg.) C3

JORDAN

GOVERNORATES

Amman 1,000,000 ....D4
El Balqa 113,000 ....D4
El Karak 93,000 ....E5
Irbid 506,000 ....D3
Ma'an 62,000 ....D5

CITIES and TOWNS

'Ajlun ⊙ 42,000 ....D3
Amman (cap.) 711,850 ....D4
'Anjara 3,163 ....D4
Aqaba 15,000 ....D6
Bal'ama 769 ....E3
Baqura 3,042 ....D2
Damiya 483 ....D3
Dana 844 ....E5
Deir Abu Sa'id 1,927 ....D3
El 'Al 492 ....D4
El Husn 3,728 ....D3
El Karak 10,000 ....E4
El Kitta 987 ....D2
El Mafraq 15,500 ....E3
Er Ramtha 19,000 ....E2
Er Rafid 787 ....D2
Er Ruseifa 6,200 ....D4
Es Sahab 2,580 ....E4
Es Salt 24,000 ....D3
Es Sukhna 649 ....E3
Esh Shaubak 4,634 ....D5
Et Tafila 17,000 ....E5
Et Taiyiba 2,606 ....D3
Ez Zarqa 263,400 ....E3
Harima 635 ....D2
Hawara 2,342 ....D2
Hisban 718 ....D4
'Ibbin 1,364 ....D3
Irbid 136,770 ....D3
Jarash 29,000 ....D3
Kitim 1,026 ....D3
Kufrinja 3,922 ....D3
Ma'ad 125 ....D2
Ma'an 50,000 ....E5
Ma'daba 22,600 ....D4
Ma'in 1,271 ....D4
Mazra' D5
Na'ur 2,382 ....D4
Qumeim 955 ....D2
Ra's en Naqb 225 ....E5
Safi E5
Safut 4,210 ....D3
Samar 716 ....D2
Sarih 3,390 ....D3
Subeihi 514 ....D3
Suweilih 3,457 ....D3
Suweima 315 ....D4
Um Jauza 582 ....D3
Wadi es Sir 4,455 ....D4
Wadi Musa 654 ....E5
Waqqas 2,321 ....D2

OTHER FEATURES

'Ajlun, Jebel (range) D3
Aqaba (gulf) D6
'Araba, Wadi (valley) D5
Dead (sea) D4
Hasa, Wadi el (dry riv.) E5
Jordan (riv.) D4
Nebo (mt.) D4
Petra (ruins) D5
Ramm, Jebel (mt.) D5
Shallala, Wadi esh (dry riv.) ..D4
Shu'eib, Wadi (dry riv.) D4
Zarqa' (riv.) D3

*City and suburbs
⊙ Population of subdivision.

Israel and Jordan

CYLINDRICAL PROJECTION

© Copyright HAMMOND INCORPORATED, Maplewood, N.J.

SCALE OF MILES
0 5 10 15 20 25 30

SCALE OF KILOMETERS
0 5 10 15 20 25 30

Capitals of Countries ....☆
Internal Capitals ....⊙
International Boundaries _____
Internal Boundaries _____

IRAN

INTERNAL DIVISIONS

Azerbaijan, East (prov.)
3,194,543 ....E1
Azerbaijan, West (prov.)
1,404,875 ....D1
Bakhtaran (prov.) 1,016,199 ..E3
Bakhtiari (governorate)
394,300 ....F4
Bushehr (prov.) 345,427 ..G6
Central (Markazi) (prov.)
6,921,283 ....G3
Esfahan (Isfahan) (prov.)
1,974,938 ....H4
Fars (prov.) 2,020,947 ..H6
Gilan (prov.) 1,577,800 ..F2
Hamadan (governorate)
1,086,512 ....F3
Hormozgan (prov.) 463,419 ..J7
Ilam (governorate) 244,222 ..E4
Isfahan (prov.) 1,974,938 ..H4
Kerman (prov.) 1,088,045 ..K6
Khorasan (prov.) 3,266,650 ..K3
Khuzestan (prov.) 2,176,612 ..F5
Kohkiluyeh and Boyer
Ahmediyeh (governorate)
244,750 ....G5
Kordestan (Kurdistan) (prov.)
781,889 ....E3

Lorestan (Luristan)
(governorate) 924,848 ......F4
Mazandaran (prov.)
2,384,226 ....H2
Semnan (governorate)
485,875 ....J3
Sistan and Baluchestan
(prov.) 659,297 ....M6
Yazd (governorate) 356,218 ..J5
Zanjan (governorate) 579,000..F2

CITIES and TOWNS

Abadan 296,081 ....F6
Abadeh 16,000 ....H5
Abhar 24,000 ....F4
Agha Jari 24,195 ....F5
Ahar 24,000 ....E1
Ahvaz (Ahwaz) 329,006 ..F5
Amol 68,782 ....H2
Andimeshk 16,000 ....F4
Arak 114,507 ....F3
Ardabil 147,404 ....F1
Asterabad (gangav) 88,348 ..J2
Babol 67,790 ....H2
Bakhtaran (Kermanshah)
290,861 ....E3
Bam 40,200 ....L6
Bandar 'Abbas 89,103 ..J7
Bandar Behesti (Bahar)
1,800 ....M8

Bandar-e Anzali (Enzeli)
55,978 ....F2
Bandar-e Bushehr (Bushire)
57,681 ....G6
Bandar-e Khomeyni 6,000 ..F5
Bandar-e Lingeh 4,920 ..J7
Bandar-e Ma'shur 17,000 ..F5
Bandar-e Torkeman 13,000 ..H2
Behbehan 39,874 ....G5
Behshahr 26,032 ....H2
Birjand 25,854 ....L4
Bojnurd 31,248 ....L2
Borazjan 20,000 ....G6
Borujerd 100,103 ....F4
Bostan 4,619 ....F5
Chalus 15,000 ....G2
Damghan 13,000 ....J2
Dasht-e Azadegan
(Susangerd) 21,000 ....F5
Dizful (Dezful) 110,287 ..F4
Duzdab (Zahedan) 92,628..M6
Emamshahr (Shahrud)
30,767 ....J2
Enzeli 55,978 ....F2
Esfahan (Isfahan) 671,825 ..G4
Eslamabad 12,000 ....E3
Estahbanat 18,187 ....J6
Fahrej (Iranshahr) 5,000 ..M7
Fasa 19,000 ....H6
Ganaveh 9,000 ....G6
Garmsar 4,723 ....H3

Ghaemshahr 63,289 ....H2
Golpayegan 20,515 ....G4
Golshan (Tabas) 10,000 ..K4
Gonbad-e Kavus 59,868 ..J2
Gorgan (Gurgan) 88,348 ..J2
Hamadan 155,846 ....F3
Hormoz 2,569 ....J7
Iranshahr 5,000 ....M7
Isfahan 671,825 ....G4
Jahrom 38,236 ....H6
Karaj 138,774 ....G3
Kashan 84,545 ....G3
Kashmar 17,000 ....L3
Kazerun 51,309 ....G6
Kazvin (Qazvin) 138,527 ..F2
Kerman 140,309 ....K5
Khomeinishar 46,836 ....G4
Khorramabad 104,928 ..F4
Khorramshahr 146,709 ..F5
Khvoy (Khoi) 70,040 ....D1
Lahijan 25,725 ....F2
Lar 22,000 ....J7
Malayer 28,434 ....F3
Mahabad 28,610 ....D2
Maragheh 60,820 ....E2
Marand 24,000 ....E1
Marv Dasht 25,498 ....H6
Masjed Soleyman 77,161 ..F5
Mashhad (Meshed) 670,180 ..L2
Miandoab 19,000 ....E2
Mianeh 28,447 ....E2

Nahavand 24,000 ....F3
Najafabad 76,236 ....G4
Nasratabad (Zabol) 20,000 ..M5
Neyriz 16,114 ....H6
Nishapur (Neyshabur) 59,101..L2
Nosratabad 20,000 ....L6
Orumiyeh (Urmia) 163,991 ..D2
Pahlevi (Enzeli) 55,978 ..F2
Qayen 6,000 ....L4
Qazvin 138,527 ....F2
Quchan 29,133 ....L2
Qum (Qom) 246,831 ....G3
Rafsanjan 21,000 ....K5
Resht (Rasht) 187,203 ..F2
Rey 102,825 ....G3
Reza'iyeh (Urmia) D2
Sa'idabad 20,000 ....J6
Sabzevar 69,174 ....L2
Sakht-Sar 12,000 ....G2
Salmas 13,161 ....D1
Sanandaj 95,834 ....E3
Saqqez 17,000 ....E3
Sari 70,936 ....H2
Savanat (Estahbanat) 18,187 ..J6
Saveh 17,565 ....G3
Semnan 31,058 ....H3
Shahr Kord 24,000 ....G4
Shahreza 34,220 ....H4
Shahrud 30,767 ....J2
Shiraz 416,408 ....H6
Shushtar 24,000 ....F4

Sinneh (Sanandaj) 95,834 ..E3
Sirjan (Sai'dabad) 20,000 ..J6
Sultanabad (Kashmar)
17,000 ....L3
Susanged 21,000 ....F5
Tabas 10,000 ....K4
Tabriz 598,576 ....D2
Tajrish 157,486 ....G3
Tehran (cap.) 4,496,159 ..G3
Torbat-e Heydariyeh 30,106..L3
Urmia 163,991 ....D2
Yazd (Yezd) 135,978 ....J5
Zabol 20,000 ....M5
Zahedan 92,628 ....M6
Zenjan (Zanjan) 99,967 ..F2

OTHER FEATURES

'Arabi (isl.) G7
Araks (Aras) (riv.) E1
Atrak (Atrek) (riv.) J2
Azerbaijan (reg.) D1
Bakhtegan (lake) J6
Baluchistan (reg.) M7
Bampur (riv.) M7
Behistun (ruins) E3
Caspian Sea (sea) G1
Damavand (Demavend)
(mt.) H2
Daryacheh-ye Namak
(salt lake) G3

Daryacheh-ye Sistan
(salt lake) M5
Dasht-e Kavir (salt des.) ..J3
Dasht-e Lut (des.) L5
Dez (riv.) F4
Elburz (mts.) G2
Farsi (isl.) G7
Gabrik (riv.) L7
Gamas Ab (riv.) E3
Gavkhuni (marsh) H4
Gorgan (riv.) J2
Hamun-e Saberi (lake) M5
Harirud (riv.) M3
Hormoz (isl.) K7
Hormoz (str.) K7
Jaba Rud (riv.) H3
Joveyn (riv.) K2
Kabir Kuh (mts.) E4
Karkheh (riv.) E4
Karun (riv.) F5
Khark (Kharg) (isl.) G6
Khusf Rud (riv.) L4
Khvojeh Lak, Kuh-e (mt.) ..E3
Kor (riv.) H6
Laristan (reg.) J7
Makran (reg.) M8
Mand (riv.) H6
Mand (riv.) H6
Mashkid (riv.) N7
Mehran (riv.) J7
Nahang (riv.) N7

Namaksar (lake) M4
Namakzar-e Shahdad
  (salt lake) L5
Oman (gulf) M8
Pasargadae (ruins) H5
Persepolis (ruins) H6
Persian (gulf) F6
Qaranqu (riv.) E2
Qareh Dagh (mts.) E1
Qareh Su (riv.) E1
Qeshm (isl.) J7
Qezel Owzam (riv.) F2
Ras al Kuh (cape) K8
Ras-e Meydani (cape) L8
Safid Rud (riv.) F2
Seistan (reg.) M5
Shatt-al- 'Arab (riv.) F5
Shelagh (riv.) M5
Shirvan (riv.) E3
Shur (riv.) J7
Sirri (isl.) J8
Susa (ruins) F4
Talab (riv.) N6
Talkheh (riv.) E1
Tashk (lake) J6
Urmia (lake) D2
Zagros (mts.) E4
Zarineh (riv.) E2
Zayandeh (riv.) H4
Zilbir (riv.) D1
Zohreh (riv.) F5

IRAQ
GOVERNORATES

Anbar 535,627 ....B4
An Najaf 438,971 ....C5
Babil 680 700 ....D4
Baghdad 4,038,430 ....D4
Basra 1,184,500 ....E5
Dhi Qar 683,537 ....E5
Diyala 650,211 ....D4
Dohuk 296,339 ....C2
Erbil 657,294 ....C3
Karbala 305,627 ....B4
Maysan 395,666 ....E5
Muthanna 239,044 ....D5
Ninawa 1,258,001 ....B3
Qadisiya 475,676 ....D4
Salahuddin 411,734 ....C3
Sulaimaniya 816,406 ....D3
Tamin 587,079 ....C3
Wasit 455,853 ....D4

CITIES and TOWNS

Ad Diwaniya 60,553 ....D5
'Afaq 5,390 ....D4
Al 'Aziziya 7,450 ....D4
Al Falluja 38,072 ....C4
Al Fathat 15,329 ....C3
'Ali Gharbi 15,456 ....E4

'Ali Sharqi 8,398 ....E4
Al Kufa 30,862 ....D4
Al Musaiyib 15,955 ....D4
'Amara 64,847 ....E5
'Ana 15,729 ....B3
An Najaf 128,096 ....D5
An Nasiriya 60,405 ....D5
Arbela (Erbil) 90,320 ....D2
Ar Rumaila 1,439 ....E5
'Aqra 8,659 ....D2
Az Zubair 41,408 ....E5
Baghdad (cap.) 502,503 ...D4
Ba'quba 34,575 ....D4
Basra 313,327 ....E5
Dohuk 16,998 ....C2
Erbil 90,320 ....D2
Fao 15,399 ....F6
Habbaniya 14,405 ....C4
Hai 16,988 ....E4
Halabja 11,206 ....D3
Hilla 84,717 ....D4
Hindiya 16,436 ....C4
Hit 9,131 ....C4
Karbal'a 83,301 ....C4
Khanaqin 23,522 ....D3
Kifri 8,500 ....D3
Kirkuk 167,413 ....D3
Kut 42,116 ....D4
Mandali 11,262 ....D4
Mosul 315,157 ....C2
Muqdadiyah 12,181 ....D4
N'amaniya 11,943 ....D4
Qal'at Diza 6,250 ....D2
Ramadi 28,723 ....C4
Rumaitha 10,222 ....D5
Samarra 24,746 ....C3
Samawa 33,473 ....D5
Shatra 18,822 ....E5
Sinjar 7,942 ....B2
Sulaimaniya 86,822 ....D3
Tal Kaif 7,482 ....C2
Taza Khurmatu 2,681 ....D3
Tikrit 9,921 ....C3
Tuz Khurmatu 13,860 ......D3
Zakho 14,790 ....C2

OTHER FEATURES

Adhaim (riv.) D3
Al Hajara (plain) D5
'Aneiza, Jebel (mt.) A4
'Ar'ar, Wadi (dry riv.) B5
Babylon (ruins) D4
Batin, Wadi al (dry riv.) E6
Ctesiphon (ruins) D4
Dalmaj, Hor (lake) D4
Darbandikhan (dam) D3
Diyala (riv.) D4
Euphrates (riv.) D4
Great Zab (riv.) C2
Habbaniya, Hor al (lake) ...C4
Haji Ibraham (mt.) D2
Hammar, Hor al (lake) E5
Hamrin, Jabal (mts.) D3
Hauran, Wadi (dry riv.) B4
Little Zab (Riv.) C3
Mesopotamia (reg.) B3
Nineveh (ruins) C2
Razaza (res.) C4
Sa'diya, Hor (lake) E4
Saniya, Hor (lake) E5
Sha'ib Hisb, Wadi (dry riv.) .C5
Shatt-al-'Arab (riv.) F5
Sinjar, Jebel (mts.) B2
Siyah Kuh (mt.) D2
Suwaiqiya, Hor as (lake) ...D4
Tharthar (res.) C3
Tharthar, Wadi (dry riv.) C3
Tigris (riv.) E4
Tubal, Wadi al (dry riv.) B4
Ubaiyidh, Wadi (dry riv.) ...B5
Ur (ruins) E5

† Population of commune.

IRAN

IRAQ

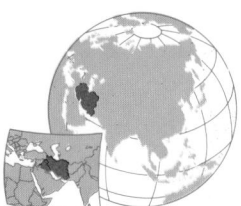

AREA 636,293 sq. mi. (1,648,000 sq. km.)
POPULATION 55,208,000
CAPITAL Tehran
LARGEST CITY Tehran
HIGHEST POINT Damavand 18,605 ft. (5,671 m.)
MONETARY UNIT Iranian rial
MAJOR LANGUAGES Persian, Azerbaijani, Kurdish
MAJOR RELIGION Islam

AREA 172,476 sq. mi. (446,713 sq. km.)
POPULATION 16,335,000
CAPITAL Baghdad
LARGEST CITY Baghdad
HIGHEST POINT Haji Ibrahim 11,811 ft.
  (3,600 m.)
MONETARY UNIT Iraqi dinar
MAJOR LANGUAGES Arabic, Kurdish
MAJOR RELIGION Islam

Topography

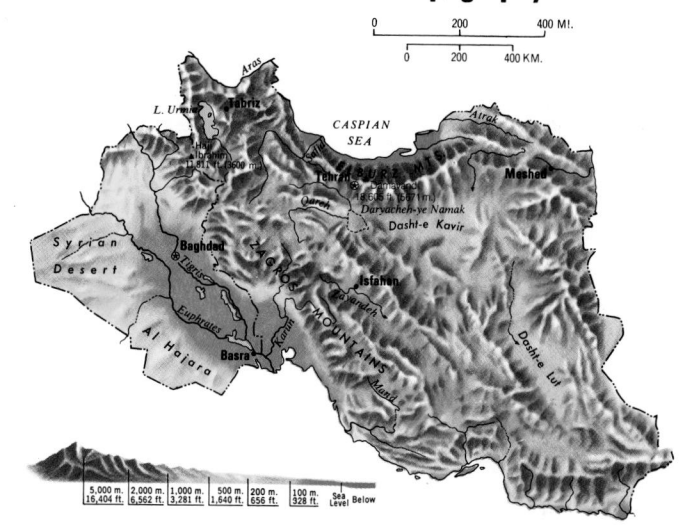

Agriculture, Industry and Resources

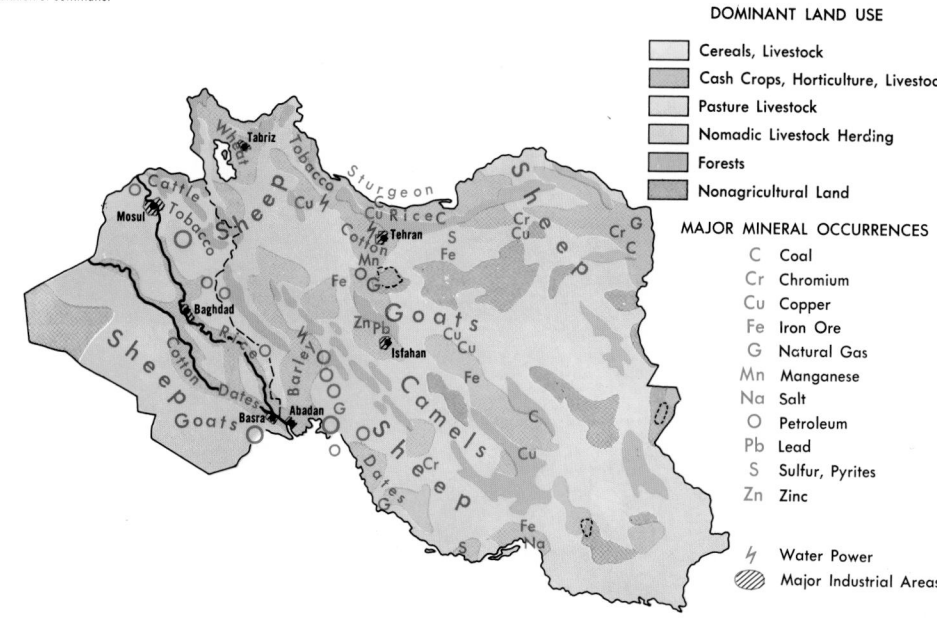

DOMINANT LAND USE

Cereals, Livestock
Cash Crops, Horticulture, Livestock
Pasture Livestock
Nomadic Livestock Herding
Forests
Nonagricultural Land

MAJOR MINERAL OCCURRENCES

C Coal
Cr Chromium
Cu Copper
Fe Iron Ore
G Natural Gas
Mn Manganese
Na Salt
O Petroleum
Pb Lead
S Sulfur, Pyrites
Zn Zinc

Water Power
Major Industrial Areas

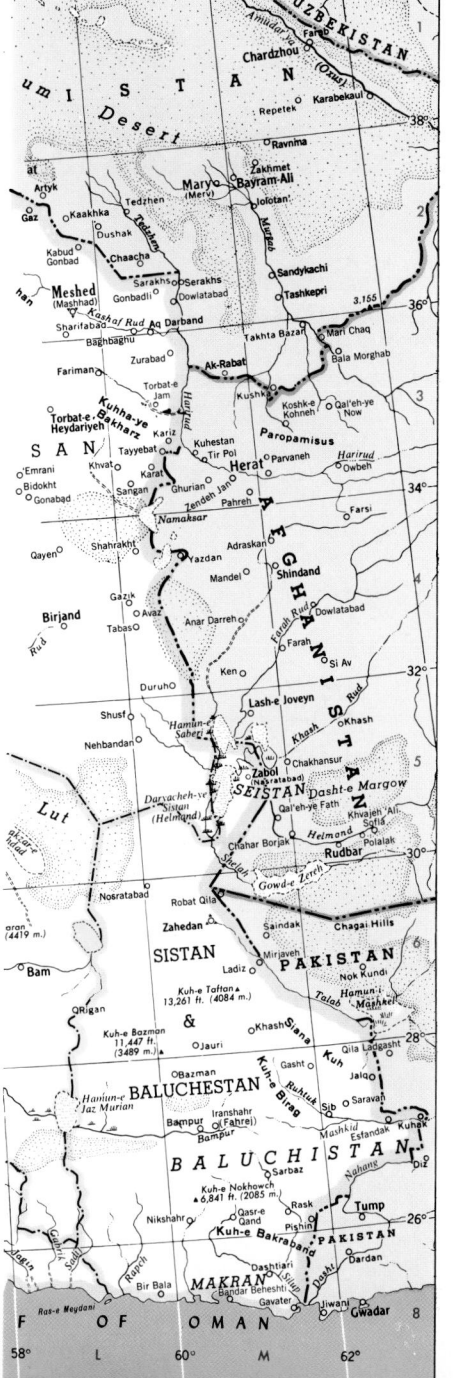

AREA 145,730 sq. mi. (377,441 sq. km.)
POPULATION 123,116,000
CAPITAL Tokyo
LARGEST CITY Tokyo
HIGHEST POINT Fuji 12,389 ft. (3,776 m.)
MONETARY UNIT yen
MAJOR LANGUAGE Japanese
MAJOR RELIGIONS Buddhism, Shintoism

AREA 46,540 sq. mi. (120,539 sq. km.)
POPULATION 22,419,000
CAPITAL P'yŏngyang
LARGEST CITY P'yŏngyang
HIGHEST POINT Paektu 9,003 ft. (2,744 m.)
MONETARY UNIT won
MAJOR LANGUAGE Korean
MAJOR RELIGIONS Confucianism, Buddhism, Ch'ondogyo

AREA 38,175 sq. mi. (98,873 sq. km.)
POPULATION 42,793,000
CAPITAL Seoul
LARGEST CITY Seoul
HIGHEST POINT Halla 6,398 ft. (1,950 m.)
MONETARY UNIT won
MAJOR LANGUAGE Korean
MAJOR RELIGIONS Confucianism, Buddhism, Ch'ondogyo, Christianity

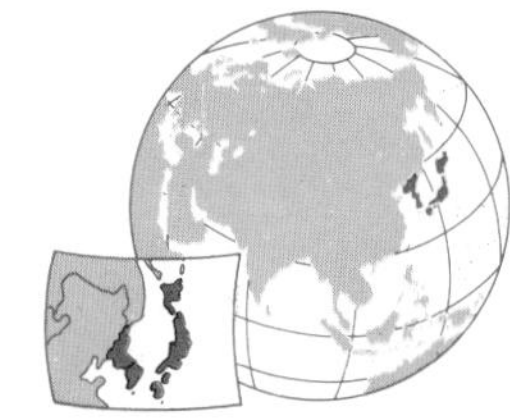

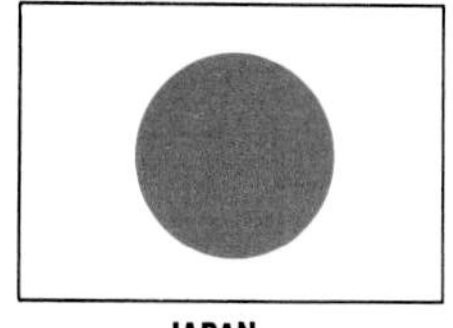

JAPAN

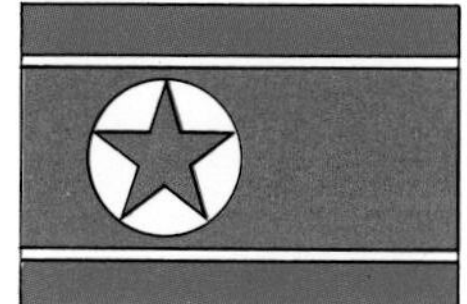

NORTH KOREA

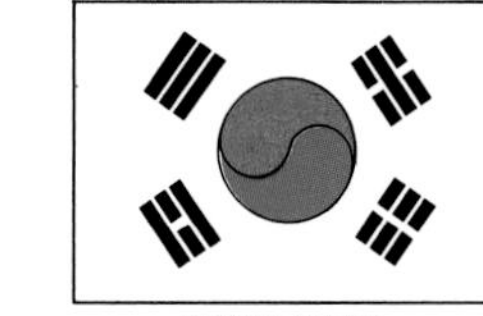

SOUTH KOREA

JAPAN

PREFECTURES

Aichi 6,221,638 ...H6
Akita 1,256,745 ...J4
Aomori 1,523,907 ...K3
Chiba 4,735,424 ...P2
Ehime 1,506,637 ...F7
Fukui 794,354 ...G5
Fukuoka 4,553,461 ...D7
Fukushima 2,035,272 ...K5
Gifu 1,960,107 ...H6
Gumma 1,848,562 ...J5
Hiroshima 2,739,161 ...E6
Hokkaido 5,575,989 ...K2
Hyogo 5,144,892 ...H7
Ibaraki 2,558,007 ...K5
Ishikawa 1,119,304 ...H5
Iwate 1,421,927 ...K4
Kagawa 999,864 ...G6
Kagoshima 1,784,623 ...E8
Kanagawa 6,924,348 ...O2
Kochi 831,275 ...F7
Kumamoto 1,790,327 ...E7
Kyoto 2,527,330 ...J7
Mie 1,686,936 ...H6
Miyagi 2,082,320 ...K4
Miyazaki 1,151,587 ...E8
Nagano 2,083,934 ...J5

CITIES and TOWNS

Abashiri 44,777 ...M1
Ageo 166,243 ...O2
Aizuwakamatsu 114,528 ...J5
Akashi 254,869 ...H8
Akita 284,863 ...J4
Amagasaki 523,650 ...H8

Nagasaki 1,590,564 ...D7
Nara 1,209,365 ...J8
Niigata 2,451,357 ...J5
Oita 1,228,913 ...E7
Okayama 1,871,023 ...F6
Okinawa 1,106,559 ...N6
Osaka 8,473,446 ...J8
Saga 865,574 ...E7
Saitama 5,420,480 ...J8
Shiga 1,079,898 ...J7
Shimane 784,795 ...F6
Shizuoka 3,446,804 ...H6
Tochigi 1,792,201 ...K5
Tokushima 825,261 ...G7
Tokyo 11,618,281 ...O1
Tottori 604,221 ...G6
Toyama 1,103,459 ...H5
Wakayama 1,087,012 ...G6
Yamagata 1,251,917 ...K4
Yamaguchi 1,587,079 ...E6
Yamanashi 804,256 ...J6

CITIES and TOWNS

Abashiri 44,777 ...M1
Ageo 166,243 ...O2
Aizuwakamatsu 114,528 ...J5
Akashi 254,869 ...H8
Akita 284,863 ...J4
Amagasaki 523,650 ...H8

Amagi 42,863 ...E7
Anan 61,253 ...G7
Aomori 287,594 ...K3
Asahi 35,721 ...K6
Asahikawa 352,619 ...L2
Ashikaga 165,756 ...J5
Ashiya 81,745 ...H8
Atami 50,082 ...J6
Atsugi 145,392 ...O2
Ayabe 42,552 ...G6
Beppu 136,485 ...E7
Chiba 746,430 ...P2
Chichibu 61,285 ...J5
Chigasaki 171,016 ...O3
Chitose 66,788 ...K2
Chofu 180,548 ...O2
Choshi 89,416 ...K6
Daito 116,635 ...J8
Ebetsu 86,349 ...K2
Eniwa 42,911 ...K2
Fuchu, Hiroshima 49,026 ...F6
Fuchu, Tokyo 192,198 ...O2
Fuji 205,751 ...J6
Fujieda 103,225 ...J6
Fujisawa 300,248 ...O3
Fukagawa 35,376 ...L2
Fukuchiyama 63,788 ...G6
Fukue 32,135 ...D7
Fukui 240,962 ...G5
Fukuoka 1,088,588 ...D7

Fukushima 262,837 ...K5
Fukuyama 346,030 ...F6
Funabashi 479,439 ...P2
Furukawa 57,060 ...K4
Gifu 410,357 ...H6
Goshogawara 50,632 ...K3
Habikino 103,181 ...J8
Hachinohe 238,179 ...K3
Hachioji 387,178 ...O2
Hadano 123,133 ...J6
Hagi 53,693 ...E6
Hakodate 320,154 ...K3
Hamada 50,799 ...E6
Hamamatsu 490,824 ...H6
Hanamaki 68,873 ...K4
Hanno 61,179 ...O2
Haramachi 46,052 ...K5
Higashiosaka 521,558 ...J8
Hikone 89,701 ...H6
Himeji 446,256 ...G6
Himi 62,413 ...H5
Hirakata 353,358 ...J7
Hiratsuka 214,293 ...O3
Hirosaki 175,330 ...K3
Hiroshima 899,399 ...E6
Hitachi 204,596 ...K5
Hitoyoshi 42,236 ...E7
Hofu 111,468 ...E6
Hondo 42,460 ...E7

Honjo 42,962 ...J4
Hyuga 58,347 ...E7
Ibaraki 234,062 ...J7
Ichihara 216,394 ...P3
Ichikawa 364,244 ...P2
Ichinomiya 253,139 ...H6
Ichinoseki 60,214 ...K4
Iida 78,515 ...H6
Iizuka 80,288 ...E7
Ikeda 101,121 ...H7
Ikoma 70,461 ...J8
Imabari 123,234 ...F6
Imari 61,243 ...D7
Ina 56,086 ...H6
Isahaya 83,723 ...D7
Ise 105,621 ...H6
Ishinomaki 120,699 ...K4
Ishioka 47,829 ...K5
Itami 178,228 ...H7
Ito 69,638 ...J6
Itoman 42,239 ...N6
Iwaki 342,074 ...K5
Iwakuni 112,525 ...E6
Iwamizawa 78,311 ...L2
Iwata 75,810 ...H6
Iwatsuki 94,696 ...O2
Izumi 124,323 ...J8
Izumiotsu 67,474 ...J8
Izumisano 90,684 ...G6
Izumo 77,303 ...F6

Joetsu 127,842 ...H5
Joyo 74,350 ...J7
Kadoma 138,902 ...J7
Kaga 65,282 ...H5
Kagoshima 505,360 ...E8
Kaizuka 81,162 ...H8
Kakamigahara 212,233 ...H6
Kakegawa 69,410 ...J7
Kakogawa 212,233 ...J6
Kamaishi 65,250 ...L4
Kamakura 172,629 ...O3
Kameoka 69,410 ...J7
Kanazawa 417,684 ...H5
Kanonji 44,927 ...F6
Kanoya 73,242 ...E8
Kanuma 85,159 ...J5
Karatsu 77,710 ...D7
Kaseda 25,392 ...D8
Kashihara 107,316 ...J8
Kashima 239,198 ...P2
Kashiwa 239,198 ...P2
Kashiwazaki 83,499 ...J5
Kasugai 244,119 ...H6
Kasukabe 155,555 ...O2
Katsuta 92,621 ...K5
Kawachinagano 78,572 ...J8
Kawagoe 259,314 ...O2
Kawaguchi 379,360 ...J6
Kawanishi 129,834 ...H7
Kawasaki 1,040,802 ...O2
Kesennuma 68,551 ...K4
Kimitsu 77,286 ...O3

Kiryu 132,889 ...J5
Kisarazu 110,711 ...P3
Kishiwada 180,317 ...J8
Kitaibaraki 47,670 ...K5
Kitakami 53,647 ...K4
Kitakyushu 1,065,078 ...E6
Kitami 102,915 ...L2
Kobayashi 40,033 ...E8
Kobe 1,367,390 ...H7
Kochi 300,822 ...F7
Kodaira 154,610 ...O2
Kofu 199,262 ...J6
Koga 56,657 ...J5
Koganei 102,456 ...O2
Komatsu 104,329 ...H5
Koriyama 286,451 ...K5
Koshigaya 223,241 ...P2
Kuki 54,410 ...O2
Kumagaya 136,806 ...J5
Kumamoto 525,662 ...E7
Kurashiki 403,785 ...F6
Kurayoshi 52,270 ...F6
Kure 234,549 ...E6
Kuroiso 46,574 ...K5
Kurume 216,972 ...E7
Kushiro 214,694 ...M2
Kyoto 1,473,065 ...J7
Machida 295,405 ...O2
Maebashi 265,169 ...J5
Maizuru 97,578 ...G6
Masuda 52,756 ...E6
Matsubara 135,849 ...H8
Matsudo 400,863 ...P2
Matsue 135,568 ...F6
Matsumoto 192,085 ...H5
Matsusaka 113,481 ...H6
Matsuto 43,766 ...H5
Matsuyama 401,703 ...F7
Mihara 84,450 ...F6
Miki 70,201 ...H7
Minoo 104,112 ...J7
Mitaka 164,526 ...O2
Mito 215,566 ...K5
Mitsukaido 40,435 ...P2
Miura 48,687 ...O3
Miyako 62,478 ...L4
Miyakonojo 129,009 ...E8
Miyazaki 264,855 ...E8
Mizusawa 55,226 ...K4
Mobara 71,521 ...K6
Mooka 52,764 ...K5
Moriguchi 165,630 ...J7
Morioka 229,114 ...K4
Muko 50,604 ...J7
Muroran 150,199 ...K2
Musashino 136,910 ...O2
Mutsu 47,610 ...K3
Nagahama 54,935 ...H6
Nagano 324,360 ...J5
Nagaoka 180,259 ...J5
Nagaokakyo 71,445 ...J7
Nagasaki 447,091 ...D7
Nago 45,991 ...N6
Nagoya 2,087,902 ...H6
Naha 295,778 ...N6
Nakatsu 63,941 ...E7
Nanao 50,394 ...H5
Nankoku 44,866 ...F7
Nara 297,953 ...J8
Narashino 125,155 ...P2
Naze 49,021 ...O5
Nemuro 42,880 ...M2
Neyagawa 255,859 ...J7
Nichinan 52,949 ...E8
Niigata 457,785 ...J5
Niihama 132,339 ...F6
Niitsu 62,282 ...J5
Nishinomiya 410,329 ...H8
Nobeoka 136,598 ...E7
Noboribetsu 56,503 ...K2
Noda 93,958 ...P2
Nogata 62,595 ...E7
Noshiro 60,674 ...J3
Noto 15,480 ...H5
Numata 47,150 ...J5
Numazu 203,695 ...J6
Obihiro 153,861 ...L2
Oda 38,026 ...F6

(continued on following page)

Agriculture, Industry and Resources

DOMINANT LAND USE

Cereals, Cash Crops
Truck Farming, Horticulture
Mixed Farming, Dairy
Rice
Forests, Scrub

MAJOR MINERAL OCCURRENCES

Ag Silver
Au Gold
C Coal
Cu Copper
Fe Iron Ore
G Natural Gas
Gr Graphite
Mg Magnesium
Mn Manganese
Mo Molybdenum
O Petroleum
Pb Lead
Py Pyrites
U Uranium
W Tungsten
Zn Zinc

⚡ Water Power
▨ Major Industrial Areas

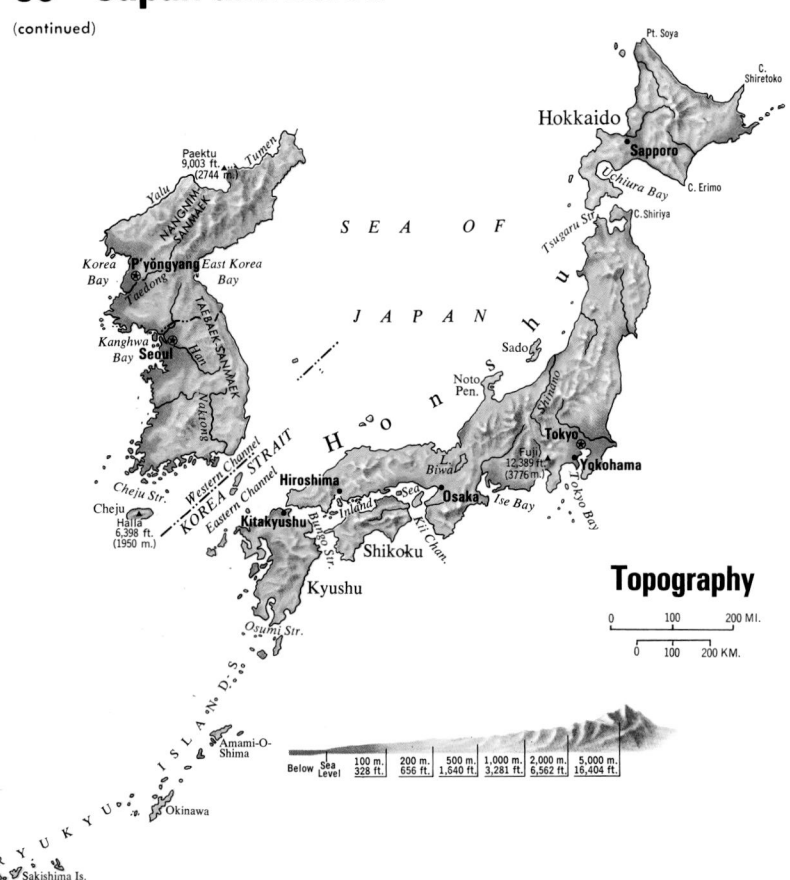

Topography

0 100 200 MI.

0 100 200 KM.

| Below Sea Level | 100 m. 328 ft. | 200 m. 656 ft. | 500 m. 1,640 ft. | 1,000 m. 3,281 ft. | 2,000 m. 6,562 ft. | 5,000 m. 16,404 ft. |

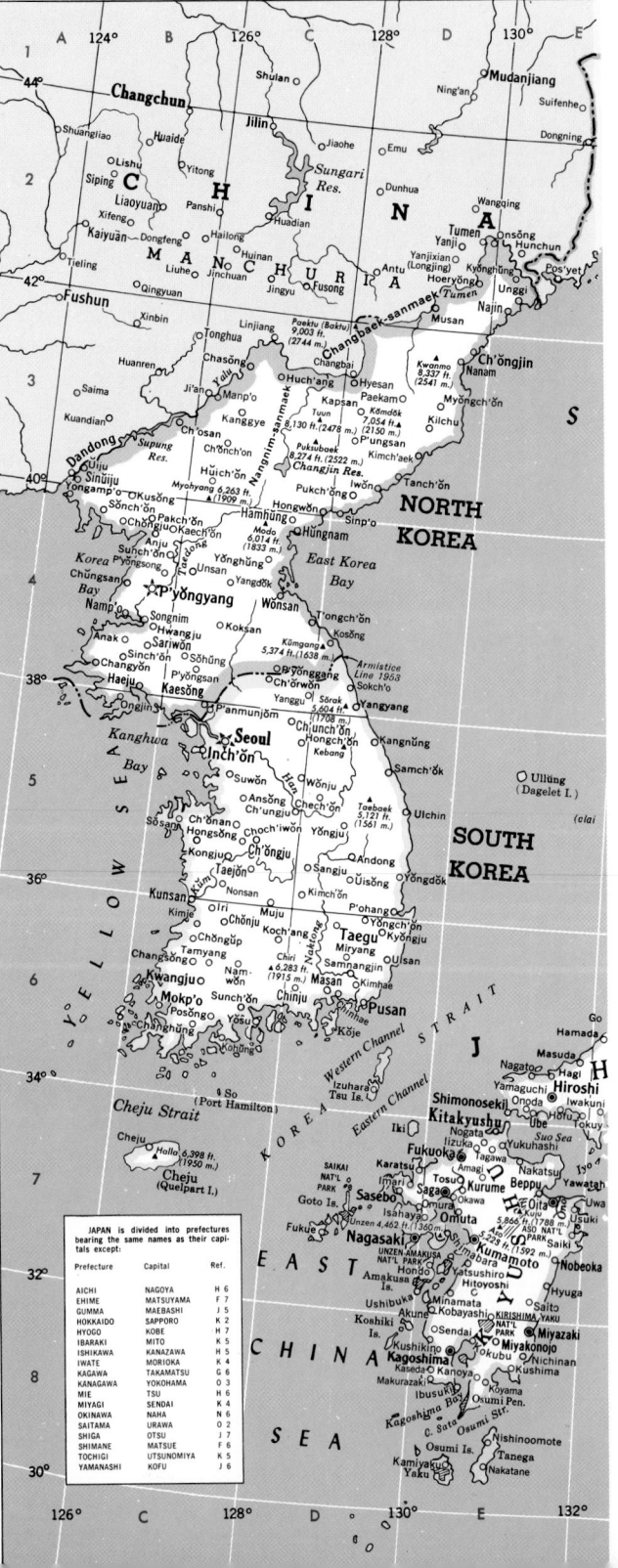

Sata (cape)............E8
Shikoku (isl.)..........F7
Shikotan (isl.).........N2
Shikotsu (lake)........K2
Shimane (pen.).........F6
Shimokita (pen.)......K3
Shinano (riv.)..........J5
Shiono (cape)..........H7
Shiragami (cape).......J3
Shirane (mt.)..........H6
Shiretoko (cape).......M1
Shiriya (cape).........K3
Soya (pt.).............L1
Suo (sea)..............E7
Suruga (bay)..........J6
Suzu (cape)...........H5
Takeshima (isls.)......F5
Tanega (isl.)..........E8
Tappi (cape)..........K3
Teshio (riv.)..........L1

Tokachi (riv.)..........L2
Tokachi (mt.)..........L2
Tokara (isls.)..........O5
Tokuno (isl.)..........O5
Tokyo (bay)...........O2
Tone (riv.)............K6
Tosa (bay)............F7
Towada (lake).........K3
Toya (lake)...........K2
Toyama (bay).........H5
Tsu (isls.)............D6
Tsugaru (strait).......K3
Tsurugi (mt.)..........G7
Uchiura (bay).........K2
Volcano (isls.)........M4
Wakasa (bay).........G6
Western Channel (strait)...D6
Yaeyama (isls.).......K7
Yaku (isl.)...........E8
Yonaguni (isl.).......K7

Yoshino (riv.)..................G6

KOREA (NORTH)

CITIES and TOWNS

Anju..........................B4
Ch'ŏngjin 306,000........E3
Ch'osan......................C3
Changyŏn....................C3
Chasŏng......................C3
Chŏngju......................B4
Haeju 140,000.............B4
Hamhŭng 484,000.........D3
Heiju (P'yŏngyang) (cap.)
  1,250,000...............C4
Hongwŏn.....................C4
Hŭich'ŏn.....................C4
Hŭngnam.....................C4
Hyesan.......................D3

Kaesŏng 175,000..........C4
Kapsan.......................C3
Kimch'aek 100,000........D3
Koksan.......................C4
Kosŏng.......................D4
Manp'o.......................C3
Musan........................D3
Najin.........................E2
Namp'o 140,000............C4
Nanam........................D3
Ongjin.......................B5
Onsŏng.......................E2
P'anmunjŏm.................C5
P'ungsan....................D3
P'yŏngyang (cap.)
  1,250,000...............C4
Pukch'ŏng..................D3
Sariwŏn.....................B4
Sinp'o.......................D4

OTHER FEATURES

Baktu (Paektu) (mt.)......C3
Changbaek-sanmaek (mts.)...D2
Changjin (res.)............C3

Sinŭiju 300,000...........B3
Sŏhŭng......................C4
Sŏnch'ŏn....................B4
Songnim.....................B4
Sunch'ŏn....................B4
Tanch'ŏn....................D3
T'ongch'ŏn..................D4
Ŭiju.........................B3
Unggi........................E2
Unsan........................C4
Wŏnsan 275,000............C4
Yangdŏk.....................C4
Yŏnghŭng....................C4
Yongamp'o...................B4

KOREA (SOUTH)

CITIES and TOWNS

Andong 102,024............D5
Chech'ŏn 74,239...........D5

East Korea (bay)..........D4
Japan (sea)...............G4
Kanghwa (bay).............B5
Korea (bay)...............B4
Kwanmo (mt.)..............D3
Nangnim-sanmaek (range)...C3
Paektu (mt.)..............C3
Puksubaek (mt.)...........B3
Supung (res.).............B3
Taedong (riv.)............C4
Tumen (riv.)..............D2
Yalu (riv.)...............C3
Yellow (sea)..............B6

Cheju 167,546.............C7
Chinhae 112,098...........D6
Chinju 202,753............D6
Ch'ŏnan 120,618...........C5
Ch'ŏngju 252,985..........C5
Chŏngup 54,864............C6
Chŏnju 366,997............C6
Ch'unch'ŏn 155,247........C5
Ch'ungju 113,138..........C5
Inch'ŏn 1,084,730.........C5
Iri 145,358...............C6
Kangnŭng 116,903..........D5
Kimch'ŏn 72,229...........C5
Kimhae 203,428............D6
Kimje 221,414.............C6
Kohŭng 217,446............C6
Kongju 39,756.............C5
Kunsan 165,318............C6
Kwangju 727,627...........C6
Kyŏngju 122,038...........D6

Masan 386,773.............D6
Miryang 42,951............D6
Mokp'o 221,856............C6
Namwŏn 50,857.............C6
Nonsan 226,429............C6
P'anmunjŏm................C5
P'ohang 201,355...........D5
Pusan 3,160,276...........D6
Samch'ŏk 42,526...........D5
Sangju 52,839.............C5
Seoul (cap.) 8,366,756....C5
Sŏkch'o 65,798............D4
Sŏsan 38,081..............C5
Sunch'ŏn 114,223..........C6
Suwŏn 310,757.............C5
Taegu 1,607,458...........D6
Taejŏn 651,642............C5
Ulsan 418,415.............D6
Wŏnju 136,961.............D5
Yanggu 277,986............C4

Yŏngch'ŏn 50,765..........D6
Yŏngju 77,890.............D5
Yŏsu 161,009..............C6

OTHER FEATURES

Cheju (isl.)..............C7
Dagelet (Ullŭng) (isl.)...E5
East China (sea)..........C8
Halla (mt.)...............C7
Han (riv.)................C5
Japan (sea)...............G4
Kanghwa (bay).............B5
Kŏje (isl.)...............D6
Korea (strait)............D6
Naktong (riv.)............D6
Quelpart (Cheju) (isl.)...C7
Ullŭng (isl.).............E5
Yellow (sea)..............B6

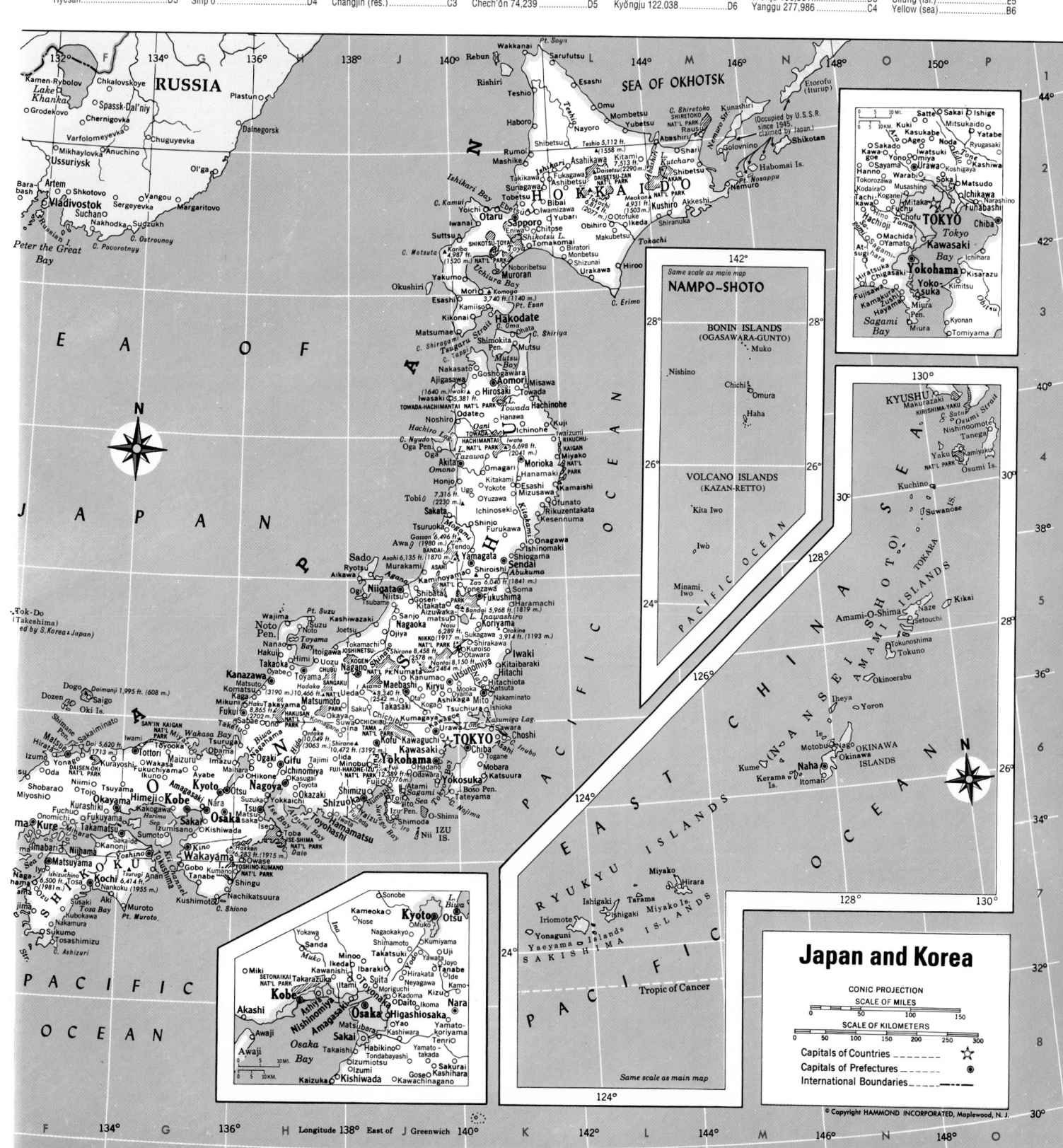

NAMPO-SHOTO

BONIN ISLANDS
(OGASAWARA-GUNTO)

VOLCANO ISLANDS
(KAZAN-RETTO)

Japan and Korea

CONIC PROJECTION

SCALE OF MILES

SCALE OF KILOMETERS

Capitals of Countries ....☆
Capitals of Prefectures ....◉
International Boundaries ....

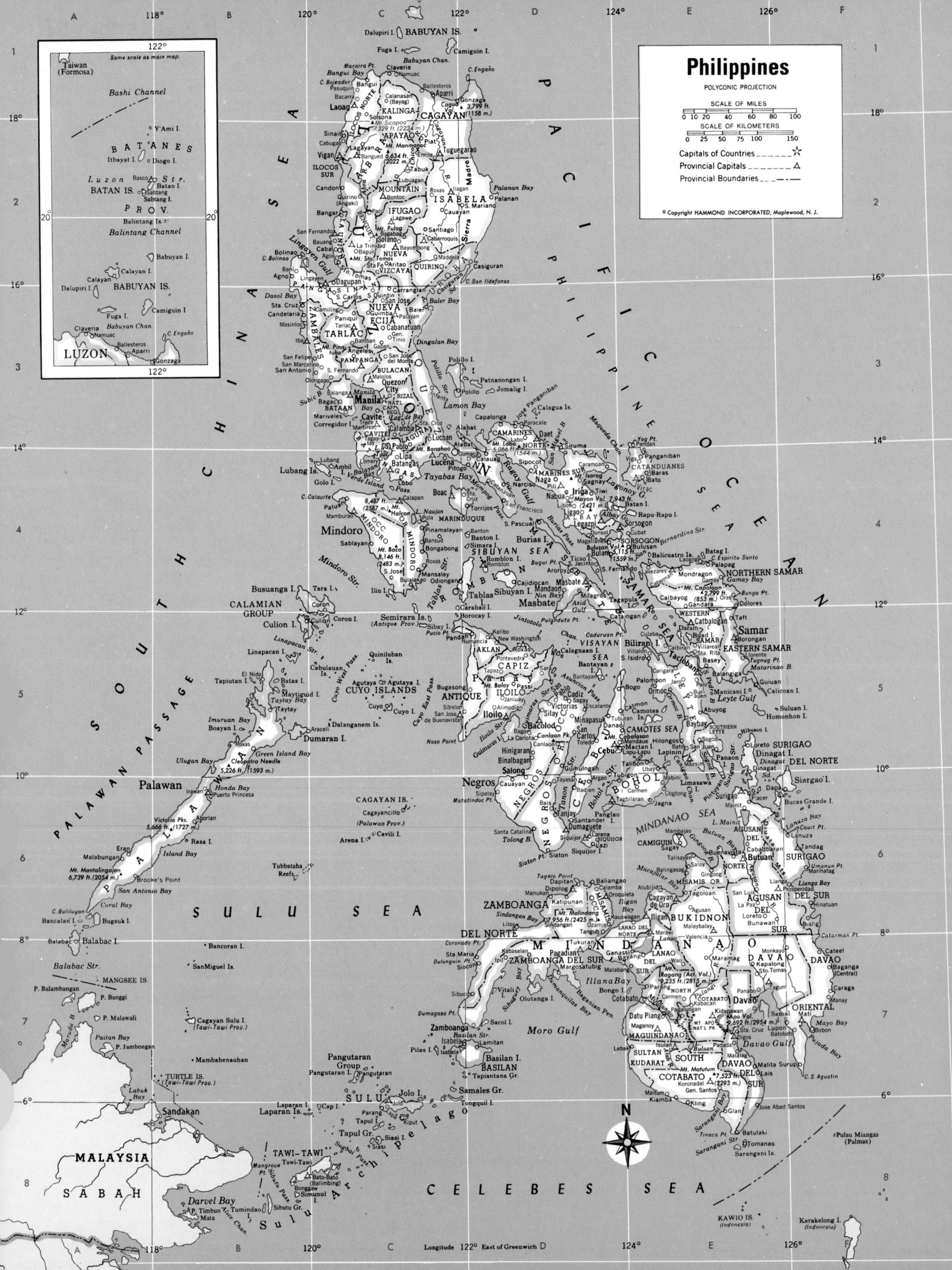

Philippines

POLYCONIC PROJECTION

SCALE OF MILES

0 10 20 40 60 80 100

SCALE OF KILOMETERS

0 25 50 75 100 150

Capitals of Countries _____ ☆
Provincial Capitals _____ △
Provincial Boundaries ____-____

® Copyright HAMMOND INCORPORATED, Maplewood, N. J.

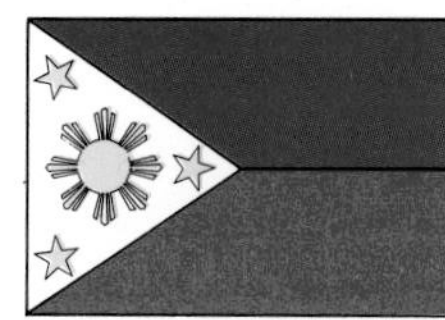

AREA 115,707 sq. mi. (299,681 sq. km.)
POPULATION 60,097,000
CAPITAL Manila
LARGEST CITY Manila
HIGHEST POINT Apo 9,692 ft. (2,954 m.)
MONETARY UNIT peso
MAJOR LANGUAGES Pilipino (Tagalog), English, Spanish, Bisayan, Ilocano, Bikol
MAJOR RELIGIONS Roman Catholicism, Islam, Protestantism, tribal religions

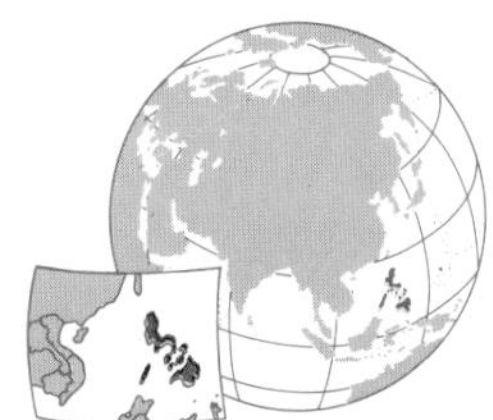

PROVINCES

Abra 160,198 . . . . C2
Agusan del Norte 365,421 . . E6
Agusan del Sur 631,634 . . . . E6
Aklan 324,563 . . . . D5
Albay 809,177 . . . . D4
Antique 344,879 . . . . D5
Aurora 107,145 . . . . C3
Basilan 201,407 . . . . D7
Bataan 323,254 . . . . C3
Batanes 12,091 . . . . A2
Batangas 1,174,201 . . . . C4
Benguet 354,751 . . . . C2
Bohol 806,031 . . . . E6
Bukidnon 631,634 . . . . E6
Bulacan 1,098,046 . . . . C3
Cagayan 711,476 . . . . C1
Camarines Norte 368,007 . . . D3
Camarines Sur 1,099,346 . . D4
Camiguin 57,126 . . . . E6
Capiz 492,231 . . . . D5
Catanduanes 175,247 . . . . . . E4
Cavite 771,320 . . . . C3
Cebu 2,091,602 . . . . D5
Davao 725,153 . . . . E7
Davao del Sur 1,133,599 . . . E7
Davao Oriental 339,931 . . . . . F7
Eastern Samar 320,637 . . . . E5
Ifugao 111,368 . . . . C2
Ilocos Norte 390,666 . . . . . . C1
Ilocos Sur 443,591 . . . . C2
Iloilo 1,433,641 . . . . D5
Isabela 870,604 . . . . C2
Kalinga-Apayao 185,063 . . . . C1
Laguna 973,104 . . . . C3
Lanao del Norte 461,049 . . . E6
Lanao del Sur 404,971 . . . . . E7
La Union 452,578 . . . . C2
Leyte 1,302,648 . . . . E5
Maguindanao 536,546 . . . . . E7
Manila 5,925,884 . . . . C3
Marinduque 173,715 . . . . . . C4
Masbate 584,526 . . . . D4
Misamis Occidental 386,328 D6
Misamis Oriental 690,032 . . . E6
Mountain 103,052 . . . . C2
National Capital Region (Manila) 5,925,884 . . . . . . C3
Negros Occidental 1,930,301 . . . . D6
Negros Oriental 819,399 . . . D6
North Cotabato 564,599 . . . . E7
Northern Samar 378,516 . . . E4
Nueva Ecija 1,069,409 . . . . . C3
Nueva Vizcaya 241,690 . . . . . C2
Occidental Mindoro 222,431 C4
Oriental Mindoro 448,938 . . . C4
Palawan 371,782 . . . . B6
Pampanga 1,181,590 . . . . . . C3
Pangasinan 1,636,057 . . . . . C3
Quezon 1,129,277 . . . . C3
Quirino 83,230 . . . . C2
Rizal 555,533 . . . . C3
Romblon 193,174 . . . . D4
Siquijor 70,300 . . . . D6
Sorsogon 500,685 . . . . E4
South Cotabato 770,473 . . . . E7
Southern Leyte 298,294 . . . . E5
Sultan Kudarat 303,784 . . . . E7
Sulu 360,588 . . . . C7
Surigao del Norte 363,414 . . F5
Surigao del Sur 377,647 . . . . F6
Tarlac 638,457 . . . . C3
Tawi-Tawi 194,651 . . . . B8
Western Samar 501,439 . . . . E5
Zambales 444,037 . . . . C3
Zamboanga del Norte 588,015 . . . . D6
Zamboanga del Sur 1,183,845 . . . . D7

CITIES and TOWNS

Angeles 188,834 . . . . C3
Aparri 45,070 . . . . C1
Bacolod 262,415 . . . . D5
Bagac 13,109 . . . . C3
Bago 99,631 . . . . D5
Baguio 119,009 . . . . C2
Balanga 39,132 . . . . C3
Baler 18,349 . . . . C3
Balimbing (Bato-Bato) 22,189 . . . . C8
Bamban 26,072 . . . . C3
Basco 4,341 . . . . A2
Batangas 143,570 . . . . C4
Bato-Bato 22,189 . . . . C8
Baybay 74,640 . . . . E5
Bislig 81,615 . . . . F6
Boac 37,005 . . . . C4
Bontoc 17,091 . . . . C2
Burauen 48,058 . . . . E5
Butuan 172,489 . . . . E6
Cabanatuan 138,298 . . . . C3
Cabarroquis 17,450 . . . . C2
Cadiz 129,632 . . . . D5
Cagayan de Oro 227,312 . . . E6
Calamba 121,175 . . . . C3
Calbayog 106,719 . . . . E4
Carigara 34,377 . . . . E5
Cauayan 70,017 . . . . D6
Cavite 87,666 . . . . C3
Cebu 490,281 . . . . D5
Cotabato 83,871 . . . . D7
Dagupan 98,344 . . . . C2
Davao 610,375 . . . . E7
Digos 70,065 . . . . E7
Escalante 71,293 . . . . D5
General Santos 149,396 . . . . E7
Gingoog 79,937 . . . . E6
Guihulngan 84,156 . . . . D5
Guimba 58,847 . . . . C3
Iba 22,791 . . . . B3
Ilagan 79,336 . . . . C2
Iligan 167,358 . . . . E6
Iloilo 244,827 . . . . D5
Infanta 27,914 . . . . C3
Jaro 29,739 . . . . E5
Jolo 52,429 . . . . C8
Koronadal 80,566 . . . . E7
Lagawe 15,075 . . . . C2
Lapu-Lapu 98,723 . . . . E5
Legazpi 99,766 . . . . D4
Ligao 69,860 . . . . D4
Lingayen 65,187 . . . . C2
Lipa 121,166 . . . . C4
Lucena 107,880 . . . . C4
Maganoy 45,845 . . . . E7
Mainit 18,078 . . . . E6
Malabang 18,955 . . . . D7
Malolos 95,699 . . . . C3
Mandaue 110,590 . . . . E5
Manila (cap.) 1,630,485 . . . . . C3
Mariveles 48,594 . . . . C3
Mati 78,178 . . . . F7
Naga 90,712 . . . . D4
Olongapo 156,430 . . . . C3
Ormoc 104,978 . . . . E5
Ozamis 77,832 . . . . D6
Pagadian 80,861 . . . . D7
Palo 31,124 . . . . E5
Palompon 40,242 . . . . E5
Panabo 71,098 . . . . E7
Prosperidad 33,824 . . . . F6
Puerto Princesa 60,234 . . . . . B6
Quezon City 1,165,865 . . . . . . C3
Romblon 24,251 . . . . D4
Roxas 81,183 . . . . D5
Sagay 99,118 . . . . D5
San Antonio 42,969 . . . . B3
San Carlos, Negros Occ. 91,627 . . . . D5
San Carlos Pangasinan 101,243 . . . . C3
San Fernando, La Union 68,410 . . . . C2
San Fernando, Pampanga 110,891 . . . . C3
San Jose 64,254 . . . . C3
San Jose del Monte 90,732 . . C3
San Pablo ı31,655 . . . . C3
Santa Fe 6,338 . . . . C2
Santiago 69,877 . . . . C2
Silay 111,131 . . . . D5
Siquijor 17,533 . . . . D6
Surigao 79,745 . . . . E6
Tacloban 102,523 . . . . E5
Tagaytay 16,322 . . . . C3
Tagum 86,201 . . . . E7
Tarlac 175,691 . . . . C3
Toledo 91,668 . . . . D5
Tuguegarao 73,507 . . . . C2
Zamboanga 343,722 . . . . C7

OTHER FEATURES

Agusan (riv.) E6
Alabat (isl.) D3
Apo (vol.) E7
Babuyan (isl.) B2
Balabac (isl.) A7
Balayan (bay) C4
Balintang (chan.) A2
Baloy (mt.) D5
Bantayan (isl.) D5
Banton (isl.) D4
Bashi (chan.) A1
Basilan (isl.) D7
Batan, Albay (isl.) E4
Batan, Batanes (isl.) B2
Batan (isls.) A2
Bay, Laguna de (lake) C3
Biliran (isl.) E5
Bohol (isl.) E6
Bojeador (cape) C1
Borocay (isl.) D5
Bucas Grande (isl.) F6
Bugsuk (isl.) A6
Buliluyan (cape) A6
Bunga (pt.) E4
Burias (isl.) D4
Busuanga (isl.) B4
Cabalasan (mt.) E5
Cabulauan (isls.) C5
Cagayan (isls.) C6
Cagayan (riv.) C2
Cagayan Sulu (isl.) B7
Cagua (vol.) D1
Calagua (isls.) D3
Calamian Group (isls.) B4
Calayan (isl.) A2
Calicoan (isl.) E5
Camiguin, Cagayan (isl.) . . . B3
Camiguin, Camiguin (isl.) . . . E6
Camotes (isls.) E5
Camotes (sea) E5
Canigao (chan.) E5
Canlaon (peak) D5
Capotoan (mt.) E4
Carabao (isl.) D4
Catanduanes (isl.) E4
Cebu (isl.) D5
Celebes (sea) D8
Cleopatra Needle (mt.) B5
Coron (isl.) C5
Corregidor (isl.) C3
Culion (isl.) B5
Cuyo (isl.) C5
Cuyo (isls.) C5
Daram (isl.) E5
Davao (gulf) E7
Dinagat (isl.) E5
Diuata (mts.) E6
Dumanquilas (bay) D7
Dumaran (isl.) C5
Engaño (cape) D1
Espiritu Santo (cape) E4
Fuga (isl.) A3
Guimaras (isl.) D5
Halcon (mt.) C4
Hibuson (isl.) E5
Homonhon (isl.) E5
Honda (bay) B6
Iligan (bay) E6
Ilin (isl.) C4
Illana (bay) D7
Imuruan (bay) B5
Island (bay) B6
Itbayat (isl.) A2
Jintotolo (chan.) D5
Jolo (isl.) C7
Jomalig (isl.) D3
Lagonoy (gulf) E4
Lamon (bay) C3
Lanao (lake) E7
Laparan (isls.) B8
Lapinin (isl.) E5
Leyte (gulf) E5
Leyte (isl.) E5
Limasawa (isl.) E6
Linapacan (isl.) B5
Lingayen (gulf) C2
Lubang (isls.) B4
Luzon (isl.) C3
Luzon (str.) A2
Macajalar (bay) E6
Malindang (mt.) D6
Mangsee (isls.) A7
Manila (bay) C3
Mantalingajan (mt.) A6
Maqueda (chan.) D3
Maraira (pt.) C1
Marinduque (isl.) C4
Masbate (isl.) D4
Mayon (vol.) D4
Maytiguid (isl.) B5
Mindanao (isl.) D7
Mindanao (riv.) E7
Mindoro (isl.) C4
Mindoro (str.) C4
Mompog (passg.) D4
Moro (gulf) D7
Mount Apo National Park . . . E7
Naso (pt.) C5
Negros (isl.) D6
Olutanga (isl.) D7
Pacsan (mt.) C2
Palawan (isl.) B6
Palawan (passg.) A6
Panaon (isl.) E5
Panay (isl.) D5
Panglao (isl.) D6
Pangutaran (isl.) C7
Pangutaran Group (isls.) . . . C7
Patnanongan (isl.) D3
Philippine (sea) D3
Pilas (isl.) C7
Pinatubo (mt.) C3
Polillo (isl.) C3
Pujada (bay) F7
Pulangi (riv.) E7
Ragang (vol.) E7
Ragay (gulf) D4
Rapu-Rapu (isl.) E4
Romblon (isl.) D4
Sabtang (isl.) B2
Sacol (isl.) D7
Samal (isl.) E7
Samales Group (isls.) D7
Samar (isl.) E5
Samar (sea) E4
San Agustin (cape) F7
San Bernardino (str.) E4
San Miguel (bay) D3
San Pedro (bay) E5
Santo Tomas (mt.) C2
Semirara (isls.) C5
Siargao (isl.) F6
Sibay (isl.) C5
Sibuguey (bay) D7
Sibutu Group (isls.) B8
Sibuyan (isl.) D4
Sibuyan (sea) D4
Sierra Madre (mt.) D2
Simunul (isl.) B8
Siquijor (isl.) D6
South China (sea) B3
Subic (bay) C3
Sulu (arch.) B8
Sulu (sea) B6
Suluan (isl.) F5
Surigao (str.) E6
Taal (lake) C4
Tablas (isl.) D4
Tablas (str.) C4
Tagapula (isl.) E4
Tagolo (pt.) D6
Tanon (str.) D6
Tapul (isl.) C8
Tapul Group (isls.) C8
Tara (isl.) C4
Tawi-Tawi (isl.) B8
Tayabas (bay) C4
Ticao (isl.) D4
Tinaca (pt.) E8
Tongquil (isl.) D8
Tumindao (isl.) B8
Turtle (isls.) B7
Verde Island (passg.) C4
Victoria (peaks) B6
Visayan (sea) D5

Topography

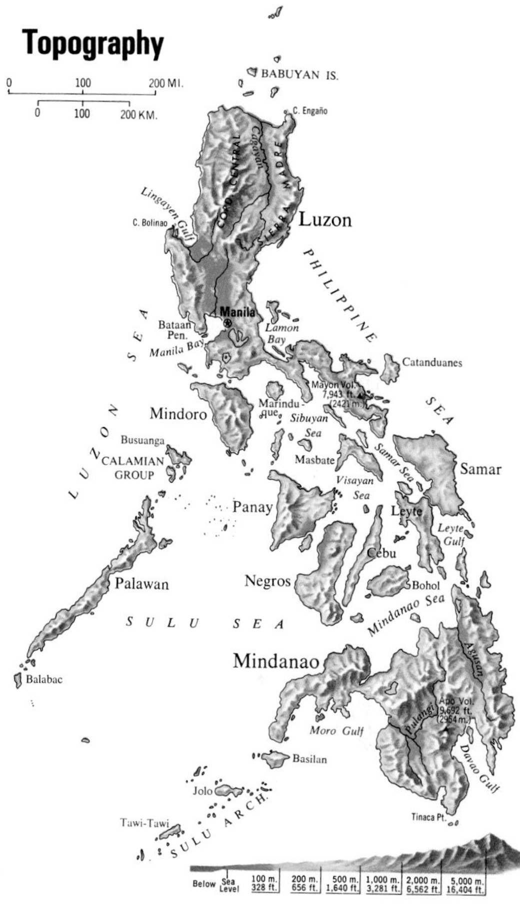

Agriculture, Industry and Resources

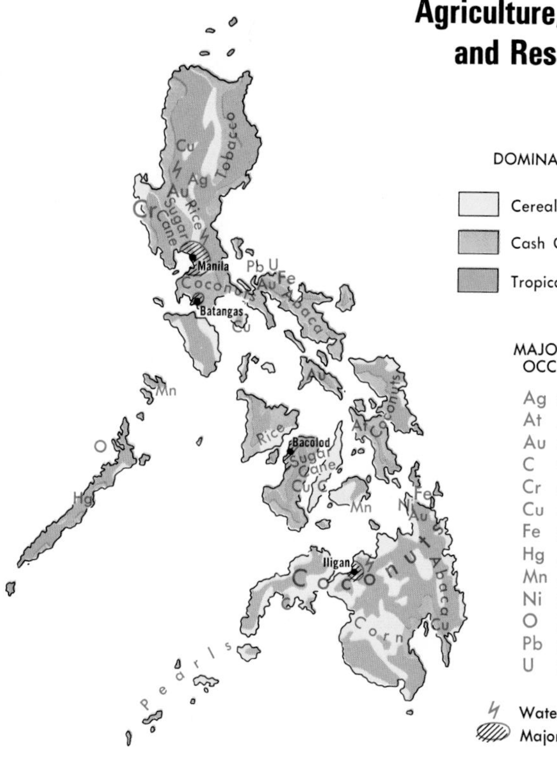

DOMINANT LAND USE

- Cereals (chiefly rice, corn)
- Cash Crops
- Tropical Forests

MAJOR MINERAL OCCURRENCES

- Ag Silver
- At Asphalt
- Au Gold
- C Coal
- Cr Chromium
- Cu Copper
- Fe Iron
- Hg Mercury
- Mn Manganese
- Ni Nickel
- O Petroleum
- Pb Lead
- U Uranium

- Water Power
- Major Industrial Areas

84 Southeast Asia

BRUNEI

CITIES and TOWNS

Bandar Seri Begawan 63,868 . . . E4
Seria 23,511 . . . E5

INDONESIA

CITIES and TOWNS

Adaut . . . J7
Agats . . . K7
Ambon (Amboina) 208,898 . . . H6
Amuntai . . . F6
Amurang . . . G5
Atambua . . . G7
Aubá . . . H7
Baa . . . G8
Bagansiapiapi . . . C5
Balikpapan 280,675 . . . F6
Banda Aceh 72,090 . . . A4
Bandanaira . . . H6
Bandung 1,462,637 . . . H2
Banggai . . . G6
Banjarmasin 381,286 . . . E6
Banyumas . . . J2
Batang . . . J2
Batavia (Jakarta) (cap.) 6,503,449 . . . H1
Baukau . . . H7
Bekasi . . . H2
Belawan . . . B5
Bengkulu 64,783 . . . C6
Beo . . . H5
Biak . . . K6
Binjai 76,464 . . . B5
Bintuhan . . . C6
Blitar 78,503 . . . K2
Bogor 247,409 . . . H2
Bojonegoro . . . J2
Bukittinggi 70,771 . . . B6
Bula . . . J6
Bulukumba . . . G7
Buntok . . . F6
Cianjur . . . H2
Cimahi . . . H2
Cirebon 223,776 . . . H2
Demta . . . L6
Denpasar . . . E7
Dili . . . H7
Djambi (Jambi) 230,373 . . . C6
Djokjakarta (Yogyakarta) 398,727 . . . J2
Dobo . . . J7
Donggala . . . F6
Enaratoli . . . K6
Ende . . . G7
Fakfak . . . J6
Garut . . . H2
Gorontalo 97,628 . . . G5
Hollandia (Jayapura) . . . K6
Indramayu . . . H2
Jailolo . . . H5
Jakarta (cap.) 6,503,449 . . . H1
Jambi 230,373 . . . C6
Jayapura (Hollandia) . . . K6
Jogjakarta (Yogyakarta) 398,727 . . . J2
Jombang . . . K2
Kaimana . . . J6
Kampung Baru (Tolitoli) . . . G5
Kediri 221,820 . . . K2
Kendari . . . G6
Kepi . . . K7
Ketapang . . . E6
Kokonau . . . K6
Kolonodale . . . G6
Kotabaharu . . . E6
Kotabaru . . . F6
Kotawaringin . . . E6
Kragen . . . K2
Kupang . . . G8
Kutaraja (Banda Aceh) 72,090 . . . A4
Labuha . . . H6
Labuhan . . . G2
Laiwui . . . H6
Larantuka . . . G7
Lekitobi . . . G6
Longiram . . . F5
Madiun 150,562 . . . K2
Magelang 123,484 . . . J2
Majalengka . . . H2
Makassar (Ujung Pandang) 709,038 . . . F7
Malang 511,780 . . . K2
Malili . . . G6
Manado 217,159 . . . G5
Manokwari . . . J6
Maumere . . . G7
Medan 1,378,955 . . . B5
Menggala . . . D6
Merauke . . . K7
Mindiptana . . . L7
Mojokerto 68,849 . . . K2
Muarasiberut . . . B6
Nangatayap . . . E6
Pacitan . . . J2
Padang 480,922 . . . B6
Padangpanjang 34,517 . . . B6
Padangsidempuan . . . B5
Pakanbaru 186,262 . . . C5
Palangkaraya 60,447 . . . E6
Palembang 787,187 . . . D6
Pangkalanbuun . . . E6
Pangkalpinang 90,096 . . . D6
Parepare 86,450 . . . F6
Pasangkayu . . . F6
Pasuruan 95,864 . . . K2
Payakumbuh 78,836 . . . C6
Pekalongan 132,558 . . . J2
Pemalang . . . J2
Pematangsiantar 150,376 . . . B5
Pinrang . . . F6
Plaju . . . D6
Pontianak 304,778 . . . D6
Probolinggo 100,296 . . . K2
Purbolinggo . . . J2
Raha . . . G6
Rantauprapat . . . C5
Rembang . . . K2
Sabang, Celebes . . . F5
Sabang, Weh 23,821 . . . B4
Salatiga 85,849 . . . J2
Samarinda 264,718 . . . F6
Sampit . . . E6
Sarmi . . . K6
Sawahlunto 13,561 . . . C6
Seba . . . G8
Semarang 1,026,671 . . . J2
Semitau . . . E5
Serui . . . K6
Sibolga 59,897 . . . B5
Sigli . . . B4
Sinabang . . . B5
Singaraja . . . F7
Solo (Surakarta) 469,888 . . . J2
Solok 31,724 . . . C6
Sorong . . . J6
Sragen . . . J2
Subang . . . H2
Sukabumi 109,994 . . . H2
Sumbawa Besar . . . F7
Sumedang . . . H2
Surabaya 2,027,913 . . . K2
Surakarta 469,888 . . . J2
Tanahmerah . . . K7
Tanjungbalai 41,894 . . . C5
Tanjungkarang 284,275 . . . D7
Tanjungpinang . . . C5
Tanjungselor . . . F5
Tarakan . . . F5
Tebingtinggi 92,087 . . . B5
Tegal 131,728 . . . J2
Telukbayur . . . C6
Tepa . . . H7
Terempa . . . D5
Tjilatjap (Cilicap) . . . H2
Tjirebon (Cirebon) 223,776 . . . H2
Tolitoli . . . G5
Tuban . . . K2
Ujung Pandang 709,038 . . . F7
Vikeke . . . H7
Wahai . . . H6
Waigama . . . H6
Wajabula . . . H5
Waren . . . K6
Weda . . . H5
Wonreli . . . H7
Yogyakarta 398,727 . . . J2

OTHER FEATURES

Anambas (isls.) 29,572 . . . D5
Arafura (sea) . . . J8
Aru (isls.) 34,195 . . . K7
Babar (isl.) . . . H7
Bali (isl.) 2,074,438 . . . F7
Banda (sea) . . . H7
Banggai (arch.) 169,025 . . . G6
Bangka (isl.) 298,017 . . . D6
Banyak (isls.) 1,980 . . . B5
Barisan (mts.) . . . C6
Barito (riv.) . . . E6
Batu (isls.) 16,390 . . . B6
Bawean (isl.) 64,551 . . . K1
Belitung (Billiton) (isl.) 128,694 . . . D6
Berau (bay) . . . J6
Biak (isl.) . . . K6
Billiton (isl.) 128,694 . . . D6
Binongko (isl.) 11,549 . . . G7
Bone (gulf) . . . G7
Borneo (isl.) . . . E5
Bosch, van den (cape) . . . J6
Bunguran (Great Natuna) (isl.) . . . D5
Buru (isl.) 23,034 . . . H6
Butung (isl.) 188,173 . . . G6
Celebes (Sulawesi) (isl.) 7,732,383 . . . G5
Celebes (sea) . . . G5
Cenderawasih (bay) . . . K6
Dampier (str.) . . . J6
Digul (riv.) . . . K7
Doberai (pen.) . . . J6
Enggano (isl.) 1,082 . . . C7
Ewab (Kai) (isls.) 108,328 . . . J7
Flores (isl.) 860,328 . . . G7
Flores (sea) . . . F7
Frederik Hendrik (Kolepom) (isl.) . . . K7
Geelvink (Cenderawasih) (bay) . . . K6
Great Kai (isl.) 38,748 . . . J7
Halmahera (isl.) 122,521 . . . H5
Irian Jaya (reg.) 923,440 . . . J6
Jambuair (cape) . . . B4
Jamursba (cape) . . . J5
Java (head) . . . C7
Java (isl.) 73,712,411 . . . J2
Java (sea) . . . D6
Jaya, Puncak (mt.) . . . K6
Jayawijaya (range) . . . K6
Jemaja (isl.) 5,628 . . . D5
Kabaena (isl.) . . . G7
Kai (isls.) 108,328 . . . J7
Kalao (isl.) . . . G7
Kalaotoa (isl.) . . . G5
Kalimantan (reg.) 4,956,865 . . . E5
Kangean (isl.) . . . F7
Kapuas (riv.) . . . D6
Karakelong (isl.) . . . H5
Karimata (arch.) 9,398 . . . D6
Karimunjawa (isls.) 5,025 . . . J1
Kerinci (mt.) . . . C6
Kisar (isl.) . . . H7
Komodo (isl.) 30,407 . . . F7
Krakatau (Rakata) (isl.) . . . C7
Laut (isl.) 55,711 . . . F6
Leuser (mt.) . . . B5
Lingga (arch.) 46,658 . . . D5
Lingga (isl.) 18,027 . . . D6
Lombok (isl.) 1,581,193 . . . F7
Madura (isl.) 1,509,774 . . . K2
Mahakam (riv.) . . . F6
Makassar (str.) . . . F6
Malacca (str.) . . . C5
Mamberamo (riv.) . . . K6
Maoke (mts.) . . . K6
Mapia (isls.) . . . J5
Mentawai (isls.) 30,107 . . . B6
Misool (isl.) . . . J6
Molucca (sea) . . . H6
Moluccas (isls.) 944,240 . . . H6
Morotai (isl.) 27,333 . . . H5
Muli (str.) . . . K7
Müller (mts.) . . . E5
Muna (isl.) 156,186 . . . G7
Musi (riv.) . . . C6
Natuna (isls.) 23,893 . . . D5
Ngunju (cape) . . . F8
Nias (isl.) 356,093 . . . B5
Numfoor (isl.) . . . J6
Obi (isls.) 12,437 . . . H6
Ombai (str.) . . . H7
Pantar (isl.) 28,259 . . . G7
Perkam (cape) . . . K6
Puting, Borneo (cape) . . . E6
Puting, Sumatra (cape) . . . C7
Raja Ampat Group (isls.) . . . H6
Rakata (isl.) . . . C7
Rantekombola (mt.) . . . F6
Raya (mt.) . . . E6
Riau (arch.) 483,230 . . . C5
Rokan (riv.) . . . C5
Roti (isl.) 76,270 . . . G8
Salawati (isl.) . . . J6
Sangihe (isl.) . . . H5
Sangihe (isls.) 183,000 . . . G5
Sawu (isls.) 51,002 . . . G8
Sawu (sea) . . . G7
Schouten (isls.) 110,148 . . . K6
Schwaner (mts.) . . . E6
Sebuku (bay) . . . F5
Selatan (cape) . . . E6
Selayar (isl.) 92,342 . . . G7
Semeru (mt.) . . . K2
Siau (isl.) 46,801 . . . H5
Siberut (str.) . . . B6
Simeulue (isl.) 29,147 . . . A5
Singkep (isl.) 28,631 . . . D6
Sipura (isl.) 6,051 . . . B6
Slamet (mt.) . . . J2
Sorikmerapi (mt.) . . . B5
South Natuna (isls.) . . . D5
Sudirman (range) . . . K6
Sula (isls.) 36,922 . . . H6
Sulawesi (isl.) 7,732,383 . . . G6
Sumatra (isl.) 19,360,400 . . . B5
Sumba (isl.) 291,190 . . . F7
Sumba (str.) . . . F7
Sumbawa (isl.) 621,140 . . . F7
Sunda (str.) . . . C7
Tahulandang (isl.) 21,493 . . . H5
Talaud (isls.) 46,395 . . . H5
Taliabu (isl.) 18,303 . . . G6
Tambelan (isls.) 4,032 . . . D5
Tanimbar (isls.) 55,405 . . . J7
Tariku (riv.) . . . K6
Tidore (isl.) 28,655 . . . H5
Timor (reg.) 1,435,527 . . . H7
Timor (sea) . . . H7
Toba (lake) . . . B5
Tolo (gulf) . . . G6
Tomini (gulf) . . . G6
Tukangbesi (isls.) 73,106 . . . G7
Vals (cape) . . . K7
Vogelkop (Doberai) (pen.) . . . J6
Waigeo (isl.) . . . J5
Wakde (isl.) . . . K6
Wangiwangi (isl.) 28,469 . . . G7
We (isl.) . . . B4
Wetar (isl.) . . . H7
Yapen (isl.) 50,888 . . . K6

MALAYSIA

STATES

North Borneo (Sabah) 1,002,608 . . . F3
Sarawak 1,294,753 . . . E5

CITIES and TOWNS

Beaufort 2,709 . . . F4
Bintulu 4,424 . . . E5
Kabong . . . E5
Kampong Sibuti . . . E5
Kapit 1,929 . . . E5
Keningau 2,037 . . . F4
Kota Kinabalu 40,939 . . . F4
Kuching 63,535 . . . E5
Kudat 5,089 . . . F4
Labuan 7,216 . . . E4
Lahad Datu 5,169 . . . F5
Lamag . . . F4
Marudi 4,700 . . . E5
Miri 35,702 . . . E5
Mukah 1,717 . . . E5

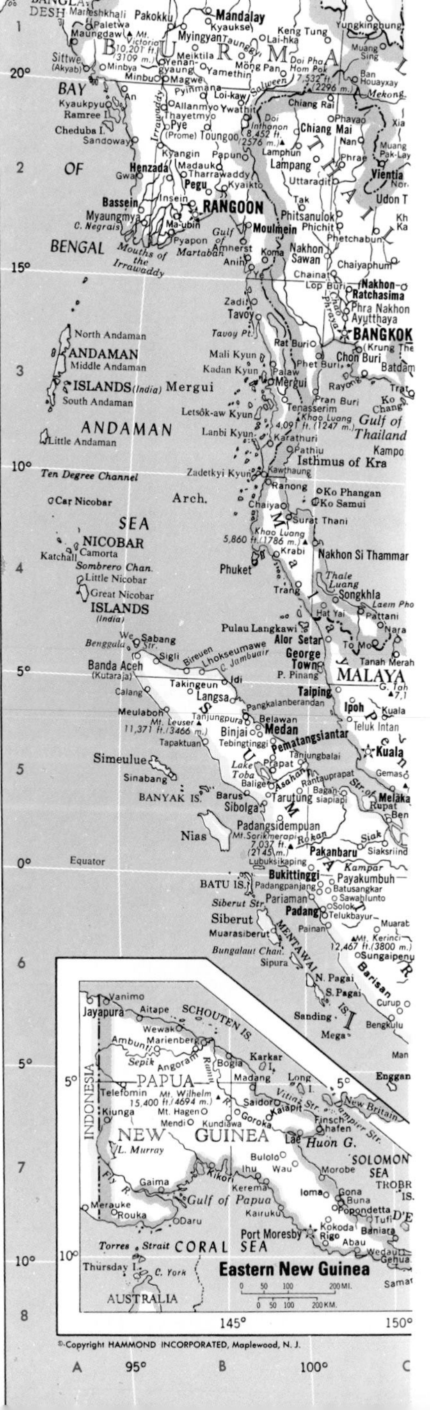

©Copyright HAMMOND INCORPORATED, Maplewood, N. J.

Topography

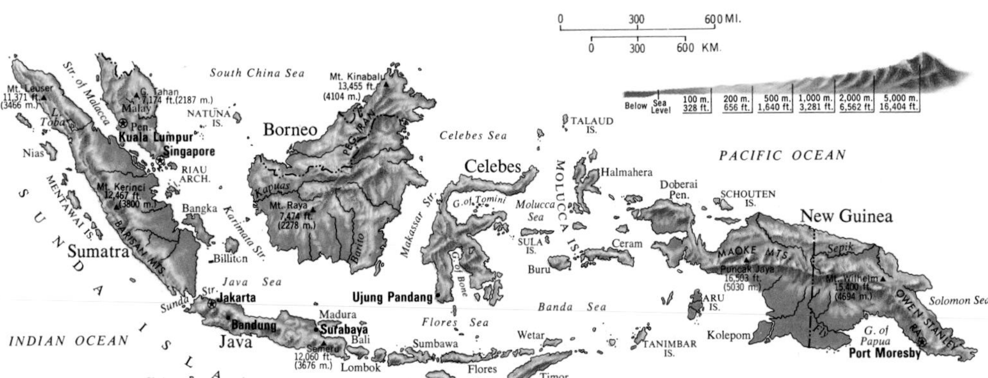

Agriculture, Industry and Resources

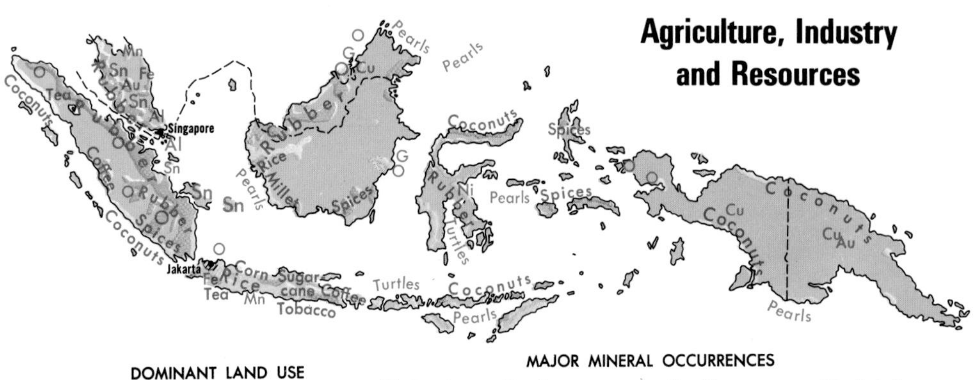

DOMINANT LAND USE

Cereals (chiefly rice, corn)
Diversified Tropical Crops
Forests

MAJOR MINERAL OCCURRENCES

Al Bauxite
Au Gold
C Coal
Cu Copper
Fe Iron Ore
G Natural Gas
Mn Manganese
Ni Nickel
O Petroleum
Sn Tin

Major Industrial Areas

Papar 1,855 . . . . . F4
Ranau 2,024 . . . . . F4
Sandakan 42,413 . . . . . F4
Sematan D5
Semporna 3,371 . . . . . F5
Serian 2,209 . . . . . E5
Sibu 50,635 . . . . . E5
Simanggang 8,445 . . . . . E5
Suai E5
Tawau 24,247 . . . . . F5
Weston F4

OTHER FEATURES

Balambangan (isl.) F4
Banggi (isl.) F4
Iran (mts.) E5
Kinabalu (mt.) F4
Labuan (isl.) 17,189 . . . . . E4
Labuk (bay) F4
Rajang (riv.) E5
Sirik (cape) E5

PAPUA NEW GUINEA

CITIES and TOWNS

Abau C7
Aitape 3,368 . . . . . B6
Ambunti 1,035 . . . . . B6
Angoram 1,846 . . . . . B6
Baniara C7
Bogia 755 . . . . . B6
Bulolo 6,730 . . . . . B7
Buna C7
Daru 7,127 . . . . . B7
Finschhaffen 756 . . . . . C7
Gaima B7
Gehua C8
Gona C7
Goroka 18,511 . . . . . B7
Ihu 541 . . . . . B7
Ioma C7
Kaiapit 515 . . . . . B7
Kairuku B7
Kerema 3,389 . . . . . B7
Kikori 763 . . . . . B7
Kiunga 1,407 . . . . . B7
Kokoda C7
Kundiawa 4,299 . . . . . B7
Lae 61,617 . . . . . B7
Madang 21,335 . . . . . B7
Marienberg B6
Mendi 4,130 . . . . . B7
Morobe C7
Mount Hagen 13,441 . . . . . B7
Popondetta 6,429 . . . . . C7
Port Moresby (cap.) 123,624 . . . . . B7
Rouka B7
Saidor 500 . . . . . B7
Samarai 864 . . . . . C8
Telefomin B7
Vanimo 3,071 . . . . . B6
Wau 2,349 . . . . . B7
Wedau C7
Wewak 19,890 . . . . . B6

OTHER FEATURES

Dampier (str.) C7
D'Entrecasteaux (isls.) C7
Fly (riv.) A7
Huon (gulf) C7
Karkar (isl.) B6
Kiriwina (isl.) C7
Long (isl.) B7
Louisiade (arch.) D8
Milne (bay) C8
Misima (isl.) C8
New Britain (isl.) 148,773 . . . . . C7
Ramu (riv.) B7
Rossel (isl.) D8
Schouten (isls.) B6
Sepik (riv.) B6
Solomon (sea) C7
Tagula (isl.) C8
Torres (str.) A7
Trobriand (isls.) C7
Vitiaz (str.) B7
Woodlark (isl.) C7

★See page 74 for other Malaysian entries.

INDONESIA

AREA 788,430 sq. mi. (2,042,034 sq. km.)
POPULATION 179,136,000
CAPITAL Jakarta
LARGEST CITY Jakarta
HIGHEST POINT Puncak Jaya 16,503 ft. (5,030 m.)
MONETARY UNIT rupiah
MAJOR LANGUAGES Bahasa Indonesia, Indonesian and Papuan languages, English
MAJOR RELIGIONS Islam, tribal religions, Christianity, Hinduism

PAPUA NEW GUINEA

AREA 183,540 sq. mi. (475,369 sq. km.)
POPULATION 3,593,000
CAPITAL Port Moresby
LARGEST CITY Port Moresby
HIGHEST POINT Mt. Wilhelm 15,400 ft. (4,694 m.)
MONETARY UNIT kina
MAJOR LANGUAGES pidgin English, Hiri Motu, English
MAJOR RELIGIONS Tribal religions, Christianity

BRUNEI

AREA 2,226 sq. mi. (5,765 sq. km.)
POPULATION 249,000
CAPITAL Bandar Seri Begawan
LARGEST CITY Bandar Seri Begawan
HIGHEST POINT Pagon 6,070 ft. (1,850 m.)
MONETARY UNIT Brunei Dollar
MAJOR LANGUAGES Malay, English, Chinese
MAJOR RELIGIONS Islam, Buddhism, Christianity, tribal religions

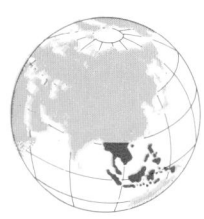

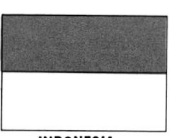

INDONESIA

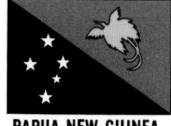

PAPUA NEW GUINEA

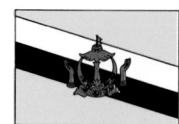

BRUNEI

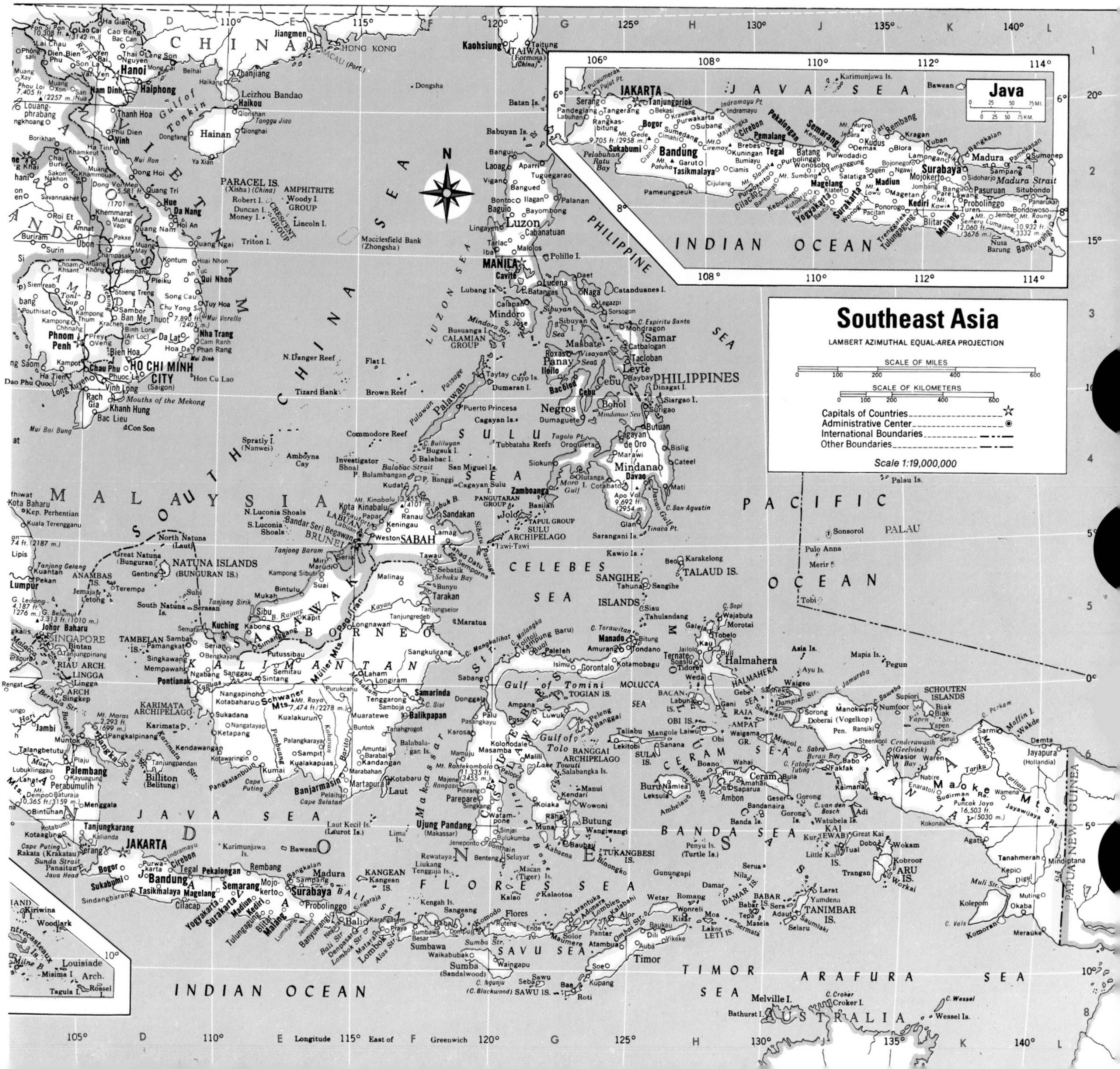

Southeast Asia

LAMBERT AZIMUTHAL EQUAL-AREA PROJECTION

SCALE OF MILES
0 100 200 400 600

SCALE OF KILOMETERS
0 100 200 400 600

Capitals of Countries ☆
Administrative Center ◉
International Boundaries
Other Boundaries

Scale 1:19,000,000

FIJI

AREA 7,055 sq. mi. (18,272 sq. km.)
POPULATION 764,000
CAPITAL Suva
LARGEST CITY Suva
HIGHEST POINT Tomaniivi 4,341 ft. (1,323 m.)
MONETARY UNIT Fijian dollar
MAJOR LANGUAGES Fijian, Hindi, English
MAJOR RELIGIONS Protestantism, Hinduism

KIRIBATI

AREA 291 sq. mi. (754 sq. km.)
POPULATION 78,000
CAPITAL Tarawa
HIGHEST POINT (on Banaba I.) 285 ft. (87 m.)
MONETARY UNIT Australian dollar
MAJOR LANGUAGES I-Kiribati, English
MAJOR RELIGIONS Protestantism, Roman Catholicism

NAURU

AREA 7.7 sq. mi. (20 sq. km.)
POPULATION 10,000
CAPITAL Yaren (district)
MONETARY UNIT Australian dollar
MAJOR LANGUAGES Nauruan, English
MAJOR RELIGION Protestantism

MARSHALL ISLANDS

AREA 70 sq. mi. (181 sq. km.)
POPULATION 54,000
CAPITAL Majuro
MONETARY UNIT U.S. dollar
MAJOR LANGUAGES English, Marshallese, Japanese
MAJOR RELIGION Protestantism

SOLOMON ISLANDS

AREA 11,500 sq. mi. (29,785 sq. km.)
POPULATION 386,000
CAPITAL Honiara
LARGEST CITY Honiara
HIGHEST POINT Mount Popomanatseu 7,647 ft. (2,331 m.)
MONETARY UNIT Solomon Islands dollar
MAJOR LANGUAGES English, pidgin English, Melanesian dialects
MAJOR RELIGIONS Tribal religions, Protestantism, Roman Catholicism

TONGA

AREA 270 sq. mi. (699 sq. km.)
POPULATION 105,000
CAPITAL Nuku'alofa
HIGHEST POINT Kao Island 3,389 ft. (1,033 m.)
MONETARY UNIT pa'anga
MAJOR LANGUAGES Tongan, English
MAJOR RELIGION Protestantism

TUVALU

AREA 9.78 sq. mi. (25.33 sq. km.)
POPULATION 10,000
CAPITAL Funafuti
MONETARY UNIT Australian dollar
MAJOR LANGUAGES English, Tuvaluan
MAJOR RELIGION Protestantism

MICRONESIA

AREA 271 sq. mi. (702 sq. km.)
POPULATION 120,347
CAPITAL Palikir
MONETARY UNIT U.S. dollar
MAJOR LANGUAGES English, Trukese, Pohnpeian, Yapese, Kosrean
MAJOR RELIGIONS Roman Catholicism, Protestantism

Abaiang (atoll) 3,296 . . . . H 5
Abemama (atoll) 2,300 . . . . H 5
Adamstown (cap.), Pitcairn Is. 54 . . . . N 8
Admiralty (isls.) . . . . E 6
Agaña (cap.), Guam 896 . . . . . . E 4
Agrihan (isl.) . . . . E 4
Ailinglapalap (atoll) 1,385 . . . . . . G 5
Ailuk (atoll) 413 . . . . G 4
Aitutaki (atoll) 2,348 . . . . K 7
Alofi (cap.), Niue 960 . . . . K 7
Alotau 4,310 . . . . E 7
Ambrym (isl.) 6,324 . . . . G 7
American Samoa 32,297 . . . . J 7
Anaa (atoll) 444 . . . . M 7
Angaur (isl.) 243 . . . . D 5
Apataki (atoll) . . . . M 7
Apia (cap.), W. Samoa 33,100 . . . . J 7
Arno (atoll) 1,487 . . . . H 5
Arorae (atoll) 1,626 . . . . H 6
Atafu (atoll) 577 . . . . J 6
Atiu (isl.) 1,225 . . . . L 8
Austral (isls.) 5,208 . . . . L 8
Avarua (cap.), Cook Is. . . . . L 8
Babelthuap (isl.) 10,391 . . . . D 5
Baker (isl.) . . . . J 5
Banaba (isl.) 2,314 . . . . G 6
Banks (isls.) 3,158 . . . . G 7
Belep (isls.) 624 . . . . F 7
Bellona (reefs) . . . . G 8
Beru (atoll) 2,318 . . . . H 6
Bikini (atoll) . . . . G 4
Bismarck (arch.) 218,339 . . . . . . E 6
Bonin (isls.) 1,879 . . . . L 3
Bora-Bora (isl.) 2,572 . . . . L 7
Bougainville (isl.) 71,761 . . . . . . F 6
Bounty (isls.) . . . . H 10
Bourail 3,149 . . . . G 8
Butaritari (atoll) 2,971 . . . . H 5
Caroline (isl.) . . . . M 7
Caroline (isls.) . . . . E 5
Chichi (isl.) 1,879 . . . . E 3
Choiseul (isl.) 10,349 . . . . F 6
Christmas (Kiritimati) (isl.) 674 . . L 5
Cook (isls.) 17,695 . . . . K 7
Coral (sea) . . . . F 7
Danger (Pukapuka) (atoll) 797 . . . . K 7
Daru 7,127 . . . . E 6
Disappointment (isls.) 373 . . . . . N 7
Ducie (isl.) . . . . O 8
Easter (isl.) 1,598 . . . . Q 8
Ebon (atoll) 887 . . . . G 5
Efate (isl.) 18,038 . . . . G 7
Enderbury (isl.) . . . . J 6
Enewetak (Eniwetok) (atoll) 542 . . . . G 4
Erromanga (isl.) 945 . . . . H 7
Espiritu Santo (isl.) 16,220 . . . . G 7
Fais (isl.) 207 . . . . E 5
Fakaofo (atoll) 654 . . . . J 6
Fanning (Tabuaeran) (isl.) 340 . . L 5
Faraulep (atoll) 132 . . . . E 5
Fatuhiva (isl.) 386 . . . . N 7
Fiji 588,068 . . . . H 8
Flint (isl.) . . . . L 7
Fly (riv.) . . . . E 6
Funafuti (cap.), Tuvalu . . . . H 6
Funafuti (atoll) 2,120 . . . . H 6
Futuna (Hoorn) (isls.) 3,173 . . . . J 7
Gambier (isls.) 556 . . . . N 8
Gardner (Nukumaroro)(isl.) . . . . J 6
Gilbert (isls.) 47,711 . . . . H 5
Greenwich (Kapingamarangi) (atoll) 508 . . . . F 5
Guadalcanal (isl.) 46,619 . . . . . . F 7
Guam 105,979 . . . . E 4
Hall (isls.) 647 . . . . F 5
Hawaiian (isls.) 964,691 . . . . J 3
Henderson (isl.) . . . . O 8
Hivaoa (isl.) 1,159 . . . . N 7
Honiara (cap.), Solomon Is. 14,942 . . . . F 6
Hoorn (isls.) 3,173 . . . . J 7
Howland (isl.) . . . . J 5
Huahine (isl.) 3,140 . . . . L 7
Hull (Orona)(isl.) . . . . J 6
Huon (gulf) . . . . E 6
Ifalik (atoll) 389 . . . . E 5
Iwo (isl.) . . . . E 3
Jaluit (atoll) 1,450 . . . . G 5
Jarvis (isl.) . . . . K 6
Johnston (isl.) 327 . . . . J 4
Kadavu (Kandavu) (isl.) 8,699 . . H 7
Kanton (isl.) . . . . J 6
Kapingamarangi (atoll) 508 . . . . . F 5
Kavieng 4,633 . . . . E 6
Kermadec (isls.) 5 . . . . J 9
Kieta 3,491 . . . . F 6
Kimbe 4,662 . . . . F 6
Kingman (reef) . . . . K 5
Kiribati 57,500 . . . . J 6
Kiritimati (isl.) 674 . . . . L 5
Koror (cap.), Palau 6,222 . . . . . . D 5
Kosrae (isl.) 5,491 . . . . G 5
Kwajalein (atoll) 6,624 . . . . G 5
Lae 61,617 . . . . E 6
Lau Group (isls.) 14,452 . . . . J 7
Lavongai (isl.) . . . . F 6
Lifu (isl.) 7,585 . . . . G 8
Line (isls.) . . . . K 5
Little Makin (atoll) 1,445 . . . . . . H 5
Lord Howe (Ontong Java) (isl.) 1,082 . . . . G 6
Lord Howe (isl.) 287 . . . . G 9
Lorengau 3,986 . . . . E 6
Louisiade (arch.) . . . . F 7
Loyalty (isls.) 14,518 . . . . G 8
Luganville 4,935 . . . . G 7
Madang 21,335 . . . . E 6

Majuro (atoll) (cap.), Marshall Is. 8,583 . . . . H 5
Makin (Butaritari) (atoll) 2,971 . . H 5
Malaita (isl.) 50,912 . . . . G 6
Malden (isl.) . . . . L 6
Malekula (isl.) 15,931 . . . . G 7
Maloelap (atoll) 763 . . . . H 5
Mangaia (isl.) 1,364 . . . . L 8
Mangareva (isl.) 556 . . . . N 8
Manihiki (atoll) 405 . . . . K 7
Manua (isls.) 1,459 . . . . K 7
Manus (isl.) 25,844 . . . . E 6
Maré (isl.) 4,156 . . . . G 8
Marianas, Northern 16,780 . . . . . E 4
Mariana Trench . . . . E 4
Marquesas (isls.) 5,419 . . . . N 6
Marshall Islands 30,873 . . . . G 4
Marutea (atoll) . . . . M 7
Mata Utu (cap.), Wallis and Futuna 558 . . . . J 7
Mauke (isl.) 684 . . . . L 8
Melanesia (reg.) . . . . E 5
Micronesia (reg.) . . . . E 4
Micronesia, Federated States of 73,160 . . . . F 5
Midway (isls.) 453 . . . . J 3
Mili (atoll) 763 . . . . H 5
Moen (isl.) 10,351 . . . . F 5
Moorea (isl.) 5,788 . . . . L 7

Mururoa (isl.) . . . . M 8
Nadi 6,938 . . . . H 7
Namonuito (atoll) 783 . . . . E 5
Namorik (atoll) 617 . . . . G 5
Nanumea (atoll) 844 . . . . H 6
Nauru 7,254 . . . . G 6
Ndeni (isl.) 4,854 . . . . G 7
New Britain (isl.) 148,773 . . . . . . F 6
New Caledonia 133,233 . . . . G 8
New Caledonia (isl.) 118,715 . . . . G 8
New Georgia (isl.) 16,472 . . . . . . F 6
New Guinea (isl.) . . . . E 6
New Ireland (isl.) 65,657 . . . . F 6
Ngatik (atoll) 560 . . . . F 5
Ngulu (atoll) 21 . . . . D 5
Niuatoputapu (isl.) 1,650 . . . . . . J 7
Niue (isl.) 3,578 . . . . K 7
Niutao (atoll) 866 . . . . H 6
Nomoi (isls.) 1,879 . . . . F 5
Nonouti (atoll) 2,223 . . . . H 6
Norfolk Island (terr.) 2,175 . . . . . G 8
Northern Marianas 116,780 . . . . E 4
Nouméa (cap.), New Caled. 56,078 . . . . G 8
Nouméa *74,335 . . . . G 8
Nui (atoll) 603 . . . . H 6
Nuku'alofa (cap.), Tonga 18,356 . . . . J 8
Nukuhiva (isl.) 1,484 . . . . M 6

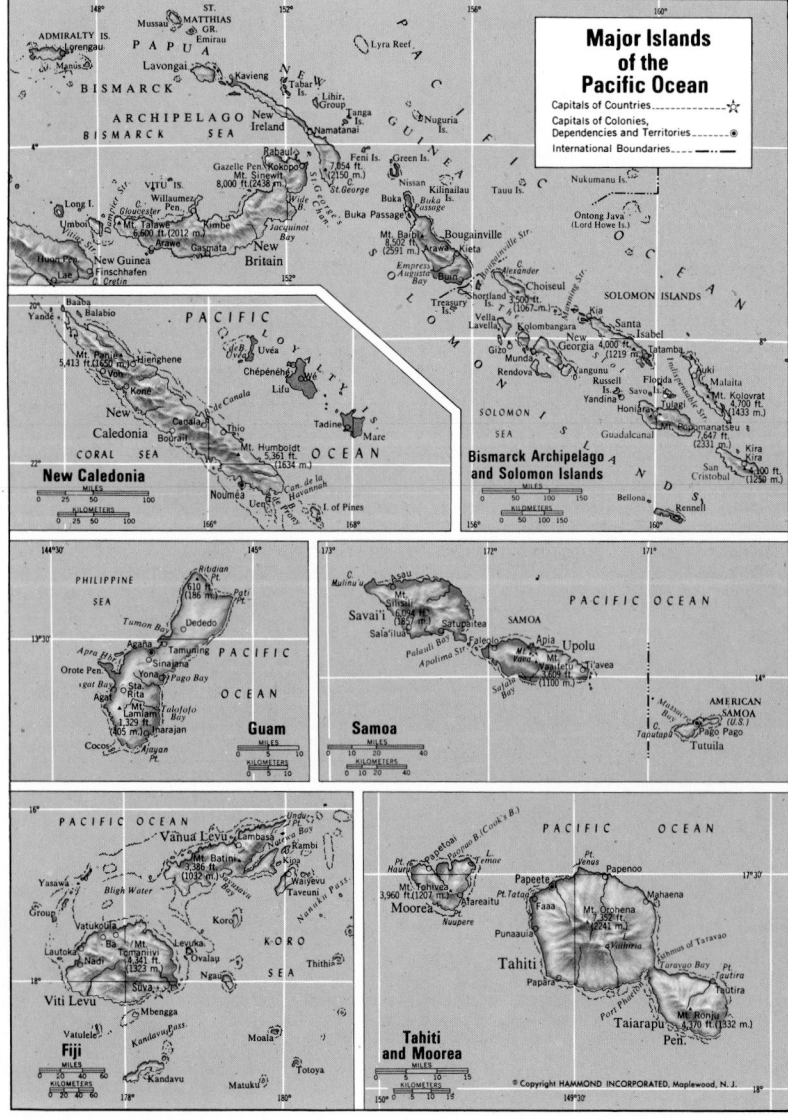

Major Islands of the Pacific Ocean

Capitals of Countries . . . . ☆
Capitals of Colonies, Dependencies and Territories . . . . . ◉
International Boundaries . . . .

Bismarck Archipelago and Solomon Islands

New Caledonia

Guam

Samoa

Fiji

Tahiti and Moorea

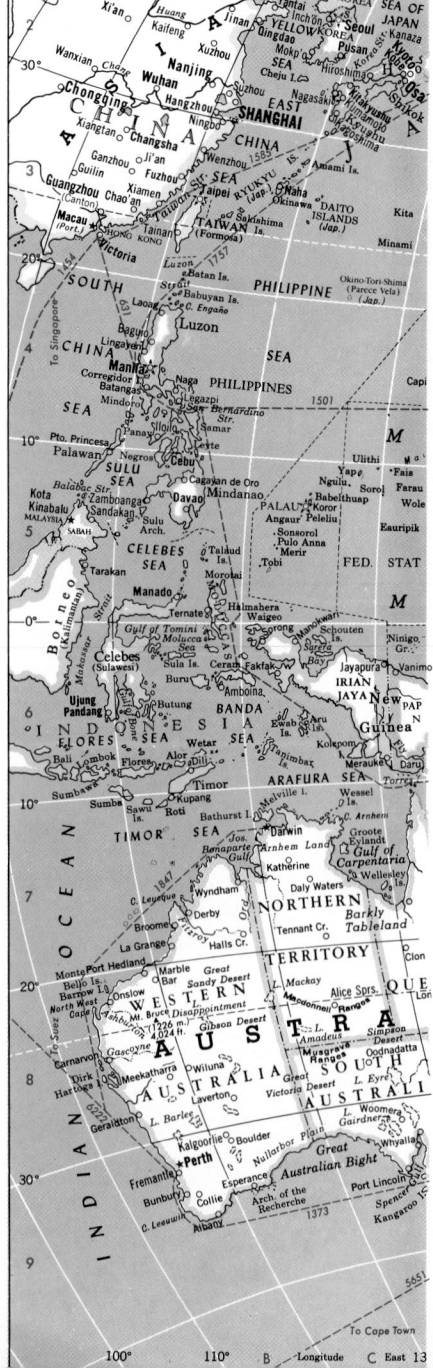

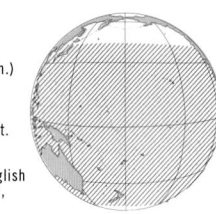

Ocean (Banaba) (isl.) 2,314 . . . G 6
Oeno (isl.) . . . . O 8
Onotoa (atoll) 1,997 . . . . H 6
Onlong Java (isl.) 1,082 . . . . . . G 6
Pagan (isl.) . . . . E 4
Pago Pago (cap.), Amer. Samoa 3,075 . . . . J 7
Palau 12,116 . . . . D 5
Palikir (cap.), Micronesia 5,549 . . . . F 5
Palmyra (atoll) . . . . K 5
Papeete (cap.), Fr. Poly. 22,967 . . . . M 7
Papetee •51,987 . . . . M 7
Papua (gulf) . . . . E 6
Papua New Guinea 3,010,727 . . E 6
Peleliu (isl.) 609 . . . . D 5
Penrhyn (Tongareva) (atoll) 608 . . . . L 6
Phoenix (isls.) . . . . J 6
Pines (isl.) 1,095 . . . . G 8
Pitcairn (isl.) 54 . . . . O 8
Pohnpei (isl.) 19,935 . . . . F 5
Polynesia (reg.) . . . . K 7
Popondetta 6,429 . . . . E 6
Port Moresby (cap.), Papua N.G. 123,624 . . . . E 6
Port-Vila (cap.), Vanuatu 4,729 . G 7
Port-Vila*14,797 . . . . G 7
Pukapuka (atoll) 797 . . . . K 7
Pulap (atoll) 427 . . . . E 5
Puluwat (atoll) 441 . . . . E 5
Rabaul 14,954 . . . . F 6
Raiatea (isl.) 2,517 . . . . L 7
Raivavae (isl.) 1,023 . . . . M 8
Rakahanga (atoll) 269 . . . . K 7
Ralik Chain (isls.) . . . . G 5
Rangiroa (atoll) . . . . M 7
Rapa (isl.) 398 . . . . M 8
Rarotonga (isl.) 9,477 . . . . K 8
Ratak Chain (isls.) . . . . G 5
Reao (atoll) 424 . . . . N 7
Rennell (isl.) 1,132 . . . . F 7
Rikitea . . . . N 8
Rimatara (isl.) 813 . . . . L 8
Rongelap (atoll) 235 . . . . G 4
Rota (isl.) 1,261 . . . . E 4
Rotuma (isl.) 2,805 . . . . H 7
Rurutu (isl.) 1,555 . . . . L 8
Saipan (cap), No. Marianas 14,549 . . . . E 4
Sala y Gomez (isl.) . . . . P 8
Samarai 869 . . . . E 7
Samoa 204,000 . . . . J 7
Samoa (isls.) . . . . J 7
San Cristobal (isl.) 11,212 . . . . G 7
Santa Cruz (isls.) 5,421 . . . . . . G 6
Santa Isabel (isl.) 10,420 . . . . . G 6
Savai'i (isl.) 43,150 . . . . J 7
Senyavin (isls.) 20,035 . . . . F 5
Society (isls.) 117,703 . . . . L 7
Solomon (isls.) . . . . F 6
Solomon (sea) . . . . F 6
Solomon Islands 221,000 . . . . . G 6
Starbuck (isl.) . . . . L 6
Suva (cap.), Fiji 63,628 . . . . . . H 7
Suva *117,827 . . . . H 7
Swains (isl.) 27 . . . . K 7
Sydney (isl.) . . . . K 6
Tabiteuea (atoll) 3,942 . . . . H 6
Tabuaeran (isl.) 340 . . . . L 5
Tahaa (isl.) 3,513 . . . . L 7
Tahiti (isl.) 95,604 . . . . L 7
Takaroa (atoll) 337 . . . . M 7
Tanna (isl.) 15,715 . . . . H 7
Tarawa (cap.), Kiribati 17,129 . . H 5
Tasman (sea) . . . . G 9
Teraina (isl.) 458 . . . . L5
Tinian (isl.) 866 . . . . E 4
Tokelau (isls.) 1,575 . . . . J 6
Tonga 90,128 . . . . J 8
Tongareva (atoll) 608 . . . . L 6
Tongatapu (isls.) 57,130 . . . . . . J 8
Torres (isls.) 325 . . . . G 7
Torres (strait) . . . . E 7
Trobriand (isls.) . . . . F 6
Truk (isls.) 37,488 . . . . F 5
Tuamotu (arch.) 9,052 . . . . M 7
Tubuai (Austral) (isls.) 5,208 . . M 8
Tubuai (isl.) 1,419 . . . . M 8

VANUATU

AREA 5,700 sq. mi. (14,763 sq. km.)
POPULATION 170,000
CAPITAL Port-Vila
LARGEST CITY Port-Vila
HIGHEST POINT Mt. Tabwemasana 6,165 ft. (1,879 m.)
MONETARY UNIT Vatu
MAJOR LANGUAGES Bislama, English, French
MAJOR RELIGIONS Christian, animist

SAMOA

AREA 1,133 sq. mi. (2,934 sq. km.)
POPULATION 204,000
CAPITAL Apia
LARGEST CITY Apia
HIGHEST POINT Mt. Silisili 6,094 ft. (1,857 m.)
MONETARY UNIT tala
MAJOR LANGUAGES Samoan, English
MAJOR RELIGIONS Protestantism, Roman Catholicism

Tutuila (isl.) 30,538 . . . . J 7
Tuvalu 7,349 . . . . H 6
Uapou (isl.) 1,563 . . . . M 6
Ujelang (atoll) 309 . . . . F 5
Ulithi (atoll) 710 . . . . D 4
Upolu (isl.) 114,620 . . . . J 7
Uturoa 2,517 . . . . L 7
Uvéa (isl.) 2,777 . . . . G 7
Vaitupu (atoll) 1,273 . . . . H 6
Vanikoro (isl.) 267 . . . . G 7
Vanimo 3,071 . . . . E 6
Vanua Levu (isl.) 103,122 . . . . . H 7
Vanuatu 170,000 . . . . G 7
Viti Levu (isl.) 445,422 . . . . . . H 7
Volcano (isls.) . . . . E 3
Vostok (isl.) . . . . L 7
Wake (isl.) 302 . . . . G 4
Wallis (isls.) 8,973 . . . . J 7
Wallis and Futuna 13,705 . . . . . J 7
Washington (Teraina) (isl.) 458 . L 5
Wau 2,349 . . . . E 6
Wewak 23,224 . . . . E 6
Woleai (isl.) 638 . . . . E 5
Wotje (atoll) 535 . . . . H 5
Yap (isl.) 6,670 . . . . D 5

*City and suburbs.
•Population of urban area.

PALAU

AREA 177 sq. mi. (458 sq. km.)
POPULATION 15,122
CAPITAL Koror
HIGHEST POINT Mt. Makelulu 804 ft. (242 m.)
MONETARY UNIT U.S. dollar
MAJOR LANGUAGES English, Sonsorolese, Angaur, Japanese, Tobi, Palauan
MAJOR RELIGIONS Christian, Modekngei

FIJI
TONGA
KIRIBATI
TUVALU
NAURU
VANUATU
SOLOMON ISLANDS
SAMOA
MARSHALL ISLANDS
MICRONESIA
PALAU

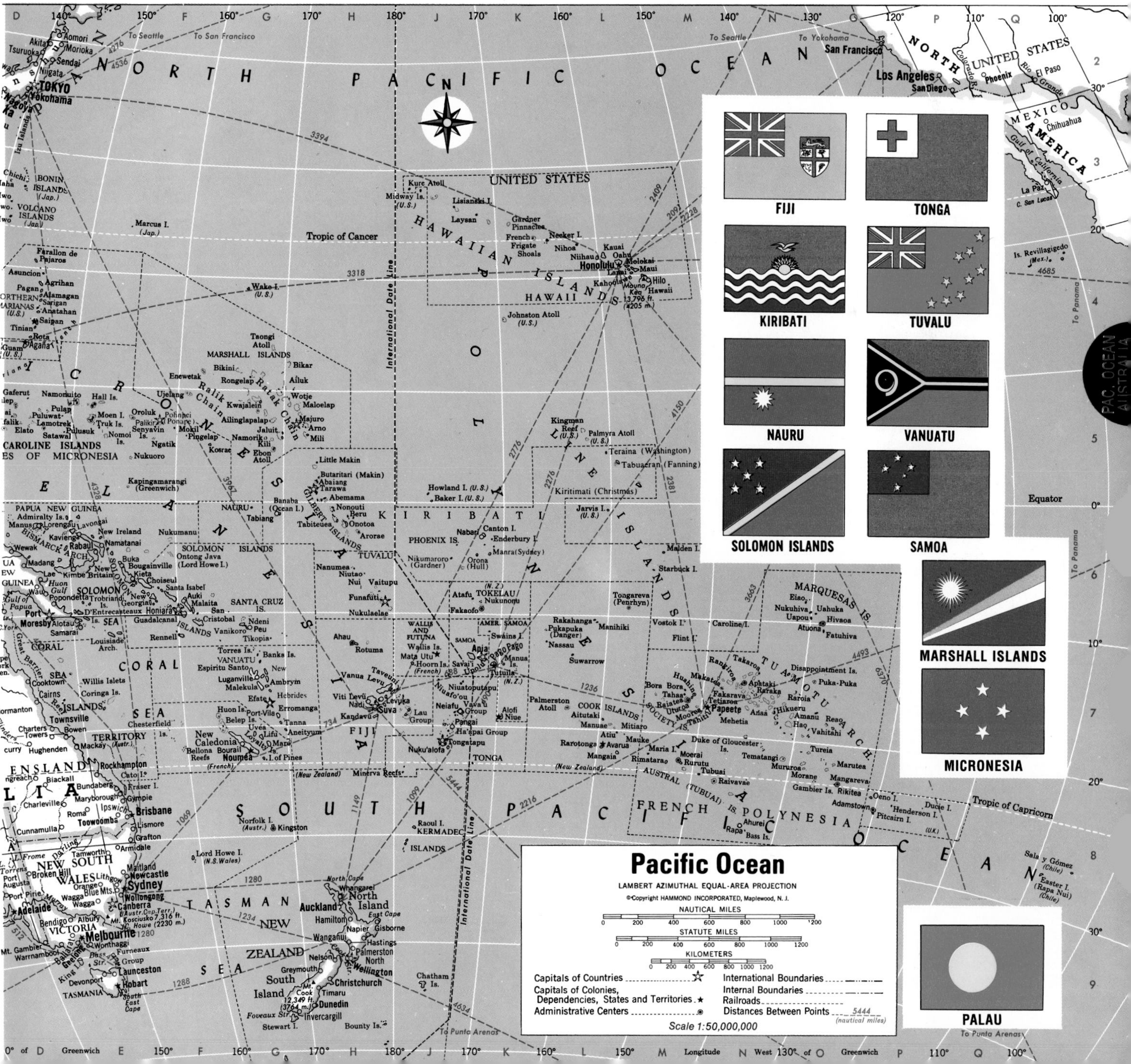

Pacific Ocean

LAMBERT AZIMUTHAL EQUAL-AREA PROJECTION

NAUTICAL MILES 0 200 400 600 800 1000 1200
STATUTE MILES 0 200 400 600 800 1000 1200
KILOMETERS 0 200 400 600 800 1000 1200

Capitals of Countries ☆
Capitals of Colonies, Dependencies, States and Territories ★
Administrative Centers ⊛
International Boundaries
Internal Boundaries
Railroads
Distances Between Points 5444 (nautical miles)

Scale 1:50,000,000

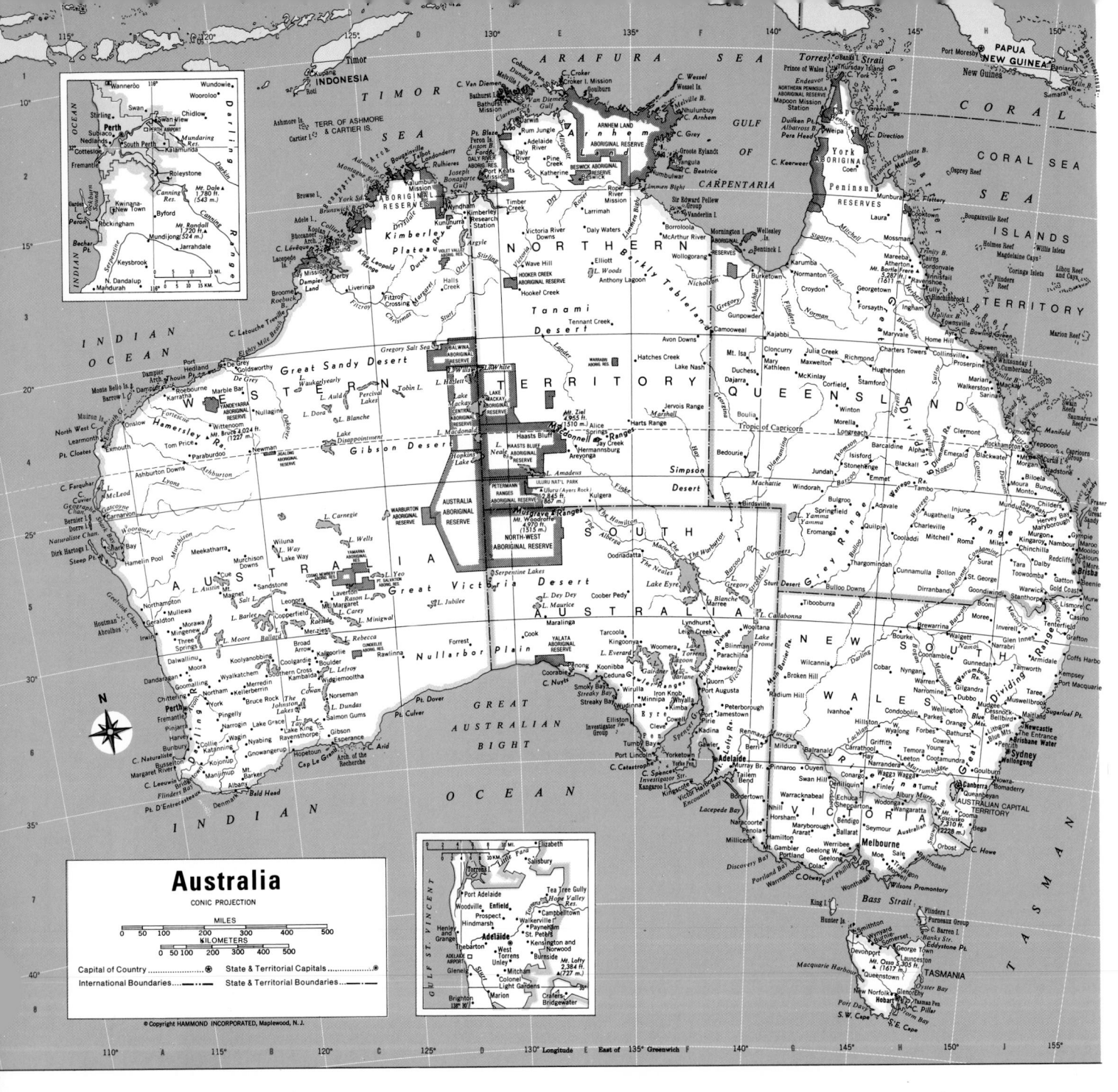

Australia

CONIC PROJECTION

MILES
0 50 100   200   300   400   500

KILOMETERS
0 100 200   300   400   500

Capital of Country .... ⊛   State & Territorial Capitals .... ⊛
International Boundaries ...._____   State & Territorial Boundaries ...._____

© Copyright HAMMOND INCORPORATED, Maplewood, N.J.

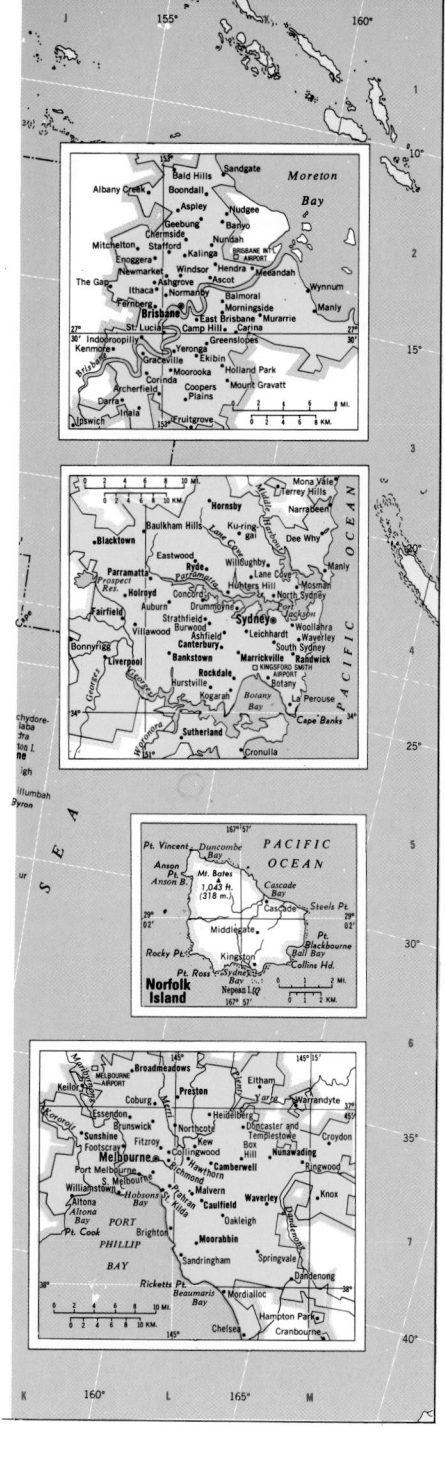

AREA 2,966,136 sq. mi. (7,682,300 sq. km.)
POPULATION 15,602,156
CAPITAL Canberra
LARGEST CITY Sydney
HIGHEST POINT Mt. Kosciusko 7,310 ft.
(2,228 m.)
LOWEST POINT Lake Eyre -39 ft. (-12 m.)
MONETARY UNIT Australian dollar
MAJOR LANGUAGE English
MAJOR RELIGIONS Protestantism,
Roman Catholicism

Population Distribution

• Cities with over 500,000 inhabitants (including suburbs)

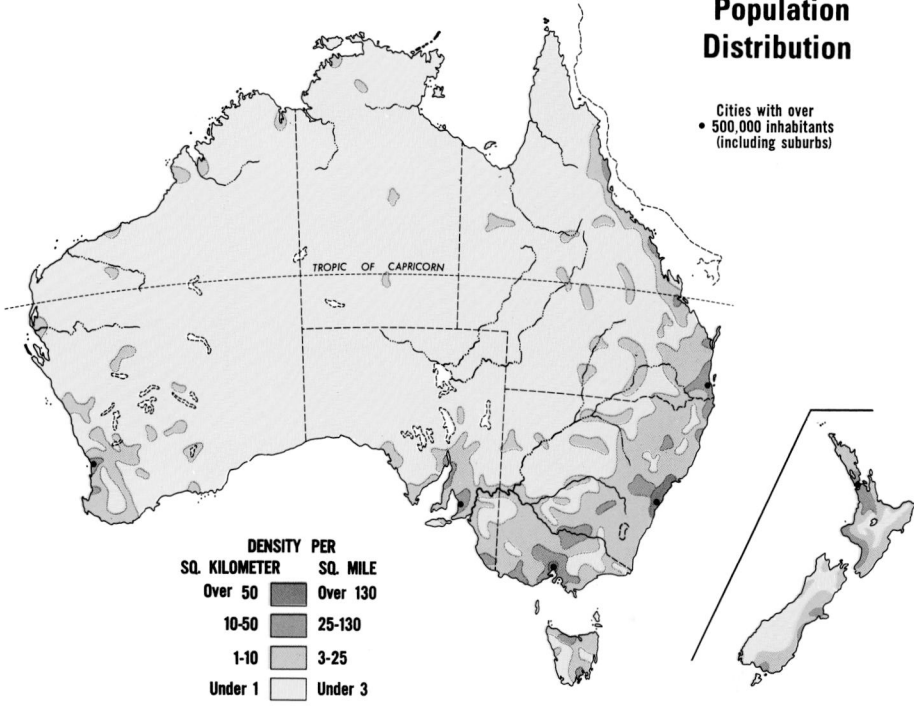

DENSITY PER

SQ. KILOMETER	SQ. MILE
Over 50	Over 130
10-50	25-130
1-10	3-25
Under 1	Under 3

Vegetation

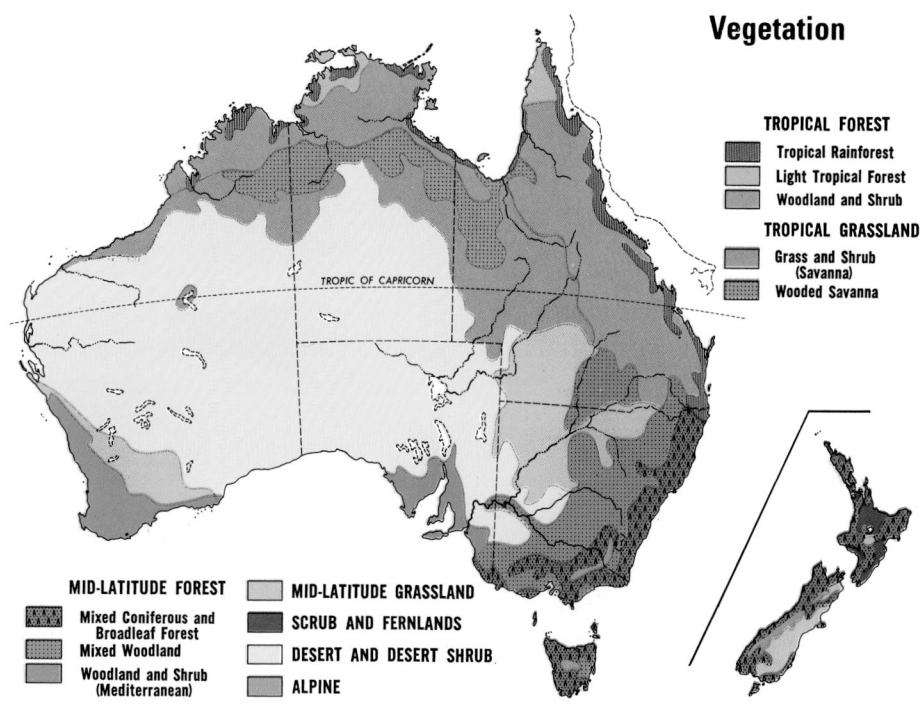

TROPICAL FOREST
Tropical Rainforest
Light Tropical Forest
Woodland and Shrub

TROPICAL GRASSLAND
Grass and Shrub (Savanna)
Wooded Savanna

MID-LATITUDE FOREST
Mixed Coniferous and Broadleaf Forest
Mixed Woodland
Woodland and Shrub (Mediterranean)

MID-LATITUDE GRASSLAND
SCRUB AND FERNLANDS
DESERT AND DESERT SHRUB
ALPINE

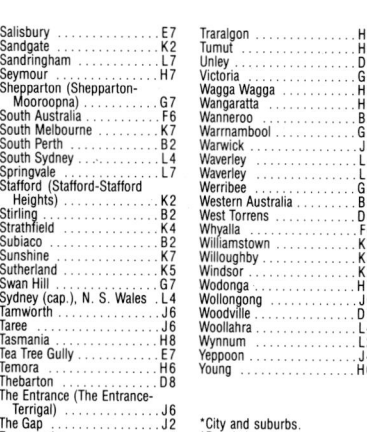

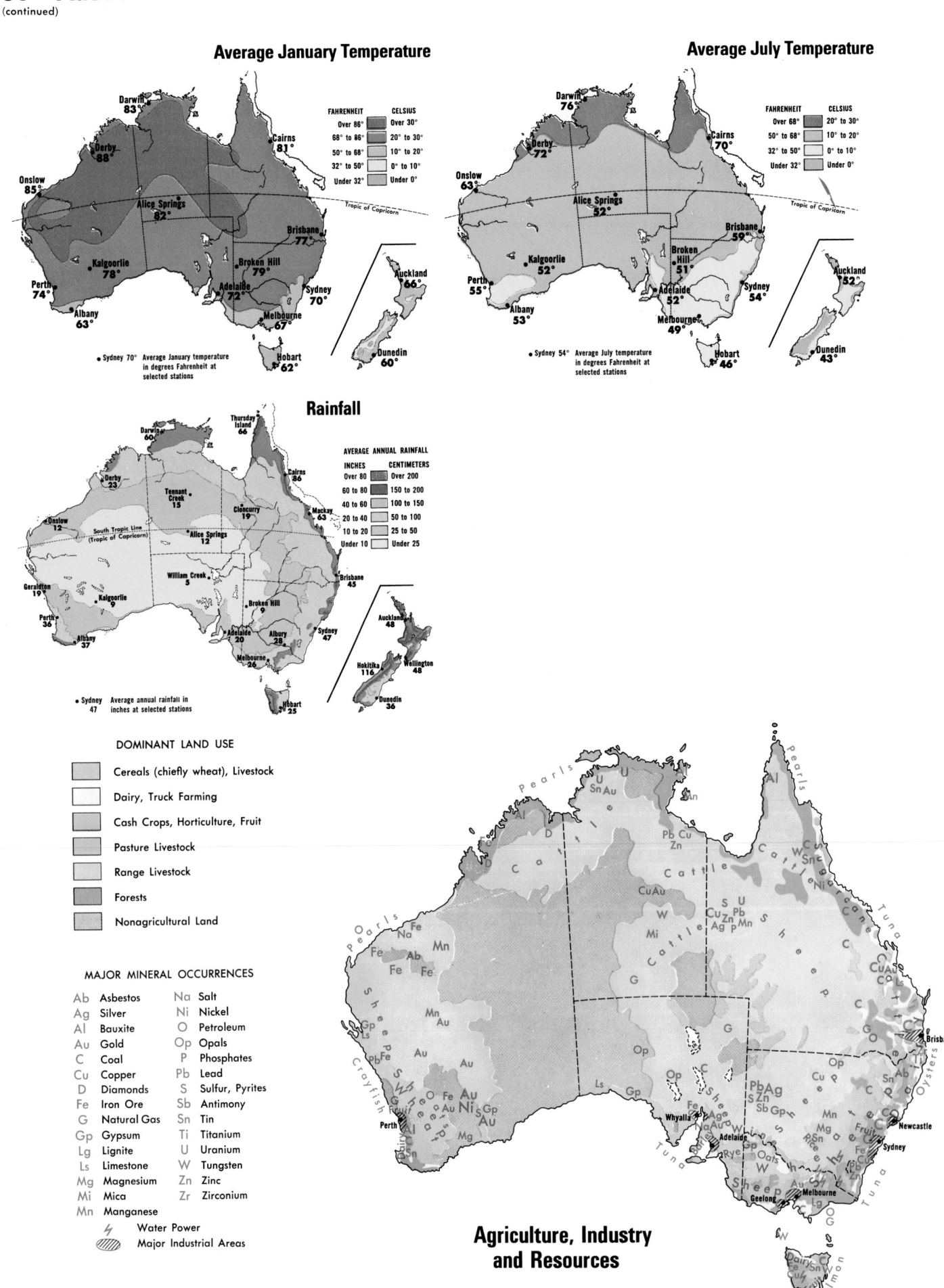

Average January Temperature

FAHRENHEIT	CELSIUS
Over 86°	Over 30°
68° to 86°	20° to 30°
50° to 68°	10° to 20°
32° to 50°	0° to 10°
Under 32°	Under 0°

Darwin 83°
Derby 88°
Onslow 85°
Alice Springs 82°
Cairns 81°
Brisbane 77°
Kalgoorlie 78°
Broken Hill 79°
Perth 74°
Adelaide 72°
Sydney 70°
Albany 63°
Melbourne 67°
Hobart 62°
Auckland 66°
Dunedin 60°

Tropic of Capricorn

• Sydney 70°   Average January temperature in degrees Fahrenheit at selected stations

Average July Temperature

FAHRENHEIT	CELSIUS
Over 68°	20° to 30°
50° to 68°	10° to 20°
32° to 50°	0° to 10°
Under 32°	Under 0°

Darwin 76°
Derby 72°
Onslow 63°
Alice Springs 52°
Cairns 70°
Brisbane 59°
Kalgoorlie 52°
Broken Hill 51°
Perth 55°
Adelaide 52°
Sydney 54°
Albany 53°
Melbourne 49°
Hobart 46°
Auckland 52°
Dunedin 43°

Tropic of Capricorn

• Sydney 54°   Average July temperature in degrees Fahrenheit at selected stations

Rainfall

AVERAGE ANNUAL RAINFALL	
INCHES	CENTIMETERS
Over 80	Over 200
60 to 80	150 to 200
40 to 60	100 to 150
20 to 40	50 to 100
10 to 20	25 to 50
Under 10	Under 25

Darwin 60
Thursday Island 66
Derby 23
Tennant Creek 15
Cairns 36
Cloncurry 19
Mackay 63
Onslow 12
Alice Springs 12
South Tropic Line (Tropic of Capricorn)
William Creek 5
Brisbane 45
Geraldton 19
Kalgoorlie 9
Broken Hill
Perth 36
Adelaide 20
Albury 28
Sydney 47
Albany 37
Melbourne 26
Hobart 25
Auckland 48
Hokitika 116
Wellington 48
Dunedin 36

• Sydney 47   Average annual rainfall in inches at selected stations

DOMINANT LAND USE

- Cereals (chiefly wheat), Livestock
- Dairy, Truck Farming
- Cash Crops, Horticulture, Fruit
- Pasture Livestock
- Range Livestock
- Forests
- Nonagricultural Land

MAJOR MINERAL OCCURRENCES

Ab	Asbestos	Na	Salt
Ag	Silver	Ni	Nickel
Al	Bauxite	O	Petroleum
Au	Gold	Op	Opals
C	Coal	P	Phosphates
Cu	Copper	Pb	Lead
D	Diamonds	S	Sulfur, Pyrites
Fe	Iron Ore	Sb	Antimony
G	Natural Gas	Sn	Tin
Gp	Gypsum	Ti	Titanium
Lg	Lignite	U	Uranium
Ls	Limestone	W	Tungsten
Mg	Magnesium	Zn	Zinc
Mi	Mica	Zr	Zirconium
Mn	Manganese		

⚡ Water Power
▨ Major Industrial Areas

Agriculture, Industry and Resources

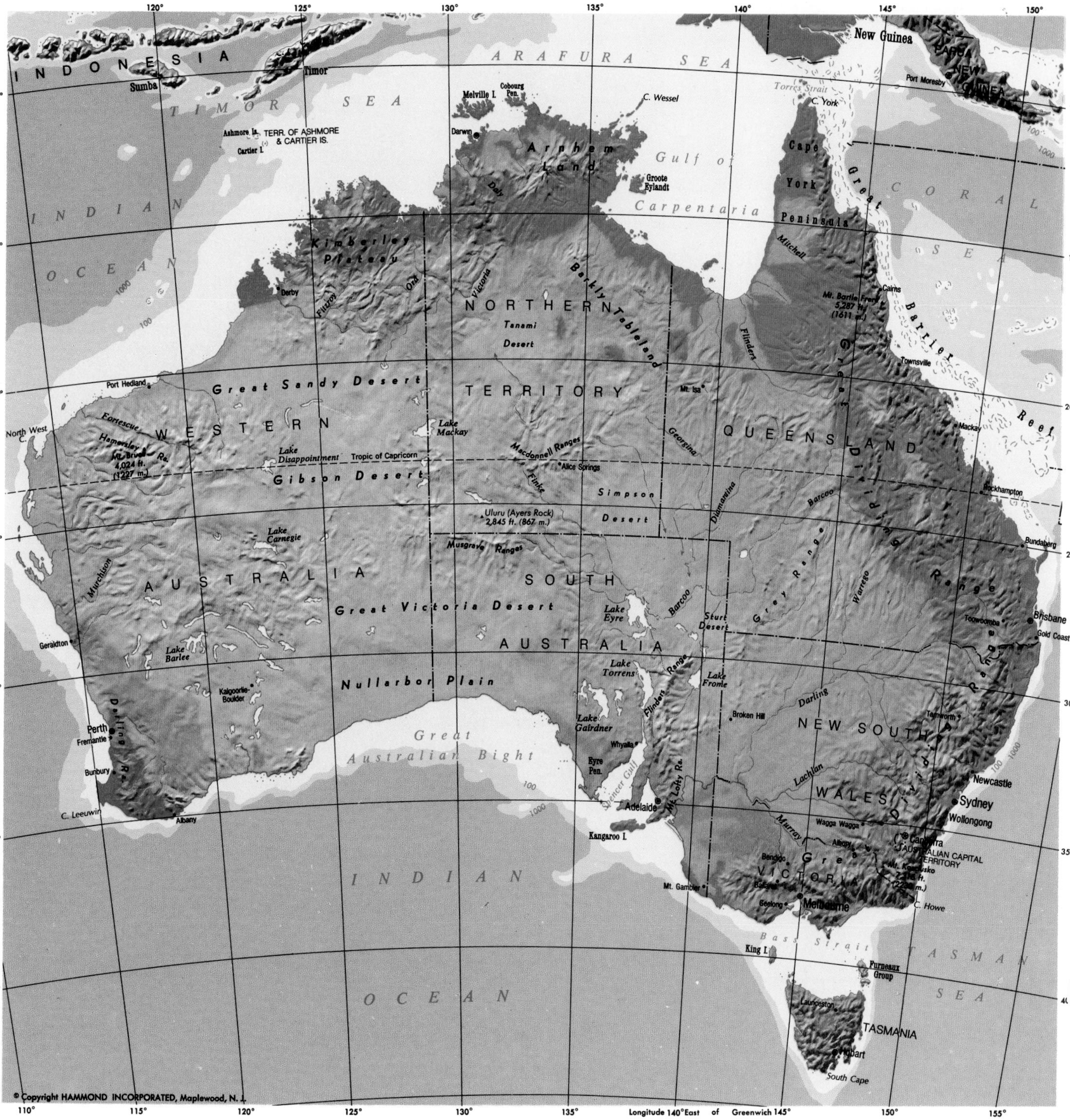

Vegetation/Relief

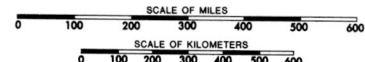

SCALE OF MILES
0   100   200   300   400   500   600

SCALE OF KILOMETERS
0   100   200   300   400   500   600

Capital of Country.................................⊛
State and Territorial Capitals....................●
International Boundaries..........................
State and Territorial Boundaries...............

Elevations in Feet   Depths in Fathoms

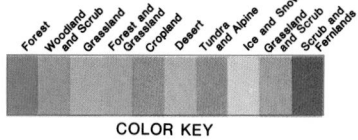

Forest | Woodland and Scrub | Grassland | Forest and Grassland | Grassland Cropland | Desert | Tundra and Alpine | Ice and Snow | Grassland and Scrub | Scrub and Fernlands

COLOR KEY

© Copyright HAMMOND INCORPORATED, Maplewood, N. J.

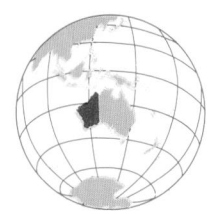

AREA 975,096 sq. mi.
(2,525,500 sq. km.)
POPULATION 1,406,929
CAPITAL Perth
LARGEST CITY Perth
HIGHEST POINT Mt. Bruce 4,024 ft.
(1,227 m.)

Topography

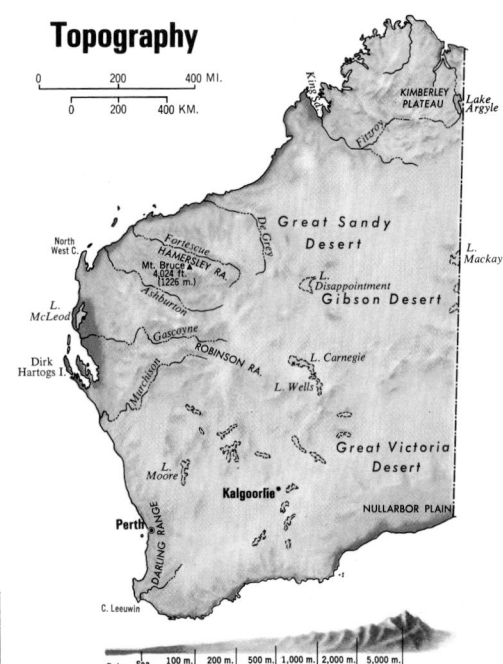

CITIES and TOWNS

Albany 15,222 . . . . B6
Augusta 588 . . . . A6
Australind 1,681 . . . . A2
Balladonia D6
Beverley 756 . . . . B1
Boddington 367 . . . . B2
Boulder-Kalgoorlie 19,848 . . C5
Boyanup 365 . . . . A2
Bridgetown 1,521 . . . . . . B6
Brookton 595 . . . . B2
Broome 3,666 . . . . C2
Bruce Rock 565 . . . . B5
Brunswick Junction 889 . . . A2
Bunbury 21,749 . . . . A2
Busselton 6,463 . . . . A6
Canning 52,816 . . . . A1
Capel 680 . . . . A2
Carnamah 422 . . . . A5
Carnarvon 5,053 . . . . A4
Collie 7,667 . . . . B2
Coolgardie 891 . . . . C5

Coorow 226 . . . . B5
Corrigin 841 . . . . B6
Cranbrook 316 . . . . B6
Cuballing ○647 . . . . B2
Cue 320 . . . . B4
Cunderdin 731 . . . . B5
Dalwallinu 639 . . . . B5
Dampier 2,471 . . . . A3
Dandaragan ○1,748 . . . . . A5
Darkan 242 . . . . B6
Denham 402 . . . . A4
Denmark 985 . . . . B6
Derby 2,933 . . . . C2
Dongara-Port Denison 1,155 A5
Donnybrook 1,197 . . . . . . A2
Dwellingup 453 . . . . A2
Esperance 6,375 . . . . C6
Eucla E5
Exmouth 2,583 . . . . A3
Fitzroy Crossing D2
Fremantle 22,484 . . . . . . A1
Geraldton 20,895 . . . . . . A5
Gingin 382 . . . . A1
Gnowangerup 872 . . . . . . B6

Goldsworthy 923 . . . . B3
Goomalling 600 . . . . B1
Halls Creek 966 . . . . D2
Harvey 2,479 . . . . A2
Hopetoun C6
Hyden B5
Jarrahdale 315 . . . . B2
Kalbarri 820 . . . . A4
Kalgoorlie 9,145 . . . . C5
Kalgoorlie-Boulder 19,848 . . C5
Kambalda 4,463 . . . . C5
Karratha 8,341 . . . . A3
Katanning 4,413 . . . . B6
Kellerberrin 1,091 . . . . . . B5
Kojonup 544 . . . . B6
Koolyanobbing 277 . . . . . . B5
Kununurra 2,081 . . . . E2
Kwinana New Town 12,355 . A1
Lake Grace 575 . . . . B6
Laverton 872 . . . . C5
Learmonth A3
Leonora 524 . . . . C5
Madura D5
Mandurah 10,978 . . . . . . A2

Manjimup 4,150 . . . . B6
Marble Bar 357 . . . . C3
Margaret River 798 . . . . . A6
Meekatharra 989 . . . . B4
Melville 61,211 . . . . A1
Menzies 232 . . . . C5
Merredin 3,520 . . . . B5
Mingenew 368 . . . . A5
Moora 1,677 . . . . B5
Morawa 694 . . . . B5
Mount Barker 1,519 . . . . . B6
Mount Magnet 618 . . . . . . B5
Mukinbudin 370 . . . . B5
Mullewa 918 . . . . A5
Mundijong 356 . . . . A2
Nannup 552 . . . . B6
Narrogin 4,969 . . . . B2
Nedlands 20,257 . . . . A1
Newman 5,466 . . . . B3
New Norcia A5
Norseman 1,895 . . . . C6
Northam 6,791 . . . . B1
Northampton 750 . . . . . . A5
Northcliffe B6
Nungarin ○332 . . . . B5
Onslow 594 . . . . A3
Pannawonica 1,170 . . . . . B3
Paraburdoo 2,357 . . . . . . B3
Pardoo A6
Pemberton 871 . . . . A6
Perenjori 257 . . . . B5
Perth (cap.) 809,035 . . . . . A1
Perth *898,918 . . . . A1
Pingelly 937 . . . . B2
Pinjarra 1,336 . . . . A2
Port Denison-Dongara 1,155 A5
Port Hedland 12,948 . . . . B3
Quairading 911 . . . . B1
Ravensthorpe 327 . . . . . . B6
Rockingham 24,932 . . . . . A2
Roebourne 1,688 . . . . B3

Sandstone ○133 . . . . B4
Shay Gap 853 . . . . C3
Southern Cross 798 . . . . . B5
South Perth 31,524 . . . . . A1
Stirling 161,858 . . . . A1
Three Springs 638 . . . . . . A5
Tom Price 3,540 . . . . B3
Toodyay 560 . . . . B1
Turkey Creek 212 . . . . . . E2
Wagin 1,488 . . . . B2
Walpole 291 . . . . B6
Wandering ○470 . . . . . . B2
Wanneroo 6,745 . . . . A1
Waroona 1,462 . . . . A2
Wickepin 267 . . . . B2
Wickham 2,387 . . . . B3
Williams 453 . . . . B2
Wiluna 221 . . . . C4
Wittenoom 247 . . . . B3
Wongan Hills 947 . . . . . . B5
Wundowie 720 . . . . B1
Wyalkatchem 453 . . . . . . B5
Wyndham 1,509 . . . . E1
Yalgoo ○315 . . . . B5
Yampi Sound C2
York 1,136 . . . . B1

OTHER FEATURES

Adele (isl.) C1
Admiralty (gulf) D1
Aloysius (mt.) E4
Argyle (lake) E2
Arid (cape) C6
Ashburton (riv.) A3
Augustus (mt.) B4
Austin (lake) B4
Australia Aboriginal Res. . . E4
Bald (head) B6
Balwina Aboriginal Res. . . . E3
Barlee (lake) B5
Barrow (isl.) A3
Beaglebay Aboriginal Res. . . C2
Bluff Knoll (mt.) B6
Bonaparte (arch.) D1
Bougainville (cape) D1
Brassey (range) C4
Bruce (mt.) B3
Brunswick (bay) D1
Buccaneer (arch.) C2
Carey (lake) C5
Carnegie (lake) C4
Central Aboriginal Res. . . . E3
Churchman (mt.) B5
Collier (bay) C2
Cosmo Newbery Aboriginal
Res. C5
Cowan (lake) C5
Cundeelee Aboriginal Res. . . C5
Dale (mt.) B1
Dampier (arch.) B3
Dampier Land (reg.) C2
Darling (range) A1
De Grey (riv.) B3
D'Entrecasteaux (pt.) A6
Dirk Hartogs (isl.) A4
Disappointment (lake) C3
Drysdale (riv.) D1
Dundas (lake) C6
Egerton (mt.) B4
Eighty Mile (beach) C2
Enid (mt.) B3
Esperance (bay) C6

Exmouth (gulf) A3
Fitzroy (riv.) D2
Flinders (bay) A6
Forrest River Aboriginal Res. D1
Fortescue (riv.) B3
Garden (isl) A1
Gascoyne (riv.) B4
Geelvink (chan.) A5
Geographe (bay) A6
Geographe (chan.) A4
Gibson (des.) D3
Great Australian (bight) . . . E6
Great Sandy (des.) C3
Great Victoria (des.) D5
Hamersley (range) B3
Hann (mt.) D1
Hopkins (lake) E4
Houtman Abrolhos (isls.) . . A5
Indian Ocean A5
Johnston, The (lakes) C6
Joseph Bonaparte (gulf) . . . E1
Kimberley (plat.) D2
King (sound) C2
King Leopold (range) D2
Koolan (isl.) C1
Leeuwin (cape) A6
Le Grand (cape) C6
Lévêque (cape) C2
Londonderry (cape) D1
Lyons (riv.) A4
Macdonald (lake) E3
Mackay (lake) E3
McLeod (lake) A4
Minigwal (lake) C5
Monte Bello (isls.) A3
Moore (lake) B5
Murchison (riv.) B4
Murray (riv.) A2
Naturaliste (cape) A6
Naturaliste (chan.) A4
North West (cape) A3
North-West Aboriginal Res. . E4
Nullarbor (plain) D5
Oakover (riv.) C3
Ord (mt.) D2
Ord (riv.) E2
Percival (lakes) D3
Peron (pen.) A4
Petermann (ranges) E4
Rason (lake) D5
Rebecca (lake) C5
Recherche (arch.) C6
Robinson (ranges) B4
Roebuck (bay) C2
Rottnest (isl.) A1
Saint George (ranges) D2
Shark (bay) A4
Southesk Tablelands D3
Sturt (creek) D2
Swan (riv.) A1
Timor (sea) D1
Tomkinson (ranges) E4
Wanna (lake) E5
Warburton Aboriginal Res. . D4
Way (lake) C4
Weld (range) B4
Wells (lake) C4
Whaleback (mt.) B3
Wooramel (riv.) A4
York (sound) D1

○ Population of district.
*Population of met. area.

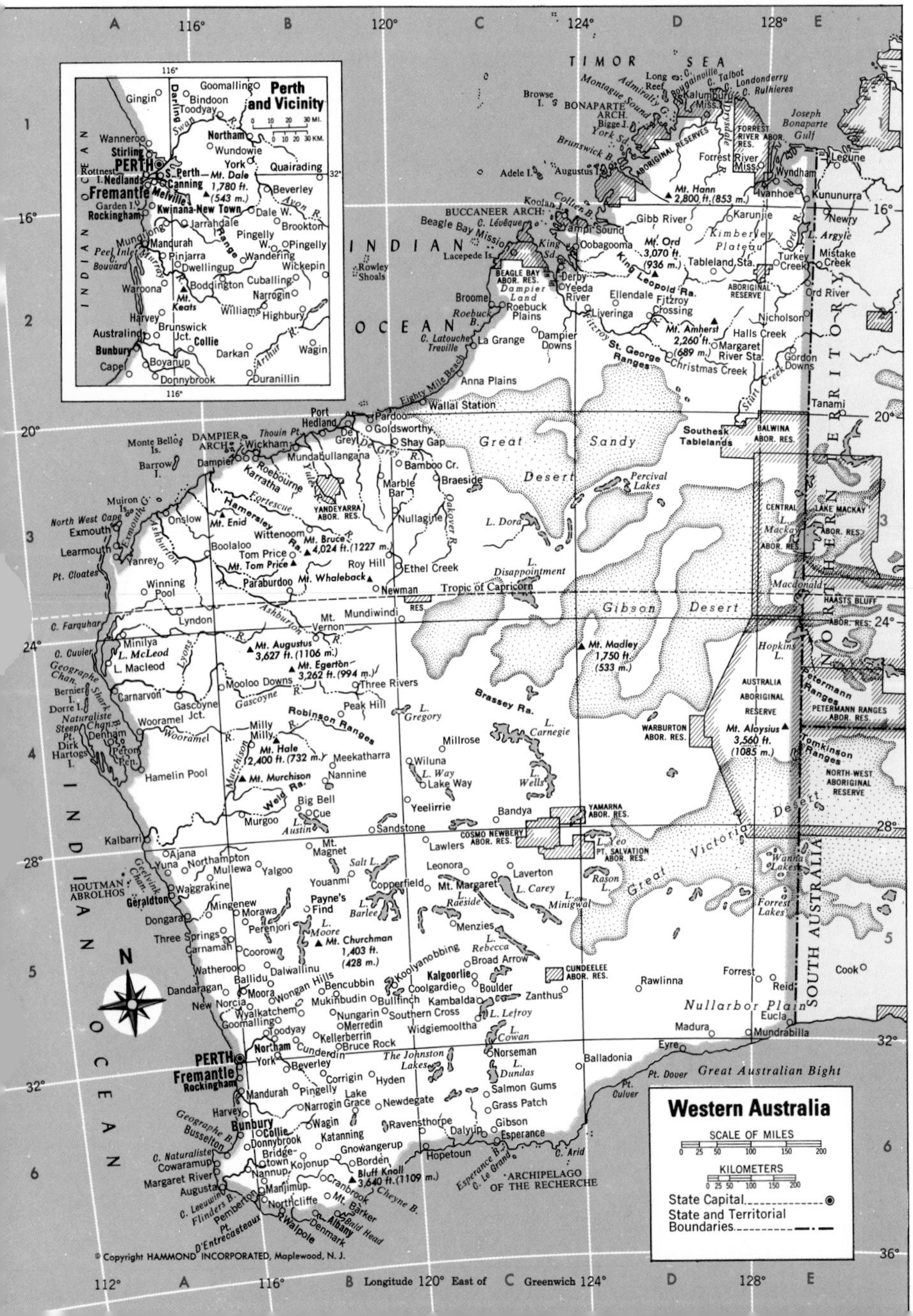

CITIES and TOWNS

Adelaide River B2
Aileron C7
Alice Springs 18,395 . . . . C7
Alyangula 1,181 . . . . E2
Angurugu 597 . . . . E3
Anthony Lagoon D4
Areyonga C8
Arltunga D7
Avon Downs E5
Bamyili-Beswick 685 . . . . C3
Banka Banka C5
Barrow Creek D6
Batchelor B2
Bathurst Island 1,032 . . . . B1
Birdum C3
Birrimbah C3
Birrindudu A5
Borroloola 420 . . . . E4
Bundooma D8
Burramurra E6
Charlotte Waters D8
Claravale B3
Coniston C7
Coolibah B3
Creswell Downs E4
Croker Island Mission C1
Daly River B2
Daly Waters C4
Darwin (cap.) 56,482 . . . . B2
Docker River 217 . . . . A8
Elliott C4
Epenarra D6
Erldunda C8
Eva Downs D5

Ewaninga D7
Goulburn Island 277 . . . . C1
Gove (Nhulunbuy) 3,879 . . . . . E2
Harts Range D7
Hatches Creek D6
Helen Springs C5
Henbury C8
Hermannsburg 541 . . . . C7
Hooker Creek 671 . . . . B5
Humpty Doo B2
Katherine 3,737 . . . . B3
Kildurk A4
Koolpinyah B2
Kulgera C8
Kurundi D6
Lake Nash E6
Larrimah C3
Legune A3
Limbunya B4
Lucy Creek E7
Mainoru C3
Maningrida 702 . . . . C2
Mataranka C3
Milingimbi 564 . . . . D2
Mistake Creek A4
Montejinnie B4
Mount Cavenagh C8
Mount Doreen C7
Murray Downs D6
Napperby C7
Newcastle Waters C4
Nhulunbuy 3,879 . . . . E2
Numbulwar 422 . . . . D3
Oenpelli 452 . . . . C2
O. T. Downs D4
Papunya 635 . . . . B7
Pine Creek 214 . . . . C2

Plenty River Mine D7
Port Keats 819 . . . . A3
Powell Creek C5
Rankine Store E5
Robinson River E4
Rockhampton Downs D5
Rodinga C8
Rum Jungle B2
Santa Teresa 479 . . . . C8
Soudan E6
Stirling Station C7
Tanami A5
Tarlton Downs E7
Tea Tree Well C7
Tempe Downs C8
Tennant Creek 3,118 . . . . C5
The Granites B6
Top Springs C4
Ucharonidge C5
Umbakumba 247 . . . . E3
Umbeara C8
Urapunga D3
Utopia D7
Victoria River Downs B4
Warrabri 459 . . . . C5
Warrego 991 . . . . C5
Wave Hill B4
White Quartz Hill D7
Willeroo B3
Willowra C6
Wollogorang F4
Yambah C7
Yirrkala 543 . . . . E2
Yuendumu 687 . . . . B7

OTHER FEATURES

Amadeus (lake) B8

Arafura (sea) D1
Arnhem (cape) E2
Arnhem Land (reg.) D2
Arnhem Land Aboriginal
  Res. C2
Arnold (riv.) D3
Barkly Tableland D4
Bathurst (isl.) A1
Beagle (gulf) A2
Beatrice (cape) E3
Bennett (lake) B7
Beswick Aboriginal Res. C3
Bickerton (Isl.) E2
Blaze (pt.) A2
Carpentaria (gulf) E3
Central Wedge (mt.) C7
Clarence (str.) B2
Cobourg (pen.) C1
Conner (mt.) B8
Croker (cape) C1
Daly (riv.) B2
Daly River Aboriginal Res. A2
Davenport (mt.) B7
Dundas (str.) B1
East Alligator (riv.) C2
Ehrenberg (range) B7
Elcho (isl.) D1
Finke (riv.) C8
Fitzmaurice (riv.) B3
Ford (cape) A2
Georgina (riv.) E6
Goulburn (isls.) C1
Goyder (riv.) D2
Groote Eylandt (isl.) 2,230 . . . . E3
Haasts Bluff Aboriginal
  Res. B7
Hale (riv.) D8

Hanson (riv.) C6
Hay (dry riv.) E7
Hogarth (mt.) E6
Hopkins (lake) A8
Joseph Bonaparte (gulf) A3
Kata Tjuta
  (Olga) (mt.) B8
Katherine (riv.) C3
Lake MacKay Aboriginal
  Res. A6
Lander (riv.) C6
Leisler (mt.) A7
Limmen Bight (riv.) D4
Macdonald (lake) B7
Macdonnell (ranges) C7
MacKay (lake) A7
Mann (riv.) D2
Marshall (riv.) D7
Melville (bay) E2
Melville (isl.) B1

Murchison (range) D6
Napier (mt.) A4
Neale (lake) A8
Newcastle (creek) C4
Nicholson (riv.) E5
Peron (isls.) A2
Petermann (ranges) A8
Petermann Ranges
  Aboriginal Res. A8
Port Darwin (inlet) B2
Ranken (riv.) E6
Robinson (riv.) E4
Roper (riv.) C3
Sandover (des.) D6
Simpson (des.) C7
Singleton (mt.) B6
Sir Edward Pellew Group
  (isls.) E3
South Alligator (riv.) C2
Stanley (mt.) B7

Stewart (cape) D1
Stirling (creek) A4
Sturt (plain) C4
Tanami (des.) C5
Timor (sea) A2
Todd (riv.) D8
Uluru Nat'l Park B8
Vanderlin (isl.) E3
Van Diemen (cape) A1
Van Diemen (gulf) B1
Victoria (riv.) B3
Wagait Aboriginal Res B2
Warwick (chan.) E3
Wessel (cape) E1
Wessel (isls.) E1
West Baines (riv.) A4
White (lake) A6
Woods (lake) C4
Young (riv.) D3
Ziel (mt.) C7

AREA 519,768 sq. mi.
  (1,346,200 sq. km.)
POPULATION 154,848
CAPITAL Darwin
LARGEST CITY Darwin
HIGHEST POINT Mt. Ziel 4,955 ft.
  (1,510 m.)

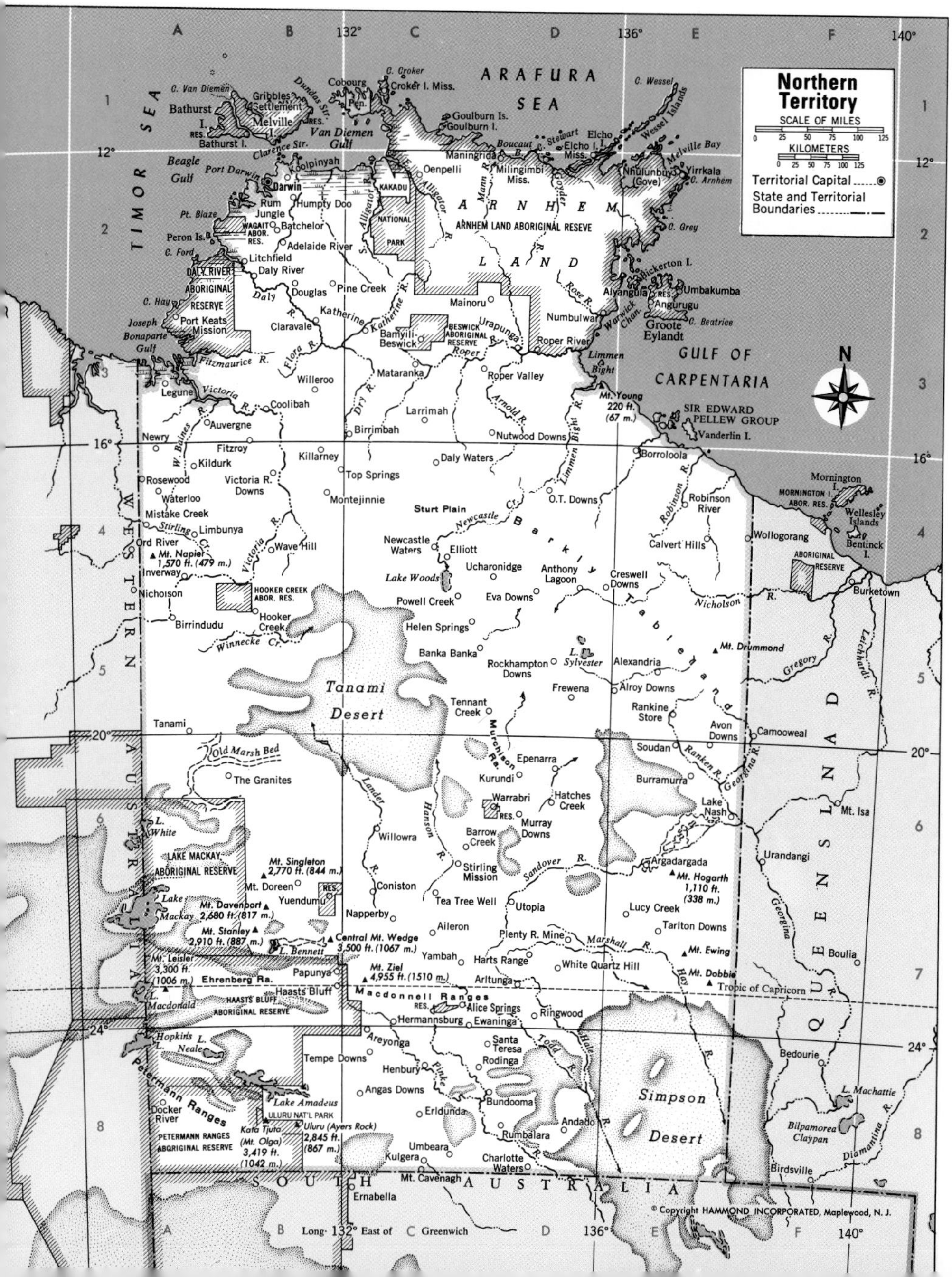

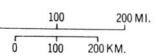

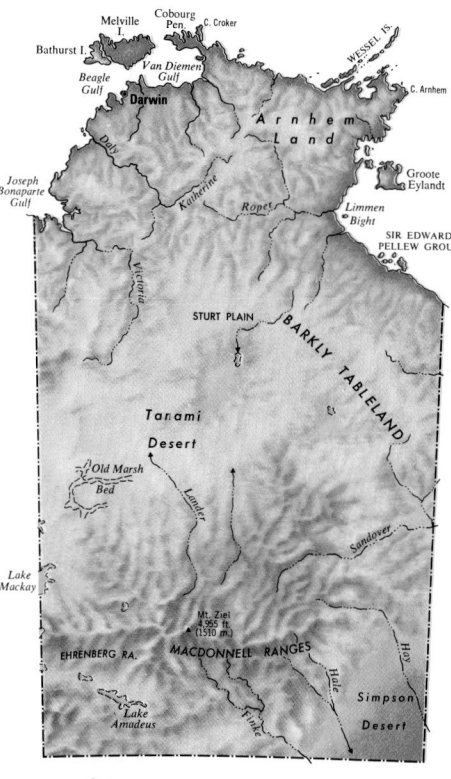

Topography

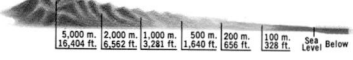

© Copyright HAMMOND INCORPORATED, Maplewood, N.J.

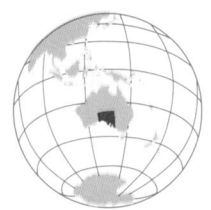

AREA 379,922 sq. mi. (984,000 sq. km.)
POPULATION 1,345,945
CAPITAL Adelaide
LARGEST CITY Adelaide
HIGHEST POINT Mt. Woodroffe 4,970 ft.
(1,515 m.)

CITIES and TOWNS

Adelaide (cap.) 882,520	B6
Adelaide *931,886	B6
Andamooka 402	E4
Angaston 1,753	F6
Balaklava 1,306	F6
Barmera 2,014	G6
Beachport 357	F7
Berri 3,419	G6
Birdwood 397	C7
Blinman	F4
Bordertown 2,138	G7
Brighton 19,441	A8
Burnside 37,593	B8
Burra 1,222	F5
Campbelltown 43,084	B7
Ceduna 2,794	D5
Clare 2,381	F5
Cleve 827	E5
Coober Pedy 2,078	D3
Cowell 626	E5
Crafters-Bridgewater 9,764	B8
Crystal Brook 1,240	E5
Cummins 767	D6
Edithburgh 359	E6
Elizabeth 32,608	B7
Elliston ○1,345	D5
Enfield 66,797	B7
Gawler 9,433	B6
Gladstone 680	F5
Glenelg 13,306	A8
Gumeracha 387	C7
Hahndorf 1,274	C8
Hawker 351	F4
Hindmarsh 7,593	A7
Iron Knob 398	E5
Jamestown 1,384	F5
Kadina 2,943	E5
Kapunda 1,340	F6
Keith 1,147	G7
Kensington and Norwood 8,950	B8
Kimba 862	E5
Kingscote 1,236	E6
Kingston 1,325	G7
Lameroo 599	G6
Laura 504	F5
Leigh Creek 1,635	F4
Lobethal 1,522	C7
Lock 213	D5
Loxton 3,100	G6
Lyndoch 539	C6
Maitland 1,085	E6
Mannum 1,984	F6
Marion 66,580	A8
Marree	E3
Meadows 388	B8
Meningie 807	F6
Millicent 5,255	F7
Minlaton 865	E6
Mitcham 60,309	B8
Moonta 1,751	E5
Mount Barker 4,190	C8
Mount Gambier 18,193	G7
Murray Bridge 8,664	F6
Nairne 706	C8
Nangwarry 758	G7

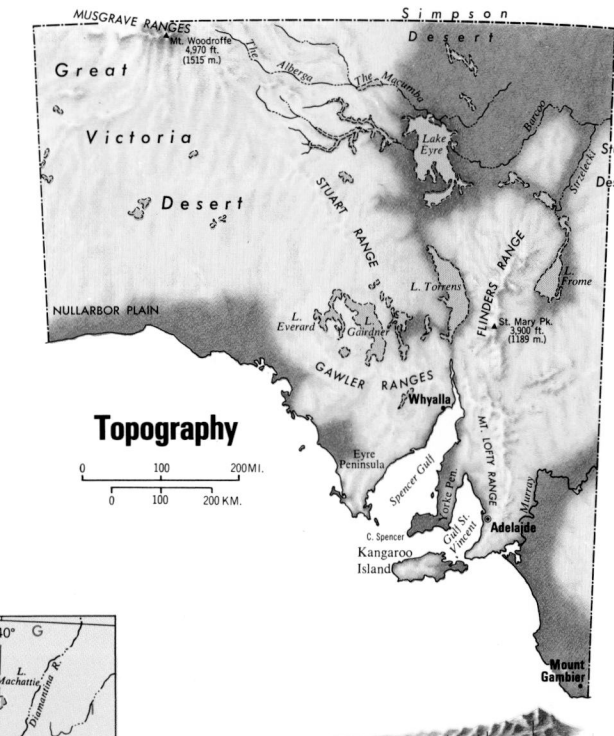

Topography

Scale: 0 — 100 — 200 MI.
0 — 100 — 200 KM.

Below Sea Level | 100 m. 328 ft. | 200 m. 656 ft. | 500 m. 1,640 ft. | 1,000 m. 3,281 ft. | 2,000 m. 6,562 ft. | 5,000 m. 16,404 ft.

Naracoorte 4,758	G7
Noarlunga 60,928	A8
Nuriootpa 2,851	F6
Oodnadatta	D2
Orroroo 604	F5
Payneham 16,502	B7
Penola 1,205	G7
Peterborough 2,575	F5
Pinnaroo 731	G6
Port Adelaide 35,407	A7
Port Augusta 15,566	E5
Port Broughton 587	F5
Port Lincoln 9,846	E6
Port Pirie 14,695	E5
Prospect 18,591	B7
Quorn 1,049	F5
Renmark 3,475	G5
Robe 590	F7
Salisbury 86,451	B7
Snowtown 492	E5
Strathalbyn 1,756	F6
Streaky Bay 985	D5
Tailem Bend 1,677	F6
Tanunda 2,621	C6
Tea Tree Gully 67,237	B7
Thebarton 9,208	A7
Tumby Bay 933	E6
Unley 35,844	B8
Uraidla 303	B8
Victor Harbor 4,522	F6
Virginia 353	B7
Waikerie 1,629	F6
Wallaroo 2,043	E5
West Torrens 45,099	A8
Whyalla 30,518	E5
Williamstown 495	C7
Willunga 667	F6
Wilmington 227	F6
Woodside 724	C8
Woodville 77,634	A7
Woomera 1,658	E4
Wudinna 572	D5
Yorketown 713	E6

OTHER FEATURES

Acraman (lake)	D5
Alberga, The (riv.)	D2
Alexandrina (lake)	F6
Anxious (bay)	D5
Arckaringa (creek)	D2
Barcoo (creek)	F3
Birksgate (range)	A2
Blanche (lake)	F3
Brady (mt.)	D3
Cadibarrawirracanna (lake)	D3
Callabonna (lake)	F3
Catastrophe (cape)	D6
Coffin (bay)	D6
Coffin Bay (pen.)	D6
Coopers (Barcoo) (creek)	F3
Coorong, The (lag.)	F6
Dey Dey (lake)	B3
Encounter (bay)	F6
Everard (lake)	D4
Everard (ranges)	C2
Eyre (pen.)	D5
Eyre North (lake)	E3
Eyre South (lake)	E3
Finke (riv.)	C1
Flinders (range)	F4
Frome (lake)	G4
Gairdner (lake)	D4
Gawler (ranges)	E5
Gawler (riv.)	B6
Gilles (lake)	E5
Goyders (lag.)	F2
Great Australian (bight)	A5
Great Victoria (des.)	B3
Gregory (lake)	F3
Hack (mt.)	F4
Hamilton, The (riv.)	D2
Harris (lake)	D4
Head of Bight (bay)	B4
Indian Ocean	E7
Investigator (str.)	E6
Investigator Group (isls.)	D5
Island (lag.)	E4
Jaffa (cape)	F7
Kangaroo (isl.) 3,515	E7
Lacepede (bay)	F7
Lofty (mt.)	B8
Macfarlane (lake)	E5
Macumba, The (riv.)	E2
Maurice (lake)	B3
Meramangye (lake)	C3
Morris (lake)	B2
Murray (res.)	F6
Musgrave (ranges)	B2
Neales, The (riv.)	E3
Northumberland (cape)	F8
Nukey Bluff (mt.)	D5
Nullarbor (plain)	A4
Nuyts (arch.)	C5
Nuyts (cape)	C5
Peera Peera Poolanna (lake)	F2
Saint Mary (peak)	F4
Saint Vincent (gulf)	F6
Serpentine (lakes)	A3
Simpson (des.)	E1
Sir Joseph Banks Group (isls.)	E6
Spencer (cape)	E6
Spencer (gulf)	E6
Stevenson, The (riv.)	D2
Streaky (bay)	C5
Strzelecki (creek)	G3
Stuart (range)	D3
Sturt (des.)	G3
The Alberga (riv.)	D2
The Coorong (lag.)	F6
The Hamilton (riv.)	D2
The Macumba (riv.)	E2
The Neales (riv.)	E3
The Stevenson (riv.)	D2
The Warburton (riv.)	F2
Thistle (isl.)	E6
Torrens (lake)	E4
Torrens (riv.)	C7
Warburton, The (riv.)	F2
Wilkinson (lakes)	B4
Woodroffe (mt.)	B2
Yalata Aboriginal Res.	B4
Yarle (lakes)	B4
Yorke (pen.)	E6

○ Population of district.
*Population of met. area.

Adelaide and Vicinity

South Australia

SCALE OF MILES
0 — 25 — 50 — 100 — 150

KILOMETERS
0 — 50 — 100 — 150

State Capital
State and Territorial Boundaries

Longitude D East 136° of E Greenwich

CITIES and TOWNS

Aramac 428 . . . . C4
Archerfield 785 . . . . D3
Ascot 4,298 . . . . E2
Atherton 4,196 . . . . C3
Ayr 8,787 . . . . C3
Balmoral 2,915 . . . . E2
Barcaldine 1,432 . . . . C4
Beaudesert 3,780 . . . . . . E6
Biloela 4,643 . . . . D5
Birdsville A5
Blackall 1,609 . . . . C5
Blackwater 5,434 . . . . . . D4
Boulia 292 . . . . A4
Bowen 7,663 . . . . D3
Brisbane (cap.) 689,378 . . D2
Brisbane *1,028,527 . . . . . D2
Bucasia 1,356 . . . . D4
Bundaberg 32,560 . . . . . . D5
Burketown 210 . . . . A3
Cairns 48,557 . . . . C3
Caloundra 16,758 . . . . . . E5
Camooweal 251 . . . . A3
Camp Hill 8,999 . . . . E3
Capella 660 . . . . D4
Cardwell 1,249 . . . . C3
Charleville 3,523 . . . . C5
Charters Towers 6,823 . . . C4
Cherbourg 963 . . . . D5
Chermside 6,892 . . . . D2
Clermont 1,659 . . . . C4
Cloncurry 1,961 . . . . B4
Collinsville 2,756 . . . . C4
Cooktown 913 . . . . C2
Coopers Plains 4,492 . . . . D3
Corinda 4,894 . . . . D3
Croydon ○255 . . . . B3
Cunnamulla 1,627 . . . . . . C5
Dalby 8,784 . . . . D5
Dirranbandi 480 . . . . D6
East Brisbane 4,853 . . . . . E3
Eidsvold 613 . . . . D5
Emerald 4,628 . . . . C4
Esk 676 . . . . E5
Gatton 4,190 . . . . E5
Gayndah 1,708 . . . . D5
Geebung 4,850 . . . . E2
Georgetown 319 . . . . B3
Gladstone 22,083 . . . . . . D4
Gold Coast 135,437 . . . . . E6
Goondiwindi 3,576 . . . . . . D6
Gordonvale 2,375 . . . . . . C3
Greenslopes 7,219 . . . . . . E3
Gympie 10,768 . . . . E5

Hervey Bay 13,569 . . . . . . E5
Holland Park 7,363 . . . . . . E3
Home Hill 3,138 . . . . C3
Hughenden 1,657 . . . . B4
Inala 17,383 . . . . D3
Indooroopilly 7,959 . . . . . D3
Ingham 5,598 . . . . C3
Innisfail 7,933 . . . . C3
Ipswich 68,297 . . . . E5
Isisford ○605 . . . . C5
Jandowae 781 . . . . D5
Jericho ○1,177 . . . . C4
Julia Creek 602 . . . . B4
Karumba 670 . . . . B3
Kilcoy 1,257 . . . . E5
Kingaroy 5,134 . . . . D5
Longreach 2,971 . . . . B4
Mackay 35,361 . . . . D4
Mareeba 6,309 . . . . C3
Marian 796 . . . . D4
Maroochydore-Mooloolaba
   17,460 . . . . E5
Maryborough 20,111 . . . . . E5
Mary Kathleen 830 . . . . . . A4
McKinlay ○1,477 . . . . A4
Millmerran 1,107 . . . . D5
Mitchell 1,171 . . . . C5
Mitchelton 5,810 . . . . D2
Monto 1,397 . . . . D5
Moorooka 8,740 . . . . D3
Moranbah 4,362 . . . . C9
Mossman 1,614 . . . . C3
Moura 2,871 . . . . D4
Mount Isa 23,679 . . . . A4
Murgon 2,327 . . . . D5
Nambour 7,965 . . . . E5
Newmarket 3,520 . . . . E2
Normanton 926 . . . . B3
Nundah 7,358 . . . . E2
Proserpine 3,058 . . . . C4
Quilpie 694 . . . . C5
Ravenshoe 915 . . . . C3
Redcliffe 42,223 . . . . E5
Richmond 784 . . . . B4
Rockhampton 50,146 . . . . D4
Roma 5,706 . . . . D5
Saint George 2,204 . . . . . D5
Saint Lucia 6,075 . . . . D3
Sandgate 6,776 . . . . D2
Sarina 2,815 . . . . D4
Springsure 774 . . . . D4
Stafford (Stafford Heights)
   13,731 . . . . D2
Stanthorpe 3,966 . . . . D6
Tara 864 . . . . D5

Taroom 688 . . . . D5
Tewantin-Noosa 9,965 . . . E5
Theodore 643 . . . . D5
Thursday Island 2,283 . . . B1
Toowoomba 63,401 . . . . . D5
Townsville 86,112 . . . . . . C3
Tully 2,728 . . . . C3
Walkerston 1,277 . . . . . . D4
Warwick 8,853 . . . . D6
Weipa 2,433 . . . . B2
Windsor 6,119 . . . . D2
Winton 1,259 . . . . B4
Wynnum 10,794 . . . . E5

Yeppoon 6,447 . . . . D4
Yeronga 4,579 . . . . D3

OTHER FEATURES

Albatross (bay) B2
Archer (riv.) B2
Balonne (riv.) D6
Banks (isl.) B1
Barcoo (creek) B5
Barkly Tableland A4
Bartle Frere (mt.) C3
Beal (range) B5

AREA 666,872 sq. mi. (1,727,200 sq. km.)
POPULATION 2,587,315
CAPITAL Brisbane
LARGEST CITY Brisbane
HIGHEST POINT Mt. Bartle Frere 5,287 ft.
   (1,611 m.)

Topography

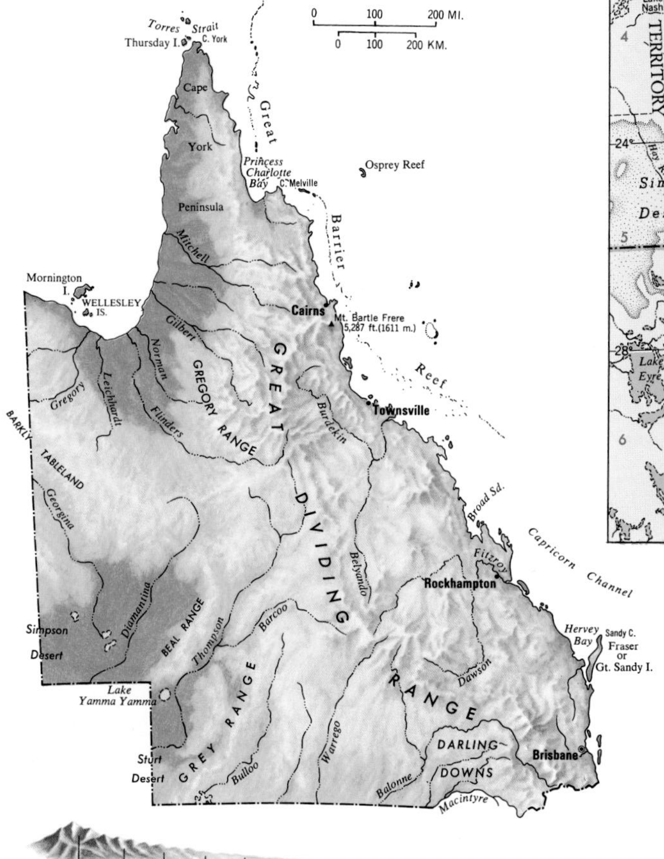

Belyando (riv.) C4
Broad (sound) D4
Bulloo (lake) B6
Bulloo (riv.) B6
Bunker Group (isls.) E4
Burdekin (riv.) C3
Cape York (pen.) B2
Capricorn (chan.) D4
Capricorn Group (isls.) . . . E4
Carnarvon (range) C5
Carpentaria (gulf) A2
Cloncurry (riv.) B4
Coopers (Barcoo) (creek) . B5
Coral (sea) C1
Culgoa (riv.) C6
Cumberland (isls.) D4
Curtis (isl.) D4
Darling Downs D5
Dawson (riv.) D5
Diamantina (riv.) B4
Drummond (range) C4
Duifken (pt.) B2
Endeavour (str.) B1

Fitzroy (riv.) D4
Flinders (riv.) B3
Fraser (isl.) E5
Georgina (riv.) A4
Gilbert (riv.) B3
Great Dividing (range) . . . C4
Gregory (range) B3
Gregory (riv.) A3
Grey (range) B5
Hamilton (riv.) A4
Hervey (bay) E5
Hinchinbrook (isl.) C3
Hook (isl.) D4
Leichhardt (riv.) A3
Machattie (lake) A4
Macintyre (riv.) D6
Maranoa (riv.) C5
Mary (riv.) D5
Melville (cape) C2
Mitchell (riv.) B2
Moreton (bay) E5
Moreton (isl.) E5
Mornington (isl.) A3

Norman (riv.) B3
Northern Peninsula
   Aboriginal Res. B1
Prince of Wales (isl.) B1
Princess Charlotte (bay) . . C2
Sandy (cape) E5
Selwyn (range) B4
Simpson (des.) A5
Sturt (des.) B3
Suttor (riv.) C4
Swain (reefs) D4
Thompson (riv.) B5
Torres (str.) B1
Warrego (range) C5
Warrego (riv.) C5
Wellesley (isls.) A3
Whitsunday (isl.) C3
Willies (range) C6
Yamma Yamma (lake) . . . B5
York (cape) B1

○ Population of district.
*Population of met. area.

NEW SOUTH WALES

AREA 309,498 sq. mi.
(801,600 sq. km.)
POPULATION 5,401,881
CAPITAL Sydney
LARGEST CITY Sydney
HIGHEST POINT Mt. Kosciusko
7,310 ft. (2,228 m.)

VICTORIA

AREA 87,876 sq. mi.
(227,600 sq. km.)
POPULATION 4,019,478
CAPITAL Melbourne
LARGEST CITY Melbourne
HIGHEST POINT Mt. Bogong
6,508 ft. (1,984 m.)

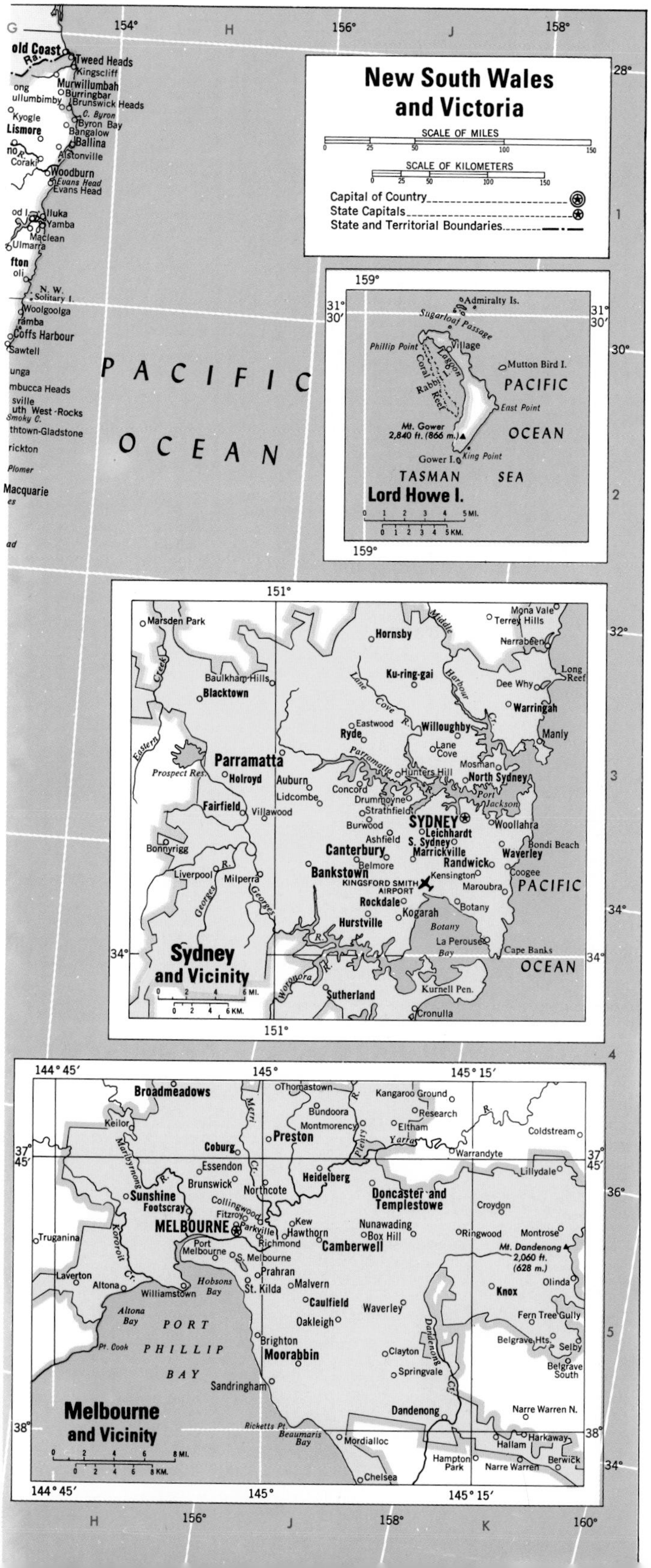

Topography

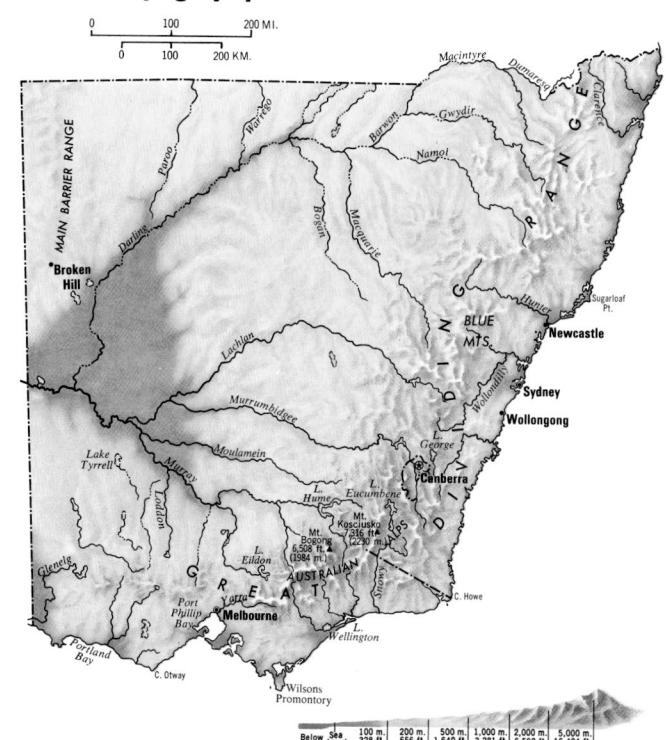

(continued on following page)

Irrigation Areas and Artesian Basins in Australia

Darwin

TANAMI DESERT

GREAT SANDY DESERT

GREAT ARTESIAN BASIN

GREAT VICTORIA DESERT

SOMERSET

Brisbane

L. Eyre

L. Torrens

L. Gairdner

MENINDEE

BURRENDONG

Perth

Darling

WARRAGAMBA

Adelaide

L. ALEXANDRINA

BURRINJUCK

Sydney

Murray

Canberra

HUME

Melbourne

ADAMINABY

BIG EILDON

Snowy

Hobart

→ Permanent Rivers
∴ Flowing Water Bores
⇢ Non-Permanent Rivers
⟶ Major Dams

Major Irrigation and Other Water Supply Areas

Basins Where Artesian Water Is Generally Available

Prepared from Atlas of Australian Resources.

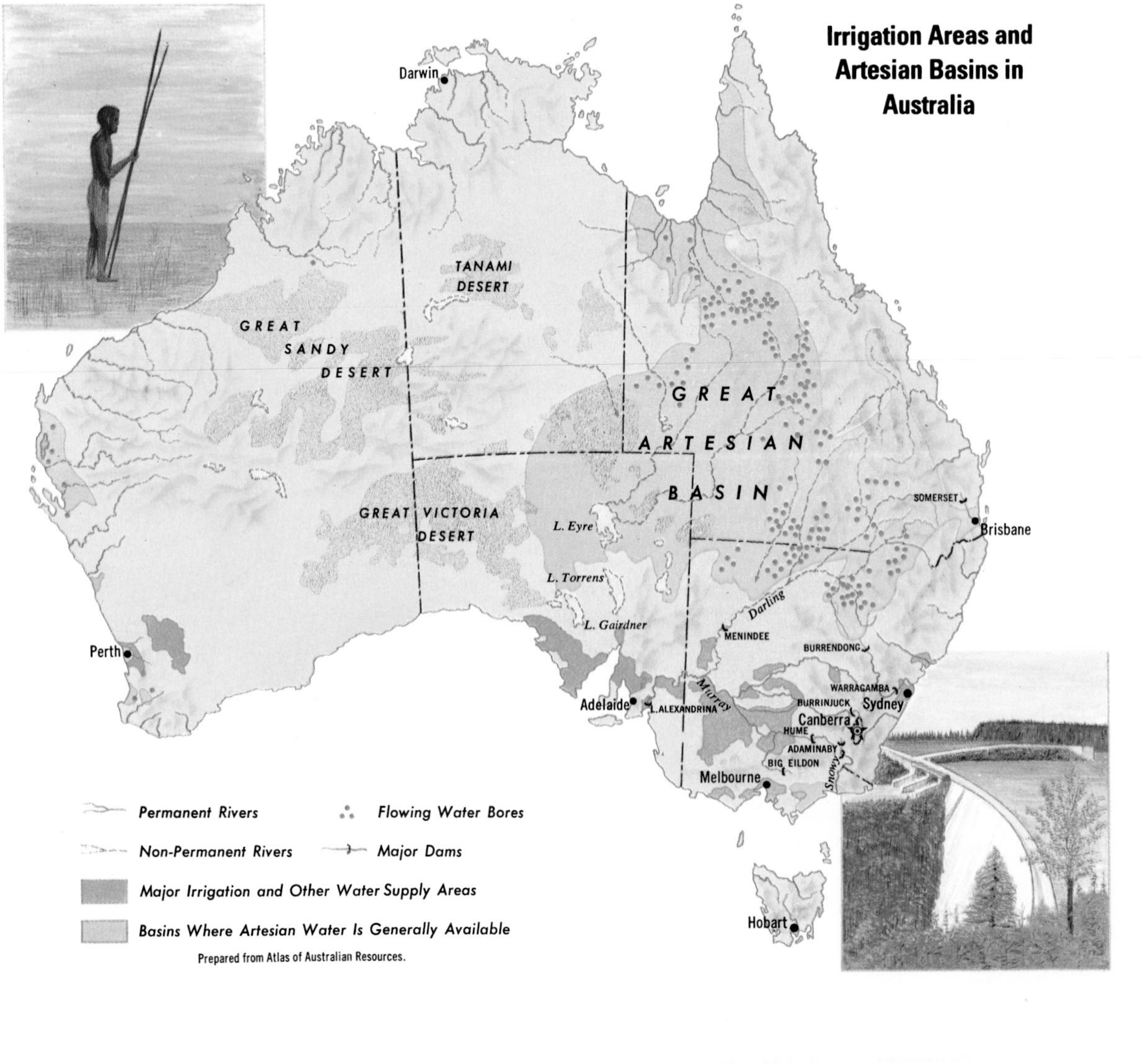

Topography

0   30   60 MI.
0   30   60 KM.

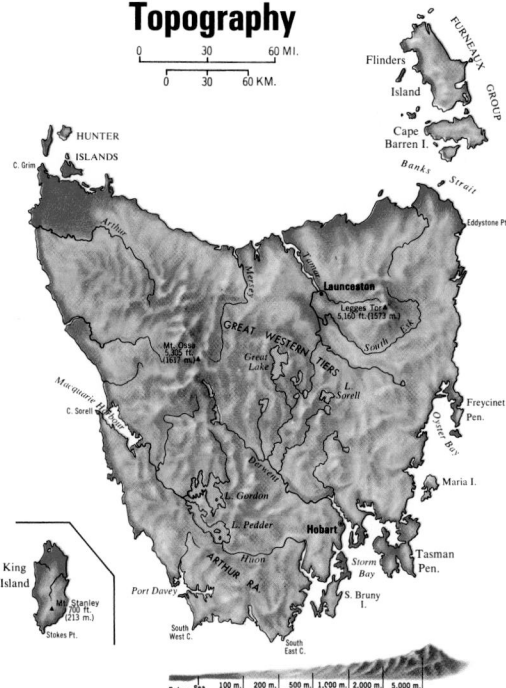

TASMANIA

AREA 26,178 sq. mi. (67,800 sq. km.)
POPULATION 436,353
CAPITAL Hobart
LARGEST CITY Hobart
HIGHEST POINT Mt. Ossa 5,305 ft.
(1,617 m.)

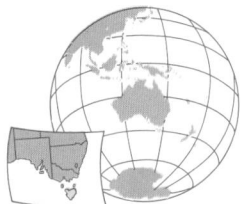

Forth (riv.)	C3
Frankland (cape)	D1
Frankland (range)	B4
Franklin (riv.)	B4
Frenchmans Cap (mt.)	B4
Freycinet (pen.)	E4
Furneaux Group (isls.) 1,039	E1
Gordon (lake)	B4
Gordon (riv.)	B4
Great (lake)	C3
Great Western Tiers (mts.)	C3
Grim (cape)	A2
Hartz (mt.)	C5
Hibbs (pt.)	B4
Hogan Group (isl.)	D1
Hummock (isl.)	D2
Hunter (isl.)	A2
Hunter (isls.)	B2
Huon (riv.)	C5
Indian Ocean	A4
Kent Group (isls.)	D1
King (isl.) 2,592	A1

King (riv.)	B4
King William (lake)	C4
Lake (riv.)	D3
Legges Tor (mt.)	D3
Leven (riv.)	B3
Lofty (range)	B3
Low Rocky (pt.)	B4
Lyell (mt.)	B4
Maatsuyker (isls.)	C5
Macquarie (harb.)	B4
Macquarie (riv.)	D3
Maria (isl.)	E4
Marion (bay)	E4
Mersey (riv.)	C3
Munro (mt.)	E2
Naturaliste (cape)	E2
Nive (riv.)	C4
Norfolk (bay)	D4
North (pt.)	E1
North Bruny (isl.)	D5
North Esk (riv.)	D3
Ossa (mt.)	C3

Ouse (riv.)	C4
Oyster (bay)	E4
Pedder (riv.)	B4
Phoques (bay)	A1
Picton (mt.)	C5
Pieman (riv.)	B3
Pillar (cape)	E5
Port Davey (inlet)	B5
Portland (cape)	D2
Ramsey (mt.)	B3
Raoul (cape)	D5
Reid (rapid)	B1
Ringarooma (bay)	D2
Robbins (isl.)	B2
Saint Clair (lake)	C4
Saint Helens (pt.)	E3
Saint Vincent (cape)	B5
Savage (riv.)	B3
Schouten (isl.)	E4
Sorell (cape)	B4
Sorell (lake)	D4
South (cape)	C5

South Bruny (isl.)	D5
South East (cape)	C5
South Esk (riv.)	D3
South West (cape)	B5
Stanley (mt.)	A1
Stokes (pt.)	A1
Storm (bay)	D5
Strzelecki (mt.)	D2
Tamar (riv.)	D3
Tasman (head)	D5
Tasman (pen.)	E5
Tasman (sea)	E4
Three Hummock (isl.)	B2
Vansittart (isl.)	E2
West (pt.)	A2
West Sister (isl.)	D1
Wickham (cape)	A1

○ Population of district.
*Population of met. area.

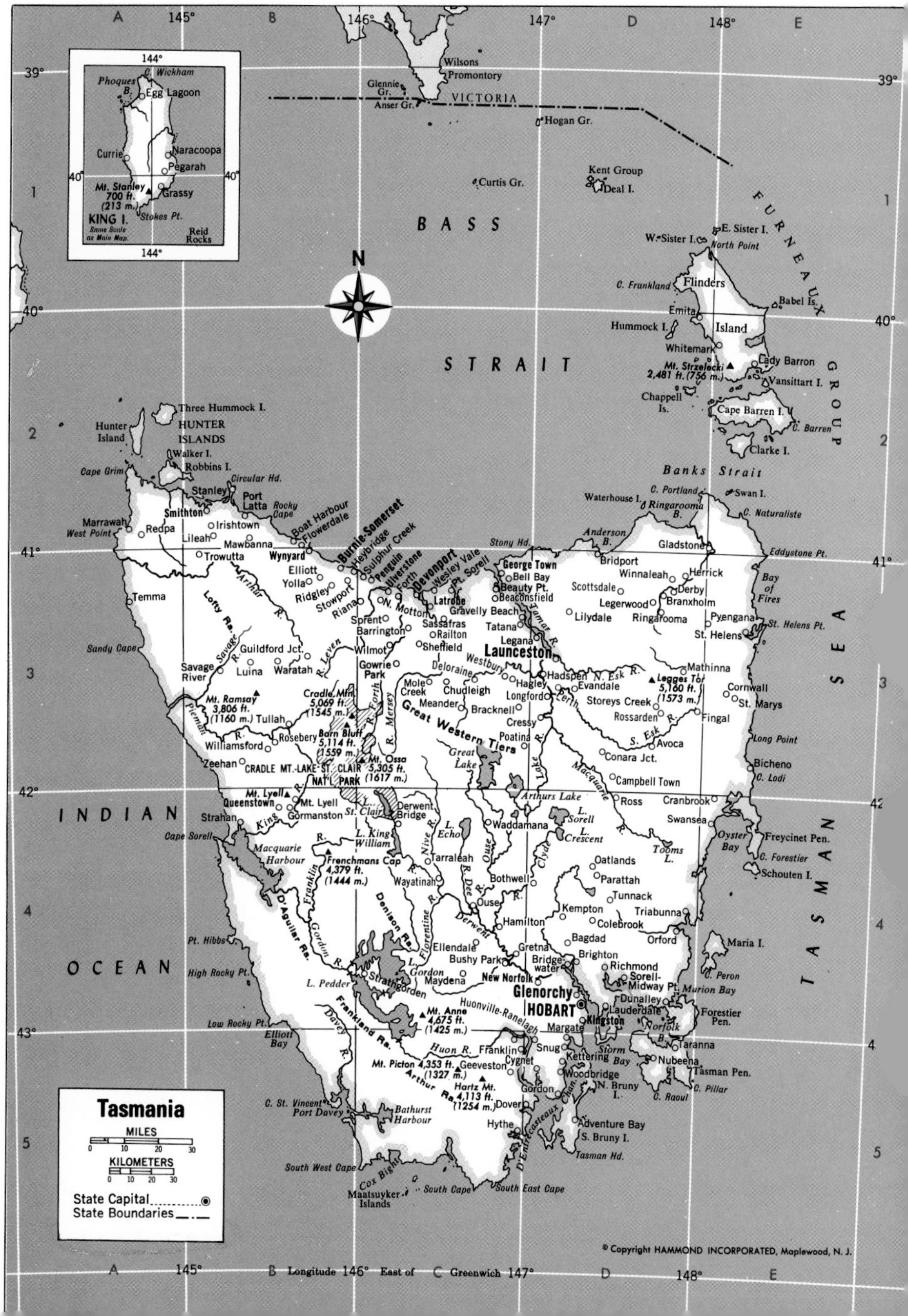

CITIES and TOWNS

Adventure Bay	D5
Avoca	D3
Bagdad	D4
Beaconsfield 898	C3
Beauty Point 998	C3
Bell Bay	C3
Bicheno 674	E3
Boat Harbour	B2
Bothwell 356	C4
Bracknell 347	C3
Branxholm 273	D3
Bridgewater 6,880	D4
Bridport 885	D3
Brighton 9,441	D4
Burnie 19,994	B3
Campbell Town 879	D3
Chudleigh	C3
Colebrook	D4
Cressy 640	C3
Currie 859	A1
Cygnet 715	C5
Deloraine 1,923	C3
Derwent Bridge	C4
Devonport 21,424	C3
Dover 570	C5
Dunalley 203	D4
Evandale 614	D3
Exeter 353	C3
Fingal 424	E3
Forth 273	C3
Franklin 479	C5
Geeveston 860	C5
George Town 5,592	C3
Glenorchy 41,019	D4
Gormanston 126	B4
Gowrie Park	C3
Grassy 780	B1
Gravelly Beach 535	C3
Hadspen 908	D3
Hagley 232	C3
Hamilton 2,488	C4
Heybridge 395	C3
Hobart (cap.) 128,603	D4
Hobart *168,359	D4
Huonville-Ranelagh 1,347	C5
Kettering 288	D4
Kingston 8,556	D4
Latrobe 2,401	C3
Lauderdale 2,117	D4
Launceston 31,273	D3
Launceston *64,555	D3
Legana 964	C3
Lilydale 308	D3
Longford 2,027	C3
Luina 522	B3
Margate 476	D4
Maydena 461	C4
Meander	C3
Mole Creek 303	C3
New Norfolk 6,243	C4
Nubeena 225	D5
Oatlands 545	D4
Orford 378	D4
Penguin 2,616	C3
Perth 1,229	D3
Poatina	C3
Port Sorell 859	C3
Queenstown 3,714	B4
Railton 857	C3
Richmond 587	D4
Ridgley 452	B3

Ringarooma 223	D3
Rosebery 2,675	B3
Ross 289	D4
Rossarden 365	D3
Saint Helens 1,005	E3
Saint Marys 653	E3
Sassafras	C3
Savage River 1,141	B3
Scottsdale 2,002	D3
Sheffield 945	C3
Smithton 3,378	A2
Snug 684	D5
Sorell-Midway Point 2,544	D4
Stanley 603	B2
Storeys Creek	D3
Strahan 402	B4
Strathgordon	C4
Sulphur Creek 367	C3
Swansea 428	D4
Tarraleah 498	C4
Temma	A3
Triabunna 924	D4
Tullah 1,894	B3
Ulverstone 9,413	C3
Waratah 342	B3
Wesley Vale	C3
Westbury 1,161	C3
Whitemark	D2
Woodbridge 259	D5
Wynyard 4,582	B3
Zeehan 1,750	B3

OTHER FEATURES

Anderson (bay)	D2
Anne (mt.)	C4
Anser Group (isls.)	C1
Arthur (lake)	D4
Arthur (range)	C5
Arthur (riv.)	B3
Babel (isl.)	E1
Banks (str.)	D2
Barn Bluff (mt.)	B3
Barren (cape)	E2
Bass (str.)	C1
Bathurst (gulf)	C5
Cape Barren (isl.)	D2
Chappell (isls.)	D2
Circular (gulf)	B2
Clarke (isl.)	E2
Clyde (riv.)	D4
Cox (bight)	C5
Cradle (mt.)	B3
Cradle Mt. Lake St. Clair Nat'l Park	B3
Crescent (lake)	D4
Curtis Group (isls.)	C1
D'Aguilar (range)	B4
Davey (riv.)	B4
Deal (isl.)	D1
Dee (riv.)	C4
Denison (range)	C4
Derwent (riv.)	C4
D'Entrecasteaux (chan.)	D5
East Sister (isl.)	E1
Echo (lake)	C4
Eddystone (pt.)	E2
Elliott (bay)	B5
Fires (bay)	E3
Flinders (isl.) 2,150	D1
Florence (lake)	C4
Forestier (chan.)	E4
Forestier (pen.)	E4

New Zealand

CONIC PROJECTION

SCALE OF MILES
0   50   100   150

SCALE OF KILOMETERS
0   50   100   150

Capital of Country .... ☆

© Copyright HAMMOND INCORPORATED, Maplewood, N. J.

Topography

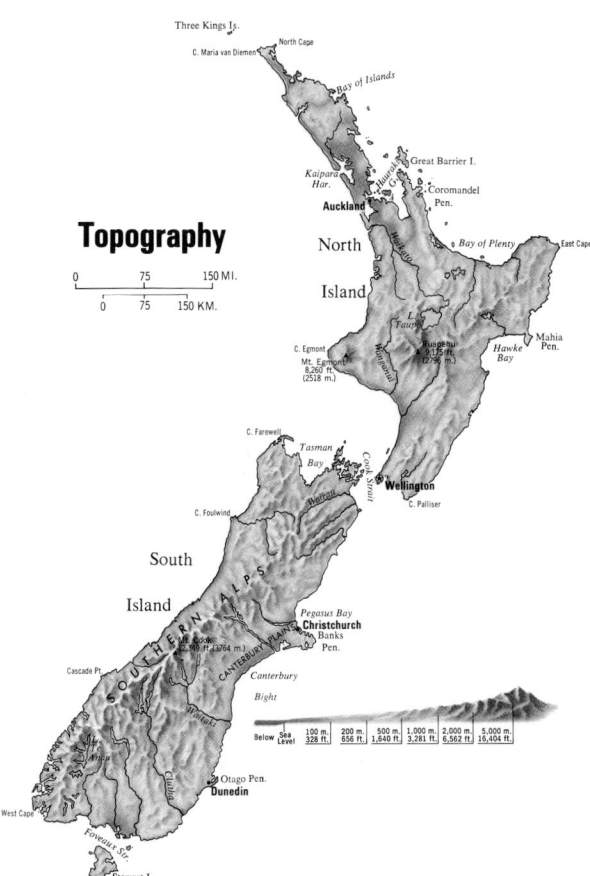

0   75   150 MI.

0   75   150 KM.

North Island

South Island

Below Sea Level | 100 m. 328 ft. | 200 m. 656 ft. | 500 m. 1,640 ft. | 1,000 m. 3,281 ft. | 2,000 m. 6,562 ft. | 5,000 m. 16,404 ft.

AREA 103,736 sq. mi. (268,676 sq. km.)
POPULATION 3,389,000
CAPITAL Wellington
LARGEST CITY Auckland
HIGHEST POINT Mt. Cook 12,349 ft.
  (3,764 m.)
MONETARY UNIT New Zealand dollar
MAJOR LANGUAGES English, Maori
MAJOR RELIGIONS Protestantism,
  Roman Catholicism

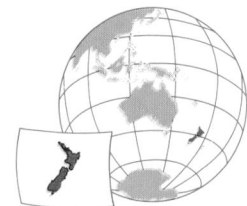

Agriculture, Industry and Resources

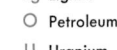

CITIES and TOWNS

Albany 2,001	B1
Alexandra 4,348	B6
Ashburton 14,151	C5
Ashhurst 1,906	E4
Auckland 144,963	B1
Auckland †769,558	B1
Balclutha 4,495	B7
Belmont 2,402	B2
Birkenhead 21,324	B1
Blenheim 17,849	D4
Bluff 2,720	B7
Bulls 1,839	E4
Cambridge 8,514	E2
Carterton 3,971	E4
Christchurch 164,680	D5
Christchurch †289,959	D5
Cromwell 2,364	B6
Dannevirke 5,663	F4
Dargaville 4,747	D1
Devonport 10,410	C1
Dunedin 77,176	C6
Dunedin †107,445	C6
Eastbourne 4,561	B3
East Coast Bays 28,866	B1
Edgecumbe 1,929	F2
Ellerslie 5,404	C1
Eltham 2,411	E3
Fairfield 1,849	C6
Featherston 2,458	E4
Feilding 11,522	E4
Foxton 2,719	E4
Geraldine 2,128	C6
Gisborne 29,986	G3
Gisborne †32,062	G3
Glen Eden 9,406	B1
Glenfield 3,691	B1
Gore 9,185	B7
Green Bay 3,035	B1
Green Island 6,899	C7
Greymouth 8,103	C5
Greytown 1,797	E4
Half Moon Bay (Oban) 2,448	B7
Hamilton 91,109	E2
Hamilton †97,907	E2
Hastings 36,083	F3
Hastings †52,563	F3
Havelock North 8,507	F3
Hawera 8,400	E3
Helensville 1,360	E1
Henderson 6,645	B1
Heretaunga-Pinehaven 6,171	C2
Hokitika 3,414	C5
Hornby 8,215	D5
Howick 13,866	C1
Huntly 6,534	E2
Hutt (Upper and Lower) †131,257	B2
Inglewood 2,839	E3

Invercargill 49,446	B7
Invercargill †53,868	B7
Kaiapoi 4,894	D5
Kaikohe 3,663	D1
Kaikoura 2,180	D5
Kaitaia 4,737	D1
Kawerau 8,593	F3
Kumeu 3,414	B1
Levin 14,652	E4
Lower Hutt 63,245	B2
Lyttelton 3,184	D5
Manukau 159,362	C1
Marton 4,858	E4
Masterton 18,785	E4
Mataura 2,345	B7
Milton 2,193	B7
Morrinsville 5,080	E2
Mosgiel 9,264	C6
Motueka 4,693	D4
Mount Albert 26,462	B1
Mount Eden 18,305	B1
Mount Maunganui 11,391	E2
Mount Roskill 33,577	B1
Mount Wellington 19,528	C1
Murupara 2,964	F3
Napier 48,314	F3
Napier †51,330	F3
Nelson 33,304	D4
Nelson †43,121	D4
New Lynn 10,445	B1
New Plymouth 36,048	D3
New Plymouth †44,095	D3
Ngaruawahia 4,435	E2
Northcote 10,061	B1
Oamaru 13,043	C6
Oban (Half Moon Bay) 2,448	B7
Onehunga 15,386	B1
One Tree Hill 11,078	C1
Opotiki 3,388	F3
Orewa 5,552	C1
Otahuhu 10,298	C1
Otaki 4,301	E4
Otorohanga 2,574	E3
Paeroa 3,702	E2
Pahiatua 2,599	F4
Paihia 1,740	D1
Palmerston North 60,105	E4
Palmerston North †66,691	E4
Papakura 22,473	E2
Papatoetoe 21,700	C1
Patea 1,938	E3
Petone 8,113	B2
Picton 3,220	D4
Pinehaven (Heretaunga-Pinehaven) 6,171	C2
Porirua 41,104	B2
Port Chalmers 2,917	C6
Pukekohe 9,070	E2
Putaruru 4,222	E3
Queenstown 3,367	B6

Raetihi 1,247	E3
Raglan 1,414	E2
Rangiora 6,385	D5
Reefton 1,200	C5
Richmond 6,847	D4
Riverton 1,479	B7
Rotorua 38,157	F3
Rotorua †48,314	F3
Runanga 1,264	C5
Russell 932	E1
Saint Kilda 6,147	C7
Shannon 1,465	E4
Stratford 5,518	E3
Taihape 2,586	E3
Takapuna 64,844	B1
Tapanui 1,042	B6
Taradale 4,681	F3
Taumarunui 6,541	E3
Taupo 13,651	F3
Tauranga 37,099	F2
Tauranga †53,097	F2
Tawa 12,216	B2
Te Anau 2,610	A6
Te Aroha 3,331	E2
Te Atatu 14,713	B1
Te Awamutu 7,922	E2
Te Kauwhata 842	E2
Te Kuiti 4,795	E3
Temuka 3,771	C6
Te Puke 4,577	F2
Thames 6,456	E2
Timaru 28,412	C6
Timaru †29,225	C6
Titirangi 8,426	B1
Tokoroa 18,713	F3
Tuakau 1,982	E2
Tuatapere 884	A7
Turangi 5,517	E3
Upper Hutt 31,405	B2
Waihi 3,538	E2
Waikanae 4,818	E4
Waikouaiti 858	C6
Waimate 3,393	C6
Wainuiomata 19,192	B3
Waipawa 1,732	F4
Waipukurau 3,648	F4
Wairoa 5,439	F3
Waitangi	D7
Waitara 6,012	E3
Waitemata 87,452	B1
Waiuku 3,654	E2
Wanaka 1,155	B6
Wanganui 37,012	E3
Wanganui †39,595	E3
Warkworth 1,734	E2
Washdyke 949	C6
Waverley 1,239	E3
Wellington (cap.) 135,688	A3

Wellington †321,004	A3
Wellsford 1,621	E2
Westport 4,686	C4
Whakatane 12,286	F2
Whangamata 1,566	F2
Whangarei 36,550	E1
Whangarei †40,212	E1
Whitianga 1,960	E2
Winton 2,035	B7
Woodville 1,647	F4

OTHER FEATURES

Arthur's (pass)	C5
Aspiring (mt.)	B6
Banks (pen.)	D5
Bream (bay)	E1
Brett (cape)	E1
Buller (riv.)	D4
Campbell (cape)	E4
Canterbury (bight)	D6
Cascade (pt.)	B6
Chatham (isls.) 751	D7
Cloudy (bay)	E4
Clutha (riv.)	B6
Coleridge (lake)	C5
Colville (cape)	E2
Cook (mt.)	C5
Cook (str.)	E4
Coromandel (pen.)	F2
Devil River (peak)	D4
D'Urville (isl.)	D4
Dusky (sound)	A6
East (cape)	G2
Egmont (cape)	D3
Egmont (mt.)	D3
Ellesmere (lake)	D5
Farewell (cape)	D4
Foulwind (cape)	C4
Fournier (cape)	E7
Foveaux (str.)	A7
Golden (bay)	D4
Great Barrier (isl.) 572	E2
Haast (pass)	B6
Hauraki (gulf)	C1
Hawke (bay)	F3
Hikurangi (mt.)	G2
Hokianga (harb.)	D1
Huiarau (range)	F3
Hutt (riv.)	C2
Islands (bay)	E1
Jackson (bay)	B5
Kaikoura (range)	D5
Kaimanawa (range)	E3
Kaipara (harb.)	D2
Karamea (bight)	C4
Kawhia (harb.)	E3
Kidnappers (cape)	F3
Mahia (pen.)	G3
Manapouri (lake)	A6
Manukau (harb.)	B1
Maria van Diemen (cape)	D1
Mataura (riv.)	B6
Mercury (isls.)	F2
Milford (sound)	A6
Needles (pt.)	E2
Nicholson, Port (inlet)	B3
Ninety Mile (beach)	D1
North (cape)	D1
North (isl.) 2,322,989	F1
North Taranaki (bight)	D3
Otago (pen.)	C6
Owen (mt.)	D4
Palliser (cape)	E4
Pegasus (bay)	D5
Pitt (isl.)	E7
Plenty (bay)	F2
Port Nicholson (inlet)	B3
Port Pegasus (inlet)	B7
Pukaki (lake)	B6
Puysegur (pt.)	A7
Rakaia (riv.)	C5
Rangitata (riv.)	C5
Rangitikei (riv.)	E3
Raukumara (range)	F3
Reinga (cape)	D1
Resolution (isl.)	A6
Richmond (range)	D4
Rocks (pt.)	C4
Rotorua (lake)	F3
Ruahine (range)	F4
Ruapehu (mt.)	E3
Ruapuke (isl.)	B7
South (cape)	A7
South (isl.) 852,748	B5
Southern Alps (range)	C5
South Taranaki (bight)	D3
Spenser (mts.)	D5
Stewart (isl.) 600	A7
Tararua (range)	E4
Tasman (bay)	D4
Tasman (mt.)	C5
Tasman (mts.)	D4
Tasman (sea)	B4
Taupo (lake)	F3
Tauroa (pt.)	D1

Te Anau (lake)	A6
Tekapo (lake)	C5
Terawhiti (cape)	A3
Thames (firth)	E2
Three Kings (isls.)	D1
Turakirae (head)	B3
Una (mt.)	D5
Waiheke (isl.) 3,223	E2
Waikato (riv.)	E2
Waimakariri (riv.)	D5
Waipa (riv.)	E2
Wairau (riv.)	D4
Waitaki (riv.)	C6
Waitemata (harb.)	B1
Wakatipu (lake)	B6
Wanaka (lake)	B6
Wanganui (riv.)	E3
West (cape)	A6
Whitcombe (mt.)	C5

†Population of urban area.

DOMINANT LAND USE

Mixed Farming, Livestock
Dairy
Truck Farming, Horticulture
Pasture Livestock (chiefly sheep)
Livestock Herding
Forests
Nonagricultural Land

MAJOR MINERAL OCCURRENCES

C Coal
G Natural Gas
J Jade
Ka Kaolin
Lg Lignite
O Petroleum
U Uranium

⚡ Water Power
▨ Major Industrial Areas

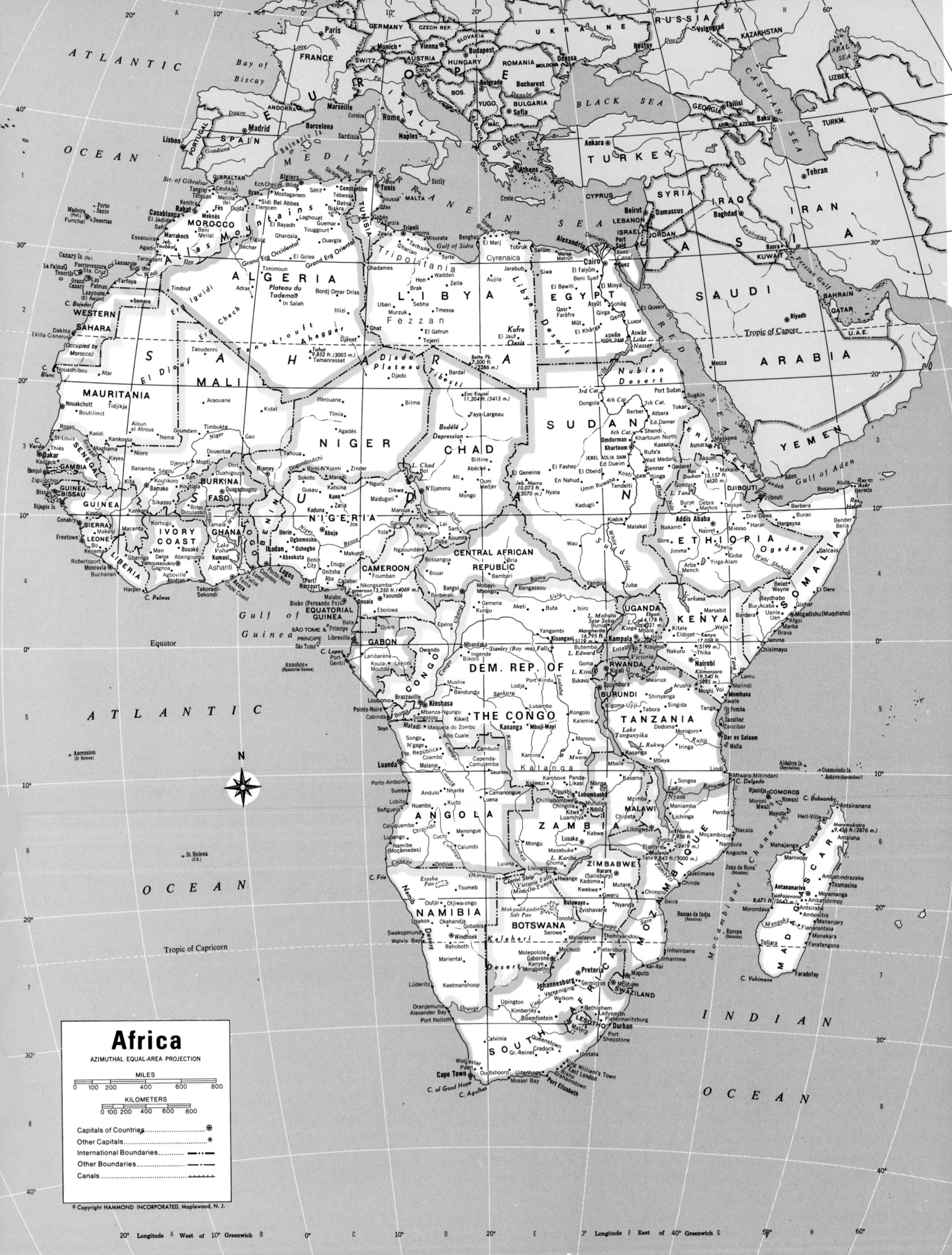

Africa

AZIMUTHAL EQUAL-AREA PROJECTION

MILES

0 100 200 400 600 800

KILOMETERS

0 100 200 400 600 800

Capitals of Countries .... ⊛
Other Capitals .... ⊛
International Boundaries .... ▬ ▬ ▬
Other Boundaries .... ▬ · ▬ ·
Canals .... ⊢⊣⊢⊣⊢

© Copyright HAMMOND INCORPORATED, Maplewood, N.J.

AREA 11,707,000 sq. mi. (30,321,130 sq. km.)
POPULATION 648,000,000
LARGEST CITY Cairo
HIGHEST POINT Kilimanjaro 19,340 ft. (5,895 m.)
LOWEST POINT Lake Assal, Djibouti -512 ft. (-156 m.)

Population Distribution

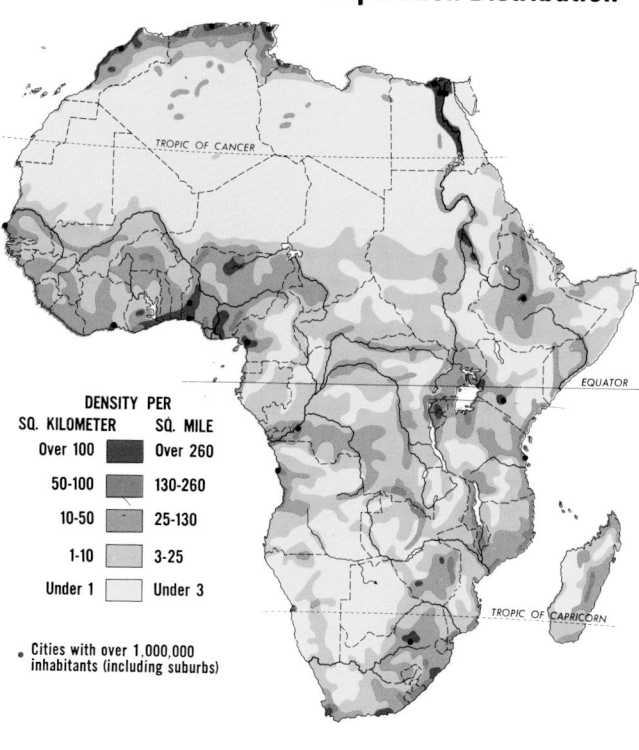

DENSITY PER

SQ. KILOMETER	SQ. MILE
Over 100	Over 260
50-100	130-260
10-50	25-130
1-10	3-25
Under 1	Under 3

● Cities with over 1,000,000 inhabitants (including suburbs)

Vegetation

TROPICAL FOREST
- Tropical Rainforest
- Light Tropical Forest
- Woodland and Shrub

TROPICAL GRASSLAND
- Grass and Shrub (Savanna)
- Wooded Savanna

MID-LATITUDE FOREST
- Mixed Coniferous and Broadleaf Forest
- Woodland and Shrub (Mediterranean)

MID-LATITUDE GRASSLAND
- Short Grass (Steppe)

RIVER VALLEY AND OASIS

DESERT AND DESERT SHRUB

UNCLASSIFIED HIGHLANDS

ERITREA
AREA 45,410 sq. mi. (117,600 sq. km.)
POPULATION 2,614,700
CAPITAL Asmara
LARGEST CITY Asmara
HIGHEST POINT Mount Soira 9,885 ft. (3,013 m.)
MONETARY UNIT birr
MAJOR LANGUAGES Arabic, English, Tigre, Afar
MAJOR RELIGIONS Coptic Christianity, Islam

DJIBOUTI

LIBYA
AREA 679,358 sq. mi. (1,759,537 sq. km.)
POPULATION 3,773,000
CAPITAL Tripoli
LARGEST CITY Tripoli
HIGHEST POINT Bette Pk. 7,500 ft. (2,286 m.)
MONETARY UNIT Libyan dinar
MAJOR LANGUAGES Arabic, Berber
MAJOR RELIGION Islam

EGYPT
AREA 386,659 sq. mi. (1,001,447 sq. km.)
POPULATION 53,080,000
CAPITAL Cairo
LARGEST CITY Cairo
HIGHEST POINT Jeb. Katherina 8,651 ft. (2,637 m.)
MONETARY UNIT Egyptian pound
MAJOR LANGUAGE Arabic
MAJOR RELIGIONS Islam, Coptic Christianity

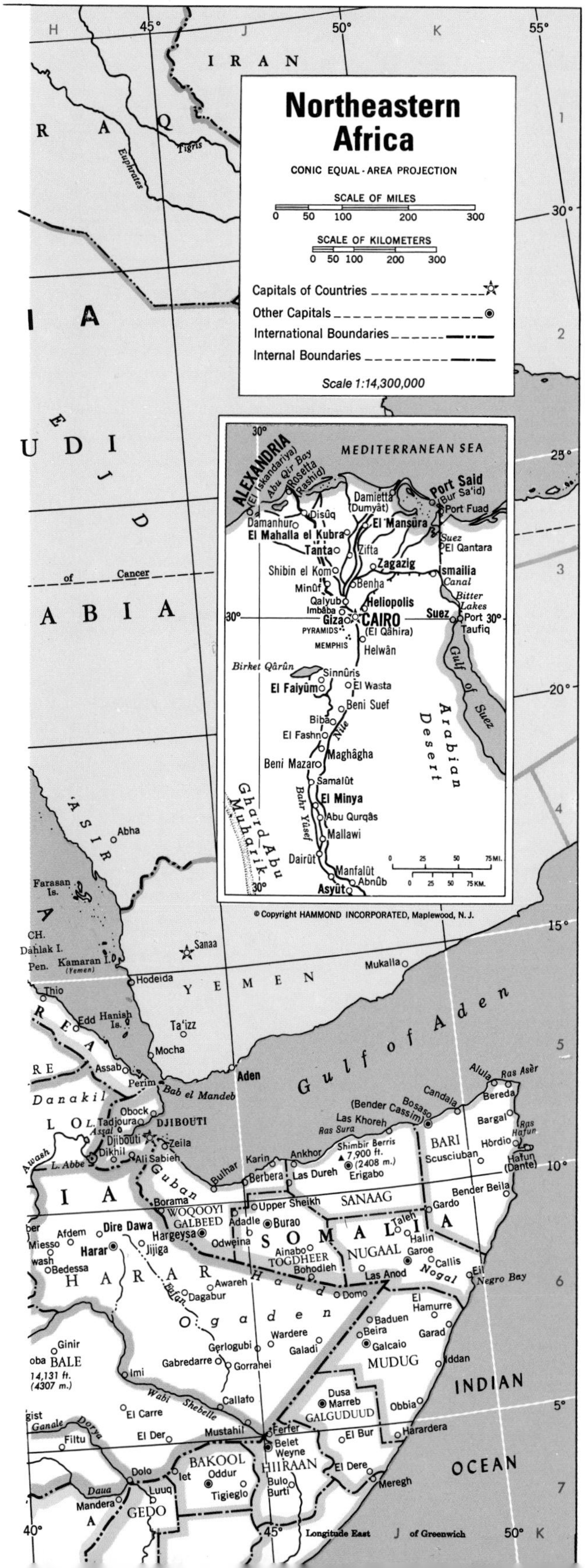

CHAD
AREA 495,752 sq. mi. (1,283,998 sq. km.)
POPULATION 5,538,000
CAPITAL N'Djamena
LARGEST CITY N'Djamena
HIGHEST POINT Emi Koussi 11,204 ft. (3,415 m.)
MONETARY UNIT CFA franc
MAJOR LANGUAGES Arabic, Bagirmi, French, Sara, Massa, Moudang
MAJOR RELIGIONS Islam, tribal religions

SUDAN
AREA 967,494 sq. mi. (2,505,809 sq. km.)
POPULATION 24,485,000
CAPITAL Khartoum
LARGEST CITY Khartoum
HIGHEST POINT Jeb. Marra 10,073 ft. (3,070 m.)
MONETARY UNIT Sudanese pound
MAJOR LANGUAGES Arabic, Dinka, Nubian, Beja, Nuer
MAJOR RELIGIONS Islam, tribal religions

ETHIOPIA
AREA 426,366 sq. mi. (1,104,300 sq. km.)
POPULATION 50,576,300
CAPITAL Addis Ababa
LARGEST CITY Addis Ababa
HIGHEST POINT Ras Dashan 15,157 ft. (4,620 m.)
MONETARY UNIT birr
MAJOR LANGUAGES Amharic, Gallinya, Tigrinya, Somali, Sidamo, Arabic, Ge'ez
MAJOR RELIGIONS Coptic Christianity, Islam

DJIBOUTI
AREA 8,880 sq. mi. (23,000 sq. km.)
POPULATION 456,000
CAPITAL Djibouti
LARGEST CITY Djibouti
HIGHEST POINT Moussa Ali 6,768 ft. (2,063 m.)
MONETARY UNIT Djibouti franc
MAJOR LANGUAGES Arabic, Somali, Afar, French
MAJOR RELIGIONS Islam, Roman Catholicism

Northeastern Africa
CONIC EQUAL-AREA PROJECTION

SCALE OF MILES
0 50 100   200   300

SCALE OF KILOMETERS
0 50 100   200   300

Capitals of Countries _ _ _ _ _ _ _ _ ☆
Other Capitals _ _ _ _ _ _ _ _ _ ◉
International Boundaries _ _ _ _ _ ▬▬
Internal Boundaries _ _ _ _ _ _ _ ▬▬

Scale 1:14,300,000

© Copyright HAMMOND INCORPORATED, Maplewood, N.J.

CHAD
CITIES and TOWNS

Abéché 28,100	D5
Abou Deïa	C5
Adré	D5
Am-Timan 4,200	D5
Arada	D4
Ati 7,500	C5
Baibokoum 5,500	C6
Biltine 3,900	D5
Bitkine 5,000	C5
Bokoro 6,500	C5
Bol 2,500	B5
Bongor 14,300	C5
Bousso 4,500	C5
Doba 13,300	C6
Fada	D4
Faya-Largeau 6,800	C4
Fianga 10,000	C6
Goré	C6
Goz Beïda	D5
Guéréda	D5
Iriba	D4
Kélo 16,800	C6
Koumra 17,000	C6
Kouno	C6

Kyabé 5,000	C6
Laï 10,400	C6
Léré	B6
Mangueigne	D5
Mao 4,900	C5
Massakory	C5
Massénya	C5
Melfi	C5
Mogororo	D5
Moissala 5,100	C6
Mongo 8,300	C5
Moundou 39,600	C6
Moussoro 7,700	C5
N'Djamena (cap.) 179,000	C5
Oum Hadjer 5,600	C5
Ounianga-Kébir	D4
Pala 13,200	B6
Sarh 43,700	C6
Wour	C3
Zouar	C3

OTHER FEATURES

Aouk, Bahr (riv.)	D5
Azoum, Bahr (riv.)	D5
Baguirmi (reg.)	C5
Bahr el Ghazal (dry riv.)	C4
Batha (riv.)	C5

Bodélé (depr.)	C4
Borku (reg.)	C4
Chad (lake)	C5
Emi Koussi (mt.)	C4
Ennedi (plat.)	D4
Fittri (lake)	C5
Kanem (reg.)	C5
Logone (reg.)	C5
Maro (riv.)	C4
Mbéré (dry riv.)	C6
Mourdi (riv.)	D4
Ouham (depr.)	C6
Pendé (riv.)	C6
Sahara (riv.)	C3
Salamat, Bahr (des.)	C6
Shari (riv.)	C5
Sudan (riv.)	C5
Tibesti (mts.)	C3
Wadai (reg.)	D5

DJIBOUTI
CITIES and TOWNS

Ali Sabieh	H5
Dikhil	H5
Djibouti (cap.) 96,000	H5
Obock	H5

Tadjoura	H5

OTHER FEATURES

Abbe (lake)	H5
Aden (gulf)	J5
Bab el Mandeb (strait)	H5

EGYPT
CITIES and TOWNS

Abnûb 39,343	J4
Akhmim 53,234	F2
Alexandria 2,318,655	J2
Aswân 144,377	F3
Asyût 213,983	J4
Benha 88,992	J3
Beni Mazar 39,373	J4
Beni Suef 118,148	J3
Biba 33,074	J4
Bur Sa'id (Port Said) 262,620	K2
Cairo (cap.) 5,084,463	J3
Dairût 31,624	J4
Damanhur 188,927	J3
Damietta 93,546	J3
Disûq 58,650	J3

(continued on following page)

Topography

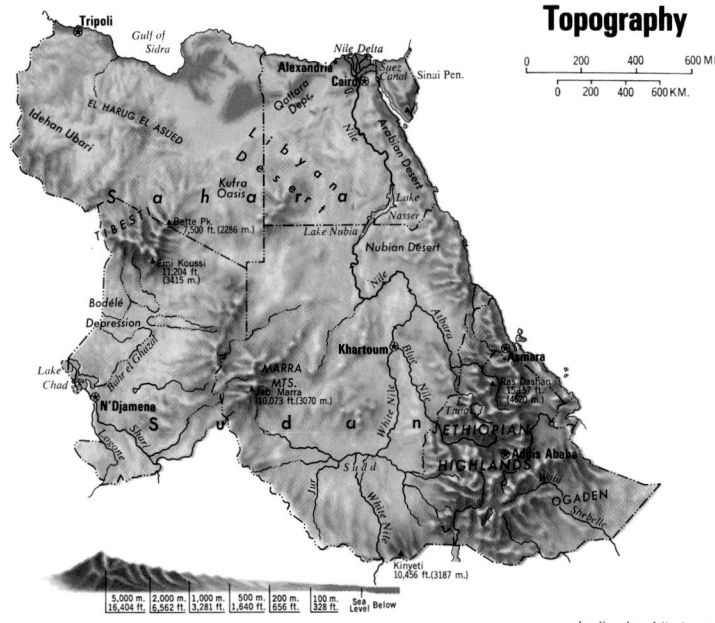

5,000 m.	2,000 m.	1,000 m.	500 m.	200 m.	100 m.	Sea Level	Below
16,404 ft.	6,562 ft.	3,281 ft.	1,640 ft.	656 ft.	328 ft.	Level	Below

0   200   400   600 MI.
0   200   400   600 KM.

(continued on following page)

Dumyât (Damietta) 93,546 ...... J3
El 'Alamein E1
El 'Arish F1
El Faiyûm 167,081 ...... J3
El Fashn 33,506 ...... J4
El Iskendariya (Alexandria) 2,318,655 ...... J2
El Karnak F2
El Khârga 26,375 ...... F2
El Mahalla el Kubra 292,853 ...... J3
El Mansûra 257,866 ...... K3
El Minya 146,423 ...... J4
El Qahira (Cairo) (cap.) 5,084,463 ...... J3
El Qantara 919 ...... K3
El Quseir 12,297 ...... F2
El Wasta 17,659 ...... J3
Girga 51,110 ...... F2
Giza 1,246,713 ...... J3
Heliopolis J3
Helwân J3
Idfu 34,858 ...... F3
Ismailia 145,978 ...... K3
Isna 34,186 ...... F2
Karnak (El Karnak) F2
Kôm Ombo 44,531 ...... F3
Luxor 92,748 ...... F2
Maghâgha 40,802 ...... J4
Mallawi 74,256 ...... J4
Manfalût 41,126 ...... J4
Mersá Matrûh 27,857 ...... E1
Minûf 55,131 ...... J3
Mût 8,032 ...... E2
Port Fuad K3
Port Safâga F2
Port Said 262,620 ...... K2
Port Taufiq K3
Qalyub 62,739 ...... J3
Qena 94,013 ...... F2
Rashid (Rosetta) 42,962 ...... J2
Rudeis F2
Salûm 4,161 ...... E1
Samalût 48,146 ...... J4
Shibin el Kom 102,844 ...... J3
Sidi Barrani 1,574 ...... E1
Sinnûris 42,022 ...... J3
Sohâg 101,758 ...... F2
Suez 194,001 ...... K3
Tahta 45,242 ...... F2
Tanta 284,636 ...... J3
Zagazig 202,637 ...... J3
Zifta 50,410 ...... J3

OTHER FEATURES

Abu Qir (bay) J2
Abydos (ruins) F2
Aqaba (gulf) G2
Arabian (des.) F2
Aswân (dam) F3
Aswân High (dam) F3
Bahariya (oasis) E2
Bânâs, Ras (cape) G3
Berenice (ruins) F3
Birket Qârûn (lake) J3
Bitter (lakes) K3
Dakhla (oasis) E2
Eastern (Arabian) (des.) F2
Farâfra (oasis) E2
Foul (bay) G3
Gilf Kebir (plat.) E3
Great Sand Sea (des.) D2
Katherina, Jebel (mt.) F2
Khârga (oasis) F2
Libyan (des.) E2
Libyan (plat.) E1
Mediterranean (sea) E1
Memphis (ruins) J3
Muhammad, Ras (cape) F2
Nasser (lake) F3
Nile (riv.) F2
Pyramids (ruins) J3
Qattara (depr.) E2
Sahara (des.) E3
Sinai (mt.) F2
Sinai (pen.) F2
Siwa (oasis) E2
Suez (canal) K3
Suez (gulf) F2
Tiran (strait) F2
'Uweinat, Jebel (mt.) E3

ERITREA

CITIES and TOWNS

Adi Ugri 12,800 ...... G5
Asmara (cap.) 393,800 ...... G4
Assab 16,000 ...... H5
Karkabat G4
Keren G4
Massawa 19,800 ...... G4
Mersa Fatma H5
Nakfa G4
Tessenei G4
Thio H5
Umm Hajar G5
Zula G4

OTHER FEATURES

Baraka (riv.) G4
Buri (pen.) H4
Dahlak (arch.) H4
Dahlak (isl.) H4
Kasar, Ras (cape) G4
Takkaze (riv.) G5

ETHIOPIA

PROVINCES

Arusi 852,900 ...... G6
Bale 707,800 ...... H6
Gamu-Gofa 698,800 ...... G6
Gojjam 1,750,100 ...... G5
Gondar 1,355,800 ...... G5
Harar 3,359,200 ...... H6
Ilubabor 688,800 ...... F6
Kaffa 1,693,000 ...... G6
Shoa 5,369,500 ...... G6
Sidamo 2,479,800 ...... G7
Tigre 1,828,900 ...... H5
Wallaga 1,269,100 ...... G6
Wallo 2,459,900 ...... H5

CITIES and TOWNS

Addis Ababa (cap.) 1,196,300 ...... G6
Addis Alam 5,500 ...... G6
Adigrat 9,400 ...... G5
Adwa 16,400 ...... G5
Aksum 12,800 ...... G5
Ankober H6
Arba Mench 7,660 ...... G6
Asselle 19,390 ...... G6
Awareh H6
Axum (Aksum) 12,800 ...... G5
Bahir Dar 25,100 ...... G5
Dagabur H6
Dangila G5
Debra Birhan 16,700 ...... G6
Debra Markos 30,260 ...... G5
Debra Tabor 8,700 ...... G5
Dembidollo 7,600 ...... F6
Dessye 49,750 ...... G5
Dilla 13,800 ...... G6
Dire Dawa 63,700 ...... H6
El Carre H6
Gabredarre H6
Galadi J6
Gambela F6
Gardula 5,800 ...... G6
Gerlogubi H6
Ghimbi 8,300 ...... G6
Ginir H6
Goba 13,500 ...... H6
Gondar 38,600 ...... G5
Gore 8,500 ...... G6
Gorrahei H6
Harar 48,440 ...... H6
Hosseina 8,500 ...... G6
Jijiga 8,000 ...... H6
Jimma 47,360 ...... G6
Jiran G6
Kibre Mengist 8,300 ...... G6
Lalibela G5
Magdala G5
Maji G6
Makale 30,780 ...... G5
Metamma G5
Metu 6,860 ...... G6
Miesso H6
Mizan Teferi G6
Moyale G7
Murle G6
Mustahil H6
Nakamti 18,310 ...... G6
Nazret 42,900 ...... G6
Negelli 8,800 ...... G6
Nejo G6
Saio (Dembidollo) 7,600 ...... F6
Soddu 11,900 ...... G6
Sokota G5
Tori F6
Waka G6
Waldia 9,600 ...... G5
Wardere J6
Wolta G6
Yaballo G7

OTHER FEATURES

Abay (riv.) G5
Abaya (lake) G6
Abbe (lake) H5
Akobo (riv.) F6
Assal (lake) H5
Assale (lake) H5
Atbara (riv.) G4
Awash (riv.) H5
Bale (mt.) G6
Blue Nile (Abay) (riv.) G5
Chamo (lake) G6
Danakil (reg.) H5
Dawa (riv.) G7
Dinder (riv.) F5
Fafan (riv.) H6
Ganale Dorya (riv.) H6
Gughe (mt.) G6
Haud (reg.) J6
Ogaden (reg.) H6
Omo (riv.) G6
Ras Dashan (mt.) G5
Red (sea) H4
Rudolf (Turkana) (lake) G7
Simen (mts.) G5
Takkaze (riv.) G5
Tana (lake) G5
Tisisat (fall) G5
Turkana (lake) G7
Zwai (lake) G6

LIBYA

CITIES and TOWNS

Ajedabia◦ 53,170 ...... D1
Aujila◦ 6,695 ...... D2
Baida◦ 59,765 ...... D1
Barce (El Marj)◦ 55,444 ...... D1
Benghazi 286,943 ...... C1
Beni Ulid◦ 19,113 ...... B1
Brak◦ 16,307 ...... B2
Cyrene (Shahat)◦ 17,157 ...... D1
Derj◦ 2,152 ...... B1
Derna◦ 44,145 ...... D1
El Abiar◦ 17,685 ...... D1
El Agheila 3 ...... C1
El Azizia◦ 34,077 ...... B1
El Bardi◦ 4,330 ...... D1
El Barkat◦ 2,139 ...... B3
El Gatrun B3
El Jauf◦ 6,481 ...... D3
El Marj◦ 55,444 ...... D1
Es Sidr◦ 706 ...... C1
Ez Zuetina◦ 7,256 ...... D1
Ghadames◦ 6,172 ...... A2
Gharian◦ 65,224 ...... B1
Ghat◦ 6,924 ...... B3
Ghemines◦ 4,313 ...... C1
Homs◦ 66,890 ...... B1
Hon◦ 2,766 ...... C2
Jaghbub (Jarabub)◦ 1,436 ...... D2
Jarabub◦ 1,436 ...... D2
Marada◦ 3,201 ...... C2
Marsa el Brega◦ 2,618 ...... D1
Marsa el Hariga◦ 5,043 ...... D1
Misurata◦ 102,439 ...... C1
Mizda◦ 11,472 ...... B1
Murzuk◦ 22,185 ...... B2
Nalut◦ 23,535 ...... B1
Ras Lanuf◦ 1,990 ...... C1
Sabrathaa◦ 30,836 ...... B1
Sebha◦ 35,879 ...... B2
Shahat◦ 17,157 ...... D1
Sinawen◦ 1,549 ...... B1
Sokna◦ 3,757 ...... C2
Soluk◦ 6,501 ...... D1
Syrte◦ 22,797 ...... C1
Tarhuna◦ 52,657 ...... B1
Tobruk◦ 58,384 ...... D1
Tokra◦ 10,714 ...... D1
Tripoli (cap.)◦ 550,438 ...... B1
Ubari◦ 19,132 ...... B2
Waddan◦ 5,347 ...... C2
Wau el Kebir C2
Zawia◦ 72,092 ...... B1
Zella◦ 72,092 ...... C2
Zliten◦ 58,981 ...... B1
Zwara◦ 15,078 ...... B1

OTHER FEATURES

Akhdar, Jebel (mts.) D1
Barqa (Cyrenaica) (reg.) D1
Ben Ghnema, Jebel (mts.) C2
Bette (peak) C3
Bey el Kebir, Wadi (dry riv.) B1
Bir Hakeim (ruins) D1
Bomba (gulf) D1
Buzeima (well) D3
Calansho Sand Sea (des.) D2
Calansho, Serir (des.) D2
Cyrenaica (reg.) D1
Fezzan (reg.) B2
Great Sand Sea (des.) D2
Harug el Asued, El (mts.) C2
Homra, Hamada el (des.) B2
Idehan Murzuk (des.) B2
Idehan Ubari (des.) B2
Jalo (oasis) D2
Jefara (reg.) B1
Jef Jef es Seghin (plat.) D3
Jofra (oasis) C2
Kufra (oasis) D3
Leptis Magna (ruins) B1
Libyan (des.) D2
Libyan (plat.) D1
Mediterranean (sea) C1
Nefusa, Jebel (mts.) B1
Rebiana (oasis) D3
Rebiana Sand Sea (des.) D3
Sahara (des.) C3
Shati, Wadi esh (dry riv.) B2
Sidra (gulf) C1
Soda, Jebel es (mts.) C2
Tazerbo (oasis) D2
Tibesti, Serir (des.) C3
Tinghert Hamada (Tinrhert) (des.) B2
Tripolitania (reg.) B1
'Uweinat, Jebel (mt.) E3
Zelten, Jebel (mts.) D2

SUDAN

PROVINCES

Central F5
Darfur D5
Eastern G4
Khartoum F4
Kordofan E5
Northern E3
Southern E6

CITIES and TOWNS

'Abri F3
Abu Hamed F4
Adok F6
Akobo F6
Amadi F6
Argo F4
Aroma G4
Atbara 66,000 ...... F4
Babanusa E5
Bara F5
Bentiu E6
Berber F4
Bor F6
Buram E5
Damazin (Ed Damazin) 12,000 ...... F5
Deim Zubeir E6
Dongola 6,000 ...... F4
Dungunab G3
Ed Damazin 12,000 ...... F5
Ed Damer 17,000 ...... F4
Ed Dueim 27,000 ...... F5
El Fasher 52,000 ...... E5
El Geneina 33,000 ...... D5
El Obeid 90,000 ...... E5
El Odaiya E5
En Nahud 23,000 ...... E5
Er Roseires F5
Fashoda (Kodok) F6
Gedaref 92,000 ...... G5
Gogrial E6
Goz Regeb G4
Haiya Junction G4
Halaib G3
Jonglei F6
Juba 57,000 ...... F7
Kadugli 18,000 ...... E5
Kaka F5
Karima F4
Kassala 99,000 ...... G4
Kerma F4
Khartoum (cap.) 334,000 ...... F4
Khartoum North 151,000 ...... F4
Khashm el Girba G5
Kodok F6
Kosti 57,000 ...... F5
Kurmuk F5
Kutum D5
Malakal 35,000 ...... F6
Maridi E7
Melut F5
Merowe F4
Meshra er Req E6
Mongalla F6
Muglad E5
Muhammad Qol G3
Nagishot F7
Nasir F6
Nyala 60,000 ...... D5
Nyamlell E6
Nyerol F6
Omdurman 299,000 ...... F4
Opari F7
Pibor Post F6
Port Sudan 133,000 ...... G4
Qala'en Nahl F5
Raga E6
Rashad F5
Rejaf F7
Renk F5
Rufa'a F5
Rumbek 17,000 ...... E6
Sennar F5
Shambe F6
Shendi F4
Shereik F4
Showak G5
Singa F5
Sinkat G4
Sodiri E5
Suakin G4
Suki F5
Tali Post F6
Talodi F5
Tambura E6
Tendelti F5
Tokar G4
Tombe F6
Tonga F6
Tonj E6
Torit F7
Trinkitat G4
Umm Keddada E5
Umm Ruwaba F5
Wadi Halfa F3
Wad Medani 107,000 ...... F5
Wankai E6
Wau 53,000 ...... E6
Yambio 7,000 ...... E7
Yei F7
Yirol F6
Zalingei D5

OTHER FEATURES

Abu Habl, Wadi (dry riv.) F5
Abu Shagara, Ras (cape) G3
Adda (riv.) D6
Atbara (riv.) G4
Bahr Azoum (riv.) D5
Bahr el 'Arab (riv.) E6
Bahr ez Zeraf (riv.) F6
Blue Nile (riv.) F5
Dar Hamid (reg.) F5
Dar Masalit (reg.) D5
Dinder (riv.) F5
El 'Atrun (oasis) E4
Fifth Cataract (falls) F4
Fourth Cataract (falls) F4
Gabgaba, Wadi (dry riv.) F3
Ghalla, Wadi el (dry riv.) E5
Hadarba, Ras (cape) G3
Howar, Wadi (dry riv.) E4
Ibra, Wadi (dry riv.) D5
Jebel Aulia (dam) F4
Jonglei (canal) F6
Jur (riv.) E6
Kinyeti (mt.) F7
Libyan (des.) E3
Lol (dry riv.) E6
Lotagipi Swamp (plain) F6
Marra, Jebel (mt.) D5
Meroe (ruins) F4
Milk, Wadi el (dry riv.) E4
Muqaddam, Wadi (dry riv.) F4
Napata (ruins) F4
Naqa (ruins) F4
Nile (riv.) F4
Nuba (mts.) E5
Nubia (lake) F3
Nubian (des.) F3
Nukheila (oasis) E4
Nuri (ruins) F4
Oda, Jebel (mt.) G3
Pibor (riv.) F6
Red (sea) G3
Red Sea (hills) G3
Sahara (des.) E3
Selima (oasis) E3
Sennar (dam) F5
Setit (riv.) G5
Sixth Cataract F4
Sobat (riv.) F6
Suakin (arch.) G4
Sudan (reg.) E5
Sudd (swamp) F6
Sue (riv.) E6
Third Cataract (falls) E4
'Uweinat, Jebel (mt.) E3
White Nile (riv.) F5

◦ Population of sub-district or division

Agriculture, Industry and Resources

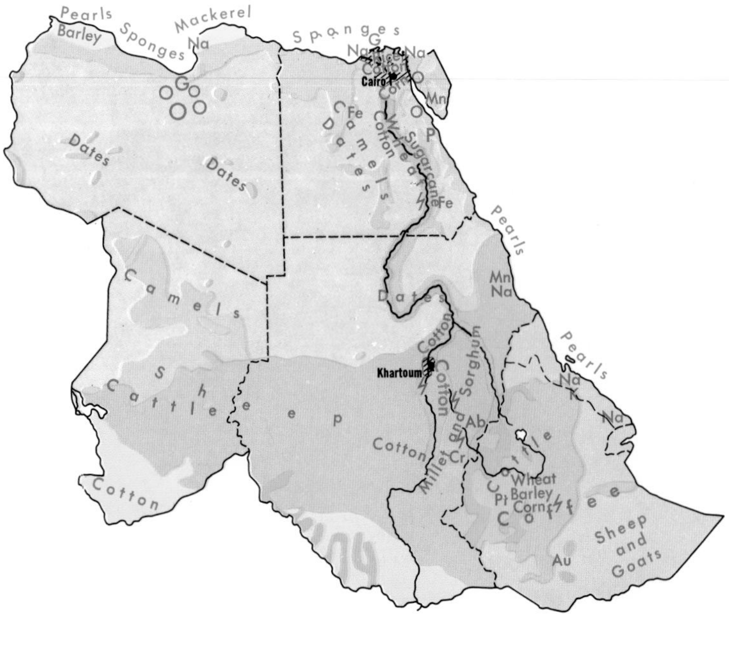

DOMINANT LAND USE

- Cereals, Horticulture, Livestock
- Cash Crops, Mixed Cereals
- Cotton, Cereals
- Market Gardening, Diversified Tropical Crops
- Plantation Agriculture
- Oases
- Pasture Livestock
- Nomadic Livestock Herding
- Forests
- Nonagricultural Land

MAJOR MINERAL OCCURRENCES

Ab	Asbestos	Mn	Manganese
Au	Gold	Na	Salt
Cr	Chromium	O	Petroleum
Fe	Iron Ore	P	Phosphates
G	Natural Gas	Pt	Platinum
K	Potash		

Water Power

Major Industrial Areas

ANGOLA

AREA 481,351 sq. mi. (1,246,700 sq. km.)
POPULATION 9,747,000
CAPITAL Luanda
LARGEST CITY Luanda
HIGHEST POINT Mt. Moco 8,593 ft. (2,620 m.)
MONETARY UNIT kwanza
MAJOR LANGUAGES Mbundu, Kongo, Lunda, Portuguese
MAJOR RELIGIONS Tribal religions, Roman Catholicism

BURUNDI

AREA 10,747 sq. mi. (27,835 sq. km.)
POPULATION 5,302,000
CAPITAL Bujumbura
LARGEST CITY Bujumbura
HIGHEST POINT 8,858 ft. (2,700 m.)
MONETARY UNIT Burundi franc
MAJOR LANGUAGES Kirundi, French, Swahili
MAJOR RELIGIONS Tribal religions, Roman Catholicism, Islam

CAMEROON

AREA 183,568 sq. mi. (475,441 sq. km.)
POPULATION 11,540,000
CAPITAL Yaoundé
LARGEST CITY Douala
HIGHEST POINT Cameroon 13,350 ft. (4,069 m.)
MONETARY UNIT CFA franc
MAJOR LANGUAGFS Fang, Bamileke, Fulani, Duala, French, English
MAJOR RELIGIONS Tribal religions, Christianity, Islam

CENTRAL AFRICAN REP.

AREA 242,000 sq. mi. (626,780 sq. km.)
POPULATION 2,740,000
CAPITAL Bangui
LARGEST CITY Bangui
HIGHEST POINT Gao 4,659 ft. (1,420 m.)
MONETARY UNIT CFA franc
MAJOR LANGUAGES Banda, Gbaya, Sangho, French
MAJOR RELIGIONS Tribal religions, Christianity, Islam

CONGO, REP. OF THE

AREA 132,046 sq. mi. (342,000 sq. km.)
POPULATION 1,843,000
CAPITAL Brazzaville
LARGEST CITY Brazzaville
HIGHEST POINT Leketi Mts. 3,412 ft. (1,040 m.)
MONETARY UNIT CFA franc
MAJOR LANGUAGES Kikongo, Bateke, Lingala, French
MAJOR RELIGIONS Christianity, tribal religions, Islam

EQUATORIAL GUINEA

AREA 10,831 sq. mi. (28,052 sq. km.)
POPULATION 341,000
CAPITAL Malabo
LARGEST CITY Malabo
HIGHEST POINT 9,868 ft. (3,008 m.)
MONETARY UNIT CFA franc
MAJOR LANGUAGES Fang, Bubi, Spanish
MAJOR RELIGIONS Tribal religions, Christianity

GABON

AREA 103,346 sq. mi. (267,666 sq. km.)
POPULATION 1,206,000
CAPITAL Libreville
LARGEST CITY Libreville
HIGHEST POINT Ibounzi 5,165 ft. (1,574 m.)
MONETARY UNIT CFA franc
MAJOR LANGUAGES Fang and other Bantu languages, French
MAJOR RELIGIONS Tribal religions, Christianity, Islam

KENYA

AREA 224,960 sq. mi. (582,646 sq. km.)
POPULATION 24,872,000
CAPITAL Nairobi
LARGEST CITY Nairobi
HIGHEST POINT Kenya 17,058 ft. (5,199 m.)
MONETARY UNIT Kenya shilling
MAJOR LANGUAGES Kikuyu, Luo, Kavirondo, Kamba, Swahili, English
MAJOR RELIGIONS Tribal religions, Christianity, Hinduism, Islam

MALAWI

AREA 45,747 sq. mi. (118,485 sq. km.)
POPULATION 8,022,000
CAPITAL Lilongwe
LARGEST CITY Blantyre
HIGHEST POINT Mulanje 9,843 ft. (3,000 m.)
MONETARY UNIT Malawi kwacha
MAJOR LANGUAGES Chichewa, Yao, English, Nyanja, Tumbuka, Tonga, Ngoni
MAJOR RELIGIONS Tribal religions, Islam, Christianity

RWANDA

AREA 10,169 sq. mi. (26,337 sq. km.)
POPULATION 6,274,000
CAPITAL Kigali
LARGEST CITY Kigali
HIGHEST POINT Karisimbi 14,780 ft. (4,505 m.)
MONETARY UNIT Rwanda franc
MAJOR LANGUAGES Kinyarwanda, French, Swahili
MAJOR RELIGIONS Tribal religions, Roman Catholicism, Islam

SOMALIA

AREA 246,200 sq. mi. (637,658 sq. km.)
POPULATION 7,339,000
CAPITAL Mogadishu
LARGEST CITY Mogadishu
HIGHEST POINT Surud Ad 7,900 ft. (2,408 m.)
MONETARY UNIT Somali shilling
MAJOR LANGUAGES Somali, Arabic, Italian, English
MAJOR RELIGION Islam

TANZANIA

AREA 363,708 sq. mi. (942,003 sq. km.)
POPULATION 24,802,000
CAPITAL Dar es Salaam
LARGEST CITY Dar es Salaam
HIGHEST POINT Kilimanjaro 19,340 ft. (5,895 m.)
MONETARY UNIT Tanzanian shilling
MAJOR LANGUAGES Nyamwezi-Sukuma, Swahili, English
MAJOR RELIGIONS Tribal religions, Christianity, Islam

UGANDA

AREA 91,076 sq. mi. (235,887 sq. km.)
POPULATION 17,804,000
CAPITAL Kampala
LARGEST CITY Kampala
HIGHEST POINT Margherita 16,795 ft. (5,119 m.)
MONETARY UNIT Ugandan shilling
MAJOR LANGUAGES Luganda, Acholi, Teso, Nyoro, Soga, Nkole, English, Swahili
MAJOR RELIGIONS Tribal religions, Christianity, Islam

CONGO, DEM. REP. OF THE

AREA 905,063 sq. mi. (2,344,113 sq. km.)
POPULATION 34,491,000
CAPITAL Kinshasa
LARGEST CITY Kinshasa
HIGHEST POINT Margherita 16,795 ft. (5,119 m.)
MONETARY UNIT zaire
MAJOR LANGUAGES Tshiluba, Mongo, Kikongo, Kingwana, Zande, Lingala, Swahili, French
MAJOR RELIGIONS Tribal religions, Christianity

ZAMBIA

AREA 290,586 sq. mi. (752,618 sq. km.)
POPULATION 8,073,000
CAPITAL Lusaka
LARGEST CITY Lusaka
HIGHEST POINT Sunzu 6,782 ft. (2,067 m.)
MONETARY UNIT Zambian kwacha
MAJOR LANGUAGES Bemba, Tonga, Lozi, Luvale, Nyanja, English
MAJOR RELIGIONS Tribal religions

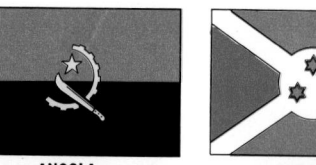 ANGOLA
 BURUNDI
 CAMEROON
 CENTRAL AFRICAN REP.
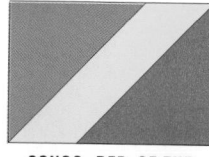 CONGO, REP. OF THE
EQUATORIAL GUINEA
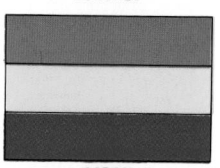 GABON
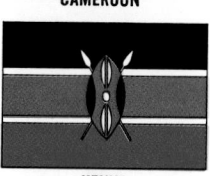 KENYA
 MALAWI
 RWANDA
 SOMALIA
 TANZANIA
 UGANDA
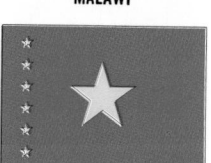 CONGO, DEM. REP. OF THE
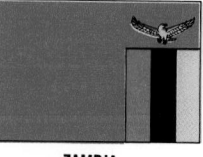 ZAMBIA
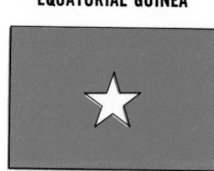

ANGOLA

PROVINCES

Bengo 68,885 ....B5
Benguela 474,897 ....B6
Bie 650,337 ....C6
Cabinda 80,857 ....B5
Cuando Cubango 112,073 .....C7
Cuanza-Norte 298,062 ....B5
Cuanza-Sul 458,592 ....C6
Cunene 147,394 ....C7
Huambo 837,627 ....C6
Huíla 497,470 ....B7
Luanda 491,704 ....B5
Lunda Norte 210,000 ....C5
Lunda Sul 98,000 ....D5
Malanje 558,630 ....C6
Moxico 213,119 ....D6
Namibe 53,058 ....B7
Uíge 386,037 ....B5
Zaire 41,766 ....B5

CITIES and TOWNS

Ambriz B5
Baía dos Tigres B7
Baia Farta B6
Bembe B5
Benguela 40,996 ....B6
Caála 8,894 ....C6
Cabinda 21,124 ....B5
Caconda B6
Caiundo C7
Camacupa 5,740 ....C6
Camanongue D6
Cambundi-Catembo C5
Capelongo C6
Cassinga C7
Catumbela B6
Caxito B5
Chinguar C6
Chitado D5
Cuango C5
Cuito-Cuanavale C7
Dondo B5
Forte República B7
Foz do Cunene B7
Gabela 6,930 ....B6
Ganda 2,538 ....B6
Golungo Alto B5
Huambo 61,885 ....C6
Katchiungo C6
Kuito 18,941 ....C6
Kuvango C6
Lobito 59,528 ....B6
Longa C6

Lóvua D5
Luacano D6
Luanda (cap.) 475,328 ....B5
Luau D6
Lubango 31,674 ....B6
Lucapa D5
Luena 2,539 ....C6
Luiana D7
Malanje 31,599 ....C6
Maquela do Zombo C5
Massango (Forte República) ...C5
Mbanza Congo 4,002 ....B5
Menongue 3,023 ....C6

Moçâmedes (Namibe) 12,076 ...B7
Namibe 12,076 ....B7
N'dalatando 7,342 ....B5
N'gage 2,548 ....C5
Ngunza (Sumbe) 7,911 ....B6
N'zeto B5
Ondjiva C7
Porto Amboim B6
Saurimo 12,901 ....D5
Soyo B5
Sumbe 7,911 ....B6
Tombua 8,235 ....B7
Uíge 11,972 ....C5
Waku Kungo 2,784 ....C6

OTHER FEATURES

Bero (riv.) B7
Chicapa (riv.) D5
Chiumbe (riv.) D5
Congo (riv.) C4
Coporolo (riv.) B6
Cuando (riv.) C7
Cuango (riv.) C5
Cuanza (riv.) C5
Cubango (riv.) C7
Cuito (riv.) C7
Cunene (dam) B7
Cunene (riv.) B7

Cuvo (riv.) B6
Kasai (riv.) D5
Kwilu (riv.) C5
Loange (riv.) C5
Loge (riv.) B5
Lungwebungu (riv.) D6
Matala (dam) B6
M'Bridge (riv.) B5
Moco (mt.) C6
Negro (cape) B7
Palmeirinhas (pt.) B5
Ruacana Falls (dam) B7
Santa Maria (cape) B6
Zambezi (riv.) D6

BURUNDI

CITIES and TOWNS

Bujumbura (cap.) 141,040 ....E4
Bururi 7,800 ....E4
Gitega 19,500 ....F4

OTHER FEATURES

Ruzizi (riv.) E4
Tanganyika (lake) E5

CAMEROON

CITIES and TOWNS

Bafia 17,855 ....B3
Bafoussam 62,239 ....B2
Bamenda 48,111 ....B2
Banyo 10,293 ....B2
Bertoua 13,985 ....B3
Bétaré-Oya B2
Bonabéri A3
Buea 24,584 ....A3
Djoum C6
Douala 458,426 ....A3
Dschang 16,629 ....A2

(continued on following page)

OTHER FEATURES

Bamingui (riv.)........C2
Bomu (riv.)...........D3
Dar Rounga (reg.)......C2
Gao (mt.)............C3
Kadei (riv.)..........C2
Kotto (riv.)..........D2
Lobaye (riv.)........C2
Mbéré (riv.)........B2
Ouham (riv.)........C2
Pendé (riv.)........C2

Sangha (riv.).........C3
Shari (riv.)..........C2
Shinko (riv.).........D2
Ubangi (riv.).........C3

CONGO, REP. OF THE
CITIES and TOWNS

Abala...............C4
Boundji............C4
Brazzaville (cap.) 298,967...C4

Djambala.............B4
Impfondo............C3
Kinkala.............B4
Loubomo 29,600......B4
Makoua.............C3
Mbinda.............B3
Mossaka.............C4
Mossendjo............B4
Nkayi 30,600........B4
Ouesso.............C3
Owando.............C3
Pointe-Noire 141,700...B4

OTHER FEATURES

Alima (riv.).........B4
Congo (riv.).........C4
Crystal (mts.).......B3
Dja (riv.)...........B3
Ivindo (riv.)........B3
Kadei (riv.).........C3
Kouilou (riv.).......C3
Likouala (riv.)......C3
N'Gounié (riv.)......B4
Niari (riv.)..........B4

EQUATORIAL GUINEA
TERRITORIES

Bioko 78,000.........A3
Río Muni 203,000......B3

CITIES and TOWNS

Bata 270,241........A3
Luba 19,933.........A3
Malabo (cap.) 37,237...A3
Mbini 14,503........A3

OTHER FEATURES

Biafra (bight)........A3
Corisco (isl.)........A3
Elobey (isls.)........A3
Fernando Po (Bioko) (isl.)...A3

GABON
CITIES and TOWNS

Bitam 5,936.........B3
Cocobeach...........A3
Fougamou...........B4
Franceville 9,345.....B4
Kango.............B3
Koula-Moutou 8,032....B4
Lambaréné 17,770.....B4
Lastoursville........B4
Libreville (cap.) 105,080...A3
Makokou 5,005.......B3
Mayumba...........B4
M'Bigou.............B4
Médouneu...........B3
Mekambo...........B3
Mimongo...........B4
Minvoul............B3
Moanda 10,709......B4
Mouila 15,016.......B4
Mounana 4,000.......B4
N'Dendé............B4
N'Djolé.............B4
Okondja.............B4
Omboué.............A3
Owendo.............A3
Oyem 12,455........B3
Port-Gentil 48,190....A4
Tchibanga 14,001.....B4

OTHER FEATURES

Crystal (mts.)........B4
Ibounzi (mt.)........B4
Ivindo (riv.).........B3
Lopez (cape).........A3
N'Dogo (lag.)........B4
N'Gounié (riv.)......B4
N'Komi (lag.)........A4
Ogooué (riv.).........A4
Pongara (pt.)........A3

KENYA
PROVINCES

Central 1,675,647....G4
Coast 944,082.......G4
Eastern 1,907,301....G4
Nairobi 509,286......G4
North-Eastern 245,757...G4
Nyanza 2,122,045.....F4
Rift Valley 2,210,289...G3
Western 1,328,298....G3

CITIES and TOWNS

Baragoi 2,383.......G3
Bunyala.............F3
Eldoret 18,196......G3
Embu 3,928.........G4
Fort Hall 4,750......G4
Galole 3,609........G4
Garissa.............G4
Gilgil 4,178.........G3
Isiolo 8,201.........G3
Kajiado 1,755........G4
Kakamega 6,244......F3
Kaningo 2,460.......G4
Kapenguria 1,790.....G3
Kericho 10,144......F4
Kiambu 2,776........G4
Kilifi 2,662.........G4
Kisii 6,080.........G4
Kisumu 32,431.......F3
Kitale 11,573........G3
Kitui 3,071.........G4
Kwale 1,092........G4
Lamu 7,403.........H4
Lokitaung 4,090......G3
Machakos 6,312......G4
Mado Gashi 1,003....G4
Malindi 10,757.......G4
Maralal 3,878........G3
Marsabit 6,635......G3
Migori 2,066.......F4
Mombasa 247,073.....G4
Nairobi (cap.) 509,286...G4
Naivasha 6,920......G3
Nakuru 47,151.......G3
Nanyuki 11,624......G3
Narok 2,608........G4
Ngong 1,583........G4
Nyeri 2,436........G4
Rumuruti 1,484......G3
Thika 18,387........G4
Thomson's Falls 7,602...G3
Vanga.............G4
Voi 5,313..........G4
Wajir..............H3
Wamba 2,650........G3

OTHER FEATURES

Daua (riv.).........H3
Elgon (mt.).........F3
Formosa (bay).......H4
Galana (riv.).......G4
Gedi (ruins)........G4
Kenya (mt.)........G4
Lak Dera (dry riv.)...H3
Lorian (swamp)......G3
Natron (lake).......G4
Nyiru (mt.).........G3
Patta (isl.)........H4
Rudolf (Turkana) (lake)...G3
Tana (riv.).........G4
Tsavo Nat'l Park.....G4
Turkana (lake)......G3
Victoria (lake)......F4
Winam (bay)........F4

MALAWI
CITIES and TOWNS

Blantyre 222,153.....F7
Chitipa 3,079.......F5
Dedza 5,448........F6
Dowa 2,067.........F6
Karonga 11,873......F5
Lilongwe (cap.) 102,924...F6
Mangochi 3,341......G6
Mchinji 1,962.......F6
Mwanza 2,271.......F7
Mzimba 4,962.......F6

Ncheu 1,326........F6
Nkhata Bay 4,024....F6
Nkhotakota 10,312....F6
Nsanje 6,091.......G7
Rumphi 3,998.......F6
Salima 4,646........F6
Thyolo 4,186.......F7
Zomba 21,000.......G7

OTHER FEATURES

Chilrua (pt.).........G7
Malawi (Nyasa) (lake)...G7
Mulanje (mts.).......G7
Nyasa (lake).........F6
Shire (riv.).........G7

RWANDA
CITIES and TOWNS

Butare 21,691.......E4
Cyangugu 7,042......E4
Gisenyi 12,436......E4
Kigali (cap.) 117,749...E4
Nyabisindu 8,587.....F4

OTHER FEATURES

Kagera Nat'l Park.....F4
Karisimbi (mt.)......E4
Kivu (lake).........E4
Ruzizi (riv.)........E4
Virunga (range)......E4

SOMALIA
PROVINCES

Bakool 100,000......H3
Bari 155,000........J1
Bay 302,000........H3
Galguduud 182,000....J2
Gedo 202,800........H3
Hiiraan 147,000......J3
Jubbada Hoose 246,000...H3
Mogadiscio 371,000....J3
Mudug 215,000......J2
Nugaal 85,000.......J2
Sanaag 369,000......J1
Shabeellaha Dhexe 237,000...J3
Shabeellaha Hoose 398,000...H3
Togdheer 258,000....J2
Woqooyi Galbeed 440,000...H1

CITIES and TOWNS

Afgoi..............J3
Afmadu 2,580.......H3
Alula..............K1
Ankhor.............J1
Balad 1,233........J3
Barawa (Brava) 6,167...H3
Baydhabo 14,962.....H3
Belet Weyne 11,426...J3
Bender Cassim.......J1
Berbera 12,219......J1
Borama 3,244.......H1
Bosaso.............J1
Brava 6,167........H3
Bulo Burti 5,247.....J3
Bur Acaba..........H3
Burao 12,617.......J2
Candala............J1
Chisimayu 17,872....H4
Coriole 4,341.......H3
Dante (Hafun)......K1
Dusa Mareb........J2
Eil................J2
El Athale (Itala).....J3
Erigabo 4,279.......J1

(continued on following page)

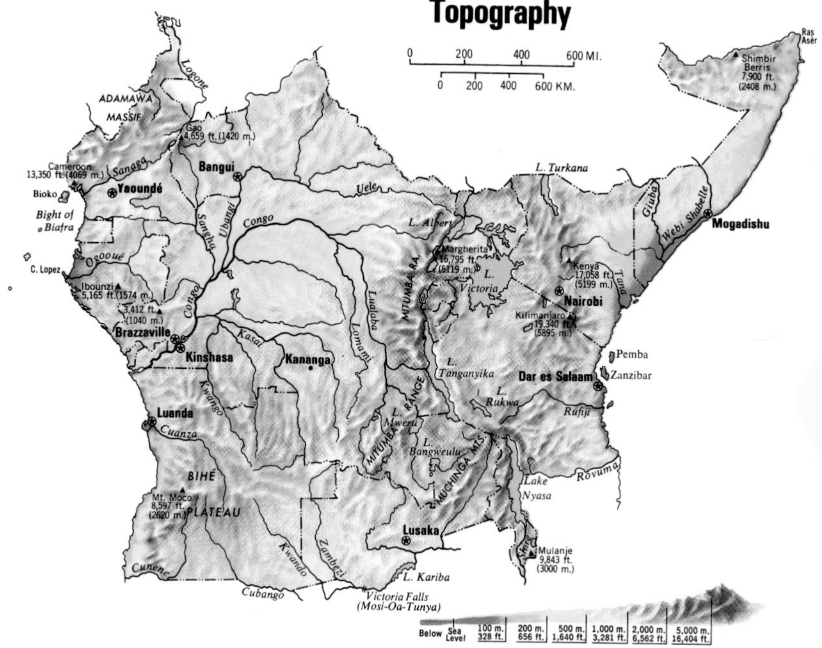

(continued)

Galcaio J2
Garbahaarrey H3
Garoe J2
Giohar 13,156 J3
Hafun K1
Hargeysa 40,254 H2
Itala J3
Jamama 5,408 H3
Jilib 3,232 H3
Kismayu (Chisimayu) 17,872 H4
Las Anod 2,441 J2
Las Khoreh 2,245 J1
Luuq H3
Margherita (Jamama) H3
Marka (Merka) 17,708 H3
Mogadishu (cap.) 371,000 J3
Muqdisho (Mogadishu) (cap.) 371,000 J3
Oddur H3
Odweina 1,422 J2
Uanle Uen H3
Villabruzzi (Johar) J3
Zeila 1,226 H1

OTHER FEATURES

Aden (gulf) J1
Asèr, Ras (cape) K1
Giuba (riv.) H3
Guban (reg.) H1
Haud (plat.) J2
Lak Dera (dry riv.) H3
Negro (bay) J2
Shimbir Berris (mt.) J1
Sura, Ras (cape) J1
Webi Shabelle (riv.) H3

TANZANIA

PROVINCES

Arusha 928,478 G4
Dar es Salaam G5
Dodoma 971,921 G5
Iringa 922,801 G5
Kagera 1,009,379 F4
Kigoma 648,950 F4
Kilimanjaro 902,394 G4
Lindi 527,902 G5
Mara 723,295 F4
Mbeya 1,080,241 F5
Morogoro 939,190 G5
Mtwara 771,726 G5
Mwanza 1,443,418 F4
Pemba 205,870 H5
Pwani (Coast) 516,949 G5
Rukwa 451,897 F5
Ruvuma 564,113 G6
Shinyanga 1,323,482 F4
Singida 614,030 F5
Tabora 818,049 F5
Tanga 1,088,592 G5
Zanzibar Mjini 143,616 G5
Zanzibar Shambani North 77,424 G5
Zanzibar Shambani South 52,325 G5

CITIES and TOWNS

Arusha 55,281 G4
Bagamoyo 5,112 G5
Biharamulo 1,011 F4
Bukene 2,288 F4
Bukoba 20,430 F4
Chake Chake 4,862 H5
Chunya 2,398 F5
Dar es Salaam (cap.) 757,346 G5
Dodoma 45,703 G5
Geita 3,066 F4
Iringa 57,182 G5
Kahama 3,211 F4
Kasulu F4
Kibondo F4
Kigoma-Ujiji 50,044 E4
Kilosa 4,458 G5
Kilwa Kivinje 2,790 G5
Kilwa Masoko G5
Koani 1,102 G5
Kondoa 4,514 G4
Kongwa G5
Korogwe 6,675 G5
Lindi 27,308 G6
Lushoto 1,803 G4
Mahenge G5
Manyoni F5
Masasi G6
Mbeya 76,606 F5
Mbulu G4
Mchinga G5
Mkokotoni 2,220 G5
Morogoro 61,890 G5
Moshi 52,223 G4
Mpanda F5
Mpwapwa 2,429 G5
Mtwara-Mikindani 48,510 H6
Musoma 32,658 F4
Mwadui 7,383 F4
Mwanza 110,611 F4
Nachingwea 3,751 G6
Newala G6
Ngara F4
Njombe F5
Nzega 2,386 F4
Pangani 2,955 G5
Shinyanga 21,703 F4
Singida 29,252 F4
Songea 17,954 G6
Sumbawanga 28,586 F5
Tabora 67,392 F5
Tanga 103,409 G4
Tukuyu 4,089 F5
Tunduru G6
Utete G5
Wete 8,469 G4
Zanzibar 110,669 G5

OTHER FEATURES

Eyasi (lake) F4
Great Ruaha (riv.) G5
Juani (isl.) G5
Kagera Nat'l Park F4
Kalambo (falls) F5
Kilimanjaro (mt.) G4
Kilombero (riv.) G5
Mafia (isl.) H5
Manyara (lake) G4
Masai (steppe) G4
Mbarangandu (riv.) G5
Mbemkuru (riv.) G5
Meru (mt.) G4
Mikumi Nat'l Park G5
Natron (lake) G4
Ngorongoro (crater) F4
Njombe (riv.) F5
Nyasa (lake) F6
Olduvai Gorge (canyon) G4
Pangani (riv.) G4
Pemba (isl.) H5
Ras Kanzi (cape) G5
Rovuma (riv.) G6
Ruaha Nat'l Park F5
Rufiji (riv.) G5
Rukwa (lake) F5
Rungwa (riv.) F5
Rungwe (mt.) F5
Serengeti Nat'l Park F4
Tanganyika (lake) E5
Tarangire Nat'l Park G4
Victoria (lake) F4
Wami (riv.) G5
Wembere (riv.) F4
Zanzibar (isl.) G5

UGANDA

CITIES and TOWNS

Arua 10,837 F3
Butiaba 261 F3
Entebbe 21,096 F3
Fort Portal 7,947 F3
Gulu 18,170 F3
Hoima 2,339 F3
Jinja 52,509 F3
Kabale 8,234 E4
Kampala (cap.) 478,895 F3
Kasese 7,213 F3
Kitgum 3,242 F3
Lira 7,340 F3
Masaka 12,987 F4
Masindi 2,100 F3
Mbale 23,544 F3
Mbarara 16,078 F4
Moroto 5,488 F3
Moyo 266 F3
Mubende 6,004 F3
Rhino Camp 198 F3
Soroti 8,130 F3
Tororo 15,977 F3

OTHER FEATURES

Albert (Mobuto Sese Seko) (lake) F3
Edward (lake) E4
Elgon (mt.) F3
George (lake) F4
Kabalega (falls) F3
Kagalega Nat'l Park F3
Kidepo Nat'l Park F3
Kioga (lake) F3
Margherita (mt.) E3
Mobuto Sese Seko (lake) F3
Owen Falls (dam) F3
Ruwenzori (range) E3
Sese (isls.) F4
Victoria (lake) F4
Virunga (range) E4
Virunga Nat'l Park F4

CONGO, DEM. REP. OF THE

PROVINCES

Bandundu 2,600,556 C4
Bas-Zaïre 1,504,361 B5
Equateur 2,431,812 D3
Haut-Zaïre 3,356,419 E3
Kasai-Occidental 2,433,861 D4
Kasai-Oriental 1,872,231 D5
Kinshasa 1,323,039 C4
Kivu 3,361,883 E4
Shaba 2,753,714 E5

CITIES and TOWNS

Aba 7,600 F3
Aketi 17,200 D3
Bambesa E3
Banalia E3
Banana B5
Bandundu 74,467 C4
Basankusu C3
Basoko 9,100 D3
Befale D3
Beni 22,800 E3
Bikoro C4
Boende 12,800 D4
Bokungu D4
Bolobo 10,300 C4
Bolomba 7,200 C3
Boma 61,100 B5
Bomongo C3
Bondo 10,000 D3
Bongandanga 12,900 D3
Bosobolo 11,100 C3
Budjala C3
Bukama E5
Bukavu 134,861 E4
Bulungu 16,300 C4
Bumba 34,700 D3
Bunia 28,800 E3
Bunkeya 5,100 E6
Businga 11,000 D3
Busu-Djanoa D3
Buta 19,800 D3
Butembo 27,800 E3
Dekese D4
Demba 22,000 D5
Dibaya 11,400 D5
Dibaya-Lubue 7,900 C4
Dilolo 14,000 D6
Dimbelenge D5
Djolu D3
Djugu F3
Dungu 9,100 E3
Faradje 10,400 E3
Feshi C5
Fizi E4
Gandâjika 60,100 D5
Gemena 37,300 D3
Goma 48,600 E4
Gungu C5
Idiofa C4
Ikela D4
Ilebo 32,200 D4
Ingende C4
Inongo 14,800 C4
Irumu 9,300 E3
Isangi D3
Isiro 49,300 E3
Kabalo 22,600 E5
Kabambare E4
Kabare 12,600 E4
Kabinda 60,500 D5
Kabongo 6,500 E5
Kahemba C5
Kalehe E4
Kalemie 62,300 E5
Kalima 27,500 E4
Kama 69,100 E4
Kambove 18,900 E6
Kamina 56,300 D5
Kampene 14,600 E4
Kananga 428,960 D5
Kaniama D5
Kapanga D5
Kasangulu 11,900 C4
Kasenga E6
Kasese E4
Kasongo 37,800 E4
Kasongo-Lunda C5
Katako-Kombe D4
Kazumba D5
Kenge 17,500 C4
Kibombo E4
Kikwit 111,960 C5
Kinshasa (cap.) 1,323,039 C4
Kipushi 32,900 E6
Kisangani 229,596 E3
Kolwezi 81,600 E6
Kongolo 14,800 E5
Kutu 10,000 C4
Libenge 13,000 C3
Lisala D3
Lodja 20,300 D4
Lomela D4
Lubefu D4
Lubudi 6,000 E5
Lubumbashi 318,000 E6
Lubutu E4
Luebo 21,800 D5
Lukula 9,400 B5
Luozi 7,000 B5
Lusambo 13,100 D4
Mambasa 7,400 E3
Mangai 41,200 C4
Manono 44,500 E5
Masi-Manimba 6,300 C4
Masisi E4
Matadi 110,436 B5
Mbandaka 107,910 C3
Mbanza-Ngungu 55,800 C5
Mbuji-Mayi 256,154 D5
Mitwaba E5
Monkoto D4
Muanda 6,400 B5
Mungbere E3
Mushie 13,700 C4
Muyumba E5
Mweka 24,900 D4
Mwene-Ditu 71,200 D5
Mwenga E4
Niangara 9,200 E3
Nyunzu 11,300 E5
Opala D4
Oshwe C4
Panda-Likasi 146,394 E6
Pangi E4
Poko E3
Popokabaka C5
Port Kindu 42,800 E4
Punia E4
Rutshuru E4
Sakania E6
Sandoa D5
Sentery 24,300 E5
Shabunda 6,900 E4
Songololo 4,600 B5
Tshela 10,700 B4
Tshikapa 38,900 D5
Ubundu 630 E4
Uvira 15,900 E4
Virunga 21,900 E5
Wamba 11,500 E3
Watsa 21,250 E3
Yangambi 22,600 D3

OTHER FEATURES

Albert (Mobuto Sese Seko) (lake) F3
Aruwimi (riv.) E3
Bomu (riv.) D3
Boyoma (Stanley) (falls) D3
Chicapa (riv.) D5
Congo (riv.) C4
Edward (lake) E4
Elila (riv.) E4
Fimi (riv.) C4
Garamba Nat'l Park E3
Giri (riv.) C3
Itimbiri (riv.) D3
Ituri (for.) E3
Karisimbi (mt.) E4
Kasai (riv.) C4
Kivu (lake) E4
Kwa (riv.) C4
Kwango (riv.) C5
Kwilu (riv.) C5
Lindi (riv.) E3
Livingstone (falls) B5
Loange (riv.) C5
Lokoro (riv.) C4
Lomami (riv.) D4
Lomela (riv.) D4
Lowa (riv.) E4
Lua (riv.) C3
Lualaba (riv.) E4
Luapula (riv.) E6
Lubilash (riv.) D5
Lufira (riv.) E5
Luilaka (riv.) C4
Lukenie (riv.) D4
Lukuga (riv.) E5
Lulua (riv.) D5
Luvua (riv.) E5
Mai-Ndombe (lake) C4
Malebo (Stanley Pool) (lake) C4
Margherita (mt.) E3
Marungu (mts.) E5
Mobuto Sese Seko (lake) F3
Mweru (lake) E5
Ruwenzori (range) E3
Ruzizi (riv.) E4
Salonga Nat'l Park D4
Sankuru (riv.) D4
Stanley (falls) D3
Stanley Pool (lake) C4
Tanganyika (lake) E5
Tshuapa (riv.) D4
Tumba (lake) C4
Ubangi (riv.) C3
Uele (riv.) E3
Ulindi (riv.) E4
Upemba (lake) E5
Upemba Nat'l Park E5
Virunga (range) E4
Virunga Nat'l Park E4

ZAMBIA

CITIES and TOWNS

Abercorn (Mbala) 11,179 F5
Bancroft (Chililabombwe) 61,928 E6
Broken Hill (Kabwe) 143,635 E6
Chilanga 12,503 E6
Chililabombwe 61,928 E6
Chingola 145,869 E6
Chipata 32,291 F6
Choma 17,943 E7
Fort Rosebery (Mansa) 34,801 E6
Isoka 6,832 F6
Kabompo 5,357 D6
Kabwe 143,635 E6
Kafue 29,794 E7
Kalabo 7,398 D6
Kalomo 5,878 E7
Kaoma 6,731 D6
Kapiri Mposhi 13,677 E6
Kasama 38,093 F6
Kawambwa 7,235 E5
Kitwe 314,794 E6
Livingstone 71,987 E7
Luanshya 132,164 E6
Lusaka (cap.) 538,469 E7
Mansa 34,801 E6
Mazabuka 29,602 E7
Mbala 11,179 F5
Mongu 24,919 D7
Monze 13,141 E7
Mpika 25,880 F6
Mporokoso 6,008 F5
Mpulungu 6,354 F5
Mufulira 149,778 E6
Mumbwa 7,570 E6
Ndola 282,439 E6
Petauke 7,531 F6
Senanga 7,204 D7
Serenje 6,008 F6
Solwezi 15,032 E6
Zambezi 8,166 D6

OTHER FEATURES

Bangweulu (lake) F6
Barotseland (reg.) D7
Chambeshi (riv.) F6
Cuando (riv.) D7
Dongwe (riv.) D6
Kabompo (riv.) D6
Kafue (riv.) E7
Kafue Nat'l Park E6
Kalambo (falls) F5
Kariba (dam) E7
Kariba (lake) E7
Luangwa (riv.) F6
Luapula (riv.) E6
Lungwebungu (riv.) D6
Mosi-Oa-Tunya (Victoria) (falls) E7
Mulungushi (dam) E6
Mweru (lake) E5
Sunzu (mt.) F5
Tanganyika (lake) E5
Victoria (falls) E7
Zambezi (riv.) D7

Agriculture, Industry and Resources

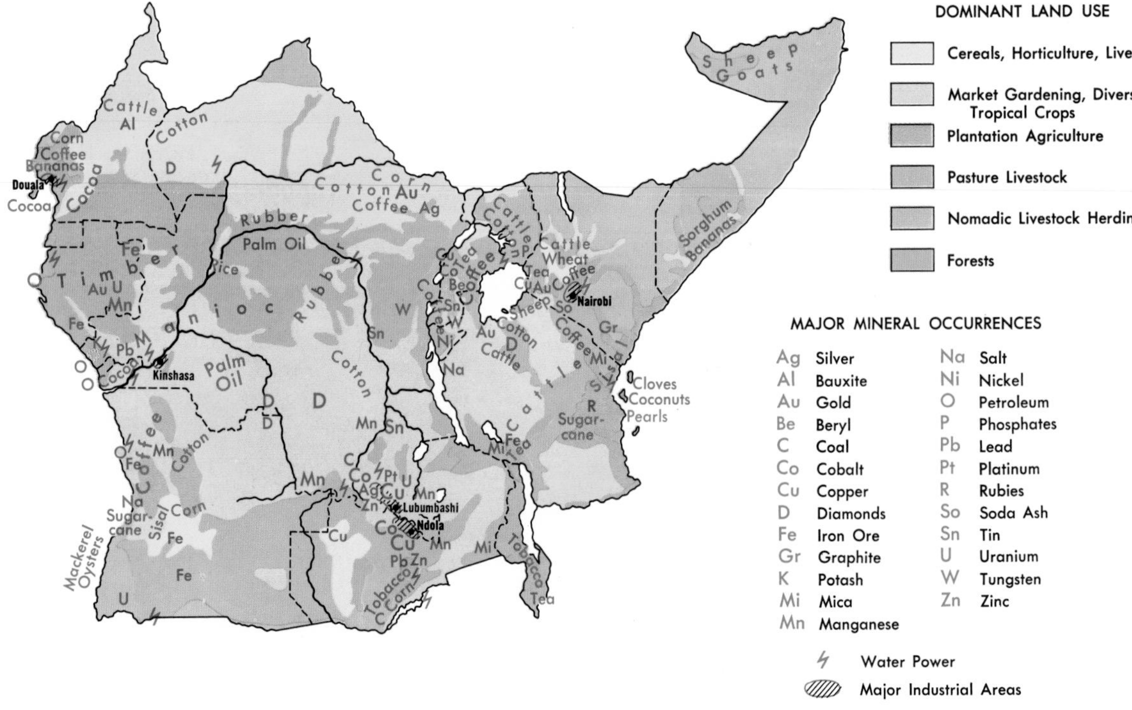

DOMINANT LAND USE
Cereals, Horticulture, Livestock
Market Gardening, Diversified Tropical Crops
Plantation Agriculture
Pasture Livestock
Nomadic Livestock Herding
Forests
MAJOR MINERAL OCCURRENCES
Ag Silver
Al Bauxite
Au Gold
Be Beryl
C Coal
Co Cobalt
Cu Copper
D Diamonds
Fe Iron Ore
Gr Graphite
K Potash
Mi Mica
Mn Manganese
Na Salt
Ni Nickel
O Petroleum
P Phosphates
Pb Lead
Pt Platinum
R Rubies
So Soda Ash
Sn Tin
U Uranium
W Tungsten
Zn Zinc
Water Power
Major Industrial Areas
Douala
Kinshasa
Nairobi
Lubumbashi
Ndola
Cattle
Cotton
Corn
Coffee
Bananas
Cocoa
Rubber
Palm Oil
Timber
Rice
Manioc
Sheep
Goats
Sorghum
Wheat
Cloves
Coconuts
Pearls
Sugar-cane
Sisal
Tobacco
Tea
Mackerel
Oysters

NAMIBIA

AREA 317,827 sq. mi. (823,172 sq. km.)
POPULATION 1,818,000
CAPITAL Windhoek
LARGEST CITY Windhoek
HIGHEST POINT Brandberg 8,550 ft.
(2,606 m.)
MONETARY UNIT rand
MAJOR LANGUAGES Ovambo, Hottentot,
Herero, Afrikaans, English
MAJOR RELIGIONS Tribal religions,
Protestantism

SOUTH AFRICA

AREA 455,318 sq. mi. (1,179,274 sq. km.)
POPULATION 34,492,000
CAPITALS Cape Town, Pretoria
LARGEST CITY Johannesburg
HIGHEST POINT Injasuti 11,182 ft. (3,408 m.)
MONETARY UNIT rand
MAJOR LANGUAGES Afrikaans, English,
Xhosa, Zulu, Sesotho
MAJOR RELIGIONS Protestantism,
Roman Catholicism, Islam, Hinduism,
tribal religions

LESOTHO

AREA 11,720 sq. mi. (30,355 sq. km.)
POPULATION 1,700,000
CAPITAL Maseru
LARGEST CITY Maseru
HIGHEST POINT 11,425 ft. (3,482 m.)
MONETARY UNIT loti
MAJOR LANGUAGES Sesotho, English
MAJOR RELIGIONS Tribal religions,
Christianity

BOTSWANA

AREA 224,764 sq. mi. (582,139 sq. km.)
POPULATION 1,256,000
CAPITAL Gaborone
LARGEST CITY Francistown
HIGHEST POINT Tsodilo Hill 5,922 ft.
(1,805 m.)
MONETARY UNIT pula
MAJOR LANGUAGES Setswana, Shona,
Bushman, English, Afrikaans
MAJOR RELIGIONS Tribal religions,
Protestantism

MOZAMBIQUE

AREA 303,769 sq. mi. (786,762 sq. km.)
POPULATION 15,326,000
CAPITAL Maputo
LARGEST CITY Maputo
HIGHEST POINT Mt. Binga 7,992 ft.
(2,436 m.)
MONETARY UNIT metical
MAJOR LANGUAGES Makua, Thonga,
Shona, Portuguese
MAJOR RELIGIONS Tribal religions,
Roman Catholicism, Islam

SWAZILAND

AREA 6,705 sq. mi. (17,366 sq. km.)
POPULATION 681,000
CAPITAL Mbabane
LARGEST CITY Manzini
HIGHEST POINT Emlembe 6,109 ft.
(1,862 m.)
MONETARY UNIT lilangeni
MAJOR LANGUAGES siSwati, English
MAJOR RELIGIONS Tribal religions,
Christianity

ZIMBABWE

AREA 150,803 sq. mi. (390,580 sq. km.)
POPULATION 9,122,000
CAPITAL Harare
LARGEST CITY Harare
HIGHEST POINT Mt. Inyangani 8,517 ft.
(2,596 m.)
MONETARY UNIT Zimbabwe dollar
MAJOR LANGUAGES English, Shona,
Ndebele
MAJOR RELIGIONS Tribal religions,
Protestantism

MADAGASCAR

AREA 226,657 sq. mi. (587,041 sq. km.)
POPULATION 9,985,000
CAPITAL Antananarivo
LARGEST CITY Antananarivo
HIGHEST POINT Maromokotro 9,436 ft.
(2,876 m.)
MONETARY UNIT Madagascar franc
MAJOR LANGUAGES Malagasy, French
MAJOR RELIGIONS Tribal religions,
Roman Catholicism, Protestantism

COMOROS

AREA 719 sq. mi. (1,862 sq. km.)
POPULATION 484,000
CAPITAL Moroni
LARGEST CITY Moroni
HIGHEST POINT Karthala 7,746 ft.
(2,361 m.)
MONETARY UNIT CFA franc
MAJOR LANGUAGES Arabic, French,
Swahili
MAJOR RELIGION Islam

MAURITIUS

AREA 790 sq. mi. (2,046 sq. km.)
POPULATION 1,068,000
CAPITAL Port Louis
LARGEST CITY Port Louis
HIGHEST POINT 2,711 ft. (826 m.)
MONETARY UNIT Mauritian rupee
MAJOR LANGUAGES English, French,
French Creole, Hindi, Urdu
MAJOR RELIGIONS Hinduism, Christianity,
Islam

SEYCHELLES

AREA 145 sq. mi. (375 sq. km.)
POPULATION 67,000
CAPITAL Victoria
LARGEST CITY Victoria
HIGHEST POINT Morne Seychellois
2,993 ft. (912 m.)
MONETARY UNIT Seychellois rupee
MAJOR LANGUAGES English, French,
Creole
MAJOR RELIGION Roman Catholicism

REUNION

AREA 969 sq. mi. (2,510 sq. km.)
POPULATION 570,000
CAPITAL St-Denis

MAYOTTE

AREA 144 sq. mi. (373 sq. km.)
POPULATION 47,300
CAPITAL Mamoutzou

ZIMBABWE

BOTSWANA

SOUTH AFRICA

LESOTHO

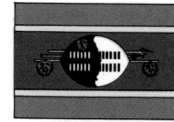
SWAZILAND

MOZAMBIQUE

COMOROS

MADAGASCAR

MAURITIUS

SEYCHELLES

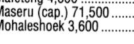
NAMIBIA

Agriculture, Industry and Resources

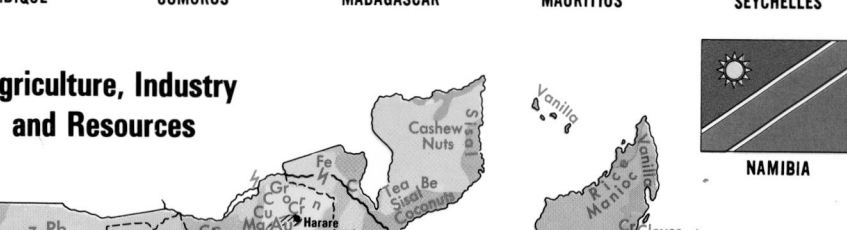

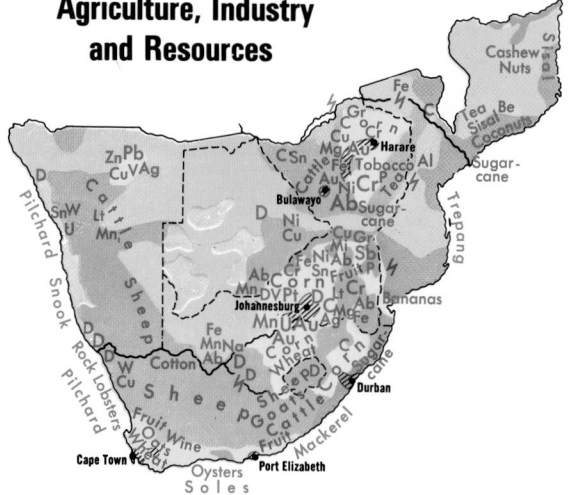

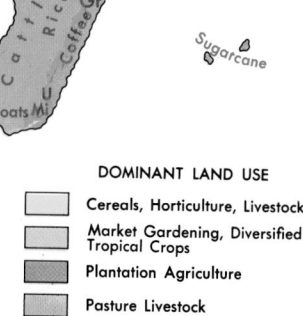

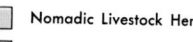

DOMINANT LAND USE

	Cereals, Horticulture, Livestock
	Market Gardening, Diversified Tropical Crops
	Plantation Agriculture
	Pasture Livestock
	Nomadic Livestock Herding
	Forests
	Nonagricultural Land

MAJOR MINERAL OCCURRENCES

Ab	Asbestos	Cu	Copper	Mn	Manganese	Sb	Antimony
Ag	Silver	D	Diamonds	Na	Salt	Sn	Tin
Al	Bauxite	Fe	Iron Ore	Ni	Nickel	U	Uranium
Au	Gold	Gr	Graphite	P	Phosphates	V	Vanadium
Be	Beryl	Lt	Lithium	Pb	Lead	W	Tungsten
C	Coal	Mg	Magnesium	Pt	Platinum	Zn	Zinc
Cr	Chromium	Mi	Mica				

⚡ Water Power

Major Industrial Areas

BOTSWANA

CITIES and TOWNS

Dinokwe 560	D4
Francistown 22,000	D4
Gaborone (cap.) 21,000	D4
Ghanzi 1,198	C4
Kanye 10,664	D5
Kasane 1,476	D3
Lobatse 11,936	D5
Mahalapye 12,056	D4
Maun 9,614	C4
Mochudi 6,945	D4
Molepolole 9,448	D4
Palapye 5,217	D4
Ramotswa 7,991	D4
Selebi-Pikwe 20,572	D4
Serowe 15,723	D4

OTHER FEATURES

Chobe (riv.)	C3
Chobe Nat'l Park	D3
Dau (lake)	C4
Kalahari (des.)	C4
Kaukauveld (mts.)	C3
Limpopo (riv.)	D4
Mababe (depr.)	C3
Makgadikgadi (salt pan)	D3
Molopo (riv.)	C5
Ngami (lake)	C4
Ngamiland (reg.)	C3
Nossob (riv.)	B4
Okovango (riv.)	C3
Okovango (swamps)	C3
Orange (riv.)	B5
Shashe (riv.)	D4
Tati (riv.)	D4
Tsodilo Hill (mt.)	C3
Xau (Dau) (lake)	C4

COMOROS

CITIES and TOWNS

Fomboni 3,229	G2
Mitsamiouli 3,196	G2
Moroni (cap.) 12,000	G2
Mutsamudu 7,652	G2

OTHER FEATURES

Mwali (Mohéli) (isl.)	G2
Njazidja (Grand Comoro) (isl.)	G2
Nzwani (Anjouan) (isl.)	G2

LESOTHO

CITIES and TOWNS

Leribe 5,200	D5
Mafeteng 4,600	D5
Maseru (cap.) 71,500	D5
Mohaleshoek 3,600	D6

MADAGASCAR

PROVINCES

Antananarivo 2,167,973	H3
Antsiranana 597,982	H2
Fianarantsoa 1,804,365	H4
Mahajanga 819,750	H3
Toamasina 1,179,660	H3
Toliara 1,034,114	G4

CITIES and TOWNS

Ambalavao 6,988	H4
Ambanja 12,258	H2
Ambatolampy 11,539	H3
Ambatondrazaka 18,044	H3
Ambilobe 9,415	H2
Ambodifototra 1,112	J3
Ambositra 16,780	H4
Andapa 6,275	H2
Antalaha 17,541	J2
Antananarivo (cap.) 451,808	H3
Antsirabe 32,979	H3
Antsiranana 40,443	H2
Antsohihy 8,721	H2
Arivonimamo 8,497	H3
Belo-Tsiribihina 4,403	G3
Brickaville (Vohibinany) 1,741	H3
Diégo-Suarez (Antsiranana) 40,443	H2
Faradofay 19,605	H5
Farafangana 10,817	H4
Fenoarivo, Toamasina 7,696	H3
Fianarantsoa 68,054	H4
Fort-Dauphin (Faradofay) 19,605	H5
Foulpointe	H3
Hell-Ville 6,183	H2
Ihosy 4,521	H4
Maevatanana 7,197	H3
Maintirano 6,375	G3
Majunga 65,864	H3
Manakara 19,768	H4
Mananjary 14,638	H4
Mandritsara 6,826	H3
Maroantsetra 6,645	J3
Marovoay 20,253	H3
Moramanga 10,806	H3
Morombe 6,967	G4
Morondava 19,061	G4
Port-Bergé 4,734	H2
Sambava 6,215	J2
Sosumav 10,946	H2
Tamatave (Toamasina) 77,395	H3

(continued on following page)

Topography

Below Sea Level | 100 m. 328 ft. | 200 m. 656 ft. | 500 m. 1,640 ft. | 1,000 m. 3,281 ft. | 2,000 m. 6,562 ft. | 5,000 m. 16,404 ft.

Graaff-Reinet 22,392 ....C6	Matatiele 3,853 ....D6	Port Elizabeth 392,231 ....D6	
Grahamstown 41,302 ....D6	Messina 21,121 ....D4	Port Nolloth 2,893 ....B5	
Grassy Park 32,709 ....E6	Middelburg, Cape Prov.	Port Saint Johns	
Griquatown 2,996 ....C5	12,121 ....D6	(Umzimbuvu) 1,817.........D6	
Harrismith 16,082 ....D5	Middelburg, Transvaal	Potchefstroom 57,443 ....D5	
Heidelberg 12,521 ....J7	26,942 ....E5	Pretoria (cap.) 525,583 ....D5	
Hermanus 4,956 ....G7	Milnerton 10,893 ....F6	Queenstown 39,304 ....D6	
Howick 12,429 ....E5	Mmabatho D5	Randburg 43,257 ....H6	
Johannesburg 654,232 ....H6	Mossel Bay 17,574 ....C6	Randfontein 50,481 ....G6	
Kempton Park 37,205 ....J6	Nelspruit 25,092 ....E5	Richards Bay 598 ....E5	
Kimberley 105,258 ....C5	Newcastle 14,407 ....E5	Robertson 10,237 ....C6	
King William's Town 15,798 ...D6	Nigel 41,179 ....J7	Roodepoort 115,366 ....H6	
Klerksdorp 63,558 ....D5	Nyanga 15,655 ....F6	Rustenburg 22,303 ....D5	
Knysna 13,479 ....C6	Odendaalsrus 15,603 ....D5	Saldanha 4,994 ....B6	
Kokstad 10,227 ....D6	Oudtshoorn 26,907 ....C6	Simonstown 12,137 ....E7	
Kraaifontein 10,286 ....F6	Paarl 49,244 ....F6	Sishen 2,692 ....C5	
Kroonstad 51,988 ....D5	Parow 60,768 ....F6	Somerset East 10,383 ....C6	
Krugersdorp 92,725 ....H6	Parys 17,447 ....D5	Somerset West 11,828 ....F6	
Ladybrand 8,757 ....D5	Pietermaritzburg 114,822 .....E5	Soweto 602,043 ....H6	
Ladysmith 28,920 ....D5	Pietersburg 27,174 ....D4	Springs 142,812 ....J6	
Lambert's Bay 3,247 ....B6	Pinelands 11,769 ....F6	Standerton 21,038 ....D5	
Mafikeng (Mafeking) 6,515...D5	Pinetown 22,721 ....E6	Stanger 11,064 ....E5	

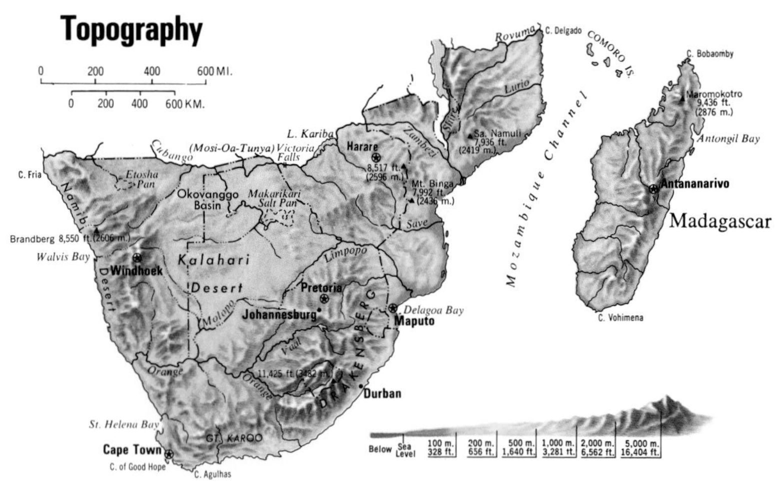

Tananarive (Antananarivo)
451,808 ....H3
Tanganiony 6,952 ....H4
Toamasina 77,395 ....H3
Toliara (Tuléar) 45,676 ....H3
Tsiroanomandidy 11,444 ....H3
Vangaindrano 3,249 ....H4
Vohibinany 1,741 ....H4
Vohimarina (Vohémar) 4,289..J2
Vohipeno 2,736 ....H4

OTHER FEATURES

Alaotra (lake) H3
Amber (Bobaomby) (cape) H2
Antongil (bay) J3
Barren (isls.) G3
Betsiboka (riv.) H3
Bobaomby (Amber) (cape) H2
Boby, Pic (mt.) H4
Chesterfield (isl.) G3
Ikopa (riv.) H3
Itasy (lake) H3
Mahajanga (bay) H4
Mananara (riv.) H4
Mananbo (riv.) G4
Mangoky (riv.) H4
Mangoro (riv.) H3
Maromokotro (mt.) H2
Masoala (pen.) J3
Menarandra (riv.) H4
Mozambique (chan.) G3
Nosy Be (isl.) J3
Nosy Boraha (isl.) J3
Onilahy (riv.) G4
Pangalanes (canal) H4
Radama (isls.) G3
Saint-André (cape) G3
Saint-Marie (Nosy Boraha)
(isl.) J3
Saint-Marie (Vohimena)
(cape) H5
Saint-Sébastien (cape) H2
Sofia (riv.) H3
Tsiafajavona (mt.) H3
Tsiribihina (riv.) G3
Vohimena (cape) H5

MAURITIUS

CITIES and TOWNS

Curepipe 52,709 ....G5
Mahébourg 15,463 ....G5
Port Louis (cap.) 141,022.....G5
Quatre Bornes 51,638 ....G5
Souillac 3,361 ....G5

OTHER FEATURES

Mascarene (isls.)................F5

MAYOTTE

CITIES and TOWNS

Mamoutzou (cap.) 196.........H2

MOZAMBIQUE

PROVINCES

Cabo Delgado 940,000......F2
Gaza 999,900 ....E4
Inhambane 977,000.............E4
Manica 541,200 ....E4
Maputo 491,800 ....E5
Maputo (city) 755,300 ....E5
Nampula 2,402,700............F2
Niassa 514,100 ....E2
Sofala 1,055,200................E3
Tete 831,000 ....E3
Zambézia 2,500,000............F3

CITIES and TOWNS

Angoche 1,714 ....G3
Bartolomeu Dias ○ 6,102.....F4
Beira 46,293 ....F3
Beira* 130,398...................F3
Chibuto 23,763 ....E4
Chicualacuala 2,050 ....E4
Chimoio 4,507 ....E4
Chinde 747 ....F3
Dona Ana (Mutarara) 686....F3
Dondo 2,112 ....F3
Funhalouro ○ 42,366 ....F4
Ibo 1,015 ....G2
Inhambane 4,975 ....F4
Inhaminga 1,607 ....F3
Inharrime 856 ....F4
Lichinga 3,011 ....F2
Lumbo ○ 11,080 ....G2
Lúrio ○ 13,417 ....G2
Mabalane ○ 13,158.............E4
Mabote ○ 28,970 ....E4
Machanga ○ 15,754 ....E4
Machaze ○ 42,255 ....E4
Mandié ○ 24,382 ....E3
Mandimba ○ 7,634 ....F2
Manhiça ○ 1,680 ....E5
Maniamba ○ 2,045 ....F2
Maputo (cap.) 755,300 ....E5
Massangena ○ 3,301 ....E4
Massinga 517....................F4
Moçambique 5,181 ....G3
Moçimboa da Praia 935........G2
Mocuba 2,293 ....F3
Montepuez 2,837 ....F2
Mualama ○ 34,992 ....F3
Mucujo ○ 15,867.................F2
Mueda 1,583 ....F2
Mutarara (Dona Ana) 686.....F3
Nacala 4,601 ....G2
Nampula 23,072 ....F3
Pafúri ○ 2,599 ....E4
Pemba 3,629 ....G2
Quelimane 10,522 ....F3
Quionga ○ 3,181 ....G2
Quissico 2,615 ....E4
Songo 2,230 ....E3
Tete 4,549 ....E3
Vila de Sena ○ 21,074 ....E3
Xai-Xai 5,234 ....E5

OTHER FEATURES

Angoche (isl.) G3
Bazaruto, Ilha do (isl.) F4
Binga (mt.) E3
Cabora Bassa (dam) E3
Changane (riv.) E4
Chirua (lake) F3
Delagoa (bay) E5
Delgado (cape) G2
Gorongosa Nat'l Park F3
Ligonha (riv.) F3
Limpopo (riv.) E4
Lugenda (riv.) F2
Lúrio (riv.) F2
Mazoe (riv.) E3
Mozambique (chan.) G3
Namuli, Serra (mt.) F3
Nyasa (lake) E2
Olifants (riv.) D4
Pungwe (riv.) F2
São Sebastião (pt.) F4
Save (riv.) E4
Shire (riv.) F3
Zambezi (riv.) E3

NAMIBIA

CITIES and TOWNS

Aroab 783 ....B5
Aus 767 ....B5

Berseba B5
Bethanie 1,207 ....B5
Gibeon B5
Gobabis 4,428 ....B4
Grootfontein 4,627 ....B4
Kalkfeld 587 ....B4
Kamanjab 713 ....B4
Karasburg 2,693 ....B5
Karibib 1,653 ....B4
Keetmanshoop 10,297 ....B5
Koes 514 ....B5
Lüderitz 6,642 ....A5
Maltahöhe 1,313 ....B4
Mariental 4,629 ....B4
Okahandja 1,688 ....B4
Omaruru 2,783 ....B4
Ondangwa B3
Opuno A3
Oranjemund 2,594 ....B5
Oshakati B3
Otavi 1,814 ....B3
Otjiwarongo 8,018 ....B4
Outjo 2,545 ....B4
Rehoboth 5,363 ....B4
Rundu 521 ....B3
Stampriet 271 ....B4
Swakopmund 5,681 ....A4
Tsumeb 12,338 ....B3
Usakos 2,334 ....B4
Walvis Bay 21,725 ....A4
Warmbad 810 ....B5
Windhoek (cap.) ○ 61,369 .....B4
Witvlei 303 ....B4

OTHER FEATURES

Brandberg (mt.) A4
Caprivi Strip (reg.) C3
Chobe (riv.) C3
Cross (bay) A4
Cubango (riv.) A3
Cunene (riv.) A3
Damaraland (reg.) B4
Diamond Coast (reg.) A5
Elephant (riv.) B4
Etosha Pan (salt pan) B3
Fish (riv.) B5
Fria (cape) A3
Great Namaland (reg.) B4
Hollam's Bird (isl.) A4
Hottentot (bay) A5
Kalahari (des.) C4
Kaokoveld (reg.) A3
Kaukauveld (mts.) C3
Kuiseb (riv.) A4
Lüderitz (bay) A5
Namib (des.) A4
Nossob (riv.) B4
Okovango (riv.) B3
Omatako (riv.) B3
Ovamboland (reg.) B3
Ruacana Falls (falls) A3
Skeleton Coast (reg.) A3
Swakop (riv.) A4
Ugab (riv.) A4
Zambezi (riv.) C3

RÉUNION

CITIES and TOWNS

Le Port 21,564 ....F5
Saint-Benoît 7,778 ....F5
Saint-Denis (cap.) 80,075 .....F5
Saint-Denis* 104,603...........F5
Saint-Joseph 8,928 ....G6
Saint-Louis 10,252 ....F5
Saint-Pierre 21,817 ....F6

OTHER FEATURES

Bassas da India (isl.) F4
Europa (isl.) G4

Glorioso (isls.) H2
Juan de Nova (isl.) G3
Mascarene (isls.) F5
Piton des Neiges (mt.) G5

SEYCHELLES

CITIES and TOWNS

Anse Boileau† 3,420 ....H5
Anse Royale† 3,182 ....H5
Cascade† 2,600 ....H5
Victoria (cap.) 15,559 ....H5
Victoria* 23,012 ....H5

OTHER FEATURES

Aldabra (isls.) H1
Assumption (isl.) H2
Astove (isl.) H2
Cerf (isl.) H5
Cosmoledo (isls.) H1
Curieuse (isl.) H5
Félicité (isl.) J5
Frigate (isl.) J5
La Digue (isl.) J5
Mahé (isl.) H5
Morne Seychellois (mt.) H5
North (isl.) H5
Praslin (isl.) J5
Sainte Anne (isl.) H5
Silhouette (isl.) H5

SOUTH AFRICA

PROVINCES

Eastern Cape 6,665,400 ....D6
Free State 2,804,600 ....D5
Gauteng 6,847,000 ....D5
KwaZulu Natal 8,549,000......E5
Mpumalanga 2,838,500........D5
Northern Cape 763,900 ....B5
Northern Province
5,120,600 ....D4
North-West 3,506,800 ....C5
Western Cape 3,620,200 ......C6

CITIES and TOWNS

Alberton 23,988 ....H6
Alexandra 57,040................H6
Aliwal North 12,311 ....D6
Barberton 12,382 ....E5
Beaufort West 17,862 ....C6
Bellville 49,026 ....F6
Benoni 151,294 ....J6
Bethlehem 29,918 ....D5
Bisho D6
Bloemfontein 149,836 ....D5
Boksburg 106,126...............J6
Brakpan 73,210 ....J6
Brits 12,182 ....D5
Butterworth (Gcuwa) 2,769...D6
Cape Town (cap.) 854,616....E6
Carltonville 40,641...............G7
Cradock 20,822 ....D6
De Aar 18,057 ....C6
Dundee 17,162 ....E5
Durban 736,852 ....E5
East London 119,727 ....D6
Edenale 41,194 ....D6
Edenvale 25,126 ....H6
Edensrivier 63,706..............H6
Ermelo 19,036 ....E5
Eshowe 4,952 ....E5
Estcourt 10,922 ....D5
Fort Beaufort 11,640...........D6
Gcuwa 2,769 ....D6
George 24,625 ....C6
Germiston 221,972..............H6
Glencoe 10,513 ....E5
Goodwood 31,592...............F6

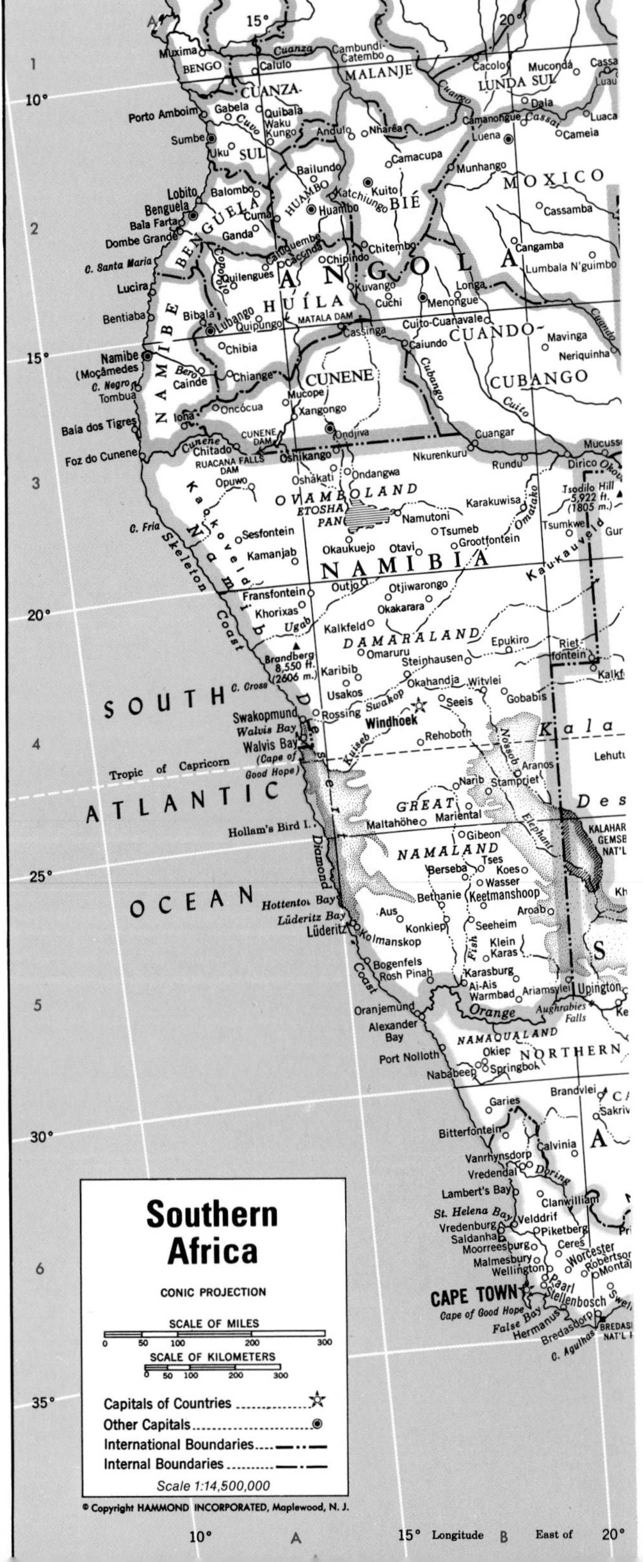

Stellenbosch 29,955....F6
Strand 24,503....F7
Stutterheim 12,077....D6
Taung 1,316....C5
Tembisa 81,821....H6
Thabazimbi 6,711....D4
Thohoyandou....C6
Uitenhage 70,517....C6
Umtata 25,216....D6
Umzimbuvu 1,817....D6
Upington 28,632....C5
Vanderbijl Park 78,754....D5
Venterspos....G6
Vereeniging 172,549....D5
Volksrust 10,238....D5
Vryburg 16,916....C5
Vryheid 16,992....E5
Warmbad 8,343....D5
Welkom 67,472....D5
Wellington 17,092....B6
Westonaria 36,253....H7
Witbank 37,456....D5

Worcester 41,198....B6
Zeerust 6,972....D5

OTHER FEATURES

Addo Nat'l Park....D6
Agulhas (cape)....B6
Algoa (bay)....D6
Aughrabies (falls)....B5
Blesbok (riv.)....J7
Bot (riv.)....F7
Bredasdorp Nat'l Park....C6
Cape (pen.)....F7
Cape (pt.)....F7
Crocodile (riv.)....H6
Diep (riv.)....F6
Doring (riv.)....B5
Drakensberg (range)....D6
Duiker (pt.)....F7
False (bay)....F7
Good Hope (cape)....F7
Great Fish (riv.)....D6

Great Karoo (reg.)....C6
Great Kei (riv.)....D6
Griqualand West (reg.)....C5
Groote (riv.)....C6
Hangklip (cape)....F7
Hartbees (riv.)....C5
Hout (bay)....E6
Jukskei (riv.)....H6
Kalahari Gemsbok Nat'l Park....C5
King George's (falls)....B5
Klip (riv.)....H6
Kruger Nat'l Park....E4
Kruis (riv.)....F6
Limpopo (riv.)....D4
Maclear (cape)....F7
Molopo (riv.)....C5
Mountain Zebra Nat'l Park....C6
Namaqualand (reg.)....B5
Nieuwveld (range)....C6
Olifants (riv.)....D4
Orange (riv.)....B5
Palmiet (riv.)....F7

Plettenberg (bay)....C6
Pondoland (reg.)....D6
Robben (isl.)....E6
Royal Natal Nat'l Park....D5
Saint Francis (bay)....D6
Saint Helena (bay)....B6
Saint Lucia (cape)....E5
Saint Lucia (lake)....E5
Sak (riv.)....C6
Sand (riv.)....D4
Sandown (bay)....F7
Seal (isl.)....F7
Slangkop (pt.)....E7
Sneeuwkop (mt.)....F6
Stettyn (mt.)....F6
Table (bay)....E6
Table (mt.)....E6
Vaal (riv.)....D5
Verwoerd (dam)....D5
Walvis (bay)....A4
Witwatersberg (range)....G6
Witwatersrand....H7

Zonderend (riv.)....G6
Zululand (reg.)....E5
Zwart (riv.)....G7

SWAZILAND

CITIES and TOWNS

Manzini 28,837....E5
Mbabane (cap.) 23,109....E5
Siteki 1,362....E5

ZIMBABWE

CITIES and TOWNS

Bindura 17,000....E3
Bulawayo 359,000....D3
Chegutu 12,000....E3
Chinhoyi 25,000....E3
Gweru 68,000....D3
Harare (cap.) 601,000....E3

Hwange 33,000....D3
Kadoma 32,000....D3
Kwekwe 54,000....D3
Marondero 23,000....E3
Masvingo 22,000....E4
Matopos° 11,330....D4
Mutare 61,000....E3
Mwenezi° 7,830....E4
Rusape 5,286....E3
Salisbury (Harare) (cap.)
601,000....E3
Shurugwi 8,387....D3
Tuli° 340....D4
Zvishavane 20,000....D3

Matabeleland (reg.)....D3
Mazowe (riv.)....E3
Mushandike Nat'l Park....D4
Sabi (riv.)....E3
Sanyati (riv.)....D3
Shangani (riv.)....D3
Shashe (riv.)....D4
Victoria (falls)....C3
Zambezi (riv.)....E3
Zimbabwe Nat'l Park....E4

OTHER FEATURES

Inyanga Nat'l Park....E3
Kariba (dam)....D3
Kariba (lake)....D3
Lundi (riv.)....E4
Mashonaland (reg.)....E3

*City and suburbs.
†Population of parish.
°Population of subdivision.

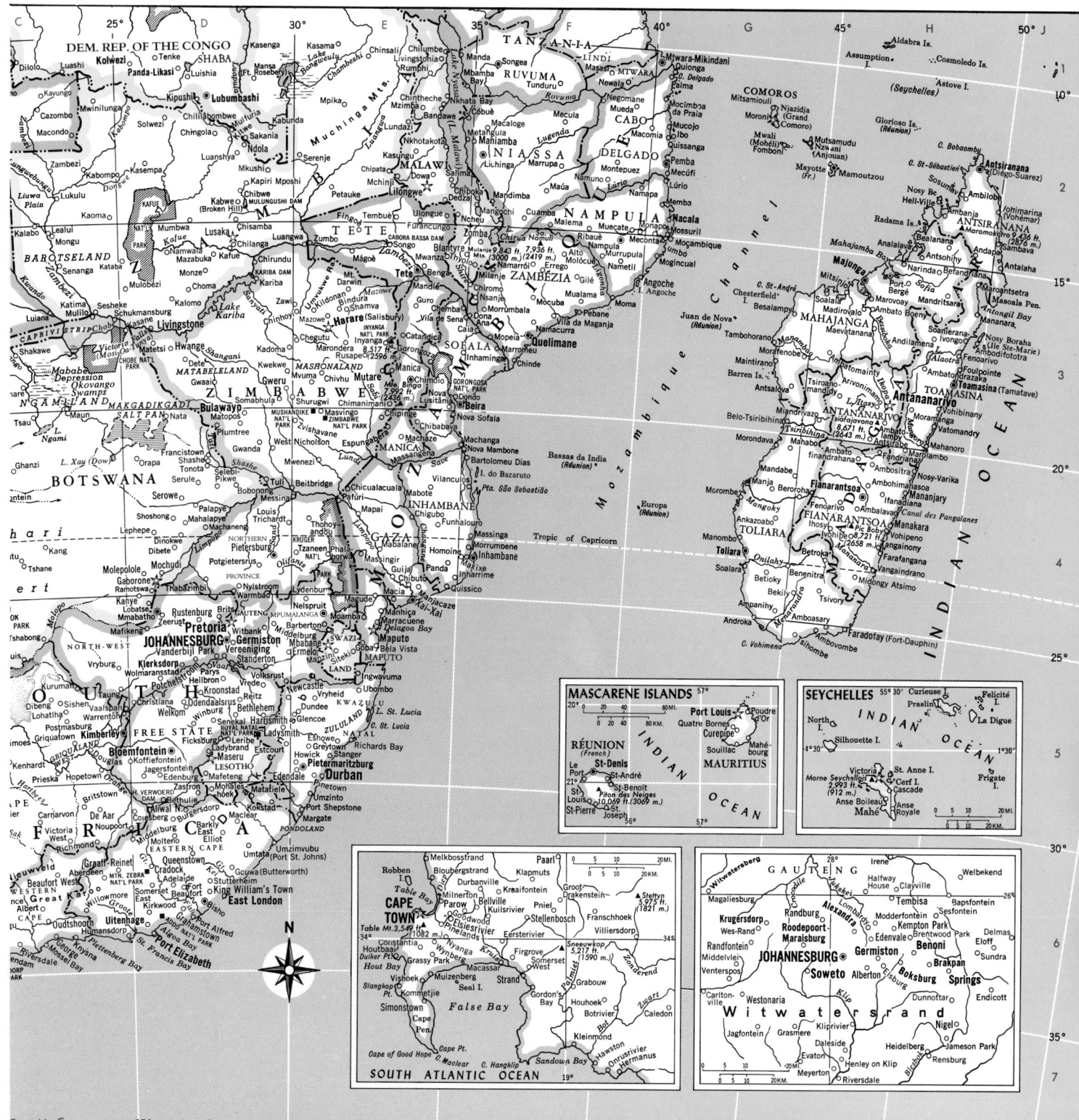

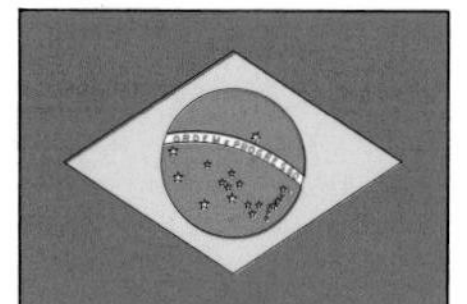

AREA 3,284,426 sq. mi. (8,506,663 sq. km.)
POPULATION 150,368,000
CAPITAL Brasília
LARGEST CITY São Paulo (greater)
HIGHEST POINT Pico da Neblina 9,889 ft.
  (3,014 m.)
MONETARY UNIT cruzado
MAJOR LANGUAGE Portuguese
MAJOR RELIGION Roman Catholicism

STATES and TERRITORIES

Acre 301,605 ....G10
Alagoas 1,987,581 ......G5
Amapá (terr.) 175,634 ....D2
Amazonas 1,432,066 .....G9
Bahia 9,474,263 ....F6
Ceará 5,294,876 ....G4
Espírito Santo 2,023,821 ..F7
Federal District 1,177,393 ..E6
Goiás 3,865,482 ....D6
Maranhão 4,002,599 .....E4
Mato Grosso 1,141,661 ...B6
Mato Grosso do Sul
  1,370,333 ....C7
Minas Gerais 13,390,805 ..E7
Pará 3,411,868 ....C4
Paraíba 2,772,600 ......G4
Paraná 7,630,466 ....D9
Pernambuco 6,147,102 ...G5
Piauí 2,140,066 ....F4
Rio de Janeiro 11,297,327 .F8
Rio Grande do Norte
  1,899,720 ....G4
Rio Grande do Sul
  7,777,212 ....C10
Rondônia 492,810 ....H10
Roraima (terr.) 79,153 ...H8
Santa Catarina 3,628,751 .D9
São Paulo 25,040,698 ....D8
Sergipe 1,141,834 ......G5
Tocantins D5

CITIES and TOWNS

Abaeté 12,861 ....E7
Abaetetuba 33,031 .....D3
Acaraú 7,144 ....F3
Acopiara 10,747 ....G4
Açu 20,544 ....G4
Agudos 18,790 ....*B3
Alagoa Grande 14,204 ..H4
Alagoinhas 76,377 .....G6
Alcobaça 3,430 ....G7
Alegre 9,441 ....*F2
Alegrete 54,786 ....B10
Além Paraíba 23,028 ...*E2
Alenquer 16,477 ....C3
Alfenas 31,815 ....*D2
Altamira 24,846 ....C3
Altos 13,621 ....F4
Amambaí 12,507 ....C8
Amapá 2,676 ....D2
Amarante 6,848 ....F4
Amargosa 11,118 ......F6
Americana 121,794 ....*C3
Amparo 26,970 ....*C3
Anápolis 160,520 ......D7
Anchieta 5,741 ....F8
Andaraí 2,476 ....F6
Andradina 42,036 .....D8
Andrelândia 8,737 .....*D2
Angra dos Reis 24,894 .*D3
Antonina 11,950 ....*B4
Aparecida 27,265 ......*D3
Apiaí 7,809 ....*B4
Aquidauana 21,514 ....C8
Aracaju 288,106 ....G5
Aracati 20,282 ....G4
Araçatuba 113,486 .....*A2
Araçuaí 12,292 ....F7
Araguari 73,302 ....D7
Araquari 22,468 ....D10
Araraquara 77,202 .....*B2
Araras 54,323 ....*C3
Araxá 51,339 ....E7
Arcoverde 40,646 ......G5
Areia Branca 12,979 ...G4
Assis 57,217 ....*A3
Avaré 40,716 ....*B3
Bacabal 43,229 ....E4
Bagé 66,743 ....C10
Bahia (Salvador) 1,496,276 ..G6
Baixo Guandu 13,714 ...F7
Balsas 13,566 ....E4
Bambuí 14,172 ....*C2
Barão de Cocais 11,950 .*E1
Barbacena 69,675 .....F7
Bariri 15,372 ....*B3
Barra 10,809 ....F5
Barra do Corda 19,280 .E4
Barra do Piraí 51,214 ..*E3
Barra Mansa 123,421 ..*E3
Barras 8,904 ....F4
Barreiras 30,355 ......E5
Barreiros 19,419 ......H5
Barretos 65,294 ....*B2
Batatais 30,478 ....*C2
Baturité 12,388 ....G4
Bauru 178,861 ....*B3
Bebedouro 39,070 .....*B2
Bela Vista 11,936 .....C8
Belém 758,117 ....E3
Belém †1,000,349 .....E3
Belo Horizonte 1,442,483 .*D1
Belo Horizonte †2,541,788 *D1
Benjamin Constant 6,563 .G9
Bento Gonçalves 40,323 .C10
Betim 71,599 ....*D2
Bicas 8,611 ....*E2
Birigui 45,348 ....*A2
Blumenau 144,819 .....D9
Boa Esperança 17,394 .*D2
Boa Vista 43,131 ......H8
Bocaiúva 16,616 ......E7
Bom Conselho 13,196 ..G5
Bom Despacho 22,941 .*D1
Bom Jesus da Lapa 19,978 .F6
Bom Sucesso 10,331 ...*D2
Borba 5,366 ....H9
Bragança Paulista 61,021 .*C3
Brasiléia 4,835 ....G10
Brasília (cap.) 411,305 ..E6
Brasília de Minas 10,171 .E7
Brejo 5,859 ....F3
Breves 31,452 ....D3
Brumado 24,663 ......F6
Brusque 37,898 ....D9

Cabedelo 18,581 ......H4
Cabo Frio 40,668 ......*F3
Caçador 25,287 ....D9
Caçapava 45,258 ......*D3
Caçapava do Sul 15,180 ..C10
Cáceres 33,472 ....B7
Cachoeira 11,520 .....G6
Cachoeira do Sul 59,967 .C10
Cachoeiro de Itapemirim
  84,994 ....G8
Caeté 23,331 ....*E1
Caetité 8,823 ....F6
Caiaponia 9,358 ....C7
Caicó 30,777 ....G4
Cajazeiras 30,834 .....G4
Cajuru 9,670 ....*C2
Camaquã 28,078 ......C10
Cambará 13,218 ......*A3
Cambuí 8,552 ....*C3
Cametá 15,539 ....D3
Camocim 19,921 ......F3
Campina Grande 222,229 .G4
Campinas 566,517 .....*C3
Campo Belo 30,392 ....*D2
Campo Formoso 10,324 .F5
Campo Grand 282,844 ..C8
Campo Largo 34,506 ...*B4
Campo Major 24,009 ...F4
Campos 174,218 ....*F2
Cananéia 5,581 ....*C4
Canavieiras 14,076 ....G6
Canindé 18,573 ....G4
Canoas 214,115 ....D10
Canoinhas 25,880 .....D9
Capanema 28,272 .....E3
Capão Bonito 24,081 ..*B4
Caraguatatuba 22,932 .*D3
Carangola 15,621 .....*E2
Caratinga 39,621 .....*E1
Caravelas 3,704 ......G7
Carazinho 41,913 .....C10
Carolina 10,136 ......E4
Caruaru 137,636 ......G5
Casa Banca 13,739 ....*C2
Cascavel 16,238 ......G4
Cássia 10,701 ....*C2
Castanhal 51,797 .....E3
Castelo 9,162 ....F8
Castro 21,079 ....*B4
Castro Alves 11,286 ...G6
Cataguases 40,659 ....*E2
Catalão 30,516 ....E7
Catanduva 64,813 .....*B2
Catolé do Rocha 12,165 .G4
Caxambu 16,221 ......*D2
Caxias 56,755 ....F4
Caxias do Sul 198,824 .D10
Ceará (Fortaleza) 648,815 .G3
Ceará-Mirim 17,097 ...H4
Ceres 13,671 ....D6
Chapecó 53,198 ......C9
Coari 14,841 ....H9
Codajás 4,923 ....H9
Codó 11,593 ....E4
Colatina 61,057 ......F7
Conceição do Araguaia
  18,143 ....D5
Concórdia 17,973 .....D9
Conselheiro Lafaiete 66,262 .E7
Corinto 17,056 ....E7
Cornélio Procópio 31,201 .D8
Coroatá 16,070 ......F3
Corumbá 66,014 .....B7
coromandel 11,604 ....F7
Coxim 14,876 ....C7
Crateús 29,905 ....F4
Crato 49,244 ....G4
Criciúma 74,003 ......D10
Cristalina 10,521 .....E7
Cruz Alta 53,315 .....C10
Cruzeiro 55,175 ......*D3
Cruzeiro do Sul 11,189 .G10
Cubatão 78,327 ......*C3
Cuiabá 167,894 ......C6
Curitiba 843,733 .....*B4
Curitiba †1,441,743 ..*B4
Currais Novos 25,663 .G4
Cururupu 10,358 .....E3
Curvelo 37,734 ......E7
Diamantina 20,197 ....E7
Divinópolis 108,344 ..*D2
Dois Córregos 11,811 .*B3
Dom Pedrito 25,773 ...C10
Dores do Indaiá 13,058 .*D1
Dourados 76,838 .....C8
Duque de Caxias 306,057 .*E3
Erexim 46,927 ....C9
Esperança 12,964 ....G4
Esplanada 9,822 .....G5
Estancia 26,527 ......G5
Feira de Santana 225,003 .G5
Fernandópolis 39,737 .*A2
Floriano 35,761 ......F4
Florianópolis 153,547 .E9

Fonte Boa 3,278 ......G9
Formiga 36,681 ......*D2
Formosa 29,304 ......E6
Fortaleza 648,815 ....G3
Fortaleza †1,581,588 .G3
Foz do Iguaçu 93,619 .C9
Franca 143,630 ......*C2
Frutal 22,955 ....*B2
Garanhuns 64,854 ....G5
Garca 26,527 ....*B3
Goiana 30,108 ....H4
Goiânia 703,263 .....D7
Goiás 15,768 ....D6
Governador Valadares
  173,699 ....F7
Grajaú 11,147 ....E4
Guaçui 12,715 ....*F2
Guajará-Mirim 19,992 .H10
Guarapuava 17,189 ...C9
Guarantiguetá 68,370 .*D3
Guarujá 67,730 ......C4
Guarulhos 395,117 ...*C3
Guaxupé 23,637 .....*C2
Guirantinga 8,981 ....D7
Gurupi 27,39 ....D5
Humaitá 10,004 ......H10
Ibaiti 11,352 ....*A3
Ibiá 11,161 ....D7
Ibicaraí 18,202 ......G6
Ibitinga 23,359 ......*B2
Icó 13,007 ....G4
Igarapava 15,342 ....*C2
Igarapé-Miri 12,172 ..D3
Iguape 16,827 ....*C4
Iguatu 39,611 ....G4
Ijui 51,925 ....C10
Ilhéus 71,240 ....G6
Imbituba 9,998 ......D10
Imperatriz 111,818 ...E4
Inhumas 23,455 .....D7
Ipameri 14,163 ......D7
Ipu 12,787 ....F4
Irati 21,956 ....*A4
Itabaiana, Paraíba 17,843 .H4

Itabaiana, Sergipe 26,055 ..G5
Itaberaba 27,590 .....F6
Itabira 57,691 ....F7
Itabirito 22,978 ......*E2
Itabuna 129,938 .....G6
Itacoatiara 26,737 ...B3
Itaituba 19,644 ......C4
Itajaí 78,867 ....D9
Itajubá 53,506 ....*D3
Itanhaem 26,181 .....C4
Itapecerica 10,234 ...*C3
Itapecuru-Mirim 12,216 .F3
Itapemirim 16,829 ....F8
Itapetinga 36,897 ....G6
Itapetininga 61,344 ...*B3
Itapeva 36,551 ......*B3
Itapipoca 19,463 .....G3
Itapira 36,308 ....*C3
Itápolis 13,750 ......*B2
Itaporanga 8,988 ....G4
Itaqui 23,136 ....B10
Itararé 24,368 ......*B4
Itatiba 35,537 ....*C3
Itaúna 49,372 ....*D2
Itu 62,211 ....*C3
Ituaçu 1,749 ....F6
Ituiutaba 65,178 .....D7
Itumbiara 56,602 ....D7
Iturama 12,363 ......*A1
Ituverava 21,323 ....*C2
Jaboatao 67,129 .....H5
Jaboticabal 40,276 ...*B2
Jacarel 103,652 .....*D3
Jacarezinho 23,684 ..*A3
Jacobina 26,723 .....F5
Jacupiranga 7,044 ...*C4
Jaguaquara 11,336 ..F6
Jaguarao 18,165 .....C11
Jaguaripe 8,566 .....*A4
Januária 20,484 .....E7
Jatai 40,957 ....D7
Jaú 59,522 ....*B3
Jequié 84,792 ....F6

Jequitinhonha 10,900 .....F7
Ji-Paraná 31,724 ....H10
Joaçaba 16,195 ....D9
João Pessoa 290,424 ....H4
João Pinheiro 17,013 ....E7
Joinville 217,074 ....D9
Juazeiro 60,940 ....F5
Juazeiro do Norte 125,248 .F4
Juiz de Fora 299,728 ....*E2
Jundiaí 210,015 ....*C3
Lages 108,768 ....D9
Laguna 27,743 ....D10
Lambari 9,722 ....*D2
Lapa 13,344 ....D9
Laranjeiras do Sul 19,329 ..C9
Lavras 35,345 ....*C2
Leme 40,155 ....*C3
Leopoldina 28,554 .....*E2
Limeira 137,812 ....*C3
Limoeiro 36,088 ....H4
Limoeiro do Norte 13,112 ..G4
Linhares 51,575 ....F7
Lins 44,633 ....*B2
Londrina 258,054 ......D8
Lorena 51,276 ....*D3
Luis Correia 3,576 ....F3
Luz 10,068 ....*D1
Luziania 67,284 ....E7
Macaé 39,644 ....*F3
Macalba 17,036 ....H4
Macapá 89,081 ....D2
Macau 17,543 ....G4
Maceio 376,479 ....H5
Machado 16,164 ......*D2
Mafra 26,226 ....D9
Magé 37,597 ....*E3
Mamanguape 16,321 ..H4
Manacapuru 17,016 ...H9
Manaus 613,068 ......H9
Manhuacu 22,678 ....*E2
Manhumirim 11,085 ..*E2
Manicoré 9,532 ....H9
Marabá 41,564 ....D4
Maracaju 9,699 ....C8

Maragogipe 13,512 ....G6
Maranguape 20,098 ......G3
Marechal Deodoro 9,400 ..H5
Mariana 11,785 ....*E2
Marília 103,904 ....*B3
Maringá 158,047 ....D8
Mata de São João 23,741 ..G6
Mato Grosso (Vila Bela da
  Santíssima Trindade)
  1,401 ....B6
Maués 10,846 ....H9
Mineiros 16,844 ....C7
Miracema 15,545 ....*E2
Miracema do Norte D5
Mirassol 25,173 ....*B2
Mococa 33,682 ....*C2
Mogi das Cruzes 122,265 ..*C3
Mogi-Mirim 41,827 .....*C3
Monte Alegre 10,646 ...C3
Monte Aprazível 9,767 ..*A2
Monteiro 11,051 ....G4
Montenegro 27,246 ....D10
Montes Claros 151,881 ..E7
Morrinhos 20,154 ......D7
Mossoró 118,007 ......G4
Muriaé 50,040 ....*E2
Muzambinho 8,803 .....*C2
Nanuque 34,445 ......F7
Natal 376,552 ....H4
Nazaré 18,068 ....G6
Niquelandia 8,828 .....D6
Niterói 386,185 ....*E3
Nova Cruz 12,824 .....H4
Nova Era 11,126 ......*E1
Nova Friburgo 88,943 ..*E3
Nova Iguaçu 491,802 ...*E3
Nova Lima 35,035 .....*E2
Nova Russas 10,021 ...F4
Novo Cruzeiro 18,439 .*E2
Novo Hamburgo 132,066 .D10
Novo Horizonte 18,439 .*B2
Óbidos 17,143 ....C3
Oeiras 12,406 ....F4
Olimpia 24,376 ....*B2
Olinda 266,392 ....H4

Oliveira 22,642 ....*D2
Oriximiná 12,078 ....C3
Orlândia 22,924 ....*C2
Osasco 376,689 ....*C3
Ourinhos 52,698 ....*B3
Ouro Preto 27,821 .....*E2
Palmares 40,624 ....H5
Palmas 15,823 ....C9
Palmeira 11,521 ....*B4
Palmeira das Missões
  23,943 ....C9
Pará (Belém) 758,117 ...E3
Paracatu 29,911 ....E7
Pará de Minas 37,127 ..*D1
Paraguaçu Paulista
  17,399 ....D8
Paraíba do Sul 13,510 ..*E3
Paranaíba 31,305 ......D7
Paranaguá 68,366 .....*B4
Parati 8,684 ....*D3
Parintins 29,369 ....C3
Parnaíba 78,718 ....F3
Passo Fundo 103,121 ..D10
Passos 56,998 ....*C2
Patos 58,735 ....G4
Patos de Minas 59,896 .E7
Patrocínio 29,520 ......E7
Pau dos Ferros 12,985 .G4
Paulo Afonso 62,066 ...G5
Pederneiras 18,864 ....*B3
Pedra Azul 13,615 .....F6
Pedreiras 30,843 ......E4
Pedro Segundo 9,693 ..F4
Pelotas 197,092 ....C10
Penápolis 32,168 ......*A2
Penedo 27,064 ....G5
Pernambuco (Recife)
  1,184,215 ....H5
Petrolina 73,436 ....G5
Petrópolis 149,427 ....*E3
Picos 33,098 ....F4
Piedade 12,406 ....*C4
Pilar 14,778 ....H5
Pindamonhangaba 51,174 .*D3

(continued on following page)

Topography

5,000 m. / 16,404 ft.   2,000 m. / 6,562 ft.   1,000 m. / 3,281 ft.   500 m. / 1,640 ft.   200 m. / 656 ft.   100 m. / 328 ft.   Sea Level   Below

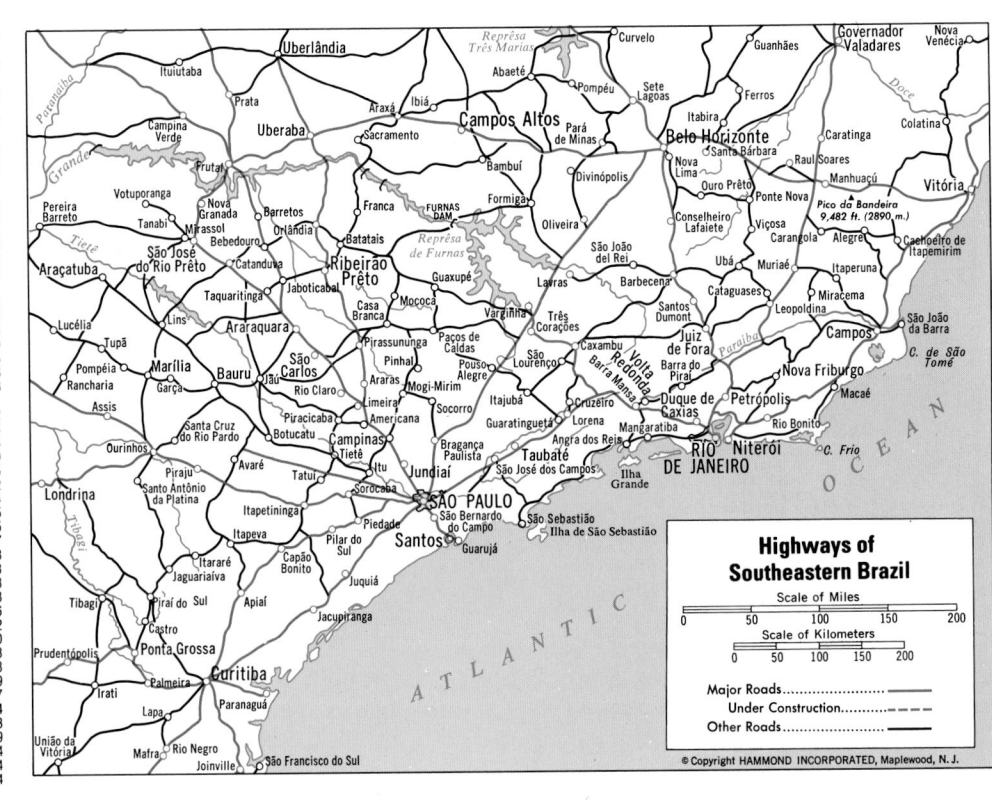

Highways of
Southeastern Brazil
Scale of Miles
0   50   100   150   200
Scale of Kilometers
0   50   100   150   200

Major Roads ....
Under Construction ....
Other Roads ....
© Copyright HAMMOND INCORPORATED, Maplewood, N. J.

Agriculture, Industry and Resources

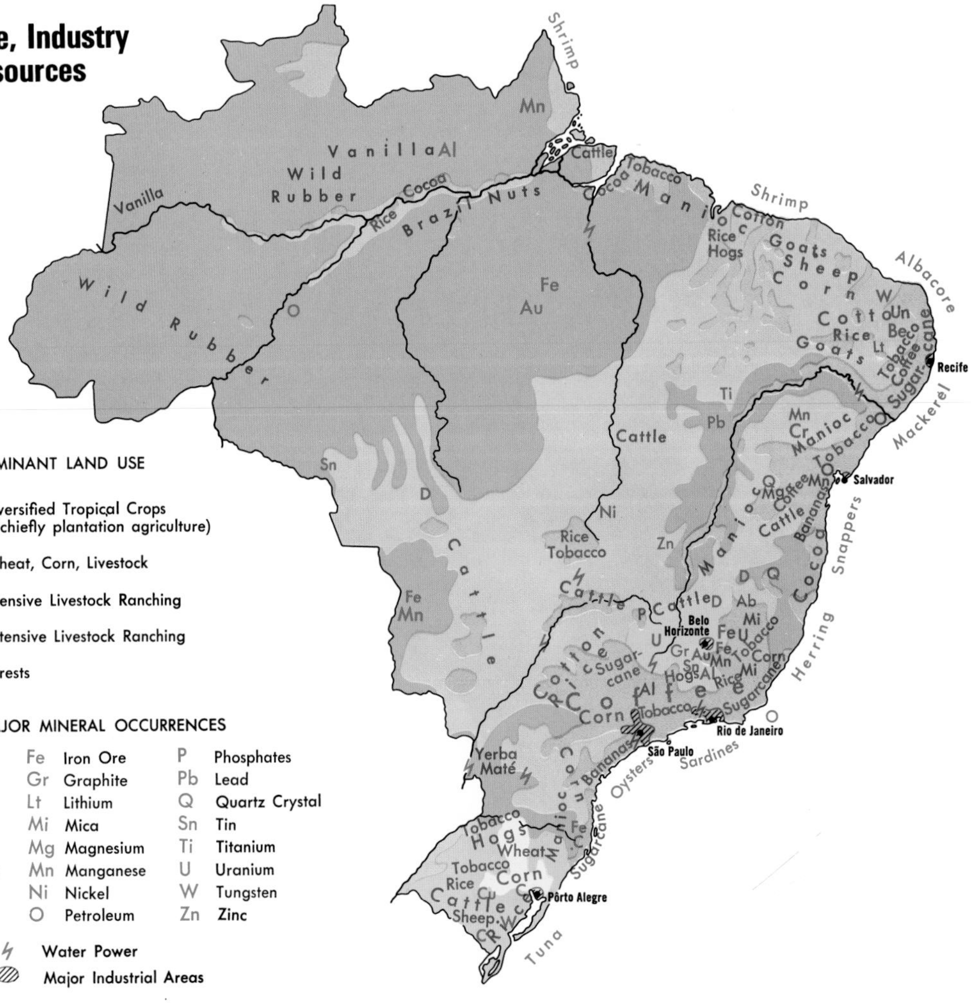

DOMINANT LAND USE

Diversified Tropical Crops
(chiefly plantation agriculture)

Wheat, Corn, Livestock

Intensive Livestock Ranching

Extensive Livestock Ranching

Forests

MAJOR MINERAL OCCURRENCES

Ab Asbestos
Al Bauxite
Au Gold
Be Beryl
C   Coal
Cr Chromium
Cu Copper
D   Diamonds

Fe Iron Ore
Gr Graphite
Lt Lithium
Mi Mica
Mg Magnesium
Mn Manganese
Ni Nickel
O   Petroleum

P   Phosphates
Pb Lead
Q   Quartz Crystal
Sn Tin
Ti Titanium
U   Uranium
W   Tungsten
Zn Zinc

⚡ Water Power

▨ Major Industrial Areas

Três Corações 36,179 . . . . *D2
Três Lagoas 45,171 . . . . C8
Três Pontas 24,225 . . . . *E2
Três Rios 47,497 . . . . *E3
Trindade 22,321 . . . . D7
Tubarão 64,585 . . . . D10
Tucuruí 27,209 . . . . D3
Tupã 44,450 . . . . *A2
Tupanciretã 13,103 . . . . C10
Tutóia 4,766 . . . . D2
Ubá 43,080 . . . . *E2
Ubaitaba 9,413 . . . . G6
Ubatuba 23,078 . . . . *D3
Uberaba 180,296 . . . . *C1
Uberlândia 230,400 . . . . E7
Unaí 28,148 . . . . D7
União 9,396 . . . . F4
União da Vitória 22,682 . . . . C9
União dos Palmares 20,876 . . . . H5
Uruaçu 19,607 . . . . D6
Uruçuí 6,047 . . . . E4
Uruguaiana 79,059 . . . . B10
Vacaria 37,370 . . . . D10
Valença 34,231 . . . . *E3
Varginha 57,448 . . . . *D2
Viana 9,753 . . . . E3
Viçosa 9,843 . . . . G5
Viçosa 29,198 . . . . *E2
Vigia 14,749 . . . . E3
Vila Velha Argolas 74,166 . . . . F8
Vilhena 12,565 . . . . H10
Viscondé dos Rio Branco 17,295 . . . . *E2
Vitória 144,143 . . . . G8
Vitória da Conquista 125,717 F6
Vitória de Santo Antão 62,890 . . . . G4
Volta Redonda 177,772 . . . . *D3
Votuporanga 44,169 . . . . *B2
Xapuri 3,122 . . . . G10
Xique-Xique 17,625 . . . . F5

OTHER FEATURES

Abacaxis (riv.) B4
Abunã (riv.) G10
Acaraí, Serra do (range) B2
Acre (riv.) G10
Aiama (lake) H9
Amambaí, Serra de (range) C7
Amapari (riv.) C2
Amazon (riv.) C3

Anauá (riv.) B2
Aporé (riv.) D7
Araguaia (riv.) D4
Araguari (riv.) D2
Araruama (lake) *E3
Arinos (riv.) B5
Aripuanã (riv.) A4
Armando Laydner (res.) *B3
Bailique (isl.) D2
Balsas (riv.) E5
Bananal (isl.) D2
Bandeira, Pico da (mt.) *E2, F8
Braço Maior do Araguaia (riv.) D5
Braço Menor do Araguaia (riv.) D6
Branco (riv.) H8
Buzios (cape) *F3
Canumã (riv.) B4
Capim (riv.) D3
Carajás, Serra dos (range) D4
Cardoso (isl.) *C4
Cassiporé (cape) D2
Caviana (isl.) D2
Chavantes, Serra dos (range) D5
Claro (riv.) D7
Comprida (isl.) *C4
Cuiabá (riv.) B7
Culuene (riv.) C6
Curuá (riv.) C3
Doce (riv.) *E2, F7
Dois Irmãos, Serra (range) F5
Espigão Mestre (Geral de Goiás) (range) E6
Espinhaço, Serra do (range) F7
Estrondo, Serra do (range) D5
Feia (lake) *F3
Feio (riv.) *B2
Formosa, Serra (range) C5
Frio (cape) *F3
Furnas (dam) *C2
Geral de Goiás, Serra (range) E6
Gi-Paraná (riv.) H10
Gradaús, Serra do (range) D4
Grajaú (riv.) E4
Grande (isl.) *D3
Grande (riv.) *B2, E8
Guanabara (bay) *E3
Guaporé (riv.) H10

Gurguéia (riv.) E5
Gurupi, Serra da (range) E4
Gurupi (riv.) E3
Ibicuí (riv.) C10
Içá (riv.) G9
Iguaçu (riv.) C9
Iguazú (falls) C9
Ilha Grande (bay) *D3
Iriri (riv.) C4
Itaipu (dam) C9
Itaipú (riv.) C9
Itapecuru (riv.) F4
Itapi (riv.) B3
Itapicuru (riv.) G5
Itararé (riv.) *B3
Ival (riv.) C8
Jaculpe (riv.) F5
Jaguaribe (riv.) G5
Jamanxim (riv.) C4
Japurá (riv.) G9
Jari (riv.) C3
Jauari, Serra (mts.) C3
Javari (riv.) F9
Jequitinhonha (riv.) F7
Juruá (riv.) G10
Juruena (riv.) B5
Jutaí (riv.) G9
Lombarda, Serra (mts.) D2
Madeira (riv.) A4
Mangueira (lag.) D11
Manso (riv.) C6
Mantiqueira (range) *D3
Mapuera (riv.) B3
Mar, Serra do (range) *C4, E9
Maracá (isl.) C2
Marajó (bay) E2
Marajó (isl.) 147,895 . . . . D3
Mato Grosso, Planalto de (plat.) B6
Maués-Açu (riv.) B4
Mearim (riv.) E4
Mexiana (isl.) D2
Miranda (riv.) B8
Mirim (lag.) C11
Mogi Guaçu (riv.) *C2
Mortes (Manso) (riv.) D6
Neblina, Pico da (peak) H9
Negro (riv.) H9
Nhamundá (riv.) B3
Norte, Serra do (range) B5
Oiapoque (Oyapock) (riv.) C2

Orange (cape) D1
Órgãos (range) *E3
Oyapock (riv.) C2
Pacajá Grande (riv.) D4
Pacaraimã, Serra da (mts.) H8
Papagaio (riv.) B6
Pará (riv.) D3
Paracatu (riv.) E7
Paraguaçu (riv.) F6
Paraguaí (riv.) B8
Paraíba (riv.) *E2
Paraná (riv.) C8
Paraná (riv.) C8
Paraná (riv.) C8
Paranapanema (riv.) *B3, C8
Paranapiacaba (range) *B4
Paranatinga (riv.) C6
Pardo (riv.) *B2, D8
Pardo (riv.) C8
Pardo (riv.) F6
Parecis, Serra dos (range) B6
Parnaíba (riv.) F3
Paru (riv.) C3
Patos (riv.) D10
Penitente, Serra do (range) E5
Piauí, Serra do (range) F5
Piauí (riv.) F5
Purus (riv.) H9
Ribeira (riv.) *B4
Roncador, Serra do (range) D5
Ronuro (riv.) C6
Roosevelt (riv.) A4
Santa Catarina (isl.) 138,556 E9
São Lourenço (riv.) C7
São Marcos (bay) D3
São Roque (cape) H4
São Francisco (riv.) *D2, G5
São Sebastião (isl.) 5,724 . . . . *D3, E8
São Tomé (cape) F8
Sapucaí (riv.) *D2
Sepetiba (bay) *D3
Sete Quedas (falls) C9
Sete Quedas (Grande) (isl.) C8
Sobradino (res.) F5
Sono (riv.) E5
Sul (chan.) D2
Tacutu (riv.) B2
Tapajós (riv.) B4
Taquari (riv.) C7
Tefé (riv.) G9
Teles Pires (riv.) B5

Tibagi (riv.) *A4
Tietê (riv.) *B2, D8
Tiracambu, Serra (range) E3
Tocantins (riv.) D3
Tombador, Serra do (range) B6
Trombetas (riv.) B3
Tucuruí (res.) D4
Tumucumaque, Serra de (range) C2

Turvo (riv.) *B2
Uaupés (riv.) G9
Uraricoera (riv.) H8
Urubu (riv.) A3
Urubupungá (dam) B2
Urucún, Morro do (mt.) B7
Uruguai (riv.) B9
Vasa Barris (riv.) G5
Velhas (riv.) E7

Verde (riv.) C7
Verdinho (riv.) D7
Xavantes (res.) *B3
Xingu (riv.) C3

†Population of met. area.
*preceding reference indicates that the name will be found on S.E. Brazil map, page 135.

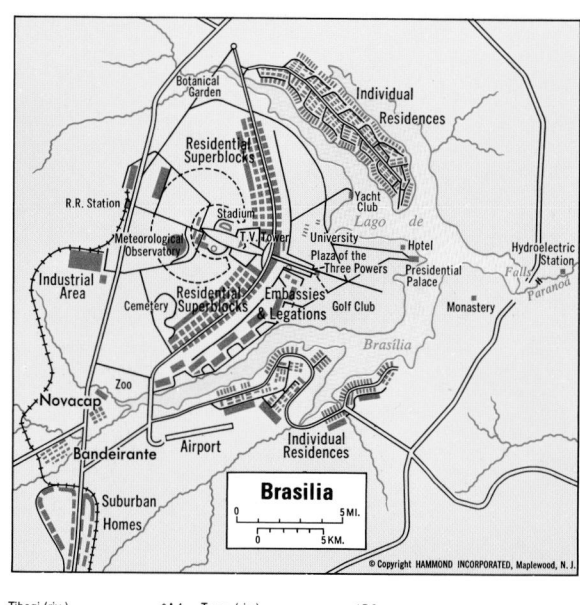

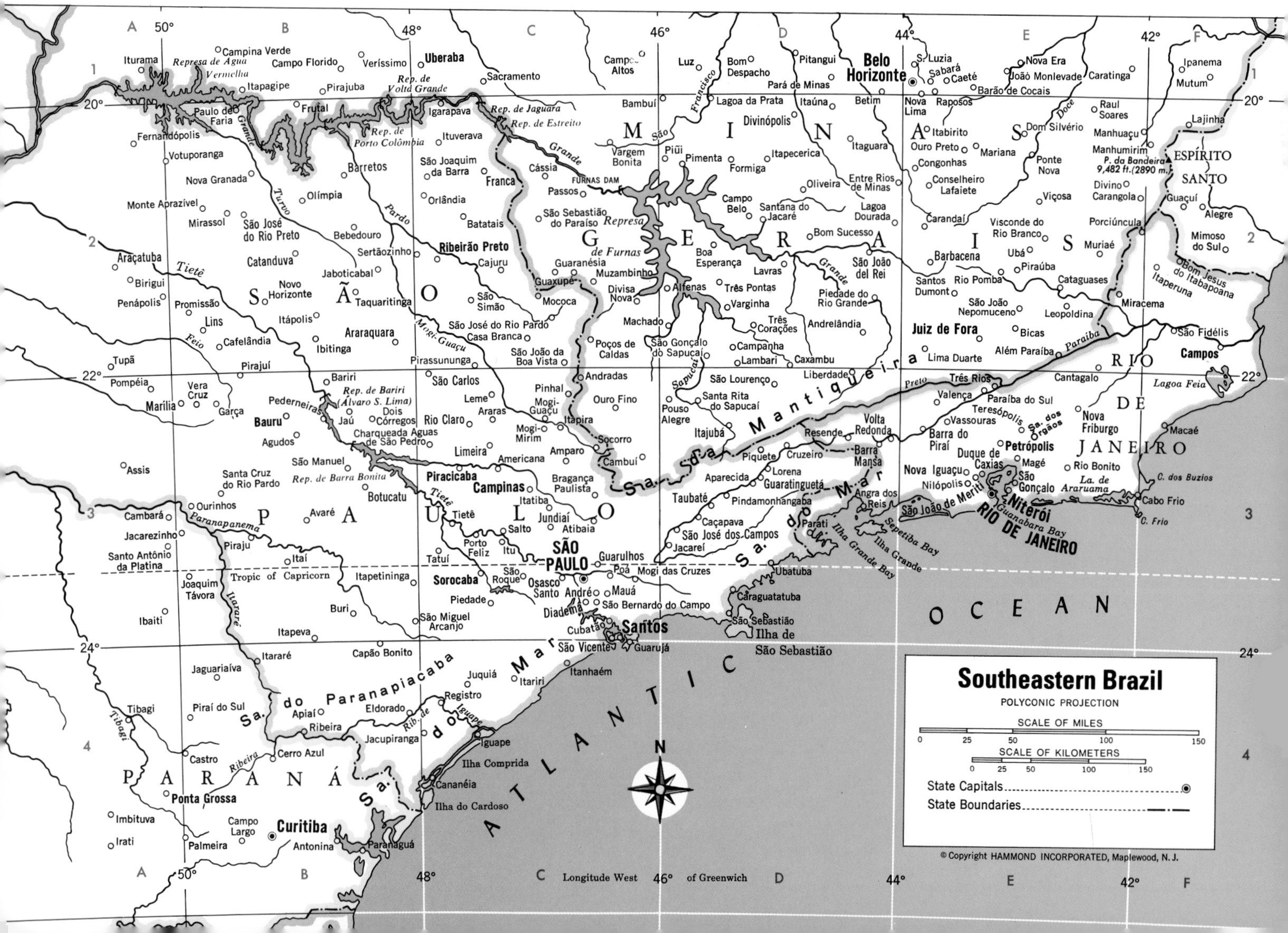

Brasilia

Southeastern Brazil
POLYCONIC PROJECTION

SCALE OF MILES
0   25   50   100   150

SCALE OF KILOMETERS
0   25   50   100   150

State Capitals . . . . ◉
State Boundaries . . . . —— ——

© Copyright HAMMOND INCORPORATED, Maplewood, N.J.

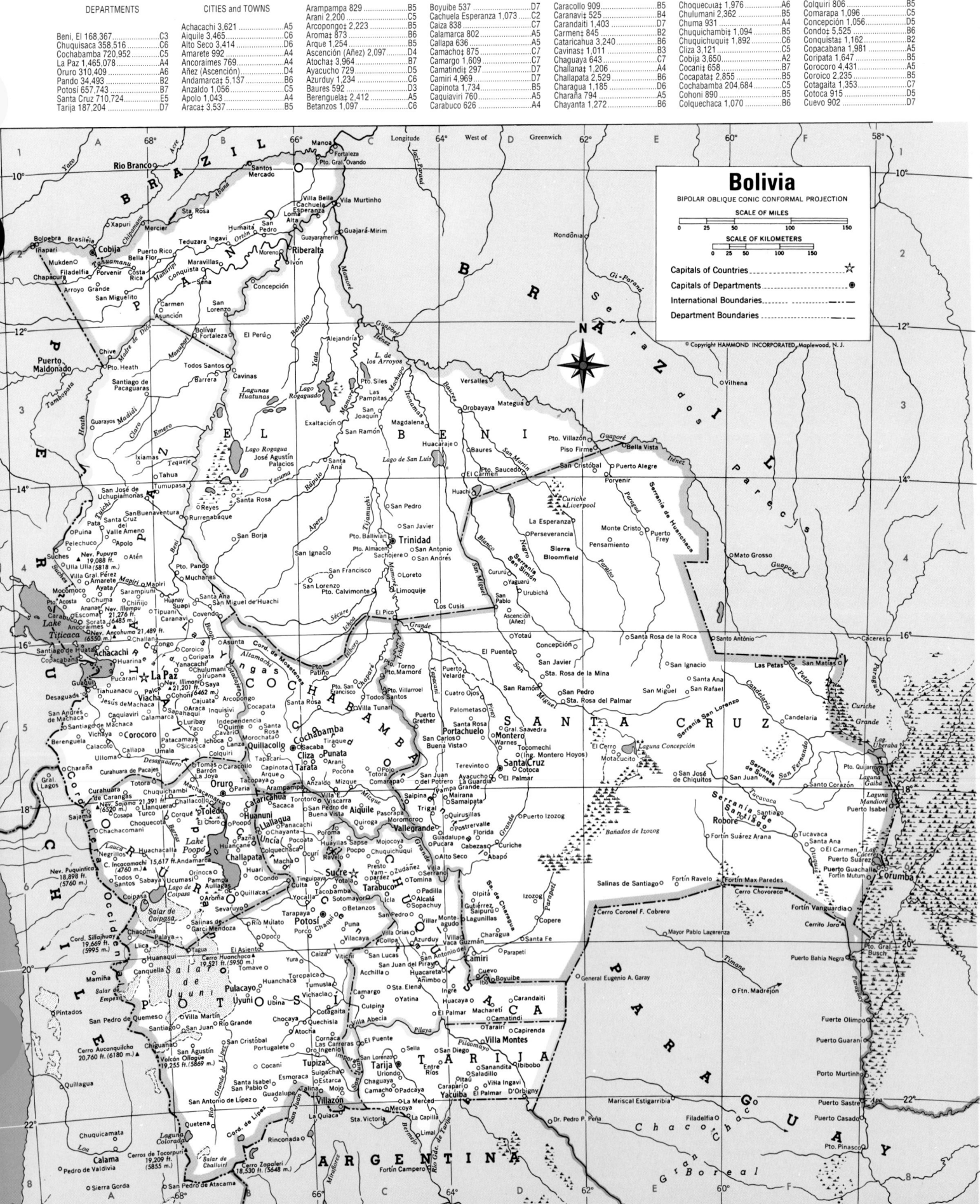

Culpina 981....C7
Culta‡ 4,412....B6
Curahuara de Pacajes 510....A5
El Palmar, Chuquisaca‡ 772....D7
El Palmar, Tarija 832....D7
El Puente, Santa Cruz‡ 1,185....D5
El Puente, Tarija‡ 1,310....C7
Entre Ríos 1,011....C7
Esmorac‡ 1,137....B7
Estarca‡ 2,331....C7
Filadelfia‡ 942....A2
Fortaleza‡ 765....B3
Fortín Mutum....F6
General Saavedra 1,006....D5
Guadalupe 2,355....C6
Guaqui 2,266....A5
Guayaramerín 1,470....C2
Huacaraje 673....D3
Huachacalla 801....A6
Huanay 574....B4
Huanchaca....B7
Huanuni 5,696....B6
Huari 1,070....B6
Huarina 1,151....A5
Ichoca 591....B5
Independencia 1,742....B5
Ingeniero Montero Hoyos (Tocomechi) 575....D5
Inquisivi 530....B5
Irupana 1,937....B5
Ivón‡ 772....C2
Izozog‡ 2,759....D6
Jesús de Machaca 529....A5
José Agustín Palacios‡ 2,273....B3
La Capilla‡ 1,870....C8
Lagunillas 840....D6
La Merced‡ 688....C6
Lanza 526....B5
La Paz (cap.) 635,283....B5
Limal‡ 524....C6
Llallagua 6,719....B6
Llanquera 613....A6
Llica 560....A6
Loreto 589....C4
Macha 1,050....B6
Machacamarca 1,746....B5
Macharetí‡ 1,164....D7
Magdalena 1,724....C3
Mairana 508....C4
Mecoya‡ 585....C8
Mizque 870....C6
Mocomechi 977....A4
Mojo 469....C8
Mojocoya 498....C6
Monteagudo 971....D6
Montero 2,713....D5
Morochata 461....B5
Moromoro 556....C6
Motacucito‡ 585....C6
Ocuri 1,531....C6
Orinoca‡ 2,380....B6
Orobayaya‡ 1,132....D3
Oro Ingenio‡ 945....C7
Oruro 124,213....B5
Padcaya 877....C7
Padilla 2,462....C6
Palaya 300....A6
Palca 887....A5
Palometas‡ 3,453....D5
Pampa Aullagas‡ 1,834....B6
Pampa Grande 727....D6
Panacachi 952....B6
Paria 335....B5
Pasorapa 1,016....C6
Pata 122....A4
Patacamaya 1,278....B5
Pazña 871....B6
Pelechuco 873....A4
Pocoata 859....B6
Pocona 518....C5

Pocpo‡ 2,791....C6
Pojo 1,047....C5
Poopó 736....B6
Porco 817....B6
Poroma 171....C6
Portachuelo 2,456....D5
Portugalete‡ 1,590....B7
Porvenir‡ 846....A2
Postrervalle 750....D6
Potosí 77,397....C6
Presto 725....C6
Pucara 762....C6
Pucarani 1,041....A5
Puerto Acosta 1,302....A4
Puerto Almacen 358....C4
Puerto General Ovando 658....C1
Puerto Heath‡ 570....A3
Puerto Rico‡ 539....B2
Puerto Siles 357....C3
Puerto Suárez 1,159....F6
Pulacayo 7,984....B7
Puna 852....C6
Punata 5,014....C5
Quechisla 171....C7
Queteña 183....B8
Quillacas 1,170....B6
Quillacollo 9,123....B5
Quime 1,256....B5
Quiroga‡ 3,467....C6
Quirusillas 433....D6
Ravelo 907....C6
Reyes 1,404....B4
Riberalta 6,549....C2
Río Grande 281....B7
Río Mulato 381....B6
Roboré 3,715....F6
Rurrenabaque 1,225....B4
Sabaya 649....A6
Sacaba 2,752....C5
Sacaca 1,778....B6
Sachojere 401....C4
Saipina 573....C6
Sajama 231....A5
Saladillo‡ 1,315....D7
Salinas de Garci Mendoza 335....B6
Samaipata 1,656....D6
San Agustín‡ 810....B7
Sanandita 379....D7
San Andrés 399....C4
San Andrés de Machaca 101....A5
San Antonio, El Beni 436....C4
San Antonio de López‡ 177....B7
San Antonio del Parapetí 497....D7
San Borja 708....B4
San Buenaventura 307....A4
San Carlos 570....D5
San Cristóbal‡ 1,200....B7
San Diego‡ 773....D7
San Francisco 185....C4
San Ignacio, El Beni 1,757....C4
San Ignacio, Santa Cruz 1,819....E5
San Javier, El Beni 294....C4
San Javier, Santa Cruz 564....D5
San Joaquín 1,959....C2
San José de Chiquitos 1,933....E5
San José de Uchupiamonas 277....A4
San Juan, Potosí 131....B7
San Juan, Santa Cruz‡ 1,482....F5
San Juan del Piray 541....C7
San Juan del Potrero 263....C5
San Lorenzo, El Beni 496....C4
San Lorenzo, Pando‡ 317....B2
San Lorenzo, Tarija 785....C7
San Lucas 925....C7
San Matías 887....F5
San Miguel 502....E5
San Miguel de Huachi 25....B4
San Pablo 11....B7

San Pedro, Chuquisaca 182....C6
San Pedro, El Beni 262....C4
San Pedro, Pando‡ 312....B2
San Pedro, Santa Cruz 80....D5
San Pedro de Buena Vista 1,094....C6
San Pedro de Quemes‡ 290....A7
San Rafael‡ 1,282....E5
San Ramón, El Beni 1,161....C3
San Ramón, Santa Cruz 379....D5
Santa Ana, El Beni 2,225....C3
Santa Ana, La Paz 171....B4
Santa Ana, Santa Cruz 275....C5
Santa Ana, Santa Cruz 2,225....F6
Santa Cruz 254,682....D5
Santa Cruz del Valle Ameno 442....A4
Santa Elena‡ 4,474....C5
Santa'Isabel‡ 323....C6
Santa Rosa, Cochabamba‡ 942....B5
Santa Rosa, Cochabamba‡ 276....C5
Santa Rosa, El Beni 765....B4
Santa Rosa, Pando‡ 105....B5
Santa Rosa, Santa Cruz 995....D5
Santa Rosa de la Mina 99....D5
Santa Rosa de la Roca 101....E5
Santa Rosa del Palmar 441....E5
Santiago, Potosí 172....A7
Santiago, Santa Cruz 765....F6
Santiago de Huata 948....A5
Santiago de Machaca 218....A5
Santo Corazón‡ 963....F5
Sapahaqui 55....B5
Sapsei 89....C6
Sarampiuni 138....A4
Saya 339....B5
Sena‡ 660....B2
Sevaruyo 475....B6
Sicasica 1,486....B5
Sopachuy 713....C6
Sorata 2,764....A4
Sotomayor 510....C6
Suapi‡ 1,750....B4
Suches‡ 231....A4
Sucre (cap.) 63,625....C6
Suipacha‡ 2,701....C7
Tacobamba‡ 6,933....C6
Tacopaya 795....B5
Talina 122....B7
Tapacarí 980....B5
Tarabuco 2,833....C6
Tararirí 394....D7
Tarapaya 357....B6
Tarata 3,016....C5
Tarija 38,916....C7
Teduzara‡ 271....B2
Terevinto‡ 3,790....D5
Tiahuanaco 1,227 *....A5

Tinguipaya 766....C6
Tipuani‡ 1,216....B4
Tirague 1,390....C5
Tocomechi 575....D5
Todos Santos, Cochabamba 408....C5
Todos Santos, Oruro 68....A6
Toledo 3,273....B6
Tomás Barrón 1,852....B5
Tomave 201....B7
Tomina 708....C6
Toropalca‡ 199....B7
Torotoro 1,233....C6
Totora....C5
Trigal 749....C6
Trinidad 14,505....C4
Tumupasa 349....B4
Tumusla‡ 526....C7
Tupiza 8,248....C7
Turco 131....A6
Ubina‡ 462....B7
Ucumasi‡ 1,040....B6
Ulla Ulla 52....A4
Ulloma 116....A5
Umala 481....B5
Uncía 4,507....B6
Uriondo 86....C7
Urubichá 1,369....D4
Uyuni 6,968....B7
Vallegrande 5,094....C6
Versalles 83....D3
Viacha 6,607....A5
Vichacla 317....C7
Vichaya 422....A5
Vilacaya 200....C6
Villa Abecia 539....C7
Villa Bella 88....C2
Villa E. Viscarra 658....C6
Villa General Pérez 802....A4
Villa Ingavi 122....D7
Villa Martín 543....B7
Villa Montes 3,105....D7
Villa Orías 404....C6
Villar 322....C6
Villa Serrano 1,570....C6
Villa Tunari 510....C5
Villa Vaca Guzmán 699....D6
Villazón 6,261....C7
Vitichi 1,515....C7
Warnes 1,571....D5
Yaco 835....B5
Yacuiba 5,027....D7
Yamparaéz 725....C6
Yanacachi 1,964....B5
Yatina‡ 1,850....C7
Yocalla 1,814....B6
Yotala 1,554....C6
Yura 136....B7
Zongo 141....B5
Zudáñez 1,868....C6

OTHER FEATURES

Abuná (riv.)....B2
Altamachi (riv.)....B5
Ancohuma, Nevada (mt.)....A4
Apere (riv.)....C4
Arroyas, Los (lake)....C3
Barras (riv.)....B6
Baures (riv.)....D3
Beni (riv.)....B3
Benicito (riv.)....C3
Bermejo (riv.)....C8
Blanco (riv.)....D4

Bloomfield, Sierra (mts.)....D4
Boopi (riv.)....B4
Cáceres (lag.)....G6
Candelaria (riv.)....F5
Capitán Ustarés, Cerro (mt.)....E8
Central, Cordillera (range)....C6
Chalíviri (salt dep.)....B8
Chaparé (riv.)....C5
Charagua, Sierra de (mt.)....D6
Chipamanu (riv.)....A3
Chovoreca, Cerro (mt.)....F6
Claro (riv.)....A3
Coipasa (lake)....A6
Coipasa (salt dep.)....A6
Colorada (lag.)....A8
Concepción (lag.)....E6
Coronel F. Gabrera (riv.)....E6
Cotacajes (riv.)....B5
Desaguadero (riv.)....B5
Emero (riv.)....A4
Empexa (salt dep.)....A7
Gaiba (lag.)....F5
Grande (marsh)....F5
Grande (riv.)....C4
Grande (riv.)....C6
Grande de Lipez (riv.)....B7
Guaporé (riv.)....C3
Heath (riv.)....A3
Huanchaca, Cerro (mt.)....B7
Huanchaca, Serranía de (mts.)....E4
Huatunas (lag.)....B3
Ichilo (riv.)....C5
Ichoa (riv.)....C5
Illampu, Nevada (mt.)....A4
Illimani, Nevada (mt.)....B5
Incacamachi, Cerro (mt.)....A6
Isiboro (riv.)....C5
Iténez (Guaporé) (riv.)....C3
Itonamas (riv.)....C3
Izozog (swamp)....E6
Jara, Cerrito (mt.)....F6
Lauca (riv.)....A5
López, Cordillera de (range)....B8
Liverpool (swamp)....D4
Machupo (riv.)....C3
Madidi (riv.)....A3
Madre de Diós (riv.)....A3
Mamoré (riv.)....C2
Mandioré (lag.)....F6
Manupari (riv.)....B3
Manuripi (riv.)....B2
Mapiri (riv.)....A4
Mizque (riv.)....C6

Mosetenes, Cordillera de (range)....B5
Negro (riv.)....D4
Occidental, Cordillera (range)....A6
Ollagüe (vol.)....B7
Oriental, Cordillera (range)....C5
Ortón (riv.)....B2
Otuquis (riv.)....F6
Paraguá (riv.)....E4
Paraguay (riv.)....F7
Paraíso (riv.)....E4
Parapetí (riv.)....D6
Petas, Las (riv.)....F5
Pilaya (riv.)....C7
Pilcomayo (riv.)....D7
Piray (riv.)....D5
Poopó (lake)....B6
Pupuya, Nevada (mt.)....A4
Puquintica, Nevado (mt.)....A6
Rápulo (riv.)....C4
Real, Cordillera (range)....A5
Rogagua (lake)....B3
Rogaguado (lake)....B3
Sajama, Nevada (mt.)....A6
San Fernando (riv.)....C7
San Juan (riv.)....C7
San Lorenzo, Serranía (mts.)....E5
San Luis (lake)....C3
San Martín (riv.)....D3
San Miguel (riv.)....D4
San Simón, Serranía (mts.)....D4
Santiago, Serranía de (mts.)....F6
Sécure (riv.)....C4
Sillajhuay, Cordillera (mt.)....A6
Suches (riv.)....A4
Sunsas, Serranía de (mts.)....A2
Tahuamanu (riv.)....A2
Tarija, Río Grande de (riv.)....C8
Tequeje (riv.)....B3
Tijamuchi (riv.)....C4
Titicaca (lake)....A4
Tocorpuri, Cerros de (mt.)....A8
Tucavaca (riv.)....F6
Tuichi (riv.)....A4
Uberaba (lag.)....G5
Uyuni (salt dep.)....B7
Yacuma (riv.)....B3
Yapacani (riv.)....C5
Yata (riv.)....C3
Yungas, Las (reg.)....B5
Zapaleri, Cerro (mt.)....B8

‡Population of canton.

AREA 424,163 sq. mi. (1,098,582 sq. km.)
POPULATION 7,193,000
CAPITALS La Paz, Sucre
LARGEST CITY La Paz
HIGHEST POINT Nevada Ancohuma 21,489 ft. (6.550 m.)
MONETARY UNIT Bolivian peso
MAJOR LANGUAGES Spanish, Quechua, Aymara
MAJOR RELIGION Roman Catholicism

Topography

0   100   200 MI.
0   100   200 KM.

Below Sea Level / 100 m. 328 ft. / 200 m. 656 ft. / 500 m. 1,640 ft. / 1,000 m. 3,281 ft. / 2,000 m. 6,562 ft. / 5,000 m. 16,404 ft.

Agriculture, Industry and Resources

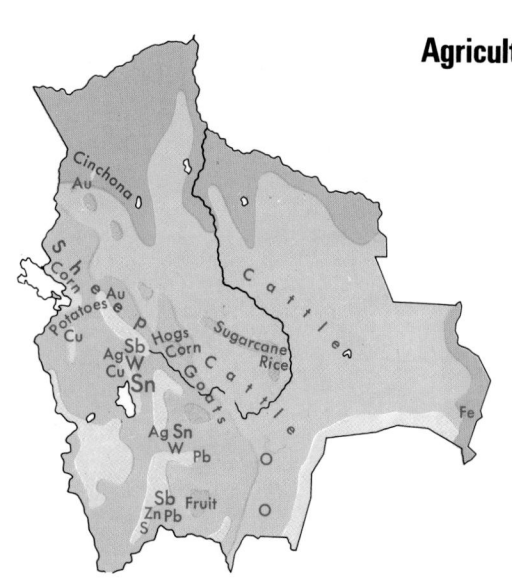

DOMINANT LAND USE

- Diversified Tropical Crops (chiefly plantation agriculture)
- Upland Cultivated Areas
- Upland Livestock Grazing, Limited Agriculture
- Extensive Livestock Ranching
- Forests
- Nonagricultural Land

MAJOR MINERAL OCCURRENCES

Ag	Silver	G	Natural Gas	Sb	Antimony
Au	Gold	O	Petroleum	Sn	Tin
Cu	Copper	Pb	Lead	W	Tungsten
Fe	Iron Ore	S	Sulfur	Zn	Zinc

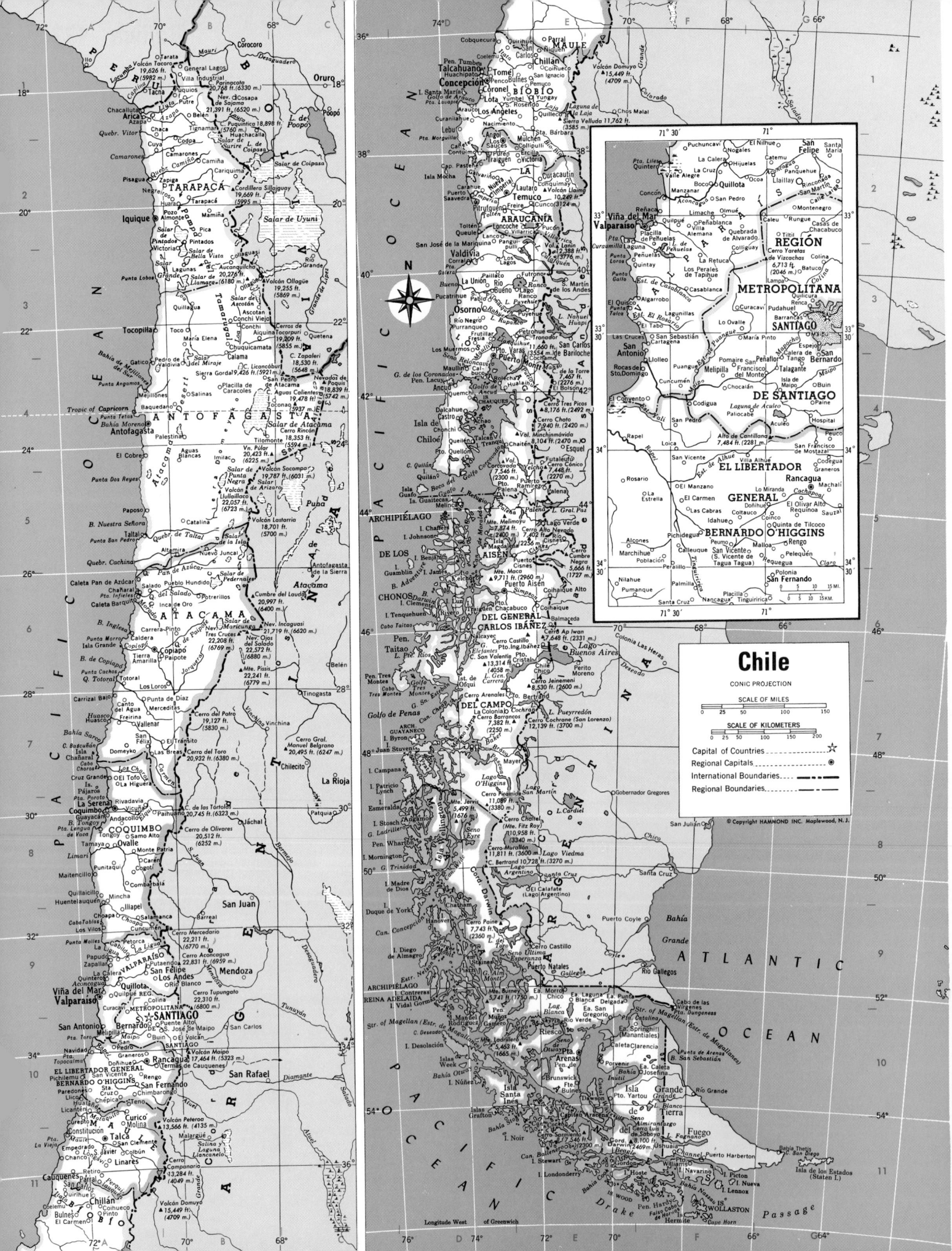
Chile
CONIC PROJECTION
SCALE OF MILES
0 25 50 100 150
SCALE OF KILOMETERS
0 25 50 100 150 200
Capital of Countries
Regional Capitals
International Boundaries
Regional Boundaries
© Copyright HAMMOND INC. Maplewood, N. J.
REGIÓN METROPOLITANA DE SANTIAGO
EL LIBERTADOR GENERAL BERNARDO O'HIGGINS
VALPARAÍSO
SANTIAGO
Viña del Mar
Valparaíso
San Antonio
Rancagua
San Fernando
Quillota
San Felipe
Los Andes
Melipilla
Talagante
Puente Alto
San Bernardo
Maipú
Buin
Paine
PERU
BOLIVIA
ARGENTINA
PACIFIC OCEAN
ATLANTIC OCEAN
TARAPACÁ
ANTOFAGASTA
ATACAMA
COQUIMBO
MAULE
BÍOBÍO
ARAUCANÍA
LOS LAGOS
AISÉN DEL GENERAL CARLOS IBÁÑEZ DEL CAMPO
MAGALLANES
Arica
Iquique
Tocopilla
Antofagasta
Tropic of Capricorn
Copiapó
La Serena
Coquimbo
Ovalle
Talca
Curicó
Chillán
Concepción
Talcahuano
Los Ángeles
Temuco
Valdivia
Osorno
Puerto Montt
Isla de Chiloé
Puerto Aisén
Coihaique
Punta Arenas
Puerto Natales
Isla Grande de Tierra del Fuego
Estrecho de Magallanes
Drake Passage
Cape Horn
Longitude West of Greenwich

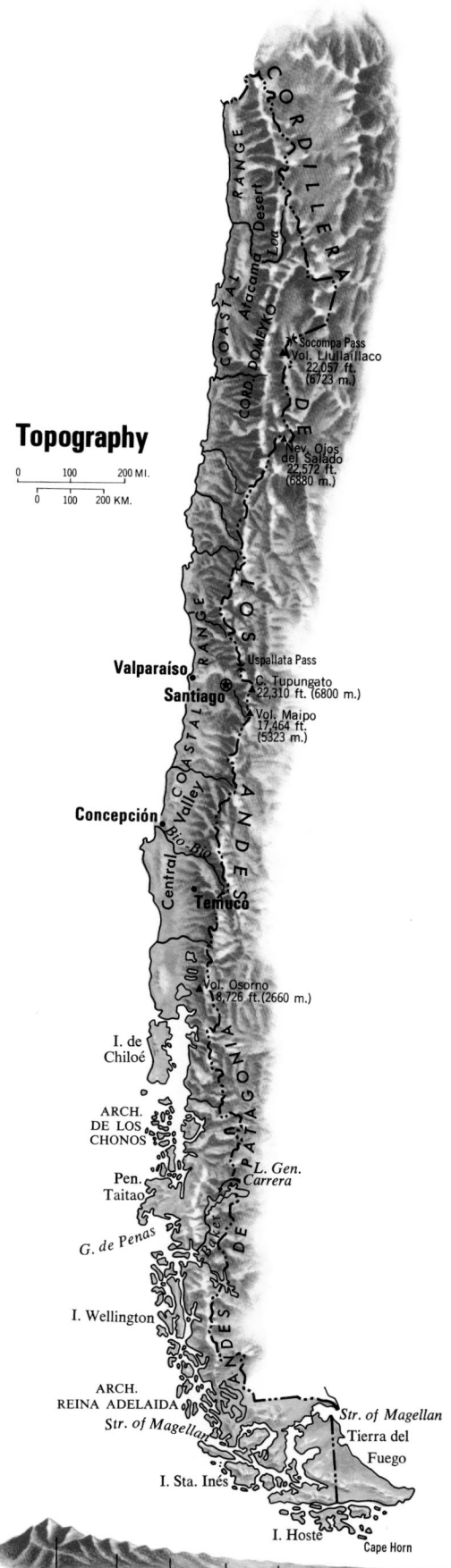

Topography

0   100   200 MI.

0   100   200 KM.

CORDILLERA
COASTAL RANGE
CORD. DOMEYKO
COASTAL RANGE
Atacama Desert
Atacama Desert
Loa

Socompa Pass
Vol. Llullaillaco
22,057 ft.
(6723 m.)

Nev. Ojos
del Salado
22,572 ft.
(6880 m.)

Valparaíso
Santiago

Uspallata Pass
C. Tupungato
22,310 ft. (6800 m.)
Vol. Maipo
17,464 ft.
(5323 m.)

Ascotán

Concepción
Central Valley
Bío-Bío

Temuco

COASTAL RANGE
ANDES

Vol. Osorno
8,726 ft. (2660 m.)

I. de
Chiloé

ARCH.
DE LOS
CHONOS

Pen.
Taitao

L. Gen.
Carrera

G. de Penas

I. Wellington

ANDES DE PATAGONIA

ARCH.
REINA ADELAIDA

Str. of Magellan
Str. of Magellan

Tierra del
Fuego

I. Sta. Inés

I. Hoste
Cape Horn

5,000 m.	2,000 m.	1,000 m.	500 m.	200 m.	100 m.	Sea	Below
16,404 ft.	6,562 ft.	3,281 ft.	1,640 ft.	656 ft.	328 ft.	Level	

AREA 292,257 sq. mi. (756,946 sq. km.)
POPULATION 12,961,000
CAPITAL Santiago
LARGEST CITY Santiago
HIGHEST POINT Ojos del Salado 22,572 ft.
(6,880 m.)
MONETARY UNIT Chilean peso
MAJOR LANGUAGE Spanish
MAJOR RELIGION Roman Catholicism

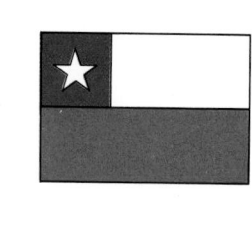

REGIONS

Aisén del General Carlos
  Ibáñez del Campo
  65,478 . . . . E6
Antofagasta 341,203 . . . . . B4
Atacama 183,071 . . . . B6
Bíoblo 1,516,552 . . . . E1
Coquimbo 419,178 . . . . . . A8
El Libertador General
  Bernardo O'Higgins
  584,989 . . . . A10
La Araucanía 692,924 . . . . E2
Los Lagos 843,430 . . . . . . D3
Magallanes 132,333 . . . . . E10
Maule 723,224 . . . . A11
Santiago, Región
  Metropolitana de (Santiago
  Metropolitan Region)
  4,294,938 . . . . A9
Tarapacá 273,427 . . . . B2
Valparaíso 1,204,693 . . . . A9

CITIES and TOWNS

Achao ○11,501 . . . . D4
Aguas Blancas ○203 . . . . . B4
Algarrobo ○3,941 . . . . F3
Ancud 11,900 . . . . D4
Andacollo 6,000 . . . . A8
Angol 42,670 . . . . D1
Antofagasta 125,100 . . . . . A4
Arauco 5,400 . . . . D1
Arica 87,700 . . . . A1
Ascotán B3
Barrancas ○184,241 . . . . . G3
Belén ○925 . . . . B1
Buin 11,800 . . . . G4
Bulnes 6,900 . . . . E1
Cabildo 5,800 . . . . A9
Calama 45,900 . . . . B3
Calbuco ○21,673 . . . . D4
Caldera ○3,268 . . . . A6
Calera de Tango ○6,198 . . . G4
Calle Larga ○7,172 . . . . . . G2
Cañete 7,900 . . . . D2
Carahue ○12,733 . . . . D2
Cartagena ○7,124 . . . . F3
Casablanca 5,500 . . . . F3
Casas de Chacabuco G2
Castro 11,200 . . . . D4
Catalina ○1,637 . . . . B5
Catemu ○8,728 . . . . G2
Cauquenes 20,200 . . . . . . A11
Cerro Castillo ○537 . . . . . . E9
Cerro Manantiales F10
Chaitén ○4,067 . . . . E4
Chañaral ○36,949 . . . . A6
Chanco ○12,433 . . . . A11
Chépica ○11,199 . . . . A10
Chillán 128,515 . . . . A11
Chimbarongo 5,300 . . . . . . A10
Chonchi ○8,911 . . . . D4
Chuquicamata 22,100 . . . . . B3
Cobquecura ○6,298 . . . . . . D1
Cochamó ○5,042 . . . . E3
Codegua ○6,757 . . . . G4
Codpa ○950 . . . . B1
Coelemu 5,400 . . . . D1
Coihaique 32,129 . . . . E6
Coihueco ○17,276 . . . . . . A11
Coinco ○4,942 . . . . G5
Colbún ○12,924 . . . . A11
Colina 7,400 . . . . G3
Collipulli 7,200 . . . . D2
Coltauco ○11,857 . . . . F5
Combarbalá ○17,332 . . . . . A8
Concepción 206,226 . . . . . D1
Constitución 11,500 . . . . . A11
Contulmo ○13,987 . . . . . . D2
Copiapó 45,200 . . . . B6
Coquimbo 73,953 . . . . A8
Coronel 37,300 . . . . D1
Corral ○5,533 . . . . D3
Cunco ○18,836 . . . . E2
Curacautín 9,800 . . . . E2
Curacaví 5,800 . . . . G3
Curanilahue 13,200 . . . . . . D1
Curepto ○13,020 . . . . A10
Curicó 41,300 . . . . A10
Dalcahue ○7,084 . . . . D4
Domeiko A7
Doñihue ○8,837 . . . . G4
El Carmen ○13,226 . . . . . . A11
El Monte 7,000 . . . . G3
El Quisco ○2,152 . . . . E3
El Tabo ○2,180 . . . . F3
El Tofo A7
Empedrado ○7,887 . . . . . . A11
Ercilla ○8,061 . . . . E2
Estancia Caleta
  Josefina ○1,042 . . . . . . F10
Estancia Morro Chico ○785 . E9
Estancia San Gregorio
  ○1,156 . . . . E9
Estancia Springhill
  (Cerro Manantiales) F10

Freire ○23,313 . . . . E2
Freirina ○5,523 . . . . A7
Fresia 15,359 . . . . D3
Frutillar ○12,721 . . . . D3
Futaleufú ○2,366 . . . . E4
Futrono ○7,109 . . . . E3
Galvarino ○9,495 . . . . D2
General Lagos ○810 . . . . . . B1
Graneros 8,900 . . . . G5
Guayacán A8
Hijuelas ○7,128 . . . . F2
Hualañé ○6,912 . . . . A10
Huara ○1,934 . . . . B2
Huasco ○4,971 . . . . A7
Illapel 12,200 . . . . A8
Inca de Oro 1,406 . . . . B6
Iquique 64,500 . . . . A2
Isla de Maipo ○12,903 . . . . G4
La Calera 24,600 . . . . F2
La Cruz ○8,907 . . . . F2
La Estrella ○3,707 . . . . . . F5
Lago Ranco ○12,767 . . . . . E3
Lagunas ○5,653 . . . . B3
La Higuera ○6,991 . . . . . . A7
La Ligua 7,500 . . . . A9
Lampa ○10,220 . . . . G3
Lanco 5,200 . . . . D2
Las Cabras ○12,119 . . . . . F5
La Serena 99,908 . . . . A8
La Unión 15,200 . . . . D3
Lautaro 11,900 . . . . E2
Lebu 12,500 . . . . D1
Licantén ○6,354 . . . . A10
Limache 15,200 . . . . F2
Linares 37,900 . . . . A11
Llay-Llay 9,700 . . . . G2
Loica F4
Loncoche ○17,539 . . . . D2
Longaví ○15,909 . . . . A11
Longuimay ○9,524 . . . . . . E2
Los Andes 23,500 . . . . B9
Los Ángeles 49,500 . . . . . . D1
Los Lagos ○14,934 . . . . . . D3
Los Muermos ○9,296 . . . . . D3
Los Sauces ○7,613 . . . . . . D1
Los Vilos ○10,453 . . . . . . A9
Lota 48,100 . . . . D1
Machalí 5,800 . . . . G5
Maipú ○117,872 . . . . G3
Malloa ○9,742 . . . . G5
Marchigüe ○4,451 . . . . . . F5
María Elena 5,900 . . . . B3
María Pinto ○5,980 . . . . . . G3
Maullín ○14,544 . . . . D4
Mejillones ○3,333 . . . . A4
Melipilla 23,900 . . . . F4
Mincha ○11,329 . . . . A8
Molina 9,400 . . . . A10
Monte Patria ○18,927 . . . . A8
Mulchén 13,700 . . . . E1
Nacimiento ○17,651 . . . . . D1
Nancagua ○11,076 . . . . . . F6
Navidad ○6,618 . . . . A10
Negreiros ○1,144 . . . . B2
Niquén ○13,640 . . . . E1
Nogales ○18,529 . . . . F2
Nueva Imperial 8,000 . . . . . D2
Olivar Alto ○5,414 . . . . . . G5
Ollagüe B3
Olmué ○8,804 . . . . F2
Osorno 68,800 . . . . D3
Ovalle 31,700 . . . . A8
Paihuano ○6,048 . . . . B8
Paillaco ○11,308 . . . . D3
Paine ○21,876 . . . . G4
Palena ○2,508 . . . . E4
Palmilla ○7,965 . . . . F6
Panguipulli 5,700 . . . . E2
Panquehue ○4,230 . . . . . . G2
Papudo ○2,594 . . . . A9
Paredones ○7,404 . . . . . . A10
Parral 17,000 . . . . A11
Pedro de Valdivia 6,200 . . . B4
Pemuco ○7,577 . . . . E1
Peñaflor 15,500 . . . . G4
Penco ○33,962 . . . . D1
Peñuelas F3
Petorca ○8,343 . . . . A9
Petrohué E3
Peumo ○11,308 . . . . F5
Pica ○1,487 . . . . B2
Pichidegua ○13,550 . . . . . F5
Pichilemu ○8,042 . . . . A10
Pinto ○8,687 . . . . A11
Pisagua ○1,880 . . . . A2
Pitrufquén 7,800 . . . . D2
Placilla ○6,441 . . . . F6
Porvenir ○4,000 . . . . E10
Potrerillos 5,800 . . . . B6
Pozo Almonte ○1,798 . . . . B2
Puchuncaví ○7,542 . . . . . . F2
Pucón 18,000 . . . . E2
Pudahuel G3
Pueblo Hundido 6,200 . . . . B6
Puente Alto 65,100 . . . . . . B10
Puerto Aisén 17,848 . . . . . E6
Puerto Cisnes ○2,800 . . . . E5

Puerto Ingeniero
  Ibáñez ○1,900 . . . . E6
Puerto Montt 119,059 . . . . E4
Puerto Natales 17,280 . . . . E9
Puerto Quellón ○7,734 . . . . D4
Puerto Varas 10,900 . . . . . E3
Puerto Williams ○949 . . . . F11
Pumanque ○3,137 . . . . . . F6
Punitaqui ○16,167 . . . . . . A8
Punta Arenas 2,140 . . . . . . E10
Purén ○11,604 . . . . D2
Purranque 5,900 . . . . D3
Putaendo ○12,806 . . . . . . A9
Putre ○855 . . . . B1
Puyehue E3
Queilén ○6,055 . . . . D4
Quemchi ○6,707 . . . . D4
Quilicura 8,100 . . . . G3
Quillagua B3
Quilleco ○16,043 . . . . E1
Quillota 36,500 . . . . F2
Quilpué 40,600 . . . . F2
Quinta de Tilcoco ○6,513 . . G5
Quintero 9,900 . . . . F2
Quirihue ○11,178 . . . . E1
Rancagua 140,589 . . . . . . G5
Renca ○67,168 . . . . G3
Rengo 12,400 . . . . G5
Requínoa ○10,730 . . . . . . G5
Retiro ○15,146 . . . . A11
Rinconada San Martín
  ○4,118 . . . . G2
Río Blanco B9
Río Bueno 9,600 . . . . D3
Río Negro 5,100 . . . . D3
Río Verde ○554 . . . . E10
Rocas de Santo
  Domingo ○4,114 . . . . . . F4
Rosario ○3,383 . . . . F5
Salamanca ○18,741 . . . . . A9
Samo Alto ○5,689 . . . . . . A8
San Antonio 46,700 . . . . . . F3
San Bernardo ○117,766 . . . G4
San Carlos 17,000 . . . . E1
San Clemente ○23,273 . . . A11
San Felipe 26,100 . . . . G2
San Fernando 23,600 . . . . . G5
San Francisco de
  Mostazal ○11,439 . . . . . G4
San Ignacio ○13,523 . . . . . E1
San Javier 10,800 . . . . A11
San José de
  Maipo ○9,601 . . . . B10
San Pablo ○7,978 . . . . D3
San Pedro ○8,255 . . . . . . F4
San Pedro de Atacama C4
San Rosendo ○14,337 . . . . E1
Santa Bárbara ○14,345 . . . E1
Santa Cruz 8,600 . . . . F6
Santa María ○8,162 . . . . . . G2
Santiago (cap.) 3,614,947 . . G3
Santiago *3,672,374 . . . . . G3
San Vicente F4
San Vicente (San Vicente
  de Tagua Tagua) ○28,333 F5
Sierra Gorda ○8,805 . . . . . B4
Talagante 16,500 . . . . G4
Talca 133,160 . . . . A11
Talcahuano 148,300 . . . . . D1
Taltal 6,400 . . . . A5
Tamaya A8
Tarapacá B2
Temuco 197,232 . . . . E2
Teno ○17,675 . . . . A10
Termas de Cauquenes B10
Tierra Amarilla ○7,899 . . . . A6
Tiltil ○9,198 . . . . G2
Toco ○8,734 . . . . B3
Toconao C4
Tocopilla 22,000 . . . . A3
Toltén ○16,265 . . . . D2
Tomé 29,600 . . . . D1
Traiguén 11,400 . . . . D2
Valdivia 115,536 . . . . D3
Vallenar 26,800 . . . . A7
Valparaíso 271,580 . . . . . . E2

Victoria 16,500 . . . . D2
Vicuña 5,100 . . . . A8
Villa Alemana 29,600 . . . . . F2
Villa Alhué ○5,078 . . . . . . G4
Villarrica 25,091 . . . . E2
Viña del Mar 281,361 . . . . F2
Yumbel ○21,858 . . . . E1
Yungay ○10,725 . . . . E1
Zapallar ○2,894 . . . . A9
Zapiga B2

OTHER FEATURES

Aconcagua (riv.) F2
Aculeo (lag.) G4
Adventure (bay) D5
Aguas Calientes, Cerro (mt.) C4
Almirantazgo (bay) F11
Almirante Montt (gulf) D9
Ancud (gulf) D4
Angamos (isl.) D8
Angamos (pt.) A4
Ap Iwan, Cerro (mt.) E6
Arauco (gulf) D1
Arenales, Cerro (mt.) D7
Atacama (des.) B4
Atacama, Salar de
  (salt dep.) C4
Aucanquilcha, Cerro (mt.) . . B3
Azapa, Quebrada (riv.) B1
Baker (riv.) D7
Ballenero (chan.) E11
Bascuñán (cape) A7
Beagle (chan.) E11
Bella Vista, Salar de
  (salt dep.) B3
Benjamín (isl.) D5
Bío-Bío (riv.) E2
Blanca (lag.) E10
Blanco (lake) F10
Bravo (riv.) D7
Brunswick (pen.) E10
Bueno (riv.) D3
Buenos Aires (lake) E6
Byron (isl.) D7
Cachapoal (riv.) G5
Cachina, Quebrada (riv.) . . . A5
Cachos (pt.) A6
Calafquén (lake) E3
Calbuco (vol.) E4
Camarones (riv.) A2
Camiña, Quebrada (riv.) . . . B2
Campana (isl.) D7
Campanario, Cerro (mt.) . . . A10
Capitán Aracena (isl.) E10
Carmen (riv.) B7
Castillo, Cerro (mt.) E6
Catalina (pt.) F10
Chaffers (isl.) D5
Chaltel, Cerro (mt.) E8
Chañaral (isl.) A7
Chatham (isl.) D9
Chauques (isls.) D4
Cheap (chan.) D7
Chiloé (isl.) 119,286. . . . . . D4
Choapa (riv.) A9
Chonos (arch.) D6
Choros (cape) A7
Cisnes (riv.) E5
Clarence (isl.) E10
Clemente (isl.) D6
Cochrane (lake) E7
Cochrane, Cerro (mt.) E7
Cockburn (chan.) E11
Concepción (chan.) D9
Cónico, Cerro (mt.) E4
Contreras (isl.) D9
Cook (bay) E11
Copiapó (bay) A6
Copiapó (riv.) A6
Corcovado (gulf) D4
Corcovado (vol.) D4
Coronados (gulf) D4
Curaumilla (pt.) E2
Darwin (bay) D6
Darwin, Cordillera (mts.) . . . D8
Darwin, Cordillera (mts.) . . . E11

(continued on following page)

Dawson (isl.) E10
Deseado (cape) D10
Desolación (isl.) D10
Diego de Almagro (isl.) . . D9
Domeyko, Cordillera (mts.) . B4
Dos Reyes (pt.) A5
Drake (passg.) E11
Dungeness (pt.) F10
Duque de York (isl.) C9
Elefantes (gulf) D6
Elqui (riv.) A8
Esmeralda (isl.) C8
Eyre (bay) D8
Fagnano (lake) F11
Fitz Roy (Chaltel) (mt.) . . . E8
Galera (pt.) D3
General Paz (lake) E5
Gordon (isl.) E11
Grafton (isl.) D10
Grande (isl.) A6
Grande (riv.) F10
Grande, Salar (salt dep.) . . B3
Grande de Tierra
  del Fuego (isl.) E11

Guafo (gulf) D5
Guafo (isl.) D5
Guaitecas (isls.) D5
Guamblin (isl.) D5
Guayaneco (arch.) D7
Hanover (isl.) D9
Hardy (pen.) F11
Hermite (isls.) F11
Horn (cape) F11
Hornos, Falso (cape) F11
Hoste (isl.) F11
Huasco (riv.) A7
Imperial (riv.) D2
Incaguasi, Nevada (mt.) . . C6
Infieles (pt.) A6
Inglesa (bay) A6
Inútil (bay) E10
James (isl.) D5
Johnson (isl.) D5
Jorge Montt (isl.) D9
Juan Stuven (isl.) D7
Lacuy (pen.) D4
Ladrillero (gulf) C8
Ladrillero (mt.) E10

Laja (riv.) E1
La Laja (lag.) E1
La Ligua (riv.) A9
Lanín (vol.) E2
Lastarria (vol.) B5
Lauca (riv.) B1
Lavapie (pt.) D1
La Vieja (pt.) A11
Lengua de Vaca (pt.) A8
Lennox (isl.) F11
Liles (pt.) F2
Limarí (riv.) A8
Llaima (vol.) E2
Llamara, Salar de (salt dep.) B3
Llanquihue (lake) E3
Llullaillaco (vol.) B5
Lluta (riv.) B1
Loa (riv.) B3
Lobos (pt.) A3
Londonderry (isl.) E11
Loros (pt.) E3
Luz (isl.) D6
Macá (mt.) D5
Madre de Dios (isl.) D8

Agriculture, Industry and Resources

DOMINANT LAND USE

Cereals, Livestock

Mediterranean Agriculture (cereals, fruit, livestock)

Pasture Livestock

Extensive Livestock Ranching

Limited Seasonal Grazing

Forests

Nonagricultural Land

MAJOR MINERAL OCCURRENCES

Ag Silver
Au Gold
C   Coal
Cu Copper
Fe Iron Ore
G   Natural Gas
Gp Gypsum

Hg Mercury
Id Iodine
Mn Manganese
Mo Molybdenum
N   Nitrates
Na Salt
O   Petroleum
S   Sulfur

⚡ Water Power   ▨ Major Industrial Areas

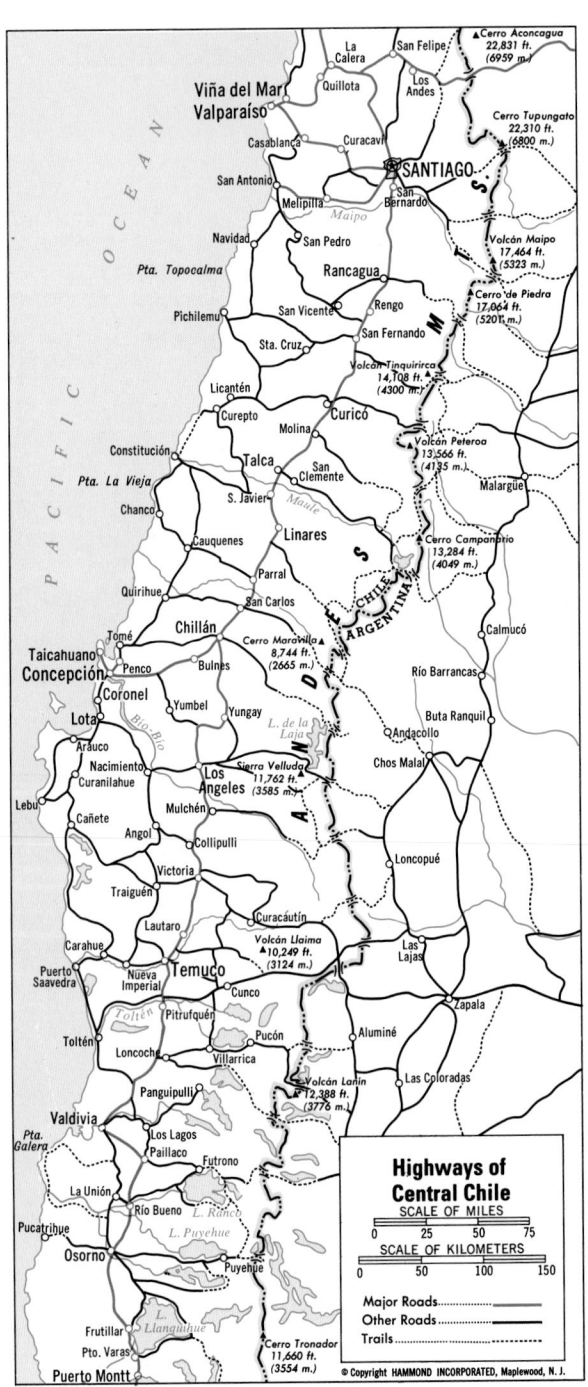

Highways of Central Chile

SCALE OF MILES
0   25   50   75

SCALE OF KILOMETERS
0   50   100   150

Major Roads . . . .
Other Roads . . . .
Trails . . . .

© Copyright HAMMOND INCORPORATED, Maplewood, N.J.

Magallanes (Magellan)
  (str.) D10
Magdalena (isl.) D5
Magellan (str.) D10
Maipo (riv.) F4
Maipú (vol.) B10
Manso (riv.) E4
Manuel Rodríguez (isl.) . . D10
Mapocho (riv.) G3
Mataquito (riv.) A10
Maule (riv.) A11
Maullín (riv.) D3
Mejillones del Sur (bay) . . A4
Melchor (isl.) D6
Melimoyu (mt.) D5
Merino Jarpa (isl.) D7
Minchinmávida (mt.) E4
Miraje, Salar del (salt dep.) B3
Mocha (isl.) B2
Molles (pt.) A9
Morado, Quebrado (riv.) . . A6
Moraleda (chan.) D5
Moreno (bay) A4
Mornington (isl.) D8
Morro (pt.) A6
Muñoz Gamero (pen.) . . . D10
Murallón, Cerro (mt.) D8
Naicayec (isl.) D6
Nassau (bay) F11
Navarino (isl.) F11
Nelson (str.) D9
Nuestra Señora (bay) A5
Nueva (isl.) F11
Núñez (isl.) D10
O'Higgins (lake) D7
Ojos del Salado,
  Nevado (mt.) B6
Otway (bay) D10
Otway (sound) E10
Oyahue (vol.) C3
Paine, Cerro (mt.) D9
Pájaros (isls.) A7
Palena (lake) E5
Palena (riv.) D5
Pan de Azúcar,
  Quebrado (riv.) B5
Parinacota, Cerro (mt.) . . . B1
Pascua (riv.) D7
Patricio Lynch (isl.) D7
Peñas (gulf) D7
Perquilauquén (riv.) A11
Piazzl (isl.) D9
Picton (isl.) F11
Pilmaiquén (riv.) D3
Pintados, Salar de
  (salt dep.) B2
Poroto (pt.) A7
Potro, Cerro del (mt.) B7
Prat (isl.) D7
Presidente Ríos (lake) . . . D6
Puangue, Estero de (riv.) . . F3
Puelo (riv.) E4
Púlar, Cerro (mt.) B4
Puquintica, Cerro (mt.) . . . B1
Puyehue (lake) E3
Quilán (cape) D4
Ranco (lake) E3
Rapel (riv.) F4
Refugio (isl.) D5
Reina Adelaida (arch.) . . . D9
Reloncaví (bay) D4

Riesco (isl.) E10
Rincón, Cerro (mt.) C4
Rivero (isl.) D6
Rupanco (lake) D3
San Esteban (gulf) D7
San Lorenzo, Cerro
  (Cochrane) (mt.) E7
San Martín (lake) E7
San Pedro (pt.) A5
Santa Inés (isl.) D10
Santa María (isl.) D1
San Valentín, Cerro (mt.) . . D6
Sarco (bay) A7
Sarmiento, Cerro (mt.) . . . E11
Sillajiguay, Cordillera (range) B2
Simpson (riv.) E6
Skyring (lake) E10
Socompa (vol.) B4
Staines (pen.) D9
Stewart (isl.) E11
Stokes (bay) D10
Stosch (isl.) C8
Surire, Salar de (salt dep.) . B1
Tablas (cape) A9
Tacora (vol.) B1
Taitao (cape) D6
Taitao (pen.) D6
Talca (pt.) E3
Taltal, Quebrada de (riv.) . . B5
Tamarugal, Pampa del
  (plain) B3
Tenquehuen (isl.) D6
Tetas (pt.) A4
Tierra del Fuego,
  Grande de (isl.) E11
Tinguiririca (riv.) F5
Toltén (riv.) D2
Tongoy (bay) A8
Topocalma (pt.) A10
Toro (lake) D9
Toro, Cerro del (mt.) B7
Toro (pt.) A10
Tórtolas, Cerro de las (mt.) . B8
Totoral, Quebrada (riv.) . . . A7
Traiguén (isl.) D6
Tranqui (isl.) D4
Tres Cruces, Nevada (mt.) . B6
Tres Montes (cape) C7
Tres Montes (gulf) C6
Tres Montes (pen.) C6
Trinidad (gulf) D8
Tronador, Cerro (mt.) E3
Tumbes (pt.) D1
Tupungato, Cerro (mt.) . . . B9
Última Esperanza (sound) . E9
Vidal Gormaz (isl.) D9
Villarrica (lake) E2
Vitor, Quebrado (riv.) A1
Week (isls.) D10
Wellington (isl.) D8
Wharton (pen.) D8
Whiteside (chan.) E10
Wollaston (isl.) F11
Wood (isls.) E11
Yelcho (lake) E4
Zapaleri, Cerro (mt.) C4

*City and suburbs.
○ Population of commune.

PROVINCES

Buenos Aires 10,796,036 ...D4
Catamarca 206,204 ...C2
Chaco 692,410 ...D2
Chubut 262,196 ...C5
Córdoba 2,407,135 ...D3
Corrientes 657,716 ...E2
Distrito Federal 2,908,001 ...H7
Entre Ríos 902,241 ...E3
Formosa 292,479 ...D1
Jujuy 408,514 ...C1
La Pampa 207,132 ...C4
La Rioja 163,342 ...C2
Mendoza 1,187,305 ...C4
Misiones 579,579 ...F2
Neuquén 241,904 ...C4
Río Negro 383,896 ...C5
Salta 662,369 ...D1
San Juan 469,973 ...C3
San Luis 212,837 ...C3
Santa Cruz 114,479 ...C6
Santa Fe 2,457,188 ...D3
Santiago del Estero 652,318 ...D2
Tierra del Fuego, Antártida, e Islas del Atlántico Sur 29,451 ...C7
Tucumán 968,066 ...C2

CITIES and TOWNS

Abra Pampa 2,929 ...C1
Adolfo Alsina 7,707 ...D4
Aguaray 4,802 ...D1
Aguilares 20,286 ...C2
Aimogasta 4,640 ...C2
Alberti 6,440 ...G7
Alcorta 5,818 ...F6
Algarrobo del Águila ...C4
Allen 14,041 ...C4
Alpachiri 1,657 ...D4
Alta Gracia 30,628 ...D3
Alumine 1,560 ...B4
Alvear 5,419 ...E2
Ameghino 2,775 ...D3
Añatuya 15,025 ...D2
Andalgalá 6,853 ...C2
Antofagasta de la Sierra ...C2
Apóstoles 11,252 ...E2
Arrecifes 17,719 ...F7
Arroyo Seco 12,886 ...F6
Ascensión 3,031 ...F7
Avellaneda 330,654 ...G7
Ayacucho 12,363 ...E4
Azul 43,582 ...E4
Bahía Blanca 220,765 ...D4
Bahía Bustamante ...C6
Bahía Thetis ...C7
Balcarce 28,985 ...E4
Balnearia 4,531 ...D3
Baradero 20,103 ...G6
Barrancas 3,602 ...F6
Barranqueras ...E2
Barreal 2,739 ...C3
Basavilbaso 7,657 ...G6
Belén 7,411 ...C2

Bella Vista, Corrientes 14,229 ...E2
Bella Vista, Tucumán 9,177 ...D2
Bell Ville 26,559 ...D3
Bolívar 16,382 ...D4
Bovril 4,735 ...G5
Bragado 27,101 ...F7
Buenos Aires (cap.) 2,908,001 ...H7
Buenos Aires *9,927,404 ...H7
Cafayate 5,048 ...C2
Calafate ...B7
Calchaquí 5,958 ...F5
Caleta Olivia 20,141 ...C6
Camarones ...C5
Campana 51,498 ...G6
Cañada de Gómez 24,706 ...F6
Canals 6,627 ...D3
Cañuelas 14,831 ...G7
Carcaraña 11,121 ...F6
Carlos Casares 13,286 ...F7
Carlos Tejedor 4,421 ...D4
Carmen de Areco 7,882 ...F7
Carmen de Patagones 13,981 ...C6
Casilda 23,492 ...F6
Castelli 4,507 ...H7
Catamarca 88,432 ...C2
Caucete 14,512 ...C3
Ceres 10,743 ...D2
Chabás 5,156 ...F6
Chacabuco 26,492 ...F7
Chajarí 15,242 ...G5

Chamical 6,333 ...C3
Charadai 1,078 ...D2
Charata 13,070 ...D2
Chascomús 21,864 ...H7
Chepes 4,775 ...C3
Chicoana 1,844 ...C2
Chilecito 14,010 ...C2
Chivilcoy 43,779 ...F7
Choele-Choel 6,191 ...C4
Chos-Malal 4,823 ...C4
Cinco Saltos 15,094 ...C4
Cipolletti 40,123 ...C4
Clorinda 21,008 ...E2
Colón, Buenos Aires 16,070 ...F6
Colón, Entre Ríos 11,648 ...G6
Colonia Las Heras 3,176 ...C6
Comandante Fontana 4,468 ...D2
Comandante Luis Piedrabuena 2,492 ...C6
Comodoro Rivadavia 96,865 ...C6
Concepción 29,355 ...C2
Concepción de la Sierra 2,778 ...E2
Concepción del Uruguay 46,065 ...G6
Concordia 93,618 ...G5
Constanza 1,313 ...G6
Córdoba 982,018 ...D3
Coronda 11,554 ...F6
Coronel Brandsen 10,484 ...H7
Coronel Dorrego 10,661 ...D4
Coronel Pringles 16,592 ...D4
Coronel Suárez 16,359 ...D4

AREA 1,072,070 sq. mi. (2,776,661 sq. km.)
POPULATION 31,929,000
CAPITAL Buenos Aires
LARGEST CITY Buenos Aires
HIGHEST POINT Cerro Aconcagua 22,831 ft. (6,959 m.)
MONETARY UNIT austral
MAJOR LANGUAGE Spanish
MAJOR RELIGION Roman Catholicism

Agriculture, Industry and Resources

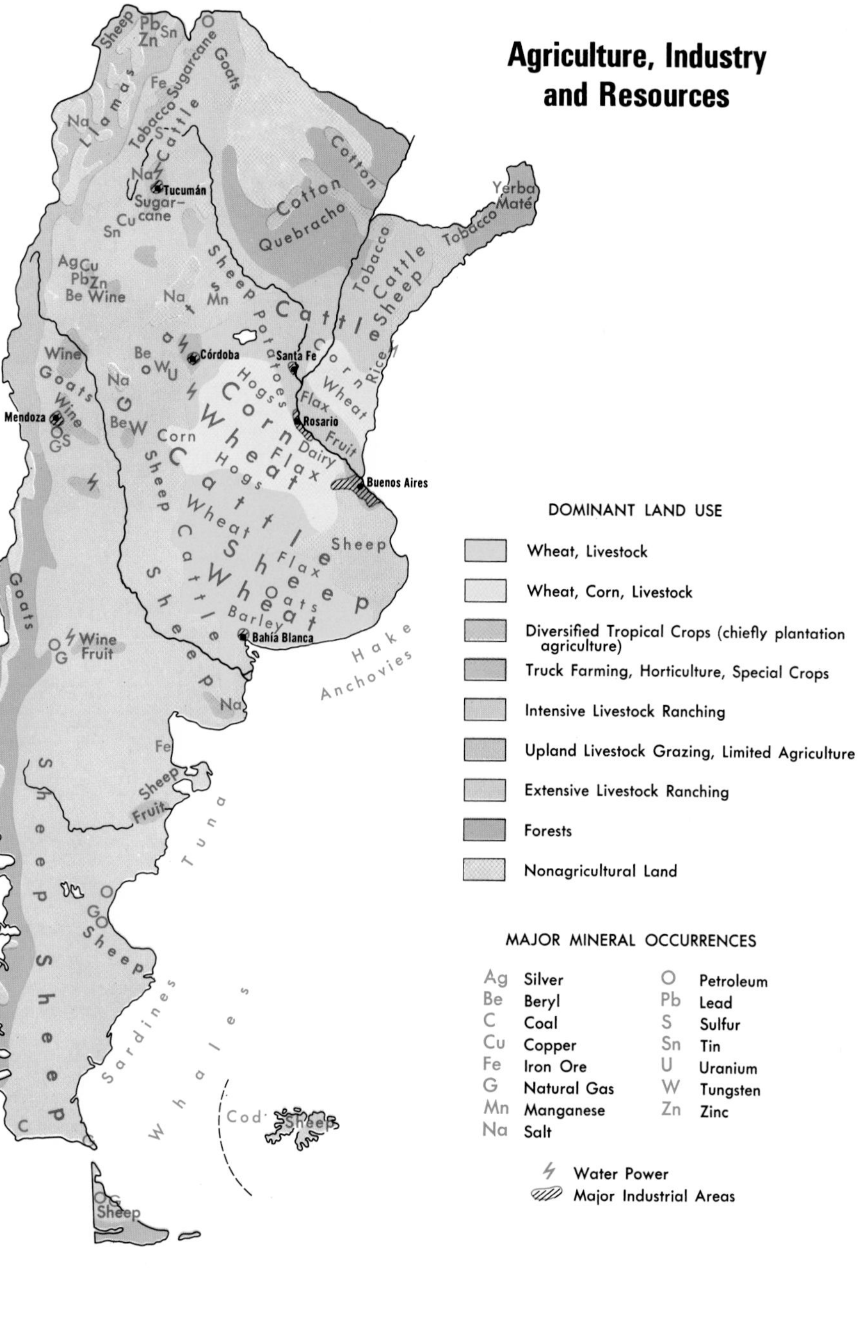

DOMINANT LAND USE

Wheat, Livestock

Wheat, Corn, Livestock

Diversified Tropical Crops (chiefly plantation agriculture)

Truck Farming, Horticulture, Special Crops

Intensive Livestock Ranching

Upland Livestock Grazing, Limited Agriculture

Extensive Livestock Ranching

Forests

Nonagricultural Land

MAJOR MINERAL OCCURRENCES

Ag Silver
Be Beryl
C Coal
Cu Copper
Fe Iron Ore
G Natural Gas
Mn Manganese
Na Salt
O Petroleum
Pb Lead
S Sulfur
Sn Tin
U Uranium
W Tungsten
Zn Zinc

⚡ Water Power
▨ Major Industrial Areas

Coronel Vidal 4,774 ...E4
Corral de Bustos 8,613 ...D3
Corrientes 179,590 ...E2
Cosquín 13,929 ...D3
Crespo 10,668 ...F6
Cruz del Eje 23,473 ...C3
Curuzú Cuatiá 24,955 ...G5
Cutral-Có 25,870 ...C4
Daireaux 8,150 ...D4
Deán Funes 16,306 ...D3
Diamante 13,464 ...F6
Dolavon 1,778 ...C5
Dolores 19,307 ...E4
Eduardo Castex 5,397 ...D4
El Bolsón 5,001 ...B5
Eldorado 22,821 ...F2
El Maitén 2,350 ...B5
Elortondo 4,939 ...F6
El Quebrachal 2,202 ...D2
Embarcación 9,016 ...D1
Empedrado 4,732 ...E2
Escobar 70,829 ...G7
Esperanza 22,838 ...F5
Esquel 17,228 ...B5
Esquina 10,380 ...G5
Famatina 1,237 ...C2
Federación 7,259 ...G5
Felipe Yofré 1,140 ...G4
Fernández 6,062 ...D2
Firmat 13,588 ...F6
Firmat 1,201 ...F5
Formosa 95,067 ...E2
Fortín Olmos 1,101 ...F4
Frías 20,901 ...D2
Gaiman 2,651 ...C5
Gálvez 14,711 ...F6
General Acha 7,647 ...C4
General Alvear, Buenos Aires 5,481 ...F7
General Alvear, Mendoza 21,250 ...C3
General Arenales 3,332 ...F7
General Belgrano 10,909 ...G7
General Conesa 3,566 ...C5
General Galarza 3,057 ...G6
General Güemes 15,534 ...D1
General José de San Martín 16,296 ...E2
General Juan Madariaga 13,409 ...E4
General La Madrid 5,154 ...D4
General Las Heras 6,005 ...G7
General Paz 5,127 ...H7
General Pico 30,180 ...D4
General Ramírez 5,393 ...F6
General Roca 38,296 ...C4
General San Martín, Buenos Aires 384,306 ...G7
General San Martín, La Pampa 2,168 ...D4
General Viamonte 10,112 ...F7
General Villegas 11,307 ...D4
Gobernador Crespo 2,972 ...F5
Godoy Cruz 141,553 ...C3
Goya 47,357 ...G4
Gualeguay 24,883 ...G6
Gualeguaychú 51,057 ...G6
Guandacol 1,351 ...C2
Hasenkamp 2,804 ...F5
Helvecia 3,927 ...F5
Hernandarias 3,002 ...F5
Hernando 8,619 ...D3
Huinca Renancó 7,187 ...D3
Humahuaca 3,963 ...C1
Humberto (Humberto Primo) 4,163 ...F5
Ibarreta 5,262 ...D2
Ibicuy 3,082 ...G6
Ingeniero Huergo 3,385 ...C4
Ingeniero Jacobacci 4,045 ...C5
Ingeniero Luiggi 3,002 ...D4
Intendente Alvear 3,640 ...D4
Itatí 3,269 ...E2

Ituzaingó 8,687 ...E2
Jáchal 8,832 ...C3
Jesús María 17,594 ...D3
Joaquín V. González 6,054 ...D2
Juárez 11,798 ...E4
Jujuy 124,487 ...C1
Junín 62,080 ...F7
Junín de los Andes 5,638 ...B4
La Banda 46,994 ...D2
Laboulaye 16,883 ...D3
La Carlota 8,614 ...D3
La Cruz 4,132 ...E2
La Cumbre 6,110 ...C3
La Falda 12,502 ...D3
Laguna Paiva 11,129 ...F5
Lanús 465,891 ...H7
La Paz, Entre Ríos 14,920 ...G5
La Paz, Mendoza 4,604 ...C3
La Plata 560,341 ...H7
Laprida 6,495 ...D4
La Quiaca 8,289 ...C1
La Rioja 66,826 ...C2
Larroque 3,147 ...F5
Las Flores 18,287 ...E4
Las Lomitas 4,047 ...D1
Las Palmas 5,061 ...E2
Las Parejas 7,430 ...F6
Las Rosas 9,725 ...F6
Las Varillas 10,605 ...D3
La Toma 4,325 ...C3
Lincoln 19,009 ...F7
Loberia 8,898 ...E4
Lobos 20,798 ...G7
Lomas de Zamora 508,620 ...G7
Lucas González 3,015 ...G6
Luján 38,919 ...G7
Lules 11,391 ...C2
Maciel 4,066 ...F6
Magdalena 7,135 ...H7
Maipú 8,279 ...E4
Malabrigo 3,294 ...F4
Malargüe 9,496 ...C4
Maquinchao 1,299 ...C5
Marcos Juárez 19,827 ...D3
Mar del Plata 407,024 ...E4
Máximo Paz 3,216 ...F6
Mburucuyá 3,044 ...E2
Médanos 4,511 ...D4
Mendoza 596,796 ...C3
Mercedes, Buenos Aires 46,581 ...G7
Mercedes, Corrientes 20,603 ...G4
Mercedes, San Luis 50,856 ...C3
Mercedes, San Luis 50,856 ...C3
Mercedes 293,059 ...G7
Metán 18,928 ...D2
Miramar 15,473 ...E4
Monte Caseros 18,247 ...G5
Monte Quemado 4,707 ...D2
Monteros 15,832 ...C2
Morón 596,769 ...G7
Morteros 11,456 ...D3
Navarro 7,176 ...G7
Necochea 50,939 ...E4
Neuquén 90,037 ...C4
Nogoyá 15,862 ...F6
Norquincó ...B5
Nueve de Julio 26,608 ...F7
Oberá 27,311 ...F2
Olavarría 63,686 ...D3
Oliva 9,231 ...D3
Palo Santo 3,088 ...E1
Paraná 159,581 ...F5
Paso de Los Libres 24,112 ...E2
Pedro Luro 3,142 ...D4
Pehuajó 25,613 ...D4
Pellegrini 3,940 ...D4
Pergamino 68,989 ...F6
Pico Truncado 9,626 ...C6
Pigüé 10,793 ...D4
Pilar 3,805 ...F5
Pirané 9,039 ...D2
Plaza Huincul 7,988 ...B4

(continued on following page)

Posadas 139,941 .... E2
Presidencia de
  la Plaza 4,904 .... D2
Presidencia Roque
  Sáenz Peña 49,261 .... D2
Puán 4,148 .... D4
Puerto Deseado 4,017 .... D6
Puerto Harberton C7
Puerto Iguazú 10,250 .... F2
Puerto Madryn 20,709 .... C5
Puerto Rico 8,195 .... D1
Punta Alta 54,375 .... D4
Quequén 11,737 .... E4
Quimili 8,972 .... D2
Quines 3,352 .... C3
Quitilipi 9,937 .... D2
Rafaela 53,132 .... F5
Ramallo 8,248 .... F6
Rauch 8,348 .... E4
Rawson 12,981 .... D5
Reconquista 32,442 .... F4
Recreo 3,502 .... C2
Resistencia 218,438 .... E2
Rinconada C1
Río Colorado 7,361 .... D4
Río Cuarto 110,148 .... D3
Río Gallegos 43,479 .... C7
Río Grande 13,271 .... C7
Río Segundo 12,839 .... D3
Río Tercero 34,735 .... D3
Rivadavia 10,953 .... C3
Rojas 14,247 .... F7
Romang 4,077 .... F4
Roque Pérez 5,434 .... G7
Rosario 954,606 .... F6
Rosario de la
  Frontera 13,531 .... D2
Rosario de Lerma 9,540 .... C1
Rosario del Tala 9,552 .... G6
Rufino 15,306 .... D3
Saladas 7,345 .... E2
Saladillo 14,806 .... G7
Salliqueló 5,479 .... D4
Salta 260,323 .... C1
Salto 18,462 .... F7
San Antonio de
  Areco 12,932 .... G7
San Antonio de
  los Cobres 2,357 .... C1
San Antonio Oeste 8,690 .... C5
San Carlos 7,613 .... F6
San Carlos de
  Bariloche 48,222 .... B5
San Cayetano 5,960 .... E4

San Cristóbal 13,345 .... F5
San Fernando 128,939 .... G7
San Francisco, Córdoba
  58,616 .... D3
San Francisco, San Luis
  2,448 .... C3
San Genaro 2,977 .... F6
San Ignacio 3,437 .... E2
San Jaime de la
  Frontera 2,811 .... G5
San José de Feliciano 4,986 .. G5
San Juan 290,479 .... C3
San Julián 4,278 .... C7
San Justo 14,135 .... F5
San Luis 70,632 .... C3
San Martín 29,746 .... C3
San Martín de
  los Andes 9,507 .... C5
San Miguel del Monte 8,414 G7
San Miguel de
  Tucumán 496,914 .... D2
San Nicolás 96,313 .... F6
San Pedro, Buenos Aires
  27,058 .... F6
San Pedro, Jujuy 36,907 .... D1
San Rafael 70,477 .... C3
San Ramón de la
  Nva. Orán 32,955 .... D1
San Salvador 4,342 .... G5
San Sebastián C7
Santa Cruz 2,353 .... C7
Santa Elena 14,655 .... F5
Santa Lucía 4,452 .... E2
Santa María 5,380 .... C2
Santa Rosa, Córdoba 4,306 .. D3
Santa Rosa, La Pampa
  51,689 .... C4
Santa Victoria D1
Santa Rosa, San Luis 2,878 .. C3
Santiago del Estero 148,357 D2
Santo Tomé, Corrientes
  14,352 .... F2
Santo Tomé, Santa Fe
  35,363 .... F5
Sarmiento 6,313 .... B6
Sauce 4,677 .... G5
Sierra Grande 9,585 .... C5
Suipacha 4,505 .... G7
Sunchales 12,493 .... F5
Suncho Corral 3,837 .... D2

Tapalqué 5,356 .... E4
Tartagal 31,367 .... D1
Tigre 199,366 .... G7
Tinogasta 7,829 .... C2
Toay 3,617 .... D4
Tornquist 4,696 .... D4
Tostado 10,492 .... D2
Trelew 52,073 .... D5
Trenque Lauquen 22,504 .... D4
Tres Arroyos 42,118 .... D4
Trevelin 2,935 .... B5
Tunuyán 14,665 .... C3
Urdinarrain 5,472 .... G6
Ushuaia 10,988 .... C7
Valcheta 2,994 .... C5
Vedia 6,273 .... F7
Veinticinco de Mayo 18,936 .. F7
Venado Tuerto 46,775 .... D3
Vera 13,555 .... E2
Verónica 5,657 .... H7
Viale 5,635 .... F5
Vicente López 289,815 .... G7
Victoria 18,883 .... F6
Victorica 3,895 .... C4
Viedma 24,338 .... D5
Vicuña Mackenna 5,665 .... D3
Villa Ángela 25,586 .... D2
Villa Atuel 2,774 .... C3
Villa Cañas 7,303 .... F6
Villa Constitución 36,157 .... F6
Villa del Rosario 10,133 .... D3
Villa Dolores 21,508 .... C3
Villa Elisa 4,106 .... G6
Villa Federal 9,222 .... G5
Villaguay 18,699 .... G5
Villa Guillermina 2,971 .... D2
Villa Huidobro 4,154 .... D3
Villa María 67,490 .... D3
Villa María Grande 4,517 .... F5
Villa Nueva 4,604 .... C3
Villa Ocampo 9,162 .... D2
Villa Regina 14,017 .... C4
Villa San José 6,800 .... G6
Villa San Martín 6,237 .... D2
Vinchina 1,070 .... C2
Zapala 18,293 .... B4
Zárate 65,504 .... G6
Zavalla 3,800 .... F6

OTHER FEATURES

Aconcagua, Cerro (mt.) C3
Andes, Cordillera
  de los (mts.) C2

Argentino (lake) B7
Arizaro, Salar de (salt dep.) .. C2
Arrecifes (riv.) G6
Atacama, Puna de (reg.) C2
Atuel (riv.) C4
Bermejo (riv.) E2
Blanca (bay) D4
Brazo Sur, Pilcomayo (riv.) .. E1
Buenos Aires (lake) B6
Campanario, Cerro (mt.) C4
Chaco Austral (reg.) D2
Chaco Central (reg.) D1
Chico (riv.) C6
Chico (riv.) C6
Chubut (riv.) C5
Colhué Huapi (lake) C6
Colorado (riv.) D4
Cónico, Cerro (mt.) B5
Corrientes (riv.) E2
Coyle (riv.) B7
Delgada (pt.) D5
Desaguadero (riv.) C3
Deseado (riv.) C6
Diamante (riv.) C3
Domuyo (vol.) B4
Dos Bahías (cape) D5
Dulce (riv.) D2
Dungeness (pt.) C7
El Chocón (res.) C4
Estados, Los (isl.) D7
Fagnano (lake) C7
Famatina, Sierra de (mts.) .. C2
Feliciano (riv.) G5
Gallegos (riv.) B7
General Manuel Belgrano,
  Cerro (mt.) C2
Gran Chaco (reg.) D1
Grande (bay) C7
Grande (falls) E3
Grande (falls) F5
Grande de Tierra del
  Fuego (isl.) C7
Gualeguay (riv.) G5
Gualeguaychú (riv.) G5
Iguazú (falls) F2
Iguazú Nat'l Park E2
Lanín (vol.) B4
Lanín Nat'l Park B4
Lechiguanas (isls.) G6
Lennox (isl.) C8
Limay (riv.) C4
Llancanelo, Salina y
  Laguna (salt lake) C4
Llullaillaco (vol.) C1
Magallanes (Magellan) (str.) .. C7

Maipo (vol.) C3
Mar Chiquita (lake) D3
Mendoza (riv.) C3
Mercedario, Cerro (mt.) B3
Mogotes (pt.) E4
Montemayor (plat.) C5
Nahuel Huapi (lake) B5
Nahuel Huapi Nat'l Park B5
Negro (riv.) D4
Neuquén (riv.) C4
Ninfas (pt.) D5
Norte (pt.) C3
Nuevo (gulf) D5
Ojos del Salado, Cerro (mt.) .. C2
Pampa de las Tres
  Hermanas (plain) C4
Pampas (plain) D4
Paraná (riv.) E2
Patagonia (reg.) C5
Peteroa (vol.) B4
Pilcomayo (riv.) E1
Pissis (mt.) C2
Plata, Río de la (est.) E4
Pueyrredón (lake) B6
Puna de Atacama (reg.) C2
Quinto (riv.) D3
Rincón, Cerro (mt.) C1
Saladillo (riv.) D2
Salado (riv.) C4
Salado (riv.) H7
Salado del Norte (riv.) D2
Salí (riv.) D2
Salto (riv.) F7
Samborombón (bay) E4
San Antonio (cape) E4
San Diego (cape) C7
San Jorge (gulf) C6
San Juan (riv.) C3
San Lorenzo, Cerro (mt.) B6
San Martín (lake) B6
San Matías (gulf) D5
Santa Cruz (riv.) B7

Senguerr (riv.) B6
Staten (Los Estados) (isl.) .. D7
Tarija (riv.) D1
Tercero (riv.) D3
Teuco (riv.) D1
Tierra del Fuego,
  Grande de (isl.) C7
Toro, Cerro del (mt.) B2
Tres Puntas (cape) D6
Trinidad (isl.) D4
Tronador (mt.) B5
Tunuyán (riv.) C3
Tupungato, Cerro (mt.) B3
Uruguay (riv.) E3
Valdés (pen.) D5
Viedma (lake) B6
Zapaleri, Cerro (mt.) C1

FALKLAND ISLANDS

CITIES and TOWNS

Stanley (cap.) 1,050 .... E7

OTHER FEATURES

Adventure (sound) E7
Choiseul (sound) E7
East Falkland (isl.) 1,491 .... D7
Falkland (isls.) D7
Falkland (sound) E7
George (isl.) E7
Jason (isls.) E7
Lively (isl.) E7
Malvinas (Falkland) (isls.) .. D7
Pebble (isl.) E7
Saunders (isl.) D7
Weddel (isl.) D7
West Falkland (isl.) 322 .... D7

*City and suburbs.

Topography

0   150   300 MI.

0   150   300 KM.

5,000 m. / 16,404 ft. | 2,000 m. / 6,562 ft. | 1,000 m. / 3,281 ft. | 500 m. / 1,640 ft. | 200 m. / 656 ft. | 100 m. / 328 ft. | Sea Level | Below

Highways of Central Argentina

MILES
0   25   50   75

KILOMETRES
0   50   100   150

Major Roads _____
Other Roads _____

© HAMMOND INCORPORATED, Maplewood, N.J.

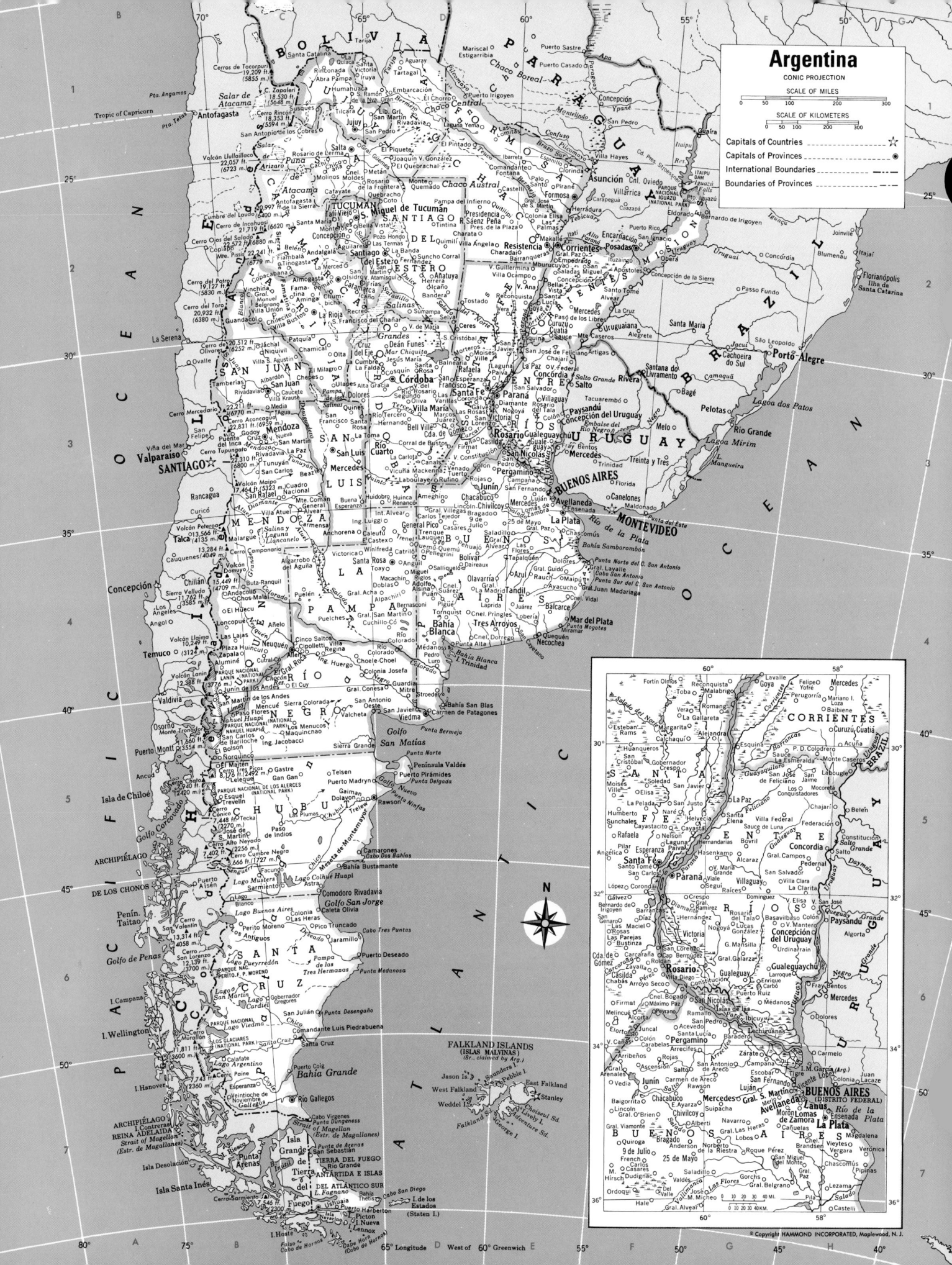

Argentina

CONIC PROJECTION

SCALE OF MILES

SCALE OF KILOMETERS

Capitals of Countries	------------	☆
Capitals of Provinces	------------	◉
International Boundaries	------------	— ·· —
Boundaries of Provinces	------------	— · —

® Copyright HAMMOND INCORPORATED, Maplewood, N. J.

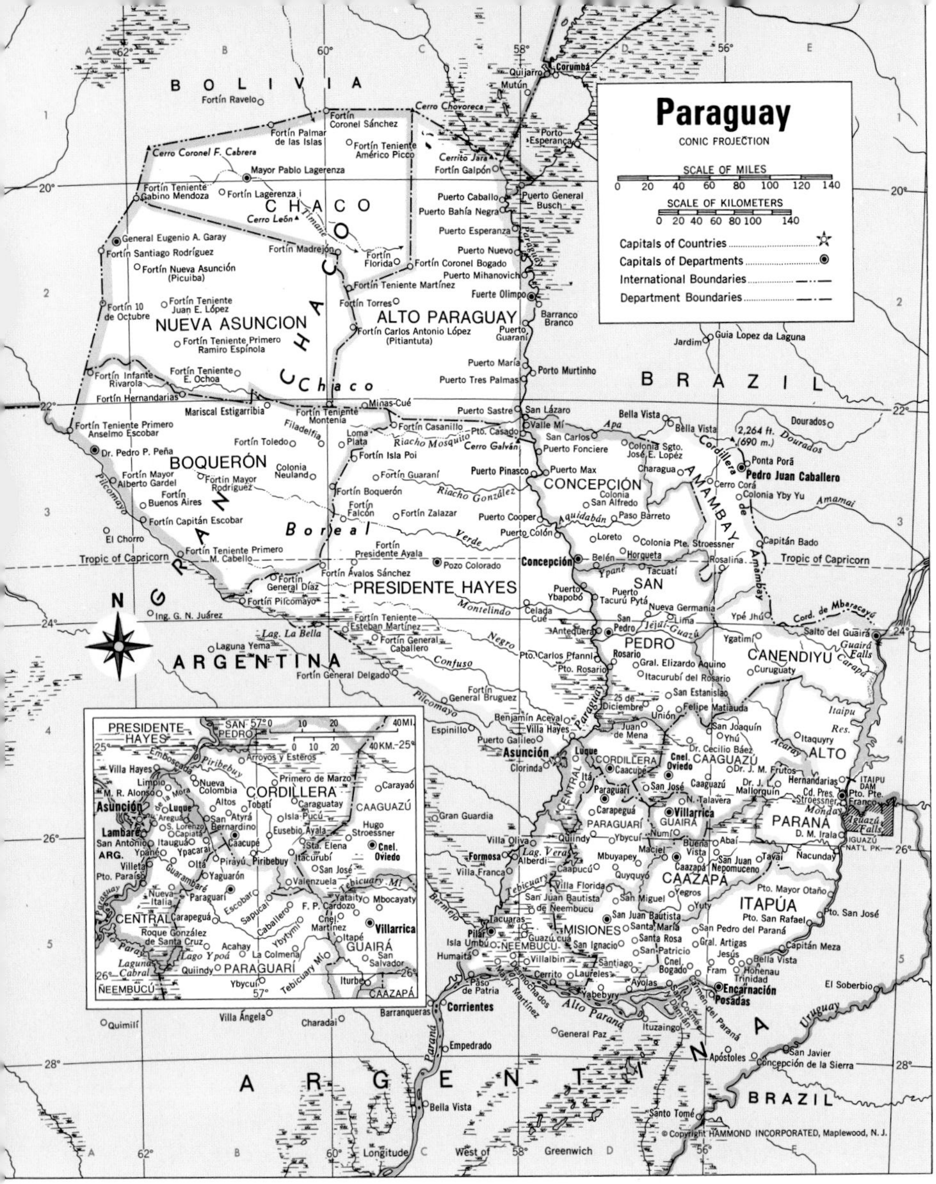

Paraguay
CONIC PROJECTION
SCALE OF MILES
0 20 40 60 80 100 120 140
SCALE OF KILOMETERS
0 20 40 60 80 100 140
Capitals of Countries
Capitals of Departments
International Boundaries
Department Boundaries
© Copyright HAMMOND INCORPORATED, Maplewood, N. J.

PARAGUAY

DEPARTMENTS

Alto Paraguay C2
Alto Paraná E4
Amambay D3
Asunción................................A4
Boquerón B3
Caaguazú............................D-E4
Caazapá..............................D-E5
Canendiyu E4
Central D4
Chaco B-C2
Concepción............................D3
Cordillera...............................D4
Guaira....................................D4
Itapúa.....................................E5
Misiones................................D5
Ñeembucú..........................C-D5
Nueva Asunción.....................B2
Paraguarí..........................D 4-5
Presidente Hayes...................C3
San Pedro ....D 4-5

CITIES and TOWNS

Abaí 1,507..............................E4
Acahay 1,937 ....B5
Alberdi 2,346 ....D5
Altos 1,441 ....B4
Antequera 1,281 ....D4
Areguá 3,941 ....B4
Arroyos y Esteros 1,253 ....B4
Asunción (cap.) 387,676 ....A4
Atyrá 1,427 ....B4
Belén 1,219 ....D3
Bella Vista 3,101 ....D3
Bella Vista 1,421 ....E5
Benjamín Aceval 2,877 ....C4
Buena Vista 1,353..................D5
Caacupé 7,278 ....B5
Caaguazú 7,950 ....D4
Caapucú 1,400........................D5
Caazapá 3,132 ....D5
Capiatá 2,827.........................B4
Carapeguá 3,416.....................B5
Carmen del Paraná 1,980 ....D5
Ciudad Presidente
Stroessner 7,085 ....E4
Concepción 19,392.................D3
Coronel Bogado 3,973............D5
Coronel Martínez 1,598...........B5
Coronel Oviedo 13,786 ....C5
Doctor Cecilio Báez 1,300.......D4
Doctor Juan L. Mallorquín
1,913.................................E4
Doctor Juan Manuel Frutos
1,494.................................E4
Encarnación 23,343 ....E5
Eusebio Ayala 4,328 ....B4
Fernando de la Mora 36,834...B4
Filadelfia 1,438.......................B3
Fuerte Olimpo 3,063 ....C2
General Artigas 3,542 ....D5
General Elizardo Aquino
1,304 ....D4
Guarambaré 3,640..................B5
Hernandarias 3,898.................E4
Horqueta 4,328.......................D3
Isla Pucú 1,766.......................B4
Itá 7,041 ....B5
Itacurubí 1,997 ....B5
Itacurubí del Rosario 2,467 ....D4
Itapé 1,376.............................C5
Itauguá 3,767..........................B5
Iturbe 3,413 ....C5
Jesús 1,495 ....E5
La Colmena 1,804...................B5
Lambaré 31,656......................A4
Limpio 2,219 ....B4
Loreto 1,258...........................D3
Luque 13,921..........................B4
Mariano Roque Alonso 1,492 .A4
Mariscal Estigarribia 3,150 .....B3
Mbuyapey 1,560......................D5
Natalicio Talavera 1,228 ....D4
Nueva Italia 1,517...................B5
Paraguarí 5,036 ....B5
Pedro Juan Caballero 21,033 ..E3
Pilar 12,506 ....C5
Pirayú 2,698 ....B5
Piribebuy 4,497 ....B5
Primero de Marzo 696 ....B4
Puerto Casado 4,078 ....C3
Puerto Guaraní 302.................C2
Puerto Pinasco 5,477 ....C3
Puerto Presidente Franco
4,152.................................E4
Quiindy 2,664 ....B5
Roque González de
Santa Cruz 1,375 ....B5
Rosario 4,165.........................D4
San Antonio 4,906 ....A5
San Estanislao 4,753 ....D4
San Ignacio 6,116...................D5
San José 3,102 ....B5
San Juan Bautista 6,457.........D5
San Juan Nepomuceno 2,974 .E5
San Lázaro 1,767....................D3
San Lorenzo 11,616................B4
San Pedro 3,186.....................D3
San Pedro del Paraná 2,723 ...D5
San Salvador 1,393.................C5
Santa Elena 1,439...................B5
Santa Rosa 3,736 ....D5
Santiago 1,265 ....D5
Sapucaí 1,864.........................B5
Tobatí 4,983............................B4
Unión 1,286............................D4
Valenzuela 1,108.....................B5
Valle Mí 1,318.........................D3
Villa Florida 1,261 ....D5
Villa Hayes 4,749 ....A4
Villarrica 17,687......................C5
Villeta 3,156...........................A5
Yaguarón 3,368 ....B5
Ybycuí 1,736...........................B5
Ypacaraí 5,195........................B5
Ypané 1,474............................B5
Yuty 2,392 ....D5

OTHER FEATURES

Acaray (riv.) E4
Alto Paraná (riv.) D5
Amambay, Cordillera de
(mts.) D3
Ao Paray (riv.)........................A5
Apa (riv.) D3
Aquidabán (riv.)......................D3
Cabral (lake) A5
Carapa (riv.) E4
Chaco Boreal (reg.)................B2
Chovoreca (mt.).....................C1
Confuso (riv.).........................C4
Coronel F. Cabrera (mt.) B1
Galván (mt.)...........................C3
González, Riacho (riv.)...........C3
Gran Chaco (reg.) B2
Itaipu (dam) E4
Itaipu (res.) E4
Jara (hill) C1
Jejuí-Guazú (riv.) D4
La Bella (lag.).........................B4
León (mt.)..............................B2
Mbaracayú, Cordillera de
(mts.)................................E3
Monday (riv.) E4
Montelindo (riv.).....................C3
Mosquito, Riacho (riv.)...........C3
Negro (riv.) C4
Paraguy (riv.).........................D4
Pilcomayo (riv.) C4
Piribebuy (riv.).......................B4
Tebicuary (riv.) C5
Tebicuary Mí (riv.) C5
Tímane (riv.) B2
Vera (lag.)..............................D5
Verde (riv.).............................C3
Ypané (riv.)............................D3
Ypoá (lake) B5

Agriculture, Industry and Resources

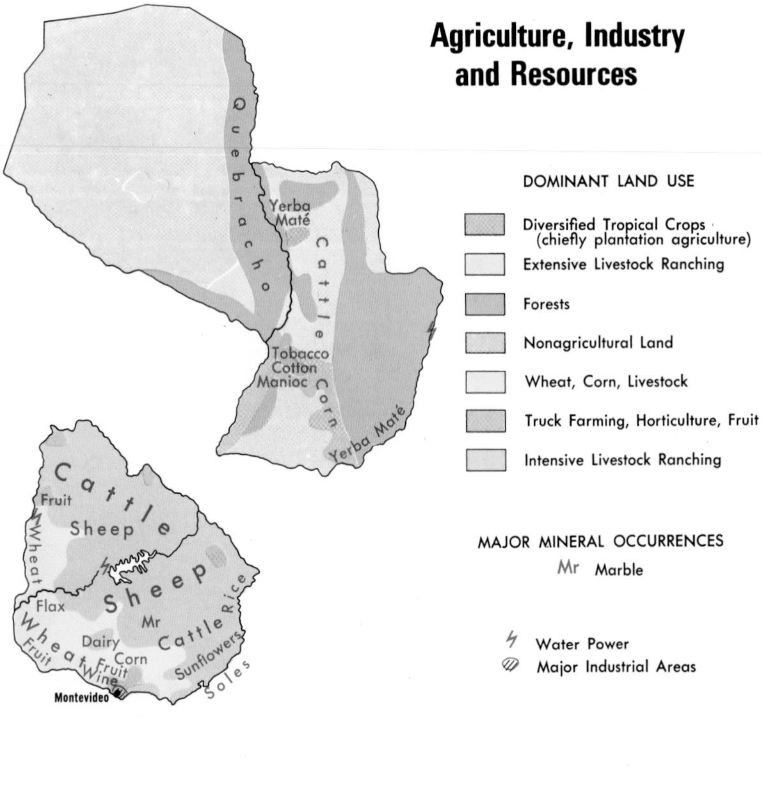

DOMINANT LAND USE
Diversified Tropical Crops (chiefly plantation agriculture)
Extensive Livestock Ranching
Forests
Nonagricultural Land
Wheat, Corn, Livestock
Truck Farming, Horticulture, Fruit
Intensive Livestock Ranching
MAJOR MINERAL OCCURRENCES
Mr Marble
Water Power
Major Industrial Areas

Topography

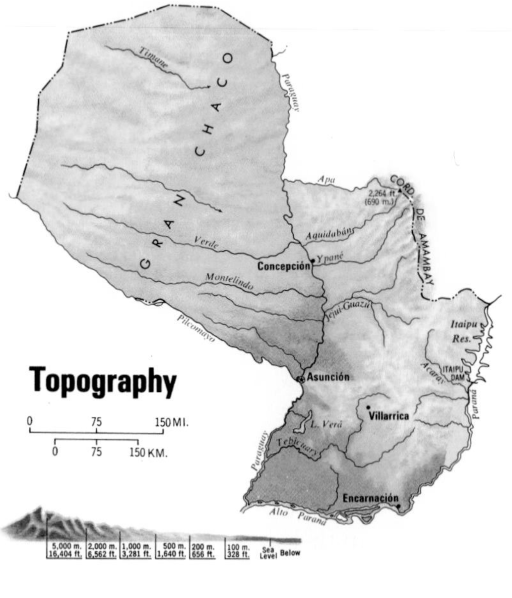

0 75 150 MI.
0 75 150 KM.
5,000 m. 16,404 ft.
2,000 m. 6,562 ft.
1,000 m. 3,281 ft.
500 m. 1,640 ft.
200 m. 656 ft.
100 m. 328 ft.
Sea Level
Below

URUGUAY

DEPARTMENTS

Artigas 52,843	B1
Canelones 258,195	D5
Cerro Largo 71,023	E3
Colonia 105,350	B5
Durazno 53,635	C3
Flores 23,530	C4
Florida 63,987	D4
Lavalleja 65,823	D5
Maldonado 61,259	E5
Montevideo 1,202,757	B7
Paysandú 88,029	B3
Río Negro 46,861	B3
Rivera 77,086	D2
Rocha 55,097	E4
Salto 92,183	B2
San José 79,563	C5
Soriano 77,906	B4
Tacuarembó 76,964	D3
Treinta y Tres 43,419	E4

CITIES and TOWNS

Aceguá 930	E2
Achar 606	C3
Agraciada 638	A4
Aguas Corrientes 992	A6
Aiguá 2,470	E5
Algorta 1,372	B3
Artigas 29,256	C1
Atlántida 2,268	B6
Balneario Solís 288	D5
Baltasar Brum 1,753	B1
Belén 2,129	B1
Bella Unión 7,778	B1
Bernabé Rivera 540	B1
Blanquillo 1,053	D3
Cañada Nieto 503	B4
Canelones 15,938	B6
Cardal 847	C5
Cardona 4,126	B4
Carlos Reyles 961	C4
Carmelo 13,631	A4
Carmen 2,318	D4
Casupá 2,265	D5
Cebollatí 1,233	F4
Cerrillos 1,690	A6
Cerro Chato, Treinta y Tres 1,850	D4
Chamizo 486	D5
Chuy 4,472	F4
Colón, Lavalleja 367	E4
Colonia 16,895	B5
Colonia Valdense 2,113	B5
Conchillas 748	B5
Constitución 3,217	A2
Costa Azul 453	E5
Cufré 430	B5
Curtina 723	C3
Diez y Nueve (19) de Abril 308	E5
Diez y Ocho (18) de Julio 742	F4
Dolores 12,771	A4
Durazno 25,811	C4
Egaña 667	B4
Empalme Olmos 2,084	B6
Estación Atlántida 1,845	B6
Estación Migues 241	C6
Florida 25,030	C5
Fraile Muerto 2,468	E3
Fray Bentos 19,569	A4
Fray Marcos 1,573	D5
Garzón 258	E5
General Enrique Martínez 973	F4
Goñi 278	C4
Grecco 447	B3
Guichón 4,720	B3
Ituzaingó 717	A6
Javier de Viana 286	C1
Joanico 692	B6
Joaquín Suárez, Canelones 3,517	B6
José Batlle y Ordóñez 2,044	D4
José Enrique Rodó 1,334	B4
José Pedro Varela 3,541	E4
Juan L. Lacaze 11,133	B5
La Coronilla 571	F4
La Cruz 633	C4
La Paloma 1,558	F5
La Paz, Canelones 14,402	B6
Lascano 6,043	E4
Las Flores 403	D5
Las Piedras 53,983	B6
Las Toscas 893	E3
Libertad 6,071	C5
Lorenzo Geyres 474	B3
Mal Abrigo 209	C5
Maldonado 22,159	D6
Mariscala 1,393	E5
Melo 38,260	E3
Mercedes 34,667	B4
Merinos 403	C3
Miguelete 533	B5
Migues 2,183	C6
Minas 35,433	D5
Minas de Corrales 2,518	D2
Montes 2,217	D5
Montevideo (cap.) 1,173,254	B7
Nueva Helvecia 8,598	B5
Nueva Palmira 6,934	A4
Nuevo Berlín 1,970	B3
Ombúes de Lavalle 1,689	B4
Palmitas 1,332	B4
Pan de Azúcar 4,862	D5
Pando 16,184	B6
Paso del Cerro 317	C2
Paso de los Toros 13,178	C3
Paysandú 62,412	A3
Piedras Coloradas 487	B3
Piedra Sola 233	C3
Piñera 261	C3
Piraraja 774	E4
Piriápolis 5,221	D5
Porvenir 705	B3
Progreso 8,257	B6
Punta del Este 6,914	E6
Quebracho 1,514	B2
Reboledo 373	D4
Río Branco 5,697	F3
Rivera 49,013	D1
Rocha 21,612	E5
Rodríguez 1,575	C5
Rosario 8,302	B5
Salto 72,948	B2
San Antonio, Canelones 1,122	B6
San Bautista 1,472	B6
San Carlos 16,883	E5
San Gregorio, Tacuarembó 2,892	D3
San Jacinto 2,292	C6
San Javier 1,583	A3
San José de Mayo 28,427	C5
San Ramón 6,570	D5
Santa Catalina 885	B4
Santa Clara de Olimar 2,867	D3
Santa Lucía 14,101	B6
Santa Rosa 2,736	B6
Santiago Vázquez 1,323	A7
Sarandí del Yi 6,326	D4
Sarandí de Navarro 259	C3
Sarandí Grande 5,598	C4
Solís 356	D5
Solís de Mataojo 1,763	D5
Soriano 1,125	A4
Tacuarembó 34,152	D2
Tala 3,611	D5
Tambores 1,534	C2
Toledo 3,127	B6
Tomás Gomensoro 2,105	B1
Tranqueras 3,922	D2
Treinta y Tres 25,757	E4
Trinidad 17,598	B4
Tupambaé 1,039	E3
Valentines 153	E4
Veinticinco (25) de Agosto 1,891	A6
Veinticinco (25) de Mayo 1,744	C5
Velázquez 1,042	E5
Vergara 2,822	E3
Vichadero 1,989	E2
Villa Darwin 507	B4
Young 11,080	B3
Zapicán 764	E4
Zapucay	D2

OTHER FEATURES

Arapey Grande (riv.)	B2
Bonete (dam)	C3
Brava (pt.)	B7
Cañas (range)	C2
Caraguatá (riv.)	D3
Castillos (lag.)	F5
Cebollatí (riv.)	F4
Cordobés (riv.)	D3
Cuareim (riv.)	B1
Cuñapirú, Arroyo (riv.)	D2
Daymán (riv.)	B2
Durazno, Grande del (range)	D4
Este (pt.)	D6
Grande (range)	D4
Haedo (range)	C2
India Muerta (riv.)	E4
Lobos (isl.)	E6
Merín (lag.)	F4
Mirador Nacional (mt.)	D5
Negra (lag.)	F5
Negro (riv.)	B4
Negro, Arroyo (riv.)	B3
Olimar Grande (riv.)	E4
Plata, La (riv.)	B5
Polonio (cape)	F5
Quequay Grande (riv.)	B3
Río Negro (res.)	D3
Rocha (lag.)	E5
Salto Grande (falls)	A2
San José (riv.)	C4
San Miguel (swamp)	F4
San Salvador (riv.)	B4
Santa Ana (range)	D2
Santa Lucía (riv.)	D5
Santa María (cape)	F5
Tacuarembó (riv.)	D2
Tacuarí (riv.)	E3
Uruguay (riv.)	A3
Yaguarón (riv.)	F3
Yí (riv.)	B4

PARAGUAY

AREA 157,047 sq. mi. (406,752 sq. km.)
POPULATION 4,157,000
CAPITAL Asunción
LARGEST CITY Asunción
HIGHEST POINT Amambay Range 2,264 ft. (690 m.)
MONETARY UNIT guaraní
MAJOR LANGUAGES Spanish, Guaraní
MAJOR RELIGION Roman Catholicism

URUGUAY

AREA 72,172 sq. mi. (186,925 sq. km.)
POPULATION 3,077,000
CAPITAL Montevideo
LARGEST CITY Montevideo
HIGHEST POINT Mirador Nacional 1,644 ft. (501 m.)
MONETARY UNIT Uruguayan peso
MAJOR LANGUAGE Spanish
MAJOR RELIGION Roman Catholicism

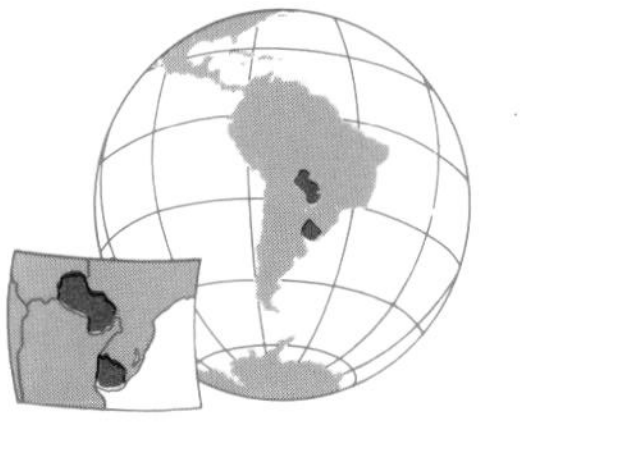

PARAGUAY

URUGUAY

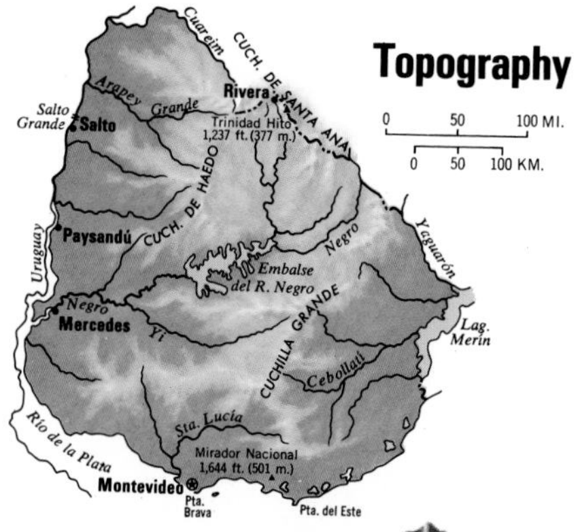

Topography
0 50 100 MI.
0 50 100 KM.
Salto Grande
Salto
Rivera
Trinidad Hills
1,237 ft. (377 m.)
CUCH. DE SANTA ANA
CUCH. DE HAEDO
Paysandú
Embalse del R. Negro
Mercedes
CUCHILLA GRANDE
Lag. Merín
Río de la Plata
Mirador Nacional
1,644 ft. (501 m.)
Montevideo
Pta. Brava
Pta. del Este

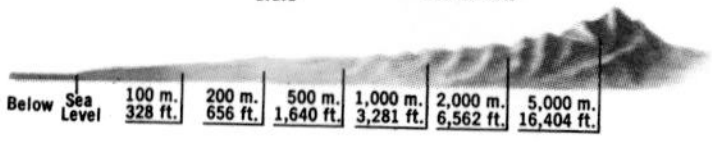

Below Sea Level
100 m. 328 ft.
200 m. 656 ft.
500 m. 1,640 ft.
1,000 m. 3,281 ft.
2,000 m. 6,562 ft.
5,000 m. 16,404 ft.

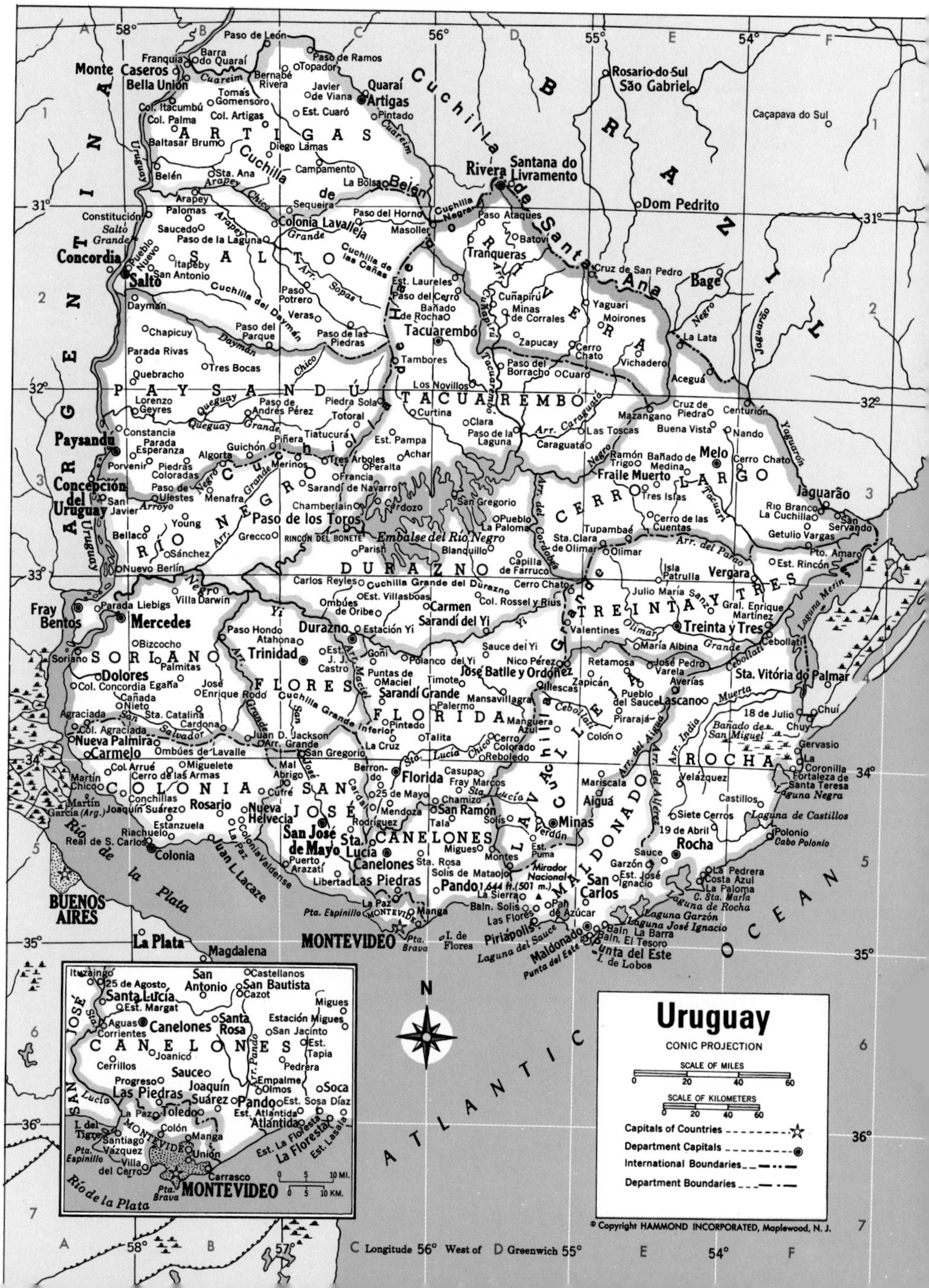

Uruguay
CONIC PROJECTION
SCALE OF MILES
0 20 40 60
SCALE OF KILOMETERS
0 20 40 60
Capitals of Countries
Department Capitals
International Boundaries
Department Boundaries
MONTEVIDEO
BUENOS AIRES
ATLANTIC OCEAN
Río de la Plata
Longitude 56° West of Greenwich 55°

North America

LAMBERT AZIMUTHAL EQUAL-AREA PROJECTION

MILES
0 100 200 400 600 800

KILOMETERS
0 100 200 400 600 800

Capitals of Countries .... ⊛
Other Capitals .... ⊛
International Boundaries .... – – –
Other Boundaries ....

© Copyright HAMMOND INCORPORATED, Maplewood, N.J.

Population Distribution

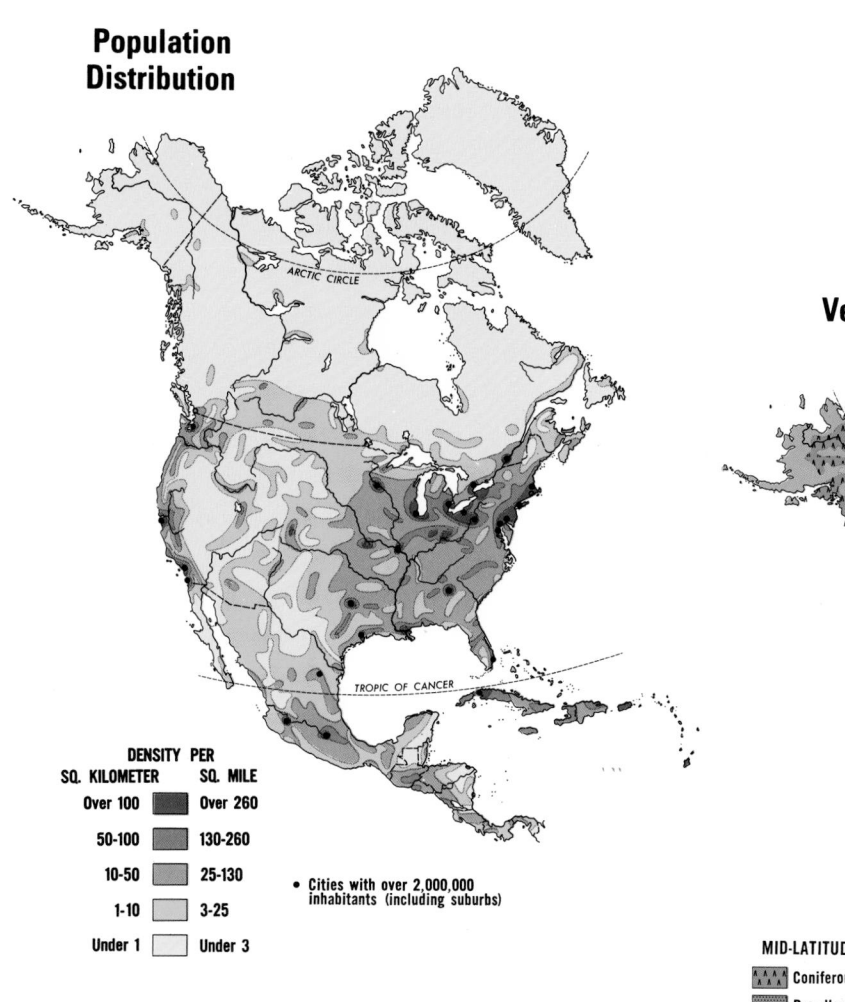

AREA 9,363,000 sq. mi.
(24,250,170 sq. km.)
POPULATION 427,000,000
LARGEST CITY New York
HIGHEST POINT Mt. McKinley 20,320 ft.
(6,194 m.)
LOWEST POINT Death Valley -282 ft.
(-86 m.)

Vegetation

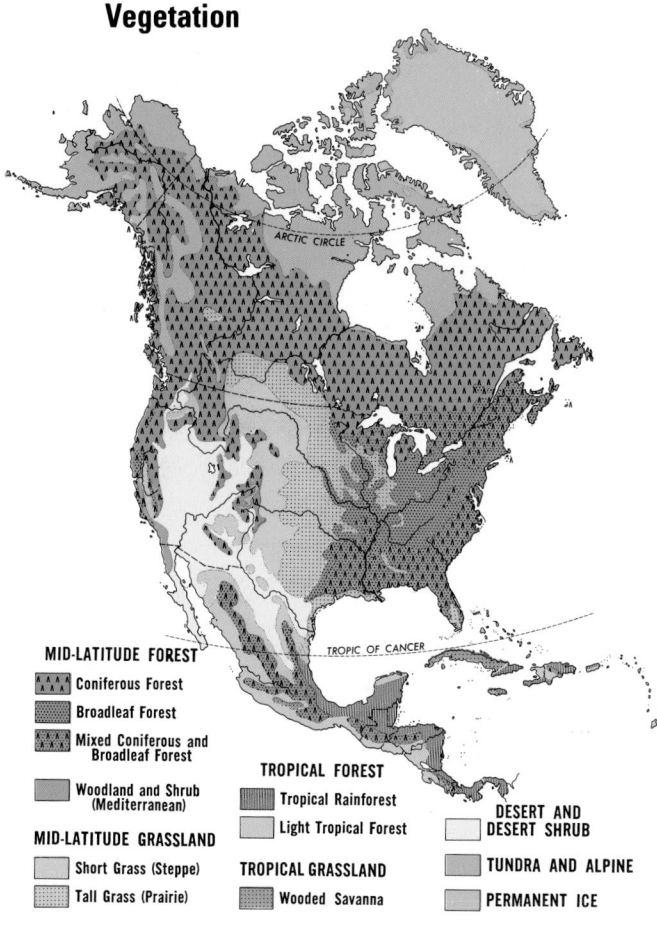

DENSITY PER

SQ. KILOMETER	SQ. MILE
Over 100	Over 260
50-100	130-260
10-50	25-130
1-10	3-25
Under 1	Under 3

• Cities with over 2,000,000 inhabitants (including suburbs)

MID-LATITUDE FOREST

- Coniferous Forest
- Broadleaf Forest
- Mixed Coniferous and Broadleaf Forest
- Woodland and Shrub (Mediterranean)

MID-LATITUDE GRASSLAND

- Short Grass (Steppe)
- Tall Grass (Prairie)

TROPICAL FOREST

- Tropical Rainforest
- Light Tropical Forest

TROPICAL GRASSLAND

- Wooded Savanna

DESERT AND DESERT SHRUB

- TUNDRA AND ALPINE
- PERMANENT ICE

NORTH AMERICA

Average January Temperature

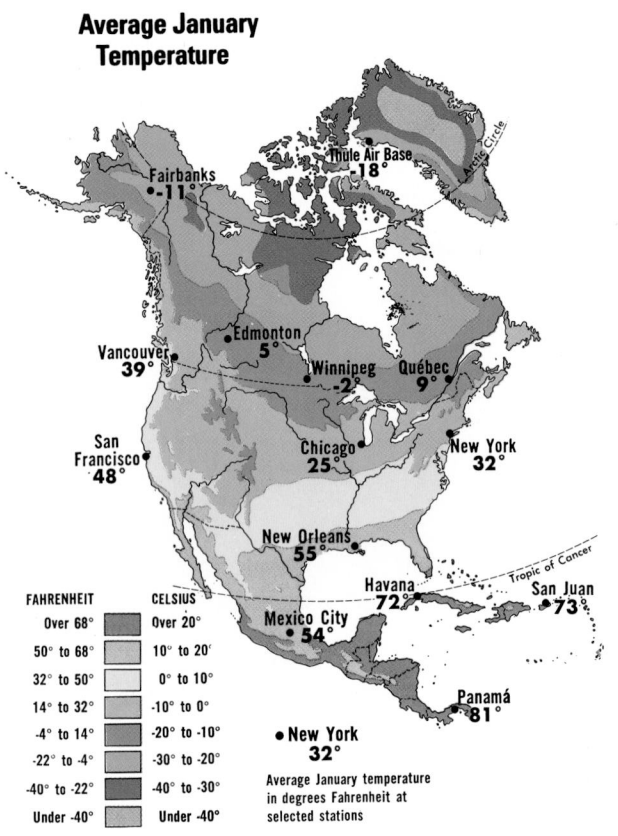

Thule Air Base -18°
Fairbanks -11°
Edmonton 5°
Vancouver 39°
Winnipeg -2°
Québec 9°
San Francisco 48°
Chicago 25°
New York 32°
New Orleans 55°
Havana 72°
San Juan 73°
Mexico City 54°
Panamá 81°

FAHRENHEIT	CELSIUS
Over 68°	Over 20°
50° to 68°	10° to 20°
32° to 50°	0° to 10°
14° to 32°	-10° to 0°
-4° to 14°	-20° to -10°
-22° to -4°	-30° to -20°
-40° to -22°	-40° to -30°
Under -40°	Under -40°

● New York
32°

Average January temperature
in degrees Fahrenheit at
selected stations

Average July Temperature

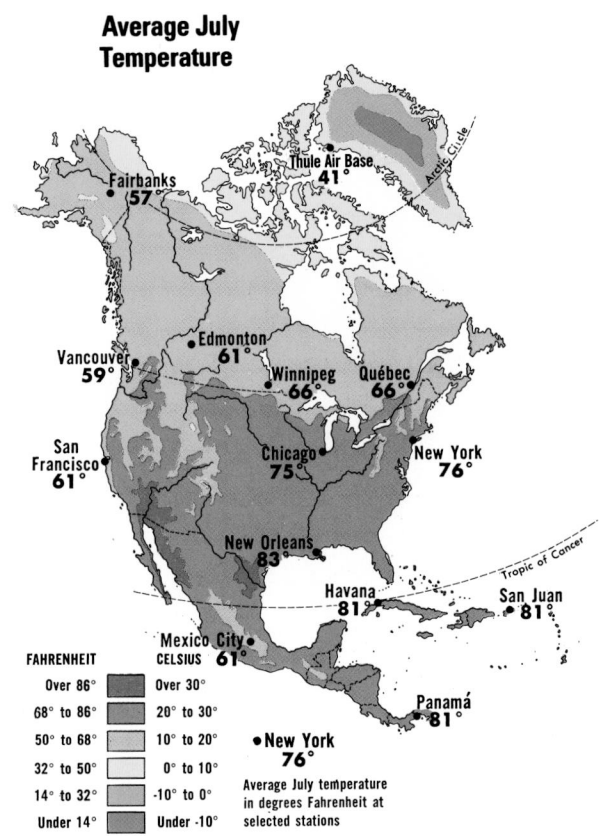

Thule Air Base 41°
Fairbanks 57°
Edmonton 61°
Vancouver 59°
Winnipeg 66°
Québec 66°
San Francisco 61°
Chicago 75°
New York 76°
New Orleans 83°
Havana 81°
San Juan 81°
Mexico City 61°
Panamá 81°

FAHRENHEIT	CELSIUS
Over 86°	Over 30°
68° to 86°	20° to 30°
50° to 68°	10° to 20°
32° to 50°	0° to 10°
14° to 32°	-10° to 0°
Under 14°	Under -10°

● New York
76°

Average July temperature
in degrees Fahrenheit at
selected stations

Rainfall

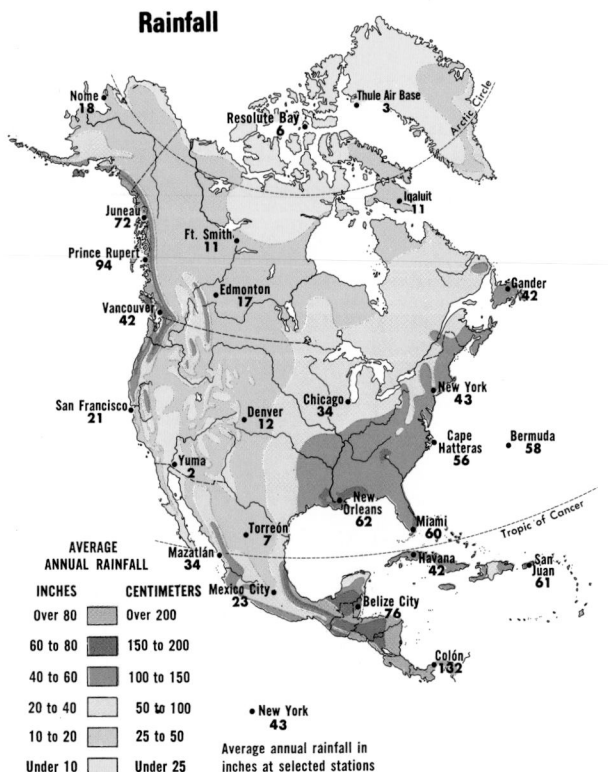

Nome 18
Resolute Bay 6
Thule Air Base 3
Iqaluit 11
Juneau 72
Ft. Smith 11
Prince Rupert 94
Gander 42
Vancouver 42
Edmonton 17
San Francisco 21
Denver 12
Chicago 34
New York 43
Cape Hatteras 56
Bermuda 58
Yuma 2
New Orleans 62
Miami 60
Torreón 7
Havana 42
San Juan 61
Mazatlán 34
Mexico City 23
Belize City 76
Colón 132

AVERAGE ANNUAL RAINFALL	
INCHES	CENTIMETERS
Over 80	Over 200
60 to 80	150 to 200
40 to 60	100 to 150
20 to 40	50 to 100
10 to 20	25 to 50
Under 10	Under 25

● New York
43

Average annual rainfall in
inches at selected stations

Vegetation/Relief

SCALE OF MILES
0 200 400 600 800 1000

SCALE OF KILOMETERS
0 200 400 600 800 1000

Capitals of Countries.......................... ⊕
Other Capitals .... ◉
International Boundaries .... –––––
Canals..

Depths in Fathoms

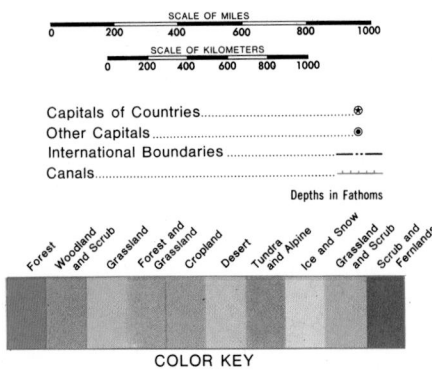

Forest | Woodland and Scrub | Grassland | Forest and Grassland | Cropland | Desert | Tundra and Alpine | Ice and Snow | Grassland and Scrub | Scrub and Fernlands

COLOR KEY

North Pole
ARCTIC OCEAN
CANADA
UNITED STATES
MEXICO
GREENLAND
(Den.)
RUSSIA
ICELAND
Reykjavik
Queen Elizabeth Islands
Hudson Bay
Laurentian Plateau
Gulf of Mexico
Bay of Campeche
CARIBBEAN SEA
PACIFIC OCEAN
ATLANTIC OCEAN
LABRADOR SEA
BEAUFORT SEA
EAST SIBERIAN SEA
BERING SEA
GREENLAND SEA
Gulf of Alaska
Gulf of California
West Indies
Greater Antilles
BAHAMAS
CUBA
Havana
JAMAICA
Kingston
HAITI
Port-au-Prince
DOMINICAN REPUBLIC
Santo Domingo
PUERTO RICO
San Juan
BELIZE
GUATEMALA
Guatemala
HONDURAS
Tegucigalpa
EL SALVADOR
San Salvador
NICARAGUA
Managua
COSTA RICA
San José
PANAMA
Panamá
VENEZUELA
Caracas
COLOMBIA
Bogotá
SOUTH AMERICA
Barranquilla
NETHERLANDS ANTILLES
ARUBA (Neth.)
Curaçao
Bonaire
Willemstad
Turks and Caicos Is. (U.K.)
Bermuda (U.K.)
Tropic of Cancer
Arctic Circle
Montréal
Ottawa
Québec
Toronto
Boston
New York
Philadelphia
Washington
Chicago
Detroit
Milwaukee
Minneapolis
Houston
Dallas
Los Angeles
San Francisco
San Diego
Mexico City
Guadalajara
Monterrey
Vancouver
Seattle
Portland
Edmonton
Calgary
Winnipeg
Regina
Saskatoon
Yellowknife
Denver
Kansas City
St. Louis
New Orleans
Atlanta
Miami
Jacksonville
Tampa
Nashville
Memphis
Cincinnati
Cleveland
Pittsburgh
Buffalo
Indianapolis
Columbus
Norfolk
Charlotte
Birmingham
Oklahoma City
Tulsa
Wichita
Omaha
Fort Worth
San Antonio
Corpus Christi
El Paso
Ciudad Juárez
Chihuahua
Phoenix
Tucson
Albuquerque
Las Vegas
Salt Lake City
Great Salt Lake
Tampico
Veracruz
Acapulco
Mérida
Yucatán Pen.
Culiacán
Halifax
St. John's
St. John
Sudbury
Thunder Bay
Duluth
Nuuk
Anchorage
Nome
Inuvik
Prince Rupert
Victoria
Popocatépetl 17,887 ft. (5452 m.)
Mt. Mitchell 6,684 ft. (2037 m.)
Pikes Peak 14,110 ft. (4301 m.)
Mt. Whitney 14,494 ft. (4418 m.)
Mt. Rainier 14,410 ft. (4392 m.)
Rocky Mountains
Appalachian Mts.
Great Plains
Great Basin
Ozark Plateau
Sierra Madre Occidental
Sierra Madre Oriental
Sierra Nevada
Coast Ranges
Brooks Range
Alaska Range
Alaska Pen.
Kodiak I.
Alexander Arch.
Queen Charlotte Is.
Vancouver I.
Victoria I.
Banks I.
Melville I.
Devon I.
Ellesmere I.
Baffin Bay
Davis Strait
Denmark Strait
Bering Strait
St. Lawrence I.
Pt. Barrow
C. Farewell
C. Chidley
C. Race
C. Cod
C. Hatteras
C. Canaveral
C. Mendocino
C. San Lucas
Cape Breton I.
Newfoundland
Gulf of St. Lawrence
Ungava Peninsula
Labrador
James Bay
Great Bear L.
Great Slave L.
L. Athabasca
L. Winnipeg
L. Superior
L. Michigan
L. Huron
L. Erie
L. Ontario
Mississippi
Missouri
Ohio
Arkansas
Red
Colorado
Snake
Rio Grande
Saskatchewan
Nelson
Churchill
Mackenzie
Yukon
Lower California
Panama Canal
© Copyright HAMMOND INCORPORATED, Maplewood, N. J.
Longitude 90° West of Greenwich

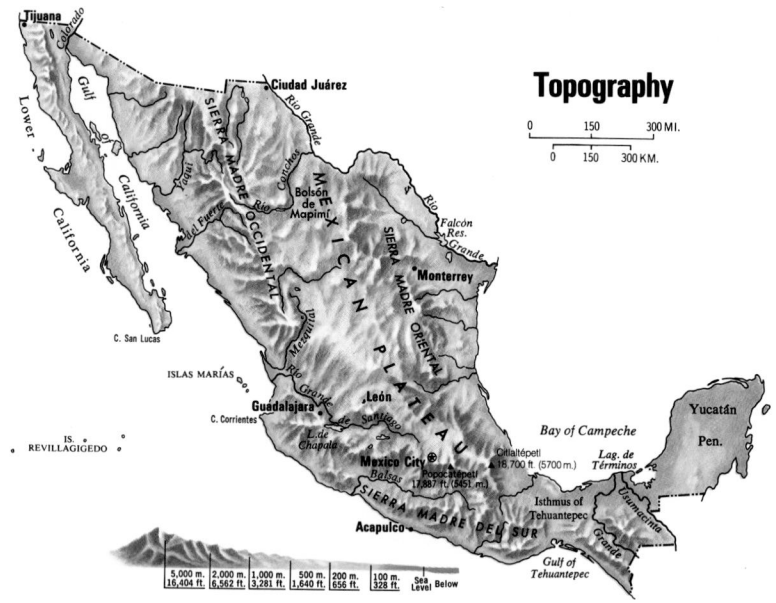

Topography

0   150   300 MI.

0   150   300 KM.

5,000 m. | 2,000 m. | 1,000 m. | 500 m. | 200 m. | 100 m. | Sea Level | Below
16,404 ft. | 6,562 ft. | 3,281 ft. | 1,640 ft. | 656 ft. | 328 ft. | |

Monterrey 1,006,221 ....J4	Nuevo Ideal 5,252 ....G4
Morelia 199,099 ....J7	Nuevo Laredo 184,622 ....J3
Moroleón 25,620 ....J6	Oaxaca de Juárez 114,948 ....L8
Motozintla de Mendoza 4,682.N9	Ocampo 4,801 ....K8
Motul de Felipe Carrillo	Ocotlán 35,361 ....H6
Puerto 12,949 ....P6	Ocotlán de Morelos 5,882 ....L8
Muna 5,491 ....P6	Ojinaga 12,757 ....G2
Naica 7,190 ....G2	Ojocaliente 7,582 ....H5
Namiquipa 4,875 ....F2	Ometepec 7,342 ....K8
Nanacamilpa 6,356 ....M1	Oriental 6,009 ....O1
Naranjos 14,732 ....L6	Orizaba 105,150 ....P2
Naucalpan de Juárez 9,425 ...L1	Oxkutzcab 8,182 ....P6
Navojoa 43,817 ....E3	Ozumba de Alzate 6,876 ....M1
Navolato 12,799 ....E4	Pachuca de Soto 83,892 ....K6
Netzahualcóyotl 580,436 ......L1	Padilla 4,581 ....K5
Nochistlán 8,780 ....H6	Palenque 2,595 ....O8
Nogales 14,254 ....P2	Pánuco 14,277 ....L6
Nogales 35,361 ....P2	Papantla de Olarte 26,773 ....L6
Nueva Casas Grandes 20,023..F1	Paraíso 7,561 ....N7
Nueva Italia de Ruiz 14,718....J7	Parral 57,619 ....G3
Nueva Rosita 34,706 ....J2	

Parras de la Fuente 18,207 ....H4	
Paso de Ovejas 4,371 ....Q2
Pátzcuaro 17,299 ....J7
Pedro Montoya 4,563 ....K6
Pénjamo 9,245 ....J6
Pericos 4,445 ....F4
Perote 12,742 ....O1
Petatlán 9,419 ....J8
Peto 8,362 ....P6
Pichucalco 4,615 ....N8
Piedras Negras, Coahuila 41,033 ....J2
Piedras Negras, Veracruz 4,099 ....Q2
Pijijiapan 5,053 ....N9
Poza Rica de Hidalgo 152,276 ....L6
Profesor Rafael Ramírez 5,338 ....O1
Progreso 17,518 ....P6

STATES

Aguascalientes 504,300 ....H6	
Baja California 1,227,400 ....B1
Baja California Sur 221,000 ....C3
Campeche 371,800 ....O7
Chiapas 2,097,500 ....N8
Chihuahua 1,935,100 ....F2
Coahuila 1,561,000 ....H3
Colima 339,400 ....G7
Distrito Federal 9,377,300 ......L1
Durango 1,160,300 ....G4
Guanajuato 3,045,600 ....J6
Guerrero 2,174,200 ....J8
Hidalgo 1,518,200 ....K6
Jalisco 4,296,500 ....H6
México 7,542,300 ....K7
Michoacán 3,049,400 ....H7
Morelos 931,400 ....K7
Nayarit 729,500 ....G6
Nuevo León 2,463,500 ....K4
Oaxaca 2,517,500 ....L8
Puebla 3,285,300 ....L7
Querétaro 730,900 ....J6
Quintana Roo 209,900 ....P7
San Luis Potosí 1,669,900 .....J5
Sinaloa 1,882,200 ....E4
Sonora 1,498,100 ....D2
Tabasco 1,150,000 ....N7
Tamaulipas 1,924,900 ....K4
Tlaxcala 548,500 ....N1
Veracruz 5,263,800 ....L7
Yucatán 1,034,300 ....P6
Zacatecas 1,144,700 ....H5

CITIES and TOWNS

Acala 11,483 ....N8	
Acámbaro 32,257 ....J7
Acaponeta 11,844 ....G6
Acapulco de Juárez 309,254...K8
Acatlán de Osorio 7,624 ....K7
Acatzingo de Hidalgo 6,905 ...N2
Acayucan 21,173 ....M8
Actopan 11,037 ....K6
Agua Dulce 21,060 ....M7
Agua Prieta 20,754 ....E1
Aguascalientes 181,277 ....H6
Aguililla 5,715 ....H7
Ahuacatitlán 6,436 ....L1
Ahuacatlán 5,350 ....G6
Ahumada 6,466 ....F1
Ajalpan 8,238 ....L7
Alamo 9,954 ....L6
Aldama 6,047 ....L2
Allende, Coahuila 11,076 ......J2
Allende, Nuevo León 9,914 ....J4
Altamira 6,053 ....L5
Altepexi 6,661 ....L7
Altotonga 6,754 ....P1
Alvarado 15,792 ....M7
Ameca 21,018 ....H6
Amecameca de Juárez 16,276 ....L1
Amozoc de Mota 9,203 ....N2
Anáhuac, Chihuahua 10,886...F2
Anáhuac, Nuevo León 8,168 ...J3
Apan 13,705 ....M1
Apatzingán de la Constitución 44,849 ....H7
Apizaco 21,189 ....N1
Arandas 18,934 ....H6
Arcelia 10,024 ....J7
Ario de Rosales 8,774 ....J7
Armería 10,616 ....G7
Arriaga 13,193 ....N8
Arteaga 5,324 ....H7
Atlixco 41,967 ....M2
Atotonilco el Alto 16,271 ....H6
Atoyac de Álvarez 8,874 ....J8
Autlán de Navarro 20,398 ......G7
Axochiapan 8,283 ....M2

Azcapotzalco 534,554 ....L1	
Bamoa 5,866 ....E4
Benjamín Hill 5,366 ....D1
Bernardino de Sahagún 12,327 ....M1
Cabo San Lucas 1,534 ....E5
Cacahoatán 5,079 ....N9
Cadereyta Jiménez 13,586 .....K4
Calkiní 6,870 ....O6
Calpulálpan 8,659 ....M1
Calvillo 6,453 ....H6
Campeche 69,506 ....O7
Cananea 17,518 ....D1
Canatlán 5,983 ....G4
Cancún 326 ....Q6
Cañitas de Felipe Pescador 4,885 ....H5
Capulhuac de Mirafuentes 8,289 ....K1
Cárdenas, San Luis Potosí 12,020 ....K6
Cárdenas, Tabasco 15,643 .....N8
Castaños 8,996 ....J3
Catemaco 11,786 ....M7
Celaya 79,977 ....J6
Cerritos 10,421 ....J5
Cerro Azul 20,259 ....L6
Chahuites 5,218 ....M8
Chalco de Díaz Covarrubias 12,172 ....L1
Champotón 6,606 ....O7
Charcas 10,491 ....J5
Chetumal 23,685 ....Q7
Chiapa de Corzo 8,571 ....N8
Chiautempan 12,327 ....N1
Chietla 4,602 ....M2
Chihuahua 327,313 ....F2
Chilapa de Álvarez 9,204 ......K8
Chilpancingo de los Bravos 36,193 ....K8
China, Nuevo León 4,958 ......K4
Chocomán 5,114 ....P2
Cholula de Rivadavia 15,399..M1
Cihuatlán 9,451 ....G7
Cintalapa de Figueroa 12,456.N8
Ciudad Acuña (Villa Acuña) 30,276 ....H2
Ciudad Altamirano 8,694 ....J7
Ciudad Camargo, Chihuahua 24,030 ....G3
Ciudad Camargo, Tamaulipas 5,953 ....K3
Ciudad de Río Grande 11,651.H5
Ciudad del Carmen 34,656 .....N7
Ciudad del Maíz 5,241 ....K5
Ciudad Delicias 52,446 ....G2
Ciudad Guzmán 48,166 ....H7
Ciudad Hidalgo, Chiapas 4,105 ....N9
Ciudad Hidalgo, Michoacán 24,692 ....J7
Ciudad Juárez 424,135 ....F1
Ciudad Lerdo 19,803 ....H4
Ciudad Madero 115,302 ....L5
Ciudad Mante 51,247 ....K5
Ciudad Mendoza 18,696 ....O2
Ciudad Miguel Alemán 11,259 ....K3
Ciudad Obregón 144,795 ....E3
Ciudad Río Bravo 39,018 ....K4
Ciudad Satélite 35,083 ....L1
Ciudad Serdán 9,581 ....O2
Ciudad Valles 47,587 ....K5
Ciudad Victoria 83,897 ....K5
Coalcomán de Matamoros 4,875 ....H7
Coatepec 21,542 ....P1
Coatetelco 5,268 ....L2
Coatzacoalcos 69,753 ....M7
Cocorit 4,478 ....E3
Colima 58,450 ....H7
Colotlán 6,135 ....H5

Comala 5,592 ....H7	
Comalcalco 14,963 ....N7
Comitán de Domínguez 21,249 ....O8
Compostela 9,801 ....G6
Concepción del Oro 8,144....J4
Contla 7,517 ....N1
Coquimatlán 6,212 ....G7
Córdoba 78,495 ....P2
Cosamaloapan de Carpio 19,766 ....M7
Coscomatepec de Bravo 6,023 ....P2
Costa Rica 11,795 ....F4
Cotija de la Paz 9,178 ....H7
Coyoacán 339,446 ....L1
Coyotepec 8,888 ....L1
Coyuca de Benítez 6,328 ....J8
Cozumel 5,858 ....Q6
Cuatrociénagas de Carranza 5,523 ....H3
Cuauhtémoc 26,598 ....F2
Cuautepec de Hinojosa 5,501.K6
Cuautitlán de Romero Rubio 11,439 ....L1
Cuautla Morelos 13,946 ....L2
Cuernavaca 239,813 ....L2
Cuitlahuac 4,813 ....P2
Culiacán 228,001 ....F4
Dolores Hidalgo de la Independencia Naci 16,849.J6
Durango 182,633 ....G4
Dzidzantún 7,064 ....P6
Dzitbalché 4,393 ....P6
Ebano 17,489 ....L5
Ecatepec de Morelos 11,899...L1
Ejutla de Crespo 5,263 ....L8
Eldorado 8,115 ....E4
El Fuerte 7,179 ....E3
El Salto 7,818 ....G5
Empalme 24,927 ....D2
Encarnación de Díaz 10,474 ...H6
Ensenada 77,687 ....A1
Escárcega 7,248 ....O7
Escuinapa de Hidalgo 6,442.G5
Escuintla 4,111 ....N9
Esperanza, Sonora 11,762 ......E3
Espita 5,394 ....Q6
Fortín de las Flores 9,358 ......P2
Francisco I. Madero 12,613....H4
Fresnillo de González Echeverría 44,475 ....H5
Frontera 10,066 ....N7
General Terán 5,354 ....K4
Gómez Palacio 79,650 ....G4
González 6,440 ....K5
Guadalajara 1,478,383 ....H6
Guadalupe, Nuevo León 51,899 ....K4
Guadalupe, Zacatecas 13,246.H5
Guadalupe Victoria, Durango 7,931 ....H4
Guamúchil 17,151 ....E4
Guanajuato 36,809 ....J6
Guasave 26,080 ....E4
Guaymas 57,492 ....D3
Gustavo Díaz Ordaz 10,154...K3
Gutiérrez Zamora 9,099 ....L6
Halachó 4,804 ....O6
Hermosillo 232,691 ....D2
Heroica Caborca 20,721 ....C1
Heroica Nogales 52,108 ....D1
Hidalgo del Parral (Parral) 57,619 ....G3
Huachinango 16,826 ....K7
Huajuapan de León 13,822 ....L8
Huamantla 15,565 ....N1
Huatabampo 18,506 ....D3
Huatusco de Chicuellar 9,501.P2
Huauchinango 16,826 ....L6
Huautla de Jiménez 6,132......L7
Huejotzingo 8,552 ....M1

Huejutla 6,854 ....K6	
Huetamo 9,333 ....J7
Huimanguillo 7,075 ....N8
Huitzuco de los Figueroa 9,406 ....K7
Huixtepec 5,927 ....L8
Huixtla 15,737 ....N9
Hunucmá 8,020 ....O6
Iguala de la Independencia 45,355 ....K7
Irapuato 135,596 ....J6
Isla, Veracruz 8,075 ....M7
Isla Mujeres 2,663 ....Q6
Ixmiquilpan 6,048 ....K6
Ixtapa J8
Ixtapalapa 522,095 ....L1
Ixtenco 5,035 ....N1
Ixtepec 14,025 ....M8
Ixtlán del Río 10,986 ....G6
Izamal 9,749 ....P6
Izúcar de Matamoros 21,164.M2
Jala 4,535 ....G6
Jalapa Enríquez 161,352 ......P1
Jalpa 9,904 ....H6
Jalpa de Méndez 4,785 ....N7
Jáltipan de Morelos 15,170...M8
Jerez de García Salinas 20,325 ....H5
Jico 7,269 ....P1
Jiménez, Chihuahua 18,095...G3
Jojutla de Juárez 14,438 ....L2
José Cardel 5,396 ....Q1
Juan Aldama 9,667 ....H4
Juchipila 6,328 ....H6
Juchitán de Zaragoza 30,218.M8
La Barca 18,055 ....H6
Lagos de Moreno 33,782 ....J6
La Paz 46,011 ....D5
La Piedad Cavadas 34,963......H6
Las Choapas 20,166 ....M7
Las Rosas 7,658 ....N8
León 468,887 ....J6
Lerdo de Tejada 11,628 ....M8
Libres 4,830 ....O1
Linares 24,456 ....K4
Loma Bonita 15,804 ....M7
Loreto 7,132 ....J5
Los Mochis 67,953 ....E4
Los Reyes de Salgado 19,452 ....H7
Macuspana 12,293 ....N8
Madera 9,759 ....F2
Magdalena de Kino 10,281....J1
Maltrata 5,457 ....O2
Manzanillo 20,777 ....G7
Mapastepec 5,907 ....N9
Martínez de la Torre 17,203...L6
Mascota 5,674 ....G6
Matamoros, Coahuila 15,125..H4
Matamoros, Tamaulipas 165,124 ....L4
Matehuala 28,799 ....J5
Matías Romero 13,200 ....M8
Maxcanú 6,505 ....O6
Mazatlán 147,010 ....F5
Melchor Múzquiz 18,868 ....H3
Melchor Ocampo del Balsas 4,766 ....H8
Meoqui 12,308 ....G2
Mérida 233,912 ....P6
Metepec 4,625 ....M2
Mexicali 317,228 ....B1
Mexico City (cap.) 9,377,300..L1
Miahuatlán de Porfirio Díaz 5,714 ....L8
Mier 5,636 ....K3
Miguel Auza 9,303 ....H4
Minatitlán 68,397 ....M8
Mineral del Monte 8,887 ....K6
Misantla 8,799 ....P1
Monclova 78,134 ....J3
Montemorelos 18,642 ....K4

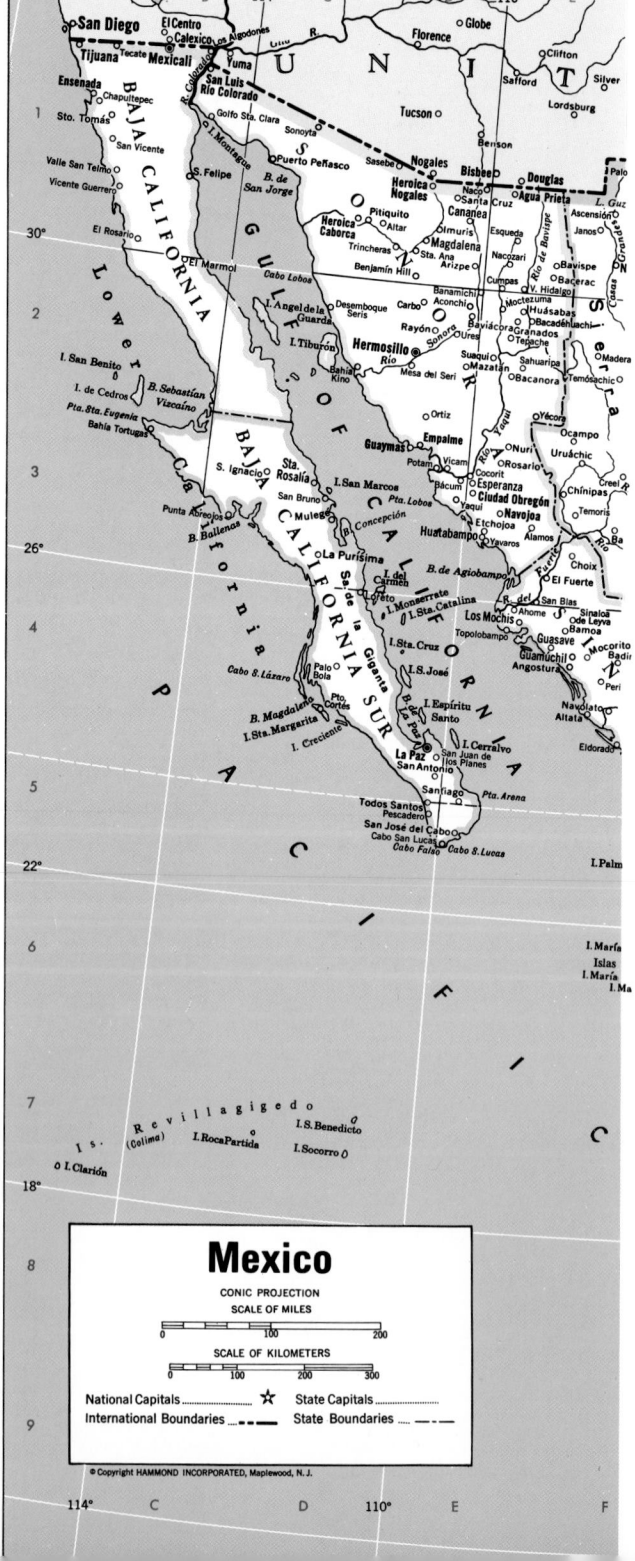

Mexico

CONIC PROJECTION

SCALE OF MILES

0   100   200

SCALE OF KILOMETERS

0   100   200   300

National Capitals .... ☆	State Capitals ⊙
International Boundaries – – –	State Boundaries ———

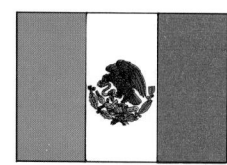

AREA 761,601 sq. mi. (1,972,546 sq. km.)
POPULATION 86,154,000
CAPITAL Mexico City
LARGEST CITY Mexico City
HIGHEST POINT Citlaltépetl 18,700 ft. (5,700 m.)
MONETARY UNIT Mexican peso
MAJOR LANGUAGE Spanish
MAJOR RELIGION Roman Catholicism

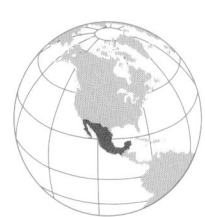

States Indicated by Numbers
1 Tlaxcala   6 Querétaro
2 Morelos   7 Guanajuato
3 Distrito Federal 8 Aguascalientes
4 México   9 Nayarit
5 Hidalgo   10 Colima

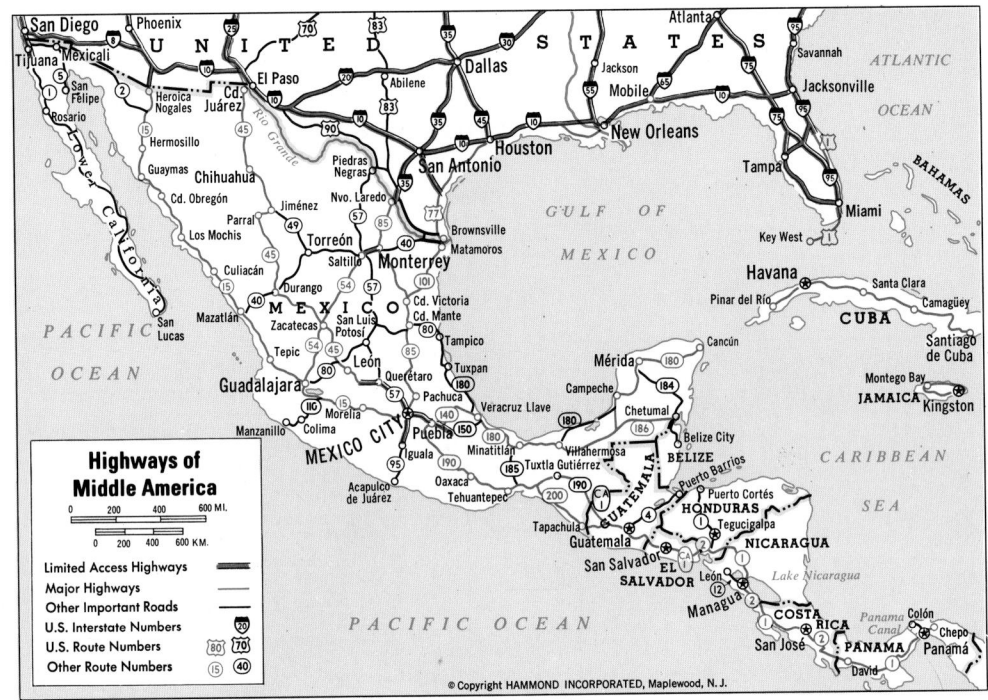

Highways of Middle America

0   200   400   600 MI.

0   200   400   600 KM.

Limited Access Highways
Major Highways
Other Important Roads
U.S. Interstate Numbers
U.S. Route Numbers
Other Route Numbers

© Copyright HAMMOND INCORPORATED, Maplewood, N.J.

Agriculture, Industry and Resources

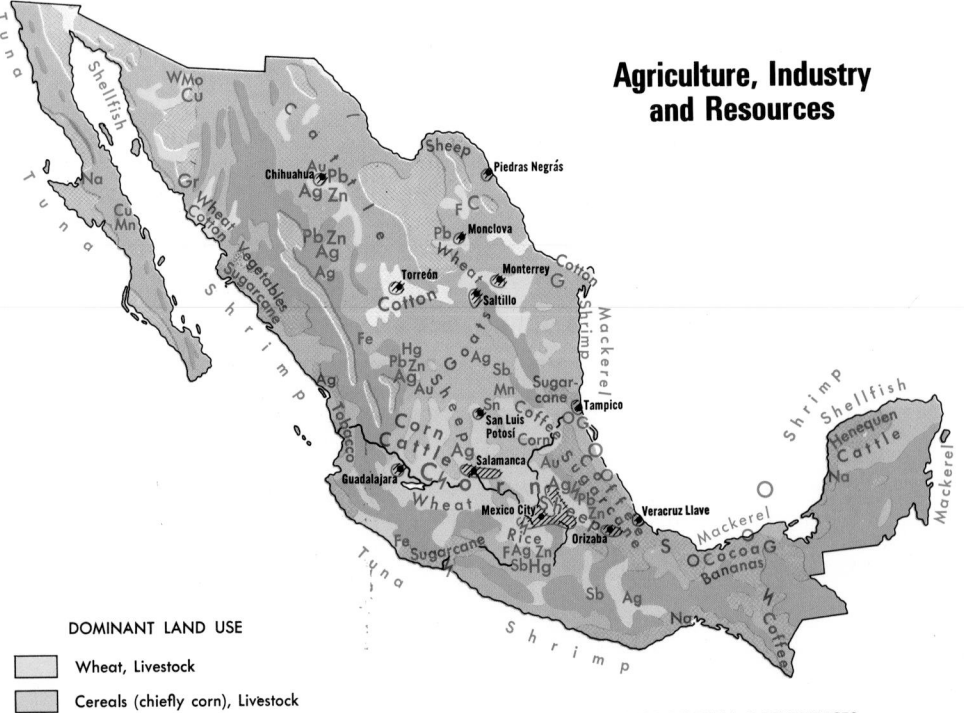

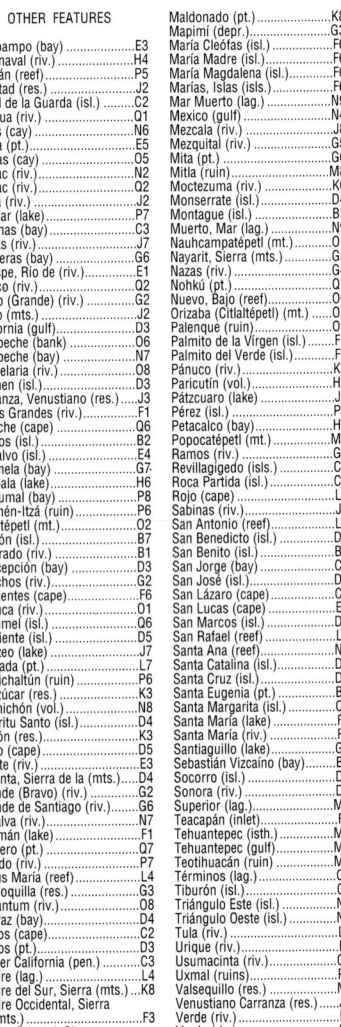

DOMINANT LAND USE

- Wheat, Livestock
- Cereals (chiefly corn), Livestock
- Diversified Tropical Cash Crops
- Cotton, Mixed Cereals
- Livestock, Limited Agriculture
- Range Livestock
- Forests
- Nonagricultural Land

MAJOR MINERAL OCCURRENCES

Ag	Silver	G	Natural Gas	O	Petroleum
Au	Gold	Gr	Graphite	Pb	Lead
C	Coal	Hg	Mercury	S	Sulfur
Cu	Copper	Mn	Manganese	Sb	Antimony
F	Fluorspar	Mo	Molybdenum	Sn	Tin
Fe	Iron Ore	Na	Salt	W	Tungsten
				Zn	Zinc

Water Power
Major Industrial Areas

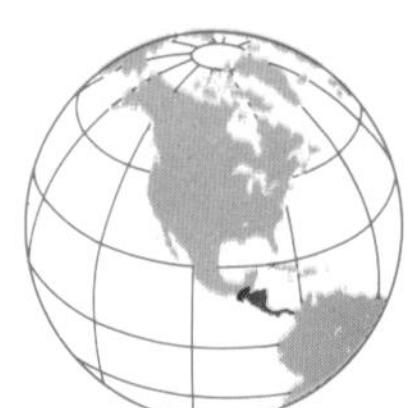

GUATEMALA
AREA 42,042 sq. mi. (108,889 sq. km.)
POPULATION 9,197,000
CAPITAL Guatemala
LARGEST CITY Guatemala
HIGHEST POINT Tajumulco 13,845 ft.
(4,220 m.)
MONETARY UNIT quetzal
MAJOR LANGUAGES Spanish, Quiché
MAJOR RELIGION Roman Catholicism

BELIZE
AREA 8,867 sq. mi. (22,966 sq. km.)
POPULATION 180,000
CAPITAL Belmopan
LARGEST CITY Belize City
HIGHEST POINT Victoria Peak 3,681 ft. (1,122 m.)
MONETARY UNIT Belize dollar
MAJOR LANGUAGES English, Spanish, Mayan
MAJOR RELIGIONS Roman Catholicism, Protestantism

EL SALVADOR
AREA 8,260 sq. mi. (21,393 sq. km.)
POPULATION 5,207,000
CAPITAL San Salvador
LARGEST CITY San Salvador
HIGHEST POINT Santa Ana 7,825 ft.
(2,385 m.)
MONETARY UNIT colón
MAJOR LANGUAGE Spanish
MAJOR RELIGION Roman Catholicism

HONDURAS
AREA 43,277 sq. mi. (112,087 sq. km.)
POPULATION 4,951,000
CAPITAL Tegucigalpa
LARGEST CITY Tegucigalpa
HIGHEST POINT Las Minas 9,347 ft.
(2,849 m.)
MONETARY UNIT lempira
MAJOR LANGUAGE Spanish
MAJOR RELIGION Roman Catholicism

NICARAGUA
AREA 45,698 sq. mi. (118,358 sq. km.)
POPULATION 3,384,000
CAPITAL Managua
LARGEST CITY Managua
HIGHEST POINT Cerro Mocotón 6,913 ft.
(2,107 m.)
MONETARY UNIT córdoba
MAJOR LANGUAGE Spanish
MAJOR RELIGION Roman Catholicism

COSTA RICA
AREA 19,575 sq. mi. (50,700 sq. km.)
POPULATION 2,959,000
CAPITAL San José
LARGEST CITY San José
HIGHEST POINT Chirripó Grande
12,530 ft. (3,819 m.)
MONETARY UNIT colón
MAJOR LANGUAGE Spanish
MAJOR RELIGION Roman Catholicism

PANAMA
AREA 29,761 sq. mi. (77,082 sq. km.)
POPULATION 2,418,000
CAPITAL Panamá
LARGEST CITY Panamá
HIGHEST POINT Vol. Baru 11,401 ft.
(3,475 m.)
MONETARY UNIT balboa
MAJOR LANGUAGE Spanish
MAJOR RELIGION Roman Catholicism

Agriculture, Industry and Resources

DOMINANT LAND USE
- Cereals (chiefly corn) Livestock
- Diversified Tropical Cash Crops
- Livestock, Limited Agriculture
- Forests
- Nonagricultural Land

MAJOR MINERAL OCCURRENCES
Ag Silver
Au Gold
Cu Copper
O Petroleum
Pb Lead
Zn Zinc

⚡ Water Power
▨ Major Industrial Areas

GUATEMALA

HONDURAS

BELIZE

NICARAGUA

EL SALVADOR

COSTA RICA

PANAMA

BELIZE

CITIES and TOWNS

Belize City 39,887 ....C2
Belmopan (cap.) 2,932 ....C2
Corozal Town 6,862 ....C1
Hattieville 904 ....C2
Independence 225 ....C2
Libertad 856 ....C1

Orange Walk Town 8,441.......C1
Punta Gorda 2,219.................C2
San Ignacio 5,606.................C2
San José 420.........................C2
San Pedro 213.......................D2
Stann Creek Town 6,627........C2

OTHER FEATURES

Ambergris (cay).....................D1

Belize (riv.)............................C2
Glover (reef)..........................D2
Half Moon (cay)....................D2
Hondo (riv.)...........................C1
Honduras (gulf).....................D2
Mauger (cay).........................C2
Mya (riv.)...............................C2
New (riv.)...............................C2
Saint Georges (cay)..............D2
Sarstún (riv.).........................C3

Turneffe (isls.).......................D2

COSTA RICA

CITIES and TOWNS

Alajuela 33,122 ....E6
Atenas 1,728 ....E6
Bagaces 2,129 ....E5
Boruca 1,892 ....F6

Buenos Aires 302 ....F6
Cañas 6,053 ....E5
Cartago 21,753......................F6
Ciudad Quesada 9,754 ....E5
Esparta 4,699........................E5
Filadelfia 2,958......................E5
Golfito 6,962 ....F6
Grecia 8,355...........................E5
Guácimo 1,168 ....F5
Guápiles 3,524.......................F5

Heredia 22,700......................E5
Las Juntas 1,129...................E5
Liberia 10,802........................E5
Limón 29,621.........................F6
Miramar 1,673........................E5
Nicoya 7,474..........................E5
Orotina 3,170..........................E6
Palmares 3,083......................F6
Paquera...................................F6
Paraíso 8,446.........................F6

Playa Bonita E6
Puerto Cortés 2,070..............F6
Puntarenas 26,331.................E6
Quepos 2,155.........................E6
San Ignacio 446.....................E6
San José (cap.) 215,441........F5
San Marcos 917.....................F6
San Ramón 9,245...................E5
Santa Cruz 5,777...................E5
Santa Rosa.............................E5

(continued on following page)

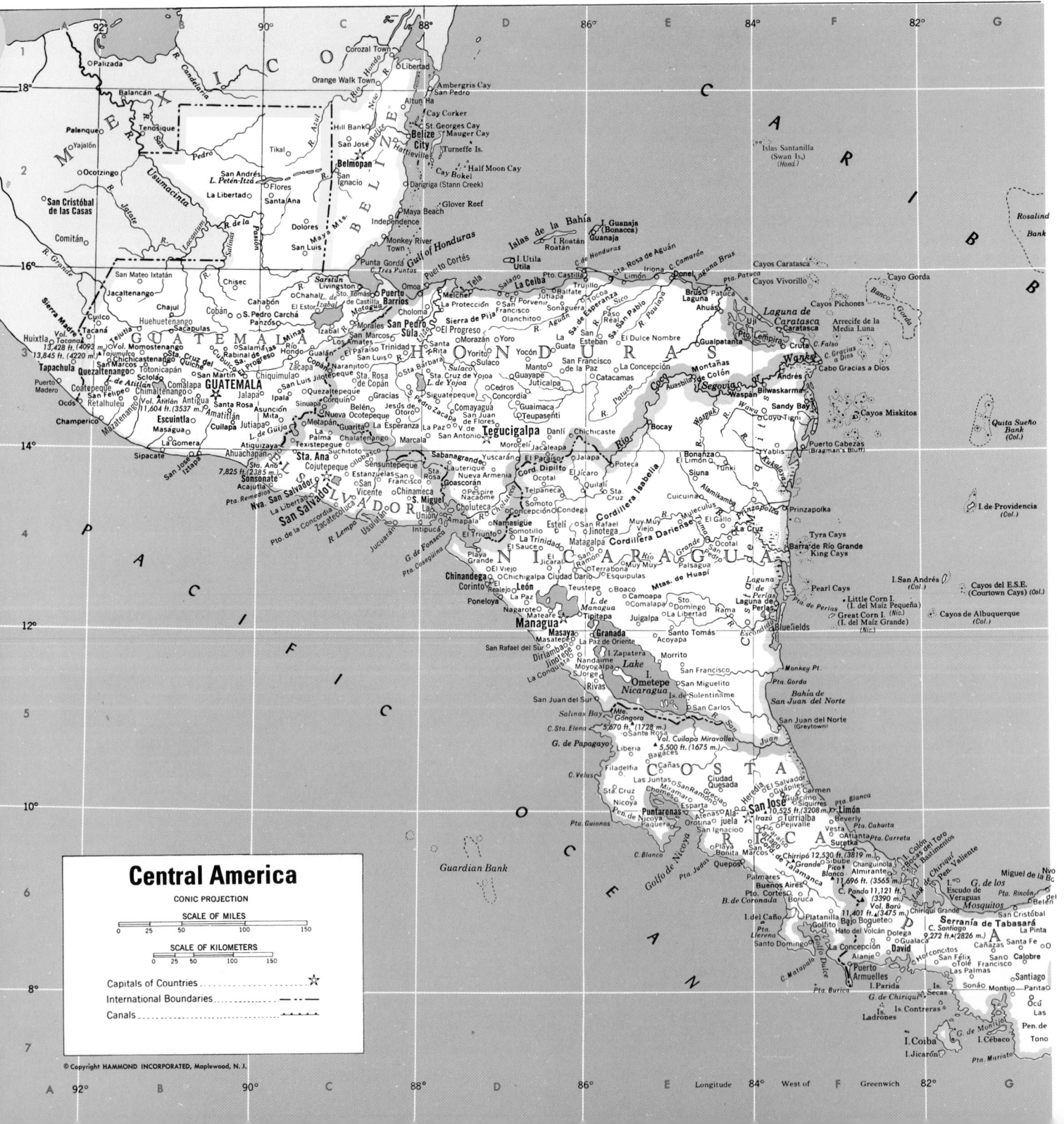

PRINCE EDWARD ISLAND

AREA 2,184 sq. mi. (5,657 sq. km.)
POPULATION 126,646
CAPITAL Charlottetown
LARGEST CITY Charlottetown
HIGHEST POINT 465 ft. (142 m.)
SETTLED IN 1720
ADMITTED TO CONFEDERATION 1873
PROVINCIAL FLOWER Lady's Slipper

NOVA SCOTIA

AREA 21,425 sq. mi. (55,491 sq. km.)
POPULATION 873,176
CAPITAL Halifax
LARGEST CITY Halifax
HIGHEST POINT Cape Breton Highlands
  1,747 ft. (532 m.)
SETTLED IN 1605
ADMITTED TO CONFEDERATION 1867
PROVINCIAL FLOWER Trailing Arbutus or
  Mayflower

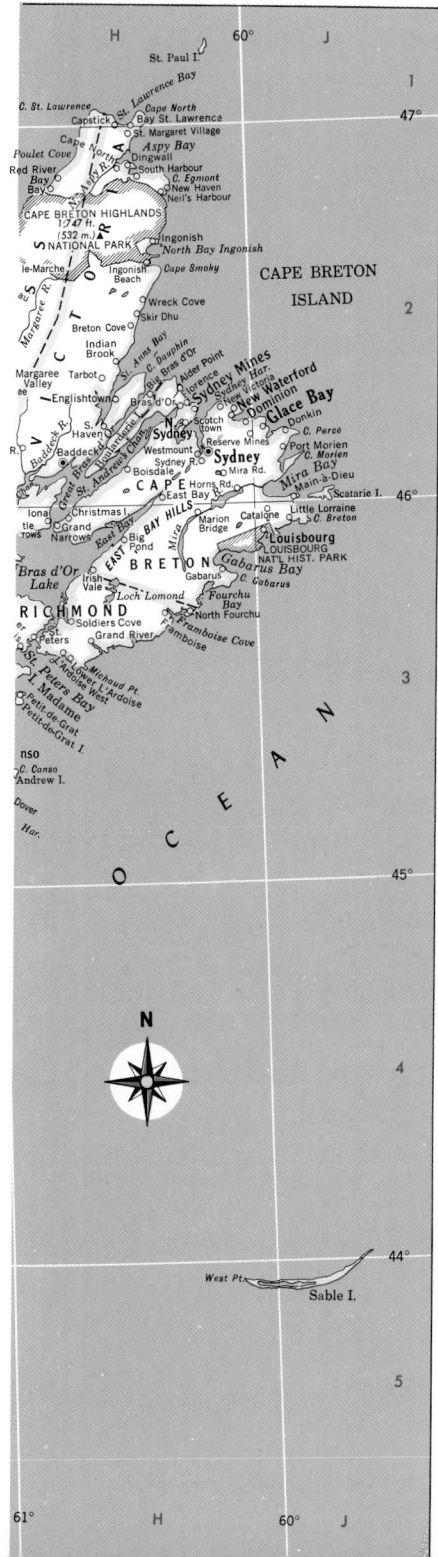

Agriculture, Industry and Resources

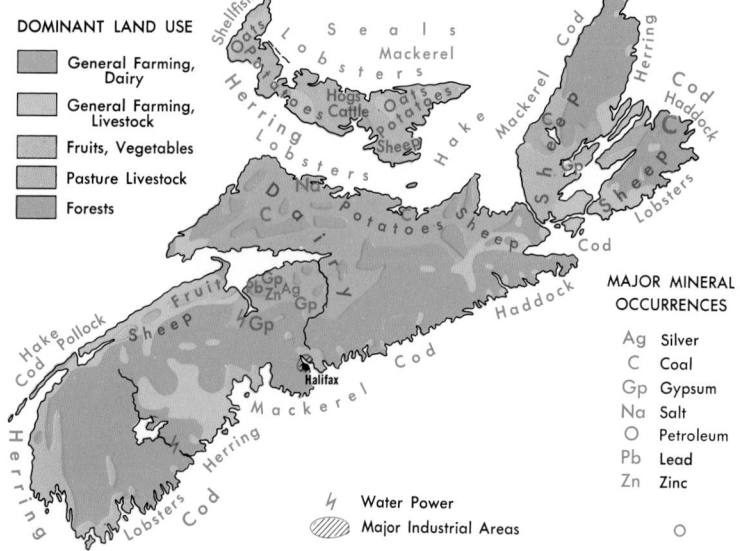

DOMINANT LAND USE

- General Farming, Dairy
- General Farming, Livestock
- Fruits, Vegetables
- Pasture Livestock
- Forests

MAJOR MINERAL OCCURRENCES

Ag   Silver
C   Coal
Gp   Gypsum
Na   Salt
O   Petroleum
Pb   Lead
Zn   Zinc

⚡ Water Power
▨ Major Industrial Areas

170 New Brunswick

COUNTIES

Albert 23,632 . . . . F 3
Carleton 24,659 . . . . C 2
Charlotte 26,571 . . . . C 3
Gloucester 86,156 . . . . E 1
Kent 30,799 . . . . E 2
King's 51,114 . . . . E 3
Madawaska 34,892 . . . . B 1
Northumberland 54,134 . . . . . D 2
Queen's 12,485 . . . . D 3
Restigouche 40,593 . . . . D 1
Saint John 86,148 . . . . D 3
Sunbury 21,012 . . . . D 3
Victoria 20,815 . . . . C 2
Westmorland 107,640 . . . . . . F 2
York 74,213 . . . . C 3

CITIES and TOWNS

Acadie Siding 64 . . . . E 2
Acadieville 176 . . . . E 2
Adamsville 94 . . . . E 2
Albert Mines 120 . . . . F 3
Alcida 59 . . . . E 1
Aldouane 64 . . . . E 2
Allardville 478 . . . . E 1
Alma 329 . . . . F 3
Anagance 114 . . . . E 3
Anse-Bleue 562 . . . . E 1
Apohaqui 341 . . . . E 3
Argyle 63 . . . . C 2
Armstrong Brook 191 . . . . E 1
Aroostook 403 . . . . C 2
Arthurette 178 . . . . C 2
Astle 201 . . . . D 1
Atholville 1,694 . . . . D 1
Aulac 113 . . . . F 3
Back Bay 455 . . . . C 3
Baie-Sainte-Anne 709 . . . . . . F 1
Baie-Verte 175 . . . . D 1
Bairdsville 81 . . . . C 2
Baker Brook 527 . . . . B 1
Balmoral 1,823 . . . . D 1
Barachois 686 . . . . F 2
Barnaby River 38 . . . . E 2
Barnettville 117 . . . . E 2
Bartibog Bridge 122 . . . . E 1
Bas-Caraquet 1,859 . . . . E 1
Bass River 112 . . . . E 2
Bath 794 . . . . C 2
Bathurst⊛ 15,705 . . . . E 1
Bayfield 81 . . . . G 2
Bayside . . . . C 3
Beaubois 211 . . . . E 1
Beaver Brook Station 95 . . . . . E 2
Beaver Harbour 316 . . . . D 3
Beechwood 111 . . . . C 2
Beersville 52 . . . . E 2
Belledune 690 . . . . D 1

Belleneur 83 . . . . C 1
Bellefond 243 . . . . E 1
Belleisle Creek 145 . . . . E 3
Benjamin River 171 . . . . D 1
Ben Lomond . . . . D 3
Benton 101 . . . . C 3
Beresford 3,652 . . . . E 1
Berry Mills 238 . . . . E 2
Bertrand 1,268 . . . . E 1
Berwick 129 . . . . E 3
Black Point 131 . . . . D 1
Black River 150 . . . . E 3
Blacks Harbour 1,356 . . . . D 3
Blackville 892 . . . . E 2
Blissfield 119 . . . . E 2
Bloomfield Ridge 153 . . . . D 2
Bloomfield Station 62 . . . . E 3
Bocabec 34 . . . . C 3
Boiestown 299 . . . . D 2
Bonny River 153 . . . . D 3
Bossé 193 . . . . B 1
Bourgeois 215 . . . . F 2
Brantville 1,066 . . . . E 1
Breau-Village 293 . . . . F 2
Brest 94 . . . . E 1
Brewers Mills 199 . . . . C 2
Briggs Corner 89 . . . . D 2
Bristol 824 . . . . C 2
Brockway (Lower Brockway-
  Brockway) 97 . . . . C 3

Browns Flat 295 . . . . D 3
Buctouche 2,476 . . . . F 2
Burnsville 156 . . . . E 1
Burton 291 . . . . D 3
Burtts Corner 484 . . . . D 2
Cambridge-Narrows 433 . . . . . E 3
Campbellton 9,818 . . . . D 1
Canaan 115 . . . . E 2
Canaan Forks 78 . . . . E 2
Canaan Road 86 . . . . E 2
Canterbury 474 . . . . C 3
Cap-Bateau 417 . . . . E 1
Cape Tormentine 229 . . . . G 2
Cap Lumière 262 . . . . F 2
Cap-Pelé 2,199 . . . . F 2
Caraquet 4,315 . . . . E 1
Carlingford 229 . . . . C 2
Carlisle 75 . . . . C 2
Caron Brook 171 . . . . B 1
Carrolls Crossing 119 . . . . D 2
Castalia 145 . . . . D 4
Central Blissville 155 . . . . D 3
Centre-Saint-Simon (St.
  Simon) 991 . . . . E 1
Centreville 577 . . . . C 2
Chance Harbour 63 . . . . D 3
Charlo 1,603 . . . . D 1
Chatham 6,779 . . . . E 1
Chatham Head . . . . E 1
Chipman 1,829 . . . . E 2

Clair 915 . . . . B 1
Clarendon 80 . . . . D 3
Cliffordvale (Limestone-
  Cliffordvale) 69 . . . . C 2
Clifton 194 . . . . E 1
Coal Branch 90 . . . . E 2
Coal Creek 61 . . . . E 2
Cocagne Cape 278 . . . . F 2
Cocagne-Cocagne Sud 600 . . . F 2
Codys 125 . . . . E 3
Coldstream 217 . . . . C 2
Coles Island 160 . . . . E 3
College Bridge 536 . . . . F 3
Collette 198 . . . . E 2
Connell 58 . . . . C 2
Connors 96 . . . . B 1
Cork 54 . . . . D 3
Cornhill 111 . . . . E 3
Coughlan 181 . . . . E 2
Cross Creek 192 . . . . D 2
Cumberland Bay 231 . . . . E 2
Dalhousie⊛ 4,958 . . . . D 1
Dalhousie Junction 105 . . . . . . D 1
Darlington 749 . . . . D 1
Daulnay 398 . . . . E 1
Dawsonville 278 . . . . C 1
Debec 200 . . . . C 2
Dieppe 8,511 . . . . F 2
Dipper Harbour 166 . . . . D 3
Doaktown 1,009 . . . . D 2

Dorchester⊛ 1,101 . . . . F 3
Dorchester Crossing 605 . . . . . F 2
Douglastown 1,091 . . . . E 1
Drummond 849 . . . . C 1
Duguayville 337 . . . . E 1
Dumfries 150 . . . . C 3
Dupuis Corner 303 . . . . F 2
Durham Bridge 255 . . . . D 2
East Riverside-Kingshurst
  989 . . . . E 3
Edmundston⊛ 12,044 . . . . B 1
Eel River Bridge 377 . . . . E 1
Eel River Crossing 1,431 . . . . . D 1
Elgin 301 . . . . E 3
Enniskillen 63 . . . . D 3
Escuminac 194 . . . . F 1
Evandale 58 . . . . E 3
Evangeline 356 . . . . F 1
Everett 48 . . . . C 1
Fairfield 250 . . . . E 3
Fairhaven 142 . . . . C 4
Fairisle 415 . . . . E 1
Fairvale 3,960 . . . . E 3
Ferry Road 325 . . . . E 1
Fielding 197 . . . . C 2
Five Fingers 189 . . . . C 1
Flatlands 249 . . . . D 1
Florenceville 705 . . . . C 2
Forest City 25 . . . . C 3
Fosterville 58 . . . . C 3

Four Falls 69 . . . . C 2
Fredericton (cap.)⊛ 43,723 . . . D 3
Fredericton Junction 711 . . . . . D 3
Gagetown⊛ 618 . . . . D 3
Gardner Creek 56 . . . . E 3
Geary 654 . . . . D 3
Germantown 62 . . . . F 3
Gillespie 96 . . . . C 2
Glassville 147 . . . . C 2
Glencoe 147 . . . . D 1
Glenlivet 284 . . . . D 1
Gloucester Junction 36 . . . . . . E 1
Gondola Point 3,076 . . . . E 3
Grafton 385 . . . . C 2
Grand Bay 3,173 . . . . D 3
Grande-Anse 817 . . . . E 1
Grand Falls 6,203 . . . . C 1
Grand Falls Hill 152 . . . . C 1
Grand Harbour 614 . . . . D 4
Gray Rapids 266 . . . . E 2
Hammondvale 72 . . . . E 3
Hampstead 87 . . . . D 3
Hampton⊛ 3,141 . . . . E 3
Harcourt 127 . . . . E 2
Hardwicke 114 . . . . E 1
Hardwood Ridge 191 . . . . E 2
Hartland 846 . . . . C 2
Harvey, Albert 58 . . . . F 3
Harvey, York 356 . . . . D 3
Hatfield Point 176 . . . . E 3

New Brunswick

SCALE
0 5 10   20   30   40 MI.
0 5 10   20   30   40 KM.

Provincial Capitals . . . . ⊛
County Seats . . . . ◉
International Boundaries . . . . . . _ · · _
Provincial Boundaries . . . . _ · _
County Boundaries . . . . _ _ _

© Copyright HAMMOND INCORPORATED, Maplewood, N.J.

AREA 28,354 sq. mi. (73,437 sq. km.)
POPULATION 709,442
CAPITAL Fredericton
LARGEST CITY Saint John
HIGHEST POINT Mt. Carleton 2,690 ft. (820 m.)
SETTLED IN 1611
ADMITTED TO CONFEDERATION 1867
PROVINCIAL FLOWER Purple Violet

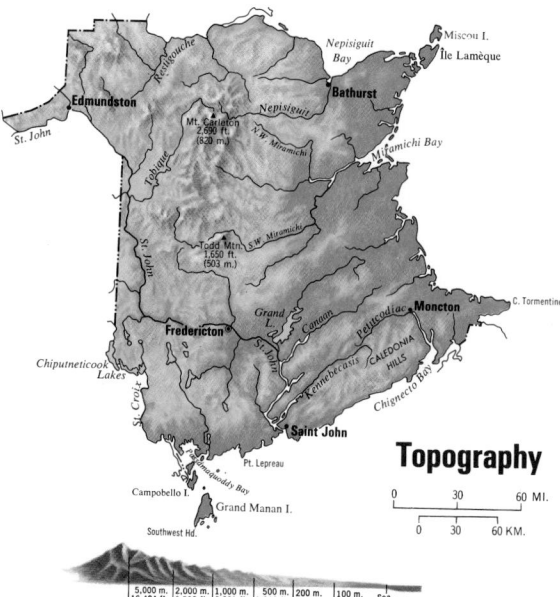

Topography

0   30   60 MI.
0   30   60 KM.

| 5,000 m. 16,404 ft. | 2,000 m. 6,562 ft. | 1,000 m. 3,281 ft. | 500 m. 1,640 ft. | 200 m. 656 ft. | 100 m. 328 ft. | Sea Level | Below |

Agriculture, Industry and Resources

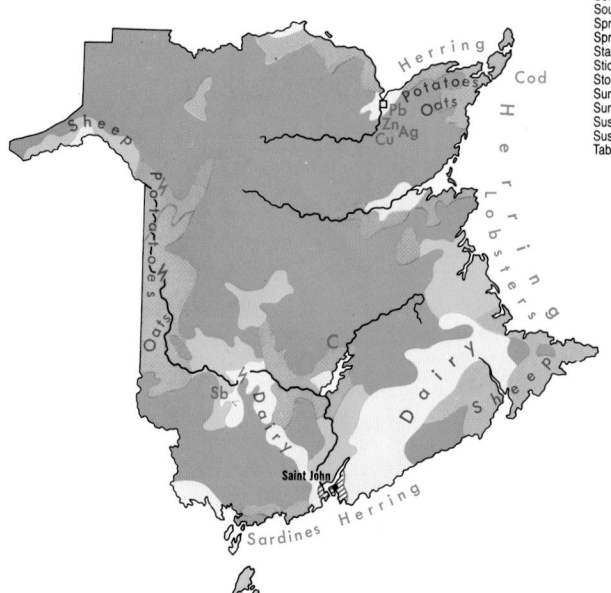

DOMINANT LAND USE

- Cereals, Livestock
- Dairy
- Potatoes
- General Farming, Livestock
- Pasture Livestock
- Forests

MAJOR MINERAL OCCURRENCES

- Ag Silver
- C Coal
- Cu Copper
- Pb Lead
- Sb Antimony
- Zn Zinc
- ⚡ Water Power
- Major Industrial Areas

Topography

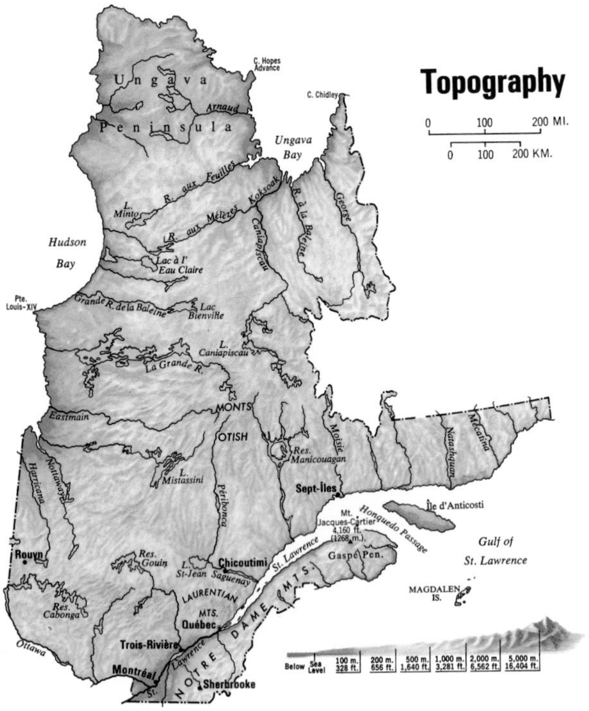
0 100 200 MI.
0 100 200 KM.
Ungava
Peninsula
C. Hopes Advance
C. Chidley
Ungava Bay
Hudson Bay
Pte. Louis-XIV
Arnaud
R. aux Feuilles
R. aux Mélèzes
Koksoak
R. à la Baleine
George
Caniapiscau
L. Minto
Lac à l'Eau Claire
Grande R. de la Baleine
Lac Bienville
L. Caniapiscau
La Grande R.
Eastmain
MONTS
OTISH
Res. Manicouagan
Moisie
Natashquan
Mécatina
L. Mistassini
Nottaway
Harricana
Péribonca
Sept-Îles
Île d'Anticosti
Honguedo Passage
Mt. Jacques-Cartier 4,160 ft. (1268 m.)
Gulf of St. Lawrence
Gaspé Pen.
MAGDALEN IS.
Rouyn
Res. Gouin
L. St-Jean
Saguenay
Chicoutimi
St. Lawrence
LAURENTIAN MTS.
Québec
Res. Cabonga
Trois-Rivières
NOTRE DAME MTS.
Ottawa
Montréal
Sherbrooke
Below Sea Level
100 m. 328 ft.
200 m. 656 ft.
500 m. 1,640 ft.
1,000 m. 3,281 ft.
2,000 m. 6,562 ft.
5,000 m. 16,404 ft.

COUNTIES

Argenteuil 32,454 . . . . C 4
Arthabaska 59,277 . . . . E 4
Bagot 26,840 . . . . E 4
Beauce 73,427 . . . . G 3
Beauharnois 54,034 . . . . C 4
Bellechasse 23,559 . . . . G 3
Berthier 31,096 . . . . C 3
Bonaventure 40,487 . . . . C 2
Brome 17,436 . . . . E 4
Chambly 307,090 . . . . J 4
Champlain 119,595 . . . . E 2
Charlevoix-Est 17,448 . . . . . . G 2
Charlevoix-Ouest 14,172 . . . . G 2
Châteauguay 59,968 . . . . D 4
Chicoutimi 174,441 . . . . G 1
Compton 20,536 . . . . F 4
Deux-Montagnes 71,252 . . . . . C 4
Dorchester 33,949 . . . . C 3
Drummond 69,770 . . . . E 4
Frontenac 26,814 . . . . G 4
Gaspé-Est 41,173 . . . . D 1
Gaspé-Ouest 18,943 . . . . C 1
Gatineau 54,229 . . . . B 3
Hull 131,213 . . . . B 4
Huntingdon 16,953 . . . . C 4
Iberville 23,180 . . . . D 4
Île-de-Montréal 1,760,122 . . . . H 4
Île-Jésus 268,335 . . . . H 4
Joliette 60,384 . . . . C 3
Kamouraska 28,642 . . . . H 2
Labelle 34,395 . . . . B 3
Lac-Saint-Jean-Est 47,891 . . . F 1
Lac-Saint-Jean-Ouest 62,952 . E 1
Laprairie 105,962 . . . . H 4
L'Assomption 109,705 . . . . D 4
Lévis 94,104 . . . . J 3
L'Islet 22,062 . . . . G 2
Lotbinière 29,653 . . . . F 3
Maskinongé 20,763 . . . . D 3
Matane 29,955 . . . . B 1
Matapédia 23,715 . . . . B 2
Mégantic 57,892 . . . . F 3
Missisquoi 36,161 . . . . D 4
Montcalm 27,557 . . . . C 3
Montmagny 25,622 . . . . G 3
Montmorency No. 1 23,048 . . . F 2
Montmorency No. 2 6,436 . . . . G 3
Napierville 13,562 . . . . D 4
Nicolet 33,513 . . . . E 3
Papineau 37,975 . . . . B 4
Pontiac 20,283 . . . . A 3
Portneuf 58,843 . . . . E 3
Québec 458,980 . . . . F 3
Richelieu 53,058 . . . . D 4
Richmond 40,871 . . . . E 4
Rimouski 69,099 . . . . J 1
Rivière-du-Loup 41,250 . . . . . . H 2
Rouville 42,391 . . . . D 4
Saguenay 115,881 . . . . H 1
Saint-Hyacinthe 55,888 . . . . . . D 4
Saint-Jean 55,576 . . . . D 4
Saint-Maurice 107,703 . . . . D 3
Shefford 70,733 . . . . E 4
Sherbrooke 115,983 . . . . E 4
Soulanges 15,429 . . . . C 4
Stanstead 38,186 . . . . F 4
Témiscouata 52,570 . . . . J 2
Terrebonne 193,865 . . . . H 4
Vaudreuil 50,043 . . . . C 4
Verchères 63,353 . . . . J 4
Wolfe 15,635 . . . . F 4
Yamaska 14,797 . . . . E 3

CITIES and TOWNS

Acton Vale 4,371 . . . . E 4
Albanel 992 . . . . E 1
Alma◎ 26,322 . . . . F 1
Amqui◎ 4,048 . . . . B 2
Ancienne-Lorette 12,935 . . . . . H 3
Angers . . . . B 4
Anjou 37,346 . . . . H 4
Annaville 712 . . . . E 3
Armagh 878 . . . . G 3
Arthabaska◎ 6,827 . . . . F 3
Arvida . . . . F 1
Asbestos 7,967 . . . . F 4
Ascot Corner 847 . . . . F 4
Audet 760 . . . . G 4
Ayer's Cliff◎ 810 . . . . E 4
Aylmer 26,695 . . . . B 4
Baie-Comeau 12,866 . . . . A 1
Baie-d'Urfé 3,674 . . . . G 4
Baie-Saint-Paul◎ 3,961 . . . . . . G 2
Baie-Trinité 749 . . . . B 1
Beaconsfield 19,613 . . . . H 4
Beauceville 4,302 . . . . G 3
Beauharnois◎ 7,025 . . . . D 4
Beaumont 791 . . . . F 3
Beauport 60,447 . . . . J 3
Beaupré 2,740 . . . . G 2
Bécancour◎ 10,247 . . . . E 3
Bedford◎ 2,832 . . . . E 4
Beebe Plain 1,072 . . . . E 4
Bélair (Val-Bélair) 12,695 . . . . H 3
Beloeil 17,540 . . . . D 4
Bernierville 2,120 . . . . F 3
Berthier-en-Bas 562 . . . . G 3
Berthierville◎ 4,049 . . . . D 3
Bic 2,994 . . . . J 1
Biencourt 824 . . . . J 2
Black Lake 5,148 . . . . F 3
Blainville 14,682 . . . . H 4
Boischatel 3,345 . . . . J 3
Bois-des-Filion 4,943 . . . . H 4
Bolduc 1,565 . . . . G 4
Bonaventure 1,371 . . . . C 2
Boucherville 29,704 . . . . J 4
Bromont 2,731 . . . . E 4
Bromptonville 3,035 . . . . F 4
Brossard 52,232 . . . . H 4
Brownsburg 2,875 . . . . C 4
Buckingham 7,992 . . . . B 4
Cabano 3,291 . . . . J 2
Cacouna 1,160 . . . . H 2
Calumet 729 . . . . C 4
Candiac 8,502 . . . . J 4
Cap-à-l'Aigle 819 . . . . G 2
Cap-Chat 3,464 . . . . B 1
Cap-de-la-Madeleine 32,626 . E 3
Caplan-Rivière Caplan 1,139 . C 2
Cap-Saint-Ignace 1,485 . . . . . . G 2
Cap-Santé◎ 671 . . . . F 3
Carignan 4,544 . . . . J 4
Carleton 2,710 . . . . C 2
Causapscal 2,501 . . . . B 2
Chambly 12,190 . . . . J 4
Chambord 961 . . . . E 1
Chandler 3,946 . . . . D 2
Charlemagne 4,827 . . . . H 4
Charlesbourg 68,326 . . . . J 3
Charny 8,240 . . . . J 3
Châteauguay 36,928 . . . . H 4
Château-Richer◎ 3,628 . . . . . . F 3
Chénéville 633 . . . . B 4
Chicoutimi◎ 60,064 . . . . G 1
Chicoutimi-Jonquière *135,172 . . . . G 1
Chute-aux-Outardes 2,280 . . . A 1
Clermont 3,621 . . . . G 2
Coaticook 6,271 . . . . F 4
Coleraine 1,660 . . . . F 4
Compton 728 . . . . F 4
Contrecoeur 5,449 . . . . D 4
Cookshire◎ 1,480 . . . . F 4
Coteau-du-Lac 1,247 . . . . C 4
Coteau-Landing◎ 1,386 . . . . . . C 4
Côte-Saint-Luc 27,531 . . . . H 4
Courcelles 608 . . . . G 4
Courville . . . . J 3
Cowansville 12,240 . . . . E 4
Crabtree 1,950 . . . . D 4
Danville 2,200 . . . . E 4
Daveluyville 1,257 . . . . E 3
Deauville 942 . . . . E 4
Dégelis 3,477 . . . . J 2
Delisle 4,011 . . . . F 1
Delson 4,935 . . . . H 4
Desbiens 1,541 . . . . E 1
Deschaillons-sur-Saint-Laurent 950 . . . . E 3
Deschambault 977 . . . . E 3
Deschênes . . . . B 4
Deux-Montagnes 9,944 . . . . . . H 4
Didyme 667 . . . . E 1
Disraëli 3,181 . . . . F 4
Dolbeau 8,766 . . . . E 1
Dollard-des-Ormeaux 39,940 . H 4
Donnacona 5,731 . . . . F 3
Dorion 5,749 . . . . C 4
Dorval 17,727 . . . . H 4
Dosquet 703 . . . . F 3
Douville . . . . D 4
Drummondville◎ 27,347 . . . . . E 4
Drummondville-Sud 9,220 . . . . E 4
Dunham 2,887 . . . . E 4
Durham-Sud 1,045 . . . . E 4
East Angus 4,016 . . . . F 4
East Broughton 1,397 . . . . F 3
East Broughton Station 1,302 . F 3
Eastman 612 . . . . E 4
Entrelacs 1,735 . . . . C 3
Farnham 6,498 . . . . E 4
Ferme-Neuve 2,266 . . . . B 3
Forestville 4,271 . . . . H 1
Frampton 684 . . . . G 3
Francoeur 1,422 . . . . F 3
Gaspé 17,261 . . . . D 1
Gatineau 74,988 . . . . B 4
Giffard . . . . J 3
Girardville 1,128 . . . . E 1
Gracefield 869 . . . . A 3
Granby 38,069 . . . . E 4
Grand'Mère 15,442 . . . . E 3
Grande-Rivière 4,420 . . . . D 2
Grandes-Bergeronnes 748 . . . H 1
Grande-Vallée 700 . . . . D 1
Greenfield Park 18,527 . . . . . . J 4
Grenville 1,417 . . . . C 4
Gros-Morne 672 . . . . C 1
Hampstead 7,598 . . . . H 4
Ham-Sud◎ 62 . . . . F 4
Hauterive 13,995 . . . . A 1
Hébertville 2,515 . . . . F 1
Hébertville-Station 1,442 . . . . . F 1
Hemmingford 737 . . . . D 4
Henryville 595 . . . . D 4
Howick 639 . . . . D 4
Hudson 4,414 . . . . C 4
Hull◎ 56,225 . . . . B 4
Huntingdon◎ 3,018 . . . . C 4
Île-Perrot 5,945 . . . . G 4
Iberville◎ 8,587 . . . . D 4
Inverness◎ 329 . . . . F 3
Joliette◎ 16,987 . . . . D 3
Jonquière 60,354 . . . . F 1
Jonquière-Chicoutimi *135,172 . . . . F 1
Kingsey Falls 818 . . . . E 4
Kirkland 10,476 . . . . H 4
Knowlton (Lac-Brome)◎ 4,316 . . . . E 4
La Baie 20,935 . . . . G 1
Labelle 1,534 . . . . C 3
Lac-à-la-Croix 1,017 . . . . F 1
Lac-Alouette-Lac-Brière 1,356 D 4
Lac-au-Saumon 1,332 . . . . B 2
Lac-aux-Sables 838 . . . . E 3
Lac-Beaufort . . . . F 3
Lac-Bouchette 1,703 . . . . E 1
Lac-Carré 717 . . . . C 3
Lac-des-Écorces 766 . . . . B 3
Lac-Drolet 1,120 . . . . G 4
Lac-Etchemin 2,729 . . . . G 3
Lachenaie 8,631 . . . . D 4
Lachine 37,521 . . . . H 4
Lachute◎ 11,729 . . . . C 4
Lac-Mégantic◎ 6,119 . . . . G 4
Lacolle 1,319 . . . . D 4
Lac-Saint-Charles 5,837 . . . . . H 3
Lafontaine 4,799 . . . . C 4
La Guadeloupe 1,692 . . . . F 4
La Malbaie◎ 4,030 . . . . G 2
Lambton 1,559 . . . . F 4
L'Annonciation 2,384 . . . . C 3
Lanoraie (Lanoraie-d'Autry) 1,613 . . . . D 4
La Pêche 4,977 . . . . B 4
La Pérade 1,039 . . . . E 3
La Pocatière 4,560 . . . . H 2
La Prairie◎ 10,627 . . . . J 4
La Providence . . . . E 4
Larouche 662 . . . . F 1
La Salle 76,299 . . . . H 4
L'Ascension 1,287 . . . . F 1
L'Assomption◎ 4,844 . . . . D 4
La Station-du-Coteau 892 . . . . C 4
Laterrière 788 . . . . F 1
La Tuque 11,556 . . . . E 2
Laurentides 1,947 . . . . D 4
Laurier-Station 1,123 . . . . F 3
Laurierville 939 . . . . F 3
Lauzon 13,362 . . . . J 3
Laval 268,335 . . . . H 4
Lavaltrie 2,053 . . . . D 4
L'Avenir 1,116 . . . . E 4
Lawrenceville 562 . . . . E 4
Le Moyne 6,137 . . . . J 4
L'Épiphanie 2,971 . . . . D 4
Léry 2,239 . . . . H 4
Lévis 17,895 . . . . J 3
Lennoxville 3,922 . . . . F 4
Les Méchins 803 . . . . B 1
Linière 1,168 . . . . G 3
L'Islet 1,070 . . . . G 2
L'Islet-sur-Mer 774 . . . . G 2
L'Isle-Verte 1,142 . . . . G 1
Longueuil◎ 124,320 . . . . J 4
Loretteville◎ 15,060 . . . . H 3
Lorraine 6,881 . . . . H 4
Louiseville◎ 3,735 . . . . E 3
Luceville 1,524 . . . . J 1
Lyster 830 . . . . F 3
Magog 13,604 . . . . E 4
Maniwaki◎ 5,424 . . . . B 3
Manseau 626 . . . . E 3
Maple Grove 2,009 . . . . H 4
Maria 1,178 . . . . C 2
Marieville◎ 4,877 . . . . D 4
Mascouche 20,345 . . . . H 4
Maskinongé 1,005 . . . . E 3
Masson 4,264 . . . . B 4
Massueville 671 . . . . E 4
Matane◎ 13,612 . . . . B 1
Matapédia 586 . . . . B 2
Melocheville 1,892 . . . . C 4
Mercier 6,352 . . . . H 4
Metabetchouan 3,406 . . . . F 1
Mirabel◎ 14,080 . . . . H 4
Mistassini 6,682 . . . . E 1
Montauban 557 . . . . E 3
Mont-Carmel 807 . . . . H 2
Montcerf 570 . . . . A 3
Montebello 1,229 . . . . B 4
Mont-Joli 6,359 . . . . J 1
Mont-Laurier◎ 8,405 . . . . B 3
Mont-Louis 756 . . . . C 1
Montmagny◎ 12,405 . . . . G 3
Montréal◎ 980,354 . . . . H 4
Montréal *2,828,349 . . . . H 4
Montréal-Est 3,778 . . . . J 4
Montréal-Nord 94,914 . . . . H 4
Mont-Rolland 1,517 . . . . C 4
Mont-Royal 19,247 . . . . H 4
Mont-Saint-Hilaire 10,066 . . . . D 4
Morin Heights 592 . . . . C 4
Murdochville 3,396 . . . . C 1
Nantes 1,167 . . . . F 4

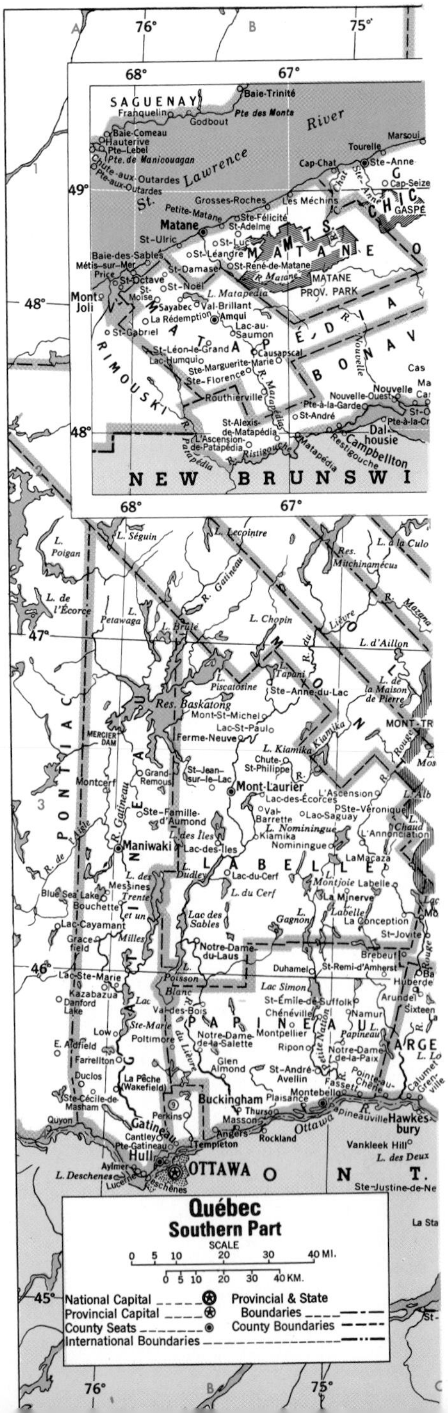
76°
75°
68°
67°
SAGUENAY
Baie-Trinité
Godbout
Pte des Monts
River
St. Lawrence
Baie-Comeau
Hauterive
Matane
Cap-Chat
Ste-Anne
Les Méchins
Mont-Joli
Amqui
Causapscal
Rimouski
MATANE PROV. PARK
NEW BRUNSWICK
Campbellton
Dalhousie
49°
48°
47°
46°
45°
Maniwaki
Mont-Laurier
Res. Baskatong
PONTIAC
LABELLE
PAPINEAU
Buckingham
Gatineau
Hull
OTTAWA
Montebello
Hawkesbury
Québec
Southern Part
SCALE
0 5 10 20 30 40 MI.
0 5 10 20 30 40 KM.
National Capital
Provincial Capital
County Seats
International Boundaries
Provincial & State Boundaries
County Boundaries

Agriculture, Industry and Resources

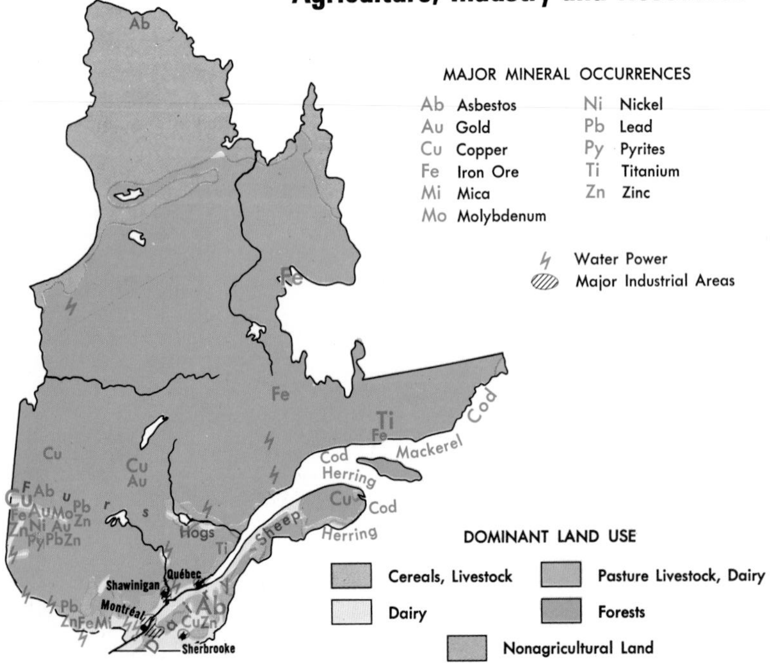
MAJOR MINERAL OCCURRENCES
Ab Asbestos
Au Gold
Cu Copper
Fe Iron Ore
Mi Mica
Mo Molybdenum
Ni Nickel
Pb Lead
Py Pyrites
Ti Titanium
Zn Zinc
Water Power
Major Industrial Areas
DOMINANT LAND USE
Cereals, Livestock
Dairy
Pasture Livestock, Dairy
Forests
Nonagricultural Land
Mackerel
Cod
Herring
Sheep
Hogs
Shawinigan
Québec
Montréal
Sherbrooke

Napierville⊕ 2,343 .... D 4
Neuville 996 .... F 3
New Carlisle⊕ 1,292 .... C 2
New Richmond 4,257 .... C 2
Nicolet 4,880 .... D 4
Nominingue 881 .... B 3
Normandin 4,041 .... E 1
North Hatley 689 .... H 4
Notre-Dame-de-la-Doré 1,064 E 1
Notre-Dame-des-Laurentides H 3
Notre-Dame-des-Prairies
6,150 .... D 3
Notre-Dame-du-Bon-Conseil
1,089 .... D 3
Notre-Dame-du-Lac⊕ 2,258 . J 2
Nouvelle 669 .... C 2
Oka 1,538. .... C 4
Omerville 1,398. .... E 4
Ormstown 1,659 .... D 4
Orsainville .... H 3
Otis 673 .... J 1
Otterburn Park 4,268 ...... D 4
Outremont 24,338 .... H 4
Pabos 1,295. .... D 2
Pabos-Mills 1,565 .... D 2
Papineauville⊕ 1,481 ...... C 4
Paspébiac 1,914 .... C 2
Percé⊕ 4,839. .... D 1
Petit-Cap 1,023. .... D 1
Petite-Matane 1,065 .... B 1
Petit-Saguenay (Saint-
François-d'Assise) 804 .. G 1
Pierrefonds 38,390 .... H 4
Pierreville 1,212 .... E 3

Pincourt 8,750 .... D 4
Pintendre 1,849. .... J 3
Plaisance 748 .... B 4
Plessisville 7,249 .... F 3
Pohénégamook 3,702 ...... H 2
Pointe-à-la-Croix 1,481 .... C 2
Pointe-au-Père 796. .... J 1
Pointe-au-Pic 1,054 .... G 2
Pointe-aux-Outardes 1,056 . A 1
Pointe-aux-Trembles 36,270 . J 4
Pointe-Calumet 2,935 ..... C 4
Pointe-Claire 24,571 ...... H 4
Pointe-du-Lac 5,359 ...... D 3
Pointe-Gatineau .... B 4
Pointe-Lebel 1,573 .... A 1
Pont-Rouge 3,580 .... F 3
Port-Alfred 8,621 .... G 1
Portneuf 1,333. .... F 3
Portneuf-sur-Mer (Rivière-
Portneuf-sur-Mer) 1,255 . H 1
Price 2,273. .... A 1
Princeville 4,023 .... F 3
Proulxville 588 .... E 3
Québec (cap.) 166,474 .... H 3
Québec *576,075 .... H 3
Quyon 744 .... A 4
Rawdon 2,958 .... D 3
Repentigny 34,419 .... J 4
Richelieu 1,832. .... D 4
Richmond 3,568 .... E 4
Rigaud 2,268 .... C 4
Rimouski⊕ 29,120 .... J 1
Rimouski-Est 2,506 .... J 1
Ripon 620. .... B 4

Rivière-à-Pierre 615 .... E 3
Rivière-au-Renard 2,211 ... D 1
Rivière-Bleue 1,690 .... J 2
Rivière-Bois-Clair 604 ..... F 3
Rivière-du-Loup 13,459 .... H 2
Rivière-du-Moulin .... G 1
Rivière-Éternité 659 .... G 1
Rivière-Portneuf-Portneuf-sur-
Mer 1,255 .... H 1
Robertsonville 1,987 ...... F 3
Roberval⊕ 11,429 .... E 1
Rock Island 1,179 .... E 4
Rosemère 7,778 .... H 4
Rougemont 972. .... D 4
Roxboro 6,292. .... H 4
Roxton Falls 1,245 .... E 4
Sacré-Coeur-de-Saguenay
1,678 .... H 1
Saint-Adelme 618 .... B 1
Saint-Adelphe 1,159 ...... E 3
Saint-Adolphe-d'Howard
1,686. .... C 4
Saint-Adrien 587 .... F 4
Saint-Agapito 2,954 ...... F 3
Saint-Aimé-des-Lacs 861 .. G 2
Saint-Alban 673 .... E 3
Saint-Alexandre-de-
Kamouraska 1,048. ..... H 2
Saint-Alexis-des-Monts 1,984. D 3
Saint-Amable 2,424 .... J 4
Saint-Ambroise 3,606. ..... F 1
Saint-Anaclet 1,377 .... J 1
Saint-André-Avellin 1,312 .. B 4
Saint-André-Est 1,293 ..... C 4

Saint-Anselme 1,808 ...... F 3
Saint-Antonin 941. .... H 2
Saint-Aubert 884. .... G 2
Saint-Augustin-de-Québec
2,475 .... E 3
Saint-Basile-Sud 1,719 .... F 3
Saint-Basile-le-Grand 7,658 . J 4
Saint-Benjamin 1,027. ..... G 3
Saint-Bernard 585 .... F 3
Saint-Bernard-sur-Mer 711 . G 2
Saint-Boniface-de-Shawinigan
3,164 .... D 3
Saint-Bruno 2,580. .... F 1
Saint-Bruno-de-Montarville
22,880 .... J 4
Saint-Camille-de-Bellechasse
1,744 .... G 3
Saint-Casimir 1,133 .... E 3
Saint-Césaire 2,935 .... D 4
Saint-Charles 1,019 .... G 3
Saint-Charles-de-Mandeville
1,392 .... D 3
Saint-Chrysostome 1,018 .. D 4
Saint-Côme 660 .... D 3
Saint-Constant 9,938 ...... H 4
Saint-Cyprien 860. .... J 2
Saint-Cyrille 1,041 .... E 4
Saint-Damien-de-Buckland
1,522 .... G 3
Saint-David 5,380 .... J 3
Saint-David-de-Falardeau
1,876 .... F 1
Saint-Denis 861 .... D 4

Saint-Dominique 2,068 .... E 4
Saint-Donat-de-Montcalm
1,521 .... C 3
Sainte-Adèle 4,675 .... C 4
Sainte-Agathe 709 .... F 3
Sainte-Agathe-des-Monts
5,641 .... C 3
Sainte-Anne-de-Beaupré
3,292 .... F 2
Sainte-Anne-de-Bellevue
3,981 .... H 4
Sainte-Anne-des-Monts⊕
6,062 .... C 1
Sainte-Anne-des-Plaines
4,258 .... J 4
Sainte-Anne-du-Lac 686 ... B 3
Sainte-Aurélie 1,045. ..... G 3
Sainte-Blandine 849. ...... J 1

Sainte-Catherine 1,474 .... F 3
Sainte-Claire 1,566. .... G 3
Sainte-Croix⊕ 1,814 .... F 3
Sainte-Félicité 711 .... B 1
Sainte-Foy 68,883 .... H 3
Sainte-Geneviève 2,573 ... H 4
Sainte-Geneviève-de-
Batiscan⊕ 356 .... E 3
Sainte-Hélène-de-Bagot
1,328 .... E 4
Sainte-Hénédine⊕ 639. .... F 3
Sainte-Julie-de-Verchères
14,243 .... J 4
Sainte-Julienne⊕ 750 ..... D 4
Sainte-Justine 1,080 ...... G 3
Saint-Élie 639 .... E 3
Saint-Elzéar 743 .... F 3
Sainte-Marie 8,937 .... G 3

Sainte-Martine⊕ 2,196. .... D 4
Saint-Émile 5,216 .... H 3
Sainte-Monique 705. ...... F 1
Sainte-Pétronille 982 ..... J 3
Sainte-Perpétue-de-L'Islet
1,232 .... H 2
Saint-Éphrem-de-Tring 973 . G 3
Saint-Épiphane 647 .... H 2
Sainte-Pudentienne 866 ... E 4
Sainte-Rosalie 2,862 ...... E 4
Saint-Esprit 1,068. .... D 4
Sainte-Thérèse 18,750. .... H 4
Sainte-Thérèse-Ouest
(Boisbriand) 13,471 .... H 4
Sainte-Thècle 1,703. ...... E 3
Saint-Étienne-de-Grès 845 . E 3
Saint-Étienne-de-Lauzon
1,218 .... J 3

AREA 594,857 sq. mi. (1,540,680 sq. km.)
POPULATION 6,532,461
CAPITAL Québec
LARGEST CITY Montréal
HIGHEST POINT Mont D'Iberville 5,420 ft.
(1.652 m.)
SETTLED IN 1608
ADMITTED TO CONFEDERATION 1867
PROVINCIAL FLOWER White Garden Lily

COUNTIES
indicated by numbers:
1 Iberville   D4
2 Napierville   D4
3 Rouville   D4
4 St-Hyacinthe   D4
5 Chambly   D4
6 Deux-Montagnes   D4
7 Laval   D4
8 Soulanges   C4
9 Beauharnois   D4
10 Hull   B4
11 Richelieu   D4
12 Vaudreuil   C4

Internal divisions represent Municipal Counties

© Copyright HAMMOND INCORPORATED, Maplewood, N.J.

Saint-Eustache 29,716......H 4
Saint-Fabien 1,361......J 1
Saint-Félicien 9,058......E 1
Saint-Félix-de-Valois 1,462......D 3
Saint-Ferréol-les-Neiges 1,758......G 2
Saint-Flavien 734......F 3
Saint-François-de-Sales 831......E 1
Saint-François-du-Lac® 942......D 4
Saint-Fulgence 950......G 1
Saint-Gabriel 3,161......D 3
Saint-Gabriel-de-Rimouski 779......J 1
Saint-Gédéon, Frontenac 1,569......G 4
Saint-Gédéon, Lac-St-Jean-E. 1,000......F 1
Saint-Georges, Beauce 10,342......G 4
Saint-Georges, Champlain 3,344......E 3
Saint-Georges-Ouest 6,378......G 4
Saint-Germain-de-Grantham 1,373......E 4
Saint-Gervais 973......G 3
Saint-Gilles 912......F 3
Saint-Grégoire (Mont-St-Grégoire) 740......D 4
Saint-Henri 1,970......J 3
Saint-Honoré, Beauce 1,116......G 4
Saint-Honoré, Chicoutimi 1,790......F 1
Saint-Hubert 60,573......J 4
Saint-Hubert-de-Témiscouata 871......J 2
Saint-Hyacinthe® 38,246......D 4
Saint-Isidore 811......J 3
Saint-Isidore-de-Laprairie 769......D 4
Saint-Jacques 2,152......D 4
Saint-Jacques-le-Mineur 1,203......H 4
Saint-Jean-Chrysostome 6,930......J 3
Saint-Jean-de-Dieu 1,377......J 1
Saint-Jean-de-Matha 931......D 3
Saint-Jean-Port-Joli 1,813......G 2
Saint-Jean-sur-Richelieu® 35,640......D 4
Saint-Jérôme 25,123......H 4
Saint-Joachim 1,139......G 2
Saint-Joseph-de-Beauce 3,216......G 3
Saint-Joseph-de-Sorel 2,545......D 3
Saint-Jovite 3,841......C 3
Saint-Lambert 20,557......J 4
Saint-Laurent 65,900......H 4

Saint-Lazare 731......G 3
Saint-Léonard 79,429......H 4
Saint-Léonard-d'Aston 992......E 3
Saint-Léonard-de-Chicoutimi 749......F 1
Saint-Léon-de-Standon 816......G 3
Saint-Léon-le-Grand 722......B 2
Saint-Liboire® 746......D 4
Saint-Louis-de-Gonzague 615......D 4
Saint-Louis-de-Terrebonne 14,172......H 4
Saint-Louis-du-Ha! Ha! 809......H 2
Saint-Luc 8,815......D 4
Saint-Luc-de-Matane 598......B 1
Saint-Marc-des-Carrières 2,822......E 3
Saint-Méthode-de-Frontenac 925......F 3
Saint-Michel-de-Bellechasse 963......G 3
Saint-Michel-des-Saints 1,584......D 3
Saint-Nazaire-de-Chicoutimi 962......F 1
Saint-Nérée 970......G 3
Saint-Nicolas 5,074......F 3
Saint-Noël 666......B 1
Saint-Odilon 580......G 3
Saint-Omer 718......C 2
Sorel® 20,347......D 4
Saint-Ours 625......D 4
Saint-Pacôme 1,996......H 2
Saint-Pamphile 3,428......H 3
Saint-Pascal 2,763......H 2
Saint-Paulin 663......D 3
Saint-Paul-de-Montminy 602......G 3
Saint-Paul-l'Ermite (Le Gardeur) 8,312......J 4
Saint-Philippe-de-Néri 715......H 2
Saint-Pie 1,725......D 4
Saint-Pierre 5,305......H 4
Saint-Pierre-d'Orléans 880......G 3
Saint-Polycarpe 602......C 4
Saint-Prime 2,522......E 1
Saint-Prosper-de-Dorchester 2,150......G 3
Saint-Raphaël 1,346......G 3
Saint-Raymond 3,605......E 3
Saint-Rédempteur 4,463......J 3
Saint-Régis 1,370......C 4
Saint-Rémi 5,146......D 4
Saint-Roch-de-l'Achigan 1,160......D 4
Saint-Roch-de-Richelieu 1,650......D 4
Saint-Romuald-d'Etchemin® 9,849......J 3

Saint-Sauveur-des-Monts 2,348......C 4
Saint-Siméon 1,152......G 2
Saint-Simon 602......H 1
Saint-Stanislas 1,443......E 3
Saint-Sylvère 1,006......E 3
Saint-Timothée 2,113......C 4
Saint-Tite 3,031......E 3
Saint-Tite-des-Caps 626......G 2
Saint-Ubald 1,605......E 3
Saint-Ulric 792......B 1
Saint-Urbain-de-Charlevoix 1,079......G 2
Saint-Victor 1,304......G 3
Saint-Zacharie 1,284......G 3
Saint-Zotique 1,774......C 4
Sault-au-Mouton 828......H 1
Sawyerville 939......F 4
Sayabec 1,721......B 1
Scotstown 762......F 4
Senneville 1,221......H 4
Shannon 3,488......F 3
Shawbridge 942......C 4
Shawinigan 23,011......E 3
Shawinigan-Sud 11,325......E 3
Shawville 1,006......A 4
Sherbrooke® 74,075......E 4
Sherrington 614......D 4
Sillery 12,825......J 3
Squatec 1,000......J 2
Stanstead Plain 1,093......F 4
Sutton 1,599......E 4
Tadoussac® 900......H 1
Templeton......E 4
Terrebonne 11,769......H 4
Thetford Mines 19,965......F 3
Thurso 2,780......B 4
Tourelle (Tourelle-Grand-Tourelle) 942......C 1
Tourville 659......H 2
Tracy 12,843......D 3
Tring-Jonction 1,315......G 3
Trois-Pistoles 4,445......H 1
Trois-Rivières 50,466......E 3
Trois-Rivières *111,453......E 3
Trois-Rivières-Ouest 13,107......E 3
Upton 926......E 4
Val-Barrette 609......C 3
Val-Brillant 687......B 1
Valcourt 2,601......E 4
Val-David 2,336......C 3
Vallée-Jonction 1,200......G 3
Valleyfield (Salaberry-de-Valleyfield) 29,574......C 4
Vanier 10,725......J 3

Varennes 8,764......J 4
Vaudreuil® 7,608......C 4
Verchères 4,473......D 4
Verdun 61,287......H 4
Victoriaville 21,838......F 3
Villeneuve......J 3
Warwick 2,847......E 4
Waterloo® 4,664......E 4
Waterville 1,397......E 4
Weedon-Centre 1,263......F 4
Westmount 20,480......H 4
Wickham 2,043......E 4
Windsor 5,233......E 4
Wottonville 673......E 4
Yamachiche® 1,258......E 3

OTHER FEATURES

Alma (isl.)......F 1
Aylmer (lake)......A 3
Baskatong (res.)......B 3
Batiscan (riv.)......E 2
Bécancour (riv.)......F 3
Bonaventure (isl.)......D 1
Bonaventure (riv.)......C 1
Brome (lake)......E 4
Brompton (lake)......E 4
Cascapédia (riv.)......C 1
Chaleur (bay)......C 1
Champlain (lake)......D 4
Chaudière (riv.)......G 4
Chic-Chocs (mts.)......B 1
Chicoutimi (riv.)......F 2
Coudres (isl.)......G 2
Deschênes (lake)......A 4
Deux Montagnes (lake)......H 4
Ditton (riv.)......F 4
Forillon Nat'l Park......D 1
Fort Chambly Nat'l Hist. Park......J 4
Gaspé (bay)......D 1
Gaspé (cape)......D 1
Gaspé (pen.)......D 1
Gaspésie Prov. Park......C 1
Gatineau (riv.)......B 3
Îles (lake)......C 1
Jacques-Cartier (mt.)......C 1
Jacques-Cartier (riv.)......E 3
Kénogami (lake)......F 1
Kiamika (lake)......B 3
La Vérendrye Nat'l Park......D 3
Laurentides Prov. Park......F 2
Lièvre (riv.)......B 3
Lièvres (isl.)......H 2
Maskinongé (riv.)......D 3
Matane (riv.)......B 1
Matane Prov. Park......B 1

Matapédia (riv.)......B 2
Mégantic (lake)......G 4
Memphremagog (lake)......E 4
Mercier (dam)......A 3
Métabetchouane (riv.)......E 1
Mille Îles (riv.)......H 4
Montmorency (riv.)......F 2
Mont-Tremblant Prov. Park......C 3
Nicolet (riv.)......E 3
Nominingue (lake)......B 3
Nord (riv.)......C 3
Orléans (isl.)......F 3
Ottawa (riv.)......B 4
Ouareau (riv.)......D 3
Ouelle (riv.)......H 2
Patapédia (riv.)......C 1
Péribonca (riv.)......F 1
Petite Nation (riv.)......B 4
Prairies (riv.)......H 4
Rimouski (riv.)......J 1
Ristigouche (riv.)......B 2
Saguenay (riv.)......G 1
Sainte-Anne (riv.)......E 3
Sainte-Anne (riv.)......G 2
Saint-François (lake)......F 4
Saint-François (riv.)......E 4
Saint-Jean (lake)......E 1
Saint Lawrence (gulf)......D 2
Saint Lawrence (riv.)......H 1
Saint-Louis (lake)......H 4
Saint-Maurice (riv.)......E 3
Saint-Pierre (lake)......E 3
Shawinigan (riv.)......E 3
Shipshaw (riv.)......F 1
Soeurs (isl.)......H 4
Témiscouata (lake)......H 2
Tremblant (lake)......C 3
Trente et un Milles (lake)......B 3
Verte (isl.)......H 1
Yamaska (riv.)......D 4
York (riv.)......D 1

® County seat.
*Population of metropolitan area.

QUÉBEC, NORTHERN

INTERNAL DIVISIONS

Abitibi (county) 93,529......B 2
Abitibi (terr.)......B 3
Berthier (county) 31,096......B 3
Bonaventure (county) 40,487......D 3
Champlain (county) 119,595......C 3
Charlevoix-Est (co.) 17,448......C 3

Charlevoix-Ouest (county) 14,712......C 3
Chicoutimi (county) 174,441......C 2
Gaspé-Est (county) 41,173......E 3
Gaspé-Ouest (county) 18,943......D 3
Gatineau (county) 54,229......B 3
Joliette (county) 60,384......B 3
Lac-St-Jean-Est (county) 47,891......C 3
Lac-St-Jean-Ouest (county) 62,952......C 2
Maskinongé (county) 20,763......C 3
Matane (county) 29,955......D 3
Matapédia (county) 23,715......D 3
Mistassini (terr.)......C 2
Montcalm (county) 27,557......C 3
Montmorency No. 1 (county) 23,048......C 3
Nouveau-Québec (terr.)......E 1
Pontiac (county) 20,283......B 3
Portneuf (county) 58,843......C 3
Québec (county) 458,980......C 3
Rimouski (county) 69,099......D 3
Saguenay (county) 115,881......C 2
Saint-Maurice (co.) 107,703......C 3
Témiscamingue (co.) 52,570......B 3

CITIES and TOWNS

Alma® 26,322......C 3
Amos® 9,421......C 2
Baie-du-Poste 1,690......D 3
Baie-du-Poste 1,690......C 2
Chicoutimi® 60,064......C 3
Gaspé 17,261......E 3
Hauterive 13,995......D 3
Jonquière 60,354......C 3
Lévis 17,895......C 3
La Tuque 11,556......C 3
Manicouagan......D 2
Maniwaki® 5,424......C 3
Matane® 13,612......D 3
Mistassini (Baie-du-Poste)......C 2
Mont-Laurier® 8,405......C 3
Montmagny® 12,405......C 3
New Carlisle 781......E 3
Percé 4,839......E 3
Port-Cartier-Ouest......D 3
Port-Menier® 275......D 3
Povungnituk 745......E 1
Rimouski® 29,120......D 3
Rivière-au-Tonnerre 480......D 3
Rivière-du-Loup 13,459......D 3
Rouyn 17,224......B 3

Sept-Îles 29,262......D 2
Shawinigan 23,011......C 3
Tadoussac 900......C 3
Val d'Or 21,371......B 3
Ville-Marie 2,651......B 3
Wemindji......B 2

OTHER FEATURES

Allard (lake)......E 2
Anticosti (isl.)......E 3
Baleine, Grand Rivière de la (riv.)......B 1
Bell (riv.)......B 2
Betsiamites (riv.)......C 2
Bienville (lake)......C 2
Broadback (riv.)......B 2
Cabonga (res.)......B 3
Caniapiscau (riv.)......D 1
Eastmain (riv.)......C 2
Eau Claire (lake)......C 1
Feuilles (riv.)......C 1
Gaspésie Prov. Park......D 3
George (riv.)......F 2
Gouin (res.)......C 3
Grande Rivière, La (riv.)......B 2
Honguedo (passage)......E 3
Hudson (bay)......A 1
Hudson (str.)......F 1
Jacques-Cartier (passage)......D 3
James (bay)......A 2
Koksoak (riv.)......D 1
Laurentides Prov. Park......C 3
Louis-XIV (pt.)......B 2
Manicouagan (res.)......D 2
Minto (lake)......C 1
Mistassibi (riv.)......C 2
Mistassini (lake)......C 2
Moisie (riv.)......D 2
Natashquan (riv.)......D 2
Nottaway (riv.)......B 2
Nouveau-Québec (crater)......F 1
Otish (mts.)......C 2
Ottawa (riv.)......B 3
Péribonca (riv.)......C 3
Plétipi (lake)......C 2
Saguenay (riv.)......C 3
Saint-Jean (lake)......C 3
Saint Lawrence (gulf)......E 3
Saint Lawrence (riv.)......D 3
Ungava (pen.)......E 1

® County seat.
*Population of metropolitan area.

ONTARIO, NORTHERN

INTERNAL DIVISIONS

Algoma (terr. dist.) 133,553 . . . D 3
Cochrane (terr. dist.) 96,875 . . D 2
Kenora (terr. dist.) 59,421 . . . . C 2
Manitoulin (terr. dist.) 11,001 . D 3
Nipissing (terr. dist.) 80,268 . . E 3
Parry Sound (terr. dist.) 33,528 . . . . E 3
Rainy River (terr. dist.) 22,798 B 3
Renfrew (county) 87,484 . . . . . E 3
Sudbury (reg. munic.) 159,779 . . . . D 3
Sudbury (terr. dist.) 27,068 . . . D 3
Thunder Bay (terr. dist.) 153,997 . . . . C 3
Timiskaming (terr. dist.) 41,288 . . . . D 3

CITIES and TOWNS

Chalk River 1,010 . . . . E 3
Elliot Lake 16,723 . . . . D 3
Fort Albany 482 . . . . D 2
Fort Frances⊙ 8,906 . . . . B 3
Kapuskasing 12,014 . . . . D 3
Kenora⊙ 9,817 . . . . B 3
Kirkland Lake 12,219 . . . . D 3
Moose Factory 1,452 . . . . D 2
Moosonee 1,433 . . . . D 2
Nickel Centre 12,318 . . . . D 3
North Bay⊙ 51,268 . . . . E 3
Pembroke⊙ 14,026 . . . . E 3
Sault Sainte Marie⊙ 82,697 . . D 3
Sudbury 91,829 . . . . D 3
Thunder Bay⊙ 112,486 . . . . . . C 3
Timmins 46,114 . . . . D 3
Valley East 20,433 . . . . D 3

OTHER FEATURES

Abitibi (lake) . . . . E 3
Abitibi (riv.) . . . . D 2
Albany (riv.) . . . . C 2
Algonquin Prov. Park . . . . E 3
Asheweig (riv.) . . . . C 2
Attawapiskat (lake) . . . . C 2
Attawapiskat (riv.) . . . . C 2
Basswood (lake) . . . . B 3
Berens (riv.) . . . . A 2
Big Trout (lake) . . . . B 2
Black Duck (riv.) . . . . C 1
Bloodvein (riv.) . . . . A 2
Caribou (isl.) . . . . C 3
Cobham (riv.) . . . . A 2
Eabamet (lake) . . . . C 2
Ekwan (riv.) . . . . C 2
English (riv.) . . . . B 2
Fawn (riv.) . . . . C 2
Finger (lake) . . . . B 2
Georgian (bay) . . . . D 3
Hannah (bay) . . . . D 2
Henrietta Maria (cape) . . . . D 1
Hudson (bay) . . . . D 1
Huron (lake) . . . . D 3
James (bay) . . . . D 2
Kapiskau (riv.) . . . . D 2
Kapuskasing (riv.) . . . . D 3
Kenogami (riv.) . . . . C 2
Kesagami (riv.) . . . . E 2
Lake of the Woods (lake) . . . . . B 3
Lake Superior Prov. Park . . . . . D 3
Little Current (riv.) . . . . C 2
Long (lake) . . . . C 3
Manitoulin (isl.) . . . . D 3
Mattagami (riv.) . . . . D 3
Michipicoten (isl.) . . . . C 3
Mille Lacs (lake) . . . . B 3
Missinaibi (lake) . . . . D 3
Missinaibi (riv.) . . . . D 2
Missisa (lake) . . . . D 2
Nipigon (lake) . . . . C 3
Nipissing (lake) . . . . E 3
North (chan.) . . . . D 3
North Caribou (lake) . . . . B 2
Nungesser (lake) . . . . B 2
Ogidaki (mt.) . . . . D 3
Ogoki (riv.) . . . . C 2
Opazatika (riv.) . . . . D 3
Opinnagau (riv.) . . . . D 2
Otoskwin (riv.) . . . . B 2
Ottawa (riv.) . . . . E 3
Pipestone (riv.) . . . . B 2
Polar Bear Prov. Park . . . . D 2
Pukaskwa Prov. Park . . . . C 3
Quetico Prov. Park . . . . B 3
Rainy (lake) . . . . B 3
Red (lake) . . . . B 2
Sachigo (riv.) . . . . B 2
Saganaga (lake) . . . . B 3
Saint Ignace (isl.) . . . . C 3
Saint Joseph (lake) . . . . B 2
Sandy (lake) . . . . B 2
Savant (lake) . . . . B 2
Seine (riv.) . . . . B 3
Seul (lake) . . . . B 2
Severn (lake) . . . . B 2
Severn (riv.) . . . . B 2
Shamattawa (riv.) . . . . C 2
Shibogama (lake) . . . . C 2
Sibley Prov. Park . . . . C 3
Slate (isls.) . . . . C 3
Stout (lake) . . . . B 2
Superior (lake) . . . . C 3
Sutton (lake) . . . . D 2
Sutton (riv.) . . . . D 2
Temigami (lake) . . . . D 3
Timiskaming (lake) . . . . E 3
Trout (lake) . . . . B 2
Wabuk (pt.) . . . . D 1
Winisk (lake) . . . . C 2
Winisk (riv.) . . . . C 2
Winnipeg (riv.) . . . . A 2
Woods (lake) . . . . B 3

ONTARIO

INTERNAL DIVISIONS

Algoma (terr. dist.) 133,553 . . . J 5
Brant (county) 104,427 . . . . . . D 4
Bruce (county) 60,020 . . . . C 3
Cochrane (terr. dist.) 96,875 . . J 4
Dufferin (county) 31,145 . . . . . D 3
Dundas (county) 18,946 . . . . . J 2
Durham (reg. munic.) 283,639 F 3
Elgin (county) 69,707 . . . . C 5
Essex (county) 312,467 . . . . . . B 5
Frontenac (county) 108,133 . . H 3
Glengarry (county) 20,254 . . . K 2
Grenville (county) 27,176 . . . . J 3
Grey (county) 73,824 . . . . D 3
Haldimand-Norfolk (reg. munic.) 89,456 . . . . E 5
Haliburton (county) 11,361 . . . F 2
Halton (reg. munic.) 253,883 . E 4
Hamilton-Wentworth (reg. munic.) 411,445 . . . . D 4
Hastings (county) 106,883 . . . G 3
Huron (county) 56,127 . . . . C 4
Kenora (terr. dist.) 59,421 . . . . G 5
Kent (county) 107,022 . . . . B 5
Lambton (county) 123,445 . . . B 5
Lanark (county) 45,676 . . . . . . H 3
Leeds (county) 53,765 . . . . H 3
Lennox and Addington (county) 33,040 . . . . G 3
Manitoulin (terr. dist.) 11,001 . B 2
Middlesex (county) 318,184 . . C 4
Muskoka (dist. munic.) 38,370 . . . . E 3
Niagara (reg. munic.) 368,288 E 4
Nipissing (terr. dist.) 80,268 . . F 2
Northumberland (county) 64,966 . . . . G 3
Ottawa-Carleton (reg. munic.) 546,849 . . . . J 2
Oxford (county) 85,920 . . . . . . D 4
Parry Sound (terr. dist.) 33,528 . . . . D 2
Peel (reg. munic.) 490,731 . . . E 4
Perth (county) 66,096 . . . . C 4
Peterborough (county) 102,452 . . . . F 3
Prescott (county) 30,365 . . . . . K 2
Prince Edward (county) 22,336 . . . . G 3
Rainy River (terr. dist.) 22,798 G 5
Renfrew (county) 87,484 . . . . . G 2
Russell (county) 22,412 . . . . . . J 2
Simcoe (county) 225,071 . . . . . E 3
Stormont (county) 61,927 . . . . K 2
Sudbury (reg. munic.) 159,779 . . . . K 6
Sudbury (terr. dist.) 27,068 . . . J 5
Thunder Bay (terr. dist.) 153,997 . . . . H 5
Timiskaming (terr. dist.) 41,288 . . . . K 5
Toronto (metro. munic.) 2,137,395 . . . . K 4
Victoria (county) 47,854 . . . . . . F 3
Waterloo (reg. munic.) 305,496 . . . . D 4
Wellington (county) 129,432 . . D 4
York (reg. munic.) 252,053 . . . E 4

CITIES and TOWNS

Ailsa Craig 765 . . . . C 4
Ajax 25,475 . . . . E 4
Alban 342 . . . . D 1
Alexandria 3,271 . . . . K 2
Alfred 1,057 . . . . K 2
Alliston 4,712 . . . . E 3
Almonte 3,855 . . . . H 2
Alvinston 736 . . . . B 5
Amherstburg 5,685 . . . . A 5
Amherst View 6,110 . . . . H 3
Ancaster 14,428 . . . . D 4
Angus 3,085 . . . . E 3
Apsley 264 . . . . F 3
Arkona 473 . . . . C 4
Armstrong 378 . . . . H 4
Arnprior 5,828 . . . . H 2
Aroland 291 . . . . H 4
Arthur 1,700 . . . . D 4
Astorville 340 . . . . E 1
Athens 948 . . . . J 3
Atherley 366 . . . . E 3
Atikokan 4,452 . . . . G 5

AREA 412,580 sq. mi. (1,068,582 sq. km.)
POPULATION 9,101,694
CAPITAL Toronto
LARGEST CITY Toronto
HIGHEST POINT in Timiskaming Dist. 2,275 ft. (693 m.)
SETTLED IN 1749
ADMITTED TO CONFEDERATION 1867
PROVINCIAL FLOWER White Trillium

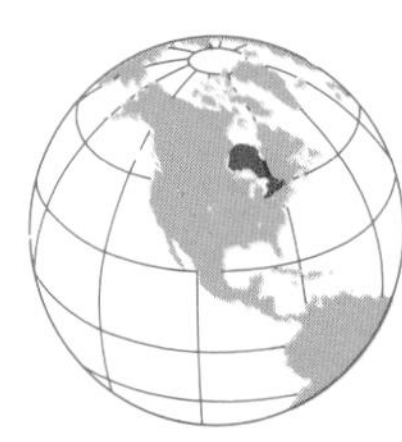

Atwood 723 . . . . D 4
Aurora 16,267 . . . . J 3
Avonmore 273 . . . . K 2
Aylmer 5,254 . . . . C 5
Ayr 1,295 . . . . D 4
Ayton 424 . . . . D 3
Baden 945 . . . . D 4
Bala 577 . . . . E 2
Bancroft 2,329 . . . . G 2
Barrie⊙ 38,423 . . . . E 3
Barry's Bay 1,216 . . . . G 2
Batawa 430 . . . . G 3
Bath 1,071 . . . . H 3
Bayfield 649 . . . . C 4
Beachburg 682 . . . . H 2
Beachville 917 . . . . D 4
Beardmore 583 . . . . H 5
Beaverton 1,952 . . . . E 3
Beeton 1,989 . . . . E 3
Belle River 3,568 . . . . B 5
Belleville⊙ 34,881 . . . . G 3
Belmont 831 . . . . C 5
Bethany 365 . . . . F 3
Bewdley 508 . . . . F 3
Binbrook 306 . . . . E 4
Blackstock 720 . . . . F 3
Blenheim 4,044 . . . . C 5
Blind River 3,444 . . . . J 5
Bloomfield 718 . . . . G 4
Blyth 926 . . . . C 4
Bobcaygeon 1,625 . . . . F 3
Bonfield 540 . . . . E 1
Bothwell 915 . . . . C 5
Bourget 1,057 . . . . J 2
Bracebridge⊙ 9,063 . . . . E 2
Bradford 7,370 . . . . E 3
Braeside 492 . . . . H 2
Brampton⊙ 149,030 . . . . J 4
Brantford⊙ 74,315 . . . . D 4
Bridgenorth 1,633 . . . . F 3
Brigden 635 . . . . B 5
Brighton 3,147 . . . . G 3
Britt 419 . . . . D 2
Brockville⊙ 19,896 . . . . J 3
Bruce Mines 635 . . . . J 5
Brussels 962 . . . . C 4
Burford 1,461 . . . . D 4
Burgessville 302 . . . . D 4
Burk's Falls 922 . . . . E 2
Burlington 114,853 . . . . E 4
Cache Bay 665 . . . . D 1
Caesarea 551 . . . . F 3
Calabogie 256 . . . . H 2
Caledon 26,645 . . . . E 4
Callander 1,158 . . . . E 1
Cambridge 77,183 . . . . D 4
Campbellford 3,409 . . . . G 3
Cannington 1,623 . . . . E 3
Capreol 3,845 . . . . K 5
Caramat 265 . . . . H 5
Cardinal 1,753 . . . . J 3
Carleton Place 5,626 . . . . H 2
Carlisle 781 . . . . D 4
Carlsbad Springs 616 . . . . J 2
Carp 707 . . . . H 2
Cartier 590 . . . . J 5
Casselman 1,675 . . . . J 2
Castleton 346 . . . . F 3
Chalk River 1,010 . . . . G 1
Chapleau 3,243 . . . . J 5
Charing Cross 443 . . . . B 5
Chatham⊙ 40,952 . . . . B 5
Chatsworth 383 . . . . D 3
Cherry Valley 289 . . . . G 4
Chesley 1,840 . . . . C 3
Chesterville 1,430 . . . . J 2
Chute-à-Blondeau 365 . . . . K 2
City View . . . . J 2
Clarence Creek 796 . . . . J 2
Clarksburg 508 . . . . D 3
Clifford 645 . . . . D 4
Clinton 3,081 . . . . C 4
Cobalt 1,759 . . . . K 5
Cobden 997 . . . . H 2
Coboconk 426 . . . . F 3
Cobourg⊙ 11,385 . . . . F 4
Cochrane⊙ 4,848 . . . . K 5
Colborne 1,796 . . . . G 4
Colchester 711 . . . . B 6
Coldwater 964 . . . . E 3
Collingwood 12,064 . . . . D 3
Comber 667 . . . . B 5
Consecon 295 . . . . G 3
Cookstown 918 . . . . E 3
Cornwall⊙ 46,144 . . . . K 2
Cottam 404 . . . . B 5
Courtland 647 . . . . D 5
Courtright 1,024 . . . . B 5
Crediton 370 . . . . C 4
Creemore 1,182 . . . . D 3
Crysler 540 . . . . J 2
Cumberland 518 . . . . J 2
Cumberland Beach-Bramshot-Buena Vista 679 . . . . E 3
Dashwood 426 . . . . C 4
Deep River 5,095 . . . . G 1
Delaware 481 . . . . C 5
Delhi 4,043 . . . . D 5
Delta 360 . . . . H 3
Deseronto 1,740 . . . . G 3
Douglas 303 . . . . H 2
Drayton 809 . . . . D 4
Dresden 2,550 . . . . B 5
Drumbo 476 . . . . D 4
Dryden 6,640 . . . . G 4
Dublin 295 . . . . C 4
Dubreuilville △988 . . . . J 5
Dundalk 1,250 . . . . D 3
Dundas 19,586 . . . . D 4
Dungannon 284 . . . . C 4
Dunnville 11,353 . . . . E 5
Durham 2,458 . . . . D 3
Dutton 1,115 . . . . C 5
Earlton 1,028 . . . . K 5
East York 101,974 . . . . J 4
Echo Bay 786 . . . . J 5
Eden Mills 318 . . . . D 4
Eganville 1,245 . . . . G 2
Egmondville 465 . . . . C 4
Elgin 327 . . . . H 3
Elk Lake 526 . . . . K 5
Elliot Lake 16,723 . . . . B 1
Elmira 7,063 . . . . D 4
Elmvale 1,183 . . . . E 3
Elmwood 364 . . . . C 3
Elora 2,666 . . . . D 4
Embro 727 . . . . C 4
Embrun 1,883 . . . . J 2
Emeryville-Puce 1,611 . . . . B 5
Emo 762 . . . . F 5
Englehart 1,689 . . . . K 5
Enterprise 357 . . . . H 3
Erieau 430 . . . . C 5
Erin 2,313 . . . . D 4
Espanola 5,836 . . . . J 5
Essex 6,295 . . . . B 5
Etobicoke 298,713 . . . . J 4
Everett 570 . . . . E 3
Exeter 3,732 . . . . C 4
Fauquier 561 . . . . J 5
Fenelon Falls 1,701 . . . . F 3
Fergus 6,064 . . . . D 4
Field 462 . . . . E 1
Finch 353 . . . . J 2
Fingal 380 . . . . C 5
Fitzroy Harbour 446 . . . . H 2
Flesherton 565 . . . . D 3
Foleyet 484 . . . . J 5
Fordwich 365 . . . . C 4
Forest 2,671 . . . . C 4
Formosa 393 . . . . C 3
Fort Erie 24,096 . . . . E 5
Fort Frances⊙ 8,906 . . . . F 5
Foxboro 597 . . . . G 3
Frankford 1,919 . . . . G 3
Fraserdale 303 . . . . J 5
Freelton 307 . . . . D 4
Gananoque 4,863 . . . . H 3
Garden Village 270 . . . . E 1
Geraldton 2,956 . . . . H 5
Glencoe 1,694 . . . . C 5
Glen Miller 639 . . . . G 3
Glen Robertson 378 . . . . K 2
Glen Walter 710 . . . . K 2
Goderich⊙ 7,322 . . . . C 4
Gogama 652 . . . . J 5
Goodwood 335 . . . . E 3
Gore Bay⊙ 777 . . . . B 2
Gorrie 468 . . . . C 4
Grafton 409 . . . . G 4
Grand Bend 680 . . . . C 4
Grand Valley 1,226 . . . . D 4
Granton 315 . . . . C 4
Gravenhurst 8,532 . . . . E 3
Greely 567 . . . . J 2
Green Valley 459 . . . . K 2
Grimsby 15,797 . . . . E 4
Guelph⊙ 71,207 . . . . D 4

(continued on following page)

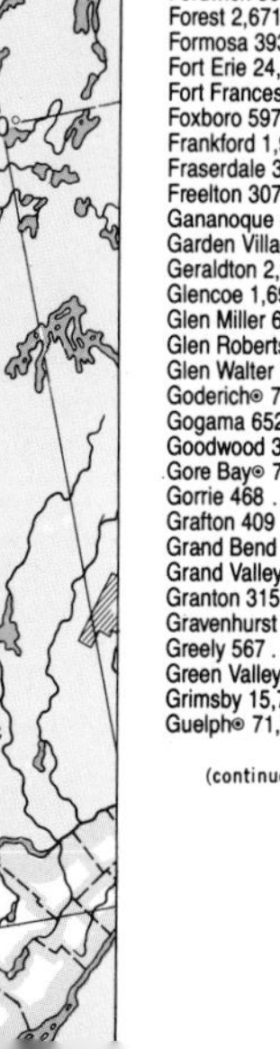

Northern Ontario

SCALE
0 25 50 100 150 200 MI.
0 25 50 100 150 200 KM.

Provincial Capital ⊛ · County Seats ⊙ · International Boundaries · Provincial and State Boundaries · County Boundaries

All islands in Hudson Bay, James Bay, Hudson Strait and Ungava Bay lie within the Northwest Territories.

© Copyright HAMMOND INCORPORATED, Maplewood, N. J.

Longitude West B of Greenwich

Haileybury® 4,925 . . . . K 5	Iroquois 1,211 . . . . J 3	Lisle 265 . . . . E 3	Maynooth 277 . . . . G 2	Napanee 4,803 . . . . G 3	Ottawa® (cap.), Canada	Port Rowan 811 . . . . D 5
Haldimand 16,866 . . . . E 5	Iroquois Falls 6,339 . . . . J 5	Listowel 5,026 . . . . D 4	McGregor 1,145 . . . . C 5	Navan 419 . . . . J 2	295,163 . . . . J 2	Port Stanley 1,891 . . . . C 5
Haliburton 1,443 . . . . F 2	Johnstown 789 . . . . J 3	Little Britain 265 . . . . F 3	McKerrow 260 . . . . C 1	Neustadt 511 . . . . D 4	Ottawa-Hull *717,978 . . . . J 2	Pottageville 286 . . . . J 3
Halton Hills 35,190 . . . . E 4	Kakabeka Falls 300 . . . . G 5	Little Current 1,507 . . . . B 2	Meaford 4,367 . . . . D 3	Newboro 260 . . . . H 3	Otterville 776 . . . . D 5	Powassan 1,169 . . . . E 1
Hamilton® 306,434 . . . . E 4	Kanata 19,728 . . . . J 2	London® 254,280 . . . . C 4	Melbourne 346 . . . . C 4	Newburgh 617 . . . . H 3	Owen Sound® 19,883 . . . . D 3	Prescott® 4,670 . . . . J 3
Hamilton *542,095 . . . . E 4	Kapuskasing 12,014 . . . . J 5	London *283,668 . . . . C 4	Merlin 745 . . . . C 5	Newbury 441 . . . . C 5	Paincourt 414 . . . . B 5	Princeton 462 . . . . D 4
Hanover 6,316 . . . . C 3	Kars 449 . . . . J 2	Longlac 2,431 . . . . H 5	Merrickville 984 . . . . J 3	Newcastle 32,229 . . . . F 4	Paisley 1,039 . . . . C 3	Puce-Emeryville 1,611 . . . . B 5
Harriston 1,954 . . . . D 4	Kearney 538 . . . . E 2	Long Sault 1,227 . . . . K 2	Metcalfe 687 . . . . J 2	New Hamburg 3,923 . . . . D 4	Pakenham 367 . . . . H 2	Rainy River 1,061 . . . . F 5
Harrow 2,274 . . . . B 5	Keene 353 . . . . F 3	L'Orignal 1,819 . . . . K 2	Midhurst 1,457 . . . . E 3	New Liskeard 5,551 . . . . K 5	Palmerston 1,989 . . . . D 4	Ramore 382 . . . . K 5
Harrowsmith 599 . . . . H 3	Keewatin 1,863 . . . . F 5	Lucan 1,616 . . . . C 4	Midland 12,132 . . . . D 3	Newmarket® 29,753 . . . . E 3	Paris 7,485 . . . . D 4	Rayside-Balfour 15,017 . . . . K 5
Harwood 332 . . . . F 3	Kemptville 2,362 . . . . J 2	Lucknow 1,088 . . . . C 3	Mildmay 928 . . . . D 4	Niagara Falls 70,960 . . . . E 4	Parkhill 1,358 . . . . C 4	Red Rock 1,260 . . . . H 5
Hastings 975 . . . . G 3	Kenora® 9,817 . . . . F 4	Lyn 518 . . . . J 3	Milford Bay 401 . . . . E 2	Niagara-on-the-Lake 12,186 . . . . E 4	Parry Sound® 6,124 . . . . E 2	Renfrew 8,283 . . . . H 2
Havelock 1,385 . . . . G 3	Killaloe Station 634 . . . . G 2	Lynden 451 . . . . D 4	Millbank 337 . . . . D 4	Nickel Centre 12,318 . . . . C 1	Pefferlaw 857 . . . . E 3	Richards Landing 405 . . . . J 5
Hawkesbury 9,877 . . . . K 2	Killarney 433 . . . . C 2	Lynhurst 685 . . . . G 2	Millbrook 927 . . . . F 3	Nipigon 2,377 . . . . H 5	Pelham 11,104 . . . . E 4	Richmond 2,880 . . . . J 2
Hawkestone 275 . . . . E 3	Kincardine 5,778 . . . . C 3	MacGregor's Bay 861 . . . . E 2	Milton® 28,067 . . . . E 4	Nobel 386 . . . . E 2	Pembroke® 14,026 . . . . G 2	Richmond Hill 37,778 . . . . J 4
Hawk Junction 349 . . . . J 5	Kingston 52,616 . . . . H 3	MacTier 647 . . . . E 2	Milverton 1,463 . . . . D 4	Nobleton 1,861 . . . . J 3	Penetanguishene 5,315 . . . . D 3	Ridgetown 3,062 . . . . C 5
Hearst 5,533 . . . . J 5	Kingsville 5,134 . . . . B 6	Madawaska 264 . . . . G 3	Minaki 319 . . . . F 4	Noelville 702 . . . . C 1	Perth® 5,655 . . . . J 2	Ripley 591 . . . . C 3
Hensall 973 . . . . C 4	Kinmount 262 . . . . F 3	Madoc 1,249 . . . . G 3	Mindemoya 376 . . . . B 2	North Bay® 51,268 . . . . E 1	Petawawa 5,520 . . . . G 2	River Valley 275 . . . . D 1
Hepworth 393 . . . . C 3	Kirkland Lake 12,219 . . . . K 5	Maitland 947 . . . . J 3	Minden® 838 . . . . F 2	North Cower 818 . . . . J 2	Peterborough® 60,620 . . . . F 3	Rockcliffe Park 1,869 . . . . J 2
Hickson 263 . . . . D 4	Kitchener® 139,734 . . . . D 4	Mallorytown 368 . . . . J 3	Mississauga 315,056 . . . . J 4	North York 559,521 . . . . J 4	Petrolia 4,234 . . . . B 5	Rockland 3,961 . . . . J 2
Highgate 435 . . . . C 5	Kitchener *287,801 . . . . D 4	Manitouwadge 3,155 . . . . H 5	Mitchell 2,777 . . . . C 4	Norwich 2,117 . . . . D 5	Pickering 37,754 . . . . K 4	Rockwood 1,068 . . . . D 4
Hillsburgh 1,065 . . . . D 4	Komoka 1,152 . . . . C 4	Manitowaning 518 . . . . C 2	Monkton 520 . . . . C 4	Norwood 1,278 . . . . F 3	Picton® 4,361 . . . . G 3	Rodney 1,007 . . . . C 5
Hillsdale 197 . . . . E 3	Lakefield 2,374 . . . . F 3	Manotick-Hillside Gardens	Moonbeam 838 . . . . J 5	Nottawa 360 . . . . D 3	Pioton® 4,361	Rosslyn Village 362 . . . . G 5
Holland Landing 2,771 . . . . E 3	Lanark 753 . . . . H 2	2,694 . . . . J 2	Moorefield 308 . . . . D 4	Oakville 75,773 . . . . J 4	Plantagenet 870 . . . . K 2	Round Lake Centre 255 . . . . G 2
Honey Harbour 505 . . . . E 2	Lancaster 637 . . . . K 2	Marathon 2,271 . . . . H 5	Mooretown 344 . . . . B 5	Oakwood 404 . . . . F 3	Plattsville 495 . . . . D 4	Russell 1,099 . . . . J 2
Hornepayne 1,848 . . . . J 5	Langton 348 . . . . E 1	Markdale 1,289 . . . . D 3	Moose Creek 393 . . . . K 2	Odessa 849 . . . . H 3	Point Edward 2,383 . . . . B 4	Ruthven 649 . . . . B 6
Hudson 515 . . . . G 4	Lansdowne 540 . . . . H 3	Markham 77,037 . . . . D 1	Morewood 264 . . . . J 3	Oil City 266 . . . . B 5	Pontypool 759 . . . . F 3	Saint Albert 254 . . . . K 2
Huntsville 11,467 . . . . E 2	Larder Lake 1,084 . . . . K 5	Markstay 444 . . . . C 1	Morpeth 284 . . . . C 5	Oil Springs 627 . . . . B 5	Port Burwell 655 . . . . D 5	Saint Catharines® 124,018 . . . . E 4
Huron Park 1,104 . . . . C 4	Latchford 397 . . . . K 5	Marmora 1,304 . . . . G 3	Morrisburg 2,308 . . . . J 3	Omemee 819 . . . . F 3	Port Carling 629 . . . . E 2	Saint Catharines-Niagara
Ignace 2,499 . . . . G 5	Leamington 12,528 . . . . B 6	Martintown 388 . . . . K 2	Mount Albert 1,165 . . . . E 3	Onaping Falls 6,198 . . . . J 5	Port Colborne 19,225 . . . . E 5	*304,353 . . . . E 4
Ilderton 301 . . . . C 4	Limoges 930 . . . . J 2	Massey 1,274 . . . . C 1	Mount Brydges 1,557 . . . . C 4	Opasatika 413 . . . . J 5	Port Elgin 6,131 . . . . C 3	Saint Charles 382 . . . . D 1
Ingersoll 8,494 . . . . D 4	Lincoln 14,196 . . . . B 6	Matachewan 444 . . . . J 5	Mount Forest 3,474 . . . . D 4	Orangeville® 13,740 . . . . D 4	Port Franks 557 . . . . C 4	Saint Clair Beach 2,845 . . . . B 5
Ingleside 1,400 . . . . J 2	Linden Beach 579 . . . . B 6	Matheson 966 . . . . F 1	Mount Hope 557 . . . . E 4	Orillia 23,955 . . . . E 3	Port Hope 9,992 . . . . F 4	Saint Clements 890 . . . . D 4
Innerkip 715 . . . . D 4	Lindsay® 13,596 . . . . F 3	Mattawa 2,652 . . . . F 1	Munster 1,531 . . . . J 2	Osgoode 1,381 . . . . J 2	Port Lambton 921 . . . . B 5	Saint-Eugène 470 . . . . K 2
Inverhuron 438 . . . . A 1	Linwood 450 . . . . D 4	Mattice 803 . . . . J 5	Nakina 936 . . . . H 4	Oshawa 117,519 . . . . F 4	Port McNicoll 1,883 . . . . E 3	Saint George 865 . . . . D 4
Iron Bridge 821 . . . . A 1	Lion's Head 467 . . . . C 2	Maxville 836 . . . . K 2	Nanticoke 19,816 . . . . E 5	Oshawa *154,217 . . . . F 4	Port Perry 4,712 . . . . E 3	Saint Isidore de Prescott 746 . . . . K 2

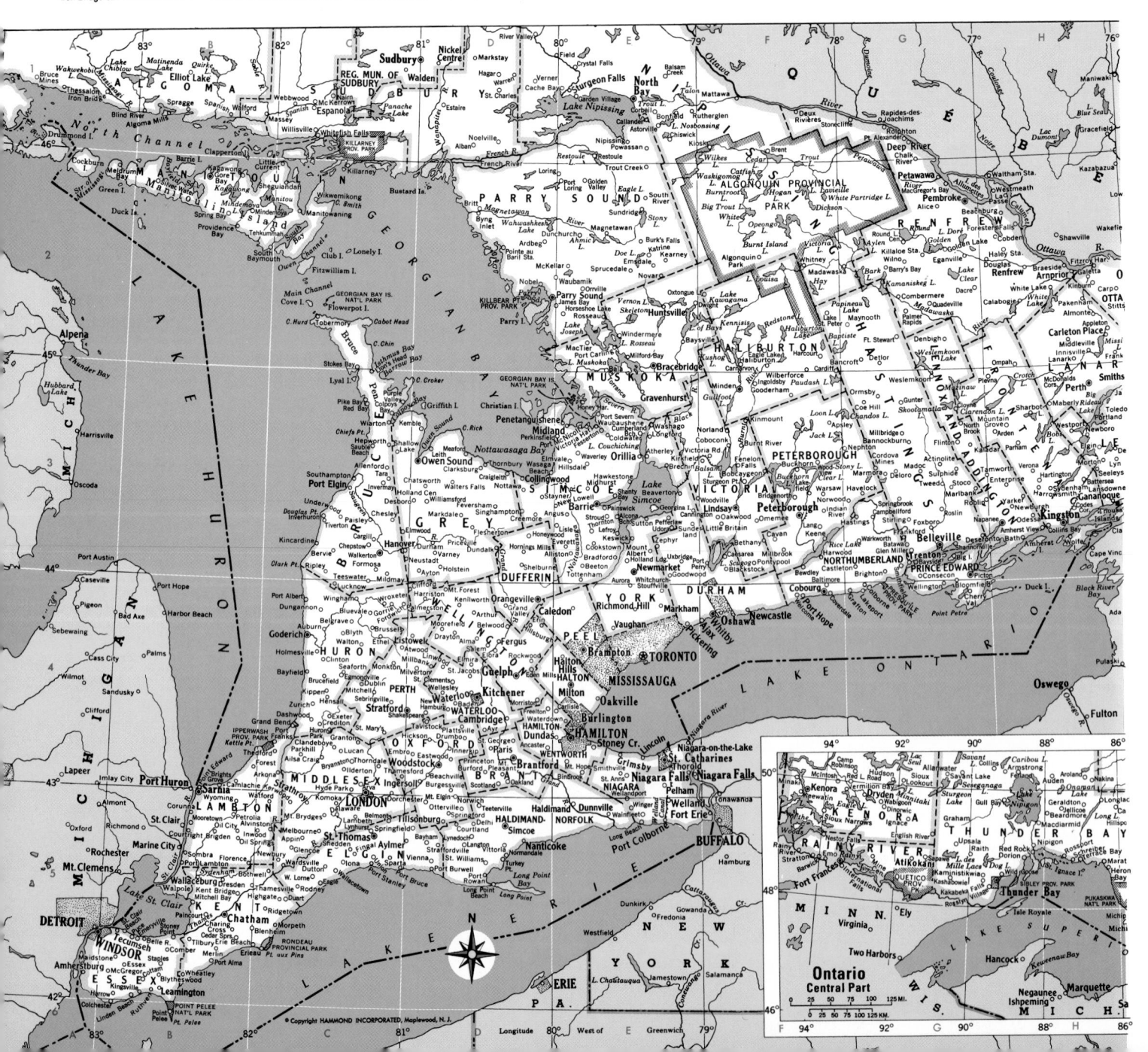

Ontario
Central Part

0 25 50 75 100 125 MI.
0 25 50 75 100 125 KM.

© Copyright HAMMOND INCORPORATED, Maplewood, N.J.

Saint Jacobs 1,189 . . . D 4
Saint Mary's 4,883 . . . C 4
Saint Thomas⊙ 28,165 . . . C 5
Saint Williams 442 . . . D 5
Salem 825 . . . D 4
Sarnia⊙ 50,892 . . . B 5
Sauble Beach 729 . . . C 3
Sault Sainte Marie⊙ 82,697 . . J 5
Scarborough 443,353 . . . K 4
Schomberg 923 . . . J 3
Schreiber 1,968 . . . H 5
Scotland 600 . . . D 4
Seaforth 2,114 . . . C 4
Searchmont 384 . . . J 5
Sebringville 579 . . . C 4
Seeleys Bay 503 . . . H 3
Shakespeare 602 . . . D 4
Shallow Lake 418 . . . C 3
Shannonville 314 . . . G 3
Shanty Bay 358 . . . E 3
Sharbot Lake 495 . . . H 3
Shedden 292 . . . C 5
Shelburne 2,862 . . . D 3
Simcoe⊙ 14,326 . . . D 5
Sioux Lookout 3,074 . . . G 4
Sioux Narrows 394 . . . F 5
Smithfield 349 . . . G 3
Smiths Falls 8,831 . . . H 3
Smithville 1,936 . . . E 4
Smooth Rock Falls 2,352 . . . J 5
Sombra 420 . . . B 5
Southampton 2,830 . . . C 3
South Mountain 285 . . . J 3
South River 1,109 . . . E 2
Spanish 1,063 . . . J 5
Sparta 283 . . . C 5
Spencerville 438 . . . J 3
Springfield 555 . . . C 5
Springford 309 . . . D 5
Stayner 2,530 . . . E 3
Stirling 1,638 . . . G 3
Stittsville 2,652 . . . J 2
Stoney Creek 36,762 . . . E 4
Stoney Point 1,090 . . . B 5
Straffordville 752 . . . D 5
Stratford⊙ 26,262 . . . C 4
Strathroy 8,748 . . . C 5
Sturgeon Falls 6,045 . . . E 1
Sudbury⊙ 91,829 . . . K 5
Sudbury *149,923 . . . K 5
Sunderland 703 . . . E 3
Sundridge 734 . . . E 2
Sydenham 595 . . . H 3
Tamworth 402 . . . H 3
Tara 687 . . . C 3
Tavistock 1,885 . . . D 4
Tecumseh 6,364 . . . B 5
Teeswater 1,026 . . . C 3
Terrace Bay 2,639 . . . H 5
Thamesford 1,920 . . . C 4
Thamesville 961 . . . C 5
Thedford 694 . . . C 4
Thessalon 1,620 . . . J 5
Thornbury 1,435 . . . D 3
Thorndale 581 . . . C 4
Thornton 414 . . . E 3
Thorold 15,412 . . . E 4
Thunder Bay⊙ 112,486 . . . H 5
Thunder Bay *121,379 . . . H 5
Tilbury 4,298 . . . B 5
Tillsonburg 10,487 . . . D 5
Timmins 46,114 . . . J 5

Tiverton 806 . . . C 3
Tobermory 282 . . . C 2
Toronto (cap.)⊙ 599,217 . . . K 4
Toronto *2,998,947 . . . K 4
Tottenham 3,022 . . . E 3
Trenton 15,085 . . . G 3
Trout Creek 652 . . . E 2
Turkey Point 407 . . . D 5
Tweed 1,574 . . . G 3
Udora 375 . . . E 3
Union 485 . . . C 5
Uxbridge 4,209 . . . E 3
Valley East 20,433 . . . J 5
Vanier 18,792 . . . J 2
Vankleek Hill 1,774 . . . K 2
Vars 527 . . . J 2
Vaughan 29,674 . . . J 4
Vermilion Bay 505 . . . G 4
Verner 1,076 . . . D 1
Vernon 303 . . . J 2
Verona 754 . . . H 3
Victoria Harbour 1,125 . . . E 3
Vienna 369 . . . D 5
Virginiatown 1,010 . . . K 5
Vittoria 420 . . . D 5
Wabigoon 268 . . . G 5
Walden 10,139 . . . J 5
Walkerton⊙ 4,682 . . . C 3
Wallaceburg 11,506 . . . B 5
Wardsville 450 . . . C 5
Warkworth 618 . . . G 3
Warren 579 . . . D 1
Warsaw 314 . . . F 3
Wasaga Beach 4,705 . . . D 3
Washago 569 . . . E 3
Waterloo 49,428 . . . D 4
Watford 1,402 . . . C 5
Waubaushene 878 . . . E 3
Wawa 4,206 . . . J 5
Webbwood 519 . . . C 1
Welcome 293 . . . F 4
Welland 454,448 . . . E 5
Wellesley 997 . . . D 4
Wellington 1,082 . . . G 4
Wendover 326 . . . J 2
West Lorne 1,258 . . . C 5
Westmeath 262 . . . H 2
Westport 621 . . . H 3
Wheatley 1,638 . . . B 5
Whitby⊙ 36,698 . . . F 4
Whitchurch-Stouffville 13,557 . J 3
White River △1,006 . . . J 5
Whitney 766 . . . F 2
Wiarton 2,074 . . . C 3
Wikwemikong 1,030 . . . C 2
Williamsburg 407 . . . J 3
Williamsford 256 . . . D 3
Williamstown 328 . . . K 2
Winchester 2,001 . . . J 2
Windsor⊙ 192,083 . . . B 5
Windsor *246,110 . . . B 5
Wingham 2,897 . . . C 4
Wolfe Island 271 . . . H 3
Woodstock⊙ 26,603 . . . D 4
Woodville 575 . . . F 3
Wroxeter 350 . . . C 4
Wyoming 1,682 . . . B 5
Yarker 319 . . . H 3
York 134,617 . . . J 4
Zephyr 330 . . . E 3
Zurich 795 . . . C 4

Ontario
Southern Part

SCALE
0 10 20 30 40 50 MI.
0 10 20 30 40 50 KM.

National Capital ⊛
Provincial Capital ⊛
County Seats ⊙
International Boundaries
Provincial & State Boundaries
County Boundaries
Canals

OTHER FEATURES

Abitibi (riv.) . . . J 5
Algonquin Prov. Park . . . F 2
Amherst (isl.) . . . H 3
Balsam (lake) . . . F 3
Barrie (isl.) . . . B 1
Bays (lake) . . . F 2
Big Rideau (lake) . . . H 3
Black (riv.) . . . E 3
Bruce (pen.) . . . C 2
Buckhorn (lake) . . . F 3
Cabot (head) . . . C 2
Charleston (lake) . . . J 3
Christian (isl.) . . . D 3
Clear (lake) . . . F 3
Cockburn (isl.) . . . A 2
Couchiching (lake) . . . E 3
Croker (cape) . . . D 3
Don (riv.) . . . J 4
Doré (lake) . . . G 2
Douglas (pt.) . . . C 3
Erie (lake) . . . E 5
Flowerpot (isl.) . . . C 2
French (riv.) . . . D 1
Georgian (bay) . . . D 2
Georgian Bay Is. Nat'l Park . . . C 2, D 3
Georgina (isl.) . . . E 3
Grand (riv.) . . . D 4
Humber (riv.) . . . J 3
Hurd (cape) . . . C 2
Huron (lake) . . . B 3
Ipperwash Prov. Park . . . C 4
Joseph (lake) . . . E 2
Killarney Prov. Park . . . C 1
Killbear Point Prov. Park . . . D 2
Lake of the Woods (lake) . . . F 5

Lake Superior Prov. Park . . . J 5
Lonely (isl.) . . . C 2
Long (pt.) . . . D 5
Long Point (bay) . . . D 5
Madawaska (riv.) . . . G 2
Magnetawan (riv.) . . . D 2
Main (chan.) . . . C 2
Manitou (lake) . . . C 2
Manitoulin (isl.) . . . B 2
Mattagami (riv.) . . . J 5
Michipicoten (isl.) . . . H 5
Missinaibi (riv.) . . . J 5
Mississagi (riv.) . . . A 1
Mississippi (lake) . . . H 2
Muskoka (lake) . . . E 2
Niagara (riv.) . . . E 4
Nipigon (lake) . . . H 5
Nipissing (lake) . . . E 1
North (chan.) . . . A 1
Nottawasaga (bay) . . . D 3
Ogidaki (mt.) . . . J 5
Ontario (lake) . . . G 4
Opeongo (lake) . . . F 2
Ottawa (riv.) . . . H 2
Owen (sound) . . . D 3
Panache (lake) . . . C 1
Parry (isl.) . . . D 2
Parry (sound) . . . D 2
Pelee (pt.) . . . B 6
Petre (pt.) . . . G 4
Point Pelee Nat'l Park . . . B 5
Presqu'ile Prov. Park . . . G 4
Pukaskwa Prov. Park . . . H 5
Quetico Prov. Park . . . G 5
Rainy (lake) . . . G 5
Rice (lake) . . . F 3
Rideau (lake) . . . H 3
Rondeau Prov. Park . . . C 5
Rosseau (lake) . . . E 2
Saint Clair (lake) . . . B 5
Saint Clair (riv.) . . . B 5
Saint Lawrence (lake) . . . K 3
Saint Lawrence (riv.) . . . J 3
Saint Lawrence Is. Nat'l Park . J 3
Saugeen (riv.) . . . C 3
Scugog (lake) . . . F 3
Seul (lake) . . . G 4
Severn (riv.) . . . E 3
Sibley Prov. Park . . . H 5
Simcoe (lake) . . . E 3
South (bay) . . . C 2
Spanish (riv.) . . . C 1
Stony (lake) . . . G 3
Superior (lake) . . . H 5
Sydenham (riv.) . . . B 5
Thames (riv.) . . . B 5
Theano (pt.) . . . J 5
Thousand (isls.) . . . H 3
Timagami (lake) . . . K 5
Trout (lake) . . . E 1
Vernon (lake) . . . E 2
Walpole (isl.) . . . B 5
Welland (canal) . . . E 5
Woods (lake) . . . F 5

⊙County seat.
*Population of metropolitan area.
△Population of town or township.

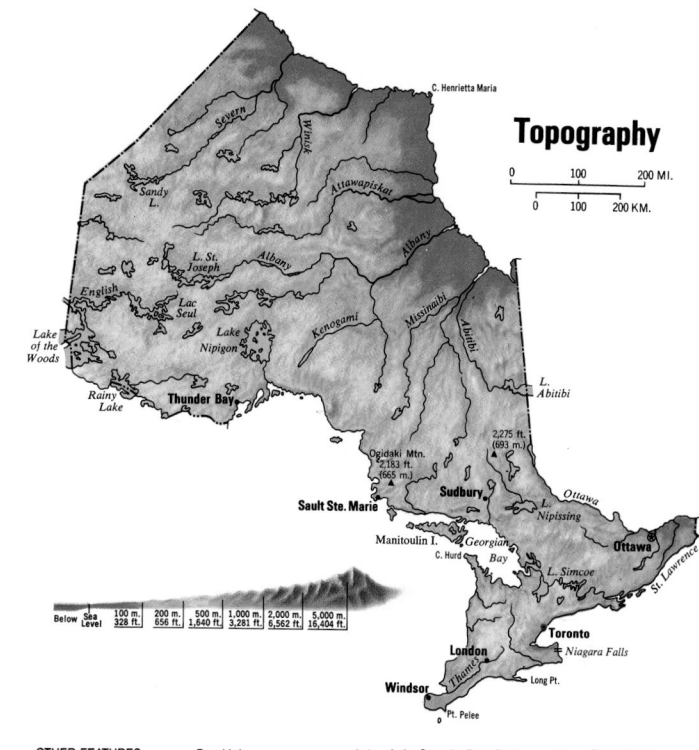

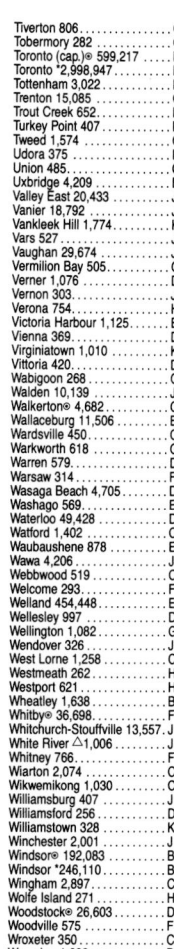

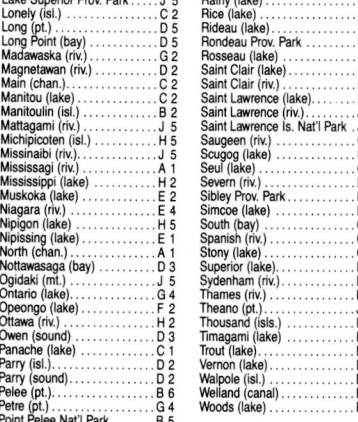

Agriculture, Industry and Resources

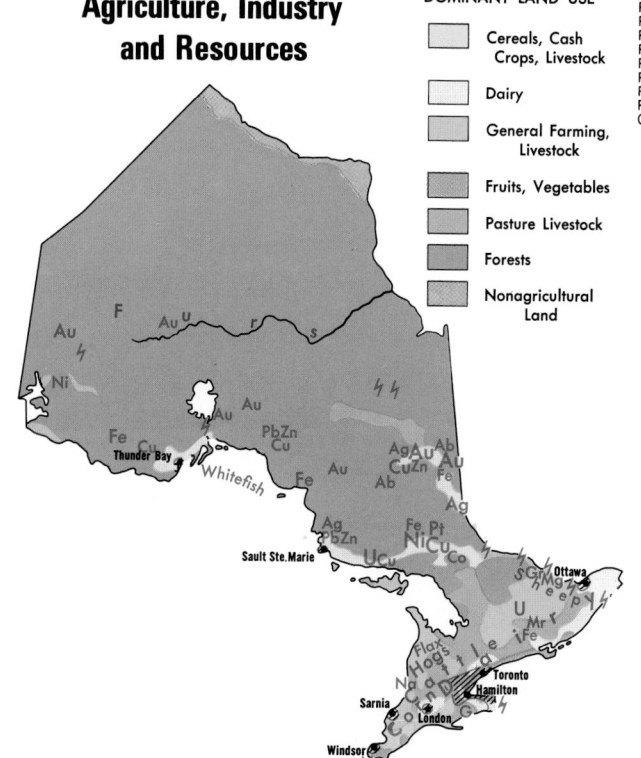

DOMINANT LAND USE

Cereals, Cash Crops, Livestock
Dairy
General Farming, Livestock
Fruits, Vegetables
Pasture Livestock
Forests
Nonagricultural Land

MAJOR MINERAL OCCURRENCES

Ab	Asbestos	Mg	Magnesium
Ag	Silver	Mr	Marble
Au	Gold	Na	Salt
Co	Cobalt	Ni	Nickel
Cu	Copper	Pb	Lead
Fe	Iron Ore	Pt	Platinum
G	Natural Gas	U	Uranium
Gr	Graphite	Zn	Zinc

Water Power
Major Industrial Areas

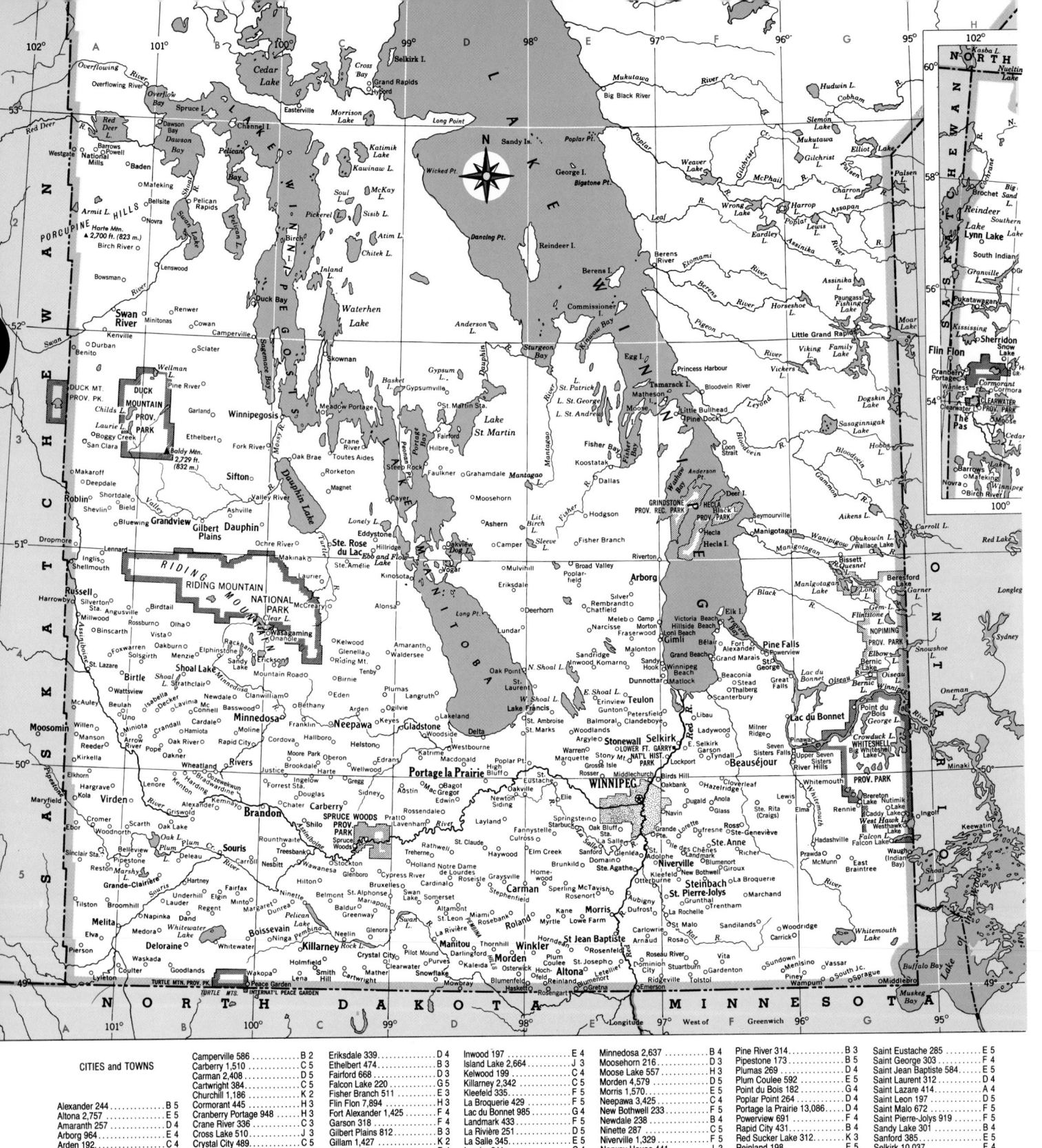

CITIES and TOWNS

Alexander 244 .... B 5
Altona 2,757 .... E 5
Amaranth 257 .... D 4
Arborg 964 .... E 4
Arden 314 .... C 4
Ashern 570 .... D 3
Austin 416 .... D 5
Baldur 344 .... C 5
Barrows 199 .... A 2
Beauséjour 2,462 .... F 4
Belmont 314 .... C 5
Benito 441 .... A 3
Berens River 681 .... F 2
Binscarth 472 .... A 4
Birch River 597 .... A 2
Birds Hill 711 .... F 4
Birtle 887 .... B 4
Bloodvein River 413 .... F 3
Blumenort 533 .... C 5
Boissevain 1,660 .... B 5
Bowsman 454 .... A 2
Brandon 36,242 .... B 5
Brochet 215 .... H 2

Camperville 586 .... B 2
Carberry 1,510 .... C 5
Carman 2,408 .... D 5
Cartwright 384 .... C 5
Churchill 1,186 .... K 2
Cormorant 445 .... H 3
Cranberry Portage 948 .... H 3
Crane River 336 .... C 3
Cross Lake 510 .... J 3
Crystal City 489 .... C 5
Cypress River 260 .... D 5
Darlingford 170 .... D 5
Dauphin 8,971 .... B 3
Deloraine 1,136 .... B 5
Dominion City 437 .... E 5
Douglas 170 .... C 5
Duck Bay 594 .... B 2
Dugald 410 .... F 5
Dunnottar 287 .... E 4
East Selkirk 985 .... F 4
Easterville 589 .... C 1
Elgin 172 .... B 5
Elie 450 .... E 5
Elkhorn 549 .... A 5
Elm Creek 293 .... D 5
Elphinstone 201 .... B 4
Emerson 762 .... E 5
Erickson 540 .... C 4

Eriksdale 339 .... D 4
Ethelbert 474 .... B 3
Fairford 668 .... D 3
Falcon Lake 220 .... G 5
Fisher Branch 511 .... E 3
Flin Flon 7,894 .... H 3
Fort Alexander 1,425 .... F 4
Garson 318 .... F 4
Gilbert Plains 812 .... B 3
Gillam 1,427 .... K 2
Gimli 1,550 .... F 4
Gladstone 964 .... D 4
Glenboro 741 .... C 5
Grand Marais 207 .... F 4
Grand Rapids 567 .... C 1
Grandview 1,013 .... B 3
Great Falls 272 .... F 4
Gretna 545 .... E 5
Grosse Isle 171 .... E 4
Grunthal 572 .... F 5
Hamiota 728 .... B 4
Hartney 465 .... B 5
Haywood 240 .... D 5
Hillridge 201 .... C 3
Hochfeld 187 .... E 5
Ile des Chênes 814 .... F 5
Inglis 209 .... A 4

Inwood 197 .... E 4
Island Lake 2,664 .... J 3
Kelwood 199 .... C 4
Killarney 2,342 .... C 5
Kleefeld 335 .... F 5
La Broquerie 429 .... F 5
Lac du Bonnet 985 .... G 4
Landmark 433 .... F 5
La Rivière 251 .... D 5
La Salle 345 .... E 5
Laurier 241 .... C 4
Letellier 178 .... E 5
Little Grand Rapids 559 .... G 2
Lockport 212 .... F 4
Lorette 1,092 .... F 5
Lowe Farm 241 .... E 5
Lundar 634 .... D 4
Lynn Lake 2,087 .... H 2
MacGregor 795 .... D 5
Mafeking 266 .... A 2
Manigotagan 216 .... F 3
Manitou 861 .... D 5
McCreary 618 .... C 4
Melita 1,156 .... A 5
Miami 401 .... D 5
Middlechurch 342 .... A 4
Miniota 247 .... A 4
Minitonas 628 .... B 2

Minnedosa 2,637 .... B 4
Mooseshorn 216 .... D 3
Moose Lake 557 .... H 3
Morden 4,579 .... D 5
Morris 1,570 .... E 5
Neepawa 3,425 .... C 4
New Bothwell 233 .... F 5
Newdale 238 .... B 4
Ninette 287 .... C 5
Niverville 1,329 .... F 5
Norway House 441 .... J 3
Notre Dame de Lourdes 627 ... D 5
Oakbank 1,277 .... F 5
Oakburn 255 .... B 4
Oak Lake 369 .... B 5
Oak River 179 .... B 4
Oakville 383 .... D 5
Ochre River 284 .... C 3
Onanole 386 .... C 4
Oozewekwun 453 .... B 5
Paungassi 296 .... G 2
Pelican Rapids 178 .... B 2
Petersfield 170 .... E 4
Pierson 201 .... A 5
Pilot Mound 838 .... D 5
Pinawa 2,006 .... G 4
Pine Falls 885 .... F 4

Pine River 314 .... B 3
Pipestone 173 .... B 5
Plumas 269 .... D 4
Plum Coulee 592 .... E 5
Point du Bois 182 .... G 4
Poplar Point 264 .... D 5
Portage la Prairie 13,086 .... D 4
Powerview 691 .... F 4
Rapid City 431 .... B 4
Red Sucker Lake 312 .... K 3
Reinland 198 .... E 5
Reston 589 .... A 5
Richer 288 .... F 5
Riding Mountain 168 .... C 4
Rivers 1,107 .... B 4
Riverton 657 .... E 3
Roblin 1,953 .... A 3
Roland 301 .... D 5
Rorketon 229 .... C 3
Rosenfeld 263 .... E 5
Rossburn 696 .... B 4
Russell 1,660 .... A 4
Saint Adolphe 928 .... E 5
Saint Ambroise 263 .... E 4
Saint Claude 592 .... D 5
Sainte Agathe 326 .... E 5
Sainte Anne 1,338 .... F 5
Sainte Rose du Lac 1,090 .... C 3

Saint Eustache 285 .... E 5
Saint George 303 .... F 4
Saint Jean Baptiste 584 .... E 5
Saint Laurent 312 .... D 4
Saint Lazare 414 .... A 4
Saint Leon 197 .... D 5
Saint Malo 672 .... F 5
Saint Pierre-Jolys 919 .... F 5
Sandy Lake 301 .... B 4
Sanford 385 .... E 5
Selkirk 10,037 .... F 4
Sherridon 138 .... H 3
Shoal Lake 835 .... B 4
Sifton 210 .... B 3
Somerset 596 .... D 5
Snow Lake 1,853 .... H 3
Souris 1,731 .... B 5
South Indian Lake 770 .... H 2
Split Lake 985 .... J 2
Sprague 199 .... G 5
Starbuck 224 .... E 5
Steinbach 6,676 .... F 5
Stonewall 2,210 .... E 4
Stony Mountain 1,313 .... E 4
Strathclair 390 .... B 4
Swan Lake 367 .... D 5
Swan River 3,782 .... A 2
Teulon 925 .... E 4

Manitoba
Northern Part

0   40   80   120 MI.

0   40   80   120 KM.

W E S T   T E R R S

HUDSON BAY

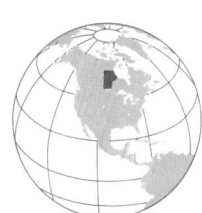

Manitoba
Southern Part

SCALE

0 5 10   20   40   60 MI.

0 5 10   20   40   60 KM.

Provincial Capital ⊛
International Boundaries ▬ ∙ ▬ ∙
Provincial Boundaries ▬ ▬ ▬

© Copyright HAMMOND INCORPORATED, Maplewood, N.J.

The Pas 6,390 .... H 3
Thicket Portage 195........ J 3
Thompson 14,288......... J 2
Treherne 743 .... D 5
Tyndall 421............... F 4
Virden 2,940 .... A 5
Vita 364 .... F 5
Wabowden 655 .... J 3
Wallace Lake ●2,044..... G 3
Wanless 193 .... H 3
Warren 459............... E 4
Waskada 239............. B 5
Wawanesa 492 .... C 5
Whitemouth 320 .... F 5
Whitewater ●856 .... B 5
Winkler 5,046............. D 5
Winnipeg (cap.) 564,473.. E 5
Winnipeg *584,842....... E 5
Winnipeg Beach 565 ..... F 4
Winnipegosis 855......... B 3
Woodlands 185........... E 4
Wooodridge 170.......... G 5
York Landing 229......... J 2

OTHER FEATURES

Aikens (lake) .... G 3
Anderson (lake).......... D 2
Anderson (pt.)........... F 3
Armit (lake) .... A 2
Assapan (riv.)........... G 2
Assiniboine (riv.) .... C 5
Assinika (lake).......... G 2
Assinika (riv.)........... C 2
Atim (lake) .... C 2
Baldy (mt.) .... B 3
Basket (lake) .... C 3
Beaverhill (lake) .... J 3
Berens (isl.).............. E 2
Berens (riv.)............. F 2
Bernic (lake) .... G 4
Big Sand (lake)......... H 2
Bigstone (lake) .... J 3
Bigstone (pt.)........... E 2
Bigstone (lake) .... J 3
Birch (lake) .... C 2
Black (isl.).............. F 3
Black (riv.)............. F 4
Bloodvein (riv.) .... F 3
Bonnet (lake) .... G 4
Buffalo (bay) .... G 5
Burntwood (riv.)........ J 2
Caribou (riv.)........... J 1
Carroll (lake) .... G 3
Cedar (lake) .... B 1
Channel (isl.)........... B 2
Charron (lake) .... G 2
Childs (lake) .... A 3
Chitek (lake) .... C 2
Churchill (cape)......... K 2
Churchill (riv.) .... J 2
Clear (lake) .... C 4
Clearwater Lake Prov. Park .. H 3
Cobham (riv.) .... G 1
Cochrane (riv.) .... H 2
Commissioner (isl.)...... E 2
Cormorant (lake)........ H 3
Cross (bay) .... C 1
Cross (lake) .... J 3
Crowduck (lake) .... G 4
Dancing (pt.)........... D 2
Dauphin (lake) .... C 3
Dauphin (riv.) .... D 3
Dawson (bay)........... B 2
Dog (lake) .... D 3
Dogskin (lake) .... F 3
Duck Mountain Prov. Park .. B 3
Eardley (lake) .... F 2

East Shoal (lake) .... E 4
Ebb and Flow (lake) ..... C 3
Egg (isl.)................ E 3
Elbow (lake) .... G 4
Elk (isl.)................ F 4
Elliot (lake) .... G 2
Etawney (lake).......... J 2
Etomami (riv.) .... F 2
Falcon (lake) .... G 5
Family (lake) .... G 3
Fisher (bay)............. E 3
Fisher (riv.)............. E 3
Fishing (lake) .... G 2
Flintstone (lake) .... G 4
Fox (riv.) .... K 2
Gammon (riv.) .... G 3
Garner (lake) .... G 4
Gem (lake) .... G 4
George (isl.)............. E 2
George (lake) .... E 3
Gilchrist (creek) .... F 2
Gilchrist (lake).......... G 2
Gods (lake) .... K 3
Gods (riv.).............. K 3
Granville (lake) .... H 2
Grass (riv.)............. H 2
Grass River Prov. Park ... H 3
Grindstone Prov. Rec. Park .. F 3
Gunisao (lake)........... J 3
Gypsum (lake) .... D 3
Harrop (lake) .... G 2
Harte (mt.) .... A 2
Hayes (riv.) .... K 3
Hecla (isl.) .... F 3
Hecla Prov. Park .... F 3
Hobbs (lake) .... K 2
Horseshoe (lake) .... G 2
Hubbart (pt.) .... K 2
Hudson (bay)........... K 2
Hudwin (lake) .... G 1
Inland (lake) .... C 2
International Peace Garden .. B 5
Island (lake) .... K 3
Katimik (lake) .... C 2
Kawinaw (lake) .... C 2
Kinwow (bay) .... E 2
Kississing (lake) .... H 2
Knee (lake) .... J 2
Lake of the Woods (lake) .. H 5
La Salle (riv.)........... E 5
Laurie (lake) .... A 3
Leaf (riv.) .... F 2
Lewis (lake) .... G 2
Leyond (riv.) .... F 3
Little Birch (lake) .... E 3
Lonely (lake) .... C 3
Long (lake) .... G 4
Long (pt.) .... D 1
Long (pt.) .... D 4
Manigotagan (lake)....... G 4

Manigotagan (riv.)......... G 3
Manitoba (lake) .... D 4
Mantagao (riv.) .... E 3
Marshy (lake) .... B 5
McKay (lake) .... C 2
McPhail (riv.) .... F 2
Minnedosa (riv.) .... B 4
Moar (lake) .... G 2
Molson (lake)............ J 3
Moose (lake) .... E 3
Morrison (lake) .... C 1
Mossy (riv.)............. C 3
Mukutawa (lake) .... D 3
Mukutawa (riv.) .... E 1
Muskeg (bay)........... G 6
Nejanilini (lake) .... J 1
Nelson (riv.) .... J 2
Nopiming Prov. Park ...... G 4
Northern Indian (lake) .... J 2
North Knife (lake) .... J 2
North Seal (riv.) .... H 2
North Shoal (lake) .... E 4
Nueltin (lake)............ H 1
Oak (lake) .... B 5
Obukowin (lake) .... G 4
Oiseau (lake) .... G 4
Oiseau (riv.) .... G 4
Overflow (bay) .... A 1
Overflowing (riv.) .... A 1
Owl (riv.) .... K 2
Oxford (lake) .... J 3
Paint (lake) .... J 2
Palsen (riv.) .... J 2
Pelican (bay) .... B 2
Pelican (lake) .... B 2
Pelican (lake) .... C 5
Pembina (hills).......... C 5
Pembina (riv.)........... C 5
Peonan (pt.) .... D 3
Pickerel (lake) .... C 2
Pigeon (riv.)............ F 2
Pipestone (creek) .... A 5
Plum (creek) .... B 5
Plum (lake)............. B 5
Poplar (riv.) .... E 2
Porcupine (hills) .... A 2
Portage (bay) .... D 3
Punk (isl.) .... F 3
Quesnel (lake) .... G 4
Rat (riv.) .... G 5
Red (riv.) .... F 4
Red Deer (lake) .... A 2
Red Deer (riv.) .... A 2
Reindeer (isl.) .... E 2
Reindeer (lake) .... H 2
Riding (mt.) .... B 4
Riding Mountain Nat'l Park .. B 4
Rock (lake) .... C 5
Ross (isl.) .... J 3
Sagemace (bay) .... B 3

Saint Andrew (lake) ...... E 3
Saint George (lake) ...... E 3
Saint Martin (lake) ...... D 3
Saint Patrick (lake) ...... E 3
Sale (riv.) .... E 5
Sandy (isls.)............ D 2
Sasaginnigak (lake) ..... G 3
Seal (riv.) .... J 2
Selkirk (lake) .... C 1
Setting (lake) .... H 3
Shoal (lake) .... G 5
Shoal (riv.) .... B 2
Sipiwesk (lake) .... J 3
Sisib (lake)............. C 2
Sleeve (lake) .... E 3
Slemon (lake) .... G 1
Snowshoe (lake) .... G 4
Soul (lake).............. C 2
Souris (riv.)............. B 5
Southern Indian (lake) ... H 2
South Knife (riv.) .... J 2
South Seal (riv.) .... J 2
Split (lake) .... J 2
Spruce (isl.) .... B 1
Spruce Woods Prov. Park .. C 5
Stevenson (lake).......... J 3
Sturgeon (bay)........... B 2
Swan (lake) .... A 3
Swan (lake) .... D 5
Swan (riv.) .... A 3
Tadoule (lake) .... J 2
Tamarack (isl.)........... F 3
Tatnam (cape).......... K 2
Traverse (bay) .... F 4
Turtle (mts.)............. B 5
Turtle (riv.)............. C 3
Turtle Mountain Prov. Park .. B 5
Valley (riv.) .... B 3
Vickers (lake) .... G 3
Viking (lake) .... G 3
Wanipigow (riv.)......... G 3
Washow (bay) .... F 3
Watenhen (lake) .... F 2
Weaver (lake) .... F 2
Wellman (lake) .... B 3
West Hawk (lake) ...... G 5
West Shoal (lake) .... E 4
Whitemouth (lake)....... G 5
Whitemouth (riv.) .... G 5
Whiteshell Prov. Park .... G 4
Whitewater (lake) .... B 5
Wicked (pt.) .... D 2
Winnipeg (lake) .... E 2
Winnipeg (riv.) .... G 4
Winnipegosis (lake) ..... C 2
Woods (lake) .... H 5
Wrong (lake) .... F 2

*Population of metropolitan area.
●Population of rural municipality.

AREA 250.999 sq. mi. (650,087 sq. km.)
POPULATION 1,063,016
CAPITAL Winnipeg
LARGEST CITY Winnipeg
HIGHEST POINT Baldy Mtn. 2,729 ft.
(832 m.)
SETTLED IN 1812
ADMITTED TO CONFEDERATION 1870
PROVINCIAL FLOWER Prairie Crocus

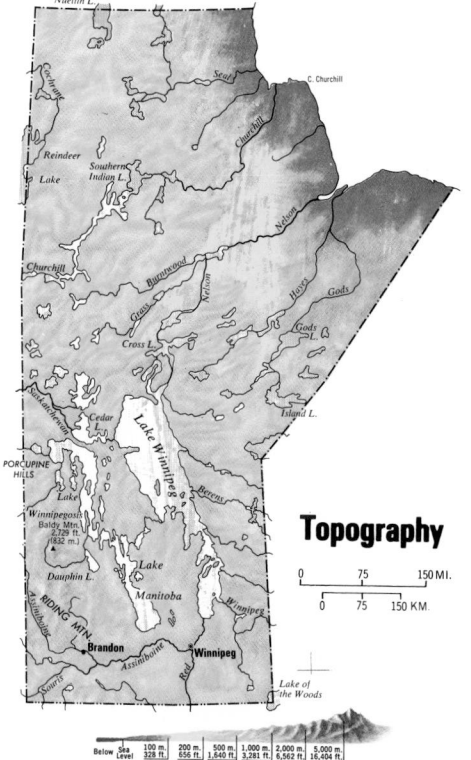

Topography

0   75   150 MI.

0   75   150 KM.

Below Sea Level | 100 m. 328 ft. | 200 m. 656 ft. | 500 m. 1,640 ft. | 1,000 m. 3,281 ft. | 2,000 m. 6,562 ft. | 5,000 m. 16,404 ft.

Agriculture, Industry and Resources

DOMINANT LAND USE

▢ Cereals (chiefly barley, oats)
▢ Cereals, Livestock
▢ Dairy
▢ Livestock
▢ Forests
▢ Nonagricultural Land

MAJOR MINERAL OCCURRENCES

Au Gold
Co Cobalt
Cu Copper
Na Salt

Ni Nickel
O   Petroleum
Pb Lead
Pt Platinum
Zn Zinc

⚡ Water Power
▨ Major Industrial Areas

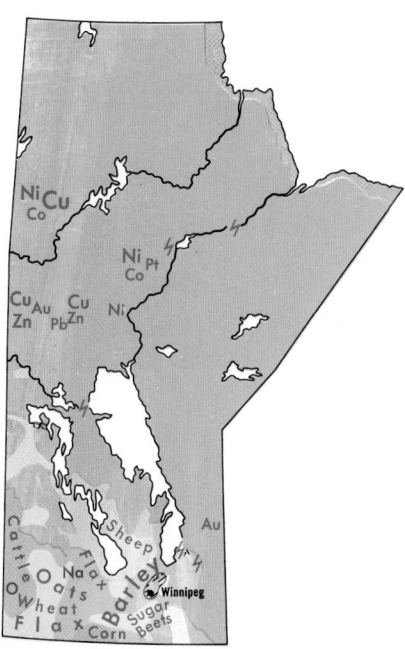

Topography

0 60 120 MI.
0 60 120 KM.

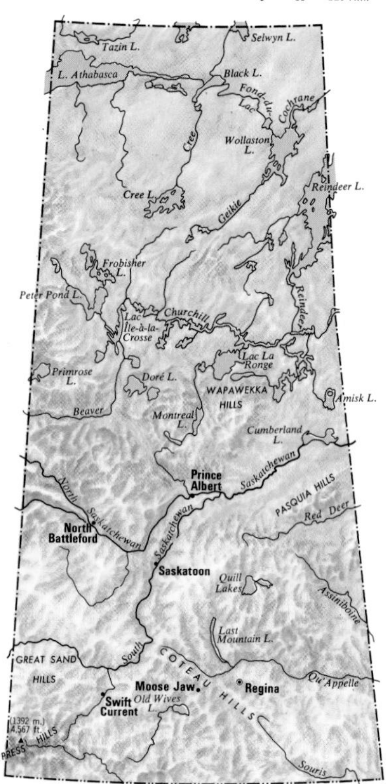

5,000 m. 16,404 ft. | 2,000 m. 6,562 ft. | 1,000 m. 3,281 ft. | 500 m. 1,640 ft. | 200 m. 656 ft. | 100 m. 328 ft. | Sea Level | Below

CITIES and TOWNS

Abbey 218 C 5
Aberdeen 496 E 3
Abernethy 300 H 5
Air Ronge 557 M 3
Alameda 318 J 6
Alida 169 K 6
Allan 871 E 4
Alsask 652 B 4
Annaheim 209 G 3
Antelope •231 C 5
Arborfield 439 H 2
Archerwill 286 H 3
Arcola 493 J 6
Arlington Beach •432 F 4
Asquith 507 D 3
Assiniboia 2,924 E 6
Avonlea 442 G 5
Baildon •799 F 5
Balcarres 739 H 5
Balgonie 777 G 5
Batoche E 3
Battleford 3,565 C 3
Beauval 606 L 3
Beechy 279 D 5
Bengough 536 F 6
Bethune 369 F 5
Bienfait 835 J 6
Biggar 2,561 C 3
Big River 819 D 2
Birch Hills 957 F 3
Bjorkdale 269 H 3
Blaine Lake 653 D 3
Borden 197 D 3
Brabant Lake 245 M 3
Bradwell 168 E 4
Bredenbury 467 K 5
Briercrest 151 F 5
Broadview 840 J 5
Brock 184 C 4
Browning •687 J 6
Bruno 772 F 3
Buchanan 392 J 4
Buffalo Gap •598 F 6
Buffalo Narrows 1,088 L 3
Burstall 550 B 5
Cabri 632 C 5
Cadillac 173 D 6
Calder 164 K 4
Cana •1,238 J 5
Candle Lake 219 F 2
Cando 163 C 3
Canoe Lake 182 L 3
Canora 2,667 J 4
Canwood 340 E 2
Carievale 246 K 6
Carlyle 1,074 J 6
Carnduff 1,043 K 6
Carrot River 1,169 H 2
Central Butte 548 E 5
Ceylon 184 G 6
Chaplin 389 E 5
Chitek Lake 170 D 2
Choiceland 543 G 2
Christopher Lake 227 F 2
Churchbridge 972 J 5
Clavet 234 E 4
Climax 293 C 6
Cochin 221 C 2
Codette 236 H 2
Coleville 383 B 4
Colonsay 594 F 4
Connaught Heights •982 G 3
Conquest 256 D 4
Consul 153 B 6
Coronach 1,032 F 6
Craik 565 F 4
Craven 206 G 5
Creelman 184 H 6
Creighton 1,636 N 4
Cudworth 947 F 3
Cumberland House 831 J 2
Cupar 669 G 5
Cut Knife 624 B 3
Dalmeny 1,064 E 3
Davidson 1,166 E 4
Debden 403 E 2
Delisle 980 D 4
Denare Beach 592 M 4
Denzil 199 B 3
Deschambault Lake 386 M 3
Dinsmore 398 D 4
Dodsland 272 C 4
Domremy 209 F 3
Drake 211 G 4
Duck Lake 699 E 3
Dundurn 531 E 4
Dysart 275 H 5
Earl Grey 303 G 5
Eastend 723 C 6
Eatonia 528 B 4
Ebenezer 164 J 4
Edam 384 C 2
Edenwold 143 G 5
Elbow 313 E 4
Eldorado 229 L 2
Elfros 199 H 4
Elrose 624 D 4
Elstow 143 E 4
Endeavour 199 J 3
Englefeld 271 G 3
Erwood 149 J 3
Esterhazy 3,065 K 5
Estevan 9,174 J 6
Eston 1,413 C 4
Eyebrow 168 E 5
Fillmore 396 H 6
Fleming 141 K 5
Flin Flon 367 N 4
Foam Lake 1,452 H 4
Fond du Lac 494 L 2
Fort Qu'Appelle 1,827 H 5
Fox Valley 380 B 5
Francis 182 H 5
Frobisher 166 J 6
Frontier 619 C 6
Gainsborough 308 K 6
Gerald 197 K 5
Glaslyn 430 C 2
Glenavon 284 J 5
Glen Ewen 168 K 6
Goodsoil 263 L 4
Govan 394 G 4
Grand Coulee 208 G 5
Gravelbourg 1,338 E 6
Grayson 264 J 5
Green Acres 139 F 2
Green Lake 634 L 4
Grenfell 1,307 J 5
Guernsey 198 F 4
Gull Lake 1,095 C 5
Hafford 557 D 3
Hague 625 E 3
Hanley 484 E 4
Harris 259 D 4
Hawarden 137 E 4
Hearts Hill •552 B 3
Hepburn 411 E 3
Herbert 1,019 D 5
Hodgeville 329 E 5
Holdfast 297 F 5
Hudson Bay 2,361 J 3
Humboldt 4,705 F 3
Hyas 165 J 4
Île-à-la-Crosse 1,035 L 3
Imperial 501 F 4
Indian Head 1,889 H 5
Invermay 353 J 4
Ituna 870 H 4
Jansen 223 G 4
Jasmin •14 H 4
Kamsack 2,688 K 4
Kelliher 397 H 4
Kelvington 1,054 H 3
Kenaston 345 E 4
Kennedy 275 J 5
Kerrobert 1,141 C 4
Kincaid 256 D 6
Kindersley 3,969 B 4
Kinistino 783 F 3
Kipling 1,016 J 5
Kisbey 228 J 6
Kronau 154 G 5
Kyle 516 C 5
Lac Pelletier •586 C 6
Lafleche 583 E 6
Laird 233 E 3
Lake Lenore 361 G 3
La Loche 1,632 L 3
Lampman 651 J 6
Lancer 156 C 5
Landis 277 C 3
Lang 219 G 6
Langenburg 1,324 K 5
Langham 1,151 E 3
Lanigan 1,732 F 4
La Ronge 2,579 L 3
Lashburn 813 B 2
Leader 1,108 B 5
Leask 478 E 2
Lebret 274 H 5
Lemberg 414 H 5
Leoville 393 D 2
Leroy 504 G 4
Lestock 402 G 4
Limerick 164 E 6
Lintlaw 234 H 3
Lipton 364 H 5
Lloydminster 6,034 A 2
Loon Lake 369 B 1
Loreburn 201 E 4
Lucky Lake 333 D 5
Lumsden 1,303 G 5
Luseland 704 B 3
Macdowall 171 E 2
Macklin 976 A 3
Macoun 190 H 6
Maidstone 1,001 B 2
Mankota 375 D 6
Manor 368 K 6
Maple Creek 2,470 B 6
Marcelin 238 E 3
Margo 153 H 4
Marriott •627 D 4
Marsden 229 B 3
Marshall 453 B 2
Martensville 1,966 E 3
Maryfield 431 K 6
Maymont 212 D 3
McLean 189 G 5
Meacham 178 F 3
Meadow Lake 3,857 C 1
Meath Park 262 F 2
Medstead 163 C 2
Melfort 6,010 G 3
Melville 5,092 J 5
Meota 235 C 2
Mervin 155 C 2
Midale 564 H 6
Middle Lake 275 F 3
Milden 251 D 4
Milestone 602 G 5
Montmartre 544 H 5
Montreal Lake 448 F 1
Moose Jaw 33,941 F 5
Moose Range •679 H 2
Moosomin 2,579 K 5
Morse 416 D 5
Mortlach 293 E 5
Mossbank 464 E 6
Muenster 385 F 3
Naicam 886 G 3
Neilburg 354 B 3
Neuanlage 144 E 3
Neudorf 425 J 5
Neuhorst 146 E 3
Nipawin 4,376 H 2
Nokomis 524 F 4
Norquay 552 J 4
North Battleford 14,030 C 3
North Portal 164 J 6
Odessa 232 H 5
Ogema 441 G 6
Osler 527 E 3
Outlook 1,976 E 4
Oxbow 1,191 J 6
Paddockwood 211 F 2
Pangman 227 G 6
Paradise Hill 421 B 2
Patuanak 173 L 3
Paynton 210 B 2
Pelican Narrows 331 N 3
Pelly 391 K 4
Pennant 202 C 5
Pense 472 G 5
Perdue 407 D 3
Pierceland 425 K 4
Pilger 150 F 3
Pilot Butte 1,255 G 5
Pine House 612 M 3
Plenty 175 C 4
Plunkett 150 F 4
Ponteix 769 D 6
Porcupine Plain 937 H 3
Preeceville 1,243 J 4
Prelate 317 B 5
Prince Albert 31,380 F 2
Prud'homme 222 F 3
Punnichy 394 G 4
Qu'Appelle 653 H 5
Quill Lake 514 G 3
Quinton 169 G 4
Rabbit Lake 159 D 2
Radisson 439 D 3
Radville 1,012 G 6
Rama 133 H 4
Raymore 635 G 4
Redvers 859 K 6
Regina (cap.) 162,613 G 5
Regina *164,313 G 5
Regina Beach 603 F 5
Rhein 271 J 4
Richmound 188 B 5
Riverhurst 193 E 5
Rocanville 934 K 5
Roche Percé 142 J 6
Rockglen 511 F 6
Rosetown 2,664 D 4
Rose Valley 538 H 3
Rosthern 1,609 E 3
Rouleau 443 G 5
Saint Benedict 157 F 3
Saint Brieux 401 G 3
Saint Louis 448 F 3
Saint Philips •538 K 4
Saint Walburg 802 B 2
Saltcoats 549 J 4
Sandy Bay 756 N 3
Saskatoon 154,210 E 3
Saskatoon *154,210 E 3
Sceptre 169 B 5
Scott 203 C 3
Sedley 373 H 5
Semans 344 G 4
Shaunavon 2,112 C 6
Sheho 285 H 4
Shell Lake 220 D 2
Shellbrook 1,228 E 2
Simpson 231 F 4
Sintaluta 215 H 5
Smeaton 246 G 2
Southey 697 G 5
Spalding 337 G 3
Spiritwood 926 D 2
Springside 533 J 4
Spy Hill 354 K 5
Star City 527 G 3
Stenen 143 J 4
Stockholm 391 J 5
Stonehenge •701 F 6
Storthoaks 142 K 6
Stoughton 716 J 6
Strasbourg 842 G 4
Sturgis 789 J 4
Swift Current 14,747 D 5
Tantallon 196 K 5
Theodore 473 J 4
Timber Bay 152 F 1
Tisdale 3,107 H 3
Togo 181 K 4
Tompkins 275 C 5
Torch River •2,440 G 2
Torquay 311 H 6
Tramping Lake 178 B 3
Tugaske 175 E 5
Turnor Lake 166 L 3
Turtleford 505 B 2
Unity 2,408 B 3
Uranium City 2,507 L 2
Val Marie 236 D 6
Vanguard 292 D 6
Vanscoy 298 D 4
Vibank 369 H 5
Viscount 386 F 4
Vonda 313 F 3
Wadena 1,495 H 4
Wakaw 1,030 F 3
Waldeck 292 D 5
Waldheim 758 E 3
Walpole •711 K 6
Wapella 487 K 5
Warman 2,076 E 3
Waseca 169 B 2
Waskesiu Lake 176 E 2
Watrous 1,830 F 4
Watson 901 G 3
Wawota 622 J 6
Weldon 279 F 2
Welwyn 170 K 5
Weyburn 9,523 H 6
White City 602 G 5
White Fox 394 H 2
Whitewood 1,003 J 5
Wilcox 202 G 5
Wilkie 1,501 C 3
Willow Bunch 494 F 6
Willow Creek •1,218 B 6
Windthorst 254 J 5
Wiseton 195 D 4
Wishart 212 H 4
Wollaston Lake 248 N 2
Wolseley 904 H 5
Wymark 162 D 5
Wynyard 2,147 G 4
Yarbo 158 K 5
Yellow Grass 477 H 6
Yorkton 15,339 J 4
Young 456 F 4
Zenon Park 273 H 2

OTHER FEATURES

Allan (hills) E 4
Amisk (lake) M 4
Antelope (lake) C 5
Antler (riv.) K 6
Arm (riv.) F 5
Assiniboine (riv.) J 3
Athabasca (lake) L 2
Bad (lake) C 4
Bad (hills) C 4
Basin (lake) F 3
Batoche Nat'l Hist. Site E 3
Battle (creek) B 6
Battle (riv.) B 3
Bear (hills) C 4
Beaver (hills) H 4
Beaver (riv.) L 4
Beaverlodge (lake) L 2
Big Muddy (lake) G 6
Bigstick (lake) B 5
Birch (lake) C 2
Bitter (lake) B 5
Black (lake) M 2
Boundary (plat.) B 6
Brightsand (lake) B 2
Bronson (lake) B 2

Agriculture, Industry and Resources

DOMINANT LAND USE

Wheat
Cereals (chiefly barley, oats)
Cereals, Livestock
Livestock
Forests

MAJOR MINERAL OCCURRENCES

Au Gold
Cu Copper
G Natural Gas
He Helium
K Potash
Lg Lignite
Na Salt
O Petroleum
S Sulfur
U Uranium
Zn Zinc

Water Power
Major Industrial Areas

Furs
Oats
Rye
Hogs
Barley
Cattle
Wheat
Sheep
Flax
Regina

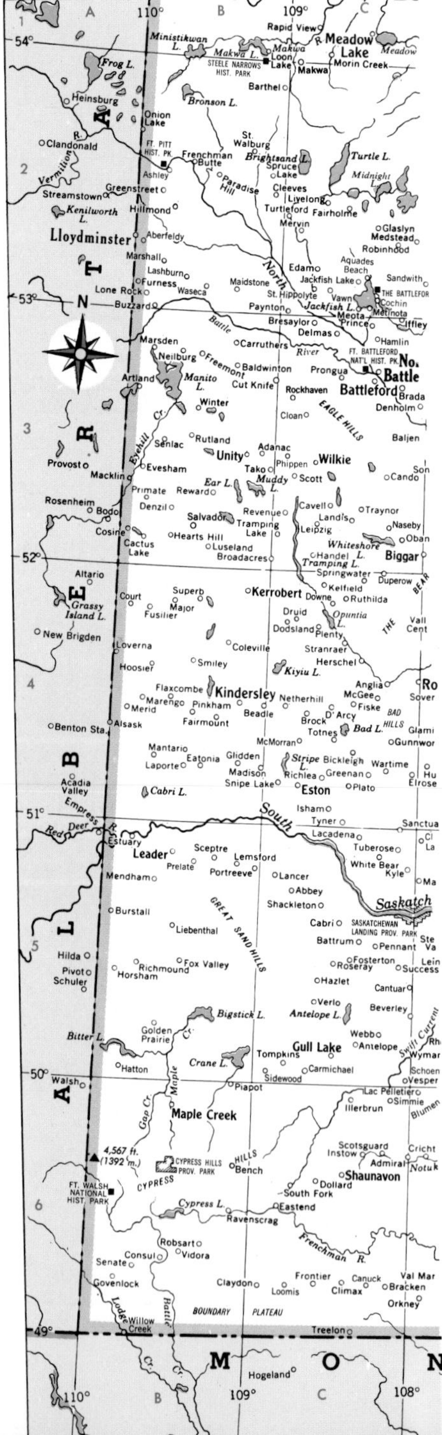

Buffalo Pound Prov. Park	F 5	Ear (lake)	B 3
Cabri (lake)	B 4	Echo Valley Prov. Park	G 5
Cactus (hills)	F 5	Etomami (riv.)	J 3
Candle (lake)	F 2	Eyebrow (lake)	E 5
Cannington Manon Hist. Park	J 6	Eyehill (creek)	B 3
Canoe (lake)	L 3	Fife (lake)	E 6
Carrot (riv.)	J 2	File (lake)	H 5
Chaplin (lake)	E 5	Fir (riv.)	J 2
Chipman (riv.)	M 2	Fond du Lac (riv.)	M 2
Chitek (lake)	D 2	Forrest (lake)	L 3
Churchill (riv.)	M 3	Fort Battleford Nat'l Hist. Park	C 3
Clearwater (riv.)	L 3	Fort Carlton Hist. Park	E 3
Cochrane (riv.)	N 2	Fort Pitt Hist. Park	B 3
Coteau (hills)	D 4	Fort Walsh Nat'l Hist. Park	A 6
Cowan (lake)	D 2	Foster (lake)	M 3
Crane (lake)	B 5	Frenchman (riv.)	C 6
Crean (lake)	E 1	Frobisher (lake)	L 3
Cree (lake)	L 3	Gap (lake)	B 6
Cree (riv.)	M 2	Gardiner (dam)	D 4
Cumberland (lake)	J 1	Geikie (riv.)	M 3
Cypress (hills)	B 6	Good Spirit (lake)	J 4
Cypress (lake)	B 6	Goodspirit Lake Prov. Park	J 4
Cypress Hills Prov. Park	B 6	Great Sand (hills)	B 5
Danielson Prov. Park	E 1	Green (lake)	D 1
Delaronde (lake)	E 1	Greenwater Lake Prov. Park	H 3
Diefenbaker (lake)	D 4	Haultain (riv.)	L 3
Doré (lake)	L 3	Île-à-la-Crosse (lake)	L 3
Douglas Prov. Park	E 4	Ironspring (creek)	G 3
Duck Lake Hist. Park	E 3	Jackfish (lake)	C 3
Duck Mountain Prov. Park	J 4	Katepwa Prov. Park	H 5
Eagle (hills)	C 3	Kingsmere (lake)	E 1
Eaglehill (creek)	D 4	Kiyiu (lake)	C 4

Lac La Ronge Prov. Park	M 3	Oldman (riv.)	L 2
Lanigan (creek)	F 4	Old Wives (lake)	E 5
Last Mountain (lake)	F 4	Opuntia (lake)	C 4
Leaf (lake)	J 2	Overflowing (riv.)	K 2
Leech (lake)	L 2	Pasquia (hills)	J 2
Lenore (lake)	G 3	Pasquia (riv.)	K 2
Little Manitou (lake)	F 4	Pelican (lake)	E 5
Lodge (creek)	B 6	Pelican (lake)	L 3
Long (creek)	E 6	Peter Pond (lake)	L 3
Long (creek)	G 4	Pheasant (hills)	J 5
Makwa (lake)	B 1	Pine Lake Prov. Park	E 4
Makwa (riv.)	B 1	Pinto (creek)	D 6
Manito (lake)	B 3	Pipestone (creek)	K 6
Maple (creek)	B 6	Pipestone (riv.)	L 2
McFarlane (riv.)	L 2	Ponass (hills)	H 3
Meadow (lake)	L 2	Poplar (riv.)	E 6
Meadow Lake Prov. Park	K 4	Porcupine (hills)	K 3
Meeting (lake)	D 2	Primrose (lake)	L 3
Midnight (lake)	C 3	Primrose Lake Air Weapons Range	L 3
Ministikwan (lake)	B 3		
Missouri Coteau (hills)	F 5	Prince Albert Nat'l Park	E 1
Montreal (lake)	E 1	Qu'Appelle (lake)	J 5
Moose (mt.)	J 6	Quill (lakes)	G 4
Moose Jaw (riv.)	G 5	Red Deer (lake)	K 3
Moose Mountain (creek)	J 6	Reindeer (lake)	N 3
Moose Mountain Prov. Park	J 6	Reindeer (riv.)	M 3
Mossy (riv.)	H 1	Riou (lake)	M 2
Muddy (lake)	B 3	Ronge, La (lake)	M 3
Mudjatik (riv.)	L 3	Rivers (lake)	F 6
Nipawin Prov. Park	G 1	Rowans Ravine Prov. Park	G 5
North Saskatchewan (riv.)	D 1	St. Victor Petroglyphs Hist. Park	E 6
Notukeu (creek)	D 6		

AREA 251,699 sq. mi. (651,900 sq. km.)
POPULATION 1,009,613
CAPITAL Regina
LARGEST CITY Regina
HIGHEST POINT Cypress Hills 4,567 ft. (1,392 m.)
SETTLED IN 1774
ADMITTED TO CONFEDERATION 1905
PROVINCIAL FLOWER Prairie Lily

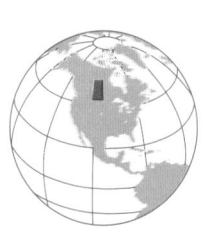

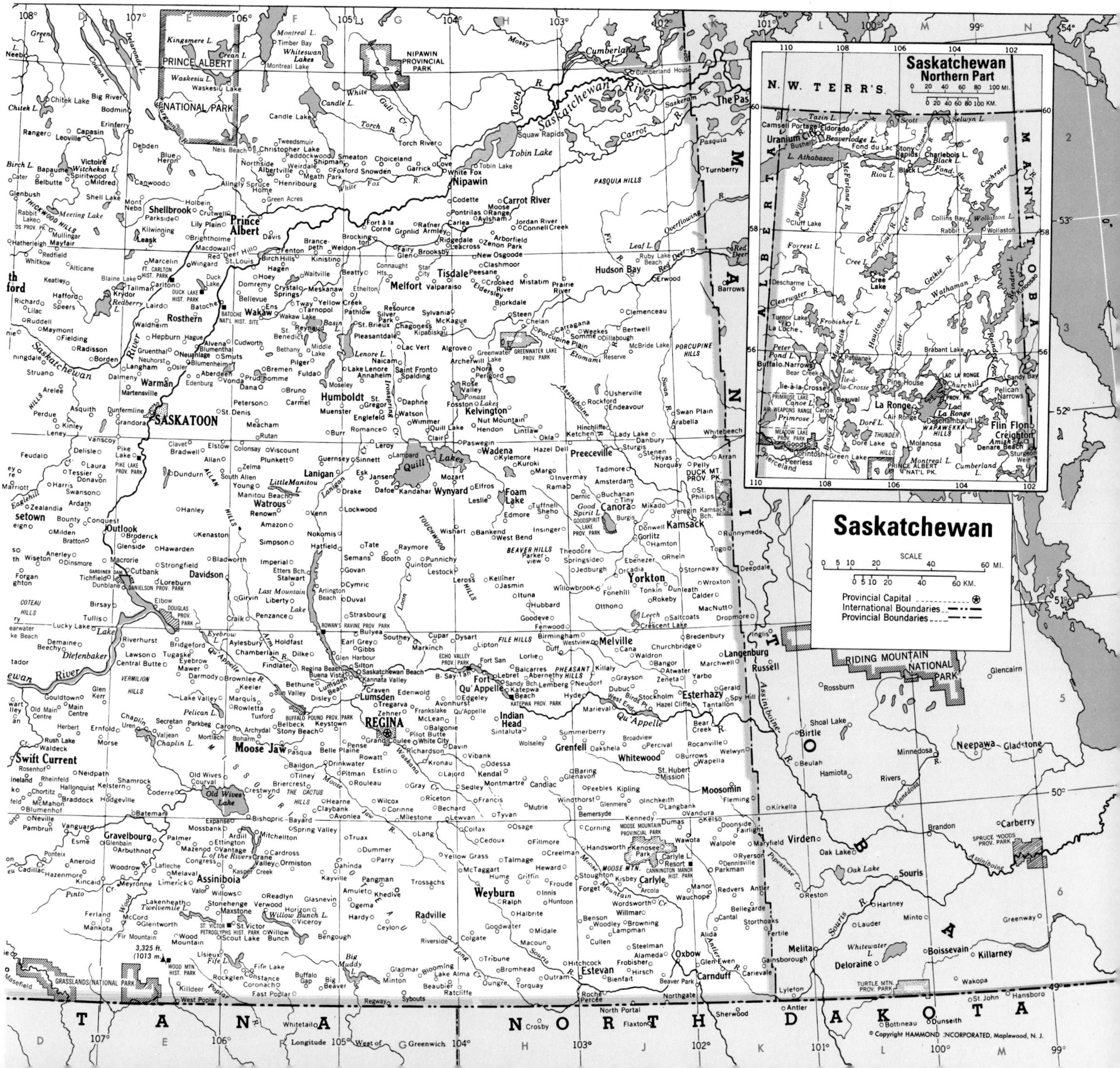

Saskatchewan (riv.)	H 2	Thickwood (hills)	D 2	White Fox (riv.)	G 2
Saskatchewan Landing Prov. Park	C 5	Thunder (lake)	L 4	White Gull (creek)	G 2
Saskeram (riv.)	J 2	Tobin (lake)	H 2	Whiteshore (lake)	C 3
Scott (lake)	M 2	Torch (riv.)	H 2	Whiteswan (lakes)	F 1
Selwyn (lake)	M 2	Touchwood (hills)	G 4	William (riv.)	L 2
South Saskatchewan (riv.)	C 5	Tramping (lake)	C 3	Willow Bunch (lake)	F 6
Steele Narrows Hist. Park	B 2	Trout (lake)	L 2	Witchekan (lake)	D 2
Stripe (lake)	C 4	Turtle (lake)	C 2	Wollaston (lake)	N 2
Sturgeon (riv.)	E 2	Twelvemile (lake)	E 6	Wood (mt.)	E 6
Swan (lake)	J 3	Vermilion (hills)	E 5	Wood (riv.)	E 6
Swift Current (creek)	D 5	Wapawekka (hills)	M 4	Wood Mountain Hist. Park	E 6
Tazin (riv.)	L 2	Waskana (creek)	G 5		
The Battlefords Prov. Park	C 2	Waskesiu (lake)	E 2		
		Watham (riv.)	M 3		
		Weed (lake)	J 5		

*Population of metropolitan area.
●Population of rural municipality.

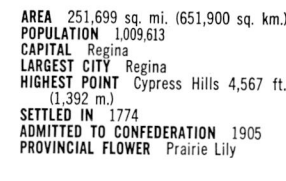

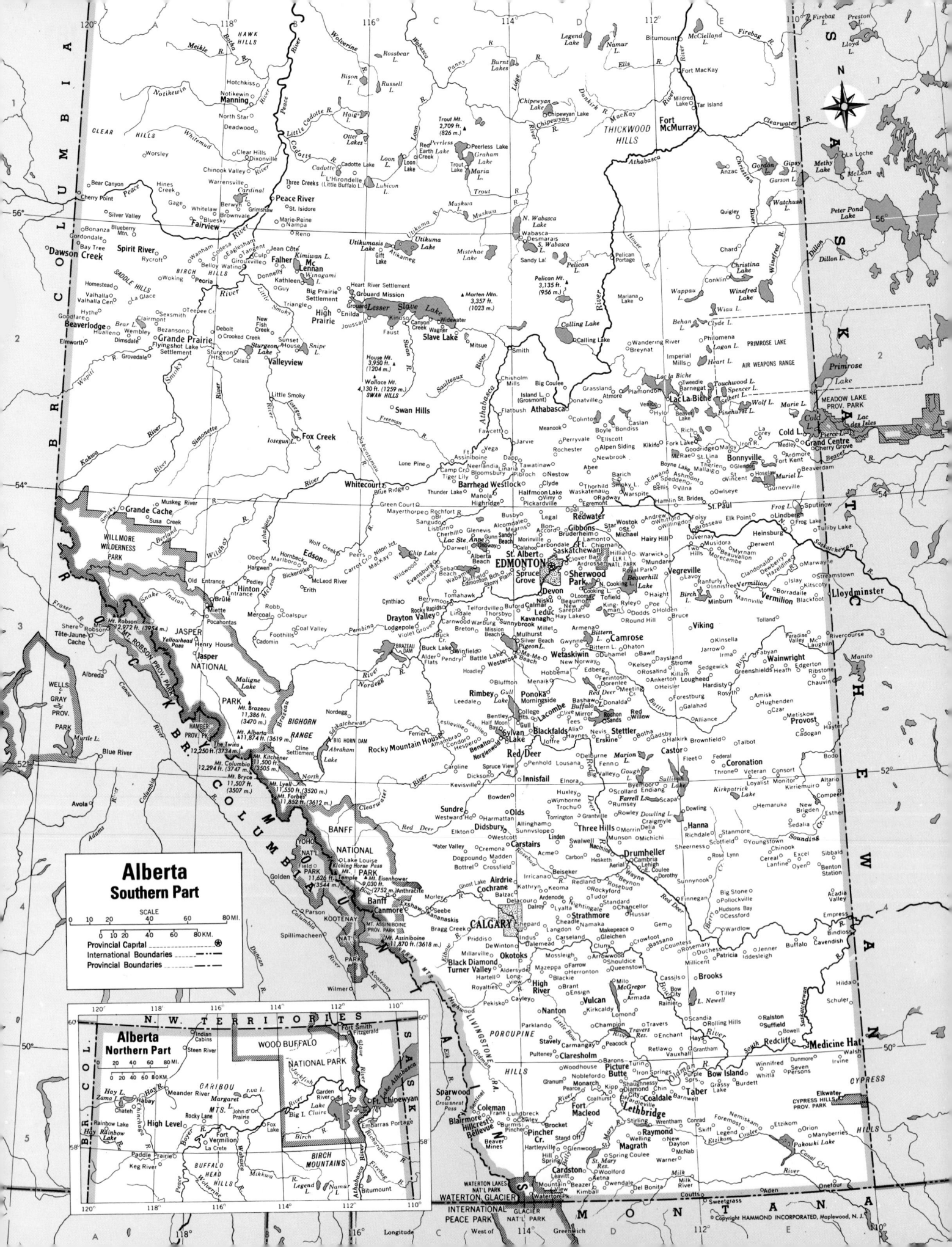

Alberta
Southern Part
SCALE
0 10 20 40 60 80 MI.
0 10 20 40 60 80 KM.
Provincial Capital
International Boundaries
Provincial Boundaries
Alberta
Northern Part
0 20 40 60 80 MI.
0 20 40 60 80 KM.
N. W. TERRITORIES
WOOD BUFFALO
NATIONAL PARK
CARIBOU MTS.
BIRCH MOUNTAINS
BUFFALO HEAD HILLS
High Level
Fort Chipewyan
Lake Athabasca
BR. COL.
SASK.
BRITISH COLUMBIA
SASKATCHEWAN
MONTANA
ROCKY MTS.
COLUMBIA MTS.
EDMONTON
CALGARY
Red Deer
Lethbridge
Medicine Hat
Fort McMurray
Grande Prairie
Peace River
Lloydminster
Lesser Slave Lake
Athabasca
Lac La Biche
PRIMROSE LAKE AIR WEAPONS RANGE
JASPER NATIONAL PARK
BANFF NATIONAL PARK
WILLMORE WILDERNESS PARK
WATERTON LAKES NAT'L PARK
WATERTON GLACIER INTERNATIONAL PEACE PARK
GLACIER NAT'L PARK
CYPRESS HILLS PROV. PARK
MEADOW LAKE PROV. PARK
THICKWOOD HILLS
SWAN HILLS
BIRCH HILLS
SADDLE HILLS
CLEAR HILLS
HAWK HILLS
PORCUPINE HILLS
CYPRESS HILLS
Longitude West of Greenwich
© Copyright HAMMOND INCORPORATED, Maplewood, N. J.

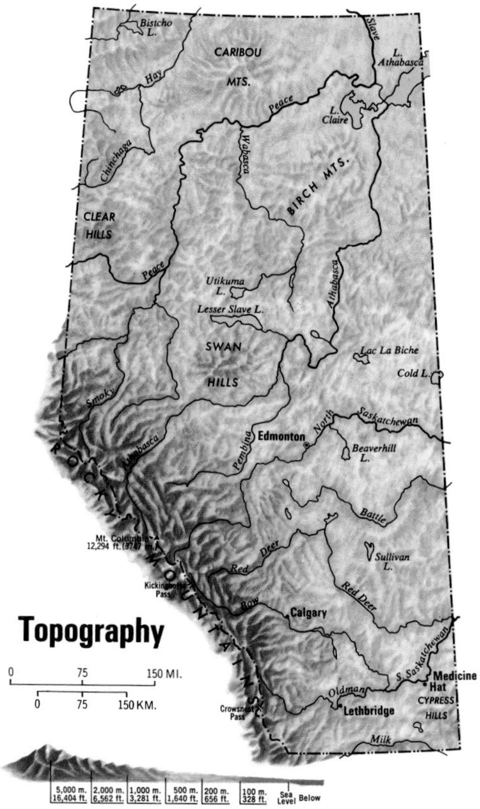
Bistcho L.
CARIBOU
MTS.
L. Athabasca
Slave
Hay
Peace
L. Claire
Chinchaga
Wabasca
BIRCH MTS.
CLEAR HILLS
Peace
Utikuma L.
Lesser Slave L.
Athabasca
SWAN HILLS
Lac La Biche
Cold L.
Smoky
Athabasca
Pembina
Edmonton
North Saskatchewan
Beaverhill L.
Battle
Mt. Columbia 12,294 ft. (3,747 m.)
Red Deer
Sullivan L.
Kickinghorse Pass
Bow
Calgary
Red Deer
S. Saskatchewan
Medicine Hat
Oldman
Lethbridge
CYPRESS HILLS
Crowsnest Pass
Milk
0 75 150 MI.
0 75 150 KM.
5,000 m. 16,404 ft.
2,000 m. 6,562 ft.
1,000 m. 3,281 ft.
500 m. 1,640 ft.
200 m. 656 ft.
100 m. 328 ft.
Sea Level
Below

Topography

AREA 255,285 sq. mi. (661,185 sq. km.)
POPULATION 2,365,825
CAPITAL Edmonton
LARGEST CITY Edmonton
HIGHEST POINT Mt. Columbia 12,294 ft. (3,747 m.)
SETTLED IN 1861
ADMITTED TO CONFEDERATION 1905
PROVINCIAL FLOWER Wild Rose

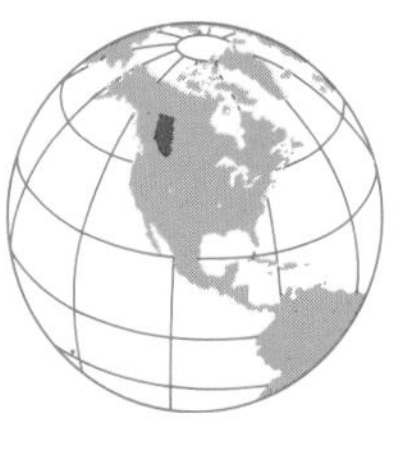

CITIES and TOWNS

Acme 457 .... D 4
Airdrie 8,414 .... C 4
Alberta Beach 485 .... C 3
Alix 837 .... D 3
Andrew 548 .... D 3
Antler Lake 334 .... D 3
Ardmore 224 .... E 2
Arrowwood 156 .... D 4
Athabasca 1,731 .... D 2
Banff 4,208 .... C 4
Barnwell 359 .... D 5
Barons 315 .... D 4
Barrhead 3,736 .... C 2
Bashaw 875 .... D 3
Bassano 1,200 .... D 4
Bawlf 350 .... D 3
Beaumont 2,638 .... D 3
Beaverlodge 1,937 .... A 2
Beiseker 580 .... D 4
Bentley 823 .... C 3
Berwyn 557 .... B 1
Big Valley 360 .... D 3
Black Diamond 1,444 .... C 4
Blackfalds 1,488 .... D 3
Blackfoot 220 .... E 3
Blackie 298 .... D 4
Bon Accord 1,376 .... D 3
Bonnyville 4,454 .... E 2
Bowden 989 .... C 4
Bow Island 1,491 .... E 5
Boyle 638 .... D 2
Bragg Creek 505 .... C 4
Breton 552 .... C 3
Brooks 9,421 .... E 4
Bruce 88 .... E 3
Bruderheim 1,136 .... D 3
Burdett 220 .... E 5
Calgary 592,743 .... C 4
Calgary *592,743 .... C 4
Calmar 1,003 .... D 3
Camrose 12,570 .... D 3
Canmore 3,484 .... C 4
Carbon 434 .... D 4
Cardston 3,267 .... D 5
Carmangay 266 .... D 4
Caroline 436 .... C 3
Carseland 484 .... D 4
Carstairs 1,587 .... D 4
Castor 1,123 .... D 3
Cereal 249 .... E 4
Champion 339 .... D 4
Chauvin 298 .... E 3
Chipman 266 .... D 3
Clairmont 469 .... A 2
Claresholm 3,493 .... D 4
Clive 364 .... D 3
Clyde 364 .... D 2
Coaldale 4,579 .... D 5
Coalhurst 882 .... D 5
Cochrane 3,544 .... C 4
Cold Lake 2,110 .... E 2
College Heights 267 .... D 3
Consort 632 .... E 3
Cooking Lake 218 .... D 3
Coronation 1,309 .... E 3
Coutts 400 .... D 5
Cowley 304 .... D 5
Cremona 382 .... C 4
Crossfield 1,217 .... C 4
Daysland 679 .... D 3
Delburne 574 .... D 3
Desmarais 260 .... D 2
Devon 3,885 .... D 3
Didsbury 3,095 .... C 4
Donalda 280 .... D 3
Donnelly 336 .... B 2
Drayton Valley 5,042 .... C 3
Drumheller 6,508 .... D 4
Duchess 429 .... E 4
East Coulee 218 .... D 4
Eckville 870 .... C 3
Edgerton 387 .... E 3
Edmonton (cap.) 532,246 .... D 3
Edmonton *657,057 .... D 3
Edmonton Beach 280 .... C 3
Edson 5,835 .... B 3
Elk Point 1,022 .... E 3
Elnora 249 .... D 3
Entwistle 462 .... C 3
Erskine 259 .... D 3
Evansburg 779 .... C 3
Exshaw 353 .... C 4
Fairview 2,869 .... A 1
Falher 1,102 .... B 2
Faust 399 .... C 2
Foremost 568 .... E 5
Forestburg 924 .... E 3
Fort Assiniboine 207 .... C 2
Fort Chipewyan 944 .... C 5
Fort Macleod 3,139 .... D 5
Fort McKay 267 .... E 1
Fort McMurray 31,000 .... E 1
Fort Saskatchewan 12,169 .... D 3
Fort Vermilion 752 .... B 5
Fox Creek 1,978 .... B 2
Fox Lake 634 .... B 5
Gibbons 2,276 .... D 3
Gift Lake 428 .... C 2
Girouxville 325 .... B 2
Gleichen 381 .... D 4
Glendon 430 .... E 2
Glenwood 259 .... D 5
Grand Centre 3,146 .... E 2
Grande Cache 4,523 .... A 3
Grande Prairie 24,263 .... A 2
Granum 399 .... D 5
Grimshaw 2,316 .... B 1
Grouard Mission 221 .... C 2
Hanna 2,806 .... E 4
Hardisty 641 .... E 3
Hay Lakes 302 .... D 3
Heisler 212 .... D 3
High Level 2,194 .... A 5
High Prairie 2,506 .... B 2
High River 4,792 .... D 4
Hines Creek 575 .... A 1
Hinton 8,342 .... B 3
Holden 430 .... D 3
Hughenden 267 .... E 3
Hythe 639 .... A 2
Innisfail 5,247 .... D 3
Innisfree 255 .... E 3
Irma 474 .... E 3
Irricana 558 .... D 4
Irvine 360 .... E 5
Jasper 3,269 .... B 3
John d'Or Prairie 437 .... B 5
Joussard 330 .... B 2
Killam 1,005 .... E 3
Kinuso 285 .... C 2
Kitscoty 497 .... E 3
Lac La Biche 2,007 .... E 2
Lacombe 5,591 .... D 3
La Crete 479 .... B 5
Lake Louise 355 .... B 4
Lamont 1,563 .... D 3
Leduc 12,471 .... D 3
Legal 1,022 .... D 3
Lethbridge 54,072 .... D 5
Linden 407 .... D 4
Little Buffalo Lake 253 .... B 1
Lloydminster 8,997 .... E 3
Longview 301 .... C 4
Lougheed 226 .... E 3
Lundbreck 244 .... C 5
Magrath 1,576 .... D 5
Manning 1,173 .... B 1
Mannville 788 .... E 3
Marlboro 211 .... B 3
Marwayne 500 .... E 3
Mayerthorpe 1,475 .... C 3
McLennan 1,125 .... B 2
Medicine Hat 40,380 .... E 4
Milk River 894 .... D 5
Millet 1,120 .... D 3
Mirror 507 .... D 3
Monarch 212 .... D 5
Morinville 4,657 .... D 3
Morrin 244 .... D 4
Mundare 604 .... D 3
Myrnam 397 .... E 3
Nacmine 369 .... D 4
Nampa 334 .... B 1
Nanton 1,641 .... D 4
New Norway 291 .... D 3
New Sarepta 417 .... D 3
Nobleford 534 .... D 5
North Calling Lake 234 .... D 2
Okotoks 3,847 .... C 4
Olds 4,813 .... D 4
Onoway 621 .... C 3
Oyen 975 .... E 4
Peace River 5,907 .... B 1
Penhold 1,531 .... D 3
Picture Butte 1,404 .... D 5
Pincher Creek 3,757 .... D 5
Plamondon 259 .... D 2
Pollockville 19 .... E 4
Ponoka 5,221 .... D 3
Provost 1,645 .... E 3
Rainbow Lake 504 .... A 5
Ralston 357 .... E 4
Raymond 2,837 .... D 5
Redcliff 3,876 .... E 4
Red Deer 46,393 .... D 3
Redwater 1,932 .... D 3
Rimbey 1,685 .... C 3
Robb 230 .... B 3
Rockyford 329 .... D 4
Rocky Mountain House 4,698 .... C 3
Rosemary 328 .... E 4
Rycroft 649 .... A 2
Ryley 483 .... D 3
Saint Albert 31,996 .... D 3
Saint Paul 4,884 .... E 3
Sangudo 398 .... C 3
Sedgewick 879 .... E 3
Sexsmith 1,180 .... A 2
Shaughnessy 270 .... D 5
Sherwood Park 29,285 .... D 3
Slave Lake 4,506 .... C 2
Smith 216 .... D 2
Smoky Lake 1,074 .... D 2
Spirit River 1,104 .... A 2
Spruce Grove 10,326 .... D 3
Standard 379 .... D 4
Stavely 504 .... D 4
Stettler 5,136 .... D 3
Stirling 688 .... D 5
Stony Plain 4,839 .... C 3
Strathmore 2,986 .... D 4
Strome 281 .... E 3
Sundre 1,742 .... C 4
Swan Hills 2,497 .... C 2
Sylvan Lake 3,779 .... C 3
Taber 5,988 .... E 5
Thorhild 576 .... D 2
Thorsby 737 .... C 3
Three Hills 1,787 .... D 4
Tilley 345 .... E 4
Tofield 1,504 .... D 3
Trochu 880 .... D 4
Turner Valley 1,311 .... C 4
Two Hills 1,193 .... E 3
Valleyview 2,061 .... B 2
Vauxhall 1,049 .... D 4
Vegreville 5,251 .... E 3
Vermilion 3,766 .... E 3
Veteran 314 .... E 3
Viking 1,232 .... E 3
Vilna 345 .... E 2
Vulcan 1,489 .... D 4
Wabamun 662 .... C 3
Wabasca 701 .... D 2
Wainwright 4,266 .... E 3
Warburg 501 .... C 3
Warner 477 .... D 5
Waskatenau 290 .... D 2
Wembley 1,169 .... A 2
Westlock 4,424 .... C 2
Wetaskiwin 9,597 .... D 3
Whitecourt 5,585 .... C 2
Wildwood 441 .... C 3
Willingdon 366 .... E 3
Youngstown 297 .... E 4

OTHER FEATURES

Abraham (lake) .... B 3
Alberta (mt.) .... B 3
Assiniboine (mt.) .... C 4
Athabasca (lake) .... C 5
Athabasca (riv.) .... D 1
Banff Nat'l Park .... B 4
Battle (riv.) .... D 3
Bear (lake) .... A 2
Beaver (riv.) .... E 2
Beaverhill (lake) .... D 3
Behan (lake) .... E 2
Belly (riv.) .... D 5
Berland (riv.) .... A 3
Berry (creek) .... E 4
Biche (lake) .... E 2
Big (isl.) .... B 5
Big Horn (dam) .... B 3
Bighorn (range) .... B 3
Birch (hills) .... A 2
Birch (lake) .... E 3
Birch (mts.) .... B 5
Birch (riv.) .... B 5
Bison (lake) .... B 1
Bittern (lake) .... D 3
Botha (riv.) .... B 1
Bow (riv.) .... D 4
Boyer (riv.) .... A 5
Brazeau (mt.) .... B 3
Brazeau (riv.) .... B 3
Buffalo (lake) .... D 3
Buffalo Head (hills) .... B 5
Burnt (lakes) .... C 1
Cadotte (lake) .... B 1
Cadotte (riv.) .... B 1
Calling (lake) .... D 2
Canal (creek) .... E 5
Cardinal (lake) .... B 1
Caribou (mts.) .... B 5
Chinchaga (riv.) .... A 5
Chip (lake) .... C 3
Chipewyan (lake) .... D 1
Chipewyan (riv.) .... D 1
Christina (lake) .... E 2
Christina (riv.) .... E 1
Claire (lake) .... B 5
Clear (hills) .... A 1
Clearwater (riv.) .... C 4
Clearwater (riv.) .... E 1
Clyde (lake) .... E 2
Cold (lake) .... E 2
Columbia (mt.) .... B 3
Crowsnest (pass) .... C 5
Cypress (hills) .... E 5
Cypress Hills Prov. Park .... E 5
Dillon (riv.) .... E 2
Dowling (lake) .... D 4
Dunkirk (riv.) .... D 1
Eisenhower (mt.) .... C 4
Elbow (riv.) .... C 4
Elk Island Nat'l Park .... D 3
Ells (riv.) .... D 1
Etzikom Coulee (riv.) .... E 5
Eva (lake) .... B 5
Farrell (lake) .... D 4
Firebag (riv.) .... E 1
Forbes (mt.) .... B 4
Freeman (riv.) .... C 2
Frog (lake) .... E 3
Garson (lake) .... E 1
Gipsy (lake) .... E 1
Gordon (lake) .... E 1
Gough (lake) .... D 3
Graham (lake) .... C 1
Gull (lake) .... C 3
Haig (lake) .... B 1
Hawk (hills) .... B 1
Hay (lake) .... A 5
Hay (riv.) .... A 5
Heart (lake) .... E 2
Highwood (riv.) .... C 4
House (mt.) .... C 2
House (riv.) .... D 2
Iosegun (lake) .... B 2
Iosegun (riv.) .... B 2
Jackfish (riv.) .... B 5
Jasper Nat'l Park .... A 3
Kakwa (riv.) .... A 2
Kickinghorse (pass) .... B 4
Kimiwan (lake) .... B 2
Kirkpatrick (lake) .... E 4
Kitchener (mt.) .... B 3
Legend (lake) .... D 1
Lesser Slave (lake) .... C 2
Liége (riv.) .... D 1
Little Bow (riv.) .... D 4
Little Cadotte (riv.) .... B 1
Little Smoky (riv.) .... B 2
Livingstone (range) .... C 4
Logan (lake) .... E 2
Loon (lake) .... C 1
Loon (riv.) .... C 1
Lubicon (lake) .... C 1
Lyell (mt.) .... B 4
MacKay (riv.) .... D 1
Maligne (lake) .... B 3
Margaret (lake) .... B 5
Marie (lake) .... E 2
Marion (lake) .... D 3
Marten (mt.) .... C 2
McClelland (lake) .... E 1
McGregor (lake) .... D 4
McLeod (riv.) .... B 3
Meikle (riv.) .... A 1
Mikkwa (riv.) .... B 5
Milk (riv.) .... D 5
Mistehae (lake) .... C 2
Muriel (lake) .... E 2
Muskwa (lake) .... C 1
Muskwa (riv.) .... C 1
Namur (lake) .... D 1
Newell (lake) .... E 4
Nordegg (riv.) .... C 3
North Saskatchewan (riv.) .... E 3
North Wabasca (lake) .... D 1
Notikewin (riv.) .... A 1
Oldman (riv.) .... D 5
Otter (lakes) .... B 1
Pakowki (lake) .... E 5
Panny (riv.) .... C 1
Peace (riv.) .... B 1
Peerless (lake) .... C 1
Pelican (lake) .... D 2
Pelican (mts.) .... D 2
Pembina (riv.) .... C 3
Pigeon (lake) .... D 3
Pinehurst (lake) .... E 2
Porcupine (hills) .... C 4
Primrose (lake) .... E 2
Rainbow (lake) .... A 5
Red Deer (lake) .... D 3
Red Deer (riv.) .... D 4
Richardson (riv.) .... C 5
Rocky (mts.) .... B-C 4
Rosebud (riv.) .... D 4
Russell (lake) .... C 1
Saddle (hills) .... A 2
Sainte Anne (lake) .... C 3
Saint Mary (res.) .... D 5
Saint Mary (riv.) .... D 5
Saulteaux (riv.) .... C 2
Seibert (lake) .... E 2
Simonette (riv.) .... A 2
Slave (riv.) .... C 5
Smoky (riv.) .... A 2
Snake Indian (riv.) .... A 3
Snipe (lake) .... B 2
Sounding (creek) .... E 4
South Saskatchewan (riv.) .... E 4
South Wabasca (lake) .... D 2
Spencer (lake) .... E 2
Spray (mts.) .... C 4
Sturgeon (lake) .... B 2
Súllivan (lake) .... D 3
Swan (hills) .... C 2
Swan (riv.) .... C 2
Temple (mt.) .... B 4
The Twins (mt.) .... B 3
Thickwood (hills) .... D 1
Touchwood (lake) .... E 2
Travers (res.) .... D 4
Trout (mt.) .... C 1
Trout (riv.) .... C 1
Utikuma (lake) .... C 2
Utikuma (riv.) .... C 1
Utikumasis (lake) .... C 2
Vermilion (riv.) .... E 3
Wabasca (riv.) .... C 1
Wallace (mt.) .... C 2
Wapiti (riv.) .... A 2
Wappau (lake) .... E 2
Watchusk (lake) .... E 1
Waterton-Glacier Int'l Peace Park .... C 5
Waterton Lakes Nat'l Park .... C 5
Whitemud (riv.) .... A 1
Wildhay (riv.) .... B 3
Willmore Wilderness Prov. Park .... A 3
Winagami (lake) .... B 2
Winefred (lake) .... E 2
Winefred (riv.) .... E 2
Wolf (lake) .... E 2
Wolverine (riv.) .... B 1
Wood Buffalo Nat'l Park .... B 5
Yellowhead (pass) .... A 3
Zama (lake) .... A 5

*Population of metropolitan area.

Agriculture, Industry and Resources

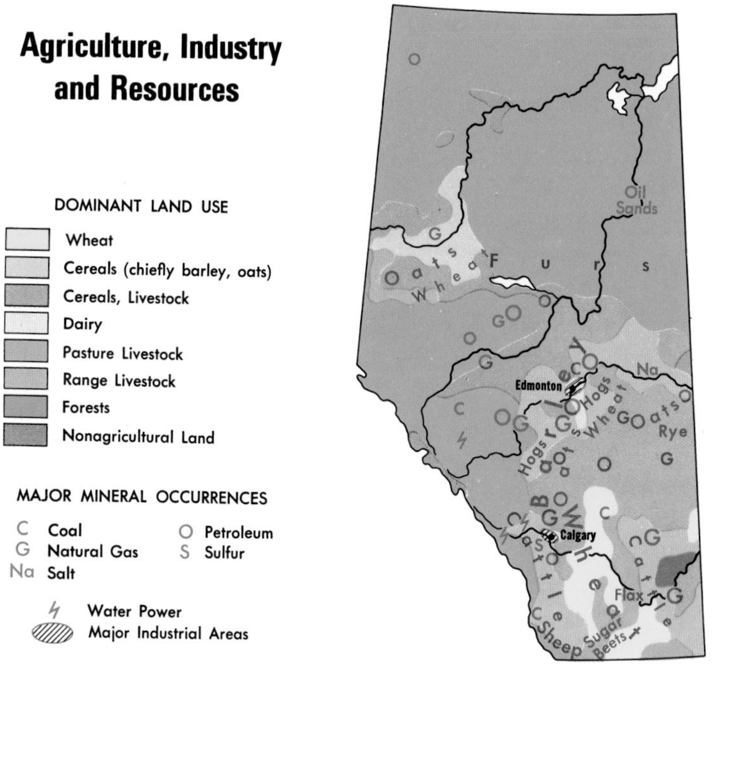
DOMINANT LAND USE
Wheat
Cereals (chiefly barley, oats)
Cereals, Livestock
Dairy
Pasture Livestock
Range Livestock
Forests
Nonagricultural Land
MAJOR MINERAL OCCURRENCES
C Coal
G Natural Gas
Na Salt
O Petroleum
S Sulfur
Water Power
Major Industrial Areas
Oil Sands
Furs
Oats
Wheat
Edmonton
Hogs
Wheat
Oats
Rye
Calgary
Flax
Sheep
Sugar Beets

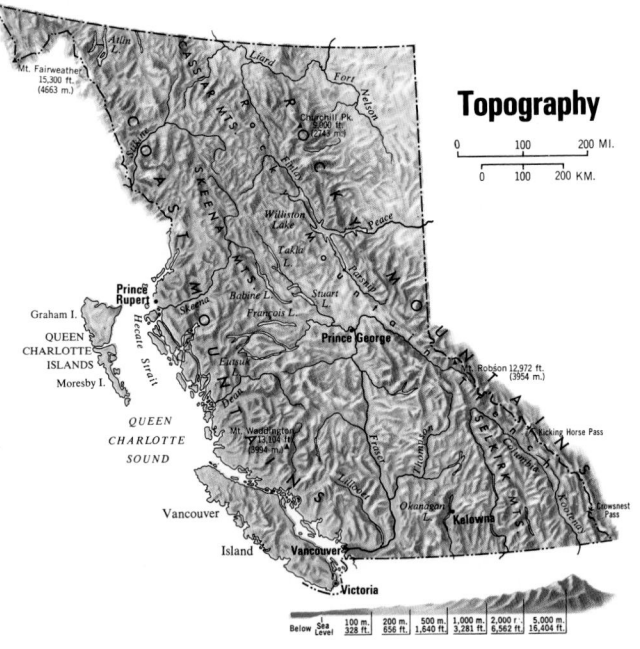

Topography

0   100   200 MI.

0   100   200 KM.

Below Sea Level | 100 m. 328 ft. | 200 m. 656 ft. | 500 m. 1,640 ft. | 1,000 m. 3,281 ft. | 2,000 m. 6,562 ft. | 5,000 m. 16,404 ft.

CITIES and TOWNS

Abbotsford 12,745 .... L 3
Alert Bay 626 .... D 5
Armstrong 2,683 .... H 5
Ashcroft 2,156 .... G 5
Ashton Creek 452 .... H 5
Balfour .... J 5
Barlow 472 .... F 3
Barrière 1,370 .... H 4
Blueberry Creek 635 .... J 5
Blue River 384 .... H 4
Boston Bar 498 .... G 5
Bowen Island 1,125 .... K 3
Brackendale 1,719 .... F 5
Burnaby ○136,494 .... K 3
Burns Lake 1,777 .... D 3
Cache Creek 1,308 .... G 5
Campbell River 15,370 .... D 5
Canal Flats 919 .... K 5
Canyon 698 .... J 5
Cassiar 1,045 .... K 2
Castlegar 6,902 .... J 5
Cawston 785 .... H 5
Central Saanich ○9,890 ... K 3
Chase 1,777 .... H 5
Chemainus 2,069 .... J 3
Cherry Creek 450 .... G 5
Chetwynd 2,553 .... G 2
Chilliwack ○40,642 .... M 3
Clearwater 1,461 .... H 4
Clinton 804 .... G 4
Coldstream ○6,450 .... H 5
Comox 6,607 .... H 2
Coquitlam ○61,077 .... K 3
Courtenay 8,992 .... E 5
Cranbrook 15,915 .... K 5
Creston 4,190 .... J 5
Crofton 1,303 .... J 3
Cultus Lake 481 .... M 3
Cumberland 1,947 .... E 5
Dawson Creek 11,373 .... G 2
Delta ○74,692 .... K 3
Duncan 4,228 .... J 3
Elkford 3,126 .... K 5
Enderby 1,816 .... H 5
Erickson 972 .... J 5
Errington 609 .... J 3
Esquimalt ○15,870 ...... K 4
Falkland 478 .... H 5
Fernie 5,444 .... K 5
Forest Grove 444 ...... G 4
Fort Fraser 574 .... E 3
Fort Langley 2,326 ..... L 3
Fort Nelson 3,724 ..... M 2
Fort Saint James 2,284 . E 3
Fort Saint John 13,891 . G 2
Fraser Lake 1,543 ..... E 3
Fruitvale 1,904 .... J 5
Gabriola 1,627 .... J 3
Galiano 669 .... K 3
Ganges 1,118 .... K 3
Gibsons 2,594 .... K 3
Gold River 2,225 ...... D 5
Golden 3,476 .... J 5
Grand Forks 3,486 .... H 6
Granisle 1,430 ...... D 3
Greenwood 856 ...... H 5
Hagensborg 350 ..... D 4
Harrison Hot Springs 569 M 3
Hatzic 1,055 .... L 3

Hazelton 393 .... D 2
Hedley 426 .... G 5
Holberg 444 .... C 5
Honeymoon Bay 474 ...... J 3
Hope 3,205 .... M 3
Hornby Island 474 ...... H 2
Horsefly 430 .... G 4
Houston 1,714 .... D 3
Hudson Hope 984 ...... F 2
Invermere 1,969 .... J 5
Kaleden 998 .... H 5
Kamloops 64,048 ...... G 5
Kaslo 854 .... J 5
Kelowna 59,196 .... H 5
Kent ○3,394 .... M 3
Keremeos 830 .... G 5
Kimberley 7,375 ...... K 5
Kitimat 12,462 ...... C 3
Kitsault 554 .... C 2
Kitwanga 369 .... D 2
Lac La Hache 647 .... G 4
Ladysmith 4,558 ..... J 3
Lake Cowichan 2,391 . J 4
Langley 15,124 ...... L 3
Lantzville 969 ...... J 3
Likely 425 .... G 4
Lillooet 1,725 ...... G 5
Lion's Bay 1,078 .... K 3
Logan Lake 2,637 ... G 5
Lumby 1,266 .... H 5
Lytton 428 .... G 5
Mackenzie 5,797 ... F 2
Mackenzie ○5,890 .. F 2
Malakwa 392 ...... H 5
Maple Bay 393 .... K 3
Maple Ridge ○32,232 . L 3
Masset 1,569 ..... B 3
Matsqui ○42,001 .. L 3
Mayne 546 .... K 3
McBride 641 ..... G 3
Merritt 6,110 .... G 5
Midway 633 ..... H 5
Mill Bay 583 .... K 3
Mission ○20,056 . L 3
Mission City 9,948 . L 3
Montrose 1,229 .. J 5
Nakusp 1,495 ... J 5
Nanaimo 47,069 . J 3
Naramata 876 .. H 5
Nelson 9,143 .. J 5
New Denver 642 . J 5
New Hazelton 792 . D 2
New Westminster 38,550 . K 3
Nicomen Island 360 . L 3
Nootka .... D 5
North Cowichan ○18,210 . J 3
North Pender Island 906 . K 3
North Saanich ○6,117 . K 3
North Vancouver 33,952 . K 3
North Vancouver ○65,367 . K 3
Oak Bay ○16,990 . K 4
Okanagan Falls 1,030 . H 5
Okanagan Landing 834 . H 5
Okanagan Mission . H 5
Old Barkerville 11 . G 3
Oliver 1,893 . H 5
One Hundred Mile House
    1,925 .... G 4
Osoyoos 2,738 . H 5
Oyama 430 .... H 5
Parksville 5,216 . J 3
Peachland ○2,865 . H 5

Penticton 23,181 .... H 5
Pitt Meadows ○6,209 .... L 3
Port Alberni 19,892 ..... H 3
Port Alice 1,668 .... D 5
Port Clements 380 ..... C 2
Port Coquitlam 27,535 . L 3
Port Edward 989 ...... B 3
Port Hardy ○3,778 .... D 5
Port McNeill 2,474 ... D 5
Port Moody 14,917 ... L 3
Pouce-Coupe 821 .... G 2
Powell River ○13,423 . E 5
Prince George 67,559 . F 3
Prince Rupert 16,197 . B 3
Princeton 3,051 ..... G 5
Qualicum Beach 2,844 . J 3
Queen Charlotte 1,070 . A 3
Quesnel 8,240 ..... F 4
Radium Hot Springs 419 . J 5
Revelstoke 5,544 .... H 5
Richmond ○96,154 ... K 3
Roberts Creek 926 .. J 3
Robson 1,008 ...... H 6
Rossland 3,967 .... H 6
Royston 754 ...... H 5
Saanich ○78,710 ... K 3
Salmo 1,100 ...... J 5
Salmon Arm 1,946 . H 5
Salmon Arm ○10,780 . H 5
Saltair 1,356 ..... J 3
Sandspit 794 ..... B 3
Sayward 482 ..... D 5
Sechelt 1,096 .... J 3
Shawnigan Lake 419 . J 3
Shoreacres 555 ... J 5
Sicamous 1,057 .. H 5
Sidney 7,946 .... K 3
Slocan 351 ..... J 5
Slocan Park 414 . J 5
Smithers 4,570 . D 3
Sointula 567 ... D 5
Sooke 852 ..... J 4
Sorrento 659 .. H 5
South Hazelton 500 . D 2
South Wellington 620 . J 3
Spallumcheen 4,213 . H 5
Sparwood 3,267 ... K 5
Sproat Lake 440 .. H 3
Squamish 1,590 .. F 5
Stewart ○1,456 .. C 2
Summerland ○7,473 . H 5
Surrey ○147,138 .. K 3
Tahsis 1,739 ..... D 5
Taylor 966 ...... G 2
Telkwa 840 .... D 3
Terrace 8,893 .. C 3
Terrace ○10,914 . C 3
Thornhill 4,281 . C 3
Thrums 360 ... J 5
Tofino 705 ... E 5
Trail 9,599 ... J 6
Ucluelet 1,593 . H 2
Union Bay 601 . H 2
Valemount 1,130 . H 4
Vancouver 414,281 . K 3
Vancouver (Greater)
    *1,169,831 ...... K 3
Vanderhoof 2,323 . E 3
Vavenby 479 ... H 4
Vernon 19,987 .. H 5
Victoria (cap.) 64,379 . K 4
Victoria ○233,481 . K 4
Warfield 1,969 . J 5
Wasa 345 .... K 5
Wells 417 .... H 5
Westbank 1,271 . H 5
West Vancouver ○35,728 . K 3
Westwold 409 . H 5
Whistler ○1,365 . F 5
White Rock 13,550 . K 3
Williams Lake 8,362 . F 4
Wilson Creek 611 . J 2
Windermere 611 . K 5
Winlaw 435 ... J 5
Woss Lake 395 . D 5
Wynndel 566 .. J 5
Yarrow 1,201 .. M 3
Youbou 965 ... J 3

OTHER FEATURES

Adams (lake) .... H 4
Adams (riv.) .... H 3
Alberni (inlet) .... H 1
Alsek (riv.) .... C 4
Aristazabal (isl.) .... C 4
Assiniboine (mt.) .... K 5
Atlin (lake) .... J 1
Azure (lake) .... G 4
Babine (lake) .... E 3
Babine (riv.) .... D 2
Banks (isl.) .... B 3
Barkley (sound) .... E 6
Beale (cape) .... E 6
Beatton (riv.) .... G 1
Bella Coola (riv.) .... D 4
Bennett, W.A.C. (dam) . G 2
Birkenhead Lake Prov. Park F 5
Bowron Lake Prov. Park . G 3
Bowser (lake) .... C 2
Brooks (pen.) .... C 4
Browning Entrance (str.) . B 3
Bryce (mt.) .... J 4
Bugaboo Glacier Prov. Park J 5
Bulkley (riv.) ...... D 2
Burke (chan.) ..... D 4
Burnaby (isl.) .... B 4
Bute (inlet) ...... E 5
Caamaño (sound) . C 4
Calvert (isl.) .... C 4
Canim (lake) .... G 4
Canoe Reach (riv.) . H 4
Cariboo (mts.) ... G 3
Carpenter (lake) . F 5
Carp Lake Prov. Park . F 3
Cassiar (mts.) ... K 2
Castle (mt.) .... J 4
Cathedral Prov. Park . H 5
Charlotte (lake) . D 4
Chatham (sound) . B 3

Chehalis (lake) .... L 3
Chilcotin (riv.) .... E 4
Chilko (lake) .... F 4
Chilko (riv.) .... E 4
Chilkoot (pass) .... J 1
Chuchi (lake) .... E 2
Churchill (peak) ..... L 2
Clayoquot (sound) ... D 5
Clearwater (lake) ... H 4
Clearwater (riv.) ... H 4
Coast (mts.) .... D 3
Columbia (lake) .... K 5
Columbia (mt.) .... J 4
Columbia (riv.) ... H 4
Columbia Reach (riv.) . H 4
Cook (cape) .... C 5
Cowichan (lake) ... J 3
Cowichan (riv.) ... J 3
Crowsnest (pass) . K 5
Cypress Prov. Park . K 3
Dean (chan.) ..... D 4
Dean (riv.) ...... D 4
Dease (lake) .... K 2
Dease (riv.) .... K 2
Devils Thumb (mt.) . A 1
Dixon Entrance (chan.) . A 3
Douglas (chan.) . C 3
Duncan (riv.) ... J 5
Dundas (isl.) ... B 3
Elk (riv.) ..... K 5
Elk Lakes Prov. Park . K 5
Eutsuk (lake) ... D 3
Fairweather (mt.) . H 1
Finlay (riv.) ... E 1

Fitzhugh (sound) .... D 4
Flathead (riv.) .... K 6
Flores (isl.) .... D 5
Fontas (riv.) .... M 2
Forbes (mt.) .... J 4
Fort Nelson (riv.) .... M 2
François (lake) ...... D 3
Fraser (lake) .... E 3
Fraser (riv.) ...... F 4
Fraser Reach (chan.) . C 3
Galiano (isl.) ..... K 3
Gardner (canal) ... C 3
Garibaldi Prov. Park . F 5
Georgia (str.) .... J 3
Germansen (lake) . E 2
Gil (isl.) .... C 3
Glacier Nat'l Park . J 4
Golden Ears Prov. Park . L 2
Gordon (riv.) ... H 3
Graham (isl.) ... A 3
Graham Reach (chan.) . C 3
Grenville (chan.) . C 3
Gil (isl.) ...... C 3
Halfway (riv.) .. F 2
Hamber Prov. Park . H 4
Harrison (lake) . M 2
Hawkesbury (isl.) . C 3
Hazelton (mts.) . C 2
Hecate (str.) ... B 3
Hobson (lake) .. H 4
Homathko (riv.) . E 4
Horsefly (lake) . G 4
Howe (sound) ... K 2
Hunter (isl.) ... C 4

Agriculture, Industry and Resources

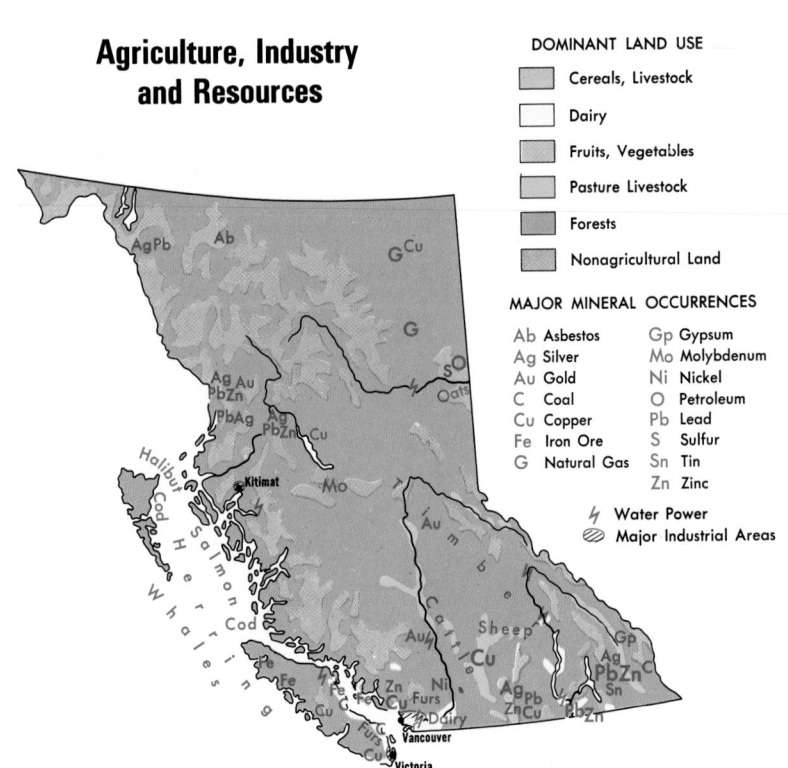

DOMINANT LAND USE

- Cereals, Livestock
- Dairy
- Fruits, Vegetables
- Pasture Livestock
- Forests
- Nonagricultural Land

MAJOR MINERAL OCCURRENCES

Ab	Asbestos	Gp	Gypsum
Ag	Silver	Mo	Molybdenum
Au	Gold	Ni	Nickel
C	Coal	O	Petroleum
Cu	Copper	Pb	Lead
Fe	Iron Ore	S	Sulfur
G	Natural Gas	Sn	Tin
	Zn	Zinc

⚡ Water Power
🌀 Major Industrial Areas

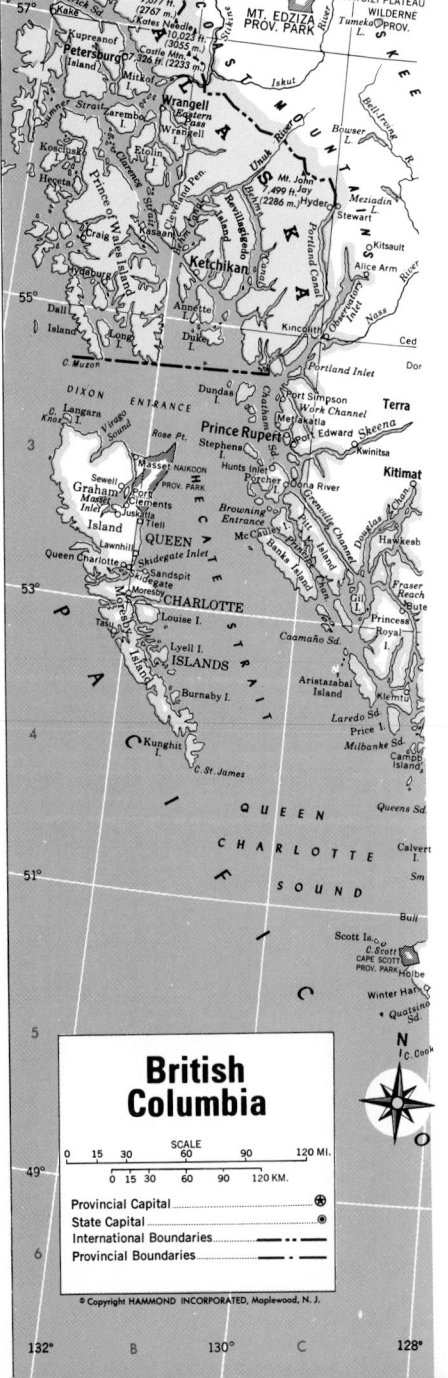

British Columbia

SCALE

0 15 30   60   90   120 MI.

0 15 30   60   90   120 KM.

Provincial Capital .... ⊛
State Capital .... ⊛
International Boundaries .... — ·· —
Provincial Boundaries ...... — — —

© Copyright HAMMOND INCORPORATED, Maplewood, N.J.

Inzana (lake) . . . . . E 3
Isaac (lake) . . . . . G 3
Iskut (riv.) . . . . . B 2
Jervis (inlet) . . . . . E 5
John Jay (mt.) . . . . . B 2
Johnstone (str.) . . . . . D 5
Juan de Fuca (str.) . . . . . J 3
Kates Needle (mt.) . . . . . A 1
Kechika (riv.) . . . . . L 2
Kenney (dam) . . . . . E 3
Kettle (riv.) . . . . . H 5
Kicking Horse (pass) . . . . . J 4
Kinbasket (lake) . . . . . H 4
King (isl.) . . . . . D 4
Klinaklini (riv.) . . . . . E 4
Kloch (lake) . . . . . E 2
Knight (inlet) . . . . . E 5
Knox (cape) . . . . . A 3
Kokanee Glacier Prov. Park . . J 5
Koocanusa (lake) . . . . . K 6
Kootenay (lake) . . . . . J 5
Kootenay (riv.) . . . . . K 5
Kootenay Nat'l Park . . . . . J 4
Kotcho (lake) . . . . . M 2
Kotcho (riv.) . . . . . M 2
Kunghit (isl.) . . . . . B 4
Kyuquot (sound) . . . . . D 5
Langara (isl.) . . . . . A 3
Laredo (sound) . . . . . C 4
Liard (riv.) . . . . . L 2
Lillooet (riv.) . . . . . F 5
Louise (isl.) . . . . . B 4
Lower Arrow (lake) . . . . . H 5
Lyell (isl.) . . . . . B 4
Lyell (mt.) . . . . . J 4
Mabel (lake) . . . . . H 5
Mahood (lake) . . . . . G 4
Malaspina (str.) . . . . . J 2
Manning Prov. Park . . . . . G 5
Masset (inlet) . . . . . A 3
McCauley (isl.) . . . . . B 3
McGregor (riv.) . . . . . G 3
Meziadin (lake) . . . . . C 2
Mica (dam) . . . . . H 4
Milbanke (sound) . . . . . C 4
Moberly (lake) . . . . . F 2
Monashee (mts.) . . . . . H 4
Moresby (isl.) . . . . . B 4
Morice (lake) . . . . . D 3
Morice (riv.) . . . . . D 3
Mount Assiniboine Prov. Park K 5
Mount Edziza Prov. Park and Rec. Area . . . . . B 1
Mount Revelstoke Nat'l Park H 4
Mount Robson Prov. Park . . H 3
Muncho Lake Prov. Park . . L 2
Murray (riv.) . . . . . G 3
Murtle (lake) . . . . . H 4
Muskwa (riv.) . . . . . M 2
Nanika (dam) . . . . . D 3
Nass (riv.) . . . . . C 2
Nation (riv.) . . . . . F 2
Nechako (riv.) . . . . . E 3
Nitinat (lake) . . . . . H 3
Nootka (isl.) . . . . . D 5
Nootka (sound) . . . . . D 5
Nootka (sound) . . . . . D 5
North Thompson (riv.) . . . . . G 4
Observatory (inlet) . . . . . C 2
Okanagan (lake) . . . . . H 5
Okanagan Mtn. Prov. Park . . G 5
Okanogan (riv.) . . . . . H 6
Omineca (mts.) . . . . . E 2
Omineca (riv.) . . . . . E 2
Ootsa (lake) . . . . . D 3
Owikeno (lake) . . . . . D 4
Pacific Rim Nat'l Park . . . . . E 6
Parsnip (riv.) . . . . . F 3
Peace (riv.) . . . . . G 2
Pend Oreille (riv.) . . . . . J 6
Petitot (riv.) . . . . . M 2
Pinchi (lake) . . . . . E 3
Pine (riv.) . . . . . G 2
Pitt (isl.) . . . . . C 3
Pitt (lake) . . . . . L 2
Porcher (isl.) . . . . . B 3
Portland (canal) . . . . . B 2
Portland (inlet) . . . . . C 3
Price (isl.) . . . . . C 4
Princess Royal (isl.) . . . . . C 3
Principe (chan.) . . . . . C 3
Prophet (riv.) . . . . . M 2
Purcell (mts.) . . . . . J 5
Quatsino (sound) . . . . . C 5
Queen Charlotte (isls.) . . . . . B 3
Queen Charlotte (sound) . . . . . C 4
Queen Charlotte (str.) . . . . . D 5
Queens (sound) . . . . . C 4
Quesnel (lake) . . . . . G 4
Quesnel (riv.) . . . . . F 4
Rivers (inlet) . . . . . D 4
Robson (mt.) . . . . . H 3
Rocky (mts.) . . . . . F 2
Roderick (isl.) . . . . . C 4
Rose (pt.) . . . . . B 3
Saint James (cape) . . . . . B 4
Salmon (riv.) . . . . . F 3
Salmon Arm (inlet) . . . . . J 2
San Juan (riv.) . . . . . J 3
Schoen Lake Prov. Park . . . E 5
Scott (cape) . . . . . C 5
Scott (isls.) . . . . . C 5
Seechelt (inlet) . . . . . J 2
Seechelt (pen.) . . . . . J 2
Selkirk (mts.) . . . . . H 4
Seymour (inlet) . . . . . D 4
Sheslay (riv.) . . . . . J 2
Shuswap (lake) . . . . . H 4
Sikanni Chief (riv.) . . . . . F 1
Silver Star Prov. Park . . . . . H 5
Sir Sandford (mt.) . . . . . H 4
Skagit (riv.) . . . . . G 6
Skeena (mts.) . . . . . C 2
Skeena (riv.) . . . . . C 3
Skidegate (inlet) . . . . . B 3
Slocan (lake) . . . . . J 5
Smith (sound) . . . . . C 4
South Bentinck Arm (inlet) . . D 4
Stave (lake) . . . . . L 3
Stephens (isl.) . . . . . B 3
Stikine (riv.) . . . . . B 1
Stone Mountain Prov. Park . . . L 2

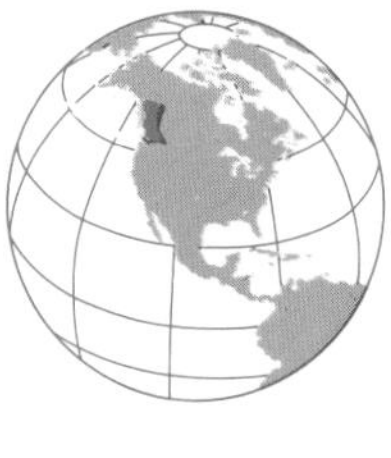

AREA 366,253 sq. mi. (948,596 sq. km.)
POPULATION 2,883,367
CAPITAL Victoria
LARGEST CITY Vancouver
HIGHEST POINT Mt. Fairweather 15,300 ft. (4,663 m.)
SETTLED IN 1806
ADMITTED TO CONFEDERATION 1871
PROVINCIAL FLOWER Dogwood

Strathcona Prov. Park . . . . . E 5
Stuart (lake) . . . . . E 3
Sustut (riv.) . . . . . D 2
Tagish (lake) . . . . . J 1
Tahtsa (lake) . . . . . D 3
Takla (lake) . . . . . D 2
Taku (riv.) . . . . . J 2
Tatlatui (lake) . . . . . D 2
Tatlayoko (lake) . . . . . E 4
Tchentlo (lake) . . . . . E 2
Teslin (lake) . . . . . K 1
Tetachuck (lake) . . . . . E 3
Texada (isl.) . . . . . J 2
Tezzeron (lake) . . . . . E 3
Thompson (riv.) . . . . . G 5
Three Guardsmen (mt.) . . . . . H 1
Thutade (lake) . . . . . D 2
Tiedemann (mt.) . . . . . E 4
Toad (riv.) . . . . . L 2
Toba (inlet) . . . . . E 5
Tochcha (lake) . . . . . E 5
Top Of The World Prov. Park . K 5
Trembleur (lake) . . . . . E 3
Troitsa (lake) . . . . . D 3
Tumeka (lake) . . . . . C 1
Turnagain (riv.) . . . . . K 2
Tuya (riv.) . . . . . K 2
Tweedsmuir Prov. Park . . . . . D 3
Upper Arrow (lake) . . . . . H 5
Valdes (isl.) . . . . . K 3
Vancouver (isl.) . . . . . D 5
Virago (sound) . . . . . A 3
Waddington (mt.) . . . . . E 4
Wapiti (riv.) . . . . . H 3
Wells Gray Prov. Park . . . . . H 4
West Road (riv.) . . . . . E 3
Whitesail (lake) . . . . . D 3
Williston (lake) . . . . . F 2
Work (chan.) . . . . . C 3
Yellowhead (pass) . . . . . H 4
Yoho Nat'l Park . . . . . J 4

*Population of metropolitan area.
○Population of municipality.

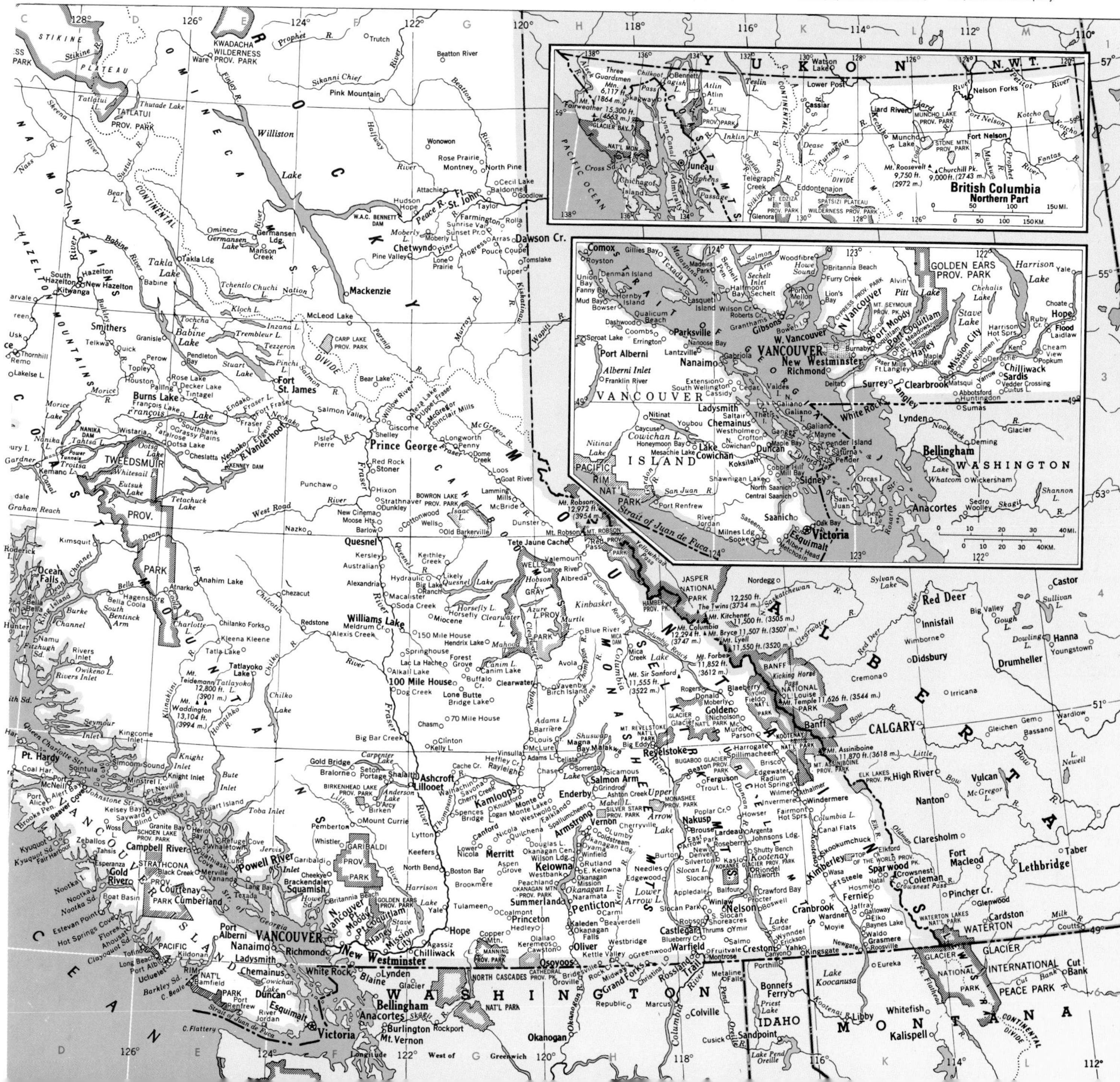

NORTHWEST TERRITORIES

REGIONS

Baffin 8,300 .... J2
Fort Smith 22,384 .... G3
Inuvik 7,485 .... F3
Keewatin 4,327 .... J3
Kitikmeot 3,245 .... G2

CITIES and TOWNS

Aklavik 721 .... E3
Alert M1
Amadjuak L3
Arctic Bay 375 .... K2
Arctic Red River 120 .... E3
Baker Lake 954 .... J3
Bathurst Inlet 20 .... H3
Bell Rock G3
Broughton Island 378 .... M3
Buffalo River Junction G3
Cambridge Bay 815 .... H3
Cape Dorset 784 .... L3
Cape Dyer M3
Cape Smith L3
Chesterfield Inlet 249 .... K3
Clyde River 443 .... M2
Colville Lake 57 .... F3
Coppermine 809 .... G3
Coral Harbour 429 .... K3
Detah 143 .... G3
Dory Point G3
Echo Bay (Port Radium) 56 .... G3
Enterprise 46 .... G3
Eskimo Point 1,022 .... J3
Eureka K2
Fort Franklin 521 .... F3
Fort Good Hope 463 .... F3
Fort Liard 405 .... F3
Fort McPherson 632 .... E3
Fort Norman 286 .... F3
Fort Providence 605 .... G3
Fort Resolution 480 .... G3
Fort Simpson 980 .... F3
Fort Smith 2,298 .... G4
Gjoa Haven 523 .... J3
Grise Fiord 106 .... K2
Hall Beach 349 .... K3
Hay River 2,863 .... G3
Holman 300 .... G2
Igloolik 746 .... K3
Inuvik 3,147 .... E3
Iqaluit 2,333 .... M3
Isachsen H2
Jean-Marie River 69 .... F3
Kakisa 36 .... G3
Kipisa 43 .... M3
Lac la Martre 268 .... G3
Lake Harbour 252 .... L3
Mould Bay F2
Nahanni Butte 85 .... F3
Nanisivik 261 .... K2
Norman Wells 420 .... F3
Pangnirtung 839 .... M3
Paulatuk 174 .... F3
Pelly Bay 257 .... K3
Pine Point 1,861 .... G3
Pond Inlet 705 .... L2
Port Burwell M3
Rae-Edzo 1,378 .... G3
Rae Lakes 200 .... G3
Rankin Inlet 1,109 .... G3
Reliance 15 .... H3
Repulse Bay 352 .... K3
Resolute 168 .... J2
Resolution Island M3
Rocher River G3
Sachs Harbour 161 .... F2
Salt River G3
Sawmill Bay G3
Snare Lake 69 .... G3
Snowdrift 253 .... G3
Spence Bay 431 .... J3
Trout Lake 59 .... F3
Tuktoyaktuk 772 .... E3
Tungsten 320 .... F3
Umingmaktok 60 .... H3
Whale Cove 188 .... J3
Wrigley 137 .... F3
Yellowknife (cap.) 9,483 .... G3

OTHER FEATURES

Adelaide (pen.) J3
Admiralty (inlet) K2
Air Force (isl.) L3
Akpatok (isl.) M3
Amadjuak (lake) L3
Amund Ringnes (isl.) J2
Amundsen (gulf) F2
Anderson (riv.) F3
Arctic Red (riv.) E3
Artillery (lake) H3
Auyuittug Nat'l Park M3
Axel Heiberg (isl.) J2
Aylmer (lake) H3
Back (riv.) J3
Baffin (bay) M2
Baffin (isl.) L2
Baker (lake) J3
Banks (isl.) F2
Barbeau (peak) L1
Barrow (str.) J2
Bathurst (cape) F2
Bathurst (inlet) H3
Bathurst (isl.) H2
Beaufort (sea) D2
Bellot (str.) J2
Boothia (gulf) K3
Boothia (pen.) J2
Borden (isl.) G2
Borden (pen.) K2
British Empire (range) L1
Brodeur (pen.) K2
Bruce (mts.) L2
Buchan (gulf) L2
Burnside (riv.) G3
Byam Martin (chan.) H2
Byam Martin (isl.) H2
Bylot (isl.) L2
Camsell (riv.) G3
Chantrey (inlet) J3
Chesterfield (inlet) J3
Chidley (cape) M3
Clinton-Colden (lake) H3
Clyde (inlet) M2
Coats (isl.) K3
Coburg (isl.) L2
Columbia (cape) M1
Colville (lake) F3
Committee (bay) K3
Contwoyto (lake) H3
Coppermine (riv.) G3
Cornwall (isl.) J2
Cornwallis (isl.) J2
Coronation (gulf) G3
Croker (bay) K2
Crown Prince Frederik (isl.) K3
Cumberland (pen.) M3
Cumberland (sound) M3
Dalhousie (cape) E2
Davis (str.) M3
Dease (str.) H3
Denmark (bay) H2
Devon (isl.) K2
Dolphin and Union (str.) G3
Dubawnt (lake) H3
Dubawnt (riv.) H3
Dundas (pen.) G2
Dyer (cape) M3
Eclipse (sound) L2
Eglinton (isl.) F2
Ellef Ringnes (isl.) H2
Ellesmere (isl.) K2
Ellesmere Is. Nat'l Park Res. L1
Ennadai (lake) H3
Eskimo (lakes) E3
Eureka (sound) K2
Evans (str.) K3
Exeter (sound) M3
Fisher (str.) K3
Fosheim (pen.) K1
Foxe (basin) L3
Foxe (chan.) K3
Foxe (pen.) L3
Franklin (bay) F2
Franklin (mts.) F3
Franklin (str.) J2
Frobisher (bay) M3
Frozen (str.) K3
Fury and Hecla (str.) K3
Gabriel (str.) M3
Garry (lake) H3
Gods Mercy (bay) K3
Great Bear (lake) F3
Great Bear (riv.) F3
Great Slave (lake) G3
Greely (fjord) K1
Grinnell (pen.) J2
Hadley (bay) H2
Hall (basin) M1
Hall (pen.) M3
Hayes (riv.) J3
Hazen (lake) L1
Hazen (str.) G2
Henik (lakes) J3
Henry Kater (cape) M3
Home (bay) M3
Hood (riv.) G3
Horn (mts.) G3
Hornaday (riv.) F3
Horton (riv.) F3
Hottah (lake) G3
Hudson (bay) K3
Hudson (str.) L3
Isachsen (cape) H2
James Ross (str.) J3
Jenny Lind (isl.) H3
Jens Munk (isl.) K3
Jones (sound) K2
Kaminuriak (lake) J3
Kane (basin) L2
Kasba (lake) H3
Kazan (riv.) H3
Keele (riv.) F3
Keith Arm (inlet) F3
Kellett (cape) F2
Kellett (str.) G2
Kennedy (chan.) M1
Kent (pen.) H3
King Christian (isl.) H2
King William (isl.) J3
Lady Ann (str.) K2
La Martre (lake) G3
Lancaster (sound) K2
Lands End (cape) F2
Larsen (sound) J2
Liard (riv.) F4
Lincoln (sea) M1
Liverpool (bay) E2

Topography

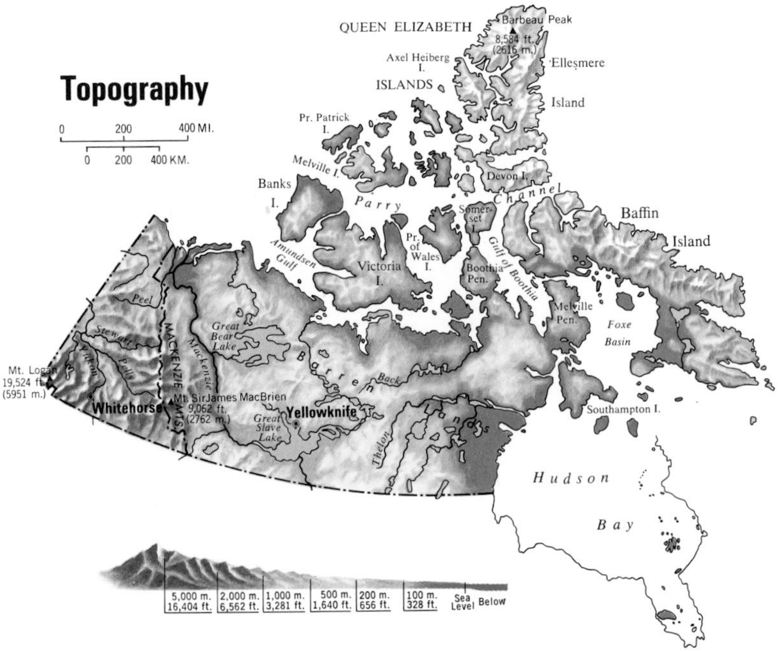

Lockhart (riv.) H3
Lougheed (isl.) H2
Lyon (inlet) K3
MacKay (lake) G3
Mackenzie (bay) E3
Mackenzie (mts.) E3
Mackenzie (riv.) F3
Mackenzie King (isl.) G2
Macmillan (pass) F3
Maguse (lake) J3
Makinson (inlet) L2
Mansel (isl.) K3
Marian (lake) G3
Markham (inlet) L1
McLeod (bay) G3
M'Clintock (chan.) H2
M'Clure (str.) G2
McTavish Arm (inlet) G3
Melghen (isl.) H1
Melville (isl.) G2
Melville (pen.) K3
Mercy (cape) M3
Mills (lake) G3
Minto (inlet) G2
Mistake (bay) J3
Nahanni Nat'l Park F3
Nansen (sound) J1
Nares (str.) L2
Navy Board (inlet) K2
Nelson Head (prom.) F2
Nettilling (lake) L3
Nonacho (lake) H3
North Arm (inlet) G3
North Magnetic Pole H2
Norwegian (bay) J2
Nottingham (isl.) L3
Nueltin (lake) H3
Ommanney (bay) H2
Padloping (isl.) M3
Parry (bay) K3
Parry (chan.) G2
Parry (isls.) G2
Parry (pen.) F2
Peary (chan.) H2
Peel (sound) J2
Pelly (bay) J3
Penny (str.) J2
Point (lake) G3
Pond (inlet) L2
Prince Albert (pen.) G2
Prince Albert (sound) G2
Prince Charles (isl.) L3
Prince Gustav Adolf (sea) H2
Prince of Wales (isl.) J2
Prince of Wales (str.) G2
Prince Patrick (isl.) F2
Prince Regent (inlet) J2
Queen Elizabeth (isls.) H1
Queen Maud (gulf) H3
Queens (chan.) J2

Agriculture, Industry and Resources

DOMINANT LAND USE

Forests
Nonagricultural Land

MAJOR MINERAL OCCURRENCES

Ab	Asbestos	G	Natural Gas
Ag	Silver	O	Petroleum
Au	Gold	Pb	Lead
C	Coal	W	Tungsten
Cu	Copper	Zn	Zinc
Fe	Iron Ore		

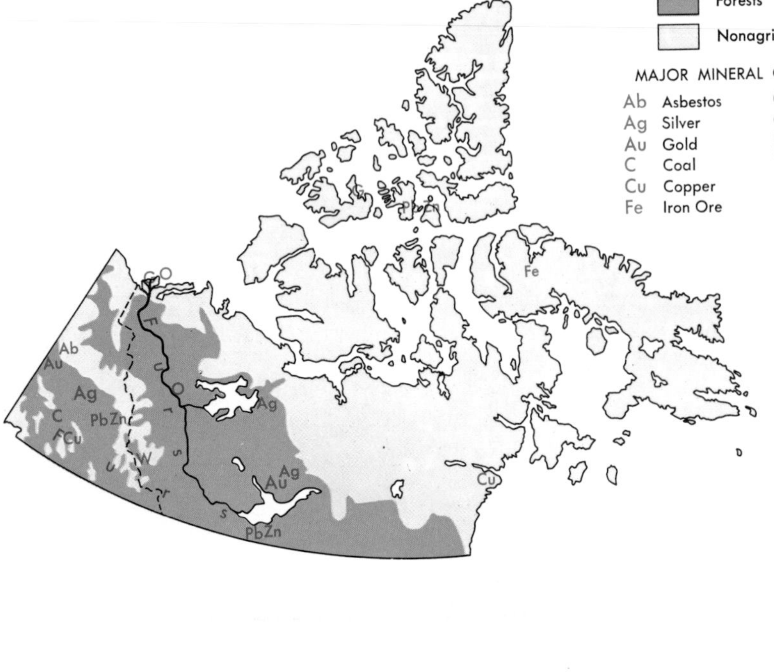

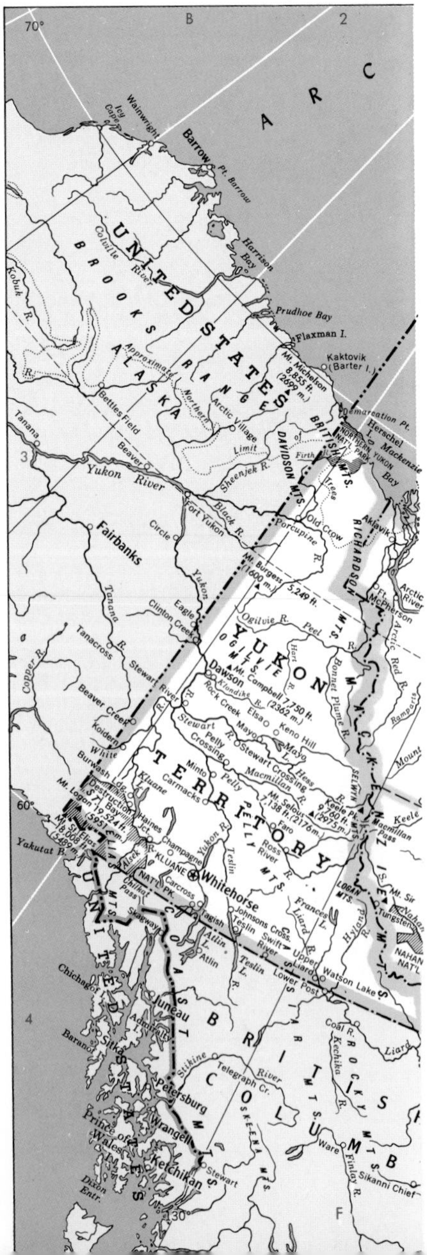

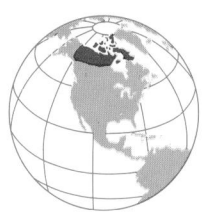

Raanes (pen.)...........K2	Stefansson (isl.)...........H2		
Rae (isth.)...............K3	Sverdrup (chan.)..........J1		
Rae (riv.)...............G3	Sverdrup (isls.)...........J2		
Rae (str.)...............J3	Takijug (lake)............G3		
Ramparts (riv.)..........E3	Talbot (inlet)............L2		
Resolution (isl.).........M3	Taltson (riv.)............G3		
Richard Collinson (inlet).G2	Tathlina (lake)...........G3		
Richards (isl.)...........E3	Tha-anne (riv.)...........J3		
Richardson (mts.)........E3	Thelon (riv.)............H3		
Robeson (chan.).........M1	Thlewiaza (riv.)..........J3		
Roes Welcome (sound)...K3	Trout (lake).............F3		
Rowley (isl.)............K3	Ungava (bay)............M4		
Royal Geographical	Vansittart (isl.).........K3		
Society (isls.).........J3	Victoria (isl.)...........G2		
Russell (isl.)............J2	Victoria (str.)...........H3		
Sabine (pen.)...........H2	Viscount Melville (sound)..G2		
Salisbury (isl.)..........L3	Wager (bay)............K3		
Seahorse (pt.)..........L3	Wales (isl.).............K3		
Selwyn (lake)...........H4	Walsingham (cape).......M3		
Sherman (inlet).........J3	Wellington (chan.).......J2		
Simpson (pen.)..........K3	Wholdaia (lake).........H3		
Sir James MacBrien (mt.).F3	Winter (harb.)..........H2		
Slave (riv.).............G3	Wollaston (pen.).........G3		
Smith (bay).............L2	Wood Buffalo Nat'l Park...G3		
Smith (cape)............L3	Wynniatt (bay)..........G2		
Smith (sound)...........L2	Yathkyed (lake)..........J3		
Snare (riv.).............G3	Yellowknife (riv.).........G3		
Snowbird (lake).........H3			
Somerset (isl.)..........J2			
South (bay).............K3			
Southampton (isl.).......K3			
South Nahanni (riv.).....F3			
Stallworthy (cape).......J1			
Steensby (inlet).........L2			

YUKON TERRITORY

AREA 207,075 sq. mi.
(536,324 sq. km.)
POPULATION 23,504
CAPITAL Whitehorse
LARGEST CITY Whitehorse
HIGHEST POINT Mt. Logan 19,524 ft.
(5,951 m.)
SETTLED IN 1897
ADMITTED TO CONFEDERATION 1898
PROVINCIAL FLOWER Fireweed

NORTHWEST TERRITORIES

AREA 1,304,896 sq. mi. (3,379,683 sq. km.)
POPULATION 52,238
CAPITAL Yellowknife
LARGEST CITY Yellowknife
HIGHEST POINT Mt. Sir James MacBrien
9,062 ft. (2,762 m.)
SETTLED IN 1800
ADMITTED TO CONFEDERATION 1870
PROVINCIAL FLOWER Mountain Avens

YUKON TERRITORY
CITIES and TOWNS

Beaver Creek 90.........D3	
Burwash Landing 73......D3	
Carcross 216...........E3	

Carmacks •256.........E3	Minto.................E3
Champagne............E3	Old Crow 243.........E3
Clinton Creek..........D3	Pelly Crossing 182.....E3
Cowley...............E3	Rock Creek 59.........E3
Dawson 697..........E3	Ross River 294........E3
Destruction Bay 45.....E3	Stewart Crossing 20....E3
Elsa 336.............E3	Stewart River.........D3
Faro 1,652...........E3	Swift River 24........E3
Haines Junction •366...E3	Tagish 89............E3
Johnson's Crossing 13...E3	Teslin •310...........E3
Keno Hill 88..........E3	Upper Liard 130.......F3
Koidern..............D3	Watson Lake •748.....F3
Mayo 398............E3	Whitehorse (cap.) 14,814..E3

OTHER FEATURES

Alsek (riv.)...........E3	Kluane Nat'l Park.......E3	Porcupine (riv.).......E3	
Bonnet Plume (riv.).....E3	Liard (riv.)............D3	Richardson (mts.).....E3	
British (mts.).........D3	Logan (mt.)...........E3	Rocky (mts.)..........F4	
Campbell (mt.).........E3	Logan (mts.)..........F3	Saint Elias (mt.)......D3	
Cassiar (mts.).........E3	Mackenzie (mts.)......E3	Saint Elias (mts.)......D3	
Frances (lake).........E3	Macmillan (riv.)......E3	Selous (mt.)..........E3	
Herschel (isl.).........E3	Mayo (lake)..........E3	Selwyn (mts.)........E3	
Hess (riv.)...........E3	Northern Yukon Nat'l Pk..E3	Stewart (riv.).........E3	
Hyland (riv.)..........F3	Ogilvie (mts.).........E3	Teslin (lake).........E4	
Keele (peak)..........E3	Ogilvie (riv.).........E3	Teslin (riv.)..........E3	
Klondike (riv.)........E3	Peel (riv.)...........E3	White (riv.)..........D3	
Kluane (lake).........E3	Pelly (mts.)..........E3	Yukon (riv.).........E3	
	Pelly (riv.)..........E3	• Population of district.	

Yukon and Northwest Territories

SCALE
0 50 100   200   300 MI.
0 50 100   200   300 KM.

Territorial Capitals .... ⊗
Regional Capitals .... ⊙
International Boundaries .... ━ ∙ ━
Provincial & Territorial Boundaries ━ ∙∙ ━
Regional Boundaries .... ━ ━

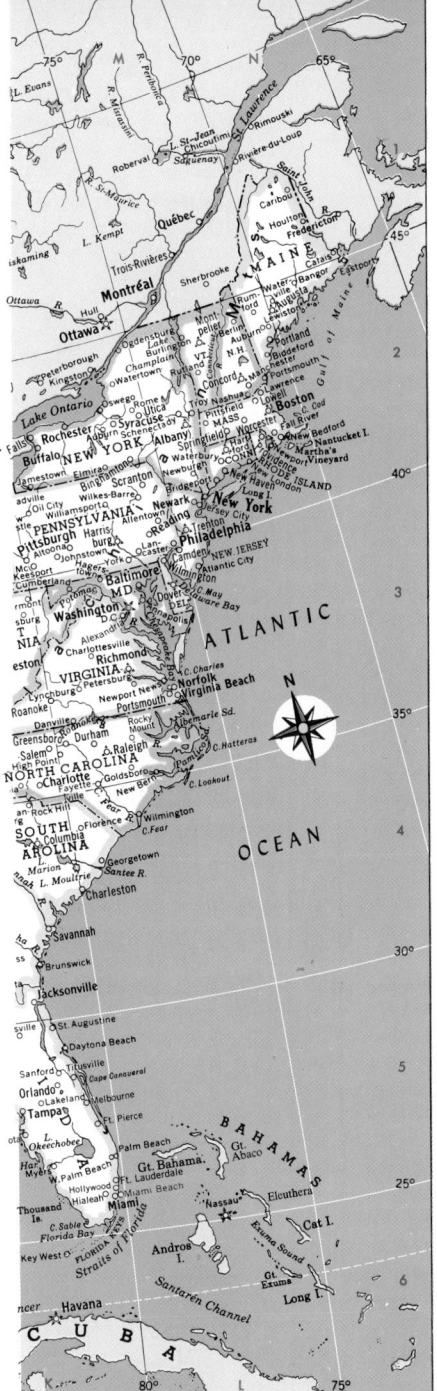

AREA 3,623,420 sq. mi.
     (9,384,658 sq. km.)
POPULATION   249,632,692
CAPITAL Washington
LARGEST CITY New York
HIGHEST POINT Mt. McKinley 20,320 ft.
     (6,194 m.)
MONETARY UNIT U.S. dollar
MAJOR LANGUAGE English
MAJOR RELIGIONS Protestantism,
     Roman Catholicism, Judaism

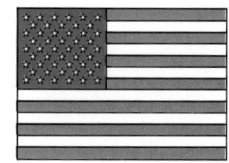

Population Distribution

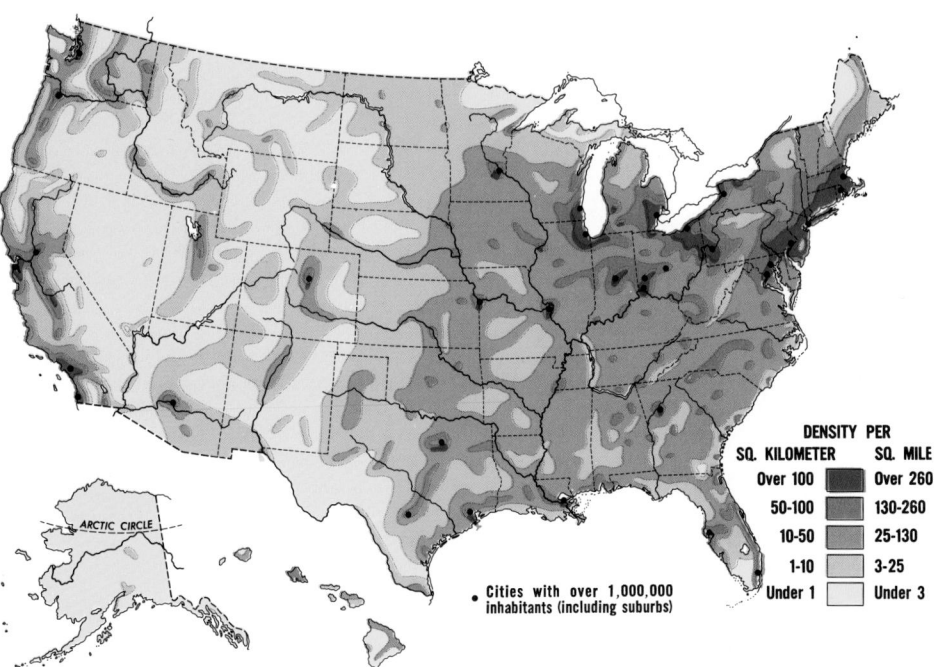

DENSITY PER

SQ. KILOMETER	SQ. MILE
Over 100	Over 260
50-100	130-260
10-50	25-130
1-10	3-25
Under 1	Under 3

● Cities with over 1,000,000
   inhabitants (including suburbs)

Vegetation

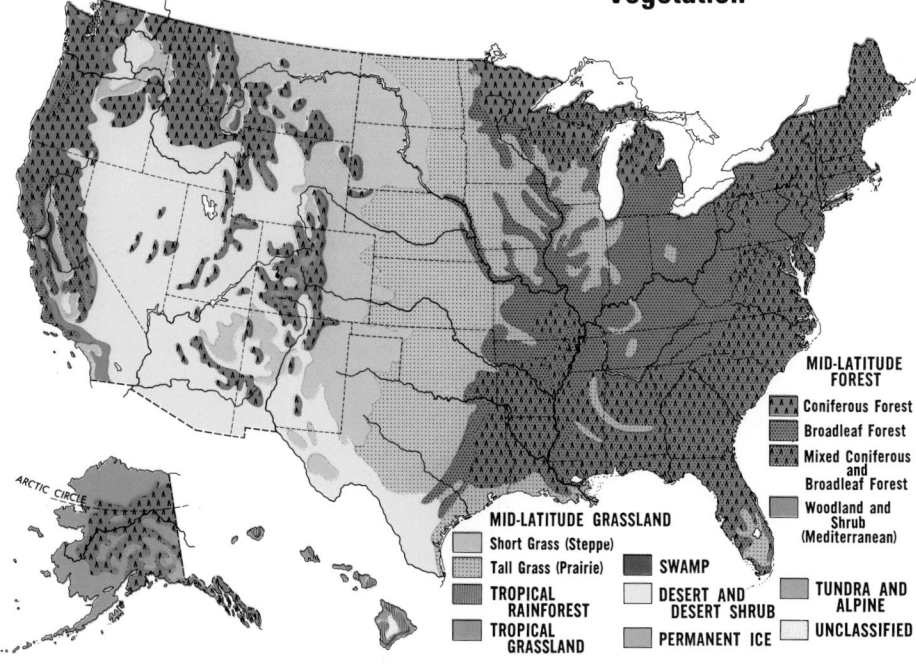

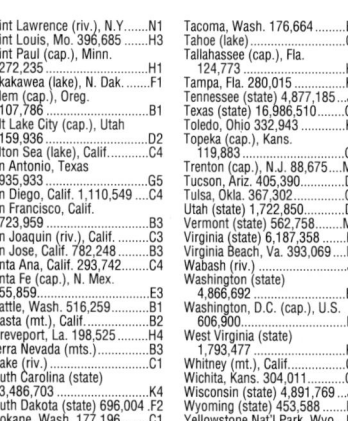

MID-LATITUDE GRASSLAND
Short Grass (Steppe)
Tall Grass (Prairie)
TROPICAL RAINFOREST
TROPICAL GRASSLAND

SWAMP
DESERT AND DESERT SHRUB
PERMANENT ICE

MID-LATITUDE FOREST
Coniferous Forest
Broadleaf Forest
Mixed Coniferous and Broadleaf Forest
Woodland and Shrub (Mediterranean)
TUNDRA AND ALPINE
UNCLASSIFIED

Rainfall

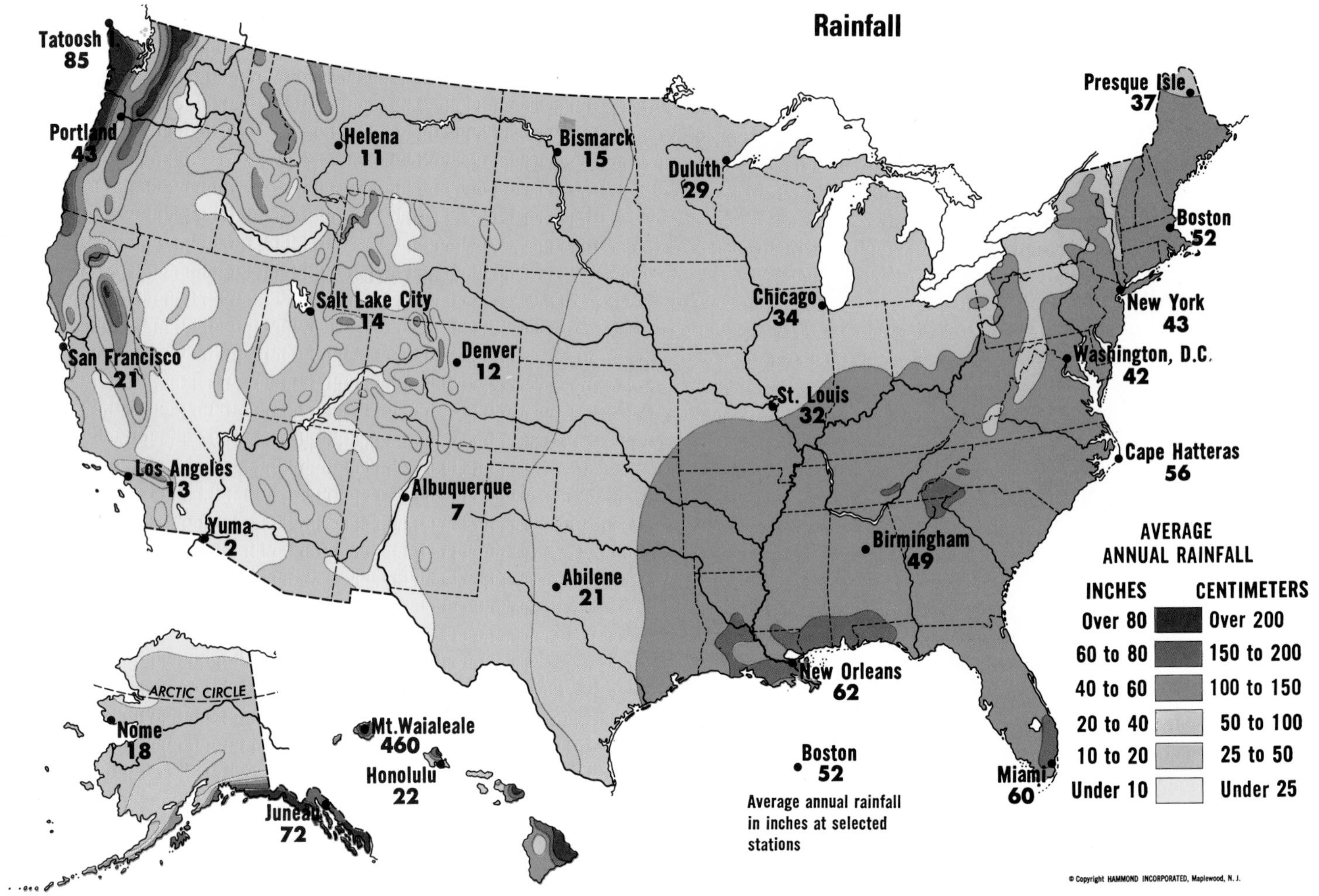

Tatoosh
85

Portland
43

Helena
11

Bismarck
15

Duluth
29

Presque Isle
37

Boston
52

Salt Lake City
14

Denver
12

Chicago
34

New York
43

San Francisco
21

St. Louis
32

Washington, D.C.
42

Los Angeles
13

Albuquerque
7

Birmingham
49

Cape Hatteras
56

Yuma
2

Abilene
21

New Orleans
62

Miami
60

ARCTIC CIRCLE

Nome
18

Mt.Waialeale
460

Honolulu
22

Boston
52

Average annual rainfall
in inches at selected
stations

Juneau
72

AVERAGE ANNUAL RAINFALL	
INCHES	CENTIMETERS
Over 80	Over 200
60 to 80	150 to 200
40 to 60	100 to 150
20 to 40	50 to 100
10 to 20	25 to 50
Under 10	Under 25

© Copyright HAMMOND INCORPORATED, Maplewood, N.J.

Average January Temperature

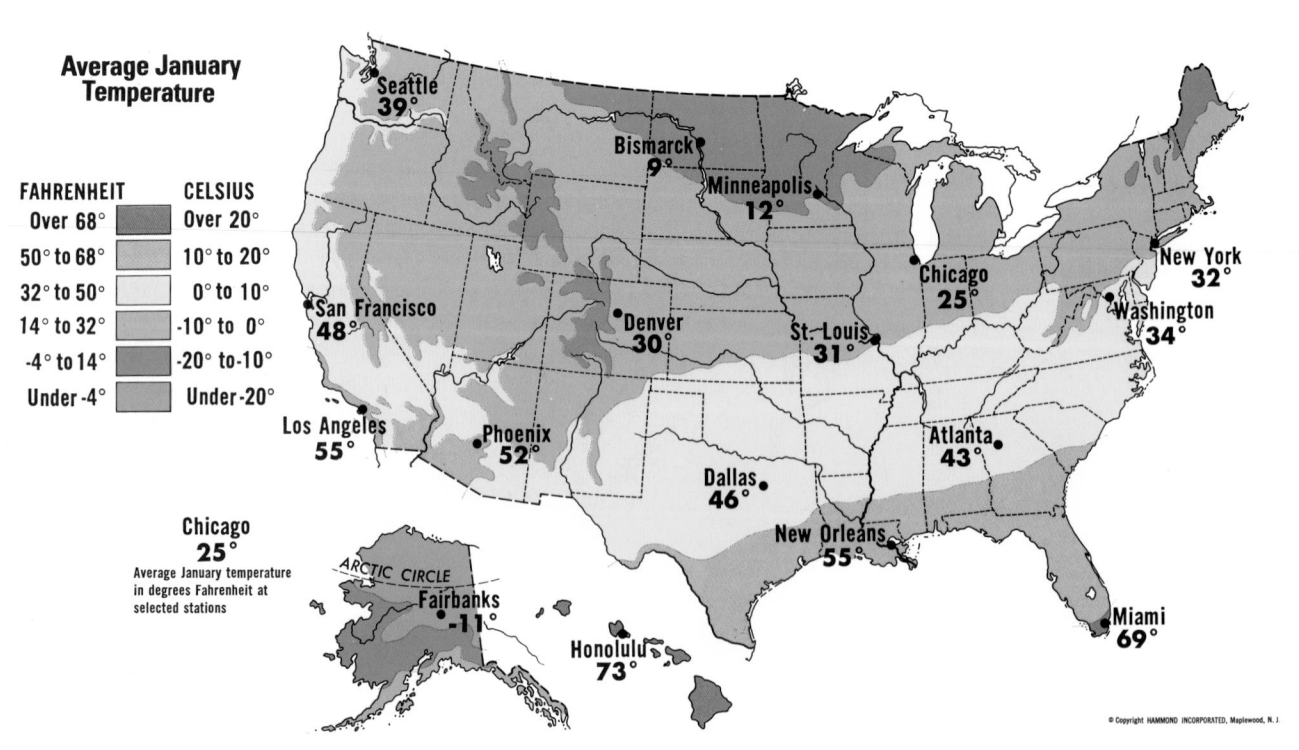

Seattle
39°

Bismarck
9°

Minneapolis
12°

FAHRENHEIT	CELSIUS
Over 68°	Over 20°
50° to 68°	10° to 20°
32° to 50°	0° to 10°
14° to 32°	-10° to 0°
-4° to 14°	-20° to -10°
Under -4°	Under -20°

San Francisco
48°

Denver
30°

St. Louis
31°

Chicago
25°

New York
32°

Washington
34°

Los Angeles
55°

Phoenix
52°

Dallas
46°

Atlanta
43°

New Orleans
55°

Chicago
25°

Average January temperature
in degrees Fahrenheit at
selected stations

ARCTIC CIRCLE

Fairbanks
-11°

Honolulu
73°

Miami
69°

© Copyright HAMMOND INCORPORATED, Maplewood, N.J.

Topography

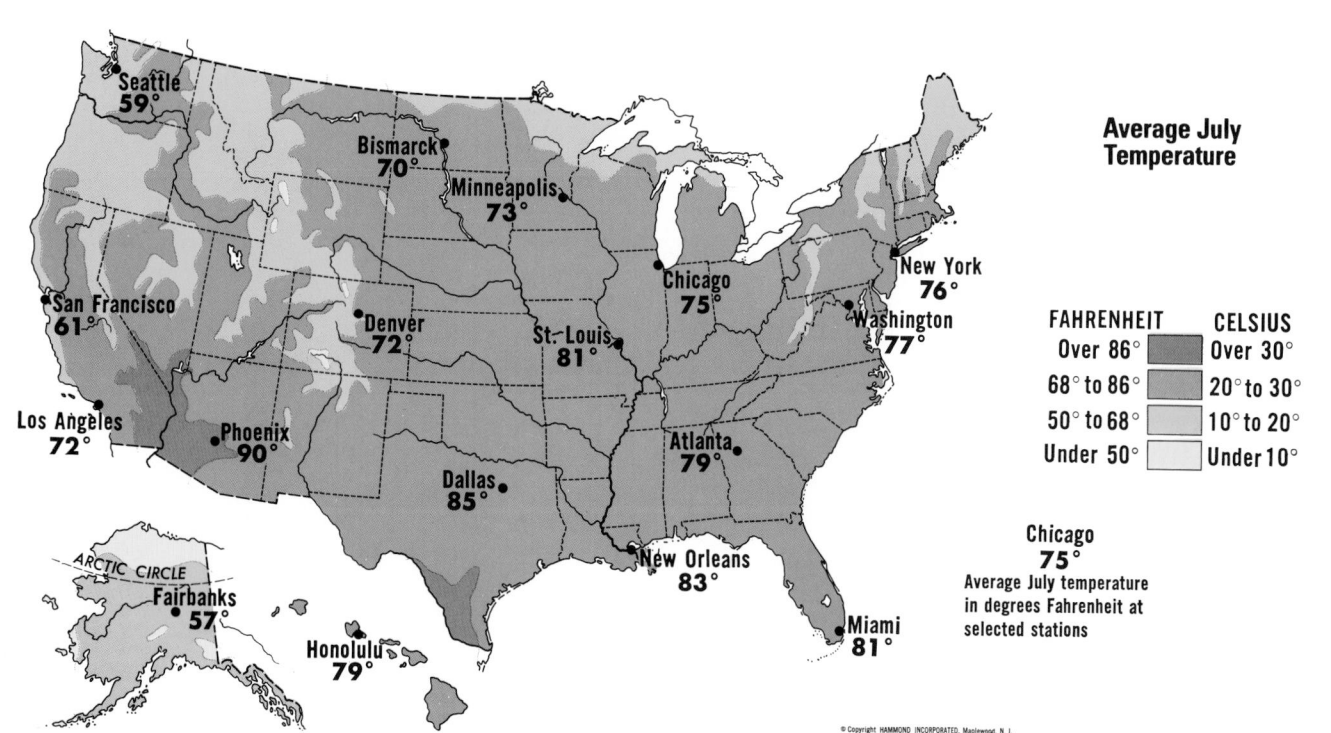

Average July Temperature

FAHRENHEIT	CELSIUS
Over 86°	Over 30°
68° to 86°	20° to 30°
50° to 68°	10° to 20°
Under 50°	Under 10°

Chicago
75°

Average July temperature
in degrees Fahrenheit at
selected stations

Seattle 59°
Bismarck 70°
Minneapolis 73°
Chicago 75°
New York 76°
Washington 77°
San Francisco 61°
Denver 72°
St. Louis 81°
Los Angeles 72°
Phoenix 90°
Dallas 85°
Atlanta 79°
New Orleans 83°
Fairbanks 57°
Honolulu 79°
Miami 81°

© Copyright HAMMOND INCORPORATED, Maplewood, N. J.

United States Standard Time Zones

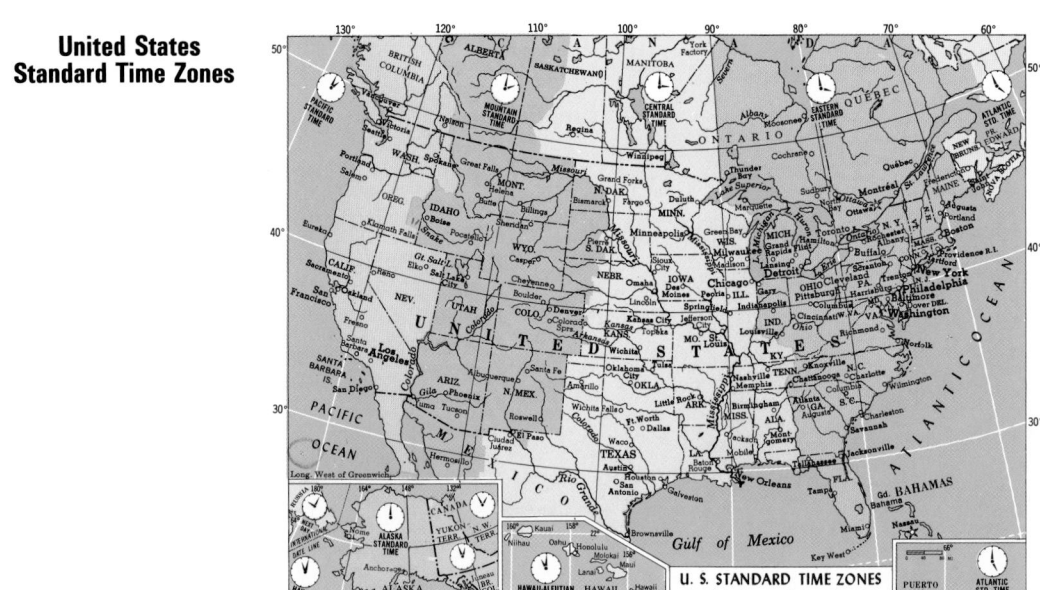

U. S. STANDARD TIME ZONES
Established by the Uniform Time Act

SCALE OF MILES

Agriculture, Industry and Resources

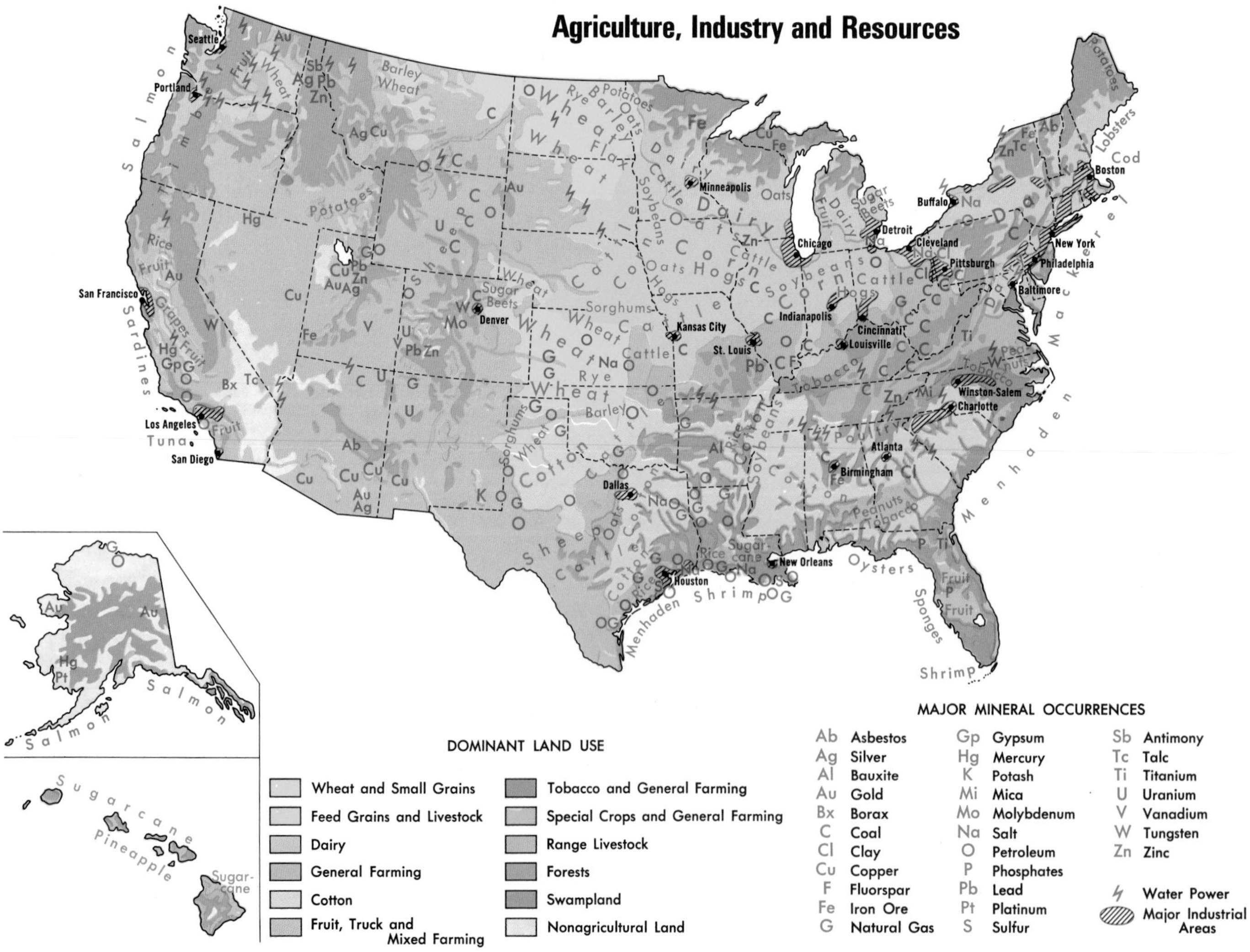

MAJOR MINERAL OCCURRENCES

Ab	Asbestos	Gp	Gypsum	Sb	Antimony
Ag	Silver	Hg	Mercury	Tc	Talc
Al	Bauxite	K	Potash	Ti	Titanium
Au	Gold	Mi	Mica	U	Uranium
Bx	Borax	Mo	Molybdenum	V	Vanadium
C	Coal	Na	Salt	W	Tungsten
Cl	Clay	O	Petroleum	Zn	Zinc
Cu	Copper	P	Phosphates		
F	Fluorspar	Pb	Lead	⚡	Water Power
Fe	Iron Ore	Pt	Platinum	▨	Major Industrial Areas
G	Natural Gas	S	Sulfur		

DOMINANT LAND USE

- Wheat and Small Grains
- Feed Grains and Livestock
- Dairy
- General Farming
- Cotton
- Fruit, Truck and Mixed Farming
- Tobacco and General Farming
- Special Crops and General Farming
- Range Livestock
- Forests
- Swampland
- Nonagricultural Land

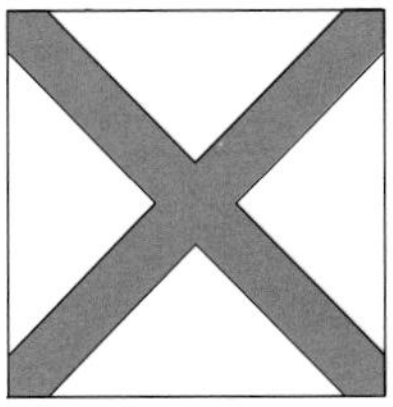

AREA 51,705 sq. mi. (133,916 sq. km.)
POPULATION 4,062,608
CAPITAL Montgomery
LARGEST CITY Birmingham
HIGHEST POINT Cheaha Mtn. 2,407 ft. (734 m.)
SETTLED IN 1702
ADMITTED TO UNION December 14, 1819
POPULAR NAME Heart of Dixie; Cotton State; Yellowhammer State
STATE FLOWER Camellia
STATE BIRD Yellowhammer

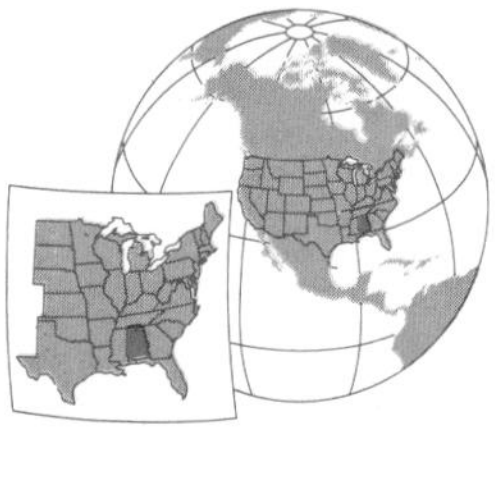

COUNTIES

Autauga 34,222 E5
Baldwin 98,280 C9
Barbour 25,417 H7
Bibb 16,576 D5
Blount 39,248 E2
Bullock 11,042 G6
Butler 21,892 E7
Calhoun 116,034 G3
Chambers 36,876 H5
Cherokee 19,543 G2
Chilton 32,458 E5
Choctaw 16,018 B6
Clarke 27,240 C7
Clay 13,252 G4
Cleburne 12,730 G3
Coffee 40,240 G8
Colbert 51,666 C1
Conecuh 14,054 E8
Coosa 11,063 F5
Covington 36,478 F8
Crenshaw 13,635 F7
Cullman 67,613 E2
Dale 49,633 G8
Dallas 48,130 D6
De Kalb 53,658 G2
Elmore 49,210 F5
Escambia 35,518 D8
Etowah 99,840 F2
Fayette 17,962 C3
Franklin 27,814 C2
Geneva 23,647 G8
Greene 10,153 C5
Hale 15,498 C5
Henry 15,374 H7
Houston 81,331 H8
Jackson 47,796 F1
Jefferson 651,525 E3
Lamar 15,715 B3
Lauderdale 79,661 C1
Lawrence 31,513 D1
Lee 87,146 H5
Limestone 54,135 E1
Lowndes 12,658 E6
Macon 24,928 G6
Madison 238,912 E1
Marengo 23,084 C6
Marion 29,830 C2
Marshall 70,832 F2
Mobile 378,643 B9
Monroe 23,968 D7
Montgomery 209,085 F6
Morgan 100,043 E2
Perry 12,759 D5
Pickens 20,699 B4
Pike 27,595 G7
Randolph 19,881 H4
Russell 46,860 H6
Saint Clair 41,205 F3
Shelby 99,358 E4
Sumter 16,174 B5
Talladega 74,107 F4
Tallapoosa 38,826 G5
Tuscaloosa 150,522 C4
Walker 67,670 D3
Washington 16,694 B8
Wilcox 13,568 D7
Winston 22,053 D2

CITIES and TOWNS

Abbeville▲ 3,173 H7
Abernant 405 D4
Adamsville 4,161 D3
Addison 626 D2
Adger 400 D4
Akron 468 C5
Alabaster 14,732 E4
Albertville 14,507 F2
Aldrich 500 E4
Alexander City 14,917 G5
Alexandria 600 G3
Aliceville 3,009 B4
Allgood 464 F3
Allsboro 300 B1
Alma 500 C8
Altoona 960 F2
Andalusia▲ 9,269 E8
Anderson 339 D1
Anniston▲ 26,623 G3
Arab 6,321 E2
Ardmore 1,090 E1
Argo 930 E3
Ariton 743 G7
Arley 338 D2
Ashby 500 E4
Ashford 1,926 H8
Ashland▲ 2,034 G4
Ashville▲ 1,494 F3
Athens▲ 16,901 E1
Atmore 8,046 C8
Attalla 6,859 F2
Auburn 33,830 H5
Autaugaville 681 E6
Avon 462 H8
Axis 500 B9
Babbie 576 F8
Baileyton 352 E2
Baker Hill 300 H7
Banks 195 G7
Barnwell 700 C10
Bay Minette▲ 7,168 C9
Bayou La Batre 2,456 B10
Bear Creek 913 C2
Beatrice 454 D7
Beaverton 319 B3
Belgreen 500 C2
Belk 255 C3
Bellamy 700 B6
Belle Mina 675 E1
Bellwood 400 G8
Benton 48 E6
Berry 1,218 C3
Bessemer 33,497 D4
Beulah 500 H5
Billingsley 150 E5
Birmingham▲ 265,968 D3
Black 174 G8
Blountsville 1,527 E2
Blue Mountain 221 G3
Blue Springs 108 G7
Boaz 6,928 F2
Boligee 268 C5
Bon Air 91 F4
Bon Secour 850 C10
Branchville 370 F3
Brantley 1,015 F7
Brent 2,776 D5
Brewton▲ 5,885 D8
Bridgeport 2,936 G1
Brighton 4,518 D4
Brilliant 751 C2
Brookside 1,365 E3
Brookwood 658 D4
Browns 375 D6
Brownville 2,386 C4
Brundidge 2,472 G7
Butler▲ 1,872 B6
Cahaba 4,778 D6
Calera 2,136 E4
Calhoun 950 F6
Calvert 600 B8
Camden▲ 2,414 D7
Camp Hill 1,415 G5
Canoe 560 D8
Carbon Hill 2,115 D3
Cardiff 72 E3
Carolina 201 E8
Carrollton▲ 1,170 B4
Carrville 820 G5
Carson 400 C8
Castleberry 669 D8
Cedar Bluff 1,174 G2
Centre▲ 2,893 G2
Centreville▲ 2,508 D5
Chatom▲ 1,094 B8
Chelsea 1,329 E4
Cherokee 1,479 C1
Chickasaw 6,649 B9
Childersburg 4,579 F4
Choccolocco 500 G3
Choctaw 600 B6
Chrysler 400 C8
Chunchula 700 B9
Citronelle 3,671 B8
Clanton▲ 7,669 E5
Clayhatchee 411 G8
Clayton▲ 1,564 G7
Cleveland 739 E3
Clio 1,365 G7
Coaling 400 D4
Coden 600 B10
Coffee Springs 294 G8
Coffeeville 431 B7
Coker 800 C4
Collinsville 1,429 G2
Columbia 922 H8
Columbiana▲ 2,968 E4
Coosada 912 F5
Cordova 2,623 D3
Cottondale 500 D4
Cottonton 324 H6
Cottonwood 1,385 H8
County Line 124 F8
County Line 199 E3
Courtland 803 D1
Cowarts 1,400 H8
Coy 950 D7
Crane Hill 355 D2
Creola 1,896 B9
Cromwell 650 B6
Crossville 1,350 G2
Cuba 390 B6
Cullman▲ 13,367 E2
Cullomburg 325 B7
Cusseta 650 H5
Dadeville▲ 3,276 G5
Daleville 5,117 G8
Daphne 11,290 C9
Dauphin Island 824 B10
Daviston 261 G4
Dayton 77 C6
De Armanville 350 G3
Decatur▲ 48,761 D1
Demopolis 7,512 C6
Detroit 291 B2
Dolomite D4
Dora 2,214 D3
Dothan▲ 53,589 H8
Double Springs▲ 1,138 D2
Douglas 474 F2
Dozier 483 F7
Dutton 243 G1
East Brewton 2,579 E8
Eclectic 1,087 F5
Edwardsville 118 H3
Elba▲ 4,011 F8
Elberta 458 C10
Eldridge 225 C3
Elkmont 389 E1
Elmore 600 F5
Elrod 746 C4
Emelle 44 B5
Empire 600 D3
Enterprise 20,123 G8
Epes 267 B5
Ethelsville 52 B4
Eufaula 13,220 H7
Eunola 199 G8
Eutaw▲ 2,281 C5
Eva 438 E2
Evergreen▲ 3,911 E8
Excel 571 D8
Fairfield 12,200 E4
Fairhope 8,485 C10
Fairview 383 E2
Falkville 1,337 E2
Faunsdale 96 C6
Fayette▲ 4,909 C3
Five Points 200 H4
Flat Rock 750 G1
Flint City 1,033 D1
Flomaton 1,811 D8
Florala 2,075 F8
Florence▲ 36,426 C1
Foley 4,937 C10
Forestdale 10,395 E3
Forkland 667 C5
Fort Davis 500 G6
Fort Deposit 1,240 E7
Fort Mitchell 900 H6
Fort Payne▲ 11,838 G2
Fosters 400 C4
Franklin 133 G6
Franklin 152 D7
Frisco City 1,581 D8
Fruitdale 500 B8
Fruithurst 177 G3
Fulton 384 C7
Fultondale 6,400 E3
Fyffe 1,094 G2
Gadsden▲ 42,523 G2
Gainesville 449 B5
Gallant 475 F2
Gantt 265 E8
Gantt's Quarry F4
Garden City 578 E2
Gardendale 9,251 E3
Gaylesville 149 G2
Geiger 270 B5
Geneva▲ 4,681 G8
Georgiana 1,933 E7
Geraldine 801 G2
Gilbertown 235 B7
Glen Allen 350 C3
Glencoe 4,670 G3
Glenwood 208 F7
Goldville 61 G4
Good Hope 1,700 E2
Goodsprings 360 D3
Goodwater 1,840 F4
Gordo 1,918 C4
Gordon 493 H8
Gorgas 500 D3
Goshen 302 F7
Gosport 500 C7
Grand Bay 3,383 B10
Grant 638 F1
Graysville 2,241 D3
Green Pond 750 D4
Greensboro▲ 3,047 C5
Greenville▲ 7,492 E7
Grimes 443 H8
Grove Hill▲ 1,551 C7
Gu-Win 243 C3
Guin 2,464 C3
Gulf Shores 3,261 C10
Guntersville▲ 7,038 F2
Gurley 1,007 F1
Hackleburg 1,161 C2
Haleburg 97 H8

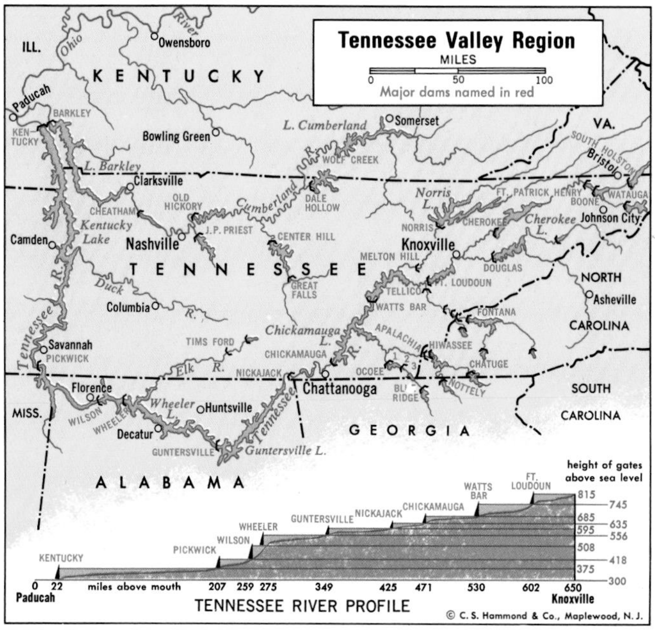

Tennessee Valley Region
MILES
0 50 100
Major dams named in red
ILL.
KENTUCKY
VA.
TENNESSEE
NORTH CAROLINA
SOUTH CAROLINA
GEORGIA
ALABAMA
MISS.
Owensboro
Paducah
Bowling Green
Somerset
L. Cumberland
Clarksville
Nashville
Knoxville
Bristol
Johnson City
Asheville
Camden
Columbia
Savannah
Florence
Huntsville
Decatur
Chattanooga
Kentucky Lake
L. Barkley
Guntersville L.
Wheeler L.
Chickamauga L.
Norris L.
Cherokee L.
height of gates above sea level
KENTUCKY
PICKWICK
WILSON
WHEELER
GUNTERSVILLE
NICKAJACK
CHICKAMAUGA
WATTS BAR
FT. LOUDOUN
0 22 miles above mouth 207 259 275 349 425 471 530 602 650
Paducah
Knoxville
TENNESSEE RIVER PROFILE
815
745
685
635
595
556
508
418
375
300
© C. S. Hammond & Co., Maplewood, N. J.

Haleyville 4,452 C2
Hamilton▲ 5,787 C2
Hammondville 420 G1
Hanceville 2,246 E2
Hardaway 600 G6
Harpersville 772 F4
Hartford 2,448 G8
Hartselle 10,795 E2
Harvest 1,922 E1
Hatchechubbee 840 H6
Hatton 950 D1
Hayden 385 E3
Hayneville▲ 969 E6
Hazel Green 2,208 E1
Headland 3,266 H8
Heath 182 F8
Heflin▲ 2,906 G3
Heiberger 310 D5
Helena 3,918 E4
Henagar 1,934 G1
Higdon 925 G1
Highland Lake 304 F3
Hillsboro 587 D1
Hobson City 794 G3
Hodges 272 C2
Hokes Bluff 3,739 G3
Hollins 500 F4
Holly Pond 602 E2
Hollywood 916 G1
Holt 4,125 D4
Holy Trinity 400 H6
Homewood 22,922 E4
Hoover 39,788 E4
Hope Hull 975 F6
Horn Hill 186 F8
Hueytown 15,280 D4
Huntsville▲ 159,789 E1
Hurtsboro 707 H6
Hytop 350 F1
Ider 671 G1
Inverness 2,528 G6
Irondale 9,454 E3
Jack 5,819 F7
Jackson 789 C8
Jacksons Gap 800 G5
Jacksonville 10,283 G3
Jasper▲ 13,553 D3
Jemison 1,898 E5
Kansas 230 C3
Kellyton 375 F5
Kennedy 523 B3
Key 400 G2
Killen 1,047 D1
Kimberly 1,096 E3
Kinsey 1,679 H8
Kinston 595 F8
Laceys Spring 400 E1
Lafayette▲ 3,151 H5
Lakeview 166 G2
Lanett 8,985 H5
Langdale 2,034 H5
Langston 207 G1
Larkinsville 425 F1
Lavaca 500 B6
Leeds 9,946 E3
Leesburg 218 G2
Leighton 988 D1
Leroy 699 B8
Lester 89 D1
Level Plains 1,473 G8
Lexington 821 D1
Libertyville 133 F8
Lillian 350 D10
Lincoln 2,941 F3
Linden▲ 2,548 C6
Lineville 2,394 G4
Lipscomb 2,892 E4
Lisman 481 B6
Little River 400 C8
Little Shawmut 2,793 H5
Littleville 925 C1
Livingston▲ 3,530 B5
Loachapoka 259 G5
Lockhart 484 F8
Locust Fork 342 E3
Longview 475 E4
Louisville 728 G7
Lower Peach Tree 926 C7
Lowndesboro 139 E6
Loxley 1,161 C9
Luverne▲ 2,555 F7
Lynn 611 C2
Madison 14,904 E1
Madrid 211 H8
Magnolia Springs 800 C10
Malvern 570 G8
Manchester 400 D3
Maplesville 725 E5
Margaret 616 F3
Marion Junction 400 D6
Marion▲ 4,211 D5
Maylene 500 E4
McCalla 657 E4
McCullough 500 D8
McIntosh 250 B8
McKenzie 464 E7
McWilliams 305 D7
Memphis 54 B4
Mentone 474 G1
Meridianville 2,852 F1
Midfield 5,559 E4
Midland City 1,819 H8
Midway 455 H6
Mignon 1,548 F4
Millbrook 6,050 F6
Millerville 345 G4
Millport 1,203 B3
Millry 781 B7
Minter 450 D6
Mobile▲ 196,278 B9
Monroeville▲ 6,993 D7
Monrovia 500 E1
Montevallo 4,239 E4
Montgomery (cap.)▲ 187,106 F6
Montrose 750 C9
Moody 4,921 F3
Mooresville 54 E1
Morris 1,136 E3
Morvin 355 C7
Moulton▲ 3,248 D2
Moundville 1,348 C5
Mount Vernon 902 B8
Mountain Brook 19,810 E4
Mountainboro 261 F2
Munford 700 F3
Muscle Shoals 9,611 C1
Myrtlewood 197 C6
Nanafalia 500 B6
Napier Field 462 H8
Nauvoo 240 D3
Nectar 238 E3
Needham 99 B7
New Brockton 1,184 G8
New Hope 2,248 F1
New Market 1,094 F1
New Site 669 G4
Newbern 222 C5
Newton 1,580 G8
Newville 531 H8
North Johns 177 D4
Northport 17,366 C4
Notasulga 979 G5
Oak Grove 436 B9
Oak Grove 638 F4
Oak Hill 28 D7
Oakman 846 D3
Odenville 796 F3
Ohatchee 1,042 G3
Oneonta▲ 4,844 E3
Onycha 150 F8
Opelika▲ 22,122 H5
Opp 6,985 F8
Orange Beach 2,253 C10
Orrville 234 D6
Owens Cross Roads 695 E1
Oxford 9,362 G3
Ozark▲ 12,922 G8
Paint Rock 214 F1
Parrish 1,433 D3
Pelham 9,765 E4
Pell City▲ 8,118 F3
Pennington 302 B6
Perdido 500 C8
Peterman 600 D7
Peterson D4
Petrey 80 F7
Phenix City▲ 25,312 H6
Phil Campbell 1,317 C2
Pickensville 169 B4
Piedmont 5,288 G3
Pinckard 618 G8
Pine Apple 365 E7
Pine Hill 481 C7
Pinson 10,987 E3
Pisgah 652 G1
Plantersville 650 E5
Pleasant Grove 8,458 D4
Point Clear 2,125 C10
Pollard 100 D8
Powell's Crossroads 636 G1
Prattville▲ 19,587 E6
Priceville 1,323 E1
Prichard 34,311 B9
Providence 307 C6
Ragland 1,807 F3
Rainbow City 7,673 F3
Rainsville 3,875 G2
Ramer 680 F6
Ranburne 447 H3
Red Bay 3,451 B2
Red Level 588 E8
Reece City 657 G2
Reform 2,105 C4
Remlap 800 E3
Renfroe 400 F4
Repton 293 D8
Republic 500 E3
River Falls 710 E8

(continued on following page)

Agriculture, Industry and Resources

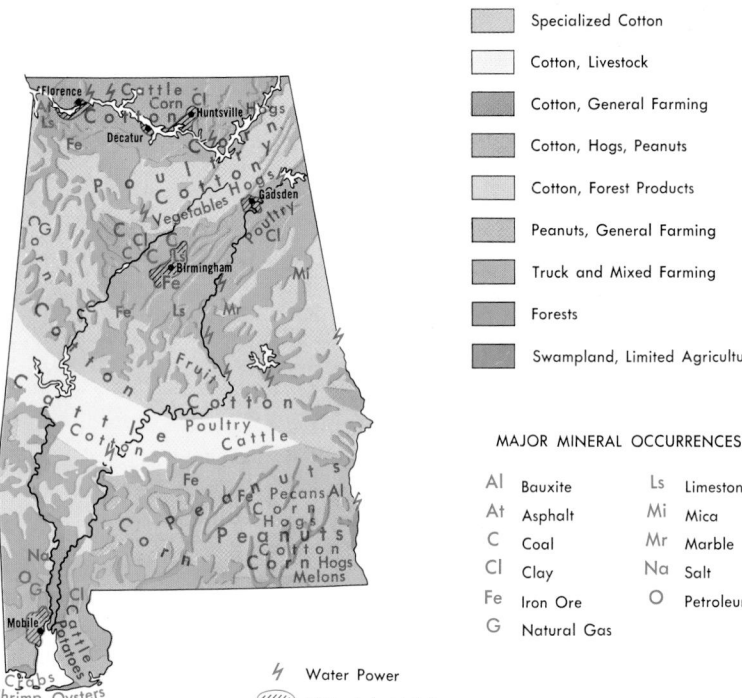

DOMINANT LAND USE

- Specialized Cotton
- Cotton, Livestock
- Cotton, General Farming
- Cotton, Hogs, Peanuts
- Cotton, Forest Products
- Peanuts, General Farming
- Truck and Mixed Farming
- Forests
- Swampland, Limited Agriculture

MAJOR MINERAL OCCURRENCES

Al	Bauxite	Ls	Limestone
At	Asphalt	Mi	Mica
C	Coal	Mr	Marble
Cl	Clay	Na	Salt
Fe	Iron Ore	O	Petroleum
G	Natural Gas		

⚡ Water Power
▨ Major Industrial Areas

Topography

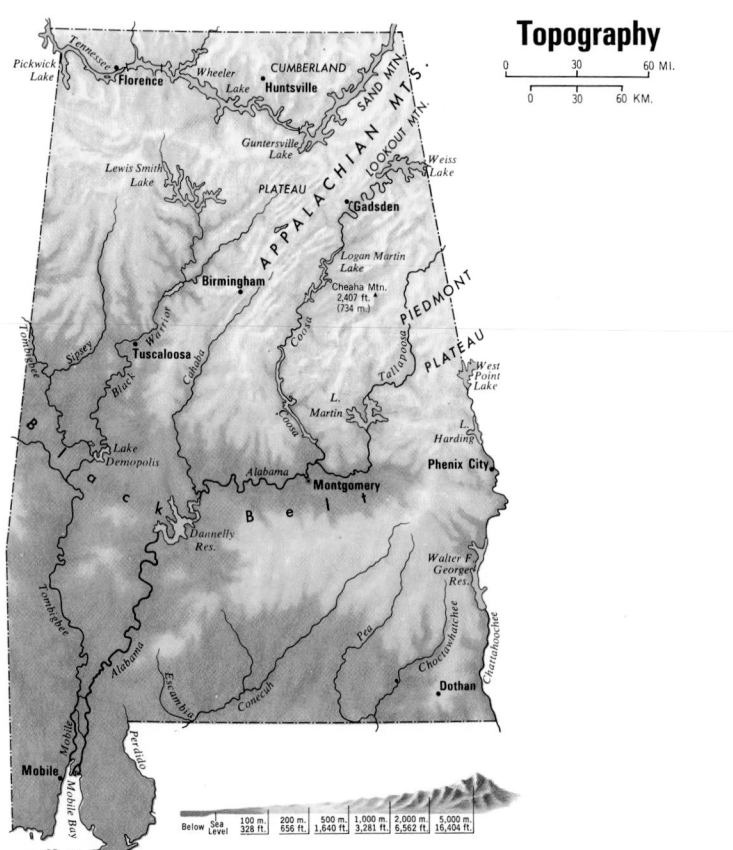

Scale: 0 — 30 — 60 MI.
0 — 30 — 60 KM.

Elevation legend: Below Sea Level | 100 m. 328 ft. | 200 m. 656 ft. | 500 m. 1,640 ft. | 1,000 m. 3,281 ft. | 2,000 m. 6,562 ft. | 5,000 m. 16,404 ft.

River View 1,314 ....H5
Riverside 1,004 ....F3
Riverview 90 ....D8
Roanoke 6,362 ....H4
Robertsdale 2,401 ....C9
Rock Mills 600 ....H4
Rockford 461 ....F5
Rogersville 1,125 ....D1
Roosevelt City 3,352 ....E4
Rosa 139 ....E3
Rural C7
Russellville▲ 7,812 ....C2
Rutledge 473 ....F7
Saginaw 475 ....E4
Saint Elmo 700 ....B10
Saint Florian 388 ....C1
Saint Stephens 700 ....B7
Salem 350 ....H5
Salitpa 550 ....C7
Samantha 400 ....C4
Samson 2,190 ....F8
Sanford 282 ....F8
Saraland 11,751 ....B9
Sardis 1,301 ....E6
Sardis 883 ....F2
Satsuma 5,194 ....B9
Sayre 700 ....E3
Scottsboro▲ 13,786 ....F1
Seale 350 ....H6
Section 777 ....G1
Selma▲ 23,755 ....E6
Selmont 3,823 ....E6
Shady Grove F7
Shawmut 2,284 ....H5
Sheffield 10,380 ....C1
Shelby 500 ....E4
Shiloh 252 ....C6
Shiloh 297 ....G2
Shorter 461 ....G6
Shorterville 400 ....H7
Silas 245 ....B7
Silverhill 556 ....C9
Sipsey 568 ....D3
Slocomb 1,906 ....G8
Smiths 3,456 ....H5
Snead 632 ....F2
Somerville 211 ....E2
South 543 ....E8
Southside 5,580 ....F3
Spanish Fort 3,732 ....C9
Spring Valley 600 ....C1
Springville 1,910 ....E3
Stapleton 975 ....C9
Steele 1,046 ....F3
Sterrett 350 ....F4
Stevenson 2,046 ....G1
Stewart 450 ....C5
Stockton 500 ....C9
Suggsville 400 ....C7
Sulligent 1,886 ....B3
Sumiton 2,604 ....D3
Summerdale 559 ....C10
Sunny South 350 ....C7
Sweet Water 243 ....C6
Sycamore 800 ....F4
Sylacauga 12,520 ....F4
Sylvania 932 ....G1
Talladega Springs 148 ....F4
Talladega▲ 18,175 ....F4
Tallassee 5,112 ....G5
Tanner 600 ....E1
Tarrant 8,046 ....E3
Taylor 1,352 ....H8
Theodore 6,509 ....B9
Thomaston 497 ....C6
Thomasville 4,301 ....C7
Thorsby 1,465 ....E5
Tibbie 675 ....B8
Town Creek 1,379 ....D1
Townley 500 ....D3
Toxey 211 ....B7
Trafford 739 ....E3
Triana 499 ....E1
Trinity 1,380 ....D1
Troy▲ 13,051 ....G7
Trussville 8,266 ....E3
Tuscaloosa▲ 77,759 ....C4
Tuscumbia▲ 8,413 ....C1
Tuskegee Institute G6
Tuskegee▲ 12,257 ....G6
Union 321 ....C5
Union Grove 119 ....E2
Union Springs▲ 3,975 ....G6
Uniontown 1,730 ....D6
Uriah 450 ....D8
Valhermoso Springs 500 ....E2
Valley 8,173 ....H5
Valley Head 577 ....G1
Vance 248 ....D4
Vandiver 700 ....F4
Verbena 500 ....E5
Vernon▲ 2,247 ....B3
Vestavia Hills 19,749 ....E4
Vina 356 ....B2
Vincent 1,767 ....F4
Vinemont E2
Vredenburgh 313 ....D7
Wadley 517 ....G4
Wadsworth 500 ....E5
Wagarville 550 ....B8
Waldo 309 ....F4
Walker Springs 500 ....C7
Walnut Grove 717 ....F2
Warrior 3,280 ....E3
Waterloo 250 ....B1
Wattsville 550 ....F3
Waverly 152 ....G5
Weaver 2,715 ....G3
Webb 1,039 ....H8
Wedowee▲ 796 ....H4
Wegra D3
Weogufka 500 ....F4
West Blocton 1,468 ....D4
West Jefferson 388 ....D3
West Point 257 ....D2
West Selmont 5,255 ....E6
Weston 384 ....B2

Westover 500 ....E4
Wetumpka▲ 4,670 ....F5
Whatley 800 ....C7
White Hall 814 ....E6
White Plains 350 ....G3
Whites Chapel 336 ....F3
Wicksburg 400 ....G8
Wilmer 494 ....B9
Wilsonville 1,185 ....E4
Wilton 602 ....E4
Winfield 3,689 ....C3
Woodland 189 ....H4
Woodstock 340 ....D4
Woodville 687 ....F1
Yantley 500 ....B6
Yellow Bluff 245 ....C7
Yellow Pine 350 ....B8
York 3,160 ....B6

OTHER FEATURES

Alabama (riv.) C8
Aliceville (dam) B4
Anniston Army Depot F3
Bankhead (lake) D4
Bartletts Ferry (dam) H5
Big Canoe (creek) F3
Big Creek (lake) B9
Black Warrior (riv.) C5
Bon Secour (bay) C10
Brookley Air Force Base B9
Buttahatchee (riv.) B3
Cahaba (riv.) D5
Cedar (pt.) B10
Chattahoochee (riv.) H8
Chattooga (riv.) H2
Cheaha (mt.) G4
Choctawhatchee (riv.) H8
Coffeeville (dam) B7
Conecuh (riv.) D8
Coosa (riv.) F4
Cowikee, North Fork (creek) H6
Cumberland (plat.) F1
Dannelly (res.) D6
Demopolis (dam) C5
Elk (riv.) D1
Escambia (creek) D8
Escambia (riv.) D9
Escatawpa (riv.) B9
Fort Gaines B10
Fort McClellan
   Military Reservation 4,128 ....G3
Fort Morgan C10
Fort Rucker 7,593 ....G8
Gainesville (dam) B5
Goat Rock (dam) H5
Goat Rock (lake) H5
Grants Pass (chan.) B10
Gunter Air Force Base F6
Guntersville (dam) F2
Guntersville (lake) F2
Harding (lake) H5
Herbes (isl.) B10
Holt (dam) D4
Horseshoe Bend
   Nat'l Mil. Park G5
Inland (lake) E3
Jordan (dam) F5
Jordan (lake) F5
Lay (dam) E5
Lewis Smith (dam) D3
Lewis Smith (lake) D2
Little (riv.) G2
Little (riv.) C8
Locust Fork (riv.) E3
Logan Martin (lake) F4
Lookout (mt.) G2
Martin (dam) G5
Martin (lake) G5
Maxwell Air Force Base F6
Mexico (gulf) E10
Mississippi (sound) B10
Mitchell (dam) F5
Mobile (bay) B10
Mobile (pt.) B10
Mobile (riv.) C9
Mulberry (creek) E5
Mulberry Fork (riv.) E3
Neely Henry (lake) F3
Oakmulgee (creek) D5
Oliver (dam) J5
Paint Rock (riv.) F1
Patsaliga (creek) F7
Pea (riv.) F8
Perdido (bay) D10
Perdido (riv.) C9
Pickwick (lake) B1
Pigeon (creek) E7
Redstone Arsenal E1
Russell Cavp Nat'l Mon. G1
Sand (mt.) G1
Sandy (creek) H7
Sepulga (riv.) E7
Sipsey (riv.) B4
Sipsey Fork (riv.) D2
Tallapoosa (riv.) G4
Tennessee (riv.) C1
Tennessee-Tombigbee
   Waterway B4
Tensaw (riv.) C9
Thurlow (dam) G6
Tombigbee (riv.) B7
Town (creek) C1
Tuscaloosa (lake) D4
Tuskegee Institute
   Nat'l Hist. Site G6
Walter F. George (dam) H7
Walter F. George (res.) H7
Warrior (dam) C5
Weiss (lake) G2
West Point (dam) H4
Wheeler (dam) D1
Wheeler (lake) D1
Wilson (dam) C1
Yates (dam) G5

▲County seat.

Alabama
SCALE
0 5 10 20 30 40 MI.
0 10 20 30 40 KM.
State Capitals
County Seats
Major Limited Access Hwys.
© Copyright HAMMOND INCORPORATED, Maplewood, N. J.
TENNESSEE
GEORGIA
FLORIDA
MISSISSIPPI
GULF OF MEXICO
Longitude West of Greenwich
LAUDERDALE
LIMESTONE
MADISON
JACKSON
COLBERT
LAWRENCE
MORGAN
MARSHALL
DEKALB
FRANKLIN
WINSTON
CULLMAN
ETOWAH
CHEROKEE
MARION
BLOUNT
LAMAR
FAYETTE
WALKER
JEFFERSON
ST. CLAIR
CALHOUN
CLEBURNE
PICKENS
TUSCALOOSA
SHELBY
TALLADEGA
CLAY
RANDOLPH
BIBB
COOSA
TALLAPOOSA
CHAMBERS
GREENE
HALE
CHILTON
PERRY
AUTAUGA
ELMORE
LEE
SUMTER
MARENGO
DALLAS
RUSSELL
MACON
LOWNDES
MONTGOMERY
BULLOCK
CHOCTAW
WILCOX
BUTLER
CRENSHAW
PIKE
BARBOUR
CLARKE
MONROE
CONECUH
HENRY
WASHINGTON
COFFEE
DALE
COVINGTON
ESCAMBIA
GENEVA
HOUSTON
MOBILE
BALDWIN
MONTGOMERY
BIRMINGHAM
Huntsville
Mobile
Tuscaloosa
Gadsden
Anniston
Decatur
Florence
Dothan
Selma
Auburn
Opelika
Bessemer
Prichard
Phenix City
CHATTANOOGA
ATLANTA
COLUMBUS
PENSACOLA
Cheaha Mtn. 2,407 ft. (734 m.)
Mobile Bay
Walter F. George Res. (Lake Eufaula)
Lake Martin
Lewis Smith Lake
Guntersville L.
Wheeler Lake
Weiss Lake
Tennessee-Tombigbee Waterway
Gulf Islands National Seashore

CITIES and TOWNS

Akiachak 481 ....F2
Akolmiut (Kasigluk) F2
Akutan 589 ....E4
Alakanuk 544 ....E2
Anchor Point 866 ....B2
Anchorage 226,338 ....B1
Anderson 628 ....H2
Angoon 638 ....M1
Aniak 540 ....G2
Barrow 3,469 ....G1
Bethel 4,674 ....F2
Big Lake 1,477 ....B1
Butte 2,039 ....C1
Chevak 598 ....E2
Clear 504 ....J2
Clover Pass 451 ....N2
Cohoe 508 ....B1
College 11,249 ....J1
Copper Center 449 ....J2
Cordova 2,110 ....D1
Craig 1,260 ....M2
Delta Junction 652 ....J2
Dillingham 2,017 ....G3
Emanguk (Emmonak) 567 ....F2
Fairbanks 30,843 ....J2
Fort Yukon 580 ....J1
Fritz Creek 1,426 ....B2
Galena 833 ....G2
Gambell 525 ....D1
Glennallen 451 ....J2
Haines 1,238 ....M1
Healy 487 ....J2

Homer 3,660 ....B2
Hoonah 795 ....M1
Hooper Bay 845 ....E2
Houston 697 ....B1
Hydaburg 384 ....M2
Juneau (cap.) 26,751 ....M1
Kachemak City 365 ....B2
Kake 700 ....M1
Kasigluk 425 ....F2
Kasilof 383 ....B1
Kenai 6,327 ....B1
Ketchikan 8,263 ....N2
Kiana 385 ....F1
King Cove 451 ....F4
King Salmon 696 ....G3
Kipnuk 470 ....F2
Klawock (Klawak) 722 ....M2
Kodiak 6,365 ....H3
Kotlik 461 ....F2
Kotzebue 2,751 ....F1
Kwethluk 558 ....F2
Manokotak 385 ....G3
McGrath 528 ....H2
Metlakatla 1,407 ....N2
Mountain Point 396 ....N2
Mountain Village 674 ....E2
Naknek 575 ....G3
Nenana 393 ....J2
New Stuyahok 391 ....G3
Ninilchik 456 ....B1
Nome 3,500 ....E2
Noorvik 531 ....G2
North Pole 1,456 ....J2
Nulato 359 ....G2

Nunapitchuk 378 ....F2
Palmer 2,866 ....C1
Petersburg 3,207 ....N2
Pilot Station 463 ....E2
Point Hope 639 ....E1
Quinhagak 501 ....F3
Saint Marys (Andreafski) 441 .F2
Saint Paul Island 763 ....D3
Sand Point 878 ....G3
Savoonga 519 ....E2
Saxman 369 ....N2
Selawik 596 ....G1
Seward 2,699 ....C1
Shishmaref 456 ....E1
Sitka 8,588 ....M1
Skagway 692 ....M1
Soldotna 3,482 ....B1
Stebbins 400 ....F2
Sterling 3,802 ....B1
Thorne Bay 569 ....M2
Togiak 613 ....F3
Tok 935 ....K2
Toksook Bay 420 ....F2
Unalakleet 714 ....G2
Unalaska 3,089 ....E4
Valdez 4,068 ....D1
Wainwright 492 ....F1
Wasilla 4,028 ....C1
Wrangell 2,479 ....N2
Yakutat 534 ....L3

OTHER FEATURES

Adak (isl.) L4

Admiralty (isl.) M1
Afognak (isl.) H3
Agattu (isl.) J3
Akutan (isl.) E4
Alaska (gulf) K3
Alaska (range) H2
Aleutian (isls.) J4
Aleutian (range) G3
Alexander (arch.) L1
Amchitka (isl.) K4
Amlia (passage) L1
Amukta (isl.) D4
Andreanof (isls.) L4
Atka (isl.) L4
Attu (isl.) J3
Baird (mts.) F1
Baranof (isl.) M1
Barrow (pt.) G1
Bear (mt.) K2
Beaufort (sea) K1
Becharof (lake) G3
Bering (glac.) K2
Bering (sea) D2
Bering (str.) E1
Blackburn (mt.) K2
Bona (mt.) K2
Bristol (bay) F3
British (mts.) K1
Brooks (range) G1
Chandalar (riv.) J1
Chatham (str.) M1
Chichagof (isl.) M1
Chignik (bay) G3
Chilkoot (pass) M1

Chirikof (isl.) G3
Chitina (riv.) K2
Christian (sound) M2
Chugach (mts.) C1
Chukchi (sea) E1
Clarence (str.) N2
Clark (lake) H2
Clear (cape) D1
Coast (mts.) N1
Columbia (glac.) C1
Colville (riv.) G1
Constantine (cape) G3
Cook (inlet) B1
Cook (mt.) J2
Copper (riv.) J2
Cordova (bay) M2
Coronation (isl.) M2
Cross (sound) L1
Dease (str.) H1
Decision (cape) M2
Denali Nat'l Park H2
Devils Paw (mt.) N1
Dixon Entrance (chan.) M2
Douglas (cape) L3
Dry (bay) L3
Eielson A.F.B. 5,251 ....J2
Elmendorf A.F.B. B1
Endicott (mts.) H1
Etolin (isl.) N2
Fairweather (cape) L1
Fairweather (mt.) L1
Firth (riv.) K1
Foraker (mt.) H2
Fort Davis E2

Fort Greely 1,147 ....J2
Fort Richardson C1
Fort Wainwright J1
Four Mountains (isls.) E4
Fox (isls.) E4
Frederick (sound) N1
Gates of the Arctic Nat'l Park .H1
Glacier (bay) M1
Glacier Bay Nat'l Park M1
Goodhope (bay) F1
Great Sitkin (isl.) L4
Guyot (glac.) K2
Hagemeister (isl.) F3
Halkett (cape) H1
Hall (isl.) D2
Harding Icefield C2
Harrison (bay) H1
Hayes (mt.) J2
Hazen (bay) E2
Hinchinbrook (isl.) D1
Hoonah (sound) M1
Hope (pt.) E1
Howard (pass) G1
Icy (bay) K3
Icy (cape) F1
Icy (pt.) L1
Icy (str.) M1
Iliamna (lake) G3
Iliamna (vol.) H2
Innoko (riv.) G2
Kachemak (bay) B2
Kanaga (isl.) L4
Kates Needle (mt.) N1
Katmai (vol.) H3

Katmai Nat'l Park H3
Kayak (isl.) K3
Kenai (lake) C1
Kenai (mts.) C2
Kenai (pen.) C2
Kenai Fjords Nat'l Park C3
Kennedy Entrance (str.) H3
King (isl.) E1
Kiska (isl.) J4
Kiska (vol.) J4
Klondike Gold Rush Nat'l
  Hist. Park N1
Knight (isl.) D1
Knik Arm (inlet) B1
Kobuk (riv.) G1
Kobuk Valley Nat'l Park F1
Kodiak (isl.) H3
Kotzebue (sound) F1
Koyukuk (riv.) G1
Krusenstern (cape) F1
Kuiu (isl.) M2
Kuk (riv.) G1
Kuskokwim (bay) F3
Kuskokwim (mts.) G2
Kuskokwim (riv.) G2
Kvichak (bay) G3
Lake Clark Nat'l Park H2
Lisburne (cape) E1
Little Diomede (isl.) E1
Little Sitkin (isl.) K4
Lynn Canal (inlet) M1
Makushin (vol.) E4
Malaspina (glac.) K3
Marcus Baker (mt.) C1

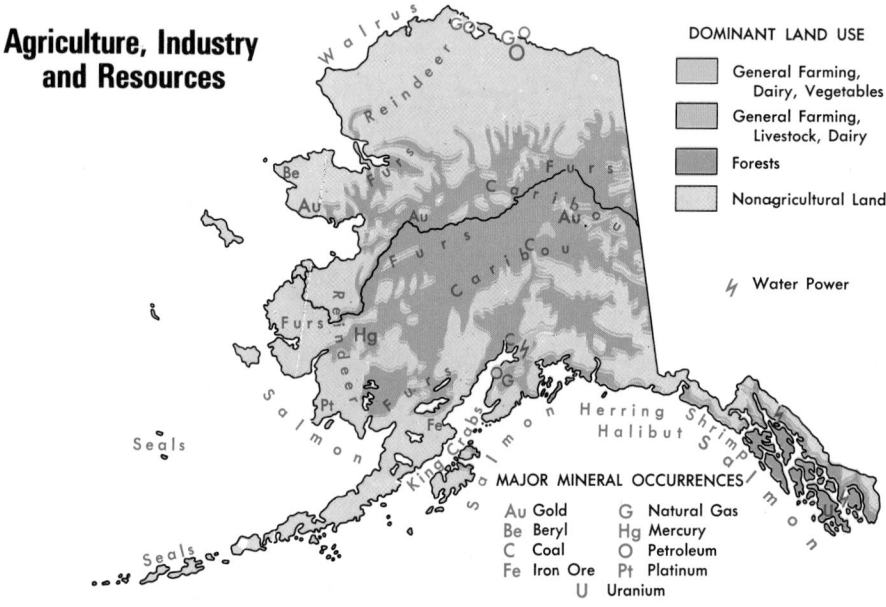

Agriculture, Industry and Resources

DOMINANT LAND USE

- General Farming, Dairy, Vegetables
- General Farming, Livestock, Dairy
- Forests
- Nonagricultural Land

Water Power

MAJOR MINERAL OCCURRENCES

- Au Gold
- Be Beryl
- C Coal
- Fe Iron Ore
- U Uranium
- G Natural Gas
- Hg Mercury
- O Petroleum
- Pt Platinum

Topography

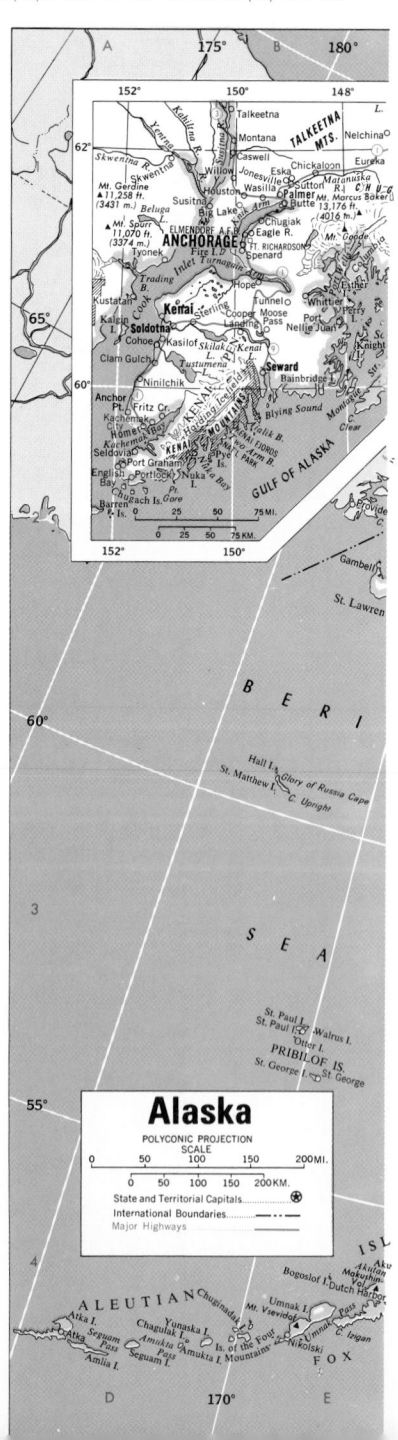

Alaska

POLYCONIC PROJECTION
SCALE

State and Territorial Capitals
International Boundaries
Major Highways

Marmot (isl.) ...H3	Port Clarence (inlet) ...E1	Shemya (isl.) ...J3	Tugidak (isl.) ...G3
Matanuska (riv.) ...C1	Port Heiden (inlet) ...G3	Shishaldin (vol.) ...E4	Turnagain Arm (inlet) ...B1
McKinley (mt.) ...H2	Portland Canal (inlet) ...N2	Shumagin (isl.) ...G4	Tustumena (lake) ...C1
Meade (riv.) ...G1	Port Moller (inlet) ...F3	Shuyak (isl.) ...H3	Two Arm (bay) ...C2
Mendenhall (cape) ...E3	Port Wells (inlet) ...C1	Sitka (sound) ...M1	Ugashik (lakes) ...G3
Mentasta (pass) ...K2	Pribilof (isls.) ...D3	Sitka Nat'l Hist. Park ...M1	Umnak (isl.) ...E4
Merrill (pass) ...H2	Prince of Wales (cape) ...E1	Sitkinak (str.) ...H3	Umnak (passage) ...E4
Michelson (pass) ...K1	Prince of Wales (isl.) ...N2	Skilak (lake) ...C1	Unalaska (isl.) ...E4
Middleton (isl.) ...J3	Prince William (sound) ...D1	Skwentna (riv.) ...A1	Unga (isl.) ...F4
Misty Fjords Nat'l Mon. ...N2	Prudhoe (bay) ...J1	Smith (bay) ...H1	Unimak (isl.) ...E4
Mitkof (isl.) ...N2	Rat (isls.) ...K4	Spencer (cape) ...L1	Unimak (passage) ...F4
Montague (isl.) ...D1	Redoubt (vol.) ...H2	Stephens (passage) ...N1	Utukok (riv.) ...F1
Muir (glac.) ...M1	Revillagigedo (chan.) ...N2	Stevenson Entrance (str.) ...H3	Valley of Ten
Mulchatna (riv.) ...G2	Revillagigedo (isl.) ...N2	Stikine (riv.) ...N2	Thousand Smokes ...G3
Muzon (cape) ...M2	Romanzof (cape) ...E2	Stikine (str.) ...N2	Vancouver (isl.) ...L2
Naknek (lake) ...G3	Sagavanirktok (riv.) ...J1	Stony (riv.) ...G2	Veniaminof (crater) ...F3
Near (isls.) ...H3	Saint Elias (cape) ...K3	Stuart (isl.) ...F2	Vsevidof (mt.) ...E4
Nelson (isl.) ...E2	Saint Elias (mt.) ...K2	Suemez (isl.) ...M2	Walrus (isl.) ...E3
Newenham (cape) ...F3	Saint George (isl.) ...D3	Sumner (str.) ...M2	Walrus (isls.) ...F3
Noatak (riv.) ...F1	Saint Lawrence (isl.) ...D2	Susitna (riv.) ...B1	Waring (mts.) ...G1
Norton (bay) ...F2	Saint Matthew (isl.) ...D2	Sutwik (isl.) ...G3	West Point (mt.) ...K2
Norton (sound) ...E2	Saint Paul (isl.) ...D3	Taku (glac.) ...N1	White (pass) ...N1
Nowitna (riv.) ...H2	Salisbury (sound) ...M1	Taku (riv.) ...N1	White (riv.) ...K2
Nuka (bay) ...C2	Sanak (isl.) ...F4	Talkeetna (mts.) ...J2	White Mountains Nat'l
Nunivak (isl.) ...E3	Sanford (mt.) ...K2	Tanaga (isl.) ...K4	Rec. Area ...J1
Nushagak (riv.) ...G2	Schwatka (mts.) ...G1	Tanaga (vol.) ...K4	Witherspoon (mt.) ...C1
Nuyakuk (riv.) ...F3	Seguam (isl.) ...D4	Tanana (riv.) ...J2	Wrangell (cape) ...H3
Ommaney (cape) ...M2	Selawik (lake) ...F1	Taylor (mts.) ...G2	Wrangell (isl.) ...N2
Otter (isl.) ...D3	Semichi (isls.) ...J3	Tazlina (lake) ...D1	Wrangell (mt.) ...K2
Pastol (bay) ...F2	Semidi (isls.) ...G3	Tazlina (riv.) ...D1	Wrangell-St. Elias Nat'l Park ...K2
Pavlof (isl.) ...F3	Semisopochnoi (isl.) ...K4	Teshekpuk (lake) ...H1	Yakobi (isl.) ...M1
Pavlof (vol.) ...F3	Seward (pen.) ...E1	Tigalda (isl.) ...F4	Yakutat (bay) ...K3
Philip Smith (mts.) ...J1	Sheenjek (riv.) ...K1	Tikchik (lakes) ...G2	Yentna (riv.) ...A1
Porcupine (riv.) ...K1	Shelikof (str.) ...H3	Togiak (bay) ...F3	Yukon (riv.) ...F2

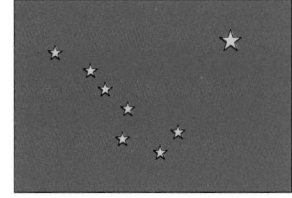

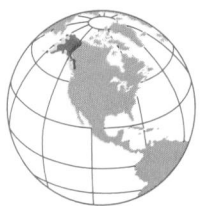

AREA 591,004 sq. mi. (1,530,700 sq. km.)
POPULATION 551,947
CAPITAL Juneau
LARGEST CITY Anchorage
HIGHEST POINT Mt. McKinley 20,320 ft.
  (6194 m.)
SETTLED IN 1801
ADMITTED TO UNION January 3, 1959
POPULAR NAME Great Land; Last Frontier
STATE FLOWER Forget-me-not
STATE BIRD Willow Ptarmigan

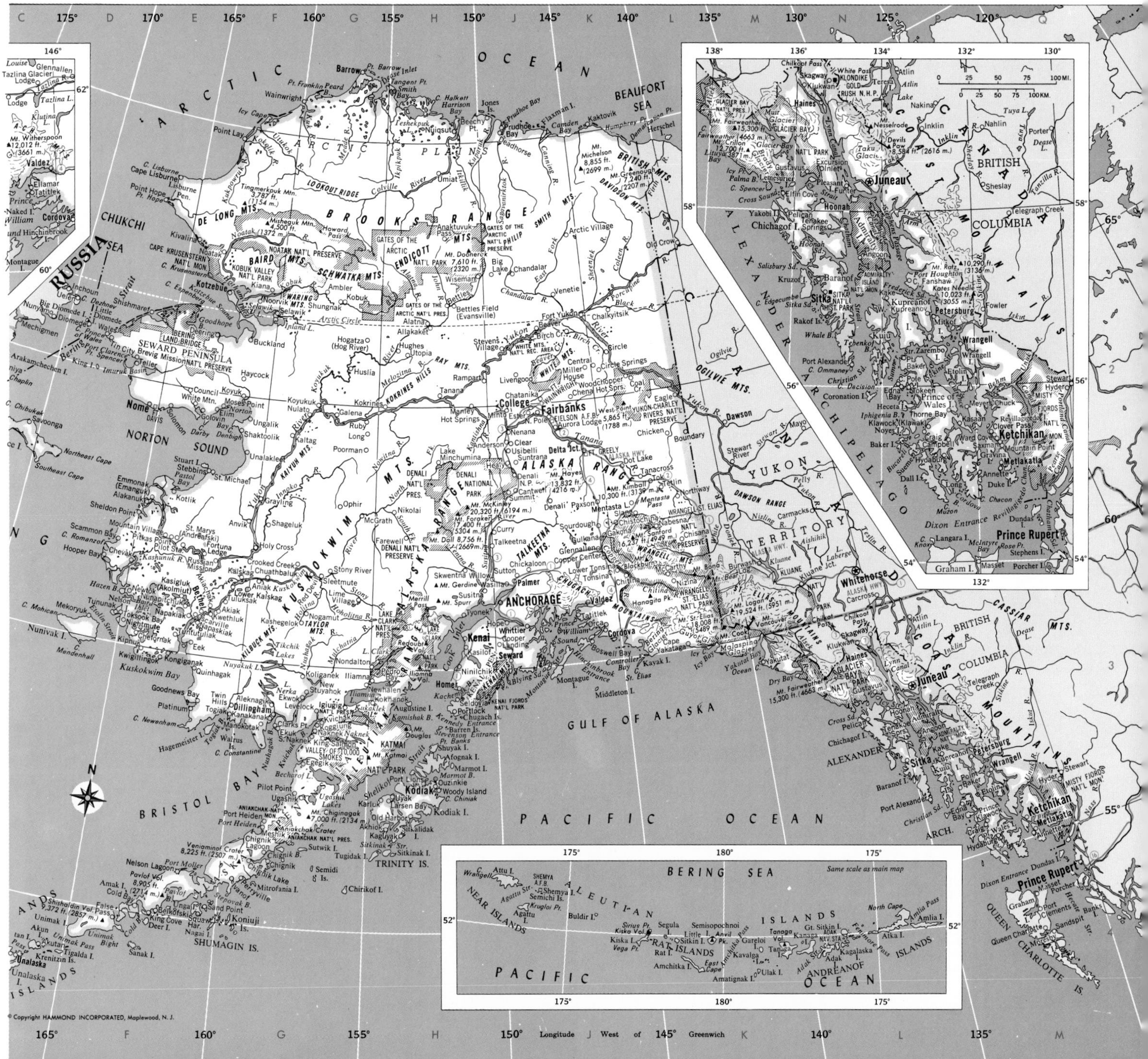

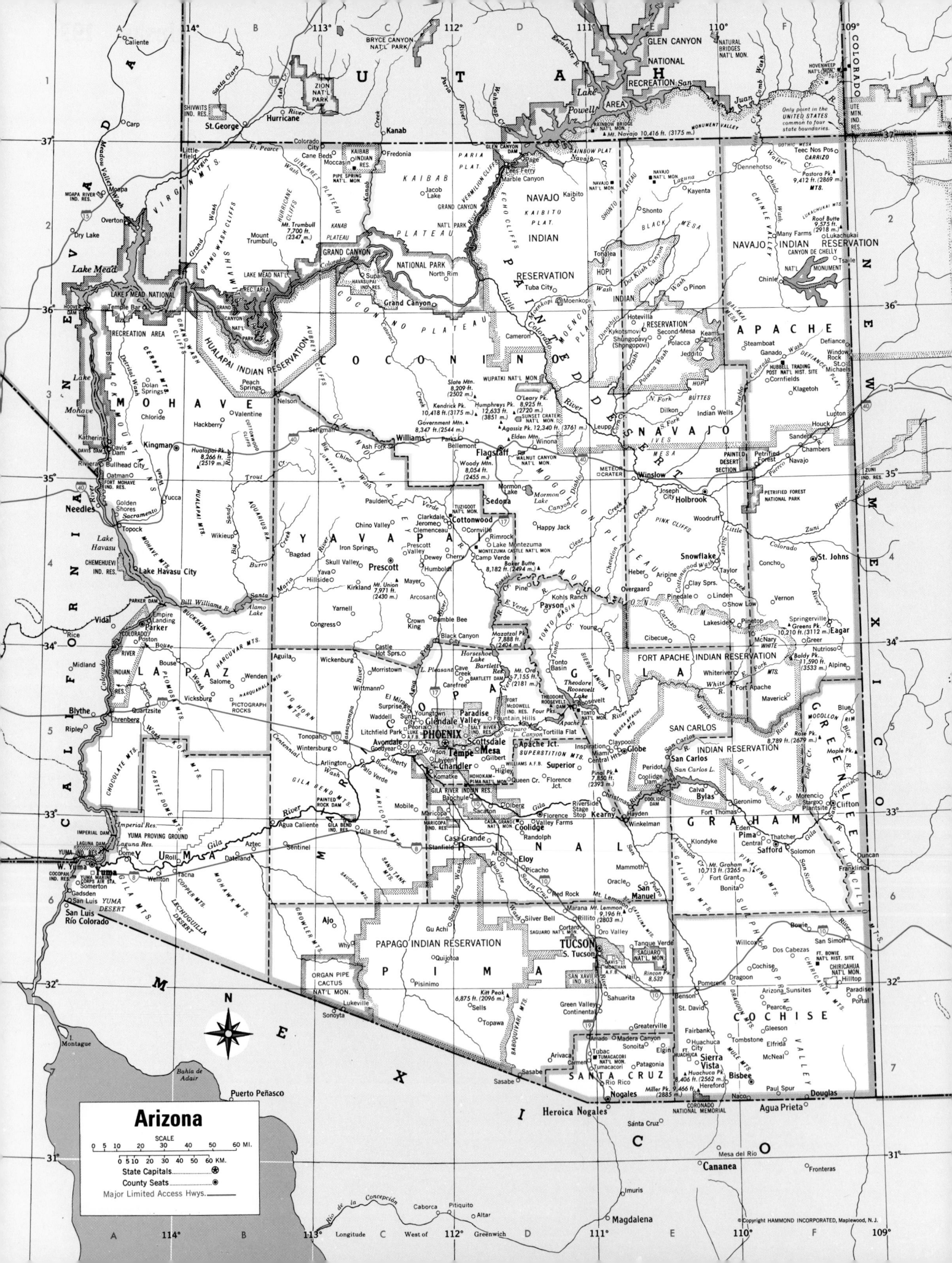
Arizona
SCALE
0 5 10 20 30 40 50 60 MI.
0 5 10 20 30 40 50 60 KM.
State Capitals
County Seats
Major Limited Access Hwys.
UTAH
NEVADA
CALIFORNIA
NEW MEXICO
COLORADO
MEXICO
MOHAVE
COCONINO
NAVAJO
APACHE
YAVAPAI
LA PAZ
MARICOPA
GILA
GREENLEE
GRAHAM
PINAL
YUMA
PIMA
SANTA CRUZ
COCHISE
PHOENIX
Tucson
Flagstaff
Prescott
Kingman
Yuma
Holbrook
St. Johns
Globe
Florence
Safford
Clifton
Nogales
Bisbee
Parker
GLEN CANYON NATIONAL RECREATION AREA
Lake Powell
GRAND CANYON NATIONAL PARK
LAKE MEAD NATIONAL RECREATION AREA
Lake Mead
HUALAPAI INDIAN RESERVATION
NAVAJO INDIAN RESERVATION
HOPI INDIAN RESERVATION
FORT APACHE INDIAN RESERVATION
SAN CARLOS INDIAN RESERVATION
PAPAGO INDIAN RESERVATION
GILA RIVER INDIAN RES.
ORGAN PIPE CACTUS NAT'L MON.
PAINTED DESERT
PETRIFIED FOREST NATIONAL PARK
Only point in the UNITED STATES common to four state boundaries.
Humphreys Pk. 12,633 ft. (3851 m.)
Heroica Nogales
Agua Prieta
Puerto Peñasco
Bahía de Adair
Longitude West of Greenwich
©Copyright HAMMOND INCORPORATED, Maplewood, N. J.

AREA 114,000 sq. mi. (295,260 sq. km.)
POPULATION 3,677,985
CAPITAL Phoenix
LARGEST CITY Phoenix
HIGHEST POINT Humphreys Pk. 12,633 ft.
(3851 m.)
SETTLED IN 1752
ADMITTED TO UNION February 14, 1912
POPULAR NAME Grand Canyon State
STATE FLOWER Saguaro Cactus Blossom
STATE BIRD Cactus Wren

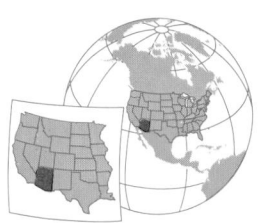

Agriculture, Industry and Resources

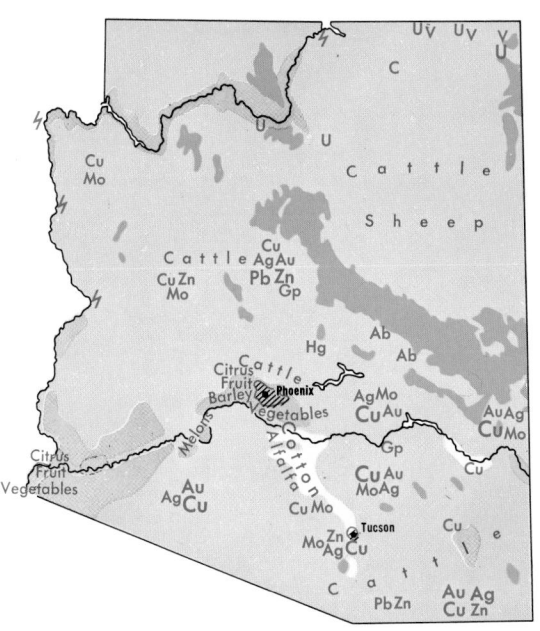

MAJOR MINERAL OCCURRENCES

Ab	Asbestos	Cu	Copper	Pb	Lead
Ag	Silver	Gp	Gypsum	U	Uranium
Au	Gold	Hg	Mercury	V	Vanadium
C	Coal	Mo	Molybdenum	Zn	Zinc

DOMINANT LAND USE

Fruit, Truck and Mixed Farming

Cotton and Alfalfa

General Farming, Livestock, Special Crops

Range Livestock

Forests

Nonagricultural Land

⚡ Water Power

▨ Major Industrial Areas

(continued on following page)

Topography

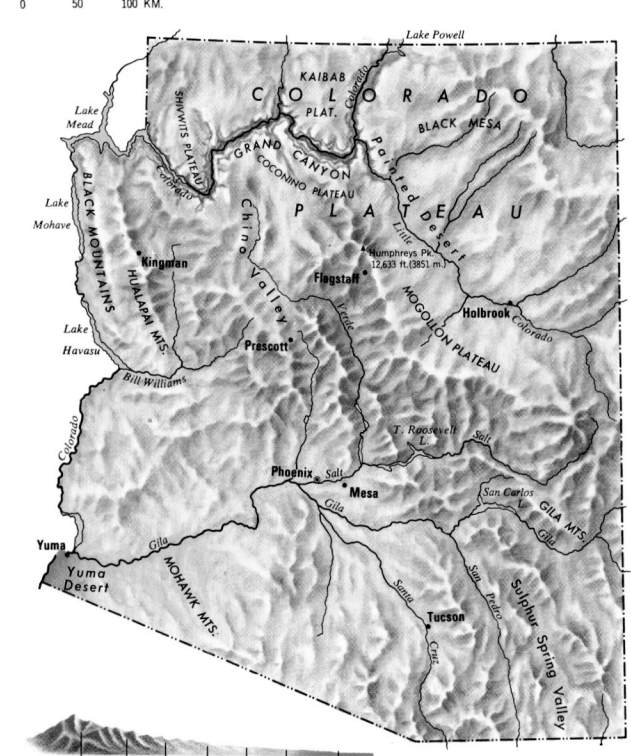

5,000 m. 16,404 ft.	2,000 m. 6,562 ft.	1,000 m. 3,281 ft.	500 m. 1,640 ft.	200 m. 656 ft.	100 m. 328 ft.	Sea Level	Below

▲County seat.

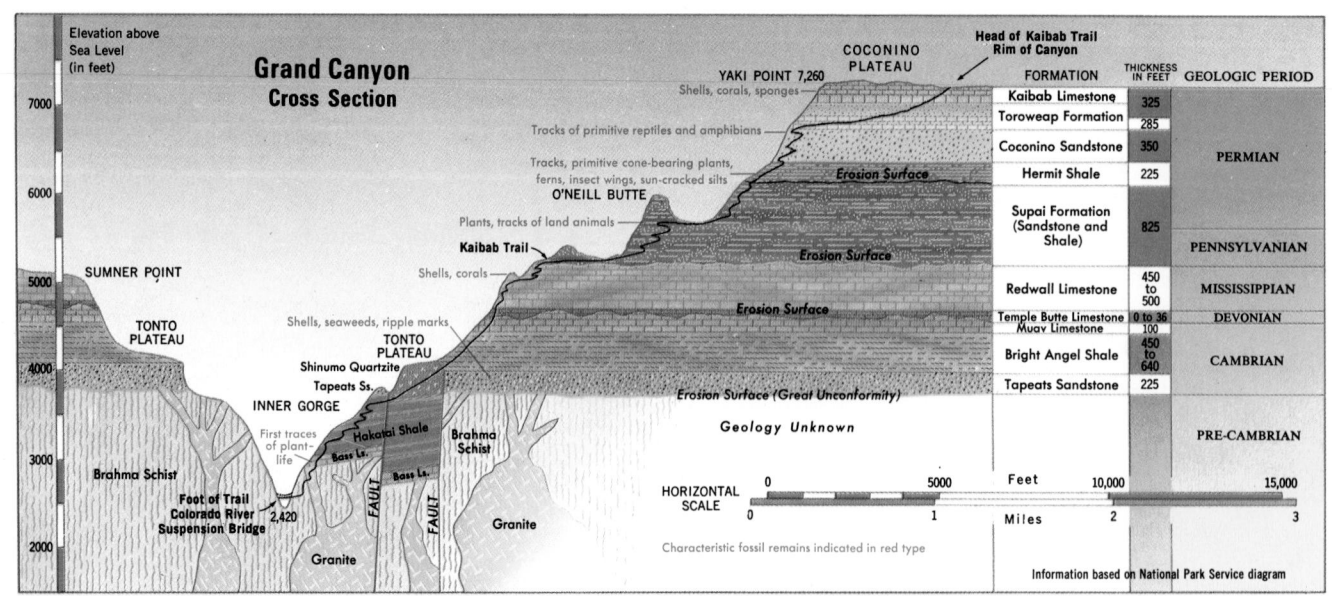
Elevation above Sea Level (in feet)
Grand Canyon Cross Section
7000
6000
5000
4000
3000
2000
COCONINO PLATEAU
Head of Kaibab Trail Rim of Canyon
YAKI POINT 7,260
Shells, corals, sponges
Tracks of primitive reptiles and amphibians
Tracks, primitive cone-bearing plants, ferns, insect wings, sun-cracked silts
O'NEILL BUTTE
Erosion Surface
Plants, tracks of land animals
Kaibab Trail
Shells, corals
SUMNER POINT
TONTO PLATEAU
Shells, seaweeds, ripple marks
TONTO PLATEAU
Shinumo Quartzite
Tapeats Ss.
INNER GORGE
Erosion Surface (Great Unconformity)
Geology Unknown
First traces of plant-life
Hakatai Shale
Bass Ls.
Brahma Schist
Brahma Schist
Foot of Trail Colorado River Suspension Bridge
2,420
FAULT
FAULT
Granite
Granite
HORIZONTAL SCALE
Feet 0 5000 10,000 15,000
Miles 0 1 2 3
Characteristic fossil remains indicated in red type
FORMATION
THICKNESS IN FEET
GEOLOGIC PERIOD
Kaibab Limestone 325
Toroweap Formation 285
Coconino Sandstone 350
Hermit Shale 225
PERMIAN
Supai Formation (Sandstone and Shale) 825
PENNSYLVANIAN
Redwall Limestone 450 to 500
MISSISSIPPIAN
Temple Butte Limestone 0 to 36
DEVONIAN
Muav Limestone 100
Bright Angel Shale 450 to 640
CAMBRIAN
Tapeats Sandstone 225
PRE-CAMBRIAN
Information based on National Park Service diagram

CALIFORNIA REPUBLIC

AREA 158,706 sq. mi. (411,049 sq. km.)
POPULATION 29,839,250
CAPITAL Sacramento
LARGEST CITY Los Angeles
HIGHEST POINT Mt. Whitney 14,494 ft. (4418 m.)
SETTLED IN 1769
ADMITTED TO UNION September 9, 1850
POPULAR NAME Golden State
STATE FLOWER Golden Poppy
STATE BIRD California Valley Quail

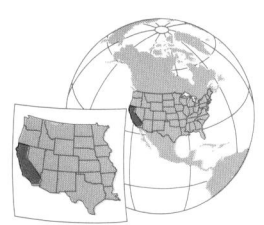

COUNTIES

Alameda 1,279,182 ....D6
Alpine 1,113 ....F5
Amador 30,039 ....E5
Butte 182,120 ....D4
Calaveras 31,998 ....E5
Colusa 16,275 ....C4
Contra Costa 803,732 ....D6
Del Norte 23,460 ....B2
El Dorado 125,995 ....E5
Fresno 667,490 ....E7
Glenn 24,798 ....C4
Humboldt 119,118 ....B3
Imperial 109,303 ....K1
Inyo 18,281 ....H7
Kern 543,477 ....G8
Kings 101,469 ....E8
Lake 50,631 ....C4
Lassen 27,598 ....E3
Los Angeles 8,863,164 ....G9
Madera 88,090 ....F6
Marin 230,096 ....C6
Mariposa 14,302 ....E6
Mendocino 80,345 ....B4
Merced 178,403 ....E6
Modoc 9,678 ....E2
Mono 9,956 ....F5
Monterey 355,660 ....D7
Napa 110,765 ....C5
Nevada 78,510 ....E4
Orange 2,410,556 ....H1
Placer 172,796 ....E4
Plumas 19,739 ....E4
Riverside 1,170,413 ....J1
Sacramento 1,041,219 ....D5
San Benito 36,697 ....D7
San Bernardino 1,418,380 ...J9
San Diego 2,498,016 ....J12
San Francisco 723,959 ....J2
San Joaquin 480,628 ....D5
San Luis Obispo 217,162 .....E8
San Mateo 649,623 ....J3
Santa Barbara 369,608 ....E9
Santa Clara 1,497,577 ....D6
Santa Cruz 229,734 ....C6
Shasta 147,036 ....C3
Sierra 3,318 ....E4
Siskiyou 43,531 ....C2
Solano 340,421 ....D5
Sonoma 388,222 ....C5
Stanislaus 370,522 ....D6
Sutter 64,415 ....D4
Tehama 49,625 ....C3
Trinity 13,063 ....B3
Tulare 311,921 ....G7
Tuolumne 48,456 ....F5
Ventura 669,016 ....F9
Yolo 141,092 ....D5
Yuba 58,228 ....D4

CITIES and TOWNS

Adelanto 8,517 ....H9
Alameda 76,459 ....J2
Alamo 12,277 ....K2
Albany 16,327 ....J2
Alhambra 82,106 ....C10
Alpine 9,695 ....J11
Alta Loma E10
Altadena 42,658 ....C10
Alturas▲ 3,231 ....E2
Amador City 196 ....C9
Anaheim 266,406 ....D11
Anderson 8,299 ....C3
Angels Camp 2,302 ....E5
Angwin 3,503 ....C5
Antioch 62,195 ....L1
Apple Valley 46,079 ....H9
Aptos 9,061 ....K4
Arbuckle 1,912 ....C4
Arcadia 48,290 ....C10
Arcata 15,197 ....A3
Arden-Arcade 92,040 ....B8
Armona 3,122 ....F7
Arnold 3,788 ....E5
Aromas 2,275 ....D7
Arroyo Grande 14,378 ....E8
Artesia 15,464 ....C11
Arvin 9,286 ....G8
Ashland 16,590 ....K2
Asti 75 ....C9
Atascadero 23,138 ....E8
Atherton 7,163 ....K3
Atwater 22,282 ....E6
Auberry 1,866 ....F6
Auburn▲ 10,592 ....C8
Avalon 2,918 ....G10
Avenal 9,770 ....E8
Azusa 41,333 ....D10
Baker 174,820 ....J8
Bakersfield▲ 105,611 ....G8
Baldwin Park 69,330 ....D10
Banning 20,570 ....J10
Barstow 21,472 ....H9
Bayview 1,318 ....A3
Baywood Park (Baywood Park-
   Los Osos) 10,933 ....E8
Beaumont 9,685 ....J10
Bell 34,365 ....C11
Bell Gardens 42,355 ....C11
Bellflower 61,815 ....C11
Belmont 24,127 ....J3
Belvedere 2,147 ....H2
Ben Lomond 7,884 ....K4
Benicia 24,437 ....K1
Berkeley 102,724 ....J2
Bethel Island 2,115 ....L1
Beverly Hills 31,971 ....B10
Big Bear City (Sugarloaf
   Post Office) 4,920 ....J9
Big Bear Lake 5,351 ....J9

Big Pine 1,158 ....G6
Biggs 1,581 ....D4
Bishop 3,475 ....G6
Bloomington 15,116 ....E10
Blue Lake 1,235 ....B3
Blythe 8,428 ....L10
Bodfish 1,283 ....G8
Bolinas 1,098 ....H1
Boron 2,101 ....H8
Borrego Springs 2,244 ....J10
Boulder Creek 6,725 ....J4
Bowman C7
Brawley 18,923 ....K11
Brea 32,873 ....D11
Brentwood 7,563 ....L2
Bridgeport▲ 525 ....F5
Brisbane 2,952 ....J2
Broderick (Broderick-Bryte)
   10,194 ....B8
Bryte (Bryte-Broderick)
   10,194 ....B8
Buellton 3,506 ....E9
Buena Park 68,784 ....D11
Burbank 93,643 ....C10
Burlingame 26,801 ....J2
Burney 3,423 ....D3
Buttonwillow 1,301 ....F8
Cabazon 1,588 ....J10
Calabasas 1,588 ....B10
Calexico 18,633 ....K11
California City 5,955 ....H8
Calimesa 2,690 ....K10
Calistoga 4,468 ....C5
Calwa 6,640 ....F7
Camarillo 52,303 ....G9
Cambria 5,382 ....D8
Campbell 36,048 ....K3
Canoga Park B10
Canyon 7,938 ....K2
Capistrano Beach 6,168 .....H10
Capitola 10,171 ....K4
Cardiff-by-the-Sea 10,054 ..H10
Carlsbad 63,126 ....H10
Carmel 4,407 ....D7
Carmel Valley 4,013 ....D7
Carmichael 48,702 ....C8
Carpinteria 13,747 ....F9
Carson 83,995 ....C11
Caruthers 1,603 ....E7
Casitas Springs 1,038 ....F9
Castro Valley 48,619 ....K2
Castroville 5,272 ....D7
Cathedral City 30,085 ....J10
Cayucos 2,960 ....E8
Central Valley 4,340 ....C3
Ceres 26,314 ....D6
Cerritos 53,240 ....C11
Chatsworth B10
Chemeketa Park (Chemeketa
   Park-Redwood Estates)
   1,847 ....K4
Cherryland 11,088 ....K2
Chester 2,082 ....D3
Chico 40,079 ....D4

China Lake 4,275 ....H8
Chinese Camp 150 ....E6
Chino 59,682 ....D10
Chowchilla 5,930 ....E6
Chula Vista 135,163 ....J11
Citrus Heights 107,439 ......C8
Claremont 32,503 ....D10
Clay 7,317 ....C9
Clayton 4,325 ....K2
Clearlake 11,804 ....C5
Clearlake Oaks 2,419 ....C4
Cloverdale 4,924 ....B5
Clovis 50,323 ....F7
Coachella 16,896 ....J10
Coalinga 8,212 ....F7
Colfax 1,306 ....E4
Colton 40,213 ....E10
Columbia 1,799 ....E5
Colusa▲ 4,934 ....C4
Commerce 12,135 ....C10
Compton 90,454 ....C11
Corcoran 13,364 ....F7
Corning 5,870 ....C4
Corona 76,095 ....E11
Coronado 26,540 ....H11
Corralitos 2,513 ....L4
Corte Madera 8,272 ....J2
Costa Mesa 96,357 ....D11
Cotati 5,714 ....C5
Cottonwood 1,747 ....C3
Covina 43,207 ....D10
Crescent City▲ 4,380 ....A2
Crestline 8,594 ....H9
Crockett 3,228 ....J1
Crowley Lake G6
Cudahy 22,817 ....C11
Culver City 38,793 ....B10
Cupertino 40,263 ....K3
Cutler 4,450 ....F7
Cutten 1,516 ....A3
Cypress 42,655 ....D11
Daly City 92,311 ....H2
Dana Point 31,896 ....H10
Danville 31,306 ....K2
Davis 46,209 ....B8
Death Valley Junction J7
Deer Park 1,825 ....C5
Del Mar 4,860 ....H11
Del Rey Oaks 1,661 ....D7
Del Rosa F10
Delano 22,762 ....F8
Delhi 3,280 ....E6
Desert Hot Springs 11,668 ..J9
Desert View Highlands 2,154 .G9
Diamond Springs 2,872 ......D8
Dinuba 12,743 ....F7
Dixon 10,401 ....B9
Dorris 892 ....D2
Dos Palos 4,196 ....E6
Downey 91,444 ....C11
Downieville▲ 500 ....E4
Duarte 20,688 ....D10

Dublin 23,229 ....K2
Dunsmuir 2,129 ....C2
Durham 4,784 ....D4
Earlimart 5,881 ....F8
East Blythe 1,511 ....L10
East Los Angeles 126,379 ..C10
Easton 1,877 ....F7
Edgemont E11
Edison G8
El Cajon 88,693 ....J11
El Centro▲ 31,384 ....K11
El Cerrito 4,924 ....J2
El Dorado 6,395 ....C8
El Dorado Hills 3,453 ....C8
El Granada 4,426 ....H3
El Monte 106,209 ....D10
El Rio 6,419 ....F9
El Segundo 15,223 ....B11
El Toro 62,685 ....E11
Elk 17,483 ....B4
Elk Grove 10,959 ....B9
Emeryville 5,740 ....J2
Empire D6
Encinitas 55,386 ....H10
Encino B10
Enterprise C3
Escalon 4,437 ....D6
Escondido 108,635 ....J10
Esparto 1,487 ....C5
Eureka▲ 27,025 ....A3
Exeter 7,276 ....F7
Fair Oaks 26,867 ....C8
Fairfax 6,931 ....H1
Fairfield▲ 77,211 ....K1
Fallbrook 22,095 ....H10
Farmersville 6,235 ....F7
Felton 5,350 ....K4
Ferndale 1,331 ....A3
Fillmore 11,992 ....F9
Firebaugh 4,429 ....E7
Florin 24,330 ....B9
Folsom 29,802 ....C8
Fontana 87,535 ....E10
Forest Knolls (Forest Knolls-
   Lagunitas) H1
Foresthill 1,409 ....F4
Fort Bragg 6,078 ....B4
Fortuna 8,788 ....A3
Foster City 28,176 ....J2
Fountain Valley 53,691 ......D11
Fowler 3,208 ....F7
Frazier Park 2,201 ....F9
Freedom 8,361 ....L4
Fremont 173,339 ....K3
Fresno▲ 354,202 ....F7
Fullerton 114,144 ....D11
Galt 8,889 ....C9
Garden Grove 143,050 ......D11
Gardena 49,847 ....C11
Gilroy 31,487 ....D6
Glen Avon Heights 8,444 ...E10
Glendale 180,038 ....C10
Glendora 47,828 ....D10
Goleta F9
Gonzales 4,660 ....D7
Goshen 1,809 ....F7
Granada Hills B10
Grand Terrace 10,946 ....E10
Grass Valley 9,048 ....D4
Graton 1,409 ....C5
Greenacres 7,378 ....F8
Greenfield 7,464 ....D7
Greenville 1,396 ....E3
Gridley 4,631 ....D4
Groveland 2,753 ....E6
Grover City 11,656 ....E9
Guadalupe 5,479 ....E9
Guerneville 1,966 ....B5
Gustine 3,931 ....D6
Half Moon Bay 8,886 ....H3
Hamilton City 1,811 ....C4
Hanford▲ 30,897 ....F7
Harbor City C11
Hawthorne 71,349 ....C11
Hayfork 2,605 ....B3
Hayward 111,498 ....K2
Healdsburg 9,469 ....B5
Heber 2,566 ....K11
Hemet 36,094 ....H10
Hercules 16,829 ....J1
Herlong 1,188 ....E3
Hermosa Beach 18,219 .....B11
Hesperia 50,418 ....H9
Hidden Hills 1,729 ....B10
Highgrove 3,175 ....E10
Highland 34,439 ....H9
Hillsborough 10,667 ....J2
Hollister (Hilmar-Irwin) 3,392 .E6
Hollister▲ 19,212 ....D7
Hollywood C10
Holt 4,820 ....C10
Holtville 4,399 ....K11
Home Gardens 7,780 ....E11
Homeland 3,312 ....H10
Hughson 3,259 ....E6
Huntington Beach 181,519 .C11

Huntington Park 56,065 .....C11
Huron 4,766 ....E7
Idyllwild (Idyllwild-
   Pine Cove) 2,853 ....J10
Imperial 4,113 ....K11
Imperial Beach 26,512 ......H11
Independence▲ 748 ....H7
Indian Wells 2,647 ....J10
Indio 36,793 ....J10
Inglewood 109,602 ....B11
Inverness 1,422 ....C5
Ione 6,516 ....C9
Irvine 110,330 ....E11
Isla Vista 20,395 ....E9
Ivanhoe 3,293 ....F7
Jackson▲ 3,545 ....C9
Jamestown 2,178 ....E5
Joshua Tree 3,898 ....J9
Julian 1,284 ....J10
Kelseyville 2,861 ....C5
Kensington 4,974 ....J2
Kerman 5,448 ....E7
Kernville 1,656 ....G8
Kettleman City 1,411 ....E7
Keyes 2,878 ....D6
King City 7,634 ....D7
Kings Beach 2,796 ....E4
Kingsburg 7,205 ....F7
La Cañada Flintridge 19,378 .C10
La Crescenta (La Crescenta-
   Montrose) 16,968 ....C10
La Habra 51,266 ....D11
La Mesa 52,931 ....H11
La Mirada 40,452 ....D11
La Puente 36,955 ....D10
La Selva Beach 1,603 ....K4
La Verne 30,897 ....D10
Lafayette 23,501 ....K2
Laguna Beach 23,170 ....G10
Laguna Hills 46,731 ....D11
Laguna Niguel 44,400 ....H10
Lagunitas (Lagunitas-
   Forest Knolls) 1,821 ....H1
Lake Arrowhead 6,539 ....H9
Lake Elsinore 18,285 ....H10
Lake Isabella 3,323 ....G8
Lakeland Village 5,159 ......L11
Lakeport▲ 4,390 ....C4
Lakewood 73,557 ....C11
Lamont 11,517 ....G8
Lancaster 97,291 ....H9
Larkspur 11,070 ....H1
Lathrop 6,841 ....D6
Lawndale 27,331 ....B11
Le Grand 1,205 ....E6
Lemon Grove 23,984 ....J11
Lemoore 13,622 ....F7
Lenwood 3,190 ....H9
Leucadia 9,478 ....H10
Lewiston 1,187 ....C3
Lincoln 7,248 ....B8
Linda 13,033 ....D4
Linden 1,339 ....D5
Lindsay 8,338 ....F7
Live Oak 11,482 ....K4
Live Oak 3,103 ....D4
Live Oak 4,320 ....K4
Livermore 56,741 ....K3
Livingston 7,317 ....E6
Locke 2,722 ....B9
Lockeford 1,852 ....C9
Lodi 51,874 ....D5
Loma Linda 17,400 ....F10
Lomita 19,382 ....C11
Lompoc 37,649 ....E9
Lone Pine 1,818 ....H7
Long Beach 429,433 ....C11
Loomis 5,705 ....C8
Los Alamitos 11,676 ....D11
Los Altos 26,303 ....K3
Los Altos Hills 7,514 ....J3
Los Angeles▲ 3,485,398 ...C10
Los Banos 14,519 ....E6
Los Gatos 27,357 ....K4
Los Molinos 1,709 ....D3
Los Osos (Los Osos-
   Baywood Park) 10,933 ...E8
Lost Hills 1,212 ....F8
Lower Lake 1,217 ....C5
Lucerne 2,011 ....C4
Lucerne Valley 61,945 ......C11
Madera▲ 29,281 ....E7
Magalia 8,987 ....D4
Mammoth Lakes 4,785 ......G6
Manhattan Beach 32,063 ...B11
Manteca 40,773 ....D6
Maricopa 1,193 ....F8
Marina 26,436 ....D7
Mariposa▲ 1,152 ....F6
Markleeville▲ 500 ....F5
Martinez▲ 31,808 ....K1
Marysville▲ 12,324 ....D4
Maywood 27,850 ....C10
McCloud 1,555 ....C2
McFarland 7,005 ....F8
McKinleyville 10,749 ....A3

Mecca 1,966 ....K10
Meiners Oaks (Meiners Oaks-
   Mira Monte) 3,329 ....F9
Mendota 6,821 ....E7
Menlo Park 28,040 ....J3
Mentone 5,675 ....H9
Merced▲ 56,216 ....E6
Mill Valley 13,038 ....H2
Millbrae 20,412 ....J2
Milpitas 50,686 ....L3
Mira Loma 15,786 ....E10
Mission Viejo 72,820 ....D11
Modesto▲ 164,730 ....D6
Mojave 3,763 ....G8
Monrovia 35,761 ....D10
Montague 1,415 ....C2
Montara 2,552 ....H3
Montclair 28,434 ....D10
Monte Sereno 3,287 ....K4
Montebello 59,564 ....C10
Monterey 31,954 ....D7
Monterey Park 60,738 ....C10
Montrose (Montrose-La
   Crescenta) C10
Moorpark 25,494 ....G9
Moraga 15,852 ....K2
Moreno Valley 118,779 ......H10
Morgan Hill 23,928 ....L4
Morro Bay 9,664 ....D8
Moss Beach 3,002 ....H3
Mount Shasta 3,460 ....C2
Mountain View 67,460 ....K3
Mulberry 1,946 ....F7
Murphys 1,517 ....E5
Murrieta 1,628 ....H10
Muscoy 7,541 ....E10
Napa▲ 61,842 ....C5
National City 54,249 ....J11
Needles 5,191 ....L9
Nevada City▲ 2,855 ....D4
Newark 37,861 ....K3
Newhall 12,029 ....G9
Newman 4,151 ....D6
Newport Beach 66,643 ......D11
Nipomo 7,109 ....E8
Norco 23,302 ....E11
North Edwards 1,259 ....H8
North Highlands 42,105 .....B8
Norwalk 94,279 ....C11
Novato 47,585 ....H1
Oak View 3,606 ....F9
Oakdale 11,961 ....E6
Oakhurst 2,602 ....F6
Oakland▲ 372,242 ....J2
Oakley 18,374 ....L1
Oceano 6,169 ....E8
Oceanside 128,398 ....H10
Oildale 26,553 ....F8
Ojai 7,613 ....F9
Ontario 133,179 ....D10
Opal Cliffs 5,940 ....K4
Orange 110,658 ....D11
Orange Cove 5,604 ....F7
Orinda 16,642 ....J2
Orland 5,052 ....C4
Orosi 5,486 ....F7
Oroville▲ 11,960 ....D4
Oxnard 142,216 ....F9
Pacheco (Pacheco-Vine Hill)
   3,325 ....K1
Pacific Grove 16,117 ....C7
Pacifica 37,670 ....H2
Pajaro 3,332 ....D7
Palermo 5,260 ....D4
Palm Desert 23,252 ....J10
Palm Springs 40,181 ....J10
Palmdale 68,842 ....G9
Palo Alto 55,900 ....K3
Palos Verdes Estates
   13,512 ....B11
Paradise 25,408 ....D4
Paramount 47,669 ....C11
Parlier 7,938 ....F7
Pasadena 131,591 ....C10
Paso Robles 18,583 ....E8
Patterson 8,626 ....D6
Pebble Beach C7
Pedley 8,869 ....E10
Perris 21,460 ....F11
Petaluma 43,184 ....H1
Pico Rivera 59,177 ....C10
Piedmont 10,602 ....J2
Pine Valley 1,297 ....J11
Pinole 17,460 ....J1
Piru 1,157 ....G9
Pismo Beach 7,669 ....E8
Pittsburg 47,564 ....L1
Pixley 2,457 ....F8
Placentia 41,259 ....D11
Placerville▲ 8,355 ....C8
Planada 3,531 ....E6
Pleasant Hill 31,585 ....K2
Pleasanton 50,553 ....L2
Pollock Pines 4,291 ....E5
Pomona 131,723 ....D10
Poplar (Poplar-Cotton Center)
   1,901 ....F7

(continued on following page)

Topography

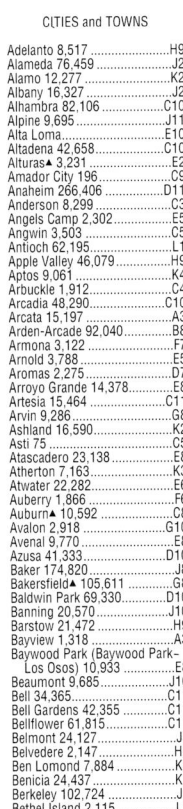

0   50   100 MI.

0   50   100 KM.

| 5,000 m. | 2,000 m. | 1,000 m. | 500 m. | 200 m. | 100 m. | Sea | Below |
| 16,404 ft. | 6,562 ft. | 3,281 ft. | 1,640 ft. | 656 ft. | 328 ft. | Level | |

Agriculture, Industry and Resources

DOMINANT LAND USE

Wheat, Small Grains
Fruit and Mixed Farming
General Farming, Livestock, Special Crops
Specialized Dairy
Fruit, Truck and Mixed Farming
Cotton, Alfalfa
Potatoes, General Farming
Range Livestock
Forests
Urban Areas
Nonagricultural Land

MAJOR MINERAL OCCURRENCES

Ab Asbestos
Ag Silver
Au Gold
Bx Borax
Cl Clay
Cu Copper
Fe Iron Ore
G   Natural Gas
Gp Gypsum
Hg Mercury
K   Potash
Lt Lithium
Mg Magnesium
Mo Molybdenum
Mr Marble
Na Salt
O   Petroleum
Pb Lead
Pt Platinum
Tc Talc
W   Tungsten
Zn Zinc

⚡ Water Power
Major Industrial Areas

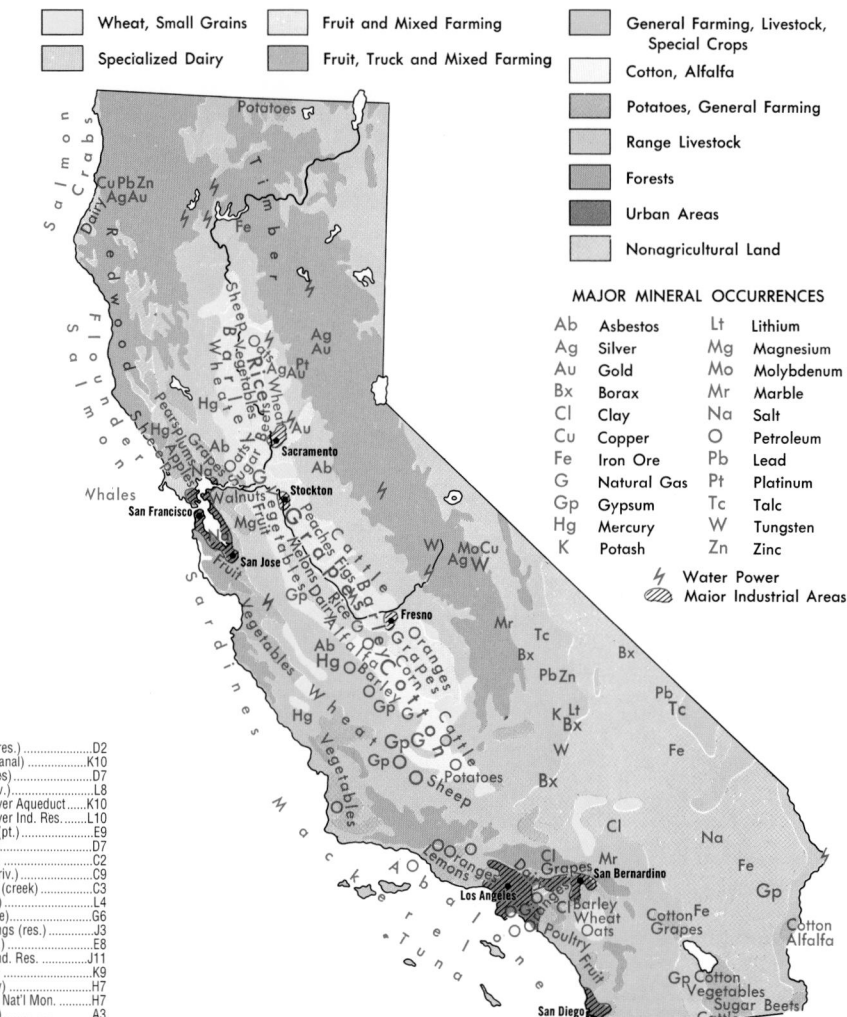

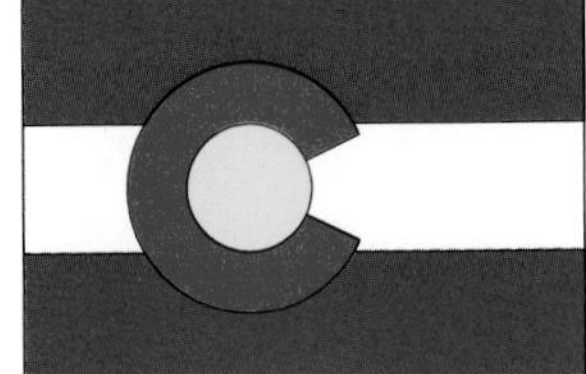

AREA 104,091 sq. mi. (269,596 sq. km.)
POPULATION 3,307,912
CAPITAL Denver
LARGEST CITY Denver
HIGHEST POINT Mt. Elbert 14,433 ft. (4399 m.)
SETTLED IN 1858
ADMITTED TO UNION August 1, 1876
POPULAR NAME Centennial State
STATE FLOWER Rocky Mountain Columbine
STATE BIRD Lark Bunting

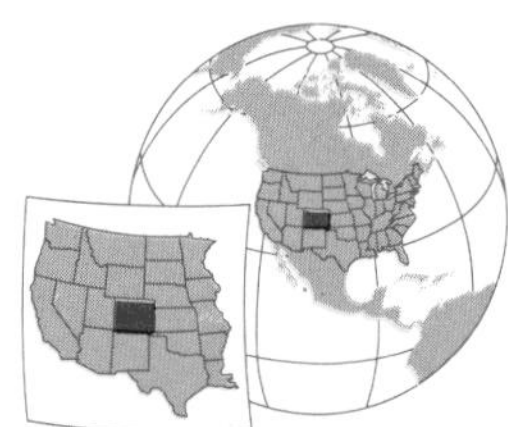

COUNTIES

Adams 265,038 L3
Alamosa 13,617 H7
Arapahoe 391,511 L3
Archuleta 5,345 E8
Baca 4,556 O8
Bent 5,048 N7
Boulder 225,339 J2
Chaffee 12,684 G5
Cheyenne 2,397 O5
Clear Creek 7,619 H3
Conejos 7,453 G8
Costilla 3,190 J8
Crowley 3,946 M6
Custer 1,926 J6
Delta 20,980 D5
Denver 467,610 K3
Dolores 1,504 C7
Douglas 60,391 K4
Eagle 21,928 F3
El Paso 397,014 K5
Elbert 9,646 L4
Fremont 32,273 J5
Garfield 29,974 C3
Gilpin 3,070 H3
Grand 7,966 G2
Gunnison 10,273 E5
Hinsdale 467 E7
Huerfano 6,009 K7
Jackson 1,605 G1
Jefferson 438,430 J3
Kiowa 1,688 O6
Kit Carson 7,140 O4
La Plata 32,284 D8
Lake 6,007 G4
Larimer 186,136 H1
Las Animas 13,765 L8
Lincoln 4,529 M5
Logan 17,567 N1
Mesa 93,145 B5
Mineral 558 F7
Moffat 11,357 C1
Montezuma 18,672 B8
Montrose 24,423 C6
Morgan 21,939 M2
Otero 20,185 M7
Ouray 2,295 D6
Park 7,174 H4
Phillips 4,189 P1
Pitkin 12,661 F4
Prowers 13,347 P7
Pueblo 123,051 K6
Rio Blanco 5,972 C3
Rio Grande 10,770 G7
Routt 14,088 E1
Saguache 4,619 G6
San Juan 745 D7
San Miguel 3,653 C6
Sedgwick 2,690 P1
Summit 12,881 G3
Teller 12,468 J5
Washington 4,812 N3
Weld 131,821 L1
Yuma 8,954 P2

CITIES and TOWNS

Agate 90 M4
Aguilar 520 K8
Akron▲ 1,599 N2
Alamosa▲ 7,579 H8
Allenspark 200 J2
Alma 148 G4
Almont 135 F5
Amherst 85 P1
Anton 875 N3
Antonito 1,103 H8
Arapahoe 300 P5
Arlington 37 N6
Arriba 220 N4
Arriola 5,672 B8
Arvada 89,235 J3
Aspen▲ 5,049 F4
Atwood 100 N1
Ault 1,107 K1
Aurora 222,103 K3
Austin D5
Avon 1,798 F3
Avondale 750 L6
Bailey 150 H4
Barnesville 20 L2
Basalt 1,128 E4
Bayfield 1,090 D8
Bedrock 45 B6
Beecher Island 5 P3
Bellvue 250 J1
Bennett 1,757 L3
Berthoud 2,990 J2
Berthoud Pass 40 H3
Bethune 173 P4
Beulah 650 K6
Black Forest 8,143 K4
Black Hawk 227 J3
Blanca 272 H8
Blue River 440 G4
Bonanza 16 G6
Boncarbo 200 K8
Bond 65 F3
Boone 341 L6
Boulder▲ 83,312 J2
Bowie 18 D5
Boyero 12 N5
Brandon 30 P6
Branson 58 M8
Breckenridge▲ 1,285 G4
Briggsdale 85 L1
Brighton▲ 14,203 K3
Bristol 200 P6
Brookside 183 J6
Broomfield 24,638 J3
Brush 4,165 M2
Buckingham 5 L1
Buena Vista 1,752 G5
Buffalo Creek 150 J4
Burlington▲ 2,941 P4
Burns 100 F3
Byers 1,065 L3
Cahone 200 B7
Calhan 562 L4
Campo 121 O8
Canon City▲ 12,687 J6
Capulin 600 G8
Carbondale 3,004 E4
Carr 49 K1
Cascade 1,479 K5
Castle Rock▲ 8,708 K4
Cedaredge 1,380 D5
Center 1,963 G7
Central City▲ 335 J3
Chama 239 J8
Cheraw 265 N6
Cheyenne Wells▲ 1,128 P5
Chimney Rock 76 E8
Chivington 20 O6
Chromo 115 F8
Cimarron 50 D6
Clark 20 F1
Clifton 12,671 C4
Climax 975 G4
Coal Creek 157 J6
Coaldale 153 H6
Coalmont 50 F1
Cokedale 116 K8
Collbran 228 C4
Colona 54 D6
Colorado City 1,149 K6
Colorado Springs▲ 281,140 K5
Columbine 23,969 E1
Commerce City 16,466 K3
Como 30 H4
Conejos▲ 200 G8
Cope 110 O3
Cornish 15 L2
Cortez▲ 7,284 B8
Cotopaxi 250 H6
Cowdrey 80 G1
Craig▲ 8,091 D2
Crawford 221 D5
Creede▲ 362 E7
Crested Butte 878 E5
Crestone 39 H7
Cripple Creek▲ 584 J5
Crook 148 O1
Crowley 225 M6
Cuchara 43 J8
Dacono 2,228 K2
Dailey 20 O1
De Beque 257 C4
Deckers 4 J4
Deer Trail 476 M3
Del Norte▲ 1,674 G7
Delhi 10 M7
Delta▲ 3,789 D5
Denver (cap.)▲ 467,610 K3
Deora 2 O7
Dillon 553 H3
Dinosaur 324 B2
Divide 700 J5
Dolores 866 C8
Dove Creek▲ 643 A7
Doyleville 75 F6
Drake 300 J2
Durango▲ 12,430 D8
Eads▲ 780 O6
Eagle▲ 1,580 F3
Eaton 1,959 K1
Eckley 211 P2
Edgewater 4,613 J3
Edwards 250 F3
Egnar 50 B7
Elbert 200 L4
Eldora 100 H3
Elizabeth 818 K4
Elk Springs 18 C2
Empire 401 H3
Englewood 29,387 K3
Erie 1,258 K2
Estes Park 3,184 J2
Eureka 25 D7
Evans 5,877 K2
Evergreen 7,582 J3
Fairplay▲ 387 H4
Farisita 116 J7
Federal Heights 9,342 J3
Firestone 1,358 K2
Firstview 6 O5
Flagler 564 N4
Fleming 344 O1
Florence 2,987 J6
Florissant 130 J5
Fort Collins▲ 87,758 J1
Fort Garland 700 J8
Fort Lupton 5,159 K2
Fort Lyon 500 N6
Fort Morgan▲ 9,068 M2
Fountain 9,984 K5
Fowler 1,154 L6
Foxton 12 J4
Franktown 200 K4
Fraser 575 H3
Frederick 988 K2
Freshwater (Guffey) 24 H5
Frisco 1,601 G3
Fruita 4,045 B4
Galeton 200 K1
Garcia 75 J8
Gardner 100 J7
Garfield 30 G5
Gateway 7,510 B5
Genoa 167 N4
Georgetown▲ 891 H3
Gilcrest 1,084 K2
Gill 250 L2
Gilman 160 G3
Glade Park 100 B5
Glen Haven 110 H2
Glendevey 50 H1
Glenwood Springs▲ 6,561 E4
Golden▲ 13,116 J3
Goodrich 85 M2
Gould 12 G2
Granada 513 P6
Granby 966 H2
Grand Junction▲ 29,034 B4
Grand Lake 259 H2
Granite 47 G4
Grant 50 H4
Greeley▲ 60,536 K2
Green Mountain Falls 663 K5
Greenland 21 K4
Greystone 2 B1
Grover 135 L1
Guffey 24 H5
Gulnare 6 K8
Gunnison▲ 4,636 E5
Gypsum 1,750 F3
Hale 4 P3
Hamilton 100 D2
Hartman 108 P6
Hartsel 69 H4
Hasty 150 O6
Haswell 62 N6
Haxtun 952 O1
Hayden 1,444 E2
Hereford 50 L1
Hesperus 250 C8
Hillrose 169 N2
Hillside 79 H6
Hoehne 400 L8
Holly 877 P6
Holyoke▲ 1,931 P1
Hooper 112 H7
Hot Sulphur Springs▲ 347 H2
Hotchkiss 744 D5
Howard 200 H6
Hoyt 60 L2
Hudson 918 K2
Hugo▲ 660 N4
Hygiene 450 J2
Idaho Springs 1,834 H3
Idalia 125 P3
Ignacio 720 D8
Iliff 174 N1
Jamestown 251 J2
Jansen 267 K8
Jaroso 50 H8
Jefferson 50 H4
Joes 100 O3
Johnstown 1,579 K2
Julesburg▲ 1,295 P1
Karval 51 N5
Keenesburg 570 L2
Keota 5 L1
Kersey 980 L2
Kim 76 N8
Kiowa▲ 275 L4
Kirk 30 P3
Kit Carson 305 O5
Kremmling 1,166 G2
Kutch 2 M5
La Garita 10 G7
La Jara 725 H8
La Junta▲ 7,637 M7
La Salle 1,783 K2
La Veta 726 J8
Lafayette 14,548 K3
Laird 105 P2
Lake City▲ 223 E6
Lake George 500 J5
Lakewood 126,481 J3
Lamar▲ 8,343 O6
Laporte 950 J1
Larkspur 232 K4
Las Animas▲ 2,481 N6
Lasauces 150 H8
Lavalley 237 J8
Lawson 108 H3
Lay 40 D2
Lazear 60 D5
Leadville▲ 2,629 G4
Lebanon 50 B8
Lewis 150 B8
Limon 1,831 M4
Lincoln Park 3,728 J6
Lindon 60 N3
Littleton▲ 33,685 K3
Livermore 150 J1
Lochbuie 1,168 K2
Log Lane Village 667 M2
Loma 265 B4
Longmont 42,942 J2
Longview 10 J4
Louisville 12,361 J3
Louviers 300 K4
Loveland 37,352 J2
Lucerne 135 K2
Lycan 4 P7
Lyons 1,227 J2
Mack 380 B4
Maher 75 D5
Malta 200 G4
Manassa 988 H8
Mancos 842 C8
Manitou Springs 4,535 J5
Manzanola 437 M6
Marble 64 E4
Marvel 176 C8
Masonville 200 J2
Masters 50 L2

(continued on following page)

Agriculture, Industry and Resources

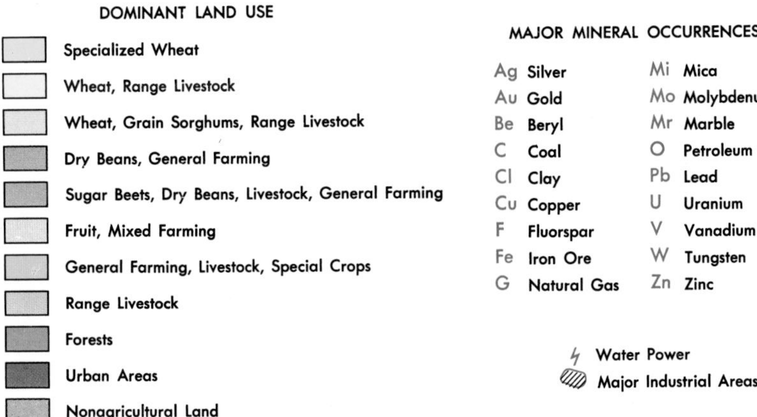
DOMINANT LAND USE
Specialized Wheat
Wheat, Range Livestock
Wheat, Grain Sorghums, Range Livestock
Dry Beans, General Farming
Sugar Beets, Dry Beans, Livestock, General Farming
Fruit, Mixed Farming
General Farming, Livestock, Special Crops
Range Livestock
Forests
Urban Areas
Nonagricultural Land
MAJOR MINERAL OCCURRENCES
Ag Silver
Au Gold
Be Beryl
C Coal
Cl Clay
Cu Copper
F Fluorspar
Fe Iron Ore
G Natural Gas
Mi Mica
Mo Molybdenum
Mr Marble
O Petroleum
Pb Lead
U Uranium
V Vanadium
W Tungsten
Zn Zinc
Water Power
Major Industrial Areas

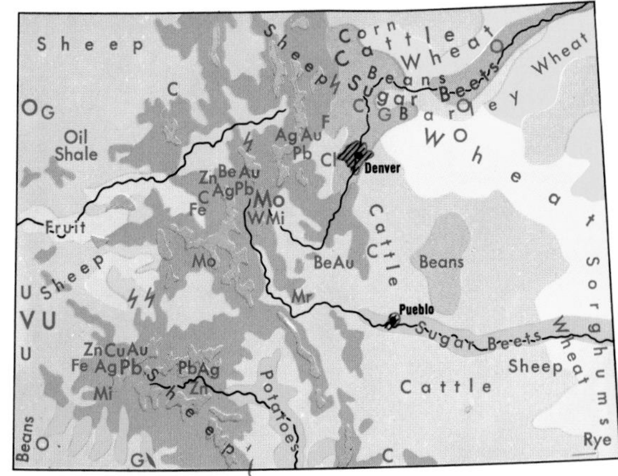
Sheep
Corn
Cattle
Wheat
Sugar Beets
Barley
Oil Shale
Denver
Fruit
Beans
Pueblo
Sorghums
Potatoes
Rye

Topography

0   50   100 MI.

0   50   100 KM.

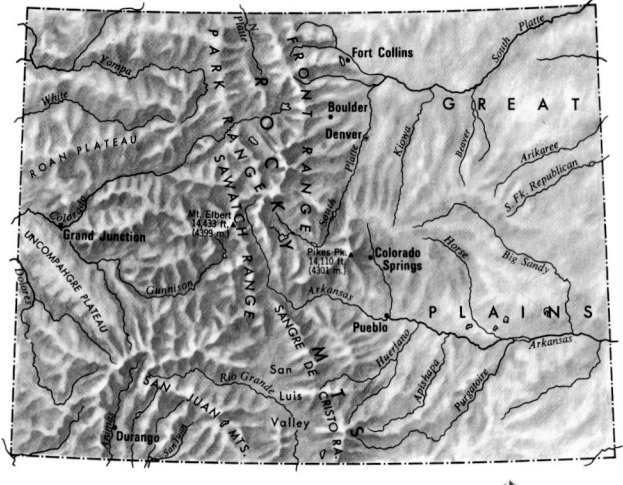

Below Sea Level | 100 m. 328 ft. | 200 m. 656 ft. | 500 m. 1,640 ft. | 1,000 m. 3,281 ft. | 2,000 m. 6,562 ft. | 5,000 m. 16,404 ft.

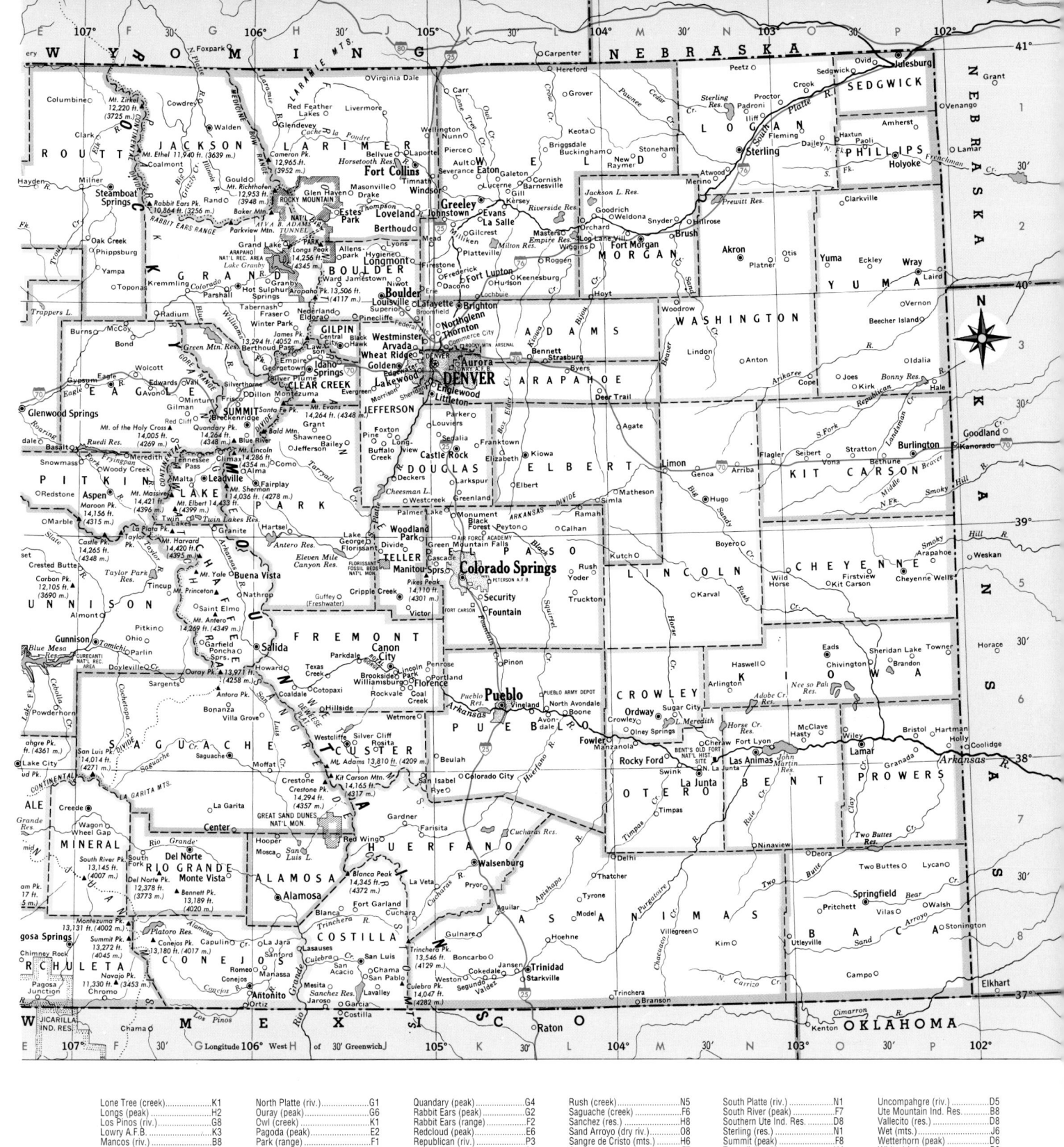

Lone Tree (creek)............K1
Longs (peak)...............H2
Los Pinos (riv.)............G8
Lowry A.F.B................K3
Mancos (riv.)..............B8
Maroon (peak)..............F4
Massive (mt.)..............F4
McElmo (creek).............B8
Medicine Bow (range).......G1
Meredith (lake)............M6
Mesa Verde Nat'l Park......C8
Middle Beaver (creek)......P4
Milton (res.)..............K2
Montezuma (peak)...........F8
Morrow Point (res.)........E6
Muddy (creek)..............E4
Navajo (peak)..............F8
Navajo (res.)..............E8
Nee so Pah (res.)..........D6
North Carrizo (creek)......N8

North Platte (riv.)........G1
Ouray (peak)...............G6
Owl (creek)................K1
Pagoda (peak)..............E2
Park (range)...............F1
Parkview (mt.).............G2
Pawnee (creek).............M1
Peterson A.F.B.............K5
Piceance (creek)...........C3
Piedra (riv.)..............E8
Pikes (peak)...............J5
Pinos (riv.)...............D8
Plateau (creek)............C4
Platoro (res.).............F8
Pot (creek)................A1
Prewitt (res.).............N2
Princeton (mt.)............G5
Pueblo (res.)..............K6
Pueblo Army Depot..........L6
Purgatoire (riv.)..........M8

Quandary (peak)............G4
Rabbit Ears (peak).........F2
Rabbit Ears (range)........F2
Redcloud (peak)............E6
Republican (riv.)..........P3
Richthofen (mt.)...........G2
Rifle (creek)..............D3
Rio Grande (res.)..........E7
Rio Grande (riv.)..........H8
Rio Grande Pyramid (mt.)...E7
Riverside (res.)...........L2
Roan (creek)...............C4
Roan (plat.)...............B3
Roaring Fork, Colorado (riv.)..E4
Rocky (mt.)................F1
Rocky Mountain Arsenal.....K3
Rocky Mountain Nat'l Park..H2
Royal Gorge (canyon).......J6
Ruedi (res.)...............F4

Rush (creek)...............N5
Saguache (creek)...........F6
Sanchez (res.).............H8
Sand Arroyo (dry riv.).....O8
Sangre de Cristo (mts.)....H6
San Juan (mts.)............F7
San Juan (riv.)............E8
San Luis (creek)...........H6
San Luis (lake)............H7
San Luis (riv.)............F6
San Miguel (mts.)..........C7
San Miguel (riv.)..........B6
Santa Fe (riv.)............H4
Sawatch (range)............G4
Sheep (creek)..............E6
Sherman (mt.)..............G4
Slate (riv.)...............E5
Smoky Hill (riv.)..........P5
Smoky Hill, North Fork (riv.)..P4
Sneffels (mt.).............D7

South Platte (riv.)........N1
South River (peak).........F7
Southern Ute Ind. Res......D8
Sterling (res.)............N1
Summit (peak)..............F8
Tarryall (creek)...........H4
Taylor (peak)..............F5
Taylor (riv.)..............F5
Taylor Park (res.).........F5
Timpas (creek).............M7
Tomichi (creek)............F5
Trappers (lake)............E3
Trinchera (peak)...........J8
Trinchera (riv.)...........H8
Trout (creek)..............E2
Twin Lakes (res.)..........G4
Two Butte (creek)..........N7
Two Buttes (res.)..........O7
Uncompahgre (peak).........E6
Uncompahgre (plat.)........B5

Uncompahgre (riv.).........D5
Ute Mountain Ind. Res......B8
Vallecito (res.)...........D8
Wet (mts.).................J6
Wetterhorn (peak)..........D6
White (riv.)...............B2
Williams Fork, Colorado (riv.)..C3
Williams Fork, Yampa (riv.)..E2
Wilson (mt.)...............C7
Windom (peak)..............D7
Yale (mt.).................G5
Yampa (riv.)...............B2
Yellow (creek).............C3
Yucca House Nat'l Mon......B8
Zenobia (peak).............B1
Zirkel (mt.)...............F1

▲County seat

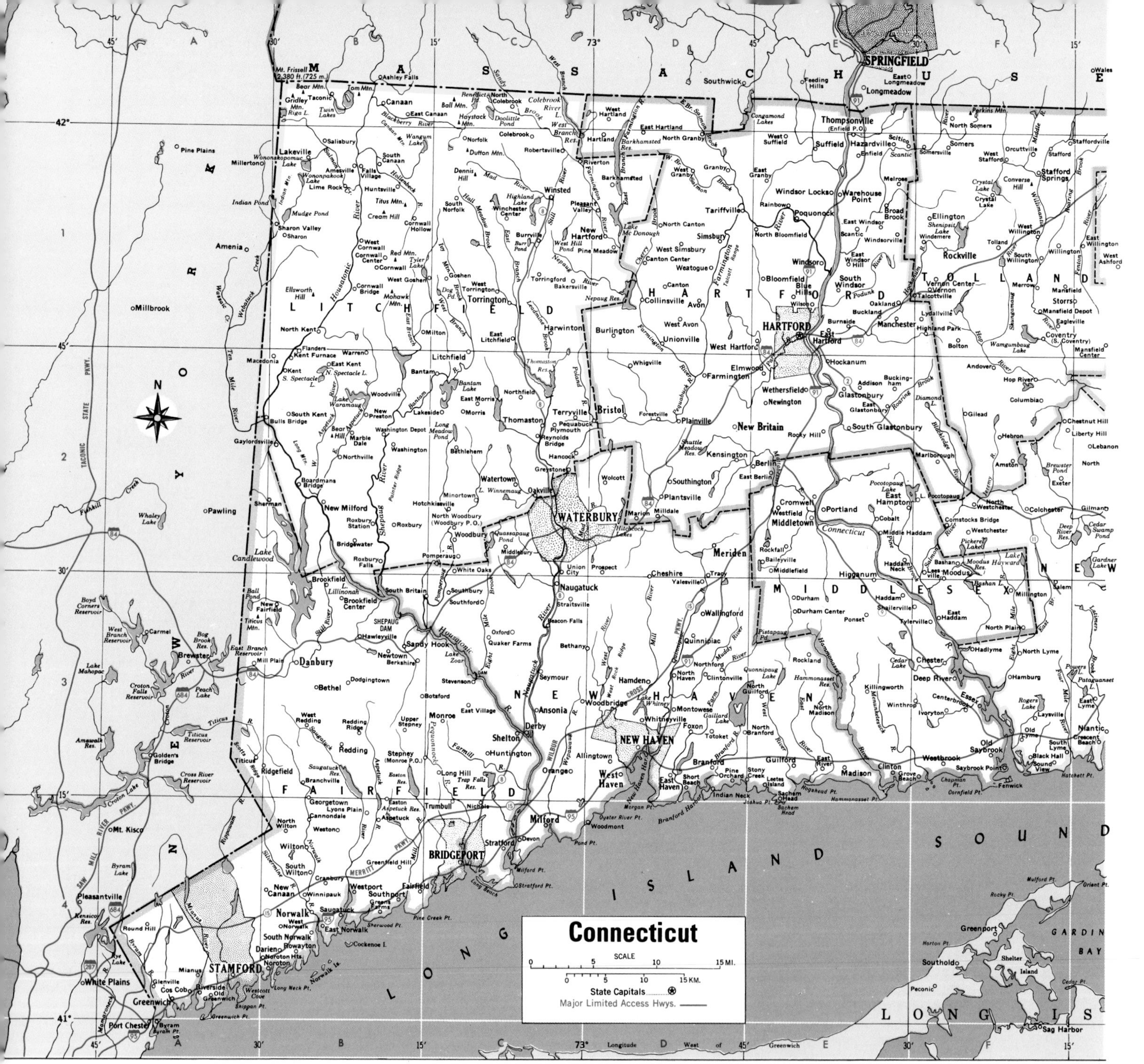

Connecticut

SCALE

0 ___ 5 ___ 10 ___ 15 MI.

0 ___ 5 ___ 10 ___ 15 KM.

State Capitals .... ⊛

Major Limited Access Hwys. ———

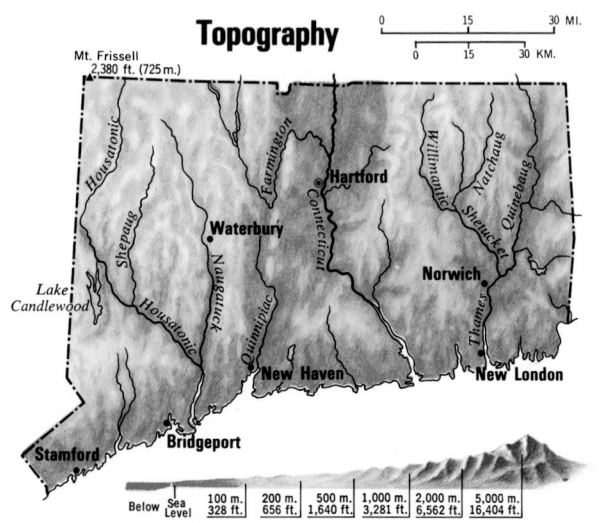

Topography

Mt. Frissell
2,380 ft. (725 m.)

0 ___ 15 ___ 30 MI.

0 ___ 15 ___ 30 KM.

Below Sea Level	100 m. 328 ft.	200 m. 656 ft.	500 m. 1,640 ft.	1,000 m. 3,281 ft.	2,000 m. 6,562 ft.	5,000 m. 16,404 ft.

COUNTIES

Fairfield 827,645 .... B3
Hartford 851,783 .... D1
Litchfield 174,092 .... C1
Middlesex 143,196 .... E3
New Haven 804,219 .... D3
New London 254,957 .... G2
Tolland 128,699 .... F1
Windham 102,525 .... H1

CITIES and TOWNS

Abington 600 .... G1
Addison 700 .... E2
Allingtown D3
Amston 900 .... F2
Andover • 2,540 .... F2
Ansonia 18,403 .... C3
Ashford P.O. (Warrenville)
  500 .... G1
Ashford • 3,765 .... G1
Avon 1,434 .... D1
Avon • 13,937 .... D1
Bakersville 750 .... C1
Ballouville 800 .... H1
Baltic G2
Bantam 757 .... B2
Barkhamsted • 3,369 .... D1
Beacon Falls • 5,083 .... C3
Berkshire 500 .... B3
Berlin • 16,787 .... E2

Bethany • 4,608 .... C3
Bethel 8,835 .... B3
Bethel • 17,541 .... B3
Bethlehem 1,762 .... C2
Bethlehem • 3,071 .... C2
Bloomfield 19,483 .... E1
Blue Hills 3,206 .... E1
Bolton • 4,575 .... F1
Branchville 600 .... B3
Branford 5,688 .... D3
Branford • 27,603 .... D3
Bridgeport 141,686 .... C4
Bridgewater • 1,654 .... B3
Bristol 60,640 .... D2
Broad Brook 3,585 .... E1
Brookfield • 14,113 .... B3
Brookfield Center B3
Brooklyn • 6,681 .... H1
Buckingham 800 .... E2
Burlington • 7,026 .... D1
Burnside E1
Byram A4
Canaan 1,057 .... B1
Canaan • 1,194 .... B1
Canterbury • 4,467 .... H2
Canton 1,680 .... D1
Canton • 8,268 .... D1
Center Groton 600 .... G3
Centerbrook 800 .... F3
Central Village 950 .... H2
Chaplin • 2,048 .... G1
Cheshire 5,759 .... D2

Cheshire • 25,684 .... D2
Chester 1,563 .... F3
Chester • 3,417 .... F3
Clinton 3,439 .... E3
Clinton • 12,767 .... E3
Clintonville D3
Cobalt 700 .... E2
Colchester 3,212 .... F2
Colchester • 10,980 .... F2
Colebrook 1,365 .... C1
Collinsville 2,591 .... D1
Columbia • 4,510 .... F2
Cornwall • 1,414 .... C1
Cos Cob A4
Coventry 3,769 .... F1
Coventry • 10,063 .... F1
Cranbury 700 .... B4
Cromwell • 12,286 .... E2
Crystal Lake 1,175 .... F1
Danbury 65,585 .... B3
Danielson 4,441 .... H1
Darien • 18,196 .... B4
Dayville H1
Deep River 2,520 .... F3
Deep River • 4,332 .... F3
Derby 12,199 .... C3
Devon C4
Durham 2,650 .... E3
Durham • 5,732 .... E3
Durham Center 500 .... E3
East Berlin 950 .... E2
East Brooklyn 1,481 .... H1

East Canaan 800 .... B1
East Granby • 4,302 .... E1
East Haddam • 6,676 ...... F3
East Hampton 2,167 .... E2
East Hampton • 10,428 ... E2
East Hartford 50,452 ...... E1
East Hartland 900 .... D1
East Haven • 26,144 .... D3
East Killingly 900 .... H1
East Lyme • 15,340 .... G3
East Morris 800 .... C2
East Norwalk B4
East Putnam 500 .... H1
East River 500 .... E3
East Windsor • 10,081 ... E1
East Windsor Hill 500 .... E1
Eastford • 1,314 .... G1
Easton • 6,303 .... B4
Ellington • 11,197 .... F1
Elmwood D2
Enfield 8,151 .... E1
Enfield • 45,532 .... E1
Essex 2,500 .... F3
Essex • 5,904 .... F3
Fabyan 600 .... H1
Fairfield • 53,418 .... B4
Falls Village 600 .... B1
Farmington • 20,608 ...... D1
Fenwick 89 .... F3
Forestville D2
Foxon D3
Franklin • 1,810 .... G2

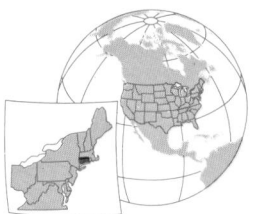

AREA 5,018 sq. mi. (12,997 sq. km.)
POPULATION 3,295,669
CAPITAL Hartford
LARGEST CITY Bridgeport
HIGHEST POINT Mt. Frissell (S. Slope) 2,380 ft.
   (725 m.)
SETTLED IN 1635
ADMITTED TO UNION January 9, 1788
POPULAR NAME Constitution State; Nutmeg State
STATE FLOWER Mountain Laurel
STATE BIRD Robin

Milldale 975	D2	Poquonock Bridge 2,770	G3	Thompson • 8,668	H1	Colebrook River (lake)	C1

Milldale 975 ....D2
Milton 600 ....C1
Mohegan 700 ....G3
Monroe • 16,896 ....C3
Monroe P.O. (Stepney) B3
Montowese D3
Montville 1,711 ....G3
Montville • 16,673 ....G3
Moodus 1,170 ....F2
Moosup 3,289 ....H2
Morningside Park G3
Morris • 2,039 ....C2
Mystic 2,618 ....H3
Naugatuck 30,625 ....C3
New Canaan • 17,864 ....B4
New Fairfield • 12,911 ....B3
New Hartford 1,269 ....C1
New Hartford • 5,769 ....C1
New Haven 130,474 ....D3
New London 28,540 ....G2
New Milford 5,775 ....B2
New Milford • 23,629 ....B2
New Preston 1,217 ....B2
Newington • 29,208 ....E2
Newtown 1,800 ....B3
Newtown • 20,779 ....B3
Niantic 3,048 ....G3
Nichols C4
Noank 1,406 ....G3
Norfolk • 2,060 ....C1
Noroton B4
Noroton Heights B4
North Bloomfield 500 ....E1
North Branford • 12,996 ....E3
North Franklin 500 ....G2
North Granby 1,455 ....D1
North Grosvenor Dale 1,705 ....H1
North Guilford E3
North Haven • 22,249 ....D3
North Lyme F3
North Stonington • 4,884 ....H3
North Wilton 900 ....B4
North Woodbury 900 ....C2
Northfield 600 ....C2
Northford D3
Northville 700 ....B2
Norwalk 78,331 ....B4
Norwich 37,391 ....G2
Norwichtown G2
Oakdale 608 ....G3
Oakville 8,741 ....C2
Occum G2
Old Greenwich A4
Old Lyme • 6,535 ....F3
Old Mystic 600 ....H3
Old Saybrook 1,820 ....F3
Old Saybrook • 9,552 ....F3
Oneco 550 ....H2
Orange • 12,830 ....C3
Oxford • 8,685 ....C3
Pawcatuck 5,289 ....H3
Pequabuck 642 ....C2
Plainfield 2,856 ....H2
Plainfield • 14,363 ....H2
Plainville • 17,392 ....D2
Plantsville D2
Pleasure Beach 1,356 ....G3
Plymouth • 11,822 ....C2
Pomfret • 3,102 ....H1
Poquonock E1

Poquonock Bridge 2,770 ....G3
Portland 5,645 ....E2
Portland • 8,418 ....E2
Preston 5,006 ....H2
Prospect • 7,775 ....D2
Putnam 6,835 ....H1
Putnam • 9,031 ....H1
Putnam Heights 500 ....H1
Quaker Hill 2,052 ....G3
Quinebaug 1,031 ....H1
Quinnipiac D3
Redding • 7,927 ....B3
Redding Ridge 550 ....B3
Ridgefield 6,363 ....B3
Ridgefield • 20,919 ....B3
Riverside A4
Rockfall 900 ....E2
Rockville F1
Rocky Hill • 16,554 ....E2
Rogers 650 ....H1
Round Hill 900 ....A4
Rowayton B4
Roxbury • 1,825 ....B2
Salem • 3,310 ....F3
Salisbury • 4,090 ....B1
Sandy Hook B3
Saugatuck B4
Saybrook Point 700 ....F3
Scantic 500 ....E1
Scotland • 1,215 ....G2
Seymour • 14,288 ....C3
Sharon • 2,928 ....B1
Shelton 35,418 ....C3
Sherman • 2,809 ....B2
Short Beach D3
Simsbury 5,577 ....D1
Simsbury • 22,023 ....D1
Somers 1,643 ....F1
Somers • 9,108 ....F1
Somersville 750 ....F1
South Coventry (Coventry)
   1,257 ....F1
South Glastonbury E2
South Killingly 500 ....H1
South Norwalk B4
South Wilton B4
South Windham 1,644 ....G2
South Windsor • 22,090 ....E1
South Woodstock 1,112 ....G1
Southbury • 15,818 ....C3
Southington • 38,518 ....D2
Southport B4
Stafford • 11,091 ....F1
Stafford Springs 4,100 ....F1
Staffordville 500 ....G1
Stamford 108,056 ....A4
Stepney B3
Sterling • 2,357 ....H2
Stonington 1,100 ....H3
Stonington • 16,919 ....H3
Stony Creek E3
Storrs 12,198 ....F1
Stratford • 49,389 ....C4
Suffield 1,353 ....E1
Suffield • 11,427 ....E1
Taftville G2
Talcottville 875 ....F1
Tariffville • 1,477 ....D1
Terryville 5,426 ....C2
Thamesville G2
Thomaston • 6,947 ....C2

Thompson • 8,668 ....H1
Thompsonville 8,458 ....E1
Tolland 11,001 ....F1
Torrington C1
Torrington 33,687 ....C1
Totoket 950 ....D3
Trumbull • 32,016 ....C4
Uncasville 1,597 ....G3
Union • 612 ....G1
Union City C2
Unionville D1
Vernon Center F1
Vernon • 29,841 ....F1
Versailles 540 ....G2
Voluntown • 2,113 ....H2
Wallingford 17,827 ....D3
Wallingford • 40,822 ....D3
Warehouse Point E1
Warren • 1,226 ....B2
Washington • 3,905 ....B2
Washington Depot 900 ....B2
Waterbury 108,961 ....C2
Waterford 2,736 ....G3
Waterford • 17,930 ....G3
Watertown • 20,456 ....C2
Wauregan 1,079 ....H2
Weatogue 2,521 ....D1
West Avon D1
West Granby 567 ....D1
West Hartford • 60,110 ....D1
West Haven 54,021 ....D3
West Mystic 3,595 ....H3
West Norwalk 950 ....B4
West Simsbury 2,149 ....D1
West Suffield E1
Westbrook 2,060 ....F3
Westbrook • 5,414 ....F3
Westfield E2
Weston • 8,648 ....B4
Westport • 24,410 ....B4
Wethersfield • 25,651 ....D2
Whitneyville D3
Willimantic 14,746 ....G2
Willington • 5,979 ....F1
Wilton 15,989 ....B4
Winchester • 11,524 ....C1
Windham • 22,039 ....G2
Windsor 17,517 ....E1
Windsor • 27,817 ....E1
Windsor Locks • 12,358 ....E1
Winnipauk 650 ....B4
Winsted 8,254 ....C1
Winthrop 750 ....E3
Wolcott • 13,700 ....D2
Woodbridge • 7,924 ....D3
Woodbury 1,212 ....C2
Woodbury • 8,131 ....C2
Woodmont 1,770 ....D4
Woodstock • 6,008 ....H1
Yalesville D3
Yantic G2

OTHER FEATURES

Aspetuck (res.) B4
Bantam (lake) C2
Barkhamsted (res.) D1
Bear (mt.) B1
Byram (riv.) A4
Candlewood (lake) A2
Coast Guard Academy G3

Colebrook River (lake) C1
Congamond (lakes) E1
Connecticut (riv.) E2
Dennis (hill) C1
Easton (res.) B3
Eight Mile (riv.) F3
Farmington (riv.) D1
French (riv.) H1
Frissell (mt.) B1
Gaillard (lake) D3
Gardner (lake) G2
Hammonasset (pt.) E3
Hammonasset (riv.) E3
Haystack (mt.) C1
Highland (lake) C1
Hockanum (riv.) E1
Hop (riv.) F1
Housatonic (riv.) C3
Lillinonah (lake) B3
Little (riv.) G2
Long Island (sound) C4
Mad (riv.) C2
Mashapaug (lake) G1
Mason (isl.) H3
Mattabesset (riv.) E2
Mianus (riv.) A4
Mohawk (mt.) B1
Moosup (riv.) H2
Mount Hope (riv.) G1
Mudge (pond) B1
Mystic (riv.) H3
Natchaug (riv.) G1
Naugatuck (riv.) C3
Nepaug (riv.) D1
Niantic (riv.) G3
Norwalk (riv.) B4
Pachaug (pond) H2
Pawcatuck (riv.) H3
Pequabuck (riv.) D2
Pequonnock (riv.) C3
Pocotopaug (lake) E2
Quaddick (lake) H1
Quinebaug (riv.) H2
Quinnipiac (riv.) D3
Rippowam (riv.) A4
Sachem (head) E4
Salmon (brook) D1
Salmon (riv.) F2
Saugatuck (res.) B3
Scantic (riv.) E1
Shenipsit (lake) F1
Shepaug (riv.) B2
Shetucket (riv.) G2
Silvermine (riv.) B4
Spectacle (lakes) B2
Still (riv.) B3
Still (riv.) C1
Talcott (range) D1
Thames (riv.) G3
Thomaston (res.) C2
Titicus (riv.) A3
Trap Falls (res.) C3
Twin (lakes) B1
Wamgumbaug (lake) F1
Waramaug (lake) B2
West Rock Ridge (hills) D3
Willimantic (riv.) F1
Wononskopomuc (lake) B1
Yantic (riv.) G2

• Population of town or township

Gales Ferry 1,191 ....G3
Gaylordsville 960 ....A2
Georgetown 1,694 ....B4
Glastonbury 7,082 ....E2
Glastonbury • 27,901 ....E2
Glenville A4
Goshen • 2,329 ....C1
Granby 1,912 ....D1
Granby • 9,369 ....D1
Greenfield Hill B4
Greenwich 58,441 ....A4
Grosvenor Dale 700 ....H1
Groton 9,837 ....G3
Groton • 45,144 ....G3
Guilford 2,588 ....E3
Guilford • 19,848 ....E3
Haddam • 6,769 ....E2
Hamden • 52,434 ....D3
Hampton • 1,578 ....G1
Hanover 500 ....G2
Hartford (cap.) 139,739 ....E1
Hartland • 1,866 ....D1
Harwinton 3,293 ....C1
Harwinton • 5,228 ....C1
Hawleyville 600 ....B3
Hazardville 5,179 ....E1
Hebron • 7,079 ....F2
Higganum 1,692 ....E2
Highland Park 500 ....F1
Hockanum E2
Huntington C3
Indian Neck D3

Ivoryton F3
Jewett City 3,349 ....H2
Kensington 8,306 ....D2
Kent • 2,918 ....B2
Killingly • 15,889 ....H1
Killingworth • 4,814 ....E3
Lakeville B1
Lebanon 6,041 ....G2
Ledyard • 14,913 ....G3
Leetes Island 500 ....E3
Litchfield 1,378 ....C2
Litchfield 8,365 ....C2
Long Hill C3
Lords Point 500 ....H3
Lyons Plain 700 ....B4
Madison 2,139 ....E3
Madison • 15,485 ....E3
Manchester 31,058 ....E1
Manchester 51,618 ....E1
Mansfield • 21,103 ....F1
Mansfield Center 1,043 ....G1
Marion 900 ....D2
Marlborough 1,039 ....F2
Marlborough • 5,535 ....F2
Meriden 59,479 ....D2
Middlebury • 6,145 ....C2
Middlefield • 3,925 ....E2
Middletown 42,762 ....E2
Milford 48,168 ....C4
Mill Plain 750 ....A3

Agriculture, Industry and Resources

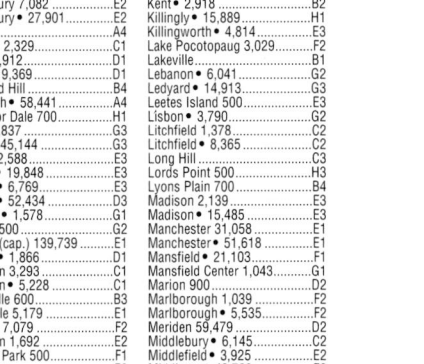

DOMINANT LAND USE

Specialized Dairy

Dairy, Poultry, Mixed Farming

Forests

Urban Areas

MAJOR MINERAL OCCURRENCES

Cl   Clay   Mi   Mica

Major Industrial Areas

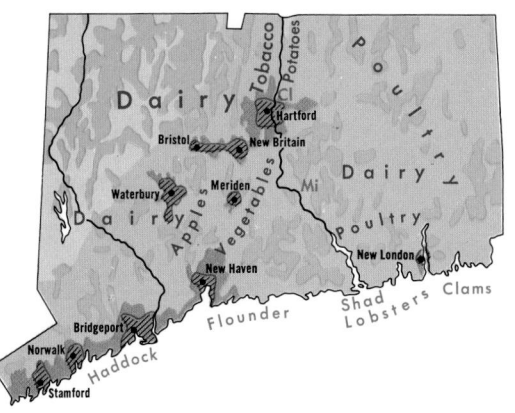

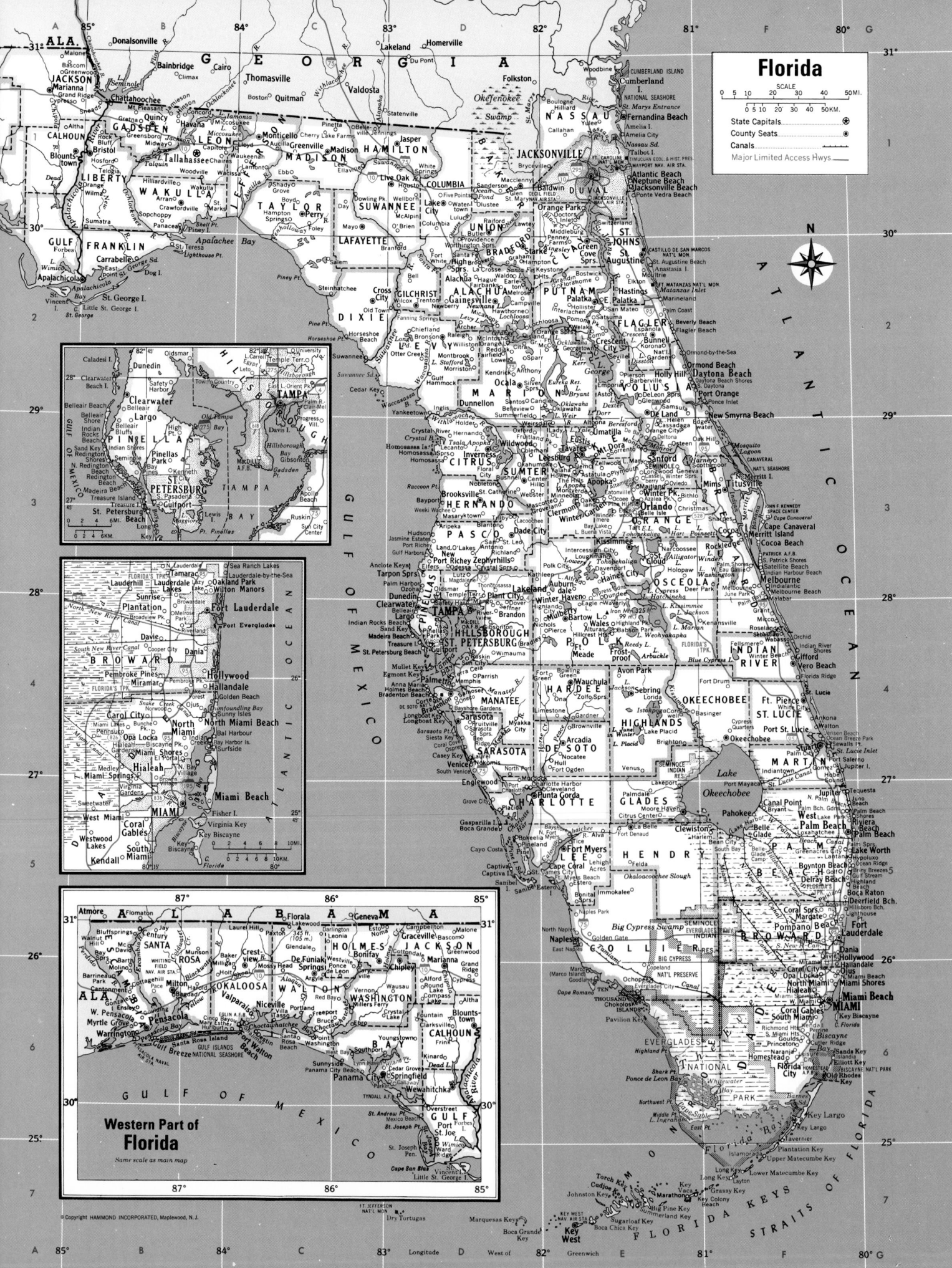

Florida

SCALE

State Capitals .... ⊛
County Seats .... ◉
Canals ....
Major Limited Access Hwys. ....

Western Part of Florida

Same scale as main map

Copyright HAMMOND INCORPORATED, Maplewood, N.J.

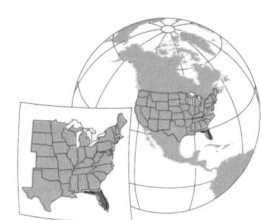

AREA 58,664 sq. mi. (151,940 sq. km.)
POPULATION 13,003,362
CAPITAL Tallahassee
LARGEST CITY Jacksonville
HIGHEST POINT (Walton County) 345 ft. (105 m.)
SETTLED IN 1565
ADMITTED TO UNION March 3, 1845
POPULAR NAME Sunshine State; Peninsula State
STATE FLOWER Orange Blossom
STATE BIRD Mockingbird

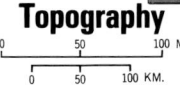

Topography

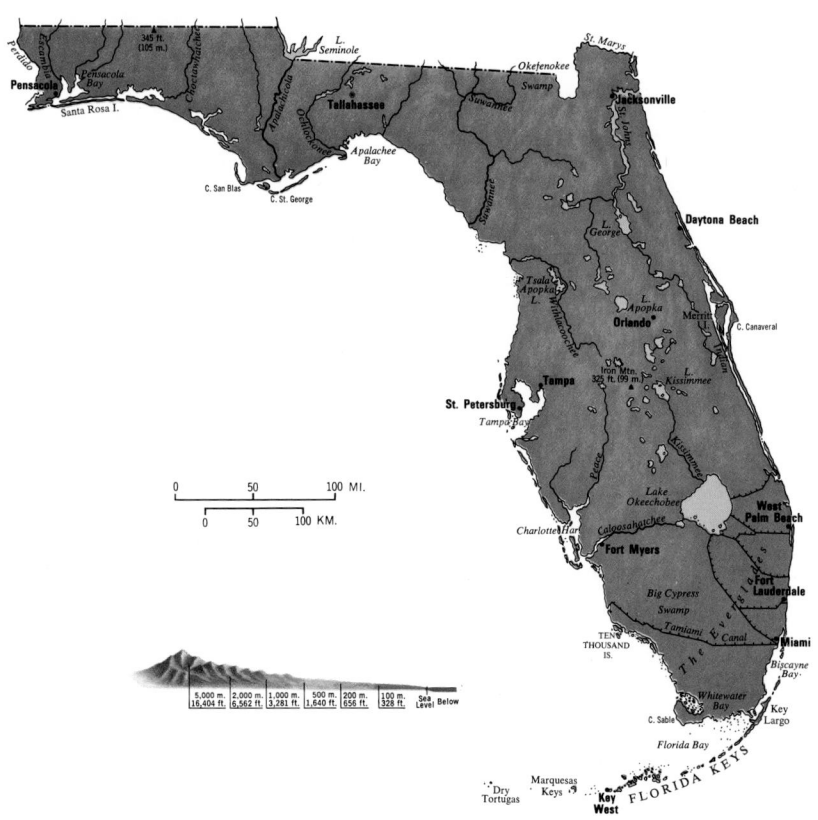

Daytona Beach 2,335	F2
Daytona Beach Shores 1,324	F2
De Bary 7,176	E3
De Funiak Springs▲ 5,120	C6
De Land▲ 16,491	E2
De Leon Springs 1,481	E2
Deer Park 250	F3
Deerfield Beach 46,325	F5
Delray Beach 47,181	F5
Deltona 50,828	E3
Destin 8,080	C6
Doctors Inlet 800	E1
Dover 2,606	D4
Dowling Park 250	C1
Dundee 2,335	E3
Dunedin 34,012	B2
Dunnellon 1,624	D2
Eagle Lake 1,758	E4
Earleton 350	D2
East Lake-Orient Park 6,171	C2
East Naples 22,951	E5
East Palatka 1,989	E2
Eastpoint 1,577	B2
Eatonville 2,170	E3
Ebro 255	C6
Edgewater 15,337	F3
Edgewood 1,062	E3
Egypt Lake 14,580	C2
El Portal 2,457	B4
Elfers 12,356	D3
Elkton 240	E2
Englewood 15,025	D5
Ensley 16,362	B6
Espanola 300	E2
Estero 3,177	E5
Esto 253	C5
Eustis 12,967	E3
Everglades City 524	E6
Fairbanks 300	D2
Fairfield 450	D2
Fanning Springs 493	C2
Felda 500	E5
Fellsmere 2,179	F4
Fernandina Beach▲ 8,765	E1
Five Points 1,136	D1
Flagler Beach 3,820	E2
Florahome 400	E2
Floral City 2,609	D3
Florida City 5,806	F6
Florida Ridge 12,218	F4
Foley 525	C1
Fort Denaud 600	E5
Fort Green 300	E4
Fort Lauderdale▲ 149,377	C4
Fort McCoy 600	E2
Fort Meade 4,976	E4
Fort Myers Beach 9,284	E5
Fort Myers▲ 45,206	E5
Fort Ogden 900	E4
Fort Pierce▲ 36,830	F4
Fort Walton Beach 21,471	C6
Fort White 268	D2
Fountain 900	D6
Freeport 843	C6
Frink 275	D6
Frostproof 2,808	E4
Fruitland Park 2,754	D3
Fruitville 9,808	D4
Gainesville▲ 84,770	D2
Geneva 1,120	E3
Georgetown 687	E2
Gibsonton 7,706	C3
Gifford 6,278	F4
Glen Saint Mary 462	D1
Glenwood 400	E2
Golden Beach 774	C4
Golden Gate 14,148	E5
Golf 234	F5
Gomez 400	F4
Gonzalez 7,669	B6
Goodland 600	E6
Goulding 4,159	B6
Goulds 7,284	F6
Graceville 2,675	D5
Graham 225	D2
Grand Ridge 536	A1
Grandin 250	E2
Grant 500	F4
Green Cove Springs▲ 4,497	E2
Greenacres City 18,683	F5
Greensboro 586	B1
Greenville 950	C1
Greenwood 474	A1
Gretna 1,981	B1
Grove City 2,374	D5
Groveland 2,300	E3
Gulf Breeze 5,530	B6
Gulf Hammock 325	D2
Gulf Harbors	D3
Gulf Stream 690	F5
Gulfport 11,727	B3
Haines City 11,683	E3
Hallandale 30,996	B4
Hampton 296	D2
Harlem 2,826	E5
Harold 500	B6

Hastings 595	E2
Havana 1,654	B1
Hawthorne 1,305	D2
Hernando 2,103	D3
Hialeah 188,004	B4
Hialeah Gardens 7,713	B4
High Point 2,288	B3
High Springs 3,144	D2
Highland Beach 3,209	F5
Highland City 1,919	E4
Highland Park 155	E4
Hiland Park 3,865	C6
Hilcrest Heights 221	E4
Hilliard 1,751	E1
Hillsboro Beach 1,748	F5
Hinson 250	B1
Hobe Sound 11,507	F4
Holder 350	D3
Holly Hill 11,141	E2
Hollywood 121,697	B4
Holmes Beach 4,810	D4
Holt 850	C6
Homestead 26,866	F6
Homosassa 2,113	D3
Homosassa Springs 6,271	D3
Horseshoe Beach 252	C2
Hosford 750	B1
Howey In The Hills 724	E3
Hudson 7,344	D3
Hurlburt	B6
Hypoluxo 830	F5
Immokalee 14,120	E5
Indialantic 2,844	F3
Indian Creek 44	B4
Indian Harbour Beach 6,933	F3
Indian River Shores 2,278	F4
Indian Rocks Beach 3,963	B3
Indian Shores 1,405	B3
Indiantown 4,794	F4
Inglis 1,241	D2
Intercession City 600	E3
Interlachen 1,160	E2
Inverness▲ 5,797	D3
Islamorada 1,220	F5
Islandia 13	F6
Jacksonville Beach 17,839	E1
Jacksonville▲ 672,971	E1
Jasmine Estates 17,136	D3
Jasper▲ 2,099	D1
Jay 666	B5
Jennings 712	C1
Jensen Beach 9,884	F4
June Park 4,080	F3
Juno Beach 2,121	F5
Jupiter 24,986	F5
Jupiter Island 549	F4
Kathleen 2,743	D3
Kenansville 650	F4
Kendall 87,271	B5
Kenneth City 4,462	B3
Key Biscayne 8,854	B5
Key Colony Beach 977	F7
Key Largo 11,336	F6
Key West▲ 24,832	D6
Keystone Heights 1,315	E2
Kinard 295	D6
Kissimmee▲ 30,050	E3
La Belle▲ 2,703	E5
La Crosse 122	D2
Lacoochee 2,072	D3
Lady Lake 8,071	E3
Lake Alfred 3,622	E3
Lake Buena Vista 1,776	E3
Lake Butler▲ 2,116	D1
Lake Carroll 13,012	C2
Lake City▲ 10,005	D1
Lake Como 340	E2
Lake Forest	B4
Lake Harbor 600	F5
Lake Helen 2,344	E3
Lake Jem 314	E3
Lake Magdalene 15,973	D3
Lake Mary 5,929	E3
Lake Monroe 500	E3
Lake Park 6,704	F5
Lake Placid 1,158	E4
Lake Wales 9,670	E4
Lake Worth 28,564	G5
Lakeland 70,576	D3
Lakeport 375	E4
Lakewood 7,211	C5
Land O'Lakes 7,892	D3
Lantana 8,392	F5
Largo 65,674	B3
Lauderdale Lakes 27,341	B3
Lauderdale-by-the-Sea 2,990	C3
Lauderhill 49,708	B3
Laurel 8,245	D4
Laurel Hill 543	C5
Lawtey 676	D1
Layton 183	F7
Lazy Lake 38	B3
Lecanto 1,243	D3
Lee 350	C1
Leesburg 14,903	E3

(continued on following page)

COUNTIES

Alachua 181,596	D2
Baker 18,486	D1
Bay 126,994	C6
Bradford 22,515	D2
Brevard 398,978	F3
Broward 1,255,488	F5
Calhoun 11,011	D6
Charlotte 110,975	E5
Citrus 93,515	D3
Clay 105,986	E2
Collier 152,099	E5
Columbia 42,613	D1
Dade 1,937,094	F6
De Soto 19,039	E4
Dixie 10,585	C2
Duval 672,971	E1
Escambia 262,798	B6
Flagler 28,701	E2
Franklin 8,967	B2
Gadsden 41,105	B1
Gilchrist 9,667	D2
Glades 7,591	E5
Gulf 11,504	D7
Hamilton 10,930	D1
Hardee 19,499	E4
Hendry 25,773	E5
Hernando 101,115	D3
Highlands 68,432	E4
Hillsborough 834,054	D4
Holmes 15,778	C5
Indian River 90,208	F4
Jackson 41,375	D5
Jefferson 11,296	C1
Lafayette 5,578	C2
Lake 152,104	E3
Lee 335,113	E5
Leon 192,493	B1
Levy 25,923	D2
Liberty 5,569	B1
Madison 16,569	C1

Manatee 211,707	D4
Marion 194,833	D2
Martin 100,900	F4
Monroe 78,024	E7
Nassau 43,941	E1
Okaloosa 143,776	C6
Okeechobee 29,627	F4
Orange 677,491	E3
Osceola 107,728	E3
Palm Beach 863,518	F5
Pasco 281,131	D3
Pinellas 851,659	D4
Polk 405,382	E4
Putnam 65,070	E2
Saint Johns 51,303	E2
Saint Lucie 87,182	F4
Santa Rosa 81,608	B6
Sarasota 277,776	D4
Seminole 287,529	E3
Sumter 31,577	D3
Suwannee 26,780	C1
Taylor 17,111	C1
Union 10,252	D1
Volusia 370,712	E2
Wakulla 14,202	B1
Walton 27,760	C6
Washington 16,919	C6

CITIES and TOWNS

Alachua 4,529	D2
Alford 472	D6
Altamonte Springs 34,879	E3
Altha 497	A1
Altoona 800	E3
Alturas 900	E4
Alva 1,036	E5
Anna Maria 1,744	D4
Anthony 500	D2
Apalachicola▲ 2,602	A2
Apollo Beach 6,025	C3
Apopka 13,512	E3

Arcadia▲ 6,488	E4
Archer 1,372	D2
Aripeka 450	D3
Astatula 981	E3
Astor 1,273	E2
Atlantic Beach 11,636	E1
Auburndale 8,858	E3
Avon Park 8,042	E4
Azalea Park 8,926	E3
Babson Park 1,125	E4
Bagdad 1,457	B6
Baker 500	C5
Bal Harbour 3,045	C4
Baldwin 1,450	E1
Barberville 500	E2
Bartow▲ 14,716	E4
Bascom 90	A1
Basinger 300	F4
Bay Harbor Islands 4,703	B4
Bay Lake	E3
Bay Pines 4,171	B3
Bayshore 17,062	E5
Bayshore Gardens 14,945	D4
Bee Ridge 6,406	D4
Bell 267	C2
Belle Glade 16,177	F5
Belle Glade Camp 1,616	F5
Belle Isle 5,272	E3
Belleair 3,968	B2
Belleair Beach 2,070	B2
Belleair Bluffs 2,128	B3
Belleair Shore 80	B3
Belleview 2,666	D2
Beverly Beach 312	E2
Biscayne Park 3,068	B4
Bithlo 4,834	E3
Blountstown▲ 2,404	A1
Boca Grande 900	D5
Boca Raton 61,492	F5
Bokeelia 750	D5
Bonifay▲ 2,612	C5
Bonita Sings 5,435	E5

Bostwick 500	E2
Boulogne	E1
Bowling Green 1,836	E4
Boynton Beach 46,194	F5
Bradenton Beach 1,657	D4
Bradenton▲ 43,779	D4
Bradley 1,108	E4
Branford 670	C2
Briny Breezes 400	G5
Bristol▲ 937	B1
Broadview Park-Rock Hill 6,022	B4
Bronson▲ 875	D2
Brooker 312	D2
Brooksville▲ 7,440	D3
Browardale 6,257	B4
Browns Village	B5
Bruce 221	C6
Bunche Park 4,388	B4
Bunnell▲ 1,873	E2
Bushnell▲ 1,998	D3
Callahan 946	E1
Callaway 12,253	D6
Campbellton 202	D5
Canal Point 900	F5
Candler 275	E2
Cantonment	B6
Cape Canaveral 8,014	F3
Cape Coral 74,991	E5
Carol City 53,331	B4
Carrabelle 1,200	B2
Caryville 631	C6
Cassadaga 325	E3
Casselberry 18,911	E3
Cedar Grove 1,479	D6
Cedar Key 668	C2
Center Hill 735	D3
Century 1,989	B5
Charlotte Harbor 3,327	D5
Chattahoochee 4,382	B1
Cherry Lake Farms 400	C1

Chiefland 1,917	D2
Chipley▲ 3,866	D6
Chokoloskee 600	E6
Christmas 800	E3
Cinco Bayou 322	B6
Citra 500	D2
Clarksville 350	D6
Clearwater▲ 98,784	B2
Clermont 6,910	E3
Cleveland 2,896	E5
Clewiston 6,085	E5
Cocoa 17,722	F3
Cocoa Beach 12,123	F3
Coconut Creek 27,485	F5
Coleman 857	D3
Compass Lake 296	D6
Concord 350	B1
Cooper City 20,791	B4
Copeland 350	E6
Coral Cove 2,042	F4
Coral Gables 40,091	B5
Coral Springs 79,443	F5
Cornwell 700	E4
Cortez 4,509	D4
Cottagehill 500	B6
Cottondale 900	D6
Crawfordville▲ 1,110	B1
Crescent City 1,859	E2
Crestview▲ 9,886	C6
Cross City▲ 2,041	C2
Crystal Lake 5,300	D3
Crystal River 4,044	D3
Crystal Springs 800	D3
Cutler Ridge 21,268	F6
Cypress 9,188	A1
Cypress Gardens 8,043	E4
Cypress Quarters 1,343	F4
Dade City▲ 5,633	D3
Dania 13,024	B4
Davenport 1,529	E3
Davie 47,217	B4
Day 61,921	C1

(continued)

Lehigh Acres 13,611 E5
Leisure City 19,379 F6
Leonia 350 C5
Leto 9,003 C2
Lighthouse Point 10,378 F5
Live Oak▲ 6,332 D1
Lloyd 500 C1
Lochloosa 400 E2
Longboat Key 5,937 D4
Longwood 13,316 E3
Lorida 950 E4
Loughman 1,214 E3
Lowell 250 D2
Loxahatchee 950 F5
Lutz 10,552 D3
Lynn Haven 9,298 C6
Macclenny▲ 3,966 D1
Madeira Beach 4,225 B3
Madison▲ 3,345 C1
Maitland 9,110 E3
Malabar 1,977 F3
Malone 765 A1
Mango 8,700 D4
Marathon 8,857 E7
Marco (Marco Island) 9,493 E6
Margate 42,985 F5
Marianna▲ 6,292 A1
Marineland 21 E2
Mary Esther 4,139 B6
Masaryktown 389 D3
Mascotte 1,761 E3
Mayo▲ 917 C1
McDavid 500 B5
McIntosh 411 D2
Medley 663 B4
Melbourne 59,646 F3
Melbourne Beach 3,021 F3
Melrose 6,477 D2
Melrose Park 5,672 B4
Memphis 6,760 D4
Merritt Island 32,886 F3
Mexico Beach 992 D6
Miami Beach 92,639 C5
Miami Lakes 12,750 B4
Miami Shores 10,084 B4
Miami Springs 13,268 B5
Miami▲ 358,548 B5
Micanopy 612 D2
Micco 8,757 F4
Miccosukee 300 B1
Middleburg 6,223 E1
Midway 852 B1
Milligan 950 C6
Milton▲ 7,216 B6
Mims 9,412 F3
Minneola 1,515 E3
Miramar 40,663 B4
Molino 1,207 B6
Montbrook 250 D2
Monticello▲ 2,573 C1
Montverde 890 E3
Moore Haven▲ 1,432 E5
Mossy Head 280 C6
Mount Dora 7,196 E3
Mulberry 2,988 E4
Murdock 272 D4
Myakka City 672 D4
Myrtle Grove 17,402 B6
Naples Park 8,002 E5
Naples▲ 19,505 E5
Naranja 5,790 F6
Neptune Beach 6,816 E1
New Port Richey 14,044 D3
New Smyrna Beach 16,543 F2
Newberry 1,644 D2
Niceville 10,507 C6
Nichols 300 E4
Nocatee 950 E4
Nokomis 3,448 D4
Noma 207 C5
Norland 22,109 B4
North Bay Village 5,383 B4
North Fort Myers 30,027 E5
North Lauderdale 26,506 B3
North Miami 49,998 B4
North Miami Beach 35,359 C4
North Naples 13,422 E5
North Palm Beach 11,343 F5
North Port 11,973 D4
North Redington Beach 1,135 B3
Oak Hill 917 F3
Oakland 700 E3
Oakland Park 1,743 B3
Ocala▲ 42,045 D2
Ocean Breeze Park 519 F4
Ocean Ridge 1,570 F5
Ochopee 750 E6
Ocoee 12,778 E3
Odessa 500 D3
Ojus 15,519 B4
Okahumpka 900 D3
Okeechobee▲ 4,943 F4
Oklawaha 700 E2
Old Town 850 C2
Oldsmar 8,361 B2
Olustee 400 D1
Ona E4
Oneco 6,417 D4
Opa Locka 14,460 B4
Orange 5,347 B1
Orange City 2,795 E3
Orange Lake 900 D2
Orange Park 9,488 E1
Orange Springs 500 E2
Orchid 10 F4
Orlando▲ 164,693 E3
Ormond Beach 29,721 E2
Ormond-by-the-Sea 7,665 E2
Osprey 2,597 D4
Osteen 875 E3
Otter Creek 136 D2
Oviedo 11,114 E3
Oxford D3
Ozona 900 D3
Pace 6,277 B6
Pahokee 6,822 F5
Palatka▲ 10,201 E2
Palm Bay 62,632 F3
Palm Beach 9,814 G5
Palm Beach Gardens 22,965 F5
Palm Beach Shores 1,040 G5
Palm City 3,925 F4
Palm Coast 14,287 E2
Palm Harbor 50,256 D3
Palm River-Clair Mel 14,447 C3
Palm Shores 210 F3
Palm Springs 9,763 F5
Palmetto 9,268 D4
Panacea 950 B1
Panama City Beach 4,051 C6
Panama City▲ 34,378 C6
Parker 4,598 C6
Parkland 3,558 F5
Parrish 950 D4
Paxton 600 C5
Pembroke Park 4,933 B4
Pembroke Pines 65,452 B4
Penney Farms 609 E2
Pennsuco 15 B4
Pensacola▲ 58,165 B6
Perrine 15,576 F6
Perry▲ 7,151 C1
Pierce 500 E4
Pierson 2,988 E2
Pine Hills 35,322 E3
Pineland 700 D5
Pinellas Park 43,426 D5
Placida 250 D5
Plant City 22,754 D3
Plantation 1,885 B4
Plymouth 950 E3
Polk City 1,439 E3
Pomona Park 663 E2
Pompano Beach 72,411 F5
Ponce Inlet 1,704 F2
Ponce de Leon 406 C6
Ponte Vedra Beach E1
Port Charlotte 41,535 D5
Port Mayaca 400 F5
Port Orange 35,317 F2
Port Richey 2,523 D3
Port Saint Joe 4,044 D6
Port Saint Lucie 55,866 F4
Port Salerno 7,786 F4
Portland 300 C6
Princeton 7,073 F6
Progress Village C3
Punta Gorda▲ 10,747 E5
Quincy▲ 7,444 B1
Raiford 198 D1
Raleigh 275 D2
Red Bay 300 C6
Reddick 554 D2
Redington Beach 1,626 B3
Redington Shores 2,366 B3
Richland 250 D3
Richmond Heights 8,583 F6
Riverland 5,919 B4
Riverview 6,478 D4
Riviera Beach 27,639 G5
Rockledge 16,023 F3
Roseland 1,379 F4
Round Lake 275 D6
Ruskin 6,046 C3
Safety Harbor 15,124 B2
Saint Augustine Beach 3,657 E2
Saint Augustine▲ 11,692 E2
Saint Catherine 486 D3
Saint Cloud 12,453 E3
Saint James City 1,904 D5
Saint Leo 1,009 D3
Saint Lucie 584 F4
Saint Marks 307 B1
Saint Petersburg 238,629 B3
Saint Petersburg Beach 9,200 B3
Samoset 3,119 D4
Samsula (Samsula-Spruce Creek) 3,404 E2
San Antonio 776 D3
San Mateo 975 E2
Sanderson 800 D1
Sanford▲ 32,387 E3
Sanibel 5,468 D5
Sarasota Springs 16,088 D4
Sarasota▲ 50,961 D4
Satellite Beach 9,889 F3
Satsuma 610 E2
Scottsmoor 900 F3
Sea Ranch Lakes 619 C3
Sebastian 10,205 F4
Sebring▲ 8,900 E4
Seffner 5,371 D4
Seminole 9,251 B3
Seville 500 E2
Sewalls Point 1,187 F4
Shalimar 341 C6
Sharpes 3,348 F3
Siesta Key 7,772 D4
Silver Springs 6,421 D2
Sneads 1,746 B1
Sopchoppy 367 B1
Sorrento 500 E3
South Bay 3,558 F5
South Daytona 12,482 F2
South Miami 10,404 B5
South Miami Heights 30,030 F6
South Pasadena 5,644 B3
South Patrick Shores 10,249 F3
South Venice 11,951 D4
Southport 1,992 C6
Sparr 902 D2
Springfield 8,715 D6
Starke▲ 5,226 D2
Steinhatchee 800 C2
Stuart▲ 11,936 F4
Summerfield 780 D2
Summerland Key 350 E7
Sun City 8,326 D4
Sun City Center 5,605 C3
Sunny Isles 11,772 C4
Sunnyside 1,008 C6
Sunrise 64,407 B4
Surfside 4,108 B4
Suwannee 365 C2
Sweetwater 13,909 B5
Switzerland 3,906 E1
Taft 900 E3
Tallahassee (cap.)▲ 124,773 B1
Tamarac 44,822 B3
Tampa▲ 280,015 C2
Tarpon Springs 17,906 D3
Tavares▲ 7,383 E3
Tavernier 2,433 F6
Telogia 400 B1
Temple Terrace 16,444 C2
Tequesta 4,499 F5
Terra Ceia 450 D4
Thonotosassa 900 D3
Tice 3,971 E5
Titusville▲ 39,394 F3
Town'n Country 60,946 B2
Treasure Island 7,266 B3
Trenton▲ 1,287 D2
Trilby 930 D3
Umatilla 2,350 E3
University 23,760 C2
Valparaiso 4,672 C6
Venice 16,922 D4
Venus 500 E4
Vernon 778 C6
Vero Beach▲ 17,350 F4
Villa Tasso 365 C6
Virginia Gardens 2,212 B5
Wabasso 1,145 F4
Wacissa 350 B1
Wakulla 225 B1
Waldo 1,017 D2
Walnut Hill 500 B5
Ward Ridge 104 D7
Warrington 16,040 B6
Watertown 3,340 D1
Wauchula▲ 3,253 E4
Wausau 313 D6
Waverly 2,071 E4
Webster 746 D3
Weeki Wachee 53 D3
Weirsdale 995 D3
Welaka 533 E2
Wellborn 500 D1
West Bay 500 C6
West Eau Gallie 2,591 F3
West Melbourne 8,399 F3
West Miami 5,727 B5
West Palm Beach▲ 67,643 F5
West Pensacola 22,107 B6
Westville 257 C6
Westwood Lakes 11,522 B5
Wewahitchka▲ 1,779 D6
White City 4,645 F4
White Springs 704 D1
Wildwood 3,421 D3
Williston 2,179 D2
Wilton Manors 11,804 B3
Wimauma 2,932 D4
Windermere 1,371 E3
Winter Beach 350 F4
Winter Garden 9,745 E3
Winter Haven 24,725 E3
Winter Park 22,242 E3
Winter Springs 22,151 E3
Woodville 2,760 B1
Worthington Springs 178 D2
Yalaha 1,168 E3
Yankeetown 635 D2
Youngstown 900 D6
Yulee 6,915 E1
Zellwood 1,760 E3
Zephyrhills 8,220 D3
Zolfo Springs 1,219 E4

OTHER FEATURES

Alapaha (riv.) C1
Alligator (lake) E3
Amelia (isl.) E1
Anastasia (isl.) E2
Anclote (keys) D3
Apalachee (bay) B2
Apalachicola (bay) B2
Apalachicola (riv.) A1
Apopka (lake) E3
Arbuckle (lake) E4
Aucilla (riv.) C1
Banana (riv.) F3
Beresford (lake) E3
Big Cypress (swamp) E5
Big Cypress Nat'l Preserve E5
Biscayne (bay) F6
Biscayne (key) B5
Biscayne Nat'l Park F6
Blackwater (riv.) B6
Blue Cypress (lake) F4
Boca Chica (key) E7
Boca Ciega (key) B3
Boca Grande (key) D7
Bryant (lake) E2
Caloosahatchee (riv.) E5
Canaveral (cape) F3
Captiva (isl.) D5
Casey (key) D4
Castillo de San Marcos Nat'l Mon. E2
Cecil Field Naval Air Sta. E1
Charlotte (harb.) D5
Chattahoochee (riv.) B1
Chipola (riv.) D6
Choctawhatchee (riv.) C6
Crescent (lake) E2
Cumberland Island Nat'l Seashore E1
Cypress (lake) E3
De Soto Nat'l Mem. D4
Dead (lake) D6
Dexter (lake) E2
Dog (isl.) B2
Dorr (lake) E2
Dry Tortugas (keys) D7
Dumfoundling (bay) C4
East (pt.) E6
Eglin A.F.B 8,347 C6
Egmont (key) D4
Elliott (key) F6
Escambia (riv.) B6
Estero (isl.) E5
Eureka (res.) E2
Everglades, The (swamp) F6
Everglades Nat'l Park E6
Fenholloway (riv.) C1
Florida (bay) F6
Florida (cape) F6
Florida (keys) E7
Florida (strs.) F7
Fort Caroline Nat'l Mem. E1
Fort Jefferson Nat'l Mon. C7
Fort Matanzas Nat'l Mon. E2
Gasparilla (isl.) D5
George (lake) E2
Grassy (key) F7
Gulf Islands Nat'l Seashore B6
Harney (lake) F3
Hart (lake) E3
Hillsborough (bay) C3
Hillsborough (canal) F5
Hillsborough (riv.) C2
Homestead A.F.B 5,153 F6
Homosassa (isls.) D3
Iamonia (lake) B1
Indian (riv.) F3
Iron (mt.) E4
Istokpoga (lake) E4
Jackson (lake) B1
Jackson (lake) E4
Jacksonville Naval Air Sta. E1
John F. Kennedy Space Center F3
June in Winter (lake) E4
Kerr (lake) E2
Key Largo (key) F6
Key Vaca (key) E7
Key West Naval Air Sta. E7
Kissimmee (lake) E4
Kissimmee (riv.) E4
Largo (key) F6
Levy (lake) D2
Lochloosa (lake) D2
Long (key) B3
Long (key) F7
Longboat (key) D4
Lower Matecumbe (key) F7
Lowery (lake) E3
MacDill A.F.B. C3
Manatee (riv.) D4
Marco (isl.) E6
Marian (lake) E4
Marquesas (keys) D7
Matanzas (inlet) E2
Mayport Naval Air Sta. E1
McCoy A.F.B. E3
Merritt (isl.) F3
Mexico (gulf) C4
Miami (canal) F5
Miami (riv.) B5
Miccosukee (lake) B1
Monroe (lake) E3
Mosquito (lag.) F3
Mullet (key) D4
Myakka (riv.) D4
Nassau (riv.) E1
Nassau (sound) E1
New (riv.) B1
New (riv.) D1
Newnans (lake) D2
North Merritt (isl.) F3
North New River (canal) F5
Ochlockonee (riv.) B1
Okaloacoochee Slough (swamp) E5
Okeechobee (lake) F5
Okefenokee (swamp) D1
Oklawaha (riv.) E2
Old Rhodes (key) F6
Old Tampa (bay) B3
Olustee (riv.) D1
Orange (lake) D2
Patrick A.F.B. F3
Peace (riv.) E4
Pensacola (bay) B6
Pensacola Naval Air Sta. B6
Perdido (riv.) B6
Pine (isl.) D5
Pine Island (sound) D5
Pinellas (pt.) B3
Piney (isl.) B1
Piney (pt.) C2
Placid (lake) E4
Plantation (key) F7
Poinsett (lake) F3
Ponce de Leon (bay) E6
Port Everglades (harb.) C4
Poet Tampa (harb.) B3
Raccoon (pt.) D3
Reedy (lake) E4
Romano (cape) E6
Sable (cape) E6
Saint Andrew (pt.) D6
Saint George (cape) A2
Saint George (isl.) B2
Saint George (sound) B2
Saint Johns (riv.) E2
Saint Joseph (bay) D6
Saint Joseph (pt.) D6
Saint Lucie (canal) F4
Saint Lucie (inlet) F4
Saint Marys (riv.) D1
Saint Marys Entrance (inlet) E1
Saint Vincent (isl.) D7
San Blas (cape) D7
Sand (key) B3
Sands (key) F6
Sanibel (isl.) D5
Santa Fe (lake) D2
Santa Fe (riv.) D2
Santa Rosa (isl.) B6
Santa Rosa (sound) B6
Sarasota (pt.) D4
Seminole (lake) B1
Seminole Ind. Res. E4
Seminole Ind. Res. E5
Shark (pt.) E6
Shoal (riv.) C6
Snake Creek (canal) B4
South New River (canal) F5
Stafford (lake) D2
Sugarloaf (key) E7
Suwannee (riv.) C2
Suwannee (sound) C2
Talbot (isl.) E1
Talquin (lake) B1
Tamiami (canal) E5
Tampa (bay) D4
Ten Thousand (isls.) E6
Torch (key) E7
Treasure (isl.) B3
Tsala Apopka (lake) D3
Tyndall A.F.B. C6
Upper Matecumbe (key) F7
Vaca (key) E7
Virginia (key) B5
Waccasassa (bay) D2
Waccasassa (riv.) D2
Washington (lake) F3
Weir (lake) E2
Weohyakapka (lake) E4
West Palm Beach (canal) F5
Whitewater (bay) F6
Whiting Field Naval Air Sta. B6
Wimico (lake) A2
Winder (lake) F3
Withlacoochee (riv.) C1
Withlacoochee (riv.) D2
Yale (lake) E3
Yellow (riv.) B6

▲County seat

Agriculture, Industry and Resources

Pensacola
Jacksonville
Orlando
Tampa
St. Petersburg
W. Palm Beach
Miami

DOMINANT LAND USE

- Fruit, Truck & Mixed Farming
- Truck & Mixed Farming
- Truck Farming
- Cotton, Tobacco, Hogs, Peanuts
- Peanuts, General Farming
- General Farming, Forest Products, Truck Farming, Cotton
- Livestock Grazing
- Forests
- Swampland, Limited Agriculture
- Urban Areas
- Nonagricultural Land

MAJOR MINERAL OCCURRENCES

Cl Clay
Ls Limestone
O Petroleum
P Phosphates
Pe Peat
Ti Titanium
Zr Zirconium

Water Power
Major Industrial Areas

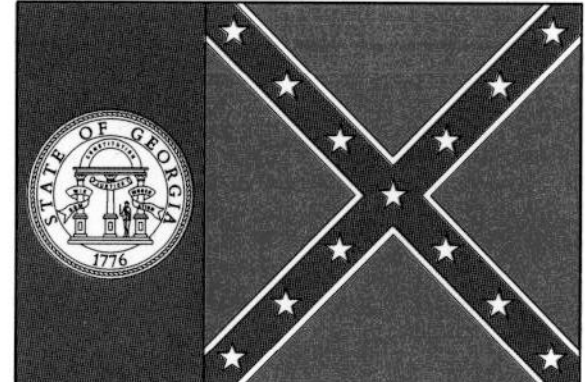

AREA 58,910 sq. mi. (152,577 sq. km.)
POPULATION 6,508,419
CAPITAL Atlanta
LARGEST CITY Atlanta
HIGHEST POINT Brasstown Bald 4,784 ft. (1458 m.)
SETTLED IN 1733
ADMITTED TO UNION January 2, 1788
POPULAR NAME Empire State of the South; Peach State
STATE FLOWER Cherokee Rose
STATE BIRD Brown Thrasher

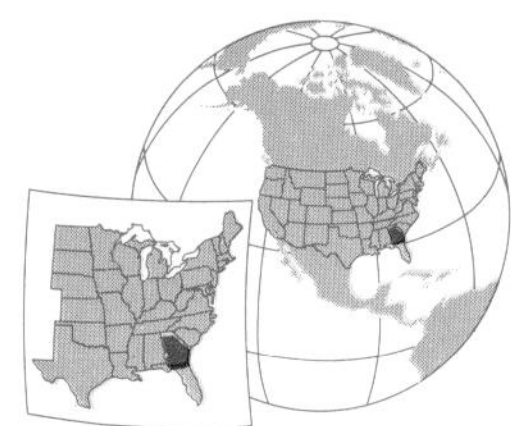

COUNTIES

Appling 15,744 H7
Atkinson 6,213 G8
Bacon 9,566 G7
Baker 3,615 D8
Baldwin 39,530 F4
Banks 10,308 E2
Barrow 29,721 E2
Bartow 55,911 C2
Ben Hill 16,245 F7
Berrien 14,153 F8
Bibb 149,967 E5
Bleckley 10,430 F6
Brantley 11,077 J8
Brooks 15,398 E9
Bryan 15,438 K6
Bulloch 43,125 J6
Burke 20,579 J4
Butts 15,326 E4
Calhoun 5,013 C7
Camden 30,167 J9
Candler 7,744 H6
Carroll 71,422 B3
Catoosa 42,464 B1
Charlton 8,496 H9
Chatham 216,935 K6
Chattahoochee 16,934 C6
Chattooga 22,242 B1
Cherokee 90,204 D2
Clarke 87,594 F3
Clay 3,364 B7
Clayton 182,052 D3
Clinch 6,160 G9
Cobb 447,745 C3
Coffee 29,592 G8
Colquitt 36,645 E8
Columbia 66,031 H3
Cook 13,456 F8
Coweta 53,853 C4
Crawford 8,991 E5
Crisp 20,011 E7
Dade 13,147 A1
Dawson 9,429 D2
De Kalb 483,024 D3
Decatur 25,511 C9
Dodge 17,607 F6
Dooly 9,901 E6
Dougherty 96,311 D7
Douglas 71,120 C3
Early 11,854 C8
Echols 2,334 G9
Effingham 25,687 K6
Elbert 18,949 G2
Emanuel 20,546 H5
Evans 8,724 J6
Fannin 15,992 D1
Fayette 62,415 C4
Floyd 81,251 B2
Forsyth 44,083 D2
Franklin 16,650 F2
Fulton 648,951 D3
Gilmer 13,368 D1
Glascock 2,357 G4
Glynn 62,496 J8
Gordon 35,072 C2
Grady 20,279 D9
Greene 11,793 F3
Gwinnett 352,910 D2
Habersham 27,621 E1
Hall 95,428 E2
Hancock 8,908 G4
Haralson 21,966 B3
Harris 17,788 C5
Hart 19,712 G2
Heard 8,628 B4
Henry 58,741 D4
Houston 89,208 E6
Irwin 8,649 F7
Jackson 30,005 E2
Jasper 8,453 E4
Jeff Davis 12,032 G7
Jefferson 17,408 H4
Jenkins 8,247 J5
Johnson 8,329 G5
Jones 20,739 E5
Lamar 13,038 D4
Lanier 5,531 F8
Laurens 39,988 G6
Lee 16,250 D7
Liberty 52,745 J7
Lincoln 7,442 H3
Long 6,202 J7
Lowndes 75,981 F9
Lumpkin 14,573 D1
Macon 13,114 D6
Madison 21,050 F2
Marion 5,590 C6
McDuffie 20,119 H4
McIntosh 8,634 K7
Meriwether 22,411 C4
Miller 6,280 C8
Mitchell 20,275 D8
Monroe 17,113 E4
Montgomery 7,163 G6
Morgan 12,883 F3
Murray 26,147 C1
Muscogee 179,278 C6
Newton 41,808 E3
Oconee 17,618 F3
Oglethorpe 8,929 F3
Paulding 41,611 C3
Peach 21,189 E5
Pickens 14,432 D2
Pierce 13,328 H8
Pike 10,224 D4
Polk 33,815 B3
Pulaski 8,108 E6
Putnam 14,137 F4
Quitman 2,209 B7
Rabun 11,648 F1
Randolph 8,023 C7
Richmond 189,719 H4
Rockdale 54,091 D3
Schley 3,588 D6
Screven 13,842 J5
Seminole 9,010 C9
Spalding 54,457 D4
Stephens 23,257 F1
Stewart 5,654 C6
Sumter 30,228 D6
Talbot 6,524 C5
Taliaferro 1,915 G3
Tattnall 17,722 H6
Taylor 7,642 D5
Telfair 11,000 G7
Terrell 10,653 D7
Thomas 38,986 E9
Tift 34,998 E7
Toombs 24,072 H6
Towns 6,754 E1
Treutlen 5,994 G6
Troup 55,536 B4
Turner 8,703 E7
Twiggs 9,806 F5
Union 11,993 E1
Upson 26,300 D5
Walker 58,340 B1
Walton 38,586 E3
Ware 35,471 H8
Warren 6,078 G4
Washington 19,112 G4
Wayne 22,356 J7
Webster 2,263 C6
Wheeler 4,903 G6
White 13,006 E1
Whitfield 72,462 B1
Wilcox 7,008 F7
Wilkes 10,597 G3
Wilkinson 10,228 F5
Worth 19,745 E8

CITIES and TOWNS

Abbeville▲ 907 F7
Acworth 4,519 C2
Adairsville 2,131 C2
Adel▲ 5,093 F8
Adrian 615 G5
Ailey 579 G6
Alamo▲ 855 G6
Alapaha 812 F8
Albany▲ 78,122 D7
Aldora 127 D4
Allenhurst 594 J7
Allentown 273 F5
Alma▲ 3,663 G7
Alpharetta 13,002 D2
Alston 160 H6
Alto 651 E2
Alvaton 91 C4
Ambrose 288 G7
Americus▲ 16,512 D6
Andersonville 277 D6
Appling▲ 150 H3
Arabi 433 E7
Aragon 902 B2
Arcade 697 E2
Arco 6,189 J8
Argyle 206 G8
Arlington 1,513 C8
Armuchee 600 B2
Arnoldsville 275 F3
Ashburn▲ 4,827 E7
Athens▲ 45,734 F3
Atlanta (cap.)▲ 394,017 K1
Attapulgus 380 D9
Auburn 3,139 E2
Augusta▲ 44,639 J4
Austell 4,173 J1
Avalon 159 F1
Avera 215 G4
Avondale Estates 2,209 L1
Baconton 623 D8
Bainbridge▲ 10,712 C9
Baldwin 1,439 E2
Ball Ground 905 D2
Barnesville▲ 4,747 D4
Barney 146 E8
Bartow 292 G5
Barwick 385 E9
Baxley▲ 3,841 H7
Bellville 192 H6
Belvedere 18,089 L1
Benevolence 138 C7
Berkeley Lake 791 D3
Berlin 480 E8
Bethlehem 348 E3
Between 82 E3
Bibb City 597 B5
Bishop 158 F3
Blackshear▲ 3,263 H8
Blairsville▲ 564 E1
Blakely▲ 5,595 C8
Bloomingdale 2,271 K6
Blue Ridge▲ 1,336 D1
Bluffton 138 C7
Blythe 300 H4
Bogart 1,018 E3
Boston 1,395 E9
Bostwick 307 E3
Bowdon 1,981 B3
Bowersville 311 F2
Bowman 791 G2
Box Springs 518 C5
Braselton 418 E2
Braswell 247 C3
Bremen 4,356 B3
Brinson 238 C9
Bronwood 513 D7
Brookfield 600 F8
Brookhaven K1
Brooklet 1,013 J6
Brooks 328 D4
Broxton 1,211 G7
Brunswick▲ 16,433 K8
Buchanan▲ 1,009 B3
Buckhead 176 F3
Buena Vista▲ 1,472 D6
Buford 8,771 D2
Butler▲ 1,673 D5
Byromville 452 E6
Byron 2,276 E5
Cadwell 458 G6
Cairo▲ 9,035 D9
Calhoun▲ 7,135 C1
Calvary 500 D9
Camak 220 G4
Camilla▲ 5,008 D8
Campton E3
Canon 737 F2
Canton▲ 4,817 C2
Carl 263 E3
Carlton 282 F2
Carnesville▲ 514 F2
Carrollton▲ 16,029 C3
Carters 12,035 C1
Cartersville▲ 9,247 C2
Cataula 500 C5
Cave Spring 950 B2
Cecil 376 F8
Cedar Grove A1
Cedartown▲ 7,978 B2
Center 3,251 F2
Centerville 2,622 E5
Centralhatchee 301 B4
Chalybeate Springs 265 C5
Chamblee 7,668 K1
Charles H6
Chatsworth▲ 2,865 C1
Chauncey 312 F6
Chester 1,072 F6
Chickamauga 2,149 B1
Chula 500 E7
Clarkesville▲ 1,151 F1
Clarkston 5,385 L1
Claxton▲ 2,464 J6
Clayton▲ 1,613 F1
Clermont 402 E2
Cleveland▲ 1,653 E1
Climax 226 D9
Clyattville 500 F9
Cobb 338 E7
Cobbtown 494 H6
Cochran▲ 4,390 F6
Cohutta 529 C1
Colbert 443 F2
Coleman 137 C7
Colemans Lake H5
College Park 20,457 K2
Collins 528 H6
Colquitt▲ 1,991 C8
Columbus▲ 179,278 C6
Comer 939 F2
Commerce 4,108 E2
Concord 211 D4
Conley 5,528 K2
Constitution K2
Conyers▲ 7,380 D3
Coolidge 610 E8
Coosa 600 B2
Cordele▲ 10,321 E7
Corinth 136 B4
Cornelia 3,219 E1
Cotton 122 D8
Covington▲ 10,026 E3
Crandall C1
Crawford 694 F3
Crawfordville▲ 577 G3
Crosland E8
Crystal Springs 500 B2
Culloden 242 D5
Cumming▲ 2,828 D2
Cusseta▲ 1,107 C6
Cuthbert▲ 3,730 C7
Dacula 2,217 E3
Dahlonega▲ 3,086 D1
Daisy 138 J6
Dallas▲ 2,810 C3
Dalton▲ 21,761 C1
Damascus 290 C8
Danielsville▲ 318 F2
Danville 480 F5
Darien▲ 1,783 K8
Dasher 659 F9
Davisboro 407 G5
Dawson▲ 5,295 D7
Dawsonville▲ 467 D2
De Soto 258 D7
Dearing 547 H4
Decatur▲ 17,336 K1
Deenwood 2,055 H8
Deepstep 111 G4
Demorest 1,088 F1
Denton 335 G7
Dexter 475 G6
Dickey C7
Dillard 199 F1
Dixie 259 E9
Dock Junction (Arco) J8
Doerun 899 E8
Donalsonville▲ 2,761 C8
Dooling 28 E6
Doraville 7,626 K1
Douglas▲ 10,464 G7
Douglasville▲ 11,635 C3
Dry Branch 700 F5
Du Pont 177 G9
Dublin▲ 16,312 G5
Ducktown D2
Dudley 430 F5
Duluth 9,029 D2
Dunwoody 26,302 K1
Durand 206 C5
East Dublin 2,524 G5
East Ellijay 303 C1
East Juliette E4
East Newnan 1,173 C4
East Point 34,402 K2
Eastman▲ 5,153 F6
Eastville E3
Eatonton▲ 4,737 F4
Eden 990 K6
Edge Hill 22 G4
Edison 1,182 C7
Elberta 1,559 E5
Elberton▲ 5,682 G2
Elizabeth 950 J1
Ellabell 500 K6
Ellaville▲ 1,724 D6
Ellenton 227 E8
Ellenwood L2
Ellerslie 700 C5
Ellijay▲ 1,178 C1
Emerson 1,201 C2
Enigma 611 F8
Ephesus 324 B4

(continued on following page)

Agriculture, Industry and Resources

DOMINANT LAND USE

- Specialized Cotton
- Cotton, General Farming
- Cotton, Tobacco, Hogs, Peanuts
- Peanuts, General Farming
- General Farming, Livestock, Fruit, Tobacco
- General Farming, Forest Products, Cotton, Truck Farming
- Forests
- Swampland, Limited Agriculture
- Urban Areas

MAJOR MINERAL OCCURRENCES

- Al Bauxite
- Ba Barite
- C Coal
- Cl Clay
- Fe Iron Ore
- Gn Granite
- Mi Mica
- Mn Manganese
- Mr Marble
- Sl Slate
- Tc Talc
- Ti Titanium

Water Power

Major Industrial Areas

Eton 315 ...C1
Euharlee 850 ...C2
Evans 13,713 ...H3
Experiment 3,762 ...D4
Fair Oaks 6,996 ...J1
Fairburn 4,013 ...J2
Fairmount 657 ...C2
Fargo 800 ...G9
Farmington ...F3
Farrar ...E4
Fayetteville▲ 5,827 ...C4
Felton 500 ...B3
Finleyson 101 ...F6
Fitzgerald▲ 8,612 ...F7
Fleming 279 ...K7
Flemington 440 ...K7
Flippen 600 ...D3
Flovilla 602 ...E4
Flowery Branch 1,251 ...E2
Floyd ...J1
Folkston▲ 2,285 ...H9
Forest Park 16,925 ...K2
Forsyth▲ 4,268 ...E4
Fort Gaines▲ 1,248 ...C7
Fort Oglethorpe 5,880 ...B1
Fort Valley▲ 8,198 ...E5
Franklin Springs 475 ...F2
Franklin▲ 876 ...B4
Funston 248 ...E8
Gainesville▲ 17,885 ...E2
Garden City 7,410 ...K6
Garfield 255 ...H5
Gay 133 ...C4
Geneva 182 ...C5
Georgetown▲ 913 ...B7
Gibson▲ 679 ...G4
Gillsville 113 ...E2
Gilmore ...J1
Girard 195 ...J4
Glenn 3,676 ...B4
Glennville 4,144 ...J7
Glenwood 824 ...G6
Glenwood 881 ...L1
Glynco ...J8
Good Hope 181 ...E3
Gordon 2,468 ...F5
Grantville 1,180 ...C4
Gray▲ 2,189 ...F4
Grayson 529 ...E3
Graysville 193 ...B1
Greensboro▲ 2,860 ...F3
Greenville▲ 1,167 ...C4
Griffin▲ 21,347 ...D4
Grovetown 3,596 ...H4
Gumbranch 291 ...J7
Guyton 740 ...K6
Haddock 800 ...F4
Hagan 787 ...J6
Hahira 1,353 ...F9
Hamilton▲ 454 ...C5

Hampton 2,694 ...D4
Hapeville 5,483 ...K2
Haralson 139 ...C4
Hardwick (Midway-Hardwick) 8,977 ...F4
Harlem 2,199 ...H4
Harrison 414 ...G5
Hartwell▲ 4,555 ...G2
Hawkinsville▲ 3,527 ...E6
Hazlehurst▲ 4,202 ...G7
Helen 300 ...E1
Helena 1,256 ...G6
Hephzibah 2,466 ...H4
Hiawassee▲ 547 ...E1
Higgston 274 ...G6
Hilltonia 402 ...H5
Hinesville▲ 21,603 ...J7
Hiram 1,389 ...C3
Hoboken 440 ...H8
Hogansville 2,976 ...C4
Holly Springs 2,406 ...D2
Homeland 981 ...H9
Homer▲ 742 ...F2
Homerville▲ 2,560 ...G8
Hoschton 642 ...E2
Howell ...F9
Hull 156 ...F2
Ideal 554 ...D6
Ila 297 ...F2
Indian Springs 1,273 ...E4
Industrial City 1,054 ...C1
Inman 500 ...D4
Iron City 503 ...C8
Irwinton▲ 641 ...F5
Ivey 1,053 ...F5
Jackson▲ 4,076 ...E4
Jacksonville 128 ...G7
Jakin 137 ...C8
Jasper▲ 1,772 ...D2
Jefferson▲ 2,763 ...E2
Jeffersonville▲ 1,545 ...F5
Jenkinsburg 213 ...E4
Jersey 149 ...E3
Jesup▲ 8,958 ...J7
Jonesboro▲ 3,635 ...D4
Juliette 600 ...E4
Junction City 182 ...C5
Juno 522 ...D4
Kennesaw 8,936 ...C2
Keysville 284 ...H4
Kingsland 4,699 ...J9
Kingston 616 ...C2
Kite 297 ...G5
Knoxville▲ 75 ...E5
La Fayette▲ 6,313 ...B1
La Grange▲ 25,597 ...B4
Lake City 2,733 ...K2
Lake Park 500 ...F9
Lakeland▲ 2,467 ...F8

Lavonia 1,840 ...F2
Lawrenceville▲ 16,848 ...D3
Leary 701 ...C8
Lebanon 800 ...D2
Leesburg▲ 1,452 ...D7
Leland ...J1
Lenox 783 ...F8
Leslie 445 ...D7
Lexington▲ 230 ...F3
Lilburn 9,301 ...D3
Lilly 138 ...E6
Lincoln Park 1,755 ...D4
Lincolnton▲ 1,476 ...G3
Lindale 4,187 ...B2
Linwood 342 ...B1
Lithia Springs 11,403 ...C3
Lithonia 2,448 ...D3
Lizella 975 ...E5
Locust Grove 1,681 ...D4
Loganville 3,180 ...E3
Lollie ...G6
Lone Oak 161 ...C4
Lookout Mountain 1,636 ...B1
Louisville▲ 2,429 ...H4
Lovejoy 754 ...D4
Lovett ...G5
Ludowici▲ 1,291 ...J7
Lula 1,018 ...E2
Lumber City 1,429 ...G7
Lumpkin▲ 1,250 ...C6
Luthersville 741 ...C4
Lyerly 493 ...B2
Lyons▲ 4,502 ...H6
Mableton 25,725 ...J1
Macon▲ 106,612 ...E5
Madison▲ 3,483 ...F3
Manassas 123 ...H6
Manchester 4,104 ...C5
Mansfield 341 ...E4
Marietta▲ 44,129 ...J1
Marlow 500 ...K6
Marshallville 1,457 ...D6
Martin 243 ...F2
Martinez 33,731 ...H3
Matthews ...H4
Maxeys 180 ...F3
Maysville 728 ...E2
McCaysville 1,065 ...D1
McDonough▲ 2,929 ...D4
McIntosh 500 ...K7
McIntyre 552 ...F5
McRae▲ 3,007 ...G6
Meansville 250 ...D4
Mechanicsville ...L1
Meigs 1,120 ...D8
Meldrim 510 ...K6
Menlo 538 ...B2
Merrillville ...E9
Metcalf ...E9
Metter▲ 3,707 ...H6

Middleton ...G2
Midville 620 ...H5
Midway 863 ...K7
Milan 1,056 ...G6
Milledgeville▲ 17,727 ...F4
Millen▲ 3,808 ...J5
Milner 321 ...D4
Milstead ...D3
Mineral Bluff 153 ...D1
Mitchell 181 ...G4
Modoc ...H5
Molena 439 ...D4
Monroe▲ 9,759 ...E3
Montezuma 4,506 ...E6
Monticello▲ 2,289 ...E4
Montrose 117 ...F5
Moreland 366 ...C4
Morgan▲ 252 ...D7
Morganton 295 ...D1
Morrow 5,168 ...K2
Morven 536 ...E9
Moultrie▲ 14,865 ...E8
Mount Airy 543 ...F1
Mount Berry ...B2
Mount Bethel ...K1
Mount Vernon▲ 1,914 ...G6
Mount Zion 511 ...B3
Mountain City 784 ...F1
Mountain Park 554 ...D2
Mountain View ...K2
Mountville 168 ...C4
Murrayville 550 ...E2
Nahunta▲ 1,049 ...H8
Nashville▲ 4,782 ...F8
Naylor 111 ...F9
Nelson 486 ...D2
New Holland 950 ...E2
Newborn 404 ...E3
Newington 319 ...J5
Newnan▲ 12,497 ...C4
Newton▲ 703 ...D8
Nicholls 1,003 ...G7
Nicholson 555 ...F2
Norcross 5,947 ...D3
Norman Park 711 ...E8
Normantown ...H6
North Canton 950 ...C2
North High Shoals 268 ...F3
Norwood 238 ...G4
Nunez 135 ...H5
Oak Park 269 ...H6
Oakfield 113 ...E7
Oakman 150 ...C1
Oakwood 1,464 ...E2
Ochlocknee 588 ...E9
Ocilla▲ 3,182 ...F7
Oconee 234 ...G5
Odessadale 142 ...C5
Odum 388 ...H7
Oglethorpe▲ 1,302 ...D6

Ohoopee ...H6
Oliver 242 ...J5
Omaha 116 ...C6
Omega 912 ...E8
Orchard Hill 239 ...D4
Oxford 1,945 ...E3
Palmetto 2,612 ...C3
Panthersville 9,874 ...L1
Parrott 140 ...D7
Patterson 626 ...H8
Pavo 774 ...E9
Payne 192 ...E5
Peachtree City 19,027 ...C4
Pearson▲ 1,714 ...G8
Pelham 3,869 ...D8
Pembroke▲ 1,503 ...J6
Pendergrass 298 ...E2
Penfield ...F3
Perry▲ 9,452 ...E6
Phillipsburg 1,044 ...E8
Piedmont ...D4
Pine Lake 810 ...D3
Pine Mountain 875 ...C5
Pine Park ...E9
Pinehurst 388 ...E6
Pineora 387 ...K6
Pineview 594 ...F6
Pitts 214 ...F6
Pittsburg ...L1
Plainfield 128 ...F6
Plains 716 ...D6
Plainville 231 ...B2
Pocotaligo ...F2
Pooler 4,453 ...K6
Port Wentworth 4,012 ...K6
Portal 522 ...J5
Porterdale 1,278 ...E3
Poulan 962 ...E8
Powder Springs 6,893 ...C3
Preston▲ 388 ...C6
Primrose 30 ...A4
Pulaski 264 ...J6
Putney 3,108 ...D8
Quitman▲ 5,292 ...E9
Raleigh ...C5
Ranger 153 ...C2
Ray City 603 ...F8
Rayle 107 ...G3
Rebecca 148 ...E7
Red Oak 953 ...J2
Register 195 ...J6
Reidsville▲ 2,469 ...H6
Remerton 463 ...F9
Reno ...D9
Rentz 364 ...G5
Resaca 410 ...C1
Rest Haven 176 ...E2
Reynolds 1,166 ...D5
Rhine 466 ...F7
Riceboro 745 ...K7

Richland 1,668 ...C6
Richmond Hill 2,934 ...K7
Riddleville 79 ...G5
Rincon 2,697 ...K6
Ringgold▲ 1,675 ...B1
Riverdale 9,359 ...K2
Riverside 74 ...B2
Riverside 99 ...E8
Roberta▲ 939 ...D5
Rochelle 1,510 ...F7
Rockmart 3,356 ...B2
Rocky Face 500 ...C1
Rocky Ford 197 ...J5
Rocky Mount 56 ...C4
Rome▲ 30,326 ...B2
Roopville 248 ...B4
Rossville 3,601 ...B1
Roswell 47,923 ...D2
Royston 2,758 ...F2
Ruckersville ...F2
Russell 871 ...E3
Rutledge 659 ...E3
Saint George 600 ...H9
Saint Marks 36 ...C4
Saint Marys 8,187 ...J9
Saint Simons Island 12,026 ...K8
Sale City 324 ...D8
Sandersville▲ 6,290 ...G5
Sandy Springs 67,842 ...K1
Santa Claus 154 ...H6
Sardis 1,116 ...J5
Sargent 800 ...C4
Sasser 335 ...D7
Savannah▲ 137,560 ...L6
Scotland 244 ...G6
Scott 8,636 ...H5
Scottdale 8,770 ...L1
Screven 819 ...H7
Sea Island 600 ...K8
Senoia 956 ...C4
Seville 209 ...E7
Shady Dale 180 ...E4
Shannon 1,703 ...B2
Sharon 94 ...G3
Sharpsburg 224 ...C4
Shellman 1,162 ...C7
Shiloh 329 ...C5
Siloam 329 ...F3
Silver Creek 500 ...B2
Six Flags Over Georgia ...J1
Sky Valley 187 ...F1
Smithonia ...F2
Smithville 804 ...D7
Smyrna 30,981 ...K1
Snellville 12,084 ...D3
Social Circle 2,755 ...E3
Soperton▲ 2,797 ...G6
Sparks 1,205 ...F8
Sparta▲ 1,710 ...F4
Spring Place 246 ...C1
Springfield▲ 1,415 ...K6
Stapleton 330 ...H4
Statenville▲ 700 ...G9
Statesboro▲ 15,854 ...J6
Statham 1,360 ...E3
Stillmore 615 ...H6
Stockbridge 3,359 ...D3
Stockton 532 ...G9
Stone Mountain 6,494 ...D3
Stonewall 950 ...J2
Sugar Hill 4,557 ...C1
Sugar Valley ...C1
Summertown 153 ...H5
Summerville▲ 5,025 ...B2
Sumner 209 ...E7
Sunny Side 215 ...D4
Surrency 253 ...H7
Suwanee 2,412 ...D2
Swainsboro▲ 7,361 ...H5
Sycamore 417 ...E7
Sylvania▲ 2,871 ...J5
Sylvester▲ 5,702 ...E7
Talbotton▲ 1,046 ...D5
Talking Rock 62 ...D1
Tallapoosa 2,805 ...B3
Tallulah Falls 147 ...F1
Talmo 189 ...E2
Tarrytown 130 ...H6
Tate 950 ...D2
Taylorsville 269 ...C2
Tazewell ...D6
Tell ...J2
Temple 1,870 ...B3
Tennille 1,552 ...G5
The Rock 88 ...D5
Thomaston▲ 9,127 ...D5
Thomasville▲ 17,457 ...E9
Thomson▲ 6,862 ...H4
Thunderbolt 2,786 ...K6
Tifton▲ 14,215 ...F8
Tiger 301 ...F1
Tignall 711 ...G3
Toccoa▲ 8,266 ...F1
Toco Hills ...K1
Toomsboro 617 ...F5
Towns ...G7
Trenton▲ 1,994 ...A1
Trion 1,661 ...B1
Tunnel Hill 970 ...C1
Turin 189 ...C4
Twin City 1,466 ...H5
Ty Ty 579 ...E8
Tybee Island 2,842 ...L6
Tyrone 2,724 ...C4
Unadilla 1,620 ...E6
Union City 8,375 ...J2
Union Point 1,753 ...F3
Unionville 2,710 ...F8
Uvalda 561 ...H6
Valdosta▲ 39,806 ...F9
Van Wert 303 ...B3
Vanna ...F2
Varnell 358 ...C1
Vernonburg 74 ...K7
Vidalia 11,078 ...H6
Vidette ...H4

Vienna▲ 2,708 ...E6
Villa Rica 6,542 ...C3
Vinings 7,417 ...K1
Waco 461 ...B3
Wadley 2,473 ...H5
Waleska 700 ...D2
Walnut Grove 458 ...E3
Walthourville 2,024 ...J7
Waresboro 582 ...H8
Warm Springs 407 ...C5
Warner Robins 43,726 ...E5
Warrenton▲ 2,056 ...G4
Warwick 501 ...E7
Watkinsville▲ 1,600 ...E3
Waverly 769 ...J8
Waverly Hall 913 ...C5
Waycross▲ 16,410 ...H8
Waynesboro▲ 5,701 ...J4
Welcome All ...J2
Wesley ...H6
West Point 3,571 ...B5
Weston 42 ...C7
Whigham 605 ...D9
White 542 ...C2
White Plains 286 ...F4
White Sulphur Springs 118 ...C5
Whitesburg 643 ...B4
Willacoochee 1,205 ...G8
Williamson 295 ...D4
Wilmington Island 11,230 ...L7
Winder▲ 7,373 ...E3
Winterville 886 ...F3
Woodbine▲ 1,212 ...J9
Woodbury 1,429 ...C5
Woodland 552 ...D5
Woodstock 4,361 ...D2
Woodville 415 ...F3
Woolsey 120 ...D4
Wrens 2,414 ...H4
Wrightsville▲ 2,331 ...G5
Yatesville 409 ...D5
Young Harris 604 ...E1
Zebulon▲ 1,035 ...D4

OTHER FEATURES

Alapaha (riv.) ...F7
Allatoona (lake) ...C2
Altamaha (riv.) ...H7
Andersonville Nat'l Hist. Site ...D6
Atlanta Naval Air Sta. ...J1
Banks (lake) ...F9
Bartletts Ferry (dam) ...B5
Blackshear (lake) ...E7
Blue Ridge (mts.) ...D1
Brasstown Bald (mt.) ...E1
Burton (lake) ...E1
Carters (lake) ...C1
Chattahoochee (riv.) ...B8
Chattahoochee River Nat'l Rec. Area ...K1
Chattooga (riv.) ...A2
Chattooga (riv.) ...F1
Chatuge (lake) ...E1
Chickamauga and Chattanooga Nat'l Mil. Park ...B1
Coosa (riv.) ...A2
Coosawattee (riv.) ...C1
Cumberland (isl.) ...K9
Cumberland Island Nat'l Seashore ...K9
Dobbins A.F.B. ...J1
Doboy (sound) ...K8
Etowah (riv.) ...C2
Flint (riv.) ...D8
Fort Benning ...B6
Fort Frederica Nat'l Mon. ...K8
Fort Gordon 9,140 ...H4
Fort McPherson ...K1
Fort Pulaski Nat'l Mon. ...L6
Fort Stewart 13,774 ...J7
Goat Rock (lake) ...B5
Harding (lake) ...B5
Hartwell (lake) ...G2
Jekyll (isl.) ...K8
Jimmy Carter Nat'l Hist. Site ...D6
Kennesaw Mtn. Nat'l Battlefield Park ...J1
Martin Luther King, Jr., Nat'l Hist. Site ...K1
Moody A.F.B. 1,288 ...F9
Morgan Falls (dam) ...K1
Nottely (lake) ...D1
Ochlockonee (riv.) ...10
Ocmulgee (riv.) ...E5
Ocmulgee Nat'l Mon. ...F5
Oconee (riv.) ...F5
Ogeechee (riv.) ...J5
Okefenokee (swamp) ...H9
Oliver (lake) ...B5
Oostanaula (riv.) ...B2
Ossabaw (sound) ...K7
Rabun (lake) ...E1
Robins A.F.B. 3,092 ...F5
Saint Andrew (sound) ...K9
Saint Catherines (isl.) ...K7
Saint Mary's (riv.) ...J9
Saint Simons (isl.) ...K8
Sapelo (isl.) ...K8
Satilla (riv.) ...G8
Savannah (riv.) ...K5
Sea (isls.) ...K9
Seminole (lake) ...B9
Sidney Lanier (lake) ...D2
Sinclair (lake) ...F4
Skidaway (isl.) ...L7
Springer (mt.) ...D1
Strom Thurmond (lakes) ...H3
Suwannee (riv.) G ...10
Walter F. George (res.) ...B7
Wassaw (sound) ...L7
West Point (lake) ...B4

▲County seat

Scale: 0 — 40 — 80 MI. / 0 — 40 — 80 KM.

Elevation key: 5,000 m. (16,404 ft.); 2,000 m. (6,562 ft.); 1,000 m. (3,281 ft.); 500 m. (1,640 ft.); 200 m. (656 ft.); 100 m. (328 ft.); Sea Level; Below

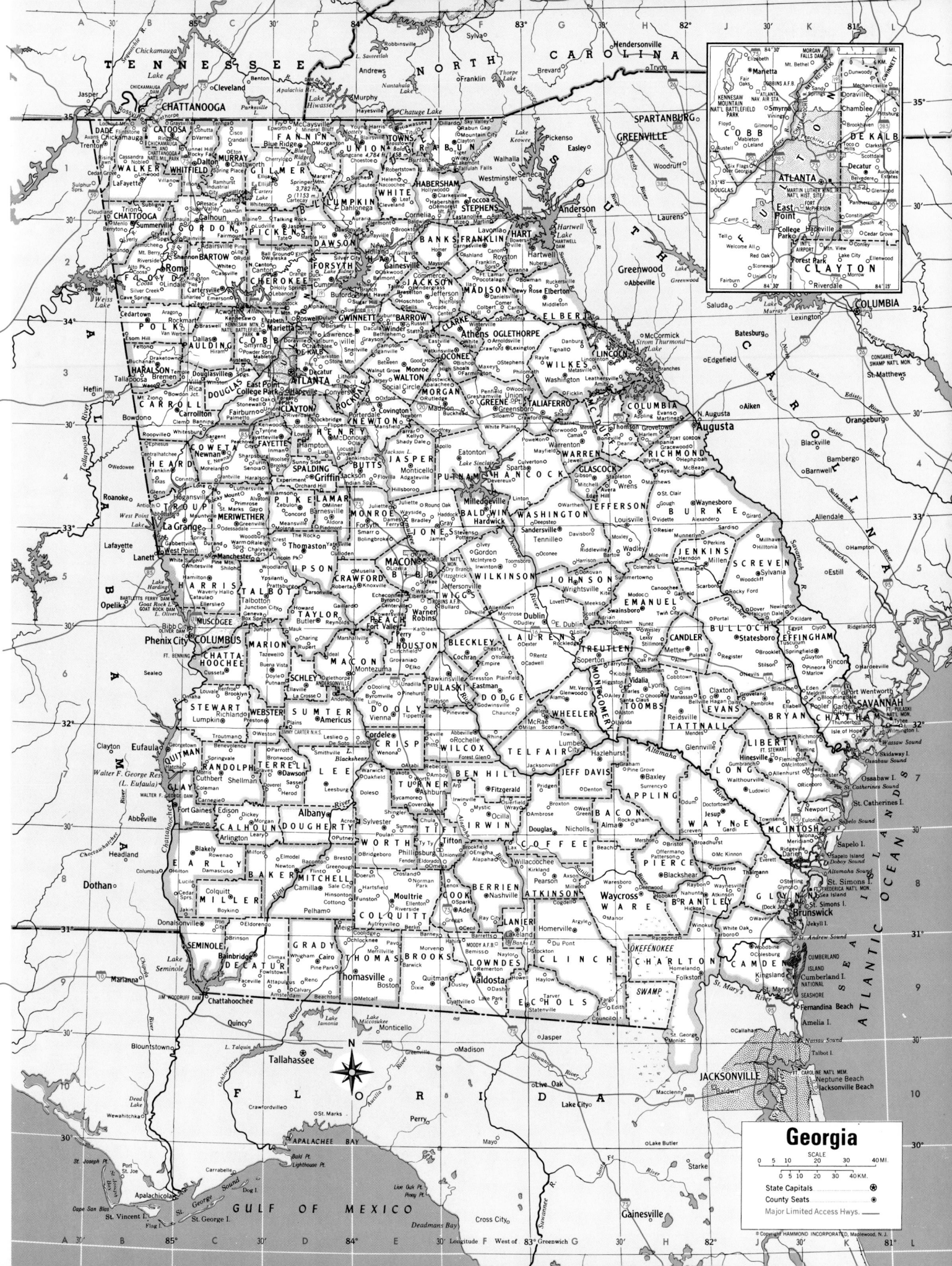

Georgia

SCALE

0 5 10   20   30   40 MI.

0 5 10   20   30   40 KM.

State Capitals .... ✪

County Seats .... ●

Major Limited Access Hwys. _____

© Copyright HAMMOND INCORPORATED, Maplewood, N. J.

COUNTIES

Hawaii 120,317	K7
Honolulu 836,231	D3
Kalawao 130	G1
Kauai 51,177	A1
Maui 100,374	J1

CITIES and TOWNS

Aiea 8,906	B3
Aina Haina	F2
Ala Moana	C4
Anahola 1,181	C1
Barbers Point 2,218	E2
Captain Cook 2,595	G5
Eleele 1,489	C2
Ewa 14,315	A4
Ewa Beach 14,369	A4
Haena 200	C1
Haiku 4,509	J2
Haina 333	H3
Hakalau	J4
Halawa Heights	B3
Halawa, Hawaii 50	J1
Haleiwa 2,442	E1
Halfway House 150	H6
Haliimaile 841	J2
Hana 683	K2
Hanalei 461	C1
Hanamaulu 3,611	C1
Hanapepe 1,395	C2
Hauula 3,479	E1
Hawaii 924	G3
Hawaii National Park 250	J6
Hawi 924	G3
Hickam Housing 6,553	B4
Hilo▲ 37,808	J5
Holualoa 3,834	G5
Honaunau 2,373	G6
Honohina 125	J4
Honokaa 2,186	H4
Honokahua 309	H1
Honokohau 200	G5
Honokohau 309	J1
Honolulu (cap.)▲ 365,272	C4
Honomu 532	J4
Honouliuli 600	A3
Hoolehua	A2
Huehue 100	G5
Hulopoe Bay	H2
Huumalu 50	H5
Iroquois Point 4,188	A4
Iwilei	C4
Kaaawa 1,138	E1
Kaanapali 579	H2
Kahakuloa 75	J1
Kahala	D5
Kahaluu 3,068	E2
Kahana 200	E1
Kahuku 2,063	E1
Kahului 16,889	J2
Kailua (Kailua Kona), Hawaii 9,126	F5
Kailua Kona	F5
Kailua, Oahu 36,818	F2
Kaimuki	D4
Kainaliu 512	G5
Kalae 150	G1
Kalaheo 3,592	C2
Kalaoa 4,490	G5
Kalapana 75	J6
Kalaupapa▲ 170	G1
Kalihi 435	C4
Kamalo 60	H1
Kamuela 1,179	G3
Kaneohe 35,448	F2
Kapaa 8,149	C1
Kapaahu 850	J6
Kapaau 1,083	G3
Kapalama	C4
Kapoho 300	K5
Kapulena 125	H4
Kaumakani 803	C2
Kaumalapau Harbor	G2
Kaunakakai 2,658	G1
Kaupakulua 600	K2
Kaupo 65	K2
Kawaihae 50	G4
Kawailoa 200	E1
Keaau 1,584	J5
Kealakekua 1,453	G5
Kealia 550	G6
Kealia, Kauai 300	D1
Keanae 280	K2
Keauhou	F5
Kekaha 3,506	B2
Keokea 500	K2
Keokea 750	J2
Kihei 11,107	J2
Kilauea 1,685	C1
Kipahulu 75	K2
Koali 60	K2
Kohala (Kapaau)	F2
Kokomo 500	K2
Koloa 1,791	C2
Koloa Landing	C2
Kualapuu 1,661	G1
Kukaiau 75	H4
Kukuihaele 316	H3
Kula 800	J2
Kunia 75	B3
Kurtistown 910	J5
Lahaina 9,073	H2
Laie 5,577	E1
Lanai City 2,400	H2
Laupahoehoe 508	J4
Lawai 1,787	C2
Lihue▲ 5,536	C2
Lower Paia 1,500	J1
Maalaea 443	J2
Maili 6,059	D2
Makaha 7,990	D2
Makakilo 9,828	E2
Makaiwa	B2
Makapala	J4
Makawao 5,405	K2
Makaweli 500	B2
Makena 100	J2
Makiki	B4
Mana	B2
Manele Bay	G2
Maunaloa 405	G1
Maunawili 4,847	F2
Mililani Town 29,359	E2
Milolii 120	C2
Moiliili	C4
Mokapu 11,615	F2
Mokuleia 1,776	D1
Mountain View 3,075	J5
Naalehu 1,027	H7
Nanakuli 9,575	D2
Napili-Honokowai 4,332	H1
Ninole 75	J4
Olowalu 750	H2
Ookala 401	J4
Opihikao 125	K6
Paauhau 350	H4
Paauilo 620	H4
Pacific Heights 5,305	C4
Pacific Palisades	E2
Pahala 1,520	H6
Pahoa 1,027	J5
Paia 2,091	J2
Papa 1,634	G6
Papaaloa	J4
Papaikou 1,567	J5
Paukaa 495	J5
Pauwela 468	K2
Peahi 308	K2
Pearl City 30,993	B3
Pepeekeo 1,813	J4
Poipu 975	C2
Princeville 1,244	C1
Puako 397	G4
Puhi 1,210	C2
Pukalani 5,879	J2
Punaluu 672	H7
Puuanahulu 56	G4
Puuiki 75	K2
Puunene 572	J2
Puunui	C4
Puuwai 200	A2
Schofield Barracks 19,597	E2
Spreckelsville 350	J1
Sunset Beach	E1
Ulumalu 201	K2
Ulupalakua 75	J2
Volcano 1,516	J6
Wahiawa 17,386	E2
Waiakoa	J2
Waialae	D4
Waialua, Oahu 3,943	E1
Waianae 8,758	D2
Waihee 4,004	J2
Waikane 717	E2
Waikapu 729	J2
Waikiki 50	H4
Waikiki	C4
Wailea, Hawaii 150	J4
Wailea-Makena, Maui 3,799	J2
Wailua 2,018	D2
Wailuku▲ 10,688	J2
Waimalu 29,967	B3
Waimanalo 3,508	F2
Waimanalo Beach 4,185	F2
Waimea (Kamuela), Hawaii 1,840	G3
Waimea 200	E1
Waimea, Kauai 5,972	B2
Wainaku 1,243	J5
Wainiha 175	C1
Waipio 11,812	H3
Waipio Acres 5,304	E2
Whitmore Village 3,373	E1

OTHER FEATURES

Alalakeiki (chan.)	J3

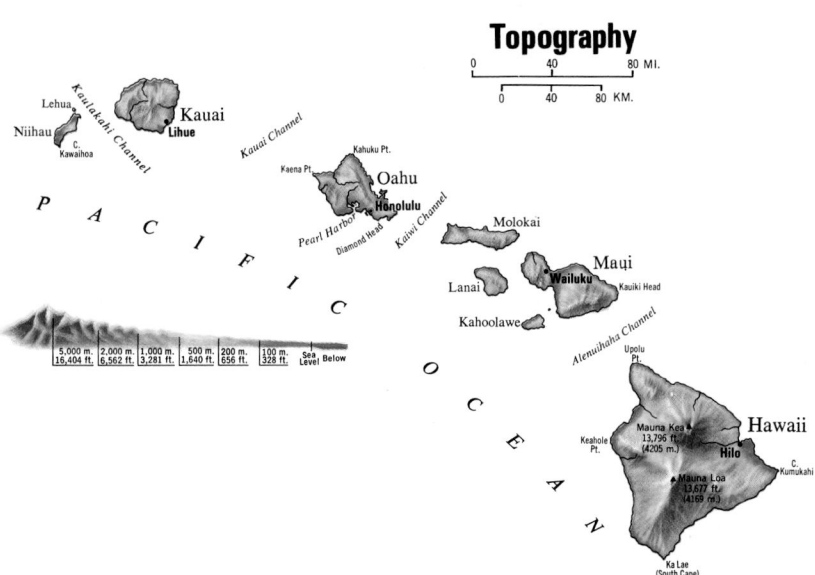

Topography

0 40 80 MI.
0 40 80 KM.

5,000 m. | 2,000 m. | 1,000 m. | 500 m. | 200 m. | 100 m. | Sea Level | Below
16,404 ft. | 6,562 ft. | 3,281 ft. | 1,640 ft. | 656 ft. | 328 ft.

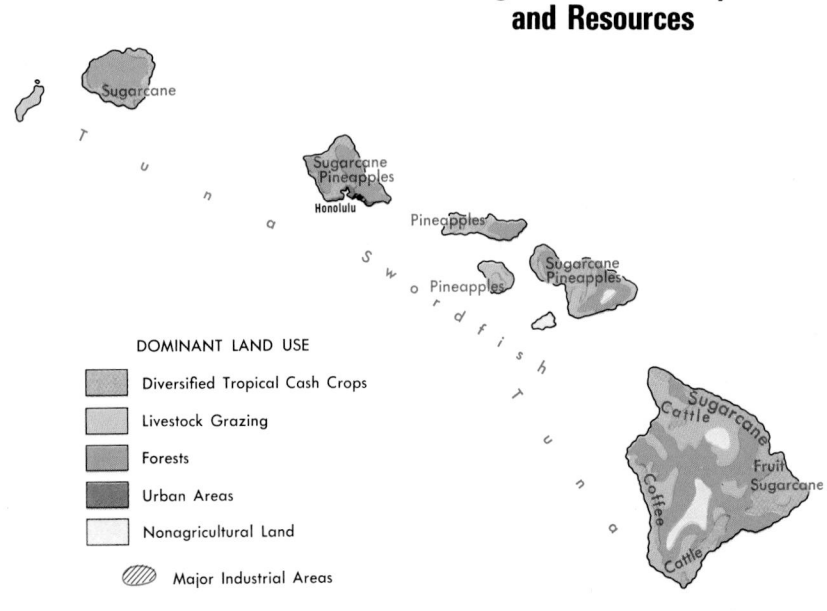

Agriculture, Industry and Resources

DOMINANT LAND USE

- Diversified Tropical Cash Crops
- Livestock Grazing
- Forests
- Urban Areas
- Nonagricultural Land

Major Industrial Areas

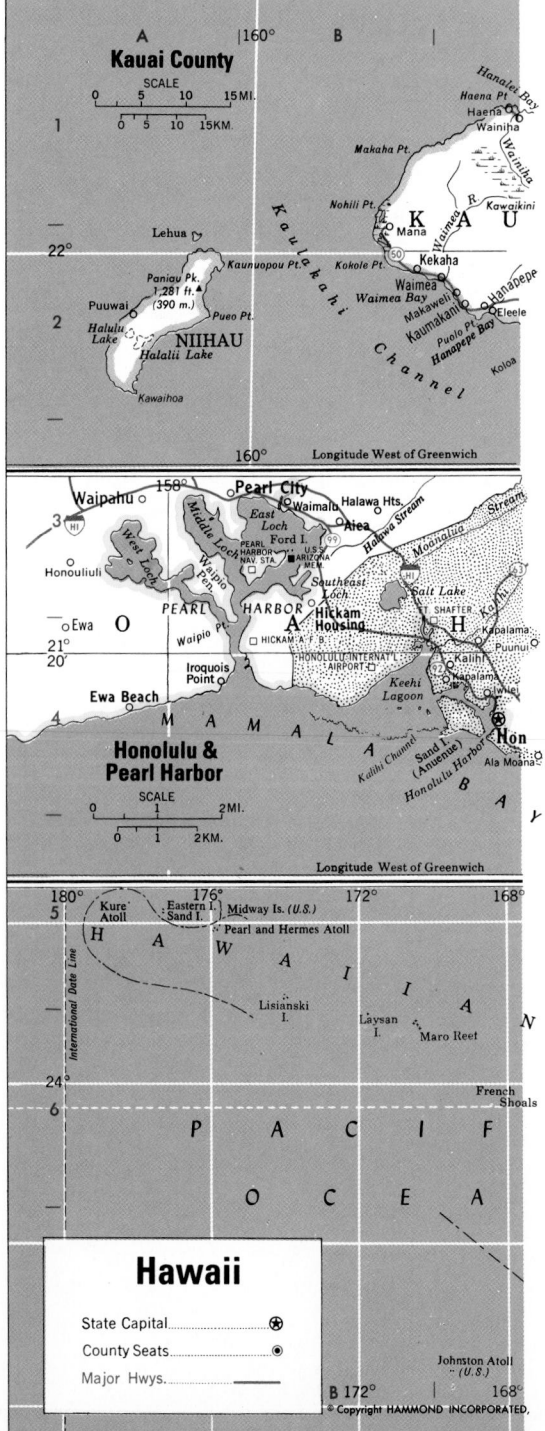

Kauai County

SCALE
0 5 10 15 MI.
0 5 10 15 KM.

Longitude West of Greenwich

Honolulu & Pearl Harbor

SCALE
0 1 2 MI.
0 1 2 KM.

Longitude West of Greenwich

Hawaii

State Capital .... ✪
County Seats .... ⊛
Major Hwys. ——

© Copyright HAMMOND INCORPORATED

▲County seat

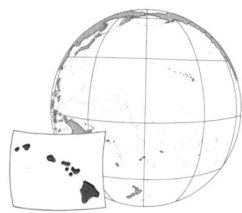

HAWAII

AREA 6,471 sq. mi. (16,760 sq. km.)
POPULATION 1,115,274
CAPITAL Honolulu
LARGEST CITY Honolulu
HIGHEST POINT Mauna Kea 13,796 ft. (4205 m.)
SETTLED IN —
ADMITTED TO UNION August 21, 1959
POPULAR NAME Aloha State
STATE FLOWER Hibiscus
STATE BIRD Nene (Hawaiian Goose)

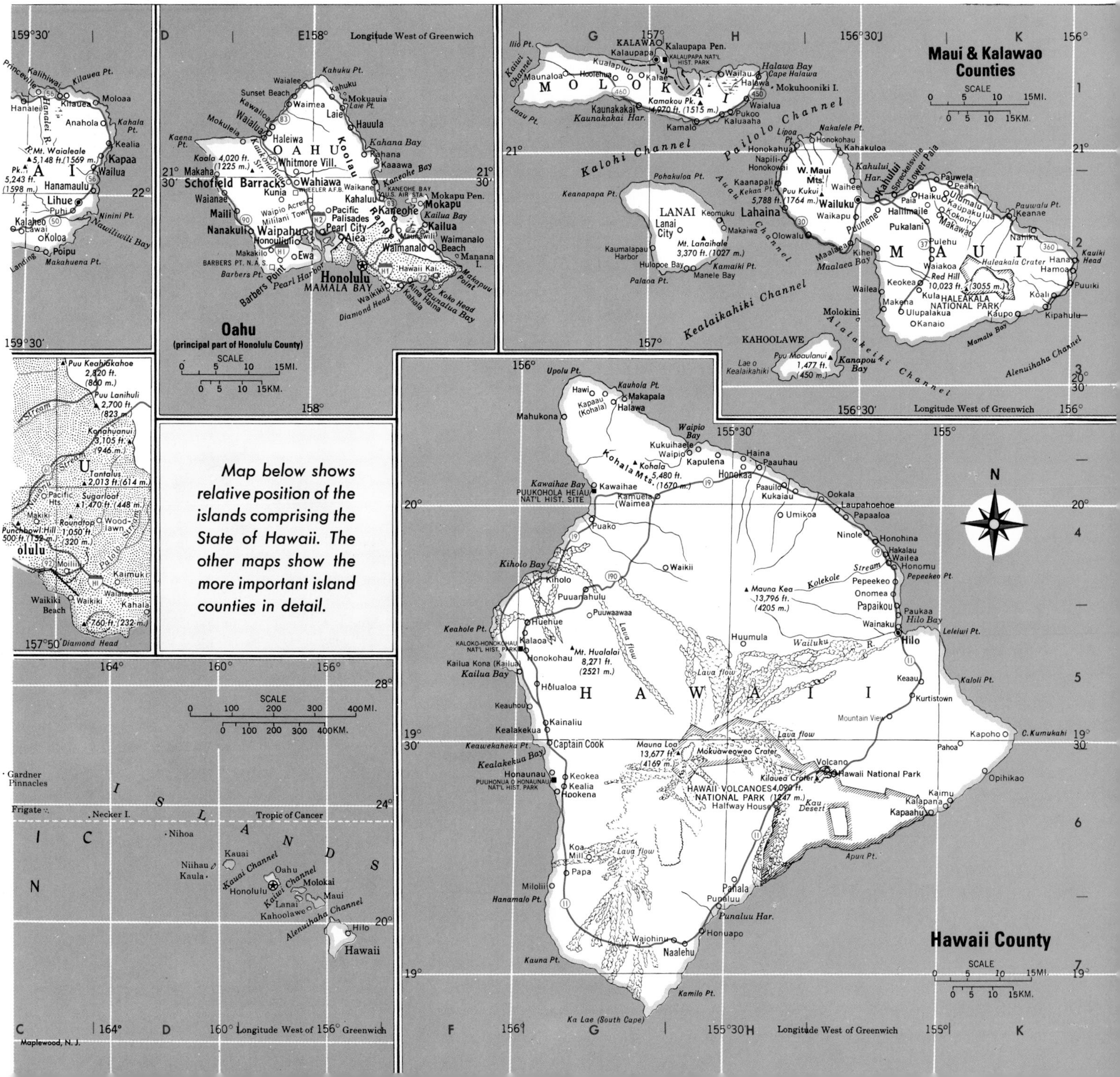

Map below shows relative position of the islands comprising the State of Hawaii. The other maps show the more important island counties in detail.

Maplewood, N.J.

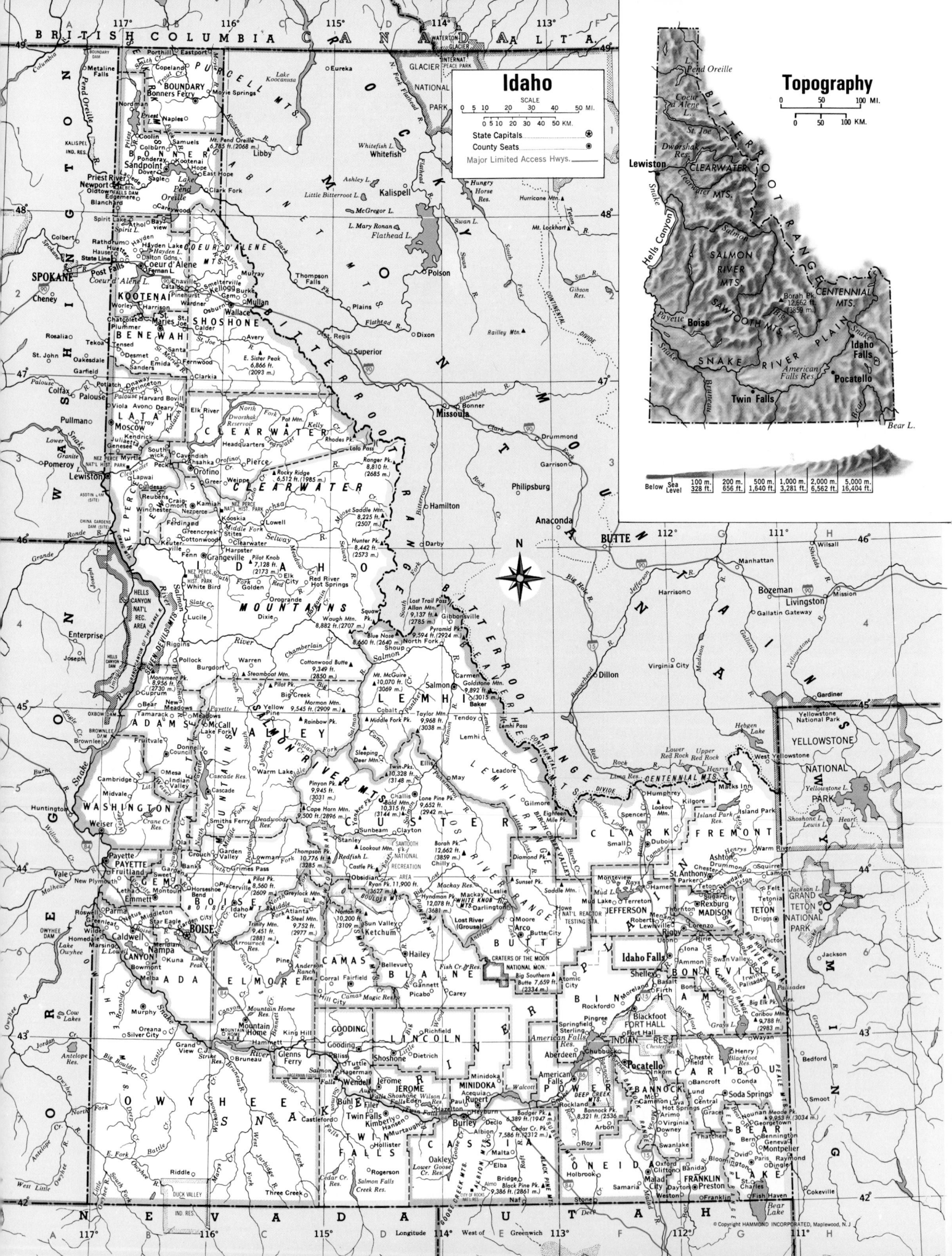

Idaho

SCALE
0 5 10   20   30   40   50 MI.
0 5 10 20 30 40 50 KM.

State Capitals .... ⊗
County Seats .... ◉
Major Limited Access Hwys. _____

Topography

0   50   100 MI.
0   50   100 KM.

Below Sea Level	100 m. 328 ft.	200 m. 656 ft.	500 m. 1,640 ft.	1,000 m. 3,281 ft.	2,000 m. 6,562 ft.	5,000 m. 16,404 ft.

© Copyright HAMMOND INCORPORATED, Maplewood, N.J.

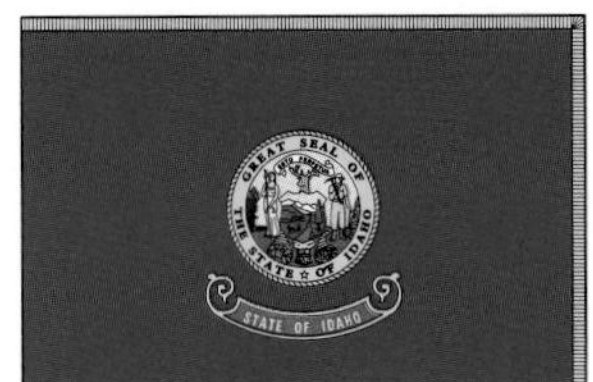
STATE OF IDAHO

AREA 83,564 sq. mi. (216,431 sq. km.)
POPULATION 1,011,986
CAPITAL Boise
LARGEST CITY Boise
HIGHEST POINT Borah Pk. 12,662 ft. (3859 m.)
SETTLED IN 1842
ADMITTED TO UNION July 3, 1890
POPULAR NAME Gem State
STATE FLOWER Syringa
STATE BIRD Mountain Bluebird

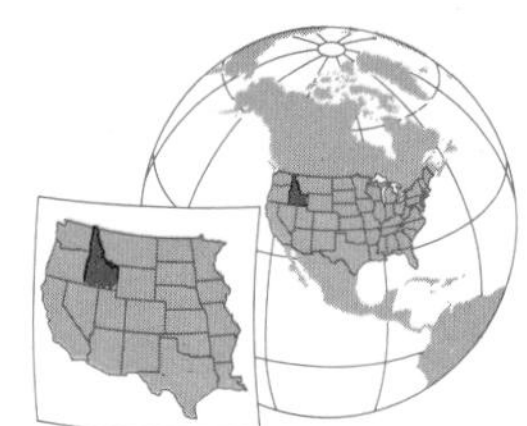

COUNTIES

Ada 205,775 .... B6
Adams 3,254 .... B5
Bannock 66,026 .... F7
Bear Lake 6,084 .... G7
Benewah 7,937 .... B2
Bingham 37,583 .... F6
Blaine 13,552 .... D6
Boise 3,509 .... C6
Bonner 26,622 .... B1
Bonneville 72,207 .... G6
Boundary 8,332 .... B1
Butte 2,918 .... E6
Camas 727 .... D6
Canyon 90,076 .... B6
Caribou 6,963 .... G7
Cassia 19,532 .... E7
Clark 762 .... F5
Clearwater 8,505 .... C3
Custer 4,133 .... D5
Elmore 21,205 .... C6
Franklin 9,232 .... G7
Fremont 10,937 .... G5
Gem 11,844 .... B6
Gooding 11,633 .... D6
Idaho 13,783 .... C4
Jefferson 16,543 .... F6
Jerome 15,138 .... D7
Kootenai 69,795 .... B2
Latah 30,617 .... B3
Lemhi 6,899 .... D4
Lewis 3,516 .... B3
Lincoln 3,308 .... D6
Madison 23,674 .... G6
Minidoka 19,361 .... E7
Nez Perce 33,754 .... B3
Oneida 3,492 .... F7
Owyhee 8,392 .... B7
Payette 16,434 .... B5
Power 7,086 .... F7
Shoshone 13,931 .... B2
Teton 3,439 .... G6
Twin Falls 53,580 .... D7
Valley 6,109 .... C5
Washington 8,550 .... B5

CITIES and TOWNS

Aberdeen 1,406 .... F7
Acequia 106 .... E7
Ahsahka 160 .... B3
Albion 305 .... E7
American Falls▲ 3,757 .... E7
Ammon 5,002 .... G6
Arco▲ 1,016 .... E6
Arimo 311 .... F7
Ashton 1,114 .... G5
Athol 346 .... B2
Atomic City 25 .... F6
Bancroft 393 .... G7
Basalt 407 .... F6
Bayview 350 .... B2
Bellevue 1,275 .... D6
Bern 154 .... G7
Blackfoot▲ 9,646 .... F6
Bliss 185 .... D7
Bloomington 197 .... G7
Boise (cap.)▲ 102,160 .... B6
Bonners Ferry▲ 2,193 .... B1
Bovill 256 .... B3
Bruneau 160 .... C7
Buhl 3,516 .... D7
Burgdorf B4
Burke 150 .... C2
Burley▲ 8,702 .... E7
Butte City 59 .... E6
Calder 200 .... B2
Caldwell▲ 18,400 .... B6
Cambridge 374 .... B5
Carey 800 .... E6
Cascade▲ 877 .... C5
Castleford 179 .... C7
Cataldo 150 .... B2
Challis▲ 1,073 .... D5
Chatcolet 72 .... B2
Chester 300 .... G5
Chilly E5
Chubbuck 7,791 .... F7
Clark Fork 448 .... B1
Clarkia 175 .... B2
Clayton 26 .... D5
Clifton 228 .... F7
Coeur d'Alene▲ 24,563 .... B2
Colburn 250 .... B1
Conda 200 .... G7
Coolin 150 .... B1
Cottonwood 822 .... B3
Council▲ 831 .... B5
Craigmont 542 .... B3
Crouch 75 .... B5
Culdesac 280 .... B3
Dalton Gardens 1,951 .... B2
Dayton 357 .... F7
Deary 529 .... B3
Declo 279 .... E7
Dietrich 127 .... D7
Dingle 300 .... G7
Donnelly 135 .... B5
Dover 294 .... B1
Downey 626 .... F7
Driggs▲ 846 .... G6
Drummond 37 .... G5
Dubois▲ 420 .... F5
Eagle 3,327 .... B6
East Hope 215 .... B1
Eden 314 .... D7
Elk City 500 .... C4
Elk River 149 .... B3
Emida 175 .... B2
Emmett▲ 4,601 .... B6
Fairfield▲ 371 .... D6
Ferdinand 135 .... B3
Fernan Lake 178 .... B2
Fernwood 608 .... B2
Filer 1,511 .... D7
Firth 429 .... F6
Fort Hall 2,681 .... F6
Franklin 478 .... G7
Fruitland 2,400 .... B6
Fruitvale 200 .... B5
Garden City 6,369 .... B6
Garden Valley 250 .... C5
Genesee 725 .... B3
Geneva 220 .... G7
Georgetown 558 .... G7
Gilmore E5
Glenns Ferry 1,304 .... C7
Gooding▲ 2,820 .... D7
Grace 973 .... G7
Grand View 330 .... B7
Grangeville▲ 3,226 .... B4
Greenleaf 648 .... B6
Grimes Pass C5
Hagerman 600 .... D7
Hailey▲ 3,687 .... D6
Hamer 79 .... F6
Hammett 180 .... C7
Hansen 848 .... D7
Harrison 226 .... B2
Hauser 380 .... A2
Hayden 3,744 .... B2
Hayden Lake 338 .... B2
Hazelton 394 .... E7
Headquarters 165 .... C3
Heise 84 .... G6
Heyburn 2,714 .... E7
Hollister 144 .... D7
Homedale 1,963 .... A6
Hope 99 .... B1
Horseshoe Bend 643 .... B6
Huetter 82 .... B2
Idaho City▲ 322 .... C6
Idaho Falls▲ 43,929 .... F6
Inkom 769 .... F7
Iona 1,049 .... G6
Irwin 108 .... G6
Island Park 159 .... G5
Jerome▲ 6,529 .... D7
Juliaetta 488 .... B3
Kamiah 1,157 .... B3
Kellogg 2,591 .... B2
Kendrick 325 .... B3
Ketchum 2,523 .... D6
Kimberly 2,367 .... D7
Kooskia 692 .... C3
Kootenai 327 .... B1
Kuna 1,955 .... B6
Laclede 400 .... B1
Lake Fork 250 .... B5
Lapwai 932 .... B3
Lava Hot Springs 420 .... F7
Leadore 74 .... E5
Lewiston▲ 28,082 .... A3
Lewisville 471 .... F6
Lost River (Grouse) 29 .... E6
Lowman 180 .... C5
Mackay 574 .... E6
Macks Inn 200 .... G5
Malad City▲ 1,946 .... F7
Malta 171 .... E7
Marsing 798 .... B6
McCall 2,005 .... C5
McCammon 722 .... F7
Meadows 250 .... B5
Melba 252 .... B6
Menan 601 .... F6
Meridian 9,596 .... B6
Middleton 1,851 .... B6
Midvale 110 .... B5
Minidoka 67 .... E7
Monteview 200 .... F6
Montpelier 2,656 .... G7
Moore 190 .... E6
Moreland 600 .... F6
Moscow▲ 18,519 .... B3
Mountain Home▲ 7,913 .... C6
Moyie Springs 415 .... B1
Mud Lake 179 .... F6
Mullan 821 .... C2
Murphy▲ 200 .... B6
Murtaugh 114 .... D7
Nampa 28,365 .... B6
Naples 250 .... B1
New Meadows 534 .... B4
New Plymouth 1,313 .... B6
Newdale 377 .... G6
Nezperce▲ 453 .... B3
Nordman 300 .... B1
North Fork 250 .... D4
Notus 380 .... B6
Oakley 635 .... D7
Ola 175 .... B5
Oldtown 151 .... A1
Onaway 203 .... B3
Orofino▲ 2,868 .... B3
Osburn 1,579 .... B2
Oxford 44 .... F7
Paris▲ 581 .... G7
Parker 288 .... G6
Parma 1,597 .... B6
Patterson 4 .... E5
Paul 901 .... E7
Payette▲ 5,592 .... B5
Pearl 8 .... B6
Peck 160 .... B3
Pierce 746 .... C3
Pinehurst 1,722 .... B2
Placerville 14 .... C6
Plummer 804 .... B2
Pocatello▲ 46,080 .... F7
Ponderay 449 .... B1
Post Falls 7,349 .... A2
Potlatch 790 .... A3
Preston▲ 3,710 .... G7
Priest River 1,560 .... A1
Rathdrum 2,000 .... A2
Reubens 46 .... B3
Rexburg▲ 14,302 .... G6
Richfield 383 .... D6
Rigby▲ 2,681 .... F6
Riggins 443 .... B4
Ririe 596 .... G6
Roberts 557 .... F6
Rockland 264 .... F7
Rupert▲ 5,455 .... E7
Sagle 600 .... B1
Saint Anthony▲ 3,010 .... G6
Saint Charles 211 .... G7
Saint Maries▲ 2,442 .... B2
Salmon▲ 2,941 .... D4
Samuels 467 .... B1
Sandpoint▲ 5,203 .... B1
Shelley 3,536 .... F6
Shoshone▲ 1,249 .... D7
Silver City 1 .... B6
Smelterville 464 .... B2
Soda Springs▲ 3,111 .... G7
Spencer 11 .... F5
Spirit Lake 790 .... A2
Stanley 71 .... D5
Star 500 .... B6
State Line 26 .... A2
Stites 204 .... C3
Sugar City 1,275 .... G6
Sun Valley 938 .... D6
Swan Valley 141 .... G6
Sweet 290 .... B6
Tendoy 155 .... E5
Tensed 90 .... B2
Terreton 400 .... F6
Teton 570 .... G6
Tetonia 132 .... G6
Thatcher 300 .... G7
Thornton 177 .... G6
Troy 699 .... B3
Twin Falls▲ 27,591 .... D7
Ucon 895 .... F6
Victor 292 .... G6
Wallace▲ 1,010 .... C2
Wardner 246 .... B2
Warm Lake 200 .... C5
Warm River 9 .... G5
Wayan 175 .... G7
Weippe 532 .... C3
Weiser▲ 4,571 .... B5
Wendell 1,963 .... D7
Weston 390 .... F7
White Bird 108 .... B4
Wilder 1,232 .... A6
Winchester 262 .... B3
Worley 182 .... B2

OTHER FEATURES

Albeni Falls (dam) B1
Albion (mts.) E7
Allan (mt.) D4
American Falls (res.) F6
Anderson Ranch (res.) C6
Antelope (creek) E6
Arrowrock (res.) C6
Auger (falls) D7
Badger (peak) E7
Bald (mt.) D5
Bannock (creek) F7
Bannock (peak) F7
Bannock (range) F7
Bargamin (creek) C4
Battle (creek) B7
Bear (lake) G7
Bear (riv.) G7
Bear River (range) G7
Beaver (creek) F5
Beaverhead (mts.) E4
Big (creek) C4
Big Boulder (creek) B7
Big Elk (peak) G6
Big Hole (mts.) G6
Big Lost (riv.) E6
Big Southern (butte) E6
Big Wood (riv.) D6
Birch (creek) F5
Birch Creek (valley) E5
Bitterroot (range) D3
Blackfoot (res.) G7
Black Pine (mts.) E7
Blue Nose (mt.) D4
Boise (mts.) B6
Boise (riv.) B6
Borah (peak) E5
Boulder (mts.) D6
Brownlee (dam) B5
Bruneau (riv.) C7
Camas (creek) D5
Camas (creek) D6
Camas (creek) F5
Canyon (creek) C6
Cape Horn (mt.) C5
Caribou (mt.) G6
Caribou (range) G6
Cascade (res.) C5
Castle (creek) B7
Castle (peak) D5
Cedar Creek (peak) E7
Cedar Creek (res.) D7
Centennial (mts.) F5
Chesterfield (res) F7
Clearwater (mts.) C3
Clearwater (riv.) B3
Coeur d'Alene (lake) B2
Coeur d'Alene (mts.) C2
Coeur d'Alene (riv.) B2
Cottonwood (butte) C4
Craig (mts.) B4
Crane Creek (res.) B5
Craters of the Moon Nat'l Mon. E6
Deadwood (res.) C5
Deep (creek) B7
Deep (creek) F7
Deep Creek (mts.) F7
Diamond (peak) E5
Duck Valley Ind. Res. B7
Dworshak (res.) C3
East Sister (peak) C2
Eighteen Mile (peak) E5
Fish Creek (res.) E6
Fort Hall Ind. Res. F6
Goldstone (mt.) E4
Goose (creek) E7
Goose Creek (mts.) E7
Grand Canyon of the Snake River (canyon) B4
Grays (lake) G6
Grays Lake Outlet (creek) G6
Greylock (mt.) C6
Hayden (lake) B2
Hells (canyon) B4
Hells Canyon Nat'l Rec. Area B4
Henrys (lake) G5
Henrys Fork, Snake (riv.) G5
Hunter (peak) D3
Hyndman (peak) D6
Indian (creek) C5
Island Park (res.) G5
Jarbidge (riv.) C7
Johnson (creek) C5
Jordan (creek) A7
Kootenai (riv.) C1
Lemhi (pass) E5
Lemhi (range) E5
Lemhi (riv.) E5
Little Lost (riv.) E5
Little Owyhee (riv.) B7
Little Salmon (riv.) B4
Little Weiser (riv.) B5
Little Wood (riv.) D6
Lochsa (riv.) C3
Lolo (creek) C3
Lolo (pass) D3
Lone Pine (peak) D5
Lookout (mt.) D5
Lookout (mt.) F5
Lost River (range) D5
Lost Trail (pass) D4
Lowell (lake) B6
Lower Goose Creek (res.) D7
Lower Granite (lake) A3
Lucky Peak (lake) B6
Mackay (res.) E6
Magic (res.) D6
Malad (riv.) F7
Marsh (creek) F7
McGuire (mt.) D4
Meade (peak) G7
Meadow (creek) C4
Medicine Lodge (creek) F5
Middle Fork (peak) D5
Monument (peak) B4
Moose (creek) D3
Mores (creek) C6
Mormon (mt.) C4
Mountain Home (res.) C6
Mountain Home A.F.B. 5,936 .... C6
Moyie (riv.) B1
Mud (lake) F6
National Reactor Testing Sta. F6
Nez Perce Nat'l Hist. Park C3
Norton (peak) D6
Orofino (creek) C3
Owyhee (mts.) B6
Owyhee, East Fork (riv.) B7
Oxbow (dam) B5
Pack (riv.) B1
Pahsimeroi (riv.) E5
Palisades (res.) G6
Palouse (riv.) B3
Panther (creek) D4
Payette (lake) C4
Payette (mts.) B5
Payette (riv.) B6
Peale (mts.) G7
Pend Oreille (lake) B1
Pend Oreille (mt.) B1
Pend Oreille (riv.) A1
Pilot (peak) C4
Pilot (peak) C6
Pilot Knob (mt.) C4
Pinyon (peak) C5
Pioneer (mts.) D6
Pot (mt.) C3
Potlatch (riv.) B3
Priest (lake) B1
Priest (riv.) B1
Purcell (mts.) B1
Pyramid (peak) E4
Raft (riv.) E7
Rainbow (mt.) C5
Ranger (peak) D3
Rays (lake) F6
Red (riv.) C4
Redfish (lake) D5
Reynolds (creek) B6
Rhodes (peak) D3
Rock (creek) F7
Rocky (mts.) D1
Rocky Ridge (mt.) C3
Ryan (peak) D6
Saddle (mt.) D3
Saddle (mt.) F6
Sailor (creek) C7
Saint Joe (riv.) B2
Saint Maries (riv.) B2
Salmon (falls) C7
Salmon (riv.) B4
Salmon Falls (creek) D7
Salmon Falls Creek (res.) D7
Salmon River (mts.) C5
Sawtooth (range) C6
Sawtooth Nat'l Rec. Area D5
Secesh (riv.) C4
Selkirk (mts.) B1
Selway (riv.) C3
Seven Devils (mts.) B4
Shoshone (falls) D7
Sleeping Deer (mt.) D5
Smith (creek) B1
Smoky (mts.) D6
Snake (riv.) A3
Snake River (plain) D7
Snake River (range) G6
Spirit (lake) B2
Squaw (creek) B5
Squaw (peak) D4
Steamboat (mt.) C4
Steel (mt.) C6
Strike, C.J. (res.) C7
Sublett (mts.) E7
Sunset (peak) E6
Taylor (mt.) D5
Teton (riv.) G6
Thompson (peak) C5
Trinity (mt.) C6
Trout (creek) B1
Twin (falls) D7
Twin Peaks (mt.) D5
Walcott (lake) E7
Waugh (mt.) D4
Weiser (riv.) B5
White Knob (mts.) E6
Wickahoney (creek) C7
Willow (creek) G6
Wilson Lake (res.) D7
Yankee Fork, Salmon (riv.) D5
Yellowstone Nat'l Park H5

▲County seat

Agriculture, Industry and Resources

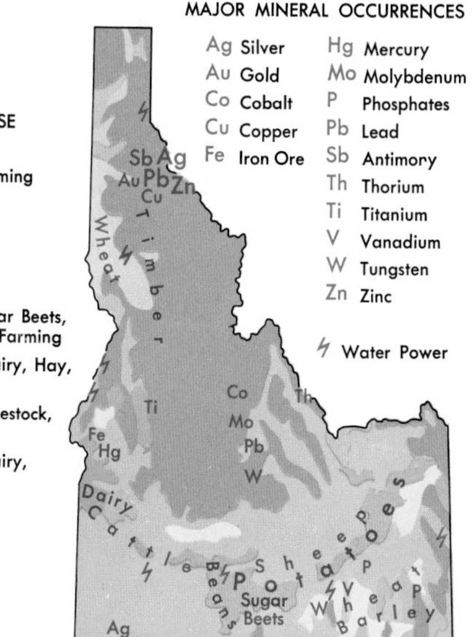
MAJOR MINERAL OCCURRENCES
Ag Silver
Au Gold
Co Cobalt
Cu Copper
Fe Iron Ore
Hg Mercury
Mo Molybdenum
P Phosphates
Pb Lead
Sb Antimony
Th Thorium
Ti Titanium
V Vanadium
W Tungsten
Zn Zinc
Water Power
DOMINANT LAND USE
Wheat, General Farming
Wheat, Peas
Specialized Dairy
Potatoes, Beans, Sugar Beets, Livestock, General Farming
General Farming, Dairy, Hay, Sugar Beets
General Farming, Livestock, Special Crops
General Farming, Dairy, Range Livestock
Range Livestock
Forests
Wheat
Timber
Dairy
Cattle
Sheep
Potatoes
Beans
Sugar Beets
Wheat
Barley

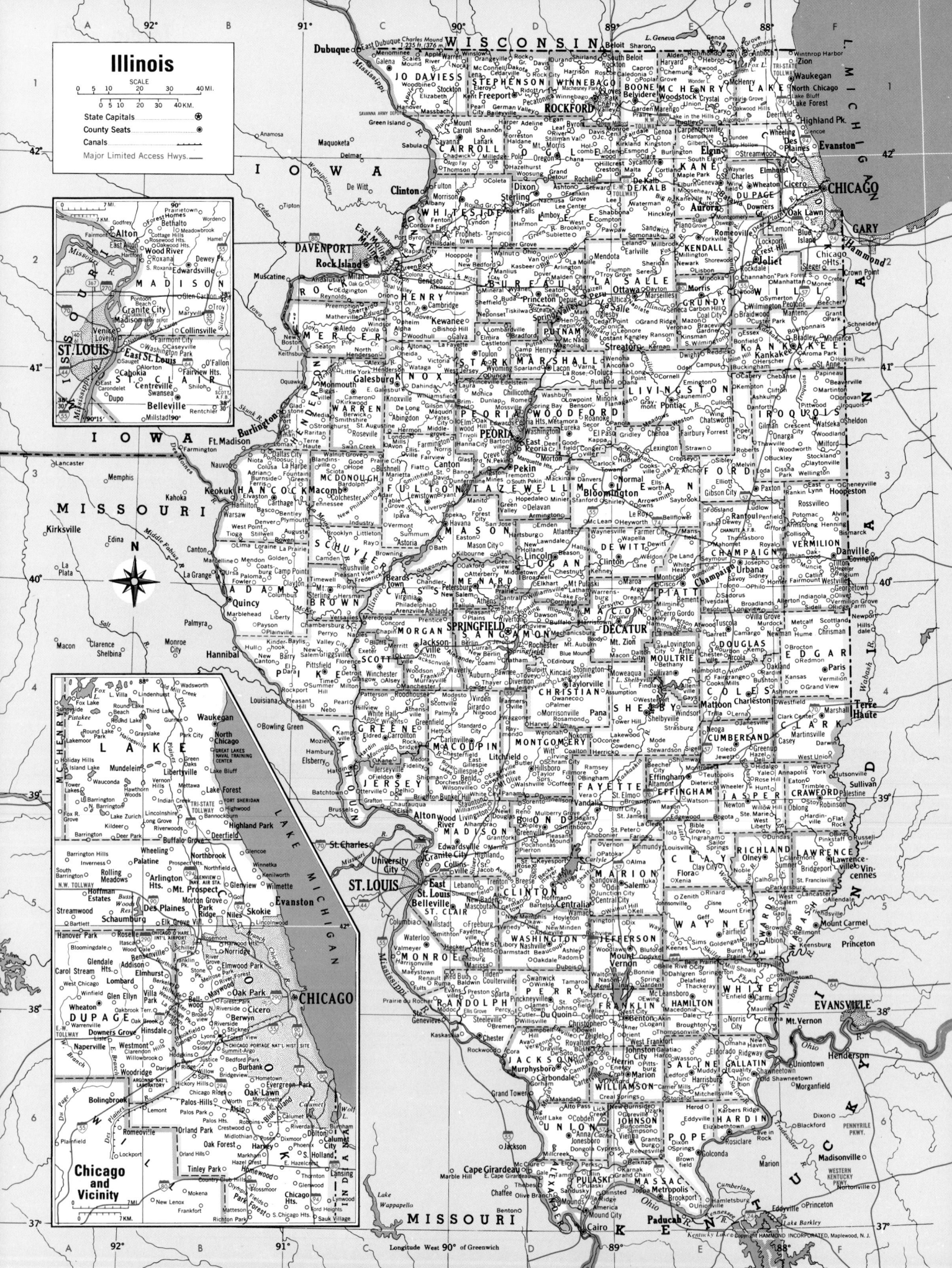

Illinois
SCALE
0 5 10 20 30 40 MI.
0 5 10 20 30 40 KM.
State Capitals
County Seats
Canals
Major Limited Access Hwys.
WISCONSIN
IOWA
MISSOURI
KENTUCKY
INDIANA
L. MICHIGAN
LAKE MICHIGAN
Chicago and Vicinity
CHICAGO
SPRINGFIELD
ROCKFORD
PEORIA
DECATUR
ST. LOUIS
EAST ST. LOUIS
JO DAVIESS
STEPHENSON
WINNEBAGO
BOONE
MCHENRY
LAKE
CARROLL
OGLE
DE KALB
KANE
COOK
DU PAGE
WHITESIDE
LEE
KENDALL
WILL
ROCK ISLAND
HENRY
BUREAU
LA SALLE
GRUNDY
KANKAKEE
MERCER
PUTNAM
STARK
MARSHALL
LIVINGSTON
IROQUOIS
KNOX
WARREN
HENDERSON
PEORIA
WOODFORD
MCDONOUGH
FULTON
TAZEWELL
MCLEAN
FORD
HANCOCK
SCHUYLER
MASON
DE WITT
CHAMPAIGN
VERMILION
ADAMS
BROWN
CASS
MENARD
LOGAN
PIATT
MACON
DOUGLAS
EDGAR
PIKE
SCOTT
MORGAN
SANGAMON
CHRISTIAN
MOULTRIE
COLES
CLARK
CALHOUN
GREENE
MACOUPIN
MONTGOMERY
SHELBY
CUMBERLAND
JERSEY
MADISON
BOND
FAYETTE
EFFINGHAM
JASPER
CRAWFORD
ST. CLAIR
CLINTON
MARION
CLAY
RICHLAND
LAWRENCE
MONROE
WASHINGTON
JEFFERSON
WAYNE
EDWARDS
WABASH
RANDOLPH
PERRY
FRANKLIN
HAMILTON
WHITE
JACKSON
WILLIAMSON
SALINE
GALLATIN
UNION
JOHNSON
POPE
HARDIN
ALEXANDER
PULASKI
MASSAC
DAVENPORT
Rock Island
Moline
Galesburg
Quincy
Bloomington
Normal
Champaign
Urbana
Danville
Joliet
Aurora
Elgin
Waukegan
Evanston
GARY
Hammond
Terre Haute
Vincennes
EVANSVILLE
Paducah
Cairo
Cape Girardeau
Hannibal
Burlington
Keokuk
Dubuque
Clinton
Kankakee
Pekin
Alton
Belleville
Carbondale
Mt. Vernon
Centralia
Effingham
Mattoon
Charleston
Jacksonville
Ottawa
Streator
Pontiac
Kewanee
Macomb
Freeport
Sterling
Dixon
Longitude West 90° of Greenwich
© Copyright HAMMOND INCORPORATED, Maplewood, N. J.

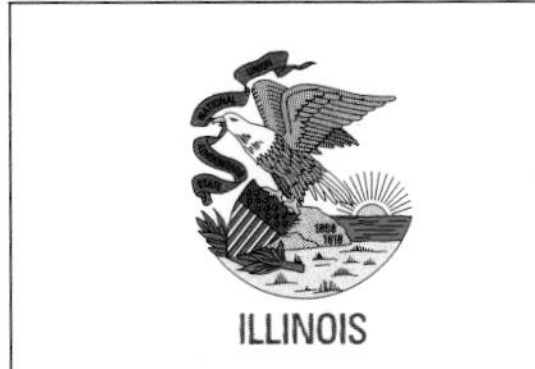

ILLINOIS

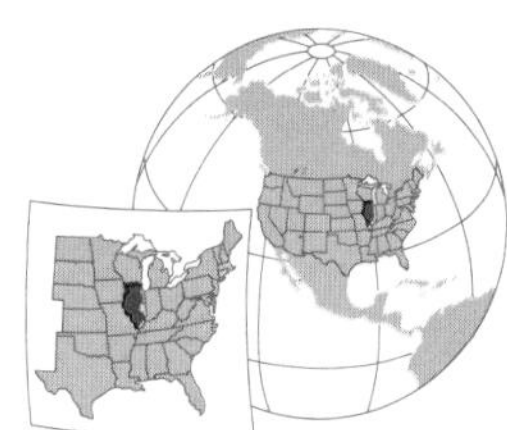

AREA 56,345 sq. mi. (145,934 sq. km.)
POPULATION 11,466,682
CAPITAL Springfield
LARGEST CITY Chicago
HIGHEST POINT Charles Mound 1,235 ft. (376 m.)
SETTLED IN 1720
ADMITTED TO UNION December 3, 1818
POPULAR NAME Prairie State; Land of Lincoln
STATE FLOWER Native Violet
STATE BIRD Cardinal

COUNTIES

Adams 66,090 ....B4
Alexander 10,626 ....D6
Bond 14,991 ....D5
Boone 30,806 ....E1
Brown 5,836 ....C4
Bureau 35,688 ....D2
Calhoun 5,322 ....C4
Carroll 16,805 ....D1
Cass 13,437 ....C4
Champaign 173,025 ....E3
Christian 34,418 ....D4
Clark 15,921 ....F4
Clay 14,460 ....E5
Clinton 33,944 ....D5
Coles 51,644 ....E4
Cook 5,105,067 ....F2
Crawford 19,464 ....F4
Cumberland 10,670 ....E4
De Kalb 74,624 ....E2
De Witt 16,516 ....E3
Douglas 19,464 ....E4
Du Page 658,858 ....E2
Edgar 19,595 ....F4
Edwards 7,440 ....E5
Effingham 31,704 ....E4
Fayette 20,893 ....D4
Ford 14,275 ....E3
Franklin 40,319 ....E5
Fulton 38,080 ....C3
Gallatin 6,909 ....E6
Greene 15,317 ....C4
Grundy 32,337 ....E2
Hamilton 8,499 ....E5
Hancock 21,373 ....B3
Hardin 5,189 ....E6
Henderson 8,096 ....C3
Henry 51,159 ....C2
Iroquois 30,787 ....F3

Jackson 61,067 ....D6
Jasper 10,609 ....E4
Jefferson 37,020 ....E5
Jersey 20,539 ....C4
Jo Daviess 21,821 ....C1
Johnson 11,347 ....E6
Kane 317,471 ....E2
Kankakee 96,255 ....F2
Kendall 39,413 ....E2
Knox 56,393 ....C3
La Salle 106,913 ....E2
Lake 516,418 ....E1
Lawrence 15,972 ....F5
Lee 34,392 ....D2
Livingston 39,301 ....E3
Logan 30,798 ....D3
Macon 117,206 ....E4
Macoupin 47,679 ....D4
Madison 249,238 ....D5
Marion 41,561 ....E5
Marshall 12,846 ....D2
Mason 16,269 ....D3
Massac 14,752 ....E6
McDonough 35,244 ....C3
McHenry 183,241 ....E1
McLean 129,180 ....E3
Menard 11,164 ....D3
Mercer 17,290 ....C2
Monroe 22,422 ....C5
Montgomery 30,728 ....D4
Morgan 36,397 ....C4
Moultrie 13,930 ....E4
Ogle 45,957 ....D1
Peoria 182,827 ....D3
Perry 21,412 ....D5
Piatt 15,548 ....E4
Pike 17,577 ....C4
Pope 4,373 ....E6
Pulaski 7,523 ....D6
Putnam 5,730 ....D2

Randolph 34,583 ....D5
Richland 16,545 ....E5
Rock Island 148,723 ....C2
Saint Clair 267,531 ....C5
Saline 26,551 ....E6
Sangamon 178,386 ....D4
Schuyler 7,498 ....C3
Scott 5,644 ....C4
Shelby 22,261 ....E4
Stark 6,534 ....D2
Stephenson 48,052 ....D1
Tazewell 123,692 ....D3
Union 17,619 ....D6
Vermilion 88,257 ....F3
Wabash 13,111 ....F5
Warren 19,181 ....C3
Washington 14,965 ....D5
Wayne 17,241 ....E5
White 16,522 ....E5
Whiteside 60,186 ....D2
Will 357,313 ....F2
Williamson 57,733 ....E6
Winnebago 252,913 ....D1
Woodford 32,653 ....D3

CITIES and TOWNS

Abingdon 3,597 ....C3
Addison 32,058 ....B5
Albany 835 ....C2
Albers 700 ....D5
Albion▲ 2,116 ....E5
Aledo▲ 3,681 ....C2
Alexis 908 ....C2
Algonquin 11,663 ....E1
Alhambra 709 ....D5
Allendale 476 ....F5
Alorton 2,960 ....B2
Alpha 753 ....C2
Alsip 18,227 ....B6

Altamont 2,296 ....E4
Alton 32,905 ....A2
Altona 559 ....C2
Amboy 2,377 ....D2
Andalusia 1,052 ....C2
Andover 579 ....C2
Anna 4,805 ....D6
Annawan 802 ....C2
Antioch 6,105 ....E1
Arcola 2,678 ....E4
Arenzville 432 ....C4
Argenta 940 ....E4
Arlington Heights 75,460 ....B5
Aroma Park 690 ....F2
Arthur 2,112 ....E4
Ashkum 650 ....E3
Ashland 1,257 ....C4
Ashley 583 ....D5
Ashmore 800 ....F4
Ashton 1,042 ....D2
Assumption 1,244 ....E4
Astoria 1,205 ....C3
Athens 1,404 ....D4
Atkinson 950 ....C2
Atlanta 1,616 ....D3
Atwood 1,253 ....E4
Auburn 3,724 ....D4
Augusta 614 ....C3
Aurora 99,581 ....E2
Ava 674 ....D5
Aviston 924 ....D5
Avon 957 ....C3
Baldwin 426 ....D5
Bannockburn 1,388 ....B5
Barrington 9,504 ....A5
Barrington Hills 4,202 ....A5
Barry 1,391 ....B4
Bartlett 19,373 ....A5
Bartonville 5,643 ....D3
Batavia 17,076 ....E2
Beardstown 5,270 ....C3
Beckemeyer 1,070 ....D5
Bedford Park 566 ....B6
Beecher 2,032 ....F2
Beecher City 437 ....E4
Belgium 511 ....F3
Belleville▲ 42,785 ....B3
Bellwood 20,241 ....B5
Belvidere▲ 15,958 ....E1
Bement 1,668 ....E4
Bensenville 17,767 ....B5
Benton▲ 7,216 ....E6
Berkeley 5,137 ....B5
Berwyn 45,426 ....B6
Bethalto 9,507 ....B2
Bethany 1,369 ....E4
Blandinsville 762 ....C3
Bloomingdale 16,614 ....A5
Bloomington▲ 51,972 ....D3
Blue Island 21,203 ....B6
Blue Mound 1,161 ....D4
Bluffs 774 ....C4
Bluford 747 ....E5
Bolingbrook 40,843 ....A6
Bourbon 13,934 ....E4
Bourbonnais 13,280 ....F2
Bowen 462 ....B4
Braceville 587 ....E2
Bradford 678 ....D2
Bradley 10,792 ....F2
Braidwood 3,584 ....E2
Breese 3,567 ....D5
Bridgeport 2,118 ....F5
Bridgeview 14,402 ....B6
Brighton 2,270 ....C4
Brimfield 797 ....D3
Broadview 8,713 ....B6
Brookfield 18,876 ....B6
Brooklyn (Lovejoy) 1,144 ....A2
Brookport 1,070 ....E6
Brownstown 668 ....E5
Buckley 557 ....F3
Buckner 478 ....E6
Buda 563 ....D2
Buffalo 503 ....D4
Buffalo Grove 36,427 ....B5
Bunker Hill 1,722 ....D4
Burbank 27,600 ....B6
Burnham 3,916 ....C6

Burr Ridge 7,669 ....B6
Bushnell 3,288 ....C3
Byron 2,284 ....D1
Cahokia 17,550 ....A3
Cairo▲ 4,846 ....D6
Calumet City 37,840 ....C6
Calumet Park 8,418 ....C6
Cambria 1,230 ....D6
Cambridge▲ 2,124 ....C2
Camp Point 1,230 ....B3
Canton 13,922 ....C3
Capron 682 ....E1
Carbon Cliff 1,492 ....C2
Carbondale 27,033 ....D6
Carlinville 5,416 ....D4
Carlyle▲ 3,474 ....D5
Carmi▲ 5,564 ....E5
Carol Stream 31,716 ....A5
Carpentersville 23,049 ....E1
Carrier Mills 2,268 ....E6
Carrollton▲ 2,507 ....C4
Carterville 3,630 ....D6
Carthage▲ 2,657 ....B3
Cary 10,043 ....E1
Casey 2,914 ....F4
Caseyville 4,419 ....B2
Catlin 2,173 ....F3
Cave in Rock 381 ....E6
Cedarville 751 ....D1
Central City 1,390 ....D5
Centralia 14,274 ....D5
Centreville 7,489 ....B3
Cerro Gordo 1,436 ....E4
Chadwick 557 ....D1
Champaign 63,502 ....E3
Chandlerville 689 ....C3
Channahon 4,266 ....E2
Chapin 632 ....C4
Charleston▲ 20,398 ....E4
Chatham 6,074 ....D4
Chatsworth 1,186 ....E3
Chebanse 1,082 ....F3
Chenoa 1,732 ....E3
Cherry 487 ....D2
Cherry Valley 1,615 ....D1
Chester▲ 8,194 ....D6
Chicago Heights 33,072 ....C6
Chicago Ridge 13,643 ....B6
Chicago▲ 2,783,726 ....C5
Chillicothe 5,959 ....D3
Chrisman 1,136 ....F4
Christopher 2,774 ....D6
Cicero 67,436 ....B5
Cisne 645 ....E5
Cissna Park 805 ....F3
Clarendon Hills 6,994 ....B6
Clay City 929 ....E5
Clayton 726 ....B3
Clifton 1,347 ....F3
Clinton▲ 7,437 ....E3
Coal City 3,907 ....E2
Coal Valley 2,683 ....C2
Cobden 1,090 ....D6
Coffeen 704 ....D4
Colchester 1,645 ....C3
Colfax 854 ....E3
Collinsville 22,446 ....B2
Colona 2,237 ....C2
Columbia 5,524 ....C5
Cordova 638 ....C2
Cornell 556 ....E3
Cortland 963 ....E2
Coulterville 984 ....D5
Country Club Hills 15,431 ....B6
Countryside 5,716 ....B6
Cowden 599 ....E4
Creal Springs 791 ....E6
Crescent City 541 ....F3
Crest Hill 10,643 ....E2
Creston 535 ....D2
Crestwood 10,823 ....B6
Crete 6,773 ....C6
Creve Coeur 5,938 ....D3
Crossville 805 ....F5
Crystal Lake 24,512 ....E1
Cuba 1,440 ....C3
Cullom 568 ....E3
Cutler 523 ....D5
Dahlgren 512 ....E5
Dakota 549 ....D1
Dallas City 1,037 ....B3
Dalton City 573 ....E4
Dalzell 587 ....D2
Danforth 491 ....F3
Danvers 981 ....D3
Danville▲ 33,828 ....F3
Darien 18,341 ....B6
Davis 541 ....D1
Dawson 536 ....D4
De Kalb 34,925 ....E2
De Land 458 ....E3
De Soto 1,500 ....D6
Decatur▲ 83,885 ....E4
Deer Creek 630 ....D3
Deer Park 2,887 ....A5
Deerfield 17,327 ....B5
Delavan 1,642 ....D3
Depue 1,729 ....D2

Des Plaines 53,223 ....B5
Dieterich 568 ....E4
Diveron 1,178 ....D4
Dix 456 ....E5
Dixmoor 3,647 ....C6
Dixon▲ 15,144 ....D2
Dolton 23,930 ....C6
Dongola 728 ....D6
Dow 465 ....C4
Dowell 480 ....D6
Downers Grove 46,858 ....A6
Downs 620 ....E3
Du Quoin 6,697 ....D5
Dundee (East and West Dundee) 6,169 ....E1
Dunlap 851 ....D3
Dupo 3,164 ....A3
Durand 1,100 ....D1
Dwight 4,230 ....E2
Earlville 1,435 ....E2
East Alton 7,063 ....A2
East Cape Girardeau 451 ....D6
East Carondelet 630 ....A3
East Dubuque 1,914 ....C1
East Dundee (Dundee) 2,721 ....E1
East Galesburg 813 ....C3
East Hazelcrest 1,570 ....C6
East Moline 20,147 ....C2
East Peoria 21,378 ....D3
East Saint Louis 40,944 ....A2
Edgewood 502 ....E5
Edinburg 982 ....D4
Edwards 14,579 ....D3
Edwardsville▲ 12,480 ....D2
Effingham▲ 11,851 ....E4
El Paso 2,499 ....D3
Elburn 1,275 ....E2
Eldorado 4,536 ....E6
Elgin 77,010 ....E1
Elizabeth 641 ....C1
Elizabethtown▲ 427 ....E6
Elk Grove Village 33,429 ....B5
Elkhart 475 ....D3
Elkville 958 ....D6
Elmhurst 42,029 ....B5
Elmwood 1,841 ....D3
Elmwood Park 23,206 ....B5
Elsah 851 ....A2
Elwood 951 ....E2
Emden 459 ....D3
Energy 1,106 ....E6
Enfield 683 ....E5
Equality 748 ....E6
Erie 1,572 ....C2
Essex 482 ....E2
Eureka▲ 4,435 ....D3
Evanston 73,233 ....B5
Evansville 844 ....D5
Evergreen Park 20,874 ....B6
Fairbury 3,643 ....E3
Fairfield▲ 5,439 ....E5
Fairmont 2,894 ....A2
Fairmont City 2,140 ....B2
Fairmount 678 ....F3
Fairview 510 ....C3
Fairview Heights 14,351 ....B3
Farina 575 ....E5
Farmer City 2,114 ....E3
Farmersville 698 ....D4
Farmington 2,535 ....C3
Findlay 787 ....E4
Fisher 1,526 ....E3
Fithian 512 ....F3
Flanagan 847 ....E3
Flat Rock 421 ....F5
Flora 5,054 ....E5
Flossmoor 8,651 ....B6
Ford Heights 4,259 ....C6
Forest City 541 ....D3
Forest Park 14,918 ....B5
Forest View 743 ....B6
Forrest 1,124 ....E3
Forreston 1,361 ....D1
Forsyth 1,275 ....D4
Fox Lake 7,478 ....A4
Fox River Grove 3,551 ....A5
Frankfort 7,180 ....B6
Franklin 634 ....C4
Franklin Grove 968 ....D2
Franklin Park 18,485 ....B5
Freeburg 3,115 ....D5
Freeport▲ 25,840 ....D1
Fulton 3,698 ....C2
Galatia 983 ....E6
Galena▲ 3,876 ....C1
Galesburg▲ 33,530 ....C3
Galva 2,742 ....D2
Gardner 1,237 ....E2
Geneseo 5,990 ....C2
Geneva▲ 12,617 ....E2
Genoa 3,083 ....E1
Georgetown 3,678 ....F4
German Valley 480 ....D1
Germantown 1,167 ....D5
Gibson City 3,498 ....E3
Gifford 845 ....E3
Gilberts 987 ....E1

Gillespie 3,645 ....D4
Gilman 1,816 ....E3
Glasford 1,115 ....D3
Glen Carbon 7,731 ....B2
Glen Ellyn 24,944 ....A5
Glencoe 8,499 ....B5
Glendale Heights 27,973 ....A5
Glenview 37,093 ....B5
Glenwood 9,289 ....C6
Godfrey 5,436 ....A2
Golconda▲ 823 ....E6
Golden 565 ....B3
Golf 454 ....B5
Goodfield 454 ....D3
Goreville 872 ....E6
Grafton 918 ....C5
Grand Ridge 560 ....E2
Grand Tower 775 ....D6
Grandview 1,647 ....D4
Granite City 32,862 ....A2
Grant Park 1,024 ....F2
Granville 1,407 ....D2
Grayslake 7,388 ....B4
Grayville 2,043 ....F5
Green Oaks 2,101 ....B4
Green Rock 2,615 ....C2
Green Valley 745 ....D3
Greenfield 1,162 ....C4
Greenup 1,616 ....E4
Greenview 848 ....D3
Greenville▲ 4,806 ....D5
Gridley 1,304 ....E3
Griggsville 1,218 ....C4
Gurnee 13,701 ....B4
Hamel 530 ....B2
Hamilton 3,281 ....B3
Hammond 527 ....E4
Hampshire 1,843 ....E1
Hampton 1,601 ....C2
Hanna City 1,205 ....D3
Hanover 908 ....C1
Hanover Park 32,895 ....A5
Hardin▲ 1,071 ....C4
Harrisburg▲ 9,289 ....E6
Harristown 1,319 ....D4
Hartford 1,676 ....A2
Harvard 5,975 ....E1
Harvey 29,771 ....B6
Harwood Heights 7,680 ....B5
Havana▲ 3,610 ....C3
Hawthorn Woods 4,423 ....B5
Hazel Crest 13,334 ....B6
Hebron 809 ....E1
Hecker 534 ....D5
Hegeler 1,853 ....F3
Hennepin▲ 669 ....D2
Henry 2,591 ....D2
Herrick 466 ....D4
Herrin 10,857 ....E6
Herscher 1,278 ....E3
Heyworth 1,627 ....E3
Hickory Hills 13,021 ....B6
Highland 7,525 ....D5
Highland Park 30,575 ....B5
Highwood 5,331 ....B5
Hillcrest 828 ....D1
Hillsboro▲ 4,400 ....D4
Hillsdale 489 ....C2
Hillside 7,672 ....B5
Hinckley 1,682 ....E2
Hinsdale 16,029 ....B6
Hodgkins 1,963 ....B6
Hoffman 492 ....D5
Hoffman Estates 46,561 ....A5
Holiday Hills 807 ....A4
Homer 1,264 ....F3
Hometown 4,769 ....B6
Homewood 19,278 ....B6
Hoopeston 5,871 ....F3
Hopedale 805 ....D3
Hopkins Park 601 ....F2
Hoyleton 508 ....D5
Hudson 1,006 ....E3
Hull 514 ....B4
Humboldt 470 ....E4
Hunt 2,453 ....E4
Huntley 1,646 ....E1
Hurst 842 ....E6
Hutsonville 622 ....F4
Illiopolis 934 ....D4
Ina 489 ....E5
Industry 571 ....C3
Inverness 6,503 ....A5
Ipava 483 ....C3
Irving 516 ....D4
Irvington 827 ....D5
Island Lake 4,449 ....A4
Itasca 6,947 ....B5
Jacksonville▲ 19,324 ....C4
Jerome 1,206 ....D4
Jerseyville▲ 7,382 ....C4
Johnston City 3,706 ....E6
Joliet▲ 76,836 ....E2
Jonesboro▲ 1,728 ....D6
Joppa 492 ....E6
Joy 452 ....C2
Junction City 539 ....D5
Justice 11,137 ....B6

(continued on following page)

Topography

5,000 m. / 16,404 ft. 2,000 m. / 6,562 ft. 1,000 m. / 3,281 ft. 500 m. / 1,640 ft. 200 m. / 656 ft. 100 m. / 328 ft. Sea Level Below

0   40   80 MI.

0   40   80 KM.

Charles Mound 1,235 ft. (376 m.)
Fox L.
Rockford
Evanston
Chicago
Mississippi
Rock Island
Joliet
Peoria
Champaign
Quincy
Springfield
Decatur
Macoupin
Carlyle L.
East St. Louis
Rend L.

Agriculture, Industry and Resources

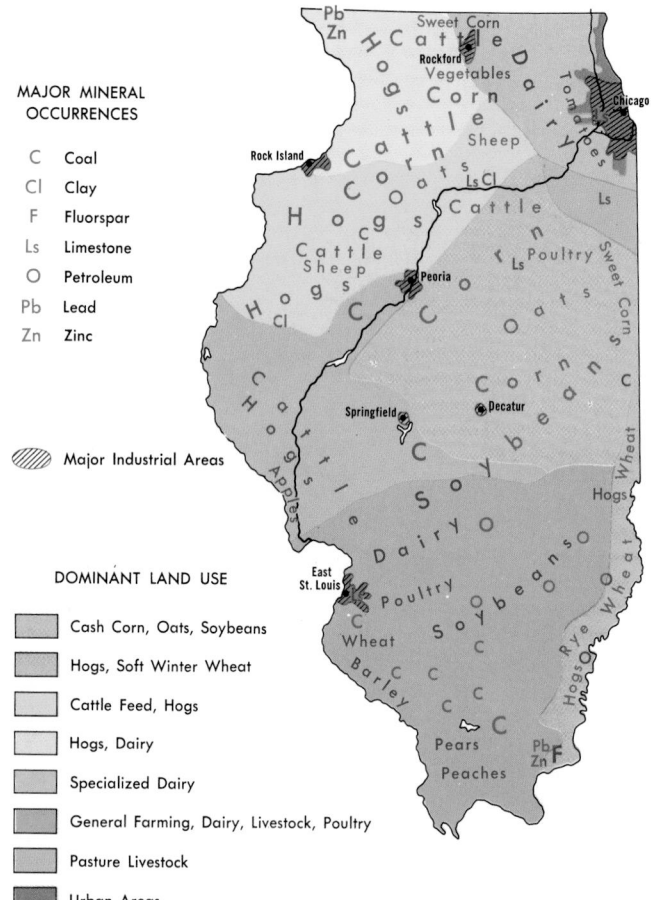

MAJOR MINERAL OCCURRENCES

- C Coal
- Cl Clay
- F Fluorspar
- Ls Limestone
- O Petroleum
- Pb Lead
- Zn Zinc

Major Industrial Areas

DOMINANT LAND USE

- Cash Corn, Oats, Soybeans
- Hogs, Soft Winter Wheat
- Cattle Feed, Hogs
- Hogs, Dairy
- Specialized Dairy
- General Farming, Dairy, Livestock, Poultry
- Pasture Livestock
- Urban Areas

East St. Louis

Springfield · Decatur · Peoria · Rock Island · Rockford · Chicago

Pears · Peaches

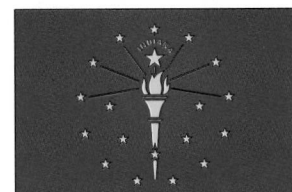

AREA 36,185 sq. mi. (93,719 sq. km.)
POPULATION 5,564,228
CAPITAL Indianapolis
LARGEST CITY Indianapolis
HIGHEST POINT 1,257 ft. (383 m.) (Wayne County)
SETTLED IN 1730
ADMITTED TO UNION December 11, 1816
POPULAR NAME Hoosier State
STATE FLOWER Peony
STATE BIRD Cardinal

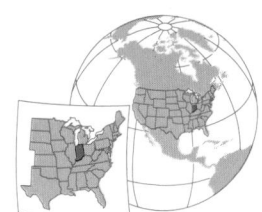

COUNTIES

Adams 31,095	H3
Allen 300,836	G2
Bartholomew 63,657	F6
Benton 9,441	C3
Blackford 14,067	G4
Boone 38,147	E4
Brown 14,080	E6
Carroll 18,809	D3
Cass 38,413	E3
Clark 87,777	F8
Clay 24,705	C6
Clinton 30,974	E4
Crawford 9,914	E8
Daviess 27,533	C7
De Kalb 35,324	H2
Decatur 23,645	G6
Delaware 119,659	G4
Dubois 36,616	D8
Elkhart 156,198	F1
Fayette 26,015	G5
Floyd 64,404	F8
Fountain 17,808	C4
Franklin 19,580	G6
Fulton 18,840	E2
Gibson 31,913	B8
Grant 74,169	F3
Greene 30,410	D6
Hamilton 108,936	E4
Hancock 45,527	F5
Harrison 29,890	E8
Hendricks 75,717	D5
Henry 48,139	G5
Howard 80,827	E4
Huntington 35,427	G3
Jackson 37,730	E7
Jasper 24,960	C2
Jay 21,512	G4
Jefferson 29,797	G7
Jennings 23,661	F7
Johnson 88,109	E6
Knox 39,884	C7
Kosciusko 65,294	F2
LaPorte 108,632	D1
Lagrange 29,477	G1
Lake 475,594	C2
Lawrence 42,836	E7
Madison 130,669	F4
Marion 797,159	E5
Marshall 42,182	E2
Martin 10,369	D7
Miami 36,897	E3
Monroe 108,978	D6
Montgomery 34,436	D4
Morgan 55,920	E6
Newton 13,551	C3
Noble 37,877	G2
Ohio 5,315	H7
Orange 18,409	E7
Owen 17,281	D6
Parke 15,410	C5
Perry 19,107	D8
Pike 12,509	C8
Porter 128,932	C2
Posey 25,968	B8
Pulaski 12,643	D2
Putnam 30,315	D5
Randolph 27,148	G4
Ripley 24,616	G6
Rush 18,129	G5
Saint Joseph 241,617	E1
Scott 20,991	F7
Shelby 40,307	F5
Spencer 19,490	C9
Starke 22,747	D2
Steuben 27,446	G1
Sullivan 18,993	C6
Switzerland 7,738	G7
Tippecanoe 130,598	D4
Tipton 16,119	E4
Union 6,976	H5
Vanderburgh 165,058	B8
Vermillion 16,773	C5
Vigo 106,107	C6
Wabash 35,069	F3
Warren 8,176	C4
Warrick 44,920	C8
Washington 23,717	E7
Wayne 71,951	H5
Wells 25,948	G3
White 23,265	D3
Whitley 27,651	F2

CITIES and TOWNS

Abington 200	H5
Adams 250	F6
Adamsboro 325	E3
Advance 520	D5
Akron 1,001	E2
Alamo 112	C5
Albany 2,357	G4
Albion▲ 1,823	G2
Alexandria 5,709	F4
Altona 156	G2
Ambia 249	C4
Amboy 370	F3
Americus 150	D3
Amity 200	E6
Amo 380	D5
Anderson▲ 59,459	F4
Andersonville 225	G5
Andrews 1,118	F3
Angola▲ 5,824	G1
Anthony 130	G4
Arcadia 1,468	E4
Arcola 300	G2
Ardmore 800	E1
Argos 1,642	E2
Arlington 500	F5
Ashley 767	G1
Athens 145	E2
Atlanta 703	E4
Attica 3,457	C4
Atwood 300	F2
Auburn▲ 9,379	G2
Aurora 3,825	H6
Austin 4,310	F7
Avilla 1,366	G2
Avoca 400	D7
Azalia 194	F6
Bainbridge 682	D5
Bargersville 1,681	E6
Batesville 4,720	G6
Battle Ground 806	D3
Bear Branch 150	G7
Bedford▲ 13,817	E7
Beech Grove 13,383	E5
Bellmore 160	C5
Bennetts Switch 138	E3
Benton 220	F2
Berne 3,559	H3
Bethany 90	E5
Beverly Shores 622	D1
Bicknell 3,357	C7
Bippus 300	F3
Birdseye 472	D8
Black Oak	C1
Blanford 500	B5
Blocher 400	F7
Bloomfield▲ 2,592	D6
Blooming Grove 300	G5
Bloomingdale 341	C5
Bloomington▲ 60,633	D6
Blountsville 155	G4
Blue Ridge 219	F5
Bluffton▲ 9,020	G3
Boggstown 200	F5
Boone Grove 220	C2
Boonville▲ 6,724	C8
Borden	F8
Boston 159	H5
Boswell 767	C3
Bourbon 1,672	E2
Bowling Green 200	D6
Bradford 350	E8
Brazil▲ 7,640	C5
Bremen 4,725	E2
Bridgeton 250	C5
Bright 2,690	H6
Brimfield 292	G2
Bringhurst 275	E3
Bristol 1,133	F1
Brook 899	C3
Brooklyn 1,162	E5
Brooksburg 79	G7
Brookston 1,804	D3
Brookville▲ 2,529	G6
Brownsburg 7,628	E5
Brownstown▲ 2,872	F7
Brownsville 250	H5
Bruceville 471	C7
Bryant 273	G3
Buck Creek 225	D4
Buckskin 200	C8
Buffalo 200	D3
Bunker Hill 1,010	E3
Burket 200	F2
Burlington 568	E4
Burnettsville 401	D3
Burney 300	F6
Burns City 140	D7
Burns Harbor 788	C1
Burrows 250	E3
Butler 2,601	H2
Butlerville 300	F6
Byron 200	C5
Cadiz 202	G5
Cambridge City 2,091	G5
Camden 607	D3
Cammack 250	G4
Campbellsburg 606	E7
Cannelburg 97	C7
Cannelton▲ 1,786	D9
Carbon 350	C5
Carefree 200	E8
Carlisle 613	C7
Carmel 25,380	E5
Cartersburg 300	E5
Carthage 887	F5
Cassville 159	E3
Cates 125	C4
Cayuga 1,083	C5
Cedar Grove 246	H6
Cedar Lake 8,885	C2
Celestine 150	D8
Centenary 150	B5
Center 278	E4
Centerpoint 242	C6
Centerton 250	E5
Centerville 2,398	H5
Chalmers 525	D3
Chandler 3,099	C8
Chapel Hill 175	E6
Charlestown 5,889	F8
Charlottesville 300	F5
Chelsea 200	F7
Chester 2,730	E8
Chesterfield 2,701	F4
Chesterton 9,124	D1
Chili 280	F3
Chrisney 511	C9
Churubusco 1,781	G2
Cicero 3,268	E4
Clarks Hill 716	D4
Clarksburg 300	G6
Clarksville 19,833	F8
Clay City 929	C6
Claypool 411	F2
Clayton 610	E5
Clear Creek 200	C6
Clear Lake 272	H1
Clifford 308	F6
Clinton 5,040	C5
Cloverdale 1,681	D5
Cloverland 175	C6
Clymers 150	E3
Coal City 225	D6
Coalmont 450	C6
Coatesville 469	D5
Coesse 150	G2
Colburn 300	D3
Colfax 727	D4
Collegeville 993	C3
Columbia City▲ 5,706	G2
Columbus▲ 31,802	E6
Commiskey 150	F7
Connersville▲ 15,550	G5
Converse 1,144	F3
Correct 131	G7
Cortland 175	F7
Corunna 241	G2
Cory 2,661	C6
Corydon▲ 2,724	E8
Covington▲ 2,747	C4
Cowan 428	G4
Craigville 130	G3
Crandall 147	E8
Crane 216	D7
Crawfordsville▲ 13,584	C4
Cromwell 520	F2
Cross Plains 254	G7
Crothersville 1,687	F7
Crown Point▲ 17,728	C2
Crumstown 175	E1
Culver 1,404	E2
Cumberland 1,624	F5
Cutler 140	D4
Cynthiana 669	B8
Dale 1,553	D8
Daleville 1,681	F4
Dana 612	C5
Danville▲ 4,345	D5
Darlington 740	D4
Darmstadt 1,346	B8
Dayton 996	D4
Decatur▲ 8,644	H3
Decker 281	B7
Deer Creek 250	E3
Deerfield 300	H4
Delaware 135	G6
Delong 156	E2
Delphi▲ 2,531	D3
Demotte 2,482	C2
Denham 140	D2
Denver 504	E3
Depauw 150	E8
Deputy 200	F7
Desoto 385	G4
Dillsboro 1,200	G6
Donaldson 320	E2
Doolittle Mills 200	D8
Dublin 805	G5
Dubois 550	D8
Dugger 936	C6
Dundee 160	F4
Dune Acres 263	C1
Dunkirk 2,739	G4
Dunlap 5,705	F1
Dunreith 205	G5
Dupont 391	G7
Dyer 10,923	C1
Eagletown 306	E4
Earl Park 443	C3
East Chicago 33,892	C1
East Enterprise 250	H7
East Germantown (Pershing) 372	G5
Eaton 1,614	G4
Economy 151	G4
Edgewood 2,057	F4
Edinburg 4,536	E6
Edwardsport 380	C7
Edwardsville 700	F8
Elberfeld 635	C8
Elizabeth 153	F8
Elizabethtown 495	F6
Elkhart 43,627	F1
Ellettsville 3,275	D6
Elnora 679	C7
Elrod 200	G6
Elston 500	D4
Elwood 9,494	F4
Eminence 200	D6
English▲ 614	E8
Etna 578	F2
Etna Green 522	E2
Eugene 400	B5
Evansville▲ 126,272	C9
Everton 500	H7
Fair Oaks 175	C2
Fairbanks 165	B6
Fairland 1,348	F5
Fairmount 3,130	F4
Fairview 1,446	G7
Fairview Park 1,545	C5
Farmersburg 1,159	C6
Farmland 1,412	G4
Fayetteville 180	D7
Ferdinand 2,318	D8
Fillmore 497	D5
Finly 400	F5
Fishers 7,508	E5
Flat Rock 323	F6
Flora 2,179	E3
Florence 155	H7
Floyds Knobs 500	F8
Fontanet 325	C6
Forest 400	E4
Fort Branch 2,447	C8
Fort Wayne▲ 173,072	G2
Fortville 2,690	F5
Fountain 766	C4
Fountain City 839	H5
Fountaintown 225	F5
Fowler▲ 2,333	C3
Fowlerton 306	F4
Francesville 969	D3
Francisco 560	B8
Frankfort▲ 14,754	E4
Franklin▲ 12,907	E6
Frankton 1,736	F4
Fredericksburg 155	E8
Freelandville 600	C7
Freetown 600	E7
Fremont 1,407	H1
French Lick 2,087	D7
Fulton 371	E3
Galena 1,231	F8
Galveston 1,609	E3
Garrett 5,349	G2
Gary 116,646	C1
Gas City 6,296	F4
Gaston 979	G4
Geneva 1,280	H3
Gentryville 277	C8
Georgetown 2,092	F8
Gessie 144	C4
Glenwood 285	G5
Glezen 300	C8
Goldsmith 235	E4
Goodland 1,033	C3
Goshen▲ 23,797	F1
Gosport 764	D6
Grabill 751	H2
Grandview 761	C9
Granger 20,241	E1
Grantsburg 189	E8
Gravelton 150	F2
Greencastle▲ 8,984	D5
Greendale 3,881	H6
Greenfield▲ 11,657	F5

(continued on following page)

Agriculture, Industry and Resources

DOMINANT LAND USE

- Cash Corn, Oats, Soybeans
- Livestock, Dairy, Soybeans, Cash Grain
- Hogs, Soft Winter Wheat
- Specialized Dairy
- General Farming, Livestock, Tobacco
- Pasture Livestock
- Forests
- Urban Areas

MAJOR MINERAL OCCURRENCES

- C   Coal
- Cl   Clay
- G   Natural Gas
- Gp   Gypsum
- Ls   Limestone
- O   Petroleum

- ////   Major Industrial Areas

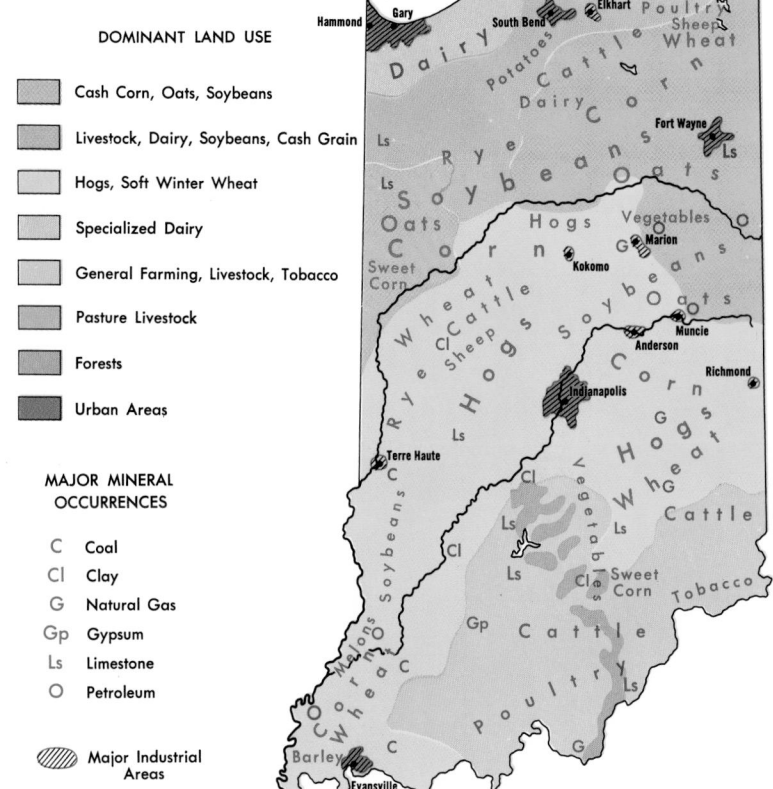

Greens Fork 416 H5
Greensboro 204 G5
Greensburg▲ 9,286 G6
Greentown 2,172 E4
Greenville 508 F8
Greenwood 26,265 E5
Griffin 171 B8
Griffith 17,916 C1
Grovertown 150 D2
Gwynneville 250 F5
Hagerstown 1,835 G5
Hamilton 684 H1
Hamlet 789 D2
Hammond 84,236 B1
Hanna 550 D2
Hanover 3,610 F7
Hardinsburg 322 E8
Harlan 840 H2
Harmony 645 C5
Harrodsburg 400 D6
Hartford City▲ 6,960 G4
Hartsville 391 F6
Hatfield 800 C9
Haubstadt 1,455 B8
Hayden 300 F7
Haysville 600 D8
Hazelwood 650 D5
Hazleton 357 B8
Hebron 3,183 C2
Helmsburg 150 E6
Heltonville 400 E7
Hemlock 300 F4
Henryville 1,132 F7
Hibbard 150 E2
Highland 23,696 B1
Hillisburg 180 E4
Hillsboro 499 C4
Hillsdale 500 C5
Hoagland 600 H3
Hobart 21,822 C1
Hobbs 200 F4
Holland 675 C8
Hollandsburg 150 C5
Holton 451 G6
Homer 235 F5
Hope 2,171 F6
Hortonville 240 E4
Houston 200 E6
Howe 800 G1
Hudson 438 G1
Hudson Lake 1,347 D1
Huntertown 1,330 G2
Huntingburg 5,242 D8
Huntington▲ 16,389 G3
Huntsville 1,200 G4
Huron 250 D7
Hymera 771 C6
Idaville 655 D3
Independence 150 C4
Indian Village 142 E1
Indianapolis (cap.)▲ 741,952 E5
Ingalls 889 F5
Inglefield 378 B8
Inwood 150 E2
Ireland 600 C8
Jamestown 764 D5
Jasonville 2,200 C6
Jasper▲ 10,030 D8
Jefferson 21,841 D4
Jeffersonville▲ 21,220 F8
Jolietville 300 E4
Jonesboro 2,073 F4
Jonesville 221 F6
Kempton 362 E4
Kendallville 7,773 G2
Kennard 382 G5
Kent 1,798 F7
Kentland▲ 1,936 C3
Kewanna 542 E2
Keystone 204 G3
Kimmell 250 F2
Kingman 561 C5
Kingsbury 258 D1
Kingsford Heights 1,486 D2
Kirklin 707 E4
Knightstown 2,048 F5
Knightsville 740 C5
Knox▲ 3,705 D2
Kokomo▲ 44,962 E4
Koontz Lake 1,615 D2
Kouts 1,603 C2
La Crosse 677 D2
La Fontaine 909 F3
Ladoga 1,124 D5
Lafayette▲ 43,764 D4
Lagrange▲ 2,382 F1
Lagro 496 F3
Lake Bruce 160 E2
Lake James 400 H1
Lake Station 13,899 C1
Lake Village 900 C2
Laketon 500 F3
Lakeville 655 E1
Lancaster 275 F7
Landess 150 F3
Lanesville 512 E8
Laotto 361 G2
Lapaz 562 E2
Lapel 1,742 F4
LaPorte▲ 21,507 D1
Laconia 75 E8
Larwill 219 F2
Laurel 544 G6
Lawrence 26,763 E5
Lawrenceburg▲ 4,375 H6
Leavenworth 320 E8
Lebanon▲ 12,059 D4
Lee 584 D3
Leesburg 629 F2
Leesville 164 E7
Leiters Ford 280 E2
Leo 500 G2
Leopold 175 D8
Leroy 400 C2
Letts 247 F6
Lewis 437 C6
Lewisville 577 G5
Lexington F7
Liberty Center 275 G3
Liberty Mills 200 F2
Liberty▲ 2,051 H5
Ligonier 3,443 F2
Lincoln City 160 C8
Lincolnville 150 F3
Linden 718 D4
Linn Grove 175 H3
Linton 5,814 C6
Linwood 157 F4
Lisbon 200 G2
Little York 155 F7
Livonia 136 E7
Lizton 410 D5
Logan 16,812 H6
Logansport▲ 17,731 E3
Long Beach 2,044 D1
Loogootee 2,884 D7
Losantville 253 G4
Lowell 6,430 C2
Lucerne 135 E3
Lydick E1
Lyford 400 C5
Lynn 1,183 H4
Lynnville 640 C8
Lyons 753 C7
Mackey 89 C8
Macy 218 E3
Madison▲ 12,006 G7
Majenica 150 G3
Manchester 250 H6
Manilla 350 F5
Mansfield 200 C5
Marco 150 C7
Marengo 856 E8
Mariah Hill 300 D8
Marietta 234 F6
Marion▲ 32,618 F3
Markle 1,208 G3
Markleville 412 F5
Marshall 379 C5
Martinsburg 200 E8
Martinsville▲ 11,677 D6
Matthews 571 F4
Mauckport 95 E8
Maxinkuckee 150 E2
Maxwell 300 F5
Mays 156 G5
McCordsville 684 F5
Mecca 331 C5
Mechanicsburg 150 G5
Medaryville 689 D2
Medora 805 E7
Mellott 222 C4
Memphis 300 F8
Mentone 912 E2
Merom 257 B6
Merrillville 27,257 C2
Metamora 350 G6
Metz 200 H1
Mexico 1,003 E3
Miami 350 E3
Michiana Shores 378 D1
Michigan City 33,822 C1
Michigantown 472 E4
Middlebury 2,004 F1
Middletown 2,333 F5
Midland 250 C6
Milan 1,529 G6
Milford 126 F2
Milford 177 F2
Mill Creek 208 D1
Millersburg 854 F1
Millhousen 151 G6
Milltown 917 E8
Millville 275 G5
Milroy 750 G6
Milton 634 G5
Mishawaka 42,608 E1
Mitchell 4,669 E7
Modoc 218 G4
Mongo 225 G1
Monon 1,585 D3
Monroe 788 H3
Monroe City 538 C7
Monroeville 1,232 H3
Monrovia 800 E5
Monterey 230 D2
Montezuma 1,134 C5
Montgomery 351 C7
Monticello▲ 5,237 D3
Montmorenci 300 D4
Montpelier 1,880 G3
Mooreland 465 G5
Moores Hill 649 G6
Mooresville 5,541 E5
Morgantown 978 E6
Morocco 1,044 C3
Morris 980 G6
Morristown 989 F5
Mount Auburn 138 G5
Mount Ayr 151 C3
Mount Carmel 108 H6
Mount Etna 111 F3
Mount Summit 238 G4
Mount Vernon▲ 7,217 B9
Mulberry 1,262 D4
Muncie▲ 71,035 G4
Munster 19,949 B1
Murray 136 G3
Nabb 150 F7
Napoleon 238 G6
Nappanee 5,510 F2
Nashville▲ 873 E6
Needmore 200 E7
New Albany▲ 36,322 F8
New Amsterdam 30 E8
New Carlisle 1,446 E1
New Castle▲ 17,753 G5
New Chicago 2,066 C1
New Goshen 500 B5
New Harmony 846 B8
New Haven 9,320 H2
New Lebanon 150 C6
New Lisbon 300 G5
New London 200 E4
New Marion 200 G6
New Market 614 D5
New Middletown 82 E8
New Palestine 671 F5
New Paris 1,007 F2
New Pekin 1,095 F7
New Point 296 G6
New Providence (Borden) 270 F8
New Richmond 312 D4
New Ross 331 D5
New Salem 200 G5
New Salisbury 350 E8
New Trenton 200 H6
New Washington 800 F7
New Waverly 162 E3
New Whiteland 4,097 E5
New Winchester 180 D5
Newbern 150 F6
Newberry 207 C7
Newburgh 2,880 C9
Newport▲ 627 C5
Newtonville 136 D8
Newtown 243 C4
Newville 150 H2
Noblesville▲ 17,655 F4
North Grove 91 F3
North Judson 1,582 D2
North Liberty 1,366 E1
North Manchester 6,383 F3
North Salem 499 D5
North Terre Haute 4,331 C5
North Vernon 5,311 F6
North Webster 881 F2
Norway 300 D3
Notre Dame E1
Nulltown 235 G5
Oakford 325 E4
Oakland City 2,810 C8
Oaktown 655 C7
Oakville 220 G4
Odon 1,475 C7
Ogden Dunes 1,499 C1
Oldenburg 715 G6
Onward 63 E3
Oolitic 1,424 E7
Ora 200 D2
Orange 200 G5
Orestes 458 F4
Orland 361 G1
Orleans 2,083 D7
Osceola 1,999 E1
Osgood 1,688 G6
Ossian 2,428 G3
Oswego 150 F2
Otis 250 D1
Otisco 425 F7
Otterbein 1,291 C4
Otwell 600 C8
Owensburg 785 D7
Owensville 1,053 B8
Oxford 1,273 C3
Packertown 150 F2
Palestine 800 F2
Palmyra 621 E8
Paoli▲ 3,542 E7
Paragon 515 D6
Parker City 1,323 G4
Patoka 704 B8
Patricksburg 250 D6
Patriot 190 H7
Paxton 200 C6
Pekin 950 E7
Pendleton 2,309 F5
Pennville 637 G4
Perkinsville 175 F4
Perrysville 443 C4
Pershing 425 E2
Pershing G5
Peru▲ 12,843 E3
Petersburg▲ 2,449 C7
Petroleum 212 G3
Pierceton 1,030 F2
Pilot Knob 150 E8
Pimento 150 C6
Pine Lake 1,676 D1
Pine Village 134 C4
Pittsboro 815 D5
Pittsburg 175 D3
Plainfield 10,433 E5
Plainville 444 C7
Pleasant Lake 800 H1
Pleasant Mills 175 H3
Plymouth▲ 8,303 E2
Poe 162 G3
Poland 230 C6
Poneto 236 G3
Portage 29,060 C1
Porter 3,118 C1
Portland▲ 6,483 H4
Poseyville 1,089 B8
Pottawattomie Park 281 C1
Prairie Creek 275 C6
Prairieton 200 B6
Preble 150 H3
Princes Lakes 1,055 E6
Princeton▲ 8,127 B8
Providence 250 E6
Putnamville 250 D5
Quincy 250 D6
Ragsdale 135 C7
Ramsey 550 E8
Ray 200 H1
Rays Crossing 157 F5
Reddington 400 F6
Redkey 1,383 G4
Reelsville 210 D5
Remington 1,247 C3
Rensselaer▲ 5,045 C3
Reynolds 528 D3
Richland 500 C9
Richmond▲ 38,705 H5
Ridgeville 808 G4
Rigdon 150 F4
Riley 232 C6
Rising Sun▲ 2,311 H7
Roachdale 902 D5
Roann 447 F3
Roanoke 1,018 G3
Rochester▲ 5,969 E2
Rockfield 300 D3
Rockport▲ 2,315 C9
Rockville▲ 2,706 C5
Rolling Prairie 550 D1
Rome 1,138 D9
Rome City 1,319 G1
Romney 250 D4
Rosedale 783 C5
Roseland 706 E1
Roselawn 200 C2
Rossville 1,175 D4
Royal Center 859 E3
Royerton 300 G4
Rushville▲ 5,533 G5
Russellville 336 D5
Russiaville 988 E4
Saint Anthony 470 D8
Saint Bernice 500 C5
Saint Henry 560 D8
Saint Joe 452 H2
Saint John 4,921 C2
Saint Leon 493 H6
Saint Louis Crossing 150 F6
Saint Mary-of-the-Woods 920 B6
Saint Marys E1
Saint Meinrad 910 D8
Saint Paul 1,032 F6
Saint Peter 175 H6
Saint Philip 400 B9
Saint Wendel 250 B8
Salamonia 138 H4
Salem 5,619 H3
Salem▲ 5,290 E7
Saltillo 117 E7
San Pierre 325 D2
Sandborn 455 C7
Santa Claus 927 D8
Saratoga 266 H4
Sardinia 133 F6
Schererville 19,926 C2
Schneider 310 C2
Schnellville 250 D8
Scipio 200 F6
Scott 5,334 F1
Scottsburg▲ 5,068 F7
Sedalia 160 E4
Seelyville 1,090 C6
Sellersburg 5,745 F8
Selma 800 G4
Servia 212 F3
Seymour 15,576 F7
Shadeland 1,674 C4
Shamrock Lakes 207 G4
Sharpsville 769 E4
Shelburn 1,147 C6
Shelby 15,336 C2
Shelbyville▲ 14,989 F6
Shepardsville 325 B5
Sheridan 2,046 E4
Shideler 275 G4
Shipshewana 524 F1
Shirley 817 F5
Shirley City (Woodburn) H2
Shoals▲ 853 D7
Sidney 167 F2
Silver Lake 528 F3
Sims 250 F3
Smith Valley E5
Smithville 500 D6
Solsberry 200 D6
Somerset 350 F3
Somerville 223 C8
South Bend▲ 105,511 E1
South Milford 270 G1
South Whitley 1,482 F2
Southport 1,969 E5
Spartanburg 201 H4
Speed 13,092 F8
Speedway 12,641 E5
Spelterville 200 C5
Spencer▲ 2,609 D6
Spencerville 400 G2
Spiceland 757 F5
Spring Grove 420 H5
Spring Lake 216 F5
Springport 194 G4
Springville 279 D7
Spurgeon 149 C8
Stanford 200 D6
Star City 351 D3
State Line 182 C4
Staunton 592 C6
Stendal 175 C8
Stewartsville 225 B8
Stilesville 298 D5
Stillwell 225 D1
Stinesville 204 D6
Stockwell 310 D4
Straughn 318 G5
Stroh 350 G1
Sullivan▲ 4,663 C6
Sulphur 257 E8
Sulphur Springs 345 G4
Sumava Resorts 300 C2
Summitville 1,010 F4
Sunman 623 G6
Swayzee 1,059 F4
Sweetser 924 F3
Switz City 257 C6
Syracuse 2,729 F2
Talma 170 E2
Taylorsville 1,044 F6
Tell City 8,088 D9
Tennyson 267 C8
Terhune 150 E4
Terre Haute▲ 57,483 C6
Thayer 350 C2
Thorntown 1,506 D4
Tippecanoe 320 E2
Tipton▲ 4,751 E4
Tocsin 160 G3
Topeka 912 F1
Town of Pines 789 D1
Trafalgar 531 E6
Trail Creek 2,463 D1
Tri Lakes 3,299 G2
Troy 465 D9
Tunnelton 150 E7
Twelve Mile 240 E3
Tyner 245 E2
Underwood 550 F7
Union 3,612 C8
Union City 3,908 H4
Union Mills 650 D2
Uniondale 289 G3
Unionville 225 E6
Universal 392 C5
Upland 3,295 F4
Urbana 400 F3
Utica 411 F8
Valeene 150 E8
Vallonia 550 E7
Valparaiso▲ 24,414 C2
Van Buren 934 F3
Veedersburg 2,192 C4
Velpen 375 C8
Vera Cruz 83 G3
Vernon▲ 370 F7
Versailles▲ 1,791 G6
Vevay▲ 1,393 G7
Vicksburg 175 C6
Vienna 175 F7
Vincennes▲ 19,859 C7
Wabash▲ 12,127 F3
Wadesville 450 B8
Wakarusa 1,667 F1
Waldron 850 F6
Walesboro 214 F6
Walkerton 2,061 E2
Wallace 89 C5
Wallen 945 G2
Walton 1,053 E3
Wanatah 852 D2
Warren 1,185 G3
Warrington 200 F5
Warsaw▲ 10,968 F2
Washington▲ 10,838 C7
Waterloo 2,040 G2
Watson 200 F8
Waveland 474 D5
Wawaka 320 F2
Wawasee 600 F2
Wawpecong 175 F3
Waynetown 911 C4
Webster 350 H5
West Baden Springs 675 D7
West College Corner 686 H5
West Harrison 318 H6
West Lafayette 25,907 D4
West Lebanon 760 C4
West Middleton 327 E4
West Terre Haute 2,495 B6
Westfield 3,304 E4
Westphalia 300 C7
Westpoint 375 C4
Westport 1,478 F6
Westville 5,255 D1
Wheatfield 621 C2
Wheatland 439 C7
Wheeler 540 C1
Wheeling 180 G4
Wheeling 500 C8
Whiteland 2,446 E5
Whitestown 476 E5
Whitewater 111 H5
Whiting 5,155 C1
Wilkinson 446 F5
Williams 425 D7
Williamsport▲ 1,798 C4
Willow Branch 145 F5
Wilmington 600 H6
Winamac▲ 2,262 D2
Winchester▲ 5,095 G4
Windfall 779 F4
Windsor 150 G4
Wingate 275 C4
Winona Lake 4,053 F2
Winslow 875 C8
Wirt 150 G7
Wolcott 886 C3
Wolcottville 879 G1
Wolflake 230 F2
Woodburn 1,321 H2
Woodland 400 E1
Woodlawn Heights 109 F4
Worthington 1,473 C6
Wyandotte 26 E8
Wyatt 250 E1
Yankeetown 250 C9
Yeoman 131 D3
Yoder 250 G3
Yorktown 4,106 G4
Young America 259 E3
Youngstown 350 C6
Zanesville 575 G3
Zenas 225 G6
Zionsville 5,281 E5

OTHER FEATURES

Anderson (riv.) D8
Bass (lake) D2
Beanblossom (creek) D6
Big (creek) B8
Big Blue (riv.) F5
Big Pine (creek) C3
Big Raccoon (creek) C5
Big Walnut (creek) D5
Blue (riv.) E8
Brookville (lake) G6
Buck (creek) E8
Busseron (creek) C7
Camp (creek) E6
Cedar (creek) G2
Clifty (creek) F6
Coal (coal) C4
Crooked (creek) D2
Cypress (pond) B8
Deer (creek) E3
Deer (creek) D5
Eagle (creek) E4
Eel (riv.) C6
Eel (riv.) F3
Elkhart (riv.) F1
Fawn (riv.) G1
Flatrock (creek) F5
Fort Benjamin Harrison E5
Freeman (lake) D3
Geist (res.) F5
George Rogers Clark Nat'l Hist. Park B7
Graham (creek) F7
Grissom A.F.B. 4,271 E3
Huntington (lake) F3
Indian (creek) D6
Indian (creek) E8
Indiana Dunes Nat'l Lakeshore C1
Iroquois (riv.) B3
Jefferson Proving Ground G7
Kankakee (riv.) C2
Lemon (lake) E6
Lincoln Boyhood Nat'l Mem. C8
Little (riv.) G3
Little Elkhart (riv.) F1
Little Pigeon (creek) C9
Little Vermilion (riv.) B5
Lost (riv.) D7
Maria (creek) C7
Maumee (riv.) H2
Maxinkuckee (lake) E2
Michigan (lake) C1
Mill (creek) D5
Mississinewa (lake) F3
Mississinewa (riv.) F3
Monroe (lake) E6
Morse (res.) E4
Muscatatuck (riv.) E7
Ohio (riv.) B9
Patoka (riv.) C8
Pigeon (creek) C8
Pigeon (riv.) F1
Pipe (creek) F4
Prairie (creek) C7
Richland (creek) D6
Saint Joseph (riv.) E1
Saint Joseph (riv.) H2
Saint Marys (lake) H3
Saint Marys (riv.) H3
Salamonie (lake) F3
Salamonie (riv.) G4
Salt (creek) E6
Sand (creek) F6
Shafer (lake) D3
Silver (creek) F8
Sugar (creek) B3
Sugar (creek) C5
Sugar (creek) F5
Tippecanoe (riv.) E2
Vermilion (riv.) B4
Vernon Fork (creek) F7
Wabash (riv.) B7
Wawasee (lake) F2
White (riv.) B8
White, East Fork (riv.) C7
White, West Fork (riv.) C7
Whitewater (riv.) H6
Wildcat (creek) E4

▲County seat

Topography

0 40 80 MI.
0 40 80 KM.

Below Sea Level 100 m. 328 ft. 200 m. 656 ft. 500 m. 1,640 ft. 1,000 m. 3,281 ft. 2,000 m. 6,562 ft. 5,000 m. 16,404 ft.

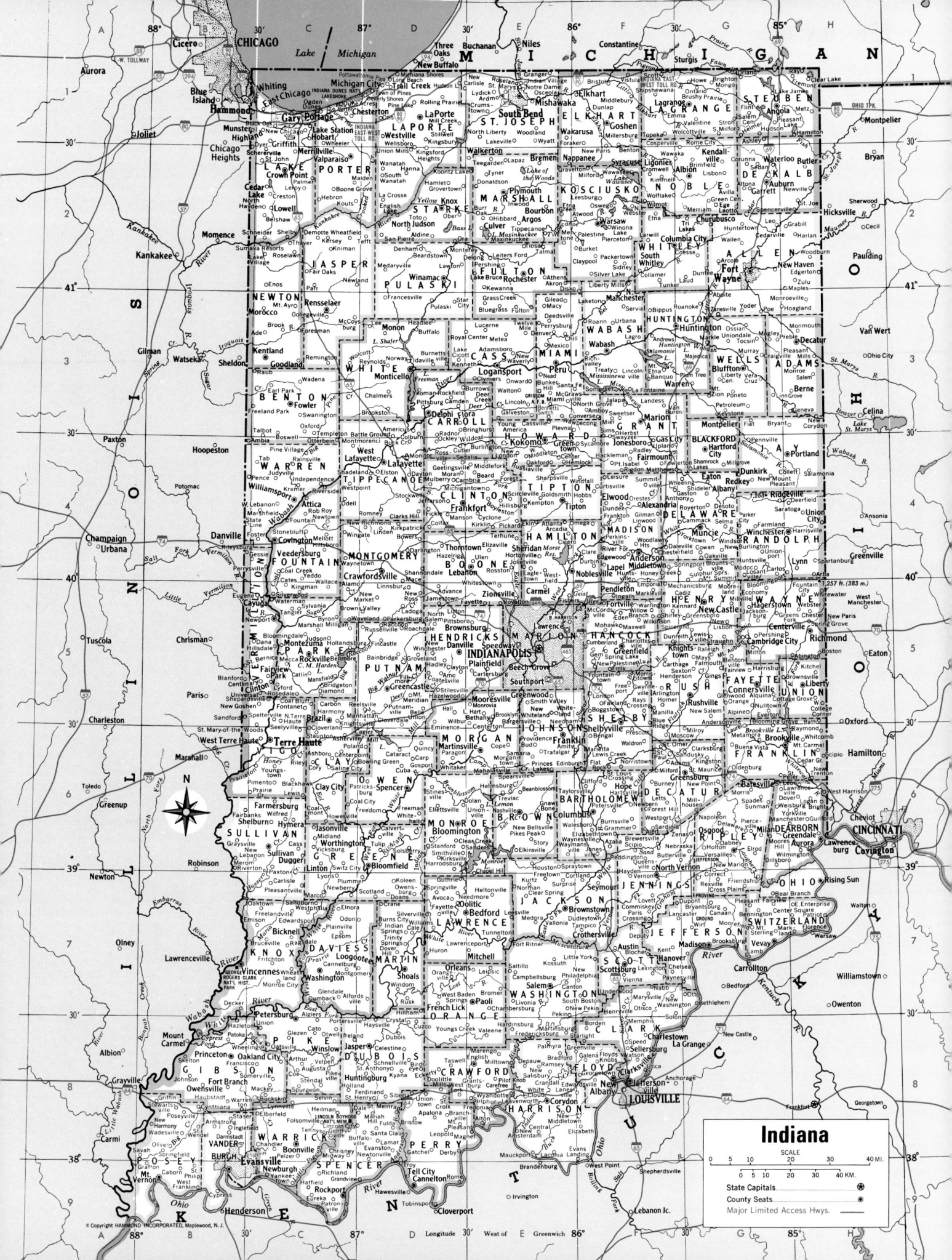
Indiana
SCALE
0 5 10 20 30 40 MI.
0 5 10 20 30 40 KM.
State Capitals
County Seats
Major Limited Access Hwys.
MICHIGAN
ILLINOIS
OHIO
KENTUCKY
Lake Michigan
CHICAGO
INDIANAPOLIS
CINCINNATI
LOUISVILLE
LAKE
PORTER
LAPORTE
ST. JOSEPH
ELKHART
LAGRANGE
STEUBEN
NEWTON
JASPER
STARKE
MARSHALL
KOSCIUSKO
NOBLE
DE KALB
PULASKI
FULTON
WHITLEY
ALLEN
BENTON
WHITE
CASS
MIAMI
WABASH
HUNTINGTON
WELLS
ADAMS
WARREN
TIPPECANOE
CARROLL
HOWARD
GRANT
BLACKFORD
JAY
FOUNTAIN
MONTGOMERY
CLINTON
TIPTON
MADISON
DELAWARE
RANDOLPH
VERMILLION
PARKE
BOONE
HAMILTON
HENRY
WAYNE
PUTNAM
HENDRICKS
MARION
HANCOCK
RUSH
FAYETTE
UNION
VIGO
CLAY
MORGAN
JOHNSON
SHELBY
DECATUR
FRANKLIN
OWEN
MONROE
BROWN
BARTHOLOMEW
SULLIVAN
GREENE
JENNINGS
RIPLEY
DEARBORN
OHIO
KNOX
DAVIESS
MARTIN
LAWRENCE
JACKSON
JEFFERSON
SWITZERLAND
SCOTT
ORANGE
WASHINGTON
CLARK
GIBSON
PIKE
DUBOIS
CRAWFORD
HARRISON
FLOYD
POSEY
VANDERBURGH
WARRICK
SPENCER
PERRY
Longitude West of Greenwich

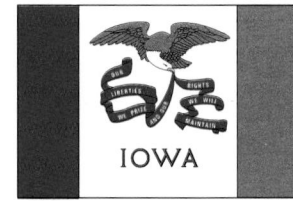

IOWA

AREA 56,275 sq. mi. (145,752 sq. km.)
POPULATION 2,787,424
CAPITAL Des Moines
LARGEST CITY Des Moines
HIGHEST POINT (Osceola Co.) 1670 ft.
(509 m.)
SETTLED IN 1788
ADMITTED TO UNION December 28, 1846
POPULAR NAME Hawkeye State
STATE FLOWER Wild Rose
STATE BIRD Eastern Goldfinch

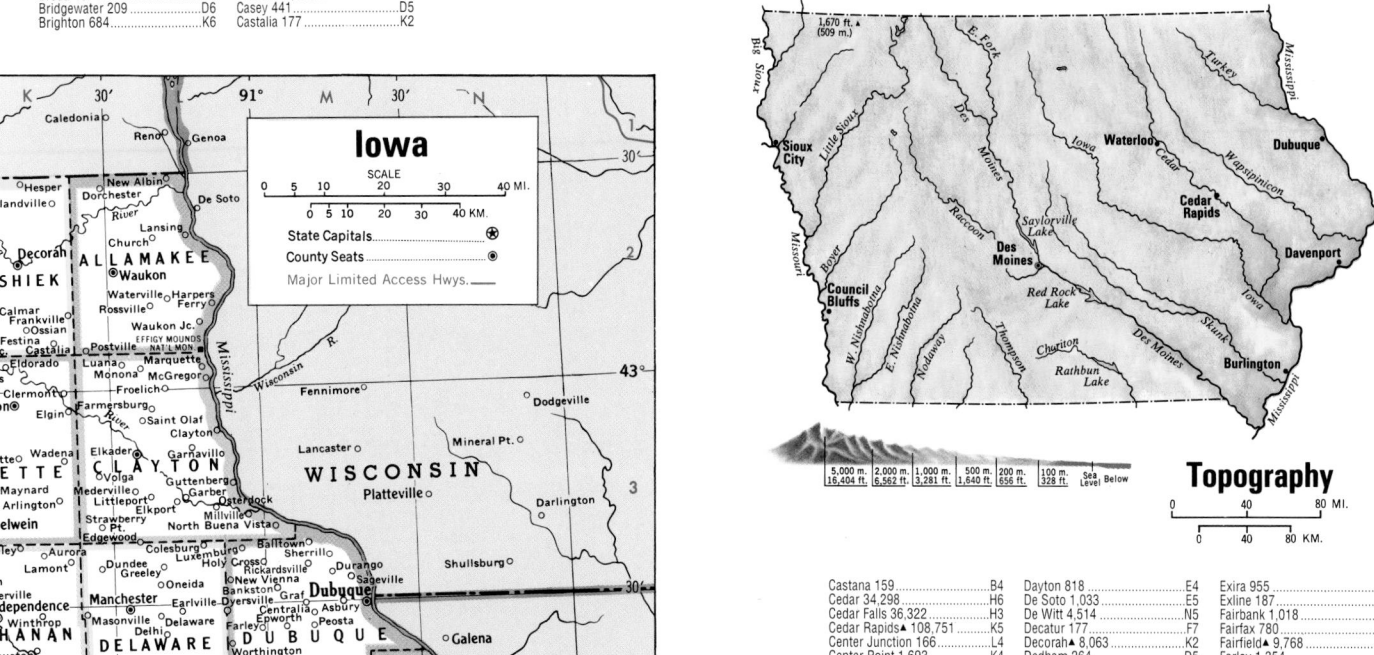

Topography

(continued on following page)

Agriculture, Industry and Resources

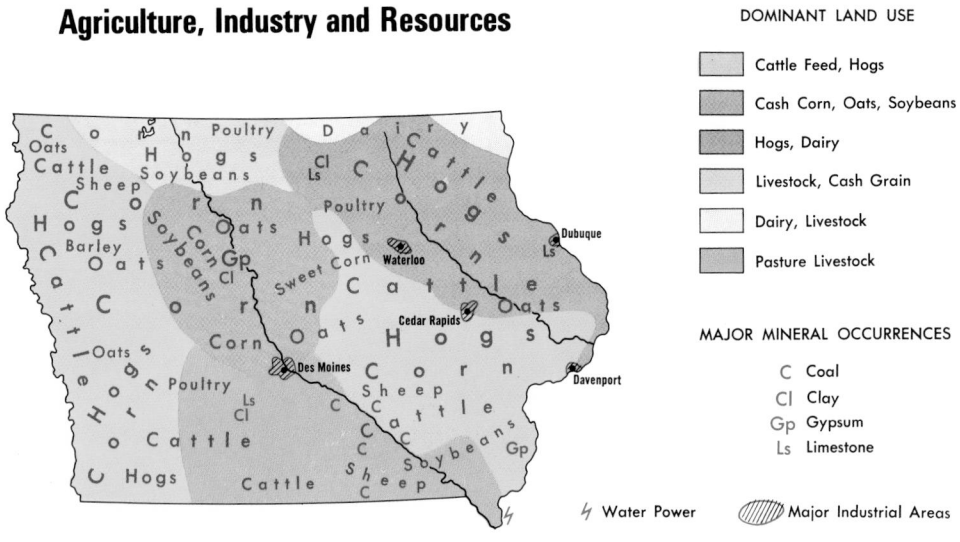

DOMINANT LAND USE

- Cattle Feed, Hogs
- Cash Corn, Oats, Soybeans
- Hogs, Dairy
- Livestock, Cash Grain
- Dairy, Livestock
- Pasture Livestock

MAJOR MINERAL OCCURRENCES

- C Coal
- Cl Clay
- Gp Gypsum
- Ls Limestone

⚡ Water Power   ⬭ Major Industrial Areas

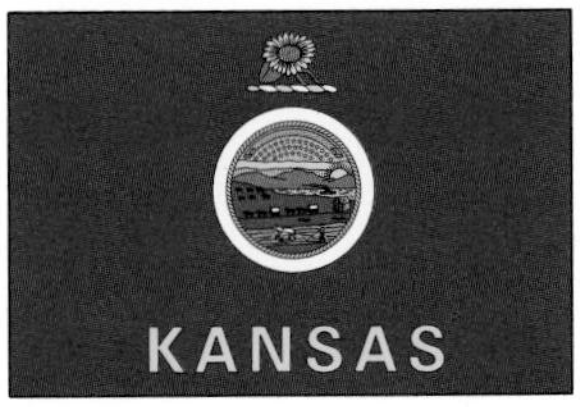

AREA 82,277 sq. mi. (213,097 sq. km.)
POPULATION 2,485,600
CAPITAL Topeka
LARGEST CITY Wichita
HIGHEST POINT Mt. Sunflower 4,039 ft. (1231 m.)
SETTLED IN 1831
ADMITTED TO UNION January 29, 1861
POPULAR NAME Sunflower State
STATE FLOWER Sunflower
STATE BIRD Western Meadowlark

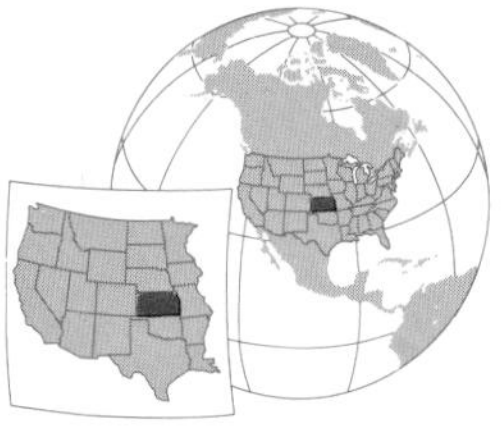

COUNTIES

Allen 15,654 ... G4
Anderson 7,803 ... G3
Atchison 16,932 ... G2
Barber 5,874 ... D4
Barton 29,382 ... D3
Bourbon 14,966 ... H4
Brown 11,128 ... G2
Butler 50,580 ... F4
Chase 3,021 ... F3
Chautauqua 4,407 ... F4
Cherokee 21,374 ... H4
Cheyenne 3,243 ... A2
Clark 2,418 ... C4
Clay 9,158 ... E2
Cloud 11,023 ... E2
Coffey 8,404 ... G3
Comanche 2,313 ... C4
Cowley 36,915 ... F4
Crawford 35,568 ... H4
Decatur 4,021 ... B2
Dickinson 18,958 ... E3
Doniphan 8,134 ... G2
Douglas 81,798 ... G3
Edwards 3,787 ... C4
Elk 3,327 ... F4
Ellis 26,004 ... C3
Ellsworth 6,586 ... D3
Finney 33,070 ... B3
Ford 27,463 ... C4
Franklin 21,994 ... G3
Geary 30,453 ... F3
Gove 3,231 ... B3
Graham 3,543 ... C2
Grant 7,159 ... A4
Gray 5,396 ... B4
Greeley 1,774 ... A3
Greenwood 7,847 ... F4
Hamilton 2,388 ... A3
Harper 7,124 ... D4
Harvey 31,028 ... E3
Haskell 3,886 ... B4
Hodgeman 2,177 ... C3
Jackson 11,525 ... G2
Jefferson 15,905 ... G2
Jewell 4,251 ... D2
Johnson 355,054 ... H3
Kearny 4,027 ... A3
Kingman 8,292 ... D4
Kiowa 3,660 ... C4
Labette 23,693 ... G4
Lane 2,375 ... B3
Leavenworth 64,371 ... G2
Lincoln 3,653 ... D2
Linn 8,254 ... H3
Logan 3,081 ... A3
Lyon 34,732 ... F3
Marion 12,888 ... E3
Marshall 11,705 ... F2
McPherson 27,268 ... E3
Meade 4,247 ... B4
Miami 23,466 ... H3
Mitchell 7,203 ... D2
Montgomery 38,816 ... G4
Morris 6,198 ... F3
Morton 3,480 ... A4
Nemaha 10,446 ... F2
Neosho 17,035 ... G4
Ness 4,033 ... C3
Norton 5,947 ... C2
Osage 15,248 ... G3
Osborne 4,867 ... D2
Ottawa 5,634 ... E2
Pawnee 7,555 ... C3
Phillips 6,590 ... C2
Pottawatomie 16,128 ... F2
Pratt 9,702 ... D4
Rawlins 3,404 ... A2
Reno 62,389 ... D4
Republic 6,482 ... E2
Rice 10,610 ... D3
Riley 67,139 ... F2
Rooks 6,039 ... C2
Rush 3,842 ... C3
Russell 7,835 ... D3
Saline 49,301 ... E3
Scott 5,289 ... B3
Sedgwick 403,662 ... E4
Seward 18,743 ... B4
Shawnee 160,976 ... G2
Sheridan 3,043 ... B2
Sherman 6,926 ... A2
Smith 5,078 ... D2
Stafford 5,365 ... D3
Stanton 2,333 ... A4
Stevens 5,048 ... A4
Sumner 25,841 ... E4
Thomas 8,258 ... A2
Trego 3,694 ... C3
Wabaunsee 6,603 ... F3
Wallace 1,821 ... A3
Washington 7,073 ... E2
Wichita 2,758 ... A3
Wilson 10,289 ... G4
Woodson 4,116 ... G4
Wyandotte 161,993 ... H2

CITIES and TOWNS

Abbyville 123 ... D4
Abilene▲ 6,242 ... E3
Ada 120 ... E2
Admire 147 ... F3
Agenda 81 ... E2
Agra 322 ... C2
Alamota 50 ... B3
Albert 229 ... C3
Alden 182 ... D3
Alexander 85 ... C3
Aliceville 60 ... G3
Allen 191 ... F3
Alma▲ 871 ... F2
Almena 423 ... C2
Alta Vista 477 ... F3
Altamont 1,048 ... G4
Alton 115 ... D2
Altoona 456 ... G4
Americus 891 ... F3
Ames 65 ... E2
Andale 566 ... E4
Andover 4,047 ... E4
Angola 55 ... G4
Anthony▲ 2,516 ... D4
Arcadia 338 ... H4
Argonia 529 ... E4
Arkansas City 12,762 ... E4
Arlington 457 ... D4
Arma 1,542 ... H4
Ash Valley 50 ... C3
Ashland▲ 1,032 ... C4
Assaria 387 ... E3
Atchison▲ 10,656 ... G2
Athol 86 ... D2
Atlanta 232 ... F4
Attica 716 ... D4
Atwood▲ 1,388 ... B2
Auburn 908 ... G3
Augusta 7,876 ... F4
Aurora 101 ... E2
Axtell 432 ... F2
Baileyville 130 ... F2
Baldwin City 2,961 ... G3
Barnard 129 ... D2
Barnes 167 ... F2
Bartlett 107 ... G4
Basehor 1,591 ... G2
Bassett 20 ... G4
Bavaria 100 ... E3
Baxter Springs 4,351 ... H4
Bazine 373 ... C3
Beagle 88 ... G3
Beattie 221 ... F2
Beaumont 112 ... F4
Beaver 57 ... D3
Beeler 80 ... B3
Belle Plaine 1,649 ... E4
Belleville▲ 2,517 ... E2
Beloit▲ 4,066 ... D2
Belpre 116 ... C4
Belvue 207 ... F2
Bendena 125 ... G2
Benedict 16 ... G4
Bennington 568 ... E2
Bentley 360 ... E4
Benton 669 ... E4
Bern 190 ... F2
Berryton 150 ... G3
Beverly 131 ... E2
Big Bow 55 ... A4
Bird City 467 ... A2
Bison 252 ... C3
Blaine 50 ... F2
Bloom 65 ... C4
Blue Mound 251 ... H3
Blue Rapids 1,131 ... F2
Bluff City 69 ... E4
Bogue 150 ... C2
Bonner Springs 6,413 ... H2
Brazilton 91 ... H4
Bremen 60 ... F2
Brewster 296 ... A2
Bridgeport 95 ... E3
Bronson 343 ... H4
Brookville 226 ... E3
Brownell 44 ... C3
Bucklin 710 ... C4
Bucyrus 135 ... H3
Buffalo 293 ... G4
Buhler 1,277 ... E3
Bunker Hill 111 ... D3
Burden 518 ... F4
Burdett 248 ... C3
Burdick 100 ... F3
Burlingame 1,074 ... G3
Burlington▲ 2,735 ... G3
Burns 226 ... F3
Burr Oak 278 ... D2
Burrton 866 ... E3
Bushong 57 ... F3
Bushton 341 ... D3
Byers 46 ... D4
Caldwell 1,351 ... E4
Cambridge 74 ... F4
Caney 2,062 ... G4
Canton 794 ... E3
Carbondale 1,526 ... G3
Carlton 39 ... E3
Carlyle 75 ... G4
Cassoday 95 ... F3
Catharine 121 ... C3
Cawker City 588 ... D2
Cedar 25 ... D2
Cedar Point 39 ... F3
Cedar Vale 760 ... F4
Centerville 104 ... H3
Centralia 452 ... F2
Chanute 9,488 ... G4
Chapman 1,264 ... E3
Chase 577 ... D3
Chautauqua 132 ... F4
Cheney 1,560 ... E4
Cherokee 651 ... H4
Cherryvale 2,464 ... G4
Chetopa 1,357 ... G4
Chicopee 300 ... H4
Cimarron▲ 1,626 ... B4
Circleville 153 ... G2
Claflin 678 ... D3
Clay Center▲ 4,613 ... E2
Clayton 91 ... B2
Clearview City ... G3
Clearwater 1,875 ... E4
Clifton 561 ... E2
Climax 57 ... F4
Clyde 793 ... E2
Coats 127 ... D4
Codell 90 ... C2
Coffeyville 12,917 ... G4
Colby▲ 5,396 ... A2
Coldwater▲ 939 ... C4
Collyer 144 ... B2
Colony 447 ... G3
Columbus▲ 3,268 ... H4

Agriculture, Industry and Resources

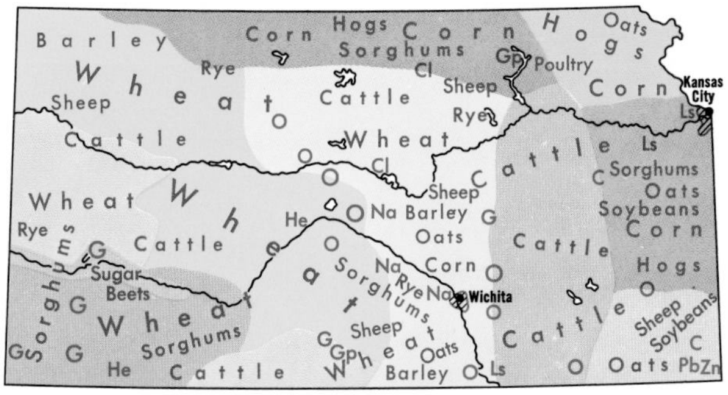

DOMINANT LAND USE

- Specialized Wheat
- Wheat, General Farming
- Wheat, Range Livestock
- Wheat, Grain Sorghums, Range Livestock
- Cattle Feed, Hogs
- Livestock, Cash Grain
- Livestock, Cash Grain, Dairy
- General Farming, Livestock, Cash Grain
- General Farming, Livestock, Special Crops
- Range Livestock

MAJOR MINERAL OCCURRENCES

C	Coal	Ls	Limestone
Cl	Clay	Na	Salt
G	Natural Gas	O	Petroleum
Gp	Gypsum	Pb	Lead
He	Helium	Zn	Zinc

Major Industrial Areas

Colwich 1,091 ... E4
Concordia▲ 6,167 ... E2
Conway 1,384 ... E3
Conway Springs 1,313 ... E4
Coolidge 90 ... A3
Copeland 290 ... B4
Corning 142 ... F2
Cottonwood Falls▲ 889 ... F3
Council Grove▲ 2,228 ... F3
Courtland 343 ... E2
Coyville 78 ... G4
Crestline 85 ... H4
Cuba 242 ... E2
Cullison 120 ... D4
Culver 162 ... E3
Cummings 150 ... G2
Cunningham 535 ... D4
Damar 112 ... C2
Danville 56 ... E4
De Soto 2,291 ... H3
Dearing 428 ... G4
Deerfield 677 ... A4
Delia 172 ... G2
Delphos 494 ... E2
Denison 225 ... G2
Dennis 96 ... G4
Denton 166 ... G2
Derby 14,699 ... E4
Detroit 90 ... E3
Devon 108 ... H4
Dexter 320 ... F4
Dighton▲ 1,361 ... B3
Dodge City▲ 21,129 ... B4
Dorrance 195 ... D3
Douglass 1,722 ... F4
Dover 192 ... G3
Downs 1,119 ... D2
Dresden 73 ... B2
Dunlap 65 ... F3
Durham 119 ... E3
Dwight 365 ... F3
Earlton 69 ... G4
Eastborough 896 ... E4
Easton 405 ... G2
Edgerton 1,244 ... H3
Edmond 37 ... C2
Edna 438 ... G4
Edson 55 ... A2
Edwardsville 3,979 ... H2
Effingham 540 ... G2
El Dorado▲ 11,504 ... F4
Elbing 184 ... E3
Elgin 118 ... F4
Elk City 334 ... G4
Elk Falls 122 ... F4
Elkhart▲ 2,318 ... A4
Ellinwood 2,329 ... D3
Ellis 1,814 ... C3
Ellsworth▲ 2,294 ... D3
Elmdale 83 ... F3
Elmont 112 ... G2
Elsmore 91 ... G4
Elwood 1,079 ... H2
Elyria 100 ... E3
Emmett 165 ... F2
Emporia▲ 25,512 ... F3
Englewood 96 ... C4
Ensign 192 ... B4
Enterprise 865 ... E3
Erie▲ 1,276 ... G4
Esbon 167 ... D2
Eskridge 518 ... F3
Eudora 3,006 ... G3
Eureka▲ 2,974 ... F4
Everest 310 ... G2
Fairview 306 ... G2
Fairway 4,173 ... H2
Fall River 113 ... G4
Falun 89 ... E3
Farlington 80 ... H4
Florence 636 ... E3
Fontana 131 ... H3
Ford 247 ... C4
Formoso 128 ... D2
Fort Dodge 400 ... C4
Fort Leavenworth ... H2
Fort Scott▲ 8,362 ... H4
Fowler 571 ... B4
Frankfort 927 ... F2
Franklin 400 ... H4
Frederick 18 ... D3
Fredonia▲ 2,599 ... G4
Freeport 8 ... E4
Frontenac 2,588 ... H4
Fulton 191 ... H4
Galatia 47 ... D3
Galena 3,308 ... H4
Galesburg 160 ... G4
Galva 651 ... E3
Garden City▲ 24,097 ... B4
Garden Plain 731 ... E4
Gardner 3,191 ... H3
Garfield 236 ... C3
Garland 112 ... H4
Garnett▲ 3,210 ... G3
Gas 505 ... G4
Gaylord 173 ... D2
Gem 104 ... B2
Geneseo 382 ... D3
Geuda Springs 219 ... E4
Girard▲ 2,794 ... H4
Glade 101 ... C2
Glasco 556 ... E2
Glen Elder 448 ... D2
Goddard 1,804 ... E4
Goessel 506 ... E3
Goff 156 ... G2
Goodland▲ 4,983 ... A2
Gorham 284 ... D3
Gove▲ 103 ... B3
Grainfield 357 ... B2
Grandview Plaza 1,233 ... F2
Grantville 220 ... G2
Great Bend▲ 15,427 ... D3
Greeley 339 ... G3
Green 150 ... E2
Greenleaf 353 ... E2
Greensburg▲ 1,792 ... C4
Grenola 256 ... F4
Gridley 356 ... G3

(continued on following page)

232 Kansas
(continued)

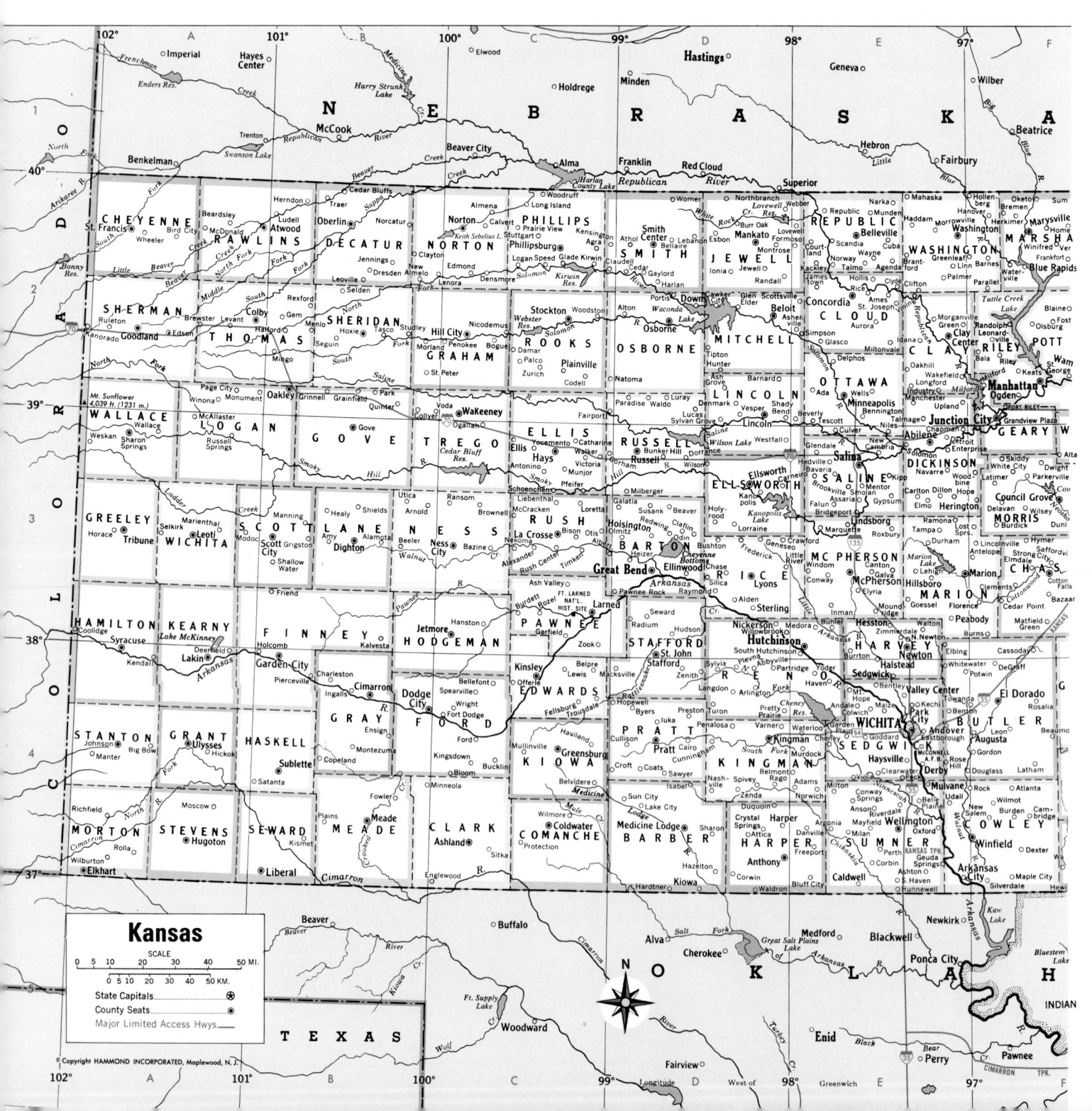

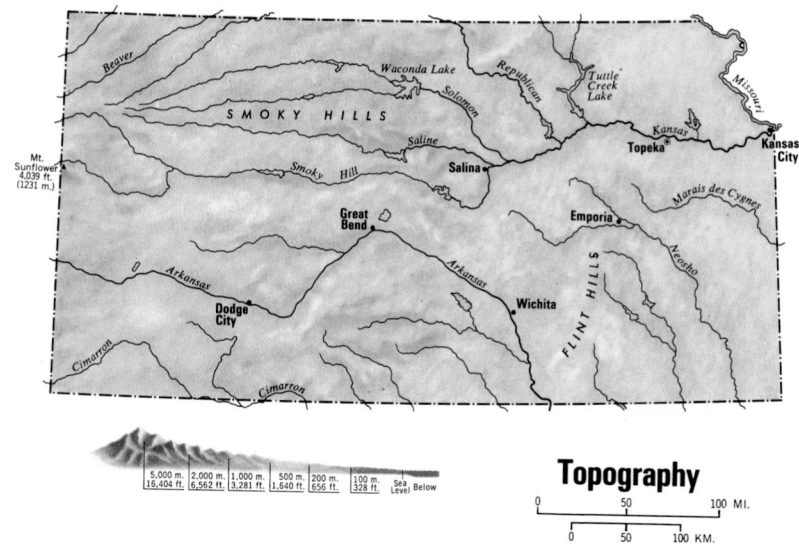

Topography

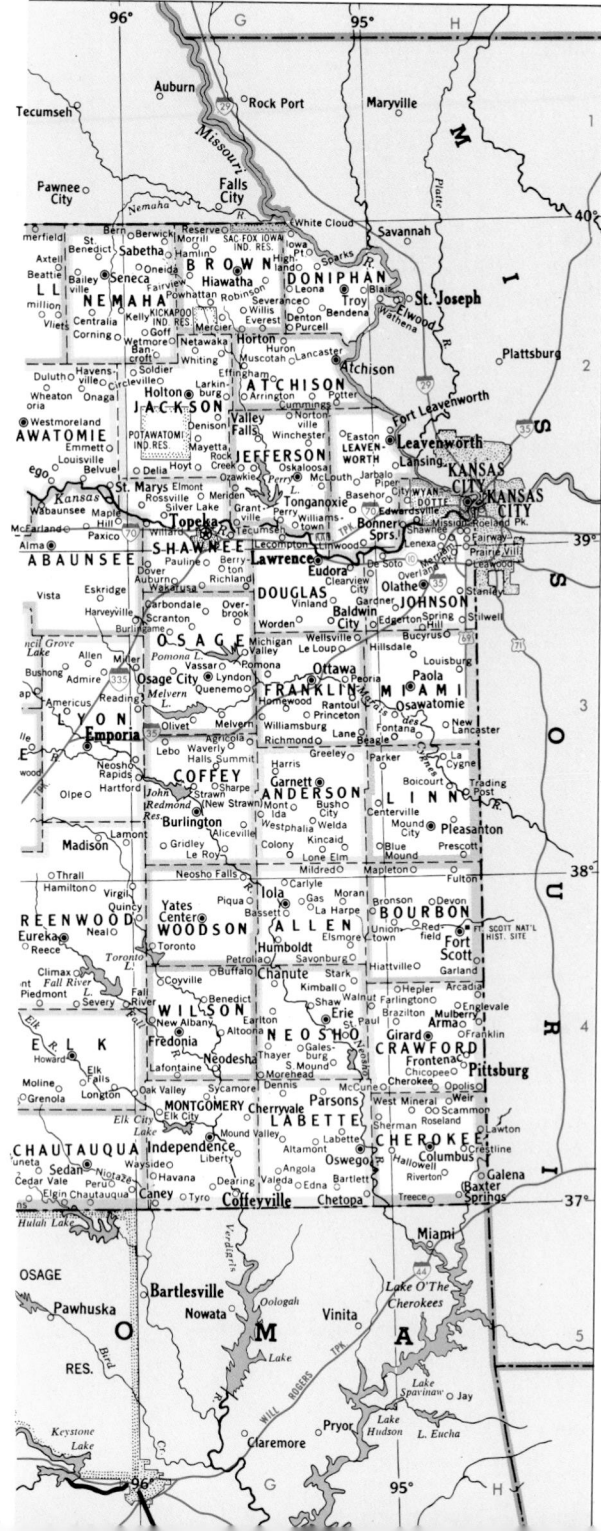

KENTUCKY

COUNTIES

Adair 15,360 ... L6
Allen 14,628 ... J7
Anderson 14,571 ... M5
Ballard 7,902 ... C6
Barren 34,001 ... K7
Bath 9,692 ... O4
Bell 31,506 ... O7
Boone 57,589 ... M3
Bourbon 19,236 ... N4
Boyd 51,150 ... R4
Boyle 25,641 ... M5
Bracken 7,766 ... N3
Breathitt 15,703 ... P5
Breckinridge 16,312 ... J5
Bullitt 47,567 ... K5
Butler 11,245 ... H6
Caldwell 13,232 ... F6
Calloway 30,735 ... E7
Campbell 83,866 ... N3
Carlisle 5,238 ... C7
Carroll 9,292 ... L3
Carter 24,340 ... P4
Casey 14,211 ... M6
Christian 68,941 ... F7
Clark 29,496 ... N4
Clay 21,746 ... O6
Clinton 9,135 ... L7
Crittenden 9,196 ... E6
Cumberland 6,784 ... L7
Daviess 87,189 ... G5
Edmonson 10,357 ... J6
Elliott 6,455 ... P4
Estill 14,614 ... O5
Fayette 225,366 ... M5
Fleming 12,292 ... O4
Floyd 43,586 ... R5
Franklin 43,781 ... M4
Fulton 8,271 ... C7
Gallatin 5,393 ... M3
Garrard 11,579 ... M5
Grant 15,737 ... M3
Graves 33,550 ... D7
Grayson 21,050 ... J5
Green 10,371 ... K6
Greenup 36,742 ... R3
Hancock 7,864 ... H5
Hardin 89,240 ... K5
Harlan 36,574 ... P7
Harrison 16,248 ... N4
Hart 14,890 ... K6
Henderson 43,044 ... F5
Henry 12,823 ... L4
Hickman 5,566 ... C7
Jackson 11,955 ... N6
Jefferson 664,937 ... K4
Jessamine 30,508 ... M5
Johnson 23,248 ... R5
Kenton 142,031 ... M3
Knott 17,906 ... R6
Knox 29,676 ... O7
Larue 11,679 ... K5
Laurel 43,438 ... N6
Lawrence 13,998 ... R4
Lee 7,422 ... O5
Leslie 13,642 ... P6
Letcher 27,000 ... R6
Lewis 13,029 ... P3
Lincoln 20,045 ... M6
Livingston 9,062 ... E6
Logan 24,416 ... H7
Lyon 6,624 ... E7
Madison 57,508 ... N5
Magoffin 13,077 ... P5
Marion 16,499 ... L5
Marshall 27,205 ... E7
Martin 12,526 ... R5
Mason 16,666 ... O3
McCracken 62,879 ... D6
McCreary 15,603 ... N7
McLean 9,628 ... G5
Meade 24,170 ... J5
Menifee 5,092 ... O5
Mercer 19,148 ... M5
Metcalfe 8,963 ... K7
Monroe 11,401 ... K7
Montgomery 19,561 ... O4
Morgan 11,648 ... P5
Muhlenberg 31,318 ... G6
Nelson 29,710 ... K5
Nicholas 6,725 ... N4
Ohio 21,105 ... H6
Oldham 33,263 ... L4
Owen 9,035 ... M3
Owsley 5,036 ... O6
Pendleton 12,036 ... N3
Perry 30,283 ... P6
Pike 72,583 ... S6
Powell 11,686 ... O5
Pulaski 49,489 ... M6
Robertson 2,124 ... N3
Rockcastle 14,803 ... N6
Rowan 20,353 ... P4
Russell 14,716 ... L6
Scott 23,867 ... M4
Shelby 24,824 ... L4
Simpson 15,145 ... H7
Spencer 6,801 ... L4
Taylor 21,146 ... L6
Todd 10,940 ... G7
Trigg 10,361 ... F7
Trimble 6,090 ... L3
Union 16,557 ... F5
Warren 76,673 ... H6
Washington 10,441 ... L5
Wayne 17,468 ... M7
Webster 13,955 ... F5
Whitley 33,326 ... N7
Wolfe 6,503 ... O5
Woodford 19,955 ... M4

CITIES and TOWNS

Adairville 906 ... H7
Ages 500 ... P7
Albany▲ 2,062 ... L7
Alexandria▲ 5,592 ... N3
Allen 229 ... R5
Allensville 218 ... G7
Amburgey 500 ... R6
Anchorage 2,082 ... L2
Annville 470 ... O6
Arjay 975 ... O7
Arlington 449 ... D7
Ashland 23,622 ... R4
Auburn 1,273 ... H7
Audubon Park 1,520 ... J2
Augusta 1,336 ... N3
Austin 500 ... K7
Auxier 900 ... R5
Bancroft 582 ... K1
Banner 950 ... R5
Barbourmeade 1,402 ... K1
Barbourville▲ 3,658 ... O7
Bardstown▲ 6,801 ... L5
Bardwell▲ 819 ... D7
Barlow 706 ... D6
Baskett 550 ... F5
Beattyville▲ 1,131 ... O5
Beauty 800 ... S5
Beaver Dam 2,904 ... H6
Bedford▲ 761 ... L3
Bee Spring 500 ... J6
Beechwood Village 1,263 ... K2
Belcher 500 ... S6
Belfry 800 ... S5
Bellemeade 927 ... L2
Bellevue 6,997 ... S1
Benham 717 ... R7
Benton▲ 3,899 ... E7
Berea 9,126 ... N5
Berry 240 ... N3
Betsy Layne 975 ... R5
Big Creek 700 ... O6
Blaine 271 ... R4
Blandville 95 ... D7
Bloomfield 845 ... L5
Blue Ridge Manor 565 ... L2
Boldman 510 ... R5
Bonnieville 300 ... K6
Bonnyman 800 ... P6
Boone 232 ... N5
Booneville▲ 191 ... O6
Bowling Green▲ 40,641 ... H7
Bradford 199 ... N3
Bradfordsville 331 ... L6
Brandenburg▲ 1,857 ... J4
Bremen 267 ... G6
Briensburg ... E7
Broadfields 273 ... K2
Brodhead 1,140 ... N6
Bromley 1,137 ... S2
Brooks 2,464 ... K4
Brooksville▲ 670 ... N3
Brownsboro Farm 670 ... L1
Brownsville 897 ... J6
Buechel 7,081 ... K2
Buffalo ... K6
Bulan 800 ... P6
Burgin 1,009 ... M5
Burkesville▲ 1,815 ... L7
Burlington▲ 6,070 ... R2
Burnside 695 ... M6
Butler 625 ... N3
Cadiz▲ 2,148 ... F7
Calhoun▲ 854 ... G5
California 130 ... N3
Calvert City 2,531 ... E6
Camargo 1,022 ... O4
Campbellsburg 604 ... L3
Campbellsville▲ 9,577 ... L6
Campton▲ 484 ... O5
Caney 549 ... P5
Caneyville 642 ... J6
Cannel City 600 ... P5
Carlisle▲ 1,639 ... N4
Carrollton▲ 3,715 ... L3
Carter ... P4
Catlettsburg▲ 2,231 ... R4
Cave City 1,953 ... K6
Cawood 800 ... P7
Center 383 ... K6
Centertown 462 ... G6
Centerville ... S6
Central City 4,979 ... G6
Cerulean ... F7
Clarkson 611 ... J6
Clay 1,173 ... F6
Clay City 1,258 ... O5
Clearfield 1,250 ... P4
Clinton▲ 1,547 ... D7
Clover Bottom 600 ... N5
Cloverport 1,207 ... H5
Coal Run 262 ... R5
Cold Spring 2,880 ... T2
Columbia▲ 3,845 ... L6
Columbus 252 ... C7
Combs 900 ... P6
Corbin 7,419 ... N7
Corinth 137 ... M3
Corydon 790 ... F5
Covington 43,264 ... S2
Crab Orchard 825 ... M6
Crescent Springs 2,179 ... R2
Crestview 356 ... S2
Crestview Hills 2,546 ... R2
Crestwood 1,435 ... L4
Crittenden 731 ... M3
Crofton 699 ... G6
Cumberland 3,112 ... R6
Cynthiana▲ 6,497 ... N4
Danville▲ 12,420 ... M5
Dawson Springs 3,129 ... F6
Dayton 6,576 ... T1
Devondale 1,164 ... K2
Dexter ... E7
Dixon▲ 552 ... F5
Dorton 750 ... R6
Douglass Hills 5,549 ... L2
Dover 297 ... O3
Drakesboro 565 ... H6
Dry Ridge 1,601 ... M3
Earlington 1,833 ... F6
East Bernstadt 550 ... N6
Echols 576 ... H6
Eddyville▲ 1,889 ... E6
Edgewood 8,143 ... S2
Edmonton▲ 1,477 ... K7
Elizabethtown▲ 18,167 ... K5
Elkhorn City 813 ... S6
Elkton▲ 1,789 ... G7
Elsmere 6,847 ... R2
Eminence 2,055 ... L4
Eolia 875 ... R6
Erlanger 15,979 ... R2
Essie 650 ... P6
Eubank 354 ... M6
Evarts 1,063 ... P7
Ewing 268 ... O4
Fairdale 6,563 ... K4
Fairfield 142 ... L5
Fairview 119 ... G7
Fairview 198 ... S2
Fallsburg ... R4
Falmouth▲ 2,378 ... N3
Fancy Farm 800 ... D7
Farmington 600 ... D7
Fedscreek 950 ... S6
Ferguson 934 ... M6
Fincastle 838 ... L1
Flat 7,799 ... O5
Flat Lick 600 ... O7
Flatwoods 8,354 ... R4
Fleming (Fleming-Neon) 759 ... R6
Flemingsburg▲ 3,071 ... O4
Florence 18,624 ... R2
Ford 522 ... N5
Fordsville 561 ... H5
Forest Hills 454 ... L2
Fort Knox 21,495 ... K5
Fort Mitchell 7,438 ... S2
Fort Thomas 16,032 ... S2
Fort Wright 6,570 ... S2
Fountain Run 259 ... K7
Frankfort (cap.)▲ 25,968 ... M4
Franklin▲ 7,607 ... J7
Fredonia 490 ... E6
Frenchburg▲ 625 ... O5
Fullerton 950 ... P3
Fulton 3,078 ... D7
Gamaliel 462 ... K7
Garrison 700 ... P3
Georgetown▲ 11,414 ... M4
Germantown 213 ... O3
Ghent 365 ... L3
Gilbertsville ... E7
Glasgow▲ 12,351 ... J7
Glencoe 257 ... M3
Glenview 653 ... K1
Goose Creek 321 ... L1
Goshen 2,447 ... K4
Gramoor 1,167 ... K1
Grand Rivers 351 ... E7
Gray 2,911 ... O7
Grayson▲ 3,510 ... R4
Greensburg▲ 1,990 ... K6
Greenup▲ 1,158 ... R3
Greenville▲ 4,689 ... G6
Guthrie 1,504 ... G7
Hammond 510 ... O7
Hanson 450 ... G6
Hardin 595 ... E7
Hardinsburg▲ 1,906 ... H5
Hardy 900 ... S5
Harlan▲ 2,686 ... P7
Harold 520 ... R5
Harrodsburg▲ 7,335 ... M5
Hartford▲ 2,532 ... H6
Hatfield 700 ... S5
Hawesville▲ 998 ... H5
Hazard▲ 5,416 ... P6
Hazel 460 ... E7
Hebron 930 ... R2
Helton 600 ... P7
Henderson▲ 25,945 ... F5
Hickman▲ 2,689 ... C7
Hickory 152 ... D7
Highland Heights 4,223 ... T2
Hima 600 ... O6
Himyar 545 ... O7
Hindman▲ 798 ... R6
Hiseville 220 ... K6
Hitchins 750 ... R4
Hodgenville▲ 2,721 ... K5
Hollow Creek 991 ... K4
Hopkinsville▲ 29,809 ... F7
Horse Cave 2,284 ... K6
Houston Acres 496 ... K2
Hustonville 313 ... M6
Hyden▲ 375 ... P6
Independence▲ 10,444 ... M3
Indian Hills 1,074 ... K1
Inez▲ 511 ... S5
Irvine▲ 2,836 ... O5
Irvington 1,180 ... J5
Island 446 ... G6
Ivel 850 ... R5
Jackson▲ 2,466 ... P5
Jamestown▲ 1,641 ... L7
Jeff 23,221 ... P6
Jeffersontown 15,795 ... L2
Jeffersonville 1,854 ... O5
Jenkins 2,751 ... R6
Junction City 1,983 ... M5
Keavy 900 ... N6
Keene 393 ... M5
Kenton 358 ... N3
Kenton Vale 145 ... S2
Kenvir 800 ... P7
Kevil 337 ... D6
King 399 ... O7
Kingsley 464 ... K2
Kitts 800 ... P7
Kuttawa 535 ... E6
La Center 1,040 ... C6
La Fayette 106 ... F7
La Grange▲ 3,853 ... L4
Lackey ... R6
Lake 3,131 ... O6
Lakeside Park 3,062 ... R2
Lancaster▲ 3,421 ... M5
Lawrenceburg▲ 5,911 ... M4
Leatherwood 800 ... P6
Lebanon Junction 1,741 ... K5
Lebanon▲ 5,695 ... L5
Leitchfield▲ 4,965 ... J6
Lejunior 597 ... P7
Lewisburg 772 ... G6
Lewisport 1,778 ... H5
Lexington▲ 204,165 ... N4
Liberty▲ 1,937 ... M6
Littcarr 645 ... R6
Livermore 1,534 ... G5
Livingston 241 ... N6
Lockport 84 ... M4
London▲ 5,757 ... N6
Lone Oak 465 ... D6
Lookout 600 ... S6
Lookout Heights ... S2
Loretto 820 ... L5
Lothair 600 ... P6
Louisa▲ 1,990 ... R4
Louisville▲ 269,063 ... J2
Loyall 1,100 ... P7
Ludlow 4,736 ... S2
Lynch 1,166 ... R7
Mackville 200 ... L5
Madisonville▲ 16,200 ... F6
Majestic 600 ... S5
Manchester▲ 1,634 ... O6
Marion▲ 3,320 ... E6
Marshes Siding 800 ... M7
Martha 650 ... R4
Martin 694 ... R5
Mary 177 ... O5
Mason 1,119 ... M3
Mayfield▲ 9,935 ... D7
Maysville▲ 7,169 ... O3
McAndrews 975 ... S5
McCarr 592 ... S5
McHenry 414 ... H6
McKee▲ 870 ... O6
McRoberts 1,101 ... R6
McVeigh 650 ... S5
Meadow Vale 798 ... L1
Meally 550 ... R5
Melbourne 660 ... T2
Mentor 169 ... N3
Meta 600 ... S5
Middlesboro 11,328 ... O7
Middletown 5,016 ... L2
Midway 1,290 ... M4
Millersburg 937 ... N4
Millstone 550 ... R6
Milton 563 ... L3
Minor Lane Heights 1,675 ... K4
Monterey 164 ... M4
Monticello▲ 5,357 ... M7
Moorland 467 ... L2
Morehead▲ 8,357 ... P4
Morgan 3,776 ... N3
Morganfield▲ 3,781 ... E5
Morgantown▲ 2,284 ... H6
Mortons Gap 987 ... F6
Mount Olivet▲ 384 ... N3
Mount Sterling▲ 5,362 ... N4
Mount Vernon▲ 2,654 ... N6
Mount Washington 5,226 ... K4
Mouthcard 900 ... S6
Muldraugh 1,376 ... J5
Munfordville▲ 1,556 ... J6
Murray▲ 14,439 ... E7
Nebo 227 ... F6
Neon (Neon-Fleming) ... R6
New Castle▲ 893 ... L4
New Concord 800 ... E7
New Haven 796 ... K5
New Hope ... L5
Newport 18,871 ... S2
Nicholasville▲ 13,603 ... N5
North Middletown 602 ... N4
Northfield 898 ... K1
Nortonville 1,209 ... G6
Oak Grove 2,863 ... G7
Oakland 202 ... J6
Oil Springs 900 ... P5
Okolona 18,902 ... K4
Oldtown 570 ... R4
Olive Hill 1,809 ... P4
Owensboro▲ 53,549 ... G5
Owenton▲ 1,306 ... M3
Owingsville▲ 1,491 ... O4
Paducah▲ 27,256 ... D6
Paintsville▲ 4,354 ... R5
Paris▲ 8,730 ... N4
Park City 549 ... J6
Park Hills 3,321 ... S2
Parksville 560 ... M5
Parkway Village 707 ... J2
Pembroke 640 ... G7
Perryville 815 ... M5
Petersburg ... M2
Pewee Valley 1,283 ... L4
Phelps 1,298 ... S6
Philpot 700 ... H5
Pikeville▲ 6,324 ... S6
Pine Knot 1,549 ... M7
Pineville▲ 2,198 ... O7
Pittsburg ... N6
Plantation 830 ... K1
Pleasure Ridge Park 25,131 ... J4
Pleasureville 761 ... L4
Plum Springs 361 ... J7
Powderly 748 ... G6
Premium 729 ... R6
Preston 3,558 ... O4
Prestonsburg▲ 4,011 ... R5
Prestonville 205 ... L3
Princeton▲ 6,940 ... F6
Prospect 2,788 ... K4
Providence 4,123 ... F6
Raceland 2,256 ... R3
Radcliff 19,772 ... K5
Ravenna 804 ... O5
Raywick 157 ... L5
Richmond▲ 21,155 ... N5
Riverwood 506 ... K1
Robards 701 ... F5
Rochester 191 ... H6
Rockholds 775 ... N7
Rockport 385 ... H6
Rolling Fields 593 ... K2
Rolling Hills 1,135 ... L1
Russell 4,014 ... R3
Russell Springs 2,363 ... L6
Russellville▲ 7,454 ... H7
Ryland Heights 279 ... M3
Sacramento 563 ... G6
Sadieville 255 ... M4
Saint Charles 316 ... F6
Saint Matthews 15,800 ... K2

Agriculture, Industry and Resources

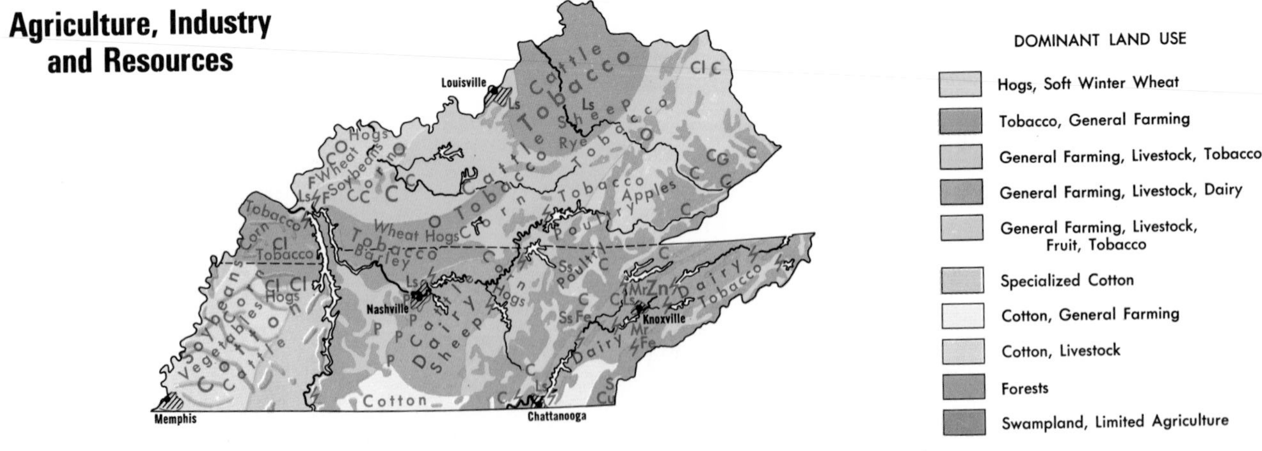

Louisville
Nashville
Knoxville
Memphis
Chattanooga
DOMINANT LAND USE
Hogs, Soft Winter Wheat
Tobacco, General Farming
General Farming, Livestock, Tobacco
General Farming, Livestock, Dairy
General Farming, Livestock, Fruit, Tobacco
Specialized Cotton
Cotton, General Farming
Cotton, Livestock
Forests
Swampland, Limited Agriculture

MAJOR MINERAL OCCURRENCES

C Coal
Cl Clay
Cu Copper
F Fluorspar
Fe Iron Ore
G Natural Gas
Ls Limestone
Mr Marble
O Petroleum
P Phosphates
S Pyrites
Ss Sandstone
Zn Zinc

Water Power

Major Industrial Areas

Saint Regis Park 1,756 .... K2
Salem 770 .... E6
Salt Lick 342 .... O4
Salyersville▲ 1,917 .... P5
Sanders 231 .... M3
Sandy Hook▲ 548 .... P4
Sardis 171 .... O3
Science Hill 628 .... M6
Scottsville▲ 4,278 .... J7
Sebree 1,510 .... F5
Seco R6
Sedalia D7
Seneca Gardens 684 .... K2
Sextons Creek 975 .... O6
Sharpsburg 315 .... O4
Shelbyville▲ 6,238 .... L4
Shepherdsville▲ 4,805 .... K4
Shively 15,535 .... K4
Silver Grove 1,102 .... T2
Simpson 907 .... P5
Simpsonville 642 .... L4
Slaughters 235 .... F6
Smilax 987 .... P6
Smithfield 115 .... L4
Smithland▲ 384 .... E6
Smiths Grove 703 .... J6
Somerset▲ 10,733 .... M6
Sonora 295 .... K5
South 202 .... J6
South Carrollton 262 .... G6
South Portsmouth 900 .... P3
South Shore 1,318 .... R3
South Williamson 1,016 .... S5
Southgate 3,266 .... T2
Sparta 133 .... M3
Spottsville 914 .... G5
Springfield▲ 2,875 .... L5
Springlee 451 .... K2
Staffordsville 700 .... R5
Stamping Ground 698 .... M4
Stanford▲ 2,686 .... M5
Stanton▲ 2,795 .... O5
Stearns 1,550 .... N7
Stone 900 .... S5
Strathmoor Village 361 .... K2
Sturgis 2,184 .... F5
Tateville 680 .... M7
Taylor Mill 5,530 .... S2
Taylorsville▲ 774 .... L4
Thealka 600 .... R5
Thornhill 146 .... K1
Tollesboro 808 .... O3
Tompkinsville▲ 2,861 .... K7
Trenton 378 .... G7
Tyner 590 .... O6
Union 1,001 .... M3
Uniontown 1,008 .... F5
Upton 719 .... K6
Valley Station 22,840 .... K4
Van 1,050 .... R6
Van Lear 2,035 .... R5
Vanceburg▲ 1,713 .... P3
Verda 1,133 .... P7
Versailles▲ 7,269 .... M4
Vicco 244 .... P6
Villa Hills 7,739 .... R2
Vine Grove 3,586 .... K5
Virgie 600 .... R6
Visalia 190 .... N3
Wallins Creek 261 .... O7
Walton 2,034 .... M3
Warfield 364 .... S5
Warsaw▲ 1,202 .... M3
Washington 795 .... O3
Water Valley 321 .... D7
Waverly 345 .... F5
Wayland 359 .... R6
Weeksbury 850 .... R6
Wellington 593 .... O5
Wellington 653 .... K2
West Buechel 1,587 .... K2
West Liberty▲ 1,887 .... P5
West Point 1,216 .... J4
West Somerset 850 .... M6
Westwood 734 .... R4
Westwood 826 .... L1
Wheatcroft 206 .... F5
Wheelwright 721 .... R6
White Plains 598 .... G6
Whitesburg▲ 1,636 .... R6
Whitesville 682 .... H5
Whitley City▲ 1,133 .... N7
Wickliffe▲ 851 .... C7
Wilders 633 .... S2
Willard R4
Williamsburg▲ 5,493 .... N7
Williamstown▲ 3,023 .... M3
Willisburg 223 .... L5
Wilmore 4,215 .... M5
Winchester▲ 15,799 .... N5
Windy Hills 2,452 .... K1
Wingo 568 .... D7
Winston Park S2
Wolf Creek 600 .... J4
Woodbine 900 .... N7
Woodburn 343 .... J7
Woodbury 117 .... H6
Woodland Hills 714 .... L2
Woodlawn (Oakdale) 308 .... D6
Woodlawn 331 .... T2
Woodlawn Park 1,099 .... K2
Wooton 750 .... P6
Worthington 1,751 .... R3
Worthville 191 .... L3
Wurtland 1,221 .... R3
Zebulon 750 .... S5

OTHER FEATURES

Abraham Lincoln Birthplace Nat'l Hist. Site K5
Barkley (dam) E6
Barkley (lake) F7
Barren (riv.) H6
Barren River (lake) J7
Beech Fork (riv.) L5
Big Sandy (riv.) R4
Black (mt.) R7
Buckhorn (lake) O6
Chaplin (riv.) L5
Clarks, East Fork (riv.) E7
Cove Run (lake) P4
Cumberland (lake) M7
Cumberland (mt.) P7
Cumberland (riv.) K8
Cumberland Gap Nat'l Hist. P7
Dale Hollow (lake) L7
Dewey (lake) R5
Dix (riv.) M5
Drakes (creek) J7
Dry (creek) R2
Eagle (creek) M3
Fishtrap (lake) S6
Fort Campbell G7
Grayson (lake) P4
Green (riv.) G6
Green River (lake) L6
Herrington (lake) M5
Hinkston (creek) N4
Kentucky (dam) E7
Kentucky (lake) E8
Kentucky (riv) M3
Land Between The Lakes Rec. Area E7
Laurel River (lake) N6
Lexington Blue Grass Army Depot N4
Licking (riv.) N3
Mammoth Cave Nat'l Park J6
Mayfield (creek) C7
Mississippi (riv.) 10
Mud (riv.) H7
Nolin (lake) K6
Nolin (riv.) J6
Obion (creek) C7
Ohio (riv.) F5
Paint Lick (riv.) M5
Panther (creek) G5
Pine (mt.) O7
Pond (riv.) G6
Red (riv.) G7
Red (riv.) O5
Rockcastle (riv.) N6
Rolling Fork (riv.) K5
Rough (riv.) H5
Rough River (lake) J5
Salt (riv.) K5
Tennessee (riv.) D6
Tradewater (riv.) F6
Tug Fork (riv.) S5

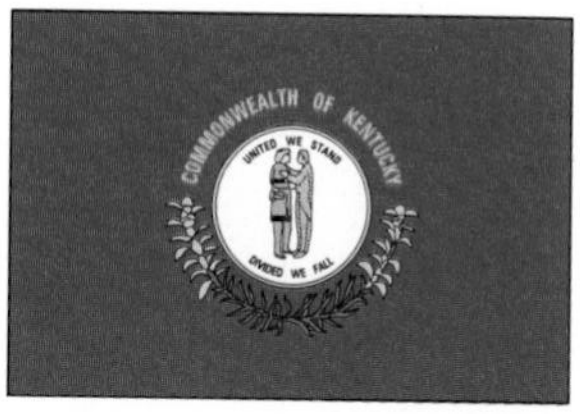

KENTUCKY

KENTUCKY

AREA 40,409 sq. mi. (104,659 sq. km.)
POPULATION 3,698,969
CAPITAL Frankfort
LARGEST CITY Louisville
HIGHEST POINT Black Mtn. 4,145 ft. (1263 m.)
SETTLED IN 1774
ADMITTED TO UNION June 1, 1792
POPULAR NAME Bluegrass State
STATE FLOWER Goldenrod
STATE BIRD Cardinal

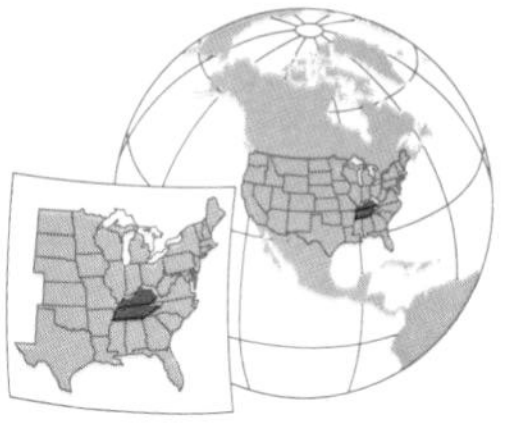

TENNESSEE

COUNTIES

Anderson 68,250 .... N8
Bedford 30,411 .... J9
Benton 14,524 .... E8
Bledsoe 9,669 .... L9
Blount 85,969 .... O9
Bradley 73,712 .... M1
Campbell 35,079 .... N8
Cannon 10,467 .... J9
Carroll 27,514 .... E9
Carter 51,505 .... S8
Cheatham 27,140 .... G8
Chester 12,819 .... D1
Claiborne 26,137 .... O8
Clay 7,238 .... K7
Cocke 29,141 .... P9
Coffee 40,339 .... J9
Crockett 13,378 .... C9
Cumberland 34,736 .... L9
Davidson 510,784 .... H8
De Kalb 13,589 .... K9
Decatur 10,472 .... E9
Dickson 35,061 .... G8
Dyer 34,854 .... C8
Fayette 25,559 .... C1
Fentress 14,669 .... M8
Franklin 34,725 .... J1
Gibson 46,315 .... D9
Giles 25,741 .... G1
Grainger 17,095 .... O8
Greene 55,853 .... R8
Grundy 13,362 .... K1
Hamblen 50,480 .... P8
Hamilton 285,536 .... L1
Hancock 6,739 .... P7
Hardeman 23,377 .... C1
Hardin 22,633 .... E1
Hawkins 44,565 .... P8
Haywood 19,437 .... C9
Henderson 21,844 .... E9
Henry 27,888 .... E8
Hickman 16,754 .... G9
Houston 7,018 .... F8
Humphreys 15,795 .... F8
Jackson 9,297 .... K8
Jefferson 33,016 .... P8
Johnson 13,766 .... T7
Knox 335,749 .... O9
Lake 7,129 .... B8
Lauderdale 23,491 .... B9
Lawrence 35,303 .... G1
Lewis 9,247 .... F9
Lincoln 28,157 .... H1
Loudon 31,255 .... N9
Macon 15,906 .... J7
Madison 77,982 .... D9
Marion 24,860 .... K1
Marshall 21,539 .... H1
Maury 54,812 .... G9
McMinn 42,383 .... M1
McNairy 22,422 .... D1
Meigs 8,033 .... M9
Monroe 30,541 .... N1
Montgomery 100,498 .... G8
Moore 4,721 .... J1
Morgan 17,300 .... M8
Obion 31,717 .... C8
Overton 17,636 .... L8
Perry 6,612 .... F9
Pickett 4,548 .... M7
Polk 13,643 .... N1
Putnam 51,373 .... K8
Rhea 24,344 .... M9
Roane 47,227 .... M9
Robertson 41,494 .... H7
Rutherford 118,570 .... J9
Scott 18,358 .... M8
Sequatchie 8,863 .... L1
Sevier 51,043 .... O9
Shelby 826,330 .... B1
Smith 14,143 .... J8
Stewart 9,479 .... F7
Sullivan 143,596 .... S7
Sumner 103,281 .... J8
Tipton 37,568 .... B9
Trousdale 5,920 .... J8
Unicoi 16,549 .... S8
Union 13,694 .... O8
Van Buren 4,846 .... L9
Warren 32,992 .... K9
Washington 92,315 .... R8
Wayne 13,935 .... F1
Weakley 31,972 .... D8
White 20,090 .... L9
Williamson 81,021 .... H9
Wilson 67,675 .... J8

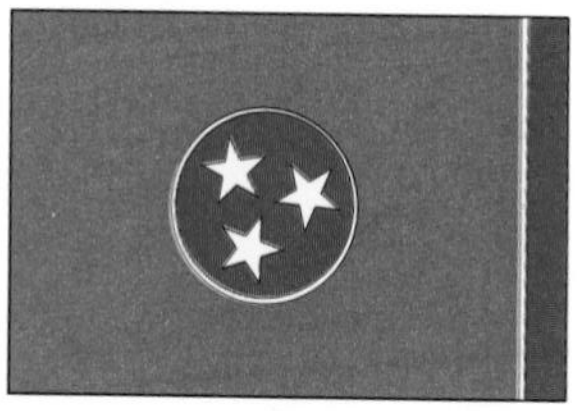

TENNESSEE

TENNESSEE

AREA 42,144 sq. mi. (109,153 sq. km.)
POPULATION 4,896,641
CAPITAL Nashville
LARGEST CITY Memphis
HIGHEST POINT Clingmans Dome 6,643 ft. (2025 m.)
SETTLED IN 1757
ADMITTED TO UNION June 1, 1796
POPULAR NAME Volunteer State
STATE FLOWER Iris
STATE BIRD Mockingbird

CITIES and TOWNS

Adams 587 .... G7
Adamsville 1,745 .... E10
Afton 800 .... R8
Alamo▲ 2,426 .... C9
Alcoa 6,400 .... N9
Alexandria 730 .... J8
Algood 2,399 .... K8
Allardt 609 .... M8
Allons 600 .... L8
Altamont▲ 679 .... K10
Apison 750 .... L10
Ardmore 866 .... H10
Arlington 1,541 .... B10
Armathwaite 700 .... M8
Arthur 500 .... O7
Ashland City▲ 2,552 .... G8
Athens▲ 12,054 .... M10
Atoka 659 .... B10
Atwood 1,066 .... D9
Auburntown 240 .... J9
Baileyton 309 .... R8
Banner Hill 1,717 .... R8
Bartlett 26,989 .... B10
Bath Springs 800 .... E10
Baxter 1,289 .... K8
Bean Station 500 .... P8
Beechgrove 550 .... J9
Beersheba Springs 596 .... K10
Bell Buckle 326 .... J9
Belle Meade 2,839 .... H8
Bells 1,643 .... C9
Benton▲ 992 .... M10
Berry Hill 802 .... H8
Berry's Chapel 2,703 .... H9
Bethel Springs 755 .... D10
Big Sandy 505 .... E8
Birchwood 550 .... M10
Blaine 1,326 .... O8
Bloomingdale 10,953 .... R7
Bloomington Springs 800 .... K8
Blountville▲ 2,605 .... S7
Bluff City 1,390 .... S8
Bolivar▲ 5,969 .... C10
Braden 354 .... B10
Bradford 1,154 .... D8
Braemar S8
Brentwood 16,392 .... H8
Briceville 850 .... N8
Brighton 717 .... B10
Bristol 23,421 .... S7
Brownsville▲ 10,019 .... C9
Bruceton 1,586 .... E8
Buena Vista 500 .... E9
Bulls Gap 659 .... P8
Burlison 394 .... B9
Burns 1,127 .... G8
Butler 500 .... T8
Byrdstown▲ 998 .... L7
Calhoun 552 .... M10
Camden▲ 3,643 .... E8
Carthage▲ 2,386 .... K8
Caryville 1,751 .... N8
Castalian Springs 650 .... J8
Cedar Hill 347 .... H7
Celina▲ 1,493 .... K7
Centertown 332 .... K9
Centerville▲ 3,616 .... G9
Chapel Hill 833 .... H9
Charleston 653 .... M10
Charlotte▲ 854 .... G8
Chattanooga▲ 152,466 .... K10
Chuckey 500 .... R8
Church Hill 4,834 .... R7
Clairfield 650 .... O7
Clarksburg 321 .... E9
Clarksville▲ 75,494 .... G7
Cleveland▲ 30,354 .... M10
Clifton 620 .... F10
Clinton▲ 8,972 .... N8
Coalfield 712 .... N8
Coalmont 813 .... K10
Cokercreek 500 .... N10
College Grove 580 .... H9
Collegedale 5,048 .... M10
Collierville 14,427 .... B10
Collinwood 1,014 .... F10
Colonial Heights 6,716 .... R8
Columbia▲ 28,583 .... G9
Concord 8,569 .... N9
Cookeville▲ 21,744 .... L8
Copperhill 362 .... N10
Cordova 600 .... B10
Cornersville 683 .... H10
Corryton 500 .... O8
Counce 975 .... E10
Covington▲ 7,487 .... B9
Cowan 1,738 .... K10
Crab Orchard 876 .... M9
Crockett Mills 500 .... C9
Cross Plains 1,025 .... H7
Crossville▲ 6,930 .... L9
Crump 2,028 .... E10
Cumberland City 319 .... F8
Cumberland Gap 210 .... O8
Cypress Inn 500 .... F10
Dandridge▲ 1,540 .... O8
Dayton▲ 5,671 .... L9
Decatur▲ 1,361 .... M9
Decaturville▲ 879 .... E9
Decherd 2,196 .... J10
Dickson 8,791 .... G8
Dover▲ 1,341 .... F8
Dowelltown 308 .... K8
Doyle 345 .... K9
Dresden▲ 2,488 .... D8
Drummonds 800 .... A10
Duck River 750 .... G9
Ducktown 421 .... N10
Dunlap▲ 3,731 .... L10
Dyer 2,204 .... D8
Dyersburg▲ 16,317 .... C8
Eads 550 .... B10
Eagleton Village 5,169 .... O9
Eagleville 462 .... H9
East Ridge 21,101 .... L11
Eastview 563 .... D10
Elgin 700 .... M8
Elizabethton▲ 11,931 .... S8
Elk Valley 750 .... N7
Elkton 448 .... H10
Ellendale 850 .... B10
Embreeville Junction R8
Emory Gap 500 .... M9
Englewood 1,611 .... M10
Enville 211 .... E10
Erin▲ 1,586 .... F8
Erwin▲ 5,015 .... S8
Estill Springs 1,408 .... J10
Ethridge 565 .... G10
Etowah 3,815 .... M10
Eva 500 .... E8
Fairfield 2,209 .... J9
Fairview 4,210 .... G9
Fall Branch 1,203 .... R8
Farner 750 .... N10
Fayetteville▲ 6,921 .... H10
Finger 279 .... D10
Finley 1,014 .... B8
Flintville 500 .... H10
Forest Hills 4,231 .... H8
Fort Pillow 700 .... B9
Fowlkes 700 .... C9
Franklin▲ 20,098 .... H9
Friendship 467 .... C9
Friendsville 792 .... N9
Gadsden 561 .... D9
Gainesboro▲ 1,002 .... K8
Gallatin▲ 18,794 .... H8
Gallaway 762 .... B10
Garland 194 .... B9
Gates 608 .... C9
Gatlinburg 3,417 .... O9
Germantown 32,893 .... B10
Gibson 281 .... D9
Gilt Edge 447 .... B9
Gleason 1,402 .... D8
Goodlettsville 8,177 .... H8
Gordonsville 891 .... K8
Grand Junction 365 .... C10
Grandview M9
Graysville 1,301 .... L10
Greenback 611 .... N9
Greenbrier 2,873 .... H8
Greeneville▲ 13,532 .... R8
Greenfield 2,105 .... D8
Grimsley 650 .... L8
Gruetli 1,810 .... K10
Guys 497 .... D10
Habersham 750 .... N8
Halls 2,431 .... C9
Halls Crossroads O8
Hampshire 788 .... G9
Hampton 2,236 .... S8
Harriman 7,119 .... M9
Harris 7,191 .... C8
Harrison 6,206 .... L10
Harrogate (Shawanee) 2,657 .... O8
Hartsville▲ 2,188 .... J8
Helenwood 675 .... M8
Henderson▲ 4,760 .... D10
Hendersonville 32,188 .... H8
Henning 802 .... B9
Henry 317 .... E8
Hickory Valley 159 .... C10
Hixson L10
Hohenwald▲ 3,760 .... F9
Hollow Rock 902 .... E8
Hornbeak 445 .... C8
Hornsby 313 .... D10
Humboldt 9,651 .... D9
Huntingdon▲ 4,180 .... E8
Huntland 885 .... J10
Huntsville▲ 660 .... N8
Hurricane Mills 850 .... F9
Iron City 402 .... F10
Jacksboro▲ 1,568 .... N8
Jackson▲ 48,949 .... D9
Jamestown▲ 1,862 .... M8
Jasper▲ 2,780 .... K10
Jefferson City 5,494 .... P8
Jellico 2,447 .... N7
Johnson City 49,381 .... S8
Jones 3,091 .... C9
Jonesborough▲ 2,829 .... R8
Karns 1,458 .... N9
Kenton 1,366 .... C8
Kimball 1,243 .... K10
Kimberlin Heights 500 .... O9
Kingsport 36,365 .... R7
Kingston Springs 1,529 .... G8
Kingston▲ 4,552 .... N9
Knoxville▲ 165,121 .... O9
Kodak 700 .... O9
La Follette 7,192 .... N8
La Grange 167 .... C10
La Vergne 7,499 .... H9
Laager 675 .... K10
Lafayette▲ 3,641 .... J7
Lake City 2,166 .... N8
Lakeland 1,204 .... B10
Lakesite 732 .... L10
Lakewood 2,009 .... H8
Lawrenceburg▲ 10,412 .... G10
Lebanon▲ 15,208 .... J8
Lenoir City 6,147 .... N9
Leoma 600 .... G10
Lewisburg▲ 9,879 .... H10
Lexington▲ 5,810 .... E9
Liberty 391 .... K8
Linden▲ 1,099 .... F9
Livingston▲ 3,809 .... L8
Lobelville 830 .... F9
Long Island S7
Lookout Mountain 1,901 .... L11
Loretto 1,515 .... G10
Loudon▲ 4,026 .... N9
Louisville 500 .... N9
Luttrell 812 .... O8
Lutts 740 .... F10
Lyles 500 .... G9
Lynchburg▲ 668 .... J10
Lynnville 344 .... G10
Madisonville▲ 3,033 .... N9
Malesus 600 .... D9
Manchester▲ 7,709 .... J10
Martel 500 .... N9
Martin 8,600 .... D8
Maryville▲ 19,208 .... O9
Mascot 2,138 .... O8
Mason 337 .... B10
Maury City 782 .... C9
Maynardville▲ 1,298 .... O8
McDonald 500 .... M10
McEwen 1,442 .... F8
McKenzie 5,168 .... E8
McLemoresville 280 .... D9
McMinnville▲ 11,194 .... K9
Medina 658 .... D9
Medon 137 .... D10
Memphis▲ 610,337 .... B10
Michie 677 .... E10
Middleton 536 .... D10
Midway 2,953 .... P8
Milan 7,512 .... D9
Milledgeville 279 .... E10
Milligan College 600 .... S8
Millington 17,866 .... B10
Minor Hill 372 .... G10
Mitchellville 193 .... J7
Monteagle 1,138 .... K10
Monterey 2,559 .... L8
Morley 600 .... N7
Morrison 570 .... K9
Morrison City 2,032 .... R7
Morristown▲ 21,385 .... P8
Moscow 384 .... C10
Mosheim 1,451 .... R8
Mount Carmel 4,082 .... R8
Mount Juliet 5,389 .... H8
Mount Pleasant 4,278 .... G9
Mountain City▲ 2,169 .... T8
Munford 2,326 .... B10
Murfreesboro▲ 44,922 .... J9
Murray Lake Hills L10
Nashville (cap.)▲ 488,374 .... H8
Neubert 800 .... O9
New Hope 854 .... K11
New Johnsonville 1,643 .... E8
New Market 1,086 .... O8
New Tazewell 1,864 .... O8
Newbern 2,515 .... C8
Newport▲ 7,123 .... P9
Niota 745 .... M9
Norma 118 .... N8
Normandy 118 .... J10
Norris 1,303 .... N8
Oak Hill 4,301 .... H8
Oak Ridge 27,310 .... N8
Oakdale 268 .... M9
Oakland 392 .... B10
Obion 1,241 .... C8
Oliver Springs 3,433 .... N8
Oneida 3,502 .... N7
Ooltewah 4,903 .... M10
Orebank 1,284 .... R7
Orlinda 469 .... H7
Orme 150 .... K10
Pall Mall 750 .... M7
Palmer 769 .... K10
Paris▲ 9,332 .... E8
Parrotsville 121 .... P8
Parsons 2,033 .... E9
Pegram 1,371 .... H8
Petersburg 514 .... H10
Petros 1,286 .... M8
Philadelphia 463 .... M9
Pickwick Dam 650 .... E10
Pigeon Forge 3,027 .... O9
Pikeville▲ 1,771 .... L9
Piperton 612 .... B10
Pittman Center 478 .... P9
Pleasant Hill 494 .... L9
Pleasant View 625 .... G8
Portland 5,165 .... H7
Powder Springs 600 .... O8
Powell 7,534 .... N8
Powells Crossroads 1,098 .... L10
Primm Springs 750 .... G9
Pulaski▲ 7,895 .... G10
Puryear 592 .... E8
Ramer 337 .... D10
Red Bank 12,322 .... L10
Red Boiling Springs 905 .... K7
Rheatown R8
Ridgely 1,775 .... B8
Ridgeside 400 .... L10
Ripley▲ 6,188 .... B9
Rives 344 .... C8
Roan Mountain 1,220 .... S8
Rockford 646 .... O9
Rockwood 5,348 .... M9
Rogersville▲ 4,149 .... P8
Rosemark 950 .... B10
Rossville 291 .... B10
Russellville 1,069 .... P8
Rutherford 1,303 .... C8
Rutledge▲ 903 .... P8
Saint Joseph 789 .... G10
Sale Creek 900 .... L10
Saltillo 383 .... E10
Samburg 374 .... C8
Sardis 305 .... E10
Saulsbury 106 .... C10
Saundersville H8
Savannah▲ 6,547 .... E10
Scotts Hill 594 .... E10
Selmer▲ 3,838 .... D10
Sequatchie 800 .... K10
Sevierville▲ 7,178 .... P9
Sewanee 2,128 .... K10
Seymour 7,026 .... O9
Sharon 1,047 .... D8
Shelbyville▲ 14,049 .... H10
Sherwood 900 .... K10
Signal Mountain 7,034 .... L10
Smithville▲ 3,791 .... K9
Smyrna 13,647 .... H9
Sneedville▲ 1,446 .... P7
Soddy-Daisy (Daisy-Soddy) 8,240 .... L10
Somerville▲ 2,047 .... C10
South Carthage 851 .... K8
South Cleveland 5,372 .... M10
South Clinton 1,671 .... N8
South Fulton 2,688 .... D8
South Pittsburg 3,295 .... K10
Southside 800 .... G8
Sparta▲ 4,681 .... K9
Spencer▲ 1,125 .... L9
Spring City 2,199 .... M9
Spring Hill 1,464 .... H9
Springfield▲ 11,227 .... H8
Stanton 487 .... C10
Stantonville 264 .... E10
Strawberry Plains 680 .... O8
Sullivan Gardens 2,513 .... R8
Summertown 850 .... G10
Surgoinsville 1,499 .... R8
Sweetwater 5,066 .... N9
Talbott 975 .... P8
Tazewell▲ 2,150 .... O8
Tellico Plains 657 .... N10
Ten Mile 700 .... M9
Tennessee Ridge 1,271 .... F8
Tiftona L11
Tipton 2,149 .... B10
Tiptonville▲ 2,438 .... B8
Toone 279 .... D10
Townsend 329 .... O9
Tracy City 1,556 .... K10
Treadway 712 .... P8
Trenton▲ 4,836 .... D9
Trezevant 874 .... D8
Trimble 694 .... C8
Troy 1,047 .... C8
Tullahoma 16,761 .... J10
Tusculum 1,918 .... R8
Union City▲ 10,513 .... C8
Vanleer 369 .... G8
Victoria 800 .... K10
Viola 123 .... K9
Vonore 605 .... N9
Walden 1,523 .... L10
Walterhill 1,043 .... J9
Wartburg▲ 932 .... M8
Wartrace 494 .... J9

(continued on following page)

▲ County seat.

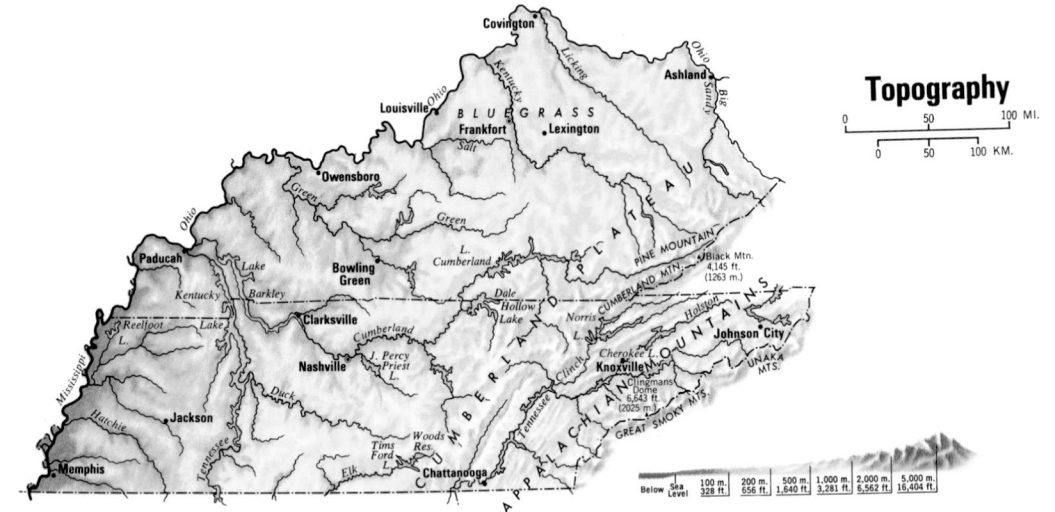

Topography

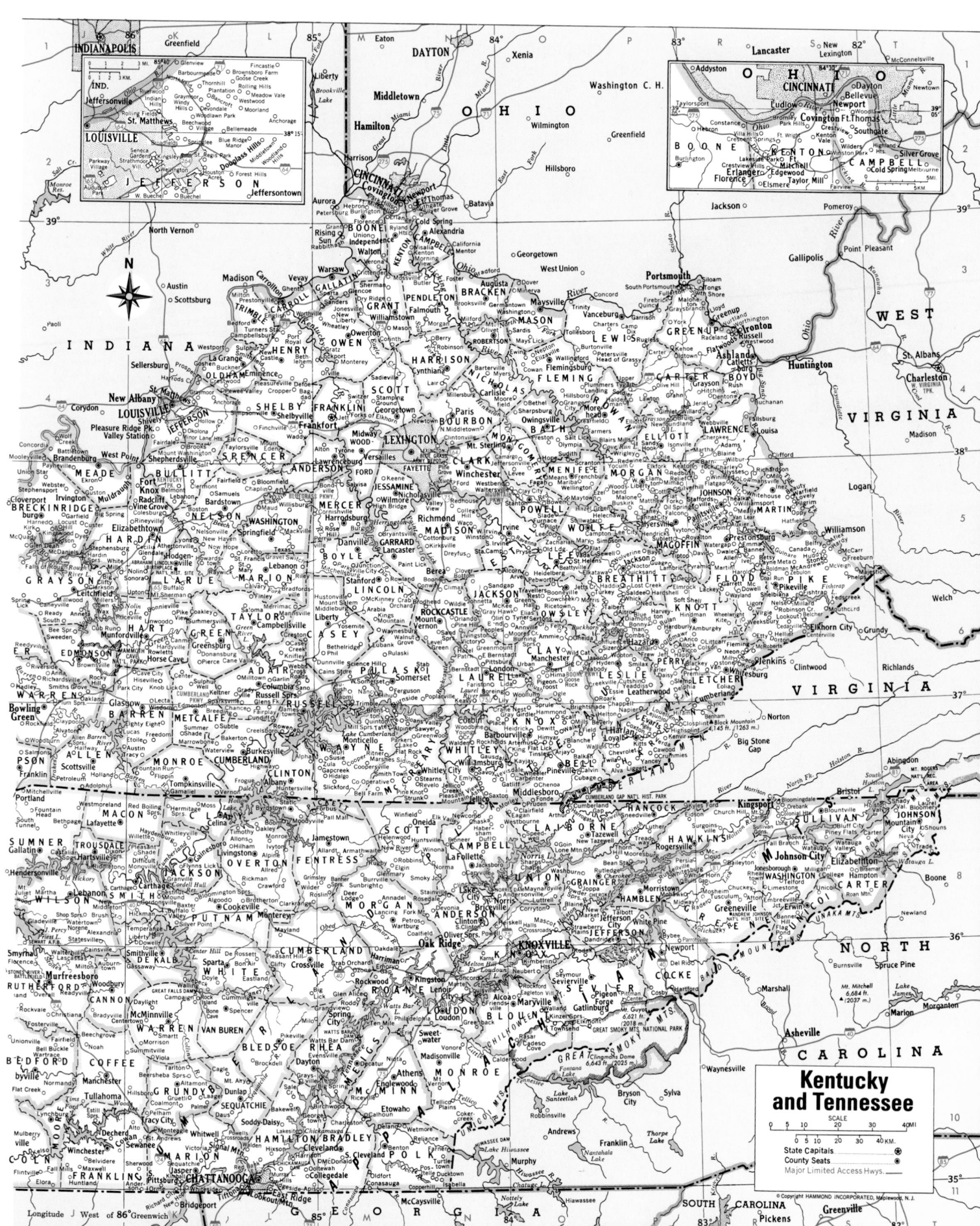

Kentucky
and Tennessee

SCALE
0   5   10   20   30   40MI
0 5 10   20   30   40 KM
State Capitals............................⊛
County Seats.............................◉
Major Limited Access Hwys.

© Copyright HAMMOND INCORPORATED, Maplewood, N.J.

Topography

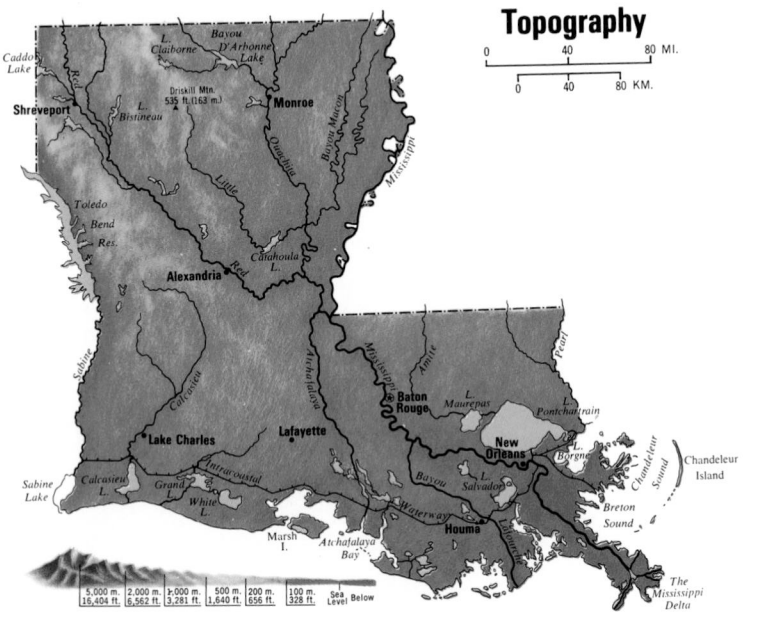

0   40   80 MI.

0   40   80 KM.

5,000 m. | 2,000 m. | 1,000 m. | 500 m. | 200 m. | 100 m. | Sea
16,404 ft. | 6,562 ft. | 3,281 ft. | 1,640 ft. | 656 ft. | 328 ft. | Level
| | | | | | Below

PARISHES

Acadia 56,427 ....F6
Allen 21,390 ....E5
Ascension 50,068 ....L3
Assumption 22,084 ....H7
Avoyelles 41,393 ....G4
Beauregard 29,692 ....D5
Bienville 16,387 ....D2
Bossier 80,721 ....C1
Caddo 252,437 ....C1
Calcasieu 167,223 ....D6
Caldwell 10,761 ....F2
Cameron 9,336 ....D7
Catahoula 12,287 ....G3
Claiborne 17,095 ....D1
Concordia 22,981 ....G4
De Soto 25,727 ....C2
East Baton Rouge 366,191 ....K1
East Carroll 11,772 ....H1
East Feliciana 19,015 ....H5
Evangeline 33,343 ....F5
Franklin 24,141 ....G2
Grant 16,703 ....E3
Iberia 63,752 ....G7
Iberville 32,159 ....H6
Jackson 17,321 ....E2
Jefferson 454,592 ....L6
Jefferson Davis 32,168 ....E6
La Salle 17,004 ....F3
Lafayette 150,017 ....F6
Lafourche 82,483 ....K7
Lincoln 39,763 ....E1
Livingston 58,806 ....L2
Madison 15,682 ....H2
Morehouse 34,803 ....G1
Natchitoches 39,863 ....D3
Orleans 557,927 ....L6
Ouachita 139,241 ....F2
Plaquemines 26,049 ....L8
Pointe Coupee 24,045 ....G5
Rapides 135,282 ....E4
Red River 10,433 ....D2
Richland 22,187 ....G2
Sabine 25,280 ....C3
Saint Bernard 64,097 ....L7
Saint Charles 37,259 ....K7
Saint Helena 9,827 ....J5
Saint James 21,495 ....L3
Saint John the Baptist
  31,924 ....M3
Saint Landry 84,128 ....F5
Saint Martin 40,214 ....G6
Saint Mary 64,253 ....H7
Saint Tammany 110,869 ....L6
Tangipahoa 80,698 ....K5
Tensas 8,525 ....H2
Terrebonne 94,393 ....J8
Union 21,167 ....F1
Vermilion 48,458 ....F7
Vernon 53,475 ....D4
Washington 44,207 ....K5
Webster 43,631 ....D1
West Baton Rouge 19,086 ....H6
West Carroll 12,922 ....H1
West Feliciana 12,186 ....H5
Winn 17,253 ....E3

CITIES and TOWNS

Abbeville▲ 11,187 ....F7
Abita Springs 1,296 ....L6
Acme 235 ....G4
Acy 570 ....L3
Addis 1,222 ....J2
Adeline 200 ....G7

Akers 150 ....N2
Albany 645 ....M1
Alberta 150 ....D2
Alexandria▲ 49,188 ....E4
Allen 175 ....D3
Alto 132 ....G2
Alton 500 ....L6
Amelia 2,447 ....H7
Amite▲ 4,301 ....K5
Anacoco 823 ....D4
Anandale F4
Andrew 100 ....F6
Angie 235 ....L5
Angola 600 ....G5
Ansley 100 ....E2
Arabi 8,787 ....P4
Arbroth 250 ....H5
Arcadia▲ 3,079 ....E1
Archibald 425 ....G2
Archie 280 ....G3
Arcola 250 ....K5
Arnaudville 1,444 ....G6
Ashland 289 ....D2
Athens 278 ....E1
Atlanta 118 ....E3
Avery Island 500 ....G7
Bains 400 ....H5
Baker 13,233 ....K1
Baldwin 2,379 ....G7
Ball 3,305 ....F4
Bancroft 114 ....C5
Baptist 150 ....M1
Barataria 1,160 ....K7
Basile 1,808 ....E5
Baskin 243 ....G2
Bastrop▲ 13,916 ....G1
Batchelor 500 ....G5
Baton Rouge (cap.)▲ 219,531 ....K2
Bayou Barbary 200 ....M2
Bayou Cane 15,876 ....J7
Bayou Goula 850 ....J3
Bayou Vista 4,733 ....H7
Baywood 100 ....K1
Beaver 350 ....E5
Beekman 150 ....G1
Bel 150 ....D6
Belcher 249 ....C1
Bell City 400 ....D6
Belle Alliance H6
Belle Chasse 8,512 ....O4
Belle D'Eau 120 ....F4
Bellevue 150 ....D3
Bellwood 150 ....D3
Belmont 350 ....C3
Benson 200 ....C3
Bentley 120 ....E3
Benton▲ 2,047 ....C1
Bernice 1,543 ....E1
Bertrandville 175 ....L7
Berwick 4,375 ....H7
Bethany 300 ....B2
Bienville 316 ....D2
Blanchard 1,175 ....C1
Bogalusa 14,280 ....L5
Bolinger 200 ....C1
Bonita 265 ....G1
Boothville 300 ....M8
Bordelonville 350 ....G4
Bosco 480 ....F2
Bossier City 52,721 ....C1
Boudreaux 275 ....J8
Bourg 2,073 ....J7
Boutte 2,702 ....N4
Boyce 1,361 ....E4
Braithwaite 350 ....P4
Branch 200 ....F6

Breaux Bridge 6,515 ....G6
Brittany 475 ....L3
Broussard 3,213 ....G6
Brusly 1,824 ....J2
Bryceland 103 ....F4
Buckeye 280 ....F4
Bunkie 5,044 ....F5
Buras (Buras-Triumph) 4,137 ....L8
Burnside 500 ....L5
Bush 275 ....L5
Cade 175 ....E4
Calcasieu 400 ....E4
Calhoun 350 ....F2
Calumet 100 ....H7
Calvin 207 ....E3
Cameron▲ 2,041 ....D7
Campti 929 ....D3
Cankton 323 ....F6
Carencro 5,429 ....G6
Carlisle 975 ....L7
Carville 1,108 ....K3
Castor 196 ....D2
Cecelia 550 ....G6
Center Point 850 ....F4
Centerville 500 ....H7
Central 546 ....L3
Chacahoula 150 ....J7
Chalmette▲ 31,860 ....P4
Charenton 1,584 ....H7
Chase 200 ....G2
Chataignier 281 ....F5
Chatham 617 ....F2
Chauvin 3,375 ....J8
Cheneyville 1,005 ....F4
Chopin 175 ....E4
Choudrant 557 ....F1
Church Point 4,677 ....F6
Clarence 577 ....E3
Clarks 650 ....F2
Clay 400 ....E2
Clayton 917 ....H3
Clear Lake 100 ....E3
Clinton▲ 1,904 ....J5
Clio 125 ....M2
Cloutierville 100 ....E3
Colfax▲ 1,696 ....E3
Collinston 300 ....G1
Columbia▲ 386 ....F2
Convent▲ 300 ....L3
Converse 436 ....C3
Corey 110 ....F2
Cotton Valley 1,130 ....D1
Cottonport 2,600 ....F5
Couchwood 150 ....D1
Coushatta▲ 1,845 ....D2
Covington▲ 7,691 ....K5
Cow Island 200 ....F7
Cravens 200 ....E5
Creole 300 ....D7
Crescent 300 ....J2
Creston 135 ....E3
Crowley▲ 13,983 ....F6
Crowville 400 ....G2
Cullen 1,642 ....D1
Curtis 110 ....C2
Cut Off 5,325 ....K7
Dalcour 275 ....P4
Danville 100 ....E2
Darrow 500 ....K3
Davant 600 ....L7
De Quincy 3,474 ....D6
De Ridder▲ 9,868 ....D5
Deerford 150 ....K1
Delcambre 1,978 ....G7
Delhi 3,169 ....H2
Delta 234 ....J2

Denham Springs 8,381 ....L2
Des Allemands 2,504 ....N4
Destrehan 8,031 ....N4
Deville 1,113 ....F4
Diamond 370 ....L7
Dixie 330 ....C1
Dixie Inn 347 ....D1
Dodson 350 ....E2
Donaldsonville▲ 7,949 ....K3
Donner 500 ....J7
Downsville 101 ....F1
Doyline 884 ....D1
Dry Creek 300 ....D5
Dry Prong 380 ....E3
Dubach 843 ....E1
Dubberly 253 ....D1
Dulac 3,273 ....J8
Dunn 225 ....G2
Duplessis 500 ....K2
Duson 1,465 ....F6
East Hodge 421 ....E2
East Point 100 ....D2
Easton 365 ....F5
Echo 525 ....F4
Edgard▲ 2,753 ....M3
Edgefield 207 ....D2
Edgerly 250 ....C6
Effie 300 ....F4
Elizabeth 414 ....E5
Elm Grove 100 ....C2
Elm Park 200 ....H5
Elmer 200 ....E4
Elton 1,277 ....E6
Empire 2,654 ....L8
Enterprise 375 ....G3
Epps 541 ....G1
Erath 2,428 ....F7
Eros 177 ....F2
Erwinville 790 ....H5
Esther 745 ....F7
Estherwood 745 ....F6
Ethel 250 ....H5
Eunice 11,162 ....F6
Eva 100 ....G4
Evangeline 400 ....F6
Evans 500 ....D5
Evergreen 283 ....F5
Extension 950 ....G3
Fairbanks 300 ....F1
Farmerville▲ 3,334 ....F1
Fenton 365 ....E6
Ferriday 4,111 ....G3
Fields 125 ....C5
Fisher 277 ....D4
Flatwoods 360 ....E4
Flora 300 ....D3
Florien 626 ....D4
Fluker 400 ....K5
Folsom 465 ....K5
Forbing 100 ....C2
Fordoche 869 ....G5
Forest 263 ....H1
Forest Hill 408 ....E4
Fort Jesup 100 ....C3
Fort Necessity 150 ....G2
Franklin▲ 9,004 ....G7
Franklinton▲ 4,007 ....K5
French Settlement 829 ....L2
Frierson 700 ....L2
Frost 500 ....L2
Fullerton 120 ....D4
Galliano 4,294 ....K8
Galvez 200 ....L2
Garden City 225 ....H7
Garyville 3,181 ....M3

(continued)

Louisiana

SCALE

0 5 10   20   30   40 MI.

0 5 10   20   30   40 KM.

State Capitals ....⊛
Parish Seats ....◉
Canals ....
Major Limited Access Hwys. ......▬▬▬

AREA 47,752 sq. mi. (123,678 sq. km.)
POPULATION 4,238,216
CAPITAL Baton Rouge
LARGEST CITY New Orleans
HIGHEST POINT Driskill Mtn. 535 ft. (163 m.)
SETTLED IN 1699
ADMITTED TO UNION April 30, 1812
POPULAR NAME Pelican State
STATE FLOWER Magnolia
STATE BIRD Eastern Brown Pelican

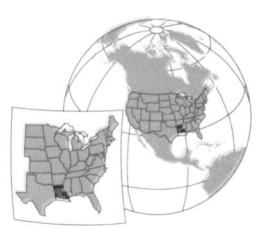

New Orleans, Baton Rouge and Vicinity

© Copyright HAMMOND INCORPORATED, Maplewood, N.J.

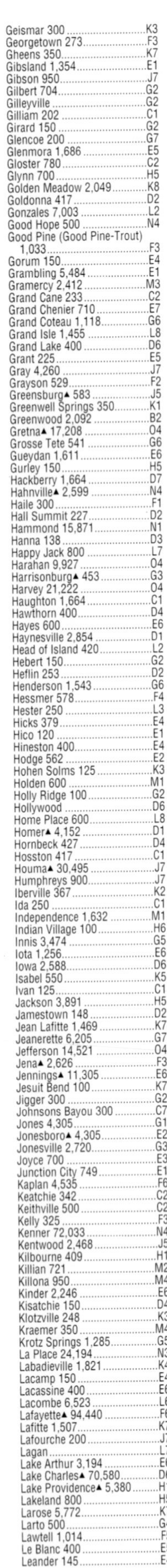

Geismar 300 K3
Georgetown 273 F3
Gheens 350 K7
Gibsland 1,354 E1
Gibson 950 J7
Gilbert 704 G2
Gilleyville G2
Gilliam 202 C1
Girard 150 G2
Glencoe 200 G7
Glenmora 1,686 E5
Gloster 780 C2
Glynn 700 H5
Golden Meadow 2,049 K8
Goldonna 417 D2
Gonzales 7,003 L2
Good Hope 500 N4
Good Pine (Good Pine-Trout) 1,033 F3
Gorum 150 E4
Grambling 5,484 E1
Gramercy 2,412 M3
Grand Cane 233 C2
Grand Chenier 710 E7
Grand Coteau 1,118 G6
Grand Isle 1,455 L8
Grand Lake 400 D6
Grant 225 E5
Gray 4,260 J7
Grayson 529 F2
Greensburg▲ 583 J5
Greenwell Springs 350 K1
Greenwood 2,092 B2
Gretna▲ 17,208 O4
Grosse Tete 541 G6
Gueydan 1,611 E6
Gurley 150 H5
Hackberry 1,664 D7
Hahnville▲ 2,599 N4
Haile 300 F1
Hall Summit 227 D2
Hammond 15,871 N1
Hanna 138 D3
Happy Jack 800 L7
Harahan 9,927 O4
Harrisonburg▲ 453 G3
Harvey 21,222 O4
Haughton 1,664 C1
Hawthorn 400 D4
Hayes 600 E6
Haynesville 2,854 D1
Head of Island 420 L2
Hebert 150 G2
Heflin 253 D2
Henderson 1,543 G6
Hessmer 578 F4
Hester 250 L3
Hicks 379 E4
Hico 120 E1
Hineston 400 E4
Hodge 562 E2
Hohen Solms 125 K3
Holden 600 M1
Holly Ridge 100 G2
Hollywood D6
Home Place 600 L8
Homer▲ 4,152 D1
Hornbeck 427 D4
Hosston 417 C1
Houma▲ 30,495 J7
Humphreys 900 J7
Iberville 367 K2
Ida 250 C1
Independence 1,632 M1
Indian Village 100 H6
Innis 3,474 G5
Iota 1,256 E6
Iowa 2,588 D6
Isabel 550 K5
Ivan 125 C1
Jackson 3,891 H5
Jamestown 148 D2
Jean Lafitte 1,469 K7
Jeanerette 6,205 G7
Jefferson 14,521 O4
Jena▲ 2,626 F3
Jennings▲ 11,305 E6
Jesuit Bend 100 K7
Jigger 300 G2
Johnsons Bayou 300 C7
Jones 4,305 G1
Jonesboro▲ 4,305 E2
Jonesville 2,720 G3
Joyce 700 E3
Junction City 749 E1
Kaplan 4,535 F6
Keatchie 342 C2
Keithville 500 C2
Kelly 325 F3
Kenner 72,033 N4
Kentwood 2,468 J5
Kilbourne 409 H1
Killian 721 M2
Killona 950 M4
Kinder 2,246 E6
Kisatchie 150 D4
Klotzville 248 K3
Kraemer 350 M4
Krotz Springs 1,285 G5
La Place 24,194 N3
Labadieville 1,821 K4
Lacamp 150 E4
Lacassine 400 E6
Lacombe 6,523 L6
Lafayette▲ 94,440 F6
Lafitte 1,507 K7
Lafourche 200 J7
Lagan L7
Lake Arthur 3,194 E6
Lake Charles▲ 70,580 D6
Lake Providence▲ 5,380 H1
Lakeland 800 H5
Larose 5,772 K7
Larto 500 G4
Lawtell 1,014 F5
Le Blanc 400 E5
Leander 145 E4

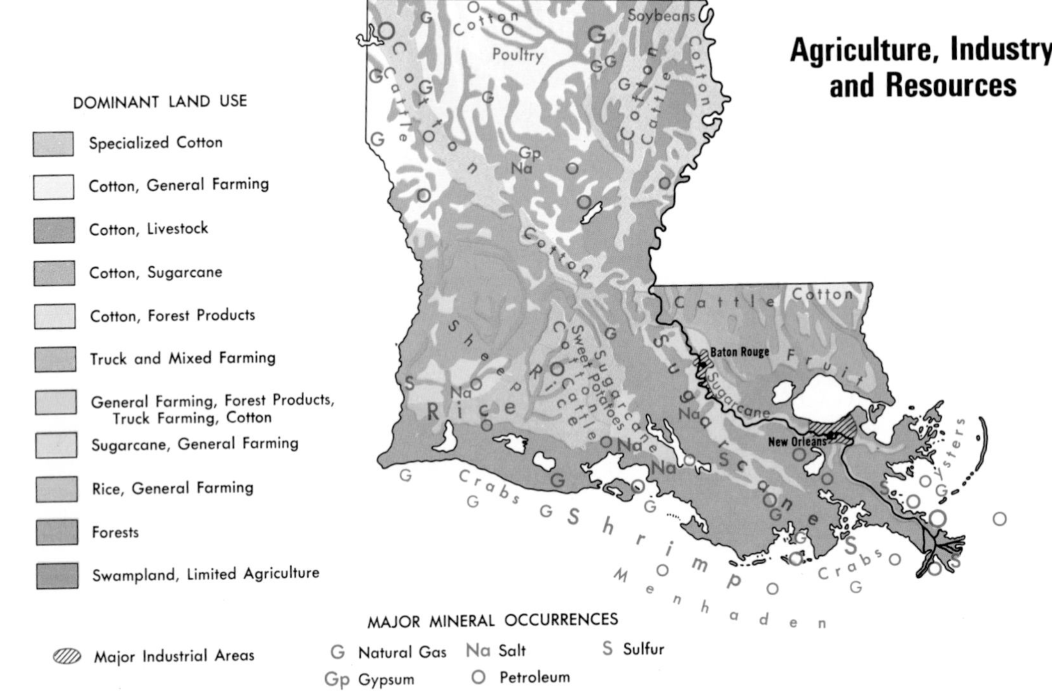

Lebeau 200 F5
Lecompte 1,661 F4
Leesville▲ 7,638 D4
Lena 300 E4
Leonville 825 G6
Leton 125 D1
Lettsworth 200 G5
Lewisburg 265 F6
Libuse 500 F4
Lillie 145 E1
Linville 150 F1
Lisbon 160 E1
Lismore 380 G3
Little Farms N4
Livingston▲ 999 L1
Livonia 970 G5
Lobdell 200 J1
Lockport 2,503 K7
Logansport 1,390 C3
Lonepine 850 F5
Longstreet 189 B2
Longville 300 D5
Loranger 250 N1
Loreauville 860 G6
Lottie 400 G5
Lucky 342 E2
Lucy 825 M3
Luling 2,803 N4
Lunita 100 C6
Lutcher 3,907 L3
Madisonville 659 K6
Mamou 3,483 F5
Mandeville 7,083 L6
Mangham 598 G2
Mansfield▲ 5,389 C2
Mansura 1,601 G4
Many▲ 3,112 C3
Maplewood D6
Maringouin 1,149 G6
Marion 775 F1
Marksville▲ 5,526 G4
Marrero 36,671 O4
Marthaville 150 D3
Martin 545 D2
Mathews 3,009 J7
Maurepas 200 M2
Maurice 432 F6
Mayna 122 G4
McCall 150 K3
McNary 248 E5
Melder 150 E4
Melrose 500 E3
Melville 1,562 G5
Mer Rouge 586 G1
Mermentau 760 E6
Merryville 1,235 D5
Metairie 149,428 O4
Midland 560 F6
Milton 450 F6
Mimosa Park 4,516 N4
Minden▲ 13,661 D1
Mira 354 C1
Mitchell 155 C3
Mix 150 G5
Modeste 225 K3
Monroe▲ 54,909 F1
Montegut 1,784 J8
Monterey 800 G4
Montgomery 645 E3
Montpelier 247 M1
Montz 200 M3

Mooringsport 873 B1
Mora 427 E4
Moreauville 919 G4
Morgan City 14,531 H7
Morganza 759 G5
Morrow 600 F5
Morse 782 F6
Mound 16 H2
Mount Airy 700 M3
Mount Hermon 170 K5
Mount Lebanon 102 D2
Myrtle Grove 100 K7
Nairn 500 L8
Napoleonville▲ 802 K4
Natalbany 1,289 N1
Natchez 434 D3
Natchitoches▲ 16,609 D3
Nebo 200 F3
Negreet 400 C4
New Era 200 G4
New Iberia▲ 31,828 G6
New Orleans▲ 496,938 O4
New Roads▲ 5,303 G5
New Sarpy 2,946 N4
Newellton 1,576 H2
Newllano 2,660 D4
Noble 225 C3
Norco 3,385 N3
North Hodge 477 E2
Norwood 317 H5
Oak Grove▲ 2,126 H1
Oak Ridge 174 G1
Oakdale 6,832 E5
Oberlin▲ 1,808 E5
Odenburg 175 G5
Oil City 1,282 C1
Olivier 300 G7
Olla 1,410 F3
Opelousas▲ 18,151 G5
Oretta 110 D5
Oscar 650 H5
Otis 400 E4
Oxford 125 C3
Paincourtville 1,550 K3
Palmetto 229 G5
Paradis 750 M4
Parhams 100 G4
Parks 400 G6
Patoutville 230 G7
Patterson 4,736 H7
Paulina 500 L3
Pearl River 1,507 L6
Peason 120 D4
Pecan Island 480 F7
Pelican 250 C3
Perry 230 F7
Perryville 100 G1
Phoenix 525 L7
Pilottown 175 M8
Pine Grove 570 J5
Pine Prairie 713 E5
Pineville 12,251 F4
Pioneer 116 H1
Pitkin 600 E5
Plain Dealing 1,074 C1
Plaquemine▲ 7,186 J2
Plattenville 205 K4
Plaucheville 187 G5
Pleasant Hill 824 C3
Pointe a la Hache▲ 750 L7
Pollock 330 F3

Ponchatoula 5,425 N2
Port Allen▲ 6,277 J2
Port Barre 2,144 G5
Port Hudson 200 J1
Port Sulphur 3,523 L8
Port Vincent 446 L2
Powhatan 147 D3
Prairieville 500 K2
Pride 100 K1
Princeton 350 C1
Provencal 538 D3
Quitman 162 E2
Raceland 5,564 J7
Rayne 8,502 F6
Rayville▲ 4,411 G2
Reddell 500 F5
Reeves 188 D5
Reggio 400 L7
Remy 850 L3
Reserve 8,847 M3
Richmond 447 H2
Richwood 1,253 F2
Ridgecrest 804 G3
Ringgold 1,655 D2
Rio 400 L5
Roanoke 800 E6
Robeline 149 D3
Robert 600 N1
Rocky Mount 150 C1
Rodessa 294 B1
Rogers 150 F3
Romeville 133 L3
Rosa 300 G5
Rosedale 807 G6
Roseland 1,093 J5
Rosepine 1,135 D5
Ruby 400 F4
Ruston▲ 20,027 E1
Saint Amant 900 L2
Saint Benedict 190 K5
Saint Bernard 750 L7
Saint Francisville▲ 1,700 H5
Saint Gabriel 975 K2
Saint James 600 L3
Saint Joseph▲ 1,517 H3
Saint Landry 550 F5
Saint Martinville▲ 7,137 G6
Saint Maurice 560 E3
Saint Rose 6,259 N4
Saint Tammany 150 L6
Saline 272 E2
Samtown F4
Sarepta 886 D1
Schriever 4,958 J7
Scotlandville 15,113 J1
Scott 4,912 F6
Seymourville 2,891 J2
Shongaloo 161 D1
Shreveport▲ 198,525 C2
Sibley 997 D1
Sicily Island 421 G3
Sieper 226 E4
Sikes 120 F2
Simmesport 2,092 G5
Simpson 536 D4
Simsboro 634 E1
Singer 250 D5
Slagle 650 D4
Slaughter 827 H5
Slidell 24,124 L6
Smoke Bend 300 K3

Sondheimer 225 H1
Sorrento 1,119 L3
South Mansfield 407 C3
Spearsville 132 E1
Springfield 439 M2
Springhill 5,668 D1
Standard 190 F3
Stanley 131 C3
Starks 750 C6
Start 200 G2
Sterlington 1,140 F1
Stonewall 1,266 C2
Sugartown 375 D5
Sulphur 20,125 D6
Summerfield 170 E1
Sun 429 L5
Sunset 2,201 F6
Sunshine 900 K2
Supreme 1,020 K4
Swartz 3,698 G1
Sweet Lake 300 D7
Talisheek 315 L5
Tallulah▲ 8,526 H2
Tangipahoa 569 J5
Taylor 500 D1
Taylortown 150 C2
Temple 250 E4
Tendal 200 H2
Terry Town 23,548 O4
Theriot 450 J8
Thibodaux▲ 14,035 J7
Tickfaw 565 M1
Tioga 457 F4
Toro 100 C4
Transylvania 400 H1
Trees 327 B1
Triumph (Triumph-Buras) 4,137 L8
Trout (Trout-Good Pine) 1,033 F3
Tullos 427 F3
Tunica 500 G5
Turkey Creek 283 F5
Union 665 L3
Urania 782 F3
Vacherie 2,169 L3
Valverda 200 G5
Varnado 236 L5
Venice 900 M8
Vernon 150 E2
Vick 500 F4
Vidalia▲ 4,953 G3
Vienna 404 E1
Ville Platte▲ 9,037 F5
Vinton 3,154 C6
Violet 8,574 P4
Vivian 4,156 B1
Wadesboro 125 M2
Wakefield 400 H5
Walker 3,727 L1
Wallace 200 M3
Walters 500 G3
Warden 130 H1
Wardville F4
Washington 1,253 G5
Waterproof 1,080 H3
Watson 800 L1
Waverly 350 H2
Weeks 400 G7
Welcome 450 L3
Welsh 3,299 E6
West Monroe 14,096 F1

West Pointe a la Hache 250 L7
Westlake 5,007 D6
Westwego 11,218 O4
Weyanoke 500 H5
White Castle 2,102 J3
Whitehall 380 M2
Whiteville 150 F5
Wildsville 800 G3
Wills Point 150 L7
Wilson 707 H5
Winnfield▲ 6,138 E3
Winnsboro▲ 5,755 G2
Wisner 1,153 G3
Woodhaven M1
Woodlawn 150 E6
Woodworth 754 E4
Youngsville 1,195 G6
Zachary 9,036 K1
Zwolle 1,779 C3

OTHER FEATURES

Allemands (lake) M4
Alligator (pt.) L6
Amite (riv.) L2
Anacoco (lake) D4
Atchafalaya (bay) H8
Atchafalaya (riv.) G6
Barataria (bay) L8
Barataria (passage) L8
Barksdale A.F.B. C2
Bayou D'Arbonne (lake) E1
Bird (isl.) M8
Bistineau (lake) D2
Black (lake) D3
Black Lake (bayou) D1
Boeuf (lake) J7
Boeuf (riv.) G1
Bonnet Carré Spillway and Floodway N3
Borgne (lake) L7
Boudreau (bay) M7
Boudreaux (lake) J8
Breton (isl.) M8
Breton (sound) M7
Bundick (lake) D5
Caddo (lake) B1
Caillou (bay) J8
Calcasieu (lake) D7
Calcasieu (passage) D7
Calcasieu (riv.) E5
Catahoula (lake) F4
Cataouatche (lake) N4
Cat Island (chan.) M6
Cat Island (passage) J8
Chandeleur (isls.) N7
Chandeleur (sound) M7
Chenier (lake) F2
Chicot (pt.) M7
Claiborne (lake) E1
Clear (lake) D3
Cocodrie (lake) E5
Cotile (lake) E4
Cross (lake) C2
Curlew (isls.) M7
Dernieres (isls.) J8
Door (pt.) M6
Driskill (mt.) E2
Drum (bay) M7
East (bay) M8
East Cote Blanche (bay) G7

Edwards (lake) C2
Eloi (bay) M7
England A.F.B. E4
Fields (lake) J7
Fort Polk 14,730 D4
Free Mason (isls.) M7
Garden Island (bay) M8
Grand (lake) E7
Grand (lake) H7
Grand Terre (isls.) L8
Iatt (lake) E3
Jean Lafitte Nat'l Hist. Park P4
Lafourche (bayou) K8
Little (riv.) F3
Louisiana (pt.) C7
Macon (bayou) H1
Main (passage) M8
Manchac (passage) N2
Marsh (isl.) G7
Maurepas (lake) M2
Mermentau (riv.) E7
Mexico (gulf) F8
Mississippi (delta) M8
Mississippi (riv.) H3
Mississippi (sound) M6
Mississippi River Gulf Outlet (canal) L7
Mozambique (pt.) M7
Mud (lake) D7
Naval Air Sta. O4
North (isls.) M7
North (pass) N8
North (pt.) M7
Northeast (pass) M8
Ouachita (riv.) F1
Palourde (lake) H7
Pearl (riv.) L5
Point au Fer (isl.) H8
Point au Fer (pt.) H8
Pontchartrain (lake) O3
Pontchartrain Causeway O3
Poverty Pt. Nat'l Mon H1
Raccoon (pt.) H8
Red (riv.) G4
Sabine (lake) C7
Sabine (passage) C7
Sabine (riv.) C5
Saline (lake) E3
Salvador (lake) K7
Smithport (lake) C2
South (pass) M8
South (pt.) G8
Southeast (pass) M8
Southwest (pass) L8
Tangipahoa (riv.) N1
Tensas (riv.) G3
Terrebonne (bay) J8
Tickfaw (riv.) M1
Timbalier (bay) K8
Timbalier (isl.) K8
Toledo Bend (res.) C3
Turkey Creek (lake) G3
Vermilion (bay) F7
Vernon (lake) D4
Verret (lake) H7
Wallace (lake) C2
West (bay) M8
West Cote Blanche (bay) G7
White (lake) E7

▲ Parish seat

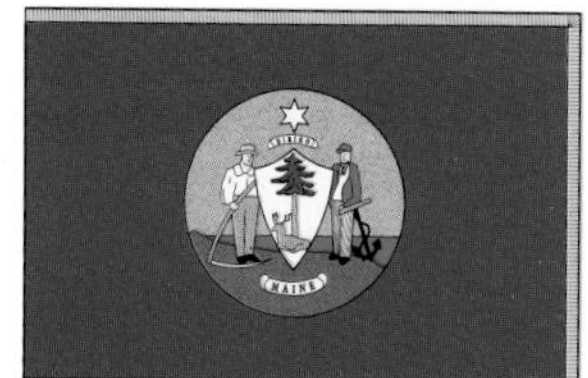
MAINE

AREA 33,265 sq. mi. (86,156 sq. km.)
POPULATION 1,233,223
CAPITAL Augusta
LARGEST CITY Portland
HIGHEST POINT Katahdin 5,268 ft. (1606 m.)
SETTLED IN 1624
ADMITTED TO UNION March 15, 1820
POPULAR NAME Pine Tree State
STATE FLOWER White Pine Cone & Tassel
STATE BIRD Chickadee

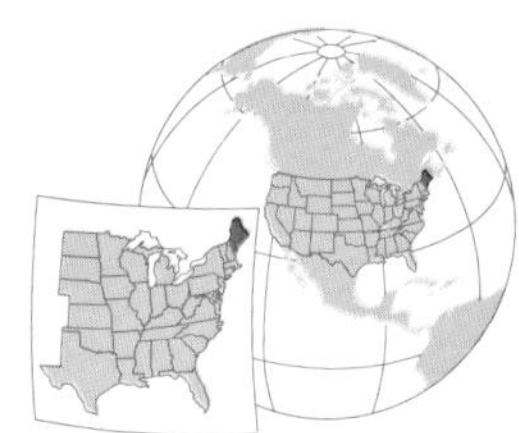

COUNTIES

Androscoggin 105,259 .... C7
Aroostook 86,936 .... F2
Cumberland 243,135 .... C8
Franklin 29,008 .... B5
Hancock 46,948 .... G6
Kennebec 115,904 .... D7
Knox 36,310 .... E7
Lincoln 30,357 .... D7
Oxford 52,602 .... B7
Penobscot 146,601 .... F5
Piscataquis 18,653 .... E4
Sagadahoc 33,535 .... D7
Somerset 49,767 .... C4
Waldo 33,018 .... E6
Washington 35,308 .... H6
York 164,587 .... B9

CITIES and TOWNS

Abbot Village• 576 .... D5
Acton 850 .... B8
Acton• 1,727 .... B8
Addison 350 .... H6
Addison• 1,114 .... H6
Albion• 1,736 .... E6
Alexander• 478 .... H5
Alfred 1,890 .... B9
Alfred• 2,238 .... B9
Allagash• 359 .... F1
Alna• 571 .... D7
Alton• 771 .... F5
Amherst• 226 .... G6
Andover 350 .... B6
Andover• 953 .... B6
Anson 950 .... D6
Anson• 2,382 .... D6
Appleton• 1,069 .... E7
Argyle 202 .... F5
Ashland 750 .... G2
Ashland• 1,542 .... G2
Athens 300 .... D6
Athens• 897 .... D6
Atkinson• 332 .... E5
Auburn▲ 24,309 .... C7
Augusta (cap.)▲ 21,325 .... D7
Aurora• 82 .... G6
Bailey Island 500 .... D8
Bancroft H4
Bancroft• 66 .... H4
Bangor▲ 33,181 .... F6
Bar Harbor 2,685 .... G7
Bar Harbor• 2,768 .... G7
Bar Mills 800 .... C8
Baring 235 .... J5
Baring• 275 .... J5
Bass Harbor 450 .... G7
Bath▲ 9,799 .... D8
Bayside F7
Beals• 667 .... H7
Beddington• 43 .... H6
Belfast▲ 6,355 .... F7
Belgrade 950 .... D7
Belgrade• 2,375 .... D7
Belgrade Lakes 700 .... D6
Belmont• 652 .... E7
Benedicta• 225 .... G4
Benton• 2,312 .... D6
Berwick 2,378 .... B9
Berwick• 5,995 .... B9
Bethel 750 .... B7
Bethel• 2,329 .... B7
Biddeford 20,710 .... B9
Biddeford Pool 500 .... C9
Bingham 1,074 .... D5
Bingham• 1,071 .... D5
Birch Harbor 300 .... H7
Blaine-Mars Hill 1,921 .... H2
Blaine• 784 .... H2
Blanchard 78 .... D5
Blue Hill 850 .... F7
Blue Hill• 1,941 .... F7
Bolsters Mills 150 .... B7
Boothbay 200 .... D8
Boothbay• 2,648 .... D8
Boothbay Harbor 1,267 .... D8
Bowdoinham• 2,192 .... D7
Bowerbank• 72 .... E5
Bradford 150 .... F5
Bradford• 1,103 .... F5
Bradley• 1,136 .... F6
Brewer 9,021 .... F6
Bridgewater• 647 .... H3
Bridgton 1,639 .... B7
Bridgton• 2,195 .... B7
Brighton• 94 .... D5
Bristol 450 .... D8
Bristol• 2,326 .... D8
Brooklin• 785 .... F7
Brooks 900 .... E6
Brooksville• 760 .... F7
Brookton 175 .... H4
Brownfield 300 .... B8
Brownfield• 1,034 .... B8
Brownville 600 .... E5
Brownville• 1,506 .... E5
Brownville Junction 950 .... E5
Brunswick 10,990 .... C8
Brunswick• 14,683 .... C8
Bryant Pond 600 .... B7
Buckfield• 1,566 .... C7
Bucks Harbor 300 .... J6
Bucksport 2,853 .... F6
Bucksport• 2,989 .... F6
Burlington• 360 .... G5
Burnham• 961 .... E6
Buxton• 6,494 .... C8
Byron• 111 .... B6
Calais 3,963 .... J5
Cambridge• 490 .... E5
Camden 3,743 .... F7
Camden• 4,022 .... F7
Canaan• 1,636 .... D6
Canton• 951 .... C7
Cape Neddick 2,193 .... B9
Cape Porpoise 500 .... C9
Caratunk 98 .... C5
Cardville 223 .... F5
Caribou 9,415 .... G2
Carmel• 1,906 .... E6
Carrabassett Valley• 325 .... C5
Carroll• 185 .... G5
Carthage• 458 .... C6
Cary• 235 .... H4
Casco 400 .... B7
Casco• 3,018 .... B7
Castine• 1,161 .... F7
Centerville• 30 .... H6
Chapman• 422 .... G2
Charleston• 1,187 .... F5
Charlotte• 271 .... J5
Chebeague Island 900 .... C8
Chelsea• 2,497 .... D7
Cherryfield• 1,183 .... H6
Chester• 442 .... F5
Chesterville• 1,012 .... C6
China 2,918 .... E7
China• 3,713 .... E7
Chisholm 1,653 .... C7
Clifton• 607 .... G6
Clinton 1,305 .... D6
Clinton• 1,485 .... D6
Columbia• 437 .... H6
Columbia Falls• 552 .... H6
Cooper• 124 .... H6
Coopers Mills 200 .... E7
Corea 375 .... H7
Corinna• 2,196 .... E6
Cornish• 1,178 .... B8
Cornville• 1,008 .... D6
Costigan 200 .... F5
Cranberry Isles• 189 .... G7
Crawford• 89 .... H5
Crescent Lake 325 .... C7
Criehaven F8
Crouseville 450 .... G2
Crystal• 303 .... G4
Cumberland Center 2,015 .... C8
Cumberland Center• 1,890 .... C8
Cundys Harbor 150 .... D8
Cushing• 988 .... E7
Cutler 400 .... J6
Cutler• 779 .... J6
Damariscotta• 1,811 .... E7
Damariscotta-Newcastle 1,567 .... E7
Danforth 650 .... H4
Danforth• 710 .... H4
Deblois• 73 .... H6
Dedham• 1,229 .... F6
Deer Isle 600 .... F7
Deer Isle• 1,829 .... F7
Denmark• 855 .... B8
Dennysville• 355 .... J6
Derby 300 .... E5
Detroit• 751 .... E6
Dexter 3,118 .... E5
Dexter• 2,650 .... E5
Dixfield 1,725 .... C6
Dixfield• 1,300 .... C6
Dixmont• 1,007 .... E6
Dover-Foxcroft▲ 2,974 .... E5
Dover-Foxcroft• 3,077 .... E5
Dresden• 1,332 .... D7
Dry Mills 700 .... C8
Dryden 675 .... C6
Dyer Brook• 243 .... G3
Eagle Lake 675 .... F1
Eagle Lake• 942 .... F1
East Andover 250 .... B6
East Baldwin 175 .... B8
East Blue Hill 150 .... G7
East Boothbay 800 .... D8
East Corinth 525 .... F5
East Dixfield 250 .... C6
East Eddington 200 .... F6
East Hiram 198 .... B8
East Holden 600 .... F6
East Lebanon 950 .... B9
East Limington 200 .... B8
East Livermore 500 .... C7
East Machias 850 .... J6
East Machias• 1,218 .... J6
East Madison 400 .... D6
East Millinocket 2,361 .... F4
East Millinocket• 2,075 .... F4
East Parsonfield 400 .... B8
East Peru 200 .... C7
East Poland 200 .... C7
East Stoneham 300 .... B7
East Sullivan 496 .... G6
East Vassalboro 300 .... D7
East Waterboro 365 .... B8
East Wilton 650 .... C6
Easton• 1,291 .... H2
Eastport 1,965 .... K6
Eddington 250 .... F6
Eddington• 1,947 .... F6
Edgecomb• 993 .... D8
Edmunds 430 .... J6
Eliot• 5,329 .... B9
Ellsworth▲ 5,975 .... F6
Enfield 150 .... F5
Enfield• 1,476 .... F5
Etna• 977 .... E6
Eustis• 616 .... B5
Exeter• 937 .... E6
Fairbanks 400 .... C6
Fairfield 3,169 .... D6
Fairfield Center 975 .... D6
Fairfield• 2,794 .... D6
Falmouth 1,655 .... C8
Falmouth• 7,610 .... C8
Farmingdale 2,014 .... D7
Farmingdale• 2,070 .... D7
Farmington▲ 3,583 .... C6
Farmington• 4,197 .... C6
Farmington Falls 500 .... C6
Fayette• 855 .... C7
Five Islands 225 .... D8
Fort Fairfield 2,282 .... H2
Fort Fairfield• 1,729 .... H2
Fort Kent 2,375 .... F1
Fort Kent• 2,123 .... F1
Fort Kent Mills 200 .... F1
Foxcroft 2,974 .... E5
Frankfort• 1,020 .... F6
Franklin 350 .... G6
Franklin• 1,141 .... G6
Freedom• 593 .... E7
Freeport 1,906 .... C8
Freeport• 1,829 .... C8
Frenchboro• 44 .... G7
Frenchville 980 .... G1
Frenchville• 1,338 .... G1
Friendship 700 .... E7
Friendship• 1,099 .... E7
Fryeburg 1,644 .... A7
Fryeburg• 1,580 .... A7
Gardiner• 6,746 .... D7
Garland 300 .... E5
Garland• 1,064 .... E5
Georgetown 190 .... D8
Georgetown• 914 .... D8
Gilead• 204 .... B7
Glen Cove 250 .... E7
Glenburn• 3,198 .... F6
Goodwins Mills 340 .... B8
Goose Rocks Beach 200 .... C9
Gorham 4,052 .... C8
Gorham• 3,618 .... C8
Gouldsboro 498 .... H7
Gouldsboro• 1,986 .... H7
Grand Isle 600 .... G1
Grand Isle• 558 .... G1
Grand Lake Stream• 174 .... H5
Gray 525 .... C8
Gray• 5,904 .... C8
Great Pond• 59 .... G6
Greene• 3,661 .... C7
Greenville• 1,839 .... D5
Greenville 1,601 .... D5
Greenville Junction 650 .... D5
Guilford 1,235 .... E5
Guilford• 1,082 .... E5
Hallowell 2,534 .... D7
Hamlin• 204 .... H1
Hampden 3,538 .... F6
Hampden• 3,895 .... F6
Hampden Highlands 950 .... F6
Hancock• 1,757 .... G6
Hanover• 272 .... B7
Harmony 450 .... D6
Harmony• 838 .... D6
Harpswell• 5,012 .... D8
Harrington• 893 .... H6
Harrison• 1,951 .... B7
Hartford• 722 .... C7
Hartland 1,041 .... D6
Hartland• 1,038 .... D6
Haynesville• 243 .... G4
Hebron• 878 .... C7
Hermon• 3,755 .... F6
Highland Lake 600 .... C8
Hiram 175 .... B8
Hiram• 1,260 .... B8
Hodgdon• 1,257 .... H3
Hollis Center• 2,892 .... B8
Hope 175 .... E7
Hope• 1,017 .... E7
Houlton▲ 5,730 .... H3
Houlton• 5,627 .... H3
Howland 1,502 .... F5
Howland• 1,304 .... F5
Hudson• 1,048 .... F5
Hulls Cove 200 .... G7
Island Falls• 897 .... G3
Isle Au Haut• 57 .... F7
Islesboro 200 .... F7
Islesboro• 579 .... F7
Jackman 700 .... C4
Jackman• 920 .... C4
Jacksonville 200 .... J6
Jay 850 .... C7
Jay• 5,080 .... C7
Jefferson• 2,111 .... D7
Jonesboro• 585 .... J6
Jonesport 1,050 .... H6
Jonesport• 1,525 .... H6
Keegan 450 .... G1
Kenduskeag• 1,234 .... E6
Kennebunk 3,294 .... B9
Kennebunk• 4,206 .... B9
Kennebunk Beach 200 .... C9
Kennebunkport 1,685 .... C9
Kennebunkport• 1,100 .... C9
Kents Hill 300 .... D7
Kezar Falls 680 .... B8
Kingfield• 1,114 .... C6
Kingman 246 .... G4
Kingsbury• 13 .... D5
Kittery 5,465 .... B9
Kittery• 5,151 .... B9
Kittery Point 1,093 .... B9
Knox• 681 .... E6
Lagrange 250 .... F5
Lagrange• 509 .... F5
Lake View• 23 .... F5
Lamoine• 1,311 .... G7
Lee• 832 .... G5
Leeds• 1,669 .... C7
Levant• 1,627 .... F6
Lewiston 39,757 .... C7
Liberty 200 .... E7
Liberty• 790 .... E7
Lille 300 .... G1
Limerick• 1,688 .... B8
Limestone 1,334 .... H2
Limestone• 1,245 .... H2
Limington• 2,796 .... B8
Lincoln 3,524 .... G5
Lincoln• 3,399 .... G5
Lincoln Center 325 .... G5
Lincolnville 800 .... E7
Lincolnville• 1,809 .... E7
Lincolnville Center 200 .... E7
Linneus• 810 .... H3
Lisbon• 9,457 .... C7
Lisbon Falls 4,674 .... D7
Lisbon-Lisbon Center 1,865 .... C7
Litchfield• 2,650 .... D7
Little Deer Isle 475 .... F7
Little Falls-South Windham 1,715 .... C8
Littleton• 956 .... H3
Livermore 280 .... C7
Livermore• 1,950 .... C7
Livermore Falls 2,441 .... C7
Livermore Falls• 1,935 .... C7
Locke Mills 600 .... B7
Lovell 180 .... B7
Lovell• 888 .... B7
Lowell• 267 .... F5
Lubec 900 .... K6
Lubec• 1,853 .... K6
Ludlow• 430 .... G3
Machias▲ 1,277 .... J6
Machias• 1,773 .... J6
Machiasport 374 .... H6
Machiasport• 1,166 .... H6
Macwahoc• 114 .... G4
Madawaska 4,165 .... G1
Madawaska• 3,653 .... G1
Madison 2,788 .... D6
Madison• 2,956 .... D6
Madrid• 178 .... B6
Manchester• 2,099 .... D7
Mapleton• 1,853 .... G2
Mars Hill• 1,760 .... H2
Mars Hill-Blaine 1,717 .... H2
Masardis• 305 .... G3

(continued on following page)

Agriculture, Industry and Resources

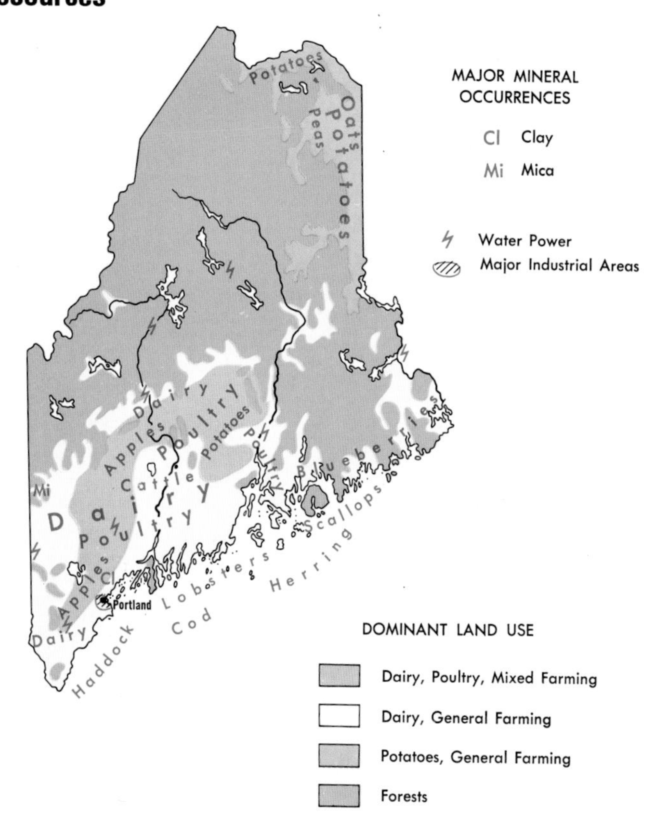
Potatoes
Oats
Peas
Potatoes
Potatoes
Dairy
Poultry
Potatoes
Apples
Cattle
Poultry
Blueberries
Scallops
Dairy
Poultry
Apples
Mi
Cl
Portland
Lobsters
Herring
Cod
Haddock
Dairy
MAJOR MINERAL OCCURRENCES
Cl Clay
Mi Mica
Water Power
Major Industrial Areas
DOMINANT LAND USE
Dairy, Poultry, Mixed Farming
Dairy, General Farming
Potatoes, General Farming
Forests

Topography

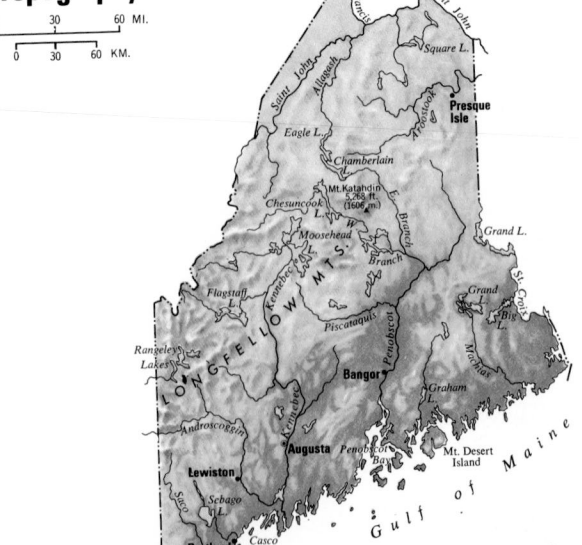

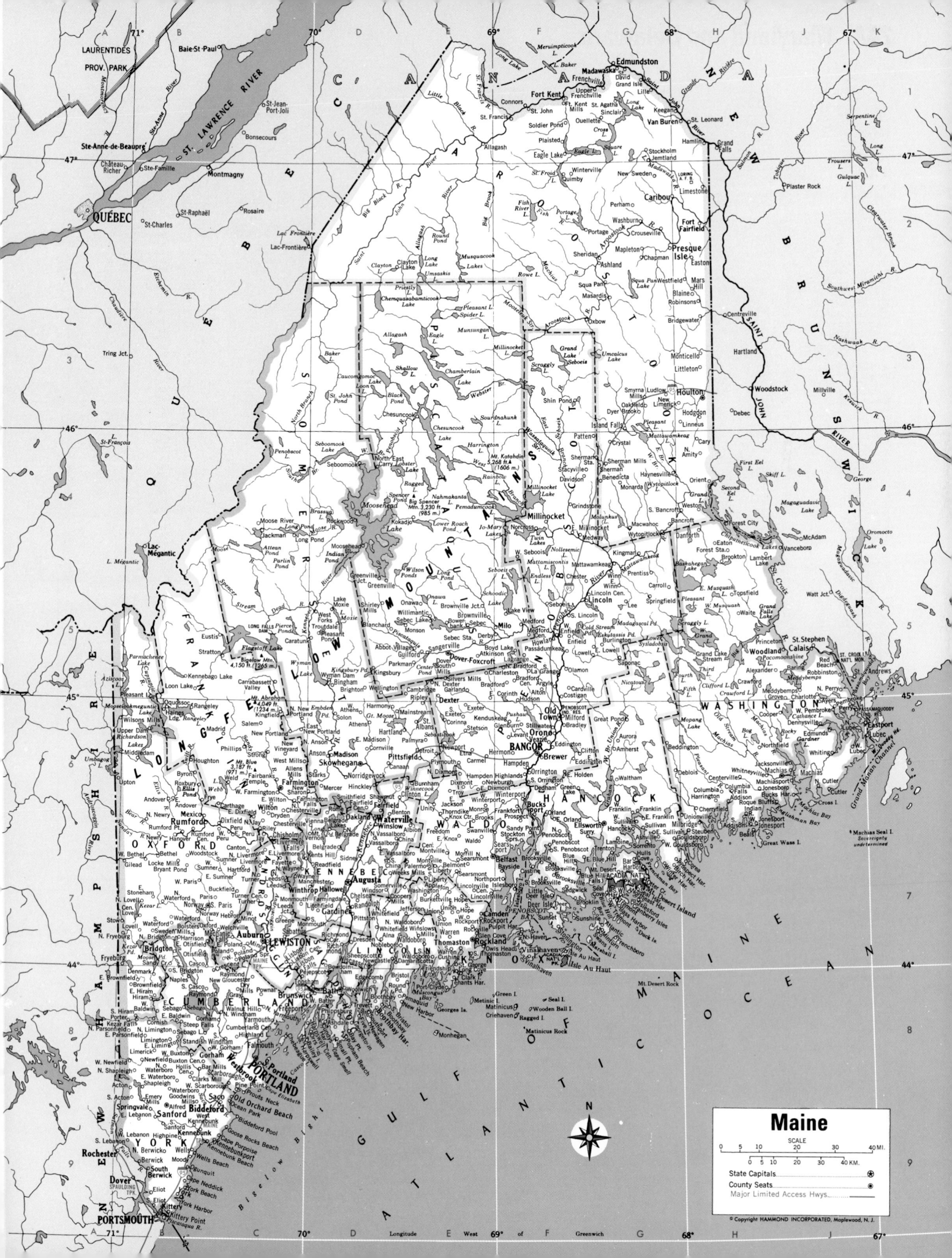

Maine

SCALE

0   5   10   20   30   40 MI.

0 5 10   20   40 KM.

State Capitals .... ⊛

County Seats .... ●

Major Limited Access Hwys. ....

© Copyright HAMMOND INCORPORATED, Maplewood, N.J.

MARYLAND

COUNTIES

Allegany 74,946 ....C2
Anne Arundel 427,239 ....M4
Baltimore 692,134 ....M3
Baltimore (city county)
  736,775 ....M3
Calvert 51,372 ....M6
Caroline 27,035 ....P5
Carroll 123,372 ....K2
Cecil 71,347 ....P2
Charles 101,154 ....K6
Dorchester 30,236 ....O7
Fredrick 114,792 ....J3
Garrett 28,138 ....A2
Harford 182,132 ....N2
Howard 187,328 ....L4
Kent 17,842 ....O3
Montgomery 757,027 ....J4
Prince Georges 665,071 ...L5
Queen Annes 25,508 ....P4
Saint Marys 59,895 ....M7
Somerset 23,440 ....R8
Talbot 30,549 ....O5
Washington 121,393 ....G2
Wicomico 74,339 ....R7
Worcester 35,028 ....S8

CITIES and TOWNS

Aberdeen 13,087 ....O2
Abingdon 500 ....N3
Accident 349 ....A2
Accokeek 4,477 ....L6
Adamstown 300 ....H3
Allen 250 ....R7
Annapolis (cap.)▲ 33,187 ..M5
Annapolis Junction 775 ....M4
Aquasco 950 ....L6
Arbutus 19,750 ....M3
Ardmore 500 ....G4
Aspen Hill 45,494 ....K4
Baltimore 736,014 ....M3
Barclay 170 ....P4
Barnesville 170 ....J4
Barstow 500 ....M6
Barton 530 ....B2
Bayview 200 ....P2
Beaver Creek 290 ....H2
Bel Air▲ 8,860 ....N2
Bel Alton 800 ....L7
Bellevue 300 ....O6
Beltsville 14,476 ....G3
Benedict 850 ....M6
Berlin 2,616 ....T7
Berwyn Heights 2,952 .....G4
Bethesda 62,936 ....E4
Bethlehem 500 ....P6
Betterton 360 ....O3
Bishops Head 250 ....O7
Bishopville 300 ....T7
Bivalve 175 ....P7
Bladensburg 8,064 ....G4
Bloomington 486 ....B3
Boonsboro 2,445 ....B2
Borden Shaft 200 ....B2
Boring 290 ....L2
Boulevard Heights 500 ....F5
Bowens 250 ....M6
Bowie 37,589 ....J4
Boyds 300 ....J4
Bozman 700 ....N5
Brandywine 1,406 ....L6
Brentwood 3,005 ....F4
Brooklyn Park 10,987 ......M4
Brownsville 190 ....H3
Brunswick 5,117 ....H3
Buckeystown 400 ....J3
Burkittsville 194 ....H3
Bushwood 750 ....L7
Butler 200 ....M2
Cabin John (Cabin John-
  Brookmont) 5,341 ....D4
California 7,626 ....M7
Calvert 1,728 ....O2
Calverton 12,046 ....L4
Cambridge▲ 11,514 ....O6
Camp Springs 16,392 .....G6
Cape Saint Claire 7,878 ...N4
Capitol Heights 3,633 ......F5
Cardiff 475 ....N2
Carmody Hills (Carmody Hills-
  Pepper Mill Village) 4,815 ..G5
Cascade (Cascade-Highfield)
  1,096 ....J2
Castleton 750 ....N2
Catoctin Furnace 516 ......J2
Catonsville 35,233 ....M3
Cavetown 1,533 ....H2
Cecilton 489 ....P3
Cedar Grove 300 ....K4
Cedar Heights G5
Cedarville 200 ....L6
Centreville▲ 2,097 ....O4
Chance 600 ....P8
Chaptico 300 ....M7
Charlestown 578 ....P2
Charlotte Hall 1,992 ....M7
Chase 900 ....N3
Cheltenham 950 ....L6
Cherry Hill 250 ....P2
Chesapeake Beach 2,403 ..N6
Chesapeake City 735 ......P2
Chester 349 ....N5
Chestertown▲ 3,300 ....O4
Cheverly 6,023 ....G4
Chevy Chase 2,675 ....E4
Chevy Chase Section Four
  2,903 ....E4
Chewsville 300 ....H2
Chillum 31,309 ....F4
Church Hill 481 ....O4
Churchville 500 ....N2
Claiborne 225 ....N5
Clarksburg 400 ....J4

Clarksville 500 ....L4
Clear Spring 415 ....G2
Clements 800 ....L7
Clinton 19,987 ....G6
Cockeysville 18,668 ....M3
Colesville 18,819 ....K4
College Park 21,927 ....G4
Colmar Manor 1,249 ....F4
Coltons Point 600 ....M8
Columbia 75,883 ....L4
Compton 500 ....M7
Cooksville 497 ....K3
Coral Hills 11,032 ....G5
Cordova 365 ....O4
Corriganville 1,020 ....C2
Cottage City 1,236 ....F4
Cox Station (Bel Alton) 800 ..L7
Creagerstown 240 ....J2
Crellin 275 ....A3
Cresaptown 4,586 ....C2
Crisfield 2,880 ....P9
Crofton 12,781 ....M4
Crownsville 1,514 ....M4
Crumpton 350 ....P4

Cumberland▲ 23,706 .....D2
Damascus 9,817 ....K3
Dames Quarter 250 ....P8
Dargan 352 ....H3
Darlington 850 ....N2
Darnestown 950 ....J4
Davidsonville 250 ....M5
Deal Island 800 ....P8
Deale 4,151 ....M5
Deer Park 419 ....A3
Defense Heights G4
Delmar 1,430 ....R7
Denton▲ 2,977 ....P5
Derwood 413 ....K4
Dickerson 530 ....J4
Doubs 200 ....J3
Downsville 255 ....G2
Drayden 400 ....N8
Dublin 366 ....N2
Dundalk 65,800 ....N3
Eagle Harbor 38 ....M6
East New Market 153 .....P6

Easton▲ 9,372 ....O5
Eckhart Mines 1,333 ......C2
Eden 800 ....R7
Edgemere 9,226 ....N4
Edgewood 23,903 ....N3
Edmonston 851 ....F4
Eldersburg 9,720 ....L3
Elk Mills 550 ....P2
Elk Neck 700 ....P2
Elkridge 12,953 ....M4
Elkton▲ 9,073 ....P2
Ellerslie 950 ....C2
Ellicott City▲ 41,396 ......L3
Emmitsburg 1,688 ....J2
Essex 40,872 ....N3
Ewell 595 ....O9
Fair Hill 250 ....P2
Fairlee 300 ....O4
Fairmount 1,238 ....P8
Fairmount Heights 1,616 ..G5
Fallston 5,730 ....N2
Federalsburg 2,365 ....P6
Ferndale 16,355 ....M4
Finksburg 950 ....L3

Fishing Creek 595 ....N7
Flintstone 400 ....D2
Forest Heights 2,859 ......F5
Forest Hill 450 ....N2
Forestville 16,731 ....G5
Fort Foote 700 ....F6
Fort Howard N4
Fountain Head 1,745 ......G2
Foxville 175 ....H2
Frederick▲ 40,148 ....J3
Freeland 500 ....M2
Friendship 600 ....M6
Friendsville 577 ....A2
Frizzellburg 300 ....K2
Frostburg 8,075 ....C2
Fruitland 3,511 ....R7
Funkstown 1,136 ....H2
Gaithersburg 39,542 ......K4
Galena 324 ....P3
Galesville 123 ....M5
Galestown 600 ....L3
Gamber 500 ....L3
Gambrills 460 ....M4
Garrett Park 884 ....E3

Garrison 5,045 ....L3
Germantown 41,145 ....J4
Girdletree 350 ....S8
Glen Arm 350 ....N3
Glen Burnie 37,305 ....M4
Glen Echo 234 ....E4
Glenarden 5,025 ....G4
Glenelg 400 ....L3
Goldsboro 185 ....P4
Good Luck G4
Graceham 300 ....J2
Granite 950 ....L3
Grantsville 505 ....B2
Grasonville 2,439 ....O5
Green Haven 14,416 ......M4
Greenbelt 21,096 ....G4
Greenmount 325 ....L2
Greensboro 1,441 ....P5
Hagerstown▲ 35,445 .....G2
Halfway 8,873 ....G2
Hampstead 2,608 ....L2
Hancock 1,926 ....F2
Hanover 500 ....M4

Harmans 400 ....M4
Harney 270 ....K2
Havre de Grace 8,952 ....O2
Hebron 665 ....R7
Helen 300 ....M7
Henryton 300 ....L3
Hereford 680 ....M2
Hillandale 10,318 ....F4
Hillcrest Heights 17,136 ..F5
Hillsboro 164 ....P5
Hollywood 500 ....M7
Hoopersville 180 ....O7
Hughesville 1,319 ....L6
Huntingtown 450 ....M6
Hurlock 1,706 ....P6
Hyattsville 13,864 ....F4
Indian Head 3,531 ....K6
Island Creek 400 ....M7
Issue 250 ....L7
Jacksonville 172 ....M2
Jarrettsville 2,148 ....M2
Jefferson 300 ....J3
Jennings 172 ....B2
Johnsville 200 ....K2

(continued)

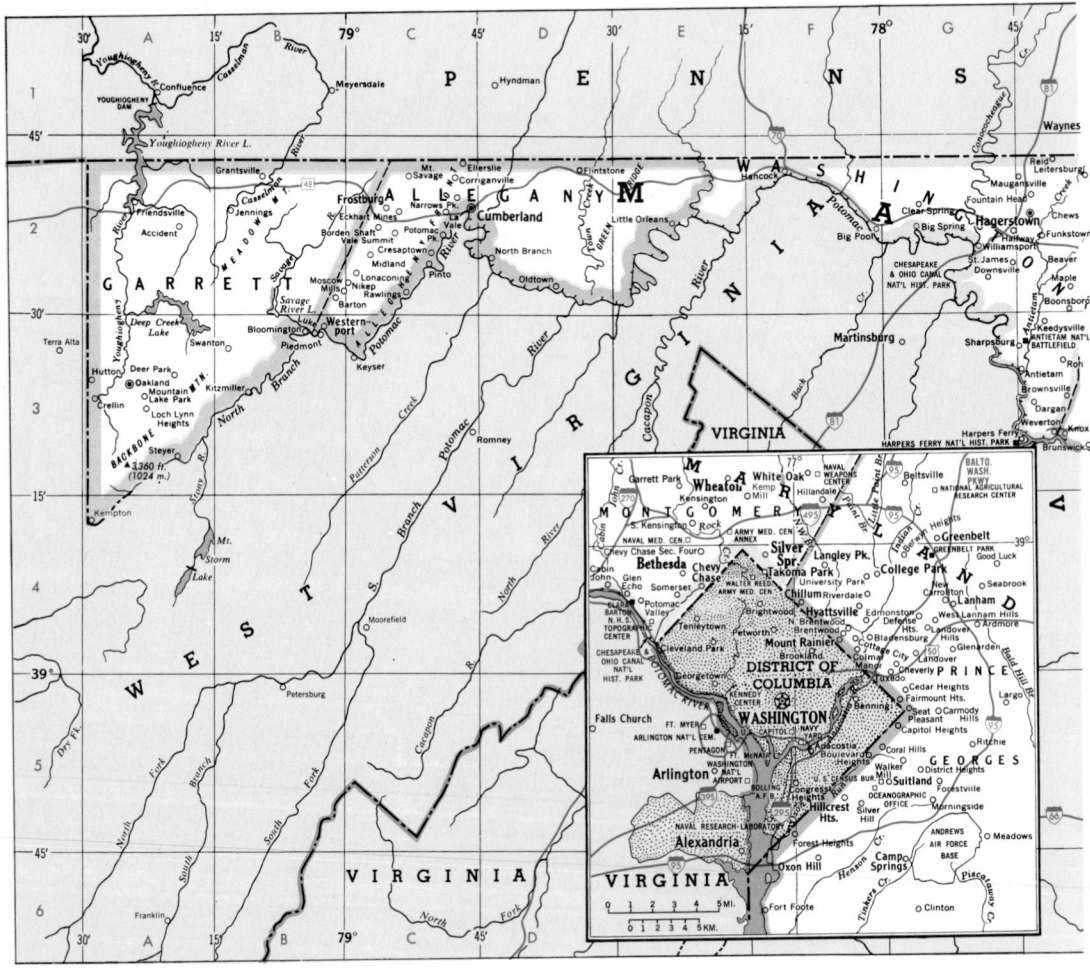

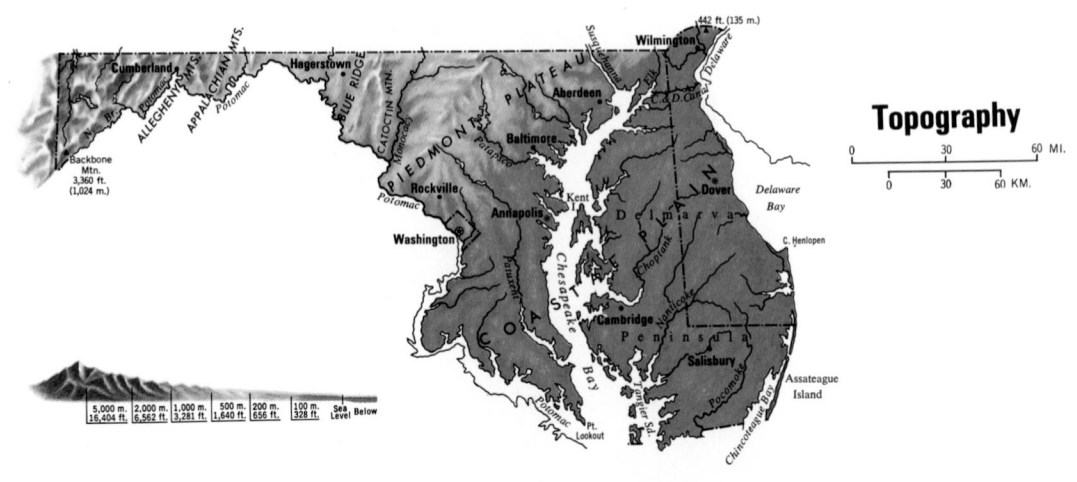

Topography

MARYLAND

AREA 10,460 sq. mi. (27,091 sq. km.)
POPULATION 4,798,622
CAPITAL Annapolis
LARGEST CITY Baltimore
HIGHEST POINT Backbone Mtn. 3,360 ft.
(1024 m.)
SETTLED IN 1634
ADMITTED TO UNION April 28, 1788
POPULAR NAME Old Line State; Free State
STATE FLOWER Black-eyed Susan
STATE BIRD Baltimore Oriole

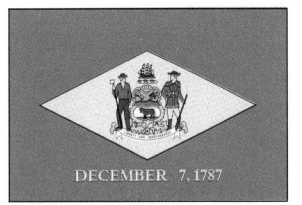

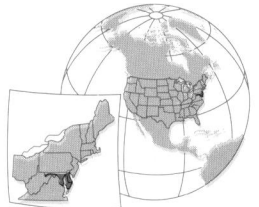

DELAWARE

AREA 2,044 sq. mi. (5,294 sq. km.)
POPULATION 668,696
CAPITAL Dover
LARGEST CITY Wilmington
HIGHEST POINT Ebright Road 442 ft. (135 m.)

SETTLED IN 1627
ADMITTED TO UNION December 7, 1787
POPULAR NAME First State; Diamond State
STATE FLOWER Peach Blossom
STATE BIRD Blue Hen Chicken

Maryland
and Delaware

SCALE

0   5   10   20   30MI.

0 5 10   20   30 KM.

National Capital .... ⊛
State Capitals .... ⊛
County Seats .... ◉
Canals ....

Major Limited Access Hwys. ....

© Copyright HAMMOND INCORPORATED, Maplewood, N.J.

Joppatowne 11,084 ... N3
Keedysville 464 ... H3
Kemp Mill ... F3
Kemptown 250 ... J3
Kennedyville 225 ... P3
Kensington 1,713 ... E4
Keymar 200 ... K2
Kingsville 3,550 ... N3
Kitzmiller 275 ... B3
Knoxville 500 ... H3
La Plata▲ 5,841 ... L6
La Vale (La Vale-Narrows Park) 4,694 ... C2
Landover 5,052 ... G4
Landover Hills 2,074 ... G4
Langley Park 17,474 ... F4
Lanham (Lanham-Seabrook) 16,792 ... G4
Lansdowne (Lansdowne-Baltimore Highlands) 15,509 ... M3
Largo 9,475 ... G5
Laurel 19,438 ... L4
Laytonsville 248 ... K4
Le Gore 500 ... J2
Leeds 177 ... P2
Leitersburg 350 ... H2
Leonardtown▲ 1,475 ... M7
Level 250 ... O2
Lewistown 600 ... J2
Lexington Park 9,943 ... M7
Libertytown 400 ... J3
Lime Kiln 230 ... J3
Lineboro 300 ... L2
Linkwood 250 ... P6
Linthicum Heights 7,547 ... M4
Little Orleans 600 ... E2
Loch Lynn Heights 461 ... A3
Lonaconing 1,122 ... C2
Londontowne 6,992 ... M5
Long Green 1,626 ... M3
Loveville 600 ... M7
Luke 184 ... B3
Lutherville (Lutherville-Timonium) 16,442 ... M3
Madison 350 ... O6
Manchester 2,810 ... L2
Manokin 270 ... P8
Mapleville 200 ... H2
Marbury 1,244 ... K6
Mardela Springs 360 ... P7
Marion Station 400 ... R8
Marshall Hall 325 ... K6
Marydel 143 ... P4
Maryland City 6,813 ... L4
Maryland Line 281 ... M2
Massey 280 ... P3
Maugansville 1,707 ... H2
Mayo 2,537 ... M5
McDaniel 275 ... N5
Meadows 200 ... G5
Mechanicsville 784 ... M7
Middle River 24,616 ... N3
Middleburg 200 ... K2
Middletown 1,834 ... J3
Midland 574 ... C2
Millersville 380 ... M4
Millington 409 ... P3
Monkton 307 ... M2
Montrose ... K4
Morningside 930 ... G5
Moscow Mills 260 ... B2
Mount Airy 3,730 ... K3
Mount Pleasant 400 ... J3
Mount Rainier 7,954 ... F4
Mount Savage 1,640 ... C2
Mount Vernon 900 ... P8
Mountain Lake Park 1,938 ... A3
Mountaindale 400 ... J2
Muirkirk 950 ... L4
Myersville 464 ... H3
Nanjemoy 238 ... K7
Nanticoke 450 ... P7
Narrows Park (Narrows Park-La Vale) ... C2
Neavitt 300 ... N6
New Carrollton 12,002 ... G4
New Market 328 ... J3
New Windsor 757 ... K2
Newark 900 ... S7
Newburg 550 ... L7
Nikep 200 ... C2
North Beach 1,173 ... N6
North Brentwood 512 ... F4
North East 1,913 ... P2
North Potomac 18,456 ... K4
Oakland 2,242 ... L3
Oakland▲ 1,741 ... A3
Ocean City 5,146 ... T7
Odenton 12,833 ... M4
Oella 600 ... L3
Oldtown 200 ... D2
Olivet 200 ... N7
Olney 23,019 ... K4
Orchard Beach 200 ... M4
Overlea 12,137 ... N3
Owings 9,474 ... M6
Owings Mills 9,526 ... L3
Oxford 699 ... O6
Oxon Hill 35,794 ... F6
Park Hall 775 ... N8
Parkton 290 ... M2
Parkville 31,617 ... M3
Parran 200 ... M6
Parsonsburg 200 ... R7
Pasadena 10,012 ... M4
Perry Hall 22,723 ... N3
Perryman 2,160 ... O3
Perryville 2,456 ... O2
Petersville 320 ... H3
Phoenix 165 ... M2
Pikesville 24,815 ... M3
Piney Point 950 ... M8
Pinto 175 ... C2
Piscataway 500 ... L6
Pisgah 650 ... K6
Pittsville 602 ... S7
Pleasant Hills 2,591 ... N3
Pleasant Valley 200 ... L2
Plum Point 200 ... N6
Pocomoke City 3,922 ... R8
Point of Rocks 210 ... J3
Pomfret 600 ... L6
Pomonkey 410 ... K6
Poolesville 3,796 ... J4
Port Deposit 685 ... O2
Potomac Heights 1,524 ... K6
Potomac Park (Potomac Park-Bowling Green) 2,275 ... C2
Potomac Valley ... E4
Powellville 400 ... S7
Preston 437 ... P6
Prince Frederick▲ 1,885 ... M6
Princess Anne▲ 1,666 ... P8
Pumphrey 5,483 ... M4
Quantico 200 ... R7
Queen Anne 250 ... O5
Queenstown 453 ... O5
Randallstown 26,277 ... L3
Randolph ... K4
Rawlings 500 ... C2
Reid 320 ... H2
Reisterstown 19,314 ... L3
Ridge 1,034 ... N8
Ridgely 933 ... P5
Ringgold 200 ... H2
Rising Sun 1,263 ... O2
Ritchie 950 ... G5
Riverdale 5,185 ... F4
Riviera Beach 11,376 ... N4
Rock Hall 1,584 ... O4
Rocks 450 ... N2
Rockville▲ 44,835 ... K4
Rohrersville 525 ... H3
Rosedale 18,703 ... M3
Rosemont 256 ... H3
Royal Oak 600 ... O6
Rumbley 200 ... P8
Sabillasville 450 ... J2
Saint Inigoes 750 ... N8
Saint Leonard 244 ... N7
Saint Marys City ... N8
Saint Michaels 1,301 ... N5
Salisbury▲ 20,592 ... R7
Sandy Spring (Sandy Spring-Ashton) 2,659 ... K4
Savage (Savage-Guilford) 9,669 ... L4
Scotland 475 ... N8
Seabrook (Seabrook-Lanham) ... G4
Seat Pleasant 5,359 ... G5
Secretary 528 ... P6
Selby-on-the-Bay 3,101 ... N5
Severn 24,499 ... M4
Severna Park 25,879 ... M4
Shady Side 4,107 ... M5
Sharpsburg 659 ... G3
Sharptown 609 ... R6
Silver Run 350 ... K2
Silver Spring 76,046 ... F4
Smithsburg 1,221 ... H2
Snow Hill▲ 2,217 ... S8
Solomons 250 ... N7
Somerset 993 ... E4
South Gate 27,564 ... M4
South Kensington 8,777 ... E4
South Laurel 18,591 ... L4
Sparrows Point ... N4
Stevensville 1,862 ... N5
Still Pond 350 ... O3
Stockton 400 ... S8
Street 200 ... N2
Sudlersville 428 ... P4
Suitland (Suitland-Silver Hill) 35,111 ... F5
Swanton 223 ... A3
Sykesville 2,303 ... K3
Takoma Park 16,700 ... F4
Taneytown 3,695 ... K2
Taylors Island 400 ... N7
Texas 300 ... M3
Thurmont 3,398 ... J2
Tilghman 979 ... N6
Timonium (Timonium-Lutherville) ... M3
Toddville 500 ... O7
Tompkinsville 200 ... L7
Towson▲ 49,445 ... M3
Trappe 974 ... O6
Tuxedo 500 ... G5
Union Bridge 910 ... K2
Union Mills 225 ... K2
Uniontown 250 ... K2
Unionville 200 ... K3
University Park 2,243 ... F4
Upper Fairmount 500 ... P8
Upper Falls 550 ... N3
Upper Marlboro▲ 745 ... M5
Upperco 500 ... L2
Vale Summit 175 ... C2
Valley Lee 600 ... M8
Vienna 264 ... P7
Waldorf 15,058 ... L6
Walker Mill 10,920 ... F5
Walkersville 4,145 ... J3
Warwick 550 ... P3
Washington Grove 434 ... K4
Welcome 438 ... K7
Wenona 270 ... P8
West Lanham Hills 350 ... G4
West Laurel 4,151 ... L4
West River 300 ... M5
Westernport 2,454 ... B3
Westminster▲ 13,068 ... L2
Westover 450 ... R8
Wheaton (Wheaton-Glenmont) 53,720 ... E3
White Hall 360 ... M2
White Marsh 8,183 ... N3
White Oak 18,671 ... F3
White Plains 3,560 ... L6
Whiteford 500 ... N2
Wicomico 210 ... L7
Willards 708 ... S7
Williamsport 2,103 ... G2
Willows 250 ... M6
Winfield 200 ... K3
Wingate 225 ... O7
Wittman 544 ... N5
Woodbine 872 ... K3
Woodlawn 5,329 ... M3
Woodmoor ... L3
Woodsboro 513 ... J2
Woolford 330 ... O7
Worton 200 ... O3
Wye Mills 315 ... O5
Wynne 450 ... N8
Yellow Springs 940 ... H3
Zion 225 ... P2

OTHER FEATURES

Aberdeen Proving Ground 5,267 ... N3
Allegheny Front (mts.) ... C2
Andrews A.F.B. 10,228 ... G5
Antietam (creek) ... H2
Antietam Nat'l Battlefield ... H3
Back (riv.) ... N4
Backbone (mt.) ... A3
Bainbridge N.T.C. ... O2
Bald Hill Branch (riv.) ... G4
Big Annemessex (riv.) ... P8
Big Pipe (creek) ... K2
Bloodsworth (isl.) ... O8
Blue Ridge (mts.) ... H3
Bodkin (pt.) ... N4
Bush (creek) ... J3
Cabin John (creek) ... D4
Camp David ... J2
Casselman (riv.) ... B2
Catoctin (creek) ... H3
Catoctin Mt. Park ... J2
Cedar (pt.) ... N7
Census Bureau ... F5
Chesapeake (bay) ... N7
Chesapeake and Delaware (canal) ... R2
Chesapeake and Ohio Canal Nat'l Hist. Park ... J4
Chester (riv.) ... O4
Chicamacomico (riv.) ... P7
Chincoteague (bay) ... S8
Choptank (riv.) ... O6
Clara Barton Nat'l Hist. Site ... E4
Conococheague (bay) ... G1
Conowingo (dam) ... O2
Cove (pt.) ... N7
Deep Creek (lake) ... A3
Deer (creek) ... N2
Dividing (creek) ... R8
Eastern (bay) ... N5
Elk (riv.) ... P3
Fishing (bay) ... O7
Fort Detrick ... J3
Fort George G. Meade 12,509 ... L4
Fort McHenry Nat'l Mon. ... M3
Fort Ritchie 1,249 ... H2
Fort Washington Park ... L6
Great Seneca (creek) ... J4
Greenbelt Park ... G4
Green Ridge (mts.) ... E2
Gunpowder (riv.) ... N3
Gunpowder Falls (creek) ... M2
Hampton Nat'l Hist. Site ... M3
Harpers Ferry Nat'l Hist. Park ... G3
Henson (creek) ... F6
Honga (riv.) ... O7
Hooper (str.) ... O8
Indian (creek) ... G4
James (pt.) ... N6
Kedges (strs) ... O8
Kent (isl.) ... N5
Kent (pt.) ... N5
Liberty (lake) ... L3
Linganore (creek) ... J3
Little Choptank (riv.) ... N6
Little Gunpowder Falls (creek) ... M2
Little Paint Branch (riv.) ... F4
Little Patuxent (riv.) ... L4
Loch Raven (res.) ... M3
Lookout (pt.) ... N8
Manokin (riv.) ... P8
Marshyhope (creek) ... P6
Mattawoman (creek) ... K6
Meadow (mt.) ... B2
Middle Patuxent (riv.) ... L3
Monocacy (riv.) ... J3
Monocacy Nat'l Battlefield ... J3
Nanticoke (riv.) ... P7
Nassawango (creek) ... S8
National Agricultural Research Center ... G3
Naval Academy, U.S. 5,420 ... N5
Naval Medical Center ... E4
Naval Weapons Center ... F3
North (pt.) ... N4
Oceanographic Office ... F5
Oxon Run (riv.) ... F5
Paint Branch (riv.) ... F4
Patapsco (riv.) ... M4
Patuxent (riv.) ... M7
Patuxent River Nav. Air Test Ctr. ... N7
Piscataway (creek) ... G6
Piscataway Park ... K6
Pocomoke (riv.) ... S8
Pocomoke (sound) ... P9
Pooles (isl.) ... O3
Poplar (isl.) ... N5
Potomac (riv.) ... M8
Prettyboy (res.) ... M2
Rock (creek) ... K4
Rocky Gorge (res.) ... L4
Saint George (isl.) ... M8
Saint Marys (riv.) ... N8
Sassafras (riv.) ... P3
Savage (riv.) ... B2
Savage River (lake) ... B2
Severn (riv.) ... N4
Sharps (isl.) ... N6
Smith (isl.) ... O8
South Marsh (isl.) ... O8
Susquehanna (riv.) ... N1
Tangier (sound) ... P8
Thomas Stone Nat'l Hist. Site ... K6
Tinkers (creek) ... F6
Topographic Center ... E4
Town (creek) ... D2
Transquaking (riv.) ... P7
Triadelphia (lake) ... L4
Tuckahoe (creek) ... P5
Walter Reed Army Medical Center Annex ... E4
Wicomico (riv.) ... L7
Wicomico (riv.) ... R7
Winters Run (creek) ... N2
Youghiogheny (riv.) ... A3
Youghiogheny River (lake) ... A2
Zekiah Swamp (riv.) ... L7

DELAWARE

COUNTIES

Kent 110,993 ... R4
New Castle 441,946 ... R2
Sussex 113,229 ... S6

CITIES and TOWNS

Arden 477 ... R1
Ardencroft 282 ... R1
Ardentown 325 ... S1
Bear 200 ... R2
Bellefonte 1,243 ... S1
Bethany Beach 326 ... T6
Bethel 178 ... R6
Blades 834 ... R6
Bowers Beach 198 ... S4
Bridgeville 1,210 ... R6
Brookside 15,307 ... R2
Camden 1,899 ... R4
Centerville 800 ... R1
Cheswold 321 ... R4
Christiana 500 ... R2
Clarksville 350 ... T6
Claymont 9,800 ... S1
Clayton 1,163 ... R3
Concord 200 ... R6
Cool Spring 200 ... T6
Dagsboro 398 ... S6
Delaware City 1,682 ... R2
Delmar 962 ... R7
Dover (cap.)▲ 27,630 ... R4
Dupont Manor 1,059 ... R4
Edgemoor 5,853 ... S1
Ellendale 313 ... S5
Elsmere 5,935 ... R2
Farmington 122 ... R5
Felton 683 ... R4
Fenwick Island 186 ... T7
Frankford 591 ... S6
Frederica 761 ... S4
Georgetown▲ 3,732 ... S6
Glasgow 350 ... R2
Greenville 230 ... R1
Greenwood 578 ... R5
Harbeson 300 ... S6
Harrington 2,311 ... R5
Hockessin 950 ... R1
Houston 487 ... S5
Kenton 232 ... R4
Kirkwood 350 ... R2
Laurel 3,226 ... R6
Leipsic 236 ... S4
Lewes 2,295 ... T5
Lincoln 757 ... S5
Little Creek 167 ... S4
Magnolia 211 ... R4
Middletown 3,834 ... R3
Midway 250 ... T6
Milford 6,040 ... S5
Millsboro 1,643 ... S6
Millville 206 ... T6
Milton 1,417 ... S5
New Castle 4,837 ... R2
Newark 25,098 ... P2
Newport 1,240 ... R2
Oak Orchard 350 ... T6
Ocean View 606 ... T6
Odessa 303 ... R3
Port Penn 300 ... R2
Rehoboth Beach 1,234 ... T6
Rodney Village 1,745 ... R4
Roxana 250 ... T6
Saint Georges 450 ... R2
Seaford 5,689 ... R6
Selbyville 1,335 ... S7
Smyrna 5,231 ... R3
South Bethany 148 ... T6
Townsend 322 ... R3
Viola 153 ... R4
Wilmington▲ 71,529 ... R2
Woodside 140 ... R4
Wyoming 977 ... R4

OTHER FEATURES

Broad (creek) ... R6
Broadkill (riv.) ... S5
Chesapeake and Delaware (canal) ... R2
Choptank (riv.) ... P5
Deep Water (pt.) ... S4
Delaware (bay) ... T5
Delaware (riv.) ... R3
Dover A.F.B. ... S4
Henlopen (cape) ... T5
Indian (riv.) ... S6
Indian River (bay) ... T6
Indian River (inlet) ... T6
Leipsic (riv.) ... R4
Mispillion (riv.) ... S5
Murderkill (riv.) ... R5
Nanticoke (riv.) ... R6
Saint Jones (riv.) ... R4
Smyrna (res.) ... R3

DISTRICT OF COLUMBIA

CITIES and TOWNS

Georgetown ... E5
Washington D.C. (cap), U.S. 609,909 ... F5

OTHER FEATURES

Anacostia (riv.) ... F5
Bolling A.F.B. ... F5
Fort Lesley J. McNair ... E5
Kennedy Center ... A5
Naval Yard ... F5
U.S. Capitol ... F5
Walter Reed Army Med. Ctr. ... E4

▲County seat.

Agriculture, Industry and Resources

DOMINANT LAND USE

- Dairy, General Farming
- Fruit and Mixed Farming
- Truck and Mixed Farming
- Tobacco, General Farming
- Forests
- Swampland, Limited Agriculture
- Urban Areas

MAJOR MINERAL OCCURRENCES

- C Coal
- Cl Clay
- G Natural Gas
- Ls Limestone

- Water Power
- Major Industrial Areas

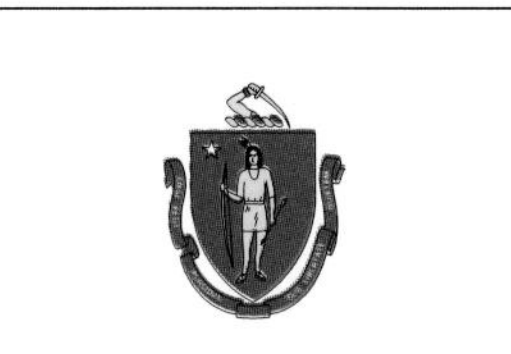

MASSACHUSETTS

AREA 8,284 sq. mi. (21,456 sq. km.)
POPULATION 6,029,051
CAPITAL Boston
LARGEST CITY Boston
HIGHEST POINT Mt. Greylock 3,491 ft. (1064 m.)
SETTLED IN 1620
ADMITTED TO UNION February 6, 1788
POPULAR NAME Bay State; Old Colony
STATE FLOWER Mayflower
STATE BIRD Chickadee

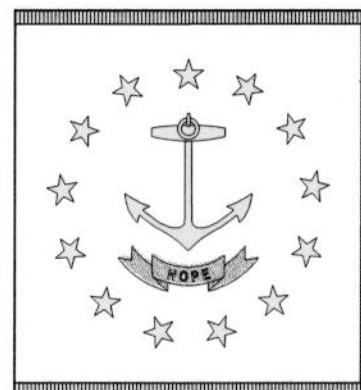

RHODE ISLAND

AREA 1,212 sq. mi. (3,139 sq. km.)
POPULATION 1,005,984
CAPITAL Providence
LARGEST CITY Providence
HIGHEST POINT Jerimoth Hill 812 ft. (247 m.)
SETTLED IN 1636
ADMITTED TO UNION May 29, 1790
POPULAR NAME Little Rhody; Ocean State
STATE FLOWER Violet
STATE BIRD Rhode Island Red

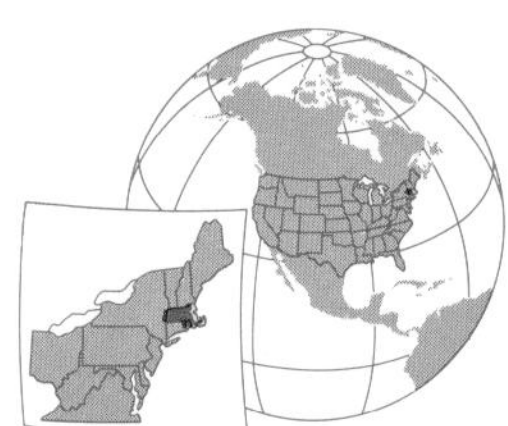

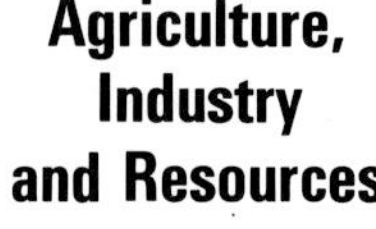

Agriculture, Industry and Resources

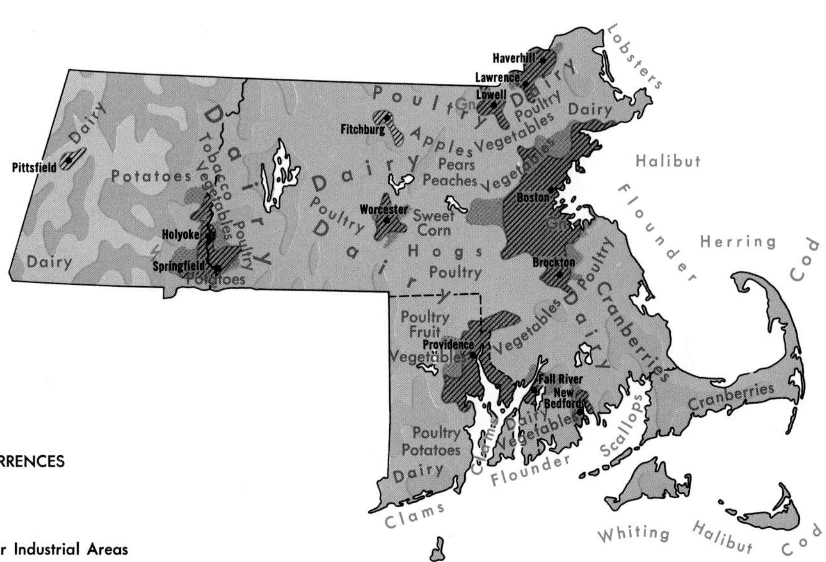

DOMINANT LAND USE

- Specialized Dairy
- Dairy, Poultry, Mixed Farming
- Forests
- Urban Areas

MAJOR MINERAL OCCURRENCES

Gn Granite

Water Power

Major Industrial Areas

MASSACHUSETTS

COUNTIES

Barnstable 186,605 … N6
Berkshire 139,352 … B3
Bristol 506,325 … K5
Dukes 11,639 … M7
Essex 670,080 … L2
Franklin 70,092 … D2
Hampden 456,310 … D4
Hampshire 146,568 … D3
Middlesex 1,398,468 … J3
Nantucket 6,012 … O7
Norfolk 616,087 … K4
Plymouth 435,276 … L5
Suffolk 663,906 … K3
Worcester 709,705 … G3

CITIES and TOWNS

Abington• 13,817 … L4
Acton• 17,872 … J3
Acushnet• 9,554 … L6
Adams 6,356 … B2
Adams• 9,445 … B2
Agawam• 27,323 … D4
Alford• 418 … A4
Allerton 900 … E7
Amesbury 12,109 … L1
Amesbury• 14,997 … L1
Amherst 17,824 … E3
Amherst• 35,228 … E3
Andover 8,242 … K2
Andover• 29,151 … K2
Arlington• 44,630 … C6
Ashburnham 900 … G2
Ashburnham• 5,433 … G2
Ashby• 2,717 … G2
Ashfield• 1,715 … C2
Ashland• 12,066 … J3
Ashley Falls 600 … A4
Assinippi 950 … E8
Assonet 950 … K5
Athol 8,732 … F2
Athol• 11,451 … F2
Attleboro 38,383 … J5
Attleboro Falls … J5
Auburn• 15,005 … G4
Auburndale … B7
Avon• 4,558 … K4
Ayer 2,889 … H2
Ayer• 6,871 … H2
Baldwinville 1,795 … F2
Ballardvale … K2
Barnstable▲ 2,790 … N6
Barnstable• 30,898 … N6
Barre 1,094 … F3
Barre• 4,546 … F3
Barrowsville 500 … K5
Becket• 1,481 … B3
Bedford• 12,996 … B6
Belchertown 2,339 … E3
Belchertown• 10,579 … E3
Bellingham 4,535 … J4
Bellingham• 14,877 … J4
Belmont• 24,720 … C6
Berkley• 4,237 … K5
Berlin• 2,293 … H3
Bernardston• 2,048 … D2
Beverly 38,195 … E5
Billerica• 37,609 … J2
Blackstone• 8,023 … H4
Blandford• 1,187 … C4
Bolton• 3,134 … H3
Bondsville 1,992 … E4
Boston (cap.)▲ 574,283 … D7
Bourne 1,284 … M6
Bourne• 16,064 … M6
Boxborough• 3,343 … H3
Boxford 2,072 … L2
Boxford• 6,266 … L2
Boylston• 3,517 … H3
Braintree• 33,836 … D8
Brant Rock-Ocean Bluff … M4
Brewster 1,818 … O5
Brewster• 8,440 … O5
Bridgewater 7,242 … K5
Bridgewater• 21,249 … K5
Brimfield• 3,001 … F4
Brockton 92,788 … K4
Brookfield 2,968 … F4
Brookfield• 2,397 … F4
Brookline• 54,718 … C7
Brookville … K4
Buckland• 1,928 … C2
Burlington• 23,302 … C5
Buzzards Bay 3,250 … M5
Byfield 950 … L1
Cambridge▲ 95,802 … C7
Canton• 18,530 … C8
Carlisle• 4,333 … J2
Carver• 10,590 … M5
Cataumet 650 … M6
Centerville 9,190 … N6
Central Village 800 … K6
Charlemont• 1,249 … C2
Charlton• 9,576 … F4
Charlton City 950 … F4
Chartley 950 … K5
Chatham 1,916 … P6
Chatham• 6,579 … P6
Chelmsford• 32,388 … J2
Chelsea 28,710 … D6
Cherry Valley … G3
Cheshire• 3,479 … B2
Chester• 1,280 … C3
Chesterfield• 1,048 … C3
Chicopee 56,632 … D4
Chilmark• 650 … M7
Chiltonville 600 … M5
City Mills 500 … J4
Clicquot-Millis … A8
Clinton• 7,943 … H3
Cochituate 6,046 … A7
Cohasset• 7,075 … F7
Collinsville … J2
Colrain• 1,757 … D2
Concord• 17,076 … B6
Conway• 1,529 … D2
Cordaville 1,530 … H3
Cotuit 2,364 … N6
Cummington• 785 … C3
Dalton• 7,155 … B3
Danvers• 24,174 … D5
Danversport … E5
Dartmouth• 27,244 … K6
Dedham▲ 23,782 … C7
Deerfield• 5,018 … D2
Dennis• 2,633 … O5
Dennis Port 2,775 … O6
Dighton• 5,631 … K5
Dorchester … D7
Douglas• 5,438 … H4
Dover 2,163 … B7
Dover• 4,915 … B7
Dracut• 25,594 … J2
Dudley• 9,540 … G4
Dunstable• 2,236 … J2
Duxbury 1,637 … M4
Duxbury• 13,895 … M4
East Braintree … D8
East Brewster 900 … O5
East Bridgewater• 11,104 … L4
East Brookfield 1,396 … G4
East Brookfield• 2,033 … G4
East Dedham … C8
East Dennis 2,584 … O5
East Douglas 1,945 … G4
East Falmouth (Teaticket) 5,577 … M6
East Foxboro 750 … K4
East Freetown 600 … L5
East Harwich 3,828 … O6
East Longmeadow• 13,367 … E4
East Milton … D7
East Norton 750 … K5
East Orleans 600 … P5
East Otis 600 … B4
East Pembroke 582 … M4
East Pepperell 2,296 … H2
East Sandwich 3,171 … N6
East Templeton 950 … G2
East Walpole … C8
East Wareham 950 … M5
East Weymouth … E8
East Whately 650 … D3
Eastham• 4,462 … O5
Easthampton• 15,537 … D3
Easton 19,807 … K4
Eastondale 600 … K4
Edgartown▲ 3,062 … M7
Edgartown• 2,204 … M7
Erving• 1,372 … E2
Essex 1,507 … L2
Essex• 3,260 … L2
Everett 35,701 … D6
Fairhaven• 16,132 … L6
Fall River 92,703 … K6
Falmouth 4,047 … M6
Falmouth• 27,960 … M6
Fayville 975 … H3
Feeding Hills … D4
Fisherville … H4
Fiskdale 2,189 … F4
Fitchburg▲ 41,194 … G2
Florida• 742 … B2
Forge Village 925 … H2
Foxboro 5,706 … J4
Foxboro• 14,148 … J4
Framingham• 64,994 … A7
Framingham Center 16,000 … J3
Franklin 9,965 … J4
Franklin• 22,095 … J4
Gardner 20,125 … G2
Gay Head• 201 … L7
Georgetown• 6,384 … L2
Gilbertville 1,029 … F3
Gill• 1,583 … D2
Gloucester 28,716 … M2
Goshen• 830 … C3
Grafton• 13,035 … H4
Granby 1,327 … E3
Granby• 5,565 … E3
Graniteville 970 … J2
Granville• 1,403 … C4
Great Barrington 2,810 … A4
Great Barrington• 7,725 … A4
Green Harbor 2,002 … M4
Greenbush 950 … F8
Greenfield▲ 14,016 … D2
Greenfield• 18,666 … D2
Greenwood … D6
Groton 1,044 … H2
Groton• 7,511 … H2
Groveland• 5,214 … L1
Hadley• 4,231 … D3
Halifax• 6,526 … L5
Hamilton• 7,280 … L2
Hampden• 4,709 … E4
Hancock• 628 … A2
Hanover• 11,912 … L4
Hanson 2,188 … L4
Hanson• 9,028 … L4
Hardwick• 2,385 … F3
Harvard• 12,329 … H2
Harwich 10,275 … O6
Harwich• 1,668 … O6
Harwich Port 1,742 … O6
Hatfield 1,234 … D3
Hatfield• 3,184 … D3
Haverhill 51,418 … K1
Haydenville 900 … C3
Heath• 716 … C2
Hingham 5,454 … E8
Hingham• 19,821 … E8
Hinsdale• 1,959 … B3
Holbrook• 11,041 … D8
Holden• 14,628 … G3
Holland• 1,331 … F4
Holliston• 12,926 … A8
Holyoke 43,704 … D4
Hopedale 3,961 … H4
Hopedale• 5,666 … H4
Hopkinton 2,305 … J4
Hopkinton• 9,191 … J4
Housatonic 1,184 … A3
Hubbardston• 2,797 … F3
Hudson 14,267 … H3
Hudson• 17,233 … H3
Hull• 10,466 … E7
Huntington• 1,987 … C4
Hyannis 14,120 … N6
Hyannis Port 750 … N6
Hyde Park … C7
Interlaken 700 … A3
Ipswich 4,132 … L2
Ipswich• 11,873 … L2
Islington … C8
Jamaica Plain … C7
Jefferson … G3
Kingston 4,774 … M5
Kingston• 9,045 … M5
Lakeville 7,785 … L5
Lakeville• 5,931 … L5
Lancaster• 6,661 … H3
Lanesboro• 3,131 … A2
Lawrence▲ 70,207 … K2
Lee 2,020 … B3
Lee• 5,849 … B3
Leicester• 10,191 … G4
Lenox 1,687 … A3
Lenox• 5,069 … A3
Lenox Dale 600 … B3
Leominster 38,145 … G2
Leverett• 1,785 … E3
Lexington• 28,974 … B6
Leyden• 662 … D2
Lincoln• 7,666 … B6
Lincoln Center 945 … B6
Linwood 995 … H4
Littleton Common 2,867 … J2
Littleton• 7,051 … H2
Longmeadow• 15,467 … D4
Lowell▲ 103,439 … J2
Ludlow• 18,820 … E4
Ludlow Center 750 … E4
Lunds Corner … L6
Lunenburg 1,694 … H2
Lunenburg• 9,117 … H2
Lynn 81,245 … D6
Lynnfield• 11,274 … C5
Malden 53,884 … D6
Manchaug 975 … G4
Manchester-by-the-Sea• 5,286 … F5
Manomet 950 … M5
Mansfield 7,170 … J4
Mansfield• 13,453 … J4
Marblehead• 19,971 … E7
Marion 1,426 … L6
Marion• 3,932 … L6
Marlborough 31,813 … H3
Marshfield 4,002 … M4
Marshfield• 21,531 … M4
Marshfield Hills 2,201 … M4
Marstons Mills 8,017 … N6
Mashpee• 7,884 … M6
Mattapan … C7
Mattapoisett 2,949 … L6
Mattapoisett• 5,597 … L6
Maynard• 10,325 … J3
Medfield 5,985 … B8
Medfield• 10,531 … B8
Medford 57,407 … C6
Medway• 9,931 … J4
Melrose 28,150 … D6
Mendon• 4,010 … H4
Merino Village … G4
Merrimac• 5,166 … L1
Methuen• 39,990 … K2
Middleboro 6,837 … L5
Middleboro• 16,404 … L5
Middlefield• 392 … B3
Middleton• 4,921 … K2
Milford 23,339 … H4
Milford• 25,355 … H4
Millbury• 12,228 … H4
Millers Falls 1,084 … E2
Millis-Clicquot 4,081 … A8
Millis• 7,613 … A8
Millville• 2,236 … H4
Milton• 25,725 … D7
Monson 2,101 … E4
Monson• 7,315 … E4
Montague• 8,316 … E2
Monterey• 805 … B4
Monument Beach 1,842 … M6
Moores Corner … E2
Mount Washington• 135 … A4
Nabnasset 975 … J2
Nahant• 3,828 … E6
Nantasket Beach … E7
Nantucket▲ 3,069 … O7
Nantucket• 6,012 … O7
Natick• 30,510 … A7
Needham Heights … B7
Needham• 27,557 … B7
Neponset … D7
New Bedford▲ 99,922 … K6
New Braintree• 881 … F3
New Marlborough• 1,240 … B4
New Salem• 802 … E2
Newbury• 5,623 … L1
Newburyport▲ 16,317 … L1
Newton 82,585 … C7
Newton Center … C7
Newton Highlands … C7
Newton Lower Falls 950 … B7
Newton Upper Falls … C7
Newtonville … C7
Norfolk• 9,270 … J4
North Abington … L4
North Adams 16,797 … B2
North Amherst 6,239 … E3
North Andover• 22,792 … K2
North Attleboro• 16,178 … J5
North Billerica … J2
North Brookfield 2,635 … F3
North Brookfield• 4,708 … F3
North Chelmsford … J2
North Dartmouth … K6
North Dighton 1,174 … K5
North Eastham 1,570 … O5
North Easton … K4
North Falmouth 2,625 … M6
North Grafton … H4
North Hadley 600 … D3
North Hanover 950 … L4
North Oxford … G4
North Pembroke 2,485 … M4
North Plymouth 3,450 … L5
North Reading• 12,002 … C5
North Scituate 4,891 … F8
North Truro 675 … O4
North Uxbridge … H4
North Waltham … B6
North Weymouth … D8
North Wilbraham … E4
Northampton▲ 29,289 … D3
Northborough 5,761 … H3
Northborough• 11,929 … H3
Northbridge• 13,371 … H4
Northfield 1,322 … E2
Northfield• 2,838 … E2
Norton 1,899 … K5
Norton• 12,690 … K5
Norwell• 9,279 … F8
Norwood• 28,700 … B8
Nutting Lake … B5
Oak Bluffs 2,804 … M7
Oak Bluffs• 1,984 … M7
Oakdale 850 … G3
Oakham• 1,503 … F3
Ocean Bluff-Brant Rock 4,541 … M4
Ocean Grove 3,169 … K6
Old Sturbridge Village 500 … F4
Onset 1,461 … M6
Orange 3,791 … E2
Orange• 7,312 … E2
Orleans 1,699 … O5
Orleans• 5,838 … O5
Osterville 2,911 … N6
Otis• 1,073 … B4
Otter River 700 … F2
Oxford 5,969 … G4
Oxford• 12,588 … G4
Palmer 4,069 … E4
Palmer• 12,054 … E4
Paxton• 4,047 … G3
Peabody 47,039 … E5
Pelham• 1,373 … E3

(continued on following page)

(continued)

Pembroke • 14,544 ....L4
Pepperell 2,350 ....H2
Pepperell • 10,098..................H2
Petersham • 1,131 ....F3
Phillipston • 1,485 ....F2
Pigeon Cove...........................M2
Pinehurst 6,614 ....B5
Pittsfield ▲ 48,622 ....A3
Plainfield • 571 ....C2
Plainville • 6,871 ....J4
Pleasant Lake 525 ....O6
Plymouth ▲ 7,258 ....M5
Plymouth • 45,608...................M5
Plympton • 2,384......................L5
Pocasset 2,756 ....M6
Princeton • 3,189 ....G3
Provincetown 3,374..................O4
Provincetown • 3,561 ....O4
Quincy 84,985 ....D7
Randolph • 30,093 ....D8
Raynham Center 3,709 ....K5
Raynham • 9,867.....................K5
Reading • 22,539.....................C5
Readville C8
Rehoboth • 8,656 ....K5
Revere 42,786 ....D6
Richmond • 1,677 ....A3
Rochdale 1,105 ....G4
Rochester • 3,921 ....L6
Rockland • 16,123 ....L4
Rockport • 5,448 ....M2
Rowe • 378..............................C2
Rowley 1,144 ....L2
Rowley • 4,452 ....L2
Roxbury C7
Royalston • 1,147 ....F2
Russell • 1,594 ....C4
Rutland 2,145...........................G3
Rutland • 4,936 ....G3
Sagamore 2,589 ....M5
Salem ▲ 38,091 ....E5
Salisbury 3,729..........................L1
Salisbury • 6,882 ....L1
Salisbury Beach 950 ....L1
Sand Hills...............................M4
Sandisfield • 667 ....B4
Sandwich 2,998........................N5
Sandwich • 15,489 ....N5
Saugus • 25,549.......................D6
Saundersville 975 ....G4
Savoy • 634 ....B2
Saxonville A7
Scituate 5,180 ....F8
Scituate • 16,786 ....F8
Seekonk • 13,046......................J5
Sharon 5,893 ....K4
Sharon • 15,517 ....K4
Shawsheen Village K2
Sheffield • 2,910.......................A4
Shelburne Falls 1,996 ....D2
Sherborn • 3,989......................A8
Shirley 1,559 ....H2
Shirley • 6,118 ....H2
Shore Acres.............................F8
Shrewsbury • 24,146 ....H3
Shutesbury • 1,561...................E3
Somerset • 17,655 ....K5
Somerville 76,210....................C6
South Acton 950 ....J3
South Amherst 5,053................E3
South Ashburnham 1,110.......G2
South Barre 900 ....F3
South Braintree.......................D8
South Carver 750....................M5
South Chatham 725................O6
South Dartmouth L6
South Deerfield 1,906.............D3
South Dennis 3,559.................O6
South Duxbury 3,017.............M4
South Easton K4
South Egremont 700...............A4
South Grafton (Fisherville)......H4
South Groveland 950 ....L2
South Hadley Falls D4
South Hadley • 16,685 ....D4
South Hanover L4
South Harwich 875.................O6
South Lancaster 1,772 ....H3
South Lee 600 ....A3
South Lynnfield D5
South Middleboro 600 ....L5
South Natick A7
South Orleans 800.................O5
South Sudbury J3
South Walpole K4
South Wellfleet 583 ....P5
South Weymouth E8
South Yarmouth 10,358 ....O6
Southampton • 4,478 ....C4
Southborough • 6,628...........H3
Southbridge 13,631...............G4
Southbridge • 17,816............G4
Southville 600........................H3
Southwick • 7,667 ....C4
Spencer 6,306........................F3
Spencer • 11,645 ....F3
Springfield ▲ 156,983............D4
Sterling • 6,481 ....G3
Stockbridge 2,408 ....A3
Stockbridge • 2,328...............A3
Stoneham • 22,203................C6
Stoughton • 26,777 ....K4
Stow • 5,328 ....H3
Sturbridge 2,093 ....F4
Sturbridge • 7,775 ....F4
Sudbury • 14,358 ....A6
Sunderland • 3,399 ....D3
Sutton 6,824.........................G4
Swampscott • 13,650 ....E6
Swansea • 15,411.................K5
Swansea Center 950 ....K5
Taunton ▲ 49,832 ....K5
Teaticket 1,856 ....M6
Templeton • 6,438 ....F2
Tewksbury 27,266 ....K2
Thorndike 900.........................E4
Three Rivers 3,006..................E4
Tolland • 289 ....B4
Topsfield 2,711 ....L2
Topsfield • 5,754 ....L2
Townsend 1,164......................H2
Townsend • 8,496 ....H2
Townsend Harbor 600 ....G2
Truro • 1,573..........................O5
Turners Falls 4,731 ....D2
Tyngsboro • 5,683 ....J2
Tyringham • 369......................A4
Upton-West Upton 2,347........H4
Upton • 4,677 ....H4
Uxbridge • 10,415 ....H4

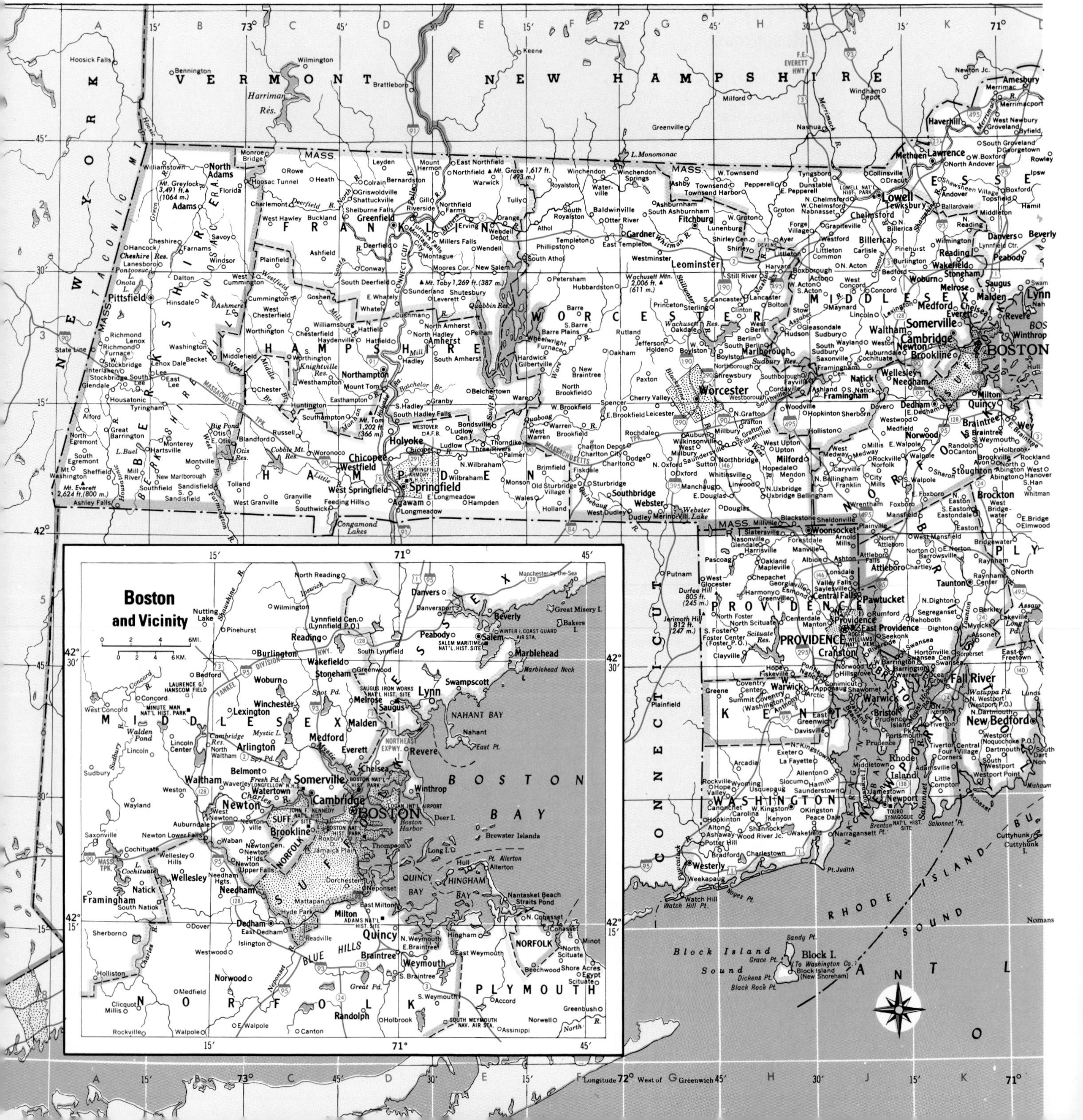

Vineyard Haven 1,762 ... M7
Waban ... B7
Wakefield • 24,825 ... C5
Wales • 1,566 ... F4
Walpole 5,495 ... B8
Walpole • 20,212 ... B8
Waltham 57,878 ... B6
Ware 6,533 ... E3
Ware • 9,808 ... E3
Wareham 19,232 ... L5
Wareham • 18,457 ... L5
Wareham Center 2,607 ... L5
Warren 1,516 ... F4
Warren • 4,437 ... F4
Warwick • 740 ... E2
Washington • 615 ... B3
Watertown • 33,284 ... C6
Waverley ... B6
Wayland • 11,874 ... A7
Webster 11,849 ... G4
Webster • 16,196 ... G4
Wellesley • 26,615 ... B7
Wellesley Hills ... B7
Wellfleet • 2,493 ... O5
Wendell • 899 ... E2
Wenham • 4,212 ... L2
West Acton 975 ... H3
West Barnstable 1,508 ... N6
West Boxford 950 ... K2
West Boylston • 6,611 ... G3
West Bridgewater • 6,389 ... K4
West Brookfield 1,419 ... F4
West Brookfield • 3,532 ... F4
West Chatham 1,504 ... O6
West Chelmsford ... J2
West Concord 5,761 ... A6
West Dennis 2,307 ... O6
West Falmouth 1,752 ... M6
West Groton 950 ... H2
West Hanover ... L4
West Harwich 883 ... O6
West Mansfield 950 ... K5
West Medway ... J4
West Newbury • 3,421 ... L1
West Newton ... B7
West Springfield • 27,537 ... D4
West Stockbridge • 1,483 ... A3
West Tisbury • 1,704 ... M7
West Townsend 950 ... H2
West Upton-Upton ... H4
West Wareham 2,059 ... L5
West Warren ... F4
West Yarmouth 5,409 ... N6
Westborough 3,917 ... H3
Westborough • 14,133 ... H3
Westfield • 38,372 ... D4
Westford • 16,392 ... J2
Westhampton • 1,327 ... C3
Westminster • 6,191 ... G2
Weston • 10,200 ... B6
Westport 13,852 ... K6
Westport • 13,763 ... K6
Westwood • 12,557 ... B8
Weymouth 54,063 ... D8
Whately • 1,375 ... D3
Whitinsville 5,639 ... H4
Whitman • 13,240 ... L4
Wilbraham 3,352 ... E4
Wilbraham • 12,635 ... E4
Williamsburg • 2,515 ... C3
Williamstown 4,791 ... B2
Williamstown • 8,220 ... B2
Wilmington • 17,654 ... C5
Winchendon 4,316 ... F2
Winchendon • 8,805 ... F2
Winchester • 20,267 ... C6
Windsor • 770 ... B2
Winthrop • 18,127 ... D6
Woburn 35,943 ... C6
Woods Hole 1,080 ... M6
Worcester▲ 169,759 ... H3
Worthington • 1,156 ... C3
Wrentham • 9,006 ... J4
Yarmouth Port 4,271 ... N6
Yarmouth • 21,174 ... O6

OTHER FEATURES

Adams Nat'l Hist. Site ... D7
Agawam (riv.) ... M5
Allerton (pt.) ... E7
Ann (cape) ... M2
Ashmere (lake) ... B3
Assabet (riv.) ... H3
Assawompset (pond) ... L5
Batchelor (brook) ... D3
Berkshire (hills) ... B4
Big (pond) ... B4
Bigelow (bight) ... M1
Blackstone (riv.) ... G3
Blue (hills) ... C8
Boston (bay) ... E6
Boston (harb.) ... D7
Boston Nat'l Hist. Park ... D6
Brewster (isls.) ... E7
Buel (lake) ... A4
Buzzards (bay) ... L7
Cambridge (res.) ... B6
Cape Cod (bay) ... N5
Cape Cod (canal) ... N5
Cape Cod Nat'l Seashore ... P5
Chappaquiddick (isl.) ... N7
Charles (riv.) ... C7
Chicopee (riv.) ... D4
Cobble Mountain (res.) ... C4
Cochituate (lake) ... A7
Cod (cape) ... O4
Concord (riv.) ... J2
Congamond (lakes) ... D4
Connecticut (riv.) ... D2
Cuttyhunk (isl.) ... L7
Deer (isl.) ... E7
Deerfield (riv.) ... C2
East (pt.) ... E6
East Chop (pt.) ... M7
Eastern (pt.) ... M2
Elizabeth (isls.) ... L7
Everett (mt.) ... A4
Falls (riv.) ... D2
Fort Devens 8,973 ... H2
Fresh (pond) ... C6
Gammon (pt.) ... N6
Gay Head (prom.) ... L7
Grace (mt.) ... E2
Great (pt.) ... O7
Green (riv.) ... B2
Greylock (mt.) ... B2
Gurnet (pt.) ... M4
Hingham (bay) ... E7
Holyoke (range) ... D3
Hoosac (mts.) ... B2
Hoosic (riv.) ... A1
Housatonic (riv.) ... A4
Ipswich (riv.) ... L2
John F. Kennedy Nat'l Hist. Site ... C7
Knightville (res.) ... C3
Laurence G. Hanscom Field ... B6
Little (riv.) ... C4
Logan Int'l Airport ... D7
Long (isl.) ... E7
Long (pt.) ... O4
Long (pond) ... L5
Longfellow Nat'l Hist. Site ... C6
Lowell Nat'l Hist. Park ... J2
Maine (gulf) ... M2
Manhan (riv.) ... D4
Manomet (pt.) ... N5
Marblehead (neck) ... F6
Martha's Vineyard (isl.) ... M7
Massachusetts (bay) ... M4
Merrimack (riv.) ... K1
Mill (riv.) ... C3
Mill (riv.) ... D3
Millers (riv.) ... E2
Minute Man Nat'l Hist. Park ... B6
Mishaum (pt.) ... L6
Monomonac (lake) ... G2
Monomoy (isl.) ... O6
Monomoy (pt.) ... O6
Mount Hope (bay) ... K6
Muskeget (chan.) ... N7
Muskeget (isl.) ... N7
Mystic (lake) ... C6
Mystic (riv.) ... C6
Nahant (bay) ... E6
Nantucket (isl.) ... O8
Nantucket (sound) ... N6
Nashawena (isl.) ... L7
Nashua (riv.) ... H3
Naushon (isl.) ... L7
Neponset (riv.) ... C8
Nomans Land (isl.) ... L7
Nonamesset (isl.) ... M6
North (riv.) ... D2
North (riv.) ... L4
Onota (lake) ... A3
Otis (res.) ... B4
Otis A.F.B. ... M6
Pasque (isl.) ... L7
Plum (isl.) ... L2
Plymouth (bay) ... M5
Poge (cape) ... N7
Pontoosuc (lake) ... A3
Quabbin (res.) ... E3
Quaboag (riv.) ... F4
Quincy (bay) ... D7
Quinebaug (riv.) ... F4
Race (pt.) ... N4
Salem Maritime Nat'l Hist. Site ... E5
Saugus Iron Works Nat'l Hist. Site ... D6
Shawshine (riv.) ... K2
Silver (lake) ... L4
South (riv.) ... D2
South Weymouth Nav. Air Sta. ... E8
Springfield Armory Nat'l Hist. Site ... D4
Squibnocket (pt.) ... M7
Stillwater (riv.) ... G3
Sudbury (res.) ... H3
Sudbury (riv.) ... A6
Swift (riv.) ... E4
Taconic (mts.) ... A2
Taunton (riv.) ... K5
Thompson (isl.) ... D7
Toby (mt.) ... E3
Tom (mt.) ... D4
Tuckernuck (isl.) ... N7
Vineyard (sound) ... L7
Wachusett (mt.) ... G3
Wachusett (res.) ... G3
Walden (pond) ... A6
Ware (riv.) ... F3
Watuppa (pond) ... K6
Webster (lake) ... G4
Wellfleet (harb.) ... O5
West (riv.) ... H4
West Chop (pt.) ... M7
Westfield (riv.) ... C3
Westover A.F.B. ... D4
Weweantic (riv.) ... L5
Whitman (riv.) ... G2
Winter I. Coast Guard Air Sta. ... E5

RHODE ISLAND

COUNTIES

Bristol 48,859 ... J6
Kent 161,135 ... H6
Newport 87,194 ... K6
Providence 596,270 ... H5
Washington 110,006 ... H7

CITIES and TOWNS

Anthony ... H6
Apponaug ... J6
Arctic ... J6
Arnold Mills ... J5
Ashaway 1,584 ... G7
Ashton ... J5
Barrington • 15,849 ... J6
Block Island • ... H8
Bradford 1,604 ... H7
Bristol▲• 21,625 ... J6
Centerdale ... H5
Central Falls 17,637 ... J5
Charlestown 6,478 ... H7
Conimicut ... J6
Coventry (Washington) 31,083 ... H6
Coventry Center ... H6
Cranston 76,060 ... J5
East Greenwich▲• 11,865 ... H6
East Providence 50,380 ... J5
Esmond ... H5
Exeter • 5,461 ... H6
Georgiaville ... H5
Greenville 8,303 ... H5
Harrisville 1,654 ... H5
Hillsgrove ... J6
Hope Valley 1,446 ... H6
Hopkinton • 6,873 ... H7
Island Park ... J6
Jamestown 4,999 ... J6
Jamestown • 4,040 ... J6
Kingston 6,504 ... J7
La Fayette ... H6
Little Compton • 3,339 ... K6
Lonsdale ... J5
Manville ... H5
Middletown • 19,460 ... J6
Narragansett 14,985 ... J7
Narragansett • 12,088 ... J7
Natick ... H6
New Shoreham (Block Island) • 836 ... H8
Newport▲ 28,227 ... J7
North Kingstown • 23,786 ... J6
North Providence • 32,090 ... J5
North Tiverton ... K6
Norwood ... J6
Oakland Beach ... J6
Pascoag 5,011 ... H5
Pawtucket 72,644 ... J5
Peace Dale-Wakefield 7,134 ... J7
Pontiac ... J6
Portsmouth • 16,857 ... J6
Providence (cap.)▲ 160,728 ... H5
Riverside ... J5
Rumford ... J5
Tiverton 7,259 ... K6
Tiverton • 14,312 ... K6
Valley Falls 11,175 ... J5
Wakefield-Peace Dale 7,134 ... J7
Warren • 11,385 ... J6
Warwick 85,427 ... J6
Watch Hill 300 ... G7
West Kingston 950 ... H7
West Warwick 29,268 ... H6
Westerly▲ 16,477 ... G7
Westerly • 21,605 ... G7
Woonsocket▲ 43,877 ... J4

OTHER FEATURES

Black Rock (pt.) ... H8
Block (isl.) ... H8
Block Island (sound) ... H8
Brenton (pt.) ... J7
Conanicut (isl.) ... J6
Dickens (pt.) ... H8
Durfee (hill) ... G5
Grace (pt.) ... H8
Jerimoth (hill) ... G5
Judith (pt.) ... J7
Mount Hope (bay) ... K6
Narragansett (bay) ... J6
Noyes (pt.) ... H7
Pawcatuck (riv.) ... G7
Prudence (isl.) ... J6
Rhode Island (isl.) ... J6
Rhode (sound) ... J7
Roger Williams Nat'l Mem. ... J5
Sakonnet (pt.) ... K7
Sakonnet (riv.) ... K7
Sandy (pt.) ... H8
Scituate (res.) ... H5
Touro Synagogue Nat'l Hist. Site ... J7
Watch Hill (pt.) ... G7

▲County seat or Shire town
• Population of town or township

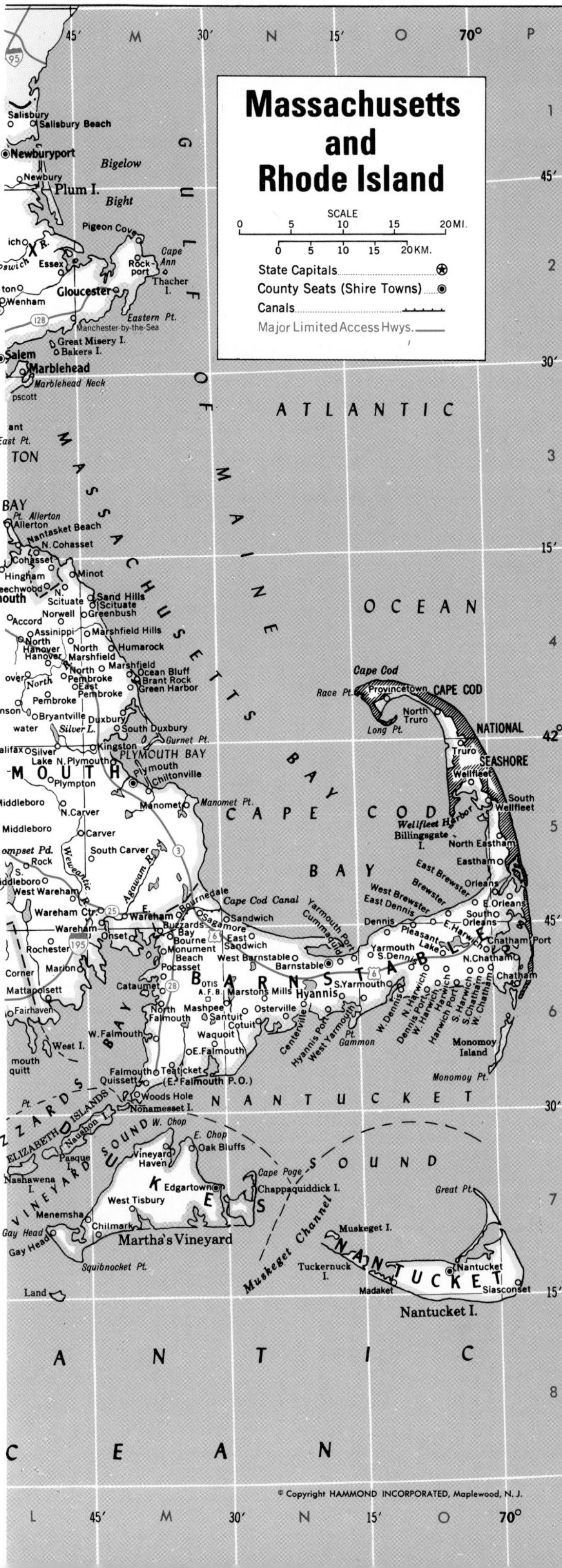

Topography

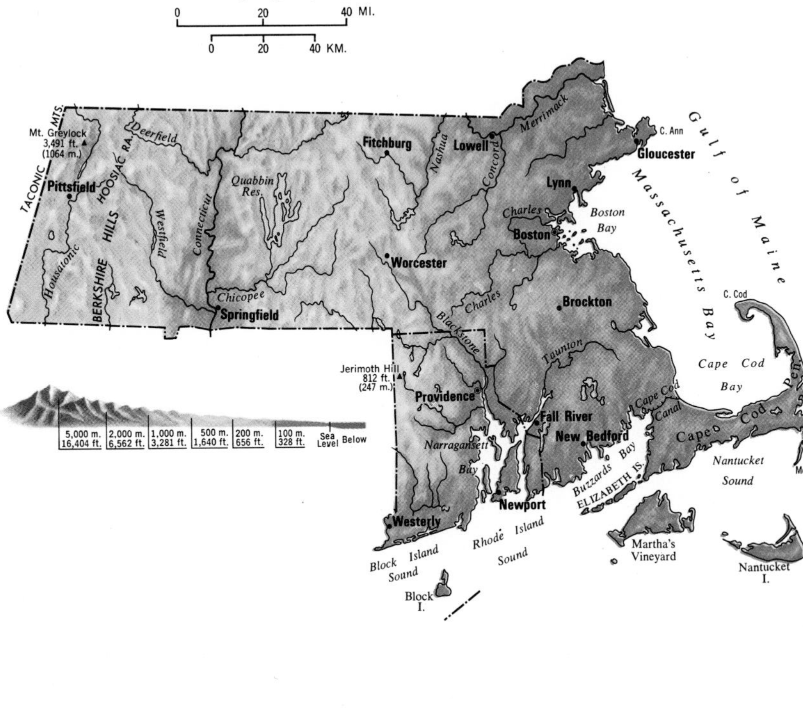

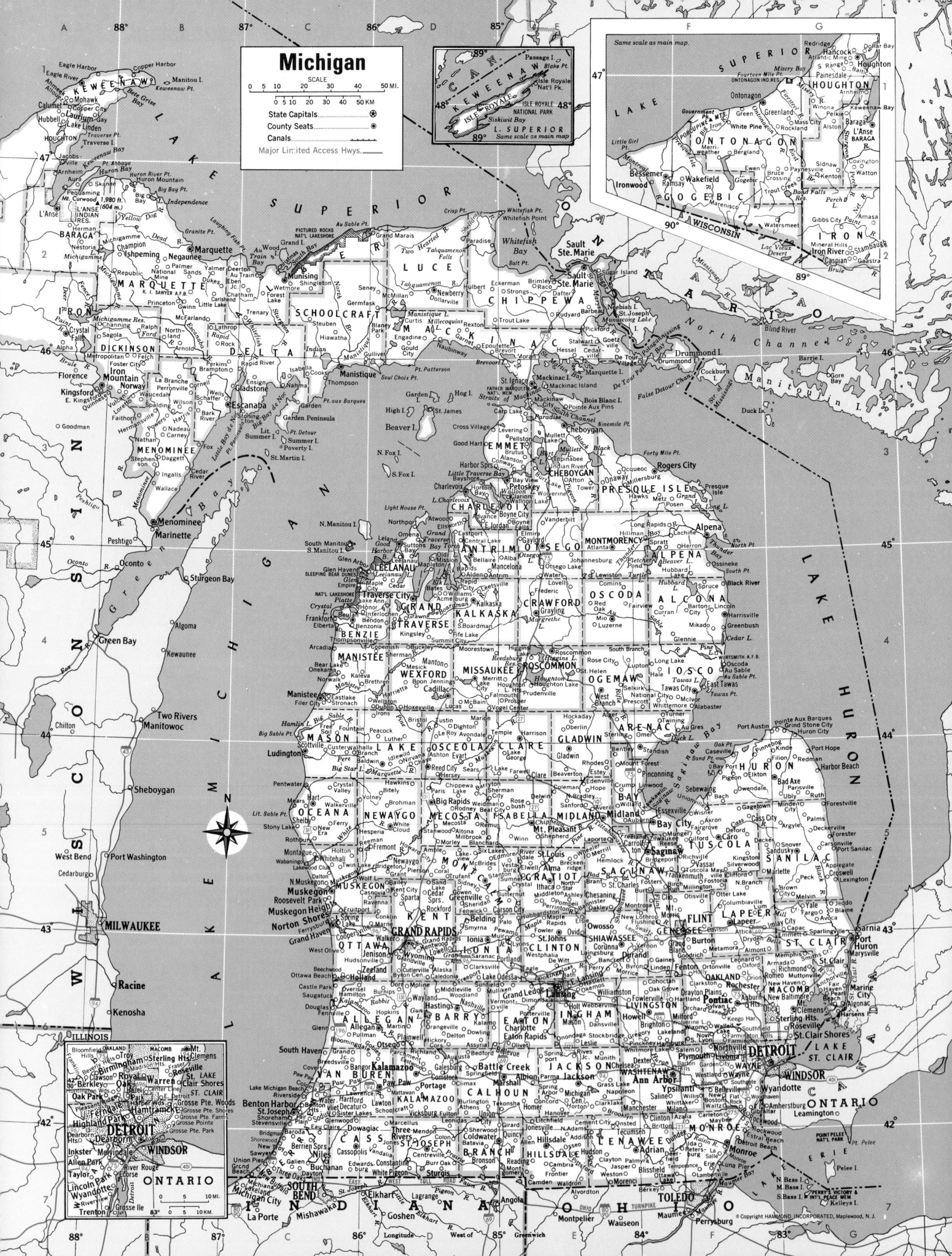
Michigan
SCALE
0 5 10 20 30 40 50 MI.
0 5 10 20 30 40 50 KM.
State Capitals
County Seats
Canals
Major Limited Access Hwys.
Same scale as main map.
LAKE SUPERIOR
LAKE MICHIGAN
LAKE HURON
LAKE ERIE
LAKE ST. CLAIR
ONTARIO
WISCONSIN
ILLINOIS
INDIANA
OHIO
ISLE ROYALE NATIONAL PARK
KEWEENAW
HOUGHTON
ONTONAGON
GOGEBIC
IRON
BARAGA
MARQUETTE
ALGER
LUCE
CHIPPEWA
SCHOOLCRAFT
MACKINAC
DELTA
DICKINSON
MENOMINEE
EMMET
CHEBOYGAN
PRESQUE ISLE
CHARLEVOIX
ANTRIM
OTSEGO
MONTMORENCY
ALPENA
LEELANAU
GRAND TRAVERSE
KALKASKA
CRAWFORD
OSCODA
ALCONA
BENZIE
MANISTEE
WEXFORD
MISSAUKEE
ROSCOMMON
OGEMAW
IOSCO
MASON
LAKE
OSCEOLA
CLARE
GLADWIN
ARENAC
HURON
OCEANA
NEWAYGO
MECOSTA
ISABELLA
MIDLAND
BAY
TUSCOLA
SANILAC
MUSKEGON
MONTCALM
GRATIOT
SAGINAW
GENESEE
LAPEER
ST. CLAIR
OTTAWA
KENT
IONIA
CLINTON
SHIAWASSEE
OAKLAND
MACOMB
ALLEGAN
BARRY
EATON
INGHAM
LIVINGSTON
WAYNE
VAN BUREN
KALAMAZOO
CALHOUN
JACKSON
WASHTENAW
CASS
ST. JOSEPH
BRANCH
HILLSDALE
LENAWEE
MONROE
Lansing
Detroit
Grand Rapids
Flint
Saginaw
Kalamazoo
Ann Arbor
Marquette
Sault Ste. Marie
Milwaukee
Toledo
Windsor
South Bend
© Copyright HAMMOND INCORPORATED, Maplewood, N.J.

Michigan 251

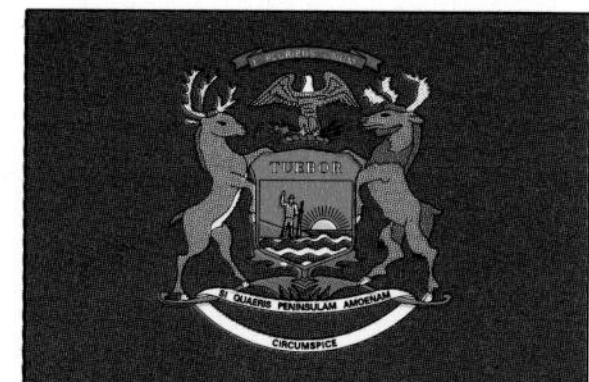

AREA 58,527 sq. mi. (151,585 sq. km.)
POPULATION 9,328,784
CAPITAL Lansing
LARGEST CITY Detroit
HIGHEST POINT Mt. Curwood 1,980 ft. (604 m.)
SETTLED IN 1650
ADMITTED TO UNION January 26, 1837
POPULAR NAME Wolverine State
STATE FLOWER Apple Blossom
STATE BIRD Robin

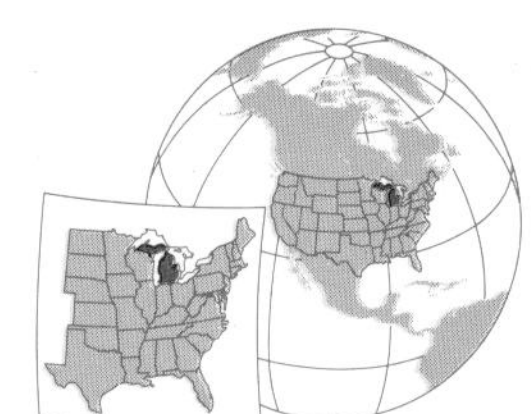

Topography

COUNTIES

Alcona 10,145 .... F4
Alger 8,972 .... C2
Allegan 90,509 .... D6
Alpena 30,605 .... F4
Antrim 18,185 .... D3
Arenac 14,931 .... F4
Baraga 7,954 .... A2
Barry 50,057 .... D6
Bay 111,723 .... E5
Benzie 12,200 .... C4
Berrien 161,378 .... C7
Branch 41,502 .... D7
Calhoun 135,982 .... D6
Cass 49,477 .... C7
Charlevoix 21,468 .... D3
Cheboygan 21,398 .... E3
Chippewa 34,604 .... E2
Clare 24,952 .... E5
Clinton 57,883 .... E6
Crawford 12,260 .... E4
Delta 37,780 .... C2
Dickinson 26,831 .... B2
Eaton 92,879 .... E6
Emmet 25,040 .... E3
Genesee 430,459 .... F5
Gladwin 21,896 .... E4
Gogebic 18,052 .... F2
Grand Traverse 64,273 .... D4
Gratiot 38,982 .... E5
Hillsdale 43,431 .... E7
Houghton 35,446 .... G1
Huron 34,951 .... F5
Ingham 281,912 .... E6
Ionia 57,024 .... D6
Iosco 30,209 .... F4
Iron 13,175 .... G2
Isabella 54,624 .... E5
Jackson 149,756 .... E6
Kalamazoo 223,411 .... D6
Kalkaska 13,497 .... D4
Kent 500,631 .... D5
Keweenaw 1,701 .... A1
Lake 8,583 .... D5
Lapeer 74,768 .... F5
Leelanau 16,527 .... D4
Lenawee 91,476 .... E7
Livingston 115,645 .... F6
Luce 5,763 .... D2
Mackinac 10,674 .... D2
Macomb 717,400 .... G6
Manistee 21,265 .... C4
Marquette 70,887 .... B2
Mason 25,537 .... C4
Mecosta 37,308 .... D5
Menominee 24,920 .... B3
Midland 75,651 .... E5
Missaukee 12,147 .... D4
Monroe 133,600 .... F7
Montcalm 53,059 .... D5
Montmorency 8,936 .... E3
Muskegon 158,983 .... C5
Newaygo 38,202 .... D5
Oakland 1,083,592 .... F6
Oceana 22,454 .... C5
Ogemaw 18,681 .... E4
Ontonagon 8,854 .... F1
Osceola 20,146 .... D5
Oscoda 7,842 .... E4
Otsego 17,957 .... E3
Ottawa 187,768 .... C6
Presque Isle 13,743 .... F3
Roscommon 19,776 .... E4
Saginaw 211,946 .... E5
Saint Clair 138,802 .... G6
Saint Joseph 56,083 .... D7
Sanilac 39,928 .... G5
Schoolcraft 8,302 .... C2
Shiawassee 69,770 .... E6
Tuscola 55,498 .... F5
Van Buren 66,814 .... C6
Washtenaw 282,937 .... F6
Wayne 2,111,687 .... F6
Wexford 26,360 .... D4

CITIES and TOWNS

Addison 632 .... E7
Adrian▲ 22,097 .... F7
Akron 421 .... F5
Alabaster 46 .... F4
Alanson 677 .... E3
Albion 10,066 .... E6
Algonac 4,551 .... G6
Allegan▲ 4,547 .... D6
Allen 201 .... E7
Allen Park 31,092 .... B7
Alma 9,034 .... E5
Almont 2,354 .... F6
Alpena▲ 11,354 .... F3
Alpha 219 .... A2
Anchorville 3,202 .... G6
Ann Arbor▲ 109,592 .... F6
Applegate 297 .... G5
Arcadia 780 .... C4
Armada 1,548 .... G6
Ashley 518 .... E5
Athens 990 .... D6
Atlanta▲ 475 .... E3
Atlantic Mine 809 .... G1
Au Gres 838 .... F4
Au Sable 1,542 .... F4
Auburn 1,855 .... F5
Auburn Heights 7,500 .... F6
Augusta 927 .... D6
Averill 800 .... E5
Bad Axe▲ 3,484 .... G5
Baldwin▲ 821 .... D5
Bancroft 599 .... E6
Bangor 1,922 .... C6
Baraga 1,231 .... G1
Bark River 800 .... B3
Baroda 657 .... C7
Barryton 393 .... D5
Barton Hills 320 .... F6
Battle Creek 53,540 .... D6
Bay City▲ 38,936 .... F5
Bay Port 750 .... F5
Beal City 345 .... D5
Bear Lake 339 .... C4
Beaverton 1,150 .... E5
Beechwood 2,676 .... C6
Belding 5,969 .... D5
Bellaire▲ 1,104 .... D4
Belleville 3,270 .... F6
Bellevue 1,401 .... E6
Benton Harbor 12,818 .... C6
Benton Heights 5,465 .... C6
Benzonia 449 .... D4
Berkley 16,960 .... B6
Berrien Springs 1,927 .... C7
Bessemer▲ 2,272 .... F2
Beulah▲ 421 .... C4
Beverly Hills 10,610 .... B6
Big Rapids▲ 12,603 .... D5
Birch Run 992 .... F5
Birmingham 19,997 .... B6
Bitely 750 .... D5
Blissfield 3,172 .... F7
Bloomfield Hills 4,288 .... B6
Bloomingdale 503 .... C6
Boyne City 3,478 .... E3
Boyne Falls 369 .... E3
Breckenridge 1,301 .... E5
Breedsville 213 .... C6
Bridgeport 8,569 .... F5
Bridgman 2,140 .... C7
Brighton 5,686 .... F6
Britton 694 .... F6
Bronson 2,342 .... D7
Brooklyn 1,027 .... E6
Brown City 1,244 .... G5
Buchanan 4,992 .... C7
Buckley 402 .... D4
Burlington 294 .... D6
Burr Oak 882 .... D7
Burt 1,169 .... F5
Burton 27,617 .... F6
Byron 573 .... E6
Byron Center 900 .... D6
Cadillac▲ 10,104 .... D4
Caledonia 885 .... D6
Calumet 818 .... A1
Camden 482 .... E7
Capac 1,583 .... G5
Carleton 2,770 .... F6
Carney 197 .... B3
Caro▲ 4,054 .... F5
Carrollton 6,521 .... E5
Carson City 1,158 .... E5
Carsonville 583 .... G5
Caseville 857 .... F5
Casnovia 376 .... D5
Caspian 1,031 .... G2
Cass City 2,276 .... F5
Cassopolis▲ 1,822 .... C7
Cedar Springs 2,600 .... D5
Cement City 493 .... E6
Center Line 9,026 .... B6
Central Lake 954 .... D3
Centreville▲ 1,516 .... D7
Charlevoix▲ 3,116 .... D3
Charlotte▲ 8,083 .... E6
Chatham 268 .... B2
Cheboygan▲ 4,999 .... E3
Chelsea 3,772 .... E6
Chesaning 2,567 .... E5
Clare 3,021 .... E5
Clarkston 1,005 .... F6
Clarksville 360 .... D6
Clawson 13,874 .... B6
Clayton 384 .... E7
Clifford 354 .... F5
Climax 677 .... D6
Clinton 2,475 .... F6
Clio 2,629 .... F5
Coldwater▲ 9,607 .... D7
Coleman 1,237 .... E5
Coloma 1,679 .... C6
Colon 1,224 .... D7
Columbiaville 934 .... F5
Comstock• 11,162 .... D6
Concord 944 .... E6
Constantine 2,032 .... D7
Coopersville 3,421 .... C5
Copemish 222 .... D4
Copper City 198 .... A1
Corunna▲ 3,091 .... E6
Croswell 2,174 .... G5
Crystal 800 .... E5
Crystal Falls▲ 1,922 .... A2
Curtis 800 .... D2
Custer 312 .... C5
Cutlerville 11,228 .... D6
Daggett 260 .... B3
Dansville 437 .... E6
Davison 5,693 .... F5
De Tour Village 407 .... E3
De Witt 3,964 .... E6
Dearborn 89,286 .... B7
Dearborn Heights 60,838 .... B7
Decatur 1,760 .... C6
Deckerville 1,015 .... G5
Deerfield 922 .... F7
Detroit Beach 2,113 .... F7
Detroit▲ 1,027,974 .... B7
Dexter 1,497 .... F6
Dimondale 1,247 .... E6
Dollar Bay 950 .... G1
Douglas 1,040 .... C6
Dowagiac 6,409 .... D6
Drayton Plains F6
Drummond Island• 746 .... F3
Dryden 628 .... F6
Dundee 2,664 .... F7
Durand 4,283 .... E6
Eagle River▲ 20 .... A1
East Detroit 35,283 .... B6
East Grand Rapids 10,807 .... D6
East Jordan 2,240 .... D3
East Kingsford A3
East Lansing 50,677 .... E6
East Tawas 2,887 .... F4
Eastlake 473 .... C4
Eastwood 6,340 .... D6
Eaton Rapids 4,695 .... E6
Eau Claire 494 .... C6
Ecorse 12,180 .... B7
Edmore 1,126 .... E5
Edwardsburg 1,142 .... C7
Elberta 478 .... C4
Elk Rapids 1,626 .... D4
Elkton 958 .... F5
Ellsworth 418 .... D3
Elsie 957 .... E5
Emmett 297 .... G6
Empire 355 .... C4
Erie 750 .... F7
Escanaba▲ 13,659 .... C3
Essexville 4,088 .... F5
Estral Beach 430 .... F7
Evart 1,744 .... D5
Ewen 821 .... F2
Fair Haven 1,505 .... G6
Fair Plain 8,051 .... C6
Fairgrove 592 .... F5
Farmington 10,132 .... F6
Farmington Hills 74,652 .... F6
Farwell 851 .... E5
Fennville 1,023 .... C6
Fenton 8,444 .... F6
Ferndale 25,084 .... B6
Ferrysburg 2,919 .... C5
Fife Lake 394 .... D4
Flat Rock 7,290 .... F6
Flint▲ 140,761 .... F5
Flushing 8,542 .... F5
Fountain 165 .... C4
Fowler 912 .... E5
Fowlerville 2,648 .... F6
Frankenmuth 4,408 .... F5
Frankfort 1,546 .... C4
Franklin 2,626 .... B6
Fraser 13,899 .... B6
Freeland 1,421 .... E5
Freeport 458 .... D6
Fremont 3,875 .... D5
Fruitport 1,090 .... C5
Gaastra 376 .... G2
Gagetown 337 .... F5
Gaines 427 .... F6
Galesburg 1,863 .... D6
Galien 596 .... C7
Garden 268 .... C3
Garden City 31,846 .... F6
Gaylord▲ 3,256 .... E3
Gibraltar 4,297 .... F6
Gladstone 4,565 .... C3
Gladwin▲ 2,682 .... E5
Gobles 769 .... D6
Goodrich 916 .... F6
Grand Blanc 7,760 .... F6
Grand Haven▲ 11,951 .... C5
Grand Ledge 7,579 .... E6
Grand Rapids▲ 189,126 .... D5
Grandville 15,624 .... D6
Grant 764 .... D5
Grass Lake 903 .... E6
Grayling▲ 1,944 .... E4
Greenville 8,101 .... D5
Grosse Ile 9,781 .... B7
Grosse Pointe 5,681 .... B7
Grosse Pointe Farms 10,092 .... B6
Grosse Pointe Park 12,857 .... B7
Grosse Pointe Shores 2,955 .... B6
Grosse Pointe Woods 17,715 .... B6
Gulliver 962 .... D2
Gwinn 2,370 .... B2
Hamilton 950 .... C6
Hamtramck 18,372 .... B6
Hancock 4,547 .... G1
Hanover 481 .... E6
Harbor Beach 2,089 .... G5
Harbor Springs 1,540 .... D3
Harper Woods 14,903 .... B6
Harrison▲ 1,835 .... E4
Harrisville▲ 470 .... F4
Hart▲ 1,942 .... C5
Hartford 2,341 .... C6
Haslett 10,230 .... E6
Hastings▲ 6,549 .... D6
Hazel Park 20,051 .... B6
Hemlock 1,601 .... E5
Hermansville 950 .... B3
Hersey 354 .... D5
Hesperia 846 .... D5
Highland Park 20,121 .... B6
Hillman 643 .... F3
Hillsdale▲ 8,170 .... E7
Holland 30,745 .... C6
Holly 5,595 .... F6
Holt 11,744 .... E6
Homer 1,758 .... E6
Honor 292 .... D4
Hopkins 546 .... D6
Houghton Lake 3,353 .... E4
Houghton Lake Heights E4
Houghton▲ 7,498 .... G1
Howard City 1,351 .... D5
Howell▲ 8,184 .... E6
Hubbardston 404 .... E5
Hubbell 1,174 .... A1
Hudson 2,580 .... E7
Hudsonville 6,170 .... D6
Huntington Woods 6,419 .... B6
Ida 970 .... F7
Imlay City 2,921 .... F5
Indian River 950 .... E3
Inkster 30,772 .... B7
Interlochen 600 .... D4
Ionia▲ 5,935 .... D6
Iron Mountain▲ 8,525 .... B3
Iron River 2,095 .... G2
Ironwood 6,849 .... F2
Ishpeming 7,200 .... B2
Isle Royale National Park E1
Ithaca▲ 3,009 .... E5
Jackson▲ 37,446 .... E6
Jenison 17,882 .... D6
Jonesville 2,283 .... E6
Kalamazoo▲ 80,277 .... D6
Kaleva 484 .... C4
Kalkaska▲ 1,952 .... D4
Keego Harbor 2,932 .... F6
Kent City 899 .... D5
Kentwood 37,826 .... D6
Kinde 473 .... G5
Kingsford 5,480 .... A3
Kingsley 738 .... D4
Kingston 439 .... F5
L'Anse▲ 2,151 .... G1
Laingsburg 1,148 .... E6
Lake Ann 217 .... D4
Lake City▲ 858 .... D4
Lake George 950 .... E5
Lake Linden 1,203 .... A1
Lake Michigan Beach 1,694 .... C6
Lake Odessa 2,256 .... D6
Lake Orion 3,057 .... F6
Lakeview 1,108 .... D5
Lakewood Club 659 .... C5

(continued on following page)

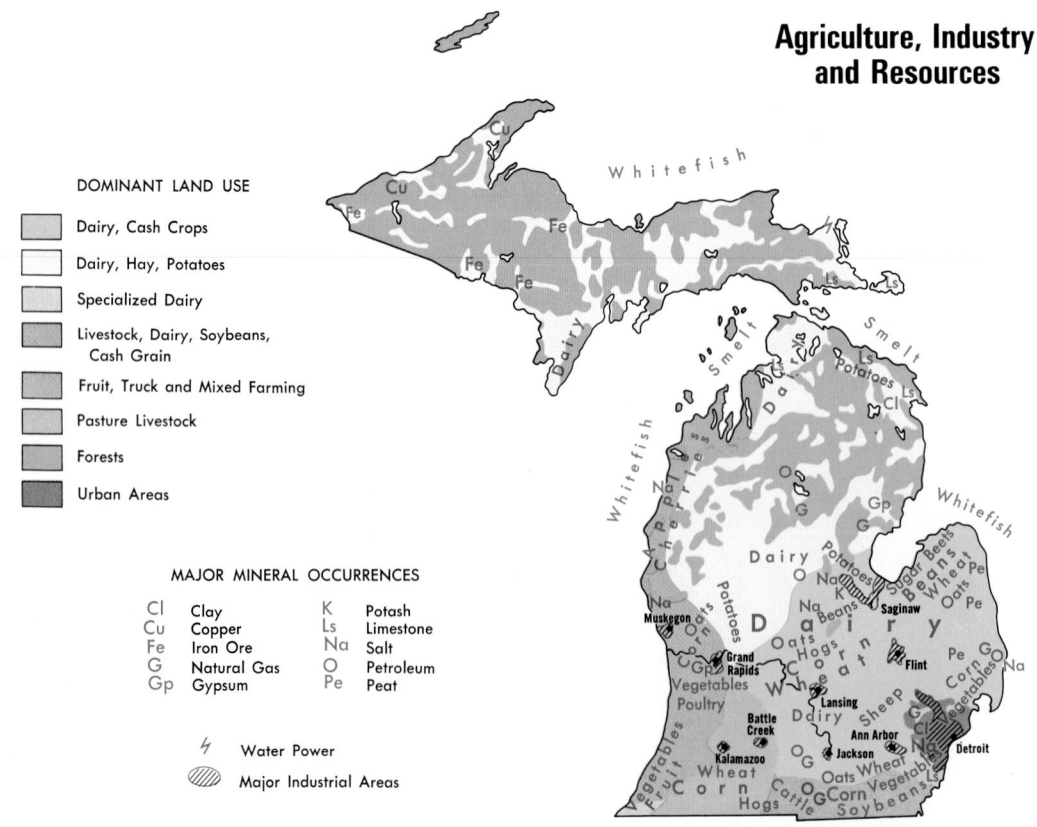

Agriculture, Industry and Resources

DOMINANT LAND USE

- Dairy, Cash Crops
- Dairy, Hay, Potatoes
- Specialized Dairy
- Livestock, Dairy, Soybeans, Cash Grain
- Fruit, Truck and Mixed Farming
- Pasture Livestock
- Forests
- Urban Areas

MAJOR MINERAL OCCURRENCES

Cl	Clay	K	Potash
Cu	Copper	Ls	Limestone
Fe	Iron Ore	Na	Salt
G	Natural Gas	O	Petroleum
Gp	Gypsum	Pe	Peat

⚡ Water Power

▨ Major Industrial Areas

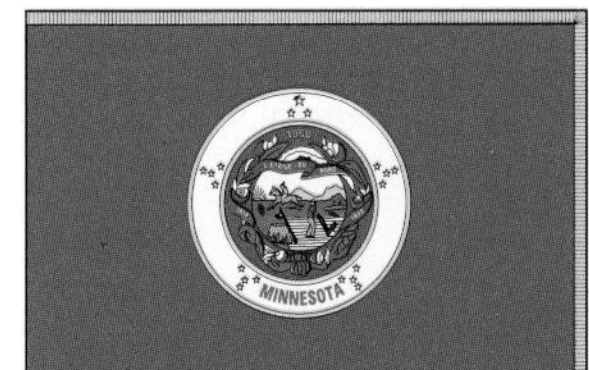

AREA 84,402 sq. mi. (218,601 sq. km.)
POPULATION 4,387,029
CAPITAL St. Paul
LARGEST CITY Minneapolis
HIGHEST POINT Eagle Mtn. 2,301 ft. (701 m.)
SETTLED IN 1805
ADMITTED TO UNION May 11, 1858
POPULAR NAME North Star State; Gopher State
STATE FLOWER Pink & White Lady's-Slipper
STATE BIRD Common Loon

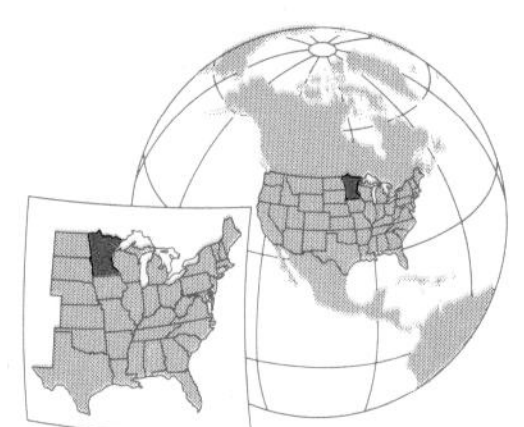

COUNTIES

Aitkin 12,425	E4
Anoka 243,641	E5
Becker 27,881	C3
Beltrami 34,384	C2
Benton 30,185	D5
Big Stone 6,285	B5
Blue Earth 54,044	D6
Brown 26,984	D6
Carlton 29,259	E4
Carver 47,915	E6
Cass 21,791	D4
Chippewa 13,228	C5
Chisago 30,521	F5
Clay 50,422	B4
Clearwater 8,309	C3
Cook 3,868	H3
Cottonwood 12,694	C6
Crow Wing 44,249	D4
Dakota 275,227	E6
Dodge 15,731	F7
Douglas 28,674	C4
Faribault 16,937	D7
Fillmore 20,777	F7
Freeborn 33,060	E7
Goodhue 40,690	F6
Grant 6,246	B5
Hennepin 1,032,431	E5
Houston 18,497	G7
Hubbard 14,939	D3
Isanti 25,921	E5
Itasca 40,863	E3
Jackson 11,677	C7
Kanabec 12,802	E5
Kandiyohi 38,761	C5
Kittson 5,767	B2
Koochiching 16,299	E2
Lac qui Parle 8,924	B6
Lake 10,415	G3
Lake of the Woods 4,076	D2
Le Sueur 23,239	E6
Lincoln 6,890	B6
Lyon 24,789	C6
Mahnomen 5,044	C3
Marshall 10,993	B2
Martin 22,914	D7
McLeod 32,030	D6
Meeker 20,846	D5
Mille Lacs 18,670	E5
Morrison 29,604	D4
Mower 37,385	F7
Murray 9,660	C6
Nicollet 28,076	D6
Nobles 20,098	C7
Norman 7,975	B3
Olmsted 106,470	F6
Otter Tail 50,714	C4
Pennington 13,306	B2
Pine 21,264	F4
Pipestone 10,491	B6
Polk 32,498	B3
Pope 10,745	C5
Ramsey 485,765	E5
Red Lake 4,525	B3
Redwood 17,254	C6
Renville 17,673	C6
Rice 49,183	E6
Rock 9,806	B7
Roseau 15,026	C2
Saint Louis 222,229	F3
Scott 57,846	E6
Sherburne 41,945	E5
Sibley 14,366	D6
Stearns 118,791	D5
Steele 30,729	E7
Stevens 10,634	C5
Swift 10,724	C5
Todd 23,363	D4
Traverse 4,463	B5
Wabasha 19,744	F6
Wadena 13,154	D4
Waseca 18,079	E6
Washington 145,896	F5
Watonwan 11,682	D7
Wilkin 7,516	B4
Winona 47,828	G6
Wright 68,710	D5
Yellow Medicine 11,684	B6

CITIES and TOWNS

Ada▲ 1,708	B3
Adams 756	F7
Adrian 1,141	C7
Afton 2,645	F6
Aitkin▲ 1,698	E4
Akeley 393	D3
Albany 1,548	D5
Albert Lea▲ 18,310	E7
Alberta 136	C5
Albertville 1,251	E5
Alborn 500	F4
Alden 623	E7
Aldrich 70	D4
Alexandria▲ 7,838	C5
Alpha 105	D7
Altura 349	G6
Alvarado 356	B2
Amboy 517	D7
Andover 15,216	E5
Annandale 2,054	D5
Anoka▲ 17,192	E5
Apple Valley 34,598	G6
Appleton 1,552	C5
Arco 104	B6
Argyle 636	B2
Arlington 1,886	D6
Arnold 2,891	F4
Ashby 469	C4
Askov 343	F4
Atwater 1,053	D5
Audubon 411	C4
Aurora 1,965	F3
Austin▲ 21,907	E7
Avoca 150	C7
Avon▲ 970	D5
Babbitt 1,562	G3
Backus 240	D4
Badger 381	B2
Bagley▲ 1,388	C3
Balaton 737	C6
Barnesville 2,066	B4
Barrett 350	B5
Barry 40	B5
Battle Lake 698	C4
Baudette▲ 1,146	D2
Baxter 3,695	D4
Bayport 3,200	F5
Beardsley 297	B5
Beaver Bay 147	G3
Beaver Creek 249	B7
Becker 902	E5
Bejou 110	B3
Belgrade 700	C5
Belle Plaine 3,149	E6
Bellechester 110	F6
Bellingham 247	B5
Beltrami 137	B3
Belview 383	C6
Bemidji▲ 11,245	D3
Bena 147	D3
Benson▲ 3,235	C5
Bertha 507	C4
Bethel 394	E5
Big Falls 341	E2
Big Lake 3,113	E5
Bigelow 232	C7
Bigfork 384	E3
Bingham Lake 155	C7
Bird Island 1,326	D6
Biscay 113	D6
Biwabik 1,097	F3
Blackduck 718	D3
Blaine 38,975	G5
Blomkest 183	D6
Blooming Prairie 2,043	E7
Bloomington 86,335	G6
Blue Earth▲ 3,745	D7
Bluffton 187	D4
Bock 115	E5
Borup 119	B3
Bovey 662	E3
Bowlus 260	D5
Boy River 43	D3
Boyd 251	C6
Braham 1,139	E5
Brainerd▲ 12,353	D4
Branch 2,400	F5
Brandon 441	C5
Breckenridge▲ 3,708	B4
Breezy Point 432	D4
Brewster 532	C7
Bricelyn 426	D7
Brook Park 125	F5
Brooklyn Center 28,887	G5
Brooklyn Park 56,381	G5
Brooks 158	B3
Brookston 107	F4
Brooten 589	C5
Browerville 782	D4
Browns Valley 804	B5
Brownsdale 695	F7
Brownsville 415	G7
Brownton 781	D6
Bruno 89	F4
Buckman 201	D5
Buffalo Lake 734	C6
Buffalo▲ 6,856	E5
Buhl 915	F3
Burnsville 51,288	E6
Burtrum 172	D5
Butterfield 509	D7
Byron 2,441	F6
Caledonia▲ 2,846	G7
Callaway 212	C3
Calumet 382	E3
Cambridge▲ 5,094	E5
Campbell 233	B4
Canby 1,826	B6
Cannon Falls 3,232	F6
Canton 362	F7
Carlos 361	C5
Carlton▲ 923	F4
Carver 744	E6
Cass Lake 923	D3
Cedar Mills 80	D6
Center City▲ 451	F5
Centerville 1,633	E5
Ceylon 461	D7
Champlin 16,849	G5
Chandler 316	C7
Chanhassen 11,732	F6
Chaska▲ 11,339	F6
Chatfield 2,226	F7
Chickamaw Beach 132	D4
Chisago City 2,009	E5
Chisholm 5,290	F3
Chokio 521	B5
Circle Pines 4,704	G5
Clara City 1,307	C6
Claremont 530	F6
Clarissa 637	C4
Clarkfield 924	C6
Clarks Grove 675	E7
Clear Lake 315	E5
Clearbrook 560	C3
Clearwater 597	D5
Clements 191	D6
Cleveland 699	E6
Climax 264	B3
Clinton 574	B5
Clitherall 109	C4
Clontarf 172	C5
Cloquet 10,885	E6
Coates 186	E6
Cobden 62	E6
Cohasset 2,180	E3
Cokato 2,180	D5
Cold Spring 2,459	D5
Coleraine 1,041	E3
Cologne 563	E6
Columbia Heights 18,910	G5
Comfrey 433	D6
Comstock 123	B4
Conger 143	E7
Cook 680	F3
Coon Rapids 52,978	G5
Corcoran 5,199	F5
Correll 60	B5
Cosmos 610	D6
Cottage Grove 22,935	F6
Cotton 982	F4
Cottonwood 924	C6
Courtland 412	D6
Cromwell 221	F4
Crookston▲ 8,119	B3
Crosby 2,073	D4
Crosslake 1,132	D4
Crystal 23,788	G5
Currie 303	C6
Cuyuna 172	E4
Cyrus 328	C5
Dakota 360	G7
Dalton 234	C4
Danube 562	C6
Danvers 98	C5
Darfur 128	D6
Darwin 252	D5
Dassel 1,082	D5
Dawson 1,626	B6
Day 4,443	E5
Dayton 4,070	F5
De Graff 149	C5
Deephaven 3,653	F6
Deer Creek 303	C4
Deer River 838	E3
Deerwood 524	E4
Delano 2,709	E5
Delavan 245	D7
Delhi 69	C6
Dellwood 887	F5
Denham 36	F4
Dennison 152	E6
Dent 177	C4
Detroit Lakes▲ 6,635	C4
Dexter 303	F7
Dilworth 2,562	B4
Dodge Center 1,954	F6
Donaldson 57	B2
Donnelly 221	C5
Doran 78	B4
Dover 416	F7
Dovray 60	C6
Duluth▲ 85,493	F4
Dumont 126	B5
Dundas 473	E6
Dundee 107	C7
Dunnell 187	D7
Eagan 47,409	G6
Eagle Bend 524	D4
Eagle Lake 1,703	E6
East Bethel 8,050	E5
East Grand Forks 8,658	B3
East Gull Lake 687	D4
Easton 229	E7
Echo 304	C6
Eden Prairie 39,311	G6
Eden Valley 732	D5
Edgerton 1,106	B7
Edina 46,070	G6
Effie 130	E3
Eitzen 221	G7
Elba 220	F6
Elbow Lake▲ 1,186	B5
Elgin 733	F6
Elizabeth 152	B4
Elk River▲ 11,143	E5
Elko 223	E6
Elkton 142	F7
Ellendale 549	E7
Ellsworth 580	C7
Elmdale 130	D5
Elmore 709	D7
Elrosa 205	C5
Ely 3,968	G3
Elysian 445	E6
Emily 613	E4
Emmons 439	E7
Erhard 181	B4
Erskine 422	B3
Esko 500	F4
Evan 83	D6
Evansville 566	C4
Eveleth 4,064	F3
Excelsior 2,367	E6
Eyota 1,448	F7
Fairfax 1,276	D6
Fairmont▲ 11,265	D7
Falcon Heights 5,380	G5
Faribault▲ 17,085	E6
Farmington 5,940	E6
Farwell 74	C5
Federal Dam 118	D3
Felton 211	B3
Fergus Falls▲ 12,362	B4
Fertile 853	B3
Fifty Lakes 299	D4
Finlayson 242	F4
Fisher 413	B3
Flensburg 213	D5
Floodwood 574	E4
Florence 53	B6
Florenton 635	F3
Foley▲ 1,854	D5
Forada 171	C5
Forest Lake 5,833	F5
Foreston 354	E5
Fort Ripley 92	D4
Fosston 1,529	C3
Fountain 327	F7
Foxhome 160	B4
Franklin 512	D6
Frazee 1,176	C4
Freeborn 301	E7
Freeport 556	D5
Fridley 28,335	G5
Frost 236	D7
Fulda 1,212	C7
Garfield 203	C5
Garrison 138	E4
Garvin 149	C6
Gary 200	B3
Gaylord▲ 1,935	D6
Geneva 444	E7
Genola 85	D5
Georgetown 107	B3
Ghent 316	C6
Gibbon 712	D6
Gilbert 1,934	F3
Gilman 192	E5
Glen 4,648	E4
Glencoe▲ 4,396	D6
Glenville 778	E7
Glenwood▲ 2,573	C5
Glyndon 862	B4
Golden Valley 20,971	G5
Gonvick 302	C3
Good Thunder 561	D6
Goodhue 533	F6
Goodridge 115	C2
Goodview 2,878	G6
Graceville 671	B5
Granada 347	D7
Grand Marais▲ 1,171	G2
Grand Meadow 967	F7
Grand Rapids▲ 7,976	E3
Granite Falls▲ 3,083	C6
Grasston 119	E5
Green Isle 239	E6
Greenbush 800	B2
Greenfield 1,450	F5
Greenwald 209	D5
Grey Eagle 353	D5
Grove City 547	D5
Grygla 220	C2
Gully 128	C3
Hackensack 245	D4
Hadley 94	C7
Hallock▲ 1,304	A2
Halma 73	B2
Halstad 611	B3
Ham Lake 8,924	E5
Hamburg 492	D6
Hamel	F5
Hammond 205	F6
Hampton 363	E6
Hancock 723	C5
Hanley Falls 246	C6
Hanover 787	E5
Hanska 443	D6
Harding 73	E4
Hardwick 234	B7
Harmony 1,081	F7
Harris 843	F5
Hartland 270	E7
Hastings▲ 15,445	F6
Hatfield 66	B7
Hawley 1,655	B4
Hayfield 1,283	F7
Hayward 246	E7
Hazel Run 81	C6
Hector 1,145	D6
Heidelberg 73	E6
Henderson 746	E6
Hendricks 684	B6
Hendrum 309	B3
Henning 738	C4
Henriette 78	E5
Herman 485	B5
Hermantown 6,761	F4
Heron Lake 730	C7
Hewitt 269	C4
Hibbing 18,046	F3

(continued on following page)

Agriculture, Industry and Resources

DOMINANT LAND USE

- Wheat, General Farming
- Dairy, Livestock
- Dairy, Hay, Potatoes
- Cattle Feed, Hogs
- Livestock, Cash Grain
- Forests
- Swampland, Limited Agriculture
- Urban Areas

MAJOR MINERAL OCCURRENCES

Cl	Clay	Gn	Granite
Fe	Iron Ore	Ls	Limestone
		Mn	Manganese

⚡ Water Power

▨ Major Industrial Areas

Topography

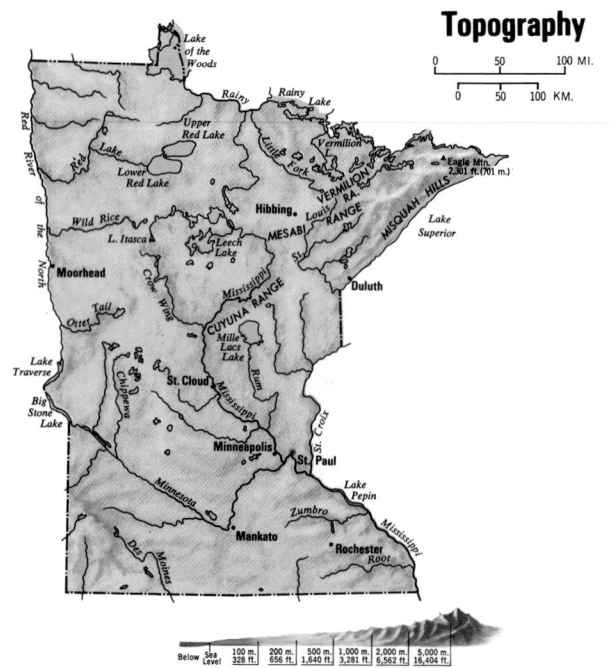

0   50   100 MI.

0   50   100 KM.

Below Sea Level | 100 m. 328 ft. | 200 m. 656 ft. | 500 m. 1,640 ft. | 1,000 m. 3,281 ft. | 2,000 m. 6,562 ft. | 5,000 m. 16,404 ft.

Minnesota

SCALE
0 5 10   20   30   40   50 MI.
0 5 10   20   30   40   50 KM.

State Capitals .... ⊛
County Seats .... ⊙
Major Limited Access Hwys. ——

Northeastern Part
of Minnesota

Copyright HAMMOND INCORPORATED, Maplewood, N.J.

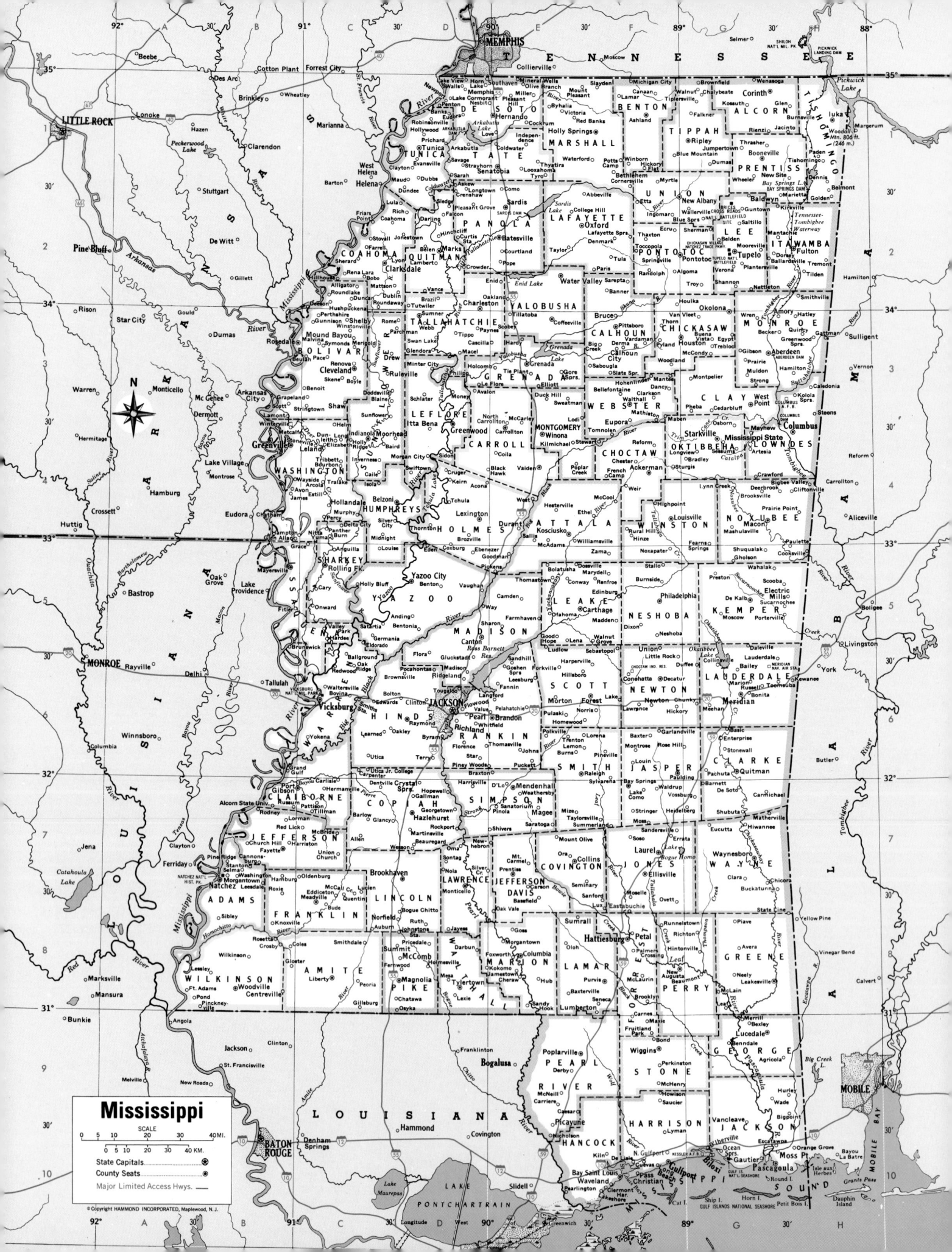

Mississippi
SCALE
0 5 10 20 30 40 MI.
0 5 10 20 30 40 KM.
State Capitals
County Seats
Major Limited Access Hwys.
© Copyright HAMMOND INCORPORATED, Maplewood, N. J.
TENNESSEE
ARKANSAS
LOUISIANA
ALABAMA
MISSISSIPPI SOUND
MEMPHIS
LITTLE ROCK
JACKSON
MONROE
BATON ROUGE
MOBILE
DE SOTO
MARSHALL
BENTON
TIPPAH
ALCORN
TISHOMINGO
TUNICA
TATE
PANOLA
LAFAYETTE
UNION
PONTOTOC
LEE
PRENTISS
ITAWAMBA
COAHOMA
QUITMAN
TALLAHATCHIE
YALOBUSHA
CALHOUN
CHICKASAW
MONROE
BOLIVAR
SUNFLOWER
GRENADA
WEBSTER
CLAY
LEFLORE
CARROLL
MONTGOMERY
CHOCTAW
OKTIBBEHA
LOWNDES
WASHINGTON
HUMPHREYS
HOLMES
ATTALA
WINSTON
NOXUBEE
SHARKEY
ISSAQUENA
YAZOO
MADISON
LEAKE
NESHOBA
KEMPER
WARREN
HINDS
RANKIN
SCOTT
NEWTON
LAUDERDALE
CLAIBORNE
COPIAH
SIMPSON
SMITH
JASPER
CLARKE
JEFFERSON
LINCOLN
LAWRENCE
JEFFERSON DAVIS
COVINGTON
JONES
WAYNE
ADAMS
FRANKLIN
AMITE
PIKE
WALTHALL
MARION
LAMAR
FORREST
PERRY
GREENE
WILKINSON
PEARL RIVER
STONE
GEORGE
HANCOCK
HARRISON
JACKSON
Mississippi River
LAKE PONTCHARTRAIN
Tupelo
Columbus
Meridian
Hattiesburg
Gulfport
Biloxi
Pascagoula
Vicksburg
Natchez
Greenville
Greenwood
Oxford
Starkville
Laurel

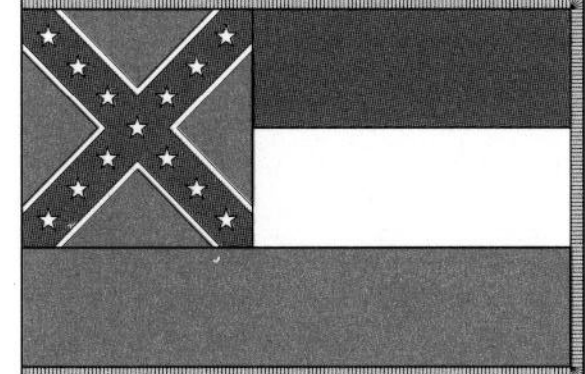

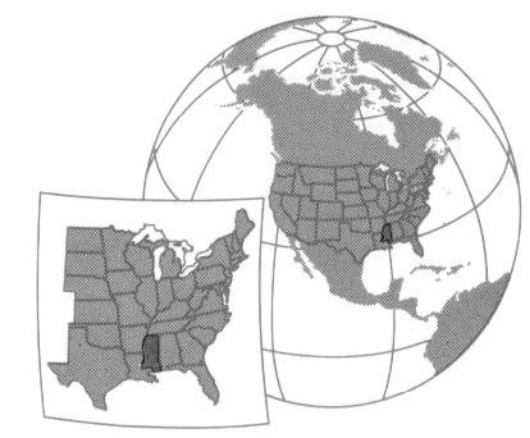

AREA 47,689 sq. mi. (123,515 sq. km.)
POPULATION 2,586,443
CAPITAL Jackson
LARGEST CITY Jackson
HIGHEST POINT Woodall Mtn. 806 ft.
(246 m.)
SETTLED IN 1716
ADMITTED TO UNION December 10, 1817
POPULAR NAME Magnolia State
STATE FLOWER Magnolia
STATE BIRD Mockingbird

COUNTIES

Adams 35,356 ....B8
Alcorn 31,722 ....G1
Amite 13,328 ....C8
Attala 18,481 ....E4
Benton 8,046 ....F1
Bolivar 41,875 ....C3
Calhoun 14,908 ....F3
Carroll 9,237 ....E4
Chickasaw 18,085 ....G3
Choctaw 9,071 ....F4
Claiborne 11,370 ....C7
Clarke 17,313 ....G6
Clay 21,120 ....G3
Coahoma 31,665 ....C2
Copiah 27,592 ....D7
Covington 16,527 ....E7
De Soto 53,930 ....E1
Forrest 68,314 ....F8
Franklin 8,377 ....C8
George 16,673 ....G9
Greene 10,220 ....G8
Grenada 21,555 ....E3
Hancock 31,760 ....E10
Harrison 165,365 ....F10
Hinds 254,441 ....D6
Holmes 21,604 ....D4
Humphreys 12,134 ....C4
Issaquena 1,909 ....B5
Itawamba 20,017 ....H2
Jackson 115,243 ....G9
Jasper 17,114 ....F6
Jefferson 8,653 ....B7
Jefferson Davis 14,051 ....E7
Jones 62,031 ....F7
Kemper 10,356 ....G5
Lafayette 31,826 ....E2
Lamar 30,424 ....E8
Lauderdale 75,555 ....G6
Lawrence 12,458 ....D7
Leake 18,436 ....E5
Lee 65,581 ....G2
Leflore 37,341 ....D3
Lincoln 30,278 ....D8
Lowndes 59,308 ....H4
Madison 53,794 ....D5
Marion 25,544 ....E8
Marshall 30,361 ....E1
Monroe 36,582 ....H3
Montgomery 12,388 ....E4
Neshoba 24,800 ....F5
Newton 20,291 ....F6
Noxubee 12,604 ....G4
Oktibbeha 38,375 ....G4
Panola 29,996 ....E2
Pearl River 38,714 ....E9
Perry 10,865 ....G8
Pike 36,882 ....D8
Pontotoc 22,237 ....F2
Prentiss 23,278 ....G1
Quitman 10,490 ....D2
Rankin 87,161 ....E6
Scott 24,137 ....E6
Sharkey 7,066 ....C5
Simpson 23,953 ....E7
Smith 14,798 ....E6
Stone 10,750 ....F9
Sunflower 32,867 ....C3
Tallahatchie 15,210 ....D3
Tate 21,432 ....E1
Tippah 19,523 ....G1
Tishomingo 17,683 ....H1
Tunica 8,164 ....D1
Union 22,085 ....F2
Walthall 14,352 ....D8
Warren 47,880 ....C6
Washington 67,935 ....C4
Wayne 19,517 ....G7
Webster 10,222 ....F3
Wilkinson 9,678 ....B8
Winston 19,433 ....F4
Yalobusha 12,033 ....E2
Yazoo 25,506 ....D5

CITIES and TOWNS

Abbeville 399.......................F2
Aberdeen▲ 6,837 ....H3
Ackerman▲ 1,573.................F4
Acona 200 ....D4
Agricola 200 ....G9
Alcorn State University........B7
Algoma 420 ....G2
Alligator 187 ....C2
Amory 7,093 ....H3
Anguilla 883 ....C5
Arcola 564 ....C4
Arkabutla 400 ....D1
Artesia 484 ....G4
Ashland▲ 490......................F1
Askew 300 ....D1
Auburn 500 ....C8
Avalon 100 ....D3
Avera 150 ....G8
Avon 400 ....B4
Bailey 320 ....G6
Baird 150 ....C4
Baldwyn 3,204 ....G2
Ballardsville 105 ....H2
Banks 100 ....D1
Banner 120 ....F2
Bassfield 249 ....E8
Batesville▲ 6,403 ....E2
Baxterville 100 ....E8
Bay Saint Louis▲ 8,063 ....F10
Bay Springs▲ 1,729 ....F7
Beaumont 1,054 ....G8
Beauregard 206 ....D7
Becker 350 ....G3
Belden 241 ....G2
Belen 400 ....D2
Bellefontaine 400.................F3
Belmont 1,554 ....H1
Belzoni▲ 2,536.....................C4
Benndale 500.......................G9
Benoit 641 ....C3

Benton 390 ....D5
Bentonia 518 ....D5
Bethlehem 210 ....F1
Beulah 460 ....B3
Bexley 130 ....G9
Big Creek 123.......................F3
Bigbee Valley 370 ....H4
Bigpoint 350 ....H9
Biloxi 46,319 ....G10
Blue Mountain 667 ....G1
Blue Springs 140 ....G2
Bobo 200 ....C2
Bogue Chitto 689 ....D8
Bolatusha 87 ....E5
Bolton 637 ....D6
Bonita 300 ....G6
Bond 350 ....F9
Bonita 200 ....C4
Booneville▲ 7,955.................G1
Bourbon 200 ....C4
Boyle 651 ....C3
Brandon▲ 11,077.................E6
Braxton 141 ....D6
Brazil 229 ....D2
Brookhaven▲ 10,243 ....C7
Brooklyn 450........................F8
Brooksville 1,098.................G4
Brownfield 125 ....G1
Brownsville 200 ....D6
Brozville 150 ....D4
Bruce 2,127 ....F3
Brunswick 90 ....C5
Buckatunna 500 ....G7
Bude 969 ....C8
Burns 949 ....E6
Burnsville 889 ....H1
Byhalia 955 ....E1
Byram 250 ....D6
Caesar 80 ....E9
Caledonia 821 ....H3
Calhoun City 1,838 ....F3
Camden 150 ....E5
Canaan 200 ....F1
Cannonsburg 240 ....B7
Canton▲ 10,062...................D5
Carlisle 425 ....C7
Carpenter 200 ....C6
Carriere 900 ....E9
Carrollton▲ 221....................E4
Carson 400 ....E7
Carthage▲ 3,819..................E5
Cary 392 ....C5
Cascilla 230 ....D3
Cedarbluff 175.....................G3
Centreville 1,771..................B8
Chalybeate 200 ....G1
Charleston▲ 2,328...............D2
Chatawa 300 ....D8
Chatham 150 ....B4
Cheraw 100 ....E8
Chunky 292 ....G6
Church Hill 350.....................B7
Clara 275 ....G7
Clarksdale▲ 19,717...............D2
Clarkson 100 ....F3
Clermont Harbor 550 ....F10
Cleveland▲ 15,384...............C3
Cliftonville 280.....................H4
Clinton 21,847 ....D6
Coahoma 254 ....C2
Cockrum 150 ....E1
Coffeeville▲ 825...................E3
Coldwater 1,502...................E1
Coles 150 ....C8
College Hill 150.....................E2
Collins▲ 2,541......................E7
Collinsville 1,364.................G6
Columbia▲ 6,815..................E8
Columbus▲ 23,799...............H3
Como 1,387 ....E1
Conehatta 925 ....F6
Corinth▲ 11,820...................G1
Courtland 329 ....E2
Coxburg 300 ....D5
Crawford 668 ....G4
Crenshaw 978......................D2
Crosby 465 ....B8
Crowder 758 ....D2
Cruger 548 ....D4
Crystal Springs 5,643 ....D7
Cuevas 200 ....F10
Curtis Station 350 ....D2
D'Iberville 6,566 ....G10
D'Lo 421 ....E7
Daleville 210 ....G5
Dancy 116 ....F3
Darbun 80 ....D8
Darling 275 ....D2
De Kalb▲ 1,073....................G5
De Lisle 450 ....F10
Decatur▲ 1,248....................F6
Delta City 310 ....C4
Dennis 150 ....H1
Dentville 175 ....C7
Derby 298 ....F5
Derma 959 ....F3
Dixon 125 ....F5
Doddsville 149 ....C3
Dorsey 100 ....H2
Drew 2,349 ....C3
Dublin 100 ....C2
Duck Hill 586 ....E3
Duffee 175 ....G6
Dumas 407 ....G1
Duncan 416 ....C2
Dundee 600 ....D1
Dunleith 140 ....C2
Durant 2,838 ....E4
Eastabuchie 200 ....F8
Ebenezer 200 ....D5
Ecru 696 ....F2
Eden 88 ....D5
Edinburg 200 ....F5
Edwards 1,279 ....C6
Egypt 100 ....G1
Electric Mills 100 ....G5
Elizabeth 500 ....C4

Elliott 200 ....E3
Ellisville▲ 3,634...................F7
Enid 100 ....E2
Enterprise 477 ....G6
Errata 85 ....F7
Escatawpa 3,902 ....G10
Estill 100 ....C4
Ethel 454 ....F4
Eudora 200 ....D1
Eupora 2,145 ....F3
Falcon 167 ....D2
Falkner 232 ....G1
Fannin 250 ....E6
Farrell 300 ....C2
Fayette▲ 1,853.....................B7
Fernwood 500 ....D8
Fitler 175 ....B5
Flora 1,482 ....D5
Florence 1,831 ....D6
Flowood 2,860......................D6
Forest▲ 5,060.......................F6
Forkville 185 ....E6
Foxworth 800 ....E8
French Camp 320 ....F4
Friars Point 1,334 ....C2
Fulton▲ 3,387.......................H2
Gallman D7
Garlandville 150 ....F6
Gattman 120 ....H3
Gautier 10,088.....................G10
Georgetown 332 ....D7
Glen 165 ....H1
Glen Allan 650 ....B4
Glendora 220 ....D3
Gloster▲ 1,323.....................B8
Gluckstadt 150 ....D5
Golden 202 ....H2
Good Hope 125 ....E5
Goodman 1,256 ....E5
Gore Springs 125 ....E3
Goshen Springs 100 ....E6
Goss 100 ....E8
Grace 325 ....C5
Grapeland 200 ....B3
Greenville▲ 45,226..............B4
Greenwood Springs 170.......H3
Greenwood▲ 18,906............D4
Grenada▲ 10,864.................E3
Gulfport▲ 40,775..................F10
Gunnison 611 ....C3
Guntown 692 ....G2
Hamburg 150 ....B7
Hamilton 500 ....H3
Hampton 200 ....B4
Hardee 100 ....C5
Harperville 200.....................E6
Harriston 500 ....C7
Harrisville 500 ....D7
Hatley 529 ....H3
Hattiesburg▲ 41,882.............F8
Hazlehurst▲ 4,221...............D7
Heidelberg 981.....................F7
Helm 80 ....C4
Hermanville 750...................C7
Hernando▲ 3,125.................E1
Hickory 493 ....F6
Hickory Flat 535...................F1
Hillsboro 800 ....E6
Hintonville 300.....................F8
Hiwannee 250......................G7
Hohenlinden 90....................F3
Hollandale 3,576..................C4
Holly Bluff 700......................C5
Holly Ridge 350....................C4
Holly Springs▲ 7,261............E1
Hollywood 80 ....D1
Hopewell 250 ....D7
Horn Lake 9,069...................D1
Houlka 800 ....G2
Houston▲ 3,903...................G3
Howison 300 ....F9
Hub 80 ....E8
Hurley 500 ....H9
Independence 150 ....E1
Indianola▲ 11,809................C4
Ingomar 150 ....F2
Inverness 1,174 ....C4
Isola 732 ....C4
Itta Bena 2,377 ....D4
Iuka▲ 3,122..........................H1
Jackson (cap.)▲ 196,637......D6
James 100 ....B4
Jayess 300 ....D8
Johns 90 ....E6
Jonestown 1,467 ....D2
Jumpertown 438 ....G1
Kewanee 250 ....H6
Kilmichael 826 ....E4
Kiln 1,262 ....F10
Kirkville 200 ....H2
Kokomo 250 ....D8
Kolola Springs 100 ....H3
Kosciusko▲ 6,986.................E4

Kossuth 245 ....G1
Lafayette Springs 80 ....F2
Lake 369 ....F6
Lake Como 150 ....E1
Lake Cormorant 300 ....D1
Lake View 125 ....H1
Lakeshore 550......................F10
Lamar 200 ....F1
Lambert 1,131 ....D2
Lamont 400 ....B3
Langford 100 ....E6
Laurel▲ 18,827.....................F7
Lawrence 250 ....E6
Le Flore 99 ....D3
Leaf 250 ....G8
Leakesville▲ 1,129...............G8
Learned 111 ....C6
Leland 6,366 ....C4
Lemon 90 ....E3
Lena 175 ....E5
Lessley 100 ....B8
Lexington▲ 2,227.................D4
Liberty▲ 624.........................C8
Long 15,804 ....C4
Long Beach 17,967 ....F10
Longtown 150 ....D1
Longview 800 ....G4
Looxahoma 200 ....E1
Lorena 90 ....F6
Lorman 350 ....B7
Louin 289 ....F6
Louise 343 ....C5
Louisville▲ 7,169..................G4
Lucedale▲ 2,592...................G9
Ludlow 300 ....E5
Lula 224 ....C2
Lumberton 2,121 ....E8
Lyman 1,117 ....F10
Lyon 446 ....C2
Maben 752 ....F3
Macon▲ 2,256......................G4

Madden 450 ....F5
Madison 7,471 ....D6
Magee 3,607 ....E7
Magnolia▲ 2,245..................D8
Malvina 100 ....C3
Mantachie 651 ....H2
Mantee 134 ....F3
Marietta 287 ....H2
Marion 1,359 ....G6
Marks▲ 1,758.......................D2
Marydell 99 ....F5
Mashulaville 227..................G4
Matherville 150 ....G7
Mathiston 818 ....F4
Mattson 200 ....C2
Maxie 233 ....F9
Mayersville▲ 329..................B5
Mayhew 150 ....G4
McAdams 350 ....E4
McCall Creek 250 ....C7
McCarley 250 ....E3
McComb 11,591 ....D8
McCondy 150 ....G3
McCool 169 ....F4
McHenry 660 ....F9
McLain 536 ....G8
McLaurin 100 ....F8
McNeill 800 ....E9
Meadville▲ 453.....................C8
Meehan 100 ....G6
Mendenhall▲ 2,463...............E7
Meridian▲ 41,036..................G6
Merigold 572 ....C3
Merrill 100 ....G9
Metcalfe 1,092 ....B4
Michigan City 350 ....F1
Midnight 500 ....C4
Mineral Wells 250 ....F1
Minter City 150 ....D3
Mississippi State G4
Mize 312 ....E7
Money 350 ....D3

Monticello▲ 1,755.................D7
Montpelier 175 ....G3
Montrose 106 ....F6
Mooreville 200 ....G2
Moorhead 2,417...................C4
Morgan City 139..................D4
Morgantown 32,880 ....B7
Morgantown 325..................E8
Morton 3,212 ....E6
Moselle 525 ....F8
Moss 17,837 ....F7
Moss Point 18,998 ....G10
Mound Bayou 2,222 ....C3
Mount Olive 914...................E7
Mount Pleasant 250 ....E1
Murphy 100 ....C4
Myrtle 358 ....F1
Natchez▲ 19,460..................B7
Neely 270 ....G8
Nesbit 366 ....D1
Neshoba 250 ....F5
New Albany▲ 6,775..............G2
New Augusta▲ 668...............G8
New Houlka (Houlka) 558.....G2
New Site 100 ....H1
Newhebron 470....................D7
Newton 3,701 ....F6
Nicholson 400 ....E10
Nitta Yuma 150....................C4
Nola 120 ....D7
North Carrollton 578 ....E3
North Gulfport 4,966 ....F10
Noxapater 441 ....F5
Oak Ridge 350.....................C6
Oak Vale 100 ....E8
Oakland 553 ....E2
Oakley 133 ....D6
Ocean Springs 14,658 ....G10
Ofahoma 350 ....E5
Okolona▲ 3,267...................G2
Olive Branch 3,567..............E1

Oloh 93 ....E8
Oma 200 ....D7
Ora 15,676 ....E7
Orange Grove H10
Ovett 600 ....F8
Oxford▲ 9,984......................F2
Pace 354 ....C3
Pachuta 268 ....G6
Paden 123 ....H1
Palmers Crossing 2,765.......F8
Panther Burn 300.................C4
Parchman 200 ....D3
Paris 253 ....F2
Pascagoula▲ 25,899............G10
Pass Christian 5,557 ....F10
Pattison 540 ....C7
Paulding▲ 630......................F6
Paulette 230 ....H4
Paynes 100 ....D3
Pearl 19,588 ....D6
Pearlington 1,603................E10
Pelahatchie 1,553................E6
Penton 175 ....D1
Peoria 100 ....C8
Perkinston 950.....................F9
Petal 7,883 ....F8
Pheba 280 ....G3
Philadelphia▲ 6,758.............F5
Philipp 975 ....D3
Piave 150 ....G8
Picayune 10,633 ....E9
Pickens 1,285 ....E5
Pine Ridge 175 ....B7
Pineville 80 ....F6
Piney Woods 450 ....D6
Pinola E7
Pittsboro▲ 277.....................F3
Plantersville 1,046...............G2
Pleasant Grove 100 ....D2
Pleasant Hill 400 ....E1
Polkville 129 ....E6

(continued on following page)

Topography

0 40 80 MI.
0 40 80 KM.

5,000 m. 2,000 m. 1,000 m. 500 m. 200 m. 100 m. Sea
16,404 ft. 6,562 ft. 3,281 ft. 1,640 ft. 656 ft. 328 ft. Level
Below

Mississippi-Missouri River System

MILES
0 100 200 300

Navigable Waterways over 9 feet deep
Major River Ports..........⊙

©Copyright HAMMOND INCORPORATED.

Agriculture, Industry and Resources

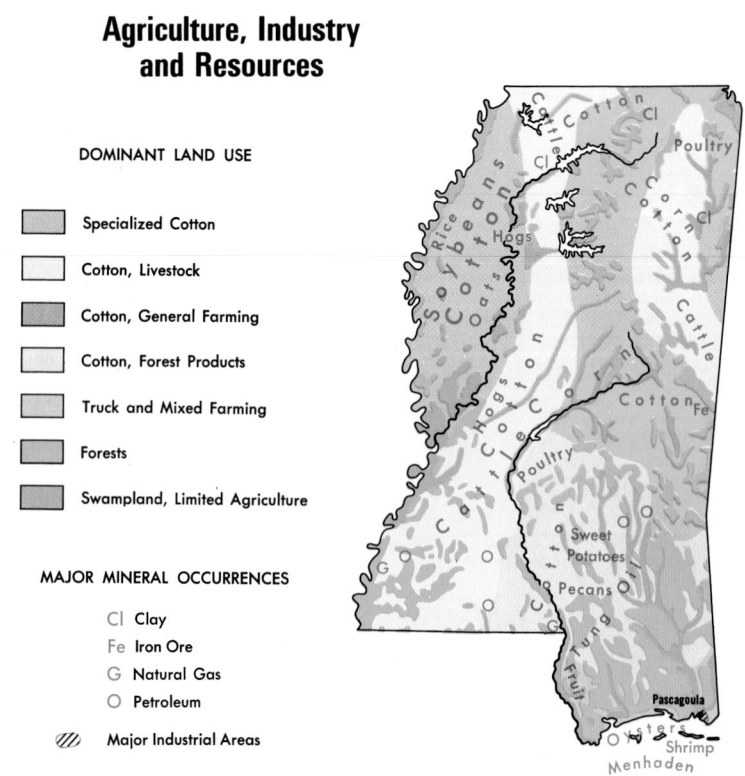

DOMINANT LAND USE

- Specialized Cotton
- Cotton, Livestock
- Cotton, General Farming
- Cotton, Forest Products
- Truck and Mixed Farming
- Forests
- Swampland, Limited Agriculture

MAJOR MINERAL OCCURRENCES

- Cl Clay
- Fe Iron Ore
- G Natural Gas
- O Petroleum
- ⫽ Major Industrial Areas

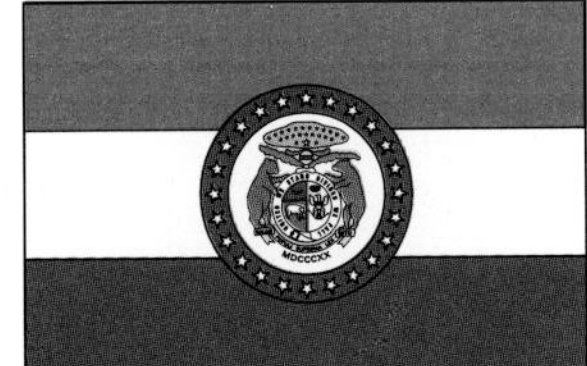

AREA 69,697 sq. mi. (180,515 sq. km.)
POPULATION 5,137,804
CAPITAL Jefferson City
LARGEST CITY St. Louis
HIGHEST POINT Taum Sauk Mtn. 1,772 ft. (540 m.)
SETTLED IN 1764
ADMITTED TO UNION August 10, 1821
POPULAR NAME Show Me State
STATE FLOWER Hawthorn
STATE BIRD Bluebird

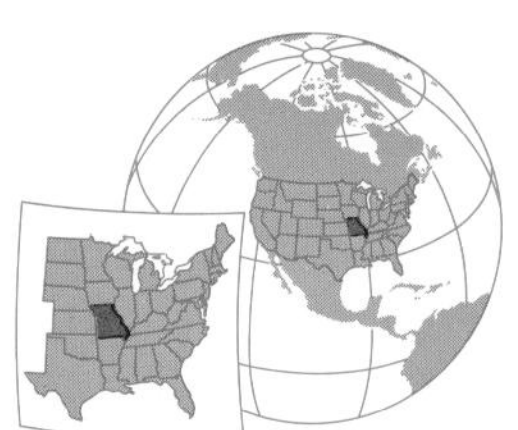

COUNTIES

Adair 24,577 ... G2
Andrew 14,632 ... C3
Atchison 7,457 ... B2
Audrain 23,599 ... J4
Barry 27,547 ... E9
Barton 11,312 ... D7
Bates 15,025 ... D6
Benton 13,859 ... F6
Bollinger 10,619 ... M8
Boone 112,379 ... H4
Buchanan 83,083 ... C3
Butler 38,765 ... M9
Caldwell 8,380 ... E3
Callaway 32,809 ... J5
Camden 27,495 ... G6
Cape Girardeau 61,633 ... N8
Carroll 10,748 ... F4
Carter 5,515 ... L9
Cass 63,808 ... D5
Cedar 12,093 ... E7
Chariton 9,202 ... F3
Christian 32,644 ... F9
Clark 7,547 ... J2
Clay 153,411 ... D4
Clinton 16,595 ... D3
Cole 63,579 ... H6
Cooper 14,835 ... G5
Crawford 19,173 ... K7
Dade 7,449 ... E8
Dallas 12,646 ... F7
Daviess 7,865 ... E3
De Kalb 8,222 ... D3
Dent 13,702 ... J7
Douglas 11,876 ... G9
Dunklin 33,112 ... M1
Franklin 80,603 ... K6
Gasconade 14,006 ... J6
Gentry 6,848 ... D2
Greene 207,949 ... F8
Grundy 10,536 ... E2
Harrison 8,469 ... E2
Henry 20,044 ... E6
Hickory 7,335 ... F7
Holt 6,034 ... B2
Howard 9,631 ... G4
Howell 31,447 ... J9
Iron 10,726 ... L7
Jackson 633,232 ... R5
Jasper 90,465 ... D8
Jefferson 171,380 ... L6
Johnson 42,514 ... E5
Knox 4,482 ... H2
Laclede 27,158 ... G7
Lafayette 31,107 ... E4
Lawrence 30,236 ... E8
Lewis 10,233 ... J2
Lincoln 28,892 ... L4
Linn 13,885 ... F3
Livingston 14,592 ... E3
Macon 15,345 ... G3
Madison 11,127 ... M8
Maries 7,976 ... J6
Marion 27,682 ... J3
McDonald 16,938 ... D9
Mercer 3,723 ... E2
Miller 20,700 ... H6
Mississippi 14,442 ... O9
Moniteau 12,298 ... G5
Monroe 9,104 ... H3
Montgomery 11,355 ... K5
Morgan 15,574 ... G6
New Madrid 20,928 ... N9
Newton 44,445 ... D9
Nodaway 21,709 ... C2
Oregon 9,470 ... K9
Osage 12,018 ... J6
Ozark 8,598 ... H9
Pemiscot 21,921 ... N1
Perry 16,648 ... N7
Pettis 35,437 ... F5
Phelps 35,248 ... J7
Pike 15,969 ... K4
Platte 57,867 ... C4
Polk 21,826 ... F7
Pulaski 41,307 ... H7
Putnam 5,079 ... F2
Ralls 8,476 ... J3
Randolph 24,370 ... G3
Ray 21,971 ... E4
Reynolds 6,661 ... L8
Ripley 12,303 ... L9
Saint Charles 144,107 ... M2
Saint Clair 8,622 ... E6
Saint Francois 42,600 ... M7
Saint Louis 974,180 ... O3
Saint Louis (city county) 452,801 ... P3
Sainte Genevieve 15,180 ... M7
Saline 23,523 ... F4
Schuyler 4,236 ... G2
Scotland 4,822 ... H2
Scott 39,376 ... N8
Shannon 7,613 ... K8
Shelby 6,942 ... H3
Stoddard 28,895 ... N9
Stone 19,078 ... F9
Sullivan 6,326 ... F2
Taney 25,561 ... F9
Texas 21,476 ... J8
Vernon 19,041 ... D7
Warren 19,534 ... K5
Washington 20,380 ... L7
Wayne 11,543 ... L8
Webster 23,753 ... G8
Worth 2,440 ... D2
Wright 16,758 ... H8

CITIES and TOWNS

Adrian 1,582 ... D6
Advance 1,139 ... N8
Affton 21,106 ... P4
Agency 642 ... C3
Alba 465 ... D8
Albany▲ 1,958 ... D2
Alexandria 341 ... K2
Alma 446 ... E4
Altamont 188 ... D3
Altenburg 307 ... O7
Alton▲ 692 ... K9
Amazonia 257 ... C3
Amoret 212 ... C6
Amsterdam 237 ... D6
Anderson 1,432 ... D9
Annapolis 363 ... L8
Anniston 288 ... O9
Appleton City 1,280 ... D6
Arbyrd 597 ... M10
Arcadia 609 ... L7
Archie 799 ... D5
Argyle 178 ... J6
Armstrong 310 ... G4
Arnold 18,828 ... M6
Asbury 220 ... C8
Ash Grove 1,128 ... E8
Ashland 1,252 ... H5
Atlanta 411 ... H3
Augusta 263 ... L5
Aurora 6,459 ... E9
Auxvasse 821 ... J4
Ava▲ 2,938 ... G9
Avondale 550 ... P5
Bakersfield 292 ... H9
Ballwin 21,816 ... N3
Baring 182 ... H2
Barnard 234 ... C2
Barnett 215 ... G6
Bates City 197 ... E5
Battlefield 1,526 ... F8
Bel-Nor 2,935 ... P2
Bel-Ridge 3,199 ... P2
Bell City 469 ... N8
Bella Villa 708 ... R4
Belle 1,218 ... J6
Bellefontaine 10,922 ... N2
Bellefontaine Neighbors 12,082 ... R2
Bellflower 413 ... K4
Belton 18,150 ... C5
Benton City 139 ... J4
Benton▲ 575 ... O8
Berger 247 ... K5
Berkeley 12,450 ... P2
Bernie 1,847 ... M9
Bertrand 692 ... O9
Bethany▲ 3,005 ... E2
Beverly 660 ... O4
Bevier 643 ... G3
Billings 989 ... F8
Birch Tree 599 ... K9
Birmingham 222 ... R5
Bismarck 1,579 ... L7
Black 6,128 ... L7
Black Jack 5,293 ... R1
Blackburn 308 ... F4
Blackwater 221 ... G5
Blairstown 185 ... E5
Bland 651 ... J6
Blodgett 202 ... O8
Bloomfield▲ 1,800 ... M9
Bloomsdale 353 ... M6
Blue Springs 40,153 ... R6
Bogard 228 ... E4
Bolckow 253 ... C2
Bolivar▲ 6,845 ... F7
Bonne Terre 3,871 ... L7
Boonville▲ 7,095 ... G5
Bosworth 334 ... F4
Bourbon 1,188 ... K6
Bowling Green▲ 2,976 ... K4
Brandsville 167 ... J9
Branson 3,706 ... F9
Brashear 318 ... H2
Braymer 886 ... E3
Breckenridge 418 ... E3
Breckenridge Hills 5,404 ... O2
Brentwood 8,150 ... P3
Bridgeton 17,779 ... O2
Bridgeton Terrace 334 ... O2
Bronaugh 211 ... C7
Brookfield 4,888 ... F3
Browning 331 ... F2
Brunswick 1,074 ... F4
Bucklin 616 ... G3
Buckner 2,873 ... R5
Buffalo▲ 2,414 ... F7
Bunceton 341 ... G5
Bunker 390 ... K8
Burlington Junction 634 ... B2
Butler▲ 4,099 ... D6
Butterfield 248 ... E9
Cabool 2,006 ... H8
Cainsville 387 ... E2
Cairo 282 ... H4
Caledonia 142 ... L7
Calhoun 450 ... E6
California▲ 3,465 ... H5
Callao 332 ... G3
Calverton Park 1,404 ... P2
Camden 238 ... D4
Camden Point 373 ... C4
Camdenton▲ 2,561 ... G6
Cameron 4,831 ... D3
Campbell 2,165 ... M9
Canalou 319 ... N9
Canton 2,623 ... J2
Cape Girardeau 34,438 ... O8
Cardwell 792 ... M10
Carl Junction 4,123 ... C8
Carrollton▲ 4,406 ... E4
Carterville 2,013 ... D8
Carthage▲ 10,747 ... D8
Caruth 7,389 ... N10
Caruthersville▲ 7,958 ... N10
Carytown 149 ... D8
Cassville▲ 2,371 ... E9
Cedar City 427 ... H5
Cedar Hill Lakes 227 ... L6
Center 552 ... J3
Centertown 356 ... H5
Centerview 214 ... E5
Centerville▲ 89 ... L8
Centralia 3,414 ... H4
Chaffee 3,059 ... N8
Chamois 449 ... J5
Charlack 1,388 ... P2
Charleston▲ 5,085 ... O9
Chesterfield 37,991 ... N2
Chilhowee 335 ... E5
Chillicothe▲ 8,804 ... E3
Chula 183 ... F3
Circle City 154 ... N9
Clarence 1,026 ... H3
Clark 257 ... H4
Clarksburg 358 ... G5
Clarksdale 287 ... D3
Clarkson Valley 2,508 ... N3
Clarksville 480 ... K4
Clarkton 1,113 ... M10
Claycomo 1,668 ... P5
Clayton▲ 13,874 ... P3
Clearmont 175 ... C1
Cleveland 506 ... C5
Clever 580 ... F8
Clinton▲ 8,703 ... E6
Cobalt City 254 ... M7
Cole Camp 1,054 ... F6
Collins 144 ... E7
Columbia▲ 69,101 ... H5
Commerce 173 ... O8
Conception Junction 236 ... C2
Concord 19,859 ... P4
Concordia 2,160 ... E5
Conway 629 ... G7
Cool Valley 1,407 ... P2
Cooter 451 ... N10
Corder 485 ... E4
Cottleville 2,936 ... M2
Country Club Village 1,234 ... C3
Cowgill 257 ... E3
Craig 346 ... B2
Crane 1,218 ... E9
Creighton 289 ... D6
Crestwood 11,234 ... O3
Creve Coeur 12,304 ... O2
Crocker 1,077 ... H7
Cross Timbers 168 ... F6
Crystal City 4,088 ... M6
Crystal Lake Park 506 ... O3
Cuba 2,537 ... K6
Curryville 261 ... K4
Dadeville 220 ... E8
De Kalb 222 ... C3
De Soto 5,993 ... L6
Dearborn 480 ... C3
Deepwater 441 ... E6
Dellwood 5,245 ... R2
Delta 450 ... N8
Des Arc 173 ... L8
Des Peres 8,395 ... O3
Desloge 4,150 ... M7
Dexter 7,559 ... N9
Diamond 775 ... D9
Diehlstadt 145 ... N9
Diggins 258 ... G8
Dixon 1,585 ... H6
Doniphan▲ 1,713 ... L9
Doolittle 599 ... J7
Downing 359 ... H2
Drexel 936 ... C6
Dudley 271 ... M9
Duenweg 940 ... D8
Duquesne 1,229 ... D8
Eagleville 275 ... D2
East Lynne 289 ... D5
East Prairie 3,416 ... O9
Easton 232 ... C3
Edgar Springs 215 ... J7
Edgerton 565 ... C3
Edina▲ 1,283 ... H2
Edmundson 1,111 ... O2
El Dorado Springs 3,830 ... E7
Eldon 4,419 ... G6
Ellington 994 ... L8
Ellisville 7,545 ... M3
Ellsinore 405 ... L9
Elmo 179 ... B1
Elsberry 1,898 ... L4
Elvins 1,391 ... L7
Eminence▲ 582 ... K8
Emma 194 ... F5
Eolia 389 ... L4
Essex 531 ... N9
Esther 1,071 ... M7
Eugene 141 ... H6
Eureka 4,683 ... M4
Everton 325 ... E8
Ewing 463 ... J2
Excelsior Springs 10,354 ... R4
Exeter 597 ... D9
Fair Grove 919 ... F8
Fair Play 442 ... E7
Fairfax 699 ... B2
Fairview 298 ... D9
Farber 418 ... J4
Farley 217 ... O4
Farmington▲ 11,598 ... M7
Fayette▲ 2,888 ... G4
Fenton 3,346 ... O4
Ferguson 22,286 ... P2
Ferrelview 338 ... O4
Festus 8,105 ... M6
Fillmore 256 ... C2
Fisk 422 ... M9
Flat 4,823 ... J7
Flat River 4,443 ... M7
Fleming 130 ... D4
Flemington 141 ... F7
Flinthill 219 ... L5
Florissant 51,206 ... P1
Foley 209 ... L4
Fordland 523 ... G8
Forest City 380 ... B3
Foristell 144 ... L5
Forsyth▲ 1,175 ... F9
Foster 161 ... D6
Frankford 396 ... K4
Franklin 181 ... G4
Fredericktown▲ 3,950 ... M7
Freeburg 446 ... J6
Freeman 480 ... C5
Freistatt 166 ... E8
Fremont 201 ... K9
Frohna 162 ... N7
Frontenac 3,374 ... O3
Fulton▲ 10,033 ... J5
Gainesville▲ 659 ... G9
Galena▲ 401 ... F9
Gallatin▲ 1,864 ... E3
Galt 296 ... F2
Garden City 1,225 ... D5
Gasconade 253 ... J5
Gerald 888 ... K6
Gideon 1,104 ... N10
Gilliam 212 ... F4
Gilman City 393 ... D2
Gladstone 26,243 ... P5
Glasgow 1,295 ... G4
Glenaire 597 ... R5
Glendale 5,945 ... P3
Glenwood 195 ... G1
Golden 794 ... E9
Golden City 900 ... D8
Goodman 1,094 ... C9
Gordonville 345 ... N8
Gower 1,249 ... C3
Graham 204 ... C2
Grain Valley 1,898 ... S6
Granby 1,945 ... D9
Grandin 233 ... L9
Grandview 24,967 ... P6
Grant City▲ 998 ... D2
Grantwood 904 ... O4
Gray Summit 2,505 ... L6
Green Castle 285 ... G2
Green City 671 ... F2
Green Ridge 452 ... F5
Greenfield▲ 1,416 ... E8
Greentop 425 ... H2
Greenville▲ 437 ... M8
Greenwood 1,505 ... R6
Hale 480 ... F3
Half Way 157 ... F7
Hallsville 917 ... H4
Halltown 161 ... E8
Hamilton 1,737 ... E3
Hanley Hills 2,325 ... P2
Hannibal 18,004 ... K3
Hardin 598 ... E4
Harrisburg 169 ... H4
Harrisonville▲ 7,683 ... D5
Hartville▲ 495 ... G8
Hawk Point 472 ... K5
Hayti 3,280 ... N10
Hayti Heights 893 ... N10
Haywood City 263 ... N9
Hazelwood 15,324 ... P2
Henrietta 412 ... E4
Herculaneum 2,263 ... M6
Hermann▲ 2,754 ... K5
Hermitage▲ 512 ... F7
Higbee 639 ... H4
Higginsville 4,693 ... E4
High Hill 204 ... K5

(continued on following page)

Agriculture, Industry and Resources

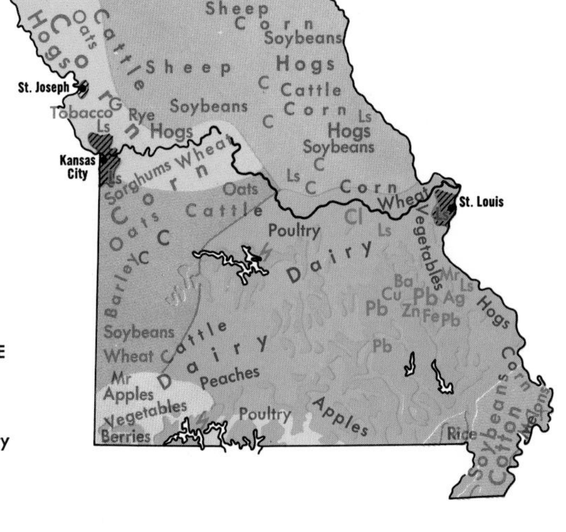

DOMINANT LAND USE

- Cattle Feed, Hogs
- Livestock, Cash Grain, Dairy
- Pasture Livestock
- Specialized Cotton
- General Farming, Dairy, Livestock, Poultry
- General Farming, Livestock, Truck Farming, Cotton
- Fruit and Mixed Farming
- Forests
- Urban Areas

MAJOR MINERAL OCCURRENCES

Ag	Silver	G	Natural Gas
Ba	Barite	Ls	Limestone
C	Coal	Mr	Marble
Cl	Clay	Pb	Lead
Cu	Copper	Zn	Zinc
Fe	Iron Ore		

Water Power — Major Industrial Areas

High Ridge 4,423 .... M6
Hillsboro▲ 1,625 .... L6
Hillsdale 1,948 .... R2
Holcomb 531 .... N10
Holden 2,389 .... E5
Holland 237 .... N10
Holliday 139 .... H3
Hollister 2,628 .... F9
Holt 311 .... D4
Holts Summit 2,292 .... H5
Homestown 230 .... N10
Hopkins 575 .... C1
Horine 1,043 .... M6
Hornersville 629 .... M10
Houston Lake 303 .... O5
Houston▲ 2,118 .... J8
Houstonia 283 .... F5
Howardville 440 .... N9
Hughesville 174 .... F5
Humansville 1,084 .... E7
Hume 287 .... C6
Hunnewell 219 .... J3
Huntleigh 392 .... O3
Huntsville▲ 1,567 .... H4
Hurdland 212 .... H2
Hurricane Deck 210 .... G6
Iberia 650 .... H6
Illmo 1,368 .... O8
Imperial 4,156 .... M6
Independence▲ 112,301 .... R5
Iron Gates 309 .... C8
Irondale 474 .... L7
Ironton▲ 1,539 .... L7
Jackson▲ 9,256 .... N8
Jameson 149 .... E2
Jamesport 570 .... E3
Jamestown 298 .... G5
Jasper 994 .... D8
Jefferson City (cap.)▲ 35,481 .H5
Jennings 15,905 .... R2
Jerico Springs 247 .... E7
Jonesburg 630 .... K5
Joplin 40,961 .... C8
Junction City 326 .... M7
Kahoka▲ 2,195 .... J2
Kansas City 435,146 .... P5
Kearney 1,790 .... D4
Kelso 526 .... O8
Kennett▲ 10,941 .... M10
Keytesville▲ 564 .... G4
Kidder 241 .... D3
Kimberling City 1,590 .... F9
Kimmswick 135 .... M6
King City 986 .... D2
Kingston▲ 279 .... E3
Kingsville 279 .... D5
Kinloch 2,702 .... P2
Kirksville▲ 17,152 .... H2
Kirkwood 27,291 .... O3
Knob Noster 2,261 .... E5
Knox City 262 .... H2
Koshkonong 198 .... J9
La Belle 655 .... J2
La Grange 1,102 .... K2
La Monte 995 .... F5
La Plata 1,401 .... H2
Laclede 410 .... F3
Laddonia 581 .... J4
Ladue 8,847 .... P3
Lake Lotawana 2,141 .... R6
Lake Ozark 681 .... G6
Lake Saint Louis 7,400 .... L5
Lake Tapawingo 761 .... R6
Lake Waukomis 1,027 .... P5
Lake Winnebago 748 .... R6
Lakeshire 1,467 .... P4
Lamar Heights 176 .... D8
Lamar▲ 4,168 .... D8
Lanagan 501 .... C9
Lancaster▲ 785 .... H1
Laredo 205 .... E2
Lathrop 1,794 .... D3
Laurie 507 .... G6
Lawson 1,876 .... D4
Leadington 201 .... M7
Leadwood 1,247 .... L7
Leasburg 289 .... K6
Lebanon▲ 9,983 .... G7
Lee's Summit 46,418 .... R6
Leeton 632 .... E5
Lemay 18,005 .... R4
Levasy 279 .... S5
Lewis 142 .... E6
Lewis and Clark Village 131 .... C3
Lewistown 453 .... J2
Lexington▲ 4,860 .... E4
Liberal 684 .... D7
Liberty▲ 20,459 .... R5
Licking 1,328 .... J8
Lilbourn 1,378 .... N9
Lincoln 874 .... F6
Linn Creek 232 .... G6
Linn▲ 1,148 .... J5
Linneus▲ 364 .... F3
Lockwood 1,041 .... E8
Lohman 154 .... H5
Lone Jack 392 .... S6
Louisiana 3,967 .... K4
Lowry City 723 .... E6
Ludlow 147 .... E3
Lutesville 865 .... M8
Mackenzie 148 .... P3
Macks Creek 272 .... G7
Macon▲ 5,571 .... H3
Madison 518 .... H4
Maitland 338 .... B2
Malden 5,123 .... M9
Malta Bend 289 .... F4
Manchester 6,542 .... O3
Mansfield 1,429 .... G8
Maplewood 9,962 .... P3
Marble Hill▲ 1,447 .... N8
Marceline 2,645 .... F3
Marionville 1,920 .... E8
Marlborough 1,949 .... P3
Marquand 278 .... M8
Marshall▲ 12,711 .... F4
Marshfield▲ 4,374 .... G8
Marston 691 .... N9
Marthasville 674 .... L5
Martinsburg 337 .... J4
Maryland Heights 25,407 .... O2
Maryville▲ 10,663 .... C2
Matthews 614 .... N9
Maysville▲ 1,176 .... D3
Mayview 279 .... E4
McFall 142 .... D2
Meadville 360 .... F3
Mehlville 27,557 .... P4
Memphis▲ 2,094 .... H2
Mendon 207 .... F3
Mercer 297 .... F2
Meta 249 .... H6
Mexico▲ 11,290 .... J4
Miami 142 .... F4
Middletown 217 .... J4
Milan▲ 1,767 .... F2
Mill Spring 252 .... L8
Miller 753 .... E8
Mindenmines 346 .... C8
Mine La Motte 125 .... M7
Miner 1,218 .... N9
Mineral Point 384 .... L7
Missouri City 348 .... R5
Moberly 12,839 .... G4
Mokane 186 .... J5
Moline Acres 2,710 .... R2
Monett 6,529 .... E9
Monroe City 2,701 .... J3
Montgomery City▲ 2,281 .... K5
Monticello▲ 106 .... J2
Montrose 440 .... E6
Morehouse 1,068 .... N9
Morley 683 .... N8
Morrison 160 .... J5
Morrisville 293 .... F8
Mosby 194 .... R4
Moscow Mills 924 .... K5
Mound City 1,273 .... B2
Moundville 140 .... C7
Mount Vernon▲ 3,726 .... E8
Mountain Grove 4,182 .... H8
Mountain View 2,036 .... J8
Murphy 9,342 .... O4
Napoleon 233 .... E4
Naylor 642 .... L9
Neelyville 381 .... M9
Nelson 181 .... F4
Neosho▲ 9,254 .... D9
Nevada▲ 8,597 .... D7
New Bloomfield 480 .... J5
New Cambria 223 .... G3
New Florence 801 .... K5
New Franklin 1,107 .... G4
New Hampton 320 .... D2
New Haven 1,757 .... K5
New London▲ 988 .... K3
New Madrid▲ 3,350 .... O9
New Melle 486 .... L5
Newburg 589 .... J7
Newtonia 204 .... D9
Niangua 459 .... G8
Nixa 4,707 .... F8
Noel 1,169 .... D9
Norborne 856 .... E4
Normandy 4,480 .... R2
North Kansas City 4,130 .... P5
Northmoor 441 .... P5
Northwoods 5,106 .... R2
Norwood 449 .... H8
Novelty 143 .... H2
Novinger 542 .... G2
O'Fallon 18,698 .... L5
Oak Grove 4,067 .... S6
Oak Grove 402 .... K6
Oak Ridge 202 .... N7
Oakland 1,593 .... P3
Oaks 130 .... P5
Oakview 351 .... P5
Oakwood 212 .... P5
Oakwood Manor 137 .... P5
Oakwood Park 213 .... P5
Odessa 3,695 .... E5
Old Monroe 242 .... L5
Olivette 7,573 .... O2
Olympian Village 752 .... M6
Oran 1,164 .... N8
Oregon▲ 935 .... B2
Oronogo 595 .... D8
Orrick 935 .... D4
Osage Beach 2,599 .... G6
Osborn 400 .... D3
Osceola▲ 755 .... E6
Otterville 507 .... G5
Overland 17,987 .... O2
Owensville 2,325 .... K6
Ozark▲ 4,243 .... F8
Pacific 4,350 .... L5
Pagedale 3,771 .... P2
Palmyra▲ 3,371 .... J3
Paris▲ 1,486 .... J4
Parksdale 270 .... F6
Parkville 2,402 .... O5
Parkway 277 .... L6
Parma 995 .... N9
Parnell 157 .... C2
Patton 414 .... M8
Pattonsburg 502 .... D2
Peculiar 1,777 .... D5
Perry 711 .... J4
Perryville▲ 6,933 .... N7
Pevely 2,831 .... M6
Phillipsburg 170 .... G7
Pickering 171 .... C2
Piedmont 2,166 .... L8
Pierce City 1,382 .... E8
Pilot Grove 714 .... G5
Pilot Knob 783 .... L7
Pine 5,092 .... K9
Pine Lawn 6,600 .... R2
Pineville▲ 580 .... D9
Platte City▲ 2,947 .... C4
Platte Woods 427 .... O5
Plattsburg▲ 2,248 .... D3
Pleasant Hill 3,827 .... D5
Pleasant Hope 360 .... F8
Pleasant Valley 2,731 .... R5
Polo 539 .... D3
Poplar Bluff▲ 16,996 .... L9
Portage Des Sioux 503 .... M5
Portageville 3,401 .... N10
Potosi▲ 2,683 .... L7
Prairie Home 215 .... G5
Princeton▲ 1,021 .... E2
Purcell 359 .... D8
Purdin 217 .... F3
Purdy 977 .... E9
Puxico 819 .... M9
Queen City 704 .... H2
Qulin 384 .... M9
Ravenwood 409 .... C2
Raymondville 425 .... J8
Raymore 5,592 .... D5
Raytown 30,601 .... P6
Rayville 170 .... E4
Reeds Spring 411 .... F9
Renick 195 .... H4
Republic 6,292 .... E8
Rhineland 157 .... J5
Rich Hill 1,317 .... D6
Richland 2,029 .... H7
Richmond Heights 10,448 .... P3
Richmond▲ 5,738 .... D4
Ridgeway 379 .... D2
Risco 434 .... N9
Rivermines 459 .... L7
Riverside 3,010 .... O5
Riverview 3,242 .... R2
Rocheport 255 .... H5
Rock Hill 5,217 .... P3
Rock Port▲ 1,438 .... B2
Rockaway Beach 275 .... F9
Rockville 193 .... D6
Rogersville 995 .... G8
Rolla▲ 14,090 .... J7
Rosebud 380 .... K6
Rosendale 186 .... C2
Rushville 306 .... B3
Russellville 869 .... H6
Saginaw 384 .... C8
Saint Ann 14,489 .... O2
Saint Charles▲ 54,555 .... N1
Saint Clair 3,917 .... K6
Saint Elizabeth 257 .... H6
Saint George 1,270 .... P4
Saint James 3,256 .... J6
Saint John 7,466 .... P2
Saint Joseph▲ 71,852 .... C3
Saint Louis▲ 396,685 .... R3
Saint Martins 717 .... H5
Saint Marys 461 .... M7
Saint Paul 1,192 .... L5
Saint Peters 45,779 .... M1
Saint Robert 1,730 .... H7
Saint Thomas 263 .... H6
Sainte Genevieve▲ 4,411 .... M6
Salem▲ 4,486 .... J7
Salisbury 1,881 .... G4
Sappington 10,917 .... O4
Sarcoxie 1,330 .... D8
Savannah▲ 4,352 .... C3
Schell City 292 .... D6
Scott City 4,292 .... O8
Sedalia▲ 19,800 .... F5
Sedgewickville 138 .... N7
Seligman 593 .... D9
Senath 1,622 .... M10
Seneca 1,885 .... C9
Seymour 1,636 .... G8
Shelbina 2,172 .... H3
Shelbyville▲ 582 .... H3
Sheldon 464 .... D7
Sheridan 174 .... C1
Shrewsbury 6,416 .... P3
Sibley 367 .... S5
Sikeston 17,641 .... N9
Silex 197 .... K4
Skidmore 404 .... B2
Slater 2,186 .... G4
Smithton 532 .... F5
Smithville 2,525 .... D4
South West City 600 .... D9
Spanish Lake 20,322 .... R1
Sparta 751 .... F9
Spickard 326 .... F2
Springfield▲ 140,494 .... F8
Stanberry 1,310 .... C2
Steele 2,395 .... N10
Steelville▲ 1,465 .... K7
Stewartsville 732 .... C3
Stockton▲ 1,579 .... E7
Stotts City 235 .... E8
Stoutland 207 .... G7
Stover 964 .... G6
Strafford 1,166 .... F8
Sturgeon 838 .... H4

Topography

0 40 80 MI.
0 40 80 KM.

5,000 m. 16,404 ft. | 2,000 m. 6,562 ft. | 1,000 m. 3,281 ft. | 500 m. 1,640 ft. | 200 m. 656 ft. | 100 m. 328 ft. | Sea Level Below

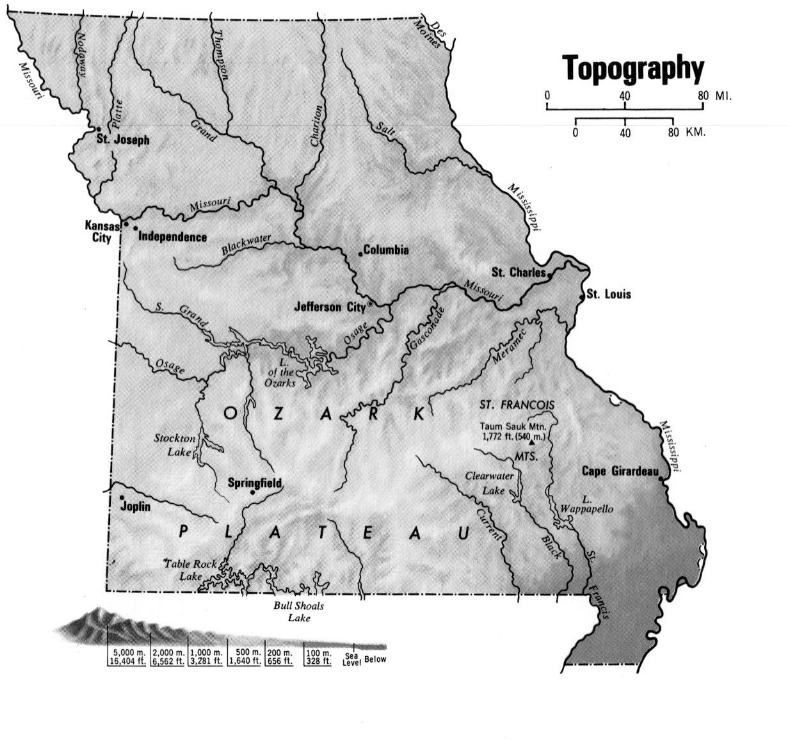

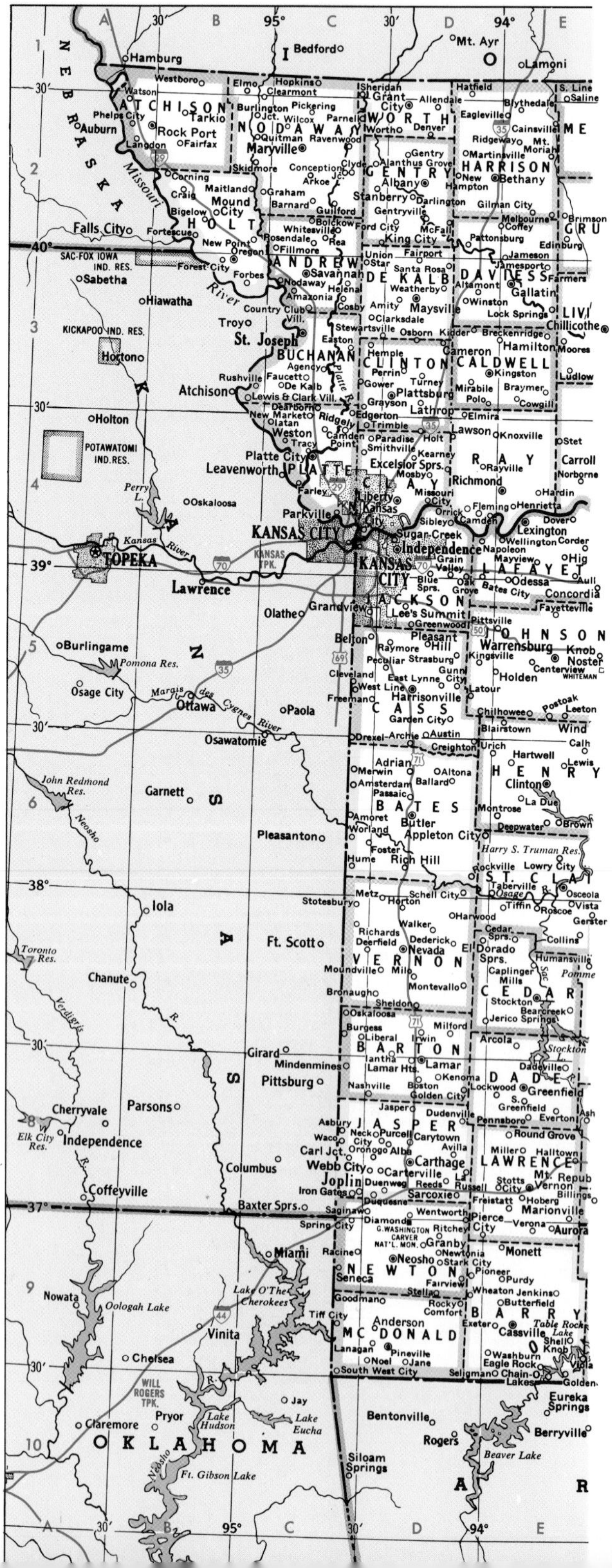

▲County seat

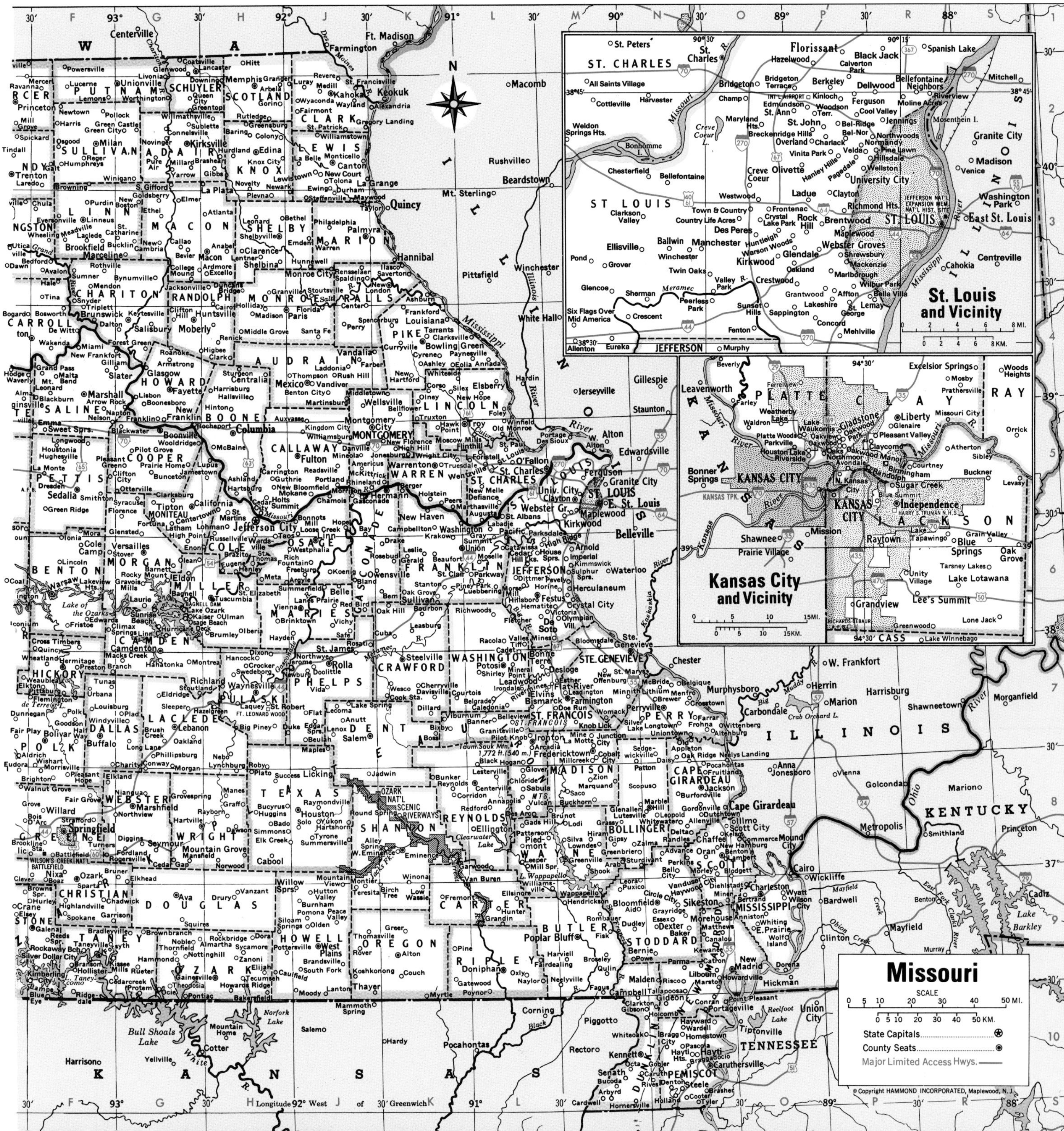
Missouri
SCALE
0 5 10 20 30 40 50 MI.
0 5 10 20 30 40 50 KM.
State Capitals
County Seats
Major Limited Access Hwys.
St. Louis and Vicinity
Kansas City and Vicinity
Longitude 92° West of 30′ Greenwich
KENTUCKY
TENNESSEE
ILLINOIS

Agriculture, Industry and Resources

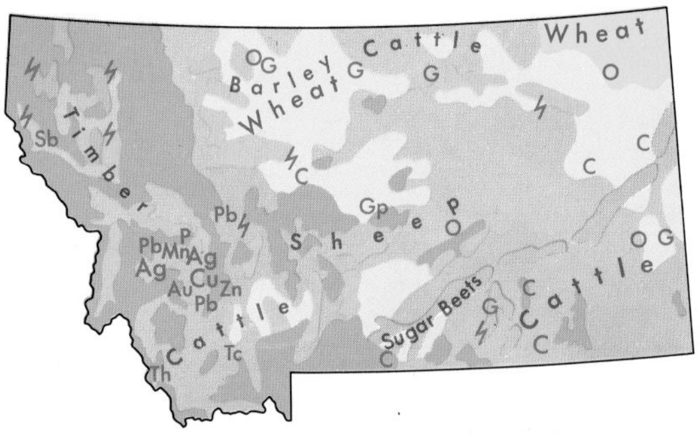
Wheat
Cattle
Barley
Wheat
Timber
Sheep
Cattle
Sugar Beets
Cattle
Sb
Pb
Ag
Mn
Cu
Zn
Au
Gp
Tc
Th

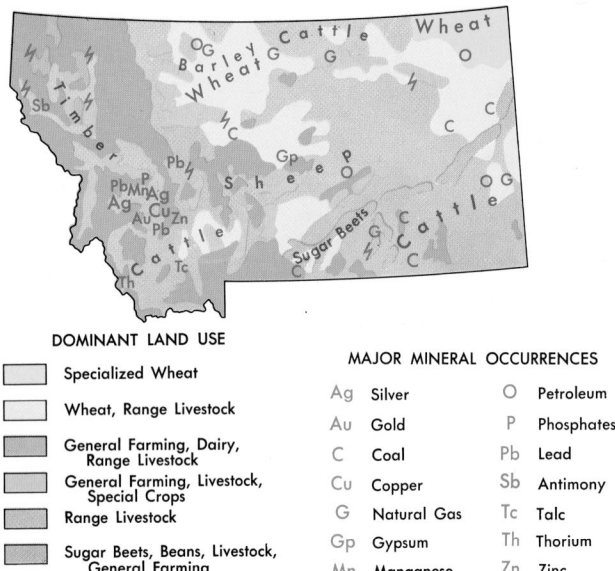

DOMINANT LAND USE

- Specialized Wheat
- Wheat, Range Livestock
- General Farming, Dairy, Range Livestock
- General Farming, Livestock, Special Crops
- Range Livestock
- Sugar Beets, Beans, Livestock, General Farming
- Forests

MAJOR MINERAL OCCURRENCES

Ag	Silver	O	Petroleum
Au	Gold	P	Phosphates
C	Coal	Pb	Lead
Cu	Copper	Sb	Antimony
G	Natural Gas	Tc	Talc
Gp	Gypsum	Th	Thorium
Mn	Manganese	Zn	Zinc

ϟ Water Power

COUNTIES

Beaverhead 8,424 .... C5
Big Horn 11,337 .... J5
Blaine 6,728 .... G2
Broadwater 3,318 .... E4
Carbon 8,080 .... G5
Carter 1,503 .... M5
Cascade 77,691 .... E3
Chouteau 5,452 .... F3
Custer 11,697 .... L4
Daniels 2,266 .... L2
Dawson 9,505 .... M3
Deer Lodge 10,278 .... C5
Fallon 3,103 .... M4
Fergus 12,083 .... G3
Flathead 59,218 .... B2
Gallatin 50,463 .... E5
Garfield 1,589 .... J3
Glacier 12,121 .... C2
Golden Valley 912 .... G4
Granite 2,548 .... C4
Hill 17,654 .... F2
Jefferson 7,939 .... D4
Judith Basin 2,282 .... F4
Lake 21,041 .... B3
Lewis and Clark 47,495 .... D3
Liberty 2,295 .... E2
Lincoln 17,481 .... A2
Madison 5,989 .... D5
McCone 2,276 .... L3
Meagher 1,819 .... F4
Mineral 3,315 .... B3
Missoula 78,687 .... C3
Musselshell 4,106 .... H4
Park 14,562 .... F5
Petroleum 519 .... H3
Phillips 5,163 .... J2
Pondera 6,433 .... D2
Powder River 2,090 .... L5
Powell 6,620 .... D4
Prairie 1,383 .... L4
Ravalli 25,010 .... B4
Richland 10,716 .... M3
Roosevelt 10,999 .... L2
Rosebud 10,505 .... K4
Sanders 8,669 .... A3
Sheridan 4,732 .... M2
Silver Bow 33,941 .... D5
Stillwater 6,536 .... G5
Sweet Grass 3,154 .... G5
Teton 6,271 .... D3
Toole 5,046 .... E2
Treasure 874 .... J4
Valley 8,239 .... K2
Wheatland 2,246 .... G4
Wibaux 1,191 .... M4
Yellowstone 113,419 .... H4

CITIES and TOWNS

Absarokee 1,067 .... G5
Acton 50 .... H5
Alberton 354 .... B3
Alder 120 .... D5
Alzada 52 .... M5
Amsterdam 130 .... E5
Anaconda-Deer Lodge County▲ C4
Angela 50 .... K4
Antelope 83 .... M2
Apgar 25 .... B2
Arlee 489 .... B3
Armington 75 .... F3
Ashland 484 .... K5
Augusta 497 .... D3
Avon 125 .... D4
Babb 150 .... C2
Bainville 165 .... M2
Baker▲ 1,818 .... M4
Ballantine 380 .... J5
Bannack 2 .... C5
Basin 350 .... D4
Bearcreek 37 .... G5
Becket 35 .... G4
Belfry 300 .... H5
Belgrade 3,411 .... E5
Belt 571 .... E3
Biddle 28 .... L5
Big Arm 250 .... B3
Big Sandy 740 .... G2
Big Sky 50 .... E5
Big Timber▲ 1,557 .... G5
Bigfork 1,080 .... C2
Billings▲ 81,151 .... H5
Birney 100 .... K5
Black Eagle 1,500 .... E3
Blackfoot 100 .... D2
Bloomfield 28 .... M3
Bonner-West Riverside 1,669 .... C4
Boulder▲ 1,316 .... E4
Box Elder 300 .... F2
Boyd 32 .... G5
Bozeman▲ 22,660 .... E5
Brady 450 .... E2
Bridger 692 .... H5
Broadus▲ 572 .... L5
Broadview 133 .... H4
Brockton 365 .... M2
Brockway 55 .... L3
Browning 1,170 .... C2
Busby 409 .... J5
Butte-Silver Bow County▲ 33,336 .... D5
Bynum 49 .... D3
Camas Prairie 160 .... B3
Cameron 150 .... E5
Canyon Creek 100 .... D4
Canyon Ferry 100 .... E4
Cardwell 34 .... E5
Carter 70 .... E3
Cartersville 115 .... K4
Cascade 729 .... E3
Charlo 358 .... B3
Chester▲ 942 .... E2
Chinook▲ 1,512 .... G2
Choteau▲ 1,741 .... D3
Christina 60 .... G3
Circle▲ 805 .... L3
Clancy 550 .... E4
Clinton 250 .... C4
Clyde Park 282 .... F5
Coffee Creek 62 .... F3
Colstrip 3,035 .... K5
Columbia Falls 2,942 .... B2
Columbus▲ 1,573 .... G5
Condon 300 .... C3
Conner 420 .... B5
Conrad▲ 2,891 .... D2
Cooke City 120 .... G5
Coram 450 .... C2
Corvallis 500 .... C4
Craig 100 .... D3
Crane 163 .... M3
Creston 60 .... C2
Crow Agency 1,446 .... J5
Culbertson 796 .... M2
Custer 300 .... J4
Cut Bank▲ 3,329 .... D2
Dagmar 35 .... M2

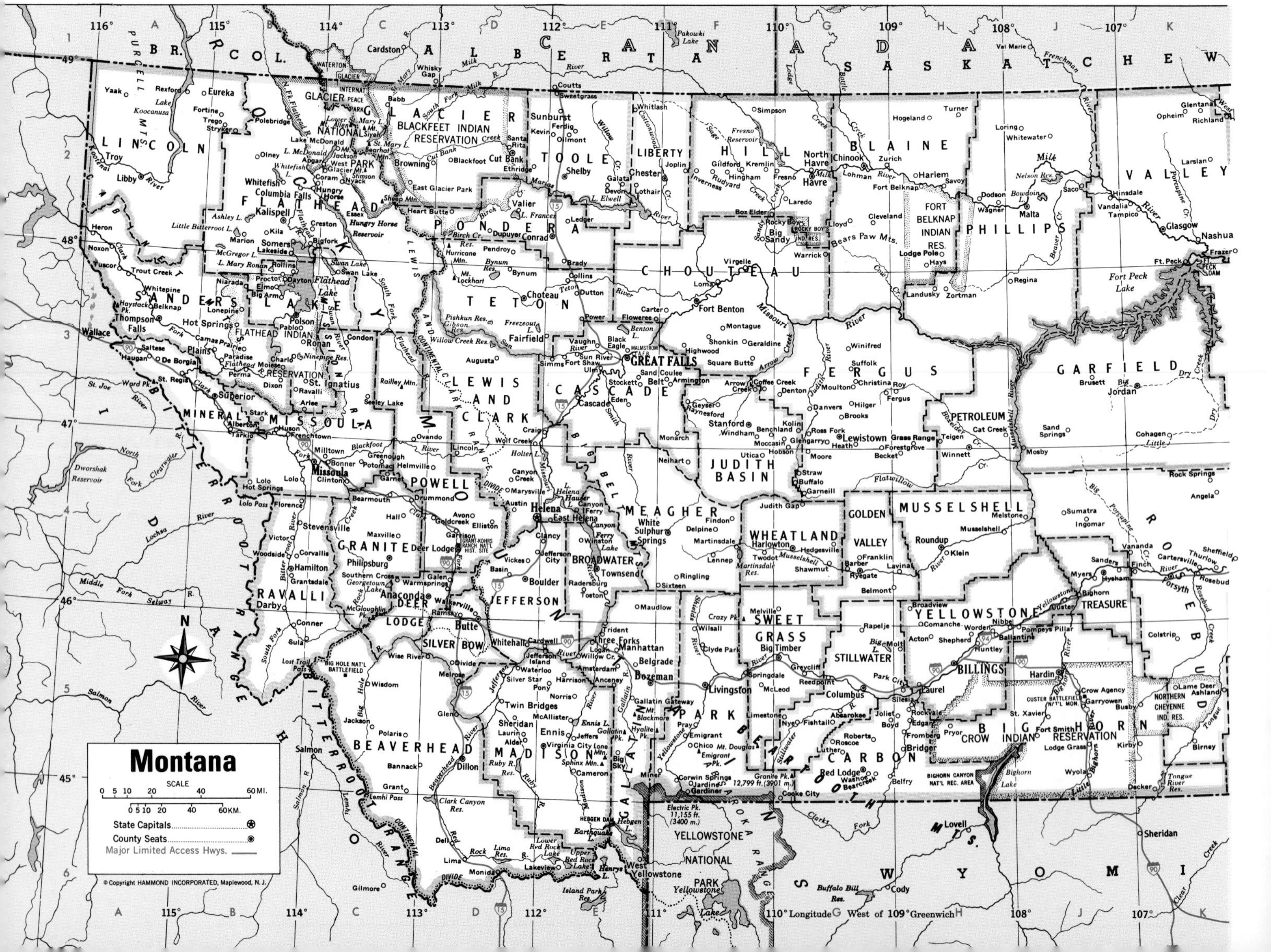
Montana
SCALE
0 5 10 20 40 60 MI.
0 5 10 20 40 60 KM.
State Capitals
County Seats
Major Limited Access Hwys.
© Copyright HAMMOND INCORPORATED, Maplewood, N. J.
ALBERTA
SASKATCHEWAN
BR. COL.
IDAHO
WYOMING
LINCOLN
FLATHEAD
GLACIER
TOOLE
LIBERTY
HILL
BLAINE
PHILLIPS
VALLEY
PONDERA
TETON
CHOUTEAU
SANDERS
LAKE
MINERAL
MISSOULA
LEWIS AND CLARK
CASCADE
FERGUS
PETROLEUM
GARFIELD
JUDITH BASIN
POWELL
GRANITE
MEAGHER
WHEATLAND
GOLDEN VALLEY
MUSSELSHELL
RAVALLI
JEFFERSON
BROADWATER
SWEET GRASS
STILLWATER
YELLOWSTONE
TREASURE
ROSEBUD
SILVER BOW
BEAVERHEAD
MADISON
GALLATIN
PARK
CARBON
BIG HORN
GREAT FALLS
Helena
Missoula
Billings
Bozeman
Butte
Havre
Kalispell
Livingston
Lewistown
Fort Peck Lake
YELLOWSTONE NATIONAL PARK
GLACIER NATIONAL PARK
110° Longitude West of 109° Greenwich

Montana 263

Topography

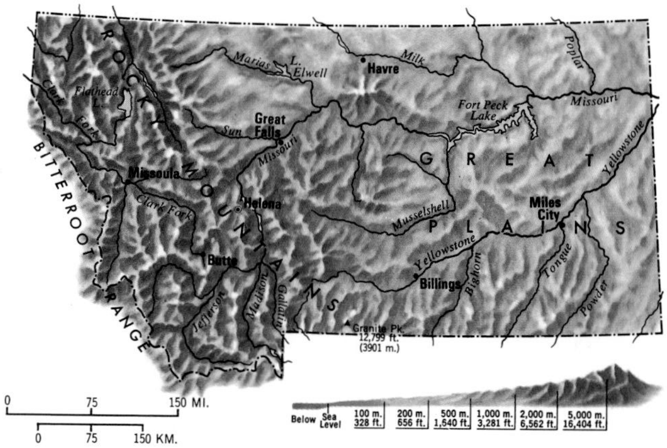
Marias
L. Elwell
Havre
Milk
Poplar
Flathead
Great Falls
Fort Peck Lake
Missouri
Sun
BITTERROOT RANGE
Missoula
Helena
Clark Fork
GREAT PLAINS
Miles City
Musselshell
Yellowstone
Butte
Billings
Bighorn
Tongue
Powder
Jefferson
Madison
Gallatin
Granite Pk. 12,799 ft. (3901 m.)
0 75 150 MI.
0 75 150 KM.
Below Sea Level
100 m. 328 ft.
200 m. 656 ft.
500 m. 1,640 ft.
1,000 m. 3,281 ft.
2,000 m. 6,562 ft.
5,000 m. 16,404 ft.

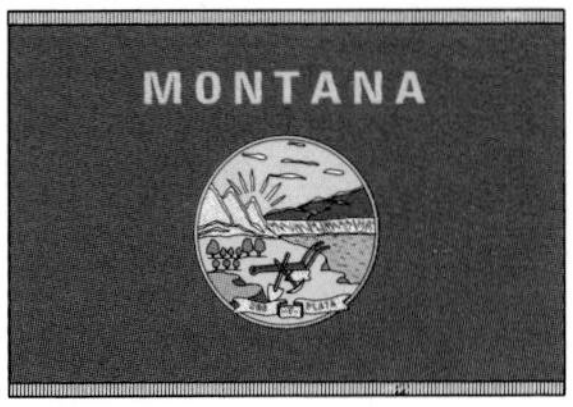
MONTANA

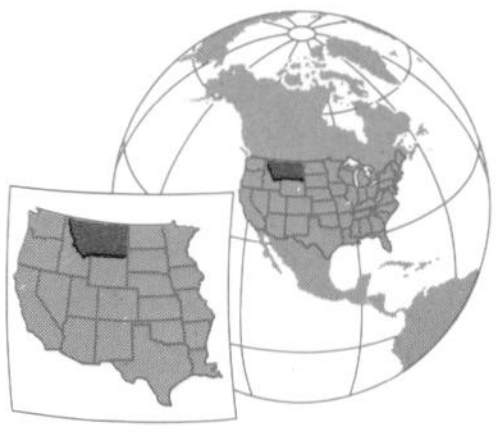

AREA 147,046 sq. mi. (380,849 sq. km.)
POPULATION 803,655
CAPITAL Helena
LARGEST CITY Billings
HIGHEST POINT Granite Pk. 12,799 ft. (3901 m.)
SETTLED IN 1809
ADMITTED TO UNION November 8, 1889
POPULAR NAME Treasure State; Big Sky Country
STATE FLOWER Bitterroot
STATE BIRD Western Meadowlark

Darby 625 B4
Dayton 140 B3
De Borgia 300 A3
Decker 150 K5
Deer Lodge▲ 3,378 D4
Dell 29 D6
Delpine 33 F4
Denton 350 G3
Dillon▲ 3,991 D5
Divide 275 D5
Dixon 550 B3
Dodson 137 H2
Drummond 264 D4
Dupuyer 105 D2
Dutton 392 E3
East Glacier Park 326 C2
East Helena 1,538 E4
Edgar 220 H5
Ekalaka▲ 439 M5
Elliston 250 D4
Elmo 250 B3
Emigrant 80 F5
Ennis 773 E5
Epsie 60 L5
Essex 48 C2
Eureka 1,043 B2
Fairfield 660 D3
Fairview 869 M3
Fallon 225 L4
Fishtail 46 G5
Flaxville 88 L2
Florence 700 B4
Floweree 48 E3
Forestgrove 100 H3
Forsyth▲ 2,178 K4
Fort Belknap 422 H2
Fort Benton▲ 1,660 F3
Fort Peck 325 K2
Fort Shaw 200 E3
Fort Smith 300 J5
Fortine 250 A2
Four Buttes 50 L2
Frazer 403 K2
Frenchtown 300 B3
Froid 195 M2
Fromberg 370 H5
Galata 100 E2
Galen 210 D4
Gallatin Gateway 600 E5
Gardiner 600 F5
Garneill 61 G4
Garrison 300 D4
Garryowen 200 J5
Geraldine 299 F3
Geyser 125 F3
Gildford 250 F2
Glasgow▲ 3,572 K2
Glen 4,802 D5
Glendive▲ 5,978 M3
Goldcreek 100 D4
Grant 25 C5
Grantsdale 500 B4
Grass Range 159 H3
Great Falls▲ 55,097 E3
Greenough 120 C4
Greycliff 37 G5
Hall 130 C4
Hamilton▲ 2,737 B4
Hardin▲ 2,940 J5
Harlem 882 H2
Harlowton▲ 1,049 F4
Harrison 94 E5
Hathaway 55 K4
Haugan 90 A3
Havre▲ 10,201 G2
Hays 333 H2
Heart Butte 499 C2
Helena (cap.)▲ 24,569 E4
Helmville 250 C4
Heron 79 A2
Highwood 150 F3
Hilger 38 G3
Hingham 181 F2
Hinsdale 260 K2
Hobson 226 G4
Hodges 50 M4
Hogeland 35 H2
Homestead 50 M2
Hot Springs 411 B3
Hungry Horse 700 C2
Huntley 250 H5
Huson 97 B3
Hysham▲ 361 J4
Ingomar 48 J4
Intake 60 M3
Inverness 150 F2
Jackson 210 C5
Jardine 30 F5
Jeffers 70 E5
Jefferson City 162 E4
Jefferson Island 25 E5
Joliet 522 G5
Joplin 300 F2
Jordan▲ 494 J3
Judith Gap 133 G4
Kalispell▲ 11,917 B2
Kevin 185 D2
Kila 350 B2
Kinsey 100 L4
Kirby 30 J5
Klein 250 H4
Kremlin 304 F2
Lakeside 663 B2
Lakeview 28 E6
Lambert 203 M3
Lame Deer 1,918 K5
Landusky 40 H3
Laurel 5,686 H5
Laurin 60 D5
Lavina 151 H4
Lewistown▲ 6,051 G3
Libby▲ 2,532 A2
Lima 265 D6
Lincoln 473 D4
Lindsay 50 L3
Livingston▲ 6,701 F5
Locate 55 L4
Lodge Grass 517 J5
Lodge Pole 292 H2
Logan 53 E5
Lohman 25 G2
Lolo 2,746 B4
Lolo Hot Springs 25 B4
Loma 200 F3
Lonepine 50 B3
Lothair 29 E2
Malta▲ 2,340 J2
Manhattan 1,034 E5
Marion 450 B2
Martinsdale 75 F4
Marysville 76 D4
Maxville 44 C4
McAllister 55 E5
McLeod 150 G5
Medicine Lake 357 M2
Melrose 350 D5
Melstone 166 H4
Melville 100 F4
Miles City▲ 8,461 L4
Mill Iron 66 M5
Milltown 300 C4
Missoula▲ 42,918 C4
Moccasin 57 F3
Molt 31 H5
Monarch 120 F3
Moore 211 G4
Musselshell 117 H4
Myers 120 J4
Nashua 375 K2
Neihart 53 F4
Nibbe 30 H4
Norris 55 E5
North Havre 1,230 G2
Noxon 800 A3
Nye 50 G5
Oilmont 50 E2
Olney 200 B2
Opheim 145 K2
Oswego 75 L2
Outlook 109 M2
Ovando 300 C3
Pablo 1,298 B3
Paradise 400 B3
Park City 800 H5
Peerless 110 L2
Pendroy 100 D2
Perma 50 B3
Philipsburg▲ 925 C4
Plains 992 B3
Plentywood▲ 2,136 M2
Plevna 140 M4
Polaris 53 C5
Polson▲ 3,283 B3
Pompeys Pillar 300 J5
Pony 130 E5
Poplar 881 L2
Potomac 80 C4
Power 159 E3
Pray 40 F5
Proctor 150 B3
Pryor 654 H5
Radersburg 104 E4
Ramsay 95 D4
Rapelje 50 G5
Ravalli 150 B3
Raymond 26 M2
Raynesford 35 F3
Red Lodge▲ 1,958 G5
Redstone 40 M2
Reedpoint 160 G5
Regina 83 J3
Reserve 80 M2
Rexford 132 A2
Richey 259 L3
Richland 48 K2
Ringling 102 F4
Roberts 312 G5
Rocky Boy 150 G2
Rollins 200 B3
Ronan 1,547 C3
Roscoe 40 G5
Rosebud 259 K4
Roundup▲ 1,808 H4
Roy 200 H3
Rudyard 450 F2
Ryegate▲ 260 G4
Saco 261 J2
Saint Ignatius 778 C3
Saint Regis 500 A3
Saint Xavier 200 J5
Saltese 90 A3
Sand Coulee 600 E3
Sanders 50 J4
Santa Rita 120 D2
Savage 300 M3
Scobey▲ 1,154 L2
Seeley Lake 900 C3
Shawmut 66 G4
Sheffield 49 K4
Shelby▲ 2,763 E2
Shepherd 200 H5
Sheridan 652 D5
Sidney▲ 5,217 M3
Silesia 90 H5
Silver Star 125 D5
Simms 200 E3
Simpson 70 F2
Somers 700 B2
Sonnette 42 L5
Springdale 45 F5
Square Butte 48 F3
Stanford▲ 529 F3
Stark 51 B3
Stevensville 1,221 C4
Stockett 500 E3
Stryker 96 B2
Suffolk 45 G3
Sula 200 B5
Sun River 300 E3
Sunburst 437 E2
Superior▲ 881 B3
Swan Lake 100 C3
Sweetgrass 250 E2
Terry▲ 659 L4
Thompson Falls▲ 1,319 A3
Three Forks 1,203 E5
Thurlow 84 K4
Toston 70 E4
Townsend▲ 1,635 E4
Trego 50 B2
Trident 50 E5
Trout Creek 300 A3
Troy 953 A2
Turner 150 H2
Twin Bridges 374 D5
Twodot 285 F4
Ulm 450 E3
Utica 30 F4
Valier 519 D2
Vananda 50 K4
Vandalia 35 J2
Vaughn 2,270 E3
Victor 700 B4
Vida 50 L3
Virgelle 28 F2
Virginia City▲ 142 E5
Volborg 125 L5
Wagner 32 H2
Walkerville 605 D4
Warmsprings 500 D4
Waterloo 102 D5
West Glacier 150 C2
West Yellowstone 913 E6
Westby 253 M2
White Sulphur Springs▲ 963 E4
Whitefish 4,368 B2
Whitehall 1,067 D5
Whitetail 150 L2
Whitewater 100 J2
Whitlash 50 E2
Wibaux▲ 628 M3
Wickes 60 D4
Willow Creek 150 E5
Wilsall 250 F5
Windham 63 F3
Winifred 150 G3
Winnett▲ 188 H4
Winston 120 E4
Wisdom 140 C5
Wise River 150 C5
Wolf Creek 500 D3
Wolf Point▲ 2,880 L2
Woodside 75 B4
Worden 600 H5
Wyola 350 J5
Zurich 60 G2

OTHER FEATURES

Absaroka (range) F5
Allen (mt.) C2
Arrow (creek) F3
Ashley (lake) B2
Battle (creek) G1
Bearhat (mt.) C2
Bears Paw (mts.) G2
Beartooth (mts.) G5
Beaver (creek) J2
Beaverhead (riv.) D5
Benton (lake) E3
Big (lake) G5
Big Belt (mts.) E4
Big Dry (creek) K3
Big Hole (riv.) C5
Big Hole Nat'l Battlefield C5
Bighorn (lake) H5
Bighorn (riv.) J5
Bighorn Canyon Nat'l Rec. Area H5
Big Muddy (riv.) M2
Big Porcupine (creek) J4
Birch (creek) D2
Birch Creek (res.) D2
Bitterroot (range) B4
Bitterroot (riv.) B4
Blackfeet Ind. Res. D2
Blackfoot (riv.) C4
Blackmore (mt.) F5
Bowdoin (lake) J2
Boxelder (creek) H3
Boxelder (creek) M5
Bynum (res.) D2
Cabinet (mts.) A2
Canyon Ferry (lake) E4
Clark Canyon (res.) D6
Clark Fork (riv.) A3
Clarks Fork, Yellowstone (riv.) G6
Cottonwood (creek) E2
Cow (creek) G2
Crazy peak) F4
Crow Ind. Res. H5
Cut Bank (creek) D2
Douglas (mt.) F5
Earthquake (lake) E6
Electric (peak) F6
Elwell (lake) E2
Emigrant (peak) F5
Ennis (lake) E5
Flathead (lake) C3
Flathead (riv.) B2
Flathead, North Fork (riv.) B2
Flathead, South Fork (riv.) C3
Flathead Ind. Res. B3
Flatwillow (creek) H4
Fort Belknap Ind. Res. H2
Fort Peck (lake) K3
Fort Union Trading Post Nat'l Hist. Site N2
Frances (lake) D2
Freezeout (lake) D3
Frenchman (riv.) J1
Fresno (res.) F2
Gallatin (peak) E5
Gallatin (riv.) E5
Georgetown (lake) C4
Gibson (res.) D3
Glacier Nat'l Park C2
Granite (peak) F5
Grant-Kohrs Ranch Nat'l Hist. Site D4
Hauser (lake) E4
Haystack (peak) A3
Hebgen (lake) E6
Helena (lake) E4
Holter (lake) D4
Hungry Horse (res.) C2
Hurricane (mt.) D2
Hyalite (peak) E5
Jackson (mt.) C2
Jefferson (riv.) D5
Judith (riv.) G3
Koocanusa (lake) A2
Kootenai (riv.) A2
Lemhi (pass) C6
Lewis and Clark (range) C3
Lima (res.) D6
Little Bighorn (riv.) J5
Little Bitterroot (lake) B2
Little Dry (creek) K3
Little Missouri (riv.) M5
Lockhart (mt.) D3
Lodge (creek) G1
Lolo (pass) B4
Lone (mt.) E5
Lost Trail (pass) B5
Lower Red Rock (lake) E6
Lower Saint Mary (lake) C2
Madison (riv.) E5
Malmstrom A.F.B. 5,938 E3
Marias (riv.) D2
Martinsdale (res.) F4
Mary Ronan (lake) B3
McDonald (lake) B2
McGloughlin (peak) C4
McGregor (lake) B3
Medicine (lake) M2
Milk (riv.) J2
Mission (range) C3
Missouri (riv.) L3
Musselshell (riv.) J3
Nelson (res.) J2
Ninepipe (res.) C3
Northern Cheyenne Indian Reservation K5
O'Fallon (creek) L4
Pishkun (res.) D3
Poplar (riv.) L2
Porcupine (creek) K2
Powder (riv.) L4
Purcell (mts.) A2
Railley (mt.) C3
Red Rock (lakes) E6
Red Rock (riv.) D6
Redwater (riv.) L3
Rock (creek) C4
Rocky (mts.) D4
Rocky Boy's Ind. Res. G2
Rosebud (creek) K4
Ruby (riv.) D5
Ruby River (res.) D5
Sage (creek) F2
Saint Mary (lake) C2
Saint Mary (riv.) C1
Sandy (creek) F2
Sheep (mt.) C2
Shields (riv.) F4
Siyeh (mt.) C2
Smith (riv.) E3
Sphinx (mt.) E5
Stillwater (riv.) G5
Stimson (mt.) C2
Sun (riv.) D3
Swan (lake) C3
Teton (riv.) E3
Tongue (riv.) K5
Upper Red Rock (lake) E6
Ward (peak) A3
Waterton-Glacier Int'l Peace Park C2
Whitefish (lake) B2
Willow (creek) E2
Willow Creek (res.) D3
Yellowstone (riv.) M3
Yellowstone National Park F6

▲County seat

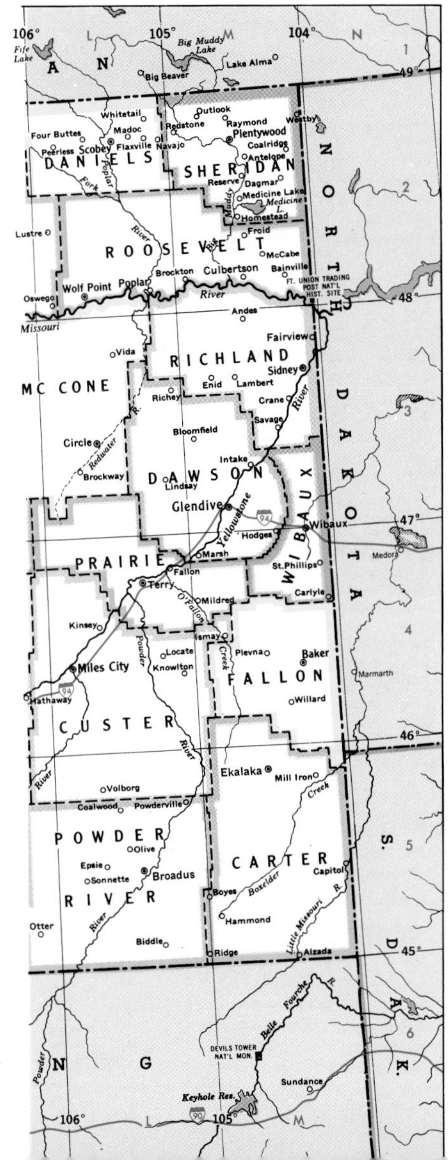
106°
105°
104°
Fife Lake
Big Muddy Lake
Lake Alma
Big Beaver
DANIELS
SHERIDAN
Whitetail
Outlook
Raymond
Westby
Plentywood
Four Buttes
Scobey
Redstone
Medicine Lake
Homestead
ROOSEVELT
Lustre
Froid
Wolf Point
Poplar
Brockton
Culbertson
Bainville
FT. UNION TRADING POST NAT'L HIST. SITE
Oswego
Missouri
River
Andes
Fairview
RICHLAND
Sidney
MC CONE
Vida
Richey
Enid
Lambert
Crane
Savage
Bloomfield
Circle
Brockway
Intake
DAWSON
Lindsay
Glendive
Wibaux
Hodges
WIBAUX
PRAIRIE
Marsh
Fallon
Terry
St. Phillips
Carlyle
Mildred
Kinsey
Ismay
Miles City
Locate
Knowlton
Plevna
Baker
FALLON
Marmarth
Hathaway
Willard
CUSTER
Ekalaka
Mill Iron
Volborg
Coalwood
Powderville
POWDER
RIVER
Olive
Epsie
Sonnette
Broadus
CARTER
Capitol
Boyes
Hammond
Otter
Biddle
Ridge
Alzada
NORTH DAKOTA
SOUTH DAKOTA
Medora
DEVILS TOWER NAT'L MON.
Sundance
Keyhole Res.
49°
48°
47°
46°
45°

COUNTIES

Adams 29,625 F4
Antelope 7,965 F2
Arthur 462 C3
Banner 852 A3
Blaine 675 E3
Boone 6,667 F3
Box Butte 13,130 A2
Boyd 2,835 F2
Brown 3,657 E2
Buffalo 37,447 E4
Burt 7,868 H3
Butler 8,601 G3
Cass 21,318 H4
Cedar 10,131 G2
Chase 4,381 C4
Cherry 6,307 C2
Cheyenne 9,494 A3
Clay 7,123 F4
Colfax 9,139 G3
Cuming 10,117 H3
Custer 12,270 E3
Dakota 16,742 H2
Dawes 9,021 A2
Dawson 19,940 E4
Deuel 2,237 B3
Dixon 6,143 H2
Dodge 34,500 H3
Douglas 416,444 H3
Dundy 2,582 C4
Fillmore 7,103 G4
Franklin 3,938 F4
Frontier 3,101 D4
Furnas 5,553 E4
Gage 22,794 H4
Garden 2,460 B3
Garfield 2,141 F3
Gosper 1,928 E4
Grant 769 C3
Greeley 3,006 F3
Hall 48,925 F4
Hamilton 8,862 F4
Harlan 3,810 E4
Hayes 1,222 C4
Hitchcock 3,750 C4
Holt 12,599 F2
Hooker 793 C3
Howard 6,055 F3
Jefferson 8,759 G4
Johnson 4,673 H4
Kearney 6,629 F4
Keith 8,584 C3
Keya Paha 1,029 E2
Kimball 4,108 A3
Knox 9,534 G2
Lancaster 213,641 H4
Lincoln 32,508 D4
Logan 878 D3
Loup 683 E3
Madison 32,655 G3
McPherson 546 C3
Merrick 8,042 F3
Morrill 5,423 A3
Nance 4,275 F3
Nemaha 7,980 J4
Nuckolls 5,786 F4
Otoe 14,252 H4
Pawnee 3,317 H4
Perkins 3,367 C4
Phelps 9,715 E4
Pierce 7,827 G2
Platte 29,820 G3
Polk 5,675 G3
Red Willow 11,705 D4
Richardson 9,937 J4
Rock 2,019 E2
Saline 12,715 G4
Sarpy 102,583 H3
Saunders 18,285 H3
Scotts Bluff 36,025 A3
Seward 15,450 G4
Sheridan 6,750 B2
Sherman 3,718 F3
Sioux 1,549 A2
Stanton 6,244 G3
Thayer 6,635 G4
Thomas 851 D3
Thurston 6,936 H2
Valley 5,169 E3
Washington 16,607 H3
Wayne 9,364 G2
Webster 4,279 F4
Wheeler 948 F3
York 14,428 G4

CITIES and TOWNS

Adams 472 H4
Ainsworth▲ 1,870 D2
Albion▲ 1,916 F3
Alda 540 F4
Alexandria 224 G4
Allen 331 H2
Alliance▲ 9,765 A2
Alma▲ 1,226 E4
Alvo 164 H4
Amherst 231 E4
Anselmo 189 E3
Ansley 555 E3
Arapahoe 1,001 E4
Arcadia 385 F3
Arlington 1,178 H3
Arnold 679 D3
Arthur▲ 128 C3
Ashland 2,136 H3
Ashton 251 F3
Atkinson 1,380 E2
Auburn▲ 3,443 J4
Aurora▲ 3,810 F4
Avoca 254 H4
Axtell 707 E4
Bancroft 494 H2
Bartlett▲ 131 F3
Bartley 339 D4
Bassett▲ 739 E2
Battle Creek 997 G3
Bayard 1,196 A3
Beatrice▲ 12,354 H4
Beaver City▲ 707 E4
Beaver Crossing 448 G4
Bee 209 H3
Beemer 672 H3
Belden 149 G2
Belgrade 157 G3
Bellevue 30,982 J3
Bellwood 395 G3
Benedict 230 G3
Benkelman▲ 1,193 C4
Bennet 544 H4
Bennington 866 H3
Bertrand 708 E4
Big Springs 495 B3
Bladen 280 F4
Blair▲ 6,860 H3
Bloomfield 1,181 G2
Blue Hill 810 F4
Blue Springs 431 H4
Boys Town 794 H3
Bradshaw 330 G4
Brady 331 D3
Brainard 326 G3
Brewster▲ 22 D3
Bridgeport▲ 1,581 A3
Broadwater 160 B3
Brock 143 H4
Broken Bow▲ 3,778 E3
Brownville 148 J4
Brule 411 C3
Bruning 332 G4
Bruno 141 G3
Brunswick 182 G2
Burwell▲ 1,278 E3
Butte▲ 452 F2
Cairo 733 F3
Callaway 539 D3
Cambridge 1,107 D4
Campbell 432 F4
Carleton 144 G4
Carroll 237 G2
Cedar Bluffs 591 H3
Cedar Creek 334 H3
Cedar Rapids 396 F3
Center▲ 112 G2
Central City▲ 2,868 F3
Ceresco 825 H3
Chadron▲ 5,588 B2
Chambers 341 F2
Chapman 292 F3
Chappell▲ 979 B3
Chester 351 G4
Clarks 379 G3
Clarkson 699 G3
Clatonia 296 H4
Clay Center▲ 825 F4
Clearwater 401 F2
Cody 177 C2
Coleridge 596 G2
Columbus▲ 19,480 G3
Concord 156 H2
Cook 333 H4
Cordova 147 G4
Cortland 393 H4
Cozad 3,823 E4
Craig 228 H3
Crawford 1,115 A2
Creighton 1,223 G2
Creston 220 G3
Crete 4,841 G4
Crofton 820 G2
Culbertson 795 C4
Curtis 791 D4
Dakota City▲ 1,470 H2
Dalton 282 B3
Dannebrog 324 F3
Davenport 383 G4
Davey 160 H4
David City▲ 2,522 G3
Dawson 157 J4
Daykin 188 G4
De Witt 598 G4
Decatur 641 H2
Denton 161 H4
Deshler 892 G4
Diller 298 H4
Dix 229 A3
Dodge 693 H3
Doniphan 736 F4
Dorchester 614 G4
Douglas 199 H4
Dunbar 171 J4
Duncan 387 G3
Dwight 227 G3
Eagle 1,047 H4
Edgar 600 F4
Edison 148 E4
Elba 196 F3
Elgin 731 F3
Elkhorn 1,398 H3
Elm Creek 852 E4
Elmwood 584 H4
Elsie 153 C4
Elwood▲ 679 E4
Emerson 791 H2
Endicott 163 G4
Eustis 452 D4
Ewing 449 F2
Exeter 661 G4
Fairbury▲ 4,335 G4
Fairfield 458 G4
Fairmont 708 G4
Falls City▲ 4,769 J4
Farnam 188 D4
Farwell 152 F3
Filley 157 H4
Firth 471 H4
Fordyce 190 G2
Fort Calhoun 648 J3
Franklin▲ 1,112 E4
Fremont▲ 23,680 H3
Friend 1,111 G4
Fullerton▲ 1,452 F3
Funk 198 E4
Garland 247 G4
Geneva▲ 2,310 G4
Genoa 1,082 G3
Gering▲ 7,946 A3
Gibbon 1,525 F4
Giltner 367 F4
Glenvil 304 F4
Goehner 192 G4
Gordon 1,803 B2
Gothenburg 3,232 D4
Grafton 167 G4
Grand Island▲ 39,386 F4
Grant▲ 1,239 C4
Greeley▲ 562 F3
Greenwood 531 H3
Gresham 253 G3
Gretna 2,249 H3
Guide Rock 290 F4
Gurley 198 B3
Hadar 291 G2
Haigler 225 C4
Hallam 309 H4
Hampton 432 G4
Hardy 206 G4
Harrisburg▲ 75 A3
Harrison▲ 291 A2
Hartington▲ 1,583 G2
Harvard 976 F4
Hastings 22,837 F4
Hay Springs 693 B2
Hayes Center▲ 259 C4
Hebron▲ 1,765 G4
Hemingford 953 A2
Henderson 999 G4
Henry 145 A2
Herman 186 H3
Hershey 579 D3
Hickman 1,081 H4
Hildreth 364 E4
Holbrook 233 D4
Holdrege▲ 5,671 E4
Holstein 207 F4
Homer 553 H2
Hooper 850 H3
Hordville 164 G3
Hoskins 307 G2
Howells 615 H3
Hubbard 199 H2
Humboldt 1,003 J4
Humphrey 741 G3
Hyannis▲ 210 C3
Imperial▲ 2,007 C4
Indianola 672 D4
Inglewood 286 H3
Inman 159 F2
Jackson 230 H2
Johnson 323 J4
Juniata 811 F4
Kearney▲ 24,396 E4
Kenesaw 818 F4
Kennard 371 H3
Kimball▲ 2,574 A3
La Vista 9,840 J3
Laurel 981 G2
Lawrence 323 F4
Leigh 447 G3
Lewellen 307 B3
Lexington▲ 6,601 E4
Lincoln (cap.)▲ 191,972 H4
Lindsay 321 G3
Litchfield 314 E3
Lodgepole 368 B3
Long Pine 396 E2
Loomis 376 E4
Louisville 998 H3
Loup City▲ 1,104 E3
Lyman 452 A3
Lynch 296 F2
Lyons 1,144 H3
Macy 836 H2
Madison▲ 2,135 G3
Madrid 288 C4
Malcolm 181 H4
Manley 170 H4
Marquette 211 G4
Mason City 160 E3
Max 285 C4
Maxwell 410 D3
Maywood 313 D4
McCook▲ 8,112 D4
McCool Junction 372 G4
Mead 513 H3
Meadow Grove 332 G2
Merna 377 E3
Merriman 151 C2
Milford 1,886 H4
Milligan 328 G4
Minatare 807 A3
Minden▲ 2,749 F4
Mitchell 1,743 A3
Monroe 309 G3
Morrill 974 A3
Mullen▲ 554 C2
Murdock 267 H4
Murray 418 J4
Nebraska City▲ 6,547 J4
Nehawka 260 H4
Neligh▲ 1,742 G2
Nelson▲ 627 F4
Nemaha 188 J4
Newcastle 271 H2
Newman Grove 787 G3
Newport 136 E2
Nickerson 291 H3
Niobrara 376 G2
Norfolk 21,476 G2
North Bend 1,249 H3
North Loup 361 F3
North Platte▲ 22,605 D3
O'Neill▲ 4,049 F2
Oakdale 362 F2
Oakland 1,279 H3
Oconto 147 E3
Odell 291 H4
Ogallala▲ 5,095 C3
Ohiowa 146 G4
Omaha▲ 335,795 J3
Orchard 439 F2
Ord▲ 2,481 F3
Orleans 490 E4
Osceola▲ 879 G3
Oshkosh▲ 986 B3
Osmond 774 G2
Otoe 196 H4
Overton 547 E4
Oxford 949 E4
Page 191 F2
Palisade 381 C4
Palmer 753 F3
Palmyra 545 H4
Panama 207 H4
Papillion▲ 10,372 J3
Pawnee City▲ 1,008 H4
Paxton 536 C3
Pender▲ 1,208 H2
Peru 1,110 J4
Petersburg 388 G3
Phillips 316 F4
Pickrell 201 H4
Pierce▲ 1,615 G2
Pilger 361 G2
Plainview 1,333 G2
Platte Center 387 G3
Plattsmouth▲ 6,412 J3
Pleasant Dale 253 G4
Pleasanton 372 E4
Plymouth 455 G4
Polk 345 G3
Ponca▲ 877 H2
Potter 388 A3
Prague 282 H3
Ralston 6,236 J3
Randolph 983 G2
Ravenna 1.317 F4
Raymond 167 H4
Red Cloud▲ 1,204 F4
Republican City 199 E4
Rising City 341 G3
Riverdale 208 E4
Riverton 162 F4
Rosalie 178 H2
Rose 247 E2
Roseland 254 F4
Rulo 191 J4
Rushville▲ 1,127 B2
Ruskin 187 G4
Saint Edward 822 G3
Saint Paul▲ 2,009 F3
Salem 160 J4
Santee 365 G2
Sargent 710 E3
Schuyler▲ 4,052 G3
Scotia 318 F3
Scottsbluff 13,711 A3
Scribner 950 H3
Seward▲ 5,634 H4
Shelby 690 G3
Shelton 954 F4
Shickley 360 G4
Shubert 237 J4
Sidney▲ 5,959 B3
Silver Creek 625 G3
Snyder 280 H3
South Sioux City 9,677 H2
Spalding 592 F3
Spencer 536 F2
Sprague 157 H4
Springfield 1,426 H3
Springview▲ 304 E2
Stamford 188 E4
Stanton▲ 1,549 G3
Staplehurst 281 G4
Stapleton▲ 299 D3
Stella 248 J4
Sterling 451 H4
Stockville▲ 32 D4
Stratton 427 C4
Stromsburg 1,241 G3
Stuart 650 E2
Sumner 210 E4
Superior 2,397 F4
Sutherland 1,032 C3
Sutton 1,353 G4
Swanton 145 H4
Syracuse 1,646 H4
Table Rock 308 H4
Talmage 246 H4
Taylor▲ 186 E3
Tecumseh▲ 1,702 H4
Tekamah▲ 1,852 H3
Terrytown 656 A3
Thedford▲ 243 D3
Tilden 895 G2

Agriculture, Industry and Resources

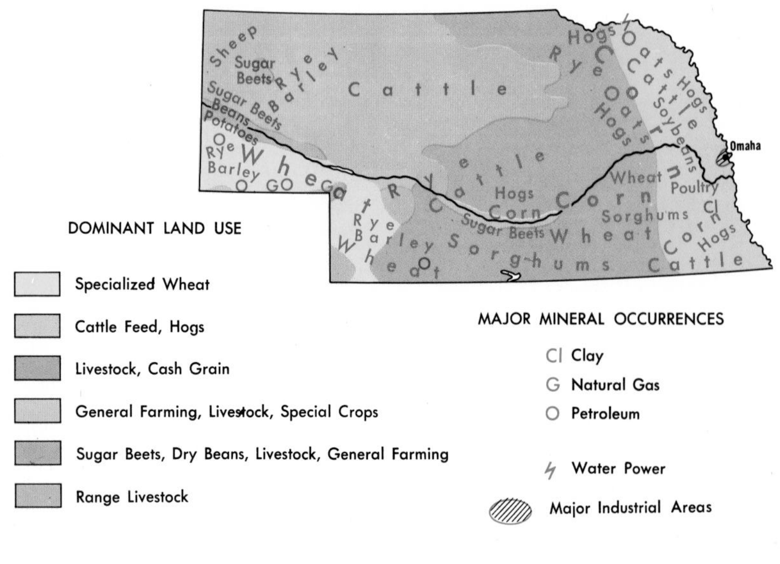
Cattle
Sheep
Sugar Beets
Rye
Barley
Potatoes
Wheat
Hogs
Oats
Corn
Soybeans
Poultry
Sorghums
Omaha
DOMINANT LAND USE
Specialized Wheat
Cattle Feed, Hogs
Livestock, Cash Grain
General Farming, Livestock, Special Crops
Sugar Beets, Dry Beans, Livestock, General Farming
Range Livestock
MAJOR MINERAL OCCURRENCES
Cl Clay
G Natural Gas
O Petroleum
Water Power
Major Industrial Areas

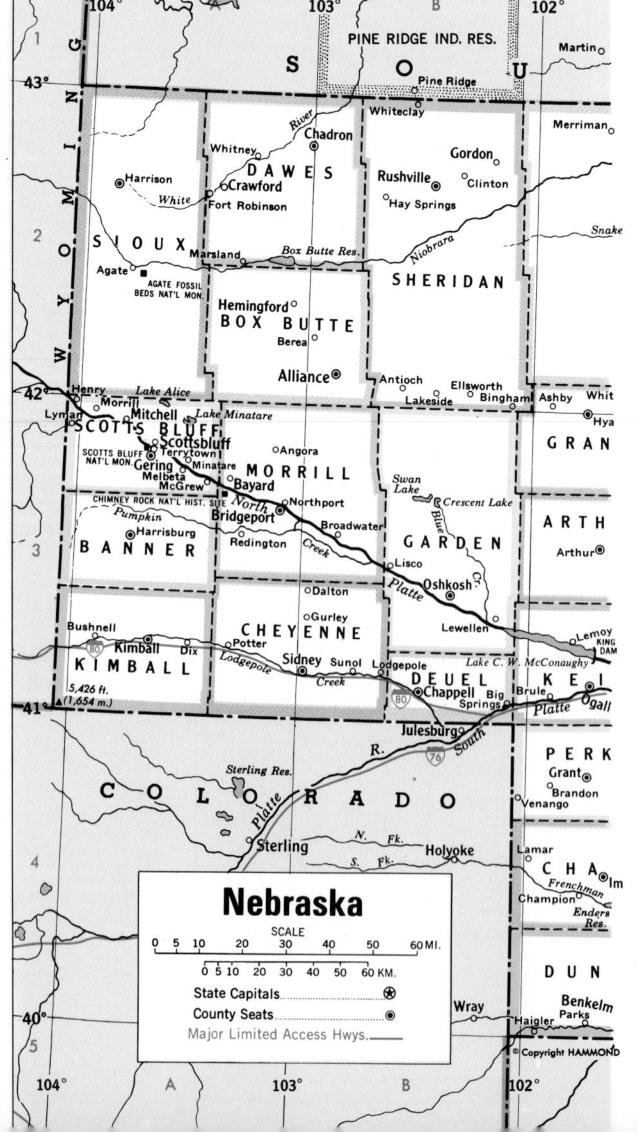
Nebraska
SCALE
0 5 10 20 30 40 50 60 MI.
0 5 10 20 30 40 50 60 KM.
State Capitals
County Seats
Major Limited Access Hwys.
© Copyright HAMMOND
PINE RIDGE IND. RES.
DAWES
SHERIDAN
BOX BUTTE
SCOTTS BLUFF
MORRILL
BANNER
GARDEN
CHEYENNE
KIMBALL
DEUEL
COLORADO
WYOMING

Trenton▲ 656 ..... D4
Trumbull 225 ..... F4
Tryon▲ 139 ..... C3
Uehling 273 ..... H3
Ulysses 256 ..... G3
Unadilla 294 ..... H4
Union 299 ..... J4
Upland 169 ..... F4
Utica 718 ..... G4
Valentine▲ 2,826 ..... D2
Valley 1,775 ..... H3
Valparaiso 481 ..... H3
Venango 192 ..... C4
Verdigre 607 ..... F2
Verdon 242 ..... J4
Waco 211 ..... G4
Wahoo▲ 3,681 ..... H3
Wakefield 1,082 ..... H2
Wallace 308 ..... C4
Walthill 747 ..... H2
Waterloo 479 ..... H3
Wauneta 675 ..... C4
Wausa 598 ..... G2
Waverly 1,869 ..... H4
Wayne▲ 5,142 ..... G2
Weeping Water 1,008 ..... J4
West Point▲ 3,250 ..... H3
Western 264 ..... G4
Weston 299 ..... H3
Wilber▲ 1,527 ..... G4
Wilcox 349 ..... E4
Wilsonville 136 ..... D4
Winnebago 705 ..... H2
Winside 434 ..... G2
Wisner 1,253 ..... H3
Wolbach 280 ..... F3
Wood River 1,156 ..... F4
Wymore 1,611 ..... H4
Wynot 213 ..... G2
York▲ 7,884 ..... G4
Yutan 626 ..... H3

OTHER FEATURES

Agate Fossil Beds Nat'l Mon. .. A2
Alice (lake) A2
Beaver (creek) D5
Big Blue (riv.) H4
Blue (creek) B3
Box Butte (res.) A2
Cedar (riv.) F3
Chimney Rock Nat'l Hist. Site . A3
Colamus (riv.) E2
Crescent (lake) B3
Dads (lake) D2
Dismal (riv.) C3
Elkhorn (riv.) G3
Enders (res.) C4
Frenchman (creek) C4
Gavins Point (dam) G2
Harlan County (lake) E5
Harry Strunk (lake) D4
Homestead Nat'l Mon. H4
Hugh Butler (lake) D4
Jeffrey (res.) D4
Johnson (lake) E4
Keya Paha (riv.) D1
Kingsley (dam) C3
Lewis and Clark (lake) G2
Little Blue (riv.) H5
Lodgepole (creek) A3
Logan (creek) H2
Loup (riv.) F3
Maloney (res.) D3
McConaughy, C. W. (lake) C3
Medicine (creek) D4
Medicine Creek (dam) D4
Merritt (res.) D2
Middle Loup (riv.) D3
Minatare (lake) A3
Missouri (riv.) H3
Moon (lake) E2
Niobrara (riv.) E2
North Loup (riv.) E3
North Platte (riv.) B3
Offutt A.F.B. J3
Omaha Ind. Res. H2
Pelican (lake) D2
Platte (riv.) E4
Pumpkin (creek) A3
Republican (riv.) G5
Santee Ind. Res. G2
Scotts Bluff Nat'l Mon. A3
Sherman (res.) E3
Snake (riv.) C2
South Loup (riv.) E3
South Platte (riv.) C3
Sutherland (res.) C3
Swan (lake) B3
Swanson (lake) D4
White (riv.) A2
Winnebago Ind. Res. H2

▲County seat

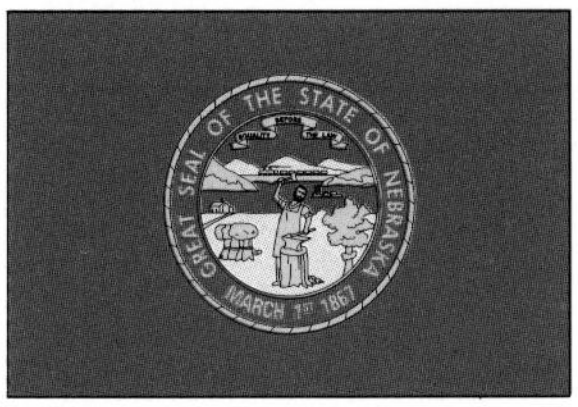

AREA 77,355 sq. mi. (200,349 sq. km.)
POPULATION 1,584,617
CAPITAL Lincoln
LARGEST CITY Omaha
HIGHEST POINT (Kimball Co.) 5,246 ft. (1654 m.)
SETTLED IN 1847
ADMITTED TO UNION March 1, 1867
POPULAR NAME Cornhusker State
STATE FLOWER Goldenrod
STATE BIRD Western Meadowlark

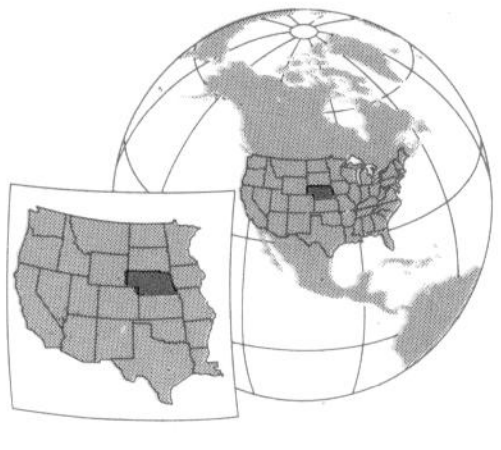

Topography

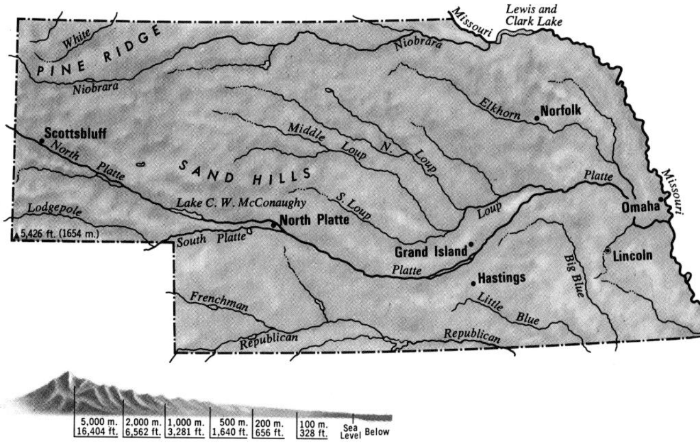

0 50 100 MI.
0 50 100 KM.

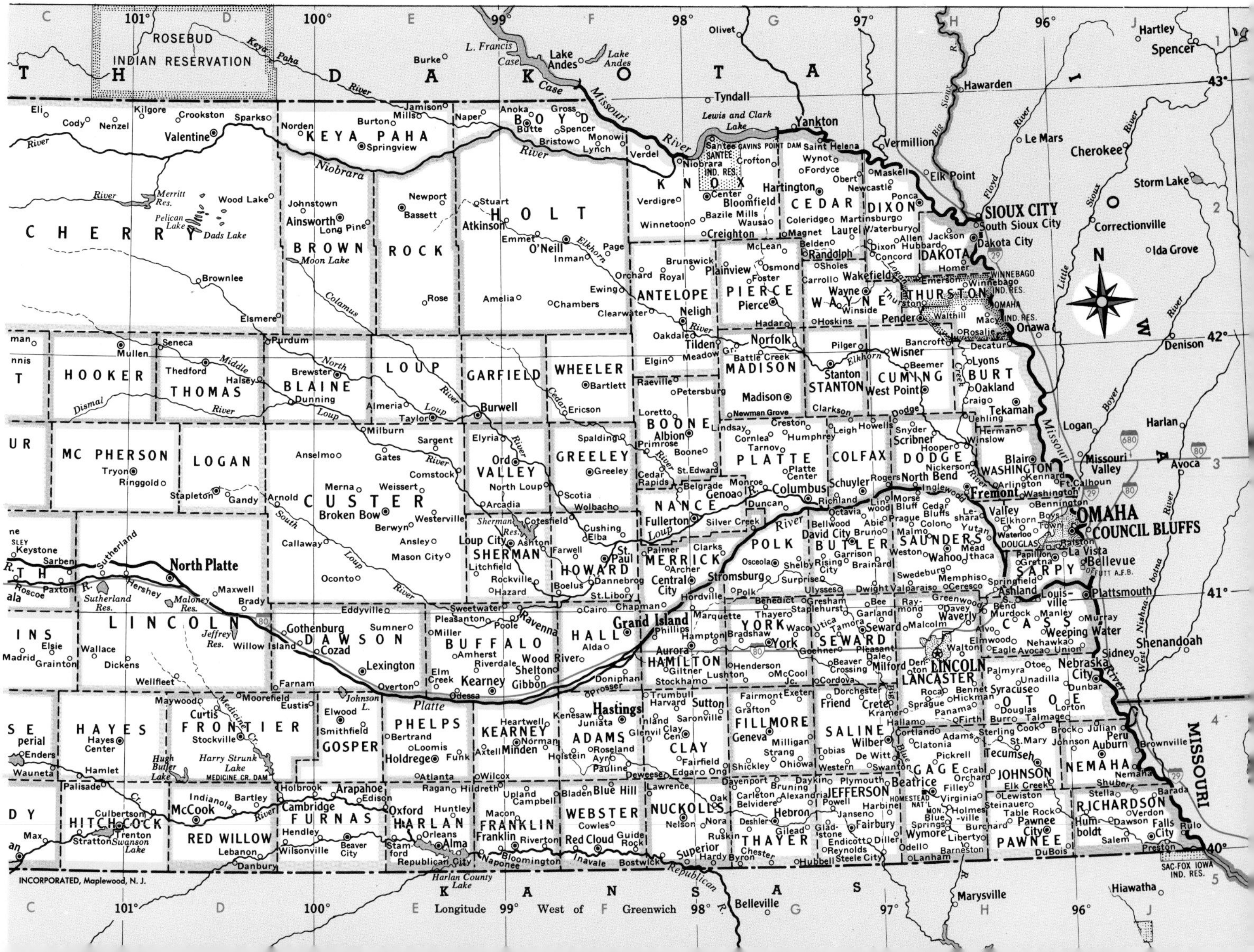

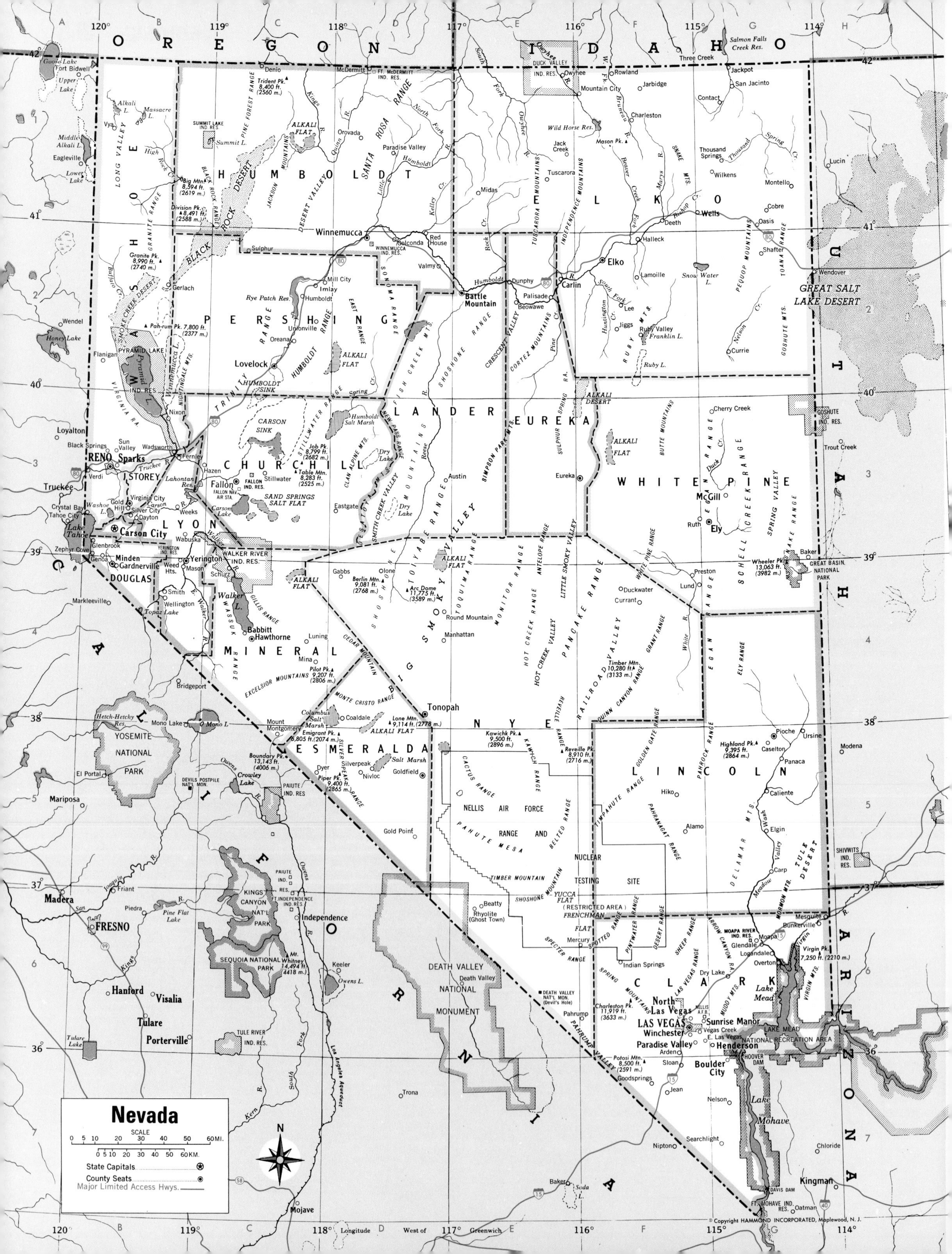

Nevada
SCALE
0 5 10 20 30 40 50 60 MI.
0 5 10 20 30 40 50 60 KM.
State Capitals
County Seats
Major Limited Access Hwys.
OREGON
IDAHO
UTAH
ARIZONA
CALIFORNIA
WASHOE
HUMBOLDT
ELKO
PERSHING
LANDER
EUREKA
WHITE PINE
CHURCHILL
STOREY
LYON
DOUGLAS
MINERAL
ESMERALDA
NYE
LINCOLN
CLARK
Carson City
RENO
Sparks
Winnemucca
Elko
Lovelock
Battle Mountain
Eureka
Ely
Fallon
Yerington
Minden
Hawthorne
Tonopah
Goldfield
Pioche
LAS VEGAS
North Las Vegas
Henderson
Boulder City
Austin
Wells
Carlin
McGill
Lake Tahoe
Pyramid Lake
Walker L.
Lake Mead
Lake Mohave
GREAT SALT LAKE DESERT
BLACK ROCK DESERT
NELLIS AIR FORCE RANGE AND NUCLEAR TESTING SITE
DEATH VALLEY NATIONAL MONUMENT
YOSEMITE NATIONAL PARK
SEQUOIA NATIONAL PARK
KINGS CANYON NAT'L PARK
GREAT BASIN NATIONAL PARK
LAKE MEAD NATIONAL RECREATION AREA
Wheeler Pk. 13,063 ft. (3982 m.)
Boundary Pk. 13,143 ft. (4006 m.)
Charleston Pk. 11,919 ft. (3633 m.)
Mt. Whitney 14,494 ft. (4418 m.)
FRESNO
Madera
Hanford
Visalia
Tulare
Porterville
Kingman
Independence
Mojave
Truckee
120°
119°
118°
117°
116°
115°
114°
42°
41°
40°
39°
38°
37°
36°
Longitude West of Greenwich
© Copyright HAMMOND INCORPORATED, Maplewood, N. J.

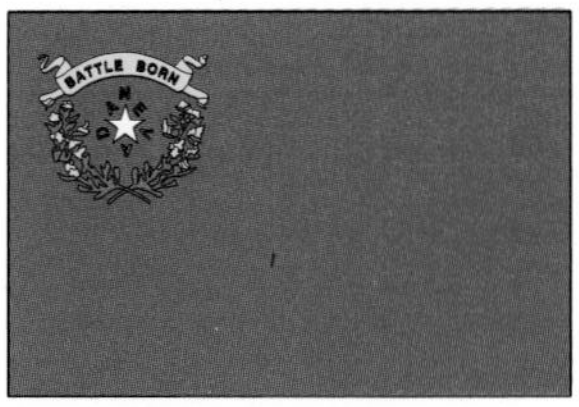
BATTLE BORN

AREA 110,561 sq. mi. (286,353 sq. km.)
POPULATION 1,206,152
CAPITAL Carson City
LARGEST CITY Las Vegas
HIGHEST POINT Boundary Pk. 13,143 ft. (4006 m.)
SETTLED IN 1850
ADMITTED TO UNION October 31, 1864
POPULAR NAME Silver State; Sagebrush State
STATE FLOWER Sagebrush
STATE BIRD Mountain Bluebird

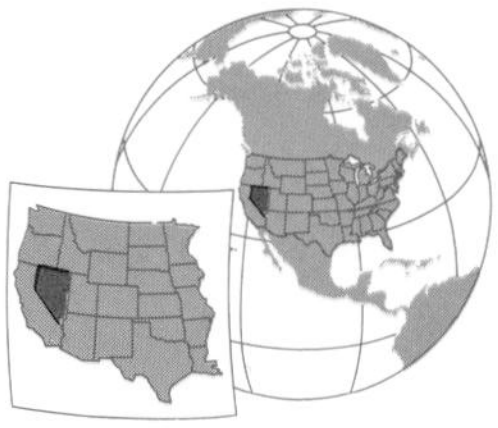

MAJOR MINERAL OCCURRENCES

- Ag Silver
- Au Gold
- Ba Barite
- Cu Copper
- Gp Gypsum
- Hg Mercury
- Lt Lithium
- Mg Magnesium
- Mo Molybdenum
- Na Salt
- O Petroleum
- Pb Lead
- S Sulfur
- W Tungsten
- Zn Zinc
- ϟ Water Power

DOMINANT LAND USE

- General Farming, Dairy, Livestock
- General Farming, Livestock, Special Crops
- Range Livestock
- Forests
- Nonagricultural Land

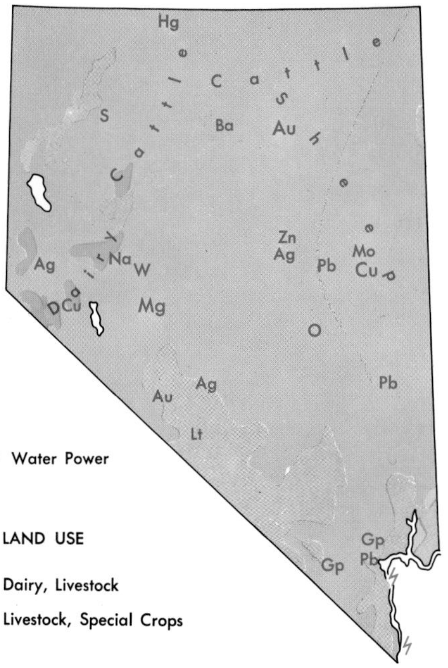
Cattle
Sheep
Dairy
Hg
S
Ba
Au
Zn
Ag
Mo
Pb
Cu
Na
W
Mg
O
Lt
Gp

Agriculture, Industry and Resources

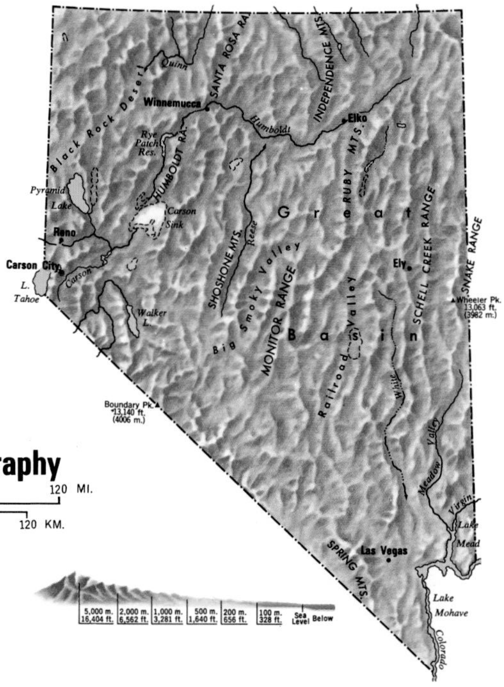
Winnemucca
Elko
Reno
Carson City
Ely
Las Vegas
Great Basin
Black Rock Desert
SANTA ROSA RA.
INDEPENDENCE MTS.
HUMBOLDT RA.
RUBY MTS.
SHOSHONE MTS.
MONITOR RANGE
SCHELL CREEK RANGE
SNAKE RANGE
SPRING MTS.
Humboldt
Quinn
Reese
Carson
Walker
Virgin
Colorado
Pyramid Lake
Carson Sink
Rye Patch Res.
L. Tahoe
Walker L.
Lake Mead
Lake Mohave
Big Smoky Valley
Railroad Valley
Meadow Valley
Wheeler Pk. 13,063 ft. (3982 m.)
Boundary Pk. 13,140 ft. (4006 m.)
5,000 m. 16,404 ft.
2,000 m. 6,562 ft.
1,000 m. 3,281 ft.
500 m. 1,640 ft.
200 m. 656 ft.
100 m. 328 ft.
Sea Level
Below

Topography

0 60 120 MI.
0 60 120 KM.

COUNTIES

Carson City (city) 40,443 .... B3
Churchill 17,938 .... C3
Clark 741,459 .... F6
Douglas 27,637 .... B4
Elko 33,530 .... F1
Esmeralda 1,344 .... D5
Eureka 1,547 .... E3
Humboldt 12,844 .... C1
Lander 6,266 .... D3
Lincoln 3,775 .... F5
Lyon 20,001 .... B3
Mineral 6,475 .... C4
Nye 17,781 .... E4
Pershing 4,336 .... C2
Storey 2,526 .... B3
Washoe 254,667 .... B2
White Pine 9,264 .... F3

CITIES and TOWNS

Alamo 300 .... F5
Austin 300 .... E3
Babbitt C4
Baker 140 .... G3
Battle Mountain▲ 3,542 .... E2
Beatty 1,623 .... E6
Beowawe 77 .... E2
Black Springs 180 .... B3
Boulder City 12,567 .... G7
Bunkerville 300 .... G6
Caliente 1,111 .... G5
Carlin 2,220 .... E2
Carp 30 .... G5
Carson City (cap.) 40,443 .... B3
Caselton G5
Cherry Creek 80 .... G3
Coaldale 31 .... D4
Crystal Bay 6,225 .... A3
Currant 30 .... F4
Dayton 2,217 .... B3
Deeth 125 .... F1
Denio 35 .... C1
Duckwater 80 .... F4
Dunphy 25 .... E2
Dyer 56 .... C5
East Las Vegas 11,087 .... F6
Elko▲ 14,736 .... F2
Ely▲ 4,756 .... G3
Eureka▲ 300 .... E3
Fallon▲ 6,438 .... C3
Fernley 5,164 .... B3
Gabbs 667 .... D4
Gardnerville 2,177 .... B4
Genoa 254 .... B4
Gerlach 400 .... B2
Glenbrook 800 .... B3
Glendale 25 .... G6
Golconda 275 .... D2
Gold Hill 80 .... B3
Goldfield▲ 500 .... D5
Goodsprings 80 .... F7
Halleck 68 .... F2
Hawthorne▲ 4,162 .... C4
Hazen 76 .... C3
Henderson 64,942 .... G6
Hiko 210 .... F5
Imlay 250 .... C2
Indian Springs 1,164 .... F6
Jack Creek E1
Jackpot 400 .... G1
Jean 125 .... F7
Lamoille 100 .... F2
Las Vegas▲ 258,295 .... F6
Lee 125 .... F2
Logandale 410 .... G6
Lovelock▲ 2,069 .... C2
Lund 380 .... F4
Luning 90 .... C4
Manhattan 93 .... E4
Mason 200 .... B4
McDermitt 373 .... D1
McGill 1,258 .... G3
Mercury 900 .... E6
Mesquite 1,871 .... G6
Mina 450 .... C4
Minden▲ 1,441 .... B4
Moapa 3,444 .... G6
Montello 100 .... G1
Mountain City 100 .... F1
Nelson 75 .... G7
Nixon 400 .... B3
North Las Vegas 47,707 .... F6
Oreana 45 .... C2
Orovada 200 .... D1
Overton 1,111 .... G6
Owyhee 908 .... F1
Pahrump 7,424 .... E6
Panaca 650 .... G5
Paradise Valley 115 .... D1
Paradise Valley 84,818 .... F6
Pioche▲ 850 .... G5
Preston 50 .... G4
Reno▲ 133,850 .... B3
Round Mountain 400 .... E4
Ruby Valley 150 .... F2
Ruth 455 .... F3
Schurz 617 .... C4
Searchlight 500 .... F7
Silver City 150 .... B3
Silverpeak 100 .... D5
Sloan 30 .... F7
Smith 1,033 .... B4
Sparks 53,367 .... B3
Stillwater 150 .... C3
Sulphur C2
Sun Valley 11,391 .... B3
Sunrise Manor 95,362 .... F6
Thousand Springs G1
Tonopah▲ 3,616 .... D4
Ursine 45 .... G5
Valmy 200 .... D2
Vegas Creek G6
Verdi 100 .... B3
Virginia City▲ 750 .... B3
Wabuska 150 .... B3
Wadsworth 640 .... B3
Wellington 505 .... B4
Wells 1,256 .... G1
Winchester 23,365 .... F6
Winnemucca▲ 6,134 .... D2
Yerington▲ 2,367 .... B4
Zephyr Cove 1,434 .... A3

OTHER FEATURES

Alkali (lake) B1
Antelope (range) E3
Arc Dome (mt.) D4
Arrow Canyon (range) G6
Beaver Creek Fork, Humboldt (riv.) F1
Belted (range) E5
Berlin (mt.) D4
Big (mt.) B1
Big Smoky (valley) D4
Bishop (creek) F1
Black Rock (des.) B2
Black Rock (range) B1
Boundary (peak) C5
Buffalo (creek) B2
Butte (mts.) F3
Cactus (range) E5
Carson (lake) C3
Carson (riv.) B3
Carson (sink) C3
Cedar (mt.) D4
Charleston (peak) F6
Clan Alpine (mts.) D3
Columbus (salt marsh) C4
Cortez (mts.) E2
Crescent (valley) E2
Davis (dam) G7
Death Valley Nat'l Mon. E6
Delamar (mts.) G5
Desatoya (mts.) D3
Desert (range) F6
Desert (valley) C1
Devil's Hole (Death Valley Nat'l Mon.) E6
Division (peak) B1
Duck (creek) G3
Duck Valley Ind. Res. E1
East (range) D2
East Walker (riv.) B4
Egan (range) G4
Ely (range) G4
Emigrant (peak) C5
Excelsior (mts.) C4
Fallon Ind. Res. C3
Fallon Nav. Air Sta. C3
Fish Creek (mts.) D2
Fort McDermitt Ind. Res. D1
Fort Mohave Ind. Res. G7
Franklin (lake) F2
Frenchman Flat (basin) F6
Gillis (range) C4
Golden Gate (range) F5
Goshute (mts.) G2
Goshute Ind. Res. G3
Granite (peak) B2
Granite (range) B2
Grant (range) F4
Great Basin Nat'l Park G4
Great Salt Lake (des.) H2
High Rock (creek) B1
Highland (peak) G5
Hoover (dam) G7
Hot Creek (range) E4
Hot Creek (valley) E4
Humboldt (range) C2
Humboldt (riv.) E2
Humboldt (salt marsh) D3
Humboldt (sink) C2
Huntington (creek) F2
Independence (mts.) E1
Jackson (mts.) C1
Job (peak) C3
Kawich (range) E5
Kelley (creek) D1
Kings (riv.) C1
Lahontan (res.) B3
Lake Mead National Rec. Area G6
Las Vegas (range) F6
Little Humboldt (riv.) D1
Little Smoky (valley) E4
Lone (mt.) D4
Long (valley) B1
Marys (riv.) F1
Mason (peak) F1
Massacre (lake) B1
Mead (lake) G6
Meadow Valley Wash (riv.) G5
Moapa River Ind. Res. G6
Mohave (lake) G7
Monitor (range) E4
Monte Cristo (range) D4
Mormon (mts.) G5
Muddy (mts.) G6
Nellis A.F.B. 8,377 .... F6
Nellis Air Force Range and Nuclear Test Site E5
Nelson (creek) G2
New Pass (range) D3
Nightingale (mts.) B2
Owyhee (riv.) E1
Pahranagat (range) F5
Pahrock (range) F5
Pah-rum (peak) B2
Pahrump (valley) F6
Pahute (mesa) E5
Pancake (range) F4
Pequop (mts.) G2
Pilot (peak) C4
Pine (creek) E2
Pine Forest (range) C1
Pintwater (range) F6
Piper (peak) D5
Potosi (mt.) F7
Pyramid (lake) B2
Pyramid Lake Ind. Res. B2
Quinn (riv.) D1
Quinn Canyon (range) F4
Railroad (valley) F4
Reese (riv.) D3
Reveille (peak) E5
Reveille (range) E4
Ruby (lake) F2
Ruby (mts.) F2
Rye Patch (res.) C2
Sand Springs (salt flat) C3
Santa Rosa (range) D1
Schell Creek (range) G3
Sheep (range) F6
Shoshone (mt.) E6
Shoshone (mts.) D3
Shoshone (range) E2
Silver Peak (range) D5
Simpson Park (mts.) E3
Smith Creek (valley) D3
Smoke Creek (des.) B2
Snake (mts.) F1
Snake (range) G3
Snow Water (lake) G2
Sonoma (range) D2
Specter (range) E6
Spotted (range) F6
Spring (creek) D2
Spring (mts.) F6
Spring (valley) G3
Stillwater (range) C3
Sulphur Spring (range) E3
Summit (lake) C1
Summit Lake Ind. Res. B1
Table (mt.) C3
Tahoe (lake) B3
Thousand Spring (creek) G1
Timber (mt.) E5
Timber (mt.) F4
Timpahute (range) F5
Toana (range) G2
Toiyabe (range) D3
Topaz (lake) B4
Toquima (range) E4
Trident (peak) C1
Trinity (range) C2
Truckee (riv.) B3
Tule (des.) G5
Tuscarora (mts.) E1
Virgin (mts.) G6
Virgin (peak) G6
Virgin (riv.) G6
Virginia (range) B3
Walker (lake) C4
Walker (riv.) C3
Walker River Ind. Res. C3
Washoe (lake) B3
Wassuk (range) C4
Wheeler (peak) G4
White (riv.) F4
White Pine (range) F3
Wild Horse (res.) E1
Winnemucca (lake) B2
Winnemucca Ind. Res. D2
Yerington Ind. Res. B3
Yucca Flat (basin) E6

▲County seat

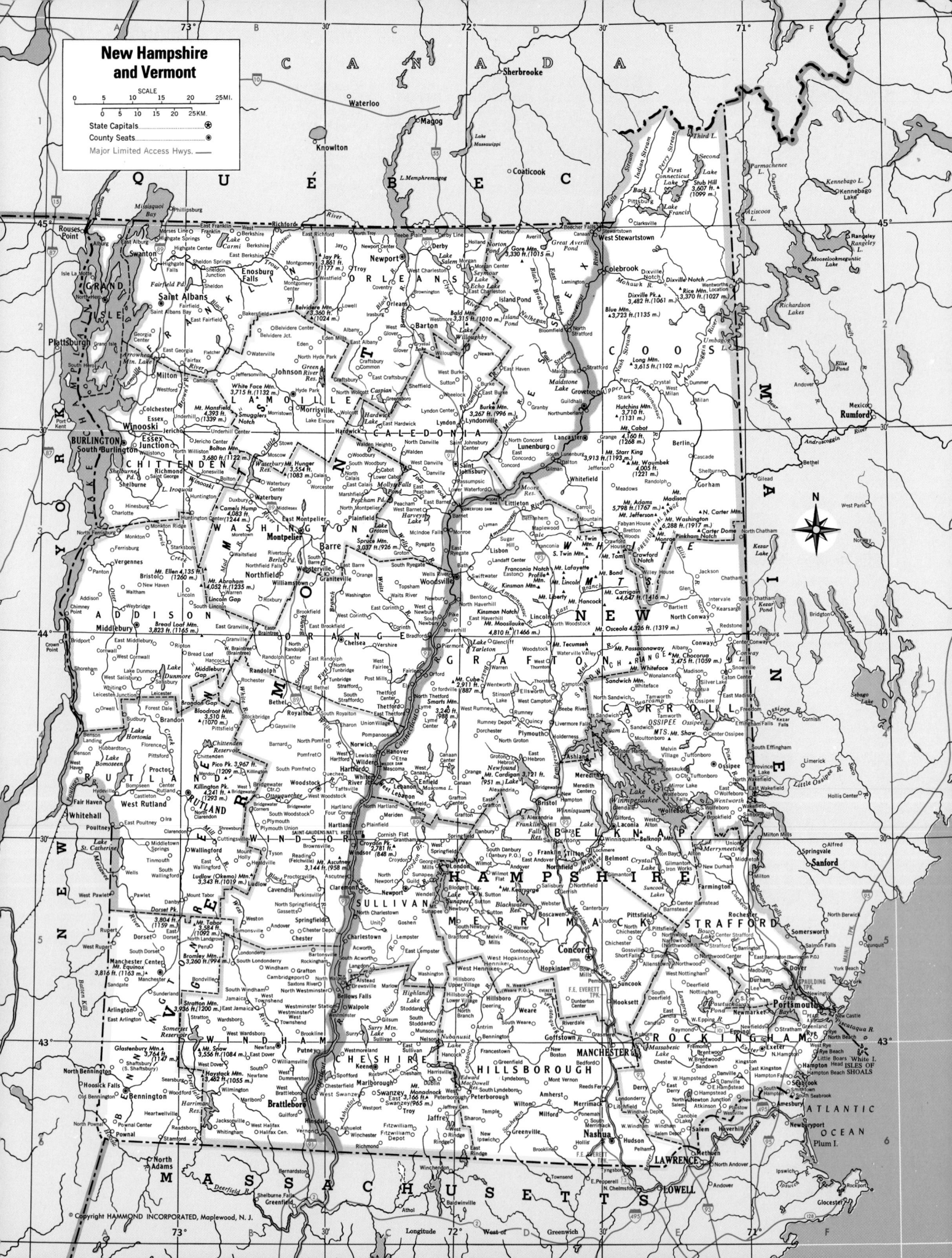

New Hampshire and Vermont
SCALE
0 5 10 15 20 25 MI.
0 5 10 15 20 25 KM.
State Capitals
County Seats
Major Limited Access Hwys.
C A N A D A
Q U É B E C
M A I N E
N E W Y O R K
M A S S A C H U S E T T S
ATLANTIC OCEAN
GRAND ISLE
FRANKLIN
ORLEANS
ESSEX
LAMOILLE
CALEDONIA
CHITTENDEN
WASHINGTON
ADDISON
ORANGE
RUTLAND
WINDSOR
BENNINGTON
WINDHAM
COOS
GRAFTON
CARROLL
BELKNAP
SULLIVAN
MERRIMACK
STRAFFORD
CHESHIRE
HILLSBOROUGH
ROCKINGHAM
NEW HAMPSHIRE
VERMONT
Montpelier
Concord
BURLINGTON
MANCHESTER
Nashua
Portsmouth
LAWRENCE
LOWELL
Sherbrooke
Rumford
Mt. Washington 6,288 ft. (1917 m.)
PRESIDENTIAL RANGE
WHITE MTS.
Lake Winnipesaukee
Lake Champlain
Connecticut R.
Longitude 72° West of Greenwich
73° 30' 72° 30' 71°
45° 44° 43°
© Copyright HAMMOND INCORPORATED, Maplewood, N. J.

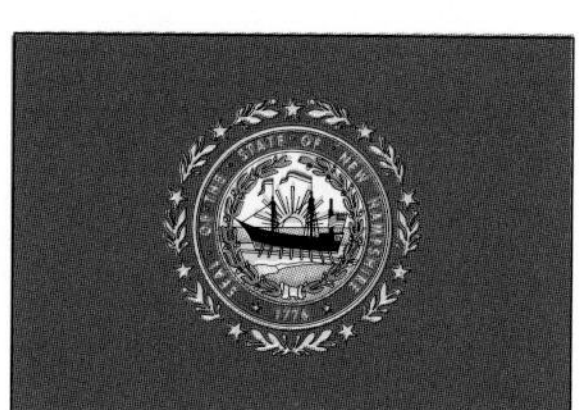

NEW HAMPSHIRE
AREA 9,279 sq. mi. (24,033 sq. km.)
POPULATION 1,113,915
CAPITAL Concord
LARGEST CITY Manchester
HIGHEST POINT Mt. Washington 6,288 ft. (1917 m.)
SETTLED IN 1623
ADMITTED TO UNION June 21, 1788
POPULAR NAME Granite State
STATE FLOWER Purple Lilac
STATE BIRD Purple Finch

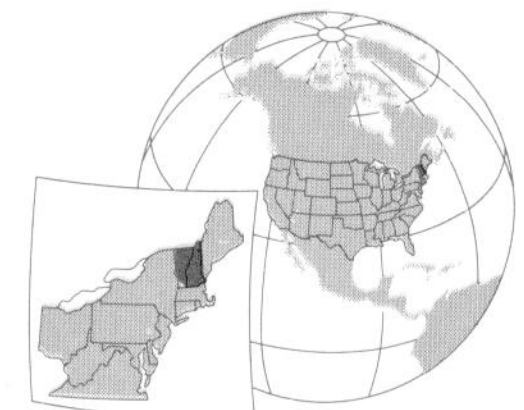

VERMONT
AREA 9,614 sq. mi. (24,900 sq. km.)
POPULATION 564,964
CAPITAL Montpelier
LARGEST CITY Burlington
HIGHEST POINT Mt. Mansfield 4,393 ft. (1339 m.)
SETTLED IN 1764
ADMITTED TO UNION March 4, 1791
POPULAR NAME Green Mountain State
STATE FLOWER Red Clover
STATE BIRD Hermit Thrush

Topography

NEW HAMPSHIRE

COUNTIES

Belknap 49,216 D4
Carroll 35,410 E4
Cheshire 70,121 C6
Coos 34,828 E2
Grafton 74,929 D4
Hillsborough 336,073 D6
Merrimack 120,005 D5
Rockingham 245,845 E5
Strafford 104,233 E5
Sullivan 38,592 C5

CITIES and TOWNS

Acworth• 776 C5
Albany• 536 E4
Alexandria• 1,190 D4
Allenstown• 4,649 E5
Alstead• 1,721 C5
Alton Bay 500 E5
Alton• 3,286 E5
Amherst• 9,068 D6
Andover• 1,883 D5
Antrim 1,325 D5
Antrim• 2,360 D5
Ashland 1,915 D4
Ashland• 1,807 D4
Ashuelot 810 C6
Atkinson• 5,188 E6
Auburn• 4,085 E5
Barnstead• 3,100 E5
Barrington• 6,164 F5
Bartlett• 2,290 E3
Bath• 784 D3
Bedford• 12,563 D6
Beebe River 355 D4
Belmont• 5,796 E5
Bennington• 1,236 D5
Benton• 330 D3
Berlin 11,824 E3
Bethlehem• 2,033 D3
Boscawen• 3,586 D5
Bow Mills 802 D5
Bradford• 1,405 D5
Brentwood• 2,590 E6
Bretton Woods E3
Bridgewater• 796 D4
Bristol 1,483 D4
Bristol• 2,537 D4
Brookfield• 518 E4
Brookline• 2,410 D6
Campton• 2,377 D4
Canaan• 3,045 C4
Candia• 3,557 E5
Canobie Lake 500 E6
Canterbury• 1,687 D5
Carroll• 528 D3
Cascade 350 E3
Center Barnstead 400 E5
Center Conway 558 E4
Center Harbor• 996 E4
Center Ossipee• 800 E4
Center Tuftonboro 300 E4
Charlestown 1,173 C5
Charlestown• 4,630 C5
Chatham• 268 E3
Chester• 2,691 E6
Chesterfield• 3,112 C6
Chichester• 1,942 E5
Chocorua 575 E4
Claremont 13,902 C5
Clarksville• 232 E1
Colebrook 2,444 E2
Colebrook• 2,459 E2
Concord• (cap.) 36,006 D5
Contoocook 1,334 D5
Conway 1,604 E4
Conway• 7,940 E4
Cornish Flat 450 C4
Croydon• 627 C5
Dalton• 827 D3
Danbury• 881 D4
Danville• 2,534 E6
Deerfield• 3,124 E5
Deering• 1,707 D5
Derry 20,446 E6
Derry• 29,603 E6
Dorchester• 392 D4
Dover▲ 25,042 F5
Dublin• 1,474 C6
Dummer• 327 E2
Durham 9,236 F5
Durham• 11,818 F5
East Andover 500 D5
East Hampstead 900 E6
East Kingston• 1,352 F6
East Lempster 300 C5
East Sullivan 300 C6
East Swanzey 500 C6
East Wolfeboro 400 E4
Easton• 223 D3
Eaton (Eaton Center) 362 E4
Ellsworth• 74 D4
Enfield 1,560 C4
Enfield• 3,979 C4
Epping 1,384 E5
Epping• 5,162 E5
Epsom• 3,591 E5
Errol• 292 E2
Etna 550 C4
Exeter▲ 9,556 F6
Exeter• 12,481 F6
Farmington 3,567 E5
Farmington• 5,739 E5
Fitzwilliam• 2,011 C6
Fitzwilliam Depot 350 C6
Francestown• 1,217 D6
Franconia• 811 D3
Franklin 8,304 D5
Freedom• 935 E4
Fremont• 2,576 E6
Georges Mills 375 C5
Gerrish 500 D5
Gilford• 5,867 E4
Gilmanton• 2,609 E5
Gilmanton Iron Works 300 E5
Gilsum• 745 C5
Glen 600 E3
Goffstown• 14,621 D5
Gorham 1,910 E3
Gorham• 3,173 E3
Goshen• 742 C5
Grafton• 923 D4
Grantham• 1,247 C5
Grasmere 400 D5
Greenfield• 1,519 D6
Greenland• 2,768 F5
Greenville 1,135 D6
Greenville• 2,231 D6
Groton• 318 D4
Groveton 1,255 D2
Guild 500 C5
Hampstead• 6,732 E6
Hampton 7,989 F6
Hampton• 12,278 F6
Hampton Beach 975 F6
Hampton Falls• 1,503 F6
Hancock• 1,604 C6
Hanover 6,538 C4
Hanover• 9,212 C4
Harrisville• 981 C6
Haverhill• 4,164 C3
Hebron• 386 D4
Henniker 1,693 D5
Henniker• 4,151 D5
Hill• 814 D4
Hillsboro 1,826 D5
Hillsboro• 4,498 D5
Hinsdale 1,718 C6
Hinsdale• 3,936 C6
Holderness• 1,694 D4
Hollis• 5,705 D6
Hooksett 2,573 E5
Hooksett• 8,767 E5
Hopkinton• 4,806 D5
Hudson 7,626 E6
Hudson• 19,530 E6
Intervale 725 E3
Jackson• 678 E3
Jaffrey 2,558 C6
Jaffrey• 5,361 C6
Jaffrey Center 340 C6
Jefferson• 965 E3
Kearsarge 350 E3
Keene▲ 22,430 C6
Kingston• 5,591 E6
Laconia▲ 15,743 E4
Lancaster▲ 1,859 D3
Lancaster• 3,522 D3
Landaff• 350 D3
Langdon• 580 C5
Lebanon 12,183 C4
Lee• 3,729 F5
Lempster• 947 C5
Lincoln• 1,229 D3
Lisbon 1,246 D3
Lisbon• 1,664 D3
Litchfield• 5,516 E6
Littleton 4,633 D3
Littleton• 5,827 D3
Lochmere 300 D5
Londonderry• 19,781 E6
Loudon• 4,114 E5
Lyman• 388 D3
Lyme• 1,496 C4
Lyndeborough• 1,294 D6
Madbury• 1,404 F5
Madison• 1,704 E4
Manchester 99,567 E6
Marlborough 1,211 C6
Marlborough• 1,927 C6
Marlow• 650 C5
Melvin Village 450 E4
Meredith 1,654 D4
Meredith• 4,837 D4
Meriden 800 C4
Merrimack• 22,156 D6
Middleton• 1,183 E5
Milan• 1,295 E2
Milford 8,015 D6
Milford• 11,795 D6
Milton• 3,691 F5
Milton Mills 450 F4
Mirror Lake 350 E4
Monroe• 746 C3
Mont Vernon• 1,812 D6
Moultonboro• 2,956 E4
Nashua▲ 79,662 D6
Nelson• 535 C5
New Boston• 3,214 D6
New Castle• 840 F5
New Durham• 1,974 E5
New Hampton• 1,606 D4
New Ipswich• 4,014 D6
New London 3,180 D5
New London• 2,935 D5
Newbury• 1,347 C5
Newfields• 888 F5
Newington• 990 F5
Newmarket 4,917 F5
Newmarket• 7,157 F5
Newport▲ 3,772 C5
Newport• 6,110 C5
Newton Junction 450 E6
Newton• 3,473 E6
North Chichester 450 E5
North Conway 2,032 E3
North Hampton• 3,637 F6
North Haverhill 400 D3
North Stratford 600 D2
North Walpole 950 C5
North Weare 400 D5
North Woodstock 750 D3
Northfield-Tilton D5
Northfield• 4,263 D5
Northumberland• 2,492 D2
Northwood• 3,124 E5
Northwood Narrows 325 E5
Nottingham• 2,939 E5
Orange• 237 D4
Orford• 1,008 C4
Ossipee 3,309 E4
Pelham• 9,408 E6
Pembroke• 6,561 E5
Peterborough 2,685 D6
Peterborough• 5,239 D6
Piermont• 624 C4
Pike 433 C3
Pittsburg• 901 E1
Pittsfield 1,717 E5
Pittsfield• 3,701 E5
Plainfield• 2,056 C4
Plaistow• 7,316 E6
Plymouth 3,967 D4
Plymouth• 5,811 D4
Portsmouth 25,925 F5
Randolph• 371 E3
Raymond 2,516 E5
Raymond• 8,713 E5
Redstone 300 E3
Richmond• 877 C6
Rindge• 4,941 C6
Rochester 26,630 E5
Roxbury• 248 C6
Rumney• 1,446 D4
Rye• 4,612 F5
Rye Beach 600 F6
Rye North Beach 700 F5
Salem• 25,746 E6
Salem Depot 975 E6
Salisbury• 1,061 D5
Salmon Falls 950 F5
Sanbornton• 2,136 D5
Sanbornville 750 F4
Sandown• 4,060 E6
Sandwich• 1,066 E4
Seabrook• 6,503 F6
Sharon• 299 D6
Shelburne 437 E3
Shelburne• 318 E3
Silver Lake 350 E4
Somersworth 11,249 F5
South Deerfield 500 E5
South Hampton• 740 F6
South Lyndeboro 300 D6
South Merrimack 650 D6
South Seabrook 500 F6
South Weare 400 D5
Spofford 750 C6
Springfield• 788 C4
Stark• 518 E2
Stewartstown• 1,048 E2
Stoddard• 622 C5
Strafford• 2,965 E5
Stratford• 927 D2
Stratham• 4,955 F5
Sugar Hill• 464 D3
Sullivan• 706 C5
Sunapee• 2,559 C5
Suncook 5,214 E5
Surry• 667 C5
Sutton• 1,457 D5
Swanzey• 6,236 C6
Tamworth• 2,165 E4
Temple• 1,194 D6
Thornton• 1,505 D4
Tilton-Northfield 3,081 D5
Tilton• 3,240 D5
Troy 2,097 C6
Troy• 2,131 C6
Tuftonboro• 1,842 E4
Twin Mountain 500 D3
Unity• 1,341 C5
Wakefield• 3,057 F4
Walpole• 3,210 C5
Warner• 2,250 D5
Warren• 820 D4
Washington• 628 C5
Waterville Valley• 151 D4
Weare• 6,193 D5
Webster• 1,405 D5
Wentworth• 630 D4
Wentworths Location 53 E2
West Campton 400 D4
West Epping 400 E5
West Henniker 500 D5
West Lebanon C4
West Milan 350 E2
West Rye 350 F6
West Stewartstown 700 E2
West Swanzey 1,055 C6
Westmoreland• 1,596 C6
Westville 750 E6
Whitefield 1,041 D3
Whitefield• 1,909 D3
Wilmot Flat 450 D5
Wilmot• 935 D5
Wilton 1,165 D6
Wilton• 3,122 D6
Winchester• 1,735 C6
Windham• 9,000 E6
Winnisquam 500 E5
Wolfeboro 2,783 E4
Wolfeboro• 4,807 E4
Wolfeboro Falls 600 E4
Woodstock• 1,167 D4
Woodsville▲ 1,122 C3

OTHER FEATURES

Adams (mt.) E3
Ammonoosuc (riv.) D3
Androscoggin (riv.) E2
Ashuelot (riv.) C6
Back (lake) E1
Baker (riv.) D4
Bearcamp (riv.) E4
Beaver (brook) E6
Belknap (mt.) E5
Blackwater (res.) D5
Blue (mt.) E2
Bond (mt.) E3
Bow (lake) E5
Cabot (mt.) E2
Cannon (mt.) D3
Cardigan (mt.) D4
Carrigain (mt.) E3
Carter Dome (mt.) E3
Chocorua (mt.) E4
Cocheco (riv.) E5
Cold (riv.) C5
Comerford (dam) D3
Connecticut (riv.) B6
Contoocook (riv.) D6
Conway (lake) E4
Crawford Notch (pass) E3
Croydon (peak) C5
Croydon Branch, Sugar (riv.) C5
Crystal (lake) E5
Cube (mt.) D4
Dixville (peak) E2
Dixville Notch (pass) E2
Edward MacDowell (res.) D6
Ellis (riv.) E3
Everett (dam) D5
Exeter (riv.) E6
First Connecticut (lake) E1
Francis (lake) E1
Franconia Notch (pass) D3
Franklin Falls (res.) D4
Gale (riv.) D3
Great (bay) F5
Halls (stream) E1
Hancock (mt.) D3
Highland (lake) C5
Hutchins (mt.) E2
Indian (stream) E1
Jefferson (mt.) E3
Kearsarge (mt.) D5
Kinsman (mt.) D3
Kinsman Notch (pass) D3
Lafayette (mt.) D3
Lamprey (riv.) E5
Liberty (mt.) D3
Lincoln (mt.) D3
Long (mt.) E2
Mad (riv.) D4
Madison (mt.) E3
Mascoma (lake) C4
Massabesic (lake) E6
Merrimack (riv.) D5
Merrymeeting (lake) E5
Mohawk (riv.) E2
Monadnock (mt.) C6
Monroe (mt.) E3
Moore (dam) D3
Moore (res.) D3
Moosilauke (mt.) D3
Nash (stream) E2
Newfound (lake) D4
North Carter (mt.) E3
North Twin (mt.) D3
Nubanusit (lake) C5
Osceola (mt.) E3
Ossipee (lake) E4
Ossipee (mts.) E4
Ossipee (riv.) F4
Passaconaway (mt.) E4
Pawtuckaway (pond) E5
Pease A.F.B. F5
Pemigewasset (riv.) D4
Perry (stream) E1
Pine (riv.) E4
Pinkham Notch (pass) E3
Piscataqua (riv.) F5
Piscataquog (riv.) D5
Presidential (range) E3
Rice (mt.) E2
Saco (riv.) E3

Agriculture, Industry and Resources

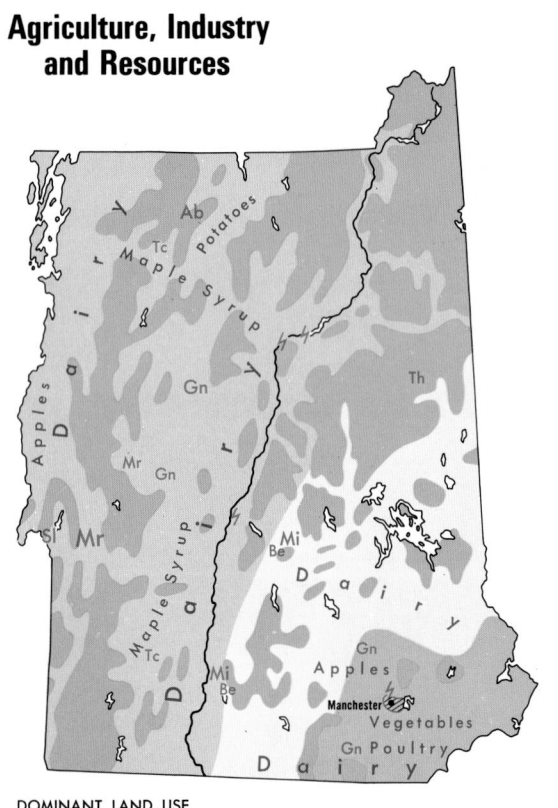

DOMINANT LAND USE

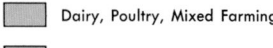

- Specialized Dairy
- Dairy, General Farming
- Dairy, Poultry, Mixed Farming
- Forests
- ⚡ Water Power
- ▨ Major Industrial Areas

MAJOR MINERAL OCCURRENCES

Ab	Asbestos	Mr	Marble
Be	Beryl	Sl	Slate
Gn	Granite	Tc	Talc
Mi	Mica	Th	Thorium

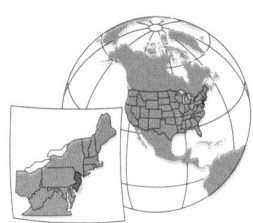

AREA 7,787 sq. mi. (20,168 sq. km.)
POPULATION 7,748,634
CAPITAL Trenton
LARGEST CITY Newark
HIGHEST POINT High Point 1,803 ft. (550 m.)
SETTLED IN 1617
ADMITTED TO UNION December 18, 1787
POPULAR NAME Garden State
STATE FLOWER Purple Violet
STATE BIRD Eastern Goldfinch

Agriculture, Industry and Resources

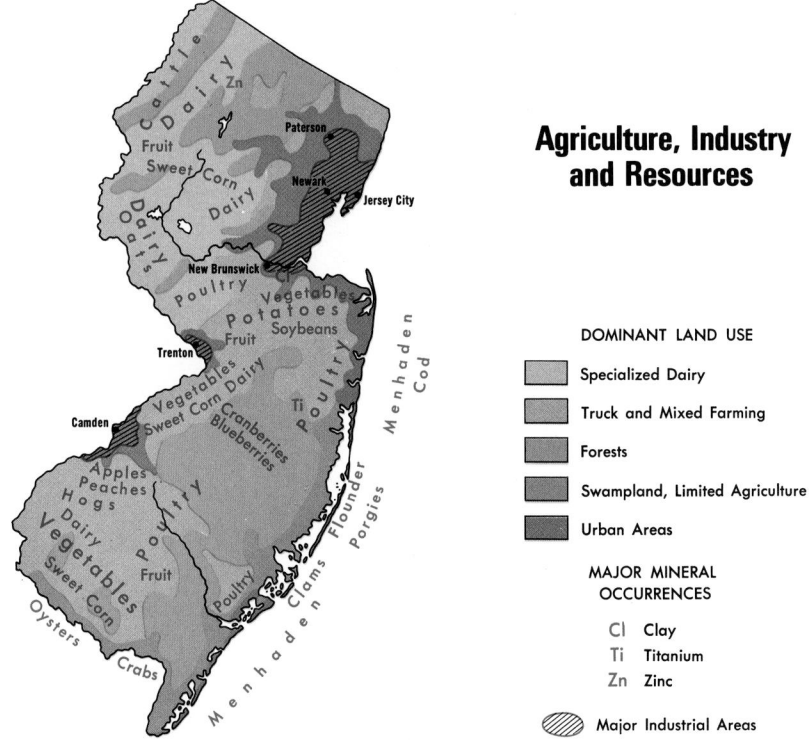

DOMINANT LAND USE

Specialized Dairy

Truck and Mixed Farming

Forests

Swampland, Limited Agriculture

Urban Areas

MAJOR MINERAL OCCURRENCES

Cl   Clay

Ti   Titanium

Zn   Zinc

Major Industrial Areas

The Urban Northeast

Urbanized Areas
● Places with more than 10,000 inhabitants
• Places with 5,000-10,000 inhabitants
· Places with 2,500-5,000 inhabitants

© Copyright HAMMOND INCORPORATED, Maplewood, N. J.

COUNTIES

Atlantic 224,327	D5
Bergen 825,380	E2
Burlington 395,066	D4
Camden 502,824	D4
Cape May 95,089	D5
Cumberland 138,053	C5
Essex 778,206	E2
Gloucester 230,082	C4
Hudson 553,099	E2
Hunterdon 107,776	D2
Mercer 325,824	D3
Middlesex 671,780	E3
Monmouth 553,124	E3
Morris 421,353	D2
Ocean 433,203	E4
Passaic 453,060	E1
Salem 65,294	C4
Somerset 240,279	D2
Sussex 130,943	D1
Union 493,819	E2
Warren 91,607	C2

CITIES and TOWNS

Aberdeen 17,235	E3
Absecon 7,298	D5
Allamuchy 600	D2
Allendale 5,900	B1
Allenhurst 759	F3
Allentown 1,828	D3
Allenwood	E3
Alloway 1,371	C4
Alpha 2,530	C2
Alpine 1,716	C1
Andover 700	D2
Annandale 1,074	D2
Asbury Park 16,799	F3
Ashland	B3
Atlantic City 37,986	E5
Atlantic Highlands 4,629	F3
Audubon 9,205	B3
Audubon Park 1,150	B3
Augusta 500	D1
Aura 500	C4
Avalon 1,809	D5
Avenel 15,504	E2
Avon By The Sea 2,165	E3
Barnegat 1,160	E4
Barnegat Light 675	E4
Barrington 6,774	B3
Basking Ridge	D2
Bay Head 1,226	E3
Bayonne 61,444	B2
Beach Haven 1,475	E4
Beach Haven Crest 500	E4
Beach Haven Terrace 500	E4
Beachwood 9,324	E4
Bedminster● 2,469	D2
Belford	E3
Belle Mead	D3
Belleplain 500	D5
Belleville 34,213	B2
Bellmawr 12,603	B3
Belmar 5,877	E3
Belvidere▲ 2,669	C2
Bergenfield 24,458	C1
Berkeley Heights● 11,980	E2
Berlin 5,672	D4
Bernardsville 6,597	D2
Beverly 2,973	D3
Blackwood 5,120	C4
Blackwood Terrace	C4
Blairstown● 4,360	C2
Bloomfield 45,061	B2
Bloomingdale 7,530	E1
Bloomsbury 890	C2
Bogota 7,824	B2
Boonton 8,343	E2
Bordentown 4,341	D3
Bound Brook 9,487	D2
Bradley Beach 4,475	F3
Branchville 851	D1
Brant Beach 500	E4
Breton Woods	E3
Brick● 66,473	E3
Bridgeport 750	C4
Bridgeton▲ 18,942	C5
Bridgewater● 29,175	D2
Brielle 4,406	E3
Brigantine 11,354	E5
Brooklawn 1,805	B3
Brookside	D2
Browns Mills 11,429	D4
Budd Lake 7,272	D2
Buena 4,441	D4
Burlington 9,835	D3
Butler 7,392	E2
Caldwell 7,549	B2
Califon 1,073	D2
Camden▲ 87,492	B3
Candlewood 6,750	E3
Cape May 4,668	D6
Cape May Court House▲ 4,426	D5

Cape May Point 248	D6
Carlstadt 5,510	B2
Carneys Point 7,686	C4
Carteret 19,025	E2
Cedar Brook 600	D4
Cedar Grove▲ 12,053	B2
Cedar Knolls	E2
Cedarville 900	C5
Cedarwood Park	E3
Chatham 8,007	E2
Chatsworth 700	D4
Cheesequake	E3
Cherry Hill● 69,319	B3
Chesilhurst 1,526	D4
Chester 1,214	D2
Chesterfield● 3,867	D3
Cinnaminson● 14,583	B3
Clark● 14,629	A3
Clarksboro	C4
Clarksburg 800	E3
Clayton 6,155	C4
Clementon 5,601	D4
Cliffside Park 20,393	C2
Cliffwood	E3
Clifton 71,742	B2
Clinton 2,054	D2
Closter 8,094	C1
Cold Spring 500	D6
Collingswood 15,289	B3
Cologne 800	D4
Colonia 18,238	E2
Colts Neck 950	E3
Columbia 600	C2
Columbus 800	D3
Convent Station	E2
Corbin City 412	D5
Cranberry Lake 500	D2
Cranbury 1,255	E3
Cranford● 22,624	E2
Cresskill 7,558	C1
Dayton 4,321	D3
Deal 1,179	F3
Deepwater 800	C4
Delanco● 3,316	D3
Delran● 14,811	B3
Demarest 4,800	C1
Dennisville 890	D5
Denville● 14,380	E2
Deptford● 23,473	B4
Dividing Creek 500	C5
Dorchester 500	D5
Dorothy 900	D5
Dover 15,115	D2
Dumont 17,187	C1
Dunellen 6,528	D2
East Brunswick● 43,548	E3
East Hanover● 9,926	E2
East Keansburg	E3
East Millstone 950	D3
East Newark 2,157	B2
East Orange 73,552	B2
East Rutherford 7,902	B2
Eatontown 13,800	E3
Edgewater 5,001	C2
Edgewater Park● 8,388	D3
Edison● 88,680	E2
Egg Harbor City 4,583	D4
Elberon	F3
Elizabeth▲ 110,002	B2
Elmer 1,571	C4
Elmwood Park 17,623	B2
Elwood 1,538	D4
Emerson 6,930	B1
Englewood 24,850	C2
Englewood Cliffs 5,634	C2
English Creek 500	D5
Englishtown 1,268	E3
Essex Fells 2,363	B2
Estell Manor 1,404	D5
Ewan 610	C4
Ewing 34,185	D3
Fair Haven 5,270	E3
Fair Lawn 30,548	B1
Fairfield● 7,615	A2
Fairton 1,359	C5
Fairview 10,733	C2
Fanwood 7,115	E2
Far Hills 657	D2
Farmingdale 1,462	E3
Fieldsboro 579	D3
Flagtown 800	D2
Flanders	D2
Flemington▲ 4,047	D2
Florence-Roebling 8,564	D3
Florham Park 8,521	E2
Folsom 2,181	D4
Fords 14,392	E2
Forked River 4,243	E4
Fort Lee 31,997	C2
Franklin 4,977	D1
Franklin Lakes 9,873	B1
Franklin Park● 31,358	D3
Franklinville	C4
Freehold▲ 10,742	E3
Frenchtown 1,528	C2
Garfield 26,727	B2

(continued on following page)

Garwood 4,227 E2
Gibbsboro 2,383 B4
Gibbstown 3,902 C4
Gilford Park 8,668 E4
Gillette E2
Glassboro 15,614 C4
Glasser D2
Glen Gardner 1,665 D2
Glen Ridge 7,076 B2
Glen Rock 10,883 B1
Glendora 5,201 B4
Glenwood 500 D1
Gloucester City 12,649 B3
Green Brook D2
Green Creek 600 D5
Green Pond 800 E1
Green Village 800 D2
Greenwich• 973 C5
Grenloch 700 C4
Greystone Park D2
Groveville D3
Guttenberg 8,268 C2
Hackensack▲ 37,049 B2
Hackettstown 8,120 D2
Haddon Heights 7,860 B3
Haddonfield 11,628 B3
Hainesport• 3,236 D4
Haledon 6,951 B1
Hamburg 2,566 D1
Hamilton Square-Mercerville D3
Hammonton 12,208 D4
Hampton 1,515 D2
Harrington Park 4,623 C1
Harrison 13,425 B2
Hartford 650 D4
Harvey Cedars 362 E4
Hasbrouck Heights 11,488 B2
Haskell A1
Haworth 3,384 C1
Hawthorne 17,084 B2
Hazlet 23,013 E3
Helmetta 1,211 E3
Hewitt 950 E1
Hi-Nella 1,045 B4
High Bridge 3,886 D2
Highland Lakes 4,550 E1
Highland Park 13,279 D2
Highlands 4,849 F3
Hightstown 5,126 D3
Hillsdale 9,750 B1
Hillside• 21,044 B2
Ho Ho Kus 3,935 B1
Hoboken 33,397 C2
Holmdel• 8,447 E3
Hopatcong 15,586 D2
Hopewell 1,968 D3
Howell• 25,065 E3
Huntington C2
Interlaken 910 E3
Ironia D2
Irvington 59,774 B2
Iselin 16,141 E2
Island Heights 1,470 E4
Jackson• 25,644 E3
Jamesburg 5,294 E3
Jersey City▲ 228,537 B2
Johnsonburg 600 D2
Juliustown 500 D3
Keansburg 11,069 E3
Kearny 34,874 B2
Keasbey E2
Kendall Park 7,127 D3
Kenilworth 7,574 E2
Keyport 7,586 E3
Kingston 1,047 D3
Kinnelon 8,470 E2
Kirkwood 800 B4
Lafayette 900 D1
Lake Hiawatha E2
Lake Hopatcong D2
Lake Mohawk 8,930 D1
Lakehurst 3,078 E3
Lakewood 26,095 E3
Lambertville 3,927 D3
Landisville D4
Lanoka Harbor E4
Laurel Springs 2,341 B4
Laurence Harbor 6,361 E3
Lavallette 2,299 E4
Lawnside 2,841 B3
Lawrenceville 6,446 D3
Layton 700 D1
Lebanon 1,036 D2
Ledgewood D2
Leeds Point 500 E4
Leesburg 700 D5
Leonardo 3,788 E3
Leonia 8,365 C2
Liberty Corner D2
Lincoln Park 10,978 A1
Lincroft 6,193 E3
Linden 36,701 A3
Lindenwold 18,734 B4
Linwood 6,866 D5
Little Falls• 11,294 B2
Little Ferry 9,989 B2
Little Silver 5,721 F3
Livingston• 26,609 E2
Lodi 22,355 B2
Long Branch 28,658 F3
Long Valley 1,744 D2
Longport 1,224 D5
Lumberton 600 D4
Lyndhurst• 18,262 B2
Lyons D2
Madison 15,850 E2
Magnolia 4,861 B3
Mahwah• 12,127 E1
Malaga 950 C4
Manahawkin 1,594 E4
Manasquan 5,369 E3
Mantoloking 334 E3
Mantua• 9,193 C4
Manville 10,567 D2
Maple Shade• 19,211 B3
Maplewood• 21,756 E2
Marcella 540 E2
Margate City 8,431 E5
Marlboro• 17,560 E3
Marlton 10,228 D4
Marmora 650 D5
Martinsville D2
Matawan 9,270 E3
Mays Landing▲ 2,090 D5
Maywood 9,473 B2
McAfee 800 D1
McKee City 950 D5
Medford D4
Medford Lakes 4,462 D4
Mendham 4,890 D2
Menlo Park E2
Mercerville-Hamilton Square 26,873 D3
Merchantville 4,095 B3
Metuchen 12,804 E2
Mickleton 950 C4
Middlesex 13,055 E2
Middletown• 62,298 E3
Midland Park 7,047 B1
Milford 1,273 C2
Millburn• 18,630 E2
Millington 975 D2
Millstone 450 D2
Milltown 6,968 E3
Millville 25,992 C5
Milmay 798 D5
Milton D1
Mine Hill• 3,325 D2
Minotola D4
Mizpah 900 D5
Monmouth Beach 3,303 F3
Monmouth Junction 1,570 D3
Monroe• 15,858 D1
Montague 750 D1
Montclair 37,729 B2
Montvale 6,946 B1
Montville• 14,290 E2
Moonachie 2,817 B2
Moorestown 13,695 B3
Morganville E3
Morris Plains 5,219 D2
Morristown▲ 16,189 D2
Mount Arlington 3,630 D2
Mount Ephraim 4,517 B3
Mount Freedom D2
Mount Holly 10,639 D4
Mount Hope D2
Mount Laurel• 17,614 D4
Mount Olive• 18,748 D2
Mount Royal 900 C4
Mountain Lakes 3,847 E2
Mountain View B2
Mountainside 6,657 E2
Mullica Hill 1,117 C4
Mystic Islands 7,400 E4
National Park 3,413 B3
Navesink E3
Neptune City 4,997 E3
Neshanic Station D3
Netcong 3,311 D2
New Brunswick▲ 41,711 E3
New Egypt 2,327 E3
New Gretna 800 E4
New Milford 15,990 B1
New Providence 11,439 E2
New Vernon D2
Newark▲ 275,221 B2
Newfield 1,592 D4
Newfoundland 900 D1
Newport 700 C5
Newton▲ 7,521 D1
Newtonville 950 D4
Nixon E2
North Arlington 13,790 B2
North Bergen• 48,414 B2
North Branch 610 D2
North Brunswick• 31,287 D3
North Caldwell 6,706 B2
North Cape May 3,574 C6
North Haledon 7,987 B1
North Plainfield 18,820 E2
North Wildwood 5,017 D6
Northfield 7,305 D5
Northvale 4,563 F1
Norwood 4,858 C1
Nutley 27,099 B2
Oak Ridge 750 E1
Oakhurst 4,130 E3
Oakland 11,997 B1
Oaklyn 4,430 B3
Ocean City 15,512 D5
Ocean Gate 2,078 E4
Ocean Grove 4,818 F3
Ocean View 950 D5
Oceanport 6,146 F3
Oceanville 600 D5
Ogdensburg 2,722 D1
Old Bridge 22,151 E3
Old Tappan 4,254 C1
Oradell 8,024 B1
Orange 29,925 B2
Osbornsville E3
Oxford 1,767 C2
Packanack Lake B1
Palermo 600 D5
Palisades Park 14,536 C2
Palmyra 7,056 B3
Paramus 25,067 B1
Park Ridge 8,102 B1
Parsippany-Troy Hills• 48,478 E2
Passaic 58,041 B2
Paterson▲ 140,891 B2
Paulsboro 6,577 C4
Peapack-Gladstone 2,111 D2
Pedricktown C4
Pemberton 1,367 D4
Pennington 2,537 D3
Penns Grove 5,228 C4
Pennsauken• 34,733 B3
Pennsville 12,218 C4
Pequannock• 12,844 B1
Perth Amboy 41,967 E2
Petersburg 750 D5
Phillipsburg 15,757 C2
Pine Beach 1,954 E4
Pine Brook E2
Pine Hill 9,854 D4
Piscataway• 42,223 D2
Pitman 9,365 C4
Plainfield 46,567 E2
Plainsboro D3
Pleasantville 16,027 D5
Point Pleasant 18,177 E3
Point Pleasant Beach 5,112 E3
Pomona 2,624 D5
Pompton Lakes 10,539 A1
Pompton Plains B1
Port Monmouth 3,558 E3
Port Morris 616 D2
Port Norris 1,701 C5
Port Reading 3,977 E2
Port Republic 992 D4
Princeton 12,016 D3
Princeton Junction 2,362 D3
Prospect Park 5,053 B1
Quinton 750 C4
Rahway 25,325 E2
Ralston 650 D2
Ramblewood 6,181 D4
Ramsey 13,228 B1
Randolph• 17,828 D2
Raritan 5,798 D2
Red Bank 10,636 E3
Richland 950 D5
Ridgefield 9,996 B2
Ridgefield Park 12,454 B2
Ridgewood 24,152 B1
Ringoes 682 D3
Ringwood 12,623 E1
Rio Grande 2,505 D5
River Edge 10,603 B1
River Vale• 9,410 B1
Riverdale 2,370 A1
Riverside• 7,974 B3
Riverton 2,775 B3
Robbinsville 650 D3
Rochelle Park• 5,587 B2
Rockaway 6,243 D2
Rockleigh 270 C1
Rocky Hill 693 D3
Roebling-Florence D3
Roosevelt 884 E3
Roseland 4,847 A2
Roselle 20,314 B2
Roselle Park 12,805 A2
Rosenhayn 1,053 C5
Roxbury• 18,878 D2
Rumson 6,701 F3
Runnemede 9,042 B3
Rutherford 17,790 B2
Saddle Brook• 13,296 B1
Saddle River 2,950 B1
Salem▲ 6,883 C4
Sayreville 34,986 E3
Scotch Plains• 21,160 E2
Sea Bright 1,693 F3
Sea Girt 2,099 E3
Sea Isle City 2,692 D5
Seabrook 1,457 C5
Seaside Heights 2,366 E4
Seaside Park 1,871 E4
Secaucus 14,061 B2
Sewaren 2,569 E2
Sewell C4
Shiloh 408 C5
Ship Bottom 1,352 E4
Shore Acres E3
Short Hills E2
Shrewsbury 3,096 E3
Sicklerville D4
Singac B2
Skillman D3
Smithburg 750 E3
Somerdale 5,440 B4
Somers Point 11,216 D5
Somerville▲ 11,632 D2
South Amboy 7,863 E3
South Belmar 1,482 E3
South Bound Brook 4,185 E2
South Brunswick• 17,127 E3
South Orange• 16,390 A2
South Plainfield 20,489 E2
South River 13,692 E3
South Seaville 600 D5
South Toms River 3,869 E4
Sparta• 13,333 D1
Spotswood 7,983 E3
Spring Lake 3,499 F3
Spring Lake Heights 5,341 E3
Springfield• 13,420 E2
Stanhope 3,393 D2
Stanton 700 D2
Stewartsville 950 C2
Stirling E2
Stockholm D1
Stockton 629 D3
Stone Harbor 1,025 D5
Stratford 7,614 B4
Strathmore 7,060 E3
Succasunna 10,931 D2
Summit 19,757 E2
Surf City 1,375 E4
Sussex 2,201 D1
Swedesboro 2,024 C4
Teaneck• 37,825 B2
Tenafly 13,326 C1
Teterboro 22 B2
Thorofare B4
Three Bridges 750 D2
Tinton Falls 12,361 E3
Titusville 900 D3
Toms River▲ 7,524 E4
Totowa 10,177 B1
Towaco E2
Townsends Inlet D5
Trenton (cap.)▲ 88,675 D3
Tuckerton 3,048 E4
Turnersville 3,843 C4
Union Beach 6,156 E3

Topography

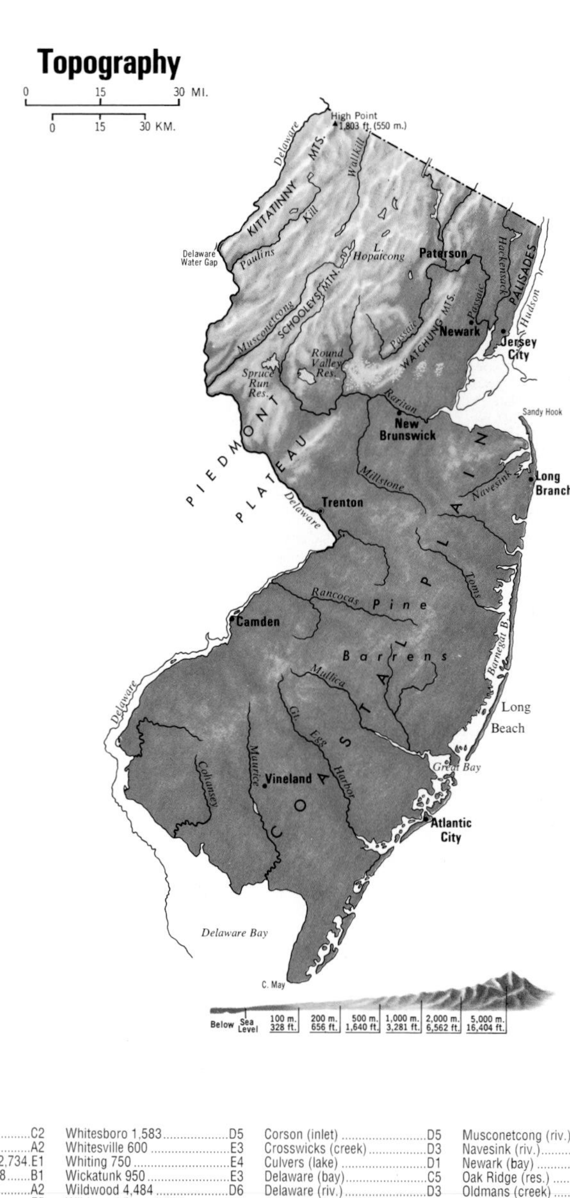

Union City 58,012 C2
Union• 50,024 A2
Upper Greenwood Lake 2,734 E1
Upper Saddle River 7,198 B1
Vauxhall A2
Ventnor City 11,005 E5
Vernon 800 E1
Verona 13,597 B2
Villas 8,136 D5
Vincentown 900 D4
Vineland 54,780 C5
Voorhees• 12,919 B3
Waldwick 9,757 B1
Wall• 18,952 E3
Wallington 10,828 B2
Wanamassa 4,530 E3
Wanaque 9,711 B1
Waretown 1,283 E4
Warren• 9,805 D2
Washington 6,474 D2
Watchung 5,110 E2
Waterford Works 950 D4
Wayne• 47,025 A1
Weehawken• 12,385 C2
Wenonah 2,331 C4
West Berlin D4
West Caldwell 10,422 A2
West Cape May 1,026 D6
West Creek 827 E4
West Deptford• 18,002 B3
West Long Branch 7,690 F3
West Milford 25,430 E1
West New York 38,125 C2
West Orange 39,103 A2
West Paterson 10,982 B2
West Trenton D3
West Wildwood 453 D6
Westfield 28,870 E2
Westmont 15,875 B3
Westville 4,573 B3
Westwood 10,446 B1
Wharton 5,405 D2
Whippany E2
White House Station 1,287 D2
White Meadow Lake 8,002 D2
Whitehouse 852 D2
Whitesboro 1,583 D5
Whitesville 600 E3
Whiting 750 E4
Wickatunk 950 E3
Wildwood 4,484 D6
Wildwood Crest 3,631 D6
Williamstown 10,891 D4
Willingboro• 36,291 D3
Winfield• 1,785 B2
Winslow 950 D4
Wood-Lynne 2,578 B3
Wood-Ridge 7,506 B2
Woodbine 2,678 D5
Woodbridge• 90,074 E2
Woodbury Heights 3,392 B4
Woodbury▲ 10,904 B4
Woodcliff Lake 5,303 B1
Woodport D2
Woodstown 3,154 C4
Wrightstown 3,843 D3
Wyckoff• 15,372 B1
Yardville 9,414 D3

OTHER FEATURES

Absecon (inlet) E5
Alloways (creek) C4
Arthur Kill (str.) B3
Atlantic Highlands (ridge) E3
Barnegat (bay) E4
Batsto (riv.) D4
Bayonne Military Ocean Terminal B2
Beach Haven (inlet) E4
Beaver (brook) C2
Ben Davis (pt.) C5
Big Flat (brook) D1
Big Timber (creek) C4
Boonton (res.) E2
Brigantine (inlet) E5
Budd (lake) D2
Canistear (res.) E1
Cedar (creek) E4
Clinton (res.) E1
Cohansey (riv.) C5
Cooper (riv.) B3
Corson (inlet) D5
Crosswicks (creek) D3
Culvers (lake) D1
Delaware (bay) C5
Delaware (riv.) D3
Delaware Water Gap Nat'l Rec. Area C1
Earle Naval Weapons Sta. E3
Echo (lake) E1
Edison Nat'l Hist. Site A2
Egg Island (pt.) C5
Fort Dix 10,205 D3
Fort Hancock F3
Fort Monmouth E3
Gateway Nat'l Rec. Area E2
Great (bay) E4
Great Egg Harbor (inlet) E5
Greenwood (lake) E1
Hackensack (riv.) C1
Hereford (inlet) D5
High Point (mt.) D1
Hopatcong (lake) D2
Hudson (riv.) C1
Island (beach) E4
Kill Van Kull (str.) B2
Kittatinny (mts.) D1
Lakehurst Naval Air-Engineering Center E3
Lamington (riv.) D2
Landing (creek) D4
Little Egg (harb.) E4
Lockatong (creek) C3
Long (beach) E4
Long Beach (isl.) E4
Lower New York (bay) E2
Manasquan (riv.) E3
Manumuskin (riv.) D5
Maurice (riv.) C4
May (cape) C6
McGuire A.F.B. 7,580 D3
Metedeconk (riv.) E3
Mill (creek) E4
Millstone (riv.) D3
Mohawk (lake) D1
Morristown Nat'l Hist. Park D2
Mullica (riv.) D4
Musconetcong (riv.) C2
Navesink (riv.) E3
Newark (bay) B2
Oak Ridge (res.) D1
Oldmans (creek) C4
Oradell (res.) B1
Oswego (riv.) E4
Owassa (lake) D1
Palisades (cliffs) C1
Passaic (riv.) E2
Paulins Kill (riv.) D1
Pennsauken (creek) B3
Pequest (riv.) D2
Picatinny Arsenal D2
Pohatcong (creek) C2
Pompton (lake) B1
Raccoon (creek) C4
Ramapo (riv.) E1
Rancocas (creek) D3
Raritan (bay) E3
Raritan (riv.) D2
Ridgeway Branch, Toms (riv.) E3
Round Valley (res.) D2
Saddle (riv.) B1
Salem (riv.) C4
Sandy Hook (split) F3
Shoal Branch, Wading (riv.) D4
Spruce Run (res.) D2
Statue of Liberty Nat'l Mon. B2
Stony (brook) D3
Stow (creek) C5
Swartswood (lake) D1
Tappan (lake) C1
The Narrows (str.) E2
Toms (riv.) E3
Townsend (inlet) D5
Tuckahoe (riv.) D5
Union (lake) C5
Upper New York (bay) B2
Wading (riv.) D4
Wallkill (riv.) D1
Wanaque (res.) E1
Wawayanda (lake) E1

▲County Seat
•Population of town or township

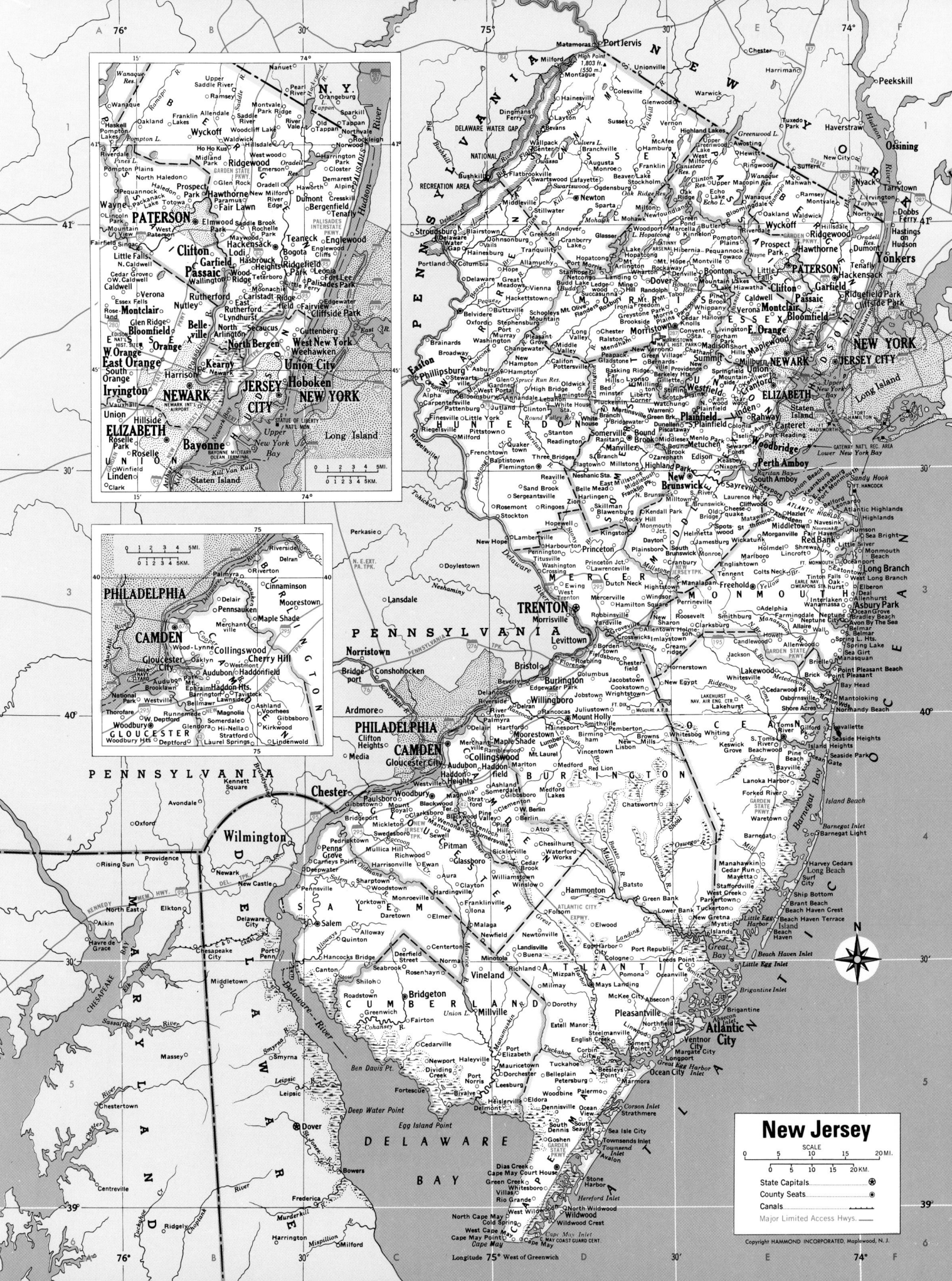

New Jersey
SCALE
0 5 10 15 20 MI.
0 5 10 15 20 KM.
State Capitals
County Seats
Canals
Major Limited Access Hwys.
Copyright HAMMOND INCORPORATED, Maplewood, N. J.
Longitude 75° West of Greenwich
PENNSYLVANIA
NEW YORK
DELAWARE
MARYLAND
DELAWARE BAY
ATLANTIC OCEAN
SUSSEX
WARREN
HUNTERDON
MORRIS
PASSAIC
BERGEN
ESSEX
HUDSON
UNION
SOMERSET
MIDDLESEX
MERCER
MONMOUTH
OCEAN
BURLINGTON
CAMDEN
GLOUCESTER
SALEM
CUMBERLAND
ATLANTIC
CAPE MAY
TRENTON
NEWARK
JERSEY CITY
PATERSON
ELIZABETH
PHILADELPHIA
CAMDEN
Atlantic City

274 New Mexico

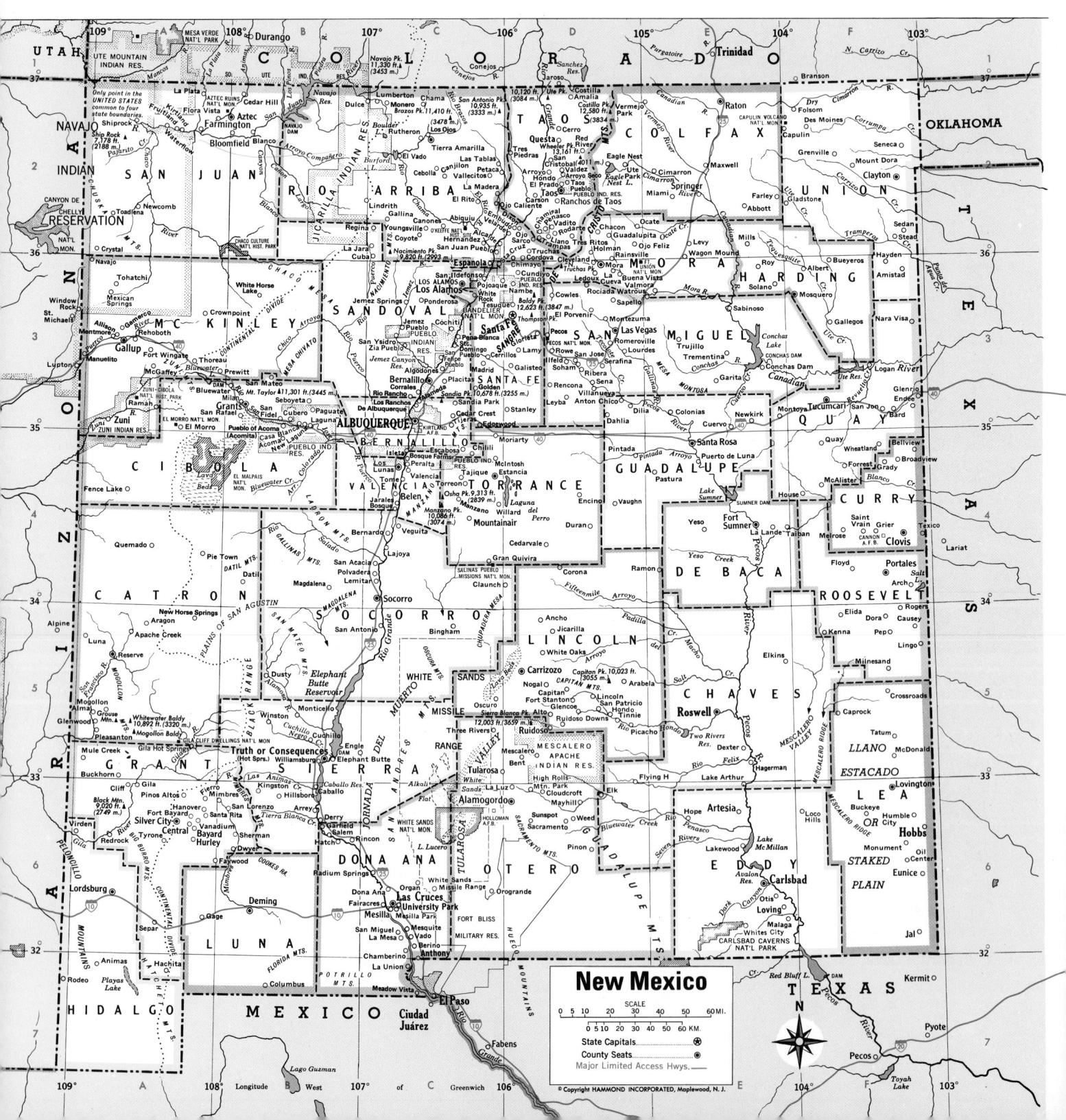

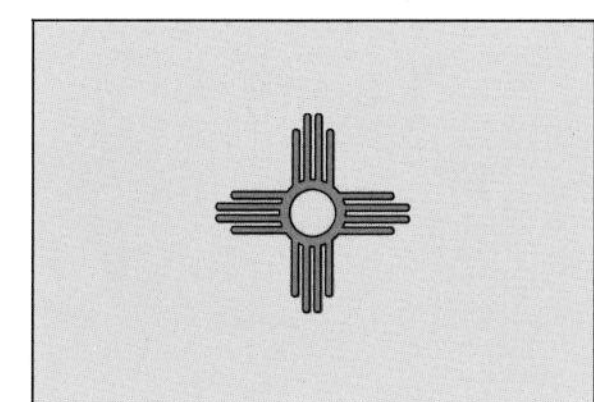

AREA 121,593 sq. mi. (314,926 sq. km.)
POPULATION 1,521,779
CAPITAL Santa Fe
LARGEST CITY Albuquerque
HIGHEST POINT Wheeler Pk. 13,161 ft. (4011 m.)
SETTLED IN 1605
ADMITTED TO UNION January 6, 1912
POPULAR NAME Land of Enchantment
STATE FLOWER Yucca
STATE BIRD Road Runner

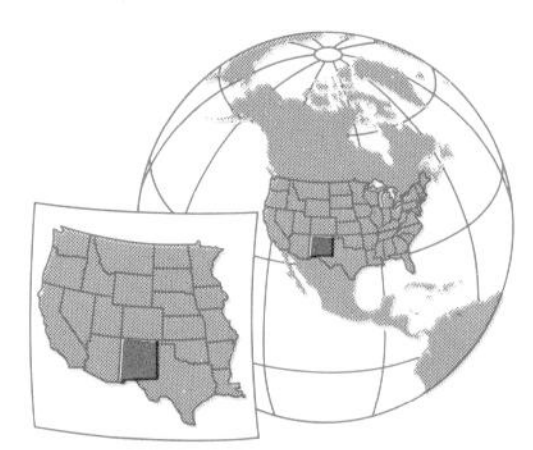

Espanola 8,389 C3
Estancia▲ 792 D4
Eunice 2,676 F6
Fairacres 700 C6
Farmington 33,997 A2
Faywood 100 B6
Fence Lake 150 A4
Fierro 200 A6
Flora Vista 1,021 A2
Floyd 117 F4
Folsom 71 F2
Fort Bayard 400 A6
Fort Stanton 80 D5
Fort Sumner▲ 1,269 E4
Fort Wingate 800 A3
Fruitland 800 A2
Galisteo 125 D3
Gallina 420 C2
Gallup▲ 19,154 A3
Gamerco 800 A3
Garfield 600 B6
Garita 66 E3
Gila 350 A6
Glencoe 125 D5
Glenwood 220 A5
Glorieta 300 D3
Golden 100 C3
Grady 110 F4
Grants▲ 8,626 B3
Guadalupita 300 D2
Hachita 75 A7
Hagerman 961 E5
Hanover 300 A6
Hatch 1,136 B6
Hernandez 500 C2
High Rolls-Mountain Park 555 D5
Hillsboro 175 B6
Hobbs 29,115 F6
Holman 400 D2
Hondo 425 D5
Hope 101 E6
Hot Springs▲ (Truth or Consequences) 6,221 B5
House 85 F4
Humble City 65 F6
Hurley 1,534 A6
Ilfeld 68 D3
Isleta 1,703 C4
Jal 2,156 F6
Jarales 700 C4
Jemez Pueblo 1,301 C3
Jemez Springs 413 C3
Kenna 100 F5
Kirtland 3,552 A2
La Cueva 200 D3
La Jara 210 B2
La Luz 1,625 C6
La Madera 200 C2
La Mesa 900 C6
La Plata 150 A2
La Union 200 C7
Laguna 434 B3
Lajoya 97 C4
Lake Arthur 336 E5
Lamy 66 D3
Las Cruces▲ 62,126 C6
Las Vegas▲ 14,753 D3
Ledoux 300 D3
Lemitar 800 B4
Lincoln 100 D5
Lindrith 349 C2
Llano 325 D2
Loco Hills 375 F6
Logan 870 F3
Lordsburg▲ 2,951 A6
Los Alamos▲ 11,455 C3
Los Lunas▲ 6,013 C4
Los Ojos C2
Los Ranchos de Albuquerque 3,955 C3
Loving 1,243 E6
Lovington▲ 9,322 F6
Lumberton 175 C2
Luna 200 A5
Magdalena 861 B4
Malaga 300 E6
Manuelito 200 A3
Manzano 65 C4
Maxwell 247 E2
Mayhill 300 D6
McAlister 320 F4
McDonald 65 F5
McIntosh 325 D4
Meadow Vista 3,377 C7
Melrose 662 F4
Mentmore 315 A3
Mescalero 1,159 D5
Mesilla 1,975 C6
Mesilla Park C6
Mesquite 500 C6
Mexican Springs 242 A3
Miami 112 E2
Milan 1,911 B3
Mimbres 300 B6
Montezuma 250 D3
Monticello 125 B5
Monument 300 F6
Mora▲ D3
Moriarty 1,399 D4
Mosquero▲ 164 F3
Mountainair 926 C4
Mule Creek 62 A5
Nambe 1,246 D3
Nara Visa 250 F3
Navajo 1,985 A3
New Laguna 250 B4
Newcomb 388 A2
Newkirk 54 E3
Nogal 150 D5
Ocate 75 E2
Oil Center 236 F6
Ojo Caliente 600 D2
Ojo Feliz 133 E2
Ojo Sarco 380 D2
Organ 300 C6
Orogrande 80 D6
Otis 200 E6
Paguate 492 B3
Pecos 1,012 D3
Pena Blanca 300 C3
Penasco 648 D2
Peralta 3,182 C4
Petaca 84 C2
Picacho 100 D5
Pie Town 90 A4
Pinos Altos 250 A6
Placitas 1,611 C3
Pleasanton 70 A5
Pojoaque 1,037 C3
Ponderosa 300 C3
Portales▲ 10,690 F4
Prewitt 300 B3
Puerto de Luna 175 E4
Questa 1,707 D2
Radium Springs 150 B6
Rainsville 350 D2
Ramah 574 A3
Ranchos de Taos 1,779 D2
Raton▲ 7,372 E2
Red River 387 D2
Regina 80 B2
Rehoboth 200 A3
Reserve▲ 319 A5
Ribera 84 D3
Rincon 300 C6
Rio Rancho 32,505 C3
Rociada 140 D3
Rodarte 650 D2
Rodeo 200 A7
Roswell▲ 44,654 E5
Rowe 290 D3
Roy 362 E3
Ruidoso 4,600 D5
Ruidoso Downs 920 D5
Rutheron 95 C2
Salem 400 B6
San Acacia 286 B4
San Antonio 359 B5
San Cristobal 350 D2
San Felipe Pueblo 1,557 C3
San Fidel 150 B3
San Ildefonso 447 C3
San Jon 277 F3
San Jose 150 D3
San Juan Pueblo 4,107 C2
San Lorenzo 200 B6
San Mateo 200 B3
San Miguel 400 C6
San Patricio 300 D5
San Rafael 300 A3
San Ysidro 233 C3
Sandia Park 450 C3
Santa Cruz 2,504 D2
Santa Fe (cap.)▲ 55,859 C3
Santa Rita 600 B6
Santa Rosa▲ 2,263 E4
Santo Domingo Pueblo 2,866 C3
Sapello 600 D3
Seboyeta 125 B3
Sedan 60 F2
Sena 150 D3
Serafina 225 D3
Sherman 100 B6
Shiprock 7,687 A2
Silver City▲ 10,683 A6
Socorro▲ 8,159 C4
Soham 104 D3
Solano 114 E3
Springer 1,262 E2
Sunspot 78 D6
Taiban 120 F4
Tajique 145 C4
Taos Pueblo 1,187 D2
Taos▲ 4,065 D2
Tatum 768 F5
Tesuque 1,490 C3
Texico 966 F4
Thoreau 1,099 A3
Tierra Amarilla▲ 850 C2
Tijeras 340 C3
Tinnie 100 D5
Toadlena 200 A2
Tohatchi 661 A3
Tome 500 C4
Torreon 200 C4
Trampas 76 D2
Trementina 80 E3
Tres Piedras 200 D2
Truchas 275 D2
Trujillo 148 E3
Truth or Consequences▲ 6,221 B5
Tucumcari▲ 6,831 F3
Tularosa 2,615 C5
Tyrone 100 A6
University Park 4,520 C6
Ute Park 67 D2
Vadito 283 D2
Vado 325 C6
Valdez 300 D2
Valencia 3,917 C4
Vallecitos 450 C2
Vanadium 150 A6
Vaughn 633 D4
Velarde 950 C2
Vermejo Park 85 D2
Villanueva 500 D3
Virden 108 A6
Wagon Mound 319 E2
Waterflow 475 A2
Watrous 175 D3
White Horse Lake B3
White Rock 6,192 C3
White Sands Missile Range 2,616 C6
Willard 183 D4
Williamsburg 456 B5
Yeso 200 E4
Youngsville 125 C2
Zia Pueblo 637 C3
Zuni 5,551 A3

OTHER FEATURES

Abiquiu (res.) C2
Alamosa (riv.) B5
Animas (riv.) B1
Avalon (res.) E6
Aztec Ruins Nat'l Mon. A2
Baldy (peak) D3
Bandelier Nat'l Mon. C3
Big Burro (mts.) A6
Black (mt.) A6
Black (range) B5
Blanco (creek) F4
Bluewater (creek) B4
Bluewater (creek) D6
Bluewater (lake) A3
Boulder (lake) C2
Brazos (peak) C2
Burford (lake) C2
Caballo (res.) B6
Canadian (riv.) F3
Cannon A.F.B. 3,312 F4
Canyon Blanco (creek) B2
Capitan (mts.) D5
Capitan (peak) D5
Capulin Volcano Nat'l Mon. E2
Carlsbad Caverns Nat'l Park E6
Carrizo (creek) F2
Chaco (mesa) B3
Chaco (riv.) A2
Chaco Culture Nat'l Hist. Park B2
Chico Arroyo (creek) B3
Chivato (mesa) B3
Chupadera (mesa) C5
Chuska (mts.) A2
Cimarron (riv.) E2
Colorado, Arroyo (riv.) B4
Compañero, Arroyo (creek) B2
Conchas (lake) E3
Conchas (riv.) E3
Cookes (range) B6
Corrumpa (creek) F2
Costilla (peak) D2
Cuchillo Negro (creek) B5
Cuervo (creek) E3
Dark Canyon (creek) E6
Datil (mts.) B4
Dry Cimarron (riv.) F2
Eagle Nest (lake) D2
Elephant Butte (res.) B5
El Morro Nat'l Mon. A3
El Rito (riv.) C2
Fifteenmile Arroyo (creek) D4
Florida (mts.) B7
Fort Bliss Mil. Res. C6
Fort Union Nat'l Mon. E3
Gallinas (mts.) B4
Gallinas (riv.) E3
Gila (riv.) A6
Gila Cliff Dwellings Nat'l Mon. A5
Grouse (mt.) A5
Guadalupe (mts.) D6
Hatchet (mts.) A7
Holloman A.F.B. 5,891 C6
Hueco (mts.) D6
Jemez (riv.) C3
Jemez Canyon (res.) C3
Jicarilla Ind. Res. B2
Jornada del Muerto (valley) C5
Kirtland A.F.B. C3
Ladron (mts.) B4
La Plata (riv.) A1
Lake Avalon (res.) E6
Largo, Cañon (creek) B2
Las Animas (creek) B5
Llano Estacado (Staked) (plain) F5
Lucero (lake) C6
Macho, Arroyo del (creek) D5
Magdalena (mts.) B4
Manzano (mts.) C4
Manzano (peak) C4
McMillan (lake) E6
Mescalero (ridge) F6
Mescalero (valley) F5
Mescalero Apache Ind. Res. D5
Mimbres (mts.) B6
Mimbres (riv.) B6
Mogollon (mts.) A5
Mogollon Baldy (peak) A5
Montosa (mesa) E3
Mora (riv.) E3
Nacimiento (mts.) C3
Nacimiento (peak) C2
Navajo (res.) B2
Navajo Ind. Res. A2
North Truchas (peak) D3
Ocate (creek) E2
O'Keeffe Nat'l Hist. Site C2
Oscura (mts.) C5
Osha (peak) C4
Padilla (creek) D5
Pajarito (creek) A2
Pecos (riv.) E5
Pecos Nat'l Mon. D3
Peloncillo (mts.) A6
Perro (lake) D4
Pinos, Rio de los (riv.) B2
Pintada Arroyo (creek) E4
Playas (lake) A7
Potrillo (mts.) B7
Pueblo Ind. Res. B4
Pueblo Ind. Res. C4
Pueblo Ind. Res. D2
Pueblo Ind. Res. D3
Puerco (riv.) A3
Red Bluff (lake) E7
Revuelto (creek) F3
Rio Brazos (riv.) C2
Rio Chama (riv.) C2
Rio Felix (riv.) E5
Rio Grande (riv.) C5
Rio Hondo (riv.) E5
Rio Penasco (riv.) E6
Rio Puerco (riv.) C4
Rio Salado (riv.) B4
Rocky (mts.) C1
Sacramento (mts.) D6
Salinas Pueblo Missions Nat'l Mon. C4
Salt (creek) E5
Salt (lake) F4
San Agustin (plains) B5
San Andres (mts.) C6
San Antonio (peak) C2
Sandia (peak) C3
San Francisco (riv.) A5
Sangre de Cristo (mts.) D3
San Jose (riv.) B3
San Juan (riv.) B2
San Mateo (mts.) B5
Seven Rivers (riv.) E6
Ship Rock (peak) A2
Sierra Blanca (peak) C5
Staked (Llano Estacado) (plain) F5
Sumner (lake) E4
Taylor (mt.) B3
Tecolote (creek) D3
Tequesquite (creek) E2
Thompson (peak) D3
Tierra Blanca (creek) B6
Tramperos (creek) F2
Tularosa (valley) C6
Ute (creek) F3
Ute (peak) D2
Ute (res.) F3
Ute Mountain Ind. Res. A1
Vermejo (riv.) E2
Wheeler (peak) D2
White Sands (des.) C5
White Sands Missile Range C5
White Sands Nat'l Mon. C6
Whitewater Baldy (mt.) A5
Wingate Army Depot A3
Yeso (creek) E4
Zuni (mts.) A3
Zuni (riv.) A3
Zuni-Cibola Nat'l Hist. Park A3
Zuni Ind. Res. A3

▲County seat

Topography

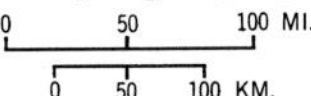

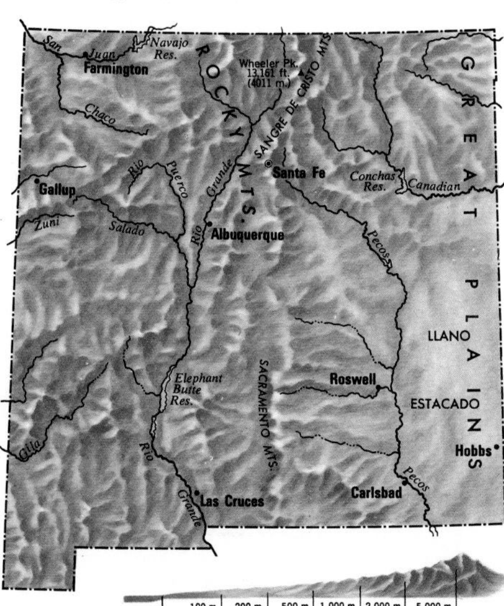

Agriculture, Industry and Resources

DOMINANT LAND USE

- Wheat, Grain Sorghums, Range Livestock
- General Farming, Livestock, Special Crops
- General Farming, Livestock, Cash Grain
- Dry Beans, General Farming
- Cotton, Forest Products
- Range Livestock
- Forests
- Nonagricultural Land

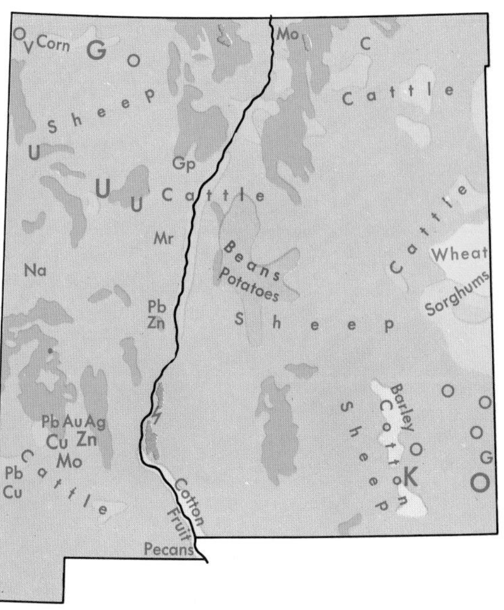

MAJOR MINERAL OCCURRENCES

Ag Silver
Au Gold
C Coal
Cu Copper
G Natural Gas
Gp Gypsum
K Potash
Mo Molybdenum
Mr Marble
Na Salt
O Petroleum
Pb Lead
U Uranium
V Vanadium
Zn Zinc
Water Power

New York

SCALE
0 5 10 20 30 40 MI.
0 5 10 20 30 40 KM.

State Capitals..............⊛
County Seats..............◉
Canals.....................
Major Limited Access Hwys. ___

AREA 49,108 sq. mi. (127,190 sq. km.)
POPULATION 18,044,505
CAPITAL Albany
LARGEST CITY New York
HIGHEST POINT Mt. Marcy 5,344 ft.
   (1629 m.)
SETTLED IN 1614
ADMITTED TO UNION July 26, 1788
POPULAR NAME Empire State
STATE FLOWER Rose
STATE BIRD Bluebird

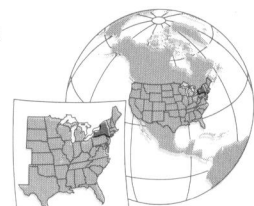

Topography

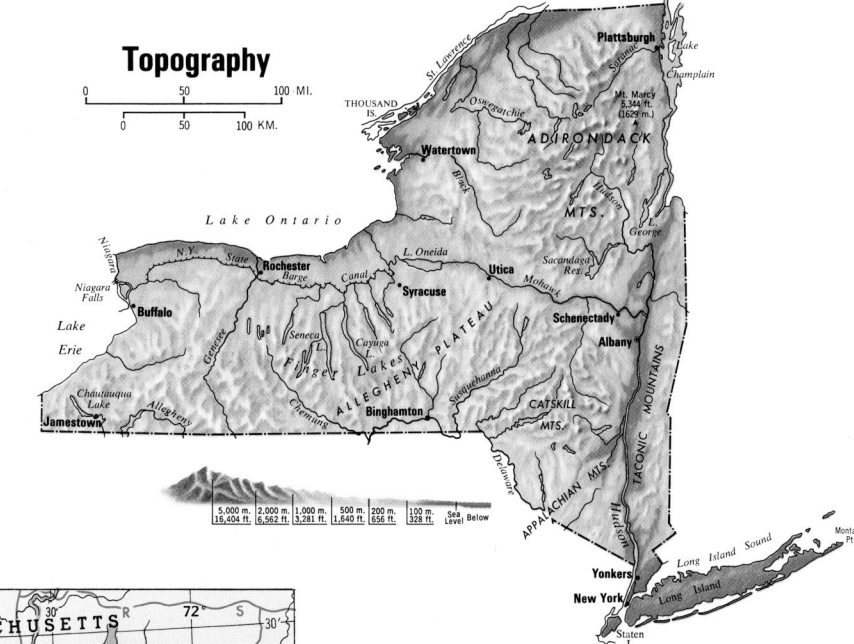

Dix Hills 25,849	O9	Gasport 1,336	C4
Dobbs Ferry 9,940	O6	Geneseo▲ 7,187	E5
Dolgeville 2,452	L4	Geneva 14,143	G5
Dover Plains 1,847	O7	Glasco 1,538	M6
Dryden 1,908	H6	Glen Cove 24,149	R6
Dundee 1,588	B5	Glens Falls 15,023	N4
Dunkirk 13,989	A5	Gloversville 16,656	M4
Earlville 883	J5	Golden's Bridge 1,589	N8
East Aurora 6,647	C5	Goshen▲ 5,255	M8
East Greenbush 3,784	N5	Gouverneur 4,604	K2
East Hampton 1,402	R9	Gowanda 2,901	B6
East Hills 6,746	R7	Granville 2,646	O4
East Meadow 36,909	R7	Great Neck 8,745	P6
East Moriches 4,021	P9	Greece 15,632	E4
East Northport 20,411	O9	Green Island 2,490	N5
East Rochester 6,932	F4	Greene 1,812	J6
East Rockaway 10,152	R7	Greenport 2,070	P8
East Syracuse 3,343	H4	Greenwich 1,961	O4
Eastchester 18,537	P6	Greenwood Lake 3,208	M8
Eden 3,088	C5	Groton 2,398	H5
Elba 703	D4	Hadley-Lake Luzerne 1,988	N4
Elbridge 1,099	G5	Hagaman 1,377	M5
Elizabethtown▲ 659	N2	Hamburg 10,442	C5
Ellenville 4,243	M7	Hamilton 3,790	J5
Elma 2,354	C5	Hammondsport 929	F6
Elmira Heights 4,359	G6	Hampton Bays 7,893	R9
Elmira▲ 33,724	G6	Hancock 1,330	K7
Elmont 28,612	P7	Hannibal 680	G4
Elmsford 3,938	O6	Harriman 2,288	M8
Elwood 10,916	O9	Harrison 23,308	P6
Endicott 13,531	H6	Harrisville 703	K2
Endwell 12,602	H6	Hartsdale 5,587	P6
Evans Mills 661	J2	Hastings On Hudson 8,000	O6
Fair Haven 895	G4	Hauppauge 19,750	O9
Fairport 5,943	F4	Haverstraw 9,438	M8
Fairview 4,811	N7	Hawthorne 4,764	O6
Falconer 2,653	A6	Hempstead 49,453	R7
Farmingdale 8,022	O9	Herkimer▲ 7,945	L4
Fayetteville 4,248	J4	Heuvelton 771	K1
Fernwood 3,640	N4	Hewlett 6,620	P7
Fishkill 1,957	N7	Hewlett Harbor 1,193	P7
Flanders-Riverside 5,400	P9	Hicksville 40,174	R7
Floral Park 15,947	P7	Highland 4,492	M8
Florida 2,497	M8	Highland Falls 3,937	M8
Fonda▲ 1,007	L5	Hillburn 892	M8
Forestville 738	B6	Hillcrest 6,447	K8
Fort Covington▲ 1,804	M1	Hilton 5,216	E4
Fort Edward 3,561	O4	Holcomb 790	F5
Fort Johnson 615	L5	Holland 1,288	C5
Fort Plain 2,416	L5	Holley 1,802	D4
Frankfort 2,693	K4	Homer 3,476	H5
Franklin Square 28,205	R7	Honeoye Falls 2,340	F5
Franklinville 1,739	D6	Hoosick Falls 3,490	O5
Fredonia 10,436	B6	Hopewell Junction 1,786	N7
Freeport 39,894	R7	Hornell 9,877	E6
Frewsburg 1,817	B6	Horseheads 6,802	G6
Friendship 1,423	D6	Houghton 1,740	D6
Fulton 12,929	H4	Hudson Falls▲ 7,651	O4
Fultonville 748	M5	Hudson▲ 8,034	N6
Garden City 21,686	R7	Huntington 18,243	R6

(continued on following page)

Huntington Station 28,247 ... R6
Hurley 4,644 ... M7
Hyde Park 2,550 ... N6
Ilion 8,888 ... K5
Interlaken 680 ... G5
Inwood 7,767 ... P7
Irondequoit 52,322 ... E4
Irvington 6,348 ... O6
Island Park 4,860 ... R7
Islip 18,924 ... O9
Ithaca▲ 29,541 ... G6
Jamestown 34,681 ... B6
Jericho 13,141 ... R6
Johnson City 16,890 ... J6
Johnstown▲ 9,058 ... M4
Jordan 1,325 ... H4
Keeseville 1,854 ... O2
Kenmore 17,180 ... C5
Kerhonkson 1,629 ... M7
Keuka Park 1,153 ... F5
Kinderhook 1,293 ... N6
Kings Park 17,773 ... O9
Kings Point 4,843 ... P6
Kingston▲ 23,095 ... M7
Lackawanna 20,585 ... B5
Lake Carmel 8,489 ... N8
Lake Erie Beach 4,509 ... B5
Lake George▲ 933 ... N4
Lake Katrine 1,998 ... M7
Lake Luzerne-Hadley 2,042 ... N4
Lake Placid 2,485 ... N2
Lake Pleasant▲ 700 ... M4
Lake Success 2,484 ... P7
Lakewood 3,564 ... B6
Lancaster 11,940 ... C5
Lansing 3,281 ... H5
Larchmont 6,181 ... P7
Latham 10,131 ... N5
Lattingtown 1,859 ... R6
Lawrence 6,513 ... P7
Le Roy 4,974 ... E5
Levittown 53,286 ... R7
Lewiston 3,048 ... B4
Liberty 4,128 ... L7
Lima 2,165 ... E5
Lindenhurst 26,879 ... O9
Little Falls 5,829 ... L4
Little Valley▲ 1,188 ... C6
Liverpool 2,624 ... H4
Livingston Manor 1,482 ... L7
Livonia 1,434 ... E5
Lloyd Harbor 3,343 ... R6
Lockport▲ 24,426 ... C4
Locust Grove 9,670 ... R6
Long Beach 33,510 ... R7
Lowville▲ 3,632 ... J3
Lynbrook 19,208 ... P7
Lyndonville 953 ... D4
Lyons Falls 698 ... K3
Lyons▲ 4,280 ... F4
Macedon 1,400 ... F4
Machias 1,191 ... D6
Mahopac 7,755 ... N8
Malone▲ 6,777 ... M1
Malverne 9,054 ... R7
Mamaroneck 17,325 ... P7
Manchester 1,598 ... F5
Manhasset 7,718 ... P7
Manhattan (borough) ... M9
Manlius 4,764 ... J5
Manorville 6,198 ... P9
Marathon 1,107 ... J6
Marcellus 1,840 ... H5
Margaretville 639 ... L6
Marion 1,080 ... F4
Marlboro 2,200 ... M7
Massapequa 22,018 ... R7
Massapequa Park 18,044 ... R7
Massena 11,719 ... L1
Mastic Beach 10,293 ... P9
Mattituck 3,902 ... P9
Maybrook 2,802 ... M8
Mayfield 817 ... M4
Mayville▲ 1,636 ... A6
McGraw 1,074 ... H5
Mechanicville 5,249 ... N5
Medina 6,686 ... D4
Melrose Park 2,091 ... G5
Melville 12,586 ... S7
Menands 4,333 ... N5
Merrick 23,042 ... R7
Mexico 1,555 ... H4
Middle Hope 3,229 ... M7
Middleburgh 1,436 ... M5
Middleport 1,876 ... C4
Middletown 24,160 ... L8
Middleville 624 ... K4
Mill Neck 977 ... R6
Millbrook 1,339 ... N7
Millerton 884 ... O7
Milton 1,140 ... M7
Milton 2,063 ... N4
Mineola▲ 18,994 ... R7
Minetto 1,252 ... H4
Mineville-Witherbee 1,740 ... O2
Minoa 3,745 ... H4
Mohawk 2,986 ... L4
Monroe 6,672 ... M8
Monsey 13,986 ... J8
Montauk 3,001 ... S8
Montgomery 2,696 ... M7
Monticello▲ 6,597 ... L7
Montour Falls 1,845 ... G6
Moravia 1,559 ... H5
Morris 642 ... K5
Morrisonville 1,742 ... N1
Morrisville 2,732 ... J5
Mount Kisco 9,108 ... N8
Mount Morris 3,102 ... E5
Mount Vernon 67,153 ... O7
Nanuet 14,065 ... K8
Napanoch 1,068 ... M7
Naples 1,237 ... F5
Nassau 1,254 ... N5
New Berlin 1,220 ... K5
New City▲ 33,673 ... K8
New Hartford 2,111 ... K4
New Hyde Park 9,728 ... P7
New Paltz 5,463 ... M7
New Rochelle 67,265 ... P7
New Square 2,605 ... K8
New Windsor 8,898 ... N8
New York Mills 3,534 ... K4
New York▲ 7,322,564 ... M9
Newark 9,849 ... G4
Newark Valley 1,082 ... H6
Newburgh 26,454 ... M7
Newfane 3,001 ... C4
Newport 676 ... K4
Niagara Falls 61,840 ... C4
Nichols 573 ... H6
Niskayuna 4,942 ... N5
Norfolk 1,412 ... K1
North Boston 2,581 ... C5
North Collins 1,335 ... C5
North Hornell 822 ... E6
North Syracuse 7,363 ... H4
North Tarrytown 8,152 ... O6
North Tonawanda 34,989 ... C4
Northport 7,572 ... O9
Northville 1,180 ... M4
Norwich▲ 7,613 ... J5
Norwood 1,841 ... L1
Nunda 1,347 ... E5
Nyack 6,558 ... K8
Oakfield 1,818 ... D4
Oceanside 32,423 ... R7
Odessa 986 ... G6
Ogdensburg 13,521 ... K1
Olcott 1,432 ... C4
Old Forge 1,061 ... L3
Olean 16,946 ... D6
Oneida 10,850 ... J4
Oneonta 13,954 ... K6
Orangeburg 3,583 ... K8
Orchard Park 3,280 ... C5
Oriskany 1,450 ... K4
Oriskany Falls 795 ... J5
Ossining 22,582 ... N8
Oswego▲ 19,195 ... G4
Otego 1,068 ... K6
Otisville 1,078 ... L8
Ovid 660 ... G5
Owego▲ 4,442 ... H6
Oxford 1,738 ... J6
Oyster Bay 6,687 ... R6
Painted Post 1,950 ... F6
Palmyra 3,566 ... F4
Patchogue 11,060 ... P9
Pawling 1,974 ... N7
Pearl River 15,314 ... K8
Peconic 1,100 ... P8
Peekskill 19,536 ... N8
Pelham 6,413 ... O7
Pelham Manor 5,443 ... O7
Penn Yan▲ 5,248 ... F5
Perry 4,219 ... D5
Peru 1,565 ... N1
Phelps 1,978 ... F5
Philadelphia 1,478 ... J2
Philmont 1,623 ... N6
Phoenix 2,435 ... H4
Piermont 2,163 ... K8
Pine Bush 1,445 ... M7
Pine Plains 1,312 ... N7
Pine Valley 1,486 ... G6
Pittsford 1,488 ... E4
Plainview 26,207 ... R7
Plattsburgh▲ 21,255 ... O1
Pleasantville 6,592 ... N8
Port Byron 1,359 ... G4
Port Chester 24,728 ... P7
Port Dickinson 1,785 ... J6
Port Ewen 3,444 ... N7
Port Henry 1,263 ... O2
Port Jefferson 7,455 ... P9
Port Jervis 9,060 ... L8
Port Leyden 723 ... K3
Port Washington 15,387 ... R6
Portville 1,040 ... D6
Potsdam 10,251 ... K1
Poughkeepsie▲ 28,844 ... N7
Prattsburg• 1,657 ... F5
Pulaski 2,525 ... H3
Putnam Valley• 8,994 ... N8
Queens (borough) ... N9
Quogue 898 ... P9
Randolph 1,298 ... C6
Ransomville 1,542 ... C4
Ravena 3,547 ... N6
Red Hook 1,794 ... N7
Red Oaks Mill 4,906 ... N7
Rensselaer 8,255 ... N5
Rhinebeck 2,725 ... N7
Richfield Springs 1,565 ... K5
Richmond (borough) (Staten Island) ... M9
Richmondville 843 ... M5
Ripley 1,189 ... A6
Riverhead▲ 8,814 ... P9
Rochester▲ 231,636 ... E4
Rockville Centre 24,727 ... R7
Rome 44,350 ... J4
Ronkonkoma 20,391 ... O9
Roosevelt 15,030 ... R7
Rosendale 1,134 ... M7
Roslyn 1,965 ... R6
Rotterdam Junction 1,010 ... N5
Round Lake 765 ... N5
Rouses Point 2,377 ... O1
Rye 14,936 ... P6
Sackets Harbor 1,313 ... H3
Sag Harbor 2,134 ... R8
Saint James 12,703 ... O9
Saint Johnsville 1,825 ... L5
Salamanca 6,566 ... C6
Salem 958 ... O4
Sand Ridge 1,312 ... H4
Sands Point 2,477 ... P6
Sandy Creek 793 ... H3
Saranac Lake 5,377 ... M2
Saratoga Springs 25,001 ... N4
Saugerties 3,915 ... M6
Savannah• 1,905 ... G4
Savona 974 ... F6
Sayville 16,550 ... O9
Scarsdale 16,987 ... P6
Schaghticoke 794 ... N5
Schenectady▲ 65,566 ... M5
Schoharie▲ 1,045 ... M5
Schuylerville 1,364 ... N4
Scotia 7,359 ... N5
Scottsville 1,912 ... E4
Sea Cliff 5,054 ... R6
Seaford 15,597 ... R7
Seneca Falls 7,370 ... G5
Sherburne 1,531 ... K5
Sherman 694 ... A6
Sherrill 2,864 ... J4
Shortsville 1,485 ... F5
Sidney 4,720 ... K6
Silver Creek 2,927 ... B5
Silver Springs 852 ... E5
Sinclairville 708 ... B6
Skaneateles 2,724 ... H5
Sloan 3,830 ... C5
Sloatsburg 3,035 ... M8
Smithtown 25,638 ... O9
Sodus 1,904 ... G4
Sodus Point 1,190 ... G4
Solvay 6,717 ... H4
South Corning 1,025 ... F6
South Fallsburg 2,115 ... L7
South Glens Falls 3,506 ... N4
South Nyack 3,352 ... K8
Southampton 1,302 ... R9
Southold 5,192 ... P8
Southport 7,753 ... G6
Sparrow Bush 1,049 ... L8
Spencer 815 ... H6
Spencerport 3,606 ... E4
Spring Valley 21,802 ... K8
Springville 4,310 ... C5
Stamford 1,211 ... L6
Stannards 1,028 ... E6
Star Lake 1,092 ... K2
Staten Island (borough) ... M9
Stillwater 1,531 ... N5
Stony Brook 13,726 ... O9
Stony Point 10,587 ... M8
Stottville 1,369 ... N6
Suffern 11,055 ... J8
Sylvan Beach 1,119 ... J4
Syosset 18,967 ... R6
Syracuse▲ 163,860 ... H4
Tappan 6,867 ... K8
Tarrytown 10,739 ... O6
Theresa 889 ... J2
Thomaston 2,612 ... P7
Ticonderoga 2,770 ... N3
Tillson 1,688 ... M7
Tivoli 1,035 ... N6
Tonawanda 17,284 ... B4
Troy▲ 54,269 ... N5
Trumansburg 1,611 ... G5
Tuckahoe 6,302 ... O7
Tully 911 ... H5
Tupper Lake 4,087 ... M2
Tuxedo Park 706 ... M8
Unadilla 1,265 ... K6
Union Springs 1,142 ... G5
Uniondale 20,328 ... R7
Utica▲ 68,637 ... K4
Valatie 1,487 ... N6
Valley Cottage 9,007 ... K8
Valley Stream 33,946 ... P7
Vestal• 27,238 ... H6
Victor 2,308 ... F5
Victory Mills 571 ... N4
Viola 4,504 ... J8
Voorheesville 3,225 ... M5
Waddington 944 ... K1
Wading River 5,317 ... P9
Walden 5,836 ... M7
Wallkill 2,125 ... M7
Walton 3,326 ... K6
Wampsville▲ 501 ... J4
Wantagh 18,567 ... R7
Wappingers Falls 4,605 ... N7
Warrensburg 3,204 ... N3
Warsaw▲ 3,830 ... D5
Warwick 5,984 ... M8
Washingtonville 4,906 ... M8
Waterford 2,370 ... N5
Waterloo▲ 5,116 ... G5
Watertown▲ 29,429 ... J3
Waterville 1,664 ... K5
Watervliet 11,061 ... N5
Watkins Glen▲ 2,207 ... G6
Waverly 4,787 ... G7
Wayland 1,976 ... E5
Webster 5,464 ... F4
Weedsport 1,996 ... G4
Wellsburg 617 ... G6
Wellsville 5,241 ... E6
West Carthage 2,166 ... J3
West Elmira 5,218 ... G6
West Glens Falls 5,964 ... N4
West Hurley 2,252 ... M6
West Nyack 3,437 ... K8
West Point 8,024 ... M8
West Sayville 4,680 ... O9
West Seneca 47,866 ... C5
West Winfield 871 ... K5
Westbury 13,060 ... R7
Westfield 3,451 ... A6
Westhampton 2,129 ... P9
Westhampton Beach 1,571 ... P9
Westons Mills 1,837 ... D6
White Plains▲ 48,718 ... P6
Whitehall 3,071 ... O3
Whitesboro 4,195 ... K4
Whitney Point 1,054 ... J6
Willard 1,339 ... G5
Williamson 1,768 ... F4
Williamsville 5,583 ... C5
Williston Park 7,516 ... R7
Wilson 1,307 ... C4
Windsor 1,051 ... J6
Witherbee-Mineville 1,925 ... N2
Wolcott 1,544 ... G4
Woodmere 15,578 ... P7
Woodridge 783 ... L7
Woodstock 1,870 ... M6
Wurtsboro 1,048 ... L7
Wyandanch 8,950 ... N9
Yonkers 188,082 ... O6
Yorkshire 1,340 ... D5
Yorktown Heights 7,690 ... N8
Yorkville 2,972 ... K4
Youngstown 2,075 ... C4

OTHER FEATURES

Adirondack (mts.) ... M3
Algonquin (peak) ... M2
Allegany Ind. Res. ... C6
Allegheny (res.) ... C7
Allegheny (riv.) ... C6
Ashokan (res.) ... M7
Ausable (riv.) ... N2
Batten Kill (riv.) ... O4
Beaver (riv.) ... K3
Big Moose (lake) ... L3
Black (lake) ... J1
Black (riv.) ... K3
Block Island (sound) ... S8
Blue Mountain (lake) ... M3
Bonaparte (lake) ... K2
Brandreth (lake) ... L3
Brant (lake) ... N3
Brookhaven Nat'l Lab. ... P9
Butterfield (lakes) ... J2
Canandaigua (lake) ... F5
Canisteo (riv.) ... F6
Cannonsville (res.) ... K6
Catskill (lake) ... L6
Cattaraugus (creek) ... C6
Cattaraugus Ind. Res. ... C5
Cayuga (lake) ... G5
Champlain (lake) ... O1
Chateaugay, Upper (lake) ... M1
Chautauqua (lake) ... A6
Chazy (lake) ... N1
Chenango (riv.) ... J6
Cohocton (riv.) ... F6
Conesus (lake) ... E5
Conewango (creek) ... B6
Cranberry (lake) ... L2
Deer (riv.) ... J3
Deer (riv.) ... L1
Delaware (riv.) ... K7
East (riv.) ... N9
Erie (lake) ... A5
Fire Island Nat'l Seashore ... P9
Fishers (isl.) ... S8
Forked (lake) ... L3
Fort Drum 11,578 ... J2
Fort Niagara ... C4
Fort Stanwix Nat'l Mon. ... J4
Fulton Chain (lakes) ... K3
Galloo (isl.) ... H3
Gardiners (bay) ... R8
Gardiners (isl.) ... R8
Gateway Nat'l Rec. Area ... M9
Genesee (riv.) ... E5
George (lake) ... N4
Grand (isl.) ... B5
Grass (riv.) ... K1
Great Sacandaga (lake) ... M4
Great South (bay) ... O9
Great South (beach) ... O9
Greenwood (lake) ... M8
Grenadier (isl.) ... H2
Griffiss A.F.B. ... K4
Haystack (mt.) ... N2
Hemlock (lake) ... E5
Hinckley (res.) ... K4
Honeoye (lake) ... F5
Honnedaga (lake) ... L3
Hudson (riv.) ... N7
Hunter (mt.) ... M6
Indian (lake) ... M3
Jones (beach) ... R7
Keuka (lake) ... F5
Lila (lake) ... L2
Little Tupper (lake) ... L2
Long (isl.) ... P9
Long (lake) ... M2
Long Island (sound) ... P9
Lower Saranac (lake) ... M2
Manhattan (isl.) ... M9
Marcy (mt.) ... N2
Martin Van Buren Nat'l Hist. Site ... N6
Meacham (lake) ... M1
Mohawk (riv.) ... L5
Montauk (pt.) ... S8
Moose (riv.) ... K3
Neversink (res.) ... L7
New York State Barge (canal) ... C4
Niagara (riv.) ... B4
Oil Spring Ind. Res. ... D6
Oneida (lake) ... J4
Onondaga Ind. Res. ... H5
Ontario (lake) ... F3
Orient (pt.) ... R8
Oswegatchie (riv.) ... K2
Oswego (riv.) ... H4
Otisco (lake) ... H5
Otsego (lake) ... L5
Otselic (riv.) ... J5
Owasco (lake) ... G5
Peconic (bay) ... R9
Peninsula (pt.) ... H3
Pepacton (res.) ... L6
Piseco (lake) ... M4
Placid (lake) ... N2
Plattsburgh A.F.B. 5,483 ... N1
Pleasant (lake) ... M4
Plum (isl.) ... R8
Poosepatuck Ind. Res. ... P9
Raquette (lake) ... L3
Rondout (pt.) ... M7
Round (lake) ... L2
Sacandaga (lake) ... L3
Sackets (harb.) ... H3
Sagamore Hill Nat'l Hist. Site ... R6
Saint Lawrence (lake) ... K1
Saint Lawrence (riv.) ... J2
Saint Regis (riv.) ... L1
Saint Regis Ind. Res. ... M1
Salmon (res.) ... J3
Salmon (riv.) ... H3
Salmon (riv.) ... M1
Saranac (lakes) ... M2
Saranac (riv.) ... N1
Saratoga (lake) ... N4
Saratoga Nat'l Hist. Park ... N4
Schoharie (res.) ... M6
Schroon (lake) ... N3
Seneca (lake) ... G5
Seneca (riv.) ... G5
Shelter (isl.) ... R8
Shinnecock Ind. Res. ... R9
Silver (lake) ... N1
Skaneateles (lake) ... H5
Skylight (mt.) ... M2
Slide (mt.) ... L6
Staten (isl.) ... M9
Statue of Liberty Nat'l Mon. ... M9
Stony (isl.) ... H3
Stony (pt.) ... H3
Susquehanna (riv.) ... H6
Thousand (isls.) ... H2
Tioughnioga (riv.) ... H6
Titus (lake) ... M1
Tomhannock (res.) ... O5
Tonawanda Ind. Res. ... D4
Toronto (res.) ... L7
Tupper (lake) ... M2
Tuscarora Ind. Res. ... B4
Unadilla (riv.) ... K5
Upper Chateaugay (lake) ... M1
Valcour (isl.) ... N1
Wallkill (riv.) ... L8
Whiteface (mt.) ... N2
Whitney Point (lake) ... J6
Woodhull (lake) ... L3

▲County seat
•Population of town or township

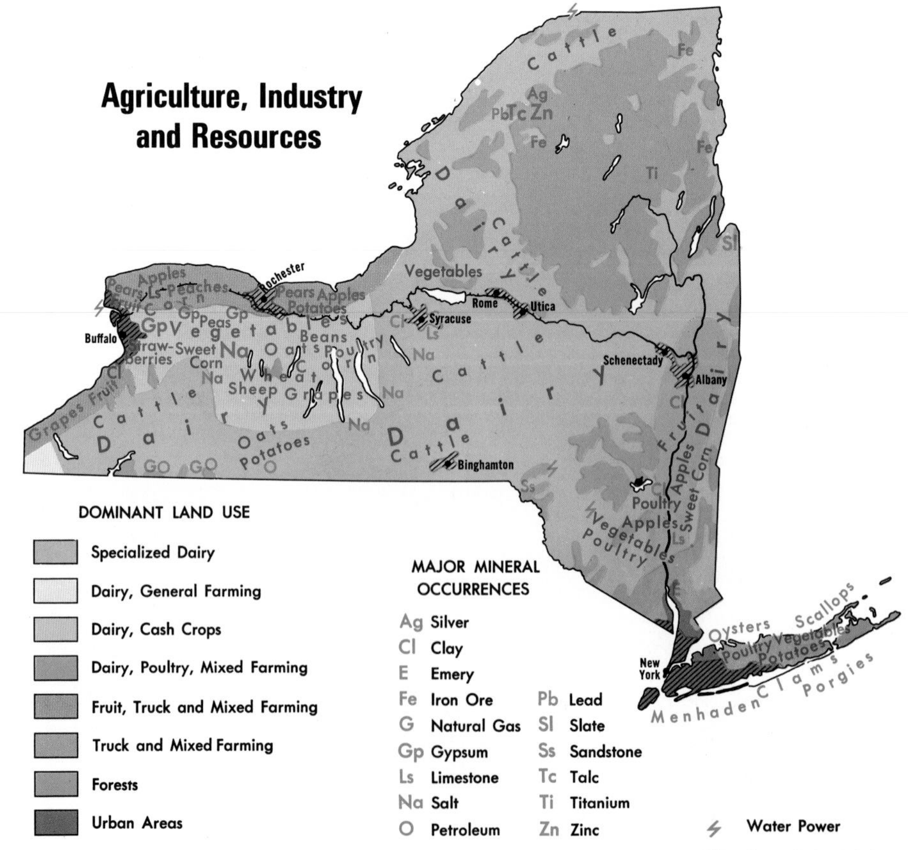
Agriculture, Industry and Resources
Rochester
Buffalo
Syracuse
Rome
Utica
Schenectady
Albany
Binghamton
New York
Vegetables
Pears Apples Potatoes
Beans
Poultry
Sheep
Grapes
Fruit
Dairy
Cattle
Oats
Potatoes
Sweet Corn
Oysters
Scallops
Menhaden
Clams
Porgies
DOMINANT LAND USE
Specialized Dairy
Dairy, General Farming
Dairy, Cash Crops
Dairy, Poultry, Mixed Farming
Fruit, Truck and Mixed Farming
Truck and Mixed Farming
Forests
Urban Areas
MAJOR MINERAL OCCURRENCES
Ag Silver
Cl Clay
E Emery
Fe Iron Ore
G Natural Gas
Gp Gypsum
Ls Limestone
Na Salt
O Petroleum
Pb Lead
Sl Slate
Ss Sandstone
Tc Talc
Ti Titanium
Zn Zinc
Water Power
Major Industrial Areas

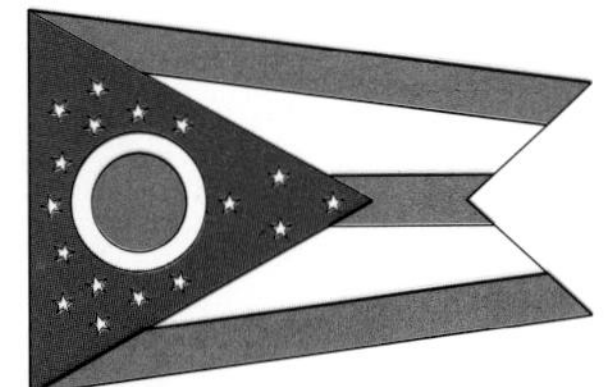
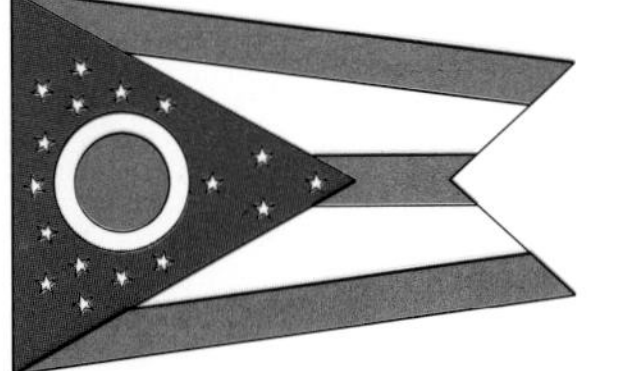

AREA 41,330 sq. mi. (107,045 sq. km.)
POPULATION 10,887,325
CAPITAL Columbus
LARGEST CITY Cleveland
HIGHEST POINT Campbell Hill 1,550 ft. (472 m.)
SETTLED IN 1788
ADMITTED TO UNION March 1, 1803
POPULAR NAME Buckeye State
STATE FLOWER Scarlet Carnation
STATE BIRD Cardinal

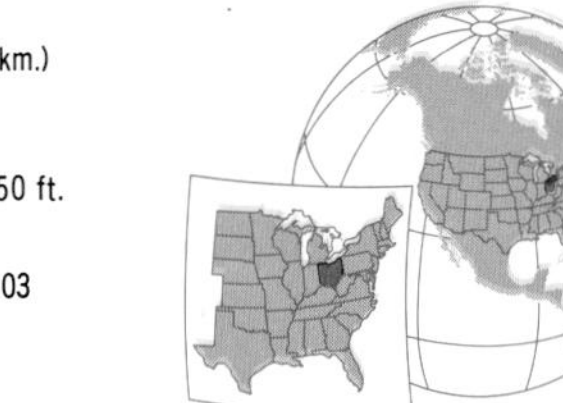

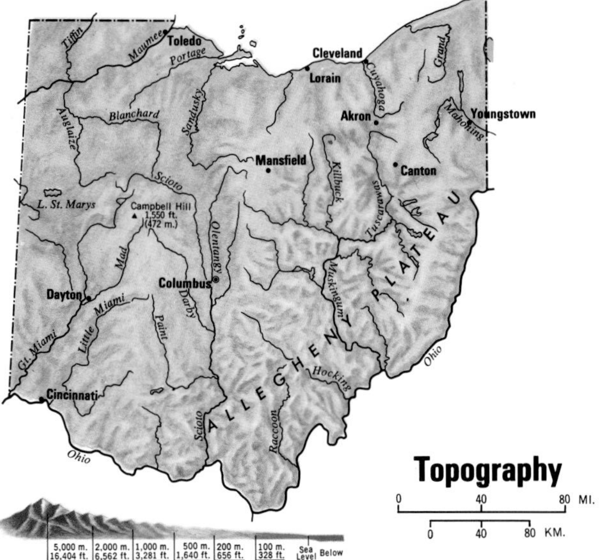
Toledo
Cleveland
Lorain
Akron
Youngstown
Mansfield
Canton
Dayton
Columbus
Cincinnati
Campbell Hill 1,550 ft. (472 m.)
Tiffin
Maumee
Portage
Auglaize
Blanchard
Sandusky
Cuyahoga
Grand
Mahoning
Scioto
L. St. Marys
Olentangy
Kilbuck
Tuscarawas
Muskingum
Mad
Miami
Little Miami
Gt. Miami
Paint
Darby
Hocking
Raccoon
Ohio
ALLEGHENY PLATEAU
Topography
0 40 80 MI.
0 40 80 KM.
5,000 m. 16,404 ft.
2,000 m. 6,562 ft.
1,000 m. 3,281 ft.
500 m. 1,640 ft.
200 m. 656 ft.
100 m. 328 ft.
Sea Level
Below

COUNTIES

Adams 25,371 D8
Allen 109,755 B4
Ashland 47,507 F4
Ashtabula 99,821 J2
Athens 59,549 F7
Auglaize 44,585 B4
Belmont 71,074 J5
Brown 34,966 C8
Butler 291,479 A7
Carroll 26,521 H4
Champaign 36,019 C5
Clark 147,548 C6
Clermont 150,187 B7
Clinton 35,415 C7
Columbiana 108,276 J4
Coshocton 35,427 G5
Crawford 47,870 E4
Cuyahoga 1,412,140 G3
Darke 53,619 A5
Defiance 39,350 A3
Delaware 66,929 D5
Erie 76,779 E3
Fairfield 103,461 E6
Fayette 27,466 D6
Franklin 961,437 E5
Fulton 38,498 B2
Gallia 30,954 F8
Geauga 81,129 H3
Greene 136,731 C6
Guernsey 39,024 H5
Hamilton 866,228 A7
Hancock 65,536 C3
Hardin 31,111 C4
Harrison 16,085 H5
Henry 29,108 B3
Highland 35,728 C7
Hocking 25,533 F6
Holmes 32,849 G4
Huron 56,240 E3
Jackson 30,230 E7
Jefferson 80,298 J5
Knox 47,473 F5
Lake 215,499 H2
Lawrence 61,834 E8
Licking 128,300 F5
Logan 42,310 C5
Lorain 271,126 F3
Lucas 462,361 C2
Madison 37,068 D6
Mahoning 264,806 J4
Marion 64,274 D4
Medina 122,354 G3
Meigs 22,987 F7
Mercer 39,443 A4
Miami 93,182 B5
Monroe 15,497 H6
Montgomery 573,809 B6
Morgan 14,194 G6
Morrow 27,749 E4
Muskingum 82,068 G5
Noble 11,336 G6
Ottawa 40,029 D2
Paulding 20,488 A3
Perry 31,557 F6
Pickaway 48,255 D6
Pike 24,249 D7
Portage 142,585 H3
Preble 40,113 A6
Putnam 33,819 B3
Richland 126,137 E4
Ross 69,330 D7
Sandusky 61,963 D3
Scioto 80,327 D8
Seneca 59,733 D3
Shelby 44,915 B5
Stark 367,585 H4
Summit 514,990 G3
Trumbull 227,813 J3
Tuscarawas 84,090 H5
Union 31,969 D5
Van Wert 30,464 A4
Vinton 11,098 E7
Warren 113,909 B7
Washington 62,254 H7
Wayne 101,461 G4
Williams 36,956 A2
Wood 113,269 C3
Wyandot 22,254 D4

CITIES and TOWNS

Aberdeen 1,329 C8
Ada 5,413 C4
Adamsville 151 G5
Addyston 1,198 B9
Adelphi 398 E7
Adena 842 J5
Akron▲ 223,019 G3
Albany 795 F7
Alexandria 468 E5
Alger 864 C4
Alliance 23,376 H4
Alvordton 298 A2
Amanda 729 E6
Amberley 3,108 C9
Amelia 1,837 D10
Amesville 250 F7
Amherst 10,332 F3
Amsterdam 669 J5
Andover 1,216 J2
Anna 1,164 B5
Ansonia 1,279 A5
Antioch 68 H6
Antwerp 1,677 A3
Apple Creek 860 G4
Aquilla 360 H2
Arcadia 546 D3
Arcanum 1,953 A6
Archbold 3,440 B2
Arlington 1,267 C4
Arlington Heights 1,084 C9
Ashland▲ 20,079 F4
Ashley 1,059 E5
Ashtabula 21,633 J2
Ashville 2,254 E6
Athalia 346 F8
Athens▲ 21,265 F7
Attica 944 E3
Aurora 9,192 H3
Austintown 32,371 J3
Avon 7,337 F3
Avon Lake 15,066 F2
Bailey Lakes 367 F4
Bainbridge 968 D7
Bairdstown 130 C3
Ballville 3,083 D3
Baltic 659 G5
Baltimore 2,971 E6
Barberton 27,623 G4
Barnesville 4,326 H6
Barnhill 313 H5
Barton 1,039 J5
Batavia▲ 1,700 B7
Batesville 95 H6
Bay View 739 E3
Bay Village 17,000 G9
Beach City 1,051 G4
Beachwood 10,677 J9
Beallsville 464 J6
Beaver 336 E7
Beavercreek 33,626 C6
Beaverdam 467 C4
Bedford 14,822 H9
Bedford Heights 12,131 J9
Bellaire 6,028 J5
Bellbrook 6,511 C6
Belle Center 796 C4
Belle Valley 267 G6
Bellefontaine▲ 12,142 C5
Bellevue 8,146 E3
Bellville 1,568 E4
Belmont 471 J5
Belmore 161 B3
Beloit 1,037 J4
Belpre 6,796 G7
Bentleyville 674 J9
Benton 351 G4
Benton Ridge 343 C4
Berea 19,051 G10
Bergholz 713 J4
Berkey 264 C2
Berlin 691 G4
Berlin Heights 756 F3
Bethel 2,407 B8
Bethesda 1,161 H5
Bettsville 752 D3
Beverly 1,444 G6
Bexley 13,088 E6
Blakeslee 128 A2
Blanchester 4,206 B7
Bloomdale 632 D3
Bloomingburg 769 D6
Bloomingdale 227 J5
Bloomville 949 D3
Blue Ash 11,860 C9
Bluffton 3,367 C4
Boardman 38,596 J3
Bolivar 914 G4
Boston Heights 733 J10
Botkins 1,340 B5
Bowerston 343 H5
Bowersville 225 C6
Bowling Green▲ 28,176 C3
Bradford 2,005 B5
Bradner 1,093 C3
Brady Lake 490 H3
Brecksville 11,818 H10
Bremen 1,386 F6
Brewster 2,307 G4
Brice 109 E6
Bridgeport 2,318 J5
Bridgetown 11,748 B9
Brilliant 1,672 J5
Brimfield 3,223 H3
Broadview Heights 12,219 H10
Brook Park 22,865 G9
Brookfield 1,396 J3
Brooklyn 11,706 H9
Brooklyn Heights 1,450 H9
Brookside 703 J5
Brookville 4,621 B6
Broughton 151 B3
Brunswick 28,230 G3
Bryan▲ 8,348 A3
Buchtel 640 F7
Buckeye Lake 2,986 F6
Buckland 239 B4
Bucyrus▲ 13,496 E4
Burbank 289 F4
Burgoon 224 D3
Burkettsville 268 A5
Burlington 3,003 F9
Burton 1,349 H3
Butler 968 F4
Butlerville 188 B7
Byesville 2,435 G6
Cadiz▲ 3,439 J5
Cairo 473 B4
Calcutta 1,212 J4
Caldwell▲ 1,786 G6
Caledonia 644 D4
Cambridge▲ 11,748 G5
Camden 2,210 A6
Campbell 10,038 J3
Canal Fulton 4,157 H4
Canal Winchester 2,617 E6
Canfield 5,409 J3
Canton▲ 84,161 H4
Cardington 1,770 E5
Carey 3,684 D4
Carlisle 4,872 B6
Carroll 558 E6
Carrollton▲ 3,042 J4
Casstown 246 B5
Castalia 915 E3
Castine 163 A6
Catawba 268 C6
Cecil 249 A3
Cedarville 3,210 C6
Celina▲ 9,650 A4
Centerburg 1,323 E5
Centerville 128 B6
Chagrin Falls 4,146 J9
Chardon▲ 4,446 H2
Chatfield 206 E4
Chauncey 980 F7
Cherry Fork 178 C8
Cherry Grove 4,972 C10
Chesapeake 1,073 E9
Cheshire 250 F8
Chester 309 G7
Chesterhill 395 G6
Chesterland 2,078 H2
Chesterville 286 E5
Cheviot 9,616 B9
Chickasaw 378 A5
Chillicothe▲ 21,923 E7
Chilo 130 B8
Christiansburg 599 C5
Cincinnati▲ 364,040 B9
Circleville▲ 11,666 D6
Clarington 406 J6
Clark 523 G5
Clarksburg 483 D7
Clarksville 485 C7
Clay Center 289 D2
Clayton 713 B6
Cleveland Heights 54,052 H9
Cleveland▲ 505,616 H9
Cleves 2,208 B9
Clinton 1,175 G4
Cloverdale 270 B3
Clyde 5,776 E3
Coal Grove 2,251 E9
Coalton 553 E7
Coldwater 4,335 A5
College Corner 379 A6
Columbiana 4,961 J4
Columbus (cap.)▲ 632,910 E6
Columbus Grove 2,231 B4
Commercial Point 405 D6
Conesville 420 G5
Congress 162 F4
Conneaut 13,241 J2
Continental 1,214 B3
Convoy 1,200 A4
Coolville 663 G7
Corning 703 F6
Cortland 5,666 J3
Corwin 225 B6
Coshocton▲ 12,193 G5
Cove 6,669 E8
Covedale 5,830 B10
Covington 2,603 B5
Craig Beach 1,402 H3
Crestline 4,934 E4
Creston 1,848 G3
Cridersville 1,885 B4
Crooksville 2,601 F6
Crown City 445 F8
Cumberland 318 G6
Custar 209 C3
Cuyahoga Falls 48,950 G3
Cuyahoga Heights 682 H9
Cygnet 560 C3
Dalton 1,377 G4
Danville 1,001 F5
Darbydale 825 D6
Darbyville 272 D6
Dayton▲ 182,044 B6
Deer Park 6,181 C9
Deersville 86 H5
Defiance▲ 16,768 B3
Degraff 1,331 C5
Delaware▲ 20,030 E5
Dellroy 314 H4
Delphos 7,093 B4
Delta 2,849 B2
Dennison 3,282 H5
Dent 6,416 B9
Deshler 1,876 C3
Devola 2,736 H7
Dexter City 161 G6
Dillonvale 857 J5
Dover 11,329 G4
Doylestown 2,668 G4
Dresden 1,581 G5
Dublin 16,366 D5
Dunkirk 869 C4
Dupont 279 B3
East Canton 1,742 H4
East Cleveland 33,096 H9
East Liverpool 13,654 J4
East Palestine 5,168 J4
East Sparta 771 H4
Eastlake 21,161 J8
Eaton Estates 1,586 G3
Eaton▲ 7,396 A6
Edgerton 1,896 A3
Edgewood 5,189 J2
Edison 488 E4
Edon 880 A2
Eldorado 549 A6
Elgin 71 A4
Elida 1,486 B4
Elmore 1,334 D3
Elmwood Place 2,937 B9
Elyria▲ 56,746 F3
Empire 364 J5
Englewood 11,432 B6
Euclid 54,875 J9
Evendale 3,175 C9
Fairborn 31,300 B6
Fairfax 2,029 C9
Fairfield 39,729 A7
Fairlawn 5,779 G3
Fairport Harbor 2,978 H2
Fairview Park 18,028 G9
Farmer 932 A3
Farmersville 950 A6
Fayette 1,248 B2
Fayetteville 393 C7
Felicity 856 B8
Findlay▲ 35,703 C3
Fletcher 545 B5
Florida 304 B3
Flushing 1,042 J5
Forest 1,594 C4
Forest Park 18,609 B9
Forestville 9,185 C10
Fort Jennings 436 B4
Fort Loramie 1,042 B5
Fort McKinley 9,740 B6
Fort Recovery 1,313 A5
Fort Shawnee 4,128 B4
Fostoria 14,983 D3
Frankfort 1,065 D7
Franklin 11,026 B6
Franklin Furnace 1,212 E8
Frazeysburg 1,165 F5
Fredericksburg 502 G4
Fredericktown 2,443 F5
Freeport 475 H5
Fremont▲ 17,648 D3
Fulton 325 E5
Fultonham 178 F6
Gahanna 27,791 E5
Galena 361 E5
Galion 11,859 E4
Gallipolis▲ 4,831 F8
Gambier 2,073 F5
Garfield Heights 31,739 J9
Garrettsville 2,014 H3
Gates Mills 2,508 J9
Geneva 6,597 J2
Geneva-on-the-Lake 1,626 H2
Genoa 2,262 D2
Georgetown▲ 3,627 C8
Germantown 4,916 B6
Gettysburg 539 A5
Gibsonburg 2,579 D3
Gilboa 208 C3
Girard 11,304 J3
Glandorf 829 B3
Glendale 2,445 C9
Glenford 208 F6
Glenmont 233 F4
Glenwillow 455 J10
Glouster 2,001 F6
Gnadenhutten 1,226 G5
Golf Manor 4,154 C9
Gordon 206 B6
Grafton 3,344 F3
Grand Rapids 955 C3
Grand River H2
Grandview 1,301 H7
Grandview Heights 7,010 D6
Granville 4,353 E5
Gratiot 195 F6
Gratis 998 A6
Green Camp 393 D4
Green Springs 1,446 E3
Greenfield 5,172 D7
Greenhills 4,393 B9
Greensburg 3,306 G4
Greentown 1,856 H4
Greenville▲ 12,863 A5
Greenwich 1,442 E3
Groesbeck 6,684 B9
Grove City 19,661 D6
Groveport 2,948 E6
Grover Hill 518 B3
Hamden 877 F7
Hamersville 586 C8
Hamilton▲ 61,368 A7
Hamler 623 B3
Hanging Rock 306 E8
Hanover 803 F5
Hanoverton 434 J4
Harbor View 122 C2
Harpster 233 D4
Harrisburg 340 D6
Harrison 7,518 A9
Harrisville 308 J5
Harrod 537 C4
Hartford 418 J3
Hartford 444 E5
Hartville 2,031 H4
Harveysburg 437 C7
Haskins 549 C3
Haviland 210 A3
Hayesville 457 F4
Heath 7,231 F5
Hebron 2,076 E6
Helena 267 D3
Hemlock 203 F6
Hicksville 3,664 A3
Higginsport 298 C8
Highland 275 C7
Highland Heights 6,249 J9
Hilliard 11,796 D5
Hillsboro▲ 6,235 C7
Hiram 1,330 H3
Holgate 1,290 B3
Holland 1,210 C2
Hollansburg 300 A5
Holloway 354 H5
Holmesville 419 G4
Hopedale 685 J5
Hoytville 301 C3
Hubbard 8,248 J3
Huber Heights 38,696 B6
Hudson 5,159 H3
Hunting Valley 799 J9
Huntsville 343 C5
Huron 7,030 E3
Independence 6,500 H9
Indian Hill 5,383 C9
Irondale 382 J4
Ironton▲ 12,751 E8
Ithaca 119 A6
Jackson Center 1,398 B5
Jackson▲ 6,144 E7
Jacksonville 544 F7
Jamestown 1,794 C6
Jefferson (West Jefferson) 3,331 D6
Jefferson▲ 2,952 J2
Jeffersonville 1,281 C6
Jenera 285 C4
Jeromesville 582 F4
Jerry City 517 C3
Jerusalem 144 H6
Jewett 778 H5
Johnstown 3,237 E5
Junction City 770 F6
Kalida 947 B4
Kelleys Island 172 E2
Kent 28,835 H3
Kenton▲ 8,356 C4
Kettering 60,569 B6
Kettlersville 194 B5
Killbuck 809 G5
Kimbolton 134 G5
Kingston 1,153 E7
Kingsville 1,243 J2
Kipton 283 F3
Kirby 155 D4
Kirkersville 563 E6
Kirtland 5,881 H2
Kirtland Hills 628 H2
La Rue 802 D4
Lafayette 449 C4
Lagrange 1,199 F3
Lakeline 210 J8
Lakemore 2,684 H3
Lakeview 1,056 C4
Lakewood 59,718 G9
Lancaster▲ 34,507 E6
Latty 205 A3
Laura 483 B6
Laurelville 605 E7
Lawrenceville 304 C6
Lebanon▲ 10,453 B7
Leesburg 1,063 D7
Leesville 156 H5
Leetonia 2,070 J4
Leipsic 2,203 C3
Lewisburg 1,584 A6
Lewisville 261 H6
Lexington 4,124 E4
Liberty Center 1,084 B3
Lima▲ 45,549 B4
Limaville 152 H4
Lincoln Heights 4,805 C9
Lindsey 529 D3
Linndale 159 G9
Lisbon▲ 3,037 J4
Lithopolis 563 E6
Lockbourne 173 E6
Lockington 214 B5
Lockland 4,357 C9
Lodi 3,042 F3
Logan▲ 6,725 F6
London▲ 7,807 C6
Lorain 71,245 F3
Lordstown 3,404 J3
Lore City 384 H6
Loudonville 2,915 F4
Louisville 8,087 H4
Loveland 9,990 D9
Lowell 617 H6
Lowellville 1,349 J3
Lower Salem 103 H6
Lucas 730 F4
Lucasville 1,575 E8
Luckey 848 D3
Ludlow Falls 300 B6
Lynchburg 1,212 C7
Lyndhurst 15,982 J9
Lyons 579 B2
Macedonia 7,509 J10
Mack 2,816 B9
Macksburg 218 G6
Madeira 9,141 C9
Madison 2,477 H2
Magnetic Springs 373 D5
Magnolia 937 H4
Maineville 359 C9
Malinta 294 B3

(continued on following page)

Agriculture, Industry and Resources

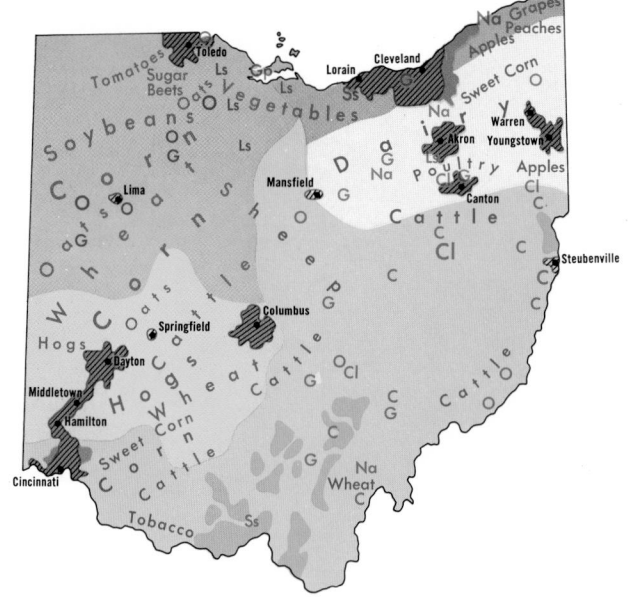

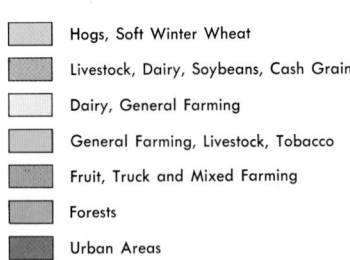

DOMINANT LAND USE

- Hogs, Soft Winter Wheat
- Livestock, Dairy, Soybeans, Cash Grain
- Dairy, General Farming
- General Farming, Livestock, Tobacco
- Fruit, Truck and Mixed Farming
- Forests
- Urban Areas

MAJOR MINERAL OCCURRENCES

- C   Coal
- Cl   Clay
- G   Natural Gas
- Gp   Gypsum
- Ls   Limestone
- Na   Salt
- O   Petroleum
- Ss   Sandstone

▨ Major Industrial Areas

Malta 802 .... G6	Mount Healthy 7,580 .... B9	Olmsted Falls 6,741 .... G9
Malvern 1,112 .... H4	Mount Orab 1,929 .... C7	Ontario 4,026 .... E4
Manchester 2,223 .... C8	Mount Pleasant 498 .... J5	Orange 2,810 .... J9
Mansfield▲ 50,627 .... F4	Mount Sterling 1,647 .... D6	Orangeville 253 .... J3
Mantua 1,178 .... H3	Mount Vernon▲ 14,550 .... E5	Oregon 18,334 .... D2
Maple Heights 27,089 .... H9	Mount Victory 551 .... D5	Orient 273 .... D6
Marblehead 745 .... E2	Mowrystown 460 .... C7	Orrville 7,712 .... G4
Marengo 393 .... E5	Mulberry 2,856 .... B7	Orwell 1,258 .... J2
Mariemont 3,118 .... C9	Munroe Falls 5,359 .... H3	Osgood 255 .... A5
Marietta▲ 15,026 .... G7	Murray City 499 .... F6	Ostrander 431 .... D5
Marion▲ 34,075 .... D4	Mutual 126 .... C5	Ottawa Hills 4,543 .... C2
Marseilles 130 .... D4	Napoleon▲ 8,884 .... B3	Ottawa▲ 3,999 .... B3
Marshall 758 .... C7	Nashville 181 .... F4	Ottoville 842 .... B4
Marshallville 788 .... G4	Navarre 1,635 .... H4	Otway 105 .... D8
Martin 7,990 .... D2	Neffs 1,213 .... J5	Owensville 1,019 .... B7
Martins Ferry 9,331 .... J5	Nellie 130 .... F5	Oxford 18,937 .... A6
Martinsburg 213 .... F5	Nelsonville 4,563 .... F7	Painesville▲ 15,699 .... H2
Martinsville 476 .... C7	Nevada 849 .... D4	Palestine 197 .... A5
Marysville▲ 9,656 .... D5	Neville 226 .... B8	Pandora 1,009 .... C4
Mason 11,452 .... B7	New Alexandria 257 .... J5	Parma 87,876 .... H9
Massillon 31,007 .... H4	New Albany 1,621 .... E5	Parma Heights 21,448 .... G9
Masury 1,836 .... J3	New Athens 370 .... H5	Parral 255 .... G4
Maumee 15,561 .... C2	New Bloomington 282 .... D4	Pataskala 5,046 .... E6
Mayfield 3,462 .... J9	New Boston 2,717 .... E8	Patterson 145 .... C4
Mayfield Heights 19,847 .... J9	New Bremen 2,558 .... B5	Paulding▲ 2,605 .... A3
McArthur▲ 1,541 .... F7	New Carlisle 6,049 .... C6	Payne 1,244 .... A3
McClure 781 .... C3	New Concord 2,086 .... G6	Peebles 1,782 .... D8
McComb 1,544 .... C3	New Holland 841 .... D6	Pemberville 1,279 .... C3
McConnelsville▲ 1,804 .... G6	New Knoxville 838 .... B5	Peninsula 562 .... G3
McDonald 3,526 .... J3	New Lebanon 4,323 .... B6	Pepper Pike 6,185 .... J9
McGuffey 550 .... C4	New Lexington▲ 5,117 .... F6	Perry 1,012 .... H2
Mechanicsburg 1,803 .... D5	New London 2,642 .... F3	Perrysburg 12,551 .... C2
Medina▲ 19,231 .... G3	New Madison 928 .... A6	Perrysville 467 .... F4
Melrose 307 .... B3	New Miami 2,555 .... A7	Phillipsburg 644 .... B6
Mendon 717 .... A4	New Middletown 1,912 .... J4	Philo 810 .... G6
Mentor 47,358 .... H2	New Paris 1,801 .... A6	Pickerington 5,668 .... E6
Mentor-on-the-Lake 8,271 .... G2	New Philadelphia▲ 15,698 .... G5	Piketon 1,717 .... E7
Metamora 543 .... C1	New Richmond 2,408 .... B8	Pioneer 1,287 .... A2
Meyers Lake 493 .... H4	New Riegel 298 .... D3	Piqua 20,612 .... B5
Miamisburg 17,834 .... B6	New Straitsville 865 .... F6	Pitsburg 425 .... A6
Middle Point 639 .... B4	New Vienna 932 .... C7	Plain City 2,278 .... D5
Middleburg 14,702 .... C5	New Washington 1,057 .... D4	Plainfield 178 .... G5
Middleburg Heights 16,218 .... G10	New Waterford 1,278 .... J4	Pleasant City 419 .... G6
Middlefield 1,898 .... H3	New Weston 148 .... A5	Pleasant Hill 1,066 .... B5
Middleport 2,725 .... F7	Newark▲ 44,389 .... F5	Pleasant Plain 138 .... B7
Middletown 46,022 .... A6	Newburgh Heights 2,310 .... H9	Pleasantville 926 .... E6
Midland 319 .... C7	Newcomerstown 4,012 .... G5	Plymouth 1,942 .... E4
Midvale 575 .... H5	Newton Falls 4,866 .... J3	Poland 2,992 .... J3
Mifflin 162 .... F4	Newtonsville 427 .... B7	Polk 355 .... F4
Milan 1,464 .... E3	Newtown 1,589 .... C10	Pomeroy▲ 2,259 .... G7
Milford 5,660 .... C9	Ney 331 .... B3	Port Clinton▲ 7,106 .... E2
Milford Center 651 .... D5	Niles 21,128 .... J3	Port Jefferson 381 .... C5
Millbury 1,081 .... D2	North Baltimore 3,139 .... C3	Port Washington 513 .... G5
Milledgeville 120 .... C6	North Bend 541 .... B9	Port William 242 .... C6
Miller 173 .... F8	North Canton 14,748 .... H4	Portage 469 .... C3
Miller City 168 .... B3	North College Hill 11,002 .... B9	Portsmouth▲ 22,676 .... E8
Millersburg▲ 3,051 .... F4	North Fairfield 504 .... E3	Potsdam 250 .... B6
Millersport 1,010 .... E6	North Hampton 417 .... C5	Powell 2,154 .... D5
Millville 755 .... A7	North Kingsville 2,672 .... J2	Powhatan Point 1,807 .... J6
Milton Center 200 .... C3	North Lewisburg 1,160 .... C5	Proctorville 765 .... F9
Mineral 725 .... F7	North Madison 8,699 .... H2	Prospect 1,148 .... D5
Mineral City 884 .... H4	North Olmsted 34,204 .... G9	Put-in-Bay 141 .... E2
Minerva 4,318 .... H4	North Perry 824 .... H2	Quaker City 560 .... H6
Minerva Park 1,463 .... E5	North Randall 977 .... J9	Quincy 697 .... C5
Mingo 4,297 .... C5	North Ridgeville 21,564 .... F3	Racine 729 .... G8
Mingo Junction 4,834 .... J5	North Robinson 216 .... E4	Rarden 184 .... E7
Minster 2,650 .... B5	North Royalton 23,197 .... H10	Ravenna▲ 12,069 .... H3
Mogadore 4,008 .... H3	North Star 246 .... A5	Rawson 482 .... C4
Monroe 279 .... B7	North Zanesville 2,121 .... G6	Ray 490 .... F7
Monroeville 1,381 .... E3	Northfield 3,624 .... J10	Rayland 566 .... J5
Montezuma 199 .... A4	Northwood 5,506 .... D2	Reading 12,038 .... C9
Montgomery 9,753 .... C9	Norton 11,477 .... G3	Reminderville 2,163 .... J10
Montpelier 4,299 .... A2	Norwalk▲ 14,731 .... E3	Republic 611 .... D3
Moraine 5,989 .... C6	Norwich 133 .... G6	Reynoldsburg 25,748 .... E6
Moreland Hills 3,354 .... J9	Norwood 23,674 .... C9	Richfield 3,117 .... G3
Morral 373 .... D4	Oak Harbor 2,637 .... D2	Richmond (Grand River) H2
Morristown 296 .... H5	Oak Hill 1,831 .... F8	Richmond 624 .... J5
Morrow 1,206 .... B7	Oakwood 709 .... H9	Richmond Heights 9,611 .... H9
Moscow 279 .... B8	Oakwood 886 .... C6	Richwood 2,186 .... D5
Mount Blanchard 491 .... D4	Oakwood 9,372 .... B6	Ridgeway 378 .... D4
Mount Carmel 4,462 .... C10	Oberlin 8,191 .... F3	Rio Grande 995 .... F8
Mount Cory 245 .... C4	Obetz 3,167 .... E6	Ripley 1,816 .... C8
Mount Eaton 236 .... G4	Ohio City 899 .... A4	Risingsun 659 .... C3
Mount Gilead▲ 2,846 .... E4		Rittman 6,147 .... G4
Riverlea 503 .... D5	Steubenville▲ 22,125 .... J5	Waverly▲ 4,477 .... D7	Chagrin (riv.) J8
Rochester 206 .... F3	Stockport 462 .... G6	Wayne 803 .... C3	Clear Fork (res.) E4
Rock Creek 553 .... J2	Stone Creek 181 .... G5	Waynesburg 1,068 .... H4	Clear Fork, Mohican (riv.) F4
Rockford 1,119 .... A4	Stout 518 .... D8	Waynesfield 831 .... C4	Clendening (lake) H5
Rocky Ridge 425 .... D2	Stoutsville 537 .... E6	Waynesville 1,949 .... B6	Cuyahoga (riv.) H10
Rocky River 20,410 .... G9	Stow 27,702 .... H3	Wellington 4,140 .... F3	Cuyahoga Valley
Rogers 247 .... J4	Strasburg 1,995 .... G4	Wellston 6,049 .... F7	Nat'l Rec. Area H10
Rome 99 .... J2	Stratton 278 .... J4	Wellsville 4,532 .... J4	Darby (creek) D5
Rosemount 1,926 .... D8	Streetsboro 9,932 .... H3	West Alexandria 1,460 .... A6	Deer (creek) D6
Roseville 1,847 .... F6	Strongsville 35,308 .... G10	West Carrollton 14,403 .... B6	Deer Creek (lake) D6
Ross 2,124 .... B9	Struthers 12,284 .... J3	West Elkton 208 .... A6	Delaware (lake) E5
Rossburg 250 .... A5	Stryker 1,468 .... B3	West Farmington 542 .... J3	Dillon (lake) F5
Rossford 5,861 .... C2	Sugar Grove 465 .... E6	West Jefferson 4,331 .... D6	Dover (lake) H4
Roswell 257 .... H5	Sugarcreek 2,062 .... G5	West Lafayette 2,129 .... G5	Duck (creek) H6
Rushsylvania 573 .... C5	Summerfield 295 .... H6	West Leipsic 244 .... B3	Erie (lake) H1
Rushville 229 .... F6	Summitville 125 .... J4	West Liberty 1,613 .... C5	Grand (riv.) H2
Russells Point 1,504 .... C5	Sunbury 2,046 .... E5	West Manchester 464 .... A6	Great Miami (riv.) A7
Russellville 459 .... C8	Swanton 3,557 .... C2	West Mansfield 830 .... D5	Hocking (riv.) F7
Russia 442 .... B5	Sycamore 919 .... D4	West Millgrove 171 .... C3	Hoover (res.) E5
Rutland 469 .... F7	Sylvania 17,301 .... C1	West Milton 4,348 .... B6	Huron (riv.) E3
Sabina 2,662 .... C7	Syracuse 827 .... G7	West Portsmouth 3,551 .... D8	Indian (lake) C5
Saint Bernard 5,344 .... B9	Tallmadge 14,870 .... H3	West Rushville 134 .... F6	James A. Garfield Nat'l
Saint Clairsville▲ 5,162 .... J5	Tarlton 315 .... E6	West Salem 1,534 .... F4	Hist. Site G2
Saint Henry 1,907 .... A5	Taylorsville (Philo) F6	West Union▲ 3,096 .... C8	Kelleys (isl.) E2
Saint Louisville 372 .... F5	Terrace Park 2,133 .... D9	West Unity 1,677 .... B2	Killbuck (creek) G4
Saint Martin 141 .... C7	The Plains 2,644 .... F7	Westerville 30,269 .... D5	Kokosing (creek) E5
Saint Marys 8,441 .... B4	Thornville 758 .... F6	Westfield Center 784 .... G3	Leesville (lake) H5
Saint Paris 1,842 .... C5	Thurston 539 .... E6	Westlake 27,018 .... G9	Licking (riv.) F5
Salem 12,233 .... J4	Tiffin▲ 18,604 .... D3	Weston 1,716 .... C3	Little Beaver (creek) J4
Salineville 1,474 .... J4	Tiltonsville 1,517 .... J5	Wharton 378 .... D4	Little Miami (riv.) B6
Sandusky▲ 29,764 .... E3	Timberlake 833 .... J8	Wheelersburg 5,113 .... E8	Little Miami, East Fork (riv.) C7
Sarahsville 162 .... H6	Tipp City 6,027 .... B6	Whitehall 20,572 .... E6	Little Muskingum (riv.) H6
Sardinia 792 .... C7	Tiro 246 .... E4	Whitehouse 2,528 .... C2	Loramie (lake) B5
Savannah 363 .... F4	Toledo▲ 332,943 .... C2	Wickliffe 14,558 .... J8	Mad (riv.) C6
Scio 856 .... H5	Tontogany 364 .... C3	Wilberforce 2,639 .... C6	Maumee (bay) D2
Sciotodale 1,128 .... E8	Toronto 6,127 .... J5	Wilkesville 151 .... F7	Maumee (riv.) A3
Scott 339 .... A4	Tremont City 493 .... C5	Willard 6,210 .... E3	Middle Bass (isl.) E2
Seaman 1,013 .... C8	Trenton 6,189 .... B7	Williamsburg 2,322 .... B7	Mohican (riv.) F4
Sebring 4,848 .... H4	Trimble 441 .... F7	Williamsport 851 .... D6	Mosquito Creek (lake) J3
Senecaville 434 .... H6	Trotwood 8,816 .... B6	Willoughby 20,510 .... J8	Mound City Group Nat'l Mon. E7
Seven Hills 12,339 .... H9	Troy▲ 19,478 .... B5	Willoughby Hills 8,427 .... J9	Muskingum (riv.) G6
Seven Mile 804 .... A7	Tuscarawas 826 .... H5	Willowick 15,269 .... J8	North Bass (isl.) E2
Seville 1,810 .... G3	Twinsburg 9,606 .... J10	Willshire 541 .... A4	Ohio (riv.) B8
Shadyside 3,934 .... J6	Uhrichsville 5,604 .... H5	Wilmington▲ 11,199 .... C7	Ohio Brush (creek) D8
Shaker Heights 30,831 .... H9	Union 5,501 .... A6	Wilmot 261 .... G4	Olentangy (riv.) D4
Sharon 13,153 .... G6	Union City 1,984 .... A5	Wilson 136 .... H4	Paint (creek) D7
Sharonville 10,108 .... C9	Uniontown 3,074 .... H4	Winchester 978 .... C8	Perry's Victory and
Shawnee 742 .... F6	Unionville 238 .... J2	Windham 2,943 .... H3	Int'l Peace Mem. E2
Shawnee Hills 423 .... D5	Unionville Center 272 .... D5	Wintersville 4,102 .... J5	Piedmont (lake) H5
Sheffield 1,943 .... F3	Uniopolis 261 .... C4	Withamsville 2,834 .... C9	Portage (riv.) D3
Sheffield Lake 9,825 .... F3	University Heights 14,790 .... H9	Woodlawn 2,674 .... C9	Pymatuning (res.) J2
Shelby 9,564 .... E4	Upper Arlington 34,128 .... D6	Woodmere 834 .... J9	Raccoon (creek) F8
Sherrodsville 284 .... H4	Upper Sandusky▲ 5,906 .... D4	Woodsfield▲ 2,832 .... H6	Rattlesnake (creek) C7
Sherwood 828 .... A3	Urbana▲ 11,353 .... C5	Woodstock 296 .... C5	Rickenbacker A.F.B. E6
Shiloh 778 .... E4	Urbancrest 862 .... D6	Woodville 1,953 .... D3	Rocky (riv.) G9
Shreve 1,584 .... F4	Utica 1,997 .... F5	Wooster▲ 22,191 .... F4	Rocky Fork (lake) D7
Sidney▲ 18,710 .... B5	Valley Hi 217 .... C5	Worthington 14,869 .... E5	Saint Joseph (riv.) A3
Silver Lake 3,052 .... G3	Valley View 2,137 .... H9	Wren 190 .... A4	Saint Marys (lake) A4
Silverton 5,859 .... C9	Valley View 730 .... C6	Wyoming 8,128 .... C9	Saint Marys (riv.) A4
Sinking Spring 189 .... D7	Van Buren 337 .... C3	Xenia▲ 24,664 .... C6	Salt Fork (creek) H5
Smithfield 762 .... J5	Van Wert▲ 10,891 .... A4	Yankee Lake 88 .... J3	Sandusky (bay) E3
Smithville 1,354 .... G4	Vandalia 13,882 .... C6	Yellow Springs 3,973 .... C6	Sandusky (riv.) D3
Solon 18,548 .... J10	Vanlue 373 .... D4	Yorkshire 126 .... B5	Scioto (riv.) D8
Somerset 1,390 .... F6	Venedocia 158 .... B4	Yorkville 1,246 .... J5	Senecaville (lake) H6
Somerville 279 .... A6	Vermilion 11,127 .... F3	Youngstown▲ 95,732 .... J3	Sevenmile (creek) A6
South Amherst 1,765 .... F3	Verona 472 .... A6	Zaleski 294 .... F7	South Bass (isl.) E2
South Bloomfield 900 .... D6	Versailles 2,351 .... A5	Zanesfield 183 .... C5	Stillwater (riv.) B5
South Charleston 1,626 .... C6	Vienna 1,067 .... J3	Zanesville▲ 26,778 .... G6	Symmes (creek) F8
South Euclid 23,866 .... H9	Vinton 293 .... G7	Zoar 284 .... H4	Tappan (lake) H5
South Lebanon 2,696 .... B7	Wadsworth 15,718 .... G3		Tiffin (riv.) B3
South Point 3,823 .... F9	Waite Hill 454 .... H2	**OTHER FEATURES**	Tuscarawas (riv.) H5
South Russell 3,402 .... H3	Wakeman 948 .... F3		Vermilion (riv.) F3
South Salem 227 .... D7	Walbridge 2,736 .... C2	Atwood (lake) H5	Wabash (riv.) A5
South Solon 379 .... C6	Waldo 340 .... D5	Auglaize (riv.) B4	West Sister (isl.) D2
South Vienna 550 .... C6	Walton Hills 2,371 .... J10	Berlin (lake) H4	Whiteoak (creek) C7
South Webster 806 .... E8	Wapakoneta▲ 9,214 .... B4	Big Walnut (creek) E5	William H. Taft
South Zanesville 1,969 .... F6	Warren▲ 50,793 .... J3	Black Fork, Mohican (riv.) F3	Nat'l Hist. Site C10
Sparta 201 .... E5	Warrensville Heights 15,745 .... H9	Blanchard (riv.) C3	Wills (creek) G5
Spencer 726 .... F3	Warsaw 699 .... F5	Blennerhassett (isl.) G7	Wright-Patterson A.F.B.
Spencerville 2,288 .... B4	Washington Court House▲	Buckeye (lake) F6	8,579 .... B6
Spring Valley 507 .... C6	12,682 .... D6	Campbell (hill) C5	Yellow (creek) J4
Springboro 6,590 .... B6	Washingtonville 894 .... J4	Captina (creek) J6	
Springdale 10,621 .... B9	Waterville 4,517 .... C3	Cedar (pt.) D2	▲County seat
Springfield▲ 70,487 .... C6	Wauseon▲ 6,322 .... B2		

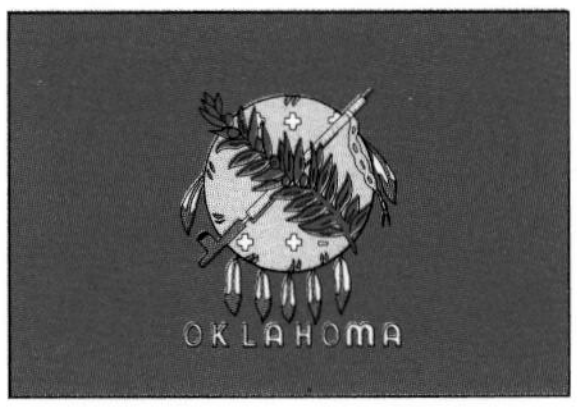

AREA 69,956 sq. mi. (181,186 sq. km.)
POPULATION 3,157,604
CAPITAL Oklahoma City
LARGEST CITY Oklahoma City
HIGHEST POINT Black Mesa 4,973 ft. (1516 m.)
SETTLED IN 1889
ADMITTED TO UNION November 16, 1907
POPULAR NAME Sooner State
STATE FLOWER Mistletoe
STATE BIRD Scissor-tailed Flycatcher

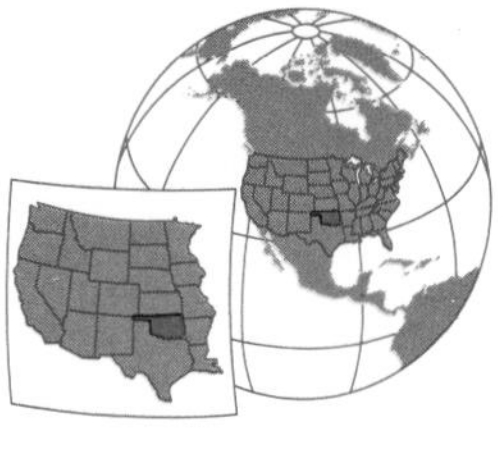

COUNTIES

Adair 18,421 ... S3
Alfalfa 6,416 ... K1
Atoka 12,778 ... O6
Beaver 6,023 ... E1
Beckham 18,812 ... G4
Blaine 11,470 ... K3
Bryan 32,089 ... O7
Caddo 29,550 ... K4
Canadian 74,409 ... K3
Carter 42,919 ... M6
Cherokee 34,049 ... R3
Choctaw 15,302 ... P6
Cimarron 3,301 ... A1
Cleveland 174,253 ... M4
Coal 5,780 ... O5
Comanche 111,486 ... K5
Cotton 6,651 ... K6
Craig 14,104 ... R1
Creek 60,915 ... O3
Custer 26,897 ... H3
Delaware 28,070 ... S2
Dewey 5,551 ... H2
Ellis 4,497 ... G2
Garfield 56,735 ... L2
Garvin 26,605 ... M5
Grady 41,747 ... L5
Grant 5,689 ... L1
Greer 6,559 ... G5
Harmon 3,793 ... G5
Harper 4,063 ... G1
Haskell 10,940 ... R4
Hughes 13,023 ... O4
Jackson 28,764 ... H5
Jefferson 7,010 ... L6
Johnston 10,032 ... N6
Kay 48,056 ... M1
Kingfisher 13,212 ... L3
Kiowa 11,347 ... J5
Latimer 10,333 ... R5
Le Flore 43,270 ... S5
Lincoln 29,216 ... N3
Logan 29,011 ... M3
Love 8,157 ... M7
Major 8,055 ... K2
Marshall 10,829 ... N6
Mayes 33,366 ... R2
McClain 22,795 ... L5
McCurtain 33,433 ... S6
McIntosh 16,779 ... P4
Murray 12,042 ... M6
Muskogee 68,078 ... R3
Noble 11,045 ... M2
Nowata 9,992 ... P1
Okfuskee 11,551 ... O3
Oklahoma 599,611 ... M3
Okmulgee 36,490 ... P3
Osage 41,645 ... O1
Ottawa 30,561 ... S1
Pawnee 15,575 ... N2
Payne 61,507 ... N2
Pittsburg 40,581 ... P5
Pontotoc 34,119 ... N5
Pottawatomie 58,760 ... N4
Pushmataha 10,997 ... R6
Roger Mills 4,147 ... G3
Rogers 55,170 ... P2
Seminole 25,412 ... N4
Sequoyah 33,828 ... S3
Stephens 42,299 ... L6
Texas 16,419 ... C1
Tillman 10,384 ... J6
Tulsa 503,341 ... P2
Wagoner 47,883 ... P3
Washington 48,066 ... P1
Washita 11,441 ... J4
Woods 9,103 ... J1
Woodward 18,976 ... H2

CITIES and TOWNS

Achille 491 ... O7
Ada▲ 15,820 ... N5
Adair 685 ... R2
Adams 150 ... D1
Adamson 150 ... P5
Addington 100 ... L6
Afton 915 ... S1
Agra 334 ... N3
Akins 250 ... S3
Albany 65 ... O7
Albert 100 ... K4
Albion 88 ... R5
Alderson 395 ... P5
Alex 639 ... L5
Alfalfa 70 ... J4
Aline 295 ... K1
Allen 972 ... O5
Altus▲ 21,910 ... H5
Alva▲ 5,495 ... J1
Amber 418 ... L4
Ames 268 ... K2
Amorita 56 ... K1
Anadarko▲ 6,586 ... K4
Antlers▲ 2,524 ... P6
Apache 1,591 ... K5
Apperson 30 ... N1
Aqua Park ... R3
Arapaho▲ 802 ... H3
Arcadia 320 ... M3
Ardmore▲ 23,079 ... M6
Arkoma 2,393 ... T4
Arnett▲ 547 ... G2
Asher 449 ... N5
Ashland 56 ... O5
Atoka▲ 3,298 ... O6
Atwood 225 ... O5
Avant 369 ... O2
Avard 37 ... J1
Avery 35 ... N3
Bache 100 ... P5
Bacone 786 ... R3
Baker 70 ... D1
Balko 100 ... E1
Barnsdall 1,316 ... O1
Baron 300 ... S3
Bartlesville▲ 34,256 ... O1
Battiest 250 ... S6
Bearden 142 ... O4
Beaver▲ 1,584 ... F1
Beggs 1,150 ... P3
Belzoni 50 ... R6
Bengal 300 ... R5
Bennington 251 ... P7
Bentley 75 ... O6
Berlin 50 ... G4
Bernice 330 ... S1
Bessie 248 ... H4
Bethany 20,075 ... L3
Bethel 2,505 ... S6
Bethel Acres 2,314 ... M4
Big Cabin 271 ... R1
Billings 555 ... M1
Binger 724 ... K4
Bison 103 ... L2
Bixby 9,502 ... P3
Blackburn 110 ... N2
Blackgum 150 ... S3
Blackwell 7,538 ... M1
Blair 922 ... H5
Blanchard 1,922 ... L4
Blanco 215 ... P5
Blocker 135 ... P4
Blue 175 ... O7
Bluejacket 247 ... R1
Boggy Depot 100 ... O6
Boise City▲ 1,509 ... B1
Bokchito 576 ... O6
Bokhoma 35 ... S7
Bokoshe 403 ... S4
Boley 908 ... O4
Boswell 643 ... P6
Bowlegs 398 ... N4
Bowring 115 ... O1
Boyd 10 ... E1
Boynton 391 ... P3
Braden 15 ... S4
Bradley 166 ... L5
Braggs 308 ... R3
Braman 251 ... M1
Bray 925 ... L5
Breckinridge 261 ... L2
Briartown 55 ... R4
Bridgeport 137 ... K3
Brinkman ... G4
Bristow 4,062 ... O3
Broken Arrow 58,043 ... P2
Broken Bow 3,961 ... S7
Bromide 162 ... N6
Brooksville 69 ... M4
Bryant 74 ... P4
Buffalo▲ 1,312 ... G1
Bunch 64 ... S3
Burbank 165 ... N1
Burlington 169 ... K1
Burneyville 150 ... M7
Burns Flat 1,027 ... H4
Butler 341 ... H3
Byars 263 ... N5
Byng 755 ... N5
Byron 57 ... K1
Cache 2,251 ... J5
Caddo 918 ... O6
Cairo 50 ... O5
Calera 1,536 ... O7
Calumet 560 ... K3
Calvin 251 ... O5
Camargo 185 ... H2
Cameron 327 ... T4
Canadian 261 ... P4
Canadian City ... L4
Caney 184 ... O6
Canton 632 ... J2
Canute 538 ... H4
Capron 38 ... J1
Cardin 165 ... S1
Carmen 459 ... J1
Carnegie 1,593 ... J4
Carney 558 ... N3
Carrier 171 ... K2
Carter 286 ... H4
Cartersville 79 ... S4
Cashion 430 ... L3
Castle 94 ... O4
Catoosa 2,954 ... P2
Cement 642 ... K5
Center 100 ... N5
Centrahoma 106 ... O5
Centralia ... R1
Chandler▲ 2,596 ... N3
Chattanooga 437 ... J6
Checotah 3,290 ... R4
Chelsea 1,620 ... P1
Cherokee▲ 1,787 ... K1
Chester 104 ... J2
Cheyenne▲ 948 ... G3
Chickasha▲ 14,988 ... L4
Chilocco 400 ... M1
Choctaw 8,545 ... M3
Chouteau 1,771 ... R2
Christie 375 ... S3
Cimarron 71 ... L3
Claremore▲ 13,280 ... R2
Clarita 72 ... O6
Clayton 636 ... R5
Clearview 47 ... O4
Clemscot 52 ... L6
Cleo Springs 359 ... K2
Cleora 45 ... S1
Cleveland 3,156 ... O2
Clinton 9,298 ... H3
Cloud Chief 12 ... J4
Cloudy 175 ... R6
Coalgate▲ 1,895 ... O5
Cogar 40 ... K4
Colbert 1,043 ... O7
Colcord 628 ... S2
Cold Springs 24 ... J5
Cole 355 ... L4
Coleman 200 ... O6
Collinsville 3,612 ... P2
Colony 163 ... J4
Comanche 1,695 ... L6
Commerce 2,426 ... R1
Concho 300 ... L3
Connerville 150 ... N6
Cooperton 15 ... J5
Copan 809 ... P1
Cordell▲ ... H4
Corinne 100 ... R6
Corn 548 ... J4
Cornish 164 ... L6
Council Hill 139 ... P3
Countyline 550 ... L6
Courtney 12 ... L7
Covington 590 ... L2
Coweta 6,159 ... P3
Cowlington 756 ... S4
Cox City 285 ... L5
Coyle 289 ... M3
Crawford 53 ... G3
Crescent 1,236 ... L3
Cromwell 268 ... N4
Crowder 339 ... P4
Cumberland 100 ... N6
Curtis 30 ... H2
Cushing 7,218 ... N3
Custer City 443 ... J3
Cyril 1,072 ... K5
Dacoma 182 ... J1
Daisy 250 ... P5
Dale 160 ... M4
Darwin 50 ... P6
Davenport 979 ... N3
Davidson 473 ... J6
Davis 2,543 ... M5
Deer Creek 124 ... L1
Del City 23,928 ... L4
Dela 434 ... P6
Delaware 544 ... P1
Delhi 41 ... G4
Depew 502 ... O3
Devol 165 ... J6
Dewar 921 ... P4
Dewey 3,326 ... P1
Dibble 181 ... L4
Dickson 942 ... M6
Dill City 622 ... H4
Disney 257 ... S2
Dougherty 138 ... M6
Douglas 55 ... L2
Douthat 30 ... S1
Dover 376 ... L3
Dow 300 ... P5
Driftwood ... K1
Drummond 408 ... L2
Drumright 2,799 ... N3
Duke (E. Duke) 360 ... G5
Duncan▲ 21,732 ... L5
Durant▲ 12,823 ... O6
Durham 30 ... G3
Dustin 429 ... O4
Eagle City 56 ... J3
Eagletown 650 ... S6
Eakly 277 ... K4
Earlsboro 535 ... N4
Edmond 52,315 ... M3
El Reno▲ 15,414 ... K3
Eldorado 573 ... G6
Elgin 975 ... K5
Elk City 10,428 ... G4
Elmer 132 ... H6
Elmore City 493 ... M5
Elmwood 300 ... F1
Empire City 219 ... L6
Enid▲ 45,309 ... L2
Enterprise 130 ... R4
Erick 1,083 ... G4
Eucha 210 ... S2
Eufaula▲ 2,652 ... P4
Fair Oaks 1,133 ... P2
Fairfax 1,749 ... N1
Fairland 916 ... S1
Fairmont 129 ... L2
Fairview▲ 2,936 ... J2
Fallis 49 ... M3
Fanshawe 331 ... S5
Fargo 299 ... G2
Farris 100 ... P6
Faxon 127 ... J6
Fay 140 ... J3
Featherston 75 ... P4
Felt 120 ... A1
Fillmore 60 ... N6
Finley 350 ... R6
Fittstown 500 ... N5
Fitzhugh 196 ... N5
Fleetwood 12 ... L7
Fletcher 1,002 ... K5
Foraker 25 ... O1
Forest Park 1,249 ... M3
Forgan 489 ... E1
Fort Cobb 663 ... K4
Fort Gibson 3,359 ... R3
Fort Supply 369 ... G1
Fort Towson 568 ... R7
Foss 148 ... H4
Foster 100 ... M5
Fox 400 ... M6
Foyil 86 ... R2
Francis 346 ... N5
Frederick▲ 5,221 ... H6
Freedom 264 ... H1
Gage 473 ... G2
Gans 218 ... S4
Garber 959 ... M2
Garvin 128 ... S7
Gate 159 ... F1
Geary 1,347 ... K3
Gene Autry 97 ... N6
Geronimo 990 ... K6
Gerty 95 ... O5
Glencoe 473 ... M2
Glenpool 6,688 ... P3
Glover 244 ... S6
Golden 300 ... S6
Goldsby 816 ... L4
Goltry 297 ... K1
Goodwater 240 ... S7
Goodwell 1,065 ... C1
Gore 690 ... R3
Gotebo 370 ... J4
Gould 237 ... G5
Gowen 75 ... R5
Gracemont 339 ... K4
Grady 85 ... L6
Graham 200 ... M6
Grainola 58 ... N1
Grand Lake Towne 58 ... S1
Grandfield 1,224 ... J6
Granite 1,844 ... H5
Grant ... R7
Gray Horse 60 ... N1
Grayson 66 ... P3
Greenfield 200 ... K3
Griggs 15 ... B1
Grove 4,020 ... S1
Guthrie▲ 10,518 ... M3
Guymon▲ 7,803 ... D1
Haileyville 918 ... P5
Hall Park 1,090 ... M4
Hallett 159 ... N2
Hammon 611 ... H3
Hanna 99 ... P4
Hanson 250 ... S4
Harden City 250 ... N5
Hardesty 228 ... D1
Hardy ... N1
Harjo 35 ... N4
Harmon 27 ... G2
Harrah 4,206 ... M4
Harris 192 ... S7
Hartshorne 2,120 ... R5
Haskell 2,143 ... P3
Hastings 164 ... K6
Haworth 293 ... S7
Haywood 175 ... P5
Headrick 183 ... H5
Healdton 2,872 ... M6
Heavener 2,601 ... S5
Helena 1,043 ... K1
Hendrix 108 ... O7
Hennepin 300 ... M5
Hennessey 1,902 ... L2
Henryetta 5,872 ... O4
Herd 18 ... O1
Hess 29 ... H6
Hester 25 ... H5
Hickory 77 ... N5
Hillsdale 96 ... K1
Hinton 1,233 ... K4
Hitchcock 139 ... K3
Hitchita 118 ... P3
Hobart▲ 4,305 ... J5
Hockerville 125 ... S1
Hodgen 150 ... S5
Hoffman 175 ... P4
Holdenville▲ 4,792 ... O4
Hollis▲ 2,584 ... G5
Hollister 59 ... J6
Homestead 35 ... K2
Hominy 2,342 ... O2
Honobia 80 ... R5
Hooker 1,551 ... D1
Hoot Owl 5 ... R2
Hopeton 42 ... J1
Howe 510 ... S5
Hoyt 160 ... R4
Hugo▲ 5,978 ... P7
Hulah 50 ... O1
Hulbert 499 ... R3
Humphreys 68 ... H5
Hunter 218 ... L1
Hydro 977 ... J3
Idabel▲ 6,957 ... S7
Indiahoma 337 ... J5

(continued on following page)

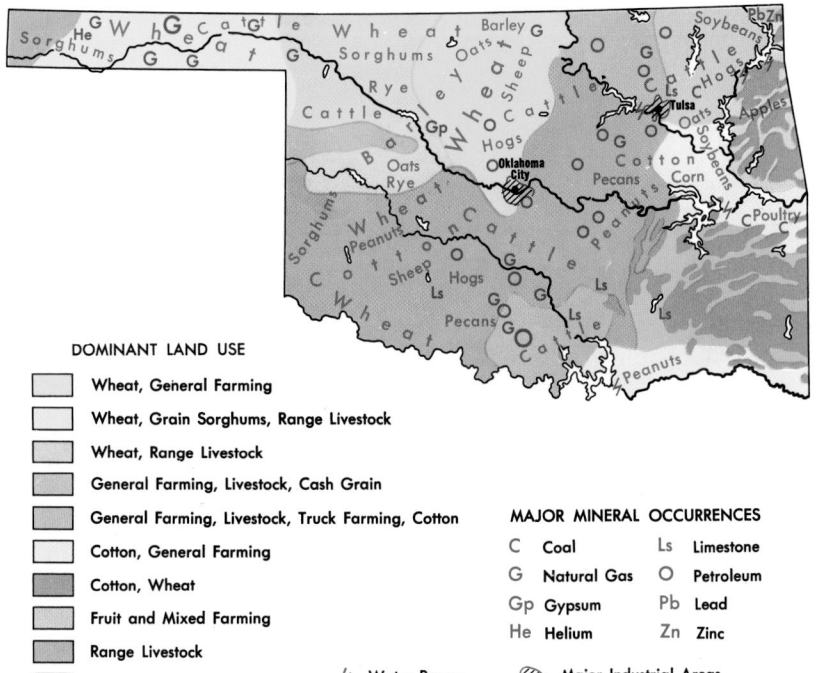

Agriculture, Industry and Resources

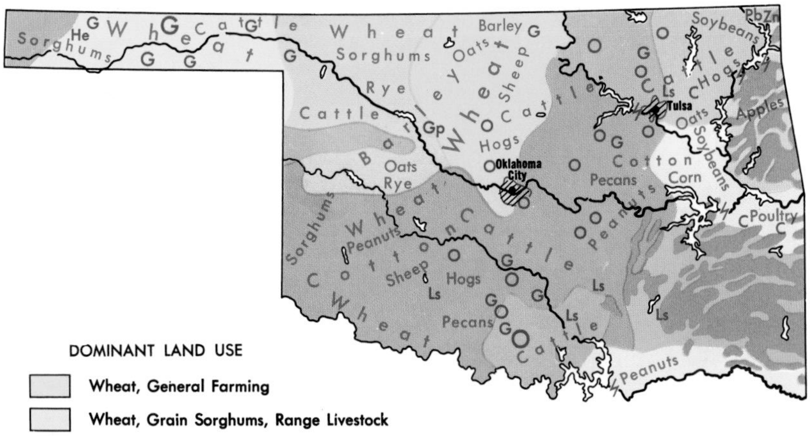

DOMINANT LAND USE

- Wheat, General Farming
- Wheat, Grain Sorghums, Range Livestock
- Wheat, Range Livestock
- General Farming, Livestock, Cash Grain
- General Farming, Livestock, Truck Farming, Cotton
- Cotton, General Farming
- Cotton, Wheat
- Fruit and Mixed Farming
- Range Livestock
- Forests

MAJOR MINERAL OCCURRENCES

- C Coal
- G Natural Gas
- Gp Gypsum
- He Helium
- Ls Limestone
- O Petroleum
- Pb Lead
- Zn Zinc

Water Power

Major Industrial Areas

Indianola 171 P4
Inola 1,444 P2
Isabella 113 K2
Jay▲ 2,220 S2
Jefferson 36 L1
Jenks 7,493 P2
Jennings 381 N2
Jet 272 K1
Jones 2,424 M3
Jumbo 40 P6
Kansas 556 S2
Kaw City 314 N1
Keefton 75 R3
Kellyville 984 O3
Kemp 138 O7
Kemp City (Hendrix) 106 O7
Kendrick 171 N3
Kenefic 147 O6
Kenton 21 A1
Kenwood 400 S2
Keota 625 S4
Ketchum 263 R1
Keyes 454 B1
Kiamichi 43 R5
Kiefer 962 O3
Kildare 94 M1
Kingfisher▲ 4,095 L3
Kingston 1,237 N7
Kinta 233 R4
Kiowa 718 P5
Knowles 18 F1
Konawa 1,508 N5
Kosoma 50 P6
Krebs 1,955 P5
Kremlin 243 L1
Lahoma 645 K2
Lamar 97 O4
Lambert 11 J1
Lamont 454 L1
Lane 218 O6
Langley 526 R2
Langston 1,471 M3
Laverne 1,269 G1
Lawton▲ 80,561 K5
Leach 350 S2
Lebanon 382 N7
Leedey 468 H3
Leflore 119 S5
Lehigh 303 O6
Lela 35 N2
Lenapah 253 P1
Leon 101 M7
Leonard 400 P3
Lequire 250 R4
Lexington 1,776 M4
Lima (New Lima) 133 O4
Lindsay 2,947 L5
Little Chief 35 N1
Loco 160 L6
Locust Grove 1,326 R2
Lone Grove 4,114 M6
Lone Wolf 576 H5
Longdale 281 K2
Lookeba 141 K4
Lotsee 7 O2
Loveland 13 J6
Lovell L2
Loyal 76 K3
Lucien 350 M2
Lula 100 O5
Luther 1,560 M3
Lutie 100 R5
Macomb 64 M4
Madill▲ 3,069 N6
Manchester 106 L1
Mangum▲ 3,344 G5
Manitou 244 J5
Mannford 1,826 O2
Mannsville 396 N6
Maramec 110 N2
Marble City 232 S3
Marietta▲ 2,306 M7
Marland 280 M1
Marlow 4,416 K5
Marshall 288 L2
Martha 217 H5
Mason 75 O3
Maud 1,204 N4
May 42 G1
Mayfield 17 G4
Maysville 1,203 M5
Mazie 118 R2

McAlester▲ 16,370 P5
McBride 80 N7
McCurtain 465 R4
McLoud 2,493 M4
McMillan 50 M6
Mead 109 O7
Medford▲ 1,172 L1
Medicine Park 285 J5
Meeker 1,003 N4
Mehan 60 M2
Meno 155 K2
Meridian 45 M3
Miami▲ 13,142 S1
Micawber 18 N3
Midwest City 52,267 M4
Milburn 264 O6
Milfay 200 N3
Mill Creek 336 N6
Millerton 234 S7
Milo 25 M6
Milton 55 S4
Minco 1,411 L4
Moffett 219 S4
Monroe 150 S4
Moodys 250 S2
Moon 50 S7
Moore 40,318 M4
Mooreland 1,157 H2
Morris 1,216 P3
Morrison 640 M2
Mounds 980 O3
Mountain Park 473 J5
Mountain View 1,086 J4
Moyers 312 P6

Muldrow 2,889 S4
Mulhall 199 M2
Muse 350 S5
Muskogee▲ 37,708 R3
Mustang 10,434 L4
Mutual 68 H2
Narcissa 100 S1
Nardin 75 M1
Nash 281 K1
Nashoba 50 R6
Nelagoney 62 O1
New Alluwe 83 R1
New Cordell▲ (Cordell) 2,903 H4
New Lima O4
New Prue (Prue) 554 O2
New Tulsa 272 P2
Newalla 350 M4
Newcastle 4,214 L4
Newkirk▲ 2,168 N1
Nichols Hills 4,020 L3
Nicoma Park 2,353 M4
Noble 4,710 M4
Norge 97 K4
Norman▲ 80,071 M4
North Enid 874 L2
North Miami 450 R1
Nowata▲ 3,896 P1
Oakhurst 3,030 P2
Oakland 602 N6
Oaks 431 S2
Oakwood 107 J3
Ochelata 441 P1
Octavia 30 S5
Oilton 1,060 N2

Okarche 1,160 L3
Okay 528 R3
Okeene 1,343 K2
Okemah▲ 3,085 O4
Okesa 165 O1
Oklahoma City (cap.)▲ 444,719 L4
Okmulgee▲ 13,441 O3
Oktaha 266 R3
Oleta 50 R6
Olive 100 O2
Olney 125 O6
Olustee 701 H5
Omega 50 K3
Oologah 828 P2
Optima 92 D1
Orienta 25 J2
Orlando 198 M2
Osage 163 O2
Oscar 60 L7
Overbrook 443 M6
Owasso 11,151 P2
Paden 400 N3
Page 20 S5
Panama 1,528 S4
Panola 75 R5
Paoli 574 M5
Paradise Hill 88 R3
Park Hill 200 R3
Parkland 60 N3
Pauls Valley▲ 6,150 M5
Pawhuska▲ 3,825 O1
Pawnee▲ 2,197 N2
Pearson 30 N4

Peckham 65 M1
Peggs R2
Pensacola 69 R2
Peoria 136 S1
Perkins 1,925 M3
Pernell 110 M5
Perry▲ 4,978 M2
Pershing 27 O1
Pharoah 100 O4
Phillips 161 O6
Picher 1,714 S1
Pickens 525 S6
Piedmont 2,522 L3
Pink 1,020 M4
Pittsburg 249 P5
Platter 275 O7
Plunkettville 125 S6
Pocasset 220 L4
Pocola 3,664 T4
Ponca City 26,359 M1
Pond Creek 982 L1
Pontotoc 150 N6
Pooleville 75 M6
Porter 588 R3
Porum 851 R4
Poteau▲ 7,210 S4
Prague 2,308 N4
Preston 350 P3
Proctor 175 S3
Prue 346 O2
Pryor▲ 8,327 R2
Purcell▲ 4,784 M4
Putnam 44 J3
Quapaw 928 S1

Quay 59 N2
Quinlan 23 J2
Quinton 1,133 R4
Ralston 405 N2
Ramona 508 P1
Ranchwood Manor 296 L4
Randlett 458 K6
Ratliff City 157 M6
Rattan 257 R6
Ravia 404 N6
Reagan 25 N6
Red Oak 602 R5
Red Rock 321 M2
Redbird 166 P3
Reed 48 G5
Remus N4
Renfrow 19 L1
Rentiesville 66 R4
Reydon 200 G3
Ringling 1,250 L6
Ringold 200 R6
Ringwood 394 K2
Ripley 376 N2
Rock Island 478 T4
Rocky 181 J4
Roff 717 N5
Roland 2,481 S4
Roosevelt 323 J5
Rose 48 R2
Rosedale 97 M5
Rosston 54 G1
Rubottom 35 M7
Rufe 150 R6
Rush Springs 1,229 L5

Ryan 945 L6
Saddle Mountain 16 J5
Saint Louis 181 N4
Salina 1,153 R2
Sallisaw▲ 7,122 S4
Sand Point 179 N7
Sand Springs 15,346 O2
Sapulpa▲ 18,074 O3
Sardis 58 R5
Sasakwa 169 N5
Savanna 869 P5
Sawyer 200 R7
Sayre▲ 2,881 G4
Schulter 600 P3
Scipio 100 P4
Scraper 80 S2
Scullin N5
Seiling 1,031 J2
Selman 25 H1
Seminole 7,071 N4
Sentinel 960 H4
Seward M3
Shady Point 597 S4
Shamrock 95 N3
Sharon 108 H2
Shattuck 1,454 G2
Shawnee▲ 26,017 N4
Sherwood 60 S6
Shidler 487 N1
Short 200 S3
Silo 249 N6
Skedee 96 N2
Skiatook 4,910 O2
Slaughterville 1,843 M4

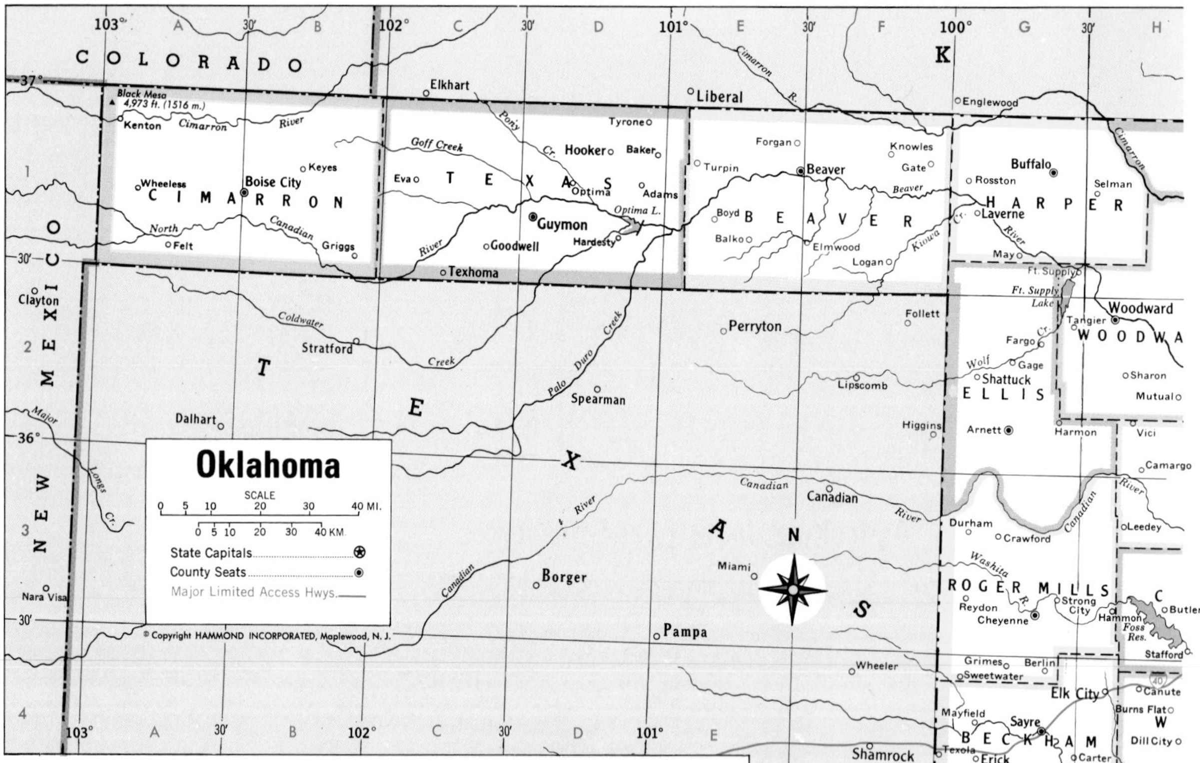
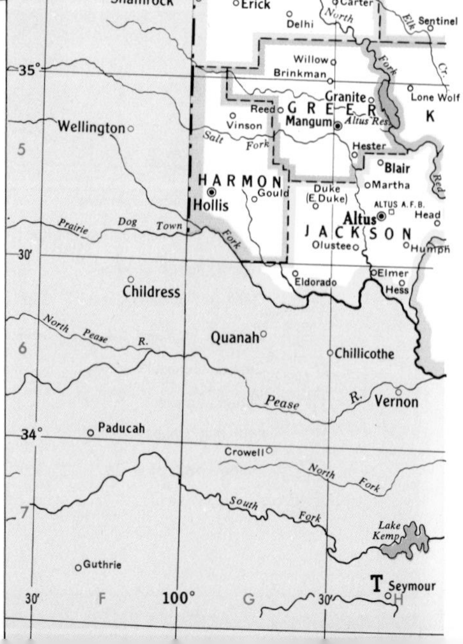

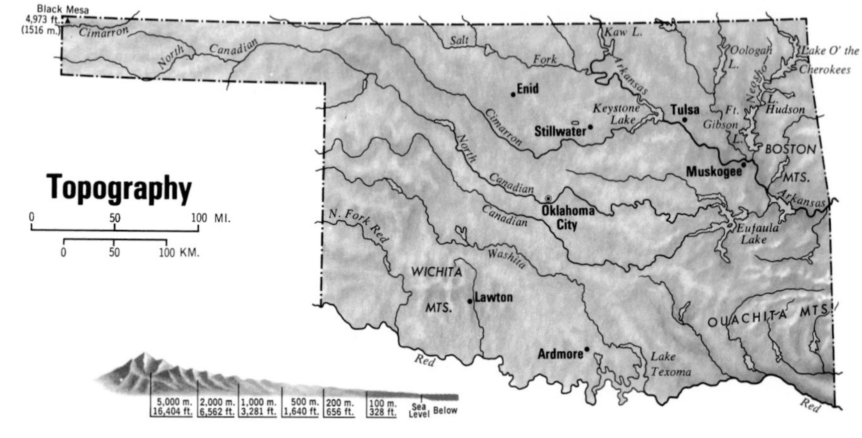

Slick 124 .... O3
Smithville 111 .... S6
Snow 200 .... R6
Snyder 1,619 .... J5
Soper 305 .... P6
South Coffeyville 791 .... P1
Southard 130 .... K2
Sparks 202 .... N3
Spavinaw 432 .... R2
Spencer 3,972 .... M3
Spencerville 275 .... R6
Sperry 937 .... P2
Spiro 2,146 .... S4
Springer 485 .... M6
Stafford 18 .... H3
Stanley 30 .... R5
Sterling 684 .... K5
Stidham 48 .... P4
Stigler▲ 2,574 .... R4
Stillwater▲ 36,676 .... N2
Stilwell▲ 2,663 .... S3
Stonebluff 50 .... P3
Stonewall 519 .... O5
Strang 141 .... R2
Stratford 1,404 .... M5
Stringtown 366 .... P6
Strong City 49 .... G3
Stroud 2,666 .... N3
Stuart 228 .... O5
Sugden 65 .... L6
Sulphur▲ 4,824 .... N5
Summerfield 150 .... S5
Sweetwater 85 .... G4
Swink R6
Tabler 28 .... L4
Taft 400 .... R3
Tahlequah▲ 10,398 .... R3
Talala 206 .... P1
Talihina 1,297 .... S5
Tallant 14 .... O1
Taloga▲ 415 .... J2
Tamaha 188 .... S4
Tatums 176 .... M6
Tecumseh 5,750 .... N4
Temple 1,223 .... K6
Terlton 121 .... O2
Terral 469 .... L7
Texhoma 746 .... C1
Texola 45 .... G4
Thackerville 290 .... M7
The Village 10,353 .... L3
Thomas 1,246 .... J3
Tiawah 125 .... P2
Tipton 1,043 .... H6
Tishomingo▲ 3,116 .... N6
Tom 600 .... S7
Tonkawa 3,127 .... M1
Tribbey 288 .... M4
Trousdale 38 .... M4
Troy 92 .... N6
Trpin 450 .... E1
Tryon 514 .... N3
Tullahassee 92 .... P3
Tulsa▲ 367,302 .... O2
Tupelo 323 .... O5
Tushka 256 .... O6
Tuskahoma 168 .... R5
Tussy 150 .... L6
Tuttle 2,807 .... L4
Tyrone 880 .... D1
Union City 1,000 .... L4
Utica 38 .... O7
Valley Brook 744 .... M4
Valliant 873 .... R6
Vanoss 130 .... N5
Velma 661 .... L6
Vera 167 .... P2
Verden 546 .... K4
Verdigris 150 .... P2
Vernon 100 .... P4
Vian 1,414 .... S4
Vici 751 .... H2
Vinita▲ 5,804 .... R1
Vinson 42 .... G5
Wade 50 .... O7
Wagoner▲ 6,894 .... R3
Wainwright 223 .... R3
Wakita 453 .... L1
Walters▲ 2,519 .... K6
Wanette 346 .... M5
Wann 126 .... P1
Wapanucka 402 .... N6
Wardville 52 .... P5
Warner 1,479 .... R4
Warr Acres 9,288 .... L3
Warwick 160 .... M3
Washington 279 .... L4
Washita 180 .... K4
Watonga▲ 3,408 .... K3
Watova 35 .... P1
Watson 48 .... S6
Watts 303 .... S2
Waukomis 1,322 .... K2
Waurika▲ 2,088 .... L6
Wayne 519 .... M5
Waynoka 947 .... J1
Weatherford 10,124 .... J4
Weathers 100 .... P5
Webb City 99 .... N1
Webbers Falls 722 .... R3
Welch 499 .... R1
Weleetka 1,112 .... O4
Welling 115 .... S3
Wellston 912 .... M3
Welty 80 .... O3
West Siloam Springs 539 .... S2
Westport 326 .... O2
Westville 1,374 .... S2
Wetumka 1,427 .... O4
Wewoka▲ 4,050 .... O4
White Oak 200 .... R1
Whitefield 253 .... R4
Whitesboro 450 .... S5
Wilburton▲ 3,092 .... R5
Williams 110 .... T4
Willis 250 .... N7
Willow 142 .... G4
Wilson 1,639 .... M6
Wirt 350 .... L6
Wister 956 .... S5
Wolco 14 .... O1
Wolf 200 .... N4
Woodford 30 .... M6
Woodville 31 .... N7
Woodward▲ 12,340 .... H2
Wright City 836 .... R6
Wyandotte 366 .... S1
Wynnewood 2,451 .... M5
Wynona 531 .... O1
Yale 1,392 .... N2
Yanush 123 .... R5
Yeager 40 .... O4
Yuba 63 .... O7
Yukon 20,935 .... L3

OTHER FEATURES

Altus (res.) H5
Altus A.F.B. H5
Arbuckles, Lake of the (lake) M6
Arbuckle Nat'l Rec. Area N6
Arkansas (riv.) S4
Atoka (res.) P5
Beaver (creek) K6
Beaver (riv.) F1
Bird (creek) O1
Black Bear (creek) M2
Black Mesa (mt.) A1
Blue (riv.) O6
Bluestem (lake) O1
Boston (mts.) S3
Broken Bow (lake) S6
Cache (creek) K6
Canadian (riv.) O4
Caney (riv.) O1
Canton (lake) J2
Carl Blackwell (lake) M2
Cherokees, Lake O'The (lake) S1
Chickasaw Nat'l Rec. Area N6
Chickasha (lake) K4
Cimarron (riv.) N2
Clear Boggy (creek) O6
Deep Fork, North Canadian (riv.) N3
Denison (dam) O7
Elk (creek) H4
Ellsworth (lake) K5
Eucha (lake) S2
Eufaula (lake) P4
Fort Cobb (res.) J4
Fort Gibson (lake) R2
Fort Sill 12,107 .... K5
Fort Supply (lake) G1
Foss (res.) H3
Great Salt Plains (lake) K1
Heyburn (res.) O3
Hudson (lake) R2
Hugo (lake) R6
Hulah (lake) O1
Illinois (riv.) S3
Jackfork (mt.) P5
Kaw (lake) N1
Kerr, Robert S. (res.) S4
Keystone (lake) O2
Kiamichi (mts.) R5
Kiamichi (riv.) R6
Kiowa (creek) F1
Lawtonka (lake) K5
Little (riv.) R6
McAlester (lake) P4
Mountain Fork (riv.) S6
Mud (creek) L6
Muddy Boggy (creek) O5
Murray (lake) M6
Neosho (riv.) R1
North Canadian (riv.) K3
North Carrizo (riv.) A1
Oologah (lake) P1
Optima (lake) D1
Osage Ind. Res. O1
Ouachita (mts.) R5
Pine Creek (lake) R6
Poteau (riv.) S5
Prairie Dog Town Fork Red (riv.) F5
Red (riv.) R7
Red, North Fork (riv.) H4
Salt Fork, Arkansas (riv.) J1
Salt Fork, Red (riv.) G5
Sans Bois (mts.) R4
Scott (mt.) K5
Spavinaw (lake) S2
Tenkiller Ferry (lake) S3
Texoma (lake) N7
Thunderbird (lake) M4
Tinker A.F.B. M4
Tom Steed (res.) J5
Vance A.F.B. K2
Verdigris (riv.) P2
Washita (riv.) M5
Waurika (lake) K6
Webbers Falls (res.) R3
Wichita (mts.) J5
Wildhorse (creek) L5
Wister (lake) S5
Wolf (creek) G2

▲County seat.

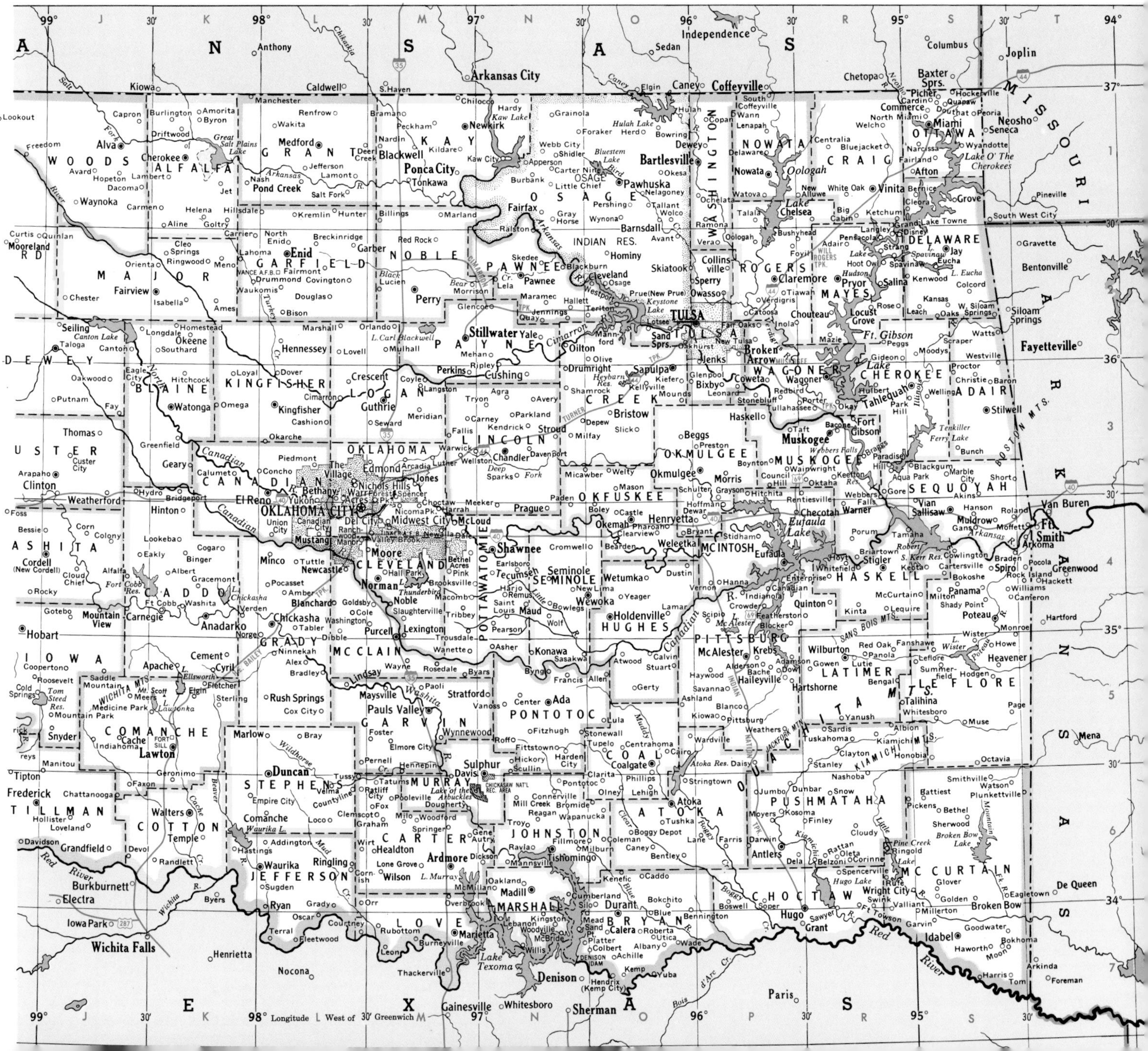

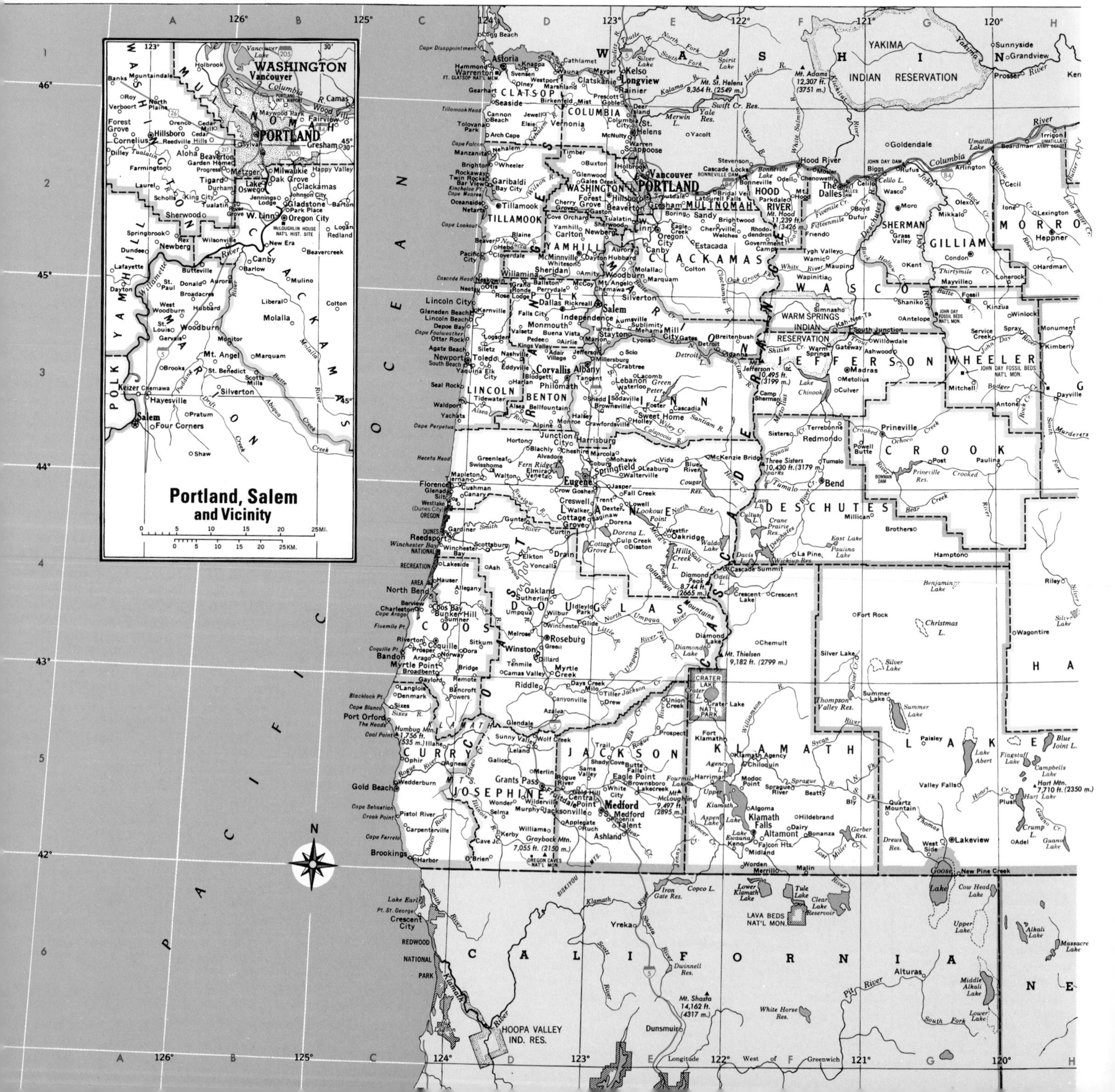

Portland, Salem and Vicinity
WASHINGTON
PORTLAND
Salem
PACIFIC OCEAN
WASHINGTON
CALIFORNIA
CLATSOP
COLUMBIA
TILLAMOOK
WASHINGTON
MULTNOMAH
HOOD RIVER
SHERMAN
GILLIAM
MORROW
YAMHILL
CLACKAMAS
WASCO
POLK
MARION
LINCOLN
BENTON
LINN
JEFFERSON
WHEELER
CROOK
LANE
DESCHUTES
DOUGLAS
COOS
CURRY
JOSEPHINE
JACKSON
KLAMATH
LAKE
YAKIMA INDIAN RESERVATION
WARM SPRINGS INDIAN RESERVATION
Portland
Salem
Eugene
Corvallis
Albany
Medford
Roseburg
Bend
Astoria
Klamath Falls
Lakeview
Mt. Hood 11,239 ft. (3426 m.)
Mt. St. Helens 8,364 ft. (2549 m.)
Mt. Jefferson 10,495 ft. (3199 m.)
Three Sisters 10,430 ft. (3179 m.)
Mt. Thielsen 9,182 ft. (2799 m.)
Mt. Shasta 14,162 ft. (4317 m.)
CRATER LAKE NAT'L PARK
LAVA BEDS NAT'L MON.
REDWOOD NATIONAL PARK
HOOPA VALLEY IND. RES.
Longitude West of Greenwich

Crabtree 200 .... E3
Crane 84 .... J4
Crater Lake 36 .... E5
Crawfordsville 350 .... E3
Crescent 750 .... F4
Crescent Lake 120 .... F4
Creswell 2,431 .... D4
Crow 200 .... D4
Culp Creek 600 .... E4
Culver 570 .... F3
Curtin 350 .... D4
Cushman 175 .... D4
Dairy 80 .... F5
Dale 85 .... J3
Dallas▲ 9,422 .... D3
Dalles, The▲ 11,060 .... F2
Danner 12 .... K5
Days Creek 550 .... D5
Dayton 1,526 .... A3
Dayville 144 .... H3
Deer Island 225 .... E2
Denmark 15 .... C5
Depoe Bay 870 .... C3
Detroit 331 .... E3
Dexter 500 .... E4
Diamond 6 .... J4
Diamond Lake 56 .... E4
Dillard 602 .... D4
Dilley 250 .... A2
Disston 123 .... E4
Donald 316 .... A3
Dora 100 .... D4
Dorena 200 .... E4
Drain 1,011 .... D4
Drew 60 .... E5
Drewsey J4
Dufur 527 .... F2
Dundee 1,663 .... A2
Dunes City (Westlake) C4
Durham 748 .... A2
Durkee 158 .... K3
Eagle Creek 250 .... E2
Eagle Point 3,008 .... E5
Echo 499 .... H2
Eddyville 564 .... D3
Elgin 1,586 .... K2
Elk City 30 .... D3
Elkton 172 .... D4

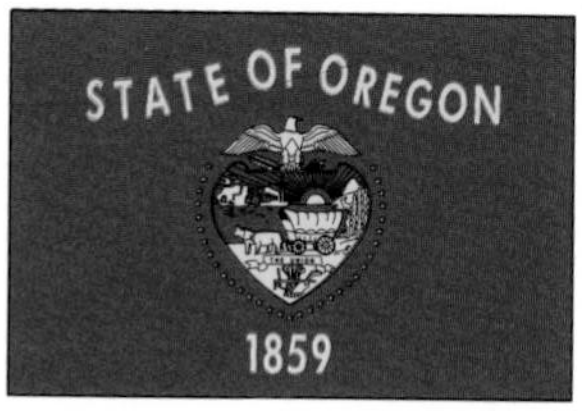
STATE OF OREGON
1859

AREA 97,073 sq. mi. (251,419 sq. km.)
POPULATION 2,853,733
CAPITAL Salem
LARGEST CITY Portland
HIGHEST POINT Mt. Hood 11,239 ft. (3426 m.)
SETTLED IN 1810
ADMITTED TO UNION February 14, 1859
POPULAR NAME Beaver State
STATE FLOWER Oregon Grape
STATE BIRD Western Meadowlark

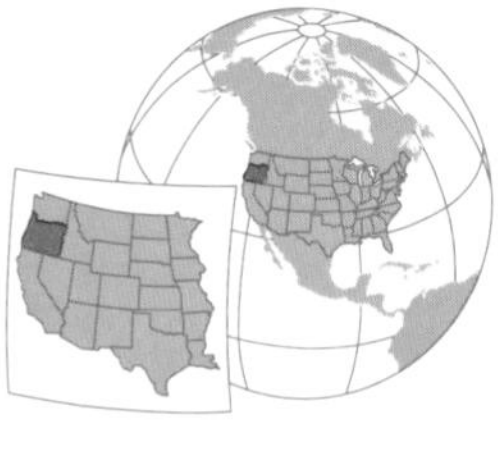

Topography

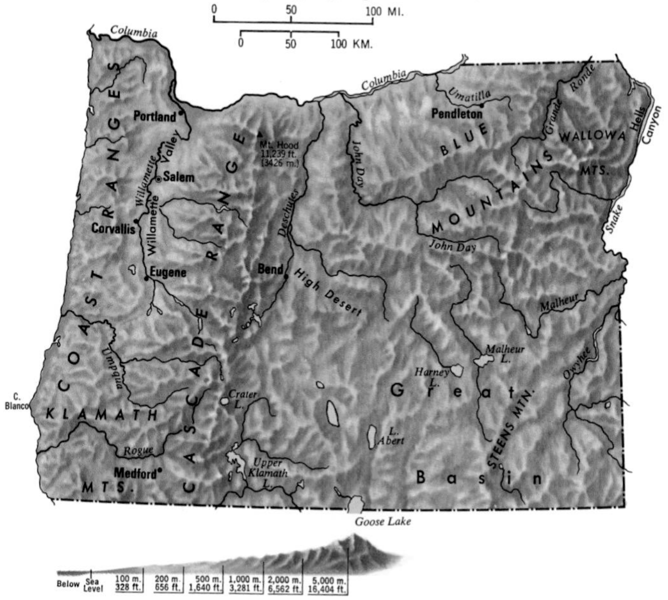
0 50 100 MI.
0 50 100 KM.
Columbia
Portland
Salem
Corvallis
Eugene
Bend
Medford
Pendleton
Mt. Hood 11,239 ft. (3426 m.)
COAST RANGES
CASCADE RANGE
KLAMATH MTS.
BLUE MOUNTAINS
WALLOWA MTS.
STEENS MIN.
Great Basin
High Desert
Willamette Valley
Willamette
Deschutes
John Day
Umatilla
Grande Ronde
Hells Canyon
Snake
Malheur
Owyhee
Malheur L.
Harney L.
L. Abert
Crater L.
Upper Klamath L.
Umpqua
Rogue
Goose Lake
C. Blanco
Below Sea Level
100 m. 328 ft.
200 m. 656 ft.
500 m. 1,640 ft.
1,000 m. 3,281 ft.
2,000 m. 6,562 ft.
5,000 m. 16,404 ft.

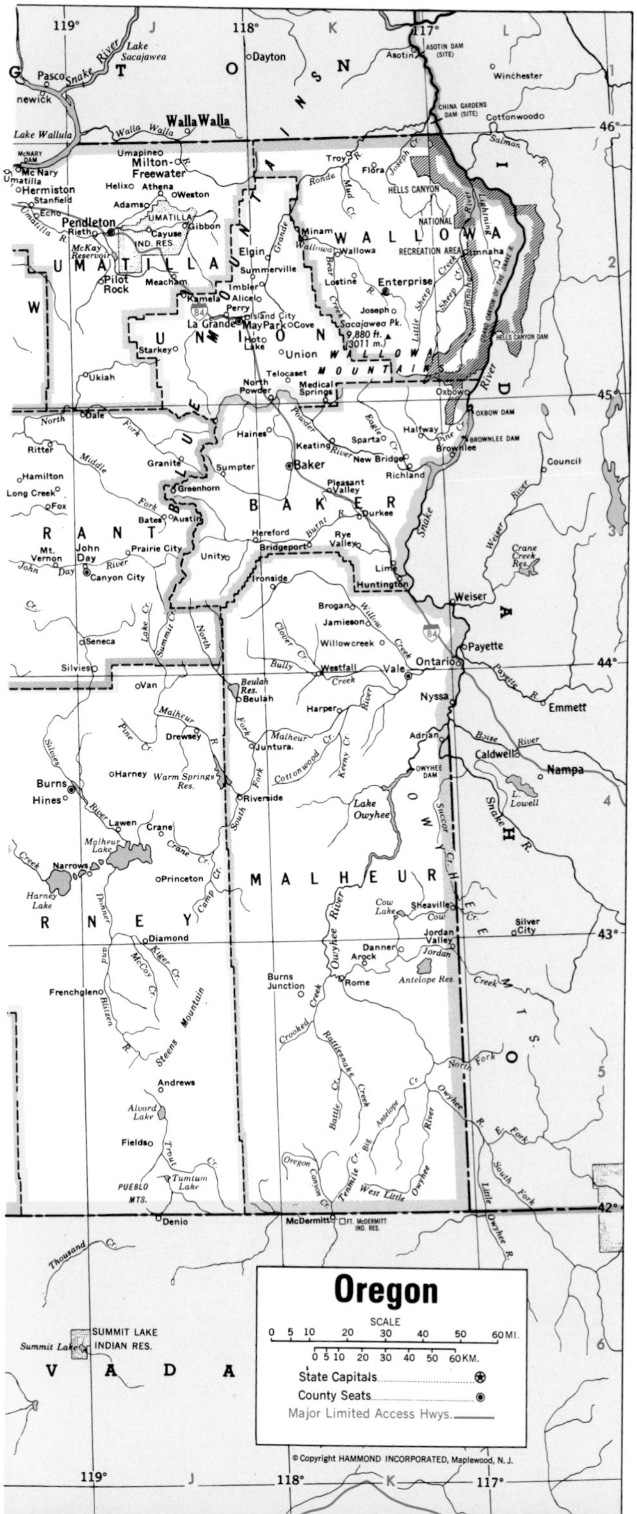
119°
118°
117°
Walla Walla
Pendleton
Milton-Freewater
Hermiston
Baker
La Grande
Enterprise
Ontario
Nyssa
Burns
Hines
Vale
Weiser
Payette
Caldwell
Nampa
UMATILLA
UNION
WALLOWA
BAKER
MALHEUR
WALLOWA MOUNTAINS
HELLS CANYON NATIONAL RECREATION AREA
Lake Owyhee
Malheur Lake
Harney Lake
Alvord Lake
Steens Mountain
McDermitt
Denio
46°
45°
44°
43°
42°
Oregon
SCALE
0 5 10 20 30 40 50 60 MI.
0 5 10 20 30 40 50 60 KM.
State Capitals
County Seats
Major Limited Access Hwys.
© Copyright HAMMOND INCORPORATED, Maplewood, N. J.

Elmira 900 .... D3
Elsie 30 .... D2
Enterprise▲ 1,905 .... K2
Estacada 1,419 .... E2
Eugene▲ 112,669 .... D3
Fairview 2,391 .... B2
Falcon Heights F5
Fall Creek 58 .... E4
Falls City 818 .... D3
Farmington 100 .... A2
Fields 150 .... J5
Flora 45 .... K2
Florence 5,162 .... C4
Forest Grove 13,559 .... A2
Fort Klamath 200 .... E5
Fort Rock 150 .... G4
Fossil▲ 399 .... G2
Foster 850 .... E3
Four Corners 12,156 .... A3
Fox 30 .... H3
Frenchglen 45 .... H5
Fruitdale-Harbeck 4,733 .... D5
Gales Creek 150 .... D2
Galice 30 .... D5
Garden Home-Whitford 6,652 .... A2
Gardiner 750 .... C4
Garibaldi 877 .... D2
Gaston 563 .... D2
Gates 499 .... E3
Gateway 108 .... F3
Gaylord 80 .... C5
Gearhart 1,027 .... C1
Gervais 992 .... A3
Gibbon 100 .... J2
Gladstone 10,152 .... B2
Glenada 300 .... C4
Glendale 707 .... D5
Gleneden Beach 400 .... C3
Glenwood 225 .... D2
Glide 470 .... D4
Goble 108 .... E1
Gold Beach▲ 1,546 .... C5
Gold Hill 964 .... D5
Goshen 200 .... D4
Government Camp 230 .... F2
Grand Ronde 289 .... D2
Granite 8 .... J3
Grants Pass▲ 17,488 .... D5
Grass Valley 160 .... G2
Green 5,076 .... D4
Greenhorn 0 .... J3
Greenleaf 60 .... D3
Gresham 68,235 .... B2
Gunter 8 .... D4
Haines 405 .... J3
Halfway 311 .... K3
Halsey 667 .... D3
Hamilton 12 .... H3
Hammond 589 .... C1
Hampton 24 .... G4
Happy Valley 1,519 .... B2
Harbor 2,143 .... C5
Hardman H2
Harlan 200 .... D3
Harney 15 .... J4
Harper 400 .... K4
Harriman 250 .... E5
Harrisburg 1,939 .... D3
Hauser 400 .... C4
Hayesville 14,318 .... A3
Hebo 400 .... D2
Helix 150 .... J2
Heppner▲ 1,412 .... H2
Hereford 128 .... K3
Hermiston 10,040 .... H2
Hildebrand 50 .... F5
Hillsboro▲ 37,520 .... A2
Hines 1,452 .... H4
Holbrook 494 .... A1
Holley 75 .... E3
Hood River▲ 4,632 .... F2
Horton 175 .... D3
Hubbard 1,881 .... A3
Huntington 522 .... K3
Idanha 289 .... E3
Idleyld Park 300 .... D4
Illahe 30 .... C5
Imbler 299 .... J2
Imnaha 150 .... L2
Independence 4,425 .... D3
Ione 255 .... H2
Ironside 50 .... K3
Irrigon 737 .... H2
Island City 696 .... K2
Jacksonville 1,896 .... D5
Jamieson 120 .... K3
Jasper 231 .... E3
Jefferson 1,805 .... D3
Jennings Lodge 6,530 .... B2
Jewell 10 .... D2
John Day 2,012 .... J3
Johnson City 586 .... B2
Jordan Valley 364 .... K5
Joseph 1,073 .... K2
Junction City 3,670 .... D3
Juntura K4
Kah-Nee-Ta 100 .... F3
Kamela 11 .... J2
Keizer 21,884 .... A3
Keno 500 .... F5
Kent 200 .... G2
Kerby 650 .... D5
Kernville 450 .... D3
Kimberly 14 .... H3
King City 2,060 .... A2
Kings Valley 50 .... D3
Klamath Agency 10 .... F5
Klamath Falls▲ 17,737 .... F5
Knappa 950 .... D1
La Grande▲ 11,766 .... J2
La Pine 850 .... F4
Lacomb 425 .... E3
Lafayette 1,292 .... A2
Lake Oswego 30,576 .... B2
Lakecreek 160 .... E5
Lakeside 1,437 .... C4
Lakeview▲ 2,526 .... G5
Langlois 150 .... C5
Latourell Falls 40 .... E2
Lawen 95 .... J4
Leaburg 150 .... E3
Lebanon 10,950 .... E3
Leland 70 .... D5
Lexington 286 .... H2
Liberal 300 .... B3
Lime 25 .... K3
Lincoln Beach 1,507 .... C3
Lincoln City 5,892 .... C3
Logan 450 .... B2
Logsden 55 .... D3
Lonerock 11 .... H2
Long Creek 249 .... H3
Lostine 231 .... K2
Lowell 785 .... E4
Lyons 938 .... E3
Madras▲ 3,443 .... F3
Malin 725 .... F5
Manzanita 513 .... C2
Mapleton 950 .... C3
Marcola 900 .... E3
Marion 300 .... D3
Marquam 40 .... B3
Marshland 30 .... D1
Maupin 456 .... F2
May Park J2
Mayger 35 .... D1
Mayville 25 .... G2
Maywood Park 781 .... B2
McCoy 40 .... D2
McKenzie Bridge 500 .... E3
McMinnville▲ 17,894 .... D2
McNary 330 .... H2
McNulty 1,805 .... E2
Meacham 150 .... J2
Medford▲ 46,951 .... E5
Mehama 250 .... E3
Melrose 30 .... D4
Merlin 500 .... D5
Merrill 837 .... F5
Metolius 450 .... F3
Metzger 3,149 .... A2
Midland 520 .... F5
Mikkalo 40 .... G2
Mill City 1,555 .... E3
Millersburg 715 .... E3
Milo 600 .... E5
Milton-Freewater 5,533 .... J2
Milwaukie 18,692 .... B2
Mist 40 .... D1
Mitchell 163 .... G3
Modoc Point 65 .... F5
Mohawk 50 .... E3
Molalla 3,651 .... B3
Monitor 82 .... B3
Monmouth 6,288 .... D3
Monroe 448 .... D3
Monument 162 .... H3
Moro▲ 292 .... G2
Mosier 244 .... F2
Mount Angel 2,778 .... B3
Mount Hood 2,234 .... F2
Mount Vernon 538 .... H3
Mountaindale 25 .... A1
Mulino 720 .... B2
Murphy 500 .... D5
Myrtle Creek 3,063 .... D4
Myrtle Point 2,712 .... C4
Nashville 23 .... D3
Nehalem 232 .... D2
Neotsu 300 .... C2
Neskowin 250 .... D2
Netarts 975 .... C2
New Bridge 28 .... K3
New Era 27 .... B2
New Pine Creek 400 .... G5
Newberg 13,086 .... A2
Newport▲ 8,437 .... C3
North Bend 9,614 .... C4
North Plains 972 .... A2
North Powder 448 .... K2
Norway 150 .... C4
Nyssa 2,629 .... K4
O\'Brien 850 .... D5
Oak Grove 12,576 .... B2
Oakland 844 .... D4
Oakridge 3,063 .... E4
Oceanside 300 .... C2
Odell 450 .... F2
Olex 40 .... G2
Olney 75 .... D1
Ontario 9,392 .... K3
Ophir 275 .... C5
Oregon City▲ 14,698 .... B2
Orenco 220 .... A2
Otis 200 .... D2
Otter Rock 450 .... C3
Oxbow 100 .... L2
Pacific City 500 .... C2
Paisley 350 .... G5
Park Place 500 .... B2
Parkdale 350 .... F2
Paulina 80 .... G3
Pedee 45 .... D3
Pendleton▲ 15,126 .... J2
Perry 50 .... J2
Perrydale 200 .... D2

(continued on following page)

Agriculture, Industry and Resources

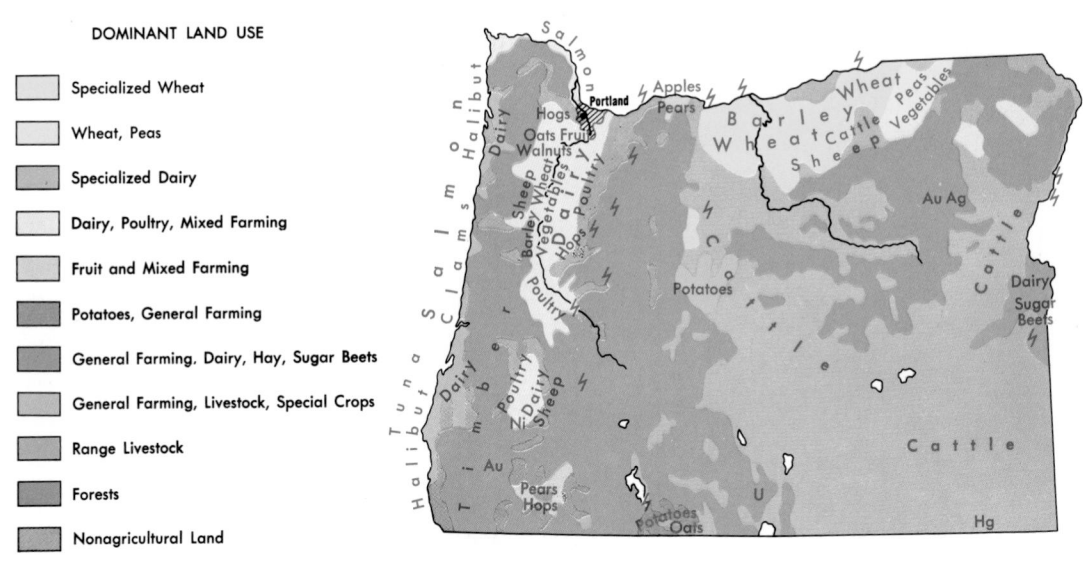

DOMINANT LAND USE

- Specialized Wheat
- Wheat, Peas
- Specialized Dairy
- Dairy, Poultry, Mixed Farming
- Fruit and Mixed Farming
- Potatoes, General Farming
- General Farming, Dairy, Hay, Sugar Beets
- General Farming, Livestock, Special Crops
- Range Livestock
- Forests
- Nonagricultural Land

MAJOR MINERAL OCCURRENCES

Ag Silver   Hg Mercury   ⚡ Water Power

Au Gold   Ni Nickel   ▨ Major Industrial Areas

U Uranium

DOMINANT LAND USE

- Specialized Dairy
- Dairy, General Farming
- Fruit and Mixed Farming
- Fruit, Truck and Mixed Farming
- General Farming, Livestock, Tobacco
- General Farming, Livestock, Fruit, Tobacco
- Forests
- Urban Areas

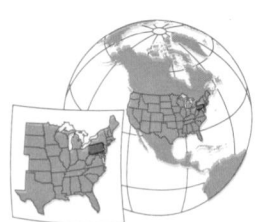

AREA 45,308 sq. mi. (117,348 sq. km.)
POPULATION 11,924,710
CAPITAL Harrisburg
LARGEST CITY Philadelphia
HIGHEST POINT Mt. Davis 3,213 ft. (979 m.)
SETTLED IN 1682
ADMITTED TO UNION December 12, 1787
POPULAR NAME Keystone State
STATE FLOWER Mountain Laurel
STATE BIRD Ruffed Grouse

MAJOR MINERAL OCCURRENCES

C	Coal	G	Natural Gas	Sl	Slate
Cl	Clay	Ls	Limestone	Ss	Sandstone
Co	Cobalt	O	Petroleum	Zn	Zinc
Fe	Iron Ore				

⚡ Water Power
▨ Major Industrial Areas

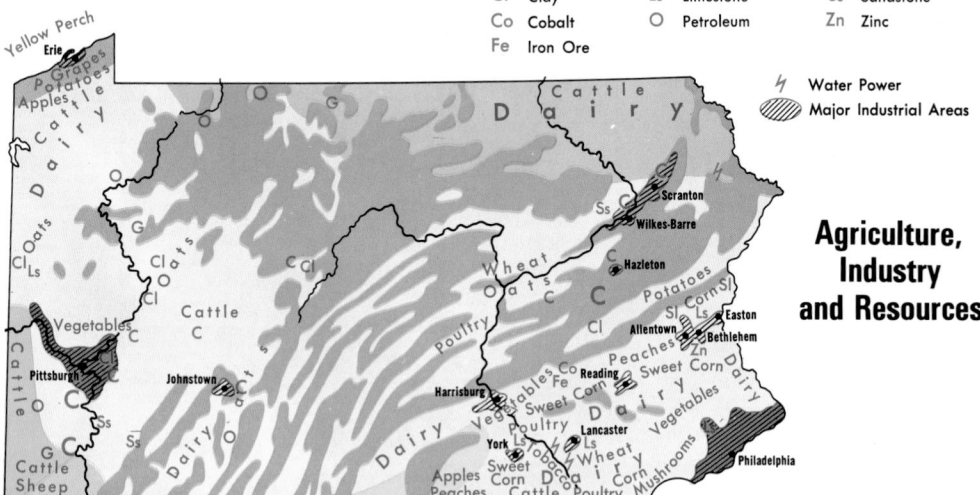

Agriculture, Industry and Resources

COUNTIES

Adams 78,274 ....H6
Allegheny 1,336,449 ....B5
Armstrong 73,478 ....D4
Beaver 186,093 ....B4
Bedford 47,919 ....E6
Berks 336,523 ....K5
Blair 130,542 ....F4
Bradford 60,967 ....J2
Bucks 541,174 ....M5
Butler 152,013 ....C4
Cambria 163,029 ....E4
Cameron 5,913 ....F3
Carbon 56,846 ....L4
Centre 123,786 ....G4
Chester 376,396 ....L6
Clarion 41,699 ....D3
Clearfield 78,097 ....F3
Clinton 37,182 ....G3
Columbia 63,202 ....K3
Crawford 86,169 ....B2
Cumberland 195,257 ....H5
Dauphin 237,813 ....J5
Delaware 547,651 ....M6
Elk 34,878 ....E3
Erie 275,572 ....B2
Fayette 145,351 ....C6
Forest 4,802 ....D2
Franklin 121,082 ....G6
Fulton 13,837 ....F6
Greene 39,550 ....B6
Huntingdon 44,164 ....F5
Indiana 89,994 ....D4
Jefferson 46,083 ....D3
Juniata 20,625 ....H4
Lackawanna 219,039 ....L3
Lancaster 422,822 ....K5
Lawrence 96,246 ....B4
Lebanon 113,744 ....K5
Lehigh 291,130 ....L4
Luzerne 328,149 ....L3
Lycoming 118,710 ....H3
McKean 50,635 ....E2
Mercer 121,003 ....B3
Mifflin 46,197 ....G4
Monroe 95,709 ....M3
Montgomery 678,111 ....M5
Montour 17,735 ....J3
Northampton 247,105 ....M4
Northumberland 96,771 ....J4
Perry 41,172 ....H5
Philadelphia (city county) 1,688,210 ....M6
Pike 27,966 ....M3
Potter 16,717 ....G2
Schuylkill 152,585 ....K4
Snyder 36,680 ....H4
Somerset 78,218 ....D6
Sullivan 6,104 ....J3
Susquehanna 40,380 ....L2
Tioga 41,126 ....H2
Union 36,176 ....H4
Venango 59,381 ....C3
Warren 45,050 ....D2
Washington 204,584 ....B5
Wayne 39,944 ....M2
Westmoreland 370,321 ....D5
Wyoming 28,076 ....L3
York 339,574 ....J6

CITIES and TOWNS

Abbottstown 539 ....J6
Abington • 58,836 ....M5
Adamstown 1,108 ....K5
Akron 3,869 ....K5
Albion 1,575 ....B2
Alburtis 1,415 ....L5
Aldan 4,549 ....M7
Alexandria 411 ....F4
Aliquippa 13,374 ....B4
Allentown▲ 105,090 ....L4
Allison Park 10,000 ....C4
Altoona 51,881 ....F4
Ambler 6,609 ....M5
Ambridge 8,133 ....B4
Annville 4,294 ....J5
Apollo 1,895 ....C4
Archbald 6,291 ....F6
Ardmore 12,646 ....M6
Arendtsville 693 ....H6
Arnold 6,113 ....C4
Ashland 3,859 ....K4
Ashley 3,291 ....E7
Aspinwall 2,880 ....C4
Atglen 825 ....K6
Athens 3,468 ....K2
Atlas 1,162 ....K4
Auburn 913 ....K4
Austin 569 ....F2
Avalon 5,784 ....B6
Avella 900 ....B5
Avis 1,506 ....H3
Avoca 2,897 ....F7
Avondale 954 ....L6
Avonmore 1,089 ....C4
Baden 5,028 ....B4
Bala-Cynwyd N6
Baldwin 21,923 ....C8
Bally 973 ....L5
Bangor 5,383 ....M4
Barnesboro 2,530 ....E4
Bath 2,358 ....M4
Beallsville 530 ....C5
Beaver Falls 10,687 ....B4
Beaver Meadows 985 ....L4
Beaver▲ 5,028 ....B4
Beaverdale 1,187 ....E5
Beavertown 853 ....H4

Bedford▲ 3,137 ....F5
Beech Creek 716 ....G3
Belle Vernon 1,213 ....C5
Bellefonte▲ 6,358 ....G4
Belleville 1,589 ....H4
Bellevue 9,126 ....B6
Bellwood 1,976 ....F4
Ben Avon 2,096 ....B6
Bendersville 560 ....H6
Bentleyville 2,673 ....B5
Benton 958 ....K3
Berlin 2,064 ....E6
Bernville 789 ....K5
Berrysburg 376 ....J4
Berwick 10,976 ....K3
Berwyn Devon 5,019 ....L5
Bessemer 1,196 ....B4
Bethel Park 33,823 ....B7
Bethlehem 71,428 ....M4
Big Run 699 ....E4
Biglerville 993 ....H6
Birdsboro 4,222 ....L5
Black Lick 1,100 ....D4
Blairsville 3,595 ....D5
Blakely 7,222 ....F7
Blawnox 1,626 ....C4
Bloomfield (New Bloomfield)▲ 1,092 ....H5
Blooming Valley 391 ....C2
Bloomsburg▲ 12,439 ....J3
Blossburg 1,571 ....H2
Boalsburg 2,206 ....G4
Bobtown 1,008 ....C6
Boiling Springs 1,978 ....H5
Bolivar 544 ....D5
Boothwyn 5,069 ....L7
Boswell 1,485 ....E5
Bowmanstown 888 ....L4
Boyertown 3,759 ....L5
Brackenridge 3,784 ....C4
Braddock 4,682 ....C7
Bradford 9,625 ....E2
Brentwood 10,823 ....C8
Briar Creek 616 ....K3
Brickerville 1,268 ....K5
Bridgeport 4,292 ....M6
Bridgeville 5,445 ....B5
Bridgewater 751 ....B4
Brisbin 369 ....F4
Bristol 10,405 ....N5
Bristol • 587,330 ....N5
Broad Top 331 ....F5
Brockway 2,207 ....E3
Brodheadsville 1,389 ....M4
Brookhaven 8,567 ....M7
Brookville▲ 4,184 ....D3
Broomall 10,930 ....M6
Brownstown 937 ....K5
Brownsville 3,164 ....C5
Bruin 646 ....C3

Bryn Athyn 1,081 ....M5
Bryn Mawr 3,271 ....M5
Burgettstown 1,634 ....A5
Burlington 479 ....J2
Burnham 2,197 ....H4
Burnside 350 ....E4
Butler▲ 15,714 ....C4
Cadogan • 459 ....C4
Cairnbrook 1,081 ....E5
California 5,748 ....C5
Callery 420 ....C4
Cambridge Springs 1,837 ....C2
Camp Hill 7,831 ....H5
Canonsburg 9,200 ....B5
Canton 1,966 ....H3
Carbondale 10,664 ....L2
Carlisle▲ 18,419 ....H5
Carmichaels 532 ....B6
Carnegie 9,278 ....B7
Carroll Valley 1,457 ....H6
Carrolltown 1,286 ....E4
Castle Shannon 9,135 ....B7
Catasauqua 6,662 ....M4
Catawissa 1,683 ....K4
Centerville 4,207 ....B6
Central City 1,246 ....E5
Centre Hall 1,203 ....G4
Chalfont 3,069 ....M5
Chambersburg▲ 16,647 ....G6
Charleroi 5,014 ....C5
Cherry Tree 431 ....E4
Chester 41,856 ....L7
Chester Heights 2,273 ....L7
Chester Hill 945 ....F4
Cheswick 1,971 ....C6
Chicora 1,058 ....C4
Christiana 1,045 ....K6
Churchill 3,883 ....C7
Clairton 9,656 ....C7
Clarendon 650 ....D2
Clarion▲ 6,457 ....D3
Clark (Clarksville) 610 ....A3
Clarks Green 1,603 ....F6
Clarks Summit 5,433 ....L3
Claysburg 1,399 ....F5
Claysville 962 ....A5
Clearfield▲ 6,633 ....F3
Clifton Heights 7,111 ....M7
Clintonville 520 ....C3
Clymer 1,499 ....D4
Coalport 578 ....E4
Coatesville 11,038 ....L5
Cochranton 1,174 ....C2
Codorus (Jefferson) 685 ....J6
Cokeburg 724 ....B5
Collegeville 4,227 ....M5
Collingdale 9,175 ....N7
Columbia 10,701 ....K5
Colver 1,024 ....E4

Colwyn 2,613 ....N7
Confluence 873 ....D6
Conneaut Lake 699 ....B2
Conneautville 822 ....A2
Connellsville 9,229 ....C5
Connoquenessing 507 ....B4
Conshohocken 8,064 ....M5
Conway 2,424 ....B4
Conyngham 2,060 ....K3
Coopersburg 2,599 ....M5
Cooperstown 506 ....C2
Coplay 3,267 ....L4
Coraopolis 6,747 ....B4
Cornwall 3,231 ....K5
Corry 7,216 ....C1
Coudersport▲ 2,854 ....G2
Crabtree 900 ....D5
Crafton 7,188 ....B7
Cranesville 598 ....B2
Cresson 1,784 ....E5
Cressona 1,694 ....K4
Cross Roads 521 ....J6
Curwensville 2,924 ....E4
Dale 1,642 ....E5
Dallas 2,567 ....L3
Dallastown 3,974 ....J6
Dalton 1,369 ....L2
Danville▲ 5,165 ....J4
Darby 10,955 ....M7
Dauphin 845 ....J5
Dayton 572 ....D4
Delaware Water Gap 733 ....M4
Delmont 2,041 ....D5
Delta 761 ....K6
Denver 2,861 ....K5
Derry 2,950 ....D5
Dickson City 6,276 ....F7
Dillsburg 1,925 ....J5
Donora 5,928 ....C5
Dormont 9,772 ....B7
Dover 1,884 ....J6
Downingtown 7,749 ....L5
Doylestown▲ 8,575 ....M5
Dravosburg 2,377 ....C7
Drexel Hill 29,744 ....M6
Drifton 1,786 ....L3
DuBois 8,286 ....E3
Dublin 1,985 ....M5
Duboistown 1,201 ....H3
Dunbar 1,213 ....C6
Duncannon 1,450 ....H5
Duncansville 1,309 ....F5
Dunmore 15,403 ....F7
Dupont 3,006 ....F7
Duquesne 8,525 ....C7
Duryea 4,869 ....F7
Dushore 738 ....K2
East Bangor 1,006 ....M4
East Berlin 1,175 ....J6
East Berwick 2,128 ....K3

East Brady 1,047 ....C3
East Butler 725 ....C4
East Conemaugh 1,470 ....E5
East Faxon 3,951 ....J3
East Greenville 3,117 ....L5
East Lansdowne 2,691 ....M7
East Petersburg 4,197 ....K5
East Pittsburgh 2,160 ....C7
East Prospect 558 ....J6
East Stroudsburg 8,781 ....M4
East Washington 2,126 ....B5
Easton▲ 26,276 ....M4
Eau Claire 371 ....C3
Ebensburg▲ 3,872 ....E5
Economy 9,519 ....B4
Eddystone 2,446 ....M7
Edgewood 2,719 ....C7
Edgeworth 1,670 ....B4
Edinboro 7,736 ....B2
Edwardsville 5,399 ....E7
Elderton 371 ....D4
Eldred 869 ....F2
Elizabeth 1,610 ....C5
Elizabethtown 9,952 ....J5
Elizabethville 1,467 ....J4
Elkland 1,849 ....H1
Ellsworth 1,048 ....C5
Ellwood City 8,894 ....B4
Elverson 470 ....L5
Elysburg 1,890 ....K4
Emigsville 2,580 ....J6
Emlenton 834 ....C3
Emmaus 11,157 ....M4
Emporium▲ 2,513 ....F2
Emsworth 2,892 ....B7
Enola 5,961 ....H5
Enon Valley 355 ....B4
Ephrata 12,133 ....K5
Erie▲ 108,718 ....B1
Ernest 492 ....D4
Espy 1,430 ....K3
Etna 4,200 ....B6
Etters (Goldsboro) 477 ....J5
Evans City 2,054 ....B4
Everett 1,777 ....F5
Everson 939 ....C5
Exeter 5,691 ....F7
Export 981 ....C5
Factoryville 1,310 ....L2
Fairchance 1,918 ....C6
Fairfield 524 ....H6
Fairless Hills 9,026 ....N5
Falls Creek 1,087 ....E3
Farrell 6,841 ....A3
Fawn Grove 489 ....J6
Fayette City 713 ....C5
Fayetteville 3,033 ....G6
Felton 438 ....J6
Ferndale 2,020 ....E5
Finleyville 446 ....B5

Fleetwood 3,478 ....L5
Fleming (Unionville) 361 ....G4
Flemington 1,321 ....G3
Folcroft 7,506 ....M7
Folsom 8,173 ....M7
Ford City 3,413 ....D4
Ford Cliff 450 ....D4
Forest City 1,846 ....L2
Forest Hills 7,335 ....C7
Forty Fort 5,049 ....F7
Fountain Hill 4,637 ....L4
Fox Chapel 5,319 ....C6
Frackville 4,700 ....K4
Franklin▲ 7,329 ....C3
Franklintown 373 ....H5
Fredericksburg 1,269 ....B2
Fredericktown 1,052 ....C6
Fredonia 683 ....B3
Freeburg 640 ....H4
Freedom 1,897 ....B4
Freeland 3,909 ....L3
Freemansburg 1,946 ....M4
Freeport 1,983 ....C4
Galeton 1,370 ....G2
Gallitzin 2,003 ....E4
Gap 1,226 ....L6
Garden View 2,687 ....H3
Garrett 520 ....D6
Geistown 2,749 ....E5
Gettysburg▲ 7,025 ....H6
Gilberton 953 ....K4
Girard 2,879 ....B2
Girardville 1,889 ....K4
Glassport 5,582 ....C7
Glen Lyon 2,082 ....E7
Glen Rock 1,688 ....J6
Glenolden 7,260 ....M7
Glenside 8,704 ....M5
Grampian 395 ....E4
Gratz 696 ....J4
Great Bend 704 ....L2
Greencastle 3,600 ....G6
Greensburg▲ 16,318 ....D5
Greentree 4,905 ....B7
Greenville 6,734 ....B3
Grove City 8,240 ....B3
Halifax 911 ....J5
Hallstead 1,274 ....L2
Hamburg 3,987 ....L4
Hanover 14,399 ....J6
Harmony 1,054 ....B4
Harrisburg (cap.)▲ 52,376 ....H5
Harrisville 862 ....B3
Harveys Lake 2,746 ....E7
Hastings 1,431 ....E4
Hatboro 7,382 ....M5
Hatfield 2,650 ....M5
Haverford • 52,371 ....M6
Havertown M6
Hawley 1,279 ....M3
Hawthorn 528 ....D3
Hazleton 24,730 ....L4
Heidelberg 1,238 ....B7
Hellam (Hallam) 1,428 ....J6
Hellertown 5,662 ....M4
Herndon 422 ....J4
Hershey 11,860 ....J5
Highland Park 1,583 ....H4
Highspire 2,668 ....J5
Hollidaysburg▲ 5,624 ....F5
Homer City 1,809 ....D4
Homestead 4,179 ....C7
Honesdale▲ 4,972 ....M2
Honey Brook 1,184 ....L5
Hooversville 731 ....E5
Hop Bottom 345 ....L2
Hopwood 2,021 ....C6
Houston 1,445 ....B5
Houtzdale 1,204 ....F4
Howard 749 ....G3
Hughestown 1,734 ....F7
Hughesville 2,049 ....J3
Hummelstown 3,981 ....J5
Huntingdon▲ 6,843 ....G5
Hyde 1,643 ....F4
Hyde Park 542 ....D4
Hydetown 681 ....C2
Hyndman 1,019 ....E6
Imperial-Enlow 3,449 ....B5
Indian Lake 388 ....E5
Indiana▲ 15,174 ....D4
Industry 2,124 ....B4
Ingram 3,901 ....B7
Irvona 669 ....E4
Irwin 4,604 ....C5
Jacobus 1,370 ....J6
Jamestown 761 ....A3
Jeannette 11,221 ....C5
Jenkintown 4,574 ....M5
Jennerstown 635 ....D5
Jermyn 2,263 ....L3
Jerome 1,074 ....E5
Jersey Shore 4,353 ....H3
Jessup 4,605 ....L3
Jim Thorpe (Mauch Chunk)▲ 5,048 ....L4

(continued on following page)

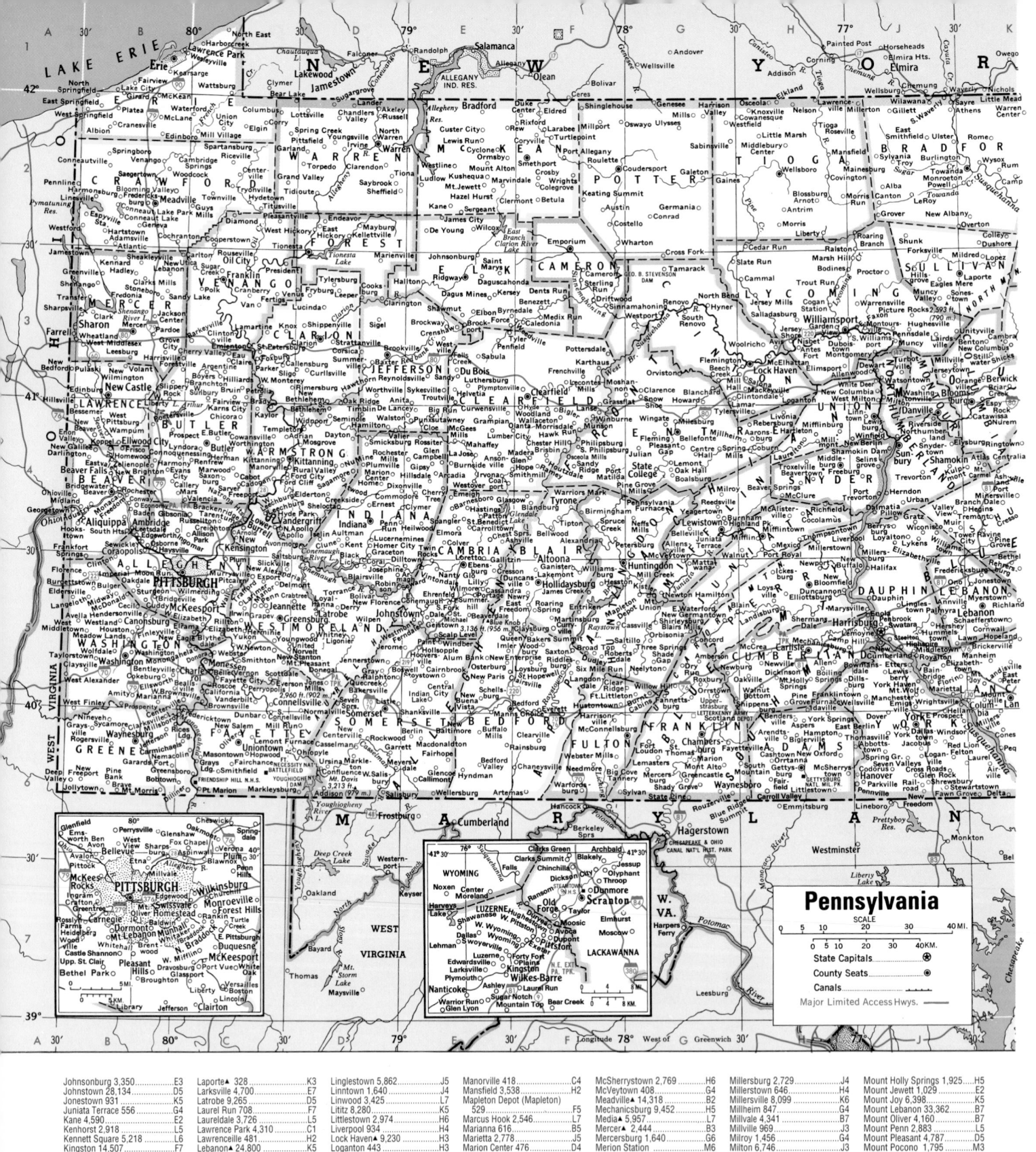

Index (continued)

Petersburg 469 ...G4
Philadelphia▲ 1,585,577 ...N6
Philipsburg 3,048 ...F4
Phoenixville 15,066 ...L5
Picture Rocks 660 ...J3
Pillow 341 ...J4
Pine Grove 2,118 ...K4
Pine Grove Mills 1,129 ...G4
Pitcairn 4,087 ...C5
Pittsburgh▲ 369,879 ...B7
Pittston 9,389 ...F7
Plains 4,693 ...F7
Platea 467 ...B2
Pleasant Gap 1,699 ...G4
Pleasant Hills 8,884 ...B7
Plum 25,609 ...C5
Plumville 390 ...D4
Plymouth 7,134 ...E7
Plymptonville 1,074 ...E3
Pocono Pines 824 ...M3
Point Marion 1,344 ...C6
Polk 1,267 ...C3
Port Allegany 2,391 ...F2
Port Carbon 2,134 ...K4
Port Matilda 669 ...F4
Port Royal 836 ...H4
Port Vue 4,641 ...C7
Portage 3,105 ...E5
Portland 516 ...M4
Pottstown 21,831 ...L5
Pottsville▲ 16,603 ...K4
Prospect 1,122 ...B4
Prospect Park 6,764 ...M7
Punxsutawney 6,782 ...E4
Quakertown 8,982 ...M5
Quarryville 1,642 ...K6
Ramey 536 ...F4
Rankin 2,503 ...C7
Reading▲ 78,380 ...L5
Reamstown 2,649 ...K5
Red Hill 1,794 ...L5
Red Lion 6,130 ...J6
Reedsville 1,023 ...G4
Renovo 1,526 ...G3
Reynoldsville 2,818 ...D3
Rices Landing 457 ...C6
Richland 1,457 ...K5
Richlandtown 1,195 ...M5
Ridgway▲ 4,793 ...E3
Ridley Park 7,592 ...M7
Riegelsville 912 ...M4
Rimersburg 1,053 ...D3
Ringtown 853 ...K4
Riverside 1,991 ...J4
Roaring Spring 2,615 ...F5
Robesonia 1,944 ...K5
Rochester 4,156 ...B4
Rockledge 2,679 ...M5
Rockwood 1,014 ...D6
Rome 475 ...K2
Roscoe 872 ...C5
Rose Valley 982 ...L7
Roseto 1,555 ...M4
Rosslyn Farms 483 ...B7
Rouseville 583 ...C2
Rouzerville 1,188 ...G6
Royalton 1,120 ...J5
Royersford 4,458 ...L5
Rural Valley 957 ...C4
Russellton 1,691 ...C4
Rutledge 843 ...M7
Saegertown 1,066 ...B2
Saint Clair 3,524 ...K4
Saint Marys 5,511 ...E3
Saint Michael-Sidman 1,189 ...E5
Saint Petersburg 349 ...C3
Salisbury 716 ...D6
Saltillo 347 ...G5
Saltsburg 990 ...D5
Sandy 1,795 ...E3
Sandy Lake 722 ...B3
Saxonburg 1,345 ...C4
Saxton 838 ...F5
Sayre 5,791 ...K2
Scalp Level 1,158 ...E5

Schnecksville 1,780 ...L4
Schuylkill Haven 5,610 ...K4
Schwenksville 1,326 ...L5
Scottdale 5,184 ...C5
Scranton▲ 81,805 ...F7
Selinsgrove 5,384 ...J4
Sellersville 4,479 ...M5
Seven Valleys 483 ...J6
Seward 522 ...E5
Sewickley 4,134 ...B4
Shamokin 9,184 ...J4
Shamokin Dam 1,690 ...J4
Sharon 17,493 ...B3
Sharon Hill 5,771 ...N7
Sharpsburg 3,781 ...B6
Sharpsville 4,729 ...A3
Sheffield 1,294 ...D2
Shenandoah 6,221 ...K4
Shickshinny 1,108 ...K3
Shillington 5,062 ...K5
Shinglehouse 1,243 ...F2
Shippensburg 5,331 ...H5
Shippenville 474 ...D3
Shoemakersville 1,443 ...K4
Shrewsbury 2,672 ...J6
Sinking Spring 2,467 ...K5
Skippack 2,042 ...M5
Slatington 4,678 ...L4
Slickville 1,178 ...C5
Sligo 706 ...C3
Slippery Rock 3,008 ...B3
Smethport▲ 1,734 ...F2
Smithfield 1,000 ...C6
Smithton 388 ...C5
Snow Shoe 800 ...G3
Snydertown 416 ...J4
Somerset▲ 6,454 ...D6
Souderton 5,957 ...M5
South Bethlehem 479 ...D4
South Connellsville 2,204 ...C6
South Fork 1,197 ...E5
South Heights 647 ...B4
South Philipsburg 438 ...F4
South Renovo 597 ...G3
South Waverly 1,049 ...J2
South Williamsport 6,496 ...J3
Spangler 2,068 ...E4
Spartansburg 403 ...C2
Spring City 3,433 ...L5
Spring Grove 1,863 ...J6
Springboro 527 ...B2
Springdale 3,992 ...C6
Springfield 24,160 ...M7
State College 38,923 ...G4
State Line 5,152 ...G6
Steelton 5,152 ...J5
Stewartstown 1,308 ...K6
Stockertown 641 ...M4
Stoneboro 1,091 ...B3
Stoystown 389 ...E5
Strasburg 2,568 ...K6
Strattanville 490 ...D3
Straussbtown 353 ...K5
Stroudsburg▲ 5,312 ...M4
Sturgeon 1,312 ...B4
Sugar Creek 5,532 ...C3
Sugar Notch 1,044 ...E7
Sugargrove 430 ...D1
Summerhill 614 ...E5
Summerville 675 ...D3
Summit Hill 3,332 ...L4
Sunbury▲ 11,591 ...J4
Susquehanna 1,994 ...L2
Swarthmore 6,157 ...M7
Swatara▲ 8,796 ...J5
Swissvale 10,637 ...C7
Swoyerville 5,630 ...E7
Sykesville 1,387 ...E3
Tamaqua 7,943 ...L4
Tarentum 5,674 ...C4
Tatamy 873 ...M4
Taylor 6,941 ...F7
Telford 4,238 ...M5
Temple 1,491 ...L5

Terre Hill 1,282 ...L5
Thompsontown 582 ...H4
Three Springs 422 ...F5
Throop 4,070 ...F7
Tidioute 791 ...D2
Tioga 638 ...H2
Tionesta▲ 634 ...C2
Tipton 1,194 ...F4
Titusville 6,434 ...C2
Topton 1,987 ...L5
Towanda▲ 3,242 ...J2
Tower City 1,518 ...J4
Townville 358 ...C2
Trafford 3,345 ...C5
Trainer 2,271 ...L7
Tremont 1,814 ...K4
Tresckow 1,033 ...K4
Trevorton 2,058 ...J4
Troy 1,262 ...J2
Trumbauersville 894 ...M5
Tullytown 2,339 ...N5
Tunkhannock▲ 2,251 ...J3
Turtobville 675 ...J3
Turtle Creek 6,556 ...C7
Tyrone 5,743 ...F4
Ulysses (Lewisville) 653 ...G2
Union City 3,537 ...C2
Uniontown▲ 12,034 ...C6
Upland 3,334 ...L7
Upper Darby 84,054 ...M6
Upper Saint Claire▲ 19,023 ...B7
Valencia 364 ...C4
Valley Forge 400 ...L5
Valley View 1,749 ...J4
Vanderbilt 545 ...C5
Vandergrift 5,904 ...D4
Vandling 660 ...F7
Verona 3,260 ...C7
Versailles 2,150 ...C7
Villanova ...M6
Vintondale 582 ...E5
Wall 853 ...C5
Walnutport 2,055 ...L4
Wampum 666 ...B4
Warren▲ 11,122 ...D2
Warrior Run 656 ...E7
Washington▲ 15,864 ...B5
Waterford 1,492 ...B2
Watsontown 2,310 ...J3
Wattsburg 486 ...C1
Waymart 1,337 ...F7
Wayne ...M6
Waynesboro 9,578 ...G6
Waynesburg▲ 4,270 ...B6
Weatherly 2,640 ...L4
Wellsboro▲ 3,430 ...H2
Wernersville 1,934 ...K5
Wesleyville 3,655 ...C1
West Brownsville 1,170 ...C6
West Chester▲ 18,041 ...L6
West Elizabeth 634 ...C5
West Grove 2,128 ...L6
West Hazleton 4,136 ...L4
West Kittanning 1,253 ...C4
West Lawn 1,606 ...K5
West Leechburg 1,359 ...C4
West Middlesex 982 ...B3
West Mifflin 23,644 ...C7
West Newton 3,152 ...C5
West Pittsburg 1,133 ...B4
West Pittston 5,590 ...F7
West View 7,734 ...B6
West Wyoming 3,117 ...E7
West York 4,283 ...J6
Westfield 1,119 ...H2
Westmont 5,789 ...D5
Westover 446 ...E4
Wheatland 960 ...B3
Whitaker 1,416 ...C7
White Haven 1,132 ...L3
White Oak 8,761 ...C7
Whitehall 14,451 ...B7
Wiconisco 1,321 ...J4
Wilkes-Barre▲ 47,523 ...F7

Wilkinsburg 21,080 ...C7
Williamsburg 1,456 ...F5
Williamsport▲ 31,933 ...H3
Williamstown 1,509 ...J4
Willow Grove 16,325 ...M5
Wilmerding 2,421 ...C5
Wilson 7,830 ...M4
Windber 4,756 ...E5
Windgap 2,651 ...M4
Windsor 1,355 ...J6
Wolfdale 2,906 ...B5
Womelsdorf 2,270 ...K5
Woodlyn 10,151 ...M7
Worthington 713 ...C4
Wrightsville 2,396 ...J5
Wyalusing 686 ...K2
Wyoming 3,255 ...E7
Wyomissing 7,332 ...K5
Yardley 2,288 ...N5
Yeadon 11,980 ...N7
York▲ 42,192 ...J6
York Haven 758 ...J5
York Springs 547 ...H6
Youngstown 1,775 ...D5
Youngwood 3,372 ...D5
Zelienople 4,158 ...B4

OTHER FEATURES

Allegheny (res.) ...E2
Allegheny (riv.) ...D2
Allegheny Front (mts.) ...E5
Appalachian (mts.) ...H4
Ararat (mt.) ...M2
Arthur (lake) ...C4
Beaver (riv.) ...B4
Blue (mt.) ...G5
Blue Knob (mt.) ...E5
Casselman (riv.) ...D6
Clarion (riv.) ...D3
Conemaugh (riv.) ...D5
Conemaugh River (lake) ...D4
Conewango (creek) ...D1
Davis (mt.) ...D6
Delaware (riv.) ...N3
Delaware Water Gap
   Nat'l Rec. ...N3
Erie (lake) ...B1
Fort Necessity Nat'l
   Battlefield ...D6
George B. Stevenson (dam) ...G3
Gettysburg Nat'l Mil. Park ...H6
Glendale (lake) ...F4
Juniata (riv.) ...G5
Laurel Hill (mt.) ...D5
Lehigh (riv.) ...L3
Letterkenny Army Depot ...G6
Licking (creek) ...F6
Little Tinicum (isl.) ...M7
Lycoming (creek) ...H3
Monongahela (riv.) ...C6
North (mt.) ...K3
Ohio (riv.) ...A4
Oil (creek) ...C2
Pine (creek) ...H2
Pine Grove (res.) ...K6
Pocono (mts.) ...M3
Pymatuning (res.) ...A2
Redbank (creek) ...E3
Schuylkill (riv.) ...M5
Shenango River (lake) ...B3
Sinnemahoning (creek) ...F3
South (mt.) ...H6
Steamtown Nat'l Hist. Site ...F7
Susquehanna (riv.) ...K6
Tioga (riv.) ...H1
Tionesta Creek (lake) ...D3
Towanda (creek) ...J2
Tuscarora (mt.) ...G5
Wallenpaupack (lake) ...M3
Youghiogheny River (lake) ...D6

▲County seat
• Population of town or township

Bottom index

New Beaver 1,736 ...B4
New Berlin 892 ...J4
New Bethlehem 1,151 ...D3
New Bloomfield ...H5
New Brighton 6,854 ...B4
New Britain 2,174 ...M5
New Castle▲ 28,334 ...A4
New Cumberland 7,665 ...J5
New Eagle 2,172 ...B5
New Florence 854 ...D5
New Freedom 2,920 ...J6
New Galilee 500 ...A4
New Holland 4,484 ...K5
New Hope 1,400 ...N5
New Kensington 15,894 ...C4
New Milford 953 ...L2
New Oxford 1,617 ...H6
New Philadelphia 1,283 ...K4
New Salem (Delmont) 669 ...D5
New Stanton 2,081 ...C5
New Wilmington 2,706 ...B3
Newport 1,568 ...H5
Newtown 2,565 ...N5
Newtown Square • 11,775 ...L6

Newville 1,349 ...H5
Nicholson 857 ...L2
Norristown▲ 30,749 ...M5
North Apollo 1,391 ...D4
North Braddock 7,036 ...C7
North Catasauqua 2,867 ...L4
North East 4,617 ...C1
North Wales 3,802 ...M5
North Warren 1,232 ...D2
Northampton 8,717 ...M4
Northumberland 3,860 ...J4
Norvelt 2,541 ...D5
Norwood 6,162 ...M7
Nuangola 701 ...L3
Oakdale 1,752 ...B4
Oakland 641 ...L2
Oakmont 6,961 ...C4
Ohioville 3,865 ...B4
Oil City 11,949 ...C3
Old Forge 8,834 ...F7
Oliver 3,271 ...C6
Olyphant 5,222 ...F7
Orangeville 504 ...K3
Orbisonia 447 ...G5

Orwigsburg 2,780 ...K4
Osborne 565 ...B4
Osceola Mills 1,310 ...F4
Oxford 3,769 ...K6
Paint 1,091 ...E5
Palmerton 5,394 ...L4
Palmyra 6,910 ...J5
Paoli 5,603 ...M5
Paradise 1,107 ...K5
Parker 853 ...C3
Parkesburg 2,981 ...L6
Parkside 2,369 ...M7
Parkville 6,014 ...J6
Patton 2,206 ...E4
Pen Argyl 3,492 ...M4
Penbrook 2,791 ...J5
Penn 511 ...C5
Penn Hills 51,430 ...C7
Penn Wynne 5,807 ...M6
Penndel 2,703 ...N5
Pennsburg 2,460 ...M5
Pennville 1,559 ...J6
Perkasie 7,878 ...M5
Perryopolis 1,833 ...C5

Topography

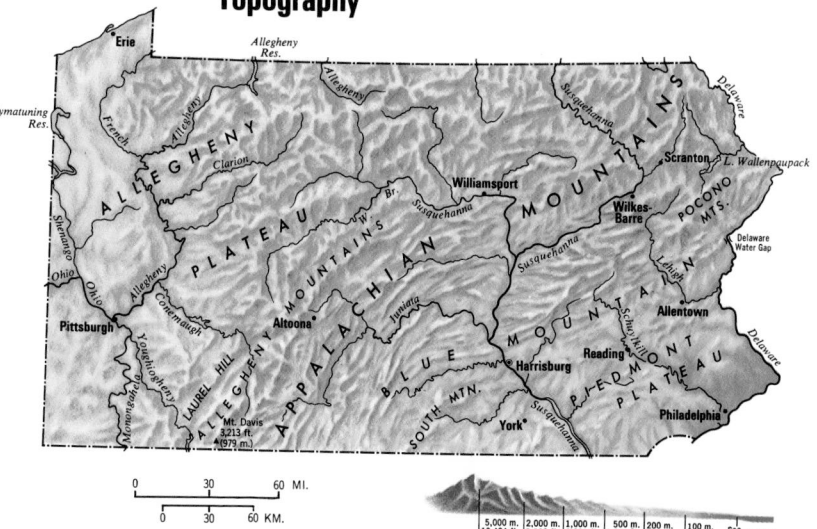

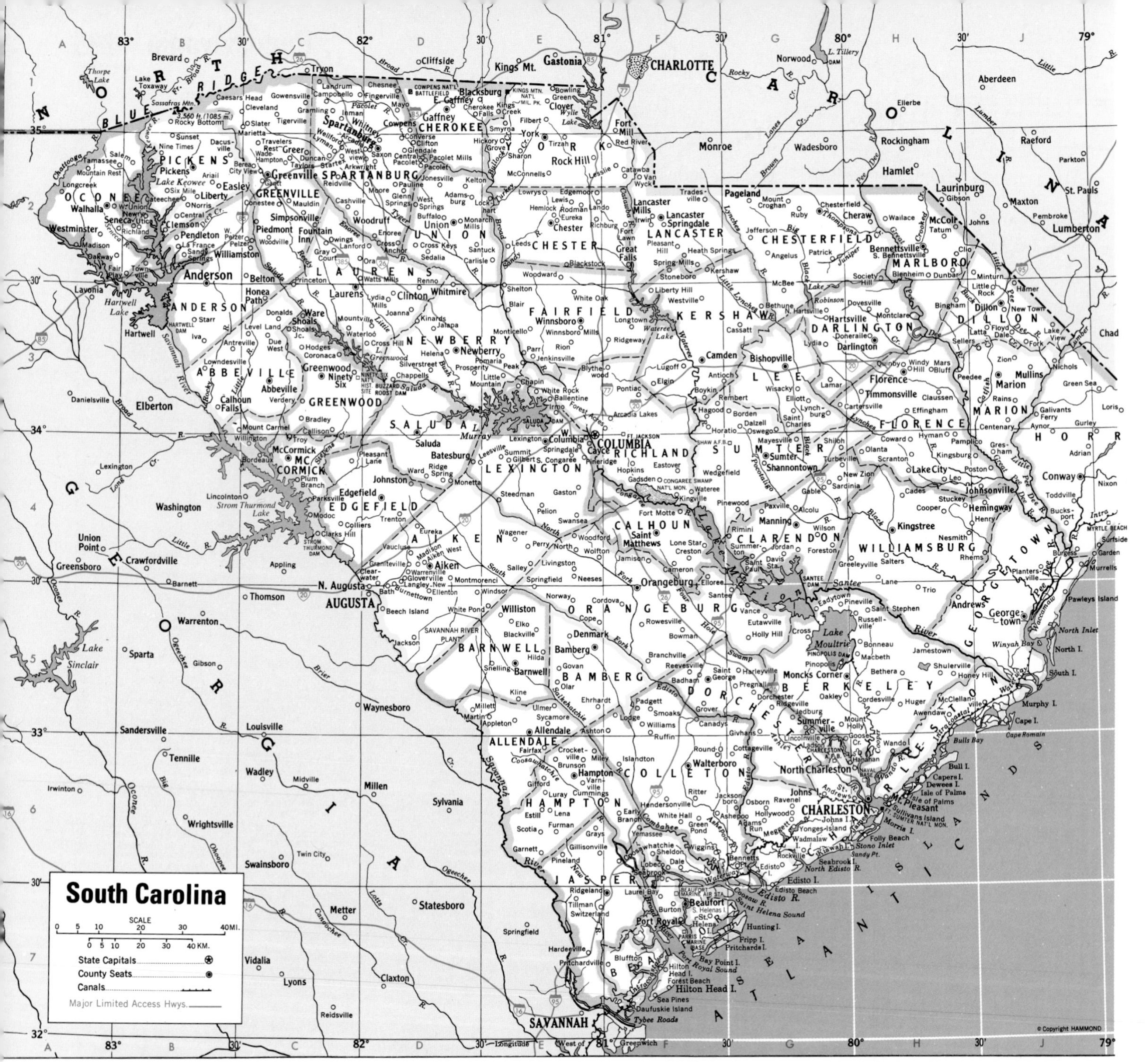

South Carolina

Map Legend

SCALE
0 5 10 20 30 40 MI.
0 5 10 20 30 40 KM.

State Capitals .... ⊛
County Seats .... •
Canals
Major Limited Access Hwys. _____

© Copyright HAMMOND

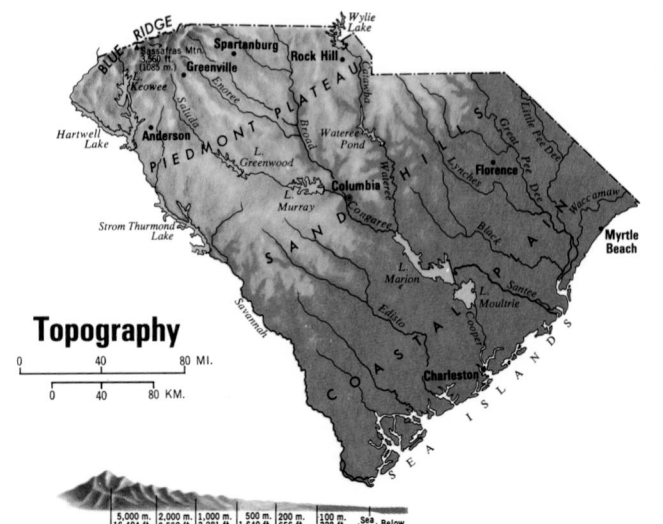

Topography

0 40 80 MI.
0 40 80 KM.

5,000 m. 2,000 m. 1,000 m. 500 m. 200 m. 100 m. Sea Level Below
16,404 ft. 6,562 ft. 3,281 ft. 1,640 ft. 656 ft. 328 ft.

COUNTIES

Abbeville 23,862	B3	
Aiken 120,940	D4	
Allendale 11,722	E6	
Anderson 145,196	B2	
Bamberg 16,902	E5	
Barnwell 20,293	E5	
Beaufort 86,425	F7	
Berkeley 128,776	G5	
Calhoun 12,753	F4	
Charleston 295,039	H6	
Cherokee 44,506	D1	
Chester 32,170	E2	
Chesterfield 38,577	G2	
Clarendon 28,450	G4	
Colleton 34,377	F6	
Darlington 61,851	H3	
Dillon 29,114	J3	
Dorchester 83,060	G5	
Edgefield 18,375	C4	
Fairfield 22,295	E3	
Florence 114,344	H3	
Georgetown 46,302	J5	
Greenville 320,167	C2	
Greenwood 59,567	C3	
Hampton 18,191	E6	
Horry 144,053	J4	
Jasper 15,487	E6	
Kershaw 43,599	F3	
Lancaster 54,516	F2	
Laurens 58,092	D2	
Lee 18,437	G3	

Lexington 167,611	E4	
Marion 33,899	J3	
Marlboro 29,361	H2	
McCormick 8,868	C4	
Newberry 33,172	D3	
Oconee 57,494	A1	
Orangeburg 84,803	F5	
Pickens 93,894	B2	
Richland 285,720	F4	
Saluda 16,357	D3	
Spartanburg 226,800	D2	
Sumter 102,637	G4	
Union 30,337	D2	
Williamsburg 36,815	H4	
York 131,497	F2	

CITIES and TOWNS

Abbeville▲ 5,778	C3	
Adams Run 500	G6	
Adamsburg 300	D2	
Aiken West 3,083	D4	
Aiken▲ 19,872	D4	
Alcolu 600	G4	
Allendale▲ 4,410	E6	
Allsbrook 100	K3	
Anderson 26,184	B2	
Andrews 3,050	H5	
Antioch 500	F3	
Antreville 500	B3	
Appleton 200	E5	
Arcadia 899	C2	
Arcadia Lakes 611	F3	

Ariail 2,419	B2	
Arkwright 2,623	C2	
Atlantic Beach 446	K4	
Awendaw 200	H5	
Aynor 470	J3	
Ballentine 550	E4	
Bamberg▲ 3,843	E5	
Barnwell▲ 5,255	E5	
Batesburg 4,082	D4	
Bath 2,242	D5	
Beaufort▲ 9,576	F7	
Beech Island 400	D5	
Belton 4,646	B2	
Bennettsville 9,345	H2	
Berea 13,535	C2	
Bethera 265	H5	
Bethune 405	F3	
Bingham 200	H3	
Bishopville▲ 3,560	G3	
Blacksburg 1,907	D1	
Blackville 2,688	E5	
Blenheim 191	H2	
Bluffton 738	F7	
Blythewood 164	E3	
Bonneau 374	G5	
Bowman 1,063	F5	
Boykin 350	F4	
Branchville 1,107	F5	
Brunson 587	E6	
Bucksport 1,022	J4	
Buffalo 1,569	D2	
Burgess 250	J4	
Burnettown 493	D5	

Burton 6,917	F7	
Calhoun Falls 2,328	B3	
Camden▲ 6,696	F3	
Cameron 504	F4	
Campobello 465	C1	
Canadys 130	F5	
Carlisle 470	D2	
Cashville 200	C2	
Catawba 607	F2	
Cateechee 225	B2	
Cayce 11,163	E4	
Central 2,438	B2	
Central Pacolet 257	D2	
Chapin 282	D3	
Chappells 45	D3	
Charleston▲ 80,414	G6	
Cheraw 5,505	H2	
Cherokee Falls 250	D1	
Chesnee 1,280	D1	
Chester▲ 7,158	E2	
Chesterfield▲ 1,373	G2	
City View 1,490	C2	
Clarks Hill 200	C4	
Clearwater 4,731	D4	
Clemson 11,096	B2	
Cleveland 800	C1	
Clifton 950	D2	
Clinton 7,987	D3	
Clio 882	H2	
Clover 3,422	E1	
Columbia (cap.)▲ 98,052	F4	

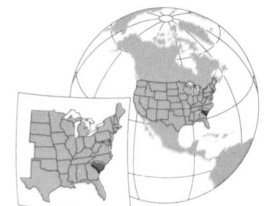

AREA 31,113 sq. mi. (80,583 sq. km.)
POPULATION 3,505,707
CAPITAL Columbia
LARGEST CITY Columbia
HIGHEST POINT Sassafras Mtn. 3,560 ft.
(1085 m.)
SETTLED IN 1670
ADMITTED TO UNION May 23, 1788
POPULAR NAME Palmetto State
STATE FLOWER Carolina (Yellow)
Jessamine
STATE BIRD Carolina Wren

Agriculture, Industry and Resources

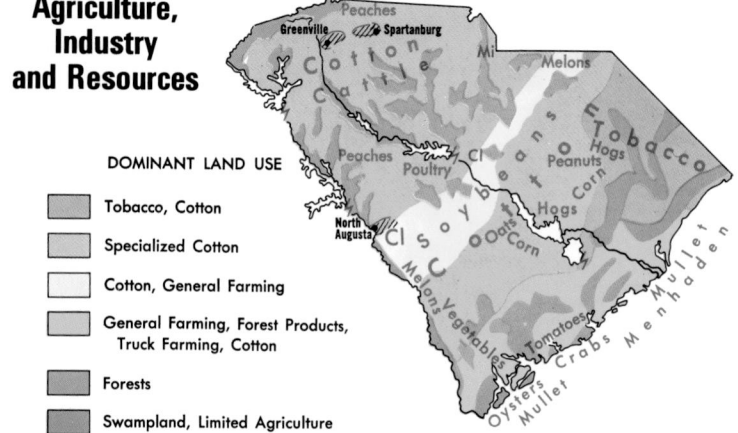

DOMINANT LAND USE

- Tobacco, Cotton
- Specialized Cotton
- Cotton, General Farming
- General Farming, Forest Products, Truck Farming, Cotton
- Forests
- Swampland, Limited Agriculture

MAJOR MINERAL OCCURRENCES

Cl Clay
Mi Mica

/// Major Industrial Areas
⚡ Water Power

298 South Dakota

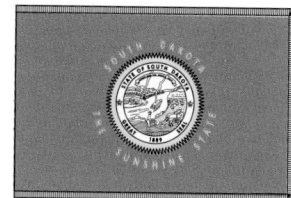

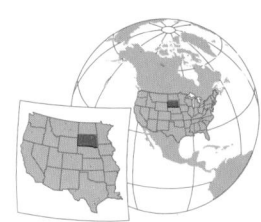

AREA 77,116 sq. mi. (199,730 sq. km.)
POPULATION 699,999
CAPITAL Pierre
LARGEST CITY Sioux Falls
HIGHEST POINT Harney Pk. 7,242 ft. (2207 m.)
SETTLED IN 1856
ADMITTED TO UNION November 2, 1889
POPULAR NAME Coyote State; Sunshine State
STATE FLOWER Pasqueflower
STATE BIRD Ring-necked Pheasant

Topography

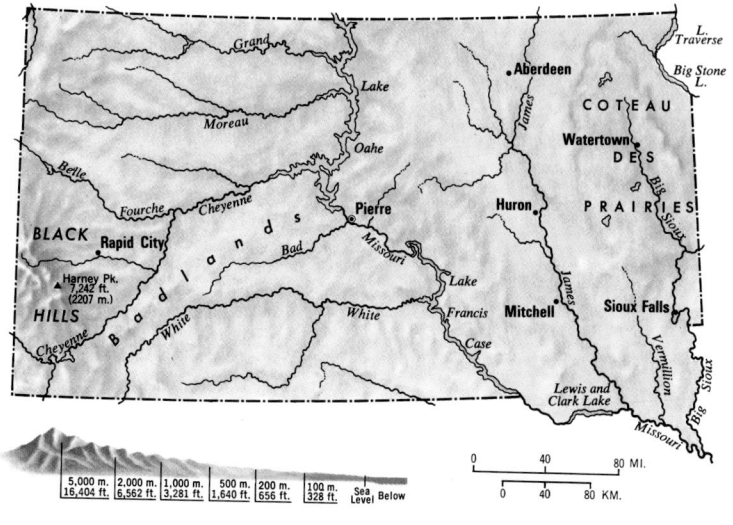

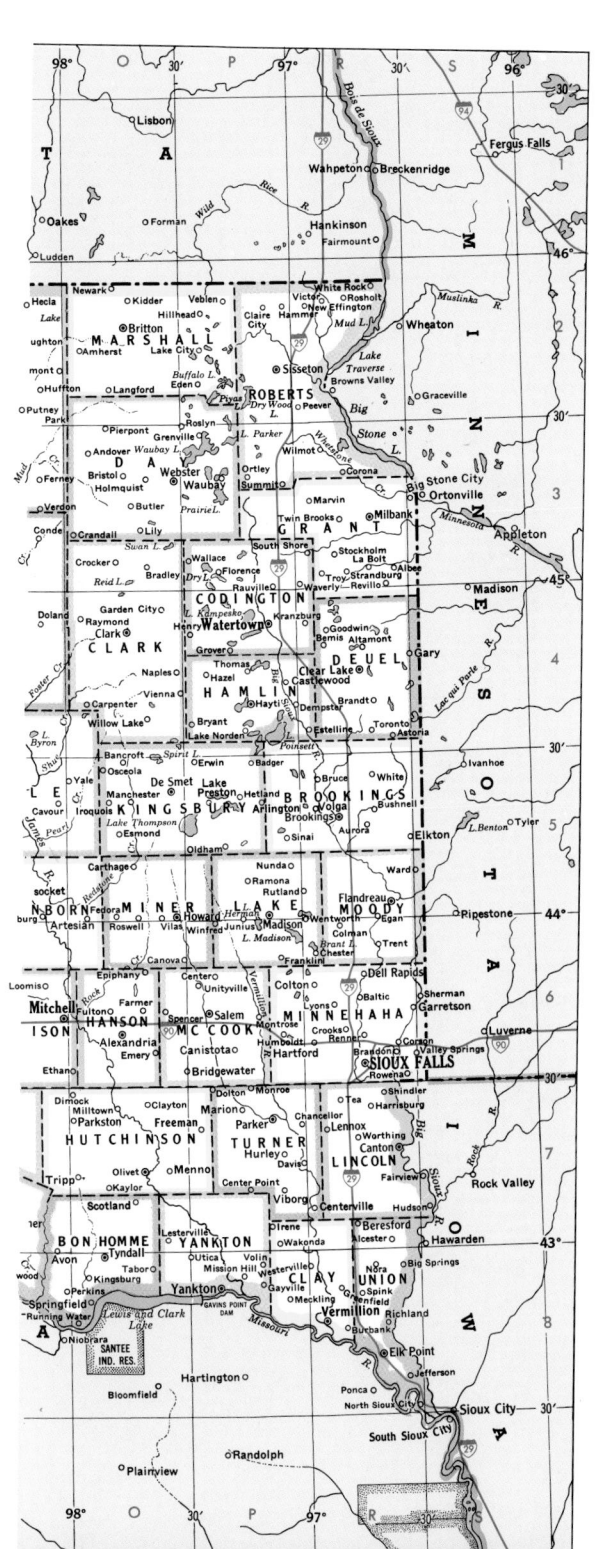

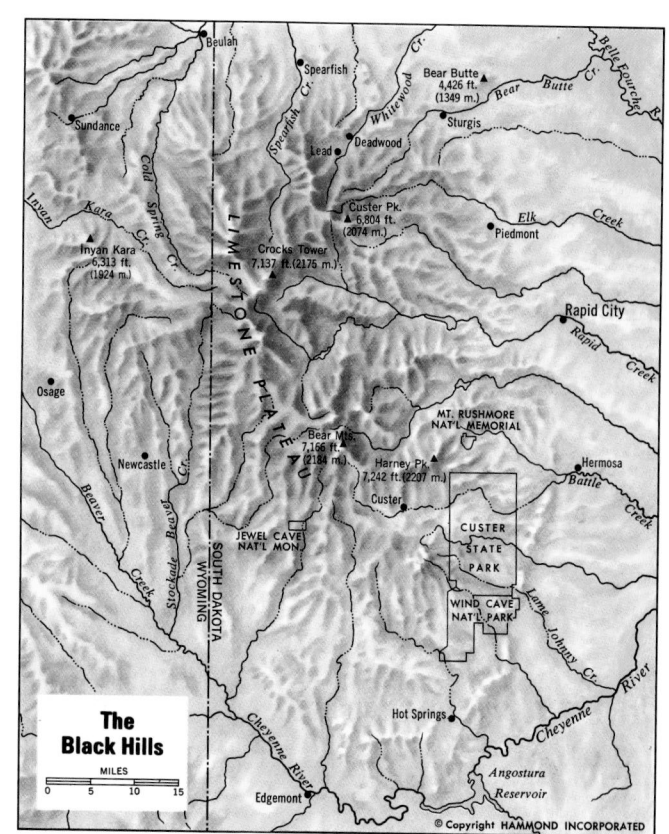

The Black Hills

MILES

© Copyright HAMMOND INCORPORATED

Agriculture, Industry and Resources

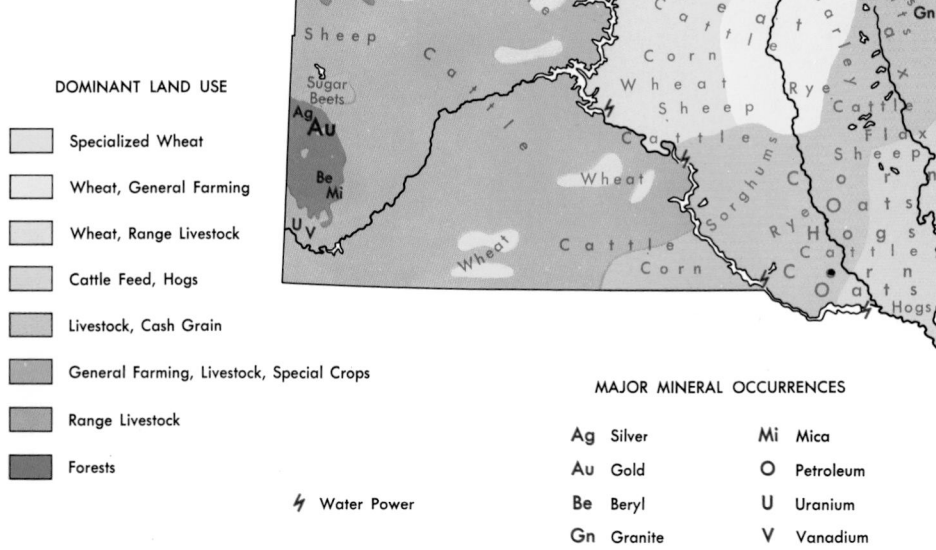

DOMINANT LAND USE

- ▢ Specialized Wheat
- ▢ Wheat, General Farming
- ▢ Wheat, Range Livestock
- ▢ Cattle Feed, Hogs
- ▢ Livestock, Cash Grain
- ▢ General Farming, Livestock, Special Crops
- ▢ Range Livestock
- ▢ Forests

⚡ Water Power

MAJOR MINERAL OCCURRENCES

Ag	Silver	Mi	Mica
Au	Gold	O	Petroleum
Be	Beryl	U	Uranium
Gn	Granite	V	Vanadium

Texas 301

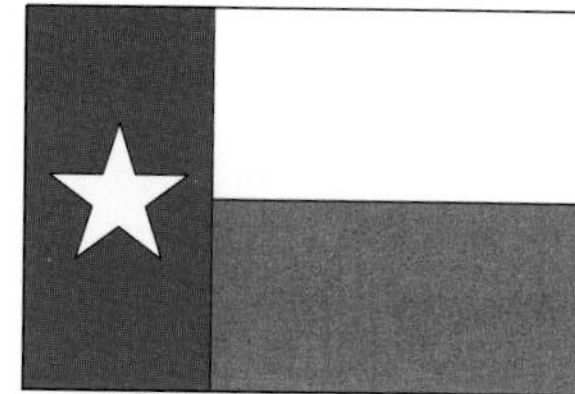

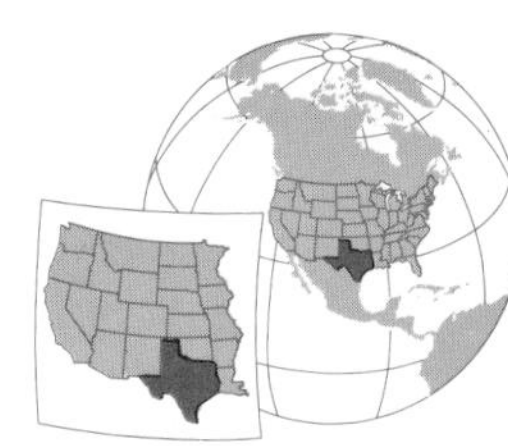

AREA 266,807 sq. mi. (691,030 sq. km.)
POPULATION 17,059,805
CAPITAL Austin
LARGEST CITY Houston
HIGHEST POINT Guadalupe Pk. 8,749 ft. (2667 m.)
SETTLED IN 1686
ADMITTED TO UNION December 29, 1845
POPULAR NAME Lone Star State
STATE FLOWER Bluebonnet
STATE BIRD Mockingbird

COUNTIES

Anderson 48,024 ......J6
Andrews 14,338 ......B5
Angelina 69,884 ......K6
Aransas 17,892 ......H10
Archer 7,973 ......F4
Armstrong 2,021 ......C3
Atascosa 30,533 ......F9
Austin 19,832 ......H8
Bailey 7,064 ......B3
Bandera 10,562 ......E8
Bastrop 38,263 ......G7
Baylor 4,385 ......E4
Bee 25,135 ......G9
Bell 191,088 ......G6
Bexar 1,185,394 ......F8
Blanco 5,972 ......F8
Borden 799 ......C5
Bosque 15,125 ......G6
Bowie 81,665 ......K4
Brazoria 191,707 ......J8
Brazos 121,862 ......H7
Brewster 8,681 ......A8
Briscoe 1,971 ......C3
Brooks 8,204 ......F11
Brown 34,371 ......F6
Burleson 13,625 ......H7
Burnet 22,677 ......F7
Caldwell 26,392 ......G8
Calhoun 19,053 ......H9
Callahan 11,859 ......E5
Cameron 260,120 ......G11
Camp 9,904 ......K5
Carson 6,576 ......C2
Cass 29,982 ......K4
Castro 9,070 ......B3
Chambers 20,088 ......K8
Cherokee 41,049 ......J6
Childress 5,953 ......D3
Clay 10,024 ......F4
Cochran 4,377 ......B4
Coke 3,424 ......D6
Coleman 9,710 ......E6
Collin 264,036 ......H4
Collingsworth 3,573 ......D3
Colorado 18,383 ......H8
Comal 51,832 ......F8
Comanche 13,381 ......F5
Concho 3,044 ......E6
Cooke 30,777 ......G4
Coryell 64,213 ......G6
Cottle 2,247 ......D3
Crane 4,652 ......B6
Crockett 4,078 ......C7
Crosby 7,304 ......C4
Culberson 3,407 ......C11
Dallam 5,461 ......B1
Dallas 1,852,810 ......H5
Dawson 14,349 ......C5
De Witt 18,903 ......G9
Deaf Smith 19,153 ......B3
Delta 4,857 ......J4
Denton 273,525 ......G4
Dickens 2,571 ......D4
Dimmit 10,433 ......E9
Donley 3,696 ......D2
Duval 12,918 ......F10
Eastland 18,488 ......F5
Ector 118,934 ......B6
Edwards 2,266 ......D7
El Paso 591,610 ......A10
Ellis 85,167 ......H5
Erath 27,991 ......F5
Falls 17,712 ......H6
Fannin 24,804 ......H4
Fayette 20,095 ......H8
Fisher 4,842 ......D5
Floyd 8,497 ......C3
Foard 1,794 ......E3
Fort Bend 225,421 ......J8
Franklin 7,802 ......J4
Freestone 15,818 ......H6
Frio 13,472 ......E9
Gaines 14,123 ......B5
Galveston 217,399 ......K8
Garza 5,143 ......C4
Gillespie 17,204 ......F7
Glasscock 1,447 ......C6
Goliad 5,980 ......G9
Gonzales 17,205 ......G8
Gray 23,967 ......D2
Grayson 95,021 ......H4
Gregg 104,948 ......K5
Grimes 18,828 ......J7
Guadalupe 64,873 ......G8
Hale 34,671 ......C3
Hall 3,905 ......D3
Hamilton 7,733 ......F6
Hansford 5,848 ......C1
Hardeman 5,283 ......E3
Hardin 41,320 ......K7
Harris 2,818,199 ......J8
Harrison 57,483 ......K5
Hartley 3,634 ......B2
Haskell 6,820 ......E4
Hays 65,614 ......F7
Hemphill 3,720 ......D2
Henderson 58,543 ......J5
Hidalgo 383,545 ......F11
Hill 27,146 ......G5
Hockley 24,199 ......B4
Hood 28,981 ......G5
Hopkins 28,833 ......J4
Houston 21,375 ......J6
Howard 32,343 ......C5
Hudspeth 2,915 ......B10
Hunt 64,343 ......H4
Hutchinson 25,689 ......C2
Irion 1,629 ......C6
Jack 6,981 ......F4
Jackson 13,039 ......H9
Jasper 31,102 ......K7
Jeff Davis 1,946 ......C11
Jefferson 239,397 ......K8
Jim Hogg 5,109 ......F11
Jim Wells 37,679 ......F10
Johnson 97,165 ......G5
Jones 16,490 ......E5
Karnes 12,455 ......G8
Kaufman 52,220 ......H5
Kendall 14,589 ......F8
Kenedy 460 ......G11
Kent 1,010 ......D4
Kerr 36,304 ......E7
Kimble 4,122 ......E7
King 354 ......D4
Kinney 3,119 ......D8
Kleberg 30,274 ......G10
Knox 4,837 ......E4
La Salle 5,254 ......E9
Lamar 43,949 ......J4
Lamb 15,072 ......B3
Lampasas 13,521 ......F6
Lavaca 18,690 ......H8
Lee 12,854 ......H7
Leon 12,665 ......J6
Liberty 52,726 ......K7
Limestone 20,946 ......H6
Lipscomb 3,143 ......D1
Live Oak 9,556 ......F9
Llano 11,631 ......F7
Loving 107 ......A6
Lubbock 222,636 ......C4
Lynn 6,758 ......C4
Madison 10,931 ......J6
Marion 9,984 ......K5
Martin 4,956 ......C5
Mason 3,423 ......E7
Matagorda 36,928 ......H9
Maverick 36,378 ......D9
McCulloch 8,778 ......E6
McLennan 189,123 ......H6
McMullen 817 ......F9
Medina 27,312 ......E8
Menard 2,252 ......E7
Midland 106,611 ......B6
Milam 22,946 ......H7
Mills 4,531 ......F6
Mitchell 8,016 ......D5
Montague 17,274 ......G4
Montgomery 182,201 ......J7
Moore 17,865 ......C2
Morris 13,200 ......K4
Motley 1,532 ......D3
Nacogdoches 54,753 ......K6
Navarro 39,926 ......H5
Newton 13,569 ......L7
Nolan 16,594 ......D5
Nueces 291,145 ......G10
Ochiltree 9,128 ......D1
Oldham 2,278 ......B2
Orange 80,509 ......L7
Palo Pinto 25,055 ......F5
Panola 22,035 ......K5
Parker 64,785 ......G5
Parmer 9,863 ......B3
Pecos 14,675 ......B7
Polk 30,687 ......K7
Potter 97,874 ......C2
Presidio 6,637 ......C12
Rains 6,715 ......J5
Randall 89,673 ......C2
Reagan 4,514 ......C6
Real 2,412 ......E8
Red River 14,317 ......J4
Reeves 15,852 ......D11
Refugio 7,976 ......G9
Roberts 1,025 ......D2
Robertson 15,511 ......H6
Rockwall 25,604 ......H5
Runnels 11,294 ......E6
Rusk 43,735 ......K5
Sabine 9,586 ......L6
San Augustine 7,999 ......K6
San Jacinto 16,372 ......J7
San Patricio 58,749 ......G10
San Saba 5,401 ......F6
Schleicher 2,990 ......D7
Scurry 18,634 ......D5
Shackelford 3,915 ......E5
Shelby 22,034 ......K6
Sherman 2,858 ......C1
Smith 151,309 ......J5
Somervell 5,360 ......G5
Starr 40,518 ......F11
Stephens 9,010 ......F5
Sterling 1,438 ......C6
Stonewall 2,013 ......D4
Sutton 4,135 ......D7
Swisher 8,133 ......C3
Tarrant 1,170,103 ......G5
Taylor 119,655 ......E5
Terrell 1,410 ......C7
Terry 13,218 ......B4
Throckmorton 1,880 ......E4
Titus 24,009 ......K4
Tom Green 98,458 ......D6
Travis 576,407 ......G7
Trinity 11,445 ......J6
Tyler 16,646 ......K7
Upshur 31,370 ......K5
Upton 4,447 ......B6
Uvalde 23,340 ......E8
Val Verde 38,721 ......C8
Van Zandt 37,944 ......J5
Victoria 74,361 ......H9
Walker 50,917 ......J7
Waller 23,390 ......J8
Ward 13,115 ......A6
Washington 26,154 ......H7
Webb 133,239 ......E10
Wharton 39,955 ......H8
Wheeler 5,879 ......D2
Wichita 122,378 ......F3
Wilbarger 15,121 ......E3
Willacy 17,705 ......G11
Williamson 139,551 ......G7
Wilson 22,650 ......F8
Winkler 8,626 ......A6
Wise 34,679 ......G4
Wood 29,380 ......J5
Yoakum 8,786 ......B4
Young 18,126 ......F4
Zapata 9,279 ......E11
Zavala 12,162 ......E9

CITIES and TOWNS

Abernathy 2,720 ......B4
Abilene▲ 106,654 ......E5
Addison 8,783 ......G2
Alamo 8,210 ......F11
Alamo Heights 6,502 ......K10
Albany▲ 1,962 ......E5
Alice▲ 19,788 ......F10
Allen 18,309 ......H1
Alpine▲ 5,637 ......D12
Alvarado 2,918 ......G5
Alvin 19,220 ......J3
Amarillo▲ 157,615 ......C2
Anahuac▲ 1,993 ......K8
Anderson 500 ......J7
Andrews▲ 10,678 ......B5
Angleton▲ 17,140 ......J8
Anson▲ 2,644 ......E5
Anthony 3,328 ......A10
Aransas Pass 7,180 ......G10
Archer City▲ 1,748 ......F4
Arlington 261,721 ......F2
Aspermont▲ 1,214 ......D4
Athens▲ 10,967 ......J5
Atlanta 6,118 ......K4
Austin (cap.)▲ 465,622 ......G7
Azle 8,868 ......E2
Bacliff 5,549 ......K2
Baird▲ 1,658 ......E5
Balch Springs 17,406 ......H2
Balcones Heights 3,022 ......J10
Ballinger▲ 3,975 ......E6
Bandera▲ 877 ......F8
Barrett 3,052 ......K1
Bastrop▲ 4,044 ......G7
Bay City▲ 18,170 ......H9
Baytown 63,850 ......L2
Beaumont▲ 114,323 ......K7
Bedford 43,762 ......F2
Beeville▲ 13,547 ......G9
Bellaire 13,842 ......J2
Bellmead 8,336 ......H6
Bellville▲ 3,378 ......H8
Belton▲ 12,476 ......G7
Benavides 1,788 ......F10
Benbrook 19,564 ......E2
Benjamin▲ 225 ......E4
Big Lake▲ 3,672 ......C6
Big Spring▲ 23,093 ......C5
Bishop 3,337 ......G10
Bloomington 1,888 ......H9
Blue Mound 2,133 ......E2
Boerne▲ 4,274 ......J10
Bonham▲ 6,686 ......H4
Borger 15,675 ......C2
Boston▲ 400 ......K4
Bowie 4,990 ......G4
Brackettville▲ 1,740 ......D8
Brady▲ 5,946 ......E6
Brazoria 2,717 ......J9
Breckenridge▲ 5,665 ......F5
Brenham▲ 11,952 ......H7
Briar 3,899 ......E1
Bridge City 8,034 ......L7
Bridgeport 3,581 ......G4
Brookshire 2,922 ......J8
Brownfield▲ 9,560 ......B4
Brownsville▲ 98,962 ......G12
Brownwood▲ 18,387 ......F6
Bryan▲ 55,002 ......H7
Buda 1,795 ......G7
Buna 2,127 ......L7
Bunker Hill Village 3,391 ......J1
Burkburnett 10,145 ......F3
Burleson 16,113 ......F3
Burnet▲ 3,423 ......F7
Caldwell▲ 3,181 ......H7
Cameron▲ 5,580 ......H7
Canadian▲ 2,417 ......D2
Canton▲ 2,949 ......J5
Canutillo 4,442 ......A10
Canyon▲ 11,365 ......C3
Carrizo Springs▲ 5,745 ......E9
Carrollton 82,169 ......G2
Carthage▲ 6,496 ......K5
Castle Hills 4,198 ......J10
Castroville 2,159 ......J11
Cedar Hill 19,976 ......G3
Cedar Park 5,161 ......G7
Center▲ 4,950 ......K6
Centerville 812 ......H6
Channelview 25,564 ......K1
Channing 277 ......B2
Childress▲ 5,055 ......D3
Cisco 3,813 ......E5
Clarendon▲ 2,067 ......C3
Clarksville▲ 4,311 ......K4
Claude▲ 1,199 ......C2
Clear Lake Shores 1,096 ......K2
Cleburne▲ 22,205 ......G5
Cleveland 7,124 ......K7
Clifton 3,195 ......G6
Clute 8,910 ......J9
Clyde 3,002 ......E5
Cockrell Hill 3,746 ......G2
Coldspring▲ 538 ......J7
Coleman▲ 5,410 ......E6
College Station▲ 52,456 ......H7
Colleyville 12,724 ......F2
Colorado City▲ 4,749 ......C5
Columbus▲ 3,367 ......H8
Comanche▲ 4,087 ......F6
Commerce 6,825 ......J4
Conroe▲ 27,610 ......J7
Converse 8,887 ......K11
Cooper▲ 2,153 ......J4
Coppell 16,881 ......G2
Copperas Cove 24,079 ......G6
Corpus Christi▲ 257,453 ......G10
Corsicana▲ 22,911 ......H5
Cotulla▲ 3,694 ......E9
Crane▲ 3,533 ......B6
Crockett▲ 7,024 ......J6
Crosby 1,811 ......J8
Crosbyton▲ 2,026 ......C4
Crowell▲ 1,230 ......E4
Crowley 6,974 ......E3
Crystal City▲ 8,263 ......E9
Cuero▲ 6,700 ......G8
Daingerfield▲ 2,572 ......K4
Dalhart▲ 6,246 ......B1
Dallas▲ 1,006,877 ......G2
Dalworthington Gardens 1,758 ......F2
Dayton 5,151 ......J7
De Kalb 1,976 ......K4
De Leon 2,190 ......F5
De Soto 30,544 ......G3
Decatur▲ 4,252 ......G4
Deer Park 27,652 ......K2
Del Rio▲ 30,705 ......D8
Denison 21,505 ......H4
Denton▲ 66,270 ......G4
Denver City 5,145 ......B4
Devine 3,928 ......E8
Diboll 4,341 ......K6
Dickens▲ 322 ......D4
Dickinson 9,497 ......K3
Dilley 2,632 ......E9
Dimmitt▲ 4,408 ......B3
Donna 12,652 ......F11
Double Oak 1,664 ......F1

DOMINANT LAND USE

- Wheat, Grain Sorghums, Range Livestock
- Cotton, Wheat
- Specialized Cotton
- Cotton, General Farming
- Cotton, Forest Products
- Cotton, Range Livestock
- Rice, General Farming
- Peanuts, General Farming
- General Farming, Livestock, Cash Grain
- General Farming, Forest Products, Truck Farming, Cotton
- Fruit, Truck and Mixed Farming
- Range Livestock
- Forests
- Swampland, Limited Agriculture
- Nonagricultural Land
- Urban Areas

MAJOR MINERAL OCCURRENCES

At Asphalt
Cl Clay
Fe Iron Ore
G Natural Gas
Gn Granite
Gp Gypsum
Gr Graphite
He Helium
Ls Limestone
Na Salt
O Petroleum
S Sulfur
Tc Talc
U Uranium

⚡ Water Power
Major Industrial Areas

Agriculture, Industry and Resources

(continued on following page)

Topography

| 0 | 90 | 180 MI. |
| 0 | 90 | 180 KM. |

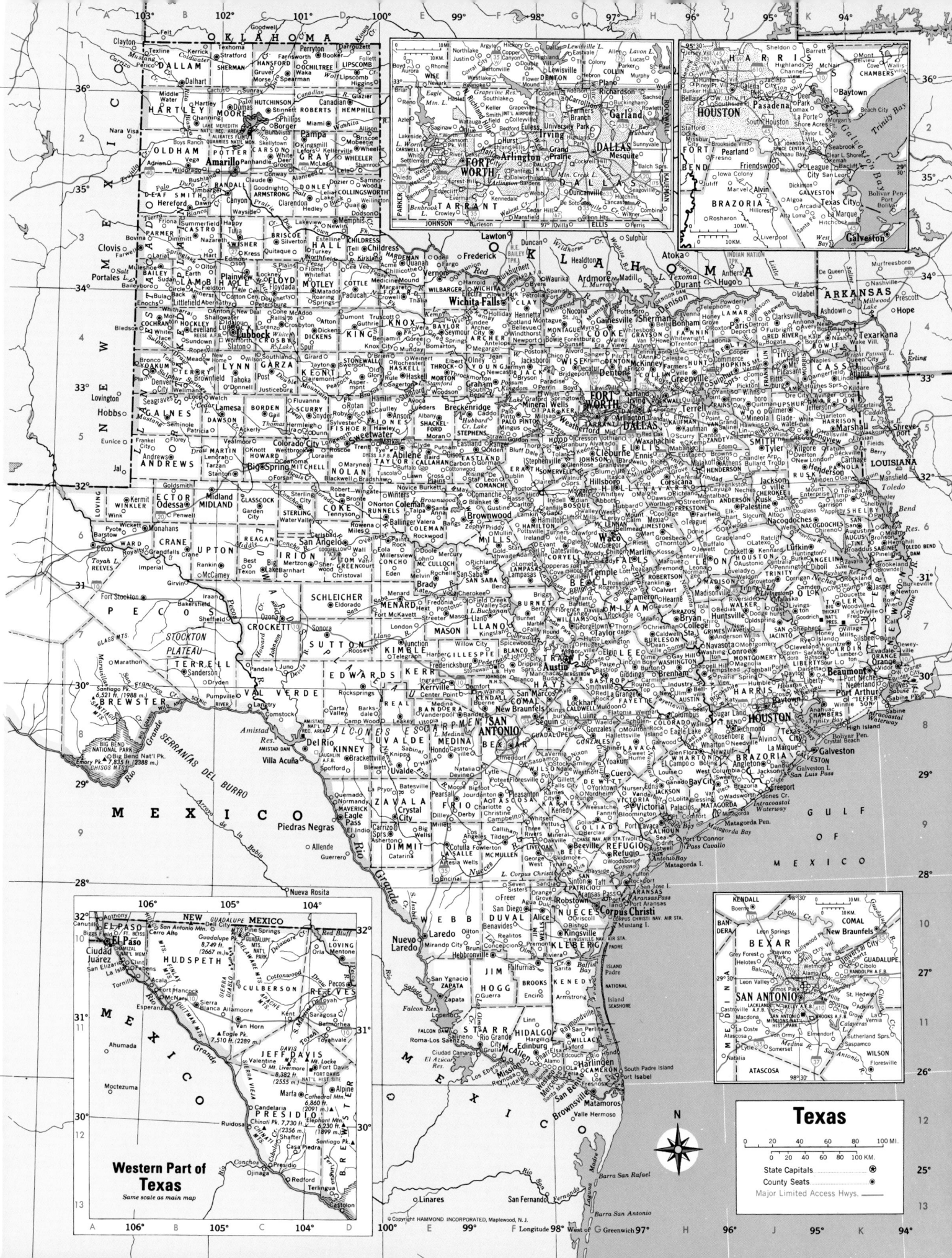
Texas
0 20 40 60 80 100 MI.
0 20 40 60 80 100 KM.
State Capitals
County Seats
Major Limited Access Hwys.
Western Part of Texas
Same scale as main map
© Copyright HAMMOND INCORPORATED, Maplewood, N.J.
Longitude 98° West of Greenwich 97°
OKLAHOMA
NEW MEXICO
MEXICO
ARKANSAS
LOUISIANA
GULF OF MEXICO
HOUSTON
DALLAS
FORT WORTH
SAN ANTONIO
AUSTIN
El Paso
Corpus Christi
Galveston
Amarillo
Lubbock
Laredo
Brownsville

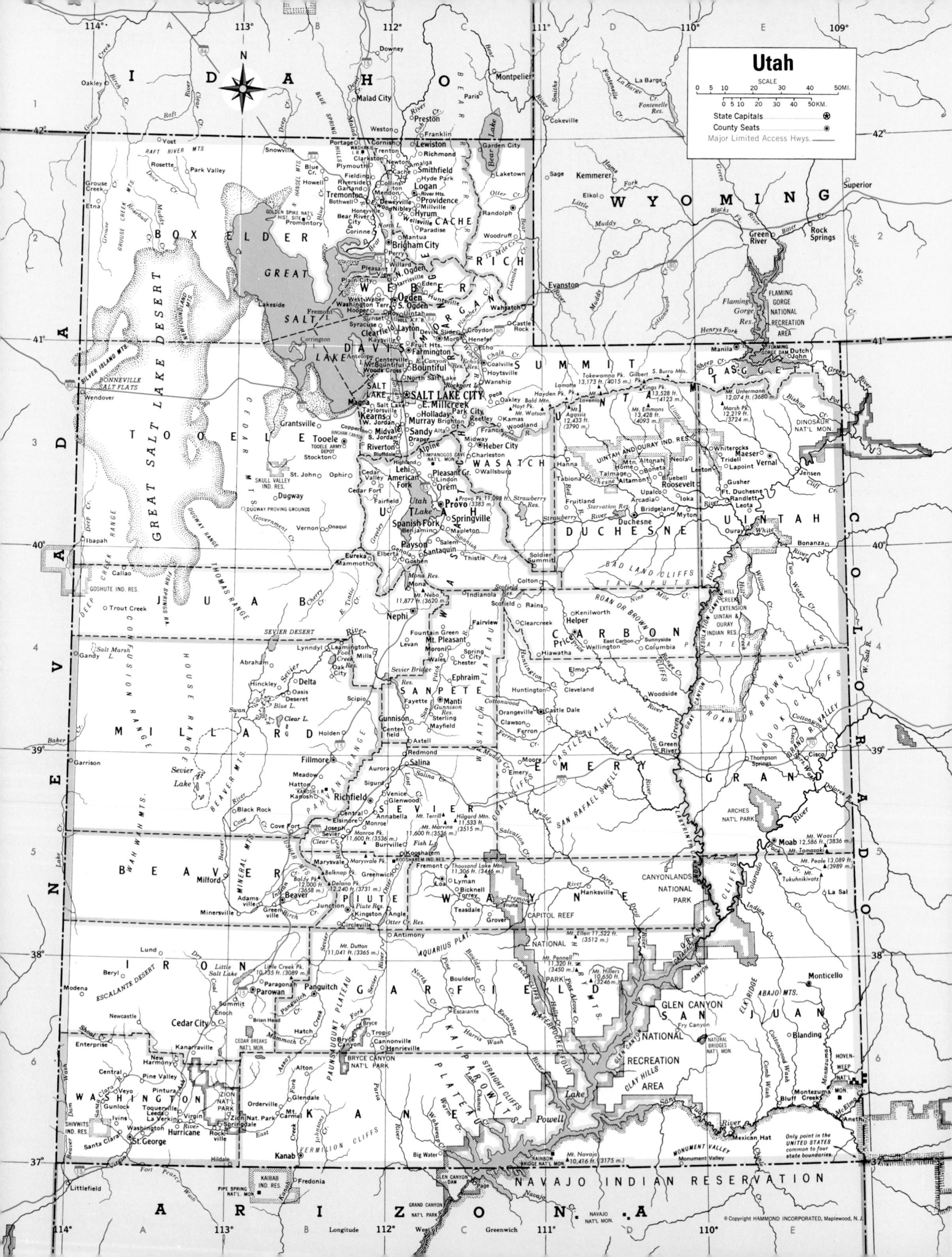

Utah
SCALE
0 5 10 20 30 40 50MI.
0 5 10 20 30 40 50KM.
State Capitals
County Seats
Major Limited Access Hwys.
IDAHO
WYOMING
NEVADA
COLORADO
ARIZONA
BOX ELDER
CACHE
RICH
WEBER
MORGAN
DAVIS
SUMMIT
DAGGETT
SALT LAKE
TOOELE
WASATCH
UTAH
DUCHESNE
UINTAH
JUAB
CARBON
SANPETE
MILLARD
EMERY
GRAND
SEVIER
BEAVER
PIUTE
WAYNE
IRON
GARFIELD
SAN JUAN
WASHINGTON
KANE
SALT LAKE CITY
GREAT SALT LAKE
GREAT SALT LAKE DESERT
BONNEVILLE SALT FLATS
Ogden
Logan
Brigham City
Provo
Orem
Tooele
Heber City
Coalville
Farmington
Nephi
Manti
Price
Castle Dale
Duchesne
Vernal
Fillmore
Richfield
Junction
Beaver
Loa
Parowan
Panguitch
Moab
Monticello
Kanab
St. George
Manila
Randolph
Morgan
Cedar City
Utah Lake
Lake Powell
FLAMING GORGE NATIONAL RECREATION AREA
DINOSAUR NAT'L MON.
ARCHES NAT'L PARK
CANYONLANDS NATIONAL PARK
CAPITOL REEF NATIONAL PARK
GLEN CANYON NATIONAL RECREATION AREA
BRYCE CANYON NAT'L PARK
ZION NAT'L PARK
CEDAR BREAKS NAT'L MON.
NATURAL BRIDGES NAT'L MON.
HOVENWEEP NAT'L MON.
NAVAJO INDIAN RESERVATION
UINTAH AND OURAY IND. RES.
Kings Pk. 13,528 ft. (4123 m.)
Only point in the UNITED STATES common to four state boundaries.
Longitude
West of
Greenwich
114°
113°
112°
111°
110°
109°
42°
41°
40°
39°
38°
37°
© Copyright HAMMOND INCORPORATED, Maplewood, N.J.

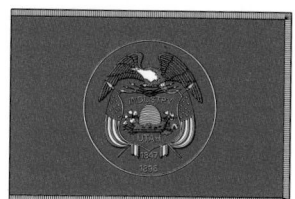

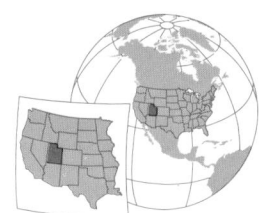

AREA 84,899 sq. mi. (219,888 sq. km.)
POPULATION 1,727,784
CAPITAL Salt Lake City
LARGEST CITY Salt Lake City
HIGHEST POINT Kings Pk. 13,528 ft. (4123 m.)
SETTLED IN 1847
ADMITTED TO UNION January 4, 1896
POPULAR NAME Beehive State
STATE FLOWER Sego Lily
STATE BIRD Sea Gull

COUNTIES

Beaver 4,765................A5
Box Elder 36,485............A2
Cache 70,183...............C2
Carbon 20,228..............D4
Daggett 690................E3
Davis 187,941..............B3
Duchesne 12,645............D3
Emery 10,332...............D4
Garfield 3,980.............C6
Grand 6,620................E5
Iron 20,789................A6
Juab 5,817.................A4
Kane 5,169.................B6
Millard 11,333.............A4
Morgan 5,528...............C2
Piute 1,277................B5
Rich 1,725.................C2
Salt Lake 725,956..........B3
San Juan 12,621............E6
Sanpete 16,259.............C4
Sevier 15,431..............C4
Summit 15,518..............C3
Tooele 26,601..............A3
Uintah 22,211..............E3
Utah 263,590...............C3
Wasatch 10,089.............C3
Washington 48,560..........A6
Wayne 2,177................C5
Weber 158,330..............B2

CITIES and TOWNS

Alpine 3,492...............C3
Alta 397...................C3
Amalga 366.................C2
American Fork 15,696.......C3
Annabella 487..............B5
Aurora 911.................B5
Bear River City 700........B2
Beaver▲ 1,998..............B5
Bicknell 327...............C5
Big Water 326..............C6
Blanding 3,162.............E6
Bluffdale 2,152............B3
Bountiful 36,659...........C2
Brigham City▲ 15,644.......C2
Brighton 150...............C3
Castle Dale▲ 1,704.........D4
Castle Rock................C2
Cedar City 13,443..........A6
Cedar Fort 284.............C3
Centerfield 766............C4
Centerville 11,500.........C3
Charleston 336.............C3
Circleville 417............B5
Clarkston 645..............B2
Clearfield 21,435..........B2
Cleveland 522..............D4
Coalville▲ 1,065...........C3
Corinne 639................B2
Delta 2,998................B4
Deweyville 318.............B2
Draper 7,257...............C3
Duchesne▲ 1,308............D3
Dugway 1,761...............B3
East Carbon 1,270..........D4
East Millcreek 21,184......C3
Elmo 267...................D4
Elsinore 608...............B5
Elwood 575.................B2
Emery 300..................C5
Enoch 1,947................A6
Enterprise 936.............A6
Ephraim 3,363..............C4
Escalante 818..............C6
Eureka 562.................B4
Fairview 960...............C4
Farmington▲ 9,028..........C4
Ferron 1,606...............C4
Fielding 422...............B2
Fillmore▲ 1,956............B5
Fort Duchesne 655..........E3
Fountain Green 578.........C4
Francis 381................C3
Fruit Heights 3,900........C2
Garden City 193............C2
Garland 1,637..............B2
Genola 803.................C4
Glendale 282...............B6
Glenwood 437...............C5
Goshen 578.................C4
Grantsville 4,500..........B3
Green River 866............D4
Gunnison 1,298.............C4
Harrisville 3,004..........C2
Heber City▲ 4,782..........C3
Helper 2,148...............D4
Henefer 554................C2
Highland 5,002.............C3
Hildale 1,325..............A6
Hinckley 658...............B4
Holden 402.................B4
Holladay 22,189............C3
Honeyville 1,112...........B2
Hooper 3,468...............B2
Howell 237.................B2
Huntington 1,875...........C4
Huntsville 566.............C2
Hurricane 3,915............A6
Hyde Park 2,190............C2
Hyrum 4,829................C2
Ivins 1,630................A6
Joseph 198.................C5
Junction▲ 132..............B5
Kamas 1,061................C3
Kanab▲ 3,289...............B6
Kanarraville 228...........A6
Kanosh 386.................B5
Kaysville 13,961...........B2
Kearns 28,374..............B3
Koosharem 266..............C5
La Verkin 1,771............A6
Laketown 261...............C2
Layton 41,784..............C2
Leamington 253.............B4
Leeds 254..................A6
Lehi 8,475.................C3
Levan 416..................C4
Lewiston 1,532.............C2
Lindon 3,818...............C3
Loa▲ 444...................C5
Logan▲ 32,762..............C2
Lyman 198..................C5
Maeser 2,598...............E3
Magna 17,829...............B3
Manila▲ 207................E3
Manti▲ 2,268...............C4
Mantua 665.................C2
Mapleton 3,572.............C3
Marysvale 364..............B5
Mayfield 438...............C4
Meadow 250.................B5
Mendon 684.................B2
Mexican Hat 259............E6
Midvale 11,886.............B3
Midway 1,554...............C3
Milford 1,107..............A5
Millville 1,202............C2
Minersville 608............A5
Moab▲ 3,971................E5
Mona 584...................C4
Monroe 1,472...............B5
Montezuma Creek 345........E6
Monticello▲ 1,806..........E6
Morgan▲ 2,023..............C2
Moroni 1,115...............C4
Mount Pleasant 2,092.......C4
Murray 31,282..............C3
Myton 468..................D3
Neola 511..................D3
Nephi▲ 3,515...............C4
Newton 600.................C2
Nibley 1,167...............C2
North Ogden 11,668.........C2
North Salt Lake 6,474......C3
Oak City 587...............B4
Oakley 522.................C3
Ogden▲ 63,909..............C2
Orangeville 1,459..........C4
Orderville 422.............B6
Orem 67,561................C3
Panguitch▲ 1,444...........B6
Paradise 561...............C2
Paragonah 307..............B6
Park City 4,468............C3
Parowan▲ 1,873.............B6
Payson 9,510...............C3
Perry 1,211................C2
Plain City 2,722...........B2
Pleasant Grove 13,476......C3
Pleasant View 3,603........B2
Plymouth 267...............B2
Price▲ 8,712...............D4
Providence 3,344...........C2
Provo▲ 86,835..............C3
Randlett 283...............E3
Randolph▲ 488..............C2
Redmond 648................C4
Richfield▲ 5,593...........B5
Richmond 1,955.............C2
River Heights 1,274........C2
Riverton 11,261............B3
Roosevelt 3,915............D3
Roy 24,603.................B2
Saint George▲ 28,502.......A6
Salem 2,284................C3
Salina 1,943...............C5
Salt Lake City (cap.)▲
 159,936...................C3
Sandy 75,058...............C3
Santa Clara 2,322..........A6
Santaquin 2,386............C4
Scipio 291.................B4
Sigurd 385.................B5
Smithfield 5,566...........C2
South Jordan 12,220........B3
South Ogden 12,105.........C2
South Salt Lake 10,129.....C3
Spanish Fork 11,272........C3
Spring City 715............C4
Springdale 275.............B6
Springville 13,950.........C3
Stockton 426...............B3
Sunnyside 339..............D4
Sunset 5,128...............B2
Syracuse 4,658.............B2
Taylorsville-Bennion 52,351..B3
Tooele▲ 13,887.............B3
Toquerville 488............A6
Tremonton 4,264............B2
Trenton 464................B2
Tropic 374.................B6
Uintah 760.................C2
Vernal▲ 6,644..............E3
Wallsburg 252..............C3
Washington 4,198...........A6
Washington Terrace 8,189...B2
Wellington 1,632...........D4
Wellsville 2,206...........C2
Wendover 1,127.............A3
West Bountiful 4,477.......B3
West Jordan 42,892.........B3
Whiterocks 312.............E3
Willard 1,298..............C2
Woods Cross 5,384..........B3

OTHER FEATURES

Abajo (mts.)...............E6
Agassiz (mt.)..............D3
Antelope (isl.)............B3
Aquarius (plat.)...........C5
Arches Nat'l Park..........E5
Assay (creek)..............B6
Bad Land (cliffs)..........D4
Baldy (peak)...............B5
Bear (lake)................C2
Bear (riv.)................B2
Beaver (mts.)..............A5
Beaver (riv.)..............A5
Beaver Dam Wash (creek)....A6
Birch (creek)..............B5
Blue (creek)...............B2
Bonneville (salt flats)....A3
Book (cliffs)..............E4
Bryce Canyon Nat'l Park....B6
Canyonlands Nat'l Park.....D5
Capitol Reef Nat'l Park....C5
Castle (valley)............D4
Cedar (mts.)...............B3
Cedar Breaks Nat'l Mon.....B6
Chalk (creek)..............C3
Chinle (creek).............E6
Clear (lake)...............B4
Cliff (creek)..............E3
Coal (cliffs)..............C5
Colorado (riv.)............E5
Confusion (range)..........A4
Cottonwood (creek).........C4
Cub (creek)................C1
Deep (creek)...............B1
Deep Creek (range).........A4
Delano (peak)..............B5
Desolation (canyon)........E4
Dinosaur Nat'l Mon.........E3
Dirty Devil (riv.).........D5
Dolores (riv.).............E5
Dry Coal (creek)...........A6
Duchesne (riv.)............D3
Dugway (range).............A3
Dugway Proving Grounds.....B3
Dutton (mt.)...............B5
East Canyon (res.).........C3
Echo (res.)................C3
Elk (ridge)................E6
Ellen (mt.)................D5
Emmons (mt.)...............D3
Escalante (des.)...........A6
Escalante (riv.)...........C6
Fish (lake)................C5
Fish Springs (range).......A4
Flaming Gorge (res.).......E3
Flaming Gorge Nat'l
 Rec. Area.................E2
Fool Creek (res.)..........B4
Fremont (isl.).............B2
Fremont (riv.).............C5
Glen Canyon Nat'l Rec. Area..D6
Golden Spike Nat'l Hist. Site..B2
Goshute Ind. Res...........A4
Gray (canyon)..............D4
Great Salt (lake)..........B2
Great Salt Lake (des.).....A3
Greeley (creek)............B3
Green (riv.)...............D4
Grouse (creek).............A2
Grouse Creek (mts.)........A2
Gunnison (res.)............C4
Henry (mts.)...............D6
Hilgard (mt.)..............C5
Hill (creek)...............E4
Hill A.F.B.................C2
Hill Creek Extension, Uintah
 and Ouray Ind. Res........E4
Hillers (mt.)..............D6
Hovenweep Nat'l Mon........E6
Hoyt (peak)................C3
Huntington (creek).........C4
Indian (creek).............B5
Jordan (riv.)..............C3
Kaiparowits (plat.)........C6
Kanab (riv.)...............B7
Kanosh Ind. Res............B5
Kings (peak)...............D3
Koosharem Ind. Res.........C5
Little Creek (peak)........B6
Little Salt (lake).........A6
Malad (riv.)...............B1
Marsh (peak)...............E3
Marvine (mt.)..............C5
Mineral (mts.).............B5
Mona (res.)................C4
Monroe (peak)..............B5
Montezuma (creek)..........E6
Monument (valley)..........D6
Muddy (creek)..............C4
Natural Bridges Nat'l Mon..E6
Navajo (mt.)...............D6
Navajo Ind. Res............D7
Nebo (mt.).................C4
Newfoundland (mts.)........A2
Nine Mile (creek)..........D3
North (lake)...............B2
Orange (cliffs)............D5
Otter (creek)..............C5
Otter Creek (res.).........C5
Paria (riv.)...............B6
Paunsaugunt (plat.)........B6
Pahvant (range)............B5
Peale (mt.)................E5
Pennell (mt.)..............D6
Piute (res.)...............B5
Plumber (creek)............C2
Powell (lake)..............D6
Price (riv.)...............D4
Provo (peak)...............C3
Provo (riv.)...............C3
Raft River (mts.)..........A2
Rainbow Bridge Nat'l Mon...C6
Roan (cliffs)..............E4
Rockport (lake)............C3
Salvation (creek)..........C5
San Juan (riv.)............D6
San Pitch (riv.)...........C4
San Rafael (riv.)..........D4
San Rafael Swell (mts.)....D5
Santa Clara (riv.).........A6
Sevier (des.)..............B4
Sevier (lake)..............A5
Sevier (riv.)..............B4
Sevier (riv.)..............C4
Shivwits Ind. Res..........A6
Silver Island (mts.).......A3
Skull Valley Ind. Res......B3
Spanish Fork (riv.)........C3
Strait (cliffs)............C6
Strawberry (res.)..........C3
Strawberry (riv.)..........D3
Swan (lake)................B4
Tavaputs (plat.)...........D4
Thomas (range).............A4
Thousand Lake (mt.)........C5
Timpanogos Cave Nat'l Mon...C3
Tokewamna (mt.)............D3
Tooele Army Depot..........B3
Two Water (creek)..........E4
Uinta (mts.)...............D3
Uinta (riv.)...............D3
Uintah and Ouray Ind. Res...D3
Utah (lake)................C3
Virgin (riv.)..............A6
Waas (mt.).................E5
Wah Wah (mts.).............A5
Wasatch (range)............C3
Washakie Ind. Res..........B2
Waterpocket Fold (cliffs)..D6
Weber (riv.)...............C3
White (riv.)...............E3
Willow (creek).............E4
Zion Nat'l Park............A6

▲County seat

Agriculture, Industry and Resources

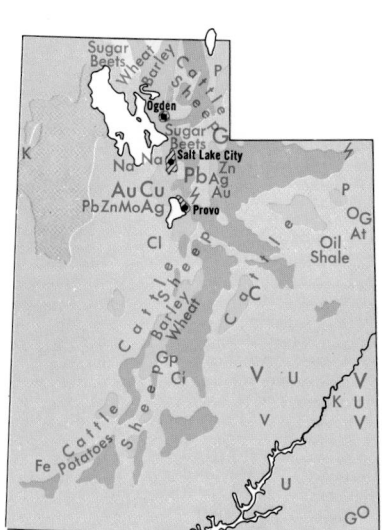

DOMINANT LAND USE

- Wheat, General Farming
- General Farming, Livestock, Special Crops
- Range Livestock
- Forests
- Nonagricultural Land

MAJOR MINERAL OCCURRENCES

Ag Silver
At Asphalt
Au Gold
C Coal
Cl Clay
Cu Copper

Fe Iron Ore
G Natural Gas
Gp Gypsum
K Potash
Mo Molybdenum
Na Salt

O Petroleum
P Phosphates
Pb Lead
U Uranium
V Vanadium
Zn Zinc

⚡ Water Power
▨ Major Industrial Areas

Topography

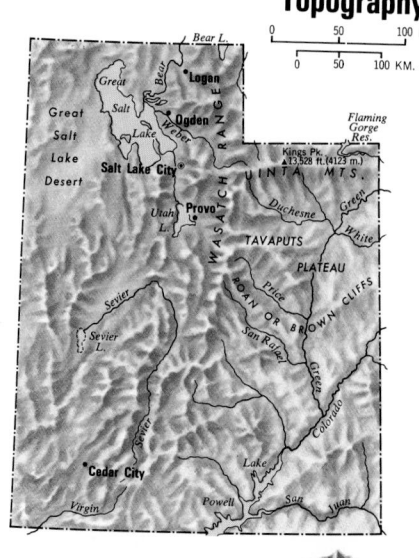

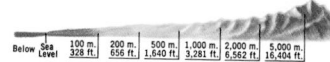

Topography

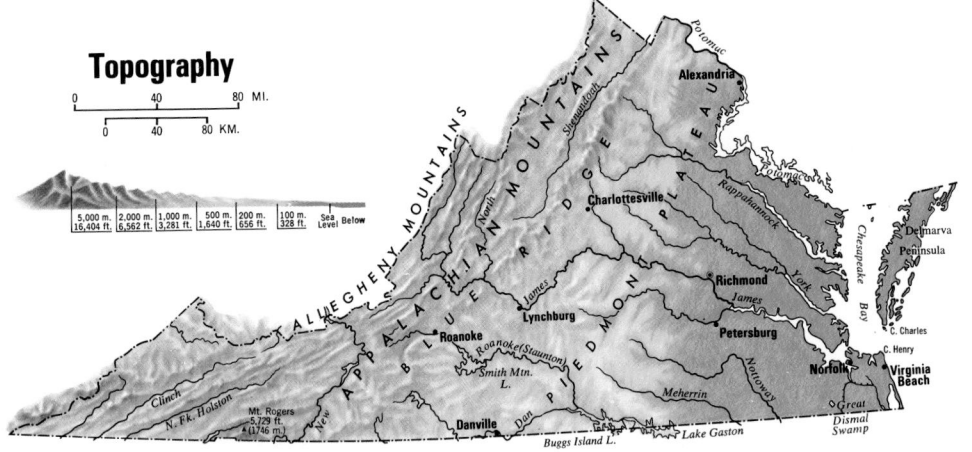

40   80 MI.
0   40   80 KM.

5,000 m. 2,000 m. 1,000 m. 500 m. 200 m. 100 m. Sea Level Below
16,404 ft. 6,562 ft. 3,281 ft. 1,640 ft. 656 ft. 328 ft.

ALLEGHENY MOUNTAINS
APPALACHIAN MOUNTAINS
BLUE RIDGE
PIEDMONT PLATEAU
Shenandoah
Potomac R.
Alexandria
Delmarva Peninsula
Chesapeake Bay
Charlottesville
Rappahannock
Richmond
York
James R.
Lynchburg
Petersburg
Roanoke
Roanoke/Staunton
James
C. Charles
C. Henry
Norfolk
Virginia Beach
Smith Mtn. L.
Clinch
Mt. Rogers 5,729 ft. 4,(1746 m.)
N. Fk. Holston
New
Dan
Danville
Meherrin
Nottoway
Buggs Island L.
Lake Gaston
Great Dismal Swamp

COUNTIES

Accomack 31,703 ....S5
Albemarle 68,040 ....L5
Alleghany 13,176 ....H5
Amelia 8,787 ....M6
Amherst 28,578 ....K6
Appomattox 12,298 ....L6
Arlington 170,936 ....N2
Augusta 54,677 ....K4
Bath 4,799 ....J4
Bedford 45,656 ....J6
Bland 6,514 ....F6
Botetourt 24,992 ....J5
Brunswick 15,987 ....N7
Buchanan 31,333 ....D6
Buckingham 12,873 ....L5
Campbell 47,572 ....K6
Caroline 19,217 ....O4
Carroll 26,594 ....G7
Charles City 6,282 ....O6
Charlotte 11,688 ....L7
Chesterfield 209,274 ....N6
Clarke 12,101 ....M2
Craig 4,372 ....H6
Culpeper 27,791 ....M3
Cumberland 7,825 ....M6
Dickenson 17,620 ....D6
Dinwiddie 20,960 ....N6
Essex 8,689 ....P5
Fairfax 818,584 ....O3
Fauquier 35,889 ....N3
Floyd 12,005 ....H7
Fluvanna 12,429 ....M5
Franklin 39,549 ....J6
Frederick 45,723 ....M2
Giles 16,366 ....G6
Gloucester 30,131 ....P6
Goochland 14,163 ....N5
Grayson 16,278 ....F7
Greene 10,297 ....M4
Greensville 8,853 ....N7
Halifax 29,033 ....L7
Hanover 63,306 ....N5
Henrico 217,881 ....O6
Henry 56,942 ....J7
Highland 2,635 ....J4
Isle of Wight 25,053 ....P7
James City 34,859 ....P6
King George 13,527 ....O4
King William 10,913 ....O5
King and Queen 6,289 ......P5
Lancaster 10,896 ....R5
Lee 24,496 ....B7
Loudoun 86,129 ....N2
Louisa 20,325 ....N5
Lunenburg 11,419 ....M7
Madison 11,949 ....M4
Mathews 8,348 ....R6
Mecklenburg 29,241 ....M7
Middlesex 8,653 ....R5
Montgomery 73,913 ....H6
Nelson 12,778 ....L5
New Kent 10,445 ....P5
Northampton 13,061 ....S6
Northumberland 10,524 ...R5
Nottoway 14,993 ....M6
Orange 21,421 ....M4
Page 21,690 ....M3
Patrick 17,473 ....H7
Pittsylvania 55,655 ....K7
Powhatan 15,328 ....N5
Prince Edward 17,320 ......M6
Prince George 27,394 ......O6
Prince William 215,686 ....O3
Pulaski 34,496 ....G6
Rappahannock 6,622 ....M3
Richmond 7,273 ....P5
Roanoke 79,332 ....H6
Rockbridge 18,350 ....K5
Rockingham 57,482 ....L4
Russell 28,667 ....D7
Scott 23,204 ....C7
Shenandoah 31,636 ....L3
Smyth 32,370 ....E7
Southampton 17,550 ....O7
Spotsylvania 57,403 ....N4
Stafford 61,236 ....O4
Surry 6,145 ....P6
Sussex 10,248 ....O7
Tazewell 45,960 ....E6
Warren 26,142 ....M3

Washington 45,887 ....D7
Westmoreland 15,480 ......P4
Wise 39,573 ....C6
Wythe 25,466 ....F7
York 42,422 ....P6

CITIES and TOWNS

Abingdon▲ 7,003 ....D7
Accomac▲ 466 ....S5
Achilles 525 ....R6
Afton 350 ....L4
Alberene 200 ....L5
Alberta 337 ....N7
Allisonia 325 ....K6
Alton 180 ....K7
Altavista 3,686 ....K6
Altavista 3,686 ....K6
Amelia Court House▲ 500 .N6
Amherst▲ 1,060 ....K5
Ammissville 150 ....M3
Amonate 350 ....E6
Andover 180 ....C7
Annandale 50,975 ....S3
Appalachia 1,994 ....C7
Appomattox▲ 1,707 ....L6
Ararat 500 ....G7
Arlington▲ 170,936 ....T3
Arrington 500 ....L5
Arvonia 500 ....M5
Ashburn 3,393 ....O2
Ashland 5,864 ....N5
Atkins 1,130 ....F7
Augusta Springs 600 ....K4
Austinville 750 ....F7
Axton 540 ....J7
Bailey's Crossroads 19,507 .S3
Ballsville 150 ....M6
Bandy 200 ....E6
Banner 327 ....D7
Barboursville 600 ....M4
Barren Springs 125 ....G7
Bassett 1,579 ....J7
Bastian 600 ....F6
Batesville 575 ....L5
Bealeton 200 ....N3
Beaverdam 500 ....N5
Beaverlett 200 ....R6
Bedford (I.C.)▲ 6,073 ......J6
Belle Haven 526 ....S5
Belle View T3
Ben Hur 400 ....B7

Bent Mountain 140 ....H6
Bentonville 500 ....M3
Bergton 150 ....L3
Berryville▲ 3,097 ....M2
Big Island 500 ....K5
Big Rock 900 ....D6
Big Stone Gap 4,748 ....C7
Birchleaf 650 ....D6
Birdsnest 736 ....S6
Bishop 600 ....E6
Blacksburg 34,590 ....H6
Blackstone 3,497 ....N6
Blackwater 130 ....H7
Blairs 500 ....K7
Bland▲ 950 ....F6
Bloxom 357 ....S5
Blue Grass 200 ....J4
Blue Ridge 2,840 ....J6
Bluefield 5,363 ....F6
Bluemont 200 ....N2
Boissevain 975 ....E6
Bolar 135 ....J4
Bon Air 16,413 ....N6
Boones Mill 239 ....J6
Boston 300 ....M3
Bowling Green▲ 727 ....O4

Boyce 520 ....M2
Boydton▲ 453 ....M7
Boykins 658 ....O7
Brandy Station 400 ....N4
Breaks 550 ....D6
Bremo Bluff 200 ....M5
Bridgewater 3,918 ....K4
Bristol (I.C.) 18,426 ....D7
Broadford 500 ....F6
Broadway 1,209 ....L3
Brodnax 388 ....N7
Brooke 245 ....O4
Brookneal 1,344 ....L6
Brownsburg 300 ....K5
Browntown 300 ....M3
Brucetown 250 ....M2
Buchanan 1,222 ....J6
Buckingham▲ 200 ....L5
Buena Vista (I.C.) 6,406 ...L5
Buffalo Junction 300 ....L7
Burgess 200 ....R5
Burke 57,734 ....R3
Burkes Garden 2,687 ......F6
Burkeville 535 ....M6
Burnsville 140 ....J4
Callao 500 ....P5

Callaway 225 ....H7
Calverton 500 ....N3
Cana 168 ....G7
Cape Charles 1,398 ....R6
Capeville 325 ....O7
Capron 144 ....N5
Cardwell 200 ....P7
Carrsville 300 ....O6
Carson 500 ....O6
Casanova 370 ....N3
Cascade 835 ....D7
Castlewood 2,110 ....D7
Catawba 350 ....H6
Catlett 300 ....N3
Cedar Bluff 1,290 ....E6
Cedar Springs 200 ....F7
Cedarville 200 ....M3
Center Cross 360 ....P5
Ceres 200 ....F6
Champlain 160 ....O4
Chancellorsville 40 ....N4
Chantilly 29,337 ....O3
Charles City▲ 5 ....O6
Charlotte Court House▲ 531 .L6
Charlottesville (I.C.)▲ 40,341 .M4
Chase City 2,442 ....M7

Chatham▲ 1,354 ....K7
Cheriton 515 ....R6
Chesapeake 151,976 ....R7
Chester 14,986 ....N6
Chester Gap 400 ....M3
Chesterfield▲ 950 ....N6
Chilhowie 1,971 ....E7
Chincoteague 3,572 ....T5
Christiansburg▲ 15,004 ...H6
Chula 150 ....N6
Church View 200 ....P5
Churchville 250 ....K4
Claremont 380 ....P6
Clarksville 1,243 ....M7
Claudville 180 ....H7
Clay Bank 200 ....P6
Clayville 200 ....N6
Clear Brook 300 ....M2
Cleveland 214 ....D7
Clifford 150 ....K5
Clifton Forge (I.C.)▲ 4,679 ..J5
Clinchburg 250 ....E7
Clinchco 900 ....D6
Clintwood▲ 1,542 ....D6
Clover 198 ....L7
Cloverdale 1,689 ....J6
Cluster Springs 350 ....L7
Cobbs Creek 700 ....R6
Coeburn 2,165 ....D7
Coleman Falls 250 ....K6
Collierstown 300 ....J5
Collinsville 7,280 ....J7
Colonial Beach 3,132 ......P4
Colonial Heights (I.C.) 16,064 ...O6
Concord 500 ....K6
Copper Valley 425 ....G7
Courtland 819 ....O7
Covesville 475 ....L5
Covington (I.C.)▲ 6,991 ...H5
Craigsville 812 ....J4
Crandon 250 ....G6
Crewe 2,276 ....M6
Crimora 1,752 ....L4
Cripple Creek 200 ....F7
Critz 125 ....H7
Crockett 200 ....F7
Cross Junction 125 ....M2
Crozet 2,256 ....L4
Crozier 300 ....N5
Crystal Hill 475 ....L7
Cullen 725 ....L6
Culpeper▲ 8,581 ....M4
Cumberland▲ 300 ....M6
Dahlgren 950 ....O4
Dale City 47,170 ....O3
Daleville 1,163 ....J6
Damascus 918 ....E7
Dante 1,083 ....D7
Danville (I.C.) 53,056 ......J7
Davenport 230 ....D6

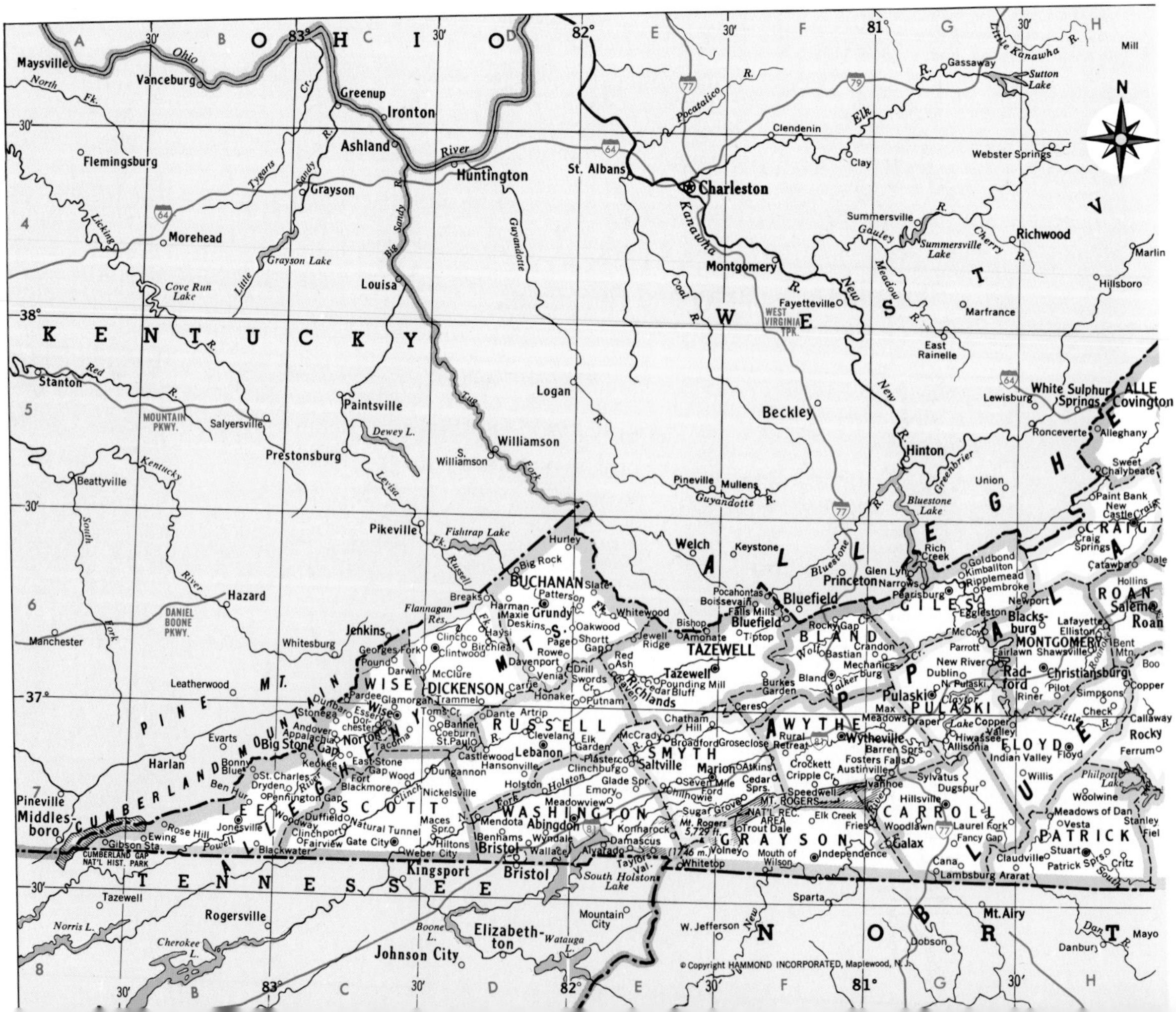

(MAP)
Maysville
Ohio R.
Vanceburg
Greenup
Ironton
Ashland
Huntington
St. Albans
Charleston
WEST VIRGINIA
Clendenin
Gassaway
Sutton Lake
Little Kanawha R.
Webster Springs
Flemingsburg
Grayson
Big Sandy River
Clay
Summersville
Summersville Lake
Richwood
Marlin
Morehead
Hillsboro
Cove Run Lake
Grayson Lake
Louisa
Montgomery
Fayetteville
Marfrance
KENTUCKY
East Rainelle
Paintsville
Logan
Beckley
White Sulphur Springs
ALLE
Covington
Salyersville
Williamson
New R.
Lewisburg
Alleghany
Roncevente
Sweet Chalybeate
Beattyville
Prestonsburg
Hinton
Paint Bank
New Castle
Pikeville
Mullens
Bluestone Lake
CRAIG
Craig Springs
Fishtrap Lake
Pineville
Guyandotte
Union
Welch
Keystone
Rich Creek
Narrows
Pearisburg
Newport
Catawba
Dale
Hazard
BUCHANAN
Grundy
Bluefield
Princeton
GILES
Blacksburg
Salem
Roanoke
Jenkins
TAZEWELL
Tazewell
BLAND
Christiansburg
Radford
Pilot
Copper
Leatherwood
WISE
DICKENSON
RUSSELL
SMYTH
WYTHE
PULASKI
Rocky
Callaway
Whitesburg
Norton
Lebanon
Saltville
Marion
Wytheville
Austinville
FLOYD
Ferrum
Harlan
SCOTT
WASHINGTON
Abingdon
MT. ROGERS
CARROLL
GRAYSON
PATRICK
Stuart
PINE MT.
Middlesboro
CUMBERLAND
LEE
Jonesville
Gate City
Bristol
Independence
Galax
Woolwine
Meadows of Dan
Vesta
Stanley
TENNESSEE
Kingsport
Bristol
South Holston Lake
Mouth of Wilson
Whitetop
Lambsburg
Ararat
Patrick Springs
Critz
Rogersville
Norris L.
Mountain City
Sparta
Mt. Airy
NORTH
Cherokee L.
Boone
Watauga
Elizabethton
W. Jefferson
Dobson
Mayo
Johnson City
Danbury
© Copyright HAMMOND INCORPORATED, Maplewood, N.J.

Dayton 921 L4
Deerfield 500 K4
Deltaville 1,082 R5
Dendron 305 P6
Denniston 200 L7
Dewitt 140 N6
Dillwyn 458 M5
Dinwiddie▲ 500 N6
Disputanta 800 O6
Drakes Branch 565 L7
Drewryville 200 O7
Drill 192 E6
Dry Fork 200 K7
Dryden 400 B7
Dublin 2,012 G6
Duffield 54 C7
Dumfries 4,282 O3
Dundas 200 M7
Dungannon 250 D7
Dunn Loring 6,509 S2
Dunnsville 800 P5
Eagle Rock 750 J5
Earlysville 210 M4
East Stone Gap 240 C7
Eastville▲ 185 R6
Ebony 400 N7
Edinburg 860 M3
Eggleston 350 G6
Elkton 1,935 L4
Elliston-Lafayette 1,243 H6
Emory-Meadowview 2,292 E7
Emporia (I.C.)▲ 5,306 N7
Esmont 950 L5
Esserville 750 C2
Ettrick 5,290 O6
Evergreen 300 L6
Evington 175 K6
Ewing 800 B7
Exmore 1,115 S5
Faber 125 L5
Fairfax (I.C.)▲ 19,622 R3
Fairfax Station R3
Fairfield 465 K5
Fairlawn 2,399 G6
Fairport 175 R5
Falls Church (I.C.) 9,578 S2
Falls Mills 800 F6
Falmouth 3,541 O4
Fancy Gap 200 G7
Farmville▲ 6,046 M6
Farnham 150 P5
Ferrum 1,514 H7
Fieldale 1,018 H7
Fincastle▲ 236 J6
Fishersville 3,230 K4
Flint Hill 750 M3
Floyd▲ 396 H7
Forest 5,624 K6
Fork Union 350 M5
Fort Blackmore 150 C7
Fort Defiance 600 L4
Fort Mitchell 125 M7

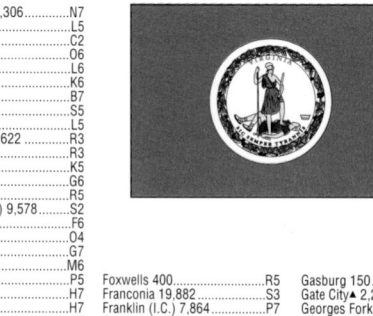

AREA 40,767 sq. mi. (105,587 sq. km.)
POPULATION 6,216,568
CAPITAL Richmond
LARGEST CITY Norfolk
HIGHEST POINT Mt. Rogers 5,729 ft. (1746 m.)
SETTLED IN 1607
ADMITTED TO UNION June 26, 1788
POPULAR NAME Old Dominion
STATE FLOWER Dogwood
STATE BIRD Cardinal

Foxwells 400 R5
Franconia 19,882 S3
Franklin (I.C.) 7,864 P7
Franktown 500 S6
Fredericksburg (I.C.) 19,027 N4
Free Union 121 L4
Fries 690 F7
Front Royal▲ 11,880 M3
Fulks Run 130 L3
Gainesville 600 N3
Galax (I.C.) 6,617 G7
Garrisonville 200 N4
Gasburg 150 N7
Gate City▲ 2,214 C7
Georges Fork 200 C6
Gibson Station 150 A7
Glade Spring 1,435 E7
Gladehill 150 J7
Gladys 500 K6
Glasgow 1,140 K5
Glen Allen 9,010 N5
Glen Lyn 170 G6
Glen Wilton 190 J5
Glenwood 2,276 K7
Gloucester▲ 1,545 P6
Gloucester Point 8,509 R6
Goldbond 250 G6
Goldvein 500 N4
Goochland▲ 800 N5
Goode 200 K6
Gordonsville 1,351 M4
Gore 500 M2
Goshen 366 K5
Grafton 500 P6
Green Bay 500 M6
Greenbackville 300 T5
Greenbush 200 S5
Greenville 400 K5
Greenwood 800 L4
Gretna 1,339 K7
Grottoes 1,455 L4
Groveton 19,997 T3
Grundy▲ 1,305 D6
Gum Spring 125 N5
Gwynn 205 R5
Hague 425 P4
Halifax▲ 772 L7
Hallwood 228 S5
Hamilton 700 N2
Hampden-Sydney 1,240 L6
Hampton (I.C.) 133,793 R6
Hanover▲ 500 O5
Hansonville 150 D7
Harborton 200 S5
Hardy 325 J6
Harman-Maxie 650 D6
Harrisonburg (I.C.)▲ 30,707 K4
Hartfield 700 R5
Haymarket 483 N3
Haynesville 500 P5

(continued on following page)

Virginia

SCALE
0 5 10 20 30 40 MI.
0 5 10 20 30 40 KM.

National Capital
State Capitals
County Seats
Canals
Major Limited Access Hwys.

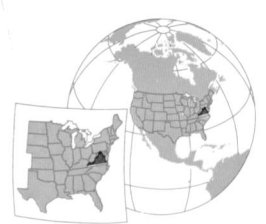

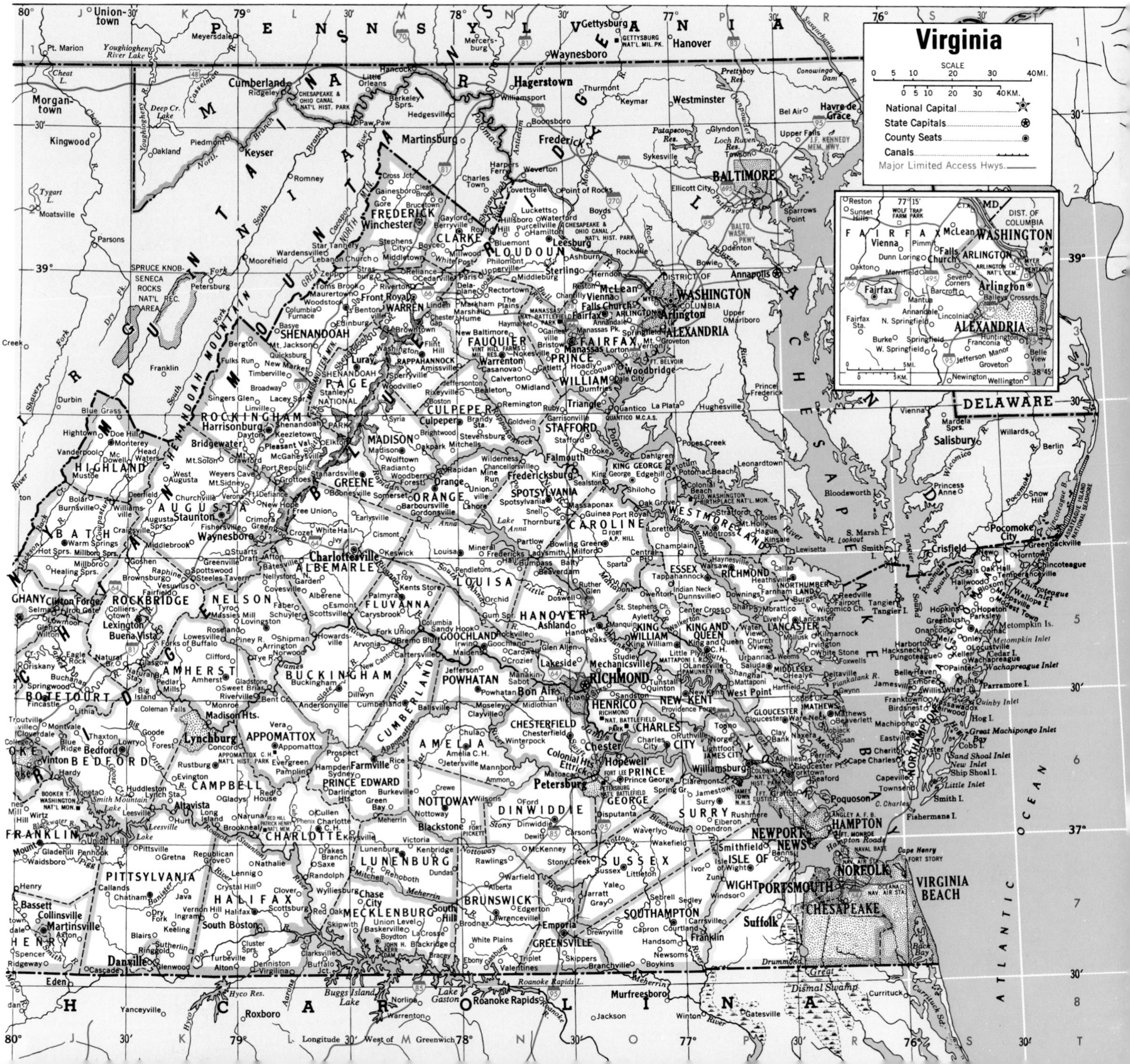

Agriculture, Industry and Resources

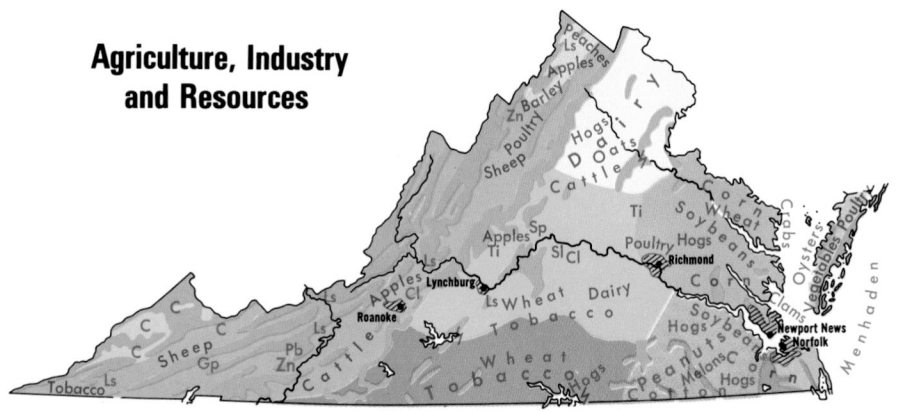

MAJOR MINERAL OCCURRENCES

C	Coal	Sl	Slate
Cl	Clay	Sp	Soapstone
Gp	Gypsum	Ti	Titanium
Ls	Limestone	Zn	Zinc
Pb	Lead		

⚡ Water Power

▨ Major Industrial Areas

DOMINANT LAND USE

- Dairy, General Farming
- General Farming, Livestock, Dairy
- General Farming, Livestock, Tobacco
- General Farming, Livestock, Fruit, Tobacco
- General Farming, Truck Farming, Tobacco, Livestock
- Tobacco, General Farming
- Peanuts, General Farming
- Fruit and Mixed Farming
- Truck and Mixed Farming
- Forests
- Swampland, Limited Agriculture

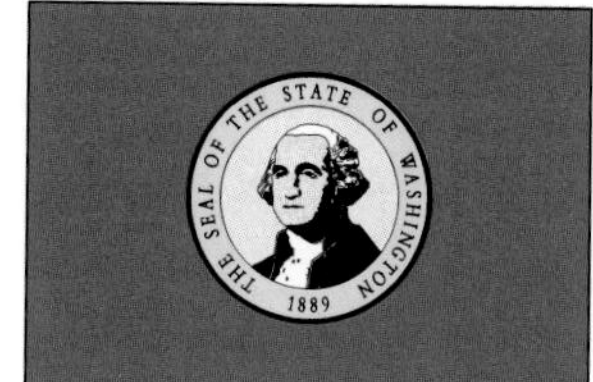

AREA 68,139 sq. mi. (176,480 sq. km.)
POPULATION 4,887,941
CAPITAL Olympia
LARGEST CITY Seattle
HIGHEST POINT Mt. Rainier 14,410 ft. (4392 m.)
SETTLED IN 1811
ADMITTED TO UNION November 11, 1889
POPULAR NAME Evergreen State
STATE FLOWER Western Rhododendron
STATE BIRD Willow Goldfinch

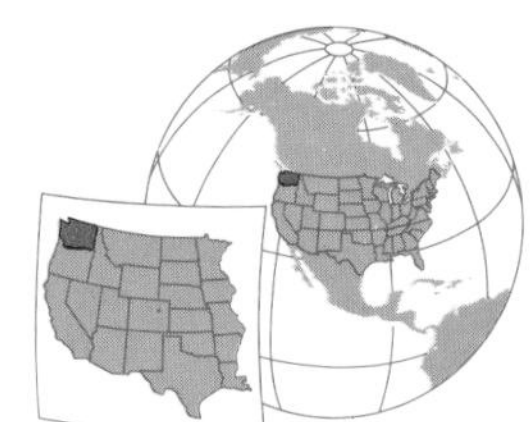

COUNTIES

Adams 13,603 G3
Asotin 17,605 H4
Benton 112,560 F4
Chelan 52,250 E3
Clallam 56,464 B2
Clark 238,053 C5
Columbia 4,024 H4
Cowlitz 82,119 C4
Douglas 26,205 F3
Ferry 6,295 G2
Franklin 37,473 G4
Garfield 2,248 H4
Grant 54,758 F3
Grays Harbor 64,175 B3
Island 60,195 C2
Jefferson 20,146 B3
King 1,507,319 D3
Kitsap 189,731 C3
Kittitas 26,725 E3
Klickitat 16,616 E5
Lewis 59,358 C4
Lincoln 8,864 G3
Mason 38,341 B3
Okanogan 33,350 F2
Pacific 18,882 B4
Pend Oreille 8,915 H2
Pierce 586,203 C3
San Juan 10,035 C2
Skagit 79,555 D2
Skamania 8,289 D5
Snohomish 465,642 D2
Spokane 361,364 H3
Stevens 30,948 H2
Thurston 161,238 C4
Wahkiakim 3,832 B4
Walla Walla 48,439 G4
Whatcom 127,780 D2
Whitman 38,775 H4
Yakima 188,823 E4

CITIES and TOWNS

Aberdeen 16,565 B3
Acme 500 C2
Addy 180 H2
Airway Heights 1,971 H3
Albion 632 H4
Alder 300 C4
Algona 1,694 C3
Allyn 850 C3
Almira 310 G3
Aloha 140 A3
Amanda Park 495 A3
Amboy 480 C5
Anacortes 11,451 C2
Appleton 120 D5
Ardenvoir 150 E3
Ariel 386 C5
Arlington 4,037 C2
Ashford 300 C4
Asotin▲ 981 H4
Auburn 33,102 C3
Azwell 152 F3
Bainbridge Island-Winslow (Winslow) A2
Baring 200 D3
Battle Ground 3,758 C5
Bay Center 187 A4
Bay City 187 B4
Beaux Arts Village 303 B2
Beaver 450 A2
Belfair 500 C3
Bellevue 86,874 B2
Bellingham▲ 52,179 C2
Benton City 1,806 F4
Beverly 200 F4
Biglake 105 C2
Bingen 645 D5
Black Diamond 1,422 D3
Blaine 2,489 C2
Blanchard 125 C2
Bonney Lake 7,494 C3
Bothell 12,345 B1
Bow 200 C2
Boyds 125 G2
Bremerton 38,142 A2
Brewster 1,633 F2
Bridgeport 1,498 F3
Brier 5,633 C3
Brinnon 500 B3
Brownstown 200 E4
Brush Prairie 2,650 C5
Bryn Mawr-Skyway 12,514 B2
Buckley 3,516 C3
Bucoda 536 C4
Buena 590 E4
Burbank 1,745 G4
Burien 25,089 A2
Burley 300 C3
Burlington 4,349 C2
Burton 650 C3
Camas 6,442 C5
Carbonado 495 D3
Carlsborg 500 B2
Carlton 410 F2
Carnation 1,243 D3
Carson 500 D5
Cashmere 2,544 E3
Castle Rock 2,067 B4
Cathlamet▲ 508 B4
Cedar Falls 200 D3
Central Park 2,669 B3
Centralia 12,101 C4
Chattaroy 250 H3
Chehalis▲ 6,527 C4
Chelan 2,969 E3
Chelan Falls 250 E3
Cheney 7,723 H3
Chewelah 1,945 H2
Chimacum 275 C3
Chinook 928 B4
Cinebar 200 C4
Clallam Bay 600 A2
Clarkston 6,753 H4
Clayton 175 H3
Cle Elum 1,778 E3
Clearlake 750 C2
Clearwater 194 A3
Clinton 1,564 C3
Clyde F4
Clyde Hill 2,972 B2
Coalfield 500 B2
Colbert 225 H3
Colby 150 A2
Colfax▲ 2,713 H4
College Place 6,308 G4
Colton 325 H4
Columbia Heights 2,515 C4
Colville▲ 4,360 H2
Conconully 153 F2
Concrete 735 D2
Connell 2,005 G4
Conway 150 C2
Copalis Beach 600 A3
Copalis Crossing 500 B3
Cosmopolis 1,372 B4
Coulee City 568 F3
Coulee Dam 1,087 G3
Coupeville▲ 1,377 C2
Cowiche 150 E4
Creston 230 G3
Cumberland 250 D3
Curlew 168 G2
Cusick 195 H2
Custer 300 C2
Dallesport 600 D5
Danville 215 G2
Darrington 1,042 D2
Davenport▲ 1,502 G3
Dayton▲ 2,468 H4
Deer Harbor 400 B2
Deer Park 2,278 H3
Deming 200 C2
Des Moines 17,283 B2
Dishman 9,671 H3
Dixie 210 G4
Doe Bay 150 C2
Doty 245 B4
Dryad 125 B4
Dryden 500 E3
Du Pont 592 C3
Dungeness 675 B2
Duvall 2,770 D3
East Olympia 300 B4
East Wenatchee 2,701 E3
Easton 250 D3
Eastsound 800 B2
Eatonville 1,374 C4
Edison 250 C2
Edmonds 30,744 C3
Edwall 150 H3
Electric City 910 F3
Ellensburg▲ 12,361 E3
Elma 3,011 B4
Elmer City 290 G2
Eltopia 200 G4
Endicott 320 H4
Enetai 2,638 A2
Entiat 449 E3
Enumclaw 7,227 D3
Ephrata▲ 5,349 F3
Erlands Point 1,254 A2
Ethel 180 C4
Everett▲ 69,961 C3
Everson 1,490 C2
Fairfield 446 H3
Fairview-Sumach 2,749 E4
Fall City 1,582 D3
Farmington 126 H3
Ferndale 5,398 C2
Fife 3,864 C3
Finley 4,897 F4
Fircrest 5,258 C3
Fords Prairie 2,480 B4
Forks 2,862 A3
Four Lakes 500 H3
Frances 144 B4
Freeland 1,278 C2
Freeman 150 H3
Friday Harbor▲ 1,492 B2
Fruitland 150 G2
Fruitvale 4,125 E4
Galvin 250 B4
Garfield 544 H3
Garrett 1,004 G4
Geiger Heights H3
George 253 F3
Gig Harbor 3,236 C3
Glacier 150 D2
Glenoma 500 C4
Glenwood 626 D4
Gold Bar 1,078 D3
Goldendale▲ 3,319 E5
Gorst 750 C3
Grand Coulee 984 G3
Grand Mound 1,394 C4
Grandview 7,169 F4
Granger 2,053 E4
Granite Falls 1,060 D2
Grapeview 250 C3
Grayland 750 A4
Grays River 350 B4
Greenacres 4,626 J3
Greenbank 600 C2
Hadlock-Irondale 2,742 C2
Hamilton 228 D2
Hansville 250 C3
Harper 300 A2
Harrah 341 E4
Harrington 449 G3
Hartline 176 F3
Hatton 71 F4
Heisson 200 C5
Hobart 500 D3
Hoodsport 500 B3
Hoquiam 8,972 A3
Humptulips 275 A3
Hunters 200 G2
Hunts Point 513 B2
Husum 200 D5
Ilwaco 815 A4
Inchelium 393 G2
Index 139 D3
Indianola 1,729 A1
Ione 507 H2
Issaquah 7,786 C3
Joyce 375 B2
Juanita 17,232 B1
Kahlotus 167 B4
Kalama 1,210 C4
Kapowsin 500 C4
Keller 195 G2
Kelso▲ 11,820 C4
Kenmore 8,917 B1
Kennewick 42,155 F4
Kent 37,960 C3
Kettle Falls 1,272 H2
Keyport 900 A2
Kingston 1,270 C3
Kiona 230 F4
Kirkland 40,052 B2
Kittitas 843 E4
Klickitat 750 D5
Krupp (Marlin) 53 F3
La Center 451 C5
La Conner 656 C2
La Push 500 A3
Lacey 19,279 C3
Lacrosse 336 H4
Lake Forest Park 4,031 B1
Lake Stevens 3,380 D3
Lakewood 58,412 C2
Lamont 91 H3
Langley 845 C2
Latah 175 H3
Laurel 972 D5
Leavenworth 1,692 E3
Lebam 275 B4
Liberty Lake 2,015 J3
Lind 472 G4
Littlerock 850 B4
Long Beach 1,236 A4
Longbranch 640 C3
Longview 31,499 B4
Loomis 150 F2
Loon Lake 500 H2
Lummi Island 675 C2
Lyle 580 D5
Lyman 275 D2
Lynden 5,709 C2
Lynnwood 28,695 C3
Mabton 1,482 E4
Malaga 125 E3
Malden 189 H3
Malo 240 G2
Malone 175 B4
Malott 350 F2
Manchester 4,031 A2
Mansfield 311 F3
Manson 220 E3
Maple Falls 300 D2
Maple Valley 1,211 C3
Marblemount 300 D2
Marcus 135 H2
Marietta-Alderwood 2,766 C2
Markham 117 B4
Marlin F3
Marysville 10,328 C2
Matlock 255 B3
Mattawa 941 F4
McCleary 1,235 B3
McKenna 300 C4
Mead H3
Medical Lake 3,664 H3
Medina 2,981 B2
Menlo 237 B4
Mercer Island (city) 20,816 B2
Mesa 252 G4
Metaline 198 H2
Metaline Falls 210 H2
Mica 105 H3
Milan 150 H3
Millwood 1,559 H3
Milton 4,995 C3
Mineral 550 C4
Moclips 500 A3
Monitor 650 E3
Monroe 4,278 D3
Montesano▲ 3,064 B4
Moses Lake 11,235 F3
Mossyrock 452 C4
Mount Vernon▲ 17,647 C2
Mountlake Terrace 19,320 B1
Moxee City 814 E4
Mukilteo 7,007 C3
Naches 596 E4
Nahcotta 200 A4
Napavine 745 C4
Naselle 500 B4
Navy Yard City 2,905 A2
Neah Bay 916 A2
Neilton 250 B3
Nespelem 291 G2
Newhalem 350 D2
Newman Lake 102 J3
Newport▲ 1,691 H2
Nine Mile Falls 150 H3
Nisqually 558 C3
Nooksack 584 C2
Nordland 706 C2
Normandy Park 6,709 A2
North Bend 2,578 D3
North Bonneville 411 C5
Northport 308 H2
Oak Harbor 17,176 C2
Oakesdale 346 H3
Oakville 493 B4

(continued on following page)

Agriculture, Industry and Resources

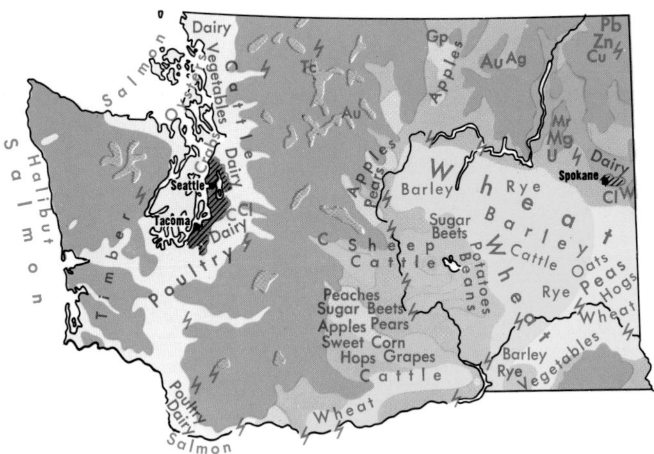

DOMINANT LAND USE

- Specialized Wheat
- Wheat, Peas
- Dairy, Poultry, Mixed Farming
- Fruit and Mixed Farming
- General Farming, Dairy, Range Livestock
- General Farming, Livestock, Special Crops
- Range Livestock
- Forests
- Urban Areas
- Nonagricultural Land

MAJOR MINERAL OCCURRENCES

- Ag Silver
- Au Gold
- C Coal
- Cl Clay
- Cu Copper
- Gp Gypsum
- Mg Magnesium
- Mr Marble
- Pb Lead
- Tc Talc
- U Uranium
- W Tungsten
- Zn Zinc

- Water Power
- Major Industrial Areas

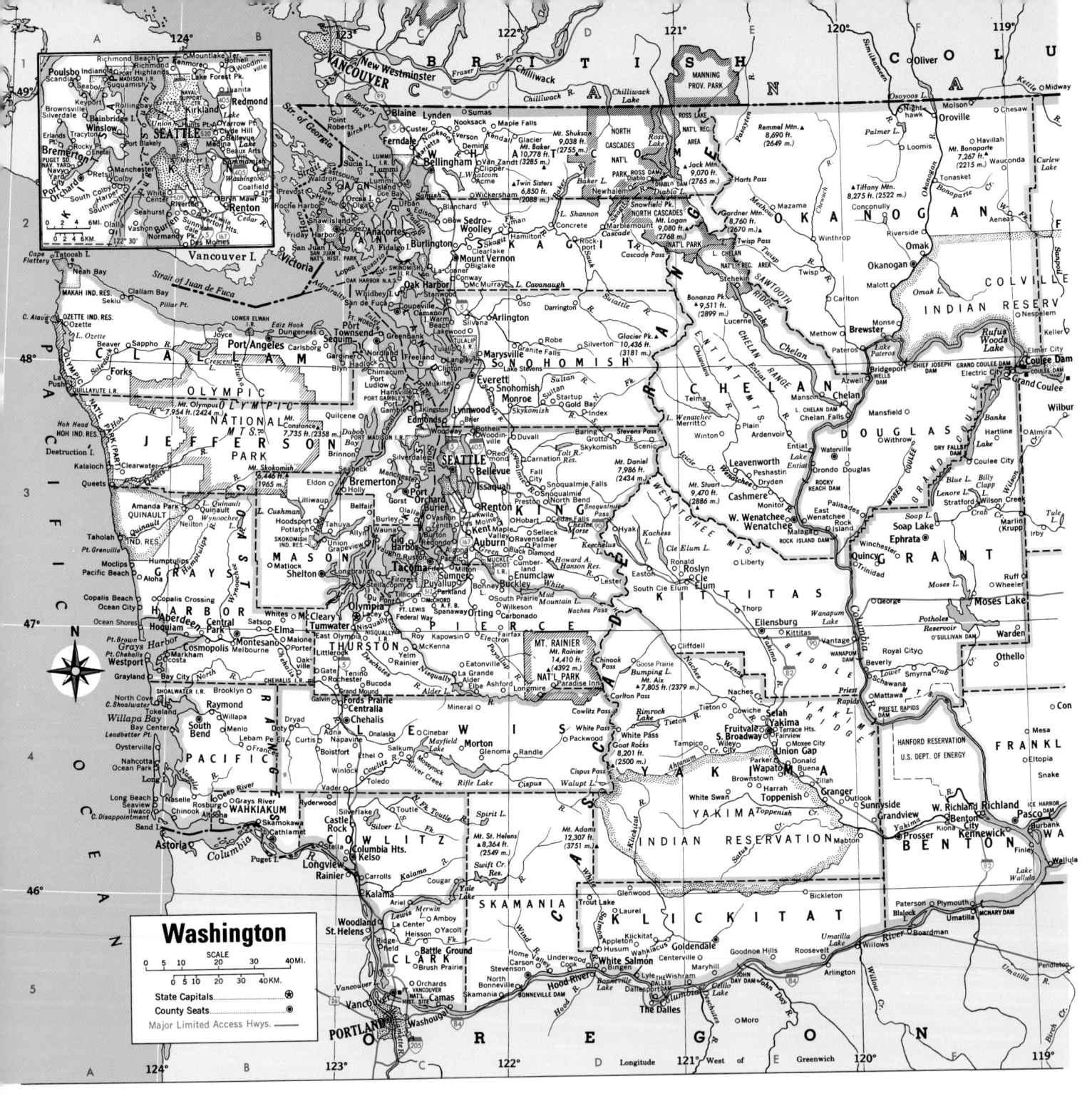

Washington

SCALE
0 5 10   20   30   40 MI.
0 5 10 20   30   40 KM.

State Capitals..............⊛
County Seats..............◉
Major Limited Access Hwys.———

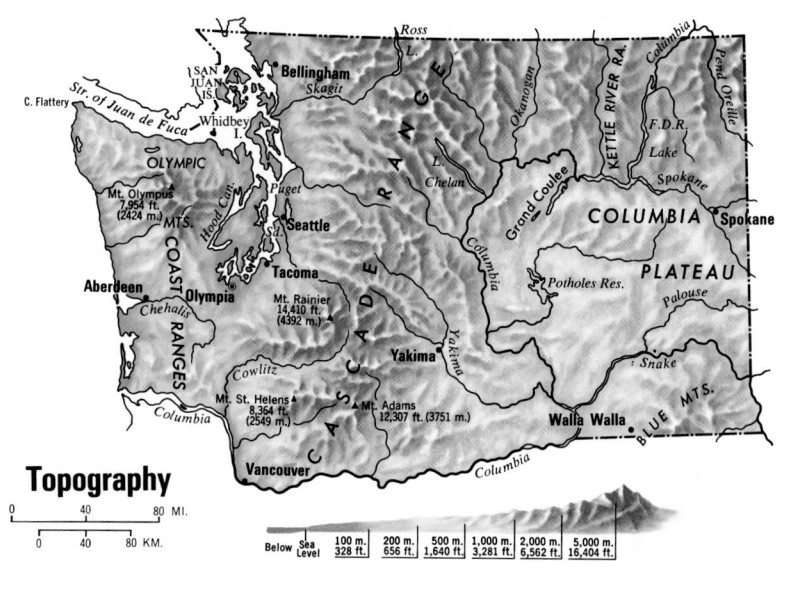

Topography

0   40   80 MI.

0   40   80 KM.

	Below Sea Level	100 m. 328 ft.	200 m. 656 ft.	500 m. 1,640 ft.	1,000 m. 3,281 ft.	2,000 m. 6,562 ft.	5,000 m. 16,404 ft.

Banks (lake) F3
Birch (pt.) C2
Blalock (isl.) F5
Blue (lake) F3
Blue (mts.) H4
Bonanza (peak) E2
Bonaparte (creek) F2
Bonaparte (mt.) F2
Bonneville (dam) D5
Bonneville (lake) D5
Boundary (bay) C1
Boundary (dam) H2
Boundary (mt.) H2
Box Canyon (dam) H2
Brown (pt.) A4
Bumping (lake) D4
Camano (isl.) C2
Carlton (pass) D4
Cascade (pass) D2
Cascade (range) D4
Cascade (pass) D2
Cavanaugh (lake) D2
Cedar (riv.) B2
Celilo (lake) E5
Chehalis (pt.) A4
Chehalis (riv.) B4
Chehalis Ind. Res. B4
Chelan (lake) E3
Chelan (lake) E2
Chelan (range) E2
Chester Morse (lake) D3
Chewuch (riv.) E2
Chief Joseph (dam) F3
China Gardens (dam) J4
Chinook (pass) D4
Chiwawa (riv.) E2
Cispus (pass) D4
Cispus (riv.) D4
Cle Elum (lake) E3
Coal (creek) G3
Coast (ranges) B3
Columbia (riv.) B4
Colville (riv.) H2
Colville Ind. Res. G2
Constance (mt.) B3
Coulee Dam Nat'l Rec. Area..G2
Cow (creek) F3
Cowlitz (pass) D4
Cowlitz (riv.) C4
Crab (creek) F3
Crescent (lake) B3
Curlew (lake) G2
Cushman (lake) B3

Dabob (bay) C3
Dalles, The (dam) D5
Daniel (mt.) D3
Deadman (creek) H4
Deer (lake) H2
Deschutes (riv.) C4
Destruction (isl.) A3
Diablo (lake) D2
Diamond (lake) H2
Disappointment (cape)...A5
Dry Falls (dam) F3
Ediz Hook (pen.) B2
Elwha (riv.) B3
Entiat (lake) E2
Entiat (mts.) E2
Entiat (riv.) E3
Fairchild A.F.B. 4,854 ...H3
Fidalgo (isl.) C2
Flattery (cape) A2
Fort Lewis (mil.) C3
Fort Vancouver Nat'l
  Hist. Site C5
Fort Worden C2

Franklin D. Roosevelt (lake)....G2
Gardner (mt.) E2
Georgia (str.) B2
Glacier (peak) D2
Goat Rocks (mts.) D4
Grand Coulee (canyon)....F3
Grand Coulee (dam) F3
Grande Ronde (riv.) H5
Grays (harb.) A4
Green (lake) A2
Green (riv.) C3
Grenville (pt.) A3
Hanford Reservation-U.S.
  Dept. of Energy F4
Hangman (creek) H3
Haro (str.) B2
Harts (pass) E2
Hells Canyon
  Nat'l Rec. Area H5
Hoh (head) A3
Hoh (riv.) A3
Hoh Ind. Res. A3
Hood Canal (inlet) B3
Howard A. Hanson (res.)...D3
Humptulips (riv.) B3
Ice Harbor (dam) G4
Icicle (creek) E3
Jack (mt.) E2
John Day (dam) E5
Juan de Fuca (str.) A2
Kachess (lake) D3
Kalama (riv.) C4
Kalispel Ind. Res. H2
Keechelus (lake) D3
Kettle (riv.) G2
Kettle River (range) G2
Klickitat (riv.) D5
Lake (creek) G3
Lake Chelan Nat'l Rec. Area..E2
Leadbetter (pt.) A4
Lenore (lake) F3
Lewis (riv.) C5
Little Goose (dam) G4
Little Spokane (riv.) H3
Logan (mt.) D2
Long (isl.) A4
Long (lake) H3
Loon (lake) H2
Lopez (isl.) C2
Lower Crab (creek) F4
Lower Elwha Ind. Res. ...B2
Lower Granite (lake) H4
Lower Monumental (lake)...G4
Lummi (isl.) C2
Lummi Ind. Res. C2
Makah Ind. Res. A2
Mayfield (lake) C4
McChord A.F.B. 4,538 ...C3
McNary F5
Merwin (lake) C5
Methow (riv.) E2
Moses (lake) F3
Moses Coulee (canyon)...F3
Mount Rainier Nat'l Park...D4
Muckleshoot Ind. Res. ...C3
Mud Mountain (lake) D3
Naches (pass) D3
Naches (riv.) E4
Naselle (riv.) B4
Naval Support Ctr. B1
Nisqually (riv.) C4
Nisqually Ind. Res. C4
Nooksack (riv.) C2
North (riv.) B4
North Cascades Nat'l Park...D2

Oak Harbor Naval Air Sta...C2
Okanogan (riv.) F2
Olympic (mts.) B3
Olympic Nat'l Park B3
Olympus (mt.) B3
Omak (lake) F2
Orcas (isl.) C2
Osoyoos (lake) F1
O'Sullivan (dam) F4
Ozette (lake) A2
Ozette Ind. Res. A2
Padilla (bay) C2
Palmer (lake) F2
Pasayten (riv.) E2
Pataha (creek) H4
Pateros (creek) F2
Pend Oreille (riv.) H2
Pillar (pt.) A2
Pine (creek) H3
Port Angeles Ind. Res. ...B2
Port Gamble Ind. Res. C3
Port Madison Ind. Res. ...A1
Potholes (res.) E4
Priest Rapids (lake) E4
Puget (isl.) B4
Puget (sound) C3
Puget Sound Navy Yard...C3
Puyallup (riv.) C4
Queets (riv.) A3
Quillayute Ind. Res. A3
Quinault (lake) A3
Quinault (riv.) A3
Quinault Ind. Res. A3
Rainier (mt.) D4
Remmel (mt.) E2
Rifle (lake) C4
Rimrock (lake) D4
Rock (creek) H3
Rock (lake) H3
Rock Island (dam) E3
Rocky (mts.) E2
Rocky Reach (dam) E3
Rosario (str.) C2
Ross (dam) D2
Ross (lake) D2
Ross Lake Nat'l Rec. Area..E2
Rufus Woods (lake) F2
Sacajawea (lake) G4
Sacheen (lake) H2
Saddle (mts.) E4
Saint Helens (mt.) C4
Samish (lake) C2
Sammamish (lake) B2
Sand (isl.) A4
San Juan (isl.) B2
San Juan Island
  Nat'l Hist. Park B2
Sanpoil (riv.) G2
Satus (creek) E4
Sauk (riv.) D2
Sawtooth (ridge) D2
Shannon (lake) D2
Shoalwater (cape) A4
Shoalwater Ind. Res. B4
Shuksan (mt.) D2
Silver (lake) C4
Similkameen (riv.) F1
Skagit (riv.) C2
Skokomish (mt.) B3
Skokomish Ind. Res. B3
Skykomish (riv.) C2
Snake (riv.) G4
Snohomish (riv.) C2
Snoqualmie (pass) D3
Snoqualmie (riv.) D3
Snow (peak) G2

Snowfield (peak) D2
Soap (lake) F3
Soleduck (riv.) A3
Spirit (lake) C4
Spokane (mt.) H3
Spokane (riv.) H3
Spokane Ind. Res. G3
Sprague (lake) G3
Stevens (pass) D3
Stuart (mt.) E3
Sucia (isl.) C2
Suiattle (riv.) D2
Sullivan (lake) H2
Sultan (riv.) D3
Swift Creek (res.) C4
Swinomish Ind. Res. C2
Sylvan (lake) G3
Tatoosh (isl.) A2
The Dalles (dam) D5
Tieton (riv.) D4
Tiffany (mt.) F2
Tolt River (res.) D3
Toppenish (creek) E4
Touchet (riv.) G4
Toutle, North Fork (riv.)...C4
Toutle, South Fork (riv.)...C4
Tucannon (riv.) G4
Tulalip Ind. Res. C2
Tule (lake) C2
Twin (lakes) G2
Twin Sisters (mt.) E2
Twisp (pass) E2
Twisp (riv.) E2
Umatilla (riv.) E5
Union (lake) B2
Vancouver (lake) C5
Walla Walla (riv.) G4
Wallula (riv.) F4
Walupt (lake) D4
Wanapum (lake) E3
Washington (lake) B2
Wells (dam) F3
Wenas (creek) E4
Wenatchee (lake) E3
Wenatchee (mts.) E3
Wenatchee (riv.) E3
Whatcom (lake) C2
Whidbey (isl.) C2
White (lake) G2
White (riv.) D3
White Salmon (riv.) D4
Whitman Mission Nat'l
  Hist. Site G4
Willapa (bay) A4
Wilson (creek) F3
Wind (riv.) D5
Wynoochee (lake) B3
Wynoochee (riv.) B3
Yakima (ridge) E4
Yakima (riv.) F4
Yakima Ind. Res. E4
Yale (lake) C4

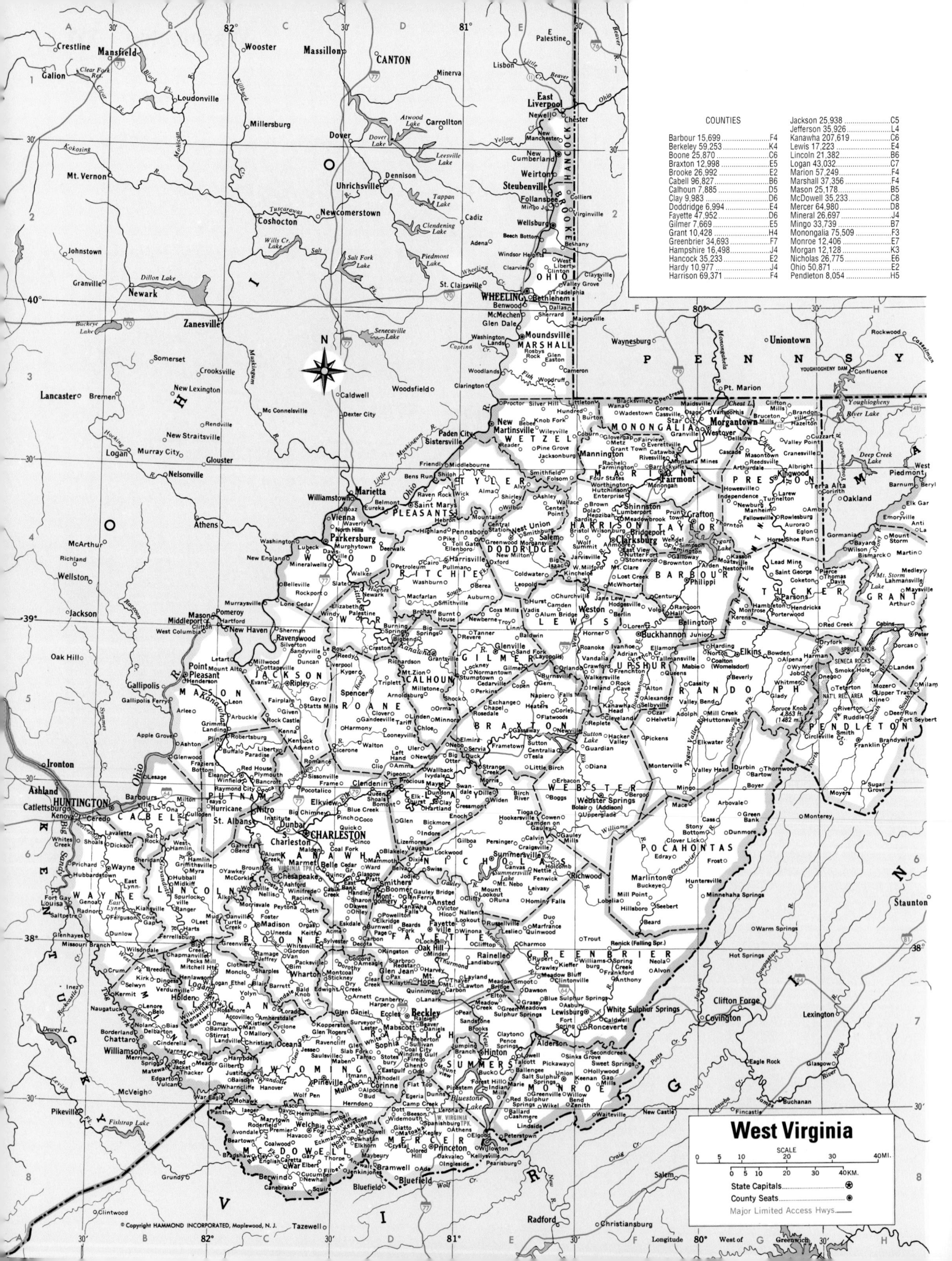

County	Population	Grid
Barbour	15,699	F4
Berkeley	59,253	K4
Boone	25,870	C6
Braxton	12,998	E5
Brooke	26,992	E2
Cabell	96,827	B6
Calhoun	7,885	D5
Clay	9,983	D6
Doddridge	6,994	E4
Fayette	47,952	D6
Gilmer	7,669	E5
Grant	10,428	H4
Greenbrier	34,693	F7
Hampshire	16,498	J4
Hancock	35,233	E2
Hardy	10,977	J4
Harrison	69,371	F4
Jackson	25,938	C5
Jefferson	35,926	L4
Kanawha	207,619	C6
Lewis	17,223	E4
Lincoln	21,382	B6
Logan	43,032	C7
Marion	57,249	F4
Marshall	37,356	F4
Mason	25,178	B5
McDowell	35,233	C8
Mercer	64,980	D8
Mineral	26,697	J4
Mingo	33,739	B7
Monongalia	75,509	F3
Monroe	12,406	E7
Morgan	12,128	K3
Nicholas	26,775	E6
Ohio	50,871	E2
Pendleton	8,054	H5

West Virginia

SCALE

0 5 10   20   30   40 MI.

0 5 10   20   30   40 KM.

State Capitals .... ✪

County Seats .... ◉

Major Limited Access Hwys. ────

© Copyright HAMMOND INCORPORATED, Maplewood, N.J.

Pleasants 7,546 .... D4
Pocahontas 9,008 .... F6
Preston 29,037 .... G4
Putnam 42,835 .... C6
Raleigh 76,819 .... D7
Randolph 27,803 .... G5
Ritchie 10,233 .... D4
Roane 15,120 .... D5
Summers 14,204 .... E7
Taylor 15,144 .... F4
Tucker 7,728 .... F4
Tyler 9,796 .... E4
Upshur 22,867 .... F5
Wayne 41,636 .... B6
Webster 10,729 .... F6
Wetzel 19,258 .... E3
Wirt 5,192 .... D4
Wood 86,915 .... D4
Wyoming 28,990 .... C7

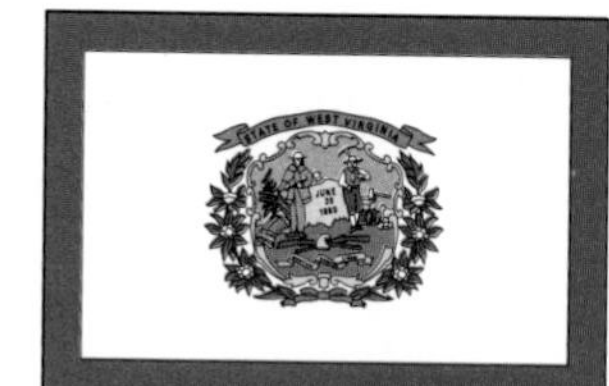

AREA 24,231 sq. mi. (62,758 sq. km.)
POPULATION 1,801,625
CAPITAL Charleston
LARGEST CITY Charleston
HIGHEST POINT Spruce Knob 4,863 ft. (1482 m.)
SETTLED IN 1774
ADMITTED TO UNION June 20, 1863
POPULAR NAME Mountain State
STATE FLOWER Big Rhododendron
STATE BIRD Cardinal

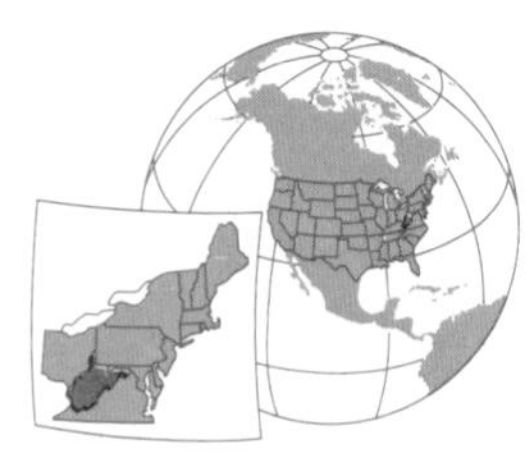

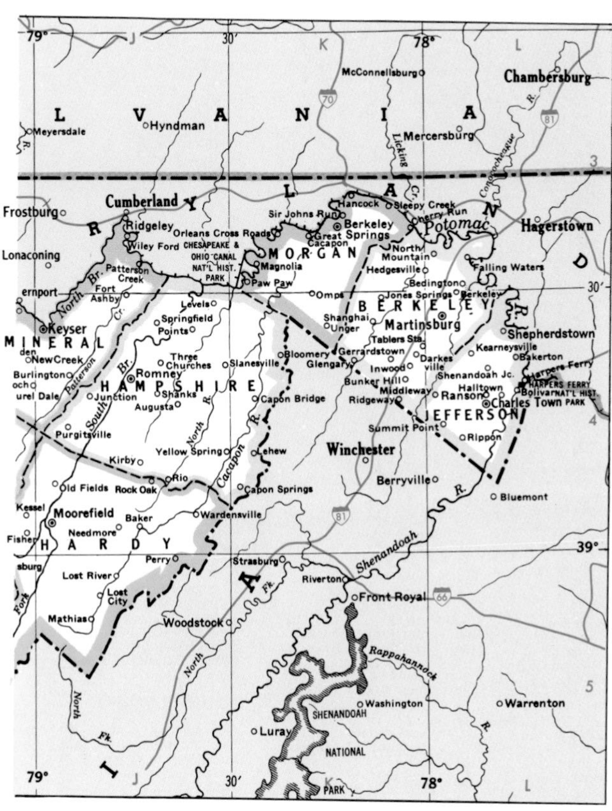
Chambersburg
McConnellsburg
Mercersburg
Hyndman
Meyersdale
Frostburg
Cumberland
Hagerstown
Hancock
Berkeley Springs
Paw Paw
Martinsburg
Shepherdstown
Keyser
Romney
Charles Town
Winchester
Berryville
Moorefield
Front Royal
Woodstock
Strasburg
Luray
Washington
Warrenton
MORGAN
BERKELEY
HAMPSHIRE
JEFFERSON
MINERAL
HARDY

Topography

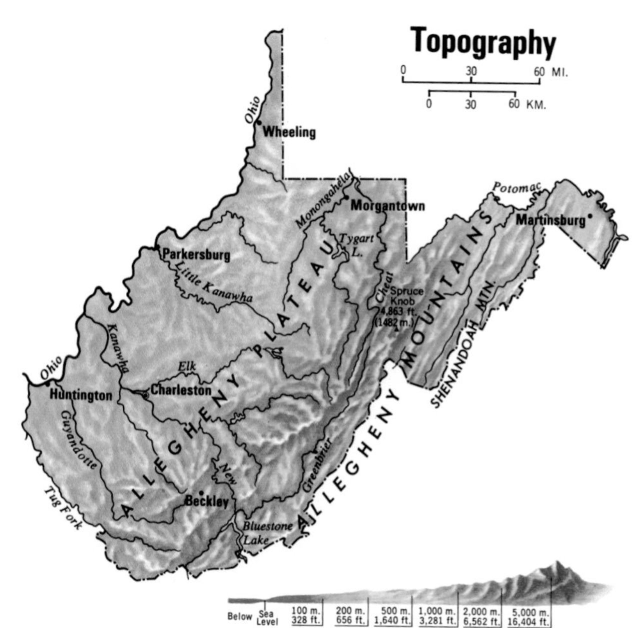
Topography
0 30 60 MI.
0 30 60 KM.
Wheeling
Morgantown
Martinsburg
Parkersburg
Charleston
Huntington
Beckley
Spruce Knob 4,863 ft. (1482 m.)
ALLEGHENY PLATEAU
ALLEGHENY MOUNTAINS
SHENANDOAH MTN.
Ohio
Monongahela
Potomac
Little Kanawha
Kanawha
Elk
Guyandotte
Tug Fork
New
Greenbrier
Cheat
Tygart L.
Bluestone Lake
Below Sea Level
100 m. 328 ft.
200 m. 656 ft.
500 m. 1,640 ft.
1,000 m. 3,281 ft.
2,000 m. 6,562 ft.
5,000 m. 16,404 ft.

CITIES and TOWNS

Accoville 975 .... C7
Acme 165 .... D6
Ada 250 .... D8
Addison▲ (Webster Springs) 674 .... F6
Adrian 510 .... F5
Albright 195 .... G3
Alderson 1,152 .... E7
Algoma 200 .... D8
Alkol 500 .... C6
Alma 197 .... E4
Alpoca 200 .... D7
Alum Bridge 150 .... F5
Alum Creek 1,602 .... C6
Alvy 150 .... E4
Ameagle 230 .... D7
Amherstdale 1,057 .... C7
Amma 200 .... D5
Anawalt 329 .... D8
Anmoore 686 .... F4
Ansted 1,643 .... D6
Apple Grove 900 .... B5
Arbovale 610 .... G6
Arden 130 .... G4
Arnett 300 .... D7
Arnoldsburg 175 .... D5
Arthur 350 .... H4
Arthurdale 1,063 .... G3
Asbury 280 .... E7
Asco 175 .... C8
Ashford 400 .... C6
Ashton 259 .... B5
Athens 741 .... E8
Auburn 89 .... E4
Augusta 750 .... J4
Aurora 250 .... G4
Avondale 250 .... C8
Baisden 500 .... C7
Baker 200 .... J4
Bakerton 125 .... L4
Bald Knob 356 .... C7
Ballard 220 .... E8
Ballengee 170 .... E7
Bancroft 381 .... C5
Barboursville 2,774 .... B6
Barnabus 750 .... C7
Barrackville 1,443 .... F3
Barrett 950 .... C7
Bartley 900 .... C8
Bartow 500 .... G5
Bayard 414 .... H4
Beards Fork 400 .... D6
Beartown 500 .... C8
Beaver (Glen Hedrick) 1,244 ... D7
Bebee 125 .... E3
Beckley▲ 18,296 .... D7
Bedington 150 .... L3
Beech Bottom 415 .... E2
Beeson 300 .... D8
Belington 1,850 .... F4
Belle 1,421 .... C6
Belmont 912 .... D4
Belva 275 .... D6
Benwood 1,669 .... E2
Bergoo 220 .... F6
Berkeley 600 .... L4
Berkeley Springs▲ 789 .... K3
Berwind 615 .... C8
Bethany 1,139 .... E2
Bethlehem 2,694 .... E2
Beverly 696 .... G5
Bickmore 300 .... D6
Big Chimney 450 .... C6
Big Creek 500 .... B7
Big Four 150 .... C8
Big Otter 150 .... D5
Big Springs 485 .... D5
Bim 500 .... C7
Birch River 650 .... E6
Blacksville 168 .... F3
Blair 800 .... C7
Bloomery 200 .... K4
Blue Creek 650 .... D6
Bluefield 12,756 .... D8
Boaz 1,137 .... D4
Boggs 131 .... E6
Bolair 450 .... F6
Bolivar 1,013 .... L4
Bomont 170 .... D6
Boomer 1,051 .... D6
Borderland 250 .... B7
Bowden 135 .... G5
Bradshaw 394 .... C8
Bramwell 620 .... D8
Brandonville 73 .... G3
Brandywine 300 .... H5
Breeden 600 .... B7
Bridgeport 6,739 .... F4
Brooks 196 .... E7
Brounland 900 .... C6
Brownton 400 .... F4
Bruceton Mills 132 .... G3
Buck 150 .... E7
Buckhannon▲ 5,909 .... F5
Bud 400 .... D7
Buffalo 969 .... C5
Bunker Hill 600 .... K4
Burlington 300 .... J4
Burning Springs 137 .... D5
Burnsville 495 .... E5
Burnt House 175 .... D4
Burnwell 140 .... D6
Burton 200 .... F3
Cabin Creek 900 .... C6
Cabins 300 .... H4
Cairo 290 .... D4
Caldwell 795 .... F7
Calvin 400 .... E6
Camden on Gauley 171 .... E6
Cameron 1,177 .... E3
Camp Creek 200 .... D7
Canebrake 300 .... C8
Canvas 300 .... E6
Capon Bridge 192 .... K4
Capon Springs 580 .... K4
Carbon 300 .... D6
Caretta 650 .... C8
Cass 148 .... G6
Cassity 150 .... F5
Cassville 1,458 .... F3
Catawba 186 .... F3
Cedar Grove 1,213 .... D6
Center Point 250 .... E4
Central Station 200 .... E4
Ceredo 1,916 .... F4
Chapmanville 1,110 .... B7
Charles Town▲ 3,122 .... L4
Charleston (cap.)▲ 57,287 .... C6
Charmco 800 .... E6
Chattaroy 1,182 .... B7
Chesapeake 1,896 .... C6
Chester 2,905 .... E1
Christian 200 .... C7
Cinco 500 .... D6
Circleville 180 .... H5
Clarksburg▲ 18,059 .... F4
Clay▲ 592 .... D6
Clear Creek 300 .... D7
Clearview 622 .... E2
Clendenin 1,203 .... D5
Clifton 325 .... B5
Clifton Mills 136 .... G3
Clifty 250 .... E6
Clinton 350 .... E2
Clintonville 250 .... E7
Clio 300 .... D5
Clothier 900 .... C7
Clover 350 .... D5
Clover Lick 250 .... F6
Coal City 1,876 .... D7
Coal Fork 2,100 .... D6
Coalton 277 .... G5
Coalwood 650 .... C8
Coburn 230 .... F3
Colcord 600 .... D7
Colliers 864 .... E2
Colored Hill 900 .... D8
Core 250 .... F3
Corinne 900 .... D7
Corinth 195 .... H4
Costa 250 .... C6
Cottageville 300 .... C5
Cove Gap 650 .... B6
Cowen 549 .... E6
Coxs Mills 275 .... E4
Craigsville 1,955 .... E6
Cranberry 315 .... D7
Crawley 395 .... E7
Crum 500 .... B7
Crystal 150 .... D8
Cucumber 274 .... C8
Culloden 2,907 .... B6
Cyclone 500 .... C7
Dallas 450 .... E2
Daniels 1,714 .... D7
Danville 595 .... C6
Darkesville 150 .... L4
Davis 799 .... H4
Davisville 200 .... C4
Davy 403 .... C8
Dawes 800 .... D6
Dawson 300 .... E7
Decota 800 .... D6
Deerwalk 150 .... D4
Delbarton 705 .... B7
Dellslow 300 .... G3
Diana 300 .... F5
Dickson 200 .... B6
Dille 300 .... E6
Dingess 600 .... B7
Dixie 985 .... D6
Dola 200 .... F4
Dorothy 400 .... D7
Dry Creek 441 .... D7
Dryfork 425 .... H5
Dunbar 8,697 .... C6
Dunlow 169 .... B6
Dunmore 280 .... G6
Durbin 278 .... G5
East Bank 892 .... D6
East Lynn 150 .... B6
East View 1,222 .... F4
Eastgulf 300 .... D7
Eccles 1,162 .... D7
Eckman 750 .... C8
Edgarton 415 .... B7
Edray 175 .... F6
Egeria 150 .... D7
Elbert 400 .... C8
Eleanor 1,256 .... C5
Elizabeth▲ 900 .... D4
Elk Garden 261 .... H4
Elkhorn 150 .... D8
Elkins▲ 7,420 .... G5
Elkridge 500 .... D6
Elkview 1,047 .... C6
Ellenboro 453 .... F5
Elton 200 .... E7
English 500 .... C8
Enterprise 1,058 .... F4
Erbacon 350 .... E6
Eskdale 400 .... D6
Ethel 450 .... C7
Evans 400 .... C5
Everettville 175 .... F3
Fairmont 20,210 .... F4
Fairplain 200 .... C5
Fairview 513 .... F3
Falling Spring (Renick) 191 .... F6
Falling Waters 130 .... L3
Farmington 414 .... F3
Fayetteville▲ 2,182 .... D6
Fenwick 500 .... E6
Ferguson 150 .... B6
Ferrellsburg 300 .... B6
Filbert 130 .... D8
Fireco 200 .... D7
Fisher 500 .... H4
Flat Top 550 .... D7
Flatwoods 324 .... E5
Flemington 352 .... F4
Follansbee 3,339 .... E2
Folsom 360 .... E4
Forest Hill 314 .... E7
Fort Ashby 1,288 .... J4
Fort Gay 852 .... A6
Fort Seybert 200 .... H5
Fort Spring 250 .... E7
Foster 500 .... C6
Four States 500 .... F4
Frametown 150 .... E5
Frankford 200 .... F7
Franklin▲ 914 .... H5
Fraziers Bottom 250 .... B5
French Creek 200 .... F5
Friendly 146 .... D3
Gallipolis Ferry 325 .... B5
Galloway 500 .... F4
Gandeeville 150 .... D5
Gap Mills 300 .... F7
Gary 1,355 .... C8
Gassaway 946 .... E5
Gauley Bridge 691 .... D6
Gauley Mills 165 .... E6
Gay 300 .... C5
Gerrardstown 240 .... K4
Ghent 500 .... D7
Giatto 400 .... D8
Gilbert 456 .... C7
Gilboa 500 .... E6
Glady 175 .... G5
Glasgow 906 .... D6
Glen 175 .... D6
Glen Dale 1,612 .... E3
Glen Daniel 300 .... D7
Glen Ferris 200 .... D6
Glen Hedrick (Beaver) B7
Glen Jean D7
Glen Rogers 500 .... D7
Glen White 300 .... D7
Glengary 250 .... K4
Glenhayes 175 .... A6
Glenville▲ 1,923 .... E5
Glenwood 400 .... B5
Gordon 300 .... C7
Grafton▲ 5,524 .... G4
Grant Town 694 .... F3
Grantsville▲ 671 .... D5
Granville 798 .... F3
Great Cacapon 750 .... K3
Green Bank 115 .... G6
Green Sulphur Springs 225 .... E7
Greenview 250 .... C6
Greenwood 750 .... E4
Griffithsville 300 .... B6
Grimms Landing 350 .... B5
Guardian 175 .... F5
Hacker Valley 440 .... F5
Halltown 375 .... L4
Hambleton 265 .... G4
Hamlin▲ 1,030 .... B6
Hampden 300 .... C7
Hancock 175 .... K3
Handley 334 .... D6
Hanover 300 .... C7
Harman 128 .... G5

(continued on following page)

Agriculture, Industry and Resources

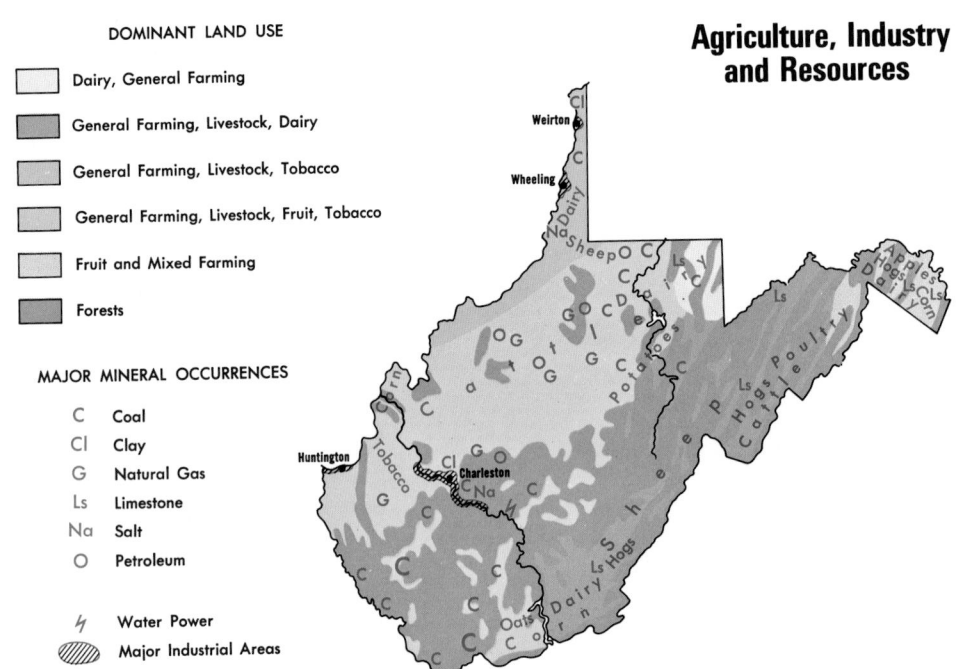

DOMINANT LAND USE

- Dairy, General Farming
- General Farming, Livestock, Dairy
- General Farming, Livestock, Tobacco
- General Farming, Livestock, Fruit, Tobacco
- Fruit and Mixed Farming
- Forests

MAJOR MINERAL OCCURRENCES

- C — Coal
- Cl — Clay
- G — Natural Gas
- Ls — Limestone
- Na — Salt
- O — Petroleum

- ⚡ Water Power
- ▨ Major Industrial Areas

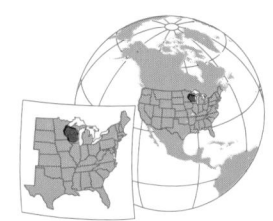

AREA 56,153 sq. mi. (145,436 sq. km.)
POPULATION 4,906,745
CAPITAL Madison
LARGEST CITY Milwaukee
HIGHEST POINT Timms Hill 1,951 ft. (595 m.)
SETTLED IN 1670
ADMITTED TO UNION May 29, 1848
POPULAR NAME Badger State
STATE FLOWER Wood Violet
STATE BIRD Robin

COUNTIES

Adams 15,682	G7
Ashland 16,307	E3
Barron 40,750	C5
Bayfield 14,008	D3
Brown 194,594	L7
Buffalo 13,584	C7
Burnett 13,084	B4
Calumet 34,291	K7
Chippewa 52,360	D5
Clark 31,647	E6
Columbia 45,088	H9
Crawford 15,940	E9
Dane 367,085	H9
Dodge 76,559	J9
Door 25,690	M6
Douglas 41,758	C3
Dunn 35,909	C6
Eau Claire 85,183	D6
Florence 4,590	K4
Fond du Lac 90,083	K8
Forest 8,776	J4
Grant 49,264	E10
Green 30,339	G10
Green Lake 18,651	H8
Iowa 20,150	F9
Iron 6,153	F3
Jackson 16,588	F3
Jefferson 67,783	J9
Juneau 21,650	F8
Kenosha 128,181	K10
Kewaunee 18,878	L6
La Crosse 97,904	D8
Lafayette 16,076	F10
Langlade 19,505	H5
Lincoln 26,993	G5
Manitowoc 80,421	L7
Marathon 115,400	G6
Marinette 40,548	K5
Marquette 12,321	H8
Menominee 3,890	J5
Milwaukee 959,275	L9
Monroe 36,633	E8
Oconto 30,226	K6
Oneida 31,679	G4
Outagamie 140,510	K7
Ozaukee 72,831	L9
Pepin 7,107	C6
Pierce 32,765	B6
Polk 34,773	B5
Portage 61,405	G6
Price 15,600	F4
Racine 175,034	K10
Richland 17,521	F9
Rock 139,510	H10
Rusk 15,079	D5
Saint Croix 43,262	B5
Sauk 46,975	G9
Sawyer 14,181	D4
Shawano 37,157	J6
Sheboygan 103,877	L8
Taylor 18,901	E5
Trempealeau 25,263	D7
Vernon 25,617	E8
Vilas 17,707	G3
Walworth 75,000	J10
Washburn 13,772	C4
Washington 95,328	K9
Waukesha 304,715	K9
Waupaca 46,104	J6
Waushara 19,385	H7
Winnebago 140,320	J8
Wood 73,605	F7

CITIES and TOWNS

Abbotsford 1,916	F6
Abrams 300	L6
Adams 1,715	G8
Adell 510	L8
Afton 225	H10
Albany 1,140	G10
Albion 300	H10
Algoma 3,353	M6
Allenton 915	K9
Allouez 14,431	L7
Alma Center 416	E7
Alma▲ 790	C7
Almena 625	B5
Almond 455	G7
Alto 235	J8
Altoona 5,889	C6
Alvin 160	J4
Amberg 875	K5
Amery 2,657	B5
Amherst 792	H7
Amherst Junction 269	H7
Angelica 200	K6
Angelo 100	E3
Aniwa 249	H6
Antigo▲ 8,276	H5
Appleton▲ 65,695	J7
Arbor Vitae 900	G4
Arcadia 2,166	D7
Arena 525	G9

Argonne 600	G9
Argyle 798	G10
Arkansaw 400	B6
Arlington 440	H9
Armstrong Creek 615	K4
Arpin 312	G6
Ashippun 750	H1
Ashland▲ 8,695	E2
Ashwaubenon 16,376	K7
Athens 951	G5
Auburndale 665	F6
Augusta 1,510	D6
Auroraville 250	H7
Avoca 474	F9
Avon 120	H10
Babcock 250	F7
Bagley 306	D10
Baileys Harbor 250	M5
Baldwin 2,022	B6
Balsam Lake▲ 792	B5
Bancroft 355	G7
Bangor 1,076	E8
Baraboo▲ 9,203	G9
Barnes 225	D3
Barneveld 660	F10
Barron▲ 2,986	C5
Barronett 575	B4
Batavia 125	K8
Bay City 578	B6
Bayfield 686	E2
Bayside 4,789	M1
Bear Creek 418	J6
Beaver 100	K5
Beaver Dam 14,196	J9
Beetown 150	E10
Beldenville 175	A6
Belgium 928	L8
Bell Center 127	E9
Belleville 1,456	G10
Belmont 823	F10
Beloit 35,573	H10
Bennett 350	C3
Benton 898	F10
Berlin 5,371	H8
Bethel 210	F6
Bevent 200	H6
Big Bend 1,299	K2
Birchwood 443	C4
Birnamwood 693	H6
Biron 794	G7
Black Creek 1,342	K7
Black Earth 1,248	G9
Black River Falls▲ 3,490	E7
Blackwell 550	K4
Blair 1,126	D7
Blanchardville 802	G10
Bloom City 167	E8
Bloomer 3,085	D5
Bloomington 776	E10
Blue Mounds 446	G9
Blue River 438	E9
Boardman 100	A5
Boaz 131	E9
Bohners Lake 1,553	K10
Bonduel 1,210	K6
Boscobel 2,706	E9
Boulder Junction 780	G3
Bowler 279	J6
Boyceville 913	C5
Boyd 683	E6
Brackett 150	D6
Bradley 100	G4
Branch 300	L7
Brandon 872	J8
Brantwood 500	F4
Bridgeport 250	D9
Briggsville 250	H8
Brighton 100	K3
Brill 200	C4
Brillion 2,840	L7
Brodhead 3,165	G10
Brokaw 224	G5
Brookfield 35,184	K1
Brooklyn 789	H10
Brooks 103	G8
Brothertown 100	K7
Brown Deer 12,236	L1
Brown's Lake 1,725	K3
Brownsville 415	J8
Browntown 256	G10
Bruce 844	D5
Brule 335	C2
Brussels 500	L6
Buffalo 915	C7
Burlington 8,855	K10
Burnett 260	J9
Butler 2,079	K1
Butte Des Morts	J7
Butternut 416	E3
Cable 227	D3
Cadott 1,328	D6
Caldwell 101	J2
Caledonia 100	L2
Cambria 768	H8
Cambridge 963	H9
Cameron 1,273	C5

Camp Douglas 512	F8
Camp Lake 2,291	K10
Campbellsport 1,732	K8
Canton 100	C5
Caroline 450	J6
Carter 100	J5
Cascade 620	K8
Casco 544	L6
Cashton 780	E8
Cassville 1,144	E10
Cataract 200	E7
Catawba 178	E4
Cazenovia 288	F8
Cecil 373	K6
Cedar Grove 1,521	L8
Cedarburg 9,895	L9
Centuria 790	A5
Chaseburg 365	D8
Chelsea 120	F5
Chenequa 601	J1
Chetek 1,953	C5
Chili 185	F6
Chilton▲ 3,240	K7
Chippewa Falls▲ 12,727	D6
City Point 110	F7
Clam Lake 140	E3
Clayton 450	B5
Clear Lake 932	B5
Clearwater Lake 200	H4
Cleveland 1,398	L8
Clinton 1,849	J10
Clintonville 4,351	J6
Clyman 370	J9
Cobb 440	F10
Cochrane 475	C7
Colby 1,532	F6
Coleman 839	L5
Colfax 1,110	C6
Coloma 383	H7
Columbus 4,093	H9
Combined Locks 2,190	K7
Como 1,353	K10
Comstock 160	C5
Concord 200	H1
Conover 480	H3
Conrath 92	E5
Coon Valley 817	E8
Cornell 1,541	D5
Cornucopia 250	D2
Couderay 92	D4
Crandon▲ 1,958	H4
Cream 120	C7
Crivitz 996	L5
Cross Plains 2,098	G9
Cuba City 2,024	F10
Cudahy 18,659	M2
Cumberland 2,163	C4
Curtiss 173	F6
Cushing 150	A4
Cylon 100	B5
Dale 410	J7
Dallas 452	C5
Dalton 300	H8
Danbury 350	B3
Dane 621	G9
Darien 1,158	J10
Darlington▲ 2,235	F10
De Forest 4,882	H9
De Pere 16,569	K7
De Soto 326	D9
Deer Park 237	B5
Deerfield 1,617	H9
Delafield 5,347	J1
Delavan 6,073	J10
Delavan Lake 2,177	J10
Dellwood 120	G7
Denmark 1,612	L7
Dexterville 100	F7
Diamond Bluff 100	A6
Dickeyville 862	E10
Dodge 185	D7
Dodgeville▲ 3,882	F10
Dorchester 697	F5
Dousman 1,277	J1
Downing 200	B5
Downsville 200	C6
Doylestown 316	H9
Draper 125	D4
Dresser 614	A5
Drummond 200	D3
Dunbar 106	K4
Durand▲ 2,003	C6
Dyckesville 300	L6
Eagle 1,182	J2
Eagle River▲ 1,374	H4
East Troy 2,664	J2
Eastman 369	D9
Easton 130	G8
Eau Claire▲ 56,856	D6
Eden 610	K8
Edgar 1,318	G6
Edgerton 4,254	H10
Egg Harbor 183	M5
Eland 247	H6
Elcho 500	H5

Elderon 175	H6
Eldorado 200	J8
Eleva 491	D6
Elk Mound 765	C6
Elkhart Lake 1,019	L8
Elkhorn▲ 5,337	J10
Ellison Bay 112	M5
Ellsworth▲ 2,706	A6
Elm Grove 6,261	K1
Elmwood 775	B6
Elmwood Park 534	M3
Elroy 1,533	F8
Elton 150	J5
Embarrass 461	J6
Emerald 128	B5
Endeavor 316	G8
Ephraim 261	M5
Ettrick 461	D7
Evansville 3,174	H10
Exeland 180	D4
Fair Water 310	J8
Fairchild 504	D6
Fall Creek 1,034	D6
Fall River 842	H9

Fence 200	K4
Fennimore 2,378	E9
Fenwood 214	F6
Ferryville 154	D9
Fifield 310	F4
Fish Creek 119	M5
Florence▲ 780	K4
Fond du Lac▲ 37,757	K8
Fontana 1,635	J10
Footville 764	H10
Forest Junction 140	K7
Forestville 470	L6
Fort Atkinson 10,227	J10
Fountain City 938	C7
Fox Lake 1,269	J8
Fox Point 7,238	M1
Foxboro 360	B2
Francis Creek 562	L7
Franklin 21,855	L2
Franksville 375	M3
Frederic 1,124	B4
Fredonia 1,558	L8
Fremont 632	J7
Friendship▲ 728	G8

Friesland 271	H8
Galesville 1,278	D7
Galloway 200	H6
Gays Mills 578	E9
Genesee 375	J2
Genesee Depot 350	J2
Genoa 266	D8
Genoa City 1,277	K11
Germantown 13,658	K1
Gibbsville 408	L8
Gillett 1,303	K6
Gilman 412	E5
Gilmanton 300	C7
Gleason 200	G5
Glen Flora 108	E4
Glen Haven 160	E10
Glenbeulah 386	L8
Glendale 14,088	M1
Glenwood City 1,026	B5
Glidden 940	E3
Goodman 875	K4
Gordon 600	C3
Gotham 250	F9
Grafton 9,340	L9

Grand Marsh 725	G8
Grand View 447	D3
Granton 379	E6
Grantsburg▲ 1,144	A4
Gratiot 207	F10
Green Bay▲ 96,466	K6
Green Lake▲ 1,064	H8
Green Valley 104	K6
Greendale 15,128	L2
Greenfield 33,403	L2
Greenleaf 300	L7
Greenville 900	J7
Greenwood 969	E6
Gresham 515	J6
Gurney 145	F3
Hager City 110	A6
Hales Corners 7,623	K2
Hallie	D6
Hamburg 170	G5
Hammond 1,097	A6
Hancock 382	G7
Hartford 8,188	K9
Hartland 6,906	J1
Hatfield 500	E7

(continued on following page)

Agriculture, Industry and Resources

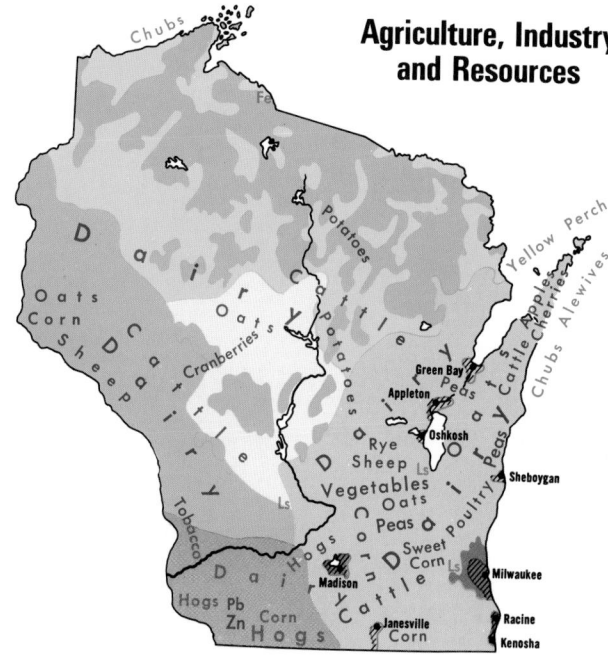

DOMINANT LAND USE

- Specialized Dairy
- Dairy, Hay, Potatoes
- Dairy, General Farming
- Hogs, Dairy
- Dairy, Livestock
- Forests
- Urban Areas

MAJOR MINERAL OCCURRENCES

Fe	Iron Ore	Pb	Lead
Ls	Limestone	Zn	Zinc

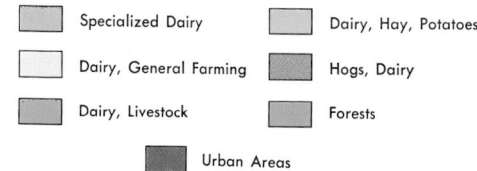 Major Industrial Areas

Hatley 295 H6
Haugen 305 C4
Hawkins 375 E4
Hawthorne 200 C3
Hayward▲ 1,897 D3
Hazel Green 1,171 F11
Hazelhurst 630 G4
Heafford Junction 110 G4
Hebron 450 J10
Helenville 300 J10
Hersey 125 B6
Hewitt 595 F6
High Bridge 525 E3
Highland 799 F9
Hilbert 1,211 K7
Hiles 350 J4
Hillsboro 1,288 F8
Hillsdale 160 C5
Hingham 250 K8
Hixton 345 E7
Holcombe 200 D5
Hollandale 256 G10
Holmen 3,220 D8
Holy Cross 150 L9
Honey Creek 300 J3
Horicon 3,873 J9
Hortonville 2,029 J7
Houlton 915 A5
Howard 9,874 K6
Howards Grove-Millersville 1,838 L8
Hubertus 600 K1
Hudson▲ 6,378 A6
Humbird 190 E6
Hurley▲ 1,782 F3
Hustisford 979 J9
Hustler 156 F8
Independence 1,041 D7
Ingram 91 E5
Iola 1,125 H6
Iron Belt 300 F3
Iron Ridge 887 K9
Iron River 878 D2
Ironton 200 F8
Ithaca 160 F9
Ixonia 525 H1
Jackson 2,486 K9
Jacksonport 150 M6
Janesville▲ 52,133 H10
Jefferson▲ 6,078 J10
Johnson Creek 1,259 J9
Juda 500 H10
Junction City 502 G6
Juneau▲ 2,157 J9
Kansasville 150 L3
Kaukauna 11,982 K7
Kekoskee 188 J8
Kellnersville 350 L7
Kempster 121 H5
Kendall 453 F8
Kennan 169 F5
Kenosha▲ 80,352 M3
Keshena▲ 685 J6
Kewaskum 2,515 K8
Kewaunee▲ 2,750 M7
Kiel 2,910 L8
Kieler 800 E10
Kimberly 5,406 K7
King H7
Kingston 346 H8
Knapp 419 B6
Knowlton 127 G6
Kohler 1,817 L8
Krakow 345 K6
La Crosse▲ 51,003 D8
La Farge 766 E8
La Pointe 300 E2
La Valle 446 F8
Lac La Belle 258 H1
Lac du Flambeau 1,423 G4
Ladysmith▲ 3,938 D5
Lake Church 175 L9
Lake Delton 1,470 G8
Lake Geneva 5,979 K10
Lake Mills 4,143 H9
Lake Nebagamon 900 C3
Lake Tomahawk 600 H4
Lake Wazeecha 2,278 G7
Lake Wissota 2,175 D6
Lakewood 425 K5
Lamartine 190 J8
Lancaster▲ 4,192 E10
Land O'Lakes 786 H3
Lannon 924 K1
Lebanon 250 H1
Lena 590 K6
Leopolis 200 J6
Lewis 200 B4
Lily 125 J5
Lima Center 175 J10
Limeridge 152 F9
Linden 429 F10
Little Chute 9,207 K7
Little Suamico 190 L6
Livingston 576 E10
Lodi 2,093 G9
Loganville 228 F9
Lohrville 368 H7
Lomira 1,542 J8
London 317 H9
Lone Rock 641 F9
Long Lake 150 J4
Loretta 200 E4
Lowell 300 J9
Loyal 1,244 E6
Lublin 129 E5
Luck 1,022 B4
Luxemburg 1,151 L6
Lyndon Station 474 F8
Lynn 117 F6
Lynxville 153 D9
Lyons 550 K10
Madison (cap.)▲ 191,262 H9
Maiden Rock 146 B6
Manawa 1,169 J7
Manchester 160 J8
Manitowoc▲ 32,520 L7
Maple 596 C2
Maplewood 200 M6
Marathon 1,606 G6
Marengo 130 E3
Maribel 372 L7
Marinette▲ 11,843 L5
Marion 1,242 J6
Markesan 1,496 J8
Marquette 182 H8
Marshall 2,329 H9
Marshfield 19,291 F6
Martell 200 B6
Mason 102 D3
Mattoon 431 J5
Mauston▲ 3,439 F8
Mayville 4,374 K9
Mazomanie 1,377 G9
McFarland 5,232 H10
McNaughton 450 H4
Medford▲ 4,283 F5
Mellen 935 E3
Melrose 551 E7
Melvina 115 E8
Menasha 14,711 J7
Menomonee Falls 26,840 K1
Menomonie▲ 13,547 C6
Mequon 18,885 L1
Mercer V3
Merrill▲ 9,860 G5
Merrillan 553 E7
Merrimac 392 G9
Merton 1,199 K1
Middle Inlet 200 K5
Middleton 13,289 G9
Mikana 200 C4
Milan 153 F6
Milladore 314 G6
Millston 110 E7
Milltown 786 J10
Milton 4,434 J10
Milwaukee▲ 628,088 M1
Mindoro 200 D7
Mineral Point 2,428 F10
Minocqua 950 G4
Minong 521 C3
Mishicot 1,296 L7
Mondovi 2,491 C6
Monico 250 H4
Monona 8,637 G10
Monroe▲ 10,241 G10
Montello▲ 1,329 H8
Monterey 150 J1
Montfort 676 E10
Monticello 1,140 G10
Montreal 838 F3
Morrisonville 375 G9
Mosinee 3,820 G6
Mount Calvary 558 K8
Mount Hope 173 D10
Mount Horeb 4,182 G10
Mount Sterling 217 D9
Mount Vernon 138 G10
Mountain 250 K5
Mukwonago 4,457 J2
Muscoda 1,287 F9
Muskego 16,813 K2
Nashotah 567 J1
Navarino 140 J6
Necedah 743 F7
Neenah 23,219 J7
Neillsville▲ 2,680 E6
Nekoosa 2,557 G7
Nelson 388 C7
Nelsonville 171 H7
Neopit 615 J6
Neosho 658 J9
Neshkoro 384 H8
New Amsterdam 120 C8
New Auburn 485 D5
New Berlin 33,592 K2
New Franken 150 L6
New Glarus 1,899 G10
New Holstein 3,342 K8
New Libson 1,491 F8
New London 6,658 J7
New Richmond 5,106 A5
Newald 375 J4
Newburg 875 K9
Niagara 1,999 K4
Nichols 254 K6
North Bay 246 M3
North Bend 200 D7
North Fond du Lac 4,292 J8
North Freedom 591 G9
North Hudson 3,101 A5
North Lake 400 J1
North Prairie 1,322 J2
North Shore 14,272 M1
Norwalk 564 E8
Oak Creek 19,513 M2
Oakdale 162 F8
Oakfield 1,003 J8
Oconomowoc 10,993 H1
Oconomowoc Lake 493 H1
Oconto Falls 2,584 K6
Oconto▲ 4,474 L6
Odanah 190 E2
Ogdensburg 220 J7
Ogema 238 F5
Okauchee 3,958 J1
Okee 250 H9
Oliver 265 B2
Omro 2,836 J7
Onalaska 11,284 D8
Oneida 808 K7
Ontario 407 E8
Oostburg 1,931 L8
Oregon 4,519 H10
Orfordville 1,219 H10
Osceola 2,075 A5
Oshkosh▲ 55,006 J8
Osseo 1,551 D6
Owen 895 F6
Oxford 499 H8
Packwaukee 271 G8
Paddock Lake 2,662 K10
Palmyra 1,539 H2
Pardeeville 1,630 H8
Park Falls 3,104 F4
Park Ridge 546 H6
Patch Grove 202 D10
Pearson 102 H5
Peeksville 250 E3
Pell Lake 2,018 K10
Pembine 500 L4
Pence 234 F3
Pensaukee 225 L6
Pepin 873 B7
Perrygo Place J10
Peshtigo 3,154 L5
Pewaukee 4,941 K1
Phelps 950 H3
Phillips▲ 1,592 E4
Phlox 150 J5
Pickerel 107 J5
Pickett 120 J8
Pigeon Falls 289 D7
Pine River 110 H7
Pittsville 838 F7
Plain 691 F9
Plainfield 839 G7
Plat 120 K1
Platteville 9,708 F10
Pleasant Prairie 11,961 L10
Plover 8,176 G7
Plum City 534 B6
Plymouth 6,769 L8
Polonia 200 H6
Poplar 516 C2
Port Edwards 1,848 G7
Port Washington▲ 9,338 L9
Port Wing 290 D2
Portage▲ 8,640 G8
Potosi 654 E10
Potter 252 K7
Pound 434 L5
Poy Sippi 425 J7
Poynette 1,662 G9
Prairie Farm 494 C5
Prairie du Chien▲ 5,659 D9
Prairie du Sac 2,380 G9
Prentice 571 F4
Prescott 3,243 A6
Presque Isle 251 G3
Princeton 1,458 H8
Pulaski 2,200 K6
Racine▲ 84,298 M3
Radisson 237 D4
Randolph 1,729 H8
Random Lake 1,439 K8
Raymond 300 L2
Readfield 200 J7
Readstown 420 E9
Red Cliff 250 E2
Redgranite 1,009 H7
Reedsburg 5,834 G8
Reedsville 1,182 L7
Reeseville 673 J9
Reserve 371 D4
Rewey 220 F10
Rhinelander▲ 7,427 H4
Rib Falls 145 G6
Rice Lake 7,998 F5
Richfield 247 K1
Richland Center▲ 5,018 F9
Ridgeland 246 B5
Ridgeway 577 F10
Rio 768 H9
Rio Creek 200 L6
Ripon 7,241 J8
River Falls 10,610 A6
River Hills 1,612 M1
Roberts 1,043 A6
Rochester 978 K3
Rock Falls 200 C6
Rock Springs 432 F8
Rockdale 235 J10
Rockfield 200 L1
Rockland 509 D8
Rome 200 H1
Rosendale 777 J8
Rosholt 512 H6
Rothschild 3,310 G6
Roxbury 260 G9
Royalton 200 J7
Rozellville 150 G6
Rubicon 261 K9
Rudolph 451 G7
Saint Cloud 494 K8
Saint Croix Falls 1,640 A5
Saint Francis 9,245 M2
Saint Joseph Ridge 450 D8
Saint Nazianz 693 L7
Sand Creek 225 C5
Sauk City 3,019 G9
Saukville 3,695 L9
Saxon 375 F3
Sayner 300 H4
Scandinavia 298 H7
Schofield 2,415 H6
School Hill 228 L8
Seneca 235 E9
Sextonville 225 F9
Seymour 1,557 K6
Sharon 1,250 J11
Shawano▲ 7,598 J6
Sheboygan▲ 49,676 L8
Sheboygan Falls 5,823 L8
Sheldon 268 D5
Shell Lake▲ 1,161 C4
Sherry 115 G6
Sherwood 837 K7
Shiocton 805 K7
Shopiere 350 H10
Shorewood 14,116 M1
Shorewood Hills 1,680 G9
Shullsburg 1,236 F10
Silver Lake 1,801 K10
Siren 863 B4
Sister Bay 675 M5
Slinger 2,340 K9
Soldiers Grove 564 E9
Solon Springs 575 C3
Somers 400 M3

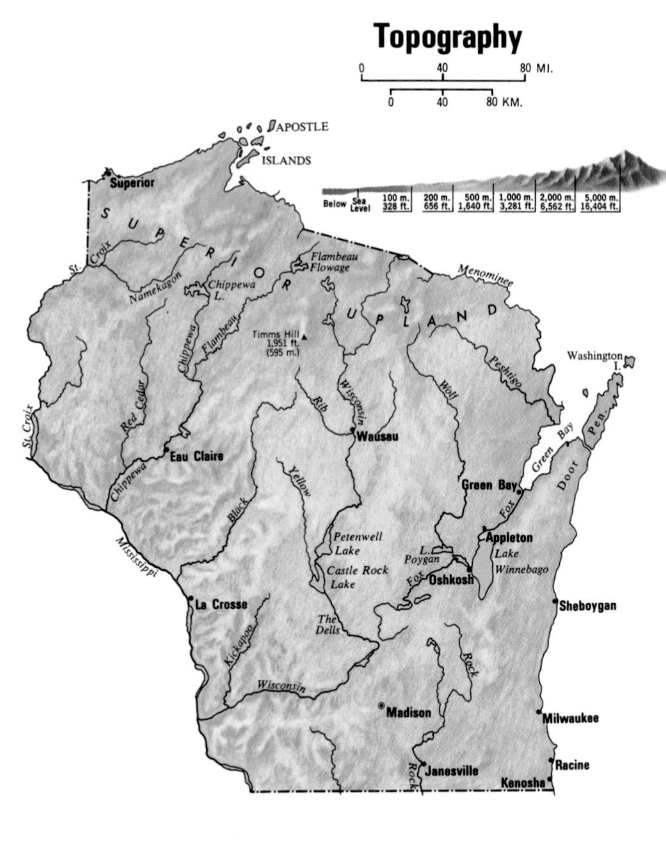

Somerset 1,065 A5
South Milwaukee 20,958 M2
South Range 149 B2
South Wayne 478 G10
Sparta▲ 7,788 E8
Spencer 1,757 F6
Spirit 400 F5
Spooner 2,464 B4
Spring Green 1,283 G9
Spring Valley 1,051 B6
Springbrook 150 C4
Stangelville 150 L7
Stanley 2,011 E6
Star Prairie 507 A5
Stetsonville 511 F5
Steuben 161 E9
Stevens Point▲ 23,006 G7
Stiles 300 L6
Stitzer 190 E10
Stockbridge 579 K7
Stoddard 775 D8
Stone Bank 390 J1
Stone Lake 210 C4
Stoughton 8,786 H10
Stratford 1,515 F6
Strum 949 D6
Sturgeon Bay▲ 9,176 M6
Sturtevant 3,803 M3
Suamico 900 K6
Sullivan 432 H1
Summit Lake 250 H5
Sun Prairie 15,333 H9
Superior▲ 27,134 C2
Superior Village 481 B2
Suring 626 K5
Sussex 5,039 K1
Symco 102 J6
Taycheedah 350 K8
Taylor 419 E7
Tennyson 378 E10
Theresa 771 K8
Thiensville 3,301 L1
Thorp 1,657 E6
Three Lakes 950 H4
Tichigan Lake 500 K2
Tigerton 815 H6
Tilleda 102 J6
Tisch Mills 315 L7
Tomah 7,570 F8
Tomahawk 3,328 G5
Tony 114 E5
Townsend 450 K5
Trego 280 C4
Trempealeau 1,039 C8
Troy Center 250 J2
Tunnel City 200 E7
Turtle Lake 817 B5
Tustin 101 J7
Twin Lakes 3,989 K11
Two Rivers 13,030 M7
Union Center 197 F8
Union Grove 3,669 L3
Unity 452 F6
Upson 115 F3
Valders 905 L7
Verona 5,374 G9
Vesper 598 F7
Viola 644 E8
Viroqua▲ 3,922 D8
Wabeno 800 J5
Waldo 442 L8
Wales 2,471 J1
Walworth 1,614 J10
Warrens 343 E7
Washburn▲ 2,285 D2
Washington Island 550 M5
Waterford 2,431 K3
Waterloo 2,712 J9
Watertown 19,142 J9
Waubeka 450 L9
Waukesha▲ 56,958 K1
Waumandee 115 C7
Waunakee 5,897 G9
Waupaca▲ 4,957 H7
Waupun 8,207 J8
Wausau▲ 37,060 G6
Wausaukee 656 K5
Wautoma▲ 1,784 H7
Wauwatosa 49,366 L1
Wauzeka 595 E9
Wayside 140 L7
Webster 623 B4
West Allis 63,221 L1
West Baraboo 1,021 G9
West Bend▲ 23,916 K9
West Milwaukee 3,973 L1
West Salem 3,611 D8
Westboro 750 F5
Westby 1,866 E8
Westfield 1,125 H8
Weston 8,775 G6
Weston 9,714 C6
Weyauwega 1,665 H7
Weyerhaeuser 283 D5
Wheeler 348 C5
White Lake 304 J5
Whitefish Bay 14,272 M1
Whitehall▲ 1,494 D7
Whitelaw 700 L7
Whitewater 12,636 J10
Whiting 1,838 H7
Wild Rose 676 H7
Williams Bay 2,108 J10
Wilson 163 B6
Wilton 478 F8
Winchester 300 G3
Wind Lake 3,748 K2
Wind Point 1,941 M2
Windsor 2,182 H9
Winnebago 1,433 J7
Winneconne 2,059 J7
Winter 383 E4
Wiota 125 G10
Wisconsin Dells 2,393 G8
Wisconsin Rapids▲ 18,245 G7
Withee 503 E6
Wittenberg 1,145 H6
Wonewoc 793 F8
Woodford 107 G10
Woodman 120 E9
Woodruff 850 G4
Woodville 942 B6
Wrightstown 1,262 K7
Wyeville 154 F7
Wyocena 620 H9
Yuba 77 F8

OTHER FEATURES

Apostle (isls.) F2
Apostle Islands Nat'l Lakeshore E1
Apple (riv.) A5
Bad River Ind. Res. E2
Bardon (lake) E2
Bear (isl.) E1
Beaver Dam (lake) J9
Beulah (lake) J2
Big Eau Pleine (res.) G6
Big Muskego (lake) L2
Big Rib (riv.) G5
Black (riv.) E7
Butternut (lake) J4
Castle Rock (lake) G8
Cat (isl.) E1
Chambers (isl.) M5
Chequamegon (bay) E2
Chetac (lake) D4
Chippewa (lake) D4
Chippewa (riv.) D6
Clam (lake) B4
Clam (riv.) A4
Dells, The (valley) G8
Denoon (lake) K2
Door (pen.) M6
Du Bay (lake) G6
Eagle (lake) H2
Eagle (lake) K3
Eau Claire (riv.) D6
Flambeau (riv.) E4
Flambeau Flowage (res.) F3
Fox (riv.) K2
Fox (riv.) K7
General Mitchell Field M2
Geneva (lake) K10
Golden (lake) H1
Green (bay) L6
Grindstone (lake) C4
Holcombe Flowage (res.) D5
Jump (riv.) E5
Kegonsa (lake) H10
Kickapoo (riv.) E9
Koshkonong (lake) H10
La Belle (lake) H1
Lac Court Oreilles Ind. Res. D4
Lac du Flambeau Ind. Res. G3
Long (lake) C4
Madeline (isl.) E2
Mendota (lake) H9
Menominee (riv.) L5
Menominee Ind. Res. J5
Metonga (lake) J4
Michigan (isl.) F2
Michigan (lake) M9
Mississippi (riv.) D10
Montreal (riv.) F2
Moose (lake) E3
Moose (lake) F3
Nagawicka (lake) J1
Namekagon (lake) D3
Namekagon (riv.) C3
North (lake) J1
Oak (isl.) E2
Oconomowoc (lake) H1
Oconto (riv.) K5
Okauchee (lake) J1
Outer (isl.) F1
Owen (lake) D3
Pecatonica (riv.) H11
Pelican (lake) H4
Pepin (lake) B7
Peshtigo (riv.) K5
Petenwell (lake) G7
Pewaukee (lake) K1
Phantom (lake) J2
Pine (lake) J1
Porte des Morts (str.) N5
Poygan (lake) J7
Puckaway (lake) H8
Red Cedar (riv.) C5
Red Cliff Ind. Res. E2
Rock (riv.) J9
Round (lake) F4
Round (lake) D3
Saint Croix (lake) A6
Saint Croix (riv.) A4
Saint Croix Flowage (res.) C3
Saint Louis (riv.) A2
Sand (isl.) D2
Shawano (lake) K6
Shell (lake) C4
Spider (lake) D3
Stockbridge Ind. Res. J6
Stockton (isl.) F2
Sugar (riv.) H10
Sugarbush Hill (mt.) J4
Superior (lake) F1
Thunder (lake) H4
Tichigan (lake) K2
Timms Hill (mt.) F5
Trempealeau (riv.) C7
Trout (lake) G3
Washington (isl.) M5
Willow (res.) F4
Wind (lake) K2
Winnebago (lake) K7
Wisconsin (riv.) E9
Wolf (riv.) J5
Yellow (lake) B4
Yellow (riv.) F7

▲County seat

Wisconsin

SCALE
0 5 10   20   30   40 MI.

0 5 10 20   30   40 KM.

State Capitals...............⊛
County Seats..................◉
Canals.....................
Major Limited Access Hwys.........

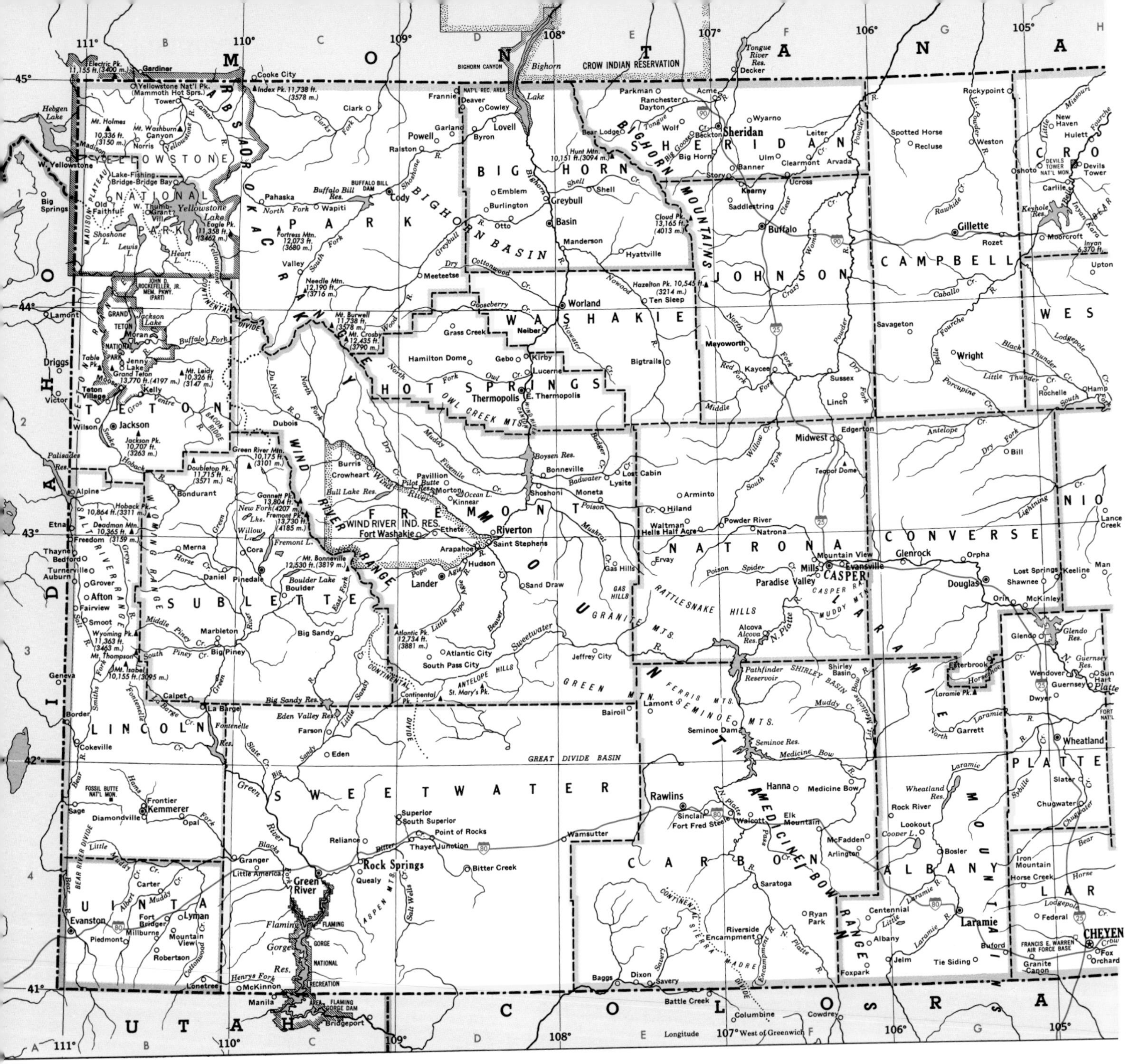

MONTANA

IDAHO

UTAH

COLORADO

45°
44°
43°
42°
41°

111° 110° 109° 108° 107° 106° 105°

Longitude 107° West of Greenwich

Counties and major places (map labels):

YELLOWSTONE NATIONAL PARK
GRAND TETON NATIONAL PARK
PARK
BIG HORN
SHERIDAN
JOHNSON
CAMPBELL
CROOK
WESTON
WASHAKIE
HOT SPRINGS
TETON
FREMONT
NATRONA
CONVERSE
NIOBRARA
SUBLETTE
LINCOLN
SWEETWATER
CARBON
NATRONA
ALBANY
PLATTE
GOSHEN
UINTA
LARAMIE
CHEYENNE

Agriculture, Industry and Resources

DOMINANT LAND USE

- Specialized Wheat
- Specialized Dairy
- General Farming, Livestock, Special Crops
- Sugar Beets, Dry Beans, Livestock, General Farming
- Range Livestock
- Forests
- Nonagricultural Land

MAJOR MINERAL OCCURRENCES

- C Coal
- Cl Clay
- Fe Iron Ore
- G Natural Gas
- O Petroleum
- P Phosphates
- So Soda Ash
- U Uranium
- V Vanadium
- ⚡ Water Power

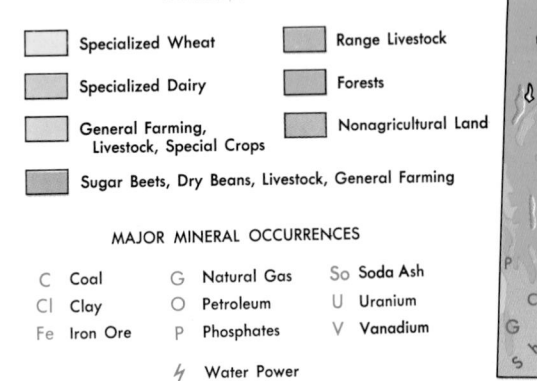

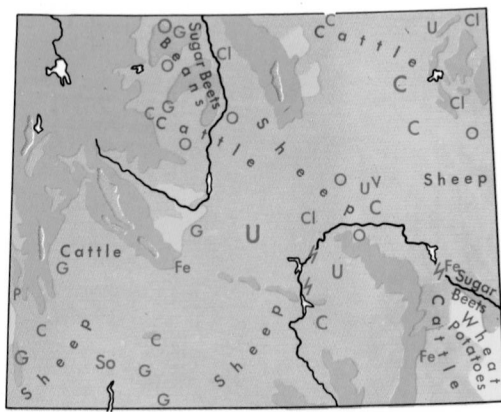

Wyoming

SCALE
0 5 10 20 30 40 MI.
0 5 10 20 30 40 KM.

State Capitals
County Seats
Major Limited Access Hwys.

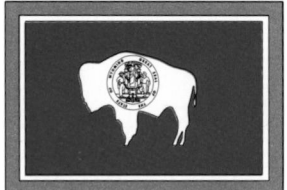

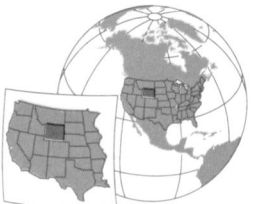

AREA 97,809 sq. mi. (253,325 sq. km.)
POPULATION 455,975
CAPITAL Cheyenne
LARGEST CITY Casper
HIGHEST POINT Gannett Pk. 13,804 ft. (4207 m.)
SETTLED IN 1834
ADMITTED TO UNION July 10, 1890
POPULAR NAME Equality State
STATE FLOWER Indian Paintbrush
STATE BIRD Meadowlark

Topography

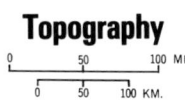
0 50 100 MI.
0 50 100 KM.

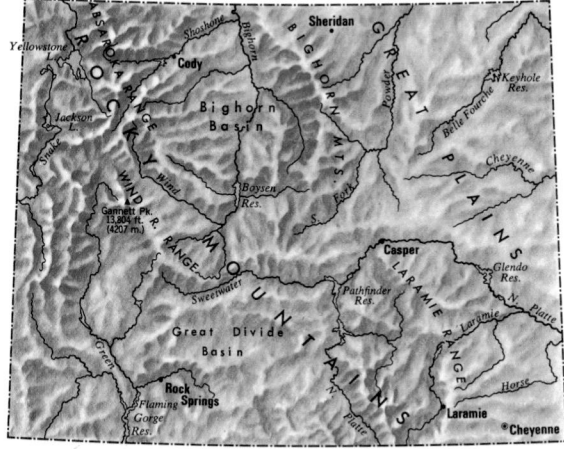
Sheridan
Cody
Yellowstone L.
Jackson L.
Bighorn Basin
BIGHORN MTS.
GREAT PLAINS
ROCKY MOUNTAINS
ABSAROKA RANGE
WIND R. RANGE
Gannett Pk. 13,804 ft. (4207 m.)
Boysen Res.
Keyhole Res.
Casper
Glendo Res.
Pathfinder Res.
LARAMIE RANGE
Great Divide Basin
Rock Springs
Flaming Gorge Res.
Laramie
Cheyenne

5,000 m. 16,404 ft.
2,000 m. 6,562 ft.
1,000 m. 3,281 ft.
500 m. 1,640 ft.
200 m. 656 ft.
100 m. 328 ft.
Sea Level
Below

Alcova 275 ... F3
Alpine 200 ... B2
Alva 50 ... H1
Arapahoe 393 ... D3
Arvada 30 ... F1
Atlantic City 25 ... D3
Auburn 360 ... A3
Baggs 272 ... E4
Bairoil 228 ... E3
Banner 40 ... F1
Basin▲ 1,180 ... E1
Beckton 110 ... E1
Bedford 350 ... A3
Beulah 184 ... H1
Big Horn 350 ... E1
Big Piney 454 ... B3
Bondurant 90 ... B2
Border 25 ... B3
Bosler 195 ... G4
Boulder 50 ... C3
Buffalo▲ 3,302 ... F1
Buford 36 ... G4
Burlington 184 ... D1
Burns 254 ... H4
Burris 30 ... C2
Byron 470 ... D1
Carpenter 75 ... H4
Carter 33 ... B4
Casper▲ 46,742 ... F3
Centennial 140 ... F4
Cheyenne (cap.)▲ 50,008 ... H4
Chugwater 192 ... H4
Clearmont 119 ... F1
Cody▲ 7,897 ... D1
Cokeville 493 ... B3
Colony 50 ... H1
Cowley 477 ... D1
Crowheart 200 ... C2
Daniel 130 ... B3
Dayton 565 ... E1
Deaver 199 ... D1
Devils Tower 28 ... H1
Diamondville 864 ... B4
Dixon 70 ... E4
Douglas▲ 5,076 ... G3
Dubois 895 ... C2
East Thermopolis 221 ... D2
Eden 198 ... C3
Edgerton 247 ... F2
Egbert 75 ... H4
Elk Mountain 174 ... F4
Encampment 611 ... F4
Ethete 1,059 ... D2
Etna 200 ... A2
Evanston▲ 10,903 ... B4
Evansville 1,403 ... F3
Fairview 150 ... B3
Farson 350 ... C3
Fort Bridger 300 ... B4
Fort Laramie 243 ... H3
Fort Washakie 1,334 ... C2
Fox Farm 2,850 ... H4
Foxpark 78 ... F4
Frannie 148 ... D1
Freedom 400 ... B3
Frontier 150 ... B4
Garland 57 ... D1
Gas Hills 150 ... E3
Gillette▲ 17,635 ... G1
Glendo 195 ... G3
Glenrock 2,153 ... G3
Granger 126 ... C4
Granite Canon 80 ... G4
Grass Creek 152 ... D2
Green River▲ 12,711 ... C4
Greybull 1,789 ... E1
Grover 425 ... B3
Guernsey 1,155 ... H3
Hamilton Dome 80 ... D2
Hanna 1,076 ... F4
Hartville 78 ... H3
Hawk Springs 84 ... H4
Hillsdale 160 ... H4
Horse Creek 225 ... G4
Hudson 392 ... D3
Hulett 429 ... H1
Huntley 50 ... H4
Hyattville 110 ... E1
Iron Mountain 45 ... G4
Jackson▲ 4,472 ... B2
Jeffrey City 1,882 ... E3
Jelm 29 ... G4
Kaycee 256 ... F2
Kearny 49 ... F1
Kelly 100 ... B2
Kemmerer▲ 3,020 ... B4
Kinnear 145 ... D2
Kirby 59 ... D2
La Barge 493 ... B3
Lagrange 224 ... H4
Lamont 30 ... E3
Lance Creek 100 ... H2
Lander▲ 7,023 ... D3
Laramie▲ 26,687 ... G4
Leiter 46 ... F1
Linch 187 ... F2
Lingle 473 ... H3
Little America 175 ... C4
Lost Cabin 25 ... E2
Lovell 2,131 ... D1
Lucerne 240 ... D2
Lusk▲ 1,504 ... H3
Lyman 1,896 ... B4
Lysite 175 ... E2
Mammoth Hot Springs (Yellowstone Nat'l Park) 350 ... B1
Manderson 83 ... E1
Manville 97 ... H3
Marbleton 634 ... B3
Mayoworth ... F2
McFadden 47 ... F4
McKinnon 135 ... C4
Medicine Bow 389 ... F4
Meeteetse 368 ... D1
Meriden 55 ... H4
Midwest 495 ... F2
Millburne 54 ... B4
Mills 1,574 ... F3
Moorcroft 768 ... H1
Moose 150 ... B2
Moran 200 ... B2
Morrisey 28 ... H2
Morton 35 ... D2
Mountain View 1,345 ... B4
Mountain View 76 ... F3
Neiber ... D2
New Haven 35 ... H1
Newcastle▲ 3,003 ... H2
Old Faithful 75 ... B1
Opal 95 ... B4
Orchard Valley 3,327 ... H4
Osage 500 ... H2
Otto 50 ... D1
Pahaska 75 ... C1
Paradise Valley ... F3
Parkman 30 ... E1
Pavillion 126 ... D2
Piedmont 25 ... B4
Pine Bluffs 1,054 ... H4
Pinedale▲ 1,181 ... C3
Point of Rocks 425 ... D4
Powder River 70 ... F2
Powell 5,292 ... D1
Ralston 109 ... D1
Ranchester 676 ... E1
Rawlins▲ 9,380 ... E4
Recluse 225 ... G1
Reliance 325 ... C4
Riverside 85 ... F4
Riverton 9,202 ... D2
Robertson 142 ... B4
Rock River 190 ... G4
Rock Springs 19,050 ... C4
Rozet 30 ... G1
Saddlestring 100 ... F1
Sage 45 ... B4
Saint Stephens 80 ... D3
Sand Draw 40 ... D3
Saratoga 1,969 ... F4
Savageton 30 ... G2
Savery 29 ... E4
Shell 80 ... E1
Sheridan▲ 13,900 ... F1
Shirley Basin 400 ... F3
Shoshoni 497 ... D2
Sinclair 500 ... E4
Smoot 310 ... B3
South Superior 586 ... D4
Story 637 ... F1
Sundance▲ 1,139 ... H1
Sunrise 29 ... H3
Superior 273 ... D4
Sussex 25 ... F2
Ten Sleep 311 ... E1
Teton Village ... B2
Thayne 267 ... A3
Thermopolis▲ 3,247 ... D2
Torrington▲ 5,651 ... H3
Turnerville 65 ... A3
Ulm 25 ... F1
Upton 980 ... H1
Veteran 60 ... H4
Walcott 200 ... F4
Wamsutter 240 ... E4
Wapiti 130 ... C1
Wheatland▲ 3,271 ... H3
Wilson 480 ... B2
Worland▲ 5,742 ... E1
Wright 1,236 ... G2
Wyarno 101 ... F1
Yellowstone National Park 350 ... B1
Yoder 136 ... H4

OTHER FEATURES

Absaroka (range) ... C1
Antelope (creek) ... G2
Antelope (hills) ... D3
Aspen (mts.) ... C4
Atlantic (peak) ... D3
Bear (creek) ... H4
Bear (riv.) ... B4
Bear Lodge (mts.) ... H1
Bear River Divide (mts.) ... B4
Beaver (creek) ... D3
Beaver (creek) ... H2
Belle Fourche (riv.) ... H1
Big Goose (creek) ... E1
Bighorn (basin) ... D1
Bighorn (lake) ... D1
Bighorn (mts.) ... E1
Bighorn (riv.) ... D1
Bighorn Canyon Nat'l Rec. Area ... D1
Big Sandy (riv.) ... C3
Bitter (creek) ... C4
Blacks Fork, Green (riv.) ... C4
Black Thunder (creek) ... G2
Bonneville (mt.) ... C3
Boysen (res.) ... D2
Buffalo Bill (dam) ... C1
Buffalo Bill (res.) ... C1
Buffalo Fork, Snake (riv.) ... B2
Burwell (mt.) ... C2
Caballo (creek) ... G1
Casper (range) ... F3
Cheyenne (riv.) ... H2
Chugwater (creek) ... H4
Clarks Fork (riv.) ... C1
Clear (creek) ... F1
Cloud (peak) ... E1
Cottonwood (creek) ... B4
Crazy Woman (creek) ... F1
Crosby (mt.) ... C2
Crow (creek) ... H4
Deadman (mt.) ... B2
Devils Tower Nat'l Mon. ... H1
Doubletop (peak) ... B2
Dry (creek) ... C2
Dry Cottonwood (creek) ... D1
Eagle (peak) ... B1
Fivemile (creek) ... D2
Flaming Gorge (res.) ... C4
Flaming Gorge Nat'l Rec. Area ... C4
Fontenelle (creek) ... B3
Fontenelle (res.) ... B3
Fort Laramie Nat'l Hist. Site ... H3
Fortress (mt.) ... C1
Fossil Butte Nat'l Mon. ... B4
Francis E. Warren A.F.B. 3,832 ... G4
Fremont (lake) ... C3
Fremont (peak) ... C2
Gannett (peak) ... C2
Gas (hills) ... E3
Glendo (res.) ... H3
Gooseberry (creek) ... D1
Grand Teton (mt.) ... B2
Grand Teton Nat'l Park ... B2
Granite (mts.) ... E3
Great Divide (basin) ... E3
Green (mt.) ... E3
Green (riv.) ... C4
Green, East Fork (riv.) ... C3
Green River (mt.) ... C2
Greybull (riv.) ... D1
Greys (riv.) ... B3
Gros Ventre (riv.) ... B2
Guernsey (res.) ... H3
Hams Fork (riv.) ... B4
Hazelton (peak) ... E1
Henrys Fork, Green (riv.) ... C4
Hoback (peak) ... B2
Hoback (riv.) ... B2
Holmes (mt.) ... B1
Horse (creek) ... H4
Horseshoe (creek) ... G3
Hunt (mt.) ... E1
Index (peak) ... C1
Inyan Kara (creek) ... H1
Inyan Kara (mt.) ... H1
Isabel (mt.) ... B3
Jackson (lake) ... B2
Jackson (peak) ... B2
John D. Rockefeller, Jr., Mem. Pkwy. ... B1
Keyhole (res.) ... H1
Lamar (riv.) ... B1
Lance (creek) ... H2
Laramie (mts.) ... G3
Laramie (peak) ... G3
Laramie (riv.) ... G4
Leidy (mt.) ... B2
Lewis (lake) ... B1
Lightning (creek) ... G2
Little Missouri (riv.) ... H1
Little Muddy (creek) ... B4
Little Powder (riv.) ... G1
Little Sandy (creek) ... C3
Little Thunder (creek) ... G2
Lodgepole (creek) ... H2
Lodgepole (creek) ... H4
Madison (plat.) ... B1
Medicine Bow (range) ... F4
Medicine Bow (riv.) ... F3
Middle Piney (creek) ... B3
Muddy (creek) ... D2
Muskrat (creek) ... E2
Needle (mt.) ... C1
Niobrara (riv.) ... J3
North Laramie (riv.) ... G3
North Platte (riv.) ... H3
Nowater (creek) ... E2
Nowood (riv.) ... E1
Owl, North Fork (creek) ... D2
Owl Creek (mts.) ... D2
Palisades (res.) ... A2
Pass (creek) ... F4
Pathfinder (res.) ... F3
Poison (creek) ... E2
Poison Spider (creek) ... F3
Popo Agie (riv.) ... D3
Powder (riv.) ... F2
Rattlesnake (hills) ... E3
Rawhide (creek) ... G1
Rocky (mts.) ... C1
Salt (riv.) ... B3
Salt River (range) ... B3
Salt Wells (creek) ... D4
Seminoe (mts.) ... E3
Seminoe (res.) ... F3
Shell (creek) ... E1
Shirley (basin) ... F3
Shoshone (lake) ... B1
Shoshone (riv.) ... D1
Sierra Madre (mts.) ... E4
Slate (creek) ... C3
Smiths Fork (riv.) ... B3
Snake (riv.) ... B2
South Cheyenne (riv.) ... H2
South Piney (creek) ... B3
Sweetwater (riv.) ... D3
Sybille (creek) ... G4
Teapot Dome (mt.) ... F2
Teton (range) ... B2
Tongue (riv.) ... E1
Washburn (mt.) ... B1
Wheatland (res.) ... G4
Willow (creek) ... F2
Wind (riv.) ... C2
Wind River (canyon) ... D2
Wind River (range) ... C2
Wind River Ind. Res. ... C2
Wood (riv.) ... C2
Wyoming (peak) ... B3
Wyoming (range) ... B2
Yellowstone (lake) ... B1
Yellowstone (riv.) ... B1
Yellowstone Nat'l Park ... B1

▲County seat

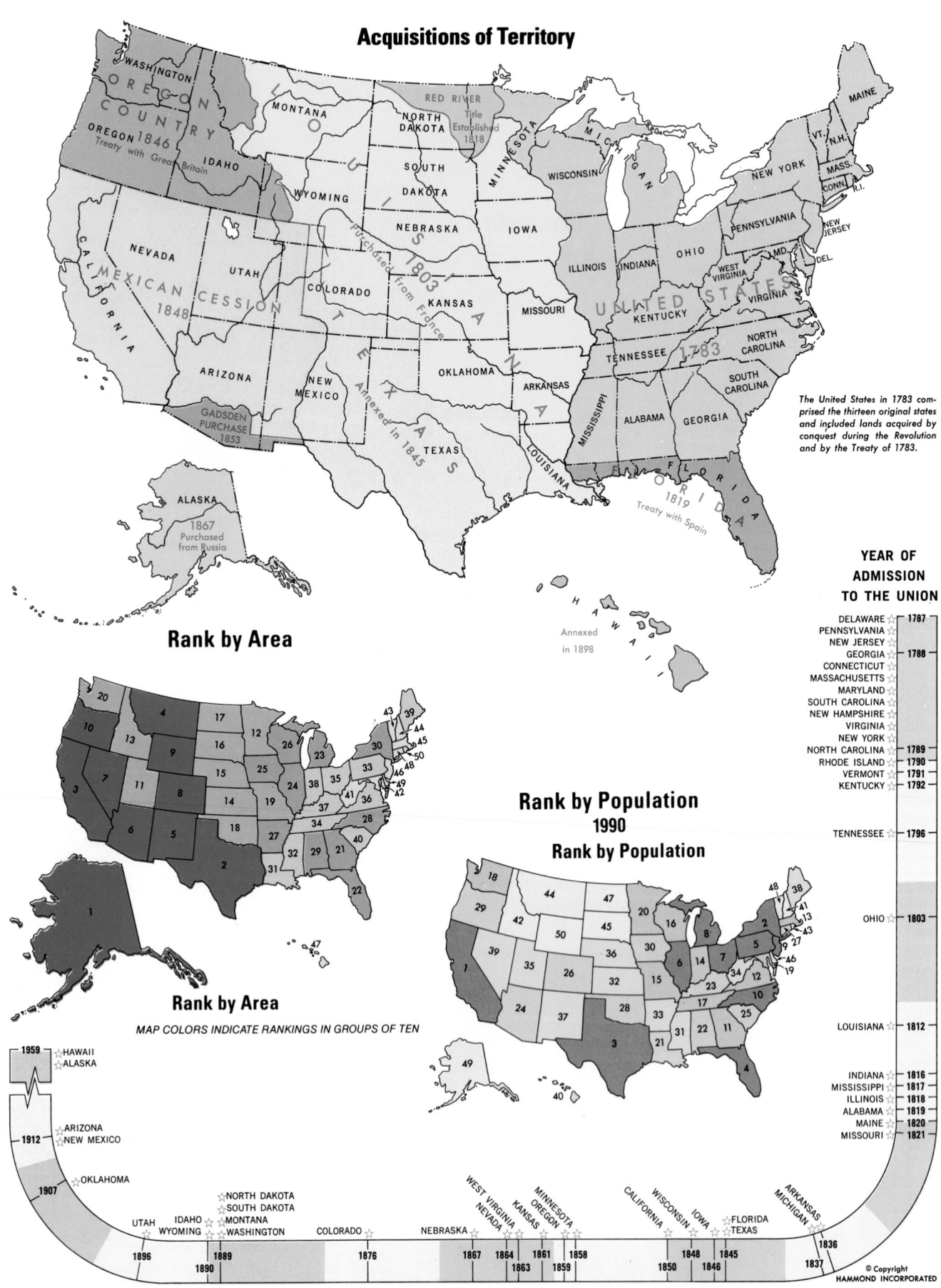

Acquisitions of Territory

The United States in 1783 comprised the thirteen original states and included lands acquired by conquest during the Revolution and by the Treaty of 1783.

Rank by Area

Rank by Population
1990
Rank by Population

MAP COLORS INDICATE RANKINGS IN GROUPS OF TEN

YEAR OF ADMISSION TO THE UNION

DELAWARE ☆	1787
PENNSYLVANIA ☆	
NEW JERSEY ☆	
GEORGIA ☆	1788
CONNECTICUT ☆	
MASSACHUSETTS ☆	
MARYLAND ☆	
SOUTH CAROLINA ☆	
NEW HAMPSHIRE ☆	
VIRGINIA ☆	
NEW YORK ☆	1789
NORTH CAROLINA ☆	1790
RHODE ISLAND ☆	1791
VERMONT ☆	1792
KENTUCKY ☆	
TENNESSEE ☆	1796
OHIO ☆	1803
LOUISIANA ☆	1812
INDIANA ☆	1816
MISSISSIPPI ☆	1817
ILLINOIS ☆	1818
ALABAMA ☆	1819
MAINE ☆	1820
MISSOURI ☆	1821

© Copyright
HAMMOND INCORPORATED

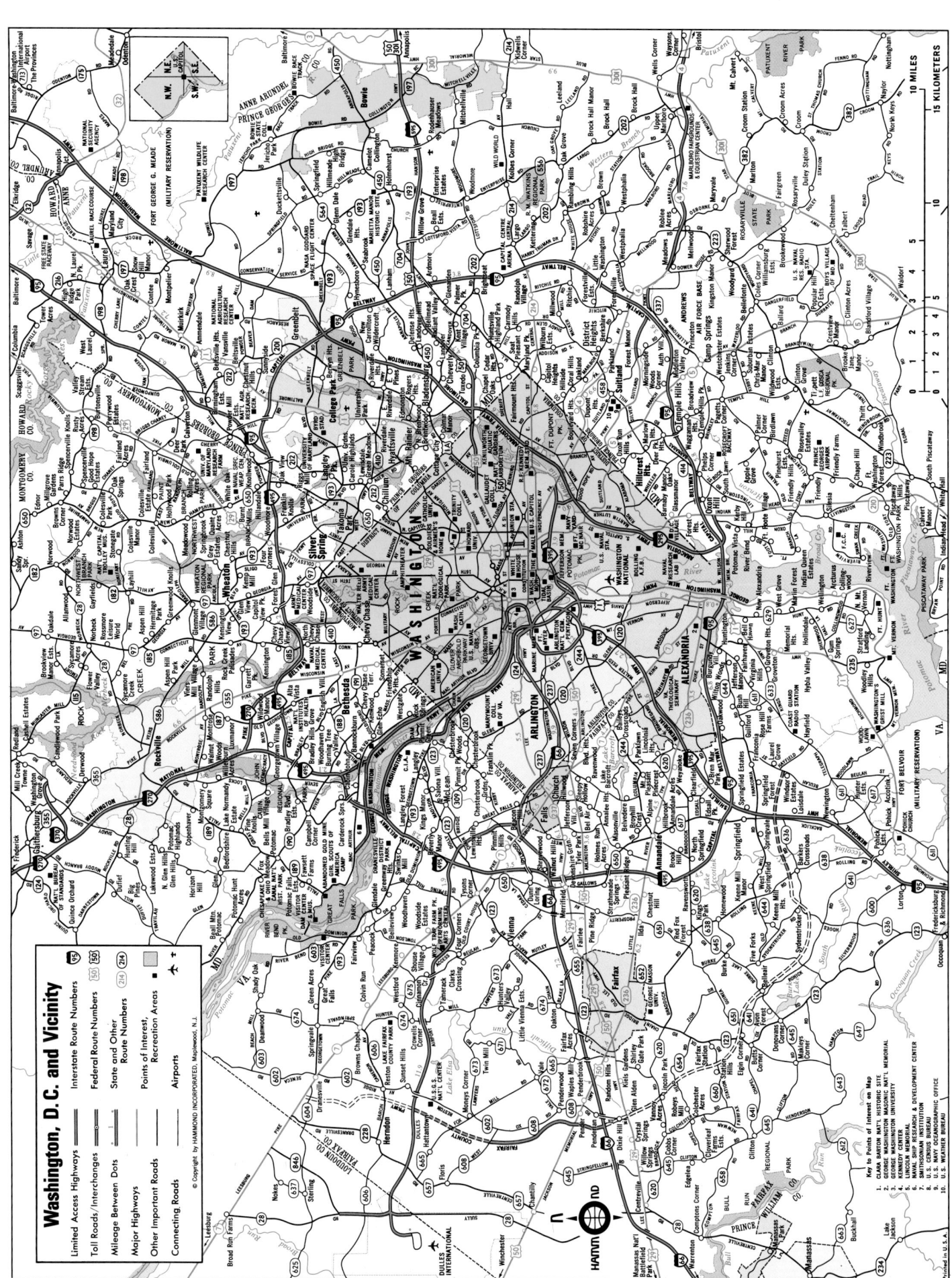

Washington, D.C. and Vicinity

Key to Points of Interest on Map
1. CLARA BARTON NAT'L HISTORIC SITE
2. GEORGE WASHINGTON MASONIC NAT'L MEMORIAL
3. KENNEDY CENTER
4. LINCOLN MEMORIAL
5. NAVAL SHIP RESEARCH & DEVELOPMENT CENTER
6. SMITHSONIAN INSTITUTION
7. U.S. CENSUS BUREAU
8. U.S. NAVY OCEANOGRAPHIC OFFICE
9. U.S. SOLDIERS' HOME
10. U.S. WEATHER BUREAU

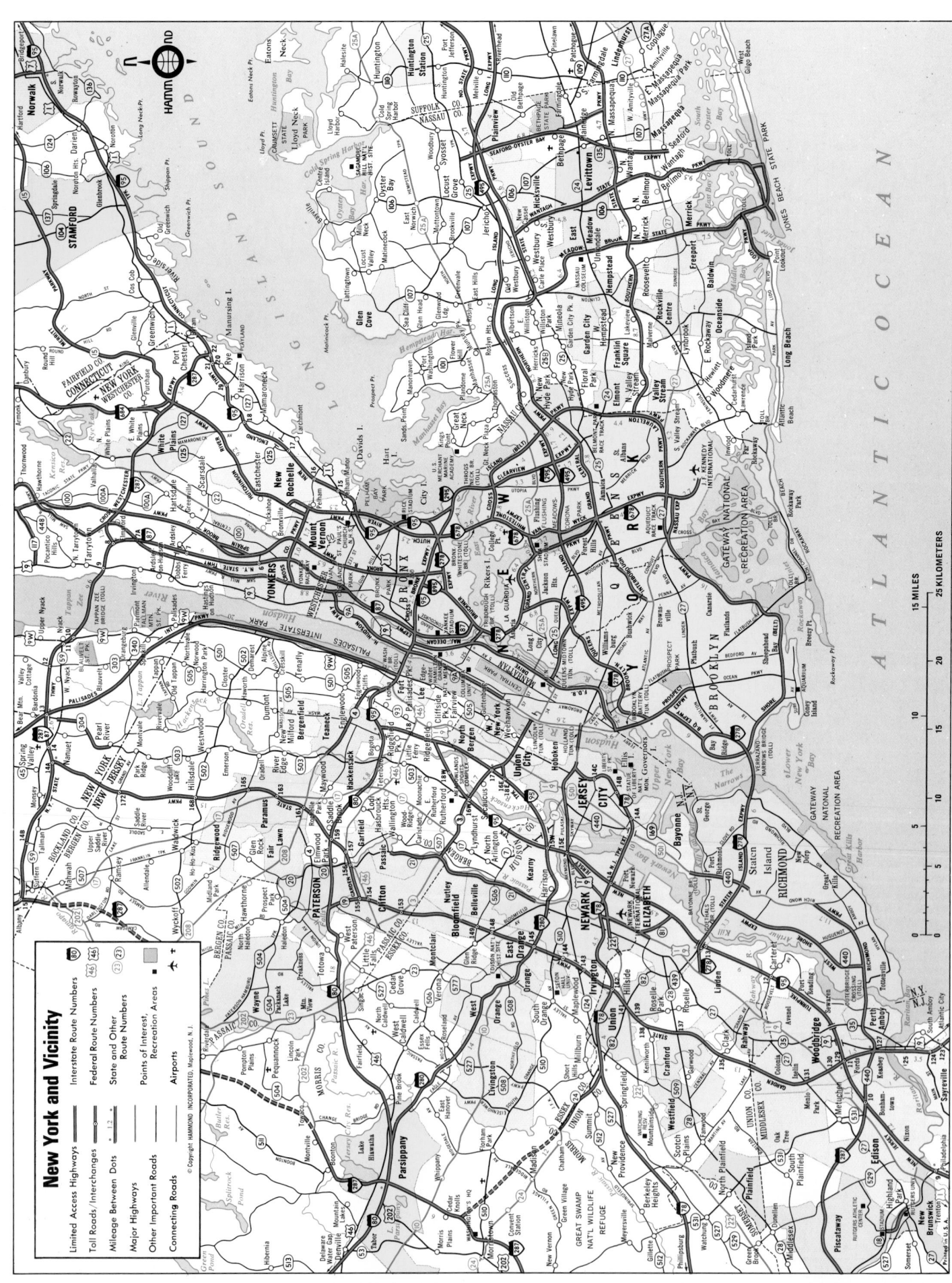

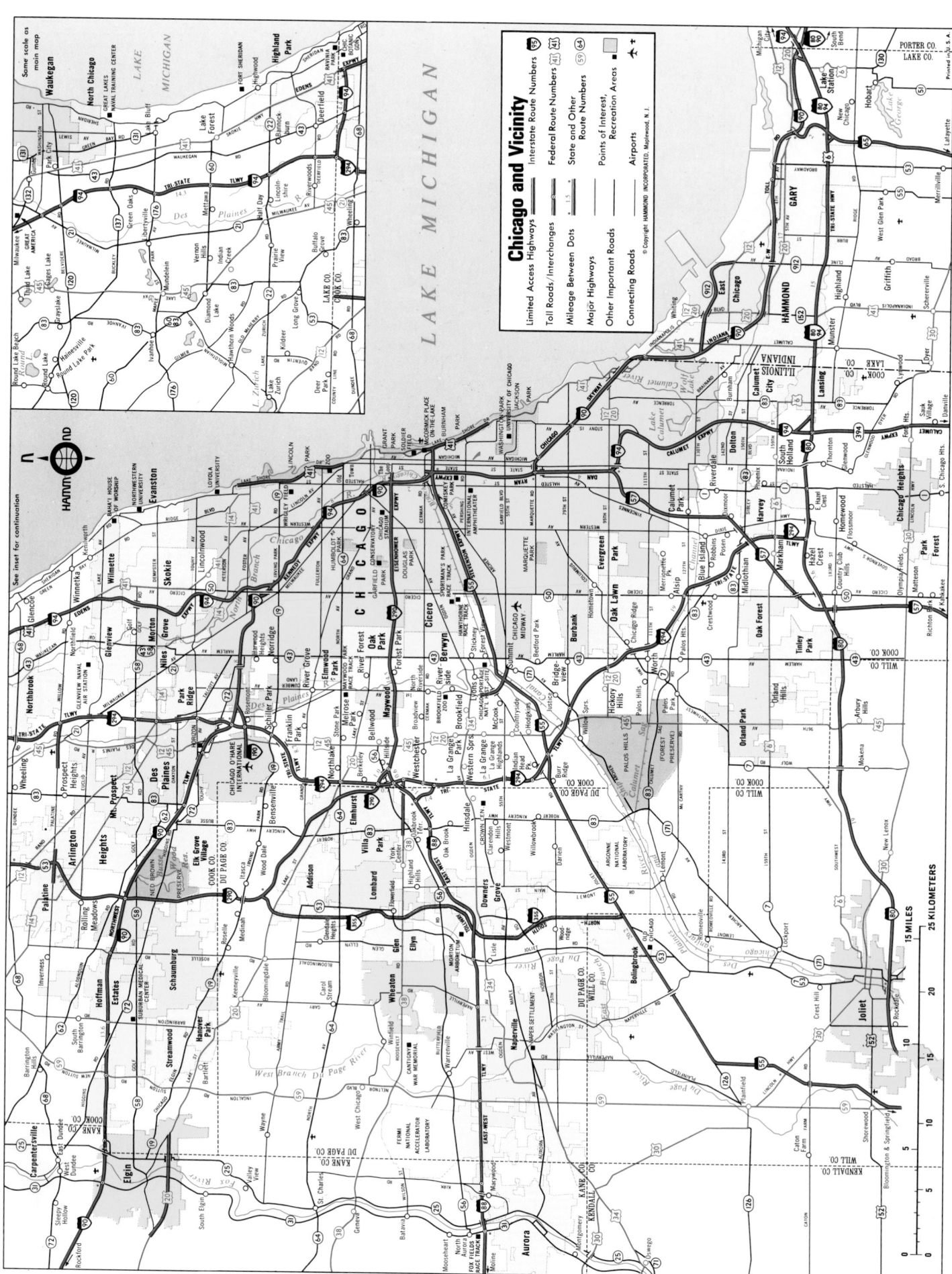
Chicago and Vicinity
Limited Access Highways
Interstate Route Numbers
Toll Roads/Interchanges
Federal Route Numbers
Mileage Between Dots
State and Other Route Numbers
Major Highways
Points of Interest, Recreation Areas
Other Important Roads
Airports
Connecting Roads
© Copyright HAMMOND INCORPORATED, Maplewood, N. J.
HAMMOND
See inset for continuation
Same scale as main map
LAKE MICHIGAN
CHICAGO
Evanston
Skokie
Wilmette
Oak Park
Cicero
Berwyn
Des Plaines
Elgin
Aurora
Joliet
Naperville
Wheaton
Hammond
Gary
East Chicago
Waukegan
North Chicago
Highland Park
Lake Forest
Deerfield
CHICAGO O'HARE INTERNATIONAL
CHICAGO MIDWAY
ILLINOIS
INDIANA
COOK CO.
DU PAGE CO.
WILL CO.
KANE CO.
LAKE CO.
PORTER CO.
15 MILES
25 KILOMETERS
Printed in U.S.A.

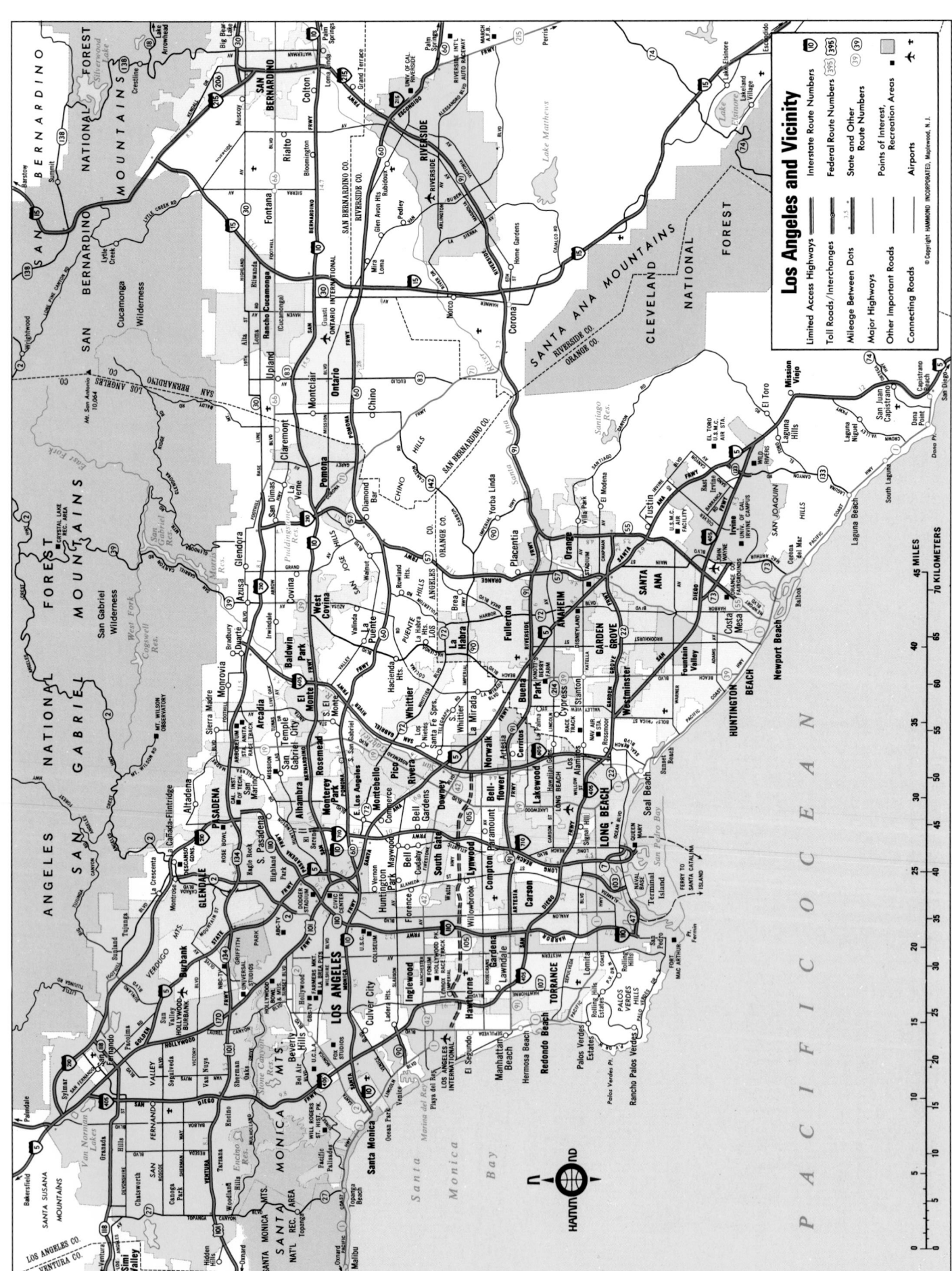

Los Angeles and Vicinity

Limited Access Highways	Interstate Route Numbers
Toll Roads/Interchanges	Federal Route Numbers
Mileage Between Dots	State and Other Route Numbers
Major Highways	Points of Interest, Recreation Areas
Other Important Roads	Airports
Connecting Roads	

© Copyright HAMMOND INCORPORATED, Maplewood, N.J.

INDEX OF THE WORLD

Introduction

This index contains a complete alphabetical listing of more than one hundred thousand names shown on all the maps included in this atlas. Names not found in the individual indexes accompanying the maps appear here. The user who is unfamiliar with the location of a country, town, or physical feature, or who is in doubt as to which country, state or province a place belongs will find the answers to his questions in this index. Entries are indexed to all maps or insets showing the place.

The name of the feature sought will be found in its proper alphabetical sequence, followed by the name of the political division in which it is located, the page number of the map on which it will be found, and the key reference necessary for finding its location on the map. After noting the key reference letter-number combination for the place name, turn to the page number indicated. The place name will be found within the square formed by the two lines of latitude and the two lines of longitude which enclose the coordinates–i.e., the marginal letters and numbers. A bullet (●) after the name signifies a township–better known as a town–in the northeastern U.S.

Because of limitations of space on the map, place names do not always appear in their complete form on the map. The complete forms are, however, given in the index. Variant spellings of names and alternate names are also given in this index. The alternate form or spelling of the name appears first, followed in parentheses by the name as it appears on the map. Physical features are usually listed under their proper names and not according to their generic terms; that is to say, Rio Negro will be found under Negro and not under Rio Negro. Exceptions are familiar names such as Rio Grande.

The abbreviations for the political division names and geographical features are explained on page VI of the atlas. In addition, reference can be made to the Gazetteer-Index appearing on pages I through V in which area, population, capital, map reference and type of government may be found for all major political and physical divisions of the world. Population figures for most entries are also included in the comprehensive individual indexes accompanying each map.

A

Aa (riv.), Switzerland 39/F3
Aachen, Germany 22/B3
Aadorf, Switzerland 39/G2
Aalen, Germany 22/D4
Aalsmeer, Netherlands 27/F4
Aalst, Belgium 27/D7
Aalten, Netherlands 27/K5
Aalter, Belgium 27/C6
Äänekoski, Finland 18/O5
Aarau, Switzerland 39/F2
Aarberg, Switzerland 39/D2
Aarburg, Switzerland 39/E2
Aardenburg, Netherlands 27/C6
Aare (riv.), Switzerland 39/E3
Aargau (canton), Switzerland 39/F2
Aarlen (Arlon), Belgium 27/H9
Aarons (creek), Va. 307/L7
Aaronsburg, Pa. 294/H4
Aarschot, Belgium 27/F7
Aat (Ath), Belgium 27/D7
Aba, China 77/F5
Aba, Hungary 41/E3
Aba, Nigeria 106/F7
Aba, Nigeria 102/C4
Aba, D.R. Congo 115/F3
Aba as Sa'ud, Saudi Arabia 59/D6
Abacaxis (riv.), Brazil 132/B4
Abadan, Iran 54/F6
Abadan, Iran 66/F5
Abadan, Iran 59/E3
Abadeh, Iran 66/H5
Abadeh, Iran 59/F3
Abadla, Algeria 106/D2
Abádszalók, Hungary 41/F3
Abaeté, Brazil 132/E7
Abaetetuba, Brazil 132/D3
Abaetetuba, Brazil 120/E3
Abagnar (Silinhot), China 77/J3
Abaí, Paraguay 144/E4
Abaiang (atoll), Kiribati 87/H5
'Abaila, Saudi Arabia 59/F5
Abajo (mts.), Utah 304/E6
Abakan, Russia 54/L4
Abakan, Russia 48/K4
Abala, Congo 115/C4
Abalos (pt.), Cuba 158/A2
Abana, Turkey 63/F2
Abancay, Peru 120/B4
Abancay, Peru 128/F9
Abapó, Bolivia 136/D6
Abaq, China 77/J3
Abarqu, Iran 59/F3
Abarqu, Iran 66/H5
'Abasan, Gaza Strip 65/A5
Abashiri, Japan 81/M1
Abashiri (riv.), Japan 81/M1
Abau, Papua N.G. 85/C7
Abaújszántó, Hungary 41/F2
Abay (riv.), Ethiopia 111/G5
Abay, Kazakhstan 48/H5
Abaya (lake), Ethiopia 111/G6
Abaza, Russia 48/J4
Abbaye (pt.), Mich. 250/B2
Abbe (lake), Djibouti 111/H5
Abbeville, Ala. 195/H7
Abbeville, France 28/D2
Abbeville, Ga. 217/F7
Abbeville, La. 238/F7
Abbeville, Miss. 256/F2
Abbeville (co.), S.C. 296/B3
Abbeville, S.C. 296/C3
Abbey, Sask. 181/C5
Abbey (head), Scotland 15/E6
Abbeydorney, Ireland 17/B7
Abbeyfeale, Ireland 10/B4
Abbeyfeale, Ireland 17/C7
Abbeylara, Ireland 17/F4
Abbeyleix, Ireland 17/G6
Abbotsford, Br. Col. 184/L3
Abbotsford, Wis. 317/F6
Abbott, Ark. 202/B3
Abbott, N. Mex. 274/E2
Abbott, Texas 303/G6
Abbottabad, Pakistan 68/C2
Abbottabad, Pakistan 59/K3
Abbottsburg, N.C. 281/M5
Abbottsford, Ga. 217/B4
Abbottstown, Pa. 294/J6
Abbot Village•, Maine 243/D5
Abbyville, Kansas 232/D4
'Abdul 'Aziz, Jebel (mts.), Syria 63/J4
Abdulino, Russia 52/H4
Abéché, Chad 102/D3
Abéché, Chad 111/D5
Abee, Alberta 182/D2
Abell, Md. 245/M8
Abemama (atoll), Kiribati 87/H5
Abengourou, Ivory Coast 106/D7
Abengourou, Ivory Coast 102/B4
Åbenrå, Denmark 18/F9
Åbenrå, Denmark 21/C7
Abeokuta, Niger 106/E7
Abeokuta, Nigeria 102/C4
Aberaeron, Wales 13/C5
Aberaeron, Wales 10/D4
Abercarn, Wales 13/B6
Aberchirder, Scotland 15/F3
Abercorn, Québec 172/E4
Abercorn (Mbala), Zambia 115/F5
Abercrombie, N. Dak. 282/S7
Abercrombie, Nova Scotia 168/F3
Abercrombie (mt.), Wash. 310/H2
Aberdare, Wales 13/A6
Aberdare, Wales 10/E5
Aberdaron, Wales 13/C5
Aberdeen, Idaho 220/F7
Aberdeen, Ky. 237/H6
Aberdeen, Md. 245/O2
Aberdeen, Miss. 256/H3
Aberdeen (dam), Miss. 256/H3
Aberdeen•, N.J. 273/E3
Aberdeen, N.S. Wales 97/F3
Aberdeen, N.C. 281/L4
Aberdeen (lake), N.W.T. 187/J3
Aberdeen, Ohio 284/C8
Aberdeen, Sask. 181/E3
Aberdeen, Scotland 7/D3
Aberdeen, Scotland 15/F3
Aberdeen, Scotland 10/F2
Aberdeen (trad. co.), Scotland 15/B5
Aberdeen, S. Africa 118/C6
Aberdeen, S. Dak. 146/J5
Aberdeen, S. Dak. 188/G1
Aberdeen, S. Dak. 298/M3
Aberdeen, Wash. 188/B1
Aberdeen, Wash. 310/B3
Aberdeen Proving Ground, Md. 245/N3
Aberdour, Scotland 15/D1
Aberfeldy, Sask. 181/B2
Aberfeldy, Scotland 10/D2
Aberfeldy, Scotland 15/E4
Aberfoyle, Scotland 15/D4
Abergavenny, Wales 13/B6
Abergavenny, Wales 10/E5
Abergele, Wales 13/D4
Aberlady, Scotland 15/F4
Aberlour, Scotland 15/E3
Abernant, Ala. 195/D4
Abernathy, Texas 303/B4
Abernethy, Sask. 181/H5
Abernethy, Scotland 15/E4
Aberporth, Wales 13/C5
Abert (lake), Oreg. 188/C2
Abert (lake), Oreg. 291/G5
Abertillery, Wales 13/B6
Abertillery, Wales 10/E5
Aberystwyth, Wales 13/C5
Aberystwyth, Wales 10/D4
Abez', Russia 52/K1
Abha, Saudi Arabia 59/D6
Abha, Saudi Arabia 54/F8
Abhar, Iran 66/F2
Abiad, Ras el (Blanc) (cape), Tunisia 106/G1
Abibe, Serraniá de (mts.), Colombia 126/B3
'Abidiya, Sudan 59/B6
Abidjan, Ivory Coast 2/J5
Abidjan, Ivory Coast 102/B4
Abidjan, Ivory Coast 106/D7
Abie, Nebr. 264/H3
Abilene, Kansas 232/E3
Abilene, Texas 146/J6
Abilene, Texas 303/E5
Abilene, Texas 188/G4
Abingdon, England 10/F5
Abingdon, England 13/F6
Abingdon, Ill. 222/C3
Abingdon, Iowa 229/J6
Abingdon, Md. 245/N3
Abingdon, Va. 307/D7
Abingdon Downs, Queensland 95/B3
Abington, Conn. 210/G1
Abington, Ind. 227/H5
Abington•, Mass. 249/L4
Abington, Pa. 294/M5
Abington, Scotland 15/E5
Abiqua (creek), Oreg. 291/B3
Abiquiu, N. Mex. 274/C2
Abiquiu (res.), N. Mex. 274/C2
Abita Springs, La. 238/L6
Abitibi (lake), Ont. 162/H6
Abitibi (lake), Ontario 175/E3
Abitibi (riv.), Ontario 162/H5
Abitibi (riv.), Ontario 175/D2
Abitibi (riv.), Ontario 177/J5
Abitibi (county), Québec 174/B2
Abitibi (terr.), Québec 174/B3
Abkhaz Aut. Rep., Georgia 48/E5
Abkhaz Aut. Rep., Georgia 52/F6
Abminga, S. Australia 94/D2
Abner, N.C. 281/K4
Abnûb, Egypt 111/J4
Åbo (Turku), Finland 18/N6
Aboisso, Ivory Coast 106/D7
Aboite, Ind. 227/G3
Abomey, Benin 106/E7
Abong-Mbang, Cameroon 115/B3
Abony, Hungary 41/E3
Abor (hills), India 68/G3
Aborlan, Philippines 82/B6
Abou Deïa, Chad 111/C5
Aboyne, Scotland 15/F3
Abqaiq, Saudi Arabia 59/E4
Abra (prov.), Philippines 82/C2
Abra (riv.), Philippines 82/C2
Abraham (lake), Alberta 182/B3
Abraham (mt.), Maine 243/C5
Abraham, Utah 304/B4
Abraham (mt.), Vt. 268/B3
Abraham Lincoln Birthplace Nat'l Hist. Site, Ky. 237/K5
Abrams, Wis. 317/L6
Abrantes, Portugal 33/B3
Abra Pampa, Argentina 143/C1
Abreus, Cuba 158/D2
'Abri, Sudan 111/F3
Abricots, Haiti 158/A6
Abruzzi (reg.), Italy 34/D3
Absaraka, N. Dak. 282/P6
Absaroka (range), Mont. 262/F5
Absaroka (range), Wyo. 319/C1
Absarokee, Mont. 262/G5
Absecon, N.J. 273/D5
Absecon (inlet), N.J. 273/E5
Abu, India 68/C4
Abu 'Arish, Saudi Arabia 59/D6
Abu Dara, Ras (cape), Sudan 59/C5
Abu Dara, Ras (cape), Sudan 111/G3
Abu Deleiq, Sudan 59/B6
Abu Dhabi (cap.), U.A.E. 54/G7
Abu Dhabi (cap.), U.A.E. 59/F5
Abu ed Duhur, Syria 63/G5
Abu Habl, Wadi (dry riv.), Sudan 111/F5
Abu Hadriya, Saudi Arabia 59/E4
Abu Hamed, Sudan 111/F4
Abu Hamed, Sudan 59/B6
Abuja (cap.), Nigeria 102/C4
Abuja (cap.), Nigeria 106/F7
Abuja Cap. Terr., Nigeria 106/F7
Abu Kemal, Syria 59/D3
Abu Kemal, Syria 63/J5
Abukuma (riv.), Japan 81/K4
Abu-Mad, Ras (cape), Saudi Arabia 59/C5
Abu Matariq, Sudan 111/E5
Abumombazi, D.R. Congo 115/D3
Abuná (riv.), Bolivia 136/B2
Abunã, Brazil 132/H10
Abunã (riv.), Brazil 132/G10
Abu Qir (bay), Egypt 111/J2
Abu Qurqâs, Egypt 111/J4
Abu Road, India 68/C4
Abu Rujmein, Jebel (mts.), Syria 63/H5
Abu Shagara, Ras (cape), Sudan 111/G3
Abu Shagara, Ras (cape), Sudan 59/C5
Abut (head), N. Zealand 100/B5
Abu Tabari (well), Sudan 111/E4
Abuyog, Philippines 82/E5
Abu Zabad, Sudan 59/A7
Abu Zabad, Sudan 111/E5
Abwong, Sudan 111/F6
Aby (lag.), Ivory Coast 106/D8
Åbybro, Denmark 21/C3
Abydos (ruins), Egypt 111/F2
Abydos (ruins), Turkey 63/B6
Abyei, Sudan 111/E6
Acaciás, Colombia 126/D6
Acaciaville, Nova Scotia 168/C4
Academy, S. Dak. 298/M7
Acadia (par.), La. 238/F6
Acadia Nat'l Park, Maine 243/G7
Acadia Valley, Alberta 182/E4
Acadie Siding, New Bruns. 170/E2
Acadieville, New Bruns. 170/E2
Acahay, Paraguay 144/B5
Acajutla, El Salvador 154/B4
Acala, Mexico 150/N8
Acala, Texas 303/B10
Acámbaro, Mexico 150/J7
Acampo, Calif. 204/C9
Acandí, Colombia 126/B3
Acaponeta, Mexico 150/G5
Acapulco de Juárez, Mexico 146/H8
Acapulco de Juárez, Mexico 150/K8
Acaraí, Serra do (range), Brazil 132/B2
Acarai (mts.), Guyana 131/B5
Acaraú, Brazil 132/F3
Acaray (riv.), Paraguay 144/E4
Acarí, Peru 128/E10
Acarí (riv.), Peru 128/E10
Acarigua, Venezuela 124/D3
Acatlán de Osorio, Mexico 150/K7
Acatzingo de Hidalgo, Mexico 150/N2
Acayucan, Mexico 150/M8
Acchilla, Bolivia 136/C7
Accident, Md. 245/A2
Accokeek, Md. 245/L6
Accomac, Va. 307/S5
Accomack (co.), Va. 307/S5
Accord, Mass. 249/E8
Accord, N.Y. 276/M7
Accoville, W. Va. 312/C7
Accra (cap.), Ghana 102/B4
Accra (cap.), Ghana 106/D7
Accra (cap.), Ghana 2/J5
Accrington, England 10/G1
Accrington, England 13/H1
Aceguá, Uruguay 145/E2
Acequia, Idaho 220/E7
Acevedo, Argentina 143/F6
Achacachi, Bolivia 136/A5
Achaguas, Venezuela 124/D4
Achalpur, India 68/D4
Achao, Chile 138/D4
Achar, Uruguay 145/C3
Acharacle, Scotland 15/C4
Achégour (well), Niger 106/G5
Achenkirch, Austria 41/A3
Achill (head), Ireland 10/A4
Achill (head), Ireland 17/A4
Achill (isl.), Ireland 10/A4
Achill (isl.), Ireland 17/A4
Achille, Okla. 288/O7
Achilles, Va. 307/R6
Achill Sound, Ireland 17/B4
Achiltibuie, Scotland 15/C3
Achinsk, Russia 48/K4
Achnasheen (butte), Scotland 10/D2
Achnasheen, Scotland 15/C3
Achourat (well), Mali 106/D4
A'Chralaig (mt.), Scotland 15/C3
Acı (lake), Turkey 63/C4
Acıgöl, Turkey 63/F3
Acıpayam, Turkey 63/C4
Acireale, Italy 34/E6
Ackerly, Texas 303/C5
Ackerman, Miss. 256/F4
Ackerville, Ala. 195/D6
Ackley, Iowa 229/G3
Acklins (isl.), Bahamas 146/L7
Acklins (isl.), Bahamas 156/C2
Ackworth, Iowa 229/G6
Aclare, Ireland 17/D3
Acle, England 13/J5
Acme, Alberta 182/D4
Acme, La. 238/G4
Acme, Mich. 250/D4
Acme, N.C. 281/N6
Acme, Texas 303/E3
Acme, Wash. 310/C2
Acme, W. Va. 312/D6
Acme, Wyo. 319/E1
Acoaxet, Mass. 249/K7
Acobamba, Peru 128/E9
Acolla, Peru 128/E8
Acoma, N. Mex. 274/B4
Acomayo, Cuzco, Peru 128/G9
Acomayo, Huánuco, Peru 128/E7
Acomita (Pueblo of Acoma), N. Mex. 274/B3
Acona, Miss. 256/D4
Aconcagua (mt.) 120/C6
Aconcagua, Cerro (mt.), Argentina 143/C3
Aconcagua, Chile 138/A9
Aconcagua (riv.), Chile 138/F2
Aconchi, Mexico 150/D2
Acopiara, Brazil 132/G4

326 Acora

Acora, Peru 128/H11
Acorizal, Brazil 132/C6
Acoyapa, Nicaragua 154/E5
Acqui Terme, Italy 34/B2
Acraman (lake), S. Australia 94/D5
Acre (state), Brazil 132/G10
Acre (riv.), Brazil 132/G10
Acre, Israel 65/C2
Acree, Ga. 217/D7
Acri, Italy 34/F5
Ács, Hungary 41/E3
Actinolite, Ontario 177/G3
Acton, Maine 243/B8
Acton•, Maine 243/B8
Acton•, Mass. 249/J3
Acton, Mont. 262/H5
Acton Vale, Québec 172/E4
Actopan, Hidalgo, Mexico 150/K6
Actopan, Veracruz, Mexico 150/Q1
Açu, Brazil 120/F3
Açu, Brazil 132/G4
Aculeo, Chile 138/G4
Aculeo (lag.), Chile 138/G4
Acuña, Argentina 143/G5
Acuracay, Peru 128/F5
Acushnet•, Mass. 249/L6
Acworth, Ga. 217/C2
Acworth•, N.H. 268/C5
Acy, La. 238/L3
Ada, Ghana 106/E7
Ada (co.), Idaho 220/B6
Ada, Kansas 232/E2
Ada, Minn. 255/B3
Ada, Ohio 284/C4
Ada, Okla. 188/G4
Ada, Okla. 288/N5
Ada, W. Va. 312/D8
Adadle, Somalia 115/H2
Adafer (reg.), Mauritania 106/B5
Adair, Ill. 222/C3
Adair (co.), Iowa 229/E6
Adair, Iowa 229/D6
Adair (co.), Ky. 237/L6
Adair (co.), Mo. 261/G2
Adair (cape), N.W.T. 187/L2
Adair (co.), Okla. 288/S3
Adair, Okla. 288/R2
Adair, Tenn. 237/D9
Adairsville, Ga. 217/C2
Adair Village, Oreg. 291/D3
Adairville, Ky. 237/H7
Adaja (riv.), Spain 33/D2
Adak (isl.), Alaska 196/L4
Adak (str.), Alaska 196/K4
Adak Naval Air Station, Alaska 196/L4
Adalar (isl.), Turkey 63/D6
Adalia (Antalya), Turkey 63/D4
Adam, Oman 59/G5
Adamawa (reg.), Cameroon 115/B2
Adamawa (reg.), Nigeria 106/G7
Adaminaby, N.S. Wales 97/E5
Adams (lake), Br. Col. 184/H4
Adams (riv.), Br. Col. 184/H4
Adams (co.), Colo. 208/L3
Adams (mt.), Colo. 208/H6
Adams (co.), Idaho 220/B5
Adams (co.), Ill. 222/B4
Adams (co.), Ind. 227/H3
Adams, Ind. 227/F6
Adams (co.), Iowa 229/D6
Adams, Kansas 232/E4
Adams, Ky. 237/R4
Adams, Mass. 249/B2
Adams•, Mass. 249/B2
Adams, Minn. 255/F7
Adams (co.), Miss. 256/B8
Adams (co.), Nebr. 264/F4
Adams, Nebr. 264/H4
Adams (mt.), N.H. 268/E3
Adams, N.Y. 276/J3
Adams (co.), N. Dak. 282/F7
Adams, N. Dak. 282/O3
Adams (co.), Ohio 284/D8
Adams, Okla. 288/D1
Adams, Oreg. 291/J2
Adams (co.), Pa. 294/H6
Adam's (peak), Sri Lanka 68/E7
Adams, Tenn. 237/G7
Adams (co.), Wash. 310/G3
Adams (mt.), Wash. 310/D4
Adams (co.), Wis. 317/G7
Adams, Wis. 317/G8
Adamsboro, Ind. 227/E3
Adam's Bridge (sound), India 68/D7
Adam's Bridge (shoals), Sri Lanka 68/D7
Adamsburg, S.C. 296/D2
Adams Center, N.Y. 276/H3
Adams Lake, Br. Col. 184/G5
Adams Mills, Ohio 284/G5
Adams Nat'l Hist. Site, Mass. 249/D7
Adamson, Okla. 288/P5
Adams Run, S.C. 296/G6
Adamstown, Md. 245/H3
Adamstown, Pa. 294/K5
Adamstown (cap.), Pitcairn Is. 87/N8
Adamsville, Ala. 195/D3
Adamsville, New Bruns. 170/E2
Adamsville, Ohio 284/G5
Adamsville, Pa. 294/B2
Adamsville, Québec 172/E4
Adamsville, R.I. 249/K6
Adamsville, Tenn. 237/E10
Adamsville, Texas 303/F6
Adamsville, Utah 304/B5
Adana (prov.), Turkey 63/F4
Adana, Turkey 59/C2
Adana, Turkey 63/F4
Adana, Turkey 54/E6
Adanac, Sask. 181/B3
Adapazarı, Turkey 63/D2
Adapazarı, Turkey 59/B1
Adarama, Sudan 111/G4
Adarama, Sudan 59/C6
Adare (cape), Ant. 2/T10
Adare (cape), Ant. 5/B9
Adare, Ireland 17/D6
Adar Qaga, Jebel (mt.), Sudan 59/C5
Adaut, Indonesia 85/J7
Adavale, Queensland 88/G5
Adavale, Queensland 95/C5
Adaza, Iowa 229/E4
Adda (riv.), Italy 34/B2
Adda (riv.), Sudan 111/D6
Addanki, India 68/D5
Addieville, Ill. 222/D5
Addington, Okla. 288/L6
Addis, La. 238/J2
Addis Ababa (cap.), Ethiopia 102/F4
Addis Ababa (cap.), Ethiopia 2/L5
Addis Ababa (cap.), Ethiopia 111/G6
Addis Alam, Ethiopia 111/G6
Addison, Ala. 195/D2
Addison, Conn. 210/E2
Addison, Ill. 222/B5
Addison, Maine 243/H6
Addison•, Maine 243/H6
Addison, Mich. 250/E7
Addison, N.Y. 276/F6
Addison, Ohio 284/F8
Addison, Pa. 294/D6
Addison, Texas 303/G2
Addison (co.), Vt. 268/A3
Addison, Vt. 268/A3
Addison (Webster Springs), W. Va. 312/F6
Addi Ugri, Eritrea 59/C7
Ad Diwaniya, Iraq 66/D5
Addo Nat'l Park, S. Africa 118/D6
Addor, N.C. 281/L4
Addy, Wash. 310/H2
Addyston, Ohio 284/B9
Ade, Ind. 227/C3
Adel, Ga. 217/F8
Adel, Iowa 229/E5
Adel, Oreg. 291/H5
Adelaide (isl.), Ant. 5/C15
Adelaide, Australia 87/D9
Adelaide, Australia 2/S7
Adelaide (pen.), N.W.T. 187/J3
Adelaide, S. Africa 118/D6
Adelaide (cap.), S. Australia 88/D8
Adelaide Airport, Australia 88/D8
Adelaide River, North. Terr. 88/E2
Adelaide River, North. Terr. 93/B2
Adelanto, Calif. 204/H9
Adelboden, Switzerland 39/E3
Adele (isl.), W. Australia 88/C3
Adele (isl.), W. Australia 92/C1
Adélie Coast (reg.), Ant. 5/C7
Adeline, Ill. 222/D1
Adeline, La. 238/G7
Adell, Wis. 317/L8
Adelong, N.S. Wales 97/D4
Adelphi, Jamaica 158/H5
Adelphi, Ohio 284/E7
Adelphia, N.J. 273/E3
Aden (gulf) 54/F8
Aden (gulf) 2/M5
Aden (gulf) 102/G3
Aden, Alberta 182/E5
Aden (gulf), Djibouti 111/J5
Aden (gulf), Somalia 115/J1
Aden, Yemen 54/F8
Aden, Yemen 59/E7
Adena, Ohio 284/J5
Adenau, Germany 22/B3
Adger, Ala. 195/D4
Adhaim (riv.), Iraq 66/D3
Adi (isl.), Indonesia 85/J6
Adícora, Venezuela 124/D2
Adige (riv.), Italy 34/C2
Adigrat, Ethiopia 111/G5
Adilabad, India 68/D5
Adilcevaz, Turkey 63/K3
Adin, Calif. 204/E2
Adirondack, N.Y. 276/N3
Adirondack (mts.), N.Y. 276/M3
Adi Ugri, Eritrea 111/G5
Adıyaman (prov.), Turkey 63/H4
Adıyaman, Turkey 63/H4
Adjuntas, P. Rico 161/B2
Adjuntas, P. Rico 156/F1
Adkins, Texas 303/K11
Adlatok (bay), Newf. 166/B2
Adlavik (isls.), Newf. 166/C2
Adliswil, Switzerland 39/F2
Admiral, Sask. 181/C6
Admiral's Beach, Newf. 166/D2
Admiral's Cove, Newf. 166/D2
Admiralty (inlet) 162/H1
Admiralty (isl.), Alaska 196/M1
Admiralty (isls.), N.S. Wales 97/J1
Admiralty (inlet), N.W.T. 187/K2
Admiralty, Papua N.G. 86/A1
Admiralty (isls.), Papua N.G. 87/E6
Admiralty (inlet), Wash. 310/B2
Admiralty (gulf), W. Australia 88/D2
Admiralty (gulf), W. Australia 92/D1
Admiralty Island Nat'l Mon., Alaska 196/M1
Admire, Kansas 232/F3
Admont, Austria 41/C3
Adna, Wash. 310/B4
Ado, Nigeria 106/E7
Adobe Creek (res.), Colo. 208/N6
Adok, Sudan 111/F6
Adolfo Alsina, Argentina 143/D4
Adolph, Minn. 255/F4
Adolph, W. Va. 312/F5
Adolphus, Ky. 237/J7
Adona, Ark. 202/E3
Adonara (isl.), Indonesia 85/G7
Adoni, India 68/D5
Adorf, Germany 22/E3
Adour (riv.), France 28/C6
Adra, Spain 33/E4
Adrano, Italy 34/E6
Adrar, Algeria 102/B2
Adrar, Algeria 106/D3
Adrar (reg.), Mauritania 106/B4
Adrar des Iforas (plat.), Algeria 106/E5
Adrar des Iforas (plat.), Mali 106/E5
Adré, Chad 111/D5
Adria, Italy 34/D2
Adrian, Ga. 217/G5
Adrian, Ill. 222/B3
Adrian, Mich. 250/F7
Adrian, Minn. 255/C7
Adrian, Mo. 261/D6
Adrian, N. Dak. 282/O6
Adrian, Ohio 284/D3
Adrian, Oreg. 291/K4
Adrian, Pa. 294/D4
Adrian, S.C. 296/J4
Adrian, Texas 303/B2
Adrian, W. Va. 312/F5
Adriatic (sea) 7/F4
Adriatic (sea), Albania 45/B4
Adriatic (sea), Croâtia 45/B4
Adriatic (sea), Italy 34/E3
Aduwa, Ethiopia 59/C7
Advance, Ind. 227/D5
Advance, Mich. 250/D3
Advance, Mo. 261/N8
Advance, N.C. 281/J3
Advent, W. Va. 312/C5
Adventure (sound), 143/E7
Adventure (bay), Chile 138/D5
Adventure, Guyana 131/B2
Adventure Bay, Tasmania 99/D5
Advocate (bay), Nova Scotia 168/D3
Advocate Harbour, Nova Scotia 168/D3
Adwa, Ethiopia 111/G5
Adwick le Street, England 13/K2
Adygey Aut. Obl., Russia 52/F6
Adygey Aut. Obl., Russia 48/D5
Adzhar Aut. Rep., Georgia 52/F6
Adzhar Aut. Rep., Georgia 48/E5
Ae, Scotland 15/E5
Aeber (creek), S. Dak. 298/G4
Aegean (sea), Greece 7/G5
Aegean (sea), Greece 45/G6
Aegean (sea), Turkey 63/A3
Aegean Islands (reg.), Greece 45/G6
Aeneas, Wash. 310/F2
Aerial, Alberta 182/D4
AErø (isl.), Denmark 21/D8
AErøskøbing, Denmark 21/D8
Aeschi bei Spiez, Switzerland 39/E3
Aetna, Alberta 182/D5
Aetna, Tenn. 237/G9
Afaq, Iraq 66/D4
Afareaitu, Fr. Poly. 86/S13
Afayan (pt.), Guam 86/K7
Afdem, Ethiopia 111/H6
Afflolé (reg.), Mauritania 106/B5
Affoltern am Albis, Switzerland 39/F2
Affoltern im Emmental, Switzerland 39/E2
Affric, Loch (lake), Scotland 15/D3
Affton, Mo. 261/P4
Afghanistan 2/N4
Afghanistan 54/H6
AFGHANISTAN 68/A2
Afgoi, Somalia 102/G4
Afgoi, Somalia 115/J3
Afif, Saudi Arabia 59/D5
Afikpo, Nigeria 106/F7
Afiqim, Israel 65/D2
Åfjord, Norway 18/G5
Aflex, Ky. 237/S5
Afmadu, Somalia 115/H3
Afognak (isl.), Alaska 196/H3
Africa 2/K4
AFRICA 102
Afşin, Turkey 63/G3
Afton, Iowa 229/E6
Afton, La. 238/H2
Afton, Mich. 250/E3
Afton, Minn. 255/F6
Afton, N.Y. 276/J6
Afton, Okla. 288/S1
Afton, Tenn. 237/R8
Afton, Texas 303/D4
Afton, Va. 307/L4
Afton, Wis. 317/H10
Afton, Wyo. 319/B3
Afuá, Brazil 132/D3
'Afula, Israel 65/C2
Afyonkarahisar (prov.), Turkey 63/D3
Afyonkarahisar, Turkey 63/D3
Afyonkarahisar, Turkey 59/A2
Agadem (well), Niger 106/G5
Agadès, Niger 106/F5
Agadès, Niger 102/C3
Agadir, Morocco 106/C2
Agadir, Morocco 102/A1
Agaña (cap.), Guam 87/E4
Agaña (cap.), Guam 86/K7
Agano (riv.), Japan 81/J4
Agar, S. Dak. 298/J4
Agartala, India 68/G4
Agassiz (peak), Ariz. 198/D3
Agassiz (mt.), Utah 304/D3
Agat, Guam 86
Agat (bay), Guam 86/K7
Agata, Russia 48/K3
Agate, Colo. 208/M4
Agate, Nebr. 264/A2
Agate, N. Dak. 282/L2
Agate Beach, Oreg. 291/C3
Agate Fossil Beds Nat'l Mon., Nebr. 264/A2
Agats, Indonesia 85/K7
Agatti (isl.), India 68/C6
Agattu (isl.), Alaska 196/J3
Agattu (str.), Alaska 196/J3
Agawa Bay, Ontario 177/J5
Agawa Bay, Ontario 175/D3
Agawam•, Mass. 249/D4
Agawam (riv.), Mass. 249/M5
Agboville, Ivory Coast 102/B4
Agboville, Ivory Coast 106/D7
Agdam, Azerbaijan 52/G6
Agde, France 28/E6
Agen, France 28/D5
Agency, Iowa 229/J7
Agency, Mo. 261/C3
Agency (lake), Oreg. 291/E5
Agenda, Kansas 232/E2
Ageo, Japan 81/O2
Agerbaek, Denmark 21/B6
Ägerisee (lake), Switzerland 39/G2
Ages, Ky. 237/P7
Aghada-Farsid-Rostellan, Ireland 17/E8
Aghadoe, Ireland 17/B7
Aghagower, Ireland 17/C4
Agha Jari, Iran 66/F5
Aginsk Buryat Aut. Okr., Russia 48/M4
Aginskoye, Russia 48/M4
Agiobampo (bay), Mexico 150/E3
Agira, Italy 34/E6
Ağlasun, Turkey 63/D4
Ağlı, Turkey 63/E2
Agness, Oreg. 291/C5
Agno, Philippines 82/B2
Agnone, Italy 34/E4
Agnos, Ark. 202/G1
Agoo, Philippines 82/C2
Agordat, Eritrea 111/G4
Agordat, Eritrea 59/C6
Agra, India 54/J7
Agra, India 68/D3
Agra, Kansas 232/C2
Agra, Okla. 288/N3
Agraciada, Uruguay 145/A4
Agrado, Colombia 126/C6
Agramonte, Cuba 158/D1
Ágreda, Spain 33/E2
Ağrı (prov.), Turkey 63/K3
Ağrı, Büyuk (Ararat) (mt.), Turkey 63/L3
Ağrı (Karaköse), Turkey 63/K3
Agricola, Kansas 232/G3
Agricola, Miss. 256/G9
Agrigento (prov.), Italy 34/D6
Agrigento, Italy 34/D6
Agrihan (isl.), No. Marianas 87/E4
Agrínion, Greece 45/E6
Agropoli, Italy 34/E4
Agryz, Russia 52/H3
Agua Caliente, Ariz. 198/B6
Agua Caliente Ind. Res., Calif. 204/J10
Aguachica, Colombia 126/D3
Aguada, P. Rico 161/A1
Aguada de Pasajeros, Cuba 158/D2
Aguada Grande, Venezuela 124/D2
Aguadas, Colombia 126/C5
Agua de Dios, Colombia 126/C5
Aguadilla (dist.), P. Rico 161/A1
Aguadilla, P. Rico 156/F1
Aguadilla, P. Rico 161/A1
Aguadilla (bay), P. Rico 161/A1
Agua Dulce, Mexico 150/M7
Aguadulce, Panama 154/G6
Agua Dulce, Texas 303/F10
Agua Fria (riv.), Ariz. 198/C5
Agua Fría, Venezuela 124/D2
Agualeguas, Mexico 150/J3
Agua Linda, Venezuela 124/E5
Aguán (riv.), Honduras 154/D3
Aguanaval (riv.), Mexico 150/H4
Aguanish, Québec 174/E2
Aguanus (riv.), Newf. 166/B3
Aguanus (riv.), Québec 174/E2
Agua Prieta, Mexico 150/E1
Aguaray, Argentina 143/D1
Aguarico (riv.), Colombia 126/B7
Aguarico (riv.), Ecuador 128/D3
Aguasay, Venezuela 124/G3
Aguas Blancas, Chile 138/B4
Aguas Buenas, P. Rico 161/E2
Aguas Calientes, Cerro (mt.), Chile 138/C4
Aguascalientes (state), Mexico 150/H6
Aguascalientes, Mexico 150/H6
Aguascalientes, Mexico 146/H7
Aguas Corrientes, Uruguay 145/A6
Agua Vermelha (res.), Brazil 135/B1
Aguaytía (riv.), Peru 128/E7
Agudos, Brazil 135/B3
Agueda, Portugal 33/B2
Agueda (riv.), Spain 33/C2
Aguedaueda (riv.), Portugal 33/C2
Agueraktem (well), Mali 106/C4
Agueraktem (well), Mauritania 106/C4
Aguila, Ariz. 198/B5
Aguilar, Colo. 208/K8
Aguilar, Spain 33/D4
Aguilares, Argentina 143/C2
Aguilas, Spain 33/F4
Aguililla, Mexico 150/H7
Aguja, La (cape), Colombia 126/C2
Aguja (pt.), Peru 2/E6
Aguja (pt.), Peru 120/A3
Aguja (pt.), Peru 128/B5
Agulhas (cape), S. Africa 102/D8
Agulhas (cape), S. Africa 118/B6
Agusan (riv.), Philippines 82/E6
Agusan, Philippines 82/E6
Agusan del Norte (prov.), Philippines 82/E6
Agusan del Sur (prov.), Philippines 82/E6
Agustín Codazzi, Colombia 126/D3
Agutaya, Philippines 82/C5
Agutaya (isl.), Philippines 82/C5
Ahaggar (range), Algeria 102/C2
Ahaggar (range), Algeria 106/F4
Ahangaran, Afghanistan 59/J3
Ahar, Iran 66/E1
Ahascragh, Ireland 17/E5
Ahau, Fiji 87/H7
Ahaura, N. Zealand 100/C5
Ahaus, Germany 22/B2
Aherlow (riv.), Ireland 17/E7
Ah-Gwah-Ching, Minn. 255/D3
Ahipara, N. Zealand 100/D1
Ahlat, Turkey 63/K3
Ahlbeck, Germany 22/F2
Ahlen, Germany 22/B3
Ahmadabad, India 2/N4
Ahmadabad, India 68/C4
Ahmadabad, India 54/J7
Ahmadnagar, India 68/C5
Ahmadpur East, Pakistan 68/C3
Ahmeek, Mich. 250/A1
Ahmic (lake), Ontario 177/E2
Ahoghill, N. Ireland 17/J2
Ahome, Mexico 150/E4
Ahoskie, N.C. 281/P2
Ahousat, Br. Col. 184/D5
Ahrensburg, Germany 22/D2
Ahsahka, Idaho 220/B3
Ahtanum (creek), Wash. 310/D4
Ähtäri, Finland 18/N5
Ahuacatitlán, Mexico 150/L1
Ahuacatlán, Mexico 150/G6
Ahuachapán, El Salvador 154/B4
Ahuás, Honduras 154/E3
Ahumada, Mexico 150/F1
Ahurei, Fr. Poly. 87/M8
Åhus, Sweden 18/J9
Ahuzzam, Israel 65/B4
Ahvaz, Iran 54/F6
Ahvaz, Iran 59/E3
Ahvaz (Ahwaz), Iran 66/F5
Ahvenanmaa (prov.), Finland 18/L6
Ahwahnee, Calif. 204/F6
Ahwar, Yemen 59/E7
Ai-Ais, Namibia 118/B5
Aialik (bay), Alaska 196/C1
Aiama (lake), Brazil 132/H9
Aibonito, P. Rico 161/D2
Aichi (pref.), Japan 81/H6
Aid, Mo. 261/M9
Aid, Ohio 284/F8
Aiea, Hawaii 218/B3
Aigen im Mühlkreis, Austria 41/B2
Aigle (riv.), Québec 172/A3
Aigle, Switzerland 39/C4
Aiguá, Uruguay 145/E5
Aiguá (riv.), Uruguay 145/E4
Aigues-Mortes, France 28/F6
Aiguille d'Argentière (mt.), Switzerland 39/C5
Aihui (Aigun) (Heihe), China 77/L1
Aija, Peru 128/D7
Aikawa, Japan 81/H4
Aiken (co.), S.C. 296/D4
Aiken, S.C. 296/D4
Aikens (lake), Manitoba 179/G3
Aiken West, S.C. 296/D4
Aikin, Md. 245/O2
Aileron, North. Terrs. 93/C7
Ailey, Ga. 217/G6
Ailinglapalap (atoll), Marshall Is. 87/G5
Aillon (lake), Québec 172/C2
Ailsa Craig, Ontario 177/C4
Ailsa Craig (isl.), Scotland 15/C5
Ailuk (atoll), Marshall Is. 87/H4
Aimogasta, Argentina 143/C2
Aimwell, La. 238/G3
Ain (dept.), France 28/F4
Ain (riv.), France 28/F4
Ainabo, Somalia 115/J2
Aina Haina, Hawaii 218/F2
'Ain al Mubarrak, Saudi Arabia 59/C5
Ainaži, Latvia 53/C2
Aïn Beïda, Algeria 106/F1
Aïn ben Tili (well), Mauritania 106/C3
'Ain el 'Arab, Syria 63/H4
Ain-Galakka, Chad 111/C4
Aïn Sefra, Algeria 106/D2
Ainslie (lake), Nova Scotia 168/G2
Ainsworth, Br. Col. 184/J5
Ainsworth, Iowa 229/K6
Ainsworth, Nebr. 264/D2
Aïn Temouchent, Algeria 106/D1
Ain Zueiya (well), Libya 111/D3
Aïoun el Atrous, Mauritania 106/C5
Aïoun el Atrous, Mauritania 102/B3
Aipe, Colombia 126/C6
Aiquile, Bolivia 136/C6
Aiquina, Chile 138/B3
Air (mts.), Niger 106/F5
Airdrie, Alberta 182/C4
Airdrie, Scotland 10/B1
Airdrie, Scotland 15/C2
Aire (riv.), England 10/F4
Aire (riv.), England 13/F4
Aire-sur-l'Adour, France 28/C6
Airey, Md. 245/O6
Air Force (isl.), N.W.T. 187/L3
Air Force Academy, Colo. 208/K5
Airlie, Oreg. 291/D3
Airolo, Switzerland 39/G3
Air Ronge, Sask. 181/M3
Airville, Pa. 294/K6
Airway Heights, Wash. 310/H3
Aisén del General Carlos Ibáñez del Campo (reg.), Chile 138/E6
Aišiškes, Lithuania 53/C3
Aisne (dept.), France 28/E3
Aisne (riv.), France 28/E3
Aitape, Papua N.G. 85/B6
Aith, Scotland 15/G2
Aitkin (co.), Minn. 255/E4
Aitkin, Minn. 255/E4
Aitutaki (atoll), Cook Is. 87/K7
Aiud, Romania 45/F2
Aix, France 7/E4
Aix (mt.), Wash. 310/D4
Aix-en-Provence, France 28/F6
Aix-les-Bains, France 28/G5
Aíyina, Greece 45/F7
Aíyion, Greece 45/F6
Aizpute, Latvia 53/A2
Aizuwakamatsu, Japan 81/J5
Aizwal, India 68/G4
Ajaccio, France 7/E4
Ajaccio, France 28/B7
Ajaccio (gulf), France 28/B7
Ajalpan, Mexico 150/L7
Ajana, W. Australia 92/A5
Ajanta, India 68/D4
Ajax, La. 238/D3
Ajax, Ontario 177/E4
Ajedabia, Libya 111/D1
Aji Chai (riv.), Iran 66/E1
Ajigasawa, Japan 81/J3
'Ajja, West Bank 65/C3
Ajka, Hungary 41/D3
'Ajlun, Jordan 65/D3
'Ajlun (range), Jordan 65/D3
'Ajman, U.A.E. 59/G4
Ajmer, India 68/C3
Ajmer, India 54/J7
Ajo, Ariz. 198/C6
Ajoewa, Suriname 131/C4
Ajoupa-Bouillon, Martinique 161/C5
Akan National Park, Japan 81/M2
Akaroa, N. Zealand 100/D5
Akasha, Sudan 111/F3
Akashi, Japan 81/H8
Akaska, S. Dak. 298/J3
Akbaba Tepesi (mt.), Turkey 63/H3
Akçaabat, Turkey 63/H2
Akçadağ, Turkey 63/G3
Akçakale, Turkey 63/H4
Akçakoca, Turkey 63/D2
Akçay, Turkey 63/C4
Akçay (riv.), Turkey 63/C4
Akdağ (mt.), Turkey 59/A2
Akdağ (mt.), Turkey 63/E4
Akdağ (mt.), Turkey 63/C4
Akdağmadeni, Turkey 63/F3
Akeley, Minn. 255/D3
Akeley, Pa. 294/D2
Aken, Germany 22/D3
Akers, La. 238/N2
Akershus (co.), Norway 18/G6
Aketi, D.R. Congo 102/E4
Aketi, D.R. Congo 115/D3
Akhaltsikhe, Georgia 52/F6
Akhdar, Jebel (mts.), Libya 111/D1
Akhdar, Jebel (range), Oman 59/G5
Akhdar, Saudi Arabia 59/C4
Akhiok, Alaska 196/H3
Akhisar, Turkey 63/B3
Akhmim, Egypt 111/F2
Akhmim, Egypt 59/B4
Akhtopol, Bulgaria 45/H4
Akhtubinsk, Russia 52/G5
Akhty, Russia 52/G6
Akhtyrka, Ukraine 52/E4
Aki, Japan 81/F7
Akiachak, Alaska 196/F2
Akiak, Alaska 196/F2
Akimiski (isl.), N.W.T. 162/H5
Akin, Ill. 222/E6
Akins, Okla. 288/S3
Åkirkeby, Denmark 21/F9
Akita (pref.), Japan 81/J4
Akita, Japan 81/J4
Akita, Japan 54/P6
Akitio, N. Zealand 100/F4
Akjoujt, Mauritania 106/B5
Akkerman (Belgorod-Dnestrovskiy), Ukraine 52/D5
Akkeshi, Japan 81/M2
Akko (Acre), Israel 65/C2
Akkrum, Netherlands 27/H2
Aklan (prov.), Philippines 82/D5
Aklavik, Canada 4/C16
Aklavik, N.W.T. 146/E3
Aklavik, N.W.T. 162/C2
Aklavik, N.W.T. 187/E3
Akobo (riv.), Ethiopia 111/F6
Akobo, Sudan 111/F6
Akobo (riv.), Sudan 111/F6
Akola, India 68/D4
Akolmiut (Kasigluk), Alaska 196/F2
Akpatok (isl.), N.W.T. 162/K3
Akpatok (isl.), N.W.T. 187/M3
Akpazar, Turkey 63/H3
Akpınar, Turkey 63/D5
Akqi, China 77/A3
Akra, N. Dak. 282/P2
Akranes, Iceland 21/B1
Akreïjit, Mauritania 106/C5
Akritas (cape), Greece 45/E7
Akron, Ala. 195/C5
Akron, Colo. 208/N2
Akron, Ind. 227/E2
Akron, Iowa 229/A3
Akron, Mich. 250/F5
Akron, N.Y. 276/C4
Akron, Ohio 188/K2
Akron, Ohio 284/G3
Akron, Ohio 146/K5
Akron, Pa. 294/K5
Aksai Chin (reg.), Pakistan 68/D2
Aksaray, Turkey 63/F3
Aksay, China 77/D4
Aksay, Kazakhstan 48/F4
Akşehir, Turkey 63/D3
Akşehir, Turkey 59/B2
Akşehir (lake), Turkey 63/D3
Akseki, Turkey 63/D4
Aksu, China 54/K5
Aksu (riv.), Turkey 63/D4
Aksum, Ethiopia 102/F3
Aksum, Ethiopia 111/G5
Aksum, Ethiopia 59/C7
Aktas, Kazakhstan 48/G5
Aktash, Russia 48/J4
Aktí (pen.), Greece 45/G5
Aktyubinsk, Kazakhstan 54/G4
Aktyubinsk, Kazakhstan 48/F4
Aku, Nigeria 106/F7
Akun (isl.), Alaska 196/E4
Akune, Japan 81/E7
Akure, Nigeria 106/F7
Akureyri, Ice. 4/C10
Akureyri, Iceland 21/C1
Akureyri, Iceland 7/C2
Akuse, Ghana 106/E7
Akutan, Alaska 196/E4
Akutan (isl.), Alaska 196/E4
Akutan (passage), Alaska 196/E4
Akviran, Turkey 63/E4
Akyab (Sittwe), Burma 72/B2
Akyazı, Turkey 63/D2
Ål, Norway 18/F6
Alabam, Ark. 202/C1
Alabama 188/J4
ALABAMA 195
Alabama (riv.), Ala. 188/J4
Alabama (riv.), Ala. 195/C8
Alabama (state), U.S. 146/K6
Alabaster, Ala. 195/E4
Alabaster, Mich. 250/F4

Alliance 327

Alabat, Philippines 82/D3
Alabat (isl.), Philippines 82/D3
Alaca, Turkey 63/F2
Alacahan, Turkey 63/G3
Alaçam, Turkey 63/F2
Alachua (co.), Fla. 212/D2
Alachua, Fla. 212/D2
Alacrán (reef), Mexico 150/P5
Alacranes, Cuba 158/D1
Aladağ (mt.), Turkey 63/F4
Aladagh, Kuh-e (mts.), Iran 66/K2
Aladagh, Kuh-i- (mt.), Iran 59/G2
Aladdin, Wyo. 319/H1
Alaejos, Spain 33/D2
Alagir, Russia 52/F6
Alagoa Grande, Brazil 132/H4
Alagoas (state), Brazil 132/G5
Alagoinhas, Brazil 120/F4
Alagoinhas, Brazil 132/G6
Alagón, Spain 33/F2
Alagón (riv.), Spain 33/C2
Alah (riv.), Philippines 82/E7
Al Ahqaf (Bahr es Safi) (des.), Saudi Arabia 59/E6
Al 'Ain, Saudi Arabia 59/C4
Alajuela, C. Rica 154/E6
Alakanuk, Alaska 196/E2
Alakol' (lake), Kazakhstan 48/J5
Al 'Ala, Saudi Arabia 59/C4
Alalakeiki (chan.), Hawaii 218/J3
Alalapadu, Suriname 131/C4
Alamagan (isl.), No. Marianas 87/E4
Alamance (co.), N.C. 281/L3
Alamance, N.C. 281/K2
Alameda (co.), Calif. 204/D6
Alameda, Calif. 204/J2
Alameda (creek), Calif. 204/K3
Alameda, N. Mex. 274/C3
Alameda, Sask. 181/J6
Alamikamba, Nicaragua 154/E4
Alamo (lake), Ariz. 198/B4
Alamo (riv.), Calif. 204/K10
Alamo, Ga. 217/G6
Alamo, Ind. 227/C5
Alamo, Mexico 150/L6
Alamo, Nev. 266/F5
Alamo, N. Dak. 282/D2
Alamo, Tenn. 237/C9
Alamo, Texas 303/F11
Ala Moana, Hawaii 218/C4
Alamo-Danville, Calif. 204/K2
Alamogordo, N. Mex. 188/E4
Alamogordo, N. Mex. 274/C6
Alamo Heights, Texas 303/K10
Álamos, Mexico 150/E3
Alamosa (co.), Colo. 208/H7
Alamosa, Colo. 208/H8
Alamosa (creek), Colo. 208/G8
Alamosa (riv.), N. Mex. 274/B5
Alamota, Kansas 232/B3
Åland (Ahvenanmaa) (prov.), Finland 18/L6
Åland (isls.), Finland 7/F2
Åland (isls.), Finland 18/L6
Alanje, Panama 154/F6
Alanreed, Texas 303/D2
Alanson, Mich. 250/E3
Alanthus Grove, Mo. 261/D2
Alanya, Turkey 59/B2
Alanya, Turkey 63/D4
Alaotra (lake), Madagascar 118/H3
Alapaha (riv.), Fla. 212/C1
Alapaha, Ga. 217/F8
Alapaha (riv.), Ga. 217/F7
Alaqua (creek), Fla. 212/C6
Alarcón (res.), Spain 33/E3
Alarka, N.C. 281/C4
Alas (str.), Indonesia 85/F7
Alaşehir, Turkey 63/C3
Alashtar, Iran 66/E4
Alaska (reg.) 4/C17
Alaska 188/C5
ALASKA 196
Alaska (gulf), Alaska 146/D4
Alaska (gulf), Alaska 188/D6
Alaska (gulf), Alaska 196/K3
Alaska (pen.), Alaska 188/C6
Alaska (pen.), Alaska 146/C4
Alaska (pen.), Alaska 196/G3
Alaska (range), Alaska 188/C6
Alaska (range), Alaska 146/C3
Alaska (range), Alaska 196/H2
Alaska, Mich. 250/D6
Alaska (state), U.S. 2/B2
Alaska (state), U.S. 146/C3
Alaska (gulf), U.S. 4/D17
Alaska (pen.), U.S. 4/D18
Alaska (range), U.S. 4/C17
Alaska Highway, Yukon 187/E3
Alassio, Italy 34/A2
Alatna, Alaska 196/H1
Alatna (riv.), Alaska 196/H1
Alatri, Italy 34/D4
Alatyr', Russia 52/G4
Al 'Auda, Saudi Arabia 59/E4
Alausí, Ecuador 128/C4
Alava (prov.), Spain 33/E1
Alava (cape), Wash. 188/A1
Alava (cape), Wash. 310/A2
Alaverdi, Armenia 52/F6
Alavus, Finland 18/N5
Alayor, Spain 33/J3
Al 'Azair, Iraq 66/E5
Alazeya (riv.), Russia 48/Q3
Al 'Aziziya, Iraq 59/E3
Al 'Aziziya, Iraq 66/D4
Alba, Italy 34/B2
Alba, Mich. 250/E4
Alba, Mo. 261/D8
Alba, Pa. 294/J2
Alba, Texas 303/J5
Albacete (prov.), Spain 33/E3
Albacete, Spain 7/D5
Albacete, Spain 33/F3
Alba de Tormes, Spain 33/D2
Albaida, Spain 33/F3
Alba Iulia, Romania 45/F2
Albalate del Arzobispo, Spain 33/F2
Alban, Ontario 177/D1
Albanel, Québec 172/E1
Albanel (lake), Québec 174/C2
Albania 2/K3
Albania 7/G4
ALBANIA 45/E5
Albano (lake), Italy 34/F7
Albano Laziale, Italy 34/F7
Albany, Australia 87/B9
Albany, Calif. 204/J2
Albany, Ga. 146/K6
Albany, Ga. 217/D7
Albany, Ill. 222/C2
Albany, Ind. 227/G4
Albany, Jamaica 158/J6
Albany, Ky. 237/L7
Albany, La. 238/M1
Albany, Minn. 255/D5
Albany, Mo. 261/D2
Albany•, N.H. 268/E4
Albany (cap.), N.Y. 188/M2
Albany (cap.), N.Y. 146/L5
Albany (co.), N.Y. 276/M5
Albany (cap.), N.Y. 276/N5
Albany, N. Zealand 100/B1
Albany, Nova Scotia 168/C4
Albany, Ohio 284/F7
Albany, Okla. 288/O7
Albany (riv.), Ont. 146/K4
Albany (riv.), Ont. 162/H5
Albany (riv.), Ontario 175/C2
Albany, Oreg. 188/B2
Albany, Oreg. 291/D3
Albany, Pr. Edward I. 168/E2
Albany, Texas 303/E5
Albany, Vt. 268/C2
Albany•, Vt. 268/C2
Albany, W. Australia 88/B6
Albany, W. Australia 92/B6
Albany, Wis. 317/G10
Albany (co.), Wyo. 319/G4
Albany, Wyo. 319/F4
Albany Creek, Queensland 88/J2
Albardon, Argentina 143/C3
Albarracín, Spain 33/F2
Albatross (pt.), N. Zealand 100/E3
Albatross (bay), Queensland 88/G2
Albatross (bay), Queensland 95/B2
Albay (prov.), Philippines 82/D4
Albay (gulf), Philippines 82/D4
Albee, S. Dak. 298/S3
Albemarle (pt.), Ecuador 128/B9
Albemarle (sound), N.C. 188/L3
Albemarle, N.C. 281/J4
Albemarle (sound), N.C. 281/S2
Albemarle (co.), Va. 307/L5
Albenga, Italy 34/B3
Albeni Falls (dam), Idaho 220/B1
Alberdi, Paraguay 144/D5
Alberene, Va. 307/L5
Alberga, S. Australia 94/D2
Alberga, The (riv.), S. Australia 94/D2
Alberga, The (riv.), S. Australia 88/E5
Alberhill, Calif. 204/E11
Alberni (inlet), Br. Col. 184/H3
Albers, Ill. 222/D5
Albert (canal), Belgium 27/F6
Albert, France 28/E2
Albert, Kansas 232/C3
Albert (co.), New Bruns. 170/F3
Albert, N. Mex. 274/F3
Albert, N.S. Wales 97/D3
Albert, Okla. 288/K4
Albert (lake), Québec 172/C3
Albert (Mobuto Sese Seko) (lake), Uganda 115/F3
Albert (creek), Wyo. 319/B4
Albert (Mobuto Sese Seko) (lake), D.R. Congo 115/F3
ALBERTA 182
Alberta (prov.) 162/E5
Alberta, Ala. 195/D6
Alberta (mt.), Alberta 182/B3
Alberta (mt.), Alta. 162/E5
Alberta (prov.), Canada 146/G4
Alberta, La. 238/D2
Alberta, Minn. 255/B5
Alberta, Va. 307/N7
Alberta Beach, Alberta 182/C3
Albert City, Iowa 229/C3
Albert Edward (bay), N.W.T. 187/H3
Albert Head, Br. Col. 184/J4
Alberti, Argentina 143/G7
Albertirsa, Hungary 41/E3
Albert Lea, Minn. 255/E7
Albert Mines, New Bruns. 170/F3
Alberton, Mont. 262/B3
Alberton, Pr. Edward I. 168/E2
Alberton, S. Africa 118/H6
Albert Town, Jamaica 158/H6
Albertville, Ala. 195/F2
Albertville, France 28/G5
Albertville, Minn. 255/E5
Albertville, Sask. 181/F2
Albeuve, Switzerland 39/D3
Albi, France 28/E6
Albia, Iowa 229/H6
Albin, Wyo. 319/H4
Albina, Suriname 131/D3
Albino, Italy 34/B2
Albion, Calif. 204/B4
Albion, Idaho 220/E7
Albion (mts.), Idaho 220/E7
Albion, Ill. 222/E5
Albion, Ind. 227/G2
Albion, Iowa 229/H4
Albion•, Maine 243/E6
Albion, Mich. 250/E6
Albion, Nebr. 264/F3
Albion, N.Y. 276/D4
Albion, Okla. 288/R5
Albion, Pa. 294/B2
Albion, R.I. 249/H5
Albion, Wash. 310/H4
Albion, Wis. 317/H10
Al Birk, Saudi Arabia 59/D6
Albocácer, Spain 33/F2
Alborán (isl.), Spain 7/D5
Alborán (isl.), Spain 33/E5
Ålborg, Denmark 7/F3
Ålborg, Denmark 18/G8
Ålborg,Ålborg (bay), Denmark 21/D4
Alborn, Minn. 255/F4
Albox, Spain 33/E4
Albreda, Br. Col. 184/H4
Albright, W. Va. 312/G3
Albrightsville, Pa. 294/L3
Albristhorn (mt.), Switzerland 39/D4
Albstadt, Germany 22/C4
Albufeira, Portugal 33/B4
Albuñol, Spain 33/E4
Albuquerque (cays), Colombia 126/A10
Albuquerque, N. Mex. 146/H6
Albuquerque, N. Mex. 188/E3
Albuquerque, N. Mex. 274/C3
Alburg, Vt. 268/A2
Alburg•, Vt. 268/A2
Alburnett, Iowa 229/K4
Alburquerque, Spain 33/C3
Alburtis, Pa. 294/L5
Albury, Australia 87/E9
Albury, N. S. Wales 88/H7
Albury, N.S. Wales 97/D5
Albury, N. Zealand 100/C6
Alca, Peru 128/F10
Alcácer do Sal, Portugal 33/B3
Alcalá, Bolivia 136/C6
Alcalá de Chivert, Spain 33/G2
Alcalá de Guadaira, Spain 33/D4
Alcalá de Henares, Spain 33/G4
Alcalá de los Gazules, Spain 33/D4
Alcalá la Real, Spain 33/E4
Alcalde, N. Mex. 274/C2
Alcamo, Italy 34/D6
Alcanar, Spain 33/G2
Alcañices, Spain 33/C2
Alcañiz, Spain 33/F2
Alcàntara, Portugal 33/A1
Alcántara, Spain 33/C3
Alcántara (res.), Spain 33/C3
Alcántaratara (res.), Portugal 33/C3
Alcantarilla, Spain 33/F4
Alcaraz, Argentina 143/G5
Alcaraz, Spain 33/E3
Alcaraz, Sierra de (range), Spain 33/E3
Alcatraz (isl.), Calif. 204/J2
Alcaudete, Spain 33/E4
Alcázar de San Juan, Spain 33/E3
Alcester, S. Dak. 298/R7
Alcida, New Bruns. 170/E1
Alcira, Spain 33/F3
Alco, Ark. 202/F2
Alco, La. 238/D4
Alcoa, Tenn. 237/N9
Alcobaça, Brazil 132/G7
Alcobaça, Portugal 33/B3
Alcolu, S.C. 296/G4
Alcomdale, Alberta 182/C3
Alcona (co.), Mich. 250/F4
Alcona Beach, Ontario 177/E3
Alcones, Chile 138/F5
Alcony, Ohio 284/B5
Alcora, Spain 33/F2
Alcorisa, Spain 33/F2
Alcorn, Ky. 237/O5
Alcorn (co.), Miss. 256/G1
Alcorn State University, Miss. 256/B7
Alcorta, Argentina 143/F6
Alcoutim, Portugal 33/C4
Alcova, Wyo. 319/F3
Alcova (res.), Wyo. 319/F3
Alcoy, Spain 33/F3
Alcudia (bay), Spain 33/H3
Alda, Nebr. 264/F4
Aldabra (isls.), Seychelles 102/G5
Aldabra (isls.), Seychelles 118/H1
Aldama, Chihuahua, Mexico 150/G2
Aldama, Tamaulipas, Mexico 150/L5
Aldan, Pa. 294/M7
Aldan, Russia 48/N4
Aldan, Russia 54/O4
Aldan (plat.), Russia 48/N4
Aldan (riv.), Russia 48/O3
Aldan (riv.), Russia 54/P3
Aldeburgh, England 13/J5
Aldeburgh, England 10/G4
Aldeia Carajá, Brazil 132/D6
Aldeia Nova de São Bento, Portugal 33/C4
Alden, Ill. 222/E1
Alden, Iowa 229/G4
Alden, Kansas 232/D3
Alden, Mich. 250/D4
Alden, Minn. 255/E7
Alden, N.Y. 276/C5
Alden Bridge, La. 238/C1
Aldenville, Pa. 294/M2
Alder, Mont. 262/D5
Alder, Wash. 310/C4
Alder (lake), Wash. 310/C4
Alder Creek, N.Y. 276/K4
Alder Flats, Alberta 182/C3
Alderley, Wis. 317/J1
Alderney (isl.), Chan. Is. 10/E6
Alderney (isl.), Chan. Is. 13/E8
Alderpoint, Calif. 204/B3
Alder Point, Nova Scotia 168/H2
Aldershot, England 10/F5
Aldershot, England 13/G8
Aldershot, Nova Scotia 168/D3
Alderson, Okla. 288/P5
Alderson, W. Va. 312/E7
Aldersyde, Alberta 182/C4
Aldine, Ind. 227/D2
Aldora, Ga. 217/D4
Aldouane, New Bruns. 170/E2
Aldrich, Ala. 195/E4
Aldrich, Minn. 255/C4
Aldrich, Mo. 261/F7
Aldridge Brownhills, England 10/G3
Aldridge Brownhills, England 13/E5
Aledo, Ill. 222/C2
Aledo, Texas 303/E2
Aleg, Mauritania 106/B5
Alegre, Brazil 135/F2
Alegre, Brazil 132/F8
Alegrete, Brazil 132/B10
Alegrete, Brazil 120/D5
'Aleih, Lebanon 63/F6
Alejandra, Argentina 143/F5
Alejandría, Bolivia 136/C3
Alejandro Selkirk (isl.), Chile 120/A6
Aleknagik, Alaska 196/G3
Aleksandriya, Ukraine 52/D5
Aleksandrov Gay, Russia 52/G4
Aleksandrovsk, Russia 52/J3
Aleksandrovsk-Sakhalinskiy, Russia 48/P5
Aleksandrovsk-Sakhalinsky, Russia 54/R4
Aleksandrów Kujawski, Poland 47/D2
Aleksandrów Łodzki, Poland 47/D3
Alekseyevka, Kazakhstan 48/H4
Alekseyevka, Russia 52/E4
Aleksin, Russia 52/E4
Aleksinac, Yugoslavia 45/E4
Além Paraíba, Brazil 135/E2
Alençon, France 28/D3
Alenquer, Brazil 132/C3
Alenquer, Brazil 120/D3
Alenuihaha (chan.), Hawaii 218/E7
Aleppo (prov.), Syria 63/G4
Aleppo, Syria 54/E6
Aleppo, Syria 59/C2
Aleppo, Syria 63/G4
Aléria, France 28/B6
Alert, Canada 4/A12
Alert, Ind. 227/F6
Alert, N.C. 281/N2
Alert, N.W.T. 162/N3
Alert, N.W.T. 187/M1
Alert (pt.), N.W.T. 187/K1
Alert Bay, Br. Col. 184/D5
Alès, France 28/E5
Alessandria (prov.), Italy 34/B2
Alessandria, Italy 34/B2
Ålestrup, Denmark 21/C4
Ålesund, Norway 7/E2
Ålesund, Norway 18/D5
Aletschhorn (mt.), Switzerland 39/F4
Aleutian (isls.), Alaska 188/D6
Aleutian (isls.), Alaska 196/J4
Aleutian (range), Alaska 196/G3
Aleutian (isls.), U.S. 4/D18
Aleutian (isls.), U.S. 2/A3
Alex, Okla. 288/L5
Alexander (arch.), Alaska 146/E4
Alexander (arch.), Alaska 196/L1
Alexander (isl.), Ant. 5/B15
Alexander, Ark. 202/F4
Alexander (lake), Conn. 210/H1
Alexander, Ga. 217/J4
Alexander (co.), Ill. 222/D6
Alexander, Ill. 222/D4
Alexander, Iowa 229/G3
Alexander, Kansas 232/C3
Alexander•, Maine 243/H5
Alexander, Manitoba 179/B5
Alexander, N.Y. 276/D5
Alexander (co.), N.C. 281/G3
Alexander, N. Dak. 282/C4
Alexander (cape), Solomon Is. 86/D2
Alexander (arch.), U.S. 4/D16
Alexander, W. Va. 312/F5
Alexander Bay, S. Africa 102/D7
Alexander Bay, S. Africa 118/B5
Alexander City, Ala. 195/G5
Alexander Mills, N.C. 281/F4
Alexandra, N. Zealand 100/B6
Alexandra, S. Africa 118/H6
Alexandra, Victoria 97/C5
Alexandra Land (isl.), Russia 4/A8
Alexandra Land (isl.), Russia 48/E1
Alexandretta (İskenderun), Turkey 63/G4
Alexandretta (gulf), Turkey 63/F4
Alexandria, Ala. 195/G3
Alexandria, Br. Col. 184/F4
Alexandria, Egypt 2/L4
Alexandria, Egypt 102/E1
Alexandria, Egypt 59/A3
Alexandria, Egypt 111/J2
Alexandria, Ind. 227/F4
Alexandria, Jamaica 158/J6
Alexandria, Ky. 237/N3
Alexandria, La. 146/J6
Alexandria, La. 188/H4
Alexandria, La. 238/E4
Alexandria, Minn. 255/C5
Alexandria, Mo. 261/K2
Alexandria, Nebr. 264/G4
Alexandria•, N.H. 268/D4
Alexandria, North. Terr. 93/E5
Alexandria, Ohio 284/E5
Alexandria, Ontario 177/K2
Alexandria, Pa. 294/F4
Alexandria, Romania 45/G3
Alexandria, Scotland 15/A1
Alexandria, Scotland 10/A1
Alexandria, S. Dak. 298/O6
Alexandria, Tenn. 237/J8
Alexandria, Va. 188/L3
Alexandria (I.C.), Va. 307/S3
Alexandria Bay, N.Y. 276/J2
Alexandrina (lake), S. Australia 94/F6
Alexandroúpolis, Greece 45/H5
Alexis, Ill. 222/C2
Alexis (riv.), Newf. 166/C3
Alexis Creek, Br. Col. 184/F4
Aleysk, Russia 48/J4
Aleza Lake, Br. Col. 184/G3
Alfalfa (co.), Okla. 288/K1
Alfalfa, Okla. 288/J4
Al Falluja, Iraq 59/D3
Al Falluja, Iraq 66/C4
Alfaro, Spain 33/F1
Alfatar, Bulgaria 45/H4
Al Fatha, Iraq 59/D2
Al Fatha, Iraq 66/C3
Alfeld, Germany 22/C2
Alfenas, Brazil 135/D2
Alférez (riv.), Uruguay 145/E5
Alford, England 13/H4
Alford, Fla. 212/D6
Alford•, Mass. 249/A4
Alford, Scotland 15/F3
Alford, Scotland 10/E2
Alfordsville, Ind. 227/C7
Alfred, Maine 243/B9
Alfred•, Maine 243/B9
Alfred, N.Y. 276/E6
Alfred, N. Dak. 282/N6
Alfred, Ontario 177/K2
Alfredton, N. Zealand 100/F4
Alfreton, England 13/F4
Alga, Kazakhstan 48/F5
Algård, Norway 18/D7
Algarrobo, Chile 138/F3
Algarrobo (pt.), P. Rico 161/A2
Algarrobo del Águila, Argentina 143/C4
Algeciras, Colombia 126/C6
Algeciras, Spain 33/D4
Algemesí, Spain 33/F3
Alger (co.), Mich. 250/C2
Alger, Mich. 250/E4
Alger, Ohio 284/C4
Algeria 2/J4
Algeria 102/C2
ALGERIA 106/D3
Algés, Portugal 33/A1
Algete, Spain 33/G4
Alghero, Italy 34/B4
Algiers (cap.), Algeria 102/C1
Algiers (cap.), Algeria 106/E1
Algiers (cap.), Algeria 2/K4
Algiers, Ind. 227/C7
Algoa, Ark. 202/H3
Algoa (bay), S. Africa 118/D6
Algoa, Texas 303/K3
Algodones, N. Mex. 274/C3
Algoma, Miss. 256/G2
Algoma (terr. dist.), Ontario 177/J5
Algoma (terr. dist.), Ontario 175/D3
Algoma, Oreg. 291/F5
Algoma, W. Va. 312/D8
Algoma, Wis. 317/M6
Algoma Mills, Ontario 177/B1
Algona, Iowa 229/E2
Algona, Wash. 310/C3
Algonac, Mich. 250/G6
Algonquin, Ill. 222/E1
Algonquin (peak), N.Y. 276/M2
Algonquin Park, Ontario 177/F2
Algonquin Prov. Park, Ontario 177/F2
Algonquin Prov. Park, Ontario 175/E3
Algood, Tenn. 237/K8
Algorta, Uruguay 145/B3
Algrove, Sask. 181/H3
Alhama de Granada, Spain 33/E4
Alhama de Murcia, Spain 33/F4
Alhambra, Alberta 182/C3
Alhambra, Calif. 204/C10
Alhambra, Ill. 222/D5
Al Hawtiah, Yemen 59/E6
Al Hilla, Saudi Arabia 59/E5
Al Hoceima, Morocco 106/D1
Alhos Vedros, Portugal 33/B3
Alhué, Estero de (riv.), Chile 138/F4
Alia, Spain 33/D3
'Aliabad, Kuh-e (mt.), Iran 59/F3
'Aliabad, Kuh-e (mt.), Iran 66/G3
Aliağa, Turkey 63/B3
Alibag, India 68/C5
Alibates Flint Quarries Nat'l Mon., Texas 303/C2
Ali-Bayramly, Azerbaijan 52/G7
Alibeyköyü, Turkey 63/D6
Alicante (prov.), Spain 33/F3
Alicante, Spain 33/F3
Alicante, Spain 7/D5
Alice (lake), Nebr. 264/A2
Alice, N. Dak. 282/P6
Alice (lake), N. Dak. 282/M3
Alice, Ontario 177/G2
Alice (chan.), Philippines 82/B8
Alice (riv.), Queensland 95/C4
Alice, Texas 303/F10
Alice Arm, Br. Col. 184/C2
Alicel, Oreg. 291/J2
Alice Springs, Australia 87/D8
Alice Springs, North. Terr. 88/E4
Alice Springs, North. Terr. 93/D7
Aliceville, Ala. 195/B4
Aliceville (dam), Ala. 195/B4
Aliceville, Kansas 232/G3
Alicia, Ark. 202/H2
Alicia (bank), Colombia 126/B8
Alicudi (isl.), Italy 34/E5
Alida, Minn. 255/C3
Alida, Sask. 181/K6
Aligarh, India 68/D3
'Ali Gharbi, Iraq 66/E4
Alijó, Portugal 33/C2
Alima (riv.), Congo 115/B4
Alimodian, Philippines 82/D5
Alindao, Cent. Afr. Rep. 115/D2
Aline, Ga. 217/H6
Aline, Okla. 288/K1
Alingly, Sask. 181/E2
Alingsås, Sweden 18/H7
Alipore, India 68/F2
Aliquippa, Pa. 294/B4
Ali Sabieh, Djibouti 111/H5
'Ali Sharqi, Iraq 66/E4
Aliskerovo, Russia 48/R3
Alivérion, Greece 45/G6
Aliwal North, S. Africa 118/D6
Alix, Alberta 182/D3
Alix, Ark. 202/C3
Aljezur, Portugal 33/B4
Aljojuca, Mexico 150/O1
Aljustrel, Portugal 33/B4
Alkabo, N. Dak. 282/C2
Alkali (lakes), Calif. 204/E2
Alkali (lake), Nev. 266/B1
Alkali (lakes), N. Dak. 282/L3
Alkali Lake, Br. Col. 184/F4
Alkaline (lake), N. Dak. 282/L6
Alken, Belgium 27/G7
Alkmaar, Netherlands 27/F3
Alkmaardermeer (lake), Netherlands 27/F3
Alkol, W. Va. 312/C6
Al Kufa, Iraq 66/D4
Al Kumait, Iraq 66/E4
Al Kuwait (cap.), Kuwait 59/E4
Al Kuwait (cap.), Kuwait 54/F7
Allagash•, Maine 243/F1
Allagash (lake), Maine 243/D3
Allagash (riv.), Maine 243/E2
Allahabad, India 68/E3
Allahabad, India 54/K7
Allaine (riv.), Switzerland 39/D2
Allaire, N.J. 273/E3
Allakaket, Alaska 196/H1
Allakh-Yun', Russia 48/O3
Allamakee (co.), Iowa 229/L2
Allaman, Switzerland 39/B4
All American (canal), Calif. 204/K11
Allamoore, Texas 303/C11
Allamuchy, N.J. 273/D2
Allan (mt.), Idaho 220/D4
Allan, Sask. 181/E4
Allan (hills), Sask. 181/E4
Allanmyo, Burma 72/B3
Allanwater, Ontario 175/C2
Allanwater, Ontario 177/G4
'Allaqi, Wadi (dry riv.), Egypt 111/F3
Allard (lake), Québec 174/E2
Allardt, Tenn. 237/M8
Allardville, New Bruns. 170/E1
Allariz, Spain 33/C1
Allatoona (lake), Ga. 217/C2
Alle, Switzerland 39/D2
Alleene, Ark. 202/B6
Allegan (co.), Mich. 250/D6
Allegan, Mich. 250/D6
Allegany (co.), Md. 245/C2
Allegany (co.), N.Y. 276/D6
Allegany, N.Y. 276/C6
Allegany, Oreg. 291/D4
Allegany Ind. Res., N.Y. 276/C6
Alleghany, Calif. 204/E4
Alleghany (co.), N.C. 281/G1
Alleghany (co.), Va. 307/H5
Alleghany, Va. 307/H5
Allegheny (res.), N.Y. 276/C7
Allegheny (riv.), N.Y. 276/C6
Allegheny (co.), Pa. 294/B5
Allegheny (res.), Pa. 294/E2
Allegheny (riv.), Pa. 294/D2
Allegheny (mts.), Va. 307/H5
Allegheny Front (mts.), Md. 245/C2
Allegheny Front (mts.), Pa. 294/E5
Allègre (pt.), Guadeloupe 161/A6
Allegre, Ky. 237/G7
Alleman, Iowa 229/F5
Allemands (lake), La. 238/M4
Allen, Ala. 195/C7
Allen, Argentina 143/C4
Allen (co.), Ind. 227/G2
Allen, Lough (lake), Ireland 10/C3
Allen (lake), Ireland 17/E3
Allen, Bog of (marsh), Ireland 17/H5
Allen (co.), Kansas 232/G4
Allen, Kansas 232/F3
Allen (co.), Ky. 237/J7
Allen, Ky. 237/R5
Allen (par.), La. 238/E5
Allen, La. 238/D3
Allen, Md. 245/R7
Allen, Mich. 250/E7
Allen, Miss. 256/C7
Allen (mt.), Mont. 262/C2
Allen, Nebr. 264/H2
Allen (co.), Ohio 284/B4
Allen, Okla. 288/O5
Allen, Pa. 294/H5
Allen, S. Dak. 298/F7
Allen, Texas 303/H1
Allendale, England 13/E3
Allendale, Ill. 222/F5
Allendale, Mo. 261/D2
Allendale, N.J. 273/B1
Allendale (co.), S.C. 296/E6
Allendale, S.C. 296/E5
Allende, Coahuila, Mexico 150/J2
Allende, Nuevo León, Mexico 150/J4
Allendorf, Iowa 229/B2
Allenford, Ontario 177/C3
Allenhurst, Ga. 217/J7
Allenhurst, N.J. 273/F3
Allen Park, Mich. 250/B7
Allens Mills, Maine 243/C6
Allenspark, Colo. 208/J2
Allen Springs, Ky. 237/J7
Allenstein (Olsztyn), Poland 47/E2
Allenstown•, N.H. 268/E5
Allensville, Ky. 237/G7
Allensville, Ohio 284/E7
Allensville, Pa. 294/G4
Allenton, Mo. 261/M4
Allenton, R.I. 249/H6
Allenton, Wis. 317/K9
Allentown, Ga. 217/F5
Allentown, N.J. 273/D3
Allentown, N.Y. 276/E6
Allentown, Ohio 284/B4
Allentown, Pa. 188/L2
Allentown, Pa. 294/L4
Allentsteig, Austria 41/C2
Allenville, Ill. 222/E4
Allenville, Mo. 261/N8
Allenwood, N.J. 273/E3
Allenwood, Pa. 294/H3
Alleppey-Cochin, India 68/D7
Aller (riv.), Germany 22/C2
Allerton, Ill. 222/F4
Allerton, Iowa 229/G7
Allerton, Mass. 249/E7
Allerton (pt.), Mass. 249/E7
Alley, Jamaica 158/J7
Alley Spring, Mo. 261/J8
Allgäu (reg.), Germany 22/D5
Allgäu Alps (mts.), Austria 41/A3
Allgood, Ala. 195/F3
Alliance, Alberta 182/E3
Alliance, Nebr. 264/A2
Alliance, N.C. 281/R4
Alliance, Ohio 284/H4

332 Athelstan

Athelstan, Québec 172/C4
Athelstane, Wis. 317/K5
Athena, Oreg. 291/J2
Athenry, Ireland 17/D5
Athens, Ala. 195/E1
Athens, Ark. 202/C5
Athens, Ga. 188/K4
Athens, Ga. 217/F3
Athens (cap.), Greece 7/G5
Athens (cap.), Greece 45/F7
Athens (cap.), Greece 2/K4
Athens, Greater, Greece 45/F7
Athens, Ill. 222/D4
Athens, Ind. 227/E2
Athens, La. 238/E1
Athens, Maine 243/D6
Athens•, Maine 243/D6
Athens, Mich. 250/D6
Athens, N.Y. 276/N6
Athens (co.), Ohio 284/F7
Athens, Ohio 284/F7
Athens, Ontario 177/J3
Athens, Pa. 294/K2
Athens, Tenn. 237/M10
Athens, Texas 303/J5
Athens, W. Va. 312/E8
Athens, Wis. 317/G5
Athensville, Ill. 222/C4
Atherley, Ontario 177/E3
Atherton, Calif. 204/K3
Atherton, Mo. 261/R5
Atherton, Queensland 95/C3
Atherton, Queensland 88/G3
Athertonville, Ky. 237/K5
Athleague, Ireland 17/E4
Athlone, Ireland 10/C4
Athlone, Ireland 17/F5
Athok, Burma 72/B3
Athol, Idaho 220/B2
Athol, Kansas 232/D2
Athol, Mass. 249/F2
Athol•, Mass. 249/F2
Athol, N.Y. 276/N4
Athol, N. Zealand 100/B6
Athol, Nova Scotia 168/D3
Athol (dist.), Scotland 15/D4
Athol, S. Dak. 298/M3
Atholville, New Bruns. 170/D1
Áthos (mt.), Greece 45/G5
Athy, Ireland 17/H6
Athy, Ireland 10/C4
Ati, Chad 111/C5
Ati, Chad 102/D3
Atibaia, Brazil 135/C3
Atico, Peru 128/F11
Atienza, Spain 33/E2
Atikameg, Alberta 182/C2
Atikokan, Ont. 162/G6
Atikokan, Ontario 177/G5
Atikokan, Ontario 175/B3
Atikonak (lake), Newf. 166/B3
Atim (lake), Manitoba 179/C2
Atiquizaya, El Salvador 154/C3
Atitlán (lake), Guatemala 154/B3
Atitlán (vol.), Guatemala 154/B3
Atiu (isl.), Cook Is. 87/L8
Atka, Alaska 196/D4
Atka, Alaska 188/D6
Atka (isl.), Alaska 196/L4
Atka, Russia 48/Q3
Atkarsk, Russia 52/G4
Atkins, Ark. 202/E3
Atkins, Iowa 229/K4
Atkins, Va. 307/F7
Atkinson (co.), Ga. 217/G8
Atkinson, Ga. 217/J8
Atkinson, Ill. 222/C2
Atkinson•, Maine 243/E5
Atkinson, Minn. 255/F4
Atkinson, Nebr. 264/E2
Atkinson•, N.H. 268/E6
Atkinson, N.C. 281/N5
Atkinson (pt.), N.W.T. 187/E2
Atlanta, Ark. 202/D7
Atlanta, C. Rica 154/F6
Atlanta (cap.), Ga. 188/K4
Atlanta (cap.), Ga. 146/K6
Atlanta (cap.), Ga. 217/K1
Atlanta, Idaho 220/C6
Atlanta, Ill. 222/D3
Atlanta, Ind. 227/E4
Atlanta, Kansas 232/F4
Atlanta, La. 238/E3
Atlanta, Mich. 250/E3
Atlanta, Mo. 261/H3
Atlanta, Nebr. 264/E4
Atlanta, N.Y. 276/F5
Atlanta, Ohio 284/D6
Atlanta, Texas 303/K4
Atlanta, U.S. 2/E4
Atlanta Nav. Air Sta., Ga. 217/J1
Atlantic (ocean) 102/B5
Atlantic (ocean) 146/M6
Atlantic, Iowa 229/D6
Atlantic, Maine 243/G7
Atlantic (co.), N.J. 273/D5
Atlantic, N.C. 281/S5
Atlantic, Pa. 294/B3
Atlantic (peak), Wyo. 319/D3
Atlantic Beach, Fla. 212/E1
Atlantic Beach, N.Y. 276/P7
Atlantic Beach, N.C. 281/R5
Atlantic Beach, S.C. 296/K4
Atlantic City, N.J. 188/M3
Atlantic City, N.J. 273/E5
Atlantic City, Wyo. 319/D3
Atlantic Highlands, N.J. 273/F3
Atlantic Highlands (ridge), N.J. 273/E3
Atlantic Mine, Mich. 250/G1
Atlántico (dept.), Colombia 126/C2
Atlantic Ocean 4/D11
Atlantic Ocean 7/C4
Atlantic Ocean 13/A7
Atlantic Ocean 15/B2
Atlantic Ocean 33/A3
Atlántida, Uruguay 145/B6
Atlas (mts.) 102/B1
Atlas (mts.), Algeria 106/E2
Atlas (mts.), Morocco 106/C2
Atlas, Pa. 294/K4
Atlas, Wis. 317/A4
Atlin, Br. Col. 184/J1
Atlin (lake), Br. Col. 184/J1
Atlit, Israel 65/B2
Atlixco, Mexico 150/M2
Atmore, Ala. 195/C8
Atmore, Alberta 182/D2
Atnarko, Br. Col. 184/E4
Atocha, Bolivia 136/B7
Atoka (co.), Okla. 288/O6
Atoka, Okla. 288/O6
Atoka (res.), Okla. 288/P5
Atoka, Tenn. 237/B10
Atomic City, Idaho 220/F6
Atotonilco el Alto, Mexico 150/H6
Atoui, Wadi (dry riv.), Mauritania 106/B4
Atoui, Wadi (dry riv.), Western Sahara 106/B4
Atoyac (riv.), Mexico 150/N2
Atoyac (riv.), Mexico 150/Q2
Atoyac de Álvarez, Mexico 150/J8
Atrak (Atrek) (riv.), Iran 66/J2
Atrato (riv.), Colombia 126/B4
Atrek (riv.), Iran 59/G2
Atrek (Atrak) (riv.), Iran 66/J2
Atrek (riv.), Turkmenistan 48/F6
Atri, Italy 34/D3
Atsugi, Japan 81/O2
Atsumi (bay), Japan 81/H6
Attachie, Br. Col. 184/G2
Attala (co.), Miss. 256/E4
Attalens, Switzerland 39/C3
Attalla, Ala. 195/F2
Attapu, Laos 72/E4
Attapulgus, Ga. 217/D9
Attawapiskat (riv.), Ont. 146/K4
Attawapiskat (riv.), Ont. 162/H5
Attawapiskat, Ontario 175/D2
Attawapiskat (lake), Ontario 175/C2
Attawapiskat (riv.), Ontario 175/C2
Attawaugan, Conn. 210/H1
Atteam (pond), Maine 243/C4
Attebubu, Ghana 106/D7
Atterberry, Ill. 222/D3
Atter See (lake), Austria 41/B3
Attert, Belgium 27/H9
Attica, Ind. 227/C4
Attica, Iowa 229/G6
Attica, Kansas 232/D4
Attica, Mich. 250/F5
Attica, N.Y. 276/D5
Attica, Ohio 284/E3
Attikamagen (lake), Newf. 166/A3
'Attil, West Bank 65/C3
Attleboro, Mass. 249/J5
Attleboro Falls, Mass. 249/J5
Attleborough, England 13/H5
Attnang-Puchheim, Austria 41/B2
Attock, Pakistan 68/C2
Attu (isl.), Alaska 188/D6
Attu (isl.), Alaska 196/J3
Attu (isl.), U.S. 4/D1
Attunga, N.S. Wales 97/F2
Atuel (riv.), Argentina 143/C4
Atuntaqui, Ecuador 128/C2
Atuona, Fr. Poly. 87/M7
Atura, Uganda 115/F3
Atushi (Artux), China 77/A4
Åtvidaberg, Sweden 18/K7
Atwater, Calif. 204/E6
Atwater, Minn. 255/D5
Atwater, Ohio 284/H3
Atwater, Sask. 181/J5
Atwood (Samana) (cay), Bahamas 156/D2
Atwood, Colo. 208/N1
Atwood, Ill. 222/E4
Atwood, Ind. 227/F2
Atwood, Kansas 232/B2
Atwood, Mich. 250/D3
Atwood (lake), Ohio 284/H4
Atwood, Okla. 288/O5
Atwood, Ontario 177/D4
Atwood, Pa. 294/D4
Atwood, Tenn. 237/D9
Atwoodville, Conn. 210/G1
Atyrá, Paraguay 144/B4
Au, Switzerland 39/J2
Auasbila, Honduras 154/E3
Auau (chan.), Hawaii 218/H2
Aubá, Indonesia 85/H7
Aubagne, France 28/F6
Aubange, Belgium 27/H9
Aube (dept.), France 28/E3
Aube (riv.), France 28/F3
Aubenas, France 28/F5
Auberry, Calif. 204/F6
Aubervilliers, France 28/B1
Aubigny, Manitoba 179/E5
Aubonne, Switzerland 39/B4
Aubrey (cliffs), Ariz. 198/B3
Aubrey, Ark. 202/J4
Auburn, Ala. 195/H5
Auburn, Calif. 204/C8
Auburn, Ga. 217/E2
Auburn, Ill. 222/D4
Auburn, Ind. 227/G2
Auburn (mt.), Ind. 227/G5
Auburn, Iowa 229/D4
Auburn, Kansas 232/G3
Auburn, Ky. 237/H7
Auburn, Maine 243/C7
Auburn, Maine 188/M2
Auburn•, Mass. 249/G4
Auburn, Mich. 250/F5
Auburn, Miss. 256/C8
Auburn, Nebr. 264/J4
Auburn•, N.H. 268/E5
Auburn, N.S. Wales 88/K4
Auburn, N.S. Wales 97/J3
Auburn, N.Y. 188/L2
Auburn, N.Y. 276/G5
Auburn, N. Dak. 282/R2
Auburn, Nova Scotia 168/D3
Auburn, Ontario 177/C4
Auburn, Pa. 294/K4
Auburn, Wash. 310/C3
Auburn, W. Va. 312/E4
Auburn, Wyo. 319/A3
Auburndale, Fla. 212/E3
Auburndale, Mass. 249/B7
Auburndale, Wis. 317/F6
Auburn Heights, Mich. 250/F6
Auburntown, Tenn. 237/J9
Aubusson, France 28/E4
Aucanquilcha, Cerro (mt.), Chile 138/B3
Auce, Latvia 53/B2
Auch, France 28/D6
Auchenblae, Scotland 15/F4
Auchencairn, Scotland 15/E6
Auchinleck, Scotland 15/D5
Auchterarder, Scotland 10/D2
Auchterarder, Scotland 15/E4
Auchtermuchty, Scotland 15/E4
Aucilla, Fla. 212/C1
Aucilla (riv.), Fla. 212/C1
Auckland (isls.), N. Zealand 2/S8
Auckland, N. Zealand 2/T7
Auckland, N. Zealand 100/B1
Auckland, N. Zealand 87/B1
Auclair, Québec 172/J2
Aude (dept.), France 28/E6
Audegle, Somalia 115/J3
Auden, Ontario 177/H4
Auden, Ontario 175/C2
Audenarde (Oudenaarde), Belgium 27/D7
Auderghem, Belgium 27/C9
Audet, Québec 172/G4
Audincourt, France 28/G4
Audrain (co.), Mo. 261/J4
Audubon (co.), Iowa 229/D5
Audubon, Iowa 229/D5
Audubon, Minn. 255/C4
Audubon, N.J. 273/B3
Audubon (lake), N. Dak. 282/H4
Audubon Park, Ky. 237/J2
Audubon Park, N.J. 273/B3
Aue, Germany 22/E3
Auerbach, Germany 22/E3
Augathella, Queensland 95/C5
Augathella, Queensland 88/H5
Auger (falls), Idaho 220/D7
Augher, N. Ireland 17/G3
Aughnacloy, N. Ireland 17/H3
Aughrabies (falls), S. Africa 118/B5
Aughrim, Ireland 17/J6
Auglaize (co.), Ohio 284/B4
Auglaize (riv.), Ohio 284/B4
Au Gres, Mich. 250/F4
Augsburg, Germany 7/E4
Augsburg, Germany 22/D4
Augusta, Ark. 202/H3
Augusta (cape), Colombia 126/C2
Augusta, Ga. 188/K4
Augusta, Ga. 146/K6
Augusta, Ga. 217/J4
Augusta, Ill. 222/C3
Augusta, Ind. 227/C8
Augusta, Iowa 229/L7
Augusta, Italy 34/E6
Augusta, Kansas 232/F4
Augusta, Ky. 237/N3
Augusta (cap.), Maine 146/M5
Augusta (cap.), Maine 243/D7
Augusta (cap.), Maine 188/N2
Augusta, Mich. 250/D6
Augusta, Mo. 261/L5
Augusta, Mont. 262/D3
Augusta, N.J. 273/D1
Augusta, Ohio 284/J4
Augusta (co.), Va. 307/K4
Augusta, W. Australia 92/A6
Augusta, W. Va. 312/J4
Augusta, Wis. 317/D6
Augusta Springs, Va. 307/K4
Augustenborg, Denmark 21/D8
Augustine (isl.), Alaska 196/H3
Augustów, Poland 47/F2
Augustus (isl.), W. Australia 92/D1
Augustus (mt.), W. Australia 92/B4
Aujila, Libya 102/E2
Aujila, Libya 111/D2
Auki, Solomon Is. 86/E3
Auki, Solomon Is. 87/G6
Aulac, New Bruns. 170/F3
Aulander, N.C. 281/P2
Auld (lake), W. Australia 88/C4
Auldearn, Scotland 15/E3
Aulencia (riv.), Spain 33/F4
Aullville, Mo. 261/E4
Aulnay-sous-Bois, France 28/B1
Ault, Colo. 208/K1
Ault (peak), Switzerland 39/H3
Aultbea, Scotland 15/C3
Aultman, Pa. 294/D4
Aumsville, Oreg. 291/E3
Auning, Denmark 21/D5
Aunis (trad. prov.), France 29
Aur, Pulau (isl.), Malaysia 72/E7
Aura, Mich. 250/A2
Aura, N.J. 273/C4
Aurangabad, Bihar, India 68/E4
Aurangabad, Maharashtra, India 68/D5
Auraria, Ga. 217/E1
Auray, France 28/B4
Aurelia, Iowa 229/C3
Aurès (lag.), Algeria 106/F1
Aurich, Germany 22/B2
Aurignac, France 28/D6
Aurillac, France 28/E5
Aurland, Norway 18/E6
Aurora, Ark. 202/C2
Aurora, Brazil 132/G4
Aurora, Colo. 188/F3
Aurora, Colo. 208/K3
Aurora, Guyana 131/B2
Aurora, Ill. 222/E2
Aurora, Ind. 227/H6
Aurora, Iowa 229/K3
Aurora, Kansas 232/E2
Aurora•, Maine 243/G6
Aurora, Minn. 255/F3
Aurora, Mo. 261/E9
Aurora, Nebr. 264/F4
Aurora, N.Y. 276/G5
Aurora, N.C. 281/R4
Aurora, Ohio 284/H3
Aurora, Ontario 177/J3
Aurora, Oreg. 291/B2
Aurora, Philippines 82/D4
Aurora, Philippines 82/C3
Aurora (co.), S. Dak. 298/M6
Aurora, S. Dak. 298/R5
Aurora, Texas 303/E1
Aurora, Utah 304/B5
Aurora, W. Va. 312/G4
Aurora Lodge, Alaska 196/J2
Auroraville, Wis. 317/H7
Aus, Namibia 118/B5
Au Sable, Mich. 250/F4
Au Sable (pt.), Mich. 250/F4
Au Sable (pt.), Mich. 250/C2
Au Sable (riv.), Mich. 250/E4
Ausable (riv.), N.Y. 276/N2
Au Sable Forks, N.Y. 276/N2
Auschwitz (Oświęcim), Poland 47/D3
Ausert (well), Western Sahara 106/B4
Auskerry (isl.), Scotland 15/F1
Aust-Agder (co.), Norway 18/E7
Austell, Ga. 217/J1
Austerlitz (Slavkov), Czech Rep. 41/D2
Austin, Ark. 202/G4
Austin, Colo. 208/D5
Austin, Ind. 227/F7
Austin, Ky. 237/K7
Austin, Manitoba 179/D5
Austin, Minn. 188/H2
Austin, Minn. 255/E7
Austin, Mo. 261/D5
Austin, Mont. 262/D4
Austin, Nev. 188/C3
Austin, Nev. 266/E3
Austin, Oreg. 291/J3
Austin, Pa. 294/F2
Austin (co.), Texas 303/H8
Austin (cap.), Texas 146/J6
Austin (cap.), Texas 303/G7
Austin (cap.), Texas 188/G4
Austin (lake), W. Australia 88/B5
Austin (lake), W. Australia 92/B4
Austinburg, Ohio 284/J2
Austintown, Ohio 284/J3
Austinville, Iowa 229/H3
Austinville, Va. 307/F7
Austonio, Texas 303/J6
Austral (isls.), Fr. Polynesia 2/B7
Austral (isls.), Fr. Poly. 87/L8
Australia 2/R7
Australia 87/C8
AUSTRALIA 88
Australia Aboriginal Reserve, W. Australia 88/D5
Australia Aboriginal Res., W. Australia 92/E4
Australian, Br. Col. 184/F4
Australian Alps (mts.), N.S. Wales 97/D5
Australian Alps (mts.), Victoria 97/D5
Australian Alps (mts.), Victoria 88/H7
Australian Capital Territory 88/H7
AUSTRALIAN CAPITAL TERRITORY 97/E4
Australian Capital Terr., Australia 87/F9
Australind, W. Australia 92/A2
Austria 2/K3
Austria 7/F4
AUSTRIA 41
Austwell, Texas 303/H9
Autauga (co.), Ala. 195/E5
Autaugaville, Ala. 195/E6
Autlán de Navarro, Mexico 150/G7
Au Train, Mich. 250/C2
Au Train (bay), Mich. 250/C2
Autreyville, Ga. 217/E8
Autryville, N.C. 281/M4
Autun, France 28/F4
Auvelais, Belgium 27/F8
Auvergne, Ark. 202/H2
Auvergne (mts.), France 28/E5
Auvergne (trad. prov.), France 29
Auvergne, North. Terr. 93/B3
Auvergne, Québec 172/F3
Auxerre, France 28/E4
Auxier, Ky. 237/R5
Auxonne, France 28/F4
Auxvasse, Mo. 261/J4
Auyantepui (mt.), Venezuela 124/G5
Auyuittuq Nat'l Park, N.W.T. 187/M3
Auyuittuq Nat'l Park, Que. 162/K2
Ava, Ill. 222/D6
Ava, Mo. 261/G9
Ava, N.Y. 276/K4
Ava, Ohio 284/G6
Avallon, France 28/E4
Avalon, Calif. 204/G10
Avalon, Ga. 217/F1
Avalon, Miss. 256/D3
Avalon, Mo. 261/F3
Avalon (pen.), Newf. 166/D2
Avalon, N.J. 273/D5
Avalon (res.), N. Mex. 274/E6
Avalon, Pa. 294/B6
Avanos, Turkey 63/F3
Avans, Ga. 217/A1
Avant, Okla. 288/O2
Avard, Okla. 288/J1
Avaré, Brazil 132/D8
Avaré, Brazil 135/B3
Avarua (cap.), Cook Is. 87/L8
Avayalik (isls.), Newf. 166/B1
Avaz, Iran 66/M4
Aveiro (dist.), Portugal 33/B2
Aveiro, Portugal 33/B2
Avej, Iran 66/F3
Avella, Pa. 294/B5
Avellaneda, Argentina 143/G7
Avellino (prov.), Italy 34/E4
Avellino, Italy 34/E4
Avenal, Calif. 204/E8
Avenches, Switzerland 39/D3
Avenel, N.J. 273/E2
Aventon, N.C. 281/O2
Avera, Ga. 217/G4
Avera, Miss. 256/G8
Averiás, Uruguay 145/E4
Averill, Mich. 250/E5
Averill, Minn. 255/B4
Averill•, Vt. 268/D2
Averill Park, N.Y. 276/O5
Aversa, Italy 34/E4
Avery, Idaho 220/C2
Avery, Iowa 229/H6
Avery (co.), N.C. 281/F2
Avery, Ohio 284/E3
Avery, Okla. 288/N3
Avery, Texas 303/K4
Avery Island, La. 238/G7
Aves (Bird) (isl.), Venezuela 156/F4
Avesnes-sur-Helpe, France 28/F2
Avesta, Sweden 18/J6
Aveyron (dept.), France 28/E5
Avezzano, Italy 34/D3
Aviemore, Scotland 15/E3
Avigliano, Italy 34/E4
Avignon, France 28/F6
Avignon, France 7/E4
Avihayil, Israel 65/B3
Ávila (prov.), Spain 33/D2
Ávila de los Caballeros, Spain 33/D2
Avilés, Spain 33/C1
Avilla, Ind. 227/G2
Avilla, Mo. 261/D8
Avinger, Texas 303/K5
Avion, France 28/E2
Avis, Pa. 294/H3
Avis, Portugal 33/C3
Aviston, Ill. 222/D5
Avize, France 28/F3
Avlum, Denmark 21/B5
Avoca, Ark. 202/B1
Avoca, Ind. 227/D7
Avoca, Iowa 229/C6
Avoca, Ireland 17/J6
Avoca, Mich. 250/G5
Avoca, Minn. 255/C7
Avoca, Nebr. 264/H4
Avoca, N.Y. 276/F6
Avoca, Pa. 294/F7
Avoca (dam), Tasmania 99/D3
Avoca, Texas 303/E5
Avoca, Victoria 97/B5
Avoca (riv.), Victoria 97/B5
Avoca, Wis. 317/F9
Avoch, Scotland 15/D3
Avola, Br. Col. 184/H4
Avola, Italy 34/E6
Avon, Ala. 195/H8
Avon, Colo. 208/F3
Avon, Conn. 210/D1
Avon•, Conn. 210/D1
Avon (co.), England 13/E6
Avon (riv.), England 13/F7
Avon (riv.), England 13/F5
Avon (riv.), England 10/F4
Avon, Idaho 220/B3
Avon, Ill. 222/C3
Avon•, Mass. 249/K4
Avon, Minn. 255/D5
Avon, Miss. 256/B4
Avon, Mont. 262/D4
Avon, N.Y. 276/E5
Avon, N.C. 281/U4
Avon (riv.), Nova Scotia 168/D4
Avon, Ohio 284/F3
Avon (riv.), Scotland 15/C1
Avon (riv.), Scotland 15/E3
Avon, S. Dak. 298/N8
Avon (riv.), W. Australia 88/B6
Avon (riv.), W. Australia 92/A1
Avon, Wis. 317/H10
Avon By The Sea, N.J. 273/E3
Avondale, Ariz. 198/C5
Avondale, Colo. 208/L6
Avondale, Mich. 250/D4
Avondale, Mo. 261/P5
Avondale, Newf. 166/D2
Avondale, N.S. Wales 97/F3
Avondale, N.C. 281/F4
Avondale, Pa. 294/L6
Avondale, W. Va. 312/C8
Avondale Estates, Ga. 217/L1
Avon Downs, North. Terr. 88/F4
Avon Downs, North. Terr. 93/E5
Avonhurst, Sask. 181/G5
Avon Lake, Ohio 284/F2
Avonlea, Sask. 181/G5
Avonmore, Ontario 177/K2
Avonmore, Pa. 294/C4
Avon Park, Fla. 212/E4
Avonport, Nova Scotia 168/D3
Avon Water (riv.), Scotland 15/D5
Avoyelles (par.), La. 238/G4
Avranches, France 28/C3
Awa (isl.), Japan 81/J4
Awaji, Japan 81/H8
Awaji (isl.), Japan 81/H8
Awanui, N. Zealand 100/D1
Awareh, Ethiopia 111/H6
Awarua (bay), N. Zealand 100/A6
Awasa, Ethiopia 114/G6
Awasa, Ethiopia 102/F4
Awash, Ethiopia 111/H6
Awash (riv.), Ethiopia 111/H5
Awaso, Ghana 106/D7
Awat, China 77/A3
Awatere (riv.), N. Zealand 100/D5
Awbeg (riv.), Ireland 17/D7
Awe, Loch (lake), Scotland 10/D2
Awe, Loch (lake), Scotland 15/C4
Aweil, Sudan 111/E6
Awendaw, S.C. 296/H5
Awosting, N.J. 273/E1
Axe Edge (mt.), England 13/H2
Axel, Netherlands 27/D6
Axel Heiberg (isl.), Canada 4/A14
Axel Heiberg (isl.), N.W.T. 146/J1
Axel Heiberg (isl.), N.W.T. 187/J2
Axel Heiburg (isl.), N.W.T. 162/N3
Axim, Ghana 106/D8
Axis, Ala. 195/B9
Ax-les-Thermes, France 28/D6
Axminster, England 13/D7
Axminster, England 10/E5
Axochiapan, Mexico 150/M2
Axson, Ga. 217/G8
Axtell, Kansas 232/F2
Axtell, Nebr. 264/E4
Axtell, Utah 304/C4
Axton, Va. 307/J7
Axum (Aksum), Ethiopia 111/G5
Ayabaca, Peru 128/C5
Ayabe, Japan 81/G6
Ayacucho, Argentina 143/E4
Ayacucho, Bolivia 136/D5
Ayacucho (dept.), Peru 128/E9
Ayacucho, Peru 128/F9
Ayacucho, Peru 120/B4
Ayaguz, Kazakhstan 54/K5
Ayaguz, Kazakhstan 48/J5
Ayakkum Hu (lake), China 77/C4
Ayamonte, Spain 33/C4
Ayan, Russia 48/O4
Ayan, Russia 54/P4
Ayancık, Turkey 63/F1
Ayapel, Colombia 126/C3
Ayapel, Serranía de (mts.), Colombia 126/C4
Ayaş, Turkey 63/E2
Ayata, Bolivia 136/A4
Ayaviri, Peru 128/G10
Aybak, Afghanistan 68/B1
Aybak, Afghanistan 59/J2
Aybastı, Turkey 63/G2
Aycliffe, England 13/F3
Ayden, N.C. 281/P4
Aydın (prov.), Turkey 63/B4
Aydin, Turkey 59/A2
Aydın, Turkey 63/B4
Aydıncık, Turkey 63/E4
Aydlett, N.C. 281/T2
Aydyrlinskiy, Russia 52/K4
Ayer, Mass. 249/H2
Ayer•, Mass. 249/H2
Ayer, Switzerland 39/E4
Ayer, Wash. 310/G4
Ayers, Maine 243/J6
Ayer's Cliff, Québec 172/E4
Ayers Rock (Uluru) (mt.), North. Terr. 88/E5
Ayersville, Ohio 284/B3
Ayiá, Greece 45/F6
Áyion Óros (aut. dist.), Greece 45/G5
Áyios Evstrátios (isl.), Greece 45/G6
Áyios Kiríkos, Greece 45/H7
Áyios Matthaíós, Greece 45/D6
Áyios Nikólaos, Greece 45/G8
Áyios Yeóryios (cape), Greece 45/G5
Aykhal, Russia 48/M3
Aylen (lake), Ontario 177/G2
Aylesbury, England 13/G7
Aylesbury, England 10/F5
Aylesbury, Sask. 181/F5
Aylesford, England 13/J8
Aylesford, Nova Scotia 168/D3
Aylett, Va. 307/O5
Ayllón, Spain 33/E2
Aylmer, N. Dak. 282/K4
Aylmer (lake), N.W.T. 187/H3
Aylmer, Ontario 177/C5
Aylmer, Québec 172/B4
Aylmer (lake), Québec 172/F4
Aylsham, England 13/J5
Aylsham, Sask. 181/H2
Aynor, S.C. 296/J3
Ayod, Sudan 111/F6
Ayolas, Paraguay 144/D5
Ayon (isl.), Russia 48/R2
Ayora, Spain 33/F3
Ayr, Nebr. 264/F4
Ayr, N. Dak. 282/P5
Ayr, Ontario 177/D4
Ayr, Queensland 95/C3
Ayr, Queensland 88/H3
Ayr, Scotland 15/D5
Ayr, Scotland 10/D3
Ayr, Heads of (cape), Scotland 15/D5
Ayr (trad. prov.) Scotland 15/A5
Ayr (riv.), Scotland 15/D5
Ayrancı, Turkey 63/E4
Ayre (pt.), I. of Man 13/C3
Ayre (pt.), I. of Man 10/D3
Ayrshire, Iowa 229/D2
Ayton, Ontario 177/D3
Ayton, Scotland 15/F5
Aytos, Bulgaria 45/H4
Ayu (isls.), Indonesia 85/J5
Ayun, Saudi Arabia 59/D4
Ayutla de los Libres, Mexico 150/K8
Ayutthaya (Phra Nakhon Si Ayutthaya), Thailand 72/D4
Ayvacık, Turkey 63/B3
Ayvalık, Turkey 59/A2
Ayvalık, Turkey 63/B3
Aywaille, Belgium 27/H8
Azalea, Oreg. 291/D5
Azalea Park, Fla. 212/E3
Azalia, Ind. 227/F6
Azalia, Mich. 250/F6
Azamgarh, India 68/E3
Azángaro, Peru 128/H10
Azángaro (riv.), Peru 128/G10
Azaoua (reg.), Niger 106/E5
Azaouad (reg.), Mali 106/D5
Azaouak (dry riv.), Mali 106/E5
Azapa, Chile 138/A1
Azaran, Iran 66/E2
Azapa, Quebrada (riv.), Chile 138/B1
Azare, Nigeria 106/G6
Azaz, Syria 63/G4
Azbine (Air) (mts.), Niger 106/F5
Azcapotzalco, Mexico 150/L1
Azdavay, Turkey 63/E2
Azemmour, Morocco 106/C2
Azerbaijan 7/J4
Azerbaijan 48/E5
AZERBAIJAN 52/G6

Azerbaijan, East (prov.), Iran 66/E1
Azerbaijan, West (prov.), Iran 66/D1
Azerbaijan (reg.), Iran 66/D1
Aziscoos (lake), Maine 243/A5
Azle, Texas 303/E2
Azogues, Ecuador 128/C4
AZORES 33
Azores (isls.), Portugal 2/H4
Azores (isls.), Portugal 33/A2
Azoum, Bahr, Chad 111/D5
Azov, Russia 52/E5
Azov (sea), Russia 7/H4
Azov (sea), Russia 48/D5
Azov (sea), Russia 52/E5
Azov (sea), Ukraine 7/H4
Azov (sea), Ukraine 48/D5
Azov (sea), Ukraine 52/E5
Azoyú, Mexico 150/K8
Azpeitia, Spain 33/E1
Azrou, Morocco 106/C2
Aztec, Ariz. 198/B6
Aztec, N. Mex. 274/B2
Aztec Ruins Nat'l Mon., N. Mex. 274/A2
Azua (prov.), Dom. Rep. 158/D6
Azua, Dom. Rep. 156/D3
Azua, Dom. Rep. 158/D6
Azuaga, Spain 33/D3
Azuara, Spain 33/F2
Azuay (prov.), Ecuador 128/C4
Azuero (pen.), Panama 154/G7
Azul, Argentina 143/E4
Azul, Argentina 120/D6
Azul (riv.), Guatemala 154/C2
Azul, Cordillera (mts.), Peru 128/E7
Azurduy, Bolivia 136/C6
Azure (lake), Br. Col. 184/G4
Azusa, Calif. 204/D10
Azwell, Wash. 310/F3
Azzel Mati, Sebkha (lake), Algeria 106/E3
Az Zubair, Iraq 66/E5

B

Ba, Fiji 86/P10
Baa, Indonesia 85/G8
Baaba (isl.), New Caled. 86/G4
Ba'albek, Lebanon 63/G5
Baan Baa, N.S. Wales 97/E2
Baar, Switzerland 39/F2
Baarle-Nassau, Netherlands 27/F6
Baarn, Netherlands 27/G4
Baatsagaan, Mongolia 77/E2
Baba, Ecuador 128/C3
Baba (cape), Turkey 63/D2
Baba (cape), Turkey 63/A3
Babadag, Romania 45/J3
Babadağ, Turkey 63/C4
Babaeski, Turkey 63/B2
Babahoyo, Ecuador 128/C3
Babanusa, Sudan 111/E5
Babaomby (cape), Madagascar 102/C6
Babaomby (cape), Madagascar 118/H2
Babar (isl.), Indonesia 85/H7
Babar (isls.), Indonesia 85/H7
Babati, Tanzania 115/G4
Babayevo, Russia 52/E3
Babb, Mont. 262/C2
Babbie, Ala. 195/F8
Babbitt, Minn. 255/G3
Babbitt, Nev. 266/C4
Babcock, Wis. 317/F7
Babel (isls.), Tasmania 99/E1
Bab el Mandeb (str.) 102/G3
Bab el Mandeb (str.), Djibouti 111/H5
Babelthuap (isl.), Belau 87/D5
Babia (riv.), Mexico 150/J2
Babil (heads), Iraq 66/D4
Babine (lake), Br. Col. 162/D5
Babine, Br. Col. 184/D2
Babine (lake), Br. Col. 184/E3
Babine (riv.), Br. Col. 184/D2
Babo, Indonesia 85/K7
Babol, Iran 54/G6
Babol, Iran 59/F2
Babol, Iran 66/H2
Babol Sar, Iran 66/H2
Baboquivari (mts.), Ariz. 198/D7
Baboua, Cent. Afr. Rep. 115/C2
Babson Park, Fla. 212/E4
Babuyan (isls.), Philippines 54/O8
Babuyan (chan.), Philippines 82/A3
Babuyan (isl.), Philippines 82/B2
Babuyan (isls.), Philippines 85/G2
Babuyan (isls.), Philippines 82/A2
Babylon (ruins), Iraq 66/D4
Babylon, N.Y. 276/O9
Baca (co.), Colo. 208/O8
Bacabal, Brazil 120/E3
Bacabal, Maranhão, Brazil 132/E4
Bacabal, Pará, Brazil 132/B4
Bacadéhuachi, Mexico 150/E2
Bacalar, Mexico 150/P7
Bacalar (lake), Mexico 150/P7
Bacan (isls.), Indonesia 85/H6
Bacanora, Mexico 150/E2
Bacarra, Philippines 82/C1
Bacău, Romania 7/G4
Bacău, Romania 45/H2
Baccalieu (isl.), Newf. 166/D2
Bac Can, Vietnam 72/E2
Baccaro (pt.), Nova Scotia 168/C5
Bacchus Marsh, Victoria 97/C5
Bacerac, Mexico 150/E1
Bac Giang, Vietnam 72/E2
Bach, Mich. 250/F5
Bachaquero, Venezuela 124/C3
Bache (pen.), N.W.T. 187/L2
Bache, Okla. 288/P5
Bachíniva, Mexico 150/F2
Bach Long Vi, Dao (isl.), Vietnam 72/F2
Bachu (Maralwexi), China 77/A4
Back (bay), India 68/B7
Back (riv.), Md. 245/N4
Back (lake), N.H. 268/E1
Back (riv.), N.W.T. 146/H3
Back (riv.), N.W.T. 162/G2
Back (riv.), N.W.T. 187/J3
Back (bay), Va. 307/S7
Back (creek), Va. 307/J4
Bačka Topola, Yugoslavia 45/D3
Back Bay, New Bruns. 170/D3
Backbone (mt.), Md. 245/A3
Backnang, Germany 22/C4
Backoo, N. Dak. 282/P2
Backus, Minn. 255/D4
Backway, The (inlet), Newf. 166/C3
Bac Lieu, Vietnam 72/E5
Bacliff, Texas 303/K2
Bac Ninh, Vietnam 72/E2
Baco (mt.), Philippines 82/C4
Bacolod, Philippines 85/G3
Bacolod, Philippines 54/O8
Bacolod, Philippines 82/D5
Bacon (co.), Ga. 217/G7
Bacone, Okla. 288/R3
Bacon Ridge (mts.), Wyo. 319/B2
Bacons, Del. 245/R6
Baconton, Ga. 217/D8
Bácsalmás, Hungary 41/E3
Bács-Kiskun (co.), Hungary 41/E3
Bácum, Mexico 150/D3
Bacuna, Neth. Ant. 161/E8
Bacup, England 13/H1
Bacup, England 10/G1
Bad (riv.), Mich. 250/E5
Bad (hills), Sask. 181/C4
Bad (lake), Sask. 181/C4
Bad (riv.), S. Dak. 298/G5
Badacsonytomaj, Hungary 41/D3
Badagara, India 68/D6
Bad Aibling, Germany 22/D5
Badajoz (prov.), Spain 33/C3
Badajoz, Spain 33/C3
Badalona, Spain 33/H2
Bad Aussee, Austria 41/B3
Bad Axe, Mich. 250/G5
Bad Berleburg, Germany 22/C3
Bad Berneck, Germany 22/D3
Bad Bramstedt, Germany 22/C2
Bad Brückenau, Germany 22/C3
Baddeck, Nova Scotia 168/H2
Baddeck (riv.), Nova Scotia 168/H2
Bad Doberan, Germany 22/D1
Bad Driburg, Germany 22/C3
Bad Dürkheim, Germany 22/C4
Bad Dürrenberg, Germany 22/D3
Bad Ems, Germany 22/B3
Baden, Austria 41/D2
Baden, Manitoba 179/A2
Baden, Md. 245/M6
Baden, Ontario 177/D4
Baden, Pa. 294/B4
Baden, Switzerland 39/F2
Ba Den, Nui (mt.), Vietnam 72/E5
Baden-Baden, Germany 22/C4
Badenoch (dist.), Scotland 15/D4
Badenweiler, Germany 22/B5
Baden-Württemberg (state), Germany 22/C4
Bad Freienwalde, Germany 22/F2
Bad Gandersheim, Germany 22/D3
Badgastein, Austria 41/B3
Badger (peak), Idaho 220/E7
Badger, Iowa 229/E3
Badger, Minn. 255/B2
Badger, Newf. 166/C4
Badger (creek), Oreg. 291/H3
Badger, S. Dak. 298/P5
Badger (creek), Wyo. 319/E2
Badger's Quay, Newf. 166/D4
Bad Goisern, Austria 41/B3
Badham, S.C. 296/F5
Bad Harzburg, Germany 22/D3
Bad Hersfeld, Germany 22/C3
Badhoevedorp, Netherlands 27/B5
Bad Hofgastein, Austria 41/B3
Bad Homburg vor der Höhe, Germany 22/C3
Bad Honnef, Germany 22/B3
Badian, Philippines 82/D6
Badin, N.C. 281/J4
Badin, Pakistan 68/B4
Badiraguato, Mexico 150/F4
Bad Ischl, Austria 41/B3
Bad Kissingen, Germany 22/D3
Bad Kreuznach, Germany 22/B4
Bad Land (cliffs), Utah 304/D4
Bad Lands (reg.), N. Dak. 282/C7
Badlands Nat'l Park, S. Dak. 298/E6
Bad Langensalza, Germany 22/D3
Bad Lauterberg im Harz, Germany 22/D3
Bad Leonfelden, Austria 41/C2
Bad Liebenwerda, Germany 22/E3
Bad Lippspringe, Germany 22/C3
Bad Mergentheim, Germany 22/C4
Bad Münster-Ebernburg, Germany 22/B4
Bad Münstereifel, Germany 22/B3
Bad Muskau, Germany 22/F3
Bad Nauheim, Germany 22/C3
Bad Neuenahr-Ahrweiler, Germany 22/B3
Bad Neustadt an der Saale, Germany 22/D3
Bado, Mo. 261/H8
Bad Oldesloe, Germany 22/D2
Ba Don, Vietnam 72/E3
Bad Orb, Germany 22/C3
Bad Pyrmont, Germany 22/C3
Badr, Saudi Arabia 59/C5
Badra, Iraq 66/D4
Bad Ragaz, Switzerland 39/H2
Bad Reichenhall, Germany 22/E5
Bad River Ind. Res., Wis. 317/E2
Bad Sachsa, Germany 22/D3
Bad Salzschlirf, Germany 22/C3
Bad Salzuflen, Germany 22/C2
Bad Salzungen, Germany 22/D3
Bad Sankt-Leonhard im Lavanttal, Austria 41/C3
Bad Schwartau, Germany 22/D2
Bad Segeberg, Germany 22/D2
Bad Tölz, Germany 22/D5
Baduen, Somalia 115/J2
Badulla, Sri Lanka 68/E7
Bad Vilbel, Germany 22/C3
Bad Waldsee, Germany 22/C5
Badwater (creek), Wyo. 319/E2
Bad Wildungen, Germany 22/C3
Bad Wimpfen, Germany 22/C4
Baelum, Denmark 21/D4
Baena, Spain 33/D4
Baerle-Hertog, Belgium 27/F6
Báez, Cuba 158/E2
Baeza, Ecuador 128/D3
Baeza, Spain 33/E4
Bafa (lake), Turkey 63/B4
Baffin (bay) 4/B13
Baffin (bay) 146/M2
Baffin (bay), Canada 2/F2
Baffin (isl.), Canada 2/F2
Baffin (isl.), Canada 4/C13
Baffin (bay), N.W.T. 162/J1
Baffin (bay), N.W.T. 187/M2
Baffin (isl.), N.W.T. 146/L2
Baffin (isl.), N.W.T. 162/J1
Baffin (isl.), N.W.T. 187/L2
Baffin (reg.), N.W.T. 186/J2
Baffin (bay), Texas 303/G10
Bafia, Cameroon 115/B3
Bafing (riv.), Guinea 106/B6
Bafing (riv.), Mali 106/B6
Bafoulabé, Mali 106/B6
Bafoussam, Cameroon 115/B2
Bafq, Iran 59/G3
Bafq, Iran 66/J5
Bafra, Turkey 59/C1
Bafra, Turkey 63/F2
Bafra (cape), Turkey 59/C1
Bafra (cape), Turkey 63/G2
Baft, Iran 66/K6
Baft, Iran 59/G4
Baga, Nigeria 106/G6
Bagabag, Philippines 82/C2
Bagac, Philippines 82/C3
Bagaces, C. Rica 154/E5
Bagadó, Colombia 126/B5
Bagalkot, India 68/D5
Bagam (well), Niger 106/F5
Bagamoyo, Tanzania 115/G5
Baganga, Philippines 82/F7
Baganian (pen.), Philippines 82/D7
Bagansiapiapi, Indonesia 85/C5
Bagata, D.R. Congo 115/C4
Bagdad, Ariz. 198/B4
Bagdad, Fla. 212/B6
Bagdad, Ky. 237/L4
Bagdad, Tasmania 99/D4
Bagdarin, Russia 48/M4
Bagé, Brazil 120/D6
Bagé, Brazil 132/C10
Bagenalstown, Ireland 10/C4
Bagenalstown (Muinebeag), Ireland 17/H6
Bagenkop, Denmark 21/D8
Baggs, Wyo. 319/E4
Baghbaghu, Iran 66/M3
Baghdad (heads), Iraq 66/D4
Baghdad (cap.), Iraq 59/E3
Baghdad (cap.), Iraq 54/F6
Baghdad (cap.), Iraq 2/M4
Baghdad (cap.), Iraq 66/D4
Bagheria, Italy 34/D5
Baghlan, Afghanistan 54/H6
Baghlan, Afghanistan 59/J2
Baghlan, Afghanistan 68/B1
Baghu, Iran 66/K7
Bağırpaşa Daği (mt.), Turkey 59/D2
Bağırpaşa Daği (mt.), Turkey 63/J3
Bagley, Iowa 229/E5
Bagley, Minn. 255/C3
Bagley, N.C. 281/N3
Bagley, Wis. 317/D10
Bagnell, Mo. 261/G6
Bagnell (dam), Mo. 261/G6
Bagnères-de-Bigorre, France 28/D6
Bagnères-de-Luchon, France 28/D6
Bagnolet, France 28/B2
Bagnols-sur-Cèze, France 28/F5
Bågø (isl.), Denmark 21/C7
Bago, Philippines 82/D5
Bagoé (riv.), Ivory Coast 106/C6
Bagoé (riv.), Mali 106/C6
Bagot, Manitoba 179/D5
Bagot (co.), Québec 172/E4
Bagrax (Bosten Hu) (lake), China 77/C3
Bagua, Peru 128/C5
Báguanos, Cuba 158/J3
Baguio, Philippines 54/N8
Baguio, Philippines 85/G2
Baguio, Philippines 82/C2
Baguirmi (reg.), Chad 111/C5
Bagwell, Texas 303/J4
Bahama, N.C. 281/M2
Bahamas 2/F4
Bahamas 146/L7
BAHAMAS 156/C1
Bahariya (oasis), Egypt 111/E2
Bahariya (oasis), Egypt 59/A4
Bahawalnagar, Pakistan 68/C2
Bahawalpur, Pakistan 54/J7
Bahawalpur, Pakistan 68/C3
Bahawalpur, Pakistan 59/K4
Bahçe, Turkey 63/G4
Bahçesaray, Turkey 63/K3
Bahia (state), Brazil 132/F6
Bahia (Salvador), Brazil 132/G6
Bahía (isls.), Honduras 154/D2
Bahía Blanca, Argentina 2/F7
Bahía Blanca, Argentina 143/D4
Bahía Blanca, Argentina 120/C6
Bahía Bustamante, Argentina 143/C6
Bahía de Caráquez, Ecuador 128/B3
Bahía Honda, Cuba 158/B1
Bahía Kino, Mexico 150/C2
Bahía San Blas, Argentina 143/D5
Bahía Thetis, Argentina 143/C7
Bahía Tortugas, Mexico 150/B3
Bahir Dar, Ethiopia 111/G5
Bahomamey, P. Rico 161/A1
Bahoruco (prov.), Dom. Rep. 158/D6
Bahoruco, Sierra de (mts.), Dom. Rep. 158/D6
Bahraich, India 68/E3
Bahrain 54/G7
BAHRAIN 59/F4
Bahramabad (Rafsanjan), Iran 66/K5
Bahr Azoum (riv.), Sudan 111/D5
Bahr el 'Arab (riv.), Sudan 111/E6
Bahr el Ghazal (dry riv.), Chad 111/C5
Bahr El Ghazal (prov.), Sudan 111/E6
Bahr es Safi (des.), Saudi Arabia 59/E6
Bahr ez Zeraf (riv.), Sudan 111/F6
Bahr Yusef (stream), Egypt 111/J4
Baia de Aramă, Romania 45/F3
Baía dos Tigres, Angola 115/B7
Baia Farta, Angola 115/B6
Baia Mare, Romania 45/F2
Baião, Brazil 132/D3
Baibiene, Argentina 143/G4
Baibokoum, Chad 111/C6
Bai Bung, Mui (Ca Mau) (pt.), Vietnam 72/E5
Baicheng (Bay), Xinjiang Uygur, China 7/B3
Baicheng, Jilin, China 77/K2
Baida, Libya 102/E1
Baida, Libya 111/D1
Baidyabati, India 68/F1
Baie-Comeau, Québec 172/A1
Baie-Comeau, Québec 174/D3
Baie de Henne, Haiti 158/B5
Baie-des-Bacons, Québec 172/H1
Baie-des-Moutons, Québec 174/F2
Baie-des-Rochers, Québec 172/H2
Baie-des-Sables, Québec 172/A1
Baie-du-Poste, Québec 174/C2
Baie-d'Urfé, Québec 172/G4
Baie-du-Vieux-Fort, Québec 174/F2
Baie-Johan-Beetz, Québec 174/E2
Baie-Mahault, Guadeloupe 161/A6
Baiersbronn, Germany 22/C4
Baie-Sainte-Anne, New Bruns. 170/F1
Baie-Sainte-Catherine, Québec 172/H1
Baie-Saint-Paul, Que. 162/J6
Baie-Saint-Paul, Québec 174/C3
Baie-Saint-Paul, Québec 172/G2
Baie-Trinité, Québec 172/B1
Baie-Verte, New Bruns. 170/F2
Baie Verte, Newf. 166/C4
Baieville, Québec 172/E3
Baigorrita, Argentina 143/F7
Baiji, Iraq 66/C3
Baildon, Sask. 181/F5
Baile Átha Cliath (Dublin) (cap.), Ireland 17/K5
Baile Átha Cliath (Dublin) (cap.), Ireland 10/C4
Băile Herculane, Romania 45/F3
Bailén, Spain 33/E3
Băileşti, Romania 45/F3
Bailey, Colo. 208/H4
Bailey, Iowa 229/H2
Bailey, Mich. 250/D5
Bailey, Miss. 256/G6
Bailey, N.C. 281/N3
Bailey (co.), Texas 303/B3
Baileyboro, Texas 303/B3
Bailey Island, Maine 243/D8
Bailey Lakes, Ohio 284/F4
Bailey's Crossroads, Va. 307/S3
Baileys Harbor, Wis. 317/M5
Baileyton, Ala. 195/E2
Baileyton, Tenn. 237/R8
Baileyville, Conn. 210/E2
Baileyville, Ill. 222/D1
Baileyville, Kansas 232/F2
Bailieborough, Ireland 17/G4
Bailique (isl.), Brazil 132/D2
Bailivanish, Scotland 15/A3
Baillie (isls.), N.W.T. 187/F2
Baillieston, Scotland 15/B2
Baillif, Guadeloupe 161/A7
Bailundo, Angola 115/C6
Baima, China 77/E5
Bainbridge (isl.), Alaska 196/C1
Bainbridge, Ga. 217/C9
Bainbridge, Ind. 227/D5
Bainbridge, N.Y. 276/J6
Bainbridge (dist.), N. Ireland 17/J3
Bainbridge, Ohio 284/D7
Bainbridge, Pa. 294/J5
Bainbridge (isl.), Wash. 310/A2
Bainbridge Island-Winslow (Winslow), Wash. 310/A2
Bainbridge N.T.C., Md. 245/O2
Bainet, Haiti 158/B6
Baingoin, China 77/D5
Bains, La. 238/H5
Bainville, Mont. 262/M2
Baird (inlet), Alaska 196/F2
Baird (mts.), Alaska 196/F1
Baird, Miss. 256/C4
Baird (pen.), N.W.T. 187/L3
Baird, Texas 303/E5
Bairdstown, Ohio 284/C3
Bairdsville, New Bruns. 170/C2
Baire, Cuba 158/H4
Bairin Zuoqi, China 77/J3
Bairnsdale, Victoria 88/H7
Bairnsdale, Victoria 97/D5
Bairoil, Wyo. 319/E3
Bais, Philippines 82/D6
Baisden, W. Va. 312/C7
Baïse (riv.), France 28/D6
Baisha, China 77/G8
Baitadi, Nepal 68/E3
Bait al Faqih, Yemen 59/D7
Bai Thuong, Vietnam 72/E3
Baixa da Banheira, Portugal 33/B3
Baixoaixo (isl.), Portugal 33/B2
Baixo Guandu, Brazil 132/F7
Baja, Hungary 41/E3
Baja California (state), Mexico 150/B1
Baja California Sur (state), Mexico 150/C3
Bajadero, P. Rico 161/C1
Bajgiran, Iran 66/L2
Bajo Boquete, Panama 154/F6
Bajo Nuevo (shoal), Colombia 126/C8
Bajos de Haina, Dom. Rep. 158/E6
Bajram Curri, Albania 45/D4
Bakala, Cent. Afr. Rep. 115/D2
Bakar, Croatia 45/B3
Bakel, Senegal 106/B6
Baker (isl.), Alaska 196/M2
Baker, Calif. 204/J8
Baker (riv.), Chile 138/D7
Baker (mt.), Colo. 208/H2
Baker (co.), Fla. 212/D1
Baker, Fla. 212/C5
Baker (co.), Ga. 217/D8
Baker, Idaho 220/E4
Baker, La. 238/K1
Baker (lake), Maine 243/D3
Baker, Minn. 255/B4
Baker, Mo. 261/N9
Baker, Mont. 262/M4
Baker, Nev. 266/G3
Baker (riv.), N.H. 268/D4
Baker, N. Dak. 282/L3
Baker (lake), N.W.T. 187/J3
Baker, Okla. 288/D1
Baker, Oreg. 188/C2
Baker (co.), Oreg. 291/K3
Baker, Oreg. 291/K3
Baker (isl.), Pacific 87/J5
Baker (creek), Utah 304/A4
Baker (lake), Wash. 310/D2
Baker (mt.), Wash. 310/D2
Baker (riv.), Wash. 310/D2
Baker, W. Va. 312/J4
Baker Brook, New Bruns. 170/B1
Baker Butte (mt.), Ariz. 198/D4
Baker Hill, Ala. 195/H7
Baker Lake, N.W.T. 162/G3
Baker Lake, N.W.T. 187/J3
Bakers (isl.), Mass. 249/F5
Bakersfield, Calif. 146/G6
Bakersfield, Calif. 188/C3
Bakersfield, Calif. 204/G8
Bakersfield, Mo. 261/H9
Bakersfield, Texas 303/B7
Bakersfield•, Vt. 268/B2
Bakers Summit, Pa. 294/F5
Bakersville, Conn. 210/C1
Bakersville, N.C. 281/E2
Bakersville, Ohio 284/G5
Bakersville, Pa. 294/D5
Bakerton, Ky. 237/L7
Bakerton, W. Va. 312/L4
Bakerville, Tenn. 237/F9
Bakewell, England 10/G2
Bakewell, England 13/J2
Bakewell, Tenn. 237/L10
Bakharz, Kuhha-ye (mt.), Iran 66/M3
Bakhchisaray, Ukraine 52/D6
Bakhmach, Ukraine 52/D4
Bakhtaran (prov.), Iran 54/F6
Bakhtaran (prov.), Iran 58/E3
Bakhtaran (prov.), Iran 66/E3
Bakhtaran, Iran 54/F6
Bakhtaran, Iran 58/E3
Bakhtaran, Iran 66/E3
Bakhtegan (lake), Iran 66/J6
Bakhtiari (gov.), Iran 66/F4
Bakhun, Kuh-e (mt.), Iran 66/K6
Bakhuys (mts.), Suriname 131/C3
Bakia, Cent. Afr. Rep. 115/E2
Bakırköy, Turkey 63/D6
Baklan, Turkey 63/C4
Bako, Ethiopia 111/G6
Bakony (mts.), Hungary 41/D3
Bakool (prov.), Somalia 115/H3
Bakouma, Cent. Afr. Rep. 115/D2
Bakoy (riv.), Guinea 106/B6
Bakoy (riv.), Mali 106/B6
Bakraband, Kuh-e (mts.), Iran 66/M7
Baktalórántháza, Hungary 41/G2
Baktu (Paektu) (mt.), N. Korea 81/C3
Baku (cap.), Azerbaijan 2/M3
Baku (cap.), Azerbaijan 7/J4
Baku (cap.), Azerbaijan 48/F5
Baku (cap.), Azerbaijan 52/H6
Bala, Kansas 232/F2
Bala, Ontario 177/E2
Balâ, Turkey 63/E3
Bala, Wales 13/D5
Bala, Wales 10/E4
Balabac, Philippines 82/A7
Balabac (isl.), Philippines 85/F4
Balabac (isl.), Philippines 82/A7
Balabac (str.), Philippines 85/F4
Balabac (str.), Philippines 82/A7
Balabalagan (isls.), Indonesia 85/F6
Balabio (isl.), New Caled. 86/G4
Balaclava, Jamaica 158/H6
Bala-Cynwyd, Pa. 294/N6
Balad, Somalia 115/J3
Balaghat, India 68/E4
Balaguer, Spain 33/G2
Balaitous (mt.), Spain 33/F1
Balakai (mesa), Ariz. 198/F3
Balakhna, Russia 52/F3
Balaklava, S. Australia 94/F6
Balaklava, Ukraine 52/D6
Balakovo, Russia 7/J3
Balakovo, Russia 48/E4
Balakovo, Russia 52/G4
Balallan, Scotland 15/B2
Bal'ama, Jordan 65/E3
Balambangan (isl.), Malaysia 85/F4
Balancán de Domínguez, Mexico 150/O8
Balandra (pt.), Dom. Rep. 158/F5
Balanga, Philippines 82/C3
Balangala, D.R. Congo 115/D3
Ba Lang An, Mui (cape), Vietnam 72/F4
Balangiga, Philippines 82/E5
Balao, Ecuador 128/C4
Balashi, Neth. Ant. 161/E10
Balashov, Russia 7/J3
Balashov, Russia 48/E4
Balashov, Russia 52/F4
Balasore, India 68/F4
Balassagyarmat, Hungary 41/E2
Balaton (lake), Hungary 7/F4
Balaton (lake), Hungary 41/D3
Balaton, Minn. 255/C6
Balatonfüred, Hungary 41/D3
Balatonszentgyörgy, Hungary 41/D3
Balayan (bay), Philippines 82/C4
Balbi (mt.), Papua N.G. 86/C2
Balboa, Panama 154/H6
Balbriggan, Ireland 17/J4
Balbriggan, Ireland 10/C4
Balcarce, Argentina 143/E4
Balcarres, Sask. 181/H5
Balchik, Bulgaria 45/H4
Balch Springs, Texas 303/H2
Balclutha, N. Zealand 100/B7
Balcones Escarpment (plat.), Texas 303/E8
Balcones Heights, Texas 303/J10
Bald (mt.), Colo. 208/H4
Bald (hill), Conn. 210/G1
Bald (mt.), Idaho 220/D5
Bald (mt.), New Bruns. 170/C1
Bald (mts.), N.C. 281/D3
Bald (mts.), Tenn. 237/R9
Bald (mt.), Utah 304/C3
Bald (mt.), Vt. 268/D2
Bald (head), W. Australia 88/B7
Bald (head), W. Australia 92/B6
Bald Eagle (lake), Minn. 255/G3
Baldeggersee (lake), Switzerland 39/F2
Baldhill (Ashtabula) (res.), N. Dak. 282/P5
Bald Hill Branch (riv.), Md. 245/G4
Bald Hills, Queensland 88/K2
Bald Knob, Ark. 202/G3
Bald Knob, W. Va. 312/C7
Baldonnel, Br. Col. 184/G2
Baldur, Manitoba 179/C5
Baldwin (co.), Ala. 195/C9
Baldwin, Fla. 212/E1
Baldwin (co.), Ga. 217/F4
Baldwin, Ga. 217/E2
Baldwin, Ill. 222/D5
Baldwin, Iowa 229/M4
Baldwin, La. 238/H7
Baldwin, Mich. 250/D5
Baldwin, N.Y. 276/R7
Baldwin, N. Dak. 282/J5
Baldwin, Pa. 294/B7
Baldwin, W. Va. 312/E5
Baldwin, Wis. 317/B6
Baldwin City, Kansas 232/G3
Baldwin Park, Calif. 204/D10
Baldwinsville, N.Y. 276/H4
Baldwinton, Sask. 181/B3
Baldwinville, Mass. 249/F2
Baldwyn, Miss. 256/G2
Baldy (peak), Ariz. 198/F5
Baldy (mt.), Manitoba 179/B3
Baldy (peak), N. Mex. 274/D3
Baldy (peak), Utah 304/B5
Bale (prov.), Ethiopia 111/H6
Bale (mt.), Ethiopia 111/G6
Baleares (prov.), Spain 33/H3
Balearic (isls.), Spain 7/E5
Balearic (Baleares) (isls.), Spain 33/H3
Baleine (riv.), Québec 174/D1
Baleine, Grande R. de la (riv.), Que. 162/J4
Baleine, Grand Rivière de la (riv.), Québec 174/B1
Baleine, Petite Rivière de la (riv.), Québec 174/B1
Baleine, R. à la (riv.), Que. 162/K4
Balen, Belgium 27/G6
Baler, Philippines 82/C3
Baler (bay), Philippines 82/C3
Balerna, Switzerland 39/G5
Balerno, Scotland 15/D2
Baleshare (isl.), Scotland 15/A3
Balestrand, Norway 18/E6
Baley, Russia 48/M4
Balfate, Honduras 154/D3
Balfour, Br. Col. 184/J5
Balfour, N.C. 281/E4
Balfour, N. Dak. 282/J4
Balfron, Scotland 15/B1
Balgonie, Sask. 181/G5
Balhaf, Yemen 59/E7
Bal Harbour, Fla. 212/C4
Bali, Cameroon 115/A2
Bali (isl.), Indonesia 54/N10
Bali (isl.), Indonesia 85/F7
Bali (sea), Indonesia 85/F7
Bali (str.), Indonesia 85/E7
Baliangao, Philippines 82/D6
Balicuatro (isls.), Philippines 82/E4
Balige, Indonesia 85/B5
Balıkesir (prov.), Turkey 63/B3
Balıkesir, Turkey 63/B3
Balıkesir, Turkey 59/A2
Balikpapan, Indonesia 54/N10
Balikpapan, Indonesia 85/F6
Balık-Uzun (lake), Turkey 63/G2
Balimbing (Bato-Bato), Philippines 82/C8
Baling, Malaysia 72/D6
Balingasag, Philippines 82/E6
Balingen, Germany 22/C4
Balintang (chan.), Philippines 82/A2
Balintang (isls.), Philippines 82/A2
Baljennie, Sask. 181/C3
Balk, Netherlands 27/H3
Balkan (mts.) 7/G4
Balkan (mts.), Bulgaria 45/G4
Balkan, Ky. 237/O7
Balkány, Hungary 41/G3
Balkbrug, Netherlands 27/J3
Balkh, Afghanistan 68/B1
Balkh, Afghanistan 59/J2
Balkhash, Kazakhstan 48/H5
Balkhash, Kazakhstan 54/J5
Balkhash (lake), Kazakhstan 2/N3
Balkhash (lake), Kazakhstan 48/H5
Balkhash (lake), Kazakhstan 54/J5
Balko, Okla. 288/E1
Ball (mt.), Conn. 210/C1

Bayard 335

Baripada, India 68/F4
Bariri, Brazil 135/B3
Bariri (res.), Brazil 135/B3
Bâris, Egypt 111/F3
Barisal, Bangladesh 68/G4
Barisan (mts.), Indonesia 85/C6
Baritbog (riv.), New Bruns. 170/E1
Barito (riv.), Indonesia 85/E6
Bark (lake), Ontario 177/G2
Barkam, China 77/F5
Barker, N.Y. 276/C4
Barker Heights, N.C. 281/D4
Barkeyville, Pa. 294/C3
Barkhamsted•, Conn. 210/D1
Barkhamsted (res.), Conn. 210/D1
Barkhan, Pakistan 68/B3
Barkhan, Pakistan 59/J4
Barking, England 10/C5
Barking, England 13/H8
Barkley (sound), Br. Col. 184/E6
Barkley (dam), Ky. 237/E6
Barkley (lake), Ky. 237/F7
Barkley (lake), Tenn. 237/F7
Barkly Downs, Queensland 95/A4
Barkly East, S. Africa 118/D6
Barkly Tableland (plat.), Australia 87/D7
Barkly Tableland, North. Terr. 88/F3
Barkly Tableland, North. Terr. 93/D4
Barkly Tableland, Queensland 95/A4
Barkmere, Québec 172/C3
Barkol, China 77/D3
Bark River, Mich. 250/B3
Barksdale, Texas 303/D8
Barksdale A.F.B., La. 238/C2
Barlby, England 13/G4
Bar-le-Duc, France 28/F3
Barlee (lake), Australia 87/B8
Barlee (lake), W. Australia 88/B5
Barlee (lake), W. Australia 92/B5
Barletta, Italy 34/F4
Barlinek, Poland 47/B2
Barling, Ark. 202/B3
Barlow, Br. Col. 184/F3
Barlow, Ky. 237/D6
Barlow, Miss. 256/C7
Barlow, N. Dak. 282/M4
Barlow, Ohio 284/G7
Barlow, Oreg. 291/B2
Barlow Bend, Ala. 195/C8
Barmedman, N.S. Wales 97/D4
Barmer, India 68/C3
Barmera, S. Australia 94/G6
Bar Mills, Maine 243/C8
Barmouth, Wales 10/D4
Barmouth, Wales 13/C5
Barna, Ireland 17/C5
Barnabus, W. Va. 312/C7
Barnaby (riv.), New Bruns. 170/E2
Barnaby River, New Bruns. 170/E2
Barnard, Kansas 232/D2
Barnard, Mo. 261/C2
Barnard, N.C. 281/D3
Barnard, S. Dak. 298/N2
Barnard•, Vt. 268/B4
Barnard Castle, England 13/E3
Barnardsville, N.C. 281/E3
Barnaul, Russia 54/K4
Barnaul, Russia 48/J4
Barn Bluff (mt.), Tasmania 99/B3
Barnegat, Alberta 182/E2
Barnegat, N.J. 273/E4
Barnegat (bay), N.J. 273/E4
Barnegat (inlet), N.J. 273/E4
Barnegat Light, N.J. 273/E4
Barnes (sound), Fla. 212/F6
Barnes, Kansas 232/F2
Barnes (co.), N. Dak. 282/O5
Barnes, Wis. 317/D3
Barnesboro, Pa. 294/E4
Barnes City, Iowa 229/H6
Barnes Corners, N.Y. 276/J3
Barneston, Nebr. 264/H4
Barnesville, Colo. 208/L2
Barnesville, Ga. 217/D4
Barnesville, Md. 245/J4
Barnesville, Minn. 255/B4
Barnesville, N.C. 281/L6
Barnesville, Ohio 284/H6
Barnet, England 13/H7
Barnet, England 10/B5
Barnet•, Vt. 268/C3
Barnett, Ga. 217/G3
Barnett, Miss. 256/G7
Barnett, Mo. 261/G6
Barnettville, New Bruns. 170/E2
Barneveld, Netherlands 27/H4
Barneveld, N.Y. 276/K4
Barneveld, Wis. 317/F10
Barneville-Carteret, France 28/C3
Barney, Ga. 217/E8
Barney, N. Dak. 282/S7
Barnhart, Texas 303/C6
Barnhill, Ohio 284/H5
Barnoldswick, England 13/H1
Barnrock, Ky. 237/R5
Barnsdall, Okla. 288/O1
Barnsley, England 13/J2
Barnsley, England 10/F4
Barnstable (co.), Mass. 249/N6
Barnstable, Mass. 249/N6
Barnstable•, Mass. 249/N6
Barnstaple, England 10/E5
Barnstaple, England 13/D6
Barnstaple (bay), England 10/D5
Barnstaple (bay), England 13/C6
Barnstead•, N.H. 268/E5
Barnum, Iowa 229/E3
Barnum, Minn. 255/F4
Barnum, W. Va. 312/H4
Barnum, Wis. 317/E9
Barnwell, Ala. 195/C10
Barnwell, Alberta 182/D5
Barnwell (co.), S.C. 296/E5
Barnwell, S.C. 296/E5
Baro (riv.), Ethiopia 111/G6
Baro, Nigeria 106/F7
Baroda (Vadodara), India 68/C4
Baroda, India 54/J7
Baroda, Mich. 250/C7
Baroghil (pass), Afghanistan 68/C1
Baroghil (pass), Pakistan 68/C1
Baron, Okla. 288/S3
Baron Bluff (prom.), Virgin Is. (U.S.) 161/E3
Barons, Alberta 182/D4
Barooga, N.S. Wales 97/C4
Barossa (res.), S. Australia 94/C6
Barotseland (reg.), Zambia 115/D7
Barpeta, India 68/G3
Barqa (Cyrenaica) (reg.), Libya 111/D1
Barques (pt.), Mich. 250/C3
Barquisimeto, Venezuela 124/D2
Barquisimeto, Venezuela 120/C2
Barr, Scotland 15/D5
Barr, Tenn. 237/B9
Barra, Brazil 132/F5
Barra (head), Scotland 10/C2
Barra (head), Scotland 15/A4
Barra (isl.), Scotland 15/A4
Barra (isl.), Scotland 10/C2
Barra (isls.), Scotland 10/C2
Barra (sound), Scotland 15/A3
Barraba, N.S. Wales 97/F2
Barra Bonita (res.), Brazil 135/B3
Barrackpore, India 68/F1
Barrackville, W. Va. 312/F3
Barra de Río Grande, Nicaragua 154/F4
Barra do Bugres, Brazil 132/B6
Barra do Corda, Brazil 132/E4
Barra do Piraí, Brazil 132/E8
Barra do Piraí, Brazil 135/E3
Barra Isles (isls.), Scotland 15/A4
Barra Mansa, Brazil 135/D3
Barranca, Lima, Peru 128/C8
Barranca, Loreto, Peru 128/D5
Barrancabermeja, Colombia 126/C4
Barranca de Upía, Colombia 126/D5
Barrancas, Argentina 143/F6
Barrancas (riv.), Argentina 143/G5
Barrancas, Chile 138/G3
Barrancas, Colombia 126/D2
Barrancas, Barinas, Venezuela 124/C3
Barrancas, Monagas, Venezuela 124/G3
Barranco de Loba, Colombia 126/C3
Barrancos, Cerro (mt.), Chile 138/D7
Barrancos, Portugal 33/C3
Barranqueras, Argentina 143/E2
Barranquilla, Colombia 120/B1
Barranquilla, Colombia 126/C2
Barranquitas, P. Rico 161/D2
Barras (riv.), Bolivia 136/B6
Barras, Brazil 132/F4
Barras, Colombia 126/D8
Barraute, Québec 174/B3
Barre, Mass. 249/F3
Barre•, Mass. 249/F3
Barre, Québec 172/G3
Barre, Vt. 268/C3
Barre•, Vt. 268/C3
Barreal, Argentina 143/C3
Barreau (pt.), New Bruns. 170/F1
Barre Center, N.Y. 276/D4
Barreiras, Brazil 120/E4
Barreiras, Brazil 132/E6
Barreirinha, Brazil 132/B3
Barreirinhas, Brazil 132/F3
Barreiro, Portugal 33/B1
Barreiros, Brazil 132/H5
Barren (isls.), Alaska 196/B2
Barren (isl.), India 68/G6
Barren (co.), Ky. 237/K7
Barren (riv.), Ky. 237/H6
Barren (isls.), Madagascar 118/G3
Barren (isl.), Nova Scotia 168/G4
Barren (cape), Tasmania 99/E2
Barren Plains, Tenn. 237/H7
Barren River (lake), Ky. 237/J7
Barren Springs, Va. 307/G7
Barre Plains, Mass. 249/F3
Barrera, Bolivia 136/B3
Barretos, Brazil 132/D8
Barretos, Brazil 135/B2
Barrett, Minn. 255/B5
Barrett, Texas 303/K1
Barrett, W. Va. 312/C7
Barretts, Ga. 217/F8
Barrhead, Alberta 182/C2
Barrhead, Scotland 10/A1
Barrhead, Scotland 15/B2
Barrhill, Scotland 15/D5
Barrie, Ontario 177/E3
Barrie (isl.), Ontario 177/B1
Barrière, Br. Col. 184/H4
Barrineau Park, Fla. 212/B6
Barrington, Ill. 222/A5
Barrington•, N.H. 268/F5
Barrington, N.J. 273/B3
Barrington, Nova Scotia 168/C5
Barrington (bay), Nova Scotia 168/C5
Barrington•, R.I. 249/J6
Barrington, Tasmania 99/C3
Barrington Hills, Ill. 222/A5
Barrington P.O. (East Barrington), N.H. 268/F5
Barrington Passage, Nova Scotia 168/C5
Barrington Tops (mt.), N.S. Wales 97/F2
Barringun, N.S. Wales 97/C1
Barron (co.), Wis. 317/C5
Barron, Wis. 317/C5
Barronett, Wis. 317/B4
Barrouallie, St. Vin. & Grens. 161/A9
Barroui, Dominica 161/E6
Barrow, Alaska 196/G1
Barrow, Alaska 188/C5
Barrow, Alaska 146/C2
Barrow (pt.), Alaska 146/C2
Barrow (pt.), Alaska 196/G1
Barrow (isl.), Australia 87/B8
Barrow (co.), Ga. 217/E2
Barrow (riv.), Ireland 17/H7
Barrow (riv.), Ireland 10/C4
Barrow (str.), N.W.T. 162/G1
Barrow (str.), N.W.T. 187/J2
Barrow (bay), Ontario 177/C2
Barrow, U.S. 4/B17
Barrow (pt.), U.S. 2/B2
Barrow (pt.), U.S. 4/B18
Barrow (isl.), W. Australia 88/A4
Barrow (isl.), W. Australia 92/A3
Barrow Creek, North. Terr. 93/D6
Barrow-in-Furness, England 10/E3
Barrow-in-Furness, England 13/D3
Barrows, Manitoba 179/A2
Barrowsville, Mass. 249/K5
Barr Smith (mt.), Ant. 5/C5
Barruelo de Santullán, Spain 33/D1
Barry, Ill. 222/B4
Barry (co.), Mich. 250/D6
Barry, Minn. 255/B5
Barry (co.), Mo. 261/E9
Barry (mts.), Victoria 97/D5
Barry, Wales 13/B7
Barry, Wales 10/E5
Barry's Bay, Ontario 177/G2
Barryton, Mich. 250/D5
Barryville, N.Y. 276/L8
Barsi, India 68/D5
Barsinghausen, Germany 22/C2
Barss Corners, Nova Scotia 168/D4
Barstow, Calif. 204/H9
Barstow, Md. 245/M6
Barstow, Texas 303/A6
Bar-sur-Aube, France 28/F3
Bar-sur-Seine, France 28/F3
Bartelso, Ill. 222/D5
Barterville, Ky. 237/N4
Barth, Germany 22/E1
Barth, Fla. 212/B6
Barthel, Sask. 181/B2
Bartholomew (bayou), Ark. 202/G6
Bartholomew (co.), Ind. 227/F6
Bartibog Bridge, New Bruns. 170/E1
Bartica, Guyana 120/D2
Bartica, Guyana 131/B2
Bartın, Turkey 63/E2
Bartle, Cuba 158/H3
Bartle Frere (mt.), Queensland 88/H3
Bartle Frere (mt.), Queensland 95/C3
Bartlesville, Okla. 288/O1
Bartlett (dam), Ariz. 198/D5
Bartlett (res.), Ariz. 198/D5
Bartlett, Ill. 222/A5
Bartlett, Iowa 229/B7
Bartlett, Kansas 232/G4
Bartlett, Nebr. 264/F3
Bartlett•, N.H. 268/E3
Bartlett, N. Dak. 282/N3
Bartlett, Ohio 284/G7
Bartlett, Tenn. 237/B10
Bartlett, Texas 303/G7
Bartlett Deep, Cayman Is. 156/B3
Bartletts Ferry (dam), Ala. 195/H5
Bartletts Ferry (dam), Ga. 217/B5
Bartley, Nebr. 264/D4
Bartley, W. Va. 312/C8
Barto, Pa. 294/L5
Bartolomeu Dias, Mozambique 118/F4
Barton, Ala. 195/C1
Barton, Ark. 202/J4
Barton (co.), Kansas 232/D3
Barton, Md. 245/B2
Barton (co.), Mo. 261/D7
Barton, N. Dak. 282/K2
Barton, Ohio 284/J5
Barton, Oreg. 291/B2
Barton, Vt. 268/C2
Barton•, Vt. 268/C2
Barton (riv.), Vt. 268/C2
Barton City, Mich. 250/F4
Barton Hills, Mich. 250/F6
Bartonsville, Pa. 294/M4
Bartonsville, Vt. 268/B5
Barton-upon-Humber, England 13/G4
Barton-upon-Humber, England 10/F4
Bartonville, Ill. 222/D3
Bartonville, Texas 303/F1
Bartoszyce, Poland 47/E1
Bartow, Fla. 212/E4
Bartow (co.), Ga. 217/C2
Bartow, Ga. 217/G5
Bartow, W. Va. 312/G5
Bartra Antiguo, Peru 128/E4
Bartra Nuevo, Peru 128/E4
Barú (isl.), Colombia 126/C2
Barú (vol.), Panama 154/F6
Baruipur, India 68/F2
Barus, Indonesia 85/B5
Barut, Tanjong (cape), Malaysia 85/E5
Baruun-Urt, Mongolia 77/H2
Barvas, Scotland 10/C1
Barvas, Scotland 15/B2
Barview, Oreg. 291/C4
Bar View, Oreg. 291/C2
Barville, Québec 174/B3
Barwani, India 68/D4
Barwick, Ga. 217/E9
Barwick, Ontario 175/B3
Barwick, Ontario 177/F5
Barwon (riv.) 88/H5
Barwon (riv.), N.S. Wales 97/D2
Barysh, Russia 52/G4
Baryulgil, N.S. Wales 97/G1
Basalt, Colo. 208/E4
Basalt, Idaho 220/F6
Basankusu, D.R. Congo 115/C3
Basavilbaso, Argentina 143/G6
Bas-Caraquet, New Bruns. 170/F1
Bascharage, Luxembourg 27/H9
Basco, Ill. 222/B3
Basco, Philippines 82/A2
Bascom, Fla. 212/A1
Bascom, Ohio 284/D3
Bascuñán (cape), Chile 138/A7
Basehor, Kansas 232/G2
Basel, Switzerland 39/E1
Basel, Switzerland 7/E4
Baselland (canton), Switzerland 39/E2
Baselstadt (canton), Switzerland 39/E1
Basey, Philippines 82/E5
Bashan, Conn. 210/F2
Bashan (lake), Conn. 210/F3
Bashaw, Alberta 182/D3
Bashi, Ala. 195/C7
Bashi (chan.), China 77/K7
Bashi (chan.), Philippines 82/A1
Bashkir Aut. Rep., Russia 48/F4
Bashkir Aut. Rep., Russia 52/J4
Basht, Iran 66/G5
Basic, Miss. 256/G6
Basilan (prov.), Philippines 82/D7
Basilan (isl.), Philippines 85/G4
Basilan (isl.), Philippines 82/D7
Basilan (str.), Philippines 82/C7
Basildon, England 13/J8
Basildon, England 10/G5
Basile, La. 238/E5
Basilicata (reg.), Italy 34/F4
Basim, India 68/D4
Basin, Mont. 262/D4
Basin (lake), Sask. 181/F3
Basin, Wyo. 319/E1
Basinger, Fla. 212/F4
Basingstoke, England 10/F5
Basingstoke, England 13/F6
Basirhat, India 68/F4
Basit (cape), Syria 63/F5
Baskahegan (lake), Maine 243/H5
Başkale, Turkey 63/K3
Baskatong (res.), Que. 162/J6
Baskatong (res.), Québec 172/B3
Baskerville, Va. 307/M7
Basket (lake), Manitoba 179/C3
Baskett, Ky. 237/F5
Baskil, Turkey 63/H3
Baskin, La. 238/G2
Basking Ridge, N.J. 273/D2
Başmakçı, Turkey 63/C4
Basodino (peak), Switzerland 39/G4
Basoko, D.R. Congo 115/D3
Basom, N.Y. 276/D4
Basongo, D.R. Congo 115/D4
Basora (pt.), Neth. Ant. 161/E10
Basra (gov.), Iraq 66/E5
Basra, Iraq 2/M4
Basra, Iraq 66/E5
Basra, Iraq 59/E3
Basra, Iraq 54/F6
Bas-Rhin (dept.), France 28/G3
Bass (str.) 88/H7
Bass (str.), Australia 87/E9
Bass (isls.), Fr. Poly. 87/M8
Bass (lake), Ind. 227/D2
Bass (str.), Tasmania 99/C1
Bassano, Alberta 182/D4
Bassano del Grappa, Italy 34/C2
Bassas da India (isl.), Réunion 102/F7
Bassas da India (isl.), Réunion 118/F4
Bassecourt, Switzerland 39/D2
Bassein, Burma 54/L8
Bassein, Burma 72/B3
Bassein, India 68/C5
Basse-Pointe, Martinique 161/C5
Basse-Sambre, Belgium 27/F8
Basse Santa Su, Gambia 106/B6
Basse-Terre (cap.), Guadeloupe 161/A7
Basse-Terre (cap.), Guadeloupe 156/F4
Basse-Terre (isl.), Guadeloupe 161/A6
Basseterre (cap.), St. Kitts & Nevis 161/C10
Basseterre (cap.), St. Kitts & Nevis 156/F3
Basse Terre, Trin. & Tob. 161/B11
Bassett, Ark. 202/K2
Bassett, Iowa 229/J2
Bassett, Kansas 232/G4
Bassett, Nebr. 264/E2
Bassett, Va. 307/J7
Bassfield, Miss. 256/E8
Bass Harbor, Maine 243/G7
Bassikounou, Mauritania 106/C5
Bassin Bleu, Haiti 158/B5
Bass River, New Bruns. 170/E2
Bass River, Nova Scotia 168/E3
Bassum, Germany 22/C2
Basswood, Manitoba 179/B4
Basswood (lake), Minn. 255/G2
Basswood (lake), Ontario 175/B3
Båstad, Sweden 18/H8
Bastak, Iran 66/J7
Bastam, Iran 66/J2
Bastar, India 68/E5
Bastelica, France 28/B6
Bastenaken (Bastogne), Belgium 27/H9
Bastia, France 7/E4
Bastia, France 28/B6
Bastian, Va. 307/F6
Bastimentos (isl.), Panama 154/G6
Bastogne, Belgium 27/H9
Bastrop, La. 238/G1
Bastrop (co.), Texas 303/G7
Bastrop, Texas 303/G7
Bastuträsk, Sweden 18/L4
Basye, Va. 307/L3
Bas-Zaïre (prov.), D.R. Congo 115/B4
Bata, Equat. Guinea 102/C4
Bata, Equat. Guinea 115/B3
Bataan (prov.), Philippines 82/C3
Batabanó (gulf), Cuba 158/C2
Batabanó (gulf), Cuba 156/A2
Batag (isl.), Philippines 82/E4
Batagay, Russia 48/O3
Batala, India 68/D2
Batalha, Brazil 132/F3
Batalha, Portugal 33/B3
Batan (isls.), Philippines 54/O7
Batan, Albay (isl.), Philippines 82/E4
Batan, Batanes (isl.), Philippines 82/B2
Batan (isls.), Philippines 85/G1
Batan (isls.), Philippines 82/A2
Batanes (prov.), Philippines 82/A2
Batang, China 77/E5
Batang, China 54/L6
Batang, Indonesia 85/J2
Batangafo, Cent. Afr. Rep. 115/C2
Batangas (prov.), Philippines 82/C4
Batangas, Philippines 82/C4
Batangas, Philippines 85/G3
Batas (isl.), Philippines 82/B5
Bátaszék, Hungary 41/E3
Batatais, Brazil 135/C2
Batavia, Ill. 222/E2
Batavia (Jakarta) (cap.), Indonesia 85/H1
Batavia, Iowa 229/J7
Batavia, Mich. 250/D7
Batavia, N.Y. 276/D5
Batavia, Ohio 284/B7
Batavia, Wis. 317/K8
Batawa, Ontario 177/G3
Bataysk, Russia 52/E5
Bat Cave, N.C. 281/E4
Batchelor, La. 238/G5
Batchelor (brook), Mass. 248/D3
Batchelor, North. Terr. 93/B2
Batchtown, Ill. 222/C4
Batchwana Bay, Ontario 177/J5
Batdambang, Cambodia 54/M8
Batdambang (Battambang), Cambodia 72/D4
Bateman, Sask. 181/E5
Batemans Bay, N.S. Wales 97/F4
Bates, Ark. 202/B4
Bates, Mich. 250/D4
Bates (co.), Mo. 261/D6
Bates (mt.), Norfolk I. 88/L5
Bates, Oreg. 291/J3
Batesburg, S.C. 296/D4
Bates City, Mo. 261/E5
Batesland, S. Dak. 298/E7
Batesville, Ala. 195/H6
Batesville, Ark. 202/G2
Batesville, Ind. 227/G6
Batesville, Miss. 256/E2
Batesville, Ohio 284/H6
Batesville, Texas 303/E9
Batesville, Va. 307/L5
Bath, England 13/E6
Bath, England 10/E5
Bath, Ill. 222/C3
Bath, Ind. 227/H5
Bath, Jamaica 158/K6
Bath (co.), Ky. 237/O4
Bath, Maine 243/D8
Bath, Mich. 250/E6
Bath, Netherlands 27/E6
Bath, New Bruns. 170/C2
Bath•, N.H. 268/D3
Bath, N.Y. 276/F6
Bath, N.C. 281/R4
Bath, Ontario 177/H3
Bath, Pa. 294/M4
Bath, S.C. 296/D5
Bath, S. Dak. 298/N3
Bath (co.), Va. 307/J4
Batha (riv.), Chad 111/C5
Bathgate, N. Dak. 282/P2
Bathgate, Scotland 15/C2
Bathgate, Scotland 10/C1
Bathsheba, Barbados 161/B8
Bath Springs, Tenn. 237/E10
Bathurst (isl.), Australia 87/C7
Bathurst (isl.), Canada 4/B14
Bathurst (Banjul) (cap.), Gambia 106/A6
Bathurst, N. Br. 162/K6
Bathurst, New Bruns. 170/E1
Bathurst, N.S. Wales 88/H6
Bathurst, N.S. Wales 97/E3
Bathurst (isl.), North. Terr. 88/D2
Bathurst (isl.), North. Terr. 93/A1
Bathurst (cape), N.W.T. 162/D1
Bathurst (cape), N.W.T. 187/F2
Bathurst (inlet), N.W.T. 187/H3
Bathurst (isl.), N.W.T. 162/F1
Bathurst (isl.), N.W.T. 146/H2
Bathurst (isl.), N.W.T. 187/H2
Bathurst (harb.), Tasmania 99/C5
Bathurst Inlet, N.W.T. 187/H3
Bathurst Island, North. Terr. 93/B1
Bathurst Island Mission, North. Terr. 88/E2
Bathurst Mines, New Bruns. 170/E1
Batié, Burkina Faso 106/D7
Batı Fırat (riv.), Turkey 63/H3
Batin, Wadi al (dry riv.), Iraq 59/E4
Batin, Wadi al (dry riv.), Iraq 66/E6
Batin, Wadi al (dry riv.), Saudi Arabia 59/E4
Batina (reg.), Oman 59/G5
Batini (mt.), Fiji 86/Q10
Batiscan, Québec 172/E3
Batiscan (lake), Québec 172/E2
Batiscan (riv.), Québec 172/E2
Batley, England 13/J1
Batlow, N.S. Wales 97/E4
Batman, Turkey 63/J4
Batna, Algeria 102/C1
Batna, Algeria 106/F1
Bato, Catanduanes, Philippines 82/E4
Bato, Leyte, Philippines 82/E5
Bato-Bato, Philippines 82/C8
Batobato, Philippines 82/E7
Batoche, Sask. 181/E3
Batoche Nat'l Hist. Site, Sask. 181/E3
Baton Rouge (cap.), La. 146/J6
Baton Rouge (cap.), La. 188/H4
Baton Rouge (cap.), La. 238/K2
Bátonyterenye, Hungary 40/E3
Batopilas, Mexico 150/F3
Batouri, Cameroon 115/B3
Batovi, Uruguay 145/D2
Batrun, Lebanon 63/F5
Bat Shelomo, Israel 65/B2
Batson, Texas 303/K7
Batsto, N.J. 273/D4
Batsto (riv.), N.J. 273/D4
Batten Kill (riv.), N.Y. 276/O4
Batten Kill (riv.), Vt. 268/A5
Batterbee (cape), Ant. 2/N9
Batterbee (cape), Ant. 5/C3
Bätterkinden, Switzerland 39/E2
Battersea, Ontario 177/H3
Batticaloa, Sri Lanka 68/E7
Battiest, Okla. 288/S6
Batti Malv (isl.), India 68/G7
Battle (riv.) 162/E5
Battle (riv.), Alberta 182/D3
Battle, England 13/H7
Battle, England 10/G5
Battle (creek), Idaho 220/B7
Battle (riv.), Minn. 255/D3
Battle (creek), Mont. 262/G1
Battle (creek), Oreg. 291/K5
Battle (creek), Sask. 181/B6
Battle (riv.), Sask. 181/B3
Battle (creek), S. Dak. 298/C6
Battleboro, N.C. 281/O2
Battle Creek, Iowa 229/B4
Battle Creek, Mich. 188/J2
Battle Creek, Mich. 250/D6
Battle Creek, Nebr. 264/G3
Battlefield, Mo. 261/F8
Battleford, Sask. 162/E5
Battleford, Sask. 181/C3
Battle Ground, Ind. 227/D3
Battle Ground, Wash. 310/C5
Battle Harbour, Newf. 166/C3
Battle Harbour, Newf. 162/L5
Battle Lake, Alberta 182/C3
Battle Lake, Minn. 255/C4
Battle Mountain, Nev. 266/E2
Battles Wharf, Ala. 195/C10
Battletown, Ky. 237/J4
Battleview, N. Dak. 282/E2
Battock (mt.), Scotland 15/F4
Battonya, Hungary 41/F3
Battrum, Sask. 181/C5
Batu (isls.), Indonesia 85/B6
Batuco, Chile 138/G3
Batu Gajah, Malaysia 72/D6
Batulaki, Philippines 82/E8
Batumi, Georgia 7/J4
Batumi, Georgia 48/E5
Batumi, Georgia 52/F6
Batu Pahat, Malaysia 72/D7
Baturaja, Indonesia 85/C6
Baturité, Brazil 132/G4
Batusangkar, Indonesia 85/C6
Bat Yam, Israel 65/B3
Bauang, Philippines 82/C2
Baubau, Indonesia 85/G7
Bauchi (state), Nigeria 106/F6
Bauchi, Nigeria 106/F6
Baudette, Minn. 255/D2
Baudette (riv.), Minn. 255/D2
Baudh, India 68/E4
Baudó, Serranía de (mts.), Colombia 126/B5
Baudó (riv.), Colombia 126/B5
Baugé, France 28/D4
Baukau, Indonesia 85/H7
Bauld (cape), Newf. 166/C3
Bauld (cape), Newf. 162/L5
Bauline, Newf. 166/D2
Baulkham Hills, N.S. Wales 88/K4
Baulkham Hills, N.S. Wales 97/H3
Baulmes, Switzerland 39/C3
Bauma, Switzerland 39/G2
Baumann (fjord), N.W.T. 187/K2
Baume-les-Dames, France 28/G4
Baures, Bolivia 136/D3
Baures (riv.), Bolivia 136/D3
Bauria, India 68/E2
Baurtregaum (mt.), Ireland 17/A7
Bauru, Brazil 120/E5
Bauru, Brazil 135/B3
Bauru, Brazil 132/D8
Bauska, Latvia 53/B2
Bauta, Cuba 158/C1
Bauta (riv.), P. Rico 161/C2
Bautzen, Germany 22/F3
Bauxite, Ark. 202/F4
Bavaria, Kansas 232/E3
Bavaria (state), Germany 22/D4
Bavarian (for.), Germany 22/E4
Bavarian Alps (mts.), Austria 41/A3
Bavarian Alps (range), Germany 22/D5
Baviácora, Mexico 150/E2
Bavispe, Mexico 150/E1
Bavispe, Río de (riv.), Mexico 150/E1
Bawean (isl.), Indonesia 85/K1
Bawku, Ghana 106/D6
Bawlf, Alberta 182/D3
Ba Xian, China 77/J4
Baxley, Ga. 217/H7
Baxoi, China 77/E5
Baxter (co.), Ark. 202/F1
Baxter, Iowa 229/G5
Baxter, Minn. 255/D4
Baxter, Miss. 256/F6
Baxter, Pa. 294/D3
Baxter, Tenn. 237/K8
Baxter Springs, Kansas 232/H4
Baxterville, Miss. 256/E8
Bay, Ark. 202/J2
Bay (Baicheng), China 77/B3
Bay (co.), Fla. 212/C6
Bay (co.), Mich. 250/E5
Bay, Mo. 261/J5
Bay, Laguna de (lake), Philippines 82/C3
Bay (prov.), Somalia 115/H3
Bayag (Calanasan), Philippines 82/C1
Bayaguana, Dom. Rep. 158/E6
Bayamhongor, Mongolia 77/E2
Bayamo, Cuba 156/C2
Bayamo, Cuba 158/H4
Bayamón (dist.), P. Rico 161/D1
Bayamón, P. Rico 161/D1
Bayamón, P. Rico 156/G1
Bayamón (riv.), P. Rico 161/D1
Bayanbaraat, Mongolia 77/G2
Bayandalay, Mongolia 77/F3
Bayan Dobo Suma, Mongolia 77/G3
Bayang, Philippines 82/E7
Bayangovĭ, Mongolia 77/F3
Bayan Har Shan (range), China 77/E5
Bayanhongor, Mongolia 77/E2
Bayan Mod, China 77/F3
Bayan Obo, China 77/G3
Bayan-Ölgiy, Mongolia 77/C2
Bayan-Öndör, Mongolia 77/E3
Bayan-Uul, Mongolia 77/E2
Bayard, Del. 245/T6
Bayard, Iowa 229/D5
Bayard, Nebr. 264/A3
Bayard, N. Mex. 274/A6

Blind River 339

Bikoro, D.R. Congo 115/C4
Bikoro, D.R. Congo 102/D5
Bilaspur, India 68/E4
Bilauktaung (range), Burma 72/C4
Bilauktaung (range), Thailand 72/C4
Bilbao, Spain 33/E1
Bilbao, Spain 7/D4
Bilecá, Bos. 45/D4
Bilecik (prov.), Turkey 63/D2
Bilecik, Turkey 59/A1
Bilecik, Turkey 63/D2
Biłgoraj, Poland 47/F3
Bilibino, Russia 4/C1
Bilibino, Russia 48/R3
Bilin, Burma 72/C3
Bílina, Czech Rep. 41/B1
Biliran (isl.), Philippines 82/E5
Bill, Wyo. 319/G2
Billate (riv.), Ethiopia 111/G6
Billerica•, Mass. 249/J2
Billings (lake), Conn. 210/H2
Billings, Mo. 261/F8
Billings, Mont. 146/H5
Billings, Mont. 188/E1
Billings, Mont. 262/H5
Billings (co.), N. Dak. 282/D5
Billings, Okla. 288/M1
Billingsgate (isl.), Mass. 249/O5
Billingshurst, England 13/G6
Billingsley, Ala. 195/E5
Billiton (isl.), Indonesia 54/M10
Billiton (isl.), Indonesia 85/D6
Bill Williams (riv.), Ariz. 198/B4
Billy Clapp (lake), Wash. 310/F3
Bilma, Niger 102/D3
Bilma, Niger 106/G5
Biloela, Queensland 88/J4
Biloela, Queensland 95/D5
Biloku, Guyana 131/B5
Biloxi, Miss. 146/K6
Biloxi, Miss. 188/J4
Biloxi, Miss. 256/G10
Biltine, Chad 111/D5
Biltine, Chad 102/D3
Biltmore Forest, N.C. 281/E3
Bilwaskarma, Nicaragua 154/F3
Bilzen, Belgium 27/G7
Bim, W. Va. 312/C7
Biminis, The (isls.), Bahamas 156/B1
Bina-Itawa, India 68/D4
Binalbagan, Philippines 82/D5
Binalong, N.S. Wales 97/E4
Binboğa (mts.), Turkey 63/G3
Binbrook, Ontario 177/E4
Binche, Belgium 27/E8
Binda, N.S. Wales 97/E4
Bindloss, Alberta 182/E4
Bindoon, W. Australia 92/B1
Bindura, Zimbabwe 118/E3
Binéfar, Spain 33/G2
Binevenagh (mt.), N. Ireland 17/H1
Binford, N. Dak. 282/O4
Binga (mt.), Mozambique 118/E3
Bingara, N.S. Wales 97/F1
Bingen, Wash. 310/D5
Bingen, Germany 22/B4
Binger, Okla. 288/K4
Bingerville, Ivory Coast 106/D7
Bingham (co.), Idaho 220/F6
Bingham, Ill. 222/D4
Bingham, Maine 243/D5
Bingham•, Maine 243/D5
Bingham, Nebr. 264/B2
Bingham, N. Mex. 274/C5
Bingham, S.C. 296/H3
Bingham (canyon), Utah 304/B3
Bingham Lake, Minn. 255/C7
Binghamton, N.Y. 188/L2
Binghamton, N.Y. 276/J6
Bingöl (prov.), Turkey 63/J3
Bingöl (Çapakçur), Turkey 63/J3
Bingöl Dağları (mts.), Turkey 63/J3
Binhai, China 77/K5
Binh Long (An Loc), Vietnam 72/E5
Binh Son, Vietnam 72/F4
Binjai, Indonesia 85/B5
Binn, Switzerland 39/F4
Binnaway, N.S. Wales 97/E2
Binningen, Switzerland 39/D1
Binongko (isl.), Indonesia 85/G7
Binscarth, Manitoba 179/A4
Bintan (isl.), Indonesia 85/C5
Bintuhan, Indonesia 85/C6
Bintulu, Malaysia 85/E5
Binyamina, Israel 65/B2
Binyang, China 77/G7
Biobío (reg.), Chile 138/E1
Bio-Bío (riv.), Chile 138/E2
Biograd, Croatia 45/B4
Bioko (isl.), Equat. Guinea 102/C4
Bioko (isl.), Equat. Guinea 115/A3
Bioko (terr.), Equat. Guinea 115/A3
Biola, Calif. 204/E7
Bippus, Ind. 227/F3
Bir, India 68/D5
Bira, Russia 48/O5
Birag, Kuh-e (mts.), Iran 66/M7
Bir 'Ali, Yemen 59/E7
Birama (pt.), Cuba 158/G4
Birao, Cent. Afr. Rep. 115/D1
Biratnagar, Nepal 68/F3
Biratori, Japan 81/L2
Bir Bala, Iran 66/L8
Bir Bala, Iran 59/G4
Bircao, Somalia 115/H4
Birch (creek), Alaska 196/J1
Birch (hills), Alberta 182/A2
Birch (lake), Alberta 182/E3
Birch (mts.), Alberta 182/B5
Birch (riv.), Alberta 182/B5
Birch (creek), Idaho 220/F5
Birch (isl.), Manitoba 179/C2
Birch (lake), Minn. 255/G3
Birch (creek), Mont. 262/D2
Birch (lake), Sask. 181/C2
Birch (creek), Utah 304/B5
Birch (pt.), Wash. 310/C2
Birch Creek, Alaska 196/J1
Birch Creek (valley), Idaho 220/E5
Birch Creek (res.), Mont. 262/D2
Birchdale, Minn. 255/D2
Birch Harbor, Maine 243/H7
Birch Hills, Sask. 181/F3
Birchip, Victoria 97/B4
Birch Island, Br. Col. 184/H4
Birchleaf, Va. 307/D6
Birch River, Manitoba 179/A2
Birch River, W. Va. 312/E6
Birch Run, Mich. 250/F5
Birchtown, Nova Scotia 168/C5
Birch Tree, Mo. 261/K9
Birchwood, Tenn. 237/M10
Birchwood, Wis. 317/C4
Birchy Bay, Newf. 166/D4
Bird (isl.), La. 238/M8
Bird (creek), Okla. 288/O1
Bird City, Kansas 232/A2
Bird Cove, Newf. 166/C3
Bird Island, Minn. 255/D6
Birds, Ill. 222/F5
Birdsboro, Pa. 294/L5
Birdseye, Ind. 227/D8
Birds Hill, Manitoba 179/F4
Birdsnest, Va. 307/S6
Birdsong, Ark. 202/K3
Birdsville, Ky. 237/D6
Birdsville, Queensland 88/F5
Birdsville, Queensland 95/A5
Birdtail, Manitoba 179/B4
Birdum, North. Terr. 93/C3
Birdwood, S. Australia 94/C7
Birecik, Turkey 63/H4
Bir el Khzaim (well), Mauritania 106/C4
Bireuen, Indonesia 85/B4
Bir Ganduz (well), Western Sahara 106/A4
Birganj, Nepal 68/F3
Bir Hakeim (ruins), Libya 111/D1
Birigui, Brazil 135/A2
Birjand, Iran 66/L4
Birjand, Iran 59/G3
Birjand, Iran 54/G6
Birken, Br. Col. 184/F5
Birkenfeld, Oreg. 291/D1
Birkenfeld, Germany 22/B4
Birkenhead, England 13/G2
Birkenhead, England 10/F2
Birkenhead, N. Zealand 100/B1
Birkenhead Lake Prov. Park, Br. Col. 184/F5
Birkerød, Denmark 21/F6
Birket Qârûn (lake), Egypt 111/J3
Bir Ksaib Ounane (well), Mali 106/C4
Birksgate (range), S. Australia 94/A2
Bîrlad, Romania 45/H2
Bîrlad (riv.), Romania 45/H2
Birmingham, Ala. 146/K6
Birmingham, Ala. 188/J4
Birmingham, Ala. 195/D3
Birmingham, England 7/D3
Birmingham, England 10/G3
Birmingham, England 13/F5
Birmingham, Iowa 229/K7
Birmingham, Mich. 250/B6
Birmingham, Mo. 261/R5
Birmingham, N.J. 273/D4
Birmingham, Ohio 284/F3
Birmingham, Pa. 294/F4
Birmingham, Sask. 181/H5
Birmitrapur, India 68/E4
Bir Mogreïn, Mauritania 106/B3
Birnam, Scotland 15/E4
Birnamwood, Wis. 317/H6
Birney, Mont. 262/K5
Birnie, Manitoba 179/C4
Birnin Kebbi, Nigeria 106/E6
Birni-N'Konni, Niger 106/E6
Birni-N'Konni, Niger 102/C3
Bir Nzaran (well), Western Sahara 106/B4
Birobidzhan, Russia 54/O5
Birobidzhan, Russia 48/O5
Biron, Wis. 317/G7
Bir Ounane (well), Mali 106/D4
Birqin, West Bank 65/C3
Birr, Ireland 17/F5
Birr, Ireland 10/B4
Birregurra, Victoria 97/B6
Birrie (riv.), N.S. Wales 88/H5
Birrie (riv.), N.S. Wales 97/D1
Birrimbah, North. Terr. 93/C3
Birrindudu, North. Terr. 93/A5
Birriwa, N.S. Wales 97/E3
Birs (riv.), Switzerland 39/D2
Birsay, Sask. 181/D4
Birsk, Russia 52/J3
Birta, Ark. 202/D3
Bir Taba, Egypt 59/B4
Bir Taba (well), Egypt 111/F2
Birtle, Manitoba 179/B4
Biru, China 77/D5
Biruaca, Venezuela 124/E4
Biržai, Lithuania 53/C2
Bir Zeit, West Bank 65/C4
Bisbee, Ariz. 188/E4
Bisbee, Ariz. 198/F7
Bisbee, N. Dak. 282/M2
Biscarrosse (lake), France 28/C5
Biscay (bay) 2/J3
Biscay (bay) 7/D4
Biscay (bay), France 28/B5
Biscay, Minn. 255/D6
Biscay (bay), Spain 33/E1
Biscay Bay (riv.), Newf. 166/D2
Biscayne (bay), Fla. 212/F6
Biscayne (key), Fla. 212/B5
Biscayne Nat'l Park, Fla. 212/F6
Biscayne Park, Fla. 212/B4
Bisceglie, Italy 34/F4
Bischofshofen, Austria 41/B3
Bischofswerda, Germany 22/F3
Bischofszell, Switzerland 39/H1
Biscoe (isls.), Ant. 5/C15
Biscoe, Ark. 202/H4
Biscoe, N.C. 281/K4
Biscotasing, Ontario 177/J5
Biscotasing, Ontario 175/D3
Biscucuy, Venezuela 124/D3
Bisha, Saudi Arabia 59/D5
Bisha, Wadi (dry riv.), Saudi Arabia 59/D5
Bishiara (well), Libya 111/D3
Bishkek (cap.), Kyrgyzstan 48/H5
Bishkek (cap.), Kyrgyzstan 54/J5
Bisho, South Africa 118/D6
Bisho (cap.), Ciskei, S. Africa 102/E8
Bishop, Calif. 204/G6
Bishop, Ga. 217/F3
Bishop, Md. 245/S7
Bishop (creek), Nev. 266/F1
Bishop, Texas 303/G10
Bishop (creek), Utah 304/E3
Bishop, Va. 307/E6
Bishop Auckland, England 10/E3
Bishop Auckland, England 13/E3
Bishopbriggs, Scotland 15/B2
Bishop Hill, Ill. 222/C2
Bishopric, Sask. 181/F5
Bishop's Falls, Newf. 166/C4
Bishops Head, Md. 245/O7
Bishops Mitre (mt.), Newf. 166/B2
Bishop's Stortford, England 10/G5
Bishop's Stortford, England 13/H6
Bishopton, Québec 172/F4
Bishopton, Scotland 15/B2
Bishopville, Md. 245/T7
Bishopville, S.C. 296/G3
Bishri, Jebel el (mts.), Syria 63/H5
Biskra, Algeria 106/F2
Biskra, Algeria 102/C1
Biskupiec, Poland 47/E2
Bislig, Philippines 85/H4
Bislig, Philippines 82/F6
Bismarck, Ark. 202/D5
Bismarck, Ill. 222/F3
Bismarck, Mo. 261/L7
Bismarck (cap.), N. Dak. 146/H5
Bismarck (cap.), N. Dak. 188/G1
Bismarck (cap.), N. Dak. 282/J6
Bismarck (arch.), Papua N.G. 2/S6
Bismarck (arch.), Papua N.G. 87/E6
Bismarck (arch.), Papua N.G. 86/B1
Bismarck (sea), Papua N.G. 86/B1
Bismarck, W. Va. 312/H4
Bismil, Turkey 63/J4
Bison (lake), Alberta 182/B1
Bison, Kansas 232/C3
Bison, Okla. 288/L2
Bison, S. Dak. 298/E2
Bispgården, Sweden 18/K5
Bissau (cap.), Guinea-Biss. 106/A6
Bissau (cap.), Guinea-Biss. 102/A3
Bissett, Manitoba 179/G4
Bistineau (lake), La. 238/D2
Bistrița, Romania 45/G2
Bita (riv.), Colombia 126/F5
Bitagron, Suriname 131/C3
Bitam, Gabon 115/B3
Bitburg, Germany 22/B4
Bitely, Mich. 250/D5
Bithlo, Fla. 212/E3
Bitkine, Chad 111/C5
Bitlis (prov.), Turkey 63/J3
Bitlis, Turkey 63/J3
Bitlis, Turkey 59/D2
Bitola, Macedonia 45/E5
Bitola, Macedonia 7/G4
Bitonto, Italy 34/F4
Bitter (lakes), Egypt 111/K3
Bitter (lake), Sask. 181/B5
Bitter (creek), Wyo. 319/C4
Bitter Creek, Wyo. 319/D4
Bitterfeld, Germany 22/E3
Bitterfontein, S. Africa 118/B6
Bittern (lake), Alberta 182/D3
Bittern Lake, Alberta 182/D3
Bitterroot (range) 188/D1
Bitterroot (range), Idaho 220/D3
Bitterroot (range), Mont. 262/B4
Bitterroot (riv.), Mont. 262/B4
Bitterroot (range), U.S. 146/G5
Bitti, Italy 34/B4
Bitumount, Alberta 182/E1
Bitung, Indonesia 85/H5
Biu, Nigeria 106/G6
Biu (plat.), Nigeria 106/G6
Bivalve, Md. 245/P7
Bivalve, N.J. 273/C5
Bivolari, Romania 45/H2
Biwa (lake), Japan 81/H6
Biwabik, Minn. 255/F3
Bixby, Minn. 255/E7
Bixby, Mo. 261/K7
Bixby, Okla. 288/P3
Biyang, China 77/H5
Biysk, Russia 54/K4
Biysk, Russia 48/J4
Bizcocho, Uruguay 145/B4
Bizerte, Tunisia 106/F1
Bizerte, Tunisia 102/C1
Bjargtangar (pt.), Iceland 21/A1
Bjelovar, Croatia 45/C3
Bjerringbro, Denmark 21/C5
Bjorkdale, Sask. 181/H3
Bjørnafjorden (fjord), Norway 18/D6
Bjorne (pen.), N.W.T. 187/K2
Bjornøya (isl.), Norway 18/D3
Blabon, N. Dak. 282/P5
Blachly, Oreg. 291/D3
Black (sea) 2/L3
Black (sea) 54/E5
Black (sea) 7/H4
Black, Ala. 195/G8
Black (riv.), Alaska 196/K1
Black (mesa), Ariz. 198/E2
Black (mts.), Ariz. 198/A3
Black (riv.), Ariz. 198/E5
Black (riv.), Ark. 202/H2
Black (sea), Bulgaria 45/J4
Black (pt.), Conn. 210/G3
Black (pond), Conn. 210/G1
Black (mts.), England 13/D6
Black (creek), Fla. 212/E1
Black (for.), Germany 22/C4
Black (head), Ireland 17/C5
Black (riv.), Jamaica 158/H6
Black (mt.), Ky. 237/R7
Black (lake), La. 238/D3
Black (pond), Maine 243/D3
Black (isl.), Manitoba 179/F3
Black (riv.), Manitoba 179/F4
Black (lake), Mich. 250/E3
Black (riv.), Mich. 250/E3
Black (riv.), Mich. 250/G5
Black (riv.), Minn. 255/D2
Black (creek), Miss. 256/F8
Black, Mo. 261/L7
Black (riv.), Mo. 261/L10
Black (mt.), N. Mex. 274/A6
Black (range), N. Mex. 274/B5
Black (lake), N.Y. 276/J1
Black (riv.), N.Y. 276/K3
Black (riv.), N.C. 281/N5
Black (riv.), Ohio 284/F3
Black (riv.), Ontario 177/E3
Black (sea), Romania 45/J4
Black (lake), Sask. 181/M2
Black (riv.), S.C. 296/H4
Black (sea), Turkey 63/E1
Black (sea), Georgia 48/D5
Black (sea), Georgia 52/D6
Black (sea), Russia 48/D5
Black (sea), Russia 52/D6
Black (sea), Ukraine 48/D5
Black (sea), Ukraine 52/D6
Black (creek), Vt. 268/B2
Black (riv.), Vt. 268/C2
Black (riv.), Vt. 268/B5
Black (riv.), Vietnam 72/D2
Black (mts.), Wales 13/D6
Black (riv.), Wis. 317/E7
Black (riv.), Yukon 187/D3
Blackall, Australia 87/E8
Blackall, Queensland 88/H4
Blackall, Queensland 95/C5
Black Bear (creek), Okla. 288/M2
Blackberry (riv.), Conn. 210/B1
Blackbird, Del. 245/R3
Blackbourne (pt.), Norfolk I. 88/L6
Black Branch, Nulhegan (riv.), Vt. 268/D2
Blackburn (mt.), Alaska 196/K2
Blackburn, England 13/H1
Blackburn, England 10/G1
Blackburn, La. 238/D1
Blackburn, Mo. 261/F4
Blackburn, Okla. 288/N2
Blackburn, Ontario 177/J2
Blackburn, Scotland 15/C2
Black Butte (lake), Calif. 204/C4
Black Canyon City, Ariz. 198/C4
Black Canyon of the Gunnison Nat'l Mon., Colo. 208/D5
Black Creek, Br. Col. 184/E5
Black Creek, N.C. 281/O3
Black Creek, Wis. 317/K7
Black Diamond, Alberta 182/C4
Black Diamond, Wash. 310/D3
Blackduck, Minn. 255/D3
Black Duck (riv.), Ontario 175/C1
Black Eagle, Mont. 262/E3
Black Earth, Wis. 317/G9
Black Elster (riv.), Germany 22/E3
Blackey, Ky. 237/R6
Blackfalds, Alberta 182/D3
Blackfeet Ind. Res., Mont. 262/D2
Blackfoot, Alberta 182/E3
Blackfoot, Idaho 220/F6
Blackfoot (res.), Idaho 220/G7
Blackfoot (riv.), Idaho 220/G6
Blackfoot, Mont. 262/D2
Blackfoot (riv.), Mont. 262/C4
Blackford (co.), Ind. 227/G4
Blackford, Ky. 237/F6
Blackford, Scotland 15/E4
Black Forest, Colo. 208/K4
Blackfork, Ohio 284/E8
Black Fork, Mohican (riv.), Ohio 284/F4
Blackgum, Okla. 288/S3
Black Hall, Conn. 210/F3
Black Hawk, Colo. 208/J3
Blackhawk, Ind. 227/C6
Black Hawk (co.), Iowa 229/J4
Black Hawk, Miss. 256/E4
Black Hawk, S. Dak. 298/C5
Blackhead (bay), Newf. 166/D2
Blackhead Road, Newf. 166/D2
Black Hills (mts.) 188/F2
Black Hills (mts.), S. Dak. 298/B5
Blackie, Alberta 182/D4
Black Isle (pen.), Scotland 15/D3
Black Jack, Mo. 261/R1
Black Lake (bayou), La. 238/D1
Black Lake, Québec 172/F3
Black Lake, Sask. 181/M2
Blackledge (riv.), Conn. 210/F2
Black Lick, Pa. 294/D4
Blacklock (pt.), Oreg. 291/C5
Black Mesa (mt.), Okla. 288/A1
Blackmore (mt.), Mont. 262/F5
Black Mountain, N.C. 281/E3
Black Oak, Ark. 202/K2
Black Oak, Ind. 227/C1
Black Pine (mts.), Idaho 220/E7
Black Pine (peak), Idaho 220/E7
Black Pine (creek), S. Dak. 298/G6
Black Point, Calif. 204/J1
Black Point, Conn. 210/G3
Black Point, New Bruns. 170/D1
Blackpool, England 13/G1
Blackpool, England 10/F1
Blackridge, Va. 307/M7
Black River, Jamaica 158/H6
Black River, Jamaica 156/B3
Black River (bay), Jamaica 158/G6
Black River, Mich. 250/F4
Black River, New Bruns. 170/E3
Black River (pond), Newf. 166/C2
Black River, N.Y. 276/J3
Black River Bridge, New Bruns. 170/E2
Black River Falls, Wis. 317/E7
Black Rock, Ark. 202/H1
Black Rock (des.), Nev. 266/B2
Black Rock (range), Nev. 266/B1
Black Rock (pt.), R.I. 249/H8
Black Rock, Utah 304/B5
Blacksburg, S.C. 296/D1
Blacksburg, Va. 307/H6
Blacks Fork, Green (riv.), Wyo. 319/C4
Blacks Harbour, New Bruns. 170/D3
Blackshear, Ga. 217/H8
Blackshear (lake), Ga. 217/E7
Blacksher, Ala. 195/C8
Blacksod (bay), Ireland 17/A3
Black Springs, Ark. 202/C5
Black Springs, Nev. 266/B3
Black Squirrel (creek), Colo. 208/L5
Blackstairs (mt.), Ireland 17/H6
Blackstock, Ontario 177/F3
Blackstock, S.C. 296/E2
Blackstone•, Mass. 249/H4
Blackstone (riv.), Mass. 249/G3
Blackstone, Va. 307/N6
Blacksville, W. Va. 312/F3
Black Thunder (creek), Wyo. 319/G2
Black Tickle, Newf. 166/C3
Blackton, Ark. 202/H4
Blacktown, N.S. Wales 88/K4
Blacktown, N.S. Wales 97/H3
Blackville, New Bruns. 170/E2
Blackville, S.C. 296/E5
Black Volta (riv.) 102/B3
Black Volta (Mouhoun) (riv.), Burkina Faso 106/D6
Black Volta (riv.), Ghana 106/D6
Black Volta (riv.), Ivory Coast 106/D6
Black Warrior (riv.), Ala. 195/C5
Blackwater (riv.), England 13/H6
Blackwater (riv.), Fla. 212/B6
Blackwater, Ireland 17/J7
Blackwater (riv.), Ireland 10/B4
Blackwater (riv.), Ireland 17/D7
Blackwater (riv.), Ireland 17/H4
Blackwater, Mo. 261/G5
Blackwater (res.), N.H. 268/D5
Blackwater (riv.), N. Ireland 17/H3
Blackwater, Queensland 95/D4
Blackwater, Queensland 88/H4
Blackwater (res.), Scotland 15/D4
Blackwater, Va. 307/B7
Blackwater (riv.), Va. 307/J6
Blackwater (riv.), Va. 307/O6
Blackwell, Ark. 202/E3
Blackwell (brook), Conn. 210/H1
Blackwell, Okla. 288/M1
Blackwell, Texas 303/D5
Blackwell, Wis. 317/J4
Blackwood (Ngundju) (cape), Indonesia 85/F8
Blackwood, N.J. 273/C4
Blackwood Terrace, N.J. 273/C4
Bladen, Nebr. 264/F4
Bladen (co.), N.C. 281/M5
Bladenboro, N.C. 281/M5
Bladensburg, Md. 245/G4
Bladensburg, Ohio 284/F5
Blades, Del. 245/R6
Bladon Springs, Ala. 195/B7
Bladworth, Sask. 181/E4
Blaeberry, Br. Col. 184/J4
Blaenavon, Wales 13/B6
Blagodarnoye, Russia 52/F5
Blagoevgrad, Bulgaria 45/F5
Blagoveshchensk, Russia 48/N4
Blagoveshchensk, Russia 52/J4
Blagoveshchensk, Russia 54/O4
Blain, France 28/C4
Blain, Pa. 294/H5
Blaine, Ga. 217/C1
Blaine (co.), Idaho 220/D6
Blaine, Kansas 232/F2
Blaine, Ky. 237/R4
Blaine•, Maine 243/H2
Blaine, Mich. 250/G5
Blaine, Minn. 255/G5
Blaine, Miss. 256/C3
Blaine (co.), Mont. 262/G2
Blaine (co.), Nebr. 264/E3
Blaine, Ohio 284/J5
Blaine (co.), Okla. 288/K3
Blaine, Oreg. 291/D2
Blaine, Tenn. 237/O8
Blaine, Wash. 310/C2
Blaine Lake, Sask. 181/D3
Blaine-Mars Hill, Maine 243/H2
Blainville, Québec 172/H4
Blair, Kansas 232/H2
Blair, Nebr. 264/H3
Blair, Okla. 288/H5
Blair (co.), Pa. 294/F4
Blair, S.C. 296/E3
Blair, W. Va. 312/C7
Blair, Wis. 317/D7
Blair Athol, Queensland 95/C4
Blair Atholl, Scotland 10/E2
Blair Atholl, Scotland 15/E4
Blairgowrie and Rattray, Scotland 15/E4
Blairgowrie and Rattray, Scotland 10/E2
Blairmore, Alberta 182/C5
Blairs, Va. 307/K7
Blairsburg, Iowa 229/F4
Blairsden, Calif. 204/E4
Blairs Mills, Ky. 237/P4
Blairs Mills, Pa. 294/G5
Blairstown, Iowa 229/J5
Blairstown, Mo. 261/E5
Blairstown•, N.J. 273/C2
Blairsville, Ga. 217/E1
Blairsville, Pa. 294/D5
Blaisdell, N. Dak. 282/F3
Blaj, Romania 45/F2
Blake (pt.), Mich. 250/E1
Blakeley, Minn. 255/E6
Blakeley, W. Va. 312/D6
Blakely, Ga. 217/C8
Blakely, Pa. 294/F6
Blakesburg, Iowa 229/H7
Blakeslee, Ohio 284/A2
Blakeslee, Pa. 294/L3
Blaketown, Newf. 166/D2
Blalock, Ala. 195/D6
Blalock, Ga. 217/E1
Blalock (isl.), Wash. 310/F5
Blanc (cape) 2/J4
Blanc (mt.), France 7/E4
Blanc (mt.), France 28/G5
Blanc (mt.), Italy 34/A2
Blanc (cape), Mauritania 102/A2
Blanc (cape), Mauritania 106/A4
Blanc (cape), Tunisia 106/G1
Blanc (cape), Western Sahara 106/A4
Blanca (bay), Argentina 120/C6
Blanca (bay), Argentina 143/D4
Blanca (lag.), Chile 138/E10
Blanca (peak), Colo. 188/F3
Blanca, Colo. 208/H8
Blanca (peak), Colo. 208/H7
Blanca (pt.), C. Rica 154/F5
Blanca, Cordillera (mts.), Peru 128/D7
Blanch, N.C. 281/L2
Blanchard, Idaho 220/A1
Blanchard, Iowa 229/C7
Blanchard, La. 238/C1
Blanchard•, Maine 243/D5
Blanchard, Mich. 250/D5
Blanchard, N. Dak. 282/R5
Blanchard (riv.), Ohio 284/C4
Blanchard, Okla. 288/L4
Blanchard, Pa. 294/G3
Blanchard, Wash. 310/C2
Blanchardstown, Ireland 17/H5
Blanchardville, Wis. 317/G10
Blanche, Ky. 237/O7
Blanche (riv.), Québec 172/E2
Blanche (lake), S. Australia 88/F5
Blanche (lake), S. Australia 94/F3
Blanche, Tenn. 237/H10
Blanche (lake), W. Australia 88/C4
Blanche Marie (fall), Suriname 131/C3
Blanchester, Ohio 284/B7
Blanchisseuse, Trin. & Tob. 161/B10
Blanco (riv.), Argentina 143/C2
Blanco (riv.), Bolivia 136/D4
Blanco (lake), Chile 138/F10
Blanco (cape), C. Rica 154/E6
Blanco (peak), C. Rica 154/F6
Blanco (riv.), Mexico 150/Q2
Blanco, N. Mex. 274/B2
Blanco (creek), N. Mex. 274/F4
Blanco, Okla. 288/P5
Blanco (cape), Oreg. 188/A2
Blanco (cape), Oreg. 291/C5
Blanco (cape), Peru 128/B5
Blanco (riv.), Peru 128/F6
Blanco (co.), Texas 303/F8
Blanco, Texas 303/F7
Blanc-Sablon, Québec 174/F2
Bland, Mo. 261/J6
Bland (co.), Va. 307/F6
Bland, Va. 307/F6
Blandburg, Pa. 294/F4
Blandford•, Mass. 249/C4
Blandford, Nova Scotia 168/D4
Blandford Forum, England 13/E7
Blandford Forum, England 10/E5
Blanding, Utah 304/E6
Blandinsville, Ill. 222/C3
Blandville, Ky. 237/D7
Blanefield, Scotland 15/B1
Blanes, Spain 33/H2
Blaney Park, Mich. 250/D2
Blanford, Ind. 227/B5
Blankenberge, Belgium 27/C6
Blankenburg am Harz, Germany 22/D3
Blanket, Texas 303/F6
Blanquillo, Uruguay 145/D3
Blansko, Czech Rep. 41/D2
Blanton, Ala. 195/H5
Blanton, Fla. 212/D3
Blantyre, Malawi 115/F7
Blantyre, Malawi 102/F6
Blantyre, Scotland 15/B2
Blarney, Ireland 10/B5
Blarney, Ireland 17/D8
Blas (peak), Switzerland 39/G3
Blasdell, N.Y. 276/C5
Blasket (isls.), Ireland 10/A4
Blasket (isls.), Ireland 17/A7
Blatná, Czech Rep. 41/B2
Blato, Croatia 45/C4
Blatten, Switzerland 39/E4
Blaubeuren, Germany 22/C4
Blauvelt, N.Y. 276/K8
Blåvands Huk (pt.), Denmark 21/A6
Blawenburg, N.J. 273/D3
Blawnox, Pa. 294/C6
Blaydon, England 10/F3
Blaydon, England 13/H3
Blaye, France 28/C5
Blayney, N.S. Wales 97/E3
Blaze (pt.), North. Terr. 88/D2
Blaze (pt.), North. Terr. 93/A2
Bleckley (co.), Ga. 217/F6
Bled, Slovenia 45/A2
Bledsoe (co.), Tenn. 237/L9
Bledsoe, Texas 303/A4
Bleecker, Ala. 195/H5
Blekinge (co.), Sweden 18/J8
Blencoe, Iowa 229/A5
Blenheim, N. Zealand 100/D4
Blenheim, Ontario 177/C5
Blenheim, S.C. 296/H2
Blenker, Wis. 317/F6
Blennerhassett (isl.), Ohio 284/G7
Blerick, Netherlands 27/J6
Blesbok (riv.), S. Africa 118/J7
Blessing, Texas 303/H9
Blessington, Ireland 17/J5
Blevins, Ark. 202/C6
Blewett, Texas 303/D8
Blida, Algeria 106/E1
Blida, Algeria 102/C1
Bligh (sound), N. Zealand 100/A6
Bligh Water (bay), Fiji 86/P10
Blind Channel, Br. Col. 184/E5
Blind River, Ont. 162/H6
Blind River, Ontario 177/J5
Blind River, Ontario 175/D3

Bradley 341

Bonhomme (isl.), Mo. 261/N2
Bon Homme (co.), S. Dak. 298/O7
Bonifacio, France 28/B7
Bonifacio (str.), France 28/B7
Bonifacio (str.), Italy 34/B4
Bonifay, Fla. 212/C5
Bönigen, Switzerland 39/E3
Bonilla, S. Dak. 298/N4
Bonin (isls.), Japan 2/S4
Bonin (isls.), Japan 54/R7
Bonin (isls.), Japan 87/E3
Bonin (isls.), Japan 81/M3
Bonita, Ariz. 198/E6
Bonita (pt.), Calif. 204/H2
Bonita, La. 238/G1
Bonita, Miss. 256/G6
Bonita Springs, Fla. 212/E5
Bonlee, N.C. 281/L3
Bonn (cap.), Germany 7/E3
Bonn (cap.), Germany 22/B3
Bonne (bay), Newf. 166/C4
Bonneau, S.C. 296/H5
Bonner (co.), Idaho 220/B1
Bonners Ferry, Idaho 220/B1
Bonner Springs, Kansas 232/H2
Bonner-West Riverside, Mont. 262/C4
Bonnet (lake), Manitoba 179/G4
Bonnétable, France 28/D3
Bonnet Carré Spillway and Floodway, La. 238/N3
Bonne Terre, Mo. 261/L7
Bonnet Plume (riv.), Yukon 187/E3
Bonneville, France 28/G4
Bonneville (co.), Idaho 220/G6
Bonneville, Oreg. 291/F2
Bonneville (dam), Oreg. 291/E2
Bonneville (salt flats), Utah 304/A3
Bonneville (dam), Wash. 310/D5
Bonneville (lake), Wash. 310/D5
Bonneville, Wyo. 319/E2
Bonneville (mt.), Wyo. 319/C3
Bonney Lake, Wash. 310/C3
Bonnie, Ill. 222/E5
Bonnieville, Ky. 237/K6
Bonnots Mill, Mo. 261/J5
Bonny (res.), Colo. 208/P3
Bonny, Nigeria 106/F8
Bonny (bight), Nigeria 106/F8
Bonnybridge, Scotland 15/C1
Bonnyman, Ky. 237/P6
Bonnyrigg, N.S. Wales 88/K4
Bonnyrigg, N.S. Wales 97/H3
Bonnyrigg and Lasswade, Scotland 10/C1
Bonnyrigg and Lasswade, Scotland 15/D2
Bonny River, New Bruns. 170/D3
Bonnyville, Alberta 182/E2
Bono, Ark. 202/J2
Bono, Ohio 284/D2
Bonorva, Italy 34/B4
Bonpas (creek), Ill. 222/F5
Bonpland (mt.), N. Zealand 100/A6
Bon Secour, Ala. 195/C10
Bon Secour (bay), Ala. 195/C10
Bonsecours, Québec 172/E4
Bonshaw, Pr. Edward I. 168/E2
Bonthain, Indonesia 85/F7
Bonthe, S. Leone 106/B7
Bontoc, Philippines 85/G2
Bontoc, Philippines 82/C2
Bon Wier, Texas 303/L7
Bonyhád, Hungary 41/E3
Boody, Ill. 222/D4
Book (cliffs), Utah 304/E4
Booker, Texas 303/D1
Booker T. Washington Nat'l Mon., Va. 307/J6
Boolaloo, W. Australia 92/B3
Booligal, N.S. Wales 97/C3
Boom, Belgium 27/E6
Boom, Tenn. 237/L7
Boomer, N.C. 281/G2
Boomer, W. Va. 312/D6
Boomi, N.S. Wales 88/H5
Boomi, N.S. Wales 97/E1
Boon (pt.), Ant. & Bar. 161/E11
Boon, Mich. 250/D4
Boondall, Queensland 88/K2
Boone (co.), Ark. 202/D1
Boone, Colo. 208/L6
Boone (co.), Ill. 222/E1
Boone (co.), Ind. 227/E4
Boone (co.), Iowa 229/F5
Boone, Iowa 229/F4
Boone (co.), Ky. 237/M3
Boone, Ky. 237/N5
Boone (co.), Mo. 261/H4
Boone (co.), Nebr. 264/F3
Boone, Nebr. 264/F3
Boone, N.C. 281/F2
Boone (lake), Tenn. 237/S8
Boone (co.), W. Va. 312/C6
Boone Grove, Ind. 227/C2
Boonesboro, Mo. 261/G4
Boones Mill, Va. 307/J6
Boonesville, Va. 307/L4
Booneville, Ark. 202/C3
Booneville, Ky. 237/O6
Booneville, Miss. 256/G1
Boonsboro, Md. 245/H2
Boonton, N.J. 273/E2
Boonton (res.), N.J. 273/E2
Boonville, Calif. 204/B5
Boonville, Ind. 227/C8
Boonville, Mo. 261/G5
Boonville, N.Y. 276/K4
Boonville, N.C. 281/H2
Boopi (riv.), Bolivia 136/B4
Boorooban, N.S. Wales 97/C4
Boorowa, N.S. Wales 97/E4
Boort, Victoria 97/B5
Booth, Ala. 195/E6
Boothbay, Maine 243/D8
Boothbay•, Maine 243/D8
Boothbay Harbor, Maine 243/D8
Boothia (pen.), Canada 4/B14
Boothia (gulf), Canada 4/B14
Boothia (gulf), N.W.T. 146/J2
Boothia (gulf), N.W.T. 162/G1
Boothia (gulf), N.W.T. 187/K3
Boothia (isthmus), N.W.T. 162/G2
Boothia (pen.), N.W.T. 146/J2
Boothia (pen.), N.W.T. 162/G1
Boothia (pen.), N.W.T. 187/J2
Boothville, La. 238/M8
Boothwyn, Pa. 294/L7
Bootle, England 10/F2
Bootle, England 13/G2
Booué, Gabon 115/B3
Boppard, Germany 22/B3
Boquerón, Cuba 158/K4
Boquerón, Cuba 156/C3
Boquerón, Paraguay 144/B3
Boquerón, El (pass), Peru 128/E7
Boquerón, P. Rico 156/F1
Boquerón, P. Rico 161/A3
Boquerón (bay), P. Rico 161/A3
Boquilla del Carmen, Mexico 150/H2
Bor, Czech Rep. 41/B2
Bor, Sudan 111/F6
Bor, Turkey 63/F4
Bor, Russia 52/F3
Bor, Yugoslavia 45/E3
Bora-Bora (isl.), Fr. Poly. 87/L7
Borah (peak), Idaho 188/D2
Borah (peak), Idaho 220/E5
Borama, Somalia 115/H1
Borås, Sweden 7/F3
Borås, Sweden 18/H8
Borazjan, Iran 66/G6
Borazjan, Iran 59/F4
Borba, Brazil 120/D3
Borba, Brazil 132/H9
Borba, Portugal 33/C3
Borbón, Venezuela 124/F4
Borçka, Turkey 63/J2
Borculo, Netherlands 27/J4
Bordeaux, France 28/C5
Bordeaux, France 7/D4
Bordeaux, S.C. 296/C4
Bordeaux (mt.), Virgin Is. (U.S.) 161/C4
Bordelonville, La. 238/G4
Borden (isl.), Canada 4/B15
Borden, Ind. 227/F8
Borden (isl.), N.W.T. 187/G2
Borden (pen.), N.W.T. 187/K2
Borden, Pr. Edward I. 168/E2
Borden, Sask. 181/D3
Borden, S.C. 296/G3
Borden (co.), Texas 303/C5
Borden, W. Australia 92/B6
Borden Shaft, Md. 245/B2
Borden Springs, Ala. 195/H3
Bordentown, N.J. 273/D3
Border, Minn. 255/D2
Border, Wyo. 319/B3
Borderland, W. Va. 312/B7
Borders (reg.), Scotland 15/E5
Bordertown, S. Australia 88/F7
Bordertown, S. Australia 94/G7
Bordighera, Italy 34/A3
Bordj Bou Arreridj, Algeria 106/E1
Bordj Fly Sainte Marie, Algeria 106/D3
Bordj Omar Driss, Algeria 106/F3
Bordj Omar Driss, Algeria 102/C2
Bordulac, N. Dak. 282/N5
Boreing, Ky. 237/N6
Boreray (isl.), Scotland 15/A2
Boreray (isl.), Scotland 15/A3
Borgå, Finland 18/O6
Borge, Norway 18/H2
Borger, Netherlands 27/K3
Borger, Texas 303/C2
Borger, Texas 188/F3
Borgerhout, Belgium 27/E6
Borgholm, Sweden 18/K8
Borghorst, Germany 22/B2
Borgloon, Belgium 27/G7
Borgne (lake), La. 238/L7
Borgne (riv.), Switzerland 39/D4
Borgo, Italy 34/C1
Borgomanero, Italy 34/B2
Borgo San Lorenzo, Italy 34/C2
Borgworm (Waremme), Belgium 27/G7
Borikan, Laos 72/D3
Boring, Md. 245/L2
Boring, Oreg. 291/E2
Borinquen (pt.), P. Rico 156/F1
Borinquen (pt.), P. Rico 161/A1
Borislav, Ukraine 52/B5
Borisoglebsk, Russia 48/E4
Borisoglebsk, Russia 52/F4
Borisov, Belarus 52/C4
Borisovka, Russia 52/E4
Bo River Post, Sudan 111/E6
Borja, Peru 128/D5
Borja, Spain 33/F2
Borjas Blancas, Spain 33/G2
Borken, Germany 22/B3
Børkop, Denmark 21/C6
Borku, Chad 111/C4
Borkum, Germany 22/B2
Borkum (isl.), Germany 22/B2
Borlänge, Sweden 18/J6
Borna, Germany 22/E3
Borndiep (chan.), Netherlands 27/H2
Borne, Netherlands 27/K4
Borneo (isl.) 2/Q6
Borneo (isl.) 54/N9
Borneo (isl.), Indonesia 85/E5
Borneo (isl.), Malaysia 85/E5
Bornheim, Germany 22/B3
Bornholm (co.), Denmark 21/F9
Bornholm (isl.), Denmark 7/F3
Bornholm (isl.), Denmark 18/J9
Bornholm (isl.), Denmark 21/F9
Borno (state), Nigeria 106/G6
Bornova, Turkey 63/B3
Borocay (isl.), Philippines 82/D5
Borojó, Venezuela 124/C2
Boron, Calif. 204/H8
Borongan, Philippines 82/E5
Borot Kidod (well), Israel 65/C5
Borovichi, Russia 52/D3
Borradaile, Alberta 182/E3
Borre, Norway 18/D4
Borrego Springs, Calif. 204/J10
Borris, Ireland 17/H6
Borris-in-Ossory, Ireland 17/F6
Borrisokane, Ireland 17/E6
Borrisoleigh, Ireland 17/E6
Borroloola, North. Terr. 88/F3
Borroloola, North. Terr. 93/E4
Borşa, Romania 45/G2
Borsod-Abaúj-Zemplén (co.), Hungary 41/F2
Bortala (Bole), China 77/B3
Borth, Wales 13/C5
Bort-les-Orgues, France 28/E5
Boruca, C. Rica 154/F6
Borujerd, Iran 59/E3
Borujerd, Iran 66/F4
Borup, Denmark 21/E7
Borup, Minn. 255/B3
Börzsöny (mts.), Hungary 41/E3
Borzya, Russia 48/M4
Bosa, Italy 34/B4
Bosanska Dubica, Bos. 45/C3
Bosanska Gradiška, Bos. 45/C3
Bosanska Kostajnica, Bos. 45/B3
Bosanska Krupa, Bos. 45/C3
Bosanski Brod, Bos. 45/D3
Bosanski Novi, Bos. 45/C3
Bosanski Petrovac, Bos. 45/C3
Bosanski Šamac, Bos. 45/D3
Bosaso, Somalia 115/J1
Bosaso, Somalia 102/G3
Boscawen•, N.H. 268/D5
Bosch, van den (cape), Indonesia 85/J6
Bosco, La. 238/F2
Boscobel, Wis. 317/E9
Bose, China 77/G7
Boshan, China 77/J4
Boskoop, Netherlands 27/F4
Boskovice, Czech Rep. 41/D2
Bosler, Wyo. 319/G4
Bosna (riv.), Bos. 45/D3
BOSNIA AND HERZEGOVINA 45/C3
Boso (pen.), Japan 81/K6
Bosobolo, D.R. Congo 115/D3
Bosporus (str.), Turkey 7/G4
Bosporus (str.), Turkey 59/A1
Bosporus (str.), Turkey 63/C2
Bosque, N. Mex. 274/C4
Bosque (co.), Texas 303/G6
Boss, Mo. 261/K7
Bossangoa, Centr. Afr. Rep. 102/D4
Bossangoa, Cent. Afr. Rep. 115/C2
Bossburg, Wash. 310/H2
Bossé, New Bruns. 170/B1
Bossembele, Cent. Afr. Rep. 115/C2
Bossier (par.), La. 238/C1
Bossier City, La. 238/C1
Bosso, Niger 106/G6
Bostan, Iran 66/F5
Bostan, Pakistan 68/B2
Bostanabad-e-Bala, Iran 66/E2
Bosten (Bagrax) Hu (lake), China 77/C3
Boston (mts.), Ark. 202/B2
Boston, England 13/G5
Boston, England 10/F4
Boston, Ga. 217/E9
Boston, Ind. 227/H5
Boston, Ky. 237/K5
Boston (cap.), Mass. 146/L5
Boston (cap.), Mass. 188/M2
Boston (cap.), Mass. 249/D7
Boston (bay), Mass. 249/E6
Boston (harb.), Mass. 249/D7
Boston, Mo. 261/D8
Boston, N.Y. 276/C5
Boston (mts.), Okla. 288/S3
Boston, Pa. 294/C7
Boston, Tenn. 237/G9
Boston, Texas 303/K4
Boston, U.S. 2/F3
Boston, Va. 307/M3
Boston Bar, Br. Col. 184/G5
Boston Heights, Ohio 284/J10
Bostonnais (isl.), Québec 172/E2
Bostonnais, Grand Lac (lake), Québec 172/E2
Bostonnais (riv.), Québec 172/E2
Boston Nat'l Hist. Park, Mass. 249/D6
Bostwick, Fla. 212/E2
Bostwick, Ga. 217/E3
Bostwick, Nebr. 264/F4
Boswell, Ark. 202/F1
Boswell, Br. Col. 184/J5
Boswell, Ind. 227/C3
Boswell, Okla. 288/P6
Boswell, Pa. 294/E5
Boswell Bay, Alaska 196/J2
Boswil, Switzerland 39/F2
Bosworth, Mo. 261/F4
Bot (riv.), S. Africa 118/G7
Botany, N.S. Wales 88/L4
Botany (bay), N.S. Wales 88/L4
Botany, N.S. Wales 97/J4
Botany (bay), N.S. Wales 97/J4
Botene, Laos 72/D3
Botetourt (co.), Va. 307/J5
Botevgrad, Bulgaria 45/F4
Botha, Alberta 182/D3
Botha (riv.), Alberta 182/B1
Bothell, Wash. 310/B1
Bothnia (gulf) 7/G2
Bothnia (gulf), Finland 18/M5
Bothnia (gulf), Sweden 18/N4
Bothwell, Ontario 177/C5
Bothwell, Tasmania 99/C4
Bothwell, Utah 304/B2
Botkins, Ohio 284/B5
Botna, Iowa 229/C5
Botoşani, Romania 45/H2
Botrange (mt.), Belgium 27/J8
Botrivier, S. Africa 118/F7
Botsford, Conn. 210/C3
Botswana 2/L7
Botswana 102/E7
BOTSWANA 118/C4
Bottesford, England 13/G4
Bottineau (co.), N. Dak. 282/J2
Bottineau, N. Dak. 282/J2
Bottrel, Alberta 182/C4
Bottrop, Germany 22/B3
Botucatu, Brazil 135/B3
Botucatu, Brazil 132/D8
Botwood, Newf. 166/C4
Bouaflé, Ivory Coast 106/C7
Bouaké, Ivory Coast 102/B4
Bouaké, Ivory Coast 106/D7
Bouali, Cent. Afr. Rep. 115/C3
Bouar, Cent. Afr. Rep. 102/D4
Bouar, Cent. Afr. Rep. 115/C2
Bou Arfa, Morocco 106/D2
Bouca, Cent. Afr. Rep. 115/C2
Boucaut (bay), North. Terr. 93/D1
Boucherville, Québec 172/J4
Boucherville (isl.), Québec 172/J4
Bouches-du-Rhône (dept.), France 28/F6
Bouchette, Québec 172/A3
Bouckville, N.Y. 276/J5
Bou Djebeha, Mali 106/D5
Boudreau (bay), La. 238/M7
Boudreaux, La. 238/J8
Boudreaux (lake), La. 238/J8
Boudry, Switzerland 39/C3
Boufarik, Algeria 106/E1
Bougainville (reef), Coral Sea Is. Terr. 95/C2
Bougainville (reef), Coral Sea Is. Terr. 88/H3
Bougainville (isl.), Papua N.G. 87/F6
Bougainville (isl.), Papua N.G. 86/C2
Bougainville (str.), Papua N.G. 86/C2
Bougainville (str.), Solomon Is. 86/D2
Bougainville (cape), W. Australia 88/D2
Bougainville (cape), W. Australia 92/D1
Bougaroun (cape), Algeria 106/F1
Boughton (isl.), Pr. Edward I. 168/F2
Bougie (Béjaïa), Algeria 106/F1
Bougouni, Mali 106/C6
Bouillante, Guadeloupe 161/A6
Bouillon, Belgium 27/G9
Bou Izakarn, Morocco 106/C3
Boujad, Morocco 106/C2
Boula, Cent. Afr. Rep. 115/C3
Boulanger, Québec 172/E1
Boularderie (isl.), Nova Scotia 168/H2
Boulder, Australia 87/C9
Boulder, Colo. 188/E2
Boulder, Colo. 146/H6
Boulder (co.), Colo. 208/J2
Boulder, Colo. 208/J2
Boulder (mts.), Idaho 220/D6
Boulder, Mont. 262/E4
Boulder (lake), N. Mex. 274/C2
Boulder, Utah 304/C6
Boulder (creek), Utah 304/C6
Boulder, W. Australia 88/C6
Boulder, Wyo. 319/C3
Boulder (lake), Wyo. 319/C3
Boulder City, Nev. 266/G7
Boulder Creek, Calif. 204/J4
Boulder Junction, Wis. 317/G3
Boulder-Kalgoorlie, W. Australia 92/C5
Boulevard, Calif. 204/J11
Boulevard Heights, Md. 245/F5
Boulia, Queensland 95/A4
Boulia, Queensland 88/F4
Boulogne, Fla. 212/E1
Boulogne-Billancourt, France 28/A2
Boulogne-sur-Mer, France 28/D2
Bouna, Ivory Coast 106/D7
Boundary, Alaska 196/K2
Boundary (co.), Idaho 220/B1
Boundary (peak), Nev. 266/C5
Boundary (plat.), Sask. 181/B6
Boundary (bay), Wash. 310/C1
Boundary (dam), Wash. 310/H2
Boundary (lake), Wash. 310/H2
Boundary Bend, Victoria 97/B4
Bound Brook, N.J. 273/D2
Boundiali, Ivory Coast 106/C7
Boundji, Congo 115/C4
Boun Nua, Laos 72/D2
Bountiful, Utah 304/C3
Bounty (isls.), N. Zealand 87/H10
Bounty, Sask. 181/D4
Bourail, New Caled. 87/G8
Bourail, New Caled. 86/G4
Bourbon, Ill. 222/E4
Bourbon, Ind. 227/E2
Bourbon (co.), Kansas 232/H4
Bourbon (co.), Ky. 237/N4
Bourbon, Miss. 256/C4
Bourbon, Mo. 261/K6
Bourbonnais (trad. prov.), France 29
Bourbonnais, Ill. 222/F2
Bourem, Mali 106/E5
Bourg, La. 238/J7
Bourganeuf, France 28/D5
Bourg-des-Saintes, Guadeloupe 161/A7
Bourg-en-Bresse, France 28/F4
Bourgeois, New Bruns. 170/F2
Bourges, France 28/E4
Bourget, Ontario 177/J2
Bourg-Léopold (Leopoldsburg), Belgium 27/G6
Bourgoin-Jallieu, France 28/F5
Bourg Saint-Pierre, Switzerland 39/D5
Bourke, N.S. Wales 88/H6
Bourke, N.S. Wales 97/D2
Bourne, England 13/G5
Bourne, Mass. 249/M6
Bourne•, Mass. 249/M6
Bournedale, Mass. 249/M5
Bournemouth, England 13/F7
Bournemouth, England 10/F5
Bourneville, Ohio 284/D7
Bou Saâda, Algeria 106/E1
Bouse, Ariz. 198/A5
Bouse Wash (dry riv.), Ariz. 198/A4
Boussac, France 28/D4
Bousso, Chad 111/C5
Boussu, Belgium 27/D8
Boutilimit, Mauritania 106/B5
Boutilimit, Mauritania 102/A3
Bouton, Iowa 229/E5
Boutte, La. 238/N4
Bouvard (cape), W. Australia 92/A2
Bouvet (isl.), Ant. 5/D1
Bouvetøya (Bouvet) (isl.), Ant. 5/D1
Boven Bolivia, Neth. Ant. 161/E8
Boves, Italy 34/A2
Bovey, Minn. 255/E3
Bovey Tracey, England 13/D7
Bovill, Idaho 220/B3
Bovina, Miss. 256/C6
Bovina, Texas 303/A3
Bovril, Argentina 143/G5
Bow (riv.), Alberta 182/D4
Bow (riv.), Alta. 162/E5
Bow (lake), N.H. 268/E5
Bow, Wash. 310/C2
Bowbells, N. Dak. 282/F2
Bow City, Alberta 182/D4
Bowden, Alberta 182/C4
Bowden, Jamaica 158/K6
Bowden, W. Va. 312/G5
Bowdens, N.C. 281/N4
Bowdle, S. Dak. 298/K3
Bowdoin (lake), Mont. 262/J2
Bowdoinham•, Maine 243/D7
Bowdon, Ga. 217/B3
Bowdon, N. Dak. 282/L5
Bowdon Junction, Ga. 217/B3
Bowell, Alberta 182/E4
Bowen, Australia 87/E7
Bowen, Ill. 222/B3
Bowen, Ky. 237/O5
Bowen, Queensland 95/D3
Bowen, Queensland 88/H3
Bowen Island, Br. Col. 184/K3
Bowens, Md. 245/M6
Bowerbank•, Maine 243/E5
Bowers, Ind. 227/D4
Bowers Beach, Del. 245/S4
Bowerston, Ohio 284/H5
Bowersville, Ga. 217/G2
Bowersville, Ohio 284/C6
Bowes, England 13/F3
Bowesmont, N. Dak. 282/R2
Bowie, Ariz. 198/F6
Bowie, Colo. 208/D5
Bowie, Md. 245/L4
Bowie (creek), Miss. 256/E7
Bowie (co.), Texas 303/K4
Bowie, Texas 303/G4
Bow Island, Alberta 182/E5
Bowkan, Iran 66/E2
Bowlegs, Okla. 288/N4
Bowler, Wis. 317/J6
Bowling Green, Fla. 212/E4
Bowling Green, Ind. 227/D6
Bowling Green, Ky. 237/H7
Bowling Green, Ky. 188/J3
Bowling Green, Mo. 261/K4
Bowling Green, Ohio 284/C3
Bowling Green (cape), Queensland 88/H3
Bowling Green (cape), Queensland 95/C3
Bowling Green, S.C. 296/E1
Bowling Green, Va. 307/O4
Bowlus, Minn. 255/D5
Bowman, Calif. 204/C8
Bowman, Ga. 217/G2
Bowman (co.), N. Dak. 282/C7
Bowman, N. Dak. 282/D7
Bowman (bay), N.W.T. 162/J2
Bowman (bay), N.W.T. 187/L3
Bowman (dam), Oreg. 291/G3
Bowman, S.C. 296/F5
Bowmansdale, Pa. 294/J5
Bowmanstown, Pa. 294/L4
Bowmansville, Pa. 294/L5
Bow Mills, N.H. 268/D5
Bowmont, Idaho 220/B6
Bowmore, Scotland 15/B5
Bowmore, Scotland 10/C3
Bowral, N.S. Wales 97/F4
Bowraville, N.S. Wales 97/G2
Bowring, Okla. 288/O1
Bowron Lake Prov. Park, Br. Col. 184/G3
Bowser, Br. Col. 184/H2
Bowser (lake), Br. Col. 184/C2
Bowsman, Manitoba 179/A2
Bowstring, Minn. 255/E3
Bowstring (lake), Minn. 255/E3
Boxborough•, Mass. 249/H3
Box Butte (co.), Nebr. 264/A2
Box Butte (res.), Nebr. 264/A2
Box Canyon (dam), Wash. 310/H2
Box Elder (creek), Colo. 208/K4
Box Elder, Mont. 262/F2
Boxelder (creek), Mont. 262/M5
Boxelder (creek), Mont. 262/H3
Box Elder, S. Dak. 298/D5
Boxelder (creek), S. Dak. 298/D5
Box Elder (co.), Utah 304/A2
Boxford, Mass. 249/L2
Boxford•, Mass. 249/L2
Box Hill, Victoria 97/J5
Box Hill, Victoria 88/L7
Boxholm, Iowa 229/E4
Bo Xian (Pohsien), China 77/J5
Boxley, Ark. 202/D2
Boxmeer, Netherlands 27/H5
Box Springs, Ga. 217/C5
Boxtel, Netherlands 27/G5
Boyabat, Turkey 63/F2
Boyacá (dept.), Colombia 126/D5
Boyama (Stanley) (falls), D.R. Congo 102/E5
Boyama (Stanley) (falls), D.R. Congo 115/D3
Boyanup, W. Australia 92/A2
Boyce, La. 238/E4
Boyce, Va. 307/M2
Boyceville, Wis. 317/C5
Boyd, Ala. 195/B5
Boyd, Fla. 212/C1
Boyd (co.), Ky. 237/R4
Boyd, Minn. 255/C6
Boyd, Mont. 262/G5
Boyd (co.), Nebr. 264/F2
Boyd, Okla. 288/E1
Boyd, Oreg. 291/F2
Boyd, Texas 303/E1
Boyd, Wis. 317/E6
Boydell, Ark. 202/H7
Boyden, Iowa 229/B2
Boyd Lake, Maine 243/F5
Boyds, Md. 245/J4
Boyds, Wash. 310/G2
Boydton, Va. 307/M7
Boyer (riv.), Alberta 182/A5
Boyer, Iowa 229/C4
Boyer (riv.), Iowa 229/B5
Boyer, W. Va. 312/G5
Boyero, Colo. 208/N5
Boyers, Pa. 294/C3
Boyertown, Pa. 294/L5
Boyes, Mont. 262/M5
Boykin, Ga. 217/C8
Boykin, S.C. 296/F3
Boykins, Va. 307/O7
Boyle, Alberta 182/D2
Boyle, Ireland 17/E4
Boyle, Ireland 10/B3
Boyle (co.), Ky. 237/M5
Boyle, Miss. 256/C3
Boyleston, Ind. 227/E4
Boylston•, Mass. 249/H3
Boylston, Nova Scotia 168/G3
Boyne (riv.), Ireland 17/J4
Boyne City, Mich. 250/E3
Boyne Falls, Mich. 250/E3
Boyne Lake, Alberta 182/E5
Boynton, Okla. 288/P3
Boynton Beach, Fla. 212/F5
Boy River, Minn. 255/D3
Boysen (res.), Wyo. 319/D2
Boysen Bay, N.Y. 276/H4
Boys Ranch, Texas 303/B2
Boys Town, Nebr. 264/H3
Boyuibe, Bolivia 136/D7
Bozcaada (isl.), Turkey 63/A3
Bozdoğan, Turkey 63/C4
Bozeman, Mont. 188/D1
Bozeman, Mont. 262/E5
Bozkır, Turkey 63/E4
Bozkurt, Turkey 63/F2
Bozman, Md. 245/N5
Bozoum, Cent. Afr. Rep. 115/C2
Bozova, Turkey 63/H4
Bozqush, Kuh-e (mts.), Iran 66/E2
Bozüyük, Turkey 59/B2
Bozüyük, Turkey 63/C3
Bra, Italy 34/A2
Brabant (prov.), Belgium 27/F7
Brabant Lake, Sask. 181/M3
Brač (isl.), Croatia 45/C4
Bracadale, Loch (inlet), Scotland 15/B3
Bracciano, Italy 34/C3
Bracciano (lake), Italy 34/D3
Bracebridge, Ontario 177/E2
Braceville, Ill. 222/E2
Bracey, Va. 307/M7
Bräcke, Sweden 18/J5
Bracken (co.), Ky. 237/N3
Bracken, Sask. 181/C6
Brackendale, Br. Col. 184/F5
Brackenridge, Pa. 294/C4
Brackett, Wis. 317/D6
Brackettville, Texas 303/D8
Brackley, England 10/F4
Brackley, England 13/F5
Bracknell, England 13/G8
Bracknell, Tasmania 99/C3
Brackney, Pa. 294/K2
Braço Maior do Araguaia (riv.), Brazil 132/D5
Braço Menor do Araguaia (riv.), Brazil 132/D6
Brad, Romania 45/F2
Bradbury, Calif. 204/D10
Braddock, N. Dak. 282/K6
Braddock, Pa. 294/C7
Braddock, Sask. 181/D5
Braddyville, Iowa 229/D7
Braden, Okla. 288/S4
Braden, Tenn. 237/B10
Bradenton, Fla. 212/D4
Bradenton Beach, Fla. 212/D4
Bradford, Ark. 202/G3
Bradford, England 13/J1
Bradford, England 10/H1
Bradford (co.), Fla. 212/D2
Bradford, Ill. 222/D2
Bradford, Ind. 227/E8
Bradford, Iowa 229/G3
Bradford, Ky. 237/N3
Bradford, Maine 243/F5
Bradford•, Maine 243/F5
Bradford•, N.H. 268/D5
Bradford, Ohio 284/B5
Bradford, Ontario 177/E3
Bradford (co.), Pa. 294/J2
Bradford, Pa. 294/E2
Bradford, R.I. 249/H7
Bradford, Tenn. 237/D8
Bradford, Vt. 268/C3
Bradford•, Vt. 268/C3
Bradford Center, Maine 243/F5
Bradford-on-Avon, England 13/E6
Bradfordsville, Ky. 237/L6
Bradgate, Iowa 229/E3
Bradley (co.), Ark. 202/F7
Bradley, Ark. 202/C7
Bradley, Calif. 204/E8
Bradley, Fla. 212/D4
Bradley, Ga. 217/E4
Bradley, Ill. 222/F2
Bradley•, Maine 243/F6
Bradley, Miss. 256/G4
Bradley, Ohio 284/J5
Bradley, Okla. 288/L5

342 Bradley

Bradley, S.C. 296/C3
Bradley, S. Dak. 298/O3
Bradley (co.), Tenn. 237/M10
Bradley, Wis. 317/G4
Bradley Beach, N.J. 273/F3
Bradleyton, Ala. 195/F7
Bradleyville, Mo. 261/F9
Bradner, Ohio 284/C3
Bradshaw, Nebr. 264/G4
Bradshaw, Texas 303/D5
Bradshaw, W. Va. 312/C8
Bradwardine, Manitoba 179/B5
Bradwell, Sask. 181/E4
Brady (glac.), Alaska 196/M1
Brady, Mont. 262/E2
Brady, Nebr. 264/D3
Brady (mt.), S. Australia 94/D3
Brady, Texas 303/E6
Brady Lake, Ohio 284/H3
Bradyville, Tenn. 237/J9
Brae, Scotland 15/G2
Braedstrup, Denmark 21/C6
Braemar, Scotland 15/E3
Braemar, Scotland 10/E2
Braemar (dist.), Scotland 15/E3
Braemar, Tenn. 237/S8
Braeside, Ontario 177/H2
Braeside, W. Australia 92/C3
Braga (dist.), Portugal 33/B2
Braga, Portugal 7/D4
Braga, Portugal 33/B2
Bragado, Argentina 143/F7
Bragança, Brazil 120/E3
Bragança, Brazil 132/E3
Bragança (dist.), Portugal 33/C2
Bragança, Portugal 33/C2
Bragança Paulista, Brazil 135/C3
Bragança Paulista, Brazil 132/E8
Braggadocio, Mo. 261/N10
Bragg City, Mo. 261/N10
Bragg Creek, Alberta 182/C4
Braggs, Ala. 195/E6
Braggs, Okla. 288/R3
Bragman's Bluff (Puerto Cabezas), Nicaragua 154/F3
Braham, Minn. 255/E5
Brahmaputra (riv.) 54/L7
Brahmaputra (riv.), Bangladesh 68/G3
Brahmaputra (riv.), India 68/G3
Braich-y-Pwll (prom.), Wales 10/D4
Braich-y-Pwll (prom.), Wales 13/C5
Braidwood, Ill. 222/E2
Braidwood, N.S. Wales 97/E4
Brăila, Romania 7/G4
Brăila, Romania 45/H3
Brăila (marshes), Romania 45/H3
Brainard, Nebr. 264/G3
Brainards, N.J. 273/C2
Braine-l'Alleud, Belgium 27/E7
Braine-le-Comte, Belgium 27/D7
Brainerd, Minn. 188/H1
Brainerd, Minn. 255/D4
Braintree•, Mass. 249/D8
Braintree (West Braintree), Vt. 268/B4
Braintree•, Vt. 268/B4
Braintree and Bocking, England 13/H6
Braintree and Bocking, England 10/G5
Braithwaite, La. 238/P4
Brak, Libya 102/D2
Brak, Libya 111/B2
Brake, Germany 22/C2
Brakna (reg.), Mauritania 106/B5
Brakpan, S. Africa 118/J6
Bralorne, Br. Col. 184/F5
Braman, Okla. 288/M1
Bramber, Nova Scotia 168/D3
Bramberg am Wildkogel, Austria 41/B3
Bramble (bay), Queensland 95/E2
Bramming, Denmark 21/B7
Bramon, Venezuela 124/B4
Brampton, England 13/E3
Brampton, Mich. 250/B3
Brampton, N. Dak. 282/P7
Brampton, Ontario 177/J4
Bramsche, Germany 22/B2
Bramwell, W. Va. 312/D8
Bran (riv.), Scotland 15/D3
Brancepeth, Sask. 181/F2
Branch, Ark. 202/C3
Branch, La. 238/F6
Branch (co.), Mich. 250/D7
Branch, Mich. 250/D5
Branch, Minn. 255/F5
Branch, Mo. 261/G7
Branch, Newf. 166/D2
Branch (riv.), Newf. 166/C2
Branch, Wis. 317/L7
Branch Dale, Pa. 294/K4
Branchport, N.Y. 276/F5
Branchton, Pa. 294/C3
Branchville, Ala. 195/F3
Branchville, Conn. 210/B3
Branchville, Ind. 227/D8
Branchville, N.J. 273/D1
Branchville, S.C. 296/F5
Branchville, Va. 307/O7
Branco (riv.), Brazil 120/C2
Branco (riv.), Brazil 132/H8
Brandberg (mt.), Namibia 118/A4
Brande, Denmark 21/B6
Brandenburg, Germany 22/E2
Brandenburg (state), Germany 22/E2
Brandenburg, Ky. 237/J4
Brandon, Colo. 208/P6
Brandon, England 13/H5
Brandon, Fla. 212/D4
Brandon, Iowa 229/K4
Brandon (bay), Ireland 17/A7
Brandon (head), Ireland 17/A7
Brandon (mt.), Ireland 17/A7
Brandon, Man. 146/H4
Brandon, Man. 162/F6
Brandon, Manitoba 179/C5
Brandon, Minn. 255/C5
Brandon, Miss. 256/E6
Brandon, Nebr. 264/C4
Brandon, Ohio 284/F5
Brandon, S. Dak. 298/R6
Brandon, Vt. 268/A4
Brandon•, Vt. 268/A4
Brandon, Wis. 317/J8
Brandon Gap (pass), Vt. 268/B4
Brandonville, W. Va. 312/G3
Brandreth (lake), N.Y. 276/L3
Brandsville, Mo. 261/J9
Brandt, Ohio 284/B6
Brandt, S. Dak. 298/R4
Brandvlei, S. Africa 118/B6
Brandýs nad Labem-Stará Boleslavv, Czech Rep. 41/C1
Brandy Station, Va. 307/N4
Brandywine, Md. 245/L6
Brandywine, W. Va. 312/H5
Branford, Conn. 210/D3
Branford•, Conn. 210/D3
Branford (harb.), Conn. 210/D4
Branford (riv.), Conn. 210/D3
Branford, Fla. 212/D2
Braniewo, Poland 47/D1
Brannock (isls.), Ireland 17/A5
Bransfield (str.), Ant. 5/C16
Branson, Colo. 208/M8
Branson, Mo. 261/F9
Brant, Alberta 182/D4
Brant, Mich. 250/E5
Brant, N.Y. 276/B5
Brant (lake), N.Y. 276/N3
Brant (county), Ontario 177/D4
Brant (lake), S. Dak. 298/R6
Brant Beach, N.J. 273/E4
Brantford, Kansas 232/E2
Brantford, N. Dak. 282/N4
Brantford, Ontario 177/D4
Brant Lake, N.Y. 276/N3
Brantley, Ala. 195/F7
Brantley (co.), Ga. 217/J8
Brant Rock-Ocean Bluff, Mass. 249/M4
Brantville, New Bruns. 170/E1
Brantwood, Wis. 317/F4
Branxholm, Tasmania 99/D3
Branxholme, Victoria 97/A5
Branxton-Greta, N.S. Wales 97/F3
Bras d'Or, Nova Scotia 168/H2
Bras d'Or (lake), Nova Scotia 168/H3
Braselton, Ga. 217/E2
Brasfield, Ark. 202/H4
Brashear, Mo. 261/H2
Brasher, Mo. 261/N10
Brasher Falls-Winthrop, N.Y. 276/L1
Brasiléia, Brazil 132/G10
Brasília (cap.), Brazil 2/G6
Brasília (cap.), Brazil 120/E4
Brasília (cap.), Brazil 132/E6
Brasília de Minas, Brazil 132/F7
Braşov, Romania 45/G3
Braşov, Romania 7/G4
Brass, Nigeria 106/F8
Brass (isls.), Virgin Is. (U.S.) 161/A4
Brassey (range), W. Australia 92/C4
Brasstown Bald (mt.), Ga. 217/E1
Brassua (lake), Maine 243/D4
Braswell, Ga. 217/C3
Brate, Norway 18/G7
Bratenahl, Ohio 284/H9
Bratislava (cap.), Slovakia 7/F4
Bratislava (city) (cap.), Slovakia 41/D2
Bratislava (cap.), Slovakia 41/D2
Bratsk, Russia 48/L4
Bratsk, Russia 54/M4
Bratsk (res.), Russia 48/L4
Brattleboro, Vt. 268/B6
Brattleboro•, Vt. 268/B6
Bratton, Sask. 181/D4
Braunau am Inn, Austria 41/B2
Braunlage, Germany 22/D3
Braunschweig (Brunswick), Germany 22/D2
Braunton, England 13/C6
Brava (isl.), C. Verde 106/B8
Brava, Somalia 115/H3
Brava, Somalia 102/G4
Brava (pt.), Uruguay 145/B7
Brave, Pa. 294/B6
Bravo (riv.), Chile 138/D7
Bravo (Grande) (riv.), Mexico 150/G2
Brawley, Calif. 188/C4
Brawley, Calif. 204/K11
Braxton, Miss. 256/D6
Braxton (co.), W. Va. 312/E5
Bray, Ireland 17/K5
Bray, Ireland 10/C4
Bray (head), Ireland 17/A8
Bray (isl.), N.W.T. 187/L3
Bray, Okla. 288/L5
Braymer, Mo. 261/E3
Brayton, Iowa 229/D5
Brazeau (dam), Alberta 182/C3
Brazeau (mt.), Alberta 182/B3
Brazeau (riv.), Alberta 182/B3
Brazil 2/F6
Brazil 120/D4
BRAZIL 132, 135
Brazil, Ind. 227/C5
Brazil, Miss. 256/D2
Brazil, Tenn. 237/C9
Brazilian Highlands (plat.), Brazil 120/E4
Brazilton, Kansas 232/H4
Brazito, Mo. 261/H6
Brazoria (co.), Texas 303/J8
Brazoria, Texas 303/J9
Brazos (peak), N. Mex. 274/C2
Brazos (co.), Texas 303/H7
Brazos (riv.), Texas 188/G4
Brazos (riv.), Texas 146/J6
Brazos (riv.), Texas 303/H7
Brazo Sur, Pilcomayo (riv.), Argentina 143/E1
Brazzaville (cap.), Congo 115/C4
Brazzaville (cap.), Congo 2/K6
Brazzaville (cap.), Congo 102/D5
Brčko, Bos. 45/D3
Brda (riv.), Poland 47/C2
Brea, Calif. 204/D11
Breadalbane (dist.), Scotland 15/D4
Bread Loaf, Vt. 268/B4
Bread Loaf (mt.), Vt. 268/A3
Breakabeen, N.Y. 276/M5
Breakeyville, Québec 172/J3
Breaks, Va. 307/D6
Breaksea (sound), N. Zealand 100/A6
Bream (bay), N. Zealand 100/E1
Breasclete, Scotland 15/B2
Breathitt (co.), Ky. 237/P5
Breau-Village, New Bruns. 170/F2
Breaux Bridge, La. 238/G6
Brebes, Indonesia 85/H2
Brébeuf, Québec 172/C3
Brébeuf (lake), Québec 172/G1
Brechin, Ontario 177/E3
Brechin, Scotland 10/E2
Brechin, Scotland 15/F4
Brecht, Belgium 27/F6
Breckenridge, Colo. 208/G4
Breckenridge, Mich. 250/E5
Breckenridge, Minn. 255/B4
Breckenridge, Mo. 261/E3
Breckenridge, Texas 303/F5
Breckenridge Hills, Mo. 261/O2
Breckinridge (co.), Ky. 237/H5
Breckinridge, Okla. 288/L2
Brecknock (Brecon), Wales 13/D6
Brecksville, Ohio 284/H10
Břeclav, Czech Rep. 41/D2
Brecon, Wales 13/D6
Brecon, Wales 10/E5
Brecon Beacons (mt.), Wales 13/D6
Brecon Beacons National Park, Wales 13/D6
Breda, Iowa 229/C4
Breda, Netherlands 27/F5
Bredasdorp, S. Africa 118/B6
Bredasdorp Nat'l Park, S. Africa 118/C6
Bredbo, N.S. Wales 97/E4
Bredbyn, Sweden 18/L5
Bredebro, Denmark 21/B7
Bredenbury, Sask. 181/K5
Bredene, Belgium 27/B6
Bredstedt, Germany 22/C1
Bree, Belgium 27/H6
Breed, Wis. 317/K5
Breeden, W. Va. 312/B7
Breeding, Ky. 237/L7
Breedsville, Mich. 250/C6
Breese, Ill. 222/D5
Breesport, N.Y. 276/G6
Breezand, Netherlands 27/F3
Breezy Point, Minn. 255/D4
Bregenz, Austria 41/A3
Bregovo, Bulgaria 45/F3
Breidhafjördhur (fjord), Iceland 7/B2
Breidhafjördhur (fjord), Iceland 21/B1
Breien, N. Dak. 282/H7
Breil-Brigels, Switzerland 39/H3
Breil-sur-Roya, France 28/G6
Breisach am Rhein, Germany 22/B4
Breisgau (reg.), Germany 22/B5
Breitenbach, Switzerland 39/E2
Breitenbush, Oreg. 291/F3
Breithorn (mt.), Switzerland 39/E5
Breithorn (mt.), Switzerland 39/E4
Brejo, Brazil 132/F3
Bremanger (isl.), Norway 18/D6
Bremen, Ala. 195/E3
Bremen, Ga. 217/B3
Bremen, Ill. 222/D6
Bremen, Ind. 227/E2
Bremen, Kansas 232/F2
Bremen, Ky. 237/G6
Bremen, N. Dak. 282/M4
Bremen, Ohio 284/F6
Bremen, Sask. 181/F3
Bremen (state), Germany 22/C2
Bremen, Germany 7/E3
Bremen, Germany 22/C2
Bremer (co.), Iowa 229/J3
Bremer, Iowa 229/J3
Bremerhaven, Germany 22/C2
Bremerton, Wash. 188/B1
Bremerton, Wash. 310/A2
Bremervörde, Germany 22/C2
Bremgarten, Switzerland 39/F2
Bremo Bluff, Va. 307/M5
Bremond, Texas 303/H6
Brenham, Texas 303/H7
Brenner (pass), Austria 41/A3
Brenner (pass), Italy 34/C1
Brent, Ala. 195/D5
Brent, England 13/H8
Brent, England 10/B5
Brent, Ontario 177/F1
Brentford, S. Dak. 298/N3
Brenton (pt.), R.I. 249/J7
Brentwood, Ark. 202/B2
Brentwood, Calif. 204/L2
Brentwood, England 10/C5
Brentwood, England 13/J8
Brentwood, Md. 245/F4
Brentwood, Mo. 261/P3
Brentwood•, N.H. 268/E6
Brentwood, N.Y. 276/O9
Brentwood, Pa. 294/B7
Brentwood, Tenn. 237/H8
Brentwood Park, S. Africa 118/J6
Brereton Lake, Manitoba 179/G5
Bresaylor, Sask. 181/C3
Brescia (prov.), Italy 34/C2
Brescia, Italy 7/E4
Brescia, Italy 34/C2
Breskens, Netherlands 27/C6
Breslau (Wrocław), Poland 47/C3
Bressanone, Italy 34/C1
Bressay (isl.), Scotland 15/G2
Bressay (isl.), Scotland 10/G1
Bressuire, France 28/C4
Brest, France 7/D4
Brest, France 28/A3
Brest, Ga. 217/D8
Brest, New Bruns. 170/E2
Brest, Belarus 7/G3
Brest, Belarus 48/C4
Brest, Belarus 52/B4
Bretaña, Peru 128/E5
Brethren, Mich. 250/D4
Breton, Alberta 182/C3
Breton (isls.), La. 238/M8
Breton (sound), La. 238/M7
Breton (cape), Nova Scotia 168/J3
Breton Cove, Nova Scotia 168/H2
Breton Woods, N.J. 273/E3
Brett (cape), N. Zealand 100/E1
Bretten, Germany 22/C4
Bretton Woods, N.H. 268/E3
Brevard (co.), Fla. 212/F3
Brevard, N.C. 281/D4
Breves, Brazil 132/D3
Brevig Mission, Alaska 196/E1
Brevik, Minn. 255/D3
Brevoort (lake), Mich. 250/D3
Brevoort (isl.), N.W.T. 187/M3
Brevort, Mich. 250/E2
Brewarrina, N. S. Wales 88/H5
Brewarrina, N.S. Wales 97/D1
Brewer, Maine 243/F6
Brewer, Mo. 261/N7
Brewers, Ky. 237/E7
Brewers Mills, New Bruns. 170/C2
Brewersville, Ind. 227/F6
Brewerton, N.Y. 276/H4
Brewster (pond), Conn. 210/F2
Brewster, Kansas 232/A2
Brewster, Mass. 249/O5
Brewster•, Mass. 249/O5
Brewster (isls.), Mass. 249/E7
Brewster, Minn. 255/C7
Brewster, Nebr. 264/D3
Brewster (lake), N.S. Wales 97/D3
Brewster, N.Y. 276/N8
Brewster, Ohio 284/G4
Brewster, Cerro (mt.), Panama 154/H6
Brewster (co.), Texas 303/A8
Brewster, Wash. 310/F2
Brewton, Ala. 195/D8
Breynat, Alberta 182/D2
Brežice, Slovenia 45/B3
Brezina, Algeria 106/E2
Březnice, Czech Rep. 41/B2
Breznik, Bulgaria 45/F4
Brezno, Slovakia 41/E2
Bria, Cent. Afr. Rep. 102/E4
Bria, Cent. Afr. Rep. 115/D2
Briançon, France 28/G5
Brian Head, Utah 304/B6
Briar, Texas 303/E1
Briar Creek, Pa. 294/K3
Briare, France 28/E4
Briartown, Okla. 288/R4
Briarwood, 282/S6
Bribbaree, N.S. Wales 97/D3
Brice, Ohio 284/E6
Bricelyn, Minn. 255/E7
Brices Cross Roads Nat'l Battlefield Site, Miss. 256/G2
Briceville, Tenn. 237/N8
Brí Chualann (Bray), Ireland 17/K5
Brick•, N.J. 273/E3
Brickaville (Vohibinany), Madagascar 118/H3
Brickerville, Pa. 294/K5
Brickeys, Ark. 202/J4
Bricks, N.C. 281/O2
Brickton, Nova Scotia 168/C4
Bridal Veil, Oreg. 291/E2
Bride (riv.), Ireland 17/E7
Bridesville, Br. Col. 184/H6
Bridge, Idaho 220/E7
Bridge, Oreg. 291/D4
Bridgeboro, Ga. 217/E8
Bridge City, Texas 303/L7
Bridgedale, New Bruns. 170/F3
Bridgeford, Sask. 181/E5
Bridgehampton, N.Y. 276/R9
Bridge Lake, Br. Col. 184/G4
Bridgeland, Utah 304/D3
Bridgend, Wales 13/A7
Bridgenorth, Ontario 177/F3
Bridge of Allan, Scotland 10/B1
Bridge of Allan, Scotland 15/C1
Bridge of Don, Scotland 15/F3
Bridge of Weir, Scotland 15/A2
Bridgeport, Ala. 195/G1
Bridgeport, Calif. 204/F5
Bridgeport, Conn. 188/M2
Bridgeport, Conn. 210/C4
Bridgeport, Ill. 222/F5
Bridgeport, Kansas 232/E3
Bridgeport, Mich. 250/F5
Bridgeport, Nebr. 264/A3
Bridgeport, N.J. 273/C4
Bridgeport, N.Y. 276/J4
Bridgeport, Ohio 284/J5
Bridgeport, Okla. 288/K3
Bridgeport, Oreg. 291/K3
Bridgeport, Pa. 294/M5
Bridgeport, Texas 303/G4
Bridgeport, Wash. 310/F3
Bridgeport, W. Va. 312/F4
Bridgeport, Wis. 317/D9
Bridger, Mont. 262/H5
Bridgeton, Ind. 227/C5
Bridgeton, Mich. 250/D5
Bridgeton, Mo. 261/O2
Bridgeton, N.J. 273/C5
Bridgeton, N.C. 281/R4
Bridgeton Terrace, Mo. 261/O2
Bridgetown (cap.), Barbados 156/G4
Bridgetown (cap.), Barbados 161/B9
Bridgetown, Md. 245/P4
Bridgetown, Nova Scotia 168/C4
Bridgetown, Ohio 284/B9
Bridgetown, W. Australia 88/B6
Bridgetown, W. Australia 92/B6
Bridgeview, Ill. 222/B6
Bridgeville, Calif. 204/B3
Bridgeville, Del. 245/R6
Bridgeville, Nova Scotia 168/F3
Bridgeville, Pa. 294/B5
Bridgeville, Québec 172/D1
Bridgewater•, Conn. 210/B2
Bridgewater, Iowa 229/D6
Bridgewater•, Maine 243/H3
Bridgewater, Mass. 249/K5
Bridgewater•, Mass. 249/K5
Bridgewater•, N.H. 268/D4
Bridgewater•, N.J. 273/D2
Bridgewater, N.Y. 276/K5
Bridgewater, N.S. 162/K7
Bridgewater, Nova Scotia 168/D4
Bridgewater, Pa. 294/B4
Bridgewater, S. Dak. 298/P6
Bridgewater, Tasmania 99/D4
Bridgewater•, Vt. 268/B4
Bridgewater (cape), Victoria 97/A6
Bridgewater, Va. 307/K4
Bridgewater Center, Vt. 268/B4
Bridgewater Corners, Vt. 268/B4
Bridgman, Mich. 250/C7
Bridgnorth, England 13/E5
Bridgnorth, England 10/E4
Bridgton, Maine 243/B7
Bridgton•, Maine 243/B7
Bridgwater, England 10/E5
Bridgwater, England 13/E6
Bridlington, England 13/G3
Bridlington, England 10/F3
Bridlington (bay), England 13/G3
Bridport, England 13/E7
Bridport, England 10/E5
Bridport, Tasmania 99/D3
Bridport•, Vt. 268/A4
Brieg (Brzeg), Poland 47/C3
Brielle, Netherlands 27/E5
Brielle, N.J. 273/E3
Briensburg, Ky. 237/E7
Brienz, Switzerland 39/F3
Brienzer Rothorn (mt.), Switzerland 39/F3
Brienzersee (lake), Switzerland 39/F3
Brier (isl.), Nova Scotia 168/B4
Brier, Wash. 310/C3
Briercrest, Sask. 181/F5
Brierfield, Ala. 195/E4
Brier Hill, N.Y. 276/J1
Brig, Switzerland 39/F4
Brigantine, N.J. 273/E5
Brigantine (inlet), N.J. 273/E5
Brigden, Ontario 177/B5
Brigg, England 13/G4
Briggs, Texas 303/F7
Briggs Corner, New Bruns. 170/E2
Briggsdale, Colo. 208/L1
Briggsville, Ark. 202/C4
Briggsville, Wis. 317/H8
Brigham City, Utah 188/D2
Brigham City, Utah 304/C2
Brighowe, England 13/J1
Bright, Ind. 227/H6
Bright, Victoria 97/D5
Brightlingsea, England 13/J6
Brightlingsea, England 10/G5
Brighton, Ala. 195/D4
Brighton, Colo. 208/K3
Brighton, England 10/F5
Brighton, England 13/G7
Brighton, Fla. 212/E4
Brighton, Ill. 222/C4
Brighton, Ind. 227/G1
Brighton, Iowa 229/K6
Brighton•, Maine 243/D5
Brighton, Mich. 250/F6
Brighton, Mo. 261/F8
Brighton, Nova Scotia 168/C4
Brighton, Ohio 284/F3
Brighton, Ontario 177/G3
Brighton, Oreg. 291/C2
Brighton, S. Australia 88/D8
Brighton, S. Australia 94/A8
Brighton, Tasmania 99/D4
Brighton, Tenn. 237/B10
Brighton, Utah 304/C3
Brighton, Victoria 97/J5
Brighton, Victoria 88/L7
Brighton, Wis. 317/K3
Brightons, Scotland 15/C1
Brightsand (lake), Sask. 181/B2
Brights Grove, Ontario 177/B4
Brightshade, Ky. 237/O7
Brightstar, Ark. 202/C7
Brightwood, D.C. 245/F4
Brightwood, Oreg. 291/E2
Brightwood, Va. 307/M4
Brignoles, France 28/G6
Brigus, Newf. 166/D2
Brihuega, Spain 33/E2
Brikama, Gambia 106/A6
Brill, Wis. 317/C4
Brilliant, Ala. 195/C2
Brilliant, Ohio 284/J5
Brillion, Wis. 317/L7
Brilon, Germany 22/C3
Brimfield, Ill. 222/D3
Brimfield, Ind. 227/G2
Brimfield•, Mass. 249/F4
Brimfield, Ohio 284/H3
Brimley, Mich. 250/E2
Brimson, Minn. 255/F3
Brimson, Mo. 261/E2
Brimstone (hill), St. Kitts & Nevis 161/C10
Brinckerhoff, N.Y. 276/N7
Brindakit, Russia 48/O4
Brindisi (prov.), Italy 34/G4
Brindisi, Italy 7/F4
Brindisi, Italy 34/G4
Bringhurst, Ind. 227/E3
Brinkhaven, Ohio 284/F5
Brinkley, Ark. 202/H4
Brinkman, Okla. 288/G4
Brinktown, Mo. 261/J6
Brinnon, Wash. 310/B3
Brinsmade, N. Dak. 282/M3
Brinson, Ga. 217/C9
Briny Breezes, Fla. 212/G5
Brione, Switzerland 39/G4
Brioude, France 28/E5
Brisbane, Australia 2/S7
Brisbane, Calif. 204/J2
Brisbane (cap.), Queensland 95/D2
Brisbane (cap.), Queensland 88/K3
Brisbane (riv.), Queensland 88/J3
Brisbane (riv.), Queensland 95/D2
Brisbane Airport, Queensland 95/E2
Brisbane International Airport, Queensland 88/K2
Brisbane Water, N.S. Wales 88/J6
Brisbane Water, N.S. Wales 97/F3
Brisbin, Pa. 294/F4
Brisco, Br. Col. 184/J5
Briscoe (co.), Texas 303/C3
Briscoe, Texas 303/D2
Brisighella, Italy 34/C2
Brissago, Switzerland 39/G4
Bristol (bay), Alaska 188/C6
Bristol (bay), Alaska 146/B4
Bristol (bay), Alaska 196/F3
Bristol (lake), Calif. 204/K9
Bristol, Colo. 208/P6
Bristol, Conn. 210/D2
Bristol, England 13/E6
Bristol, England 7/D3
Bristol, England 10/E5
Bristol (chan.), England 13/C6
Bristol (chan.), England 10/E5
Bristol, Fla. 212/B1
Bristol, Ga. 217/H8
Bristol, Ind. 227/F1
Bristol, Maine 243/D8
Bristol•, Maine 243/D8
Bristol, Md. 245/M5
Bristol (co.), Mass. 249/K5
Bristol, Mich. 250/D4
Bristol, New Bruns. 170/C2
Bristol, N.H. 268/D4
Bristol•, N.H. 268/D4
Bristol, Pa. 294/N5
Bristol•, Pa. 294/N5
Bristol (co.), R.I. 249/J6
Bristol, R.I. 249/J6
Bristol, S. Dak. 298/O3
Bristol, Tenn. 188/K3
Bristol, Tenn. 237/S7
Bristol (bay), U.S. 4/D18
Bristol, Va. 188/K3
Bristol, Vt. 268/A3
Bristol•, Vt. 268/A3
Bristol (I.C.), Va. 307/D7
Bristol (chan.), Wales 13/C6
Bristol (chan.), Wales 10/E5
Bristol, W. Va. 312/F4
Bristolville, Ohio 284/J3
Bristow, Ind. 227/D8
Bristow, Iowa 229/H3
Bristow, Nebr. 264/F2
Bristow, Okla. 288/O3
Bristow, Va. 307/N3
Britannia Beach, Br. Col. 184/K2
British (mts.), Alaska 196/K1
British (mts.), Yukon 187/D3
British Columbia (prov.) 162/D4
BRITISH COLUMBIA 184
British Columbia (prov.), Canada 146/F4
British Empire (range), N.W.T. 186/L1
British Indian Ocean Territory 2/N6
British Indian Ocean Territory 54/J10
British Isles 7/D3
Brits, S. Africa 118/D5
Britstown, S. Africa 118/C6
Britt, Iowa 229/F2
Britt, Minn. 255/F3
Britt, Ontario 177/D2
Brittany (trad. prov.), France 29
Brittany, La. 238/L3
Brittnau, Switzerland 39/E2
Britton, Mich. 250/F6
Britton, S. Dak. 298/O2
Brive-la-Gaillarde, France 28/D5
Briviesca, Spain 33/E1
Brno, Czech Rep. 7/F4
Brno, Czech Rep. 41/D2
Broa (inlet), Cuba 158/C1
Broach (Bharuch), India 68/C4
Broad (brook), Conn. 210/H2
Broad (creek), Del. 245/R6
Broad (riv.), N.C. 281/E4
Broad (sound), Queensland 88/H4
Broad (sound), Queensland 95/D4
Broad (bay), Scotland 15/B2
Broad (riv.), S.C. 296/F7
Broad (riv.), S.C. 296/E2
Broadacres, Oreg. 291/A3
Broadacres, Sask. 181/B3
Broadalbin, N.Y. 276/M4
Broad Arrow, W. Australia 88/C6
Broad Arrow, W. Australia 92/C5
Broadback (riv.), Québec 174/B2
Broadbent, Oreg. 291/C4
Broad Brook, Conn. 210/E1
Broad Cove, Newf. 166/D2
Broad Cove, Nova Scotia 168/D4
Broaddus, Texas 303/K6
Broadfields, Ky. 237/K2
Broadford, Ireland 17/C7
Broadford, Scotland 15/B3
Broadford, Victoria 97/C5
Broadford, Va. 307/E7
Broad Haven (harb.), Ireland 17/B3
Broadhurst, Ga. 217/J8
Broadkill (riv.), Del. 245/S5
Broadland, S. Dak. 298/N4
Broadlands, Ill. 222/E4
Broad Law (mt.), Scotland 15/E5
Broadmeadows, Victoria 88/L6
Broadmeadows, Victoria 97/H4
Broadstairs and Saint Peter's, England 13/J6
Broad Top, Pa. 294/F5
Broadus, Mont. 262/L5
Broad Valley, Manitoba 179/E4
Broadview, Ill. 222/B6
Broadview, Mont. 262/H4
Broadview, N. Mex. 274/F4
Broadview, Sask. 181/J5
Broadview Heights, Ohio 284/H10
Broadview Park, Fla. 212/B4
Broadwater (co.), Mont. 262/E4
Broadwater, Nebr. 264/B3
Broadway, N.J. 273/C2

Buffalo Bill 343

Broadway, N.C. 281/L4
Broadway, Ohio 284/C5
Broadway, Va. 307/L3
Broadwell, Ill. 222/D3
Broager, Denmark 21/C8
Broc, Switzerland 39/D3
Brochet, Man. 162/F4
Brochet, Manitoba 179/H2
Brock (isl.), N.W.T. 162/M3
Brock, Nebr. 264/H4
Brock (isl.), N.W.T. 187/G2
Brock, Sask. 181/C4
Brockdell, Tenn. 237/L10
Brocken (mt.), Germany 22/D3
Brocket, Alberta 182/D5
Brocket, N. Dak. 282/O3
Brockington, Sask. 181/G2
Brockport, N.Y. 276/D4
Brockport, Pa. 294/E3
Brockton, Mass. 249/K4
Brockton, Mont. 262/M2
Brockville, Ontario 177/J3
Brockway, Mont. 262/L3
Brockway, New Bruns. 170/C3
Brockway, Pa. 294/E3
Brocton, Ill. 222/F4
Brocton, N.Y. 276/B6
Broderick, Sask. 181/E4
Broderick-Bryte, Calif. 204/B8
Brodeur (pen.), Canada 4/B14
Brodeur (pen.), N.W.T. 146/K2
Brodeur (pen.), N.W.T. 162/H1
Brodeur (pen.), N.W.T. 187/K2
Brodhead, Ky. 237/N6
Brodhead, Wis. 317/G10
Brodheadsville, Pa. 294/M4
Brodick, Scotland 15/C5
Brodick, Scotland 10/D3
Brodnax, Va. 307/N7
Brodnica, Poland 47/D2
Broek in Waterland, Netherlands 27/C4
Brogan, Oreg. 291/K3
Brohard, W. Va. 312/D4
Brohman, Mich. 250/D5
Brokaw, Wis. 317/G5
Broken (bay), N.S. Wales 97/F3
Broken Arrow, Okla. 288/P2
Broken Bow, Nebr. 264/E3
Broken Bow, Okla. 288/S7
Broken Bow (lake), Okla. 288/S6
Broken Hill, Australia 87/E9
Broken Hill, N.S. Wales 88/G6
Broken Hill, N.S. Wales 97/A3
Broken Hill (Kabwe), Zambia 115/E6
Brokensword, Ohio 284/E4
Brokopondo (dist.), Suriname 131/D4
Brokopondo, Suriname 131/D3
Brome (co.), Québec 172/E4
Brome, Québec 172/E4
Brome (lake), Québec 172/E4
Bromer, Ind. 227/E7
Bromhead, Sask. 181/H6
Bromide, Okla. 288/N6
Bromley, England 13/H8
Bromley, England 10/C5
Bromley, Ky. 237/S2
Bromley (mt.), Vt. 268/B5
Bromont, Québec 172/E4
Brompton (lake), Québec 172/E4
Bromptonville, Québec 172/F4
Bromsgrove, England 13/E5
Bromyard, England 13/E5
Bronaugh, Mo. 261/C7
Bronco, Texas 303/B4
Brønderslev, Denmark 18/F8
Brønderslev, Denmark 21/C3
Brønnøysund, Norway 18/G4
Brøns, Denmark 21/B7
Bronson, Fla. 212/D2
Bronson, Iowa 229/A4
Bronson, Kansas 232/H4
Bronson, Mich. 250/D7
Bronson (lake), Sask. 181/B2
Bronson, Texas 303/L6
Bronston, Ky. 237/M7
Bronte, Italy 34/E6
Bronte, Texas 303/D6
Bronwood, Ga. 217/D7
Bronx (co.), N.Y. 276/N9
Bronx (borough), N.Y. 276/N9
Bronxville, N.Y. 276/O7
Brook, Ind. 227/C3
Brookdale, Calif. 204/J4
Brookdale, Manitoba 179/C4
Brookdale, Nova Scotia 168/D3
Brooke, Va. 307/O4
Brooke (co.), W. Va. 312/E2
Brookeborough, N. Ireland 17/G3
Brookeland, Texas 303/L6
Brooker, Fla. 212/D2
Brooke's Point, Philippines 82/A6
Brookeville, Md. 245/K4
Brookfield•, Conn. 210/B3
Brookfield, Ga. 217/F8
Brookfield, Ill. 222/B6
Brookfield, Mass. 249/F4
Brookfield•, Mass. 249/F4
Brookfield, Mo. 261/F3
Brookfield•, N.H. 268/E4
Brookfield, N.Y. 276/K5
Brookfield, Nova Scotia 168/E3
Brookfield, Ohio 284/J3
Brookfield•, Vt. 268/B3
Brookfield, Wis. 317/K1
Brookfield Center, Conn. 210/B3
Brookford, N.C. 281/G3
Brookhaven, Ga. 217/K1
Brookhaven, Miss. 256/C7
Brookhaven, Pa. 294/M7
Brookhaven Nat'l Lab., N.Y. 276/P9
Brookings, Oreg. 291/C5
Brookings (co.), S. Dak. 298/R5
Brookings, S. Dak. 298/R5
Brookland, Ark. 202/J2
Brookland, D.C. 245/F4
Brooklawn, N.J. 273/B3
Brooklet, Ga. 217/J6
Brooklin•, Maine 243/F7
Brookline•, Mass. 249/C7
Brookline•, N.H. 268/D6
Brookline•, Vt. 268/B5
Brookline Station (Brookline), Mo. 261/F8
Brooklyn, Ala. 195/E8
Brooklyn•, Conn. 210/H1
Brooklyn, Ga. 217/C6
Brooklyn (Lovejoy), Ill. 222/A2
Brooklyn, Ill. 222/C3
Brooklyn, Ind. 227/E5
Brooklyn, Iowa 229/J5
Brooklyn, Ky. 237/H6
Brooklyn, Mich. 250/E6
Brooklyn, Miss. 256/F8
Brooklyn, Newf. 166/D2
Brooklyn (borough), N.Y. 276/N9
Brooklyn, Nova Scotia 168/D4
Brooklyn, Ohio 284/H9
Brooklyn, Pa. 294/L2
Brooklyn, Wash. 310/B4
Brooklyn, Wis. 317/H10
Brooklyn Center, Minn. 255/G5
Brooklyn Heights, Ohio 284/H9
Brooklyn Park, Md. 245/M4
Brooklyn Park, Minn. 255/G5
Brookmere, Br. Col. 184/G5
Brookneal, Va. 307/L6
Brook Park, Minn. 255/F5
Brook Park, Ohio 284/G9
Brookport, Ill. 222/E6
Brooks (range), Alaska 146/C3
Brooks (range), Alaska 188/C5
Brooks (range), Alaska 196/G1
Brooks, Alberta 182/E4
Brooks (pen.), Br. Col. 184/D5
Brooks, Calif. 204/C5
Brooks (co.), Ga. 217/E9
Brooks, Ga. 217/D4
Brooks, Iowa 229/D7
Brooks, Ky. 237/K4
Brooks•, Maine 243/E6
Brooks, Minn. 255/B3
Brooks, Mont. 262/G3
Brooks, Oreg. 291/A3
Brooks (co.), Texas 303/F11
Brooks (range), U.S. 4/C17
Brooks, W. Va. 312/E7
Brooks, Wis. 317/G8
Brooks A.F.B., Texas 303/K11
Brooksburg, Ind. 227/G7
Brooksby, Sask. 181/G2
Brookshire, Texas 303/J8
Brookside, Ala. 195/E3
Brookside, Colo. 208/J6
Brookside, Del. 245/R2
Brookside, N.J. 273/D2
Brookside, Ohio 284/J5
Brookside Village, Texas 303/J2
Brookston, Ind. 227/D3
Brookston, Minn. 255/F4
Brooksville, Ala. 195/F2
Brooksville, Fla. 212/D3
Brooksville, Ky. 237/N3
Brooksville, Maine 243/F7
Brooksville•, Maine 243/F7
Brooksville, Miss. 256/G4
Brooksville, Okla. 288/M4
Brookton, Ga. 217/E2
Brookton, Maine 243/H4
Brookton, W. Australia 92/B2
Brooktondale, N.Y. 276/H6
Brookview, Md. 245/P6
Brook Village, Nova Scotia 168/G2
Brookville, Ind. 227/G6
Brookville (lake), Ind. 227/G6
Brookville, Kansas 232/E3
Brookville, Mass. 249/K4
Brookville, N.Y. 276/R6
Brookville, Ohio 284/B6
Brookville, Pa. 294/D3
Brookwood, Ala. 195/D4
Broom, Loch (inlet), Scotland 15/C3
Broomall, Pa. 294/M6
Broome, Australia 87/C7
Broome (co.), N.Y. 276/J6
Broome, W. Australia 88/C3
Broome, W. Australia 92/C2
Broomfield, Colo. 208/J3
Broomhill, Manitoba 179/B5
Brooten, Minn. 255/C5
Brora, Scotland 15/E2
Brora (riv.), Scotland 15/D2
Brørup, Denmark 21/C7
Broseley, Mo. 261/M9
Brosna, Ireland 17/C7
Brosna (riv.), Ireland 17/F5
Brossard, Québec 172/H4
Brosseau, Alberta 182/E3
Brothers, Oreg. 291/G4
Brotherton, Tenn. 237/L8
Brothertown, Wis. 317/K7
Brou, France 28/D3
Brough (head), Scotland 15/E1
Brough Ness (prom.), Scotland 15/F2
Broughshane, N. Ireland 17/J2
Broughton, Ill. 222/E6
Broughton, Ohio 284/B3
Broughton, Pa. 294/B7
Broughton, Scotland 15/E5
Broughton Island, N.W.T. 187/M3
Broumov, Czech Rep. 41/D1
Brounland, W. Va. 312/C6
Brouse, Br. Col. 184/J5
Broussard, La. 238/F6
Brouwershaven, Netherlands 27/D5
Brovst, Denmark 21/C3
Broward (co.), Fla. 212/F5
Browardale, Fla. 212/B4
Browder, Ky. 237/H6
Browerville, Minn. 255/D4
Brown (co.), Ill. 222/C4
Brown (co.), Ind. 227/E6
Brown (co.), Kansas 232/G2
Brown (co.), Minn. 255/D6
Brown (co.), Nebr. 264/E2
Brown (lake), N.W.T. 187/J3
Brown (co.), Ohio 284/C8
Brown (reefs), Philippines 85/F3
Brown (co.), S. Dak. 298/N2
Brown (co.), Texas 303/F6
Brown (Roan) (cliffs), Utah 304/E4
Brown (pt.), Wash. 310/A4
Brown, W. Va. 312/F4
Brown (co.), Wis. 317/L7
Brownbranch, Mo. 261/G9
Brown City, Mich. 250/G5
Brown Deer, Wis. 317/L1
Browndell, Texas 303/L7
Browne (bay), N.W.T. 187/J2
Brownell, Kansas 232/C3
Browney (riv.), England 13/H3
Brownfield, Alberta 182/E3
Brownfield, Ill. 222/E6
Brownfield, Maine 243/B8
Brownfield•, Maine 243/B8
Brownfield, Miss. 256/G1
Brownfield, Texas 303/B4
Browning, Ill. 222/C3
Browning, Mo. 261/F2
Browning, Mont. 262/C2
Browning, N.S. Wales 97/E4
Browning, Sask. 181/J6
Browning Entrance (str.), Br. Col. 184/B3
Brownington, Mo. 261/E6
Brownington•, Vt. 268/C2
Brownlee (dam), Idaho 220/B5
Brownlee, Nebr. 264/D2
Brownlee, Oreg. 291/L3
Brownlee (dam), Oreg. 291/L3
Brownlee, Sask. 181/F5
Browns, Ala. 195/D6
Browns, Ill. 222/F5
Brown's (riv.), Vt. 268/A2
Brownsboro, Ala. 195/F1
Brownsboro, Oreg. 291/E5
Brownsboro, Texas 303/J5
Brownsboro Farm, Ky. 237/L1
Brownsburg, Ind. 227/E5
Brownsburg, Québec 172/C4
Brownsburg, Va. 307/K5
Brownsdale, Minn. 255/F7
Brownsdale, Newf. 166/D2
Browns Flat, New Bruns. 170/D3
Brown's Lake, Wis. 317/K3
Browns Mills, N.J. 273/D4
Browns Spring, Mo. 261/F9
Browns Summit, N.C. 281/K2
Brownstown, Ill. 222/E5
Brownstown, Ind. 227/F7
Browns Town, Jamaica 158/J6
Brownstown, Pa. 294/K5
Brownstown, Wash. 310/E4
Browns Valley, Ind. 227/C5
Browns Valley, Minn. 255/B5
Browns Village, Fla. 212/B4
Brownsville, Ind. 227/H5
Brownsville, Ky. 237/J6
Brownsville, Md. 245/H3
Brownsville, Minn. 255/G7
Brownsville, Miss. 256/D6
Brownsville, Oreg. 291/E3
Brownsville, Pa. 294/C5
Brownsville, Tenn. 237/C9
Brownsville, Texas 303/G12
Brownsville, Texas 188/G5
Brownsville, Texas 146/J7
Brownsville, Vt. 268/B5
Brownsville, Wash. 310/A2
Brownsville, Wis. 317/J8
Brownton, Minn. 255/D6
Brownton, W. Va. 312/F4
Browntown, Va. 307/M3
Browntown, Wis. 317/G10
Brownvale, Alberta 182/B1
Brownville, Ala. 195/C4
Brownville, Fla. 212/E4
Brownville, Maine 243/E5
Brownville•, Maine 243/E5
Brownville, Nebr. 264/J4
Brownville, N.Y. 276/H3
Brownville Junction, Maine 243/E5
Brown Willy (mt.), England 13/C7
Brownwood, Texas 303/F6
Brownwood (lake), Texas 303/E6
Browse (isl.), W. Australia 88/C2
Browse (isl.), W. Australia 92/C1
Broxburn, Scotland 15/D1
Broxton, Ga. 217/G7
Broye (riv.), Switzerland 39/C3
Broyle (cape), Newf. 166/D2
Brozas, Spain 33/C3
Brozville, Miss. 256/D4
Brtnice, Czech Rep. 41/C2
Bruay-en-Artois, France 28/E2
Bruce, Alberta 182/E3
Bruce (mt.), Australia 87/C8
Bruce, Fla. 212/C6
Bruce, Miss. 256/F3
Bruce (mts.), N.W.T. 187/L2
Bruce (county), Ontario 177/C3
Bruce (pen.), Ontario 177/C2
Bruce, S. Dak. 298/R5
Bruce (mt.), W. Australia 88/B4
Bruce (mt.), W. Australia 92/B3
Bruce, Wis. 317/D5
Bruce Crossing, Mich. 250/G2
Brucefield, Ontario 177/C4
Bruce Lake, Ontario 175/B2
Bruce Mines, Ontario 177/J5
Bruce Mines, Ontario 175/D3
Bruce Rock, W. Australia 88/B6
Bruce Rock, W. Australia 92/B5
Bruceton, Tenn. 237/E8
Bruceton Mills, W. Va. 312/G3
Brucetown, Va. 307/M2
Bruceville, Ind. 227/C7
Bruchsal, Germany 22/C4
Bruck an der Leitha, Austria 41/D2
Bruck an der Mur, Austria 41/C3
Bruderheim, Alberta 182/D3
Bruff, Ireland 17/D7
Bruges, Belgium 27/C6
Brugg, Switzerland 39/F2
Brugge (Bruges), Belgium 27/C6
Brühl, Germany 22/B3
Bruin, Ky. 237/P4
Bruin (cape), New Bruns. 170/G2
Bruin, Pa. 294/C3
Bruins, Ark. 202/K4
Brûlé, Alberta 182/B3
Brule (riv.), Mich. 250/A3
Brule, Nebr. 264/C3
Brule, Nova Scotia 168/E3
Brûlé (lake), Québec 172/C3
Brûlé (lake), Québec 172/B2
Brule (co.), S. Dak. 298/L6
Brule (mt.), Switzerland 39/D4
Brule, Wis. 317/C2
Brumado, Brazil 120/E4
Brumado, Brazil 132/F6
Brumley, Mo. 261/H6
Brummen, Netherlands 27/J4
Brundidge, Ala. 195/G7
Bruneau, Idaho 220/C7
Bruneau (riv.), Idaho 220/C7
Brunei 2/Q5
Brunei 54/N9
BRUNEI 85/E4
Bruner, Mo. 261/F8
Brunete, Spain 33/F4
Brunette (isl.), Newf. 166/C4
Brunflo, Sweden 18/J5
Bruni, Texas 303/F10
Brunico, Italy 34/D1
Bruning, Nebr. 264/G4
Brunkild, Manitoba 179/E5
Brunner, N. Zealand 100/C5
Brunner (lake), N. Zealand 100/C5
Bruno, Ark. 202/E1
Bruno, Minn. 255/F4
Bruno, Nebr. 264/G3
Bruno, Sask. 181/F3
Brunot, Mo. 261/M8
Brunsbüttel, Germany 22/C2
Brunson, S.C. 296/E6
Brunssum, Netherlands 27/J7
Brunsville, Iowa 229/A3
Brunswick (pen.), Chile 138/E10
Brunswick, Ga. 188/K4
Brunswick, Ga. 217/K8
Brunswick, Germany 7/E3
Brunswick, Germany 22/D2
Brunswick, Maine 243/C8
Brunswick•, Maine 243/C8
Brunswick, Md. 245/H3
Brunswick, Minn. 255/E5
Brunswick, Miss. 256/C5
Brunswick, Mo. 261/F4
Brunswick, Nebr. 264/G2
Brunswick (co.), N.C. 281/N6
Brunswick, N.C. 281/M6
Brunswick, Ohio 284/G3
Brunswick, Tenn. 237/B10
Brunswick, Victoria 88/K7
Brunswick, Victoria 97/H5
Brunswick (co.), Va. 307/N7
Brunswick (bay), W. Australia 88/C3
Brunswick (bay), W. Australia 92/D1
Brunswick Heads, N.S. Wales 97/G1
Brunswick Junction, W. Australia 92/A2
Bruntál, Czech Rep. 41/D2
Bruree, Ireland 17/D7
Brus (lag.), Honduras 154/E2
Brusett, Mont. 262/J3
Brush, Colo. 208/M2
Brush Creek, Minn. 255/E7
Brush Creek, Mo. 261/G7
Brush Creek, Tenn. 237/J8
Brush Prairie, Wash. 310/C5
Brushton, N.Y. 276/L1
Brushy Prairie, Ind. 227/G1
Brusio, Switzerland 39/K4
Brus Laguna, Honduras 154/E3
Brusly, La. 238/J2
Brusque, Brazil 132/D9
Brussels (cap.), Belgium 7/E3
Brussels, Ill. 222/C5
Brussels, Ontario 177/C4
Brussels, Wis. 317/L6
Bruthen, Victoria 97/D5
Brutus, Mich. 250/E3
Bruxelles, Manitoba 179/C5
Bruzual, Venezuela 124/D3
Bryan (co.), Ga. 217/K6
Bryan, Ohio 284/A3
Bryan (co.), Okla. 288/O7
Bryan, Texas 188/G4
Bryan, Texas 303/H7
Bryan (lake), Wash. 310/H4
Bryansk, Russia 7/H3
Bryansk, Russia 48/D4
Bryansk, Russia 52/D4
Bryanston, Ontario 177/C4
Bryant, Ala. 195/G1
Bryant, Ark. 202/F4
Bryant, Fla. 212/F5
Bryant (lake), Fla. 212/E2
Bryant, Ill. 222/C3
Bryant, Ind. 227/G3
Bryant, Iowa 229/N5
Bryant, Okla. 288/P4
Bryant, S. Dak. 298/P4
Bryant, Wis. 317/J5
Bryant Pond, Maine 243/B7
Bryantsburg, Ind. 227/G7
Bryantsville, Ky. 237/M5
Bryantville, Mass. 249/L4
Bryce (mt.), Br. Col. 184/J4
Bryce, Utah 304/B6
Bryce Canyon, Utah 304/B6
Bryce Canyon Nat'l Park, Utah 304/B6
Bryceland, La. 238/E2
Bryceville, Fla. 212/D1
Bryn Athyn, Pa. 294/M5
Brynica (riv.), Poland 47/B4
Bryn Mawr, Pa. 294/M5
Brynmawr, Wales 10/E5
Brynmawr, Wales 13/B6
Bryn Mawr-Skyway, Wash. 310/B2
Bryrup, Denmark 21/C5
Bryson, Texas 303/F4
Bryson City, N.C. 281/C4
Bryte-Broderick, Calif. 204/B8
Brzeg, Poland 47/C3
Brzeg Dolny, Poland 47/C3
Brzesko, Poland 47/E4
Brzozów, Poland 47/F4
B-Say-Tah, Sask. 181/G5
Bua Chum, Thailand 72/D4
Buad (isl.), Philippines 82/E5
Buba, Guinea-Biss. 106/B6
Bubali, Neth. Ant. 161/D10
Bubaque, Guinea-Biss. 106/A6
Bubendorf, Switzerland 39/E2
Bubikon, Switzerland 39/G2
Bubiyan (isl.), Kuwait 59/E4
Bucak, Turkey 63/D4
Bucaramanga, Colombia 120/B2
Bucaramanga, Colombia 126/D4
Bucareli (bay), Alaska 196/M2
Bucas Grande (isl.), Philippines 82/F6
Bucasia, Queensland 95/D4
Buccaneer (arch.), W. Australia 88/C3
Buccaneer (arch.), W. Australia 92/C2
Buchan (gulf), N.W.T. 187/L2
Buchan (dist.), Scotland 15/F3
Buchanan, Ga. 217/B3
Buchanan (co.), Iowa 229/K4
Buchanan, Iowa 229/L5
Buchanan, Ky. 237/R4
Buchanan, Liberia 106/B7
Buchanan, Liberia 102/A4
Buchanan, Mich. 250/C7
Buchanan (co.), Mo. 261/C3
Buchanan, N.Y. 276/N8
Buchanan, N. Dak. 282/N5
Buchanan, Sask. 181/J4
Buchanan, Tenn. 237/E8
Buchanan (lake), Texas 303/F7
Buchanan (co.), Va. 307/D6
Buchanan, Va. 307/J5
Buchan Ness (prom.), Scotland 15/G3
Buchans, Newf. 166/C4
Bucharest (cap.), Romania 7/G4
Bucharest (cap.), Romania 2/L3
Bucharest (București) (cap.), Romania 45/G3
Buchegg (mts.), Switzerland 39/D2
Buchholz in der Nordheide, Germany 22/C2
Buchlyvie, Scotland 15/B1
Buchon (pt.), Calif. 204/D8
Buchs, Switzerland 39/H2
Buchtel, Ohio 284/F7
Buck (creek), Ind. 227/E8
Buck (creek), S.C. 296/J3
Buck (creek), Texas 303/D3
Buck (isl.), Virgin Is. (U.S.) 161/G3
Buck, W. Va. 312/E7
Buckatunna, Miss. 256/G7
Buck Creek, Alberta 182/C3
Buck Creek, Ind. 227/D4
Bückeburg, Germany 22/C2
Buckeye, Ariz. 198/C5
Buckeye, Iowa 229/G4
Buckeye, La. 238/F4
Buckeye, N. Mex. 274/F6
Buckeye (lake), Ohio 284/F6
Buckeye, W. Va. 312/F6
Buckeye Lake, Ohio 284/F6
Buckeystown, Md. 245/J3
Buckfastleigh, England 13/C7
Buckfield•, Maine 243/C7
Buck Grove, Iowa 229/C5
Buckhannon, W. Va. 312/F5
Buckhannon (riv.), W. Va. 312/F5
Buckhaven and Methil, Scotland 15/F4
Buckhaven and Methil, Scotland 10/E2
Buckhead, Ga. 217/F3
Buck Hollow (creek), Oreg. 291/G2
Buckholts, Texas 303/H7
Buckhorn (lake), Ky. 237/O6
Buckhorn, Mo. 261/M8
Buckhorn, N. Mex. 274/A5
Buckhorn, Ontario 177/F3
Buckhorn (lake), Ontario 177/F3
Buckie, Scotland 15/E3
Buckie, Scotland 10/E2
Buckingham, Colo. 208/L1
Buckingham, Conn. 210/E2
Buckingham, England 13/G6
Buckingham, England 10/F5
Buckingham, Ill. 222/E2
Buckingham, Iowa 229/J4
Buckingham, Québec 172/B4
Buckingham, Texas 303/H2
Buckingham (co.), Va. 307/L5
Buckingham, Va. 307/L5
Buckinghamshire (co.), England 13/G6
Buck Island (chan.), Virgin Is. (U.S.) 161/F3
Buck Island Reef Nat'l Mon., Virgin Is. (U.S.) 161/G3
Buck Lake, Alberta 182/C3
Buckland, Alaska 196/F1
Buckland, Conn. 210/E1
Buckland•, Mass. 249/C2
Buckland, Ohio 284/B4
Buckland, Québec 172/G3
Buckley, Ill. 222/F3
Buckley, Mich. 250/D4
Buckley, Wales 13/G2
Buckley, Wash. 310/C3
Bucklin, Kansas 232/C4
Bucklin, Mo. 261/G3
Buckman, Minn. 255/D5
Buckner, Ark. 202/D7
Buckner, Ill. 222/E6
Buckner, Ky. 237/L4
Buckner, Mo. 261/R5
Bucks, Ala. 195/B8
Bucks (co.), Pa. 294/M5
Bucksburn, Scotland 15/F3
Bucks Harbor, Maine 243/J6
Buckskin (mts.), Ariz. 198/B4
Buckskin, Ind. 227/C8
Bucksport, Maine 243/F6
Bucksport•, Maine 243/F6
Bucksport, S.C. 296/J4
Buckville, Ark. 202/D4
Bucoda, Mo. 261/M10
Bucoda, Wash. 310/C4
Buco-Zau, Angola 115/B4
Buctouche, New Bruns. 170/F2
Buctouche (harb.), New Bruns. 170/F2
Buctouche (riv.), New Bruns. 170/F2
București (Bucharest) (cap.), Romania 45/G3
Bucyrus, Kansas 232/H3
Bucyrus, Mo. 261/H8
Bucyrus, N. Dak. 282/E7
Bucyrus, Ohio 284/E4
Bud, Ind. 227/E6
Bud, W. Va. 312/D7
Buda, Ill. 222/D2
Buda, Texas 303/G7
Budafok, Hungary 41/E3
Budakeszi, Hungary 41/E3
Budaörs, Hungary 41/E3
Budapest (co.), Hungary 41/E3
Budapest (cap.), Hungary 41/E3
Budapest (cap.), Hungary 7/F4
Budaun, India 68/D3
Budd (lake), N.J. 273/D2
Budd Coast (reg.), Ant. 5/C6
Budd Lake, N.J. 273/D2
Buddon Ness (prom.), Scotland 15/F4
Bude (bay), England 13/C7
Bude, Miss. 256/C8
Bude-Stratton, England 13/C7
Budge-Budge, India 68/F2
Budgewoi Lake, N.S. Wales 97/F3
Budia, Spain 33/E2
Büdingen, Germany 22/C3
Budišov, Czech Rep. 41/D2
Budjala, D.R. Congo 115/C3
Budleigh Salterton, England 13/D7
Budrio, Italy 34/C2
Budva, Yugoslavia 45/D4
Buea, Cameroon 115/A3
Buechel, Ky. 237/K2
Buel (lake), Mass. 249/A4
Buellton, Calif. 204/E9
Buena, N.J. 273/D4
Buena, Wash. 310/E4
Buena Esperanza, Argentina 143/C3
Buena Park, Calif. 204/D11
Buenaventura, Colombia 126/B6
Buenaventura, Colombia 120/B2
Buenaventura (bay), Colombia 126/B6
Buenaventura, Cuba 158/H3
Buenaventura, Mexico 150/F2
Buena Vista, Ala. 195/D7
Buena Vista, Ark. 202/D7
Buena Vista, Bolivia 136/D5
Buena Vista (lake), Calif. 204/F8
Buena Vista, Colo. 208/G5
Buenavista, Cuba 158/F2
Buenavista (bay), Cuba 158/F2
Buena Vista, Ga. 217/C6
Buena Vista (co.), Iowa 229/C3
Buena Vista, Miss. 256/G3
Buena Vista, N. Mex. 274/D3
Buena Vista, Ohio 284/D8
Buena Vista, Oreg. 291/D3
Buena Vista, Paraguay 144/D5
Buenavista, Philippines 82/E6
Buena Vista, Sask. 181/F5
Buena Vista, Tenn. 237/E9
Buena Vista, Uruguay 145/E3
Buena Vista, Anzoátegui, Venezuela 124/F3
Buena Vista, Apure, Venezuela 124/D4
Buena Vista, Falcón, Venezuela 124/D2
Buena Vista (I.C.), Va. 307/K5
Buendía (res.), Spain 33/E2
Bueno (riv.), Chile 138/D3
Buenos Aires (lake) 120/B7
Buenos Aires (prov.), Argentina 143/D4
Buenos Aires (cap.), Argentina 120/C6
Buenos Aires (cap.), Argentina 143/H7
Buenos Aires (cap.), Argentina 2/F7
Buenos Aires (lake), Argentina 143/B6
Buenos Aires (lake), Chile 138/E6
Buenos Aires, Amazonas, Colombia 126/F9
Buenos Aires, Caquetá, Colombia 126/D7
Buenos Aires, C. Rica 154/F6
Buesaco, Colombia 126/B7
Buey Arriba, Cuba 158/H4
Bueyeros, N. Mex. 274/F3
Buffalo, Ala. 195/H5
Buffalo, Alberta 182/E4
Buffalo (lake), Alberta 182/D3
Buffalo (riv.), Ark. 202/E2
Buffalo, Ill. 222/D4
Buffalo, Ind. 227/D3
Buffalo, Iowa 229/M6
Buffalo, Kansas 232/G4
Buffalo, Ky. 237/K6
Buffalo (bay), Manitoba 179/G5
Buffalo, Minn. 255/E5
Buffalo (riv.), Minn. 255/B4
Buffalo, Mo. 261/F7
Buffalo, Mont. 262/G4
Buffalo (co.), Nebr. 264/E4
Buffalo (creek), Nev. 266/B2
Buffalo, N.Y. 146/L5
Buffalo, N.Y. 188/L2
Buffalo, N.Y. 276/B5
Buffalo, N. Dak. 282/R6
Buffalo, Ohio 284/G6
Buffalo, Okla. 288/G1
Buffalo, S.C. 296/D2
Buffalo (co.), S. Dak. 298/L5
Buffalo, S. Dak. 298/B2
Buffalo (creek), S. Dak. 298/F6
Buffalo (lake), S. Dak. 298/P2
Buffalo (riv.), Tenn. 237/F9
Buffalo, Texas 303/J6
Buffalo, W. Va. 312/C5
Buffalo (co.), Wis. 317/C7
Buffalo, Wis. 317/C7
Buffalo, Wyo. 319/F1
Buffalo Bill (dam), Wyo. 319/C1

Cambridge 345

Byars, Okla. 288/N5
Bybee, Tenn. 237/P8
Bydgoszcz (prov.), Poland 47/C2
Bydgoszcz, Poland 47/C2
Bydgoszcz, Poland 7/F3
Byemoor, Alberta 182/D4
Byers, Colo. 208/L3
Byers, Kansas 232/D4
Byers, Texas 303/F3
Byesville, Ohio 284/G6
Byfield, Mass. 249/L1
Byford, W. Australia 88/B2
Bygland, Minn. 255/B3
Bygland, Norway 18/F7
Byhalia, Miss. 256/E1
Bykhov, Belarus 52/C4
Bylas, Ariz. 198/E5
Bylot (isl.), N.W.T. 146/L2
Bylot (isl.), N.W.T. 162/J1
Bylot (isl.), N.W.T. 187/L2
Byng, Okla. 288/N5
Byng Inlet, Ontario 177/D2
Byng Inlet, Ontario 175/D3
Bynum, Mont. 262/D3
Bynum (res.), Mont. 262/D2
Bynum, N.C. 281/L3
Bynumville, Mo. 261/G3
Byram, Conn. 210/A4
Byram (pt.), Conn. 210/A4
Byram (riv.), Conn. 210/A4
Byram, Miss. 256/D6
Byrd Station, Ant. 5/A12
Byrdstown, Tenn. 237/L7
Byrnedale, Pa. 294/E3
Byrock, N.S. Wales 97/D2
Byromville, Ga. 217/E6
Byron, Calif. 204/L2
Byron (isl.), Chile 138/D7
Byron, Ga. 217/E5
Byron, Ill. 222/D1
Byron, Ind. 227/C5
Byron, Maine 243/B6
Byron•, Maine 243/B6
Byron, Mich. 250/E6
Byron, Minn. 255/F6
Byron, Nebr. 264/G4
Byron (bay), Newf. 166/C3
Byron (cape), N. S. Wales 88/J5
Byron (cape), N.S. Wales 97/G1
Byron, N.Y. 276/D4
Byron, Okla. 288/K1
Byron (lake), S. Dak. 298/N4
Byron, Wis. 317/K8
Byron, Wyo. 319/D1
Byron Bay, N.S. Wales 97/G1
Byron Center, Mich. 250/D6
Byrum, Denmark 21/E3
Byskeälv (riv.), Sweden 18/L4
Bystřice nad Pernštejnem, Czech Rep. 41/D2
Bystřice pod Hostýnem, Czech Rep. 41/D2
Bystrzyca Kłodzka, Poland 47/C3
Bytča, Slovakia 41/E2
Bytom, Poland 47/A3
Bytów, Poland 47/C1

C

Caacupé, Paraguay 144/B5
Caaguazú, Paraguay 144/D-E4
Caaguazú, Paraguay 144/D4
Caála, Angola 115/C6
Caamaño (sound), Br. Col. 184/C4
Caapucú, Paraguay 144/D5
Caatingas (for.), Brazil 120/E3
Caazapá, Paraguay 144/D-E5
Caazapá, Paraguay 144/D5
Caba, Philippines 82/C2
Cabadbaran, Philippines 82/E6
Cabaiguán, Cuba 158/E2
Cabalasan (mt.), Philippines 82/E5
Caballero, Paraguay 144/B5
Caballo, N. Mex. 274/B6
Caballo (res.), N. Mex. 274/B6
Caballo (creek), Wyo. 319/G1
Caballococha, Peru 128/G4
Caballones (chan.), Cuba 158/F3
Cabana, Peru 128/C7
Cabañaquinta, Spain 33/D1
Cabañas, Cuba 158/B1
Cabanatuan, Philippines 54/O8
Cabanatuan, Philippines 82/C3
Cabanatuan, Philippines 85/G2
Cabanes, Spain 33/F2
Cabano, Québec 172/J2
Cabarroguis, Philippines 82/C2
Cabarrus (co.), N.C. 281/H4
Cabazon, Calif. 204/J10
Cabbage Tree (creek), Queensland 95/D2
Cabedelo, Brazil 132/H4
Cabell (co.), W. Va. 312/B6
Cabery, Ill. 222/E3
Cabet, Pitons du (mt.), Martinique 161/C6
Cabeza del Buey, Spain 33/D3
Cabezas, Bolivia 136/D6
Cabezas, Cuba 158/D1
Cabildo, Chile 138/A9
Cabimas, Venezuela 120/B1
Cabimas, Venezuela 124/C2
Cabin Creek, W. Va. 312/C6
Cabinda (prov.), Angola 115/B5
Cabinda, Angola 115/B5
Cabinda, Angola 102/D5
Cabinet (mts.), Mont. 262/A2
Cabin John (creek), Md. 245/E4
Cabin John-Brookmont, Md. 245/E4
Cabins, W. Va. 312/H4
Cable, Minn. 255/D5
Cable, Ohio 284/C5
Cable, Wis. 317/D3
Cabo Blanco, Peru 128/B5
Cabo Delgado (prov.), Mozambique 118/F2
Cabo Frio, Brazil 132/F8
Cabo Frio, Brazil 135/F3
Cabo Gracias a Dios, Nicaragua 154/F3
Cabonga (res.), Québec 174/B3
Cabool, Mo. 261/H8
Cabora Bassa (dam), Mozambique 118/E3
Caborn, Ind. 227/B9
Cabo Rojo, P. Rico 161/A2
Cabo San Lucas, Mexico 150/E5
Cabot (str.) 162/K6
Cabot, Ark. 202/F4
Cabot (str.), Canada 146/N5
Cabot (lake), Newf. 166/B2
Cabot (str.), Newf. 166/B4
Cabot (mt.), N.H. 268/E2
Cabot (head), Ontario 177/C2
Cabot, Pa. 294/C4
Cabot, Vt. 268/C3
Cabot•, Vt. 268/C3
Cabo Vírgenes, Argentina 143/C7
Cabra, Spain 33/D4
Cabra de Santo Cristo, Spain 33/E4
Cabral, Dom. Rep. 158/D6
Cabral (lag.), Paraguay 144/A5
Cabrera, Dom. Rep. 158/E5
Cabrera (isl.), Spain 33/H3
Cabri, Sask. 181/C5
Cabri (lake), Sask. 181/B4
Cabrillo Nat'l Mon., Calif. 204/H11
Cabrits (isl.), Martinique 161/D7
Cabrón (cape), Dom. Rep. 158/F5
Cabruta, Venezuela 124/E4
Cabudare, Venezuela 124/D3
Cabugao, Philippines 82/C2
Cabulauan (isls.), Philippines 82/C5
Cabullones (pt.), P. Rico 161/C3
Caburai (mt.), Guyana 131/A3
Cabure, Venezuela 124/D2
Caçador, Brazil 132/D9
Cacahoatán, Mexico 150/N9
Čačak, Yugoslavia 45/E4
Caçapava, Brazil 135/D3
Caçapava do Sul, Brazil 132/C10
Cacapon (riv.), W. Va. 312/J4
Cáceres (lag.), Bolivia 136/G6
Cáceres, Brazil 132/B7
Cáceres, Brazil 120/D4
Cáceres, Colombia 126/C4
Cáceres (prov.), Spain 33/C3
Cáceres, Spain 33/C3
Cáceres, Spain 7/D5
Cachapoal (riv.), Chile 138/G5
Cache (riv.), Ark. 202/H3
Cache (riv.), Ill. 222/D6
Cache, Okla. 288/J5
Cache (creek), Okla. 288/K6
Cache (co.), Utah 304/C2
Cache Bay, Ontario 177/D1
Cache Creek, Br. Col. 184/G5
Cache Junction, Utah 304/C2
Cache la Poudre (riv.), Colo. 208/H1
Cacheu, Guinea-Biss. 106/A6
Cachi, Argentina 143/C2
Cachina, Quebrada (riv.), Chile 138/A5
Cachipo, Venezuela 124/G3
Cachoeira, Brazil 132/G6
Cachoeira de Itapemirim, Brazil 120/E5
Cachoeira do Arari, Brazil 132/D3
Cachoeira do Sul, Brazil 132/C10
Cachoeira do Sul, Brazil 120/D6
Cachoeiro de Itapemirim, Brazil 132/G8
Cachorras, Colombia 126/D8
Cachos (pt.), Chile 138/A6
Cachuela Esperanza, Bolivia 136/C2
Cachuma (lake), Calif. 204/F9
Cacocum, Cuba 158/H3
Cacocum, Cuba 156/C2
Cacolo, Angola 115/C6
Caconda, Angola 115/B6
Cacouna, Québec 172/H2
Cactus (range), Nev. 266/E5
Cactus (hills), Sask. 181/F5
Cactus, Texas 303/B1
Cactus Lake, Sask. 181/B3
Cacuri, Venezuela 124/F5
Cacuso, Angola 115/C5
Čadca, Slovakia 41/E2
Caddo (riv.), Ark. 202/D5
Caddo (par.), La. 238/C1
Caddo (lake), La. 238/B1
Caddo (co.), Okla. 288/K4
Caddo, Okla. 288/O6
Caddo, Texas 303/F5
Caddo (lake), Texas 303/L5
Caddo Gap, Ark. 202/C5
Caddo Valley, Ark. 202/D5
Caddy Lake, Manitoba 179/G5
Cade, La. 238/G6
Cadereyta Jiménez, Mexico 150/K4
Cades, S.C. 296/H4
Cades, Tenn. 237/D9
Cades Cove, Tenn. 237/O9
Cadet, Mo. 261/L6
Cadibarrawirracanna (lake), S. Australia 94/D3
Cadillac, Mich. 250/D4
Cadillac, Québec 174/B3
Cadillac, Sask. 181/D6
Cadiz, Calif. 204/K9
Cadiz (lake), Calif. 204/K9
Cadiz, Ind. 227/G5
Cadiz, Ky. 237/F7
Cadiz, Ohio 284/J5
Cadiz, Philippines 82/D5
Cádiz (gulf), Portugal 33/C4
Cádiz (prov.), Spain 33/D4
Cádiz, Spain 33/C4
Cádiz, Spain 7/D5
Cádiz (gulf), Spain 33/C4
Cadogan, Alberta 182/E3
Cadogan•, Pa. 294/C4
Cadomin, Alberta 182/B3
Cadott, Wis. 317/D6
Cadotte (lake), Alberta 182/B1
Cadotte (riv.), Alberta 182/B1
Cadotte Lake, Alberta 182/B1
Cadron (creek), Ark. 202/F3
Caduruan (pt.), Philippines 82/D5
Cadwell, Ga. 217/G6
Cadyville, N.Y. 276/N1
Caen, France 28/C3
Caen, France 7/D4
Caerleon, Wales 13/B6
Caernarfon, Wales 13/C4
Caernarfon, Wales 10/D4
Caernarfon (bay), Wales 13/C4
Caernarfon (bay), Wales 10/D4
Caerphilly, Wales 13/B6
Caerphilly, Wales 10/E5
Caesar, Miss. 256/E9
Caesarea, Ontario 177/F3
Caesars Head, S.C. 296/B1
Caeté, Brazil 135/E1
Caetité, Brazil 132/F6
Cafayate, Argentina 143/C2
Cafelândia, Brazil 135/B2
Cagayan (prov.), Philippines 82/C1
Cagayan (isls.), Philippines 82/C6
Cagayan (isls.), Philippines 85/F4
Cagayan (riv.), Philippines 82/C2
Cagayancillo, Philippines 82/C6
Cagayan de Oro, Philippines 82/E6
Cagayan de Oro, Philippines 85/G4
Cagayan Sulu (isl.), Philippines 85/F4
Cagayan Sulu (isl.), Philippines 82/B7
Cagle, Tenn. 237/L10
Cagles Mill (lake), Ind. 227/D6
Cagli, Italy 34/D3
Cagliari (prov.), Italy 34/B5
Cagliari, Italy 7/E5
Cagliari, Italy 34/B5
Cagliari (gulf), Italy 34/B5
Cagua (vol.), Philippines 82/D1
Cagua, Venezuela 124/E2
Caguán (riv.), Colombia 126/C7
Caguas, P. Rico 161/E2
Caguas, P. Rico 156/G1
Caha (mts.), Ireland 17/B8
Cahaba, Ala. 195/D6
Cahaba (riv.), Ala. 195/D5
Cahabón, Guatemala 154/C3
Cahir, Ireland 10/B4
Cahir, Ireland 17/F7
Cahirciveen, Ireland 17/A8
Cahirciveen, Ireland 10/A5
Cahokia, Ill. 222/A3
Cahone, Colo. 208/B7
Cahore (pt.), Ireland 17/J6
Cahors, France 28/D5
Cahuapanas, Peru 128/D5
Cahuilla Ind. Res., Calif. 204/J10
Cahuinari (riv.), Colombia 126/E8
Cahuita (pt.), C. Rica 154/F6
Caia, Mozambique 114/G7
Caia, Mozambique 118/E3
Caiapônia, Brazil 132/C7
Caibarién, Cuba 158/F2
Caibarién, Cuba 156/B2
Caibiran, Philippines 82/E5
Caicara, Venezuela 124/G3
Caicara de Orinoco, Venezuela 124/E4
Caicedonia, Colombia 126/C5
Caicó, Brazil 120/F3
Caicó, Brazil 132/G4
Caicos (passage), Bahamas 156/D2
Caicos (bank), Turks & Caicos 156/D2
Caicos (isls.), Turks & Caicos 156/D2
Caicos (passage), Turks & Caicos 156/D2
Caile, Miss. 256/C4
Cailloma, Peru 128/G10
Caillou (bay), La. 238/J8
Caimanera, Cuba 158/J4
Caimanera, Cuba 156/C3
Cain (creek), S. Dak. 298/N5
Cainde, Angola 115/B7
Cains (riv.), New Bruns. 170/D2
Cains Store, Ky. 237/M6
Cainsville, Mo. 261/E2
Cainsville, Tenn. 237/J9
Caird Coast (reg.), Ant. 5/B17
Cairnbaan, Scotland 15/C4
Cairnbrook, Pa. 294/E5
Cairndow, Scotland 15/D4
Cairn Gorm (mt.), Scotland 15/E3
Cairngorm (mts.), Scotland 15/E3
Cairnryan, Scotland 15/D6
Cairns, Australia 87/E7
Cairns, Queensland 95/C3
Cairns, Queensland 88/H3
Cairnsmore (mt.), Scotland 15/D5
Cairn Toul (mt.), Scotland 15/E3
Cairo, Egypt 59/B4
Cairo (cap.), Egypt 102/F2
Cairo (cap.), Egypt 111/J3
Cairo (cap.), Egypt 2/L4
Cairo, Ga. 217/D9
Cairo, Ill. 188/J3
Cairo, Ill. 222/D6
Cairo, Kansas 232/D4
Cairo, Mo. 261/H4
Cairo, Nebr. 264/F3
Cairo, N.Y. 276/M6
Cairo, Ohio 284/B4
Cairo, Okla. 288/O5
Cairo, W. Va. 312/D4
Caissie (pt.), New Bruns. 170/F2
Caister-on-Sea, England 13/J5
Caistor, England 13/G4
Caithness (trad. co.), Scotland 15/B4
Caiundo, Angola 102/D6
Caiundo, Angola 115/C7
Caiza, Bolivia 136/C7
Cajabamba, Ecuador 128/C3
Cajabamba, Peru 128/C6
Cajacay, Peru 128/D8
Caja de Muertos (isl.), P. Rico 161/C3
Cajamarca (dept.), Peru 128/C6
Cajamarca, Peru 128/C6
Cajamarca, Peru 120/B3
Cajatambo, Peru 128/D8
Cajazeiras, Brazil 132/G4
Cajidiocan, Philippines 82/D4
Cajuata, Bolivia 136/B5
Cajuru, Brazil 135/C2
Čakovec, Croatia 45/C2
Çal, Turkey 63/C3
Çala, Turkey 63/K2
Calabar, Nigeria 102/D4
Calabar, Nigeria 106/F7
Calabash, N.C. 281/M7
Calabazar de Sagua, Cuba 158/E1
Calabogie, Ontario 177/H2
Calabozo, Venezuela 124/E3
Calabria (reg.), Italy 34/F5
Cala Burras (pt.), Spain 33/D4
Calaceite, Spain 33/G2
Calacoto, Bolivia 136/A5
Caladesi (isl.), Fla. 212/B2
Calafat, Romania 45/F3
Calafate, Argentina 143/B7
Calafquén (lake), Chile 138/E3
Calagnaan (isl.), Philippines 82/D5
Calagua (isls.), Philippines 82/D3
Calahoo, Alberta 182/D3
Calahorra, Spain 33/E1
Calais, Alberta 182/B2
Calais, France 28/D2
Calais, France 7/E3
Calais (Dover) (str.), France 28/D2
Calais, Maine 188/N1
Calais, Maine 243/J5
Calais•, Vt. 268/B3
Calama, Brazil 132/H10
Calama, Chile 120/C5
Calama, Chile 138/B3
Calamar, Bolívar, Colombia 126/C2
Calamar, Vaupés, Colombia 126/D7
Calamarca, Bolivia 136/A5
Calamba, Laguna, Philippines 82/C3
Calamba, Misamis Occ., Philippines 82/D6
Calamian Group (isls.), Philippines 85/F3
Calamian Group (isls.), Philippines 82/B4
Calamine, Ark. 202/H1
Calamocha, Spain 33/F2
Calamus, Iowa 229/M5
Calanasan, Philippines 82/C1
Calancasca (riv.), Switzerland 39/H4
Calanda, Spain 33/F2
Calandula, Angola 114/C5
Calang, Indonesia 85/B5
Calansho, Serir (des.), Libya 111/D2
Calansho Sand Sea (des.), Libya 111/D2
Calapan, Philippines 82/C4
Calapan, Philippines 85/G3
Calapooia (riv.), Oreg. 291/E3
Calapooya (mts.), Oreg. 291/E4
Călărași, Romania 45/H3
Calarcá, Colombia 126/C5
Calasparra, Spain 33/F3
Calatayud, Spain 33/F2
Calatorao, Spain 33/F2
Calauag, Philippines 82/D4
Calaveras (co.), Calif. 204/E5
Calaveras (res.), Calif. 204/L3
Calaveras (lake), Texas 303/K11
Calavite (cape), Philippines 82/C4
Calayan, Philippines 82/A2
Calayan (isl.), Philippines 82/A2
Calbayog, Philippines 82/E4
Calbe, Germany 22/D3
Calbuco, Chile 138/D4
Calca, Peru 128/G9
Calcasieu (par.), La. 238/D6
Calcasieu, La. 238/E4
Calcasieu (lake), La. 238/D7
Calcasieu (passage), La. 238/D7
Calcasieu (riv.), La. 238/E5
Calceta, Ecuador 128/C3
Calchaquí, Argentina 143/F5
Calcis, Ala. 195/F4
Calcutta, India 68/F2
Calcutta, India 54/K7
Calcutta, India 2/P4
Calcutta, Ohio 284/J4
Calcutta, Suriname 131/C3
Caldas (dept.), Colombia 126/C5
Caldas da Rainha, Portugal 33/B3
Caldas Novas, Brazil 132/D7
Calder, Idaho 220/B2
Calder, Sask. 181/K4
Calder, Loch (lake), Scotland 15/E2
Caldera, Chile 120/B5
Caldera, Chile 138/A6
Calderas (bay), Dom. Rep. 158/D6
Calderas, Venezuela 124/C3
Calderwood, Tenn. 237/N9
Caldicot, Wales 13/E6
Çaldıran, Turkey 63/K3
Caldwell, Ark. 202/J3
Caldwell, Idaho 220/B6
Caldwell, Idaho 188/C2
Caldwell, Kansas 232/E4
Caldwell (co.), Ky. 237/F6
Caldwell (par.), La. 238/F2
Caldwell (co.), Mo. 261/E3
Caldwell, N.J. 273/B2
Caldwell (co.), N.C. 281/F3
Caldwell, Ohio 284/G6
Caldwell (co.), Texas 303/G8
Caldwell, Texas 303/H7
Caldwell, W. Va. 312/F7
Caldwell, Wis. 317/J2
Caldy (isl.), Wales 13/C6
Cale, Ark. 202/D6
Cale, Ind. 227/D7
Caledon, N. Ireland 17/H3
Caledon, Ontario 177/E4
Caledon, S. Africa 118/G7
Caledonia, Ill. 222/E1
Caledonia, Mich. 250/D6
Caledonia, Minn. 255/G7
Caledonia, Miss. 256/H3
Caledonia, Mo. 261/L7
Caledonia, N.Y. 276/E5
Caledonia, N. Dak. 282/S5
Caledonia, Guysborough, Nova Scotia 168/F3
Caledonia, Queens, Nova Scotia 168/C4
Caledonia, Ohio 284/D4
Caledonia, Pa. 294/F3
Caledonia (co.), Vt. 268/C2
Caledonia, Wis. 317/L2
Caledonian (canal), Scotland 15/D3
Calella, Spain 33/H2
Calenzana, France 28/B6
Calera, Ala. 195/E4
Calera, Okla. 288/O7
Calera de Tango, Chile 138/G4
Caleta Barquito, Chile 138/A6
Caleta Clarencia, Chile 138/E10
Caleta Olivia, Argentina 143/C6
Caleta Olivia, Argentina 120/C7
Caleta Pan de Azúcar, Chile 138/A5
Caleu, Chile 138/G2
Caleufú, Argentina 143/C4
Calexico, Calif. 204/K11
Calf of Man (isl.), I. of Man 13/C3
Calfsound, Scotland 15/F1
Calgary (cap.), Alberta 182/C4
Calgary (cap.), Alta.. 146/G4
Calgary, Alta. 162/E5
Calgary, Canada 2/D3
Calhan, Colo. 208/L4
Calheta, Portugal 33/A2
Calhoun (co.), Ala. 195/G3
Calhoun, Ala. 195/F6
Calhoun (co.), Ark. 202/E6
Calhoun (co.), Fla. 212/D6
Calhoun (co.), Ga. 217/C7
Calhoun, Ga. 217/C1
Calhoun (co.), Ill. 222/C4
Calhoun, Ill. 222/E5
Calhoun (co.), Iowa 229/D4
Calhoun, Ky. 237/G5
Calhoun, La. 238/F2
Calhoun (co.), Mich. 250/D6
Calhoun (co.), Miss. 256/F3
Calhoun, Mo. 261/E6
Calhoun (co.), S.C. 296/F4
Calhoun, Tenn. 237/M10
Calhoun (co.), Texas 303/H9
Calhoun (co.), W. Va. 312/D5
Calhoun City, Miss. 256/F3
Calhoun Falls, S.C. 296/B3
Cali, Colombia 126/B6
Cali, Colombia 120/B2
Calicito, Cuba 158/H4
Calicoan (isl.), Philippines 82/E5
Calico Rock, Ark. 202/F1
Calicut (Kozhikode), India 68/D6
Caliente, Nev. 266/G5
Califon, N.J. 273/D2
California 188/B3
CALIFORNIA 204
California, Ky. 237/N3
California, Md. 245/M7
California (gulf), Mexico 146/G7
California (gulf), Mexico 150/D3
California, Mo. 261/H5
California, Pa. 294/C5
California, Trin. & Tob. 161/A11
California (state), U.S. 146/G6
California Aqueduct, Calif. 204/E7
California City, Calif. 204/H8
California Hot Springs, Calif. 204/G8
California Junction, Iowa 229/B5
Calimete, Cuba 158/D1
Calio, N. Dak. 282/N2
Calion, Ark. 202/E7
Calipatria, Calif. 204/K10
Calistoga, Calif. 204/C5
Calixa-Lavallée, Québec 172/J4
Calkiní, Mexico 150/O6
Çalköy, Turkey 63/C3
Call, Texas 303/L7
Callabonna (lake), S. Australia 88/G5
Callabonna (lake), S. Australia 94/F3
Callafo, Ethiopia 111/H6
Callahan, Calif. 204/C2
Callahan, Fla. 212/E1
Callahan (co.), Texas 303/E5
Callalli, Peru 128/G10
Callan, Ireland 17/G7
Callan, Ireland 10/C4
Callander, Ont. 162/H6
Callander, Ontario 177/E1
Callander, Scotland 10/D2
Callander, Scotland 15/D4
Callands, Va. 307/J7
Callantsoog, Netherlands 27/F3
Callao, Mo. 261/G3
Callao (prov.), Peru 128/D9
Callao, Peru 128/D9
Callao, Peru 2/F6
Callao, Peru 120/B4
Callao, Utah 304/A4
Callao, Va. 307/P5
Callapa, Bolivia 136/A5
Callaway, Fla. 212/D6
Callaway, Minn. 255/C3
Callaway (co.), Mo. 261/J5
Callaway, Nebr. 264/D3
Callaway, Va. 307/H7
Calle Larga, Chile 138/G2
Callender, Iowa 229/E4
Callensburg, Pa. 294/D3
Callery, Pa. 294/C4
Calleuque, Chile 138/F5
Calliaqua, St. Vin. & Grens. 161/A9
Callicoon, N.Y. 276/K7
Callicoon Center, N.Y. 276/L7
Callihan, Texas 303/F9
Callimont, Pa. 294/E6
Calling (lake), Alberta 182/D2
Callis, Somalia 115/J2
Callison, S.C. 296/C3
Callosa de Ensarriá, Spain 33/G3
Calloway (co.), Ky. 237/E7
Calmar, Alberta 182/D3
Calmar, Iowa 229/K2
Calmer, Ark. 202/F6
Calnali, Mexico 150/K6
Calne, England 13/F6
Calobre, Panama 154/G6
Caloosahatchee (riv.), Fla. 212/E5
Caloundra, Queensland 88/J5
Caloundra, Queensland 95/E5
Čalovo, Czech Rep. 41/D3
Calpella, Calif. 204/B4
Calpet, Wyo. 319/B3
Calpulálpan, Mexico 150/M1
Calstock, England 13/C7
Caltagirone, Italy 34/E6
Caltanissetta (prov.), Italy 34/D6
Caltanissetta, Italy 34/D6
Caluire-et-Cuire, France 28/F5
Calulo, Angola 115/C6
Calumet (lake), Ill. 222/C6
Calumet, Iowa 229/B3
Calumet, La. 238/H7
Calumet, Mich. 188/J1
Calumet, Mich. 250/A1
Calumet, Minn. 255/E3
Calumet, Okla. 288/K3
Calumet, Québec 172/C4
Calumet (co.), Wis. 317/K7
Calumet City, Ill. 222/C6
Calumet Park, Ill. 222/C6
Calumetville, Wis. 317/K8
Caluquembe, Angola 102/D6
Caluquembe, Angola 115/B6
Calva, Ariz. 198/E5
Calvados (dept.), France 28/C3
Calvary, Ga. 217/D9
Calvary, Ky. 237/L6
Calvert, Ala. 195/B8
Calvert (isl.), Br. Col. 184/C4
Calvert, Kansas 232/C2
Calvert (co.), Md. 245/M6
Calvert, Md. 245/O2
Calvert, Newf. 166/D2
Calvert, Texas 303/H7
Calvert City, Ky. 237/E6
Calvert Hills, North. Terr. 93/E4
Calverton, Md. 245/L4
Calverton, Va. 307/N3
Calverton Park, Mo. 261/P2
Calvertville, Ind. 227/D6
Calvi, France 28/B6
Calvillo, Mexico 150/H6
Calvin, Ky. 237/O7
Calvin, La. 238/E3
Calvin, N. Dak. 282/N2
Calvin, Okla. 288/O5
Calvin, W. Va. 312/E6
Calvinia, S. Africa 102/E8
Calvinia, S. Africa 118/B6
Calwa, Calif. 204/F7
Calypso, N.C. 281/N4
Calzada de Calatrava, Spain 33/E3
Camabatela, Angola 115/C5
Camacho, Bolivia 136/C7
Camacupa, Angola 115/C6
Camaguán, Venezuela 124/E3
Camagüey (prov.), Cuba 158/G2
Camagüey, Cuba 158/G3
Camagüey, Cuba 146/L7
Camagüey, Cuba 156/B2
Camagüey (arch.), Cuba 158/G2
Camaiore, Italy 34/C3
Camajuaní, Cuba 158/E2
Camak, Ga. 217/G4
Camaná, Peru 128/F11
Camanche (res.), Calif. 204/C9
Camanche, Iowa 229/N5
Camano (isl.), Wash. 310/C2
Camanongue, Angola 115/D6
Camanongue, Angola 102/E6
Camaquã, Brazil 132/C10
Câmara de Lobos, Portugal 33/A2
Çamardı, Turkey 63/F4
Camargo, Bolivia 136/C7
Camargo, Ill. 222/E4
Camargo, Ky. 237/K4
Camargo, Okla. 288/H2
Camarillo, Calif. 204/F9
Camarines Norte (prov.), Philippines 82/D3
Camarines Sur (prov.), Philippines 82/D4
Camarón (cape), Honduras 154/E2
Camarones, Argentina 143/C5
Camarones, Chile 138/B2
Camarones (riv.), Chile 138/A2
Camas (co.), Idaho 220/D6
Camas (creek), Idaho 220/D6
Camas (creek), Idaho 220/F5
Camas (creek), Idaho 220/D5
Camas, Wash. 310/C5
Camas Prairie, Mont. 262/B3
Camas Valley, Oreg. 291/D4
Camatagua, Venezuela 124/E3
Camatindi, Bolivia 136/D7
Ca Mau (Mui Bai Bung) (pt.), Vietnam 72/E5
Cambará, Brazil 135/A3
Cambará, Brazil 132/D8
Cambay, India 68/C4
Cambay (gulf), India 54/J7
Cambay (gulf), India 68/C4
Camberwell, Victoria 88/L7
Camberwell, Victoria 97/J5
Cambodia 2/Q5
Cambodia 54/M8
CAMBODIA (KAMPUCHEA) 72
Camborne-Redruth, England 10/D5
Camborne-Redruth, England 13/B7
Cambra, Pa. 294/K3
Cambrai, France 28/E2
Cambria, Alberta 182/D4
Cambria, Calif. 204/D8
Cambria, Ill. 222/D6
Cambria, Ind. 227/D4
Cambria, Iowa 229/G7
Cambria, Mich. 250/E7
Cambria, Minn. 255/D6
Cambria (co.), Pa. 294/E4
Cambria, Wis. 317/H8
Cambrian (mts.), Wales 13/D5
Cambridge, England 13/G5
Cambridge, England 10/G4
Cambridge, Idaho 220/B5
Cambridge, Ill. 222/C2
Cambridge, Iowa 229/G5

346 Cambridge

Cambridge, Jamaica 158/H6
Cambridge, Kansas 232/F4
Cambridge•, Maine 243/E5
Cambridge, Md. 245/O6
Cambridge, Mass. 249/C7
Cambridge (res.), Mass. 249/B6
Cambridge, Minn. 255/E5
Cambridge, Nebr. 264/D4
Cambridge, N.Y. 276/O4
Cambridge, N. Zealand 100/E2
Cambridge, Ohio 284/G5
Cambridge, Ontario 177/D4
Cambridge, Tasmania 99/D4
Cambridge, Vt. 268/B2
Cambridge•, Vt. 268/B2
Cambridge, Wis. 317/H9
Cambridge Bay, Canada 4/B15
Cambridge Bay, N.W.T. 162/F2
Cambridge Bay, N.W.T. 187/H3
Cambridge City, Ind. 227/G5
Cambridge-Narrows, New Bruns. 170/E3
Cambridgeport, Vt. 268/B5
Cambridgeshire (co.), England 13/G5
Cambridge Springs, Pa. 294/C2
Cambridge Station, Nova Scotia 168/D3
Cambuí, Brazil 135/C3
Cambulo, Angola 115/D5
Cambulo, Angola 102/E5
Cambundi-Catembo, Angola 114/C5
Cambuslang, Scotland 15/B2
Camden, Ala. 195/D7
Camden (bay), Alaska 196/K1
Camden, Ark. 202/E6
Camden, Del. 245/R4
Camden, England 13/H8
Camden, England 10/B5
Camden (co.), Ga. 217/J9
Camden, Ill. 222/C3
Camden, Ind. 227/D3
Camden, Maine 243/F7
Camden•, Maine 243/F7
Camden, Mich. 250/E7
Camden, Miss. 256/E5
Camden (co.), Mo. 261/G6
Camden, Mo. 261/D4
Camden, N.J. 188/M3
Camden (co.), N.J. 273/D4
Camden, N.J. 273/B3
Camden, N.S. Wales 97/F4
Camden, N.Y. 276/J4
Camden (co.), N.C. 281/S2
Camden, N.C. 281/S2
Camden, Ohio 284/A6
Camden, S.C. 296/F3
Camden, Tenn. 237/E8
Camden, Texas 303/K7
Camden, W. Va. 312/E4
Camden Haven, N.S. Wales 97/G2
Camden on Gauley, W. Va. 312/E6
Camden Park, St. Vin. & Grens. 161/A9
Camden Point, Mo. 261/C4
Camdenton, Mo. 261/G6
Cameia, Angola 115/D6
Camelford, England 13/C7
Çameli, Turkey 63/C4
Camels Hump (mt.), Vt. 268/B3
Camerino, Italy 34/D3
Cameron, Ariz. 198/D3
Cameron (peak), Colo. 208/H1
Cameron, Ill. 222/C3
Cameron (par.), La. 238/D7
Cameron, La. 238/D7
Cameron, Mo. 261/D3
Cameron, Mont. 262/E5
Cameron, N.Y. 276/F6
Cameron (mts.), N. Zealand 100/A7
Cameron, N.C. 281/L4
Cameron (isl.), N.W.T. 187/H2
Cameron, Ohio 284/J6
Cameron, Okla. 288/T4
Cameron (co.), Pa. 294/F3
Cameron, Pa. 294/F3
Cameron, S.C. 296/F4
Cameron (co.), Texas 303/G11
Cameron, Texas 303/H7
Cameron, W. Va. 312/E3
Cameron, Wis. 317/C5
Cameron Falls, Ontario 177/H5
Cameron Highlands, Malaysia 72/D6
Cameroon 2/K5
Cameroon 102/D4
CAMEROON 115/B2
Cameroon (mt.), Cameroon 102/C4
Cameroon (mt.), Cameroon 115/A3
Camerota, Italy 34/E4
Cametá, Brazil 132/D3
Camiguin (prov.), Philippines 82/E6
Camiguin, Cagayan (isl.), Philippines 82/B3
Camiguin, Camiguin (isl.), Philippines 82/E6
Camiling, Philippines 82/C3
Camilla, Ga. 217/D8
Camillus, N.Y. 276/H4
Camiña, Chile 138/B2
Camiña, Quebrada (riv.), Chile 138/B2
Caminha, Portugal 33/B2
Camino, Calif. 204/E5
Camiri, Bolivia 120/C5
Camiri, Bolivia 136/D7
Camlachie, Ontario 177/B4
Çamlıdere, Turkey 63/E2
Cammack, Ind. 227/G4
Cammack Village, Ark. 202/E4
Cammal, Pa. 294/H3
Camoapa, Nicaragua 154/E4
Camocim, Brazil 132/F3
Camolin, Ireland 17/J6
Camooweal, Queensland 88/F3
Camooweal, Queensland 95/A3
Camopi, Fr. Guiana 131/E4
Camopi (riv.), Fr. Guiana 131/E4
Camorta (isl.), India 68/G7
Camoruco, Colombia 126/E4
Camotes (isls.), Philippines 82/E5
Camotes (sea), Philippines 82/E5
Camp (creek), Ga. 217/J2
Camp (creek), Ind. 227/E6
Camp (creek), Oreg. 291/J4
Camp (co.), Texas 303/K5
Campaign, Tenn. 237/K9
Campamento, Uruguay 145/C1
Campana, Argentina 143/G6
Campana (isl.), Chile 120/B7
Campana (isl.), Chile 138/D7
Campanario, Cerro (mt.), Argentina 143/C4
Campanario, Cerro (mt.), Chile 138/A10
Campanario, Spain 33/D3
Campanha, Brazil 135/D2
Campania, Ga. 217/H4
Campania (reg.), Italy 34/E4
Campaspe (riv.), Victoria 97/C5
Campbell, Ala. 195/C7
Campbell, Alaska 196/M2
Campbell, Calif. 204/K3
Campbell (co.), Ky. 237/N3
Campbell, Minn. 255/B4
Campbell, Mo. 261/M9
Campbell, Nebr. 264/F4
Campbell, N.Y. 276/F6
Campbell (cape), N. Zealand 100/E4
Campbell, Ohio 284/J3
Campbell (hill), Ohio 284/C5
Campbell (co.), S. Dak. 298/J2
Campbell (co.), Tenn. 237/N8
Campbell (co.), Va. 307/K6
Campbell (co.), Wyo. 319/G1
Campbell (mt.), Yukon 187/E3
Campbellford, Ontario 177/G3
Campbell Hall, N.Y. 276/M8
Campbell Hill, Ill. 222/D6
Campbell Island, Br. Col. 184/C4
Campbellpore, Pakistan 68/C2
Campbell River, Br. Col. 184/E5
Campbells (lake), Oreg. 291/H5
Campbellsburg, Ind. 227/E7
Campbellsburg, Ky. 237/L3
Campbellsport, Wis. 317/K8
Campbell Station, Ark. 202/H2
Campbellsville, Ky. 237/L6
Campbellton, Fla. 212/D5
Campbellton, Mo. 261/K5
Campbellton, N. Br. 162/K6
Campbellton, N. Br. 146/M5
Campbellton, New Bruns. 170/D1
Campbellton, Newf. 166/D4
Campbellton, Pr. Edward I. 168/D2
Campbellton, Texas 303/F9
Campbelltown, N.S. Wales 97/F4
Campbelltown, S. Australia 88/E8
Campbelltown, S. Australia 94/B7
Campbell Town, Tasmania 99/D3
Campbeltown, Scotland 15/C5
Campbeltown, Scotland 10/C3
Camp Creek, Alberta 182/C2
Camp Creek, W. Va. 312/D7
Camp Crook, S. Dak. 298/B2
Camp David, Md. 245/J2
Camp Dennison, Ohio 284/D9
Camp Dix, Ky. 237/P3
Camp Douglas, Wis. 317/F8
Campeche (state), Mexico 150/O7
Campeche, Mexico 146/J8
Campeche, Mexico 150/O7
Campeche (bank), Mexico 150/O6
Campeche (bay), Mexico 146/J7
Campeche (bay), Mexico 150/N7
Campechuela, Cuba 158/G4
Camper, Manitoba 179/D3
Camperdown, Victoria 97/C6
Camperville, Manitoba 179/B2
Camp Grove, Ill. 222/D2
Camp Hale, Colo. 208/G4
Camp Hill, Ala. 195/G5
Camp Hill, Pa. 294/H5
Camp Hill, Queensland 88/K3
Camp Hill, Queensland 95/E3
Campiglia Marittima, Italy 34/C3
Campile, Ireland 17/H7
Campillo de Altobuey, Spain 33/F3
Campillos, Spain 33/D4
Campina Grande, Brazil 120/F3
Campina Grande, Brazil 132/G4
Campinas, Brazil 120/E5
Campinas, Brazil 135/C3
Campinas, Brazil 132/E8
Campina Verde, Brazil 135/B1
Campina Verde, Brazil 132/D7
Camp Lake, Wis. 317/K10
Camp Lejeune Marine Corps Base, N.C. 281/P5
Campli, Italy 34/D3
Camp Morton, Manitoba 179/E4
Camp Nelson, Calif. 204/G7
Campo, Calif. 204/J11
Campo, Cameroon 115/B3
Campo, Colo. 208/O8
Campoalegre, Colombia 126/C6
Campobasso (prov.), Italy 34/E4
Campobasso, Italy 34/E4
Campobello (isl.), New Bruns. 170/D4
Campobello, S.C. 296/C1
Campo Belo, Brazil 132/E8
Campo Belo, Brazil 135/D2
Campo Claro, Venezuela 124/G2
Campo de Criptana, Spain 33/E3
Campo de la Cruz, Colombia 126/C2
Campo Florido, Brazil 135/B1
Campo Formoso, Brazil 132/F5
Campo Grande, Brazil 120/D5
Campo Grande, Brazil 132/C8
Campo Ind. Res., Calif. 204/J11
Campo Largo, Brazil 135/B4
Campo Maior, Brazil 132/F4
Campo Maior, Portugal 33/C3
Campos, Brazil 132/F8
Campos, Brazil 135/F2
Campos, Brazil 120/E5
Campos (reg.), Brazil 120/E4
Campos Altos, Brazil 135/C1
Campo Seco, Calif. 204/D9
Campo Tencia (peak), Switzerland 39/G4
Campo Tures, Italy 34/C1
Camp Pendleton, Calif. 204/H10
Camp Perrin, Haiti 158/A6
Camp Point, Ill. 222/B3
Camp Robinson, Ontario 177/G4
Camp Robinson, Ontario 175/B2
Camp Sherman, Oreg. 291/F3
Camp Springs, Md. 245/G6
Campti, La. 238/D3
Campton, Ga. 217/E3
Campton, Ky. 237/O5
Campton•, N.H. 268/D4
Camptown, Pa. 294/K2
Campus, Ill. 222/E2
Camp Verde, Ariz. 198/D4
Campville, Fla. 212/D2
Camp Wood, Texas 303/D8
Cam Ranh, Vietnam 72/F5
Cam Ranh, Vinh (bay), Vietnam 72/F5
Camrose, Alberta 182/D3
Camrose, Alta. 162/E5
Camsell (riv.), N.W.T. 187/G3
Camsell Portage, Sask. 181/L2
Camuy, P. Rico 161/B1
Camuy, P. Rico 156/F1
Camuy (riv.), P. Rico 161/B1
Çan, Turkey 63/B2
Cana (pt.), Dom. Rep. 158/F6
Cana, Sask. 181/J5
Čaňa, Slovakia 41/F2
Cana, Va. 307/G7
Canaan, Conn. 210/B1
Canaan•, Conn. 210/B1
Canaan (mt.), Conn. 210/B1
Canaan, Ind. 227/G7
Canaan•, Maine 243/D6
Canaan, Miss. 256/F1
Canaan, New Bruns. 170/E2
Canaan (riv.), New Bruns. 170/E2
Canaan•, N.H. 268/C4
Canaan, N.Y. 276/O6
Canaan•, Vt. 268/D2
Canaan Center, N.H. 268/C4
Canaan Forks, 170/E2
Canaan Road, New Bruns. 170/E2
Canada 2/D3
Canada 4/C13
Canada 146/G4
CANADA 163
Cañada, La (mt.), Cuba 158/B2
Canada, Ky. 237/S5
Canada (bay), Newf. 166/C3
Cañada de Gómez, Argentina 143/F6
Cañada Nieto, Uruguay 145/B4
Canadensis, Pa. 294/M3
Canadian (riv.) 188/F3
Canadian (riv.), N. Mex. 274/F3
Canadian (co.), Okla. 288/K3
Canadian, Okla. 288/P4
Canadian (riv.), Okla. 288/O4
Canadian, Texas 303/D2
Canadian (riv.), Texas 303/D1
Canadian (riv.), U.S. 146/H6
Canadian City, Okla. 288/L4
Canadice (lake), N.Y. 276/F5
Canadys, S.C. 296/F5
Canagua (riv.), Venezuela 124/C3
Canajoharie, N.Y. 276/L5
Çanakkale (prov.), Turkey 63/B2
Çanakkale, Turkey 63/B6
Çanakkale, Turkey 59/A2
Çanakkale Boğazı (Dardanelles) (str.), Turkey 63/B6
Çanakkale Boğazı (str.), Turkey 59/A2
Canal (creek), Alberta 182/E5
Canala, New Caled. 86/G4
Canala (bay), New Caled. 86/H4
Canal Flats, Br. Col. 184/K5
Canal Fulton, Ohio 284/H4
Canalou, Mo. 261/N9
Canal Point, Fla. 212/F5
Canals, Argentina 143/D3
Canal Winchester, Ohio 284/E6
Canandaigua, N.Y. 276/F5
Canandaigua (lake), N.Y. 276/F5
Cananea, Mexico 150/D1
Cananéia, Brazil 132/E9
Cananéia, Brazil 135/C4
Cananova, Cuba 158/K3
Cañar (prov.), Ecuador 128/C4
Cañar, Ecuador 128/C4
Canaries, St. Lucia 161/G6
Canaries, Piton (mt.), St. Lucia 161/G6
Canarreos, Los (arch.), Cuba 158/C2
Canary, Oreg. 291/D4
Canary (isls.), Spain 102/A2
Canary (isls.), Spain 2/H4
Canary (isls.), Spain 33/B4
Canary (isls.), Spain 106/A3
Cañas, C. Rica 154/E5
Cañas, Cuba 158/B1
Cañas (range), Uruguay 145/C2
Canaseraga, N.Y. 276/E6
Cañasgordas, Colombia 126/B4
Canasí, Cuba 158/C1
Canastota, N.Y. 276/J4
Canatlán, Mexico 150/G4
Canaveral (cape), Fla. 146/L7
Canaveral (Kennedy) (cape), Fla. 188/L5
Canaveral (cape), U.S. 2/F4
Canavieiras, Brazil 132/G6
Cañazas, Panama 154/G6
Canbelego, N.S. Wales 97/D2
Canberra (cap.), Australia 87/F9
Canberra (cap.), Australia 2/S7
Canberra (cap.), Aust. Cap. Terr. Australia 97/E4
Canby, Calif. 204/E2
Canby, Minn. 255/B6
Canby, Oreg. 291/B2
Cancún, Mexico 150/Q6
Candala, Somalia 115/J1
Candarave, Peru 128/G11
Çandarlı (gulf), Turkey 63/B3
Candás, Spain 33/D1
Candéias, Brazil 120/F4
Candela, Mexico 150/J3
Candelaria, Bolivia 136/F5
Candelaria (riv.), Bolivia 136/F5
Candelaria, Cuba 158/B1
Candelaria, Mexico 150/O7
Candelaria (riv.), Mexico 150/O8
Candelaria, Philippines 82/B3
Candelaria, Texas 303/C12
Candelaria, Venezuela 124/F4
Candeleda, Spain 33/D2
Candelero (pt.), P. Rico 161/F2
Candelo, N.S. Wales 97/E5
Candia (Iráklion), Greece 45/G8
Candia•, N.H. 268/E5
Candiac, Québec 172/J4
Candiac, Sask. 181/H5
Cândido Mendes, Brazil 132/E3
Çandır, Turkey 63/F3
Candle (lake), Sask. 181/F2
Candle Lake, Sask. 181/F2
Candler, Fla. 212/E2
Candler (co.), Ga. 217/H6
Candler, N.C. 281/D3
Candlewood (lake), Conn. 210/A2
Candlewood, N.J. 273/E3
Cando, N. Dak. 282/M3
Cando, Sask. 181/C3
Candon, Philippines 82/C2
Candor, N.Y. 276/H6
Candor, N.C. 281/K4
Cane (creek), Utah 304/E5
Canea (Khaniá), Greece 45/G8
Caneadea, N.Y. 276/D6
Canebay, Virgin Is. (U.S.) 161/E3
Cane Beds, Ariz. 198/B2
Canebrake, W. Va. 312/C8
Caneel (bay), Virgin Is. (U.S.) 161/B4
Canehill, Ark. 202/B2
Canelones (dept.), Uruguay 145/D5
Canelones, Uruguay 120/D6
Canelones, Uruguay 145/B6
Canelos, Ecuador 128/D3
Canendiyu, Paraguay 144/E4
Cañete (riv.), Peru 128/D9
Cañete, Chile 138/D2
Cañete, Spain 33/F2
Cane Valley, Ky. 237/L6
Caney, Kansas 232/G4
Caney, Ky. 237/P5
Caney, Okla. 288/O6
Caney (riv.), Okla. 288/O1
Caney Fork (riv.), Tenn. 237/L9
Caneyville, Ky. 237/J6
Canfield, Ark. 202/C7
Canfield, Ohio 284/J3
Canford, Br. Col. 184/G5
Cangallo, Peru 128/E9
Cangamba, Angola 115/C6
Cangas, Spain 33/B1
Cangas de Narcea, Spain 33/C1
Cangas de Onís, Spain 33/D1
Canguaretama, Brazil 132/H4
Cangyuan, China 77/E7
Cangzhou (Tsangchow), China 77/J4
Caniapiscau (riv.), Que. 162/K4
Caniapiscau, Québec 174/D1
Caniapiscau (res.), Québec 174/D2
Caniapiscau (riv.), Québec 174/D1
Canicattì, Italy 34/E6
Canigao (chan.), Philippines 82/E5
Canik (mts.), Turkey 63/G2
Caniles, Spain 33/E4
Canim (lake), Br. Col. 184/G4
Canim Lake, Br. Col. 184/G4
Canindé, Brazil 132/G4
Canistear (res.), N.J. 273/E1
Canisteo, N.Y. 276/E6
Canisteo (riv.), N.Y. 276/F6
Canistota, S. Dak. 298/P6
Cañitas de Felipe Pescador, Mexico 150/H5
Canjáyar, Spain 33/E4
Canje (riv.), Guyana 131/C2
Canjilon, N. Mex. 274/C2
Çankaya, Turkey 63/E3
Çankırı (prov.), Turkey 63/E2
Çankırı, Turkey 63/E2
Çankırı, Turkey 59/B1
Cankton, La. 238/F6
Canlaon, Philippines 82/D5
Canlaon (peak), Philippines 82/D5
Canmer, Ky. 237/K6
Canmore, Alberta 182/C4
Canna (isl.), Scotland 10/C2
Canna (isl.), Scotland 15/B3
Canna (sound), Scotland 15/B3
Cannalville, Ohio 284/F6
Cannanore, India 68/C6
Cannanore (Laccadive) (isls.), India 54/H8
Cannanore (Laccadive) (isls.), India 68/C6
Cannelburg, Ind. 227/C7
Cannel City, Ky. 237/P5
Cannelles (pt.), St. Lucia 161/G7
Cannelles (riv.), St. Lucia 161/G6
Cannelton, Ind. 227/D9
Cannes, France 28/G6
Cannich, Scotland 15/D3
Canning (riv.), Alaska 196/J1
Canning, Nova Scotia 168/D3
Canning, S. Dak. 298/K5
Canning (riv.), W. Australia 88/B3
Canning (res.), W. Australia 88/B2
Canning, W. Australia 92/A1
Cannington, Ontario 177/E3
Cannington Manon Hist. Park, Sask. 181/J6
Cannock, England 10/G2
Cannock, England 13/E5
Cannon, Del. 245/R6
Cannon (mt.), N.H. 268/D3
Cannon (co.), Tenn. 237/J9
Cannon A.F.B., N. Mex. 274/F4
Cannon Ball, N. Dak. 282/J7
Cannonball (riv.), N. Dak. 282/G7
Cannon Beach, Oreg. 291/D2
Cannondale, Conn. 210/B4
Cannon Falls, Minn. 255/F6
Cannonsburg, Miss. 256/B7
Cannonsville (res.), N.Y. 276/K6
Cannonville, Utah 304/B6
Cann River, Victoria 97/E5
Caño (isl.), C. Rica 154/F6
Canoas, Brazil 132/D10
Canoas, Brazil 120/D5
Canobie Lake, N.H. 268/E6
Caño Capure (riv.), Venezuela 124/H3
Canoe, Ala. 195/D8
Canoe (lake), Sask. 181/L3
Canoe Lake, Sask. 181/L3
Canoe Reach (riv.), Br. Col. 184/H4
Canoe River, Br. Col. 184/H4
Canoga Park, Calif. 204/B10
Canoinhas, Brazil 132/D9
Caño Macareo (riv.), Venezuela 124/H3
Caño Mánamo (riv.), Venezuela 124/G3
Canon, Ga. 217/F2
Canonbie, Scotland 15/F5
Canonchet, R.I. 249/H7
Canon City, Colo. 208/J6
Canones, N. Mex. 274/C2
Canonsburg, Pa. 294/B5
Canoochee, Ga. 217/H5
Canoose Flowage (lake), New Bruns. 170/C3
Canora, Sask. 181/J4
Canosa di Puglia, Italy 34/E4
Canouan (isl.), St. Vin. & Grens. 156/G4
Canova, S. Dak. 298/O6
Canovanas (riv.), P. Rico 161/E1
Canowindra, N.S. Wales 97/E3
Canquella, Bolivia 136/A7
Cansado, Mauritania 106/A4
Canso, Nova Scotia 168/H3
Canso (cape), Nova Scotia 168/H3
Canso (str.), Nova Scotia 168/G3
Canta, Peru 128/D8
Cantabrian (range), Spain 33/C1
Cantagalo, Brazil 135/E3
Cantal (dept.), France 28/E5
Cantal, Sask. 181/K6
Cantalejo, Spain 33/D2
Cantanhede, Portugal 33/B2
Cantaura, Venezuela 124/F3
Canterbury•, Conn. 210/H2
Canterbury, Del. 245/R4
Canterbury, England 10/G5
Canterbury, England 13/H6
Canterbury, New Bruns. 170/C3
Canterbury•, N.H. 268/D5
Canterbury, N. S. Wales 88/K4
Canterbury, N.S. Wales 97/J3
Canterbury (bight), N. Zealand 100/D6
Can Tho, Vietnam 72/E5
Can Tho, Vietnam 54/M9
Cantil, Calif. 204/H8
Cantiles (cay), Cuba 158/C3
Cantillana, Alto de (mt.), Chile 138/G4
Cantley, Québec 172/B4
Canto del Agua, Chile 138/A7
Canto do Buriti, Brazil 132/F5
Canton (Guangzhou), China 77/H7
Canton (Guangzhou), China 54/N7
Canton, China 2/Q4
Canton, Conn. 210/D1
Canton•, Conn. 210/D1
Canton, Ga. 217/C2
Canton, Ill. 222/C3
Canton, Ind. 227/E7
Canton, Kansas 232/E3
Canton, Ky. 237/F7
Canton (Kanton) (isl.), Kiribati 87/J6
Canton•, Maine 243/C7
Canton•, Mass. 249/C8
Canton, Minn. 255/F7
Canton, Miss. 256/D5
Canton, Mo. 261/J2
Canton, N.J. 273/C5
Canton, N.Y. 276/K1
Canton, N.C. 281/D3
Canton (Hensel), N. Dak. 282/P2
Canton, Ohio 188/K2
Canton, Ohio 284/H4
Canton, Okla. 288/J2
Canton (lake), Okla. 288/J2
Canton, Pa. 294/J2
Canton, S. Dak. 298/R7
Canton, Texas 303/J5
Canton, Wis. 317/C5
Canton-Bégin, Québec 172/F1
Canton Bend, Ala. 195/D6
Canton Center, Conn. 210/D1
Cantonment, Fla. 212/B6
Canton-Patapédia, Québec 172/B2
Cantoria, Spain 33/E4
Cantrall, Ill. 222/D4
Cantril, Iowa 229/J7
Cantù, Italy 34/B2
Cantuar, Sask. 181/C5
Cantwell, Alaska 196/J2
Canuck, Sask. 181/C6
Cañuelas, Argentina 143/G7
Canumã (riv.), Brazil 132/B4
Canutama, Brazil 132/G9
Canute, Okla. 288/H4
Canutillo, Texas 303/A10
Canvas, W. Va. 312/E6
Canvey Island, England 13/J8
Canvey Island, England 10/G5
Canwood, Sask. 181/E2
Canyon (lake), Ariz. 198/D5
Canyon, Br. Col. 184/J5
Canyon, Calif. 204/K2
Canyon (co.), Idaho 220/B6
Canyon (creek), Idaho 220/C6
Canyon, Minn. 255/F3
Canyon, Texas 303/C3
Canyon, Wyo. 319/B1
Canyon Blanco (creek), N. Mex. 274/B2
Canyon City, Oreg. 291/J3
Canyon Creek, Alberta 182/C2
Canyon Creek, Mont. 262/D4
Canyon de Chelly Nat'l Mon., Ariz. 198/F2
Canyon Ferry, Mont. 262/E4
Canyon Ferry (lake), Mont. 262/E4
Canyonlands Nat'l Park, Utah 304/D5
Canyonville, Oreg. 291/D5
Cao Bang, Vietnam 72/E2
Caol, Scotland 15/C4
Cao Lanh, Vietnam 72/E5
Caonao, Cuba 158/E2
Caonillas (lake), P. Rico 161/C2
Cap (isl.), Philippines 82/C8
Cap (pt.), St. Lucia 161/G5
Capa, S. Dak. 298/H5
Capac, Mich. 250/G5
Capachica, Peru 128/H10
Çapakçur, Turkey 59/D2
Çapakçur, Turkey 63/J3
Cap-à-l'Aigle, Québec 172/G2
Capalonga, Philippines 82/D3
Capanaparo (riv.), Venezuela 124/E4
Capanema, Brazil 132/E3
Capannori, Italy 34/C3
Capão Bonito, Brazil 132/D9
Capão Bonito, Brazil 135/B4
Caparica, Portugal 33/A1
Caparo (riv.), Venezuela 124/C4
Capasin, Sask. 181/D2
Capatárida, Venezuela 124/C2
Capay, Calif. 204/C5
Cap-Bateau, New Bruns. 170/F1
Cap-Chat, Que. 162/K6
Cap-Chat, Québec 172/B1
Cap-Chat, Québec 174/D3
Cap-de-la-Madeleine, Québec 172/E3
Cap-des-Rosiers, Québec 172/D1
Cap d'Or (cape), Nova Scotia 168/D3
Cape (pen.), S. Africa 118/E7
Cape (pt.), S. Africa 118/F7
Cape (isl.), S.C. 296/J5
Cape Barren (isl.), Tasmania 88/H8
Cape Barren (isl.), Tasmania 99/E2
Cape Breton (co.), Nova Scotia 168/H3
Cape Breton (isl.), N.S. 146/N5
Cape Breton (isl.), N.S. 162/K6
Cape Breton (isl.), Nova Scotia 168/J2
Cape Breton Highlands Nat'l Park, Nova Scotia 168/H2
Cape Broyle, Newf. 166/D2
Cape Canaveral, Fla. 212/F3
Cape Carteret, N.C. 281/P5
Cape Charles, Newf. 166/C3
Cape Charles, Va. 307/R6
Cape Coast, Ghana 106/D7
Cape Coast, Ghana 102/B4
Cape Cod (bay), Mass. 249/N5
Cape Cod (canal), Mass. 249/N5
Cape Cod Nat'l Seashore, Mass. 249/P5
Cape Coral, Fla. 212/E5
Cape Dorset, N.W.T. 162/J3
Cape Dorset, N.W.T. 187/L3
Cape Dyer, N.W.T. 187/M3
Cape Fanshaw, Alaska 196/N1
Cape Fear (riv.), N.C. 188/L4
Cape Fear (riv.), N.C. 281/M5
Cape George, Nova Scotia 168/F3
Cape Girardeau (co.), Mo. 261/N8
Cape Girardeau, Mo. 261/O8
Cape Girardeau, Mo. 188/H3
Cape Hatteras Nat'l Seashore, N.C. 281/T4
Cape Horn (mt.), Idaho 220/C5
Cape Krusenstern Nat'l Mon., Alaska 196/F1
Capel, W. Australia 92/A2
Capela, Brazil 132/G5
Cape Lisburne, Alaska 196/E1
Capella, Queensland 95/D4
Capella (isls.), Virgin Is. (U.S.) 161/B5
Capelle, Netherlands 27/F5
Capelongo, Angola 115/C7
Cape Lookout Nat'l Seashore, N.C. 281/S5
Cape May (co.), N.J. 273/D5
Cape May, N.J. 273/D6
Cape May (inlet), N.J. 273/D6
Cape May Coastguard Ctr., N.J. 273/D6
Cape May Court House, N.J. 273/D5
Cape May Point, N.J. 273/D6
Capenda-Camulemba, Angola 115/C5
Capenda-Camulemba, Angola 102/D5
Cape Neddick, Maine 243/B9
Cape Negro (isl.), Nova Scotia 168/C5
Cape North, Nova Scotia 168/H2
Cape Pole, Alaska 196/M2
Cape Porpoise, Maine 243/C9
Cape Ray, Newf. 166/C4
Capers (isl.), S.C. 296/H6
Cape Sable (isl.), Nova Scotia 168/C5
Cape Saint Claire, Md. 245/N4
Cape Smith, N.W.T. 187/L3
Capesterre, Basse-Terre, Guadeloupe 161/A7
Capesterre, Marie-Galante, Guadeloupe 161/B7
Cape Tormentine, New Bruns. 170/G2
Cape Town (cap.), S. Africa 2/L7
Cape Town (cap.), S. Africa 102/D8
Cape Town (cap.), S. Africa 118/E6
Cape Verde 2/H5
CAPE VERDE 106/A8
Capeville, Va. 307/R6
Cape Vincent, N.Y. 276/H2
Cape Yakataga, Alaska 196/K2
Cape York (pen.), Australia 87/E7
Cape York, Queensland 95/B1
Cape York (pen.), Queensland 88/G2
Cape York (pen.), Queensland 95/B2
Cap-Haïtien, Haiti 158/C5
Cap-Haïtien, Haiti 156/D3
Capiatá, Paraguay 144/B4
Capibara, Venezuela 124/E6
Capilla de Farruco, Uruguay 145/D3
Capim (riv.), Brazil 132/D3
Capinota, Bolivia 136/B5
Capira, Panama 154/G6
Capirenda, Bolivia 136/D7
Capistrano Beach, Calif. 204/H10
Capitan, N. Mex. 274/D5

348 Casamance

Casamance (riv.), Senegal 106/A6
Casanare (inten.), Colombia 126/B3
Casanare (riv.), Colombia 126/E4
Casanay, Venezuela 124/G2
Casa Nova, Brazil 132/F5
Casanova, Va. 307/N3
Casa Piedra, Texas 303/C12
Casar, N.C. 281/F3
Casar de Cáceres, Spain 33/C3
Casas Grandes (riv.), Mexico 150/F1
Casas-Ibáñez, Spain 33/F3
Cascade (range) 188/B1
Cascade (range), Calif. 204/D1
Cascade, Colo. 208/K5
Cascade, Idaho 220/C5
Cascade (res.), Idaho 220/C5
Cascade, Iowa 229/L4
Cascade, Jamaica 158/G6
Cascade (co.), Mont. 262/E3
Cascade, Mont. 262/E3
Cascade, N.H. 268/E3
Cascade (pt.), N. Zealand 100/B6
Cascade, Norfolk I. 88/L5
Cascade (bay), Norfolk I. 88/L5
Cascade (head), Oreg. 291/C2
Cascade (range), Oreg. 291/E4
Cascade, Seychelles 118/H5
Cascade (range), U.S. 146/F5
Cascade, Va. 307/J7
Cascade (pass), Wash. 310/D2
Cascade (range), Wash. 310/D4
Cascade (riv.), Wash. 310/D2
Cascade, W. Va. 312/G3
Cascade, Wis. 317/K8
Cascade Locks, Oreg. 291/E2
Cascade Summit, Oreg. 291/F4
Cascadia, Oreg. 291/E3
Cascais, Portugal 33/B3
Cascajal, Cuba 158/E1
Cascapédia (riv.), Québec 172/C1
Cascas, Peru 128/C6
Cascavel, Brazil 132/G4
Cascilla, Miss. 256/D3
Cascina-Navacchio, Italy 34/C3
Casco, Maine 243/B7
Casco•, Maine 243/B7
Casco (bay), Maine 243/C8
Casco, Wis. 317/L6
Cascorro, Cuba 158/H3
Cascumpeque (bay), Pr. Edward I. 168/E2
Caselton, Nev. 266/G5
Case-Pilote, Martinique 161/C6
Caserta (prov.), Italy 34/E4
Caserta, Italy 34/E4
Caseville, Mich. 250/F5
Casey (key), Fla. 212/D4
Casey, Ill. 222/F4
Casey, Iowa 229/D5
Casey (co.), Ky. 237/M6
Casey, Québec 174/C3
Casey Creek, Ky. 237/L6
Caseyville, Ill. 222/B2
Caseyville, Ky. 237/E5
Cash, Ark. 202/J2
Cashel, Ireland 17/F7
Cashel, Ireland 10/C4
Cashiers, N.C. 281/C4
Cashion, Ariz. 198/C5
Cashion, Okla. 288/L3
Cashmere, Wash. 310/E3
Cashmere, W. Va. 312/E8
Cashton, Wis. 317/E8
Cashtown, Pa. 294/H6
Cashville, S.C. 296/C2
Casigua, Falcón, Venezuela 124/C2
Casigua, Zulia, Venezuela 124/B3
Casiguran, Philippines 82/D2
Casiguran (sound), Philippines 82/C2
Casilda, Argentina 143/F6
Casilda, Cuba 158/E2
Casilda (pt.), Cuba 158/E2
Casino, N.S. Wales 88/J5
Casino, N.S. Wales 97/G1
Casiquiare, Brazo (riv.), Venezuela 124/E6
Casitas Springs, Calif. 204/F9
Caslan, Alberta 182/D2
Čáslav, Czech Rep. 41/C2
Casma, Peru 128/C7
Casma (riv.), Peru 128/C7
Casmalia, Calif. 204/E9
Casnovia, Mich. 250/D5
Caspar, Calif. 204/B4
Caspe, Spain 33/G2
Casper, Wyo. 188/E2
Casper, Wyo. 146/H5
Casper, Wyo. 319/F3
Casper (range), Wyo. 319/F3
Caspian (sea) 54/G5
Caspian (sea) 2/M3
Caspian (sea), Azerbaijan 48/F6
Caspian (sea), Azerbaijan 52/G6
Caspian (sea), Europe 7/J4
Caspian (sea), Iran 66/G1
Caspian (sea), Kazakhstan 48/F6
Caspian, Mich. 250/G2
Caspian (sea), Russia 48/F6
Caspian (sea), Russia 52/G6
Caspian (sea), Turkmenistan 48/F6
Caspian (lake), Vt. 268/C2
Caspiana, La. 238/C2
Cass, Ark. 202/C2
Cass (co.), Ill. 222/C4
Cass (co.), Ind. 227/E3
Cass, Ind. 227/C6
Cass (co.), Iowa 229/D6
Cass (co.), Mich. 250/C7
Cass (riv.), Mich. 250/F5
Cass (co.), Minn. 255/D4
Cass (lake), Minn. 255/D3
Cass (co.), Mo. 261/D5
Cass (co.), Nebr. 264/H4
Cass (co.), N. Dak. 282/R5
Cass (co.), Texas 303/K4
Cass, W. Va. 312/G6
Cassadaga, Fla. 212/E3
Cassadaga, N.Y. 276/B6
Cassá de la Selva, Spain 33/H2
Cassai, Angola 115/D6
Cassamba, Angola 115/D6
Cassandra, Ga. 217/B1
Cassandra, Pa. 294/E5
Cassano allo Ionio, Italy 34/F5
Cassatt, S.C. 296/G3
Cass City, Mich. 250/F5
Casscoe, Ark. 202/H4
Casselberry, Fla. 212/E3
Casselman (riv.), Md. 245/B2
Casselman, Ontario 177/J2
Casselman, Pa. 294/D6
Casselman (riv.), Pa. 294/D6
Casselton, N. Dak. 282/R6
Cássia, Brazil 135/C2
Cassia (co.), Idaho 220/E7
Cassiar, Br. Col. 184/K2
Cassiar (mts.), Br. Col. 184/K2
Cassiar (mts.), Yukon 187/E3
Cassidy, Br. Col. 184/J3
Cassilis, N.S. Wales 97/E3
Cassils, Alberta 182/D4
Cassinga, Angola 114/C7
Cassino, Italy 34/D4
Cassiporé (cape), Brazil 132/D2
Cassity, W. Va. 312/F5
Cass Lake, Minn. 255/D3
Cassoday, Kansas 232/F3
Cassopolis, Mich. 250/C7
Casstown, Ohio 284/B5
Cassville, Ga. 217/C2
Cassville, Ind. 227/E3
Cassville, Mo. 261/E9
Cassville, Pa. 294/G5
Cassville, W. Va. 312/F3
Cassville, Wis. 317/E10
Castagnola, Switzerland 39/G4
Castaic, Calif. 204/G9
Castalia, Iowa 229/K2
Castalia, New Bruns. 170/D4
Castalia, N.C. 281/O2
Castalia, Ohio 284/E3
Castalian Springs, Tenn. 237/J8
Castana, Iowa 229/B4
Castanhal, Brazil 120/E3
Castanhal, Brazil 132/E3
Castaños, Mexico 150/J3
Castelfranco Veneto, Italy 34/D2
Castel Gandolfo, Italy 34/F7
Casteljaloux, France 28/D5
Castella, Calif. 204/C2
Castellammare (gulf), Italy 34/D5
Castellammare del Golfo, Italy 34/D5
Castellammare di Stabia, Italy 34/E4
Castellane, France 28/G6
Castellanos, Uruguay 145/B6
Castelli, Buenos Aires, Argentina 143/H7
Castelli, Chaco, Argentina 143/D2
Castellón (prov.), Spain 33/G2
Castellón de la Plana, Spain 33/G2
Castellote, Spain 33/F2
Castelnaudary, France 28/E6
Castelo, Brazil 132/F8
Castelo Branco (dist.), Portugal 33/C3
Castelo Branco, Portugal 33/C3
Castelo de Vide, Portugal 33/C3
Castelo do Piauí, Brazil 132/F4
Castel San Pietro Terme, Italy 34/C2
Castelsarrasin, France 28/D6
Castelvetrano, Italy 34/D6
Casterton, Victoria 97/A5
Castiglione del Lago, Italy 34/C3
Castiglion Fiorentino, Italy 34/C3
Castile, N.Y. 276/D5
Castilletes, Venezuela 124/C2
Castillo, Cerro (mt.), Chile 138/E6
Castillo, Dom. Rep. 158/E5
Castillo de San Marcos Nat'l Mon., Fla. 212/E2
Castillos, Uruguay 145/F5
Castillos (lag.), Uruguay 145/F5
Castine•, Maine 243/F7
Castine, Ohio 284/A6
Castle (harb.), Bermuda 156/H2
Castle (mt.), Br. Col. 184/A2
Castle (peak), Colo. 208/F5
Castle (creek), Idaho 220/B7
Castle (peak), Idaho 220/D5
Castle (pt.), N. Zealand 100/F4
Castle, Okla. 288/O4
Castle (valley), Utah 304/D4
Castle A.F.B., Calif. 204/E6
Castlebar, Ireland 17/C4
Castlebar, Ireland 10/B4
Castlebay, Scotland 15/A4
Castlebellingham, Ireland 17/J4
Castleberry, Ala. 195/D8
Castleblayney, Ireland 10/C3
Castleblayney, Ireland 17/H3
Castlebridge, Ireland 17/J7
Castle Bruce, Dominica 161/F6
Castlecomer-Donaguile, Ireland 17/G6
Castlecomer-Donaguile, Ireland 10/C4
Castle Dale, Utah 304/D4
Castle Danger, Minn. 255/G3
Castledawson, N. Ireland 17/H2
Castlederg, N. Ireland 17/F2
Castledermot, Ireland 17/H6
Castle Dome (mts.), Ariz. 198/A5
Castle Douglas, Scotland 15/E6
Castle Douglas, Scotland 10/D3
Castlefin, Ireland 17/F2
Castleford, Idaho 220/C7
Castlegar, Br. Col. 184/J5
Castlegregory, Ireland 10/B4
Castlegregory, Ireland 17/A7
Castle Hayne, N.C. 281/O6
Castle Hills, Texas 303/J10
Castle Hot Springs, Ariz. 198/C5
Castleisland, Ireland 17/B7
Castle Kennedy, Scotland 15/D6
Castlemaine, Victoria 97/C5
Castlemartyr, Ireland 17/E8
Castle Park, Mich. 250/C6
Castlepollard, Ireland 17/G4
Castlerea, Ireland 17/D4
Castlerea, Ireland 10/B4
Castlereagh (riv.), N.S. Wales 97/E2
Castlereagh (dist.), N. Ireland 17/K2
Castle Rock, Colo. 208/K4
Castle Rock, Minn. 255/E6
Castle Rock, S. Dak. 298/C4
Castle Rock, Utah 304/C2
Castle Rock, Wash. 310/B4
Castle Rock (lake), Wis. 317/G8
Castle Shannon, Pa. 294/B7
Castleton, Ill. 222/D2
Castleton, Jamaica 158/J6
Castleton, Md. 245/N2
Castleton, Ontario 177/F3
Castleton•, Vt. 268/A4
Castleton-on-Hudson, N.Y. 276/N5
Castletown, Ireland 17/F6
Castletown, I. of Man 13/C3
Castletown, Scotland 15/E2
Castletownbere, Ireland 17/B8
Castletownroche, Ireland 17/D7
Castletownshend, Ireland 17/C9
Castlewellan, N. Ireland 17/K3
Castlewood, S. Dak. 298/R4
Castlewood, Va. 307/D7
Castolon, Texas 303/D12
Castor, Alberta 182/D3
Castor, La. 238/D2
Castorland, N.Y. 276/J3
Castres, France 28/E6
Castries (cap.), St. Lucia 156/G4
Castries (cap.), St. Lucia 161/G6
Castro, Brazil 135/B4
Castro, Brazil 132/D9
Castro, Chile 138/D4
Castro (co.), Texas 303/B3
Castro Alves, Brazil 132/G6
Castro Daire, Portugal 33/C2
Castro del Río, Spain 33/D4
Castrojeriz, Spain 33/E1
Castro Marim, Portugal 33/C4
Castropol, Spain 33/C1
Castrop-Rauxel, Germany 22/B3
Castroreale, Italy 34/E5
Castro-Urdiales, Spain 33/E1
Castro Valley, Calif. 204/K2
Castro Verde, Portugal 33/B4
Castrovillari, Italy 34/F5
Castroville, Calif. 204/D7
Castroville, Texas 303/J11
Castrovirreyna, Peru 128/E9
Castuera, Spain 33/D3
Casuarito, Colombia 126/G5
Casupá, Uruguay 145/D5
Caswell, Alaska 196/B1
Caswell (co.), N.C. 281/L2
Caswell Beach, N.C. 281/N7
Cat (isl.), Bahamas 146/L7
Cat (isl.), Bahamas 156/C1
Cat (isl.), Miss. 256/F10
Çat, Turkey 63/J3
Cat (isl.), Wis. 317/E1
Catacamas, Honduras 154/E3
Catacaos, Peru 128/B5
Catacocha, Ecuador 128/C5
Catadupa, Jamaica 158/H6
Cataguases, Brazil 135/E2
Catahoula (par.), La. 238/G3
Catahoula (lake), La. 238/F4
Cataingan, Philippines 82/E5
Çatak, Turkey 63/K4
Catalão, Brazil 132/D7
Çatalca, Turkey 63/C2
Cataldo, Idaho 220/B2
Catalina, Chile 138/B5
Catalina (pt.), Chile 138/F10
Catalina (isl.), Dom. Rep. 158/F6
Catalina, Newf. 166/D2
Catalone, Nova Scotia 168/H3
Catalonia (reg.), Spain 33/G2
Catalpa (creek), Miss. 256/G4
Çatalzeytin, Turkey 63/F1
Catamarca (prov.), Argentina 143/C2
Catamarca, Argentina 143/C2
Catamarca, Argentina 120/C5
Catamayo, Ecuador 128/C4
Catanauan, Philippines 82/D4
Catandica, Mozambique 118/E3
Catanduanes (prov.), Philippines 82/E4
Catanduanes (isl.), Philippines 82/E4
Catanduanes (isl.), Philippines 85/H3
Catanduva, Brazil 135/B2
Catanduva, Brazil 132/D8
Catania (prov.), Italy 34/E6
Catania, Italy 34/E6
Catania, Italy 7/F5
Cataño, P. Rico 156/G1
Cataño, P. Rico 161/D1
Catanzaro (prov.), Italy 34/F5
Catanzaro, Italy 34/F5
Cataouatche (lake), La. 238/N4
Cataract (creek), Ariz. 198/C3
Cataract, Ind. 227/D6
Cataract (canyon), Utah 304/D5
Cataract, Wis. 317/E7
Catarama, Ecuador 128/C3
Cataricahua, Bolivia 136/B6
Catarina, Texas 303/E9
Catarman, Philippines 82/E4
Catarman (pt.), Philippines 82/F7
Catasauqua, Pa. 294/M4
Catastrophe (cape), S. Australia 88/F7
Catastrophe (cape), S. Australia 94/D6
Catatumbo (riv.), Colombia 126/D3
Catatumbo (riv.), Venezuela 124/B3
Cataula, Ga. 217/C5
Cataumet, Mass. 249/M6
Catawba (co.), N.C. 281/G3
Catawba, N.C. 281/G3
Catawba (lake), N.C. 281/G4
Catawba (riv.), N.C. 281/H5
Catawba, Ohio 284/C6
Catawba, S.C. 296/F2
Catawba (riv.), S.C. 296/F2
Catawba, Va. 307/H6
Catawba, W. Va. 312/F3
Catawba, Wis. 317/E4
Catawba Island, Ohio 284/E2
Catawissa, Mo. 261/L6
Catawissa, Pa. 294/K4
Cat Ba, Dao (isl.), Vietnam 72/E2
Catbalogan, Philippines 85/H3
Catbalogan, Philippines 82/E5
Cat Creek, Mont. 262/H3
Cateechee, S.C. 296/B2
Cateel, Philippines 85/H4
Cateel, Philippines 82/F7
Catemaco, Mexico 150/M7
Catemu, Chile 138/G2
Cater, Sask. 181/C2
Caterham and Warlingham, England 13/H8
Caterham and Warlingham, England 10/B6
Cates, Ind. 227/C4
Catete, Angola 115/B5
Catfish (lake), N.C. 281/P5
Catfish (lake), Ontario 177/F2
Catfish (creek), S.C. 296/J3
Cathance (lake), Maine 243/J6
Catharine, Kansas 232/C3
Catharine Lake, N.C. 281/O5
Cathay, N. Dak. 282/M4
Cathedral (mt.), Texas 303/D12
Cathedral City, Calif. 204/J10
Cathedral Prov. Park, Br. Col. 184/H5
Catherine, Ala. 195/D6
Catherine (lake), Ark. 202/E5
Catheys Valley, Calif. 204/E6
Cathlamet, Wash. 310/B4
Cat Island (chan.), La. 238/M6
Cat Island (passage), La. 238/J8
Catlett, Va. 307/N3
Catlettsburg, Ky. 237/R4
Catlin, Ill. 222/F3
Catlin, Ind. 227/C5
Catmon, Philippines 82/E5
Cato, Ark. 202/F4
Cato (isl.), Australia 87/F8
Cato, Ind. 227/C8
Cato, N.Y. 276/G4
Cato, Wis. 317/L7
Catoche (cape), Mexico 150/Q6
Catoctin (creek), Md. 245/H3
Catoctin Furnace, Md. 245/J2
Catoctin Mt. Park, Md. 245/J2
Catolé do Rocha, Brazil 132/G4
Catonsville, Md. 245/M3
Catoosa (co.), Ga. 217/B1
Catoosa, Okla. 288/P2
Catriló, Argentina 143/D4
Catrimani, Brazil 132/H9
Catrine, Scotland 15/D5
Catron, Mo. 261/N9
Catron (co.), N. Mex. 274/A4
Catskill, N.Y. 276/N6
Catskill (mts.), N.Y. 276/L6
Cattaraugus (co.), N.Y. 276/C6
Cattaraugus, N.Y. 276/C6
Cattaraugus (creek), N.Y. 276/C6
Cattaraugus Ind. Res., N.Y. 276/C5
Catumbela, Angola 115/B6
Cauayan, Isabela, Philippines 82/C2
Cauayan, Negros Occ., Philippines 82/D6
Cauca (dept.), Colombia 126/B6
Cauca (riv.), Colombia 120/B2
Cauca (riv.), Colombia 126/C4
Caucagua, Venezuela 124/E2
Caucasia, Colombia 126/C4
Caucasus (mts.), Armenia 7/J4
Caucasus (mts.), Armenia 48/E5
Caucasus (mts.), Armenia 52/F6
Caucasus (mts.), Azerbaijan 7/J4
Caucasus (mts.), Azerbaijan 48/E5
Caucasus (mts.), Azerbaijan 52/F6
Caucasus (mts.), Georgia 7/J4
Caucasus (mts.), Georgia 48/E5
Caucasus (mts.), Georgia 52/F6
Caucasus (mts.), Russia 7/J4
Caucasus (mts.), Russia 48/E5
Caucasus (mts.), Russia 52/F6
Caucedo (cape), Dom. Rep. 158/E6
Caucete, Argentina 143/C3
Caucomgomoc (lake), Maine 243/D3
Caudete, Spain 33/F3
Caughnawaga, Québec 172/H4
Cauit (pt.), Philippines 82/F6
Cauldcleuch Head (mt.), Scotland 15/F5
Caulfield, Mo. 261/H9
Caulfield, Victoria 88/L7
Caulfield, Victoria 97/J5
Caulksville, Ark. 202/C3
Caulonia, Italy 34/F5
Caúngula, Angola 115/C5
Cauquenes, Chile 138/A11
Caura (riv.), Venezuela 120/D2
Caura (riv.), Venezuela 124/F5
Causapscal, Québec 172/B2
Causeway, Ireland 17/B7
Causey, N. Mex. 274/F5
Causses (reg.), France 28/D5
Cauterets, France 28/C6
Cauthron, Ark. 202/B4
Cauto (riv.), Cuba 158/H3
Cauto del Embarcadero, Cuba 158/H4
Cauto el Cristo, Cuba 158/J3
Cava de'Tirreni, Italy 34/E4
Cavaillon, France 28/F6
Cavaillon, Haiti 158/A6
Cavalier (co.), N. Dak. 282/N2
Cavalier, N. Dak. 282/P2
Cavalla (riv.), Liberia 106/C7
Cavalli (isls.), N. Zealand 100/E1
Cavallo (passage), Texas 303/H9
Cavally (riv.), Ivory Coast 106/C7
Cavan (co.), Ireland 17/G4
Cavan, Ireland 10/C4
Cavan, Ireland 17/G3
Cavan, Ontario 177/F3
Cavanaugh (lake), Wash. 310/D2
Cavari, Bolivia 136/B5
Cavarzere, Italy 34/D2
Cave City, Ark. 202/G2
Cave City, Ky. 237/K6
Cave Creek, Ariz. 198/D5
Cave Hill, Barbados 161/B9
Cave in Rock, Ill. 222/E6
Cave Junction, Oreg. 291/D5
Cavell, Sask. 181/C3
Cavendish, Alberta 182/E4
Cavendish, Idaho 220/B3
Cavendish, Newf. 166/D2
Cavendish•, Vt. 268/B5
Cavergno, Switzerland 39/G4
Cave Spring, Ga. 217/B2
Cave Springs, Ark. 202/B1
Cavetown, Md. 245/H2
Caviana (isl.), Brazil 120/E2
Caviana (isl.), Brazil 132/D2
Cavili (isl.), Philippines 82/C6
Cavinas, Bolivia 136/B3
Cavite (prov.), Philippines 82/C3
Cavite, Philippines 82/C3
Cavite, Philippines 85/G3
Cavour, S. Dak. 298/N5
Cavour, Wis. 317/K4
Cawdor, Scotland 15/E3
Cawker City, Kansas 232/D2
Cawndilla (lake), N.S. Wales 97/A3
Cawnpore (Kanpur), India 68/E3
Cawood, Ky. 237/P7
Cawston, Br. Col. 184/H5
Cawston, England 13/J5
Caxambu, Brazil 135/D2
Caxias, Brazil 120/E3
Caxias, Brazil 132/F4
Caxias do Sul, Brazil 120/D5
Caxias do Sul, Brazil 132/D10
Caxito, Angola 115/B5
Çay, Turkey 63/D3
Cayacoa, Dom. Rep. 158/E6
Cayamas (cays), Cuba 158/C2
Cayambe, Ecuador 128/D3
Cayambe (mt.), Ecuador 128/D2
Cayasta, Argentina 143/F5
Cayastacito, Argentina 143/F5
Cayce, Ky. 237/C7
Cayce, S.C. 296/E4
Çaycuma, Turkey 63/E2
Caycuse, Br. Col. 184/J3
Çayeli, Turkey 63/J2
Cayenne (dist.), Fr. Guiana 131/E3
Cayenne (cap.), Fr. Guiana 2/G5
Cayenne (cap.), Fr. Guiana 120/D2
Cayenne (cap.), Fr. Guiana 131/E3
Cayer, Manitoba 179/D3
Cayes Jacmel, Haiti 158/C6
Cayeux-sur-Mer, France 28/D2
Cayey, P. Rico 156/G1
Cayey, P. Rico 161/D2
Cayey, Sierra de (mts.), P. Rico 161/D2
Çayıralan, Turkey 63/F3
Çayırlı, Turkey 63/J3
Cayley, Alberta 182/D4
Cayman (isls.) 146/K8
Cayman Brac (isl.), Cayman Is. 156/B3
CAYMAN ISLANDS 156/B3
Cayo Costa (isl.), Fla. 212/D5
Cayon, St. Kitts & Nevis 161/C10
Cay Sal (bank), Bahamas 156/B2
Cayucos, Calif. 204/E8
Cayuga, Ind. 227/C5
Cayuga (co.), N.Y. 276/G4
Cayuga, N.Y. 276/G5
Cayuga (lake), N.Y. 276/G5
Cayuga, N. Dak. 282/R7
Cayuga, Texas 303/J6
Cayuga Heights, N.Y. 276/H6
Cayuse, Oreg. 291/J2
Cayuta (creek), N.Y. 276/G6
Cazadero, Calif. 204/B5
Cazalla de la Sierra, Spain 33/D4
Cazaux (lake), France 28/C5
Cazenovia, N.Y. 276/J5
Cazenovia, Wis. 317/F8
Cazin, Bos. 45/B3
Cazis, Switzerland 39/H3
Cazma (riv.), Croatia 45/C3
Cazombo, Angola 115/D6
Cazones (gulf), Cuba 158/C2
Cazorla, Spain 33/E4
Cazorla, Venezuela 124/E3
Cazot, Uruguay 145/B6
Cazueleja, Cerro (mt.), Colombia 126/C6
Ceanannus Mór, Ireland 17/G4
Ceanannus Mór, Ireland 10/C4
Ceará (state), Brazil 132/G4
Ceará (Fortaleza), Brazil 132/G3
Ceará-Mirim, Brazil 132/H4
Ceará-Mirim, Brazil 120/F3
Cébaco (isl.), Panama 154/G7
Ceballos, Mexico 150/H3
Cebeci, Turkey 63/E3
Cebolla (creek), Colo. 208/E6
Cebolla, N. Mex. 274/C2
Cebollatí, Uruguay 145/F4
Cebollatí (riv.), Uruguay 145/F4
Cebreros, Spain 33/D2
Cebu (prov.), Philippines 82/D5
Cebu, Philippines 82/D5
Cebu, Philippines 85/G3
Cebu, Philippines 54/O8
Cebu, Philippines 2/R5
Cebu (isl.), Philippines 85/G3
Cebu (isl.), Philippines 82/D5
Cecelia, La. 238/G6
Cecil, Ala. 195/F6
Cecil, Ark. 202/C3
Cecil, Ga. 217/F8
Cecil (co.), Md. 245/P2
Cecil, Ohio 284/A3
Cecil, Oreg. 291/H2
Cecil, Pa. 294/B5
Cecil, Wis. 317/K6
Cecil Field Naval Air Sta., Fla. 212/E1
Cecilia, Ky. 237/K5
Cecil Lake, Br. Col. 184/G2
Cecil M. Harden (lake), Ind. 227/C5
Cecilton, Md. 245/P3
Cecilville, Calif. 204/B2
Cecina, Italy 34/C3
Ceclavín, Spain 33/C3
Cedar (pt.), Ala. 195/B10
Cedar, Br. Col. 184/J3
Cedar (creek), Colo. 208/M1
Cedar (lake), Conn. 210/E3
Cedar (creek), Ind. 227/G2
Cedar (co.), Iowa 229/L5
Cedar, Iowa 229/H6
Cedar (riv.), Iowa 188/H2
Cedar (riv.), Iowa 229/K4
Cedar, Kansas 232/D2
Cedar (lake), Manitoba 179/B1
Cedar (pt.), Md. 245/N7
Cedar, Mich. 250/D4
Cedar (lake), Mich. 250/F4
Cedar (riv.), Minn. 255/F7
Cedar (co.), Mo. 261/E7
Cedar (co.), Nebr. 264/G2
Cedar (riv.), Nebr. 264/F3
Cedar (mt.), Nev. 266/D4
Cedar (creek), N.J. 273/E4
Cedar (creek), N. Dak. 282/G7
Cedar (pt.), Ohio 284/D2
Cedar (lake), Ontario 177/F1
Cedar (lake), Texas 303/B5
Cedar (mts.), Utah 304/B3
Cedar (isl.), Va. 307/S5
Cedar (riv.), Wash. 310/B2
Cedar Bluff, Ala. 195/G2
Cedar Bluff, Iowa 229/L5
Cedar Bluff (res.), Kansas 232/C3
Cedarbluff, Miss. 256/G3
Cedar Bluff, Va. 307/E6
Cedar Bluffs, Kansas 232/B2
Cedar Bluffs, Nebr. 264/H3
Cedar Breaks Nat'l Mon., Utah 304/B6
Cedar Brook, N.J. 273/D4
Cedarburg, Wis. 317/L9
Cedarbutte, S. Dak. 298/H6
Cedar City, Mo. 261/H5
Cedar City, Utah 188/D3
Cedar City, Utah 304/A6
Cedar Cove, Ala. 195/D4
Cedar Creek, Ark. 202/C4
Cedar Creek (peak), Idaho 220/E7
Cedar Creek (res.), Idaho 220/D7
Cedarcreek, Mo. 261/G9
Cedar Creek, Nebr. 264/J3
Cedar Crest, N. Mex. 274/C3
Cedaredge, Colo. 208/D5
Cedar Falls, Iowa 229/H3
Cedar Falls, N.C. 281/K3
Cedar Falls, Wash. 310/D3
Cedar Falls, Wis. 317/C6
Cedar Fort, Utah 304/C3
Cedar Gap, Mo. 261/G8
Cedar Grove, Ant. & Bar. 161/E11
Cedar Grove, Fla. 212/D6
Cedar Grove, Ga. 217/L2
Cedar Grove, Ind. 227/H6
Cedar Grove, Md. 245/K4
Cedar Grove•, N.J. 273/B2
Cedar Grove, N.C. 281/L2
Cedar Grove, Tenn. 237/D9
Cedar Grove, W. Va. 312/D6
Cedar Grove, Wis. 317/L8
Cedar Heights, Md. 245/G5
Cedar Hill, N. Mex. 274/B2
Cedar Hill, Tenn. 237/H7
Cedar Hill, Texas 303/G3
Cedar Hill Lakes, Mo. 261/L6
Cedar Hills, Oreg. 291/A2
Cedarhurst, N.Y. 276/P7
Cedar Island, N.C. 281/S5
Cedar Key, Fla. 212/C2
Cedar Knolls, N.J. 273/E2
Cedar Lake, Ind. 227/C2
Cedar Lake, Minn. 255/E4
Cedar Mill, Oreg. 291/A2
Cedar Mills, Minn. 255/D6
Cedar Mountain, N.C. 281/D4
Cedar Park, Texas 303/G7
Cedar Point, Ill. 222/D2
Cedar Point, Kansas 232/F3
Cedar Rapids, Iowa 188/H2
Cedar Rapids, Iowa 229/K5
Cedar Rapids, Iowa 146/J5
Cedar Rapids, Nebr. 264/F3
Cedar River, Mich. 250/B3
Cedar Run, N.J. 273/E4
Cedar Run, Pa. 294/H2
Cedar Springs, Ga. 217/C8
Cedar Springs, Mich. 250/D5
Cedar Springs, Mo. 261/E7
Cedar Springs, Ontario 177/B5
Cedar Springs, Va. 307/F7
Cedar Swamp (pond), Conn. 210/G2
Cedartown, Ga. 217/B2
Cedarvale, Br. Col. 184/C2
Cedar Vale, Kansas 232/F4
Cedarvale, N. Mex. 274/D4
Cedar Valley, Utah 304/B3
Cedarville, Ark. 202/B2
Cedarville, Calif. 204/E2
Cedarville, Ill. 222/D1
Cedarville, Ind. 227/G2
Cedarville, Ky. 237/S6
Cedarville, Md. 245/L6
Cedarville, Mich. 250/E2
Cedarville, N.J. 273/C5
Cedarville, N.Y. 276/K5
Cedarville, Ohio 284/C6
Cedarville, Va. 307/M3
Cedarville, W. Va. 312/E5
Cedarwood Park, N.J. 273/E3
Cedonia, Wash. 310/G2
Cedoux, Sask. 181/H6
Cedral, Mexico 150/J5
Cedros, Honduras 154/D3
Cedros (isl.), Mexico 146/G7
Cedros (isl.), Mexico 150/B2
Cedros, Trin. & Tob. 161/A11
Ceduna, S. Australia 88/E6
Ceduna, S. Australia 94/D5
Cee Vee, Texas 303/D3
Cefalù, Italy 34/E5
Cegléd, Hungary 41/E3
Ceglie Messapico, Italy 34/F4
Cehegín, Spain 33/F3

Charleston 349

Ceiba, P. Rico 161/F2
Çekerek, Turkey 63/F2
Çekerek (riv.), Turkey 63/F3
Celada Cué, Paraguay 144/D3
Celano, Italy 34/D3
Celanova, Spain 33/B1
Celaya, Mexico 150/J6
Celbridge, Ireland 17/H5
Celebes (sea) 54/O9
Celebes (isl.), Indonesia 54/N10
Celebes (isl.), Indonesia 2/R6
Celebes (Sulawesi) (isl.), Indonesia 85/G5
Celebes (sea), Indonesia 85/G5
Celebes (sea), Philippines 82/D8
Celendín, Peru 128/D6
Celerigna-Schlarigna, Switzerland 39/J3
Celeste, Texas 303/H4
Celestine, Ind. 227/D8
Celestún, Mexico 150/O6
Celica, Ecuador 128/B4
Céligny, Switzerland 39/B4
Çelikhan, Turkey 63/H3
Celilo, Oreg. 291/G2
Celilo (lake), Oreg. 291/G2
Celilo (lake), Wash. 310/E5
Celina, Minn. 255/E3
Celina, Ohio 284/A4
Celina, Tenn. 237/K7
Celina, Texas 303/H4
Celista, Br. Col. 184/H5
Celje, Slovenia 45/B2
Cella, Spain 33/F2
Cellar (head), Scotland 15/B2
Celldömölk, Hungary 41/D3
Celle, Germany 22/D2
Celorico da Beira, Portugal 33/C2
Celoron, N.Y. 276/B6
Cement, Okla. 288/K5
Cement City, Mich. 250/E6
Çemişkezek, Turkey 63/H3
Cemmaes (head), Wales 13/C5
Cenderawasih (bay), Indonesia 85/K6
Ceneri (mt.), Switzerland 39/G4
Cenia, Spain 33/G2
Census Bureau, Md. 245/F5
Centenary, Ind. 227/B5
Centenary, S.C. 296/J3
Centennial (mts.), Idaho 220/F5
Centennial, Wyo. 319/F4
Centennial Wash (dry riv.), Ariz. 198/B5
Center, Colo. 208/G7
Center, Ga. 217/F2
Center, Ind. 227/E4
Center, Ky. 237/K6
Center (pond), Maine 243/E5
Center, Mo. 261/J3
Center, Nebr. 264/G2
Center, N. Dak. 282/H5
Center, Okla. 288/N5
Center, S. Dak. 298/P6
Center, Texas 303/K6
Center Barnstead, N.H. 268/E5
Center Belpre, Ohio 284/G7
Centerbrook, Conn. 210/F3
Centerburg, Ohio 284/E5
Center City, Minn. 255/F5
Center Conway, N.H. 268/E4
Center Cross, Va. 307/P5
Centerdale, R.I. 249/H5
Centereach, N.Y. 276/O9
Centerfield, Utah 304/C4
Center Groton, Conn. 210/G3
Center Harbor•, N.H. 268/E4
Center Hill, Ark. 202/G3
Center Hill, Fla. 212/D3
Center Hill (lake), Tenn. 237/K9
Center Junction, Iowa 229/L4
Center Line, Mich. 250/B6
Center Lovell, Maine 243/B7
Center Montville, Maine 243/E7
Center Moreland, Pa. 294/E7
Center Moriches, N.Y. 276/P9
Center Ossipee, N.H. 268/E4
Center Point, Ark. 202/C5
Centerpoint, Ind. 227/C6
Center Point, Iowa 229/K4
Center Point, La. 238/F4
Center Point, S. Dak. 298/P7
Center Point, Texas 303/E8
Center Point, W. Va. 312/E4
Center Ridge, Ark. 202/E3
Center Rutland, Vt. 268/A4
Center Sandwich, N.H. 268/D4
Center Square, Ind. 227/H7
Center Strafford, N.H. 268/E5
Centerton, Ark. 202/B1
Centerton, Ind. 227/E5
Centerton, N.J. 273/C4
Centertown, Ky. 237/G6
Centertown, Mo. 261/H5
Centertown, Tenn. 237/K9
Center Tuftonboro, N.H. 268/E4
Centerview, Mo. 261/E5
Center Village, Ohio 284/E5
Centerville, Ark. 202/D3
Centerville, Del. 245/R1
Centerville, Ga. 217/E5
Centerville, Ind. 227/H5
Centerville, Iowa 229/H7
Centerville, Kansas 232/H3
Centerville, Ky. 237/S6
Centerville, La. 238/H7
Centerville•, Maine 243/H6
Centerville, Mass. 249/N6
Centerville, Minn. 255/E5
Centerville, Mo. 261/L8
Centerville, N.C. 281/N2
Centerville, Ohio 284/B6
Centerville, Pa. 294/B6
Centerville, Pa. 294/C2
Centerville, S. Dak. 298/R7
Centerville, Tenn. 237/G9
Centerville, Texas 303/H6
Centerville, Utah 304/C3
Centerville, Wash. 310/D5
Centrahoma, Okla. 288/O5
Central, Ala. 195/F5
Central, Alaska 196/H2
Central, Alaska 196/J1
Central, Ariz. 198/F6
Central, Cordillera (range), Bolivia 136/C6
Central, Cordillera (range), Colombia 126/C5
Central, Cordillera (range), Dom. Rep. 158/D5
Central, Idaho 220/G7
Central, Ind. 227/E8
Central (Markazi) (prov.), Iran 66/G3
Central (dist.), Israel 65/B3
Central (prov.), Kenya 115/G4
Central, La. 238/L3
Central, N. Mex. 274/A6
Central, Paraguay 144/D4
Central (Baganga), Philippines 82/F7
Central, Cordillera (range), P. Rico 161/C2
Central (reg.), Scotland 15/D4
Central, S.C. 296/B2
Central, Utah 304/A6
Central, Utah 304/B5
Central Aboriginal Res., W. Australia 88/D4
Central Aboriginal Res., W. Australia 92/E3
Central African Republic 2/K5
Central African Republic 102/D4
CENTRAL AFRICAN REPUBLIC 115/C2
Central Aguirre, P. Rico 161/D3
Central Amancio Rodríguez, Cuba 158/G3
Central America 2/E5
Central América, Cuba 158/J4
Central Bedeque, Pr. Edward I. 168/E2
Central Blissville, New Bruns. 170/D3
Central Bolivia, Cuba 158/G2
Central Brasil, Cuba 158/G2
Central Bridge, N.Y. 276/M5
Central Butte, Sask. 181/E5
Central Cándido González, Cuba 158/G3
Central City, Ark. 202/B3
Central City, Colo. 208/J3
Central City, Ill. 222/D5
Central City, Iowa 229/K4
Central City, Ky. 237/G6
Central City, Nebr. 264/F3
Central City, Pa. 294/E5
Central City, S. Dak. 298/B5
Central Colombia, Cuba 158/G3
Central Falls, R.I. 249/J5
Central Frank País, Cuba 158/K3
Central Greece and Euboea (reg.), Greece 45/F6
Central Guatemala, Cuba 158/J3
Central Haití, Cuba 158/G3
Centralhatchee, Ga. 217/B4
Central Heights-Midland City, Ariz. 198/E5
Centralia, Ill. 222/D5
Centralia, Iowa 229/M4
Centralia, Kansas 232/F2
Centralia, Mo. 261/H4
Centralia, Okla. 288/R1
Centralia, Pa. 294/K4
Centralia, Texas 303/K6
Centralia, Wash. 188/B1
Centralia, Wash. 310/C4
Centralia, W. Va. 312/E5
Central Intelligence Agency (C.I.A.), Va. 307/S2
Central Islip, N.Y. 276/O9
Central Lake, Mich. 250/D3
Central Los Reynaldos, Cuba 158/J4
Central Loynaz Echevarría, Cuba 158/J3
Central Manuel Tames, Cuba 158/K4
Central Niágara, Cuba 158/B1
Central Pacolet, S.C. 296/D2
Central Park, Wash. 310/B3
Central Patricia, Ontario 175/B2
Central Point, Oreg. 291/D5
Central Point, Va. 307/O4
Central Saanich, Br. Col. 184/K3
Central Square, N.Y. 276/H4
Central Station, W. Va. 312/E4
Central Ural (mts.), Russia 52/J2
Central Valley, Calif. 204/C3
Central Valley, N.Y. 276/M8
Central Village, Conn. 210/H2
Central Village, Mass. 249/K6
Central Wedge (mt.), North. Terr. 93/C7
Centre, Ala. 195/G2
Centre (co.), Pa. 294/G4
Centre Hall, Pa. 294/G4
Centre Island, N.Y. 276/R6
Centre-Saint-Simon, New Bruns. 170/E1
Centreville, Ala. 195/D5
Centreville, Ill. 222/B3
Centreville, Md. 245/O4
Centreville, Mich. 250/D7
Centreville, Miss. 256/B8
Centreville, New Bruns. 170/C2
Centreville, Digby, Nova Scotia 168/B4
Centreville, Kings, Nova Scotia 168/D3
Centreville (Thurman), Ohio 284/F8
Centuria, Wis. 317/A5
Centurión, Uruguay 145/F3
Century, Fla. 212/B5
Century, W. Va. 312/F4
Cephalonia (Kefallinía) (isl.), Greece 45/E6
Ceram (isl.), Indonesia 54/P10
Ceram (isl.), Indonesia 85/H6
Cerbat (mts.), Ariz. 198/A3
Cercal, Portugal 33/B4
Cerca la Source, Haiti 158/C5
Cereal, Alberta 182/E4
Ceredo, W. Va. 312/B6
Ceres, Argentina 143/D2
Ceres, Brazil 132/D6
Ceres, Brazil 120/E4
Ceres, Calif. 204/D6
Ceres, N.Y. 276/D6
Ceres, S. Africa 118/B6
Ceres, Va. 307/F6
Ceresco, Nebr. 264/H3
Céret, France 28/E6
Cereté, Colombia 126/C3
Cerf (lake), Québec 172/B3
Cerf (isl.), Seychelles 118/H5
Cerfontaine, Belgium 27/E8
Cerignola, Italy 34/E4
Çerkeş, Turkey 63/E2
Çerkezköy, Turkey 63/C2
Çermik, Turkey 63/H3
Cernavodă, Romania 45/J3
Cernier, Switzerland 39/C2
Cernobbio, Italy 34/B2
Cerralvo (isl.), Mexico 150/E4
Cerrillos, N. Mex. 274/D3
Cerrillos, Uruguay 145/A6
Cerrito, Paraguay 144/D5
Cerritos, Calif. 204/C11
Cerritos, Mexico 150/J5
Cerro, N. Mex. 274/D2
Cerro Aconcagua (mt.) 120/C6
Cerro Alto (mt.), Texas 303/B10
Cêrro Azul, Brazil 135/B4
Cerro Azul, Mexico 150/L6
Cerro Azul, Peru 128/D9
Cerro Castillo, Chile 138/E9
Cerro Chato, Cerro Largo, Uruguay 145/F3
Cerro Chato, Rivera, Uruguay 145/D2
Cerro Chato, Treinta y Tres, Uruguay 145/D2
Cerro Colorado, Uruguay 145/D4
Cerro Corá, Paraguay 144/E3
Cerro de las Armas, Uruguay 145/B5
Cerro de las Cuentas, Uruguay 145/E3
Cerro de Pasco, Peru 120/B4
Cerro de Pasco, Peru 128/D8
Cerro de San Antonio, Colombia 126/C2
Cerro Gordo, Ill. 222/E4
Cerro Gordo (co.), Iowa 229/G2
Cerro Gordo, N.C. 281/M6
Cerro Gordo (pt.), P. Rico 161/D1
Cerro Gordo, Tenn. 237/E10
Cerro Largo (dept.), Uruguay 145/E3
Cerro Manantiales, Chile 138/F10
Cerulean, Ky. 237/F7
Cervera, Spain 33/G2
Cervera del Río Alhama, Spain 33/E1
Cervera de Pisuerga, Spain 33/D1
Cerveteri, Italy 34/E6
Cervione, France 28/B6
Cesano, Italy 34/F6
Cesar (dept.), Colombia 126/D3
César (riv.), Colombia 126/D2
Cesena, Italy 34/D2
Cesenatico, Italy 34/D2
Cēsis, Latvia 52/C3
Cēsis, Latvia 53/C2
Česká Kamenice, Czech Rep. 41/C1
Česká Lípa, Czech Rep. 41/C1
Česká Třebová, Czech Rep. 41/D2
České Budějovice, Czech Rep. 41/C2
Český Brod, Czech Rep. 41/C1
Český Krumlov, Czech Rep. 41/C2
Český Těšín, Czech Rep. 41/E2
Çeşme, Turkey 63/B3
Céspedes, Cuba 158/G2
Cessford, Alberta 182/E4
Cessnock-Bellbird, N.S. Wales 88/J6
Cessnock-Bellbird, N.S. Wales 97/F3
Cestos (riv.), Liberia 106/C7
Cetinje, Yugoslavia 45/D4
Çetinkaya, Turkey 63/G3
Ceuta, Spain 106/C1
Ceuta, Spain 7/D5
Ceuta, Spain 102/B1
Ceuta, Spain 33/D5
Cévennes (mts.), France 28/E5
Cevio, Switzerland 39/G4
Cevizli, Turkey 63/D4
Ceyhan, Turkey 63/F4
Ceyhan (riv.), Turkey 63/F4
Ceyhan (riv.), Turkey 59/C2
Ceylânpınar, Turkey 63/H4
Ceylon (Sri Lanka) 54/K9
Ceylon, Minn. 255/D7
Ceylon, Sask. 181/G6
Chabás, Argentina 143/F6
Chaca, Chile 138/B1
Chacabuco, Argentina 143/F7
Chacabuco, Chile 138/G2
Chacachacare (isl.), Trin. & Tob. 161/A10
Chacahoula, La. 238/J7
Chacalluta, Chile 138/A1
Chachacomani, Bolivia 136/A6
Chachapoyas, Peru 128/D6
Chachapoyas, Peru 120/B3
Chachoengsao, Thailand 72/D4
Chachro, Pakistan 68/C3
Chaco (prov.), Argentina 143/D2
Chaco (mesa), N. Mex. 274/B3
Chaco (riv.), N. Mex. 274/A2
Chaco, Paraguay 144/B-C2
Chaco Austral (reg.), Argentina 143/D2
Chaco Boreal (reg.), Paraguay 144/B2-3
Chaco Central (reg.), Argentina 143/D1
Chaco Culture Nat'l Hist. Park, N. Mex. 274/B2
Chacoma, Bolivia 136/A6
Chacon (cape), Alaska 196/N2
Chacon, N. Mex. 274/D2
Chacuaco (creek), Colo. 208/M8
Chad 2/K5
Chad 102/D3
CHAD 111/C4
Chad (lake) 102/D3
Chad (lake), Chad 111/C5
Chad (lake), Niger 106/G6
Chad (lake), Nigeria 106/G6
Chadan, Russia 48/K4
Chadbourn, N.C. 281/M6
Chadron, Nebr. 264/B2
Chadwick, Ill. 222/D1
Chadwick, Mo. 261/G9
Chadwick Acres, N.C. 281/P6
Chadwicks, N.Y. 276/K4
Chadyr-Lunga, Moldova 52/C5
Chaffee (co.), Colo. 208/G5
Chaffee, Mo. 261/N8
Chaffee, N.Y. 276/C5
Chaffee, N. Dak. 282/R6
Chaffers (isl.), Chile 138/D5
Chafurray, Colombia 126/D6
Chagai (hills), Afghanistan 68/A3
Chagai, Pakistan 59/H4
Chagai, Pakistan 68/A3
Chagai (hills), Pakistan 68/A3
Chagai (hills), Pakistan 59/H4
Chagda, Russia 48/O4
Chaghcharan, Afghanistan 68/B2
Chagoda, Russia 52/E3
Chagoness, Sask. 181/G3
Chagos (arch.), Br. Ind. Ocean Terr. 2/N6
Chagos (arch.), Br. Ind. Ocean Terr. 54/J10
Chagrin (riv.), Ohio 284/J8
Chagrin Falls, Ohio 284/J9
Chaguanas, Trin. & Tob. 161/B10
Chaguaramas, Trin. & Tob. 161/A10
Chaguaramas, Venezuela 124/E3
Chaguaya, Bolivia 136/C7
Chagulak (isl.), Alaska 196/D4
Chahal, Guatemala 154/C3
Chahar Borjak, Afghanistan 59/H3
Chahar Borjak, Afghanistan 68/A2
Chah Bahar, Afghanistan 59/H4
Chahuites, Mexico 150/M8
Chai Badan, Thailand 72/D4
Chaibasa, India 68/F4
Chai Buri, Thailand 72/D3
Chainat, Thailand 72/D4
Chain-O-Lakes, Mo. 261/E9
Chaira, Laguna (lake), Colombia 126/C7
Chaires, Fla. 212/B1
Chaitén, Chile 138/E4
Chaiya, Thailand 72/C5
Chaiyaphum, Thailand 72/D4
Chajarí, Argentina 143/G5
Chajul, Guatemala 154/B3
Chake Chake, Tanzania 115/H5
Chala, Peru 128/E10
Chalais, Switzerland 39/E4
Chalatenango, El Salvador 154/C3
Chalchihuites, Mexico 150/G5
Chalco de Díaz Covarrubias, Mexico 150/M1
Chaleur (bay), New Bruns. 170/E1
Chaleur (bay), Québec 172/C2
Chaleur (bay), Québec 174/D3
Chalfont, Pa. 294/M5
Chalhuanca, Peru 128/F10
Chaling, China 77/H6
Chalk (creek), Utah 304/C3
Chalk River, Ontario 175/E3
Chalk River, Ontario 177/G1
Chalkyitsik, Alaska 196/K1
Challacollo, Bolivia 136/B6
Challana, Bolivia 136/A4
Challapata, Bolivia 136/B6
Challis, Idaho 220/D5
Challviri (salt dep.), Bolivia 136/B8
Chalmers, Ind. 227/D3
Chalmette, La. 238/P4
Chalna Port, Bangladesh 68/F4
Chalonnes-sur-Loire, France 28/C4
Châlons-sur-Marne, France 28/F3
Chalon-sur-Saône, France 28/F4
Chaltel, Cerro (mt.), Chile 138/E8
Chalus, Iran 59/F2
Chalus, Iran 66/G2
Chalybeate, Miss. 256/G1
Chalybeate Springs, Ga. 217/C5
Chalybeate Springs, N.C. 281/M3
Cham, Germany 22/E4
Cham, Switzerland 39/F2
Chama, Colo. 208/J8
Chama, N. Mex. 274/C2
Chaman, Pakistan 68/B2
Chaman, Pakistan 59/J3
Chamba, India 68/D2
Chambal (riv.), India 68/D3
Chambas, Cuba 158/F2
Chamberino, N. Mex. 274/C6
Chamberlain (creek), Idaho 220/C4
Chamberlain (lake), Maine 243/E3
Chamberlain, Sask. 181/F5
Chamberlain, S. Dak. 298/L6
Chamberlain, Uruguay 145/C3
Chamberlin, La. 238/J1
Chambers (co.), Ala. 195/H5
Chambers, Ariz. 198/F3
Chambers, Nebr. 264/F2
Chambers (co.), Texas 303/K8
Chambers (isl.), Wis. 317/M5
Chambersburg, Ill. 222/C4
Chambersburg, Ind. 227/E7
Chambersburg, Pa. 294/G6
Chambéry, France 28/F5
Chambeshi (riv.), Zambia 115/F6
Chambeyron (mt.), France 28/G5
Chambeyron (mt.), Italy 34/A2
Chambi, Jebel (mt.), Tunisia 106/F2
Chamblee, Ga. 217/K1
Chambly (co.), Québec 172/J4
Chambly, Québec 172/J4
Chambord, France 28/D4
Chambord, Québec 172/E1
Chamdo (Qamdo), China 77/E5
Chame (pt.), Panama 154/H6
Chamela (bay), Mexico 150/G7
Chamical, Argentina 143/C3
Chamisal, N. Mex. 274/D2
Chamizal Nat'l Mem., Texas 303/A10
Chamizo, Uruguay 145/D5
Chamo (lake), Ethiopia 111/G6
Chamois, Mo. 261/J5
Chamonix-Mont-Blanc, France 28/G5
Chamoson, Switzerland 39/D4
Champ, Mo. 261/O2
Champagne (trad. prov.), France 29
Champagne, Yukon 187/E3
Champaign (co.), Ill. 222/E3
Champaign, Ill. 188/J2
Champaign, Ill. 222/E3
Champaign (co.), Ohio 284/C5
Champasak, Laos 72/E4
Champdani, India 68/F1
Champerico, Guatemala 154/A3
Champéry, Switzerland 39/C4
Champex, Switzerland 39/D4
Champigny-sur-Marne, France 28/C2
Champion, Alberta 182/D4
Champion, Mich. 250/B2
Champion, Nebr. 264/C4
Champlain (lake) 188/M2
Champlain, N.Y. 276/N1
Champlain (lake), N.Y. 276/O1
Champlain (county), Québec 174/C3
Champlain (co.), Québec 172/E2
Champlain, Québec 172/E3
Champlain (lake), Québec 172/D4
Champlain (lake), Vt. 268/A2
Champlain, Va. 307/O4
Champlain Park, N.Y. 276/O1
Champlin, Minn. 255/G5
Champney's West, Newf. 166/D2
Champotón, Mexico 150/O7
Chamusa, Sierra (mts.), Colombia 126/C6
Chamusca, Portugal 33/B3
Chan, Ko (isl.), Thailand 72/C5
Chana, Ill. 222/D2
Chañaral, Chile 120/B5
Chañaral, Chile 138/A6
Chañaral (isl.), Chile 138/A7
Chancay, Peru 128/D8
Chance, Ala. 195/C7
Chance, Ky. 237/L7
Chance, Md. 245/P8
Chance Cove, Newf. 166/D2
Chance Cove (cape), Newf. 166/D2
Chance Harbour, New Bruns. 170/D3
Chancellor, Ala. 195/G8
Chancellor, Alberta 182/D4
Chancellor, S. Dak. 298/R7
Chancellorsville, Va. 307/N4
Chanco, Chile 138/A11
Chancy, Switzerland 39/A4
Chandalar, Alaska 196/J1
Chandalar (riv.), Alaska 196/J1
Chandalar, East Fork (riv.), Alaska 196/J1
Chandeleur (isls.), La. 238/N7
Chandeleur (sound), La. 238/M7
Chanderi, India 68/D4
Chandernagore, India 68/F1
Chandigarh (terr.), India 68/D2
Chandigarh, India 68/D2
Chandler, Ariz. 198/D5
Chandler, Ind. 227/C8
Chandler, Minn. 255/C7
Chandler, Okla. 288/N3
Chandler, Que. 162/K6
Chandler, Québec 174/E3
Chandler, Québec 172/D2
Chandler, Texas 303/J5
Chandler Springs, Ala. 195/F4
Chandlers Valley, Pa. 294/D2
Chandlersville, Ohio 284/G6
Chandlerville, Ill. 222/C3
Chandmanī, Mongolia 77/E2
Chandolin, Switzerland 39/E4
Chandos (lake), Ontario 177/G3
Chandrapur, India 68/D5
Chaneysville, Pa. 294/F6
Chang, Ko (isl.), Thailand 72/D4
Changane (riv.), Mozambique 118/E4
Changbaek-sanmaek (mts.), N. Korea 81/D2
Changchih (Changzhi), China 77/H4
Changchow (Changzhou), China 77/J5
Changchow (Zhangzhou), China 77/J7
Changchun, China 77/K3
Changchun, China 54/O5
Changchun, China 2/R3
Changde (Changteh), China 77/H6
Changde, China 54/N7
Change Islands, Newf. 166/D4
Changewater, N.J. 273/D2
Changhua, China 77/K7
Changhŭng, S. Korea 81/C6
Changji, China 77/C3
Changjiang, China 77/G8
Chang Jiang (Yangtze) (riv.), China 2/Q4
Chang Jiang (Yangtze) (riv.), China 54/N6
Chang Jiang (Yangtze) (riv.), China 77/K5
Changjin (res.), N. Korea 81/C3
Chang Khoeng, Thailand 72/C3
Changling, China 77/K3
Changsha, China 77/H6
Changsha, China 2/Q4
Changsha, China 54/N7
Changshun, China 77/G6
Changsŏng, S. Korea 81/C6
Changteh (Changde), China 77/H6
Changuinola, Panama 154/F6
Changwu, China 77/G4
Changyang, China 77/H5
Changyeh (Zhangye), China 77/F4
Changyŏn, N. Korea 81/B4
Changzhi (Changchih), China 77/H4
Changzhi, China 54/N6
Changzhou (Changchow), China 77/K5
Chanhassen, Minn. 255/F6
Chankiang (Zhanjiang), China 77/H7
Channahon, Ill. 222/E2
Channel (isls.) 7/D4
Channel (isl.), Manitoba 179/B2
CHANNEL ISLANDS 10/E6
CHANNEL ISLANDS 13/E8
Channel Islands Nat'l Park, Calif. 204/E11
Channel-Port aux Basques, Newf. 166/C4
Channel-Port aux Basques, Newf. 162/L6
Channelview, Texas 303/K1
Channing, Mich. 250/B2
Channing, Texas 303/B2
Chantada, Spain 33/C1
Chanthaburi, Thailand 72/D4
Chantilly, France 28/E3
Chantilly, Va. 307/O3
Chantonnay, France 28/C4
Chantrey (inlet), N.W.T. 187/J3
Chanute, Kansas 232/G4
Chanute A.F.B., Ill. 222/E3
Chao, Peru 128/C7
Chao'an (Chaochow), China 77/J7
Chao (isl.), Portugal 33/B2
Chao Phraya, Mae Nam (riv.), Thailand 72/D4
Chaotung (Zhaotung), China 77/F6
Chaoyang, Guangdong, China 77/J7
Chaoyang, Liaoning, China 77/J3
Chapa, Vietnam 72/E2
Chapacura, Bolivia 136/A2
Chapais, Québec 174/B3
Chapala (lake), Mexico 150/H6
Chapanoke, N.C. 281/S2
Chaparé (riv.), Bolivia 136/C5
Chaparra, Cuba 158/H3
Chaparral, Colombia 126/C6
Chapayevsk, Russia 48/F4
Chapayevsk, Russia 52/G4
Chapecó, Brazil 132/C9
Chapel, W. Va. 312/E5
Chapel Arm, Newf. 166/D2
Chapel en le Frith, England 13/J2
Chapel Hill, Ark. 202/B5
Chapel Hill, Ind. 227/E6
Chapel Hill, N.C. 281/L3
Chapel Hill, Tenn. 237/H9
Chapelton, Jamaica 158/J6
Chapicuy, Uruguay 145/B2
Chapin, Ill. 222/C4
Chapin, Iowa 229/G3
Chapin, S.C. 296/E3
Chapleau, Ont. 162/H6
Chapleau, Ontario 175/D3
Chapleau, Ontario 177/J5
Chaplin•, Conn. 210/G1
Chaplin, Ky. 237/L5
Chaplin (riv.), Ky. 237/L5
Chaplin, Sask. 181/E5
Chaplin (lake), Sask. 181/E5
Chapman, Ala. 195/E7
Chapman (pt.), Conn. 210/F3
Chapman, Kansas 232/E3
Chapman•, Maine 243/G2
Chapman, Nebr. 264/F3
Chapmansboro, Tenn. 237/G8
Chapmanville, W. Va. 312/B7
Chappaquiddick (isl.), Mass. 249/N7
Chappell, Ky. 237/P7
Chappell, Nebr. 264/B3
Chappell (isls.), Tasmania 99/D2
Chappell Hill, Texas 303/H7
Chappells, S.C. 296/D3
Chapra, India 68/F3
Chaptico, Md. 245/M7
Chapultepec, Mexico 150/A1
Chaquí, Bolivia 136/C6
Chara, Russia 48/M4
Charadai, Argentina 143/D2
Charagua, Bolivia 136/D6
Charagua, Sierra de (mts.), Bolivia 136/D6
Charagua, Paraguay 144/D3
Charak, Iran 66/J7
Charambirá (pt.), Colombia 126/B5
Charaña, Bolivia 136/A5
Charata, Argentina 143/D2
Charbon, N.S. Wales 97/F3
Charbonneau, N. Dak. 282/C4
Charcas, Mexico 150/J5
Charcot (isl.), Ant. 5/C15
Chard, Alberta 182/E2
Chard, England 13/E7
Chard, England 10/E5
Chardon, Ohio 284/H2
Chardonnière, Haiti 158/A6
Chardzhou, Turkmenistan 48/G6
Chardzhou, Turkmenistan 54/H6
Charente (dept.), France 28/D5
Charente (riv.), France 28/C5
Charente-Maritime (dept.), France 28/C5
Charenton, La. 238/H7
Charenton-le-Pont, France 28/B2
Charette, Québec 172/D3
Charikar, Afghanistan 68/B1
Charikar, Afghanistan 59/J2
Charing, Ga. 217/D6
Charing Cross, Ontario 177/B5
Chariton, Iowa 229/G6
Chariton (riv.), Iowa 229/G7
Chariton (co.), Mo. 261/F3
Chariton (riv.), Mo. 261/G1
Charity, Guyana 131/B2
Charity, Mo. 261/G7
Charkhlia (Ruoqiang), China 77/C4
Charlack, Mo. 261/P2
Charlemagne, Québec 172/H4
Charlemont•, Mass. 249/C2
Charleroi, Belgium 27/E8
Charleroi, Pa. 294/C5
Charles, Ga. 217/H6
Charles (co.), Md. 245/K6
Charles (riv.), Mass. 249/C7
Charles (isl.), N.W.T. 187/L3
Charles (cape), Va. 188/L3
Charles (cape), Va. 307/R6
Charlesbourg, Québec 172/J3
Charles City, Iowa 229/H2
Charles City (co.), Va. 307/O6
Charles City, Va. 307/O6
Charles Mix (co.), S. Dak. 298/M7
Charles Mound (hill), Ill. 222/C1
Charleston, Ark. 202/B3
Charleston, Ill. 222/E4
Charleston, Kansas 232/B4
Charleston•, Maine 243/F5
Charleston, Miss. 256/D2
Charleston, Mo. 261/O9

Cîmpulung 351

Chichi (isl.), Japan 87/E3
Chichi (isl.), Japan 81/M3
Chichibu, Japan 81/J5
Chichibu-Tama National Park, Japan 81/J6
Chichicaste, Honduras 154/E3
Chichicastenango, Guatemala 154/B3
Chichigalpa, Nicaragua 154/D4
Chichiriviche, Venezuela 124/D2
Chickalah, Ark. 202/D3
Chickaloon, Alaska 196/C1
Chickamauga, Ga. 217/B1
Chickamauga (dam), Tenn. 237/L10
Chickamauga (lake), Tenn. 188/J3
Chickamauga (lake), Tenn. 237/L10
Chickamauga and Chattanooga Nat'l Mil. Park, Ga. 217/B1
Chickamaw Beach, Minn. 255/D4
Chickasaw, Ala. 195/B9
Chickasaw (co.), Iowa 229/J2
Chickasaw (co.), Miss. 256/G3
Chickasaw, Ohio 284/A5
Chickasawhay (riv.), Miss. 256/G7
Chickasaw Village, Natchez Trace Pkwy., Miss. 256/G2
Chickasha, Okla. 188/G4
Chickasha, Okla. 288/L4
Chickasha (lake), Okla. 288/K4
Chicken, Alaska 196/K2
Chiclana de la Frontera, Spain 33/C4
Chiclayo, Peru 128/C6
Chiclayo, Peru 120/B3
Chico (riv.), Argentina 120/C7
Chico (riv.), Argentina 143/C6
Chico (riv.), Argentina 143/C5
Chico, Calif. 204/D4
Chico, Mont. 262/F5
Chico (riv.), Philippines 82/C2
Chico, Texas 303/G4
Chicoana, Argentina 143/C2
Chico Arroyo (creek), N. Mex. 274/B3
Chicopee, Kansas 232/H4
Chicopee, Mass. 249/D4
Chicopee (riv.), Mass. 249/D4
Chicora, Miss. 256/G7
Chicora, Pa. 294/C4
Chicot (co.), Ark. 202/H7
Chicot, Ark. 202/H7
Chicot (pt.), La. 238/M7
Chicoutimi, Que. 162/J6
Chicoutimi, Que. 146/L5
Chicoutimi (county), Québec 174/C2
Chicoutimi (co.), Québec 172/G1
Chicoutimi, Québec 172/G1
Chicoutimi, Québec 174/C3
Chicoutimi (riv.), Québec 172/F2
Chicoutimi-Nord, Québec 172/F1
Chicualacuala, Mozambique 118/E4
Chidambaram, India 68/E6
Chidester, Ark. 202/D6
Chidley (cape), Canada 146/M3
Chidley (cape), Newf. 166/B1
Chidley (cape), Newf. 162/K3
Chidley (cape), N.W.T. 187/M3
Chidlow, W. Australia 88/B2
Chief Joseph (dam), Wash. 310/F3
Chiefland, Fla. 212/D2
Chiefs (pt.), Ontario 177/C3
Chiemsee (lake), Germany 22/E5
Chienti (riv.), Italy 34/D3
Chieri, Italy 34/A2
Chieti (prov.), Italy 34/E3
Chieti, Italy 34/E3
Chietla, Mexico 150/M2
Chièvres, Belgium 27/D7
Chifeng, China 77/J3
Chigasaki, Japan 81/O3
Chiginagak (mt.), Alaska 196/G3
Chignahuapan, Mexico 150/N1
Chignecto (bay), New Bruns. 170/F3
Chignecto (bay), Nova Scotia 168/D3
Chignecto (cape), Nova Scotia 168/C3
Chignecto (isth.), Nova Scotia 168/D3
Chignik, Alaska 196/G3
Chignik (bay), Alaska 196/G3
Chignik Lagoon, Alaska 196/G3
Chignik Lake, Alaska 196/G3
Chiguana, Bolivia 136/A7
Chigubo, Mozambique 118/E4
Chigwell, England 13/H8
Chigwell, England 10/C5
Chihuahua (state), Mexico 150/F2
Chihuahua, Mexico 150/F2
Chihuahua, Mexico 146/H7
Chikaskia (riv.), Kansas 232/E4
Chik Ballapur, India 68/D6
Chikmagalur, India 68/D6
Chilanga, Zambia 115/E7
Chilanko Forks, Br. Col. 184/E4
Chilapa de Álvarez, Mexico 150/K8
Chilas, Pakistan 68/C1
Chilas, Pakistan 59/K2
Chilca (Pucusana), Peru 128/D9
Chilcoot, Calif. 204/E4
Chilcotin (riv.), Br. Col. 184/E4
Childers, Queensland 88/J5
Childersburg, Ala. 195/F4
Childress (co.), Texas 303/D3
Childress, Texas 303/D3
Childs (lake), Manitoba 179/A3
Childs, Md. 245/P2
Childwold, N.Y. 276/L2
Chile 2/F7
Chile 120/B5
CHILE 138
Chile Chico, Chile 138/E6
Chilecito, Argentina 143/C2
Chiles, Colombia 126/A7
Chilete, Peru 128/C6
Chilga, Ethiopia 111/G5
Chilhowee, Mo. 261/E5
Chilhowee (mt.), Tenn. 237/O9
Chilhowie, Va. 307/E7
Chili, Ind. 227/F3
Chili, Wis. 317/F6
Chililabombwe, Zambia 115/E6
Chililabombwe, Zambia 102/E6
Chilili, N. Mex. 274/C4
Chilka (lake), India 68/F5
Chilko (lake), Br. Col. 184/F4
Chilko (riv.), Br. Col. 184/E4
Chilkoot (pass), Alaska 196/M1
Chilkoot (pass), Br. Col. 184/J1
Chillán, Chile 120/B6
Chillán, Chile 138/A11
Chillicothe, Ill. 222/D3
Chillicothe, Iowa 229/J6
Chillicothe, Mo. 261/E3
Chillicothe, Ohio 284/E7
Chillicothe, Texas 303/E3
Chilliwack, Br. Col. 162/D6
Chilliwack, Br. Col. 184/M3
Chillum, Md. 245/F4
Chilmark•, Mass. 249/M7
Chilo, Ohio 284/B8
Chilocco, Okla. 288/M1
Chiloé (isl.), Chile 120/B7
Chiloé (isl.), Chile 138/D4
Chiloquin, Oreg. 291/F5
Chilpancingo de los Bravos, Mexico 150/K8
Chiltern (hills), England 13/G6
Chilton (co.), Ala. 195/E5
Chilton, Texas 303/G6
Chilton, Wis. 317/K7
Chiltonville, Mass. 249/M5
Chilumba, Malawi 115/F6
Chilwa (lake), Malawi 115/G7
Chilwa (lake), Mozambique 118/F3
Chimacum, Wash. 310/C3
Chimaltenango, Guatemala 154/B3
Chimán, Panama 154/H6
Chimanimani, Zimbabwe 118/E3
Chimantá-tepui (mt.), Venezuela 124/G5
Chimay, Belgium 27/E8
Chimayo, N. Mex. 274/D3
Chimbarongo, Chile 138/A10
Chimbay, Uzbekistan 48/F5
Chimborazo (prov.), Ecuador 128/C3
Chimborazo (mt.), Ecuador 120/B3
Chimborazo (mt.), Ecuador 128/C3
Chimbote, Peru 120/B3
Chimbote, Peru 128/C7
Chimbote (bay), Peru 128/C7
Chimichaqua, Colombia 126/D3
Chimkent, Kazakhstan 48/H5
Chimkent, Kazakhstan 54/H5
Chimney Point, Vt. 268/A3
Chimney Rock, Colo. 208/E8
Chimney Rock Nat'l Hist. Site, Nebr. 264/A3
Chimoio, Mozambique 118/E3
Chimoio, Mozambique 102/F6
Chin, Alberta 182/D5
Chin (state), Burma 72/B2
Chin (hills), Burma 72/B2
Chin (cape), Ontario 177/C2
China 2/P4
China 54/L6
CHINA 77
CHINA 85
China, Maine 243/E7
China•, Maine 243/E7
Chiná, Campeche, Mexico 150/O7
Chiná, Nuevo León, Mexico 150/K4
Chinácota, Colombia 126/D4
China Gardens (dam), Wash. 310/J4
China Grove, Ala. 195/G7
China Grove, N.C. 281/H3
China Grove, Texas 303/K11
China Lake, Calif. 204/H8
China Lake Naval Weapons Center, Calif. 204/H8
Chinameca, El Salvador 154/C4
Chinandega, Nicaragua 154/D4
Chinati (mts.), Texas 303/C12
Chinati (peak), Texas 303/C12
Chincha (isls.), Peru 128/D9
Chincha Alta, Peru 128/D9
Chincha Alta, Peru 120/B4
Chinchaga (riv.), Alberta 182/A5
Chinchilla, Pa. 294/F6
Chinchilla, Queensland 88/J5
Chinchilla de Monte-Aragón, Spain 33/F3
Chinchiná, Colombia 126/C5
Chinchón, Spain 33/G5
Chinchoua, Gabon 115/A4
Chinchow (Jinzhou), China 77/K3
Chincoteague (bay), Md. 245/S8
Chincoteague, Va. 307/T5
Chincoteague (bay), Va. 307/T4
Chincoteague (inlet), Va. 307/T5
Chinde, Mozambique 118/F3
Chinde, Mozambique 102/F6
Chindu, China 77/E5
Chindwin (riv.), Burma 72/B2
Chinese Camp, Calif. 204/E6
Chingleput, India 68/E6
Chingola, Zambia 115/E6
Chingola, Zambia 102/E6
Chinguar, Angola 115/C6
Chinguetti, Mauritania 106/B4
Chinhae, S. Korea 81/D6
Chiniak (cape), Alaska 196/H3
Chinhoyi, Zimbabwe 115/F7
Chinhoyi, Zimbabwe 118/D3
Chiñijo, Bolivia 136/A4
Chiniot, Pakistan 68/C2
Chínipas, Mexico 150/E3
Chinju, S. Korea 81/D6
Chinkapin Knob (mt.), Ark. 202/E2
Chinkiang (Zhenjiang), China 77/J5
Chinle, Ariz. 198/F2
Chinle (creek), Ariz. 198/F2
Chinle (valley), Ariz. 198/F2
Chinle (creek), Utah 304/E6
Chinle Wash (dry riv.), Ariz. 198/F2
Chino (valley), Ariz. 198/C3
Chino, Calif. 204/D10
Chinon, France 28/D4
Chinook, Alberta 182/E4
Chinook, Mont. 262/G2
Chinook (lake), Oreg. 291/F3
Chinook, Wash. 310/B4
Chinook (pass), Wash. 310/D4
Chinook Valley, Alberta 182/B1
Chino Valley, Ariz. 198/C4
Chinquapin, N.C. 281/O5
Chinsali, Zambia 115/F6
Chinsi (Jinxi), China 77/K3
Chintheche, Malawi 115/F6
Chinú, Colombia 126/C3
Chinwangtao (Qinhuangdao), China 77/K4
Chiny, Belgium 27/G9
Chioggia, Italy 34/D2
Chip (lake), Alberta 182/C3
Chipamanu (riv.), Bolivia 136/A2
Chipata, Zambia 115/F6
Chipata, Zambia 102/F6
Chipewyan (lake), Alberta 182/D1
Chipewyan (riv.), Alberta 182/D1
Chipewyan Lake, Alberta 182/D1
Chipindo, Angola 102/D6
Chipindo, Angola 115/C6
Chipinge, Zimbabwe 118/E4
Chipley, Fla. 212/D6
Chiplun, India 68/C5
Chipman, Alberta 182/D3
Chipman, New Bruns. 170/E2
Chipman (riv.), Sask. 181/M2
Chipoka, Malawi 115/F6
Chipola (riv.), Fla. 212/D6
Chipola, La. 238/J5
Chippenham, England 13/E6
Chippenham, England 10/F5
Chippewa (co.), Mich. 250/E2
Chippewa (riv.), Mich. 250/E5
Chippewa (co.), Minn. 255/C5
Chippewa (riv.), Minn. 255/C5
Chippewa (riv.), Wis. 188/H1
Chippewa (co.), Wis. 317/D5
Chippewa (lake), Wis. 317/D4
Chippewa (riv.), Wis. 317/B7
Chippewa Falls, Wis. 317/D6
Chippewa Lake, Mich. 250/D5
Chipping Norton, England 13/F6
Chippis, Switzerland 39/E4
Chiputneticook (lakes), Maine 243/H4
Chiputneticook (lakes), New Bruns. 170/C3
Chiquián, Peru 128/D8
Chiquimula, Guatemala 154/C3
Chiquinquirá, Colombia 126/C5
Chiquita (lake), Argentina 120/C6
Chir (riv.), Russia 52/F5
Chira (riv.) 120/A3
Chira (riv.), Ecuador 128/B5
Chirala, India 68/E5
Chirchik, Uzbekistan 48/H5
Chireno, Texas 303/K6
Chirfa, Niger 106/G4
Chiri (mt.), S. Korea 81/C6
Chiribiquete, Sierra de (mts.), Colombia 126/D7
Chiricahua (mts.), Ariz. 198/F6
Chiricahua Nat'l Mon., Ariz. 198/F6
Chiriguaná, Colombia 126/D3
Chirikof (isl.), Alaska 196/G3
Chirinos, Peru 128/C5
Chiriquí (gulf), Panama 154/F7
Chiriquí (lag.), Panama 154/G6
Chiriquí Grande, Panama 154/F6
Chirk, Wales 13/D5
Chirnside, Scotland 15/F5
Chiromo, Malawi 115/F7
Chironico, Switzerland 39/G4
Chirpan, Bulgaria 45/G4
Chirripó Grande (mt.), C. Rica 154/F6
Chirundu, Zimbabwe 118/D3
Chisago (co.), Minn. 255/F5
Chisago City, Minn. 255/E5
Chisamba, Zambia 115/E6
Chisana, Alaska 196/K2
Chisasibi, Québec 162/J5
Chisasibi, Québec 174/B2
Chisec, Guatemala 154/B3
Chisholm, Maine 243/C7
Chisholm, Minn. 255/E3
Chisholm Mills, Alberta 182/C2
Chishui, China 77/G6
Chisimayu, Somalia 115/H4
Chisimayu, Somalia 102/G5
Chisinau (cap.), Moldova 7/G4
Chisinau (cap.), Moldova 48/C5
Chisinau (cap.), Moldova 52/C5
Chişineu Criş, Romania 45/E2
Chismville, Ark. 202/C3
Chisos (mts.), Texas 303/A8
Chistochina, Alaska 196/K2
Chistopol', Russia 52/H3
Chiswick, Ontario 177/E1
Chita, Russia 48/M4
Chita, Russia 54/N4
Chitado, Angola 115/B7
Chitado, Namibia 118/A3
Chitato, Angola 114/D5
Chitek (lake), Manitoba 179/C2
Chitek (lake), Sask. 181/D2
Chitek Lake, Sask. 181/D2
Chitembo, Angola 115/C6
Chitina, Alaska 196/K2
Chitina (riv.), Alaska 196/K2
Chitipa, Malawi 115/F5
Chitorgarh, India 68/C4
Chitose, Japan 81/K2
Chitradurga, India 68/D6
Chitral, Pakistan 59/K2
Chitral, Pakistan 68/C1
Chitré, Panama 154/G7
Chittagong, Bangladesh 54/L7
Chittagong, Bangladesh 68/G4
Chittenango, N.Y. 276/J4
Chittenden (co.), Vt. 268/A3
Chittenden•, Vt. 268/B4
Chittenden (res.), Vt. 268/B4
Chittering, W. Australia 88/B6
Chittoor, India 68/D6
Chiumbe (riv.), Angola 115/D5
Chiva, Spain 33/F3
Chivacoa, Venezuela 124/D2
Chivapure (riv.), Venezuela 124/E4
Chivasso, Italy 34/A2
Chivato (mesa), N. Mex. 274/B3
Chivay, Peru 128/G10
Chive, Bolivia 136/A3
Chivhu, Zimbabwe 118/E3
Chivilcoy, Argentina 143/F7
Chivilcoy, Argentina 120/C6
Chivington, Colo. 208/O6
Chiwawa (riv.), Wash. 310/E2
Chixoy (riv.), Guatemala 154/B2
Chizha, Russia 52/F1
Chloe, W. Va. 312/D5
Chloride, Ariz. 198/A3
Chloride, Mo. 261/L8
Chlumec, Czech Rep. 41/C1
Choam Khsant, Cambodia 72/E4
Choapa, Chile 138/A9
Choapa (riv.), Chile 138/A9
Choate, Br. Col. 184/M3
Chobe (riv.), Botswana 118/C3
Chobe (riv.), Namibia 118/C3
Chobe Nat'l Park, Botswana 118/D3
Choc, St. Lucia 161/G5
Choc (bay), St. Lucia 161/G5
Chocalán, Chile 138/F4
Chocaya, Bolivia 136/B7
Choccolocco, Ala. 195/G3
Choceň, Czech Rep. 41/D1
Choch'iwŏn, S. Korea 81/C5
Chocó (dept.), Colombia 126/B4
Chocó (bay), Colombia 126/B6
Chocolate (mts.), Ariz. 198/A5
Chocolate (mts.), Calif. 204/K10
Chocomán, Mexico 150/P2
Choconut, Pa. 294/K2
Chocorua, N.H. 268/E4
Chocorua (mt.), N.H. 268/E4
Chocowinity, N.C. 281/P4
Choctaw (co.), Ala. 195/B6
Choctaw, Ala. 195/B6
Choctaw, Ark. 202/F2
Choctaw (co.), Miss. 256/F4
Choctaw (co.), Okla. 288/P6
Choctaw, Okla. 288/M3
Choctaw Bluff, Ala. 195/C8
Choctawhatchee (riv.), Ala. 195/H8
Choctawhatchee (bay), Fla. 212/C6
Choctawhatchee (riv.), Fla. 212/C6
Choctaw Ind. Res., Miss. 256/F6
Chodov, Czech Rep. 41/B1
Chodzież, Poland 47/C2
Choele-Choel, Argentina 143/C4
Choele-Choel, Argentina 120/C6
Choestoe, Ga. 217/E1
Chofu, Japan 81/O2
Choiceland, Sask. 181/G2
Choiseul (sound), Falkland Is. 143/E7
Choiseul, St. Lucia 161/F7
Choiseul (isl.), Solomon Is. 87/F6
Choiseul (isl.), Solomon Is. 86/D2
Choisy-le-Roi, France 28/B2
Choix, Mexico 150/E3
Chojna, Poland 47/B2
Chojnice, Poland 47/C2
Chojnów, Poland 47/B3
Chokai (mt.), Japan 81/J4
Chokio, Minn. 255/B5
Chokoloskee, Fla. 212/E6
Chokurdakh, Russia 4/B2
Chokurdakh, Russia 48/P2
Chokurdakh, Russia 54/R2
Cholame, Calif. 204/E8
Cholet, France 28/C4
Choloma, Honduras 154/C3
Cholula de Rivadavia, Mexico 150/M1
Choluteca, Honduras 154/D4
Choluteca (riv.), Honduras 154/D4
Choma, Zambia 115/E7
Choma, Zambia 102/E6
Chomes, C. Rica 154/E5
Chomo Lhari (mt.), Bhutan 68/F3
Chomutov, Czech Rep. 41/B1
Ch'ŏnan, S. Korea 81/C5
Chon Buri, Thailand 72/D4
Chonchi, Chile 138/D4
Ch'ŏnch'ŏn, N. Korea 81/C3
Chone, Ecuador 128/B3
Ch'ŏngjin, N. Korea 54/P5
Ch'ŏngjin, N. Korea 81/E3
Chŏngju, N. Korea 81/B4
Ch'ŏngju, S. Korea 81/C5
Chongqing (Chungking), China 77/G6
Chongqing, China 2/P4
Chongqing, China 54/M7
Chŏngŭp, S. Korea 81/C6
Chongyang, China 77/H6
Chongzuo, China 77/G7
Chŏnju, S. Korea 81/C6
Chon May, Vung (bay), Vietnam 72/F3
Chonos (arch.), Chile 120/B7
Chonos (arch.), Chile 138/D6
Chopin, La. 238/E4
Chopin (lake), Québec 172/B2
Choptank (riv.), Del. 245/P5
Choptank, Md. 245/P6
Choptank (riv.), Md. 245/O6
Choquecota, Bolivia 136/A6
Chorley, England 10/G2
Chorley, England 13/G2
Chorleywood, England 13/G7
Chorleywood, England 10/A5
Choroní, Venezuela 124/E2
Choros (cape), Chile 138/A7
Choros, Los (riv.), Chile 138/A7
Chortitz, Sask. 181/D5
Chortkov, Ukraine 52/B5
Ch'ŏrwŏn, S. Korea 81/C4
Chorzele, Poland 47/E2
Chorzów, Poland 47/B4
Ch'osan, N. Korea 81/C3
Choshi, Japan 81/K6
Chosica, Peru 128/D8
Chos-Malal, Argentina 143/C4
Choszczno, Poland 47/B2
Chota, Peru 128/C6
Choteau, Mont. 262/D3
Choteau (creek), S. Dak. 298/N7
Chotěboř, Czech Rep. 41/C2
Choudrant, La. 238/F1
Chouteau (co.), Mont. 262/F3
Chouteau, Okla. 288/R2
Chovoreca, Cerro (mt.), Bolivia 136/F6
Chovoreca (mt.), Paraguay 144/C1
Chowan (co.), N.C. 281/R2
Chowan (riv.), N.C. 281/R2
Chowchilla, Calif. 204/E6
Choybalsan, Mongolia 54/N5
Choybalsan, Mongolia 77/J2
Chrastava, Czech Rep. 41/C1
Chriesman, Texas 303/H7
Chrisman, Ill. 222/F4
Chrisney, Ind. 227/C8
Christchurch, England 10/F5
Christchurch, England 13/F7
Christchurch, N. Zealand 2/T8
Christchurch, N. Zealand 100/D5
Christian (sound), Alaska 196/M2
Christian (co.), Ill. 222/D4
Christian (co.), Ky. 237/F7
Christian (co.), Mo. 261/F9
Christian (cape), N.W.T. 187/M2
Christian (isl.), Ontario 177/D3
Christian, W. Va. 312/C7
Christiana, Del. 245/R2
Christiana, Jamaica 158/H6
Christiana, Pa. 294/K6
Christiana, S. Africa 118/D5
Christiana, Tenn. 237/J9
Christiansburg, Ohio 284/C5
Christiansburg, Va. 307/H6
Christiansfeld, Denmark 21/C7
Christiansted, Virgin Is. (U.S.) 156/H2
Christiansted, Virgin Is. (U.S.) 161/F4
Christiansted Nat'l Hist. Site, Virgin Is. (U.S.) 161/F4
Christie, Okla. 288/S3
Christina (lake), Alberta 182/E2
Christina (riv.), Alberta 182/E1
Christina (lake), Minn. 255/C4
Christina, Mont. 262/G3
Christina Lake, Br. Col. 184/H5
Christine, N. Dak. 282/S6
Christine, Texas 303/F9
Christmas, Ariz. 198/E5
Christmas (isl.), Australia 54/M11
Christmas (isl.), Australia 2/Q6
Christmas, Fla. 212/E3
Christmas (Kiritimati) (isl.), Kiribati 87/L5
Christmas, Mich. 250/C2
Christmas (lake), Oreg. 291/G4
Christmas (riv.), W. Australia 88/D3
Christmas Creek, W. Australia 92/D2
Christmas Island, Nova Scotia 168/H3
Christopher, Ill. 222/D6
Christopher Lake, Sask. 181/F2
Christoval, Texas 303/D6
Chromo, Colo. 208/F8
Chrudim, Czech Rep. 41/C2
Chrudimka (riv.), Czech Rep. 41/C2
Chrysler, Ala. 195/C8
Chryston, Scotland 15/C2
Chrzanów, Poland 47/B4
Chu (riv.), Kazakhstan 48/H5
Chualar, Calif. 204/D7
Chüanchow (Quanzhou), China 77/J7
Chuathbaluk, Alaska 196/G2
Chubbuck, Idaho 220/F7
Chubu-Sangaku Nat'l Park, Japan 81/H5
Chubut (prov.), Argentina 143/C5
Chubut (riv.), Argentina 120/C7
Chubut (riv.), Argentina 143/C5
Chuchi (lake), Br. Col. 184/E2
Chuchow (Zhuzhou), China 77/H6
Chuckey, Tenn. 237/R8
Chucunaque (riv.), Panama 154/J6
Chudleigh, Tasmania 99/C3
Chudovo, Russia 52/D3
Chugach (isls.), Alaska 196/B2
Chugash (mts.), Alaska 196/C1
Chugiak, Alaska 196/C1
Chuginadak (isl.), Alaska 196/D4
Chuguchak (Tacheng), China 77/B2
Chugwater, Wyo. 319/H4
Chugwater (creek), Wyo. 319/H4
Chukai, Malaysia 72/D6
Chukchi (sea) 4/C18
Chukchi (sea) 54/W3
Chukchi (sea), Alaska 196/E1
Chukchi (pen.), Russia 4/C18
Chukchi (pen.), Russia 48/T3
Chukchi (pen.), Russia 54/V3
Chukchi (sea), Russia 48/T2
Chukchi Aut. Okr., Russia 48/R3
Chukhloma, Russia 52/F3
Chula, Ark. 202/C4
Chula, Ga. 217/E7
Chula, Mo. 261/F3
Chula, Va. 307/N6
Chu Lai, Vietnam 72/F4
Chula Vista, Calif. 204/J11
Chulucanas, Peru 128/B5
Chulumani, Bolivia 136/B5
Chulym (riv.), Russia 48/J4
Chuma, Bolivia 136/A4
Chumatien (Zhumadian), China 77/H5
Chumbicha, Argentina 143/C2
Chumikan, Russia 48/O4
Chumphon, Thailand 72/C5
Chuna (riv.), Russia 48/K4
Chunchi, Ecuador 128/C4
Ch'unch'ŏn, S. Korea 81/D5
Chunchula, Ala. 195/B9
Ch'ungju, S. Korea 81/C5
Chungking (Chongqing), China 77/G6
Chŭngsan, N. Korea 81/B4
Chungshan (Zhongshan), China 77/H7
Chunky, Miss. 256/G6
Chunya, Tanzania 115/F5
Chunya (riv.), Russia 48/K3
Chupaca, Peru 128/E9
Chupadera (mesa), N. Mex. 274/C5
Chupara (pt.), Trin. & Tob. 161/B10
Chuquibamba, Peru 128/F10
Chuquibambilla, Peru 128/F9
Chuquicamata, Chile 138/B3
Chuquichambi, Bolivia 136/B5
Chuquisaca (dept.), Bolivia 136/C6
Chur, Switzerland 39/J3
Churachandpur, India 68/G4
Church, Iowa 229/L2
Churchbridge, Sask. 181/J5
Church Creek, Md. 245/O6
Church Hill, Md. 245/O4
Church Hill, Miss. 256/B7
Church Hill, Tenn. 237/R7
Churchill (riv.) 162/G4
Churchill (pk.), Br. Col. 162/D4
Churchill (peak), Br. Col. 184/L2
Churchill (riv.), Canada 146/J4
Churchill, Man. 146/J4
Churchill, Man. 162/G4
Churchill, Manitoba 179/K2
Churchill (cape), Manitoba 162/G4
Churchill (cape), Manitoba 179/K2
Churchill (riv.), Manitoba 179/J2
Churchill (co.), Nev. 266/C3
Churchill (falls), Newf. 166/B3
Churchill (riv.), Newf. 166/B3
Churchill, Pa. 294/C7
Churchill (riv.), Que. 162/K5
Churchill (riv.), Sask. 181/M3
Churchill, Victoria 97/D6
Churchill Falls, Newf. 166/B3
Churchman (mt.), W. Australia 92/B5
Church Point, La. 238/F6
Church Point, Nova Scotia 168/B4
Church's Ferry, N. Dak. 282/M3
Church Stretton, England 13/E5
Churchton, Md. 245/N5
Churchtown, Pa. 294/L5
Church View, Va. 307/P5
Churchville, Md. 245/N2
Churchville, N.Y. 276/E4
Churchville, Va. 307/K4
Churchville, W. Va. 312/E4
Churdan, Iowa 229/D4
Churfirsten (mt.), Switzerland 39/H2
Churín, Peru 128/D8
Churu, India 68/D3
Churubusco, Ind. 227/G2
Churubusco, N.Y. 276/N1
Churuguara, Venezuela 124/D2
Churwalden, Switzerland 39/J3
Chushul, India 68/D2
Chuska (mts.), N. Mex. 274/A2
Chusovoy, Russia 52/J3
Chute-à-Blondeau, Ontario 177/K2
Chute-aux-Outardes, Québec 172/A1
Chute-des-Passes, Québec 174/C3
Chute-Saint-Philippe, Québec 172/B3
Chuvash Aut Rep., Russia 48/E4
Chuvash Aut. Rep., Russia 52/G3
Chu Xian, China 77/J5
Chuxiong, China 77/F7
Chuy, Uruguay 145/F4
Chvalšiny, Czech Rep. 41/C2
Ciales, P. Rico 161/C1
Ciamis, Indonesia 85/H2
Ciampino, Italy 34/F7
Cianjur, Indonesia 85/H2
Cibecue, Ariz. 198/E4
Cibola (co.), N. Mex. 274/B3
Cibolo, Texas 303/K10
Cibolo (creek), Texas 303/K11
Çiçekdagı, Turkey 63/F3
Cicero, Ill. 222/B5
Cicero, Ind. 227/E4
Cicero Dantas, Brazil 132/G5
Cicerone, W. Va. 312/D5
Ciconsine (lake), Québec 172/D2
Cid, N.C. 281/J3
Cide, Turkey 63/E2
Cidlina (riv.), Czech Rep. 41/C1
Cidra, Cuba 158/D1
Cidra, P. Rico 161/D2
Ciechanów (prov.), Poland 47/E2
Ciechanów, Poland 47/E2
Ciechocinek, Poland 47/D2
Ciego de Ávila (prov.), Cuba 158/F2
Ciego de Ávila, Cuba 156/B2
Ciego de Ávila, Cuba 158/F2
Ciempozuelos, Spain 33/F5
Ciénaga, Colombia 120/B1
Ciénaga, Colombia 126/C2
Ciénaga de Oro, Colombia 126/C3
Cienfuegos (prov.), Cuba 158/E2
Cienfuegos, Cuba 156/B2
Cienfuegos, Cuba 146/K7
Cienfuegos, Cuba 158/D2
Cienfuegos (bay), Cuba 158/D2
Cieplice Śląskie-Zdrój, Poland 47/B3
Čierny Balog, Slovakia 41/E2
Cieszyn, Poland 47/D4
Cieza, Spain 33/F3
Çifteler, Turkey 63/D3
Cifuentes, Spain 33/E2
Cigánd, Hungary 41/F2
Cihanbeyli, Turkey 63/E3
Cihuatlán, Mexico 150/G7
Cijara (res.), Spain 33/D3
Cijulang, Indonesia 85/H2
Cilacap, Indonesia 85/H2
Çıldır, Turkey 63/K2
Çıldır (lake), Turkey 63/K2
Cilleros, Spain 33/C2
Cilo Dağı (mt.), Turkey 63/K4
Cima, Calif. 204/K8
Cimahi, Indonesia 85/H2
Cimarron (riv.) 188/G3
Cimarron, Colo. 208/D6
Cimarron, Kansas 232/B4
Cimarron (riv.), Kansas 232/B4
Cimarron, N. Mex. 274/E2
Cimarron (riv.), N. Mex. 274/E2
Cimarron (co.), Okla. 288/A1
Cimarron, Okla. 288/L3
Cimarron (riv.), Okla. 288/N2
Cimin, Turkey 63/H3
Cimone (mt.), Italy 34/C2
Cîmpeni, Romania 45/F2
Cîmpia Turzii, Romania 45/F2
Cîmpina, Romania 45/H3
Cîmpulung, Romania 45/G3

352 Cîmpulung Moldovenesc

Cîmpulung Moldovenesc, Romania 45/G2
Cinaruco (riv.), Colombia 126/F4
Cinaruco (riv.), Venezuela 124/D4
Cinca (riv.), Spain 33/G2
Cincinnati, Ark. 202/B1
Cincinnati, Iowa 229/G7
Cincinnati, Ohio 146/K6
Cincinnati, Ohio 284/B9
Cincinnati, Ohio 188/K3
Cincinnatus, N.Y. 276/H5
Cinclare, La. 238/J2
Cinco, W. Va. 312/D6
Cinco Balas (cays), Cuba 158/E3
Cinco Bayou, Fla. 212/B6
Cinco Saltos, Argentina 143/C4
Cinderella, W. Va. 312/B7
Cinderford, England 13/E6
Çine, Turkey 63/B4
Cinebar, Wash. 310/C4
Ciney, Belgium 27/G8
Cinnaminson•, N.J. 273/B3
Cintalapa de Figueroa, Mexico 150/N8
Cinto (mt.), France 28/B6
Cipolletti, Argentina 143/C4
Circeo (cape), Italy 34/D4
Circle, Alaska 196/K1
Circle, Mont. 262/L3
Circle (cliffs), Utah 304/C6
Circle Back, Texas 303/B3
Circle City, Mo. 261/N9
Circle Pines, Minn. 255/G5
Circle Springs, Alaska 196/K1
Circleville, Kansas 232/G2
Circleville, Ohio 284/D6
Circleville, Utah 304/B5
Circleville, W. Va. 312/H5
Circular (head), Tasmania 99/B2
Cirebon, Indonesia 85/H2
Cirebon, Indonesia 54/M10
Ciremay (mt.), Indonesia 85/H2
Cirencester, England 10/F5
Cirencester, England 13/E6
Cirque (mt.), Newf. 166/B2
Cisco, Ga. 217/C1
Cisco, Ill. 222/E3
Cisco, Texas 303/E5
Cisco, Utah 304/E5
Cisco Springs Wash (creek), Utah 304/E4
Cismont, Va. 307/M4
Cisnădie, Romania 45/G3
Cisne, Ill. 222/E5
Cisneros, Colombia 126/C4
Cisnes (riv.), Chile 138/E5
Cispus (pass), Wash. 310/D4
Cispus (riv.), Wash. 310/D4
Cissna Park, Ill. 222/F3
Citlaltépetl (mt.), Mexico 150/O2
Citra, Fla. 212/D2
Citronelle, Ala. 195/B8
Citrus (co.), Fla. 212/D3
Citrus Center, Fla. 212/E5
Citrus Heights, Calif. 204/C8
Cittadella, Italy 34/C2
Città di Castello, Italy 34/C3
Cittanova, Italy 34/F5
City of Rocks Nat'l Reserve, Idaho 220/E7
City Mills, Mass. 249/J4
City Point, Wis. 317/F7
City View, Ontario 177/J2
City View, S.C. 296/C2
Ciudad Acuña (Villa Acuña), Mexico 150/J2
Ciudad Altamirano, Mexico 150/J7
Ciudad Bolívar, Venezuela 120/C2
Ciudad Bolívar, Venezuela 124/G3
Ciudad Bolivia, Venezuela 124/C3
Ciudad Camargo, Chihuahua, Mexico 150/G3
Ciudad Camargo, Tamaulipas, Mexico 150/K3
Ciudad Darío, Nicaragua 154/D4
Ciudad del Carmen, Mexico 150/N7
Ciudad Delicias, Mexico 150/G2
Ciudad del Maíz, Mexico 150/K5
Ciudad de Nutrias, Venezuela 124/D3
Ciudad de Río Grande, Mexico 150/H5
Ciudadela, Spain 33/H2
Ciudad Guayana, Venezuela 120/C2
Ciudad Guayana, Venezuela 124/G3
Ciudad Guerrero, Mexico 150/F2
Ciudad Guzmán, Mexico 150/H7
Ciudad Hidalgo, Chiapas, Mexico 150/N9
Ciudad Hidalgo, Michoacán, Mexico 150/J7
Ciudad Juárez, Mexico 146/H6
Ciudad Juárez, Mexico 150/F1
Ciudad Lerdo, Mexico 150/H4
Ciudad Madero, Mexico 150/L5
Ciudad Mante, Mexico 150/K5
Ciudad Mendoza, Mexico 150/O2
Ciudad Miguel Alemán, Mexico 150/K3
Ciudad Obregón, Mexico 146/H7
Ciudad Obregón, Mexico 150/E3
Ciudad Ojeda, Venezuela 120/B2
Ciudad Ojeda, Venezuela 124/C2
Ciudad Piar, Venezuela 124/G4
Ciudad Presidente Stroessner, Paraguay 144/E4
Ciudad Quesada, C. Rica 154/E5
Ciudad Real (prov.), Spain 33/D3
Ciudad Real, Spain 33/D3
Ciudad Río Bravo, Mexico 150/K4
Ciudad-Rodrigo, Spain 33/C2
Ciudad Satélite, Mexico 150/L1
Ciudad Serdán, Mexico 150/O2
Ciudad Valles, Mexico 150/K5
Ciudad Victoria, Mexico 150/K5
Civa (cape), Turkey 63/G2
Cividale del Friuli, Italy 34/D1
Civitavecchia, Italy 34/C3
Civitella del Tronto, Italy 34/D3
Civray, France 28/D4
Çivril, Turkey 63/C3
Cizre, Turkey 63/K4
Clachan, Scotland 15/C5
Clackamas (co.), Oreg. 291/E2
Clackamas, Oreg. 291/B2
Clackamas (riv.), Oreg. 291/E2
Clackmannan, Scotland 10/B1
Clackmannan, Scotland 15/C1
Clackmannan (trad. co.), Scotland 15/E5
Clacton, England 13/J6
Clacton, England 10/G5
Claflin, Kansas 232/D3
Claiborne, Ala. 195/D7
Claiborne (par.), La. 238/D1
Claiborne (lake), La. 238/E1
Claiborne, Md. 245/N5
Claiborne (co.), Miss. 256/C7
Claiborne (co.), Tenn. 237/O8
Clair, New Bruns. 170/B1
Clair, Sask. 181/G3
Claire (lake), Alberta 182/B5
Claire (lake), Alta. 162/E4
Claire City, S. Dak. 298/P2
Clairemont, Texas 303/D4
Clair Engle (lake), Calif. 204/C3
Clairette, Texas 303/F5
Clairfield, Tenn. 237/O7
Clairmont, Alberta 182/A2
Clairmont Springs, Ala. 195/G4
Clairton, Pa. 294/C7
Clallam (co.), Wash. 310/B2
Clallam Bay, Wash. 310/A2
Clam (bay), Nova Scotia 168/F4
Clam (lake), Wis. 317/B4
Clam (riv.), Wis. 317/A4
Clamart, France 28/A2
Clamecy, France 28/E4
Clam Falls, Wis. 317/B4
Clam Gulch, Alaska 196/B1
Clam Lake, Wis. 317/E3
Clan Alpine (mts.), Nev. 266/D3
Clancy, Mont. 262/E4
Clandeboye, Manitoba 179/E4
Clandeboye, Ontario 177/C4
Clandonald, Alberta 182/E3
Clanton, Ala. 195/E5
Clanwilliam, Manitoba 179/C4
Clanwilliam, S. Africa 118/B6
Clapperton (isl.), Ontario 177/B1
Clara, Ireland 10/C4
Clara, Ireland 17/F5
Clara, Miss. 256/G7
Clara, Uruguay 145/D3
Clara Barton Nat'l Hist. Site, Md. 245/E4
Clara City, Minn. 255/C6
Claravale, North. Terr. 93/B3
Clare, Ill. 222/E1
Clare, Ind. 227/F4
Clare, Iowa 229/E3
Clare (co.), Ireland 17/D6
Clare (isl.), Ireland 10/A4
Clare (isls.), Ireland 17/A4
Clare (riv.), Ireland 17/D5
Clare (co.), Mich. 250/E5
Clare, Mich. 250/E5
Clare, N.S. Wales 97/B3
Clare, S. Australia 94/F5
Claregalway, Ireland 17/D5
Claremont, Calif. 204/D10
Claremont, Ill. 222/F5
Claremont, Jamaica 158/J6
Claremont, Minn. 255/E6
Claremont, N.H. 268/C5
Claremont, N.C. 281/G3
Claremont, S. Dak. 298/N2
Claremont, Va. 307/P6
Claremore, Okla. 288/R2
Claremorris, Ireland 17/C4
Claremorris, Ireland 10/B4
Clarence (str.), Alaska 196/N2
Clarence (isl.), Chile 120/B8
Clarence (isl.), Chile 138/E10
Clarence, Iowa 229/M5
Clarence, La. 238/E3
Clarence, Mo. 261/H3
Clarence (riv.), N.S. Wales 88/J5
Clarence (riv.), N.S. Wales 97/G1
Clarence•, N.Y. 276/C5
Clarence (riv.), N. Zealand 100/E5
Clarence (str.), North. Terr. 88/E2
Clarence (str.), North. Terr. 93/B2
Clarence (cape), N.W.T. 187/K2
Clarence (head), N.W.T. 187/L2
Clarence, Pa. 294/G3
Clarence Bridge, N. Zealand 100/E5
Clarence Creek, Ontario 177/J2
Clarenceville, Québec 172/D4
Clarendon, Ark. 202/H4
Clarendon, New Bruns. 170/D3
Clarendon, N.C. 281/M6
Clarendon (lake), Ontario 177/G3
Clarendon, Pa. 294/D2
Clarendon (co.), S.C. 296/G4
Clarendon, Texas 303/C3
Clarendon•, Vt. 268/A4
Clarendon Hills, Ill. 222/B6
Clarens, Switzerland 39/C4
Clarenville, Newf. 166/C2
Claresholm, Alberta 182/D4
Clariden (mt.), Switzerland 39/G3
Clarie Coast (reg.), Ant. 5/C7
Clarinda, Iowa 229/C7
Clarines, Venezuela 124/F3
Clarington, Ohio 284/J6
Clarington, Pa. 294/D3
Clarion, Iowa 229/F3
Clarión (isl.), Mexico 150/B7
Clarion, Mich. 250/E3
Clarion (co.), Pa. 294/D3
Clarion, Pa. 294/D3
Clarion (riv.), Pa. 294/D3
Clarion River, East Branch (lake), Pa. 294/E2
Clarissa, Minn. 255/C4
Clarita, Okla. 288/O6
Clark (lake), Alaska 196/H2
Clark (co.), Ark. 202/D5
Clark, Colo. 208/F1
Clark (co.), Idaho 220/F5
Clark (co.), Ill. 222/F4
Clark (co.), Ind. 227/F8
Clark (co.), Kansas 232/C4
Clark (co.), Ky. 237/N4
Clark (co.), Mo. 261/J2
Clark, Mo. 261/H4
Clark (co.), Nev. 266/F6
Clark•, N.J. 273/A3
Clark, N.C. 281/P4
Clark (buttes), N. Dak. 282/G7
Clark (co.), Ohio 284/C6
Clark, Ohio 284/G5
Clark (pt.), Ontario 177/C3
Clark, Pa. 294/B3
Clark (co.), S. Dak. 298/O4
Clark, S. Dak. 298/O4
Clark (co.), Wash. 310/C5
Clark (co.), Wis. 317/E6
Clark, Wyo. 319/C1
Clark Canyon (res.), Mont. 262/D6
Clark Center, Ill. 222/F4
Clarkdale, Ariz. 198/C4
Clarke (co.), Ala. 195/C7
Clarke (co.), Ga. 217/F3
Clarke (co.), Iowa 229/F6
Clarke (co.), Miss. 256/G6
Clarke (range), Queensland 95/C4
Clarke (isl.), Tasmania 99/E2
Clarke (co.), Va. 307/M2
Clarke City, Québec 174/D2
Clarkedale, Ark. 202/K3
Clarke's Beach, Newf. 166/D2
Clarkesville, Ga. 217/F1
Clarkfield, Minn. 255/C6
Clark Fork, Idaho 220/B1
Clark Fork (riv.), Mont. 188/D1
Clark Fork (riv.), Mont. 262/A3
Clarkia, Idaho 220/B2
Clark Island, Maine 243/E8
Clarklake, Mich. 250/E6
Clarkrange, Tenn. 237/L8
Clarks, East Fork (riv.), Ky. 237/E7
Clarks, La. 238/F2
Clarks, Nebr. 264/G3
Clarksboro, N.J. 273/C4
Clarksburg, Calif. 204/B9
Clarksburg, Ind. 227/G6
Clarksburg, Md. 245/J4
Clarksburg, Mo. 261/G5
Clarksburg, N.J. 273/E3
Clarksburg, Ohio 284/D7
Clarksburg, Ontario 177/D3
Clarksburg, Tenn. 237/E9
Clarksburg, W. Va. 188/K3
Clarksburg, W. Va. 312/F4
Clarks Corner, Conn. 210/G1
Clarksdale, Miss. 188/J4
Clarksdale, Miss. 256/D2
Clarksdale, Mo. 261/D3
Clarks Falls, Conn. 210/H3
Clarks Fork, Yellowstone (riv.), Mont. 262/G6
Clarks Fork (riv.), Wyo. 319/C1
Clarks Green, Pa. 294/F6
Clarks Grove, Minn. 255/E7
Clark's Harbour, Nova Scotia 168/C5
Clarks Hill, Ind. 227/D4
Clarks Hill, S.C. 296/C4
Clarks Mill, Maine 243/B8
Clarks Mills, Pa. 294/B3
Clarkson, Ky. 237/J6
Clarkson, Miss. 256/F3
Clarkson, Nebr. 264/G3
Clarkson, N.Y. 276/E4
Clarkson Valley, Mo. 261/N3
Clarks Point, Alaska 196/G3
Clarks Summit, Pa. 294/F6
Clarkston, Ga. 217/L1
Clarkston, Mich. 250/F6
Clarkston, Scotland 15/B2
Clarkston, Utah 304/B2
Clarkston, Wash. 310/H4
Clark's Town, Jamaica 158/H6
Clarksville, Ark. 202/D3
Clarksville, Del. 245/T6
Clarksville, Fla. 212/D6
Clarksville, Ind. 227/F8
Clarksville, Iowa 229/H3
Clarksville, Md. 245/L4
Clarksville, Mich. 250/D6
Clarksville, Mo. 261/K4
Clarksville•, N.H. 268/E1
Clarksville, N.Y. 276/M5
Clarksville, Ohio 284/C7
Clarksville (Clark), Pa. 294/B3
Clarksville, Pa. 294/B6
Clarksville, Tenn. 188/J3
Clarksville, Tenn. 237/G7
Clarksville, Texas 303/K4
Clarksville, Va. 307/L7
Clarkton, Mo. 261/M10
Clarkton, N.C. 281/M6
Clarno, Wis. 317/G10
Claro (riv.), Bolivia 136/A3
Claro (riv.), Brazil 132/D7
Claro (riv.), Chile 138/G5
Claro, Switzerland 39/G4
Clashmoor, Sask. 181/H3
Clashmore, Ireland 17/F8
Clatonia, Nebr. 264/H4
Clatskanie, Oreg. 291/D1
Clatsop (co.), Oreg. 291/D1
Claud, Ala. 195/F5
Claude, Texas 303/C2
Claudell, Kansas 232/C2
Claudville, Va. 307/H7
Claudy, N. Ireland 17/G2
Claunch, N. Mex. 274/C4
Claussen, S.C. 296/H3
Clausthal-Zellerfeld, Germany 22/D3
Claverack-Red Mills, N.Y. 276/N6
Claveria, Philippines 82/C1
Clavet, Sask. 181/E4
Clawson, Mich. 250/B6
Clawson, Utah 304/C4
Claxton, Ga. 217/J6
Clay (co.), Ala. 195/G4
Clay (co.), Ark. 202/K1
Clay, Calif. 204/C9
Clay (creek), Colo. 208/O7
Clay (co.), Fla. 212/E2
Clay (co.), Ga. 217/B7
Clay (co.), Ill. 222/E5
Clay (co.), Ind. 227/C6
Clay (co.), Iowa 229/C2
Clay (co.), Kansas 232/E2
Clay (co.), Ky. 237/O6
Clay, Ky. 237/F6
Clay, La. 238/E2
Clay (co.), Minn. 255/B4
Clay (co.), Miss. 256/G3
Clay (co.), Mo. 261/D4
Clay (co.), Nebr. 264/F4
Clay (co.), N.C. 281/B4
Clay (co.), S. Dak. 298/P8
Clay (co.), Tenn. 237/K7
Clay (co.), Texas 303/F4
Clay (hills), Utah 304/D6
Clay (co.), W. Va. 312/D6
Clay, W. Va. 312/D6
Claybank, Sask. 181/F5
Clay Bank, Va. 307/P6
Clay Center, Kansas 232/E2
Clay Center, Nebr. 264/F4
Clay Center, Ohio 284/D2
Clay City, Ill. 222/E5
Clay City, Ind. 227/C6
Clay City, Ky. 237/O5
Claycomo, Mo. 261/P5
Clay Cross, England 13/J2
Claydon, Sask. 181/B6
Clayhatchee, Ala. 195/G8
Claymont, Del. 245/S1
Claymour, Ky. 237/G7
Clayoquot (sound), Br. Col. 184/D5
Claypool, Ariz. 198/E5
Claypool, Ind. 227/F2
Claypool, Ky. 237/J7
Claysburg, Pa. 294/F5
Clay Springs, Ariz. 198/E4
Claysville, Ohio 284/G6
Claysville, Pa. 294/B5
Clayton, Ala. 195/G7
Clayton, Calif. 204/K2
Clayton, Del. 245/R3
Clayton (co.), Ga. 217/D3
Clayton, Ga. 217/F1
Clayton, Idaho 220/D5
Clayton, Ill. 222/B3
Clayton, Ind. 227/D5
Clayton (co.), Iowa 229/L3
Clayton, Iowa 229/L3
Clayton, Kansas 232/B2
Clayton, La. 238/H3
Clayton (lake), Maine 243/D2
Clayton, Mich. 250/E7
Clayton, Miss. 256/D1
Clayton, Mo. 261/P3
Clayton, N.J. 273/C4
Clayton, N. Mex. 274/F2
Clayton, N.Y. 276/H2
Clayton, N.C. 281/N3
Clayton, Ohio 284/B6
Clayton, Okla. 288/R5
Clayton, S. Dak. 298/O7
Clayton, Victoria 97/J5
Clayton, Wash. 310/H3
Clayton, W. Va. 312/E7
Clayton, Wis. 317/B5
Clayton Lake, Maine 243/E2
Claytonville, Ill. 222/F3
Claytor (lake), Va. 307/G6
Clayville, N.Y. 276/K5
Clayville, R.I. 249/H5
Clayville, S. Africa 118/H6
Clayville, Va. 307/N6
Clear, Alaska 196/J2
Clear (cape), Alaska 196/D1
Clear (hills), Alberta 182/A1
Clear (creek), Ariz. 198/D4
Clear (lake), Calif. 188/B3
Clear (lake), Calif. 204/C4
Clear (lake), Iowa 229/G2
Clear (cape), Ireland 7/C3
Clear (cape), Ireland 17/B9
Clear (cape), Ireland 10/B5
Clear (isl.), Ireland 17/C9
Clear (lake), La. 238/D3
Clear (lake), Manitoba 179/C4
Clear (lake), Ontario 177/F3
Clear (lake), Ontario 177/G2
Clear (creek), Utah 304/B2
Clear (lake), Utah 304/B4
Clear (creek), Wyo. 319/F1
Clear Boggy (creek), Okla. 288/O6
Clearbrook, Br. Col. 184/L3
Clearbrook, Minn. 255/C3
Clear Brook, Va. 307/M2
Clear Creek, Calif. 204/B2
Clear Creek (co.), Colo. 208/H3
Clear Creek, Ind. 227/E6
Clearcreek, Utah 304/C4
Clear Creek, W. Va. 312/D7
Clearfield, Iowa 229/D7
Clearfield, Ky. 237/P4
Clearfield (co.), Pa. 294/F3
Clearfield, Pa. 294/F3
Clearfield, S. Dak. 298/K7
Clearfield, Utah 304/B2
Clear Fork (res.), Ohio 284/E4
Clear Fork, Mohican (riv.), Ohio 284/F4
Clear Fork, Brazos (riv.), Texas 303/D5
Clear Fork, Guyandotte (riv.), W. Va. 312/C7
Clear Hills, Alberta 182/B1
Clearlake, Calif. 204/C5
Clear Lake (res.), Calif. 204/D2
Clear Lake, Ind. 227/H1
Clear Lake, Iowa 229/G2
Clear Lake, La. 238/E3
Clear Lake, Minn. 255/E5
Clear Lake, S. Dak. 298/R4
Clearlake, Wash. 310/C2
Clear Lake, Wis. 317/B5
Clearlake Oaks, Calif. 204/C4
Clear Lake Shores, Texas 303/K2
Clearmont, Mo. 261/C1
Clearmont, Wyo. 319/F1
Clear Ridge, Pa. 294/F5
Clear Spring, Ind. 227/E7
Clear Spring, Md. 245/G2
Clearview, Okla. 288/O4
Clearview, W. Va. 312/E2
Clearview City, Kansas 232/G3
Clearville, Pa. 294/F6
Clearwater (riv.), Alberta 182/C4
Clearwater (riv.), Alberta 182/E1
Clearwater, Br. Col. 184/G4
Clearwater (lake), Br. Col. 184/G4
Clearwater (riv.), Br. Col. 184/G4
Clearwater, Fla. 188/K5
Clearwater, Fla. 212/B2
Clearwater (co.), Idaho 220/C3
Clearwater, Idaho 220/C3
Clearwater (mts.), Idaho 220/C3
Clearwater (riv.), Idaho 220/B3
Clearwater, Kansas 232/E4
Clearwater, Manitoba 179/D5
Clearwater (co.), Minn. 255/C3
Clearwater, Minn. 255/D5
Clearwater (riv.), Minn. 255/C3
Clearwater (lake), Mo. 261/L8
Clearwater, Nebr. 264/F2
Clearwater (brook), New Bruns. 170/D2
Clearwater (riv.), Sask. 181/L3
Clearwater, S.C. 296/D4
Clearwater, Wash. 310/A3
Clearwater Beach (isl.), Fla. 212/B2
Clearwater Lake, Manitoba 179/H3
Clearwater Lake, Wis. 317/H4
Clearwater Lake Beach, Sask. 181/D5
Clearwater Lake Prov. Park, Manitoba 179/H3
Cleator Moor, England 13/D3
Cleburne (co.), Ala. 195/G3
Cleburne (co.), Ark. 202/F2
Cleburne, Texas 188/G4
Cleburne, Texas 303/G5
Cle Elum, Wash. 310/E3
Cle Elum (lake), Wash. 310/E3
Cleethorpes, England 13/H4
Cleethorpes, England 10/F4
Cleeves, Sask. 181/C2
Cleghorn, Iowa 229/B3
Cleghorn, Wis. 317/C6
Clem, Ga. 217/B3
Clemenceau, Ariz. 198/C4
Clemenceau, Sask. 181/J3
Clément, Fr. Guiana 131/E4
Clemente (isl.), Chile 138/D6
Clementon, N.J. 273/D4
Clements, Calif. 204/C9
Clements, Kansas 232/F3
Clements, Md. 245/L7
Clements, Minn. 255/D6
Clementson, Minn. 255/D2
Clementsport, Nova Scotia 168/C4
Clementsvale, Nova Scotia 168/C4
Clementsville, N. Dak. 282/O5
Clemmons, N.C. 281/J2
Clemons, Iowa 229/G4
Clemscot, Okla. 288/L6
Clemson, S.C. 296/B2
Clendenin, W. Va. 312/D5
Clendening (lake), Ohio 284/H5
Cleopatra Needle (mt.), Philippines 82/B5
Cleora, Okla. 288/S1
Cleo Springs, Okla. 288/K2
Clerf (riv.), Luxembourg 27/J8
Clermont, Fla. 212/E3
Clermont, France 28/E3
Clermont, Ga. 217/E2
Clermont, Iowa 229/K3
Clermont, Ky. 237/K5
Clermont, N.Y. 276/N6
Clermont (co.), Ohio 284/B7
Clermont, Pa. 294/E2
Clermont, Québec 172/G2
Clermont, Queensland 88/H4
Clermont, Queensland 95/C4
Clermont-Ferrand, France 7/E4
Clermont-Ferrand, France 28/E5
Clermont Harbor, Miss. 256/F10
Clervaux, Luxembourg 27/J8
Cleve, S. Australia 88/F6
Cleve, S. Australia 94/E5
Clevedon, England 13/D6
Cleveland, Ala. 195/E3
Cleveland (co.), Ark. 202/F6
Cleveland, Ark. 202/E3
Cleveland (co.), England 13/F3
Cleveland (hills), England 13/F3
Cleveland, Fla. 212/E5
Cleveland, Ga. 217/E1
Cleveland, Minn. 255/E6
Cleveland, Miss. 256/C3
Cleveland, Mo. 261/C5
Cleveland, Mont. 262/G2
Cleveland, N. Mex. 274/D2
Cleveland, N.Y. 276/J4
Cleveland (co.), N.C. 281/F4
Cleveland, N.C. 281/H3
Cleveland, N. Dak. 282/M6
Cleveland, Ohio 188/K2
Cleveland, Ohio 284/H9
Cleveland, Ohio 146/K5
Cleveland (co.), Okla. 288/M4
Cleveland, Okla. 288/O2
Cleveland, S.C. 296/C1
Cleveland, Tenn. 237/M10
Cleveland, Texas 303/K7
Cleveland, Utah 304/D4
Cleveland, Va. 307/D7
Cleveland, W. Va. 312/F5
Cleveland, Wis. 317/L8
Cleveland Heights, Ohio 284/H9
Cleveland-Hopkins Mun. Airport, Ohio 284/G9
Clevelândia do Norte, Brazil 132/D2
Cleveland Park, D.C. 245/E4
Clever, Mo. 261/F8
Cleves, Iowa 229/G4
Cleves, Ohio 284/B9
Clew (bay), Ireland 17/B4
Clew (bay), Ireland 10/B4
Clewiston, Fla. 212/E5
Clichy, France 28/B1
Clicquot-Millis, Mass. 249/A8
Clifden, Ireland 10/B4
Clifden, Ireland 17/B5
Cliff, N. Mex. 274/A6
Cliff (cape), Nova Scotia 168/E3
Cliff (creek), Utah 304/E3
Cliffdell, Wash. 310/E4
Clifford, Ind. 227/F6
Clifford, Ky. 237/S4
Clifford (lake), Maine 243/H5
Clifford, Mich. 250/F5
Clifford, N. Dak. 282/R5
Clifford, Ontario 177/D4
Clifford, Pa. 294/L2
Clifford, Va. 307/K5
Clifford, Wis. 317/F4
Cliffordvale, New Bruns. 170/C2
Cliffside, N.C. 281/F4
Cliffside Park, N.J. 273/C2
Clifftop, W. Va. 312/E6
Cliffwood, N.J. 273/E3
Clifton, Ariz. 198/F5
Clifton, Colo. 208/C4
Clifton, Idaho 220/F7
Clifton, Ill. 222/F3
Clifton, Kansas 232/E2
Clifton, La. 238/K5
Clifton•, Maine 243/G6
Clifton, New Bruns. 170/E1
Clifton, N.J. 273/B2
Clifton, S.C. 296/D2
Clifton, Tenn. 237/F10
Clifton, Texas 303/G6
Clifton, W. Va. 312/B5
Clifton, Wis. 317/F8
Clifton City, Mo. 261/G5
Clifton Dartmouth Hardness, England 10/E5
Clifton Dartmouth Hardness, England 13/D7
Clifton Forge (I.C.), Va. 307/J5
Clifton Heights, Pa. 294/M7
Clifton Hill, Mo. 261/G4
Clifton Hills, S. Australia 94/F2
Clifton Mills, W. Va. 312/G3
Clifton Park•, N.Y. 276/N5
Clifton Springs, N.Y. 276/F4
Cliftonville, Miss. 256/H4
Clifty, Ark. 202/C1
Clifty (creek), Ind. 227/F6
Clifty, Ky. 237/G7
Clifty, Tenn. 237/L9
Clifty, W. Va. 312/E6
Climax, Colo. 208/G4
Climax, Ga. 217/D9
Climax, Kansas 232/F4
Climax, Ky. 237/N6
Climax, Mich. 250/D6
Climax, Minn. 255/B3
Climax, N.C. 281/K3
Climax, Sask. 181/C6
Climax Springs, Mo. 261/G6
Climbing Hill, Iowa 229/B4
Clinch (co.), Ga. 217/G9
Clinch (riv.), Tenn. 237/N9
Clinch (riv.), Va. 307/C7
Clinchburg, Va. 307/E7
Clinchco, Va. 307/D6
Clinchfield, Ga. 217/E6
Clinchmore, Tenn. 237/N8
Clinchport, Va. 307/C7
Cline Settlement, Alberta 182/B3
Clingmans Dome (mt.), N.C. 281/C3
Clingmans Dome (mt.), Tenn. 237/P10
Clint, Texas 303/B10
Clinton, Ala. 195/C5
Clinton, Ark. 202/F2
Clinton, Br. Col. 184/G4
Clinton, Conn. 210/E3
Clinton•, Conn. 210/E3
Clinton (co.), Ill. 222/D5
Clinton, Ill. 222/E3
Clinton (co.), Ind. 227/E4
Clinton, Ind. 227/C5
Clinton (co.), Iowa 229/M5
Clinton, Iowa 188/J2
Clinton, Iowa 229/N5
Clinton (co.), Ky. 237/L7
Clinton, Ky. 237/D7
Clinton, La. 238/J5
Clinton, Maine 243/D6
Clinton•, Maine 243/D6
Clinton, Md. 245/G6
Clinton•, Mass. 249/H3
Clinton (co.), Mich. 250/E6
Clinton, Mich. 250/F6
Clinton, Minn. 255/B5
Clinton, Miss. 256/D6
Clinton (co.), Mo. 261/D3
Clinton, Mo. 261/E6
Clinton, Mont. 262/C4
Clinton, Nebr. 264/B2
Clinton, N.J. 273/D2
Clinton (res.), N.J. 273/E1
Clinton (co.), N.Y. 276/N1
Clinton, N.Y. 276/K4
Clinton, N. Zealand 100/B7
Clinton, N.C. 281/N5
Clinton (co.), Ohio 284/C7
Clinton, Ohio 284/G4
Clinton, Okla. 288/H3
Clinton, Ontario 177/C4
Clinton (co.), Pa. 294/G3
Clinton, Pa. 294/B5
Clinton, S.C. 296/D3
Clinton, Tenn. 237/N8
Clinton, Wash. 310/C3
Clinton, W. Va. 312/E2
Clinton, Wis. 317/J10
Clinton-Colden (lake), N.W.T. 187/H3
Clinton Corners, N.Y. 276/N7

Coutts 355

Coolaney, Ireland 17/D3
Coolatai, N.S. Wales 97/F1
Cooleemee, N.C. 281/H3
Coolgardie, W. Australia 88/C6
Coolgardie, W. Australia 92/C5
Coolgreany, Ireland 17/J6
Coolibah, North. Terr. 93/B3
Coolidge, Ariz. 198/D6
Coolidge (dam), Ariz. 198/E5
Coolidge, Ga. 217/E8
Coolidge, Kansas 232/A3
Coolidge, Texas 303/H6
Coolidge Dam, Ariz. 198/E5
Coolin, Idaho 220/B1
Cool Spring, Del. 245/T6
Cool Valley, Mo. 261/P2
Coolville, Ohio 284/G7
Cooma, N.S. Wales 88/H7
Cooma, N.S. Wales 97/E5
Coombs, Br. Col. 184/H3
Coonabarabran, N.S. Wales 97/E2
Coonamble, N.S. Wales 88/H6
Coonamble, N.S. Wales 97/E2
Coondapoor, India 68/C6
Coon Rapids, Iowa 229/D5
Coon Rapids, Minn. 255/G5
Coon Valley, Wis. 317/E8
Cooper, Ala. 195/E5
Cooper (pt.), Calif. 204/D7
Cooper, Iowa 229/E5
Cooper, Ky. 237/M7
Cooper, Maine 243/H6
Cooper•, Maine 243/H6
Cooper (co.), Mo. 261/G5
Cooper (riv.), N.J. 273/B3
Cooper, S.C. 296/H4
Cooper (riv.), S.C. 296/H6
Cooper, Texas 303/J4
Cooper (lake), Wyo. 319/G4
Co-Operative, Ky. 237/M7
Cooper City, Fla. 212/B4
Cooperdale, Ohio 284/F5
Cooper Landing, Alaska 196/C1
Coopers (Barcoo) (creek), Queensland 95/B5
Coopers (Barcoo) (creek), S. Australia 88/G5
Coopers (Barcoo) (creek), S. Australia 94/F3
Coopersburg, Pa. 294/M5
Coopers Mills, Maine 243/E7
Coopers Plains, N.Y. 276/F6
Coopers Plains, Queensland 95/D3
Coopers Plains, Queensland 88/K3
Cooperstown, N.Y. 276/L5
Cooperstown, N. Dak. 282/O5
Cooperstown, Pa. 294/C2
Coopersville, Ky. 237/M7
Coopersville, Mich. 250/C5
Cooperton, Okla. 288/J5
Coorabie, S. Australia 88/E6
Coorabie, S. Australia 94/B4
Coorong, The (lag.), S. Australia 94/F6
Coorow, W. Australia 92/B5
Coos (co.), N.H. 268/E2
Coos (co.), Oreg. 291/C4
Coos (riv.), Oreg. 291/D4
Coosa (co.), Ala. 195/F5
Coosa (riv.), Ala. 195/F4
Coosa, Ga. 217/B2
Coosa (riv.), Ga. 217/A2
Coosada, Ala. 195/F5
Coosaw (riv.), S.C. 296/G7
Coosawattee (riv.), Ga. 217/C1
Coosawhatchie, S.C. 296/F6
Coosawhatchie (riv.), S.C. 296/E6
Coos Bay, Oreg. 188/A2
Coos Bay, Oreg. 291/C4
Cootamundra, N.S. Wales 88/H6
Cootamundra, N.S. Wales 97/D4
Cootehill, Ireland 17/G3
Cootehill, Ireland 10/C3
Cooter, Mo. 261/N10
Copacabana, Argentina 143/C2
Copacabana, Bolivia 136/A5
Copake, N.Y. 276/N6
Copake Falls, N.Y. 276/N6
Copala, Mexico 150/K8
Copalis Beach, Wash. 310/A3
Copalis Crossing, Wash. 310/B3
Copan, Okla. 288/P1
Copano (bay), Texas 303/G9
Copco (lake), Calif. 204/C2
Cope, Colo. 208/O3
Cope, Ind. 227/E6
Cope, S.C. 296/E5
Cope (cape), Spain 33/F4
Copeland, Ala. 195/B7
Copeland, Fla. 212/E6
Copeland, Idaho 220/B1
Copeland, Kansas 232/B4
Copeland (isl.), N. Ireland 17/K2
Copemish, Mich. 250/D4
Copen, W. Va. 312/E5
Copenhagen (commune), Denmark 21/F6
Copenhagen (cap.), Denmark 7/F3
Copenhagen (cap.), Denmark 21/F6
Copenhagen (cap.), Denmark 18/G9
Copenhagen, N.Y. 276/J3
Copere, Bolivia 136/D6
Copiague, N.Y. 276/O9
Copiah (co.), Miss. 256/D7
Copiapó, Chile 120/B5
Copiapó, Chile 138/B6
Copiapó (bay), Chile 138/A6
Copiapó (riv.), Chile 138/A6
Copinsay (isl.), Scotland 15/F2
Coplay, Pa. 294/L4
Copley, S. Australia 94/F4
Copmanhurst, N.S. Wales 97/G1
Coporito, Venezuela 124/H3
Coporolo (riv.), Angola 115/B6
Coppell, Texas 303/G2
Coppename (riv.), Suriname 131/C3
Copper (riv.), Alaska 196/J2
Copper (mts.), Ariz. 198/B6
Copperas Cove, Texas 303/G6
Copper Canyon, Texas 303/F1
Copper Center, Alaska 196/J2
Copper City, Mich. 250/A1
Copperfield, W. Australia 88/C5
Copperfield, W. Australia 92/B5
Copper Harbor, Mich. 250/B1
Copperhill, Tenn. 237/N10
Copper Hill, Va. 307/H6
Coppermine, Canada 4/C15
Coppermine, N.W.T. 162/E2
Coppermine (riv.), N.W.T. 162/E2
Coppermine (riv.), N.W.T. 187/G3
Coppermine, N.W.T. 187/G3
Copper Mountain, Br. Col. 184/G5
Copperton, Utah 304/B3
Copper Valley, Va. 307/G7
Coppet, Switzerland 39/B4
Coppock, Iowa 229/K6
Coqên, China 77/C5
Coquet (riv.), England 13/F2
Coquí, P. Rico 161/D3
Coquille, Oreg. 291/C4
Coquille (pt.), Oreg. 291/C4
Coquimatlán, Mexico 150/G7
Coquimbo (reg.), Chile 138/A8
Coquimbo, Chile 120/B6
Coquimbo, Chile 138/A8
Coquitlam, Br. Col. 184/K3
Cora, Ill. 222/D6
Cora, Wyo. 319/C3
Corabia, Romania 45/G4
Coracora, Peru 128/F10
Corail, Haiti 158/A6
Coraki, N.S. Wales 97/G1
Coral (sea) 87/F7
Coral (sea) 88/H2
Coral (sea) 2/S6
Coral, Mich. 250/D5
Coral (sea), New Caled. 86/G4
Coral (sea), Papua N.G. 85/B7
Coral, Pa. 294/D5
Coral (bay), Philippines 82/A6
Coral (sea), Queensland 95/C1
Coral (bay), Virgin Is. (U.S.) 161/C4
Coral Cove, Fla. 212/D4
Coral Gables, Fla. 212/B5
Coral Harbour, N.W.T. 162/H2
Coral Harbour, N.W.T. 187/K3
Coral Hills, Md. 245/G5
Coral Sea Islands (terr.), Australia 87/E7
CORAL SEA ISLANDS TERR. 95/C2
Coral Sea Islands Territory, Australia 88/J3
Coral Springs, Fla. 212/F5
Coralville, Iowa 229/K5
Coralville (lake), Iowa 229/K5
Coram, Mont. 262/C2
Coramba, N.S. Wales 97/G2
Corangamite (lake), Victoria 97/B6
Corantijn (riv.), Suriname 131/C3
Coraopolis, Pa. 294/B4
Corapeake, N.C. 281/R1
Corato, Italy 34/F4
Corbeil, Ontario 177/E1
Corberrie, Nova Scotia 168/C4
Corbigny, France 28/E4
Corbin, Kansas 232/E4
Corbin, Ky. 237/N7
Corbin City, N.J. 273/D5
Corbridge, England 13/E3
Corby, England 13/G5
Corcelles-près-Payerne, Switzerland 39/C3
Corcoran, Calif. 204/F7
Corcoran, Minn. 255/F5
Corcovado (gulf), Chile 120/B7
Corcovado (gulf), Chile 138/D4
Corcovado (vol.), Chile 138/D5
Corcubión, Spain 33/B1
Cord, Ark. 202/H2
Cordaville, Mass. 249/H3
Cordele, Ga. 217/E7
Cordelia, Calif. 204/K1
Cordell, Okla. 288/H4
Cordell Hull (res.), Tenn. 237/K8
Corder, Mo. 261/E4
Cordesville, S.C. 296/H5
Cordillera, Paraguay 144/D4
Cordillo Grounds, S. Australia 94/G2
Córdoba (prov.), Argentina 143/D3
Córdoba, Argentina 2/F7
Córdoba, Argentina 143/D3
Córdoba, Argentina 120/C6
Córdoba (dept.), Colombia 126/C3
Córdoba, Mexico 150/P2
Córdoba (prov.), Spain 33/D3
Córdoba, Spain 33/D4
Córdoba, Spain 7/D5
Cordobés (riv.), Uruguay 145/D3
Cordova, Ala. 195/D3
Cordova, Alaska 196/D1
Cordova, Alaska 188/D6
Cordova, Alaska 146/D3
Cordova (bay), Alaska 196/M2
Cordova, Ill. 222/C2
Cordova, Manitoba 179/C4
Cordova, Md. 245/O5
Cordova, Nebr. 264/G4
Cordova, N. Mex. 274/D2
Córdova, Peru 128/E10
Cordova, S.C. 296/F5
Cordova, Tenn. 237/B10
Cordova, U.S. 4/C17
Cordova Mines, Ontario 177/G3
Core (banks), N.C. 281/S5
Core (sound), N.C. 281/S5
Core, W. Va. 312/F3
Corea, Maine 243/H7
Coredó (Humboldt) (bay), Colombia 126/B4
Coree South, N.S. Wales 97/C4
Corella, Spain 33/F1
Corey, La. 238/F2
Corfield, Queensland 88/G4
Corfield, Queensland 95/B4
Corfu (Kérkira) (isl.), Greece 45/D6
Corfu, N.Y. 276/D5
Corgémont, Switzerland 39/D2
Cori, Italy 34/F7
Coria, Spain 33/C3
Coria del Río, Spain 33/C4
Corigliano Calabro, Italy 34/F5
Corinda, Queensland 88/K3
Corinda, Queensland 95/A3
Corinda, Queensland 95/D3
Coringa (islets), Australia 87/F7
Coringa (isls.), Coral Sea Is. Terr. 88/H3
Corinna•, Maine 243/E6
Corinne, Okla. 288/R6
Corinne, Sask. 181/G5
Corinne, Utah 304/B2
Corinne, W. Va. 312/D7
Corinth, Ark. 202/C3
Corinth, Ga. 217/B4
Corinth, Greece 45/F7
Corinth (gulf), Greece 45/F6
Corinth, Ky. 237/M3
Corinth, Miss. 256/G1
Corinth, N.Y. 276/N4
Corinth, N. Dak. 282/D2
Corinth•, Vt. 268/C3
Corinth, W. Va. 312/H4
Corinto, Brazil 132/E7
Corinto, Colombia 126/B6
Corinto, Nicaragua 154/D4
Coriole, Somalia 115/H3
Coripata, Bolivia 136/B5
Corisco (isl.), Equat. Guinea 115/A3
Cork (co.), Ireland 17/D7
Cork, Ireland 7/D3
Cork, Ireland 10/B5
Cork, Ireland 17/E8
Cork (harb.), Ireland 17/E8
Cork (harb.), Ireland 10/B5
Cork, New Bruns. 170/D3
Corker (cay), Belize 154/D2
Corleone, Italy 34/D6
Corley, W. Va. 312/E5
Çorlu, Turkey 63/B2
Cormorant, Manitoba 179/H3
Cormorant (lake), Manitoba 179/H3
Cormorant, Minn. 255/B4
Corn (creek), Ariz. 198/E3
Corn, Okla. 288/J4
Cornaca, Bolivia 136/C7
Corncake (inlet), N.C. 281/O7
Cornelia, Ga. 217/E1
Cornélio Procópio, Brazil 132/D8
Cornelius, N.C. 281/H4
Cornelius, Oreg. 291/A2
Cornell, Ill. 222/E3
Cornell, Mich. 250/B3
Cornell, Wis. 317/D5
Corner (inlet), Victoria 97/D6
Corner Brook, Newf. 166/C4
Corner Brook, Newf. 162/K6
Cornerstone, Ark. 202/G5
Cornersville, Md. 245/O6
Cornersville, Miss. 256/F1
Cornersville, Tenn. 237/H10
Cornerville, Ark. 202/G6
Cornettes de Bise (mts.), Switzerland 39/C4
Cornfield (pt.), Conn. 210/F3
Cornfields, Ariz. 198/F3
Cornhill, New Bruns. 170/E3
Cornhill, Scotland 15/F3
Corning, Ark. 202/J1
Corning, Calif. 204/C4
Corning, Iowa 229/D7
Corning, Kansas 232/F2
Corning, Mo. 261/B2
Corning, N.Y. 276/F6
Corning, Ohio 284/F6
Corning, Sask. 181/J6
Cornish, Colo. 208/L2
Cornish•, Maine 243/B8
Cornish, Okla. 288/L6
Cornish, Utah 304/B2
Cornish Flat, N.H. 268/C4
Cornishville, Ky. 237/M5
Cornland, Ill. 222/D4
Cornlea, Nebr. 264/G3
Corno (mt.), Italy 34/D3
Cornucopia, Wis. 317/D2
Cornville, Ariz. 198/D4
Cornville•, Maine 243/D6
Cornwall•, Conn. 210/B1
Cornwall (co.), England 13/C7
Cornwall (cape), England 13/B7
Cornwall (isl.), N.W.T. 162/M3
Cornwall (isl.), N.W.T. 187/J2
Cornwall, Ont. 162/J7
Cornwall, Ontario 177/K2
Cornwall, Pa. 294/K5
Cornwall, Pr. Edward I. 168/E2
Cornwall, Tasmania 99/E3
Cornwall•, Vt. 268/A4
Cornwall Bridge, Conn. 210/B1
Cornwall Center, Conn. 210/B1
Cornwall Hollow, Conn. 210/B1
Cornwallis (isl.), N.W.T. 162/F1
Cornwallis (isl.), N.W.T. 187/J2
Cornwall On Hudson, N.Y. 276/M8
Cornwell, Fla. 212/E4
Coro, Venezuela 124/D2
Coro, Venezuela 120/C1
Coroatá, Brazil 132/F3
Corocoro, Bolivia 120/C4
Corocoro, Bolivia 136/A5
Corofin, Ireland 17/C6
Coroico, Bolivia 136/B5
Corolla, N.C. 281/T2
Coromandel, Brazil 132/E7
Coromandel, N. Zealand 100/E2
Coromandel (pen.), N. Zealand 100/F2
Coromandel (range), N. Zealand 100/E2
Coromandel Coast (reg.), India 68/E6
Coron, Philippines 82/C4
Coron (isl.), Philippines 82/C5
Corona, Ala. 195/C3
Corona, Calif. 204/E11
Corona, N. Mex. 274/D4
Corona, S. Dak. 298/R3
Coronaca, S.C. 296/C3
Coronach, Sask. 181/F6
Coronada (bay), C. Rica 154/F6
Coronado, Calif. 204/H11
Coronado (pt.), Philippines 82/C7
Coronado Nat'l Memorial, Ariz. 198/E7
Coronados (gulf), Chile 138/D4
Coronation (isl.), Alaska 196/M2
Coronation, Alberta 182/E3
Coronation (isl.), Ant. 5/C16
Coronation (gulf), N.W.T. 162/E2
Coronation (gulf), N.W.T. 187/G3
Coronda, Argentina 143/F6
Coronel, Chile 138/D1
Coronel, Chile 120/B6
Coronel Bogado, Argentina 143/F6
Coronel Bogado, Paraguay 144/D5
Coronel Brandsen, Argentina 143/H7
Coronel Dorrego, Argentina 143/D4
Coronel F. Cabrera, Bolivia 136/E6
Coronel F. Cabrera (mt.), Paraguay 144/B1
Coronel Martínez, Paraguay 144/B5
Coronel Moldes, Argentina 143/C2
Coronel Oviedo, Paraguay 144/C5
Coronel Pringles, Argentina 143/D4
Coronel Suárez, Argentina 143/D4
Coronel Vidal, Argentina 143/E4
Corongo, Peru 128/D7
Coronie (dist.), Suriname 131/C3
Coropuna, Nudo (mt.), Peru 128/F10
Cororooke, Victoria 97/B6
Çorovodë, Albania 45/E5
Corowa, N.S. Wales 97/D4
Corozal, Colombia 126/C3
Corozal, P. Rico 161/D1
Corozal Town, Belize 154/C1
Corozo Pando, Venezuela 124/E3
Corpach, Scotland 15/C4
Corpus Christi, Texas 188/G5
Corpus Christi, Texas 146/J7
Corpus Christi, Texas 303/G10
Corpus Christi (bay), Texas 188/G5
Corpus Christi (lake), Texas 303/F9
Corpus Christi N.A.S., Texas 303/G10
Corque, Bolivia 136/B6
Corquín, Honduras 154/C3
Corral, Chile 138/D3
Corral, Idaho 220/D6
Corral City, Texas 303/F1
Corral de Almaguer, Spain 33/E3
Corral de Bustos, Argentina 143/D3
Corrales, N. Mex. 274/C3
Corralillo, Cuba 158/D1
Corralitos, Calif. 204/L4
Corral Viejo, P. Rico 161/C2
Correct, Ind. 227/G7
Correctionville, Iowa 229/B4
Correggio, Italy 34/C2
Corregidor (isl.), Philippines 82/C3
Correll, Minn. 255/B5
Corrente, Brazil 132/E5
Corrente (riv.), Brazil 132/E6
Correntina, Brazil 132/E6
Corrèze (dept.), France 28/D5
Corrib (lake), Ireland 17/C5
Corrib, Lough (lake), Ireland 10/B4
Corridon, Mo. 261/L8
Corrie, Scotland 15/C5
Corrientes (prov.), Argentina 143/E2
Corrientes, Argentina 143/E2
Corrientes, Argentina 120/D5
Corrientes (riv.), Argentina 143/E2
Corrientes (cape), Colombia 120/B2
Corrientes (cape), Colombia 126/B5
Corrientes (cape), Cuba 158/A2
Corrientes (inlet), Cuba 158/A2
Corrientes (cape), Mexico 146/H7
Corrientes (cape), Mexico 150/F6
Corrientes (riv.), Peru 128/E4
Corrigan, Texas 303/K7
Corriganville, Md. 245/C2
Corrigin, W. Australia 92/B6
Corriverton, Guyana 131/C3
Corrumpa (creek), N. Mex. 274/F2
Corry, Pa. 294/C2
Corryong, Victoria 97/D5
Corryton, Tenn. 237/O8
Corse (cape), France 28/B6
Corse du Sud (dept.), France 28/B6
Corserine (mt.), Scotland 15/D5
Corsewall (pt.), Scotland 15/C5
Corsham, England 13/E6
Corsica (isl.), France 7/E4
Corsica (isl.), France 28/B6
Corsica, Pa. 294/D3
Corsica, S. Dak. 298/N7
Corsicana, Texas 188/G4
Corsicana, Texas 303/H5
Corso, Mo. 261/K4
Corson (inlet), N.J. 273/D5
Corson (co.), S. Dak. 298/G2
Corson, S. Dak. 298/R6
Cortaro, Ariz. 198/D6
Corte, France 28/B6
Corte Madera, Calif. 204/J2
Cortés, Cuba 158/A2
Cortés (isl), Cuba 158/B2
Cortez, Colo. 208/B8
Cortez, Fla. 212/D4
Cortez (mts.), Nev. 266/E2
Cortina d'Ampezzo, Italy 34/D1
Cortland, Ill. 222/E2
Cortland, Ind. 227/F7
Cortland, Nebr. 264/H4
Cortland (co.), N.Y. 276/H5
Cortland, N.Y. 276/H5
Cortland, Ohio 284/J3
Cortona, Italy 34/C3
Coruche, Portugal 33/B3
Çoruh (riv.), Turkey 59/D1
Çoruh (riv.), Turkey 63/J2
Çorum (prov.), Turkey 63/F2
Çorum, Turkey 59/B1
Çorum, Turkey 63/F2
Çorum (riv.), Turkey 63/F2
Corumbá, Brazil 120/D4
Corumbá, Brazil 132/B7
Corunna, Ind. 227/G2
Corunna, Mich. 250/E6
Corunna, Ontario 177/B5
Corvallis, Mont. 262/C4
Corvallis, Oreg. 188/B2
Corvallis, Oreg. 291/D3
Corvo (isl.), Portugal 33/A1
Corvuso, Minn. 255/D6
Corwen (delta), Wales 10/E4
Corwen, Wales 13/D5
Corwin, Kansas 232/D4
Corwin, Ohio 284/B6
Corwin Springs, Mont. 262/F5
Corwith, Iowa 229/F3
Cory, Ind. 227/C6
Corydon, Ind. 227/E8
Corydon, Iowa 229/G7
Corydon, Ky. 237/F5
Coryell (co.), Texas 303/G6
Coryville, Pa. 294/F2
Corzoneso, Switzerland 39/G4
Cosalá, Mexico 150/F4
Cosamaloapan de Carpio, Mexico 150/M7
Cosapa, Bolivia 136/A6
Cosautlán de Carvajal, Mexico 150/P1
Cosby, Mo. 261/C3
Cosby, Tenn. 237/P9
Cos Cob, Conn. 210/A4
Coscomatepec de Bravo, Mexico 150/P2
Cosegüina (pt.), Nicaragua 154/D4
Cosenza (prov.), Italy 34/F5
Cosenza, Italy 34/F5
Cosenza, Italy 7/F5
Coshocton (co.), Ohio 284/G5
Coshocton, Ohio 284/G5
Cosine, Sask. 181/A3
Cosío, Mexico 150/H5
Cosmoledo (isls.), Seychelles 102/G5
Cosmoledo (isls.), Seychelles 118/H1
Cosmo Newbery Aboriginal Res., W. Australia 88/C5
Cosmo Newbery Aboriginal Res., W. Australia 92/C5
Cosmopolis, Wash. 310/B4
Cosmos, Minn. 255/D6
Cosne-Cours-sur-Loire, France 28/E4
Cosperville, Ind. 227/F1
Cosquín, Argentina 143/D3
Cossonay, Switzerland 39/B3
Costa, W. Va. 312/C6
Costa Azul, Uruguay 145/E5
Costa Brava (reg.), Spain 33/H2
Costa da Caparica, Portugal 33/A1
Costa de Sola (Costa del Sol) (reg.), Spain 33/D4
Costa Mesa, Calif. 204/D11
Costa Rica 2/E5
Costa Rica 146/K8
COSTA RICA 154/E5
Costa Rica, Bolivia 136/A2
Costa Rica, Mexico 150/F4
Costa Smeralda (reg.), Italy 34/B4
Costa Verde (reg.), Italy 34/B5
Costello, Pa. 294/G2
Costessey, England 13/J5
Costești, Romania 45/G3
Costigan, Maine 243/F5
Costilla (co.), Colo. 208/J8
Costilla, N. Mex. 274/D2
Costilla (peak), N. Mex. 274/D2
Cosumnes (riv.), Calif. 204/C9
Coswig, Dresden, Germany 22/E3
Coswig, Halle, Germany 22/E3
Cotabato, Philippines 85/G4
Cotabato, Philippines 82/D7
Cotacajes (riv.), Bolivia 136/B5
Cotagaita, Bolivia 136/C7
Cotahuasi, Peru 128/F10
Cotati, Calif. 204/C5
Coteau, N. Dak. 282/F2
Coteau (hills), Sask. 181/D4
Coteau-du-Lac, Québec 172/C4
Coteau du Missouri (plain), N. Dak. 282/G3
Coteau-Landing, Québec 172/C4
Coteaux, Haiti 158/A6
Côte-d'Or (dept.), France 28/F4
Côte-d'Or (mts.), France 28/F4
Cotentin (pen.), France 28/C3
Côte-Saint-Luc, Québec 172/H4
Côtes de Fer, Haiti 158/B6
Côtes-du-Nord (dept.), France 28/B3
Cotesfield, Nebr. 264/F3
Cotija de la Paz, Mexico 150/H7
Cotile (lake), La. 238/E4
Coto, Argentina 143/D2
Cotoca, Bolivia 136/D5
Coto Laurel, P. Rico 161/C2
Cotonou, Benin 102/C4
Cotonou, Benin 106/E7
Cotopaxi, Colo. 208/H6
Cotopaxi (prov.), Ecuador 128/C3
Cotopaxi (mt.), Ecuador 128/C3
Cotswold (hills), England 13/E6
Cottage City, Md. 245/F4
Cottage Grove, Ala. 195/F5
Cottage Grove, Ind. 227/H5
Cottage Grove, Minn. 255/F6
Cottage Grove, Oreg. 291/D4
Cottage Grove (lake), Oreg. 291/E4
Cottage Grove, Tenn. 237/E8
Cottagehill, Fla. 212/B6
Cottage Hills, Ill. 222/B2
Cottageville, S.C. 296/G6
Cottageville, W. Va. 312/C5
Cottam, Ontario 177/B5
Cottbus, Germany 22/F3
Cotter, Ark. 202/E1
Cotter, Iowa 229/L6
Cottesloe, W. Australia 88/B2
Cottian Alps (range), France 28/G5
Cottian Alps (range), Italy 34/A2
Cottica, Suriname 131/D4
Cottica (riv.), Suriname 131/D3
Cottle, Ky. 237/P5
Cottle (co.), Texas 303/D3
Cottleville, Mo. 261/M2
Cotton, Ga. 217/D8
Cotton, Minn. 255/F3
Cotton (co.), Okla. 288/K6
Cottonburg, Ky. 237/N5
Cotton Center, Texas 303/C4
Cottondale, Ala. 195/D4
Cottondale, Fla. 212/D6
Cotton Ground, St. Kitts & Nevis 161/C11
Cotton Plant, Ark. 202/H3
Cottonport, La. 238/F5
Cottonton, Ala. 195/H6
Cottontown, Tenn. 237/H8
Cotton Valley, La. 238/D1
Cottonwood, Ala. 195/H8
Cottonwood, Ariz. 198/D4
Cottonwood (cliffs), Ariz. 198/B3
Cottonwood, Br. Col. 184/G3
Cottonwood, Calif. 204/C3
Cottonwood (creek), Calif. 204/C3
Cottonwood, Idaho 220/B3
Cottonwood (butte), Idaho 220/C4
Cottonwood (riv.), Kansas 232/F3
Cottonwood (co.), Minn. 255/C6
Cottonwood, Minn. 255/C6
Cottonwood (riv.), Minn. 255/C6
Cottonwood (creek), Mont. 262/E2
Cottonwood (creek), Oreg. 291/K4
Cottonwood, S. Dak. 298/F6
Cottonwood (creek), S. Dak. 298/E5
Cottonwood (lake), S. Dak. 298/M4
Cottonwood, Texas 303/D5
Cottonwood (creek), Utah 304/C4
Cottonwood (creek), Utah 304/E4
Cottonwood (creek), Wyo. 319/B4
Cottonwood Draw (dry riv.), Texas 303/C10
Cottonwood Falls, Kansas 232/F3
Cottonwood Wash (dry riv.), Ariz. 198/E4
Cottonwood Wash (creek), Utah 304/E6
Cotuí, Dom. Rep. 158/E5
Cotuit, Mass. 249/N6
Cotulla, Texas 303/E9
Couch, Mo. 261/K9
Couchiching (lake), Ontario 177/E3
Couchwood, La. 238/D1
Coudekerque-Branche, France 28/E2
Couderay, Wis. 317/D4
Coudersport, Pa. 294/G2
Coudres (isl.), Québec 172/G2
Cougar (res.), Oreg. 291/E3
Cougar, Wash. 310/C4
Coughlan, New Bruns. 170/E2
Coulee, N. Dak. 282/F2
Coulee City, Wash. 310/F3
Coulee Dam, Wash. 310/G3
Coulee Dam Nat'l Rec. Area, Wash. 310/G2
Coulihaut, Dominica 161/E6
Coulommiers, France 28/E3
Coulter, Iowa 229/G3
Coulter, Manitoba 179/B5
Coulterville, Calif. 204/E6
Coulterville, Ill. 222/D5
Counamama, Fr. Guiana 131/E3
Counce, Tenn. 237/E10
Council, Alaska 196/F2
Council, Ga. 217/G9
Council, Idaho 220/B5
Council, N.C. 281/M6
Council Bluffs, Iowa 229/B6
Council Bluffs, Iowa 188/G2
Council Grove, Kansas 232/F3
Council Grove (lake), Kansas 232/F3
Council Hill, Okla. 288/P3
Countess, Alberta 182/D4
Country (harb.), Nova Scotia 168/G3
Country Club Hills, Ill. 222/B6
Country Club Village, Mo. 261/C3
Country Harbour Mines, Nova Scotia 168/G3
Country Life Acres, Mo. 261/N3
Countryside, Ill. 222/B6
County Line, Ala. 195/E3
Countyline, Okla. 288/L6
Coupar Angus, Scotland 10/E2
Coupar Angus, Scotland 15/E4
Coupeville, Wash. 310/C2
Courantyne (riv.) 120/D2
Courantyne (riv.), Guyana 131/C3
Courbevoie, France 28/A1
Courcelles, Belgium 27/E8
Courcelles, Québec 172/G4
Courgenay, Switzerland 39/D2
Courmayeur, Italy 34/A2
Courrendlin, Switzerland 39/D2
Courroux, Switzerland 39/D2
Courtelary, Switzerland 39/C2
Courtenay, Br. Col. 162/D6
Courtenay, Br. Col. 184/E5
Courtenay, N. Dak. 282/N5
Courtételle, Switzerland 39/D2
Courtland, Ala. 195/D1
Courtland, Calif. 204/B9
Courtland, Kansas 232/E2
Courtland, Minn. 255/D6
Courtland, Miss. 256/E2
Courtland, Ontario 177/D5
Courtland, Va. 307/O7
Courtmacsherry, Ireland 17/D8
Courtmacsherry (bay), Ireland 17/D8
Courtney, Mo. 261/R5
Courtney, Okla. 288/L7
Courtois, Mo. 261/K7
Courtown (Este Sudeste) (cays), Colombia 126/A10
Courtown Harbour, Ireland 17/J6
Courtrai (Kortrijk), Belgium 27/C7
Courtright, Ontario 177/B5
Courval, Sask. 181/E5
Courville, Québec 172/J3
Coushatta, La. 238/D2
Coutances, France 28/C3
Coutras, France 28/C5
Coutts, Alberta 182/D5

D

360 Desolge

Desloge, Mo. 261/M7
Desmarais, Alberta 182/D2
Desmaraisville, Québec 174/B3
Desmet, Idaho 220/B2
De Smet, S. Dak. 298/O5
Desmochados, Paraguay 144/C5
Des Moines (riv.) 188/H2
Des Moines (co.), Iowa 229/L7
Des Moines (cap.), Iowa 146/J5
Des Moines (cap.), Iowa 188/H2
Des Moines (cap.), Iowa 229/G5
Des Moines (riv.), Iowa 229/J7
Des Moines (riv.), Minn. 255/C7
Des Moines (riv.), Mo. 261/J1
Des Moines, N. Mex. 274/F2
Des Moines, Wash. 310/B2
Desna (riv.), Russia 52/D4
Desna (riv.), Ukraine 52/D4
Desolación (isl.), Chile 120/B8
Desolación (isl.), Chile 138/D10
Desolation (canyon), Utah 304/E4
De Soto (co.), Fla. 212/E4
De Soto, Ga. 217/D7
De Soto, Ill. 222/D6
Desoto, Ind. 227/G4
De Soto, Iowa 229/E5
De Soto, Kansas 232/H3
De Soto (par.), La. 238/C2
De Soto (co.), Miss. 256/E1
De Soto, Miss. 256/G7
De Soto, Mo. 261/L6
De Soto, Texas 303/G3
De Soto, Wis. 317/D9
De Soto Nat'l Mem., Fla. 212/D4
Des Peres, Mo. 261/O3
Des Plaines, Ill. 222/B5
Des Plaines (riv.), Ill. 222/A6
Dessa, Niger 106/E6
Dessalines, Haiti 158/C5
Dessau, Germany 22/E3
Dessel, Belgium 27/G6
Dessye, Ethiopia 102/G3
Dessye, Ethiopia 111/G5
Destelbergen, Belgium 27/D6
Destin, Fla. 212/C6
Destrehan, La. 238/N4
Destruction (isl.), Wash. 310/A3
Destruction Bay, Yukon 187/E3
Deta, Romania 45/E3
Detah, N.W.T. 187/G3
Dete, Zimbabwe 118/D3
Detlor, Ontario 177/G2
Detmold, Germany 22/C3
De Tour (passage), Mich. 250/E3
Detour (pt.), Mich. 250/C3
De Tour Village, Mich. 250/E3
Detrital Wash (dry riv.), Ariz. 198/A3
Detroit, Ala. 195/B2
Detroit, Ill. 222/C4
Detroit, Kansas 232/E3
Detroit•, Maine 243/E6
Detroit, Mich. 146/K5
Detroit, Mich. 188/K2
Detroit, Mich. 250/B7
Detroit (riv.), Mich. 250/B7
Detroit, Oreg. 291/E3
Detroit (lake), Oreg. 291/E3
Detroit, Texas 303/J4
Detroit, U.S. 2/E3
Detroit Beach, Mich. 250/F7
Detroit Lakes, Minn. 255/C4
Detva, Slovakia 41/E2
De Twente (reg.), Netherlands 27/K4
Deuel (co.), Nebr. 264/B3
Deuel (co.), S. Dak. 298/R4
Deûle (riv.), Belgium 27/B7
Deurne, Belgium 27/F6
Deurne, Netherlands 27/H6
Deustua, Peru 128/G10
Deutsch Feistritz, Austria 41/C3
Deutschkreutz, Austria 41/D3
Deutsch Landsberg, Austria 41/C3
Deutsch Wagram, Austria 41/D2
Deux Frères, Les (isls.), Vietnam 72/E5
Deux-Montagnes (co.), Québec 172/C4
Deux-Montagnes, Québec 172/H4
Deux Montagnes (lake), Québec 172/C4
Deux Rivières, Ontario 177/F1
Deux-Sèvres (dept.), France 28/C4
Deva, Romania 45/F3
De Valls Bluff, Ark. 202/H4
Devault, Pa. 294/L5
Dévaványa, Hungary 41/F3
Devecser, Hungary 41/D3
Develi, Turkey 59/C2
Develi, Turkey 63/F3
Deventer, Netherlands 27/J4
Devenyns (lake), Québec 172/D2
Devereux, Ga. 217/F4
Deveron (riv.), Scotland 15/F3
De View (bayou), Ark. 202/J3
Deville, La. 238/F4
Devil River (peak), N. Zealand 100/D4
Devil's (isl.), Fr. Guiana 120/D2
Devil's (isl.), Fr. Guiana 131/E3
Devils (lake), N. Dak. 282/N3
Devils (riv.), Texas 303/D7
Devilsbit (mt.), Ireland 17/F6
Devil's Hole (Death Valley Nat'l Mon.), Nev. 266/E6
Devils Lake, N. Dak. 188/G1
Devils Lake, N. Dak. 282/N3
Devils Paw (mt.), Alaska 196/N1
Devils Postpile Nat'l Mon., Calif. 204/F6
Devils Slide, Utah 304/C2
Devils Thumb (mt.), Br. Col. 184/A1
Devils Tower, Wyo. 319/H1
Devils Tower Nat'l Mon., Wyo. 319/H1
Devin, Bulgaria 45/G5
Devine, Texas 303/E8
Devizes, England 13/F6
Devizes, England 10/F5
Devol, Okla. 288/J6
Devola, Ohio 284/H7
De Volet (pt.), St. Vin. & Grens. 161/A8
Devon, Alberta 182/D3
Devon (isl.), Canada 4/B14
Devon, Conn. 210/C4
Devon (co.), England 13/D7
Devon, Jamaica 158/H6
Devon, Kansas 232/H4
Devon, Mont. 262/E2
Devon (isl.), N.W.T. 162/M3
Devon (isl.), N.W.T. 146/K2
Devon (isl.), N.W.T. 187/K2
Devondale, Ky. 237/K2
Devonia, Tenn. 237/N8
Devonport, Australia 87/E10
Devonport, N. Zealand 100/C1
Devonport, Tasmania 88/H8
Devonport, Tasmania 99/C3
Devrek, Turkey 63/D2
Devrekâni, Turkey 63/E2
Devrez (riv.), Turkey 63/E2
Dewar, Iowa 229/J3
Dewar, Okla. 288/P4
Dewart, Pa. 294/J3
Dewas, India 68/D4
Dewberry, Alberta 182/E3
Dewees (isl.), S.C. 296/H6
De Weese (plat.), Colo. 208/J6
Deweese, Nebr. 264/F4
Dewey, Ariz. 198/C4
Dewey, Ill. 222/E3
Dewey (lake), Ky. 237/R5
Dewey (co.), Okla. 288/H2
Dewey, Okla. 288/P1
Dewey (Culebra), P. Rico 161/G1
Dewey (co.), S. Dak. 298/G3
Dewey Park, Ill. 222/B2
Deweyville, Texas 303/L7
Deweyville, Utah 304/B2
De Wijk, Netherlands 27/J3
De Winton, Alberta 182/C4
De Witt, Ark. 202/H5
De Witt (co.), Ill. 222/E3
Dewitt, Ill. 222/E3
De Witt, Iowa 229/N5
Dewitt, Ky. 237/O7
De Witt, Mich. 250/E6
De Witt, Mo. 261/F4
De Witt, Nebr. 264/G4
DeWitt, N.Y. 276/H4
De Witt (co.), Texas 303/G9
Dewitt, Va. 307/N6
Dewittville, Québec 172/C4
Dewsbury, England 10/H2
Dewsbury, England 13/J1
Dewy Rose, Ga. 217/G2
Dexter (lake), Fla. 212/E2
Dexter, Ga. 217/G6
Dexter, Iowa 229/E5
Dexter, Kansas 232/F4
Dexter, Ky. 237/E7
Dexter, Maine 243/E5
Dexter•, Maine 243/E5
Dexter, Mich. 250/F6
Dexter, Minn. 255/F7
Dexter, Mo. 261/N9
Dexter, N. Mex. 274/E5
Dexter, N.Y. 276/H2
Dexter, Oreg. 291/E4
Dexter City, Ohio 284/G6
Dexterville, Wis. 317/F7
Deyang, China 77/F5
Dey Dey (lake), S. Australia 88/E5
Dey Dey (lake), S. Australia 94/B3
DeYoung, Pa. 294/E2
Dez (riv.), Iran 59/E3
Dez (riv.), Iran 66/F4
De Zaan (riv.), Netherlands 27/B4
Dezful, Iran 59/E3
Dezful, Iran 54/F6
Dezful, Iran 66/F4
Dezhnev (cape), Russia 4/C18
Dezhnev (cape), Russia 48/T3
Dezhou (Tehchow), China 77/J4
Dezh Shahpur, Iran 66/E3
Dezh Shahpur, Iran 59/E2
Dhaba, Saudi Arabia 59/C4
Dhahiriya, West Bank 65/B5
Dhahran, Saudi Arabia 54/F7
Dhahran, Saudi Arabia 59/E4
Dhaka (Dacca) (cap.), Bangladesh 68/G4
Dhaka (Dacca) (cap.), Bangladesh 54/L7
Dhali, Cyprus 63/E5
Dhamar, Yemen 59/D7
Dhamtari, India 68/E4
Dhanbad, India 68/F4
Dhangarhi, Nepal 68/E3
D'Hanis, Texas 303/E8
Dhank, Oman 59/G5
Dhankuta, Nepal 68/F3
Dhar, India 68/C4
Dharma, Saudi Arabia 59/E5
Dharmsala, India 68/D2
Dharwar-Hubli, India 68/C5
Dhaulagiri (mt.), Nepal 68/E3
Dhenkanal, India 68/E4
Dhidhimótikhon, Greece 45/H5
Dhíkaia, Greece 45/H5
Dhimitsána, Greece 45/F7
Dhi Qar (heads), Iraq 66/E5
Dhira', Jordan 65/D5
Dhofar (reg.), Oman 59/F6
Dholpur, India 68/D3
Dhomokós, Greece 45/F6
Dhond, India 68/C5
Dhoraji, India 68/C4
Dhubri, India 68/G3
Dhulia, India 68/C4
Día (isl.), Greece 45/G8
Diable (pt.), Martinique 161/D5
Diablerets (mt.), Switzerland 39/D4
Diablo (canyon), Ariz. 198/D4
Diablo, Calif. 204/K2
Diablo, Sierra (mts.), Texas 303/C10
Diablo, Wash. 310/D2
Diablo (dam), Wash. 310/D2
Diablo (lake), Wash. 310/D2
Diablotin, Morne (mt.), Dominica 161/E6
Diadema, Brazil 135/C3
Diagonal, Iowa 229/E7
Dial, Ga. 217/D1
Diamant, Rocher du (isl.), Martinique 161/C7
Diamante, Argentina 143/F6
Diamante (riv.), Argentina 143/C3
Diamantina, Brazil 132/F7
Diamantina (riv.), Queensland 88/G4
Diamantina (riv.), Queensland 95/B4
Diamantina Lakes, Queensland 95/B4
Diamantino, Brazil 132/B6
Diamond (lake), Conn. 210/F2
Diamond (head), Hawaii 218/C5
Diamond (peak), Idaho 220/E5
Diamond, Ind. 227/C5
Diamond, La. 238/L7
Diamond, Mo. 261/D9
Diamond, Ohio 284/H3
Diamond, Oreg. 291/J4
Diamond (lake), Oreg. 291/E4
Diamond (peak), Oreg. 291/E4
Diamond, Pa. 294/C2
Diamond, Virgin Is. (U.S.) 161/F4
Diamond, Wash. 310/H4
Diamond (lake), Wash. 310/H2
Diamond Bluff, Wis. 317/A6
Diamond City, Alberta 182/D5
Diamond City, Ark. 202/E1
Diamond Coast (reg.), Namibia 118/A5
Diamond Lake, Oreg. 291/E4
Diamond Point, N.Y. 276/N4
Diamond Springs, Calif. 204/D8
Diamondville, Wyo. 319/B4
Diana, W. Va. 312/F5
Dian Chi (lake), China 77/F7
Dianjiang, China 77/G5
Diano Marina, Italy 34/B3
Dianópolis, Brazil 132/E5
Diapaga, Burkina Faso 106/E6
Dias Creek, N.J. 273/D5
Díaz, Argentina 143/F6
Diaz, Ark. 202/H2
Dibaya, D.R. Congo 115/D5
Dibaya-Lubue, D.R. Congo 115/C4
Dibble, Okla. 288/L4
Dibeng, S. Africa 118/C5
D'Iberville, Miss. 256/G10
Dibete, Botswana 118/D4
Diboll, Texas 303/K6
Dibrugarh, India 68/G3
Dibulla, Colombia 126/D2
Dickens, Iowa 229/C2
Dickens, Nebr. 264/C4
Dickens (pt.), R.I. 249/H8
Dickens (co.), Texas 303/D4
Dickens, Texas 303/D4
Dickenson (co.), Va. 307/D6
Dickerson, Md. 245/J4
Dickey, Ga. 217/C7
Dickey (co.), N. Dak. 282/N7
Dickey, N. Dak. 282/N6
Dickeyville, Wis. 317/E10
Dickinson, Ala. 195/C7
Dickinson (co.), Iowa 229/C2
Dickinson (co.), Kansas 232/E3
Dickinson (co.), Mich. 250/B2
Dickinson, N. Dak. 188/F1
Dickinson, N. Dak. 282/E6
Dickinson, Pa. 294/H5
Dickinson, Texas 303/K3
Dickinson Center, N.Y. 276/M1
Dickson, Alberta 182/C3
Dickson, Okla. 288/M6
Dickson (lake), Ontario 177/F2
Dickson (co.), Tenn. 237/G8
Dickson, Tenn. 237/G8
Dickson, W. Va. 312/B6
Dickson City, Pa. 294/F7
Dicle, Turkey 63/J3
Dicle (riv.), Turkey 63/J4
Didam, Netherlands 27/J5
Didcot, England 13/F6
Dido, La. 238/E5
Didsbury, Alberta 182/C4
Didsbury, Alta. 162/E5
Didyme, Québec 172/E1
Die, France 28/F5
Diébougou, Burkina Faso 106/D6
Diefenbaker (lake), Sask. 181/E4
Diego de Almagro (isl.), Chile 138/D9
Diego Garcia (isl.), Br. Ind. Ocean Terr. 54/J10
Diego Lamas, Uruguay 145/C1
Diego Pérez (cay), Cuba 158/C2
Diégo-Suarez (Antsiranana), Madagascar 118/H2
Diehlstadt, Mo. 261/N9
Diekirch, Luxembourg 27/J9
Dielsdorf, Switzerland 39/F1
Diemen, Netherlands 27/C5
Diemtigen, Switzerland 39/D3
Dien Bien Phu, Vietnam 72/D2
Diep (riv.), S. Africa 118/F6
Diepholz, Germany 22/C2
Diepoldsau, Switzerland 39/J2
Dieppe, France 28/D3
Dieppe, New Bruns. 170/F2
Dieppe Bay, St. Kitts & Nevis 161/C10
Dieren, Netherlands 27/J4
Dierks, Ark. 202/B5
Diessenhofen, Switzerland 39/G1
Diest, Belgium 27/F7
Dieterich, Ill. 222/E4
Dietikon, Switzerland 39/F2
Dietrich, Idaho 220/D7
Diever, Netherlands 27/J3
Diez y Nueve de Abril, Uruguay 145/E5
Diez y Ocho de Julio, Uruguay 145/F4
Dif, Somalia 115/H3
Diffa, Niger 106/G6
Differdange, Luxembourg 27/H9
Difficult, Tenn. 237/K8
Difficult (mt.), Victoria 97/B5
Digboi, India 68/H3
Digby (co.), Nova Scotia 168/C4
Digby, Nova Scotia 168/C4
Digby Gut (chan.), Nova Scotia 168/C4
Digby Neck (pen.), Nova Scotia 168/B4
Digdeguash (riv.), New Bruns. 170/C3
Digges (isls.), N.W.T. 187/L3
Diggins, Mo. 261/G8
Dighton, Kansas 232/B3
Dighton•, Mass. 249/K5
Dighton, Mich. 250/D4
Digne, France 28/G5
Digoin, France 28/F4
Digor, Turkey 63/K2
Digos, Philippines 82/E7
Digul (riv.), Indonesia 85/K7
Dijon, France 28/F4
Dijon, France 7/E4
Dike, Iowa 229/H4
Dikhil, Djibouti 111/H5
Dikili, Turkey 63/B3
Diksmuide, Belgium 27/B6
Dikson, Russia 4/B5
Dikson, Russia 48/J2
Dikwa, Nigeria 106/G6
Dikwa, Nigeria 102/D3
Dilam, Saudi Arabia 59/E5
Dilbeek, Belgium 27/B9
Dildo, Newf. 166/D2
Dili, Indonesia 54/O10
Dili, Indonesia 85/H7
Dilia, N. Mex. 274/D3
Diligent River, Nova Scotia 168/D3
Di Linh, Vietnam 72/F5
Dilke, Sask. 181/F5
Dilkon, Ariz. 198/E3
Dilla, Ethiopia 111/G6
Dillabough, Sask. 181/J3
Dillard, Ga. 217/F1
Dillard, Mo. 261/K7
Dillard, Oreg. 291/D4
Dill City, Okla. 288/H4
Dille, W. Va. 312/E6
Dillenburg, Germany 22/C3
Diller, Nebr. 264/H4
Dilley, Oreg. 291/A2
Dilley, Texas 303/E9
Dillia (dry riv.), Niger 106/G5
Dilliner, Pa. 294/B6
Dilling, Sudan 111/E5
Dillingen, Germany 22/B4
Dillingen an der Donau, Germany 22/D4
Dillingham, Alaska 188/C6
Dillingham, Alaska 196/G3
Dillon (riv.), Alberta 182/E2
Dillon, Colo. 208/H3
Dillon, Kansas 232/E3
Dillon, Mont. 262/D5
Dillon (lake), Ohio 284/F5
Dillon (co.), S.C. 296/J3
Dillon, S.C. 296/J3
Dillonvale, Ohio 284/J5
Dillsboro, Ind. 227/G6
Dillsboro, N.C. 281/C4
Dillsburg, Pa. 294/J5
Dilltown, Pa. 294/E5
Dillwyn, Va. 307/M5
Dilolo, D.R. Congo 115/D6
Dilsen, Belgium 27/H6
Dilworth, Minn. 255/B4
Dimas, Cuba 158/A2
Dimas, Mexico 150/F5
Dimashq (Damascus) (cap.), Syria 63/G6
Dimashq (Damascus) (cap.), Syria 59/C3
Dimbelenge, D.R. Congo 115/D5
Dimbokro, Ivory Coast 106/D7
Dimboola, Victoria 97/B5
Dime Box, Texas 303/H7
Dimitrovgrad, Bulgaria 45/G4
Dimitrovgrad, Russia 48/F4
Dimitrovgrad, Russia 52/G4
Dimitrovgrad, Yugoslavia 45/F4
Dimlang (mt.), Nigeria 106/G7
Dimmit (co.), Texas 303/E9
Dimmitt, Texas 303/B3
Dimock, Pa. 294/L2
Dimock, S. Dak. 298/O7
Dimona, Israel 65/D5
Dimona (mt.), Israel 65/C5
Dimondale, Mich. 250/E6
Dimsdale, Alberta 182/A2
Dinagat, Philippines 82/E5
Dinagat (isl.), Philippines 85/H3
Dinagat (isl.), Philippines 82/E5
Dinagat (sound), Philippines 82/E5
Dinajpur, Bangladesh 68/F3
Dinan, France 28/B3
Dinant, Belgium 27/G8
Dinar, Kuh-e (mts.), Iran 66/G5
Dinar, Turkey 63/D3
Dinard, France 28/B3
Dinaric Alps (mts.), Croatia 45/B3
Dinas Powis, Wales 13/B7
Dinder (riv.), Ethiopia 111/F5
Dinder (riv.), Sudan 59/B7
Dinder (riv.), Sudan 111/F5
Dindigul, India 68/D6
Dingalan (bay), Philippines 82/C3
Dingbian, China 77/G4
Dingess, W. Va. 312/B7
Dinggye, China 77/C6
Dinghai, China 77/K5
Dingle, Idaho 220/G7
Dingle, Ireland 10/A4
Dingle, Ireland 17/A7
Dingle (bay), Ireland 10/A4
Dingle (bay), Ireland 17/A7
Dingmans Ferry, Pa. 294/N3
Dingolfing, Germany 22/E4
Dinguiraye, Guinea 106/B6
Dingwall, Nova Scotia 168/H2
Dingwall, Scotland 15/D3
Dingwall, Scotland 10/D2
Dingxi, China 77/F4
Dingxing, China 77/H4
Dinh, Mui (cape), Vietnam 72/F5
Dinkelsbühl, Germany 22/D4
Dinnebito Wash (dry riv.), Ariz. 198/E3
Dinokwe, Botswana 118/D4
Dinorwic, Ontario 177/G5
Dinorwic, Ontario 175/B3
Dinosaur, Colo. 208/B2
Dinosaur Nat'l Mon., Colo. 208/B2
Dinosaur Nat'l Mon., Utah 304/E3
Dinsdale, Iowa 229/H4
Dinsmore, Sask. 181/D4
Dinsor, Somalia 115/H3
Dinuba, Calif. 204/F7
Dinwiddie (co.), Va. 307/N6
Dinwiddie, Va. 307/N6
Dinxperlo, Netherlands 27/K5
Diogo (isl.), Philippines 82/B2
Dioila, Mali 106/C6
Diomede, Alaska 196/E1
Diourbel, Senegal 106/A6
Diphu, India 68/G3
Dipilto, Cordillera (range), Nicaragua 154/D4
Diplo, Pakistan 68/B4
Dipolog, Philippines 82/D6
Dipper Harbour, New Bruns. 170/D3
Dir, Pakistan 68/C1
Dir, Pakistan 59/K2
Dire, Mali 106/D5
Direction (cape), Queensland 88/G2
Direction (cape), Queensland 95/B2
Dire Dawa, Ethiopia 102/G4
Dire Dawa, Ethiopia 111/H6
Diriamba, Nicaragua 154/D5
Dirico, Angola 115/D7
Dirico, Namibia 118/C3
Dirk Hartogs (isl.), Australia 87/B8
Dirk Hartogs (isl.), W. Australia 88/A5
Dirk Hartogs (isl.), W. Australia 92/A4
Dirksland, Netherlands 27/E5
Dirmil, Turkey 63/C4
Dirranbandi, Queensland 88/H5
Dirranbandi, Queensland 95/D6
Dirty Devil (riv.), Utah 304/D5
Disappointment (lake), Australia 87/C8
Disappointment (creek), Colo. 208/B7
Disappointment (isls.), Fr. Poly. 87/N7
Disappointment (lake), Newf. 166/B3
Disappointment (cape), Wash. 188/A1
Disappointment (cape), Wash. 310/A4
Disappointment (lake), W. Australia 88/C4
Disappointment (lake), W. Australia 92/C3
Discovery (bay), Victoria 88/E7
Discovery (bay), Victoria 97/A6
Discovery Bay, Jamaica 158/J5
Disentis-Mustér, Switzerland 39/G3
Dishman, Wash. 310/H3
Disko (isl.), Greenl. 4/C12
Disko (isl.), Greenland 146/N3
Disko, Ind. 227/E2
Disley, Sask. 181/F5
Dismal (riv.), Nebr. 264/C3
Dismal (Great) (swamp), N.C. 281/S1
Disney, Okla. 288/S2
Dison, Belgium 27/H7
Dispur, India 68/G3
Disputanta, Va. 307/O6
Disraeli (fiord), N.W.T. 187/L1
Disraëli, Québec 172/F4
Diss, England 13/J5
Diss, England 10/G4
Disston (lake), Fla. 212/E2
Disston, Oreg. 291/E4
District Heights, Md. 245/G5
District of Columbia 146/L6
District of Columbia 188/L3
DISTRICT OF COLUMBIA 245
Distrito Especial, Colombia 126/C5
Distrito Federal, Argentina 143/H7
Distrito Federal, Mexico 150/L1
Distrito Federal, Venezuela 124/E2
Distrito Nacional, Dom. Rep. 158/E6
Disûq, Egypt 111/J3
Dittmer, Mo. 261/L6
Ditton (riv.), Québec 172/F4
Diu (dist.), India 68/C4
Diu, India 68/C4
Diuata (mts.), Philippines 82/E6
Divernon, Ill. 222/D4
Divide, Colo. 208/J5
Divide, Mont. 262/D5
Divide (co.), N. Dak. 282/C2
Dividing (creek), Md. 245/R8
Dividing Creek, N.J. 273/C5
Divino, Brazil 135/E2
Divinópolis, Brazil 132/E8
Divinópolis, Brazil 120/E5
Divinópolis, Brazil 135/D2
Divis (mt.), N. Ireland 17/J2
Divisa Nova, Brazil 135/C2
Division (peak), Nev. 266/B1
Divo, Ivory Coast 106/C7
Divriği, Turkey 63/H3
Divriği, Turkey 59/C2
Dix, Ill. 222/E5
Dix (riv.), Ky. 237/M5
Dix, Nebr. 264/A3
Dixfield, Maine 243/C6
Dixfield•, Maine 243/C6
Dix Hills, N.Y. 276/O9
Dixie, Ala. 195/E8
Dixie (co.), Fla. 212/C2
Dixie, Ga. 217/E9
Dixie, Idaho 220/C4
Dixie, La. 238/C1
Dixie, Wash. 310/G4
Dixie, W. Va. 312/D6
Dixie Inn, La. 238/D1
Dixmont, Maine 243/E6
Dixmont•, Maine 243/E6
Dixmoor, Ill. 222/C6
Dixmude (Diksmuide), Belgium 27/B6
Dixon, Calif. 204/B9
Dixon, Ill. 222/D2
Dixon, Iowa 229/M5
Dixon, Ky. 237/F5
Dixon, Miss. 256/F5
Dixon, Mo. 261/H6
Dixon, Mont. 262/B3
Dixon (co.), Nebr. 264/H2
Dixon, Nebr. 264/H2
Dixon, N. Mex. 274/D2
Dixon, N.C. 281/O5
Dixon, Ohio 284/A4
Dixon, S. Dak. 298/L7
Dixon, Wyo. 319/E4
Dixon Entrance (chan.) 146/E4
Dixon Entrance (chan.), Alaska 196/M2
Dixon Entrance (chan.), Br. Col. 184/A3
Dixons Mills, Ala. 195/C6
Dixon Springs, Ill. 222/E6
Dixon Springs, Tenn. 237/J8
Dixonville, Ala. 195/E8
Dixonville, Alberta 182/B1
Dixonville, Pa. 294/D4
Dixville (peak), N.H. 268/E2
Dixville, Québec 172/F4
Dixville Notch, N.H. 268/E2
Dixville Notch (pass), N.H. 268/E2
Diyadin, Turkey 63/K3
Diyala (heads), Iraq 66/D4
Diyala (riv.), Iraq 66/D4
Diyarbakır (prov.), Turkey 63/H4
Diyarbakır, Turkey 54/F6
Diyarbakır, Turkey 63/H4
Diyarbakır, Turkey 59/C2
Dizful (Dezful), Iran 66/F4
Dja (riv.), Cameroon 115/B3
Dja (riv.), Congo 115/B3
Djado (plat.) 102/D2
Djado, Niger 102/D2
Djado, Niger 106/G4
Djado (plat.), Niger 106/G4
Djakarta (Jakarta) (cap.), Indonesia 85/H1
Djakovica, Yugoslavia 45/E4
Djakovo, Croatia 45/D3
Djambala, Congo 115/B4
Djambi (Jambi), Indonesia 85/C6
Djanet, Algeria 106/F4
Djanet, Algeria 102/C2
Djelfa, Algeria 106/E2
Djema, Cent. Afr. Rep. 115/E2
Djemaa, Algeria 106/F2
Djenné, Mali 102/B3
Djenné, Mali 106/D6
Djerba (isl.), Tunisia 106/G2
Djerid, Shott el (salt lake), Tunisia 106/F2
Djibo, Burkina Faso 106/D6
Djibouti 2/L5
Djibouti 102/G3
DJIBOUTI 111/H5
Djibouti (cap.), Djibouti 111/H5
Djibouti (cap.), Djibouti 102/G3
Djokjakarta (Yogyakarta), Indonesia 85/J2
Djolu, D.R. Congo 115/D3
Djouf, El (des.), Mauritania 106/C4
Djougou, Benin 106/E7
Djoum, Cameroon 115/B3
Djugu, D.R. Congo 115/F3
D'Lo, Miss. 256/E7
Dmitriya Lapteva (str.), Russia 4/B2
Dmitriya Lapteva (str.), Russia 48/O2
Dneprodzerzhinsk, Ukraine 7/H4
Dneprodzerzhinsk, Ukraine 52/D5
Dnepropetrovsk, Ukraine 7/H4
Dnepropetrovsk, Ukraine 48/D5
Dnepropetrovsk, Ukraine 52/D5
Dnieper (riv.), Ukraine 7/H3
Dnieper (riv.), Ukraine 48/D5
Dnieper (riv.), Ukraine 52/D5
Dniester (riv.), Moldova 7/G4
Dniester (riv.), Moldova 48/C5
Dniester (riv.), Moldova 52/C5
Dniester (riv.), Ukraine 7/G4
Dniester (riv.), Ukraine 48/C5
Dniester (riv.), Ukraine 52/C5
Dno, Russia 52/D3
Doaghbeg, Ireland 17/F1
Doaktown, New Bruns. 170/D2
Doans, Ind. 227/D7
Doba, Chad 111/C6
Doba, Chad 102/D4
Dobbie (mt.), North. Terr. 93/E7
Dobbin (bay), N.W.T. 187/L2
Dobbins A.F.B., Ga. 217/J1
Dobbs Ferry, N.Y. 276/O6
Dobbyn, Queensland 95/A3
Dobele, Latvia 53/B2
Döbeln, Germany 22/E3
Doberai (pen.), Indonesia 85/J6
Dobiegniew, Poland 47/B2
Doblas, Argentina 143/D4
Dobo, Indonesia 85/J7
Doboj, Bos. 45/C3
Doboy (sound), Ga. 217/K8
Dobřany, Czech Rep. 41/B2
Dobre Miasto, Poland 47/E2
Dobrich (Tolbukhin), Bulgaria 45/H4
Dobříš, Czech Rep. 41/C2
Dobrush, Belarus 52/D4
Dobruška, Czech Rep. 41/D1
Dobryanka, Russia 52/J3
Dobšiná, Slovakia 41/F2
Dobson, N.C. 281/H2
Doce (riv.), Brazil 135/E2
Doce (riv.), Brazil 132/F7
Doce Leguas (cays), Cuba 158/F3
Docker River, North. Terr. 93/A8
Docking, England 13/H5
Dock Junction (Arco), Ga. 217/J8
Doctor Arroyo, Mexico 150/K5
Doctor Cecilio Báez, Paraguay 144/D4
Doctor Juan L. Mallorquín, Paraguay 144/E4
Doctor Juan Manuel Frutos, Paraguay 144/E4
Doctor M. Irala, Paraguay 144/E4
Doctor Pedro P. Peña, Paraguay 144/A3
Doctors Inlet, Fla. 212/E1
Doctortown, Ga. 217/J7
Doddridge, Ark. 202/C7
Doddridge (co.), W. Va. 312/E4
Dodds, Alberta 182/D3
Doddsville, Miss. 256/C3

Drumhill 361

Dodecanese (isls.), Greece 45/H8
Dodge (co.), Ga. 217/F6
Dodge, Mass. 249/G4
Dodge (co.), Minn. 255/F7
Dodge (co.), Nebr. 264/H3
Dodge, Nebr. 264/H3
Dodge, N. Dak. 282/F5
Dodge, Texas 303/J7
Dodge (co.), Wis. 317/J9
Dodge, Wis. 317/D7
Dodge Center, Minn. 255/F6
Dodge City, Kans. 188/F3
Dodge City, Kansas 232/B4
Dodgeville, Wis. 317/F10
Dodgingtown, Conn. 210/B3
Dodman (pt.), England 13/C7
Dodoma (reg.), Tanzania 115/G5
Dodoma, Tanzania 102/F5
Dodoma, Tanzania 115/G5
Dodsland, Sask. 181/C4
Dodson, La. 238/E2
Dodson, Mont. 262/H2
Dodson, Texas 303/D3
Doe (lake), Ontario 177/E2
Doe (bay), Wash. 310/C2
Doe Bay, Wash. 310/C2
Doe Hill, Va. 307/K4
Doering, Wis. 317/G5
Doerun, Ga. 217/E8
Doe Run, Mo. 261/M7
Doesburg, Netherlands 27/J4
Doetinchem, Netherlands 27/J5
Dog (pond), Conn. 210/C1
Dog (isl.), Fla. 212/B2
Dog (lake), Manitoba 179/D3
Dog (isl.), Newf. 166/B2
Dog (lake), Ontario 177/G5
Dogai Coring (lake), China 77/C5
Doğanbey, Turkey 63/D4
Doğanhisar, Turkey 63/D3
Doğanşehir, Turkey 63/G3
Dog Creek, Br. Col. 184/G4
Dog Ear (creek), S. Dak. 298/K6
Döger, Turkey 63/D3
Dogo (isl.), Japan 81/F5
Dogondoutchi, Niger 106/E6
Dogondoutchi, Niger 102/C3
Dogpatch, Ark. 202/D1
Dog Pound, Alberta 182/C4
Dogskin (lake), Manitoba 179/G3
Doğubeyazıt, Turkey 63/K3
Dogwood (pt.), St. Kitts & Nevis 161/D11
Doha (cap.), Qatar 54/G7
Doha (cap.), Qatar 59/F4
Dohad, India 68/C4
Doheny, Québec 172/E2
Dohuk (gov.), Iraq 66/C2
Dohuk, Iraq 66/C2
Doi Inthanon (mt.), Thailand 72/C3
Doilungdêqên, China 77/C6
Doi Pha Hom Pok (mt.), Thailand 72/C2
Doi Pia Fai (mt.), Thailand 72/D4
Doische, Belgium 27/F8
Dois Córregos, Brazil 135/B3
Dois Irmãos, Serra (range), Brazil 132/F5
Dokkum, Netherlands 27/H2
Doksy, Czech Rep. 41/C1
Dokterstuin, Neth. Ant. 161/F8
Dola, Ohio 284/C4
Dola, W. Va. 312/F4
Dolan, Ind. 227/E6
Doland, S. Dak. 298/N4
Dolan Springs, Ariz. 198/A3
Dolavon, Argentina 143/C5
Dolbeau, Québec 174/C3
Dolbeau, Québec 172/E1
Doldenhorn (mt.), Switzerland 39/E4
Dôle, France 28/F4
Dolega, Panama 154/F6
Dolent (mt.), Switzerland 39/C5
Doles, Ga. 217/E7
Dolgellau, Wales 13/D5
Dolgellau, Wales 10/E4
Dolgeville, N.Y. 276/L4
Dolgiy (isl.), Russia 52/J1
Dolinsk, Russia 48/P5
Dollar, Scotland 10/B1
Dollar, Scotland 15/E4
Dollar Bay, Mich. 250/G1
Dollard (bay), Netherlands 27/L2
Dollard, Sask. 181/C6
Dollard-des-Ormeaux, Québec 172/H4
Dollart (est.), Germany 22/B2
Dollarville, Mich. 250/D2
Dolliver, Iowa 229/D2
Dolný Kubín, Slovakia 41/E2
Dolo, Ethiopia 111/H7
Dolomite, Ala. 195/D4
Dolomite Alps (range), Italy 34/C1
Dolores, Argentina 143/E4
Dolores, Argentina 120/D6
Dolores (co.), Colo. 208/C7
Dolores, Colo. 208/C8
Dolores (riv.), Colo. 208/B5
Dolores, Guatemala 154/C2
Dolores, Philippines 82/E4
Dolores, Spain 33/F3
Dolores, Uruguay 145/A4
Dolores (riv.), Utah 304/E5
Dolores, Venezuela 124/D3
Dolores Hidalgo de la Independencia Nacional, Mexico 150/J6
Dolphin and Union (str.), N.W.T. 187/G3
Dölsach, Austria 41/B3
Dolton, Ill. 222/C6
Dolton, S. Dak. 298/P7
Dom (mt.), Switzerland 39/E4
Domain, Manitoba 179/E5
Domaniç, Turkey 63/C3
Domar (dry riv.), Chad 111/C4
Domat-Ems, Switzerland 39/H3
Domažlice, Czech Rep. 41/B2
Dombås, Norway 18/F5
Dombe Grande, Angola 115/B6
Dombóvár, Hungary 41/E3
Dombrád, Hungary 41/F2
Dombresson, Switzerland 39/C2
Domburg, Netherlands 27/C5
Domburg, Suriname 131/D3
Dome, Ariz. 198/A6
Dome Creek, Br. Col. 184/G3
Domeiko, Chile 138/A7
Domeyko, Cordillera (mts.), Chile 138/B4
Domínguez, Argentina 143/G6
Dominica 2/F5
Dominica 146/M8
DOMINICA 156/G4
DOMINICA 161/E7
Dominica (passage), Dominica 161/E5
Dominican Republic 2/F4
Dominican Republic 146/L8
DOMINICAN REPUBLIC 156/D3
DOMINICAN REPUBLIC 158
Dominion (lake), Newf. 166/B3
Dominion (cape), N.W.T. 187/L3
Dominion, Nova Scotia 168/J2
Dominion City, Manitoba 179/E5
Domino, Newf. 166/C3
Dömitz, Germany 22/D2
Domjor, India 68/F1
Domleschg (valley), Switzerland 39/E2
Dommel (riv.), Netherlands 27/H6
Domo, Ethiopia 111/J6
Domodossola, Italy 34/A1
Dom Pedrito, Brazil 132/C10
Dompu, Indonesia 85/F7
Domremy, Sask. 181/F3
Domrémy-la-Pucelle, France 28/F3
Dom Silvério, Brazil 135/E2
Dömsöd, Hungary 41/E3
Domuyo (vol.), Argentina 143/B4
Don (riv.), England 10/F4
Don (riv.), England 13/F4
Don (riv.), Ontario 177/J4
Don (riv.), Russia 7/J4
Don (riv.), Russia 48/E5
Don (riv.), Russia 52/F5
Don (riv.), Scotland 15/F3
Don (riv.), Scotland 10/E2
Dona Ana (Mutarara), Mozambique 118/F3
Dona Ana (co.), N. Mex. 274/C6
Dona Ana, N. Mex. 274/C6
Donabate, Ireland 17/J5
Donaghadee, N. Ireland 17/K2
Donahue, Iowa 229/M5
Donald, Br. Col. 184/J4
Donald, Oreg. 291/A3
Donald, Victoria 97/B5
Donald, Wash. 310/E4
Donald, Wis. 317/E5
Donalda, Alberta 182/D3
Donalds, S.C. 296/C3
Donaldson, Ark. 202/E5
Donaldson, Ind. 227/E2
Donaldson, Minn. 255/B2
Donaldson A.F.B., S.C. 296/C2
Donaldsonville, La. 238/K3
Donalsonville, Ga. 217/C8
Donansburg, Ky. 237/K6
Donath, Switzerland 39/H3
Donatville, Alberta 182/D2
Donau (Danube) (riv.), Austria 41/D2
Donau (Danube) (riv.), Germany 22/C4
Donaueschingen, Germany 22/C5
Donauwörth, Germany 22/D4
Donavon, Sask. 181/D4
Donbar, Queensland 95/B3
Don Benito, Spain 33/C3
Doncaster, England 13/F4
Doncaster, England 10/F4
Doncaster, Md. 245/K7
Doncaster and Templestowe, Victoria 88/L7
Doncaster and Templestowe, Victoria 97/J5
Dondo, Angola 115/B5
Dondo, Mozambique 118/F3
Dondra (head), Sri Lanka 68/E7
Dondra Head (cape), Sri Lanka 54/K9
Donegal (co.), Ireland 17/K2
Donegal, Ireland 10/B3
Donegal, Ireland 17/F2
Donegal (bay), Ireland 17/D3
Donegal (bay), Ireland 10/B3
Donegal (harb.), Ireland 17/E2
Donegal (pt.), Ireland 17/B6
Donegal, Pa. 294/D5
Donel, Honduras 154/E3
Doneraile, Ireland 17/D7
Doneraile, S.C. 296/H3
Donets (riv.), Ukraine 7/H4
Donets (riv.), Ukraine 48/D5
Donets (riv.), Ukraine 52/E5
Donetsk, Ukraine 7/H4
Donetsk, Ukraine 48/D5
Donetsk, Ukraine 52/E5
Donga (riv.), Cameroon 115/B2
Donga, Nigeria 106/G7
Donga (riv.), Nigeria 106/G7
Dongara, W. Australia 92/A5
Dongchuan, China 77/F6
Dongen, Netherlands 27/F5
Dongfang, China 77/G8
Dongfanghong, China 77/M2
Donggala, Indonesia 85/F6
Dônghên, Laos 72/E3
Dong Hoi, Vietnam 72/E3
Dongio, Switzerland 39/H4
Dongning, China 77/M3
Dongo, D.R. Congo 115/C3
Dongola, Ill. 222/D6
Dongola, Sudan 102/E3
Dongola, Sudan 59/B6
Dongola, Sudan 111/F4
Dongou, Congo 115/C3
Dong Rak (mts.), Thailand 72/D4
Dongsha (isl.), China 77/J7
Dongsheng, China 77/H4
Dongtai, China 77/K5
Dongting (lake), China 54/N7
Dongting Hu (riv.), China 77/H6
Dong Ujimqin, China 77/J2
Dongwe (riv.), Zambia 115/D6
Donie, Texas 303/H6
Doñihue, Chile 138/G5
Doniphan (co.), Kansas 232/G2
Doniphan, Mo. 261/L9
Doniphan, Nebr. 264/F4
Donji Vakuf, Bos. 45/C3
Donkin, Nova Scotia 168/J2
Donley (co.), Texas 303/D2
Dønna (isl.), Norway 18/H3
Donna, Texas 303/F11
Donnacona, Québec 172/F3
Donnellson, Ill. 222/D4
Donnellson, Iowa 229/K7
Donnelly, Alberta 182/B2
Donnelly, Idaho 220/B5
Donnelly, Minn. 255/B5
Donner (pass), Calif. 204/E4
Donner, La. 238/J7
Donner and Blitzen (riv.), Oreg. 291/J4
Donnybrook, N. Dak. 282/G2
Donnybrook, Queensland 95/D5
Donnybrook, W. Australia 92/A2
Donora, Pa. 294/C5
Donovan, Ga. 217/G5
Donovan, Ill. 222/F3
Donsol, Philippines 82/D4
Donwell, Sask. 181/J4
Donzère, France 28/F5
Dooagh-Keel, Ireland 17/A4
Doole, Texas 303/E6
Dooling, Ga. 217/E6
Doolittle (pond), Conn. 210/C1
Doolittle, Mo. 261/J7
Doolittle Mills, Ind. 227/D8
Dooly (co.), Ga. 217/E6
Doon, Iowa 229/A2
Doon, Ireland 17/E6
Doon, Loch (lake), Scotland 15/D5
Doon (riv.), Scotland 15/D5
Doonerak (mt.), Alaska 196/H1
Doonside, Sask. 181/K6
Door (pt.), La. 238/M6
Door (co.), Wis. 317/M6
Door (pen.), Wis. 317/M6
Doorn, Netherlands 27/G4
Doornik (Tournai), Belgium 27/C7
Doqa, Saudi Arabia 59/D6
Dor, Israel 65/B2
Dora, Ala. 195/D3
Dora, Mo. 261/H9
Dora, N. Mex. 274/F5
Dora, Oreg. 291/D4
Dora (lake), W. Australia 88/C4
Dora (lake), W. Australia 92/C3
Dora Baltea (riv.), Italy 34/A2
Dorado, P. Rico 161/D1
Dora Lake, Minn. 255/D3
Doran, Minn. 255/B4
Dora Riparia (riv.), Italy 34/A2
Doraville, Ga. 217/K1
D'Orbigny, Bolivia 136/D7
Dorbiljin (Emin), China 77/B2
Dorbod, China 77/K2
Dorcas, W. Va. 312/H5
Dorchester, England 10/E5
Dorchester, England 13/E7
Dorchester, Ga. 217/K7
Dorchester, Ill. 222/D4
Dorchester, Iowa 229/L2
Dorchester (co.), Md. 245/O7
Dorchester, Mass. 249/D7
Dorchester, Nebr. 264/G4
Dorchester, New Bruns. 170/F3
Dorchester•, N.H. 268/D4
Dorchester, N.J. 273/D5
Dorchester (cape), N.W.T. 187/L3
Dorchester, Ontario 177/C5
Dorchester (co.), Québec 172/C3
Dorchester (co.), S.C. 296/G5
Dorchester, S.C. 296/G5
Dorchester, Wis. 317/F5
Dorchester Crossing, New Bruns. 170/F2
Dordogne (dept.), France 28/D5
Dordogne (riv.), France 7/E4
Dordogne (riv.), France 28/D5
Dordrecht, Netherlands 27/F5
Doré (lake), Ontario 177/G2
Doré (lake), Sask. 181/L3
Dore Alps (mts.), France 28/E5
Doré Lake, Sask. 181/L4
Dorena, Mo. 261/O9
Dorena, Oreg. 291/E4
Dorena (lake), Oreg. 291/E4
Dorenlee, Alberta 182/D3
Dores, Scotland 15/D3
Dores do Indaiá, Brazil 132/E7
Dorgali, Italy 34/B4
Dörgön Nuur (lake), Mongolia 77/D2
Dori, Mali 102/B3
Dori, Burkina Faso 106/D6
Doring (riv.), S. Africa 118/B6
Dorintosh, Sask. 181/L4
Dorion, Ontario 177/H5
Dorion, Québec 172/C4
Dorking, England 13/G8
Dorking, England 10/F5
Dormont, Pa. 294/B7
Dornach, Switzerland 39/E2
Dornbirn, Austria 41/A3
Dornie, Scotland 15/C3
Dornoch, Scotland 10/D2
Dornoch, Scotland 15/D3
Dornoch (firth), Scotland 15/E3
Dornoch (firth), Scotland 10/E2
Dornod, Mongolia 77/H2
Dornogovĭ, Mongolia 77/G3
Dorog, Hungary 41/E3
Dorohoi, Romania 45/H2
Dorotea, Sweden 18/K4
Dorothy, Alberta 182/D4
Dorothy, Minn. 255/B3
Dorothy, N.J. 273/D5
Dorothy, W. Va. 312/D7
Dorr (lake), Fla. 212/E2
Dorr, Mich. 250/D6
Dorrance, Kansas 232/D3
Dorre (isl.), W. Australia 88/A5
Dorre (isl.), W. Australia 92/A4
Dorreen, Br. Col. 184/C3
Dorrigo, N.S. Wales 97/G2
Dorris, Calif. 204/D2
Dorset (co.), England 13/E7
Dorset, Minn. 255/D4
Dorset, Ohio 284/J2
Dorset•, Vt. 268/A5
Dorset (peak), Vt. 268/A5
Dorset Heights (hills), England 13/E7
Dorsey, Miss. 256/H2
Dorsten, Germany 22/B3
Dortches, N.C. 281/O2
Dortmund, Germany 7/E3
Dortmund, Germany 22/B3
Dorton, Ky. 237/R6
Dörtyol, Turkey 63/F4
Doruma, D.R. Congo 115/E3
Dorval, Québec 172/H4
Dory Point, N.W.T. 187/G3
Dos Bahías (cape), Argentina 143/D5
Dos Cabezas, Ariz. 198/F6
Dos Caminos, Cuba 158/J4
Dos de Mayo, Peru 128/E6
Dos Hermanas, Spain 33/D4
Dos Palos, Calif. 204/E6
Dosquet, Québec 172/F3
Dos Reyes (pt.), Chile 138/A5
Dos Ríos, Cuba 158/J4
Dosso, Niger 106/E6
Dossor, Kazakhstan 48/F5
Dossville, Miss. 256/F5
Doswell, Va. 307/N5
Dothan, Ala. 188/J4
Dothan, Ala. 195/H8
Doti, Nepal 68/E3
Dot Klish (canyon), Ariz. 198/E2
Dot Lake, Alaska 196/K2
Dott, W. Va. 312/D8
Döttingen, Switzerland 39/F1
Doty, Wash. 310/B4
Douai, France 28/E2
Douala, Cameroon 115/B3
Douala, Cameroon 102/D4
Douarnenez, France 28/A3
Double Branches, Ga. 217/H3
Double Mer (lake), Newf. 166/C3
Double Mountain Fork, Brazos (riv.), Texas 303/C4
Double Oak, Texas 303/F1
Double Springs, Ala. 195/D2
Doubletop (peak), Wyo. 319/B2
Doubs (dept.), France 28/G4
Doubs (riv.), France 28/G4
Doubs, Md. 245/J3
Doubs (riv.), Switzerland 39/C2
Doubtful (sound), N. Zealand 100/A6
Doubtless (bay), N. Zealand 100/D1
Doucette, Texas 303/K7
Douds, Iowa 229/J7
Doué-la-Fontaine, France 28/C4
Douentza, Mali 106/D6
Douentza, Mali 102/B3
Dougherty (co.), Ga. 217/D7
Dougherty, Iowa 229/G3
Dougherty, Okla. 288/M6
Dougherty, Texas 303/C4
Douglas, Ala. 195/F2
Douglas (mt.), Alaska 196/H3
Douglas, Ariz. 146/G6
Douglas, Ariz. 188/E4
Douglas, Ariz. 198/F7
Douglas (chan.), Br. Col. 184/C3
Douglas (co.), Colo. 208/K4
Douglas (creek), Colo. 208/B3
Douglas (bay), Dominica 161/E5
Douglas (co.), Ga. 217/C3
Douglas, Ga. 217/G7
Douglas (co.), Ill. 222/E4
Douglas, Ireland 17/D8
Douglas (cap.), I. of Man 13/C3
Douglas (cap.), I. of Man 10/D3
Douglas (co.), Kansas 232/G3
Douglas, Manitoba 179/C5
Douglas•, Mass. 249/H4
Douglas, Mich. 250/C6
Douglas (co.), Minn. 255/C5
Douglas, Minn. 255/F6
Douglas (co.), Mo. 261/G9
Douglas (mt.), Mont. 262/F5
Douglas (co.), Nebr. 264/H3
Douglas, Nebr. 264/H4
Douglas (co.), Nev. 266/B4
Douglas, N. Dak. 282/G4
Douglas, North. Terr. 93/B2
Douglas, Okla. 288/L2
Douglas, Ontario 177/H2
Douglas (pt.), Ontario 177/C3
Douglas (co.), Oreg. 291/D4
Douglas, Scotland 15/E5
Douglas, S. Africa 118/C5
Douglas (co.), S. Dak. 298/N7
Douglas (lake), Tenn. 237/P9
Douglas (co.), Wash. 310/F3
Douglas, Wash. 310/F3
Douglas (co.), Wis. 317/C3
Douglas, Wyo. 319/G3
Douglas Harbour, New Bruns. 170/D3
Douglas Lake, Br. Col. 184/H5
Douglas Prov. Park, Sask. 181/E4
Douglass, Kansas 232/F4
Douglass, Texas 303/K6
Douglass Hills, Ky. 237/L2
Douglassville, Pa. 294/L5
Douglastown, New Bruns. 170/E1
Douglastown, Québec 172/D1
Douglasville, Ga. 217/C3
Doullens, France 28/E2
Doulus (head), Ireland 17/A8
Doumé, Cameroon 115/B3
Dounby, Scotland 15/E1
Doune, Scotland 15/D4
Dour, Belgium 27/D8
Dourados, Brazil 120/D5
Dourados, Brazil 132/C8
Douro (riv.), Portugal 7/D4
Douro (riv.), Portugal 33/B2
Douro (riv.), Spain 33/C2
Dousman, Wis. 317/J1
Douthat, Okla. 288/S1
Douville, Québec 172/D4
Dove (riv.), England 13/J2
Dove (creek), Utah 304/A2
Dove Creek, Colo. 208/A7
Dover, Ark. 202/D3
Dover (cap.), Del. 146/L6
Dover (cap.), Del. 188/L3
Dover (cap.), Del. 245/R4
Dover, England 7/E3
Dover, England 10/G5
Dover, England 13/J6
Dover (str.), England 13/J7
Dover (str.), England 10/G5
Dover, Fla. 212/D4
Dover, Ga. 217/J5
Dover, Idaho 220/B1
Dover, Ill. 222/D2
Dover, Ind. 227/H6
Dover, Kansas 232/G3
Dover, Ky. 237/O3
Dover, Mass. 249/B7
Dover•, Mass. 249/B7
Dover, Minn. 255/F7
Dover, Mo. 261/E4
Dover, N.H. 268/F5
Dover, N.J. 273/D2
Dover, N.C. 281/P4
Dover, Ohio 284/G4
Dover (lake), Ohio 284/H4
Dover, Okla. 288/L3
Dover, Pa. 294/J6
Dover, Tasmania 99/C5
Dover, Tenn. 237/F8
Dover (pt.), W. Australia 88/D6
Dover (pt.), W. Australia 92/D6
Dover A.F.B., Del. 245/S4
Doverel, Ga. 217/D7
Dover-Foxcroft, Maine 243/E5
Dover-Foxcroft•, Maine 243/E5
Dover Hill, Ind. 227/D7
Dover Plains, N.Y. 276/O7
Dover South Mills, Maine 243/E5
Dovesville, S.C. 296/H3
Dovey (riv.), Wales 10/D4
Dovey (riv.), Wales 13/D5
Dovns Klint (cliff), Denmark 21/D8
Dovray, Minn. 255/C6
Dovre, Norway 18/F6
Dovrefjell (hills), Norway 18/F5
Dow (Xau) (lake), Botswana 118/C4
Dow, Ill. 222/C4
Dow, Okla. 288/P5
Dowa, Malawi 115/F6
Dowagiac, Mich. 250/D6
Dow City, Iowa 229/B5
Dowell, Ill. 222/D6
Dowelltown, Tenn. 237/K8
Dowlatabad, Afghanistan 59/H3
Dowlatabad, Afghanistan 68/A2
Dowlatabad, Kerman, Iran 66/K6
Dowlatabad, Khorasan, Iran 66/M2
Dowlat Yar, Afghanistan 59/J3
Dowlat Yar, Afghanistan 68/B2
Dowling, Alberta 182/E4
Dowling (lake), Alberta 182/D4
Dowling, Mich. 250/D6
Dowling Park, Fla. 212/C1
Down (dist.), N. Ireland 17/K3
Downe, Sask. 181/C4
Downer, Minn. 255/B4
Downers Grove, Ill. 222/A6
Downey, Calif. 204/C11
Downey, Idaho 220/F7
Downey, Iowa 229/L5
Downfall (creek), Queensland 95/D2
Downham Market, England 13/H5
Downham Market, England 10/G4
Downieville, Calif. 204/E4
Downing, Mo. 261/H2
Downing, Wis. 317/B5
Downings, Va. 307/P5
Downingtown, Pa. 294/L5
Downpatrick (head), Ireland 17/C3
Downpatrick, N. Ireland 10/C3
Downpatrick, N. Ireland 17/K3
Downs, Ill. 222/E3
Downs, Kansas 232/D2
Downsville, La. 238/F1
Downsville, Md. 245/G2
Downsville, N.Y. 276/L6
Downsville, Wis. 317/C6
Downton, England 13/F6
Dows, Iowa 229/F3
Dowshi, Afghanistan 59/J2
Dowshi, Afghanistan 68/B1
Doyle, Calif. 204/E3
Doyle, Ga. 217/D6
Doyle, Tenn. 237/K9
Doylestown, Ohio 284/G4
Doylestown, Pa. 294/M5
Doylestown, Wis. 317/H9
Doyleville, Colo. 208/F6
Doyline, La. 238/D1
Doyon, N. Dak. 282/O3
Dozen (isls.), Japan 81/F5
Dozier, Ala. 195/F7
Dozier, Texas 303/D2
Dozois (res.), Québec 174/B3
Dra, Wadi (dry riv.), Morocco 106/C3
Drachten, Netherlands 27/J2
Dracut•, Mass. 249/J2
Drăgăneşti Olt, Romania 45/G3
Drăgăşani, Romania 45/F3
Dragonera (isl.), Spain 33/H3
Dragons Mouth (str.), Trin. & Tob. 156/F5
Dragons Mouth (str.), Trin. & Tob. 161/A10
Dragons Mouth (str.), Venezuela 124/H2
Dragoon, Ariz. 198/F6
Dragoon (mts.), Ariz. 198/F7
Draguignan, France 28/G6
Drain, Oreg. 291/D4
Drake (passage) 2/F8
Drake (passage), Ant. 5/C15
Drake (passage), Chile 138/E11
Drake, Colo. 208/J2
Drake, Mo. 261/K6
Drake, N. Dak. 282/K4
Drake, Sask. 181/G4
Drakensberg (range), Lesotho 118/D6
Drakensberg (range), S. Africa 118/D6
Drakensberg (range), Swaziland 118/D6
Drakes (creek), Ky. 237/J7
Drakesboro, Ky. 237/H6
Drakes Branch, Va. 307/L7
Drakesville, Iowa 229/J7
Draketown, Ga. 217/B3
Dráma, Greece 45/F5
Drammen, Norway 7/E3
Drammen, Norway 18/C4
Drance (riv.), Switzerland 39/D4
Drancy, France 28/B1
Drang, Ia (riv.), Cambodia 72/E4
Draper, S. Dak. 298/J6
Draper, Utah 304/C3
Draper, Va. 307/G7
Draper, Wis. 317/E4
Draperstown, N. Ireland 17/H2
Draperstown, N. Ireland 10/C3
Drasco, Ark. 202/G2
Drau (riv.), Austria 41/C3
Drava (riv.) 7/F4
Drava (riv.), Croatia 45/C3
Dráva (riv.), Hungary 41/D3
Dravosburg, Pa. 294/C7
Drawsko Pomorskie, Poland 47/B2
Drax Hall, Barbados 161/B8
Drayden, Md. 245/N8
Drayton, N. Dak. 282/R2
Drayton, Ontario 177/D4
Drayton Plains, Mich. 250/F6
Drayton Valley, Alberta 182/C3
Drenthe (prov.), Netherlands 27/K3
Dresbach, Minn. 255/G7
Dresden, Germany 7/F3
Dresden, Germany 22/E3
Dresden, Kansas 232/B2
Dresden•, Maine 243/D7
Dresden, Mo. 261/F5
Dresden, N.Y. 276/F5
Dresden, N. Dak. 282/O2
Dresden, Ohio 284/G5
Dresden, Ontario 177/B5
Dresden, Tenn. 237/D8
Dresden Station, N.Y. 276/O3
Dresser, Wis. 317/A5
Dreux, France 28/D3
Drew (co.), Ark. 202/G6
Drew, Miss. 256/C3
Drew, Oreg. 291/E5
Drewry, Ala. 195/D8
Drewryville, Va. 307/O7
Drews (res.), Oreg. 291/G5
Drewsey, Oreg. 291/J4
Drewsville, N.H. 268/C5
Drexel, Mo. 261/C6
Drexel, N.C. 281/F3
Drexel Hill, Pa. 294/M6
Dreyfus, Ky. 237/N5
Drezdenko, Poland 47/B2
Driebergen, Netherlands 27/G4
Driffield, England 13/G3
Driffield, England 10/F4
Drift (creek), Oreg. 291/B3
Drifton, Pa. 294/L3
Driftwood, Okla. 288/K1
Driftwood, Pa. 294/F3
Driggs, Ark. 202/C3
Driggs, Idaho 220/G6
Drill, Va. 307/E6
Drimoleague, Ireland 17/C8
Drin (riv.), Albania 45/E4
Drina (riv.), Bos. 45/D3
Drinkwater, Sask. 181/F5
Dripping Springs, Texas 303/F7
Driscoll, N. Dak. 282/K6
Driscoll, Texas 303/G10
Drishane, Ireland 17/C7
Driskill (mt.), La. 238/E2
Drøbak, Norway 18/D4
Drobeta-Turnu Severin, Romania 45/F3
Drogenbos, Belgium 27/B10
Drogheda, Ireland 17/J4
Drogheda, Ireland 10/C4
Drogobych, Ukraine 48/C5
Drogobych, Ukraine 52/B5
Droichead Nua, Ireland 10/C4
Droichead Nua, Ireland 17/H5
Droitwich, England 13/E5
Dromahair, Ireland 17/E3
Drôme (dept.), France 28/F5
Drôme (riv.), France 28/F5
Dromore, Bainbridge, N. Ireland 17/J3
Dromore, Omagh, N. Ireland 17/G3
Dromore West, Ireland 17/D3
Dronfield, England 13/J2
Drongan, Scotland 15/D5
Dronne (riv.), France 28/D5
Dronninglund, Denmark 21/D3
Dronten, Netherlands 27/H3
Dropmore, Manitoba 179/A3
Drouin, Victoria 97/C6
Druid, Sask. 181/C4
Druif, Neth. Ant. 161/D10
Drum (hills), Ireland 17/F7
Drum (bay), La. 238/M7
Drum (inlet), N.C. 281/S5
Drumaness, N. Ireland 17/K3
Drumbeg, Scotland 15/C2
Drumbo, Ontario 177/D4
Drumcar, Ireland 17/J4
Drumconrath, Ireland 17/H4
Drumheller, Alberta 182/D4
Drumheller, Alta. 162/E5
Drumhill, N.C. 281/R1

362 Drumkeerin

Drumkeerin, Ireland 17/E3
Drumlish, Ireland 17/F4
Drummond, Idaho 220/G5
Drummond (isl.), Mich. 250/F2
Drummond, Mont. 262/D4
Drummond, New Bruns. 170/C1
Drummond (mt.), North. Terr. 93/E5
Drummond, Okla. 288/L2
Drummond (co.), Québec 172/E4
Drummond (range), Queensland 88/H4
Drummond (range), Queensland 95/C5
Drummond (lake), Va. 307/P7
Drummond, Wis. 317/D3
Drummond Island, Mich. 250/F3
Drummonds, Tenn. 237/A10
Drummondville, Québec 172/E4
Drummondville-Nord, Québec 172/E4
Drummondville-Sud, Québec 172/E4
Drummore, Scotland 15/D6
Drummoyne, N.S. Wales 88/K4
Drummoyne, N.S. Wales 97/J3
Drumnadrochit, Scotland 15/D3
Drumquin, N. Ireland 17/F2
Drumright, Okla. 288/N3
Drums, Pa. 294/K3
Drumshanbo, Ireland 17/E3
Drury, Mo. 261/H9
Druskininkai, Lithuania 53/C3
Druten, Netherlands 27/H5
Druz, Jebel ed (mts.), Syria 63/G6
Druzhba, Kazakhstan 48/J5
Druzhina, Russia 48/P3
Drvar, Bos. 45/C3
Dry (bay), Alaska 196/L3
Dry (creek), Ky. 237/R3
Dry (lake), N. Dak. 282/M3
Dry (riv.), North. Terr. 88/E3
Dry (riv.), North. Terr. 93/C3
Dry (creek), S. Dak. 298/G4
Dry (lake), S. Dak. 298/P3
Dry (creek), Wyo. 319/C2
Dryad, Wash. 310/B4
Dryanovo, Bulgaria 45/G4
Dry Branch, Ga. 217/F5
Dry Cimarron (riv.), N. Mex. 274/F2
Dry Coal (creek), Utah 304/A6
Dry Cottonwood (creek), Wyo. 319/D1
Dry Creek, La. 238/D5
Dry Creek, W. Va. 312/D7
Dryden, Ark. 202/J2
Dryden, Maine 243/C6
Dryden, Mich. 250/F6
Dryden, N.Y. 276/H6
Dryden, Ontario 177/G4
Dryden, Ontario 175/B3
Dryden, Texas 303/C7
Dryden, Va. 307/B7
Dryden, Wash. 310/E3
Dry Falls (dam), Wash. 310/F3
Dry Fork, Va. 307/K7
Dryfork, W. Va. 312/H5
Dry Fork (riv.), W. Va. 312/G5
Dry Fork (riv.), W. Va. 312/C8
Dry Fork, Cheyenne (riv.), Wyo. 319/G2
Dry Fork, Powder (riv.), Wyo. 319/F2
Dry Lake, Nev. 266/G6
Drymen, Scotland 15/B1
Dry Mills, Maine 243/C8
Dry Prong, La. 238/E3
Dry Ridge, Ky. 237/M3
Dry Run, Pa. 294/G5
Drysdale (riv.), W. Australia 88/D3
Drysdale (riv.), W. Australia 92/D1
Dry Tortugas (keys), Fla. 212/D7
Drytown, Calif. 204/C8
Dry Wood (lake), S. Dak. 298/P2
Dschang, Cameroon 115/A2
Duaca, Venezuela 124/D2
Duaringa, Queensland 95/D4
Duart, Ontario 177/C5
Duarte, Calif. 204/D10
Duarte (prov.), Dom. Rep. 158/E5
Duarte (peak), Dom. Rep. 158/D5
Dubach, La. 238/E1
Dubai, U.A.E. 59/F4
Dubawnt (lake), N.W.T. 162/F3
Dubawnt (lake), N.W.T. 146/H3
Dubawnt (lake), N.W.T. 187/H3
Dubawnt (riv.), N.W.T. 162/F3
Dubawnt (riv.), N.W.T. 187/H3
Du Bay (lake), Wis. 317/G6
Dubberly, La. 238/D1
Dubbo, N. S. Wales 88/H6
Dubbo, N.S. Wales 97/E3
Dubbs, Miss. 256/D1
Dübendorf, Switzerland 39/G2
Dublin, Calif. 204/K2
Dublin, Ga. 217/G5
Dublin, Ind. 227/G5
Dublin (co.), Ireland 17/J5
Dublin (cap.), Ireland 7/D3
Dublin (cap.), Ireland 17/K5
Dublin (cap.), Ireland 10/C4
Dublin (bay), Ireland 10/C4
Dublin (bay), Ireland 17/J5
Dublin, Ky. 237/D7
Dublin, Md. 245/N2
Dublin, Mich. 250/D4
Dublin, Miss. 256/C2
Dublin•, N.H. 268/C6
Dublin, N.C. 281/M5
Dublin, Ohio 284/D5
Dublin, Ontario 177/C4
Dublin, Pa. 294/M5
Dublin, Texas 303/F5
Dublin, Va. 307/G6
Dubna, Russia 52/E4
Dubna, Russia 52/E3
Dubnica nad Váhom, Slovakia 41/E2
Dubno, Ukraine 52/C4
Dubois, Idaho 220/F5
Dubois, Ill. 222/D5
Dubois (co.), Ind. 227/D8
Dubois, Ind. 227/D8
Du Bois, Nebr. 264/H4
DuBois, Pa. 294/E3
Dubois, Wyo. 319/C2
Duboistown, Pa. 294/H3
Dubréka, Guinea 106/B7
Dubreuilville, Ontario 177/J5
Dubrovnik, Croatia 45/C4
Dubruelville, Ontario 175/D3
Dubuc, Sask. 181/J5
Dubuque (co.), Iowa 229/M4
Dubuque, Iowa 188/H2
Dubuque, Iowa 229/M3
Duchcov, Czech Rep. 41/B1
Duchesne (co.), Utah 304/D3
Duchesne, Utah 304/D3
Duchesne (riv.), Utah 304/D3
Duchess, Alberta 182/E4
Duchess, Queensland 88/F4
Duchess, Queensland 95/A4
Ducie (isl.), Pitcairn Is. 87/O8
Duck (isls.), Maine 243/G7
Duck (lake), Mich. 250/F4
Duck (creek), Nev. 266/G3
Duck, N.C. 281/T2
Duck (creek), Ohio 284/H6
Duck (isl.), Ontario 177/H4
Duck (isls.), Ontario 177/A2
Duck (riv.), Tenn. 237/F9
Duck, W. Va. 312/E5
Duck Bay, Manitoba 179/B2
Duck Hill, Miss. 256/E3
Duck Lake, Sask. 181/E3
Duck Lake Hist. Park, Sask. 181/E3
Duck Lake Post, Manitoba 179/J2
Duck Mountain Prov. Park, Manitoba 179/B3
Duck Mountain Prov. Park, Sask. 181/K4
Duck River, Tenn. 237/G9
Ducktown, Ga. 217/D2
Ducktown, Tenn. 237/N10
Duck Valley Indian Res., Idaho 220/B7
Duck Valley Indian Res., Nev. 266/E1
Duckwater, Nev. 266/F4
Duclos, Québec 172/A4
Ducor, Calif. 204/G8
Ducos, Martinique 161/D6
Dudelange, Luxembourg 27/J10
Dudenville, Mo. 261/D8
Duderstadt, Germany 22/D3
Dudhi, India 68/E4
Dudignac, Argentina 143/F7
Düdingen, Switzerland 39/D3
Dudinka, Russia 4/B5
Dudinka, Russia 48/J3
Dudinka, Russia 54/K3
Dudley, England 13/E5
Dudley, England 10/G3
Dudley, Ga. 217/F5
Dudley•, Mass. 249/G4
Dudley, Mo. 261/M9
Dudley, N.C. 281/N4
Dudley, Pa. 294/F5
Dudley (lake), Québec 172/B3
Dudleytown, Ind. 227/F7
Dudváh (riv.), Slovakia 41/D2
Dueñas, Spain 33/D2
Duenweg, Mo. 261/D8
Duero (Douro) (riv.), Spain 33/C2
Due West, S.C. 296/C3
Duff, Sask. 181/H5
Duff, Tenn. 237/N8
Duffee, Miss. 256/G6
Duffel, Belgium 27/F6
Dufferin (county), Ontario 177/D3
Duffield, Alberta 182/C3
Duffield, Va. 307/C7
Dufftown, Scotland 10/E2
Dufftown, Scotland 15/E3
Dufourspitze (mt.), Switzerland 39/E5
Dufresne, Manitoba 179/F5
Dufrost, Manitoba 179/E5
Dufur, Oreg. 291/F2
Dugald, Manitoba 179/F5
Dugger, Ind. 227/C6
Dugi Otok (isl.), Croatia 45/B3
Dugspur, Va. 307/G7
Duguayville, New Bruns. 170/E1
Du Gué (riv.), Québec 174/C1
Dugway, Utah 304/B3
Dugway (range), Utah 304/A3
Dugway Proving Grounds, Utah 304/B3
Duhamel, Alberta 182/D3
Duhamel, Québec 172/B3
Duich, Loch (inlet), Scotland 15/C3
Duida, Cerro (mt.), Venezuela 124/F6
Duifken (pt.), Queensland 88/G2
Duifken (pt.), Queensland 95/B2
Duiker (pt.), S. Africa 118/E6
Duinain (riv.), Scotland 15/D3
Duirinish (dist.), Scotland 15/B3
Duisburg, Germany 22/B3
Duitama, Colombia 126/D5
Duiveland (isl.), Netherlands 27/D5
Duivendrecht, Netherlands 27/C5
Duke, Ala. 195/G3
Duke (isl.), Alaska 196/N2
Duke, Mo. 261/H7
Duke (East Duke), Okla. 288/G5
Duke Center, Pa. 294/F2
Dukedom, Tenn. 237/D8
Duke of Gloucester (isls.), Fr. Poly. 87/M8
Dukes (co.), Mass. 249/M7
Dukes, Mich. 250/B2
Dukhan, Qatar 59/F4
Duki, Pakistan 68/B2
Dukla (pass), Poland 47/E4
Dukla (pass), Slovakia 41/F2
Dukou, China 77/F6
Dulac, La. 238/J8
Dulah, N.C. 281/M6
Dulan, China 77/E4
Dulce (riv.), Argentina 143/D2
Dulce (gulf), C. Rica 154/F6
Dulce, N. Mex. 274/B2
Duleek, Ireland 17/J4
Dulgalakh (riv.), Russia 48/O3
Dülmen, Germany 22/B3
Dulunguin (pt.), Philippines 82/C7
Duluth, Ga. 217/D2
Duluth, Kansas 232/F2
Duluth, Minn. 146/J5
Duluth, Minn. 188/H1
Duluth, Minn. 255/F4
Dulverton, England 13/D6
Duma, Syria 63/G6
Duma, West Bank 65/C3
Dumagasa (pt.), Philippines 82/C7
Dumaguete, Philippines 82/D6
Dumaguete, Philippines 85/G4
Dumanquilas (bay), Philippines 82/D7
Dumaran (isl.), Philippines 85/G3
Dumaran (isl.), Philippines 82/C5
Dumaresq (riv.), N.S. Wales 97/F1
Dumas, Ark. 202/H6
Dumas, Miss. 256/G1
Dumas, Sask. 181/J6
Dumas, Texas 303/C2
Dumbarton, New Bruns. 170/C3
Dumbarton, Scotland 10/A1
Dumbarton, Scotland 15/B1
Dum Dum, India 68/F1
Dume (pt.), Calif. 204/G10
Dumeir, Syria 63/G6
Dumfoundling (bay), Fla. 212/C4
Dumfries, New Bruns. 170/C3
Dumfries, Scotland 15/E5
Dumfries, Scotland 10/E3
Dumfries (trad. co.), Scotland, 15/B5
Dumfries, Va. 307/O3
Dumfries and Galloway (reg.), Scotland 15/E5
Dumlu, Turkey 63/J2
Dummer•, N.H. 268/E2
Dummer, Sask. 181/G6
Dümmersee (lake), Germany 22/C2
Dumont, Iowa 229/H3
Dumont, Minn. 255/B5
Dumont, N.J. 273/C1
Dumont, Texas 303/D4
Dumont d'Urville Station, Ant. 5/C7
Dumyât (Damietta), Egypt 111/J3
Dumyat (Damietta), Egypt 59/B3
Dun (isl.), Scotland 15/A2
Duna (Danube) (riv.), Hungary 41/E3
Dunaff (head), Ireland 17/F1
Dunaföldvár, Hungary 41/E3
Dunaharaszti, Hungary 41/E3
Dunajec (riv.), Poland 47/E4
Dunajec (riv.), Slovakia 41/F2
Dunajská Streda, Czech Rep. 41/D3
Dunakeszi, Hungary 41/E3
Dunalley, Tasmania 99/D4
Dunany (pt.), Ireland 17/J4
Dunaszekcső, Hungary 41/E3
Dunaújváros, Hungary 41/E3
Dunav (Danube) (riv.), Bulgaria 45/H4
Dunavecse, Hungary 41/E3
Dunbar, Iowa 229/H5
Dunbar, Nebr. 264/J4
Dunbar, Okla. 288/P6
Dunbar, Pa. 294/C6
Dunbar, Scotland 10/E2
Dunbar, Scotland 15/F4
Dunbar, S.C. 296/H2
Dunbar, W. Va. 312/C6
Dunbar, Wis. 317/K4
Dunbarton•, N.H. 268/D5
Dunbarton (trad. co.), Scotland 15/A5
Dunbarton Center, N.H. 268/D5
Dunbeath, Scotland 15/E2
Dunbeg, Scotland 15/C4
Dunblane, Sask. 181/D4
Dunblane, Scotland 15/E4
Dunblane, Scotland 10/D2
Dunbridge, Ohio 284/C3
Duncan, Ariz. 198/F6
Duncan, Br. Col. 184/J3
Duncan (riv.), Br. Col. 184/J5
Duncan (isls.), China 85/E2
Duncan, Ill. 222/D3
Duncan (passage), India 68/G6
Duncan, Miss. 256/C2
Duncan, Nebr. 264/G3
Duncan, Okla. 288/L5
Duncan (lake), Québec 174/B2
Duncan, S.C. 296/C2
Duncan, W. Va. 312/C5
Duncan Falls, Ohio 284/G6
Duncannon, Ireland 17/H7
Duncannon, Pa. 294/H5
Duncans, Jamaica 158/H5
Duncans Bridge, Mo. 261/H3
Duncansby (head), Scotland 15/F2
Duncansby (head), Scotland 10/E1
Duncansville, Pa. 294/F5
Duncanville, Ala. 195/D4
Duncanville, Texas 303/G3
Dunchurch, Ontario 177/E2
Duncombe, Iowa 229/E4
Duncombe (bay), Norfolk I. 88/L5
Dundaga, Latvia 53/B2
Dundalk, Ireland 17/H3
Dundalk, Ireland 10/C4
Dundalk (bay), Ireland 10/C4
Dundalk (bay), Ireland 17/J4
Dundalk, Md. 245/N3
Dundalk, Ontario 177/D3
Dundarrach, N.C. 281/L5
Dundas (isl.), Br. Col. 184/B3
Dundas, Ill. 222/E5
Dundas, Minn. 255/E6
Dundas (str.), North. Terr. 88/E2
Dundas (str.), North. Terr. 93/B1
Dundas (pen.), N.W.T. 187/G2
Dundas, Ohio 284/E7
Dundas (county), Ontario 177/J2
Dundas, Ontario 177/D4
Dundas, Va. 307/M7
Dundas (lake), W. Australia 88/C6
Dundas (lake), W. Australia 92/C6
Dundee, Fla. 212/E3
Dundee (East and West Dundee), Ill. 222/E1
Dundee, Ind. 227/F4
Dundee, Iowa 229/L3
Dundee, Ky. 237/H5
Dundee, Mich. 250/F7
Dundee, Minn. 255/C7
Dundee, Miss. 256/D1
Dundee, N.Y. 276/F5
Dundee, Oreg. 291/A2
Dundee, Scotland 7/D3
Dundee, Scotland 15/F4
Dundee, Scotland 10/E2
Dundee, S. Africa 118/E5
Dundee, Texas 303/F4
Dundgovĭ, Mongolia 77/G2
Dundon, W. Va. 312/D6
Dundonald, Scotland 15/D5
Dundrum, N. Ireland 17/K3
Dundrum (bay), N. Ireland 17/K3
Dundurn, Sask. 181/E4
Dundy (co.), Nebr. 264/C4
Dune Acres, Ind. 227/C1
Dunedin, Fla. 212/B2
Dunedin, N. Zealand 2/T8
Dunedin, N. Zealand 100/C6
Dunedoo, N.S. Wales 97/E3
Dunellen, N.J. 273/D2
Dunes (Westlake), Oreg. 291/C4
Dunfanaghy, Ireland 17/F1
Dunfee, Ind. 227/G2
Dunfermline, Ill. 222/D3
Dunfermline, Sask. 181/D3
Dunfermline, Scotland 15/D1
Dunfermline, Scotland 10/C1
Dungalear Station, N.S. Wales 97/D1
Dungannon (dist.), N. Ireland 17/H3
Dungannon, N. Ireland 17/H3
Dungannon, Ontario 177/C4
Dungannon, Va. 307/D7
Dungarpur, India 68/C4
Dungarvan, Ireland 10/C4
Dungarvan, Ireland 17/F7
Dungarvan (harb.), Ireland 10/C4
Dungarvan (harb.), Ireland 17/G7
Dungarvon (riv.), New Bruns. 170/D2
Dungeness (pt.), Argentina 143/C7
Dungeness (pt.), Chile 138/F10
Dungeness (prom.), England 13/J7
Dungeness (prom.), England 10/G5
Dungeness, Wash. 310/B2
Dungiven, N. Ireland 17/H2
Dungloe, Ireland 17/E2
Dungog, N.S. Wales 97/F3
Dungu, D.R. Congo 115/E3
Dungunab, Sudan 59/C5
Dungunab, Sudan 111/G3
Dunham, Québec 172/E4
Dunhua (Tunhwa), China 77/L3
Dunhuang, China 77/E3
Dunkeld, Queensland 95/D5
Dunkeld, Scotland 15/E4
Dunkeld, Victoria 97/B5
Dunkellin (riv.), Ireland 17/D5
Dunkerton, Iowa 229/J3
Dunkery (hill), England 13/D6
Dunkineely, Ireland 17/E2
Dunkirk (riv.), Alberta 182/D1
Dunkirk (Dunkerque), France 28/E2
Dunkirk, France 28/E2
Dunkirk, Ind. 227/G4
Dunkirk, N.Y. 276/B5
Dunkirk, Ohio 284/C4
Dunkley, Br. Col. 184/F3
Dunklin (co.), Mo. 261/M10
Dunkwa, Ghana 106/D7
Dún Laoghaire, Ireland 10/D4
Dún Laoghaire, Ireland 17/K5
Dunlap, Ill. 222/D3
Dunlap, Ind. 227/F1
Dunlap, Iowa 229/B5
Dunlap, Kansas 232/F3
Dunlap, Tenn. 237/L10
Dunlavin, Ireland 17/H5
Dunleath, Sask. 181/K4
Dunleer, Ireland 17/J4
Dunleith, Miss. 256/C4
Dunlow, W. Va. 312/B6
Dunloy, N. Ireland 17/J1
Dunmanus (bay), Ireland 17/B8
Dunmanway, Ireland 17/C8
Dunmanway, Ireland 10/B5
Dunmor, Ky. 237/G6
Dunmore, Alberta 182/E5
Dunmore, Ireland 17/D4
Dunmore, Pa. 294/F7
Dunmore (lake), Vt. 268/A4
Dunmore, W. Va. 312/G6
Dunmore East, Ireland 17/G7
Dunn, La. 238/G2
Dunn, N.C. 281/M4
Dunn (co.), N. Dak. 282/E5
Dunn, Texas 303/D5
Dunn (co.), Wis. 317/C6
Dunnamanagh, N. Ireland 17/G2
Dunn Center, N. Dak. 282/E5
Dunnegan, Mo. 261/E7
Dunnell, Minn. 255/D7
Dunnellon, Fla. 212/D2
Dunnet, Scotland 15/E2
Dunnet (bay), Scotland 15/E2
Dunnet (head), Scotland 10/E1
Dunnet (head), Scotland 15/E2
Dunnigan, Calif. 204/C5
Dunning, Nebr. 264/D3
Dunning, Scotland 15/E4
Dunn Loring, Va. 307/S2
Dunnottar, Manitoba 179/E4
Dunnottar, S. Africa 118/J6
Dunns, W. Va. 312/D7
Dunnsville, Va. 307/P5
Dunnville, Ky. 237/M6
Dunnville, Ontario 177/E5
Du Noir (riv.), Wyo. 319/C2
Dunolly, Victoria 97/B5
Dunoon, Scotland 15/A2
Dunoon, Scotland 10/A1
Dunphy, Nev. 266/E2
Dunragit, Scotland 15/D6
Dunrea, Manitoba 179/C5
Dunreith, Ind. 227/F5
Duns, Scotland 10/E3
Duns, Scotland 15/F5
Dunscore, Scotland 15/E5
Dunseith, N. Dak. 282/K2
Dunshaughlin, Ireland 17/H5
Dunsmuir, Calif. 204/C2
Dunstable, England 10/F5
Dunstable, England 13/G6
Dunstable•, Mass. 249/J2
Dunster, Br. Col. 184/G3
Duntochter, Scotland 15/B2
Dunure, Scotland 15/D5
Dunvegan, Nova Scotia 168/F4
Dunvegan, Scotland 15/B3
Dunvegan, Loch (inlet), Scotland 15/B3
Dunville, Newf. 166/D2
Dunwoody, Ga. 217/K1
Duo, W. Va. 312/E6
Duolun, China 77/J3
Duong Dong, Vietnam 72/D5
Du Page (co.), Ill. 222/E2
Du Page (riv.), Ill. 222/E2
Du Page, East Branch (riv.), Ill. 222/A6
Du Page, West Branch (riv.), Ill. 222/A6
Duparquet, Québec 174/B3
Duperow, Sask. 181/C4
Duplessis, La. 238/K2
Duplin (co.), N.C. 281/O5
Dupo, Ill. 222/A3
Du Pont, Ga. 217/G9
Dupont, Ind. 227/G7
Dupont, Ohio 284/B3
Dupont, Pa. 294/F7
Du Pont, Wash. 310/C3
Dupont Manor, Del. 245/R4
Dupree, S. Dak. 298/F3
Dupuis Corner, New Bruns. 170/F2
Dupuy, Québec 174/B3
Dupuyer, Mont. 262/D2
Duque de Caxias, Brazil 135/E3
Duque de York (isl.), Chile 138/C9
Duquesne, Mo. 261/D8
Duquesne, Pa. 294/C7
Duquette, Minn. 255/F4
Du Quoin, Ill. 222/D5
Duquoin, Kansas 232/D4
Dura, West Bank 65/C4
Durack (range), W. Australia 88/D3
Durağan, Turkey 63/F2
Duran, N. Mex. 274/D4
Durance (riv.), France 28/F6
Durand, Ga. 217/C5
Durand, Ill. 222/D1
Durand, Mich. 250/E6
Durand, Wis. 317/C6
Durango, Colo. 188/E3
Durango, Colo. 208/D8
Durango, Iowa 229/M3
Durango (state), Mexico 150/G4
Durango, Mexico 146/H7
Durango, Mexico 150/G4
Durango, Spain 33/E1
Duranillin, W. Australia 92/B2
Durant, Iowa 229/M5
Durant, Miss. 256/E4
Durant, Okla. 188/G4
Durant, Okla. 288/O6
Duratón (riv.), Spain 33/E2
Durazno (dept.), Uruguay 145/C3
Durazno, Uruguay 145/C4
Durazno, Grande del (range), Uruguay 145/D4
Durban, Manitoba 179/A3
Durban, S. Africa 2/L7
Durban, S. Africa 102/F7
Durban, S. Africa 118/E5
Durbanville, S. Africa 118/F6
Durbe, Latvia 53/A2
Durbin, Ind. 227/F4
Durbin, N. Dak. 282/R6
Durbin, W. Va. 312/G5
Durbuy, Belgium 27/H8
Düren, Germany 22/B3
Durfee (hill), R.I. 249/G5
Durg, India 68/E4
Durgapur, India 68/F4
Durgerdam, Netherlands 27/C4
Durham, Ark. 202/C2
Durham, Calif. 204/D4
Durham, Conn. 210/E3
Durham•, Conn. 210/E3
Durham (co.), England 13/F3
Durham, England 13/J3
Durham, England 10/F3
Durham, Kansas 232/E3
Durham, Mo. 261/J3
Durham, N.H. 268/F5
Durham•, N.H. 268/F5
Durham (pt.), N. Zealand 100/D7
Durham (co.), N.C. 281/M3
Durham, N.C. 188/L3
Durham, N.C. 281/M2
Durham, Okla. 288/G3
Durham (reg. munic.), Ontario 177/F3
Durham, Ontario 177/D3
Durham, Oreg. 291/A2
Durham Bridge, New Bruns. 170/D2
Durham Center, Conn. 210/E3
Durham Downs, Queensland 95/B5
Durham-Sud, Québec 172/E4
Durhamville, N.Y. 276/J4
Duri, N.S. Wales 97/F2
Durkee, Oreg. 291/K3
Durness, Scotland 15/D2
Durnford (pt.), Western Sahara 106/A4
Dürnten, Switzerland 39/G2
Duror, Scotland 15/C4
Durrell, Newf. 166/D4
Dürrenroth, Switzerland 39/E2
Durrës (Durazzo), Albania 45/D5
Durrës, Albania 7/F4
Durrington, England 13/F6
Durrow, Laois, Ireland 17/G6
Durrow, Offaly, Ireland 17/F5
Dursey (isl.), Ireland 17/A8
Dursunbey, Turkey 63/C3
Duruh, Iran 59/H3
Duruh, Iran 66/M4
D'Urville (isl.), N. Zealand 100/D4
Duryea, Pa. 294/F7
Dusa Marreb, Somalia 115/J2
Dûsh, Egypt 59/B5
Dûsh, Egypt 111/F3
Dushan, China 77/G6
Dushanbe (cap.), Tajikistan 2/N4
Dushanbe (cap.), Tajikistan 48/G6
Dushanbe (cap.), Tajikistan 54/H6
Dushore, Pa. 294/K2
Dusky (sound), N. Zealand 100/A6
Duson, La. 238/F6
Düsseldorf, Germany 7/E3
Düsseldorf, Germany 22/B3
Dustin, Okla. 288/O4
Dusty, N. Mex. 274/B5
Dusty, Wash. 310/H4
Dutch (creek), Ark. 202/C4
Dutch Cap (cay), Virgin Is. (U.S.) 161/A4
Dutchess (co.), N.Y. 276/N7
Dutch Flat, Calif. 204/E4
Dutch Harbor, Alaska 196/E4
Dutch John, Utah 304/E3
Dutch Mills, Ark. 202/B2
Dutch Neck, N.J. 273/D3
Dutchtown, Mo. 261/N8
Dutton, Ala. 195/G1
Dutton, Ark. 202/C2
Dutton (mt.), Conn. 210/C1
Dutton, Mont. 262/E3
Dutton, Ontario 177/C5
Dutton (mt.), Utah 304/B5
Duval (co.), Fla. 212/E1
Duval, Sask. 181/G4
Duval (co.), Texas 303/F10
Duvalierville, Haiti 158/C6
Duvall, Wash. 310/D3
Duvergé, Dom. Rep. 158/D6
Duvernay, Alberta 182/E3
Duwadami, Saudi Arabia 59/D5
Duxbury (pt.), Calif. 204/H2
Duxbury, Mass. 249/M4
Duxbury•, Mass. 249/M4
Duxbury•, Vt. 268/B3
Duyun (Tuyün), China 77/G6
Düzce, Turkey 63/D2
Duzdab (Zahedan), Iran 66/M6
Dvina (bay), Russia 52/E2
Dvina, Northern (riv.), Russia 4/C7
Dvina, Northern (riv.), Russia 7/J2
Dvina, Northern (riv.), Russia 48/E3
Dvina, Northern (riv.), Russia 52/F2
Dvina, Western (riv.), Belarus 7/G3
Dvina, Western (riv.), Belarus 48/C4
Dvina, Western (riv.), Belarus 52/C3
Dvina, Western (riv.), Latvia 7/G3
Dvina, Western (riv.), Latvia 48/C4
Dvina, Western (riv.), Latvia 52/C3
Dvina, Western (riv.), Latvia 53/C2
Dvinsk (Daugavpils), Latvia 52/C3
Dvory nad Žitavou, Slovakia 41/E3
Dvůr Králové nad Labem, Czech Rep. 41/C1
Dwale, Ky. 237/R5
Dwarka, India 68/B4
Dwellingup, W. Australia 92/B2
Dwight, Ill. 222/E2
Dwight, Kansas 232/F3
Dwight, Nebr. 264/G3
Dwight, N. Dak. 282/S7
Dwight, Ontario 177/F2
Dworshak (res.), Idaho 220/C3
Dwyer, N. Mex. 274/B6
Dwyer, Wyo. 319/G3
Dyas, Ala. 195/C9
Dyat'kovo, Russia 52/D4
Dybvad, Denmark 21/D3
Dyce, Scotland 15/F3
Dyckesville, Wis. 317/L6
Dycusburg, Ky. 237/E6
Dyer, Ark. 202/B3
Dyer, Ind. 227/C1
Dyer, Ky. 237/J5
Dyer, Nev. 266/C5
Dyer (cape), N.W.T. 162/K2
Dyer (cape), N.W.T. 187/M3
Dyer (co.), Tenn. 237/C8
Dyer, Tenn. 237/D8
Dyer Brook•, Maine 243/G3
Dyersburg, Tenn. 237/C8
Dyersville, Iowa 229/L3
Dyess, Ark. 202/K2
Dyess A.F.B., Texas 303/D5
Dyfed, Wales 13/C6
Dyje (riv.), Czech Rep. 41/D2
Dyke (lake), Newf. 166/A3
Dykh-Tau (mt.), Russia 52/F6
Dyle (riv.), Belgium 27/F7
Dysart, Iowa 229/J4
Dysart, Sask. 181/H5
Dysartsville, N.C. 281/F3
Dzamïn üüd, Mongolia 77/H3
Dzavhan, Mongolia 77/E2
Dzavhan Gol (riv.), Mongolia 77/D2
Dzerzhinsk, Russia 7/J3
Dzerzhinsk, Russia 48/E4
Dzerzhinsk, Russia 52/F3
Dzhalal-Abad, Kyrgyzstan 48/H5
Dzhalilabad, Azerbaijan 52/G7
Dzhalinda, Russia 48/N4
Dzhambul, Kazakhstan 54/J5
Dzhambul, Kazakhstan 48/H5
Dzhankoy, Ukraine 52/D5
Dzhelinda, Russia 48/M2
Dzhetygara, Kazakhstan 48/G4
Dzhezkazgan, Kazakhstan 54/H5
Dzhezkazgan, Kazakhstan 48/G5
Dzhugdzhur (range), Russia 48/O4
Dzhugdzhur (range), Russia 54/P4
Dzhul'fa, Azerbaijan 52/G7
Dzhusaly, Kazakhstan 48/G5
Działdowo, Poland 47/E2
Dzibalchén, Mexico 150/P7
Dzibichaltún (ruin), Mexico 150/P6
Dzidzantún, Mexico 150/P6
Dzierżoniów, Poland 47/C3

Fannin 367

Ether, N.C. 281/K4
Ethete, Wyo. 319/D2
Ethiopia 2/L5
ETHIOPIA 59/C7
Ethiopia 102/F4
ETHIOPIA 111/G5
Ethridge, Mont. 262/D2
Ethridge, Tenn. 237/G10
Etive, Loch (inlet), Scotland 15/C4
Etiwanda, Calif. 204/E10
Etna, Calif. 204/C2
Etna, Ind. 227/F2
Etna (vol.), Italy 7/F5
Etna (vol.), Italy 34/E6
Etna•, Maine 243/E6
Etna, N.H. 268/C4
Etna, Ohio 284/E6
Etna, Pa. 294/B6
Etna, Utah 304/A2
Etna, Wyo. 319/A2
Etna Green, Ind. 227/E2
Etobicoke, Ontario 177/J4
Etoile, Ky. 237/K7
Etoile, D.R. Congo 115/E6
Etolin (isl.), Alaska 196/N2
Etolin (str.), Alaska 196/E2
Etomami (riv.), Manitoba 179/F2
Etomami (riv.), Sask. 181/J3
Eton, England 10/F5
Eton, England 13/G8
Eton, Ga. 217/C1
Etorofu (Iturup) (isl.), Japan 81/N1
Etosha Pan (salt pan), Namibia 118/B3
Etosha Salt Pan, Namibia 102/D6
Etoumbi, Congo 115/B3
Etowah (co.), Ala. 195/F2
Etowah, Ark. 202/K2
Etowah (riv.), Ga. 217/C2
Etowah, N.C. 281/D4
Etowah, Tenn. 237/M10
Étretat, France 28/D3
Etta, Miss. 256/F2
Etta (lake), N. Dak. 282/L6
Et Tafila, Jordan 65/E5
Et Taiyiba, Jordan 65/D2
Ettelbruck, Luxembourg 27/J9
Et Tell el Abyad, Syria 63/H4
Etten-Leur, Netherlands 27/F5
Etter, Minn. 255/F6
Etterbeek, Belgium 27/B9
Etters, Pa. 294/J5
Etters Beach, Sask. 181/F4
Ettington, Sask. 181/F6
Ettlingen, Germany 22/C4
Ettrick, Scotland 15/E5
Ettrick, Va. 307/O6
Ettrick, Wis. 317/D7
Ettrick Pen (mt.), Scotland 15/E5
Etty, Ky. 237/R6
Etzatlán, Mexico 150/G6
Etzikom, Alberta 182/E5
Etzikom Coulee (riv.), Alberta 182/E5
Eu, France 28/D3
Euabalong, N.S. Wales 97/D3
Eubank, Ky. 237/M6
Euboea (Évvoia) (isl.), Greece 45/G6
Eucha, Okla. 288/S2
Eucha (lake), Okla. 288/S2
Eucla, W. Australia 92/E5
Euclid, Minn. 255/B3
Euclid, Ohio 284/J9
Eucumbene (lake), N.S. Wales 97/E5
Eucutta, Miss. 256/G7
Eudora, Ark. 202/H7
Eudora, Kansas 232/G3
Eudora, Miss. 256/D1
Eudora, Mo. 261/E7
Eufaula, Ala. 195/H7
Eufaula (Walter F. George Res.) (lake), Ala. 195/H7
Eufaula (Walter F. George Res.) (lake), Ga. 217/B7
Eufaula (res.), Ohio 284/L4
Eufaula, Okla. 288/P4
Eufaula (lake), Okla. 288/P4
Eugene, Ind. 227/B5
Eugene, Mo. 261/H6
Eugene, Oreg. 188/B2
Eugene, Oreg. 146/F5
Eugene, Oreg. 291/D3
Eugene O'Neill Nat'l Hist. Site, Calif. 204/K2
Eugowra, N.S. Wales 97/E3
Euharlee, Ga. 217/C2
Euless, Texas 303/F2
Eulo, Queensland 95/C6
Eulonia, Ga. 217/K7
Eumungerie, N.S. Wales 97/E2
Eunice, La. 238/F6
Eunice, N. Mex. 274/F6
Eunola, Ala. 195/G8
Eupen, Belgium 27/J7
Euphrates (riv.) 54/F6
Euphrates (riv.), Iran 59/E3
Euphrates (riv.), Iraq 59/E3
Euphrates (riv.), Iraq 66/D4
Euphrates (riv.), Syria 59/E3
Euphrates (El Furat) (riv.), Syria 63/H4
Euphrates (Firat) (riv.), Turkey 63/G4
Eupora, Miss. 256/F3
Eure (dept.), France 28/D3
Eure (riv.), France 28/D3
Eure, N.C. 281/R2
Eure-et-Loir (dept.), France 28/D3
Eureka, Calif. 188/B2
Eureka, Calif. 146/F5
Eureka, Calif. 204/A3
Eureka, Canada 4/A14
Eureka, Colo. 208/D7
Eureka (res.), Fla. 212/E2
Eureka, Ill. 222/D3
Eureka, Ind. 227/C9
Eureka, Kansas 232/F4
Eureka, Mo. 261/M4
Eureka, Mont. 262/B2
Eureka (co.), Nev. 266/E3
Eureka, Nev. 266/E3
Eureka, N.C. 281/O3
Eureka, N.W.T. 146/K2
Eureka, N.W.T. 162/N3
Eureka, N.W.T. 187/K2
Eureka (sound), N.W.T. 187/K2
Eureka, Nova Scotia 168/F3
Eureka, S.C. 296/E2
Eureka, S.C. 296/D4
Eureka, S. Dak. 298/K2
Eureka, Utah 304/B4
Eureka, Wash. 310/G4
Eureka, W. Va. 312/D4
Eureka Lodge, Alaska 196/C1
Eureka Springs, Ark. 202/C1
Euroa, Victoria 97/C5
Europa (pt.), Gibraltar 33/D4
Europa (isl.), Réunion 102/G7
Europa (isl.), Réunion 118/G4
Europe 2/K3
Europoort, Netherlands 27/E5
Eusebio Ayala, Paraguay 144/B4
Euskirchen, Germany 22/B3
Eustace, Texas 303/H5
Eustis, Fla. 212/E3
Eustis, Maine 243/B5
Eustis•, Maine 243/B5
Eustis, Nebr. 264/D4
Euston, N.S. Wales 97/B4
Eutaw, Ala. 195/C5
Eutawville, S.C. 296/G5
Eutin, Germany 22/D1
Eutsuk (lake), Br. Col. 184/D3
Eva, Ala. 195/E2
Eva (lake), Alberta 182/B5
Eva, La. 238/G4
Eva, Okla. 288/C1
Eva, Tenn. 237/E8
Evadale, Texas 303/L7
Eva Downs, North. Terr. 93/D5
Évain, Québec 174/B3
Evan, Minn. 255/D6
Evan (lake), Québec 174/B2
Evandale, New Bruns. 170/D3
Evandale, Tasmania 99/D3
Evangeline (par.), La. 238/F5
Evangeline, La. 238/F6
Evangeline, New Bruns. 170/F1
Evans, Colo. 208/K2
Evans (mt.), Colo. 208/H3
Evans (co.), Ga. 217/J6
Evans, Ga. 217/H3
Evans, La. 238/D5
Evans (head), N.S. Wales 97/G1
Evans (str.), N.W.T. 162/H3
Evans (str.), N.W.T. 187/K3
Evans, Wash. 310/H2
Evans, W. Va. 312/C5
Evansburg, Alberta 182/C3
Evans Center, N.Y. 276/B5
Evans City, Pa. 294/B4
Evansdale, Iowa 229/J4
Evans Head, N.S. Wales 97/G1
Evans Mills, N.Y. 276/J2
Evansport, Ohio 284/B3
Evanston, Ill. 222/B5
Evanston, Ind. 227/D8
Evanston, Wyo. 188/D2
Evanston, Wyo. 319/B4
Evansville (Bettles Field), Alaska 196/H1
Evansville, Ark. 202/B2
Evansville, Ill. 222/D5
Evansville, Ind. 188/J3
Evansville, Ind. 146/K6
Evansville, Ind. 227/C9
Evansville, Minn. 255/C4
Evansville, Miss. 256/D1
Evansville, Pa. 294/L5
Evansville, Wis. 317/H10
Evansville, Wyo. 319/F3
Evant, Texas 303/G6
Evanton, Scotland 15/D3
Evart, Mich. 250/D5
Evarts, Ky. 237/P7
Evaton, S. Africa 118/H7
Evaz, Iran 66/J7
Eveleth, Minn. 255/F3
Evelyn, La. 238/D3
Evendale, Ohio 284/C9
Evening Shade, Ark. 202/G1
Evenki Aut. Okr., Russia 48/K3
Evensk, Russia 4/C1
Evensk, Russia 48/Q3
Evensville, Tenn. 237/M9
Even Yehuda, Israel 65/B3
Everard (lake), S. Australia 88/E6
Everard (lake), S. Australia 94/D4
Everard (ranges), S. Australia 94/C2
Evere, Belgium 27/C9
Everest (mt.) 54/K7
Everest (mt.), China 77/C6
Everest, Kansas 232/G2
Everest (mt.), Nepal 68/F3
Everest, N. Dak. 282/R6
Everett, Ga. 217/J8
Everett, Mass. 249/D6
Everett (mt.), Mass. 249/A4
Everett, New Bruns. 170/C1
Everett (dam), N.H. 268/D5
Everett (mts.), N.W.T. 187/M3
Everett, Ontario 177/E3
Everett, Pa. 294/F5
Everett, Wash. 188/B1
Everett, Wash. 310/C3
Everetts, N.C. 281/P3
Everettville, W. Va. 312/F3
Evergem, Belgium 27/D6
Everglades, The (swamp), Fla. 212/F6
Everglades, The (swamp), Fla. 188/K5
Everglades City, Fla. 212/E6
Everglades Nat'l Park, Fla. 212/F6
Evergreen, Ala. 195/E8
Evergreen, Colo. 208/J3
Evergreen, La. 238/F5
Evergreen, N.C. 281/M6
Evergreen, Va. 307/L6
Evergreen Park, Ill. 222/B6
Everly, Iowa 229/C2
Everman, Texas 303/F3
Everson, Pa. 294/C5
Everson, Wash. 310/C2
Eversonville, Mo. 261/F3
Everton, Ark. 202/E1
Everton, Ind. 227/G5
Everton, Mo. 261/E8
Evesham, England 10/E4
Evesham, England 13/F5
Evesham, Sask. 181/B3
Evington, Va. 307/K6
Évolène, Switzerland 39/D4
Évora (dist.), Portugal 33/C3
Évora, Portugal 7/D5
Évora, Portugal 33/C3
Évreux, France 28/D3
Évros (riv.), Greece 45/H5
Évry, France 28/E3
Évvoia (isl.), Greece 7/G5
Évvoia (isl.), Greece 45/G6
Ewa, Hawaii 218/A4
Ewab (Kai) (isls.), Indonesia 85/J7
Ewa Beach, Hawaii 218/A4
Ewan, N.J. 273/C4
Ewan, Wash. 310/H3
Ewaninga, North. Terr. 93/D7
Ewart, Iowa 229/H5
Ewarton, Jamaica 156/C3
Ewarton, Jamaica 158/J6
Ewauna (lake), Oreg. 291/F5
Ewe, Loch (inlet), Scotland 15/C3
Ewell, Md. 245/O9
Ewen, Mich. 250/F2
Ewing, Ill. 222/E5
Ewing, Ky. 237/O4
Ewing, Mo. 261/J2
Ewing, Nebr. 264/F2
Ewing, N.J. 273/D3
Ewing (mt.), North. Terr. 93/E7
Ewing, Va. 307/B7
Ewington, Ohio 284/F8
Ewo, Congo 115/B4
Exaltación, Bolivia 136/C3
Excel, Ala. 195/D8
Excel, Alberta 182/E4
Excello, Mo. 261/H3
Excello, Ohio 284/B7
Excelsior, Minn. 255/E6
Excelsior (mts.), Nev. 266/C4
Excelsior, Wis. 317/E9
Excelsior Springs, Mo. 261/R4
Exchange, W. Va. 312/E5
Excursion Inlet, Alaska 196/M1
Exe (riv.), England 13/D7
Exe (riv.), England 10/E5
Executive Committee (range), Ant. 5/B12
Exeland, Wis. 317/D4
Exeter, Calif. 204/F7
Exeter, Conn. 210/F2
Exeter, England 13/D7
Exeter, England 10/E5
Exeter, Ill. 222/C4
Exeter, Maine 243/E6
Exeter•, Maine 243/E6
Exeter, Mo. 261/D9
Exeter, Nebr. 264/G4
Exeter, N.H. 268/F6
Exeter•, N.H. 268/F6
Exeter (riv.), N.H. 268/E6
Exeter (sound), N.W.T. 187/M3
Exeter, Ontario 177/C4
Exeter•, R.I. 249/H6
Exeter, Tasmania 99/C3
Exira, Iowa 229/D5
Exline, Iowa 229/H7
Exminster, England 13/D7
Exmoor National Park, England 13/D6
Exmore, Va. 307/S5
Exmouth, England 13/D7
Exmouth, England 10/E5
Exmouth, W. Australia 88/A4
Exmouth, W. Australia 92/A3
Exmouth (gulf), W. Australia 88/A4
Exmouth (gulf), W. Australia 92/A3
Expanse, Sask. 181/E6
Experiment, Ga. 217/D4
Exploits (riv.), Newf. 166/C4
Export, Pa. 294/C5
Exshaw, Alberta 182/C4
Extension, Br. Col. 184/J3
Extension, La. 238/G3
Exu, Brazil 132/G4
Exuma (cays), Bahamas 156/C1
Exuma (sound), Bahamas 156/C1
Eyasi (lake), Tanzania 115/F4
Eye, England 10/G4
Eye, England 13/J5
Eye (pen.), Scotland 15/B2
Eyebrow, Sask. 181/E5
Eyebrow (lake), Sask. 181/E5
Eyehill (creek), Sask. 181/B3
Eyemouth, Scotland 15/F5
Eyemouth, Scotland 10/F3
Eynesil, Turkey 63/H2
Eynhallow (sound), Scotland 15/E1
Eynort, Loch (inlet), Scotland 15/A3
Eyota, Minn. 255/F7
Eyre (lake), Australia 87/D8
Eyre (bay), Chile 138/D8
Eyre (mts.), N. Zealand 100/B6
Eyre (riv.), Queensland 88/F5
Eyre (lake), S. Australia 88/F5
Eyre (pen.), S. Australia 88/F6
Eyre (pen.), S. Australia 94/D5
Eyre, W. Australia 92/D6
Eyrecourt, Ireland 17/E5
Eyre North (lake), S. Australia 94/E3
Eyre South (lake), S. Australia 94/E3
Eysturoy (isl.), Denmark 21/B3
Eyüp, Turkey 63/D6
Ezel, Ky. 237/P5
Ezequiel Montes, Mexico 150/K6
Ezibider, Turkey 63/H2
Ezine, Turkey 63/B3
Ezna, Iran 66/F4
Ez Zababida, West Bank 65/C3
Ez Zarqa', Jordan 65/E3
Ez Zuetina, Libya 111/D1

F

Faaa, Fr. Poly. 86/S13
Fabens, Texas 303/B10
Faber (lake), N.W.T. 187/G3
Faber, Va. 307/L5
Fabius, Ala. 195/G1
Fabius, N.Y. 276/J5
Fåborg, Denmark 21/D7
Fåborg, Denmark 18/G9
Fabriano, Italy 34/D3
Fabyan, Alberta 182/E3
Fabyan, Conn. 210/H1
Fabyan House, N.H. 268/E3
Facatativá, Colombia 126/C5
Faceville, Ga. 217/C9
Fachi, Niger 106/G5
Fackler, Ala. 195/G1
Factoryville, Pa. 294/L2
Facundo, Argentina 143/C6
Fada, Chad 111/D4
Fada-N'Gourma, Burkina Faso 106/E6
Fadd, Hungary 41/E3
Faddeyevskiy (isl.), Russia 4/B2
Faddeyevskiy (isl.), Russia 48/P2
Faden, Newf. 166/A3
Faenza, Italy 34/D2
Fafan (riv.), Ethiopia 111/H6
Fafe, Portugal 33/B2
Fagan, Ky. 237/O5
Făgăraş, Romania 45/G3
Fagernes, Norway 18/F6
Fagersta, Sweden 18/J6
Fagnano (lake), Argentina 143/C7
Fagnano (lake), Chile 138/F11
Faguibine (lake), Mali 106/D5
Fagundes, Brazil 132/C4
Fagus, Mo. 261/M9
Fahan, Ireland 17/G1
Fahrej (Iranshahr), Iran 66/M7
Fahrej (Iranshahr), Iran 59/H4
Faial (isl.), Portugal 33/B1
Faid, Saudi Arabia 59/D4
Faido, Switzerland 39/G4
Fainaven (mt.), Scotland 15/D2
Fair (head), N. Ireland 17/J1
Fair (isl.), Scotland 10/F1
Fairacres, N. Mex. 274/C6
Fairbank, Ariz. 198/E7
Fairbank, Iowa 229/K3
Fairbank, Md. 245/N6
Fairbanks, Alaska 146/D3
Fairbanks, Alaska 196/J2
Fairbanks, Alaska 188/D5
Fairbanks, Fla. 212/D2
Fairbanks, Ind. 227/B6
Fairbanks, La. 238/F1
Fairbanks, Maine 243/C6
Fairbanks, Minn. 255/G3
Fairbanks, U.S. 4/C17
Fairbanks, U.S. 2/C2
Fair Bluff, N.C. 281/M6
Fairborn, Ohio 284/B6
Fairburn, Ga. 217/J2
Fairburn, S. Dak. 298/C6
Fairbury, Ill. 222/E3
Fairbury, Nebr. 264/G4
Fairchance, Pa. 294/C6
Fairchild, Wis. 317/D6
Fairchild A.F.B., Wash. 310/H3
Fairdale, Ill. 222/E1
Fairdale, Ky. 237/K4
Fairdale, N. Dak. 282/O3
Fairdealing, Mo. 261/L9
Fairfax, Calif. 204/H1
Fairfax, Iowa 229/K5
Fairfax, Manitoba 179/B5
Fairfax, Minn. 255/D6
Fairfax, Mo. 261/B2
Fairfax, Ohio 284/C9
Fairfax, Okla. 288/N1
Fairfax, S.C. 296/E6
Fairfax, S. Dak. 298/M7
Fairfax•, Vt. 268/B2
Fairfax (co.), Va. 307/O3
Fairfax (I.C.), Va. 307/R3
Fairfax, Wash. 310/C4
Fairfax Station, Va. 307/R3
Fairfield, Ala. 195/E4
Fairfield, Calif. 204/K1
Fairfield (co.), Conn. 210/B3
Fairfield•, Conn. 210/B4
Fairfield, Fla. 212/D2
Fairfield, Idaho 220/D6
Fairfield, Ill. 222/E5
Fairfield, Iowa 229/J6
Fairfield, Ky. 237/L5
Fairfield, Maine 243/D6
Fairfield•, Maine 243/D6
Fairfield, Mont. 262/D3
Fairfield, Nebr. 264/G4
Fairfield, New Bruns. 170/E3
Fairfield•, N.J. 273/A2
Fairfield, N.S. Wales 88/K4
Fairfield, N.S. Wales 97/H3
Fairfield, N. Zealand 100/C6
Fairfield, N.C. 281/S3
Fairfield, N. Dak. 282/D5
Fairfield (co.), Ohio 284/E6
Fairfield, Ohio 284/A7
Fairfield, Pa. 294/H6
Fairfield (co.), S.C. 296/E3
Fairfield, Tenn. 237/J9
Fairfield, Texas 303/H6
Fairfield, Utah 304/B3
Fairfield•, Vt. 268/B2
Fairfield (pond), Vt. 268/A2
Fairfield, Va. 307/K5
Fairfield, Wash. 310/H3
Fairfield Center, Maine 243/D6
Fairford, Ala. 195/B8
Fairford, Manitoba 179/D3
Fairgrange, Ill. 222/E4
Fairgrove, Mich. 250/F5
Fair Grove, Mo. 261/F8W
Fair Harbour, Br. Col. 184/D5
Fairhaven•, Mass. 249/L6
Fair Haven, Mich. 250/G6
Fairhaven, Minn. 255/D5
Fairhaven, New Bruns. 170/C4
Fair Haven, N.J. 273/E3
Fair Haven, N.Y. 276/G4
Fairhaven, Ohio 284/A6
Fair Haven, Vt. 268/A4
Fair Haven•, Vt. 268/A4
Fair Hill, Md. 245/P2
Fairholme, Sask. 181/C2
Fairhope, Ala. 195/C10
Fairhope, Pa. 294/E6
Fairisle, New Bruns. 170/E1
Fair Isle (isl.), Scotland 15/F3
Fairland, Ind. 227/F5
Fairland, Okla. 288/S1
Fair Lawn, N.J. 273/B1
Fairlawn, Ohio 284/G3
Fairlawn, Va. 307/G6
Fairlee, Md. 245/O4
Fairlee•, Vt. 268/C4
Fairless Hills, Pa. 294/N5
Fairlie, N. Zealand 100/C6
Fairlie, Scotland 15/D5
Fairlight, Sask. 181/K6
Fairmead, Calif. 204/E6
Fairmont, Ill. 222/A2
Fairmont, Minn. 255/D7
Fairmont, Mo. 261/J2
Fairmont, Nebr. 264/G4
Fairmont, N.C. 281/L6
Fairmont, Okla. 288/L2
Fairmont, W. Va. 188/K3
Fairmont, W. Va. 312/F4
Fairmont City, Ill. 222/B2
Fairmont Hot Springs, Br. Col. 184/J5
Fairmount, Ga. 217/C2
Fairmount, Ill. 222/F3
Fairmount, Ind. 227/F4
Fairmount, Md. 245/P8
Fairmount, N. Dak. 282/S7
Fairmount, Sask. 181/B4
Fairmount Heights, Md. 245/G5
Fair Oaks, Ark. 202/J3
Fair Oaks, Calif. 204/C8
Fair Oaks, Ga. 217/J1
Fair Oaks, Ind. 227/C2
Fair Oaks, Okla. 288/P2
Fair Plain, Mich. 250/C6
Fairplain, W. Va. 312/C5
Fairplay, Colo. 208/H4
Fairplay, Ky. 237/L7
Fair Play, Mo. 261/E7
Fair Play, S.C. 296/A2
Fairpoint, Ohio 284/J5
Fairpoint, S. Dak. 298/D4
Fairport, Iowa 229/M6
Fairport, Kansas 232/C2
Fairport, Mo. 261/D2
Fairport, N.Y. 276/F4
Fairport, Va. 307/R5
Fairport Harbor, Ohio 284/H2
Fairton, N.J. 273/C5
Fairvale, New Bruns. 170/E3
Fairview, Ala. 195/E2
Fairview, Alberta 182/A1
Fairview, Ill. 222/B3
Fairview, Ind. 227/G5
Fairview, Ind. 227/G7
Fairview, Kansas 232/G2
Fairview, Ky. 237/S2
Fairview, Ky. 237/G7
Fairview, Mich. 250/F4
Fairview, Mo. 261/D9
Fairview, Mont. 262/M3
Fairview, N.J. 273/C2
Fairview, N.Y. 276/N7
Fairview, N.C. 281/D3
Fairview, Ohio 284/H5
Fairview, Okla. 288/J2
Fairview, Oreg. 291/B2
Fairview, Pa. 294/B1
Fairview, Pa. 294/C3
Fairview, S. Dak. 298/R7
Fairview, Tenn. 237/G9
Fairview, Utah 304/C4
Fairview, W. Va. 312/F3
Fairview, Wyo. 319/B3
Fairview Heights, Ill. 222/B3
Fairview Park, Ind. 227/C5
Fairview Park, Ohio 284/G9
Fairview-Sumach, Wash. 310/E4
Fair Water, Wis. 317/J8
Fairway, Kansas 232/H2
Fairweather (cape), Alaska 196/L1
Fairweather (mt.), Alaska 196/L1
Fairweather (mt.), Br. Col. 184/H1
Fairy Glen, Sask. 181/G2
Fais (isl.), Micronesia 87/E5
Faisalabad, Pakistan 54/J6
Faisalabad, Pakistan 59/K3
Faisalabad, Pakistan 68/C2
Faison, N.C. 281/N4
Faith, Minn. 255/B3
Faith, N.C. 281/J3
Faith, S. Dak. 298/E4
Faithorn, Mich. 250/B3
Faizabad-cum-Ayodhya, India 68/E3
Fajami, Syria 63/J5
Fajardo, P. Rico 161/F1
Fajardo (riv.), P. Rico 161/F1
Fajou (isl.), Guadeloupe 161/A6
Fakaofo (atoll), Tokelau Is. 87/J6
Fakarava (atoll), Fr. Poly. 87/M7
Fakenham, England 13/H5
Fakfak, Indonesia 85/J6
Fakılı, Turkey 63/F3
Fakse, Denmark 21/F7
Fakse (bay), Denmark 21/F7
Fakse Ladeplads, Denmark 21/F7
Falaise, France 28/C3
Falam, Burma 72/B2
Falama, West Bank 65/C3
Falcarragh, Ireland 17/E1
Fălçiu, Romania 45/J2
Falcon, Ky. 237/P5
Falcon (lake), Manitoba 179/G5
Falcón (res.), Mexico 150/K3
Falcon, Miss. 256/D2
Falcon, N.C. 281/M4
Falcon (cape), Oreg. 291/C2
Falcon (dam), Texas 303/E11
Falcon (res.), Texas 188/G5
Falcon (res.), Texas 303/E11
Falcón (state), Venezuela 124/D2
Falcone (cape), Italy 34/B4
Falconer, N.Y. 276/B6
Falcon Heights, Minn. 255/G5
Falcon Heights, Oreg. 291/F5
Falcon Lake, Manitoba 179/G5
Falémé (riv.), Mali 106/B6
Falémé (riv.), Senegal 106/B6
Faleolo, Samoa 86/L8
Falfurrias, Texas 303/F10
Falher, Alberta 182/B2
Falkenberg, Sweden 18/H8
Falkensee, Germany 22/E3
Falkenstein, Germany 22/E3
Falkirk, N. Dak. 282/H5
Falkirk, Scotland 10/B1
Falkirk, Scotland 15/C1
Falkland (isls.) 2/G8
Falkland (isls.) 143/D7
Falkland (sound), Falk. Is. 143/D7
Falkland, Br. Col. 184/H5
Falkland, N.C. 281/O3
Falkland, Scotland 15/E4
Falkland Islands 120/D8
FALKLAND ISLANDS 143
Falkner, Miss. 256/G1
Falknov (Sokolov), Czech Rep. 41/B1
Falköping, Sweden 18/H7
Falkville, Ala. 195/E2
Fall (riv.), Kansas 232/G4
Falla, Cuba 158/F2
Fall Branch, Tenn. 237/R8
Fallbrook, Calif. 204/H10
Fall City, Wash. 310/D3
Fall Creek, Oreg. 291/E4
Fall Creek, Wis. 317/D6
Fallin, Scotland 15/C1
Falling Spring (Renick), W. Va. 312/F6
Falling Waters, W. Va. 312/L3
Fallis, Okla. 288/M3
Fall Mills, Tenn. 237/J10
Fallon (co.), Mont. 262/M4
Fallon, Mont. 262/L4
Fallon, Nev. 266/C3
Fallon Ind. Res., Nev. 266/C3
Fallon Nav. Air Sta., Nev. 266/C3
Fall River, Kansas 232/G4
Fall River (lake), Kansas 232/F4
Fall River, Mass. 188/M2
Fall River, Mass. 249/K6
Fall River, Nova Scotia 168/E4
Fall River (co.), S. Dak. 298/B7
Fall River, Tenn. 237/G10
Fall River, Wis. 317/H9
Fall River Mills, Calif. 204/D3
Falls (riv.), Mass. 249/D2
Falls, Pa. 294/E6
Falls (co.), Texas 303/H6
Falls Church (I.C.), Va. 307/S2
Falls City, Nebr. 264/J4
Falls City, Oreg. 291/D3
Falls City, Texas 303/G9
Falls Creek, Pa. 294/E3
Falls Mill, W. Va. 312/E5
Falls Mills, Va. 307/F6
Falls of Rough, Ky. 237/J5
Fallston, Md. 245/N2
Fallston, N.C. 281/G4
Falls Village, Conn. 210/B1
Fallsville, Ark. 202/D2
Falmouth, Ant. & Bar. 161/E11
Falmouth, Ant. & Bar. 156/F3
Falmouth, England 10/D5
Falmouth, England 13/B7
Falmouth (bay), England 13/B7
Falmouth, Ind. 227/G5
Falmouth, Jamaica 158/H5
Falmouth, Jamaica 156/C3
Falmouth, Ky. 237/N3
Falmouth, Maine 243/C8
Falmouth•, Maine 243/C8
Falmouth, Mass. 249/M6
Falmouth•, Mass. 249/M6
Falmouth, Mich. 250/E4
Falmouth, Nova Scotia 168/D3
Falmouth, Va. 307/O4
False (bay), S. Africa 118/F7
False Detour (chan.), Mich. 250/F3
False Divi (pt.), India 68/E5
False Pass, Alaska 196/F4
Falso (cape), Dom. Rep. 158/C7
Falso (cape), Honduras 154/F3
Falso (cape), Mexico 150/D5
Falster (isl.), Denmark 21/F8
Fălticeni, Romania 45/H2
Falun, Kansas 232/E3
Falun, Sweden 18/J6
Falun, Sweden 7/F2
Falun, Wis. 317/A4
Famagusta, Cyprus 63/F5
Famagusta, Cyprus 59/B3
Famagusta (bay), Cyprus 63/F5
Famaka, Sudan 111/F5
Famatina, Argentina 143/C2
Famatina, Sierra de (mts.), Argentina 143/C2
Family (lake), Manitoba 179/G3
Famoso, Calif. 204/F8
Fan (lake), N. Dak. 282/L2
Fanad (head), Ireland 17/F1
Fancy Farm, Ky. 237/D7
Fancy Gap, Va. 307/G7
Fancy Prairie, Ill. 222/D4
Fandriana, Madagascar 118/H4
Fangak, Sudan 111/F6
Fang Xian, China 77/G5
Fangzheng, China 77/L2
Fannettsburg, Pa. 294/G5
Fannich, Loch (lake), Scotland 15/D3
Fannin (co.), Ga. 217/D1
Fannin, Miss. 256/E6

Fort Apache 369

Fisher, La. 238/D4
Fisher (bay), Manitoba 179/E3
Fisher (riv.), Manitoba 179/E3
Fisher, Minn. 255/B3
Fisher (str.), N.W.T. 162/H3
Fisher (str.), N.W.T. 187/K3
Fisher (lake), Nova Scotia 168/C4
Fisher, S. Australia 94/B4
Fisher (co.), Texas 303/D5
Fisher, W. Va. 312/H4
Fisher Bay, Manitoba 179/E3
Fisher Branch, Manitoba 179/E3
Fishermans (isl.), Va. 307/S6
Fishers, Ind. 227/E5
Fishers (isl.), N.Y. 276/S8
Fishers Island, N.Y. 276/R8
Fishersville, Va. 307/K4
Fisherville (South Grafton), Mass. 249/H4
Fishguard and Goodwick, Wales 13/B5
Fishguard and Goodwick, Wales 10/D4
Fish Haven, Idaho 220/G7
Fishing (lake), Manitoba 179/G2
Fishing (bay), Md. 245/O7
Fishing (creek), N.C. 281/O2
Fishing Creek, Md. 245/N7
Fishing Lake, Alberta 182/E3
Fishing Ships Harbour, Newf. 166/C3
Fishkill, N.Y. 276/N7
Fish River (lake), Maine 243/F2
Fishs Eddy, N.Y. 276/K8
Fish Springs (range), Utah 304/A4
Fishtail, Mont. 262/G5
Fishtoft, England 13/H5
Fishtrap, Ky. 237/S6
Fishtrap (lake), Ky. 237/S6
Fisk, Mo. 261/M9
Fiskdale, Mass. 249/F4
Fiske, Sask. 181/C4
Fiskeville, R.I. 249/H6
Fitch Bay, Québec 172/E4
Fitchburg, Mass. 249/G2
Fitchville, Conn. 210/G2
Fitchville, Ohio 284/E3
Fithian, Ill. 222/F3
Fitler, Miss. 256/B5
Fittri (lake), Chad 111/C5
Fittstown, Okla. 288/N5
Fitzcarrald, Peru 128/G8
Fitzgerald, Alberta 182/C4
Fitzgerald, Ga. 217/F7
Fitzgerald, N.W.T. 162/E4
Fitzhugh (sound), Br. Col. 184/D4
Fitzhugh, Okla. 288/N5
Fitzmaurice (riv.), North. Terr. 93/B3
Fitzpatrick, Ala. 195/G6
Fitzpatrick, Ga. 217/F5
Fitzroy (riv.), Australia 87/C7
Fitz Roy (Chaltel) (mt.), Chile 138/E8
Fitzroy, North. Terr. 93/B4
Fitzroy (riv.), Queensland 88/J4
Fitzroy (riv.), Queensland 95/D4
Fitzroy, Victoria 97/H5
Fitzroy, Victoria 88/L7
Fitzroy (riv.), W. Australia 88/C3
Fitzroy (riv.), W. Australia 92/D2
Fitzroy Crossing, W. Australia 88/D3
Fitzroy Crossing, W. Australia 92/D2
Fitzroy Harbour, Ontario 177/H2
Fitzwilliam•, N.H. 268/C6
Fitzwilliam (isl.), Ontario 177/C2
Fitzwilliam Depot, N.H. 268/C6
Fiume (Rijeka), Croatia 45/B3
Fiumicino, Italy 34/F7
Five (isls.), Nova Scotia 168/D3
Five Fingers, New Bruns. 170/C1
Five Island (lake), Iowa 229/D2
Five Islands, Maine 243/D8
Five Islands, Nova Scotia 168/D3
Five Mile (riv.), Conn. 210/H1
Fivemile (creek), Oreg. 291/F2
Fivemile (pt.), Oreg. 291/C4
Fivemile (creek), Wyo. 319/D2
Fivemiletown, N. Ireland 17/G3
Five Points, Ala. 195/H4
Five Points, Fla. 212/D1
Five Points, Tenn. 237/G10
Five Stars, Guyana 131/A2
Fivizzano, Italy 34/B2
Fizi, D.R. Congo 115/E4
Fjerritslev, Denmark 21/C3
Flagler, Colo. 208/N4
Flagler (co.), Fla. 212/E2
Flagler Beach, Fla. 212/E2
Flag Pond, Tenn. 237/R8
Flagstaff, Ariz. 146/G6
Flagstaff, Ariz. 188/D3
Flagstaff, Ariz. 198/D3
Flagstaff (lake), Maine 243/C5
Flagstaff (lake), Oreg. 291/H5
Flagtown, N.J. 273/D2
Flambeau (riv.), Wis. 317/E4
Flambeau Flowage (res.), Wis. 317/F3
Flamborough (head), England 13/G3
Flamborough (head), England 10/G3
Flamenco de San Pedro, Cuba 158/F3
Flaming Gorge (dam), Utah 304/E3
Flaming Gorge (res.), Utah 304/E3
Flaming Gorge (res.), Wyo. 319/C4
Flaming Gorge Nat'l Rec. Area, Utah 304/E2
Flaming Gorge Nat'l Rec. Area, Wyo. 319/C4
Flamingo (cay), Bahamas 156/C2
Flanagan, Ill. 222/E3
Flanagan (passage), Virgin Is. (U.K.) 161/D4
Flanagan (passage), Virgin Is. (U.S.) 161/D4
Flanagin Town, Trin. & Tob. 161/B10
Flanders, Conn. 210/B1
Flanders (trad. prov.) France 29
Flanders, N.J. 273/D2
Flanders, Ontario 175/B3
Flanders-Riverside, N.Y. 276/P9
Flandreau, S. Dak. 298/R5
Flanigan, Nev. 266/B2
Flannagan (res.), Va. 307/C6
Flannan (isls.), Scotland 15/A2
Flannan (isls.), Scotland 10/C1
Flasher, N. Dak. 282/H7
Flat, Ky. 237/O5
Flat, Mo. 261/J7
Flat (isl.), Philippines 85/F3
Flat, Texas 303/G6
Flat (cays), Virgin Is. (U.S.) 161/A4
Flat (creek), Va. 307/M6
Flat Bay, Newf. 166/C4
Flatbrookville, N.J. 273/D1
Flatbush, Alberta 182/C2
Flat Creek, Tenn. 237/H10
Flat Creek-Wegra, Ala. 195/D3
Flat Fork, Ky. 237/P5
Flatgap, Ky. 237/R5
Flathead (riv.), Br. Col. 184/K6
Flathead (co.), Mont. 262/B2
Flathead (lake), Mont. 188/D1
Flathead (lake), Mont. 262/C3
Flathead (riv.), Mont. 262/B2
Flathead, North Fork (riv.), Mont. 262/B2
Flathead, South Fork (riv.), Mont. 262/C3
Flathead Ind. Res., Mont. 262/B3
Flatlands, New Bruns. 170/D1
Flat Lick, Ky. 237/O7
Flatonia, Texas 303/G8
Flat River, Mo. 261/M7
Flat Rock, Ala. 195/G1
Flat Rock, Ill. 222/F5
Flat Rock, Ind. 227/F6
Flatrock (creek), Ind. 227/F5
Flat Rock, Ky. 237/M7
Flat Rock, Mich. 250/F6
Flat Rock, Newf. 166/D2
Flat Rock, N.C. 281/E4
Flat Rock, Ohio 284/E3
Flats, N.C. 281/B4
Flattery (cape), Br. Col. 162/D6
Flattery (cape), Queensland 88/H2
Flattery (cape), Queensland 95/C2
Flattery (cape), Wash. 146/F5
Flattery (cape), Wash. 188/A1
Flattery (cape), Wash. 310/A2
Flat Top, W. Va. 312/D7
Flatwillow (creek), Mont. 262/H4
Flatwood, Ala. 195/C6
Flatwoods, Ky. 237/R4
Flatwoods, La. 238/E4
Flatwoods, Tenn. 237/F9
Flatwoods, W. Va. 312/E5
Flawil, Switzerland 39/H2
Flaxcombe, Sask. 181/B4
Flaxman (isl.), Alaska 196/J1
Flaxton, N. Dak. 282/F2
Flaxville, Mont. 262/L2
Fleet, Alberta 182/E3
Fleet, England 13/G8
Fleet, Loch (inlet), Scotland 15/D3
Fleetwood, England 10/E4
Fleetwood, England 13/D4
Fleetwood, Okla. 288/L7
Fleetwood, Pa. 294/L5
Fleischmanns, N.Y. 276/L6
Flekkefjord, Norway 18/E7
Flémalle, Belgium 27/G7
Fleming, Colo. 208/O1
Fleming, Ga. 217/K7
Fleming (co.), Ky. 237/O4
Fleming, Mo. 261/D4
Fleming, Pa. 294/G4
Fleming, Sask. 181/K5
Fleming-Neon, Ky. 237/R6
Flemingsburg, Ky. 237/O4
Flemington, Ga. 217/K7
Flemington, Mo. 261/F7
Flemington, N.J. 273/D2
Flemington, Pa. 294/G3
Flemington, W. Va. 312/F4
Flen, Sweden 18/K7
Flensburg, Minn. 255/D5
Flensburg, Germany 22/C1
Flers, France 28/C3
Flesherton, Ontario 177/D3
Flesk (riv.), Ireland 17/C7
Fleta, Ala. 195/F6
Fletcher (pond), Mich. 250/F4
Fletcher, Mo. 261/L6
Fletcher, N.C. 281/E4
Fletcher, Ohio 284/B5
Fletcher, Okla. 288/K5
Fletcher•, Vt. 268/B2
Fletschhorn (mt.), Switzerland 39/F4
Fleurance, France 28/D6
Fleur de Lys, Newf. 166/C3
Fleur-de-May (lake), Newf. 166/B3
Fleurier, Switzerland 39/C3
Fleurus, Belgium 27/E8
Flevoland Polders, Netherlands 27/G4
Flims, Switzerland 39/H3
Flinders (reef), Coral Sea Is. Terr. 88/H3
Flinders (reefs), Coral Sea Is. Terr. 95/D3
Flinders (riv.), Australia 87/E7
Flinders (riv.), Queensland 88/G3
Flinders (riv.), Queensland 95/B3
Flinders (range), S. Australia 88/F6
Flinders (range), S. Australia 94/F4
Flinders (isl.), Tasmania 88/H7
Flinders (isl.), Tasmania 99/D1
Flinders (bay), W. Australia 88/A6
Flinders (bay), W. Australia 92/A6
Flin Flon, Man. 146/H4
Flin Flon, Manitoba 179/H3
Flin Flon, Man.-Sask. 162/F4
Flin Flon, Sask. 181/N4
Flint, Ga. 217/D8
Flint (riv.), Ga. 188/K4
Flint (riv.), Ga. 217/D8
Flint, Ind. 227/G1
Flint (isl.), Kiribati 87/L7
Flint, Mich. 146/K5
Flint, Mich. 188/K2
Flint, Mich. 250/F5
Flint (riv.), Mich. 250/F5
Flint (lake), N.W.T. 187/L3
Flint, Wales 13/G2
Flint City, Ala. 195/D1
Flinthill, Mo. 261/L5
Flint Hill, Va. 307/M3
Flinton, Ontario 177/G3
Flint Rock (creek), S. Dak. 298/E3
Flintstone, Ga. 217/B1
Flintstone (lake), Manitoba 179/G4
Flintstone, Md. 245/D2
Flintville, Tenn. 237/H10
Flippen, Ga. 217/D3
Flippin, Ark. 202/E1
Flippin, Ky. 237/K7
Flix, Spain 33/G2
Flom, Minn. 255/B3
Flomaton, Ala. 195/D8
Flomot, Texas 303/D3
Flood, Br. Col. 184/M3
Floodwood, Minn. 255/E4
Flora, Ill. 222/E5
Flora, Ind. 227/E3
Flora, La. 238/D3
Flora, Miss. 256/D5
Flora, N. Dak. 282/M4
Flora (riv.), North. Terr. 93/B3
Flora, Norway 18/D6
Flora, Oreg. 291/K2
Florac, France 28/E5
Florahome, Fla. 212/E2
Floral, Ark. 202/G2
Florala, Ala. 195/F8
Floral City, Fla. 212/D3
Floral Park, N.Y. 276/P7
Floraville, Queensland 95/B3
Flora Vista, N. Mex. 274/A2
Floreana (Sta. Maria), Ecuador 128/B10
Floreana (Santa Maria) (isl.), Ecuador 128/B10
Florence, Ala. 188/J4
Florence, Ala. 195/C1
Florence, Ariz. 198/D5
Florence, Ark. 202/G6
Florence (lake), Calif. 204/G6
Florence, Colo. 208/J6
Florence, Ill. 222/C4
Florence, Ind. 227/H7
Florence (prov.), Italy 34/C3
Florence, Italy 7/F4
Florence, Italy 34/C3
Florence, Kansas 232/E3
Florence, Ky. 237/R2
Florence, Minn. 255/B6
Florence, Miss. 256/D6
Florence, Mo. 261/G5
Florence, Mont. 262/B4
Florence, N.Y. 276/J4
Florence, N.C. 281/R4
Florence, Nova Scotia 168/H2
Florence, Ontario 177/B5
Florence, Oreg. 291/C4
Florence, Pa. 294/A5
Florence (co.), S.C. 296/H3
Florence, S.C. 188/L4
Florence, S.C. 296/H3
Florence, S. Dak. 298/P3
Florence (riv.), Tasmania 99/C4
Florence, Tenn. 237/H9
Florence, Texas 303/G7
Florence, Vt. 268/A4
Florence (co.), Wis. 317/K4
Florence, Wis. 317/K4
Florence Junction, Ariz. 198/D5
Florence-Roebling, N.J. 273/D3
Florenceville, New Bruns. 170/C2
Florencia, Colombia 126/C7
Florencia, Colombia 120/B2
Florencia, Cuba 158/F2
Florennes, Belgium 27/F8
Florenton, Minn. 255/F3
Florenville, Belgium 27/G9
Flores, Las (riv.), Argentina 143/G7
Flores, Brazil 132/G4
Flores (isl.), Br. Col. 184/D5
Flores, Guatemala 154/C2
Flores (isl.), Indonesia 54/O10
Flores (isl.), Indonesia 85/G7
Flores (sea), Indonesia 2/Q6
Flores (sea), Indonesia 54/N10
Flores (sea), Indonesia 85/F7
Flores (isl.), Portugal 33/A1
Flores (dept.), Uruguay 145/C4
Flores (isl.), Uruguay 145/D5
Floresville, Texas 303/K11
Florey, Texas 303/B5
Florham Park, N.J. 273/E2
Floriano, Brazil 132/F4
Floriano, Brazil 120/E3
Florianópolis, Brazil 132/E9
Florianópolis, Brazil 120/E5
Florida 188/K5
FLORIDA 212
Florida (strs.) 146/K7
Florida, Bolivia 136/D6
Florida, Cuba 158/G3
Florida (str.), Cuba 156/B1
Florida (bay), Fla. 188/K6
Florida (bay), Fla. 212/F6
Florida (cape), Fla. 212/F6
Florida (keys), Fla. 188/K6
Florida (keys), Fla. 212/E7
Florida (strs.), Fla. 188/K6
Florida (strs.), Fla. 212/F7
Florida•, Mass. 249/B2
Florida, Mo. 261/J4
Florida (mts.), N. Mex. 274/B7
Florida, N.Y. 276/M8
Florida, Ohio 284/B3
Florida, P. Rico 161/C1
Florida (isls.), Solomon Is. 86/E3
Florida (state), U.S. 146/K7
Florida (dept.), Uruguay 145/D4
Florida, Uruguay 145/C5
Florida City, Fla. 212/F6
Florida Ridge, Fla. 212/F4
Floridia, Italy 34/E6
Florien, La. 238/D4
Florin, Calif. 204/B8
Florin, Pa. 294/J5
Flórina, Greece 45/E5
Floris, Iowa 229/J7
Florissant, Colo. 208/J5
Florissant, Mo. 261/P1
Florissant Fossil Beds Nat'l Mon., Colo. 208/J5
Flossmoor, Ill. 222/B6
Flovilla, Ga. 217/E4
Flowerdale, Tasmania 99/B2
Floweree, Mont. 262/E3
Flower Mound, Texas 303/F1
Flowerpot (isl.), Ontario 177/C2
Flowers (bay), Newf. 166/B2
Flowers Cove, Newf. 166/C3
Flowery Branch, Ga. 217/E2
Flowood, Miss. 256/D6
Floyd (co.), Ga. 217/B2
Floyd, Ga. 217/J1
Floyd (co.), Ind. 227/F8
Floyd (co.), Iowa 229/H2
Floyd, Iowa 229/H2
Floyd (riv.), Iowa 229/A3
Floyd (co.), Ky. 237/R5
Floyd, La. 238/H1
Floyd, N. Mex. 274/F4
Floyd (co.), Texas 303/C3
Floyd (co.), Va. 307/H7
Floyd, Va. 307/H7
Floydada, Texas 303/C3
Floyd Dale, S.C. 296/J3
Floyds Knobs, Ind. 227/F8
Fluchthorn (mt.), Switzerland 39/K3
Flüela (pass), Switzerland 39/J3
Flüelen, Switzerland 39/G3
Fluhberg (mt.), Switzerland 39/G2
Fluker, La. 238/K5
Flums, Switzerland 39/H2
Flushing, Mich. 250/F5
Flushing, Netherlands 27/C6
Flushing, Ohio 284/J5
Fluvanna, Texas 303/D5
Fluvanna (co.), Va. 307/M5
Fly, Ohio 284/H6
Fly (riv.), Papua N.G. 87/E6
Fly (riv.), Papua N.G. 85/A7
Fly Creek, N.Y. 276/K5
Flying H, N. Mex. 274/E5
Flying Shot, Alberta 182/A2
Flynns Lick, Tenn. 237/K8
Foam Lake, Sask. 181/H4
Foard (co.), Texas 303/E3
Foça, Turkey 63/B3
Foča, Bos. 45/D4
Fochabers, Scotland 15/E3
Focşani, Romania 45/H3
Foge (isl.), Nigeria 106/E6
Foggia (prov.), Italy 34/E4
Foggia, Italy 7/F4
Foggia, Italy 34/E4
Fogo (isl.), C. Verde 106/B8
Fogo, Newf. 166/D4
Fogo (isl.), Newf. 166/D4
Fogo (isl.), Newf. 162/L6
Fohnsdorf, Austria 41/C3
Föhr (isl.), Germany 22/C1
Foisy, Alberta 182/E3
Foix, France 28/D6
Foix (trad. prov.) France 29
Folcroft, Pa. 294/M7
Folda (fjord), Norway 18/J3
Folda (fjord), Norway 18/G4
Földeák, Hungary 41/F3
Földes, Hungary 41/F2
Foley, Ala. 195/C10
Foley, Fla. 212/C1
Foley, Minn. 255/D5
Foley, Mo. 261/L4
Foley (isl.), N.W.T. 187/L3
Foleyet, Ontario 177/J5
Foleyet, Ontario 175/D3
Foligno, Italy 34/D3
Folkestone, England 13/J6
Folkestone, England 10/G5
Folkston, Ga. 217/H9
Folkstone, N.C. 281/O5
Follansbee, W. Va. 312/E2
Follett, Texas 303/D1
Föllinge, Sweden 18/J5
Folly Beach, S.C. 296/H6
Folsom, Calif. 204/C8
Folsom (lake), Calif. 204/C8
Folsom, La. 238/K5
Folsom, N.J. 273/D4
Folsom, N. Mex. 274/E2
Folsom, Pa. 294/M7
Folsom, W. Va. 312/E4
Folsomville, Ind. 227/C8
Folteşti, Romania 45/H3
Fomboni, Comoros 118/G2
Fomento, Cuba 158/E2
Fonda, Iowa 229/D3
Fonda, N.Y. 276/M5
Fonda, N. Dak. 282/K2
Fond d'Or (bay), St. Lucia 161/G6
Fond du Lac, Sask. 181/L2
Fond-du-Lac (riv.), Sask. 162/F4
Fond du Lac (riv.), Sask. 181/M2
Fond du Lac (co.), Wis. 317/K8
Fond du Lac, Wis. 188/J2
Fond du Lac, Wis. 317/K8
Fond du Lac Ind. Res., Minn. 255/F4
Fonde, Ky. 237/O7
Fondi, Italy 34/D4
Fond-Lahaye, Martinique 161/C6
Fond-Saint-Denis, Martinique 161/C6
Fond Verrettes, Haiti 158/C6
Fonehill, Sask. 181/J4
Fongafale (cap.), Tuvalu 87/H6
Fonsagrada, Spain 33/C1
Fonseca, Colombia 126/D2
Fonseca (gulf), El Salvador 154/D4
Fonseca (gulf), Honduras 154/D4
Fonseca (gulf), Nicaragua 154/D4
Fontaine, New Bruns. 170/F2
Fontainebleau, France 28/E3
Fontainebleau, Québec 172/F4
Fontana, Calif. 204/E10
Fontana, Kansas 232/H3
Fontana (lake), N.C. 281/B4
Fontana, Wis. 317/J10
Fontanelle, Iowa 229/E6
Fontanet, Ind. 227/C5
Fontas (riv.), Br. Col. 184/M2
Fonte Boa, Brazil 132/G9
Fontein, Neth. Ant. 161/E8
Fontenay-le-Comte, France 28/C4
Fontenay-sous-Bois, France 28/C2
Fonteneau (lake), Newf. 166/B3
Fontenelle, Québec 172/D1
Fontenelle (creek), Wyo. 319/B3
Fontenelle (res.), Wyo. 319/B3
Fontibón, Colombia 126/C5
Fontur (prom.), Iceland 7/C2
Fontur (pt.), Iceland 21/D1
Fonyód, Hungary 41/D3
Foochow (Fuzhou), China 77/J6
Fool Creek (res.), Utah 304/B4
Foosland, Ill. 222/E3
Foothills, Alberta 182/B3
Footscray, Victoria 97/H5
Footscray, Victoria 88/K7
Footville, Ohio 284/J2
Footville, Wis. 317/H10
Foping, China 77/G5
Forada, Minn. 255/C5
Foraker (mt.), Alaska 196/H2
Foraker, Ind. 227/F1
Foraker, Ohio 284/C4
Foraker, Okla. 288/O1
Forbach, France 28/G3
Forbes (mt.), Alberta 182/B4
Forbes (mt.), Br. Col. 184/J4
Forbes (isl.), Fla. 212/D6
Forbes, Minn. 255/F3
Forbes, Mo. 261/B3
Forbes, N.S. Wales 88/H6
Forbes, N.S. Wales 97/E3
Forbes, N. Dak. 282/N8
Forbes (lake), Québec 172/C3
Forbing, La. 238/C2
Forbus, Tenn. 237/M7
Forcados, Nigeria 106/E7
Forcalquier, France 28/F6
Force, Pa. 294/E3
Forchheim, Germany 22/D4
Forchu (bay), Nova Scotia 168/H3
Forchu (cape), Nova Scotia 168/B5
Ford, England 13/F2
Ford (isl.), Hawaii 218/B3
Ford (co.), Ill. 222/E3
Ford (co.), Kansas 232/C4
Ford, Kansas 232/C4
Ford, Ky. 237/N5
Ford (riv.), Mich. 250/B2
Ford (cape), North. Terr. 88/D2
Ford (cape), North. Terr. 93/A2
Ford, Va. 307/N6
Ford, Wash. 310/H3
Ford City, Calif. 204/F8
Ford City, Mo. 261/C2
Ford City, Pa. 294/D4
Ford Cliff, Pa. 294/D4
Ford Heights, Ill. 222/C6
Fordland, Mo. 261/G8
Fordoche, La. 238/G5
Ford Ranges (mts.), Ant. 5/B11
Fords, N.J. 273/E2
Ford's Bridge, N.S. Wales 97/C1
Fords Prairie, Wash. 310/B4
Fordsville, Ky. 237/H5
Fordville, N. Dak. 282/P3
Fordwich, Ontario 177/C4
Fordyce, Ark. 202/F6
Fordyce, Nebr. 264/G2
Forécariah, Guinea 106/B7
Foreman, Ark. 202/B6
Foremost, Alberta 182/E5
Foresman, Ind. 227/C3
Forest, Belgium 27/B9
Forest, Ind. 227/E4
Forest, La. 238/H1
Forest, Miss. 256/F6
Forest (riv.), N. Dak. 282/P3
Forest, Ohio 284/C4
Forest, Ontario 177/C4
Forest (co.), Pa. 294/D2
Forest, Va. 307/K6
Forest (co.), Wis. 317/J4
Forest Acres, S.C. 296/E3
Forest Beach, S.C. 296/F7
Forestburg, Alberta 182/E3
Forestburg, S. Dak. 298/N5
Forestburg, Texas 303/G4
Forest City, Ill. 222/D3
Forest City, Iowa 229/F2
Forest City, Maine 243/H4
Forest City, Mo. 261/B3
Forest City, New Bruns. 170/C3
Forest City, N.C. 281/E4
Forest City, Pa. 294/L2
Forestdale, Ala. 195/E3
Forestdale, R.I. 249/H5
Forest Dale, Vt. 268/A4
Forester, Mich. 250/G5
Foresters Falls, Ontario 177/H2
Forest Glen, Ga. 217/F7
Forest Green, Mo. 261/G4
Forest Grove, Br. Col. 184/G4
Forestgrove, Mont. 262/H3
Forest Grove, Oreg. 291/A2
Forest Heights, Md. 245/F5
Foresthill, Calif. 204/E4
Forest Hill, Ind. 227/F6
Forest Hill, La. 238/E4
Forest Hill, Md. 245/N2
Forest Hill, N.S. Wales 97/D4
Forest Hill, Texas 303/F2
Forest Hill, W. Va. 312/E7
Forest Hills, Ky. 237/L2
Forest Hills, Pa. 294/C7
Forest Hills, Tenn. 237/H8
Forest Home, Ala. 195/E7
Forest Homes, Ill. 222/B2
Forestier (cape), Tasmania 99/E4
Forestier (pen.), Tasmania 99/E4
Forest Junction, Wis. 317/K7
Forest Knolls-Lagunitas, Calif. 204/H1
Forest Lake, Mich. 250/C2
Forest Lake, Minn. 255/F5
Foreston, Minn. 255/E5
Foreston, S.C. 296/G4
Forest Park, Ga. 217/K2
Forest Park, Ill. 222/B5
Forest Park, Ohio 284/B9
Forest Park, Okla. 288/M3
Forestport, N.Y. 276/K4
Forest River, N. Dak. 282/P3
Forest Station, Maine 243/H4
Forest View, Ill. 222/B6
Forestville, Conn. 210/D2
Forestville, Md. 245/G5
Forestville, Mich. 250/G5
Forestville, N.Y. 276/B6
Forestville, Ohio 284/C10
Forestville, Pa. 294/B3
Forestville, Québec 172/H1
Forestville, Québec 174/D3
Forestville, Wis. 317/L6
Forez (mts.), France 28/E5
Forfar, Scotland 10/E2
Forfar, Scotland 15/F4
Forgan, Okla. 288/E1
Forgan, Sask. 181/D4
Forget, Sask. 181/J6
Forge Village, Mass. 249/H2
Forillon Nat'l Park, Que. 162/K6
Forillon Nat'l Park, Québec 172/D1
Foristell, Mo. 261/L5
Fork, N.C. 281/J3
Fork, S.C. 296/J3
Forked (lake), N.Y. 276/L3
Forked Deer (riv.), Tenn. 237/C9
Forked Deer, Middle Fork (riv.), Tenn. 237/C9
Forked Deer, North Fork (riv.), Tenn. 237/C8
Forked Deer, South Fork (riv.), Tenn. 237/C9
Forked River, N.J. 273/E4
Fork Lake, Alberta 182/E2
Forkland, Ala. 195/C5
Fork Mountain, Tenn. 237/N8
Fork River, Manitoba 179/B3
Forks, Wash. 310/A3
Forks of Buffalo, Va. 307/K5
Forks of Elkhorn, Ky. 237/M4
Forks of Salmon, Calif. 204/B2
Forksville, Pa. 294/J3
Fork Union, Va. 307/M5
Forkville, Miss. 256/E6
Forlì (prov.), Italy 34/D2
Forlì, Italy 34/D2
Forman, N. Dak. 282/P7
Formartine (dist.), Scotland 15/F3
Formby, England 13/G2
Formby, England 10/F2
Formby (head), England 13/G2
Formentera (isl.), Spain 33/G3
Formentor (cape), Spain 33/H2
Formia, Italy 34/D4
Formiga, Brazil 135/D2
Formiga, Brazil 132/E8
Formosa (prov.), Argentina 143/D1
Formosa, Argentina 143/E2
Formosa, Argentina 120/D5
Formosa, Ark. 202/E3
Formosa, Brazil 132/E6
Formosa, Serra (range), Brazil 132/C5
Formosa (Taiwan) (isl.), China 2/R4
Formosa (Taiwan) (isl.), China 77/K7
Formosa (Taiwan) (str.), China 77/J7
Formosa (bay), Kenya 115/H4
Formosa, Ontario 177/C3
Formosa, Paraguay 144/C5
Formoso, Kansas 232/D2
Forney, Ala. 195/H2
Forney, Texas 303/H5
Forres, Scotland 10/E2
Forres, Scotland 15/E3
Forrest, Ill. 222/E3
Forrest (co.), Miss. 256/F8
Forrest, N. Mex. 274/F4
Forrest (lake), Sask. 181/L3
Forrest, W. Australia 88/D6
Forrest (lakes), W. Australia 88/D5
Forrest, W. Australia 92/D5
Forrest City, Ark. 202/J3
Forreston, Ill. 222/D1
Forrest River Aborginal Res., W. Australia 92/D1
Forrest River Mission, W. Australia 92/D1
Forrest Station, Manitoba 179/C5
Forsan, Texas 303/C5
Forsayth, Queensland 95/B3
Forsayth, Queensland 88/G3
Forshaga, Sweden 18/H7
Forssa, Finland 18/N6
Forst, Germany 22/F3
Forster-Tuncurry, N.S. Wales 97/G3
Forsyth (co.), Ga. 217/D2
Forsyth, Ga. 217/E4
Forsyth, Ill. 222/D4
Forsyth, Mo. 261/F9
Forsyth, Mont. 262/K4
Forsyth (co.), N.C. 281/J2
Fort (pt.), St. Kitts and Nevis 161/C11
Fort (mt.), Switzerland 39/D4
Fort A.P. Hill, Va. 307/O4
Fort Adams, Miss. 256/B8
Fort à la Corne, Sask. 181/G2
Fort Albany, Ont. 146/K4
Fort Albany, Ont. 162/H5
Fort Albany, Ontario 175/D2
Fort Alexander, Manitoba 179/F4
Fortaleza, Bolivia 136/C1
Fortaleza, Bolivia 136/B3
Fortaleza, Brazil 132/G3
Fortaleza, Brazil 120/F3
Fortaleza, Brazil 2/H6
Fortaleza de Santa Teresa, Uruguay 145/F5
Fort Ann, N.Y. 276/N4
Fort Apache, Ariz. 198/F5

Gäddede 371

Franklin, La. 238/G7
Franklin (co.), Maine 243/B5
Franklin, Maine 243/G6
Franklin•, Maine 243/G6
Franklin, Manitoba 179/C4
Franklin (co.), Mass. 249/D2
Franklin, Mass. 249/J4
Franklin•, Mass. 249/J4
Franklin, Mich. 250/B6
Franklin, Minn. 255/F3
Franklin, Minn. 255/D6
Franklin (co.), Miss. 256/C8
Franklin (co.), Mo. 261/K6
Franklin, Mo. 261/G4
Franklin, Mont. 262/G4
Franklin (co.), Nebr. 264/F4
Franklin, Nebr. 264/E4
Franklin (lake), Nev. 266/F2
Franklin, N.H. 268/D5
Franklin, N.J. 273/D1
Franklin (co.), N.Y. 276/M1
Franklin, N.Y. 276/K6
Franklin (co.), N.C. 281/N2
Franklin, N.C. 281/C4
Franklin (bay), N.W.T. 187/F2
Franklin (lake), N.W.T. 187/J3
Franklin (mts.), N.W.T. 187/F3
Franklin (str.), N.W.T. 162/G1
Franklin (str.), N.W.T. 187/J2
Franklin (co.), Ohio 284/E5
Franklin, Ohio 284/B6
Franklin (co.), Pa. 294/G6
Franklin, Pa. 294/C3
Franklin, S. Dak. 298/P6
Franklin, Tasmania 99/C5
Franklin (riv.), Tasmania 99/B4
Franklin (co.), Tenn. 237/J10
Franklin, Tenn. 237/H9
Franklin (co.), Texas 303/J4
Franklin, Texas 303/H7
Franklin (co.), Vt. 268/B2
Franklin•, Vt. 268/B2
Franklin (co.), Va. 307/J6
Franklin (I.C.), Va. 307/P7
Franklin (co.), Wash. 310/G4
Franklin, W. Va. 312/H5
Franklin, Wis. 317/L2
Franklin D. Roosevelt (lake), Wash. 310/G2
Franklin Falls (res.), N.H. 268/D4
Franklin Furnace, Ohio 284/E8
Franklin Grove, Ill. 222/D2
Franklin Lakes, N.J. 273/B1
Franklin Park, Ill. 222/B5
Franklin Park•, N.J. 273/D3
Franklin River, Br. Col. 184/H3
Franklin Springs, Ga. 217/F2
Franklin Square, N.Y. 276/R7
Franklinton, La. 238/K5
Franklinton, N.C. 281/N2
Franklintown, Pa. 294/H5
Franklinville, N.J. 273/C4
Franklinville, N.Y. 276/D6
Franklinville, N.C. 281/K3
Franks (pond), Newf. 166/D2
Frankslake, Sask. 181/G5
Frankston, Texas 303/J5
Franksville, Wis. 317/M3
Frankton, Ind. 227/F4
Franktown, Colo. 208/K4
Franktown, Ontario 177/H2
Franktown, Va. 307/S6
Frankville, Ala. 195/B7
Frankville, Iowa 229/K2
Frankville, Nova Scotia 168/G3
Frankville, Ontario 177/J2
Frannie, Wyo. 319/D1
Franquelin, Québec 172/B1
Franquia, Uruguay 145/B1
Franschhoek, S. Africa 118/F6
Fransfontein, Namibia 118/A4
Františkovy Lázně, Czech Rep. 41/B1
Franz, Ontario 177/J5
Franz, Ontario 175/D3
Franz Josef Land (isls.), Russia 2/L1
Franz Josef Land (isls.), Russia 4/A7
Franz Josef Land (isls.), Russia 48/F1
Frascati, Italy 34/F7
Fraser (isl.), Australia 87/F8
Fraser (lake), Br. Col. 184/E3
Fraser (riv.), Br. Col. 146/F4
Fraser (riv.), Br. Col. 162/D5
Fraser (riv.), Br. Col. 184/F4
Fraser, Colo. 208/H3
Fraser, Iowa 229/E4
Fraser, Mich. 250/B6
Fraser, Minn. 255/F3
Fraser (riv.), Newf. 166/B2
Fraser (isl.), Queensland 88/J4
Fraser (isl.), Queensland 95/E5
Fraserburgh, Scotland 15/G3
Fraserburgh, Scotland 10/E2
Fraserdale, Ontario 175/D3
Fraserdale, Ontario 177/J5
Fraser Lake, Br. Col. 184/E3
Fraser Mills, Br. Col. 184/K3
Fraser Reach (chan.), Br. Col. 184/C3
Frasertown, N. Zealand 100/F3
Fraserwood, Manitoba 179/E4
Frasnes-lez Anvaing, Belgium 27/D7
Frauenfeld, Switzerland 39/G1
Frauenkirchen, Austria 41/D3
Fray Benito, Cuba 158/J3
Fray Bentos, Uruguay 145/A4
Fray Marcos, Uruguay 145/D5
Frazee, Minn. 255/C4
Frazer, Mont. 262/K2
Frazeysburg, Ohio 284/F5
Frazier Park, Calif. 204/F9
Fraziers Bottom, W. Va. 312/B5
Frechen, Germany 22/B3
Fred, Texas 303/K7
Freda, N. Dak. 282/H7
Fredensborg, Denmark 21/F6
Fredensdal, Virgin Is. (U.S.) 161/F4
Frederic, Mich. 250/E4
Frederic, Wis. 317/B4
Frederica, Del. 245/S4
Fredericia, Denmark 21/C6
Fredericia, Denmark 18/F9
Frederick (sound), Alaska 196/N1
Frederick, Colo. 208/K2
Frederick, Ill. 222/C3
Frederick, Kansas 232/D3
Frederick (co.), Md. 245/J3
Frederick, Md. 245/J3
Frederick, Okla. 288/H6
Frederick, S. Dak. 298/N2
Frederick (co.), Va. 307/M2
Fredericksburg, Ind. 227/E8
Fredericksburg, Iowa 229/J3
Fredericksburg, Ohio 284/G4
Fredericksburg, Pa. 294/J5
Fredericksburg, Pa. 294/B2
Fredericksburg, Texas 303/E7
Fredericksburg (I.C.), Va. 307/N4
Fredericks Hall, Va. 307/N4
Frederickton, N.S. Wales 97/G2
Fredericktown, Mo. 261/M7
Fredericktown, Ohio 284/F5
Fredericktown, Pa. 294/C6
Fredericton (cap.), N. Br. 146/M5
Fredericton, N. Br. 162/K6
Fredericton (cap.), New Bruns. 170/D3
Fredericton Junction, New Bruns. 170/D3
Frederika, Iowa 229/J3
Frederik Hendrik (Kolepom) (isl.), Indonesia 85/K7
Frederiksberg (commune), Denmark 21/F6
Frederiksberg, Denmark 21/F6
Frederiksberg (co.), Denmark 21/E5
Frederikshåb (Paamiut), Greenl. 4/C12
Frederikshåb (Paamiut), Greenl. 146/N3
Frederikshavn, Denmark 18/G8
Frederikshavn, Denmark 21/D3
Frederikssund, Denmark 21/E6
Frederiksted, Virgin Is. (U.S.) 161/E4
Frederiksted, Virgin Is. (U.S.) 156/G2
Frederiksvaerk, Denmark 21/E6
Frederiksvaerk, Denmark 18/G8
Frederik Willem IV (falls), Suriname 131/C4
Fredonia, Ala. 195/H5
Fredonia, Ariz. 198/C2
Fredonia (Biscoe), Ark. 202/H4
Fredonia, Ind. 227/E8
Fredonia, Iowa 229/L6
Fredonia, Kansas 232/G4
Fredonia, Ky. 237/E6
Fredonia, N.Y. 276/B6
Fredonia, N. Dak. 282/M7
Fredonia, Pa. 294/B3
Fredonia, Texas 303/E7
Fredonia, Wis. 317/L8
Fredric, Iowa 229/H6
Fredrika, Sweden 18/L4
Fredrikstad, Norway 18/D4
Freeborn (co.), Minn. 255/E7
Freeborn, Minn. 255/E7
Freeburg, Ill. 222/D5
Freeburg, Minn. 255/G7
Freeburg, Mo. 261/J6
Freeburg, Pa. 294/H4
Freeburn, Ky. 237/S5
Freedhem, Minn. 255/D4
Freedom, Calif. 204/L4
Freedom, Ind. 227/D6
Freedom, Ky. 237/K7
Freedom•, Maine 243/E7
Freedom•, N.H. 268/E4
Freedom, Okla. 288/H1
Freedom, Pa. 294/B4
Freedom, Wyo. 319/B3
Freehold, N.J. 273/E3
Freehold, N.Y. 276/N6
Freel (peak), Calif. 204/F5
Freeland, Md. 245/M2
Freeland, Mich. 250/E5
Freeland, N.C. 281/N6
Freeland, Pa. 294/L3
Freeland, Wash. 310/C2
Freeland Park, Ind. 227/C3
Freelandville, Ind. 227/C7
Freels (cape), Newf. 166/D3
Freelton, Ontario 177/D4
Freeman (riv.), Alberta 182/C2
Freeman, Ind. 227/D6
Freeman (lake), Ind. 227/D3
Freeman, Mo. 261/C5
Freeman, S. Dak. 298/O7
Freeman, Wash. 310/H3
Freemansburg, Pa. 294/M4
Freemanville, Ala. 195/D8
Free Mason (isls.), La. 238/M7
Freemont, Calif. 188/B3
Freemont, Sask. 181/B3
Freeport, Bahamas 156/B1
Freeport, Fla. 212/C6
Freeport, Ill. 188/J2
Freeport, Ill. 222/D1
Freeport, Ind. 227/F5
Freeport, Kansas 232/E4
Freeport, Maine 243/C8
Freeport•, Maine 243/C8
Freeport, Mich. 250/D6
Freeport, Minn. 255/D5
Freeport, N.Y. 276/R7
Freeport, Nova Scotia 168/B4
Freeport, Ohio 284/H5
Freeport, Pa. 294/C4
Freeport, Texas 303/J9
Freer, Texas 303/F10
Free Soil, Mich. 250/C4
Free State (prov.), S. Africa 118/D5
Freestone (co.), Texas 303/H6
Freetown, Ant. & Bar. 161/E11
Freetown, Ind. 227/E7
Freetown, N.Y. 276/R9
Freetown (cap.), S. Leone 102/A4
Freetown (cap.), S. Leone 106/B7
Free Union, Va. 307/L4
Freeville, N.Y. 276/H5
Freezeout (lake), Mont. 262/D3
Fregenal de la Sierra, Spain 33/C3
Fregene, Italy 34/F6
Freiberg, Germany 22/E3
Freiburg, Germany 7/E4
Freiburg im Breisgau, Germany 22/B5
Freidberg, Austria 41/D3
Freienbach, Switzerland 39/G2
Freire, Chile 138/E2
Freirina, Chile 138/A7
Freising, Germany 22/D4
Freistadt, Austria 41/C2
Freistatt, Mo. 261/E8
Freital, Germany 22/E3
Freixo de Espada à Cinta, Portugal 33/C2
Fréjus, France 28/G6
Fréjus (pass), France 28/G5
Fréjus (pass), Italy 34/A2
Frelighsburg, Québec 172/E4
Fremantle, Australia 2/Q7
Fremantle, Australia 87/B9
Fremantle, W. Australia 88/B6
Fremantle, W. Australia 92/A1
Fremington, England 13/C6
Fremont, Calif. 204/K3
Fremont (peak), Calif. 204/H8
Fremont (co.), Colo. 208/J5
Fremont (co.), Idaho 220/G5
Fremont, Ind. 227/H1
Fremont (co.), Iowa 229/B7
Fremont, Iowa 229/H6
Fremont, Mich. 250/D5
Fremont, Mo. 261/K9
Fremont, Nebr. 188/G2
Fremont, Nebr. 264/H3
Fremont•, N.H. 268/E6
Fremont, N.C. 281/N3
Fremont, Ohio 284/D3
Fremont, Utah 304/C5
Fremont (isl.), Utah 304/B2
Fremont (riv.), Utah 304/C5
Fremont, Wis. 317/J7
Fremont (co.), Wyo. 319/D2
Fremont (lake), Wyo. 319/C3
Fremont (peak), Wyo. 319/C2
French, Argentina 143/F7
French (riv.), Conn. 210/H1
French (riv.), Ontario 177/D1
French (creek), Pa. 294/C2
French (creek), S. Dak. 298/C6
French (isl.), Victoria 97/C6
Frenchboro•, Maine 243/G7
French Broad (riv.), N.C. 281/D3
French Broad (riv.), Tenn. 237/R9
Frenchburg, Ky. 237/O5
French Camp, Miss. 256/F4
French Creek, W. Va. 312/F5
French Frigate (shoal), Hawaii 188/F6
French Frigate (shoals), Hawaii 87/K3
French Frigate (shoals), Hawaii 218/C6
Frenchglen, Oreg. 291/H5
French Guiana 2/G5
French Guiana 120/D2
FRENCH GUIANA 131/E3
French Lick, Ind. 227/D7
Frenchman (creek), Colo. 208/P1
Frenchman (bay), Maine 243/G7
Frenchman (riv.), Mont. 188/E1
Frenchman (riv.), Mont. 262/J1
Frenchman (creek), Nebr. 264/C4
Frenchman (riv.), Sask. 181/C6
Frenchman (cay), Virgin Is. (U.K.) 161/C4
Frenchman Butte, Sask. 181/B2
Frenchman Flat (basin), Nev. 266/F6
Frenchmans Cap (mt.), Tasmania 99/B4
Frenchmans Island, Newf. 166/C3
Frenchpark, Ireland 17/E4
French Polynesia 87/L8
French River, Minn. 255/G4
French River, Ontario 177/D1
French Settlement, La. 238/L2
Frenchton, W. Va. 312/F5
Frenchtown, Mont. 262/B3
Frenchtown, N.J. 273/C2
Frenchville, Maine 243/G1
Frenchville•, Maine 243/G1
Frenchville, Pa. 294/F3
Frenštát pod Radhoštěm, Czech Rep. 41/E2
Fresco, Ivory Coast 106/C7
Fresh (pond), Mass. 249/C6
Freshford, Ireland 17/G6
Freshwater, Calif. 204/B3
Freshwater (Guffey), Colo. 208/H5
Freshwater, England 13/F7
Freshwater, Newf. 166/D2
Fresia, Chile 138/D3
Fresillo, Mexico 146/H7
Fresnillo de González Echerrería, Mexico 150/H5
Fresno (co.), Calif. 204/E7
Fresno, Calif. 146/G6
Fresno, Calif. 188/C3
Fresno, Calif. 204/F7
Fresno (riv.), Calif. 204/E7
Fresno, Colombia 126/C5
Fresno, Mont. 262/G2
Fresno (res.), Mont. 262/F2
Fresno, Texas 303/J2
Freudenstadt, Germany 22/C4
Frew, Ky. 237/P6
Frewena, North. Terr. 93/D5
Frewsburg, N.Y. 276/B6
Freycinet (pen.), Tasmania 99/E4
Fria, Guinea 106/B6
Fria (cape), Namibia 102/D6
Fria (cape), Namibia 118/A3
Friant, Calif. 204/F7
Friant-Kern (canal), Calif. 204/F8
Friars Point, Miss. 256/C2
Frías, Argentina 143/D2
Fribourg (canton), Switzerland 39/D3
Fribourg, Switzerland 39/D3
Frick, Switzerland 39/E1
Friday Harbor, Wash. 310/B2
Fridley, Minn. 255/G5
Fried, N. Dak. 282/N5
Friedberg, Germany 22/C3
Friedland, Germany 22/E2
Friedrichshafen, Germany 22/C5
Friedrichstadt, Germany 22/C1
Friend, Kansas 232/B3
Friend, Nebr. 264/G4
Friend, Oreg. 291/F2
Friendly, W. Va. 312/D3
Friendship, Ark. 202/E5
Friendship, Ind. 227/G7
Friendship, Maine 243/E7
Friendship•, Maine 243/E7
Friendship, Md. 245/M6
Friendship, N.Y. 276/D6
Friendship, Ohio 284/D8
Friendship, Tenn. 237/C9
Friendship, Wis. 317/G8
Friendship Hill Nat'l Hist. Site, Pa. 294/C6
Friendsville, Ill. 222/F5
Friendsville, Md. 245/A2
Friendsville, Pa. 294/L2
Friendsville, Tenn. 237/N9
Friendswood, Texas 303/J2
Frienisberg (mt.), Switzerland 39/D2
Frierson, La. 238/C2
Fries, Va. 307/F7
Friesach, Austria 41/C3
Friesche Gat (chan.), Netherlands 27/J2
Friesland, Minn. 255/E4
Friesland (prov.), Netherlands 27/H2
Friesland, Wis. 317/H8
Frigate (isl.), Seychelles 118/J5
Frigate Bay, St. Kitts & Nevis 161/C10
Frimley and Camberley, England 13/G8
Frink, Fla. 212/D6
Frinton and Walton, England 10/G5
Frinton and Walton, England 13/J6
Frio (cape), Brazil 120/E5
Frio (cape), Brazil 135/F3
Frio (co.), Texas 303/E9
Frio (riv.), Texas 303/E8
Friockheim, Scotland 15/F4
Friol, Spain 33/C1
Friona, Texas 303/B3
Fripp (isl.), S.C. 296/G7
Frisches Haff (lag.), Poland 47/D1
Frisco, Colo. 208/G3
Frisco, N.C. 281/T4
Frisco, Pa. 294/B4
Frisco, Texas 303/H4
Frisco City, Ala. 195/D8
Frisian (isls.) 7/E3
Frisian, North (isls.), Denmark 21/B7
Frisian, East (isls.), Germany 22/B2
Frisian, North (isls.), Germany 22/B1
Frisian, West (isls.), Netherlands 27/G2
Frissell (mt.), Conn. 210/B1
Fristoe, Mo. 261/F6
Fritch, Texas 303/C2
Fritchton, Ind. 227/C7
Fritz Creek, Alaska 196/B2
Fritzlar, Germany 22/C3
Friuli-Venezia Giulia (reg.), Italy 34/D1
Frizzellburg, Md. 245/K2
Frobisher (bay), N.W.T. 162/K3
Frobisher (bay), N.W.T. 187/M3
Frobisher, Sask. 181/J6
Frobisher (lake), Sask. 181/L3
Froelich, Iowa 229/L2
Frog (lake), Alberta 182/E3
Frog Lake, Alberta 182/E3
Frogue, Ky. 237/L7
Frohavet (bay), Norway 18/F5
Frohna, Mo. 261/N7
Frohnleiten, Austria 41/C3
Froid, Mont. 262/M2
Froidchapelle, Belgium 27/E8
Frolovo, Russia 48/E5
Frolovo, Russia 52/F5
Fromberg, Mont. 262/H5
Frome (lake), Australia 87/E9
Frome, England 10/E5
Frome, England 13/E6
Frome, Jamaica 158/G6
Frome (lake), S. Australia 88/G6
Frome (lake), S. Australia 94/G4
Front (range), Colo. 208/H1
Fronteira, Portugal 33/C3
Fronteiras, Brazil 132/F4
Frontenac, Kansas 232/H4
Frontenac, Minn. 255/F6
Frontenac, Mo. 261/O3
Frontenac (county), Ontario 177/H3
Frontenac (co.), Québec 172/G4
Frontera, Mexico 150/N7
Frontier, Mich. 250/E7
Frontier (co.), Nebr. 264/D4
Frontier, N. Dak. 282/S6
Frontier, Sask. 181/C6
Frontier, Wyo. 319/B4
Front Royal, Va. 307/M3
Frosinone (prov.), Italy 34/D4
Frosinone, Italy 34/D4
Frösö, Sweden 18/J5
Frost, La. 238/L2
Frost, Minn. 255/D7
Frost, Texas 303/H5
Frost, W. Va. 312/G6
Frostburg, Md. 245/C2
Frostproof, Fla. 212/E4
Froude, Sask. 181/H6
Frövi, Sweden 18/J7
Frøya (isl.), Norway 18/F5
Frozen (str.), N.W.T. 162/H2
Frozen (str.), N.W.T. 187/K3
Fruita, Colo. 208/B4
Fruita, Utah 304/C5
Fruitdale, Ala. 195/B8
Fruitdale, S. Dak. 298/B4
Fruitdale-Harbeck, Oreg. 291/D5
Fruitgrove, Queensland 88/K3
Fruit Heights, Utah 304/C2
Fruithurst, Ala. 195/G3
Fruitland, Idaho 220/B6
Fruitland, Iowa 229/L6
Fruitland, Md. 245/R7
Fruitland, Mo. 261/N8
Fruitland, N. Mex. 274/A2
Fruitland, Tenn. 237/D9
Fruitland, Utah 304/D3
Fruitland, Wash. 310/G2
Fruitland Park, Fla. 212/D3
Fruitland Park, Miss. 256/F9
Fruitport, Mich. 250/C5
Fruitvale, Br. Col. 184/J5
Fruitvale, Idaho 220/B5
Fruitvale, Tenn. 237/C9
Fruitvale, Wash. 310/E4
Fruitville, Fla. 212/D4
Frunze (Bishkek) (cap.), Kyrgyzstan 48/H5
Frunze (Bishkek) (cap.), Kyrgyzstan 54/J5
Frutal, Brazil 135/B2
Frutigen, Switzerland 39/E3
Frutillar, Chile 138/D3
Fry, Ga. 217/D1
Fryburg, N. Dak. 282/D6
Fryburg, Ohio 284/B4
Fryburg, Pa. 294/D3
Fry Canyon, Utah 304/D6
Frýdek-Místek, Czech Rep. 41/E2
Frýdlant nad Ostravicí, Czech Rep. 41/E2
Frýdlant v. Čechách, Czech Rep. 41/C1
Frye, Maine 243/B6
Fryeburg, La. 238/D2
Fryeburg, Maine 243/A7
Fryeburg•, Maine 243/A7
Fu'an, China 77/K6
Fuchu, Hiroshima, Japan 81/F6
Fuchu, Tokyo, Japan 81/O2
Fuding, China 77/K6
Fuengirola, Spain 33/D4
Fuensalida, Spain 33/D2
Fuente-Álamo, Spain 33/F4
Fuente de Cantos, Spain 33/C3
Fuentelapeña, Spain 33/D2
Fuente Obejuna, Spain 33/D3
Fuenterrabiá, Spain 33/E1
Fuentesaúco, Spain 33/D2
Fuentes de Andalucía, Spain 33/D4
Fuentes de Oñoro, Spain 33/C2
Fuerte (isl.), Colombia 126/B3
Fuerte (riv.), Mexico 150/E3
Fuerte Bulnes, Chile 138/E10
Fuerte Olimpo, Argentina 120/D5
Fuerte Olimpo, Paraguay 144/C2
Fuerteventura (isl.), Spain 102/A2
Fuerteventura (isl.), Spain 106/B3
Fuerteventura (isl.), Spain 33/C4
Fuga (isl.), Philippines 82/A3
Fuglebjerg, Denmark 21/E7
Fugu, China 77/H4
Fuhai (Burultokay), China 77/C2
Fuik, Neth. Ant. 161/G9
Fujairah, U.A.E. 59/G4
Fuji, Japan 81/J6
Fuji (mt.), Japan 81/J6
Fuji (riv.), Japan 81/J6
Fujian (Fukien), China 77/J6
Fujieda, Japan 81/J6
Fuji-Hakone-Izu Nat'l Park, Japan 81/H6
Fujin, China 77/M2
Fujisawa, Japan 81/O3
Fukagawa, Japan 81/L2
Fukang, China 77/C3
Fukuchiyama, Japan 81/G6
Fukue, Japan 81/D7
Fukui (pref.), Japan 81/G5
Fukui, Japan 81/G5
Fukuoka (pref.), Japan 81/D7
Fukuoka, Japan 54/O6
Fukuoka, Japan 81/D7
Fukushima (pref.), Japan 81/K5
Fukushima, Japan 81/K5
Fukuyama, Japan 81/F6
Fulbourn, England 13/H5
Fulbright, Texas 303/J4
Fulda, Germany 22/C3
Fulda, Ind. 227/D8
Fulda, Minn. 255/C7
Fulda, Sask. 181/F3
Fulda (riv.), Germany 22/C3
Fulford, England 13/F4
Fulford Harbour, Br. Col. 184/K3
Fuling, China 77/G6
Fulks Run, Va. 307/L3
Fullarton, Trin. & Tob. 161/A11
Fullerton, Calif. 204/D11
Fullerton, Ky. 237/P3
Fullerton, La. 238/D4
Fullerton, Nebr. 264/F3
Fullerton, N. Dak. 282/O7
Fully, Switzerland 39/D4
Fulnek, Czech Rep. 41/D2
Fulpmes, Austria 41/A3
Fulton, Ala. 195/C7
Fulton (co.), Ark. 202/G1
Fulton, Ark. 202/C6
Fulton (co.), Ga. 217/D3
Fulton (co.), Ill. 222/C3
Fulton, Ill. 222/C2
Fulton (co.), Ind. 227/E2
Fulton, Ind. 227/E3
Fulton, Iowa 229/M4
Fulton, Kansas 232/H4
Fulton (co.), Ky. 237/C7
Fulton, Ky. 237/D7
Fulton, Mich. 250/D6
Fulton, Miss. 256/H2
Fulton, Mo. 261/J5
Fulton (co.), N.Y. 276/M4
Fulton, N.Y. 276/H4
Fulton (co.), Ohio 284/B2
Fulton, Ohio 284/E5
Fulton (co.), Pa. 294/F6
Fulton, S. Dak. 298/O6
Fulton, Tenn. 237/B9
Fulton, Texas 303/H9
Fulton Chain (lakes), N.Y. 276/K3
Fultondale, Ala. 195/E3
Fultonham, Ohio 284/F6
Fultonville, N.Y. 276/M5
Fults, Ill. 222/C5
Fulwood, England 10/G1
Fulwood, England 13/G1
Funabashi, Japan 81/P2
Funafuti (atoll), Tuvalu 87/H6
Funchal, Portugal 33/A2
Funchal (cap.), Madeira, Port. 102/A1
Funchal (cap.), Madeira, Port. 106/A2
Fundación, Colombia 126/C2
Fundão, Portugal 33/C2
Fundy (bay) 162/K7
Fundy (bay), New Bruns. 170/E3
Fundy (bay), Nova Scotia 168/C3
Fundy Nat'l Park, New Bruns. 170/E3
Funhalouro, Mozambique 118/E4
Funing, China 77/K5
Funk, Nebr. 264/E4
Funk (isl.), Newf. 166/D4
Funkley, Minn. 255/D3
Funkstown, Md. 245/H2
Funston, Ga. 217/E8
Funter, Alaska 196/M1
Funtua, Nigeria 106/F6
Fuping, China 77/H4
Fuquay-Varina, N.C. 281/M3
Furancungo, Mozambique 118/E2
Furka (pass), Switzerland 39/F3
Furman, Ala. 195/E6
Furman, S.C. 296/E6
Furmanov, Russia 52/F3
Furnace, Ky. 237/O5
Furnace, Mass. 249/F3
Furnace, Scotland 15/C4
Furnas (res.), Brazil 120/E5
Furnas (dam), Brazil 135/C2
Furnas (co.), Nebr. 264/E4
Furneaux Group (isls.), Australia 87/E9
Furneaux Group (isls.), Tasmania 88/H8
Furneaux Group (isls.), Tasmania 99/E1
Furnes (Veurne), Belgium 27/B6
Furness, Sask. 181/B2
Furry Creek, Br. Col. 184/K2
Fürstenberg, Germany 22/E2
Fürstenfeld, Austria 41/C3
Fürstenfeldbruck, Germany 22/D4
Fürstenwalde, Germany 22/F2
Fürth, Germany 22/D4
Furth im Wald, Germany 22/E4
Furukawa, Japan 81/K4
Fury and Hecla (str.), N.W.T. 162/H2
Fury and Hecla (str.), N.W.T. 187/K3
Fusagasugá, Colombia 126/C5
Fushun, China 77/K3
Fushun, China 54/O5
Fusilier, Sask. 181/B4
Fusin (Fuxin), China 77/K3
Fusingchen (Simao), China 77/F7
Fusio, Switzerland 39/G4
Fusong, China 77/L3
Füssen, Germany 22/D5
Futa Jallon (lag.), Guinea 106/B6
Futaleufú, Chile 138/E4
Futrono, Chile 138/E3
Futuna (Hoorn) (isls.), Wallis and Futuna 87/J7
Fu Xian, Liaoning, China 77/K4
Fu Xian, Shaanxi, China 77/G4
Fuxin (Fusin), China 77/K3
Fuxin, China 54/O5
Fuyang (Fowyang), China 77/J5
Fuyu, Heilongjiang, China 77/K2
Fuyu, Jilin, China 77/L2
Fuyuan, Heilongjiang, China 77/M2
Fuyuan, Yunnan, China 77/F6
Fuyun, China 77/C2
Füzesabony, Hungary 41/F3
Füzesgyarmat, Hungary 41/F3
Fuzhou, Jiangxi, China 77/J6
Fuzhou, China 2/R4
Fuzhou, China 54/N7
Fuzhou (Foochow), Fujian, China 77/J6
Fyffe, Ala. 195/G2
Fylingdales, England 13/G3
Fyn (co.), Denmark 21/D7
Fyn (isl.), Denmark 21/D7
Fyn (isl.), Denmark 18/G9
Fyne, Loch (inlet), Scotland 10/D2
Fyne, Loch (inlet), Scotland 15/C5
Fyns Hoved (pt.), Denmark 21/D6
Fyvie, Scotland 15/F3
Fyzabad, Trin. & Tob. 161/A11

G

Gaastra, Mich. 250/G2
Gabarus, Nova Scotia 168/H3
Gabarus (bay), Nova Scotia 168/H3
Gabarus (cape), Nova Scotia 168/J3
Gabbettville, Ga. 217/B5
Gabbs, Nev. 266/D4
Gabela, Angola 115/B6
Gabès, Tunisia 106/F2
Gabès, Tunisia 102/D1
Gabès (gulf), Tunisia 106/G2
Gabgaba, Wadi (dry riv.), Sudan 111/F3
Gable, S.C. 296/G4
Gabon 2/K6
Gabon 102/D4
GABON 115/B4
Gaborone (cap.), Botswana 2/L7
Gaborone (cap.), Botswana 118/D4
Gaborone (cap.), Botswana 102/E7
Gabras, Sudan 111/E5
Gabredarre, Ethiopia 111/H6
Gabriel (str.), N.W.T. 187/M3
Gabrik (riv.), Iran 66/L7
Gabriola, Br. Col. 184/J3
Gabrovo, Bulgaria 45/G4
Gachalá, Colombia 126/D5
Gach Saran, Iran 59/F3
Gach Saran, Iran 66/G5
Gackle, N. Dak. 282/M6
Gacko, Bos. 45/D4
Gadag-Betgeri, India 68/D5
Gäddede, Sweden 18/J4

Gadê, China 77/E5
Gadebusch, Germany 22/D2
Gadmen, Switzerland 39/F3
Gadsby, Alberta 182/D3
Gadsden, Ala. 188/J4
Gadsden, Ala. 195/G2
Gadsden, Ariz. 198/A6
Gadsden (co.), Fla. 212/B1
Gadsden, S.C. 296/F4
Gadsden, Tenn. 237/D9
Gads Hill, Mo. 261/L8
Gadston (pt.), Fla. 212/C3
Gadwal, India 68/D5
Gadyach, Ukraine 52/D4
Găeşti, Romania 45/G3
Gaeta, Italy 34/D4
Gaeta (gulf), Italy 34/D4
Gaferut (isl.), Micronesia 87/E5
Gaffney, S.C. 296/D1
Gafsa, Tunisia 106/F2
Gagarin, Russia 52/D3
Gage, Alberta 182/A1
Gage (co.), Nebr. 264/H4
Gage, N. Mex. 274/A6
Gage, Okla. 288/G2
Gagetown, Mich. 250/F5
Gagetown, New Bruns. 170/D3
Gaggenau, Germany 22/C4
Gagnoa, Ivory Coast 102/B4
Gagnoa, Ivory Coast 106/C7
Gagnon, Que. 162/K5
Gagnon, Québec 174/D2
Gagnon (lake), Québec 172/B3
Gagny, France 28/C1
Gagra, Georgia 52/E6
Gahanna, Ohio 284/E5
Gaiba (lag.), Bolivia 136/F5
Gail, Saudi Arabia 59/E5
Gail, Texas 303/C5
Gaillac, France 28/D6
Gaillard (lake), Conn. 210/D3
Gaillard, Ga. 217/D5
Gaima, Papua N.G. 85/B7
Gaiman, Argentina 143/C5
Gaines, Mich. 250/F6
Gaines, Pa. 294/G2
Gaines (co.), Texas 303/B5
Gainesboro, Tenn. 237/K8
Gainesboro, Va. 307/M2
Gainestown, Ala. 195/C8
Gainesville, Ala. 195/B5
Gainesville (dam), Ala. 195/B5
Gainesville, Fla. 188/K5
Gainesville, Fla. 212/D2
Gainesville, Ga. 217/E2
Gainesville, Mo. 261/G9
Gainesville, N.Y. 276/D5
Gainesville, Texas 303/G4
Gainesville, Va. 307/N3
Gainsborough, England 10/F4
Gainsborough, England 13/G4
Gainsborough, Sask. 181/K6
Gairdner (lake), Australia 87/D9
Gairdner (lake), S. Australia 88/F6
Gairdner (lake), S. Australia 94/D4
Gairloch, Scotland 15/C3
Gairloch, Loch (inlet), Scotland 15/C3
Gais, Switzerland 39/H2
Gaithersburg, Md. 245/K4
Gajdel, Slovakia 41/E2
Gakona, Alaska 196/K2
Galadi, Ethiopia 111/J6
Galahad, Alberta 182/E3
Galana (riv.), Kenya 115/G4
Galand, Iran 66/J2
Galanta, Slovakia 41/D2
Galápagos (isls.), Ecuador 2/E6
Galápagos (isls.), Ecuador 128/C8
Galashiels, Scotland 10/E3
Galashiels, Scotland 15/F5
Galata, Mont. 262/E2
Galata, Turkey 63/C6
Galaţi, Romania 7/G4
Galaţi, Romania 45/H3
Galatia, Ill. 222/E6
Galatia, Kansas 232/D3
Galatina, Italy 34/G4
Galatone, Italy 34/F4
Galax (I.C.), Va. 307/G7
Galbally, Ireland 17/E7
Galbraith, La. 238/E4
Galcaio, Somalia 102/G4
Galcaio, Somalia 115/J2
Galchutt, N. Dak. 282/S7
Gale, Ill. 222/D6
Gale (riv.), N.H. 268/D3
Galeana, Chihuahua, Mexico 150/F1
Galeana, Nuevo León, Mexico 150/J4
Galela, Indonesia 85/H5
Galen, Mont. 262/D4
Galena, Alaska 196/G2
Galena, Ill. 222/C1
Galena, Ind. 227/F8
Galena, Kansas 232/H4
Galena, Md. 245/P3
Galena, Mo. 261/F9
Galena, Ohio 284/E5
Galena Park, Texas 303/J1
Galeota (pt.), Trin. & Tob. 161/B11
Galera (pt.), Chile 138/D3
Galera (pt.), Ecuador 128/B2
Galera (pt.), Trin. & Tob. 161/C10
Galera (pt.), Trin. & Tob. 156/G5
Galesburg, Ill. 188/H2
Galesburg, Ill. 222/C3
Galesburg, Kansas 232/G4
Galesburg, Mich. 250/D6
Galesburg, N. Dak. 282/R5
Gales Creek, Oreg. 291/D2
Gales Ferry, Conn. 210/G3
Galestown, Md. 245/P6
Galesville, Md. 245/M5
Galesville, Wis. 317/D7
Galeton, Colo. 208/K1
Galeton, Pa. 294/G2
Galetta, Ontario 177/H2
Galgenberg (hill), Netherlands 27/H4
Galguduud (prov.), Somalia 115/J2
Galiano, Br. Col. 184/K3
Galiano (isl.), Br. Col. 184/K3
Galice, Oreg. 291/D5
Galich, Russia 52/F3
Galicia (reg.), Spain 33/B1
Galien, Mich. 250/C7
Galilee (reg.), Israel 65/C2
Galilee, Sea of (lake), Israel 59/C3
Galilee, Sea of (Tiberias) (lake), Israel 65/D2
Galilee (lake), Queensland 95/C4
Galina (pt.), Jamaica 158/J6
Galion (bay), Martinique 161/D6
Galion, Ohio 284/E4
Galisteo, N. Mex. 274/D3
Galiuro (mts.), Ariz. 198/E6
Galivants Ferry, S.C. 296/J3
Gallabat, Sudan 111/G5
Gallan (head), Scotland 15/A2
Gallant, Ala. 195/F2
Gallarate, Italy 34/B2
Gallatin (co.), Ill. 222/E6
Gallatin (co.), Ky. 237/M3
Gallatin, Mo. 261/E3
Gallatin (co.), Mont. 262/E5
Gallatin (peak), Mont. 262/E5
Gallatin (riv.), Mont. 262/E5
Gallatin, Tenn. 237/H8
Gallatin Gateway, Mont. 262/E5
Gallaway, Tenn. 237/B10
Galle, Sri Lanka 54/J9
Galle, Sri Lanka 68/D7
Gallegos (riv.), Argentina 143/B7
Gallegos, N. Mex. 274/F3
Galley (head), Ireland 17/D9
Gallia (co.), Ohio 284/F8
Galliano, La. 238/K8
Gallina, N. Mex. 274/C2
Gallinas (pt.), Colombia 120/B1
Gallinas (pt.), Colombia 126/E1
Gallinas (mts.), N. Mex. 274/B4
Gallinas (riv.), N. Mex. 274/E3
Gallion, Ala. 195/C6
Gallion, La. 238/G1
Gallipoli, Italy 34/F4
Gallipoli, Turkey 59/A1
Gallipoli, Turkey 63/C5
Gallipolis, Ohio 284/F8
Gallipolis Ferry, W. Va. 312/B5
Gallitzin, Pa. 294/E4
Gällivare, Sweden 18/M3
Gallman, Miss. 256/D7
Gallo (pt.), Chile 138/E3
Gallo (mt.), Dom. Rep. 158/D5
Gällö, Sweden 18/J5
Galloo (isl.), N.Y. 276/H3
Galloway, Ark. 202/F4
Galloway, Br. Col. 184/K5
Galloway (dist.), Scotland 15/D5
Galloway, Mull of (prom.), Scotland 15/D6
Galloway, Mull of (prom.), Scotland 10/D3
Galloway, W. Va. 312/F4
Galloway, Wis. 317/H6
Gallup, N. Mex. 188/E3
Gallup, N. Mex. 274/A3
Gallur, Spain 33/F2
Galole, Kenya 115/G4
Gal'on, Israel 65/B4
Galston, Scotland 10/D3
Galston, Scotland 15/D5
Galt, Calif. 204/C9
Galt, Iowa 229/F3
Galt, Mo. 261/F2
Galtee (mts.), Ireland 17/E7
Galtymore (mt.), Ireland 17/E7
Galva, Ill. 222/D2
Galva, Iowa 229/C3
Galva, Kansas 232/E3
Galván (mt.), Paraguay 144/C3
Galvarino, Chile 138/D2
Galveston, Ind. 227/E3
Galveston (co.), Texas 303/K8
Galveston, Texas 146/J7
Galveston, Texas 188/H5
Galveston, Texas 303/L3
Galveston (bay), Texas 188/H5
Galveston (bay), Texas 303/L2
Galveston (isl.), Texas 303/K8
Gálvez, Argentina 143/F6
Galvez, La. 238/L2
Gálvez, Spain 33/D3
Galvin, Wash. 310/B4
Galway (co.), Ireland 17/D5
Galway, Ireland 17/C5
Galway, Ireland 7/D3
Galway, Ireland 10/B4
Galway (bay), Ireland 17/C5
Galway (bay), Ireland 10/B4
Galway, N.Y. 276/N4
Gamaliel, Ky. 237/K7
Gamarra, Colombia 126/D3
Gamas Ab (riv.), Iran 66/F3
Gamay, Philippines 82/E4
Gamay (bay), Philippines 82/E4
Gamba, China 77/C6
Gambaga, Ghana 106/D6
Gambela, Ethiopia 111/F6
Gambell, Alaska 196/D2
Gamber, Md. 245/L3
Gambia 2/J5
Gambia 102/A3
GAMBIA 106/A6
Gambia (riv.), Gambia 106/B6
Gambia (riv.), Senegal 106/B6
Gambier (isls.), Fr. Poly. 87/N8
Gambier, Ohio 284/F5
Gambo, Newf. 166/D4
Gamboma, Congo 115/C4
Gambos, Angola 115/B6
Gambrills, Md. 245/M4
Gamerco, N. Mex. 274/A3
Gaming, Austria 41/C3
Gamleby, Sweden 18/J8
Gammon (riv.), Manitoba 179/G3
Gammon (pt.), Mass. 249/N6
Gampel, Switzerland 39/E4
Gamu-Gofa (prov.), Ethiopia 111/G6
Gamvik, Norway 18/Q1
Ganado, Ariz. 198/F3
Ganado, Texas 303/H8
Ganale Dorya (riv.), Ethiopia 111/H6
Gananoque, Ontario 177/H3
Ganassi, Philippines 82/D7
Ganaveh, Iran 66/G6
Ganda, Angola 115/B6
Gandajika, D.R. Congo 115/D5
Gandara, Philippines 82/E4
Gándara, Spain 33/C1
Gandava, Pakistan 68/B3
Gandava, Pakistan 59/J4
Gandeeville, W. Va. 312/D5
Gander, Newf. 162/L6
Gander, Newf. 166/D4
Gander (lake), Newf. 166/D4
Gander (riv.), Newf. 166/D4
Gandesa, Spain 33/G2
Gandhinagar, India 68/C4
Gandía, Spain 33/F3
Gandy, Nebr. 264/D3
Gandy, Utah 304/A4
Ganga (Ganges) (riv.), India 68/F3
Gan Gan, Argentina 143/C5
Ganganagar, India 68/C3
Gangapur, India 68/D3
Gangara, Niger 106/F6
Gangaw, Burma 72/B2
Gangca, China 77/F4
Gangdisê Shan (range), China 77/B5
Ganges (riv.) 54/K7
Ganges (riv.) 2/P4
Ganges, Mouths of the (delta), Bangladesh 68/F3
Ganges (riv.), Bangladesh 68/F3
Ganges, Br. Col. 184/K3
Ganges, Mouths of the (delta), India 68/F4
Ganges (riv.), India 68/F3
Gangtok, India 68/F3
Gan He (riv.), China 77/K2
Gani, Indonesia 85/H6
Ganister, Pa. 294/F5
Ganmain, N.S. Wales 97/D4
Gann (Brinkhaven), Ohio 284/F5
Gannat, France 28/E4
Gannett, Idaho 220/D6
Gannett (peak), Wyo. 188/D2
Gannett (peak), Wyo. 319/C2
Gannvalley, S. Dak. 298/L5
Ganquan, China 77/H4
Gans, Okla. 288/S4
Gänserndorf, Austria 41/D2
Gansevoort, N.Y. 276/N4
Ganshoren, Belgium 27/B9
Gansu (Kansu), China 77/E3
Gansville, La. 238/E2
Gantt, Ala. 195/E8
Gantt, S.C. 296/C2
Ganzhou (Kanchow), China 77/H6
Gao (mt.), Cent. Afr. Rep. 115/C2
Gao, Mali 102/C3
Gao, Mali 106/E5
Gao'an, China 77/H6
Gaolan, China 77/F4
Gaotai, China 77/F4
Gaoua, Burkina Faso 106/D6
Gaoual, Guinea 106/B6
Gaoyou Hu (lake), China 77/J5
Gap, France 28/G5
Gap, Pa. 294/L6
Gap (creek), Sask. 181/B6
Gapan, Philippines 82/C3
Gapcreek, Ky. 237/M7
Gap Mills, W. Va. 312/F7
Gar, China 77/B5
Gara (lake), Ireland 17/D4
Gara, Lough (lake), Ireland 10/B4
Garachiné, Panama 154/H6
Garad, Somalia 115/J2
Garadice (lake), Ireland 17/F3
Garah, N.S. Wales 97/E1
Garamba Nat'l Park, D.R. Congo 115/E3
Garanhuns, Brazil 120/F3
Garanhuns, Brazil 132/G5
Garards Fort, Pa. 294/B6
Garbahaarrey, Somalia 115/H3
Garba Tula, Kenya 115/G3
Garber, Iowa 229/L3
Garber, Okla. 288/M2
Garberville, Calif. 204/B3
Garbosh, Kuh-e (mt.), Iran 66/G4
Garbsen, Germany 22/C2
Garça, Brazil 135/B3
Garcia, Colo. 208/J8
García de Sola (res.), Spain 33/D3
Garcitas, Venezuela 124/C3
Gard (dept.), France 28/F6
Gard (riv.), France 28/F5
Garda (lake), Italy 34/C2
Gardanne, France 28/F6
Gardar, N. Dak. 282/P2
Gardelegen, Germany 22/D2
Garden, Mich. 250/C3
Garden (isl.), Mich. 250/D3
Garden (pen.), Mich. 250/C3
Garden (co.), Nebr. 264/B3
Garden (isl.), W. Australia 88/A2
Garden (isl.), W. Australia 92/A1
Gardena, Calif. 204/C11
Gardena, Idaho 220/B5
Gardena, N. Dak. 282/J2
Garden City, Ala. 195/E2
Garden City, Ga. 217/K6
Garden City, Idaho 220/B6
Garden City, Iowa 229/G4
Garden City, Kans. 188/F3
Garden City, Kansas 232/B4
Garden City, La. 238/H7
Garden City, Mich. 250/F6
Garden City, Minn. 255/D6
Garden City, Mo. 261/D5
Garden City, N.Y. 276/R7
Garden City, S. Dak. 298/O4
Garden City, Texas 303/C6
Garden City, Utah 304/C2
Garden City Beach, S.C. 296/K4
Gardendale, Ala. 195/E3
Garden Grove, Calif. 204/D11
Garden Grove, Iowa 229/F7
Garden Home-Whitford, Oreg. 291/A2
Garden Island (bay), La. 238/M8
Garden Plain, Kansas 232/E4
Garden Prairie, Ill. 222/E1
Garden Reach, India 68/F2
Garden River, Alberta 182/B5
Gardenstown, Scotland 15/F3
Gardenton, Manitoba 179/F5
Garden Valley, Idaho 220/C5
Garden View, Pa. 294/H3
Garden Village, Ontario 177/E1
Gardez, Afghanistan 59/J3
Gardez, Afghanistan 68/B2
Gardi, Ga. 217/J7
Gardiner, Maine 243/D7
Gardiner, Mont. 262/F5
Gardiner, Oreg. 291/C4
Gardiner (dam), Sask. 181/D4
Gardiner, Wash. 310/B2
Gardiners (bay), N.Y. 276/R8
Gardiners (isl.), N.Y. 276/R8
Gardner (canal), Br. Col. 184/C3
Gardner, Colo. 208/J7
Gardner (lake), Conn. 210/G2
Gardner, Fla. 212/E4
Gardner, Ill. 222/E2
Gardner, Kansas 232/H3
Gardner (Nikumaroro) (isl.), Kiribati 87/J6
Gardner (lake), Maine 243/J6
Gardner, Mass. 249/G2
Gardner, N. Dak. 282/R5
Gardner, Tenn. 237/D8
Gardner (mt.), Wash. 310/E2
Gardner Creek, New Bruns. 170/E3
Gardner Pinnacles (isls.), Hawaii 87/K3
Gardner Pinnacles (isls.), Hawaii 188/F6
Gardner Pinnacles (isls.), Hawaii 218/C6
Gardnerville, Nev. 266/B4
Gardo, Somalia 115/J2
Gardula, Ethiopia 111/G6
Gare Loch (inlet), Scotland 15/A1
Garelochhead, Scotland 15/A1
Garelochhead, Scotland 10/A1
Gareloi (isl.), Alaska 196/K4
Garessio, Italy 34/A2
Garfield, Ark. 202/C1
Garfield (co.), Colo. 208/C3
Garfield, Colo. 208/G5
Garfield, Ga. 217/H5
Garfield, Kansas 232/C3
Garfield, Ky. 237/J5
Garfield, Minn. 255/C5
Garfield (co.), Mont. 262/J3
Garfield (co.), Nebr. 264/F3
Garfield, N.J. 273/B2
Garfield, N. Mex. 274/B6
Garfield (co.), Okla. 288/L2
Garfield (co.), Utah 304/C6
Garfield (co.), Wash. 310/H4
Garfield, Wash. 310/H3
Garfield Heights, Ohio 284/J9
Gargaliánoi, Greece 45/E7
Gargunnock, Scotland 15/B1
Garibaldi, Br. Col. 184/F5
Garibaldi, Oreg. 291/D2
Garibaldi Prov. Park, Br. Col. 184/F5
Garies, S. Africa 118/B6
Garioch (dist.), Scotland 15/F3
Garissa, Kenya 115/G4
Garita, N. Mex. 274/E3
Garland, Ala. 195/E7
Garland (co.), Ark. 202/D4
Garland, Kansas 232/H4
Garland, Maine 243/E5
Garland•, Maine 243/E5
Garland, Manitoba 179/B3
Garland, Nebr. 264/G4
Garland, N.C. 281/N5
Garland, Pa. 294/C2
Garland, Tenn. 237/B9
Garland, Tex. 188/G4
Garland, Texas 303/H2
Garland, Utah 304/B2
Garland, Wyo. 319/D1
Garland City, Ark. 202/C7
Garlandville, Miss. 256/F6
Garlieston, Scotland 15/D6
Garlin, Ky. 237/L6
Garmisch-Partenkirchen, Germany 22/D5
Garmouth, Scotland 15/E3
Garmsar, Iran 59/F2
Garmsar, Iran 66/H3
Garnavillo, Iowa 229/L3
Garneill, Mont. 262/G4
Garner, Ark. 202/G3
Garner, Iowa 229/F2
Garner (lake), Manitoba 179/G4
Garner, N.C. 281/M3
Garnet, Mich. 250/D2
Garnet, Mont. 262/C4
Garnet (bay), N.W.T. 187/L3
Garnett, Kansas 232/G3
Garnett, S.C. 296/E6
Garnish, Newf. 166/C4
Garoe, Somalia 115/J2
Garonne (riv.), France 7/D4
Garonne (riv.), France 28/C5
Garoua, Cameroon 102/D4
Garoua, Cameroon 115/B2
Garrabost, Scotland 15/B2
Garrard (co.), Ky. 237/M5
Garretson, S. Dak. 298/S6
Garrett, Ill. 222/E4
Garrett, Ind. 227/G2
Garrett, Ky. 237/R6
Garrett (co.), Md. 245/A2
Garrett, Pa. 294/D6
Garrett, Wash. 310/G4
Garrett, Wyo. 319/G3
Garrett Park, Md. 245/E3
Garretts Bend, W. Va. 312/C6
Garrettsville, Ohio 284/H3
Garrick, Sask. 181/G2
Garrison, Iowa 229/J4
Garrison, Ky. 237/P3
Garrison, Md. 245/L3
Garrison, Minn. 255/E4
Garrison, Mo. 261/F9
Garrison, Mont. 262/D4
Garrison, Nebr. 264/G3
Garrison, N.Y. 276/N8
Garrison, N. Dak. 282/H4
Garrison (dam), N. Dak. 282/H5
Garrison, Texas 303/K6
Garrison, Utah 304/A5
Garrisonville, Va. 307/N4
Garron (pt.), N. Ireland 17/K1
Garrovillas, Spain 33/C3
Garry (lake), Canada 4/C14
Garry (lake), N.W.T. 162/G2
Garry (lake), N.W.T. 187/H3
Garry, Loch (lake), Scotland 15/D3
Garry (riv.), Scotland 15/D4
Garryowen, Mont. 262/J5
Garsen, Kenya 115/G4
Garske, N. Dak. 282/N3
Garson (lake), Alberta 182/E1
Garson, Manitoba 179/F4
Garstang, England 13/G1
Gartan (lake), Ireland 17/F2
Gartmore, Scotland 15/B1
Garulia, India 68/F1
Garut, Indonesia 85/H2
Garvagh, N. Ireland 17/H2
Garvan (isls.), Ireland 17/G1
Garvin, Minn. 255/C6
Garvin (co.), Okla. 288/M5
Garvin, Okla. 288/S7
Garwin, Iowa 229/H4
Garwolin, Poland 47/E3
Garwood, Mo. 261/L8
Garwood, N.J. 273/E2
Garwood, Texas 303/H8
Gary, Ind. 146/K5
Gary, Ind. 188/J2
Gary, Ind. 227/C1
Gary, Minn. 255/B3
Gary, S. Dak. 298/S4
Gary, Texas 303/K5
Gary, W. Va. 312/C8
Garyarsa (Gartok), China 77/B5
Garyarsa, China 54/K6
Garysburg, N.C. 281/O2
Garyville, La. 238/M3
Garza (co.), Texas 303/C4
Garzê, China 77/F5
Garzón, Colombia 126/C6
Garzón, Uruguay 145/E5
Garzón (lag.), Uruguay 145/E5
Gas, Kansas 232/G4
Gas (hills), Wyo. 319/E3
Gasan-Kuli, Turkmenistan 48/F6
Gasburg, Va. 307/N7
Gas City, Ind. 227/F4
Gasconade (co.), Mo. 261/J6
Gasconade, Mo. 261/J5
Gasconade (riv.), Mo. 261/H7
Gascony (trad. prov.), France 29
Gascoyne (riv.), Australia 87/B8
Gascoyne, N. Dak. 282/D7
Gascoyne (riv.), W. Australia 88/A4
Gascoyne (riv.), W. Australia 92/B4
Gascoyne Junction, W. Australia 92/A4
Gash (Mareb) (riv.), Eritrea 59/C7
Gash (Mareb) (riv.), Ethiopia 59/C7
Gash (riv.), Sudan 59/C6
Gashaka, Nigeria 106/G7
Gas Hills, Wyo. 319/E3
Gash Mareb (riv.), Eritrea 111/G5
Gash Mareb (riv.), Ethiopia 111/G5
Gasht, Iran 66/M7
Gasker (isl.), Scotland 15/A3
Gaskiers, Newf. 166/D2
Gasmata, Papua N.G. 86/B2
Gaspar, Cuba 158/F2
Gaspar Hernández, Dom. Rep. 158/E5
Gasparilla (isl.), Fla. 212/D5
Gaspé, Que. 162/K6
Gaspé, Québec 172/D1
Gaspé, Québec 174/E3
Gaspé (bay), Québec 172/D1
Gaspé (cape), Québec 172/D1
Gaspé (pen.), Québec 172/D2
Gaspé-Est (county), Québec 174/E3
Gaspé-Est (co.), Québec 172/D1
Gaspé-Ouest (co.), Québec 172/C1
Gaspé-Ouest (county), Québec 174/D3
Gaspereau (riv.), New Bruns. 170/D2
Gaspereau (lake), Nova Scotia 168/D4
Gaspésie Prov. Park, Québec 174/D3
Gaspésie Prov. Park, Québec 172/C1
Gasport, N.Y. 276/C4
Gasque, Ala. 195/C10
Gassan (mt.), Japan 81/J4
Gassaway, Tenn. 237/K9
Gassaway, W. Va. 312/E5
Gassetts, Vt. 268/B5
Gassville, Ark. 202/F1
Gaston, Ind. 227/G4
Gaston (co.), N.C. 281/G4
Gaston, N.C. 281/O1
Gaston (res.), N.C. 281/O2
Gaston, Oreg. 291/D2
Gaston, S.C. 296/E4
Gaston (lake), Va. 307/M8
Gastonburg, Ala. 195/C6
Gastonia, N.C. 188/K3
Gastonia, N.C. 281/G4
Gastre, Argentina 143/C5
Gat, Israel 65/B4
Gata (cape), Cyprus 59/B3
Gata (cape), Cyprus 63/E5
Gata (cape), Spain 33/F4
Gata (mts.), Spain 33/C2
Gatchel, Ind. 227/D8
Gatchina, Russia 52/C3
Gate, Okla. 288/F1
Gate, Wash. 310/B4
Gate City, Va. 307/C7
Gatehouse-of-Fleet, Scotland 10/E3
Gatehouse-of-Fleet, Scotland 15/D6
Gates, Nebr. 264/E3
Gates (co.), N.C. 281/R2
Gates, N.C. 281/R2
Gates, Oreg. 291/E3
Gates, Tenn. 237/C9
Gateshead, England 10/F3
Gateshead, England 13/J3
Gateshead (isl.), N.W.T. 187/J2
Gates Mills, Ohio 284/J9
Gates of the Arctic Nat'l Park, Alaska 196/H1
Gates of the Arctic Nat'l Pres., Alaska 196/H1
Gatesville, N.C. 281/R2
Gatesville, Texas 303/G6
Gateswood, Ala. 195/C9
Gateway, Ark. 202/B1
Gateway, Colo. 208/B5
Gateway, Oreg. 291/F3
Gateway Nat'l Rec. Area, N.J. 273/E2
Gateway Nat'l Rec. Area, N.Y. 276/M9
Gatewood, Mo. 261/K9
Gatico, Chile 138/A4
Gatineau (co.), Québec 172/B3
Gatineau (county), Québec 174/B3
Gatineau, Québec 172/B4
Gatineau (riv.), Québec 172/B3
Gatliff, Ky. 237/O7
Gatlinburg, Tenn. 237/O9
Gatooma (Kadoma), Zimbabwe 118/D3
Gatooma, Zimbabwe 102/E6
Gatow, Germany 22/E4
Gatteville-le-Phare, France 28/C3
Gattman, Miss. 256/H3
Gatton, Queensland 88/J5
Gatton, Queensland 95/E5
Gatun (lake), Panama 154/G6
Gatzke, Minn. 255/C2
Gaucín, Spain 33/D4
Gauhati, India 68/G3
Gauhati, India 54/L7
Gauja (riv.), Latvia 53/C2
Gauley (riv.), W. Va. 312/D6
Gauley Bridge, W. Va. 312/D6
Gauley Mills, W. Va. 312/E6
Gaultois, Newf. 166/C4
Gausdale, Ky. 237/N7
Gause, Texas 303/H7
Gaussberg (mt.), Ant. 5/C5
Gauteng (prov.), S. Africa 118/D5
Gautier, Miss. 256/G10
Gavater, Iran 59/H5
Gavater, Iran 66/M8
Gávdhos (isl.), Greece 45/F8
Gave de Pau (riv.), France 28/C6
Gavião, Portugal 33/C3
Gavins Point (dam), Nebr. 264/G2
Gavins Point (dam), S. Dak. 298/P8
Gaviota, Calif. 204/E9
Gavkhuni (lake), Iran 59/F3
Gavkhuni (marsh), Iran 66/H4
Gävle, Sweden 7/F2
Gävle, Sweden 18/K6
Gävleborg (co.), Sweden 18/K6
Gawai, Burma 72/C1
Gawler, S. Australia 88/F6
Gawler (ranges), S. Australia 88/F6
Gawler, S. Australia 94/B6
Gawler (riv.), S. Australia 94/B6
Gawler (ranges), S. Australia 94/E5
Gay, Ga. 217/C4
Gay, Mich. 250/A1
Gay, Russia 52/J4
Gay, W. Va. 312/C5
Gaya, India 68/F4
Gaya, Niger 106/E6
Gay Head•, Mass. 249/L7
Gay Head (prom.), Mass. 249/L7
Gay Hill, Texas 303/H7
Gayle, Jamaica 158/J6
Gaylesville, Ala. 195/G2
Gaylord, Kansas 232/D2
Gaylord, Mich. 250/E3
Gaylord, Minn. 255/D6
Gaylord, Oreg. 291/C5
Gaylord, Va. 307/M2
Gaylordsville, Conn. 210/A2
Gayndah, Queensland 95/D5
Gayndah, Queensland 88/J5
Gayny, Russia 52/H2
Gays, Ill. 222/E4
Gaysin, Ukraine 52/C5
Gays Mills, Wis. 317/E9
Gaysport, Ohio 284/G6
Gaysville, Vt. 268/B4
Gayville, S. Dak. 298/P8
Gaza, Cent. Afr. Rep. 115/C3
Gaza, Egypt 59/B3
Gaza, Gaza Strip 65/A5
Gaza, Iowa 229/B2
Gaza (prov.), Mozambique 118/E4
Gaza, N.H. 268/D4
Gaza Strip 65/A5
GAZA STRIP 59/B3
Gazelle, Calif. 204/C2
Gazelle (pen.), Papua N.G. 86/B2
Gaziantep (prov.), Turkey 63/G4
Gaziantep, Turkey 54/E6
Gaziantep, Turkey 63/G4
Gaziantep, Turkey 59/C2
Gazik, Iran 66/L4
Gazipaşa, Turkey 63/E4
Gbarnga, Liberia 106/C7
Gbarnga, Liberia 102/B4
Gbogo, Nigeria 106/F7
Gcuwa, S. Africa 118/D6
Gdańsk (prov.), Poland 47/D1
Gdańsk, Poland 7/F3
Gdańsk, Poland 47/D1
Gdańsk (gulf), Poland 47/D1
Gdov, Russia 52/C3
Gdynia, Poland 7/F3
Gdynia, Poland 47/D1
Gearhart, Oreg. 291/C1
Geary (co.), Kansas 232/F3

374 Gitega

Gitega, Burundi 115/F4
Giuba (riv.), Somalia 115/H3
Giubiasco, Switzerland 39/H4
Giulianova, Italy 34/E3
Giurgiu, Romania 45/G3
Giv'atayim, Israel 65/B3
Giv'at Brenner, Israel 65/B4
Giv'at Hayyim, Israel 65/B3
Give, Denmark 21/C6
Given, W. Va. 312/C5
Givet, France 28/F2
Givhans, S.C. 296/G5
Givors, France 28/F5
Giza, Egypt 111/J3
Giza, Egypt 59/B4
Gizab, Afghanistan 59/J3
Gizab, Afghanistan 68/B2
Gizhiga (bay), Russia 48/Q3
Gizo, Solomon Is. 86/D3
Giżycko, Poland 47/E1
Gjerlev, Denmark 21/D4
Gjerrild Klint (cliff), Denmark 21/D5
Gjirokastër, Albania 45/D5
Gjoa Haven, N.W.T. 162/G2
Gjoa Haven, N.W.T. 187/J3
Gjøvik, Norway 18/G6
Gjøvik, Norway 7/E2
Glace Bay, Nova Scotia 162/L6
Glace Bay, Nova Scotia 168/J2
Glacier (bay), Alaska 196/M1
Glacier, Br. Col. 184/J4
Glacier (co.), Mont. 262/C2
Glacier, Wash. 310/D2
Glacier (peak), Wash. 310/D2
Glacier Bay Nat'l Park, Alaska 196/M1
Glacier Bay Nat'l Pres., Alaska 196/L1
Glacier Nat'l Pk., Br. Col. 162/D5
Glacier Nat'l Park, Br. Col. 184/J4
Glacier Nat'l Park, Mont. 188/D1
Glacier Nat'l Park, Mont. 262/C2
Gladbrook, Iowa 229/H4
Glade, Kansas 232/C2
Glade, La. 238/G4
Gladehill, Va. 307/J7
Glade Park, Colo. 208/B5
Glades (co.), Fla. 212/E5
Glade Spring, Va. 307/E7
Glade Valley, N.C. 281/G2
Gladeville, Tenn. 237/J8
Gladewater, Texas 303/K5
Gladmar, Sask. 181/G6
Gladstone, Ill. 222/B3
Gladstone, Manitoba 179/D4
Gladstone, Mich. 250/C3
Gladstone, Mo. 261/P5
Gladstone, Nebr. 264/G4
Gladstone, N. Mex. 274/F2
Gladstone, N. Dak. 282/F6
Gladstone, Oreg. 291/B2
Gladstone, Queensland 88/J4
Gladstone, Queensland 95/D4
Gladstone, S. Australia 94/F5
Gladstone, Tasmania 99/D2
Gladstone, Va. 307/L5
Glad Valley, S. Dak. 298/F3
Gladwin (co.), Mich. 250/E4
Gladwin, Mich. 250/E5
Glady, W. Va. 312/G5
Gladys, Va. 307/K6
Glåma (riv.), Norway 7/F2
Glåma (riv.), Norway 18/G6
Glamis, Calif. 204/K11
Glamis, Sask. 181/D4
Glamis, Scotland 15/F4
Glamoč, Bos. 45/C3
Glamsbjerg, Denmark 21/D7
Glan, Philippines 85/G4
Glan, Philippines 82/E8
Glancy, Miss. 256/C7
Gland, Switzerland 39/B4
Glandore, Ireland 17/C8
Glandore (harb.), Ireland 17/C9
Glandorf, Ohio 284/B3
Glâne (riv.), Switzerland 39/C3
Glanmire-Riverstown, Ireland 17/E8
Glanworth, Ireland 17/E7
Glärnisch (mt.), Switzerland 39/H2
Glarus (canton), Switzerland 39/H3
Glarus, Switzerland 39/H2
Glarus Alps (mts.), Switzerland 39/H3
Glasco, Kansas 232/E2
Glasco, N.Y. 276/M6
Glascock (co.), Ga. 217/G4
Glasford, Ill. 222/D3
Glasgo, Conn. 210/H2
Glasgow, Del. 245/R2
Glasgow, Ill. 222/C4
Glasgow, Ky. 237/J7
Glasgow, Mo. 261/G4
Glasgow, Mont. 262/K2
Glasgow, Pa. 294/E4
Glasgow, Scotland 7/D3
Glasgow, Scotland 10/B1
Glasgow, Scotland 15/B2
Glasgow, Va. 307/K5
Glasgow, W. Va. 312/D6
Glasier (lake), New Bruns. 170/A1
Glaslyn, Sask. 181/C2
Glas Maol (mt.), Scotland 15/E4
Glasnevin, Sask. 181/F6
Glass, Manitoba 179/F5
Glass (riv.), Scotland 15/D3
Glass (mts.), Texas 303/A7
Glassboro, N.J. 273/C4
Glasscock (co.), Texas 303/C6
Glasser, N.J. 273/D2
Glassport, Pa. 294/C7
Glasston, N. Dak. 282/R2
Glassville, New Bruns. 170/C2
Glastenbury (mt.), Vt. 268/A6
Glastonbury, Conn. 210/E2
Glastonbury•, Conn. 210/E2
Glastonbury, England 13/E6
Glastonbury, England 10/E5
Glatt (riv.), Switzerland 39/G2
Glattfelden, Switzerland 39/F1
Glauchau, Germany 22/E3
Glazier, Texas 303/D2
Glazov, Russia 7/K3
Glazov, Russia 52/H3
Gleason, Tenn. 237/D8
Gleason, Wis. 317/G5
Gleasondale, Mass. 249/J3
Gleeson, Ariz. 198/F7
Gleichen, Alberta 182/D4
Gleisdorf, Austria 41/C3
Gleiwitz (Gliwice), Poland 47/A4
Glen (lake), Ireland 17/F1
Glen (lake), Mich. 250/C4
Glen, Minn. 255/E4
Glen, Miss. 256/H1
Glen, Mont. 262/D5
Glen, N.H. 268/E3
Glen (canyon), Utah 304/D6
Glen, W. Va. 312/D6
Glenada, Oreg. 291/C4
Glenaire, Mo. 261/R5
Glen Alice, Tenn. 237/M9
Glen Allan, Miss. 256/B4
Glen Allen, Ala. 195/C3
Glenallen, Mo. 261/M8
Glen Allen, Va. 307/N5
Glen Almond, Québec 172/B4
Glen Alpine, N.C. 281/F3
Glenamaddy, Ireland 17/D4
Glen Arbor, Mich. 250/C4
Glenarden, Md. 245/G4
Glen Arm, Md. 245/N3
Glenarm, N. Ireland 17/J2
Glenavon, Sask. 181/J5
Glen Avon Heights, Calif. 204/E10
Glenavy, N. Zealand 100/C6
Glenavy, N. Ireland 17/J2
Glen Bain, Sask. 181/E6
Glenbarr, Scotland 15/C5
Glenbeigh, Ireland 17/B7
Glenbeulah, Wis. 317/L8
Glenboro, Manitoba 179/C5
Glenbrook, Nev. 266/B3
Glenburn•, Maine 243/F6
Glenburn, N. Dak. 282/H2
Glen Burnie, Md. 245/M4
Glenbush, Sask. 181/D2
Glen Campbell, Pa. 294/E4
Glen Canyon (dam), Ariz. 198/D2
Glen Canyon Nat'l Rec. Area, Ariz. 198/D1
Glen Canyon Nat'l Rec. Area, Utah 304/D6
Glencaple, Scotland 15/E5
Glen Carbon, Ill. 222/B2
Glencliff, N.H. 268/D4
Glencoe, Ala. 195/G3
Glencoe, Ill. 222/B5
Glencoe, Ky. 237/M3
Glencoe, La. 238/G7
Glencoe, Minn. 255/D6
Glencoe, Mo. 261/M3
Glencoe, New Bruns. 170/D1
Glencoe, N. Mex. 274/D5
Glencoe, Ohio 284/J6
Glencoe, Okla. 288/M2
Glencoe, Ontario 177/C5
Glencoe, Pa. 294/E6
Glencoe, Scotland 15/C4
Glencoe, S. Africa 118/E5
Glencolumbkille, Ireland 17/D2
Glen Cove, Maine 243/E7
Glen Cove, N.Y. 276/R6
Glencross, S. Dak. 298/H3
Glendale, Ariz. 198/C5
Glendale, Calif. 188/C4
Glendale, Calif. 204/C10
Glendale, Fla. 212/C5
Glendale, Ind. 227/C7
Glendale, Kansas 232/E3
Glendale, Ky. 237/K5
Glendale, Mass. 249/A3
Glendale, Mo. 261/P3
Glendale, Nev. 266/G6
Glendale, N.H. 268/E4
Glendale, Nova Scotia 168/G3
Glendale, Ohio 284/C9
Glendale, Oreg. 291/D5
Glendale (lake), Pa. 294/F4
Glendale, R.I. 249/H5
Glendale, S.C. 296/D2
Glendale, Utah 304/B6
Glen Dale, W. Va. 312/E3
Glendale, Wis. 317/M1
Glendale Heights, Ill. 222/A5
Glen Daniel, W. Va. 312/D7
Glen Dean, Ky. 237/J5
Glendevey, Colo. 208/H1
Glendive, Mont. 262/M3
Glendo, Wyo. 319/G3
Glendo (res.), Wyo. 319/H3
Glendon, Alberta 182/E2
Glendon, N.C. 281/L4
Glendora, Calif. 204/D10
Glendora, Miss. 256/D3
Glendora, N.J. 273/B4
Glen Easton, W. Va. 312/E3
Glen Echo, Md. 245/E4
Glen Eden, N. Zealand 100/B1
Gleneden Beach, Oreg. 291/C3
Glen Elder, Kansas 232/D2
Glenelg, Md. 245/L3
Glenelg, Scotland 15/C3
Glenelg (cay), Scotland 10/D2
Glenelg, S. Australia 88/D8
Glenelg, S. Australia 94/A8
Glenelg (riv.), Victoria 97/A5
Glenella, Manitoba 179/C4
Glen Ellyn, Ill. 222/A5
Glenevis, Alberta 182/C3
Glen Ewen, Sask. 181/K6
Glen Ferris, W. Va. 312/D6
Glenfield, N.Y. 276/K3
Glenfield, N. Zealand 100/B1
Glenfield, N. Dak. 282/N5
Glenfield, Pa. 294/B6
Glen Flora, Texas 303/H8
Glen Flora, Wis. 317/E4
Glenford, Ohio 284/F6
Glen Gardner, N.J. 273/D2
Glengarriff, Ireland 17/C8
Glengarry, Mont. 262/G3
Glengarry (county), Ontario 177/K2
Glengary, W. Va. 312/K4
Glenham, S. Dak. 298/J2
Glen Harbour, Sask. 181/G5
Glen Haven, Colo. 208/H2
Glen Haven, Mich. 250/C4
Glen Haven, Wis. 317/E10
Glenhayes, W. Va. 312/A6
Glen Hedrick (Beaver), W. Va. 312/D7
Glen Hope, Pa. 294/F4
Glen Innes, N. S. Wales 88/J5
Glen Innes, N.S. Wales 97/F1
Glen Jean, W. Va. 312/D7
Glen Kerr, Sask. 181/D5
Glenlea, Manitoba 179/E5
Glenlivet, New Bruns. 170/D1
Glenluce, Scotland 15/D6
Glen Lyn, Va. 307/G6
Glen Lyon, Pa. 294/E7
Glenmary, Tenn. 237/M8
Glenmere, Sask. 181/J5
Glen Miller, Ontario 177/G3
Glenmont, Ohio 284/F4
Glenmora, La. 238/E5
Glen More (dist.), Scotland 15/D3
Glenmorgan, Queensland 95/D5
Glenn (co.), Calif. 204/C4
Glenn, Ga. 217/B4
Glenn, Mich. 250/C6
Glennallen, Alaska 196/D1
Glenn Heights, Texas 303/G3
Glennie, Mich. 250/F4
Glenns Ferry, Idaho 220/C7
Glenn Springs, S.C. 296/D2
Glennville, Calif. 204/G8
Glennville, Ga. 217/J7
Glenolden, Pa. 294/M7
Glenoma, Wash. 310/C4
Glenora, Br. Col. 184/K2
Glenorchy, Tasmania 88/H8
Glenorchy, Tasmania 99/D4
Glenormiston, Queensland 95/A4
Glen Park, N.Y. 276/J3
Glenpool, Okla. 288/P3
Glen Raven, N.C. 281/L2
Glenreagh, N.S. Wales 97/G2
Glen Riddle, Pa. 294/L7
Glen Ridge, N.J. 273/B2
Glenrio, N. Mex. 274/F3
Glen Robertson, Ontario 177/K2
Glen Rock, N.J. 273/B1
Glen Rock, Pa. 294/J6
Glenrock, Wyo. 319/G3
Glen Rogers, W. Va. 312/D7
Glen Rose, Texas 303/G5
Glenrothes, Scotland 15/E4
Glen Roy, Ohio 284/E7
Glen Saint Mary, Fla. 212/D1
Glens Falls, N.Y. 276/N4
Glens Fork, Ky. 237/L6
Glenshaw, Pa. 294/C6
Glenside, Pa. 294/M5
Glenside, Sask. 181/E4
Glenside-Churton Park, N. Zealand 100/B2
Glensted, Mo. 261/G5
Glentana, Mont. 262/K2
Glenties, Ireland 10/B3
Glenties, Ireland 17/E2
Glentrool, Scotland 15/D5
Glentworth, Sask. 181/E6
Glen Ullin, N. Dak. 282/G6
Glenview, Ill. 222/B5
Glenview, Ky. 237/K1
Glenview Nav. Air. Sta., Ill. 222/B5
Glenvil, Nebr. 264/F4
Glenville, Conn. 210/A4
Glenville, Ireland 17/D7
Glenville, Minn. 255/E7
Glenville, N.C. 281/C4
Glenville, W. Va. 312/E5
Glen Walter, Ontario 177/K2
Glen White, W. Va. 312/D7
Glenwillow, Ohio 284/J10
Glen Wilton, Va. 307/J5
Glenwood, Ala. 195/F7
Glenwood, Alberta 182/D5
Glenwood, Ark. 202/C5
Glenwood, Fla. 212/E2
Glenwood, Ga. 217/L1
Glenwood, Ill. 222/C6
Glenwood, Ind. 227/G5
Glenwood, Iowa 229/B6
Glenwood, Mich. 250/C6
Glenwood, Minn. 255/C5
Glenwood, Mo. 261/G1
Glenwood, Newf. 166/D4
Glenwood, N.J. 273/D1
Glenwood, N. Mex. 274/A5
Glenwood, N.C. 281/F3
Glenwood, Oreg. 291/D2
Glenwood, Utah 304/C5
Glenwood, Va. 307/K7
Glenwood, Wash. 310/D4
Glenwood, W. Va. 312/B5
Glenwood City, Wis. 317/B5
Glenwood Springs, Colo. 208/E4
Glezen, Ind. 227/C8
Glidden, Iowa 229/D4
Glidden, Sask. 181/B4
Glidden, Wis. 317/E3
Glide, Oreg. 291/D4
Glin, Ireland 17/C6
Glis, Switzerland 39/E4
Glittertinden (mt.), Norway 7/E2
Glittertinden (mt.), Norway 18/F6
Gliwice, Poland 47/A4
Globe, Ariz. 188/D4
Globe, Ariz. 198/E5
Gloggnitz, Austria 41/D3
Głogów (Glogau), Poland 47/C3
Glomawr, Ky. 237/P6
Glomfjord, Norway 18/J3
Gloria (bay), Cuba 158/G2
Glorieta, N. Mex. 274/D3
Glorioso (isls.), Réunion 118/H2
Glory, Minn. 255/E4
Glory of Russia (cape), Alaska 196/D2
Glossop, England 13/J2
Glossop, England 10/G2
Gloster, La. 238/C2
Gloster, Miss. 256/B8
Glostrup, Denmark 21/F6
Gloucester, England 13/E6
Gloucester, England 10/E5
Gloucester, Mass. 249/M2
Gloucester (co.), New Bruns. 170/E1
Gloucester (co.), N.J. 273/C4
Gloucester, N.S. Wales 97/F2
Gloucester, N.C. 281/S5
Gloucester (cape), Papua N.G. 86/B2
Gloucester (co.), Va. 307/P6
Gloucester, Va. 307/P6
Gloucester City, N.J. 273/B3
Gloucester Junction, New Bruns. 170/E1
Gloucester Point, Va. 307/R6
Gloucestershire (co.), England 13/E6
Glouster, Ohio 284/F6
Glover (reef), Belize 154/D2
Glover, Mo. 261/L8
Glover (isl.), Newf. 166/C4
Glover, N. Dak. 282/O7
Glover, Okla. 288/S6
Glover•, Vt. 268/C2
Glovergap, W. Va. 312/F3
Gloversville, N.Y. 276/M4
Glovertown, Newf. 166/C1
Gloverville, S.C. 296/D4
Głowno, Poland 47/D2
Głubczyce, Poland 47/C3
Glubokoye, Belarus 52/C3
Głuchołazy, Poland 47/C3
Glücksburg, Germany 22/C1
Glückstadt, Germany 22/C2
Gluckstadt, Miss. 256/D5
Glukhov, Ukraine 52/D4
Glumsø, Denmark 21/E7
Glyde (riv.), Ireland 17/H4
Glynco, Ga. 217/J8
Glyncorrwg, Wales 13/D6
Glyndon, Md. 245/L3
Glyndon, Minn. 255/B4
Glyngøre, Denmark 21/C4
Glynn (co.), Ga. 217/J8
Glynn, La. 238/H5
Glynn, N. Ireland 17/K2
Gmünd, Carinthia, Austria 41/B3
Gmünd, Lower Austria, Austria 41/C2
Gmunden, Austria 41/B3
Gnadenhutten, Ohio 284/G5
Gnaw Bone, Ind. 227/E6
Gnesta, Sweden 18/G2
Gniew, Poland 47/D2
Gniewkowo, Poland 47/D2
Gniezno, Poland 47/C2
Gnjilane, Yugoslavia 45/E4
Gnowangerup, W. Australia 88/B6
Gnowangerup, W. Australia 92/B6
Goa (state), India 68/C5
Goalpara, India 68/G3
Goascorán, Honduras 154/D4
Goat Fell (mt.), Scotland 15/C5
Goat River, Br. Col. 184/G3
Goat Rock (dam), Ala. 195/H5
Goat Rock (lake), Ala. 195/H5
Goat Rock (dam), Ga. 217/B5
Goat Rock (lake), Ga. 217/B5
Goat Rocks (mt.), Wash. 310/D4
Goba, Ethiopia 111/H6
Goba, Ethiopia 102/G4
Goba, Mozambique 118/E5
Gobabis, Namibia 118/B4
Gobabis, Namibia 102/D7
Gobernador Crespo, Argentina 143/F5
Gobernador Gregores, Argentina 143/C6
Gobernador Mansilla, Argentina 143/G6
Gobi (des.) 54/M5
Gobi (des.), China 77/G3
Gobi (des.), Mongolia 77/G3
Goble, Oreg. 291/E1
Gobler, Mo. 261/N10
Gobles, Mich. 250/D6
Gobo, Japan 81/G7
Gobwen, Somalia 115/H4
Goch, Germany 22/B3
Go Cong, Vietnam 72/E5
Godahl, Minn. 255/D6
Godalming, England 13/G8
Godalming, England 10/F5
Godavari (riv.), India 54/J8
Godavari (riv.), India 68/D5
Godbout, Québec 174/D3
Godbout, Québec 172/B1
Goddard, Kansas 232/E4
Godech, Bulgaria 45/F4
Goderich, Ontario 177/C4
Godfrey, Ga. 217/F4
Godfrey, Ill. 222/A2
Godhavn (Qeqertarsauq), Greenland 4/C12
Godhavn (Qeqertarsauq), Greenland 146/N3
Godhra, India 68/C4
Gödöllő, Hungary 41/E3
Godoy Cruz, Argentina 143/C3
Gods (lake), Man. 162/G5
Gods (lake), Manitoba 179/K3
Gods (riv.), Man. 162/G4
Gods (riv.), Manitoba 179/K3
Gods Mercy (bay), N.W.T. 187/K3
Gods River, Manitoba 179/K3
Godthåb (Nuuk) (cap.), Greenland 4/C12
Godthåb (Nuuk) (cap.), Greenland 2/G2
Godthåb (Nuuk) (cap.), Greenland 146/N3
Godwin, N.C. 281/M4
Godwin Austen (mt.), Pakistan 68/D1
Godwinsville, Ga. 217/F6
Goehner, Nebr. 264/G4
Goéland (lake), Québec 174/B3
Goélands (lake), Québec 174/E1
Goeree (isl.), Netherlands 27/D5
Goes, Netherlands 27/D6
Goessel, Kansas 232/E3
Goetzville, Mich. 250/E2
Goff, Kansas 232/G2
Goff (creek), Okla. 288/C1
Goffstown•, N.H. 268/D5
Gogama, Ontario 175/D3
Gogama, Ontario 177/J5
Gogebic (co.), Mich. 250/F2
Gogebic (lake), Mich. 250/F2
Gogrial, Sudan 111/E6
Goi, Ben (bay), Vietnam 72/F4
Goiana, Brazil 132/H4
Goiandira, Brazil 132/E7
Goiânia, Brazil 132/D7
Goiânia, Brazil 120/D4
Goiás (state), Brazil 132/D6
Goiás, Brazil 132/D6
Goiás, Brazil 120/D4
Goil, Loch (lake), Scotland 15/A1
Goin, Tenn. 237/O8
Goirle, Netherlands 27/G5
Góis, Portugal 33/B2
Gojjam (prov.), Ethiopia 111/G5
Gökçe, Turkey 63/B2
Gökçeada (isl.), Turkey 59/A1
Gökçeada (isl.), Turkey 63/A2
Gökırmak (riv.), Turkey 63/F2
Göksu (riv.), Turkey 63/E4
Göksun, Turkey 63/G3
Gokteik, Burma 72/C2
Gol, Norway 18/F6
Gola (isl.), Ireland 17/E1
Golan Heights, West Bank 65/D1
Gölbaşı, Turkey 63/G4
Golborne, England 13/G2
Gol'chikha, Russia 48/J2
Golconda, Ill. 222/E6
Golconda (ruins), India 68/D5
Golconda, Nev. 266/D2
Gölcük, Turkey 63/C2
Golčův Jeníkov, Czech Rep. 41/C2
Gold (riv.), Nova Scotia 168/D4
Gołdap, Poland 47/F1
Gold Bar, Wash. 310/D3
Gold Beach, Oreg. 291/C5
Goldbond, Va. 307/G6
Goldboro, Nova Scotia 168/G3
Gold Bridge, Br. Col. 184/F5
Gold Coast (reg.), Ghana 106/D8
Gold Coast, Queensland 95/E6
Gold Coast, Queensland 88/J5
Goldcreek, Mont. 262/D4
Golden, Br. Col. 184/J4
Golden, Colo. 208/J3
Golden, Idaho 220/C4
Golden, Ill. 222/B3
Golden, Ireland 17/F7
Golden, Miss. 256/H1
Golden, Mo. 261/E9
Golden, N. Mex. 274/C3
Golden (bay), N. Zealand 100/D4
Golden, Okla. 288/S6
Golden (lake), Ontario 177/G2
Golden (lake), Wis. 317/H1
Golden Beach, Fla. 212/C4
Golden City, Mo. 261/D8
Goldendale, Wash. 310/E5
Golden Ears Prov. Park, Br. Col. 184/L2
Golden Gate (chan.), Calif. 188/B3
Golden Gate (chan.), Calif. 204/H2
Golden Gate, Fla. 212/E5
Golden Gate, Ill. 222/E5
Golden Gate (range), Nev. 266/F5
Golden Gate Nat'l Rec. Area, Calif. 204/H2
Golden Grove, Jamaica 158/K6
Golden Hill, Md. 245/O7
Golden Lake, Ontario 177/G2
Golden Meadow, La. 238/K8
Golden Prairie, Sask. 181/B5
Golden Rock, St. Kitts & Nevis 161/C10
Golden's Bridge, N.Y. 276/N8
Golden Shores, Ariz. 198/A4
Golden Spike Nat'l Hist. Site, Utah 304/B2
Golden Vale (plain), Ireland 17/E7
Golden Valley, Minn. 255/G5
Golden Valley (co.), Mont. 262/G4
Golden Valley (co.), N. Dak. 282/C5
Goldenvalley, N. Dak. 282/F5
Golden Valley, Ontario 177/E2
Goldfield, Iowa 229/F3
Goldfield, Nev. 188/C3
Goldfield, Nev. 266/D5
Gold Hill, Ala. 195/G5
Gold Hill, Nev. 266/B3
Gold Hill, N.C. 281/J3
Gold Hill, Oreg. 291/D5
Goldonna, La. 238/D2
Gold Point, Nev. 266/D5
Gold River, Br. Col. 184/D5
Goldsberry, Mo. 261/G3
Goldsboro, Md. 245/P4
Goldsboro, N.C. 188/L3
Goldsboro, N.C. 281/O4
Goldsboro (Etters), Pa. 294/J5
Goldsby, Okla. 288/L4
Goldsmith, Ind. 227/E4
Goldsmith, Texas 303/B5
Goldston, N.C. 281/L3
Goldstone (mt.), Idaho 220/E4
Goldsworthy, W. Australia 88/C4
Goldsworthy, W. Australia 92/B3
Goldthwaite, Texas 303/F6
Goldvein, Va. 307/N4
Goldville, Ala. 195/G4
Göle, Turkey 63/K2
Goleniów, Poland 47/B2
Goleta, Calif. 204/F9
Golf, Fla. 212/F5
Golf, Ill. 222/B5
Golfito, C. Rica 154/F6
Golf Manor, Ohio 284/C9
Golfo Santa Clara, Mexico 150/B1
Gölhisar, Turkey 63/C4
Goliad (co.), Texas 303/G9
Goliad, Texas 303/G9
Gölköy, Turkey 63/G2
Golling an der Salzach, Austria 41/B3
Gölmarmara, Turkey 63/C3
Golmud (Golmo), China 77/D4
Golmud, China 54/L6
Golo (riv.), France 28/B6
Golo (isl.), Philippines 82/C4
Golovin, Alaska 196/F2
Golpayegan, Iran 59/F3
Golpayegan, Iran 66/G4
Gölpazarı, Turkey 63/D2
Golshan (Tabas), Iran 66/K4
Golspie, Scotland 15/E3
Goltry, Okla. 288/K1
Golts, Md. 245/P3
Golub-Dobrzyn, Poland 47/D2
Golungo Alto, Angola 115/B5
Golva, N. Dak. 282/C6
Goma, D.R. Congo 115/E4
Goma, D.R. Congo 102/E5
Gombari, D.R. Congo 115/E3
Gombe, Nigeria 106/G6
Gomel', Belarus 7/H3
Gomel', Belarus 48/D4
Gomel', Belarus 52/D4
Gomer, Ohio 284/B4
Gomera (isl.), Spain 106/A3
Gomera (isl.), Spain 33/B5
Gometra (isl.), Scotland 15/B4
Gomez, Fla. 212/F4
Gómez Farías, Mexico 150/F2
Gómez Palacio, Mexico 150/G4
Gomishan, Iran 66/J2
Goms (valley), Switzerland 39/F4
Gona, Papua N.G. 85/C7
Gonabad, Iran 59/G3
Gonabad, Iran 66/L3
Gonaïves, Haiti 158/B5
Gonaïves, Haiti 156/D3
Gonâve (gulf), Haiti 158/B5
Gonâve (isl.), Haiti 158/B6
Gonâve (isl.), Haiti 156/D3
Gonbad-e Kavus, Iran 66/J2
Gonbadli, Iran 66/M2
Gönc, Hungary 41/F2
Gonda, India 68/E3
Gondal, India 68/C4
Gondar, Ethiopia 102/F3
Gondar, Ethiopia 59/C7
Gondar, Ethiopia 111/G5
Gondia, India 68/E4
Gondola Point, New Bruns. 170/D3
Gondomar, Portugal 33/B2
Gönen, Turkey 63/B2
Gonggar, China 77/D6
Gongga Shan (mt.), China 77/F6
Gonghe, China 77/F4
Gongliu, China 77/B3
Gongola (state), Nigeria 106/G7
Gongola (riv.), Nigeria 106/G6
Gongolgan, N.S. Wales 97/D2
Góngora (mt.), C. Rica 154/E5
Goñi, Uruguay 145/C4
Gonjo, China 77/E5
Gonvick, Minn. 255/C3
Gonzaga, Philippines 82/D1
Gonzales, Calif. 204/D7
Gonzales, La. 238/L2
Gonzales (co.), Texas 303/G8
Gonzales, Texas 303/G8
Gonzalez, Fla. 212/B6
González, Mexico 150/K5
González, Riacho (riv.), Paraguay 144/C3
Goobies, Newf. 166/D2
Goochland (co.), Va. 307/N5
Goochland, Va. 307/N5
Goodbee, La. 238/K6
Goode (mt.), Alaska 196/C1
Goode, Va. 307/K6
Goodell, Iowa 229/F3
Goodenough (cape), Ant. 5/C7
Gooderham, Ontario 177/F3
Goodeve, Sask. 181/H4
Goodfare, Alberta 182/A2
Goodfellow A.F.B., Texas 303/D6
Goodfield, Ill. 222/D3
Good Harbor (bay), Mich. 250/D3
Good Hart, Mich. 250/D3
Good Hope, Ala. 195/E2
Goodhope (bay), Alaska 196/F1
Good Hope, Ga. 217/E3
Good Hope, Ill. 222/C3
Good Hope, La. 238/N3
Good Hope, Miss. 256/E5
Good Hope, Ohio 284/D7
Good Hope (cape), S. Africa 102/D8
Good Hope (cape), S. Africa 2/K7
Good Hope (cape), S. Africa 118/E7
Goodhue (co.), Minn. 255/F6
Goodhue, Minn. 255/F6
Gooding (co.), Idaho 220/D6
Gooding, Idaho 220/D7
Goodland, Fla. 212/E6
Goodland, Ind. 227/C3
Goodland, Kansas 232/A2
Goodland, Minn. 255/E3
Goodlands, Manitoba 179/B5
Goodlettsville, Tenn. 237/H8
Goodlow, Br. Col. 184/G2
Good Luck, Md. 245/G4
Goodman, Miss. 256/E5
Goodman, Mo. 261/C9
Goodman, Wis. 317/K4
Goodnews Bay, Alaska 196/F3
Goodnight, Texas 303/C3
Goodnoe Hills, Wash. 310/E5
Goodooga, N.S. Wales 97/D1
Good Pine, La. 238/F3
Goodrich, Colo. 208/M2
Goodrich, Mich. 250/F6
Goodrich, N. Dak. 282/K5
Goodrich, Texas 303/K7
Goodrich, Wis. 317/G5
Goodridge, Alberta 182/E2
Goodridge, Minn. 255/C2
Goodsoil, Sask. 181/L4
Goodson, Mo. 261/F7

Grandview Heights 375

Good Spirit (lake), Sask. 181/J4
Goodspirit Lake Prov. Park, Sask. 181/J4
Goodspring, Tenn. 237/G10
Goodsprings, Ala. 195/D3
Goodsprings, Nev. 266/F7
Good Thunder, Minn. 255/D6
Goodview, Minn. 255/G6
Goodwater, Ala. 195/F4
Goodwater, Okla. 288/S7
Goodwater, Sask. 181/H6
Goodway, Ala. 195/D8
Goodwell, Okla. 288/C1
Goodwin, Ark. 202/J4
Goodwin, S. Dak. 298/R4
Goodwins Mills, Maine 243/B8
Goodwood, Ontario 177/E3
Goodwood, S. Africa 118/F6
Goodyear, Ariz. 198/C5
Gooik, Belgium 27/E7
Goole, England 10/F4
Goole, England 13/G4
Goolgowi, N.S. Wales 97/C3
Gooloogong, N.S. Wales 97/E3
Goomalling, W. Australia 88/B6
Goomalling, W. Australia 92/B1
Goombalie, N.S. Wales 97/C1
Goondiwindi, Queensland 88/H5
Goondiwindi, Queensland 95/D6
Goor, Netherlands 27/K4
Goose (lake) 188/B2
Goose (lake), Calif. 204/E1
Goose (creek), Idaho 220/E7
Goose (riv.), Newf. 166/B3
Goose (riv.), N. Dak. 282/P4
Goose (isl.), Nova Scotia 168/F4
Goose (isl.), Nova Scotia 168/G3
Goose (lake), Oreg. 291/G5
Goose (creek), Va. 307/J6
Goose (creek), Va. 307/N3
Goose Airport P.O. (Goose Bay), Newf. 162/K5
Goose Bay, Newf. 162/K5
Goose Bay, Newf. 146/M4
Goose Bay-Happy Valley, Newf. 166/B3
Gooseberry (creek), Wyo. 319/D1
Gooseberry Cove, Newf. 166/C2
Goose Cove, Newf. 166/C2
Goose Cove, Newf. 166/C3
Goose Cove, Nova Scotia 168/H2
Goose Creek (mts.), Idaho 220/E7
Goose Creek, Ky. 237/L1
Goose Creek, S.C. 296/H6
Goose Lake, Iowa 229/N5
Goose Prairie, Wash. 310/D4
Goose Rock, Ky. 237/O6
Goose Rocks Beach, Maine 243/C9
Göppingen, Germany 22/C4
Góra, Poland 47/C3
Gorakhpur, India 68/E3
Gorchs, Argentina 143/G7
Gorda (pt.), Cuba 158/C2
Gorda (bank), Honduras 154/F3
Gorda (cay), Honduras 154/F3
Gorda (pt.), Nicaragua 154/F5
Gorda (pt.), Panama 154/H6
Gördes, Turkey 63/C3
Gordevio, Switzerland 39/G4
Gørding, Denmark 21/B7
Gordo, Ala. 195/C4
Gordola, Switzerland 39/G4
Gordon, Ala. 195/H8
Gordon (lake), Alberta 182/E1
Gordon (riv.), Br. Col. 184/H3
Gordon (isl.), Chile 138/E11
Gordon (co.), Ga. 217/C2
Gordon, Ga. 217/F5
Gordon, Kansas 232/F4
Gordon, Nebr. 264/B2
Gordon, Ohio 284/B6
Gordon, Scotland 15/F5
Gordon, Tasmania 99/G5
Gordon (lake), Tasmania 99/C4
Gordon (riv.), Tasmania 99/B4
Gordon, Texas 303/F5
Gordon, W. Va. 312/C7
Gordon, Wis. 317/C3
Gordondale, Alberta 182/A2
Gordon Downs, W. Australia 92/E2
Gordon's Bay, S. Africa 118/F7
Gordonsburg, Tenn. 237/F9
Gordonsville, Ala. 195/E6
Gordonsville, Minn. 255/E7
Gordonsville, Tenn. 237/K8
Gordonsville, Va. 307/M4
Gordonvale, Queensland 88/H3
Gordonvale, Queensland 95/C3
Gordonville, Mo. 261/N8
Gore (pt.), Alaska 196/C2
Goré, Chad 111/C6
Gore (range), Colo. 208/G3
Gore, Ethiopia 111/G6
Gore, Ethiopia 102/F4
Gore, N. Zealand 100/B7
Gore, Ohio 284/F6
Gore, Okla. 288/R3
Gore (mt.), Vt. 268/D2
Gore, Va. 307/M2
Gore Bay, Ontario 177/B2
Gorebridge, Scotland 10/C1
Gorebridge, Scotland 15/D2
Goree, Texas 303/E4
Goregaon, India 68/B7
Görele, Turkey 63/H2
Gore Springs, Miss. 256/E3
Goreville, Ill. 222/E6
Gorey, Chan. Is. 13/F8
Gorey, Ireland 17/J6
Gorey, Ireland 10/C4
Gorgan, Iran 54/G6
Gorgan, Iran 59/F2
Gorgan (Gurgan), Iran 66/J2
Gorgan (riv.), Iran 66/J2
Gorgan (riv.), Iran 59/F2
Gorgas, Ala. 195/D3
Gorgol (reg.), Mauritania 106/B5
Gorgona (isl.), Colombia 126/A6
Gorgona (isl.), Italy 34/B3
Gorham, Ill. 222/D6
Gorham, Kansas 232/D3
Gorham, Maine 243/C8
Gorham•, Maine 243/C8
Gorham, N.H. 268/E3
Gorham•, N.H. 268/E3
Gorham, N.Y. 276/F5
Gorham, N. Dak. 282/D5
Gori, Georgia 52/F6
Gorin, Mo. 261/H2
Gorinchem, Netherlands 27/G5
Gorizia (prov.), Italy 34/D2
Gorizia, Italy 34/D2
Gorki, Belarus 52/D4
Gørlev, Denmark 21/E7
Gorlice, Poland 47/E4
Görlitz, Germany 22/F3
Görlitz, Germany 7/F3
Gorlitz, Sask. 181/J4
Gorlovka, Ukraine 7/H4
Gorlovka, Ukraine 52/E5
Gorman, Calif. 204/G9
Gorman, Tenn. 237/F8
Gorman, Texas 303/F5
Gormania, W. Va. 312/H4
Gormanston, Ireland 17/J4
Gormanston, Tasmania 99/B4
Gorna Oryakhovitsa, Bulgaria 45/G4
Gornji Milanovac, Yugoslavia 45/D3
Gornji Vakuf, Bos. 45/C4
Gorno-Altay Aut. Obl., Russia 48/J4
Gorno-Altaysk, Russia 48/J4
Gorno-Badakhshan Aut. Obl., Tajikistan 48/H6
Gornyak, Russia 48/J4
Gorodets, Russia 52/F3
Gorodok, Belarus 52/D3
Goroka, Papua N.G. 85/B7
Goroke, Victoria 97/A5
Gorong (isl.), Indonesia 85/J6
Gorong (isls.), Indonesia 85/J6
Gorongosa Nat'l Park, Mozambique 118/E3
Gorongoza, Mozambique 118/E3
Gorontalo, Indonesia 85/G5
Gorrahei, Ethiopia 111/H6
Gorredijk, Netherlands 27/J2
Gorrie, Ontario 177/C4
Gort, Wash. 310/C3
Gort, Ireland 10/B4
Gort, Ireland 17/D5
Gortin, N. Ireland 17/G2
Gorum, La. 238/E4
Gorumna (isl.), Ireland 17/B5
Goryn' (riv.), Belarus 52/C4
Goryn' (riv.), Ukraine 52/C4
Gorzów (prov.), Poland 47/B2
Gorzów Wielkopolski, Poland 47/B2
Gorzów Wielkopolski, Poland 7/F3
Göschenen, Switzerland 39/G3
Gose, Japan 81/J8
Gosen, Japan 81/J5
Goshen, Ala. 195/F7
Goshen, Ark. 202/C1
Goshen, Calif. 204/F7
Goshen•, Conn. 210/C1
Goshen (pt.), Conn. 210/G3
Goshen, Ind. 227/F1
Goshen, Ky. 237/K4
Goshen•, Mass. 249/C3
Goshen•, N.H. 268/C5
Goshen, N.J. 273/D5
Goshen, N.Y. 276/M8
Goshen, Nova Scotia 168/G3
Goshen, Ohio 284/B7
Goshen, Oreg. 291/D4
Goshen, Utah 304/C4
Goshen, Va. 307/K5
Goshen (co.), Wyo. 319/H4
Goshen Springs, Miss. 256/E6
Goshogawara, Japan 81/K3
Goshute (mts.), Nev. 266/G2
Goshute Ind. Res., Nev. 266/G3
Goshute Ind. Res., Utah 304/A4
Gosier, Guadeloupe 161/B6
Goslar, Germany 22/D3
Gosnell, Ark. 202/K2
Gosper (co.), Nebr. 264/E4
Gospić, Croatia 45/B3
Gosport, Ala. 195/C7
Gosport, England 13/F7
Gosport, England 10/F5
Gosport, Ind. 227/D6
Goss, Miss. 256/E8
Gossau, Switzerland 39/H2
Gossville, N.H. 268/E5
Gostivar, Macedonia 45/E5
Gostyń, Poland 47/C3
Gostynin, Poland 47/D2
Göta (canal), Sweden 18/J7
Göta (riv.), Sweden 18/H7
Gotebo, Okla. 288/J4
Göteborg, Sweden 7/F3
Göteborg, Sweden 18/G8
Göteborg och Bohus (co.), Sweden 18/G7
Gotha, Germany 22/D3
Gotham, Wis. 317/F9
Gothenburg, Nebr. 264/D4
Gothic (mesa), Ariz. 198/F2
Gotland (co.), Sweden 18/L8
Gotland (isl.), Sweden 7/F3
Gotland (isl.), Sweden 18/L8
Goto (isls.), Japan 81/D7
Goto (lake), Neth. Ant. 161/D8
Gotse Delchev, Bulgaria 45/F5
Gotska Sandön (isl.), Sweden 18/L7
Gotsu, Japan 81/F6
Göttingen, Germany 22/D3
Gottwaldov (Zlín), Czech Rep. 41/D2
Götzis, Austria 41/A3
Goubere, Cent. Afr. Rep. 115/E2
Gouda, Netherlands 27/F4
Goudeau, La. 238/G5
Gough (lake), Alberta 182/D3
Gough, Ga. 217/H4
Gough (isl.), St. Helena 2/J8
Gouin (res.), Que. 162/J6
Gouin (res.), Québec 174/C3
Goulburn, N.S. Wales 88/J6
Goulburn, N.S. Wales 97/E4
Goulburn (isls.), North. Terr. 88/E2
Goulburn (isls.), North. Terr. 93/C1
Goulburn (riv.), Victoria 97/C5
Goulburn Island, North. Terr. 93/C1
Gould, Ark. 202/G6
Gould, Colo. 208/G2
Gould, Okla. 288/G5
Gould, Québec 172/F4
Gould City, Mich. 250/D2
Goulding, Fla. 212/B6
Goulds, Fla. 212/F6
Goulds, Newf. 166/D2
Gouldsboro, Maine 243/H7
Gouldsboro•, Maine 243/H7
Gouldsboro, Pa. 294/L3
Gouldtown, Sask. 181/D5
Goulmima, Morocco 106/C2
Goumbou, Mali 106/C6
Gounamitz (riv.), New Bruns. 170/C1
Goundam, Mali 106/D5
Goundam, Mali 102/B3
Gourara (oasis), Algeria 106/E3
Gourbeyre, Guadeloupe 161/A7
Gourdon, France 28/D5
Gouré, Niger 106/G6
Gourma-Rharous, Mali 106/D5
Gournay-en-Bray, France 28/D3
Gouro, Chad 111/C4
Gourock, Scotland 10/A1
Gourock, Scotland 15/A1
Gouveia, Portugal 33/C2
Gouverneur, N.Y. 276/K2
Gouvy, Belgium 27/H8
Gouyave, Grenada 161/C8
Gouyave, Grenada 156/F4
Govan, Sask. 181/G4
Govan, S.C. 296/E5
Gove (co.), Kansas 232/B3
Gove, Kansas 232/B3
Gove (Nhulunbuy), North. Terr. 93/E2
Govena (cape), Russia 48/R4
Govenlock, Sask. 181/B6
Governador Valadares, Brazil 132/F7
Governador Valadares, Brazil 120/E4
Government (mt.), Ariz. 198/C3
Government (peak), Mich. 250/F1
Government (creek), Utah 304/B3
Government Camp, Oreg. 291/F2
Governor (lake), Nova Scotia 168/F3
Govĭ-Altay, Mongolia 77/E3
Gowan, Minn. 255/F4
Gowanda, N.Y. 276/B6
Gowd-e Zerreh (depr.), Afghanistan 59/H4
Gowen, Mich. 250/D5
Gowen, Okla. 288/R5
Gowensville, S.C. 296/C1
Gower, Mo. 261/C3
Gower (isl.), N.S. Wales 97/J2
Gower (mt.), N.S. Wales 97/J2
Gower (pen.), Wales 13/C6
Gowna (lake), Ireland 17/G4
Gowran, Ireland 17/G6
Gowrie, Iowa 229/E4
Gowrie Park, Tasmania 99/C3
Goya, Argentina 120/D5
Goya, Argentina 143/G4
Goyave, Guadeloupe 161/A6
Goyder (riv.), North. Terr. 93/D2
Goyders (lag.), S. Australia 94/F2
Göynücek, Turkey 63/F2
Göynük, Turkey 63/D2
Goz Beïda, Chad 111/D5
Gozo (isl.), Malta 34/E6
Goz Regeb, Sudan 111/G4
Graaff-Reinet, S. Africa 118/C6
Graal-Müritz, Germany 22/E1
Graauw, Netherlands 27/E6
Grabill, Ind. 227/H2
Grabouw, S. Africa 118/F7
Grabs, Switzerland 39/H2
Gračac, Croatia 45/B3
Gračanica, Bos. 45/D3
Grace, Idaho 220/G7
Grace (mt.), Mass. 249/E2
Grace, Miss. 256/C5
Grace (pt.), R.I. 249/H8
Grace City, N. Dak. 282/N4
Gracefield, Québec 172/A3
Graceham, Md. 245/J2
Gracemont, Okla. 288/K4
Graceton, Minn. 255/D2
Graceton, Pa. 294/D4
Graceville, Fla. 212/D5
Graceville, Minn. 255/B5
Graceville, Queensland 88/K3
Gracewood, Ga. 217/H4
Gracey, Ky. 237/F7
Grächen, Switzerland 39/E4
Gracias, Honduras 154/C3
Gracias a Dios (cape), Nic. 146/K8
Gracias a Dios (cape), Nicaragua 154/F3
Graciosa (isl.), Portugal 33/C1
Gradačac, Bos. 45/D3
Gradaús, Brazil 120/D3
Gradaús, Brazil 132/D4
Gradaús, Serra dos (range), Brazil 132/D4
Grado, Spain 33/D1
Grady, Ala. 195/F7
Grady, Ark. 202/G5
Grady (co.), Ga. 217/D9
Grady (isl.), Newf. 166/C3
Grady, N. Mex. 274/F4
Grady (co.), Okla. 288/L5
Grady, Okla. 288/L6
Gradyville, Ky. 237/L6
Graeagle, Calif. 204/E4
Graested, Denmark 21/F5
Graettinger, Iowa 229/D2
Graf, Iowa 229/M3
Grafenau, Germany 22/E4
Grafenwöhr, Germany 22/D4
Graff, Mo. 261/H8
Graff-Reinet, S. Africa 102/E8
Graford, Texas 303/F5
Grafton, Australia 87/F8
Grafton (isls.), Chile 138/D10
Grafton, Ill. 222/C5
Grafton, Ind. 227/B9
Grafton, Iowa 229/G2
Grafton•, Mass. 249/H4
Grafton, Nebr. 264/G4
Grafton, New Bruns. 170/C2
Grafton (co.), N.H. 268/D4
Grafton•, N.H. 268/D4
Grafton, N.S. Wales 88/J5
Grafton, N.S. Wales 97/G1
Grafton, N.Y. 276/N5
Grafton, N. Dak. 282/R3
Grafton, Ohio 284/F3
Grafton, Ontario 177/G4
Grafton•, Vt. 268/B5
Grafton, Va. 307/P6
Grafton, W. Va. 312/G4
Grafton, Wis. 317/L9
Grafton Center, N.H. 268/D4
Graham, Ala. 195/H4
Graham (lake), Alberta 182/C1
Graham (co.), Ariz. 198/E6
Graham (mt.), Ariz. 198/F6
Graham (isl.), Br. Col. 184/A3
Graham (peak), Colo. 208/E8
Graham, Fla. 212/D2
Graham, Ga. 217/H7
Graham (creek), Ind. 227/F7
Graham (co.), Kansas 232/C2
Graham, Ky. 237/G6
Graham (lake), Maine 243/G6
Graham, Mo. 261/C2
Graham (co.), N.C. 281/B4
Graham, N.C. 281/L2
Graham (isl.), N.W.T. 162/M3
Graham (isl.), N.W.T. 187/J2
Graham, Okla. 288/M6
Graham, Ontario 175/B3
Graham, Ontario 177/G5
Graham, Texas 303/F4
Graham Bell (isl.), Russia 4/A6
Graham Bell (isl.), Russia 48/G1
Grahamdale, Manitoba 179/D3
Graham Land (reg.), Ant. 2/G9
Graham Land (reg.), Ant. 5/C15
Graham Reach (chan.), Br. Col. 184/C3
Grahamstown, S. Africa 102/E8
Grahamstown, S. Africa 118/D6
Grahamsville, N.Y. 276/L7
Grahn, Ky. 237/P4
Graian Alps (range), France 28/G5
Graian Alps (range), Italy 34/A2
Graiguenamanagh-Tinnahinch, Ireland 17/H6
Grain Coast (reg.), Liberia 106/B8
Grainfield, Kansas 232/B2
Grainger (co.), Tenn. 237/O8
Graingers, N.C. 281/O4
Grainola, Okla. 288/N1
Grainton, Nebr. 264/C4
Grain Valley, Mo. 261/S6
Grajaú, Brazil 132/E4
Grajaú (riv.), Brazil 132/E4
Grajewo, Poland 47/F2
Gram, Denmark 21/C7
Gramalote, Colombia 126/D4
Gramat, France 28/D5
Grambling, La. 238/E1
Gramercy, La. 238/M3
Gramling, S.C. 296/C1
Grammer, Ind. 227/F6
Grammont (Geraardsbergen), Belgium 27/D7
Grampian, Pa. 294/E4
Grampian (reg.), Scotland 15/F3
Grampian (mts.), Scotland 15/D4
Gramsbergen, Netherlands 27/K3
Gran, Norway 18/G6
Granada, Colo. 208/P6
Granada, Minn. 255/D7
Granada, Nicaragua 154/E5
Granada (prov.), Spain 33/E4
Granada, Spain 33/E4
Granada, Spain 7/D5
Granada Hills, Calif. 204/B10
Granados, Mexico 150/E2
Granard, Ireland 17/F4
Granbury, Texas 303/G5
Granby, Colo. 208/H2
Granby (lake), Colo. 208/G2
Granby, Conn. 210/D1
Granby•, Conn. 210/D1
Granby, Mass. 249/E3
Granby•, Mass. 249/E3
Granby, Mo. 261/D9
Granby, Québec 172/E4
Granby•, Vt. 268/D2
Gran Canaria (isl.), Spain 33/B5
Gran Chaco (reg.) 120/C5
Gran Chaco (reg.), Argentina 143/D1
Gran Chaco (reg.), Paraguay 144/B2-3
Gran Couva, Trin. & Tob. 161/B11
Grand (canal), China 54/N6
Grand (canal), China 77/J4
Grand (co.), Colo. 208/G2
Grand (bay), Dominica 161/F7
Grand (canal), Ireland 17/G5
Grand (lake), La. 188/H4
Grand (lake), La. 238/H8
Grand (lake), La. 238/E7
Grand (lake), Maine 243/H4
Grand (isl.), Mich. 250/C2
Grand (lake), Mich. 250/F3
Grand (riv.), Mich. 250/D6
Grand (riv.), Mo. 261/F3
Grand (bay), New Bruns. 170/D3
Grand (lake), New Bruns. 170/D3
Grand (lake), New Bruns. 170/C3
Grand (lake), Newf. 166/B3
Grand (lake), Newf. 166/C4
Grand (isl.), N.Y. 276/B5
Grand (riv.), Ohio 284/H2
Grand (riv.), Ontario 177/D4
Grand (riv.), S. Dak. 298/F2
Grand (co.), Utah 304/E5
Grand Anse, Grenada 161/C9
Grand Bahama (isl.), Bahamas 146/L7
Grand Bahama (isl.), Bahamas 156/B1
Grand Bank, Newf. 166/C4
Grand-Bassam, Ivory Coast 106/D7
Grand Bay, Ala. 195/B10
Grand Bay, Dominica 161/F7
Grand Bay, New Bruns. 170/D3
Grand Bayou, La. 238/C2
Grand Beach, Manitoba 179/F4
Grand Beach, Mich. 250/C7
Grand Bend, Ontario 177/C4
Grand Blanc, Mich. 250/F6
Grand-Bourg, Guadeloupe 161/B7
Grand Bruit, Newf. 166/C4
Grand Caicos (isl.), Turks & Caicos 156/D2
Grand Caille (pt.), St. Lucia 161/F6
Grand Canary (isl.), Spain 102/A2
Grand Canary (isl.), Spain 106/A3
Grand Cane, La. 238/C2
Grand Canyon, Ariz. 188/D3
Grand Canyon, Ariz. 198/C2
Grand Canyon, Snake R. (canyon), Oreg. 291/L2
Grand Canyon Nat'l Mon., Ariz. 198/C2
Grand Canyon Nat'l Park, Ariz. 188/D3
Grand Canyon Nat'l Park, Ariz. 198/C2
Grand Canyon of the Snake River (canyon), Idaho 220/B4
Grand Cayman (isl.), Cayman Is. 156/B3
Grand Centre, Alberta 182/E2
Grand Cess, Liberia 106/C8
Grand Chain, Ill. 222/E6
Grand Chenier, La. 238/E7
Grand Combin (mt.), Switzerland 39/D5
Grand Comoro (Njazidja) (isl.), Comoros 102/G6
Grand Comoro (Njazidja) (isl.), Comoros 118/G2
Grand Coteau, La. 238/G6
Grand Coulee, Sask. 181/G5
Grand Coulee, Wash. 310/G3
Grand Coulee (canyon), Wash. 310/F3
Grand Coulee (dam), Wash. 310/F3
Grandcour, Switzerland 39/C3
Grand Cul de Sac (riv.), St. Lucia 161/G6
Grand Cul-de-Sac Marin (bay), Guadeloupe 161/A6
Grand Desert, Nova Scotia 168/E4
Grand Detour, Ill. 222/D2
Grande (bay), Argentina 120/C8
Grande (bay), Argentina 143/C7
Grande (falls), Argentina 143/E3
Grande (riv.), Argentina 143/C4
Grande (marsh), Bolivia 136/F5
Grande (riv.), Bolivia 136/C6
Grande (riv.), Bolivia 136/C4
Grande (riv.), Brazil 132/C8
Grande (isl.), Brazil 135/D3
Grande (riv.), Brazil 120/E5
Grande (riv.), Brazil 132/D8
Grande (riv.), Brazil 132/E5
Grande (riv.), Brazil 135/B2
Grande (isl.), Chile 138/A6
Grande (riv.), Chile 138/F10
Grande, Salar (salt dep.), Chile 138/B3
Grande, Salto (falls), Colombia 126/B8
Grande (isl.), Colombia 126/B4
Grande (riv.), Guatemala 154/A3
Grande (riv.), Jamaica 158/K6
Grande (riv.), Mexico 150/G2
Grande (riv.), Mexico 150/N8
Grande (riv.), New Bruns. 170/C1
Grande (riv.), Nicaragua 154/E4
Grande (riv.), Peru 128/E10
Grande (range), Uruguay 145/D4
Grande, Arroyo (riv.), Uruguay 145/B4
Grande-Anse, New Bruns. 170/E1
Grande-Anse, Québec 172/E2
Grande Cache, Alberta 182/A3
Grande-Cascapédia, Québec 172/C2
Grande Cayemite (isl.), Haiti 158/B6
Grande-Clairière, Manitoba 179/B5
Grande de Añasco (riv.), P. Rico 161/B2
Grande de Arecibo (riv.), P. Rico 161/C1
Grande de Lípez (riv.), Bolivia 136/B7
Grande de Loíza (riv.), P. Rico 161/E1
Grande de Manatí (riv.), P. Rico 161/C1
Grande de Santiago (riv.), Mexico 150/G6
Grande de Tierra del Fuego (isl.), Argentina 143/C7
Grande de Tierra del Fuego (isl.), Chile 138/E11
Grande Dixence (dam), Switzerland 39/D4
Grande-Grève, Québec 172/D1
Grande Inferior (range), Uruguay 145/C4
Grande Pointe, Manitoba 179/F5
Grande Prairie, Alberta 182/A2
Grande Prairie, Alta. 162/E4
Grande-Prairie, Alta. 146/G4
Grande Prairie, Texas 303/G2
Grand Erg Occidental (des.), Algeria 102/C1
Grand Erg Occidental (des.), Algeria 106/E2
Grand Erg Oriental (des.), Algeria 102/C1
Grand Erg Oriental (des.), Algeria 106/F2
Grand Erg Oriental (des.), Tunisia 106/F2
Grande' Rivière, Martinique 161/C5
Grande-Rivière, Québec 172/D2
Grande-Rivière, La (riv.), Que. 146/L4
Grande Rivière, La (riv.), Québec 174/B2
Grande Rivière, Trin. & Tob. 161/B10
Grande Rivière du Nord, Haiti 158/C5
Grande Ronde (riv.), Oreg. 291/K2
Grande Ronde (riv.), Wash. 310/H5
Grande Saline, Haiti 158/B5
Grandes-Bergeronnes, Québec 172/H1
Grandes-Piles, Québec 172/E3
Grand-Étang, Nova Scotia 168/G2
Grande-Terre, Guadeloupe 161/B6
Grande-Vallée, Québec 172/D1
Grande Vigie, Guadeloupe 161/B5
Grand Falls (lake), Maine 243/H5
Grand Falls, New Bruns. 170/C1
Grand Falls, Newf. 166/C4
Grand Falls, Newf. 146/N5
Grand Falls, Newf. 162/L6
Grandfalls, Texas 303/B6
Grand Falls Hill, New Bruns. 170/C1
Grandfield, Okla. 288/J6
Grand Forks, Br. Col. 184/H6
Grand Forks, N. Dak. 146/J5
Grand Forks, N. Dak. 188/G1
Grand Forks (co.), N. Dak. 282/P3
Grand Forks, N. Dak. 282/R4
Grand Forks A.F.B., N. Dak. 282/R4
Grand Glaise, Ark. 202/G3
Grand Goâve, Haiti 158/B6
Grand Gorge, N.Y. 276/L6
Grand Gosier, Haiti 158/C6
Grand Gulf, Miss. 256/B6
Grand Harbour, New Bruns. 170/D4
Grand Haven, Mich. 250/C5
Grand-Îlet (isl.), Guadeloupe 161/A7
Grandin, Fla. 212/E2
Grandin, Mo. 261/L9
Grandin, N. Dak. 282/R5
Grand Island, Nebr. 146/J5
Grand Island, Nebr. 188/G2
Grand Island, Nebr. 264/F4
Grand Island, N.Y. 276/B5
Grand Isle, La. 238/L8
Grand Isle, Maine 243/G1
Grand Isle (co.), Vt. 268/A2
Grand Isle•, Vt. 268/A2
Grand Junction, Colo. 146/H6
Grand Junction, Colo. 188/E3
Grand Junction, Colo. 208/B4
Grand Junction, Iowa 229/E4
Grand Junction, Mich. 250/C6
Grand Junction, Tenn. 237/C10
Grand-Lahou, Ivory Coast 106/C8
Grand Lake, Ark. 202/H7
Grand Lake, Colo. 208/H2
Grand Lake, La. 238/D6
Grand Lake, Nova Scotia 168/E4
Grand Lake Seboeis (lake), Maine 243/F3
Grand Lake Stream•, Maine 243/H5
Grand Lake Towne, Okla. 288/S1
Grand Ledge, Mich. 250/E6
Grand-Lieu (lake), France 28/C4
Grand Manan (chan.), Maine 243/K6
Grand Manan (chan.), New Bruns. 170/C4
Grand Manan (isl.), New Bruns. 170/D4
Grand Marais, Manitoba 179/F4
Grand Marais, Mich. 250/D2
Grand Marais, Minn. 255/G2
Grand Marsh, Wis. 317/G8
Grand Meadow, Minn. 255/F7
Grand'Mère, Québec 172/E3
Grand Mound, Iowa 229/M5
Grand Mound, Wash. 310/C4
Grand Muveran (mt.), Switzerland 39/D4
Grand Narrows, Nova Scotia 168/H3
Grândola, Portugal 33/B3
Grandora, Sask. 181/E3
Grand Pass, Mo. 261/F4
Grand-Popo, Benin 106/E7
Grand Portage, Minn. 255/G2
Grand Portage Ind. Res., Minn. 255/G2
Grand Portage Nat'l Mon., Minn. 255/G2
Grand Pré, Nova Scotia 168/D3
Grand Rapids, Manitoba 179/C1
Grand Rapids, Mich. 146/K5
Grand Rapids, Mich. 188/K2
Grand Rapids, Mich. 250/D5
Grand Rapids, Minn. 255/E3
Grand Rapids, N. Dak. 282/N7
Grand Rapids, Ohio 284/C3
Grand-Remous, Québec 172/B3
Grand Ridge, Fla. 212/A1
Grand Ridge, Ill. 222/E2
Grand River, Iowa 229/F7
Grand River, Nova Scotia 168/H3
Grand River, Ohio 284/H2
Grand River (valley), Utah 304/E4
Grand Rivers, Ky. 237/E7
Grand Ronde, Oreg. 291/D2
Grand Roy, Grenada 161/C8
Grand Saline, Texas 303/J5
Grand Santi, Fr. Guiana 131/D3
Grandson, Switzerland 39/C3
Grand Terrace, Calif. 204/E10
Grand Terre (isls.), La. 238/L8
Grand Teton (mt.), Wyo. 319/B2
Grand Teton Nat'l Park, Wyo. 319/B2
Grand Tower, Ill. 222/D6
Grand Traverse (co.), Mich. 250/D4
Grand Traverse (bay), Mich. 250/D3
Grand Turk (isl.), Turks & Caicos 156/D2
Grand Valley, Ontario 177/D4
Grand Valley, Pa. 294/C2
Grandview, Ark. 202/C1
Grand View, Idaho 220/B7
Grandview, Ill. 222/D4
Grand View, Ill. 222/F4
Grandview, Ind. 227/C9
Grandview, Iowa 229/L6
Grandview, Manitoba 179/B3
Grandview, Mo. 261/P6
Grandview, Ohio 284/H7
Grandview, Tenn. 237/M9
Grandview, Texas 303/G5
Grandview, Wash. 310/F4
Grand View, Wis. 317/D3
Grandview Heights, Ohio 284/D6

378 Gulch

Gulch (cape), Newf. 166/B2
Gulen, Norway 18/D6
Gulf (co.), Fla. 212/D7
Gulf, N.C. 281/L3
Gulf Breeze, Fla. 212/B6
Gulf Crest, Ala. 195/B8
Gulf Hammock, Fla. 212/D2
Gulf Harbors, Fla. 212/D3
Gulf Island Nat'l Seashore, Fla. 212/B6
Gulf Islands Nat'l Seashore, Miss. 256/G10
Gulfport, Fla. 212/B3
Gulf Port, Ill. 222/B3
Gulfport, Miss. 188/J4
Gulfport, Miss. 256/F10
Gulf Shores, Ala. 195/C10
Gulf Stream, Fla. 212/F5
Gulgong, N.S. Wales 97/E3
Gulian, China 77/K1
Gulin, China 77/G6
Gulistan, Uzbekistan 48/G5
Gulja (Yining), China 77/B3
Gulkana, Alaska 196/J2
Gull (lake), Alberta 182/C3
Gull (lake), Minn. 255/D4
Gull (isl.), Newf. 166/D2
Gullane, Scotland 15/F4
Gull Bay, Ontario 177/H5
Gull Bay, Ontario 175/C3
Gullfoot (lake), Ontario 177/F3
Gull Island, Newf. 166/D2
Gull Island (pt.), Newf. 166/D2
Gulliver, Mich. 250/D2
Gull Lake, Alberta 182/D3
Gull Lake, Sask. 181/C5
Gully, Minn. 255/C3
Gülnar, Turkey 63/E4
Gulnare, Colo. 208/K8
Gulnare, Ky. 237/S5
Gulquac (lake), New Bruns. 170/D2
Gulquac (riv.), New Bruns. 170/C2
Gülşehir, Turkey 63/F3
Gulu, Uganda 115/F3
Gulvain (mt.), Scotland 15/C4
Guma (Pishan), China 77/A4
Gumaca, Philippines 82/D4
Gumare, Botswana 118/C3
Gumbranch, Ga. 217/J7
Gumel, Nigeria 106/F6
Gumeracha, S. Australia 94/C7
Gumma (pref.), Japan 81/J5
Gummersbach, Germany 22/B3
Gummi, Nigeria 106/F6
Gum Spring, Va. 307/N5
Gum Springs, Ark. 202/D5
Gümüş, Turkey 63/F2
Gümüşhacıköy, Turkey 63/F2
Gümüşhane (prov.), Turkey 63/H2
Gümüşhane, Turkey 59/C1
Gümüşhane, Turkey 63/H2
Gun (cay), Bahamas 156/B1
Gun (lake), Mich. 250/D6
Guna, India 68/D4
Gunbower, Victoria 97/C4
Gundagai, N.S. Wales 97/D4
Gunderbooka (ranges), N.S. Wales 97/C2
Gündoğmuş, Turkey 63/D4
Güney, Turkey 63/C3
Gunflint Trail, Minn. 255/F1
Gungu, D.R. Congo 115/C5
Gunisao (lake), Manitoba 179/J3
Gunlock, Utah 304/A6
Gunn, Alberta 182/C3
Gunna (isl.), Scotland 15/B4
Gunnbjørn (mt.), Greenl. 4/C11
Gunn City, Mo. 261/D5
Gunnedah, N. S. Wales 88/H6
Gunnedah, N.S. Wales 97/F2
Gunning, N.S. Wales 97/E4
Gunnison (co.), Colo. 208/E5
Gunnison, Colo. 208/E5
Gunnison (riv.), Colo. 208/C5
Gunnison (tunnel), Colo. 208/D6
Gunnison, Miss. 256/C3
Gunnison, Utah 304/C4
Gunnison (res.), Utah 304/C4
Gunnworth, Sask. 181/C4
Gunpowder (riv.), Md. 245/N3
Gunpowder, Queensland 95/A3
Gunpowder, Queensland 88/F3
Gunpowder Falls (creek), Md. 245/M2
Guntakal, India 68/D5
Gunter, Ontario 177/G3
Gunter, Oreg. 291/D4
Gunter Air Force Base, Ala. 195/F6
Guntersville, Ala. 195/F2
Guntersville (dam), Ala. 195/F2
Guntersville (lake), Ala. 195/F2
Gunton, Manitoba 179/E4
Guntown, Miss. 256/G2
Guntur, India 54/K8
Guntur, India 68/D5
Gunungapi (isl.), Indonesia 85/H7
Günzburg, Germany 22/D4
Gunzenhausen, Germany 22/D4
Gurabo, P. Rico 161/E2
Gurais, India 68/D2
Gurdon, Ark. 202/D6
Gurgan (Gorgan), Iran 66/J2
Gurguéia (riv.), Brazil 132/E5
Guri, Venezuela 124/G4
Guri (dam), Venezuela 120/C2
Guri (res.), Venezuela 120/C2
Guri (res.), Venezuela 124/G4
Gurk, Austria 41/C3
Gurla Mandhada (mt.), China 77/B5
Gurley, Ala. 195/F1
Gurley, La. 238/H5
Gurley, Nebr. 264/B3
Gurley, N.S. Wales 97/E1
Gurley, S.C. 296/J3
Gurleyville, Conn. 210/G1
Gurnee, Ill. 222/B4
Gurnet (pt.), Mass. 249/M4
Gurney, Wis. 317/F3
Gurneyville, Alberta 182/E2
Guro, Mozambique 118/E3
Gürpınar, Turkey 63/K3
Gurteen, Ireland 17/D3
Gurtnellen, Switzerland 39/G3
Gürün, Turkey 63/G3
Gurupá, Brazil 132/D3
Gurupi, Brazil 132/D5
Gurupi, Brazil 120/E4
Gurupi, Serra do (range), Brazil 132/E4
Gurupi (riv.), Brazil 132/E3
Gur'yev, Kazakhstan 48/F5
Gur'yev, Kazakhstan 54/G5
Gusau, Nigeria 106/F6
Gusau, Nigeria 102/C3
Gusher, Utah 304/E3
Gusinje, Yugoslavia 45/D4
Gusinoozersk, Russia 48/L4
Gus'-Khrustal'nyy, Russia 52/F3
Güssing, Austria 41/D3
Gustavo Díaz Ordaz, Mexico 150/K3
Gustavus, Alaska 196/M1
Gustavus, Ohio 284/J3
Gustine, Calif. 204/D6
Gustine, Texas 303/F6
Guston, Ky. 237/J5
Güstrow, Germany 22/E2
Gütersloh, Germany 22/C3
Guthrie, Ind. 227/D7
Guthrie (co.), Iowa 229/D5
Guthrie, Ky. 237/G7
Guthrie, Minn. 255/D3
Guthrie, Mo. 261/H5
Guthrie, Okla. 188/G3
Guthrie, Okla. 288/M3
Guthrie, Texas 303/D4
Guthrie Center, Iowa 229/D5
Gutiérrez Zamora, Mexico 150/L6
Guttannen, Switzerland 39/F3
Guttenberg, Iowa 229/L3
Guttenberg, N.J. 273/C2
Guttingen, Switzerland 39/H1
Gu-Win, Ala. 195/C3
Guy, Alberta 182/B2
Guy, Ark. 202/F3
Guyana 2/G5
Guyana 120/D2
GUYANA 131/B3
Guyandotte (riv.), W. Va. 312/B6
Guyang, China 77/G3
Guymon, Okla. 288/D1
Guyot (glac.), Alaska 196/K2
Guyot (mt.), N.C. 281/C3
Guyot (mt.), Tenn. 237/P9
Guyra, N.S. Wales 97/F2
Guys, Tenn. 237/D10
Guysborough (co.), Nova Scotia 168/F3
Guysborough, Nova Scotia 168/G3
Guysborough (riv.), Nova Scotia 168/G3
Guys Mills, Pa. 294/C2
Guysville, Ohio 284/G7
Guyton, Ga. 217/K6
Guyuan, China 77/G4
Guzmán (lake), Mexico 150/F1
Guzmán Blanco, Venezuela 124/E6
Guzmanes (cays), Cuba 158/B2
Gwa, Burma 72/B3
Gwaai, Zimbabwe 118/D3
Gwabegar, N.S. Wales 97/E2
Gwadabawa, Nigeria 106/F6
Gwadar, Pakistan 59/H5
Gwadar, Pakistan 68/A4
Gwalior, India 54/J7
Gwalior, India 68/D3
Gwanda, Zimbabwe 118/D4
Gwda (riv.), Poland 47/C2
Gweebarra (bay), Ireland 17/D2
Gweebarra (riv.), Ireland 17/E2
Gwelo, (Gweru) Zimbabwe 118/D3
Gwent, Wales 13/D6
Gwersyllt, Wales 13/E4
Gweru, Zimbabwe 118/D3
Gweru, Zimbabwe 102/F6
Gwinn, Mich. 250/B2
Gwinner, N. Dak. 282/P7
Gwinnett (co.), Ga. 217/D2
Gwydir (riv.), N.S. Wales 97/E1
Gwynedd, Wales 13/C4
Gwynn, Va. 307/R5
Gwynne, Alberta 182/D3
Gwynneville, Ind. 227/F5
Gyaca, China 77/D6
Gyandzhe, Azerbaijan 7/J4
Gyandzhe, Azerbaijan 48/E5
Gyandzhe, Azerbaijan 52/G6
Gyangzê, China 77/C6
Gyaring Co (lake), China 77/C5
Gyaring Hu (lake), China 77/E5
Gyasikan, Ghana 106/D7
Gyda, Russia 48/H2
Gyda (pen.), Russia 4/C6
Gyda (pen.), Russia 48/H2
Gyda (pen.), Russia 54/J2
Gydan (Kolyma) (range), Russia 48/Q3
Gyirong, China 77/B6
Gylling, Denmark 21/D6
Gympie, Australia 87/F8
Gympie, Queensland 88/J5
Gympie, Queensland 95/E5
Gyobingauk, Burma 72/C3
Gyoma, Hungary 41/F3
Gyöngyös, Hungary 41/E3
Gyönk, Hungary 41/E3
Győr, Hungary 7/F4
Győr, Hungary 41/D3
Győr-Sopron (co.), Hungary 41/D3
Gypsum, Colo. 208/F3
Gypsum, Kansas 232/E3
Gypsum (lake), Manitoba 179/D3
Gypsum, Ohio 284/E2
Gypsumville, Manitoba 179/D3
Gyrfalcon (isls.), N.W.T. 187/M4
Gyula, Hungary 41/F3

H

Haacht, Belgium 27/F7
Haag, Austria 41/C2
Haakon (co.), S. Dak. 298/F5
Haamstede, Netherlands 27/D5
Ha'apai Group (isls.), Tonga 87/J8
Haapajärvi, Finland 18/O5
Haapamäki, Finland 18/O5
Haapsalu, Estonia 53/B1
Haar, Germany 22/D4
Haarlem, Netherlands 27/F4
Haarlemmermeer (Hoofddorp), Netherlands 27/F4
Haarlemmermeer Polder, Netherlands 27/B5
Haast, N. Zealand 100/B5
Haast (pass), N. Zealand 100/B6
Haast (riv.), N. Zealand 100/B5
Haasts Bluff, North. Terr. 88/E4
Haasts Bluff, North. Terr. 93/B7
Haasts Bluff Aboriginal Reserve, North. Terr. 88/E5
Haasts Bluff Aboriginal Res., North. Terr. 93/B7
Hab (riv.), Pakistan 68/B3
Hab (riv.), Pakistan 59/J4
Habahe, China 77/C2
Habana, Ciudad de La (prov.), Cuba 158/C1
Habana, La (Havana) (prov.), Cuba 158/C1
Habana (Havana) (cap.), Cuba 158/C1
Habay, Alberta 182/A5
Habay, Belgium 27/H9
Habban, Yemen 59/E7
Habbaniya, Iraq 59/D3
Habbaniya, Iraq 66/C4
Habbaniya, Hor al (lake), Iraq 66/C4
Habersham (co.), Ga. 217/E1
Habersham, Ga. 217/F1
Habersham, Tenn. 237/N8
Habiganj, Bangladesh 68/G4
Habikino, Japan 81/J8
Habomai (isls.), Japan 81/N2
Habonim, Israel 65/B2
Haboro, Japan 81/K1
Hachenburg, Germany 22/B3
Hachinohe, Japan 81/K3
Hachioji, Japan 81/O2
Hachiro (lag.), Japan 81/J3
Hachita, N. Mex. 274/A7
Hacıbektaş, Turkey 63/F3
Hacılar, Turkey 63/F3
Hack (mt.), S. Australia 94/F4
Hackberry, Ariz. 198/B3
Hackberry, La. 238/D7
Hackensack, Minn. 255/D4
Hackensack, N.J. 273/B2
Hackensack (riv.), N.J. 273/C1
Hacker Valley, W. Va. 312/F5
Hacketstown, Ireland 17/H6
Hackett, Ark. 202/B3
Hacketts Cove, Nova Scotia 168/E4
Hackettstown, N.J. 273/D2
Hackleburg, Ala. 195/C2
Hackleman, Ind. 227/F4
Hackney, England 13/H8
Hackney, England 10/B5
Hacksneck, Va. 307/S5
Hacoda, Ala. 195/F8
Hadano, Japan 81/O3
Hadar, Nebr. 264/G2
Hadarba, Ras (cape), Sudan 111/G3
Hadashville, Manitoba 179/G5
Hadd, Ras al (cape), Oman 59/G5
Hadd, Ras al (cape), Oman 54/H7
Haddam•, Conn. 210/E3
Haddam, Kansas 232/E2
Haddam Neck, Conn. 210/E2
Haddar, Saudi Arabia 59/E5
Haddington, Scotland 10/E3
Haddington, Scotland 15/F5
Haddix, Ky. 237/P6
Haddock, Ga. 217/F4
Haddonfield, N.J. 273/B3
Haddon Heights, N.J. 273/B3
Hadejia, Nigeria 106/G6
Hadejia (riv.), Nigeria 106/F6
Hadensville, Ky. 237/G7
Hadera, Israel 65/B3
Hadera (dry riv.), Israel 65/B3
Haderslev, Denmark 21/C7
Haderslev, Denmark 18/F9
Hadhar, Iraq 66/C3
Hadhramaut (reg.), Yemen 54/F8
Hadhramaut (dist.), Yemen 59/E7
Hadhramaut, Wadi (dry riv.), Yemen 59/F7
Hadibu, Yemen 54/G8
Hadibu, Yemen 59/F7
Hadım, Turkey 63/E4
Haditha, Iraq 66/C3
Haditha, Iraq 59/D3
Hadiya, Saudi Arabia 59/C4
Hadleigh, England 13/H5
Hadley, Ind. 227/D5
Hadley, Ky. 237/H6
Hadley•, Mass. 249/D3
Hadley, Minn. 255/C7
Hadley (bay), N.W.T. 187/H2
Hadley, Pa. 294/B3
Hadley-Lake Luzerne, N.Y. 276/N4
Hadlock-Irondale, Wash. 310/C2
Hadlyme, Conn. 210/F3
Hadselfjorden (fjord), Norway 18/J2
Hadspen, Tasmania 99/D3
Hadsten, Denmark 21/C5
Hadsund, Denmark 21/D4
Haedo (range), Uruguay 145/C2
Haeju, N. Korea 81/B4
Haena, Hawaii 218/C1
Haena (pt.), Hawaii 218/C1
Hafar al Batin, Saudi Arabia 59/E4
Haffe, Syria 63/G5
Hafford, Sask. 181/D3
Hafik, Turkey 63/G3
Haflong, India 68/G3
Hafnarfjördhur, Iceland 21/B2
Haft Gel, Iran 66/F5
Hafun, Somalia 115/K1
Hafun, Ras (cape), Somalia 115/K1
Hagaman, N.Y. 276/M5
Hagan, Ga. 217/J6
Hagar, Ontario 177/D1
Hagari (riv.), India 68/D6
Hagarstown, Ill. 222/D5
Hagarville, Ark. 202/D2
Hagemeister (isl.), Alaska 196/F3
Hagen, Germany 22/B3
Hagen, Sask. 181/F3
Hagenow, Germany 22/D2
Hagensborg, Br. Col. 184/D4
Hager City, Wis. 317/A6
Hagerman, Idaho 220/D7
Hagerman, N. Mex. 274/E5
Hagerman Fossil Beds Nat'l Monument, Idaho 220/D7
Hagerstown, Ind. 227/G5
Hagerstown, Md. 245/G2
Hagerstown, Md. 188/L3
Hagfors, Sweden 18/H6
Hagi, Japan 81/E6
Ha Giang, Vietnam 72/E2
Hagley, Tasmania 99/C3
Hagood, S.C. 296/F3
Hags (head), Ireland 17/B6
Hague, Fla. 212/D2
Hague (cape), France 28/C3
Hague, The (cap.), Netherlands 7/E3
Hague, The (cap.), Netherlands 27/E4
Hague, N.Y. 276/N3
Hague, N. Dak. 282/L7
Hague, Sask. 181/E3
Hague, Va. 307/P4
Haguenau, France 28/G3
Haha (isl.), Japan 87/E3
Haha (isl.), Japan 81/M3
Ha! Ha! (lake), Qué. 172/G1
Ha! Ha! (riv.) Qué. 172/G1
Hahatonka, Mo. 261/G7
Hahira, Ga. 217/F9
Hahndorf, S. Australia 94/C8
Hahnville, La. 238/N4
Hai, Iraq 59/E3
Hai, Iraq 66/E4
Haifa (dist.), Israel 65/C2
Haifa, Israel 65/B2
Haifa, Israel 59/B3
Haifa (bay), Israel 65/C2
Haifeng, China 77/J7
Haig (lake), Alberta 182/B1
Haight, Alberta 182/D3
Haigler, Nebr. 264/C4
Haikang, China 77/G7
Haikou (Hoihow), China 77/H7
Haikou, China 54/N8
Haiku, Hawaii 218/J2
Hail, Saudi Arabia 54/F7
Hail, Saudi Arabia 59/D4
Hailar, China 77/J2
Hailar He (riv.), China 77/K2
Haile, La. 238/F1
Hailesboro, N.Y. 276/K2
Hailey, Idaho 220/D6
Haileybury, Ontario 177/K5
Haileybury, Ontario 175/D3
Haileyville, Okla. 288/P5
Hailong, China 77/L3
Hailsham, England 13/H7
Hailun, China 77/L2
Hailuoto, Finland 18/O4
Hailuoto (isl.), Finland 18/O4
Haina, Hawaii 218/H3
Hainan (prov.), China 77/H8
Hainan (isl.), China 2/Q5
Hainan (isl.), China 54/N8
Hainan (isl.), China 77/H8
Hainaut (prov.), Belgium 27/D7
Hainburg an der Donau, Austria 41/D2
Haines, Alaska 196/M1
Haines, Oreg. 291/J3
Hainesburg, N.J. 273/C2
Haines City, Fla. 212/E3
Haines Junction, Yukon 187/E3
Haines Landing, Maine 243/B6
Hainesport•, N.J. 273/D4
Hainesville, Ill. 222/A4
Hainesville, N.J. 273/D1
Hainfeld, Austria 41/C2
Haiphong, Vietnam 54/M7
Hairy Hill, Alberta 182/D3
Haiti 2/F5
Haiti 146/L8
HAITI 156/D3
HAITI 158
Haiwee, Calif. 204/H7
Haiya Junction, Sudan 59/C6
Haiya Junction, Sudan 111/G4
Haiyan, China 77/F4
Haiyang, China 77/K4
Haiyuan, China 77/G4
Hajara, Al (plain), Iraq 66/D5
Hajarain, Yemen 59/E6
Hajdú-Bihar (co.), Hungary 41/F3
Hajdúböszörmény, Hungary 41/F3
Hajdúdorog, Hungary 41/F3
Hajdúhadház, Hungary 41/F3
Hajdúnánás, Hungary 41/F3
Hajdúsámson, Hungary 41/F3
Hajdúszoboszló, Hungary 41/F3
Haji Ibraham (mt.), Iraq 66/D2
Hajja, Yemen 59/D6
Hajnowka, Poland 47/F2
Hajós, Hungary 41/E3
Haka, Burma 72/B2
Hakalau, Hawaii 218/J4
Hakkâri (prov.), Turkey 63/K4
Hakkâri (Çöelemerik), Turkey 63/K4
Hakkâri (mts.), Turkey 63/K4
Hakken (mt.), Japan 81/H6
Hakodate, Japan 81/K3
Hakodate, Japan 54/R5
Haku (mt.), Japan 81/H5
Hakui, Japan 81/H5
Hakusan National Park, Japan 81/H5
Hal (Halle), Belgium 27/E7
Halabja, Iraq 66/D3
Halachó, Mexico 150/O6
Halaib, Sudan 59/C5
Halaib, Sudan 111/G3
Halalii (lake), Hawaii 218/A2
Halaula, Hawaii 188/G5
Halawa, Hawaii, Hawaii 218/G3
Halawa, Molokai, Hawaii 218/H1
Halawa (bay), Hawaii 218/H1
Halawa (cape), Hawaii 218/H1
Halawa (stream), Hawaii 218/B3
Halawa Heights, Hawaii 218/B3
Halberstadt, Germany 22/D3
Halbrite, Sask. 181/H6
Halbur, Iowa 229/D4
Halcon (mt.), Philippines 82/C4
Halcyon Dale, Ga. 217/J5
Haldane, Ill. 222/D1
Haldeman, Ky. 237/P4
Halden, Norway 18/G7
Haldensleben, Germany 22/D2
Haldimand, Ontario 177/E5
Haldimand-Norfolk (reg. munic.), Ontario 177/E5
Hale (co.), Ala. 195/C5
Hale, Argentina 143/F7
Hale, Colo. 208/P3
Hale, Camp, Colo. 208/G4
Hale, England 13/H2
Hale, Iowa 229/L4
Hale, Mich. 250/F4
Hale, Mo. 261/F3
Hale (riv.), North. Terr. 93/D8
Hale (co.), Texas 303/C3
Hale (mt.), W. Australia 92/B4
Haleakala (crater), Hawaii 218/K2
Haleakala Nat'l Park, Hawaii 218/K2
Haleb (Aleppo), Syria 59/C2
Haleb (Aleppo), Syria 63/G4
Haleburg, Ala. 195/H8
Hale Center, Texas 303/C3
Haledon, N.J. 273/B1
Haleiwa, Hawaii 218/E1
Halen, Belgium 27/G7
Hales Corners, Wis. 317/K2
Halesowen, England 13/E5
Halesowen, England 10/G3
Hales Point, Tenn. 237/B9
Halesworth, England 13/J5
Haley, N. Dak. 282/D8
Haley Station, Ontario 177/H2
Haleyville, Ala. 195/C2
Haleyville, N.J. 273/C5
Half Assini, Ghana 106/D8
Halfeti, Turkey 63/H4
Half Island Cove, Nova Scotia 168/G3
Half Moon (cay), Belize 154/D2
Halfmoon Bay, Alberta 182/C3
Halfmoon Bay, Br. Col. 184/J2
Half Moon Bay, Calif. 204/H3
Half Moon Bay (Oban), N. Zealand 100/B7
Half Moon Lake, Alberta 182/D2
Halford, Kansas 232/B2
Halfway (riv.), Br. Col. 184/F2
Halfway, Ky. 237/J7
Halfway, Md. 245/G2
Half Way, Mo. 261/F7
Halfway, Oreg. 291/K3
Halfway House, Hawaii 218/H6
Halfway House, S. Africa 118/H6
Halfweg, Netherlands 27/B4
Halhul, West Bank 65/C4
Haliburton (county), Ontario 177/F2
Haliburton, Ontario 177/F2
Haliburton (lake), Ontario 177/F2
Halieli, Turkey 63/B6
Halifax, Canada 2/F3
Halifax, England 13/J1
Halifax, England 10/G1
Halifax (harb.), Grenada 161/C8
Halifax•, Mass. 249/L5
Halifax (co.), N.C. 281/O2
Halifax, N.C. 281/O2
Halifax (co.), Nova Scotia 168/E4
Halifax (cap.), Nova Scotia 162/K7
Halifax (cap.), Nova Scotia 146/M5
Halifax (cap.), Nova Scotia 168/E4
Halifax (harb.), Nova Scotia 168/E4
Halifax, Pa. 294/J5
Halifax (bay), Queensland 88/H3
Halifax (bay), Queensland 95/C3
Halifax•, Vt. 268/B6
Halifax (co.), Va. 307/L7
Halifax, Va. 307/L7
Halifax Center, Vt. 268/B6
Haliimaile, Hawaii 218/J2
Halil (riv.), Iran 59/G4
Halin, Somalia 115/J2
Halkett (cape), Alaska 196/H1
Halkirk, Alberta 182/D3
Halkirk, Scotland 10/E1
Halkirk, Scotland 15/E2
Hall (isl.), Alaska 196/D2
Hall (co.), Ga. 217/E2
Hall, Ind. 227/D5
Hall, Ky. 237/R6
Hall, Md. 245/L5
Hall (isls.), Micronesia 87/F5
Hall, Mont. 262/C4
Hall (co.), Nebr. 264/F4
Hall (basin), N.W.T. 187/M1
Hall (lake), N.W.T. 187/K3
Hall (pen.), N.W.T. 162/K3
Hall (pen.), N.W.T. 187/M3
Hall (riv.), Québec 172/C2
Hall (co.), Texas 303/D3
Hall, W. Va. 312/F4
Halla (mt.), S. Korea 81/C7
Hallam, Nebr. 264/H4
Hallam, Victoria 97/K5
Halland (co.), Sweden 18/H8
Hallandale, Fla. 212/B4
Hallandale (riv.), Scotland 15/E2
Hallaniya (isl.), Yemen 59/G6
Hallau, Switzerland 39/F1
Hall Beach, N.W.T. 187/K3
Hallboro, Manitoba 179/C4
Halle, Belgium 27/E7
Halle, Germany 7/F3
Halle, Germany 22/D3
Halleck, Nev. 266/F2
Hällefors, Sweden 18/J7
Hallein, Austria 41/B3
Halle-Neustadt, Germany 22/D3
Hallett, Okla. 288/N2
Hallettsville, Texas 303/G8
Halley, Ark. 202/H6
Halliday, N. Dak. 282/F5
Hallie, Wis. 317/D6
Halligen (isls.), Germany 22/C1
Hall Meadow (brook), Conn. 210/C1
Hallock, Minn. 255/A2
Hallonquist, Sask. 181/D5
Hallowell, Kansas 232/H4
Hallowell, Maine 243/D7
Hall Park, Okla. 288/M4
Halls (stream), N.H. 268/E1
Halls, Tenn. 237/C9
Halls (creek), Utah 304/D6
Hallsberg, Sweden 18/J7
Hallsboro, N.C. 281/M6
Halls Creek, Australia 87/C7
Halls Creek, W. Australia 88/D3
Halls Creek, W. Australia 92/D2
Halls Crossroads, Tenn. 237/O8
Hallson, N. Dak. 282/P2
Halls Summit, Kansas 232/G3
Hallstahammar, Sweden 18/K7
Hallstatt, Austria 41/B3
Hallstavik, Sweden 18/L6
Hallstead, Pa. 294/L2
Hall Summit, La. 238/D2
Hallsville, Ill. 222/D3
Hallsville, Mo. 261/H4
Hallsville, Ohio 284/E7
Hallsville, Texas 303/K5
Hallton, Pa. 294/E3
Halltown, Mo. 261/E8
Halltown, W. Va. 312/L4
Hallum, Netherlands 27/H2
Hallwilersee (lake), Switzerland 39/F2
Hallwood, Va. 307/S5
Halma, Minn. 255/B2
Halmahera (isl.), Indonesia 54/O9
Halmahera (isl.), Indonesia 85/H5
Halmahera (sea), Indonesia 85/H5
Halmstad, Sweden 18/H8
Halq el Oued, Tunisia 106/G1
Hals, Denmark 21/D3
Halsell, Ala. 195/B6
Halsey, Nebr. 264/D3
Halsey, Oreg. 291/D3
Halstad, Minn. 255/B3
Halstead, England 13/H6
Halstead, England 10/G5
Halstead, Kansas 232/E4
Haltdalen, Norway 18/G5
Haltemprice, England 13/G4
Haltemprice, England 10/F4
Haltern, Germany 22/B3
Haltiatunturi (mt.), Finland 18/M2
Haltom City, Texas 303/F2
Halton (reg. munic.), Ontario 177/E4
Halton Hills, Ontario 177/E4
Haltwhistle, England 13/E2
Halulu (lake), Hawaii 218/A2
Ham, Chad 111/C5
Ham, France 28/E3
Hama (prov.), Syria 63/G5
Hama, Syria 63/G5
Hama, Syria 59/C2
Hamada, Jebel (mt.), Egypt 59/B5
Hamada, Japan 81/E6
Hamadan (gov.), Iran 66/F3
Hamadan, Iran 66/F3
Hamadan, Iran 59/E3
Hamadan, Iran 54/F6
Hamamatsu, Japan 54/P6
Hamamatsu, Japan 81/H6
Hamar, N. Dak. 282/N4
Hamar, Norway 18/G6
Hamar, Saudi Arabia 59/E5
Hambantota, Sri Lanka 68/E7
Hamberg, N. Dak. 282/L4
Hamber Prov. Park, Br. Col. 184/H4
Hamblen (co.), Tenn. 237/P8
Hambleton, W. Va. 312/G4
Hamburg, Ark. 202/G7
Hamburg, Conn. 210/F3
Hamburg (state), Germany 22/D2
Hamburg, Germany 7/F3
Hamburg, Germany 22/D2
Hamburg, Ill. 222/C4
Hamburg, Iowa 229/B7
Hamburg, Mich. 250/F6
Hamburg, Minn. 255/D6
Hamburg, Miss. 256/B7
Hamburg, N.J. 273/D1
Hamburg, N.Y. 276/C5
Hamburg, Pa. 294/L4
Hamburg, Wis. 317/G5
Hamda, Saudi Arabia 59/D6
Hamden•, Conn. 210/D3
Hamden, N.Y. 276/K6
Hamden, Ohio 284/F7
Häme (prov.), Finland 18/O6
Hämeenlinna, Finland 18/O6
Hamel, Ill. 222/B2
Hamel, Minn. 255/F5
Hamel, Québec 172/G3
Hamelin Pool, W. Australia 88/A5
Hamelin Pool, W. Australia 92/A4
Hameln, Germany 22/C2
Hamer, Idaho 220/F6
Hamer, S.C. 296/J3
Hamersley (range), W. Australia 88/B4
Hamersley (range), W. Australia 92/B3
Hamersville, Ohio 284/C8
Hamhŭng, N. Korea 81/C4
Hami (Kumul), China 77/D3
Hami, China 54/L5
Hamill, S. Dak. 298/K6
Hamilton, Ala. 195/C2
Hamilton (lake), Ark. 202/D5
Hamilton (cap.), Bermuda 156/G3

380 Hartland

Hartland, Wis. 317/J1
Hartland Four Corners, Vt. 268/C4
Hartlepool, England 10/F3
Hartlepool, England 13/F3
Hartleton, Pa. 294/H4
Hartley, Iowa 229/C2
Hartley (co.), Texas 303/B2
Hartley, Texas 303/B2
Hartleyville, Alberta 182/D5
Hartline, Wash. 310/F3
Hartly, Del. 245/R4
Hartman, Ark. 202/C3
Hartman, Colo. 208/P6
Hartney, Manitoba 179/B5
Harts (pass), Wash. 310/E2
Harts, W. Va. 312/B6
Hartsburg, Ill. 222/D3
Hartsburg, Mo. 261/H5
Hartsdale, N.Y. 276/P6
Hartsel, Colo. 208/H4
Hartselle, Ala. 195/E2
Hartsfield, Ga. 217/E8
Hartsgrove, Ohio 284/J2
Hartshorn, Mo. 261/J8
Hartshorne, Okla. 288/R5
Harts Range, North. Terr. 88/F4
Harts Range, North. Terr. 93/D7
Hartstown, Pa. 294/B2
Hartsville, Ind. 227/F6
Hartsville, Mass. 249/B4
Hartsville, S.C. 296/G3
Hartsville, Tenn. 237/J8
Hartville, Mo. 261/G8
Hartville, Ohio 284/H4
Hartville, Wyo. 319/H3
Hartwell, Ga. 217/G2
Hartwell (dam), Ga. 217/G2
Hartwell (lake), Ga. 217/G2
Hartwell, Mo. 261/E6
Hartwell (dam), S.C. 296/B3
Hartwell (lake), S.C. 296/A3
Hartwick, Iowa 229/J5
Hartwick, N.Y. 276/K5
Hartz (mt.), Tasmania 99/C5
Harug el Asued, El (mts.), Libya 111/C2
Haruniye, Turkey 63/G4
Har Us Nuur (lake), Mongolia 77/D2
Harvard (mt.), Colo. 208/G5
Harvard, Idaho 220/B3
Harvard, Ill. 222/E1
Harvard, Iowa 229/G7
Harvard•, Mass. 249/H2
Harvard, Nebr. 264/F4
Harvel, Ill. 222/D4
Harvest, Ala. 195/E1
Harvester, Mo. 261/N2
Harvey, Ill. 222/B6
Harvey, Iowa 229/H6
Harvey (co.), Kansas 232/E3
Harvey, La. 238/O4
Harvey, Albert, New Bruns. 170/F3
Harvey, York, New Bruns. 170/D3
Harvey (lake), New Bruns. 170/C3
Harvey (mt.), New Bruns. 170/D3
Harvey, N. Dak. 282/L4
Harvey, W. Australia 88/B6
Harvey, W. Australia 92/A2
Harvey, W. Va. 312/D7
Harvey Cedars, N.J. 273/E4
Harveys (lake), Vt. 268/C3
Harveysburg, Ohio 284/C7
Harveys Lake, Pa. 294/E7
Harveyton, Ky. 237/P6
Harveyville, Kansas 232/F3
Harviell, Mo. 261/M9
Harwich, England 13/J6
Harwich, England 10/G5
Harwich, Mass. 249/O6
Harwich•, Mass. 249/O6
Harwich Port, Mass. 249/O6
Harwinton, Conn. 210/C1
Harwinton•, Conn. 210/C1
Harwood, Mo. 261/D7
Harwood, N. Dak. 282/S6
Harwood, Ontario 177/F3
Harwood, Texas 303/G8
Harwood Heights, Ill. 222/B5
Harwood Island, N.S. Wales 97/G1
Harworth, England 13/F4
Haryana (state), India 68/D3
Harz (mts.), Germany 22/D3
Harzgerode, Germany 22/D3
Hasa, Wadi el (dry riv.), Jordan 65/E5
Hasan Dağı, Büyük (mt.), Turkey 63/E3
Hasbrouck Heights, N.J. 273/B2
Hase (riv.), Germany 22/B2
Haseke (prov.), Syria 63/J4
Haselünne, Germany 22/B2
Hasenkamp, Argentina 143/F5
Hashtpar, Iran 66/F2
Haskeir (isl.), Scotland 15/A3
Haskell, Ark. 202/E4
Haskell (co.), Kansas 232/B4
Haskell, N.J. 273/A1
Haskell (co.), Okla. 288/R4
Haskell, Okla. 288/P3
Haskell (co.), Texas 303/E4
Haskell, Texas 303/E4
Haskett, Manitoba 179/D5
Haskins, Iowa 229/K6
Haskins, Ohio 284/C3
Haslach an der Mühl, Austria 41/C2
Hasle, Denmark 21/F8
Haslemere, England 13/G6
Haslemere, England 10/F5
Haslet, Texas 303/E2
Haslett, Mich. 250/E6
Haslev, Denmark 21/E7
Haslingden, England 13/H1
Hassa, Turkey 63/G4
Hassan, India 68/D6
Hassayampa (riv.), Ariz. 198/C5
Hasse, Texas 303/F6
Hassel (sound), N.W.T. 187/J2
Hassel (isl.), Virgin Is. (U.S.) 161/B4
Hassell, N.C. 281/P3
Hasselt, Belgium 27/G7
Hasselt, Netherlands 27/J3
Hassfurt, Germany 22/D3
Hassi Messaoud, Algeria 106/F2
Hassi R'Mel, Algeria 106/E2
Hässleholm, Sweden 18/H8
Hassloch, Germany 22/C4
Haster, Scotland 15/E2
Hastière, Belgium 27/F8
Hastings, England 10/G5
Hastings, England 13/H7
Hastings, Fla. 212/E2
Hastings, Iowa 229/C6
Hastings, Mich. 250/D6
Hastings, Minn. 255/F6
Hastings, Nebr. 188/G2
Hastings, Nebr. 264/F4
Hastings, N. Zealand 100/F3
Hastings, N. Dak. 282/O6
Hastings, Okla. 288/K6
Hastings (county), Ontario 177/G3
Hastings, Ontario 177/G3
Hastings, Pa. 294/E4
Hastings On Hudson, N.Y. 276/O6
Hasty, Ark. 202/D1
Hasty, Colo. 208/O6
Hasvik, Norway 18/M1
Haswell, Colo. 208/N6
Hat (peak), Calif. 204/E2
Hat (creek), S. Dak. 298/B7
Hatay (prov.), Turkey 63/G4
Hatay (Antakya), Turkey 63/G4
Hatboro, Pa. 294/M5
Hatch, N. Mex. 274/B6
Hatch, Utah 304/B6
Hatchechubbee, Ala. 195/H6
Hatcher, Ga. 217/B7
Hatches Creek, North. Terr. 88/F4
Hatches Creek, North. Terr. 93/D6
Hatchet (mts.), N. Mex. 274/A7
Hatchett (pt.), Conn. 210/G3
Hatchie (riv.), Tenn. 237/B9
Hatchineha (lake), Fla. 212/E3
Haţeg, Romania 45/F3
Hatfield, Ark. 202/B5
Hatfield, England 13/H7
Hatfield, Ind. 227/C9
Hatfield, Ky. 237/S5
Hatfield, Mass. 249/D3
Hatfield•, Mass. 249/D3
Hatfield, Minn. 255/B7
Hatfield, Mo. 261/D1
Hatfield, N.S. Wales 97/B3
Hatfield, Pa. 294/M5
Hatfield, Sask. 181/F4
Hatfield, Wis. 317/E7
Hatfield Point, New Bruns. 170/E3
Hatgal, Mongolia 77/E1
Hathaway, Mont. 262/K4
Hatherleigh, Sask. 181/C2
Hathras, India 68/D3
Hatiba, Ras (cape), Saudi Arabia 59/C5
Ha Tien, Vietnam 72/E5
Hatillo, P. Rico 161/B1
Ha Tinh, Vietnam 72/E3
Hatira (mt.), Israel 65/B6
Hatley, Miss. 256/H3
Hatley, Québec 172/F4
Hatley, Wis. 317/H6
Hato, Neth. Ant. 161/G8
Hato del Volcán, Panama 154/F6
Hato Mayor, Dom. Rep. 158/F6
Hato Rey, P. Rico 161/E1
Hatseva, Israel 65/D5
Hattem, Netherlands 27/H4
Hatteras (cape), N.C. 146/L6
Hatteras (cape), N.C. 188/M3
Hatteras, N.C. 281/T4
Hatteras (cape), N.C. 281/U4
Hatteras (inlet), N.C. 281/T4
Hatteras (isl.), N.C. 281/U4
Hatteras (cape), U.S. 2/F4
Hattiesburg, Miss. 188/H4
Hattiesburg, Miss. 256/F8
Hattieville, Ark. 202/E3
Hattieville, Belize 154/C2
Hatton, Ala. 195/D1
Hatton, N. Dak. 282/R4
Hatton, Sask. 181/B5
Hatton, Scotland 15/G3
Hatton, Utah 304/B5
Hatton, Wash. 310/G4
Hatuey, Cuba 158/G3
Hatvan, Hungary 41/E3
Hat Yai, Thailand 72/C6
Hatzic, Br. Col. 184/L3
Hau Bon, Vietnam 72/E4
Haubstadt, Ind. 227/B8
Haud (reg.), Ethiopia 111/J6
Haud (plat.), Somalia 115/J2
Haugan, Mont. 262/A3
Hauge, Norway 18/E7
Haugen, Wis. 317/C4
Haugesund, Norway 7/E3
Haugesund, Norway 18/D7
Haughton, La. 238/C1
Hauhungaroa (range), N. Zealand 100/E3
Haukivesi (lake), Finland 18/Q5
Haultain (riv.), Sask. 181/L3
Hauppauge, N.Y. 276/O9
Haura, Yemen 59/E7
Hauraki (gulf), N. Zealand 100/C1
Hauran, Wadi (dry riv.), Iraq 59/D3
Hauran, Wadi (dry riv.), Iraq 66/B4
Hauroko (lake), N. Zealand 100/A6
Hauru (pt.), Fr. Poly. 86/S12
Hauser, Idaho 220/A2
Hauser (lake), Mont. 262/E4
Hauser, Oreg. 291/C4
Hausstock (mt.), Switzerland 39/H3
Haut (isl.), Maine 243/G7
Haute (isl.), Nova Scotia 168/C3
Haute-Corse (dept.), France 28/B6
Haute-Garonne (dept.), France 28/D6
Haute-Loire (dept.), France 28/E5
Haute-Marne (dept.), France 28/F3
Hauterive, Québec 172/A1
Hauterive, Québec 174/D3
Hautes-Alpes (dept.), France 28/G5
Haute-Saône (dept.), France 28/G4
Haute-Savoie (dept.), France 28/G5
Hautes-Pyrénées (dept.), France 28/D6
Haute-Vienne (dept.), France 28/D5
Hautmont, France 28/F2
Haut-Rhin (dept.), France 28/G4
Hauts-de-Seine (dept.), France 28/A2
Haut-Zaïre (prov.), D.R. Congo 115/E3
Hauula, Hawaii 218/E1
Havaco, W. Va. 312/C8
Havana, Ala. 195/C5
Havana, Ark. 202/D3
Havana (prov.), Cuba 158/C1
Havana (cap.), Cuba 2/E4
Havana (cap.), Cuba 146/K7
Havana (cap.), Cuba 156/A2
Havana (cap.), Cuba 158/C1
Havana, Fla. 212/B1
Havana, Ill. 222/D3
Havana, Kansas 232/G4
Havana, Minn. 255/E6
Havana, N. Dak. 282/P8
Havana, Ohio 284/E3
Havannah (chan.), New Caled. 86/H5
Havant and Waterloo, England 13/G7
Havasu (lake) 188/D4
Havasu (lake), Ariz. 198/A4
Havasu (lake), Calif. 204/L9
Havasu (lake), U.S. 146/G6
Havasupai Ind. Res., Ariz. 198/C2
Havdrup, Denmark 21/F6
Havel (riv.), Germany 22/E2
Havelange, Belgium 27/G8
Havelberg, Germany 22/D2
Havelock, Iowa 229/D3
Havelock, New Bruns. 170/E3
Havelock, N. Zealand 100/D4
Havelock, N.C. 281/P5
Havelock, N. Dak. 282/E7
Havelock, Ontario 177/G3
Havelock North, N. Zealand 100/F3
Haven, Kansas 232/E4
Havensville, Kansas 232/F2
Haverford•, Pa. 294/M6
Haverfordwest, Wales 10/D5
Haverfordwest, Wales 13/B6
Haverhill, England 13/H5
Haverhill, Iowa 229/H5
Haverhill, Mass. 249/K1
Haverhill•, N.H. 268/C3
Haverhill, Ohio 284/E8
Havering, England 10/C5
Havering, England 13/J8
Haverstraw, N.Y. 276/M8
Havertown, Pa. 294/M6
Haviland, Kansas 232/C4
Haviland, Ohio 284/A3
Havillah, Wash. 310/F2
Havířov, Czech Rep. 41/E2
Havlíčkův Brod, Czech Rep. 41/C2
Havran, Turkey 63/B3
Havre, Mont. 146/G5
Havre, Mont. 188/E1
Havre, Mont. 262/G2
Havre Boucher, Nova Scotia 168/G3
Havre de Grace, Md. 245/O2
Havre-Saint-Pierre, Québec 174/E2
Havre-St-Pierre, Que. 162/K5
Havsa, Turkey 63/B2
Havza, Turkey 63/F2
Haw (riv.), N.C. 281/K2
Hawaii 188/F5
HAWAII 218
Hawaii (co.), Hawaii 218/K7
Hawaii (isl.), Hawaii 87/L4
Hawaii (isl.), Hawaii 188/F6
Hawaii (isl.), Hawaii 218/H5
Hawaii (state), U.S. 87/K4
Hawaii (state), U.S. 188/F5
Hawaiian (isls.) 87/J3
Hawaii Kai, Hawaii 218/F2
Hawaii Nat'l Park, Hawaii 218/J6
Hawaii Volcanoes Nat'l Park, Hawaii 218/H6
Hawara, Jordan 65/D2
Hawarden, Iowa 229/A2
Hawarden, N. Zealand 100/D5
Hawarden, Sask. 181/E4
Hawarden, Wales 13/G2
Hawea (lake), N. Zealand 100/B6
Hawera, N. Zealand 100/E3
Hawes, England 13/E3
Hawesville, Ky. 237/H5
Hawi, Hawaii 218/G3
Hawick, Minn. 255/D5
Hawick, Scotland 10/E3
Hawick, Scotland 15/F5
Hawk (hills), Alberta 182/B1
Hawke (hills), Newf. 166/D2
Hawke (isl.), Newf. 166/C3
Hawke (riv.), Newf. 166/C3
Hawke (bay), N. Zealand 100/F3
Hawker, S. Australia 88/F6
Hawker, S. Australia 94/F4
Hawke's Bay, Newf. 166/C3
Hawkesbury (isl.), Br. Col. 184/C3
Hawkesbury, Ontario 177/K2
Hawkestone, Ontario 177/E3
Hawkeye, Iowa 229/J3
Hawkins, Mich. 250/D5
Hawkins (co.), Tenn. 237/P8
Hawkins, Texas 303/J5
Hawkins, Wis. 317/E4
Hawkinsville, Ga. 217/E6
Hawk Junction, Ontario 175/D3
Hawk Junction, Ontario 177/J5
Hawk Point, Mo. 261/K5
Hawk Run, Pa. 294/F4
Hawks, Mich. 250/F3
Hawk Springs, Wyo. 319/H4
Hawley, Minn. 255/B4
Hawley, Pa. 294/M3
Hawley, Texas 303/E5
Hawleyville, Conn. 210/B3
Haworth, N.J. 273/C1
Haworth, Okla. 288/S7
Hawston, S. Africa 118/G7
Hawthorn, La. 238/D4
Hawthorn, Pa. 294/D3
Hawthorn, Victoria 97/J5
Hawthorne, Calif. 204/C11
Hawthorne, Fla. 212/D2
Hawthorne, Nev. 266/C4
Hawthorne, N.J. 273/B2
Hawthorne, N.Y. 276/O6
Hawthorne, Victoria 88/L7
Hawthorne, Wis. 317/C3
Hawthorn Woods, Ill. 222/B5
Haxby, England 13/F3
Haxtun, Colo. 208/O1
Hay (riv.) 162/E4
Hay (lake), Alberta 182/A5
Hay (riv.), Alberta 182/A5
Hay (riv.), Canada 146/G4
Hay, N.S. Wales 88/H6
Hay, N.S. Wales 97/C4
Hay (dry riv.), North. Terr. 88/F4
Hay (cape), North. Terr. 93/A3
Hay (dry riv.), North. Terr. 93/E7
Hay (lake), Ontario 177/F2
Hay, Wales 10/E4
Hay, Wales 13/D5
Hay, Wash. 310/H4
Hayama, Japan 81/O3
Hayange, France 28/F3
Haycock, Alaska 196/F1
Hayden, Ala. 195/E3
Hayden, Ariz. 198/E5
Hayden, Colo. 208/E2
Hayden, Idaho 220/B2
Hayden (lake), Idaho 220/B2
Hayden, Ind. 227/F7
Hayden, Mo. 261/H6
Hayden, N. Mex. 274/F3
Hayden (peak), Utah 304/C3
Haydenburg, Tenn. 237/K8
Hayden Lake, Idaho 220/B2
Haydenville, Mass. 249/C3
Haydenville, Ohio 284/F7
Hayes (mt.), Alaska 196/J2
Hayes (pen.), Greenl. 4/B13
Hayes, Jamaica 158/J6
Hayes, La. 238/E6
Hayes (riv.), Man. 162/G4
Hayes (riv.), Manitoba 179/K3
Hayes (co.), Nebr. 264/C4
Hayes (riv.), N.W.T. 187/J3
Hayes, S. Dak. 298/H5
Hayes, Wis. 317/J5
Hayes Center, Nebr. 264/C4
Hayesville, Iowa 229/J6
Hayesville, New Bruns. 170/D2
Hayesville, N.C. 281/B4
Hayesville, Ohio 284/F4
Hayesville, Oreg. 291/A3
Hayfield, Iowa 229/F2
Hayfield, Minn. 255/F7
Hayfork, Calif. 204/B3
Hay Fork, Trinity (riv.), Calif. 204/B3
Hay Lakes, Alberta 182/D3
Hayle, England 13/B7
Haylow, Ga. 217/G9
Haymana, Turkey 63/E3
Haymarket, Va. 307/N3
Hayne, N.C. 281/M5
Haynes, Alberta 182/D3
Haynes, Ark. 202/J4
Haynes, N. Dak. 282/F8
Haynesville, La. 238/D1
Haynesville•, Maine 243/G4
Haynesville, Va. 307/P5
Hayneville, Ala. 195/E6
Hayrabolu, Turkey 63/B2
Hay River, N.W.T. 162/E3
Hay River, N.W.T. 146/G3
Hay River, N.W.T. 187/G3
Hays, Alberta 182/E4
Hays, Kansas 232/C3
Hays, Mont. 262/H2
Hays, N.C. 281/G2
Hays (co.), Texas 303/F7
Haysi, Va. 307/D6
Hay Springs, Nebr. 264/B2
Haystack (mt.), Conn. 210/C1
Haystack (peak), Mont. 262/A3
Haystack (mt.), N.Y. 276/N2
Haystack (mt.), Vt. 268/B6
Haysville, Ind. 227/D8
Haysville, Kansas 232/E4
Haysville, Pa. 294/B4
Hayter, Alberta 182/E3
Hayti, Mo. 261/N10
Hayti, S. Dak. 298/P4
Hayti Heights, Mo. 261/N10
Hayton, Wis. 317/K7
Hayward, Calif. 204/K2
Hayward (lake), Conn. 210/F2
Hayward, Minn. 255/E7
Hayward, Mo. 261/N10
Hayward, Wis. 317/D3
Haywards-Manor Park, N. Zealand 100/B2
Haywood, Manitoba 179/D5
Haywood (co.), N.C. 281/C3
Haywood, N.C. 281/L3
Haywood, Okla. 288/P5
Haywood (co.), Tenn. 237/C9
Haywood City, Mo. 261/N9
Hazar (lake), Turkey 63/H3
Hazaran, Kuh-e (mt.), Iran 66/K6
Hazard, Ky. 237/P6
Hazard, Nebr. 264/F3
Hazardville, Conn. 210/E1
Hazaribagh, India 68/F4
Hazar Qadam, Afghanistan 59/J3
Hazar Qadam, Afghanistan 68/B2
Hazebrouck, France 28/E2
Hazel, Ky. 237/E7
Hazel, S. Dak. 298/P4
Hazel Cliffe, Sask. 181/J5
Hazel Crest, Ill. 222/B6
Hazeldean, New Bruns. 170/C2
Hazel Dell, Ill. 222/E4
Hazel Dell, Sask. 181/H4
Hazeldine, Alberta 182/E3
Hazel Green, Ala. 195/E1
Hazel Green, Ky. 237/O5
Hazelgreen, Mo. 261/H7
Hazel Green, Wis. 317/F11
Hazel Grove and Bramhall, England 13/H2
Hazel Hill, Nova Scotia 168/G3
Hazelhurst, Ill. 222/D2
Hazel Hurst, Pa. 294/E2
Hazelhurst, Wis. 317/G4
Hazel Park, Mich. 250/B6
Hazel Patch, Ky. 237/N6
Hazelridge, Manitoba 179/F5
Hazelrigg, Ind. 227/D4
Hazel Run, Minn. 255/C6
Hazelton, Br. Col. 162/D5
Hazelton, Br. Col. 184/D2
Hazelton (mts.), Br. Col. 184/C2
Hazelton, Idaho 220/E7
Hazelton, Kansas 232/D4
Hazelton, N. Dak. 282/K7
Hazelton, W. Va. 312/G3
Hazelton (peak), Wyo. 319/E1
Hazelwood, Ind. 227/D5
Hazelwood, Mo. 261/P2
Hazelwood, N.C. 281/C4
Hazen (bay), Alaska 196/E2
Hazen, Ark. 202/G4
Hazen, Nev. 266/C3
Hazen, N. Dak. 282/G5
Hazen (lake), N.W.T. 187/L1
Hazen (str.), N.W.T. 187/G2
Hazenmore, Sask. 181/D6
Hazerim, Israel 65/B5
Hazlehurst, Ga. 217/G7
Hazlehurst, Miss. 256/D7
Hazlet, N.J. 273/E3
Hazlet, Sask. 181/C5
Hazleton, Ind. 227/B8
Hazleton, Iowa 229/K3
Hazleton, Pa. 294/L4
Hazlett (lake), W. Australia 88/D4
Hazlettville, Del. 245/R4
Hazor Hagelilit, Israel 65/D2
Hazro, Turkey 63/J3
Heacham, England 13/H5
Headford, Ireland 17/C5
Headland, Ala. 195/H8
Headlee, Ind. 227/D3
Head of Amherst, Nova Scotia 168/E3
Head of Bay d'Espoir, Newf. 166/C4
Head of Bight (bay), S. Australia 94/B4
Head of Grassy, Ky. 237/P4
Head of Island, La. 238/L2
Head of Jeddore, Nova Scotia 168/E4
Head of Millstream, New Bruns. 170/E3
Head of Saint Margarets Bay, Nova Scotia 168/E4
Headquarters, Idaho 220/C3
Headrick, Okla. 288/H5
Heads, The (prom.), Oreg. 291/C5
Heads of Ayr (cape), Scotland 15/D5
Head Waters, Va. 307/K4
Heafford Junction, Wis. 317/G4
Healdsburg, Calif. 204/B5
Healdton, Okla. 288/M6
Healdville, Vt. 268/B5
Healesville, Victoria 97/C5
Healing Springs, Ala. 195/B7
Healing Springs, Va. 307/J5
Healy, Alaska 196/H2
Healy, Kansas 232/B3
Healys, Va. 307/R5
Heanor, England 13/F4
Heard (isl.), Australia 2/N8
Heard (co.), Ga. 217/B4
Hearne, Sask. 181/F5
Hearne, Texas 303/H7
Hearst (isl.), Ant. 5/B16
Hearst, Ont. 162/H6
Hearst, Ontario 177/J5
Hearst, Ontario 175/D3
Heart (lake), Alberta 182/E2
Heart (butte), N. Dak. 282/G6
Heart (riv.), N. Dak. 282/F6
Heart (lake), Wyo. 319/B1
Heart Butte, Mont. 262/C2
Heart River Settlement, Alberta 182/B2
Heart's Content, Newf. 166/D2
Heart's Delight, Newf. 166/D2
Heart's Desire, Newf. 166/D2
Hearts Hill, Sask. 181/B3
Heartwell, Nebr. 264/F4
Heartwellville, Vt. 268/A6
Heaters, W. Va. 312/E5
Heath, Ala. 195/F8
Heath, Alberta 182/E3
Heath (riv.), Bolivia 136/A3
Heath•, Mass. 249/C2
Heath, Mont. 262/G3
Heath, Ohio 284/F5
Heath (riv.), Peru 128/H9
Heath (pt.), Québec 174/E3
Heathcote, Victoria 97/C5
Heatherton, Newf. 166/C4
Heatherton, Nova Scotia 168/G3
Heathhall, Scotland 15/E5
Heath Springs, S.C. 296/F2
Heath Steele, New Bruns. 170/D1
Heathsville, Va. 307/P5
Heaton, N. Dak. 282/L5
Heavener, Okla. 288/S5
Hebbardsville, Ky. 237/G5
Hebbronville, Texas 303/F10
Hebbs Cross, Nova Scotia 168/D4
Hebburn, England 13/J3
Hebei (Hopei), China 77/J4
Hebel, Queensland 95/C6
Heber, Ariz. 198/E4
Heber, Calif. 204/K11
Heber City, Utah 304/C3
Heber Springs, Ark. 202/G2
Hebert, La. 238/G2
Hébert (riv.), Nova Scotia 168/D3
Hébertville, Québec 172/F1
Hébertville-Station, Québec 172/F1
Hebgen (dam), Mont. 262/E6
Hebgen (lake), Mont. 262/E6
Hebi, China 77/H4
Hebo, Oreg. 291/D2
Hebrides, Inner (isls.), Scotland 10/C2
Hebrides, Inner (isls.), Scotland 15/B4
Hebrides, Outer (isls.), Scotland 10/C2
Hebrides, Outer (isls.), Scotland 15/A3
Hebrides (sea), Scotland 15/B3
Hebrides (sea), Scotland 10/C2
Hebron•, Conn. 210/F2
Hebron, Ill. 222/E1
Hebron, Ind. 227/C2
Hebron, Ky. 237/R2
Hebron•, Maine 243/C7
Hebron, Md. 245/R7
Hebron, Nebr. 264/G4
Hebron (fjord), Newf. 166/B2
Hebron•, N.H. 268/D4
Hebron, N. Dak. 282/G6
Hebron, Nova Scotia 168/B5
Hebron, Ohio 284/E6
Hebron, Texas 303/G1
Hebron, West Bank 65/C4
Hebron, West Bank 59/C3
Hebron, W. Va. 312/D4
Hebron, Wis. 317/J10
Hecate (str.), Br. Col. 162/C5
Hecate (str.), Br. Col. 146/E4
Hecate (str.), Br. Col. 184/B3
Hecelchakán, Mexico 150/O6
Heceta (isl.), Alaska 196/M2
Heceta (head), Oreg. 291/C3
Hechi, China 77/G7
Hechingen, Germany 22/C4
Hechuan (Hochwan), China 77/G5
Hecker, Ill. 222/D5
Hecla, Manitoba 179/F3
Hecla (isl.), Manitoba 179/F3
Hecla, S. Dak. 298/N2
Hecla Prov. Park, Manitoba 179/F3
Hector, Ark. 202/E3
Hector, Minn. 255/D6
Hector, N.Y. 276/G5
Hede, Sweden 18/H5
Hedemora, Sweden 18/K6
Hedenäset, Sweden 18/N3
Hedensted, Denmark 21/C6
Hedgesville, Mont. 262/G4
Hedgesville, W. Va. 312/K3
Hedley, Br. Col. 184/G5
Hedley, Texas 303/D3
Hedmark (co.), Norway 18/G6
Hedon, England 13/G4
Hedrick, Iowa 229/J6
Hedville, Kansas 232/E3
Hedwig Village, Texas 303/H1
Heemskert, Netherlands 27/F3
Heemstede, Netherlands 27/F4
Heer, Netherlands 27/H7
Heerde, Netherlands 27/H4
Heerenveen, Netherlands 27/H3
Heerhugowaard, Netherlands 27/F3
Heerlen, Netherlands 27/J7
Heesch, Netherlands 27/G5
Hefei (Hofei), China 77/J5
Hefei, China 54/N6
Heffley Creek, Br. Col. 184/G5
Heflin, Ala. 195/G3
Heflin, La. 238/D2
Hegang (Hokang), China 77/L2
Hegang, China 54/O5
Hegau (reg.), Germany 22/C5
Hegeler, Ill. 222/F3
Hegins, Pa. 294/K4
Heiban, Sudan 111/F5
Heiberger, Ala. 195/D5
Heide, Germany 22/C1
Heidelberg, Germany 22/C4
Heidelberg, Ky. 237/O5
Heidelberg, Minn. 255/E6
Heidelberg, Miss. 256/F7
Heidelberg, Pa. 294/B7
Heidelberg, S. Africa 118/J7
Heidelberg, Victoria 97/J5
Heidelberg, Victoria 88/L7
Heiden, Switzerland 39/H2
Heidenau, Germany 22/E3
Heidenheim an der Brenz, Germany 22/D4
Heidenreichstein, Austria 41/C2
Heidrick, Ky. 237/O7
Heihe (Aihui) (Aigun), China 77/L1
Heijo (P'yŏngyang) (cap.), N. Korea 81/C4
Heil, N. Dak. 282/G7
Heilbron, S. Africa 118/D5
Heilbronn, Germany 22/C4
Heiligenblut, Austria 41/B3
Heiligenhafen, Germany 22/D1
Heiligenstadt, Germany 22/D3
Heilman, Ind. 227/C8
Heilongjiang (Heilungkiang), China 77/K2
Heilong Jiang (Amur) (riv.), China 77/L2
Heiloo, Netherlands 27/F3
Heilwood, Pa. 294/E4
Heimberg, Switzerland 39/E3
Heimdal, N. Dak. 282/L4
Heinola, Finland 18/P6
Heinola, Minn. 255/C4
Heinsburg, Alberta 182/E3
Heinze Chaung (bay), Burma 72/C4
Heise, Idaho 220/G6
Heiskell, Tenn. 237/O8
Heisler, Alberta 182/D3
Heislerville, N.J. 273/D5
Heisson, Wash. 310/C5
Heist-Knokke, Belgium 27/C6
Heist-op-den-Berg, Belgium 27/F6
Heizer, Kansas 232/D3
Hejaz (reg.), Saudi Arabia 59/C4
Hejian, China 77/J4
Hejing, China 77/C3
Hekimhan, Turkey 63/G3
Hekla (mt.), Iceland 4/C11
Hekla (mt.), Iceland 7/C2

Hudson 383

Honduras (gulf), Honduras 154/D2
Honea Path, S.C. 296/C3
Honegg (mt.), Switzerland 39/E3
Honeoye, N.Y. 276/F5
Honeoye (lake), N.Y. 276/F5
Honeoye Falls, N.Y. 276/F5
Honesdale, Pa. 294/M2
Honey (lake), Calif. 204/E3
Honey (creek), Ind. 227/C6
Honey (creek), Oreg. 291/G5
Honey Brook, Pa. 294/L5
Honey Creek, Ind. 227/F4
Honey Creek, Iowa 229/B6
Honey Creek, Wis. 317/J3
Honeydale, New Bruns. 170/C3
Honeyford, N. Dak. 282/R3
Honey Grove, Texas 303/J4
Honey Harbour, Ontario 177/E3
Honey Hill, S.C. 296/H5
Honey Island, Texas 303/K7
Honeymoon Bay, Br. Col. 184/J3
Honeyville, Utah 304/B2
Honeywood, Ontario 177/D3
Honfleur, France 28/D3
Honfleur, Québec 172/G3
Høng, Denmark 21/E7
Honga (riv.), Md. 245/O7
Hon Gai, Vietnam 72/E2
Hongch'ŏn, S. Korea 81/D5
Hong Kong 54/N7
Hong Kong 2/Q4
HONG KONG 77
Hongliuhe, China 77/E3
Hongor, Mongolia 77/H2
Hongshui He (riv.), China 77/G7
Hongsŏng, S. Korea 81/C5
Hongtong, China 77/H4
Honguedo (passage), Québec 174/E3
Hongwŏn, N. Korea 81/C3
Hongze Hu (lake), China 77/J5
Honiara (cap.), Solomon Is. 86/D3
Honiara (cap.), Solomon Is. 87/F6
Honiton, England 10/E5
Honiton, England 13/D7
Honjo, Japan 81/J4
Honnedaga (lake), N.Y. 276/L3
Honnelles, Belgium 27/D8
Honningsvag, Norway 18/O1
Honobia, Okla. 288/R5
Honohina, Hawaii 218/J4
Honokaa, Hawaii 188/G5
Honokaa, Hawaii 218/H4
Honokahua, Hawaii 218/H1
Honokohau, Hawaii, Hawaii 218/G5
Honokohau, Maui, Hawaii 218/J1
Honolulu (co.), Hawaii 218/D3
Honolulu (cap.), Hawaii 87/L3
Honolulu (cap.), Hawaii 188/F5
Honolulu (cap.), Hawaii 218/C4
Honolulu (harb.), Hawaii 218/C4
Honolulu, U.S. 2/B5
Honolulu Int'l Airport, Hawaii 218/B4
Honomu, Hawaii 218/J4
Honor, Mich. 250/D4
Honoraville, Ala. 195/F7
Honouliuli, Hawaii 218/A3
Honshu (isl.), Japan 2/S4
Honshu (isl.), Japan 54/P6
Honshu (isl.), Japan 81/J5
Honuapo, Hawaii 218/H7
Hood, Calif. 204/B9
Hood (riv.), N.W.T. 187/G3
Hood (mt.), Oreg. 291/F2
Hood (riv.), Oreg. 291/F2
Hood (co.), Texas 303/G5
Hood (canal), Wash. 310/B3
Hood River (co.), Oreg. 291/F2
Hood River, Oreg. 291/F2
Hoodsport, Wash. 310/B3
Hoofddorp (Haarlemmermeer), Netherlands 27/F4
Hoogeveen, Netherlands 27/J3
Hoogezand-Sappemeer, Netherlands 27/K2
Hooghly (riv.), India 68/F2
Hooghly-Chinsura, India 68/F1
Hoogkarspel, Netherlands 27/G3
Hoogstraten, Belgium 27/F6
Hook (head), Ireland 17/H7
Hook (isl.), Queensland 88/H4
Hook (isl.), Queensland 95/D4
Hookena, Hawaii 218/G6
Hooker (co.), Nebr. 264/C3
Hooker, Okla. 288/D1
Hooker Creek, North. Terr. 88/E3
Hooker Creek, North. Terr. 93/B5
Hooker Creek Aboriginal Reserve, North. Terr. 88/E3
Hookersville, W. Va. 312/E6
Hookerton, N.C. 281/O4
Hook of Holland, Netherlands 27/D4
Hooks, Texas 303/K4
Hooksett, N.H. 268/E5
Hooksett•, N.H. 268/E5
Hookstown, Pa. 294/B4
Hoolehua, Hawaii 188/F5
Hoolehua, Hawaii 218/G1
Hoonah, Alaska 196/M1
Hoonah (sound), Alaska 196/M1
Hoopa, Calif. 204/B2
Hoopa Valley Ind. Res., Calif. 204/A2
Hooper, Colo. 208/H7
Hooper (str.), Md. 245/O8
Hooper, Nebr. 264/H3
Hooper, Utah 304/B2
Hooper, Wash. 310/G4
Hooper Bay, Alaska 196/E2
Hooper Bay, Alaska 188/C5
Hoopersville, Md. 245/O7
Hoopeston, Ill. 222/F3
Hoople, N. Dak. 282/P2
Hooppole, Ill. 222/D2
Hoorn, Netherlands 27/G3
Hoorn (isls.), Wallis and Futuna 87/J7
Hoosac (mts.), Mass. 249/B2
Hoosac Tunnel, Mass. 249/C2
Hoosic (riv.), Mass. 249/A1
Hoosic (riv.), Vt. 268/A6
Hoosick Falls, N.Y. 276/O5
Hoosier, Sask. 181/B4
Hoot Owl, Okla. 288/R2
Hooven, Ohio 284/A9
Hoover, Ala. 195/E4
Hoover (dam), Ariz. 198/A2
Hoover (dam), Nev. 266/G7
Hoover (res.), Ohio 284/E5
Hoover, S. Dak. 298/C3
Hooversville, Pa. 294/E5
Hop (riv.), Conn. 210/F1
Hopa, Turkey 63/J2
Hopatcong, N.J. 273/D2
Hopatcong (lake), N.J. 273/D2
Hop Bottom, Pa. 294/L2
Hope, Alaska 196/C1
Hope (pt.), Alaska 196/E1
Hope (bay), Ant. 5/C16
Hope, Ark. 202/C6
Hope, Br. Col. 162/D6
Hope, Br. Col. 184/M3
Hope, Idaho 220/B1
Hope, Ind. 227/F6
Hope, Kansas 232/E3
Hope, Ky. 237/O4
Hope, Maine 243/E7
Hope•, Maine 243/E7
Hope, Mich. 250/E5
Hope, Minn. 255/E7
Hope, Mo. 261/J5
Hope (lake), Newf. 166/B3
Hope, N.J. 273/D2
Hope, N. Mex. 274/E6
Hope, N. Dak. 282/P5
Hope (isl.), Norway 4/B8
Hope, R.I. 249/H6
Hope, Loch (lake), Scotland 15/D2
Hope Bay, Jamaica 158/K6
Hopedale, Ill. 222/D3
Hopedale, Mass. 249/H4
Hopedale•, Mass. 249/H4
Hopedale, Newf. 166/B2
Hopedale, Newf. 162/L4
Hopedale, Newf. 146/N4
Hopedale, Ohio 284/J5
Hope Hull, Ala. 195/F6
Hopei (Hebei), China 77/J4
Hopeland, Pa. 294/K5
Hopelchén, Mexico 150/P7
Hopeman, Scotland 15/E3
Hope Mills, N.C. 281/M5
Hopen (isl.), Norway 18/E2
Hopes Advance (cape), Québec 174/F1
Hopeton, Okla. 288/J1
Hopeton, Va. 307/S5
Hopetoun, Victoria 97/B4
Hopetoun, W. Australia 92/C6
Hopetown, Québec 172/D2
Hopetown, S. Africa 118/C5
Hopetown, W. Australia 88/C6
Hope Valley, R.I. 249/H6
Hope Valley (res.), S. Australia 88/E7
Hopeville, Iowa 229/F7
Hopewell, Ala. 195/H3
Hopewell, Jamaica 158/G5
Hopewell, Kansas 232/D4
Hopewell, Md. 245/P8
Hopewell, Miss. 256/D7
Hopewell, N.J. 273/D3
Hopewell (isls.), N.W.T. 187/L4
Hopewell, Nova Scotia 168/F3
Hopewell, Ohio 284/F6
Hopewell, Pa. 294/F5
Hopewell (I.C.), Va. 307/O6
Hopewell Cape, New Bruns. 170/F3
Hopewell Hill, New Bruns. 170/F3
Hopewell Junction, N.Y. 276/N7
Hopfgarten in Nordtirol, Austria 41/B3
Hopi (buttes), Ariz. 198/E3
Hopi Ind. Res., Ariz. 198/E3
Hopkins (co.), Ky. 237/F6
Hopkins, Mich. 250/D6
Hopkins, Minn. 255/G5
Hopkins, Mo. 261/C1
Hopkins (lake), North. Terr. 93/A8
Hopkins, S.C. 296/F4
Hopkins (co.), Texas 303/J4
Hopkins (riv.), Victoria 97/B5
Hopkins, Va. 307/S5
Hopkins (lake), W. Australia 88/D4
Hopkins (lake), W. Australia 92/E4
Hopkins Park, Ill. 222/F2
Hopkinsville, Ky. 237/F7
Hopkinton, Iowa 229/L4
Hopkinton, Mass. 249/J4
Hopkinton•, Mass. 249/J4
Hopkinton•, N.H. 268/D5
Hopkinton, N.Y. 276/L1
Hopkinton•, R.I. 249/H7
Hopland, Calif. 204/B5
Hoppo (Hepu), China 77/G7
Hop River, Conn. 210/F2
Hopwood, Pa. 294/C6
Hoquiam, Wash. 188/B1
Hoquiam, Wash. 310/A3
Horace, Kansas 232/A3
Horace, N. Dak. 282/S6
Horasan, Turkey 63/K2
Horatio, Ark. 202/B3
Horatio, S.C. 296/F3
Horažďovice, Czech Rep. 41/B2
Horche, Spain 33/E2
Horconcitos, Panama 154/F6
Hordaland (co.), Norway 18/E6
Horden, England 13/J4
Hordio, Somalia 115/K1
Hordville, Nebr. 264/G3
Horgen, Switzerland 39/G2
Hořice v Podkrkonoší, Czech Rep. 41/C1
Horicon, Wis. 317/J9
Horine, Mo. 261/M6
Horizon, Sask. 181/F6
Horley, England 13/H8
Hormigüeros, P. Rico 161/A2
Hormoz, Iran 66/J7
Hormoz (isl.), Iran 66/K7
Hormozgan (prov.), Iran 66/J7
Hormuz (str.), Iran 59/G4
Hormuz (str.), Iran 66/K7
Hormuz (str.), Oman 59/G4
Horn (cape) 2/F8
Horn, Austria 41/C2
Horn (cape), Chile 120/C8
Horn (cape), Chile 138/F11
Horn (cape), Iceland 7/B2
Horn (cape), Iceland 21/B1
Horn (head), Ireland 17/E1
Horn (isl.), Miss. 256/G10
Horn (mts.), N.W.T. 187/G3
Horn (riv.), N.W.T. 187/G3
Hornád (riv.), Slovakia 41/F2
Hornaday (riv.), N.W.T. 187/F3
Hornafjördhur (fjord), Iceland 21/D1
Horná Štubňa, Slovakia 41/E2
Horn-Bad Meinberg, Germany 22/C3
Hornbeak, Tenn. 237/C8
Hornbeck, Alberta 182/B3
Hornbeck, La. 238/D4
Hornbrook, Calif. 204/C2
Hornby, N. Zealand 100/D5
Hornby (bay), N.W.T. 187/G3
Hornby Island, Br. Col. 184/H2
Horncastle, England 13/G4
Horncastle, England 10/F4
Horndean, Manitoba 179/E5
Hörnefors, Sweden 18/L5
Hornell, N.Y. 276/E6
Hornepayne, Ontario 175/C3
Hornepayne, Ontario 177/J5
Horner, W. Va. 312/F5
Hornerstown, N.J. 273/E3
Hornersville, Mo. 261/M10
Horní Benešov, Czech Rep. 41/D2
Hornick, Iowa 229/A4
Horní Libina, Czech Rep. 41/D2
Hornings Mills, Ontario 177/D3
Hornitos, Calif. 204/E6
Horn Lake, Miss. 256/D1
Hörnli (mt.), Switzerland 39/G2
Hornos, Falso (cape), Chile 138/F11
Hornsby, N.S. Wales 88/K3
Hornsby, N.S. Wales 97/J3
Hornsby, Tenn. 237/D10
Hornsea, England 13/G4
Hornsea, England 10/F4
Hornslandet (pen.), Sweden 18/K6
Hornslet, Denmark 21/D5
Horns Road, Nova Scotia 168/H2
Hornsund (bay), Norway 18/C2
Horntown, Va. 307/T5
Hořovice, Czech Rep. 41/C2
Horqin Youyi Qianqi (Ulanhot), China 77/K2
Horqueta, Paraguay 144/D3
Horry (co.), S.C. 296/J4
Horse (lake), Calif. 204/E3
Horse (creek), Colo. 208/M5
Horse (creek), Fla. 212/E4
Horse (isls.), Newf. 166/C3
Horse (creek), Oreg. 291/F3
Horse (creek), Wyo. 319/H4
Horse (creek), Wyo. 319/B3
Horse Branch, Ky. 237/H6
Horse Cave, Ky. 237/K6
Horse Chops (head), Newf. 166/D2
Horse Creek, Calif. 204/C2
Horse Creek (res.), Colo. 208/N6
Horse Creek, Wyo. 319/G4
Horsefly, Br. Col. 184/G4
Horsefly (lake), Br. Col. 184/G4
Horsehead (lake), N. Dak. 282/L5
Horsehead (creek), S. Dak. 298/C7
Horseheads, N.Y. 276/G6
Horsens, Denmark 18/F9
Horsens, Denmark 21/C6
Horsens (fjord), Denmark 21/D6
Horseshoe (lake), Ariz. 198/D5
Horseshoe (pt.), Fla. 212/C2
Horseshoe (lake), Manitoba 179/G2
Horse Shoe (pt.), St. Kitts and Nevis 161/C11
Horseshoe (creek), Wyo. 319/G3
Horseshoe Beach, Fla. 212/C2
Horseshoe Bend, Ark. 202/G1
Horseshoe Bend, Idaho 220/B6
Horseshoe Bend Nat'l Mil. Park, Ala. 195/G5
Horseshoe Lake, Ontario 177/E2
Horse Shoe Run, W. Va. 312/G4
Horsetooth (res.), Colo. 208/J1
Horsham, England 10/F5
Horsham, England 13/G6
Horsham, Sask. 181/B5
Horsham, Victoria 97/B5
Horsham, Victoria 88/G7
Hørsholm, Denmark 21/F6
Horšovský Týn, Czech Rep. 41/B2
Horst, Netherlands 27/H6
Horta (dist.), Portugal 33/A1
Horta, Portugal 33/B1
Hortaleza, Spain 33/G4
Horten, Norway 18/D4
Hortense, Ga. 217/J8
Hortensfjord (fjord), Norway 18/G4
Horton, Ala. 195/F2
Horton, Iowa 229/J3
Horton, Kansas 232/G2
Horton, Mich. 250/E6
Horton, Mo. 261/D7
Horton (riv.), N.S. Wales 97/F2
Horton (riv.), N.W.T. 187/F3
Horton, Oreg. 291/D3
Horton Bay, Mich. 250/D3
Hortonia (lake), Vt. 268/A4
Hortonville, Ind. 227/E4
Hortonville, Mass. 249/K5
Hortonville, Wis. 317/J7
Hørve, Denmark 21/E6
Horwich, England 10/G2
Horwich, England 13/G2
Hoschton, Ga. 217/E2
Hoselaw, Alberta 182/E2
Hosenofu (well), Libya 111/D3
Hosford, Fla. 212/B1
Hoshab, Pakistan 68/A3
Hoshab, Pakistan 59/H4
Hoshangabad, India 68/D4
Hoskins, Nebr. 264/G2
Hosmer, Br. Col. 184/K5
Hosmer, S. Dak. 298/L2
Hospental, Switzerland 39/F3
Hospers, Iowa 229/B2
Hospet, India 68/D5
Hospital, Chile 138/G4
Hospital, Ireland 17/E7
Hospitalet, Spain 33/H2
Hosseina, Ethiopia 111/G6
Hosston, La. 238/C1
Hoste (isl.), Chile 120/B8
Hoste (isl.), Chile 138/F11
Hostinné, Czech Rep. 41/C1
Hoswick, Scotland 15/G2
Hot, Thailand 72/C3
Hotan, China 77/B4
Hotan, China 54/K6
Hotan He (riv.), China 77/B4
Hotchkiss, Alberta 182/B1
Hotchkiss, Colo. 208/D5
Hotchkissville, Conn. 210/C2
Hot Creek (range), Nev. 266/E4
Hot Creek (valley), Nev. 266/E4
Hotevilla, Ariz. 198/E3
Hotham (inlet), Alaska 196/F1
Hoting, Sweden 18/K4
Hot Lake, Oreg. 291/K2
Hot Spring (co.), Ark. 202/E5
Hot Springs, Mont. 262/B3
Hot Springs (Truth or Consequences), N. Mex. 274/B5
Hot Springs, N.C. 281/D3
Hot Springs, S. Dak. 188/F2
Hot Springs, S. Dak. 298/C7
Hot Springs, Va. 307/J4
Hot Springs (co.), Wyo. 319/D2
Hot Springs Cove, Br. Col. 184/D5
Hot Springs National Park, Ark. 188/H4
Hot Springs National Park, Ark. 202/D4
Hot Springs Nat'l Park, Ark. 202/D4
Hot Sulphur Springs, Colo. 208/H2
Hottah (lake), N.W.T. 162/E2
Hottah (lake), N.W.T. 187/G3
Hottentot (bay), Namibia 118/A5
Hotton, Belgium 27/G8
Hou, Nam (riv.), Laos 72/D2
Houck, Ariz. 198/F3
Houcktown, Ohio 284/C4
Houffalize, Belgium 27/H8
Houghton, Iowa 229/K7
Houghton, Maine 243/B6
Houghton, Mich. 188/J1
Houghton (co.), Mich. 250/G1
Houghton, Mich. 250/G1
Houghton (lake), Mich. 250/E4
Houghton, N.Y. 276/D6
Houghton, S. Dak. 298/N2
Houghton Lake, Mich. 250/E4
Houghton Lake Heights, Mich. 250/E4
Houghton-le-Spring, England 13/J3
Houhoek, S. Africa 118/F7
Houlka, Miss. 256/G2
Houlton, Maine 188/N1
Houlton, Maine 243/H3
Houlton•, Maine 243/H3
Houlton, Wis. 317/A5
Houma, China 77/H4
Houma, La. 238/J7
Houndé, Burkina Faso 106/D6
Hounslow, England 13/G8
Hounslow, England 10/B5
Hourn, Loch (inlet), Scotland 15/C3
Housatonic (riv.), Conn. 210/C3
Housatonic, Mass. 249/A3
Housatonic (riv.), Mass. 249/A4
House (mt.), Alberta 182/C2
House (riv.), Alberta 182/D2
House, N. Mex. 274/F4
House (range), Utah 304/A4
House Springs, Mo. 261/L6
Houston (co.), Ala. 195/H8
Houston, Ala. 195/D3
Houston, Alaska 196/B1
Houston, Ark. 202/E3
Houston, Br. Col. 184/D3
Houston, Del. 245/S5
Houston, Fla. 212/D1
Houston (co.), Ga. 217/E6
Houston, Ind. 227/E6
Houston (co.), Minn. 255/G7
Houston, Minn. 255/G7
Houston, Miss. 256/G3
Houston, Mo. 261/J8
Houston, Ohio 284/B5
Houston, Pa. 294/B5
Houston (co.), Tenn. 237/F8
Houston (co.), Texas 303/J6
Houston, Texas 303/J2
Houston, Texas 188/G5
Houston, Texas 146/J7
Houston (lake), Texas 303/J8
Houston, U.S. 2/E4
Houston Acres, Ky. 237/K2
Houstonia, Mo. 261/F5
Houston Lake, Mo. 261/O5
Houston Ship (chan.), Texas 303/K2
Hout (bay), S. Africa 118/E6
Houtbaai, S. Africa 118/E6
Houtman Abrolhos (isls.), W. Australia 88/A5
Houtman Abrolhos (isls.), W. Australia 92/A5
Houtrak Polder, Netherlands 27/A4
Houtzdale, Pa. 294/F4
Hov, Denmark 21/D6
Hovd, Mongolia 77/D2
Hovd (Kobdo, Jirgalanta), Mongolia 77/D2
Hovd, Mongolia 54/L5
Hovd Gol (riv.), Mongolia 77/D2
Hove, England 13/G7
Hove, England 10/F5
Hoven, S. Dak. 298/K3
Hovenweep Nat'l Mon., Colo. 208/A8
Hovenweep Nat'l Mon., Utah 304/E6
Hoving, N. Dak. 282/P7
Hovland, Minn. 255/G2
Hövsgöl, Mongolia 77/E1
Hövsgöl Nuur (lake), Mongolia 77/F1
Howar, Wadi (dry riv.), Sudan 111/E4
Howard (pass), Alaska 196/G1
Howard (co.), Ark. 202/C5
Howard, Colo. 208/H6
Howard, Ga. 217/D5
Howard (co.), Ind. 227/E4
Howard (co.), Iowa 229/J2
Howard, Kansas 232/F4
Howard (co.), Md. 245/L4
Howard (co.), Mo. 261/G4
Howard (co.), Nebr. 264/F3
Howard, New Bruns. 170/E2
Howard, Ohio 284/F5
Howard, Pa. 294/G4
Howard, S. Dak. 298/P5
Howard (co.), Texas 303/C5
Howard (creek), Texas 303/C7
Howard, Wis. 317/K6
Howard A. Hanson (res.), Wash. 310/D3
Howard City, Mich. 250/D5
Howard City (Boelus), Nebr. 264/F3
Howard Lake, Minn. 255/D5
Howards Grove-Millersville, Wis. 317/L8
Howards Ridge, Mo. 261/H9
Howardstown, Ky. 237/K5
Howardsville, Va. 307/L5
Howardville, Mo. 261/N9
Howden, England 13/G4
Howe (cape), Australia 87/F9
Howe (sound), Br. Col. 184/K2
Howe, Idaho 220/F6
Howe, Ind. 227/G1
Howe (cape), N.S. Wales 88/J7
Howe (cape), N.S. Wales 97/F5
Howe, Okla. 288/S5
Howe, Texas 303/H4
Howell, Ark. 202/H3
Howell, Ga. 217/F9
Howell, Mich. 250/E6
Howell (co.), Mo. 261/J9
Howell•, N.J. 273/E3
Howell, Tenn. 237/H10
Howell, Utah 304/B2
Howells, Nebr. 264/H3
Howes, S. Dak. 298/E4
Howesville, Ind. 227/C6
Howesville, W. Va. 312/G4
Howey In The Hills, Fla. 212/E3
Howick, N. Zealand 100/C1
Howick, Québec 172/D4
Howick, S. Africa 118/E5
Howison, Miss. 256/F9
Howland, Maine 243/F5
Howland•, Maine 243/F5
Howland (isl.), Pacific 87/J5
Howland Ridge, New Bruns. 170/C2
Howley, Newf. 166/C4
Howlong, N.S. Wales 97/D4
Howrah, India 68/F2
Howrah, India 54/K7
Howser, Br. Col. 184/J5
Hoxeyville, Mich. 250/D4
Hoxie, Ark. 202/H1
Hoxie, Kansas 232/B2
Höxter, Germany 22/C3
Hoxud, China 77/C3
Hoy (isl.), Scotland 15/E2
Hoy (isl.), Scotland 10/E1
Hoy (sound), Scotland 15/E2
Hoyerswerda, Germany 22/F3
Hoylake, England 13/G2
Hoylake, England 10/F2
Hoyland Nether, England 13/J2
Hoyleton, Ill. 222/D5
Hoyos, Spain 33/C2
Hoyran (lake), Turkey 63/D3
Hoyt, Colo. 208/L2
Hoyt, Kansas 232/G2
Hoyt, New Bruns. 170/D3
Hoyt, Okla. 288/R4
Hoyt (peak), Utah 304/C3
Hoyt Lakes, Minn. 255/F3
Hoytsville, Utah 304/C3
Hoytville, Ohio 284/C3
Hozat, Turkey 59/C2
Hozat, Turkey 63/H3
Hradec Králové, Czech Rep. 41/C1
Hranice, Czech Rep. 41/D2
Hrinova, Slovakia 41/E2
Hron (riv.), Slovakia 41/E2
Hronov, Czech Rep. 41/D1
Hrubieszów, Poland 47/F3
Hrušovany, Czech Rep. 41/D2
Hsenwi, Burma 72/C2
Hsipaw, Burma 72/C2
Hsüchang (Xuchang), China 77/H5
Htawgaw, Burma 72/C1
Huacaraje, Bolivia 136/D3
Huacareta, Bolivia 136/C7
Huacaya, Bolivia 136/D7
Huachacalla, Bolivia 136/A6
Huachi, Bolivia 136/D4
Huachi, China 77/G4
Huachinango, Mexico 150/K7
Huachipato, Chile 138/D1
Huacho, Peru 120/B4
Huacho, Peru 128/D8
Huachuca (peak), Ariz. 198/E7
Huachuca City, Ariz. 198/E7
Huacrachuco, Peru 128/D7
Huade, China 77/H3
Huadian, China 77/L3
Hua Hin, Thailand 72/D4
Huahine (isl.), Fr. Poly. 87/L7
Huaibei, China 77/J5
Huaibin, China 77/H5
Huaide (Hwaiteh), China 77/K3
Huaiji, China 77/H7
Huainan, China 77/J5
Huainan, China 54/N6
Huairen, China 77/H4
Huajuapan de León, Mexico 150/L8
Hualaihué, Chile 138/E4
Hualalai (mt.), Hawaii 218/G5
Hualañé, Chile 138/A10
Hualapai (mts.), Ariz. 198/B4
Hualapai (peak), Ariz. 198/B3
Hualapai Ind. Res., Ariz. 198/B3
Hualgayoc, Peru 128/C6
Hualien, China 77/K7
Hualla, Peru 128/F9
Huallaga (riv.), Peru 120/B3
Huallaga (riv.), Peru 128/D5
Huallanca, Ancash, Peru 128/D7
Huallanca, Huánuco, Peru 128/D7
Huallen, Alberta 182/A2
Huamachuco, Peru 128/D6
Huamantla, Mexico 150/N1
Huambo (prov.), Angola 115/C6
Huambo, Angola 102/D6
Huambo, Angola 115/C6
Huambo, Angola 2/K6
Huanaqui, Bolivia 136/A7
Huanay, Bolivia 136/B4
Huancabamba, Peru 128/C5
Huancané, Bolivia 136/B6
Huancané, Peru 128/H10
Huancapi, Peru 128/E9
Huancavelica (dept.), Peru 128/E9
Huancavelica, Peru 120/B4
Huancavelica, Peru 128/E9
Huancayo, Peru 128/E9
Huancayo, Peru 120/B4
Huanchaca, Bolivia 136/B7
Huanchaca, Cerro (mt.), Bolivia 136/B7
Huanchaca, Serranía de (mts.), Bolivia 136/E4
Huanchaco, Peru 128/C7
Huanggang, China 77/J5
Huang He (riv.), China 2/Q4
Huang He (Hwang Ho) (riv.), China 54/N6
Huang He (Ma Qu) (riv.), China 77/F5
Huang He (Yellow) (riv.), China 77/J4
Huangling, China 77/G4
Huangliu, China 77/G8
Huangshi, China 77/J5
Huangzhong, China 77/F4
Huanqueros, Argentina 143/F5
Huanta, Peru 128/E9
Huánuco (dept.), Peru 128/D7
Huánuco, Peru 128/E7
Huánuco, Peru 120/B3
Huanuni, Bolivia 136/B6
Huanuni, Bolivia 120/C4
Huan Xian, China 77/G4
Huapai, N. Zealand 100/B1
Huapí (mts.), Nicaragua 154/E4
Huaquechula, Mexico 150/M2
Huara, Chile 138/B2
Huaral, Peru 128/D8
Huaráz, Peru 128/D7
Huaráz, Peru 120/B3
Huari, Bolivia 136/B6
Huari, Peru 128/D7
Huariaca, Peru 128/E8
Huarina, Bolivia 136/A5
Huarmey, Peru 128/C8
Huarochirí, Peru 128/D9
Huarocondo, Peru 128/F9
Huásabas, Mexico 150/E2
Huasaga (riv.), Peru 128/D4
Huascarán (mt.), Peru 120/B3
Huascarán (mt.), Peru 128/D7
Huasco, Chile 138/A7
Huasco (riv.), Chile 138/A7
Huatabampo, Mexico 150/D3
Huatunas (lag.), Bolivia 136/B3
Huatusco de Chicuellar, Mexico 150/P2
Huauchinango, Mexico 150/L6
Huaura, Peru 128/D8
Huautla de Jiménez, Mexico 150/L7
Huayabamba (riv.), Peru 128/D6
Huaylas, Peru 128/C7
Huayllas, Bolivia 136/C6
Hub, Miss. 256/E8
Hubball, W. Va. 312/B6
Hubbard, Iowa 229/G4
Hubbard (lake), Mich. 250/F4
Hubbard (co.), Minn. 255/D3
Hubbard, Minn. 255/C4
Hubbard, Nebr. 264/H2
Hubbard, Ohio 284/J3
Hubbard, Oreg. 291/A3
Hubbard, Sask. 181/H4
Hubbard, Texas 303/H6
Hubbard Creek (lake), Texas 303/F5
Hubbard Lake, Mich. 250/F4
Hubbards, Nova Scotia 168/D4
Hubbardston•, Mass. 249/F3
Hubbardston, Mich. 250/E5
Hubbardstown, W. Va. 312/A6
Hubbardsville, N.Y. 276/J5
Hubbardton•, Vt. 268/A4
Hubbart (pt.), Manitoba 179/K2
Hubbell, Mich. 250/A1
Hubbell, Nebr. 264/G4
Hubbell Trading Post Nat'l Hist. Site, Ariz. 198/F3
Hub City, Wis. 317/F9
Hubei (Hupei), China 77/H5
Huberdeau, Québec 172/C4
Huber Heights, Ohio 284/B6
Hubert, N.C. 281/P5
Hubertus, Wis. 317/K1
Hubli-Dharwar, India 68/C5
Hubli-Dharwar, India 54/J8
Huch'ang, N. Korea 81/C3
Hückelhoven, Germany 22/B3
Hucknall, England 13/F4
Huddersfield, England 10/G2
Huddersfield, England 13/J2
Huddinge, Sweden 18/H1
Huddleston, Va. 307/K6
Huddy, Ky. 237/S5
Hudiksvall, Sweden 18/K6
Hudson (bay) 162/H3

384 Hudson

Hudson (str.) 162/J3
Hudson (bay), Canada 2/E3
Hudson (bay), Canada 146/K3
Hudson (str.), Canada 146/L3
Hudson, Colo. 208/K2
Hudson, Fla. 212/D3
Hudson, Ill. 222/E3
Hudson, Ind. 227/G1
Hudson, Iowa 229/H4
Hudson, Kansas 232/D3
Hudson, Ky. 237/J5
Hudson•, Maine 243/F5
Hudson (bay), Manitoba 179/K2
Hudson, Md. 245/N6
Hudson, Mass. 249/H3
Hudson•, Mass. 249/H3
Hudson, Mich. 250/E7
Hudson, N.H. 268/E6
Hudson•, N.H. 268/E6
Hudson (co.), N.J. 273/E2
Hudson (riv.), N.J. 273/C1
Hudson, N.Y. 276/N6
Hudson (riv.), N.Y. 276/N7
Hudson, N.C. 281/G3
Hudson (bay), N.W.T. 187/K3
Hudson (str.), N.W.T. 187/L3
Hudson, Ohio 284/H3
Hudson (lake), Okla. 288/R2
Hudson, Ontario 175/B2
Hudson, Ontario 177/G4
Hudson (bay), Ontario 175/D1
Hudson, Québec 172/C4
Hudson (bay), Québec 174/A1
Hudson (str.), Québec 174/F1
Hudson, S. Dak. 298/R7
Hudson, Wis. 317/A6
Hudson, Wyo. 319/D3
Hudson Bay, Sask. 181/J3
Hudson Falls, N.Y. 276/O4
Hudson Hope, Br. Col. 184/F2
Hudson Lake, Ind. 227/D1
Hudsons Bay, Alberta 182/E4
Hudsonville, Mich. 250/D6
Hudspeth (co.), Texas 303/B10
Hudwin (lake), Manitoba 179/G1
Hue, Vietnam 54/M8
Hue, Vietnam 72/E3
Hueco (mts.), N. Mex. 274/D6
Hueco (mts.), Texas 303/B10
Huedin, Romania 45/F2
Huehue, Hawaii 218/G5
Huehuetenango, Guatemala 154/B3
Huehuetlán el Chico, Mexico 150/M2
Huejotzingo, Mexico 150/M1
Huejutla, Mexico 150/K6
Huelma, Spain 33/E4
Huelva (prov.), Spain 33/C4
Huelva, Spain 33/C4
Huelva, Spain 7/D5
Huelva (riv.), Spain 33/C4
Huentelauquén, Chile 138/A8
Huercal-Overa, Spain 33/F4
Huerfano (co.), Colo. 208/K7
Huerfano (riv.), Colo. 208/L7
Huesca (prov.), Spain 33/F1
Huesca, Spain 33/F1
Huéscar, Spain 33/E4
Huetamo, Mexico 150/J7
Huete, Spain 33/E2
Huetter, Idaho 220/B2
Huey, Ill. 222/D5
Hueyotlipan de Hidalgo, Mexico 150/M1
Hueytown, Ala. 195/D4
Huff, N. Dak. 282/J6
Huffman, Ark. 202/L2
Huffton, S. Dak. 298/N2
Huger, S.C. 296/H5
Huggins, Mo. 261/H8
Hugh Butler (lake), Nebr. 264/D4
Hughenden, Alberta 182/E3
Hughenden, Australia 87/E8
Hughenden, Queensland 88/G4
Hughenden, Queensland 95/B4
Hughes, Alaska 196/H1
Hughes, Ark. 202/J4
Hughes (co.), Okla. 288/O4
Hughes, S. Australia 94/A4
Hughes (co.), S. Dak. 298/J5
Hughes (riv.), W. Va. 312/D4
Hughes Springs, Texas 303/K5
Hughestown, Pa. 294/F7
Hughesville, Md. 245/L6
Hughesville, Mo. 261/F5
Hughesville, Pa. 294/J3
Hughson, Calif. 204/E6
Hughton, Sask. 181/D4
Hugh Town, England 13/A8
Hugo, Colo. 208/N4
Hugo, Minn. 255/E5
Hugo, Okla. 288/P7
Hugo (lake), Okla. 288/R6
Hugo Stroessner, Paraguay 144/C4
Hugoton, Kansas 232/A4
Huhehot (Hohhot), China 77/H3
Huiarau (range), N. Zealand 100/F3
Hŭich'ŏn, N. Korea 81/C3
Huila (prov.), Angola 115/B7
Huila (dept.), Colombia 126/C6
Huila (mt.), Colombia 120/B2
Huila, Nevado del (mt.), Colombia 126/C6
Huimanguillo, Mexico 150/N8
Huimin, China 77/J4
Huinca Renancó, Argentina 143/D3
Huining, China 77/G4
Huissen, Netherlands 27/H5
Huitzilán, Mexico 150/O1
Huitzuco de los Figueroa, Mexico 150/K7
Huixcolotla, Mexico 150/N2
Huixtepec, Mexico 150/L8
Huixtla, Mexico 150/N9
Huize, China 77/F6
Huizen, Netherlands 27/G4
Huizhou, China 77/H7
Hulaco, Ala. 195/E2
Hulah (lake), Kansas 232/F5
Hulah, Okla. 288/O1
Hulah (lake), Okla. 288/O1
Hulan, China 77/L2
Hulbert, Mich. 250/D2
Hulbert, Okla. 288/R3
Hulberton, N.Y. 276/D4
Hulett, Wyo. 319/H1
Hulin, China 77/M2
Hull, England 7/E3
Hull, England 10/F4
Hull, England 13/G4
Hull, Fla. 212/E4
Hull, Ga. 217/F2
Hull, Ill. 222/B4
Hull, Iowa 229/A2
Hull (Orono) (isl.), Kiribati 87/J6
Hull•, Mass. 249/E7
Hull, N. Dak. 282/K7
Hull, Que. 162/J6
Hull (co.), Québec 172/B4
Hull, Québec 172/B4
Hulls Cove, Maine 243/G7
Hulopoe (bay), Hawaii 218/G2
Hulopoe Bay, Hawaii 218/H2
Hulst, Netherlands 27/E6
Hultsfred, Sweden 18/K8
Hulun Nur (lake), China 77/J2
Huma, China 77/L1
Humacao (dist.), P. Rico 161/E2
Humacao, P. Rico 161/E2
Humacao, P. Rico 156/G1
Humacao (riv.), P. Rico 161/E2
Huma He (riv.), China 77/K1
Humahuaca, Argentina 143/C1
Humaitá, Bolivia 136/B2
Humaitá, Brazil 132/H10
Humaitá, Brazil 120/C3
Humaitá, Brazil 132/G10
Humaitá, Paraguay 144/C5
Humansdorp, S. Africa 118/C6
Humansville, Mo. 261/E7
Humarock, Mass. 249/M4
Humber (riv.), England 13/G4
Humber (riv.), England 10/G4
Humber (riv.), Newf. 166/C4
Humber (riv.), Ontario 177/J3
Humberside (co.), England 13/G4
Humberto, Argentina 143/F5
Humbird, Wis. 317/E6
Humble, Texas 303/J7
Humble City, N. Mex. 274/F6
Humboldt, Ariz. 198/C4
Humboldt (co.), Calif. 204/B3
Humboldt (bay), Calif. 204/A3
Humboldt (bay), Colombia 126/B4
Humboldt, Ill. 222/E4
Humboldt (co.), Iowa 229/E3
Humboldt, Iowa 229/E3
Humboldt, Kansas 232/G4
Humboldt, Minn. 255/A2
Humboldt, Nebr. 264/J4
Humboldt (co.), Nev. 266/C1
Humboldt, Nev. 266/C2
Humboldt (range), Nev. 266/C2
Humboldt (riv.), Nev. 188/C2
Humboldt (riv.), Nev. 266/E2
Humboldt (sink), Nev. 266/C2
Humboldt (mt.), New Caled. 86/H4
Humboldt, Sask. 162/F5
Humboldt, Sask. 181/F3
Humboldt, S. Dak. 298/P6
Humboldt, Tenn. 237/D9
Humboldt Salt (marsh), Nev. 266/D3
Humbug (mt.), Oreg. 291/C5
Hume, Ill. 222/F4
Hume, Mo. 261/C6
Hume (res.), N.S. Wales 97/D4
Hume, N.Y. 276/D5
Hume, Sask. 181/H6
Hume (lake), Victoria 97/D4
Hume, Va. 307/N3
Humenné, Slovakia 41/G2
Humeston, Iowa 229/G7
Humlum, Denmark 21/B4
Hummelstown, Pa. 294/J5
Hummock (isl.), Tasmania 99/D2
Humnoke, Ark. 202/G4
Humphrey (pt.), Alaska 196/K1
Humphrey, Ark. 202/G5
Humphrey, Idaho 220/F5
Humphrey, Nebr. 264/G3
Humphreys (peak), Ariz. 198/D3
Humphreys, La. 238/J7
Humphreys (co.), Miss. 256/C4
Humphreys, Mo. 261/F2
Humphreys, Okla. 288/H5
Humphreys (co.), Tenn. 237/F8
Humpolec, Czech Rep. 41/C2
Humptulips, Wash. 310/A3
Humptulips (riv.), Wash. 310/B3
Humpty Doo, North. Terr. 93/B2
Húnaflói (bay), Iceland 7/B2
Húnaflói (bay), Iceland 21/B1
Hunan, China 77/H6
Hunchun, China 77/M3
Hundested, Denmark 21/E6
Hundred, W. Va. 312/E3
Hunedoara, Romania 7/G4
Hunedoara, Romania 45/F3
Hünfeld, Germany 22/C3
Hungary 2/K3
Hungary 7/F4
HUNGARY 41
Hunger (mt.), Vt. 268/B3
Hungerford, Queensland 95/B6
Hŭngnam, N. Korea 54/O6
Hungry Horse, Mont. 262/C2
Hungry Horse (res.), Mont. 262/C2
Hungtow (isl.), China 77/K7
Hunjiang, China 77/L3
Hunmanby, England 13/G3
Hunnewell, Kansas 232/E4
Hunnewell, Mo. 261/J3
Hunse (riv.), Netherlands 27/K3
Hunsrück (mts.), Germany 22/B4
Hunstanton, England 13/H5
Hunstanton, England 10/G4
Hunt, Ill. 222/E4
Hunt (co.), Texas 303/H4
Hunt (mt.), Wyo. 319/E1
Hunte (riv.), Germany 22/C2
Hunter, Ark. 202/H3
Hunter (isl.), Br. Col. 184/C4
Hunter (peak), Idaho 220/D3
Hunter, Kansas 232/D2
Hunter, Mo. 261/L9
Hunter (riv.), N.S. Wales 97/F3
Hunter, N.Y. 276/M6
Hunter (mt.), N.Y. 276/M6
Hunter (mts.), N. Zealand 100/A6
Hunter, N. Dak. 282/R5
Hunter, Okla. 288/L1
Hunter (isls.), Tasmania 88/G8
Hunter (isl.), Tasmania 99/A2
Hunter (isls.), Tasmania 99/B2
Hunterdon (co.), N.J. 273/D2
Hunter River, Pr. Edward I. 168/E2
Hunters, Wash. 310/G2
Hunters Creek Village, Texas 303/J1
Hunters Hill, N.S. Wales 88/K4
Hunters Hill, N.S. Wales 97/J3
Huntersville, Ky. 237/L7
Huntersville, Minn. 255/D4
Huntersville, N.C. 281/H4
Huntersville, W. Va. 312/G6
Huntertown, Ind. 227/G2
Hunterville, N. Zealand 100/E3
Hunting (riv.), N.C. 281/H2
Hunting (isl.), S.C. 296/G7
Huntingburg, Ind. 227/D8
Huntingdon, Br. Col. 184/L3
Huntingdon (isl.), Newf. 166/C3
Huntingdon (co.), Pa. 294/F5
Huntingdon, Pa. 294/G5
Huntingdon (co.), Québec 172/C4
Huntingdon, Québec 172/C4
Huntingdon, Tenn. 237/E8
Huntingdon and Godmanchester, England 13/G5
Huntingdon and Godmanchester, England 10/F4
Huntington, Ark. 202/B3
Huntington, Conn. 210/C3
Huntington, England 13/G3
Huntington (co.), Ind. 227/G3
Huntington, Ind. 227/G3
Huntington (lake), Ind. 227/F3
Huntington, Iowa 229/D2
Huntington•, Mass. 249/C4
Huntington (creek), Nev. 266/F2
Huntington, N.J. 273/C2
Huntington, N.Y. 276/R6
Huntington, Oreg. 291/K3
Huntington, Texas 303/K6
Huntington, Utah 304/C4
Huntington (creek), Utah 304/C4
Huntington•, Vt. 268/B3
Huntington, Va. 307/S3
Huntington, W. Va. 188/K3
Huntington, W. Va. 312/A6
Huntington Beach, Calif. 204/C11
Huntington Center, Vt. 268/B3
Huntington Park, Calif. 204/C11
Huntington Station, N.Y. 276/R6
Huntingtown, Md. 245/M6
Hunting Valley, Ohio 284/J9
Huntland, Tenn. 237/J10
Huntleigh, Mo. 261/O3
Huntley, Ill. 222/E1
Huntley, Minn. 255/D7
Huntley, Mont. 262/H5
Huntley, Nebr. 264/E4
Huntley, Wyo. 319/H4
Huntly, N. Zealand 100/E2
Huntly, Scotland 10/E2
Huntly, Scotland 15/F3
Huntoon, Sask. 181/H6
Huntsburg, Ohio 284/H2
Hunts Inlet, Br. Col. 184/B3
Hunts Point, Nova Scotia 168/D5
Hunts Point, Wash. 310/B2
Huntsville, Ala. 188/J4
Huntsville, Ala. 195/E1
Huntsville, Ark. 202/C1
Huntsville, Conn. 210/B1
Huntsville, Ind. 227/F4
Huntsville, Ind. 227/G4
Huntsville, Ky. 237/H6
Huntsville, Mo. 261/H4
Huntsville, Ohio 284/C5
Huntsville, Ontario 177/E2
Huntsville, Ontario 175/E3
Huntsville, Tenn. 237/N8
Huntsville, Texas 303/J7
Huntsville, Utah 304/C2
Huntsville, Wash. 310/G4
Hunucmá, Mexico 150/O6
Hunza (Baltit), Pakistan 68/C1
Huocheng, China 77/B3
Huon (isls.), New Caled. 87/G7
Huon (gulf), Papua N.G. 87/E6
Huon (gulf), Papua N.G. 85/C7
Huon (pen.), Papua N.G. 86/A2
Huon (riv.), Tasmania 99/C5
Huong Khe, Vietnam 72/E3
Huonville-Ranelagh, Tasmania 99/C5
Huoshan, China 77/J5
Huot, Minn. 255/B3
Huo Xian, China 77/H4
Hupei (Hubei), China 77/H5
Hurbanovo, Slovakia 41/E3
Hurd (cape), Ontario 177/C2
Hurdland, Mo. 261/H2
Hurdle Mills, N.C. 281/L2
Hurdsfield, N. Dak. 282/L5
Hure, China 77/K3
Hureidha, Yemen 59/E6
Hurghada, Egypt 111/F2
Hurghada, Egypt 59/B4
Hurlburt, Fla. 212/B6
Hurley, Miss. 256/H9
Hurley, Mo. 261/F9
Hurley, N. Mex. 274/A6
Hurley, N.Y. 276/M7
Hurley, S. Dak. 298/P7
Hurley, Va. 307/D6
Hurley, Wis. 317/F3
Hurleyville, N.Y. 276/L7
Hurlford, Scotland 15/D5
Hurlock, Md. 245/P6
Huron (lake) 146/K5
Huron (lake) 162/H7
Huron, Calif. 204/E7
Huron, Ind. 227/D7
Huron, Kansas 232/G2
Huron (co.), Mich. 250/F5
Huron (bay), Mich. 250/A2
Huron (lake), Mich. 188/K2
Huron (lake), Mich. 250/G4
Huron (riv.), Mich. 250/F6
Huron (co.), Ohio 284/E3
Huron, Ohio 284/E3
Huron (riv.), Ohio 284/E3
Huron (co.), Ontario 177/C4
Huron (lake), Ontario 177/B3
Huron (lake), Ontario 175/D3
Huron, S. Dak. 188/G2
Huron, S. Dak. 298/N5
Huron, Tenn. 237/E9
Huron City, Mich. 250/G4
Huron Mountain, Mich. 250/B2
Huron Park, Ontario 177/C4
Huron River (pt.), Mich. 250/B2
Hurricane, Ala. 195/C9
Hurricane (cliffs), Ariz. 198/B2
Hurricane (mt.), Mont. 262/D2
Hurricane, Utah 304/A6
Hurricane, W. Va. 312/C6
Hurricane Deck, Mo. 261/G6
Hurricane Mills, Tenn. 237/F9
Hurst, Ga. 217/D1
Hurst, Ill. 222/D6
Hurst, Texas 303/F2
Hurst, W. Va. 312/E4
Hurstville, Iowa 229/M4
Hurstville, N.S. Wales 88/K4
Hurstville, N.S. Wales 97/J4
Hurt, Va. 307/K6
Hürth, Germany 22/B3
Hurtsboro, Ala. 195/H6
Hurunui (riv.), N. Zealand 100/D5
Hurup, Denmark 21/B4
Húsavík, Iceland 21/C1
Husher, Wis. 317/L2
Hushpuckena, Miss. 256/C2
Huşi, Romania 45/J2
Husk, N.C. 281/F1
Huskisson, N.S. Wales 97/F4
Huslia, Alaska 196/G1
Huson, Mont. 262/B3
Hussar, Alberta 182/D4
Hustisford, Wis. 317/J9
Hustler, Wis. 317/F8
Hustontown, Pa. 294/F5
Hustonville, Ky. 237/M6
Hustopeče, Czech Rep. 41/D2
Husum, Germany 22/C1
Husum, Sweden 18/L5
Husum, Wash. 310/D5
Hutchins (mt.), N.H. 268/E2
Hutchins, Texas 303/G3
Hutchinson, Kansas 188/G3
Hutchinson, Kansas 232/D3
Hutchinson, Kansas 146/J6
Hutchinson, Minn. 255/D6
Hutchinson (co.), S. Dak. 298/O7
Hutchinson (co.), Texas 303/C2
Hutchinson, W. Va. 312/F4
Huth, Yemen 59/D6
Hutsonville, Ill. 222/F4
Hutt (riv.), N. Zealand 100/C2
Hüttenberg, Austria 41/C3
Hutte Sauvage (lake), Québec 174/E1
Huttig, Ark. 202/F7
Hutto, Texas 303/G7
Hutton, La. 238/D4
Hutton, Md. 245/A3
Huttonsville, W. Va. 312/G5
Hutton Valley, Mo. 261/J9
Huttwil, Switzerland 39/E2
Hutubi, China 77/C3
Huumula, Hawaii 218/H5
Huutokoski, Finland 18/P5
Huwelijkszorg, Suriname 131/C2
Huxford, Ala. 195/D8
Hu Xian, China 77/G5
Huxley, Alberta 182/D4
Huxley, Iowa 229/F5
Huxley, Texas 303/L6
Huy, Belgium 27/G8
Huyton-with-Roby, England 13/G2
Huzgan, Iran 66/F5
Huzhou, China 77/K5
Hvannadalshnúkur (mt.), Iceland 21/C1
Hvar (isl.), Croatia 45/C4
Hvidbjerg, Denmark 21/B4
Hvide Sande, Denmark 21/A6
Hviding, Denmark 21/B7
Hvítá (riv.), Iceland 21/B1
Hwainan (Huainan), China 77/J5
Hwaiteh (Huaide), China 77/K3
Hwange (Wankie), Zimbabwe 118/D3
Hwange (Wankie), Zimbabwe 102/E6
Hwang Ho (riv.), China 54/N6
Hwangju, N. Korea 81/C4
Hwangshih (Huangshi), China 77/J5
Hyak, Wash. 310/D3
Hyalite (peak), Mont. 262/E5
Hyannis, Mass. 249/N6
Hyannis, Nebr. 264/C3
Hyannis Port, Mass. 249/N6
Hyargas, Mongolia 77/D2
Hyargas Nuur (lake), Mongolia 77/D2
Hyas, Sask. 181/J4
Hyattstown, Md. 245/J3
Hyattsville, Md. 245/F4
Hyattville, Wyo. 319/E1
Hybart, Ala. 195/D7
Hybord, Manitoba 179/C1
Hyco (riv.), N.C. 281/L2
Hyco (riv.), Va. 307/K8
Hydaburg, Alaska 196/M2
Hyde, England 13/H2
Hyde, England 10/G2
Hyde, N. Zealand 100/C6
Hyde (co.), N.C. 281/S3
Hyde, Pa. 294/F4
Hyde (co.), S. Dak. 298/K4
Hyden, Ky. 237/P6
Hyden, W. Australia 92/B6
Hyde Park, Mass. 249/C7
Hyde Park, N.Y. 276/N6
Hyde Park, Ontario 177/C4
Hyde Park, Pa. 294/D4
Hyde Park, Utah 304/C2
Hyde Park, Vt. 268/B2
Hyde Park•, Vt. 268/B2
Hyder, Alaska 196/P2
Hyderabad, India 2/N5
Hyderabad, India 68/D5
Hyderabad, India 54/J8
Hyderabad, Pakistan 68/B3
Hyderabad, Pakistan 59/J4
Hyderabad, Pakistan 54/H7
Hydesville, Calif. 204/B3
Hydetown, Pa. 294/C2
Hydeville, Vt. 268/A4
Hydraulic, Br. Col. 184/F4
Hydro, Okla. 288/J3
Hye, Texas 303/F7
Hyères, France 28/G6
Hyères (isls.), France 28/G6
Hyesan, N. Korea 81/D3
Hygiene, Colo. 208/J2
Hyland (riv.), Yukon 187/F3
Hylo, Alberta 182/D2
Hyltebruk, Sweden 18/H8
Hyman, S.C. 296/H4
Hymer, Kansas 232/F3
Hymera, Ind. 227/C6
Hyndman (peak), Idaho 220/D6
Hyndman, Pa. 294/E6
Hyner, Pa. 294/G3
Hynish (bay), Scotland 15/B4
Hyogo (pref.), Japan 81/H7
Hypoluxo, Fla. 212/F5
Hyrra Banda, Cent. Afr. Rep. 115/D2
Hyrum, Utah 304/C2
Hyrynsalmi, Finland 18/Q4
Hysham, Mont. 262/J4
Hythe, Alberta 182/A2
Hythe, Alta. 162/E4
Hythe, England 10/G5
Hythe, England 13/H6
Hythe, Tasmania 99/C5
Hytop, Ala. 195/F1
Hyuga, Japan 81/E7
Hyvinkää, Finland 18/O6

I

Ia Drang (riv.), Vietnam 72/E4
Iaeger, W. Va. 312/C8
Ialomiţa (marshes), Romania 45/J3
Ialomiţa (riv.), Romania 45/H3
Iamonia (lake), Fla. 212/B1
Iantha, Mo. 261/D8
Iar Connacht (dist.), Ireland 17/C5
Iaşi, Romania 7/G4
Iaşi, Romania 45/H2
Iatan, Mo. 261/C4
Iatt (lake), La. 238/E3
Iba, Philippines 85/F4
Iba, Philippines 82/B3
Ibadan, Nigeria 2/K5
Ibadan, Nigeria 102/C4
Ibadan, Nigeria 106/E7
Ibagué, Colombia 126/C5
Ibagué, Colombia 120/B2
Ibaiti, Brazil 135/A3
Ibapah, Utah 304/A3
Ibar (riv.), Yugoslavia 45/E4
Ibaraki (pref.), Japan 81/K5
Ibaraki, Japan 81/J7
Ibarra, Ecuador 128/D2
Ibarra, Ecuador 120/B2
Ibarreta, Argentina 143/D2
Ibb, Yemen 59/D7
Ibbenbüren, Germany 22/B2
'Ibbin, Jordan 65/D3
Iberia (par.), La. 238/G7
Iberia, Mo. 261/H6
Iberia, Ohio 284/E4
Iberia, Peru 128/F5
Iberville (par.), La. 238/H6
Iberville, La. 238/K2
Iberville (co.), Québec 172/D4
Iberville, Québec 172/D4
Iberville, D' (lake), Québec 174/C1
Ibi, Nigeria 106/F7
Ibiá, Brazil 132/E7
Ibibobo, Bolivia 136/D7
Ibicaraí, Brazil 132/G6
Ibicuí (riv.), Brazil 132/C10
Ibicuy, Argentina 143/G6
Ibipetuba, Brazil 132/F5
Ibitinga, Brazil 135/B2
Ibiza, Spain 33/G3
Ibiza (isl.), Spain 7/E5
Ibiza (isl.), Spain 33/G3
Ibo, Bolivia 136/D7
Ibo, Mozambique 118/G2
Ibounzi (mt.), Gabon 115/B4
Ibra, Oman 59/G5
Ibra, Wadi (dry riv.), Sudan 111/D5
Ibrány, Hungary 41/F2
'Ibri, Oman 59/G5
Ibusuki, Japan 81/E8
Içá (riv.), Brazil 120/C3
Içá (riv.), Brazil 132/G9
Ica (dept.), Peru 128/E10
Ica, Peru 128/E10
Ica, Peru 120/B4
Ica (riv.), Peru 128/E10
Icabarú, Venezuela 124/H5
Icabarú (riv.), Venezuela 124/G5
Icacos (pt.), Trin. & Tob. 161/A11
Icaña, Catamarca, Argentina 143/C2
Icaño, Santiago del Estero, Argentina 143/D2
Icard, N.C. 281/G3
Ice Harbor (dam), Wash. 310/G4
İçel (prov.), Turkey 63/F4
İçel (Mersin), Turkey 63/F4
Iceland 2/J2
Iceland 7/C2
Iceland 4/C10
ICELAND 21/B1
Ichang (Yichang), China 77/H5
Ichchapuram, India 68/F5
Ichhapur, India 68/F1
Ichihara, Japan 81/P3
Ichikawa, Japan 81/P2
Ichilo (riv.), Bolivia 136/C5
Ichinohe, Japan 81/K3
Ichinomiya, Japan 81/H6
Ichinoseki, Japan 81/K4
Ichnya, Ukraine 52/D4
Ichoa (riv.), Bolivia 136/C4
Ichoca, Bolivia 136/B5
Ichtegem, Belgium 27/B6
Ichun (Yichun), China 77/L2
Ichuña, Peru 128/G11
Icicle (creek), Wash. 310/E3
Ickesburg, Pa. 294/H5
Icla, Bolivia 136/C6
İçme, Turkey 63/H3
Icó, Brazil 132/G4
Iconium, Mo. 261/E6
Icy (bay), Alaska 196/K3
Icy (cape), Alaska 196/F1
Icy (cape), Alaska 196/K3
Icy (pt.), Alaska 196/L1
Icy (str.), Alaska 196/M1
Ida (co.), Iowa 229/C4
Ida, La. 238/C1
Ida, Mich. 250/F7
Idabel, Okla. 288/S7
Ida Grove, Iowa 229/B4
Idaho 188/D2
IDAHO 220
Idaho (co.), Idaho 220/C4
Idaho, Ohio 284/D7
Idaho (state), U.S. 146/G5
Idaho City, Idaho 220/C6
Idaho Falls, Idaho 146/G5
Idaho Falls, Idaho 188/D2
Idaho Falls, Idaho 220/F6
Idaho Springs, Colo. 208/H3
Idahue, Chile 138/F5
Idalia, Colo. 208/P3
Idalou, Texas 303/C4
Idana, Kansas 232/E2
Idanha, Oreg. 291/E3
Idanha-a-Nova, Portugal 33/C3
Idar-Oberstein, Germany 22/B4
Idaville, Ind. 227/D3
Idaville, Pa. 294/H5
Iddan, Somalia 115/J2
Iddesleigh, Alberta 182/E4
Ide, Japan 81/J7
Ideal, Ga. 217/D6
Ideal, S. Dak. 298/K6
Idehan Murzuk (des.), Libya 111/B2
Idehan Ubari (des.), Libya 111/B2
Idelès, Algeria 106/F4
Ider, Ala. 195/G1
Ider Gol (riv.), Mongolia 77/E2
Idfu, Egypt 111/F3
Idfu, Egypt 59/B5
Idhi (mt.), Greece 45/G8
Idhra, Greece 45/F7
Idi, Indonesia 85/B4
Idil, Turkey 63/J4
Idiofa, D.R. Congo 115/C4
Idlewild, Mich. 250/D5
Idlewild, Tenn. 237/D8
Idleyld Park, Oreg. 291/D4
Idlib (prov.), Syria 63/G5
Idlib, Syria 63/G5
Idna, West Bank 65/B4
Idrigill (pt.), Scotland 15/B3
Idyllwild, Calif. 204/J10
Ie (isl.), Japan 81/N6
Ieper, Belgium 27/B7
Ierápetra, Greece 45/G8
Iet, Somalia 115/H3
Ifakara, Tanzania 115/G5
Ifalik (atoll), Micronesia 87/E5
Ifanadiana, Madagascar 118/H4
Ife, Nigeria 106/E7
Iférouane, Niger 102/C3
Iférouane, Niger 106/F5
Iffley, Sask. 181/C3
Ifni (Sidi Ifni), Morocco 106/B3
Ifni (Sidi Ifni), Morocco 102/B2
Ifugao (prov.), Philippines 82/C2
Igal, Hungary 41/D3
Igara-Paraná (riv.), Colombia 126/D8
Igarapava, Brazil 135/C2
Igarapé-Miri, Brazil 132/D3
Igarka, Russia 4/C5
Igarka, Russia 48/J3
Igarka, Russia 54/K3
Iğdır, Turkey 63/K3
Iggesund, Sweden 18/K6
Igis, Switzerland 39/J3
Igiugig, Alaska 196/G3
Iglesias, Italy 34/B5
Igli, Algeria 106/D2
Igloo, S. Dak. 298/B7
Igloolik, Canada 4/B14
Igloolik, N.W.T. 162/H2
Igloolik, N.W.T. 187/K3
Iglosiatik (isl.), Newf. 166/B2
Ignace, Ont. 162/G6
Ignace, Ontario 175/B3
Ignace, Ontario 177/G5
Ignacio, Calif. 204/H1
Ignacio, Colo. 208/D8
Ignacio Agramonte, Cuba 158/G3
Ignacio de la Llave, Mexico 150/Q2
İğneada (cape), Turkey 63/C2
Igoumenítsa, Greece 45/E6
Igra, Russia 52/H3
Igrim, Russia 48/G3

Jewish Aut. Obl. 387

Jackson•, N.H. 268/E3
Jackson•, N.J. 273/E3
Jackson (bay), N. Zealand 100/B5
Jackson (co.), N.C. 281/C4
Jackson, N.C. 281/P2
Jackson (co.), Ohio 284/E7
Jackson, Ohio 284/E7
Jackson (co.), Okla. 288/H5
Jackson (co.), Oreg. 291/E5
Jackson (creek), Oreg. 291/E5
Jackson, Pa. 294/L2
Jackson, S.C. 296/D5
Jackson (co.), S. Dak. 298/F6
Jackson (co.), Tenn. 237/K8
Jackson, Tenn. 188/J3
Jackson, Tenn. 237/D9
Jackson (co.), Texas 303/H9
Jackson (riv.), Va. 307/J4
Jackson (co.), W. Va. 312/C5
Jackson (co.), Wis. 317/E7
Jackson, Wis. 317/K9
Jackson (lake), Wyo. 188/E2
Jackson, Wyo. 319/B2
Jackson (lake), Wyo. 319/B2
Jackson (peak), Wyo. 319/B2
Jacksonboro, S.C. 296/G6
Jacksonburg, Ind. 227/G5
Jacksonburg, Ohio 284/B6
Jacksonburg, W. Va. 312/E3
Jackson Center, Ohio 284/B5
Jackson Center, Pa. 294/B3
Jackson Junction, Iowa 229/K2
Jackson Lake (res.), Colo. 208/L2
Jacksonport, Ark. 202/H2
Jacksonport, Wis. 317/M6
Jackson's Arm, Newf. 166/C4
Jacksons Gap, Ala. 195/G5
Jackson Springs, N.C. 281/K4
Jacksontown, Ohio 284/F6
Jacksonville, Ala. 195/G3
Jacksonville, Ark. 202/F4
Jacksonville, Fla. 146/K6
Jacksonville, Fla. 188/K4
Jacksonville, Fla. 212/E1
Jacksonville, Ga. 217/G7
Jacksonville, Ill. 222/C4
Jacksonville, Maine 243/J6
Jacksonville, Md. 245/M2
Jacksonville, Mo. 261/G3
Jacksonville, New Bruns. 170/C2
Jacksonville, N.C. 281/O5
Jacksonville, Ohio 284/F7
Jacksonville, Oreg. 291/D5
Jacksonville (Kent), Pa. 294/D4
Jacksonville, Texas 303/J5
Jacksonville, Vt. 268/B6
Jacksonville Beach, Fla. 212/E1
Jacksonville Naval Air Sta., Fla. 212/E1
Jacmel, Haiti 158/C6
Jacmel, Haiti 156/D3
Jacobabad, Pakistan 59/J4
Jacobabad, Pakistan 68/B3
Jacobina, Brazil 120/E4
Jacobina, Brazil 132/F5
Jacob Lake, Ariz. 198/C2
Jacobson, Minn. 255/E4
Jacobstown, N.J. 273/D3
Jacobsville, Mich. 250/A1
Jacobus, Pa. 294/J6
Jacques-Cartier (lake), Québec 172/F2
Jacques-Cartier (mt.), Québec 172/C1
Jacques-Cartier (passage), Québec 174/E3
Jacques-Cartier (riv.), Québec 172/F2
Jacquet (riv.), New Bruns. 170/D1
Jacquet River, New Bruns. 170/E1
Jacquinot (bay), Papua N.G. 86/B2
Jacuípe (riv.), Brazil 132/F5
Jacumba, Calif. 204/J11
Jacupiranga, Brazil 135/B4
Jaddi, Ras (cape), Pakistan 59/H4
Jaddi, Ras (pt.), Pakistan 68/A4
Jade (bay), Germany 22/C2
Jadwin, Mo. 261/K8
Jaén, Peru 128/C5
Jaén (prov.), Spain 33/E4
Jaén, Spain 7/D5
Jaén, Spain 33/E4
Jaffa (cape), S. Australia 94/F7
Jaffna, Sri Lanka 68/E7
Jaffna, Sri Lanka 54/K9
Jaffray, Br. Col. 184/K5
Jaffrey, N.H. 268/C6
Jaffrey•, N.H. 268/C6
Jaffrey Center, N.H. 268/C6
Jafura (des.), Saudi Arabia 59/F5
Jagdalpur, India 68/E5
Jagdaqi, China 77/K1
Jagersfontein, S. Africa 118/D5
Jagfontein, S. Africa 118/G7
Jaghbub (Jarabub), Libya 111/D2
Jagin (riv.), Iran 66/L8
Jagna, Philippines 82/E6
Jagtial, India 68/D5
Jagua, Cuba 158/D2
Jaguaquara, Brazil 132/F6
Jaguara (res.), Brazil 135/C2
Jaguarão, Brazil 132/C11
Jaguariaíva, Brazil 132/D9
Jaguariaíva, Brazil 135/B4
Jaguaribe (riv.), Brazil 132/G4
Jagüey Grande, Cuba 158/D2
Jagüey Grande, Cuba 156/B2
Jahrom, Iran 59/F4
Jahrom, Iran 66/H6
Jaicoa, Cordillera (mts.), P. Rico 161/B1
Jaicós, Brazil 132/F4
Jailolo, Indonesia 85/H5
Jainca, China 77/F4
Jaipur, India 54/J7
Jaipur, India 68/D3
Jaisalmer, India 68/C3
Jajarm, Iran 66/K2
Jajce, Bos. 45/C3
Jajpur, India 68/F4
Jakarta (cap.), Indonesia 2/Q6
Jakarta (cap.), Indonesia 54/M10
Jakarta (cap.), Indonesia 85/H1
Jakin, Ga. 217/C8
Jakobstad, Finland 18/N5
Jakubany, Slovakia 41/F2
Jal, N. Mex. 274/F6
Jala, Mexico 150/G6
Jalacingo, Mexico 150/P1
Jalaid, China 77/K2
Jalalabad, Afghanistan 68/B2
Jalalabad, Afghanistan 59/K3
Jalama, West Bank 65/C3
Jalapa, Guatemala 154/B3
Jalapa, Ind. 227/F3
Jalapa, Nicaragua 154/E4
Jalapa, S.C. 296/D3
Jalapa Enríquez, Mexico 146/J8
Jalapa Enríquez, Mexico 150/P1
Jalbun, West Bank 65/C3
Jaleswar, Nepal 68/F3
Jalgaon, India 68/D4
Jalingo, Nigeria 106/G7
Jalisco (state), Mexico 150/H6
Jalkot, Pakistan 59/K2
Jalna, India 68/D4
Jalo, Libya 111/D2
Jalo (oasis), Libya 111/D2
Jalón (riv.), Spain 33/E2
Jalor, India 68/C3
Jalpa, Mexico 150/H6
Jalpa de Méndez, Mexico 150/N7
Jalpaiguri, India 68/F3
Jalpan, Mexico 150/K6
Jalq, Iran 66/N7
Jáltipan de Morelos, Mexico 150/M8
Jalud, West Bank 65/C3
Jaluit (atoll), Marshall Is. 87/G5
Jam, Iran 66/H7
Jama, Ecuador 128/B3
Jamaica 2/F5
Jamaica 146/L8
JAMAICA 158
JAMAICA 156/C3
Jamaica, Cuba 158/K4
Jamaica (chan.), Haiti 156/C3
Jamaica, Iowa 229/E5
Jamaica (chan.), Jamaica 156/C3
Jamaica, N.Y. 276/N9
Jamaica•, Vt. 268/B5
Jamaica Plain, Mass. 249/C7
Jamaiké, Suriname 131/D4
Jamalpur, Bangladesh 68/F4
Jamalpur, India 68/F3
Jamama, Somalia 115/H3
Jamanota (mt.), Neth. Ant. 161/E10
Jamanxim (riv.), Brazil 132/C4
Jambi, Indonesia 85/C6
Jambi, Indonesia 54/M10
Jambuair (cape), Indonesia 85/B4
James (bay) 162/H5
James (riv.) 188/G2
James (bay), Canada 146/K4
James (isl.), Chile 138/D5
James (peak), Colo. 208/H3
James, Ga. 217/E5
James, Iowa 229/A3
James (pt.), Md. 245/N6
James, Miss. 256/B4
James (lake), N.C. 281/E3
James (riv.), N. Dak. 282/N6
James (bay), Ontario 175/D2
James (bay), Québec 174/A2
James (isl.), S.C. 296/H6
James (riv.), S. Dak. 298/N5
James (riv.), Va. 307/O6
James A. Garfield Nat'l Hist. Site, Ohio 284/G2
James Bay, Ontario 177/E2
Jamesburg, N.J. 273/E3
James City, N.C. 281/R4
James City, Pa. 294/E2
James City (co.), Va. 307/P6
James Creek, Pa. 294/F5
Jameson, Mo. 261/E2
Jameson Park, S. Africa 118/J7
Jamesport, Mo. 261/E3
James Ross (isl.), Ant. 5/C16
James Ross (str.), N.W.T. 162/G1
James Ross (str.), N.W. Terrs. 187/J3
Jamestown, Ala. 195/G2
Jamestown, Ark. 202/G2
Jamestown, Calif. 204/E6
Jamestown, Colo. 208/J2
Jamestown, Ill. 222/D5
Jamestown, Ind. 227/D5
Jamestown, Kansas 232/E2
Jamestown, Ky. 237/L7
Jamestown, La. 238/D2
Jamestown, Miss. 256/E8
Jamestown, Mo. 261/G5
Jamestown, N.Y. 188/L2
Jamestown, N.Y. 276/B6
Jamestown, N.C. 281/K3
Jamestown, N. Dak. 188/G1
Jamestown, N. Dak. 282/N6
Jamestown (dam), N. Dak. 282/N6
Jamestown (res.), N. Dak. 282/N6
Jamestown, Ohio 284/C6
Jamestown, Pa. 294/A3
Jamestown, R.I. 249/J6
Jamestown•, R.I. 249/J6
Jamestown, S. Australia 88/F6
Jamestown, S. Australia 94/F5
Jamestown, S.C. 296/H5
Jamestown, Tenn. 237/M8
Jamestown, Va. 307/P6
Jamestown Nat'l Hist. Site, Va. 307/P6
Jamesville, N.Y. 276/H5
Jamesville, N.C. 281/R3
Jamesville, Va. 307/S5
Jamieson, Fla. 212/B1
Jamieson, Oreg. 291/K3
Jamison, Nebr. 264/E2
Jamison, S.C. 296/F4
Jamma, Somalia 102/G4
Jammerbugt (bay), Denmark 21/C3
Jammu, India 54/J6
Jammu, India 68/D2
Jammu and Kashmir (state), India 68/D2
Jamnagar, India 68/B4
Jamnagar, India 54/H7
Jampur, Pakistan 59/K4
Jämsä, Finland 18/O6
Jamshedpur, India 54/K7
Jamshedpur, India 68/F4
Jämtland (co.), Sweden 18/J5
Jamursba (cape), Indonesia 85/J5
Janakpur, Nepal 68/F3
Jandaq, Iran 66/J3
Jandowae, Queensland 95/D5
Jane, Mo. 261/D9
Jane Lew, W. Va. 312/F4
Janesville, Calif. 204/E3
Janesville, Ill. 222/E4
Janesville, Iowa 229/J3
Janesville, Minn. 255/E6
Janesville (Smithmill), Pa. 294/F4
Janesville, Wis. 188/J2
Janesville, Wis. 317/H10
Janesville-Beloit, Wis. 317/H10
Janetstown, Scotland 15/E2
Janeville, New Bruns. 170/E1
Jánico, Dom. Rep. 158/D5
Janikowo, Poland 47/C2
Janiuay, Philippines 82/D5
Jan Mayen (isl.), Norway 4/B10
Jan Mayen (isl.), Norway 7/D1
Janos, Mexico 150/F1
Jánoshalma, Hungary 41/E3
Jánosháza, Hungary 41/D3
Janów Lubelski, Poland 47/F3
Jansen, Colo. 208/K8
Jansen, Nebr. 264/G4
Jansen, Sask. 181/G4
Jantetelco, Mexico 150/L2
Januária, Brazil 120/E4
Januária, Brazil 132/E6
Janvrin (isl.), Nova Scotia 168/G3
Jaora, India 68/D4
Japan 2/S4
Japan 54/R6
JAPAN 81
Japan (sea) 2/R4
Japan (sea) 54/P6
Japan (sea), Japan 81/G4
Japan (sea), N. Korea 81/G4
Japan (sea), Russia 48/O6
Japan (sea), S. Korea 81/G4
Japurá, Brazil 132/G9
Japurá (riv.), Brazil 120/C3
Japurá (riv.), Brazil 132/G9
Jaquet (pt.), Dominica 161/E5
Jara, Cerrito (mt.), Bolivia 136/F6
Jara (hill), Paraguay 144/C1
Jarabacoa, Dom. Rep. 158/E5
Jarabub, Libya 102/E2
Jarabub, Libya 111/D2
Jaragua, Dom. Rep. 158/D6
Jaraíz de la Vera, Spain 33/D2
Jarales, N. Mex. 274/C4
Jarama (riv.), Spain 33/E2
Jaramillo, Argentina 143/C6
Jarandilla de la Vera, Spain 33/D2
Jarash, Jordan 65/D3
Jarbalo, Kansas 232/G2
Jarbidge (riv.), Idaho 220/C7
Jarbidge, Nev. 266/F1
Jardim, Brazil 132/G4
Jardine, Mont. 262/F5
Jardines de la Reina (arch.), Cuba 158/F3
Jardines de la Reina (arch.), Cuba 156/B2
Jargalant, Mongolia 77/J2
Jari (riv.), Brazil 120/D2
Jari (riv.), Brazil 132/C3
Järna, Sweden 18/G2
Jarnac, France 28/C5
Jaro, Philippines 82/E5
Jarocin, Poland 47/C3
Jaroměř, Czech Rep. 41/C1
Jarosław, Poland 47/F4
Jaroso, Colo. 208/H8
Järpen, Sweden 18/H5
Jarrahdale, W. Australia 88/B3
Jarrahdale, W. Australia 92/B2
Jarratt, Va. 307/O7
Jarrettsville, Md. 245/M2
Jarrow, Alberta 182/E3
Jarrow, England 13/J3
Jarrow, England 10/F3
Jars (plain), Laos 72/D3
Jartai, China 77/G4
Jaruco, Cuba 158/C1
Jarud, China 77/K3
Järvenpää, Finland 18/O6
Jarvie, Alberta 182/D2
Jarvis (isl.), Pacific 87/K6
Jarvisburg, N.C. 281/T2
Jarvisville, W. Va. 312/F4
Järvsö, Sweden 18/K6
Jask, Iran 59/G4
Jask, Iran 54/G7
Jask, Iran 66/K8
Jasło, Poland 47/E4
Jasmin, Sask. 181/H4
Jasmine Estates, Fla. 212/D3
Jason (isls.), Falkland Is. 143/D7
Jason, Ky. 237/O6
Jason, N.C. 281/O4
Jasonville, Ind. 227/C6
Jasper, Ala. 195/D3
Jasper, Alberta 182/B3
Jasper, Alta. 162/E5
Jasper, Ark. 202/D1
Jasper, Fla. 212/D1
Jasper (co.), Ga. 217/E4
Jasper, Ga. 217/D2
Jasper (co.), Ill. 222/E4
Jasper (co.), Ind. 227/C2
Jasper, Ind. 227/D8
Jasper (co.), Iowa 229/G5
Jasper, Mich. 250/E7
Jasper, Minn. 255/B7
Jasper (co.), Miss. 256/F6
Jasper (co.), Mo. 261/D8
Jasper, Mo. 261/D8
Jasper, N.Y. 276/F6
Jasper, Ohio 284/D7
Jasper, Ontario 177/H3
Jasper, Oreg. 291/E3
Jasper (co.), S.C. 296/E6
Jasper, Tenn. 237/K10
Jasper (co.), Texas 303/K7
Jasper, Texas 303/L7
Jasper Nat'l Park, Alberta 182/A3
Jasper Nat'l Park, Alta. 162/E5
Jastrowie, Poland 47/C2
Jastrzębie Zdroj, Poland 47/D3
Jászapáti, Hungary 41/E3
Jászárokszállás, Hungary 41/E3
Jászberény, Hungary 41/E3
Jászfényszaru, Hungary 41/E3
Jászkarajenő, Hungary 41/E3
Jászkisér, Hungary 41/F3
Jászladány, Hungary 41/F3
Jataí, Brazil 120/D4
Jataí, Brazil 132/D7
Jatibonico, Cuba 158/F2
Jatibonico del Sur (riv.), Cuba 158/F3
Játiva, Spain 33/F3
Jaú, Brazil 132/D8
Jaú, Brazil 135/B3
Jauaperi (riv.), Brazil 132/A2
Jauari, Serra (mts.), Brazil 132/C3
Jauco, Cuba 158/K4
Jauf, Saudi Arabia 54/F7
Jauf, Saudi Arabia 59/C4
Jauja, Peru 128/E8
Jaumave, Mexico 150/K5
Jaun, Switzerland 39/D3
Jaunjelgava, Latvia 53/C2
Jaunpur, India 68/E3
Jauri, Iran 66/M6
Java (head), Indonesia 85/C7
Java (isl.), Indonesia 2/Q6
Java (isl.), Indonesia 54/M10
Java (isl.), Indonesia 85/J2
Java (sea), Indonesia 2/Q6
Java (sea), Indonesia 54/M10
Java (sea), Indonesia 85/D6
Java, S. Dak. 298/K3
Java, Va. 307/K7
Javari (riv.), Brazil 132/F9
Jávea, Spain 33/G3
Javier de Viana, Uruguay 145/C1
Jaworzno, Poland 47/B4
Jay, Fla. 212/B5
Jay (co.), Ind. 227/G4
Jay, Maine 243/C7
Jay•, Maine 243/C7
Jay, N.Y. 276/N2
Jay, Okla. 288/S2
Jay•, Vt. 268/C2
Jay (peak), Vt. 268/B2
Jaya, Puncak (mt.), Indonesia 85/K6
Jayanca, Peru 128/B6
Jayapura, Indonesia 85/L6
Jayawijaya (range), Indonesia 85/K6
Jay Creek, North. Terr. 88/E4
Jay Em, Wyo. 319/H3
Jayess, Miss. 256/D8
Jayton, Texas 303/D4
Jayuya, P. Rico 156/G1
Jayuya, P. Rico 161/C2
Jaz Murian, Hamun-e (marsh), Iran 66/L7
Jaz Murian, Hamun-e (marsh), Iran 59/G4
Jean, Nev. 266/F7
Jean, Texas 303/F4
Jean Côté, Alberta 182/B2
Jeanerette, La. 238/G7
Jeanette (bay), Newf. 166/C3
Jean Lafitte, La. 238/K7
Jean Lafitte Nat'l Hist. Park, La. 238/P4
Jean-Marie River, N.W. Terrs. 187/F3
Jeanne Mance, New Bruns. 170/E1
Jeannette, Pa. 294/C5
Jean-Rabel, Haiti 158/B5
Jean-Rabel (pt.), Haiti 158/B5
Jebba, Nigeria 106/E7
Jebel Abyad (plat.), Sudan 111/E4
Jebel Aulia (dam), Sudan 102/F3
Jebel Aulia (dam), Sudan 111/F4
Jebel Dhanna, U.A.E. 59/F5
Jeberos, Peru 128/D5
Jeble, Syria 63/F5
Jedburg, S.C. 296/G5
Jedburgh, Sask. 181/J4
Jedburgh, Scotland 10/E3
Jedburgh, Scotland 15/F5
Jeddah (Jidda), Saudi Arabia 59/C5
Jeddito, Ariz. 198/E3
Jeddo, Mich. 250/G5
Jeddo, Pa. 294/L3
Jeddore (cape), Nova Scotia 168/E4
Jeddore (harb.), Nova Scotia 168/F4
Jędrzejów, Poland 47/E3
Jefara (reg.), Libya 111/B1
Jefara (reg.), Tunisia 106/G2
Jeff, Ala. 195/E1
Jeff, Ky. 237/P6
Jeff Davis (co.), Ga. 217/G7
Jeff Davis (co.), Texas 303/C11
Jeffers, Minn. 255/C6
Jeffers, Mont. 262/E5
Jefferson (co.), Ala. 195/E3
Jefferson, Ala. 195/C6
Jefferson (co.), Ark. 202/G5
Jefferson, Ark. 202/F5
Jefferson (co.), Colo. 208/J3
Jefferson, Colo. 208/H4
Jefferson (co.), Fla. 212/C1
Jefferson (co.), Ga. 217/H4
Jefferson, Ga. 217/F2
Jefferson (co.), Idaho 220/F6
Jefferson (co.), Ill. 222/E5
Jefferson (co.), Ind. 227/G7
Jefferson, Ind. 227/D4
Jefferson (co.), Iowa 229/K6
Jefferson, Iowa 229/E4
Jefferson (co.), Kansas 232/G2
Jefferson (co.), Ky. 237/K4
Jefferson (par.), La. 238/K7
Jefferson•, Maine 243/D7
Jefferson, Md. 245/J3
Jefferson, Mass. 249/G3
Jefferson (co.), Miss. 256/B7
Jefferson (co.), Mo. 261/L6
Jefferson (co.), Mont. 262/D4
Jefferson (riv.), Mont. 262/D5
Jefferson (co.), Nebr. 264/G4
Jefferson•, N.H. 268/D3
Jefferson (mt.), N.H. 268/E3
Jefferson (co.), N.Y. 276/J2
Jefferson, N.Y. 276/L6
Jefferson, N.C. 281/G2
Jefferson (co.), Ohio 284/J5
Jefferson (West Jefferson), Ohio 284/D6
Jefferson, Ohio 284/J2
Jefferson (co.), Okla. 288/L6
Jefferson, Okla. 288/L1
Jefferson (co.), Oreg. 291/F3
Jefferson, Oreg. 291/D3
Jefferson (mt.), Oreg. 291/F3
Jefferson (co.), Pa. 294/D3
Jefferson, Pa. 294/B7
Jefferson, Pa. 294/B6
Jefferson (Codorus), Pa. 294/J6
Jefferson, S.C. 296/G2
Jefferson, S. Dak. 298/S8
Jefferson (co.), Tenn. 237/P8
Jefferson (co.), Texas 303/K8
Jefferson, Texas 303/K5
Jefferson, Va. 307/N5
Jefferson (co.), Wash. 310/B3
Jefferson (co.), W. Va. 312/L4
Jefferson (co.), Wis. 317/J9
Jefferson, Wis. 317/J10
Jefferson City (cap.), Mo. 261/H5
Jefferson City (cap.), Mo. 146/J6
Jefferson City (cap.), Mo. 188/H3
Jefferson City, Mont. 262/E4
Jefferson City, Tenn. 237/P8
Jefferson Davis (par.), La. 238/E6
Jefferson Davis (co.), Miss. 256/E7
Jefferson Heights, La. 238/O4
Jefferson Island, Mont. 262/E5
Jefferson Manor, Va. 307/S3
Jefferson Nat'l Expansion Mem. Nat'l Hist. Site, Mo. 261/R3
Jefferson Proving Ground, Ind. 227/G7
Jeffersonton, Va. 307/N3
Jeffersontown, Ky. 237/L2
Jeffersonville, Ga. 217/F5
Jeffersonville, Ind. 227/F8
Jeffersonville, Ky. 237/O5
Jeffersonville, N.Y. 276/L7
Jeffersonville, Ohio 284/C6
Jeffersonville, Vt. 268/B2
Jeffrey (res.), Nebr. 264/D4
Jeffrey, W. Va. 312/C7
Jeffrey City, Wyo. 319/E3
Jeffrey's, Newf. 166/C4
Jef Jef es Seghin (plat.), Chad 111/D3
Jef Jef es Seghin (plat.), Libya 111/D3
Jega, Nigeria 106/E6
Jegenstorf, Switzerland 39/D2
Jeinemeni, Cerro (mt.), Chile 138/E6
Jeisyville, Ill. 222/D4
Jejuí-Guazú (riv.), Paraguay 144/D4
Jēkabpils, Latvia 52/C3
Jēkabpils, Latvia 53/C2
Jekyll (isl.), Ga. 217/K8
Jeleń, Poland 47/B4
Jelenia Góra (prov.), Poland 47/B3
Jelenia Góra, Poland 47/B3
Jelgava, Latvia 7/G3
Jelgava, Latvia 52/B3
Jelgava, Latvia 53/B2
Jellico, Tenn. 237/N7
Jellico Creek, Ky. 237/N7
Jellicoe, Ontario 177/H5
Jelling, Denmark 21/C6
Jelloway, Ohio 284/F4
Jelm, Wyo. 319/G4
Jelšava, Slovakia 41/F2
Jemaja (isl.), Indonesia 85/D5
Jemappes, Belgium 27/D8
Jember, Indonesia 85/K2
Jemez (riv.), N. Mex. 274/C3
Jemez Canyon (res.), N. Mex. 274/C3
Jemez Pueblo, N. Mex. 274/C3
Jemez Springs, N. Mex. 274/C3
Jeminay, China 77/C2
Jemison, Ala. 195/E5
Jemnice, Czech Rep. 41/C2
Jemseg, New Bruns. 170/D3
Jemtland, Maine 243/G1
Jena, Germany 22/D3
Jena, La. 238/F3
Jenaz, Switzerland 39/J3
Jenbach, Austria 41/A3
Jendouba, Tunisia 106/F1
Jeneponto, Indonesia 85/F7
Jenera, Ohio 284/C4
Jenifer, Ala. 195/G3
Jenin, West Bank 65/C3
Jenison, Mich. 250/D6
Jenkinjones, W. Va. 312/D8
Jenkins (co.), Ga. 217/J5
Jenkins, Ky. 237/R6
Jenkins, Minn. 255/D4
Jenkins, Mo. 261/E9
Jenkinsburg, Ga. 217/E4
Jenkinsville, S.C. 296/E3
Jenkintown, Pa. 294/M5
Jenks, Okla. 288/P2
Jenner, Alberta 182/E4
Jennersdorf, Austria 41/C3
Jennerstown, Pa. 294/D5
Jennie, Ark. 202/H7
Jennie, Suriname 131/C3
Jennings, Ant. & Bar. 161/D11
Jennings, Fla. 212/C1
Jennings (co.), Ind. 227/F7
Jennings, Kansas 232/B2
Jennings, La. 238/E6
Jennings, Md. 245/B2
Jennings, Mich. 250/D4
Jennings, Mo. 261/R2
Jennings, N.S. Wales 97/F1
Jennings, Okla. 288/N2
Jennings Lodge, Oreg. 291/B2
Jenny (creek), Oreg. 291/E5
Jenny Lake, Wyo. 319/B2
Jenny Lind, Calif. 204/C9
Jenny Lind (isl.), N.W.T. 187/H3
Jenolan Caves, N.S. Wales 97/E3
Jenpeg, Manitoba 179/J2
Jensen, Utah 304/E3
Jensen Beach, Fla. 212/F4
Jens Munk (isl.), N.W.T. 162/H2
Jens Munk (isl.), N.W.T. 187/K3
Jepara, Indonesia 85/J2
Jequié, Brazil 120/E4
Jequié, Brazil 132/F6
Jequitinhonha, Brazil 132/F7
Jequitinhonha (riv.), Brazil 120/E4
Jequitinhonha (riv.), Brazil 132/F7
Jerablus, Syria 63/G4
Jerada, Morocco 106/D2
Jerauld (co.), S. Dak. 298/M5
Jérémie, Haiti 156/C3
Jérémie, Haiti 158/A6
Jeremoabo, Brazil 132/G5
Jeremy (riv.), Conn. 210/F2
Jerez, Spain 7/D5
Jerez de García Salinas, Mexico 150/H5
Jerez de la Frontera, Spain 33/C4
Jerez de los Caballeros, Spain 33/C3
Jericho, Ark. 202/K3
Jericho, N.Y. 276/R6
Jericho, Queensland 95/C4
Jericho, Vt. 268/A2
Jericho•, Vt. 268/A2
Jericho, West Bank 65/C4
Jericho Center, Vt. 268/B3
Jerico Springs, Mo. 261/E7
Jeriel, Ky. 237/R4
Jerilderie, N.S. Wales 97/C4
Jerimoth (hill), R.I. 249/G5
Jermyn, Pa. 294/L2
Jermyn, Texas 303/F4
Jerome, Ariz. 198/C4
Jerome, Ark. 202/G7
Jerome (co.), Idaho 220/D7
Jerome, Idaho 220/D7
Jerome, Ill. 222/D4
Jerome, Mo. 261/J7
Jerome, Pa. 294/D5
Jeromesville, Ohio 284/F4
Jerry City, Ohio 284/C3
Jersey, Ark. 202/F7
Jersey (isl.), Chan. Is. 13/E8
Jersey (isl.), Chan. Is. 10/E6
Jersey, Ga. 217/E3
Jersey (co.), Ill. 222/C4
Jersey, Ohio 284/E5
Jersey (bay), Virgin Is. (U.S.) 161/B4
Jersey City, N.J. 188/M2
Jersey City, N.J. 273/B2
Jersey Mills, Pa. 294/H3
Jersey Shore, Pa. 294/H3
Jerseyside, Newf. 166/B3
Jerseytown, Pa. 294/J3
Jersey Village, Texas 303/J1
Jerseyville, Ill. 222/C4
Jerslev, Denmark 21/D3
Jerumenha, Brazil 132/F4
Jerusalem, Ark. 202/E3
Jerusalem (dist.), Israel 65/B4
Jerusalem (cap.), Israel 54/E6
Jerusalem (cap.), Israel 65/C4
Jerusalem (cap.), Israel 59/C3
Jerusalem, Ohio 284/H6
Jervis (inlet), Br. Col. 184/E5
Jervis (mt.), Chile 138/D8
Jervis Bay, Aust. Cap. Terr. 97/F4
Jervois Range, North. Terr. 88/F4
Jesenice, Slovenia 45/A2
Jeseník, Czech Rep. 41/D1
Jeseníky (mts.), Czech Rep. 41/D1
Jesenské, Slovakia 41/F2
Jesi, Italy 34/D3
Jessamine (co.), Ky. 237/M5
Jesse, W. Va. 312/C7
Jessie, N. Dak. 282/O4
Jessieville, Ark. 202/D4
Jessnitz, Germany 22/E3
Jessore, Bangladesh 68/F4
Jessup, Pa. 294/F6
Jesterville, Md. 245/P7
Jesuit Bend, La. 238/K7
Jesup, Ga. 217/J7
Jesup, Iowa 229/J4
Jesús, Paraguay 144/E5
Jesús de Machaca, Bolivia 136/A5
Jesús de Otoro, Honduras 154/C3
Jesús María, Argentina 143/D3
Jesús María (reef), Mexico 150/L4
Jet, Okla. 288/K1
Jetersville, Va. 307/M6
Jetmore, Kansas 232/B3
Jett, Ky. 237/M4
Jette, Belgium 27/B9
Jetts Creek, Ky. 237/O6
Jever, Germany 22/B2
Jevíčko, Czech Rep. 41/D2
Jewel Cave Nat'l Mon., S. Dak. 298/B6
Jewell, Ga. 217/G4
Jewell, Iowa 229/F4
Jewell (co.), Kansas 232/D2
Jewell, Kansas 232/D2
Jewell, Ohio 284/B3
Jewell, Oreg. 291/D2
Jewell Ridge, Va. 307/E6
Jewett, Ill. 222/E4
Jewett, Ohio 284/H5
Jewett, Texas 303/H6
Jewett City, Conn. 210/H2
Jewish Aut. Obl., Russia 48/O5

388 Jeypore

Jeypore, India 68/E5
Jhalawar, India 68/D4
Jhal Jhao, Pakistan 59/H4
Jhal Jhao, Pakistan 68/B3
Jhang Sadar, Pakistan 59/K3
Jhang Sadar, Pakistan 68/C2
Jhansi, India 68/D3
Jharsuguda, India 68/E4
Jhelum (riv.), India 68/C2
Jhelum, Pakistan 68/C2
Jhelum, Pakistan 59/K3
Jhelum (riv.), Pakistan 68/C2
Jhudo, Pakistan 68/B3
Jhunjhunu, India 68/D3
Jialing (riv.), China 54/M6
Jiamusi (Kiamusze), China 77/M2
Ji'an (Kian), China 77/J6
Jiande, China 77/J6
Jiangcheng, China 77/F7
Jiangmen (Kongmoon), China 77/H7
Jiangsu (Kiangsu), China 77/K5
Jiangxi (Kiangsi), China 77/J6
Jiangyou, China 77/G5
Jian'ou, China 77/J6
Jianshi, China 77/H5
Jianshui, China 77/F7
Jianyang, China 77/J6
Jiaohe, China 77/L3
Jiao Xian, China 77/K4
Jiaozuo (Tsiaotso), China 77/H4
Jiashan, China 77/J5
Jia Xian, China 77/H4
Jiaxing (Kashing), China 77/K5
Jiayin, China 77/M2
Jiayu, China 77/H6
Jiayuguan, China 77/E4
Jibaro, Cuba 158/F2
Jibhalanta (Uliastay), Mongolia 77/E2
Jibóia, Brazil 132/G8
Jibou, Romania 45/F2
Jibsh, Ras (cape), Oman 59/G5
Jicarilla, N. Mex. 274/D5
Jicarilla Ind. Res., N. Mex. 274/B2
Jicarón (isl.), Panama 154/F7
Jičín, Czech Rep. 41/C1
Jico, Mexico 150/P1
Jidda, Saudi Arabia 54/E7
Jidda, Saudi Arabia 59/C5
Jiexiu, China 77/H4
Jieyang, China 77/J7
Jifna, West Bank 65/C4
Jigalong Aboriginal Res., W. Australia 88/C4
Jigger, La. 238/G2
Jiggs, Nev. 266/F2
Jiguaní, Cuba 158/H4
Jiguero (pt.), P. Rico 156/F1
Jiguero (pt.), P. Rico 161/A1
Jigüey (bay), Cuba 158/G2
Jigzhi, China 77/F5
Jihlava, Czech Rep. 41/C2
Jihlava (riv.), Czech Rep. 41/D2
Jihočeský (reg.), Czech Rep. 41/C2
Jihomoravský (reg.), Czech Rep. 41/D2
Jijel, Algeria 106/F1
Jijia (riv.), Romania 45/H2
Jijiga, Ethiopia 111/H6
Jijona, Spain 33/F3
Jilemnice, Czech Rep. 41/C1
Jilib, Somalia 115/H3
Jilin (Kirin), China 77/L3
Jilin, China 54/O5
Jilotepec de Abasolo, Mexico 150/K7
Jim (lake), N. Dak. 282/N5
Jimaní, Dom. Rep. 158/C6
Jimbolia, Romania 45/E3
Jimena de la Frontera, Spain 33/D4
Jiménez, Chihuahua, Mexico 150/G3
Jiménez, Coahuila, Mexico 150/J2
Jim Falls, Wis. 317/D5
Jim Hogg (co.), Texas 303/F11
Jimma, Ethiopia 111/G6
Jimma, Ethiopia 102/F4
Jimmy Carter Nat'l Hist. Site, Ga. 217/D6
Jimsar, China 77/C3
Jim Thorpe, Pa. 294/L4
Jim Wells (co.), Texas 303/F10
Jim Woodruff (dam), Ga. 217/C9
Jinan (Tsinan), China 77/J4
Jinan, China 54/N6
Jincheng, China 77/H4
Jinchuan, China 77/F5
Jind, India 68/D3
Jindabyne, N.S. Wales 97/E5
Jindabyne (lake), N.S. Wales 97/E5
Jindalee, N.S. Wales 97/E4
Jindřichův Hradec, Czech Rep. 41/C2
Jingbian, China 77/G4
Jingdezhen (Kingtehchen), China 77/J6
Jingellic, N.S. Wales 97/D4
Jinggu, China 77/F7
Jinghe, China 77/B3
Jinghong, China 77/F7
Jingtai, China 77/F4
Jingxi, China 77/G7
Jing Xian, Anhui, China 77/J5
Jing Xian, Hunan, China 77/H6
Jingyuan, China 77/F4
Jinhua (Kinhwa), China 77/J6
Jining (Tsining), Nei Monggol, China 77/H3
Jining (Tsining), Shandong, China 77/J4
Jinja, Uganda 115/F3
Jinja, Uganda 102/F4
Jinmen (Quemoy) (isl.), China 77/J7
Jinotega, Nicaragua 154/E4
Jinotepe, Nicaragua 154/D5
Jinping, China 77/G6
Jinsha Jiang (Yangtze) (riv.), China 77/E5
Jinshi (Tsingshih), China 77/H6
Jintotolo (chan.), Philippines 82/D5
Jinxi (Chinsi), China 77/K3
Jin Xian, China 77/K4
Jinzhou (Chinchow), China 77/K3
Jinzhou, China 54/N5
Jipijapa, Ecuador 128/B3
Jiran, Ethiopia 111/G6
Jirgalanta (Hovd), Mongolia 77/D2
Jiřkov, Czech Rep. 41/B1
Jish, Israel 65/C1
Jishou, China 77/H6
Jisr esh Shughur, Syria 63/G5
Jiu (riv.), Romania 45/F3
Jiujiang (Kiukiang), China 77/J6
Jiulong, China 77/F6
Jiuquan (Kiuchüan), China 77/E4
Jixi (Kisi), China 77/M2
Jixi, China 54/P5
Ji Xian, China 77/H4
Jizan (Qizan), Saudi Arabia 59/D6
Jizera (riv.), Czech Rep. 41/C1
Joaçaba, Brazil 132/D9
Joachimsthal, Germany 22/E2
Joachín, Mexico 150/Q2
Joana Peres, Brazil 132/D3
Joanico, Uruguay 145/B6
Joanna, S.C. 296/D3
João Monlevade, Brazil 135/E1
João Pessoa, Brazil 120/F3
João Pessoa, Brazil 132/H4
João Pinheiro, Brazil 132/E7
Joaquim Távora, Brazil 135/B3
Joaquin, Texas 303/L5
Joaquín Suárez, Canelones, Uruguay 145/B6
Joaquín Suárez, Colonia, Uruguay 145/B5
Joaquín V. González, Argentina 143/D2
Job (peak), Nev. 266/C3
Job, W. Va. 312/G5
Jobabo, Cuba 158/H3
Jobos, P. Rico 161/D3
Jobos (bay), P. Rico 161/D3
Job's Cove, Newf. 166/D2
Jobstown, N.J. 273/D3
Joch (pass), Switzerland 39/F3
Jódar, Spain 33/E4
Jo Daviess (co.), Ill. 222/C1
Jodhpur, India 54/J7
Jodhpur, India 68/C3
Jodie, W. Va. 312/D6
Jodoigne, Belgium 27/F7
Joe Batt's Arm, Newf. 166/D4
Joensuu, Finland 7/H2
Joensuu, Finland 18/R5
Joes, Colo. 208/O3
Joes (brook), Vt. 268/C3
Joetsu, Japan 81/H5
Joffre, Alberta 182/D3
Jofra (oasis), Libya 111/C2
Jõgeva, Estonia 53/D1
Joggins, Nova Scotia 168/D3
Joghatay, Kuh-e (mts.), Iran 66/K2
Jogjakarta (Yogyakarta), Indonesia 85/J2
Jogues, Ontario 175/D3
Johannesburg, Calif. 204/H8
Johannesburg, Mich. 250/E4
Johannesburg, S. Africa 102/E7
Johannesburg, S. Africa 2/L7
Johannesburg, S. Africa 118/H6
Johanngeorgenstadt, Germany 22/E3
John (riv.), Alaska 196/H1
John (cape), Nova Scotia 168/E3
John D. Rockefeller, Jr., Mem. Pkwy., Wyo. 319/B1
John Day, Oreg. 291/J3
John Day (dam), Oreg. 291/G2
John Day (riv.), Oreg. 291/G2
John Day (dam), Wash. 310/E5
John Day Fossil Beds Nat'l Mon., Oreg. 291/G3
John d'Or Prairie, Alberta 182/B5
Johnetta, Ky. 237/N6
John F. Kennedy Space Center, Fla. 212/F3
John F. Kennedy Nat'l Hist. Site, Mass. 249/C7
John H. Kerr (dam), Va. 307/M7
John Jay (mt.), Br. Col. 184/B2
John Martin (res.), Colo. 208/N6
John Muir Nat'l Hist. Site, Calif. 204/K1
John O'Groats, Scotland 15/E2
John Redmond (res.), Kansas 232/G3
Johns, Miss. 256/E6
Johns, N.C. 281/K5
Johns (isl.), S.C. 296/G6
Johnsburg, Minn. 255/F7
Johnsburg, N.Y. 276/M3
Johnshaven, Scotland 15/F4
Johns Island, S.C. 296/G6
Johnson (co.), Ark. 202/C2
Johnson, Ark. 202/B1
Johnson (isl.), Chile 138/D5
Johnson (co.), Ga. 217/G5
Johnson (creek), Idaho 220/C5
Johnson (co.), Ill. 222/E6
Johnson (co.), Ind. 227/E6
Johnson, Ind. 227/B8
Johnson (co.), Iowa 229/K5
Johnson (co.), Kansas 232/H3
Johnson, Kansas 232/A4
Johnson (co.), Ky. 237/R5
Johnson, Minn. 255/B5
Johnson (co.), Mo. 261/E5
Johnson (co.), Nebr. 264/H4
Johnson, Nebr. 264/J4
Johnson (lake), Nebr. 264/E4
Johnson (co.), Tenn. 237/T7
Johnson (co.), Texas 303/G5
Johnson, Vt. 268/B2
Johnson•, Vt. 268/B2
Johnson (co.), Wyo. 319/F1
Johnsonburg, N.J. 273/D2
Johnsonburg, Pa. 294/E3
Johnson City, N.Y. 276/J6
Johnson City, Oreg. 291/B2
Johnson City, Tenn. 237/S8
Johnson City, Texas 303/F7
Johnson Creek, Wis. 317/J9
Johnsondale, Calif. 204/G8
Johnson Draw (dry riv.), Texas 303/C7
Johnsons (creek), Utah 304/B6
Johnsons Bayou, La. 238/C7
Johnson's Crossing, Yukon 187/E3
Johnsons Landing, Br. Col. 184/J5
Johnsons Point, Ant. & Bar. 161/D11
Johnsonville, Ill. 222/E5
Johnsonville, N.Y. 276/O5
Johnsonville, S.C. 296/J4
Johnston (key), Fla. 212/E7
Johnston, Iowa 229/F5
Johnston (co.), N.C. 281/N4
Johnston (co.), Okla. 288/N6
Johnston (atoll), Pacific 87/K4
Johnston, S.C. 296/D4
Johnston (lakes), W. Australia 88/C6
Johnston, The (lakes), W. Australia 92/C6
Johnston City, Ill. 222/E6
Johnstone (str.), Br. Col. 184/D5
Johnstone, Scotland 10/A1
Johnstone, Scotland 15/B2
Johnstons Station, Miss. 256/D8
Johnstown, Colo. 208/K2
Johnstown, Ireland 17/G6
Johnstown, Nebr. 264/D2
Johnstown, N.Y. 276/M4
Johnstown, N. Dak. 282/R3
Johnstown, Ohio 284/E5
Johnstown, Ontario 177/J3
Johnstown, Pa. 188/L2
Johnstown, Pa. 294/D5
Johnsville, Ark. 202/F7
Johnsville, Md. 245/K2
Johor (Johore) (state), Malaysia 72/D7
Johor, Sungai (riv.), Malaysia 72/F5
Johor Baharu (Johore Bharu), Malaysia 72/F5
Johore (str.), Malaysia 72/E6
Johore Baharu, Malaysia 54/M9
Joice, Iowa 229/G2
Joigny, France 28/E3
Joiner, Ark. 202/K3
Joinville, Brazil 120/E5
Joinville, Brazil 132/D9
Joinville (isl.), Ant. 5/C16
Jojutla de Juárez, Mexico 150/L2
Jokkmokk, Sweden 18/L3
Jökulsá (riv.), Iceland 21/C1
Joli (pt.), Nova Scotia 168/D5
Jolicure, New Bruns. 170/F3
Joliet, Ill. 188/J2
Joliet, Ill. 222/E2
Joliet, Mont. 262/G5
Joliette, N. Dak. 282/R2
Joliette (county), Québec 174/B3
Joliette (co.), Québec 172/C3
Joliette, Québec 172/D3
Jolietville, Ind. 227/E4
Jolley, Iowa 229/D4
Jollytown, Pa. 294/B6
Jolo, Philippines 82/C8
Jolo (isl.), Philippines 85/G4
Jolo (isl.), Philippines 82/C7
Jolon, Calif. 204/D7
Jomalig (isl.), Philippines 82/D3
Jo-Mary (lkes), Maine 243/E4
Jombang, Indonesia 85/K2
Jomda, China 77/E5
Jona, Switzerland 39/G2
Jonacatepec, Mexico 150/M2
Jonava, Lithuania 53/C3
Joncs (plain), Cambodia 72/E5
Joncs (plain), Vietnam 72/E5
Jones, Ala. 195/E5
Jones (isls.), Alaska 196/J1
Jones (co.), Ga. 217/E5
Jones (co.), Iowa 229/L4
Jones, La. 238/G1
Jones, Mich. 250/D7
Jones (co.), Miss. 256/F7
Jones (beach), N.Y. 276/R7
Jones (co.), N.C. 281/P4
Jones (sound), N.W.T. 187/K2
Jones (sound), N.W.T. 146/K2
Jones (sound), N.W.T. 162/M3
Jones, Okla. 288/M3
Jones (co.), S. Dak. 298/H6
Jones, Tenn. 237/C9
Jones (co.), Texas 303/E5
Jonesboro, Ark. 188/H3
Jonesboro, Ark. 202/J2
Jonesboro, Ga. 217/D4
Jonesboro, Ill. 222/D6
Jonesboro, Ind. 227/F4
Jonesboro, La. 238/E2
Jonesboro•, Maine 243/J6
Jonesborough, N. Ireland 17/J3
Jonesborough, Tenn. 237/R8
Jonesburg, Mo. 261/K5
Jones Creek, Texas 303/J9
Jonesdale, Wis. 317/F10
Jones Mills, Ark. 202/E5
Jones Mills, Pa. 294/D5
Jonesport, Maine 243/H6
Jonesport•, Maine 243/H6
Jones Springs, W. Va. 312/K4
Jonestown, Miss. 256/D2
Jonestown, Pa. 294/K5
Jonesville, Alaska 196/B1
Jonesville, Ind. 227/F6
Jonesville, Ky. 237/M3
Jonesville, La. 238/G3
Jonesville, Mich. 250/E6
Jonesville, N.C. 281/H2
Jonesville, S.C. 296/D2
Jonesville, Vt. 268/B3
Jonesville, Va. 307/B7
Jonglei, Sudan 111/F6
Jonglei (canal), Sudan 111/F6
Joniškis, Lithuania 53/B2
Jönköping (co.), Sweden 18/H8
Jönköping, Sweden 18/H8
Jönköping, Sweden 7/F3
Jonquière, Que. 162/J6
Jonquière, Québec 172/F1
Jonquière, Québec 174/C3
Jonuta, Mexico 150/N7
Jonzac, France 28/C5
Joplin, Mo. 261/C8
Joplin, Mo. 146/J6
Joplin, Mo. 188/H3
Joplin, Mont. 262/F2
Joppa, Ala. 195/E2
Joppa, Ill. 222/E6
Joppa, Tenn. 237/O8
Joppatowne, Md. 245/N3
Jorat (mt.), Switzerland 39/C3
Jordan 2/L4
Jordan 54/E6
JORDAN 59/C3
Jordan (dam), Ala. 195/F5
Jordan (lake), Ala. 195/F5
Jordan (creek), Idaho 220/A7
Jordan, Iowa 229/F4
Jordan (riv.), Israel 65/D3
Jordan (riv.), Jordan 65/D3
Jordan, Minn. 255/E6
Jordan, Mont. 262/J3
Jordan, N.Y. 276/H4
Jordan, B. Everett (lake), N.C. 281/M3
Jordan (bay), Nova Scotia 168/C5
Jordan (lake), Nova Scotia 168/C4
Jordan (riv.), Nova Scotia 168/C5
Jordan (creek), Oreg. 291/K5
Jordan, S.C. 296/G4
Jordan (riv.), Utah 304/C3
Jordan Falls, Nova Scotia 168/C5
Jordan River, Sask. 181/H2
Jordan Valley, Oreg. 291/K5
Jorge Montt (isl.), Chile 138/D9
Jorhat, India 68/G3
Jorm, Afghanistan 68/C1
Jorm, Afghanistan 59/K2
Jörn, Sweden 18/M4
Jornada del Muerto (valley), N. Mex. 274/C5
Jorquera (riv.), Chile 138/B6
Jõrva-Jaani, Estonia 53/D1
Jos, Nigeria 106/F7
Jos, Nigeria 102/C4
Jos (plat.), Nigeria 106/F7
Jose Abad Santos, Philippines 82/E8
José Agustín Palacios, Bolivia 136/B3
José Batlle y Ordóñez, Uruguay 145/D4
José Cardel, Mexico 150/Q1
José de San Martín, Argentina 143/B5
José Enrique Rodó, Uruguay 145/B4
José Ignacio (lag.), Uruguay 145/E5
José M. Micheo, Argentina 143/G7
Jose Panganiban, Philippines 82/D3
José Pedro Varela, Uruguay 145/E4
Joseph (lake), Newf. 166/B3
Joseph (lake), Ontario 177/E2
Joseph, Oreg. 291/K2
Joseph (creek), Oreg. 291/K2
Joseph, Utah 304/B5
Joseph Bonaparte (gulf) 88/D2
Joseph Bonaparte (gulf), Australia 87/C7
Joseph Bonaparte (gulf), North. Terr. 93/A3
Joseph Bonaparte (gulf), W. Australia 92/E1
Joseph City, Ariz. 198/E4
Josephine, Ala. 195/C10
Josephine (co.), Oreg. 291/D5
Josephine, Pa. 294/D5
Joshinetsu-Kogen National Park, Japan 81/J5
Joshua (pt.), Conn. 210/E4
Joshua Tree, Calif. 204/J9
Joshua Tree Nat'l Mon., Calif. 204/J10
Jostedal, Norway 18/E6
Jostedalsbreen (glac.), Norway 18/E6
Jost Van Dyke (isl.), Virgin Is. (U.K.) 161/C3
Jost Van Dyke (isl.), Virgin Is. (U.K.) 156/G1
Joubert, S. Dak. 298/M7
Jourdanton, Texas 303/F9
Joure, Netherlands 27/H3
Joussard, Alberta 182/B2
Joux (lake), Switzerland 39/B3
Jovellanos, Cuba 156/B2
Jovellanos, Cuba 158/D1
Joveyn (riv.), Iran 66/K2
Joy, Ill. 222/C2
Joy, Ky. 237/E6
Joyce, La. 238/E3
Joyce, Wash. 310/B2
Joyce's Country (dist.), Ireland 17/B4
Joyo, Japan 81/J7
Juab (co.), Utah 304/A4
Juana Díaz, P. Rico 161/C2
Juan Aldama, Mexico 150/H4
Juan D. Jackson, Uruguay 145/C4
Juan de Fuca (str.) 146/F5
Juan de Fuca (str.), Br. Col. 162/D6
Juan de Fuca (str.), Br. Col. 184/J4
Juan de Fuca (str.), Wash. 188/A1
Juan de Fuca (str.), Wash. 310/A2
Juan de Mena, Paraguay 144/D4
Juan de Nova (isl.), Réunion 102/G6
Juan de Nova (isl.), Réunion 118/G3
Juan Fernández (isls.), Chile 2/E7
Juan Fernández (isls.), Chile 120/B6
Juangriego, Venezuela 124/G2
Juani (isl.), Tanzania 115/G5
Juanita, N. Dak. 282/N4
Juanita, Wash. 310/B1
Juanjuí, Peru 128/D6
Juan L. Lacaze, Uruguay 145/B5
Juan Stuven (isl.), Chile 138/D7
Juárez, Argentina 143/D4
Juárez, Mexico 150/J3
Juazeiro, Brazil 132/G5
Juàzeiro, Brazil 120/E3
Juazeiro do Norte, Brazil 132/F4
Juàzeiro do Norte, Brazil 120/F3
Juba, Sudan 111/F7
Juba, Sudan 102/F4
Jubail, Saudi Arabia 59/F4
Jubba, Saudi Arabia 59/D4
Jubbada Hoose (prov.), Somalia 115/H3
Jubbulpore (Jabalpur), India 68/D4
Jubilee (lake), W. Australia 88/D5
Juby (cape), Morocco 106/B3
Júcar (riv.), Spain 7/D5
Júcar (riv.), Spain 33/F3
Júcaro, Cuba 158/F2
Juchipila, Mexico 150/H6
Juchique de Ferrer, Mexico 150/Q1
Juchitán de Zaragoza, Mexico 150/M8
Jucuarán, El Salvador 154/C4
Jud, N. Dak. 282/N6
Juda, Wis. 317/H10
Judaea (reg.), Israel 65/B5
Judaea (reg.), Jordan 65/C4
Judas (pt.), C. Rica 154/E6
Judenburg, Austria 41/C3
Judibana, Venezuela 124/C2
Judique, Nova Scotia 168/G3
Judith (riv.), Mont. 262/G3
Judith (pt.), R.I. 249/J7
Judith Basin (co.), Mont. 262/F4
Judith Gap, Mont. 262/G4
Judson, Ind. 227/C5
Judson, Minn. 255/D6
Judson, N. Dak. 282/H6
Judsonia, Ark. 202/G3
Judyville, Ind. 227/C4
Juelsminde, Denmark 21/D6
Juhu, India 68/B7
Juichin (Ruijin), China 77/J6
Juigalpa, Nicaragua 154/E4
Juist (isl.), Germany 22/B2
Juiz de Fora, Brazil 120/E5
Juiz de Fora, Brazil 135/E2
Juiz de Fora, Brazil 132/F8
Jujuy (prov.), Argentina 143/C1
Jujuy, Argentina 143/C1
Jujuy, Argentina 120/C5
Jukskei (riv.), S. Africa 118/H6
Julesburg, Colo. 208/P1
Juli, Peru 128/H11
Juliaca, Peru 120/B4
Juliaca, Peru 128/G10
Julia Creek, Queensland 88/G4
Julia Creek, Queensland 95/B4
Juliaetta, Idaho 220/B3
Julian, Calif. 204/J10
Julian, Nebr. 264/J4
Julian, N.C. 281/K3
Julian, Pa. 294/G4
Julian Alps (range), Italy 34/D1
Julianatop (mt.), Suriname 131/C4
Julianehåb (Qaqortoq), Greenl. 4/D12
Julianehåb (Qaqortoq), Greenland 2/G2
Julianehåb (Qaqortoq), Greenland 146/P3
Jülich, Germany 22/B3
Juliette, Ga. 217/E4
Juliff, Texas 303/J3
Julio María Sanz, Uruguay 145/E4
Juliustown, N.J. 273/D3
Jullundur, India 68/D2
Jumbilla, Peru 128/C5
Jumbo, Okla. 288/P6
Jumilla, Spain 33/F3
Jumla, Nepal 68/E3
Jumna (riv.), India 68/E3
Jump (riv.), Wis. 317/E5
Jumpertown, Miss. 256/G1
Jumping Branch, W. Va. 312/E7
Jump River, Wis. 317/E5
Junagadh, India 68/B4
Junaina, Saudi Arabia 59/D5
Juncal, Argentina 143/F6
Juncos, P. Rico 161/E2
Juncos, P. Rico 156/G1
Junction, Ill. 222/E6
Junction, Texas 303/E7
Junction, Utah 304/B5
Junction, W. Va. 312/J4
Junction City, Ark. 202/E7
Junction City, Ga. 217/C5
Junction City, Ill. 222/D5
Junction City, Kansas 232/E2
Junction City, Ky. 237/M5
Junction City, La. 238/E1
Junction City, Mo. 261/M7
Junction City, Ohio 284/F6
Junction City, Oreg. 291/D3
Junction City, Wis. 317/G6
Jundah, Queensland 95/B5
Jundah, Queensland 88/G4
Jundiaí, Brazil 135/C3
Jundiaí, Brazil 132/E8
Juneau (cap.), Alaska 146/E4
Juneau (cap.), Alaska 188/E6
Juneau (cap.), Alaska 196/N1
Juneau, U.S. 4/D16
Juneau, U.S. 2/C3
Juneau (co.), Wis. 317/F8
Juneau, Wis. 317/J9
Juneda, Spain 33/G2
Junee, N.S. Wales 97/D4
June in Winter (lake), Fla. 212/E4
June Lake, Calif. 204/G6
June Park, Fla. 212/F3
Jungar, China 77/H4
Jungfrau (mt.), Switzerland 39/E3
Jungfraujoch, Switzerland 39/E3
Junggar Pendi (desert basin), China 77/C2
Junglei (prov.), Sudan 111/F6
Juniata, Nebr. 264/F4
Juniata (co.), Pa. 294/H4
Juniata (riv.), Pa. 294/G5
Juniata Terrace, Pa. 294/G4
Junín, Argentina 143/F7
Junín, Argentina 120/C6
Junín (dept.), Peru 128/E8
Junín, Peru 128/E8
Junín (lake), Peru 128/E8
Junín de los Andes, Argentina 143/B4
Junior, W. Va. 312/G5
Juniper (mts.), Ariz. 198/C3
Juniper (mt.), Colo. 208/C1
Juniper, Ga. 217/C6
Juniper, New Bruns. 170/C2
Juniper (creek), S.C. 296/H2
Junius, S. Dak. 298/P6
Juniye, Lebanon 63/F5
Junlian, China 77/F6
Juno, Ga. 217/D2
Juno, North. Terr. 93/C5
Juno, Tenn. 237/E9
Juno, Texas 303/C7
Juno Beach, Fla. 212/F5
Junosuando, Sweden 18/N3
Juntura, Oreg. 291/K4
Jun Xian, China 77/H5
Juojärvi (lake), Finland 18/Q5
Jupiter, Fla. 212/F5
Jupiter, N.C. 281/D3
Jupiter Island, Fla. 212/F4
Juquiá, Brazil 135/C4
Jur (riv.), Sudan 111/E6
Jura (dept.), France 28/F4
Jura (mts.), France 28/F4
Jura (isl.), Scotland 10/D3
Jura (isl.), Scotland 15/C5
Jura (sound), Scotland 15/C5
Jura (sound), Scotland 10/D3
Jura (canton), Switzerland 39/D2
Jura (mts.), Switzerland 39/B3
Juradó, Colombia 126/B4
Jurbarkas, Lithuania 53/B3
Jurmala, Latvia 52/B3
Jurmala, Latvia 53/B2
Jurong, Singapore 72/E6
Juruá (riv.), Brazil 120/C3
Juruá (riv.), Brazil 132/G10
Juruá (riv.), Peru 128/F7
Juruena, Brazil 132/B6
Juruena (riv.), Brazil 120/D4
Juruena (riv.), Brazil 132/B5
Juruti, Brazil 132/B3
Jusepín, Venezuela 124/G3
Juskatla, Br. Col. 184/A3
Jussy, Switzerland 39/B4
Justice, Ill. 222/B6
Justice, Manitoba 179/C4
Justice, W. Va. 312/C7
Justiceburg, Texas 303/C5
Justin, Texas 303/F1
Justus, Ohio 284/G4
Jutaí (riv.), Brazil 132/G9
Jüterbog, Germany 22/E3
Jutiapa, Guatemala 154/B3
Jutiapa, Honduras 154/D3
Juticalpa, Honduras 154/D3
Jutland (pen.), Denmark 21/C5
Jutland (pen.), Denmark 18/F9
Jutland, N.J. 273/D2
Juuka, Finland 18/Q5
Juventud (municipio especial), Cuba 158/C2
Juventud (isl.), Cuba 146/K7
Juventud, Isla de la (Pines) (isl.), Cuba 158/B3
Juventud (Pines) (isl.), Cuba 156/A2
Juwara, Oman 59/G6
Ju Xian, China 77/J4
Juye, China 77/J4
Jyderup, Denmark 21/E6
Jylland (Jutland) (pen.), Denmark 21/C5
Jyske Ås (hills), Denmark 21/D3
Jyväskylä, Finland 7/G2
Jyväskylä, Finland 18/O5

K

K2 (mt.) 54/J6
K2 (mt.), Pakistan 68/D1
Kaaawa, Hawaii 218/F1
Kaabong, Uganda 115/F3
Kaala (mt.), Hawaii 218/D1
Kaanapali, Hawaii 218/H2
Kaba (Habahe), China 77/C2
Kaba, Hungary 41/F2
Kabacan, Philippines 82/E7
Kabaena (isl.), Indonesia 85/G7
Kabala, S. Leone 106/B7
Kabale, Uganda 115/E4
Kabalega (falls), Uganda 115/F3
Kabalega Nat'l Park, Uganda 115/F3
Kabalo, D.R. Congo 115/E5
Kabambare, D.R. Congo 115/E4
Kabardin-Balkar Aut. Rep., Russia 48/E5
Kabardin-Balkar Aut. Rep., Russia 52/F6
Kabare, D.R. Congo 115/E4
Kabasalan, Philippines 82/D7
Kabba, Nigeria 106/F7
Kabetogama, Minn. 255/F2
Kabetogama (lake), Minn. 255/E2
Kabinakagami (riv.), Ontario 177/J5
Kabin Buri, Thailand 72/D4
Kabinda, D.R. Congo 115/D5
Kabir Kuh (mts.), Iran 66/E4
Kabompo, Zambia 115/D6
Kabompo (riv.), Zambia 115/D6
Kabong, Malaysia 85/E5
Kabongo, D.R. Congo 115/E5
Kabud Gonbad, Iran 66/L2
Kabul (cap.), Afghanistan 68/B2
Kabul (cap.), Afghanistan 59/J3
Kabul (cap.), Afghanistan 54/H6
Kabul (cap.), Afghanistan 2/N4
Kabul (riv.), Afghanistan 68/C2
Kabul (riv.), Afghanistan 59/K3
Kabul (riv.), Pakistan 68/C2
Kabunda, D.R. Congo 115/E6
Kabwe, Zambia 102/E6
Kabwe, Zambia 115/E6
Kabylia (reg.), Algeria 106/E1
Kachchh (gulf), India 68/B4
Kachchh (reg.), India 68/B4
Kachchh, Rann of (salt marsh), India 68/B4

Kariba 389

Kachhch, Rann of (salt marsh), India 54/H7
Kachchh, Rann of (salt lake), Pakistan 59/K5
Kachchh, Rann of (salt marsh), Pakistan 68/C4
Kachemak (bay), Alaska 196/B2
Kachemak City, Alaska 196/B2
Kachess (lake), Wash. 310/D3
Kachin (state), Burma 72/C1
Kachug, Russia 48/L4
Kaçkar Dağı (mt.), Turkey 63/J2
Kackley, Kansas 232/E2
Kadaň, Czech Rep. 41/B1
Kadan Kyun (isl.), Burma 72/C4
Kadavu (Kandavu) (isl.), Fiji 87/H7
Kadayanallur, India 68/D7
Kadei (riv.), Cameroon 115/C3
Kadei (riv.), Cent. Afr. Rep. 115/C3
Kadei (riv.), Congo 115/C3
Kadıköy, Turkey 63/D6
Kadina, S. Australia 88/F6
Kadina, S. Australia 94/F5
Kadınhanı, Turkey 63/E3
Kadiolo, Mali 106/C6
Kadiri, India 68/D6
Kadirli, Turkey 63/F4
Kadiyevka (Stakhanov), Ukraine 52/E5
Kadmat (isl.), India 68/C6
Kadoka, S. Dak. 298/F6
Kadoma, Japan 81/J7
Kadoma, Zimbabwe 102/E6
Kadoma, Zimbabwe 118/D3
Kadugli, Sudan 111/E5
Kadugli, Sudan 102/E3
Kaduna (state), Nigeria 106/F6
Kaduna, Nigeria 102/C3
Kaduna, Nigeria 106/F6
Kaduna (riv.), Nigeria 106/F7
Kadzherom, Russia 52/J2
Kaech'ŏn, N. Korea 81/B4
Kaédi, Mauritania 106/B5
Kaédi, Mauritania 102/A3
Kaélé, Cameroon 115/B1
Kaena (pt.), Hawaii 218/D1
Kaeo, N. Zealand 100/D1
Kaesŏng, N. Korea 81/C4
Kaf, Saudi Arabia 59/C3
Kafan, Armenia 52/G7
Kafar Kanna, Israel 65/C2
Kaffa (prov.), Ethiopia 111/G6
Kaffrine, Senegal 106/A6
Kafia Kingi, Sudan 111/D6
Kafirévs (cape), Greece 45/G6
Kafr Yasif, Israel 65/C2
Kafue, Zambia 115/E7
Kafue (riv.), Zambia 115/E7
Kafue Nat'l Park, Zambia 115/E6
Kaga, Japan 81/H5
Kaga Bandoro, Cent. Afr. Rep. 115/C2
Kagalaska (isl.), Alaska 196/L4
Kagan, Uzbekistan 48/G6
Kagawa (pref.), Japan 81/G6
Kagawong, Ontario 177/B2
Kagawong (lake), Ontario 177/B2
Kagera (reg.), Tanzania 114/F4
Kagera Nat'l Park, Rwanda 115/F4
Kağıthane, Turkey 63/D6
Kağızman, Turkey 63/K2
Kagoshima (pref.), Japan 81/E8
Kagoshima, Japan 81/E8
Kagoshima, Japan 54/O6
Kagoshima (bay), Japan 81/E8
Kagul, Moldova 52/C5
Kaguyak, Alaska 196/H3
Kahakuloa, Hawaii 218/J1
Kahala, Hawaii 218/D5
Kahala (pt.), Hawaii 218/D1
Kahaluu, Hawaii 218/E2
Kahama, Tanzania 115/F4
Kahana, Hawaii 218/F1
Kahana (bay), Hawaii 218/F1
Kahayan (riv.), Indonesia 85/E6
Kahemba, D.R. Congo 115/C5
Kahiltna (riv.), Alaska 196/B1
Kahlotus, Wash. 310/G4
Kah-Nee-Ta, Oreg. 291/F3
Kahoka, Mo. 261/J2
Kahoolawe (isl.), Hawaii 188/F5
Kahoolawe (isl.), Hawaii 87/L4
Kahoolawe (isl.), Hawaii 218/H3
Kahouanne (isl.), Guadeloupe 161/A6
Kahramanmaraş (prov.), Turkey 63/G4
Kâhta, Turkey 63/H4
Kahuku, Hawaii 218/E1
Kahuku, Hawaii 188/F5
Kahuku (pt.), Hawaii 218/E1
Kahului, Hawaii 218/J2
Kahului, Hawaii 188/F5
Kahului (harb.), Hawaii 218/J1
Kai (isls.), Indonesia 85/J7
Kaiama, Nigeria 106/E7
Kaiapit, Papua N.G. 85/B7
Kaiapoi, N. Zealand 100/D5
Kaibab (plat.), Ariz. 198/C2
Kaibab Ind. Res., Ariz. 198/C2
Kaibito, Ariz. 198/D2
Kaibito (plat.), Ariz. 198/D2
Kaieteur (fall), Guyana 131/B3
Kaifeng, China 77/H5
Kaifeng, China 54/N6
Kaikohe, N. Zealand 100/D1
Kaikoura, N. Zealand 100/D5
Kaikoura (pen.), N. Zealand 100/E5
Kaikoura (range), N. Zealand 100/D5
Kaili, China 77/G6
Kailu, China 77/K3
Kailua (Kailua Kona), Hawaii, Hawaii 218/F5
Kailua, Oahu, Hawaii 218/F2
Kailua (bay), Hawaii 218/F2
Kailua (bay), Hawaii 218/F5
Kailua Kona, Hawaii 218/F5
Kaimana, Indonesia 85/J6
Kaimanawa (range), N. Zealand 100/E3
Kaimu, Hawaii 218/J6
Kaimuki, Hawaii 218/D4
Kainaliu, Hawaii 218/G5
Kainaliu, Hawaii 188/F6
Kainan (bay), Ant. 5/B10
Kaingaroa, N. Zealand 100/E7
Kainji (res.), Nigeria 106/E6
Kaipara (harb.), N. Zealand 100/D2
Kaipara (riv.), N. Zealand 100/A1
Kaiparowits (plat.), Utah 304/C6
Kaipokok (bay), Newf. 166/B2
Kaipokok (riv.), Newf. 166/B3
Kairouan, Tunisia 106/F1
Kairuku, Papua N.G. 85/B7
Kaiser, Mo. 261/G6
Kaiseregg (mt.), Switzerland 39/D3
Kaiserslautern, Germany 22/B4
Kaiserstuhl (mt.), Germany 22/B4
Kaitaia, N. Zealand 100/D1
Kaitangata, N. Zealand 100/C7
Kaitumälv (riv.), Sweden 18/M3
Kaiwi (chan.), Hawaii 218/E6
Kaiyuan, Liaoning, China 77/K3
Kaiyuan, Yunnan, China 77/F7
Kaiyuh (mts.), Alaska 196/G2
Kaizuka, Japan 81/H8
Kajaani, Finland 7/G2
Kajaani, Finland 18/P4
Kajabbi, Queensland 88/G3
Kajabbi, Queensland 95/A4
Kajiado, Kenya 115/G4
Kajok, Sudan 111/E6
Kaka, Cent. Afr. Rep. 115/E2
Kaka, Sudan 111/F5
Kakabeka Falls, Ontario 177/G5
Kakabeka Falls, Ontario 175/B3
Kakamega, Kenya 115/F3
Kake, Alaska 196/M1
Kakhk, Iran 66/L3
Kakhovka, Ukraine 52/D5
Kakhovka (res.), Ukraine 48/D5
Kakhovka (res.), Ukraine 52/D5
Kakinada, India 54/K8
Kakinada, India 68/E5
Kakisa, N.W.T. 187/G3
Kakkiviak (cape), Newf. 166/B1
Kakogawa, Japan 81/G6
Kaktovik, Alaska 196/K1
Kakwa (riv.), Alberta 182/A2
Kalaa-Kebira, Tunisia 106/F1
Kalaallit-Nunaat (Greenland) 2/G2
Kalaallit-Nunaat (Greenland) 4/B12
Kalaallit-Nunaat (Greenland) 146/P2
Kalabahi, Indonesia 85/G7
Kalabo, Zambia 115/D6
Kalach, Russia 52/F4
Kalachinsk, Russia 48/H4
Kalach-na-Donu, Russia 52/F5
Kaladan (riv.), Burma 72/B2
Kaladar, Ontario 177/H3
Kalae, Hawaii 218/G1
Ka Lae (cape), Hawaii 218/G7
Kalahari (des.) 102/E7
Kalahari (des.), Botswana 118/C4
Kalahari (des.), Namibia 118/C4
Kalahari Gemsbok Nat'l Park, S. Africa 118/C5
Kalaheo, Hawaii 218/C2
Kalajoki, Finland 18/N4
Kalajoki (riv.), Finland 18/O4
Kalakan, Russia 48/M4
Kalaloch, Wash. 310/A3
Kalam, Pakistan 68/C1
Kalama, Wash. 310/C4
Kalama (riv.), Wash. 310/C4
Kalámai, Greece 7/G5
Kalámai, Greece 45/F7
Kalamazoo (co.), Mich. 250/D6
Kalamazoo, Mich. 188/J2
Kalamazoo, Mich. 250/D6
Kalamazoo (riv.), Mich. 250/C6
Kalambo (falls), Tanzania 115/F5
Kalambo (falls), Zambia 115/F5
Kalamo, Mich. 250/D6
Kalampáka, Greece 45/E6
Kalamunda, W. Australia 88/B2
Kalan, Turkey 63/H3
Kalao (isl.), Indonesia 85/G7
Kalaoa, Hawaii 218/G5
Kalaotoa (isl.), Indonesia 85/G5
Kalapana, Hawaii 218/J6
Kalasin, Thailand 72/D3
Kalat (Qalat), Afghanistan 68/B2
Kalat (Qalat), Afghanistan 59/J3
Kalat, Pakistan 54/H7
Kalat, Pakistan 59/J4
Kalat, Pakistan 68/B3
Kalaupapa, Hawaii 218/G1
Kalaupapa (pen.), Hawaii 218/H1
Kalaupapa Nat'l Hist. Park, Hawaii 218/H1
Kalávrita, Greece 45/F6
Kalawao (co.), Hawaii 218/G1
Kalbarri, W. Australia 92/A4
Kale, Turkey 63/C4
Kalecik, Turkey 63/E2
Kaleden, Br. Col. 184/H5
Kalegauk (isl.), Burma 72/C4
Kalehe, D.R. Congo 115/E4
Kaleida, Manitoba 179/D5
Kalemie, D.R. Congo 115/E5
Kalemie, D.R. Congo 102/E5
Kalemyo, Burma 72/B2
Kaleva, Mich. 250/C4
Kalevala, Russia 52/D1
Kalewa, Burma 72/B2
Kalgan (Zhangjiakou), China 77/J3
Kalgin (isl.), Alaska 196/B1
Kalgoorlie, Australia 2/R7
Kalgoorlie, W. Australia 88/C6
Kalgoorlie, W. Australia 92/C5
Kalgoorlie-Boulder, W. Australia 92/C5
Kaliakra (cape), Bulgaria 45/J4
Kalianda, Indonesia 85/D7
Kalibo, Philippines 82/D5
Kalida, Ohio 284/B4
Kalihi, Hawaii 218/C4
Kalihi (channel), Hawaii 218/B4
Kalihi (stream), Hawaii 218/C3
Kalihiwai, Hawaii 218/C1
Kalima, D.R. Congo 115/E4
Kalimantan (reg.), Indonesia 85/E5
Kálimnos, Greece 45/H7
Kálimnos (isl.), Greece 45/H7
Kalinga, Queensland 88/K2
Kalinga-Apayao (prov.), Philippines 82/C1
Kalinin (Tver'), Russia 7/H3
Kalinin (Tver'), Russia 48/D4
Kalinin (Tver'), Russia 52/E3
Kaliningrad, Russia 7/G3
Kaliningrad, Russia 48/B4
Kaliningrad, Kaliningrad, Russia 52/B4
Kaliningrad, Moscow Oblast, Russia 52/E3
Kalininsk, Russia 52/F4
Kalinkovichi, Belarus 52/C4
Kalispel Ind. Res., Wash. 310/H2
Kalispell, Mont. 188/C1
Kalispell, Mont. 262/B2
Kalisz (prov.), Poland 47/D3
Kalisz, Poland 7/F3
Kalisz, Poland 47/D3
Kaliua, Tanzania 115/F5
Kalix, Sweden 18/N4
Kalixälv (riv.), Sweden 18/N3
Kalkaska (co.), Mich. 250/D4
Kalkaska, Mich. 250/D4
Kalkfeld, Namibia 118/B4
Kalkfontein, Botswana 118/C4
Kallaste, Estonia 53/D1
Kallavesi (lake), Finland 18/P5
Kallsjö (lake), Sweden 18/H5
Kalmalo, Nigeria 106/F6
Kalmar (co.), Sweden 18/K8
Kalmar, Sweden 7/F3
Kalmar, Sweden 18/K8
Kalmarsund (sound), Sweden 18/K8
Kalmthout, Belgium 27/F6
Kalmuck Aut. Rep., Russia 52/F5
Kalmuck Aut. Rep., Russia 48/E5
Kalmunai, Sri Lanka 68/E7
Kalmykovo, Kazakhstan 48/F5
Kalo, Iowa 229/E4
Kalocsa, Hungary 41/E3
Kalohi (chan.), Hawaii 218/G1
Kaloko-Honokohau Nat'l Hist. Park, Hawaii 218/F6
Kaloli (pt.), Hawaii 218/K5
Kalomo, Zambia 115/E7
Kalona, Iowa 229/K6
Kalpeni (isl.), India 68/C7
Kalpin, China 77/A3
Kalskag, Alaska 196/F2
Kaltag, Alaska 196/G2
Kaltbrunn, Switzerland 39/H2
Kaluaaha, Hawaii 218/H1
Kaluga, Russia 7/H3
Kaluga, Russia 48/D4
Kaluga, Russia 52/E4
Kalumburu Mission, W. Australia 88/D2
Kalumburu Mission, W. Australia 92/D1
Kalundborg, Denmark 21/D6
Kalundborg, Denmark 18/G9
Kalush, Ukraine 52/B5
Kalutara, Sri Lanka 68/D7
Kalvarija, Lithuania 53/B3
Kalvesta, Kansas 232/B3
Kalyan, India 68/C5
Kama, Burma 72/B3
Kama (res.), Russia 52/J3
Kama (riv.), Russia 7/K3
Kama (riv.), Russia 52/H2
Kama, D.R. Congo 115/E4
Kamaiki (pt.), Hawaii 218/H2
Kamaing, Burma 72/C1
Kamaishi, Japan 81/L4
Kamakou (peak), Hawaii 218/H1
Kamakura, Japan 81/O3
Kamakusa, Guyana 131/A3
Kamalino, Hawaii 218/A2
Kamalo, Hawaii 218/H1
Kaman, Turkey 63/E3
Kamaniskeg (lake), Ontario 177/G2
Kamanjab, Namibia 118/A3
Kamaran (isl.), Yemen 59/D6
Kamarang, Guyana 131/A3
Kamarhati, India 68/F1
Kamaria (falls), Guyana 131/B2
Kamas, Utah 304/C3
Kamay, Texas 303/F4
Kambalda, W. Australia 88/C6
Kambalda, W. Australia 92/C5
Kambia, S. Leone 106/B7
Kambove, D.R. Congo 115/E6
Kambove, D.R. Congo 102/E6
Kamchatka (pen.), Russia 2/T3
Kamchatka (pen.), Russia 48/Q4
Kamchatka (pen.), Russia 54/S4
Kamela, Oreg. 291/J2
Kamenets-Podol'skiy, Ukraine 52/C5
Kamenice, Czech Rep. 41/C2
Kamenjak (cape), Croatia 45/A3
Kamenka, Archangel, Russia 52/F1
Kamenka, Penza, Russia 52/F4
Kamen'-na-Obi, Russia 48/H4
Kamenskoye, Russia 48/R3
Kamensk-Shakhtinskiy, Russia 52/F5
Kamensk-Ural'skiy, Russia 48/G4
Kamenz, Germany 22/F3
Kameoka, Japan 81/J7
Kames, Scotland 15/C5
Kamet (mt.), India 68/D2
Kamiah, Idaho 220/B3
Kamienna Góra, Poland 47/B3
Kamień Pomorski, Poland 47/B2
Kamiisco, Japan 81/K3
Kamil, Oman 59/G5
Kamilo (pt.), Hawaii 218/H7
Kamilukuak (lake), N.W.T. 187/H3
Kamina, D.R. Congo 102/E5
Kamina, D.R. Congo 115/D5
Kaminak (lake), N.W.T. 187/J3
Kaminoyama, Japan 81/J4
Kaminuriak (lake), N.W.T. 187/J3
Kamishak (bay), Alaska 196/H3
Kamiyaku, Japan 81/E8
Kamloops, Br. Col. 162/D5
Kamloops, Br. Col. 146/G4
Kamloops, Br. Col. 184/G5
Kamo, Japan 81/J7
Kamoa (riv.), Guyana 131/B5
Kamouraska (co.), Québec 172/H2
Kamouraska, Québec 172/H2
Kamp (riv.), Austria 41/C2
Kampala (cap.), Uganda 2/L5
Kampala (cap.), Uganda 102/F4
Kampala (cap.), Uganda 115/F3
Kampar (riv.), Indonesia 85/C5
Kampar, Malaysia 72/D6
Kampen, Germany 22/C1
Kampen, Netherlands 27/H3
Kampene, D.R. Congo 115/E4
Kampeska (lake), S. Dak. 298/P4
Kamphaeng Phet, Thailand 72/C3
Kampong Cham, Cambodia 54/M8
Kampong Cham, Cambodia 72/E4
Kampong Chhnang, Cambodia 72/D4
Kampong Khleang, Cambodia 72/E4
Kampong Kuala Besut, Malaysia 72/D6
Kampong Saom, Cambodia 72/D5
Kampong Sedenak, Malaysia 72/E5
Kampong Sibuti, Malaysia 85/E5
Kampong Spoe, Cambodia 72/E5
Kampong Thum, Cambodia 72/E4
Kampong Trabek, Cambodia 72/E5
Kampot, Cambodia 72/E5
Kampsville, Ill. 222/C4
Kamptee, India 68/D4
KAMPUCHEA (CAMBODIA) 72
Kampung Baru (Tolitoli), Indonesia 85/G5
Kamrar, Iowa 229/F4
Kamsack, Sask. 162/F5
Kamsack, Sask. 181/K4
Kamsack Beach, Sask. 181/K4
Kamsar, Guinea 106/B6
Kamuela, Hawaii 218/G3
Kamui (cape), Japan 81/K2
Kamyshin, Russia 7/J3
Kamyshin, Russia 48/E4
Kamyshin, Russia 52/F4
Kanaaupscow (riv.), Québec 174/B2
Kanab (creek), Ariz. 198/C2
Kanab (plat.), Ariz. 198/C2
Kanab, Utah 304/B6
Kanab (creek), Utah 304/B7
Kanabec (co.), Minn. 255/E5
Kanaga (isl.), Alaska 196/L4
Kanagawa (pref.), Japan 81/O2
Kanaio, Hawaii 218/J3
Kanairiktok (riv.), Newf. 166/B3
Kanakanak, Alaska 196/G3
Kananaskis, Alberta 182/C4
Kananga, D.R. Congo 115/D5
Kananga, D.R. Congo 102/E5
Kanapou (bay), Hawaii 218/J3
Kanaranzi, Minn. 255/B7
Kanaranzi (creek), Minn. 255/C7
Kanarraville, Utah 304/A6
Kanash, Russia 52/G3
Kanata, Ontario 177/J2
Kanauga, Ohio 284/F8
Kanawha, Iowa 229/F3
Kanawha (co.), W. Va. 312/C6
Kanawha (riv.), W. Va. 312/C5
Kanawha Falls, W. Va. 312/D6
Kanawha Head, W. Va. 312/F5
Kanazawa, Japan 81/H5
Kanazawa, Japan 54/P6
Kanbalu, Burma 72/B2
Kanchanaburi, Thailand 72/C4
Kanchenjunga (mt.), India 68/F3
Kanchenjunga (mt.), Nepal 68/F3
Kanchipuram, India 68/E6
Kanchow (Ganzhou), China 77/H6
Kanchrapara, India 68/F1
Kandahar (Qandahar), Afghanistan 59/J3
Kandahar (Qandahar), Afghanistan 68/B2
Kandahar, Sask. 181/G4
Kanda-Kanda, D.R. Congo 115/D5
Kandalaksha, Russia 7/H2
Kandalaksha, Russia 48/C3
Kandalaksha, Russia 52/D1
Kandalaksha (gulf), Russia 52/D1
Kandangan, Indonesia 85/F6
Kándanos, Greece 45/F8
Kandava, Latvia 53/B2
Kandavu (Kadavu) (isl.), Fiji 87/H7
Kandavu (isl.), Fiji 86/Q11
Kandavu (passage), Fiji 86/Q11
Kander (riv.), Switzerland 39/C2
Kandersteg, Switzerland 39/E4
Kandi, Benin 106/E6
Kandıra, Turkey 63/D2
Kandiyohi (co.), Minn. 255/C5
Kandiyohi, Minn. 255/D5
Kandla, India 68/C4
Kandos, N.S. Wales 97/F3
Kandrach, Pakistan 68/A3
Kandrach, Pakistan 59/H4
Kandukur, India 68/E5
Kandy, Sri Lanka 54/K9
Kandy, Sri Lanka 68/E7
Kane (basin) 4/B13
Kane (co.), Ill. 222/E2
Kane, Ill. 222/C4
Kane, Manitoba 179/E5
Kane (basin), N.W.T. 162/N3
Kane (basin), N.W.T. 187/L2
Kane, Pa. 294/E2
Kane (co.), Utah 304/B6
Kanem (reg.), Chad 111/C5
Kaneohe, Hawaii 218/F2
Kaneohe (bay), Hawaii 218/F2
Kaneohe Bay U.S.M.C. Air Station, Hawaii 218/F2
Kaneville, Ill. 222/E2
Kang, Botswana 118/C4
Kanga, Tanzania 115/G5
Kangaba, Mali 106/C6
Kangal, Turkey 63/G3
Kangan, Iran 59/F4
Kangan, Iran 66/G7
Kangar, Malaysia 72/D6
Kangarilla, S. Australia 94/B8
Kangaroo (isl.), Australia 87/D9
Kangaroo (isl.), S. Australia 88/F7
Kangaroo (isl.), S. Australia 94/E7
Kangaroo Ground, Victoria 97/J4
Kangaruma, Guyana 131/B3
Kangavar, Iran 59/E3
Kangavar, Iran 66/F3
Kangding, China 77/F5
Kangean (isl.), Indonesia 85/F7
Kangean (isls.), Indonesia 85/F7
Kanggye, N. Korea 81/C3
Kanghwa (bay), N. Korea 81/B5
Kanghwa (bay), S. Korea 81/B5
Kangiqsualujuaq, Québec 162/K4
Kangiqsualujuaq, Québec 174/F2
Kangiqsujuaq, Québec 162/J3
Kangiqsujuaq, Québec 174/F1
Kangirsuk, Québec 162/J3
Kangsiruk, Québec 174/F1
Kangley, Ill. 222/E2
Kangnŭng, S. Korea 81/D5
Kango, Gabon 115/B3
Kangrinboqê Feng (mt.), China 77/B5
Kani, Burma 72/B2
Kaniama, D.R. Congo 115/D5
Kanin (pen.), Russia 4/C7
Kanin (pen.), Russia 7/J2
Kanin (pen.), Russia 48/E3
Kanin (pen.), Russia 52/G1
Kaningo, Kenya 115/G4
Kanin Nos (cape), Russia 48/E3
Kanin Nos (cape), Russia 52/F1
Kaniva, Victoria 97/A5
Kanjiža, Yugoslavia 45/D2
Kankaanpää, Finland 18/M6
Kankakee, Ill. 188/J2
Kankakee (co.), Ill. 222/F2
Kankakee, Ill. 222/F2
Kankakee (riv.), Ill. 222/F2
Kankakee (riv.), Ind. 227/C2
Kankan, Guinea 106/C6
Kankan, Guinea 102/B3
Kanker, India 68/E4
Kankossa, Mauritania 102/A3
Kankossa, Mauritania 106/B5
Kannapolis, N.C. 281/H4
Kannata Valley, Sask. 181/G5
Kannauj, India 68/D3
Kano (state), Nigeria 106/F6
Kano, Nigeria 106/F6
Kano, Nigeria 102/C3
Kanon (pt.), Neth. Ant. 161/G9
Kanona, N.Y. 276/F6
Kanonji, Japan 81/F6
Kanopolis, Kansas 232/D3
Kanopolis (lake), Kansas 232/D3
Kanorado, Kansas 232/A2
Kanosh, Utah 304/B5
Kanosh Ind. Res., Utah 304/B5
Kanoya, Japan 81/E8
Kanpur, India 54/K7
Kanpur, India 68/E3
Kanrach, Pakistan 59/H4
KANSAS 188/G3
Kansas, Ala. 195/C3
Kansas, Ill. 222/F4
Kansas (riv.), Kans. 188/G3
Kansas (riv.), Kansas 232/F2
Kansas, Ohio 284/D3
Kansas, Okla. 288/S2
Kansas (state), U.S. 146/J6
Kansas City, Kans. 188/G3
Kansas City, Kansas 232/H2
Kansas City, Mo. 261/P5
Kansas City, Mo. 188/H3
Kansas City, Mo. 146/J6
Kansasville, Wis. 317/L3
Kansk, Russia 48/K4
Kansk, Russia 54/L4
Kansu (Gansu), China 77/E3
Kantishna (riv.), Alaska 196/H2
Kanton (isl.), Kiribati 87/J6
Kantunilkin, Mexico 150/Q6
Kanturk, Ireland 10/B4
Kanturk, Ireland 17/D7
Kanuku (mts.), Guyana 131/B4
Kanuma, Japan 81/J5
Kanye, Botswana 102/E7
Kanye, Botswana 118/C5
Kanzi (cape), Tanzania 115/G5
Kaohsiung, China 77/J7
Kaohsiung, Taiwan 54/N7
Kaokoveld (reg.), Namibia 118/A3
Kaolack, Senegal 106/A6
Kaolack, Senegal 102/A3
Kaoma, Zambia 115/D6
Kao Prawa (mt.), Thailand 72/C3
Kapaa, Hawaii 218/D1
Kapaa, Hawaii 188/E5
Kapaahu, Hawaii 218/J6
Kapaau, Hawaii 218/G3
Kapalama, Hawaii 218/C4
Kapalong, Philippines 82/E7
Kapanga, D.R. Congo 115/D5
Kapchagay, Kazakhstan 48/H5
Kapellen, Belgium 27/E6
Kapenguria, Kenya 115/G3
Kapfenberg, Austria 41/C3
Kapingamarangi (atoll), Micronesia 87/F5
Kapiri Mposhi, Zambia 115/E6
Kapiskau (riv.), Ontario 175/D2
Kapit, Malaysia 85/E5
Kapiti (isl.), N. Zealand 100/E4
Kaplan, La. 238/F6
Kaplice, Czech Rep. 41/C2
Kapoeta, Sudan 111/F7
Kapoho, Hawaii 218/K5
Kapos (riv.), Hungary 41/D3
Kaposvár, Hungary 41/D3
Kapowsin, Wash. 310/C4
Kappa, Ill. 222/D3
Kappl, Austria 41/A3
Kaprun, Austria 41/B3
Kapsan, N. Korea 81/C3
Kapsukas, Lithuania 53/B3
Kapsukas, Lithuania 52/B4
Kapuas (riv.), Indonesia 85/D6
Kapulena, Hawaii 218/H4
Kapunda, S. Australia 94/F6
Kapuskasing, Ont. 162/H6
Kapuskasing, Ontario 175/D3
Kapuskasing, Ontario 177/J5
Kapuskasing (riv.), Ontario 177/J5
Kapuskasing (riv.), Ontario 175/D3
Kapuvár, Hungary 41/D3
Kapydzhik (mt.), Armenia 52/G7
Kara, Russia 48/G3
Kara, Russia 52/L1
Kara (sea), Russia 4/B6
Kara (sea), Russia 48/G2
Kara (sea), Russia 52/K1
Kara (sea), Russia 54/H2
Kara-Bogaz-Gol (gulf), Turkmenistan 48/F5
Karabük, Turkey 63/E2
Karaburun, Turkey 63/B3
Karacabey, Turkey 63/C2
Karaca Dağ (mt.), Turkey 63/H4
Karachay-Cherkess Aut. Obl., Russia 48/E5
Karachay-Cherkess Aut. Obl., Russia 52/F6
Karachayevsk, Russia 52/F6
Karachev, Russia 52/E4
Karachi, Pakistan 2/N4
Karachi, Pakistan 59/J5
Karachi, Pakistan 68/B4
Karachi, Pakistan 54/H7
Karád, Hungary 41/D3
Karad, India 68/C5
Karadağ (mt.), Turkey 59/B2
Karadağ (mt.), Turkey 63/E4
Karadeniz Boğazı (Bosporus) (str.), Turkey 63/C2
Karadeniz Boğazı (Bosporus) (str.), Turkey 59/A1
Karaganda, Kazakhstan 2/N3
Karaganda, Kazakhstan 48/H5
Karaganda, Kazakhstan 54/J5
Karaginskiy (isl.), Russia 48/R4
Karaginskiy (isl.), Russia 54/T4
Karahallı, Turkey 63/C3
Karaikudi, India 68/D7
Karaisalı, Turkey 63/F4
Karaj, Iran 66/G3
Karakalpak Aut. Rep., Uzbekistan 48/G5
Karakax (Kara Kash) (Moyu), China 77/A4
Karakax He (riv.), China 77/A4
Karakelong (isl.), Indonesia 85/H5
Karakhoto (ruins), China 77/F3
Karakoçan, Turkey 63/H3
Karakoram (mts.), India 68/D1
Karakoram (mts.), Pakistan 68/D1
Karakorum (ruins), Mongolia 54/M5
Karakorum (ruins), Mongolia 77/F2
Karaköse, Turkey 59/D2
Karaköse (Ağrı), Turkey 63/K3
Kara-Kum (canal), Turkmenistan 48/F6
Kara-Kum (des.), Turkmenistan 48/F5
Karakuwisa, Namibia 118/B3
Karaman, Turkey 59/B2
Karaman, Turkey 63/E4
Karamanlı, Turkey 63/C4
Karamay, China 77/B2
Karamay, China 54/K5
Karamea, N. Zealand 100/C4
Karamea (bight), N. Zealand 100/C4
Karamiran Shankou (pass), China 77/C4
Karan (state), Burma 72/C3
Karangasem, Indonesia 85/F7
Karanja, India 68/D4
Karapelit, Bulgaria 45/H4
Karapınar, Turkey 63/E4
Karas, Namibia 118/B5
Karasabai, Guyana 131/B4
Karasavey (cape), Russia 4/B6
Karasburg, Namibia 118/B5
Karasjok, Norway 18/O2
Karasu, Turkey 63/D2
Karasu (riv.), Turkey 63/J3
Karasu-Aras (mts.), Turkey 63/J3
Karasuk, Russia 48/H4
Karat, Iran 66/M3
Karataş, Turkey 63/F4
Karataş (cape), Turkey 63/F4
Karatau, Kazakhstan 48/H5
Karathuri, Burma 72/C5
Karatsu, Japan 81/D7
Karawanken (range), Austria 41/C3
Karayaka, Turkey 63/G2
Karayazı, Turkey 63/J3
Karazhal, Kazakhstan 48/H5
Karbala (gov.), Iraq 66/B4
Karbal'a, Iraq 59/D3
Karbala, Iraq 54/F6
Karbal'a, Iraq 66/C4
Karbers Ridge, Ill. 222/E6
Karby, Denmark 21/B4
Karcag, Hungary 41/F3
Kardhítsa, Greece 45/E6
Kärdla, Estonia 53/B1
Karelian Aut. Rep., Russia 48/D3
Karelian Aut. Rep., Russia 52/D2
Karema, Tanzania 115/F5
Karesuando, Sweden 18/M2
Kargasok, Russia 48/J4
Kargı, Turkey 63/F2
Kargil, India 68/D2
Kargopol', Russia 52/E2
Karhula, Finland 18/P6
Kariá, Greece 45/F6
Kariaí, Greece 45/G5
Kariba (lake) 102/E6
Kariba (mt.), Japan 81/K2
Kariba (dam), Zambia 115/E7
Kariba (lake), Zambia 115/E7
Kariba, Zimbabwe 118/D3

390 Kariba

Kariba (dam), Zimbabwe 118/D3
Kariba (lake), Zimbabwe 118/D3
Karibib, Namibia 118/B4
Karikal, India 68/E6
Karikari (cape), N. Zealand 100/D1
Karima, Sudan 59/B6
Karima, Sudan 111/F4
Karimata (arch.), Indonesia 85/D6
Karimata (isl.), Indonesia 85/D6
Karimata (str.), Indonesia 85/D6
Karimunjawa (isls.), Indonesia 85/J1
Karin, Somalia 115/J1
Karis, Finland 18/N6
Karise, Denmark 21/F7
Karisimbi (mt.), Rwanda 115/E4
Karisimbi (mt.), D.R. Congo 115/E4
Káristos, Greece 45/G6
Kariz, Iran 66/M3
Karjaa (Karis), Finland 18/N6
Karkabat, Eritrea 111/G4
Karkal, India 68/C6
Karkar (isl.), Papua N.G. 85/B6
Karkas, Kuh-e (mt.), Iran 66/G4
Karkheh (riv.), Iran 66/E4
Karkkila, Finland 18/N6
Karkur-Pardes Hanna, Israel 65/C3
Karlıova, Turkey 63/J3
Karlö (Hailuoto) (isl.), Finland 18/O4
Karlovac, Croatia 45/B3
Karlovo, Bulgaria 45/G4
Karlovy Vary, Czech Rep. 41/B1
Karlshamn, Sweden 18/J8
Karlskoga, Sweden 18/J7
Karlskrona, Sweden 18/J8
Karlsruhe, N. Dak. 282/J3
Karlsruhe, Germany 7/E4
Karlsruhe, Germany 22/C4
Karlstad, Germany 22/C4
Karlstad, Minn. 255/B2
Karlstad, Sweden 7/F3
Karlstad, Sweden 18/H7
Karluk, Alaska 196/H3
Karnak (El Karnak), Egypt 111/F2
Karnak, Ill. 222/E6
Karnak, N. Dak. 282/O5
Karnal, India 68/D3
Karnataka (state), India 68/D6
Karnes (co.), Texas 303/G9
Karnes City, Texas 303/G9
Karnobat, Bulgaria 45/H4
Karns, Tenn. 237/N9
Karns City, Pa. 294/C4
Karonga, Malawi 115/F5
Karora, Sudan 111/G4
Karoro, N. Zealand 100/C5
Karosa, Indonesia 85/F6
Karpakora, N.S. Wales 97/B3
Kárpathos, Greece 45/H8
Kárpathos (isl.), Greece 45/H8
Karpenísion, Greece 45/E6
Karpinsk, Russia 48/F4
Karratha, W. Australia 88/B4
Karratha, W. Australia 92/B3
Kars, Ontario 177/J2
Kars (prov.), Turkey 63/K2
Kars, Turkey 59/D1
Kars, Turkey 63/K2
Kārsava, Latvia 53/D2
Karshi, Uzbekistan 48/G6
Karşıyaka, Turkey 63/B3
Karskiye Vorota (str.), Russia 4/B7
Karskiye Vorota (str.), Russia 48/F2
Karskiye Vorota (str.), Russia 52/J1
Kartal, Turkey 63/D6
Kartaly, Russia 48/G4
Karthaus, Pa. 294/F3
Kartuzy, Poland 47/C1
Karumba, Queensland 88/G3
Karumba, Queensland 95/B3
Karun (riv.), Iran 59/E3
Karun (riv.), Iran 66/F5
Karunjie, W. Australia 92/D2
Karunki, Finland 18/O4
Karup, Denmark 21/C5
Karval, Colo. 208/N5
Karviná, Czech Rep. 41/E2
Karwar, India 68/C6
Kaş, Turkey 63/C4
Kasaan, Alaska 196/N2
Kasabonika, Ontario 175/C2
Kasai (riv.) 102/E5
Kasai (riv.), Angola 115/D5
Kasai (riv.), D.R. Congo 115/C4
Kasai-Occidental (prov.), D.R. Congo 115/D4
Kasai-Oriental (prov.), D.R. Congo 115/D5
Kasaji, D.R. Congo 115/D6
Kasama, Zambia 102/F6
Kasama, Zambia 115/F6
Kasane, Botswana 118/D3
Kasanga, Tanzania 115/F5
Kasanga, Tanzania 102/F5
Kasangulu, D.R. Congo 115/C4
Kasar, Ras (cape), Ethiopia 111/G4
Kasar, Ras (cape), Sudan 111/G4
Kasar, Ras (cape), Sudan 59/C6
Kasaragod, India 68/C6
Kasba (lake), N.W.T. 162/F3
Kasba (lake), N.W.T. 187/H3
Kasbeer, Ill. 222/D2
Kaseda, Japan 81/D8
Kasempa, Zambia 115/E6
Kasenga, D.R. Congo 115/E6
Kasenyi, D.R. Congo 115/E3
Kasese, Uganda 115/F3
Kasese, D.R. Congo 115/E4
Kasganj, India 68/D3
Kashabowie, Ontario 177/G5
Kashaf Rud (riv.), Iran 66/M2
Kashan, Iran 59/F3
Kashan, Iran 66/G3
Kashechewan, Ontario 175/D2
Kashegelok, Alaska 196/G2
Kashi, China 77/A4
Kashi, China 54/J6
Kashihara, Japan 81/J8
Kashin, Russia 52/E3
Kashing (Jiaxing), China 77/K5
Kashiwa, Japan 81/P2
Kashiwara, Japan 81/J8
Kashiwazaki, Japan 81/J5
Kashmar, Iran 66/L3
Kashmar, Iran 59/G2
Kashmor, Pakistan 68/C3
Kashunuk (riv.), Alaska 196/F2
Kasigluk, Alaska 196/F2
Kasilof, Alaska 196/B1
Kasimov, Russia 52/F4
Kaskaskia, Ill. 222/C6
Kaskaskia (riv.), Ill. 222/E4
Kaskinen (Kaskö), Finland 18/M5
Kaskö, Finland 18/M5
Kaslo, Br. Col. 162/E6
Kaslo, Br. Col. 184/J5
Kasongo, D.R. Congo 115/E4
Kasongo-Lunda, D.R. Congo 115/C5
Kásos (isl.), Greece 45/H8
Kasota, Minn. 255/D6
Kasper Creek, Sask. 181/F6
Kaspiysk, Russia 52/G6
Kaspiyskiy, Russia 52/G5
Kassala (prov.), Sudan 111/F4
Kassala, Sudan 111/G4
Kassala, Sudan 59/C6
Kassala, Sudan 102/F3
Kassándra (pen.), Greece 45/F6
Kassel, Germany 7/E3
Kassel, Germany 22/C3
Kasserine, Tunisia 106/F1
Kasson, Minn. 255/F6
Kasson, W. Va. 312/G4
Kastamonu (prov.), Turkey 63/E2
Kastamonu, Turkey 59/B1
Kastamonu, Turkey 63/F2
Kastéllion, Greece 45/G8
Kastéllion (Kíssamos), Greece 45/F8
Kasterlee, Belgium 27/F6
Kastoría, Greece 45/E5
Kastrup, Denmark 21/F6
Kastrup, Denmark 18/H9
Kasugai, Japan 81/H6
Kasukabe, Japan 81/O2
Kasulu, Tanzania 115/F4
Kasumiga (lag.), Japan 81/K5
Kasungu, Malawi 115/F6
Kasur, Pakistan 68/C2
Kasur, Pakistan 59/K3
Kataba, Zambia 115/D7
Katahdin (mt.), Maine 243/F4
Katako-Kombe, D.R. Congo 115/D4
Katákolon, Greece 45/E7
Katanga (reg.), D.R. Congo 102/E5
Katangli, Russia 48/P4
Katanning, W. Australia 88/B6
Katanning, W. Australia 92/B6
Katarnian Ghat, India 68/E3
Kata Tjuta (Mt. Olga) (mt.), North. Terr. 93/B8
Katchall (isl.), India 68/G7
Katchiungo, Angola 115/C6
Katemcy, Texas 303/E7
Katenga, D.R. Congo 115/E5
Katepwa Beach, Sask. 181/H5
Katepwa Prov. Park, Sask. 181/H5
Katerini, Greece 45/F5
Kates Needle (mt.), Alaska 196/N1
Kates Needle (mt.), Br. Col. 184/A1
Katha, Burma 72/C1
Katherina, Jebel (mt.), Egypt 111/F2
Katherina, Jebel (mt.), Egypt 59/B4
Katherine, Ariz. 198/A3
Katherine, Australia 87/D7
Katherine, North. Terr. 88/E2
Katherine, North. Terr. 93/B3
Katherine (riv.), North. Terr. 93/C3
Kathiawar (pen.), India 68/B4
Kathleen, Alberta 182/B2
Kathleen, Fla. 212/D3
Kathleen, Ga. 217/E6
Kathmandu (cap.), Nepal 54/K7
Kathmandu (cap.), Nepal 68/E3
Kathryn, Alberta 182/D4
Kathryn, N. Dak. 282/P6
Kati, Mali 106/C6
Katihar, India 68/F3
Katima Mulilo, Namibia 118/C3
Katimik (lake), Manitoba 179/C2
Katiola, Ivory Coast 106/C7
Katipunan, Philippines 82/D6
Katmai (vol.), Alaska 196/H3
Katmai Nat'l Park, Alaska 196/H3
Katmai Nat'l Pres., Alaska 196/H3
Katni (Murwara), India 68/E4
Katonah, N.Y. 276/N8
Katoomba-Wentworth Falls, N.S. Wales 97/F3
Katowice (prov.), Poland 47/D3
Katowice, Poland 7/F3
Katowice, Poland 47/B4
Katrime, Manitoba 179/D4
Katrine, Ontario 177/E2
Katrine, Loch (lake), Scotland 15/D4
Katrineholm, Sweden 18/K7
Katsina, Nigeria 102/C3
Katsina, Nigeria 106/F6
Katsina Ala, Nigeria 106/F7
Katsuta, Japan 81/K5
Katsuura, Japan 81/K6
Kattakurgan, Uzbekistan 48/G5
Kattegat (str.) 7/F3
Kattegat (str.), Denmark 21/E4
Kattegat (str.), Denmark 18/G8
Kattegat (str.), Sweden 18/G8
Katwe, Uganda 115/F4
Katwijk aan Zee, Netherlands 27/E4
Katy, Texas 303/J8
Kau (des.), Hawaii 218/J6
Kau, Indonesia 85/H5
Kauai (co.), Hawaii 218/A1
Kauai (isl.), Hawaii 87/L3
Kauai (isl.), Hawaii 188/E5
Kauai (chan.), Hawaii 218/E6
Kauai (isl.), Hawaii 218/C1
Kaufbeuren, Germany 22/D5
Kaufman (co.), Texas 303/H5
Kaufman, Texas 303/H5
Kauhola (pt.), Hawaii 218/G3
Kauiki (head), Hawaii 218/K2
Kaukauna, Wis. 317/K7
Kaukauveld (mts.), Botswana 118/C3
Kaukauveld (mts.), Namibia 118/C3
Kaukonahua (stream), Hawaii 218/E1
Kaula (isl.), Hawaii 188/F6
Kaula (isl.), Hawaii 218/D6
Kaulakahi (chan.), Hawaii 218/B2
Kauliranta, Finland 18/O3
Kaumajet (mts.), Newf. 166/B2
Kaumakani, Hawaii 218/C2
Kaumalapau (harb.), Hawaii 218/G2
Kaumalapau Harbor, Hawaii 218/G2
Kauna (pt.), Hawaii 218/G7
Kaunakakai, Hawaii 218/G1
Kaunakakai (harb.), Hawaii 218/G1
Kaunas, Lithuania 7/G3
Kaunas, Lithuania 48/C4
Kaunas, Lithuania 52/B4
Kaunas, Lithuania 53/C3
Kauniainen, Finland 18/O6
Kaunuopou (pt.), Hawaii 218/B2
Kaupakulua, Hawaii 218/K2
Kaupo, Hawaii 218/K2
Kaura Namoda, Nigeria 106/F6
Kauswagan, Philippines 82/E6
Kautokeino, Norway 18/N2
Kauttua, Finland 18/M6
Kavadarci, Macedonia 45/E5
Kavajë, Albania 45/D5
Kavak, Çanakkale, Turkey 63/C5
Kavak, Samsun, Turkey 63/F2
Kavalerovo, Russia 48/O5
Kavalga (isl.), Alaska 196/K4
Kavali, India 68/E6
Kavála, Greece 7/G4
Kavála, Greece 45/G5
Kavanagh, Alberta 182/D3
Kavanayen, Venezuela 124/H5
Kavaratti, India 68/C6
Kavarna, Bulgaria 45/J4
Kaveri (riv.), India 68/D6
Kavieng, Papua N.G. 87/E6
Kavieng, Papua N.G. 86/B1
Kavir, Dasht-e (salt des.), Iran 59/G3
Kavir, Dasht-e (salt des.), Iran 66/J3
Kavir-e Namak (salt des.), Iran 59/G3
Kavirondo (gulf), Kenya 115/F4
Kavungo, Angola 114/D6
Kaw, Fr. Guiana 131/E3
Kaw (lake), Okla. 288/N1
Kawachinagano, Japan 81/J8
Kawagama (lake), Ontario 177/F2
Kawagoe, Japan 81/O2
Kawaguchi, Japan 81/J6
Kawaihae, Hawaii 218/G4
Kawaihae (bay), Hawaii 218/G4
Kawaihoa (cape), Hawaii 218/A2
Kawaikini (peak), Hawaii 218/C1
Kawailoa, Hawaii 218/E1
Kawakawa, N. Zealand 100/E1
Kawambwa, Zambia 115/E5
Kawanishi, Japan 81/H7
Kawardha, India 68/E4
Kawasaki, Japan 81/O2
Kawau (isl.), N. Zealand 100/E2
Kaw City, Okla. 288/N1
Kawerau, N. Zealand 100/F3
Kawhia, N. Zealand 100/E3
Kawhia (harb.), N. Zealand 100/E3
Kawi (mt.), Indonesia 85/K2
Kawich (peak), Nev. 266/E5
Kawich (range), Nev. 266/E5
Kawinaw (lake), Manitoba 179/C2
Kawio (isls.), Indonesia 85/G5
Kawkawlin, Mich. 250/F5
Kawlin, Burma 72/B2
Kawludo, Burma 72/C3
Kawthaung, Burma 72/C5
Kay (co.), Okla. 288/M1
Kaya, Burkina Faso 106/D6
Kayah (state), Burma 72/C3
Kayak (isl.), Alaska 196/K3
Kayan (riv.), Indonesia 54/N9
Kayan (riv.), Indonesia 85/F5
Kaycee, Wyo. 319/F2
Kayenta, Ariz. 198/E2
Kayes, Mali 106/B6
Kayes, Mali 102/A3
Kayjay, Ky. 237/O7
Kaylor, Pa. 294/C4
Kaylor, S. Dak. 298/O7
Kayser (mts.), Suriname 131/C4
Kayseri (prov.), Turkey 63/F3
Kayseri, Turkey 63/F3
Kayseri, Turkey 59/C2
Kayseri, Turkey 54/E6
Kaysville, Utah 304/B2
Kayuagung, Indonesia 85/D6
Kayville, Sask. 181/F6
Kazabazua, Québec 172/A4
KAZAKHSTAN 48/G5
Kazakhstan 54/H5
Kazan (riv.), N.W.T. 162/F3
Kazan (riv.), N.W.T. 187/H3
Kazan', Russia 7/J3
Kazan', Russia 48/F4
Kazan', Russia 52/G3
Kazanlı, Turkey 63/F4
Kazanlŭk, Bulgaria 45/G4
Kazan-retto (Volcano) (isls.), Japan 81/M4
Kazatin, Ukraine 52/C5
Kazbek (mt.), Russia 52/F6
Kazerun, Iran 66/G6
Kazerun, Iran 59/F4
Kazhim, Russia 52/H2
Kazimierza Wielka, Poland 47/E3
Kazımkarabekir, Turkey 63/E4
Kazincbarcika, Hungary 41/F2
Kazlu-Rūda, Lithuania 53/B3
Kazumba, D.R. Congo 115/D5
Kazvin (Qazvin), Iran 66/F2
Kdyně, Czech Rep. 41/B2
Kéa, Greece 45/G7
Kéa (isl.), Greece 45/G7
Keaau, Hawaii 188/G6
Keaau, Hawaii 218/J5
Keady, N. Ireland 17/H3
Keahi (pt.), Hawaii 218/A4
Keahole (pt.), Hawaii 218/F5
Kealaikahiki (chan.), Hawaii 218/H3
Kealakekua, Hawaii 218/G5
Kealakekua (bay), Hawaii 218/F6
Kealia, Hawaii, 218/G6
Kealia, Kauai, Hawaii 218/D1
Keams Canyon, Ariz. 198/E3
Keanae, Hawaii 218/K2
Keanapapa (pt.), Hawaii 218/G2
Keansburg, N.J. 273/E3
Kearney, Mo. 261/D4
Kearney, Nebr. 188/G2
Kearney (co.), Nebr. 264/F4
Kearney, Nebr. 264/E4
Kearney, Ontario 177/E2
Kearneysville, W. Va. 312/L4
Kearns, Utah 304/B3
Kearny, Ariz. 198/E5
Kearny (co.), Kansas 232/A3
Kearny, N.J. 273/B2
Kearny, Wyo. 319/F1
Kearsarge, N.H. 268/E3
Kearsarge (mt.), N.H. 268/D5
Kearsarge, Pa. 294/B1
Keasbey, N.J. 273/E2
Keatchie, La. 238/C2
Keating, Oreg. 291/K3
Keating Summit, Pa. 294/F2
Keatley, Sask. 181/D3
Keaton, Ky. 237/P5
Keats, Kansas 232/F2
Keats (mt.), W. Australia 92/A2
Keauhou, Hawaii 218/F5
Keavy, Ky. 237/N6
Keawekaheka (pt.), Hawaii 218/F5
Keban, Turkey 63/H3
Kebang (mt.), S. Korea 81/D5
Ke Bao, Vietnam 72/E2
Kebbi (riv.), Nigeria 106/E6
Kebnekaise (mt.), Sweden 7/F2
Kebnekaise (mt.), Sweden 18/L3
Kebock (head), Scotland 15/B2
Kebumen, Indonesia 85/J2
Kecel, Hungary 41/E3
Kechi, Kansas 232/E4
Kechika (riv.), Br. Col. 184/L2
Keçiborlu, Turkey 63/D4
Kecskemét, Hungary 7/F4
Kecskemét, Hungary 41/E3
Kedah (state), Malaysia 72/D6
Kedainiai, Lithuania 53/C3
Keddie, Calif. 204/E3
Kedges (strs), Md. 245/O8
Kedgwick, New Bruns. 170/C1
Kedgwick (riv.), New Bruns. 170/C1
Kedgwick Ouest, New Bruns. 170/C1
Kedgwick River, New Bruns. 170/C1
Kediri, Indonesia 85/K2
Kédougou, Senegal 106/B6
Kedron (brook), Queensland 95/D2
Kedzierzyn-Koźle, Poland 47/C3
Keechelus (lake), Wash. 310/D3
Keedysville, Md. 245/H3
Keefers, Br. Col. 184/G5
Keefton, Okla. 288/R3
Keegan, Maine 243/G1
Keego Harbor, Mich. 250/F6
Keehi (lag.), Hawaii 218/B4
Keel-Dooagh, Ireland 17/A4
Keele (riv.), N.W.T. 187/F3
Keele (peak), Yukon 187/E3
Keeler, Calif. 204/H7
Keeler, Sask. 181/F5
Keeline, Wyo. 319/H3
Keeling (Cocos) (isls.), Australia 2/P6
Keeling, Va. 307/K7
Keels, Newf. 166/D1
Keelung, China 77/K6
Keenan, W. Va. 312/F7
Keenan Siding, New Bruns. 170/E2
Keene, Calif. 204/G8
Keene, Ky. 237/M5
Keene, N.H. 268/C6
Keene, N.Y. 276/N2
Keene, N. Dak. 282/E4
Keene, Ohio 284/G5
Keene, Ontario 177/F3
Keene, Texas 303/G5
Keener, Ala. 195/G2
Keenes, Ill. 222/E5
Keenesburg, Colo. 208/L2
Keene Valley, N.Y. 276/N2
Keensburg, Ill. 222/F5
Keeny (creek), Oreg. 291/K4
Keeper (hill), Ireland 17/E6
Keerweer (cape), Queensland 88/G2
Keerweer (cape), Queensland 95/B2
Keeseville, N.Y. 276/O2
Keesler A.F.B., Miss. 256/G10
Keetley, Utah 304/C3
Keetmanshoop, Namibia 118/B5
Keetmanshoop, Namibia 102/D7
Keewatin, Minn. 255/E3
Keewatin (reg.), N.W.T. 162/G3
Keewatin (reg.), N.W.T. 187/J3
Keewatin, Ontario 177/F5
Keewatin, Ontario 175/A3
Keewong, N.S. Wales 97/C3
Keezletown, Va. 307/L4
Kefallinía (isl.), Greece 45/E6
Kefar Blum, Israel 65/D1
Kefar Gil'adi, Israel 65/C1
Kefar Ruppin, Israel 65/D3
Kefar Sava, Israel 65/B3
Kefar Vitkin, Israel 65/B3
Kefar Zekhariya, Israel 65/B4
Keffi, Nigeria 106/F7
Keflavik, Iceland 21/B1
Kégashka, Québec 174/E2
Kegley, W. Va. 312/D8
Kegonsa (lake), Wis. 317/H10
Keg River, Alberta 182/A5
Kehl, Germany 22/B4
Kehoe, Ky. 237/P4
Kehra, Estonia 53/C1
Keila, Estonia 53/C1
Keilor, Victoria 88/K7
Keilor, Victoria 97/H5
Keimoes, S. Africa 118/C5
Keirn, Miss. 256/D4
Keiser, Ark. 202/K2
Keiss, Scotland 15/E2
Keitele (lake), Finland 18/O5
Keith (co.), Nebr. 264/C3
Keith, Scotland 10/E2
Keith, Scotland 15/F3
Keith, S. Australia 94/G7
Keith, W. Va. 312/C6
Keith Arm (inlet), N.W.T. 187/F3
Keithley Creek, Br. Col. 184/G4
Keithsburg, Ill. 222/B2
Keith Sebelius (res.), Kansas 232/C2
Keithville, La. 238/C2
Keizer, Oreg. 291/A3
Kejimkujik (lake), Nova Scotia 168/C4
Kejimkujik Nat'l Park, Nova Scotia 168/C4
Kekaa (pt.), Hawaii 218/H2
Kekaha, Hawaii 218/C2
Kekaha, Hawaii 188/E5
Kekertaluk (isl.), N.W.T. 187/M3
Kékes (mt.), Hungary 41/E3
Kekoskee, Wis. 317/J8
Kelang, Malaysia 72/D7
Kelantan (state), Malaysia 72/D6
Kelantan, Sungai (riv.), Malaysia 72/D6
Kelasa (str.), Indonesia 85/D6
Keldron, S. Dak. 298/F2
Keles, Turkey 63/C3
Kelfield, Sask. 181/C4
Kelford, N.C. 281/P2
Kelheim, Germany 22/D4
Kelkit, Turkey 63/H2
Kelkit (riv.), Turkey 59/C1
Kelkit (riv.), Turkey 63/G2
Kell, Ill. 222/E5
Kellé, Congo 115/B4
Keller (lake), N.W.T. 187/F3
Keller, Texas 303/F2
Keller, Va. 307/S5
Keller, Wash. 310/G2
Kellerberrin, W. Australia 88/B6
Kellerberrin, W. Australia 92/B5
Kellerman, Ala. 195/D4
Kellerton, Iowa 229/E7
Kellerville, Texas 303/D2
Kellett (cape), N.W.T. 162/D1
Kellett (cape), N.W.T. 187/F2
Kellett (str.), N.W.T. 187/G2
Kellettville, Pa. 294/D2
Kelley, Iowa 229/F5
Kelley (creek), Nev. 266/D1
Kelleys (isl.), Ohio 284/E2
Kelleys Island, Ohio 284/E2
Kelligrews, Newf. 166/D2
Kelliher, Minn. 255/D3
Kelliher, Sask. 181/H4
Kellnersville, Wis. 317/L7
Kellogg (mt.), Ariz. 198/E6
Kellogg, Idaho 220/B2
Kellogg, Iowa 229/H5
Kellogg, Minn. 255/G6
Kelloggsville, Ohio 284/J2
Kelloselkä, Finland 18/Q3
Kells (Ceanannus Mór), Ireland 17/G4
Kells, Ireland 17/G6
Kells, N. Ireland 17/J2
Kelly, Ga. 217/E4
Kelly (creek), Idaho 220/C3
Kelly, Kansas 232/G2
Kelly, Ky. 237/G7
Kelly, La. 238/F3
Kelly, N.C. 281/N6
Kelly, Wyo. 319/B2
Kelly A.F.B., Texas 303/J11
Kelly Lake, Br. Col. 184/G4
Kelly Lake, Minn. 255/F3
Kellys, N. Dak. 282/R4
Kellysville, W. Va. 312/E8
Kellyton, Ala. 195/F5
Kellyville, Okla. 288/O3
Kelmė, Lithuania 53/B3
Kélo, Chad 111/C6
Kélo, Chad 102/D4
Kelowna, Br. Col. 146/G4
Kelowna, Br. Col. 162/E6
Kelowna, Br. Col. 184/H5
Kelsey, Alberta 182/D3
Kelsey, Minn. 255/F3
Kelsey Bay, Br. Col. 184/D5
Kelseyville, Calif. 204/C5
Kelso, Ark. 202/H6
Kelso, Calif. 204/K8
Kelso, Mo. 261/O8
Kelso, Sask. 181/K6
Kelso, Scotland 10/E3
Kelso, Scotland 15/F5
Kelso, Tenn. 237/J10
Kelso, Wash. 310/C4
Kelstern, Sask. 181/E5
Kelston West, N. Zealand 100/B1
Keltie (cape), Ant. 5/C7
Keltner, Ky. 237/K6
Kelton, S.C. 296/D2
Kelty, Scotland 10/C1
Kelty, Scotland 15/D1
Keluang, Malaysia 72/D7
Kelvington, Sask. 181/H3
Kelwood, Manitoba 179/C4
Kem', Russia 4/C8
Kem', Russia 7/H2
Kem', Russia 48/D3
Kem', Russia 52/D2
Ké-Macina, Mali 106/C6
Kemah, Texas 303/K2
Kemah, Turkey 63/H3
Kemaliye, Turkey 63/H3
Kemalpaşa, Turkey 63/J2
Kemano, Br. Col. 184/D3
Kemasik, Malaysia 72/D6
Kembe, Cent. Afr. Rep. 115/D3
Kemble, Ontario 177/D3
Kemboma, Gabon 115/B3
Kemecse, Hungary 41/F2
Kemer, Turkey 63/D4
Kemerburgaz, Turkey 63/D5
Kemerovo, Russia 54/K4
Kemerovo, Russia 48/J4
Kemi, Finland 7/G2
Kemi, Finland 18/O4
Kemi (riv.), Finland 7/G2
Kemijärvi, Finland 18/P3
Kemijärvi (lake), Finland 18/Q3
Kemijoki (riv.), Finland 18/O3
Kemikli, Büyük (cape), Turkey 63/B6
Kemirhisar, Turkey 63/G4
Kemmerer, Wyo. 319/B4
Kemnay, Manitoba 179/B5
Kemnay, Scotland 15/F3
Kemp, Ill. 222/E4
Kemp, Okla. 288/O7
Kemp, Texas 303/H5
Kemp (lake), Texas 303/E4
Kemp City (Hendrix), Okla. 288/O7
Kemp Coast (reg.), Ant. 5/C3
Kemper (co.), Miss. 256/G5
Kemp Mill, Md. 245/F3
Kempsey, N. S. Wales 88/J6
Kempsey, N.S. Wales 97/G2
Kempster, Wis. 317/H5
Kempston, England 13/G5
Kempt, Nova Scotia 168/C4
Kempt (lake), Québec 172/C2
Kempten, Germany 22/D5
Kempton, Ill. 222/E3
Kempton, Ind. 227/E4
Kempton, Md. 245/A4
Kempton, N. Dak. 282/P4
Kempton, Pa. 294/L4
Kempton, Tasmania 99/D4
Kempton Park, S. Africa 118/J6
Kemptown, Md. 245/J3
Kemptown, Nova Scotia 168/E3
Kemptville, Nova Scotia 168/C4
Kemptville, Ontario 177/J2
Ken, Afghanistan 68/A2
Ken, Afghanistan 59/H3
Kenadsa, Algeria 106/D2
Kenai, Alaska 196/B1
Kenai (lake), Alaska 196/C1
Kenai (mt.), Alaska 196/C2
Kenai (pen.), Alaska 196/C2
Kenai Fjords Nat'l Park, Alaska 196/C3
Kenamu (riv.), Newf. 166/B3
Kenansville, Fla. 212/F4
Kenansville, N.C. 281/O5
Kenaston, N. Dak. 282/F2
Kenaston, Sask. 181/E4
Kenbridge, Va. 307/M7
Kendal, Barbados 161/B8
Kendal, England 13/E3
Kendal, England 10/E3
Kendal, Indonesia 85/J2
Kendal, Sask. 181/H5
Kendall, Fla. 212/B5
Kendall (co.), Ill. 222/E2
Kendall, Kansas 232/A4
Kendall, N.S. Wales 97/G2
Kendall, N.Y. 276/E4
Kendall (cape), N.W.T. 187/K3
Kendall (co.), Texas 303/F8
Kendall, Wash. 310/C2
Kendall, Wis. 317/F8
Kendall Park, N.J. 273/D3
Kendallville, Ind. 227/G2
Kendallville, Iowa 229/K2
Kendari, Indonesia 85/G6
Kendawangan, Indonesia 85/D6
Kendrapara, India 68/F4
Kendrick (peak), Ariz. 198/D3
Kendrick, Fla. 212/D2
Kendrick, Idaho 220/B3
Kendrick, Okla. 288/N3
Kenduskeag•, Maine 243/E6
Kenedy (co.), Texas 303/G11
Kenedy, Texas 303/G9
Kenefic, Okla. 288/O6
Kenel, S. Dak. 298/H2
Kenema, S. Leone 102/A4
Kenema, S. Leone 106/B7
Kenesaw, Nebr. 264/F4
Kengah (isls.), Indonesia 85/F7
Kenge, D.R. Congo 115/C4
Keng Hkam, Burma 72/C2
Keng Tung, Burma 72/C2
Kenhardt, S. Africa 118/C5
Kenhorst, Pa. 294/L5
Kéniéba, Mali 106/B6
Kenilworth, England 13/F5
Kenilworth, Ill. 222/B5
Kenilworth, N.J. 273/E2
Kenilworth, Ontario 177/D4
Kenilworth, Utah 304/D4
Keningau, Malaysia 85/F4
Kenitra, Morocco 102/B1
Kenitra, Morocco 106/C2
Kenli, China 77/J4
Kenly, N.C. 281/N3
Kenmare, Ireland 10/B5
Kenmare, Ireland 17/B8
Kenmare (riv.), Ireland 17/A8
Kenmare, N. Dak. 282/G2
Kenmore, N.Y. 276/C5
Kenmore, Queensland 88/J3
Kenmore, Scotland 15/E4
Kenmore, Wash. 310/B1
Kenna, N. Mex. 274/F5
Kenna, W. Va. 312/C5
Kennan, Wis. 317/F5
Kennard, Ind. 227/G5
Kennard, Nebr. 264/H3
Kennard, Pa. 294/B3
Kennard, Texas 303/J6
Kennebago Lake, Maine 243/B5
Kennebec (co.), Maine 243/D7
Kennebec (riv.), Maine 243/D7

Kilwa 391

Kennebec, S. Dak. 298/K6
Kennebecasis (bay), New Bruns. 170/E3
Kennebecasis (riv.), New Bruns. 170/E3
Kennebunk, Maine 243/B9
Kennebunk•, Maine 243/B9
Kennebunk Beach, Maine 243/C9
Kennebunkport, Maine 243/C9
Kennebunkport•, Maine 243/C9
Kennedale, Texas 303/F3
Kennedy, Ala. 195/B3
Kennedy (Canaveral) (cape), Fla. 212/F3
Kennedy, Minn. 255/B2
Kennedy, N.Y. 276/B6
Kennedy (chan.), N.W.T. 162/N3
Kennedy (chan.), N.W.T. 187/M1
Kennedy, Sask. 181/J5
Kennedy Center, D.C. 245/A5
Kennedy Entrance (str.), Alaska 196/H3
Kennedyville, Md. 245/P3
Kenner, La. 238/N4
Kennesaw, Ga. 217/C2
Kennesaw Mtn. Nat'l Battlefield Park, Ga. 217/J1
Kennet (riv.), England 13/F6
Kennetcook, Nova Scotia 168/E3
Kennetcook (riv.), Nova Scotia 168/E3
Kenneth, Ind. 227/E3
Kenneth, Minn. 255/B7
Kenneth City, Fla. 212/B3
Kennett, Mo. 261/M10
Kennett Square, Pa. 294/L6
Kennewick, Wash. 310/F4
Kenney (dam), Br. Col. 184/E3
Kenney, Ill. 222/D3
Kennisis (lake), Ontario 177/F2
Keno, Oreg. 291/F5
Kenogami (riv.), Ont. 162/H6
Kenogami (riv.), Ontario 177/H4
Kenogami (riv.), Ontario 175/J2
Kénogami (lake), Québec 172/F1
Keno Hill, Yukon 187/E3
Kenoma, Mo. 261/D8
Kenora, Ont. 146/J4
Kenora, Ont. 162/G5
Kenora (terr. dist.), Ontario 177/G5
Kenora (terr. dist.), Ontario 175/C2
Kenora, Ontario 175/B3
Kenora, Ontario 177/F4
Kenosee Park, Sask. 181/J6
Kenosha (co.), Wis. 317/K10
Kenosha, Wis. 317/M3
Kenova, W. Va. 312/A6
Kensal, N. Dak. 282/N5
Kenscoff, Haiti 158/C6
Kensett, Ark. 202/G3
Kensett, Iowa 229/G2
Kensington, Calif. 204/J2
Kensington, Conn. 210/D2
Kensington, Kansas 232/C2
Kensington, Md. 245/E4
Kensington, Minn. 255/C5
Kensington, N.S. Wales 97/J4
Kensington, Ohio 284/J4
Kensington, Pr. Edward I. 168/E2
Kensington and Chelsea, England 13/G8
Kensington and Chelsea, England 10/B5
Kensington and Norwood, S. Australia 88/E8
Kensington and Norwood, S. Australia 94/B8
Kent, Ala. 195/G5
Kent, Br. Col. 184/M3
Kent•, Conn. 210/B2
Kent (co.), Del. 245/R4
Kent (co.), England 13/H6
Kent, Ill. 222/D1
Kent, Ind. 227/F7
Kent, Iowa 229/E7
Kent (co.), Md. 245/O3
Kent (isl.), Md. 245/N5
Kent (pt.), Md. 245/N5
Kent (co.), Mich. 250/D5
Kent, Minn. 255/B4
Kent (co.), New Bruns. 170/E2
Kent (pen.), N.W.T. 187/H3
Kent, Ohio 284/H3
Kent (county), Ontario 177/B5
Kent, Oreg. 291/G2
Kent, Pa. 294/D4
Kent (co.), R.I. 249/H6
Kent (co.), Texas 303/D4
Kent, Texas 303/C11
Kent, Wash. 310/C3
Kentau, Kazakhstan 48/G5
Kent Bridge, Ontario 177/B5
Kent City, Mich. 250/D5
Kent Furnace, Conn. 210/B2
Kent Group (isls.), Tasmania 99/D1
Kent Junction, New Bruns. 170/E2
Kent Lake, New Bruns. 170/E2
Kentland, Ind. 227/C3
Kenton, Del. 245/R4
Kenton (co.), Ky. 237/M3
Kenton, Ky. 237/N3
Kenton, Manitoba 179/B5
Kenton, Mich. 250/G2
Kenton, Ohio 284/C4
Kenton, Okla. 288/A1
Kenton, Tenn. 237/C8
Kenton Vale, Ky. 237/S2
Kents Hill, Maine 243/D7
Kents Store, Va. 307/M5
Kentuck, W. Va. 312/C5
Kentucky 188/J3
KENTUCKY 237
Kentucky (lake) 188/J3
Kentucky (dam), Ky. 237/E7
Kentucky (lake), Ky. 237/E8
Kentucky (riv.), Ky. 237/M3
Kentucky (lake), Tenn. 237/E8
Kentucky (state), U.S. 146/K6
Kentville, Nova Scotia 168/D3
Kentwood, La. 238/J5
Kentwood, Mich. 250/D6
Kenville, Manitoba 179/A3
Kenvir, Ky. 237/P7
Kenwood, Ga. 217/D3
Kenwood, Okla. 288/S2
Kenya 2/L5
Kenya 102/F4
KENYA 115/G3
Kenya (mt.), Kenya 102/F4
Kenya (mt.), Kenya 115/G4
Kenyon, Minn. 255/E6
Kenyon, R.I. 249/H7
Kenyonville, Conn. 210/G1
Keo, Ark. 202/G4
Keokea, Hawaii, Hawaii 218/G6
Keokea, Maui, Hawaii 218/J2
Keokee, Va. 307/C7
Keokuk (co.), Iowa 229/J6
Keokuk, Iowa 188/H2
Keokuk, Iowa 229/L8
Keoma, Alberta 182/D4
Keomah, Iowa 229/J6
Keomuku, Hawaii 218/H2
Keonjhar, India 68/F4
Keosauqua, Iowa 229/J7
Keota, Colo. 208/L1
Keota, Iowa 229/K6
Keota, Okla. 288/S4
Keowee (lake), S.C. 296/B2
Keowee (riv.), S.C. 296/B2
Kepez, Turkey 63/B6
Kepi, Indonesia 85/K7
Kępno, Poland 47/C3
Keppel (harb.), Singapore 72/F6
Kepsut, Turkey 63/C3
Kerala (state), India 68/D6
Kerama (isls.), Japan 81/M6
Kerang, Victoria 97/B4
Kerava, Finland 18/O6
Kerby, Oreg. 291/D5
Kerch', Ukraine 7/H4
Kerch', Ukraine 52/E5
Kerchoual, Mali 106/E5
Kerema, Papua N.G. 85/B7
Keremeos, Br. Col. 184/G5
Kerempe (cape), Turkey 63/E1
Keren, Eritrea 59/C6
Keren, Eritrea 111/G4
Kerens, Texas 303/H5
Kerens, W. Va. 312/G4
Keret', Russia 52/D1
Kerguélen (isl.), (Fr.) 2/N8
Kerhonkson, N.Y. 276/M7
Kericho, Kenya 115/F4
Kerinci (mt.), Indonesia 85/C6
Keriya (Yutian), China 77/B4
Keriya He (riv.), China 77/B4
Keriya Shankou (pass), China 77/B4
Kerkdriel, Netherlands 27/G5
Kerkennah (isls.), Tunisia 106/G2
Kerkhoven, Minn. 255/C5
Kerki, Turkmenistan 48/G6
Kérkira, Greece 45/D6
Kérkira (isl.), Greece 7/F5
Kérkira (isl.), Greece 45/D6
Kerkrade, Netherlands 27/J7
Kerlin, Ark. 202/D7
Kerma, Sudan 111/F4
Kerma, Sudan 59/B6
Kermadec (isls.), N. Zealand 2/T7
Kermadec (isls.), N. Zealand 87/J9
Kerman, Calif. 204/E7
Kerman (prov.), Iran 66/K6
Kerman, Iran 54/G6
Kerman, Iran 59/G3
Kerman, Iran 66/K5
Kerme (gulf), Turkey 63/B4
Kermit, Texas 303/B6
Kermit, W. Va. 312/B7
Kern (co.), Calif. 204/G8
Kern (riv.), Calif. 204/G8
Kernan, Ill. 222/E2
Kernersville, N.C. 281/J2
Kerns, Switzerland 39/F3
Kernville, Calif. 204/G8
Kernville, Oreg. 291/D3
Kérouané, Guinea 106/C7
Kerr (lake), Fla. 212/E2
Kerr, N.C. 281/N5
Kerr, W. Scott (res.), N.C. 281/G2
Kerr, Robert S. (res.), Okla. 288/S4
Kerr (co.), Texas 303/E7
Kerrera (isl.), Scotland 15/C4
Kerrick, Minn. 255/F4
Kerrick, Texas 303/B1
Kerrobert, Sask. 181/C4
Kerrville, Tenn. 237/B10
Kerrville, Texas 303/E7
Kerry (co.), Ireland 17/B7
Kerry (head), Ireland 17/A7
Kerry, Wales 13/D5
Kersey, Colo. 208/L2
Kersey, Ind. 227/C2
Kersey, Pa. 294/E3
Kershaw (co.), S.C. 296/F3
Kershaw, S.C. 296/G2
Kersley, Br. Col. 184/F4
Kerteminde, Denmark 21/D7
Kerulen (riv.) 54/N5
Kerulen (riv.), Mongolia 77/H2
Kerwood, Ontario 177/C5
Kerzaz, Algeria 106/D3
Kerzers, Switzerland 39/D3
Kesagami (lake), Ontario 175/E2
Keşan, Turkey 63/B2
Keşap, Turkey 63/H2
Kesch (peak), Switzerland 39/J3
Kesennuma, Japan 81/K4
Kesgrave, England 13/J5
Kesh, N. Ireland 17/F3
Keshena, Wis. 317/J6
Keşiş Tepesi (mt.), Turkey 63/H3
Keskin, Turkey 63/E3
Keski-Suomi (prov.), Finland 18/O5
Kesley, Iowa 229/H3
Kessel, W. Va. 312/H4
Kesten'ga, Russia 52/D1
Kesteren, Netherlands 27/G5
Keswick, England 13/D3
Keswick, England 10/E3
Keswick, Iowa 229/J6
Keswick, New Bruns. 170/D3
Keswick (riv.), New Bruns. 170/C2
Keswick, Ontario 177/E3
Keswick, Va. 307/M4
Keswick Grove, N.J. 273/E4
Keszthely, Hungary 41/D3
Keta, Ghana 106/E7
Ketapang, Indonesia 85/E6
Ketchen, Sask. 181/J3
Ketch Harbour, Nova Scotia 168/E4
Ketchikan, Alaska 146/E4
Ketchikan, Alaska 188/E6
Ketchikan, Alaska 196/N2
Ketchum, Idaho 220/D6
Ketchum, Okla. 288/R1
Kétegyháza, Hungary 41/F3
Kete Krachi, Ghana 106/E7
Kętrzyn, Poland 47/E1
Kettering, England 13/G5
Kettering, England 10/F4
Kettering, Ohio 284/B6
Kettering, Tasmania 99/D5
Kettle (riv.), Br. Col. 184/H5
Kettle (riv.), Minn. 255/F4
Kettle (pt.), Ontario 177/B4
Kettle (riv.), Wash. 310/G2
Kettle Falls, Wash. 310/H2
Kettleman City, Calif. 204/E7
Kettle River, Minn. 255/E4
Kettle River (range), Wash. 310/G2
Kettlersville, Ohio 284/B5
Kettle Valley, Br. Col. 184/H5
Keuka (lake), N.Y. 276/F5
Keuka Park, N.Y. 276/F5
Keuterville, Idaho 220/B3
Kevelaer, Germany 22/B3
Kevil, Ky. 237/D6
Kevin, Mont. 262/D2
Kevisville, Alberta 182/C4
Kew, Victoria 88/L7
Kew, Victoria 97/J5
Kewa, Wash. 310/G2
Kewanee, Ill. 222/C2
Kewanee, Miss. 256/H6
Kewanee, Mo. 261/N9
Kewanna, Ind. 227/E2
Kewaskum, Wis. 317/K8
Kewaunee (co.), Wis. 317/L6
Kewaunee, Wis. 317/M7
Keweenaw (co.), Mich. 250/A1
Keweenaw (bay), Mich. 250/A1
Keweenaw (pt.), Mich. 250/B1
Keweenaw Bay, Mich. 250/G1
Key, Ala. 195/G2
Key (lake), Ireland 17/E3
Keya Paha (co.), Nebr. 264/E2
Keya Paha (riv.), Nebr. 264/D1
Keyapaha, S. Dak. 298/J7
Keya Paha (riv.), S. Dak. 298/K7
Key Biscayne, Fla. 212/B5
Key Colony Beach, Fla. 212/F7
Keyes, Calif. 204/E6
Keyes, Manitoba 179/C4
Keyes, Okla. 288/B1
Keyesport, Ill. 222/D5
Keyhole (res.), Wyo. 319/H1
Key Largo, Fla. 212/F6
Key Largo (key), Fla. 212/F6
Keymar, Md. 245/K2
Keynsham, England 13/E6
Keyport, N.J. 273/E3
Keyport, Wash. 310/A2
Keysbrook, W. Australia 88/B3
Keyser, W. Va. 312/J4
Keystone, Ind. 227/G3
Keystone, Iowa 229/J5
Keystone, Nebr. 264/C3
Keystone (res.), Ohio 284/K2
Keystone (lake), Okla. 288/O2
Keystone, S. Dak. 298/C6
Keystone, W. Va. 312/D8
Keystone Heights, Fla. 212/E2
Keystown, Sask. 181/F5
Keysville, Ga. 217/H4
Keysville, Va. 307/M6
Keytesville, Mo. 261/G4
Key Vaca (key), Fla. 212/E7
Key West, Fla. 146/K7
Key West, Fla. 188/K6
Key West, Fla. 212/E7
Key West Naval Air Sta., Fla. 212/E7
Kezar (lake), Maine 243/B7
Kezar (pond), Maine 243/B7
Kezar Falls, Maine 243/B8
Kežmarok, Slovakia 41/F2
Khabake (Habahe), China 77/C2
Khabarovsk, Russia 2/R3
Khabarovsk, Russia 48/O5
Khabarovsk, Russia 54/P5
Khabur (riv.), Syria 63/J5
Khabur (riv.), Syria 59/D2
Khachmas, Azerbaijan 52/G6
Khadyzhensk, Russia 52/E6
Khaf, Iran 66/L3
Khaibar, 'Asir, Saudi Arabia 59/D6
Khaibar, Hejaz, Saudi Arabia 59/C4
Khairpur, Pakistan 68/B3
Khairpur, Pakistan 59/J4
Khakass Aut. Obl., Russia 48/J4
Khalkhal, Iran 66/F2
Khálki (isl.), Greece 45/H7
Khalkis, Greece 45/F6
Khal'mer-Yu, Russia 52/K1
Khaluf, Oman 59/G5
Khamgaon, India 68/D4
Khamis Mushait, Saudi Arabia 59/D6
Khamkeut, Laos 72/E3
Khamman, India 68/D5
Khanabad, Afghanistan 59/J2
Khanabad, Afghanistan 68/B1
Khanaqin, Iraq 59/D3
Khanaqin, Iraq 66/D3
Khancoban, N.S. Wales 97/E5
Khandwa, India 68/D4
Khandyga, Russia 48/O3
Khan esh Shamat, Syria 63/G6
Khanewal, Pakistan 68/C2
Khanh Hoa, Vietnam 72/F4
Khanh Hung, Vietnam 72/E5
Khaniá, Greece 45/G8
Khaniá, Greece 7/G5
Khaniá (gulf), Greece 45/G8
Khanka (lake) 54/P5
Khanka (lake), China 77/M3
Khanka (lake), Russia 48/O5
Khanpur, Pakistan 68/C3
Khanpur, Pakistan 59/K4
Khan Sheikhun, Syria 63/G5
Khanty-Mansi Aut. Okr., Russia 48/H3
Khanty-Mansiysk, Russia 48/H3
Khanty-Mansiysk, Russia 54/J3
Khanu, Thailand 72/C3
Khan Yunis, Gaza Strip 65/A5
Khao Luang (mt.), Burma 72/C5
Khao Luang (mt.), Thailand 72/C5
Khapcheranga, Russia 48/M5
Kharagpur, India 68/F4
Kharan, Pakistan 59/J4
Kharan Kalat, Pakistan 68/A3
Kharas, West Bank 65/C4
Kharasavey (cape), Russia 48/G2
Khardah, India 68/F1
Khârga (oasis), Egypt 111/F2
Khârga (oasis), Egypt 59/B4
Khark (Kharg) (isl.), Iran 59/F4
Khark (Kharg) (isl.), Iran 66/G6
Khar'kov, Ukraine 7/H4
Khar'kov, Ukraine 2/L3
Khar'kov, Ukraine 48/D4
Khar'kov, Ukraine 52/E5
Kharmanli, Bulgaria 45/H5
Kharovsk, Russia 48/D3
Kharovsk, Russia 52/F3
Khartoum (prov.), Sudan 111/F4
Khartoum (cap.), Sudan 2/L5
Khartoum (cap.), Sudan 59/B6
Khartoum (cap.), Sudan 111/F4
Khartoum (cap.), Sudan 102/F3
Khartoum North, Sudan 102/F3
Khartoum North, Sudan 59/B6
Khartoum North, Sudan 111/F4
Khasab, Oman 59/G4
Khasavyurt, Russia 52/G6
Khash, Afghanistan 68/A2
Khash, Afghanistan 59/H3
Khash, Iran 59/H4
Khash, Iran 66/M6
Khashm el Girba, Sudan 111/G5
Khashuri, Georgia 52/F6
Khasi (hills), India 68/G3
Khaskovo, Bulgaria 45/G5
Khatanga, Russia 4/B4
Khatanga, Russia 48/L2
Khatanga, Russia 54/M2
Khatuniye, Syria 63/J4
Khay, Saudi Arabia 59/D6
Khedive, Sask. 181/G6
Khemis Miliana, Algeria 106/E1
Khemmarat, Thailand 72/E4
Khenifra, Morocco 106/C2
Kherson, Ukraine 7/H4
Kherson, Ukraine 48/D5
Kherson, Ukraine 52/D5
Khe Sanh, Vietnam 72/E3
Kheta (riv.), Russia 48/K2
Khilok, Russia 48/M4
Khíos, Greece 45/G6
Khíos (isl.), Greece 45/G6
Khirbet Qumran (site), Jordan 65/D4
Khiva, Uzbekistan 48/F5
Khiyav, Iran 66/E1
Khmel'nitskiy, Ukraine 7/G4
Khmel'nitskiy, Ukraine 52/C5
Khoai, Hon (isl.), Vietnam 72/E5
Khodzheyli, Uzbekistan 48/F5
Kholm, Afghanistan 68/B1
Kholm, Afghanistan 59/J2
Kholm, Russia 52/D3
Kholmsk, Russia 48/P5
Khoman, Iran 66/F2
Khomeinshar, Iran 66/G4
Khon Kaen, Thailand 72/D3
Khoper (riv.), Russia 52/F4
Khorasan (prov.), Iran 66/K3
Khóra Sfakíon, Greece 45/G8
Khorat (Nakhon Ratchasima), Thailand 72/D4
Khoreyver, Russia 52/J1
Khorixas, Namibia 118/A4
Khorog, Tajikistan 48/H6
Khorol, Ukraine 52/D5
Khorramabad, Iran 59/E3
Khorramabad, Iran 66/F4
Khorramshahr, Iran 59/E3
Khorramshahr, Iran 66/F5
Khotan (Hotan), China 77/B4
Khotin, Ukraine 52/C5
Khouribga, Morocco 106/C2
Khowst, Afghanistan 68/B2
Khromtau, Kazakhstan 48/F4
Khuaf, Iran 59/H3
Khudzhand, Tajikistan 48/G5
Khugiani, Afghanistan 68/B2
Khugiani, Afghanistan 59/J3
Khuis, Botswana 118/C5
Khu Khan, Thailand 72/E4
Khulna, Bangladesh 68/F4
Khurda, India 68/F4
Khurma, Saudi Arabia 59/D5
Khusf Rud (riv.), Iran 66/L4
Khushab, Pakistan 68/C2
Khust, Ukraine 52/B5
Khuzdar, Pakistan 59/J4
Khuzestan (prov.), Iran 66/F5
Khvaf, Iran 66/L3
Khvalynsk, Russia 52/G4
Khvojeh Lak, Kuh-e (mt.), Iran 66/E3
Khvonsar, Iran 66/F4
Khvor, Iran 59/G3
Khvor, Iran 66/J4
Khvoy, Iran 59/E2
Khvoy (Khoi), Iran 66/D1
Khwae Noi, Mae Nam (riv.), Thailand 72/C4
Khyber (pass) 54/J6
Khyber (pass), Pakistan 59/K3
Khyber (pass), Pakistan 68/C2
Kia, Solomon Is. 86/D2
Kiahsville, W. Va. 312/B6
Kiama, N.S. Wales 97/F4
Kiamba, Philippines 82/E8
Kiambi, D.R. Congo 115/E5
Kiambu, Kenya 115/G4
Kiamichi, Okla. 288/R5
Kiamichi (mts.), Okla. 288/R5
Kiamichi (riv.), Okla. 288/R6
Kiamika, Québec 172/B3
Kiamika (lake), Québec 172/B3
Kiamika (riv.), Québec 172/B3
Kiamusze (Jiamusi), China 77/M2
Kian (Ji'an), China 77/J6
Kiana, Alaska 196/F1
Kiangsi (Jiangxi), China 77/J6
Kiangsu (Jiangsu), China 77/K5
Kiantajärvi (lake), Finland 18/Q4
Kiáton, Greece 45/F6
Kiawah (isl.), S.C. 296/G6
Kibaek, Denmark 21/B5
Kibangou, Congo 115/B4
Kibara, Tanzania 115/F4
Kibaya, Tanzania 115/G5
Kibbee, Ga. 217/H6
Kibler, Ark. 202/B3
Kibombo, D.R. Congo 115/E4
Kibondo, Tanzania 115/F4
Kibre Mengist, Ethiopia 111/G6
Kibwezi, Kenya 115/G4
Kičevo, Macedonia 45/E5
Kickapoo (riv.), Wis. 317/E9
Kickapoo Ind. Res., Kansas 232/G2
Kickinghorse (pass), Alberta 182/B4
Kicking Horse (pass), Br. Col. 184/J4
Kidal, Mali 102/C3
Kidal, Mali 106/E5
Kidapawan, Philippines 82/E7
Kidder, Mo. 261/D3
Kidder (co.), N. Dak. 282/L6
Kidder, S. Dak. 298/O2
Kidderminster, England 10/G3
Kidderminster, England 13/E5
Kidepo Nat'l Park, Uganda 115/F3
Kidnappers (cape), N. Zealand 100/F3
Kidron, Ohio 284/G4
Kidsgrove, England 13/E4
Kidwelly, Wales 13/C6
Kidwelly, Wales 10/D5
Kief, N. Dak. 282/J4
Kiefer, Okla. 288/O3
Kieffer, W. Va. 312/E7
Kiel, Germany 7/E3
Kiel, Germany 22/D1
Kiel (bay), Germany 22/D1
Kiel (Nord-Ostsee) (canal), Germany 22/C1
Kiel, Wis. 317/L8
Kielce (prov.), Poland 47/E3
Kielce, Poland 47/E3
Kielce, Poland 7/G3
Kieler, Wis. 317/E10
Kien Hung, Vietnam 72/E5
Kienyang (Qianyang), China 77/H6
Kiester, Minn. 255/E7
Kieta, Papua N.G. 86/C2
Kieta, Papua N.G. 87/F6
Kiev (cap.), Ukraine 2/L3
Kiev (cap.), Ukraine 7/H3
Kiev (cap.), Ukraine 48/D4
Kiev (cap.), Ukraine 52/D4
Kiev (res.), Ukraine 52/C4
Kiffa, Mauritania 106/B5
Kifri, Iraq 66/D3
Kigali (cap.), Rwanda 115/F4
Kigali (cap.), Rwanda 102/F5
Kiger (creek), Oreg. 291/J5
Kiği, Turkey 63/J3
Kiglapait (cape), Newf. 166/B2
Kiglapait (mts.), Newf. 166/B2
Kigoma (reg.), Tanzania 115/F4
Kigoma-Ujiji, Tanzania 115/E4
Kigoma-Ujiji, Tanzania 102/F5
Kihei, Hawaii 218/J2
Kihnu (isl.), Estonia 53/B1
Kiholo, Hawaii 218/G4
Kiholo (bay), Hawaii 218/F4
Kii (chan.), Japan 81/G7
Kiiminki, Finland 18/P4
Kikai (isl.), Japan 81/O5
Kikiktaksoak (isl.), Newf. 166/B2
Kikinda, Yugoslavia 45/E3
Kikino, Alberta 182/D2
Kikkertavak (isl.), Newf. 166/B2
Kikoira, N.S. Wales 97/D3
Kikonai, Japan 81/K3
Kikori, Papua N.G. 85/B7
Kikwit, D.R. Congo 115/C5
Kikwit, D.R. Congo 102/D5
Kila, Mont. 262/B2
Kilafors, Sweden 18/K6
Kilauea, Hawaii 188/E5
Kilauea, Hawaii 218/C1
Kilauea (crater), Hawaii 218/H6
Kilauea (pt.), Hawaii 218/C1
Kilbaha, Ireland 17/B6
Kilbarchan, Scotland 15/A2
Kilbeggan, Ireland 17/G5
Kilbirnie, Scotland 15/A2
Kilbourne, Ill. 222/D3
Kilbourne, La. 238/H1
Kilbrannan (sound), Scotland 15/C5
Kilbride, Newf. 166/D2
Kilbuck (mts.), Alaska 196/G2
Kilburn, New Bruns. 170/C2
Kilcar, Ireland 17/D2
Kilchoan, Scotland 15/B4
Kilchu, N. Korea 81/D3
Kilcock, Ireland 17/H5
Kilconnell, Ireland 17/E5
Kilcoole, Ireland 17/K5
Kilcormac, Ireland 17/F5
Kilcoy, Queensland 95/E5
Kilcullen, Ireland 17/H5
Kildare, Ga. 217/K5
Kildare (co.), Ireland 17/H5
Kildare, Ireland 10/C4
Kildare, Ireland 17/H5
Kildare, Okla. 288/M1
Kildare (cape), Pr. Edward I. 168/E2
Kildare, Texas 303/K5
Kildeer, Ill. 222/A5
Kil'din (isl.), Russia 52/D1
Kildonan, Br. Col. 184/E5
Kildonan, Scotland 15/E2
Kildonan, Zimbabwe 118/E3
Kildurk, North. Terr. 93/A4
Kildysart, Ireland 17/C6
Kilembe, Uganda 115/F3
Kilembe, D.R. Congo 115/C5
Kilfenora, Ireland 17/C6
Kilfinane, Ireland 17/D7
Kilgarvan, Ireland 17/B8
Kilgore, Idaho 220/G5
Kilgore, Nebr. 264/D2
Kilgore, Ohio 284/H5
Kilgore, Texas 303/K5
Kili (isl.), Marshall Is. 87/G5
Kilifi, Kenya 115/G4
Kilimanjaro (reg.), Tanzania 115/G4
Kilimanjaro (mt.), Tanzania 102/F5
Kilimanjaro (mt.), Tanzania 115/G4
Kilimli, Turkey 63/D2
Kilinailau (isls.), Papua N.G. 86/C2
Kilingi-Nõmme, Estonia 53/C1
Kilis, Turkey 63/G4
Kilitbahir, Turkey 63/B6
Kiliya, Ukraine 52/C5
Kilkee, Ireland 10/B4
Kilkee, Ireland 17/B6
Kilkeel, N. Ireland 17/K3
Kilkelly, Ireland 17/D4
Kilkenny (co.), Ireland 17/G6
Kilkenny, Ireland 10/C4
Kilkenny, Ireland 17/G6
Kilkenny, Minn. 255/E6
Kilkieran (bay), Ireland 17/B5
Kilkis, Greece 45/F5
Killala, Ireland 17/C3
Killala (bay), Ireland 17/C3
Killaloe, Ireland 10/B4
Killaloe, Ireland 17/D6
Killaloe Station, Ontario 177/G2
Killaly, Sask. 181/J5
Killam, Alberta 182/E3
Killam, New Bruns. 170/E2
Killarney, Ireland 10/B4
Killarney, Ireland 17/C7
Killarney (lakes), Ireland 10/B4
Killarney, Man. 162/G6
Killarney, Manitoba 179/C5
Killarney, North. Terr. 93/B4
Killarney, Ontario 177/C2
Killarney Prov. Park, Ontario 177/C1
Killary (harb.), Ireland 17/A4
Killavullen, Ireland 17/D7
Killbear Point Prov. Park, Ontario 177/D2
Kill Buck, N.Y. 276/C6
Killbuck, Ohio 284/G5
Killbuck (creek), Ohio 284/G4
Killdeer, N. Dak. 282/E5
Killdeer, Sask. 181/E6
Kill Devil Hills, N.C. 281/T3
Killduff, Iowa 229/H5
Killearn, Scotland 15/B1
Killeen, Texas 303/G6
Killen, Ala. 195/D1
Killenaule, Ireland 17/F6
Killeshandra, Ireland 17/F3
Killian, La. 238/M2
Killimor, Ireland 17/E5
Killin, Scotland 15/D4
Killinaboy, Ireland 17/C6
Killingly•, Conn. 210/H1
Killington, Vt. 268/B4
Killington (peak), Vt. 268/B4
Killingworth•, Conn. 210/E3
Killona, La. 238/M3
Killorglin, Ireland 17/B7
Killough, N. Ireland 17/K3
Killucan-Rathwire, Ireland 17/G4
Kill Van Kull (str.), N.J. 273/B2
Killybegs, Ireland 17/E2
Killyclogher, N. Ireland 17/G2
Killyleagh, N. Ireland 17/K3
Kilmacolm, Scotland 15/A2
Kilmacrennan, Ireland 17/F1
Kilmacthomas, Ireland 17/G7
Kilmallock, Ireland 17/D7
Kilmarnock, Scotland 15/D5
Kilmarnock, Scotland 10/D3
Kilmarnock, Va. 307/R5
Kilmaurs, Scotland 15/D5
Kilmeadan, Ireland 17/G7
Kilmichael, Miss. 256/E4
Kilmihill, Ireland 17/C6
Kilmoganny, Ireland 17/G7
Kilmore, Victoria 97/C5
Kilmore Quay, Ireland 17/H7
Kilmurry, Ireland 17/C6
Kiln, Miss. 256/F10
Kilnaleck, Ireland 17/G4
Kilninver, Scotland 15/C4
Kilo, D.R. Congo 115/E3
Kilombero (riv.), Tanzania 115/G5
Kilosa, Tanzania 115/G5
Kilpisjärvi (lake), Finland 18/M2
Kilpisjärvi (lake), Sweden 18/M2
Kilrea, N. Ireland 17/H2
Kilrenny and Anstruther, Scotland 15/F4
Kilrenny and Anstruther, Scotland 10/E2
Kilronan, Ireland 17/B5
Kilrush, Ireland 10/B4
Kilrush, Ireland 17/C6
Kilsheelan, Ireland 17/F7
Kilsyth, Scotland 15/B1
Kilsyth, Scotland 10/B1
Kilsyth, W. Va. 312/D7
Kiltan (isl.), India 68/C6
Kiltimagh, Ireland 17/C4
Kilwa, D.R. Congo 115/E5

392 Kilwa Kivinje

Kilwa Kivinje, Tanzania 115/G5
Kilwa Masoko, Tanzania 115/G5
Kilwinning, Sask. 181/E2
Kilwinning, Scotland 15/D5
Kilworth, Ireland 17/E7
Kilyos, Turkey 63/D5
Kim, Colo. 208/N8
Kimba, S. Australia 88/F6
Kimba, S. Australia 94/E5
Kimball (mt.), Alaska 196/K2
Kimball, Alberta 182/D5
Kimball, Kansas 232/G4
Kimball, Minn. 255/D5
Kimball (co.), Nebr. 264/A3
Kimball, Nebr. 264/A3
Kimball, S. Dak. 298/M6
Kimball, Tenn. 237/K10
Kimball, W. Va. 312/C8
Kimballton, Iowa 229/D5
Kimballton, Va. 307/G6
Kimbe, Papua N.G. 86/B2
Kimbe, Papua N.G. 87/F6
Kimberley, Br. Col. 184/K5
Kimberley, S. Africa 102/E7
Kimberley, S. Africa 118/C5
Kimberley (plat.), W. Australia 88/D3
Kimberley (plat.), W. Australia 92/D2
Kimberley Research Station, W. Australia 88/D3
Kimberling City, Mo. 261/F9
Kimberlin Heights, Tenn. 237/O9
Kimberly, Ala. 195/E3
Kimberly, Idaho 220/D7
Kimberly, Minn. 255/E4
Kimberly, Oreg. 291/H3
Kimberly, Wis. 317/K7
Kimble (co.), Texas 303/E7
Kimbolton, Ohio 284/G5
Kimbrough, Ala. 195/C6
Kimch'aek, N. Korea 81/D3
Kimch'ŏn, S. Korea 81/D5
Kimesville, N.C. 281/L3
Kimhae, Pakistan 81/D6
Kími, Greece 45/F6
Kimitsu, Japan 81/O3
Kimiwan (lake), Alberta 182/B2
Kimje, S. Korea 81/C6
Kimmell, Ind. 227/F2
Kimmins, Tenn. 237/F9
Kimmswick, Mo. 261/M6
Kímolos (isl.), Greece 45/G7
Kimovsk, Russia 52/E4
Kimry, Russia 52/E3
Kimsquit, Br. Col. 184/D4
Kinabalu (mt.), Malaysia 85/F4
Kinalı (isl.), Turkey 63/D6
Kinalung, N.S. Wales 97/B3
Kinango, Kenya 115/G4
Kinard, Fla. 212/D6
Kinards, S.C. 296/D3
Kinbasket (lake), Br. Col. 184/H4
Kinbrace, Scotland 15/E2
Kinbrae, Minn. 255/C7
Kinburn, Ontario 177/H2
Kincaid, Ill. 222/D4
Kincaid, Kansas 232/G3
Kincaid, Sask. 181/D6
Kincardine, Ontario 177/C3
Kincardine, Scotland 10/B1
Kincardine, Scotland 15/C1
Kincheloe (pt.), Oreg. 291/C2
Kincheloe, W. Va. 312/E4
Kincolith, Br. Col. 184/B2
Kincraig, Scotland 15/E3
Kinda, D.R. Congo 115/D5
Kindama, Congo 115/C4
Kindberg, Austria 41/C3
Kinde, Mich. 250/G5
Kinder, La. 238/E6
Kinderhook, Ill. 222/B4
Kinderhook, N.Y. 276/N6
Kindersley, Sask. 162/F5
Kindersley, Sask. 181/B4
Kindia, Guinea 106/B6
Kindia, Guinea 102/A3
Kindred, N. Dak. 282/R6
Kinel', Russia 52/H4
Kinel' (riv.), Russia 52/H4
Kineshma, Russia 7/J3
Kineshma, Russia 52/F3
King (isl.), Alaska 196/E1
King (isl.), Australia 87/E10
King (isl.), Br. Col. 184/D4
King, Ky. 237/O7
King (pt.), N.S. Wales 97/J2
King (cays), Nicaragua 154/F4
King, N.C. 281/J2
King (isl.), Tasmania 88/G7
King (isl.), Tasmania 99/A1
King (riv.), Tasmania 99/B4
King (co.), Texas 303/D4
King (co.), Wash. 310/D3
King (sound), W. Australia 88/C3
King (sound), W. Australia 92/C2
King, Wis. 317/H7
King and Queen (co.), Va. 307/P5
King and Queen Court House, Va. 307/P5
Kingaroy, Queensland 95/D5
Kingaroy, Queensland 88/J5
King Christian (isl.), N.W.T. 187/H2
King Christian IX Land (reg.), Greenl. 4/C11
King Christian IX Land (reg.), Greenland 146/Q3
King Christian X Land (reg.), Greenl. 4/B11
King Christian X Land (reg.), Greenland 146/R2
King City, Calif. 204/D7
King City, Mo. 261/D2
King City, Ontario 177/J3
King City, Oreg. 291/A2
Kingcome Inlet, Br. Col. 184/D4
King Cove, Alaska 196/F4
Kingdom City, Mo. 261/J5
King Ferry, N.Y. 276/G5
Kingfield•, Maine 243/C6
Kingfisher (co.), Okla. 288/L3
Kingfisher, Okla. 288/L3
King Frederik VI Coast (reg.), Greenland 146/P3
King Frederik VIII Land (reg.), Greenl. 4/B11
King Frederik VIII Land (reg.), Greenland 146/R2
King George (isl.), Ant. 5/C16
King George (isls.), N.W.T. 187/L4
King George (co.), Va. 307/O4
King George, Va. 307/O4
King Hill, Idaho 220/C6
Kinghorn, Scotland 15/D1
Kingisepp (Kuressaare), Estonia 53/B1
King Leopold (range), W. Australia 88/D3
King Leopold (range), W. Australia 92/D2
Kingman, Alberta 182/D3
Kingman, Ariz. 198/A3
Kingman, Ind. 227/C5
Kingman (co.), Kansas 232/D4
Kingman, Kansas 232/D4
Kingman, Maine 243/G4
Kingman (reef), Pacific 87/K5
Kingoonya, S. Australia 88/E6
Kingoonyah, S. Australia 94/D4
Kings (co.), Calif. 204/G8
Kings (riv.), Calif. 204/F7
Kings (riv.), Nev. 266/C1
King's (co.), New Bruns. 170/E3
Kings (co.), N.Y. 276/N9
Kings (co.), Nova Scotia 168/D4
Kings (co.), Pr. Edward I. 168/F2
Kings (peak), Utah 304/D3
King Salmon, Alaska 196/G3
Kings Beach, Calif. 204/F4
Kingsbridge, England 13/D7
Kingsburg, Calif. 204/F7
Kingsburg, S.C. 296/H4
Kingsburg, S. Dak. 298/O8
Kingsbury, Ind. 227/D1
Kingsbury•, Maine 243/D5
Kingsbury (pond), Maine 243/D5
Kingsbury, Québec 172/E4
Kingsbury (co.), S. Dak. 298/O5
Kingsbury, Texas 303/G8
Kings Canyon Nat'l Park, Calif. 204/G7
Kingsclear, New Bruns. 170/D3
Kingscliff, N.S. Wales 97/G1
Kingscote, S. Australia 88/F7
Kingscote, S. Australia 94/E6
Kingscourt, Ireland 17/H4
Kingscourt, Ireland 10/C4
King's Cove, Newf. 166/D1
Kings Creek, N.C. 281/G3
Kings Creek, Ohio 284/C5
Kings Creek, S.C. 296/E1
Kingsdale, Minn. 255/F4
Kingsdown, Kansas 232/C4
Kingsey Falls, Québec 172/E4
Kingsford, Mich. 250/A3
Kingsford Heights, Ind. 227/D2
Kingsford Smith Airport, N.S. Wales 88/L4
Kingsford Smith Airport, N.S. Wales 97/J4
Kingsgate, Br. Col. 184/K5
Kingshill, Virgin Is. (U.S.) 161/F4
Kingsland, Ark. 202/F6
Kingsland, Ga. 217/J9
Kingsland, Texas 303/F7
Kings Landing, Ala. 195/D6
King's Landing, New Bruns. 170/C3
Kingsley (lake), Fla. 212/E2
Kingsley, Iowa 229/A3
Kingsley, Ky. 237/K2
Kingsley, Mich. 250/D4
Kingsley (dam), Nebr. 264/C3
Kingsley, New Bruns. 170/D2
King's Lynn, England 13/H5
King's Lynn, England 10/G4
Kingsmere (lake), Sask. 181/E1
Kingsmill, Texas 303/D2
Kings Mills, Ohio 284/B7
Kings Mountain, Ky. 237/M6
Kings Mountain, N.C. 281/G4
Kings Mountain Nat'l Mil. Park, S.C. 296/E1
Kings Park, N.Y. 276/O9
King's Point, Newf. 166/C4
Kings Point, N.Y. 276/P6
Kingsport, Nova Scotia 168/D3
Kingsport, Tenn. 237/R7
Kingston, Ark. 202/C1
Kingston, Australia 87/G8
Kingston, Ga. 217/C2
Kingston, Ill. 222/E1
Kingston, Ind. 227/G6
Kingston, Iowa 229/L7
Kingston (cap.), Jamaica 146/L8
Kingston (cap.), Jamaica 156/C3
Kingston (cap.), Jamaica 158/K6
Kingston, La. 238/C2
Kingston, Md. 245/R8
Kingston, Mass. 249/M5
Kingston•, Mass. 249/M5
Kingston, Mich. 250/F5
Kingston, Minn. 255/D5
Kingston, Mo. 261/E3
Kingston•, N.H. 268/E6
Kingston, N.J. 273/D3
Kingston, N. Mex. 274/B6
Kingston, N.Y. 276/M7
Kingston, N. Zealand 100/B6
Kingston, Norfolk I. 88/L6
Kingston, Nova Scotia 168/D4
Kingston, Ohio 284/E7
Kingston, Okla. 288/N7
Kingston, Ont. 162/J7
Kingston, Ont. 146/L5
Kingston, Ontario 177/H3
Kingston, Pa. 294/F7
Kingston, R.I. 249/J7
Kingston, S. Australia 94/G7
Kingston, Tasmania 99/D4
Kingston, Tenn. 237/N9
Kingston, Utah 304/B5
Kingston, Wash. 310/C3
Kingston, W. Va. 312/D7
Kingston, Wis. 317/H8
Kingston Mines, Ill. 222/D3
Kingston Springs, Tenn. 237/G8
Kingston upon Thames, England 10/B6
Kingston upon Thames, England 13/H8
Kingstown (Dún Laoghaire), Ireland 17/K5
Kingstown, N.S. Wales 97/F2
Kingstown (cap.), St. Vin. & Grens. 161/A9
Kingstown (cap.), St. Vin. & Grens. 156/G4
Kingstown (bay), St. Vin. & Grens. 161/A9
Kingstree, S.C. 296/H4
Kings Valley, Oreg. 291/D3
Kingsville, Md. 245/N3
Kingsville, Mo. 261/D5
Kingsville, Ohio 284/J2
Kingsville, Ontario 177/B6
Kingsville, Texas 303/G10
Kingsville N.A.S., Texas 303/G10
Kingswood, England 13/E6
Kingswood, Ky. 237/J5
Kingtehchen (Jingdezhen), China 77/J6
Kington, England 13/E5
Kington, England 10/E4
Kingurutik (mesa), Newf. 166/B2
Kingussie, Scotland 15/D3
Kingussie, Scotland 10/D2
Kingville, S.C. 296/F4
King William (isl.), N.W.T. 162/G2
King William (isl.), N.W.T. 187/J3
King William (lake), Tasmania 99/C4
King William (co.), Va. 307/O5
King William, Va. 307/O5
King William's Town, S. Africa 102/E8
King William's Town, S. Africa 118/D6
Kingwood, W. Va. 312/G4
Kinhwa (Jinhua), China 77/J6
Kiniama, D.R. Congo 115/E6
Kınık, Turkey 63/B3
Kinistino, Sask. 181/F3
Kinkala, Congo 115/B4
Kinkora, Pr. Edward I. 168/E2
Kinley, Sask. 181/D3
Kinloch, Mo. 261/P2
Kinlochbervie, Scotland 15/D2
Kinlochewe, Scotland 15/C3
Kinlochleven, Scotland 15/D4
Kinloch Rannoch, Scotland 15/D4
Kinloss, Scotland 15/E3
Kinlough, Ireland 17/E3
Kinmount, Minn. 255/F2
Kinmount, Ontario 177/F3
Kinmundy, Ill. 222/E5
Kinna, Sweden 18/H8
Kinnairds (head), Scotland 10/F2
Kinnairds (head), Scotland 15/G3
Kinnear, Wyo. 319/D2
Kinnegad, Ireland 17/G5
Kinnelon, N.J. 273/E2
Kinneret, Israel 65/D2
Kinney, Minn. 255/F3
Kinney (co.), Texas 303/D8
Kinnitty, Ireland 17/F5
Kino (riv.), Japan 81/G6
Kinoosao, Sask. 181/N3
Kinosota, Manitoba 179/D4
Kinrooi, Belgium 27/H6
Kinross, Iowa 229/J6
Kinross, Scotland 15/E4
Kinross, Scotland 10/E2
Kinross (trad. co.), Scotland 15/A5
Kinsale, Ireland 10/B5
Kinsale, Ireland 17/D8
Kinsale (harb.), Ireland 17/E8
Kinsale, Old Head of (head), Ireland 17/E8
Kinsale, Va. 307/P4
Kinsella, Alberta 182/E3
Kinsey, Ala. 195/H8
Kinsey, Mont. 262/L4
Kinshasa (prov.), D.R. Congo 115/C4
Kinshasa (cap.), D.R. Congo 2/K6
Kinshasa (cap.), D.R. Congo 115/C4
Kinshasa (cap.), D.R. Congo 102/D5
Kinsley, Kansas 232/C4
Kinsman, Ill. 222/E2
Kinsman (mt.), N.H. 268/D3
Kinsman, Ohio 284/J3
Kinsman Notch (pass), N.H. 268/D3
Kinston, Ala. 195/F8
Kinston, N.C. 281/O4
Kinta, Okla. 288/R4
Kintampo, Ghana 106/D7
Kintnersville, Pa. 294/M4
Kintore, Scotland 15/F3
Kintyre, N. Dak. 282/L6
Kintyre (pen.), Scotland 15/C5
Kintyre, Mull of (prom.), Scotland 15/C5
Kinuso, Alberta 182/C2
Kinvara, Ireland 17/D5
Kinwow (bay), Manitoba 179/E2
Kinyangiri, Tanzania 115/G4
Kinyeti (mt.), Sudan 111/F7
Kinzel Springs, Tenn. 237/O9
Kinzua, Oreg. 291/H3
Kioa (isl.), Fiji 86/R10
Kioga (lake), Uganda 102/F4
Kioga (lake), Uganda 115/F3
Kiona, Wash. 310/F4
Kiosk, Ontario 177/F1
Kiowa (co.), Colo. 208/O6
Kiowa, Colo. 208/L4
Kiowa (creek), Colo. 208/L3
Kiowa (co.), Kansas 232/C4
Kiowa, Kansas 232/D4
Kiowa (co.), Okla. 288/J5
Kiowa, Okla. 288/P5
Kiowa (creek), Okla. 288/F1
Kiowa (creek), Texas 303/D1
Kipabiskau, Sask. 181/G3
Kipahulu, Hawaii 218/K2
Kiparissía, Greece 45/E7
Kiparissía (gulf), Greece 45/E7
Kipawa, Québec 174/B3
Kipili, Tanzania 115/F5
Kipini, Kenya 115/H4
Kipisa, N.W.T. 187/M3
Kipling, N.C. 281/M4
Kipling, Sask. 181/J5
Kipnuk, Alaska 196/F2
Kipp, Alberta 182/D5
Kipp, Kansas 232/E3
Kippel, Switzerland 39/E4
Kippen, Scotland 15/B1
Kippens, Newf. 166/C4
Kippure (mt.), Ireland 17/J5
Kipton, Ohio 284/F3
Kipushi, D.R. Congo 115/E6
Kipushi, D.R. Congo 102/E6
Kiput, Philippines 82/C8
Kira Kira, Solomon Is. 86/E3
Kiraz, Turkey 63/C3
Kirazlı, Turkey 63/C6
Kirby, Ark. 202/C5
Kirby, Mont. 262/J5
Kirby, Ohio 284/D4
Kirby, Texas 303/K11
Kirby, W. Va. 312/J4
Kirby, Wyo. 319/D2
Kirbyville, Texas 303/K7
Kirchberg, Bern, Switzerland 39/E2
Kirchberg, St. Gallen, Switzerland 39/G2
Kirchdorf an der Krems, Austria 41/C3
Kirchheim unter Teck, Germany 22/C4
Kircubbin, N. Ireland 17/K3
Kirensk, Russia 48/L4
Kiri, D.R. Congo 115/C4
Kiribati 2/A6
KIRIBATI 87/J6
Kiribati 2/T6
Kirigalpota (mt.), Sri Lanka 68/E7
Kırıkhan, Turkey 63/G4
Kırıkkale, Turkey 63/E3
Kirillov, Russia 52/E2
Kirin (Jilin), (prov.) China 77/L3
Kirin (Jilin), China 77/L3
Kirishi, Russia 52/D3
Kirishima-Yaku Nat'l Park, Japan 81/E7
Kiritimati (isl.), Kiribati 87/L5
Kiriwina (isl.), Papua N.G. 85/C7
Kirk, Colo. 208/P3
Kirk, Ky. 237/H5
Kirk, W. Va. 312/B7
Kırkağaç, Turkey 63/B3
Kirkburton, England 13/J2
Kirkby, England 13/G2
Kirkby, England 10/F2
Kirkby Lonsdale, England 13/E3
Kirkbymoorside, England 13/F3
Kirkby Stephen, England 13/E3
Kirkcaldy, Alberta 182/D4
Kirkcaldy, Scotland 15/D1
Kirkcaldy, Scotland 10/C1
Kirkcolm, Scotland 15/C6
Kirkconnel, Scotland 15/E5
Kirkcowan, Scotland 15/D6
Kirkcudbright, Scotland 15/E6
Kirkcudbright, Scotland 10/E3
Kirkcudbright (trad. co.), Scotland 15/A5
Kirkee, India 68/C5
Kirkella, Manitoba 179/A4
Kirkenes, Norway 18/Q2
Kirkersville, Ohio 284/E6
Kirkfield, Ontario 177/E3
Kirkham, England 13/G1
Kirkham, England 10/F1
Kirkhill, Scotland 15/D3
Kirkinner, Scotland 15/D6
Kirkintilloch, Scotland 10/B1
Kirkintilloch, Scotland 15/B2
Kirkland, Ariz. 198/C4
Kirkland, Ga. 217/G8
Kirkland, Ill. 222/E1
Kirkland, New Bruns. 170/C3
Kirkland, Québec 172/H4
Kirkland, Tenn. 237/H9
Kirkland, Texas 303/D3
Kirkland, Wash. 310/B2
Kirkland Lake, Ont. 162/H6
Kirkland Lake, Ont. 146/K5
Kirkland Lake, Ontario 177/K5
Kirkland Lake, Ontario 175/D3
Kırklareli (prov.), Turkey 63/B2
Kırklareli, Turkey 63/B2
Kirklin, Ind. 227/E4
Kirkman, Iowa 229/C5
Kirkmansville, Ky. 237/G6
Kirkmuirhill, Scotland 15/E5
Kirkpatrick (lake), Alberta 182/E4
Kirkpatrick (mt.), Ant. 5/A8
Kirkpatrick, Ind. 227/D4
Kirkpatrick, Ohio 284/D4
Kirksey, Ky. 237/E7
Kirksville, Ind. 227/D6
Kirksville, Ky. 237/N5
Kirksville, Mo. 261/H2
Kirkton of Glenisla, Scotland 15/E4
Kirkuk, Iraq 54/F6
Kirkuk, Iraq 59/D2
Kirkuk, Iraq 66/D3
Kirkville, Iowa 229/H6
Kirkville, Miss. 256/H2
Kirkwall, Scotland 10/E1
Kirkwall, Scotland 15/E2
Kirkwood, Del. 245/R2
Kirkwood, Ill. 222/C3
Kirkwood, Mo. 261/O3
Kirkwood, N.J. 273/B4
Kirkwood, N.Y. 276/J6
Kirkwood, Pa. 294/K6
Kirkwood, S. Africa 118/D6
Kirmastı (riv.), Turkey 63/C3
Kirn, Germany 22/B4
Kiron, Iowa 229/C4
Kirov, Russia 7/J3
Kirov, Russia 48/E4
Kirov, Kaluga, Russia 52/D4
Kirov, Kirov, Russia 52/G3
Kirovabad (Gyandzhe), Azerbaijan 7/J4
Kirovabad (Gyandzhe), Azerbaijan 48/E5
Kirovabad (Gyandzhe), Azerbaijan 52/G6
Kirovakan, Armenia 52/G6
Kirovo-Chepetsk, Russia 52/H3
Kirovograd, Ukraine 7/H4
Kirovograd, Ukraine 48/D5
Kirovograd, Ukraine 52/D5
Kirovsk, Russia 52/D1
Kirovskiy, Kazakhstan 48/H5
Kirriemuir, Alberta 182/E4
Kirriemuir, Scotland 10/E2
Kirriemuir, Scotland 15/E4
Kirs, Russia 52/H3
Kirsanov, Russia 52/F4
Kırşehir (prov.), Turkey 63/F3
Kırşehir, Turkey 63/F3
Kırşehir, Turkey 59/B2
Kirte, Turkey 63/B6
Kirtland, N. Mex. 274/A2
Kirtland, Ohio 284/H2
Kirtland A.F.B., N. Mex. 274/C3
Kirtland Hills, Ohio 284/H2
Kirton, England 13/H5
Kiruna, Sweden 4/C8
Kiruna, Sweden 7/G2
Kiruna, Sweden 18/L3
Kirundu, D.R. Congo 115/E4
Kirwin, Kansas 232/C2
Kirwin (res.), Kansas 232/C2
Kiryu, Japan 81/J5
Kisa, Sweden 18/J7
Kisangani, D.R. Congo 115/E3
Kisangani, D.R. Congo 102/E4
Kisar (isl.), Indonesia 85/H7
Kisarazu, Japan 81/P3
Kisatchie, La. 238/D4
K.I. Sawyer A.F.B., Mich. 250/B2
Kisbér, Hungary 41/D3
Kisbey, Sask. 181/J6
Kiselevsk, Russia 48/J4
Kishangarh, India 68/D3
Kishiwada, Japan 81/J8
Kishorganj, Bangladesh 68/G4
Kishtwar, India 68/D2
Kisi (Jixi), China 77/M2
Kisii, Kenya 115/F4
Kisiju, Tanzania 115/G5
Kiska (isl.), Alaska 188/D6
Kiska (isl.), Alaska 196/J4
Kiska (vol.), Alaska 196/J4
Kiskatinaw (riv.), Br. Col. 184/G2
Kiskissink, Québec 172/E2
Kiskissink (lake), Québec 172/E2
Kiskőrös, Hungary 41/E3
Kiskunfélegyháza, Hungary 41/E3
Kiskunhalas, Hungary 41/E3
Kiskunmajsa, Hungary 41/E3
Kislovodsk, Russia 7/J4
Kislovodsk, Russia 52/F6
Kismayu (Chisimayu), Somalia 115/H4
Kismet, Kansas 232/B4
Kispest, Hungary 41/E3
Kíssamos, Greece 45/G8
Kissee Mills, Mo. 261/G9
Kissidougou, Guinea 106/B7
Kissimmee, Fla. 212/E3
Kissimmee (lake), Fla. 212/E4
Kissimmee (riv.), Fla. 212/E4
Kississing (lake), Manitoba 179/H2
Kistelek, Hungary 41/E3
Kisten (pass), Switzerland 39/H3
Kisterenye, Hungary 41/E2
Kistler, Pa. 294/G5
Kistler, W. Va. 312/C7
Kistna (riv.), India 54/J8
Kistna (Krishna) (riv.), India 68/D5
Kistrand, Norway 18/O1
Kisújszállás, Hungary 41/F3
Kisumu, Kenya 115/F3
Kisumu, Kenya 102/F5
Kisvárda, Hungary 41/G2
Kita, Mali 102/B3
Kita, Mali 106/C6
Kitaibaraki, Japan 81/K5
Kita Iwo (isl.), Japan 87/D3
Kita Iwo (isl.), Japan 81/M4
Kitakami, Japan 81/K4
Kitakami (riv.), Japan 81/K4
Kitakata, Japan 81/J5
Kitakyushu, Japan 81/E6
Kitakyushu, Japan 54/P6
Kitakyushu, Japan 2/R4
Kitale, Kenya 102/F4
Kitale, Kenya 115/G3
Kitami, Japan 81/L2
Kit Carson (co.), Colo. 208/O4
Kit Carson, Colo. 208/O5
Kit Carson (mt.), Colo. 208/H7
Kitchel, Ind. 227/H5
Kitchener (mt.), Alberta 182/B3
Kitchener, Ontario 177/D4
Kite, Ga. 217/G5
Kite, Ky. 237/R6
Kitgum, Uganda 115/F3
Kithira, Greece 45/F7
Kithira (isl.), Greece 45/F7
Kíthnos (isl.), Greece 45/G7
Kitikmeot (reg.), N.W.T. 187/G2
Kitim, Jordan 65/D3
Kitimat, Br. Col. 162/D5
Kitimat, Br. Col. 146/F4
Kitimat, Br. Col. 184/C3
Kitinen (riv.), Finland 18/P3
Kitsap (co.), Wash. 310/C3
Kitsault, Br. Col. 184/C2
Kitscoty, Alberta 182/E3
Kitt (peak), Ariz. 198/D7
Kittanning, Pa. 294/D4
Kittatinny (mts.), N.J. 273/D1
Kittery, Maine 243/B9
Kittery•, Maine 243/B9
Kittery Point, Maine 243/B9
Kittilä, Finland 18/O3
Kittitas (co.), Wash. 310/E3
Kittitas, Wash. 310/E4
Kittrell, N.C. 281/M2
Kitts, Ky. 237/P7
Kitts Hill, Ohio 284/E8
Kittson (co.), Minn. 255/B2
Kitty Hawk, N.C. 281/T2
Kitui, Kenya 115/G4
Kitunda, Tanzania 115/F5
Kitwanga, Br. Col. 184/D2
Kitwe, Zambia 115/E6
Kitwe, Zambia 102/E6
Kitzbühel, Austria 41/B3
Kitzingen, Germany 22/C4
Kitzmiller, Md. 245/B3
Kiuchüan (Jiuquan), China 77/E4
Kiukiang (Jiujiang), China 77/J6
Kiunga, Papua N.G. 85/B7
Kivalina, Alaska 196/E1
Kivijärvi (lake), Finland 18/O5
Kiviõli, Estonia 53/D1
Kivu (lake) 102/E5
Kivu (lake), Rwanda 115/E4
Kivu (prov.), D.R. Congo 115/E4
Kivu (lake), D.R. Congo 115/E4
Kiyiu (lake), Sask. 181/C4
Kizel', Russia 7/K3
Kizel, Russia 48/F4
Kizel, Russia 52/J3
Kızılcahamam, Turkey 63/E2
Kızılhisar, Turkey 63/C4
Kızılırmak (riv.), Turkey 63/F2
Kızılırmak (riv.), Turkey 59/B1
Kızıltepe, Turkey 63/J4
Kızıltoprak, Turkey 63/D6
Kızılviran, Turkey 63/E4
Kizimkazi, Tanzania 115/G5
Kizlyar, Russia 52/G6
Kizu, Japan 81/J7
Kizyl-Arvat, Turkmenistan 48/F6
Kjeller, Norway 18/E3
Kjellerup, Denmark 21/C5
Kjölen (mts.) 7/F2
Kjölen (mts.), Norway 18/K3
Kladanj, Bos. 45/D3
Kladno, Czech Rep. 41/B1
Kladovo, Yugoslavia 45/F3
Klagenfurt, Austria 41/C3
Klagetoh, Ariz. 198/F3
Klaipėda, Lithuania 7/F3
Klaipėda, Lithuania 48/B4
Klaipėda, Lithuania 52/B3
Klaipėda, Lithuania 53/A3
Klaksvík, Denmark 21/B2
Klamath (riv.), Calif. 188/B2
Klamath, Calif. 204/B2
Klamath (riv.), Calif. 204/B2
Klamath (co.), Oreg. 291/F5
Klamath (mts.), Oreg. 291/C5
Klamath (riv.), Oreg. 291/E6
Klamath Agency, Oreg. 291/F5
Klamath Falls, Oreg. 146/F5
Klamath Falls, Oreg. 188/B2
Klamath Falls, Oreg. 291/F5
Klapmuts, S. Africa 118/F6
Klar (riv.), Sweden 7/F2
Klarälv (riv.), Sweden 18/H6
Klaten, Indonesia 85/J2
Klatovy, Czech Rep. 41/B2
Klausen (pass), Switzerland 39/G3
Klawock, Alaska 196/M2
Klazienaveen, Netherlands 27/L3
Kleberg (co.), Texas 303/G10
Kleefeld, Manitoba 179/F5
Kleena Kleene, Br. Col. 184/E4
Klein, Mont. 262/H4
Klein Bonaire (isl.), Neth. Ant. 161/E8
Kleine Emme (riv.), Switzerland 39/F3
Klein Karas, Namibia 118/B5
Kleinlützel, Switzerland 39/D2
Kleinmachnow, Germany 22/E4
Kleinmond, S. Africa 118/F7
Klemme, Iowa 229/F3
Klemtu, Br. Col. 184/C4
Klerksdorp, S. Africa 118/D5
Kleve, Germany 22/B3
Klickitat (co.), Wash. 310/E5
Klickitat, Wash. 310/D5
Klickitat (riv.), Wash. 310/D4
Klides (isls.), Cyprus 63/F5
Klinaklini (riv.), Br. Col. 184/E4
Kline, S.C. 296/E5
Kline, W. Va. 312/H5
Kling, Philippines 82/E8
Klingenthal, Germany 22/E3
Klingnau, Switzerland 39/F1
Klintehamn, Sweden 18/K8
Klintsy, Russia 52/D4
Klip (riv.), S. Africa 118/H6
Kliprivier, S. Africa 118/H7
Klitmøller, Denmark 21/B3
Ključ, Bos. 45/C3
Kłobuck, Poland 47/D3
Kloch (lake), Br. Col. 184/E2
Kłodawa, Poland 47/D2
Kłodnica (riv.), Poland 47/A4
Kłodzko, Poland 47/C3
Klondike (riv.), Yukon 187/E3
Klondike Gold Rush Nat'l Hist. Park, Alaska 196/N1
Klondyke, Ariz. 198/E6
Klossner, Minn. 255/D6
Klosterneuburg, Austria 41/D2
Klosters-Serneus, Switzerland 39/J3
Kloten, N. Dak. 282/O4
Kloten, Switzerland 39/G2
Klotzville, La. 238/K3
Kluane (lake), Yukon 162/C3
Kluane (lake), Yukon 187/E3
Kluane Nat'l Park, Yukon 187/E3
Kluane Nat'l Park, Yukon 162/C3
Kluczbork, Poland 47/D3
Klukwan, Alaska 196/M1
Klutina (lake), Alaska 196/D1
Klyuchevskaya Sopka (vol.), Russia 48/Q4
Knapdale (dist.), Scotland 15/C5
Knapp, Minn. 255/D5
Knapp, Wis. 317/B6
Knappa, Oreg. 291/D1

Krishna 393

Knapp Creek, N.Y. 276/C6
Knaresborough, England 13/F4
Knaresborough, England 10/F3
Knee (lake), Manitoba 179/J3
Knierim, Iowa 229/D4
Knife (lake), Minn. 255/G2
Knife (riv.), N. Dak. 282/G5
Knife River, Minn. 255/G4
Knife R. Indian Villages Nat'l Hist. Site, N. Dak. 282/H5
Knifley, Ky. 237/L6
Knight (isl.), Alaska 196/D1
Knight (inlet), Br. Col. 184/E5
Knightdale, N.C. 281/N3
Knight Inlet, Br. Col. 184/E5
Knighton, Wales 10/E4
Knighton, Wales 13/D5
Knightsen, Calif. 204/L1
Knights Landing, Calif. 204/B8
Knightstown, Ind. 227/F5
Knightstown, Ireland 17/A8
Knightsville, Ind. 227/C5
Knightville (res.), Mass. 249/C3
Knik Arm (inlet), Alaska 196/B1
Kniman, Ind. 227/C2
Knin, Croatia 45/C3
Knippa, Texas 303/E8
Knittelfeld, Austria 41/C3
Knjaževac, Yugoslavia 45/F4
Knobel, Ark. 202/J1
Knob Fork, W. Va. 312/E3
Knob Lick, Ky. 237/K6
Knob Lick, Mo. 261/M7
Knob Noster, Mo. 261/E5
Knock, Ireland 17/D4
Knockadoon (head), Ireland 17/F8
Knockanefune (mt.), Ireland 17/C7
Knockboy (mt.), Ireland 17/B8
Knocklayd (mt.), N. Ireland 17/J1
Knocklong, Ireland 17/D7
Knockmealdown (mts.), Ireland 17/F7
Knocknagashel, Ireland 17/C7
Knoke, Iowa 229/D3
Knokke-Heist, Belgium 27/C6
Knøsen (mt.), Denmark 21/D3
Knott (co.), Ky. 237/R6
Knott, Texas 303/C5
Knotts Island, N.C. 281/T2
Knottsville, Ky. 237/H5
Knowles, Okla. 288/F1
Knowlesville, New Bruns. 170/C2
Knowlesville, N.Y. 276/D4
Knowlton, Mont. 262/L4
Knowlton, Québec 172/E4
Knowlton, Wis. 317/G6
Knox (cape), Br. Col. 162/C5
Knox (cape), Br. Col. 184/A3
Knox (co.), Ill. 222/C3
Knox (co.), Ind. 227/C7
Knox, Ind. 227/D2
Knox (co.), Ky. 237/O7
Knox (co.), Maine 243/E7
Knox•, Maine 243/E6
Knox (co.), Mo. 261/H2
Knox (co.), Nebr. 264/G2
Knox (lake), Newf. 166/A3
Knox, N. Dak. 282/L3
Knox (co.), Ohio 284/F5
Knox, Pa. 294/C3
Knox (co.), Tenn. 237/O9
Knox (co.), Texas 303/E4
Knox, Victoria 97/K5
Knox, Victoria 88/M7
Knoxboro, N.Y. 276/J5
Knox Center, Maine 243/E6
Knox City, Mo. 261/H2
Knox City, Texas 303/E4
Knox Coast (reg.), Ant. 5/C6
Knoxville, Ala. 195/C4
Knoxville, Ark. 202/D3
Knoxville, Ga. 217/E5
Knoxville, Ill. 222/C3
Knoxville, Iowa 229/G6
Knoxville, Md. 245/H3
Knoxville, Miss. 256/B8
Knoxville, Mo. 261/E4
Knoxville, Pa. 294/H2
Knoxville, Tenn. 146/K6
Knoxville, Tenn. 188/K3
Knoxville, Tenn. 237/O9
Knud Rasmussen Land (reg.), Greenl. 4/B12
Knudshoved (pt.), Denmark 21/D7
Knurów, Poland 47/A4
Knutsford, Br. Col. 184/G5
Knutsford, England 13/H2
Knutsford, England 10/G2
Knutsford, Pr. Edward I. 168/D2
Knysna, S. Africa 118/C6
Koah Kong (isl.), Cambodia 72/D5
Koah Nhek, Cambodia 72/E4
Koah Rung (isl.), Cambodia 72/D5
Koah Tang (isl.), Cambodia 72/D5
Koali, Hawaii 218/K2
Koa Mill, Hawaii 218/G6
Koani, Tanzania 115/G5
Kobayashi, Japan 81/E8
Kobbfjorden (fjord), Norway 18/O1
Kobdo (Hovd), Mongolia 77/D2
Kobe, Japan 81/H7
Kobe, Japan 54/P6
København (co.), Denmark 21/F6
København (Copenhagen) (cap.), Denmark 21/F6
København (Copenhagen) (commune), Denmark 21/F6
Koblenz, Germany 22/B3
Koblenz, Switzerland 39/F1
Kobrin, Belarus 52/B4
Kobroor (isl.), Indonesia 85/K7
Kobuk, Alaska 196/G1
Kobuk (riv.), Alaska 188/C5
Kobuk (riv.), Alaska 196/G1
Kobuk Valley Nat'l Park, Alaska 196/F1
Kobuleti, Georgia 52/F6
Koca (riv.), Turkey 63/C3
Koca (riv.), Turkey 63/C6
Koca (riv.), Turkey 63/E2
Kocaeli (prov.), Turkey 63/C2
Kocaeli (Izmit), Turkey 63/D2
Kočani, Macedonia 45/F5
Koçarlı, Turkey 63/B4
Kočevje, Slovenia 45/B3
Koch (isl.), N.W.T. 187/L3
Koch'ang, S. Korea 81/C6
Kochevo, Russia 52/J3
Kochi (pref.), Japan 81/F7
Kochi, Japan 81/F7
Kodaira, Japan 81/O2
Kodak, Tenn. 237/O9
Kodiak, Alaska 188/D6
Kodiak, Alaska 196/H3
Kodiak (isl.), Alaska 146/C4
Kodiak (isl.), Alaska 196/H3
Kodiak, U.S. 4/D17
Kodiak (isl.), U.S. 4/D17
Kodok, Sudan 111/F6
Kodok, Sudan 102/F4
Koekelare, Belgium 27/B6
Koekelberg, Belgium 27/B9
Koenig, Mo. 261/J6
Koenton, Ala. 195/B7
Koes, Namibia 118/B5
Kofa (mts.), Ariz. 198/B5
Kofçaz, Turkey 63/B2
Koffiefontein, S. Africa 118/D5
Köflach, Austria 41/C3
Koforidua, Ghana 106/D7
Kofu, Japan 81/J6
Koga, Japan 81/J5
Kogaluc (riv.), Québec 174/E1
Kogaluk (riv.), Newf. 166/B2
Koganei, Japan 81/O2
Kogarah, N. S. Wales 88/K4
Kogarah, N.S. Wales 97/J4
Køge, Denmark 21/F7
Køge (bay), Denmark 21/F7
Koggiung, Alaska 196/G3
Kogo, Equat. Guinea 106/F8
Kogo, Equat. Guinea 115/A3
Kohala (Kapaau), Hawaii 218/G3
Kohala (mts.), Hawaii 218/G4
Kohala (peak), Hawaii 218/G4
Kohat, Pakistan 59/K3
Kohat, Pakistan 68/C2
Kohila, Estonia 53/C1
Kohima, India 68/G3
Kohkiluyeh and Boyer Ahmediyeh (gov.), Iran 66/G5
Kohler, Wis. 317/L8
Kohls Ranch, Ariz. 198/D4
Kohtla-Järve, Estonia 52/C3
Kohtla-Järve, Estonia 53/D1
Kohŭng, S. Korea 81/C6
Koidern, Yukon 187/D3
Koitere (lake), Finland 18/R5
Kŏje (isl.), S. Korea 81/D6
Kojetín, Czech Rep. 41/D2
Kojonup, W. Australia 88/B6
Kojonup, W. Australia 92/B6
Kokadjo, Maine 243/E4
Kokand, Uzbekistan 48/H5
Kokanee Glacier Prov. Park, Br. Col. 184/J5
Kokava nad Rimavicou, Slovakia 41/E2
Kokchetav, Kazakhstan 48/H4
Kokchetav, Kazakhstan 54/J4
Kokemäki, Finland 18/N6
Kokish, Br. Col. 184/D5
Kokiu (Gejiu), China 77/F7
Kokkola, Finland 18/N5
Koknanok, Alaska 196/H3
Koko (head), Hawaii 218/F2
Koko, Nigeria 106/F7
Kokoda, Papua N.G. 85/C7
Kokole (pt.), Hawaii 218/B2
Kokolik (riv.), Alaska 196/F1
Kokomo, Hawaii 218/K2
Kokomo, Ind. 188/J2
Kokomo, Ind. 227/E4
Kokomo, Miss. 256/E8
Kokonau, Indonesia 85/K6
Kokopo, Papua N.G. 86/B2
Kokosing (riv.), Ohio 284/E5
Kokrines, Alaska 196/G1
Kokrines (hills), Alaska 196/H1
Koksan, N. Korea 81/C4
Koksijde, Belgium 27/B6
Koksilah, Br. Col. 184/J3
Koksoak (riv.), Que. 162/K4
Koksoak (riv.), Québec 174/D1
Kokstad, S. Africa 118/D6
Kokubu, Japan 81/E8
Kola, Manitoba 179/A5
Kola (pen.), Russia 4/C8
Kola (pen.), Russia 7/H2
Kola (pen.), Russia 48/D3
Kola (pen.), Russia 52/E1
Kolahun, Liberia 106/C7
Kolaka, Indonesia 85/G6
Kolar, India 68/D6
Kolar Gold Fields, India 68/D6
Kolari, Finland 18/O3
Kolárovo, Slovakia 41/D3
Kolašin, Yugoslavia 45/D4
Kolberg (Kołobrzeg), Poland 47/B1
Kolbio, Kenya 115/H4
Kolbuszowa, Poland 47/E3
Kolda, Senegal 106/B6
Kolding, Denmark 18/F9
Kolding, Denmark 21/C7
Kole, Haut-Zaïre, D.R. Congo 115/E3
Kole, Kasai-Oriental, D.R. Congo 115/D4
Koleen, Ind. 227/D7
Kolekole (stream), Hawaii 218/J4
Kölen (mts.), Sweden 18/K3
Kolepom (isl.), Indonesia 85/K7
Kolguyev (isl.), Russia 4/B7
Kolguyev (isl.), Russia 7/J2
Kolguyev (isl.), Russia 48/E3
Kolguyev (isl.), Russia 52/G1
Kolhapur, India 68/C5
Kolhapur, India 54/J8
Koliganek, Alaska 196/G3
Kolín, Czech Rep. 41/C1
Kolin, Mont. 262/G3
Kolind, Denmark 21/D5
Kölliken, Switzerland 39/F2
Kollum, Netherlands 27/J2
Kolmanskop, Namibia 118/B5
Köln (Cologne), Germany 22/B3
Kolno, Poland 47/F2
Koło, Poland 47/D2
Koloa, Hawaii 188/E5
Koloa, Hawaii 218/C2
Koloa Landing, Hawaii 218/C2
Kołobrzeg, Poland 47/B1
Kologriv, Russia 52/F3
Kolokani, Mali 106/C6
Kolola Springs, Miss. 256/H3
Kolombangara (isl.), Solomon Is. 86/D2
Kolomiya, Ukraine 52/B5
Kolomna, Russia 7/H3
Kolomna, Russia 48/D4
Kolomna, Russia 52/E4
Kolondiéba, Mali 106/C6
Kolonodale, Indonesia 85/G6
Kolovrat (mt.), Solomon Is. 86/E3
Kolpashevo, Russia 54/K4
Kolpashevo, Russia 48/J4
Kolpino, Russia 52/D3
Kolva (riv.), Russia 52/J1
Kolwezi, D.R. Congo 102/E6
Kolwezi, D.R. Congo 115/E6
Kolyma (range), Russia 4/C1
Kolyma (range), Russia 48/Q3
Kolyma (range), Russia 54/S3
Kolyma (riv.), Russia 4/C2
Kolyma (riv.), Russia 48/Q3
Kolyma (riv.), Russia 54/S3
Koma, Burma 72/C4
Komádi, Hungary 41/F3
Komadugu Yobe (riv.), Niger 106/G6
Komadugu Yobe (riv.), Nigeria 106/G6
Komaga (mt.), Japan 81/K2
Komagane, Japan 81/H6
Komandorskiye (isls.), Russia 2/T3
Komandorskiye (isls.), Russia 48/R4
Komandorskiye (isls.), Russia 54/T4
Komárno, Slovakia 41/D3
Komarno, Manitoba 179/E4
Komárom (co.), Hungary 41/E3
Komárom, Hungary 41/E3
Komatke, Ariz. 198/C5
Komatsu, Japan 81/H5
Komba, D.R. Congo 115/D3
Kŏmdŏk (mt.), N. Korea 81/D3
Komi Aut. Rep., Russia 48/F3
Komi Aut. Rep., Russia 52/H2
Komi-Permyak Aut. Okr., Russia 48/F4
Komi-Permyak Aut. Okr., Russia 52/H3
Komló, Hungary 41/E3
Kommetjie, S. Africa 118/E7
Kommunarsk, Ukraine 52/E5
Komodo (isl.), Indonesia 85/F7
Komoka, Ontario 177/C5
Kôm Ombo, Egypt 111/F3
Kôm Ombo, Egypt 59/B5
Komono, Congo 115/B4
Komoran (isl.), Indonesia 85/K7
Komotiní, Greece 45/G5
Komrat, Moldova 52/C5
Komsomolets (isl.), Russia 4/A5
Komsomolets (isl.), Russia 48/L1
Komsomolets (isl.), Russia 54/M1
Komsomol'sk, Russia 54/P4
Komsomol'skiy, Russia 52/K1
Komsomol'sk-na-Amure, Russia 48/O4
Kona, Ky. 237/R6
Konahuanui (peaks), Hawaii 218/C3
Konar (riv.), Afghanistan 68/C1
Konar (riv.), Afghanistan 59/K2
Konar (riv.), Pakistan 68/C1
Konawa, Okla. 288/N5
Kondoa, Tanzania 115/G4
Kondopoga, Russia 52/D2
Kondopoga, Russia 48/D3
Kondoros, Hungary 41/F3
Konduz, Afghan. 58/J2
Konduz, Afghan. 68/B1
Konduz (riv.), Afghan. 58/J2
Konduz (riv.), Afghan. 68/B1
Koné, New Caled. 86/G4
Kong, Koh (isl.), Cambodia 72/D5
Kong, Ivory Coast 106/D7
Kongiganak, Alaska 196/F3
Kongju, S. Korea 81/C5
Kong Karls Land (isl.), Norway 18/E1
Kongmoon (Jiangmen), China 77/H7
Kongolo, D.R. Congo 115/E5
Kongolo, D.R. Congo 102/E5
Kongor, Sudan 111/F6
Kongsberg, N. Dak. 282/J4
Kongsberg, Norway 18/F7
Kongsfjorden (fjord), Norway 18/B2
Kongsvinger, Norway 18/H6
Kongur Shan (mt.), China 77/A4
Kongwa, Tanzania 115/G5
Koni (pen.), Russia 48/Q4
Koniecpol, Poland 47/D3
Königsberg (Kaliningrad), Russia 52/B4
Königssee (lake), Germany 22/E5
Königswiesen, Austria 41/C2
Königswinter, Germany 22/B3
Königs Wusterhausen, Germany 22/E2
Konin (prov.), Poland 47/D2
Konin, Poland 47/D2
Kónitsa, Greece 45/E5
Koniuji (isls.), Alaska 196/G3
Köniz, Switzerland 39/D3
Konjic, Bos. 45/D4
Konkiep, Namibia 118/B5
Konnagar, India 68/F1
Konolfingen, Switzerland 39/E3
Konomoc (lake), Conn. 210/G3
Konosha, Russia 52/F2
Konotop, Ukraine 52/D4
Konqi He (riv.), China 77/C3
Końskie, Poland 47/E3
Konstantinovka, Ukraine 52/E5
Konstantynów Łódzki, Poland 47/D3
Konstanz, Germany 22/C5
Kontagora, Nigeria 106/F6
Kontcha, Cameroon 115/B2
Kontich, Belgium 27/E6
Kontiomäki, Finland 18/Q4
Kon Tum, Vietnam 72/E4
Kon Tum (plat.), Vietnam 72/E4
Konya (prov.), Turkey 63/E4
Konya, Turkey 63/E4
Konya, Turkey 59/B2
Konya, Turkey 54/E6
Konza, Kenya 115/G4
Koocanusa (lake), Br. Col. 184/K6
Koocanusa (lake), Mont. 262/A2
Koochiching (co.), Minn. 255/E2
Koog aan de Zaan, Netherlands 27/A4
Koolan (isl.), W. Australia 88/C3
Koolan (isl.), W. Australia 92/C1
Koolau (range), Hawaii 218/E2
Kooline Station, W. Australia 92/B3
Koolpinyah, North. Terr. 93/B2
Koolyanobbing, W. Australia 88/B6
Koolyanobbing, W. Australia 92/B5
Koondrook, Victoria 97/B4
Koonibba, S. Australia 88/E6
Koonibba, S. Australia 94/C4
Koontz Lake, Ind. 227/D2
Koorawatha, N.S. Wales 97/E4
Koosharem, Utah 304/C5
Koosharem Ind. Res., Utah 304/C5
Kooskia, Idaho 220/C3
Koostatak, Manitoba 179/E3
Kootenai (co.), Idaho 220/B2
Kootenai, Idaho 220/B1
Kootenai (riv.), Idaho 220/C1
Kootenai (riv.), Mont. 262/A2
Kootenay (lake), Br. Col. 162/E5
Kootenay (lake), Br. Col. 184/J5
Kootenay (riv.), Br. Col. 184/K5
Kootenay Nat'l Park, Br. Col. 184/J4
Kootenay Nat'l Pk., Br. Col. 162/E5
Kootingal, N.S. Wales 97/F2
Kópavogur, Iceland 21/B1
Köpenick, Germany 22/F4
Koper, Slovenia 45/A3
Kopervik, Norway 18/D7
Kopeysk, Russia 48/G4
Köping, Sweden 18/J7
Koppal, India 68/D5
Koppang, Norway 18/G6
Kopparberg (co.), Sweden 18/J6
Kopparberg, Sweden 18/J7
Koppel, Pa. 294/B4
Kopperston, W. Va. 312/C7
Koprivnica, Croatia 45/C2
Köprü (riv.), Turkey 63/D4
Kor (riv.), Iran 66/H6
Korab (mt.), Albania 45/E5
Korab (mt.), Macedonia 45/E5
Koraka (cape), Turkey 63/B3
Koran, La. 238/D2
Koraput, India 68/E5
Korba, India 68/E4
Korbach, Germany 22/C3
Korbel, Calif. 204/B3
Korçë, Albania 45/E5
Korčula (isl.), Croatia 45/C4
Kordestan (Kurdistan) (prov.), Iran 66/E3
Kord Kuy, Iran 66/J2
Kordofan, Southern (prov.), Sudan 111/E5
Kordofan, Northern (prov.), Sudan 111/E5
Korea (North) 2/R4
KOREA (NORTH) 81
Korea (South) 2/R4
KOREA (SOUTH) 81
Korea (bay), N. Korea 81/B4
Korea (str.), S. Korea 81/D6
Korenovsk, Russia 52/E5
Korf, Russia 4/C1
Korf, Russia 48/R3
Korf, Russia 54/T3
Korhogo, Ivory Coast 106/C7
Korhogo, Ivory Coast 102/B4
Kőrishegy (mt.), Hungary 41/D3
Koriyama, Japan 81/K5
Korkuteli, Turkey 63/D4
Korla, China 77/C3
Kormakiti (cape), Cyprus 59/B2
Kormakiti (cape), Cyprus 63/E5
Körmend, Hungary 41/D3
Kornat (isl.), Yugoslavia 45/B4
Korneuburg, Austria 41/D2
Kornsjø, Norway 18/G7
Kornwestheim, Germany 22/C4
Koro (isl.), Fiji 86/Q10
Koro (sea), Fiji 86/Q10
Köroğlu (mts.), Turkey 63/E2
Köroğlu Dağı (mt.), Turkey 63/E2
Korogwe, Tanzania 115/G5
Koroit, Victoria 97/B6
Korona, Fla. 212/E2
Koronadal, Philippines 82/E7
Koronowo, Poland 47/C2
Koropí, Greece 45/G7
Koror (cap.), Palau 87/D5
Kororoit (creek), Victoria 97/H5
Kororoit (creek), Victoria 88/K7
Körös (riv.), Hungary 41/F3
Körösladány, Hungary 41/F3
Korosten', Ukraine 52/C4
Korostyshev, Ukraine 52/C4
Koro Toro, Chad 111/C4
Korpilombolo, Sweden 18/N3
Korsakov, Russia 48/P5
Korsnäs, Finland 18/M5
Korsør, Denmark 21/E7
Korsør, Denmark 18/G9
Kortemark, Belgium 27/C6
Korti, Sudan 111/F4
Korti, Sudan 59/B6
Kortrijk, Belgium 27/C7
Korumburra, Victoria 97/D6
Koryak (range), Russia 48/S3
Koryak (range), Russia 54/U3
Koryak Aut. Okr., Russia 48/R3
Koryazhma, Russia 52/G2
Kos, Greece 45/H7
Kos (isl.), Greece 45/H7
Kościan, Poland 47/C2
Kościerzyna, Poland 47/C1
Kosciusko (mt.), Australia 87/F9
Kosciusko (co.), Ind. 227/F2
Kosciusko, Miss. 256/E4
Kosciusko (mt.), N. S. Wales 88/H7
Kosciusko (mt.), N.S. Wales 97/E5
Koshigaya, Japan 81/P2
Koshiki (isls.), Japan 81/D8
Koshk-e Kohneh, Afghanistan 68/A2
Koshkonong, Mo. 261/J9
Koshkonong (lake), Wis. 317/H10
Košice, Slovakia 7/G4
Košice, Slovakia 41/F2
Koslan, Russia 48/E3
Koslan, Russia 52/G2
Köslin (Koszalin), Poland 47/C1
Kosoma, Okla. 288/P6
Kosŏng, N. Korea 81/D4
Kosovo (aut. reg.), Yugoslavia 45/E4
Kosovska Mitrovica, Yugoslavia 45/E4
Kosrae (isl.), Micronesia 87/G5
Kosse, Texas 303/H6
Kössen, Austria 41/B3
Kossou, Lac de (lake), Ivory Coast 106/C7
Kossuth, Ind. 227/E7
Kossuth (co.), Iowa 229/E2
Kossuth, Miss. 256/G1
Kostajnica, Croatia 45/C3
Kostelec nad černými Lesy, Czech Rep. 41/C2
Kostelec nad Orlicí, Czech Rep. 41/D1
Kosti, Sudan 59/B7
Kosti, Sudan 111/F5
Kosti, Sudan 102/F3
Kostopol', Ukraine 52/C4
Kostroma, Russia 7/J3
Kostroma, Russia 48/E4
Kostroma, Russia 52/F3
Kostrzyń, Poland 47/B2
Koszalin (prov.), Poland 47/C1
Koszalin, Poland 7/F3
Koszalin, Poland 47/C1
Kőszeg, Hungary 41/D3
Koszta, Iowa 229/J5
Kota, India 68/D3
Kota, India 54/J7
Kotaagung, Indonesia 85/C7
Kotabaharu, Indonesia 85/E6
Kota Baharu, Malaysia 54/M9
Kota Baharu, Malaysia 72/D6
Kotabaru, Indonesia 85/F6
Kotabumi, Indonesia 85/C7
Kota Kinabalu, Malaysia 54/N9
Kota Kinabalu, Malaysia 85/F4
Kotamobagu, Indonesia 85/G5
Kota Tinggi, Malaysia 72/F5
Kotawaringin, Indonesia 85/E6
Kotcho (lake), Br. Col. 184/M2
Kotcho (riv.), Br. Col. 184/M2
Kotel, Bulgaria 45/H4
Kotel'nich, Russia 52/G3
Kotel'nikovo, Russia 52/F5
Kotel'nyy (isl.), Russia 4/B2
Kotel'nyy (isl.), Russia 48/O2
Köthen, Germany 22/E3
Kotido, Uganda 115/F3
Kotka, Finland 7/G2
Kotka, Finland 18/P6
Kotlas, Russia 7/J2
Kotlas, Russia 48/E3
Kotlas, Russia 52/G2
Kotlik, Alaska 196/F2
Kotor, Yugoslavia 45/D4
Kotovo, Russia 52/G4
Kotovsk, Odessa, Ukraine 52/C5
Kotovsk, Tambov, Russia 52/F4
Kotri, Pakistan 68/B3
Kötschach-Mauthen, Austria 41/B3
Kottaguden, India 68/E5
Kottayam, India 68/D7
Kotto (riv.), Cent. Afr. Rep. 115/D2
Kotturu, India 68/D6
Kotuy (riv.), Russia 4/B4
Kotuy (riv.), Russia 48/L3
Kotuy (riv.), Russia 54/M2
Kotzebue, Alaska 196/F1
Kotzebue, Alaska 146/B3
Kotzebue, Alaska 188/C5
Kotzebue (sound), Alaska 196/F1
Kotzebue, U.S. 4/C18
Kouango, Cent. Afr. Rep. 115/D2
Kouchibouguac, New Bruns. 170/F2
Kouchibouguac (bay), New Bruns. 170/F2
Kouchibouguacis (riv.), New Bruns. 170/E2
Kouchobouguac Nat'l Park, New Bruns. 170/F2
Koudougou, Burkina Faso 106/D6
Kouilou (riv.), Congo 115/B4
Koukdjuak (riv.), N.W.T. 187/L3
Kouki, Cent. Afr. Rep. 115/C2
Koula-Moutou, Gabon 115/B4
Koula-Moutou, Gabon 102/D5
Koulikoro, Mali 106/C6
Koulikoro, Mali 102/B3
Koumala, Queensland 95/D4
Koumbi Saleh (ruins), Mauritania 106/C5
Koumra, Chad 102/D4
Koumra, Chad 111/C6
Koundara, Guinea 106/B6
Kounde, Cent. Afr. Rep. 115/B2
Kouno, Chad 111/C6
Kounradskiy, Kazakhstan 48/H5
Kountze, Texas 303/K7
Koupela, Burkina Faso 106/D6
Kourou, Fr. Guiana 131/E3
Kourouba, Mali 106/B6
Kouroussa, Guinea 106/C6
Kousseri, Cameroon 115/B1
Koutiala, Mali 106/C6
Koutiala, Mali 102/B3
Kouts, Ind. 227/C2
Kouvola, Finland 18/P6
Kovdor, Russia 52/D1
Kovel', Ukraine 48/C4
Kovel', Ukraine 52/C4
Kovrov, Russia 48/E4
Kovrov, Russia 52/F3
Kovur, India 68/E6
Kovylkino, Russia 52/F4
Kowary, Poland 47/B3
Kowloon, China 77/H7
Kowst, Afghanistan 59/J3
Kowt-e 'Ashrow, Afghanistan 68/B2
Koyama, Japan 81/E8
Köyceğiz, Turkey 63/C4
Köyceğiz (lake), Turkey 63/C4
Koyuk, Alaska 196/F1
Koyukuk, Alaska 196/G1
Koyukuk (riv.), Alaska 188/C5
Koyukuk (riv.), Alaska 196/G1
Koyulhisar, Turkey 63/G2
Kozaklı, Turkey 63/F3
Kozan, Turkey 63/F4
Kozáni, Greece 45/F5
Kozhevnikovo, Russia 48/L2
Kozhikode, India 68/D6
Kozhikode, India 54/J8
Kozhva, Russia 52/J1
Kozienice, Poland 47/E3
Kozlu, Turkey 63/D2
Kozluk, Turkey 63/J3
Kozmin, Poland 47/C3
Kożuchów, Poland 47/B3
Kpalimé, Togo 106/E7
Kpandu, Ghana 106/D7
Kpémé, Togo 106/E7
Kra (isth.), Thailand 72/C5
Kraaifontein, S. Africa 118/F6
Kraainem, Belgium 27/C9
Krabi, Thailand 72/C5
Kra Buri, Thailand 72/C5
Kracheh, Cambodia 72/E4
Kraemer, La. 238/M4
Kragan, Indonesia 85/K2
Kragerø, Norway 18/F7
Kragujevac, Yugoslavia 45/E3
Kragujevac, Yugoslavia 7/G4
Krakatau (Rakata) (isl.), Indonesia 85/C7
Krakow, Mo. 261/K6
Kraków (Cracow), Poland 47/E4
Krakow, Wis. 317/K6
Kralendijk (cap.), Bonaire, Neth. Ant. 161/E8
Kralendijk, Neth. Ant. 156/E4
Králíky, Czech Rep. 41/D1
Kraljevo, Yugoslavia 45/E4
Kralovice, Czech Rep. 41/B2
Král'ovský Chlmec, Czech Rep. 41/G2
Kralupy nad Vltavou, Czech Rep. 41/C1
Kramatorsk, Ukraine 52/E5
Kramer, Ind. 227/C4
Kramer, Nebr. 264/H4
Kramer, N. Dak. 282/J2
Kramfors, Sweden 18/L5
Kranidhion, Greece 45/F7
Kranj, Slovenia 45/B2
Kranzburg, S. Dak. 298/R4
Krapkowice, Poland 47/D3
Krasino, Russia 52/H1
Krasino, Russia 48/F2
Krāslava, Latvia 53/D3
Kraslice, Czech Rep. 41/B1
Krásná Lípa, Czech Rep. 41/C1
Kraśnik Fabryczny, Poland 47/F3
Krasnoarmeysk, Russia 52/G4
Krasnoborsk, Russia 52/G2
Krasnodar, Russia 7/H4
Krasnodar, Russia 48/E5
Krasnodar, Russia 52/E6
Krasnograd, Ukraine 52/E5
Krasnokamensk, Russia 48/M4
Krasnokamsk, Russia 48/F4
Krasnokamsk, Russia 52/H3
Krasnoperekopsk, Ukraine 52/D5
Krasnoslobodsk, Russia 52/G5
Krasnotur'insk, Russia 48/G3
Krasnoural'sk, Russia 48/G4
Krasnovishersk, Russia 52/J2
Krasnovodsk, Turkmenistan 54/G5
Krasnovodsk, Turkmenistan 48/F5
Krasnoyarsk, Russia 2/P3
Krasnoyarsk, Russia 48/K4
Krasnoyarsk, Russia 54/L4
Krasnystaw, Poland 47/F3
Krasnyy Kut, Russia 52/G4
Krasnyy Luch, Ukraine 52/E5
Krasnyy Sulin, Russia 52/F5
Krasnyy Yar, Russia 52/G5
Kraulshavn (Nussaq), Greenl. 4/B13
Krause Lagoon (chan.), Virgin Is. (U.S.) 161/F4
Krawang, Indonesia 85/H2
Krebs, Okla. 288/P5
Krefeld, Germany 22/B3
Kremenchug, Ukraine 7/H4
Kremenchug, Ukraine 48/D5
Kremenchug, Ukraine 52/D5
Kremlin, Mont. 262/F2
Kremlin, Okla. 288/L1
Kremmling, Colo. 208/G2
Kremnica, Slovakia 41/E2
Krems an der Donau, Austria 41/C2
Krenitzin (isls.), Alaska 196/E4
Kresgeville, Pa. 294/L4
Kress, Texas 303/C3
Kretinga, Lithuania 53/A3
Kreutztal, Germany 22/C3
Kreuzlingen, Switzerland 39/H1
Kribi, Cameroon 115/B3
Krichev, Belarus 52/D4
Kriens, Switzerland 39/F2
Krimml, Austria 41/B3
Krimpen aan den IJssel, Netherlands 27/F5
Kriós (cape), Greece 45/F8
Krishna (Kistna) (riv.), India 68/D5

394 Krishnanagar

Krishnanagar, India 68/F4
Kristiansand, Norway 18/F8
Kristiansand, Norway 7/E3
Kristianstad (co.), Sweden 18/J8
Kristianstad, Sweden 18/J9
Kristiansund, Norway 7/E2
Kristiansund, Norway 18/E5
Kristiinankaupunki (Kristinestad), Finland 18/N5
Kristinehamn, Sweden 18/H7
Kristinestad, Finland 18/N5
Kríti (Crete) (isl.), Greece 45/G8
Krivoy Rog, Ukraine 7/H4
Krivoy Rog, Ukraine 48/D5
Krivoy Rog, Ukraine 52/D5
Križevci, Croatia 45/C2
Krk, Croatia 45/B3
Krk (isl.), Croatia 45/B3
Krnov, Czech Rep. 41/D1
Krolevets, Ukraine 52/D4
Kroměříž, Czech Rep. 41/D2
Krompachy, Slovakia 41/F2
Kronach, Germany 22/D3
Kronau, Sask. 181/G5
Krong Kaoh Kong, Cambodia 72/D4
Krong Keb, Cambodia 72/E5
Kronoberg (co.), Sweden 18/J8
Kronshtadt, Russia 52/C3
Kroonstad, S. Africa 118/D5
Kropotkin, Russia 52/F5
Kroschel, Minn. 255/E4
Krosno (prov.), Poland 47/E4
Krosno, Poland 47/E4
Krosno Odrzanskie, Poland 47/B2
Krotoszyn, Poland 47/C3
Krotz Springs, La. 238/G5
Krško, Slovenia 45/B3
Kru Coast (reg.), Liberia 106/C8
Kruger Nat'l Park, S. Africa 118/E4
Krugersdorp, S. Africa 118/H6
Krugloi (pt.), Alaska 196/J3
Kruis (riv.), S. Africa 118/F6
Krujë, Albania 45/D5
Krum, Texas 303/G4
Krumbach, Germany 22/D4
Krummenau, Switzerland 39/H2
Krumovgrad, Bulgaria 45/G5
Krung Thep (Bangkok) (cap.), Thailand 72/D4
Krupina, Slovakia 41/E2
Krupka, Czech Rep. 41/B1
Krupp (Marlin), Wash. 310/F3
Krusenstern (cape), Alaska 196/F1
Krusenstern (cape), N.W.T. 187/G3
Kruševac, Yugoslavia 45/E4
Krušné Hory (Erzgebirge) (mts.), Czech Rep. 41/B1
Kruszwica, Poland 47/D2
Kruzof (isl.), Alaska 196/M1
Krydor, Sask. 181/D3
Krymsk, Russia 52/E5
Krynica, Poland 47/E4
Krypton, Ky. 237/P6
Krzyż, Poland 47/C2
Ksar el Boukhari, Algeria 106/E1
Ksar el Kebir, Morocco 106/C2
Ktima, Cyprus 63/E5
Kuala Dungun, Malaysia 72/D6
Kualakapuas, Indonesia 85/E6
Kuala Kerai, Malaysia 72/D6
Kualakurun, Indonesia 85/E6
Kuala Lipis, Malaysia 72/D6
Kuala Lumpur (cap.), Malaysia 72/D7
Kuala Lumpur (cap.), Malaysia 54/M9
Kuala Lumpur (cap.), Malaysia 2/P5
Kuala Pilah, Malaysia 72/D7
Kualapuu, Hawaii 218/G1
Kuala Rompin, Malaysia 72/D7
Kuala Selangor, Malaysia 72/D7
Kuala Terengganu, Malaysia 72/D6
Kuancheng, China 77/J3
Kuantan, Malaysia 72/D7
Kuba, Azerbaijan 52/G6
Kubachi, Russia 52/G6
Kubaisa, Iraq 66/C4
Kuban (riv.), Russia 7/J4
Kuban' (riv.), Russia 52/E5
Kubbum, Sudan 111/D5
Kubeno (lake), Russia 52/E3
Küblis, Switzerland 39/J3
Kubohama, Japan 81/F7
Kubrat, Bulgaria 45/H4
Kuching, Malaysia 54/N9
Kuching, Malaysia 85/E5
Kuchino (isl.), Japan 81/O4
Kuçovë (Stalin), Albania 45/D5
Küçükköy, Turkey 63/C6
Kudarebe (pt.), Neth. Ant. 161/D9
Kudat, Malaysia 85/F4
Kudowa Zdroj, Poland 47/B3
Kudus, Indonesia 85/J2
Kudymkar, Russia 48/F4
Kudymkar, Russia 52/H3
Kufra (oasis), Libya 102/E2
Kufra (oasis), Libya 111/D3
Kufrinja, Jordan 65/D3
Kufstein, Austria 41/A3
Kuh (cape), Iran 66/K8
Kuhak, Iran 66/N7
Kuhestan, Afghanistan 59/H3
Kuhestan, Afghanistan 68/A2
Kühlungsborn, Germany 22/D1
Kuhmo, Finland 18/Q4
Kuhpayeh, Iran 66/H4
Kuilsrivier, S. Africa 118/F6
Kuiseb (riv.), Namibia 118/B4
Kuito, Angola 115/C6
Kuiu (isl.), Alaska 196/M2
Kuivaniemi, Finland 18/O4
Kuji, Japan 81/K3
Kuju (mt.), Japan 81/E7
Kuk (riv.), Alaska 196/G1
Kukaiau, Hawaii 218/H4
Kukaklek (lake), Alaska 196/G3
Kukalar, Kuh-e (mt.), Iran 59/F3
Kukalar, Kuh-e (mt.), Iran 66/G5
Kukalaya (riv.), Nicaragua 154/F4
Kukawa, Nigeria 106/G6
Kukës, Albania 45/E4
Kuki, Japan 81/O2
Kukpowruk (riv.), Alaska 196/F1
Kukui (riv.), Guyana 131/A3
Kukuihaele, Hawaii 218/H3
Kula, Bulgaria 45/F4
Kula, Hawaii 218/J2
Kula, Turkey 63/C3
Kulai, Malaysia 72/F5
Kula Kangri (mt.), Bhutan 68/G3
Kuldīga, Latvia 53/A2
Kuldja (Yining), China 77/B3
Kulebaki, Russia 52/F3
Kulen, Cambodia 72/E4
Kulen Vakuf, Bos. 45/B3
Kulgera, North. Terr. 88/E5
Kulgera, North. Terr. 93/C8
Kulkyne (creek), N.S. Wales 97/C1
Kulm, N. Dak. 282/N7
Kulmbach, Germany 22/D3
Kuloy, Russia 52/F2
Kulp, Turkey 63/J3
Kulpmont, Pa. 294/J4
Kulpsville, Pa. 294/M5
Kul'sary, Kazakhstan 48/F5
Kulu, India 68/D2
Kulu, Turkey 63/E3
Kulunda, Russia 48/H4
Kulyab, Tajikistan 48/H6
Kŭm (riv.), S. Korea 81/C5
Kuma (riv.), Russia 7/J4
Kuma (riv.), Russia 48/E5
Kuma (riv.), Russia 52/G5
Kumagaya, Japan 81/J5
Kumai, Indonesia 85/E6
Kumai, Indonesia 85/E6
Kumaka, Guyana 131/B4
Kumamoto (pref.), Japan 81/E7
Kumamoto, Japan 54/P6
Kumamoto, Japan 81/E7
Kumano, Japan 81/G7
Kumanovo, Macedonia 45/E4
Kumara, N. Zealand 100/C5
Kumasi, Ghana 106/D7
Kumasi, Ghana 102/B4
Kumba, Cameroon 115/A3
Kumbakonam, India 68/D6
Kumbo, Cameroon 115/B2
Kum-Dag, Turkmenistan 48/F6
Kume (isl.), Japan 81/M6
Kumertau, Russia 52/J4
Kumeu, N. Zealand 100/B1
Kŭmgang (mt.), N. Korea 81/D4
Kumiyama, Japan 81/J7
Kumkale, Turkey 63/B6
Kumköy, Turkey 63/B6
Kumla, Sweden 18/J7
Kumluca, Turkey 63/D4
Kummerowersee (lake), Germany 22/E2
Kumo (riv.), Finland 7/G2
Kumo, Nigeria 106/G7
Kumphawapi, Thailand 72/D3
Kumta, India 68/C6
Kumukahi (cape), Hawaii 218/K5
Kumul (Hami), China 77/D3
Kuna, Idaho 220/B6
Kunágota, Hungary 41/F3
Kunashiri (isl.), Japan 81/N1
Kunda, Estonia 52/C3
Kunda, Estonia 53/D1
Kundiawa, Papua N.G. 85/B7
Kundl, Austria 41/A3
Künes (Xinyuan), China 77/B3
Künes He (riv.), China 77/B3
Kungälv, Sweden 18/G8
Kunghit (isl.), Br. Col. 184/B4
Kungsbacka, Sweden 18/G8
Kungu, D.R. Congo 102/D4
Kungu, D.R. Congo 115/C3
Kungur, Russia 7/K3
Kungur, Russia 48/F4
Kungur, Russia 52/J3
Kunhegyes, Hungary 41/F3
Kunia, Hawaii 218/E2
Kuningan, Indonesia 85/H2
Kunkle, Ohio 284/A2
Kunkletown, Pa. 294/M4
Kunlong, Burma 72/C2
Kunlun (range), China 54/K6
Kunlun (range), India 68/D1
Kunlun Shan (range), China 77/B4
Kunmadaras, Hungary 41/F3
Kunming, China 77/F6
Kunming, China 2/Q4
Kunming, China 54/M7
Kunsan, S. Korea 81/C6
Kunszentmárton, Hungary 41/F3
Kunszentmiklós, Hungary 41/E3
Kununurra, W. Australia 88/D3
Kununurra, W. Australia 92/E2
Kuolayarvi, Russia 52/D1
Kuopio (prov.), Finland 18/P5
Kuopio, Finland 7/G2
Kuopio, Finland 18/Q5
Kupa (riv.), Slovenia 45/B3
Kupang, Indonesia 54/O11
Kupang, Indonesia 85/G8
Kuparuk (riv.), Alaska 196/H1
Kupino, Russia 48/H4
Kupiškis, Lithuania 53/C3
Kupreanof (isl.), Alaska 196/N1
Kupreanov, Alaska 196/M2
Kupyansk, Ukraine 52/E5
Kuqa, China 77/B3
Kur (isl.), Indonesia 85/J7
Kura (riv.), Russia 48/E6
Kura (riv.), Russia 52/G6
Kuraiyima, Jordan 65/D3
Kurang (riv.), Iran 66/G4
Kurashiki, Japan 81/F6
Kurayoshi, Japan 81/F6
Kurdistan (Kordestan) (prov.), Iran 66/E3
Kurdistan (reg.), Iran 59/D2
Kurdistan (reg.), Iran 66/D2
Kurdistan (reg.), Iraq 59/D2
Kurdistan (reg.), Iraq 66/C2
Kurdistan (reg.), Turkey 59/D2
Kŭrdzhali, Bulgaria 45/G5
Kure (atoll), Hawaii 87/J3
Kure (atoll), Hawaii 218/A5
Kure, Japan 81/F6
Küre, Turkey 63/E2
Küre (mts.), Turkey 63/E2
Kure Beach, N.C. 281/O7
Kuressaare, Estonia 53/B1
Kuressaare, Estonia 52/B3
Kurgan, Russia 54/H4
Kurgan, Russia 48/G4
Kurgan-Tyube, Tajikistan 48/G6
Kuria Muria (isls.), Oman 54/G8
Kuria Muria (isls.), Oman 59/G6
Kurikka, Finland 18/M5
Kuril (isls.), Russia 2/S3
Kuril (isls.), Russia 48/P5
Kuril (isls.), Russia 54/R5
Kuril'sk, Russia 48/P5
Ku-ring-gai, N. S. Wales 88/K4
Kurla, India 68/B7
Kurmuk, Sudan 111/F5
Kurnell (pen.), N.S. Wales 97/J4
Kurnool, India 54/J8
Kurnool, India 68/D5
Kuroiso, Japan 81/K5
Kuroki, Sask. 181/H4
Kurow, N. Zealand 100/C6
Kurri Kurri-Weston, N.S. Wales 97/F3
Kuršėnai, Lithuania 53/B2
Kursk, Russia 7/H3
Kursk, Russia 48/D4
Kursk, Russia 52/E4
Kurşunlu, Turkey 63/E2
Kurtalan, Turkey 63/J3
Kurthwood, La. 238/D4
Kurtistown, Hawaii 218/J5
Kurtz, Ind. 227/E7
Kurucaşile, Turkey 63/E2
Kuruçay (riv.), Turkey 63/K2
Kuruktag Shan (range), China 77/C3
Kuruman, S. Africa 118/C5
Kurume, Japan 81/E7
Kurundi, North. Terr. 93/D6
Kurunegala, Sri Lanka 68/E7
Kurungiku (mts.), Guyana 131/B3
Kurupukari, Guyana 131/B3
Kuş (lake), Turkey 63/B2
Kuşada (gulf), Turkey 63/B4
Kuşadası, Turkey 63/B4
Kushchevskaya, Russia 52/E5
Kushequa, Pa. 294/E2
Kushikino, Japan 81/E8
Kushima, Japan 81/E8
Kushimoto, Japan 81/G7
Kushiro, Japan 54/R5
Kushiro, Japan 81/M2
Kushka, Turkmenistan 48/G6
Kushog (lake), Ontario 177/F2
Kuskokwim (bay), Alaska 196/F3
Kuskokwim (mts.), Alaska 196/G2
Kuskokwim (riv.), Alaska 146/C3
Kuskokwim (riv.), Alaska 188/C6
Kuskokwim (riv.), Alaska 196/G2
Kuskokwim, North Fork (riv.), Alaska 196/H2
Kuskokwim, South Fork (riv.), Alaska 196/H2
Kuskokwim (riv.), U.S. 4/C17
Küsnacht, Switzerland 39/G2
Kusŏng, N. Korea 81/B4
Küssnacht am Rigi, Switzerland 39/F2
Kustanay, Kazakhstan 54/H4
Kustanay, Kazakhstan 48/G4
Kustatan, Alaska 196/B1
Küstrin, Poland 47/B2
Kut, Iraq 59/E3
Kut, Iraq 66/D4
Kut, Ko (isl.), Thailand 72/D5
Kuta, Nigeria 106/F7
Kütahya (prov.), Turkey 63/C3
Kütahya, Turkey 59/B2
Kütahya, Turkey 63/C3
Kutaisi, Georgia 7/J4
Kutaisi, Georgia 48/E5
Kutaisi, Georgia 52/F6
Kutaraja (Banda Aceh), Indonesia 85/A4
Kutari (riv.), Guyana 131/C4
Kutari (riv.), Suriname 131/C4
Kutch, Colo. 208/M5
Kutch (Kachchh), Rann of (salt marsh) 54/H7
Kutch (Kachchh) (gulf), India 68/B4
Kutch (Kachchh) (reg.), India 68/B4
Kutch (Kachchh), Rann of (salt marsh), India 68/B4
Kutch (Kachchh), Rann of (salt lake), Pakistan 59/K5
Kutch (Kachchh), Rann of (salt marsh), Pakistan 68/B4
Kutcharo (lake), Japan 81/M2
Kutina, Croatia 45/C3
Kutná Hora, Czech Rep. 41/C2
Kutno, Poland 47/D2
Kutoarjo, Indonesia 85/J2
Kuttawa, Ky. 237/E6
Küttigen, Switzerland 39/F2
Kutu, D.R. Congo 115/C4
Kutum, Sudan 111/D5
Kúty, Slovakia 41/D2
Kutztown, Pa. 294/L4
Kuujjuac (Fort-Chimo), Québec 162/K4
Kuujjuac (Fort-Chimo), Québec 174/F2
Kuujjuarapik, Québec 162/J4
Kuujjuarapik, Québec 174/B1
Kuusamo, Finland 18/Q4
Kuusamojärvi (lake), Finland 18/Q4
Kuusankoski, Finland 18/P6
Kuvandyk, Russia 52/J4
Kuwait 2/M4
Kuwait 54/F7
KUWAIT 59/E4
Kuvango, Angola 115/C6
Kuybyshev, Russia 48/H4
Kuybyshev (Samara), Russia 2/M3
Kuybyshev (Samara), Russia 7/K3
Kuybyshev (Samara), Russia 48/F4
Kuybyshev (Samara), Russia 52/H4
Kuybyshev (res.), Russia 7/K3
Kuybyshev (res.), Russia 48/F4
Kuybyshev (res.), Russia 52/G4
Kuyto (lake), Russia 52/D2
Kuytun, China 77/C3
Kuyucak, Turkey 63/C4
Kuyuwini (riv.), Guyana 131/B4
Kuznetsk, Russia 52/G4
Kuzomen', Russia 52/E1
Kvaenangen (fjord), Norway 18/N2
Kvaerndrup, Denmark 21/D7
Kvaløya (isl.), Norway 18/O1
Kvaløya (isl.), Norway 18/K2
Kvarner (gulf), Croatia 45/B3
Kvichak, Alaska 196/G3
Kvichak (bay), Alaska 196/G3
Kvikkjokk, Sweden 18/K3
Kvinnherad, Norway 18/E6
Kvissleby, Sweden 18/K5
Kviteseid, Norway 18/F7
Kwa (riv.), D.R. Congo 115/C4
Kwai (Mae Nam Khwae Noi) (riv.), Thailand 72/C4
Kwajalein (atoll), Marshall Is. 87/G5
Kwakoegron, Suriname 131/D3
Kwakwani, Guyana 131/C3
Kwale, Kenya 102/F5
Kwale, Kenya 115/G4
Kwamouth, D.R. Congo 115/C4
Kwangchow (Canton), China 77/H7
Kwangju, S. Korea 54/O6
Kwangju, S. Korea 81/C6
Kwango (riv.), D.R. Congo 115/C5
Kwangsi Chuang Aut. Reg. (Guangxi Zhuangzu), China 77/G7
Kwangtung (Guangdong), China 77/H7
Kwanmo (mt.), N. Korea 81/D3
Kwara (state), Nigeria 106/E7
KwaZulu Natal (prov.), S. Africa 118/E5
Kwekwe, Zimbabwe 118/D3
Kwekwe, Zimbabwe 102/E6
Kweichow (Guizhou), China 77/G6
Kweilin (Guilin), China 77/G6
Kweisui (Hohhot), China 77/H3
Kweiyang (Guiyang), China 77/G6
Kwethluk, Alaska 196/F2
Kwidzin, Poland 47/D2
Kwigillingok, Alaska 196/F3
Kwilu (riv.), Angola 115/C5
Kwilu (riv.), D.R. Congo 115/C5
Kwinana-Newtown, W. Australia 88/B2
Kwinana New Town, W. Australia 92/A1
Kwinitsa, Br. Col. 184/C3
Kwitaro (riv.), Guyana 131/B4
Kyabé, Chad 111/C6
Kyabram, Victoria 97/C5
Kyaikto, Burma 72/C3
Kya-in Seikkyi, Burma 72/C3
Kyakhta, Russia 48/L4
Kyakhta, Russia 54/M4
Kyalite, N.S. Wales 97/B4
Kyana, Ind. 227/D8
Kyancutta, S. Australia 94/D5
Kyangin, Burma 72/B3
Kyaukme, Burma 72/C2
Kyaukpadaung, Burma 72/B2
Kyaukpyu, Burma 72/B3
Kyaukse, Burma 72/C2
Kybartai, Lithuania 53/B3
Kyeburn, N. Zealand 100/C6
Kyger, Ohio 284/F8
Kyger, W. Va. 312/D5
Kyjov, Czech Rep. 41/D2
Kykosmovi, Ariz. 198/E3
Kyle, Sask. 181/C5
Kyle, S. Dak. 298/E7
Kyle, Texas 303/G8
Kyleakin, Scotland 15/C3
Kylemore, Sask. 181/H4
Kyle of Lochalsh, Scotland 15/C3
Kyle of Tongue (inlet), Scotland 15/D2
Kyles Ford, Tenn. 237/R7
Kylestrome, Scotland 15/D2
Kymi (prov.), Finland 18/Q6
Kyneton, Victoria 97/C5
Kynšperk, Czech Rep. 41/B1
Kynuna, Queensland 95/B4
Kyogle, N.S. Wales 97/G1
Kyonan, Japan 81/O3
Kyŏnghŭng, N. Korea 81/E2
Kyŏngju, S. Korea 81/D6
Kyoto (pref.), Japan 81/J7
Kyoto, Japan 54/P6
Kyoto, Japan 81/J7
Kyrenia, Cyprus 63/E5
KYRGYZSTAN 48/H5
Kyrgyzstan 54/J5
Kyritz, Germany 22/E2
Kysucké Nové Mesto, Slovakia 41/E2
Kythrea, Cyprus 63/E5
Kyuquot, Br. Col. 184/D5
Kyuquot (sound), Br. Col. 184/D5
Kyushu (isl.), Japan 2/R4
Kyushu (isl.), Japan 54/P6
Kyushu (isl.), Japan 81/E7
Kyustendil, Bulgaria 45/F4
Kyusyur, Russia 48/N2
Kywebwe, Burma 72/C3
Kyzyl, Russia 48/K4
Kyzyl, Russia 54/L4
Kyzyl-Kum (des.), Uzbekistan 48/G5
Kzyl-Orda, Kazakhstan 48/G5
Kzyl-Orda, Kazakhstan 54/H5

L

Laa an der Thaya, Austria 41/D2
La Aduana, Venezuela 124/D3
Laager, Tenn. 237/K10
La Aguja (cape), Colombia 126/C2
Laakirchen, Austria 41/B3
La Almunia de Doña Godina, Spain 33/F2
La Altagracia (prov.), Dom. Rep. 158/F6
La Anna, Pa. 294/M3
La Antigua Veracruz, Mexico 150/Q1
La Araucanía (reg.), Chile 138/E2
La Asunción, Venezuela 124/G2
Laau (pt.), Hawaii 218/G1
Laax, Switzerland 39/H3
Laayoune, W. Sahara 102/A2
Laayoune, Western Sahara 106/B3
Labadie, Mo. 261/L5
Labadieville, La. 238/K4
La Baie, Québec 172/G1
La Baie-de-Shawinigan, Québec 172/E3
La Banda, Argentina 143/D2
La Bandera (pt.), P. Rico 161/F1
La Bañeza, Spain 33/C1
La Barca, Mexico 150/H6
La Barge, Wyo. 319/B3
La Barge (creek), Wyo. 319/B3
La Barra de Navidad, Mexico 150/G7
Labasheeda, Ireland 17/C6
La Baule-Escoublac, France 28/B4
L'Abbaye, Switzerland 39/B3
Labe (riv.), Czech Rep. 41/C1
Labé, Guinea 106/B6
La Bella (lag.), Paraguay 144/B4
La Belle, Fla. 212/E5
La Belle, Mo. 261/J2
Labelle (co.), Québec 172/B3
Labelle, Québec 172/C3
Labelle (lake), Québec 172/C3
La Belle (lake), Wis. 317/H1
Laberge (lake), Yukon 162/C3
Laberinto de las Doce Leguas (cays), Cuba 158/F3
La Berra (mt.), Switzerland 39/D3
Labette (co.), Kansas 232/G4
Labette, Kansas 232/G4
Labinsk, Russia 52/F6
La Bisbal, Spain 33/H1
La Blanquilla (isl.), Venezuela 124/F2
Labo, Philippines 82/D3
Labo (mt.), Philippines 82/D3
La Bolsa, Uruguay 145/C1
La Bolt, S. Dak. 298/R3
La Bonita, Ecuador 128/D2
La Boquilla (res.), Mexico 150/G3
Laborec (riv.), Slovakia 41/F2
Laborie, St. Lucia 161/G7
La Bostonnais, Québec 172/E2
Labougle, Argentina 143/G5
Laboulaye, Argentina 143/D3
Labrador (sea) 146/N4
Labrador (sea) 162/L4
Labrador (reg.), Canada 2/G3
Labrador (reg.), Newf. 166/B2
Labrador (sea), Newf. 166/C2
Labrador (reg.), Newf. 146/M4
Labrador (reg.), Newf. 162/K4
Labrador City, Newf. 166/A3
La Branche, Mich. 250/B3
Lábrea, Brazil 132/G10
La Brea, Trin. & Tob. 161/A11
Labrieville, Québec 174/C3
La Broquerie, Manitoba 179/F5
Labuan, Malaysia 85/E4
Labuan (isl.), Malaysia 85/E4
Labuan (state), Malaysia 85/F4
Labuha, Indonesia 85/H6
Labuhan, Indonesia 85/G2
Labuk (bay), Malaysia 85/F4
Labutta, Burma 72/B3
Labyrinth (canyon), Utah 304/D5
Labytnangi, Russia 48/G3
Lac (bay), Neth. Ant. 161/D9
Lac-à-Beauce, Québec 172/E2
Lacadena, Sask. 181/C5
Lacadie, Québec 172/J4
La Cahouane, Haiti 158/A6
Lac-à-la-Croix, Québec 172/F1
La Calera, Chile 138/F2
Lac-Alouette, Québec 172/D4
Lacamp, La. 238/E4
La Canada Flintridge, Calif. 204/C10
Lacanau (lake), France 28/C5
La Canoa, Venezuela 124/G3
Lacantum (riv.), Mexico 150/O8
La Capilla, 136/C8
La Carlota, Argentina 143/D3
La Carlota, Philippines 82/D5
La Carlota, Spain 33/D4
La Carolina, Spain 33/E3
Lacassine, La. 238/E6
Lac-au-Saumon, Québec 172/B2
Lac-aux-Sables, Québec 172/E3
Lac Baker, New Bruns. 170/B1
Lac-Beauport, Québec 172/F3
Lac-Bouchette, Québec 172/E1
Lac-Carré, Québec 172/C3
Lac-Cayamant, Québec 172/A3
Lac-Chat, Québec 172/E2
Lac Court Oreilles Ind. Res., Wis. 317/D4
Lac de Gras (lake), N.W.T. 187/G3
Lac-Delage, Québec 172/H3
Lac-des-Aigles, Québec 172/J2
Lac des Arcs, Alberta 182/C4
Lac-des-Écorces, Québec 172/B3
Lac-des-Îles, Québec 172/B3
Lac-Drolet, Québec 172/G4
Lac du Bonnet, Manitoba 179/G4
Lac-du-Cerf, Québec 172/B3
Lac du Flambeau, Wis. 317/G4
Lac du Flambeau Ind. Res., Wis. 317/G3
Lac-Édouard, Québec 172/E2
La Ceiba, Hond. 146/K8
La Ceiba, Honduras 154/D3
La Ceiba, Apure, Venezuela 124/C4
La Ceiba, Trujillo, Venezuela 124/C3
La Center, Ky. 237/C6
La Center, Wash. 310/C5
Lacepede (bay), S. Australia 88/F7
Lacepede (bay), S. Australia 94/F7
Lacepede (range), W. Australia 88/D3
Lacepede (isls.), W. Australia 92/C2
La Cerbatana, Serranía de (mts.), Venezuela 124/E4
Lac-Etchemin, Québec 172/G3
Lacey, Ark. 202/G7
Lacey, Wash. 310/C3
Lacey Spring, Va. 307/L3
Laceys Spring, Ala. 195/E1
Laceyville, Pa. 294/K2
Lac-Frontière, Québec 172/H3
Lac Giao (Ban Me Thuot), Vietnam 72/E4
Lacha (lake), Russia 52/E2
La Chapelle, Haiti 158/C5
La Charité-sur-Loire, France 28/E4
La Châtre, France 28/D4
La Chaux-de-Fonds, Switzerland 39/C2
Lachay (pt.), Peru 128/D8
Lachen, Switzerland 39/G2
Lachenaie, Québec 172/D4
Lachine, Mich. 250/F3
Lachine, Québec 172/H4
Lachlan (riv.), N.S. Wales 88/G6
Lachlan (range), N.S. Wales 97/C3
Lachlan (riv.), N.S. Wales 97/C3
La Chorrera, Colombia 126/D8
La Chorrera, Panama 154/H6
Lac-Humqui, Québec 172/B2
Lachute, Québec 172/C4
La Ciénaga, Dom. Rep. 158/D6
La Ciotat, France 28/F6
Lackawanna, N.Y. 276/B5
Lackawanna (co.), Pa. 294/L3
Lackawaxen, Pa. 294/N3
Lackey, Ky. 237/R6
Lackland A.F.B., Texas 303/J11
Lac La Belle, Wis. 317/H1
Lac La Biche, Alberta 182/E2
Lac La Biche, Alta. 162/E5
Lac La Hache, Br. Col. 184/G4
Lac la Martre, N.W.T. 187/G3
La Clarita, Argentina 143/G5
Lac La Ronge Prov. Park, Sask. 181/M3
Laclede, Idaho 220/B1
La Clede, Ill. 222/E5
Laclede (co.), Mo. 261/G7
Laclede, Mo. 261/F3
Lac-Mégantic, Québec 172/G4
Lacolle, Québec 172/D4
La Colmena, Paraguay 144/B5
La Coloma, Cuba 158/B2
La Colonia, Chile 138/D7
Lacomb, Oreg. 291/E3
Lacombe, Alberta 182/D3
Lacombe, Alta. 162/E5
Lacombe, La. 238/L6
Lacon, Ill. 222/D2
Lacona, Iowa 229/G6
Lacona, N.Y. 276/J3
La Concepción, Honduras 154/E3
La Concepción, Panama 154/F6
La Concepción, Venezuela 124/C2
La Concepción, Venezuela 124/B2
La Conception, Québec 172/C3
La Concordia, Mexico 150/N9
Laconia, Ind. 227/E8
Laconia, N.H. 268/E4
Laconia, Tenn. 237/C10
La Conner, Wash. 310/C2
La Conquista, Nicaragua 154/D5
Lacoochee, Fla. 212/D3
La Corey, Alberta 182/E2
La Coronilla, Uruguay 145/F4
La Coruña (prov.), Spain 33/B1
La Coruña, Spain 33/B1
La Coruña, Spain 7/D4
La Coste, Texas 303/J11
La Courneuve, France 28/B1
Lacovia, Jamaica 158/H6
Lac Pelletier, Sask. 181/C6
Lac-Poulin, Québec 172/G3
Lac qui Parle (co.), Minn. 255/B6
Lac qui Parle, Minn. 255/B5
Lac qui Parle (lake), Minn. 255/C5
Lac qui Parle (riv.), Minn. 255/B6
Lacre (pt.), Neth. Ant. 161/E9
La Crescent, Minn. 255/G7
La Crescenta-Montrose, Calif. 204/C10
La Crete, Alberta 182/B5
La Croche, Québec 172/E2
La Croix (lake), Minn. 255/F2
La Crosse, Fla. 212/D2
La Crosse, Ga. 217/D6
La Crosse, Ind. 227/D2
La Crosse, Kansas 232/C3
La Crosse, Va. 307/M7
Lacrosse, Wash. 310/H4
La Crosse, Wis. 146/J5
La Crosse, Wis. 188/H2
La Crosse (co.), Wis. 317/D8
La Crosse, Wis. 317/D8
La Cruz, Argentina 143/E2
La Cruz, Chile 138/F2
La Cruz, Colombia 126/B7
La Cruz, Chihuahua, Mexico 150/G3
La Cruz, Sinaloa, Mexico 150/F5
La Cruz, Nicaragua 154/E4
La Cruz, Uruguay 145/C4
Lac-Saguay, Québec 172/B3
Lac-Saint-Charles, Québec 172/H3
Lac-Sainte-Marie, Québec 172/A4
Lac-Saint-Jean-Est (co.), Québec 172/F1
Lac-Saint-Jean-Est (county), Québec 174/C3
Lac-Saint-Jean-Ouest (co.), Québec 172/E1
Lac-Saint-Jean-Ouest (county), Québec 174/C2
Lac-Saint-Joseph, Québec 172/F3
Lac-Saint-Paul, Québec 172/B3
Lac-Sergent, Québec 172/F3
Lac Seul, Ontario 175/B2
La Cuchilla, Uruguay 145/F3
La Cueva, N. Mex. 274/D3
La Cumbre, Argentina 143/C3
La Cure, Switzerland 39/B4
Lacuy (pen.), Chile 138/D4
Lac Vert, Sask. 181/G3
La Cygne, Kansas 232/H3
Ladakh (reg.), India 68/D2
Ladd, Ill. 222/D2
Ladder (creek), Kansas 232/A3
Ladder (hills), Scotland 15/E3

Lemitar 397

La Tortuga (isl.), Venezuela 124/F2
Latouche Treville (cape), W. Australia 88/C3
Latouche Treville (cape), W. Australia 92/C2
Latour, Mo. 261/D5
La Tour-de-Peilz, Switzerland 39/C4
La Tour-du-Pin, France 28/F5
Latourell Falls, Oreg. 291/E2
La Trinidad, Nicaragua 154/D4
La Trinidad, Philippines 82/C2
La Trinidad, Venezuela 124/D3
La Trinidad de Arauca, Venezuela 124/D4
La Trinidad de Orichuna, Venezuela 124/D4
La Trinité, Martinique 161/D6
La Trinité-des-Monts, Québec 172/J1
Latrobe, Pa. 294/D5
Latrobe, Tasmania 99/C3
Latta, S.C. 296/J3
Lattimore, N.C. 281/F4
Lattingtown, N.Y. 276/R6
Latty, Ohio 284/A3
La Tuque, Que. 162/J6
La Tuque, Québec 172/E2
La Tuque, Québec 174/C3
Latur, India 68/D5
Latvia 7/G3
Latvia 52/B3
Latvia 48/C4
LATVIA 53/B2
Lauca (riv.), Bolivia 136/A6
Lauca (riv.), Chile 138/B1
Lauchhammer, Germany 22/E3
Laud, Ind. 227/G2
Laudat, Dominica 161/E6
Lauder, Manitoba 179/B5
Lauder, Scotland 10/E3
Lauder, Scotland 15/F5
Lauderdale (co.), Ala. 195/C1
Lauderdale, Minn. 255/G5
Lauderdale (co.), Miss. 256/G6
Lauderdale, Miss. 256/G5
Lauderdale, Tasmania 99/D4
Lauderdale (co.), Tenn. 237/B9
Lauderdale-by-the-Sea, Fla. 212/C3
Lauderdale Lakes, Fla. 212/B3
Lauderhill, Fla. 212/B3
Lauenburg an der Elbe, Germany 22/D2
Lauenen, Switzerland 39/D4
Lauf an der Pegnitz, Germany 22/D4
Läufelfingen, Switzerland 39/E2
Laufen, Switzerland 39/D2
Laufen, Germany 22/E5
Laufenburg, Switzerland 39/F1
Laughery (creek), Ind. 227/G6
Laughing Fish (pt.), Mich. 250/B2
Laughlin A.F.B., Texas 303/D8
Lau Group (isls.), Fiji 87/J7
Lauingen, Germany 22/D4
Launceston, England 13/C7
Launceston, England 10/D5
Launceston, Tasmania 99/C3
Launceston, Tasmania 88/H8
Laune (riv.), Ireland 17/B7
Launglon Bok (isls.), Burma 72/C4
La Unión, Chile 138/D3
La Unión, Colombia 126/B7
La Unión, El Salvador 154/D4
La Unión, Mexico 150/J8
La Union, N. Mex. 274/C7
La Unión, Peru 128/D7
La Union (prov.), Philippines 82/C2
La Unión, Spain 33/F4
La Unión, Venezuela 124/E3
Laupahoehoe, Hawaii 218/J4
Laupen, Switzerland 39/D3
Lauperswil, Switzerland 39/E3
Laura, Ill. 222/D3
Laura, Ohio 284/B6
Laura, Queensland 88/G3
Laura, Queensland 95/C2
Laura, Sask. 181/D4
Laura, S. Australia 94/F5
La Urbana, Venezuela 124/E4
Laurel, Del. 245/R6
Laurel, Fla. 212/D4
Laurel, Ind. 227/G6
Laurel, Iowa 229/H5
Laurel (co.), Ky. 237/N6
Laurel, Md. 245/L4
Laurel, Miss. 188/J4
Laurel, Miss. 256/F7
Laurel, Mont. 262/H5
Laurel, Nebr. 264/G2
Laurel, Oreg. 291/A2
Laurel, Pa. 294/K6
Laurel, Wash. 310/D5
Laurel (mt.), W. Va. 312/G4
Laurel Bay, S.C. 296/F7
Laurel Bloomery, Tenn. 237/T7
Laureldale, Pa. 294/L5
Laurel Dale, W. Va. 312/H4
Laureles, Paraguay 144/D5
Laurel Fork, Va. 307/G7
Laurel Hill, Fla. 212/C5
Laurel Hill, N.C. 281/K5
Laurel Hill (mt.), Pa. 294/D5
Laurel Park, N.C. 281/D4
Laurel River (lake), Ky. 237/N6
Laurel Run, Pa. 294/F7
Laurel Springs, N.J. 273/B4
Laurelton, Pa. 294/H4
Laurelville, Ohio 284/E7
Laurence G. Hanscom Field, Mass. 249/B6
Laurence Harbor, N.J. 273/E3
Laurencekirk, Scotland 10/E2
Laurencekirk, Scotland 15/F4
Laurens (co.), Ga. 217/G6
Laurens, Iowa 229/D3
Laurens, N.Y. 276/K5
Laurens (co.), S.C. 296/D2
Laurens, S.C. 296/C3
Laurentides, Québec 172/D4
Laurentides Prov. Park, Québec 174/C3
Laurentides Prov. Park, Québec 172/F2
Lauria, Italy 34/E4
Laurie (lake), Manitoba 179/A3
Laurie, Mo. 261/G6
Laurier, Manitoba 179/C4
Laurier, Wash. 310/G2
Laurier-Station, Québec 172/F3
Laurierville, Québec 172/F3
Laurieston, Scotland 15/D6
Laurin, Mont. 262/D5
Laurinburg, N.C. 281/K5
Lauritsala, Finland 18/Q6
Laurium, Mich. 250/A1
Laurot (Laut Kecil) (isls.), Indonesia 85/E7
Lausanne, Switzerland 39/C3
Lauscha, Germany 22/D3
Laut (isl.), Indonesia 85/F6
Laut (North Natuna) (isl.), Indonesia 85/D5
Lautaro, Chile 138/E2
Lauterbach, Germany 22/C3
Lauterbrunnen, Switzerland 39/E3
Lauterique, Honduras 154/D4
Laut Kecil (isls.), Indonesia 85/E7
Lautoka, Fiji 86/P10
Lauwers (chan.), Netherlands 27/J1
Lauwers Zee (bay), Netherlands 27/J2
Lauzon, Québec 172/J3
Lava (lake), Oreg. 291/F4
Lava Beds Nat'l Mon., Calif. 204/D2
Lavaca, Ala. 195/B6
Lavaca, Ark. 202/B3
Lavaca (co.), Texas 303/H8
Lavaca (bay), Texas 303/H9
Lava Hot Springs, Idaho 220/F7
Laval, France 28/C3
Laval, Québec 172/H4
Laval (bay), Québec 172/J1
La Vale-Narrows Park, Md. 245/C2
Lavalette, W. Va. 312/B6
Lavalle, Argentina 143/G4
La Valle, Wis. 317/F8
Lavalleja (dept.), Uruguay 145/D5
Lavallette, N.J. 273/E4
Lavalley, Colo. 208/J8
Lavaltrie, Québec 172/D4
Lavamünd, Austria 41/C3
Lavapié (pt.), Chile 138/D1
Lavaur, France 28/D6
La Vecilla de Curueño, Spain 33/D1
Laveen, Ariz. 198/C5
La Vega (prov.), Dom. Rep. 158/D6
La Vega, Dom. Rep. 158/E5
La Vega, Dom. Rep. 156/D3
La Vega, Spain 33/C1
La Vela (cape), Colombia 126/D1
La Vela de Coro, Venezuela 124/D2
Lavelanet, France 28/E6
Lavello, Italy 34/E4
Lavenham, Manitoba 179/D5
L'Avenir, Québec 172/E4
La Vergne, Tenn. 237/H9
La Verkin, Utah 304/A6
La Verne, Calif. 204/D10
Laverne, Okla. 288/G1
La Vernia, Texas 303/K11
Laverton, Australia 87/C8
Laverton, W. Australia 88/C5
Laverton, W. Australia 92/C5
La Veta, Colo. 208/J8
Lavey-Morcles, Switzerland 39/D4
Lavezares, Philippines 82/E4
La Victoria, Colombia 126/A7
La Victoria, Apure, Venezuela 124/D4
La Victoria, Aragua, Venezuela 124/E2
Lavieille (lake), Ontario 177/F2
La Vieja (pt.), Chile 138/A11
Lavik, Norway 18/D6
Lavillette, New Bruns. 170/E1
Lavina, Mont. 262/H4
Lavinia, Manitoba 179/B4
Lavinia, Tenn. 237/D9
La Vista, Nebr. 264/J3
Lavon (lake), Texas 303/H1
Lavongai (isl.), Papua N.G. 87/F6
Lavongai (isls.), Papua N.G. 86/B1
Lavonia, Ga. 217/F2
Lavos, Portugal 33/B2
Lavoy, Alberta 182/E3
Lavras, Brazil 132/E8
Lavras, Brazil 135/D2
Lávrion, Greece 45/G7
Lawa (riv.), Fr. Guiana 131/D4
Lawa (riv.), Suriname 131/D4
Lawai, Hawaii 218/C2
Lawang, Indonesia 85/K2
Lawen, Oreg. 291/J4
Lawler, Iowa 229/J2
Lawler, Minn. 255/E4
Lawlers, W. Australia 92/C5
Lawley, Ala. 195/E5
Lawn, Newf. 166/C4
Lawn, Pa. 294/J5
Lawn, Texas 303/E5
Lawndale, Calif. 204/B11
Lawndale, Ill. 222/D3
Lawndale, Minn. 255/B4
Lawndale, N.C. 281/F4
Lawnhill, Br. Col. 184/A3
Lawn Hill, Queensland 95/A3
Lawnside, N.J. 273/B3
Lawra, Ghana 106/D6
Lawrence (co.), Ala. 195/D1
Lawrence (co.), Ark. 202/H1
Lawrence (co.), Ill. 222/F5
Lawrence (co.), Ind. 227/E7
Lawrence, Ind. 227/E5
Lawrence, Kans. 188/G3
Lawrence, Kansas 232/G3
Lawrence (co.), Ky. 237/R4
Lawrence, Mass. 188/M2
Lawrence, Mass. 249/K2
Lawrence, Mich. 250/C6
Lawrence (co.), Miss. 256/D7
Lawrence, Miss. 256/F6
Lawrence (co.), Mo. 261/E8
Lawrence, Nebr. 264/F4
Lawrence, N.Y. 276/P7
Lawrence, N. Zealand 100/B6
Lawrence, N.C. 281/O2
Lawrence (co.), Ohio 284/E8
Lawrence (co.), Pa. 294/B4
Lawrence (co.), S. Dak. 298/B5
Lawrence (co.), Tenn. 237/G10
Lawrenceburg, Ind. 227/H6
Lawrenceburg, Ky. 237/M4
Lawrenceburg, Tenn. 237/G10
Lawrence Park•, Pa. 294/C1
Lawrenceport, Ind. 227/D7
Lawrence Station, New Bruns. 170/C3
Lawrencetown, Nova Scotia 168/C4
Lawrenceville, Ga. 217/D3
Lawrenceville, Ill. 222/F5
Lawrenceville, Ind. 227/H6
Lawrenceville•, N.J. 273/D3
Lawrenceville, N.Y. 276/L1
Lawrenceville, Ohio 284/C6
Lawrenceville, Pa. 294/H2
Lawrenceville, Québec 172/E4
Lawrenceville, Va. 307/N7
Lawson, Ark. 202/F7
Lawson, Colo. 208/H3
Lawson, Mo. 261/D4
Lawson, Sask. 181/E5
Lawsonville, N.C. 281/J2
Lawtell, La. 238/F5
Lawtey, Fla. 212/D1
Lawton, Ind. 227/D2
Lawton, Iowa 229/A4
Lawton, Kansas 232/H4
Lawton, Ky. 237/P4
Lawton, Mich. 250/D6
Lawton, N. Dak. 282/O3
Lawton, Okla. 146/J6
Lawton, Okla. 188/G4
Lawton, Okla. 288/K5
Lawton, Pa. 294/K2
Lawton, W. Va. 312/E7
Lawtonka (lake), Okla. 288/K5
Lawu (mt.), Indonesia 85/J2
Lax, Ga. 217/F8
Lax, Switzerland 39/F4
Laxå, Sweden 18/J7
Laxey, I. of Man 13/C3
Laxford, Loch (inlet), Scotland 15/C2
Lay (dam), Ala. 195/E5
Lay (lake), Ala. 195/F4
Lay (pt.), Alaska 196/F1
Lay, Colo. 208/D2
Lay, Mui (cape), Vietnam 72/E3
Layang Layang, Malaysia 72/E5
Layland, W. Va. 312/F7
Layopolis (Sand Fork), W. Va. 312/E5
Layou (riv.), Dominica 161/E6
Layou, St. Vin. & Grens. 161/A9
Laysan (isl.), Hawaii 87/J3
Laysan (isl.), Hawaii 188/E6
Laysan (isl.), Hawaii 218/B5
Laysville, Conn. 210/F3
Layton, Fla. 212/F7
Layton, N.J. 273/D1
Layton, Utah 304/C2
Laytonsville, Md. 245/K4
Laytonville, Calif. 204/B4
Laytown-Bettystown-Mornington, Ireland 17/J4
Lazarev Station 5/C1
Lazdijai, Lithuania 53/B3
Lazear, Colo. 208/D5
Lazi, Philippines 82/D6
Łaziska Górne, Poland 47/A4
Lazy Lake, Fla. 212/B3
Lea (riv.), England 13/G6
Lea (co.), N. Mex. 274/F6
Leaburg, Oreg. 291/E3
Leach, Okla. 288/S2
Leach, Tenn. 237/E9
Leachville, Ark. 202/K2
Leacross, Sask. 181/H2
Lead, S. Dak. 188/F2
Lead, S. Dak. 298/B5
Leadbetter (pt.), Wash. 310/A4
Leader, Minn. 255/D4
Leader, Sask. 181/B5
Lead Hill, Ark. 202/D1
Leadington, Mo. 261/M7
Leadmine (brook), Conn. 210/C1
Lead Mine, W. Va. 312/G4
Leadmine, Wis. 317/F10
Leadore, Idaho 220/E5
Leadpoint, Wash. 310/H2
Leadville, Colo. 188/E3
Leadville, Colo. 208/G4
Leadwood, Mo. 261/L7
Leaf, Ga. 217/E1
Leaf (riv.), Manitoba 179/F2
Leaf (riv.), Minn. 255/C4
Leaf, Miss. 256/G8
Leaf (riv.), Miss. 256/F8
Leaf (lake), Sask. 181/J2
Leaf River, Ill. 222/D1
Leaf Valley, Minn. 255/C4
League City, Texas 303/K2
Leah, Ga. 217/H3
Leake (co.), Miss. 256/E5
Leakesville, Miss. 256/G8
Leakey, Texas 303/E8
Leal, N. Dak. 282/O5
Lealui, Zambia 115/D6
Leamington, Ontario 177/B5
Leamington, Utah 304/B4
Leamington Spa, England 10/F4
Leander, La. 238/E4
Leane (lake), Ireland 17/G4
Leane (lake), Ireland 17/B7
Leapwood, Tenn. 237/E10
Learmonth, W. Australia 88/A4
Learmonth, W. Australia 92/A3
Learned, Miss. 256/C6
Leary, Ga. 217/C8
Leasburg, Mo. 261/K6
Leasburg, N.C. 281/L2
Leask, Sask. 181/E2
Leatherhead, England 13/G8
Leatherhead, England 10/B6
Leathersville, Ga. 217/G3
Leatherwood, Ky. 237/P6
Leavenworth, Ind. 227/E8
Leavenworth, Kans. 188/G3
Leavenworth (co.), Kansas 232/G2
Leavenworth, Kansas 232/H2
Leavenworth, Wash. 310/E3
Leavitt, Alberta 182/D5
Leavittsburg, Ohio 284/J3
Leawood, Kansas 232/H3
Łeba, Poland 47/C1
Lebak, Philippines 82/D7
Lebam, Wash. 310/B4
Lebanon 2/L4
Lebanon 54/E6
LEBANON 59/C3
LEBANON 63/F6
Lebanon, Colo. 208/B8
Lebanon•, Conn. 210/G2
Lebanon, Ga. 217/D2
Lebanon, Ill. 222/D5
Lebanon, Ind. 227/D4
Lebanon, Kansas 232/D2
Lebanon, Ky. 237/L5
Lebanon (mts.), Lebanon 63/F6
Lebanon, Mo. 261/G7
Lebanon, Nebr. 264/D4
Lebanon, N.H. 268/C4
Lebanon, N.J. 273/D2
Lebanon, Ohio 284/B7
Lebanon, Okla. 288/N7
Lebanon, Oreg. 291/E3
Lebanon (co.), Pa. 294/K5
Lebanon, Pa. 294/K5
Lebanon, S. Dak. 298/K3
Lebanon, Tenn. 237/J8
Lebanon, Va. 307/D7
Lebanon, Wis. 317/H1
Lebanon Church, Va. 307/L2
Lebanon Junction, Ky. 237/K5
Lebanon Springs, N.Y. 276/O6
Lebeau, La. 238/F5
Lebec, Calif. 204/G9
Lebedin, Ukraine 52/D4
Lebedinyy, Russia 48/N4
Lebel-sur-Quévillon, Québec 174/B3
Lébényimiklós, Hungary 41/D3
Lebesby, Norway 18/P1
Le Blanc, France 28/D4
Le Blanc, La. 238/E5
Le Blanc-Mesnil, France 28/B1
Lebo, Kansas 232/G3
Le Borgne, Haiti 158/C5
Lębork, Poland 47/C1
Le Bourget, France 28/B1
Le Brassus, Switzerland 39/B3
Lebret, Sask. 181/H5
Lebrija (riv.), Colombia 126/D4
Lebrija, Spain 33/D4
Lebu, Chile 138/D1
Lecanto, Fla. 212/D3
Le Carbet, Martinique 161/C6
Le Cateau, France 28/E2
Lecce (prov.), Italy 34/G4
Lecce, Italy 34/G4
Lecce, Italy 7/F4
Lecco, Italy 34/B2
Le Center, Minn. 255/E6
Lech (riv.), Germany 22/D4
Le Châble, Switzerland 39/D4
Le Chasseral (mt.), Switzerland 39/D2
Leche (lag.), Cuba 158/F2
Le Chenit (Le Brassus), Switzerland 39/B3
Le Chesnay, France 28/A2
Lechiguanas (isls.), Argentina 143/G6
Lechuguilla (des.), Ariz. 198/A6
Le Claire, Iowa 229/N5
Leclercville, Québec 172/F3
Lecointre (lake), Québec 172/B2
Lecoma, Mo. 261/J7
Lecompte, La. 238/F4
Lecompton, Kansas 232/G2
Lecontes Mills, Pa. 294/F3
Le Creusot, France 28/F4
Le Croisic, France 28/B4
Lecta, Ky. 237/K6
Łęczyca, Poland 47/D2
Ledang, Gunong (mt.), Malaysia 72/D7
Ledbury (cays), England 10/E5
Ledbury, England 13/E5
Lede, Belgium 27/D7
Ledeč, Czech Rep. 41/C2
Ledesma, Spain 33/C2
Ledford, Ill. 222/E6
Ledge, Bermuda 156/G2
Ledger, Mont. 262/E2
Ledgewood, N.J. 273/D2
Le Diamant, Martinique 161/D7
Ledoux, N. Mex. 274/D3
Leduc, Alberta 182/D3
Leduc, Alta. 162/E5
Ledyard•, Conn. 210/G3
Ledyard, Iowa 229/E2
Lee (co.), Ala. 195/H5
Lee (co.), Ark. 202/J4
Lee (co.), Fla. 212/E5
Lee, Fla. 212/C1
Lee (co.), Ga. 217/D7
Lee (co.), Ill. 222/D2
Lee, Ill. 222/E2
Lee, Ind. 227/D3
Lee (co.), Iowa 229/L7
Lee (riv.), Ireland 17/D8
Lee (riv.), Ireland 10/B5
Lee (co.), Ky. 237/O5
Lee•, Maine 243/G5
Lee, Mass. 249/B3
Lee•, Mass. 249/B3
Lee (co.), Miss. 256/G2
Lee, Nev. 266/F2
Lee•, N.H. 268/F5
Lee (co.), N.C. 281/L4
Lee (co.), S.C. 296/G3
Lee (co.), Texas 303/H7
Lee (co.), Va. 307/B7
Lee Bayou, La. 238/G3
Lee Center, Ill. 222/D2
Lee Center, N.Y. 276/K4
Leech (lake), Minn. 188/G1
Leech (lake), Minn. 255/D3
Leech, New Bruns. 170/E1
Leech (lake), Sask. 181/J4
Leechburg, Pa. 294/C4
Leech Lake Ind. Res., Minn. 255/D3
Leechville, N.C. 281/R3
Lee City, Ky. 237/P5
Leeco, Ky. 237/O5
Leecreek, Ark. 202/B2
Leedale, Alberta 182/C3
Leedey, Okla. 288/H3
Leeds, Ala. 195/E3
Leeds, England 13/J1
Leeds, England 7/D3
Leeds, England 10/F4
Leeds, Maine 243/C7
Leeds•, Maine 243/C7
Leeds, Md. 245/P2
Leeds, N.Y. 276/N6
Leeds, N. Dak. 282/M3
Leeds (county), Ontario 177/H3
Leeds, Québec 172/F3
Leeds, S.C. 296/E2
Leeds, Utah 304/A6
Leeds Junction, Maine 243/C7
Leeds Point, N.J. 273/E4
Leek, England 13/H2
Leek, England 10/E4
Leek, Netherlands 27/J2
Leelanau (co.), Mich. 250/D4
Leelanau (lake), Mich. 250/D4
Leenane, Ireland 17/B4
Leeper, Mo. 261/L8
Leeper, Pa. 294/D3
Leer, Germany 22/B2
Leerdam, Netherlands 27/F5
Leesburg, Ala. 195/G2
Leesburg, Fla. 212/E3
Leesburg, Ga. 217/D7
Leesburg, Ind. 227/F2
Leesburg, Miss. 256/E6
Leesburg, N.J. 273/D5
Leesburg, Ohio 284/D7
Leesburg, Pa. 294/B3
Leesburg, Va. 307/N2
Lees Creek, Ohio 284/C7
Leesdale, Miss. 256/B7
Lees Ferry, Ariz. 198/D2
Leesport, Pa. 294/K5
Lee's Summit, Mo. 261/R6
Leeston, N. Zealand 100/D5
Leesville, Conn. 210/F2
Leesville, Ind. 227/E7
Leesville, La. 238/D4
Leesville, Ohio 284/H5
Leesville (lake), Ohio 284/H5
Leesville, S.C. 296/E4
Leesville, Va. 307/K6
Leesville (lake), Va. 307/K6
Leet, W. Va. 312/B6
Leetes Island, Conn. 210/E3
Leeton, Mo. 261/E5
Leeton, N. S. Wales 88/H6
Leeton, N.S. Wales 97/D4
Leeton, Utah 304/E3
Leetonia, Ohio 284/J4
Leetsdale, Pa. 294/B4
Leetsville, Mich. 250/D4
Leeuwarden, Netherlands 27/H2
Leeuwin (cape), Australia 87/B9
Leeuwin (cape), Australia 2/O7
Leeuwin (cape), W. Australia 88/A6
Leeuwin (cape), W. Australia 92/A6
Lee Vining, Calif. 204/F6
Leeward (passage), Virgin Is. (U.S.) 161/B4
Leeward (isls.), W. Indies 156/F3
Lefaivre, Ontario 177/K2
Lefka, Cyprus 63/E5
Lefkara, Cyprus 63/E5
Leflore (co.), Miss. 256/D3
Le Flore, Miss. 256/D3
Le Flore (co.), Okla. 288/S5
Leflore, Okla. 288/S5
Lefor, N. Dak. 282/F6
Lefors, Texas 303/D2
Le François, Martinique 161/D6
Lefroy, Ontario 177/E3
Lefroy (lake), W. Australia 88/C6
Lefroy (lake), W. Australia 92/C5
Left Hand, W. Va. 312/D5
Legal, Alberta 182/D3
Legana, Tasmania 99/C3
Leganés, Spain 33/F4
Legazpi, Philippines 82/D4
Legazpi, Philippines 85/G3
Legend, Alberta 182/E5
Legend (lake), Alberta 182/D1
Léger Brook, New Bruns. 170/F2
Légerville, New Bruns. 170/F2
Legerwood, Tasmania 99/D3
Legges Tor (mt.), Tasmania 99/D3
Leggett, N.C. 281/O3
Leghorn (Livorno) (prov.), Italy 34/C3
Leghorn (Livorno), Italy 7/E4
Leghorn (Livorno), Italy 34/C3
Legionowo, Poland 47/E2
Léglise, Belgium 27/H9
Legnago, Italy 34/C2
Legnica (prov.), Poland 47/C4
Legnica, Poland 47/C3
Le Gore, Md. 245/J2
Le Goulet, New Bruns. 170/F1
Le Grand, Calif. 204/E6
Le Grand, Iowa 229/H5
Le Grand (cape), W. Australia 88/C6
Le Grand (cape), W. Australia 92/C6
Le Gros Crêt (mt.), Switzerland 39/B3
Leguan (isl.), Guyana 131/B2
Legune, North. Terr. 93/A3
Leh, India 68/D2
Le Havre, France 7/E4
Le Havre, France 28/C3
Lehew, W. Va. 312/K4
Lehi, Utah 304/C3
Lehigh, Alberta 182/D4
Lehigh, Iowa 229/E4
Lehigh, Kansas 232/E3
Lehigh, N. Dak. 282/E6
Lehigh, Okla. 288/O6
Lehigh (co.), Pa. 294/L4
Lehigh (riv.), Pa. 294/L3
Lehigh Acres, Fla. 212/E5
Lehighton, Pa. 294/L4
Lehman, Pa. 294/E7
Lehr, N. Dak. 282/M7
Lehrte, Germany 22/D2
Lehua (isl.), Hawaii 218/A2
Lehututu, Botswana 118/C4
Leiah, Pakistan 68/C2
Leibnitz, Austria 41/C3
Leicester, England 13/F5
Leicester, England 10/F4
Leicester•, Mass. 249/G4
Leicester, N.Y. 276/D5
Leicester•, Vt. 268/A4
Leicester Junction, Vt. 268/A4
Leicestershire (co.), England 13/F5
Leichhardt, N.S. Wales 88/L4
Leichhardt, N.S. Wales 97/J3
Leichhardt (range), Queensland 95/C4
Leichhardt (riv.), Queensland 88/F3
Leichhardt (riv.), Queensland 95/A3
Leiden, Netherlands 27/E4
Leidy (mt.), Wyo. 319/B2
Leigh, England 10/G2
Leigh, England 13/H2
Leigh, Nebr. 264/G3
Leigh Creek, S. Australia 88/F6
Leigh Creek, S. Australia 94/F4
Leighlindridge, Ireland 17/H6
Leighton, Ala. 195/D1
Leighton, Iowa 229/H6
Leighton-Linslade, England 13/F7
Leijun, Yemen 59/E6
Leimebamba, Peru 128/D6
Leinan, Sask. 181/D5
Leine (riv.), Germany 22/C2
Leinster (prov.), Ireland 17/G5
Leinster (trad. co.), Ireland 17
Leinster (mt.), Ireland 17/H6
Leipers Fork, Tenn. 237/G9
Leipsic, Del. 245/S4
Leipsic (riv.), Del. 245/R4
Leipsic, Ind. 227/E7
Leipsic, Ohio 284/C3
Leipzig, Germany 7/F3
Leipzig, Germany 22/E3
Leipzig, Sask. 181/C3
Leiria (dist.), Portugal 33/B3
Leiria, Portugal 33/B3
Leisler (mt.), North. Terr. 93/A7
Leiston-cum-Sizewell, England 13/J5
Leisure, Ind. 227/F4
Leisure City, Fla. 212/F6
Leitchfield, Ky. 237/J6
Leiter, Wyo. 319/F1
Leitersburg, Md. 245/H2
Leiters Ford, Ind. 227/E2
Leith, N. Dak. 282/G7
Leith, Ontario 177/D3
Leitrim (co.), Ireland 17/E3
Leitrim, Ireland 17/F3
Leivasy, W. Va. 312/E6
Leix (Laoighis) (co.), Ireland 17/G6
Leixlip, Ireland 17/H5
Leiyang, China 77/H6
Leizhou Bandao (pen.), China 77/G7
Lejunior, Ky. 237/P7
Lek (riv.), Netherlands 27/F5
Leka (isl.), Norway 18/G4
Le Kef (El Kef), Tunisia 106/F1
Lekitobi, Indonesia 85/G6
Lekoni, Gabon 102/D5
Lekoni, Gabon 115/B4
Leksand, Sweden 18/J6
Leksula, Indonesia 85/H6
Lela, Okla. 288/N2
Lela, Texas 303/D2
Le Lamentin, Martinique 161/D6
Leland, Ga. 217/J1
Leland, Ill. 222/E2
Leland, Iowa 229/F2
Leland, Mich. 250/D3
Leland, Miss. 256/C4
Leland, N.C. 281/N6
Leland, Oreg. 291/D5
Le Landeron, Switzerland 39/C2
Leleiwi (pt.), Hawaii 218/K5
Leleque, Argentina 143/B5
Lelia Lake, Texas 303/D3
Le Lieu, Switzerland 39/B3
Le Locle, Switzerland 39/C2
Le Lorrain, Martinique 161/D6
Le Loup, Kansas 232/G3
Lely (mts.), Suriname 131/D3
Lelydorp, Suriname 131/D3
Lelystad, Netherlands 27/H3
Lem, Denmark 21/B5
Léman (Geneva) (lake), Switzerland 39/C4
Le Mans, France 28/C3
Le Mans, France 7/E4
Le Marin, Martinique 161/D7
Le Mars, Iowa 229/A3
Lemasters, Pa. 294/G6
Lemay, Mo. 261/R4
Lemberg, Sask. 181/H5
Leme, Brazil 135/C3
Lemelerberg (hill), Netherlands 27/J4
Lemery, Philippines 82/C4
Lemesurier (isl.), Alaska 196/M1
Lemgo, Germany 22/C2
Lemhi (co.), Idaho 220/D4
Lemhi, Idaho 220/E5
Lemhi (pass), Idaho 220/E5
Lemhi (range), Idaho 220/E5
Lemhi (riv.), Idaho 220/E5
Lemhi (pass), Mont. 262/C6
Lemieux (isls.), N.W.T. 187/M3
Lemington•, Vt. 268/D2
Lemitar, N. Mex. 274/B4

Little Paint Branch 399

Liège, Belgium 27/H7
Liegnitz (Legnica), Poland 47/C3
Lieksa, Finland 18/R5
Lienyünkang (Lianyungang), China 77/J5
Lienz, Austria 41/B3
Liepāja, Estonia 7/F3
Liepāja, Estonia 48/B4
Liepāja, Estonia 52/B3
Liepāja, Estonia 53/A2
Lier, Belgium 27/F6
Lierneux, Belgium 27/H8
Lierre (Lier), Belgium 27/F6
Liestal, Switzerland 39/E2
Liévin, France 28/E2
Lièvre (riv.), Québec 172/B4
Lièvres (isl.), Québec 172/H2
Liezen, Austria 41/C3
Liffey (riv.), Ireland 17/H5
Liffey (riv.), Ireland 10/C4
Lifford, Ireland 10/C3
Lifford, Ireland 17/F2
Lifu (isl.), New Caled. 87/G8
Lifu (isl.), New Caled. 86/H4
Ligao, Philippines 82/D4
Līgatne, Latvia 53/C2
Liggett, Ky. 237/P7
Lightfoot, Va. 307/P6
Lighthouse (pt.), Fla. 212/B2
Light House (pt.), Mich. 250/D3
Lighthouse Point, Fla. 212/F5
Lightning (creek), Oreg. 291/L2
Lightning (creek), Wyo. 319/G2
Lightning Ridge, N.S. Wales 97/E1
Lightsville, Ohio 284/A5
Lignite, N. Dak. 282/F2
Ligon, Ky. 237/R6
Ligonha (riv.), Mozambique 118/F3
Ligonier, Ind. 227/F2
Ligonier, Pa. 294/D5
Liguria (reg.), Italy 34/B2
Ligurian (sea), Italy 34/B3
Lihir Group (isls.), Papua N.G. 86/C1
Lihou (cays), Coral Sea Is. Terr. 88/J3
Lihue, Hawaii 218/C2
Lihue, Hawaii 188/E5
Lihula, Estonia 53/C1
Lijiang, China 77/F6
Likasi, Panda-, D.R. Congo 115/E6
Likati, D.R. Congo 115/D3
Likely, Br. Col. 184/G4
Likely, Calif. 204/E2
Likhoslavl', Russia 52/E3
Likouala (riv.), Congo 115/C3
Lila (lake), N.Y. 276/L2
Lilac, Sask. 181/D3
Lilbourn, Mo. 261/N9
Lilburn, Ga. 217/D3
Lileah, Tasmania 99/B2
L'Île-Rousse, France 28/B6
Liles (pt.), Chile 138/F2
Lilesville, N.C. 281/K5
Lilienfeld, Austria 41/C3
Lille, France 7/E3
Lille, France 28/E2
Lille, Maine 243/G1
Lilleå (riv.), Denmark 21/B5
Lille Baelt (chan.), Denmark 21/C7
Lillehammer, Norway 18/F6
Lillesand, Norway 18/F7
Lillestrøm, Norway 18/E3
Lillian, Ala. 195/D10
Lillie, La. 238/E1
Lilliesleaf, Scotland 15/F5
Lillington, N.C. 281/M4
Lillinonah (lake), Conn. 210/B3
Lilliwaup, Wash. 310/B3
Lillo, Spain 33/E3
Lillooet, Br. Col. 162/D5
Lillooet, Br. Col. 184/G5
Lillooet (riv.), Br. Col. 184/F5
Lilly, Ga. 217/E6
Lilly, Ill. 222/D3
Lilly, Pa. 294/E5
Lilly Chapel, Ohio 284/D6
Lillydale, Victoria 97/J4
Lilongwe (cap.), Malawi 2/L6
Lilongwe (cap.), Malawi 102/F6
Lilongwe (cap.), Malawi 115/F6
Liloy, Philippines 82/D6
Lily, Ky. 237/N6
Lily, S. Dak. 298/O3
Lily, Wis. 317/J5
Lilydale, Minn. 255/G5
Lily Dale, N.Y. 276/B6
Lilydale, Tasmania 99/D3
Lily Plain, Sask. 181/E2
Lim (fjord), Denmark 18/E8
Lim (riv.), Yugoslavia 45/D4
Lima, Ill. 222/B3
Lima (isls.), Indonesia 85/F7
Lima, Pulau (isl.), Malaysia 72/F6
Lima, Mont. 262/D6
Lima (res.), Mont. 262/D6
Lima, N.Y. 276/E5
Lima, Ohio 284/B4
Lima, Ohio 188/K2
Lima (New Lima), Okla. 288/D4
Lima, Paraguay 144/D3
Lima, Pa. 294/L7
Lima (dept.), Peru 128/D8
Lima (cap.), Peru 2/F6
Lima (cap.), Peru 120/B4
Lima (cap.), Peru 128/D8
Lima (riv.), Portugal 33/B2
Lima (pt.), P. Rico 161/F2
Lima Center, Wis. 317/J10
Limache, Chile 138/F2
Lima Duarte, Brazil 135/E2
Limal, Bolivia 136/C8
Limanowa, Poland 47/E4
Limarí (riv.), Chile 138/A8
Limasawa (isl.), Philippines 82/E6
Limassol, Cyprus 59/B3
Limassol, Cyprus 63/E5
Limavady (dist.), N. Ireland 17/H1
Limavady, N. Ireland 10/C3
Limavady, N. Ireland 17/H1
Limaville, Ohio 284/H4
Limay (riv.), Argentina 120/C6
Limay (riv.), Argentina 143/C4
Limbach-Oberfrohna, Germany 22/E3
Limbani, Peru 128/H10
Limbaži, Latvia 53/C2
Limbe, Cameroon 106/F8
Limbe, Cameroon 115/A3
Limbé, Haiti 158/C5
Limbourg, Belgium 27/J7
Limbunya, North. Terr. 93/B4
Limburg (prov.), Belgium 27/G7
Limburg (Limbourg), Belgium 27/J7
Limburg (prov.), Netherlands 27/H6
Limburg an der Lahn, Germany 22/C3
Lime, Oreg. 291/K3
Limedsforsen, Sweden 18/H6
Limeira, Brazil 132/E8
Limeira, Brazil 135/C3
Lime Kiln, Md. 245/J3
Limekilns, Scotland 15/D1
Limenária, Greece 45/G5
Limerick (co.), Ireland 17/D7
Limerick, Ireland 17/D6
Limerick, Ireland 10/B4
Limerick, Ireland 7/D3
Limerick•, Maine 243/B8
Limerick, Sask. 181/E6
Limeridge, Wis. 317/F9
Lime Rock, Conn. 210/B1
Lime Springs, Iowa 229/J2
Limestone (co.), Ala. 195/E1
Limestone, Ark. 202/D2
Limestone, Fla. 212/E4
Limestone, Maine 243/H2
Limestone•, Maine 243/H2
Limestone, Mont. 262/F5
Limestone, N.Y. 276/C6
Limestone, Tenn. 237/R8
Limestone (co.), Texas 303/H6
Lime Village, Alaska 196/G2
Limfjorden (fjord), Denmark 21/D4
Limfjorden (fjord), Denmark 21/A4
Limington, Maine 243/B8
Limington•, Maine 243/B8
Limmat (riv.), Switzerland 39/F2
Limmen (bight), North. Terr. 88/F2
Limmen (bight), North. Terr. 93/D3
Limmen Bight (riv.), North. Terr. 88/F3
Limmen Bight (riv.), North. Terr. 93/D4
Límni, Greece 45/F6
Límnos (isl.), Greece 45/G6
Limoeiro, Brazil 132/H4
Limoeiro do Norte, Brazil 132/G4
Limoges, France 7/E4
Limoges, France 28/D5
Limoges, Ontario 177/J2
Limon, Colo. 208/M4
Limón, C. Rica 146/K8
Limón, C. Rica 154/F6
Limón, Honduras 154/E3
Limonade, Haiti 158/C5
Limonar, Cuba 158/D1
Limoquije, Bolivia 136/C4
Limousin (trad. prov.), France 29
Limousin (reg.), France 28/D5
Limoux, France 28/E6
Limpio, Paraguay 144/B4
Limpopo (riv.) 102/E7
Limpopo (riv.), Botswana 118/D4
Limpopo (riv.), Mozambique 118/E4
Limpopo (riv.), S. Africa 118/D4
Lim Rock, Ala. 195/F1
Linapacan (isl.), Philippines 82/B5
Linapacan (str.), Philippines 82/B5
Linard (peak), Switzerland 39/K3
Linares, Chile 138/A11
Linares, Chile 120/B6
Linares, Mexico 150/K4
Linares, Spain 33/E3
Linares, Spain 7/D5
Linaria, Alberta 182/C2
Lincang, China 77/E7
Linch, Wyo. 319/F2
Lincklaen, N.Y. 276/J5
Lincoln (sea) 146/M1
Lincoln (sea) 4/A12
Lincoln, Ala. 195/F3
Lincoln, Argentina 143/F7
Lincoln (co.), Ark. 202/G6
Lincoln, Ark. 202/B2
Lincoln, Calif. 204/B8
Lincoln (isl.), China 85/E2
Lincoln (co.), Colo. 208/M5
Lincoln (mt.), Colo. 208/G4
Lincoln, Del. 245/S5
Lincoln, England 13/G4
Lincoln, England 10/F4
Lincoln (co.), Ga. 217/H3
Lincoln (co.), Idaho 220/D6
Lincoln, Ill. 222/D3
Lincoln, Ind. 227/E3
Lincoln, Iowa 229/H4
Lincoln (co.), Kansas 232/D2
Lincoln, Kansas 232/D2
Lincoln (co.), Ky. 237/M6
Lincoln (par.), La. 238/E1
Lincoln (co.), Maine 243/D7
Lincoln, Maine 243/G5
Lincoln•, Maine 243/G5
Lincoln•, Mass. 249/B6
Lincoln, Mich. 250/F4
Lincoln (co.), Minn. 255/B6
Lincoln (co.), Miss. 256/D8
Lincoln (co.), Mo. 261/L4
Lincoln, Mo. 261/F6
Lincoln (co.), Mont. 262/A2
Lincoln, Mont. 262/D4
Lincoln (co.), Nebr. 264/D4
Lincoln (cap.), Nebr. 146/J5
Lincoln (cap.), Nebr. 188/G2
Lincoln (cap.), Nebr. 264/H4
Lincoln (co.), Nev. 266/F5
Lincoln•, N.H. 268/D3
Lincoln (mt.), N.H. 268/D3
Lincoln (co.), N. Mex. 274/D5
Lincoln, N. Mex. 274/D5
Lincoln (co.), N.C. 281/G3
Lincoln, N. Dak. 282/J6
Lincoln (sea), N.W.T. 187/M1
Lincoln (co.), Okla. 288/N3
Lincoln, Ontario 177/E4
Lincoln (co.), Oreg. 291/D3
Lincoln, Pa. 294/C7
Lincoln (co.), S. Dak. 298/R7
Lincoln (co.), Tenn. 237/H10
Lincoln, Texas 303/H7
Lincoln (creek), Utah 304/C2
Lincoln•, Vt. 268/B3
Lincoln (co.), Wash. 310/G3
Lincoln, Wash. 310/G3
Lincoln (co.), W. Va. 312/B6
Lincoln (co.), Wis. 317/G5
Lincoln (co.), Wyo. 319/B3
Lincoln Beach, Oreg. 291/C3
Lincoln Boyhood Nat'l Mem., Ind. 227/C8
Lincoln Center, Maine 243/G5
Lincoln Center, Mass. 249/B6
Lincoln City, Ind. 227/C8
Lincoln City, Oreg. 291/C3
Lincoln Gap (pass), Vt. 268/B3
Lincoln Heights, Ohio 284/C9
Lincolnia, Va. 307/S3
Lincoln Park, Colo. 208/J6
Lincoln Park, Ga. 217/D5
Lincoln Park, Mich. 250/B7
Lincoln Park, N.J. 273/A1
Lincolnshire (co.), England 13/G4
Lincolnshire, Ill. 222/B5
Lincolnton, Ga. 217/G3
Lincolnton, N.C. 281/G4
Lincoln University, Pa. 294/L6
Lincolnville, Ind. 227/F3
Lincolnville, Kansas 232/F3
Lincolnville, Maine 243/E7
Lincolnville•, Maine 243/E7
Lincolnville, Nova Scotia 168/G3
Lincolnville, S.C. 296/G6
Lincolnville Center, Maine 243/E7
Lincoln Wolds (hills), England 13/G4
Lincolnwood, Ill. 222/B5
Lincroft, N.J. 273/E3
L'Incudine (mt.), France 28/B7
Lind, Wash. 310/G4
Linda, Calif. 204/D4
Lindale, Alberta 182/C3
Lindale, Ga. 217/B2
Lindale, Texas 303/J5
Lindau, Germany 22/C5
Lindberg, Alberta 182/E3
Linden, Ala. 195/C6
Linden, Alberta 182/D4
Linden, Ariz. 198/E4
Linden, Calif. 204/D5
Linden, Guyana 131/L2
Linden, Ind. 227/D4
Linden, Iowa 229/E5
Linden, Mich. 250/F6
Linden, N.J. 273/A3
Linden, N.C. 281/M4
Linden (mts.), Switzerland 39/F2
Linden, Tenn. 237/F9
Linden, Texas 303/K4
Linden, Va. 307/M3
Linden, W. Va. 312/D5
Linden, Wis. 317/F10
Linden Beach, Ontario 177/B6
Lindenhurst, Ill. 222/B4
Lindenhurst, N.Y. 276/O9
Lindenwold, N.J. 273/B4
Lindenwood, Ill. 222/D1
Lindesberg, Sweden 18/J7
Lindesnes (cape), Norway 7/E3
Lindesnes (cape), Norway 18/E8
Lindi (reg.), Tanzania 115/G5
Lindi, Tanzania 102/F5
Lindi, Tanzania 115/G5
Lindi (riv.), D.R. Congo 115/E3
Lindisfarne (Holy) (dist.), England 13/F2
Lindisfarne (Holy) (isl.), England 10/F3
Lindley, N.Y. 276/F6
Lindon, Colo. 208/N3
Lindon, Utah 304/C3
Líndos, Greece 45/J7
Lindrith, N. Mex. 274/C2
Lindsay, Calif. 204/F7
Lindsay, La. 238/H5
Lindsay, Mont. 262/L3
Lindsay, Nebr. 264/G3
Lindsay, Okla. 288/L5
Lindsay, Ontario 177/F3
Lindsborg, Kansas 232/E3
Lindsey, Ohio 284/D3
Lindsey, Wis. 317/F6
Lindside, W. Va. 312/E8
Lindstrom, Minn. 255/F5
Line (isls.) 2/B6
Line (isls.), Pacific 87/K5
Lineboro, Md. 245/L2
Linesville, Pa. 294/A2
Lineville, Ala. 195/G4
Lineville, Iowa 229/G7
Linfen, China 77/H4
Linfield, Pa. 294/L5
Linganore (creek), Md. 245/J3
Lingao, China 77/G8
Lingayen, Philippines 85/F2
Lingayen, Philippines 82/C2
Lingayen (gulf), Philippines 82/C2
Lingen, Germany 22/B2
Lingga (arch.), Indonesia 85/D5
Lingga (isl.), Indonesia 85/D6
Lingle, Wyo. 319/H3
Linglestown, Pa. 294/J5
Lingling, China 77/H6
Lingo, N. Mex. 274/F5
Lingqiu, China 77/H4
Lingshan, China 77/G7
Lingshui, China 77/H8
Linguère, Senegal 106/B5
Lingwu, China 77/G4
Linhai, China 77/K6
Linhares, Brazil 132/F7
Linhe, China 77/G3
Linière, Québec 172/G3
Linkebeek, Belgium 27/C10
Linköping, Sweden 18/K7
Linköping, Sweden 7/F3
Linkou, China 77/M2
Linkwood, Md. 245/P6
Linlithgow, Scotland 10/B1
Linlithgow, Scotland 15/C1
Linn (co.), Iowa 229/K4
Linn (co.), Kansas 232/H3
Linn, Kansas 232/E2
Linn (co.), Mo. 261/F3
Linn, Mo. 261/J5
Linn (co.), Oreg. 291/E3
Linn, Texas 303/F11
Linn, W. Va. 312/E4
Linn Creek, Mo. 261/G6
Linndale, Ohio 284/G9
Linneus•, Maine 243/H3
Linneus, Mo. 261/F3
Linn Grove, Ind. 227/H3
Linn Grove, Iowa 229/C3
Linnhe, Loch (inlet), Scotland 10/D2
Linnhe, Loch (inlet), Scotland 15/C4
Linnsburg, Ind. 227/D5
Linntown, Pa. 294/J4
Lino Lakes, Minn. 255/G5
Linosa (isl.), Italy 34/D7
Linqing (Lintsing), China 77/J4
Lins, Brazil 132/D8
Lins, Brazil 135/B2
Linstead, Jamaica 158/J6
Linter, Belgium 27/G7
Linth (riv.), Switzerland 39/G3
Linthal, Switzerland 39/H3
Linthicum Heights, Md. 245/M4
Lintlaw, Sask. 181/H3
Linton, Ga. 217/F4
Linton, Ind. 227/C6
Linton, Ky. 237/F7
Linton, N. Dak. 282/K7
Linville, La. 238/F1
Linville, N.C. 281/F2
Linville, Va. 307/L3
Linville Falls, N.C. 281/F3
Linwood, Ga. 217/B1
Linwood, Ind. 227/F4
Linwood, Kansas 232/G2
Linwood, Ky. 237/K6
Linwood, Md. 245/K2
Linwood, Mass. 249/H4
Linwood, Mich. 250/F5
Linwood, Nebr. 264/H3
Linwood, N.J. 273/D5
Linwood, N.C. 281/J3
Linwood, Ontario 177/D4
Linwood, Pa. 294/L7
Linwood, Scotland 15/B2
Linxi, China 77/J3
Linxia (Linsia), China 77/F4
Linyi, China 77/J4
Linz, Austria 7/F4
Linz, Austria 41/C2
Linze, China 77/F4
Linzee (cape), Nova Scotia 168/G2
Lionel, Scotland 15/B2
Lionel Town, Jamaica 158/J7
Lions (gulf) 7/E4
Lions (gulf), France 28/F6
Lion's Bay, Br. Col. 184/K3
Lion's Head, Ontario 177/C2
Lipa, Philippines 82/C4
Lipan, Texas 303/F5
Lipari, Italy 34/E5
Lipari (isl.), Italy 34/E5
Lipari (isls.), Italy 34/E5
Lipetsk, Russia 7/H3
Lipetsk, Russia 48/E4
Lipetsk, Russia 52/E4
Lipez, Cordillera de (range), Bolivia 136/B8
Liping, China 77/G6
Lipník nad Bečvou, Czech Rep. 41/D2
Lipno (res.), Czech Rep. 41/C2
Lipno, Poland 47/D2
Lipoa (pt.), Hawaii 218/H1
Lipova, Romania 45/E2
Lippe (riv.), Germany 22/C3
Lippstadt, Germany 22/C3
Lipscomb, Ala. 195/E4
Lipscomb (co.), Texas 303/D1
Lipscomb, Texas 303/D1
Lipton, Sask. 181/H5
Liptovský Hrádok, Slovakia 41/E2
Liptovský Mikuláš, Slovakia 41/E2
Lipu, China 77/H7
Lira, Uganda 115/F3
Lircay, Peru 128/E9
Liri (riv.), Italy 34/D4
Liria, Spain 33/F3
Lisala, D.R. Congo 115/D3
Lisbellaw, N. Ireland 17/K2
Lisbon•, Conn. 210/G2
Lisbon, Ill. 222/E2
Lisbon, Ind. 227/G2
Lisbon, Iowa 229/L5
Lisbon, La. 238/E1
Lisbon•, Maine 243/C7
Lisbon, Md. 245/K3
Lisbon, Mo. 261/G4
Lisbon, N.H. 268/D3
Lisbon•, N.H. 268/D3
Lisbon, N.Y. 276/K1
Lisbon, N. Dak. 282/P7
Lisbon, Ohio 284/J4
Lisbon (dist.), Portugal 33/A1
Lisbon (cap.), Portugal 2/J4
Lisbon (cap.), Portugal 7/D5
Lisbon (Lisboa) (cap.), Portugal 33/A1
Lisbon Falls, Maine 243/D7
Lisbon-Lisbon Center, Maine 243/C7
Lisburn, Alberta 182/C3
Lisburn (dist.), N. Ireland 17/J2
Lisburn, N. Ireland 10/D3
Lisburn, N. Ireland 17/J2
Lisburne (cape), Alaska 196/E1
Lisburne (pen.), Alaska 196/E1
Liscannor (bay), Ireland 17/B6
Liscarroll, Ireland 17/D7
Lisco, Nebr. 264/B3
Liscomb, Iowa 229/H4
Liscomb (isl.), Nova Scotia 168/G4
Lisdoonvarna, Ireland 17/C5
Lishi, China 77/H4
Lishui, China 77/K6
Lisianski (isl.), Hawaii 188/E6
Lisianski (isl.), Hawaii 87/J3
Lisianski (isl.), Hawaii 218/B5
Lisichansk, Ukraine 52/E5
Lisieux, France 28/D3
Lisieux, Sask. 181/E6
Liskeard, England 13/C7
Liskeard, England 10/D5
Lisle, Ill. 222/A6
Lisle, N.Y. 276/H6
Lisle, Ontario 177/E3
L'Islet (co.), Québec 172/G2
L'Islet, Québec 172/G2
L'Islet-sur-Mer, Québec 172/G2
L'Isle-Verte, Québec 172/G1
Lisman, Ala. 195/B6
Lisman, Ky. 237/F6
Lismore, Australia 87/F8
Lismore, Ireland 10/B4
Lismore, Ireland 17/F7
Lismore, La. 238/G3
Lismore, Minn. 255/B7
Lismore, N. S. Wales 88/J5
Lismore, N.S. Wales 97/G1
Lismore (isl.), Scotland 15/C4
Lisnaskea, N. Ireland 17/G3
Lišov, Czech Rep. 41/C2
Lispeszentadorján, Hungary 41/D3
Lisse, Netherlands 27/F4
Lista (pen.), Norway 18/E7
Lister (mt.) 5/B8
Listie, Pa. 294/D5
Listowel, Ireland 17/C7
Listowel, Ireland 10/B4
Listowel, Ontario 177/D4
Litang, China 77/F6
Litani (riv.), Fr. Guiana 131/D4
Litani (riv.), Lebanon 63/F6
Litani (riv.), Suriname 131/D4
Litchfield (co.), Conn. 210/B1
Litchfield, Conn. 210/C2
Litchfield•, Conn. 210/C2
Litchfield, Ill. 222/D4
Litchfield•, Maine 243/D7
Litchfield, Mich. 250/E6
Litchfield, Minn. 255/D5
Litchfield, Nebr. 264/E3
Litchfield•, N.H. 268/E6
Litchfield, North. Terr. 93/B2
Litchfield, Ohio 284/F3
Litchfield Park, Ariz. 198/C5
Litchville, N. Dak. 282/O6
Lith, Netherlands 27/G5
Litherland, England 13/G2
Litherland, England 10/F2
Lithgow, Australia 87/F9
Lithgow, N. S. Wales 88/J6
Lithgow, N.S. Wales 97/F3
Lithia, Va. 307/J6
Lithia Springs, Ga. 217/C3
Lithium, Mo. 261/N7
Lithonia, Ga. 217/D3
Lithopolis, Ohio 284/E6
Lithuania 7/G3
Lithuania 48/C4
Lithuania 52/B3
LITHUANIA 53/B3
Lititz, Pa. 294/K5
Litókhoron, Greece 45/F5
Litoměřice, Czech Rep. 41/C1
Litomyšl, Czech Rep. 41/D2
Litovel, Czech Rep. 41/D2
Littau, Switzerland 39/F2
Littcarr, Ky. 237/R6
Little (riv.), Ala. 195/G2
Little (riv.), Ala. 195/C8
Little (riv.), Ark. 202/B6
Little (riv.), Conn. 210/G2
Little (riv.), Conn. 210/H1
Little (riv.), Ind. 227/G3
Little (riv.), La. 238/F3
Little (riv.), Mass. 249/C4
Little (riv.), New Bruns. 170/D2
Little (riv.), N.C. 281/N3
Little (riv.), N.C. 281/L4
Little (riv.), Okla. 288/R6
Little (riv.), Oreg. 291/E4
Little (riv.), S.C. 296/D3
Little (riv.), S.C. 296/C3
Little (riv.), Vt. 268/B3
Little (inlet), Va. 307/S6
Little (riv.), Va. 307/N5
Little (riv.), Va. 307/H7
Little Alföld (plain), Hungary 41/D3
Little America, Ant. 2/B10
Little America 5/B10
Little America, Wyo. 319/C4
Little Andaman (isl.), India 68/G6
Little Arkansas (riv.), Kansas 232/E3
Little Barrier (isl.), N. Zealand 100/E2
Little Bay de Noc (bay), Mich. 250/B3
Little Bay Islands, Newf. 166/C4
Little Beaver (creek), Kansas 232/A2
Little Beaver (creek), Ohio 284/J4
Little Bighorn (riv.), Mont. 262/J5
Little Birch (lake), Manitoba 179/E3
Little Birch, W. Va. 312/E5
Little Bitterroot (lake), Mont. 262/B2
Little Black (riv.), Maine 243/E1
Little Black, Wis. 317/F5
Little Blue (riv.), Kansas 232/E1
Little Blue (riv.), Nebr. 264/H5
Little Boars Head, N.H. 268/F6
Little Bow (riv.), Alberta 182/D4
Little Britain, Ontario 177/F3
Little Brook, Nova Scotia 168/B4
Little Brosna (riv.), Ireland 17/E5
Little Buffalo Lake, Alberta 182/B1
Little Bullhead, Manitoba 179/F3
Little Butter (creek), Oreg. 291/H2
Little Cadotte (riv.), Alberta 182/B1
Little Cape, New Bruns. 170/F2
Little Catalina, Newf. 166/D2
Little Cayman (isl.), Cayman Is. 156/B3
Little Cedar, Iowa 229/H2
Little Chief, Okla. 288/N1
Little Choptank (riv.), Md. 245/N6
Little Chute, Wis. 317/K7
Little Coco (isl.), Burma 72/B4
Little Colorado (riv.), Ariz. 188/D3
Little Colorado (riv.), Ariz. 198/D3
Little Compton•, R.I. 249/K6
Little Corn (isl.), Nicaragua 154/F4
Little Creek, Del. 245/S4
Little Creek, La. 238/F3
Little Creek (peak), Utah 304/B6
Little Current, Ontario 177/B2
Little Current (riv.), Ontario 175/C2
Little Deep (creek), N. Dak. 282/G2
Little Deer Isle, Maine 243/F7
Little Diomede (isl.), Alaska 196/E1
Little Dover, Nova Scotia 168/G3
Little Dry (creek), Mont. 262/K3
Little Eagle, S. Dak. 298/H2
Little Egg (harb.), N.J. 273/E4
Little Egg (inlet), N.J. 273/E5
Little Elkhart (riv.), Ind. 227/F1
Little Falls, Minn. 255/D5
Little Falls•, N.J. 273/B2
Little Falls, N.Y. 276/L4
Little Falls-South Windham, Maine 243/C8
Little Farms, La. 238/N4
Little Ferry, N.J. 273/B2
Littlefield, Ariz. 198/B2
Littlefield, Texas 303/B4
Little Flock, Ark. 202/B1
Littlefork, Minn. 255/E2
Little Fork (riv.), Minn. 255/E2
Little Genesee, N.Y. 276/D6
Little Girl (pt.), Mich. 250/E1
Little Goose (dam), Wash. 310/G4
Little Grand Rapids, Manitoba 179/G2
Little Gunpowder Falls (creek), Md. 245/M2
Littlehampton, England 13/G7
Littlehampton, England 10/F5
Little Harbour, Nova Scotia 168/D5
Little Heart's Ease, Newf. 166/D2
Little Hocking, Ohio 284/G7
Little Humboldt (riv.), Nev. 266/D1
Little Inagua (isl.), Bahamas 156/D2
Little Kai (isl.), Indonesia 85/J7
Little Kanawha (riv.), W. Va. 312/D5
Little Knife (riv.), N. Dak. 282/F3
Little Lake, Calif. 204/H8
Little Lake, Mich. 250/B2
Little Laramie (riv.), Wyo. 319/G4
Little London, Jamaica 158/G6
Little Lorraine, Nova Scotia 168/J3
Little Lost (riv.), Idaho 220/E5
Littlelot, Tenn. 237/G9
Little Lynches (riv.), S.C. 296/G3
Little Madawaska (riv.), Maine 243/G2
Little Makin (atoll), Kiribati 87/H5
Little Manitou (lake), Sask. 181/F4
Little Marais, Minn. 255/G3
Little Marsh, Pa. 294/H2
Little Meadows, Pa. 294/K2
Little Mecatina (riv.), Newf. 166/B3
Little Medicine Bow (riv.), Wyo. 319/F3
Little Miami (riv.), Ohio 284/B6
Little Minch (sound), Scotland 10/C2
Little Minch (sound), Scotland 15/B3
Little Missouri (riv.) 188/F1
Little Missouri (riv.), Ark. 202/D6
Little Missouri (riv.), Mont. 262/M5
Little Missouri (riv.), N. Dak. 282/D4
Little Missouri (riv.), S. Dak. 298/B1
Little Missouri (riv.), Wyo. 319/H1
Littlemore, England 13/F6
Little Moreau (riv.), S. Dak. 298/G3
Little Mountain, S.C. 296/E3
Little Muddy (riv.), N. Dak. 282/C3
Little Muddy (creek), Wyo. 319/B4
Little Muskingum (riv.), Ohio 284/H6
Little Narrows, Nova Scotia 168/H3
Little Nicobar (isl.), India 68/G7
Little Orleans, Md. 245/E2
Little Owyhee (riv.), Idaho 220/B7
Little Paint Branch (riv.), Md. 245/F4

400 Little Para

Little Para (riv.), S. Australia 88/D7
Little Para (riv.), S. Australia 94/B7
Little Patuxent (riv.), Md. 245/L4
Little Pee Dee (riv.), N.C. 281/L6
Little Pee Dee (riv.), S.C. 296/J4
Little Pigeon (creek), Ind. 227/C9
Little Plymouth, Va. 307/P5
Little Popo Agie (riv.), Wyo. 319/D3
Littleport, England 13/H5
Littleport, Iowa 229/L3
Little Powder (riv.), Wyo. 319/G1
Little Prairie, Wis. 317/H2
Little Red (riv.), Ark. 202/G3
Little River, Ala. 195/C8
Little River (co.), Ark. 202/B6
Littleriver, Calif. 204/B4
Little River, Kansas 232/E3
Little River, N. Zealand 100/D5
Little River, Nova Scotia 168/B4
Little River (harb.), Nova Scotia 168/B5
Little River, S.C. 296/K4
Little River (inlet), S.C. 296/L4
Little Rock (cap.), Ark. 188/H4
Little Rock (cap.), Ark. 146/J6
Little Rock (cap.), Ark. 202/F4
Little Rock, Iowa 229/B2
Little Rock, Minn. 255/D5
Little Rock (creek), Minn. 255/C7
Little Rock, Miss. 256/F5
Little Rock, S.C. 296/J3
Littlerock, Wash. 310/B4
Little Rock A.F.B., Ark. 202/F4
Little Sable (pt.), Mich. 250/C5
Little Saint Bernard (pass), France 28/G5
Little Saint George (isl.), Fla. 212/B2
Little Salmon (riv.), Idaho 220/B4
Little Salt (lake), Utah 304/A6
Little Sandy (creek), Wyo. 319/C3
Little Sauk, Minn. 255/D5
Little Sevogle (riv.), New Bruns. 170/D1
Little Sheep (creek), Oreg. 291/K2
Little Shippegan, New Bruns. 170/F1
Little Silver, N.J. 273/F3
Little Sioux, Iowa 229/B5
Little Sioux (riv.), Iowa 229/B3
Little Sitkin (isl.), Alaska 196/K4
Little Smoky, Alberta 182/B2
Little Smoky (riv.), Alberta 182/B2
Little Smoky (valley), Nev. 266/E4
Little Southwest Miramichi (riv.), New Bruns. 170/D2
Little Spokane (riv.), Wash. 310/H3
Littlestown, Pa. 294/H6
Little Suamico, Wis. 317/L6
Little Summer (isl.), Mich. 250/C3
Little Tallahatchie (riv.), Miss. 256/D2
Little Tennessee (riv.), N.C. 281/B4
Little Tennessee (riv.), Tenn. 237/N10
Little Thunder (creek), Wyo. 319/G2
Little Tinicum (isl.), Pa. 294/M7
Little Tobago (isl.), Virgin Is. (U.K.) 161/B3
Little Tobique (riv.), New Bruns. 170/C1
Littleton, Colo. 208/K3
Littleton, Ill. 222/C3
Littleton, Iowa 229/K3
Littleton, Ireland 17/F6
Littleton•, Maine 243/H3
Littleton•, Mass. 249/H2
Littleton, N.H. 268/D3
Littleton•, N.H. 268/D3
Littleton, N.C. 281/O2
Littleton, Va. 307/O7
Littleton, W. Va. 312/F3
Littleton Common, Mass. 249/J2
Little Traverse (bay), Mich. 250/D3
Little Trout River (pond), Newf. 166/C4
Little Tupper (lake), N.Y. 276/L2
Little Valley, N.Y. 276/C6
Little Vermilion (riv.), Ind. 227/B5
Littleville, Ala. 195/C1
Little Wabash (riv.), Ill. 222/E5
Little Weiser (riv.), Idaho 220/B5
Little White (riv.), S. Dak. 298/H7
Little Wood (riv.), Idaho 220/D6
Little Yenisey (riv.), Russia 48/K4
Little York, Ill. 222/C2
Little York, Ind. 227/F7
Little York, N.J. 273/C2
Little Zab (riv.), Iraq 66/C3
Lituya (bay), Alaska 196/L1
Litvínov, Czech Rep. 41/B1
Liuba, China 77/G5
Liukang Tenggaja (isls.), Indonesia 85/F7
Liuli, Tanzania 115/F6
Liuzhou (Liuchow), China 77/G7
Liuzhou, China 54/M7
Līvāni, Latvia 53/D2
Livelong, Sask. 181/C2
Lively (isl.), Falkland Is. 143/E7
Lively, Va. 307/P5
Livengood, Alaska 196/J1
Live Oak, Calif. 204/K4
Live Oak, Calif. 204/D4
Live Oak, Fla. 212/D1
Live Oak (co.), Texas 303/F9
Live Oak, Texas 303/K10
Liveringa, W. Australia 88/C3
Liveringa, W. Australia 92/D2
Livermore, Calif. 204/L2
Livermore, Colo. 208/J1
Livermore, Iowa 229/E3
Livermore, Ky. 237/G5
Livermore, Maine 243/C7
Livermore•, Maine 243/C7
Livermore (mt.), Texas 303/C11
Livermore Falls, Maine 243/C7
Livermore Falls•, Maine 243/C7
Livermore Falls, N.H. 268/D4
Liverpool (swamp), Bolivia 136/D4
Liverpool, England 10/F2
Liverpool, England 13/G2
Liverpool, England 7/D3
Liverpool (bay), England 13/D4
Liverpool, Ill. 222/C3
Liverpool, N. S. Wales 88/K4
Liverpool, N.S. Wales 97/H4
Liverpool (range), N.S. Wales 97/F2
Liverpool, N.Y. 276/H4
Liverpool (bay), N.W.T. 187/E2
Liverpool (cape), N.W.T. 187/L2
Liverpool, Nova Scotia 168/D4
Liverpool (bay), Nova Scotia 168/D5
Liverpool, Pa. 294/H4
Liverpool, Texas 303/J3
Liverpool, W. Va. 312/C5
Livia, Ky. 237/G5
Livigno, Italy 34/C1
Livingston, Ala. 195/B5
Livingston, Calif. 204/E6
Livingston, Guatemala 154/C3
Livingston (co.), Ill. 222/E3
Livingston, Ill. 222/D5
Livingston (co.), Ky. 237/E6
Livingston, Ky. 237/N6
Livingston (par.), La. 238/L2
Livingston, La. 238/L1
Livingston (co.), Mich. 250/F6
Livingston (co.), Mo. 261/E3
Livingston, Mont. 188/D1
Livingston, Mont. 262/F5
Livingston•, N.J. 273/E2
Livingston (co.), N.Y. 276/E5
Livingston, Scotland 15/C2
Livingston, Scotland 10/C1
Livingston, S.C. 296/E4
Livingston, Tenn. 237/L8
Livingston, Texas 303/K7
Livingston (lake), Texas 303/K7
Livingston, Wis. 317/E10
Livingstone (range), Alberta 182/C4
Livingstone (falls), D.R. Congo 115/B5
Livingstone, Zambia 115/E7
Livingstone, Zambia 102/E6
Livingstonia, Malawi 115/F6
Livingston Manor, N.Y. 276/L7
Livingstonville, N.Y. 276/M6
Livno, Bos. 45/C4
Livny, Russia 52/E4
Livona, N. Dak. 282/K6
Livonia, Ind. 227/E7
Livonia, La. 238/G5
Livonia, Mich. 250/F6
Livonia, Mo. 261/G1
Livonia, N.Y. 276/E5
Livonia, Pa. 294/H4
Livorno (prov.), Italy 34/C3
Livorno, Italy 7/E4
Livorno, Italy 34/C3
Livry-Gargan, France 28/C1
Liwale, Tanzania 115/G5
Li Xian, China 77/F9
Lixoúrion, Greece 45/E6
Lizard, The (dist.), England 13/B8
Lizard (pt.), England 10/D6
Lizard (pt.), England 13/B8
Lizella, Ga. 217/E5
Lizemores, W. Va. 312/D6
Lizton, Ind. 227/D5
Ljubinje, Bos. 45/D4
Ljubljana (cap.), Slovenia 7/F4
Ljubljana (cap.), Slovenia 45/B3
Ljubuški, Bos. 45/C4
Ljugarn, Sweden 18/L8
Ljungan (riv.), Sweden 18/K5
Ljungby, Sweden 18/J8
Ljusdal, Sweden 18/J6
Ljusna (riv.), Sweden 7/F2
Ljusnan (riv.), Sweden 18/H5
Ljusne, Sweden 18/K6
Llagostera, Spain 33/H2
Llaima (vol.), Chile 138/E2
Llallagua, Bolivia 136/B6
Llallagua, Bolivia 120/C4
Llamara, Salar de (salt dep.), Chile 138/B3
Llanarth, Wales 13/C5
Llancanelo (lag.), Argentina 143/C4
Llancanelo, Salina y Laguna (salt dep.), Argentina 143/C4
Llandeilo, Wales 13/C6
Llandovery, Wales 13/D5
Llandovery, Wales 10/D5
Llandrindod Wells, Wales 10/E4
Llandrindod Wells, Wales 13/D5
Llandudno, Wales 13/D4
Llandudno, Wales 10/E4
Llandybie, Wales 13/C6
Llandyssul, Wales 13/C5
Llanelli, Wales 13/C6
Llanelli, Wales 10/D5
Llanes, Spain 33/D1
Llanfair Caereinion, Wales 13/D5
Llanfairfechan, Wales 13/D4
Llanfyllin, Wales 10/E4
Llanfyllin, Wales 13/D5
Llangefni, Wales 13/C4
Llangollen, Wales 13/D5
Llangollen, Wales 10/E4
Llanguicke, Wales 13/D6
Llanidloes, Wales 13/D5
Llanidloes, Wales 10/E4
Llanllyfni, Wales 13/C4
LLannon, Wales 13/C6
Llano, N. Mex. 274/D2
Llano (co.), Texas 303/F7
Llano, Texas 303/F7
Llano (riv.), Texas 303/D7
Llano Estacado (Staked) (plain), N. Mex. 274/F5
Llano Estacado (plain), Texas 303/B4
Llanon, Wales 13/C5
Llanos (plain) 120/B2
Llanos (plains), Colombia 126/D5
Llanquera, Bolivia 136/A6
Llanquihue (lake), Chile 138/E3
Llanrhaeadr, Wales 13/D5
Llanrhystyd, Wales 13/C5
Llanrian, Wales 13/B6
Llanrwst, Wales 13/D4
Llanrwst, Wales 10/E4
Llantrisant, Wales 13/A7
Llantwit Major, Wales 13/A7
Llanwnog, Wales 13/D5
Llanwrtyd Wells, Wales 13/D5
Llata, Peru 128/D7
Llay-Llay, Chile 138/G2
Lleida (prov.), Spain 33/G2
Lleida, Spain 33/G2
Lleida, Spain 7/D4
Llera de Canales, Mexico 150/K5
Llerena (pt.), C. Rica 154/F6
Llerena, Spain 33/C3
Lleyn (pen.), Wales 13/C5
Llica, Bolivia 136/A6
Llico, Chile 138/A10
Llivia, Spain 33/G1
Llobregat (riv.), Spain 33/H2
Llodio, Spain 33/E1
Llolleo, Chile 138/F4
Llorente, Philippines 82/E5
Lloyd, Fla. 212/C1
Lloyd (res.), Ga. 188/K4
Lloyd, Ky. 237/R3
Lloyd, Mont. 262/G2
Lloyd Harbor, N.Y. 276/R6
Lloydminster, Alberta 182/E3
Lloydminster, Alta.-Sask. 162/E5
Lloydminster, Sask. 181/A2
Lluchmayor, Spain 33/H3
Lluidas Vale, Jamaica 158/J6
Llullaillaco (mt.) 120/C5
Llullaillaco (vol.), Argentina 143/C1
Llullaillaco (vol.), Chile 138/B5
Lluta (riv.), Chile 138/B1
Llwchwr, Wales 13/D6
Loa (riv.), Chile 120/C5
Loa (riv.), Chile 138/B3
Loa, Utah 304/C5
Loachapoka, Ala. 195/G5
Loami, Ill. 222/D4
Loange (riv.), Angola 115/C5
Loange (riv.), D.R. Congo 115/C5
Loanhead, Scotland 10/C1
Loanhead, Scotland 15/D2
Lobatse, Botswana 118/D5
Löbau, Germany 22/F3
Lobaye (riv.), Cent. Afr. Rep. 115/C2
Lobdell, La. 238/J1
Lobeco, S.C. 296/F6
Lobelia, W. Va. 312/F6
Lobelville, Tenn. 237/H9
Lobenstein, Germany 22/D3
Lobería, Argentina 143/E4
Lobethal, S. Australia 94/C7
Łobez, Poland 47/B2
Lobito, Angola 115/B6
Lobito, Angola 102/D6
Lobitos, Peru 128/B5
Lobo, Philippines 82/C4
Lobo (cay), P. Rico 161/G1
Lobos, Argentina 143/G7
Lobos (pt.), Chile 138/A3
Lobos (cape), Mexico 150/C2
Lobos (pt.), Mexico 150/D3
Lobos (isl.), Uruguay 145/E6
Lobos de Afuera (isls.), Peru 128/B6
Lobos de Tierra (isl.), Peru 128/B6
Lobster (lake), Maine 243/E4
Locarno, Switzerland 39/G4
Locate, Mont. 262/L4
Lochaber, Nova Scotia 168/F3
Lochaber (dist.), Scotland 15/D4
Lochailort, Scotland 15/C4
Lochaline, Scotland 15/C4
Lochans, Scotland 15/D6
Locharbriggs, Scotland 15/E5
Lochawe, Scotland 15/C4
Lochboisdale, Scotland 15/A3
Lochbuie, Colo. 208/K2
Lochcarron, Scotland 10/D2
Lochcarron, Scotland 15/C3
Lochearnhead, Scotland 15/D4
Lochem, Netherlands 27/J4
Lochend, Scotland 15/D3
Loches, France 28/D4
Lochgelly, Scotland 10/C1
Lochgelly, Scotland 15/D1
Lochgelly, W. Va. 312/D6
Lochgilphead, Scotland 10/D2
Lochgilphead, Scotland 15/C4
Lochgoilhead, Scotland 15/D4
Lochindorb (lake), Scotland 15/E3
Lochinver, Scotland 10/D1
Lochinver, Scotland 15/C2
Lochloosa, Fla. 212/E2
Lochloosa (lake), Fla. 212/D2
Loch Lynn Heights, Md. 245/A3
Lochmaben, Scotland 10/E3
Lochmaben, Scotland 15/E5
Lochmaddy, Scotland 15/A3
Lochmere, N.H. 268/D5
Lochnagar (mt.), Scotland 15/E4
Lochore, Scotland 15/D1
Lochranza, Scotland 15/C5
Loch Raven (res.), Md. 245/M3
Lochristi, Belgium 27/D6
Lochsa (riv.), Idaho 220/C3
Lochwinnoch, Scotland 15/A2
Lochy, Loch (lake), Scotland 15/D3
Lochy, Loch (lake), Scotland 10/D2
Lock, S. Australia 94/D5
Lockatong (creek), N.J. 273/C3
Lockbourne, Ohio 284/E6
Locke, Calif. 204/B9
Locke, N.Y. 276/H5
Locke (mt.), Texas 303/D11
Lockeford, Calif. 204/C9
Locke Mills, Maine 243/B7
Lockeport, Nova Scotia 168/C5
Lockerbie, Scotland 10/E3
Lockerbie, Scotland 15/E5
Lockesburg, Ark. 202/B6
Lockhart, Ala. 195/F8
Lockhart, Minn. 255/B3
Lockhart (mt.), Mont. 262/D3
Lockhart, N.S. Wales 97/D4
Lockhart (riv.), N.W.T. 187/H3
Lockhart, S.C. 296/E2
Lockhart, Texas 303/G8
Lock Haven, Pa. 294/H3
Lockington, Ohio 284/B5
Lockland, Ohio 284/C9
Lockney, Texas 303/C3
Lockney, W. Va. 312/E5
Lockport, Ill. 222/B6
Lockport, Ky. 237/M4
Lockport, La. 238/K7
Lockport, Manitoba 179/F4
Lockport, N.Y. 276/C4
Lockridge, Iowa 229/K7
Lock Springs, Mo. 261/E3
Lockwood, Mo. 261/E8
Lockwood, Sask. 181/G4
Lockwood, W. Va. 312/D6
Loc Ninh, Vietnam 72/E5
Loco, Okla. 288/L6
Loco Hills, N. Mex. 274/F6
Locumba, Peru 128/G11
Locumba (riv.), Peru 128/G11
Locust, N.C. 281/J4
Locust Bayou, Ark. 202/E6
Locust Fork, Ala. 195/E3
Locust Fork (riv.), Ala. 195/E3
Locust Grove, Ark. 202/G2
Locust Grove, Ga. 217/D4
Locust Grove, N.Y. 276/R6
Locust Grove, Ohio 284/D8
Locust Grove, Okla. 288/R2
Locust Hill, Ky. 237/J5
Locustville, Va. 307/S5
Lod (Lydda), Israel 65/B4
Loda, Ill. 222/E3
Lodar, Yemen 59/E7
Loddon, England 13/J5
Loddon (riv.), Victoria 97/B5
Loddon (riv.), Victoria 88/G7
Lodève, France 28/E6
Lodeynoye Pole, Russia52/D2
Lodge (creek), Mont. 262/G1
Lodge (creek), Sask. 181/B6
Lodge, S.C. 296/F5
Lodge Bay, Newf. 166/C3
Lodge Grass, Mont. 262/J5
Lodge Hill, Barbados 161/B8
Lodgepole, Alberta 182/C3
Lodge Pole, Mont. 262/H2
Lodgepole, Nebr. 264/B3
Lodgepole (creek), Nebr. 264/A3
Lodgepole, S. Dak. 298/D2
Lodgepole (creek), Wyo. 319/H2
Lodgepole (creek), Wyo. 319/H4
Lodi, Calif. 188/B3
Lodi, Calif. 204/C9
Lodi, Italy 34/B2
Lodi, Miss. 256/E3
Lodi, Mo. 261/M8
Lodi, N.J. 273/B2
Lodi, N.Y. 276/G5
Lodi, Ohio 284/F3
Lodi (cape), Tasmania 99/E3
Lodi, Texas 303/K5
Lodi, Wis. 317/G9
Lødingen, Norway 18/J2
Lodja, D.R. Congo 102/E5
Lodja, D.R. Congo 115/D4
Lodosa, Spain 33/E1
Lodrino, Switzerland 39/G4
Lodwar, Kenya 115/G3
Łódź (prov.), Poland 47/D3
Łódź (city prov.), Poland 47/D3
Łódź, Poland 7/F3
Łódź, Poland 47/D3
Loei, Thailand 72/D3
Loen, Norway 18/E6
Lofer, Austria 41/B3
Lofoten (isls.), Norway 4/C9
Lofoten (isls.), Norway 7/F2
Lofoten (isls.), Norway 18/H2
Loftus, England 13/G3
Loftus, England 10/F3
Lofty (mt.), S. Australia 88/E8
Lofty (mt.), S. Australia 94/B8
Lofty (range), Tasmania 99/B3
Logan, Ala. 195/E2
Logan (lake), Alberta 182/E2
Logan (co.), Ark. 202/C3
Logan (mt.), Canada 4/C17
Logan (co.), Colo. 208/N1
Logan (co.), Ill. 222/D3
Logan, Ill. 222/E6
Logan, Ind. 227/H6
Logan, Iowa 229/B5
Logan (co.), Kansas 232/A3
Logan, Kansas 232/C2
Logan (co.), Ky. 237/H7
Logan, Mont. 262/E5
Logan (co.), Nebr. 264/D3
Logan (creek), Nebr. 264/H2
Logan, N. Mex. 274/F3
Logan (co.), N. Dak. 282/L7
Logan, N. Dak. 282/H3
Logan (co.), Ohio 284/C5
Logan, Ohio 284/F6
Logan (co.), Okla. 288/M3
Logan, Okla. 288/F1
Logan, Oreg. 291/B2
Logan, Utah 304/C2
Logan, Utah 188/D2
Logan (mt.), Wash. 310/E2
Logan (co.), W. Va. 312/C7
Logan, W. Va. 312/B7
Logan (mt.), Yukon 162/B3
Logan (mt.), Yukon 187/D3
Logan (mts.), Yukon 187/F3
Logandale, Nev. 266/G6
Logan Internat'l Airport, Mass. 249/D7
Logan Lake, Br. Col. 184/G5
Logan Martin (lake), Ala. 195/F4
Logansport, Ind. 227/E3
Logansport, Ky. 237/H6
Logansport, La. 238/C3
Loganton, Pa. 294/H3
Loganville, Ga. 217/E3
Loganville, Pa. 294/J6
Loganville, Wis. 317/F9
Loge (riv.), Angola 115/B5
Loggieville, New Bruns. 170/E1
Log Lane Village, Colo. 208/M2
Logone (riv.) 102/D3
Logone (riv.), Cameroon 115/C2
Logone (riv.), Chad 111/C5
Logroño (prov.), Spain 33/E1
Logroño, Spain 7/D4
Logroño, Spain 33/E1
Logrosán, Spain 33/D3
Logsden, Oreg. 291/D3
Løgstør, Denmark 21/C4
Løgstør, Denmark 18/F8
Løgstør Bredning (fjord), Denmark 21/C4
Løgumkloster, Denmark 21/B7
Lohals, Denmark 21/D7
Lohardaga, India 68/E4
Lohatlha, S. Africa 118/C5
Lohman, Mo. 261/H5
Lohman, Mont. 262/G2
Lohn, Texas 303/E6
Löhne, Germany 22/C2
Loho (Luohe), China 77/H5
Lohr am Main, Germany 22/C4
Lohrville, Iowa 229/D4
Lohrville, Wis. 317/H7
Loica, Chile 138/F4
Loi-kaw, Burma 72/C3
Loi Leng (mt.), Burma 72/C2
Loimaa, Finland 18/N6
Loir (riv.), France 28/D4
Loire (dept.), France 28/F5
Loire (riv.), France 7/E4
Loire (riv.), France 28/C4
Loire-Atlantique (dept.), France 28/C4
Loiret (dept.), France 28/E4
Loir-et-Cher (dept.), France 28/D4
Loíza, P. Rico 161/E1
Loíza Aldea, P. Rico 161/E1
Loja (prov.), Ecuador 128/C4
Loja, Ecuador 128/C4
Loja, Ecuador 120/B3
Loja, Spain 33/D4
Løjt Kirkeby, Denmark 21/C7
Loka, Sudan 111/F7
Lokeren, Belgium 27/D6
Lokitaung, Kenya 115/G3
Lokka (res.), Finland 18/Q3
Løkken, Denmark 21/C3
Løkken, Norway 18/F5
Lokoja, Nigeria 106/F7
Lokolama, D.R. Congo 115/D4
Lokoro (riv.), D.R. Congo 115/C4
Lőkösháza, Hungary 41/F3
Lokossa, Benin 106/E7
Loksa, Estonia 53/C1
Loks Land (isl.), N.W.T. 187/M3
Lol (dry riv.), Sudan 111/E6
Lola, Ky. 237/E6
Loleta, Calif. 204/A3
Lolgorien, Kenya 115/G4
Lolita, Texas 303/H9
Lolland (isl.), Denmark 18/G9
Lolland (isl.), Denmark 21/E8
Lollie, Ga. 217/G6
Lolo (creek), Idaho 220/C3
Lolo (pass), Idaho 220/D3
Lolo, Mont. 262/B4
Lolo (pass), Mont. 262/B4
Lolo Hot Springs, Mont. 262/B4
Lom, Bulgaria 45/F4
Lom (riv.), Cameroon 115/B2
Lom, Norway 18/F6
Loma, Colo. 208/B4
Loma, Mont. 262/F3
Loma, N. Dak. 282/O2
Loma, Mansa (lag.), S. Leone 106/B7
Loma Alta, Bolivia 136/B2
Loma Bonita, Mexico 150/M7
Loma Linda, Calif. 204/F10
Loma Mar, Calif. 204/J3
Lomami (riv.), D.R. Congo 115/D4
Loman, Minn. 255/E2
Loma Plata, Paraguay 144/C3
Lomas, Peru 128/E10
Lomas de Zamora, Argentina 143/G7
Lomax, Ala. 195/E5
Lomax, Ill. 222/B3
Lomax, Texas 303/K2
Lombard, Ill. 222/B5
Lombarda, Serra (mts.), Brazil 132/D2
Lombardville, Ill. 222/D2
Lombardy (reg.), Italy 34/B2
Lombardy, S. Africa 118/H6
Lombez, France 28/D6
Lomblen (isl.), Indonesia 85/G7
Lombok (isl.), Indonesia 54/N10
Lombok (isl.), Indonesia 85/F7
Lombok (str.), Indonesia 85/E7
Lomé (cap.), Togo 102/C4
Lomé (cap.), Togo 106/E7
Lomela, D.R. Congo 115/D4
Lomela (riv.), D.R. Congo 115/D4
Lometa, Texas 303/F6
Lomié, Cameroon 115/B3
Lomira, Wis. 317/J8
Lo Miranda, Chile 138/G5
Lomita, Calif. 204/C11
Lommel, Belgium 27/G6
Lomnice, Czech Rep. 41/C2
Lomond, Alberta 182/D4
Lomond, Loch (lake), Nova Scotia 168/H3
Lomond, Loch (lake), Scotland 15/D4
Lomond, Loch (lake), Scotland 10/A1
Lompoc, Calif. 204/E9
Lom Sak, Thailand 72/D3
Łomża (prov.), Poland 47/F2
Łomża, Poland 47/F2
Lonaconing, Md. 245/C2
Loncoche, Chile 138/D2
Loncopué, Argentina 143/B4
London, Ark. 202/D3
London, Greater, England 13/H8
London (cap.), England 7/D3
London (cap.), England 10/B5
London (cap.), England 13/H8
London, Ind. 227/F5
London, Ky. 237/N6
London, Minn. 255/E7
London, Ohio 284/C6
London, Ont. 146/K5
London, Ont. 162/H7
London, Ontario 177/C5
London, Texas 303/E7
London (cap.), U.K. 2/J3
London, Wis. 317/H9
Londonderry (isl.), Chile 138/E11
Londonderry•, N.H. 268/E6
Londonderry, N. Ireland 7/D3
Londonderry (dist.), N. Ireland 17/G2
Londonderry (Derry), N. Ireland 10/C3
Londonderry (Derry), N. Ireland 17/G2
Londonderry, Nova Scotia 168/E3
Londonderry, Ohio 284/E7
Londonderry•, Vt. 268/B5
Londonderry (cape), W. Australia 88/D2
Londonderry (cape), W. Australia 92/D1
Londonderry Station, Nova Scotia 168/E3
London Mills, Ill. 222/C3
Londontowne, Md. 245/M4
Londrina, Brazil 132/D8
Londrina, Brazil 120/D5
Lone (mt.), Mont. 262/E5
Lone (mt.), Nev. 266/D4
Lone Butte, Br. Col. 184/G4
Lone Cedar, W. Va. 312/C4
Lone Cone (mt.), Colo. 208/C7
Lone Elm, Kansas 232/G3
Lone Grove, Okla. 288/M6
Lone Jack, Mo. 261/S6
Lonely (lake), Manitoba 179/C3
Lonely (isl.), Ontario 177/C2
Lone Mountain, Tenn. 237/O8
Lone Oak, Ga. 217/C4
Lone Oak, Ky. 237/D6
Lone Oak, Texas 303/H5
Lone Pine, Alberta 182/C2
Lone Pine, Calif. 204/H7
Lone Pine (peak), Idaho 220/D5
Lonepine, La. 238/F5
Lonepine, Mont. 262/B3
Lone Prairie, Br. Col. 184/G2
Lone Rock, Iowa 229/E2
Lonerock, Oreg. 291/H2
Lone Rock, Sask. 181/A2
Lone Rock, Wis. 317/F9
Lone Star, S.C. 296/F4
Lone Tree (creek), Colo. 208/K1
Lone Tree, Iowa 229/L6
Lonetree, N. Dak. 282/G3
Lonetree, Wyo. 319/B4
Lone Wolf, Okla. 288/H5
Long, Alaska 196/G2
Long (isl.), Alaska 196/M2
Long (isl.), Ant. & Bar. 161/E11
Long (isl.), Bahamas 146/L7
Long (cay), Bahamas 156/C2
Long (isl.), Bahamas 156/C2
Long (bay), Barbados 161/B9
Long (mt.), Conn. 210/B2
Long (pond), Conn. 210/H3
Long (key), Fla. 212/F7
Long (key), Fla. 212/B3
Long (pond), Fla. 212/D2
Long (co.), Ga. 217/J7
Long (bay), Jamaica 158/H7
Long (lake), Maine 243/E2
Long (lake), Maine 243/G1
Long (lake), Maine 243/B7
Long (pond), Maine 243/E5
Long (pond), Maine 243/D6
Long (pond), Maine 243/C4
Long (lake), Manitoba 179/G4
Long (pt.), Manitoba 179/D1
Long (pt.), Manitoba 179/D4
Long (isl.), Martinique 161/D6
Long (isl.), Mass. 249/E7
Long (pond), Mass. 249/L5
Long (pt.), Mass. 249/O4
Long (lake), Mich. 250/F3
Long (lake), Minn. 255/D4
Long (lake), Minn. 255/F3
Long, Miss. 256/C4
Long (valley), Nev. 266/B1
Long (isl.), New Bruns. 170/D3
Long (lake), New Bruns. 170/D1
Long (isl.), Newf. 166/C2
Long (isl.), Newf. 166/D2
Long (lake), Newf. 166/A3
Long (lake), Newf. 166/B3
Long (pt.), Newf. 166/C4
Long (mt.), N.H. 268/E2
Long (beach), N.J. 273/E4
Long (isl.), N.Y. 188/M2

Lowndes 401

Long (isl.), N.Y. 276/P9
Long (lake), N.Y. 276/M2
Long (isl.), N. Zealand 100/A7
Long (lake), N.C. 281/P5
Long (lake), N. Dak. 282/K6
Long (lake), N. Dak. 282/J4
Long (lake), N. Dak. 282/L2
Long (isl.), Nova Scotia 168/B4
Long (lake), Ontario 177/H5
Long (lake), Ontario 175/C3
Long (pt.), Ontario 177/D5
Long (isl.), Papua N.G. 85/B7
Long (isl.), Papua N.G. 86/A2
Long (creek), Sask. 181/H6
Long, Loch (inlet), Scotland 10/A1
Long, Loch (inlet), Scotland 15/D4
Long (lake), S. Dak. 298/L2
Long (pt.), Tasmania 99/E3
Long (str.), Russia 48/S2
Long (pt.), Virgin Is. (U.S.) 161/B4
Long (pt.), Virgin Is. (U.S.) 161/E4
Long (isl.), Wash. 310/A4
Long (lake), Wash. 310/H3
Long (reef), W. Australia 92/D1
Long (lake), Wis. 317/C4
Longa, Angola 115/C6
Longa (isl.), Scotland 15/C3
Longaví, Chile 138/A11
Long Bay, Jamaica 158/K6
Long Beach, Br. Col. 184/E5
Long Beach, Calif. 146/F6
Long Beach, Calif. 188/C4
Long Beach, Calif. 204/C11
Long Beach (pen.), Conn. 210/C4
Long Beach, Ind. 227/D1
Long Beach, Minn. 255/C5
Long Beach, Miss. 256/F10
Long Beach (isl.), N.J. 273/E4
Long Beach, N.Y. 276/R7
Long Beach, N.C. 281/N7
Long Beach, Ontario 177/E5
Long Beach, Wash. 310/A4
Longbenton, England 13/J3
Longboat (key), Fla. 212/D4
Longboat Key, Fla. 212/D4
Long Bottom, Ohio 284/G7
Long Branch, N.J. 273/F3
Longbranch, Wash. 310/C3
Longchuan, China 77/J7
Long Cove, Maine 243/E8
Long Creek, Oreg. 291/H3
Longcreek, S.C. 296/A2
Longdale, Okla. 288/K2
Longde, China 77/G4
Long Eaton, England 13/F5
Long Eddy, N.Y. 276/K7
Long Falls (dam), Maine 243/C5
Longfellow (mts.), Maine 243/B6
Longford (co.), Ireland 17/F4
Longford, Ireland 10/C4
Longford, Ireland 17/F4
Longford, Kansas 232/E2
Longford, Ontario 177/E3
Longford, Tasmania 99/C3
Longford, Virgin Is. (U.S.) 161/F4
Long Green, Md. 245/M3
Long Grove, Ill. 222/B5
Long Grove, Iowa 229/M5
Long Harbour, Newf. 166/D2
Long Hill, Conn. 210/C3
Longhua, China 77/J3
Longhui, China 77/H6
Longido, Tanzania 115/G4
Longiram, Indonesia 85/F5
Long Island (sound), Conn. 210/C4
Long Island (bay), Ireland 17/B9
Long Island, Kansas 232/C2
Long Island (sound), N.Y. 276/P9
Longisland, N.C. 281/H3
Long Island, Tenn. 237/S7
Long Island, Va. 307/K6
Longjiang, China 77/K2
Long Key, Fla. 212/F7
Longkou, China 77/J4
Longlac, Ontario 177/H5
Longlac, Ontario 175/C3
Long Lake, Mich. 250/F4
Long Lake, Minn. 255/F5
Long Lake, N.Y. 276/L3
Longlake, S. Dak. 298/L2
Long Lake, Wis. 317/J4
Long Lane, Mo. 261/G7
Longleaf, La. 238/E4
Long Meadow (pond), Conn. 210/C2
Longmeadow•, Mass. 249/D4
Longmire, Wash. 310/D4
Longmont, Colo. 188/E2
Longmont, Colo. 208/J2
Longnan, China 77/J7
Longnawan, Indonesia 85/F5
Long Neck (pt.), Conn. 210/B4
Long Pine, Nebr. 264/E2
Long Point, Ill. 222/E3
Long Point, Nova Scotia 168/G3
Long Point (bay), Ontario 177/D5
Long Point Beach, Ontario 177/D5
Long Pond, Maine 243/C4
Long Pond, Pa. 294/L3
Longport, N.J. 273/D5
Long Prairie, Minn. 255/D5
Long Prairie (riv.), Minn. 255/D4
Long Range (mts.), Newf. 166/C4
Long Rapids, Mich. 250/F3
Longreach, Australia 87/E8
Long Reach (inlet), New Bruns. 170/D3
Longreach, Queensland 88/G4
Longreach, Queensland 95/B4
Long Reef (pt.), N.S. Wales 97/K3
Longridge, England 13/H1
Longridge, England 10/G1
Longs (peak), Colo. 208/H2
Longs, S.C. 296/K4
Long Sault, Ontario 177/K2
Longshan, China 77/G6
Long Siding, Minn. 255/E5
Long Society, Conn. 210/G2
Long Spruce, Manitoba 179/K2
Longstreet, La. 238/B2
Longton, Kansas 232/F4
Longtown, Miss. 256/D1
Longtown, Mo. 261/N7
Longtown, S.C. 296/F3
Longueuil, Québec 172/J4
Long Valley, N.J. 273/D2
Longvalley, S. Dak. 298/F7
Longview, Ala. 195/E4
Longview, Alberta 182/C4
Longview, Colo. 208/J4
Longview, Ill. 222/E4
Longview, Miss. 256/G4
Longview, N.C. 281/F3
Longview, Texas 188/G4
Longview, Texas 303/K5
Longview, Wash. 188/B1
Longview, Wash. 310/B4
Longville, La. 238/D5
Longville, Minn. 255/D4
Longwood, Fla. 212/E3
Longwood, Mo. 261/F5
Longwood, N.C. 281/M7
Longwood Park, N.C. 281/K5
Longworth, Br. Col. 184/G3
Longworth, Texas 303/D5
Longwy, France 28/F3
Long Xian, China 77/G5
Long Xuyen, Vietnam 72/E5
Longyan, China 77/J6
Longyearbyen, Norway 18/D2
Longyearbyen, Norway 4/B8
Longzhen (Lungchen), China 77/L2
Loni Beach, Manitoba 179/F4
Lonigo, Italy 34/C2
Lonneker, Netherlands 27/K4
Lonoke (co.), Ark. 202/G4
Lonoke, Ark. 202/G4
Lonquimay, Chile 138/E2
Lonsdale, Ark. 202/E4
Lonsdale, Minn. 255/E6
Lonsdale, R.I. 249/J5
Lons-le-Saunier, France 28/F4
Lonton, Burma 72/B1
Lontzen, Belgium 27/H9
Looe, England 13/C7
Loogootee, Ind. 227/D7
Lookeba, Okla. 288/K4
Lookingglass (riv.), Mich. 250/E6
Lookout (mt.), Ala. 195/G2
Lookout (ridge), Alaska 196/G1
Lookout, Calif. 204/D2
Lookout (mt.), Idaho 220/F5
Lookout (mt.), Idaho 220/D5
Lookout, Ky. 237/S6
Lookout (pt.), Md. 245/N8
Lookout (cape), N.C. 188/L4
Lookout (cape), N.C. 281/S5
Lookout, Okla. 288/H1
Lookout (cape), Oreg. 188/B1
Lookout (cape), Oreg. 291/C2
Lookout, Pa. 294/M2
Lookout, W. Va. 312/E6
Lookout, Wyo. 319/G4
Lookout Mountain, Ga. 217/B1
Lookout Mountain, Tenn. 237/L11
Lookout Point (lake), Oreg. 291/E4
Looma, Alberta 182/D3
Loomis, Calif. 204/C8
Loomis, Nebr. 264/E4
Loomis, Sask. 181/C6
Loomis, S. Dak. 298/N6
Loomis, Wash. 310/F2
Loomis, Wis. 317/K5
Loon (lake), Alberta 182/C1
Loon (riv.), Alberta 182/C1
Loon (lake), Maine 243/D3
Loon (lake), Ontario 177/F3
Loon (creek), Sask. 181/G4
Loon (lake), Wash. 310/H2
Looneyville, W. Va. 312/D5
Loon Lake, Alberta 182/C1
Loon Lake, Maine 243/B5
Loon Lake, N.Y. 276/M1
Loon Lake, Sask. 181/B1
Loon Lake, Wash. 310/H2
Loon op Zand, Netherlands 27/G5
Loon Strait, Manitoba 179/F3
Loop (head), Ireland 17/A6
Loop (head), Ireland 10/A4
Loop, Texas 303/B5
Loos, Br. Col. 184/G3
Loosahatchie (riv.), Tenn. 237/B10
Loose Creek, Mo. 261/J5
Lo Ovalle, Chile 138/F3
Looxahoma, Miss. 256/E1
Looz (Borgloon), Belgium 27/G7
Lopatka (cape), Russia 48/Q4
Lopatka (cape), Russia 54/S4
Lop Buri, Thailand 72/D4
Lopeno, Texas 303/E11
Lopez (pt.), Calif. 204/D7
Lopez (cape), Gabon 102/C5
Lopez (cape), Gabon 115/A4
Lopez, Pa. 294/K3
Lopez, Wash. 310/C2
Lopez (isl.), Wash. 310/C2
Lopi, Congo 115/C3
Lop Nor (Lop Nur) (lake), China 77/D3
Lopnur (Yuli), China 77/C3
Lop Nur (lake), China 54/L5
Lopphavet (bay), Norway 18/M1
Lora, Hamun-i- (swamp), Pakistan 68/B3
Lora, Hamun-i- (swamp), Pakistan 59/J4
Lora del Río, Spain 33/D4
Lorado, W. Va. 312/C7
Lorain (co.), Ohio 284/F3
Lorain, Ohio 284/F3
Loraine, Ill. 222/B3
Loraine, N. Dak. 282/G2
Loraine, Texas 303/D5
Loraine, Wis. 317/B4
Loralai, Pakistan 68/B2
Loralai, Pakistan 59/J3
Loramie (lake), Ohio 284/B5
Loranger, La. 238/N1
Lorca, Spain 33/F4
Lord Howe (isl.), Australia 87/G9
Lord Howe (isl.), Australia 2/T7
Lord Howe (isl.), N.S. Wales 97/J2
Lord Howe (Ontong Java) (isl.), Solomon Is. 87/G6
Lord Howe (ontong Java) (isls.), Solomon Is. 86/D2
Lord Mayor (bay), N.W.T. 187/J3
Lordsburg, N. Mex. 274/A6
Lords Point, Conn. 210/H3
Lordstown, Ohio 284/J3
Lords Valley, Pa. 294/M3
Loreauville, La. 238/G6
Loreburn, Sask. 181/E4
Lore City, Ohio 284/H6
Lorena, Brazil 135/D3
Lorena, Miss. 256/F6
Lorengau, Papua N.G. 86/A1
Lorengau, Papua N.G. 87/E6
Lo-Reninge, Belgium 27/B7
Lorentz, W. Va. 312/F4
Lorenzo, Idaho 220/G6
Lorenzo, Texas 303/C4
Lorenzo Geyres, Uruguay 145/B3
Lorestan (Luristan) (governorate), Iran 66/F4
Loreto, Bolivia 136/C4
Loreto, Colombia 126/E9
Loreto, Ecuador 128/D3
Loreto, Baja California, Mexico 150/D4
Loreto, Zacatecas, Mexico 150/J5
Loreto, Paraguay 144/D3
Loreto (dept.), Peru 128/E5
Loreto, Agusan del Sur, Philippines 82/E6
Loreto, Surigao del Norte, Philippines 82/E5
Loretta, Kansas 232/C3
Loretta, Wis. 317/E4
Lorette, Manitoba 179/F5
Loretteville, Québec 172/H3
Loretto, Ky. 237/L5
Loretto, Mich. 250/B3
Loretto, Minn. 255/F5
Loretto, Nebr. 264/F3
Loretto, Pa. 294/E4
Loretto, Tenn. 237/G10
Loretto, Va. 307/O4
Lorian (swamp), Kenya 115/G3
Lorica, Colombia 126/C3
Lorida, Fla. 212/E4
Lorient, France 7/D4
Lorient, France 28/B4
L'Orignal, Ontario 177/K2
Lorimor, Iowa 229/E6
Lőrinci, Hungary 41/E3
Loring, Mont. 262/J2
Loring, Ontario 177/D2
Loring A.F.B., Maine 243/H2
Loris, S.C. 296/K3
Lorlie, Sask. 181/H5
Lorman, Miss. 256/B7
Lorne, New Bruns. 170/D1
Lorne, Nova Scotia 168/F3
Lorne (dist.), Scotland 15/C4
Lorne (firth), Scotland 10/D2
Lorne (firth), Scotland 15/C4
Loros (pt.), Chile 138/E3
Lörrach, Germany 22/B5
Lorrain (riv.), Martinique 161/D5
Lorraine, Kansas 232/D3
Lorraine, N.Y. 276/J3
Lorraine, Québec 172/H4
Lorrainville, Québec 174/B3
Lorrha, Ireland 17/E5
Lort (riv.), W. Australia 88/C6
Lorton, Nebr. 264/H4
Lorton, Va. 307/O3
Lorze (riv.), Switzerland 39/F2
Los (isls.), Guinea 106/B7
Losada (riv.), Colombia 126/C6
Los Alamitos, Calif. 204/D11
Los Alamos, Calif. 204/E9
Los Alamos, N.Mex. 188/E3
Los Alamos (co.), N. Mex. 274/C3
Los Alamos, N. Mex. 274/C3
Los Alerces Nat'l Park, Argentina 143/C5
Los Algodones, Mexico 150/B1
Los Altos, Calif. 204/K3
Los Altos Hills, Calif. 204/J3
Los Amates, Guatemala 154/C3
Los Andes, Chile 138/B9
Los Andes, Colombia 126/B7
Los Angeles, Calif. 146/G6
Los Angeles, Calif. 188/C4
Los Angeles (co.), Calif. 204/G9
Los Angeles, Calif. 204/C10
Los Ángeles, Chile 138/D1
Los Angeles, Chile 120/B6
Los Angeles, Texas 303/F9
Los Angeles, U.S. 2/D4
Los Angeles Aqueduct, Calif. 204/G8
Los Antiguos, Argentina 143/B6
Losantville, Ind. 227/G4
Los Arabos, Cuba 158/E1
Los Arroyos, Cuba 158/A2
Los Banos, Calif. 204/E6
Los Barcos (pt.), Cuba 158/B2
Los Canarreos (arch.), Cuba 158/C2
Los Castillos, Venezuela 124/G3
Los Choros (riv.), Chile 138/A7
Los Colorados (arch.), Cuba 158/A1
Los Conquistadores, Argentina 143/G5
Los Coyotes Ind. Res., Calif. 204/J10
Los Cusis, Bolivia 136/D4
Los Estados (isl.), Argentina 143/D7
Los Frailes (isl.), Dom. Rep. 158/C7
Los Fresnos, Texas 303/G11
Los Gatos, Calif. 204/K4
Los Glaciares Nat'l Park, Argentina 143/B6
Loshan (Leshan), China 77/F6
Los Hermanos (isls.), Venezuela 124/F2
Łosice, Poland 47/F2
Los Indios, Cuba 158/B2
Lošinj (isl.), Croatia 45/B3
Los Lagos (reg.), Chile 138/D3
Los Lagos, Chile 138/D3
Los Llanos, Dom. Rep. 158/F6
Los Loros, Chile 138/B6
Los Lunas, N. Mex. 274/C4
Los Menucos, Argentina 143/C5
Los Mochis, Mexico 150/E4
Los Molinos, Calif. 204/D3
Los Monjes (isls.), Venezuela 124/C1
Los Muermos, Chile 138/D3
Los Navalmorales, Spain 33/D3
Los Navalucillos, Spain 33/D3
Los Negros, Cuba 158/F2
Løsning, Denmark 21/C6
Los Novillos, Uruguay 145/D2
Los Ojos, N. Mex. 274/C2
Los Olivos, Calif. 204/E9
Los Olmos (creek), Texas 303/F10
Los Olmos (creek), Texas 303/F11
Los Osos-Baywood Park, Calif. 204/E8
Los Palacios, Cuba 158/B1
Los Palacios, Cuba 156/A2
Los Perales de Tapihue, Chile 138/F3
Los Pinos (riv.), Colo. 208/G8
Los Ranchos De Albuquerque, N. Mex. 274/C3
Los Reyes de Salgado, Mexico 150/H7
Los Ríos (prov.), Ecuador 128/C3
Los Roques (isls.), Venezuela 124/E2
Los Santos, Panama 154/G7
Los Santos de Maimona, Spain 33/C3
Los Sauces, Chile 138/D2
Losser, Netherlands 27/L4
Lossiemouth and Branderburgh, Scotland 15/E3
Lossiemouth and Branderburgh, Scotland 10/E2
Lost (riv.), Calif. 204/D1
Lost (riv.), Ind. 227/D7
Lost (riv.), Minn. 255/C3
Lost (riv.), Oreg. 291/F5
Lost (creek), Utah 304/C5
Lostallo, Switzerland 39/H4
Lostant, Ill. 222/D2
Los Taques, Venezuela 124/C2
Lost Cabin, Wyo. 319/E2
Lost City, W. Va. 312/J5
Lost Creek, Ky. 237/P6
Lost Creek, Wash. 310/H2
Lost Creek, W. Va. 312/F4
Los Teques, Venezuela 120/C2
Los Teques, Venezuela 124/E2
Los Testigos (isls.), Venezuela 124/G2
Lost Hills, Calif. 204/F8
Lostine, Oreg. 291/K2
Lost Island (lake), Iowa 229/D2
Lost Nation, Iowa 229/M5
Lost River, Idaho 220/E6
Lost River (range), Idaho 220/E5
Lost River, W. Va. 312/J5
Lost Springs, Kansas 232/E3
Lost Springs, Wyo. 319/G3
Lost Trail (pass), Idaho 220/E4
Lost Trail (pass), Mont. 262/B5
Lostwood, N. Dak. 282/F3
Los Vilos, Chile 138/A9
Los Yébenes, Spain 33/E3
Lot (dept.), France 28/D5
Lot (riv.), France 28/D5
Lota, Chile 138/D1
Lotagipi Swamp (plain), Sudan 111/F6
Lotbinière (co.), Québec 172/F3
Lotbinière, Québec 172/F3
Lot-et-Garonne (dept.), France 28/D5
Lothair, Ky. 237/P6
Lothair, Mont. 262/E2
Lothian, Md. 245/M5
Lothian (reg.), Scotland 15/E5
Loto, D.R. Congo 115/D4
Lötschberg (tunnel), Switzerland 39/E4
Lotsee, Okla. 288/O2
Lott, Texas 303/H6
Lottie, Ala. 195/C8
Lottie, La. 238/G5
Lottsville, Pa. 294/D2
Lotus, Calif. 204/C8
Lotzwil, Switzerland 39/E2
Louang Namtha, Laos 72/D2
Louangphrabang, Laos 72/D3
Louangprabang, Laos 54/M7
Louann, Ark. 202/E7
Loubomo, Congo 115/B4
Loubomo, Congo 102/D5
Loudéac, France 28/B3
Loudima, Congo 115/B4
Loudon•, N.H. 268/E5
Loudon (co.), Tenn. 237/N9
Loudon, Tenn. 237/N9
Loudonville, Ohio 284/F4
Loudoun (co.), Va. 307/N2
Loudun, France 28/D4
Louellen, Ky. 237/P7
Louga, Senegal 106/A5
Loughborough, England 13/F5
Loughborough, England 10/F4
Loughbrickland, N. Ireland 17/J3
Lougheed, Alberta 182/E3
Lougheed (isl.), N.W.T. 187/H2
Loughman, Fla. 212/E3
Loughrea, Ireland 17/E5
Loughrea, Ireland 10/B4
Loughros More (bay), Ireland 17/D2
Louin, Miss. 256/F6
Louisa (co.), Iowa 229/L6
Louisa, Ky. 237/R4
Louisa, La. 238/G7
Louisa (lake), Ontario 177/F2
Louisa (co.), Va. 307/N5
Louisa, Va. 307/M4
Louisbourg, Nova Scotia 168/J3
Louisbourg Nat'l Hist. Park, Nova Scotia 168/J3
Louisburg, Kansas 232/H3
Louisburg, Minn. 255/B5
Louisburg, Mo. 261/F7
Louisburg, N.C. 281/N2
Louisburgh, Ireland 17/B4
Louis Creek, Br. Col. 184/H4
Louisdale, Nova Scotia 168/G3
Louise (lake), Alaska 196/C1
Louise (isl.), Br. Col. 184/B4
Louise, Miss. 256/C5
Louise (lake), Québec 172/C4
Louise, Texas 303/H8
Louiseville, Québec 172/E3
Louisiade (arch.), Papua N.G. 87/F7
Louisiade (arch.), Papua N.G. 85/D8
Louisiana 188/H4
LOUISIANA 238
Louisiana (pt.), La. 238/C7
Louisiana, Mo. 261/K4
Louisiana (state), U.S. 146/J6
Louis Trichardt, S. Africa 118/E4
Louisville, Ala. 195/G7
Louisville, Colo. 208/J3
Louisville, Ga. 217/H4
Louisville, Ill. 222/E5
Louisville, Kansas 232/F2
Louisville, Ky. 237/J2
Louisville, Ky. 146/K6
Louisville, Miss. 256/G4
Louisville, Nebr. 264/H3
Louisville, Ohio 284/H4
Louisville, Tenn. 237/N9
Louisvillle, Ky. 188/J3
Louis XIV (pt.), Que. 162/H5
Louis-XIV (pt.), Québec 174/B2
Loukhi, Russia52/D1
Loulé, Portugal 33/B4
Louny, Czech Rep. 41/B1
Loup (co.), Nebr. 264/E3
Loup (riv.), Nebr. 264/F3
Loup (riv.), Québec 172/H2
Loup City, Nebr. 264/E3
Lourdes, France 28/C6
Lourdes, Newf. 166/C4
Lourdes, N. Mex. 274/D3
Lourdes, Québec 172/F3
Louriçal, Portugal 33/B3
Lourinhã, Portugal 33/B3
Lousã, Portugal 33/B2
Lousana, Alberta 182/D3
Louth, England 13/H4
Louth, England 10/F4
Louth (co.), Ireland 17/J4
Louth, Ireland 17/J4
Louth, N.S. Wales 97/C2
Loutrá Aidhipsoú, Greece 45/F6
Louvain (Leuven), Belgium 27/F7
Louvale, Ga. 217/C6
Louviers, Colo. 208/K4
Louviers, France 28/D3
Lövånger, Sweden 18/M4
Lovango (cay), Virgin Is. (U.S.) 161/C4
Lovat' (riv.), Russia 52/D3
Love, Miss. 256/D1
Love (co.), Okla. 288/M7
Love, Sask. 181/G2
Lovech, Bulgaria 45/G4
Lovejoy, Ga. 217/D4
Lovejoy, Ill. 222/A2
Lovelaceville, Ky. 237/D7
Lovelady, Texas 303/J6
Loveland, Colo. 188/E2
Loveland, Colo. 208/J2
Loveland, Iowa 229/B6
Loveland, Ohio 284/D9
Loveland, Okla. 288/J6
Lovell, Maine 243/B7
Lovell•, Maine 243/B7
Lovell, Okla. 288/L2
Lovell, Wyo. 319/D1
Lovells, Mich. 250/E4
Lovelock, Nev. 266/C2
Lovely, Ky. 237/S5
Lovenia (mt.), Utah 304/D3
Love Point, Md. 245/N4
Loverna, Sask. 181/B4
Loves Park, Ill. 222/E1
Lovett, Ga. 217/G5
Lovett, Ind. 227/F7
Lovettsville, Va. 307/N2
Love Valley, N.C. 281/H3
Loveville, Md. 245/M7
Lovewell, Kansas 232/D2
Lovewell (res.), Kansas 232/D2
Lovilia, Iowa 229/H6
Loving, N. Mex. 274/E6
Loving (co.), Texas 303/A6
Lovingston, Va. 307/L5
Lovington, Ill. 222/E4
Lovington, N. Mex. 274/F6
Lovisa, Finland 18/P6
Lövő, Hungary 41/D3
Lovosice, Czech Rep. 41/C1
Lóvua, Angola 115/D5
Low (cape), N.W.T. 162/H3
Low (cape), N.W.T. 187/K3
Low, Québec 172/B4
Lowa (riv.), D.R. Congo 115/E4
Low Bush River, Ontario 177/K5
Low Bush River, Ontario 175/E3
Lowden, Iowa 229/L5
Lowder, Ill. 222/D4
Lowe Farm, Manitoba 179/E5
Lowell, Ark. 202/B1
Lowell, Fla. 212/D2
Lowell, Idaho 220/C3
Lowell (lake), Idaho 220/B6
Lowell, Ind. 227/C2
Lowell, Iowa 229/L7
Lowell, Maine 243/F5
Lowell•, Maine 243/F5
Lowell, Mass. 188/M2
Lowell, Mass. 249/J2
Lowell, Mich. 250/D6
Lowell, N.C. 281/G4
Lowell, Ohio 284/H6
Lowell, Oreg. 291/E4
Lowell•, Vt. 268/C2
Lowell, W. Va. 312/E7
Lowell, Wis. 317/J9
Lowell Nat'l Hist. Park, Mass. 249/J2
Lowellville, Ohio 284/J3
Lower Alkali (lake), Calif. 204/E2
Lower Argyle, Nova Scotia 168/C5
Lower Arrow (lake), Br. Col. 184/H5
Lower Austria (prov.), Austria 41/C2
Lower Bank, N.J. 273/E4
Lower Barneys River, Nova Scotia 168/F3
Lower Brule, S. Dak. 298/K5
Lower Brule Ind. Res., S. Dak. 298/K5
Lower Burrell, Pa. 294/C4
Lower Cabot, Vt. 268/C3
Lower California (pen.), Mexico 2/D4
Lower California (pen.), Mexico 146/G7
Lower California (pen.), Mexico 150/C3
Lower Cloverdale, New Bruns. 170/F2
Lower Crab (creek), Wash. 310/F4
Lower Derby, New Bruns. 170/E2
Lower Durham, New Bruns. 170/D2
Lower East Pubnico, Nova Scotia 168/C5
Lower Elwah Ind. Res., Wash. 310/B2
Lower Engadine (valley), Switzerland 39/K3
Lower Goose Creek (res.), Idaho 220/D7
Lower Granite (lake), Idaho 220/A3
Lower Granite (dam), Wash. 310/H4
Lower Granite (lake), Wash. 310/H4
Lower Hainesville, New Bruns. 170/C2
Lower Hutt, N. Zealand 100/B2
Lower Island Cove, Newf. 166/D2
Lower Kalskag, Alaska 196/F2
Lower Kars, New Bruns. 170/E3
Lower Klamath (lake), Calif. 204/D2
Lower Lake, Calif. 204/C5
Lower L'Ardoise, Nova Scotia 168/H3
Lower Marlboro, Md. 245/M6
Lower Matecumbe (key), Fla. 212/F7
Lower Millstream, New Bruns. 170/E3
Lower Montague, Pr. Edward I. 168/F2
Lower Monumental (dam), Wash. 310/G4
Lower Monumental (lake), Wash. 310/G4
Lower New York (bay), N.J. 273/E2
Lower Nicola, Br. Col. 184/G5
Lower Ohio, Nova Scotia 168/C5
Lower Paia, Hawaii 218/J1
Lower Peach Tree, Ala. 195/C7
Lower Post, Br. Col. 184/K1
Lower Red (lake), Minn. 255/C3
Lower Red Rock (lake), Mont. 262/E6
Lower Rhine (riv.), Netherlands 27/H5
Lower Roach (pond), Maine 243/E4
Lower Saint Mary (lake), Mont. 262/C2
Lower Salem, Ohio 284/H6
Lower Sapin, New Bruns. 170/F2
Lower Saranac (lake), N.Y. 276/M2
Lower Saxony (state), Germany 22/C2
Lower Southampton, New Bruns. 170/C2
Lower South River, Nova Scotia 168/F3
Lower Sysladobsis (lake), Maine 243/G5
Lower Tonsina, Alaska 196/J2
Lower Tunguska (riv.), Russia 48/K3
Lower Tunguska (riv.), Russia 54/L3
Lower Waterford, Vt. 268/D3
Lower Wedgeport, Nova Scotia 168/C5
Lower West Pubnico, Nova Scotia 168/C5
Lower Woods Harbour, Nova Scotia 168/C5
Lowery, Ala. 195/F8
Lowery (lake), Fla. 212/E3
Lowes, Ky. 237/D7
Lowestoft, England 13/J5
Lowestoft, England 10/G4
Lowesville, Va. 307/K5
Lowgap, N.C. 281/H1
Łowicz, Poland 47/D2
Lowland, N.C. 281/S4
Lowman, Idaho 220/C5
Lowmansville, Ky. 237/R5
Low Moor, Iowa 229/N5
Lowmoor, Va. 307/J5
Lowndes (co.), Ala. 195/E6
Lowndes (co.), Ga. 217/F9

M

Marked Tree 405

Manners Sutton, New Bruns. 170/D3
Mannford, Okla. 288/O2
Mannheim, Germany 7/E4
Mannheim, Germany 22/C4
Manning, Alberta 182/B1
Manning, Ark. 202/E5
Manning, Iowa 229/C5
Manning, Kansas 232/B3
Manning (riv.), N.S. Wales 97/F2
Manning, N. Dak. 282/E5
Manning (cape), N.W.T. 187/F2
Manning (str.), Solomon Is. 86/D2
Manning, S.C. 296/G4
Manning Prov. Park, Br. Col. 184/G5
Mannington, Ky. 237/G6
Mannington, W. Va. 312/F3
Männlifluh (mt.), Switzerland 39/E3
Manns Choice, Pa. 294/E6
Manns Harbor, N.C. 281/T3
Mannsville, Ky. 237/L6
Mannsville, N.Y. 276/H3
Mannsville, Okla. 288/N6
Mannu (riv.), Italy 34/B5
Mannum, S. Australia 94/F6
Mannville, Alberta 182/E3
Mano (riv.), Liberia 106/B7
Mano (riv.), S. Leone 106/B7
Manoa, Bolivia 136/C1
Manokin, Md. 245/P8
Manokin (riv.), Md. 245/P8
Manokotak, Alaska 196/G3
Manokwari, Indonesia 85/J6
Manola, Alberta 182/C2
Manombo, Madagascar 118/G4
Manomet, Mass. 249/M5
Manomet (pt.), Mass. 249/N5
Manono, D.R. Congo 115/E5
Manono, D.R. Congo 102/E5
Manor, Ga. 217/G8
Manor, Pa. 294/C5
Manor, Sask. 181/K6
Manor, Texas 303/G7
Manorhamilton, Ireland 17/E3
Manori, India 68/B6
Manori (creek), India 68/B7
Manorville, N.Y. 276/P9
Manorville, Pa. 294/C4
Manosque, France 28/G6
Manotick, Ontario 177/J2
Manouane, Québec 172/C2
Manouane (lake), Québec 174/C2
Manp'o, N. Korea 81/B3
Manquin, Va. 307/O5
Manra (Sydney) (isl.), Kiribati 87/K6
Manresa, Spain 33/G2
Mansa, Zambia 115/E6
Mansa, Zambia 102/E6
Mansalay, Philippines 82/C4
Mansavillagra, Uruguay 145/D4
Manseau, Québec 172/E3
Mansel (isl.), N.W.T. 162/H3
Mansel (isl.), N.W.T. 146/K3
Mansel (isl.), N.W.T. 187/K3
Mansel'ka (mts.), Russia52/C1
Mansfield, Ark. 202/B3
Mansfield•, Conn. 210/F1
Mansfield, England 13/K2
Mansfield, England 10/F4
Mansfield, Ga. 217/E4
Mansfield, Ill. 222/E3
Mansfield, Ind. 227/C5
Mansfield, La. 238/C2
Mansfield, Mass. 249/J4
Mansfield•, Mass. 249/J4
Mansfield, Minn. 255/E7
Mansfield, Mo. 261/G8
Mansfield, Ohio 188/K2
Mansfield, Ohio 284/F4
Mansfield, Pa. 294/H2
Mansfield, S. Dak. 298/N3
Mansfield, Tenn. 237/E8
Mansfield, Texas 303/F3
Mansfield (mt.), Vt. 268/B2
Mansfield, Victoria 97/D5
Mansfield, Wash. 310/F3
Mansfield Center, Conn. 210/G1
Mansfield Depot, Conn. 210/F1
Mansfield Woodhouse, England 13/F4
Mansilla de las Mulas, Spain 33/D1
Manso (riv.), Brazil 132/C6
Manso (riv.), Chile 138/E4
Manson, Ind. 227/D4
Manson, Iowa 229/D3
Manson, Manitoba 179/A4
Manson, N.C. 281/N2
Manson, Wash. 310/E3
Manson Creek, Br. Col. 184/E2
Mansonville, Québec 172/E4
Mansura, La. 238/G4
Manta, Ecuador 128/B3
Manta, Ecuador 120/A3
Manta (bay), Ecuador 128/B3
Mantachie, Miss. 256/H2
Mantador, N. Dak. 282/R7
Mantagao (lake), Manitoba 179/E3
Mantagao (riv.), Manitoba 179/E3
Mantalingajan (mt.), Philippines 82/A6
Mantario, Sask. 181/B4
Mantaro (riv.), Peru 128/E8
Mantas (well), Niger 106/E5
Manteca, Calif. 204/D6
Mantecal, Apure, Venezuela 124/D4
Mantecal, Bolívar, Venezuela 124/F4
Mantee, Miss. 256/F3
Manteigas, Portugal 33/C2
Manteno, Ill. 222/F2
Manteo, N.C. 281/T3
Manter, Kansas 232/A4
Mantes-la-Jolie, France 28/D3
Manti, Utah 304/C4
Mantiqueira (range), Brazil 135/D3
Manto, Honduras 154/D3
Mantoloking, N.J. 273/E3
Manton, Calif. 204/D3
Manton, Mich. 250/D4
Manton, R.I. 249/J5
Mantorville, Minn. 255/F6
Mänttä, Finland 18/O6
Mantua, Ala. 195/C4
Mantua, Cuba 158/A2
Mantua (prov.), Italy 34/C2
Mantua, Italy 34/C2
Mantua•, N.J. 273/C4
Mantua, Ohio 284/H3
Mantua, Utah 304/C2
Mantua, Va. 307/S3
Manturovo, Russia52/F3
Manú, Peru 128/G9
Manú (riv.), Peru 128/G8
Manua (isls.), Amer. Samoa 87/K7
Manuae (atoll), Cook Is. 87/K7
Manuel Benavides, Mexico 150/H2
Manuelito, N. Mex. 274/A3
Manuel Rodríguez (isl.), Chile 138/D10
Manuels, New Bruns. 170/F1
Manuels, Newf. 166/D2
Manui (isl.), Indonesia 85/G6
Manukan, Philippines 82/D6
Manukau, N. Zealand 100/C1
Manukau (harb.), N. Zealand 100/B1
Manulla, Ireland 17/C4
Manumuskin (riv.), N.J. 273/D5
Manunui, N. Zealand 100/E3
Manuripi (riv.), Bolivia 136/B2
Manus (isl.), Papua N.G. 87/E6
Manus (isl.), Papua N.G. 86/A1
Manutuke, N. Zealand 100/F3
Manvel, N. Dak. 282/R3
Manvel, Texas 303/J3
Manville, N.J. 273/D2
Manville, R.I. 249/H5
Manville, Wyo. 319/H3
Many, La. 238/C3
Manyara (lake), Tanzania 115/G4
Manyas, Turkey 63/B3
Manyberries, Alberta 182/E5
Manych-Gudilo (lake), Russia 52/F5
Many Farms, Ariz. 198/F2
Manyoni, Tanzania 115/G5
Manzai, Pakistan 59/K3
Manzanar, Chile 138/F2
Manzanares, Spain 33/E3
Manzanares (riv.), Spain 33/F4
Manzanillo, Cuba 158/H4
Manzanillo, Cuba 156/C2
Manzanillo (bay), Dom. Rep. 158/C5
Manzanillo (bay), Haiti 158/C5
Manzanillo, Mexico 150/G7
Manzanillo, Mexico 146/H8
Manzanillo (pt.), Panama 154/H6
Manzanita, Oreg. 291/C2
Manzanita Ind. Res., Calif. 204/J11
Manzano, N. Mex. 274/C4
Manzano (mts.), N. Mex. 274/C4
Manzano (peak), N. Mex. 274/C4
Manzanola, Colo. 208/M6
Manzhouli (Manchouli), China 77/J2
Manzini, Swaziland 118/E5
Mao, Chad 111/C5
Mao, Dom. Rep. 158/D5
Maoke (mts.), Indonesia 85/K6
Maoming (Mowming), China 77/H7
Mapai, Mozambique 118/E4
Mapararí, Venezuela 124/D2
Mapastepec, Mexico 150/N9
Mapes, N. Dak. 282/O3
Mapia (isls.), Indonesia 85/J5
Mapimí, Mexico 150/G4
Mapimí (depr.), Mexico 150/G3
Mapire, Venezuela 124/F4
Mapiri, Bolivia 136/B4
Mapiripán, Laguna (lake), Colombia 126/E6
Maple (peak), Ariz. 198/F5
Maple (riv.), Mich. 250/E5
Maple (lake), Minn. 255/B3
Maple (riv.), Minn. 255/E7
Maple (riv.), N. Dak. 282/O8
Maple (riv.), N. Dak. 282/R6
Maple (creek), Sask. 181/B5
Maple (riv.), S. Dak. 298/M1
Maple, Wis. 317/C2
Maple Bay, Br. Col. 184/K3
Maple Bay, Minn. 255/B3
Maple City, Kansas 232/F4
Maple City, Mich. 250/D4
Maple Creek, Sask. 162/F6
Maple Creek, Sask. 181/B6
Maple Falls, Wash. 310/D2
Maple Grove, Minn. 255/G5
Maple Grove, Ontario 177/F4
Maple Grove, Québec 172/H4
Maple Heights, Ohio 284/H9
Maple Hill, Iowa 229/D2
Maple Hill, Kansas 232/F2
Maple Hill, N.C. 281/O5
Maple Island, Minn. 255/E7
Maple Lake, Minn. 255/D5
Maple Park, Ill. 222/E2
Maple Plain, Minn. 255/F5
Maple Rapids, Mich. 250/E5
Maple Ridge, Br. Col. 184/L3
Maple River, Iowa 229/D4
Maples, Ind. 227/H2
Maples, Mo. 261/J7
Maple Shade•, N.J. 273/B3
Maplesville, Ala. 195/E5
Mapleton, Iowa 229/B4
Mapleton, Kansas 232/H3
Mapleton•, Maine 243/G2
Mapleton, Mich. 250/D4
Mapleton, Minn. 255/E7
Mapleton, N.C. 281/P2
Mapleton, N. Dak. 282/R6
Mapleton, Oreg. 291/C3
Mapleton (Mapleton Depot), Pa. 294/F5
Mapleton, Utah 304/C3
Mapleton, Wis. 317/J1
Mapleton Depot, Pa. 294/F5
Maple Valley, Wash. 310/C3
Mapleview, Minn. 255/E7
Mapleview, New Bruns. 170/C2
Mapleville, Md. 245/H2
Mapleville, R.I. 249/H5
Maplewood, La. 238/D6
Maplewood, Minn. 255/G5
Maplewood, Mo. 261/P3
Maplewood, N.H. 268/D3
Maplewood•, N.J. 273/E2
Maplewood, Ohio 284/B5
Maplewood, Wis. 317/M6
Mapocho (riv.), Chile 138/G3
Mapoon Mission Station, Queensland 88/G2
Mapoon Mission Station, Queensland 95/B1
Maporal, Venezuela 124/C4
Mapos (Amazones), Cuba 158/F2
Mappsville, Va. 307/T5
Mapuera (riv.), Brazil 132/B3
Maputo (city) (prov.), Mozambique 118/E5
Maputo (prov.), Mozambique 118/E5
Maputo (cap.), Mozambique 2/L7
Maputo (cap.), Mozambique 118/E5
Maputo (cap.), Mozambique 102/F7
Maqatin (ruins), Yemen 59/E7
Maqên, China 77/F5
Maqna, Saudi Arabia 59/C4
Ma Qu (Huang He) (riv.), China 77/F5
Maquapit (lake), New Bruns. 170/D3
Maqueda (chan.), Philippines 82/D3
Maquela do Zombo, Angola 102/D5
Maquela do Zombo, Angola 115/C5
Maquereau (pt.), Québec 172/D2
Maquinchao, Argentina 143/C5
Maquoketa, Iowa 229/M4
Maquon, Ill. 222/C3
Mar (mts.), Brazil 120/E5
Mar (range), Brazil 135/C4
Mar, Serra do (range), Brazil 132/E9
Mar (dist.), Scotland 15/F3
Mara, Guyana 131/C3
Mara (reg.), Tanzania 115/F4
Marabá, Brazil 132/D4
Marabá, Brazil 120/E3
Marabahan, Indonesia 85/E6
Marabella, Trin. & Tob. 161/All
Maracá (isl.), Brazil 120/E2
Maracá (isl.), Brazil 132/D2
Maracaibo, Venezuela 124/C2
Maracaibo, Venezuela 120/B1
Maracaibo (lake), Venezuela 120/B2
Maracaibo (lake), Venezuela 124/C3
Maracaju, Brazil 132/C8
Maracas (bay), Trin & Tob. 161/C10
Maracay, Venezuela 124/E2
Marada, Libya 111/C2
Maradi, Niger 106/F6
Maradi, Niger 102/C3
Maragheh, Iran 59/E2
Maragheh, Iran 66/E2
Maragogipe, Brazil 132/G6
Maraira (pt.), Philippines 82/C1
Marajó (bay), Brazil 132/E2
Marajó (est.), Brazil 120/E2
Marajó (isl.), Brazil 120/E3
Marajó (isl.), Brazil 132/D3
Maralal, Kenya 115/G3
Maralinga, S. Australia 88/E6
Maralwexi (Bachu), China 77/A4
Maramag, Philippines 82/E7
Maramec, Okla. 288/N2
Marampa, S. Leone 106/B7
Marana, Ariz. 198/D6
Marand, Iran 59/E2
Marand, Iran 66/D1
Marang, Malaysia 72/D6
Maranguape, Brazil 132/G3
Maranhão (state), Brazil 132/E4
Maranoa (riv.), Queensland 95/C5
Marañón (riv.), Peru 120/B3
Marañón (riv.), Peru 128/E5
Marapanim, Brazil 132/E3
Maras (mt.), Indonesia 85/D6
Maraş, Turkey 59/C2
Maraş (Kahramanmaraş), Turkey 63/G4
Marathon, Fla. 212/E7
Marathón, Greece 45/G6
Marathon, Iowa 229/C3
Marathon, N.Y. 276/J6
Marathon, Ohio 284/C7
Marathon, Ont. 162/H6
Marathon, Ontario 177/H5
Marathon, Ontario 175/C3
Marathon, Texas 303/A7
Marathon (co.), Wis. 317/G6
Marathon, Wis. 317/G6
Maratua (isl.), Indonesia 85/F5
Maravillas, Bolivia 136/B2
Maravillas (creek), Texas 303/A7
Marawi, Philippines 85/G4
Marawi, Philippines 82/E6
Marbach, Switzerland 39/E3
Marbach am Neckar, Germany 22/C4
Marbella, Spain 33/D4
Marble, Ark. 202/C1
Marble, Colo. 208/E4
Marble, Minn. 255/E3
Marble, N.C. 281/B4
Marble (isl.), N.W.T. 162/G3
Marble (isl.), N.W.T. 187/J3
Marble Bar, Australia 87/C8
Marble Bar, W. Australia 88/B4
Marble Bar, W. Australia 92/C3
Marble Canyon, Ariz. 198/D2
Marble Canyon Nat'l Mon., Ariz. 198/D2
Marble City, Okla. 288/S3
Marble Dale, Conn. 210/B2
Marble Falls, Texas 303/F7
Marblehead, Ill. 222/B4
Marblehead•, Mass. 249/E7
Marblehead (neck), Mass. 249/F6
Marblehead, Ohio 284/E2
Marble Hill, Ga. 217/D2
Marble Hill, Mo. 261/N8
Marblemount, Wash. 310/D2
Marble Rock, Iowa 229/H3
Marbleton, Québec 172/F4
Marbleton, Wyo. 319/B3
Marble Valley, Ala. 195/F4
Marburg an der Lahn, Germany 22/C3
Marbury, Ala. 195/E5
Marbury, Md. 245/K6
Marcala, Honduras 154/C3
Marcali, Hungary 41/D3
Marcapata, Peru 128/G9
Marcelin, Sask. 181/E3
Marceline, Mo. 261/F3
Marcell, Minn. 255/E3
Marcella, Ark. 202/G2
Marcella, N.J. 273/E2
Marcelline, Ill. 222/B3
Marcellus, Mich. 250/D6
Marcellus, N.Y. 276/H5
Marcelville, New Bruns. 170/E2
March (riv.), Austria 41/D2
March, England 10/G4
March, England 13/H5
March A.F.B., Calif. 204/E11
Marchand, Manitoba 179/F5
Marche, Ark. 202/F4
Marche (trad. prov.) France 29
Marche (reg.), Italy 34/D3
Marche-en-Famenne, Belgium 27/G8
Marchegg, Austria 41/D2
Marchena (isl.), Ecuador 128/B9
Marchena, Spain 33/D4
Marchfield, Barbados 161/B9
Marchigüe, Chile 138/F5
Marchin, Belgium 27/G8
Mar Chiquita (lake), Argentina 143/D3
Marchwell, Sask. 181/K5
Marco (Marco Island), Fla. 212/E6
Marco (isl.), Fla. 212/E6
Marco, Ind. 227/C7
Marco, La. 238/E3
Marcola, Oreg. 291/E3
Marcona, Peru 128/E10
Marcos Juárez, Argentina 143/D3
Marcus, Iowa 229/B3
Marcus (isl.), Japan 87/F3
Marcus, S. Dak. 298/E4
Marcus, Wash. 310/H2
Marcus Baker (mt.), Alaska 196/C1
Marcus Hook, Pa. 294/L7
Marcy, N.Y. 276/K4
Marcy (mt.), N.Y. 276/N2
Mardan, Pakistan 68/C2
Mardan, Pakistan 59/K3
Mardela Springs, Md. 245/P7
Mar del Plata, Argentina 143/E4
Mar del Plata, Argentina 120/D6
Mardin (prov.), Turkey 63/J4
Mardin, Turkey 59/D2
Maré (isl.), New Caled. 87/G8
Maré (isl.), New Caled. 86/J4
Mareb (riv.), Eritrea 59/C7
Marechal Deodoro, Brazil 132/H5
Maree, Loch (lake), Scotland 10/D2
Mare, Loch (lake), Scotland 15/C3
Mareeba, Queensland 95/C3
Mareeba, Queensland 88/G3
Mare Island Navy Yard, Calif. 204/J1
Marengo (co.), Ala. 195/C6
Marengo, Ala. 195/C6
Marengo, Ill. 222/E1
Marengo, Ind. 227/E8
Marengo, Iowa 229/J5
Marengo, Ohio 284/E5
Marengo, Sask. 181/B4
Marengo, Wash. 310/G3
Marengo, Wis. 317/E3
Marenisco, Mich. 250/F2
Marennes, France 28/C5
Mareth, Tunisia 106/F2
Marettimo (isl.), Italy 34/C6
Marfa, Texas 303/C12
Marfield, N.S. Wales 97/C3
Marfrance, W. Va. 312/E6
Margai Caka (lake), China 77/C4
Marganets, Ukraine 52/E5
Margao, India 68/C5
Margaree, Nova Scotia 168/G2
Margaree (isl.), Nova Scotia 168/F4
Margaree Centre, Nova Scotia 168/H2
Margaree Forks, Nova Scotia 168/G2
Margaree Harbour, Nova Scotia 168/G2
Margaree Valley, Nova Scotia 168/H2
Margaret, Ala. 195/F3
Margaret (lake), Alberta 182/B5
Margaret, Manitoba 179/C5
Margaret, Texas 303/E3
Margaret (riv.), W. Australia 88/D3
Margaret River, W. Australia 88/A6
Margaret River, W. Australia 92/A6
Margaret River Station, W. Australia 92/D2
Margaretsville, Nova Scotia 168/C3
Margaretville, N.Y. 276/L6
Margarita, Argentina 143/F5
Margarita (isl.), Venezuela 120/C1
Margarita (isl.), Venezuela 124/F2
Margate, England 13/J6
Margate, England 10/G5
Margate, Fla. 212/F5
Margate, S. Africa 118/E6
Margate, Tasmania 99/D4
Margate City, N.J. 273/E5
Margento, Colombia 126/C4
Margerum, Ala. 195/B1
Margherita (Jamama), Somalia 115/H3
Margherita (mt.), Uganda 115/E3
Margherita (mt.), D.R. Congo 102/E4
Margherita (mt.), D.R. Congo 115/E3
Margie, Minn. 255/E2
Margo, Sask. 181/H4
Margos, Peru 128/D8
Margosatubig, Philippines 82/D7
Margow, Dasht-e (des.), Afghanistan 59/H3
Margow, Dasht-e (des.), Afghanistan 68/A2
Margraten, Netherlands 27/H7
Margret, Ga. 217/D1
Margrethe (lake), Mich. 250/E4
Marguerite (bay) 5/C15
Maria (isl.), Fr. Poly. 87/L8
Maria (creek), Ind. 227/C7
Maria, Québec 172/C2
Maria (isls.), St. Lucia 161/G7
Maria (isl.), Tasmania 99/E4
María Albina, Uruguay 145/E4
María Cleófas (isl.), Mexico 150/F6
María Elena, Chile 138/B3
Mariager, Denmark 21/D4
Mariager, Denmark 18/G8
Mariager (fjord), Denmark 21/D4
Mariah Hill, Ind. 227/D8
María Madre (isl.), Mexico 150/F6
María Magdalena (isl.), Mexico 150/F6
Marian (lake), Fla. 212/E4
Marian (lake), N.W.T. 187/G3
Marian, Queensland 88/H4
Marian, Queensland 95/D4
Mariana, Brazil 135/E2
Mariana Lake, Alberta 182/D2
Marianao, Cuba 158/C1
Marianao, Cuba 156/A2
Marianas, Northern 87/E4
Mariana Trench, Pacific 87/E4
Marianna, Ark. 202/J4
Marianna, Fla. 212/A1
Marianna, Pa. 294/B5
Mariano I. Loza, Argentina 143/G4
Mariano Roque Alonso, Paraguay 144/A4
Mariánské Lázně, Czech Rep. 41/B2
María Pinto, Chile 138/G3
Mariapolis, Manitoba 179/C5
Marias, Islas (isls.), Mexico 150/F6
Marias (riv.), Mont. 188/D1
Marias (riv.), Mont. 262/D2
Maria Stein, Ohio 284/A5
Mariato, Punta (cape), Panama 154/G7
María Trinidad Sánchez (prov.), Dom. Rep. 158/E5
Mari Aut. Rep., Russia 48/E4
Mari Aut. Rep., Russia 52/G3
Maria van Diemen (cape), N. Zealand 100/D1
Mariazell, Austria 41/C3
Marib, Saudi Arabia 59/E6
Marib, Yemen 59/E6
Mariba, Ky. 237/O5
Maribel, Wis. 317/L7
Maribo, Denmark 21/E8
Maribor, Slovenia 7/F4
Maribor, Slovenia 45/B2
Maribyrnong (riv.), Victoria 97/H5
Maribyrnong (riv.), Victoria 88/K7
Maricao, P. Rico 161/B2
Maricopa (co.), Ariz. 198/C5
Maricopa, Ariz. 198/C5
Maricopa (mts.), Ariz. 198/C5
Maricopa, Calif. 204/F8
Maricopa Ind. Res., Ariz. 198/C6
Maricunga, Salar de (salt dep.), Chile 138/B6
Maridi, Sudan 111/E7
Marie (lake), Alberta 182/E2
Marie, Ark. 202/K2
Marie, W. Va. 312/E7
Marie Byrd Land (reg.), Ant. 2/D10
Marie Byrd Land (reg.) 5/B13
Mariefred, Sweden 18/F1
Marie-Galante (isl.), Guadeloupe 161/B7
Marie-Galante (isl.), Guadeloupe 156/G4
Mariehamn, Finland 18/M7
Mariel, Cuba 158/B1
Mariemont, Ohio 284/C9
Marienberg, Papua N.G. 85/B6
Marienburg (Malbork), Poland 47/D1
Mariënburg, Suriname 131/D2
Mariental, Namibia 118/B4
Mariental, Namibia 102/D7
Marienthal, Kansas 232/A3
Marienville, Pa. 294/D3
Marie-Reine, Alberta 182/B1
Maries (co.), Mo. 261/J6
Mariestad, Sweden 18/H7
Marietta, Ga. 217/J1
Marietta, Ill. 222/C3
Marietta, Ind. 227/F6
Marietta, Minn. 255/B5
Marietta, Miss. 256/H2
Marietta, N.C. 281/L6
Marietta, Ohio 284/G7
Marietta, Okla. 288/M7
Marietta, Pa. 294/J5
Marietta-Alderwood, Wash. 310/C2
Marietta-Slater, S.C. 296/C1
Marieval, Sask. 181/J5
Marieville, Québec 172/D4
Marigot, Dominica 161/F6
Marigot, Haiti 158/C6
Marigot, Martinique 161/D5
Marigot, St. Lucia 161/G6
Marigüitar, Venezuela 124/G2
Marihatag, Philippines 82/F6
Marília, Brazil 120/D5
Marília, Brazil 135/A3
Marília, Brazil 132/D8
Marilla, N.Y. 276/C5
Marin (co.), Calif. 204/C5
Marín, Spain 33/B1
Marina, Calif. 204/D7
Marinduque (prov.), Philippines 82/C4
Marinaduque (isl.), Philippines 82/C4
Marine, Ill. 222/D5
Marine City, Mich. 250/G6
Marineland, Fla. 212/E2
Marine on Saint Croix, Minn. 255/F5
Marinette (co.), Wis. 317/K5
Marinette, Wis. 317/L5
Maringá, Brazil 120/D5
Maringá, Brazil 132/D8
Maringouin, La. 238/G6
Marinha Grande, Portugal 33/B3
Marinhas, Portugal 33/B2
Marino, Italy 34/F7
Marion (reef) 95/E3
Marion (co.), Ala. 195/C2
Marion, Ala. 195/D5
Marion (lake), Alberta 182/D3
Marion (co.), Ark. 202/E1
Marion, Ark. 202/K3
Marion, Conn. 210/D2
Marion (co.), Fla. 212/D2
Marion (co.), Ga. 217/C6
Marion (co.), Ill. 222/E5
Marion, Ill. 222/E6
Marion (co.), Ind. 227/E5
Marion, Ind. 188/J2
Marion, Ind. 227/F3
Marion (co.), Iowa 229/G8
Marion, Iowa 229/K4
Marion (co.), Kansas 232/E3
Marion, Kansas 232/F3
Marion (lake), Kansas 232/E3
Marion (co.), Ky. 237/L5
Marion, Ky. 237/E6
Marion, La. 238/F1
Marion, Mass. 249/L6
Marion•, Mass. 249/L6
Marion, Mich. 250/D4
Marion (co.), Miss. 256/E8
Marion, Miss. 256/G6
Marion (co.), Mo. 261/J3
Marion, Mont. 262/B2
Marion, N.Y. 276/F4
Marion, N.C. 281/E3
Marion, N. Dak. 282/O6
Marion (co.), Ohio 284/D4
Marion, Ohio 188/K2
Marion, Ohio 284/D4
Marion (co.), Oreg. 291/E3
Marion, Oreg. 291/D3
Marion, Pa. 294/G6
Marion (res.), Queensland 88/J3
Marion, S. Australia 88/D8
Marion, S. Australia 94/A8
Marion (lake), S.C. 188/K4
Marion (co.), S.C. 296/J3
Marion, S.C. 296/J3
Marion (lake), S.C. 296/G5
Marion, S. Dak. 298/P7
Marion (bay), Tasmania 99/E4
Marion (co.), Tenn. 237/K10
Marion (co.), Texas 303/K5
Marion, Va. 307/E7
Marion (co.), W. Va. 312/F4
Marion, Wis. 317/J6
Marion Bridge, Nova Scotia 168/H3
Marion Center, Pa. 294/D4
Marion Junction, Ala. 195/D6
Marion Station, Md. 245/R8
Marionville, Mo 261/E8
Maripa, Fr. Guiana 131/E4
Maripa, Venezuela 124/F4
Maripasoula, Fr. Guiana 131/D4
Mariposa (co.), Calif. 204/E6
Mariposa, Calif. 204/E6
Mariscala, Uruguay 145/E5
Mariscal Estigarribia, Paraguay 120/C5
Mariscal Estigarribia, Paraguay 144/B3
Marismas, Las (marsh), Spain 33/C4
Marissa, Ill. 222/D5
Maritime Alps (range), France 28/G5
Maritime Alps (range), Italy 34/A2
Maritsa, Bulgaria 45/H4
Maritsa (riv.), Bulgaria 45/G4
Mariupol', Ukraine 52/E5
Mariupol', Ukraine 48/D5
Marivan (Dezh Shahpur), Iran 66/E3
Mariveles, Philippines 82/C3
Märjamaa, Estonia 53/C1
Mark (riv.), Belgium 27/F6
Mark, Ill. 222/D2
Mark (riv.), Netherlands 27/F6
Marka (Merka), Somalia 115/H3
Marka, Somalia 102/G4
Markam, China 77/E6
Markaryd, Sweden 18/H8
Mark Center, Ohio 284/A3
Markdale, Ontario 177/D3
Marked Tree, Ark. 202/K2

406 Marken

Marken (isl.), Netherlands 27/G4
Markerwaard Polder, Netherlands 27/G3
Markesan, Wis. 317/J8
Market Drayton, England 10/E4
Market Drayton, England 13/E5
Market Harborough, England 13/G5
Markethill, N. Ireland 17/H3
Market Rasen, England 13/G4
Market Weighton, England 13/G4
Markha (riv.), Russia 48/M3
Markham (mt.) 5/A8
Markham, Ill. 222/B6
Markham (bay), N.W.T. 187/L3
Markham (inlet), N.W.T. 187/L1
Markham, Ontario 177/K4
Markham, Va. 307/N3
Markham, Wash. 310/B4
Markinch, Sask. 181/G5
Markinch, Scotland 15/E4
Markit, China 77/A4
Markkleeberg, Germany 22/E3
Markland, Ind. 227/G3
Markland, Newf. 166/D2
Markle, Ind. 227/G3
Markleeville, Calif. 204/F5
Marklesburg (James Creek), Pa. 294/F5
Markleton, Pa. 294/D6
Markleville, Ind. 227/F5
Markleysburg, Pa. 294/C6
Markounda, Cent. Afr. Rep. 115/C2
Markovo, Russia 4/C1
Markovo, Russia 48/S3
Marks, Miss. 256/D2
Marks, Russia52/G4
Markstay, Ontario 177/D1
Marksville, La. 238/G4
Marktredwitz, Germany 22/E4
Markville, Minn. 255/F4
Marl, Germany 22/B3
Marland, Okla. 288/M1
Marlbank, Ontario 177/G3
Marlboro, Alberta 182/B3
Marlboro•, N.J. 273/E3
Marlboro, N.Y. 276/M7
Marlboro (co.), S.C. 296/H2
Marlboro•, Vt. 268/B6
Marlborough, Conn. 210/F2
Marlborough•, Conn. 210/F2
Marlborough, England 13/F6
Marlborough, England 10/F5
Marlborough, Mass. 249/H3
Marlborough, Mo. 261/P3
Marlborough, N.H. 268/C6
Marlborough•, N.H. 268/C6
Marlborough, Queensland 95/D4
Marlette, Mich. 250/G5
Marlin, Texas 303/H6
Marlin, Wash. 310/F3
Marlinton, W. Va. 312/F6
Marlow, Ala. 195/C10
Marlow, England 13/G8
Marlow, Ga. 217/K6
Marlow•, N.H. 268/C5
Marlow, Okla. 288/K5
Marlton, N.J. 273/D4
Marmaduke, Ark. 202/K1
Marmagao, India 68/C5
Marmande, France 28/C5
Marmara (sea), Turkey 7/G4
Marmara (isl.), Turkey 63/B2
Marmara (sea), Turkey 63/C2
Marmara (sea), Turkey 59/A1
Marmaris, Turkey 63/C4
Marmarth, N. Dak. 282/B7
Mar Menor (lag.), Spain 33/F4
Marmet, W. Va. 312/C6
Marmolada (mt.), Italy 34/C1
Marmontana (mt.), Switzerland 39/H4
Marmora, N.J. 273/D5
Marmora, Ontario 177/G3
Marmot (bay), Alaska 196/H3
Marmot (isl.), Alaska 196/H3
Mar Muerto (lag.), Mexico 150/N9
Marne (dept.), France 28/F3
Marne (riv.), France 28/C2
Marne, Germany 22/C2
Marne, Iowa 229/C6
Marne, Mich. 250/D5
Maro (dry riv.), Chad 111/C4
Maro (reef), Hawaii 188/F6
Maro (reef), Hawaii 218/C6
Maroa, Ill. 222/E3
Maroa, Venezuela 124/E6
Maroantsetra, Madagascar 118/J3
Marolambo, Madagascar 118/H4
Maromokotro (mt.), Madagascar 102/G6
Maromokotro (mt.), Madagascar 118/H2
Marondera, Zimbabwe 118/E3
Maroni (riv.) 120/D2
Maroni (riv.), Fr. Guiana 131/D3
Maroochydore-Mooloolaba, Queensland 88/J5
Maroochydore-Mooloolaba, Queensland 95/E5
Maroon (peak), Colo. 208/F4
Maroon Town, Jamaica 158/H6
Maros (riv.), Hungary 41/F3
Maros, Indonesia 85/F6
Maroua, Cameroon 102/D3
Maroua, Cameroon 115/B1
Maroubra, N.S. Wales 97/K3
Marouini (riv.), Fr. Guiana 131/D4
Marovoay, Madagascar 102/G6
Marovoay, Madagascar 118/H3
Marowijne (dist.), Suriname 131/D4
Marowijne (riv.), Suriname 131/D3
Marquam, Oreg. 291/B3
Marquand, Mo. 261/M8
Marquesas (keys), Fla. 212/D7
Marquesas (isls.), Fr. Polynesia 2/B6
Marquesas (isls.), Fr. Poly. 87/N6
Marquette, Iowa 229/L2
Marquette, Kansas 232/E3
Marquette, Manitoba 179/E4
Marquette, Mich. 146/K5
Marquette, Mich. 188/J1
Marquette (co.), Mich. 250/B2
Marquette, Mich. 250/B2
Marquette (isl.), Mich. 250/E3
Marquette, Nebr. 264/G4
Marquette (co.), Wis. 317/H8
Marquette, Wis. 317/H8
Marquette Heights, Ill. 222/D3
Marquez, Texas 303/H6
Marquis, Grenada 161/D8
Marquis, St. Lucia 161/G6
Marquis, Sask. 181/F5
Marra, Jebel (mt.), Sudan 102/E3
Marra (creek), N.S. Wales 97/D2
Marra, Jebel (mt.), Sudan 111/D5
Marracuene, Mozambique 118/E5
Marrakech, Morocco 102/B1
Marrakech, Morocco 106/C2
Marrawah, Tasmania 99/A2
Marree, S. Australia 88/F5
Marree, S. Australia 94/E3
Marrero, La. 238/O4
Marrickville, N.S. Wales 88/L4
Marrickville, N.S. Wales 97/J3
Marriott, Sask. 181/D4
Marromeu, Mozambique 118/F3
Marrowbone, Ky. 237/K7
Marrowie (creek), N.S. Wales 97/C3
Marrupa, Mozambique 118/F2
Mars, Pa. 294/C4
Mars (riv.), Québec 172/G1
Marsabit, Kenya 115/G3
Marsabit, Kenya 102/F4
Marsa el Brega, Libya 111/D1
Marsa el Hariga, Libya 111/D1
Marsala, Italy 34/D6
Marsa Oseif, Sudan 111/G3
Mars Bluff, S.C. 296/H3
Marsciano, Italy 34/D3
Marsden, N.S. Wales 97/D3
Marsden, Sask. 181/B3
Marsden Park, N.S. Wales 97/H3
Marsdiep (chan.), Netherlands 27/F3
Marseille, France 7/E4
Marseille, France 28/F6
Marseilles, Ill. 222/E2
Marseilles, Ohio 284/D4
Marsh (creek), Idaho 220/F7
Marsh (isl.), La. 238/G7
Marsh (lake), Minn. 255/B5
Marsh, Mont. 262/M4
Marsh (peak), Utah 304/E3
Marshall (co.), Ala. 195/F2
Marshall, Ark. 202/E2
Marshall (co.), Ill. 222/D2
Marshall, Ill. 222/F4
Marshall (co.), Ind. 227/E2
Marshall, Ind. 227/C5
Marshall (co.), Iowa 229/G4
Marshall (co.), Kansas 232/F2
Marshall (co.), Ky. 237/E7
Marshall, Liberia 106/B7
Marshall (isl.), Maine 243/G7
Marshall, Mich. 250/E6
Marshall (co.), Minn. 255/B2
Marshall, Minn. 255/C6
Marshall (co.), Miss. 256/E1
Marshall, Mo. 261/F4
Marshall, N.C. 281/D3
Marshall, N. Dak. 282/F5
Marshall (riv.), North. Terr. 88/F4
Marshall (riv.), North. Terr. 93/D7
Marshall, Ohio 284/C7
Marshall (co.), Okla. 288/N6
Marshall, Okla. 288/L2
Marshall, Sask. 181/B2
Marshall (co.), S. Dak. 298/O2
Marshall (co.), Tenn. 237/H10
Marshall, Texas 188/H4
Marshall, Texas 303/K5
Marshall, Va. 307/N3
Marshall (isls.), U.S. 2/T5
Marshall (co.), W. Va. 312/E3
Marshall, Wis. 317/H9
Marshallberg, N.C. 281/S5
Marshall Hall, Md. 245/K6
Marshall Islands 87/G4
Marshalls Creeks, Pa. 294/M3
Marshallton, Del. 245/R2
Marshalltown, Iowa 229/G4
Marshalltown, Iowa 188/H2
Marshallville, Ga. 217/D6
Marshallville, Ohio 284/G4
Marshes Siding, Ky. 237/M7
Marshfield, Ind. 227/C4
Marshfield, Mass. 249/M4
Marshfield•, Mass. 249/M4
Marshfield, Mo. 261/G8
Marshfield, Vt. 268/C3
Marshfield•, Vt. 268/C3
Marshfield, Wis. 317/F6
Marshfield Hills, Mass. 249/M4
Marsh Hill, Pa. 294/H3
Mars Hill•, Maine 243/H2
Mars Hill, N.C. 281/D3
Mars Hill-Blaine, Maine 243/H2
Marshland, Oreg. 291/D1
Marshville, N.C. 281/J4
Marshy (lake), Manitoba 179/B5
Marshyhope (creek), Md. 245/P6
Marsing, Idaho 220/B6
Marsland, Nebr. 264/A2
Marsoui, Québec 172/C1
Märsta, Sweden 18/K7
Marstal, Denmark 21/D8
Marston, Mo. 261/N9
Marston, N.C. 281/K5
Marstons Mills, Mass. 249/N6
Marstrand, Sweden 18/G8
Mart, Texas 303/H6
Martaban, Burma 72/C3
Martaban (gulf), Burma 54/L8
Martaban (gulf), Burma 72/C4
Martapura, Indonesia 85/F6
Martel, Ohio 284/E4
Martel, Tenn. 237/N9
Martelange, Belgium 27/H9
Martell, Calif. 204/C9
Martell, Wis. 317/B6
Martelle, Iowa 229/L4
Marten (mt.), Alberta 182/C2
Martensdale, Iowa 229/F6
Martensville, Sask. 181/E3
Martha, Ky. 237/R4
Martha, Okla. 288/H5
Martha, Tenn. 237/J8
Marthaguy (creek), N.S. Wales 97/D2
Marthasville, Mo. 261/L5
Martha's Vineyard (isl.), Mass. 188/N2
Martha's Vineyard (isl.), Mass. 249/M7
Marthaville, La. 238/D3
Martí, Camagüey, Cuba 158/G3
Martí, Matanzas, Cuba 158/D1
Martí, Cuba 156/C2
Martigny, Switzerland 39/C4
Martigues, France 28/F6
Martin (dam), Ala. 195/G5
Martin (lake), Ala. 195/G5
Martin (co.), Fla. 212/F4
Martin•, Ga. 217/F2
Martin (co.), Ind. 227/D7
Martin (co.), Ky. 237/R5
Martin, Ky. 237/R5
Martin, La. 238/D2
Martin, Mich. 250/D6
Martin (co.), Minn. 255/D7
Martin, New Bruns. 170/E3
Martin (head), New Bruns. 170/E3
Martin (co.), N.C. 281/P3
Martin, N. Dak. 282/K4
Martin, Ohio 284/D2
Martin, Slovakia 41/E2
Martin, S.C. 296/D5
Martin, S. Dak. 298/F7
Martin, Tenn. 237/D8
Martin (co.), Texas 303/C5
Martin, W. Va. 312/H4
Martina Franca, Italy 34/F4
Martinborough, N. Zealand 100/E4
Martín Chico, Uruguay 145/A5
Martinez, Calif. 204/K1
Martinez, Ga. 217/H3
Martínez de la Torre, Mexico 150/L6
Martín García (isl.), Argentina 143/H6
Martinique (isl.) 146/M8
MARTINIQUE 161/D5
MARTINIQUE 156/G4
Martinique (passage), Dominica 161/E7
Martinique (passage), Martinique 161/C5
Martin Luther King, Jr., Nat'l Hist. Site, Ga. 217/K1
Martinsburg, Ind. 227/E8
Martinsburg, Iowa 229/J6
Martinsburg, Mo. 261/J4
Martinsburg, Nebr. 264/H2
Martinsburg, N.Y. 276/J3
Martinsburg, Ohio 284/F5
Martinsburg, Pa. 294/F5
Martinsburg, W. Va. 312/K4
Martins Creek, Pa. 294/M4
Martinsdale, Mont. 262/F4
Martinsdale (res.), Mont. 262/F4
Martins Ferry, Ohio 284/J5
Martins Mills, Tenn. 237/F10
Martins River, Nova Scotia 168/D4
Martinsville, Ill. 222/F4
Martinsville, Ind. 227/D6
Martinsville, Miss. 256/D7
Martinsville, Mo. 261/D2
Martinsville, N.J. 273/D2
Martinsville, Ohio 284/C7
Martinsville (I.C.), Va. 307/J7
Martinton, Ill. 222/F3
Martintown, Ontario 177/K2
Martin Van Buren Nat'l Hist. Site, N.Y. 276/N6
Martinville, Ark. 202/F3
Martinville, Québec 172/F4
Martock, England 13/E7
Martofte, Denmark 21/D6
Marton, N. Zealand 100/E4
Martos, Spain 33/E4
Martre, Lac la (lake), N.W.T. 162/E3
Martwick, Ky. 237/H6
Marty, S. Dak. 298/N8
Marudi (mts.), Guyana 131/B5
Marudi, Malaysia 85/E5
Ma'ruf, Afghanistan 68/B2
Ma'ruf, Afghanistan 59/J3
Maruim, Brazil 132/G5
Marulan, N.S. Wales 97/E4
Marungu (mts.), D.R. Congo 115/E5
Marutea (atoll), Fr. Poly. 87/N8
Marv Dasht, Iran 66/H6
Marvejols, France 28/E5
Marvel, Ala. 195/D4
Marvel, Colo. 208/C8
Marvell, Ark. 202/J4
Marvin, S. Dak. 298/R3
Marvindale, Pa. 294/E2
Marvine (mt.), Utah 304/C5
Marvyn, Ala. 195/H6
Marwayne, Alberta 182/E3
Marwood, Pa. 294/C4
Mary, Ky. 237/O5
Mary (lake), Minn. 255/C5
Mary (riv.), Queensland 95/E5
Mary (Merv), Turkmenistan 48/G6
Mary, Turkmenistan 54/H6
Maryborough, Australia 87/F8
Maryborough (Portlaoise), Ireland 17/G5
Maryborough (Portlaoise), Ireland 10/C4
Maryborough, Queensland 95/E5
Maryborough, Queensland 88/J5
Maryborough, Victoria 97/B5
Maryborough, Victoria 88/G7
Marydel, Md. 245/P4
Marydell, Miss. 256/F5
Mary Esther, Fla. 212/B6
Maryfield, Sask. 181/K6
Maryhill, Wash. 310/E5
Mary Kathleen, Queensland 88/G4
Mary Kathleen, Queensland 95/A4
Marykirk, Scotland 15/F4
Maryland 188/L3
MARYLAND 245
Maryland, N.Y. 276/L5
Maryland (state), U.S. 146/L6
Maryland City, Md. 245/L4
Maryland Heights, Mo. 261/O2
Maryland Line, Md. 245/M2
Maryneal, Texas 303/D5
Maryport, England 10/E3
Maryport, England 13/D3
Mary Ronan (lake), Mont. 262/B3
Marys (creek), Idaho 220/C7
Marys (riv.), Nev. 266/F1
Mary's Harbour, Newf. 166/C3
Marystown, Newf. 166/D4
Marysvale, Utah 304/B5
Marysvale (peak), Utah 304/B5
Marysville, Calif. 188/B3
Marysville, Calif. 204/D4
Marysville, Ind. 227/F7
Marysville, Iowa 229/G6
Marysville, Kansas 232/F2
Marysville, Mich. 250/G6
Marysville, Mont. 262/D4
Marysville, Ohio 284/D5
Marysville, Pa. 294/H5
Marysville, Wash. 310/C2
Marytown, W. Va. 312/C8
Maryvale, Queensland 95/C3
Maryvale, Queensland 88/H3
Maryville, Ill. 222/B2
Maryville, Mo. 261/C2
Maryville, Tenn. 237/O9
Marzo (pt.), Colombia 126/B4
Masagua, Guatemala 154/B3
Masahim, Kuh-e (mt.), Iran 66/J5
Masai (steppe), Tanzania 115/G4
Masaka, Uganda 115/F4
Masamba, Indonesia 85/G6
Masan, S. Korea 81/D6
Masardis•, Maine 243/G3
Masaryktown, Fla. 212/D3
Masasi, Tanzania 115/G6
Masatepe, Nicaragua 154/D5
Masaya, Nicaragua 154/D5
Masbate (prov.), Philippines 82/D4
Masbate, Philippines 82/D4
Masbate (isl.), Philippines 82/D4
Masbate (isl.), Philippines 85/G3
Mascara, Algeria 106/D1
Mascarene (isls.), Mauritius 118/F5
Mascarene (isls.), Réunion 118/F5
Mascoma, N.H. 268/C4
Mascoma (lake), N.H. 268/C4
Mascot, Tenn. 237/O8
Mascota, Mexico 150/G6
Mascotte, Fla. 212/E3
Mascouche, Québec 172/H4
Mascoutah, Ill. 222/D5
Masefield, Sask. 181/D6
Masela (isl.), Indonesia 85/H7
Maseru (cap.), Lesotho 102/E8
Maseru (cap.), Lesotho 118/D5
Mash'Abbe Sade, Israel 65/B6
Mashabi (isl.), Saudi Arabia 59/C4
Masham, England 13/F3
Mashapaug, Conn. 210/G1
Mashapaug (lake), Conn. 210/G1
Mashash, Wadi (dry riv.), Jordan 65/C4
Mashhad (Meshed), Iran 66/L2
Mashike, Japan 81/K2
Mashkel, Hamun-i- (swamp), Pakistan 68/A3
Mashkel, Hamun-i- (swamp), Pakistan 59/H4
Mashkid (riv.), Iran 66/N7
Mashkid (riv.), Iran 59/H4
Mashkid (riv.), Pakistan 59/H4
Mashkid (riv.), Pakistan 68/A3
Mashonaland (reg.), Zimbabwe 118/E3
Mashpee•, Mass. 249/M6
Mashulaville, Miss. 256/G4
Masi-Manimba, D.R. Congo 115/C4
Masindi, Uganda 115/F3
Masinloc, Philippines 82/B3
Masío (cay), Cuba 158/C2
Masira (isl.), Oman 54/G7
Masira (gulf), Oman 59/G6
Masira (isl.), Oman 59/G5
Masisea, Peru 128/E7
Masisi, D.R. Congo 115/E4
Masjed Soleyman, Iran 66/F5
Mask (lake), Ireland 17/C4
Mask, Lough (lake), Ireland 10/B4
Maskell, Nebr. 264/H2
Maskinongé (co.), Québec 172/D3
Maskinongé (county), Québec 174/C3
Maskinongé, Québec 172/E3
Maskinongé (riv.), Québec 172/D3
Masoala (pen.), Madagascar 118/J3
Masoller, Uruguay 145/C2
Mason (isl.), Conn. 210/H3
Mason (co.), Ill. 222/D3
Mason, Ill. 222/E5
Mason (co.), Ky. 237/O3
Mason, Ky. 237/M3
Mason (co.), Mich. 250/C4
Mason, Mich. 250/E6
Mason, Nev. 266/B4
Mason (peak), Nev. 266/F1
Mason (bay), N. Zealand 100/A7
Mason, Ohio 284/B7
Mason, Okla. 288/O3
Mason, Tenn. 237/B10
Mason (co.), Texas 303/E7
Mason, Texas 303/E7
Mason (co.), Wash. 310/B3
Mason (co.), W. Va. 312/B5
Mason, W. Va. 312/B4
Mason, Wis. 317/D3
Mason City, Ill. 222/D3
Mason City, Iowa 229/G2
Mason City, Iowa 188/H2
Mason City, Nebr. 264/E3
Mason Hall, Tenn.237/C8
Mason Springs, Md. 245/K6
Masontown, Pa. 294/C6
Masontown, W. Va. 312/G3
Masonville, Colo. 208/J2
Masonville, Iowa 229/K4
Masonville, N.Y. 276/K6
Masqat (Muscat) (cap.), Oman 59/G5
Massa, Italy 34/C2
Massabesic (lake), N.H. 268/E6
Massac (co.), Ill. 222/E6
Massa-Carrara (prov.), Italy 34/C2
Massachusetts 188/M2
MASSACHUSETTS 249
Massachusetts (bay), Mass. 249/M4
Massachusetts (state), U.S. 146/L5
Massacre (bay), Amer. Samoa 86/N9
Massacre (lake), Nev. 266/B1
Massafra, Italy 34/F4
Massakory, Chad 111/C5
Massa Marittima, Italy 34/C3
Massamgo (Forte República), Angola 115/C5
Massangena, Mozambique 118/E4
Massanutten (mt.), Va. 307/L3
Massapê, Brazil 132/G3
Massapeag, Conn. 210/G3
Massapequa, N.Y. 276/R7
Massapequa Park, N.Y. 276/R7
Massaponax, Va. 307/O4
Massawa, Eritrea 59/C6
Massawa, Eritrea 102/F3
Massawa, Eritrea 111/G4
Massbach, Ill. 222/C1
Mass City, Mich. 250/G1
Massena, Iowa 229/D6
Massena, N.Y. 276/L1
Massénya, Chad 111/C5
Masset, Br. Col. 184/B3
Masset (inlet), Br. Col. 184/A3
Massey, Md. 245/P3
Massey, N. Zealand 100/B1
Massey, Ontario 177/C1
Massies Mill, Va. 307/K5
Massillon, Ala. 195/D6
Massillon, Iowa 229/L5
Massillon, Ohio 284/H4
Massinga, Mozambique 118/F4
Massingir, Mozambique 118/E4
Massive (mt.), Colo. 208/F4
Masson, Québec 172/B4
Massueville, Québec 172/E4
Mastaba, Saudi Arabia 59/C5
Mastens Corners, Del. 245/R5
Masters, Colo. 208/L2
Masterton, N. Zealand 100/E4
Mastic Beach, N.Y. 276/P9
Mastuj, Pakistan 59/K2
Mastung, Pakistan 59/J4
Mastung, Pakistan 68/B3
Mastura, Saudi Arabia 59/C5
Masuda, Japan 81/E6
Masurian (lakes), Poland 47/E2
Masury, Ohio 284/J3
Masvingo, Zimbabwe 118/E4
Masyaf, Syria 63/G5
Matabeleland (reg.), Zimbabwe 118/D3
Matachewan, Ontario 177/J5
Matachewan, Ontario 175/D3
Mata de São João, Brazil 132/G6
Matadi, D.R. Congo 115/B5
Matadi, D.R. Congo 102/D5
Matador, Sask. 181/D5
Matador, Texas 303/D3
Matagalpa, Nicaragua 154/E4
Matagami, Québec 174/B3
Matagami (lake), Québec 174/B3
Matagorda (co.), Texas 303/H9
Matagorda, Texas 303/J9
Matagorda (bay), Texas 188/G5
Matagorda (bay), Texas 303/H9
Matagorda (isl.), Texas 303/H9
Matagorda (pen.), Texas 303/J9
Matagorda Isl. Bombing and Gunnery Range, Texas 303/H9
Matakana (isl.), N. Zealand 100/F2
Matala (dam), Angola 115/B6
Matam, Senegal 106/B5
Matamoras, Pa. 294/N3
Matamoros, Mexico 146/J7
Matamoros, Coahuila, Mexico 150/H4
Matamoros, Tamaulipas, Mexico 150/L4
Matane (co.), Québec 172/B1
Matane (county), Québec 174/D3
Matane, Québec 172/B1
Matane, Québec 174/D3
Matane (riv.), Québec 172/B1
Matane Prov. Park, Québec 172/B1
Matanuska (riv.), Alaska 196/C1
Matanza, Colombia 126/D4
Matanzas (prov.), Cuba 158/D1
Matanzas, Cuba 146/K7
Matanzas, Cuba 158/D1
Matanzas, Cuba 156/B2
Matanzas (bay), Cuba 158/C1
Matanzas (inlet), Fla. 212/E2
Mata Palacio, Dom. Rep. 158/F6
Matapalo (cape), C. Rica 154/F6
Matapan (Tainaron) (cape), Greece 45/F7
Matapédia (county), Québec 174/D3
Matapédia (co.), Québec 172/B2
Matapédia, Québec 172/B2
Matapédia (lake), Québec 172/B1
Matapédia (riv.), Québec 172/B2
Mataquito (riv.), Chile 138/A10
Matara, Sri Lanka 68/E7
Mataram, Indonesia 85/F7
Matarani, Peru 120/B4
Matarani, Peru 128/F11
Mataranka, North. Terr. 93/C3
Matarinao (bay), Philippines 82/E5
Mataró, Spain 33/H2
Matatiele, S. Africa 118/D6
Matatindoc (pt.), Philippines 82/D6
Mataura, N. Zealand 100/B7
Mataura (riv.), N. Zealand 100/B6
Mata Utu (cap.), Wallis and Futuna 87/J7
Matawai, N. Zealand 100/F3
Matawan, Minn. 255/E7
Matawan, N.J. 273/E3
Matawin (lake), Québec 172/D3
Matawin (riv.), Québec 172/C3
Mateare, Nicaragua 154/D4
Mateguá, Bolivia 136/D3
Matehuala, Mexico 150/J5
Matelot, Trin. & Tob. 161/B10
Matera (prov.), Italy 34/F4
Matera, Italy 34/F4
Maternillos (pt.), Cuba 158/H2
Mátészalka, Hungary 41/G3
Matetsi, Zimbabwe 118/D3
Mateur, Tunisia 106/F1
Matewan, W. Va. 312/B7
Matfield Green, Kansas 232/F3
Mather, Manitoba 179/C5
Mather, Wis. 317/F7
Mather A.F.B., Calif. 204/C8
Matherville, Ill. 222/C2
Matherville, Miss. 256/G7
Matheson, Colo. 208/M4
Matheson, Ontario 177/K5
Matheson Island, Manitoba 179/E3
Mathews, Ala. 195/F6
Mathews (lake), Calif. 204/E11
Mathews, La. 238/J7
Mathews (co.), Va. 307/R6
Mathews, Va. 307/R6
Mathias, W. Va. 312/J5
Mathinna, Tasmania 99/E3
Mathis, Texas 303/G9
Mathis, Texas 303/G9
Mathiston, Miss. 256/F3
Mathoura, N.S. Wales 97/C4
Mathura, India 68/D3
Mati, Philippines 85/H4
Mati, Philippines 82/F7
Matías Romero, Mexico 150/M8
Matinenda (lake), Ontario 177/B1
Matinicus, Maine 243/F8
Matinicus Rock (isl.), Maine 243/F8
Matlock, England 10/F4
Matlock, England 13/J2
Matlock, Iowa 229/A2
Matlock, Wash. 310/B3
Matoaca, Va. 307/N6
Matoaka, W. Va. 312/D8
Matochkin Shar (str.), Russia 48/F2
Mato Grosso (state), Brazil 132/B6
Mato Grosso, Brazil 120/D4
Mato Grosso, Brazil 132/B6
Mato Grosso (plat.), Brazil 120/D4
Mato Grosso, Planalto de (plat.), Brazil 132/B6
Mato Grosso do Sul (state), Brazil 132/C7
Matopos, Zimbabwe 118/D4
Matosinhos, Portugal 33/B2
Matoury, Fr. Guiana 131/E3
Mátra (mts.), Hungary 41/E3
Matrah, Oman 54/G7
Matrah, Oman 59/G5
Matrei in Osttirol, Austria 41/B3
Matruh, Egypt 59/A3
Matsqui, Br. Col. 184/L3
Matsu (Mazu) (isl.), China 77/K6
Matsubara, Japan 81/H8
Matsue, Japan 81/F6
Matsumae, Japan 81/J3
Matsumoto, Japan 81/H5
Matsusaka, Japan 81/H6
Matsuto, Japan 81/H5
Matsuyama, Japan 81/F7
Matsuyama, Japan 54/P6
Matt, Switzerland 39/H3
Mattabesset (riv.), Conn. 210/E2
Mattagami (riv.), Ontario 175/D3
Mattagami (riv.), Ontario 177/J5
Mattamiscontis (lake), Maine 243/F4
Mattamuskeet (lake), N.C. 281/S3
Mattapan, Mass. 249/C7
Mattapoisett, Mass. 249/L6
Mattapoisett•, Mass. 249/L6
Mattaponi, Va. 307/P5
Mattaponi (riv.), Va. 307/O5
Mattaponi Ind. Res., Va. 307/P5
Mattawa, Ont. 162/J6
Mattawa, Ontario 177/F1
Mattawa, Ontario 175/E3
Mattawa, Wash. 310/F4
Mattawamkeag•, Maine 243/G5
Mattawamkeag (lake), Maine 243/G4
Mattawamkeag (riv.), Maine 243/G4
Mattawan, Mich. 250/D6
Mattawana, Pa. 294/G5
Mattawoman (creek), Md. 245/K6
Matterhorn (mt.), Switzerland 39/E4
Mattersburg, Austria 41/D3
Matteson, Ill. 222/B6

Milan 409

Meridian, Ga. 217/K8
Meridian, Idaho 220/B6
Meridian, Miss. 146/K6
Meridian, Miss. 188/J4
Meridian, Miss. 256/G6
Meridian, N.Y. 276/G4
Meridian, Okla. 288/M3
Meridian, Texas 303/G6
Meridian Naval Air Sta., Miss. 256/G5
Meridianville, Ala. 195/F1
Merigold, Miss. 256/C3
Merigomish, Nova Scotia 168/F3
Merigomish (harb.), Nova Scotia 168/F3
Merimbula, N.S. Wales 97/F5
Merín (lag.), Uruguay 145/F4
Merino, Colo. 208/N2
Merino, Victoria 97/A5
Merino Jarpa (isl.), Chile 138/D7
Merinos, Uruguay 145/C3
Merino Village, Mass. 249/G4
Merion Station, Pa. 294/M6
Merir (isl.), Belau 87/D5
Meriwether (co.), Ga. 217/C4
Meriwether Lewis Park, Natchez Trace Pkwy., Tenn. 237/G10
Merj 'Uyun, Lebanon 63/F6
Mérk, Hungary 41/G3
Merkel, Texas 303/E5
Merksem, Belgium 27/E6
Merksplas, Belgium 27/F6
Merlin, Ontario 177/B5
Merlin, Oreg. 291/D5
Merlo, Argentina 143/G7
Mermentau, La. 238/E6
Mermentau (riv.), La. 238/E7
Merna, Nebr. 264/E3
Merna, Wyo. 319/B3
Meroe (ruins), Sudan 111/F4
Merom, Ind. 227/B6
Merowe, Sudan 111/F4
Merowe, Sudan 59/B6
Merredin, W. Australia 88/B6
Merredin, W. Australia 92/B5
Merri (riv.), Victoria 88/L7
Merriam, Ind. 227/G2
Merriam, Kansas 232/H3
Merrick (co.), Nebr. 264/F3
Merrick, N.Y. 276/R7
Merrick (mt.), Scotland 15/D5
Merrickville, Ontario 177/J3
Merricourt, N. Dak. 282/N7
Merrifield, Minn. 255/D4
Merrifield (bay), Newf. 166/B2
Merrifield, N. Dak. 282/R4
Merrifield, Va. 307/S3
Merrill (pass), Alaska 196/H2
Merrill, Iowa 229/A3
Merrill, Mich. 250/E5
Merrill, Miss. 256/G9
Merrill, N.Y. 276/N1
Merrill, Oreg. 291/F5
Merrill, Wis. 317/G5
Merrillan, Wis. 317/E7
Merrillville, Ga. 217/E9
Merrillville, Ind. 227/C2
Merrimac, Ky. 237/L6
Merrimac•, Mass. 249/L1
Merrimac, W. Va. 312/B7
Merrimac, Wis. 317/G9
Merrimack (riv.), Mass. 249/K1
Merrimack (co.), N.H. 268/D5
Merrimack•, N.H. 268/D6
Merrimack (riv.), N.H. 268/D5
Merrimacport, Mass. 249/L1
Merriman, Nebr. 264/C2
Merrimon, N.C. 281/R5
Merrionette Park, Ill. 222/B6
Merritt, Br. Col. 162/D5
Merritt, Br. Col. 184/G5
Merritt (isl.), Fla. 212/F3
Merritt, Ill. 222/C4
Merritt, Mich. 250/D4
Merritt (res.), Nebr. 264/D2
Merritt, Wash. 310/E3
Merritt Island, Fla. 212/F3
Merriwa, N.S. Wales 97/F3
Merriwagga, N.S. Wales 97/C3
Merriweather, Mich. 250/F1
Mer Rouge, La. 238/G1
Merrow, Conn. 210/F1
Merry Hill, N.C. 281/R2
Merrymeeting (lake), N.H. 268/E5
Merry Oaks, N.C. 281/L3
Merryville, La. 238/D5
Mersa Fatma, Eritrea 111/H5
Mersá Matrûh, Egypt 111/E1
Mersá Matrûh, Egypt 102/E1
Mersch, Luxembourg 27/J9
Mersea (dist.), England 13/J6
Merseburg, Germany 22/D3
Mersey (riv.), England 10/F2
Mersey (riv.), England 13/G2
Mersey (riv.), Nova Scotia 168/C4
Mersey (riv.), Tasmania 99/C3
Merseyside (co.), England 13/G2
Mershon, Ga. 217/H8
Mersin, Turkey 63/F4
Mersin, Turkey 59/B2
Mersin, Turkey 54/E6
Mersing, Malaysia 72/E7
Mērsrags, Latvia 53/B2
Mertert, Luxembourg 27/J9
Merthyr Tydfil, Wales 13/A6
Merthyr Tydfil, Wales 10/E5
Mértola, Portugal 33/C4
Merton, England 10/B5
Merton, England 13/H8
Merton, Wis. 317/K1
Mertz Glacier Tongue, Ant. 5/C8
Mertzon, Texas 303/C6
Mertztown, Pa. 294/L4
Meru, Kenya 115/G3
Meru (mt.), Tanzania 115/G4
Merv (Mary), Russia 48/F8
Merville, Br. Col 184/E5
Mervin, Sask. 181/C2
Merwin, Mo. 261/C6
Merwin (lake), Wash. 310/C5
Merzifon, Turkey 63/F2
Merzig, Germany 22/B4
Mesa, Ariz. 146/G6
Mesa, Ariz. 188/D4
Mesa, Ariz. 198/D5
Mesa (co.), Colo. 208/B5
Mesa, Colo. 208/C4
Mesa, Idaho 220/B5
Mesa, Miss. 256/D8
Mesa, Wash. 310/G4
Mesabi (range), Minn. 255/E3
Mesa Bolívar, Venezuela 124/C3
Mesachie Lake, Br. Col. 184/J3
Mesa del Seri, Mexico 150/D2
Mesagne, Italy 34/G4
Mesai (riv.), Colombia 126/D7
Mesará (gulf), Greece 45/G8
Mesa Verde National Park, Colo. 208/C8
Mesa Verde Nat'l Park, Colo. 208/C8
Mescalero, N. Mex. 274/D5
Mescalero (ridge), N. Mex. 274/F6
Mescalero (valley), N. Mex. 274/F5
Mescalero Apache Ind. Res., N. Mex. 274/D5
Meschede, Germany 22/C3
Mesena, Ga. 217/G4
Meservey, Iowa 229/G3
Meshed, Iran 54/G6
Meshed, Iran 66/L2
Meshed, Iran 59/H2
Meshed-i-Sar (Babol Sar), Iran 66/H2
Meshik, Alaska 196/G3
Meshoppen, Pa. 294/L2
Meshra er Req, Sudan 111/E6
Mesic, N.C. 281/R4
Mesick, Mich. 250/D4
Mesilla, N. Mex. 274/C6
Mesilla Park, N. Mex. 274/C6
Mesita, Colo. 208/H8
Meskanaw, Sask. 181/F3
Meskene, Syria 59/C2
Meskene, Syria 63/H5
Mesocco, Switzerland 39/H4
Mesolóngion, Greece 45/E6
Mesopotamia (reg.), Iraq 66/B3
Mesopotamia (reg.), Iraq 59/D3
Mesopotamia, Ohio 284/J3
Mesquite, Nev. 266/G6
Mesquite, N. Mex. 274/C6
Mesquite, Texas 303/H2
Messancy, Belgium 27/H9
Messina (prov.), Italy 34/E5
Messina, Italy 34/E5
Messina, Italy 7/F5
Messina (str.), Italy 34/E6
Messina, S. Africa 118/D4
Messines, Québec 172/B3
Messini, Greece 45/E7
Messini (gulf), Greece 45/E7
Mesta (riv.), Bulgaria 45/F5
Mestre, Italy 34/D2
Mesudiye, Turkey 63/F4
Meta (riv.) 120/B2
Meta (dept.), Colombia 126/D6
Meta (riv.), Colombia 126/D6
Meta, Ky. 237/S5
Meta, Mo. 261/H6
Meta (riv.), Venezuela 124/E4
Metabetchouan, Québec 172/F1
Métabetchouane (riv.), Québec 172/F1
Metairie, La. 238/O4
Metaline, Wash. 310/H2
Metaline Falls, Wash. 310/H2
Metamma, Ethiopia 111/G5
Metamora, Ill. 222/D3
Metamora, Ind. 227/G6
Metamora, Mich. 250/F6
Metamora, Ohio 284/C2
Metán, Argentina 143/D2
Metangula, Mozambique 118/F2
Metapán, El Salvador 154/C3
Métascouac (lake), Québec 172/F2
Metasville, Ga. 217/G3
Metauro (riv.), Italy 34/D3
Metcalf, Ga. 217/E9
Metcalf, Ill. 222/F4
Metcalfe (co.), Ky. 237/K7
Metcalfe, Miss. 256/B4
Metcalfe, Ontario 177/J2
Metchin (riv.), Newf. 166/B3
Metchosin, Br. Col. 184/K4
Metea, Ind. 227/E3
Metedeconk (riv.), N.J. 273/E3
Meteghan, Nova Scotia 168/B4
Meteghan Centre, Nova Scotia 168/B4
Meteghan River, Nova Scotia 168/B4
Meteor (crater), Ariz. 198/E3
Metepec, Mexico 150/M2
Methlick, Scotland 15/F3
Methow, Wash. 310/E2
Methow (riv.), Wash. 310/E2
Methuen•, Mass. 249/K2
Methven, N. Zealand 100/C5
Methven, Scotland 15/E4
Metica (riv.), Colombia 126/D6
Metigoshe (lake), N. Dak. 282/K2
Metinic (isl.), Maine 243/E8
Metinota, Sask. 181/C2
Metiskow, Alberta 182/E3
Métis-sur-Mer, Québec 172/A1
Metlakatla, Alaska 196/N2
Metlakatla, Br. Col. 184/B3
Metlatonoc, Mexico 150/K8
Metlili Chaamba, Algeria 106/E2
Meto (bayou), Ark. 202/H5
Metolius, Oreg. 291/F3
Metolius (riv.), Oreg. 291/F3
Metompkin (inlet), Va. 307/T5
Metompkin (isl.), Va. 307/T5
Metonga (lake), Wis. 317/J4
Metropolis, Ill. 222/E6
Metropolitan, Mich. 250/A3
Métsovon, Greece 45/E6
Mettawa, Ill. 222/B4
Mettawee (riv.), Vt. 268/A5
Metter, Ga. 217/H6
Mettet, Belgium 27/F8
Mettler, Calif. 204/G8
Metu, Ethiopia 111/G6
Metu, Ethiopia 115/G2
Metuchen, N.J. 273/E2
Metula, Israel 65/D1
Metz, France 7/E4
Metz, France 28/G3
Metz, Ind. 227/H1
Metz, Mo. 261/C6
Metz, W. Va. 312/F3
Metzger, Oreg. 291/A2
Metzingen, Germany 22/C4
Meudon, France 28/A2
Meulaboh, Indonesia 85/B5
Meulebeke, Belgium 27/C7
Meung-sur-Loire, France 28/D4
Meurthe-et-Moselle (dept.), France 28/G3
Meuse (riv.), Belgium 27/F8
Meuse (dept.), France 28/F3
Meuse (riv.), France 28/F3
Meuselwitz, Germany 22/E3
Mexia, Ala. 195/D8
Mexia, Texas 303/H6
Mexiana (isl.), Brazil 132/D2
Mexicali, Mexico 150/B1
Mexicali, Mexico 146/G6
Mexican Hat, Utah 304/E6
Mexican Springs, N. Mex. 274/A3
Mexico 2/D4
Mexico 146/H7
MEXICO 150
Mexico (gulf) 188/J5
Mexico (gulf) 2/E4
Mexico (gulf) 146/K7
Mexico (gulf), Ala. 195/E10
Mexico (gulf), Cuba 158/A1
Mexico (gulf), Fla. 212/C4
Mexico, Ind. 227/E3
Mexico, Ky. 237/E6
Mexico (gulf), La. 238/F8
Mexico, Maine 243/B6
Mexico•, Maine 243/B6
México (state), Mexico 150/K7
Mexico (gulf), Mexico 150/N4
Mexico, Mo. 261/J4
Mexico, N.Y. 276/H4
Mexico, Pa. 294/H4
Mexico (gulf), Texas 303/K9
Mexico Beach, Fla. 212/D6
Mexico City (cap.), Mexico 150/L1
Mexico City (cap.), Mexico 146/J7
Mexico City (cap.), Mexico 2/E5
Meyadin, Syria 59/C3
Meyadin, Syria 63/J5
Meybod, Iran 66/J4
Meydani, Ras-e (cape), Iran 59/G4
Meydani, Ras-e (cape), Iran 66/L8
Meyer, Iowa 229/H2
Meyers Chuck, Alaska 196/N2
Meyersdale, Pa. 294/E6
Meyers Lake, Ohio 284/H4
Meyerton, S. Africa 118/H7
Meymaneh, Afghanistan 68/A1
Meymaneh, Afghanistan 54/H6
Meymaneh, Afghanistan 59/H2
Meyrin, Switzerland 39/B4
Meyronne, Sask. 181/E6
Mezcala (riv.), Mexico 150/J8
Mezen', Russia 4/C7
Mezen', Russia 7/J2
Mezen', Russia 48/E3
Mezen', Russia 52/F1
Mezen' (bay), Russia 52/F1
Mezen' (riv.), Russia 48/E3
Mezen' (riv.), Russia 52/G1
Mézenc (mt.), France 28/E5
Mezhdurechenskiy, Russia 48/G4
Mezhdusharskiy (isl.), Russia 52/G1
Meziadin (lake), Br. Col. 184/C2
Mézin, France 28/D5
Mezőberény, Hungary 41/F3
Mezőcsát, Hungary 41/F3
Mezőfalva, Hungary 41/E3
Mezőhegyes, Hungary 41/F3
Mezőkovácsháza, Hungary 41/F3
Mezőkövesd, Hungary 41/F3
Mezőszilas, Hungary 41/E3
Mezőtúr, Hungary 41/F3
Mezquital, Mexico 150/G5
Mezquital (riv.), Mexico 150/G5
Mhor, Loch (lake), Scotland 15/D3
Mhow, India 68/D4
Miacatlán, Mexico 150/K2
Miahuatlán de Porfirio Díaz, Mexico 150/L8
Miajadas, Spain 33/D3
Miami, Ariz. 198/E5
Miami, Fla. 188/K5
Miami, Fla. 146/K7
Miami, Fla. 212/B5
Miami (canal), Fla. 212/F5
Miami (riv.), Fla. 212/B5
Miami (co.), Ind. 227/E3
Miami, Ind. 227/E3
Miami (co.), Kansas 232/H3
Miami, Manitoba 179/D5
Miami, Mo. 261/F4
Miami, N. Mex. 274/E2
Miami (co.), Ohio 284/B5
Miami, Okla. 288/S1
Miami, Texas 303/D2
Miami, U.S. 2/F4
Miami Beach, Fla. 188/L5
Miami Beach, Fla. 212/C5
Miami Lakes, Fla. 212/B4
Miamisburg, Ohio 284/B6
Miami Shores, Fla. 212/B4
Miami Springs, Fla. 212/B5
Miamitown, Ohio 284/A9
Miamiville, Ohio 284/D9
Miandowab, Iran 66/E2
Miandrivazo, Madagascar 118/G3
Mianeh, Iran 59/E2
Mianeh, Iran 66/E2
Mianus, Conn. 210/A4
Mianus (riv.), Conn. 210/A4
Mianwali, Pakistan 68/C2
Mianwali, Pakistan 59/K3
Mianyang, Hubei, China 77/H5
Mianyang, Sichuan, China 77/G5
Mianzhu, China 77/F5
Miass, Russia 48/G4
Miastko, Poland 47/C2
Miazal, Ecuador 128/D4
Mica (dam), Br. Col. 184/H4
Mica, Wash. 310/H3
Mica Creek, Br. Col. 184/H4
Micanopy, Fla. 212/D2
Micawber, Okla. 288/N3
Micay, Colombia 126/B6
Micco, Fla. 212/F4
Miccosukee, Fla. 212/B1
Miccosukee (lake), Fla. 212/B1
Michael, I. of Man 13/C3
Michael (lake), Newf. 166/C3
Michalovce, Slovakia 41/G2
Michaud (pt.), Nova Scotia 168/H3
Michelago, N.S. Wales 97/E4
Michelson (mt.), Alaska 196/K1
Michelstadt, Germany 22/C4
Miches, Dom. Rep. 158/F6
Michiana, Mich. 250/C7
Michiana Shores, Ind. 227/D1
Michichi, Alberta 182/D4
Michie, Tenn. 237/E10
Michigamme, Mich. 250/B2
Michigamme (lake), Mich. 250/A2
Michigamme (res.), Mich. 250/B2
Michigamme (riv.), Mich. 250/A2
Michigan 188/J1
MICHIGAN 250/80
Michigan (lake) 188/J2
Michigan (lake), Ill. 222/F1
Michigan (lake), Ind. 227/C1
Michigan (lake), Mich. 250/B5
Michigan, N. Dak. 282/O3
Michigan (state), U.S. 146/K5
Michigan (lake), U.S. 146/K5
Michigan (isl.), Wis. 317/F2
Michigan (lake), Wis. 317/M9
Michigan Bar, Calif. 204/C8
Michigan Center, Mich. 250/E6
Michigan City, Ind. 227/C1
Michigan City, Miss. 256/F1
Michigantown, Ind. 227/E4
Michigan Valley, Kansas 232/G3
Michipicoten (isl.), Ontario 177/H5
Michipicoten (isl.), Ontario 175/C3
Michipicoten River, Ontario 177/H5
Michipicoten River, Ontario 177/C3
Michoacán (state), Mexico 150/H7
Michurin, Bulgaria 45/H4
Michurinsk, Russia 48/E4
Michurinsk, Russia 52/F4
Mickelton, N.J. 273/C4
Micotrin (mt.), Dominica 161/F6
Micoua, Québec 174/D3
Micoud, St. Lucia 161/G6
Micro, N.C. 281/N3
Micronesia, Federated States of 2/S5
Micronesia, Federated States of 87/F5
Micronesia (reg.), Pacific 87/E4
Midale, Sask. 181/H6
Midas, Nev. 266/E1
Middelburg, Netherlands 27/C6
Middelburg, Cape Prov., S. Africa 118/D6
Middelburg, Transvaal, S. Africa 118/D5
Middelfart, Denmark 21/C7
Middelfart, Denmark 18/G9
Middelharnis, Netherlands 27/E5
Middelkerke, Belgium 27/B6
Middelvlei, S. Africa 118/G7
Middenmeer, Netherlands 27/F3
Middle (riv.), Conn. 210/F1
Middle (pt.), Fla. 212/E6
Middle, Iowa 229/K5
Middle (riv.), Minn. 255/B2
Middle Alkali (lake), Calif. 204/E2
Middle Andaman (isl.), India 68/G6
Middle Arm, Newf. 166/C4
Middle Atlas (ranges), Morocco 106/C2
Middle Bass, Ohio 284/E2
Middle Bass (isl.), Ohio 284/E2
Middle Beaver (creek), Colo. 208/P4
Middleboro, Mass. 249/L5
Middleboro•, Mass. 249/L5
Middleboro (McKean), Pa. 294/B2
Middlebourne, W. Va. 312/E3
Middlebranch, Ohio 284/H4
Middlebro, Manitoba 179/G5
Middlebrook, Va. 307/K4
Middleburg, Fla. 212/E1
Middleburg, Ky. 237/M6
Middleburg, Md. 245/K2
Middleburg, N.C. 281/N2
Middleburg, Ohio 284/C5
Middleburg, Pa. 294/H4
Middleburg, Va. 307/N3
Middleburgh, N.Y. 276/M5
Middleburg Heights, Ohio 284/G10
Middlebury•, Conn. 210/C2
Middlebury, Ind. 227/F1
Middlebury, Vt. 268/A3
Middlebury•, Vt. 268/A3
Middlebury Center, Pa. 294/H2
Middlebury Gap (pass), Vt. 268/B4
Middlebush, N.J. 273/D3
Middlechurch, Manitoba 179/E4
Middle Concho (riv.), Texas 303/C6
Middledam, Maine 243/B6
Middle Falls, N.Y. 276/O4
Middlefield•, Conn. 210/E2
Middlefield•, Mass. 249/B3
Middlefield, Ohio 284/H3
Middle Fork (peak), Idaho 220/D5
Middlefork, Ind. 227/E4
Middle Fork, Powder (riv.), Wyo. 319/F2
Middlegate, Norfolk Is. 88/L6
Middle Granville, N.Y. 276/O4
Middlegrove, Ill. 222/C3
Middle Grove, Mo. 261/H4
Middle Haddam, Conn. 210/E2
Middle Harbour (creek), N.S. Wales 88/K3
Middle Harbour (creek), N.S. Wales 97/J3
Middle Hope, N.Y. 276/M7
Middle Inlet, Wis. 317/K5
Middle Lake, Sask. 181/F3
Middle Loch (inlet), Hawaii 218/A3
Middle Loup (riv.), Nebr. 264/D3
Middlemarch, N. Zealand 100/B6
Middle Musquodoboit, Nova Scotia 168/E3
Middle Patuxent (riv.), Md. 245/L3
Middle Piney (creek), Wyo. 319/B3
Middle Point, Ohio 284/B4
Middleport, N.Y. 276/C4
Middleport, Ohio 284/F7
Middleport, Pa. 294/K4
Middle River, Md. 245/N3
Middle River, Minn. 255/B2
Middle River, Nova Scotia 168/G2
Middle Saranac (lake), N.Y. 276/M2
Middlesboro, Ky. 237/O7
Middlesboro, Ky. 188/K3
Middlesbrough, England 7/D3
Middlesbrough, England 13/F3
Middlesbrough, England 10/F3
Middlesex (co.), Conn. 210/E3
Middlesex (co.), Mass. 249/J3
Middlesex (co.), N.J. 273/E3
Middlesex, N.J. 273/E2
Middlesex, N.Y. 276/F5
Middlesex, N.C. 281/N3
Middlesex (county), Ontario 177/C4
Middlesex•, Vt. 268/B3
Middlesex (co.), Va. 307/R5
Middle Stewiacke, Nova Scotia 168/E3
Middleton (isl.), Alaska 196/J3
Middleton, England 13/H2
Middleton, England 10/G2
Middleton, Ga. 217/G2
Middleton, Idaho 220/B6
Middleton•, Mass. 249/K2
Middleton, Mich. 250/E5
Middleton•, N.H. 268/E5
Middleton, Nova Scotia 168/C4
Middleton, Tenn. 237/D10
Middleton, Wis. 317/G9
Middletown, Calif. 204/C5
Middletown, Conn. 210/E2
Middletown, Del. 245/R3
Middletown, Ill. 222/D3
Middletown, Ind. 227/F4
Middletown, Iowa 229/L7
Middletown, Ky. 237/L2
Middletown, Md. 245/J3
Middletown, Mo. 261/J4
Middletown•, N.J. 273/E3
Middletown, N.Y. 276/L8
Middletown, N.C. 281/T4
Middletown, N. Ireland 17/H3
Middletown, Ohio 284/A6
Middletown, Pa. 294/J5
Middletown•, R.I. 249/J6
Middletown, Va. 307/M2
Middletown Springs•, Vt. 268/A5
Middle Valley, N.J. 273/D2
Middleville, Mich. 250/D6
Middleville, N.J. 273/D1
Middleville, N.Y. 276/K4
Middleville, Ontario 177/H2
Middle Water, Texas 303/B2
Middleway, W. Va. 312/K4
Middlewich, England 13/H2
Middlewich, England 10/G2
Middlewood, Nova Scotia 168/D4
Midfield, Ala. 195/E4
Midgic Station, New Bruns. 170/F3
Mid Glamorgan, Wales 13/D6
Midhurst, Ontario 177/E3
Midian (dist.), Saudi Arabia 59/C4
Midkiff, W. Va. 312/B6
Midland, Ark. 202/B3
Midland, Ind. 227/C6
Midland, La. 238/F6
Midland, Md. 245/C2
Midland (co.), Mich. 250/E5
Midland, Mich. 250/E5
Midland, N.C. 281/J4
Midland, Ohio 284/C7
Midland, Ontario 177/D3
Midland, Oreg. 291/F5
Midland, Pa. 294/A4
Midland, S. Dak. 298/G5
Midland, Tex. 188/F4
Midland (co.), Texas 303/B6
Midland, Texas 303/C6
Midland, Va. 307/N3
Midland City, Ala. 195/H8
Midland Park, N.J. 273/B1
Midlandvale, Alberta 182/D4
Midleton, Ireland 17/E8
Midleton, Ireland 10/B5
Midlothian, Ill. 222/B6
Midlothian (trad. co.), Scotland 15/B5
Midlothian, Texas 303/G5
Midlothian, Va. 307/N6
Midnapore, India 68/F4
Midnight, Miss. 256/C4
Midnight (lake), Sask. 181/C2
Midongy Atsimo, Madagascar 118/H4
Midvale, Idaho 220/B5
Midvale, Ohio 284/H5
Midvale, Utah 304/B3
Midville, Ga. 217/H5
Midway (isls.) 188/E6
Midway, Ala. 195/H6
Midway, Br. Col. 184/H6
Midway, Del. 245/T6
Midway, Fla. 212/B1
Midway, Ga. 217/K7
Midway, Ind. 227/C8
Midway, Ky. 237/M4
Midway (Sedalia), Ohio 284/D6
Midway, Pa. 294/B5
Midway, Tenn. 237/P8
Midway (isls.), U.S. 87/J3
Midway, Utah 304/C3
Midway City, Calif. 204/D11
Midway Park, N.C. 281/O5
Midwest, Wyo. 319/F2
Midwest City, Okla. 288/M4
Midyat, Turkey 63/J4
Midye, Turkey 63/C2
Mid Yell, Scotland 15/G2
Midzhur (mt.), Bulgaria 45/F4
Midzhur (mt.), Yugoslavia 45/F4
Mie (pref.), Japan 81/H6
Miechów, Poland 47/E3
Międzychód, Poland 47/B2
Międzylesie, Poland 47/C3
Międzyrzec Podlaski, Poland 47/F3
Międzyrzecz, Poland 47/B2
Mielec, Poland 47/E3
Mier, Ind. 227/F3
Mier, Mexico 150/K3
Miercurea Ciuc, Romania 45/G2
Mieres, Spain 33/D1
Miesso, Ethiopia 111/H6
Miesso, Ethiopia 102/G4
Miesville, Minn. 255/F6
Miette, Alberta 182/B3
Mifflin, Ohio 284/F4
Mifflin (co.), Pa. 294/G4
Mifflin, Pa. 294/H4
Mifflin, Wis. 317/F10
Mifflinburg, Pa. 294/H4
Mifflintown, Pa. 294/H4
Miflin, Ala. 195/C10
Migdal, Israel 65/C2
Migdal Ha 'Emeq, Israel 65/C2
Mignon, Ala. 195/F4
Migori, Kenya 115/F4
Miguel Alves, Brazil 132/F4
Miguel Auza, Mexico 150/H4
Miguel de la Borda, Panama 154/G6
Miguelete, Uruguay 145/B5
Miguel Riglos, Argentina 143/D4
Migues, Uruguay 145/C6
Mihalıççık, Turkey 63/D3
Mihara, Japan 81/F6
Mikado, Mich. 250/F4
Mikado, Sask. 181/J4
Mikana, Wis. 317/C4
Mikhaylovgrad, Bulgaria 45/F4
Mikhaylovka, Russia52/F4
Mikhmoret, Israel 65/B3
Miki, Japan 81/H7
Mikínai, Greece 45/F7
Mikkalo, Oreg. 291/G2
Mikkeli (prov.), Finland 18/P6
Mikkeli, Finland 18/P6
Mikkwa (riv.), Alberta 182/B5
Miklów, Poland 47/B4
Míkonos (isl.), Greece 45/G7
Mikulov, Czech Rep. 41/D2
Mikumi Nat'l Park, Tanzania 115/G5
Mikun', Russia52/H2
Mikuni, Japan 81/G5
Milaca, Minn. 255/E5
Milagro, Ecuador 120/A3
Milagro, Ecuador 128/C4
Milagros, Philippines 82/D4
Milam (co.), Texas 303/H7
Milam, Texas 303/L6
Milam, W. Va. 312/H5
Milan, Ga. 217/G6
Milan, Ill. 222/C2
Milan, Ind. 227/G6
Milan (prov.), Italy 34/B2
Milan, Italy 2/K3
Milan, Italy 7/E4
Milan, Italy 34/B2
Milan, Kansas 232/E4
Milan, Mich. 250/F6
Milan, Minn. 255/C5
Milan, Mo. 261/F2
Milan•, N.H. 268/E2

Monhegan 411

Mirnyy, Russia 54/N3
Mirpur, Pakistan 68/C2
Mirpur Khas, Pakistan 68/B3
Mirror, Alberta 182/D3
Mirror Lake, N.H. 268/E4
Mirtóön (sea), Greece 45/F7
Miryang, S. Korea 81/D6
Mirzapur-cum-Vindhyachal, India 68/E4
Misamis Occidental (prov.), Philippines 82/D6
Misamis Oriental (prov.), Philippines 82/E6
Misantla, Mexico 150/P1
Misawa, Japan 81/K3
Miscou (isl.), New Bruns. 170/F1
Miscou (pt.), New Bruns. 170/F1
Miscou Centre, New Bruns. 170/F1
Miscouche, Pr. Edward I. 168/D2
Miscou Harbour, New Bruns. 170/F1
Misenheimer, N.C. 281/J4
Misery (bay), Mich. 250/G1
Misery (riv.), Mich. 250/G1
Misery (mt.), St. Kitts & Nevis 161/C10
Misgar, Pakistan 68/C1
Misha'ab, Ras (cape), Saudi Arabia 59/E4
Mishagua, Peru 128/F8
Mishan, China 77/M2
Mishaum (pt.), Mass. 249/L6
Mishawaka, Ind. 227/E1
Misheguk (mt.), Alaska 196/F1
Mishicot, Wis. 317/L7
Mishmar Hanegev, Israel 65/B5
Mishmar Hayarden, Israel 65/D1
Mishmi (hills), India 68/H3
Misima (isl.), Papua N.G. 85/C8
Misiones (prov.), Argentina 143/F2
Misiones (dept.), Paraguay 144/D5
Miskitos (cays), Nicaragua 1154/F3
Miskolc, Hungary 41/F2
Miskolc, Hungary 7/G4
Misool (isl.), Indonesia 85/J6
Mispec, New Bruns. 170/E3
Mispillion (riv.), Del. 245/S5
Misquah (hills), Minn. 255/F2
Missanable, Ontario 177/J5
Missanable, Ontario 175/D3
Missaukee (co.), Mich. 250/D4
Missi Falls, Manitoba 179/J2
Missinaibi (riv.), Ont. 162/H6
Missinaibi (lake), Ontario 175/D3
Missinaibi (riv.), Ontario 175/D2
Mission, Br. Col 184/L3
Mission, Kansas 232/H2
Mission (range), Mont. 262/C3
Mission, S. Dak. 298/H7
Mission, Texas 303/F11
Mission Beach, Alberta 182/C3
Mission City, Br. Col. 184/L3
Mission Hill, S. Dak. 298/P8
Mission Ridge, S. Dak. 298/H4
Mission Viejo, Calif. 204/D11
Missisa (lake), Ontario 175/D2
Missisquoi (co.), Québec 172/D4
Missisquoi (riv.), Vt. 268/B2
Mississagi (riv.), Ontario 177/A1
Mississagi (str.), Ontario 177/A2
Mississaugua, Ontario 177/J4
Mississinewa (lake), Ind. 227/F3
Mississinewa (riv.), Ind. 227/F3
Mississippi 188/J4
MISSISSIPPI 256
Mississippi (riv.) 188/H4
Mississippi (sound), Ala. 195/B10
Mississippi (co.), Ark. 202/K2
Mississippi (riv.), Ark. 202/H7
Mississippi (riv.), Ill. 222/C5
Mississippi (riv.), Iowa 229/L7
Mississippi (riv.), Ky. 237/A10
Mississippi (delta), La. 146/K7
Mississippi (delta), La. 188/J5
Mississippi (delta), La. 238/M8
Mississippi (riv.), La. 238/H3
Mississippi (sound), La. 238/M6
Mississippi (riv.), Minn. 255/D4
Mississippi (riv.), Miss. 256/A8
Mississippi (sound), Miss. 256/G10
Mississippi (co.), Mo. 261/O9
Mississippi (riv.), Mo. 261/L4
Mississippi (lake), Ontario 177/H2
Mississippi (riv.), Tenn. 237/A10
Mississippi (state), U.S. 146/K6
Mississippi (riv.), U.S. 2/E4
Mississippi (riv.), U.S. 146/J6
Mississippi (riv.), Wis. 317/D10
Mississippi River Gulf Outlet (canal), La. 238/L7
Mississippi State, Miss. 256/G4
Missoula, Mont. 146/G5
Missoula, Mont. 188/D1
Missoula (co.), Mont. 262/C3
Missoula, Mont. 262/C4
Missouri 188/H3
MISSOURI 261
Missouri (riv.) 188/H3
Missouri (riv.), Iowa 229/A4
Missouri (riv.), Kansas 232/G1
Missouri (riv.), Mo. 261/H5
Missouri (riv.), Mont. 262/L3
Missouri (riv.), Nebr. 264/H3
Missouri (riv.), N. Dak. 282/H5
Missouri (riv.), S. Dak. 298/P8
Missouri (state), U.S. 146/J6
Missouri (riv.), U.S. 2/D3
Missouri (riv.), U.S. 146/J5
Missouri Branch, W. Va. 312/A7
Missouri City, Mo. 261/R5
Missouri City, Texas 303/J2
Missouri Coteau (hills), Sask. 181/F5
Missouri Valley, Iowa 229/B5
Mist, Ark. 202/G7
Mist, Oreg. 291/D1
Mistake (bay), N.W.T. 187/J3
Mistake Creek, North. Terr. 93/A4
Mistaken (pt.), Newf. 166/D2
Mistassibi (riv.), Que. 162/J5
Mistassibi (riv.), Québec 174/C3
Mistassini (lake), Que. 162/J5
Mistassini (lake), Que. 146/L4
Mistassini (terr.), Québec 174/B2
Mistassini, Québec 172/E1
Mistassini, Québec 174/C3
Mistassini (Baie-du-Poste), Québec 174/C2
Mistassini (lake), Québec 174/C2
Mistastin (lake), Newf. 166/B2
Mistastin (riv.), Newf. 166/B2
Mistatim, Sask. 181/H3
Mistehae (lake), Alberta 182/C2
Mistelbach an der Zaya, Austria 41/D2
Misteriosa (bank), Cayman Is. 156/A3
Misti, El (mt.), Peru 120/B4
Misti, El (mt.), Peru 128/G11
Mistinippi (lake), Newf. 166/B3
Miston, Tenn. 237/B8
Mistretta, Italy 34/E6
Misty Fjords Nat'l Mon., Alaska 196/N2
Misurata, Libya 102/D1
Misurata, Libya 111/C1
Mita (pt.), Mexico 150/G6
Mitaka, Japan 81/O2
Mitcham, S. Australia 88/D8
Mitcham, S. Australia 94/B8
Mitchell (lake), Ala. 188/J4
Mitchell (dam), Ala. 195/E5
Mitchell (lake), Ala. 195/F5
Mitchell, Ark. 202/G1
Mitchell (co.), Ga. 217/D8
Mitchell, Ga. 217/G4
Mitchell, Ind. 227/E7
Mitchell (co.), Iowa 229/H2
Mitchell, Iowa 229/H2
Mitchell (co.), Kansas 232/D2
Mitchell, La. 238/C3
Mitchell, Nebr. 264/A3
Mitchell (co.), N.C. 281/E2
Mitchell (mt.), N.C. 188/K3
Mitchell (mt.), N.C. 281/E3
Mitchell, Ontario 177/C4
Mitchell, Oreg. 291/G3
Mitchell, Queensland 88/H5
Mitchell, Queensland 95/C5
Mitchell (riv.), Queensland 88/G3
Mitchell (riv.), Queensland 95/B2
Mitchell, S. Dak. 188/G2
Mitchell, S. Dak. 298/N6
Mitchell (creek), S. Dak. 298/G5
Mitchell (co.), Texas 303/D5
Mitchell (riv.), Victoria 97/D5
Mitchell Bay, Ontario 177/B5
Mitchell Heights, W. Va. 312/B7
Mitchells, Va. 307/N4
Mitchellsburg, Ky. 237/M5
Mitchellsville, Ill. 222/E6
Mitchellton, Sask. 181/F6
Mitchellville, Ark. 202/H6
Mitchellville, Iowa 229/G5
Mitchellville, Tenn. 237/J7
Mitchelstown, Ireland 10/B4
Mitchelstown, Ireland 17/E7
Mitchelton, Queensland 88/J2
Mitchelton, Queensland 95/D2
Mitchinamécus (res.), Québec 172/C2
Mithi, Pakistan 68/C4
Míthimna, Greece 45/G6
Mitiaro, Cook Is. 87/L7
Mitilíni, Greece 45/H6
Mitkof (isl.), Alaska 196/N2
Mitla (ruin), Mexico 150/M8
Mito, Japan 81/K5
Mitrofania (isl.), Alaska 196/G3
Mitsamiouli, Comoros 118/G2
Mitsinjo, Madagascar 118/H3
Mitsue, Alberta 182/C2
Mitsukaido, Japan 81/P2
Mittagong, N.S. Wales 97/F4
Mitta Mitta (riv.), Victoria 97/D5
Mittenwald, Germany 22/D5
Mittersill, Austria 41/B3
Mittie, La. 238/E5
Mittweida, Germany 22/E3
Mitú, Colombia 126/E7
Mitú, Colombia 120/B2
Mituas, Colombia 126/F6
Mitwaba, D.R. Congo 115/E5
Mitzic, Gabon 115/B3
Miura, Japan 81/O3
Miura (pen.), Japan 81/O3
Mivtahim, Israel 65/A5
Mix, La. 238/G5
Miyagi (pref.), Japan 81/K4
Miyako, Japan 81/L4
Miyako (isl.), Japan 81/L7
Miyako (isls.), Japan 81/L7
Miyakonojo, Japan 81/E8
Miyazaki (pref.), Japan 81/E8
Miyazaki, Japan 81/E8
Miyazu, Japan 81/G6
Miyoshi, Japan 81/F6
Mizan Teferi, Ethiopia 111/G6
Mizda, Libya 111/B1
Mize, Ga. 217/F2
Mize, Miss. 256/E7
Mizen (head), Ireland 10/A5
Mizen (head), Ireland 17/B9
Mizen (head), Ireland 17/K6
Mizhi, China 77/H4
Mizil, Romania 45/H3
Mizo (hill), India 68/G4
Mizoram (terr.), India 68/G4
Mizpah, Minn. 255/D3
Mizpah, N.J. 273/D5
Mizpe Ramon, Israel 65/D5
Mizque, Bolivia 136/C5
Mizque (riv.), Bolivia 136/C6
Mizusawa, Japan 81/K4
Mjölby, Sweden 18/J7
Mkokotoni, Tanzania 115/G5
Mkushi, Zambia 115/E6
Mladá Boleslav, Czech Rep. 41/C1
Mladá Vožice, Czech Rep. 41/C2
Mława, Poland 47/E2
Mljet (isl.), Croatia 45/C4
Mmabatho (cap.), Bophuthatswana, S. Africa 102/E7
Mmabatho, S. Africa 118/D5
Mnichovo Hradiště, Czech Rep. 41/C1
Mo, Norway 7/F2
Mo, Norway 18/J3
Moa, Cuba 158/K3
Moa (riv.), Guinea 106/B7
Moa (isl.), Indonesia 85/H7
Moa (riv.), S. Leone 106/B7
Moab, Utah 304/E5
Moak Lake, Manitoba 179/J2
Moala (isl.), Fiji 86/Q11
Moama, N.S. Wales 97/C5
Moamba, Mozambique 118/E5
Moanalua (stream), Hawaii 218/B3
Moanda, Gabon 115/B4
Moanda, D.R. Congo 115/B5
Moapa, Nev. 266/G6
Moapa River Ind. Res., Nev. 266/G6
Moar (lake), Manitoba 179/G2
Moark, Ark. 202/J1
Moate, Ireland 17/F5
Moatsville, W. Va. 312/G4
Mobara, Japan 81/K6
Mobaye, Cent. Afr. Rep. 115/D3
Mobayi-Mbongo, D.R. Congo 115/D3
Mobayi-Mbongo, D.R. Congo 102/E4
Mobeetie, Texas 303/D2
Moberly, Br. Col. 184/J4
Moberly (lake), Br. Col. 184/F2
Moberly, Mo. 261/G4
Moberly, Mo. 188/H3
Moberly Lake, Br. Col. 184/G2
Mobile, Ala. 146/K6
Mobile, Ala. 188/J4
Mobile, Ala. 195/B9
Mobile (bay), Ala. 188/J5
Mobile (bay), Ala. 195/B10
Mobile (co.), Ala. 195/B9
Mobile (pt.), Ala. 195/B10
Mobile (riv.), Ala. 195/C9
Mobile, Ariz. 198/C5
Mobile, Newf. 166/D2
Mobile Big (pond), Newf. 166/D2
Mobjack, Va. 307/R6
Mobjack (bay), Va. 307/R6
Mobridge, S. Dak. 298/J2
Mobuto Sese Seko (lake), Africa 102/F4
Mobuto Sese Seko (lake), Uganda 115/F3
Mobuto Sese Seko (lake), D.R. Congo 115/F3
Moca, Dom. Rep. 156/D3
Moca, Dom. Rep. 158/D5
Moca, P. Rico 161/A1
Mocajuba, Brazil 132/D3
Moçambique, Mozambique 118/G3
Moçambique, Mozambique 102/F6
Moçâmedes (Namibe), Angola 115/B7
Mocanaqua, Pa. 294/K3
Moccasin, Ariz. 198/C2
Moccasin, Mont. 262/F3
Mocha (isl.), Chile 138/B2
Mocha (isl.), Yemen 59/D7
Moc Hoa, Vietnam 72/E5
Mochudi, Botswana 118/D4
Mochudi, Botswana 102/E7
Mocímboa da Praia, Mozambique 118/G2
Mociu, Romania 45/G2
Mocksville, N.C. 281/H3
Moclips, Wash. 310/A3
Moco (mt.), Angola 115/C6
Mocoa, Colombia 126/B7
Mococa, Brazil 135/C2
Mocodome (cape), Nova Scotia 168/G3
Mocomoco, Bolivia 136/A4
Mocoretá, Argentina 143/G5
Mocorito, Mexico 150/F4
Moctezuma, San Luis Potosí, Mexico 150/J5
Moctezuma, Sonora, Mexico 150/E2
Moctezuma (riv.), Mexico 150/K6
Mocuba, Mozambique 118/F3
Modale, Iowa 229/B5
Modane, France 28/G5
Modasa, India 68/C4
Modderfontein, S. Africa 118/H6
Mode, Ill. 222/E4
Model, Colo. 208/L8
Modena (prov.), Italy 34/C2
Modena, Italy 7/F4
Modena, Italy 34/C2
Modena, Utah 304/A6
Modena, Wis. 317/C7
Modeste, La. 238/K3
Modesto, Calif. 188/B3
Modesto, Calif. 204/D6
Modesto, Ill. 222/D4
Modest Town, Va. 307/T5
Modica, Italy 34/E6
Mödling, Austria 41/D2
Modoc (co.), Calif. 204/E2
Modoc, Ga. 217/H5
Modoc, Ill. 222/C5
Modoc, Ind. 227/G4
Modoc, Kansas 232/A3
Modoc, S.C. 296/C4
Modoc Point, Oreg. 291/F5
Modra, Slovakia 41/D2
Modriča, Bos. 45/D3
Modrý Kameň, Slovakia 41/E2
Mo Duc, Vietnam 72/F4
Moe, Victoria 88/H7
Moe, Victoria 97/D6
Moen (isl.), Micronesia 87/F5
Moencopi (plat.), Ariz. 198/D3
Moengo, Suriname 131/D3
Moenkopi, Ariz. 198/D2
Moenkopi Wash (dry riv.), Ariz. 198/D2
Moerai, Fr. Poly. 87/L8
Moerdijk, Netherlands 27/F5
Moerewa, N. Zealand 100/E1
Moësa (riv.), Switzerland 39/H4
Moeskroen (Mouscron), Belgium 27/C7
Moffat (co.), Colo. 208/C1
Moffat, Colo. 208/H6
Moffat, Scotland 15/E5
Moffat, Scotland 10/E3
Moffet (peak), N. Zealand 100/B6
Moffett, Okla. 288/S4
Moffett Nav. Air Sta., Calif. 204/K3
Moffit, N. Dak. 282/K6
Mogadiscio (prov.), Somalia 115/J3
Mogadishu (cap.), Somalia 2/M5
Mogadishu (cap.), Somalia 102/G4
Mogadishu (cap.), Somalia 115/J3
Mogador (Essaouira), Morocco 106/B2
Mogadore, Ohio 284/H3
Mogadouro, Portugal 33/C2
Mogami (riv.), Japan 81/K4
Mogaung, Burma 72/C1
Møgeltønder, Denmark 21/B8
Mogi das Cruzes, Brazil 132/E9
Mogi das Cruzes, Brazil 135/C3
Mogi Guaçu (riv.), Brazil 135/C2
Mogi-Guaçu, Brazil 135/C3
Mogilev, Belarus 7/G3
Mogilev, Belarus 52/C4
Mogilev, Belarus 48/D4
Mogilev-Podol'skiy, Ukraine 52/C5
Mogil Mogil, N.S. Wales 97/E1
Mogilno, Poland 47/C2
Mogi-Mirim, Brazil 135/C3
Mogincual, Mozambique 118/G3
Mogocha, Russia 48/N4
Mogok, Burma 72/C2
Mogollon (plat.), Ariz. 198/D4
Mogollon, N. Mex. 274/A5
Mogollon (mts.), N. Mex. 274/A5
Mogollon Baldy (peak), N. Mex. 274/A5
Mogollon Rim (cliffs), Ariz. 198/D4
Mogororo, Chad 111/D5
Mogotes (pt.), Argentina 143/E4
Moguer, Spain 33/C4
Mohács, Hungary 41/E4
Mohaka (riv.), N. Zealand 100/F3
Mohaleshoek, Lesotho 118/D6
Mohall, N. Dak. 282/G2
Mohammadia, Algeria 106/D1
Mohammedia, Morocco 106/C2
Mohave (co.), Ariz. 198/A3
Mohave (lake), Ariz. 198/A3
Mohave (mts.), Ariz. 198/A4
Mohave (lake), Nev. 266/G7
Mohawk (mts.), Ariz. 198/B6
Mohawk (mt.), Conn. 210/B1
Mohawk, Ind. 227/F5
Mohawk, Mich. 250/A1
Mohawk (riv.), N.H. 268/E2
Mohawk (lake), N.J. 273/D1
Mohawk, N.Y. 276/L4
Mohawk (riv.), N.Y. 276/L5
Mohawk, Oreg. 291/E3
Mohawk, Tenn. 237/P8
Mohawk, W. Va. 312/C7
Mohe, China 77/K1
Mohegan, Conn. 210/G3
Mohéli (Mwali) (isl.), Comoros 102/G6
Mohéli (Mwali) (isl.), Comoros 118/G2
Mohelnice, Czech Rep. 41/D2
Mohenjo Daro (ruins), Pakistan 68/B3
Moher (cliffs), Ireland 17/B6
Mohican (cape), Alaska 196/E2
Mohican (riv.), Ohio 284/F4
Mohill, Ireland 17/F4
Mohler, Wash. 310/G3
Möhlin, Switzerland 39/E1
Mohnton, Pa. 294/L5
Mohnyin, Burma 72/C1
Moho, Peru 128/H10
Mohoro, Tanzania 115/G5
Mohrsville, Pa. 294/K5
Moi, Norway 18/E7
Moidart (dist.), Scotland 15/C4
Moiese, Mont. 262/B3
Moiliili, Hawaii 218/C4
Moineşti, Romania 45/H2
Moingona, Iowa 229/F4
Moira, N.Y. 276/M1
Moírai, Greece 45/G8
Moirones, Uruguay 145/E2
Mõisaküla, Estonia 53/C1
Moise (riv.), Que. 146/M4
Moisés Ville, Argentina 143/E5
Moisie (riv.), Que. 162/K5
Moisie, Québec 174/D2
Moisie (riv.), Québec 174/D2
Moissac, France 28/D5
Moissala, Chad 111/C6
Moitaco, Venezuela 124/F4
Mojácar, Spain 33/F4
Mojave, Calif. 204/G8
Mojave (des.), Calif. 204/H9
Mojave (riv.), Calif. 204/J9
Mojo, Bolivia 136/C7
Mojocoya, Bolivia 136/C6
Mojokerto, Indonesia 85/K2
Mokane, Mo. 261/J5
Mokapu, Hawaii 218/F2
Mokapu (pen.), Hawaii 218/F2
Mokau (riv.), N. Zealand 100/E3
Mokelumne (riv.), Calif. 204/C9
Mokelumne Hill, Calif. 204/E5
Mokena, Ill. 222/B6
Mokil (atoll), Micronesia 87/G5
Moknine, Tunisia 106/G1
Mokohinau (isl.), N. Zealand 100/E1
Mokokchung, India 68/G3
Mokolo, Cameroon 115/B1
Mokp'o, S. Korea 81/C6
Moksha (riv.), Russia52/F4
Mokuaulua (isl.), Hawaii 218/E1
Mokuaweoweo (crater), Hawaii 218/H6
Mokuhoonki (isl.), Hawaii 218/J1
Mokuleia, Hawaii 218/D1
Mol, Belgium 27/G6
Mola di Bari, Italy 34/F4
Molalla, Oreg. 291/B3
Molalla (riv.), Oreg. 291/B3
Moland, Minn. 255/E6
Molanosa, Sask. 181/M4
Moláoi, Greece 45/F7
Molare (peak), Switzerland 39/G3
Mold, Wales 13/G2
Moldau (Vltava) (riv.), Czech Rep. 41/C2
Moldava nad Bodvou, Slovakia 41/F2
Molde, Norway 18/E5
Moldova 7/G4
Moldova 48/C5
MOLDOVA 52/C5
Moldova Nouă, Romania 45/E3
Modoveanul (mt.), Romania 45/G3
Mole (riv.), England 13/H8
Môle (cape), Haiti 158/B5
Mole Creek, Tasmania 99/C3
Molega (lake), Nova Scotia 168/D4
Molena, Ga. 217/D4
Molenbeek-Saint-Jean, Belgium 27/B9
Molepolole, Botswana 118/C4
Molepolole, Botswana 102/E7
Môle Saint Nicolas, Haiti 158/B5
Molfetta, Italy 34/F4
Molina, Chile 138/A10
Molina, Colo. 208/D4
Molina, Spain 33/F2
Molinas, Argentina 143/C2
Moline, Ill. 188/J2
Moline, Ill. 222/C2
Moline, Kansas 232/F4
Moline, Manitoba 179/B4
Moline, Mich. 250/D6
Moline Acres, Mo. 261/R2
Molinicos, Spain 33/F3
Molinière (pt.), Grenada 161/C8
Molino, Fla. 212/B6
Molinos (pt.), P. Rico 161/G1
Moliro, D.R. Congo 115/E5
Molise (reg.), Italy 34/E4
Mollebjerg (mt.), Denmark 21/C6
Mollendo, Peru 120/B4
Mollendo, Peru 128/F11
Mollerusa, Spain 33/G2
Molles (pt.), Chile 138/A9
Mollis, Switzerland 39/H2
Mölln, Germany 22/D2
Mollusk, Va. 307/P5
Mollys Falls (pond), Vt. 268/C3
Mölndal, Sweden 18/H8
Moloaa, Hawaii 218/D1
Molodechno, Belarus 48/C4
Molodechno, Belarus 52/C4
Molokai (isl.), Hawaii 87/L3
Molokai (isl.), Hawaii 188/F5
Molokai (isl.), Hawaii 218/G1
Molokini (isl.), Hawaii 218/J2
Molong, N.S. Wales 97/E3
Molopo (riv.), Botswana 118/C5
Molopo (riv.), S. Africa 118/C5
Molotov (Perm'), Russia52/J3
Moloundou, Cameroon 115/C3
Molson (lake), Manitoba 179/J3
Molson, Wash. 310/F2
Molt, Mont. 262/H5
Molteno, S. Africa 118/D6
Molucca (isls.), Indonesia 54/O10
Molucca (sea), Indonesia 54/O10
Molucca (sea), Indonesia 85/H6
Moluccas (isls.), Indonesia 85/H6
Molunkus (lake), Maine 243/G4
Moma, Mozambique 118/F3
Mombasa, Kenya 115/G4
Mombasa, Kenya 102/G5
Mombetsu, Japan 81/L1
Mombo, Tanzania 115/G4
Momchilgrad, Bulgaria 45/G5
Momence, Ill. 222/F2
Momeyer, N.C. 281/N3
Momignies, Belgium 27/E8
Momostenango, Guatemala 154/B3
Mompog (passage), Philippines 82/D4
Mompós, Colombia 126/C3
Mon (state), Burma 72/C3
Mon (riv.), Burma 72/B2
Møn (isl.), Denmark 21/F8
Møn (isl.), Denmark 18/H9
Mona (passage) 146/M8
Mona, Cyprus 63/E5
Mona (passage), Dom. Rep. 156/E3
Mona (passage), Dom. Rep. 158/F6
Mona (isl.), P. Rico 156/E3
Mona (passage), P. Rico 156/E3
Mona (passage), P. Rico 161/A2
Mona, Utah 304/C4
Mona (res.), Utah 304/C4
Monaca, Pa. 294/B4
Monach (isls.), Scotland 15/A3
Monach (sound), Scotland 15/A3
Monaco 7/E4
MONACO 28/G6
Monadhliath (mts.), Scotland 15/D3
Monadnock (mt.), N.H. 268/C6
Monagas (state), Venezuela 124/G3
Monaghan (co.), Ireland 17/H3
Monaghan, Ireland 10/C3
Monaghan, Ireland 17/G3
Monahans, Texas 303/B6
Monango, N. Dak. 282/N7
Monapo, Mozambique 118/G2
Monar, Loch (lake), Scotland 15/C3
Monarch, Alberta 182/D5
Monarch, Mont. 262/F3
Monarch Mills, S.C. 296/D2
Monarda, Maine 243/G4
Monaro (range), N.S. Wales 97/E5
Monashee (mts.), Br. Col. 184/H4
Monasterevan, Ireland 17/H5
Monastery, Nova Scotia 168/G3
Monastir, Tunisia 106/G1
Monatélé, Cameroon 115/B3
Mona Vale, N.S. Wales 88/L3
Mona Vale, N.S. Wales 97/K2
Monaville, W. Va. 312/B7
Monavullagh (mts.), Ireland 17/F7
Monbetsu, Japan 81/L2
Moncalieri, Italy 34/A2
Monçao, Portugal 33/B1
Moncayo (mt.), Spain 33/F2
Moncayo, Sierra de (range), Spain 33/F2
Monchegorsk, Russia 7/H2
Monchegorsk, Russia 48/C3
Monchegorsk, Russia 52/D1
Mönchengladbach, Germany 22/B3
Monches, Wis. 317/J1
Monchique, Portugal 33/B4
Monchique, Serra de (mts.), Portugal 33/B4
Moncion, Dom. Rep. 158/D5
Moncks Corner, S.C. 296/G5
Monclo, W. Va. 312/C7
Monclova, Mexico 146/H7
Monclova, Mexico 150/J3
Monclova, Ohio 284/C2
Moncouche (lake), Québec 172/G1
Moncton, N. Br. 146/M5
Moncton, N. Br. 162/K6
Moncton, New Bruns. 170/F2
Moncure, N.C. 281/L3
Mondamin, Iowa 229/B5
Monday (riv.), Paraguay 144/E4
Mondego (cape), Portugal 33/B2
Mondego (riv.), Portugal 33/B2
Mondéjar, Spain 33/E2
Mondonac (lake), Québec 172/D2
Mondoñedo, Spain 33/C1
Mondovi, Wis. 317/C6
Mondovì Breo, Italy 34/A2
Mondragon, Philippines 85/H3
Mondragon, Philippines 82/E4
Mondsee, Austria 41/B3
Moneague, Jamaica 158/J6
Monee, Ill. 222/F2
Monero, N. Mex. 274/C2
Monessen, Pa. 294/C5
Monesterio, Spain 33/C3
Moneta, Iowa 229/C2
Moneta, Va. 307/J6
Moneta, Wyo. 319/E2
Monett, Mo. 261/E9
Monetta, S.C. 296/D4
Monette, Ark. 202/K2
Money (isl.), China 85/E2
Money, Miss. 256/D3
Moneygall, Ireland 17/F6
Moneymore, N. Ireland 17/H2
Monfalcone, Italy 34/D2
Monforte, Portugal 33/C3
Monforte, Spain 33/C1
Monga, D.R. Congo 115/D3
Mongalla, Sudan 111/F6
Mong Cai, Vietnam 72/E2
Möng Hsat, Burma 72/C2
Monghyr, India 68/F3
Möng Maü, Burma 72/C3
Möng Mit, Burma 72/C2
Möng Tung, Burma 72/C2
Mongo, Chad 111/C5
Mongo, Chad 102/D3
Mongo, Ind. 227/G1
MONGOLIA 77
Mongolia 2/P3
Mongolia 54/M5
Mongoumba, Cent. Afr. Rep. 115/C3
Möng Pan, Burma 72/C2
Möng Si, Burma 72/C2
Möng Tön, Burma 72/C2
Möng Tung, Burma 72/C2
Mongu, Zambia 102/E6
Mongu, Zambia 115/D7
Monhegan•, Maine 243/E8

412 Monhegan

Monhegan (isl.), Maine 243/E8
Mönhhaan, Mongolia 77/H2
Moniac, Ga. 217/H9
Moniaive, Scotland 10/D3
Moniaive, Scotland 15/E5
Monica, Ill. 222/D3
Monico, Wis. 317/H4
Monida, Mont. 262/D6
Monie, Md. 245/P8
Monifieth, Scotland 15/F4
Moniquirá, Colombia 126/D5
Moniteau (co.), Mo. 261/G5
Monitor, Alberta 182/E4
Monitor, Ind. 227/D4
Monitor (range), Nev. 266/E4
Monitor, Oreg. 291/B3
Monitor, Wash. 310/E3
Monivea, Ireland 17/D5
Monkayo, Philippines 82/E7
Monkey (pt.), Nicaragua 154/F5
Monkey (hill), St. Kitts & Nevis 161/C10
Monkey River Town, Belize 154/C2
Mońki, Poland 47/F2
Monkoto, D.R. Congo 115/D4
Monkton, Md. 245/M2
Monkton, Ontario 177/C4
Monkton•, Vt. 268/A3
Monkton Ridge, Vt. 268/A3
Monmouth, Ill. 222/C3
Monmouth, Ind. 227/H3
Monmouth, Iowa 229/M4
Monmouth, Maine 243/D7
Monmouth•, Maine 243/D7
Monmouth (co.), N.J. 273/E3
Monmouth, Oreg. 291/D3
Monmouth, Wales 13/E6
Monmouth, Wales 10/E5
Monmouth Beach, N.J. 273/F3
Monmouth Junction, N.J. 273/D3
Monnickendam, Netherlands 27/C4
Mono (riv.), Benin 106/E7
Mono (co.), Calif. 204/F5
Mono (lake), Calif. 188/C3
Mono (lake), Calif. 204/G5
Mono (riv.), Togo 106/E7
Monocacy (riv.), Md. 245/J3
Monocacy Nat'l Battlefield, Md. 245/J3
Mono Lake, Calif. 204/F5
Monolith, Calif. 204/G8
Monólithos, Greece 45/H7
Monomonac (lake), Mass. 249/G2
Monomoy (isl.), Mass. 249/O6
Monomoy (pt.), Mass. 249/O6
Monon, Ind. 227/D3
Monona (co.), Iowa 229/B4
Monona, Iowa 229/L2
Monona, Wis. 317/H9
Monongah, W. Va. 312/F4
Monongahela, Pa. 294/B5
Monongahela (riv.), Pa. 294/C6
Monongahela (riv.), W. Va. 312/G3
Monongalia (co.), W. Va. 312/F3
Monopoli, Italy 34/F4
Monor, Hungary 41/E3
Monos (isl.), Trin. & Tob. 161/A10
Monóvar, Spain 33/F3
Monoville, Tenn. 237/K8
Monowi, Nebr. 264/F2
Monreal del Campo, Spain 33/F2
Monreale, Italy 34/D5
Monroe (co.), Ala. 195/D7
Monroe (co.), Ark. 202/H4
Monroe, Ark. 202/H4
Monroe•, Conn. 210/C3
Monroe (co.), Fla. 212/E7
Monroe (lake), Fla. 212/E3
Monroe (co.), Ga. 217/E4
Monroe, Ga. 217/E3
Monroe (co.), Ill. 222/C5
Monroe (co.), Ind. 227/D6
Monroe, Ind. 227/H3
Monroe (lake), Ind. 227/E6
Monroe (co.), Iowa 229/H7
Monroe, Iowa 229/G5
Monroe (co.), Ky. 237/K7
Monroe, La. 188/H4
Monroe, La. 146/J6
Monroe, La. 238/F1
Monroe•, Maine 243/E6
Monroe (co.), Mich. 250/F7
Monroe, Mich. 250/F7
Monroe (co.), Miss. 256/H3
Monroe (co.), Mo. 261/H3
Monroe, Nebr. 264/G3
Monroe•, N.H. 268/C3
Monroe (mt.), N.H. 268/E3
Monroe•, N.J. 273/E3
Monroe (co.), N.Y. 276/E4
Monroe, N.Y. 276/M8
Monroe, N.C. 281/J5
Monroe (co.), Ohio 284/H6
Monroe, Ohio 284/B7
Monroe, Okla. 288/S4
Monroe, Oreg. 291/D3
Monroe (co.), Pa. 294/M3
Monroe (Monroeton), Pa. 294/J2
Monroe, S. Dak. 298/P7
Monroe (co.), Tenn. 237/N10
Monroe, Tenn. 237/L8
Monroe, Utah 304/B5
Monroe (peak), Utah 304/B5
Monroe, Va. 307/K6
Monroe, Wash. 310/D3
Monroe (co.), W. Va. 312/E7
Monroe (co.), Wis. 317/E8
Monroe, Wis. 317/G10
Monroe Bridge, Mass. 249/C2
Monroe Center, Ill. 222/E1
Monroe City, Ind. 227/C7
Monroe City, Mo. 261/J3
Monroe P.O. (Stepney), Conn. 210/B3
Monroeton, Pa. 294/J2
Monroeville, Ala. 195/D7
Monroeville, Ind. 227/H3
Monroeville, N.J. 273/C4
Monroeville, Ohio 284/E3
Monroeville, Pa. 294/C7
Monrovia, Ala. 195/E1
Monrovia, Calif. 204/D10
Monrovia, Ind. 227/E5
Monrovia (cap.), Liberia 106/B7
Monrovia (cap.), Liberia 2/J5
Monrovia (cap.), Liberia 102/A4
Monrovia, Md. 245/J3
Mons, Belgium 27/E8
Monsanto, Portugal 33/C2
Monschau, Germany 22/B3
Monse, Wash. 310/F2
Monsefú, Peru 128/C6
Monselice, Italy 34/C2
Montserrate (isl.), Mexico 150/D4
Monsey, N.Y. 276/J8
Møns Klint (cliff), Denmark 21/F8
Monson•, Maine 243/E5
Monson, Mass. 249/E4
Monson•, Mass. 249/E4
Mönsterås, Sweden 18/K8
Montagu, S. Africa 118/C6
Montague (isl.), Alaska 196/D1
Montague (str.), Alaska 196/D1
Montague, Calif. 204/C2
Montague•, Mass. 249/E2
Montague (isl.), Mexico 150/B1
Montague, Mich. 250/C5
Montague, Mont. 262/F3
Montague, N.J. 273/D1
Montague, N.C. 281/N6
Montague, Pr. Edward I. 168/F2
Montague (co.), Texas 303/G4
Montague, Texas 303/G4
Montague (sound), W. Australia 88/C2
Montague (sound), W. Australia 92/D1
Montague City, Mass. 249/D2
Montalba, Texas 303/J6
Montalbán, Spain 33/F2
Montalcino, Italy 34/C3
Mont Alto, Pa. 294/G6
Montalto Uffugo, Italy 34/E5
Montalvão, Portugal 33/C3
Montalvo, Calif. 204/F9
Montana 188/E1
MONTANA 262
Montana, Alaska 196/B1
Montaña, La (reg.), Peru 128/F8
Montana, Switzerland 39/D4
Montana (state), U.S. 146/H5
Montana Mines, W. Va. 312/F3
Montánchez, Spain 33/D3
Montanja di Reij, Neth. Ant. 161/G9
Montara, Calif. 204/H3
Montargil, Portugal 33/B3
Montargis, France 28/E3
Montauban, France 28/D5
Montauban, Québec 172/E3
Montauk, N.Y. 276/S8
Montauk (pt.), N.Y. 276/S8
Montbard, France 28/F4
Montbéliard, France 28/G4
Mont Belvieu, Texas 303/L1
Montblanch, Spain 33/G2
Montbrison, France 28/E5
Montbrook, Fla. 212/D2
Montcalm (co.), Mich. 250/D5
Montcalm (co.), Québec 172/C3
Montcalm (co.), Québec 174/B3
Mont-Carmel, Québec 172/H2
Montceau-les-Mines, France 28/F4
Mont Cenis (tunnel), France 28/G5
Mont Cenis (tunnel), Italy 34/A2
Montcerf, Québec 172/A3
Montclair, Calif. 204/D10
Montclair, N.J. 273/B2
Montclare, S.C. 296/H3
Montcoal, W. Va. 312/D7
Mont-de-Marsan, France 28/C6
Montdidier, France 28/E3
Mont-Dore, France 28/E5
Monteagle, Tenn. 237/K10
Monteagudo, Bolivia 136/D6
Monte Alegre, Brazil 132/C3
Montealegre del Castillo, Spain 33/F3
Monte Alegre de Minas, Brazil 132/D7
Monte Aprazível, Brazil 135/A2
Monte Azul, Brazil 132/F6
Monte Bello (isls.), Australia 87/B8
Montebello, Calif. 204/C10
Montebello, Québec 172/B4
Monte Bello (isls.), W. Australia 88/A4
Monte Bello (isls.), W. Australia 92/A3
Montebelluna, Italy 34/D2
Monte Carlo, Monaco 28/G6
Monte Caseros, Argentina 143/G5
Montecito, Calif. 204/F9
Monte Comán, Argentina 143/C3
Monte Creek, Br. Col. 184/G5
Montecristi (prov.), Dom. Rep. 158/D5
Monte Cristi, Dom. Rep. 156/D2
Montecristi, Dom. Rep. 158/C5
Montecristi, Ecuador 128/B3
Monte Cristo, Bolivia 136/E4
Montecristo (isl.), Italy 34/C3
Monte Cristo (range), Nev. 266/D4
Monte Dourado, Brazil 132/C2
Montefiascone, Italy 34/D3
Montefrío, Spain 33/D4
Montego (bay), Jamaica 158/G5
Montego Bay, Jamaica 158/H5
Montego Bay, Jamaica 156/B3
Montego Bay (pt.), Jamaica 158/G5
Montegut, La. 238/J8
Montehermoso, Spain 33/C2
Monteiro, Brazil 132/G4
Monteith, Iowa 229/D5
Montejinnie, North. Terr. 93/C4
Monte Lake, Br. Col. 184/G5
Montélimar, France 28/F5
Montelindo (riv.), Paraguay 144/C3
Montellano, Spain 33/D4
Montello, Nev. 266/G1
Montello, Wis. 317/H8
Montemayor (plat.), Argentina 143/C5
Montemorelos, Mexico 150/K4
Montemoro-o-Novo, Portugal 33/B3
Montemoro-o-Velho, Portugal 33/B2
Monte Ne, Ark. 202/B1
Montenegro, Brazil 132/D10
Montenegro, Chile 138/G2
Montenegro (rep.), Yugoslavia 45/D4
Monte Patria, Chile 138/A8
Monte Plata, Dom. Rep. 158/E6
Montepuez, Mozambique 118/F2
Montepulciano, Italy 34/C3
Monte Quemado, Argentino 143/D2
Monte Real, Brazil 132/A5
Monterey, Ala. 195/E7
Monterey (co.), Calif. 204/D7
Monterey, Calif. 188/B3
Monterey, Calif. 204/D7
Monterey (bay), Calif. 188/B3
Monterey (bay), Calif. 204/K4
Monterey, Ind. 227/D2
Monterey, Ky. 237/M4
Monterey, La. 238/G4
Monterey•, Mass. 249/B4
Monterey, Tenn. 237/L8
Monterey, Va. 307/K4
Monterey, Wis. 317/J1
Monterey Park, Calif. 204/C10
Montería, Colombia 120/B2
Montería, Colombia 126/B3
Monte Rio, Calif. 204/B5
Montero, Bolivia 136/D5
Monteros, Argentina 143/C2
Monterotondo, Italy 34/f6
Monterrey, Mexico 2/D4
Monterrey, Mexico 146/J7
Monterrey, Mexico 150/J4
Monterville, W. Va. 312/F5
Montes, Uruguay 145/D5
Montesano, Wash. 310/B4
Monte Sant'Angelo, Italy 34/F4
Monte Santo, Brazil 132/G5
Montes Claros, Brazil 120/E4
Montes Claros, Brazil 132/E7
Monte Sereno, Calif. 204/K4
Montevallo, Ala. 195/E4
Montevallo, Mo. 261/D7
Montevarchi, Italy 34/C3
Montevideo, Minn. 255/C6
Montevideo (dept.), Uruguay 145/B7
Montevideo (cap.), Uruguay 145/B7
Montevideo (cap.), Uruguay 120/D6
Montevideo (cap.), Uruguay 2/G7
Monteview, Idaho 220/F6
Monte Vista, Colo. 208/G7
Montezuma (co.), Colo. 208/B8
Montezuma, Colo. 208/H3
Montezuma (peak), Colo. 208/F8
Montezuma, Ga. 217/E6
Montezuma, Ind. 227/C5
Montezuma, Iowa 229/H5
Montezuma, Kansas 232/B4
Montezuma, N. Mex. 274/D3
Montezuma, Ohio 284/A4
Montezuma, Tenn. 237/D10
Montezuma (creek), Utah 304/E6
Montezuma Castle Nat'l Mon., Ariz. 198/D4
Montezuma Creek, Utah 304/E6
Montfoort, Netherlands 27/G4
Montfort, France 28/C3
Montfort, Wis. 317/E10
Montgomery (co.), Ala. 195/F6
Montgomery (cap.), Ala. 188/J4
Montgomery (cap.), Ala. 146/K6
Montgomery (cap.), Ala. 195/F6
Montgomery (co.), Ark. 202/C4
Montgomery (co.), Ga. 217/G6
Montgomery (co.), Ill. 222/D4
Montgomery, Ill. 222/E2
Montgomery (co.), Ind. 227/D4
Montgomery, Ind. 227/C7
Montgomery (co.), Iowa 229/C6
Montgomery, Iowa 229/C2
Montgomery (co.), Kansas 232/G4
Montgomery (co.), Ky. 237/O4
Montgomery, La. 238/E3
Montgomery (co.), Md. 245/J4
Montgomery, Mich. 250/E7
Montgomery, Minn. 255/E6
Montgomery (co.), Miss. 256/E4
Montgomery (co.), Mo. 261/K5
Montgomery (co.), N.Y. 276/M5
Montgomery, N.Y. 276/M7
Montgomery (co.), N.C. 281/K4
Montgomery (co.), Ohio 284/B6
Montgomery, Ohio 284/C9
Montgomery (co.), Pa. 294/M5
Montgomery, Pa. 294/H3
Montgomery (co.), Tenn. 237/G8
Montgomery (co.), Texas 303/J7
Montgomery, Texas 303/J7
Montgomery•, Vt. 268/B2
Montgomery (co.), Va. 307/H6
Montgomery, Wales 13/D5
Montgomery, Wales 10/E4
Montgomery, W. Va. 312/D6
Montgomery Center, Vt. 268/B2
Montgomery City, Mo. 261/K5
Monthey, Switzerland 39/C4
Monticello, Ark. 202/G6
Monticello, Fla. 212/C1
Monticello, Ga. 217/E4
Monticello, Ill. 222/E3
Monticello, Ind. 227/D3
Monticello, Iowa 229/L4
Monticello, Ky. 237/M7
Monticello•, Maine 243/H3
Monticello, Minn. 255/E5
Monticello, Miss. 256/D7
Monticello, Mo. 261/J2
Monticello, N. Mex. 274/B5
Monticello, N.Y. 276/L7
Monticello, Ohio 284/B4
Monticello, S.C. 296/E3
Monticello, Utah 304/E6
Monticello, Wis. 317/G10
Mont Ida, Kansas 232/G3
Montier, Mo. 261/J8
Montigny-les-Metz, France 28/G3
Montigny-le-Tilleul, Belgium 27/E8
Montijo, Panama 154/G6
Montijo (gulf), Panama 154/G7
Montijo, Portugal 33/B3
Montijo, Spain 33/C3
Montilla, Spain 33/D4
Montjoie (lake), Québec 172/B3
Mont-Joli, Québec 162/Kk6
Mont-Joli, Québec 174/D3
Mont-Joli, Québec 172/J1
Mont-Laurier, Québec 162/J6
Mont-Laurier, Québec 172/B3
Mont-Laurier, Québec 174/B3
Mont-Louis, Québec 172/C1
Montluçon, France 28/E4
Montmagny (co.), Québec 172/G3
Montmagny, Québec 174/C3
Montmagny, Québec 172/G3
Montmartre, Sask. 181/H5
Montmédy, France 28/F3
Montmorenci, Ind. 227/D4
Montmorenci, S.C. 296/D4
Montmorency (co.), Mich. 250/E3
Montmorency, Québec 172/J3
Montmorency (riv.), Québec 172/F2
Montmorency, Victoria 97/J4
Montmorency No. 1 (co.), Québec 172/F2
Montmorency No. 1 (co.), Québec 174/C3
Montmorency No. 2 (co.), Québec 172/G3
Montmorillon, France 28/D4
Mont Nebo, Sask. 181/E2
Montney, Br. Col. 184/G2
Monto, Queensland 95/D5
Monto, Queensland 88/J4
Montoire-sur-le-Loir, France 28/D4
Montor, Spain 33/D3
Montoso (mesa), N. Mex. 274/E3
Montour, Idaho 220/B6
Montour, Iowa 229/H5
Montour (co.), Pa. 294/J3
Montour Falls, N.Y. 276/G6
Montoursville, Pa. 294/J3
Montowese, Conn. 210/D3
Montoya, N. Mex. 274/F3
Montoz (mt.), Switzerland 39/D2
Montpelier, Idaho 188/D2
Montpelier, Idaho 220/G7
Montpelier, Ind. 227/G3
Montpelier, Iowa 229/M6
Montpelier, Jamaica 158/H6
Montpelier, La. 238/M1
Montpelier, Miss. 256/G3
Montpelier, N. Dak. 282/N6
Montpelier, Ohio 284/A2
Montpelier (cap.), Vt. 146/L5
Montpelier (cap.), Vt. 188/M2
Montpelier (cap.), Vt. 268/B3
Montpellier, France 7/E4
Montpellier, France 28/E6
Montpellier, Québec 172/B4
Montréal, Canada 2/F3
Montreal (riv.), Mich. 250/F1
Montreal, Mo. 261/G7
Montréal, Que. 146/L5
Montréal, Que. 162/J7
Montréal, Québec 172/H4
Montreal (lake), Sask. 181/F1
Montreal, Wis. 317/F3
Montreal (riv.), Wis. 317/F2
Montréal-Est, Québec 172/J4
Montreal Lake, Sask. 181/F1
Montréal-Nord, Québec 172/H4
Montreal River Harbor, Ontario 177/J5
Montreat, N.C. 281/E3
Montreuil, Pas-de-Calais, France 28/D2
Montreuil, Seine-Saint-Denis, France 28/B2
Montreux, Switzerland 39/C4
Montricher, Switzerland 39/B3
Mont-Rolland, Québec 172/C4
Montrose, Ala. 195/C9
Montrose, Ark. 202/H7
Montrose, Br. Col. 184/J5
Montrose (co.), Colo. 208/C6
Montrose, Colo. 208/D6
Montrose, Ga. 217/F5
Montrose, Ill. 222/E4
Montrose, Iowa 229/L7
Montrose, Kansas 232/D2
Montrose, La. 238/D3
Montrose, Md. 245/K4
Montrose, Mich. 250/F5
Montrose, Minn. 255/E5
Montrose, Miss. 256/F6
Montrose, Mo. 261/E6
Montrose, Pa. 294/L2
Montrose, Scotland 10/E2
Montrose, Scotland 15/F4
Montrose, S. Dak. 298/P6
Montrose, Victoria 97/K5
Montrose, W. Va. 312/G4
Montrose-La Crescenta, Calif. 204/C10
Montross, Va. 307/P4
Montrouge, France 28/B2
Mont-Royal, Québec 172/H4
Monts (pt.), Québec 172/B1
Mont-Saint-Hilaire, Québec 172/D4
Mont-Saint-Michel, France 28/C3
Mont-Saint-Michel, Québec 172/B3
Mont-Saint-Pierre, Québec 172/C1
MONTSERRAT 156/G3
Montserrat (mt.), Spain 33/G2
Montsinéry, Fr. Guiana 131/E3
Mont-Tremblant, Québec 172/C3
Mont-Tremblant Prov. Park, Québec 172/C3
Mont-Tremblant Prov. Park, Québec 174/C3
Montvale, N.J. 273/B1
Montvale, Va. 307/J6
Montverde, Fla. 212/E3
Mont Vernon•, N.H. 268/D6
Montville, Conn. 210/G3
Montville•, Conn. 210/G3
Montville, Maine 243/E7
Montville•, Maine 243/E7
Montville, Mass. 249/B4
Montville•, N.J. 273/E2
Montville, Ohio 284/H2
Montz, La. 238/M3
Monument, Colo. 208/K4
Monument (peak), Idaho 220/B4
Monument, Kansas 232/A2
Monument, N. Mex. 274/F6
Monument, Oreg. 291/H3
Monument (valley), Utah 304/D6
Monument Beach, Mass. 249/M6
Monument Valley, Utah 304/D6
Monywa, Burma 72/B2
Monza, Italy 34/B2
Monze, Zambia 115/E7
Monzón, Spain 33/G2
Mooar, Iowa 229/L8
Moodie (isl.), N.W.T. 187/M3
Moodus, Conn. 210/F2
Moodus (res.), Conn. 210/F2
Moody, Ala. 195/F3
Moody A.F.B., Ga. 217/F9
Moody, Maine 243/B9
Moody, Mo. 261/L9
Moody (co.), S. Dak. 298/R5
Moody, Texas 303/G6
Moodys, Okla. 288/S2
Moodyville, Tenn. 237/L7
Mooers, N.Y. 276/N1
Mooka, Japan 81/K5
Mooleyville, Ky. 237/H4
Mooloo Downs, W. Australia 92/B4
Moomin (creek), N.S. Wales 97/E1
Moon (lake), Calif. 204/E2
Moon (lake), Nebr. 264/E2
Moon, Okla. 288/S7
Moonachie, N.J. 273/B2
Moonah (creek), Queensland 95/A4
Moonbeam, Ontario 177/J5
Mooncoin, Ireland 17/G7
Moonie (riv.), N.S. Wales 97/E1
Moonie, Queensland 95/D5
Moon Run, Pa. 294/B5
Moonta, S. Australia 94/E5
Moora, W. Australia 88/B6
Moora, W. Australia 92/B5
Moorabbin, Victoria 88/L7
Moorabbin, Victoria 97/J5
Moorcroft, Wyo. 319/H1
Moore, Idaho 220/E6
Moore, Mont. 262/G4
Moore (dam), N.H. 268/D3
Moore (res.), N.H. 268/D3
Moore (co.), N.C. 281/L4
Moore, Okla. 288/M4
Moore, S.C. 296/D2
Moore (co.), Tenn. 237/J10
Moore (co.), Texas 303/C2
Moore, Texas 303/E9
Moore, Utah 304/C5
Moore (dam), Vt. 268/D3
Moore (res.), Vt. 268/D3
Moore (lake), W. Australia 88/B5
Moore (lake), W. Australia 92/B5
MOOREA, Fr. Poly. 86/S13
Moorea (isl.), Fr. Poly. 87/L7
Moorea (isl.), Fr. Poly. 86/S13
Moorefield, Ark. 202/G2
Moorefield, Ind. 227/G7
Moorefield, Ky. 237/O4
Moorefield, Nebr. 264/D4
Moorefield, Ontario 177/D4
Moorefield, W. Va. 312/J4
Moore Haven, Fla. 212/E5
Mooreland, Ind. 227/G5
Mooreland, Okla. 288/H2
Moore Park, Manitoba 179/C4
Mooresboro, N.C. 281/F4
Moores Bridge, Ala. 195/C4
Mooresburg, Tenn. 237/P8
Moores Creek, Ky. 237/O6
Moores Creek Nat'l Battlefield, N.C. 281/N6
Moores Hill, Ind. 227/G6
Moores Mills, New Bruns. 170/C3
Moorestown, Mich. 250/D4
Moorestown, N.J. 273/B3
Mooresville, Ala. 195/E1
Mooresville, Ind. 227/E5
Mooresville, Mo. 261/E3
Mooresville, N.C. 281/H3
Mooreton, N. Dak. 282/S7
Moore Town, Jamaica 158/K6
Mooretown, Ontario 177/B5
Mooreville, Miss. 256/G2
Moorfoot (hills), Scotland 15/E5
Moorhead, Iowa 229/B5
Moorhead, Minn. 188/G1
Moorhead, Minn. 255/B4
Moorhead, Miss. 256/C4
Mooringsport, La. 238/B1
Moorland, Iowa 229/E4
Moorland, Ky. 237/L2
Moorman, Ky. 237/G6
Moorooka, Queensland 88/K3
Moorooka, Queensland 95/D3
Mooroopna, Victoria 97/C5
Moorpark, Calif. 204/G9
Moorreesburg, S. Africa 118/B6
Moorslede, Belgium 27/B7
Moosburg an der Isar, Germany 22/D4
Moose (creek), Idaho 220/D3
Moose (pond), Maine 243/B7
Moose (riv.), Maine 243/D4
Moose (isl.), Manitoba 179/E3
Moose (riv.), Minn. 255/C2
Moose (riv.), N.Y. 276/K3
Moose (mt.), Sask. 181/J6
Moose (riv.), Vt. 268/D2
Moose (lake), Wis. 317/E3
Moose (lake), Wis. 317/F3
Moose, Wyo. 319/B2
Moose Creek, Ontario 177/K2
Moose Factory, Ontario 175/D2
Moosehead, Maine 243/D4
Moosehead (lake), Maine 243/D4
Mooseheart, Ill. 222/E2
Moose Heights, Br. Col. 184/F3
Moosehorn, Manitoba 179/D3
Moose Jaw, Sask. 146/H4
Moose Jaw, Sask. 162/F6
Moose Jaw, Sask. 181/F5
Moose Jaw (riv.), Sask. 181/G5
Moose Lake, Manitoba 179/H3
Moose Lake, Minn. 255/F4
Mooseland, Nova Scotia 168/F4
Mooseleuk (stream), Maine 243/F2
Mooselookmeguntic (lake), Maine 243/B6
Moose Mountain (creek), Sask. 181/J6
Moose Mountain Prov. Park, Sask. 181/J6
Moose Pass, Alaska 196/C1
Moose Range, Sask. 181/H2
Moose River•, Maine 243/C4
Moose River, Ontario 175/D2
Moosic, Pa. 294/F7
Moosilauke (mt.), N.H. 268/D3
Moosomin, Sask. 162/F5
Moosomin, Sask. 181/K5
Moosonee, Ont. 162/H5
Moosonee, Ont. 146/K4
Moosonee, Ontario 175/D2
Moosup, Conn. 210/H2
Moosup (riv.), Conn. 210/H2
Mopang (lake), Maine 243/H6
Mopeia, Mozambique 118/F3
Mopti, Mali 102/B3
Mopti, Mali 106/D6
Moqatta, Sudan 59/C7
Moqor, Afghanistan 68/B2
Moqor, Afghanistan 59/J3
Moquah, Wis. 317/D2
Moquegua (dept.), Peru 128/G11
Moquegua, Peru 120/B4
Moquegua, Peru 128/G11
Mór, Hungary 41/E3
Mora, Cameroon 115/B1
Mora, India 68/B7
Mora, La. 238/E4
Mora, Minn. 255/E5
Mora, Mo. 261/F5
Mora (co.), N. Mex. 274/E3
Mora, N. Mex. 274/D3
Mora (riv.), N. Mex. 274/E3
Mora, Portugal 33/B3
Mora, Spain 33/E3
Mora, Sweden 18/J6
Moradabad, India 54/J7
Moradabad, India 68/D3
Mora de Rubielos, Spain 33/F2
Morado, Quebrado (riv.), Chile 136/A6
Morafenobe, Madagascar 118/G3
Morąg, Poland 47/E2
Moraga, Calif. 204/K2
Moraine, Ohio 284/B6
Moraleda (chan.), Chile 138/D5
Morales, Guatemala 154/C3
Morales, Peru 128/D6
Moramanga, Madagascar 118/H3
Moramanga, Madagascar 102/G6
Moran, Ind. 227/D4
Moran, Kansas 232/G4
Moran, Mich. 250/E2
Moran, Texas 303/E5
Moran, Wyo. 319/B2
Moranbah, Queensland 95/C9
Morane (isl.), Fr. Poly. 87/N8
Morant (pt.), Jamaica 156/C3
Morant Bay, Jamaica 158/K7
Morar, Scotland 15/C4
Morar, Loch (lake), Scotland 15/C4
Morat (lake), Switzerland 39/D3
Morata de Tajuña, Spain 33/G4
Moratalla, Spain 33/E3
Morattico, Va. 307/P5
Moratuwa, Sri Lanka 68/D7
Morava (riv.), Czech Rep. 41/D2
Morava (riv.), Yugoslavia 45/E3
Moravia, Iowa 229/H7
Moravia, N.Y. 276/H5
Moravian Falls, N.C. 281/G2
Moravská Třebová, Czech Rep. 41/D2
Moravskaé Budějovice, Czech Rep. 41/D2
Morawa, W. Australia 88/B5

Mount Margaret 413

Morawa, W. Australia 92/B5
Morawhanna, Guyana 120/D2
Morawhanna, Guyana 131/B1
Moray (firth), Scotland 7/D3
Moray (firth), Scotland 10/E2
Moray (firth), Scotland 15/E3
Moray (trad. co.), Scotland 15/A5
Morazán, Honduras 154/D3
Morbihan (dept.), France 28/B4
Mörbylånga, Sweden 18/K8
Morden, Man. 162/G6
Morden, Manitoba 179/D5
Mordialloc, Victoria 97/J6
Mordialloc, Victoria 88/L7
Mordvinian Aut. Rep., Russia 48/E4
Mordvinian Aut. Rep., Russia 52/G4
More, Loch (lake), Scotland 15/E2
More, Loch (lake), Scotland 15/D2
Morea, Victoria 97/A5
Moreau (riv.), S. Dak. 298/G3
Moreauville, La. 238/G4
Morebattle, Scotland 15/F5
Morecambe, Alberta 182/E3
Morecambe (bay), England 10/E3
Morecambe (bay), England 13/D3
Moree, N.S. Wales 88/H5
Moree, N.S. Wales 97/E1
Morehead, Kansas 232/G4
Morehead, Ky. 237/P4
Morehead City, N.C. 281/R5
Morehouse (par.), La. 238/G1
Morehouse, Mo. 261/N9
Moreland, Ark. 202/E3
Moreland, Ga. 217/C4
Moreland, Idaho 220/F6
Moreland Hills, Ohio 284/J9
Morelia, Mexico 150/J7
Morelia, Mexico 146/H8
Morella, Queensland 95/B4
Morell, Pr. Edward I. 168/F2
Morella, Queensland 88/G4
Morella, Spain 33/F2
Morelos (state), Mexico 150/K7
Morelos, Mexico 150/J2
Morelos Cañada, Mexico 150/O2
Morena, India 68/D3
Morena, Sierra (mts.), Spain 7/D5
Morena, Sierra (range), Spain 33/E3
Morenci, Ariz. 198/F5
Morenci, Mich. 250/E7
Moreni, Romania 45/G3
Moreno, Bolivia 136/B2
Moreno, Calif. 204/H10
Moreno (bay), Chile 138/A4
Møre og Romsdal (co.), Norway 18/E5
Mores (creek), Idaho 220/C6
Moresby, Br. Col. 184/B3
Moresby (isl.), Br. Col. 184/B4
Moreton (bay), Queensland 88/K2
Moreton (bay), Queensland 95/E5
Moreton (isl.), Queensland 88/J5
Moreton (isl.), Queensland 95/E5
Moretonhampstead, England 13/C7
Moreton-in-Marsh, England 13/F6
Moretown•, Vt. 268/B3
Morewood, Ontario 177/J2
Morgan (co.), Ala. 195/E2
Morgan (co.), Colo. 208/M2
Morgan (pt.), Conn. 210/D4
Morgan (co.), Ga. 217/F3
Morgan, Ga. 217/C7
Morgan (co.), Ill. 222/C4
Morgan (co.), Ind. 227/E6
Morgan (co.), Ky. 237/P5
Morgan, Ky. 237/N3
Morgan, Minn. 255/D6
Morgan (co.), Mo. 261/G6
Morgan, Mo. 261/G7
Morgan (co.), Ohio 284/G6
Morgan (co.), Tenn. 237/M8
Morgan, Texas 303/G5
Morgan (co.), Utah 304/C2
Morgan, Utah 304/C2
Morgan•, Vt. 268/D2
Morgan (co.), W. Va. 312/K3
Morgan Center, Vt. 268/D2
Morgan City, La. 238/H7
Morgan City, Miss. 256/D4
Morgan Falls (dam), Ga. 217/K1
Morganfield, Ky. 237/E5
Morgan Hill, Calif. 204/L4
Morganito, Venezuela 124/E5
Morgans Point, Texas 303/K2
Morgansville, W. Va. 312/E4
Morganton, Ark. 202/F3
Morganton, Ga. 217/D1
Morganton, N.C. 281/F3
Morgantown, Ind. 227/E6
Morgantown, Ky. 237/H6
Morgantown, Miss. 256/E8
Morgantown, Miss. 256/B7
Morgantown, Ohio 284/D7
Morgantown, Pa. 294/L5
Morgantown, W. Va. 312/G3
Morganville, Kansas 232/E2
Morganville, N.J. 273/E3
Morganza, La. 238/G5
Morges, Switzerland 39/B3
Morguilla (pt.), Chile 138/D1
Mori, China 77/D3
Mori, Japan 81/K2
Moriah, N.Y. 276/N2
Moriah Center, N.Y. 276/N2
Moriarty, N. Mex. 274/D4
Morice (lake), Br. Col. 184/D3
Morice (riv.), Br. Col. 184/D3
Morichal, Colombia 126/E6
Morichal Largo (riv.), Venezuela 124/G3
Morien (cape), Nova Scotia 168/J2
Moriguchi, Japan 81/J7
Morin Creek, Sask. 181/C1
Morin Dawa Daurzu, China 77/K2
Morin Heights, Québec 172/C4
Morinville, Alberta 182/D3
Morioka, Japan 81/K4
Morisset, N.S. Wales 97/F3
Morisset, Québec 172/G3
Moriston (riv.), Scotland 15/D3
Morjärv, Sweden 18/N3
Morlaix, France 28/B3
Morland, Kansas 232/B2
Morley, Alberta 182/C4
Morley, Iowa 229/L4
Morley, Mich. 250/D5
Morley, Mo. 261/N8
Morley, N.Y. 276/K1
Morley, Tenn. 237/O7
Mormon (lake), Ariz. 198/D4
Mormon (mt.), Idaho 220/D4
Mormon (mts.), Nev. 266/G5
Mormon Lake, Ariz. 198/D4
Morne-à-l'Eau, Guadeloupe 161/A6
Morne Seychellois (mt.), Seychelles 118/H5
Morningside, Alberta 182/D3
Morningside, Md. 245/G5
Morningside, Queensland 88/K2
Morningside Park, Conn. 210/G3
Morning Sun, Iowa 229/L6
Mornington (isl.), Chile 138/D8
Mornington (isl.), Queensland 88/F3
Mornington (isl.), Queensland 95/A3
Mornington, Victoria 97/C6
Mornington (pen.), Victoria 97/C6
Morning View, Ky. 237/N3
Moro, Ark. 202/H4
Moro (creek), Ark. 202/F7
Moro, Oreg. 291/G2
Moro (gulf), Philippines 82/D7
Moro (gulf), Philippines 85/G4
Moro (mt.), Switzerland 39/E5
Moro Bay, Ark. 202/F7
Morobe, Papua N.G. 85/C7
Morocco 2/J4
Morocco 102/B1
MOROCCO 106/C2
Morocco, Ind. 227/C3
Moroceli, Honduras 154/D3
Morochata, Bolivia 136/B5
Morococha, Peru 128/D8
Morogoro (reg.), Tanzania 115/G5
Morogoro, Tanzania 115/G5
Morogoro, Tanzania 102/F5
Moroleón, Mexico 150/J6
Morombe, Madagascar 118/G4
Moromoro, Bolivia 136/C6
Morón, Argentina 143/G7
Morón, Cuba 158/F2
Morón, Cuba 156/B2
Moron, Haiti 158/A6
Mörön (Muren), Mongolia 77/F2
Moron (mt.), Switzerland 39/D2
Morón, Venezuela 124/D2
Morona, Ecuador 128/D4
Morona (riv.), Peru 128/D5
Morona-Santiago (prov.), Ecuador 128/C4
Morondava, Madagascar 118/G3
Morondava, Madagascar 102/G7
Morón de la Frontera, Spain 33/D4
Morongo Ind. Res., Calif. 204/J10
Moroni (cap.), Comoros 118/G2
Moroni (cap.), Comoros 102/G6
Moroni, Utah 304/C4
Moron Us He (riv.), China 77/D5
Morotai (isl.), Indonesia 54/O9
Morotai (isl.), Indonesia 85/H5
Moroto, Uganda 115/F3
Morovis, P. Rico 161/D1
Morpeth, England 13/F2
Morpeth, England 10/F3
Morpeth, Ontario 177/C5
Morphou, Cyprus 63/E5
Morphou (bay), Cyprus 63/E5
Morral, Ohio 284/D4
Morrice, Mich. 250/E6
Morrill, Kansas 232/G2
Morrill•, Maine 243/E7
Morrill, Minn. 255/E5
Morrill (co.), Nebr. 264/A3
Morrill, Nebr. 264/A3
Morrillton, Ark. 202/E3
Morrin, Alberta 182/D4
Morrinhos, Brazil 132/D7
Morrinsville, N. Zealand 100/E2
Morris, Ala. 195/E3
Morris (res.), Calif. 204/D10
Morris•, Conn. 210/C2
Morris, Ga. 217/C7
Morris, Ill. 222/E2
Morris, Ind. 227/G6
Morris (co.), Kansas 232/F3
Morris, Manitoba 179/E5
Morris, Minn. 255/C5
Morris (co.), N.J. 273/D2
Morris, N.Y. 276/K5
Morris, Okla. 288/P3
Morris, Pa. 294/H2
Morris (mt.), S. Australia 94/B2
Morris (isl.), S.C. 296/H6
Morris (co.), Texas 303/K4
Morris, W. Va. 312/E5
Morrisburg, Ontario 177/J3
Morris Chapel, Tenn. 237/E10
Morrisdale, New Bruns. 170/D3
Morrisdale, Pa. 294/F4
Morrisey, Wyo. 319/H2
Morris Fork, Ky. 237/O6
Morris Jessup (cape), Greenl. 4/A11
Morrison, Colo. 208/J3
Morrison, Ill. 222/C2
Morrison, Iowa 229/H4
Morrison (lake), Manitoba 179/C1
Morrison (co.), Minn. 255/D4
Morrison, Mo. 261/J5
Morrison, Okla. 288/M2
Morrison, Tenn. 237/K9
Morrison Bluff, Ark. 202/D3
Morrison City, Tenn. 237/R7
Morrisonville, Ill. 222/D4
Morrisonville, N.Y. 276/N1
Morrisonville, Wis. 317/G9
Morris Plains, N.J. 273/D2
Morris Run, Pa. 294/J2
Morriston, Ark. 202/G1
Morriston, Fla. 212/D2
Morriston, Ontario 177/D4
Morristown, Ariz. 198/C5
Morristown, Ill. 222/D1
Morristown, Ind. 227/F5
Morristown, Minn. 255/E6
Morristown, N.J. 273/D2
Morristown, N.Y. 276/J1
Morristown, Ohio 284/H5
Morristown, S. Dak. 298/F2
Morristown, Tenn. 237/P8
Morristown•, Vt. 268/B2
Morristown Nat'l Hist. Park., N.J. 273/D2
Morrisvale, W. Va. 312/C6
Morrisville, Mo. 261/F8
Morrisville, N.Y. 276/J5
Morrisville, N.C. 281/M3
Morrisville, Pa. 294/N5
Morrisville, Vt. 268/B2
Morrito, Nicaragua 154/E5
Morro (pt.), Chile 138/A6
Morro Bay, Calif. 204/D8
Morro do Chapéu, Brazil 132/F5
Morropón, Peru 128/C5
Morros, Brazil 132/F3
Morrosquillo (gulf), Colombia 126/C3
Morrow, Ark. 202/B2
Morrow, Ga. 217/K2
Morrow, La. 238/F5
Morrow (co.), Ohio 284/E4
Morrow, Ohio 284/B7
Morrow (co.), Oreg. 291/H2
Morrow Point (res.), Colo. 208/E6
Morrowville, Kansas 232/E2
Morrumbala, Mozambique 118/F3
Morrumbene, Mozambique 118/F4
Mors (isl.), Denmark 21/B4
Morse (res.), Ind. 227/E4
Morse, La. 238/F6
Morse, Sask. 181/D5
Morse, Texas 303/C1
Morse, Wis. 317/E3
Morse Bluff, Nebr. 264/H3
Morse Mill, Mo. 261/L6
Morses Line, Vt. 268/A2
Morshank, Russia52/F4
Mortagne-au-Perche, France 28/D3
Mortara, Italy 34/B2
Morte (pt.), England 13/C6
Morteau, France 28/G4
Morteros, Argentina 143/D3
Mortes (Manso) (riv.), Brazil 132/D6
Mortlach, Sask. 181/E5
Mortlake, Victoria 97/B6
Morton, Ill. 222/D3
Morton (co.), Kansas 232/A4
Morton, Minn. 255/C6
Morton, Miss. 256/E6
Morton (co.), N. Dak. 282/H6
Morton, Ontario 177/H3
Morton, Pa. 294/M7
Morton, Texas 303/B4
Morton, Wash. 310/C4
Morton, Wyo. 319/D2
Morton Grove, Ill. 222/B5
Morton Mills, Iowa 229/C6
Mortons Gap, Ky. 237/F6
Mortsel, Belgium 27/E6
Moruga, Trin. & Tob. 161/B11
Moruka (riv.), Guyana 131/B2
Morundah, N.S. Wales 97/D4
Moruya, N.S. Wales 97/D4
Morvan (plat.), France 28/F4
Morven, Ga. 217/E9
Morven, N. Zealand 100/C6
Morven, N.C. 281/J5
Morven, Queensland 95/C5
Morven (dist.), Scotland 15/C4
Morven (mt.), Scotland 15/E2
Morvi, India 68/C4
Morvin, Ala. 195/C7
Morwell, Victoria 97/D5
Morwell, Victoria 88/H7
Mosbach, Germany 22/C4
Mosby, Mo. 261/R4
Mosby, Mont. 262/J4
Mosca, Colo. 208/H7
Moscavide, Portugal 33/A1
Moscow, Ark. 202/G5
Moscow, Idaho 220/B3
Moscow, Idaho 188/C1
Moscow, Ind. 227/F6
Moscow, Iowa 229/L5
Moscow, Kansas 232/A4
Moscow, Ky. 237/D7
Moscow, Miss. 256/G5
Moscow, Ohio 284/B8
Moscow, Pa. 294/F7
Moscow, Tenn. 237/C10
Moscow (cap.), Russia 2/L3
Moscow (cap.), Russia 7/H3
Moscow (cap.), Russia 48/D4
Moscow (Moskva) (cap.), Russia 52/E3
Moscow, Vt. 268/B3
Moscow Mills, Md. 245/B2
Moscow Mills, Mo. 261/K5
Mosel (riv.), Germany 22/B3
Mosel (riv.), Luxembourg 27/J9
Moseley, Sask. 181/G3
Moseley, Va. 307/H6
Moselle (dept.), France 28/G3
Moselle (riv.), France 28/G3
Moselle, Miss. 256/F8
Moselle, Mo. 261/L6
Moser River, Nova Scotia 168/F4
Moses (lake), Wash. 310/F3
Moses Coulee (canyon), Wash. 310/F3
Moses Lake, Wash. 310/F3
Moses Point, Alaska 196/F2
Mosetenes, Cordillera de (range), Bolivi 136/B5
Mosgiel, N. Zealand 100/C6
Mosgrove, Pa. 294/D4
Moshannon, Pa. 294/F3
Mosheim, Tenn. 237/R8
Mosher, S. Dak. 298/J7
Moshi, Tanzania 115/G4
Moshi, Tanzania 102/F5
Mosler, Oreg. 291/F2
Mosina, Poland 47/C2
Mosinee, Wis. 317/G6
Mosi-Oa-Tunya (falls), Africa 102/E6
Mosi-Oa-Tunya (Victoria) (falls), Zambia 115/E7
Mosi-Oa-Tunya (Victoria) (falls), Zimbabwe 118/C3
Mosjøen, Norway 18/H4
Moskenesøya (isl.), Norway 18/H3
Moskva (Moscow) (cap.), U.S.S.R 52/E3
Moskva (riv.), Russia52/E3
Mosler, Oreg. 291/C2
Mosman, N.S. Wales 88/L4
Mosman, N.S. Wales 97/J3
Mosonmagyaróvár, Hungary 41/D3
Mosquera, Colombia 126/A6
Mosquero, N. Mex. 274/F3
Mosquic (lake), Québec 172/C3
Mosquito (lag.), Fla. 212/F3
Mosquito, Riacho (riv.), Paraguay 144/C3
Mosquito Creek (lake), Ohio 284/J3
Mosquitos, Costa de (reg.), Nicaragua 154/E4
Mosquitos, Golfo de los (gulf), Panama 154/G6
Moss, Miss. 256/F7
Moss, Norway 18/D4
Moss, Tenn. 237/K7
Mossaka, Congo 115/C4
Mossbank, Sask. 181/E6
Moss Beach, Calif. 204/H3
Mossel Bay, S. Africa 102/E8
Mossel Bay, S. Africa 118/C6
Mossendjo, Congo 115/B4
Mossgiel, N.S. Wales 97/C4
Moss Landing, Calif. 204/C7
Mossleigh, Alberta 182/D4
Mossman, Queensland 88/G3
Mossman, Queensland 95/C3
Mossoró, Brazil 120/F3
Mossoró, Brazil 132/G4
Moss Point, Miss. 256/G10
Mossuril, Mozambique 118/G2
Moss Vale, N.S. Wales 97/F4
Mossville, Ill. 222/D3
Mossy (riv.), Manitoba 179/C3
Mossy (riv.), Sask. 181/H1
Mossy Head, Fla. 212/C6
Mossyrock, Wash. 310/C4
Most, Czech Rep. 41/B1
Mostaganem, Algeria 102/C1
Mostaganem, Algeria 106/D1
Mostar, Bos. 7/F4
Mostar, Bos. 45/D4
Mosty, Belarus 52/B4
Mosul, Iraq 66/C2
Mosul, Iraq 59/D2
Mosul, Iraq 54/F6
Motacucito, Bolivia 136/E5
Mota del Cuervo, Spain 33/E3
Motagua (riv.), Guatemala 154/C3
Motala, Sweden 18/J7
Motherwell and Wishaw, Scotland 10/B1
Motherwell and Wishaw, Scotland 15/C2
Motilla del Palancar, Spain 33/E3
Motiti (isl.), N. Zealand 100/F2
Motley, Minn. 255/D4
Motley (co.), Texas 303/D3
Motobu, Japan 81/N6
Motozintla de Mendoza, Mexico 150/N9
Motril, Spain 33/E4
Motsuta (cape), Japan 81/J2
Mott, N. Dak. 282/F7
Motu (riv.), N. Zealand 100/F3
Motueka, N. Zealand 100/D4
Motuhora (isl.), N. Zealand 100/F2
Motuihe (isl.), N. Zealand 100/C1
Motul de Fielipe Carillo Puerto, Mexico 150/P6
Motupe, Peru 128/C6
Motutapu (isl.), N. Zealand 100/C1
Motygino, Russia 48/K4
Mouchoir (passage), Turks & Caicos 156/D2
Moúdros, Greece 45/G6
Moudjéria, Mauritania 106/B5
Moudon, Switzerland 39/C3
Mouhoun (riv.), Burkina Faso 106/D6
Mouila, Gabon 115/B4
Mouka, Cent. Afr. Rep. 115/D2
Moulamein, N.S. Wales 97/C4
Moulamein (creek), N.S. Wales 97/C4
Mould Bay, Canada 4/B16
Mould Bay, N.W.T. 187/F2
Moule, Guadeloupe 161/B6
Moule à Chique (cape), St. Lucia 161/G7
Moulin-Morneault, New Bruns. 170/B1
Moulins, France 28/E4
Moulmein, Burma 72/C3
Moulmein, Burma 54/L8
Moulouya (riv.), Morocco 106/D2
Moulton, Ala. 195/D2
Moulton, Iowa 229/H7
Moulton, Mont. 262/G3
Moulton, Texas 303/H8
Moultonboro•, N.H. 268/E4
Moultrie, Fla. 212/E2
Moultrie, Ga. 217/E8
Moultrie (co.), Ill. 222/E4
Moultrie (lake), S.C. 188/K4
Moultrie (lake), S.C. 296/G5
Mounana, Gabon 115/B4
Mound, La. 238/H2
Mound, Minn. 255/E6
Mound Bayou, Miss. 256/C3
Mound City, Ill. 222/D6
Mound City, Kansas 232/H3
Mound City, Mo. 261/B2
Mound City, S. Dak. 298/K2
Mound City Group Nat'l Mon., Ohio 284/E7
Moundou, Chad 111/C6
Moundou, Chad 102/D4
Moundridge, Kansas 232/E3
Mounds, Ill. 222/D6
Mounds, Okla. 288/O3
Mound Station (Timewell), Ill. 222/C3
Mounds View, Minn. 255/G5
Moundsville, W. Va. 312/E3
Mound Valley, Kansas 232/G4
Moundville, Ala. 195/C5
Moundville, Mo. 261/C7
Moung Roussei, Cambodia 72/D4
Mouniapamôk, Laos 72/E4
Mount (cape), Liberia 106/B7
Mountain, N. Dak. 282/P2
Mountain (riv.), N.W.T. 187/F3
Mountain, Ontario 177/J2
Mountain (prov.), Philippines 82/C2
Mountain, W. Va. 312/E4
Mountain, Wis. 317/K5
Mountainair, N. Mex. 274/C4
Mountain Ash, Ky. 237/N7
Mountain Ash, Wales 13/A6
Mountain Ash, Wales 10/E5
Mountainboro, Ala. 195/F2
Mountain Brook, Ala. 195/E4
Mountainburg, Ark. 202/B2
Mountain City, Ga. 217/F1
Mountain City, Nev. 266/F1
Mountain City, Tenn. 237/T8
Mountain Creek, Ala. 195/E5
Mountain Creek (lake), Texas 303/G2
Mountaindale, Md. 245/J2
Mountain Dale, N.Y. 276/L7
Mountaindale, Oreg. 291/A1
Mountain Fork (riv.), Ark. 202/A5
Mountain Fork (riv.), Okla. 288/S6
Mountain Grove, Mo. 261/H8
Mountain Grove, Ontario 177/H3
Mountain Home, Ark. 202/F1
Mountain Home, Idaho 220/C6
Mountain Home (res.), Idaho 220/C6
Mountainhome, Pa. 294/M3
Mountain Home, Utah 304/D3
Mountain Home A.F.B., Idaho 220/C6
Mountain Iron, Minn. 255/F3
Mountain Lake, Minn. 255/D7
Mountain Lake Park, Md. 245/A3
Mountain Lakes, N.J. 273/E2
Mountain Meadows (res.), Calif. 204/E3
Mountain Park, Ga. 217/D2
Mountain Park, Okla. 288/J5
Mountain Pine, Ark. 202/D4
Mountain Point, Alaska 196/N2
Mountain Rest, S.C. 296/A2
Mountain Road, Manitoba 179/C4
Mountainside, N.J. 273/E2
Mountain Valley, Ark. 202/D4
Mountain View, Alberta 182/D5
Mountain View, Ark. 202/F2
Mountain View, Calif. 204/K3
Mountain View, Ga. 217/K2
Mountainview, Hawaii 218/J5
Mountain View, Mo. 261/J8
Mountain View, N.J. 273/B2
Mountain View, Okla. 288/J4
Mountain View, Wyo. 319/B4
Mountain View, Wyo. 319/F3
Mountain Village, Alaska 196/E2
Mountain Zebra Nat'l Park, S. Africa 118/C6
Mount Airy, Ga. 217/F1
Mount Airy, La. 238/M3
Mount Airy, Md. 245/K3
Mount Airy, N.C. 281/H1
Mount Airy, Tenn. 237/L10
Mount Albert, N. Zealand 100/B1
Mount Albert, Ontario 177/E3
Mount Alto, W. Va. 312/C5
Mount Alton, Pa. 294/E2
Mount Andrew, Ala. 195/H7
Mount Angel, Oreg. 291/B3
Mount Apo National Park, Philippine 82/E7
Mount Arlington, N.J. 273/D2
Mount Arrowsmith, N.S. Wales 97/A2
Mount Assiniboine Prov. Park, Br. Col. 184/K5
Mount Auburn, Ill. 222/D4
Mount Auburn, Ind. 227/G5
Mount Auburn, Iowa 229/J4
Mount Aukum, Calif. 204/E5
Mount Ayr, Ind. 227/C3
Mount Ayr, Iowa 299/E7
Mount Barker, S. Australia 94/C8
Mount Barker, W. Australia 88/B6
Mount Barker, W. Australia 92/B6
Mount Beauty, Victoria 97/D5
Mount Bellew, Ireland 17/D5
Mount Berry, Ga. 217/B2
Mount Bethel, Ga. 217/K1
Mount Blanchard, Ohio 284/D4
Mount Bold (res.), S. Australia 94/B8
Mount Brydges, Ontario 177/C5
Mount Calm, Texas 303/H6
Mount Calvary, Wis. 317/K8
Mount Carbon, W. Va. 312/D7
Mount Carleton Prov. Park, New Bruns. 170/D1
Mount Carmel, Ala. 195/F6
Mount Carmel, Ill. 222/F5
Mount Carmel, Ind. 227/H6
Mount Carmel, Miss. 256/E7
Mount Carmel, Newf. 166/D2
Mount Carmel, N. Dak. 282/O2
Mount Carmel, Ohio 284/C10
Mount Carmel, Pa. 294/K4
Mount Carmel, Pr. Edward I. 168/D2
Mount Carmel, S.C. 296/C3
Mount Carmel, Tenn. 237/R8
Mount Carmel, Utah 304/B6
Mount Carroll, Ill. 222/D1
Mount Cavenagh, North. Terr. 93/C8
Mountcharles, Ireland 17/E2
Mount Clare, W. Va. 312/F4
Mount Clemens, Mich. 250/G6
Mount Cory, Ohio 284/C4
Mount Crawford, Va. 307/L4
Mount Croghan, S.C. 296/G2
Mount Currie, Br. Col. 184/F5
Mount Darwin, Zimbabwe 118/E3
Mount Desert, Maine 243/G7
Mount Desert•, Maine 243/G7
Mount Desert (isl.), Maine 243/G7
Mount Desert Rock (isl.), Maine 243/G8
Mount Dora, Fla. 212/E3
Mount Dora, N. Mex. 274/F2
Mount Doreen, North. Terr. 93/B7
Mount Douglas, Queensland 95/C4
Mount Drysdale, N.S. Wales 97/C2
Mount Eaton, Ohio 284/G4
Mount Eba, S. Australia 94/D4
Mount Eden, Ky. 237/L4
Mount Eden, N. Zealand 100/B1
Mount Edziza Prov. Park and Rec. Area Br. Col. 184/B1
Mount Elgin, Ontario 177/D5
Mount Emu (creek), Victoria 97/B5
Mount Enterprise, Texas 303/K6
Mount Ephraim, N.J. 273/B3
Mount Erie, Ill. 222/E5
Mount Etna, Ind. 227/F3
Mount Etna, Iowa 229/D6
Mount Everard, Guyana 131/B2
Mount Forest, Mich. 250/F5
Mount Forest, Ontario 177/D4
Mount Freedom, N.J. 273/D2
Mount Gambier, Australia 87/D9
Mount Gambier, S. Australia 88/G7
Mount Gambier, S. Australia 94/G7
Mount Gay, W. Va. 312/C7
Mount Gilead, N.C. 281/K4
Mount Gilead, Ohio 284/E4
Mount Gravatt, Queensland 88/K3
Mount Hagen, Papua N.G. 85/B7
Mount Hamill, Iowa 229/K7
Mount Healthy, Ohio 284/B9
Mount Hermon, Calif. 204/K4
Mount Hermon, La. 238/K5
Mount Hermon, Mass. 249/D2
Mount Holly, Ark. 202/E7
Mount Holly•, N.J. 273/D4
Mount Holly, N.C. 281/H4
Mount Holly, S.C. 296/H5
Mount Holly•, Vt. 268/B5
Mount Holly, Va. 307/P4
Mount Holly Springs, Pa. 294/H5
Mount Hood, Oreg. 291/F2
Mount Hope, Ala. 195/D2
Mount Hope (riv.), Conn. 210/G1
Mount Hope, Kansas 232/E4
Mount Hope (bay), Mass. 249/K6
Mount Hope, N.J. 273/D2
Mount Hope, N.S. Wales 97/C3
Mount Hope, Ohio 284/G4
Mount Hope, Ontario 177/E4
Mount Hope (bay), R.I. 249/K6
Mount Hope, W. Va. 312/D7
Mount Hope, Wis. 317/D10
Mount Horeb, Wis. 317/G10
Mount Ida, Ark. 202/C4
Mount Ida, Wis. 317/E10
Mount Isa, Queensland 95/A4
Mount Isa, Queensland 88/F4
Mount Jackson, Va. 307/L3
Mount Jewett, Pa. 294/E2
Mount Joy, Pa. 294/K5
Mount Judea, Ark. 202/D2
Mount Juliet, Tenn. 237/H8
Mount Kisco, N.Y. 276/N8
Mount Kuring-gai, N.S. Wales 97/J3
Mountlake Terrace, Wash. 310/B1
Mount Laurel•, N.J. 273/D4
Mount Lebanon, La. 238/D2
Mount Lebanon•, Pa. 294/B7
Mount Lemmon, Ariz. 198/E6
Mount Leonard, Mo. 261/F4
Mount Liberty, Ohio 284/E5
Mount Lofty (range), S. Australia 88/F6
Mount Lookout, W. Va. 312/E6
Mount Magnet, W. Australia 88/B5
Mount Magnet, W. Australia 92/B5
Mount Margaret, Queensland 95/A3
Mount Margaret, W. Australia 88/C5
Mount Margaret, W. Australia 92/C5

Newry 417

Neuchâtel, Switzerland 39/C3
Neuchâtel (lake), Switzerland 39/C3
Neudorf, Sask. 181/J5
Neuenegg, Switzerland 39/D3
Neuenhagen bei Berlin, Germany 22/F4
Neufchâteau, Belgium 27/G9
Neufchâteau, France 28/F3
Neufchâtel-en-Bray, France 28/D3
Neugersdorf, Germany 22/F3
Neuhausen am Rheinfall, Switzerland 39/G1
Neuhorst, Sask. 181/E3
Neuilly-sur-Seine, France 28/A1
Neu-Isenburg, Germany 22/C3
Neumarkt am Wallersee, Austria 41/B3
Neumarkt in der Oberpfalz, Germany 22/D4
Neumarkt in Steiermark, Austria 41/C3
Neumünster, Germany 22/C1
Neunkirch, Switzerland 39/F1
Neunkirchen, Austria 41/C3
Neunkirchen, Germany 22/B4
Neuquén (prov.), Argentina 143/C4
Neuquén, Argentina 143/C4
Neuquén, Argentina 120/C6
Neuquén (riv.), Argentina 143/C4
Neuruppin, Germany 22/E2
Neuse, N.C. 281/M3
Neuse (riv.), N.C. 281/R5
Neusiedl am See, Austria 41/D3
Neusiedler See (lake), Austria 41/D3
Neusiedler See (lake), Hungary 41/D3
Neuss, Germany 22/B3
Neustadt, Germany 22/D3
Neustadt, Ontario 177/D3
Neustadt (Titisee-Neustadt), Germany 22/C5
Neustadt an der Aisch, Germany 22/D4
Neustadt an der Weinstrasse, Germany 22/B4
Neustadt bei Coburg, Germany 22/D3
Neustadt-Glewe, Germany 22/D2
Neustadt in Holstein, Germany 22/D1
Neustift im Stubaital, Austria 41/A3
Neustrelitz, Germany 22/E2
NEUTRAL ZONE 59/E4
Neutral Zone 54/F7
Neu-Ulm, Germany 22/D4
Neuville, Québec 172/F3
Neuwerk (isl.), Germany 22/C2
Neuwied, Germany 22/B3
Neva, Tenn. 237/T8
Nevada 188/C3
NEVADA 266
Nevada (co.), Ark. 202/D6
Nevada (co.), Calif. 204/E4
Nevada, Sierra (mts.), Calif. 204/E4
Nevada, Iowa 229/G5
Nevada, Mo. 261/D7
Nevada, Ohio 284/D4
Nevada, Sierra (mts.), Spain 33/E4
Nevada (state), U.S. 146/G6
Nevada City, Calif. 204/D4
Nevatim, Israel 65/B5
Nevel', Russia 52/D3
Nevele, Belgium 27/D6
Nevel'sk, Russia 48/P5
Nevers, France 28/E4
Neversink (res.), N.Y. 276/L7
Nevertire, N.S. Wales 97/D2
Nevesinje, Bos. 45/D4
Neville, Ohio 284/B8
Neville, Sask. 181/D6
Nevils, Ga. 217/J6
Nevinnomyssk, Russia 52/F6
Nevinville, Iowa 229/D6
Nevis, Alberta 182/D3
Nevis, Minn. 255/D4
Nevis (isl.), St. Kitts & Nevis 161/D11
Nevis (isl.), St. Kitts & Nevis 156/F3
Nevis (peak), St. Kitts & Nevis 161/D11
Nevis, Loch (inlet), Scotland 15/C3
Nevisdale, Ky. 237/N7
Nevşehir (prov.), Turkey 63/F3
Nevşehir, Turkey 59/B2
Nevşehir, Turkey 63/F3
New (riv.), Belize 154/C2
New (riv.), Calif. 204/K11
New (for.), England 13/F6
New (riv.), Fla. 212/D1
New (riv.), Fla. 212/B1
New (riv.), Guyana 131/C4
New, South Fork (riv.), N.C. 281/G2
New (riv.), N.C. 281/O5
New (riv.), S.C. 296/E6
New (inlet), Va. 307/S6
New (riv.), Va. 307/F8
New (riv.), W. Va. 312/E7
New Abbey, Scotland 15/E6
Newagen, Maine 243/D8
Newala, Tanzania 115/G6
New Albany, Ind. 188/J3
New Albany, Ind. 227/F8
New Albany, Kansas 232/G4
New Albany, Miss. 256/G2
New Albany, Ohio 284/E5
New Albany, Pa. 294/J2
New Albin, Iowa 229/L2
Newald, Wis. 317/J4
New Alexandria, Ohio 284/J5
New Alexandria, Pa. 294/C5
Newalla, Okla. 288/M4
New Alluwe, Okla. 288/R1
New Almaden, Calif. 204/L4
New Almelo, Kansas 232/B2
New Amsterdam, Guyana 120/D2
New Amsterdam, Guyana 131/B2
New Amsterdam, Ind. 227/E8
New Amsterdam, Wis. 317/C8
New Angledool, N.S. Wales 97/E1
Newark, Ark. 202/H2
Newark, Calif. 204/K3
Newark, Del. 245/P2
Newark, England 13/G4
Newark, England 10/F4
Newark, Ill. 222/E2
Newark, Md. 245/S7
Newark, Mo. 261/H2
Newark, N.J. 188/L2
Newark, N.J. 273/B2
Newark (bay), N.J. 273/B2
Newark, N.Y. 276/G4
Newark, Ohio 284/F5
Newark, S. Dak. 298/O2
Newark, Texas 303/E1
Newark•, Vt. 268/D2
Newark, W. Va. 312/D4
Newark Int'l Airport, N.J. 273/B2
Newark Valley, N.Y. 276/H6
Newarthill, Scotland 15/C2
New Athens, Ill. 222/D5
New Athens, Ohio 284/H5
New Auburn, Minn. 255/D6
New Auburn, Wis. 317/D5
New Augusta, Miss. 256/F8
Newaygo (co.), Mich. 250/D5
Newaygo, Mich. 250/D5
New Baden, Ill. 222/D5
New Baltimore, Mich. 250/G6
New Baltimore, N.Y. 276/N6
New Baltimore, Pa. 294/E6
New Baltimore, Va. 307/N3
New Bavaria, Ohio 284/B3
New Beaver, Pa. 294/B4
New Bedford, Ill. 222/D2
New Bedford, Mass. 188/N2
New Bedford, Mass. 249/K6
New Bedford, Ohio 284/G5
New Bedford, Pa. 294/A3
New Bellsville, Ind. 227/E6
Newberg, Oreg. 291/A2
New Berlin, Ill. 222/D4
New Berlin, N.Y. 276/K5
New Berlin, Pa. 294/J4
New Berlin, Wis. 317/K2
Newbern, Ala. 195/C5
Newbern, Ind. 227/F6
New Bern, N.C. 188/L4
New Bern, N.C. 281/P4
Newbern, Tenn. 237/C8
Newberne, W. Va. 312/E4
Newberry, Fla. 212/D2
Newberry, Ind. 227/C7
Newberry, Mich. 250/D2
Newberry (co.), S.C. 296/D3
Newberry, S.C. 296/D3
Newberry Springs, Calif. 204/J9
New Bethlehem, Pa. 294/D3
Newbiggin-by-the-Sea, England 13/F2
New Blaine, Ark. 202/D3
Newbliss, Ireland 17/G3
New Bloomfield, Mo. 261/J5
New Bloomfield, Pa. 294/H5
New Bloomington, Ohio 284/D4
New Bonaventure, Newf. 166/D2
Newborn, Ga. 217/E3
Newboro, Ontario 177/H3
New Boston, Ill. 222/B2
New Boston, Mich. 250/F6
New Boston, Mo. 261/G3
New Boston•, N.H. 268/D6
New Boston, Ohio 284/E8
New Boston, Texas 303/K4
New Bothwell, Manitoba 179/F5
New Braintree•, Mass. 249/F3
New Braunfels, Texas 303/K10
New Bremen, N.Y. 276/K3
New Bremen, Ohio 284/B5
Newbridge (Droichead Nua), Ireland 17/H5
New Bridge, Oreg. 291/K3
New Brigden, Alberta 182/E4
New Brighton, Minn. 255/G5
New Brighton, Pa. 294/B4
New Britain, Conn. 210/E2
New Britain (isl.), Papua N.G. 87/F6
New Britain (isl.), Papua N.G. 85/C7
New Britain (isl.), Papua N.G. 86/B2
New Britain, Pa. 294/M5
New Brockton, Ala. 195/G8
Newbrook, Alberta 182/D2
NEW BRUNSWICK 170
New Brunswick (prov.) 162/K6
New Brunswick (prov.), Canada 146/M5
New Brunswick, N.J. 273/E3
New Buena Vista, Pa. 294/E5
New Buffalo, Mich. 250/C7
New Buffalo, Pa. 294/H5
Newburg, Ark. 202/G1
Newburg, Iowa 229/H5
Newburg, Md. 245/L7
Newburg, Mo. 261/J7
Newburg, N. Dak. 282/J2
Newburg, Pa. 294/G5
Newburg (La Jose), Pa. 294/E4
Newburg, W. Va. 312/G4
Newburg, Wis. 317/K9
Newburgh, Ind. 227/C9
Newburgh•, Maine 243/F6
Newburgh, N.Y. 188/M2
Newburgh, N.Y. 276/M7
Newburgh, Ontario 177/H3
Newburgh, Scotland 10/E2
Newburgh, Grampian, Scotland 15/G3
Newburgh, Fife, Scotland 15/E4
Newburgh Heights, Ohio 284/H9
New Burlington, Ind. 227/G4
New Burlington, Ohio 284/B9
New Burnside, Ill. 222/E6
Newbury, England 13/F6
Newbury, England 10/F5
Newbury•, Mass. 249/L1
Newbury•, N.H. 268/C5
Newbury, Ohio 284/H3
Newbury, Ontario 177/C5
Newbury, Vt. 268/C3
Newbury•, Vt. 268/C3
Newburyport, Mass. 249/L1
New Bussa, Nigeria 106/E6
NEW CALEDONIA 86/G4
New Caledonia 87/G8
New Caledonia (isl.), (Fr.) 2/T7
New Caledonia (isl.), New Caled. 87/G8
New Caledonia (isl.), New Caled. 86/G4
New Cambria, Kansas 232/E3
New Cambria, Mo. 261/G3
New Canaan•, Conn. 210/B4
New Canton, Ill. 222/B4
New Canton, Va. 307/M5
New Carlisle, Ind. 227/E1
New Carlisle, Ohio 284/C6
New Carlisle, Québec 172/D2
New Carlisle, Québec 174/E3
New Carrollton, Md. 245/G4
New Castile (reg.), Spain 33/E3
Newcastle, Australia 2/S7
Newcastle, Calif. 204/C8
New Castle, Colo. 208/E3
New Castle (co.), Del. 245/R2
New Castle, Del. 245/R2
New Castle, Ind. 227/G5
Newcastle, Ireland 10/B4
Newcastle, Ireland 17/D7
New Castle, Ky. 237/L4
Newcastle•, Maine 243/D7
Newcastle, N. Br. 162/K6
Newcastle, N.S. Wales 88/J6
Newcastle, Nebr. 264/H2
Newcastle, New Bruns. 170/E2
New Castle•, N.H. 268/F5
Newcastle, N.S. Wales 97/F3
Newcastle, N. Ireland 10/D3
Newcastle, N. Ireland 17/J3
Newcastle (creek), North. Terr. 93/C4
New Castle, Ohio 284/F5
Newcastle, Okla. 288/L4
Newcastle, Ontario 177/F4
New Castle, Pa. 188/K2
New Castle, Pa. 294/B3
Newcastle, St. Kitts & Nevis 161/D11
Newcastle, S. Africa 118/E5
Newcastle, Texas 303/F4
Newcastle, Utah 304/A6
New Castle, Va. 307/H5
Newcastle, Wyo. 319/H2
Newcastle Creek, New Bruns. 170/D2
Newcastle-Damariscotta, Maine 243/E7
Newcastle Emlyn, Wales 13/C5
Newcastleton, Scotland 15/F5
Newcastle-under-Lyme, England 13/E4
Newcastle-under-Lyme, England 10/E4
Newcastle upon Tyne, England 7/D3
Newcastle upon Tyne, England 10/E3
Newcastle upon Tyne, England 13/H3
Newcastle Waters, North. Terr. 93/C4
New Centerville, Pa. 294/D6
New Chelsea, Newf. 166/D2
New Chicago, Ind. 227/C1
New Church, Va. 307/S5
New Cinema, Br. Col. 184/F3
New City, N.Y. 276/K8
New Columbia, Pa. 294/H3
New Columbus, Pa. 294/K3
Newcomb, N. Mex. 274/A2
Newcomb, N.Y. 276/M3
Newcomb, Tenn. 237/N7
Newcomerstown, Ohio 284/G5
New Concord, Ky. 237/E7
New Concord, Ohio 284/G6
New Cordell (Cordell), Okla. 288/H4
New Corydon, Ind. 227/H3
New Court, Mo. 261/J2
New Creek, W. Va. 312/J4
New Cumberland, Pa. 294/J5
New Cumberland, W. Va. 312/E2
New Cumnock, Scotland 15/D5
Newdale, Idaho 220/G6
Newdale, Manitoba 179/B4
New Dayton, Alberta 182/D5
New Deal, Texas 303/C4
New Deer, Scotland 15/F3
Newdegate, W. Australia 92/B6
New Delhi (cap.), India 2/N4
New Delhi, India 54/J7
New Delhi (cap.), India 68/D3
New Denmark, New Bruns. 170/C1
New Denver, Br. Col. 184/J5
New Diggings, Wis. 317/F10
New Douglas, Ill. 222/D5
New Dover, Ohio 284/D5
New Durham•, N.H. 268/E5
New Eagle, Pa. 294/B5
New Edinburg, Ark. 202/F6
New Effington, S. Dak. 298/R2
New Egypt, N.J. 273/E3
Newell, Ala. 195/H4
Newell (lake), Alberta 182/E4
Newell, Iowa 229/D3
Newell, S. Dak. 298/C4
Newell, W. Va. 312/E1
New Ellenton, S.C. 296/D5
Newellton, La. 238/H2
Newellton, Nova Scotia 168/C5
New England (range), N.S. Wales 97/F1
New England, N. Dak. 282/E6
New England, W. Va. 312/C4
Newenham (cape), Alaska 196/F3
New Enterprise, Pa. 294/F5
New Era, La. 238/G4
New Era, Mich. 250/C5
New Era, Oreg. 291/B2
Newe Yam, Israel 65/B2
Newe Zohar, Israel 65/C5
New Fairfield•, Conn. 210/B3
Newfane, N.Y. 276/C4
Newfane, Vt. 268/B6
Newfane•, Vt. 268/B6
Newfield, Maine 243/B8
Newfield•, Maine 243/B8
Newfield, N.J. 273/D4
Newfield, N.Y. 276/G6
Newfields•, N.H. 268/F5
New Fish Creek, Alberta 182/B2
New Florence, Mo. 261/K5
New Florence, Pa. 294/D5
Newfolden, Minn. 255/B2
New Fork (lakes), Wyo. 319/C2
Newfound (lake), N.H. 268/D4
NEWFOUNDLAND 166
Newfoundland (prov.) 162/L5
Newfoundland (isl.) 162/L6
Newfoundland (prov.), Canada 146/M4
Newfoundland (isl.), Canada 2/G3
Newfoundland, Ky. 237/P4
Newfoundland (isl.), Newf. 166/C4
Newfoundland (isl.), Newf. 146/N5
Newfoundland, N.J. 273/D1
Newfoundland, Pa. 294/M3
Newfoundland (mts.), Utah 304/A2
New Franken, Wis. 317/L6
New Frankfort, Mo. 261/F4
New Franklin, Mo. 261/G4
New Freedom, Pa. 294/J6
New Freeport, Pa. 294/B6
New Galilee, Pa. 294/A4
New Galloway, Scotland 10/D3
New Galloway, Scotland 15/D5
Newgate, Br. Col. 184/K5
New Georgia (isl.), Solomon Is. 87/F6
New Georgia (isl.), Solomon Is. 86/D3
New Germantown, Pa. 294/G5
New Germany, Minn. 255/E6
New Germany, Nova Scotia 168/D4
New Glarus, Wis. 317/G10
New Glasgow, Nova Scotia 168/F3
New Glasgow, Québec 172/D4
New Gloucester, Maine 243/C8
New Gloucester•, Maine 243/C8
New Goshen, Ind. 227/C5
New Gretna, N.J. 273/E4
New Guinea (isl.) 2/S6
New Guinea (isl.) 54/P10
New Guinea (isl.) 87/E6
New Guinea (isl.), Papua N.G. 86/B2
Newgulf, Texas 303/J8
Newhalem, Wash. 310/D2
Newhalen, Alaska 196/H3
Newhall, Calif. 204/G9
Newhall, Iowa 229/K5
Newhall, W. Va. 312/C8
Newham, England 13/H8
Newham, England 10/B5
New Hamburg, Mo. 261/O8
New Hamburg, Ontario 177/D4
New Hampshire 188/M2
NEW HAMPSHIRE 268
New Hampshire, Ohio 284/C4
New Hampshire (state), U.S. 146/L5
New Hampton, Iowa 229/J2
New Hampton, Mo. 261/D2
New Hampton•, N.H. 268/D4
New Hampton, N.J. 273/D2
New Hanover (co.), N.C. 281/O6
New Hanover (Lavongai) (isl.), Papua N.G. 87/F6
New Hanover (isl.), Papua N.G. 86/B1
New Harbor, Maine 243/E8
New Harbour, Newf. 166/C4
New Harbour, Newf. 166/D2
New Harbour, Nova Scotia 168/G3
New Harmony, Ind. 227/B8
New Harmony, Utah 304/A6
New Hartford, Conn. 210/C1
New Hartford•, Conn. 210/C1
New Hartford, Iowa 229/H3
New Hartford, Mo. 261/K4
New Hartford, N.Y. 276/K4
New Haven (co.), Conn. 210/D3
New Haven, Conn. 188/M2
New Haven, Conn. 210/D3
New Haven (harb.), Conn. 210/D3
Newhaven, England 10/F5
Newhaven, England 13/H7
New Haven, Ill. 222/E6
New Haven, Ind. 227/H2
New Haven, Ky. 237/K5
New Haven, Mich. 250/G6
New Haven, Mo. 261/K5
New Haven, N.Y. 276/H4
New Haven, Nova Scotia 168/H2
New Haven, Ohio 284/E3
New Haven•, Vt. 268/A3
New Haven, W. Va. 312/C5
New Haven, Wyo. 319/H1
New Hazelton, Br. Col. 184/D2
New Hebrides (Vanuatu) 87/G7
Newhebron, Miss. 256/D7
New Hill, N.C. 281/M3
New Holland, Ga. 217/E2
New Holland, Ill. 222/D3
New Holland, N.C. 281/S4
New Holland, Ohio 284/D6
New Holland, Pa. 294/K5
New Holland, S. Dak. 298/M7
New Holstein, Wis. 317/K8
New Home, Texas 303/C4
New Hope, Ala. 195/F1
Newhope, Ark. 202/C5
New Hope, Ky. 237/L5
New Hope, Minn. 255/G5
New Hope, Ohio 284/A6
New Hope, Pa. 294/N5
New Hope, Tenn. 237/K11
New Hope, Va. 307/L4
New Horse Springs, N. Mex. 274/A5
New Houlka (Houlka), Miss. 256/G2
New Hradec, N. Dak. 282/E5
New Hyde Park, N.Y. 276/P7
New Iberia, La. 238/G6
Newington•, Conn. 210/E2
Newington, Ga. 217/J5
Newington•, N.H. 268/F5
Newington, Ontario 177/K2
Newington, Va. 307/S3
New Ipswich•, N.H. 268/D6
New Ireland (isl.), Papua N.G. 87/F6
New Ireland (isl.), Papua N.G. 86/B1
New Jenny Lind, Ark. 202/B3
New Jersey 188/M3
NEW JERSEY 273
New Jersey, New Bruns. 170/E1
New Jersey (state), U.S. 146/L5
New Johnsonville, Tenn. 237/E8
New Kensington, Pa. 294/C4
New Kent (co.), Va. 307/P5
New Kent, Va. 307/P5
Newkirk, N. Mex. 274/E3
Newkirk, Okla. 288/N1
New Knoxville, Ohio 284/B5
New Laguna, N. Mex. 274/B4
New Lancaster, Kansas 232/H3
Newland, Ind. 227/C2
Newland, N.C. 281/F2
New Lebanon, Ind. 227/C6
New Lebanon, N.Y. 276/O6
New Lebanon, Ohio 284/B6
New Lebanon, Pa. 294/B3
New Leipzig, N. Dak. 282/G7
New Lenox, Ill. 222/B6
New Lexington, Ohio 284/F6
New Liberty, Iowa 229/M5
New Liberty, Ky. 237/M3
New Lima, Okla. 288/O4
New Limerick•, Maine 243/G3
Newlin, Texas 303/D3
New Lisbon, Ind. 227/G5
New Lisbon, N.J. 273/D4
New Lisbon, Wis. 317/F8
New Liskeard, Ont. 162/H6
New Liskeard, Ontario 177/K5
New Liskeard, Ontario 175/E3
Newllano, La. 238/D4
New London, Ark. 202/F7
New London, Conn. 188/M2
New London (co.), Conn. 210/G2
New London, Conn. 210/G3
New London, Ind. 227/E4
New London, Iowa 229/L7
New London, Minn. 255/C5
New London, Mo. 261/K3
New London, N.H. 268/D5
New London•, N.H. 268/D5
New London, N.C. 281/J4
New London, Ohio 284/F3
New London (bay), Pr. Edward I. 168/E2
New London, Texas 303/K5
New London, Wis. 317/J7
New Lothrop, Mich. 250/F5
New Lowell, Ontario 177/E3
New Lyme, Ohio 284/J2
New Lynn, N. Zealand 100/B1
New Madison, Ohio 284/A6
New Madrid (co.), Mo. 261/N9
New Madrid, Mo. 261/O9
Newmains, Scotland 15/C2
Newman, Calif. 204/D6
Newman, Ill. 222/B6
Newman, Ky. 237/G5
Newman (sound), Newf. 166/D2
Newman, W. Australia 88/C4
Newman (lake), Wash. 310/H3
Newman, W. Australia 92/B3
New Manchester, W. Va. 312/E1
Newman Grove, Nebr. 264/G3
Newman Lake, Wash. 310/J3
Newmans Cove, Newf. 166/D2
New Marion, Ind. 227/G6
New Market, Ala. 195/F1
Newmarket, England 13/H5
Newmarket, England 10/G4
New Market, Ind. 227/D5
New Market, Iowa 229/D7
Newmarket, Ireland 10/B4
Newmarket, Ireland 17/C7
Newmarket, Jamaica 158/H6
New Market, Md. 245/J3
New Market, Minn. 255/E6
New Market, Mo. 261/C4
New Market, New Bruns. 170/D3
Newmarket, N.H. 268/F5
Newmarket•, N.H. 268/F5
New Market, Ohio 284/C7
Newmarket, Ontario 177/E3
Newmarket, Queensland 88/K2
Newmarket, Queensland 95/D2
Newmarket, Scotland 15/B2
New Market, Tenn. 237/O8
New Market, Va. 307/L3
Newmarket-on-Fergus, Ireland 17/D6
New Marlborough•, Mass. 249/B4
New Martinsburg, Ohio 284/D7
New Martinsville, W. Va. 312/E3
New Maryland, New Bruns. 170/D3
New Matamoras, Ohio 284/J6
New Meadows, Idaho 220/B5
New Melle, Mo. 261/L5
New Memphis, Ill. 222/D5
Newmerella, Victoria 97/E5
New Mexico 188/E4
NEW MEXICO 274
New Mexico (state), U.S. 146/H6
New Miami, Ohio 284/A7
New Middleton, Tenn. 237/J8
New Middletown, Ind. 227/E8
New Middletown, Ohio 284/J4
New Milford, Conn. 210/B2
New Milford•, Conn. 210/B2
New Milford, Ill. 222/D1
New Milford, N.J. 273/B1
New Milford, Ohio 284/H3
New Milford, Pa. 294/L2
Newmill, Scotland 15/E3
New Mills, England 13/J2
New Mills, England 10/G2
Newmilns and Greenholm, Scotland 15/D5
New Milton, W. Va. 312/E4
New Minas, Nova Scotia 168/D3
New Minden, Ill. 222/D5
New Mount Pleasant, Ind. 227/G4
New Munich, Minn. 255/D5
Newnan, Ga. 217/C4
Newnans (lake), Fla. 212/D2
New Norcia, W. Australia 92/A5
New Norfolk, Tasmania 88/H8
New Norfolk, Tasmania 99/C4
New Norway, Alberta 182/D3
New Offenburg, Mo. 261/M7
New Orleans, La. 188/H5
New Orleans, La. 146/K7
New Orleans, La. 238/O4
New Orleans, U.S. 2/E4
New Osgoode, Sask. 181/H3
New Oxford, Pa. 294/H6
New Palestine, Ind. 227/F5
New Pallas, Ireland 17/E6
New Paltz, N.Y. 276/M7
New Paris, Ind. 227/F2
New Paris, Ohio 284/A6
New Paris, Pa. 294/E5
New Pass (range), Nev. 266/D3
New Pekin, Ind. 227/F7
New Perlican, Newf. 166/D2
New Petersburg, Ohio 284/D7
New Philadelphia, Ill. 222/C3
New Philadelphia, Ind. 227/F7
New Philadelphia, Ohio 284/G5
New Philadelphia, Pa. 294/K4
New Pine Creek, Oreg. 291/G5
New Pitsligo, Scotland 15/F3
New Pittsburg, Ohio 284/F4
New Plymouth, Idaho 220/B6
New Plymouth, N. Zealand 100/D3
New Plymouth, Ohio 284/F7
New Point, Ind. 227/G6
New Point, Mo. 261/B2
Newport, Ark. 202/H2
Newport, Del. 245/R2
Newport, England 13/F7
Newport, England 13/E5
Newport, England 10/F5
Newport, Ind. 227/C5
Newport, Mayo, Ireland 17/C4
Newport, Tipperary, Ireland 17/E6
Newport, Ky. 237/S2
Newport, Ky. 188/K3
Newport, Maine 243/E6
Newport•, Maine 243/E6
Newport, Md. 245/L7
Newport, Minn. 255/F6
Newport, Miss. 256/D1
Newport, Nebr. 264/E2
New Port, Neth. Ant. 161/G9
Newport, N.H. 268/C5
Newport•, N.H. 268/C5
Newport, N.J. 273/C5
Newport, N.Y. 276/K4
Newport, N.C. 281/R5
Newport, Nova Scotia 168/E3
Newport, Ohio 284/C6
Newport, Ohio 284/H7
Newport, Oreg. 291/C3
Newport, Pa. 294/H5
Newport, Québec 172/D2
Newport, R.I. 188/M2
Newport (co.), R.I. 249/K6
Newport, R.I. 249/J7
Newport, Tenn. 237/P9
Newport, Texas 303/F4
Newport, Vt. 268/C2
Newport•, Vt. 268/C2
Newport, Va. 307/H6
Newport, Dyfed, Wales 13/C5
Newport, Gwent, Wales 13/B6
Newport, Wales 10/E5
Newport, Wash. 310/H2
Newport Beach, Calif. 204/D11
Newport Center, Vt. 268/C2
New Portland, Maine 243/C6
New Portland•, Maine 243/C6
Newport News, Va. 188/L3
Newport News (I.C.), Va. 307/P6
Newport-on-Tay, Scotland 15/F4
Newport Pagnell, England 13/G5
New Port Richey, Fla. 212/D3
New Prague, Minn. 255/E6
New Preston, Conn. 210/B2
New Providence (isl.), Bahamas 156/C1
New Providence (Borden), Ind. 227/F8
New Providence, Iowa 229/G4
New Providence, N.J. 273/E2
New Providence, Pa. 294/K6
New Prue (Prue), Okla. 288/O2
Newquay, England 10/D5
Newquay, England 13/B7
New Quay, Wales 10/D4
New Quay, Wales 13/C5
New Raymer, Colo. 208/M1
New Richland, Minn. 255/E7
New Richmond, Ind. 227/D4
New Richmond, Ohio 284/B8
New Richmond, Québec 172/C2
New Richmond, Wis. 317/A5
New Riegel, Ohio 284/D3
New River, N.C. 281/O5
New River (inlet), N.C. 281/P6
New River, Tenn. 237/M8
New River, Va. 307/G6
New River Beach, New Bruns. 170/D3
New Road, Nova Scotia 168/E4
New Roads, La. 238/G5
New Rochelle, N.Y. 276/P7
New Rockford, N. Dak. 282/N4
New Romney, England 13/J7
New Ross, Ind. 227/D5
New Ross, Ireland 10/C4
New Ross, Ireland 17/H7
New Ross, Nova Scotia 168/D4
Newry, Maine 243/B6
Newry•, Maine 243/B6
Newry, N. Ireland 17/J3

418 Newry

Newry, N. Ireland 10/C3
Newry, North. Terr. 93/A3
Newry, Pa. 294/F5
Newry, S.C. 296/B2
New Salem, Ill. 222/C4
New Salem, Ind. 227/G5
New Salem, Kansas 232/F4
New Salem•, Mass. 249/E2
New Salem, N. Dak. 282/G6
New Salem, Nova Scotia 168/D3
New Salem, Ohio 284/E6
New Salem, Pa. 294/C6
New Salem (Delmont), Pa. 294/D5
New Salisbury, Ind. 227/E8
New Sarepta, Alberta 182/D3
New Sarpy, La. 238/N4
New Schwabenland (reg.) 5/B1
New Scone, Scotland 15/E4
New Sharon, Iowa 229/H6
New Sharon•, Maine 243/C6
New Sharon, N.J. 273/D3
New Shoreham (Block Island)•, R.I. 249/H8
New Siberian (isls.), Russia 4/B2
New Siberian (isls.), Russia 2/S2
New Siberian (isls.), Russia 48/P2
New Siberian (isls.), Russia 54/R2
New Site, Ala. 195/G4
New Site, Miss. 256/H1
New Smyrna Beach, Fla. 212/F2
Newsoms, Va. 307/O7
New South Wales 88/H6
NEW SOUTH WALES 97
New South Wales (state), Australia 87/E9
New Spadra, Ark. 202/C3
New Square, N.Y. 276/K8
New Stanton, Pa. 294/C5
New Straitsville, Ohio 284/F6
New Strawn (Strawn), Kansas 232/G3
New Stuyahok, Alaska 196/G3
New Sweden, Maine 243/G2
New Sweden•, Maine 243/G2
New Tazewell, Tenn. 237/O8
Newtok, Alaska 196/F2
Newton, Ala. 195/G8
Newton (co.), Ark. 202/D2
Newton (co.), Ga. 217/E3
Newton, Ga. 217/D8
Newton, Ill. 222/E5
Newton (co.), Ind. 227/C3
Newton, Iowa 188/H2
Newton, Iowa 229/H5
Newton, Kansas 232/E3
Newton, Mass. 249/C7
Newton (co.), Miss. 256/F6
Newton, Miss. 256/F6
Newton (co.), Mo. 261/D9
Newton•, N.H. 268/E6
Newton, N.J. 273/D1
Newton, N.C. 281/G3
Newton, Québec 172/C4
Newton, Scotland 15/E5
Newton (co.), Texas 303/L7
Newton, Texas 303/L7
Newton, Utah 304/C2
Newton, W. Va. 312/D5
Newton Abbot, England 13/D7
Newton Abbot, England 10/E5
Newton Center, Mass. 249/C7
Newton Falls, N.Y. 276/K2
Newton Falls, Ohio 284/J3
Newtongrange, Scotland 15/D2
Newton Grove, N.C. 281/N4
Newton Hamilton, Pa. 294/G5
Newton Highlands, Mass. 249/C7
Newtonia, Mo. 261/D9
Newton Junction, N.H. 268/E6
Newton-le-Willows, England 13/H2
Newton Lower Falls, Mass. 249/B7
Newton Mearns, Scotland 15/B2
Newton Mills, Nova Scotia 168/F3
Newtonmore, Scotland 15/D3
Newton Siding, Manitoba 179/D5
Newton Stewart, Scotland 10/D3
Newton Stewart, Scotland 15/D6
Newtonsville, Ohio 284/B7
Newton Upper Falls, Mass. 249/C7
Newtonville, Ind. 227/D8
Newtonville, Mass. 249/C7
Newtonville, N.J. 273/D4
Newtown, Conn. 210/B3
Newtown•, Conn. 210/B3
Newtown, Ind. 227/C4
Newtown, Ky. 237/N4
Newtown, Mo. 261/F2
Newtown, New Bruns. 170/E3
Newtown, Newf. 166/D4
Newtown, N.S. Wales 97/C6
New Town, N. Dak. 282/F4
Newtown, Ohio 284/C10
Newtown, Pa. 294/N5
New Town, S.C. 296/J3
Newtown, Victoria 97/C6
Newtown, Wales 13/D5
Newtown, Wales 10/E4
Newtownabbey (dist.), N. Ireland 17/J2
Newtownabbey, N. Ireland 17/K2
Newtownards, N. Ireland 17/K2
Newtownbutler, N. Ireland 17/G3
Newtown Forbes, Ireland 17/F4
Newtownhamilton, N. Ireland 17/H3
Newtownmountkennedy, Ireland 17/J5
Newtown Saint Boswells, Scotland 15/F5
Newtownsandes, Ireland 17/C6
Newtown Square•, Pa. 294/L6
Newtownstewart, N. Ireland 17/G2
New Trenton, Ind. 227/H6
New Trier, Minn. 255/F6
New Tripoli, Pa. 294/L4
New Troy, Mich. 250/C7
New Tulsa, Okla. 288/P2
Newtyle, Scotland 15/E4
New Ulm, Minn. 255/D6
New Ulm, Texas 303/H8
New Underwood, S. Dak. 298/D5
New Vernon, N.J. 273/D2
New Victoria, Nova Scotia 168/H2
New Vienna, Iowa 229/L3
New Vienna, Ohio 284/C7
Newville, Ala. 195/H8
Newville, Ind. 227/H2
Newville, Pa. 294/H5
Newville, W. Va. 312/E5
New Vineyard•, Maine 243/C6
New Virginia, Iowa 229/F6
New Washington, Ind. 227/F7
New Washington, Ohio 284/E4
New Washington, Philippines 82/D5
New Waterford, Nova Scotia 168/J2
New Waterford, Ohio 284/J4
New Waverly, Ind. 227/E3
New Waverly, Texas 303/J7
New Westminster, Br. Col. 162/D6
New Westminster, Br. Col. 184/K3
New Weston, Ohio 284/A5
New Whiteland, Ind. 227/E5
New Wilmington, Pa. 294/B3
New Winchester, Ind. 227/D5
New Winchester, Ohio 284/D4
New Windsor, England 13/G8
New Windsor, England 10/F5
New Windsor, Ill. 222/C2
New Windsor, Md. 245/K2
New Windsor, N.Y. 276/N8
New Witten, S. Dak. 298/K7
New Woodstock, N.Y. 276/J5
New World (isl.), Newf. 166/C4
New York 188/L2
NEW YORK 276
New York (co.), N.Y. 276/M9
New York, N.Y. 146/L5
New York, N.Y. 188/M2
New York, N.Y. 276/M9
New York (state), U.S. 146/L5
New York, U.S. 2/F3
New York Mills, Minn. 255/C4
New York Mills, N.Y. 276/K4
New York State Barge (canal), N.Y. 276/C4
New Zealand 2/T8
New Zealand 87/G9
NEW ZEALAND 100
New Zion, New Bruns. 170/D2
New Zion, S.C. 296/H4
Ney, Ohio 284/B3
Neyagawa, Japan 81/J7
Neyland, Wales 13/B6
Neyriz, Iran 66/J6
Neyshabur, Iran 59/G2
Neyshabur, Iran 66/L2
Nezhin, Ukraine 52/D4
Nez Perce (co.), Idaho 220/B3
Nezperce, Idaho 220/B3
Nez Perce Nat'l Hist. Park, Idaho 220/B-C3
Nezwar (mt.), Iran 66/H3
Ngabang, Indonesia 85/D5
N'gage, Angola 115/C5
N'gage, Angola 102/D5
Ngahere, N. Zealand 100/C5
Ngami (lake), Botswana 118/C4
Ngamiland (reg.), Botswana 118/C3
Ngamring, China 77/C6
Ngangla Ringco (lake), China 77/B5
Ngangzê Co (lake), China 77/C5
Ngao, Thailand 72/D3
Ngaoundéré, Cameroon 115/B2
Ngaoundéré, Cameroon 102/D4
Ngapara, N. Zealand 100/C6
Ngara, Tanzania 115/F4
Ngaruawahia, N. Zealand 100/E2
Ngatapa, N. Zealand 100/F3
Ngatik (atoll), Micronesia 87/F5
Ngau (isl.), Fiji 86/Q10
Ngauruhoe (mt.), N. Zealand 100/E3
Ngawi, Indonesia 85/K2
Nghia Lo, Vietnam 72/D2
Ngoc Linh (mt.), Vietnam 72/E4
Ngom Qu (riv.), China 77/E5
Ngong, Kenya 115/G4
Ngoring Hu (lake), China 77/E4
Ngorongoro (crater), Tanzania 115/F4
N'Gounié (riv.), Congo 115/B4
N'Gounié (riv.), Gabon 115/B4
Ngourou, Cent. Afr. Rep. 115/D2
N'Guigmi, Niger 106/G6
Ngulu (atoll), Micronesia 87/D5
Ngunju (cape), Indonesia 85/F8
Ngunza (Sumbe), Angola 102/D6
Ngunza (Sumbe), Angola 115/B6
Nguru, Nigeria 102/D3
Nguru, Nigeria 106/G6
Nhâmundá (riv.), Brazil 120/D3
Nhamundá (riv.), Brazil 132/B3
Nharêa, Angola 115/C6
Nharêa, Angola 102/D6
Nha Trang, Vietnam 72/F4
Nha Trang, Vietnam 54/M8
Nhava-Sheva, India 68/B7
Nhill, Victoria 88/G7
Nhill, Victoria 97/A5
Nhulunbuy, North. Terr. 88/F2
Nhulunbuy, North. Terr. 93/E2
Ni (riv.), Va. 307/N4
Niafunké, Mali 106/D5
Niagara (co.), N.Y. 276/C4
Niagara (riv.), N.Y. 276/B4
Niagara, N. Dak. 282/P4
Niagara (reg. munic.), Ontario 177/E4
Niagara (riv.), Ontario 177/E4
Niagara, Wis. 317/K4
Niagara Falls, N.Y. 188/K2
Niagara Falls, N.Y. 276/C4
Niagara Falls, Ont. 162/J7
Niagara Falls, Ontario 177/E4
Niagara-on-the-Lake, Ontario 177/E4
Niamey (cap.), Niger 2/K5
Niamey (cap.), Niger 102/C3
Niamey (cap.), Niger 106/E6
Niangara, D.R. Congo 115/E3
Niangua, Mo. 261/G8
Niantic, Conn. 210/G3
Niantic (riv.), Conn. 210/G3
Niantic, Ill. 222/D4
Niarada, Mont. 262/B3
Niari (riv.), Congo 115/B4
Nias (isl.), Indonesia 54/L9
Nias (isl.), Indonesia 85/B5
Niassa (prov.), Mozambique 118/F2
Nibbe, Mont. 262/H4
Nibe, Denmark 21/C4
Nibe, Denmark 18/F8
Nibley, Utah 304/C2
Nicaragua 2/E5
Nicaragua 146/K8
NICARAGUA 154/E4
Nicaragua (lake), Nic. 146/K8
Nicaragua (lake), Nicaragua 154/E5
Nicaro, Cuba 158/J3
Nicasio, Calif. 204/H1
Nicastro, Italy 34/F5
Nicatous (lake), Maine 243/G5
Nice, France 7/E4
Nice, France 28/G6
Niceville, Fla. 212/C6
Nichinan, Japan 81/E8
Nichol (isl.), Nova Scotia 168/F4
Nicholas (chan.), Cuba 156/B2
Nicholas (chan.), Cuba 158/E1
Nicholas (co.), Ky. 237/N4
Nicholas (co.), W. Va. 312/E6
Nicholas Denys, New Bruns. 170/D1
Nicholasville, Ky. 237/N5
Nicholls, Ga. 217/G7
Nichols, Conn. 210/C4
Nichols, Fla. 212/E4
Nichols, Iowa 229/L6
Nichols, Minn. 255/E4
Nichols, N.Y. 276/H6
Nichols, S.C. 296/J3
Nichols, Wis. 317/K6
Nichols Hills, Okla. 288/L3
Nicholson (riv.), Australia 88/F3
Nicholson, Br. Col. 184/J4
Nicholson, Ga. 217/F2
Nicholson, Miss. 256/E10
Nicholson, Port (inlet), N. Zealand 100/B3
Nicholson (riv.), North. Terr. 93/E5
Nicholson, Pa. 294/L2
Nicholson (riv.), Queensland 95/A3
Nicholson, W. Australia 92/E2
Nicholsville, Ala. 195/C6
Nicholville, N.Y. 276/L1
Nickel Centre, Ontario 175/D3
Nickel Centre, Ontario 177/D1
Nickelsville, Va. 307/D7
Nickerie (dist.), Suriname 131/C3
Nickerie (riv.), Suriname 131/C3
Nickerson, Kansas 232/D3
Nickerson, Minn. 255/F4
Nickerson, Nebr. 264/H3
Nicobar (isls.), India 54/L9
Nicobar (isls.), India 68/G7
Nicodemus, Kansas 232/C2
Nicola, Br. Col. 184/G5
Nicolaus, Calif. 204/B8
Nicolet (co.), Québec 172/E3
Nicolet, Québec 172/E3
Nicolet (lake), Québec 172/F4
Nicolet (riv.), Québec 172/E3
Nicollet (co.), Minn. 255/D6
Nicollet, Minn. 255/D6
Nicoma Park, Okla. 288/M4
Nicomen Island, Br. Col. 184/L3
Nico Pérez, Uruguay 145/D4
Nicosia (cap.), Cyprus 63/E5
Nicosia (cap.), Cyprus 59/B2
Nicosia (cap.), Cyprus 54/E6
Nicosia, Italy 34/E6
Nicoya, C. Rica 154/E5
Nicoya (gulf), C. Rica 154/E6
Nicoya (pen.), C. Rica 154/E6
Nictau, New Bruns. 170/C1
Nictaux, Nova Scotia 168/D4
Nidau, Switzerland 39/D2
Nidd (riv.), England 10/F3
Nidwalden (canton), Switzerland 39/F3
Nidzica, Poland 47/E2
Niebüll, Germany 22/C1
Niederbipp, Switzerland 39/E2
Niedere Tauern (range), Austria 41/B3
Niederurnen, Switzerland 39/G2
Nielsville, Minn. 255/B3
Niemba, D.R. Congo 115/E5
Niemen (riv.), Lithuania 7/G3
Niemen (riv.), Lithuania 52/B4
Niemen (riv.), Lithuania 53/A3
Niemen (riv.), Russia 7/G3
Niemen (riv.), Russia 52/B4
Nienburg, Germany 22/C2
Nieuport (Nieuwpoort), Belgium 27/B6
Nieuw-Amsterdam, Suriname 131/D2
Nieuw-Buinen, Netherlands 27/K3
Nieuwegein, Netherlands 27/G4
Nieuwendam, Netherlands 27/C4
Nieuwe-Pekela, Netherlands 27/L2
Nieuweschans, Netherlands 27/L2
Nieuwkoop, Netherlands 27/F4
Nieuw-Nickerie, Suriname 120/D2
Nieuw-Nickerie, Suriname 131/C2
Nieuwpoort, Belgium 27/B6
Nieuw-Schoonebeek, Netherlands 27/L3
Nieuwveld (range), S. Africa 118/C6
Nieves, Mexico 150/H5
Nièvre (dept.), France 28/E4
Nigadoo, New Bruns. 170/E1
Niğde (prov.), Turkey 63/F4
Niğde, Turkey 59/B2
Niğde, Turkey 63/F4
Nigel, S. Africa 118/J7
Niger 2/K5
Niger 102/C3
NIGER 106/F5
Niger (riv.) 2/K5
Niger (riv.) 102/C4
Niger (riv.), Benin 106/E6
Niger (riv.), Guinea 106/C6
Niger (riv.), Mali 106/D5
Niger (riv.), Niger 106/E6
Niger (state), Nigeria 106/F7
Niger (delta), Nigeria 106/F8
Niger (riv.), Nigeria 106/F7
Nigeria 2/K5
Nigeria 102/C4
NIGERIA 106/F6
Nightcaps, N. Zealand 100/B6
Nighthawk, Wash. 310/F2
Nightingale, Alberta 182/D4
Nightingale (mts.), Nev. 266/B2
Nightingale (Bach Long Vi) (isl.), Vietnam 72/F2
Nightmute, Alaska 196/F2
Nigrita, Greece 45/F5
Nigua (riv.), P. Rico 161/D2
Nihoa (isl.), Hawaii 87/K3
Nihoa (isl.), Hawaii 188/F6
Nihoa (isl.), Hawaii 218/D6
Nii (isl.), Japan 81/J6
Niigata (pref.), Japan 81/J5
Niigata, Japan 54/P6
Niigata, Japan 81/J5
Niihama, Japan 81/F6
Niihau (isl.), Hawaii 87/K3
Niihau (isl.), Hawaii 188/E5
Niihau (isl.), Hawaii 218/A2
Niimi, Japan 81/F6
Niitsu, Japan 81/J5
Nijar, Spain 33/E4
Nijkerk, Netherlands 27/H4
Nijmegen, Netherlands 27/H5
Nijvel (Nivelles), Belgium 27/E7
Nijverdal, Netherlands 27/J4
Nikel', Russia52/C1
Nikep, Md. 245/C2
Nikki, Benin 106/E7
Nikko National Park, Japan 81/J5
Nikolai, Alaska 196/H2
Nikolayev, Ukraine 7/H4
Nikolayev, Ukraine 48/D5
Nikolayev, Ukraine 52/D5
Nikolayevsk, Russia2/S3
Nikolayevsk, Russia4/D2
Nikolayevsk, Russia52/G4
Nikolayevsk, Russia54/P4
Nikolayevsk-na-Amure, Russia 48/P4
Nikol'sk, Russia 52/G3
Nikol'sk, Russia 52/G4
Nikolski, Alaska 196/E4
Nikol'skoye, Russia 48/R4
Nikopol, Bulgaria 45/G4
Nikopol', Ukraine 52/D5
Niksar, Turkey 63/G2
Nikshahr, Iran 59/H4
Nikshahr, Iran 66/L7
Nikšić, Yugoslavia 45/D4
Nikumaroro (isl.), Kiribati 87/J6
Nila (isl.), Indonesia 85/H7
Nilahue, Chile 138/E6
Niland, Calif. 204/K10
Nilaveli, Sri Lanka 68/E7
Nile (riv.) 2/L5
Nile (riv.) 102/F2
Nile (riv.), Egypt 111/F2
Nile (riv.), Egypt 59/B4
Nile (prov.), Sudan 111/F4
Nile (riv.), Sudan 59/B6
Nile (riv.), Sudan 111/F4
Niles, Ill. 222/B5
Niles, Kansas 232/E2
Niles, Mich. 250/C7
Niles, Ohio 284/J3
Ni'lin, West Bank 65/C4
Nilópolis, Brazil 135/E3
Nilwood, Ill. 222/D4
Nimach, India 68/D4
Nimba (lag.), Guinea 106/C7
Nimba (lag.), Ivory Coast 106/C7
Nimba (lag.), Liberia 106/C7
Nîmes, France 28/F6
Nîmes, France 7/E4
Nimmitabel, N.S. Wales 97/E5
Nimmons, Ark. 202/K1
Nimnyrskiy, Russia 48/N4
Nimrod, Ark. 202/D4
Nimrod (lake), Ark. 202/D4
Nimrod, Minn. 255/D4
Nimule, Sudan 111/F7
Nin (bay), Philippines 82/D4
Nin, Croatia 45/B3
Ninaview, Colo. 208/N7
Ninawa (gov.), Iraq 66/B3
Nine Degree (chan.), India 68/C7
Ninemile (pt.), Mich. 250/E3
Nine Mile (creek), Utah 304/D4
Nine Mile Falls, Wash. 310/H3
Nine Mile River, Nova Scotia 168/E3
Ninepipe (res.), Mont. 262/C3
Nine Times, S.C. 296/B2
Ninette, Manitoba 179/C5
Ninety Mile (beach), N. Zealand 100/D1
Ninety Mile (beach), Victoria 97/D6
Ninety Six, S.C. 296/C3
Ninety Six Nat'l Hist. Site, S.C. 296/C3
Nineveh (ruins), Iraq 66/C2
Nineveh, N.Y. 276/J6
Nineveh, Pa. 294/B6
Ninfas (pt.), Argentina 143/D5
Ninga, Manitoba 179/C5
Ning'an, China 77/L3
Ningbo (Ningpo), China 77/K6
Ningbo, China 54/O7
Ningde, China 77/K6
Ningdu, China 77/J6
Ninghua, China 77/J6
Ningpo (Ningbo), China 77/K6
Ningsia (Yinchuan, Yinchwan), China 77/G4
Ningsia Hui Aut. Reg. (Ningxia Huizu), China 77/F3
Ningwu, China 77/H4
Ningxia Huizu (Ningsia Hui Aut. Reg.), China 77/F3
Ning Xian, China 77/G4
Ninh Binh, Vietnam 72/E3
Ninigo Group (isls.), Papua N.G. 87/E6
Ninilchik, Alaska 196/B1
Ninini (pt.), Hawaii 218/D2
Ninnekah, Okla. 288/L5
Ninnescah (riv.), Kansas 232/E4
Ninnis Glacier Tongue, Antarc. 5/C8
Ninole, Hawaii 218/J4
Ninove, Belgium 27/D7
Nioaque, Brazil 132/C8
Niobe, N.Y. 276/B6
Niobe, N. Dak. 282/F2
Niobrara (riv.), Nebr. 188/F2
Niobrara, Nebr. 264/G2
Niobrara (riv.), Nebr. 264/E2
Niobrara (co.), Wyo. 319/H2
Niobrara (riv.), Wyo. 319/J3
Niono, Mali 106/C6
Nioro, Mali 106/C5
Nioro, Mali 102/B3
Nioro-du-Rip, Senegal 106/A6
Niort, France 28/C4
Niota, Ill. 222/B3
Niota, Tenn. 237/M9
Niotaze, Kansas 232/F4
Nipani, India 68/C5
Nipawin, Sask. 181/H2
Nipawin Prov. Park, Sask. 181/G1
Nipe (bay), Cuba 158/J3
Nipigon, Ont. 162/H6
Nipigon, Ontario 177/H5
Nipigon, Ontario 175/C3
Nipigon (lake), Ont. 146/K5
Nipigon (lake), Ont. 162/H6
Nipigon (lake), Ontario 175/C3
Nipigon (lake), Ontario 177/H5
Nipinnawasee, Calif. 204/F6
Nipishish (lake), Newf. 166/B3
Nipissing (terr. dist.), Ontario 177/F2
Nipissing (terr. dist.), Ontario 175/E3
Nipissing, Ontario 177/E1
Nipissing (lake), Ontario 177/E1
Nipissing (lake), Ontario 175/E3
Nipomo, Calif. 204/E8
Nippers Harbour, Newf. 166/C4
Nipton, Calif. 204/K8
Niquelândia, Brazil 132/D6
Niquén, Chile 138/E1
Niquero, Cuba 158/G4
Niquero, Cuba 156/C2
Niquivil, Argentina 143/C3
Nirgua, Venezuela 124/D2
Nirmal, India 68/D5
Nirvana, Mich. 250/D5
Nir Yitzhaq, Israel 65/A5
Niš, Yugoslavia 7/G4
Niš, Yugoslavia 45/F4
Nisa, Portugal 33/C3
Nisab, Yemen 59/E7
Nisab, Saudi Arabia 59/D4
Nisbet, Pa. 294/H3
Niscemi, Italy 34/E6
Nishapur (Neyshabur), Iran 66/L2
Nishino (isl.), Japan 81/M3
Nishinomiya, Japan 81/H8
Nishinoomote, Japan 81/E8
Nisiros (isl.), Greece 45/H7
Niskayuna, N.Y. 276/N5
Nisko, Poland 47/E3
Nisku, Alberta 182/D3
Nisland, S. Dak. 298/C4
Nisqually, Wash. 310/C3
Nisqually (riv.), Wash. 310/C4
Nisqually Ind. Res., Wash. 310/C4
Nissan (isl.), Papua N.G. 86/C2
Nissum (fjord), Denmark 21/A5
Nisswa, Minn. 255/D4
Niterói, Brazil 132/F8
Niterói, Brazil 120/E5
Niterói, Brazil 135/E3
Nith (riv.), Scotland 15/E5
Nith (riv.), Scotland 10/E3
Nitil, Jordan 65/D4
Nitinat, Br. Col. 184/H3
Nitinat (lake), Br. Col. 184/H3
Niton Junction, Alberta 182/C3
Nitra, Slovakia 41/E2
Nitra (riv.), Slovakia 41/E2
Nitro, W. Va. 312/C6
Nitta Yuma, Miss. 256/C4
Nittedal, Norway 18/D3
Niuafo'ou (isl.), Tonga 87/J7
Niuatoputapu (isl.), Tonga 87/J7
Niue (isl.) 87/K7
Niue (isl.), N. Zealand 2/A6
Niutao (atoll), Tuvalu 87/H6
Nivala, Finland 18/O5
Nive (riv.), Tasmania 99/C4
Nivelles, Belgium 27/E7
Nivernais (trad. prov.), France 29
Niverville, Manitoba 179/F5
Niwot, Colo. 208/J2
Nixa, Mo. 261/F8
Nixburg, Ala. 195/F5
Nixon, Nev. 266/B3
Nixon, N.J. 273/E2
Nixon, Texas 303/G8
Nixonville, S.C. 296/K4
Niya (Minfeng), China 77/B4
Nizamabad, India 68/D5
Nizao, Dom. Rep. 158/E6
Nizhnekamsk, Russia 7/K3
Nizhnekamsk, Russia 52/H3
Nizhneudinsk, Russia 48/K4
Nizhnevartovsk, Russia 48/H3
Nizhneyansk, Russia 48/O3
Nizhniy Lomov, Russia 52/F4
Nizhniy Novgorod (Gor'kiy), Russia 48/E4
Nizhniy Novgorod (Gor'kiy), Russia 52/F3
Nizhniy Tagil, Russia 54/H4
Nizhniy Tagil, Russia 48/G4
Nizhnyaya Pesha, Russia 52/G1
Nizina, Alaska 196/K2
Nizip, Turkey 63/G4
Nizwa, Oman 59/G5
Nizza Monferrato, Italy 34/B2
Nizzanim, Israel 65/B4
Njazidja (isl.), Comoros 118/G2
Njazidja (isl.), Comoros 102/G6
Njombe, Tanzania 115/F5
Njombe (riv.), Tanzania 115/F5
Nkambe, Cameroon 115/B2
Nkayi, Congo 115/B4
Nkhata Bay, Malawi 115/F6
Nkhotakota, Malawi 115/F6
N'Komi (lag.), Gabon 115/A4
Nkongsamba, Cameroon 115/B3
Nkongsamba, Cameroon 102/D4
Nkurenkuru, Namibia 118/B3
Nkurenkuru, Namibia 115/C7
Nmai (riv.), Burma 72/C1
Nnewi, Nigeria 106/F7
Noah, Tenn. 237/J9
Noakhali, Bangladesh 68/G4
Noank, Conn. 210/G3
Noatak, Alaska 196/F1
Noatak (riv.), Alaska 196/F1
Noatak Nat'l Preserve, Alaska 196/F1
Nobel, Ontario 177/D2
Nobeoka, Japan 81/E7
Noble, Ga. 217/B1
Noble, Ill. 222/E5
Noble (co.), Ind. 227/G2
Noble, Iowa 229/K6
Noble, La. 238/C3
Noble, Mo. 261/G9
Noble (co.), Ohio 284/G6
Noble (co.), Okla. 288/M2
Noble, Okla. 288/M4
Nobleboro•, Maine 243/D7
Nobleford, Alberta 182/D5
Noble Lake, Ark. 202/G5
Nobles (co.), Minn. 255/C7
Noblesville, Ind. 227/F4
Nobleton, Fla. 212/D3
Nobleton, Ontario 177/J3
Noboribetsu, Japan 81/K2
Nocatee, Fla. 212/E4
Noccundra, Queensland 95/B5
Nocera Inferiore, Italy 34/E4
Nochistlán, Mexico 150/H6
Nocona, Texas 303/G4
Noctor, Ky. 237/P5
Noda, Japan 81/P2
Nodaway, Iowa 229/D7
Nodaway (riv.), Iowa 229/D7
Nodaway (co.), Mo. 261/C2
Nodaway, Mo. 261/C3
Node, Wyo. 319/H3
Nodine, Minn. 255/G7
Noel, Mo. 261/D9
Noel, Nova Scotia 168/E3
Noel Road, Nova Scotia 168/E3
Noelville, Ontario 177/D1
Nogal, N. Mex. 274/D5
Nogal (reg.), Somalia 115/J2
Nogales, Ariz. 188/D4
Nogales, Ariz. 198/E7
Nogales, Chile 138/F2
Nogales, Mexico 150/P2
Nogamut, Alaska 196/G2
Nogata, Japan 81/E7
Nogent-le-Rotrou, France 28/D3
Nogent-sur-Seine, France 28/E3
Nogoa (riv.), Queensland 88/H4
Nogoa (riv.), Queensland 95/C5
Nogoyá, Argentina 143/F6
Nógrád (co.), Hungary 41/E3
Nohili (pt.), Hawaii 218/B1
Nohkú (pt.), Mexico 150/Q7
Noinville, New Bruns. 170/E2
Noir (isl.), Chile 138/E11
Noires (mts.), Dom. Rep. 158/C5
Noires (mts.), Haiti 158/C5
Noirmont (mt.), Switzerland 39/B4
Noirmoutier (isl.), France 28/B4
Noisy-le-Sec, France 28/B1
Nojima (cape), Japan 81/K6
Nokesville, Va. 307/N3
Nokhowch, Kuh-e (mt.), Iran 66/M7
Nokia, Finland 18/N6
Nok Kundi, Pakistan 68/A3
Nok Kundi, Pakistan 59/H4
Nokomis, Ala. 195/D8
Nokomis, Fla. 212/D4
Nokomis, Ill. 222/D4
Nokomis, Sask. 181/F4
Nokou, Chad 111/B5
Nola, Ark. 202/C4
Nola, Cent. Afr. Rep. 115/C3
Nola, Miss. 256/D7
Nolan (co.), Texas 303/D5
Nolan, W. Va. 312/B7
Nolichucky (riv.), N.C. 281/E2
Nolichucky (riv.), Tenn. 237/R8
Nolin, Ky. 237/K5
Nolin (lake), Ky. 237/K6
Nolin (riv.), Ky. 237/J6
Nolinsk, Russia 52/H3
Nollesemic (lake), Maine 243/F4
Noma, Fla. 212/C5
Nomans Land (isl.), Mass. 249/L7

Northport 419

Nombre de Dios, Mexico 150/G5
Nome, Alaska 146/B3
Nome, Alaska 196/E2
Nome, Alaska 188/C5
Nome, Alaska 2/A2
Nome, N. Dak. 282/P6
Nome, U.S. 4/C18
Nomgon, Mongolia 77/G3
Nominingue, Québec 172/B3
Nominingue (lake), Québec 172/B3
Nomoi (isls.), Micronesia 87/F5
Nonacho (lake), N.W.T. 162/F3
Nonacho (lake), N.W.T. 187/H3
Nonamesset (isl.), Mass. 249/M6
Nondalton, Alaska 196/G2
Nong Het, Laos 72/E3
Nong Khai, Thailand 72/D3
Nong Lahan (lake), Thailand 72/D3
Nonoava, Mexico 150/F3
Nonouti (atoll), Kiribati 87/H6
Nonquitt, Mass. 249/L6
Nonsan, S. Korea 81/C5
Nontron, France 28/D5
Nooksack, Wash. 310/C2
Nooksack (riv.), Wash. 310/C2
Noonan, N. Dak. 282/D2
Noord (pt.), Neth. Ant. 161/F8
Noord (pt.), Neth. Ant. 161/D8
Noord di Salinja, Neth. Ant. 161/E8
Noordwijk, Netherlands 27/E4
Noorvik, Alaska 196/F1
Nootka, Br. Col. 184/D5
Nootka (isl.), Br. Col. 184/D5
Nootka (sound), Br. Col. 184/D5
Nopalucan de la Granja, Mexico 150/O1
Nopeming, Minn. 255/F4
Nopiming Prov. Park, Manitoba 179/G4
Nóqui, Angola 115/B5
Noquochoke P.O. (Westport), Mass. 249/K6
Nora, Ill. 222/D1
Nora, Nebr. 264/G4
Nora, Sask. 181/H3
Nora, S. Dak. 298/R8
Nora, Sweden 18/J7
Nora, Va. 307/D6
Noranda, Québec 162/J6
Noranda, Québec 174/B3
Noranside, Queensland 95/A4
Nora Springs, Iowa 229/H2
Norbeck, S. Dak. 298/L3
Norberg, Sweden 18/K6
Norberto de la Riestra, Argentina 143/G7
Norbertville, Québec 172/F3
Norborne, Mo. 261/E4
Norcatur, Kansas 232/B2
Norco, Calif. 204/E11
Norco, La. 238/N3
Norcross, Ga. 217/D3
Norcross, Maine 243/F4
Norcross, Minn. 255/B5
Nord (dept.), France 28/E2
Nord (pt.), Guadeloupe 161/B7
Nord (dept.), Haiti 158/C5
Nord (riv.), Québec 172/C4
Nordaustlandet (isl.), Norway 18/D1
Nordborg, Denmark 21/C7
Nordby, Århus, Denmark 21/D5
Nordby, Ribe, Denmark 21/B7
Norddeich, Germany 22/B2
Nordegg, Alberta 182/B3
Nordegg (riv.), Alberta 182/C3
Norden, Nebr. 264/D2
Norden, Germany 22/B2
Nordenham, Germany 22/C2
Norderney, Germany 22/B2
Norderney (isl.), Germany 22/B2
Norderstedt, Germany 22/D2
Nord-Est (bay), Guadeloupe 161/B6
Nordfjord (fjord), Norway 18/E6
Nordhausen, Germany 22/D3
Nordheim, Texas 303/G9
Nordhorn, Germany 22/B2
Nordin, New Bruns. 170/E1
Nordjylland (co.), Denmark 21/D4
Nordkapp (cape), Norway 7/G1
Nordkapp (pt.), Norway 18/C1
Nordkinn (headland), Norway 18/Q1
Nordkinn (pen.), Norway 18/P1
Nordland (co.), Norway 18/J3
Nordland, Wash. 310/C2
Nordli, Norway 18/H4
Nördlingen, Germany 22/D4
Nordmaling, Sweden 18/L5
Nordman, Idaho 220/B1
Nord-Ostsee (canal), Germany 22/C1
Nord-Ouest (dept.), Haiti 158/B5
Nordstrand (isl.), Germany 22/C1
Nord-Trøndelag (co.), Norway 18/H4
Nordvik-Ugol'naya, Russia 4/B4
Nordvik-Ugol'naya, Russia 48/M2
Nore (riv.), Ireland 10/C4
Nore (riv.), Ireland 17/G7
Norene, Tenn. 237/J8
Norfield, Miss. 256/C8
Norfolk (isl.), Australia 2/T7
Norfolk•, Conn. 210/C1
Norfolk (co.), England 13/H5
Norfolk (co.), Mass. 249/K4
Norfolk•, Mass. 249/J4
Norfolk, Nebr. 188/G2
Norfolk, Nebr. 264/G2
Norfolk, N.Y. 276/K1
Norfolk (bay), Tasmania 99/D4
Norfolk, Va. 188/L3
Norfolk, Va. 146/L6
Norfolk (I.C.), Va. 307/R7
Norfolk Island (terr.), Australia 88/L5
Norfolk Island (terr.), Australia 87/G8
Norfork, Ark. 202/F1
Norfork (lake), Ark. 202/F1
Norfork (lake), Mo. 261/H10
Norg, Netherlands 27/J2
Norge, Okla. 288/K4
Norge, Va. 307/P6
Norglenwold, Alberta 182/C3
Noril'sk, Russia 2/P2
Noril'sk, Russia 4/B5
Noril'sk, Russia 48/J3
Noril'sk, Russia 54/L3
Norland, Fla. 212/B4
Norland, Ontario 177/F3
Norlina, N.C. 281/N2
Norma, N.J. 273/C4
Norma, N. Dak. 282/G2
Norma, Tenn. 237/N8
Normal, Ill. 222/E3
Normalville, Pa. 294/D5
Norman, Ark. 202/C5
Norman, Ind. 227/E7
Norman (co.), Minn. 255/B3
Norman, Nebr. 264/F4
Norman (cape), Newf. 166/C3
Norman, N.C. 281/K4
Norman (lake), N.C. 281/H3
Norman, Okla. 288/M4
Norman (riv.), Queensland 88/G3
Norman (creek), Queensland 95/D3
Norman (riv.), Queensland 95/B3
Norman (isl.), Virgin Is. (U.K.) 161/D4
Normanby, Queensland 88/K2
Normand (lake), Québec 172/D2
Normandale, Ontario 177/D5
Normandin, Québec 172/E1
Normandy (trad. prov.), France 29
Normandy, Mo. 261/R2
Normandy (riv.), Queensland 95/C2
Normandy, Tenn. 237/J10
Normandy, Texas 303/D9
Normandy Beach, N.J. 273/E3
Normandy Park, Wash. 310/A2
Normangee, Texas 303/H6
Norman Park, Ga. 217/E8
Norman's Cove, Newf. 166/D2
Normanton, Australia 87/E7
Normanton, Queensland 95/B3
Normanton, Queensland 88/G3
Normantown, Ga. 217/H6
Normantown, W. Va. 312/E5
Norman Wells, Canada 4/C16
Norman Wells, N.W.T. 146/F3
Norman Wells, N.W.T. 162/D2
Norman Wells, N.W.T. 187/F3
Normétal, Québec 174/B3
Noroton, Conn. 210/B4
Noroton Heights, Conn. 210/B4
Norphlet, Ark. 202/E7
Norquay, Sask. 181/J4
Ñorquincó, Argentina 143/B5
Norrbotten (co.), Sweden 18/L3
Nørre Åby, Denmark 21/C7
Nørre Alslev, Denmark 21/E8
Nørre Broby, Denmark 21/D7
Nørre Nebel, Denmark 21/B6
Nørre Snede, Denmark 21/C6
Nørre Vorupør, Denmark 21/B4
Norridge, Ill. 222/B5
Norridgewock, Maine 243/D6
Norridgewock•, Maine 243/D6
Norrie, Wis. 317/H6
Norris, Ill. 222/C3
Norris, Miss. 256/F6
Norris, Mont. 262/E5
Norris, S.C. 296/B2
Norris, S. Dak. 298/G7
Norris, Tenn. 237/N8
Norris (dam), Tenn. 237/N8
Norris (lake), Tenn. 188/K3
Norris (lake), Tenn. 237/O8
Norris, Wyo. 319/B1
Norris Arm, Newf. 166/C4
Norris City, Ill. 222/E6
Norris Point, Newf. 166/C4
Norristown, Ga. 217/H5
Norristown, Ind. 227/F6
Norristown, Pa. 294/M5
Norrisville, Md. 245/N2
Norrköping, Sweden 7/F3
Norrköping, Sweden 18/K7
Norrsundet, Sweden 18/K6
Norrtälje, Sweden 18/L7
Norseland, Minn. 255/D6
Norseman, W. Australia 88/C6
Norseman, W. Australia 92/C6
Norsjö, Sweden 18/L4
Norte (pt.), Argentina 143/D5
Norte (chan.), Brazil 120/E2
Norte (chan.), Brazil 132/D2
Norte, Serra do (range), Brazil 132/B5
Norte del Cabo San Antonio (pt.), Argentina 143/E4
Norte de Santander (dept.), Colombia 126/D3
North (sea) 2/K3
North (sea) 7/E3
North (cape), Alaska 196/L4
North (pt.), Barbados 161/B8
North (sea), Belgium 27/D4
North (rocks), Bermuda 156/H2
North (sea), Denmark 21/B9
North (sea), England 13/J4
North (sea), France 28/E1
North (sea), Germany 22/B2
North (cape), Ice. 4/C11
North (Horn) (cape), Iceland 21/B1
North (sound), Ireland 17/B5
North (isls.), La. 238/M7
North (pass), La. 238/N8
North (pt.), La. 238/M7
North (pt.), Md. 245/N4
North (riv.), Mass. 249/D2
North (riv.), Mass. 249/L4
North (chan.), Mich. 250/F2
North (pt.), Mich. 250/F3
North (lake), Minn. 255/F1
North (sea), Netherlands 27/E3
North (lake), New Bruns. 170/C3
North (riv.), Newf. 166/C3
North (riv.), Newf. 166/B2
North (isl.), N. Zealand 87/H9
North (cape), N. Zealand 87/H9
North (cape), N. Zealand 100/D1
North (isl.), N. Zealand 100/F1
North (lake), N. Dak. 282/J3
North (chan.), N. Ireland 10/D3
North (chan.), N. Ireland 17/K1
North (Nordkapp) (cape), Norway 7/G1
North (cape), Norway 4/B8
North (cape), Nova Scotia 162/K6
North (cape), Nova Scotia 168/H1
North (mt.), Nova Scotia 168/D3
North (chan.), Ontario 177/A1
North (chan.), Ontario 175/D3
North (mt.), Pa. 294/K3
North (pt.), Pr. Edward I. 168/E1
North (chan.), Scotland 10/D3
North (chan.), Scotland 15/C5
North (sound), Scotland 15/G4
North (sound), Scotland 15/F1
North (isl.), Seychelles 118/H5
North, S.C. 296/E4
North (inlet), S.C. 296/J5
North (isl.), S.C. 296/J5
North (pt.), Tasmania 99/E1
North (creek), Utah 304/C6
North (lake), Utah 304/B2
North (riv.), Wash. 310/B4
North (riv.), W. Va. 312/J4
North (lake), Wis. 317/J1
North Abington, Mass. 249/L4
North Acton, Mass. 249/J2
North Adams, Mass. 249/B2
North Adams, Mich. 250/E7
Northallerton, England 10/F3
Northallerton, England 13/F3
Northam, England 13/C6
Northam, W. Australia 88/B6
Northam, W. Australia 92/B1
NORTH AMERICA 146
North America 2/C4
North Amherst, Mass. 249/E3
North Amity, Maine 243/H4
Northampton, England 13/F5
Northampton, England 10/F4
Northampton, Mass. 249/D3
Northampton (co.), N.C. 281/P2
Northampton (co.), Pa. 294/M4
Northampton, Pa. 294/M4
Northampton (co.), Va. 307/S6
Northampton, W. Australia 88/A5
Northampton, W. Australia 92/A5
Northamptonshire (co.), England 13/G5
North Andaman (isl.), India 68/G6
North Andover•, Mass. 249/K2
North Anna (riv.), Va. 307/M4
North Anson, Maine 243/D6
North Apollo, Pa. 294/D4
North Arlington, N.J. 273/B2
North Arm (inlet), N.W.T. 187/G3
North Ashford, Conn. 210/G1
North Aspy (riv.), Nova Scotia 168/H2
North Atlantic Ocean 2/H3
North Attleboro•, Mass. 249/J5
North Augusta, Ontario 177/J3
North Augusta, S.C. 296/C5
North Aulatsivik (isl.), Newf. 166/B2
North Aurora, Ill. 222/E2
North Avondale, Colo. 208/L6
North Ballachulish, Scotland 15/C4
North Baltimore, Ohio 284/C3
North Bangor, N.Y. 276/M1
North Barrington, Ill. 222/A5
North Bass (isl.), Ohio 284/E2
North Battleford, Sask. 146/H4
North Battleford, Sask. 162/F5
North Battleford, Sask. 181/C3
North Bay, N.Y. 276/J4
North Bay, Ont. 146/L5
North Bay, Ont. 162/J6
North Bay, Ontario 177/E1
North Bay, Ontario 175/E3
North Bay, Wis. 317/M3
North Bay Ingonish (bay), Nova Scotia 168/H2
North Bay Village, Fla. 212/B4
North Beach, Md. 245/N6
North Belgrade, Maine 243/D7
North Bellingham, Mass. 249/J4
North Bend, Br. Col. 184/G5
North Bend, Nebr. 264/H3
North Bend, Ohio 284/B9
North Bend, Oreg. 291/C4
North Bend, Pa. 294/G3
North Bend, Wash. 310/D3
North Bend, Wis. 317/D7
North Bennington, Vt. 268/A6
North Bergen•, N.J. 273/B2
North Berwick, Maine 243/B9
North Berwick•, Maine 243/B9
North Berwick, Scotland 15/F4
North Berwick, Scotland 10/E2
North Beveland (isl.), Netherlands 27/D5
North Billerica, Mass. 249/J2
North Bloomfield, Conn. 210/E1
North Bloomfield, Ohio 284/J3
North Bonneville, Wash. 310/C5
North Borneo (Sabah) (state), Malaysia 85/F3
Northboro, Iowa 229/C7
Northborough, Mass. 249/H3
Northborough•, Mass. 249/H3
North Boston, N.Y. 276/C5
North Bourke, N.S. Wales 97/C2
North Brabant (prov.), Netherlands 27/F5
North Braddock, Pa. 294/C7
North Bradford, Maine 243/F5
North Bradley, Mich. 250/E5
Northbranch, Kansas 232/D2
North Branch, Md. 245/D2
North Branch, Mich. 250/F5
North Branch, Minn. 255/F5
North Branch, N.H. 268/D5
North Branch, N.J. 273/D2
North Branch Oromocto (riv.), New Bruns. 170/D3
North Branford•, Conn. 210/E3
North Brentwood, Md. 245/F4
Northbridge•, Mass. 249/H4
North Bridgton, Maine 243/B7
Northbrook, Ill. 222/B5
North Brook, Ontario 177/G3
North Brookfield, Mass. 249/F3
North Brookfield•, Mass. 249/F3
North Brooksville, Maine 243/F7
North Brunswick•, N.J. 273/D3
North Bruny (isl.), Tasmania 99/D5
North Buena Vista, Iowa 229/L3
North Calais, Vt. 268/C3
North Caldwell, N.J. 273/B2
North Calling Lake, Alberta 182/D2
North Canadian (riv.) 188/G3
North Canadian (riv.), Okla. 288/K3
North Canton, Conn. 210/D1
North Canton, Ga. 217/C2
North Canton, Ohio 284/H4
North Cape (Nordkapp) (pt.), Norway 18/P1
North Cape May, N.J. 273/C6
North Caribou (lake), Ontario 175/B2
North Carolina 188/L3
NORTH CAROLINA 281
North Carolina (state), U.S. 146/K6
North Carrizo (creek), Colo. 208/N8
North Carrizo (riv.), Okla. 288/A1
North Carrollton, Miss. 256/E3
North Carter (mt.), N.H. 268/E3
North Carver, Mass. 249/L5
North Cascades Nat'l Park, Wash. 310/D2
North Catasauqua, Pa. 294/L4
North Charleston, S.C. 296/G6
North Charlestown, N.H. 268/C5
North Chatham, Mass. 249/O6
North Chatham, N.H. 268/E3
North Chelmsford, Mass. 249/J2
North Chesterville, Maine 243/C6
North Chicago, Ill. 222/B4
North Chichester, N.H. 268/E5
North Chili, N.Y. 276/E4
North City (Coello), Ill. 222/E5
North Clarendon, Vt. 268/B4
Northcliffe, W. Australia 92/B6
North Cohasset, Mass. 249/F7
North Colebrook, Conn. 210/C1
North College Hill, Ohio 284/B9
North Collins, N.Y. 276/C5
North Concho (riv.), Texas 303/C6
North Concord, Vt. 268/D3
North Conway, N.H. 268/E3
North Cooking Lake, Alberta 182/D3
North Cotabato (prov.), Philippines 82/E7
Northcote, Minn. 255/A2
Northcote, N. Zealand 100/B1
Northcote, Victoria 88/L7
Northcote, Victoria 97/J5
North Cove, N.C. 281/F3
North Cove, Wash. 310/A4
North Cowichan, Br. Col. 184/J3
North Creek, N.Y. 276/M3
North Crossett, Ark. 202/G7
North Cutler, Maine 243/J6
North Dakota 188/F1
NORTH DAKOTA 282
North Dakota (state), U.S. 146/H5
North Dandalup, W. Australia 88/B3
North Danger (reef), Philippines 85/E3
North Danville, Vt. 268/C3
North Dartmouth, Mass. 249/K6
North Dexter, Maine 243/E5
North Dighton, Mass. 249/K5
North Dixmont, Maine 243/E6
North Down (dist.), N. Ireland 17/K2
North Downs (hills), England 13/G6
North Eagle Butte, S. Dak. 298/G3
Northeast (cape), Alaska 196/E2
North East (pt.), Jamaica 158/K6
Northeast (pass), La. 238/M8
North East, Md. 245/P2
North East, Pa. 294/C1
North East Breakers, Bermuda 156/H2
North East Cape Fear (riv.), N.C. 281/O4
North East Carry, Maine 243/D4
North-Eastern (prov.), Kenya 115/G3
Northeast Foreland (pen.), Greenl. 4/A10
North Eastham, Mass. 249/O5
Northeast Harbor, Maine 243/G7
Northeast Land (isl.), Norway 4/B8
North East Margaree (riv.), Nova Scotia 168/H2
North Easton, Mass. 249/K4
North East Providence (chan.), Bahamas 156/C1
North Edisto (riv.), S.C. 296/G6
North Edwards, Calif. 204/H8
North Egremont, Mass. 249/A4
Northeim, Germany 22/C3
North English, Iowa 229/J5
North Enid, Okla. 288/L2
Northern (dist.), Israel 65/C2
Northern (head), New Bruns. 170/D4
Northern (prov.), Sudan 111/E3
Northern Cape (prov.), S. Africa 118/B5
Northern Cheyenne Ind. Res., Mont. 262/K5
Northern Dvina (riv.), Russia 48/E3
Northern Dvina (riv.), Russia 52/F2
Northern Indian (lake), Manitoba 179/J2
NORTHERN IRELAND 17
NORTHERN IRELAND, 10/C3
Northern Ireland, U.K. 7/D3
Northern Marianas 87/E4
Northern Marianas, U.S. 2/S5
Northern Peninsula Aboriginal Reserve, Queensland 88/G2
Northern Peninsula Aboriginal Res., Queensland 95/B1
Northern Province (prov.), S. Africa 118/D4
Northern Samar (prov.), Philippines 82/E4
Northern Sporades (isls.), Greece 45/F6
Northern Territory, 88/E3
NORTHERN TERRITORY 93
Northern Territory (terr.), Australia 87/D7
Northern Yukon Nat'l Park, Yukon 162/B2
Northern Yukon Nat'l Park, Yukon 187/D3
North Esk (riv.), Scotland 15/F4
North Esk (riv.), Tasmania 99/D3
North Fairfield, Ohio 284/E3
North Falmouth, Mass. 249/M6
North Ferrisburg, Vt. 268/A3
Northfield, Conn. 210/C2
Northfield, Ill. 222/B5
Northfield, Ky. 237/K1
Northfield•, Maine 243/H6
Northfield, Mass. 249/E2
Northfield•, Mass. 249/E2
Northfield, Minn. 255/E6
Northfield•, N.H. 268/D5
Northfield, N.J. 273/D5
Northfield, Ohio 284/J10
Northfield, Texas 303/D3
Northfield, Vt. 268/B3
Northfield•, Vt. 268/B3
Northfield, Wis. 317/D7
Northfield Falls, Vt. 268/B3
Northfield Farms, Mass. 249/E2
Northfield-Tilton, N.H. 268/D5
Northfleet, England 10/C5
Northfleet, England 13/J8
North Fond du Lac, Wis. 317/J8
Northford, Conn. 210/D3
North Foreland (prom.), England 10/G5
North Foreland (prom.), England 13/J6
North Fork, Calif. 204/F6
North Fork, Frenchman (creek), Colo. 208/O1
Forth Fork, Gunnison (riv.), Colo. 208/D5
North Fork, Smoky Hill (riv.), Colo. 208/P4
North Fork, Idaho 220/D4
North Fork (riv.), Idaho 220/B7
North Fork, Flathead (riv.), Mont. 262/B2
North Fork, Little Humboldt (riv.), Nev. 266/D1
North Fork, Grand (riv.), N. Dak. 282/E8
Northfork, W. Va. 312/D8
North Fork, Powder (riv.), Wyo. 319/F2
North Fork, Wind (riv.), Wyo. 319/C2
North Fork, Shoshone (riv.), Wyo. 319/C1
North Fort Myers, Fla. 212/E5
North Foster, R.I. 249/H5
North Fourchu, Nova Scotia 168/H3
North Fox (isl.), Mich. 250/D3
North Franklin, Conn. 210/G2
North Freedom, Wis. 317/G9
North Friars (bay), St. Kitts and Nevis 161/D10
North Friesland (reg.), Germany 22/C1
North Frisian (isls.), Denmark 21/B7
North Frisian (isls.), Germany 22/B1
North Fryeburg, Maine 243/B7
North Galiano, Br. Col. 184/K3
North Garden, Va. 307/L5
Northgate, N. Dak. 282/F2
Northgate, Sask. 181/J6
Northglenn, Colo. 208/K3
North Gorham, Maine 243/B8
North Gosforth, England 13/J3
North Gower, Ontario 177/J2
North Grafton, Mass. 249/H4
North Granby, Conn. 210/D1
North Grant, Nova Scotia 168/G3
North Grosvenor Dale, Conn. 210/H1
North Groton, N.H. 268/D4
North Grove, Ind. 227/F3
North Guilford, Conn. 210/E3
North Gulfport, Miss. 256/F10
North Hadley, Mass. 249/D3
North Haledon, N.J. 273/B1
North Hampton•, N.H. 268/F6
North Hampton, Ohio 284/C5
North Hanover, Mass. 249/L4
North Hansel (mts.), Utah 304/B2
North Harbour, Newf. 166/D2
North Harlowe, N.C. 281/R5
North Hartland, Vt. 268/C4
North Hartsville, S.C. 296/G3
North Harwich, Mass. 249/O6
North Hatfield, Mass. 249/D3
North Hatley, Québec 172/F4
North Haven•, Conn. 210/D3
North Haven, Maine 243/F7
North Haven•, Maine 243/F7
North Haverhill, N.H. 268/D3
North Havre, Mont. 262/G2
North Hayden, Ind. 227/B2
North Head, New Bruns. 170/D4
North Henderson, Ill. 222/C2
North Hero, Vt. 268/A2
North Highlands, Calif. 204/B8
North High Shoals, Ga. 217/F3
North Hills, W. Va. 312/D4
North Hodge, La. 238/E2
North Holland (prov.), Netherlands 27/F3
North Holland (canal), Netherlands 27/C4
North Hollywood, Calif. 204/B10
North Hornell, N.Y. 276/E6
North Horr, Kenya 115/G3
North Hudson, N.Y. 276/N3
North Hudson, Wis. 317/A5
North Hyde Park, Vt. 268/B2
North Hykeham, England 13/G4
North Industry, Ohio 284/H4
North Inishkea (isl.), Ireland 17/A3
North Java, N.Y. 276/D5
North Jay, Maine 243/C6
North Johns, Ala. 195/D4
North Judson, Ind. 227/D2
North Kansas City, Mo. 261/P5
North Kedgwick (riv.), New Bruns. 170/C1
North Kent, Conn. 210/B1
North Kent (isl.), N.W.T. 187/J2
North Kingstown•, R.I. 249/J6
North Kingsville, Ohio 284/J2
North Knife (lake), Manitoba 179/J2
North Knife Lake, Manitoba 179/J2
North Korea 54/O5
North La Junta, Colo. 208/N7
Northlake, Ill. 222/B5
Northlake, Texas 303/F1
North Lake, Wis. 317/J1
North Lakhimpur, India 68/G3
Northland, Mich. 250/B2
Northland, Wis. 317/H6
North Landgrove, Vt. 268/B5
North Laramie (riv.), Wyo. 319/G3
North Las Vegas, Nev. 266/F6
North Lauderdale, Fla. 212/B3
North Lawrence, N.Y. 276/L1
North Lawrence, Ohio 284/G4
North Leeds, Maine 243/C7
North Lewisburg, Ohio 284/C5
North Liberty, Ind. 227/E1
North Liberty, Iowa 229/K5
North Lima, Ohio 284/J4
North Limington, Maine 243/B8
North Little Rock, Ark. 202/F4
North Livermore, Maine 243/C7
North Loup, Nebr. 264/F3
North Loup (riv.), Nebr. 264/E3
North Lovell, Maine 243/B7
North Lubec, Maine 243/J6
North Luconia (shoals), Philippines 85/E4
North Madison, Conn. 210/E3
North Madison, Ohio 284/H2
North Magnetic Pole (dist.) 162/F1
North Magnetic Pole, Canada 4/B15
North Magnetic Pole, N.W.T. 187/H2
North Manchester, Ind. 227/F3
North Manitou (isl.), Mich. 250/C3
North Mankato, Minn. 255/D6
North Marshfield, Mass. 249/M4
North Merritt (isl.), Fla. 212/F3
North Miami, Fla. 212/B4
North Miami, Okla. 288/R1
North Miami Beach, Fla. 212/C4
North Middleboro, Mass. 249/L5
North Middletown, Ky. 237/N4
North Minch (sound), Scotland 10/D1
North Minch (sound), Scotland 15/B3
North Montpelier, Vt. 268/C3
Northmoor, Mo. 261/P5
North Motton, Tasmania 99/C3
North Mountain, W. Va. 312/K3
North Muskegon, Mich. 250/C5
North Myrtle Beach, S.C. 296/K4
North Naples, Fla. 212/E5
North Natuna (isl.), Indonesia 85/D4
North Negril (pt.), Jamaica 158/G6
North Newport, N.H. 268/C5
North New Portland, Maine 243/C6
North New River (canal), Fla. 212/F5
North Newry, Maine 243/B6
North Newton, Kansas 232/E3
North Oaks, Minn. 255/G5
North Ogden, Utah 304/C2
North Olmsted, Ohio 284/G9
Northome, Minn. 255/D3
North Ossetian Aut. Rep., Russia 48/E5
North Ossetian Aut. Rep., Russia 52/F6
North Oxford, Mass. 249/G4
North Pacific (ocean) 87/F4
North Pacific Ocean 2/B5
North Pacific Ocean 2/T4
North Pagai (isl.), Indonesia 85/C6
North Palm Beach, Fla. 212/F5
North Parsonfield, Maine 243/A8
North Pease (riv.), Texas 303/D3
North Pekin, Ill. 222/D3
North Pembroke, Mass. 249/M4
North Pender Island, Br. Col. 184/K3
North Penobscot, Maine 243/F7
North Perry, Maine 243/J5
North Perry, Ohio 284/H2
North Petherton, England 13/D6
North Pine, Br. Col. 184/G2
North Plain, Conn. 210/F3
North Plainfield, N.J. 273/E2
North Plains, Oreg. 291/A2
North Platte (riv.) 188/F2
North Platte (riv.), Colo. 208/G1
North Platte, Nebr. 188/F2
North Platte, Nebr. 264/D3
North Platte (riv.), Nebr. 264/B3
North Platte (riv.), U.S. 146/H5
North Platte (riv.), Wyo. 319/H3
North Plymouth, Mass. 249/L5
North Pole 4/A1
North Pole 2/F1
North Pole, Alaska 196/J2
North Pole (brook), New Bruns. 170/D1
North Pomfret, Vt. 268/B4
Northport, Ala. 195/C4
North Port, Fla. 212/D4
Northport•, Maine 243/E7
Northport, Mich. 250/D3
Northport, Nebr. 264/B3

420 Northport

Northport, N.Y. 276/O9
Northport, Nova Scotia 168/E3
Northport, Wash. 310/H2
North Portal, Sask. 181/J6
North Potomac, Md. 245/K4
North Powder, Oreg. 291/K2
North Pownal, Vt. 268/A6
North Prairie, Wis. 317/J2
North Providence•, R.I. 249/J5
North Pulaski, Va. 307/G6
North Randall, Ohio 284/H9
North Randolph, Vt. 268/B4
North Raymond, Maine 243/C8
North Reading•, Mass. 249/C5
North Redington Beach, Fla. 212/B3
North Redwood, Minn. 255/D6
North Renous (riv.), New Bruns. 170/D2
North Rhine-Westphalia (state), Germany 22/B3
North Richland Hills, Texas 303/F2
Northridge, Ohio 284/B6
North Ridgeville, Ohio 284/F3
North Rim, Ariz. 198/C2
North River, Newf. 166/D2
North River, N.Y. 276/M3
North River, N. Dak. 282/S6
North River, Nova Scotia 168/D4
North Riverside, Ill. 222/B5
North Robinson, Ohio 284/E4
North Ronaldsay (firth), Scotland 15/F1
North Ronaldsay (isl.), Scotland 15/F1
North Ronaldsay (isl.), Scotland 10/E1
Northrop, Minn. 255/D7
North Rose, N.Y. 276/G4
North Roxboro, N.C. 281/L2
North Royalton, Ohio 284/H10
North Rustico, Pr. Edward I. 168/E2
North Saanich, Br. Col. 184/K3
North Saint Paul, Minn. 255/G5
North Salem, Ind. 227/D5
North Salem, N.H. 268/E6
North Salt Lake, Utah 304/C3
North Sandwich, N.H. 268/E4
North San Juan, Calif. 204/E4
North Santiam (riv.), Oreg. 291/E3
North Saskatchewan (riv.) 162/E5
North Saskatchewan (riv.), Alberta 182/E3
North Saskatchewan (riv.), Canada 146/G4
North Saskatchewan (riv.), Sask. 181/D3
North Scituate, Mass. 249/F8
North Scituate, R.I. 249/H5
North Sea (canal), Netherlands 27/F4
North Seal (riv.), Manitoba 179/H2
North Searsmont, Maine 243/E7
North Sentinel (isl.), India 68/G6
North Sevogle (riv.), New Bruns. 170/D1
North Shapleigh, Maine 243/B8
North Shoal (lake), Manitoba 179/E4
Northside, N.C. 281/M2
Northside, Sask. 181/F2
North Sioux City, S. Dak. 298/R8
North Skunk (riv.), Iowa 229/H5
North Somercotes, England 13/H4
North Somercotes (canal), England 10/G4
North Somers, Conn. 210/F1
North Spectacle (lake), Conn. 210/B2
North Spirit Lake, Ontario 175/B2
North Springfield, Pa. 294/A1
North Springfield, Vt. 268/B5
North Springfield, Va. 307/S3
North Star, Alberta 182/B1
North Star, Mich. 250/E5
North Star, Ohio 284/A5
North Stonington•, Conn. 210/H3
North Stratford, N.H. 268/D2
North Sunderland, England 13/F2
North Sutton, N.H. 268/D5
North Swansea, Mass. 249/K5
North Sydney, N.S. Wales 88/L4
North Sydney, N.S. Wales 97/J3
North Sydney, Nova Scotia 168/H2
North Syracuse, N.Y. 276/H4
North Taranaki (bight), N. Zealand 100/D3
North Tarrytown, N.Y. 276/O6
North Terre Haute, Ind. 227/C5
North Thetford, Vt. 268/C4
North Thompson (riv.), Br. Col. 184/G4
North Tidworth, England 13/F6
North Tiverton, R.I. 249/K6
North Tolsta, Scotland 15/B2
Northton, Scotland 15/B3
North Tonawanda, N.Y. 276/C4
North Trap (isl.), N. Zealand 100/B7
North Troy, Vt. 268/C2
North Truchas (peak), N. Mex. 274/D3
North Truro, Mass. 249/O4
North Tunbridge, Vt. 268/C4
North Turner, Maine 243/C7
North Twin (mt.), N.H. 268/D3
North Tyne (riv.), England 13/E2
North Uist (isl.), Scotland 15/A3
North Uist (isl.), Scotland 10/C2
Northumberland (co.), England 13/E2
Northumberland (co.), New Bruns. 170/D2
Northumberland (str.), New Bruns. 170/F2
Northumberland•, N.H. 268/D2
Northumberland (str.), Nova Scotia 168/E2
Northumberland (county), Ontario 177/G3
Northumberland (co.), Pa. 294/J4
Northumberland, Pa. 294/J4
Northumberland (str.), Pr. Edward I. 168/D2
Northumberland (isls.), Queensland 95/D4
Northumberland (cape), S. Australia 94/F8
Northumberland (co.), Va. 307/R5
Northumberland National Park, England 13/E2
North Umpqua (riv.), Oreg. 291/E4
North Ural (mts.), Russia 52/K1
North Utica (Utica), Ill. 222/E2
North Uxbridge, Mass. 249/H4
Northvale, N.J. 273/F1
North Vancouver, Br. Col. 162/D6
North Vancouver, Br. Col. 184/K3
North Vassalboro, Maine 243/D7
North Vernon, Ind. 227/F6
Northview, Mo. 261/G8
Northville, Conn. 210/B2
Northville, Mich. 250/F6
Northville, N.Y. 276/M4
Northville, S. Dak. 298/M3
North Wabasca (lake), Alberta 182/D1
North Wakefield, N.H. 268/E4
North Waldoboro, Maine 243/E7
North Wales, Pa. 294/M5
North Walpole, N.H. 268/C5
North Walsham, England 13/J5
North Walsham, England 10/G4
North Waltham, Mass. 249/B6
North Warren, Pa. 294/D2
North Washington, Iowa 229/J2
North Waterboro, Maine 243/B8
North Waterford, Maine 243/B7
Northway, Alaska 196/K2
North Wayne, Maine 243/C7
North Weare, N.H. 268/D5
North Webster, Ind. 227/F2
Northwest (pt.), Fla. 212/E6
North West (dist.), Guyana 131/A2
North West (pt.), Jamaica 158/G5
North West (cape), Australia 87/B8
North West (cape), W. Australia 88/A4
North West (cape), W. Australia 92/A3
North-West (prov.), S. Africa 118/C5
North-West Aboriginal Reserve, S. Australia 88/E5
North-West Aboriginal Res., W. Australia 92/E4
North West Arm (inlet), Newf. 166/D2
North West Brook, Newf. 166/C2
North West Brook (riv.), Newf. 166/D2
North Westchester, Conn. 210/F2
North-West Frontier (prov.), Pakistan 68/C2
North West Gander (riv.), Newf. 166/C4
North Westminster, Vt. 268/B5
Northwest Miramichi (riv.), New Bruns. 170/D1
Northwest Oromocto (riv.), New Bruns. 170/D3
North Westport, Mass. 249/K6
North West Providence (chan.), Bahamas 156/B1
North West River, Newf. 166/B3
Northwest Territories 162/E2
NORTHWEST TERRITORIES 187
Northwest Territories (prov.), Canada 146/G3
Northwest Upsalquitch (riv.), New Bruns. 170/D1
North Weymouth, Mass. 249/D8
North Whitefield, Maine 243/D7
Northwich, England 13/H2
Northwich, England 10/G2
North Wilbraham, Mass. 249/E4
North Wildwood, N.J. 273/D6
North Wilkesboro, N.C. 281/G2
North Williston, Vt. 268/A3
North Wilton, Conn. 210/B4
North Windham, Conn. 210/G1
North Windham, Maine 243/C8
North Wolcott, Vt. 268/C2
Northwood, Iowa 229/G2
Northwood•, N.H. 268/E5
Northwood, N. Dak. 282/P4
Northwood, Ohio 284/D2
North Woodbury, Conn. 210/C2
Northwood Center, N.H. 268/E5
Northwood Narrows (Northwood P.O.), N.H. 268/E5
Northwoods, Mo. 261/R2
North Woodstock, Conn. 210/G1
North Woodstock, Maine 243/B7
North Woodstock, N.H. 268/D3
Northwye, Mo. 261/J7
North Yarmouth, Maine 243/C8
North Yarmouth•, Maine 243/C8
North York, Ontario 177/J4
North York Moors National Park, England 13/G3
North Yorkshire (co.), England 13/F3
North Zanesville, Ohio 284/G6
Norton (bay), Alaska 196/F2
Norton (sound), Alaska 146/B3
Norton (sound), Alaska 188/C5
Norton (sound), Alaska 196/E2
Norton, England 13/G3
Norton (peak), Idaho 220/D6
Norton (co.), Kansas 232/C2
Norton (res.), Kansas 232/C2
Norton, Mass. 249/K5
Norton•, Mass. 249/K5
Norton, New Bruns. 170/E3
Norton, Ohio 284/G3
Norton, Texas 303/E6
Norton (sound), U.S. 4/C18
Norton•, Vt. 268/D2
Norton (pond), Vt. 268/D2
Norton (I.C.), Va. 307/C7
Norton, W. Va. 312/G5
Norton A.F.B., Calif. 204/F10
Norton-Radstock, England 13/E6
Norton Shores, Mich. 250/C5
Nortonville, Kansas 232/G2
Nortonville, Ky. 237/G6
Nortonville, N. Dak. 282/N6
Norumbega, Argentina 143/F7
Norvegia (cape) 5/B18
Norvell, Ark. 202/K3
Norvelt, Pa. 294/D5
Norwalk, Calif. 204/C11
Norwalk, Conn. 210/B4
Norwalk (isls.), Conn. 210/B4
Norwalk (riv.), Conn. 210/B4
Norwalk, Iowa 229/F6
Norwalk, Mich. 250/C4
Norwalk, Ohio 284/E3
Norwalk, Wis. 317/E8
Norway 2/K2
Norway 4/C9
NORWAY 18
Norway 7/E2
Norway, Ind. 227/D3
Norway, Iowa 229/K5
Norway, Kansas 232/E2
Norway, Maine 243/B7
Norway•, Maine 243/B7
Norway, Mich. 250/B3
Norway (bay), N.W.T. 187/H2
Norway, Oreg. 291/C4
Norway, S.C. 296/E5
Norway House, Man. 162/G5
Norway House, Manitoba 179/J3
Norway Lake, Maine 243/B7
Norwegian (sea) 4/C10
Norwegian (sea) 7/D2
Norwegian (bay), N.W.T. 187/J2
Norwegian (sea), Norway 18/F3
Norwell•, Mass. 249/F8
Norwich, Conn. 210/G2
Norwich, England 13/J5
Norwich, England 10/G4
Norwich, Kansas 232/E4
Norwich, N.Y. 276/J5
Norwich, N. Dak. 282/J3
Norwich, Ohio 284/G6
Norwich, Ontario 177/D5
Norwich•, Vt. 268/C4
Norwichtown, Conn. 210/G2
Norwood, Colo. 208/C6
Norwood, Ga. 217/G4
Norwood, La. 238/H5
Norwood•, Mass. 249/B8
Norwood, Minn. 255/E6
Norwood, Mo. 261/H8
Norwood, N.J. 273/C1
Norwood, N.Y. 276/L1
Norwood, N.C. 281/J4
Norwood, Ohio 284/C9
Norwood, Ontario 177/F3
Norwood, Pa. 294/M7
Norwood, R.I. 249/J6
Norwood, Va. 307/L5
Nosappu (pt.), Japan 81/N2
Nosbonsing (lake), Ontario 177/E1
Nose, Japan 81/J7
Noshiro, Japan 81/J3
Nosovka, Ukraine 52/D4
Nosratabad, Iran 66/L6
Noss (head), Scotland 15/F2
Nossa Senhora do Livramento, Brazil 132/B6
Nossob (riv.), Botswana 118/B4
Nossob (riv.), Namibia 118/B4
Nosy Be (isl.), Madagascar 118/H2
Nosy Boraha (isl.), Madagascar 118/J3
Nosy-Varika, Madagascar 118/H4
Notakwanon (riv.), Newf. 166/B2
Notasulga, Ala. 195/G5
Noteć (riv.), Poland 47/B2
Notikewin, Alberta 182/B1
Notikewin (riv.), Alberta 182/A1
Noto, Italy 34/E6
Noto, Japan 81/H5
Noto (pen.), Japan 81/H5
Notodden, Norway 18/F7
Notre Dame, Ind. 227/E1
Notre-Dame, New Bruns. 170/F2
Notre Dame (bay), Newf. 166/C4
Notre-Dame-de-Ham, Québec 172/F4
Notre-Dame-de-la-Doré, Québec 172/E1
Notre-Dame-de-la-Paix, Québec 172/C4
Notre-Dame-de-la-Salette, Québec 172/B4
Notre Dame de Lourdes, Manitoba 179/D5
Notre-Dame-de-Pierreville, Québec 172/D3
Notre-Dame-des-Anges, Québec 172/E3
Notre-Dame-des-Bois, Québec 172/G4
Notre-Dame-des-Laurentides, Québec 172/H3
Notre-Dame-des-Monts, Québec 172/G2
Notre-Dame-des-Prairies, Québec 172/D3
Notre-Dame-de-Stanbridge, Québec 172/D4
Notre-Dame-du-Bon-Conseil, Québec 172/E4
Notre-Dame-du-Lac, Québec 172/J2
Notre-Dame-du-Laus, Québec 172/B3
Notre-Dame-du-Portage, Québec 172/H2
Notre-Dame-du-Rosaire, Québec 172/F1
Nottawa, Ontario 177/D3
Nottawasaga (bay), Ontario 177/D3
Nottawasaga (riv.), Ontario 177/E3
Nottaway (riv.), Que. 162/J5
Nottaway (riv.), Québec 174/B2
Nottely (lake), Ga. 217/D1
Nøtterøy, Norway 18/D4
Nottingham, Ala. 195/F4
Nottingham, England 13/F5
Nottingham, England 10/F4
Nottingham•, N.H. 268/E5
Nottingham (isl.), N.W.T. 162/H3
Nottingham (isl.), N.W.T. 187/L3
Nottinghamshire (co.), England 13/F4
Nottinghill, Mo. 261/G9
Nottoway (co.), Va. 307/M6
Nottoway, Va. 307/M6
Nottoway (riv.), Va. 307/O7
Notukeu (creek), Sask. 181/D6
Notus, Idaho 220/B6
Nouadhibou, Mauritania 106/A4
Nouadhibou, Mauritania 102/A2
Nouakchott (cap.), Mauritania 106/A5
Nouakchott (cap.), Mauritania 102/A3
Nouakchott (cap.), Mauritania 2/J5
Nouméa (cap.), New Caled. 87/G8
Nouméa (cap.), New Caledonia 2/T7
Nouméa (cap.), New Caled. 86/H5
Nounan, Idaho 220/G7
Noup (head), Scotland 15/E1
Noupoort, S. Africa 118/C6
Nouveau-Québec (terr.), Québec 174/E1
Nouveau-Québec (crater), Québec 174/F1
Nouvelle, Québec 172/C2
Nouvelle (riv.), Québec 172/C2
Nouvelle-France (cape), Québec 174/F1
Nouvelle-Ouest, Québec 172/C2
Nova, Hungary 41/D3
Nova, Ohio 284/F3
Nová Baňa, Slovakia 41/E2
Nová Bystrica, Slovakia 41/E2
Nová Bystřice, Czech Rep. 41/C2
Nova Cruz, Brazil 132/H4
Nova Era, Brazil 135/E1
Nova Friburgo, Brazil 132/F8
Nova Friburgo, Brazil 135/E3
Nova Goa (Panaji), India 68/C5
Nova Gorizia, Slovenia 45/A2
Nova Gradiška, Croatia 45/C3
Nova Granada, Brazil 135/B2
Nova Iguaçu, Brazil 120/E5
Nova Iguaçu, Brazil 135/E3
Nova Iguaçu, Brazil 132/F8
Nova Iorque, Brazil 132/E4
Nova Lima, Brazil 135/E2
Nova Lusitânia, Mozambique 118/E3
Nova Mambone, Mozambique 118/F4
Novar, Ontario 177/E2
Novara (prov.), Italy 34/B2
Novara, Italy 34/B2
Nova Russas, Brazil 132/F4
Nova Scotia (prov.) 162/K7
Nova Scotia (prov.), Canada 146/M5
NOVA SCOTIA 168
Nova Sofala, Mozambique 118/F4
Novato, Calif. 204/H1
Novaya Kakhovka, Ukraine 52/D5
Novaya Kazanka, Kazakhstan 48/F5
Novaya Sibir' (isl.), Russia 4/B2
Novaya Sibir' (isl.), Russia 48/Q2
Novaya Zemlya (isl.), Russia 2/L2
Novaya Zemlya (isls.), Russia 4/B7
Novaya Zemlya (isls.), Russia 48/F2
Novaya Zemlya (isls.), Russia 52/H1
Nova Zagora, Bulgaria 45/H4
Nové Hrady, Czech Rep. 41/C2
Novelda, Spain 33/F3
Novelty, Mo. 261/H2
Nové Město nad Váhom, Slovakia 41/D2
Nové Město na Moravě, Czech Rep. 41/D2
Nové Strašecí, Czech Rep. 41/B1
Nové Zámky, Slovakia 41/D3
Novgorod, Russia 7/H3
Novgorod, Russia 52/D3
Novgorod, Russia 48/D4
Novgorod-Severskiy, Ukraine 52/D4
Novi, Croatia 45/B3
Novi, Mich. 250/F6
Novice, Texas 303/E5
Novi Ligure, Italy 34/B2
Novinger, Mo. 261/G2
Novi Pazar, Bulgaria 45/H4
Novi Pazar, Yugoslavia 45/E4
Novi Sad, Yugoslavia 45/D3
Novi Sad, Yugoslavia 7/F4
Nóvita, Colombia 126/B5
Novoanninskiy, Russia 52/F4
Novo Aripuanã, Brazil 120/D3
Novocherkassk, Russia 7/J4
Novocherkassk, Russia 52/F5
Novodvinsk, Russia 52/F2
Novograd-Volynskiy, Ukraine 52/C4
Novogrudok, Belarus 52/C4
Novo Hamburgo, Brazil 132/D10
Novo Horizonte, Brazil 135/B2
Novokazalinsk, Kazakhstan 48/G5
Novokuybyshevsk, Russia 7/K3
Novokuybyshevsk, Russia 52/G4
Novokuznetsk, Russia 54/K4
Novokuznetsk, Russia 48/J4
Novo Mesto, Slovenia 45/B3
Novomoskovsk, Russia 7/H3
Novomoskovsk, Russia 48/E4
Novomoskovsk, Russia 52/E4
Novopolotsk, Belarus 52/C3
Novorossiysk, Russia 7/H4
Novorossiysk, Russia 48/D5
Novorossiysk, Russia 52/E6
Novosergiyevka, Russia 52/H4
Novoshakhtinsk, Russia 52/E5
Novosibirsk, Russia 54/J4
Novosibirsk, Russia 2/P3
Novosibirsk, Russia 48/J4
Novotroitsk, Russia 52/J4
Novoukrainka, Ukraine 52/D5
Novouzensk, Russia 52/G4
Novovolynsk, Ukraine 52/B4
Novovyatsk, Russia 52/G3
Novozybkov, Russia 48/D4
Novozybkov, Russia 52/D4
Novra, Manitoba 179/B2
Novska, Croatia 45/C3
Nový Bohumín, Czech Rep. 41/E2
Nový Bor, Czech Rep. 41/C1
Nový Bydžov, Czech Rep. 41/C1
Nový Hrozenkov, Czech Rep. 41/E2
Nový Jičín, Czech Rep. 41/E2
Novyy Bug, Ukraine 52/D5
Novyy Port, Russia 4/C6
Novyy Port, Russia 48/G3
Novyy Urengoy, Russia 48/H3
Novyy Uzen', Kazakhstan 48/F5
Nowa Dęba, Poland 47/E3
Nowa Nowa, Victoria 97/E5
Nowa Ruda, Poland 47/C3
Nowa Sól, Poland 47/B3
Nowata (co.), Okla. 288/P1
Nowata, Okla. 288/P1
Nowater (creek), Wyo. 319/E2
Nowe, Poland 47/D2
Nowe Miasto Lubawskie, Poland 47/D2
Nowendoc, N.S. Wales 97/F2
Nowgong, Assam, India 68/G3
Nowgong, Madhya Pradesh, India 68/D3
Nowitna (riv.), Alaska 196/H2
Nowogard, Poland 47/B2
Nowood (riv.), Wyo. 319/E1
Nowra-Bomaderry, N. S. Wales 88/J6
Nowra-Bomaderry, N.S. Wales 97/F4
Now Shahr, Iran 66/G2
Nowshera, Pakistan 59/K3
Nowshera, Pakistan 68/C2
Nowy Dwór Gdański, Poland 47/D1
Nowy Dwór Mazowiecki, Poland 47/E2
Nowy Sącz (prov.), Poland 47/E4
Nowy Sącz, Poland 47/E4
Nowy Staw, Poland 47/D1
Nowy Targ, Poland 47/E4
Nowy Tomyśl, Poland 47/C2
Now Zad, Afghanistan 68/A2
Now Zad, Afghanistan 59/H3
Noxapater, Miss. 256/F5
Noxen, Pa. 294/E7
Noxon, Mont. 262/A3
Noxubee (co.), Miss. 256/G4
Noxubee (riv.), Miss. 256/G4
Noya, Spain 33/B1
Noyes (isl.), Alaska 196/M2
Noyes, Minn. 255/A2
Noyes (pt.), R.I. 249/H7
Noyo (riv.), Calif. 204/B4
Noyon, France 28/E3
Noyon, Mongolia 77/F3
Nsanje, Malawi 115/G7
Nsawam, Ghana 106/D7
Nsukka, Nigeria 106/F7
Nsuta, Ghana 106/D7
Nuba (mts.), Sudan 111/E5
Nubanusit (lake), N.H. 268/C5
Nubeena, Tasmania 99/D5
Nuberg, Ga. 217/G2
Nubia (lake), Sudan 111/F3
Nubian (des.), Sudan 102/F2
Nubian (des.), Sudan 111/F3
Nubian (des.), Sudan 59/B5
Nubieber, Calif. 204/D2
Nuckolls (co.), Nebr. 264/F4
Nuckols, Ky. 237/G5
Nucla, Colo. 208/B6
Nudgee, Queensland 88/K2
Nueces (co.), Texas 303/G10
Nueces (riv.), Texas 188/G5
Nueces (riv.), Texas 303/F9
Nueltin (lake) 162/G3
Nueltin (lake), Manitoba 179/H1
Nueltin (lake), N.W.T. 187/H3
Nuestra Señora (bay), Chile 138/A5
Nueva (isl.), Argentina 143/C8
Nueva (isl.), Chile 138/F11
Nueva Alejandría, Peru 128/F5
Nueva Antioquia, Colombia 126/F5
Nueva Armenia, Honduras 154/D4
Nueva Asunción, Paraguay 144/B2
Nueva Casas Grandes, Mexico 150/F1
Nueva Ciudad Guerrero, Mexico 150/K3
Nueva Colombia, Paraguay 144/B4
Nueva Ecija (prov.), Philippines 82/C3
Nueva Esparta (state), Venezuela 124/G2
Nueva Germania, Paraguay 144/D3
Nueva Gerona, Cuba 156/A2
Nueva Gerona, Cuba 158/B2
Nueva Helvecia, Uruguay 145/B5
Nueva Imperial, Chile 138/D2
Nueva Italia, Paraguay 144/B5
Nueva Italia de Ruiz, Mexico 150/J7
Nueva Ocotepeque, Honduras 154/C3
Nueva Palmira, Uruguay 145/A4
Nueva Rosita, Mexico 150/J2
Nueva San Salvador, El Salvador 154/C4
Nueva Vizcaya (prov.), Philippines 82/C2
Nueve de Julio, Argentina 143/F7
Nuevitas, Cuba 156/C2
Nuevitas, Cuba 158/G2
Nuevitas (bay), Cuba 158/H2
Nuevo (gulf), Argentina 143/D5
Nuevo, Bajo (reef), Mexico 150/O6
Nuevo Berlín, Uruguay 145/B3
Nuevo Chagres, Panama 154/G6
Nuevo Ideal, Mexico 150/G4
Nuevo Juncal, Chile 138/B5
Nuevo Laredo, Mexico 146/H7
Nuevo Laredo, Mexico 150/J3
Nuevo León (state), Mexico 150/K4
Nuevo Mamo, Venezuela 124/G3
Nuevo Rocafuerte, Ecuador 128/E3
Nufenen, Switzerland 39/H3
Nugaal (prov.), Somalia 115/J2
Nugget (pt.), N. Zealand 100/C7
Nugrus, Jebel (mt.), Egypt 59/B4
Nuguria (isls.), Papua N.G. 86/C1
Nui (atoll), Tuvalu 87/H6
Nuiqsut, Alaska 196/H1
Nu Jiang (riv.), China 77/E6
Nuka (bay), Alaska 196/C2
Nuka (isl.), Alaska 196/C2
Nukey Bluff (mt.), S. Australia 94/D5
Nukheila (oasis), Sudan 111/E4
Nuku'alofa (cap.), Tonga 87/J8
Nukuhiva (isl.), Fr. Poly. 87/M6
Nukulaelae (atoll), Tuvalu 87/H6
Nukumanu (atoll), Papua N.G. 87/F6
Nukumanu (isls.), Papua N.G. 86/D2
Nukunonu (atoll), Tokelau Is. 87/J6
Nukuoro (atoll), Micronesia 87/F5
Nukus, Uzbekistan 54/H5
Nukus, Uzbekistan 48/G5
Nulato, Alaska 196/G2
Nules, Spain 33/F3
Nulhegan (riv.), Vt. 268/D2
Nulhegan, East Branch (riv.), Vt. 268/D2
Nullagine, W. Australia 88/C4
Nullagine, W. Australia 92/C3
Nullarbor (plain), Australia 88/D6
Nullarbor (plain), Australia 87/C9
Nullarbor, S. Australia 94/B4
Nullarbor (plain), S. Australia 94/A4
Nullarbor (plain), W. Australia 92/D5
Nulliberg (mt.), Virgin Is. (U.S.) 161/B4
Nulltown, Ind. 227/G5
Numa, Iowa 229/G7
Numan, Nigeria 106/G7
Numancia, Philippines 82/D5
Numansdorp, Netherlands 27/E5
Numata, Japan 81/J5
Numazu, Japan 81/J6
Numbulwar, North. Terr. 88/F2
Numbulwar, North. Terr. 93/D3
Numfoor (isl.), Indonesia 85/J6
Ñumí, Paraguay 144/D4
Nu Mine, Pa. 294/D4
Numurkah, Victoria 97/C5
Nunaksaluk (isl.), Newf. 166/B2
Nunapitchuk, Alaska 196/F2
Nunawading, Victoria 88/L7
Nunawading, Victoria 97/J5
Nunchía, Colombia 126/D5
Nunda, N.Y. 276/E5
Nunda, S. Dak. 298/P5
Nundah, Queensland 88/K2
Nundah, Queensland 95/E2
Nundle, N.S. Wales 97/F2
Nuneaton, England 13/F5
Nuneaton, England 10/F4
Núñez (isl.), Chile 138/D10
Nunez, Ga. 217/H5
Nungarin, W. Australia 92/B5
Nungesser (lake), Ontario 175/B2
Nunivak (isl.), Alaska 146/B4
Nunivak (isl.), Alaska 188/C6
Nunivak (isl.), Alaska 196/E3
Nunivak (isl.), U.S. 4/D18
Nunley, Ark. 202/B4
Nunn, Colo. 208/K1
Nunnelly, Tenn. 237/G9
Nunningen, Switzerland 39/E2
Nuñoa, Peru 128/G10
Nunspeet, Netherlands 27/H4
Nuoro (prov.), Italy 34/B4
Nuoro, Italy 34/B4
Nuqub, Yemen 59/E6
Nuquí, Colombia 126/B5
Nuremberg, Germany 7/F4
Nuremberg, Germany 22/D4
Nuremberg, Pa. 294/K4
Nurestan (reg.), Afghanistan 59/K2
Nurhak, Turkey 63/G4
Nuri, Mexico 150/E3
Nuri (ruins), Sudan 111/F4
Nuria, Sierra de (mts.), Venezuela 124/H4
Nuriootpa, S. Australia 94/F6
Nuristan (reg.), Afghanistan 68/C1
Nurlat, Russia 52/H4
Nurmes, Finland 18/Q5
Nürnberg (Nuremberg), Germany 22/D4
Nurrari (lakes), S. Australia 94/B3
Nursery, Texas 303/H9
Nürtingen, Germany 22/C4
Nuruhak Dağı (mt.), Turkey 63/G3
Nus, Ras (cape), Oman 59/G6
Nusa Barung (isl.), Indonesia 85/K3
Nusaybin, Turkey 63/J4
Nushagak (bay), Alaska 196/G3
Nushagak (riv.), Alaska 196/G2
Nushki, Pakistan 68/B3
Nushki, Pakistan 59/J4
Nussaq, Greenland 4/B12
Nutimik, Manitoba 179/G5
Nutley, N.J. 273/B2
Nut Mountain, Sask. 181/H3
Nutrioso, Ariz. 198/F5
Nuttby (mt.), Nova Scotia 168/E3
Nutter Fort, W. Va. 312/F4
Nutting Lake, Mass. 249/B5
Nutwood Downs, North. Terr. 93/D3
Nuuanu (stream), Hawaii 218/C4
Nuuk (cap.), Greenland 4/C12
Nuuk (cap.), Greenland 146/N3
Nuuk (cap.), Greenland 2/G2
Nuupere (pt.), Fr. Poly. 86/S13
Nuwara Eliya, Sri Lanka 68/E7
Nuweiba, Egypt 111/F2
Nuyakuk (lake), Alaska 196/F3
Nuyts (arch.), S. Australia 94/C5
Nuyts (cape), S. Australia 88/E6
Nuyts (cape), S. Australia 94/C5
Nyabing, W. Australia 88/B6
Nyabisindu, Rwanda 115/F4
Nyack, Mont. 262/C2
Nyack, N.Y. 276/K8
Nyah, Victoria 97/B4
Nyah West, Victoria 97/B4
Nyainqêntanglha Shan (range), China 77/D5
Nyainrong, China 77/D5
Nyala, Sudan 111/E5
Nyala, Sudan 102/E3

Ny-Ålesund, Norway 18/C2
Nyamlell, Sudan 111/E6
Nyandoma, Russia 7/J2
Nyandoma, Russia 48/E3
Nyandoma, Russia 52/F2
Nyanga, Gabon 115/A4
Nyanga, S. Africa 118/F6
Nyanza (prov.), Kenya 115/F4
Nyasa (lake) 102/F6
Nyasa (lake) 2/L6
Nyasa (lake), Malawi 115/F6
Nyasa (lake), Mozambique 118/E2
Nyasa (lake), Tanzania 115/F6
Nyborg, Denmark 21/D7
Nyborg, Denmark 18/G9
Nybro, Sweden 18/J8
Nye, Mont. 262/G5
Nye (co.), Nev. 266/E4
Nyeri, Kenya 115/G4
Nyerol, Sudan 111/F6
Nyima, China 77/C5
Nyingchi, China 77/D6
Nyírábrány, Hungary 41/G3
Nyíradony, Hungary 41/G3
Nyírbátor, Hungary 41/G3
Nyíregyháza, Hungary 41/F3
Nyírmada, Hungary 41/F2
Nyiru (mt.), Kenya 115/G3
Nykarleby, Finland 18/N5
Nykøbing, Denmark 18/H9
Nykøbing, Denmark 18/G9
Nykøbing, Denmark 18/F8
Nykøbing, Storstrøm, Denmark 21/F8
Nykøbing, Vestsjaelland, Denmark 21/E
Nykøbing, Viborg, Denmark 21/B4
Nyköping, Sweden 18/K7
Nylstroom, S. Africa 118/D4
Nymagee, N.S. Wales 97/D3
Nymboida, N.S. Wales 97/G1
Nymboida (riv.), N.S. Wales 97/G1
Nymburk, Czech Rep. 41/C1
Nynäshamn, Sweden 18/L7
Nyngan, N. S. Wales 88/H6
Nyngan, N.S. Wales 97/D2
Nyon, Switzerland 39/B4
Nyons, France 28/F5
Nýřany, Czech Rep. 41/B2
Nyrob, Russia 52/J2
Nýrsko, Czech Rep. 41/B2
Nysa, Poland 47/C3
Nysa Kłodzka (riv.), Poland 47/C3
Nysa Łużycka (Neisse) (riv.), Poland 47/B3
Nyssa, Oreg. 291/K4
Nysted, Denmark 21/E8
Nytva, Russia 52/H3
Nyudo (cape), Japan 81/J4
Nyukhcha, Russia 52/G2
Nyunzu, D.R. Congo 115/E5
Nyurba, Russia 48/M3
Nyuvchim, Russia 52/H2
Nzega, Tanzania 115/F4
N'Zérékoré, Guinea 106/C7
N'zeto, Angola 115/B5
Nzwani (isl.), Comoros 118/G2
Nzwani (isl.), Comoros 102/G6

O

Oa, Mull of (prom.), Scotland 10/C3
Oa, Mull of (prom.), Scotland 15/B5
Oacoma, S. Dak. 298/L6
Oadby, England 13/F5
Oahe (lake), N. Dak. 282/J7
Oahe (dam), S. Dak. 298/J5
Oahe (lake), S. Dak. 188/F1
Oahe (lake), S. Dak. 298/J1
Oahe (lake), U.S. 146/J5
Oahu (isl.), Hawaii 87/L3
Oahu (isl.), Hawaii 188/F5
Oahu (isl.), Hawaii 218/E2
Oak (lake), Manitoba 179/B5
Oak (pt.), Mich. 250/F5
Oak, Nebr. 264/G4
Oak (creek), N. Dak. 282/J8
Oak (isl.), Nova Scotia 168/E3
Oak (creek), S. Dak. 298/J6
Oak (creek), S. Dak. 298/H2
Oak (isl.), Wis. 317/E2
Oakbank, Manitoba 179/F5
Oak Bay, Br. Col. 184/K4
Oak Bay, New Bruns. 170/C3
Oak Bluffs, Mass. 249/M7
Oak Bluffs•, Mass. 249/M7
Oak Bluff Station, Manitoba 179/E5
Oakboro, N.C. 281/J4
Oak Brae, Manitoba 179/C3
Oak Brook, Ill. 222/B6
Oakbrook Terrace, Ill. 222/B5
Oakburn, Manitoba 179/B4
Oak Center, Minn. 255/F6
Oak City, N.C. 281/P3
Oak City, Utah 304/B4
Oak Creek, Colo. 208/F2
Oak Creek, Wis. 317/M2
Oakdale, Calif. 204/E6
Oakdale, Conn. 210/G3
Oakdale, Ill. 222/D5
Oakdale, Iowa 229/K5
Oakdale, La. 238/E5
Oakdale, Mass. 249/G3
Oakdale, Minn. 255/E5
Oakdale, Nebr. 264/F2
Oakdale, Pa. 294/B5
Oakdale, Tenn. 237/M9
Oakdale, Wis. 317/F8
Oakes, N. Dak. 282/O7
Oakesdale, Wash. 310/H3
Oakfield, Ga. 217/E7
Oakfield•, Maine 243/G3
Oakfield, N.Y. 276/D4
Oakfield, Tenn. 237/D9
Oakfield, Wis. 317/J8
Oakford, Ill. 222/D3
Oakford, Ind. 227/E4
Oak Forest, Ill. 222/B6
Oak Grove, Ala. 195/B9
Oak Grove, Ala. 195/F4
Oak Grove, Ark. 202/C1
Oak Grove, Del. 245/R6
Oak Grove, Ill. 222/C2
Oak Grove, Ky. 237/G7
Oak Grove, La. 238/H1
Oak Grove, Mich. 250/F6
Oak Grove, Mo. 261/S6
Oak Grove, Mo. 261/K6
Oak Grove, Oreg. 291/B2
Oak Grove, Va. 307/O4
Oak Grove Fork, Clackamas (riv.), Oreg. 291/F2
Oak Hall, Pa. 294/G4
Oak Hall, Va. 307/S5
Oakham, England 13/G5
Oakham, England 10/F4
Oakham•, Mass. 249/F3
Oak Harbor, Ohio 284/D2
Oak Harbor, Wash. 310/C2
Oak Harbor Naval Air Sta., Wash. 310/C2
Oakhaven, Ark. 202/C6
Oak Hill, Ala. 195/D7
Oak Hill, Fla. 212/F3
Oak Hill, Ill. 222/D3
Oakhill, Kansas 232/E2
Oak Hill, Mo. 261/K6
Oak Hill, Ohio 284/E8
Oak Hill, Tenn. 237/H8
Oak Hill, W. Va. 312/D6
Oakhurst, Calif. 204/F6
Oakhurst, N.J. 273/E3
Oakhurst, Okla. 288/P2
Oakhurst, Texas 303/J7
Oak Island, Minn. 255/D1
Oak Lake, Manitoba 179/B5
Oakland, Calif. 146/F6
Oakland, Calif. 188/B3
Oakland, Calif. 204/J2
Oakland, Conn. 210/E1
Oakland, Fla. 212/E3
Oakland, Ill. 222/F4
Oakland, Iowa 229/C6
Oakland, Ky. 237/J6
Oakland, La. 238/F1
Oakland, Maine 243/D6
Oakland•, Maine 243/D6
Oakland, Md. 245/L3
Oakland, Md. 245/A3
Oakland (co.), Mich. 250/F6
Oakland, Miss. 256/E2
Oakland, Mo. 261/P3
Oakland, Mo. 261/G7
Oakland, Nebr. 264/H3
Oakland, N.J. 273/B1
Oakland, Okla. 288/N6
Oakland, Ontario 177/D4
Oakland, Oreg. 291/D4
Oakland, Pa. 294/L2
Oakland, R.I. 249/H5
Oakland, Tenn. 237/B10
Oakland Acres, Iowa 229/H5
Oakland Army Base, Calif. 204/J2
Oakland Beach, R.I. 249/J6
Oakland City, Ind. 227/C8
Oakland Mills, Iowa 229/K7
Oakland Park, Fla. 212/B3
Oaklands, N.S. Wales 97/D4
Oak Lawn, Ill. 222/B6
Oakleigh, Victoria 88/L7
Oakleigh, Victoria 97/J5
Oakley, Calif. 204/L1
Oakley, Idaho 220/D7
Oakley, Ill. 222/E4
Oakley, Iowa 229/G6
Oakley, Kansas 232/B2
Oakley, Mich. 250/E5
Oakley, Miss. 256/D6
Oakley, N.C. 281/P3
Oakley, Scotland 15/C1
Oakley, S.C. 296/G5
Oakley, Tenn. 237/L8
Oakley, Utah 304/C3
Oaklyn, N.J. 273/B3
Oakman, Ala. 195/D3
Oakman, Ga. 217/C1
Oakmont, Pa. 294/C6
Oakmulgee (creek), Ala. 195/D5
Oakner, Manitoba 179/B4
Oak Orchard, Del. 245/T6
Oakover (riv.), W. Australia 88/C4
Oakover (riv.), W. Australia 92/C3
Oak Park, Ga. 217/H6
Oak Park, Ill. 222/B5
Oak Park, Mich. 250/B6
Oak Park, Minn. 255/E5
Oakpark, Va. 307/M4
Oak Point, Manitoba 179/B5
Oak Point, New Bruns. 170/D3
Oak Ridge, La. 238/G1
Oak Ridge, Miss. 256/C6
Oak Ridge, Mo. 261/N7
Oak Ridge, N.J. 273/E1
Oak Ridge (res.), N.J. 273/D1
Oak Ridge, N.C. 281/K2
Oakridge, Oreg. 291/E4
Oak Ridge, Pa. 294/D3
Oak Ridge, Tenn. 188/J3
Oak Ridge, Tenn. 237/N8
Oak River, Manitoba 179/D4
Oaks, Mo. 261/P5
Oaks, Okla. 288/S2
Oakshela, Sask. 181/J5
Oakton, Ky. 237/C7
Oakton, Va. 307/R3
Oaktown, Ind. 227/C7
Oak Vale, Miss. 256/E8
Oakvale, W. Va. 312/D8
Oak Valley, Kansas 232/G4
Oak View, Calif. 204/F9
Oakview, Manitoba 179/D3
Oakview, Mo. 261/P5
Oakville, Conn. 210/C2
Oakville, Ind. 227/G4
Oakville, Iowa 229/L6
Oakville, Ky. 237/H7
Oakville, Manitoba 179/D5
Oakville, Ontario 177/E4
Oakville, Pa. 294/H5
Oakville, Texas 303/G9
Oakville, Wash. 310/B4
Oakway, S.C. 296/A2
Oakwood, Ga. 217/E2
Oakwood, Ill. 222/F3
Oakwood, Mo. 261/P5
Oakwood, N. Dak. 282/R3
Oakwood, Ohio 284/H9
Oakwood, Ohio 284/B6
Oakwood, Ohio 284/B3
Oakwood, Okla. 288/J3
Oakwood, Ontario 177/F3
Oakwood, Texas 303/J6
Oakwood, Va. 307/E6
Oakwood Heights, Ill. 222/B2
Oakwood Manor, Mo. 261/P5
Oakwood Park, Mo. 261/P5
Oamaru, N. Zealand 100/C6
Oani (riv.), Japan 81/K3
Oasis, Nev. 266/G1
Oasis, Utah 304/B4
Oates Coast (reg.) 5/B8
Oatlands, Tasmania 99/D4
Oatman, Ariz. 198/A3
Oatsville, Ind. 227/C8
Oaxaca (state), Mexico 150/L8
Oaxaca, Mexico 146/J8
Oaxaca de Juárez, Mexico 150/L8
Ob' (gulf), Russia 4/B6
Ob' (gulf), Russia 48/H3
Ob' (gulf), Russia 54/J3
Ob' (riv.), Russia 2/N2
Ob' (riv.), Russia 4/C6
Ob' (riv.), Russia 48/G3
Ob' (riv.), Russia 54/H3
Oba, Ont. 162/H6
Oba, Ontario 177/J5
Oba, Ontario 175/D3
Obama, Japan 81/G6
Oban (Half Moon Bay), N. Zealand 100/B7
Oban, Sask. 181/C3
Oban, Scotland 15/C4
Oban, Scotland 10/D2
Obbia, Somalia 115/J2
Obed, Alberta 182/B3
Obed (riv.), Tenn. 237/M8
Ober, Ind. 227/D2
Oberá, Argentina 143/F2
Oberägeri, Switzerland 39/G2
Oberalp (pass), Switzerland 39/G3
Oberalpstock (mt.), Switzerland 39/G3
Oberammergau, Germany 22/D5
Oberburg, Switzerland 39/E2
Oberdiessbach, Switzerland 39/E3
Oberdorf, Switzerland 39/E2
Ober Grafendorf, Austria 41/C2
Oberhausen, Germany 22/B3
Oberhof, Germany 22/D3
Oberlin, Kansas 232/B2
Oberlin, La. 238/E5
Oberlin, Mich. 250/E4
Oberlin, Ohio 284/F3
Oberndorf bei Salzburg, Austria 41/B3
Oberon, Manitoba 179/C4
Oberon, N.S. Wales 97/E3
Oberon, N. Dak. 282/M4
Oberpfälzer Wald (for.), Germany 22/E4
Oberriet, Switzerland 39/J2
Obersaxen, Switzerland 39/H3
Obersiggenthal, Switzerland 39/F1
Oberstammheim, Switzerland 39/G1
Oberstdorf, Germany 22/D5
Obert, Nebr. 264/G2
Oberursel, Germany 22/C3
Obervellach, Austria 41/B3
Oberwald, Switzerland 39/F3
Oberwart, Austria 41/D3
Oberwil, Switzerland 39/D3
Oberwölz, Austria 41/C3
Oberzwil, Switzerland 39/H2
Obetz, Ohio 284/E6
Obi (isl.), Indonesia 85/H6
Obi (isls.), Indonesia 85/H6
Óbidos, Brazil 120/D3
Óbidos, Brazil 132/C3
Óbidos, Portugal 33/B3
Obihiro, Japan 81/L2
Obion (creek), Ky. 237/C7
Obion (co.), Tenn. 237/C8
Obion, Tenn. 237/C8
Obion, South Fork (riv.), Tenn. 237/D8
Obion, Middle Fork (riv.), Tenn. 237/D8
Obion (riv.), Tenn. 237/C8
Obion, North Fork (riv.), Tenn. 237/D8
Obispos, Venezuela 124/D3
Obitsu (riv.), Japan 81/P3
Oblong, Ill. 222/F5
Obluch'ye, Russia 48/N5
Obninsk, Russia 52/E3
Obo, Cent. Afr. Rep. 115/E2
Obock, Djibouti 111/H5
Oborniki, Poland 47/C2
Oboyan', Russia 52/E4
Obozerskiy, Russia 52/E2
O'Brien, Fla. 212/D1
O'Brien (co.), Iowa 229/B2
O'Brien, Oreg. 291/D5
O'Brien, Texas 303/E4
O'Briensbridge-Montpelier, Ireland 17/D6
Observatory (inlet), Br. Col. 184/C2
Obsidian, Idaho 220/D6
Obuasi, Ghana 106/D7
Obukowin (lake), Manitoba 179/G3
Obwalden (canton), Switzerland 39/F3
Ocala, Fla. 212/D2
Ocamo (riv.), Venezuela 124/F6
Ocampo, Chihuahua, Mexico 150/E2
Ocampo, Coahuila, Mexico 150/H3
Ocampo, Tamaulipas, Mexico 150/K5
Ocaña, Colombia 126/D3
Ocaña, Spain 33/E3
Ocate, N. Mex. 274/E2
Ocate (creek), N. Mex. 274/E2
Occidental, Cordillera (range), Bolivia 136/A6
Occidental, Cordillera (range), Colombia 126/B5
Occidental, Cordillera (range), Peru 128/F10
Occidental Mindoro (prov.), Philippines 82/C4
Occoquan, Va. 307/O3
Occum, Conn. 210/G2
Ocean (cape), Alaska 196/K3
Ocean (pond), Fla. 212/D1
Ocean (Banaba) (isl.), Kiribati 87/G6
Ocean (co.), N.J. 273/E4
Ocean (lake), Nova Scotia 168/G3
Ocean (lake), Wyo. 319/D2
Oceana (co.), Mich. 250/C5
Oceana, W. Va. 312/C7
Oceana N.A.S., Va. 307/S7
Ocean Beach, N.Y. 276/O9
Ocean Bluff-Brant Rock, Mass. 249/M4
Ocean Breeze Park, Fla. 212/F4
Ocean City, Md. 245/T7
Ocean City, N.J. 273/D5
Ocean City, Wash. 310/A3
Ocean Falls, Br. Col. 184/D4
Ocean Gate, N.J. 273/E4
Ocean Grove, Mass. 249/K6
Ocean Grove, N.J. 273/F3
Ocean Isle Beach, N.C. 281/N7
Oceano, Calif. 204/E8
Oceanographic Office, Md. 245/F5
Ocean Park, Maine 243/C9
Ocean Park, Wash. 310/A4
Oceanport, N.J. 273/F3
Ocean Ridge, Fla. 212/F5
Ocean Shores, Wash. 310/A3
Oceanside, Calif. 204/H10
Oceanside, N.Y. 276/R7
Oceanside, Oreg. 291/C2
Ocean Springs, Miss. 256/G10
Ocean View, Del. 245/T6
Ocean View, N.J. 273/D5
Oceanville, N.J. 273/D5
Oceola, Ohio 284/D4
Ochamchira, Georgia 52/F6
Ochelata, Okla. 288/P1
Ocheyedan, Iowa 229/B2
Ochil (hills), Scotland 15/E4
Ochiltree (co.), Texas 303/D1
Ochlocknee, Ga. 217/E9
Ochlockonee (riv.), Fla. 212/B1
Ochlockonee (riv.), Ga. 217/C10
Ochoco (creek), Oreg. 291/G3
Ochopee, Fla. 212/E6
Ocho Rios, Jamaica 158/J6
Ochre River, Manitoba 179/C3
Ochsen (mt.), Switzerland 39/D3
Ochsenfurt, Germany 22/D4
Ochsenkopf (mt.), Liecht. 39/J2
Ocie, Mo. 261/G9
Ocilla, Ga. 217/F7
Ockelbo, Sweden 18/K6
Ocklawaha (lake), Fla. 212/E2
Ockley, Ind. 227/D4
Ocmulgee (riv.), Ga. 217/E5
Ocmulgee Nat'l Mon., Ga. 217/F5
Ocna Mureș, Romania 45/G2
Ocoa, Chile 138/G2
Ocoa (bay), Dom. Rep. 158/D6
Ocoee, Fla. 212/E3
Ocoee (riv.), Tenn. 237/M10
Ocoña, Peru 128/F11
Ocoña (riv.), Peru 128/F11
Oconee (co.), Ga. 217/F3
Oconee, Ga. 217/G5
Oconee (riv.), Ga. 217/F5
Oconee, Ill. 222/D4
Oconee (co.), S.C. 296/A2
Oconomowoc, Wis. 317/H1
Oconomowoc (lake), Wis. 317/H1
Oconomowoc Lake, Wis. 317/H1
Oconto, Nebr. 264/E3
Oconto (co.), Wis. 317/K6
Oconto, Wis. 317/L6
Oconto (riv.), Wis. 317/K5
Oconto Falls, Wis. 317/K6
Ocós, Guatemala 154/A3
Ocosingo, Mexico 150/O8
Ocosta, Wash. 310/B4
Ocotal, Segovia, Nicaragua 154/D4
Ocotal, Zelaya, Nicaragua 154/E4
Ocotlán, Mexico 150/H6
Ocotlán de Morelos, Mexico 150/L8
Ocqueoc, Mich. 250/F3
Ocracoke, N.C. 281/T4
Ocracoke (inlet), N.C. 281/T5
Ocracoke (isl.), N.C. 281/T4
Ocre, Ala. 195/H4
Ocros, Peru 128/D8
Octa, Mo. 261/M10
Octa, Ohio 284/C6
Octagon, Ala. 195/C6
Octavia, Nebr. 264/G3
Octavia, Okla. 288/S5
October Revolution (isl.), Russia 4/B5
October Revolution (isl.), Russia 48/L2
October Revolution (isl.), Russia 54/K2
Ocú, Panama 154/G7
Ocumare de la Costa, Venezuela 124/E2
Ocumare del Tuy, Venezuela 124/E2
Ocurí, Bolivia 136/C6
Oda, Ghana 106/D7
Oda, Japan 81/F6
Oda, Jebel (mt.), Sudan 59/C5
Oda, Jebel (mt.), Sudan 111/G3
Odanah, Wis. 317/E2
Odate, Japan 81/K3
Odawara, Japan 81/J6
Odd, W. Va. 312/D7
Odda, Norway 18/E6
Odder, Denmark 21/D6
Oddur, Somalia 115/H3
Odebolt, Iowa 229/C4
Odell, Ill. 222/E2
Odell, Ind. 227/C4
Odell, Nebr. 264/H4
Odell, Oreg. 291/F2
Odell (lake), Oreg. 291/E4
Odell, Texas 303/E3
Odell River, New Bruns. 170/C2
Odemira, Portugal 33/B4
Ödemiş, Turkey 63/C3
Oden, Ark. 202/C4
Odenburg, La. 238/G5
Odendaalsrus, S. Africa 118/D5
Odense, Denmark 7/F3
Odense, Denmark 18/G9
Odense, Denmark 21/D7
Odense (fjord), Denmark 21/D7
Odenton, Md. 245/M4
Odenville, Ala. 195/F3
Odenwald (for.), Germany 22/C4
Oder (riv.) 7/F3
Oder (Odra) (riv.), Czech Rep. 41/D2
Oder (riv.), Germany 22/F2
Oder (riv.), Poland 47/B2
Oder-Haff (mts.), Germany 22/F2
Oder-Haff (lag.), Poland 47/B2
Odessa, Del. 245/R3
Odessa, Fla. 212/D3
Odessa, Minn. 255/B5
Odessa, Mo. 261/E5
Odessa, Nebr. 264/E4
Odessa, N.Y. 276/G6
Odessa, Ontario 177/H3
Odessa, Sask. 181/H5
Odessa, Tex. 188/F4
Odessa, Texas 146/H6
Odessa, Texas 303/B6
Odessa, Ukraine 2/L3
Odessa, Ukraine 7/H4
Odessa, Ukraine 48/D5
Odessa, Ukraine 52/D5
Odessa, Wash. 310/G3
Odessadale, Ga. 217/C5
Odgen, Utah 188/D2
Odgensburg, N.Y. 188/M2
Odiel (riv.), Spain 33/C4
Odienné, Ivory Coast 106/C7
Odin, Ill. 222/D5
Odin, Kansas 232/D3
Odin, Minn. 255/D7
Odiongan, Philippines 82/C4
Odivelas, Portugal 33/A1
Odobești, Romania 45/H3
Odon, Ind. 227/C7
Odongk, Cambodia 72/E5
O'Donnell, Texas 303/C5
O'Donnells, Newf. 166/D2
Odoorn, Netherlands 27/K3
Odorheiu Secuiesc, Romania 45/G2
Odra (Oder) (riv.), Poland 47/B2
Odry, Czech Rep. 41/D2
Odum, Ga. 217/H7
Odweina, Somalia 115/J2
Oebisfelde, Germany 22/D2
Oeiras, Brazil 132/F4
Oeiras, Portugal 33/B3
Oelemari (riv.), Suriname 131/D4
Oella, Md. 245/L3
Oelrichs, S. Dak. 298/C7
Oelsnitz, Germany 22/E3
Oelsnitz im Erzgebirge, Germany 22/E3
Oelwein, Iowa 229/K3
Oeno (isl.), Pitcairn Is. 87/O8
Oenpelli, North. Terr. 93/C2
Oensingen, Switzerland 39/E2
Of, Turkey 63/J2
Ofahoma, Miss. 256/E5
O'Fallon, Ill. 222/B2
O'Fallon, Mo. 261/L5
O'Fallon (creek), Mont. 262/L4
Ofanto (riv.), Italy 34/E4
Ofaqim, Israel 65/B5
Ofen (pass), Switzerland 39/K3
Ofenhorn (mt.), Switzerland 39/F4
Offa, Nigeria 106/E7
Offaly (co.), Ireland 17/F5
Offenbach am Main, Germany 22/C3
Offenburg, Germany 22/B4
Offerle, Kansas 232/C4
Offerman, Ga. 217/H8
Offutt, Ky. 237/R5
Offutt A.F.B., Nebr. 264/J3
Ofotfjorden (fjord), Norway 18/K2
Ofqui (isth.), Chile 138/D6
Oftringen, Switzerland 39/E2
Ofunato, Japan 81/K4
Oga, Japan 81/J4
Oga (pen.), Japan 81/J4
Ogaden (reg.), Ethiopia 102/G4
Ogaden (reg.), Ethiopia 111/H6
Ogaki, Japan 81/H6
Ogallah, Kansas 232/C3
Ogallala, Nebr. 264/C3
Ogasawara-gunto (Bonin) (isls.), Japan 81/M3
Ogbomosho, Nigeria 102/C4
Ogbomosho, Nigeria 106/E7
Ogden, Ark. 202/B6
Ogden, Ill. 222/F3
Ogden, Iowa 229/E4
Ogden, Kansas 232/F2
Ogden (bay), N.W.T. 187/H3
Ogden, Utah 146/G6
Ogden, Utah 304/C2
Ogden Dunes, Ind. 227/C1
Ogdensburg, N.J. 273/D1
Ogdensburg, N.Y. 276/K1
Ogdensburg, Wis. 317/J7
Ogeechee (riv.), Ga. 217/J5
Ogema, Minn. 255/C3
Ogema, Sask. 181/G6
Ogema, Wis. 317/F5
Ogemaw, Ark. 202/E7
Ogemaw (co.), Mich. 250/E4
Ogi, Japan 81/J5
Ogidaki (mt.), Ontario 175/D3
Ogidaki (mt.), Ontario 177/J5
Ogilvie, Manitoba 179/D4
Ogilvie, Minn. 255/E5
Ogilvie (mts.), Yukon 187/E3
Ogilvie (riv.), Yukon 187/E3
Oglala, S. Dak. 298/D7
Ogle (co.), Ill. 222/D1
Ogle, Ky. 237/O6
Oglesby, Ill. 222/D2
Oglesby, Texas 303/G6
Oglethorpe (co.), Ga. 217/F3
Oglethorpe, Ga. 217/D6
Oglio (riv.), Italy 34/C2
Ogmore, Queensland 88/J4
Ogmore and Garw, Wales 13/A6
Ogoja, Nigeria 106/F7
Ogoki (riv.), Ont. 162/H5
Ogoki (riv.), Ontario 175/C2
Ogooué (riv.), Congo 115/A4
Ogooué (riv.), Gabon 115/A4
Ogre, Latvia 53/C2
Ogulin, Croatia 45/B3
Ogun (state), Nigeria 106/E7
Ogunquit, Maine 243/B9
Oğuzeli, Turkey 63/G4
Ohai, N. Zealand 100/A6
Ohakune, N. Zealand 100/E3
O'Hare Field-Chicago International Airport, Ill. 222/B5
Ohariu (stream), N. Zealand 100/B2
Ohata, Japan 81/K3
Ohatchee, Ala. 195/G3
Ohaton, Alberta 182/D3
Ohau (lake), N. Zealand 100/B6
Ohaupo, N. Zealand 100/E2
Ohey, Belgium 27/G8
O'Higgins (lake), Chile 138/D7
OHIO 284
Ohio 118/K2
Ohio (riv.) 188/J3
Ohio, Colo. 208/F5
Ohio, Ill. 222/D2
Ohio (riv.), Ill. 222/E6
Ohio (co.), Ind. 227/H7
Ohio (riv.), Ind. 227/B9
Ohio (co.), Ky. 237/H6
Ohio (riv.), Ky. 237/F5
Ohio, Nova Scotia 168/F3
Ohio (riv.), Nova Scotia 168/D4
Ohio (riv.), Ohio 284/B8
Ohio (riv.), Pa. 294/A4
Ohio (state), U.S. 146/K5
Ohio (riv.), U.S. 146/K6
Ohio (riv.), U.S. 2/E4
Ohio (co.), W. Va. 312/E2
Ohio (riv.), W. Va. 312/B5
Ohio Brush (creek), Ohio 284/D8
Ohio City, Ohio 284/A4
Ohiopyle, Pa. 294/D6
Ohioville, Pa. 294/B4
Ohiowa, Nebr. 264/G4
Ohley, W. Va. 312/D6
Ohlman, Ill. 222/D4
Ohoopee, Ga. 217/H6
Ohře (riv.), Czech Rep. 41/B1
Ohrid (lake), Albania 45/E5
Ohrid, Macedonia 45/E5
Ohrid (lake), Macedonia 45/E5
Ohura, N. Zealand 100/E3
Oiapoque (Oyapock) (riv.), Brazil 132/C2
Oich, Loch (lake), Scotland 15/D3
Oich (riv.), Scotland 15/D3
Oies (isl.), Québec 172/G2
Oil (creek), Pa. 294/C2
Oil Center, N. Mex. 274/F6
Oil City, La. 238/C1
Oil City, Ontario 177/B5
Oil City, Pa. 188/L2
Oil City, Pa. 294/C3
Oildale, Calif. 204/F8
Oilmont, Mont. 262/E2
Oil Spring Ind. Res., N.Y. 276/D6
Oil Springs, Ky. 237/P5
Oil Springs, Ontario 177/B5
Oilton, Okla. 288/N2
Oilton, Texas 303/F10
Oil Trough, Ark. 202/G2
Oinói, Greece 45/F6
Oise (dept.), France 28/E3
Oise (riv.), France 28/E3
Oiseau (lake), Manitoba 179/G4
Oiseau (riv.), Manitoba 179/G4
Oisterwijk, Netherlands 27/G5
Oistins, Barbados 161/B9
Oistins (bay), Barbados 161/B9
Oita (pref.), Japan 81/E7
Oita, Japan 81/E7
Ojai, Calif. 204/F9
Ojibwa, Wis. 317/D4
Ojinaga, Mexico 150/G2
Ojiya, Japan 81/J5
Ojocaliente, Mexico 150/H5
Ojo Caliente, N. Mex. 274/D2
Ojo del Toro (mt.), Cuba 158/G4
Ojo Feliz, N. Mex. 274/E2
Ojo Sarco, N. Mex. 274/D2
Ojos del Salado (mt.) 120/C5
Ojos del Salado, Cerro (mt.), Argentina 143/C2
Ojos del Salado, Nevado (mt.), Chile 138/B6
Ojos Negros, Spain 33/F2
Ojus, Fla. 212/B4

Otuquis 423

Orange, France 28/F5
Orange, Ga. 217/D2
Orange (co.), Ind. 227/E7
Orange, Ind. 227/G5
Orange, Mass. 249/E2
Orange•, Mass. 249/E2
Orange (canal), Netherlands 27/K3
Orange•, N.H. 268/D4
Orange, N.J. 273/B2
Orange, N.S. Wales 88/H6
Orange, N.S. Wales 97/E3
Orange (co.), N.Y. 276/M8
Orange (co.), N.C. 281/L2
Orange, Ohio 284/J9
Orange (riv.), S. Africa 118/B5
Orange (mts.), Suriname 131/D4
Orange (co.), Texas 303/L7
Orange, Texas 303/L7
Orange (butte), Utah 304/D5
Orange (co.), Vt. 268/C3
Orange•, Vt. 268/C3
Orange (co.), Va. 307/M4
Orange, Va. 307/M4
Orange Beach, Ala. 195/C10
Orangeburg, N.Y. 276/K8
Orangeburg (co.), S.C. 296/F5
Orangeburg, S.C. 296/F4
Orange City, Fla. 212/E3
Orange City, Iowa 229/A2
Orange Cove, Calif. 204/F7
Orangedale, Nova Scotia 168/G3
Orange Grove, Miss. 256/H10
Orange Grove, Texas 303/F10
Orange Hill, St. Vin. & Grens. 161/A8
Orange Lake, Fla. 212/D2
Orange Park, Fla. 212/E1
Orange Springs, Fla. 212/E2
Orangeville, Ill. 222/D1
Orangeville, Ind. 227/D7
Orangeville, Mich. 250/D6
Orangeville, Ohio 284/J3
Orangeville, Ontario 177/D4
Orangeville, Pa. 294/K3
Orangeville, Utah 304/C4
Orange Walk Town, Belize 154/C1
Oranienburg, Germany 22/E2
Oranjemund, Namibia 102/D7
Oranjemund, Namibia 118/B5
Oranjestad (cap.), Aruba, Neth. Ant. 161/D10
Oranjestad, Neth. Ant. 156/D4
Oranmore, Ireland 17/D5
Orapa, Botswana 118/D4
Oras, Philippines 82/E4
Orăştie, Romania 45/F3
Orava (res.), Poland 47/D4
Orava (res.), Slovakia 41/E2
Orava (riv.), Slovakia 41/E2
Oraville, Ill. 222/D6
Oraviţa, Romania 45/E3
Orb (riv.), France 28/E6
Orbe, Switzerland 39/C3
Orbe (riv.), Switzerland 39/C3
Orbetello, Italy 34/C3
Órbigo (riv.), Spain 33/D1
Orbisonia, Pa. 294/G5
Orbost, Victoria 88/H7
Orbost, Victoria 97/E5
Orbyhus, Sweden 18/K6
Orca, Alaska 196/J2
Orcadia, Sask. 181/J4
Orcas (isl.), Wash. 310/C2
Orcera, Spain 33/E3
Orchard, Colo. 208/L2
Orchard, Iowa 229/H2
Orchard, Nebr. 264/F2
Orchard Beach, Md. 245/M4
Orchard Hill, Ga. 217/D4
Orchard Lake, Mich. 250/F6
Orchard Mesa, Colo. 208/C4
Orchard Park, N.Y. 276/C5
Orchards, Wash. 310/C5
Orchard Valley, Wyo. 319/H4
Orchid, Fla. 212/F4
Orchid, Va. 307/N5
Orchy (riv.), Scotland 15/D4
Orcotuna, Peru 128/E8
Orcutt, Calif. 204/E9
Orcuttville, Conn. 210/F1
Ord (mt.), Ariz. 198/D5
Ord (riv.), Australia 87/C7
Ord, Nebr. 264/F3
Ord (riv.), W. Australia 88/D3
Ord (mt.), W. Australia 92/D2
Ord (riv.), W. Australia 92/E2
Ordenes, Spain 33/B1
Orderville, Utah 304/B6
Ordoqui, Argentina 143/F7
Ordos (reg.), China 77/G4
Ord River, W. Australia 92/E2
Ordu (prov.), Turkey 63/G2
Ordu, Turkey 59/C1
Ordu, Turkey 63/G2
Ordway, Colo. 208/M6
Ordway, S. Dak. 298/N2
Ordzhonikidze (Vladikavkaz), Russia 7/J4
Ordzhonikidze (Vladikavkaz), Russia 48/E5
Ordzhonikidze (Vladikavkaz), Russia 52/F6
Orealla, Guyana 131/C3
Oreälv (riv.), Sweden 18/L4
Oreana, Idaho 220/B6
Oreana, Ill. 222/E4
Oreana, Nev. 266/C2
Orebank, Tenn. 237/R7
Örebro (co.), Sweden 18/J7
Örebro, Sweden 7/F3
Örebro, Sweden 18/J7
Ore City, Texas 303/K5
OREGON 291
Oregon 188/B2
Oregon, Ill. 222/D1
Oregon (co.), Mo. 261/K9
Oregon, Mo. 261/B2
Oregon (inlet), N.C. 281/U3
Oregon, Ohio 284/D2
Oregon Canyon (creek), Oreg. 291/K5
Oregon (state), U.S. 146/F5
Oregon, Wis. 317/H10
Oregon Caves Nat'l Mon., Oreg. 291/D5
Oregon City, Oreg. 188/B1
Oregon City, Oreg. 291/B2
Oregon Dunes Nat'l Rec. Area, Oreg. 291/C4
Oregonia, Ohio 284/B7
Öregrund, Sweden 18/L6
Orel, Russia 7/H3
Orel, Russia 52/E4
Orel, Russia 48/D4
Orellana, Peru 128/E6
Orellana la Vieja, Spain 33/D3
Orem, Utah 304/C3
Orenburg, Russia 7/K3
Orenburg, Russia 48/F4
Orenburg, Russia 52/J4
Orenco, Oreg. 291/A2
Orense (prov.), Spain 33/C1
Orense, Spain 33/C1
Orense, Spain 7/D4
Orestes, Ind. 227/F4
Orestías, Greece 45/H5
Øresund (sound), Denmark 21/F6
Öresund (sound), Denmark 18/H9
Öresund (sound), Sweden 18/H9
Oreti (riv.), N. Zealand 100/B6
Oretta, La. 238/D5
Orewa, N. Zealand 100/E2
Orford•, N.H. 268/C4
Orford, Tasmania 99/D4
Orford Ness (prom.), England 13/J5
Orfordville, N.H. 268/C4
Orfordville, Wis. 317/H10
Organ, N. Mex. 274/C6
Organabo, Fr. Guiana 131/E3
Organ Pipe Cactus Nat'l Mon., Ariz. 198/C6
Órgãos (range), Brazil 135/E3
Orgas, W. Va. 312/C6
Orgaz, Spain 33/E3
Orgeyev, Moldova 52/C5
Orhaneli, Turkey 63/C3
Orhangazi, Turkey 63/C2
Orhon Gol (riv.), Mongolia 77/F2
Oria, Spain 33/E4
Orick, Calif. 204/A2
Orient, Ill. 222/E6
Orient, Iowa 229/E6
Orient•, Maine 243/H4
Orient, N.Y. 276/R8
Orient (pt.), N.Y. 276/R8
Orient, Ohio 284/D6
Orient, S. Dak. 298/L4
Orient, Wash. 310/G2
Orienta, Okla. 288/J2
Oriental, Cordillera (range), Bolivia 136/C5
Oriental, Cordillera (range), Colombia 126/D5
Oriental, Cordillera (range), Dom. Rep. 158/F6
Oriental, Mexico 150/O1
Oriental, N.C. 281/R4
Oriental, Cordillera (range), Peru 128/H10
Oriental Mindoro (prov.), Philippines 82/C4
Orihuela, Spain 33/F3
Orihvesi (lake), Finland 18/Q5
Orillia, Ontario 177/E3
Orin, Wash. 310/H2
Orin, Wyo. 319/G3
Orinda, Calif. 204/J2
Orinoca, Bolivia 136/B6
Orinoco (riv.) 120/C2
Orinoco (riv.) 2/F5
Orinoco (riv.), Colombia 126/G5
Orinoco (delta), Venezuela 120/C2
Orinoco (delta), Venezuela 124/H3
Orinoco (riv.), Venezuela 124/G3
Oriole, Md. 245/P8
Orion, Ala. 195/F7
Orion, Alberta 182/E5
Orion, Ill. 222/C2
Oriska, N. Dak. 282/P6
Oriskany, N.Y. 276/K4
Oriskany, Va. 307/J5
Oriskany Falls, N.Y. 276/J5
Orissa (state), India 68/E5
Oristano, Italy 34/B5
Oristano (gulf), Italy 34/B5
Orituco (riv.), Venezuela 124/E3
Oriximiná, Brazil 132/C3
Orizaba, Mexico 146/J8
Orizaba, Mexico 150/P2
Orizaba (Citlaltépetl) (mt.), Mexico 150/O2
Órjiva, Spain 33/E4
Orkanger, Norway 18/F5
Örkény, Hungary 41/E3
Orkney, Sask. 181/D6
Orkney (islands area), Scotland 15/E1
Orkney (isls.), Scotland 7/D3
Orkney (isls.), Scotland 15/F1
Orkney (isls.), Scotland 10/E1
Orkney (trad. co.), Scotland 15/B4
Orla, Texas 303/D10
Orland, Calif. 204/C4
Orland, Ind. 227/G1
Orland, Maine 243/F6
Orland•, Maine 243/F6
Orland Hills, Ill. 222/B6
Orlândia, Brazil 135/C2
Orlando, Fla. 146/K7
Orlando, Fla. 188/K5
Orlando, Fla. 212/E3
Orlando, Ky. 237/N6
Orlando, Okla. 288/M2
Orlando, W. Va. 312/E5
Orland Park, Ill. 222/B6
Orleães, Brazil 132/D10
Orléanais (trad. prov.), France 29
Orleans, Calif. 204/B2
Orléans, France 7/E4
Orléans, France 28/D3
Orleans, Ind. 227/D7
Orleans, Iowa 229/C2
Orleans (par.), La. 238/L6
Orleans, Mass. 249/O5
Orleans•, Mass. 249/O5
Orleans, Minn. 255/B2
Orleans, Nebr. 264/E4
Orleans (co.), N.Y. 276/D4
Orleans, Ontario 177/J2
Orléans (isl.), Québec 172/F3
Orleans (co.), Vt. 268/C2
Orleans, Vt. 268/C2
Orleans Cross Roads, W. Va. 312/K3
Orléansville (El Asnam), Algeria 106/E1
Orlice (riv.), Czech Rep. 41/D1
Orlická (res.), Czech Rep. 41/C2
Orlinda, Tenn. 237/H7
Orlová, Czech Rep. 41/E2
Orly, France 28/B2
Orma, W. Va. 312/D5
Ormara, Pakistan 59/J4
Ormara, Pakistan 68/A3
Orme, Tenn. 237/K10
Ormea, Italy 34/A2
Ormiston, Sask. 181/F6
Ormoc, Philippines 82/E5
Ormoc (bay), Philippines 82/E5
Ormond Beach, Fla. 212/E2
Ormond-by-the-Sea, Fla. 212/E2
Ormont-Dessus, Switzerland 39/D4
Ormsby, Minn. 255/D7
Ormsby, Pa. 294/E2
Ormskirk, England 10/F2
Ormskirk, England 13/G2
Ormstown, Québec 172/D4
Orne (dept.), France 28/C3
Orne (riv.), France 28/C3
Orneta, Poland 47/E1
Ornö (isl.), Sweden 18/J2
Örnsköldsvik, Sweden 18/L5
Orobayaya, Bolivia 136/D3
Orocovis, P. Rico 161/C2
Orocué, Colombia 126/E5
Orofino, Idaho 220/B3
Orofino (creek), Idaho 220/C3
Oro Grande, Calif. 204/H9
Orogrande, Idaho 220/C4
Orogrande, N. Mex. 274/D6
Orohena (mt.), Fr. Poly. 86/T13
Oro Ingenio, Bolivia 136/C7
Oroluk (atoll), Micronesia 87/F5
Oromocto, New Bruns. 170/D3
Oromocto (lake), New Bruns. 170/C3
Oromocto (riv.), New Bruns. 170/D3
Oron, Israel 65/C6
Oron, Nigeria 106/F8
Orona (Hull) (isl.), Kiribati 87/J6
Orondo, Wash. 310/E3
Orongorongo (riv.), N. Zealand 100/B3
Oron-la-Ville, Switzerland 39/C3
Orono (isl.), Kiribati 87/L5
Orono, Maine 243/F6
Orono•, Maine 243/F6
Orono, Minn. 255/F5
Oronoco, Minn. 255/F6
Oronogo, Mo. 261/D8
Oronsay (isl.), Scotland 15/B4
Orontes (riv.), Syria 59/C2
Orontes (riv.), Syria 63/G5
Oropesa, Spain 33/D3
Oropuche (riv.), Trin. & Tob. 161/B10
Oroqen, China 77/K1
Oroquieta, Philippines 85/G4
Oroquieta, Philippines 82/D6
Orosei (gulf), Italy 34/B4
Orosháza, Hungary 41/F3
Orosi, Calif. 204/F7
Oroszlány, Hungary 41/E3
Orote (pen.), Guam 86/K7
Orotina, C. Rica 154/E6
Orotukan, Russia 48/Q3
Orovada, Nev. 266/D1
Oro Valley, Ariz. 198/E6
Oroville, Calif. 204/D4
Oroville (lake), Calif. 204/D4
Oroville, Wash. 310/F2
Orozco, Cuba 158/B1
Orpha, Wyo. 319/G3
Orr, Minn. 255/F2
Orr, N. Dak. 282/P3
Orr, Okla. 288/M6
Orrefors, Sweden 18/J8
Orrick, Mo. 261/D4
Orrin, N. Dak. 282/K3
Orrin (riv.), Scotland 15/D3
Orrington, Maine 243/F6
Orrington•, Maine 243/F6
Orroroo, S. Australia 94/F5
Orrs Island, Maine 243/D8
Orrstown, Pa. 294/G5
Orrtanna, Pa. 294/H6
Orrum, N.C. 281/L6
Orrville, Ala. 195/D6
Orrville, Ohio 284/G4
Orrville, Ontario 177/E2
Orsa, Sweden 18/J6
Orsainville, Québec 172/H3
Orsha, Belarus 7/G3
Orsha, Belarus 52/C4
Orsières, Switzerland 39/D4
Orsk, Russia 7/K3
Orsk, Russia 48/F4
Orsk, Russia 52/J4
Orson, Pa. 294/M2
Orsonnens, Switzerland 39/D3
Orşova, Romania 45/F3
Ørsted, Denmark 21/D5
Orta, Turkey 63/E2
Ortaca, Turkey 63/C4
Ortakaraviran, Turkey 63/E4
Ortaköy, Çorum, Turkey 63/F2
Ortaköy, Niğde, Turkey 63/F3
Ortega, Colombia 126/C6
Ortegal (cape), Spain 33/B1
Orteguaza (riv.), Colombia 126/C7
Orthez, France 28/C6
Ortigueira, Spain 33/C1
Orting, Wash. 310/C3
Ortiz, Colo. 208/H8
Ortiz, Mexico 150/D2
Ortiz, Venezuela 124/E3
Ortles (range), Italy 34/C1
Ortley, S. Dak. 298/P3
Ortoire (riv.), Trin. & Tob. 161/B11
Ortón (riv.), Bolivia 136/B2
Ortona, Italy 34/E3
Ortonville, Mich. 250/F6
Ortonville, Minn. 255/B5
Oruro (dept.), Bolivia 136/A6
Oruro, Bolivia 120/C4
Oruro, Bolivia 136/B5
Oruzgan (Hazar Qadam), Afghanistan 68/B2
Orvieto, Italy 34/D3
Orville, Ky. 237/M4
Orviston, Pa. 294/G3
Orwell, N.Y. 276/J3
Orwell, Ohio 284/J2
Orwell•, Vt. 268/A4
Orwigsburg, Pa. 294/K4
Oryakhovo, Bulgaria 45/F4
Or Yehuda, Israel 65/B4
Orzesze, Poland 47/A4
Orzysz, Poland 47/E2
Osa, Russia 52/J3
Osage (riv.) 188/H3
Osage, Ark. 202/D1
Osage, Iowa 229/H2
Osage (co.), Kansas 232/G3
Osage, Minn. 255/C4
Osage (co.), Mo. 261/J6
Osage (riv.), Mo. 261/E6
Osage (co.), Okla. 288/O1
Osage, Okla. 288/O2
Osage, Sask. 181/H6
Osage, W. Va. 312/F3
Osage, Wyo. 319/H2
Osage Beach, Mo. 261/G6
Osage City, Kansas 232/G3
Osage Ind. Res., Okla. 288/O1
Osaka (pref.), Japan 81/J8
Osaka, Japan 2/R4
Osaka, Japan 54/P6
Osaka, Japan 81/J8
Osaka (bay), Japan 81/H8
Osakis, Minn. 255/C5
Osasco, Brazil 135/C3
Osawatomie, Kansas 232/H3
Osborn, Miss. 256/G3
Osborn, Mo. 261/D3
Osborn, S.C. 296/G6
Osborne (co.), Kansas 232/D2
Osborne, Kansas 232/D2
Osborne, Pa. 294/B4
Osbornsville, N.J. 273/E3
Osburn, Idaho 220/B2
Oscar, Fr. Guiana 131/E4
Oscar, La. 238/H5
Oscar, Okla. 288/L7
Oscarville, Alaska 196/F2
Osceola, Ark. 202/K2
Osceola (co.), Fla. 212/E3
Osceola, Ind. 227/E1
Osceola (co.), Iowa 229/B2
Osceola, Iowa 229/F6
Osceola (co.), Mich. 250/D5
Osceola, Mo. 261/E6
Osceola, Nebr. 264/G3
Osceola (mt.), N.H. 268/E3
Osceola, N.Y. 276/J3
Osceola, Pa. 294/H2
Osceola, S. Dak. 298/O5
Osceola, Wis. 317/A5
Osceola Mills, Pa. 294/F4
Oschatz, Germany 22/E3
Oschersleben, Germany 22/D2
Oscoda (co.), Mich. 250/E4
Oscoda, Mich. 250/F4
Oscura (mts.), N. Mex. 274/C5
Oscuro, N. Mex. 274/C5
Ösel (Saaremaa) (isl.), Estonia 52/B3
Osgood, Ind. 227/G6
Osgood, Mo. 261/F2
Osgood, Ohio 284/A5
Osgoode, Ontario 177/J2
Osh, Kyrgyzstan 48/H5
Osh, Kyrgyzstan 54/J5
Osha (peak), N. Mex. 274/C4
Oshakat, Namibia 118/B3
Oshawa, Ontario 177/F4
Oshikango, Namibia 118/A3
O-Shima (isl.), Japan 81/J6
Oshkosh, Nebr. 264/B3
Oshkosh, Wis. 188/J2
Oshkosh, Wis. 317/J8
Oshnoviyeh, Iran 66/D2
Oshogbo, Nigeria 102/C4
Oshogbo, Nigeria 106/F7
Oshoto, Wyo. 319/G1
Oshtoran Kuh (mt.), Iran 66/F4
Oshwe, D.R. Congo 115/C4
Osierfield, Ga. 217/F7
Osijek, Croatia 7/F4
Osijek, Croatia 45/D3
Osimo, Italy 34/D3
Osipenko (Berdyansk), Ukraine 52/E5
Osipovichi, Belarus 52/C4
Oskaloosa, Iowa 229/H6
Oskaloosa, Iowa 188/H2
Oskaloosa, Kansas 232/G2
Oskaloosa, Mo. 261/D7
Oskarshamn, Sweden 18/K8
Oskélanéo, Québec 174/C3
Oslavany, Czech Rep. 41/D2
Osler, Sask. 181/E3
Oslo, Minn. 255/A2
Oslo (city county), Norway 18/D3
Oslo (cap.), Norway 2/K2
Oslo (cap.), Norway 7/F2
Oslo (cap.), Norway 18/D3
Oslofjord (fjord), Norway 18/D4
Osmanabad, India 68/D5
Osmancık, Turkey 63/F2
Osmaneli, Turkey 63/D2
Osmaniye, Turkey 63/G4
Osmond, Nebr. 264/G2
Osnabrock, N. Dak. 282/O2
Osnabrück, Germany 22/C2
Osnaburgh House, Ontario 175/B2
Oso, Wash. 310/D2
Osogna, Switzerland 39/H4
Osorno, Chile 120/B7
Osorno, Chile 138/D3
Osorno, Spain 33/D1
Osoyoos, Br. Col. 184/H5
Osoyoos (lake), Wash. 310/F1
Ospino, Venezuela 124/D3
Osprey (reef), 95/C2
Osprey, Fla. 212/D4
Osprey (reef), Queensland 88/H2
Oss, Netherlands 27/H5
Ossa, Serra da (mts.), Portugal 33/C3
Ossa (mt.), Tasmania 88/H8
Ossa (mt.), Tasmania 99/C3
Ossabaw (isl.), Ga. 217/K7
Ossabaw (sound), Ga. 217/K7
Osse (riv.), Nigeria 106/F7
Osseo, Mich. 250/E7
Osseo, Minn. 255/G5
Osseo, Wis. 317/D6
Ossian, Ind. 227/G3
Ossian, Iowa 229/K2
Ossineke, Mich. 250/F4
Ossining, N.Y. 276/N8
Ossipee, N.H. 268/E4
Ossipee (lake), N.H. 268/E4
Ossipee (mts.), N.H. 268/E4
Ossipee (riv.), N.H. 268/F4
Ossokmanuan (res.), Newf. 166/B3
Ostashkov, Russia 52/D3
Oste (riv.), Germany 22/C2
Osteen, Fla. 212/E3
Ostend, Belgium 27/B6
Osterburg, Pa. 294/E5
Österdalälven (riv.), Sweden 18/H6
Osterdock, Iowa 229/L3
Östergötland (co.), Sweden 18/J7
Osterholz-Scharmbeck, Germany 22/C2
Osterode am Harz, Germany 22/D3
Östersund, Sweden 7/F2
Östersund, Sweden 18/J5
Osterville, Mass. 249/N6
Øster Vrå, Denmark 21/D3
Osterwick, Manitoba 179/D5
Østfold (co.), Norway 18/G7
Östhammar, Sweden 18/L6
Ostia Antica, Italy 34/F7
Ostrander, Minn. 255/F7
Ostrander, Ohio 284/D5
Ostrava, Czech Rep. 7/F4
Ostrava, Czech Rep. 41/E2
Ostróda, Poland 47/D2
Ostrogozhsk, Russia 48/D4
Ostrogozhsk, Russia 52/E4
Ostrołęka (prov.), Poland 47/E2
Ostrołęka, Poland 47/E2
Ostrov, Czech Rep. 41/B1
Ostrov, Russia 52/C3
Ostrowiec Świętokrzyski, Poland 47/E3
Ostrów Mazowiecka, Poland 47/E2
Ostrów Wielkopolski, Poland 47/C3
Ostrzeszów, Poland 47/C3
Ostuni, Italy 34/F4
O'Sullivan (dam), Wash. 310/F4
Osŭm (riv.), Bulgaria 45/G4
Osumi (isls.), Japan 81/E8
Osumi (pen.), Japan 81/E8
Osumi (str.), Japan 81/E8
Osuna, Spain 33/D4
Oswaldtwistle, England 13/H1
Oswayo, Pa. 294/G2
Oswegatchie, N.Y. 276/K2
Oswegatchie (riv.), N.Y. 276/K2
Oswego, Ill. 222/E2
Oswego, Ind. 227/F2
Oswego, Kansas 232/G4
Oswego, Mont. 262/L2
Oswego (riv.), N.J. 273/E4
Oswego (co.), N.Y. 276/H4
Oswego, N.Y. 276/G4
Oswego (riv.), N.Y. 276/H4
Oswego, N.Y. 188/L2
Oswego, S.C. 296/G3
Oswestry, England 10/E4
Oswestry, England 13/E5
Oświęcim, Poland 47/D3
Osyka, Miss. 256/D8
Ota, Japan 81/J5
Otago (harb.), N. Zealand 100/C6
Otago (pen.), N. Zealand 100/C6
Otahuhu, N. Zealand 100/C1
Otaki, N. Zealand 100/E4
Otakine (mt.), Japan 81/K5
Otaru, Japan 81/K2
Otautau, N. Zealand 100/B7
Otava (riv.), Czech Rep. 41/B2
Otavalo, Ecuador 128/C2
Otavi, Namibia 118/B3
Otawara, Japan 81/K5
O. T. Downs, North. Terr. 93/D4
Oteen, N.C. 281/E3
Otego, N.Y. 276/K6
Otematata, N. Zealand 100/B6
Otero (co.), Colo. 208/M7
Otero (co.), N. Mex. 274/D6
Othello, Wash. 310/F4
Otho, Iowa 229/E4
Oti (riv.), Ghana 106/E7
Oti (riv.), Togo 106/E7
Oti (riv.), Burkina Faso 106/E7
Otira, N. Zealand 100/C5
Otis, Colo. 208/O2
Otis, Ind. 227/D1
Otis, Kansas 232/C3
Otis, La. 238/E4
Otis•, Mass. 249/B4
Otis (res.), Mass. 249/B4
Otis, N. Mex. 274/E6
Otis, Oreg. 291/D2
Otis, Québec 172/G1
Otis A.F.B., Mass. 249/M6
Otisco, Ind. 227/F7
Otisco, Minn. 255/E7
Otisco (lake), N.Y. 276/H5
Otisfield, Maine 243/B7
Otisfield•, Maine 243/B7
Otish (mts.), Québec 174/C2
Otis Orchards-East Farms, Wash. 310/H3
Otisville, Mich. 250/F5
Otisville, N.Y. 276/L8
Otjiwarongo, Namibia 102/D7
Otjiwarongo, Namibia 118/B4
Otley, Iowa 229/G6
Oto, Iowa 229/B4
Otoe (co.), Nebr. 264/H4
Otoe, Nebr. 264/H4
Otofuke, Japan 81/L2
Otog, China 77/G4
Otorohanga, N. Zealand 100/E3
Otoskwin (riv.), Ontario 175/B2
Otra (riv.), Norway 18/E7
Otrabanda, Neth. Ant. 161/F9
Otradnyy, Russia 52/H4
Otranto (str.), Albania 45/D5
Otranto, Iowa 229/H2
Otranto, Italy 34/G4
Otranto (str.), Italy 34/G5
Otsego (co.), Mich. 250/E3
Otsego, Mich. 250/D6
Otsego (lake), Mich. 250/E4
Otsego (co.), N.Y. 276/K5
Otsego (lake), N.Y. 276/L5
Otsego, Ohio 284/G5
Otsego Lake, Mich. 250/E4
Otselic (riv.), N.Y. 276/J5
Otsu, Japan 81/J7
Otta, Norway 18/F6
Ottauquechee (riv.), Vt. 268/B4
Ottawa (cap.), Canada 2/F3
Ottawa (cap.), Canada 146/L5
Ottawa (cap.), Canada 162/J6
Ottawa (riv.), Canada 146/L5
Ottawa (riv.), Canada 162/J6
Ottawa, Ill. 222/E2
Ottawa (co.), Kansas 232/E2
Ottawa, Kansas 232/G3
Ottawa (co.), Mich. 250/C6
Ottawa, Minn. 255/E6
Ottawa (isls.), N.W.T. 146/K4
Ottawa (isls.), N.W.T. 162/H4
Ottawa (isls.), N.W.T. 187/K4
Ottawa (co.), Ohio 284/D2
Ottawa, Ohio 284/B3
Ottawa (co.), Okla. 288/S1
Ottawa (cap.), Canada, Ontario 177/J2
Ottawa (riv.), Ontario 175/E3
Ottawa (riv.), Ontario 177/H2
Ottawa (riv.), Québec 172/B4
Ottawa (riv.), Québec 174/B3
Ottawa Beach, Mich. 250/C6
Ottawa-Carleton (reg. munic.), Ontario 177/J2
Ottawa Hills, Ohio 284/C2
Ottawa Lake, Mich. 250/F7
Otter (isl.), Alaska 196/D3
Otter (lakes), Alberta 182/B1
Otter, Mont. 262/K5
Otter (creek), Utah 304/C5
Otter (creek), Utah 304/C2
Otter (creek), Vt. 268/A3
Otterbein, Ind. 227/C4
Otterburne, Manitoba 179/E5
Otterburn Park, Québec 172/D4
Otter Creek, Fla. 212/D2
Otter Creek, Maine 243/G7
Otter Creek (res.), Utah 304/C5
Otter Lake, Mich. 250/F5
Otterlo, Netherlands 27/H4
Otterøya (isl.), Norway 18/E5
Otter River, Mass. 249/F2
Otter Rock, Oreg. 291/C3
Otter Tail (co.), Minn. 255/C4
Ottertail, Minn. 255/C4
Otter Tail (lake), Minn. 255/C4
Otter Tail (riv.), Minn. 255/B4
Otterup, Denmark 21/D7
Otterville, Ill. 222/C4
Otterville, Iowa 229/K3
Otterville, Mo. 261/G5
Otterville, Ontario 177/D5
Ottery Saint Mary, England 13/D7
Ottery Saint Mary, England 10/E5
Otthon, Sask. 181/J4
Ottleys (creek), N.S. Wales 97/F1
Otto, Ind. 227/G7
Otto, Mo. 261/M6
Otto, N.Y. 276/C6
Otto, N.C. 281/C4
Otto (fjord), N.W.T. 187/K1
Otto, Wyo. 319/D1
Ottosen, Iowa 229/E3
Ottoville, Ohio 284/B4
Ottsville, Pa. 294/M5
Ottumwa, Iowa 188/H2
Ottumwa, Iowa 229/J6
Ottumwa, S. Dak. 298/G5
Otumba de Gómez Farías, Mexico 150/M1
Otuquis (riv.), Bolivia 136/F6

Parrotsville 425

Palm City, Fla. 212/F4
Palm Coast, Fla. 212/E2
Palmdale, Calif. 204/G9
Palmdale, Fla. 212/E5
Palm Desert, Calif. 204/J10
Palmeira, Brazil 132/D9
Palmeira, Brazil 135/B4
Palmeira das Missões, Brazil 132/C9
Palmeiras, Brazil 132/F6
Palmeirinhas (pt.), Angola 115/B5
Palmer, Alaska 196/C1
Palmer, Alaska 188/D5
Palmer (arch.) Ant. 5/C15
Palmer, Ill. 222/D4
Palmer, Ind. 227/C2
Palmer, Iowa 229/D3
Palmer, Kansas 232/E2
Palmer, Mass. 249/E4
Palmer•, Mass. 249/E4
Palmer, Mich. 250/B2
Palmer, Nebr. 264/F3
Palmer (head), N. Zealand 100/B3
Palmer, P. Rico 161/F1
Palmer (riv.), Queensland 95/B2
Palmer, Sask. 181/E6
Palmer, Tenn. 237/K10
Palmer, Wash. 310/D3
Palmer (lake), Wash. 310/F2
Palmer Lake, Colo. 208/J4
Palmer Land (reg.), Ant. 2/F9
Palmer Land (reg.), Ant. 5/B15
Palmer Rapids, Ontario 177/G2
Palmers, Minn. 255/G4
Palmers Crossing, Miss. 256/F8
Palmer Station, Ant. 5/C15
Palmerston (atoll), Cook Is. 87/K7
Palmerston, N. Zealand 100/C6
Palmerston, Ontario 177/D4
Palmerston North, N. Zealand 87/H10
Palmerston North, N. Zealand 100/E4
Palmersville, Tenn. 237/D8
Palmerton, Pa. 294/L4
Palmerville, Queensland 95/B3
Palmetto, Fla. 212/D4
Palmetto, Ga. 217/C3
Palmetto, La. 238/G5
Palmetto (pt.), St. Kitts & Nevis 161/C10
Palm Harbor, Fla. 212/D3
Palmi, Italy 34/E5
Palmiet (riv.), S. Africa 118/F7
Palmilla, Chile 138/F6
Palmillas (pt.), Dom. Rep. 158/F6
Palmillas, Mexico 150/K5
Palmira, Colombia 120/B2
Palmira, Colombia 126/B6
Palmira, Cuba 158/E2
Palmitas, Uruguay 145/B4
Palmito de la Virgen (isl.), Mexico 150/F5
Palmito del Verde (isl.), Mexico 150/F5
Palm River-Clair Mel, Fla. 212/C3
Palms, Mich. 250/G5
Palms, Isle of (isl.), S.C. 296/H6
Palm Shores, Fla. 212/F3
Palm Springs, Calif. 188/C4
Palm Springs, Calif. 204/J10
Palm Springs, Fla. 212/F5
Palmyra, Ill. 222/C4
Palmyra, Ind. 227/E8
Palmyra•, Maine 243/E6
Palmyra, Mich. 250/E7
Palmyra, Mo. 261/J3
Palmyra, Nebr. 264/H4
Palmyra, N.J. 273/B3
Palmyra, N.Y. 276/F4
Palmyra (atoll), Pacific 87/K5
Palmyra, Pa. 294/J5
Palmyra (ruin), Syria 59/C3
Palmyra (Tadmor) (ruins), Syria 63/H5
Palmyra, Tenn. 237/G8
Palmyra (isl.), U.S. 2/A5
Palmyra, Va. 307/M5
Palmyra, Wis. 317/H2
Palmyras (pt.), India 68/F4
Palnackie, Scotland 15/E6
Palni, India 68/D6
Palo, Iowa 229/K4
Palo, Mich. 250/E5
Palo, Minn. 255/F3
Palo, Philippines 82/E5
Palo Alto, Calif. 188/B3
Palo Alto, Calif. 204/K3
Palo Alto, Cuba 158/F3
Palo Alto (co.), Iowa 229/D2
Palo Alto (lake), Iowa 229/D2
Palo Bola, Mexico 150/D4
Palo Duro (creek), Texas 303/B2
Palo Duro (creek), Texas 303/C1
Paloemeu (riv.), Suriname 131/D4
Palolo (stream), Hawaii 218/D4
Paloma, Ill. 222/B3
Palomar (mt.), Calif. 204/J10
Palomas, Mexico 150/F1
Palomas, Uruguay 145/B2
Palombara Sabina, Italy 34/F6
Palometas, Bolivia 136/D5
Palompon, Philippines 82/E5
Palo Pinto (co.), Texas 303/F5
Palo Pinto, Texas 303/F5
Palopo, Indonesia 85/F6
Palos (cape), Spain 33/F4
Palo Santo, Argentina 143/E2
Palo Seco, P. Rico 161/D1
Palo Seco, Trin. & Tob. 161/A11
Palos Heights, Ill. 222/B6
Palos Hills, Ill. 222/B6
Palos Park, Ill. 222/B6
Palos Verdes Estates, Calif. 204/B11
Palotás, Hungary 41/E3
Palourde (lake), La. 238/H7
Palouse (riv.), Idaho 220/B3
Palouse, Wash. 310/H4
Palouse (riv.), Wash. 310/G4
Palo Verde, Ariz. 198/C5
Palo Verde, Calif. 204/L10
Palpa, Nepal 68/E3
Palpa, Peru 128/E10
Palsagua, Nicaragua 154/E4
Palsen (riv.), Manitoba 179/G2
Palu, Indonesia 85/F6
Palu, Turkey 63/H3
Paluan, Philippines 82/C4
Pama, Burkina Faso 106/E6
Pamangkat, Indonesia 85/D5
Pamar, Colombia 126/E8
Pambrun, Sask. 181/D6
Pambula, N.S. Wales 97/E5
Pamekasan, Indonesia 85/L2
Pameungpeuk, Indonesia 85/H2
Pamiers, France 28/D6
Pamir (plat.) 54/J6
Pamlico (sound), N.C. 188/L3
Pamlico (co.), N.C. 281/R4
Pamlico (riv.), N.C. 281/R4
Pamlico (sound), N.C. 281/S4
Pampa, Texas 188/F3
Pampa, Texas 303/D2
Pampa Aullagas, Bolivia 136/B6
Pampachiri, Peru 128/F10
Pampacolca, Peru 128/F10
Pampa de la Salina (salt dep.), Argentina 143/C3
Pampa de las Salinas, Argentina 143/C3
Pampa de la Tres Hermanas (plain), Argentina 143/C6
Pampa del Infierno, Argentina 143/D2
Pampa Grande, Bolivia 136/D5
Pampanga (prov.), Philippines 82/C3
Pampas (plain), Argentina 120/C6
Pampas (plain), Argentina 143/D4
Pampas, Peru 128/E9
Pampas (riv.), Peru 128/E9
Pampilhosa da Serra, Portugal 33/C3
Pamplico, S.C. 296/H4
Pamplin, Va. 307/L6
Pamplona, Colombia 126/D4
Pamplona, Spain 33/F1
Pamplona, Spain 7/D4
Pamunkey (riv.), Va. 307/O5
Pamunkey Ind. Res., Va. 307/P5
Pana, Ill. 222/D4
Panabá, Mexico 150/P6
Panabo, Philippines 82/E7
Panaca, Nev. 266/G5
Panacachi, Bolivia 136/B6
Panacea, Fla. 212/B1
Panache (lake), Ontario 177/C1
Panagyurishte, Bulgaria 45/F4
Panaitan (isl.), Indonesia 85/C7
Panaji, India 68/C5
Panama 2/E5
Panama 146/K9
PANAMA 154/G6
Panama (canal) 2/E5
Panama, Ill. 222/D4
Panama, Iowa 229/B5
Panama, Nebr. 264/H4
Panama, N.Y. 276/A6
Panama, Okla. 288/S4
Panamá (cap.), Pan. 146/L9
Panamá (cap.), Panama 154/H6
Panamá (canal), Pan. 146/L8
Panamá (gulf), Pan. 146/L9
Panamá (gulf), Panama 154/H7
Panama City, Fla. 188/K4
Panama City, Fla. 212/C6
Panama City Beach, Fla. 212/C6
Panamint (range), Calif. 204/H7
Panamint (valley), Calif. 204/H7
Panao, Peru 128/E7
Panaon (isl.), Philippines 82/E5
Panarea (isl.), Italy 34/E5
Panaro (riv.), Italy 34/C2
Panarukan, Indonesia 85/K2
Panay (isl.), Philippines 54/O8
Panay (isl.), Philippines 85/G3
Panay (isl.), Philippines 82/D5
Pancake (range), Nev. 266/F4
Pančevo, Yugoslavia 45/E3
Panchor, Malaysia 72/F5
Panchur, India 68/F2
Panciu, Romania 45/H3
Panda, Mozambique 118/E4
Pandale, Texas 303/C7
Panda-Likasi, D.R. Congo 115/E6
Panda-Likasi, D.R. Congo 102/E6
Pandan, Antique, Philippines 82/C5
Pandan, Catanduanes, Philippines 82/E3
Pan de Azúcar, Quebrado (riv.), Chile 138/B5
Pan de Azúcar, Uruguay 145/D5
Pandeglang, Indonesia 85/G1
Pandharpur, India 68/D5
Pandi Pandi, S. Australia 94/F2
Pando (dept.), Bolivia 136/B2
Pando, Cerro (mt.), Panama 154/F6
Pando, Uruguay 145/B6
Pando (riv.), Uruguay 145/B6
Pandora, Ohio 284/C4
Pandrup, Denmark 21/C3
Panevėžys, Lithuania 52/B3
Panevėžys, Lithuania 53/C3
Panfilov, Kazakhstan 48/H5
Pangai, Tonga 87/J7
Pangala, Congo 115/B4
Pangalanes (canal), Madagascar 118/H4
Pangani, Tanzania 115/G5
Pangani (riv.), Tanzania 115/G4
Panganiban, Philippines 82/E4
Pangasinan (prov.), Philippines 82/C3
Pangburn, Ark. 202/G3
Pangi, D.R. Congo 115/E4
Pangkalanberandan, Indonesia 85/B5
Pangkalanbuun, Indonesia 85/E6
Pangkalpinang, Indonesia 85/D6
Pangkor, Pulau (isl.), Malaysia 72/D6
Panglao (isl.), Philippines 82/D6
Pangman, Sask. 181/G6
Pangnirtung, Canada 4/C13
Pangnirtung, N.W.T. 162/K2
Pangnirtung, N.W.T. 187/M3
Pangong Tso (lake), India 68/D2
Pangsau (pass), Burma 72/C1
Panguipulli, Chile 138/E2
Panguitch, Utah 304/B6
Panguitch (creek), Utah 304/B6
Pangutaran, Philippines 82/C7
Pangutaran (isl.), Philippines 82/C7
Pangutaran Group (isls.), Philippines 82/C7
Pangutaran Group (isls.), Philippines 85/G4
Panhandle, Texas 303/C2
Paniau (peak), Hawaii 218/A2
Panié (mt.), New Caled. 86/G4
Panihati, India 68/F1
Panipat, India 68/D3
Paniqui, Philippines 82/C3
Panj (riv.), Afghanistan 68/C1
Panjab, Afghanistan 68/B2
Panjab, Afghanistan 59/J3
Panjang, Hon (Hon Tho Chau) (isl.), Vietnam 72/D5
Panjgur, Pakistan 68/A3
Panjgur, Pakistan 59/H4
Panjim (Panaji), India 54/J8
Panjim (Panaji), India 68/C5
Pankow, Germany 22/F3
Pankshin, Nigeria 106/F7
P'anmunjŏm, N. Korea 81/C5
P'anmunjŏm, S. Korea 81/C5
Panmure (isl.), Pr. Edward I. 168/F2
Panna, India 68/E4
Pannawonica, W. Australia 92/B3
Pannonhalma, Hungary 41/D3
Panny (riv.), Alberta 182/C1
Panola, Ala. 195/B5
Panola, Ill. 222/E3
Panola (co.), Miss. 256/E2
Panola, Okla. 288/R5
Panola (co.), Texas 303/K5
Panora, Iowa 229/E5
Panorama Park, Iowa 229/N5
Panquehue, Chile 138/G2
Panruti, India 68/D6
Pansey, Ala. 195/H8
Pantanal (reg.), Brazil 120/D4
Pantar (isl.), Indonesia 85/G7
Pantego, N.C. 281/R3
Pantego, Texas 303/F2
Pantelleria, Italy 34/C6
Pantelleria (isl.), Italy 7/F5
Pantelleria (isl.), Italy 34/D6
Pantha, Burma 72/B2
Panther (creek), Idaho 220/D4
Panther (creek), Ky. 237/G5
Panther, W. Va. 312/C8
Panther Burn, Miss. 256/C4
Panthersville, Ga. 217/L1
Pantin, France 28/B1
Pantoja, Peru 128/E3
Panton•, Vt. 268/A3
Pánuco, Mexico 150/K6
Pánuco (riv.), Mexico 150/K5
Panuke (lake), Nova Scotia 168/D4
Pan Xian, China 77/G6
Panyam, Nigeria 106/F7
Panzós, Guatemala 154/C3
Pao (riv.), Venezuela 124/D3
Pao (riv.), Venezuela 124/F3
Paoki (Baoji), China 77/G5
Paola, Italy 34/E5
Paola, Kansas 232/H3
Paoli, Colo. 208/P1
Paoli, Ind. 227/E7
Paoli, Okla. 288/M5
Paoli, Pa. 294/M5
Paoli, Wis. 317/G10
Paonia, Colo. 208/D5
Paopao (bay), Fr. Poly. 86/S12
Paoting (Baoding), China 77/J4
Paotow (Baotou), China 77/G3
Paoua, Cent. Afr. Rep. 115/C2
Paoy Pet, Cambodia 72/D4
Papa, Hawaii 218/G6
Pápa, Hungary 41/D3
Papaaloa, Hawaii 218/J4
Papagaio (riv.), Brazil 132/B6
Papagayo (gulf), C. Rica 154/E5
Papago Ind. Res., Ariz. 198/C6
Papaikou, Hawaii 188/G6
Papaikou, Hawaii 218/J5
Papakura, N. Zealand 100/E2
Papallacta, Ecuador 128/D3
Papanoa, Mexico 150/J8
Papantla de Olarte, Mexico 150/L6
Papar, Malaysia 85/F4
Papara, Fr. Poly. 86/S13
Papa Stour (isl.), Scotland 10/G1
Papa Stour (isl.), Scotland 15/F2
Papatoetoe, N. Zealand 100/C1
Papa Westray (isl.), Scotland 15/F1
Papa Westray (isl.), Scotland 10/E1
Papeete (cap.), Fr. Polynesia 2/B6
Papeete (cap.), Fr. Poly. 86/S13
Papeete (cap.), Fr. Poly. 87/M7
Papelón, Venezuela 124/D3
Papenburg, Germany 22/B2
Papenoo, Fr. Poly. 86/T12
Papetoai, Fr. Poly. 86/S12
Paphos, Cyprus 63/E5
Papillion, Nebr. 264/J3
Papineau, Ill. 222/F3
Papineau (lake), Ontario 177/G2
Papineau (co.), Québec 172/B4
Papineau (lake), Québec 172/C4
Papineauville, Québec 172/C4
Paposo, Chile 138/A5
Papradno, Slovakia 41/E2
Paps, The (mt.), Ireland 17/C7
Paps of Jura (mt.), Scotland 15/C5
Papua (gulf), Papua N.G. 87/E6
Papua New Guinea 2/S6
PAPUA NEW GUINEA 86/B1
PAPUA NEW GUINEA 85/B7
Papua New Guinea 87/E6
Papudo, Chile 138/A9
Papun, Burma 72/C3
Papunáua (riv.), Colombia 126/E6
Papunya, North. Terr. 93/B7
Papurí (riv.), Colombia 126/F7
Paquera, C. Rica 154/E6
Paquette, Québec 172/F4
Paquetville, New Bruns. 170/E1
Pará (state), Brazil 132/C4
Pará (Belém), Brazil 132/E3
Pará (est.), Brazil 120/E3
Pará (riv.), Brazil 132/D3
Para (dist.), Suriname 131/D3
Paraburdoo, W. Australia 88/B4
Paraburdoo, W. Australia 92/B3
Paracale, Philippines 82/D3
Paracas (pen.), Peru 128/D9
Paracatu, Brazil 132/E7
Paracatu (riv.), Brazil 132/E7
Paracel (isls.), China 85/E2
Parachilna, S. Australia 88/F6
Parachilna, S. Australia 94/F4
Parachute, Colo. 208/C4
Paraćin, Yugoslavia 45/E4
Parada Esperanza, Uruguay 145/B3
Parada Liebigs, Uruguay 145/A4
Parada Rivas, Uruguay 145/B2
Parade, S. Dak. 298/G3
Pará de Minas, Brazil 132/E7
Pará de Minas, Brazil 135/D1
Paradip, India 68/F4
Paradis, La. 238/M4
Paradise, Ariz. 198/F7
Paradise, Calif. 204/D4
Paradise, Guyana 131/C3
Paradise, Kansas 232/D2
Paradise, Mich. 250/D2
Paradise (lake), Mich. 250/E3
Paradise, Mo. 261/D4
Paradise, Mont. 262/B3
Paradise, Newf. 166/D2
Paradise (riv.), Newf. 166/C3
Paradise, Nova Scotia 168/C4
Paradise (lake), Nova Scotia 168/C4
Paradise, Pa. 294/K5
Paradise, Texas 303/G5
Paradise, Utah 304/C2
Paradise, W. Va. 312/C5
Paradise Hill, Okla. 288/R3
Paradise Hill, Sask. 181/B2
Paradise Inn, Wash. 310/D4
Paradise River, Newf. 166/C3
Paradise Valley, Alberta 182/E3
Paradise Valley, Ariz. 198/D5
Paradise Valley, Nev. 266/F6
Paradise Valley, Nev. 266/D1
Paradise Valley, Wyo. 319/F3
Paradisino (peak), Switzerland 39/K4
Paradiso, Switzerland 39/G5
Paradox, Colo. 208/B6
Paragon, Ind. 227/D6
Paragonah, Utah 304/B6
Paragould, Ark. 202/J1
Paraguá (riv.), Bolivia 136/E4
Paragua (riv.), Venezuela 124/G4
Paraguaçu (riv.), Brazil 120/F4
Paraguaçu (riv.), Brazil 132/F6
Paraguaçu Paulista, Brazil 132/D8
Paraguai (riv.) 120/D4
Paraguai (riv.), Brazil 132/B8
Paraguaipoa, Venezuela 124/C2
Paraguaná (pen.), Venezuela 124/C1
Paraguarí (dept.), Paraguay 144/D4-5
Paraguay 2/F7
Paraguay 120/D5
PARAGUAY 144
Paraguay (riv.), Argentina 143/E1
Paraguay (riv.), Bolivia 136/F7
Paraguay (riv.), Paraguay 144/D4
Paraíba (state), Brazil 132/G4
Paraíba (riv.), Brazil 120/E5
Paraíba (riv.), Brazil 135/E2
Paraíba do Sul, Brazil 135/E3
Parainen, Finland 18/M6
Paraíso, C. Rica 154/F6
Paraíso, Dom. Rep. 158/D7
Paraíso, Mexico 150/N7
Paraíso de Chabasquén, Venezuela 124/D3
Parakou, Benin 106/E7
Parallel, Kansas 232/F2
Paraloma, Ark. 202/B6
Paramaribo (dist.), Suriname 131/D2
Paramaribo (cap.), Suriname 131/D2
Paramaribo (cap.), Suriname 2/G5
Paramaribo (cap.), Suriname 120/D2
Paramithía, Greece 45/E6
Paramonga, Peru 128/C8
Paramount, Calif. 204/C11
Paramus, N.J. 273/B1
Paramushir (isl.) 54/S5
Paramushir (isl.), Russia 48/Q4
Paran (dry riv.), Israel 65/D5
Paraná (riv.) 2/G7
Paraná (riv.) 120/D5
Paraná, Argentina 143/F5
Paraná, Argentina 120/D6
Paraná (riv.), Argentina 143/E2
Paraná (state), Brazil 132/D9
Paraná (state), Brazil 135/B4
Paranã, Brazil 132/E6
Paraná (riv.), Brazil 132/C8
Paranã (riv.), Brazil 132/E6
Paranaguá, Brazil 120/E5
Paranaguá, Brazil 132/E9
Paranaguá, Brazil 135/B4
Paranaíba, Brazil 132/D7
Paranam, Suriname 131/D3
Paranapanema (riv.), Brazil 132/C8
Paranapanema (riv.), Brazil 135/B3
Paranapiacaba (range), Brazil 135/B4
Paranatinga (riv.), Brazil 120/D4
Paranatinga (riv.), Brazil 132/C6
Parang, Maguindanao, Philippines 82/E7
Parang, Sulu, Philippines 82/C8
Parao (riv.), Uruguay 145/E3
Paraparaumu, N. Zealand 100/E4
Parapetí (riv.), Bolivia 136/D6
Para Station, N.S. Wales 97/B3
Parati, Brazil 135/D3
Paratinga, Brazil 132/F6
Paray-le-Monial, France 28/F4
Parbhani, India 68/D5
Parchim, Germany 22/D2
Parchman, Miss. 256/D3
Parchment, Mich. 250/D6
Parczew, Poland 47/F3
Pardee (res.), Calif. 204/C9
Pardee, Va. 307/C6
Pardeeville, Wis. 317/H8
Pardes Hanna-Karkur, Israel 65/B2
Parding, China 77/C5
Pardo (riv.), Brazil 132/D8
Pardo (riv.), Brazil 132/F6
Pardo (riv.), Brazil 135/B2
Pardo (riv.), Brazil 132/C8
Pardoe, Pa. 294/B3
Pardoo, W. Australia 92/B3
Pardubice, Czech Rep. 41/C1
Pare, Indonesia 85/K2
Parece Vela (isl.), Japan 54/P7
Parece Vela (isl.), Japan 87/D3
Parecis (mts.), Brazil 120/C4
Parecis, Serra dos (range), Brazil 132/B6
Paredes de Nava, Spain 33/D1
Paredones, Chile 138/A10
Parent, Québec 174/C3
Pareora, N. Zealand 100/C6
Parepare, Indonesia 85/F6
Parguera, P. Rico 161/A3
Parham, Ant. & Bar. 161/E11
Parham, Ontario 177/H3
Parhams, La. 238/G4
Paria (gulf) 120/C1
Paria (plat.), Ariz. 198/D2
Paria (riv.), Ariz. 198/D1
Paria, Bolivia 136/B5
Paria (gulf), Trin. & Tob. 156/G5
Paria (gulf), Trin. & Tob. 161/A11
Paria (riv.), Utah 304/B6
Paria (gulf), Venezuela 124/H2
Paria (pen.), Venezuela 124/G2
Pariaguán, Venezuela 124/F3
Pariaman, Indonesia 85/B6
Paricutín (vol.), Mexico 150/H7
Parida (isl.), Panama 154/F6
Parika, Guyana 131/B2
Parikkala, Finland 18/Q6
Parima, Sierra (mts.), Venezuela 124/F6
Parinacochas (lake), Peru 128/F10
Parinacota, Cerro (mt.), Chile 138/B1
Parinari, Peru 128/E5
Pariñas (pt.), Peru 128/B5
Parintins, Brazil 120/D3
Parintins, Brazil 132/B3
Paris, Ark. 202/C3
Paris (city) (dept.), France 28/B2
Paris (cap.), France 2/J3
Paris (cap.), France 7/E4
Paris (cap.), France 28/B2
Paris, Idaho 220/G7
Paris, Ill. 222/F4
Paris, Iowa 229/K4
Paris, Ky. 237/N4
Paris•, Maine 243/B7
Paris, Mich. 250/D5
Paris, Miss. 256/F2
Paris, Mo. 261/J4
Paris, Ohio 284/H4
Paris, Ontario 177/D4
Paris, Tenn. 237/E8
Paris, Texas 303/J4
Paris, Texas 188/G4
Paris, Va. 307/N3
Paris Crossing, Ind. 227/F7
Parish, N.Y. 276/H4
Parish, Uruguay 145/C3
Parishville, N.Y. 276/L1
Parisville, Mich. 250/G5
Parisville, Québec 172/F3
Parita, Panama 154/G6
Parita (bay), Panama 154/G6
Park (co.), Colo. 208/H4
Park (range), Colo. 208/F1
Park (riv.), Conn. 210/E2
Park, Kansas 232/B2
Park (co.), Mont. 262/F5
Park (riv.), N. Dak. 282/R3
Park (dist.), Scotland 15/B2
Park (co.), Wyo. 319/C1
Parkano, Finland 18/N6
Parkbeg, Sask. 181/E5
Park City, Ill. 222/B4
Park City, Kansas 232/E4
Park City, Ky. 237/J6
Park City, Mont. 262/H5
Park City, Utah 304/C3
Parkdale, Ark. 202/H7
Parkdale, Colo. 208/H6
Parkdale, Oreg. 291/F2
Parkdale, Pr. Edward I. 168/E2
Parke (co.), Ind. 227/C5
Parker, Ariz. 198/A4
Parker (dam), Ariz. 198/A4
Parker, Colo. 208/K4
Parker, Fla. 212/C6
Parker, Idaho 220/G6
Parker, Kansas 232/H3
Parker, Pa. 294/C3
Parker, S. Dak. 298/P7
Parker (lake), S. Dak. 298/P3
Parker (co.), Texas 303/G5
Parker, Texas 303/H1
Parker, Wash. 310/E4
Parker City, Ind. 227/G4
Parker Dam, Calif. 204/L9
Parkersburg, Ill. 222/F5
Parkersburg, Ind. 227/D5
Parkersburg, Iowa 229/H3
Parkersburg, W. Va. 188/K3
Parkersburg, W. Va. 312/D4
Parkers Cove, Newf. 166/D4
Parkers Cove, Nova Scotia 168/C4
Parkers Lake, Ky. 237/M7
Parkers Prairie, Minn. 255/C4
Parkertown, N.J. 273/E4
Parkerview, Sask. 181/H4
Parkerville, Kansas 232/F3
Parkes, N.S. Wales 88/H6
Parkes, N.S. Wales 97/E3
Parkesburg, Pa. 294/L6
Park Falls, Wis. 317/F4
Park Forest, Ill. 222/B6
Park Forest South, Ill. 222/F2
Park Hall, Md. 245/N8
Park Hill, Okla. 288/R3
Parkhill, Ontario 177/C4
Park Hills, Ky. 237/S2
Parkin, Ark. 202/J3
Parkland, Alberta 182/D4
Parkland, Fla. 212/F5
Parkland, Okla. 288/N3
Parkland, Wash. 310/C3
Parkman•, Maine 243/D5
Parkman, Ohio 284/H3
Parkman, Sask. 181/K6
Parkman, Wyo. 319/E1
Park Place, Oreg. 291/B2
Park Rapids, Minn. 255/D4
Park Rapids, Wash. 310/H2
Park Ridge, Ill. 222/B5
Park Ridge, N.J. 273/B1
Park Ridge, Wis. 317/H6
Park River, N. Dak. 282/P3
Parks, Ariz. 198/C3
Parks, Ark. 202/B4
Parks, La. 238/G6
Parks, Nebr. 264/C4
Parksdale, Mo. 261/L6
Parkside, Pa. 294/M7
Parkside, Sask. 181/E2
Parksley, Va. 307/S5
Parkston, S. Dak. 298/O7
Parksville, Br. Col. 184/J3
Parksville, Ky. 237/M5
Parksville, N.Y. 276/L7
Parksville, S.C. 296/C4
Parkton, Md. 245/M2
Parkton, N.C. 281/M5
Park Valley, Utah 304/A2
Parkview (mt.), Colo. 208/G2
Parkville, Md. 245/M3
Parkville, Mo. 261/O5
Parkville, Pa. 294/J6
Parkville, Victoria 97/H5
Parkway, Mo. 261/L6
Parkway Village, Ky. 237/J2
Parkwood, N.C. 281/M3
Parlakhemundi, India 68/E5
Parlier, Calif. 204/F7
Parlin, Colo. 208/F6
Parlin (pond), Maine 243/C4
Parma, Idaho 220/B6
Parma (prov.), Italy 34/C2
Parma, Italy 7/E4
Parma, Italy 34/C2
Parma (riv.), Italy 34/C2
Parma, Mich. 250/E6
Parma, Mo. 261/N9
Parma, Ohio 284/H9
Parmachenee (lake), Maine 243/B5
Parma Heights, Ohio 284/G9
Parmana, Venezuela 124/F4
Parmele, N.C. 281/P3
Parmelee, S. Dak. 298/G7
Parmer (co.), Texas 303/B3
Parnaguá, Brazil 132/E5
Parnaíba, Brazil 132/F3
Parnaíba, Brazil 120/E3
Parnaíba (riv.), Brazil 120/E3
Parnaíba (riv.), Brazil 132/F3
Parnamirim, Brazil 132/F4
Parnassus (mt.), Greece 45/F6
Parnassus, N. Zealand 100/D5
Parndana, S. Australia 94/E6
Parnell, Iowa 229/J5
Parnell, Mo. 261/C2
Pärnu, Estonia 7/G3
Pärnu, Estonia 48/C4
Pärnu, Estonia 52/C3
Pärnu, Estonia 53/C1
Paro, Bhutan 68/F3
Paron, Ark. 202/E4
Paroo (chan.), N.S. Wales 97/B2
Paroo (riv.), N.S. Wales 88/G5
Paroo (riv.), N.S. Wales 97/C1
Paroo (riv.), Queensland 95/C6
Paropamisus (mts.), Afghanistan 59/H3
Paropamisus (range), Afghanistan 68/A2
Páros (isl.), Greece 45/G7
Parow, S. Africa 118/F6
Parowan, Utah 304/B6
Parpan, Switzerland 39/J3
Parr, Ind. 227/C2
Parr, S.C. 296/E3
Parral, Chile 138/A11
Parral, Mexico 150/G3
Parral, Ohio 284/G4
Parramatta, N.S. Wales 88/K4
Parramatta, N.S. Wales 97/H3
Parramatta (riv.), N.S. Wales 88/K4
Parramatta (riv.), N.S. Wales 97/J3
Parramore (isl.), Va. 307/S5
Parran, Md. 245/M6
Parras de la Fuente, Mexico 150/H4
Parratah, Tasmania 99/D4
Parrett (riv.), England 13/E6
Parrish, Ala. 195/D3
Parrish, Fla. 212/D4
Parrish, Wis. 317/H5
Parris Island Marine Base, S.C. 296/F7
Parrotsville, Tenn. 237/P8

Point Reyes Nat'l Seashore 429

Pins (pt.), Ontario 177/C5
Pinsk, Belarus 48/C4
Pinsk, Belarus 52/C4
Pinson, Ala. 195/E3
Pinson, Tenn. 237/D10
Pinta (isl.), Ecuador 128/B9
Pintada, N. Mex. 274/D4
Pintada Arroyo (creek), N. Mex. 274/E4
Pintado, Artigas, Uruguay 145/C1
Pintado, Florida, Uruguay 145/C4
Pintados, Chile 138/B2
Pintados, Salar de (salt dep.), Chile 138/B2
Pintendre, Québec 172/J3
Pinto, Chile 138/A11
Pinto, Md. 245/C2
Pinto (creek), Sask. 181/D6
Pintura, Utah 304/A6
Pintuyan, Philippines 82/E6
Pintwater (range), Nev. 266/F6
Pinware (riv.), Newf. 166/C3
Pinware River, Newf. 166/C3
Pinyon (peak), Idaho 220/C5
Pinzón (isl.), Ecuador 128/B9
Pioche, Nev. 266/G5
Piombino, Italy 34/C3
Pioneer (mts.), Idaho 220/D6
Pioneer, Iowa 229/E3
Pioneer, La. 238/H1
Pioneer, Mo. 261/E9
Pioneer, Ohio 284/A2
Pioneer, Tenn. 237/N8
Pioner (isl.), Russia 48/J2
Pionerskiy, Russia 48/G3
Pionki, Poland 47/E3
Piopio, N. Zealand 100/E3
Piopolis, Québec 172/F4
Piotrków (prov.), Poland 47/D3
Piotrków Trybunalski, Poland 47/D3
Piove di Sacco, Italy 34/C2
Piper (creek), Ind. 227/F4
Piper (peak), Nev. 266/D5
Piper City, Ill. 222/E3
Piper City, Kansas 232/H2
Pipersville, Pa. 294/M5
Piperton, Tenn. 237/B10
Pipe Spring Nat'l Mon., Ariz. 198/C2
Pipestem (riv.), N. Dak. 282/M5
Pipestem, W. Va. 312/E7
Pipestone, Manitoba 179/B5
Pipestone (creek), Manitoba 179/A5
Pipestone (co.), Minn. 255/B6
Pipestone, Minn. 255/B7
Pipestone (riv.), Ontario 175/B2
Pipestone (creek), Sask. 181/K6
Pipestone (riv.), Sask. 181/L2
Pipestone Nat'l Mon., Minn. 255/B6
Pipinas, Argentina 143/H7
Pipinui (pt.), N. Zealand 100/B2
Pipmuacan (res.), Québec 174/D3
Piqan (Shanshan), China 77/D3
Piqua, Kansas 232/G4
Piqua, Ohio 284/B5
Piquete, Brazil 135/D3
Piquiri (riv.), Brazil 132/C7
Piquiri (riv.), Brazil 132/C9
Piracanjuba, Brazil 132/D7
Piracicaba, Brazil 120/E5
Piracicaba, Brazil 135/C3
Piracicaba, Brazil 132/E8
Piracuruca, Brazil 132/F3
Piraí do Sul, Brazil 132/D9
Piraí do Sul, Brazil 135/B4
Piraiévs, Greece 7/G5
Piraiévs (Piraeus), Greece 45/F7
Piraju, Brazil 135/B3
Pirajuba, Brazil 135/B1
Pirajuí, Brazil 135/B2
Pirámide, Cerro (mt.), Chile 138/D8
Piran, Slovenia 45/A3
Pirané, Argentina 143/E2
Pirapora, Brazil 120/E4
Pirapora, Brazil 132/E7
Piraraja, Uruguay 145/E4
Pirassununga, Brazil 135/C2
Pirata (mt.), P. Rico 161/F2
Piraúba, Brazil 135/E2
Piray (riv.), Bolivia 136/D5
Pirayú, Paraguay 144/B5
Pirdop, Bulgaria 45/G4
Pirenópolis, Brazil 132/D6
Pires do Rio, Brazil 132/D7
Pírgos, Greece 45/E7
Piriápolis, Uruguay 145/D5
Piribebuy, Paraguay 144/B5
Piribebuy (riv.), Paraguay 144/B4
Piripiri, Brazil 132/F4
Píritu, Anzoátegui, Venezuela 124/F2
Píritu, Falcón, Venezuela 124/D2
Píritu, Portuguesa, Venezuela 124/D3
Pirmasens, Germany 22/B4
Pirna, Germany 22/E3
Pirongia (mt.), N. Zealand 100/E3
Pirot, Yugoslavia 45/F4
Piru, Calif. 204/G9
Piru, Indonesia 85/H6
Piryatin, Ukraine 52/D4
Piryí, Greece 45/G6
Pisa (prov.), Italy 34/C3
Pisa, Italy 34/C3
Pisac, Peru 128/G9
Pisagua, Chile 138/A2
Piscadera (bay), Neth. Ant. 161/F9
Piscataqua (riv.), Maine 243/B9
Piscataqua (riv.), N.H. 268/F5
Piscataquis (co.), Maine 243/E4
Piscataquis (riv.), Maine 243/E5
Piscataquog (riv.), N.H. 268/D5
Piscataway, Md. 245/L6
Piscataway (creek), Md. 245/G6
Piscataway•, N.J. 273/D2
Piscataway Park, Md. 245/K6
Piscatosine (lake), Québec 172/B3
Pisco, Peru 128/D9
Pisco, Peru 120/B4
Pisco (bay), Peru 128/D9
Pisco (riv.), Peru 128/D9
Piseco, N.Y. 276/L4
Piseco (lake), N.Y. 276/M4
Písek, Czech Rep. 41/C2
Pisek, N. Dak. 282/P3
Pisgah, Ala. 195/G1
Pisgah, Iowa 229/B5
Pisgah, Md. 245/K6
Pisgah Forest, N.C. 281/D4
Pishan (Guma), China 77/A4
Pishin, Iran 66/M7
Pishin, Pakistan 68/B2
Pishin, Pakistan 59/J3
Pishkun (res.), Mont. 262/D3
Pisinimo, Ariz. 198/C6
Pismo Beach, Calif. 204/E8
Piso Firme, Bolivia 136/D3
Pisoniano, Italy 34/F6
Pissis (mt.), Argentina 143/C2
Pistakee (lake), Ill. 222/A4
Pistapaug (pond), Conn. 210/E3
Pisticci, Italy 34/F4
Pistoia (prov.), Italy 34/C2
Pistoia, Italy 34/C2
Pistolet (bay), Newf. 166/C3
Pistol River, Oreg. 291/C5
Pisz, Poland 47/E2
Pit (riv.), Calif. 204/D2
Pitalito, Colombia 126/B7
Pitangui, Brazil 135/D1
Pitarpunga (lake), N.S. Wales 97/B4
Pitcairn (isl.) 87/O8
Pitcairn (isl.), (U.K.) 2/C7
Pitcairn, Pa. 294/C5
Pitch (lake), Trin. & Tob. 161/A11
Piteå, Sweden 18/M4
Piteälv (riv.), Sweden 18/M4
Piteşti, Romania 45/G3
Piteşti, Romania 7/G4
Píthion, Greece 45/H5
Pithiviers, France 28/E3
Pitiquito, Mexico 150/D1
Pitkas Point, Alaska 196/F2
Pitkin (co.), Colo. 208/F4
Pitkin, Colo. 208/F5
Pitkin, La. 238/E5
Pitlochry, Scotland 15/E4
Pitlochry, Scotland 10/E2
Pitman, N.J. 273/C4
Pitman, Sask. 181/G5
Pitmedden, Scotland 15/F3
Pitogo, Philippines 82/C4
Piton des Neiges (mt.), Réunion 118/G5
Pitrufquén, Chile 138/D2
Pitsburg, Ohio 284/A6
Pitt (isl.), Br. Col. 184/C3
Pitt (lake), Br. Col. 184/L2
Pitt, Minn. 255/D2
Pitt (isl.), N. Zealand 100/E7
Pitt (str.), N. Zealand 100/E7
Pitt (co.), N.C. 281/P3
Pittenweem, Scotland 15/F4
Pitti (isl.), India 68/C6
Pittman Center, Tenn. 237/P9
Pitt Meadows, Br. Col. 184/L3
Pittock, Pa. 294/B7
Pitts, Ark. 202/J2
Pitts, Ga. 217/E7
Pittsboro, Ind. 227/D5
Pittsboro, Miss. 256/F3
Pittsboro, N.C. 281/L3
Pittsburg, Calif. 204/L1
Pittsburg, Ga. 217/L1
Pittsburg, Ill. 222/E6
Pittsburg, Ind. 227/D3
Pittsburg, Kansas 232/H4
Pittsburg, Ky. 237/N6
Pittsburg, Mo. 261/F7
Pittsburg•, N.H. 268/E1
Pittsburg (co.), Okla. 288/P5
Pittsburg, Okla. 288/P5
Pittsburg, Texas 303/J4
Pittsburgh, Pa. 146/K5
Pittsburgh, Pa. 188/L2
Pittsburgh, Pa. 294/B7
Pittsfield, Ill. 222/C4
Pittsfield, Maine 243/E6
Pittsfield•, Maine 243/E6
Pittsfield, Mass. 188/M2
Pittsfield, Mass. 249/A3
Pittsfield, N.H. 268/E5
Pittsfield•, N.H. 268/E5
Pittsfield, Pa. 294/D2
Pittsfield•, Vt. 268/B4
Pittsford, Mich. 250/E7
Pittsford, N.Y. 276/E4
Pittsford, Vt. 268/A4
Pittsford•, Vt. 268/A4
Pittston•, Maine 243/D7
Pittston, Pa. 294/F7
Pittstown, N.J. 273/C2
Pittsview, Ala. 195/H6
Pittsville, Md. 245/S7
Pittsville, Mo. 261/E5
Pittsville, Va. 307/K7
Pittsville, Wis. 317/F7
Pittsylvania (co.), Va. 307/K7
Pittville, Calif. 204/D2
Pittwood, Ill. 222/F3
Piúí, Brazil 132/E8
Piúí, Brazil 135/D2
Piura (dept.), Peru 128/B5
Piura, Peru 120/A3
Piura, Peru 128/B5
Piura (riv.), Peru 128/B5
Piute (co.), Utah 304/B5
Piute (res.), Utah 304/B5
Pivijay, Colombia 126/C2
Pixley, Calif. 204/F8
Piyas (lake), S. Dak. 298/P2
Pizacoma, Peru 128/H11
Pizarro, Colombia 126/B5
Pizol (peak), Switzerland 39/H3
Place, Ky. 237/N7
Placentia, Calif. 204/D11
Placentia, Newf. 166/C2
Placentia (bay), Newf. 166/C2
Placentia (sound), Newf. 166/C2
Placer (co.), Calif. 204/E4
Placer, Philippines 82/E6
Placerville, Calif. 204/C8
Placerville, Colo. 208/D6
Placerville, Idaho 220/C6
Placetas, Cuba 158/E2
Placid (lake), Fla. 212/E4
Placid (lake), N.Y. 276/N2
Placida, Fla. 212/D5
Placilla, Chile 138/F6
Placilla de Caracoles, Chile 138/B4
Placilla de Peñuelas, Chile 138/F2
Placitas, N. Mex. 274/C3
Plad, Mo. 261/G7
Pladda (isl.), Scotland 15/C5
Plaffeien, Switzerland 39/D3
Plain, Wash. 310/E3
Plain, Wis. 317/F9
Plain City, Ohio 284/D5
Plain City, Utah 304/B2
Plain Dealing, La. 238/C1
Plainfield, Ark. 202/D7
Plainfield, Conn. 210/H2
Plainfield•, Conn. 210/H2
Plainfield, Ga. 217/F6
Plainfield, Ill. 222/A6
Plainfield, Ind. 227/E5
Plainfield, Iowa 229/J3
Plainfield•, Mass. 249/C2
Plainfield•, N.H. 268/C4
Plainfield, N.J. 273/E2
Plainfield, Ohio 284/G5
Plainfield, Vt. 268/C3
Plainfield•, Vt. 268/C3
Plainfield, Wis. 317/G7
Plains, Ga. 217/D6
Plains, Kansas 232/B4
Plains, Mont. 262/B3
Plains, Pa. 294/F7
Plains, Texas 303/B4
Plainsboro, N.J. 273/D3
Plainview, Ark. 202/D4
Plain View, Iowa 229/M5
Plainview, Minn. 255/F6
Plainview, Nebr. 264/G2
Plainview, N.Y. 276/R7
Plainview, S. Dak. 298/E4
Plainview, Texas 303/C3
Plainville•, Conn. 210/D2
Plainville, Ga. 217/C2
Plainville, Ill. 222/B4
Plainville, Ind. 227/C7
Plainville, Kansas 232/C2
Plainville•, Mass. 249/J4
Plainwell, Mich. 250/D6
Plaisance, Haiti 158/C5
Plaisance, Québec 172/B4
Plaisted, Maine 243/F1
Plaistow•, N.H. 268/E6
Plaju, Indonesia 85/D6
Plamondon, Alberta 182/D2
Plana (cays), Bahamas 156/D2
Planá, Czech Rep. 41/B2
Planada, Calif. 204/E6
Planeta Rica, Colombia 126/C3
Plánice, Czech Rep. 41/B2
Plankinton, S. Dak. 298/N6
Plano, Ill. 222/E2
Plano, Iowa 229/G7
Plano, Texas 303/G1
Plant, Tenn. 237/F9
Plantagenet, Ontario 177/K2
Plantation, Fla. 212/B4
Plantation (key), Fla. 212/F7
Plantation, Ky. 237/K1
Plant City, Fla. 212/D3
Plantersville, Ala. 195/E5
Plantersville, Miss. 256/G2
Plantersville, S.C. 296/J4
Plantsite, Ariz. 198/F5
Plantsville, Conn. 210/D2
Plaquemine, La. 238/J2
Plaquemines (par.), La. 238/L8
Plasencia, Spain 33/C2
Plaster City, Calif. 204/K11
Plaster Rock, New Bruns. 170/C2
Plastun, Russia 48/O5
Plasy, Czech Rep. 41/B2
Plat, Wis. 317/K1
Plata (riv.) 2/G7
Plata, Río de la (est.), Argentina 143/E4
Plata (riv.), P. Rico 161/D2
Plata, La (riv.), Uruguay 145/B5
Platanal, Venezuela 124/F6
Platanilla, C. Rica 154/F6
Platea, Pa. 294/B2
Plateau (creek), Colo. 208/C4
Plateau (state), Nigeria 106/F7
Plateau, Nova Scotia 168/H2
Plateau City, Colo. 208/D4
Plate Cove, Newf. 166/D2
Platen, Kapp (pt.), Norway 18/D1
Platina, Calif. 204/B3
Platinum, Alaska 196/F3
Platner, Colo. 208/N2
Plato, Colombia 126/C3
Plato, Minn. 255/D6
Plato, Mo. 261/H8
Plato, Sask. 181/C4
Platoro (res.), Colo. 208/F8
Platte (riv.), Iowa 229/D8
Platte (lake), Mich. 250/C4
Platte (riv.), Mo. 261/C3
Platte (co.), Nebr. 264/G3
Platte (riv.), Nebr. 146/J5
Platte (riv.), Nebr. 188/G2
Platte (riv.), Nebr. 264/E4
Platte, S. Dak. 298/M7
Platte (lake), S. Dak. 298/M6
Platte (co.), Wyo. 319/H4
Platte Center, Nebr. 264/G3
Platte City, Mo. 261/C4
Plattenville, La. 238/K4
Platter, Okla. 288/O7
Platteville, Colo. 208/K2
Platteville, Wis. 317/F10
Platte Woods, Mo. 261/O5
Plattsburg, Mo. 261/D3
Plattsburgh, N.Y. 276/O1
Plattsburgh A.F.B., N.Y. 276/N1
Plattsmouth, Nebr. 264/J3
Plattsville, Ontario 177/D4
Plau, Germany 22/E2
Plaucheville, La. 238/G5
Plauen, Germany 22/E3
Plauersee (lake), Germany 22/E2
Plav, Yugoslavia 45/D4
Plaviņas, Latvia 53/C2
Playa (pt.), Guyana 131/B1
Playa Azul, Mexico 150/H7
Playa Bonita, C. Rica 154/E6
Playa de Fajardo, P. Rico 161/F1
Playa de Humacao, P. Rico 161/F2
Playa Grande, Nicaragua 154/D4
Playas, Ecuador 128/B4
Playas (lake), N. Mex. 274/A7
Playón Chico, Panama 154/H6
Playón Grande, Panama 154/H6
Plaza, N. Dak. 282/G3
Plaza, Wash. 310/H3
Plaza Huincul, Argentina 143/B4
Pleasant (isl.), Alaska 196/M1
Pleasant (lake), Ariz. 198/C5
Pleasant, Ind. 227/G7
Pleasant (lake), Maine 243/H5
Pleasant (lake), Maine 243/E3
Pleasant (lake), Maine 243/G3
Pleasant (riv.), Maine 243/H6
Pleasant (mt.), New Bruns. 170/D3
Pleasant (lake), N.Y. 276/M4
Pleasant (bay), Nova Scotia 168/H2
Pleasant Bay, Nova Scotia 168/H2
Pleasant City, Ohio 284/G6
Pleasant Dale, Nebr. 264/G4
Pleasantdale, Sask. 181/G3
Pleasant Gap, Ala. 195/H3
Pleasant Gap, Pa. 294/G4
Pleasant Green, Mo. 261/F5
Pleasant Grove, Ala. 195/D4
Pleasant Grove, Calif. 204/B8
Pleasant Grove, Miss. 256/D2
Pleasant Grove, N.J. 273/D2
Pleasant Grove, Utah 304/C3
Pleasant Hill, Ala. 195/E6
Pleasant Hill, Calif. 204/K2
Pleasant Hill, Ill. 222/C4
Pleasant Hill, La. 238/C3
Pleasant Hill, Miss. 256/E1
Pleasant Hill, Mo. 261/D5
Pleasant Hill, N.C. 281/O1
Pleasant Hill, Ohio 284/B5
Pleasant Hill, S.C. 296/F2
Pleasant Hill, Tenn. 237/L9
Pleasant Hills, Md. 245/N3
Pleasant Hills, Pa. 294/B7
Pleasant Hope, Mo. 261/F8
Pleasant Island, Maine 243/B5
Pleasant Lake, Ind. 227/H1
Pleasant Lake, Mass. 249/O6
Pleasant Lake, Minn. 255/D5
Pleasant Lake, N. Dak. 282/L3
Pleasant Lane, S.C. 296/D4
Pleasant Mills, Ind. 227/H3
Pleasant Mound, Ill. 222/D5
Pleasant Mount, Pa. 294/M2
Pleasanton, Calif. 204/L2
Pleasanton, Iowa 229/F7
Pleasanton, Kansas 232/H3
Pleasanton, Nebr. 264/E4
Pleasanton, N. Mex. 274/A5
Pleasanton, Texas 303/F9
Pleasant Plain, Iowa 229/K6
Pleasant Plain, Ohio 284/B7
Pleasant Plains, Ark. 202/G2
Pleasant Plains, Ill. 222/D4
Pleasant Point, N. Zealand 100/C6
Pleasant Pond, Maine 243/D5
Pleasant Prairie, Wis. 317/L10
Pleasant Ridge, Mich. 250/B6
Pleasants (co.), W. Va. 312/D4
Pleasant Shade, Tenn. 237/K8
Pleasant Valley, Conn. 210/C1
Pleasant Valley, Md. 245/L2
Pleasant Valley, Mo. 261/R5
Pleasant Valley, Oreg. 291/K3
Pleasant Valley (creek), S. Dak. 298/B6
Pleasant Valley, Va. 307/L4
Pleasant View, Colo. 208/B7
Pleasant View, Ill. 222/C3
Pleasant View, Ky. 237/N7
Pleasant View, Tenn. 237/G8
Pleasant View, Utah 304/B2
Pleasantville, Ind. 227/C7
Pleasantville, Iowa 229/G6
Pleasantville, N.J. 273/D5
Pleasantville, N.Y. 276/N8
Pleasantville, Ohio 284/F6
Pleasantville (Alum Bank), Pa. 294/E5
Pleasantville, Pa. 294/C2
Pleasantville, Tenn. 237/F9
Pleasure Beach, Conn. 210/G3
Pleasure Ridge Park, Ky. 237/J4
Pleasureville, Ky. 237/L4
Pleiku, Vietnam 72/E4
Pleniţa, Romania 45/F3
Plenty (bay), N. Zealand 100/F2
Plenty, Sask. 181/C4
Plenty (riv.), Victoria 97/J4
Plenty (riv.), Victoria 88/L6
Plenty River Mine, North. Terr. 93/D7
Plentywood, Mont. 262/M2
Plesetsk, Russia 52/F2
Plessis, N.Y. 276/J2
Plessisville, Québec 172/F3
Plessur (riv.), Switzerland 39/J3
Pleszew, Poland 47/C3
Pletcher, Ala. 195/E5
Plétipi (lake), Que. 162/J5
Plétipi (lake), Québec 174/C2
Plettenberg, Germany 22/C3
Plettenberg (bay), S. Africa 118/C6
Pleven, Bulgaria 7/G4
Pleven, Bulgaria 45/G4
Plevna, Ala. 195/F1
Plevna, Ind. 227/E3
Plevna, Kansas 232/D4
Plevna, Mo. 261/H3
Plevna, Mont. 262/M4
Plevna, Ontario 177/H3
Pliny, W. Va. 312/B5
Pljevlja, Yugoslavia 45/D4
Ploče, Croatia 45/C4
Płock (prov.), Poland 47/D2
Płock, Poland 47/D2
Plockton, Scotland 15/C3
Ploërmel, France 28/B4
Ploieşti, Romania 45/H3
Ploieşti, Romania 7/G4
Plomárion, Greece 45/H6
Plomb du Cantal (mt.), France 28/E5
Plombières, Belgium 27/H7
Plomer (pt.), N.S. Wales 97/G2
Plomosa (mts.), Ariz. 198/A5
Plön, Germany 22/D1
Płonia (riv.), Poland 47/B2
Płońsk, Poland 47/E2
Plovdiv, Bulgaria 7/G4
Plovdiv, Bulgaria 45/G4
Plover, Iowa 229/D3
Plover, Wis. 317/G7
Pluckemin, N.J. 273/D2
Plum (riv.), Ill. 222/C1
Plum (creek), Manitoba 179/B5
Plum (lake), Manitoba 179/B5
Plum (isl.), Mass. 249/L2
Plum (isl.), N.Y. 276/R8
Plum, Pa. 294/C5
Plumas (co.), Calif. 204/E4
Plumas, Manitoba 179/D4
Plumber (creek), Utah 304/C2
Plum Branch, S.C. 296/C4
Plum City, Wis. 317/B6
Plum Coulee, Manitoba 179/E5
Plumerville, Ark. 202/E3
Plummer, Idaho 220/B2
Plummer, Ind. 227/C7
Plummer, Minn. 255/B3
Plummers Landing, Ky. 237/P4
Plum Point, Md. 245/N6
Plum Springs, Ky. 237/J7
Plumsteadville, Pa. 294/M5
Plum Tree, Ind. 227/G3
Plumtree, Zimbabwe 118/D4
Plumville, Pa. 294/D4
Plumwood, Ohio 284/D6
Plungė, Lithuania 53/B3
Plunkett, Sask. 181/F4
Plunkettville, Okla. 288/S6
Plush, Oreg. 291/H5
Plymouth (cap.), 156/F3
Plymouth, Calif. 204/C8
Plymouth•, Conn. 210/C2
Plymouth, England 7/D3
Plymouth, England 10/E5
Plymouth, England 13/C7
Plymouth (sound), England 13/C7
Plymouth, Fla. 212/E3
Plymouth, Ill. 222/C3
Plymouth, Ind. 227/E2
Plymouth (co.), Iowa 229/A3
Plymouth, Iowa 229/G2
Plymouth•, Maine 243/E6
Plymouth (co.), Mass. 249/L5
Plymouth, Mass. 249/M5
Plymouth•, Mass. 249/M5
Plymouth (bay), Mass. 249/M5
Plymouth, Mich. 250/F6
Plymouth, Minn. 255/G5
Plymouth, Nebr. 264/G4
Plymouth, N.H. 268/D4
Plymouth•, N.H. 268/D4
Plymouth, N.C. 281/R3
Plymouth, Ohio 284/E4
Plymouth, Pa. 294/E7
Plymouth, Utah 304/B2
Plymouth•, Vt. 268/B4
Plymouth, Wash. 310/F5
Plymouth, W. Va. 312/C5
Plymouth, Wis. 317/L8
Plymouth Union, Vt. 268/B4
Plympton•, Mass. 249/L5
Plympton, Nova Scotia 168/C4
Plynlimon (mt.), Wales 13/D5
Plzeň, Czech Rep. 7/F4
Plzeň, Czech Rep. 41/B2
Pniel, S. Africa 118/F6
Pniewy, Poland 47/C2
Po, Burkina Faso 106/D6
Po (riv.), Italy 7/E4
Po (riv.), Italy 34/C2
Po (riv.), Va. 307/N4
Poá, Brazil 135/C3
Poatina, Tasmania 99/C3
Pobeda (peak), China 77/A3
Pobeda (peak), Kyrgyzstan 48/J5
Población, Chile 138/F5
Pobla de Segur, Spain 33/G1
Poca, W. Va. 312/C6
Pocahontas, Alberta 182/B3
Pocahontas, Ark. 202/H1
Pocahontas, Ill. 222/D5
Pocahontas (co.), Iowa 229/D3
Pocahontas, Iowa 229/D4
Pocahontas, Miss. 256/D6
Pocahontas, Mo. 261/N8
Pocahontas, Tenn. 237/D10
Pocahontas, Va. 307/F6
Pocahontas (co.), W. Va. 312/F6
Pocasset, Mass. 249/M6
Pocasset, Okla. 288/L4
Pocatalico (riv.), W. Va. 312/C5
Pocatello, Idaho 146/G5
Pocatello, Idaho 220/F7
Pocatello, Idaho 188/D2
Počátky, Czech Rep. 41/C2
Pochep, Russia 52/D4
Pöchlarn, Austria 41/C2
Pocklington, England 13/G4
Pocoata, Bolivia 136/B6
Poções, Brazil 132/F6
Pocola, Okla. 288/T4
Pocologan, New Bruns. 170/D3
Pocomoke (riv.), Md. 245/S8
Pocomoke (sound), Md. 245/P9
Pocomoke (sound), Va. 307/S5
Pocomoke City, Md. 245/R8
Pocomoonshine (lake), Maine 243/H5
Pocona, Bolivia 136/C5
Poconé, Brazil 132/B7
Pocono (mts.), Pa. 294/M3
Pocono Lake, Pa. 294/L3
Pocono Pines, Pa. 294/M3
Poços de Caldas, Brazil 120/E5
Poços de Caldas, Brazil 135/C2
Poços de Caldas, Brazil 132/E8
Pocotalago, Ga. 217/F2
Pocotalico, W. Va. 312/C6
Pocotaligo (riv.), S.C. 296/G4
Pocotopaug (lake), Conn. 210/E2
Pocpo, Bolivia 136/C6
Podbořany, Czech Rep. 41/B1
Poděbrady, Czech Rep. 41/C1
Podgorica, Yugoslavia 7/F4
Podgorica, Yugoslavia 45/D4
Podol'sk, Russia 7/H3
Podol'sk, Russia 52/E3
Podol'sk, Russia 48/D4
Podor, Senegal 106/B5
Podporozh'ye, Russia 52/D2
Podunk (riv.), Conn. 210/E1
Poe, Alberta 182/D3
Poe, Ind. 227/G3
Poel (isl.), Germany 22/D1
Poenari Burchi, Romania 45/G3
Poge (cape), Mass. 249/N7
Poggibonsi, Italy 34/C3
Pogradec, Albania 45/E5
Pohakuloa (pt.), Hawaii 218/H2
P'ohang, S. Korea 81/D5
Pohatcong (creek), N.J. 273/C2
Pohénégamooke, Québec 172/H2
Pohjois-Karjala (prov.), Finland 18/Q5
Pohnpei (isl.), Micronesia 87/F5
Pohořelice, Czech Rep. 41/D2
Pohsien (Bo Xian), China 77/J5
Poiana Mare, Romania 45/F4
Poigan (lake), Québec 172/A2
Poinsett (co.), Ark. 202/J2
Poinsett (lake), Fla. 212/F3
Poinsett (lake), S. Dak. 298/P4
Point, La. 238/F1
Point (lake), N.W.T. 187/G3
Point, Texas 303/J5
Point Alexander, Ontario 177/G1
Point Arena, Calif. 204/B5
Point au Fer (isl.), La. 238/H8
Point au Fer (pt.), La. 238/H8
Point Baker, Alaska 196/M2
Point Cedar, Ark. 202/D5
Point Clear, Ala. 195/C10
Point Comfort, Texas 303/H9
Point Cross, Nova Scotia 168/G2
Point de Bute, New Bruns. 170/F3
Point du Bois, Manitoba 179/G4
Pointe-à-la-Croix, Québec 172/C2
Pointe-à-la-Frégate, Québec 172/D1
Pointe-à-la-Garde, Québec 172/B2
Pointe a la Hache, La. 238/L7
Pointe-à-Pitre, Guadeloupe 161/B6
Pointe-à-Pitre, Guadeloupe 156/G3
Pointe à Raquette, Haiti 158/B6
Pointe au Baril Station, Ontario 177/D2
Pointe-au-Chêne, Québec 172/C4
Pointe-au-Père, Québec 172/J1
Pointe-au-Pic, Québec 172/G2
Pointe Aux Barques, Mich. 250/G4
Pointe-aux-Outardes, Québec 172/A1
Pointe Aux Pins, Mich. 250/E3
Pointe-aux-Trembles, Québec 172/J4
Pointe-Bleue, Québec 172/E1
Pointe-Calumet, Québec 172/G4
Pointe-Claire, Québec 172/H4
Pointe Coupee (par.), La. 238/G5
Pointe du Bout, Martinique 161/C6
Pointe-du-Chêne, New Bruns. 170/F2
Pointe-du-Lac, Québec 172/E3
Pointe-du-Moulin, Québec 172/H4
Point Edward, Ontario 177/B4
Pointe-Gatineau, Québec 172/B4
Pointe-Lebel, Québec 172/A1
Pointe-Noire, Congo 102/D5
Pointe-Noire, Congo 115/B4
Pointe-Noire, Guadeloupe 161/A6
Pointe-Sapin, New Bruns. 170/F2
Pointe-Verte, New Bruns. 170/E1
Point Fortin, Trin. & Tob. 161/A11
Point Harbor, N.C. 281/T2
Point Hope, Alaska 188/C5
Point Hope, Alaska 196/E1
Point Isabel, Ind. 227/F4
Point La Haye, Newf. 166/D2
Point Lance, Newf. 166/C2
Point Lay, Alaska 196/F1
Point Leamington, Newf. 166/C4
Point Marion, Pa. 294/C6
Point Mugu Pacific Missile Test Center, Calif. 204/F9
Point of Rocks, Md. 245/J3
Point of Rocks, Wyo. 319/D4
Point Pelee, Ontario 177/B6
Point Pelee Nat'l Park, Ontario 177/B5
Point Pleasant, Mo. 261/O10
Point Pleasant, N.J. 273/E3
Point Pleasant, Ohio 284/B8
Point Pleasant, Pa. 294/N5
Point Pleasant, W. Va. 312/B5
Point Pleasant Beach, N.J. 273/E3
Point Reyes Nat'l Seashore, Calif. 204/H1

Ribeira 435

Red (isl.), Newf. 166/C2
Red (bay), N. Ireland 17/K1
Red, North Fork (riv.), Okla. 288/H4
Red (riv.), Okla. 288/R7
Red (lake), Ontario 175/B2
Red (sea), Saudi Arabia 59/C5
Red (lake), S. Dak. 298/L6
Red (sea), Sudan 111/G3
Red (riv.), Tenn. 237/G7
Red (riv.), Texas 303/F3
Red (riv.), U.S. 146/J6
Red (riv.), Utah 304/D3
Red (riv.), Vietnam 72/E2
Red (pt.), Virgin Is. (U.S.) 161/D4
Red (sea), Yemen 59/C5
Reda, Poland 47/D1
Redang, Pulau (isl.), Malaysia 72/D6
Redange, Luxembourg 27/H9
Red Ash, Va. 307/E6
Red Bank, New Bruns. 170/E2
Red Bank, N.J. 273/E3
Redbank (creek), Pa. 294/E3
Red Bank, Tenn. 237/L10
Red Banks, Miss. 256/F1
Red Bay, Ala. 195/B2
Red Bay, Fla. 212/C6
Red Bay, Newf. 166/C3
Red Bay, Ontario 177/C3
Red Beach, Maine 243/J5
Red Bird, Mo. 261/J6
Redbird, Okla. 288/P3
Red Bluff, Calif. 204/C3
Red Bluff (lake), N. Mex. 274/E7
Red Bluff (lake), Texas 188/F4
Red Bluff (lake), Texas 303/A6
Red Boiling Springs, Tenn. 237/K7
Redbridge, England 13/H8
Redbridge, England 10/C5
Red Bud, Ill. 222/D5
Redbush, Ky. 237/P5
Redby, Minn. 255/D3
Redcar, England 10/F3
Redcar, England 13/F3
Red Cedar (riv.), Wis. 317/C5
Red Chute (bayou), La. 238/C1
Redcliff, Alberta 182/E4
Red Cliff, Colo. 208/G4
Red Cliff, Wis. 317/E2
Redcliffe, Queensland 95/E5
Red Cliffe, Queensland 88/J5
Red Cliff Ind. Res., Wis. 317/E2
Red Cliffs, Victoria 97/B4
Redcloud (peak), Colo. 208/E6
Red Cloud, Nebr. 264/F4
Red Creek, N.Y. 276/G4
Red Creek, W. Va. 312/H4
Redcrest, Calif. 204/A3
Red Deer, Alberta 182/D3
Red Deer (lake), Alberta 182/D3
Red Deer (riv.), Alberta 182/D4
Red Deer, Alta. 146/G4
Red Deer, Alta. 162/E5
Red Deer (lake), Manitoba 179/A2
Red Deer (riv.), Manitoba 179/A2
Red Deer (riv.), Sask. 181/K3
Red Deer (riv.), Sask. 181/A5
Red Deer Hill, Sask. 181/F2
Reddell, La. 238/F5
Redden, Del. 245/S5
Red Devil, Alaska 196/G2
Reddick, Fla. 212/D2
Reddick, Ill. 222/E2
Redding, Calif. 146/F5
Redding, Calif. 188/B2
Redding, Calif. 204/C3
Redding•, Calif. 204/80
Redding•, Conn. 210/B3
Redding, Iowa 229/E7
Redding Ridge, Conn. 210/B3
Reddington, Ind. 227/F6
Redditch, England 13/E5
Redditch, England 10/G3
Red Earth Creek, Alberta 182/C1
Red Elm, S. Dak. 298/F3
Redeye (riv.), Minn. 255/D4
Red Feather Lakes, Colo. 208/H1
Redfield, Ark. 202/F5
Redfield, Iowa 229/E5
Redfield, Kansas 232/H4
Redfield, N.Y. 276/J3
Redfield, Sask. 181/D2
Redfield, S. Dak. 298/N4
Redfish (lake), Idaho 220/D5
Redford, Mo. 261/L8
Redford, Texas 303/C12
Red Fork, Powder (riv.), Wyo. 319/F2
Redgranite, Wis. 317/J7
Redhead, Trin. & Tob. 161/B10
Red Head Cove, Newf. 166/D2
Red Hill (mt.), Hawaii 218/K2
Red Hill, Pa. 294/L5
Red Hill Patrick Henry Nat'l Mem., Va. 306/L6
Red Hook, N.Y. 276/N7
Redhouse, Ky. 237/N5
Red House, Nev. 266/D2
Red House, Va. 307/L6
Red House, W. Va. 312/C5
Redig, S. Dak. 298/C3
Red Indian (lake), Newf. 166/C4
Redington, Nebr. 264/A3
Redington Beach, Fla. 212/B3
Redington Shores, Fla. 212/B3
Red Jacket, W. Va. 312/B7
Redkey, Ind. 227/G4
Red Lake (co.), Minn. 255/B3
Redlake, Minn. 255/C3
Red Lake (riv.), Minn. 255/B2
Red Lake, Ont. 162/G6
Red Lake, Ontario 175/B2
Red Lake Falls, Minn. 255/B3
Red Lake Ind. Res., Minn. 255/C2
Red Lake Road, Ontario 177/G5
Red Lake Road, Ontario 175/B2
Redland, Alberta 182/D4
Redland, Oreg. 291/B2
Redlands, Calif. 204/H9
Red Level, Ala. 195/E8
Red Lick, Miss. 256/B7
Red Lion, Del. 245/R2
Red Lion, N.J. 273/D4
Red Lion, Ohio 284/B7
Red Lion, Pa. 294/J6
Red Lodge, Mont. 262/G5
Redman, Mich. 250/G5
Red Mesa, Colo. 208/C8
Redmon, Ill. 222/F4
Redmond, Oreg. 291/F3
Redmond, Utah 304/C4
Redmond, Wash. 310/B1
Red Mountain, Calif. 204/H8
Red Oak, Ga. 217/J2
Red Oak, Iowa 229/C6
Red Oak, Mich. 250/E4
Red Oak, N.C. 281/N2
Red Oak, Okla. 288/R5
Red Oak, Texas 303/H5
Red Oak, Va. 307/L7
Red Oaks Mill, N.Y. 276/N7
Redon, France 28/C4
Redonda (isl.), Ant. & Bar. 156/F3
Redondela, Spain 33/B1
Redondo, Portugal 33/C3
Redondo, Wash. 310/C3
Redondo Beach, Calif. 204/B11
Redoubt (vol.), Alaska 196/H2
Redowl, S. Dak. 298/D4
Red Owl (creek), S. Dak. 298/E4
Redpa, Tasmania 99/A2
Red Pass, Br. Col. 184/H4
Redridge, Mich. 250/G1
Red River (par.), La. 238/D2
Red River, N. Mex. 274/D2
Red River, Nova Scotia 168/H2
Red River, S.C. 296/F2
Red River (co.), Texas 303/J4
Red River Hot Springs, Idaho 220/C4
Red River of the North (riv.) 188/G1
Red River of the North (riv.), Minn. 255/A2
Red River of the North (riv.), N. Dak. 282/S4
Red Rock, Ariz. 198/D6
Red Rock, Br. Col. 184/F3
Red Rock (lake), Iowa 229/G6
Red Rock (lakes), Mont. 262/E6
Red Rock (riv.), Mont. 262/D6
Redrock, N. Mex. 274/A6
Red Rock, Okla. 288/M2
Red Rock, Ontario 177/H5
Red Rock, Ontario 175/C3
Red Rock, Texas 303/G8
Red Scaffold (creek), S. Dak. 298/F4
Red Sea (prov.), Sudan 111/G4
Red Sea Hills (mts.), Sudan 59/C5
Red Springs, N.C. 281/L5
Red Springs, Texas 303/E4
Redstar, W. Va. 312/D7
Redstone, Br. Col. 184/F4
Redstone, Colo. 208/E4
Redstone, Mont. 262/M2
Redstone, N.H. 268/E3
Redstone (riv.), N.W.T. 187/F3
Redstone (lake), Ontario 177/F2
Redstone (creek), S. Dak. 298/O5
Redstone Arsenal, Ala. 195/E1
Red Sucker Lake, Manitoba 179/K3
Red Sulphur Springs, W. Va. 312/E7
Redtop, Minn. 255/E4
Redvale, Colo. 208/B6
Redvers, Sask. 181/K6
Red Volta (riv.), Ghana 106/D6
Red Volta (Nazinon) (riv.), Burkina Faso 106/D6
Redwater, Alberta 182/D3
Redwater (riv.), Mont. 262/L3
Redwater (creek), S. Dak. 298/A4
Redway, Calif. 204/B3
Red Willow, Alberta 182/D3
Red Willow (co.), Nebr. 264/D4
Redwine, Ky. 237/P4
Red Wine (riv.), Newf. 166/B3
Red Wing, Colo. 208/J7
Redwing, Kansas 232/D3
Red Wing, Minn. 255/F6
Redwood (co.), Minn. 255/C6
Redwood (riv.), Minn. 255/C6
Redwood, Miss. 256/C6
Redwood, N.Y. 276/J2
Redwood City, Calif. 204/J3
Redwood Estates-Chemeketa Park, Calif. 204/K4
Redwood Falls, Minn. 255/C6
Redwood Nat'l Park, Calif. 204/A2
Redwood Valley, Calif. 204/B4
Ree, Lough (lake), Ireland 10/B4
Ree (lake), Ireland 17/F5
Reece, Kansas 232/F4
Reece City, Ala. 195/G2
Reed, Ark. 202/H6
Reed, Ky. 237/G5
Reed, Okla. 288/G5
Reed (mt.), Québec 174/D2
Reed City, Mich. 250/D5
Reeder, Manitoba 179/A4
Reeder, N. Dak. 282/E7
Reedley, Calif. 204/F7
Reedpoint, Mont. 262/G5
Reeds, Mo. 261/D8
Reedsburg (res.), Mich. 250/E4
Reedsburg, Ohio 284/F4
Reedsburg, Wis. 317/G8
Reeds Ferry, N.H. 268/D6
Reedsport, Oreg. 291/C4
Reeds Spring, Mo. 261/F9
Reedsville, Ohio 284/G7
Reedsville, Pa. 294/G4
Reedsville, W. Va. 312/G3
Reedsville, Wis. 317/L7
Reedville, Oreg. 291/A2
Reedville, Va. 307/R5
Reedy (lake), Fla. 212/E4
Reedy (riv.), S.C. 296/C2
Reedy, W. Va. 312/D5
Reedy (creek), W. Va. 312/D5
Reedyville, Ky. 237/H6
Reef (bay), Virgin Is. (U.S.) 161/C4
Reefton, N. Zealand 100/C5
Ree Heights, S. Dak. 298/L4
Reelfoot (lake), Tenn. 237/C8
Reelsville, Ind. 227/D5
Reeman, Mich. 250/D5
Reese, Mich. 250/F5
Reese (riv.), Nev. 266/D3
Reese A.F.B., Texas 303/B4
Reeseville, Wis. 317/J9
Reesville, Ohio 284/C7
Reeves, La. 238/D5
Reeves (co.), Texas 303/D11
Reeves Knob (mt.), Ark. 202/E2
Reevesville, Ill. 222/E6
Reevesville, S.C. 296/F5
Refahiye, Turkey 63/H3
Refa'i, Iraq 66/E5
Reform, Ala. 195/C4
Reform, Miss. 256/F4
Refton, Pa. 294/K6
Refuge Cove, Br. Col. 184/E5
Refugio (isl.), Chile 138/D5
Refugio (co.), Texas 303/G9
Refugio, Texas 303/G9
Rega (riv.), Poland 47/B2
Regal, Minn. 255/D5
Regan, N. Dak. 282/K5
Regen, Germany 22/E4
Regen (riv.), Germany 22/E4
Regeneração, Brazil 132/F4
Regensburg, Germany 7/F4
Regensburg, Germany 22/E4
Regensdorf, Switzerland 39/F2
Regent, Manitoba 179/B5
Regent, N. Dak. 282/E7
Reger, Mo. 261/F2
Reggane, Algeria 106/D3
Regge (riv.), Netherlands 27/K4
Reggio, La. 238/L7
Reggio di Calabria (prov.), Italy 34/E5
Reggio di Calabria, Italy 7/F5
Reggio di Calabria, Italy 34/E5
Reggio nell'Emilia (prov.), Italy 34/C2
Reggio nell'Emilia, Italy 34/C2
Reghin, Romania 45/G2
Régina, Fr. Guiana 131/E3
Regina, Mont. 262/J3
Regina, N. Mex. 274/B2
Regina (cap.), Sask. 162/F5
Regina (cap.), Sask. 146/H4
Regina (cap.), Sask. 181/G5
Regina Beach, Sask. 181/F5
Register, Ga. 217/J6
Registro, Brazil 135/C4
Regla, Cuba 158/C1
Regnitz (riv.), Germany 22/D4
Reguengos de Monsaraz, Portugal 33/C3
Regway, Sask. 181/G6
Rehau, Germany 22/D3
Rehoboth, Ala. 195/D6
Rehoboth•, Mass. 249/K5
Rehoboth, Namibia 118/B4
Rehoboth, Namibia 102/D7
Rehoboth, N. Mex. 274/A3
Rehoboth, Va. 307/M7
Rehoboth Beach, Del. 245/T6
Rehovot, Israel 65/B4
Rehrersburg, Pa. 294/K5
Reichenau an der Rax, Austria 41/C3
Reichenbach, Germany 22/E3
Reichenbach im Kandertal, Switzerland 39/E3
Reid, Md. 245/H2
Reid (lake), S. Dak. 298/O3
Reid (rocks), Tasmania 99/B1
Reid, W. Australia 92/E5
Reiden, Switzerland 39/F2
Reids Grove, Md. 245/P6
Reidsville, Ga. 217/H6
Reidsville, N.C. 281/K2
Reidville, S.C. 296/C2
Reigate, England 13/H8
Reigate, England 10/F5
Reile's Acres, N. Dak. 282/S6
Reily, Ohio 284/A7
Re'im, Israel 65/A5
Reims, France 7/E4
Reims, France 28/E3
Reina Adelaida (arch.), Chile 120/B8
Reina Adelaida (arch.), Chile 138/D9
Reinach in Aargau, Switzerland 39/F2
Reinach in Baselland, Switzerland 39/E2
Reinbeck, Iowa 229/H4
Reindeer (lake) 162/F4
Reindeer (lake), Canada 146/H4
Reindeer (isl.), Manitoba 179/E2
Reindeer (lake), Manitoba 179/H2
Reindeer (lake), Sask. 181/N3
Reindeer (riv.), Sask. 181/M3
Reinersville, Ohio 284/G6
Reinfeld, Germany 22/D2
Reinga (cape), N. Zealand 100/D1
Reinland, Manitoba 179/E5
Reinosa, Spain 33/D1
Reisaelv (riv.), Norway 18/M2
Reisduoddarhal'di (Haltiatunturi), Norway 18/M2
Reiss, Scotland 15/E2
Reisterstown, Md. 245/L3
Reitz, S. Africa 118/D5
Rejaf, Sudan 111/F7
Reliance, Md. 245/P6
Reliance, N.W.T. 187/H3
Reliance, S. Dak. 298/K6
Reliance, Tenn. 237/N10
Reliance, Va. 307/M3
Reliance, Wyo. 319/C4
Relief, Ky. 237/P5
Relizane, Algeria 106/E1
Reloncaví (bay), Chile 138/D4
Remada, Tunisia 106/F2
Remagen, Germany 22/B3
Remanso, Brazil 132/F5
Remates, Cuba 158/A2
Rembang, Indonesia 85/K2
Rembert, S.C. 296/G3
Rembrandt, Iowa 229/C3
Rembrandt, Manitoba 179/E4
Remedios, Colombia 126/C4
Remedios, Cuba 156/B2
Remedios, Cuba 158/E2
Remedios (pt.), El Salvador 154/B4
Remer, Minn. 255/E3
Remerton, Ga. 217/F9
Remich, Luxembourg 27/J9
Reminderville, Ohio 284/J10
Remington, Ind. 227/C3
Remington, Ohio 284/C9
Remington, Va. 307/N3
Rémire, Fr. Guiana 131/E3
Rémire (isls.), Fr. Guiana 131/F3
Remiremont, France 28/G3
Remlap, Ala. 195/E3
Remmel (mt.), Wash. 310/E2
Remo, Br. Col. 184/C3
Remolino, Colombia 126/C2
Remote, Oreg. 291/D5
Remscheid, Germany 22/B3
Remsen, Iowa 229/B3
Remsen, N.Y. 276/K4
Remus, Mich. 250/D5
Remus, Okla. 288/N4
Remy, La. 238/L3
Rena, Ark. 202/B3
Rena, Norway 18/G6
Reñaca, Chile 138/F2
Renaix (Ronse), Belgium 27/D7
Rena Lara, Miss. 256/C2
Renan, Switzerland 39/C2
Renault, Ill. 222/C5
Renca, Chile 138/G3
Rencona, N. Mex. 274/D3
Rencontre East, Newf. 166/C4
Rend (lake), Ill. 222/E5
Rendeux, Belgium 27/H8
Rendova (isl.), Solomon Is. 86/D3
Rendsburg, Germany 22/C1
Rendville, Ohio 284/F6
Renens, Switzerland 39/C3
Renews, Newf. 166/D2
Renforth, New Bruns. 170/E3
Renfrew, Ont. 162/J6
Renfrew (county), Ontario 177/G2
Renfrew (county), Ontario 175/E3
Renfrew, Ontario 177/H2
Renfrew, Ontario 175/E3
Renfrew, Pa. 294/C4
Renfrew, Scotland 10/A1
Renfrew, Scotland 15/B2
Renfrew (trad. co.), Scotland 15/A5
Renfroe, Ala. 195/F4
Renfroe, Ga. 217/C6
Renfroe, Miss. 256/F5
Renfrow, Okla. 288/L1
Rengam, Malaysia 72/E5
Rengat, Indonesia 85/C6
Rengo, Chile 138/G5
Reni, Ukraine 52/C5
Renick, Mo. 261/H4
Renick, W. Va. 312/F6
Renigunta, India 68/E6
Renish (pt.), Scotland 15/B3
Renk, Sudan 111/F5
Renkum, Netherlands 27/H5
Renmark, S. Australia 88/G6
Renmark, S. Australia 94/G5
Rennell (isl.), Solomon Is. 87/F7
Rennell (isl.), Solomon Is. 86/E3
Renner, S. Dak. 298/R6
Rennert, N.C. 281/L5
Rennes, France 7/D4
Rennes, France 28/C3
Rennie, Manitoba 179/G5
Rennie (lake), N.W.T. 187/H3
Renno, S.C. 296/D2
Reno, Alberta 182/B2
Reno, Ga. 217/D9
Reno, Ill. 222/D5
Reno (co.), Kansas 232/D4
Reno (lake), Minn. 255/C5
Reno, Nev. 146/G6
Reno, Nev. 188/C3
Reno, Nev. 266/B3
Reno, Ohio 284/H7
Reno, Texas 303/E2
Reno Beach, Ohio 284/D2
Renous, New Bruns. 170/E2
Renous (riv.), New Bruns. 170/D2
Renova, Miss. 256/C3
Renovo, Pa. 294/G3
Renown, Sask. 181/F4
Rensburg, S. Africa 118/J7
Rensselaer, Ind. 227/C3
Rensselaer, Mo. 261/J3
Rensselaer (co.), N.Y. 276/O5
Rensselaer, N.Y. 276/N5
Rensselaer Falls, N.Y. 276/K1
Rentchler, Ill. 222/B3
Rentiesville, Okla. 288/R4
Renton, Scotland 15/A1
Renton, Wash. 310/B2
Rentz, Ga. 217/G6
Renville (co.), Minn. 255/C6
Renville, Minn. 255/C6
Renville (co.), N. Dak. 282/G2
Renwer, Manitoba 179/B2
Renwick, Iowa 229/E3
Répcelak, 41/D3
Repentigny, Québec 172/J4
Replete, W. Va. 312/F5
Repos (lake), Québec 172/C2
Repton, Ala. 195/D8
Republic, Ala. 195/E3
Republic (co.), Kansas 232/E2
Republic, Kansas 232/E2
Republic, Mich. 250/B2
Republic, Mo. 261/E8
Republic, Ohio 284/D3
Republic, Wash. 310/G2
República Dominicana, Cuba 158/F2
Republican (riv.) 188/F2
Republican (riv.), Colo. 208/P3
Republican (riv.), Kansas 232/E2
Republican (riv.), Nebr. 264/G5
Republican City, Nebr. 264/E4
Republican Grove, Va. 307/K7
Repulse (bay), Queensland 88/H4
Repulse Bay, Canada 4/C14
Repulse Bay, N.W.T. 162/H2
Repulse Bay, N.W.T. 187/K3
Requa, Calif. 204/A2
Requegua, Chile 138/G5
Requena, Peru 128/F5
Requena, Spain 33/F3
Requínoa, Chile 138/G5
Rera, Brazil 132/A1
Resaca, Ga. 217/C1
Reşadiye, Turkey 63/G2
Research, Victoria 97/J4
Reseda, Calif. 204/B10
Resende, Brazil 135/D3
Resende, Portugal 33/B2
Reserve, Kansas 232/G2
Reserve, La. 238/M3
Reserve, Mont. 262/M2
Reserve, N. Mex. 274/A5
Reserve, Sask. 181/J3
Reserve, Wis. 317/D4
Reserve Mines, Nova Scotia 168/H2
Resht (Rasht), Iran 66/F2
Reshui, China 77/E4
Resistencia, Argentina 143/E2
Resistencia, Argentina 120/D5
Reşiţa, Romania 45/E3
Resolute, Canada 4/B14
Resolute, N.W.T. 162/G1
Resolute, N.W.T. 187/J2
Resolution (isl.), N. Zealand 100/A6
Resolution (isl.), N.W.T. 146/M3
Resolution (isl.), N.W.T. 162/K3
Resolution (isl.), N.W.T. 187/M3
Resolution Island, N.W.T. 187/M3
Resort, Loch (inlet), Scotland 15/A2
Resource, Sask. 181/G3
Respenda de la Peña, Spain 33/D1
Restauración, Dom. Rep. 158/D5
Rest Haven, Ga. 217/E2
Restigouche (co.), New Bruns. 170/C1
Restigouche (riv.), New Bruns. 170/C1
Restigouche, Québec 172/C2
Reston, Manitoba 179/A5
Reston, Va. 307/R2
Restoule, Ontario 177/E1
Restoule (lake), Ontario 177/E1
Restrepo, Colombia 126/D5
Reszel, Poland 47/E1
Retalhuleu, Guatemala 154/B3
Retamosa, Uruguay 145/E4
Rethel, France 28/F3
Réthimnon, Greece 45/G8
Retie, Belgium 27/G6
Retiro, Chile 138/A11
Retlaw, Alberta 182/D4
Rétság, Hungary 41/E3
Retsil, Wash. 310/A2
Retsof, N.Y. 276/E5
Retz, Austria 41/D2
Reubens, Idaho 220/B3
RÉUNION 118/F5
Réunion (isl.), (Fr.) 2/M7
Reus, Spain 33/G2
Reusel, Netherlands 27/G6
Reuss (riv.), Switzerland 39/F2
Reutlingen, Germany 22/C4
Reutte, Austria 41/A3
Reva, S. Dak. 298/C2
Revadim, Israel 65/B4
Reveille (peak), Nev. 266/E5
Reveille (range), Nev. 266/E4
Revel, France 28/E6
Revel (Tallinn), Estonia 52/B3
Revelo, Ky. 237/N7
Revelstoke, Br. Col. 162/E5
Revelstoke, Br. Col. 184/J5
Reventazón, Peru 128/B6
Revenue, Sask. 181/B3
Revere, Mass. 249/D6
Revere, Minn. 255/C6
Revere, Mo. 261/J2
Revere, N. Dak. 282/O5
Revere, W. Va. 312/E5
Reverie, Tenn. 237/A9
Revillagigedo (chan.), Alaska 196/N2
Revillagigedo (isl.), Alaska 196/N2
Revillagigedo (isls.), Mexico 146/G8
Revillagigedo (isls.), Mexico 2/D5
Revillagigedo (isls.), Mexico 150/C7
Revillo, S. Dak. 298/R3
Révin, France 28/F3
Revivim, Israel 65/D5
Revúca, Slovakia 41/F2
Revuelto (creek), N. Mex. 274/F3
Rew, Pa. 294/F2
Rewa, India 68/E4
Reward, Sask. 181/B3
Rewataya (reef), Indonesia 85/F7
Rewey, Wis. 317/F10
Rex, N.C. 281/M5
Rex, Oreg. 291/A2
Rexburg, Idaho 220/G6
Rexford, Kansas 232/B2
Rexford, Mont. 262/A2
Rexton, Mich. 250/D2
Rexton, New Bruns. 170/F2
Rexville, Ind. 227/G7
Rexville, N.Y. 276/E6
Rey, Iran 59/F2
Rey, Iran 66/G3
Rey (isl.), Panama 154/H6
Rey Bouba, Cameroon 115/B2
Reydell, Ark. 202/G5
Reydon, Okla. 288/G3
Reyes, Bolivia 136/B4
Reyes (pt.), Calif. 204/B6
Reyhanli, Turkey 63/G4
Reykjanestá (cape), Iceland 7/B2
Reykjanestá (cape), Iceland 21/A2
Reykjavík (cap.), Iceland 4/C11
Reykjavík (cap.), Iceland 2/J2
Reykjavík (cap.), Iceland 21/B1
Reykjavík (cap.), Iceland 7/B2
Reynaud, Sask. 181/F3
Reyno, Ark. 202/J1
Reynolds, Ga. 217/D5
Reynolds (creek), Idaho 220/B6
Reynolds, Ill. 222/C2
Reynolds, Ind. 227/D3
Reynolds (co.), Mo. 261/L8
Reynolds, Mo. 261/K8
Reynolds, Nebr. 264/G4
Reynolds, N. Dak. 282/R4
Reynolds Bridge, Conn. 210/C2
Reynoldsburg, Ohio 284/E6
Reynolds Station, Ky. 237/H5
Reynoldsville, Pa. 294/D3
Reynosa, Mexico 150/K3
Rezaiyeh (Urmia), Iran 66/D2
Reza'iyeh (Urmia), Iran 59/D2
Rezé, France 28/C4
Rēzekne, Latvia 52/C3
Rēzekne, Latvia 53/D2
Rhaetian Alps (range), Switzerland 39/J3
Rhame, N. Dak. 282/C7
Rhätikon (mts.), Liecht. 39/J2
Rhätikon (mts.), Switzerland 39/J2
Rhayader, Wales 13/D5
Rhea (creek), Oreg. 291/H2
Rhea (co.), Tenn. 237/M9
Rheatown, Tenn. 237/R8
Rheda-Wiedenbrück, Germany 22/C3
Rheden, Netherlands 27/J4
Rheims (Reims), France 28/E4
Rhein, Sask. 181/J4
Rheinau, Switzerland 39/G1
Rheine, Germany 22/B2
Rheineck, Switzerland 39/J2
Rheinfeld, Sask. 181/D5
Rheinfelden, Switzerland 39/E1
Rheinfelden, Germany 22/B5
Rheinsberg, Germany 22/E2
Rheinwaldhorn (mt.), Switzerland 39/G4
Rhems, S.C. 296/H4
Rhenen, Netherlands 27/H5
Rhéris, Wadi (dry riv.), Morocco 106/D2
Rhine (riv.) 7/E4
Rhine (riv.), Austria 41/A3
Rhine (riv.), France 28/G3
Rhine, Ga. 217/F7
Rhine (riv.), Liecht. 39/J2
Rhine (riv.), Netherlands 27/J5
Rhine (riv.), Switzerland 39/J2
Rhine (riv.), Germany 22/B3
Rhinebeck, N.Y. 276/N7
Rhinecliff, N.Y. 276/N7
Rhineland, Mo. 261/J5
Rhineland, Sask. 181/D5
Rhinelander, Wis. 317/H4
Rhineland-Palatinate (state), Germany 22/B4
Rhinns, The (pen.), Scotland 15/C6
Rhinns (pt.), Scotland 15/B5
Rhino Camp, Uganda 115/F3
Rhir, Wadi (dry riv.), Algeria 106/F2
Rhir (cape), Morocco 106/B2
Rho, Italy 34/B2
Rhode Island 188/M2
RHODE ISLAND 249
Rhode Island (isl.), R.I. 249/J6
Rhode Island (sound), R.I. 249/J7
Rhode Island (state), U.S. 146/M5
Rhodell, W. Va. 312/D7
Rhodes (Ródhos), Greece 45/J7
Rhodes (isl.), Greece 7/G5
Rhodes (isl.), Greece 45/H7
Rhodes (peak), Idaho 220/D3
Rhodes, Iowa 229/G5
Rhodes, Mich. 250/E5
Rhodes Point, Md. 245/O9
Rhodhiss, N.C. 281/F3
Rhododendron, Oreg. 291/F2
Rhodope (mts.), Bulgaria 45/G5
Rhodope (mts.), Greece 45/G5
Rhome, Texas 303/E1
Rhün (mts.), Germany 22/D3
Rhün (mts.), Germany 22/D3
Rhondda, Wales 13/A6
Rhondda, Wales 10/E5
Rhône (dept.), France 28/F5
Rhône (riv.), France 7/E4
Rhône (riv.), France 28/F5
Rhône (riv.), Switzerland 39/D4
Rhosllanerchrugog, Wales 13/D4
Rhu, Scotland 15/A1
Rhu Coigeach (cape), Scotland 15/C2
Rhyl, Wales 13/D4
Rhymney, Wales 13/A6
Rhymney (riv.), Wales 13/B6
Rhynie, Scotland 15/F3
Rhyolite (Ghost Town), Nev. 266/E6
Riachão, Brazil 132/E4
Riachuelo, Uruguay 145/B5
Rialto, Calif. 204/E10
Riana, Tasmania 99/B3
Riaño, Spain 33/D1
Riau (arch.), Indonesia 85/C5
Riaza, Spain 33/E2
Rib (mt.), Wis. 317/G6
Ribadavia, Spain 33/B1
Ribadeo, Spain 33/C1
Ribamar, Brazil 132/F3
Ribas do Rio Pardo, Brazil 132/C8
Ribat Qila, Pakistan 68/A3
Ribat Qila, Pakistan 59/H4
Ribáuè, Mozambique 118/F3
Ribble (riv.), England 10/E4
Ribble (riv.), England 13/E4
Ribe (co.), Denmark 21/B7
Ribe, Denmark 21/B7
Ribe, Denmark 18/F9
Ribeira, Brazil 135/B4
Ribeira (riv.), Brazil 135/B4

Rong Xian **437**

Riverton, Manitoba 179/E3
Riverton, Minn. 255/D4
Riverton, Nebr. 264/F4
Riverton, N.J. 273/B3
Riverton, N. Zealand 100/B7
Riverton, Nova Scotia 168/F3
Riverton, Oreg. 291/C4
Riverton, Utah 304/B3
Riverton, Vt. 268/B3
Riverton, Va. 307/M3
Riverton, Wash. 310/B2
Riverton, W. Va. 312/H5
Riverton, Wyo. 319/D2
Riverton Heights, Wash. 310/B2
Rivervale, Ark. 202/K2
River Vale•, N.J. 273/B1
River Valley, Ontario 177/D1
Riverview, Ala. 195/D8
Riverview, Fla. 212/D4
Riverview, Mich. 250/B7
Riverview, Mo. 261/R2
Riverview, New Bruns. 170/F2
Riverville, Va. 307/L5
Riverwood, Ky. 237/K1
Riverwoods, Ill. 222/B5
Rives, Mo. 261/M10
Rives, Tenn. 237/C8
Rives Junction, Mich. 250/E6
Rivesville, W. Va. 312/F3
Riviera (reg.), France 28/G6
Riviera, Texas 303/G10
Riviera Beach, Fla. 212/G5
Riviera Beach, Md. 245/N4
Riviera-Bullhead, Ariz. 198/A3
Rivière-à-Claude, Québec 172/C1
Rivière-à-Pierre, Québec 172/E3
Rivière-au-Renard, Québec 172/D1
Rivière-au-Tonnerre, Québec 174/D2
Rivière-Bleue, Québec 172/J2
Rivière-Bois-Clair, Québec 172/F3
Rivière-du-Loup (co.), Québec 172/H2
Rivière-du-Loup, Québec 172/H2
Rivière-du-Loup, Québec 174/D3
Rivière-du-Loup, Québec 172/H2
Rivière-du-Moulin, Québec 172/G1
Rivière-du-Portage, New Bruns. 170/F1
Rivière-Éternité, Québec 172/G1
Rivière-la-Madeleine, Québec 172/C1
Rivière-Matawin, Québec 172/E3
Rivière-Ouelle, Québec 172/G2
Rivière-Pentecôte, Québec 174/D3
Rivière-Pilote, Martinique 161/D7
Rivière-Port-Daniel, Québec 172/D2
Rivière-Portneuf, Québec 172/H1
Rivière-Saint-Paul, Québec 174/F2
Rivière-Salée, Martinique 161/D7
Rivière-Trois-Pistoles, Québec 172/J1
Rivière Verte, New Bruns. 170/B1
Rivière-Verte, Québec 172/H2
Riwaka, N. Zealand 100/D4
Riwoqê, China 77/E5
Rixeyville, Va. 307/M3
Rixford, Pa. 294/F2
Riyadh (cap.), Saudi Arabia 2/M4
Riyadh (cap.), Saudi Arabia 54/F7
Riyadh (cap.), Saudi Arabia 59/E5
Riyan, Yemen 59/E7
Rizal (prov.), Philippines 82/C3
Rize (prov.), Turkey 63/J2
Rize, Turkey 59/D1
Rize, Turkey 63/J2
Rizokarpasso, Cyprus 63/F5
Rjukan, Norway 18/F7
Roa, Norway 18/G6
Roa, Spain 33/E2
Roachdale, Ind. 227/D5
Road (bay), Virgin Is. (U.K.) 161/D3
Roadside, Scotland 15/F4
Roadstown, N.J. 273/C5
Road Town (cap.), Virgin Is. (U.K.) 161/D3
Road Town (cap.), Virgin Is. (U.K.) 156/H1
Roag, Loch (inlet), Scotland 15/B2
Roan (creek), Colo. 208/C4
Roan (plat.), Colo. 208/B3
Roan, Norway 18/G4
Roan (isl.), Scotland 15/D2
Roan (cliffs), Utah 304/E4
Roane (co.), Tenn. 237/M9
Roane (co.), W. Va. 312/D5
Roan Mountain, Tenn. 237/S8
Roann, Ind. 227/F3
Roanne, France 28/E4
Roanoke (riv.) 188/L3
Roanoke, Ala. 195/H4
Roanoke, Ill. 222/D3
Roanoke, Ind. 227/G3
Roanoke, La. 238/E6
Roanoke, Mo. 261/G4
Roanoke (isl.), N.C. 281/T3
Roanoke (riv.), N.C. 281/P2
Roanoke, Texas 303/F1
Roanoke, Va. 146/L6
Roanoke, Va. 188/K3
Roanoke (co.), Va. 307/H6
Roanoke (I.C.), Va. 307/H6
Roanoke (riv.), Va. 307/N8
Roanoke, W. Va. 312/F5
Roanoke Rapids, N.C. 281/O2
Roaring (brook), Conn. 210/F1
Roaring (brook), Conn. 210/E2
Roaring Branch, Pa. 294/J2
Roaring Fork, Colorado (riv.), Colo. 208/E4
Roaring Gap, N.C. 281/H2
Roaring River, N.C. 281/G2
Roaring Spring, Pa. 294/F5
Roaring Springs, Texas 303/D4
Roaringwater (bay), Ireland 17/B9
Roark, Ky. 237/P6
Roatán, Honduras 154/D2
Roatán (isl.), Honduras 154/D2
Roba, Ala. 195/G6
Robards, Ky. 237/F5
Robat Karim, Iran 66/G3
Robb, Alberta 182/B3
Robben (isl.), S. Africa 118/E6
Robbins, Calif. 204/B8
Robbins, Ill. 222/B6
Robbins, N.C. 281/K4
Robbins (isl.), Tasmania 99/B2
Robbins, Tenn. 237/M8
Robbinsdale, Minn. 255/G5
Robbinston, Maine 243/J5
Robbinston•, Maine 243/J5
Robbinsville, N.J. 273/D3
Robbinsville, N.C. 281/B4
Robe (mt.), N.S. Wales 97/A2
Robe, S. Australia 94/F7
Robe, Wash. 310/D2
Robeline, La. 238/D3
Roberdel, N.C. 281/K5
Robersonville, N.C. 281/P3
Robert (isl.), China 85/E2
Robert, La. 238/N1
Robert (harb.), Martinique 161/D6
Roberta, Ga. 217/D5
Roberta, Okla. 288/K7
Robert Lee, Texas 303/D6
Roberto Payán, Colombia 126/A7
Roberts, Idaho 220/F6
Roberts, Ill. 222/E3
Roberts, Mont. 262/G5
Roberts (co.), S. Dak. 298/P2
Roberts (co.), Texas 303/D2
Roberts, Wis. 317/A6
Robert's Arm, Newf. 166/C4
Robertsburg, W. Va. 312/C5
Roberts Creek, Br. Col. 184/J3
Robertsdale, Ala. 195/C9
Robertsdale, Pa. 294/F5
Roberts Field Int'l Airport, Liberia 106/C7
Robertsfors, Sweden 18/M4
Robertsganj, India 68/E4
Robertson (co.), Ky. 237/N3
Robertson, S. Africa 118/C6
Robertson (co.), Tenn. 237/H7
Robertson (co.), Texas 303/H6
Robertson, Wyo. 319/B4
Robertsonville, Québec 172/F3
Robertsport, Liberia 102/A4
Robertsport, Liberia 106/B7
Robertstown, Ga. 217/E1
Robertsville, Conn. 210/C1
Robertsville, Ohio 284/H4
Robertville, New Bruns. 170/E1
Roberval, Québec 162/J6
Roberval, Québec 174/C3
Roberval, Québec 172/E1
Robeson (co.), N.C. 281/L5
Robeson (chan.), N.W.T. 187/M1
Robesonia, Pa. 294/K5
Robichaud, New Bruns. 170/F2
Robinhood, Sask. 181/C2
Robins, Iowa 229/K4
Robins, Ohio 284/H6
Robins A.F.B., Ga. 217/F5
Robinson, Ill. 222/F5
Robinson, Iowa 229/K4
Robinson, Kansas 232/G2
Robinson, Ky. 237/N4
Robinson, N. Dak. 282/L5
Robinson (riv.), North. Terr. 93/E4
Robinson, Pa. 294/D5
Robinson (lake), S.C. 296/G3
Robinson (ranges), W. Australia 92/B4
Robinson Creek, Ky. 237/S6
Robinson Crusoe (isl.), Chile 120/B6
Robinson River, North. Terr. 93/E4
Robinsons, Maine 243/H3
Robinsonville, Miss. 256/D1
Robinsonville, New Bruns. 170/C1
Robinvale, Victoria 97/B4
Robles, Colombia 126/D2
Roblin, Manitoba 179/A3
Roblin, Ontario 177/G3
Roboré, Bolivia 136/F6
Roboré, Bolivia 120/D4
Rob Roy, Ind. 227/C4
Robsart, Sask. 181/B6
Robson, Br. Col. 184/J5
Robson (mt.), Br. Col. 162/D5
Robson (mt.), Br. Col. 184/H3
Robstown, Texas 303/G10
Roby, Mo. 261/H7
Roby, Texas 303/D5
Roca, Nebr. 264/H4
Roca (cape), Portugal 33/B3
Rocafuerte, Ecuador 128/B3
Rocanville, Sask. 181/K5
Roca Partida (isl.), Mexico 150/C7
Roca que Vela (cay), Colombia 126/B8
Rocas (isl.), Brazil 120/F3
Rocas de Santo Domingo, Chile 138/F4
Roccastrada, Italy 34/C3
Rocha (dept.), Uruguay 145/E4
Rocha, Uruguay 145/E5
Rocha (lag.), Uruguay 145/E5
Rochdale, England 13/H2
Rochdale, England 10/G2
Rochdale, Mass. 249/G4
Roche, Switzerland 39/C4
Rochechouart, France 28/D5
Rochefort, Belgium 27/G8
Rochefort, France 28/C4
Roche Harbor, Wash. 310/B2
Rochelle, Ga. 217/F7
Rochelle, Ill. 222/D2
Rochelle, Texas 303/E6
Rochelle, Wyo. 319/H2
Rochelle Park•, N.J. 273/B2
Roche Percé, Sask. 181/J6
Rocheport, Mo. 261/H5
Rocher River, N.W.T. 162/E3
Rocher River, N.W.T. 187/G3
Rochert, Minn. 255/C4
Rochester, Alberta 182/D2
Rochester, England 13/J8
Rochester, England 10/G5
Rochester, Ill. 222/D4
Rochester, Ind. 227/E2
Rochester, Iowa 229/L5
Rochester, Ky. 237/H6
Rochester•, Mass. 249/L6
Rochester, Mich. 250/F6
Rochester, Minn. 188/H2
Rochester, Minn. 255/F6
Rochester, N.H. 268/E5
Rochester, N.Y. 188/L2
Rochester, N.Y. 146/L5
Rochester, N.Y. 276/E4
Rochester, Ohio 284/F3
Rochester, Pa. 294/B4
Rochester, Texas 303/E4
Rochester•, Vt. 268/B4
Rochester, Victoria 97/C5
Rochester, Wash. 310/C4
Rochester, Wis. 317/K3
Rochester Mills, Pa. 294/D4
Rochford, S. Dak. 298/B5
Rochfort Bridge, Alberta 182/C3
Rochon Sands, Alberta 182/D3
Rociada, N. Mex. 274/D3
Rock (creek), Idaho 220/F7
Rock (creek), Ill. 222/D2
Rock (riv.), Ill. 222/C2
Rock (riv.), Iowa 229/A2
Rock, Kansas 232/F4
Rock (lake), Manitoba 179/C5
Rock (creek), Md. 245/K4
Rock, Mass. 249/L5
Rock, Mich. 250/B2
Rock (co.), Minn. 255/B7
Rock (riv.), Minn. 255/B7
Rock (creek), Mont. 262/C4
Rock (co.), Nebr. 264/E2
Rock (creek), Nev. 266/E2
Rock (creek), Oreg. 291/E4
Rock (creek), Oreg. 291/G2
Rock (creek), Oreg. 291/H3
Rock (creek), S. Dak. 298/O6
Rock (creek), Wash. 310/H3
Rock (lake), Wash. 310/H3
Rock (co.), Wis. 317/H10
Rock (riv.), Wis. 317/J9
Rockall (isl.), Scotland 7/C3
Rockaway, N.J. 273/D2
Rockaway, Oreg. 291/C2
Rockaway Beach, Mo. 261/F9
Rock Bluff, Fla. 212/B1
Rockbridge, Ill. 222/C4
Rockbridge, Mo. 261/H9
Rockbridge, Ohio 284/E6
Rockbridge (co.), Va. 307/K5
Rockbridge, Wis. 317/F9
Rockcastle (co.), Ky. 237/N6
Rockcastle (riv.), Ky. 237/N6
Rock Castle, W. Va. 312/C5
Rock Cave, W. Va. 312/F5
Rock City, Ill. 222/D1
Rockcliffe Park, Ontario 177/J2
Rockcorry, Ireland 17/H3
Rock Creek, Br. Col. 184/H6
Rock Creek, Kansas 232/G2
Rock Creek, Minn. 255/F5
Rock Creek, Ohio 284/J2
Rock Creek, Yukon 187/E3
Rockdale (co.), Ga. 217/D3
Rockdale, Ill. 222/E2
Rockdale, N. S. Wales 88/K4
Rockdale, N.S. Wales 97/J4
Rockdale, Texas 303/G7
Rockdale, Wis. 317/J10
Rock Dell, Minn. 255/F7
Rockerville, S. Dak. 298/C6
Rockfall, Conn. 210/E2
Rock Falls, Ill. 222/D2
Rock Falls, Iowa 229/G2
Rock Falls, Wis. 317/C6
Rockfield, Ind. 227/D3
Rockfield, Ky. 237/J7
Rockfield, Wis. 317/L1
Rockfish, N.C. 281/L5
Rockford, Ala. 195/F5
Rockford, Idaho 220/F6
Rockford, Ill. 146/K5
Rockford, Ill. 188/J2
Rockford, Ill. 222/D1
Rockford, Iowa 229/H2
Rockford, Mich. 250/D5
Rockford, Minn. 255/F5
Rockford, N.C. 281/H2
Rockford, Ohio 284/A4
Rockford, Sask. 181/J3
Rockford, Tenn. 237/O9
Rockford, Wash. 310/H3
Rock Forest, Québec 172/F4
Rock Glen, Pa. 294/K4
Rockglen, Sask. 181/F6
Rock Grove, Ill. 222/D1
Rock Hall, Md. 245/O4
Rockham, S. Dak. 298/M4
Rockhampton, Australia 2/S7
Rockhampton, Australia 87/F8
Rockhampton, Queensland 88/H4
Rockhampton, Queensland 95/D4
Rockhampton Downs, North. Terr. 93/D5
Rockhaven, Sask. 181/B3
Rock Hill, Mo. 261/P3
Rock Hill, S.C. 188/K4
Rock Hill, S.C. 296/E2
Rockholds, Ky. 237/N7
Rockingham, Ga. 217/H7
Rockingham (co.), N.H. 268/E5
Rockingham (co.), N.C. 281/K2
Rockingham, N.C. 281/K5
Rockingham•, Vt. 268/B5
Rockingham (co.), Va. 307/L4
Rockingham, W. Australia 88/B2
Rockingham, W. Australia 92/A2
Rock Island, Ill. 188/J2
Rock Island (co.), Ill. 222/C2
Rock Island, Ill. 222/C2
Rock Island, Okla. 288/T4
Rock Island, Québec 172/E4
Rock Island, Tenn. 237/K9
Rock Island, Texas 303/H8
Rock Island, Wash. 310/E3
Rock Island (dam), Wash. 310/E3
Rock Island Arsenal, Ill. 222/C2
Rocklake, N. Dak. 282/M2
Rockland, Conn. 210/E3
Rockland, Del. 245/R1
Rockland, Idaho 220/F7
Rockland, Maine 243/E7
Rockland•, Mass. 249/L4
Rockland, Mich. 250/G1
Rockland (co.), N.Y. 276/M8
Rockland, Ontario 177/J2
Rockland, Texas 303/K6
Rockland, Wis. 317/D8
Rocklands (res.), Victoria 97/B5
Rockledge, Fla. 212/F3
Rockledge, Ga. 217/G6
Rockledge, Pa. 294/M5
Rockleigh, N.J. 273/C1
Rocklin, Calif. 204/B8
Rockmart, Ga. 217/B2
Rock Mills, Ala. 195/H4
Rock Oak, W. Va. 312/J4
Rock Point, Md. 245/L7
Rockport, Ark. 202/E5
Rockport, Calif. 204/B4
Rockport, Ill. 222/B4
Rockport, Ind. 227/C9
Rockport, Ky. 237/H6
Rockport, Maine 243/F7
Rockport•, Maine 243/F7
Rockport•, Mass. 249/M2
Rockport, Miss. 256/D7
Rock Port, Mo. 261/B2
Rockport, Texas 303/H9
Rockport (lake), Utah 304/C3
Rockport, Wash. 310/D2
Rockport, W. Va. 312/C4
Rock Rapids, Iowa 229/A2
Rock River, Wyo. 319/G4
Rock Run, Ala. 195/G2
Rocks, Md. 245/N2
Rocks (pt.), N. Zealand 100/C4
Rock Springs, Mont. 262/K4
Rocksprings, Texas 303/D8
Rock Springs, Wis. 317/F8
Rock Springs, Wyo. 146/H5
Rock Springs, Wyo. 188/E2
Rock Springs, Wyo. 319/C4
Rockstone, Guyana 131/B2
Rockton, Ill. 222/E1
Rockvale, Colo. 208/J6
Rockvale, Mont. 262/H5
Rockvale, Tenn. 237/J9
Rock Valley, Iowa 229/A2
Rockville, Conn. 210/F1
Rockville, Ind. 227/C5
Rockville, Maine 243/E7
Rockville, Md. 245/K4
Rockville, Mass. 249/A8
Rockville, Minn. 255/D5
Rockville, Mo. 261/D6
Rockville, Nebr. 264/F3
Rockville, Nova Scotia 168/B5
Rockville, R.I. 249/G6
Rockville, S.C. 296/G6
Rockville, Utah 304/A6
Rockville, Va. 307/N5
Rockville, Wis. 317/E10
Rockville Centre, N.Y. 276/R7
Rockwall (co.), Texas 303/H5
Rockwall, Texas 303/H5
Rockwell, Iowa 229/G3
Rockwell, N.C. 281/J3
Rockwell City, Iowa 229/D4
Rockwood, Ala. 195/C2
Rockwood, Ill. 222/D6
Rockwood, Maine 243/D4
Rockwood, Mich. 250/F6
Rockwood, Ontario 177/D4
Rockwood, Pa. 294/D6
Rockwood, Tenn. 237/M9
Rockwood, Texas 303/E6
Rocky (mts.) 162/D4
Rocky (mts.) 146/F4
Rocky (mts.) 188/E3
Rocky (mts.), Alberta 182/BC4
Rocky (mts.), Br. Col. 184/F2
Rocky (mts.), Canada 4/D16
Rocky (mts.), Colo. 208/F1
Rocky (mts.), Idaho 220/D1
Rocky (lake), Maine 243/J6
Rocky (mts.), Mont. 262/D4
Rocky (bay), Newf. 166/C3
Rocky (riv.), Newf. 166/D2
Rocky (mts.), N. Mex. 274/C1
Rocky (pt.), Norfolk I. 88/K6
Rocky (riv.), N.C. 281/H4
Rocky (riv.), Ohio 284/G9
Rocky, Okla. 288/J4
Rocky (riv.), S.C. 296/B3
Rocky (cape), Tasmania 99/B2
Rocky (mts.), Wash. 310/H2
Rocky (mts.), Wyo. 319/C1
Rocky (mts.), Yukon 187/F4
Rocky Bottom, S.C. 296/B1
Rocky Boy, Mont. 262/G2
Rocky Boy's Ind. Res., Mont. 262/G2
Rocky Comfort, Mo. 261/D9
Rocky Face, Ga. 217/C1
Rockyford, Alberta 182/D4
Rocky Ford, Colo. 208/M6
Rocky Ford, Ga. 217/J5
Rocky Fork (lake), Ohio 284/D7
Rocky Gap, Va. 307/F6
Rocky Gorge (res.), Md. 245/L4
Rocky Harbour, Newf. 166/C4
Rocky Hill•, Conn. 210/E2
Rocky Hill, Ky. 237/J6
Rocky Hill, N.J. 273/D3
Rocky Lane, Alberta 182/B5
Rocky Mount, Ga. 217/C4
Rocky Mount, La. 238/C1
Rocky Mount, Mo. 261/G6
Rocky Mount, N.C. 188/L3
Rocky Mount, N.C. 281/O3
Rocky Mount, Va. 307/J7
Rocky Mountain Arsenal, Colo. 208/K3
Rocky Mountain House, Alberta 182/C3
Rocky Mountain House, Alta. 162/E5
Rocky Mountain Nat'l Park, Colo. 208/H2
Rocky Point, N.C. 281/O6
Rocky Point, Wash. 310/A2
Rockypoint, Wyo. 319/G1
Rocky Rapids, Alberta 182/C3
Rocky Reach (dam), Wash. 310/E3
Rocky Ridge (mt.), Idaho 220/C3
Rocky Ridge, Ohio 284/D2
Rocky River, Ohio 284/G9
Rodanthe, N.C. 281/U3
Rodarte, N. Mex. 274/D2
Rodas, Cuba 158/E2
Rødby, Denmark 21/E8
Rødby, Denmark 18/G9
Roddickton, Newf. 166/C3
Rødding, Denmark 21/B7
Roddy, Tenn. 237/M9
Rødekro, Denmark 21/C7
Roden, Netherlands 27/J2
Rodeo, Calif. 204/J1
Rodeo, Mexico 150/G4
Rodeo, N. Mex. 274/A7
Roderfield, W. Va. 312/C8
Roderick (isl.), Br. Col. 184/C4
Rodessa, La. 238/B1
Rodez, France 28/E5
Ródhos, Greece 45/J7
Roding (riv.), England 13/J7
Rodinga, North. Terr. 93/D8
Rødkaersbro, Denmark 21/C5
Rodman, Iowa 229/D2
Rodman, N.Y. 276/J3
Rodman, S.C. 296/E2
Rodney, Iowa 229/A4
Rodney, Mich. 250/D5
Rodney, Miss. 256/B7
Rodney, Ontario 177/C5
Rodney Village, Del. 245/R4
Rodrigues, Brazil 132/F10
Rodríguez, Uruguay 145/C5
Rødvig, Denmark 21/F7
Roe, Ark. 202/H4
Roe (riv.), N. Ireland 17/H1
Roebling-Florence, N.J. 273/D3
Roebourne, W. Australia 88/B4
Roebourne, W. Australia 92/B3
Roebuck (bay), W. Australia 88/C3
Roebuck (bay), W. Australia 92/C2
Roebuck Plains, W. Australia 92/C2
Roeland Park, Kansas 232/H2
Roer (riv.), Netherlands 27/J6
Roermond, Netherlands 27/J6
Roeselare, Belgium 27/C7
Roes Welcome (sound), N.W.T. 162/H2
Roes Welcome (sound), N.W.T. 187/K3
Roff, Okla. 288/N5
Rogachev, Belarus 52/D4
Rogagua (lake), Bolivia 136/B3
Rogaguado (lake), Bolivia 136/C3
Rogaland (co.), Norway 18/E7
Rogatica, Bos. 45/D4
Roger Mills (co.), Okla. 288/G3
Rogers, Ark. 202/B1
Rogers, Br. Col. 184/J4
Rogers (lake), Calif. 204/H9
Rogers, Conn. 210/H1
Rogers (lake), Conn. 210/F3
Rogers, La. 238/F3
Rogers, Minn. 255/E5
Rogers, Nebr. 264/H3
Rogers, N. Mex. 274/F5
Rogers, N. Dak. 282/O5
Rogers, Ohio 284/J4
Rogers (co.), Okla. 288/P2
Rogers, Texas 303/G7
Rogers (mt.), Va. 307/E7
Rogers City, Mich. 250/F3
Rogerson, Idaho 220/D7
Rogers Springs, Tenn. 237/D10
Rogersville, Ala. 195/D1
Rogersville, Mo. 261/G8
Rogersville, New Bruns. 170/E2
Rogersville, Pa. 294/B6
Rogersville, Tenn. 237/P8
Roger Williams Nat'l Mem., R.I. 249/J5
Roggen, Colo. 208/L2
Roggwil, Switzerland 39/E2
Rogliano, France 28/B6
Rogozno, Poland 47/C2
Rogue (riv.), Oreg. 291/C5
Rogue River, Oreg. 291/D5
Roha, India 68/C5
Rohnert Park, Calif. 204/C5
Rohnerville, Calif. 204/B3
Rohrbach in Oberösterreich, Austria 41/B2
Rohrersville, Md. 245/H3
Rohri, Pakistan 68/B3
Rohtak, India 68/C5
Rohwer, Ark. 202/H6
Roi Et, Thailand 72/D4
Roja, Latvia 53/B2
Rojas, Argentina 143/F7
Rojo (cape), Mexico 150/L6
Rojo (cape), P. Rico 161/A3
Rojo (cape), P. Rico 156/F1
Rokan (riv.), Indonesia 85/C5
Rokeby, Sask. 181/J4
Rokiškis, Lithuania 53/C2
Rokycany, Czech Rep. 41/B2
Rokytnice nad Jizerou, Czech Rep. 41/C1
Rola Co (lake), China 77/C4
Roland, Ark. 202/E4
Roland, Iowa 229/F4
Roland, Manitoba 179/D5
Roland, Okla. 288/S4
Røldal, Norway 18/E7
Roldán, Argentina 143/F6
Rolecha, Chile 138/D4
Rolesville, N.C. 281/N3
Rolette (co.), N. Dak. 282/L2
Rolette, N. Dak. 282/L2
Roleystone, W. Australia 88/B2
Rolfe, Iowa 229/D3
Roll, Ariz. 198/A6
Rolla, Ark. 202/E5
Rolla, Br. Col. 184/G2
Rolla, Kansas 232/A4
Rolla, Mo. 261/J7
Rolla, N. Dak. 282/L2
Rollag, Minn. 255/B4
Rolle, Switzerland 39/B4
Rollingbay, Wash. 310/A2
Rollingdam, New Bruns. 170/C3
Rolling Fields, Ky. 237/K2
Rolling Fork (riv.), Ky. 237/L5
Rolling Fork, Miss. 256/C5
Rolling Hills, Alberta 182/E4
Rolling Hills, Calif. 204/B11
Rolling Hills, Ky. 237/L1
Rolling Hills Estates, Calif. 204/B11
Rolling Meadows, Ill. 222/A5
Rolling Prairie, Ind. 227/D1
Rollingstone, Minn. 255/G6
Rollins, Mont. 262/B3
Rollo (bay), Pr. Edward I. 168/F2
Rolphton, Ontario 177/G1
Roma, Australia 87/E8
Roma (Rome) (cap.), Italy 34/F6
Roma, Queensland 88/H5
Roma, Queensland 95/D5
Roma, Sweden 18/L8
Romain (cape), S.C. 296/J6
Romaine (riv.), Newf. 166/B3
Romaine (riv.), Que. 162/K5
Romaine, Québec 174/E2
Romaine (riv.), Québec 174/E2
Roma-Los Saenz, Texas 303/E11
Roman, Romania 45/H2
Romance, Ark. 202/F3
Romance, Sask. 181/G3
Romance, W. Va. 312/C5
Romang, Argentina 143/F4
Romang (isl.), Indonesia 85/H7
Romania 2/L3
Romania 7/G4
ROMANIA 45/F3
Romano (cay), Cuba 158/G2
Romano (cay), Cuba 156/C2
Romano (cape), Fla. 212/E6
Romanshorn, Switzerland 39/H1
Romans-sur-Isère, France 28/F5
Romanzof (cape), Alaska 196/E2
Rombauer, Mo. 261/M9
Romblon (prov.), Philippines 82/D4
Romblon, Philippines 82/D4
Romblon (isl.), Philippines 82/D4
Rome, Ga. 188/K4
Rome, Ga. 217/B2
Rome, Ill. 222/D3
Rome, Ind. 227/D9
Rome, Iowa 229/K7
Rome (prov.), Italy 34/F6
Rome (cap.), Italy 7/F4
Rome (cap.), Italy 34/F6
Rome (cap.), Italy 2/K3
Rome•, Maine 243/D6
Rome, Miss. 256/C3
Rome, N.Y. 188/M2
Rome, N.Y. 276/J4
Rome (Stout), Ohio 284/D8
Rome, Ohio 284/J2
Rome, Oreg. 291/K5
Rome, Pa. 294/K2
Rome, Wis. 317/H1
Rome City, Ind. 227/G1
Romeo, Colo. 208/G8
Romeo, Mich. 250/F6
Romeoville, Ill. 222/B6
Romeroville, N. Mex. 274/D3
Romeville, La. 238/L3
Romilly-sur-Seine, France 28/F3
Romney, Ind. 227/D4
Romney, W. Va. 312/J4
Romny, Ukraine 52/D4
Rømø, Denmark 21/B7
Rømø (isl.), Denmark 21/B7
Rømø (isl.), Denmark 18/F9
Romont, Switzerland 39/C3
Romorantin-Lanthenay, France 28/D4
Romsdalsfjorden (fjord), Norway 18/E5
Romsey, England 10/F5
Romsey, England 13/F6
Romulus, Mich. 250/F6
Romulus, N.Y. 276/G5
Ron, Vietnam 72/E3
Ron, Mui (cape), Vietnam 72/E3
Rona (isl.), Scotland 15/B3
Ronald, Wash. 310/E3
Ronan, Mont. 262/C3
Ronay (isl.), Scotland 15/A3
Roncador, Serra do (range), Brazil 132/D5
Roncador (cays), Colombia 126/B9
Ronceverte, W. Va. 312/F7
Ronciglione, Italy 34/C3
Ronda, N.C. 281/H2
Ronda, Spain 33/D4
Rønde, Denmark 21/D5
Ronde (isl.), Grenada 161/D7
Rondeau Prov. Park, Ontario 177/C5
Rondo, Ark. 202/J4
Rondônia (state), Brazil 132/H10
Rondônia, Brazil 132/H10
Rondonópolis, Brazil 120/D4
Rondout (res.), N.Y. 276/M7
Rondu, Pakistan 68/D1
Rong, Koh (isl.), Cambodia 72/D5
Rong'an, China 77/G6
Ronge, Lac La (lake), Sask. 162/F4
Ronge, La (lake), Sask. 181/M3
Rongelap (atoll), Marshall Is. 87/G4
Rongjiang, China 77/G6
Rong Kwang, Thailand 72/D3
Rong Xian, China 77/H7

Saint-Antonin 439

Rumaitha, Iraq 66/D5
Ruman, Venezuela 124/H5
Rumania (Romania) 45
Rumbalara, North. Terr. 93/D8
Rumbek, Sudan 111/E6
Rumbley, Md. 245/P8
Rumburk, Czech Rep. 41/C1
Rumelifeneri, Turkey 63/D5
Rumford, Maine 188/M2
Rumford, Maine 243/B6
Rumford•, Maine 243/B6
Rumford, R.I. 249/J5
Rumford, S. Dak. 298/B7
Rumford Center, Maine 243/B7
Rumford Point, Maine 243/B6
Rumia, Poland 47/D1
Rum Jungle, North. Terr. 88/E2
Rum Jungle, North. Terr. 93/B2
Rumlang, Switzerland 39/G2
Rummerfield, Pa. 294/K2
Rumney•, N.H. 268/D4
Rumney Depot, N.H. 268/D4
Rumoi, Japan 81/K2
Rumphi, Malawi 115/F6
Rumsey, Alberta 182/D4
Rumsey, Ky. 237/G5
Rumson, N.J. 273/F3
Rumuruti, Kenya 115/G3
Runa, W. Va. 312/E6
Runanga, N. Zealand 100/C5
Runaway (cape), N. Zealand 100/G2
Runaway Bay, Jamaica 158/J5
Runcorn, England 10/G2
Runcorn, England 13/G2
Rundu, Namibia 118/B3
Runge, Texas 303/G9
Rungue, Chile 138/G2
Rungwa, Tanzania 115/F5
Rungwa (riv.), Tanzania 115/F5
Rungwe (mt.), Tanzania 115/F5
Runnells, Iowa 229/G5
Runnels (co.), Texas 303/E6
Runnelstown, Miss. 256/F8
Runnemede, N.J. 273/B3
Running Water, S. Dak. 298/N8
Runnymede, Sask. 181/K4
Ruoqiang (Qarkilik), China 77/C4
Rupanco (lake), Chile 138/D3
Rupat (isl.), Indonesia 85/C5
Rupel (riv.), Belgium 27/F7
Rupert, Ga. 217/D6
Rupert, Idaho 220/E7
Rupert (riv.), Québec 174/B2
Rupert•, Vt. 268/A5
Rupert, W. Va. 312/E7
Rupununi (dist.), Guyana 131/B4
Rupununi (riv.), Guyana 131/B4
Rural Hall, N.C. 281/J2
Rural Hill, Miss. 256/F4
Rural Retreat, Va. 307/F7
Rural Valley, Pa. 294/D4
Rurrenabaque, Bolivia 136/B4
Rurutu (isl.), Fr. Poly. 87/L8
Rusagonis, New Bruns. 170/D3
Rusanovo, Russia 52/J1
Rusape, Zimbabwe 118/E3
Rüschegg, Switzerland 39/D3
Ruse, Bulgaria 7/G4
Ruse, Bulgaria 45/H4
Rush, Colo. 208/L5
Rush (creek), Colo. 208/N5
Rush (co.), Ind. 227/G5
Rush, Ireland 10/C4
Rush, Ireland 17/J4
Rush (co.), Kansas 232/C3
Rush, Ky. 237/R4
Rush, N.Y. 276/E5
Rush (lake), N. Dak. 282/N2
Rush (riv.), N. Dak. 282/R5
Rush Center, Kansas 232/C3
Rush City, Minn. 255/F5
Rushden, England 13/G5
Rushden, England 10/F4
Rushford, Minn. 255/G7
Rushford, N.Y. 276/D6
Rush Hill, Mo. 261/J4
Rush Lake, Sask. 181/D5
Rush Lake, Wis. 317/J8
Rushmere, Va. 307/P6
Rushmore, Minn. 255/C7
Rushoon, Newf. 166/D4
Rush River, Minn. 255/D6
Rush Run, Ohio 284/J5
Rush Springs, Okla. 288/L5
Rushsylvania, Ohio 284/C5
Rushville, Ill. 222/C3
Rushville, Ind. 227/G5
Rushville, Mo. 261/B3
Rushville, Nebr. 264/B2
Rushville, N.Y. 276/F5
Rushville, Ohio 284/F6
Rushworth, Victoria 97/C5
Rusk, Ind. 227/D7
Rusk (co.), Texas 303/K5
Rusk, Texas 303/J6
Rusk (co.), Wis. 317/D5
Rusk, Wis. 317/C6
Ruskin, Fla. 212/C3
Ruskin, Nebr. 264/G4
Ruskington, England 13/G4
Ruso, N. Dak. 282/J4
Russas, Brazil 132/G4
Russell (co.), Ala. 195/H6
Russell (lake), Alberta 182/C1
Russell, Ark. 202/G3
Russell, Ga. 217/E3
Russell, Iowa 229/G7
Russell (co.), Kansas 232/D3
Russell, Kansas 232/D3
Russell (co.), Ky. 237/L7
Russell, Ky. 237/R3
Russell, Manitoba 179/A4
Russell•, Mass. 249/C4
Russell, Minn. 255/C6
Russell, Miss. 256/G6
Russell, N.Y. 276/K2
Russell, N. Zealand 100/E1
Russell, N. Dak. 282/J2
Russell (cape), N.W.T. 187/G2
Russell (isl.), N.W.T. 187/J2
Russell (pt.), N.W.T. 187/G2
Russell (county), Ontario 177/J2
Russell, Ontario 177/J2
Russell, Pa. 294/D2
Russell (isls.), Solomon Is. 86/D3
Russell (co.), Va. 307/D7
Russell Cave Nat'l Mon., Ala. 195/G1
Russell Fork (riv.), Va. 307/C5
Russells Point, Ohio 284/C5
Russell Springs, Kansas 232/A3
Russell Springs, Ky. 237/L6
Russellton, Pa. 294/C4
Russellville, Ala. 195/C2
Russellville, Ark. 202/D3
Russellville, Ill. 222/F5
Russellville, Ind. 227/D5
Russellville, Ky. 237/H7
Russellville, Mo. 261/H6
Russellville, Ohio 284/C8
Russellville, S.C. 296/H5
Russellville, Tenn. 237/P8
Russellville, W. Va. 312/E6
Rüsselsheim, Germany 22/C4
Russia 7/H3
RUSSIA 48/D4
RUSSIA 52/F3
Russia 54/L3
Russia 2/L2
Russia 4/C2
Russia, Ohio 284/B5
Russian (riv.), Calif. 204/B4
Russian Mission, Alaska 196/F2
Russiaville, Ind. 227/E4
Russkiy Zavorot (cape), Russia 52/H1
Russum, Miss. 256/B7
Rust, Austria 41/D3
Rustad, Minn. 255/B4
Rustavi, Georgia 52/G6
Rustburg, Va. 307/K6
Rustenburg, S. Africa 118/D5
Ruston, La. 238/E1
Ruston, Wash. 310/C3
Ruswil, Switzerland 39/F2
Rutan, Sask. 181/F3
Rutba, Iraq 59/D3
Rutba, Iraq 66/B4
Rute, Spain 33/D4
Ruteng, Indonesia 85/G7
Ruth, Mich. 250/G5
Ruth, Miss. 256/D8
Ruth, Nev. 266/F3
Ruth, N.C. 281/E4
Rutherford, Ala. 195/H6
Rutherford, N.J. 273/B2
Rutherford (co.), N.C. 281/E4
Rutherford (co.), Tenn. 237/J9
Rutherford, Tenn. 237/C8
Rutherford College, N.C. 281/F3
Rutherford Fork, Obion (riv.), Tenn. 237/D8
Rutherfordton, N.C. 281/E4
Rutherglen, Ontario 177/F1
Rutherglen, Scotland 15/B2
Rutherglen, Scotland 10/B1
Rutherglen, Victoria 97/D5
Ruther Glen, Va. 307/O5
Rutheron, N. Mex. 274/C2
Rüthi, Switzerland 39/J2
Ruthilda, Sask. 181/C4
Ruthin, Wales 10/E4
Ruthin, Wales 13/D4
Ruthsburg, Md. 245/P4
Ruthton, Minn. 255/B6
Ruthven, Iowa 229/D2
Ruthven, Ontario 177/B6
Ruthville, Va. 307/P6
Rüti, Zürich, Switzerland 39/G2
Rüti, Glarus, Switzerland 39/H3
Rutland, Br. Col. 184/H5
Rutland, Ill. 222/D3
Rutland (isl.), India 68/G6
Rutland, Iowa 229/E3
Rutland, Mass. 249/G3
Rutland•, Mass. 249/G3
Rutland, N. Dak. 282/P7
Rutland, Ohio 284/F7
Rutland, Sask. 181/B3
Rutland, S. Dak. 298/P5
Rutland (co.), Vt. 268/A4
Rutland, Vt. 268/B4
Rutland•, Vt. 268/B4
Rutland, Vt. 188/M2
Rutland Plains, Queensland 95/B2
Rutledge, Ala. 195/F7
Rutledge, Ga. 217/E3
Rutledge, Minn. 255/F4
Rutledge, Mo. 261/H2
Rutledge, Pa. 294/M7
Rutledge, Tenn. 237/P8
Rutog, China 77/A5
Rutshuru, D.R. Congo 115/E4
Rutten, Netherlands 27/H3
Ruurlo, Netherlands 27/J4
Ruus al Jibal (dist.), Oman 59/G4
Ruvo di Puglia, Italy 34/F4
Ruvuma (reg.), Tanzania 115/G6
Ruwais, U.A.E. 59/F5
Ruwandiz, Iraq 66/D2
Ruwaq, Jebel er (mts.), Syria 63/G5
Ruwenzori (range), Uganda 115/E3
Ruwenzori (range), D.R. Congo 115/E3
Ruzayevka, Russia 52/F4
Ruzizi (riv.), Burundi 115/E4
Ruzizi (riv.), Rwanda 115/E4
Ruzizi (riv.), D.R. Congo 115/E4
Ružomberok, Slovakia 41/E2
Rwanda 2/L6
Rwanda 102/F5
RWANDA 115/E4
Ry, Denmark 21/C5
Ryan (peak), Idaho 220/D6
Ryan, Iowa 229/K4
Ryan, Okla. 288/L6
Ryan, Loch (inlet), Scotland 15/C5
Ryan Park, Wyo. 319/F4
Ryans (bay), Newf. 166/B2
Ryazan', Russia 7/H3
Ryazan', Russia 48/E4
Ryazan', Russia 52/E4
Ryazhsk, Russia 52/F4
Rybachiy (pen.), Russia 48/D2
Rybachiy (pen.), Russia 52/D1
Rybinsk, Russia 7/H3
Rybinsk, Russia 48/D4
Rybinsk, Russia 52/E3
Rybinsk (res.), Russia 7/H3
Rybinsk (res.), Russia 48/D4
Rybinsk (res.), Russia 52/E3
Rybnik, Poland 47/D3
Rybnitsa, Moldova 52/C5
Rychnov nad Kněžnou, Czech Rep. 41/D1
Rycroft, Alberta 182/A2
Rydal, Ga. 217/C2
Ryde, Calif. 204/B9
Ryde, England 10/F5
Ryde, England 13/F7
Ryde, N.S. Wales 88/K4
Ryde, N.S. Wales 97/J3
Ryder, N. Dak. 282/G4
Ryderwood, Wash. 310/B4
Rye, Ark. 202/F6
Rye, Colo. 208/K7
Rye, England 13/H7
Rye, England 10/G5
Rye (bay), England 13/H7
Rye•, N.H. 268/F5
Rye, N.Y. 276/P6
Rye, Texas 303/K7
Rye Beach, N.H. 268/F6
Ryegate, Mont. 262/G4
Ryegate•, Vt. 268/C3
Rye North Beach, N.H. 268/F5
Rye Patch (res.), Nev. 266/C2
Ryerson, Sask. 181/K6
Rye Valley, Oreg. 291/K3
Ryggebyen, Norway 18/D4
Ryki, Poland 47/F3
Ryland, Ala. 195/F1
Ryland, N.C. 281/R2
Ryland Heights, Ky. 237/M3
Ryley, Alberta 182/D3
Rylstone, N.S. Wales 97/E3
Rýmařov, Czech Rep. 41/D2
Ryomgård, Denmark 21/D5
Ryotsu, Japan 81/J4
Rypin, Poland 47/D2
Rysy (mt.), Poland 47/D4
Ryton, England 13/H3
Ryugasaki, Japan 81/P2
Ryukyu (isls.), Japan 54/O7
Ryukyu (isls.), Japan 2/R4
Ryukyu (isls.), Japan 81/L7
Rzepin, Poland 47/B2
Rzeszów (prov.), Poland 47/F4
Rzeszów, Poland 47/F4
Rzhev, Russia 7/H3
Rzhev, Russia 48/D4
Rzhev, Russia 52/D3

S

Sa'ad, Israel 65/B5
Sa'ada, Yemen 59/D6
Saale (riv.), Germany 22/D3
Saalfeld, Germany 22/D3
Saalfelden am Steinernen Meer, Austria 41/B3
Saane (Sarine) (riv.), Switzerland 39/D3
Saanen, Switzerland 39/D4
Saanich, Br. Col. 184/K3
Saar (riv.), France 28/G3
Saar (riv.), Germany 22/B4
Saarbrücken, Germany 7/E4
Saarbrücken, Germany 22/B4
Saarburg, Germany 22/B4
Saaremaa (isl.), Estonia 7/G3
Saaremaa (isl.), Estonia 48/B4
Saaremaa (isl.), Estonia 52/B3
Saaremaa (isl.), Estonia 53/B1
Saarijärvi, Finland 18/O5
Saarland (state), Germany 22/B4
Saarlouis, Germany 22/B4
Saas, Switzerland 39/J3
Saas Fee, Switzerland 39/E4
Saba (isl.), Neth. Ant. 156/F3
Saba (isl.), Virgin Is. (U.S.) 161/A4
Šabac, Yugoslavia 45/D3
Sabadell, Spain 7/E4
Sabadell, Spain 33/H2
Sabae, Japan 81/H5
Sabah (reg.), Malaysia 54/N9
Sabah (state), Malaysia 2/Q5
Sabah (state), Malaysia 85/F4
Sábalo, Cuba 158/A2
Sabana, Cuba 158/K4
Sabana (arch.), Cuba 158/E1
Sabana de la Mar, Dom. Rep. 156/E3
Sabana de la Mar, Dom. Rep. 158/F5
Sabana Grande, Dom. Rep. 158/E6
Sabanagrande, Honduras 154/D4
Sabana Grande, P. Rico 161/B2
Sabanalarga, Colombia 126/C2
Sabana Seca, P. Rico 161/D1
Sabancuy, Mexico 150/O7
Sabaneta, Dom. Rep. 158/D5
Sabaneta, Barinas, Venezuela 124/D3
Sabaneta, Falcón, Venezuela 124/D2
Sabang, Celebes, Indonesia 85/F5
Sabang, Weh, Indonesia 85/B4
Şabanözü, Turkey 63/E2
Sabará, Brazil 135/E1
Sabattus, Maine 243/C7
Sabattus•, Maine 243/C7
Sabaudia, Italy 34/D4
Sabaya, Bolivia 136/A6
Saberi, Hamun-e (lake), Iran 66/M5
Sabetha, Kansas 232/G2
Sabi (riv.), Zimbabwe 118/E3
Sabile, Latvia 53/B2
Sabillasville, Md. 245/J2
Sabin, Minn. 255/B4
Sabina, Ohio 284/C7
Sabinal (cay), Cuba 158/H2
Sabinal, Texas 303/E8
Sabinas, Mexico 150/J3
Sabinas (riv.), Mexico 150/J3
Sabinas Hidalgo, Mexico 150/J3
Sabine (riv.) 188/H4
Sabine (mt.) 5/B9
Sabine (par.), La. 238/C3
Sabine (lake), La. 238/C7
Sabine (passage), La. 238/C7
Sabine (riv.), La. 238/C5
Sabine (pen.), N.W.T. 187/H2
Sabine (co.), Texas 303/L6
Sabine, Texas 303/L8
Sabine (lake), Texas 303/L8
Sabine (riv.), Texas 303/L7
Sabine Pass, Texas 303/L8
Sabinópolis, Brazil 132/F7
Sabinoso, N. Mex. 274/E3
Sabinov, Slovakia 41/F2
Sabinsville, Pa. 294/G2
Sabir, Jebel (mt.), Yemen 59/D7
Sabirabad, Azerbaijan 52/G6
Sabkha, Syria 63/H5
Sablayan, Philippines 82/C4
Sable (cape), Fla. 188/K5
Sable (cape), Fla. 212/E6
Sable (cape), N.S. 146/M5
Sable (isl.), N.S. 146/N5
Sable (cape), N.S. 162/K7
Sable (isl.), N.S. 162/L7
Sable (cape), Nova Scotia 168/C5
Sable (isl.), Nova Scotia 168/J5
Sable (riv.), Ontario 177/B1
Sable (riv.), Québec 174/D1
Sable River, Nova Scotia 168/C5
Sables (lake), Québec 172/B3
Sables (lake), Québec 172/H1
Sablé-sur-Sarthe, France 28/C4
Sabougla, Miss. 256/F3
Sabra (cape), Indonesia 85/J6
Sabrathaa, Libya 111/B1
Sabrina Coast (reg.) 5/C6
Sabtang, Philippines 82/B2
Sabtang (isl.), Philippines 82/B2
Sabugal, Portugal 33/C2
Sabula, Iowa 229/N4
Sabula, Mo. 261/L8
Sabula, Pa. 294/E3
Sabya, Saudi Arabia 59/D6
Sabzevar, Iran 54/G6
Sabzevar, Iran 59/G2
Sabzevar, Iran 66/K2
Sabzvaran, Iran 66/K6
Sabzvaran, Iran 59/G4
Sac (co.), Iowa 229/C4
Sac (riv.), Mo. 261/E7
Sacaba, Bolivia 136/C5
Sacaca, Bolivia 136/B6
Sacajawea (peak), Oreg. 291/K2
Sacajawea (lake), Wash. 310/G4
Sácama, Colombia 126/D4
Sacandaga (lake), N.Y. 276/L3
Sac and Fox Ind. Res., Iowa 229/H5
Sacapulas, Guatemala 154/B3
Sacaton, Ariz. 198/D5
Sacavém, Portugal 33/A1
Sac City, Iowa 229/C4
Sacedón, Spain 33/E2
Săcele, Romania 45/G3
Sac-Fox-Iowa Ind. Res., Kansas 232/G2
Sacheen (lake), Wash. 310/H2
Sachem (head), Conn. 210/E4
Sachem Head, Conn. 210/E3
Sachigo (riv.), Ont. 162/G5
Sachigo (riv.), Ontario 175/B2
Sachojere, Bolivia 136/C4
Sachse, Texas 303/H2
Sachseln, Switzerland 39/F3
Sachs Harbour, Canada 4/B16
Sachs Harbour, N.W.T. 162/D1
Sachs Harbour, N.W.T. 187/F2
Sackets (harb.), N.Y. 276/H3
Sackets Harbor, N.Y. 276/H3
Säckingen, Germany 22/C5
Sackville, New Bruns. 170/F3
Sackville, Nova Scotia 168/E4
Saco, Ala. 195/G7
Saco, Maine 243/C8
Saco (riv.), Maine 243/B8
Saco, Mo. 261/M8
Saco, Mont. 262/J2
Saco (riv.), N.H. 268/E3
Sacol (isl.), Philippines 82/D7
Sacramento, Brazil 132/D7
Sacramento, Brazil 135/C1
Sacramento (co.), Calif. 204/D5
Sacramento (cap.), Calif. 146/F6
Sacramento (cap.), Calif. 188/B3
Sacramento (cap.), Calif. 204/B8
Sacramento (riv.), Calif. 188/B3
Sacramento (riv.), Calif. 204/D5
Sacramento, Ky. 237/G6
Sacramento, N. Mex. 274/D6
Sacramento (mts.), N. Mex. 274/D6
Sacramento Army Depot, Calif. 204/B8
Sacramento Wash (dry riv.), Ariz. 198/A4
Sacratif (cape), Spain 33/E4
Sacré-Coeur-de-Saguenay, Québec 172/H1
Sacred Heart, Minn. 255/C6
Sacul, Texas 303/K6
Sádaba, Spain 33/F1
Sadani, Tanzania 115/G5
Saddle (hills), Alberta 182/A2
Saddle, Ark. 202/G1
Saddle (mt.), Idaho 220/F6
Saddle (mt.), Idaho 220/D3
Saddle (riv.), N.J. 273/B1
Saddle (mts.), Wash. 310/E4
Saddle Brook•, N.J. 273/B1
Saddle Mountain, Okla. 288/J5
Saddle River, N.J. 273/B1
Saddlestring, Wyo. 319/F1
Saddleworth, England 13/J2
Saddleworth, England 10/G2
Sa Dec, Vietnam 72/E5
Sadhoowa, Trin. & Tob. 161/B11
Sadieville, Ky. 237/M4
Sadij (riv.), Iran 66/L8
Sadiya, India 68/H3
Sa'diya, Iraq 66/D3
Sa'diya, Hor (lake), Iraq 66/E4
Sadlers Village, St. Kitts & Nevis 161/C10
Sadlersville, Tenn. 237/G7
Sado (isl.), Japan 81/J4
Sado (riv.), Portugal 33/B3
Sadon, Burma 72/C1
Sadorus, Ill. 222/E4
Saeby, Denmark 18/G8
Saeby, Denmark 21/D3
Saeendey, Iran 66/E2
Saegertown, Pa. 294/B2
Saetermoen, Norway 18/L2
Safad (Zefat), Israel 65/C2
Safaniya, Ras (cape), Saudi Arabia 59/E4
Šafárikovo, Slovakia 41/F2
Safata (bay), Samoa 86/M9
Safe, Mo. 261/J6
Safety Harbor, Fla. 212/B2
Säffle, Sweden 18/H7
Safford, Ala. 195/D6
Safford, Ariz. 198/F6
Saffordville, Kansas 232/F3
Saffron Walden, England 10/G4
Saffron Walden, England 13/H5
Safi, Jordan 65/E5
Safi, Morocco 102/B1
Safi, Morocco 106/C2
Safidar, Kuh-e (mt.), Iran 59/F4
Safidar, Kuh-e (mt.), Iran 66/H6
Safid Rud (riv.), Iran 66/F2
Safien, Switzerland 39/H3
Safita, Syria 63/G5
Safonovo, Russia 52/D3
Safranbolu, Turkey 63/E2
Safut, Jordan 65/D3
Saga, China 77/B6
Saga (pref.), Japan 81/E7
Saga, Japan 81/E7
Sagadahoc (co.), Maine 243/D7
Sagaing (div.), Burma 72/B1
Sagaing, Burma 72/B2
Sagami (bay), Japan 81/O3
Sagami (riv.), Japan 81/O2
Sagami (sea), Japan 81/J6
Sagamihara, Japan 81/O2
Sagamore, Mass. 249/M5
Sagamore, Pa. 294/D4
Sagamore Hill Nat'l Hist. Site, N.Y. 276/R6
Sagamore Hills, Ohio 284/J10
Saganaga (lake), Minn. 255/H2
Saganaga (lake), Ontario 175/B3
Sagar, India 68/D4
Sagavanirktok (riv.), Alaska 196/J1
Sagay, Camiguin, Philippines 82/E6
Sagay, Negros Occ., Philippines 82/D5
Sage, Ark. 202/G1
Sage (creek), Mont. 262/F2
Sage (mt.), Virgin Is. (U.K.) 161/D4
Sage, Wyo. 319/B4
Sagemace (bay), Manitoba 179/B3
Sagerton, Texas 303/E4
Sageville, Iowa 229/M3
Sag Harbor, N.Y. 276/R8
Saginaw, Ala. 195/E4
Saginaw, Mich. 188/K2
Saginaw (bay), Mich. 188/K2
Saginaw (co.), Mich. 250/E5
Saginaw, Mich. 250/F5
Saginaw (bay), Mich. 250/F5
Saginaw (riv.), Mich. 250/F5
Saginaw, Minn. 255/F4
Saginaw, Mo. 261/C8
Saginaw, Oreg. 291/E4
Saginaw, Texas 303/E2
Sagle, Idaho 220/B1
Saglek (bay), Newf. 166/B2
Saglek (fjord), Newf. 166/B2
Sagnay, Philippines 82/D4
Sagola, Mich. 250/B2
Saguache (co.), Colo. 208/G6
Saguache, Colo. 208/G6
Saguache (creek), Colo. 208/F6
Sagua de Tánamo, Cuba 158/K3
Sagua la Grande, Cuba 156/B2
Sagua la Grande, Cuba 158/E1
Sagua la Grande (riv.), Cuba 158/E1
Saguaro (lake), Ariz. 198/D5
Saguaro Nat'l Mon., Ariz. 198/E6
Saguenay (county), Québec 174/D2
Saguenay (co.), Québec 172/H1
Saguenay (riv.), Québec 174/C3
Saguenay (riv.), Québec 172/G1
Saguia el Hamra (dry riv.), Western Sahara 106/B3
Sagunto, Spain 33/F3
Sa'gya, China 77/C6
Sahagún, Colombia 126/C3
Sahagún, Spain 33/D1
Sahand, Kuh-e (mt.), Iran 66/E2
Sahara (desert) 2/J4
Sahara (des.) 102/C2
Sahara (des.), Algeria 106/E4
Sahara (des.), Chad 111/C3
Sahara (des.), Egypt 111/E3
Sahara (des.), Libya 111/C3
Sahara (des.), Mali 106/D4
Sahara (des.), Mauritania 106/C4
Sahara (des.), Niger 106/F4
Sahara (des.), Sudan 111/E3
Saharan Atlas (ranges), Algeria 106/E2
Saharanpur, India 68/D3
Saharsa, India 68/F3
Şahinli, Turkey 63/C6
Sahiwal, Pakistan 68/C2
Sahiwal, Pakistan 59/K3
Sahuaripa, Mexico 150/E2
Sahuarita, Ariz. 198/E7
Sahuayo de Díaz, Mexico 150/H7
Šahy, Slovakia 41/E2
Saïda, Algeria 106/E2
Saida, Lebanon 63/F6
Sa'idabad, Iran 66/J6
Sa'idabad, Iran 59/G4
Saïdia, Morocco 106/D2
Saidor, Papua N.G. 85/B7
Saidu, Pakistan 68/C2
Saignelégier, Switzerland 39/D2
Saigo, Japan 81/F5
Saigon (Ho Chi Minh City), Vietnam 54/M8
Saigon (Ho Chi Minh City), Vietnam 72/E5
Saihut, Yemen 54/G8
Saihut, Yemen 59/F6
Saikai Nat'l Park, Japan 81/D7
Saiki, Japan 81/E7
Sailes, La. 238/D2
Sailor (creek), Idaho 220/C7
Sailor Springs, Ill. 222/E5
Saimaa (lake), Finland 18/Q6
Saimbeyli, Turkey 63/G4
Sain Alto, Mexico 150/H5
Sain-ni, N. Korea 81/B4
Saint Abbs, Scotland 15/F5
Saint Abbs (head), Scotland 15/F5
Saint-Adalbert, Québec 172/H3
Saint-Adelme, Québec 172/B1
Saint-Adelphe, Québec 172/E3
Saint Adolphe, Manitoba 179/E5
Saint-Adolphe, Québec 172/F2
Saint-Adolphe-d'Howard, Québec 172/C4
Saint-Adrien, Québec 172/F4
Saint-Affrique, France 28/E6
Saint-Agapitville, Québec 172/F3
Saint Agatha•, Maine 243/G1
Saint Agnes, England 13/B7
Saint-Aimé-des-Lacs, Québec 172/G2
Saint-Alban, Québec 172/E3
Saint Albans, England 13/H7
Saint Albans, England 10/F5
Saint Alban's (head), England 13/F7
Saint Albans•, Maine 243/E6
Saint Albans, Mo. 261/L5
Saint Alban's, Newf. 166/C4
Saint Albans, Vt. 268/A2
Saint Albans•, Vt. 268/A2
Saint Albans, W. Va. 312/C6
Saint Albans Bay, Vt. 268/A2
Saint Albert, Alberta 182/D3
Saint Albert, Ontario 177/J2
Saint-Albert, Québec 172/E3
Saint-Alexandre, Québec 172/D4
Saint-Alexandre-de-Kamouraska, Québec 172/H2
Saint-Alexis, Québec 172/D4
Saint-Alexis-de-Matapédia, Québec 172/B2
Saint-Alexis-des-Monts, Québec 172/D3
Saint Almo, New Bruns. 170/C2
Saint Alphonse, Manitoba 179/C5
Saint-Alphonse, Québec 172/D3
Saint Alphonse de Clare, Nova Scotia 168/B4
Saint-Alphonse-de-Caplan, Québec 172/C2
Saint-Amable, Québec 172/J4
Saint-Amand-Mont-Rond, France 28/E4
Saint Amant, La. 238/L2
Saint Ambroise, Manitoba 179/E4
Saint-Ambroise, Québec 172/F1
Saint-Anaclet, Québec 172/J1
Saint-André (cape), Madagascar 118/G3
Saint-André, New Bruns. 170/C1
Saint-André, Québec 172/B2
Saint-André, Réunion 118/G5
Saint-André-Avellin, Québec 172/B4
Saint-André-de-Kamouraska, Québec 172/H2
Saint-André-du-Lac-Saint-Jean, Québec 172/E1
Saint-André-Est, Québec 172/C4
Saint Andrew (pt.), Fla. 212/D6
Saint Andrew (sound), Ga. 217/K9
Saint Andrew (lake), Manitoba 179/E3
Saint Andrew (mt.), St. Vin. & Grens. 161/A9
Saint Andrews, New Bruns. 170/C3
Saint Andrew's, Newf. 166/C4
Saint Andrews, Nova Scotia 168/F3
Saint Andrews (chan.), Nova Scotia 168/H2
Saint Andrews, Scotland 15/F4
Saint Andrews, Scotland 10/E2
Saint Andrews (bay), Scotland 15/F4
Saint Andrews, S.C. 296/G6
Saint Andrews, Tenn. 237/K10
Saint-Anicet, Québec 172/C4
Saint Ann, Mo. 261/O2
Saint Anne, Chan. Is. 13/E8
Saint Anne, Ill. 222/F2
Saint Anns (bay), Nova Scotia 168/H2
Saint Anns, Ontario 177/E4
Saint Ann's Bay, Jamaica 156/C3
Saint Ann's Bay, Jamaica 158/J5
Saint-Anselme, Québec 172/F3
Saint Ansgar, Iowa 229/H2
Saint Anthony, Idaho 220/G6
Saint Anthony, Ind. 227/D8
Saint Anthony, Iowa 229/G4
Saint Anthony, Minn. 255/D5
Saint Anthony, Minn. 255/G5
Saint Anthony, Newf. 166/C3
Saint Anthony, N. Dak. 282/H6
Saint-Antoine, New Bruns. 170/F2
Saint-Antoine, Québec 172/H4
Saint-Antoine-Abbé, Québec 172/D4
Saint-Antoine-sur-Richelieu, Québec 172/D4
Saint-Antonin, Québec 172/H2

Salem Center 441

Saint Joseph, Mo. 261/C3
Saint Joseph, Mo. 188/H3
Saint Joseph, Mo. 146/J6
Saint-Joseph, New Bruns. 170/F3
Saint Joseph (riv.), Ohio 284/A3
Saint Joseph (lake), Ont. 162/G5
Saint Joseph (lake), Ontario 175/B2
Saint-Joseph, Réunion 118/G6
Saint Joseph, Tenn. 237/G10
Saint Joseph, Trin. & Tob. 161/B10
Saint Joseph, Trin. & Tob. 161/B11
Saint-Joseph-de-Beauce, Québec 172/G3
Saint-Joseph-de-Kamouraska, Québec 172/H2
Saint-Joseph-de-la-Rive, Québec 172/G2
Saint-Joseph-de-Madawaska, New Bruns. 170/B1
Saint-Joseph-de-Mékinac, Québec 172/E3
Saint-Joseph-de-Sorel, Québec 172/D3
Saint-Joseph-du-Lac, Québec 172/C4
Saint-Joseph-du-Moine, Nova Scotia 168/G2
Saint Joseph Ridge, Wis. 317/D8
Saint Joseph's, Newf. 166/D2
Saint-Josse-ten-Noode, Belgium 27/C9
Saint-Jovite, Québec 172/C3
Saint-Jude, Québec 172/E4
Saint-Junien, France 28/D5
Saint Just, England 13/B7
Saint-Justin, Québec 172/D3
Saint Kilda, N. Zealand 100/C7
Saint Kilda (isl.), Scotland 15/A2
Saint Kilda, Victoria 88/L7
Saint Kilda, Victoria 97/J5
Saint Kilian, Minn. 255/C7
Saint Kitts (isl.), St. Kitts & Nevis 156/F3
Saint Kitts (isl.), St. Kitts & Nevis 161/D10
SAINT KITTS AND NEVIS 156/F3
SAINT KITTS AND NEVIS 161/D11
Saint-Lambert, Québec 172/J4
Saint Landry (par.), La. 238/F5
Saint Landry, La. 238/F5
Saint Laurent, Manitoba 179/D4
Saint-Laurent, Québec 172/H4
Saint-Laurent-de-la-Salanque, France 28/E6
Saint-Laurent-d'Orléans, Québec 172/G3
Saint-Laurent-du-Maroni, Fr. Guiana 120/D2
Saint-Laurent du Maroni (dist.), Fr. Guiana 131/E4
Saint-Laurent du Maroni, Fr. Guiana 131/E3
Saint Lawrence (gulf) 146/M5
Saint Lawrence (riv.) 162/K6
Saint Lawrence (riv.) 146/L5
Saint Lawrence (isl.), Alaska 146/A3
Saint Lawrence (isl.), Alaska 196/D2
Saint Lawrence, Barbados 161/B9
Saint Lawrence (gulf), Canada 2/G3
Saint Lawrence (riv.), N.Y. 188/N1
Saint Lawrence (gulf), New Bruns. 170/F1
Saint Lawrence, Newf. 166/C4
Saint Lawrence (gulf), Newf. 166/B4
Saint Lawrence (co.), N.Y. 276/K2
Saint Lawrence (lake), N.Y. 276/K1
Saint Lawrence (riv.), N.Y. 276/J2
Saint Lawrence (bay), Nova Scotia 168/H1
Saint Lawrence (cape), Nova Scotia 168/H1
Saint Lawrence (lake), Ontario 177/K3
Saint Lawrence (riv.), Ontario 177/J3
Saint Lawrence (gulf), Pr. Edward I. 168/F2
Saint Lawrence (gulf), Que. 162/K6
Saint Lawrence (gulf), Québec 172/D2
Saint Lawrence (gulf), Québec 174/E3
Saint Lawrence (riv.), Québec 174/D3
Saint Lawrence (riv.), Québec 172/H1
Saint Lawrence, Queensland 95/D4
Saint Lawrence, S. Dak. 298/M4
Saint Lawrence (isl.), U.S. 4/C18
Saint Lawrence Is. Nat'l Park, Ontario 177/J3
Saint Lazare, Manitoba 179/A4
Saint-Lazare, Québec 172/G3
Saint-Léandre, Québec 172/B1
Saint-Léger, Belgium 27/H9
Saint-Légier-La Chiésaz, Switzerland 39/C4
Saint Leo, Fla. 212/D3
Saint Leo, Minn. 255/C6
Saint-Léolin, New Bruns. 170/E1
Saint Leon, Ind. 227/H6
Saint Leon, Manitoba 179/D5
Saint-Léon, Québec 172/D3
Saint Leonard, Md. 245/N7
Saint Leonard, New Bruns. 170/C1
Saint-Léonard, Québec 172/H4
Saint-Léonard-d'Aston, Québec 172/E3
Saint-Léonard-de-Noblat, France 28/D5
Saint-Léonard-de-Portneuf, Québec 172/E3
Saint-Léon-de-Chicoutimi, Québec 172/F1
Saint-Léon-de-Standon, Québec 172/G3
Saint-Léon-le-Grand, Québec 172/B2
Saint Lewis (cape), Newf. 166/C3
Saint Lewis (riv.), Newf. 166/C3
Saint-Liboire, Québec 172/E4
Saint Libory, Ill. 222/D5
Saint Libory, Nebr. 264/F3
Saint Lina, Alberta 182/E2
Saint-Lô, France 28/C3
Saint-Louis, Guadeloupe 161/B7
Saint Louis, Mich. 250/E5
Saint Louis (co.), Minn. 255/F3
Saint Louis (riv.), Minn. 255/F4
Saint Louis (bay), Miss. 256/F10
Saint Louis (co.), Mo. 261/O3
Saint Louis (city county), Mo. 261/P3
Saint Louis, Mo. 261/R3
Saint Louis, Mo. 146/K6
Saint Louis, Mo. 188/H3
Saint Louis, Okla. 288/N4
Saint Louis, Oreg. 291/A3
Saint Louis, Pr. Edward I. 168/D2
Saint-Louis (lake), Québec 172/H4
Saint-Louis, Réunion 118/F5
Saint Louis, Sask. 181/F3
Saint-Louis, Senegal 102/A3
Saint-Louis, Senegal 106/A5
Saint Louis, U.S. 2/E4
Saint Louis (riv.), Wis. 317/A2
Saint Louis Crossing, Ind. 227/F6
Saint-Louis-de-Gonzague, Québec 172/D4
Saint-Louis-de-Kent, New Bruns. 170/F2
Saint-Louis-de-Terrebonne, Québec 172/H4
Saint-Louis-du-Ha! Ha!, Québec 172/H2
Saint-Louis du Nord, Haiti 158/B5
Saint-Louis du Sud, Haiti 158/B6
Saint Louis Park, Minn. 255/G5
Saint Louisville, Ohio 284/F5
Saint-Luc, Québec 172/D4
Saint Lucas, Iowa 229/K2
Saint-Luc-de-Matane, Québec 172/B1
Saint Lucia 2/G5
Saint Lucia 146/M8
SAINT LUCIA 161/G5
SAINT LUCIA 156/G4
Saint Lucia, Queensland 88/K3
Saint Lucia, Queensland 95/D3
Saint Lucia (chan.), St. Lucia 156/G4
Saint Lucia (chan.), St. Lucia 161/G5
Saint Lucia (cape), S. Africa 118/E5
Saint Lucia (lake), S. Africa 118/E5
Saint Lucie (co.), Fla. 212/F4
Saint Lucie, Fla. 212/F4
Saint Lucie (canal), Fla. 212/F4
Saint Lucie (inlet), Fla. 212/F4
Saint-Ludger, Québec 172/G4
Saint Lunaire-Griquet, Newf. 166/C3
Saint-Magloire, Québec 172/G3
Saint Magnus (bay), Scotland 10/G1
Saint Magnus (bay), Scotland 15/F2
Saint-Malachie, Québec 172/G3
Saint-Malo, France 28/B3
Saint-Malo (gulf), France 28/B3
Saint Malo, Manitoba 179/F5
Saint-Malo, Québec 172/F4
Saint-Mandé, France 28/B2
Saint-Marc, Haiti 158/B5
Saint-Marc, Haiti 156/D3
Saint-Marc (chan.), Haiti 158/B6
Saint-Marc (pt.), Haiti 158/B5
Saint-Marc, Québec 172/D4
Saint-Marc-des-Carrières, Québec 172/E3
Saint-Marcel (mt.), Fr. Guiana 131/E4
Saint-Marcel-de-L'Islet, Québec 172/G3
Saint-Marcellin, France 28/F5
Saint Margarets, New Bruns. 170/E2
Saint Margarets (bay), Nova Scotia 168/E4
Saint Margaret's Bay, Jamaica 158/K6
Saint Margaret's Hope, Scotland 15/F2
Saint Margaret Village, Nova Scotia 168/H2
Saint Maries, Idaho 220/B2
Saint Maries (riv.), Idaho 220/B2
Saint Marks, Fla. 212/B1
Saint Marks, Ga. 217/C4
Saint Marks, Manitoba 179/E4
Saint Martin (isl.), Guadeloupe 156/F3
Saint Martin (par.), La. 238/G6
Saint Martin (lake), Manitoba 179/D3
Saint-Martin (cape), Martinique 161/C5
Saint Martin, Md. 245/T7
Saint Martin (bay), Mich. 250/E3
Saint Martin (isl.), Mich. 250/C3
Saint Martin, Minn. 255/D5
Saint Martin (Sint Maarten) (isl.), Neth. Ant. 156/F3
Saint Martin, Ohio 284/C7
Saint-Martin, Switzerland 39/E4
Saint Martin de Restigouche, New Bruns. 170/C1
Saint Martins, Barbados 161/C9
Saint Martin's (isl.), England 13/A8
Saint Martins, Mo. 261/H5
Saint Martins, New Bruns. 170/E3
Saint Martin Station, Manitoba 179/D3
Saint Martinville, La. 238/G6
Saint Mary (res.), Alberta 182/D5
Saint Mary (riv.), Alberta 182/D5
Saint Mary, Ky. 237/L5
Saint Mary (par.), La. 238/H7
Saint Mary, Iowa 229/L7
Saint Mary (lake), Mont. 262/C2
Saint Mary (riv.), Mont. 262/C1
Saint Mary, Nebr. 264/H4
Saint Mary (cape), Nova Scotia 168/B4
Saint Mary (peak), S. Australia 94/F4
Saint Mary-of-the-Woods, Ind. 227/B6
Saint Marys, Alaska 196/F2
Saint Mary's (isl.), England 13/A8
Saint Marys (riv.), Fla. 212/D1
Saint Marys, Ga. 217/J9
Saint Marys (riv.), Ga. 217/J9
Saint Marys, Ind. 227/E1
Saint Marys (lake), Ind. 227/H3
Saint Marys (riv.), Ind. 227/H3
Saint Marys, Iowa 229/F6
Saint Marys, Kansas 232/G2
Saint Marys (co.), Md. 245/M7
Saint Marys (riv.), Md. 245/N8
Saint Marys (riv.), Mich. 250/E2
Saint Marys, Mo. 261/M7
Saint Mary's, Newf. 166/D2
Saint Mary's (bay), Newf. 166/C2
Saint Mary's (cape), Newf. 166/C2
Saint Marys (bay), Nova Scotia 168/B4
Saint Mary's (riv.), Nova Scotia 168/F3
Saint Marys, Ohio 284/B4
Saint Marys (lake), Ohio 284/A4
Saint Marys (riv.), Ohio 284/A4
Saint Mary's, Ontario 177/C4
Saint Marys, Pa. 294/E3
Saint Mary's, Scotland 15/F2
Saint Mary's (lake), Scotland 15/E5
Saint Marys, Tasmania 99/E3
Saint Marys, W. Va. 312/D4
Saint Marys (peak), Wyo. 319/D3
Saint Marys City, Md. 245/N8
Saint Marys Entrance (inlet), Fla. 212/E1
Saint-Mathieu, Québec 172/J1
Saint-Mathieu (lake), Québec 172/J1
Saint Matthew (isl.), Alaska 188/C5
Saint Matthew (isl.), Alaska 146/A4
Saint Matthew (isl.), Alaska 196/D2
Saint Matthew (isl.), U.S. 4/C18
Saint Matthews, Ky. 237/K2
Saint Matthews, S.C. 296/F4
Saint Matthias Group (isls.), Papua N.G. 86/B1
Saint-Maur-des-Fossés, France 28/B2
Saint Maurice, Ind. 227/G6
Saint Maurice, La. 238/E3
Saint-Maurice (co.), Québec 172/D3
Saint-Maurice (county), Québec 174/C3
Saint-Maurice (riv.), Québec 172/E2
Saint-Maurice, Switzerland 39/C4
Saint-Médard, Québec 172/J1
Saint Meinrad, Ind. 227/D8
Saint-Méthode, Québec 172/E1
Saint-Méthode-de-Frontenac, Québec 172/F3
Saint Michael, Alaska 196/F2
Saint Michael, Alberta 182/D3
Saint Michael, Minn. 255/E5
Saint Michael, N. Dak. 282/N4
Saint Michael, Pa. 294/E5
Saint Michaels, Ariz. 198/F3
Saint Michaels, Md. 245/N5
Saint Michaels (bay), Newf. 166/C3
Saint-Michel-de-Bellechasse, Québec 172/G3
Saint-Michel de l'Atalaye, Haiti 158/C5
Saint-Michel-des-Saints, Québec 172/D3
Saint-Michel du Sud, Haiti 158/B6
Saint-Mihiel, France 28/F3
Saint-Modeste, Québec 172/H2
Saint-Moïse, Québec 172/B1
Saint Monance, Scotland 15/F4
Saint Moritz, Switzerland 39/J3
Saint-Narcisse-de-Rimouski, Québec 172/J1
Saint-Nazaire, France 7/D4
Saint-Nazaire, France 28/B4
Saint-Nazaire, Fr. Guiana 131/E3
Saint-Nazaire, Québec 172/E4
Saint-Nazaire-de-Buckland, Québec 172/G3
Saint-Nazaire-de-Chicoutimi, Québec 172/F1
Saint Nazianz, Wis. 317/L7
Saint Neots, England 13/G5
Saint Neots, England 10/F4
Saint-Nérée, Québec 172/G3
Saint-Nicolas, Belgium 27/G7
Saint Niklaus, Switzerland 39/E4
Saint-Noël, Québec 172/B1
Saint-Octave, Québec 172/B1
Saint-Odilon, Québec 172/G3
Saint Olaf, Iowa 229/L3
Saint-Omer, France 28/E2
Saint Omer, Ind. 227/F6
Saint-Omer, Québec 172/C2
Saint-Onésime, Québec 172/H2
Saintonge (trad. prov.), France 29
Saint Onge, S. Dak. 298/B4
Saint-Ouen, France 28/B1
Saint-Ours, Québec 172/D4
Saint-Pacôme, Québec 172/G2
Saint-Pamphile, Québec 172/H3
Saint Paris, Ohio 284/C5
Saint-Pascal, Québec 174/D3
Saint-Pascal, Québec 172/H2
Saint-Patrice-de-Beaurivage, Québec 172/F3
Saint Patrick (lake), Manitoba 179/E3
Saint Patrick, Mo. 261/J2
Saint Patrick (chan.), Nova Scotia 168/G3
Saint Paul (isl.), (Fr.) 2/P7
Saint Paul (isl.), Alaska 196/D3
Saint Paul, Alberta 182/E3
Saint Paul, Alta. 162/E5
Saint Paul, Ark. 202/C2
Saint Paul (cape), Ghana 106/E7
Saint Paul, Ind. 227/F6
Saint Paul, Iowa 229/L7
Saint Paul, Kansas 232/G4
Saint Paul (cap.), Minn. 188/H1
Saint Paul (cap.), Minn. 146/J5
Saint Paul (cap.), Minn. 255/G6
Saint Paul, Mo. 261/L5
Saint Paul, Nebr. 264/F3
Saint-Paul, New Bruns. 170/E2
Saint Paul (riv.), Newf. 166/C3
Saint Paul (isl.), Nova Scotia 168/H1
Saint Paul, Oreg. 291/A3
Saint-Paul, Québec 172/E4
Saint Paul (riv.), Québec 174/F2
Saint Paul, S.C. 296/G4
Saint Paul, Texas 303/H1
Saint Paul, Va. 307/D7
Saint-Paul-de-Montminy, Québec 172/G3
Saint-Paul-du-Nord, Québec 172/H1
Saint-Paulin, Québec 172/D3
Saint Paul Island, Alaska 196/D3
Saint-Paul-l'Ermite, Québec 172/J4
Saint Paul Park, Minn. 255/G6
Saint Paul's, Newf. 166/C4
Saint Pauls, N.C. 281/M5
Saint Peter, Ill. 222/E5
Saint Peter, Ind. 227/H6
Saint Peter, Kansas 232/C2
Saint Peter, Minn. 255/E6
Saint Peter Port (cap.), Guernsey, Chan. Is. 13/E8
Saint Peter Port (cap.), Guernsey, Chan. Is. 10/E6
Saint Peters, Mo. 261/M1
Saint Peters, Nova Scotia 168/H3
Saint Peters (bay), Nova Scotia 168/H3
Saint Peters, Pr. Edward I. 168/F2
Saint Peters (bay), Pr. Edward I. 168/F2
Saint Peters (isl.), Pr. Edward I. 168/E2
Saint Peters, S. Australia 88/E8
Saint Petersburg, Fla. 188/K5
Saint Petersburg, Fla. 146/K7
Saint Petersburg, Fla. 212/B3
Saint Petersburg, Pa. 294/C3
St. Petersburg, Russia 2/L3
St. Petersburg, Russia 7/H3
St. Petersburg, Russia 48/D4
St. Petersburg, Russia 52/C3
Saint Petersburg Beach, Fla. 212/B3
Saint-Petronille, Québec 172/J3
Saint-Philémon, Québec 172/G3
Saint Philip, Ind. 227/B9
Saint-Philippe-de-Laprairie, Québec 172/J4
Saint-Philippe-de-Néri, Québec 172/H2
Saint Philips, Sask. 181/K4
Saint Phillips, Mont. 262/M4
Saint Phillips, Newf. 166/D2
Saint-Pie, Québec 172/E4
Saint-Pierre, Martinique 161/C6
Saint-Pierre, Martinique 156/G4
Saint-Pierre (bay), Martinique 161/C6
Saint-Pierre, Île-de-Mont., Québec 172/H4
Saint-Pierre, Joliette, Québec 172/D3
Saint-Pierre (lake), Québec 172/E3
Saint-Pierre (pt.), Québec 172/D1
Saint-Pierre, Réunion 118/F6
Saint-Pierre (cap.), Saint Pierre & Miquelon 166/C4
Saint-Pierre (isl.), Saint-Pierre & Miquelon 166/C4
SAINT PIERRE AND MIQUELON 166/C4
Saint Pierre & Miquelon (isls.) (Fr.) 162/L6
Saint Pierre and Miquelon (isls.) (Fr.) 146/N5
Saint-Pierre-Baptiste, Québec 172/F3
Saint-Pierre-de-Broughton, Québec 172/F3
Saint-Pierre-d'Orléans, Québec 172/G3
Saint-Pierre-Jolys, Manitoba 179/F5
Saint-Pierre-Montmagny, Québec 172/G3
Saint-Placide, Québec 172/C4
Saint-Pol-de-Léon, France 28/A3
Saint-Pol-sur-Ternoise, France 28/E2
Saint-Polycarpe, Québec 172/C4
Saint-Pons, France 28/E6
Saint-Prex, Switzerland 39/B4
Saint-Prime, Québec 172/E1
Saint-Prosper-de-Dorchester, Québec 172/G3
Saint-Quentin, France 28/E3
Saint Quentin, New Bruns. 170/C1
Saint-Raphaël, France 28/G6
Saint-Raphaël, Haiti 158/C5
Saint-Raphaël, Québec 172/G3
Saint-Raphaël-sur-Mer, New Bruns. 170/F1
Saint-Raymond, Québec 172/F3
Saint-Rédempteur, Québec 172/J3
Saint Regis, Mont. 262/A3
Saint Regis (riv.), N.Y. 276/L1
Saint-Régis, Québec 172/C4
Saint Regis Falls, N.Y. 276/M1
Saint Regis Ind. Res., N.Y. 276/M1
Saint Regis Park, Ky. 237/K2
Saint-Rémi, Québec 172/D4
Saint-Rémi-d'Amherst, Québec 172/C3
Saint-Rémi-de-Tingwick, Québec 172/F4
Saint-René-de-Matane, Québec 172/B1
Saint Robert, Mo. 261/H7
Saint-Roch-de-l'Achigan, Québec 172/D4
Saint-Roch-de-Mékinac, Québec 172/E3
Saint-Roch-de-Richelieu, Québec 172/D4
Saint-Romain, Québec 172/F4
Saint-Romuald-d'Etchemin, Québec 172/J3
Saint Rosa, Minn. 255/D5
Saint Rose, Ill. 222/D5
Saint Rose, La. 238/N4
Saint Sampson's, Chan. Is. 13/E8
Saints-Anges, Québec 172/G3
Saint Sauveur, New Bruns. 170/E1
Saint-Sauveur-des-Monts, Québec 172/C4
Saint-Sébastien (cape), Madagascar 118/H2
Saint-Sébastien, Frontenac, Québec 172/G4
Saint-Sébastien, Iberville, Québec 172/D4
Saint-Sever, France 28/C6
Saint-Séverin-de-Beaurivage, Québec 172/G3
Saint Shotts, Newf. 166/D2
Saint-Siméon, Québec 172/G2
Saint-Siméon-de-Bonaventure, Québec 172/C2
Saint-Simon, Québec 172/H1
Saint-Simon-de-Bagot, Québec 172/E4
Saint Simons, Ga. 217/K8
Saint Simons Island, Ga. 217/K8
Saint-Stanislas, Québec 172/E3
Saint Stephan, Switzerland 39/D3
Saint Stephen, Minn. 255/D5
Saint Stephen, N. Bruns. 162/K6
Saint Stephen, New Bruns. 170/C3
Saint Stephen, S.C. 296/H5
Saint Stephen-in-Brannel, England 13/B7
Saint Stephens, Ala. 195/B7
Saint Stephens, Wyo. 319/D3
Saint Stephens Church, Va. 307/O5
Saint-Sylvère, Québec 172/E3
Saint-Sylvestre, Québec 172/F3
Saint Tammany (par.), La. 238/L6
Saint Tammany, La. 238/L6
Saint Teresa, Fla. 212/B2
Saint-Théodore, Québec 172/D3
Saint-Théodore-d'Acton, Québec 172/E4
Saint-Théophile, Québec 172/G4
Saint Theresa Point, Manitoba 179/J3
Saint Thomas, Mo. 261/H6
Saint Thomas, N. Dak. 282/R2
Saint Thomas, Ontario 177/C5
Saint Thomas, Pa. 294/G6
Saint Thomas (harb.), Virgin Is. (U.S.) 161/B4
Saint Thomas (isl.), Virgin Is. (U.S.) 156/G1
Saint Thomas (isl.), Virgin Is. (U.S.) 161/A4
Saint-Thomas-de-Joliette, Québec 172/D3
Saint-Thuribe, Québec 172/E3
Saint-Timothée, Québec 172/D4
Saint-Tite, Québec 172/E3
Saint-Tite-des-Caps, Québec 172/G2
Saint-Trond (Sint-Truiden), Belgium 27/G7
Saint-Tropez, France 28/G6
Saint-Ubald, Québec 172/E3
Saint-Ulric, Québec 172/B1
Saint-Urbain-de-Charlevoix, Québec 172/G2
Saint-Ursanne, Switzerland 39/D2
Saint-Valentin, Québec 172/D4
Saint-Valère-de-Bulstrode, Québec 172/E3
Saint-Valérien, Québec 172/E4
Saint-Valérien-de-Rimouski, Québec 172/J1
Saint-Valéry-sur-Somme, France 28/D2
Saint-Vallier, France 28/F5
Saint-Vallier, Québec 172/G3
Saint-Victor, Québec 172/G3
Saint Victor, Sask. 181/F6
Saint Victor Petroglypths Hist. Park, Sask. 181/E6
Saint Vincent, Alberta 182/E2
Saint Vincent (isl.), Fla. 212/D7
Saint Vincent, Italy 34/A2
Saint Vincent, Minn. 255/A2
Saint Vincent (São Vincente) (cape), Portugal 33/B4
Saint Vincent (chan.), St. Lucia 161/G7
Saint Vincent (isl.), St. Vin. & Grens. 156/G4
Saint Vincent (passage), St. Vin. & Grens. 156/G4
Saint Vincent (passage), St. Vin. & Grens. 161/A8
Saint Vincent (gulf), S. Australia 88/D8
Saint Vincent (gulf), S. Australia 94/F6
Saint Vincent (cape), Tasmania 99/B5
Saint Vincent and The Grenadines 2/F5
Saint Vincent and The Grenadines 146/M8
SAINT VINCENT AND THE GRENADINES 156/G4
SAINT VINCENT AND THE GRENADINES 161/A8
Saint Vincent's, Newf. 166/D2
Saint-Vith (Sankt Vith), Belgium 27/J8
Saint Vrain, N. Mex. 274/F4
Saint Walburg, Sask. 162/F5
Saint Walburg, Sask. 181/B2
Saint-Wenceslas, Québec 172/E3
Saint Wendel, Ind. 227/B8
Saint Wilfred, New Bruns. 170/E1
Saint Williams, Ontario 177/D5
Saint Xavier, Mont. 262/J5
Saint-Yrieix-la-Perche, France 28/D5
Saint-Yvon, Québec 172/D1
Saint-Zacharie, Québec 172/G3
Saint-Zénon, Québec 172/D3
Saint-Zéphirin, Québec 172/E3
Saint-Zotique, Québec 172/C4
Saio (Dembidollo), Ethiopia 111/F6
Saipan (cap.), No. Marianas 87/E4
Saipina, Bolivia 136/C6
Saitama (pref.), Japan 81/O2
Saito, Japan 81/E7
Sajama, Bolivia 136/A6
Sajama, Nevada (mt.), Bolivia 136/A6
Sajó (riv.), Hungary 41/F2
Sajószentpéter, Hungary 41/F2
Sak (riv.), S. Africa 118/C6
Sakado, Japan 81/O2
Sakai, Ibaraki, Japan 81/P1
Sakai, Osaka, Japan 81/J8
Sakaide, Japan 81/G6
Sakaiminato, Japan 81/F6
Sakaka, Saudi Arabia 59/D4
Sakakawea (lake), N. Dak. 146/H5
Sakakawea (lake), N. Dak. 188/F1
Sakakawea (lake), N. Dak. 282/G5
Sakami (lake), Québec 174/B2
Sakami (riv.), Québec 174/B2
Sakania, D.R. Congo 115/E6
Sakarya (prov.), Turkey 63/D2
Sakarya (Adapazarî), Turkey 63/D2
Sakarya (riv.), Turkey 59/B1
Sakarya (riv.), Turkey 63/D2
Sakata, Japan 81/J4
Sakhalin (gulf), Russia 48/P4
Sakhalin (isl.), Russia 2/S3
Sakhalin (isl.), Russia 48/P4
Sakhalin (isl.), Russia 54/R4
Sakhar, Afghanistan 68/B2
Sakhar, Afghanistan 59/J3
Sakht-Sar, Iran 66/G2
Sakhnin, Israel 65/C2
Saki, Ukraine 52/D5
Šakiai, Lithuania 53/B3
Sakishima (isls.) Japan 54/O7
Sakishima (isls.), Japan 81/K7
Sakon Nakhon, Thailand 72/E3
Sakonnet (pt.), R.I. 249/K7
Sakonnet (riv.), R.I. 249/K6
Sakrivier, S. Africa 118/C6
Saksaul'skiy, Kazakhstan 48/F5
Sakskøbing, Denmark 21/E8
Saku, Japan 81/J5
Sakurai, Japan 81/J8
Sakwatamau (riv.), Alberta 182/C2
Sal (isl.), C. Verde 106/B7
Šal'a, Slovakia 41/D2
Sala, Sweden 18/K7
Salabangka (isls.), Indonesia 85/G6
Salacgrīva, Latvia 53/C2
Sala Consilina, Italy 34/E4
Saladas, Argentina 143/E2
Saladillo, Argentina 143/G7
Saladillo (riv.), Argentina 143/D2
Saladillo, Bolivia 136/D7
Salado (riv.), Argentina 120/C6
Salado (riv.), Argentina 143/H7
Salado (riv.), Argentina 143/C4
Salado, Ark. 202/G2
Salado, Chile 138/A6
Salado, Quebrado del (riv.), Chile 138/B6
Salado, Cuba 158/H3
Salado, Honduras 154/D3
Salado del Norte (riv.), Argentina 120/C5
Salado del Norte (riv.), Argentina 143/D2
Salaga, Ghana 106/D7
Salahuddin (gov.), Iraq 66/C3
Sala'ilua, Samoa 86/L8
Salala, Oman 59/F6
Salala, Oman 54/G8
Salamá, Guatemala 154/B3
Salamanca, Chile 138/A9
Salamanca, Mexico 150/J6
Salamanca, N.Y. 276/C6
Salamanca (prov.), Spain 33/C2
Salamanca, Spain 33/D2
Salamanca, Spain 7/D4
Salamat, Bahr (riv.), Chad 111/C6
Salamina, Colombia 126/C5
Salamis, Greece 45/F6
Salamonia, Ind. 227/H4
Salamonie (lake), Ind. 227/F3
Salamonie (riv.), Ind. 227/G4
Salas, Spain 33/C1
Salas de los Infantes, Spain 33/E2
Salatiga, Indonesia 85/J2
Salavat, Russia 7/K3
Salavat, Russia 52/H4
Salaverry, Peru 128/C7
Salawati (isl.), Indonesia 85/J6
Salay, Philippines 82/E6
Sala y Gómez (isl.), Chile 2/D7
Sala y Gómez (isl.), Chile 87/P8
Salazar, Colombia 126/D4
Salcantay (mt.), Peru 128/F9
Salcedo (prov.), Dom. Rep. 158/E5
Salcedo, Dom. Rep. 158/E5
Salcombe, England 13/D7
Salcombe, England 10/D5
Saldaña (riv.), Colombia 126/C6
Saldaña, Spain 33/D1
Saldanha, S. Africa 118/B6
Saldee, Ky. 237/P6
Saldus, Latvia 53/B2
Sale, England 13/H2
Sale (riv.), Manitoba 179/E5
Salé, Morocco 106/C2
Sale, Victoria 88/H7
Sale, Victoria 97/D6
Sale City, Ga. 217/D8
Sale Creek, Tenn. 237/L10
Salée (riv.), Guadeloupe 161/A6
Salekhard, Russia 2/N2
Salekhard, Russia 4/C6
Salekhard, Russia 48/G3
Salekhard, Russia 54/H3
Salem, Ala. 195/H5
Salem, Ark. 202/G1
Salem•, Conn. 210/F3
Salem, Fla. 212/C2
Salem, Ill. 222/E5
Salem, India 54/J8
Salem, India 68/D6
Salem, Ind. 227/E7
Salem, Ind. 227/H3
Salem, Iowa 229/K7
Salem, Ky. 237/E6
Salem, Maine 243/C6
Salem, Md. 245/P7
Salem, Mass. 249/E5
Salem, Mich. 250/F6
Salem, Mo. 261/J7
Salem, Nebr. 264/J4
Salem•, N.H. 268/E6
Salem (co.), N.J. 273/C4
Salem, N.J. 273/C4
Salem (riv.), N.J. 273/C4
Salem, N. Mex. 274/B6
Salem, N.Y. 276/O4
Salem, Ohio 284/J4
Salem, Ontario 177/D4
Salem (cap.), Oreg. 146/F5
Salem (cap.), Oreg. 188/B1
Salem (cap.), Oreg. 291/A3
Salem, S.C. 296/A2
Salem, S. Dak. 298/P6
Salem, Utah 304/C3
Salem (lake), Vt. 268/C2
Salem (I.C.), Va. 307/H6
Salem, W. Va. 312/E4
Salemburg, N.C. 281/N4
Salem Center, Ind. 227/G1

Santa Bárbara 443

Sandy (isls.), Manitoba 179/D2
Sandy (creek), Mont. 262/F2
Sandy (lake), Newf. 166/C4
Sandy (lake), Ont. 162/G5
Sandy (lake), Ontario 175/B2
Sandy, Oreg. 291/E2
Sandy, Pa. 294/E3
Sandy (cape), Queensland 88/J4
Sandy (cape), Queensland 95/E5
Sandy (pt.), R.I. 249/H8
Sandy (pt.), S.C. 296/H6
Sandy (riv.), S.C. 296/E2
Sandy (cape), Tasmania 99/A3
Sandy, Utah 304/C3
Sandy (pt.), Virgin Is. (U.S.) 161/D4
Sandy Bay, Jamaica 158/G5
Sandy Bay, Nicaragua 154/F3
Sandy Bay, Sask. 181/N3
Sandy Beach, Alberta 182/C3
Sandy Beach, Sask. 181/H5
Sandy Cove, Nova Scotia 168/B4
Sandy Creek, Maine 243/B7
Sandy Creek, N.Y. 276/H3
Sandy Hook, Conn. 210/B3
Sandy Hook, Ky. 237/P4
Sandy Hook, Manitoba 179/E4
Sandy Hook, Miss. 256/E8
Sandy Hook (spit), N.J. 273/F3
Sandy Hook, Va. 307/M5
Sandy Lake, Alberta 182/D2
Sandy Lake, Manitoba 179/B4
Sandy Lake, Pa. 294/B3
Sandy Point, Maine 243/F7
Sandy Point, Nova Scotia 168/C5
Sandy Point, St. Kitts & Nevis 161/C10
Sandy Ridge, Ala. 195/E6
Sandy Ridge, N.C. 281/J1
Sandy Ridge, Pa. 294/F4
Sandy Spring-Ashton, Md. 245/K4
Sandy Springs, Ga. 217/K1
Sandy Springs, S.C. 296/B2
Sandyville, Iowa 229/G6
Sandyville, Ohio 284/H4
Sandyville, W. Va. 312/C5
San Elizario, Texas 303/A10
San Estanislao, Paraguay 144/D4
San Esteban (gulf), Chile 138/D7
San Esteban, Honduras 154/D3
San Esteban de Gormaz, Spain 33/E2
San Felipe, Chile 138/G2
San Felipe, Colombia 126/G7
San Felipe (cays), Cuba 156/A2
San Felipe (cays), Cuba 158/B2
San Felipe, Guatemala 154/B3
San Felipe, Baja California, Mexico 150/B1
San Felipe, Guanajuato, Mexico 150/J6
San Felipe, Philippines 82/B3
San Felipe, Yaracuy, Venezuela 124/D2
San Felipe, Zulia, Venezuela 124/B3
San Felipe Pueblo, N. Mex. 274/C3
San Feliu de Guíxols, Spain 33/H2
San Félix, Chile 138/A7
San Félix (isl.), Chile 120/A5
San Félix, Panama 154/G6
San Félix, Venezuela 124/C2
San Fernando, Argentina 143/G7
San Fernando (riv.), Bolivia 136/F5
San Fernando, Calif. 204/C10
San Fernando, Chile 138/G6
San Fernando, Tamaulipas, Mexico 150/L4
San Fernando, La Union, Philippines 82/C2
San Fernando, Masbate, Philippines 82/D4
San Fernando, Pampanga, Philippines 82/C3
San Fernando, Spain 33/C4
San Fernando, Trin. & Tob. 161/A11
San Fernando, Trin. & Tob. 156/G5
San Fernando, Venezuela 120/C2
San Fernando de Apure, Venezuela 124/E4
San Fernando de Atabapo, Venezuela 124/E5
San Fidel, N. Mex. 274/B3
Sanford, Ala. 195/F8
Sanford (mt.), Alaska 196/K2
Sanford, Colo. 208/H8
Sanford, Fla. 188/K5
Sanford, Fla. 212/E3
Sanford, Maine 243/B9
Sanford•, Maine 243/B9
Sanford, Manitoba 179/E5
Sanford, Mich. 250/E5
Sanford, Miss. 256/F8
Sanford, N.C. 281/L4
Sanford, Nova Scotia 168/B5
San Francique, Trin. & Tob. 161/A11
San Francisco, Argentina 120/C6
San Francisco, San Luis, Argentina 143/C3
San Francisco, Córdoba, Argentina 143/D3
San Francisco (riv.), Ariz. 198/F5
San Francisco, Bolivia 136/C4
San Francisco (city county), Calif. 204/J2
San Francisco, Calif. 146/F6
San Francisco, Calif. 188/B3
San Francisco, Calif. 204/H2
San Francisco (bay), Calif. 204/J2
San Francisco, Colombia 126/B7
San Francisco (cape), Ecuador 128/B2
San Francisco, Honduras 154/D3
San Francisco (riv.), N. Mex. 274/A5
San Francisco, Nicaragua 154/E5
San Francisco, Panama 154/G6
San Francisco (creek), Texas 303/B8
San Francisco, U.S. 2/C4
San Francisco, Lara, Venezuela 124/C2
San Francisco de la Paz, Honduras 154/D3
San Francisco del Chañar, Argentina 143/C2
San Francisco del Oro, Mexico 150/F3
San Francisco del Rincón, Mexico 150/H6
San Francisco de Macorís, Dom. Rep. 158/E5
San Francisco de Macorís, Dom. Rep. 156/E3
San Francisco de Mostazal, Chile 138/G4
San Francisco Gotera, El Salvador 154/C4
Sanga (riv.), Cameroon 115/C3
Sanga (riv.), Cent. Afr. Rep. 115/C3
San Gabriel, Calif. 204/C10
San Gabriel (res.), Calif. 204/D10
San Gabriel, Ecuador 128/D2
San Gabriel Chilac, Mexico 150/K7
San Gallán (isl.), Peru 128/D9
Sangamner, India 68/C5
Sangamon (co.), Ill. 222/D4
Sangamon (riv.), Ill. 222/C3
Sangan, Iran /M3
Sangar, Russia 48/N3
Sangar, Russia 54/O3
Sangaredyi, Guinea 106/B6
Sangay (mt.), Ecuador 128/C4
Sangeang (isl.), Indonesia 85/F7
San Genaro, Argentina 143/F6
Sanger, Calif. 204/F7
Sanger, N. Dak. 282/H5
Sanger, Texas 303/G4
Sangerhausen, Germany 22/D3
San Germán, Cuba 158/J3
San Germán, P. Rico 161/A2
San Germán, P. Rico 156/F1
Sangerville•, Maine 243/E5
Sangestan, Kuh-e (mt.), Iran 66/H5
Sanggabuwana (mt.), Indonesia 85/G2
Sanggau, Indonesia 85/E5
Sangha (riv.), Congo 115/C3
Sangihe (isls.), Indonesia 54/O9
Sangihe (isl.), Indonesia 85/H5
Sangihe (isls.), Indonesia 85/G5
San Gil, Colombia 126/D4
San Giovanni in Fiore, Italy 34/F5
San Giovanni in Persiceto, Italy 34/C2
San Giuliano Terme, Italy 34/C3
Sangju, S. Korea 81/D5
Sangkulirang, Indonesia 85/F5
Sangli, India 68/C5
Sangmélima, Cameroon 115/B3
Sangolquí, Ecuador 128/C3
Sangre de Cristo (mts.), Colo. 208/H6
Sangre de Cristo (mts.), N. Mex. 274/D3
San Gregorio, Calif. 204/J3
San Gregorio, San José, Uruguay 145/C4
San Gregorio, Tacuarembó, Uruguay 145/D3
Sangre Grande, Trin. & Tob. 161/B10
Sangre Grande, Trin. & Tob. 156/G5
Sangri, China 77/D6
Sangro (riv.), Italy 34/E4
Sangudo, Alberta 182/C3
Sangue (riv.), Brazil 132/B6
Sangüesa, Spain 33/F1
Sanhe, China 77/K1
Sanibel, Fla. 212/D5
Sanibel (isl.), Fla. 212/D5
San Ignacio, Argentina 143/E2
San Ignacio, Belize 154/C2
San Ignacio, El Beni, Bolivia 136/C4
San Ignacio, Santa Cruz, Bolivia 136/E5
San Ignacio, Chile 138/E1
San Ignacio, C. Rica 154/E6
San Ignacio, Baja California Sur, Mexico 150/C3
San Ignacio, Sinaloa, Mexico 150/F5
San Ignacio, Paraguay 144/D5
San Ignacio, Venezuela 124/B2
Sanilac (co.), Mich. 250/G5
San Ildefonso, N. Mex. 274/C3
San Ildefonso (cape), Philippines 82/D2
San Ildefonso, Spain 33/E2
San'in Kaigan National Park, Japan 81/G6
San Isabel, Colo. 208/K7
Sanish, N. Dak. 282/E4
San Isidro, Argentina 143/C2
San Isidro, Philippines 82/E5
Saniya, Hor (lake), Iraq 66/E5
San Jacinto, Calif. 204/H10
San Jacinto, Colombia 126/C3
San Jacinto, Nev. 266/G1
San Jacinto, Philippines 82/D4
San Jacinto (co.), Texas 303/J7
San Jacinto, Uruguay 145/C6
San Jaime de la frontera, Argentina 143/G5
San Javier, Río Negro, Argentina 143/D5
San Javier, Santa Fe, Argentina 143/F5
San Javier, Santa Cruz, Bolivia 136/D5
San Javier, El Beni, Bolivia 136/C4
San Javier, Chile 138/A11
San Javier, Uruguay 145/A3
San Jerónimo de Juárez, Mexico 150/J8
Sanjo, Japan 81/J5
San Joaquín, Bolivia 136/C3
San Joaquin (riv.), Calif. 188/C3
San Joaquin (co.), Calif. 204/D6
San Joaquin, Calif. 204/E7
San Joaquin (riv.), Calif. 204/E6
San Joaquin (valley), Calif. 204/D6
San Joaquín, Paraguay 144/E4
San Jon, N. Mex. 274/F3
San Jorge (gulf), Argentina 120/C7
San Jorge (gulf), Argentina 143/C6
San Jorge (riv.), Colombia 126/C3
San Jorge (bay), Mexico 150/C1
San Jorge, Nicaragua 154/E5
San Jorge (gulf), Spain 33/G2
San José, Belize 154/C2
San Jose, Calif. 146/F6
San Jose, Calif. 188/B3
San Jose, Calif. 204/L3
San José, Colombia 126/F6
San José (cap.), C. Rica 146/K9
San José (cap.), C. Rica 154/F5
San José, Guatemala 154/B4
San Jose, Ill. 222/D3
San José (isl.), Mexico 150/D4
San Jose, N. Mex. 274/D3
San Jose (riv.), N. Mex. 274/B3
San José (isl.), Panama 154/H6
San José, Paraguay 144/B5
San José, Peru 128/B6
San Jose, Philippines 85/G3
San Jose, Nueva Ecija, Philippines 82/C3
San Jose, Occ. Mindoro, Philippines 82/C4
San José (lag.), P. Rico 161/E1
San Jose (isl.), Texas 303/H9
San José (dept.), Uruguay 145/C5
San José (riv.), Uruguay 145/C4
San José, Amazonas, Venezuela 124/E5
San José, Zulia, Venezuela 124/B3
San José de Amacuro, Venezuela 124/H3
San José de Areocuar, Venezuela 124/G2
San Jose de Buenavista, Philippines 82/C5
San José de Chiquitos, Bolivia 136/E5
San José de Feliciano, Argentina 143/G5
San José de Guanipa, Venezuela 124/G3
San José de la Costa, Venezuela 124/D2
San José de la Mariquina, Chile 138/D2
San José de las Lajas, Cuba 158/C1
San José de las Matas, Dom. Rep. 158/D5
San José del Cabo, Mexico 150/D5
San José del Guaviare, Colombia 126/D6
San Jose del Monte, Philippines 82/C3
San José del Ocune, Colombia 126/E5
San José de los Ramos, Cuba 158/D1
San José de Maipo, Chile 138/B10
San José de Mayo, Uruguay 145/C5
San José de Ocoa, Dom. Rep. 158/E6
San José de Río Chico, Venezuela 124/F2
San José de Sisa, Peru 128/D6
San José de Tiznados, Venezuela 124/E3
San José de Uchupiamonas, Bolivia 136/A4
San Juan (riv.) 188/E3
San Juan (prov.), Argentina 143/C3
San Juan, Argentina 143/C3
San Juan, Argentina 120/C6
San Juan (riv.), Argentina 143/C3
San Juan, Potosí, Bolivia 136/B7
San Juan, Santa Cruz, Bolivia 136/F5
San Juan (riv.), Bolivia 136/C7
San Juan (riv.), Br. Col. 184/J3
San Juan (creek), Calif. 204/E8
San Juan (riv.), Colombia 126/B5
San Juan (co.), Colo. 208/D7
San Juan (mts.), Colo. 208/F7
San Juan (riv.), Colo. 208/E8
San Juan (riv.), C. Rica 154/E5
San Juan (prov.), Dom. Rep. 158/D6
San Juan, Dom. Rep. 158/D6
San Juan, Mexico 150/K6
San Juan (co.), N. Mex. 274/A2
San Juan (riv.), N. Mex. 274/B2
San Juan (riv.), Nicaragua 154/E5
San Juan, Peru 128/E10
San Juan, Philippines 82/E5
San Juan (dist.), P. Rico 161/D1
San Juan (cap.), P. Rico 146/M8
San Juan (cap.), P. Rico 161/E1
San Juan (cap.), P. Rico 156/G1
San Juan (cape), P. Rico 156/G1
San Juan, Cabezas de (prom.), P. Rico 161/F1
San Juan, Texas 303/F11
San Juan, Trin. & Tob. 161/A10
San Juan (co.), Utah 304/E6
San Juan (riv.), Utah 304/D6
San Juan (co.), Wash. 310/C2
San Juan (isl.), Wash. 310/B2
San Juan Bautista, Calif. 204/D7
San Juan Bautista, Paraguay 144/D5
San Juan Bautista de Neembucú, Paraguay 144/D5
San Juan Capistrano, Calif. 204/H10
San Juan de Colón, Venezuela 124/B3
San Juan de Flores, Honduras 154/D3
San Juan de las Galdonas, Venezuela 124/G2
San Juan del César, Colombia 126/D2
San Juan del Norte, Nicaragua 154/F5
San Juan del Norte (bay), Nicaragua 154/F5
San Juan de los Cayos, Venezuela 124/D2
San Juan de los Lagos, Mexico 150/H6
San Juan de los Morros, Venezuela 124/E3
San Juan de los Planes, Mexico 150/D4
San Juan del Piray, Bolivia 136/C7
San Juan del Potrero, Bolivia 136/C5
San Juan del Sur, Nicaragua 154/D5
San Juan de Manapiare, Venezuela 124/E5
San Juan de Payara, Venezuela 124/E4
San Juan Island Nat'l Hist. Park, Wash. 310/B2
San Juan Nat'l Hist. Site, P. Rico 161/D1
San Juan Nepomuceno, Paraguay 144/E5
San Juan Pueblo, N. Mex. 274/C2
San Juan Xiutetelco, Mexico 150/O1
San Juan y Martínez, Cuba 158/B2
San Julián, Argentina 143/C6
San Julián, Argentina 120/C7
San Justo, Argentina 143/F5
Sankrail, India 68/E2
Sankt Aegyd am Neuwalde, Austria 41/C3
Sankt Anton am Arlberg, Austria 41/A3
Sankt Blasien, Germany 22/C5
Sankt Gallen (canton), Switzerland 39/H2
Sankt Gallen, Switzerland 39/H2
Sankt Goar, Germany 22/B3
Sankt Ingbert, Germany 22/B4
Sankt Johann in Tirol, Austria 41/B3
Sankt Margrethen, Switzerland 39/J2
Sankt Michael im Lungau, Austria 41/B3
Sankt Michael in Obersteiermark, Austria 41/C3
Sankt Paul im Lavanttal, Austria 41/C3
Sankt Peter-Ording, Germany 22/C1
Sankt Pülten, Austria 41/C2
Sankt Valentin, Austria 41/C2
Sankt Veit an der Glan, Austria 41/C3
Sankt Vith, Belgium 27/J8
Sankt Wendel, Germany 22/B4
Sankt Wolfgang im Dalzkammergut, Austria 41/B3
Sankuru (riv.), D.R. Congo 102/E5
Sankuru (riv.), D.R. Congo 115/D4
San Lázaro (cape), Mexico 150/C4
San Lázaro, Paraguay 144/D3
San Leandro, Calif. 204/J2
San Leon, Texas 303/L2
San Lorenzo, Argentina 143/F6
San Lorenzo, Cerro (mt.), Argentina 143/B6
San Lorenzo, El Beni, Bolivia 136/C4
San Lorenzo, Pando, Bolivia 136/B2
San Lorenzo, Tarija, Bolivia 136/C7
San Lorenzo, Serranía (mts.), Bolivia 136/E5
San Lorenzo, Calif. 204/K2
San Lorenzo (riv.), Calif. 204/K4
San Lorenzo, Cerro (Cochrane) (mt.), Chile 138/E7
San Lorenzo, Ecuador 128/C2
San Lorenzo (cape), Ecuador 128/B3
San Lorenzo, N. Mex. 274/B6
San Lorenzo, Paraguay 144/B4
San Lorenzo, Peru 128/H8
San Lorenzo (isl.), Peru 128/D9
San Lorenzo, P. Rico 161/E2
San Lorenzo, P. Rico 156/G1
San Lorenzo, Falcón, Venezuela 124/D2
San Lorenzo, Zulia, Venezuela 124/C3
San Lorenzo de El Escorial, Spain 33/E2
Sanlúcar de Barrameda, Spain 33/C4
Sanlúcar la Mayor, Spain 33/C4
San Lucas, Bolivia 136/C7
San Lucas, Calif. 204/E7
San Lucas (cape), Mexico 146/G7
San Lucas (cape), Mexico 2/D4
San Lucas (cape), Mexico 150/E5
San Luis (prov.), Argentina 143/C3
San Luis, Argentina 143/C3
San Luis, Argentina 120/C6
San Luis, Ariz. 198/A6
San Luis (lake), Bolivia 136/C3
San Luis (res.), Calif. 204/E7
San Luis, Colo. 208/J8
San Luis (creek), Colo. 208/H6
San Luis (lake), Colo. 208/H7
San Luis (peak), Colo. 208/F6
San Luis, Cuba 156/C2
San Luis, Pinar del Río, Cuba 158/B2
San Luis, Santiago de Cuba, Cuba 158/J4
San Luis, Guatemala 154/C2
San Luis, Honduras 154/C3
San Luis, Philippines 82/E6
San Luis (passage), Texas 303/K8
San Luis, Venezuela 124/D2
San Luis de la Paz, Mexico 150/J6
San Luis del Cordero, Mexico 150/H4
San Luis Jilotepeque, Guatemala 154/C3
San Luis Obispo, Calif. 188/B3
San Luis Obispo, Calif. 146/F6
San Luis Obispo (co.), Calif. 204/E8
San Luis Obispo, Calif. 204/E8
San Luis Potosí (state), Mexico 150/J5
San Luis Potosí, Mexico 150/J5
San Luis Potosí, Mexico 146/H7
San Luis Río Colorado, Mexico 150/B1
San Manuel, Ariz. 198/E6
San Marcelino, Philippines 82/B3
San Marco in Lamis, Italy 34/E4
San Marcos, Calif. 204/H10
San Marcos, Colombia 126/C3
San Marcos, C. Rica 154/E6
San Marcos, Guatemala 154/B3
San Marcos, Honduras 154/C3
San Marcos, Mexico 150/K8
San Marcos (isl.), Mexico 150/D3
San Marcos, Texas 303/F8
San Mariano, Philippines 82/D2
San Marino 7/F4
SAN MARINO 34
San Marino, Calif. 204/D10
San Marino (cap.), San Marino 34/D3
San Martín (lake) 120/B7
San Martín, Argentina 143/C3
San Martín (lake), Argentina 143/B6
San Martín (riv.), Bolivia 136/D3
San Martin, Calif. 204/L4
San Martin (cape), Calif. 204/D8
San Martín (lake), Chile 138/E7
San Martín, Colombia 126/D6
San Martín (dept.), Peru 128/D6
San Martín, Peru 128/E3
San Martín de las Pirámides, Mexico 150/M1
San Martín de los Andes, Argentina 143/C5
San Martín de Valdeiglesias, Spain 33/D2
San Martine Draw (dry riv.), Texas 303/C11
San Martín Jilotepeque, Guatemala 154/B3
San Martín Texmelucan, Mexico 150/M1
San Mateo (co.), Calif. 204/C3
San Mateo, Calif. 204/J3
San Mateo, Fla. 212/E2
San Mateo, N. Mex. 274/B3
San Mateo (mts.), N. Mex. 274/B5
San Mateo, Spain 33/F2
San Mateo, Venezuela 124/F3
San Mateo Ixtatán, Guatemala 154/B3
San Matías (gulf), Argentina 120/C7
San Matías (gulf), Argentina 143/D5
San Matías, Bolivia 136/F5
Sanmaur, Québec 174/C3
San Mauricio, Venezuela 124/E3
Sanmenxia, China 77/H5
San Miguel, Argentina 143/E2
San Miguel, Bolivia 136/E5
San Miguel (riv.), Bolivia 136/D4
San Miguel, Calif. 204/E8
San Miguel (isl.), Calif. 204/E9
San Miguel (riv.), Colombia 126/B7
San Miguel (co.), Colo. 208/C6
San Miguel (mts.), Colo. 208/C7
San Miguel (riv.), Colo. 208/B6
San Miguel, Cuba 158/H3
San Miguel, Ecuador 128/C3
San Miguel (riv.), Ecuador 128/D2
San Miguel, El Salvador 154/D4
San Miguel (co.), N. Mex. 274/D3
San Miguel, N. Mex. 274/C6
San Miguel, Golfo de (bay), Panama 154/H6
San Miguel, Paraguay 144/D5
San Miguel, Ayacucho, Peru 128/F9
San Miguel, Cajamarca, Peru 128/C6
San Miguel (bay), Philippines 82/D3
San Miguel (isls.), Philippines 85/F4
San Miguel (isls.), Philippines 82/B7
San Miguel (swamp), Uruguay 145/F4
San Miguel de Allende, Mexico 150/J6
San Miguel de Huachi, Bolivia 136/B4
San Miguel del Monte, Argentina 143/G7
San Miguel de Salcedo, Ecuador 128/C3
San Miguel de Tucumán, Argentina 143/D2
San Miguel de Tucumán, Argentina 120/C5
San Miguelito, Bolivia 136/A2
San Miguelito, Nicaragua 154/E5
San Miguel Nuevo, Colombia 126/B7
Sanming, China 77/J6
San Miniato, Italy 34/C3
San Narciso, Philippines 82/D4
Sannicandro Garganico, Italy 34/E4
San Nicolás, Argentina 143/F6
San Nicolás, Argentina 120/D6
San Nicolas (isl.), Calif. 204/F10
San Nicolás, Cuba 158/C1
San Nicolás (bay), Peru 128/E10
San Nicolás de los Garza, Mexico 150/J3
Sannikova (str.), Russia 48/O2
San Nua (Sam Neua), Laos 72/E2
Sano, Ky. 237/L6
Sanok, Poland 47/F4
San Onofre, Colombia 126/C3
San Pablo, Potosí, Bolivia 136/B7
San Pablo, Santa Cruz, Bolivia 136/D4
San Pablo, Calif. 204/J1
San Pablo (bay), Calif. 204/J1
San Pablo, Chile 138/D3
San Pablo, Colombia 126/B7
San Pablo, Colo. 208/J8
San Pablo, Sierra (mts.), Honduras 154/E3
San Pablo, Laguna, Philippines 82/C3
San Pablo, Negros Occ., Philippines 82/D5
San Pascual, Philippines 82/D4
San Patricio, N. Mex. 274/D5
San Patricio, Paraguay 144/D5
San Patricio (co.), Texas 303/G10
San Pedro, Buenos Aires, Argentina 143/F6
San Pedro, Jujuy, Argentina 143/D1
San Pedro (riv.), Ariz. 188/D4
San Pedro (riv.), Ariz. 198/E6
San Pedro, Belize 154/D2
Saa Pedro, Chuquisaca, Bolivia 136/C6
San Pedro, El Beni, Bolivia 136/C4
San Pedro, Pando, Bolivia 136/B2
San Pedro, Santa Cruz, Bolivia 136/D5
San Pedro, Calif. 204/C11
San Pedro (bay), Calif. 204/C11
San Pedro (chan.), Calif. 204/G10
San Pedro, Santiago, Chile 138/F4
San Pedro, Valparaíso, Chile 138/F2
San Pedro (pt.), Chile 138/A5
San Pedro, Colombia 126/E5
San Pedro, Cuba 158/B2
San Pedro (riv.), Cuba 158/G3
San Pedro (riv.), Guatemala 154/B2
San Pedro, Ivory Coast 106/C8
San Pedro, Nicaragua 154/E4
San Pedro, Paraguay 144/D4-5
San Pedro, Paraguay 144/D3
San Pedro (bay), Philippines 82/E5
San Pedro, Sierra de (range), Spain 33/C3
San Pedro Carchá, Guatemala 154/B3
San Pedro de Arimena, Colombia 126/E5
San Pedro de Atacama, Chile 138/C4
San Pedro de Buena Vista, Bolivia 136/C6
San Pedro de las Bocas, Venezuela 124/G4
San Pedro de las Colonias, Mexico 150/H4
San Pedro del Gallo, Mexico 150/G4
San Pedro de Lloc, Peru 128/C6
San Pedro del Paraná, Paraguay 144/D5
San Pedro de Macorís (prov.), Dom. Rep. 158/F6
San Pedro de Macorís, Dom. Rep. 156/E3
San Pedro de Macorís, Dom. Rep. 158/F6
San Pedro de Quemes, Bolivia 136/A7
San Pedro Pochutla, Mexico 150/L9
San Pedro Sula, Honduras 154/C3
San Pedro Zacapa, Honduras 154/D3
San Perlita, Texas 303/G11
Sanpete (co.), Utah 304/C4
San Pierre, Ind. 227/D2
San Pietro (isl.), Italy 34/B5
San Pitch (riv.), Utah 304/C4
Sanpoil (riv.), Wash. 310/G2
San Quentin, Calif. 204/H1
Sanquhar, Scotland 15/D5
San Quintin, Philippines 82/C3
San Rafael, Argentina 143/C3
San Rafael, Argentina 120/C6
San Rafael, Bolivia 136/E5
San Rafael, Calif. 204/J1
San Rafael (cape), Dom. Rep. 158/F5
San Rafael, Mexico 150/M1
San Rafael (reef), Mexico 150/L4
San Rafael, N. Mex. 274/A3
San Rafael (riv.), Utah 304/D4
San Rafael, Venezuela 124/C2
San Rafael de Atamaica, Venezuela 124/E4
San Rafael del Norte, Nicaragua 154/E4
San Rafael del Sur, Nicaragua 154/D5
San Rafael del Yuma, Dom. Rep. 158/F6
San Rafael de Orituco, Venezuela 124/E3
San Rafael Swell (mts.), Utah 304/D5
San Ramón, El Beni, Bolivia 136/C3
San Ramón, Santa Cruz, Bolivia 136/D5
San Ramon, Calif. 204/K2
San Ramón, C. Rica 154/E5
San Ramón, Cuba 158/H4
San Ramón, Nicaragua 154/E4
San Ramón, Peru 128/E8
San Ramón, Uruguay 145/D5
San Ramon de la Nva. Orán, Argentina 143/D1
San Remo, Italy 34/A3
San Roque, Colombia 126/C4
San Roque, Spain 33/D4
San Rosendo, Chile 138/E1
San Saba (co.), Texas 303/F6
San Saba, Texas 303/F6
San Saba (riv.), Texas 303/D7
San Salvador, Argentina 143/G5
San Salvador (isl.), Bahamas 156/D1
San Salvador (isl.), Ecuador 128/B9
San Salvador (cap.), El Salvador 154/C4
San Salvador (cap.), El Salvador 146/J8
San Salvador, Paraguay 144/C5
San Salvador (riv.), Uruguay 145/B4
San Salvador el Seco, Mexico 150/O1
Sans Bois (mts.), Okla. 288/R4
San Sebastián, Argentina 143/C7
San Sebastián, Chile 138/F3
San Sebastián, P. Rico 161/B1
San Sebastián, Spain 7/D4
San Sebastián, Spain 33/E1
San Sebastián, Venezuela 124/E2
Sansepolcro, Italy 34/C3
San Servando, Uruguay 145/F3
San Severino Marche, Italy 34/D3
San Severo, Italy 34/E4
San Simeon, Calif. 204/D8
San Simon, Ariz. 198/F6
San Simon (riv.), Ariz. 198/F6
San Simón, Serranía (mts.), Bolivia 136/D4
San Simón del Cocuy, Venezuela 124/E3
Sanski Most, Bos. 45/C3
Sansom Park Village, Texas 303/E2
Sans Souci, Trin. & Tob. 161/B10
Sans Toucher (mt.), Guadeloupe 161/A6
Santa, Idaho 220/B2
Santa, Peru 128/C7
Santa (riv.), Peru 128/C7
Santa Ana, El Beni, Bolivia 136/C3
Santa Ana, La Paz, Bolivia 136/B4
Santa Ana, Santa Cruz, Bolivia 136/E5
Santa Ana, Santa Cruz, Bolivia 136/F6
Santa Ana, Calif. 188/C4
Santa Ana, Calif. 204/D11
Santa Ana (riv.), Calif. 204/E11
Santa Ana, Colombia 126/F6
Santa Ana, Ecuador 128/B3
Santa Ana, El Salvador 154/C4
Santa Ana (mt.), El Salvador 154/C4
Santa Ana, Guatemala 154/C2
Santa Ana, Mexico 150/D1
Santa Ana (reef), Mexico 150/N7
Santa Ana, Uruguay 145/B1
Santa Ana (range), Uruguay 145/D2
Santa Ana, Anzoátegui, Venezuela 124/F3
Santa Ana, Táchira, Venezuela 124/B4
Santa Ana Chiautempan (Chiautempan), Mexico 150/N1
Santa Anna, Texas 303/E6
Santa Barbara (co.), Calif. 204/E9
Santa Barbara, Calif. 204/F9
Santa Barbara, Calif. 146/F6
Santa Barbara, Calif. 188/C4
Santa Barbara (chan.), Calif. 204/E9
Santa Barbara (isls.), Calif. 146/F6
Santa Barbara (isls.), Calif. 188/C4
Santa Barbara (isl.), Calif. 204/G10
Santa Barbara (isls.), Calif. 204/F10
Santa Bárbara, Chile 138/E1
Santa Bárbara, Colombia 126/C5
Santa Bárbara, Cuba 158/B2
Santa Bárbara, Honduras 154/C3
Santa Bárbara, Mexico 150/F3
Santa Barbara, Neth. Ant. 161/G9
Santa Bárbara, Amazonas, Venezuela 124/E6
Santa Bárbara, Barinas, Venezuela 124/C4

Searchlight 445

Sarthe (dept.), France 28/D3
Sarthe (riv.), France 28/D4
Sartrouville, France 28/A1
Sarufutsu, Japan 81/L1
Sarur, Oman 59/G5
Sárvár, Hungary 41/D3
Sarver, Pa. 294/C4
Sárviz csatorna (canal), Hungary 41/E3
Saryshagan, Kazakhstan 48/H5
Sary Su (riv.), Kazakhstan 48/H5
Sasabe, Ariz. 198/D7
Sasabe, Mexico 150/C1
Sasaginnigak (lake), Manitoba 179/G3
Sasakwa, Okla. 288/N5
Sasaram, India 68/E4
Sasebo, Japan 81/D7
Saseenos, Br. Col. 184/J3
SASKATCHEWAN 181
Saskatchewan (prov.) 162/F5
Saskatchewan (riv.) 162/F5
Saskatchewan (prov.), Canada 146/H4
Saskatchewan (riv.), Canada 2/D3
Saskatchewan (riv.), Sask. 181/H2
Saskatchewan Beach, Sask. 181/G5
Saskatchewan Landing Prov. Park, Sask. 181/C5
Saskatoon, Sask. 162/F5
Saskatoon, Sask. 146/H4
Saskatoon, Sask. 181/E3
Saskeram (riv.), Sask. 181/K2
Sason, Turkey 63/J3
Sasovo, Russia 52/F4
Saspamco, Texas 303/K11
Sassafras, Md. 245/P3
Sassafras (riv.), Md. 245/P3
Sassafras (mt.), S.C. 296/B1
Sassafras, Tasmania 99/C3
Sassandra, Ivory Coast 106/C8
Sassandra (riv.), Ivory Coast 106/C7
Sassari (prov.), Italy 34/B4
Sassari, Italy 34/B4
Sassari, Italy 7/E4
Sasseneire (mt.), Switzerland 39/E4
Sasser, Ga. 217/D7
Sassnitz, Germany 22/E1
Sasstown, Liberia 106/C8
Sassuolo, Italy 34/C2
Sástago, Spain 33/F2
Sasu (mt.), N. Korea 81/C4
Sata (cape), Japan 81/E8
Satadougou, Mali 106/B6
Satanta, Kansas 232/B4
Satara, India 68/C5
Satartia, Miss. 256/C5
Satawal (isl.), Micronesia 87/E5
Satellite Beach, Fla. 212/F3
Säter, Sweden 18/J6
Saticoy, Calif. 204/F9
Satigny, Switzerland 39/A4
Satilla (riv.), Ga. 217/G8
Satipo, Peru 128/E8
Satluj (Sutlej) (riv.), 68/C3
Satna, India 68/E4
Sátoraljaújhely, Hungary 41/F2
Satpayev, Kazakhstan 48/G5
Satpura (range), India 68/D4
Satsop, Wash. 310/B3
Satsuma, Ala. 195/B9
Satsuma, Fla. 212/E2
Satsuma, La. 238/L1
Satte, Japan 81/O1
Satu Mare, Romania 45/F2
Satu Mare, Romania 7/G4
Satun, Thailand 72/C6
Satupaitea, Samoa 86/L8
Saturna Island, Br. Col. 184/K3
Saturnia, Italy 34/C3
Satus (creek), Wash. 310/E4
Sauble Beach, Ontario 177/C3
Sauce, Argentina 143/G5
Sauce, Peru 128/D6
Sauce, Canelones, Uruguay 145/B6
Sauce, Rocha, Uruguay 145/B6
Sauce (lag.), Uruguay 145/D5
Sauceda (mts.), Ariz. 198/C6
Sauce de Luna, Argentina 143/G5
Sauce del Yi, Uruguay 145/D4
Saucedo, Uruguay 145/B2
Sauchie, Scotland 15/C1
Saucier, Miss. 256/F9
Saucillo, Mexico 150/G2
Sauda, Qurnet es (mt.), Lebanon 63/G5
Saudhárkrókur, Iceland 21/B1
Saudi Arabia 2/M4
Saudi Arabia 54/F7
SAUDI ARABIA 59/D4
Sauer (riv.), Germany 22/B4
Sauer (riv.), Luxembourg 27/J9
Sauerland (reg.), Germany 22/B3
Saugatuck, Conn. 210/B4
Saugatuck (res.), Conn. 210/B3
Saugatuck (riv.), Conn. 210/B3
Saugatuck, Mich. 250/C6
Saugeen (riv.), Ontario 177/C3
Saugerties, N.Y. 276/M6
Sauget, Ill. 222/A2
Saugus•, Mass. 249/D6
Saugus Iron Works Nat'l Hist. Site, Mass. 249/D6
Sauiá, Brazil 132/B3
Sauk (riv.), Wash. 310/D2
Sauk (co.), Wis. 317/G9
Sauk Centre, Minn. 255/C5
Sauk City, Wis. 317/G9
Sauk Rapids, Minn. 255/D5
Sauk Village, Ill. 222/C6
Saukville, Wis. 317/L9
Saül, Fr. Guiana 131/E4
Saulgau, Germany 22/C5
Saulkrasti, Latvia 53/C2
Saulnierville, Nova Scotia 168/B4
Saulsbury, Tenn. 237/C10
Saulsville, W. Va. 312/C7
Sault-au-Mouton, Québec 172/H1
Sault au Mouton (riv.), Québec 172/H1
Saulteaux (riv.), Alberta 182/C2
Sault Sainte Marie, Mich. 188/J1
Sault Sainte Marie, Mich. 250/E2
Sault Sainte Marie, Ont. 162/H6
Sault Sainte Marie, Ontario 177/J5
Sault Sainte Marie, Ontario 175/D3
Sault Ste. Marie, Ont. 146/K5
Saum, Minn. 255/D3
Saumarez (reef) 95/E4
Saumarez (reef), Coral Sea Is. Terr. 88/J4
Saumarez, New Bruns. 170/E1
Saumâtre (lake), Haiti 158/C6
Saumlaki, Indonesia 85/J7
Saumur, France 28/D4
Saunders (isl.), 143/E7
Saunders (co.), Nebr. 264/H3
Saunderstown, R.I. 249/J6
Saundersville, Mass. 249/G4
Saunemin, Ill. 222/E3
Sauqira (bay), Oman 59/G6
Sauqira, Ras (cape), Oman 59/G6
Sauquoit, N.Y. 276/K5
Saurimo, Angola 115/D5
Saurimo, Angola 102/E6
Sausalito, Calif. 204/H2
Sautee-Nacoochee, Ga. 217/E1
Sauteurs, Grenada 161/D8
Saut-Tigre, Fr. Guiana 131/E3
Sauzal, Chile 138/G5
Sava (riv.) 7/F4
Sava (riv.), Yugoslavia 45/D3
Savage (riv.), Md. 245/B2
Savage, Minn. 255/G6
Savage, Miss. 256/D1
Savage, Mont. 262/M3
Savage (harb.), Pr. Edward I. 168/F2
Savage (riv.), Tasmania 99/B3
Savage-Guilford, Md. 245/L4
Savage River (lake), Md. 245/B2
Savage River, Tasmania 99/B3
Savageton, Wyo. 319/G2
Savah, Ind. 227/B8
Savai'i (isl.), Samoa 87/J7
Savai'i (isl.), Samoa 86/L8
Savalou, Benin 106/E7
Savana (isl.), Virgin Is. (U.S.) 161/A4
Savanat (Estahbanat), Iran 66/J6
Savaneta, Neth. Ant. 161/E10
Savanette, Haiti 158/C6
Savanna, Ill. 222/C1
Savanna, Okla. 288/P5
Savanna Army Depot, Ill. 222/C1
Savannah (riv.) 188/K4
Savannah, Ga. 146/K6
Savannah, Ga. 188/K4
Savannah, Ga. 217/L6
Savannah (riv.), Ga. 217/K5
Savannah, Mo. 261/C3
Savannah•, N.Y. 276/G4
Savannah, Ohio 284/F4
Savannah (riv.), S.C. 296/E6
Savannah, Tenn. 237/E10
Savannah, U.S. 2/F4
Savannah (riv.), U.S. 146/K6
Savannah River Plant Atomic Energy Commission, S.C. 296/D5
Savannakhét, Laos 72/E3
Savanna-la-Mar, Jamaica 158/G6
Savanna-la-Mar, Jamaica 156/B3
Savannes (bay), St. Lucia 161/G7
Savant (lake), Ontario 177/G4
Savant (lake), Ontario 175/B2
Savant Lake, Ontario 177/G4
Savant Lake, Ontario 175/B2
Savantvadi, India 68/C5
Savanur, India 68/D6
Savaştepe, Turkey 63/B3
Save (riv.) 102/F7
Savé, Benin 106/E7
Save (riv.), Mozambique 118/E4
Saveh, Iran 59/F2
Saveh, Iran 66/G3
Săveni, Romania 45/H1
Saverne, France 28/G3
Saverton, Mo. 261/K3
Savery, Wyo. 319/E4
Savery (creek), Wyo. 319/E4
Savièse, Switzerland 39/D4
Savigliano, Italy 34/A2
Savo (isl.), Solomon Is. 86/D3
Savognin, Switzerland 39/J3
Savoie (dept.), France 28/G5
Savona, Br. Col. 184/G5
Savona (prov.), Italy 34/B2
Savona, Italy 34/B2
Savona, N.Y. 276/F6
Savonburg, Kansas 232/G4
Savonet, Neth. Ant. 161/F8
Savonlinna, Finland 18/Q6
Savoonga, Alaska 196/E2
Savoy, Ill. 222/E3
Savoy, Ky. 237/N7
Savoy•, Mass. 249/B2
Savoy, Mont. 262/H2
Savoy, S. Dak. 298/B5
Şavşat, Turkey 63/K2
Sävsjö, Sweden 18/J8
Savu (sea), Indonesia 54/O10
Savukoski, Finland 18/Q3
Savur, Turkey 63/J4
Savusavu (bay), Fiji 86/Q10
Sawahlunto, Indonesia 85/C6
Sawankhalok, Thailand 72/C3
Sawara, Japan 81/K6
Sawatch (range), Colo. 208/G4
Sawbill, Newf. 166/A3
Sawbill Landing, Minn. 255/G3
Sawbridgeworth, England 13/H7
Saweba (cape), Indonesia 85/J6
Sawi, India 68/G7
Sawmill Bay, N.W.T. 187/G3
Sawpit, Colo. 208/D7
Sawston, England 13/H5
Sawtell, N.S. Wales 97/G2
Sawtooth (range), Idaho 220/C6
Sawtooth (ridge), Wash. 310/E2
Sawtooth Nat'l Rec. Area, Idaho 220/D5
Sawu (isl.), Indonesia 85/G8
Sawu (isls.), Indonesia 85/G8
Sawu (sea), Indonesia 85/G7
Sawyer, Kansas 232/D4
Sawyer, Ky. 237/N7
Sawyer, Mich. 250/C7
Sawyer, Minn. 255/F4
Sawyer, N. Dak. 282/H3
Sawyer, Okla. 288/R7
Sawyer (co.), Wis. 317/D4
Sawyers Bar, Calif. 204/B2
Sawyerville, Ala. 195/C5
Sawyerville, Ill. 222/D4
Sawyerville, Québec 172/F4
Saxapahaw, N.C. 281/L3
Saxe, Va. 307/L7
Saxeville, Wis. 317/H7
Saxis, Va. 307/S5
Saxman, Alaska 196/N2
Saxmundham, England 13/J5
Saxon, S.C. 296/D2
Saxon, Switzerland 39/D4
Saxon, Wis. 317/F3
Saxonburg, Pa. 294/C4
Saxonville, Mass. 249/A7
Saxony (state), Germany 22/E3
Saxony-Anhalt (state), Germany 22/D2
Saxton, Ky. 237/N7
Saxton, Pa. 294/F5
Saxtons River, Vt. 268/B5
Say, Niger 106/E6
Saya, Bolivia 136/B5
Sayabec, Québec 172/B2
Sayaboury (Muang Xaignabouri), Laos 72/D3
Sayama, Japan 81/O2
Sayán, Peru 128/D8
Sayan (mts.), Russia 48/K4
Saybrook, Ill. 222/E3
Saybrook, Pa. 294/D2
Saybrook Point, Conn. 210/F3
Sayhan-Ovoo, Mongolia 77/F2
Saylesville, R.I. 249/J5
Saylorsburg, Pa. 294/M4
Saylorville (lake), Iowa 229/F5
Sayner, Wis. 317/H4
Saynshand, Mongolia 77/H3
Saynshand, Mongolia 54/M5
Sayre, Ala. 195/E3
Sayre, Okla. 288/G4
Sayre, Pa. 294/K2
Sayreville, N.J. 273/E3
Sayula, Mexico 150/H7
Sayula de Alemán, Mexico 150/M8
Sayville, N.Y. 276/O9
Sayward, Br. Col. 184/D5
Sazan (isl.), Albania 45/D5
Sázava (riv.), Czech Rep. 41/C2
Sbaa, Algeria 106/D3
Sbeitla, Tunisia 106/F1
Scafell Pike (mt.), England 13/D3
Scafell Pike (mt.), England 10/E3
Scalasaig, Scotland 15/B4
Scalby, England 13/G3
Scales Mound, Ill. 222/C1
Scaletta (pass), Switzerland 39/J3
Scalf, Ky. 237/O7
Scalloway, Scotland 10/G1
Scalloway, Scotland 15/G2
Scalpay (isl.), Scotland 15/B3
Scalpay (isl.), Scotland 15/C3
Scalp Level, Pa. 294/E5
Scaly Mountain, N.C. 281/C4
Scammon, Kansas 232/H4
Scammon Bay, Alaska 196/E2
Scandia, Alberta 182/E4
Scandia, Kansas 232/E2
Scandia, Minn. 255/F5
Scandia, Wash. 310/A1
Scandinavia 18
Scandinavia, Wis. 317/H7
Scanlon, Minn. 255/F4
Scanterbury, Manitoba 179/F4
Scantic, Conn. 210/E1
Scantic (riv.), Conn. 210/E1
Scapa, Alberta 182/D4
Scapa Flow (chan.), Scotland 15/E2
Scapa Flow (chan.), Scotland 10/E1
Scappoose, Oreg. 291/E2
Scarba (isl.), Scotland 15/C4
Scarboro, Barbados 161/B9
Scarboro, Ga. 217/J5
Scarborough, England 10/F3
Scarborough, England 13/G3
Scarborough, Maine 243/C8
Scarborough•, Maine 243/C8
Scarborough, Ontario 177/K4
Scarborough, Trin. & Tob. 156/G5
Scarbro, W. Va. 312/D7
Scarinish, Scotland 15/B4
Scarp (isl.), Scotland 15/A2
Scarriff, Ireland 17/E6
Scarriff (isl.), Ireland 17/A8
Scarsdale, N.Y. 276/P6
Scarth, Manitoba 179/B5
Scarville, Iowa 229/F2
Scatarie (isl.), Nova Scotia 168/J2
Scavaig, Loch (inlet), Scotland 15/B3
Sceaux, France 28/A2
Scenic, S. Dak. 298/D6
Scenic, Wash. 310/D3
Sceptre, Sask. 181/B5
Schaal, Ark. 202/C6
Schaalsee (lake), Germany 22/D2
Schaan, Liecht. 39/H2
Schaefferstown, Pa. 294/K5
Schaerbeek, Belgium 27/C9
Schaffer, Mich. 250/B3
Schaffhausen (canton), Switzerland 39/G1
Schaffhausen, Switzerland 39/G1
Schagen, Netherlands 27/F3
Schaghticoke, N.Y. 276/N5
Schaller, Iowa 229/C4
S-chanf, Switzerland 39/J3
Schangnau, Switzerland 39/E3
Schänis, Switzerland 39/H2
Scharans, Switzerland 39/J3
Schärding, Austria 41/B2
Scharhörn (isl.), Germany 22/C2
Schattdorf, Switzerland 39/G3
Schaumburg, Ill. 222/A5
Schawana, Wash. 310/F4
Schefferville, Que. 146/L4
Schefferville, Que. 162/K5
Schefferville, Québec 174/D2
Scheibbs, Austria 41/C2
Scheinfeld, Germany 22/D4
Schelde (Scheldt) (riv.), Belgium 27/C7
Scheldt (riv.), Belgium 27/C7
Schell City, Mo. 261/D6
Schell Creek (range), Nev. 266/G3
Schellsburg, Pa. 294/E5
Schellville, Calif. 204/J1
Schenectady (co.), N.Y. 276/M5
Schenectady, N.Y. 188/M2
Schenectady, N.Y. 276/M5
Schenevus, N.Y. 276/L5
Schererville, Ind. 227/C2
Scherhorn (mt.), Switzerland 39/G3
Schertz, Texas 303/K10
Scherzingen, Switzerland 39/H1
Schesaplana (mt.), Switzerland 39/J2
Scheveningen, Netherlands 27/E4
Schichallion (mt.), Scotland 15/D4
Schiedam, Netherlands 27/E5
Schiermonnikoog, Netherlands 27/J1
Schiermonnikoog (isl.), Netherlands 27/J1
Schiers, Switzerland 39/J3
Schijndel, Netherlands 27/G5
Schiller Park, Ill. 222/B5
Schinznach-Dorf, Switzerland 39/F2
Schio, Italy 34/C2
Schiphol, Netherlands 27/B5
Schkeuditz, Germany 22/E3
Schladming, Austria 41/B3
Schlater, Miss. 256/D3
Schlei (inlet), Germany 22/C1
Schleicher (co.), Texas 303/D7
Schleitheim, Switzerland 39/G1
Schleswig, Germany 22/C1
Schleswig, Iowa 229/B4
Schleswig-Holstein (state), Germany 22/C1
Schleusingen, Germany 22/D3
Schley (co.), Ga. 217/D6
Schley, Minn. 255/D3
Schlieren, Switzerland 39/F2
Schliersee, Germany 22/D5
Schlitz, Germany 22/C3
Schlüchtern, Germany 22/C3
Schmalkalden, Germany 22/D3
Schmölln, Germany 22/E3
Schnecksville, Pa. 294/L4
Schneeberg, Germany 22/E3
Schneeberg (mt.), Germany 22/D3
Schnee Eifel (plat.), Belgium 27/J8
Schneidemühl (Piła), Poland 47/C2
Schneider, Ind. 227/C2
Schnellville, Ind. 227/D8
Schoelcher, Martinique 161/C6
Schoenchen, Kansas 232/C3
Schoenfeld, Sask. 181/D5
Schoen Lake Prov. Park, Br. Col. 184/E5
Schofield, Wis. 317/H6
Schofield Barracks, Hawaii 218/E2
Schoharie (co.), N.Y. 276/M5
Schoharie, N.Y. 276/M5
Schoharie (creek), N.Y. 276/M6
Schoharie (res.), N.Y. 276/M6
Scholle, N. Mex. 274/C4
Scholls, Oreg. 291/A2
Schomberg, Ontario 177/J3
Schönberg, Germany 22/D2
Schönberg, Germany 22/D1
Schönebeck, Germany 22/D2
Schöneberg, Germany 22/E4
Schöneiche, Germany 22/E2
Schönenwerd, Switzerland 39/E2
Schongau, Germany 22/D5
Schöningen, Germany 22/D2
Schoodic (lake), Maine 243/F5
Schoolcraft (co.), Mich. 250/C2
Schoolcraft, Mich. 250/D6
Schoolcraft (riv.), Minn. 255/C3
Schooleys Mountain, N.J. 273/D2
School Hill, Wis. 317/L8
Schoonhoven, Netherlands 27/F5
Schoten, Belgium 27/F6
Schottegat (bay), Neth. Ant. 161/G9
Schouten (isls.), Indonesia 85/K6
Schouten (isls.), Papua N.G. 85/B6
Schouten (isl.), Tasmania 99/E4
Schouwen (isl.), Netherlands 27/D5
Schramberg, Germany 22/C4
Schram City, Ill. 222/D4
Schreckhorn (mt.), Switzerland 39/F3
Schreiber, Ontario 177/H5
Schreiber, Ontario 175/C3
Schrems, Austria 41/C2
Schriever, La. 238/J7
Schroeder, Minn. 255/G3
Schroon (lake), N.Y. 276/N3
Schroon (riv.), N.Y. 276/N3
Schroon Lake, N.Y. 276/N3
Schruns, Austria 41/A3
Schübelbach, Switzerland 39/G2
Schulenburg, Texas 303/H8
Schuler, Alberta 182/E4
Schull, Ireland 10/B5
Schull, Ireland 17/B8
Schulter, Okla. 288/P3
Schultz (lake), N.W.T. 187/J3
Schumacher, Ontario 175/D3
Schüpfheim, Switzerland 39/F3
Schurz, Nev. 266/C4
Schussenried, Germany 22/C4
Schuyler (co.), Ill. 222/C3
Schuyler (co.), Mo. 261/G2
Schuyler, Nebr. 264/G3
Schuyler (co.), N.Y. 276/G6
Schuyler, Va. 307/L5
Schuyler Lake, N.Y. 276/L5
Schuylerville, N.Y. 276/N4
Schuylkill (co.), Pa. 294/K4
Schuylkill (riv.), Pa. 294/M5
Schuylkill Haven, Pa. 294/K4
Schwaan, Germany 22/E2
Schwabach, Germany 22/D4
Schwäbisch Gmünd, Germany 22/C4
Schwäbisch Hall, Germany 22/C4
Schwalmstadt, Germany 22/C3
Schwanden, Switzerland 39/H2
Schwandorf im Bayern, Germany 22/E4
Schwaner (mts.), Indonesia 85/E6
Schwarzach im Pongau, Austria 41/B3
Schwarzenburg, Switzerland 39/D3
Schwarzhorn (mt.), Switzerland 39/E4
Schwarzhorn (mt.), Switzerland 39/F3
Schwarzwald (Black) (for.), Germany 22/C4
Schwatka (mts.), Alaska 196/G1
Schwaz, Austria 41/A3
Schwechat, Austria 41/D2
Schwedt, Germany 22/F2
Schweidnitz (Świdnica), Poland 47/C3
Schweinfurt, Germany 22/D3
Schwelm, Germany 22/B3
Schwenksville, Pa. 294/L5
Schwerin, Germany 22/D2
Schwerinersee (lake), Germany 22/D2
Schwertberg, Austria 41/C2
Schwetzingen, Germany 22/C4
Schwyz (canton), Switzerland 39/G2
Schwyz, Switzerland 39/G2
Sciacca, Italy 34/D6
Scicli, Italy 34/E6
Science Hill, Ky. 237/M6
Scilly, England 13/A7
Scilly (isls.), England 10/C6
Scio, N.Y. 276/E6
Scio, Ohio 284/H5
Scio, Oreg. 291/E3
Sciota, Ill. 222/C3
Sciota, Pa. 294/M4
Scioto (co.), Ohio 284/D8
Scioto (riv.), Ohio 284/D8
Sciotodale, Ohio 284/E8
Scioto Furnace, Ohio 284/E8
Scipio, Ind. 227/F6
Scipio, Ind. 227/H6
Scipio, Okla. 288/P4
Scipio, Utah 304/B4
Scircleville, Ind. 227/E4
Scitico, Conn. 210/E1
Scituate, Mass. 249/F8
Scituate•, Mass. 249/F8
Scituate (res.), R.I. 249/H5
Sclater, Manitoba 179/B3
Scobey, Miss. 256/E3
Scobey, Mont. 262/L2
Scofield, Utah 304/C4
Scofield (res.), Utah 304/C4
Scollard, Alberta 182/D4
Scone, N.S. Wales 97/F3
Scooba, Miss. 256/G5
Scopi (mt.), Switzerland 39/G3
Scopus, Mo. 261/N8
Scoresby (sound), Greenl. 4/B10
Scoresbysund (Ittoqqortoormiit), Greenl. 4/B10
Scotch Grove, Iowa 229/L4
Scotch Plains•, N.J. 273/E2
Scotchtown, Nova Scotia 168/H2
Scotch Village, Nova Scotia 168/E3
Scotfield, Alberta 182/E4
Scotia (sea) 2/G8
Scotia (sea) 5/D16
Scotia, Calif. 204/A3
Scotia, Nebr. 264/F3
Scotia, N.Y. 276/N5
Scotia, S.C. 296/E6
SCOTLAND 10/D2
SCOTLAND 15
Scotland, Ark. 202/E2
Scotland•, Conn. 210/G2
Scotland, Ga. 217/G6
Scotland, Ind. 227/D7
Scotland, Md. 245/N8
Scotland (co.), Mo. 261/H2
Scotland (co.), N.C. 281/L5
Scotland, Ontario 177/D4
Scotland, Pa. 294/G6
Scotland, S. Dak. 298/O7
Scotland, Texas 303/F4
Scotland, U.K. 7/D3
Scotland Neck, N.C. 281/P2
Scotlandville, La. 238/J1
Scots (bay), Nova Scotia 168/D3
Scots Bay, Nova Scotia 168/D3
Scotsburn, Nova Scotia 168/F3
Scotsguard, Sask. 181/C6
Scotstown, Ireland 17/H3
Scotstown, Québec 172/F4
Scotsville, Nova Scotia 168/G2
Scott (isl.), Ant. 2/A9
Scott (isl.) 5/C10
Scott (co.), Ark. 202/B4
Scott, Ark. 202/F4
Scott (cape), Br. Col. 162/D5
Scott (cape), Br. Col. 184/C5
Scott (isls.), Br. Col. 184/C5
Scott (riv.), Calif. 204/B2
Scott, Ga. 217/G5
Scott (co.), Ill. 222/C4
Scott (co.), Ind. 227/F7
Scott, Ind. 227/F1
Scott (co.), Iowa 229/M5
Scott (co.), Kansas 232/B3
Scott (co.), Ky. 237/M4
Scott, La. 238/F6
Scott (co.), Minn. 255/E6
Scott (co.), Miss. 256/E6
Scott, Miss. 256/B3
Scott (co.), Mo. 261/N8
Scott, Ohio 284/A4
Scott (mt.), Okla. 288/K5
Scott, Sask. 181/C3
Scott (lake), Sask. 181/M2
Scott (co.), Tenn. 237/M8
Scott (co.), Va. 307/C7
Scott A.F.B., Ill. 222/B3
Scott City, Kansas 232/B3
Scott City, Mo. 261/O8
Scottdale, Ga. 217/L1
Scottdale, Pa. 294/C5
Scott-Jonction, Québec 172/F3
Scottland, Ill. 222/F4
Scotts (head), Dominica 161/E7
Scotts, N.C. 281/H3
Scottsbluff, Nebr. 188/F2
Scottsbluff, Nebr. 146/H5
Scotts Bluff (co.), Nebr. 264/A3
Scottsbluff, Nebr. 264/A3
Scotts Bluff Nat'l Mon., Nebr. 264/A3
Scottsboro, Ala. 195/F1
Scottsburg, Ind. 227/F7
Scottsburg, Ky. 237/F6
Scottsburg, Oreg. 291/D4
Scottsburg, Va. 307/L7
Scottsdale, Ariz. 198/D5
Scottsdale, Tasmania 99/D3
Scotts Hill, N.C. 281/O6
Scotts Hill, Tenn. 237/E10
Scotts Mills, Oreg. 291/B3
Scottsmoor, Fla. 212/F3
Scotts Ridge (hills), Conn. 210/A3
Scott Station, Ant. 5/B9
Scotts Valley, Calif. 204/K4
Scottsville, Ark. 202/D3
Scottsville, Kansas 232/D2
Scottsville, Ky. 237/J7
Scottsville, N.Y. 276/E4
Scottsville, Va. 307/L5
Scottville, Ill. 222/C4
Scottville, Mich. 250/C5
Scoudouc, New Bruns. 170/F2
Scourie, Scotland 15/C2
Scout Lake, Sask. 181/F6
Scrabster, Scotland 15/E2
Scraggly (lake), Maine 243/H5
Scraggly (lake), Maine 243/F3
Scranage, Ala. 195/C8
Scranton, Ark. 202/C3
Scranton, Iowa 229/D4
Scranton, Kansas 232/G3
Scranton, Ky. 237/O5
Scranton, N.Y. 276/C5
Scranton, N.C. 281/S4
Scranton, N. Dak. 282/D7
Scranton, Pa. 188/L2
Scranton, Pa. 146/L5
Scranton, Pa. 294/F7
Scranton, S.C. 296/H4
Scraper, Okla. 288/S2
Screven (co.), Ga. 217/J5
Screven, Ga. 217/H7
Scriba, N.Y. 276/H4
Scribner, Nebr. 264/H3
Scridain, Loch (inlet), Scotland 15/B4
Scugog (lake), Ontario 177/F3
Scullin, Okla. 288/N5
Scunthorpe, England 10/F4
Scunthorpe, England 13/G4
Scuol, Switzerland 39/K3
Scurdie Ness (prom.), Scotland 15/F4
Scurrival (pt.), Scotland 15/A3
Scurry (co.), Texas 303/D5
Scurry, Texas 303/H5
Scusciuban, Somalia 115/J1
Scutari (lake), Albania 45/D4
Scutari (lake), Yugoslavia 45/D4
Scyrene, Ala. 195/C7
Sea (isls.), Ga. 217/K9
Sea (isls.), S.C. 296/G7
Seabeck, Wash. 310/C3
Seaboard, N.C. 281/O1
Seabold, Wash. 310/A1
Sea Breeze, N.Y. 276/F4
Sea Bright, N.J. 273/F3
Seabrook•, N.H. 268/F6
Seabrook, N.J. 273/C5
Seabrook, S.C. 296/F6
Seabrook (isl.), S.C. 296/G6
Seabrook, Texas 303/K2
Seabrook-Lanham, Md. 245/G4
Sea Cliff, N.Y. 276/R6
Seadrift, Texas 303/H9
Seaford, Del. 245/R6
Seaford, England 10/G5
Seaford, England 13/H7
Seaford, N.Y. 276/R7
Seaford, Va. 307/R6
Seaforth, Minn. 255/C6
Seaforth, Ontario 177/C4
Seaforth, Loch (inlet), Scotland 15/B3
Sea Girt, N.J. 273/E3
Seagoville, Texas 303/H3
Seagraves, Texas 303/B5
Seagrove, N.C. 281/K3
Seaham, England 10/F3
Seaham, England 13/J3
Seahorse (lake), Newf. 166/A3
Seahorse (pt.), N.W.T. 187/L3
Seahurst, Wash. 310/A2
Sea Island, Ga. 217/K8
Sea Isle City, N.J. 273/D5
Seal (isls.), Maine 243/F8
Seal (riv.), Man. 162/G4
Seal (riv.), Manitoba 179/J2
Seal (lake), Newf. 166/B3
Seal (isl.), Nova Scotia 168/B5
Seal (isl.), S. Africa 118/F7
Sea Lake, Victoria 97/B4
Seal Beach, Calif. 204/C11
Seal Cove, Maine 243/G7
Seal Cove, New Bruns. 170/D4
Seal Cove, Newf. 166/C4
Seal Cove, Newf. 166/C3
Seale, Ala. 195/H6
Sealevel, N.C. 281/S5
Seal Harbor, Maine 243/G7
Seal Rock, Oreg. 291/C3
Sealston, Va. 307/O4
Sealy, Texas 303/H8
Seaman, Ohio 284/C8
Seamer, England 13/G3
Sea Pines, S.C. 296/F7
Sea Ranch Lakes, Fla. 212/C3
Searchlight, Nev. 266/F7

Shoal 447

Shady Cove, Oreg. 291/E5
Shady Dale, Ga. 217/E4
Shady Grove, Ala. 195/F7
Shady Grove, Fla. 212/C1
Shady Grove, Ky. 237/F6
Shady Grove, Pa. 294/G6
Shady Point, Okla. 288/S4
Shady Side, Md. 245/M5
Shadyside, Ohio 284/J6
Shady Valley, Tenn. 237/T7
Shafer (lake), Ind. 227/D3
Shafer, Minn. 255/F5
Shafter, Calif. 204/F8
Shafter, Nev. 266/G2
Shafter, Texas 303/C12
Shaftesbury, England 13/E7
Shaftesbury, England 10/E5
Shaftsbury•, Vt. 268/A6
Shageluk, Alaska 196/G2
Shag Harbour, Nova Scotia 168/C5
Shahat, Libya 102/E1
Shahat, Libya 111/D1
Shahbandar, Pakistan 68/B4
Shahdad, Iran 59/G3
Shahdad, Iran 66/K5
Shahdol, India 68/E4
Shahistan (Saravan), Iran 66/N7
Shah Jahan, Kuh-e (mts.), Iran 66/L2
Shahjahanpur, India 68/E3
Shah Juy, Afghanistan 59/J3
Shahrakht, Iran 66/M4
Shahreza, Iran 59/F3
Shahreza, Iran 66/H4
Shahr Kord, Iran 66/G4
Shahrud, Iran 59/G2
Shahrud, Iran 66/J2
Shaibara (isl.), Saudi Arabia 59/C4
Sha'ib Hisb, Wadi (dry riv.), Iraq 66/C5
Shaikh Sa'ad, Iraq 66/E4
Shaikh Shu'aib (isl.), Iran 66/H7
Shaikh Shu'aib (isl.), Iran 59/F4
Shailerville, Conn. 210/E3
Shajapur, India 68/D4
Shakawe, Botswana 118/C3
Shaker Heights, Ohio 284/H9
Shakespeare, Ontario 177/D4
Shakhtinsk, Kazakhstan 48/H5
Shakhty, Russia 7/J4
Shakhty, Russia 48/E5
Shakhty, Russia 52/F5
Shakhun'ya, Russia 52/G3
Shaki, Nigeria 106/E7
Shâkir (isl.), Egypt 59/B4
Shakopee, Minn. 255/F6
Shakopee (creek), Minn. 255/C5
Shaktoolik, Alaska 196/F2
Shalalth, Br. Col. 184/F5
Shaler (mts.), N.W.T. 187/G2
Shalimar, Fla. 212/C6
Shallala, Wadi esh (dry riv.), Jordan 65/D2
Shallotte, N.C. 281/N7
Shallow (lake), Maine 243/E3
Shallowater, Texas 303/B4
Shallow Lake, Ontario 177/C3
Shallow Water, Kansas 232/B3
Sham, Jebel (mt.), Oman 59/G5
Shamattawa, Manitoba 179/K2
Shamattawa (riv.), Ontario 175/C2
Shambaugh, Iowa 229/D7
Shambe, Sudan 111/F6
Shamil, Iran 66/K7
Shammar, Jebel (plat.), Saudi Arabia 59/D4
Shamokin, Pa. 294/J4
Shamokin Dam, Pa. 294/J4
Shamrock, Okla. 288/N3
Shamrock, Sask. 181/E5
Shamrock, Texas 303/D2
Shamrock Lakes, Ind. 227/G4
Shamva, Zimbabwe 118/E3
Shan (state), Burma 72/C2
Shan (plat.), Burma 72/C2
Shanagolden, Ireland 17/C6
Shandan, China 77/F4
Shandon, Calif. 204/E8
Shandong (Shantung) (prov.), China 77/J4
Shangani (riv.), Zimbabwe 118/D3
Shangdu, China 77/H3
Shanghai, China 2/R4
Shanghai, China 54/O6
Shanghai, China 77/K5
Shanghai, Va. 307/P5
Shanghai, W. Va. 312/K4
Shanghang, China 77/J6
Shangnan, China 77/H5
Shangqui (Shangkiu), China 77/J5
Shangrao (Shangjao), China 77/J6
Shangshui, China 77/J5
Shang Xian, China 77/H5
Shangzhi, China 77/L2
Shaniko, Oreg. 291/G3
Shanks, W. Va. 312/J4
Shanksville, Pa. 294/E5
Shannock, R.I. 249/H7
Shannon, Ga. 217/B2
Shannon (isl.), Greenl. 4/B10
Shannon, Ill. 222/D1
Shannon, Mouth of the (est.), Ireland 17/B6
Shannon (riv.), Ireland 10/B4
Shannon (riv.), Ireland 17/E6
Shannon, Miss. 256/G2
Shannon (co.), Mo. 261/K8
Shannon, New Bruns. 170/E3
Shannon, N. Zealand 100/E4
Shannon, N.C. 281/L5
Shannon, Québec 172/F3
Shannon (co.), S. Dak. 298/D7
Shannon (lake), Wash. 310/D2
Shannon Airport, Ireland 17/D6
Shannon Bridge, Ireland 17/F5
Shannon City, Iowa 229/E7
Shannondale, Ind. 227/D4
Shannon Hills, Ark. 202/F4
Shannontown, S.C. 296/G4
Shannonville, Ontario 177/G3
Shanshan (Piqan), China 77/D3
Shansi (Shanxi) (prov.), China 77/H4
Shantar (isls.), Russia 48/O4
Shantar (isls.), Russia 54/P4
Shantou (Swatou), China 77/J7
Shantou, China 54/N7
Shantung (Shandong) (prov.), China 77/J4
Shanty Bay, Ontario 177/E3
Shanxi (Shansi) (prov.), China 77/H4
Shanyang, China 77/G5
Shanyin, China 77/H4
Shaoguan (Shiukwan), China 77/H7
Shaowu, China 77/J6
Shaoxing (Shaohing), China 77/K5
Shaoyang, China 77/H6
Shap, England 13/E3
Shapinsay (isl.), Scotland 15/F1
Shapio (lake), Newf. 166/B3
Shapleigh, Maine 243/B8
Shapleigh•, Maine 243/B8
Shaqlawa, Iraq 66/D2
Shaqra, Saudi Arabia 54/F7
Shaqra, Saudi Arabia 59/D4
Sharafkhaneh, Iran 66/D1
Sharbatat, Ras (cape), Oman 59/G6
Sharbot Lake, Ontario 177/H3
Shari (riv.) 102/D4
Shari (riv.), Cent. Afr. Rep. 115/C2
Shari (riv.), Chad 111/C5
Shari, Japan 81/M2
Sharifabad, Iran 66/L2
Sharjah, U.A.E. 59/F4
Shark (pt.), Fla. 212/E6
Shark (bay), W. Australia 88/A5
Shark (bay), W. Australia 92/A4
Shark Bay, W. Australia 88/A5
Sharkey (co.), Miss. 256/C5
Sharlyk, Russia 52/H4
Sharon•, Conn. 210/B1
Sharon, Ga. 217/G3
Sharon, Kansas 232/D4
Sharon, Mass. 249/K4
Sharon•, Mass. 249/K4
Sharon, Miss. 256/E5
Sharon•, N.H. 268/D6
Sharon, N. Dak. 282/P4
Sharon, Ohio 284/G6
Sharon, Okla. 288/H2
Sharon, Pa. 294/B3
Sharon, S.C. 296/E2
Sharon, Tenn. 237/D8
Sharon•, Vt. 268/C4
Sharon, W. Va. 312/D6
Sharon, Wis. 317/J11
Sharon Center, Ohio 284/G3
Sharon Grove, Ky. 237/G7
Sharon Hill, Pa. 294/N7
Sharon Springs, Kansas 232/A3
Sharon Springs, N.Y. 276/L5
Sharon Valley, Conn. 210/B1
Sharonville, Ohio 284/C9
Sharp (co.), Ark. 202/G1
Sharpe, Kansas 232/G3
Sharpe (lake), S. Dak. 298/J5
Sharpe Army Depot, Calif. 204/D6
Sharpes, Fla. 212/F3
Sharples, W. Va. 312/C7
Sharps (isl.), Md. 245/N6
Sharps, Va. 307/P5
Sharpsburg, Ga. 217/C4
Sharpsburg, Iowa 229/D7
Sharpsburg, Ky. 237/O4
Sharpsburg, Md. 245/G3
Sharpsburg, N.C. 281/O3
Sharpsburg, Pa. 294/B6
Sharps Chapel, Tenn. 237/O8
Sharpsville, Ind. 227/E4
Sharpsville, Pa. 294/A3
Sharptown, Md. 245/R6
Sharptown, N.J. 273/C4
Shar'ya, Russia 48/E4
Shar'ya, Russia 52/G3
Shashe, Botswana 118/D4
Shashe (riv.), Botswana 118/D4
Shashe (riv.), Zimbabwe 118/D4
Shashi (Shasi), China 77/H5
Shasta, Calif. 204/C3
Shasta (co.), Calif. 204/C3
Shasta (dam), Calif. 204/C3
Shasta (lake), Calif. 204/C3
Shasta (mt.), Calif. 188/B2
Shasta (mt.), Calif. 204/C2
Shasta (res.), Calif. 188/B2
Shasta (riv.), Calif. 204/C2
Shati, Wadi esh (dry riv.), Libya 111/B2
Shatra, Iraq 66/E5
Shattuc, Ill. 222/D5
Shattuck, Okla. 288/G2
Shattuckville, Mass. 249/D2
Shauck, Ohio 284/E4
Shaughnessy, Alberta 182/D5
Shaunavon, Sask. 162/F6
Shaunavon, Sask. 181/C6
Shavano Park, Texas 303/J10
Shaver Lake, Calif. 204/F6
Shavers Fork (riv.), W. Va. 312/G5
Shave Ziyyon, Israel 65/B2
Shaw, Kansas 232/G4
Shaw, La. 238/G4
Shaw, Minn. 255/F3
Shaw, Miss. 256/C3
Shaw (mt.), N.H. 268/E4
Shaw, Oreg. 291/A3
Shaw A.F.B., S.C. 296/F4
Shawan, China 77/B3
Shawanese, Pa. 294/E7
Shawano (co.), Wis. 317/J6
Shawano, Wis. 317/J6
Shawano (lake), Wis. 317/K6
Shawboro, N.C. 281/S2
Shawbost, Scotland 15/B2
Shawbridge, Québec 172/C4
Shawinigan, Que. 162/J6
Shawinigan, Québec 174/C3
Shawinigan, Québec 172/E3
Shawinigan (riv.), Québec 172/E3
Shawinigan-Sud, Québec 172/E3
Shaw Island, Wash. 310/B2
Shawmut, Maine 243/D6
Shawmut, Mont. 262/G4
Shawmut, Pa. 294/E3
Shawnee, Colo. 208/H4
Shawnee (co.), Kansas 232/G2
Shawnee, Kansas 232/H2
Shawnee, Ohio 284/F6
Shawnee, Okla. 188/G3
Shawnee, Okla. 288/N4
Shawnee, Wyo. 319/G3
Shawnee Hills, Ohio 284/D5
Shawnee on Delaware, Pa. 294/N3
Shawneetown, Ill. 222/E6
Shawnigan Lake, Br. Col. 184/J3
Shawomet, R.I. 249/J6
Shawsheen Village, Mass. 249/K2
Shawshine (riv.), Mass. 249/K2
Shawsville, Md. 245/M2
Shawsville, Va. 307/H6
Shawville, Québec 172/A4
Shay Gap, W. Australia 92/C3
Shayib, Jebel (mt.), Egypt 59/B4
Shay Juy, Afghanistan 68/B2
Shchekino, Russia 52/E4
Shchel'yayur, Russia 52/H1
Shchigry, Russia 52/E4
Shchuchinsk, Kazakhstan 48/H4
Sheakleyville, Pa. 294/B3
Sheaville, Oreg. 291/K4
Shebandowan, Ontario 177/G5
Sheberghan, Afghanistan 54/H6
Sheberghan, Afghanistan 68/B1
Sheberghan, Afghanistan 59/H2
Sheboygan, Wis. 188/J2
Sheboygan (co.), Wis. 317/L8
Sheboygan, Wis. 317/L8
Sheboygan Falls, Wis. 317/L8
Shedd, Oreg. 291/D3
Shedden, Ontario 177/C5
Shediac, New Bruns. 170/F2
Shediac (isl.), New Bruns. 170/F2
Shediac Bridge, New Bruns. 170/F2
Sheeffry (hills), Ireland 17/B4
Sheelin (lake), Ireland 17/G4
Sheenjek (riv.), Alaska 196/K1
Sheep (mt.), Colo. 208/E6
Sheep (mt.), Mont. 262/C2
Sheep (range), Nev. 266/F6
Sheep (creek), Oreg. 291/L2
Sheep (creek), Utah 304/E3
Sheep Creek, Alberta 182/A2
Sheep Haven (harb.), Ireland 17/F1
Sheeps (head), Ireland 17/B8
Sheepscott, Maine 243/D7
's Heerenberg, Netherlands 27/J5
Sheerness, Alberta 182/E4
Sheet (harb.), Nova Scotia 168/F4
Sheet Harbour, Nova Scotia 168/F4
Shefar'am, Israel 65/C2
Shefayim, Israel 65/B3
Sheffield, Ala. 195/C1
Sheffield, England 7/D3
Sheffield, England 10/F4
Sheffield, England 13/J2
Sheffield, Ill. 222/D2
Sheffield, Iowa 229/G3
Sheffield•, Mass. 249/A4
Sheffield, Mont. 262/K4
Sheffield, New Bruns. 170/D3
Sheffield, Ohio 284/F3
Sheffield, Pa. 294/D2
Sheffield, Tasmania 99/C3
Sheffield, Texas 303/B7
Sheffield•, Vt. 268/C2
Sheffield Lake, Ohio 284/F3
Shefford (co.), Québec 172/E4
Sheguiandah, Ontario 177/C2
Sheho, Sask. 181/H4
Shehy (mts.), Ireland 17/C8
Sheikh Sa'id, Yemen 59/D7
Sheila, New Bruns. 170/F1
Sheki, Azerbaijan 52/G6
Shelagh (riv.), Iran 66/M5
Shelagskiy (cape), Russia 48/R2
Shelbiana, Ky. 237/R6
Shelbina, Mo. 261/H3
Shelburn, Ind. 227/C6
Shelburne, N.H. 268/E3
Shelburne•, N.H. 268/E3
Shelburne (co.), Nova Scotia 168/C5
Shelburne, Nova Scotia 168/C5
Shelburne, Ontario 177/D3
Shelburne•, Vt. 268/A3
Shelburne (pond), Vt. 268/A3
Shelburne Falls, Mass. 249/D2
Shelby (co.), Ala. 195/E4
Shelby, Ala. 195/E4
Shelby (co.), Ill. 222/E4
Shelby (co.), Ind. 227/F5
Shelby, Ind. 227/C2
Shelby (co.), Iowa 229/C5
Shelby, Iowa 229/C5
Shelby (co.), Ky. 237/L4
Shelby, Mich. 250/C5
Shelby, Miss. 256/C3
Shelby (co.), Mo. 261/H3
Shelby, Mont. 262/E2
Shelby, Nebr. 264/G3
Shelby, N.C. 281/G4
Shelby (co.), Ohio 284/B5
Shelby, Ohio 284/E4
Shelby (co.), Tenn. 237/B10
Shelby (co.), Texas 303/K6
Shelby Center, N.Y. 276/D4
Shelbyville, Ill. 222/E4
Shelbyville (lake), Ill. 222/E4
Shelbyville, Ind. 227/F6
Shelbyville, Ky. 237/L4
Shelbyville, Mo. 261/H3
Shelbyville, Tenn. 237/H10
Shelbyville, Texas 303/L6
Sheldahl, Iowa 229/F5
Sheldon, Ill. 222/F3
Sheldon, Iowa 229/B2
Sheldon, Minn. 255/G7
Sheldon, Mo. 261/D7
Sheldon, N. Dak. 282/P6
Sheldon, S.C. 296/F6
Sheldon, Texas 303/K1
Sheldon•, Vt. 268/B2
Sheldon, Wis. 317/D5
Sheldon Junction, Vt. 268/B2
Sheldon Point, Alaska 196/E2
Sheldon Springs, Vt. 268/A2
Sheldonville, Mass. 249/J4
Shelekhov (gulf), Russia 48/Q4
Shelekhov (gulf), Russia 54/S3
Shelikof (str.), Alaska 196/H3
Shell (pt.), Fla. 212/B1
Shell (riv.), Minn. 255/C4
Shell (creek), N. Dak. 282/F3
Shell, Loch (inlet), Scotland 15/B3
Shell (lake), Wis. 317/C4
Shell, Wyo. 319/E1
Shell (creek), Wyo. 319/E1
Shellbrook, Sask. 162/F5
Shellbrook, Sask. 181/E2
Shelldrake (riv.), Mich. 250/D2
Shelley, Br. Col. 184/F3
Shelley, Idaho 220/F6
Shellharbour, N.S. Wales 97/F4
Shell Knob, Mo. 261/E9
Shell Lake, Sask. 181/D2
Shell Lake, Wis. 317/C4
Shellman, Ga. 217/C7
Shellmouth, Manitoba 179/A4
Shell Rock, Iowa 229/H3
Shellsburg, Iowa 229/K4
Shelltown, Md. 245/R9
Shelly, Minn. 255/B3
Shelmerdine, N.C. 281/P4
Shelocta, Pa. 294/D4
Shelter (isl.), N.Y. 276/R8
Shelton, Conn. 210/C3
Shelton, Nebr. 264/F4
Shelton, S.C. 296/E3
Shelton, Wash. 310/B3
Shemakha, Azerbaijan 52/G6
Shemogue, New Bruns. 170/F2
Shemya (isl.), Alaska 196/J3
Shemya Air Force Base, Alaska 196/J3
Shenandoah, Iowa 229/C7
Shenandoah, Pa. 294/K4
Shenandoah (co.), Va. 307/L3
Shenandoah, Va. 307/L4
Shenandoah (mt.), Va. 307/K3
Shenandoah (riv.), Va. 307/N2
Shenandoah (riv.), W. Va. 312/K4
Shenandoah Junction, W. Va. 312/L4
Shenandoah Nat'l Park, Va. 307/L3
Shenango, Pa. 294/A3
Shenango River (lake), Pa. 294/B3
Shendam, Nigeria 106/F7
Shendi, Sudan 59/B6
Shendi, Sudan 102/F3
Shendi, Sudan 111/F4
Shëngjin, Albania 45/D5
Sheng Xian, China 77/K6
Shenipsit (lake), Conn. 210/F1
Shenkursk, Russia 48/E3
Shenkursk, Russia 52/F2
Shenmu, China 77/G4
Shennington, Wis. 317/F7
Shennongjia, China 77/H5
Shensi (Shaanxi) (prov.), China 77/G5
Shenyang (Mukden), China 77/K3
Shenyang, China 54/O5
Shenyang, China 2/R3
Sheopur, India 68/D3
Shepard, Alberta 182/D4
Shepardsville, Ind. 227/B5
Shepaug (dam), Conn. 210/B3
Shepaug (riv.), Conn. 210/B2
Shepetovka, Ukraine 52/C4
Shepherd, Mich. 250/E5
Shepherd, Mont. 262/H5
Shepherd (bay), N.W.T. 187/J3
Shepherd, Texas 303/K7
Shepherdstown, W. Va. 312/L4
Shepherdsville, Ky. 237/K4
Shepody, New Bruns. 170/F3
Shepody (bay), New Bruns. 170/F3
Sheppard A.F.B., Texas 303/F3
Shepparton, Victoria 88/G7
Shepparton, Victoria 97/C5
Sheppey (isl.), England 13/J6
Sheppton, Pa. 294/K4
Shepshed, England 13/F5
Shepton Mallet, England 13/E6
Shepton Mallet, England 10/E5
Sheqi, China 77/H5
Sherack, Minn. 255/B3
Sherard, Miss. 256/C2
Sherard (cape), N.W.T. 187/L2
Sherborn•, Mass. 249/A8
Sherborne, England 10/E5
Sherborne, England 13/E7
Sherbro (isl.), S. Leone 106/B7
Sherbrooke, Nova Scotia 168/G3
Sherbrooke (lake), Nova Scotia 168/D4
Sherbrooke (riv.), Nova Scotia 168/D4
Sherbrooke, Que. 162/J7
Sherbrooke (co.), Québec 172/E4
Sherbrooke, Québec 172/E4
Sherburn, Minn. 255/D7
Sherburne (co.), Minn. 255/E5
Sherburne, N.Y. 276/K5
Shercock, Ireland 17/G4
Shereik, Sudan 111/F4
Sheridan, Ark. 202/F5
Sheridan, Calif. 204/D5
Sheridan, Colo. 208/J3
Sheridan, Ill. 222/E2
Sheridan, Ind. 227/E4
Sheridan (co.), Kansas 232/B2
Sheridan, Maine 243/F2
Sheridan, Mich. 250/D5
Sheridan, Mo. 261/C1
Sheridan (co.), Mont. 262/M2
Sheridan, Mont. 262/D5
Sheridan (co.), Nebr. 264/B2
Sheridan, N.Y. 276/B5
Sheridan (co.), N. Dak. 282/K4
Sheridan, Oreg. 291/D2
Sheridan, W. Va. 312/B6
Sheridan, Wis. 317/H7
Sheridan, Wyo. 188/E2
Sheridan, Wyo. 146/H5
Sheridan (co.), Wyo. 319/F1
Sheridan, Wyo. 319/F1
Sheridan Lake, Colo. 208/P6
Sheringham, England 13/J5
Sheringham, England 10/G4
Sherkin (isl.), Ireland 17/C9
Sherman (mt.), Colo. 208/G4
Sherman•, Conn. 210/B2
Sherman, Ill. 222/D4
Sherman (co.), Kansas 232/A2
Sherman, Kansas 232/H4
Sherman, Ky. 237/M3
Sherman, Maine 243/G4
Sherman•, Maine 243/G4
Sherman, Mich. 250/D4
Sherman, Miss. 256/G2
Sherman, Mo. 261/N3
Sherman (co.), Nebr. 264/F3
Sherman (res.), Nebr. 264/E3
Sherman, N. Mex. 274/B6
Sherman, N.Y. 276/A6
Sherman (inlet), N.W.T. 187/J3
Sherman (co.), Oreg. 291/G2
Sherman, S. Dak. 298/S6
Sherman (co.), Texas 303/C1
Sherman, Texas 303/H4
Sherman, Texas 188/G4
Sherman, W. Va. 312/C5
Sherman City, Mich. 250/D5
Sherman Mills, Maine 243/G4
Shermans Dale, Pa. 294/H5
Sherman Station, Maine 243/F4
Sherrard, Ill. 222/C2
Sherrard, W. Va. 312/E3
Sherridon, Man. 162/G4
Sherridon, Manitoba 179/H3
Sherrill, Ark. 202/F5
Sherrill, Iowa 229/M3
Sherrill, N.Y. 276/J4
Sherrington, Québec 172/D4
Sherrodsville, Ohio 284/H4
Sherry, Wis. 317/G6
's Hertogenbosch, Netherlands 27/G5
Sherwood, Ark. 202/F4
Sherwood (pt.), Conn. 210/B4
Sherwood (for.), England 13/F4
Sherwood, Mich. 250/D6
Sherwood, N. Dak. 282/G2
Sherwood, Ohio 284/A3
Sherwood, Okla. 288/S6
Sherwood, Oreg. 291/A2
Sherwood, Pr. Edward I. 168/E2
Sherwood, Tenn. 237/K10
Sherwood, Texas 303/D6
Sherwood, Wis. 317/K7
Sherwood Park, Alberta 182/D3
Sheslay (riv.), Br. Col. 184/J2
Shetek (lake), Minn. 255/C6
Shetland (islands area), Scotland 15/F2
Shetland (isls.), Scotland 7/D2
Shetland (isls.), Scotland 10/G1
Shetland (isls.), Scotland 15/G2
Shetucket (riv.), Conn. 210/G2
Shevchenko, Kazakhstan 48/F5
Shevchenko, Kazakhstan 54/G5
Shevlin, Manitoba 179/A3
Shevlin, Minn. 255/C3
Sheyenne, N. Dak. 282/M4
Sheyenne (riv.), N. Dak. 188/G1
Sheyenne (riv.), N. Dak. 282/O6
Sheykh Sho'eyb (isl.), Iran 66/H7
Shiant (isls.), Scotland 15/B3
Shiant (sound), Scotland 15/B3
Shiawassee (co.), Mich. 250/E6
Shiawassee (riv.), Mich. 250/E5
Shibam, Yemen 59/E6
Shibata, Japan 81/J5
Shibetsu, Japan 81/M2
Shibin el Kom, Egypt 111/J3
Shibogama (lake), Ontario 175/C2
Shickley, Nebr. 264/G4
Shickshinny, Pa. 294/K3
Shideler, Ind. 227/G4
Shidler, Okla. 288/N1
Shiel, Loch (lake), Scotland 10/D2
Shiel, Loch (lake), Scotland 15/C4
Shieldaig, Scotland 15/C3
Shields, Kansas 232/B3
Shields (riv.), Mont. 262/F4
Shields, N. Dak. 282/H7
Shieldsville, Minn. 255/E6
Shifnal, England 13/E5
Shiga (pref.), Japan 81/J7
Shigatse (Xigazê), China 77/C6
Shigawake, Québec 172/D2
Shihezi (Shihhotzu), China 77/C3
Shihr, Yemen 59/E7
Shijak, Albania 45/D5
Shijiazhuang (Shihkiachwang), China 77/J4
Shijiazhuang, China 54/N6
Shikarpur, Pakistan 68/B3
Shikarpur, Pakistan 59/J4
Shikoku, Japan 54/P6
Shikoku (isl.), Japan 2/R4
Shikoku (isl.), Japan 81/F7
Shikotan (isl.), Japan 81/N2
Shikotsu (lake), Japan 81/K2
Shikotsu-Toya Nat'l Park, Japan 81/K2
Shilbottle, England 13/F2
Shildon, England 13/F3
Shilka, Russia 48/M4
Shilka (riv.), Russia 54/N4
Shillelagh, Ireland 17/J6
Shillelagh, Ireland 10/C4
Shillington, Pa. 294/K5
Shillong, India 68/G3
Shilo, Manitoba 179/C5
Shiloh, Ala. 195/G2
Shiloh, Ala. 195/C6
Shiloh, Ga. 217/C5
Shiloh, Ill. 222/B3
Shiloh, N.J. 273/C5
Shiloh, Ohio 284/E4
Shiloh, S.C. 296/G4
Shiloh, Tenn. 237/E10
Shiloh, Va. 307/O4
Shiloh Nat'l Mil. Park, Tenn. 237/E10
Shilovo, Russia 52/F4
Shimabara, Japan 81/E7
Shimamoto, Japan 81/J7
Shimane (pref.), Japan 81/F6
Shimane (pen.), Japan 81/F6
Shimanovsk, Russia 48/N4
Shimbir Berris (mt.), Somalia 115/J1
Shimizu, Japan 81/J6
Shimoda, Japan 81/J6
Shimoga, India 68/D6
Shimokita (pen.), Japan 81/K3
Shimonoseki, Japan 81/E6
Shin (falls), Scotland 15/D3
Shin, Loch (lake), Scotland 15/D2
Shin, Loch (lake), Scotland 10/D1
Shin (riv.), Scotland 15/D3
Shinano (riv.), Japan 81/J5
Shinas, Oman 59/G5
Shindand, Afghanistan 59/H3
Shindand, Afghanistan 68/A2
Shindler, S. Dak. 298/R7
Shiner, Texas 303/G8
Shingbwiyang, Burma 72/B1
Shinglehouse, Pa. 294/F2
Shingler, Ga. 217/E7
Shingle Springs, Calif. 204/C8
Shingleton, Mich. 250/C2
Shingu, Japan 81/H7
Shining Tree, Ontario 177/J5
Shinjo, Japan 81/K4
Shinko (riv.), Cent. Afr. Rep. 115/D2
Shinnecock Ind. Res., N.Y. 276/R9
Shinnston, W. Va. 312/F4
Shin Pond, Maine 243/F3
Shinrone, Ireland 17/F5
Shinyanga (reg.), Tanzania 115/F4
Shinyanga, Tanzania 115/F4
Shinyanga, Tanzania 102/F5
Shiocton, Wis. 317/K7
Shiogama, Japan 81/K4
Shiono (cape), Japan 81/H7
Ship (isl.), Miss. 256/G10
Ship Bottom, N.J. 273/E4
Ship Harbour, Newf. 166/D2
Ship Harbour, Nova Scotia 168/F4
Shiping, China 77/F7
Shipki (pass), India 68/D2
Shipman, Ill. 222/C4
Shipman, Sask. 181/F2
Shipman, Va. 307/L5
Shippan (pt.), Conn. 210/A4
Shippegan, New Bruns. 170/F1
Shippegan (bay), New Bruns. 170/E1
Shippegan (gully), New Bruns. 170/F1
Shippensburg, Pa. 294/H5
Shippenville, Pa. 294/D3
Shiprock, N. Mex. 274/A2
Ship Rock (peak), N. Mex. 274/A2
Shipshaw (riv.), Québec 172/F1
Shipshewana, Ind. 227/F1
Ship Shoal (isl.), Va. 307/S6
Shipston on Stour, England 13/F5
Shiqian, China 77/G6
Shiqma (riv.), Israel 65/B4
Shiquan, China 77/G5
Shiquanhe, China 77/A5
Shiragami (cape), Japan 81/J3
Shirakawa, Japan 81/K5
Shirane (mt.), Japan 81/H6
Shirane (mt.), Japan 81/J5
Shiranuka, Japan 81/M2
Shiraz, Iran 54/G7
Shiraz, Iran 66/H6
Shiraz, Iran 59/F4
Shire (riv.), Malawi 115/G7
Shire (riv.), Mozambique 118/E3
Shiretoko (cape), Japan 81/M1
Shiriya (cape), Japan 81/K3
Shir Kuh (mt.), Iran 59/F3
Shir Kuh (mt.), Iran 66/J5
Shirland, Ill. 222/D1
Shirley, Ark. 202/F2
Shirley, Ill. 222/E3
Shirley, Ind. 227/F5
Shirley, Mass. 249/H2
Shirley•, Mass. 249/H2
Shirley, Mo. 261/L7
Shirley, W. Va. 312/E4
Shirley (basin), Wyo. 319/F3
Shirley Basin, Wyo. 319/F3
Shirley Center, Mass. 249/H2
Shirley City (Woodburn), Ind. 227/H2
Shirley Mills, Maine 243/D5
Shirley Mills•, Maine 243/D5
Shirleysburg, Pa. 294/G5
Shiro, Texas 303/J7
Shiroishi, Japan 81/K4
Shirvan, Iran 59/G2
Shirvan, Iran 66/K2
Shirvan (riv.), Iran 66/E3
Shishaldin (vol.), Alaska 196/E4
Shishmaref, Alaska 196/E1
Shithatha, Iraq 59/D3
Shithatha, Iraq 66/C4
Shitike (creek), Oreg. 291/F3
Shiukwan (Shaoyuan), China 77/H7
Shively, Calif. 204/B3
Shively, Ky. 237/K4
Shivers, Miss. 256/E7
Shivpuri, India 68/D3
Shivwits (plat.), Ariz. 198/B2
Shivwits Ind. Res., Utah 304/A6
Shiyan, China 77/H5
Shizuishan (Shihsuishan), China 77/G4
Shizunai, Japan 81/L2
Shizuoka (pref.), Japan 81/H6
Shizuoka, Japan 54/P6
Shizuoka, Japan 81/H6
Shkodër, Albania 7/F4
Shkodër, Albania 45/D5
Shoa (prov.), Ethiopia 111/G6
Shoal (riv.), Fla. 212/C6
Shoal (creek), Ill. 222/D5
Shoal (lake), Manitoba 179/B4

Summerville Centre 453

Stony Gorge (res.), Calif. 204/C4
Stony Island, Nova Scotia 168/C5
Stony Lake, Mich. 250/C5
Stony Mountain, Manitoba 179/E4
Stony Plain, Alberta 182/C3
Stony Point, N.Y. 276/M8
Stony Point, N.C. 281/G3
Stony Rapids, Sask. 181/M2
Stony River, Alaska 196/G2
Stony Tunguska (riv.), Russia 48/K3
Stony Tunguska (riv.), Russia 54/L3
Stony Wold, N.Y. 276/M1
Storå (riv.), Denmark 21/B5
Stora Lulevatten (lake), Sweden 18/L3
Storden, Minn. 255/C6
Store Baelt (chan.), Denmark 18/G9
Store Baelt (chan.), Denmark 21/D6
Store Heddinge, Denmark 21/F7
Store-Heddinge, Denmark 18/H9
Stor-Elvdal, Norway 18/G6
Støren, Norway 18/F5
Storey (co.), Nev. 266/B3
Storeys Creek, Tasmania 99/D3
Storeytown, New Bruns. 170/D2
Storfjorden (fjord), Norway 18/D2
Storjorm (lake), Sweden 18/J4
Storkerson (bay), N.W.T. 187/F2
Storla, S. Dak. 298/M6
Storm (lake), Iowa 229/C3
Storm (bay), Tasmania 99/D5
Storm Lake, Iowa 229/C3
Stormont (county), Ontario 177/K2
Stornoway, Québec 172/F4
Stornoway, Sask. 181/K4
Stornoway, Scotland 15/B2
Stornoway, Scotland 10/C1
Stornoway (harb.), Scotland 15/B2
Storøya (isl.), Norway 18/E1
Storozhevsk, Russia 52/H2
Storr, The (mt.), Scotland 15/B3
Storrs, Conn. 210/F1
Storsjön (lake), Sweden 18/J5
Storstrøm (co.), Denmark 21/E7
Stort (riv.), England 13/H7
Storthoaks, Sask. 181/K6
Storuman, Sweden 18/K4
Storuman (lake), Sweden 18/K4
Storvik, Sweden 18/K6
Story, Ind. 227/E6
Story (co.), Iowa 229/G4
Story, Wyo. 319/F1
Story City, Iowa 229/F4
Stosch (isl.), Chile 138/C8
Stotesbury, Mo. 261/C7
Stotesbury, W. Va. 312/D7
Stotts City, Mo. 261/E8
Stottville, N.Y. 276/N6
Stoughton•, Mass. 249/K4
Stoughton, Sask. 181/J6
Stoughton, Wis. 317/H10
Stoumont, Belgium 27/H8
Stour (riv.), England 13/J6
Stour (riv.), England 13/H6
Stour (riv.), England 13/E7
Stour (riv.), England 10/G4
Stourbridge, England 13/E5
Stourbridge, England 10/G3
Stourport-on-Severn, England 10/G3
Stourport-on-Severn, England 13/E5
Stout, Iowa 229/H3
Stout, Ohio 284/D8
Stout (lake), Ontario 175/B2
Stoutland, Mo. 261/G7
Stoutsville, Mo. 261/J3
Stoutsville, Ohio 284/E6
Stovall, Miss. 256/C2
Stovall, N.C. 281/M2
Stover, Mo. 261/G6
Støvring, Denmark 21/C4
Stow•, Maine 243/A7
Stow•, Mass. 249/H3
Stow (creek), N.J. 273/C5
Stow, Ohio 284/H3
Stow, Scotland 15/F5
Stowe, Pa. 294/L5
Stowe, Vt. 268/B3
Stowe•, Vt. 268/B3
Stowmarket, England 13/J5
Stowmarket, England 10/G4
Stowport, Tasmania 99/B3
Stoy, Ill. 222/F5
Stoystown, Pa. 294/E5
Strabane (dist.), N. Ireland 17/G2
Strabane, N. Ireland 17/G2
Strabane, N. Ireland 10/C3
Strachan, Scotland 15/F3
Strachur Bay, Scotland 15/C4
Stradbally, Laois, Ireland 17/G5
Stradbally, Waterford, Ireland 17/F7
Strafford, Mo. 261/F8
Strafford (co.), N.H. 268/E5
Strafford•, N.H. 268/E5
Strafford•, Vt. 268/C4
Straffordville, Ontario 177/D5
Strahan, Iowa 229/B7
Strahan, Tasmania 99/B4
Strait (butte), Utah 304/C6
Straits, N.C. 281/R5
Straits Pond, Mass. 249/F7
Straitsville, Conn. 210/C3
Strakonice, Czech Rep. 41/B2
Stralsund, Germany 22/E1
Strand, S. Africa 118/F7
Strandburg, S. Dak. 298/R3
Strandby, Denmark 21/D3
Strandquist, Minn. 255/B2
Strang, Nebr. 264/G4
Strang, Okla. 288/R2
Strange Creek, W. Va. 312/E5
Strangford, N. Ireland 17/K3
Strangford (inlet), N. Ireland 17/K3
Strängnäs, Sweden 18/F1
Stranraer, Sask. 181/C4
Stranraer, Scotland 10/D3
Stranraer, Scotland 15/C6
Strasbourg, France 28/H3
Strasbourg, France 7/E4
Strasbourg, Sask. 181/G4
Strasburg, Colo. 208/L3
Strasburg, Ill. 222/E4
Strasburg, Mo. 261/D5
Strasburg, N. Dak. 282/K7
Strasburg, Ohio 284/G4
Strasburg, Pa. 294/K6
Strasburg, Va. 307/M3
Strassburg, Austria 41/C3
Stratford, Calif. 204/F7
Stratford•, Conn. 210/C4
Stratford (pt.), Conn. 210/C4
Stratford, Iowa 229/F4
Stratford•, N.H. 268/D2
Stratford, N.J. 273/B4
Stratford, N.Y. 276/L4
Stratford, N. Zealand 100/E3
Stratford, Okla. 288/M5
Stratford, Ontario 177/C4
Stratford, S. Dak. 298/N3
Stratford, Texas 303/C1
Stratford, Va. 307/P4
Stratford, Wash. 310/F3
Stratford, Wis. 317/F6
Stratford-Centre, Québec 172/F4
Stratford-upon-Avon, England 13/F5
Stratford-upon-Avon, England 10/F4
Strathalbyn, S. Australia 94/F6
Stratham•, N.H. 268/F5
Strathaven, Scotland 15/D5
Strathbogie (dist.), Scotland 15/F3
Strathclair, Manitoba 179/B4
Strathclyde (reg.), Scotland 15/C4
Strathcona, Minn. 255/B2
Strathcona Prov. Park, Br. Col. 184/E5
Strathfield, N. S. Wales 88/K4
Strathfield, N.S. Wales 97/J3
Strathfoyle, N. Ireland 17/G1
Strathgordon, Tasmania 99/C4
Strathlorne, Nova Scotia 168/G2
Strathmere, N.J. 273/D5
Strathmoor Village, Ky. 237/J2
Strathmore, Alberta 182/D4
Strathmore, Calif. 204/F7
Strathmore, N.J. 273/E3
Strathmore, Scotland 15/E4
Strathnaver, Br. Col. 184/F3
Strathpeffer, Scotland 15/D3
Strathroy, Ontario 177/C5
Strathspey (dist.), Scotland 15/E3
Strathy (pt.), Scotland 15/E2
Strathy (pt.), Scotland 10/D1
Strathyre, Scotland 15/D4
Strattanville, Pa. 294/D3
Stratton, Colo. 208/O4
Stratton, Maine 243/B5
Stratton, Nebr. 264/C4
Stratton, Ohio 284/J4
Stratton, Ontario 177/F5
Stratton, Ontario 175/B3
Stratton•, Vt. 268/B5
Stratton (mt.), Vt. 268/B5
Straubing, Germany 22/E4
Straubville, N. Dak. 282/O7
Straughn, Ind. 227/G5
Strausberg, Germany 22/F2
Strausstown, Pa. 294/K5
Straw, Mont. 262/G4
Strawberry, Ark. 202/H2
Strawberry (lake), N. Dak. 282/J4
Strawberry (res.), Utah 304/C3
Strawberry (riv.), Utah 304/D3
Strawberry Plains, Tenn. 237/O8
Strawberry Point, Iowa 229/K3
Strawn, Ill. 222/E3
Strawn, Kansas 232/G3
Strawn, Texas 303/F5
Strayhorn, Miss. 256/D1
Strážnice, Czech Rep. 41/D2
Streaky (bay), S. Australia 88/E6
Streaky (bay), S. Australia 94/C5
Streaky Bay, S. Australia 88/E6
Streaky Bay, S. Australia 94/D5
Streamstown, Alberta 182/E3
Streamwood, Ill. 222/A5
Streator, Ill. 222/E2
Středočeský (reg.), Czech Rep. 41/C2
Středoslovenský (reg.), Slovakia 41/E2
Street, England 10/E5
Street, England 13/E6
Street, Md. 245/N2
Streeter, N. Dak. 282/M6
Streeter, Texas 303/E7
Streetman, Texas 303/H6
Streetsboro, Ohio 284/H3
Strehaia, Romania 45/F3
Stresa, Italy 34/B2
Stretford, England 13/H2
Stretford, England 10/G2
Streymoy (isl.), Denmark 21/B3
Strezhevoy, Russia 48/H3
Stříbro, Czech Rep. 41/B2
Strichen, Scotland 15/F3
Strickler, Ark. 202/B2
Strike, C.J. (res.), Idaho 220/C7
Strimón (gulf), Greece 45/G5
Stringer, Miss. 256/F7
Stringtown, Miss. 256/C3
Stringtown, Okla. 288/P6
Stripe (lake), Sask. 181/C4
Striven, Loch (inlet), Scotland 15/A2
Stroeder, Argentina 143/D5
Strofádhes (isls.), Greece 45/E7
Stroh, Ind. 227/G1
Strokestown, Ireland 17/E4
Stroma (isl.), Scotland 15/E2
Stromboli (isl.), Italy 34/E5
Strome, Alberta 182/E3
Stromeferry, Scotland 15/C3
Stromness, Scotland 10/E1
Stromness, Scotland 15/E2
Stromsburg, Nebr. 264/G3
Strümstad, Sweden 18/G7
Strümsund, Sweden 18/K5
Strom Thurmond (lake), Ga. 217/H3
Strom Thurmond (dam), S.C. 296/C4
Strom Thrumond (lake), S.C. 296/C4
Stronach, Mich. 250/C4
Strong, Ark. 202/F7
Strong•, Maine 243/C6
Strong (riv.), Miss. 256/D7
Strong City, Kansas 232/F3
Strong City, Okla. 288/G3
Strongfield, Sask. 181/E4
Stronghurst, Ill. 222/C3
Strongs, Mich. 250/E2
Strongs, Miss. 256/G3
Strongsville, Ohio 284/G10
Stronsay (firth), Scotland 15/F1
Stronsay (isl.), Scotland 10/E1
Stronsay (isl.), Scotland 15/F1
Strontian, Scotland 15/C4
Stropkov, Slovakia 41/F2
Stroud, Ala. 195/H4
Stroud, England 13/E6
Stroud, England 10/E5
Stroud, N.S. Wales 97/G3
Stroud, Okla. 288/N3
Stroud, Ontario 177/E3
Stroudsburg, Pa. 294/M4
Struan, Sask. 181/D3
Struan, Scotland 15/B3
Struble, Iowa 229/A3
Struer, Denmark 21/B5
Struer, Denmark 18/F8
Struga, Macedonia 45/E5
Strum, Wis. 317/D6
Struma (riv.), Bulgaria 45/F5
Strumble (head), Wales 13/B5
Strumica, Macedonia 45/F5
Strunk, Ky. 237/N7
Struthers, Ohio 284/J3
Stryker, Mont. 262/B2
Stryker, Ohio 284/B3
Strykersville, N.Y. 276/C5
Strzegom, Poland 47/C3
Strzelce Krajeńskie, Poland 47/B2
Strzelce Opolskie, Poland 47/D3
Strzelecki (creek), S. Australia 88/G5
Strzelecki (creek), S. Australia 94/G3
Strzelecki (mt.), Tasmania 99/D2
Strzelin, Poland 47/C3
Strzelno, Poland 47/D2
Strzyżów, Poland 47/E4
Stuart (isl.), Alaska 196/F2
Stuart (lake), Br. Col. 184/E3
Stuart, Fla. 212/F4
Stuart, Iowa 229/E6
Stuart, Nebr. 264/E2
Stuart, Okla. 288/O5
Stuart (range), S. Australia 94/D3
Stuart, Va. 307/H7
Stuart (mt.), Wash. 310/E3
Stuartburn, Manitoba 179/F5
Stuart Island, Br. Col. 184/E5
Stuarts Draft, Va. 307/L4
Stuart Town, N.S. Wales 97/E3
Stubbekøbing, Denmark 21/F8
Stubbenkammer (pt.), Germany 22/E1
Stub Hill (mt.), N.H. 268/E1
Stuckey, S.C. 296/H4
Studénka, Czech Rep. 41/D2
Studley, Kansas 232/B2
Studley, Va. 307/O5
Stukely-Sud, Québec 172/E4
Stump (lake), N. Dak. 282/O4
Stumptown, W. Va. 312/E5
Stumpy Point, N.C. 281/T3
Stupino, Russia 52/E4
Stura (riv.), Italy 34/A2
Sturbridge, Mass. 249/F4
Sturbridge•, Mass. 249/F4
Sturdivant, Mo. 261/M8
Sturgeon (lake), Alberta 182/B2
Sturgeon (bay), Manitoba 179/E3
Sturgeon (riv.), Mich. 250/C2
Sturgeon (riv.), Minn. 255/F3
Sturgeon, Mo. 261/H4
Sturgeon (lake), Ontario 177/G5
Sturgeon, Pa. 294/B5
Sturgeon, Pr. Edward I. 168/F2
Sturgeon (riv.), Sask. 181/E2
Sturgeon Bay, Wis. 317/M6
Sturgeon Falls, Ont. 162/H6
Sturgeon Falls, Ontario 175/E3
Sturgeon Falls, Ontario 177/E1
Sturgeon Heights, Alberta 182/B2
Sturgeon Lake, Minn. 255/F4
Sturgeon Point, Ontario 177/F3
Sturgeon Weir, Sask. 181/N4
Sturgis, Ky. 237/F5
Sturgis, Mich. 250/D7
Sturgis, Miss. 256/G4
Sturgis, Sask. 181/J4
Sturgis, S. Dak. 298/B5
Štúrovo, Slovakia 41/E3
Sturt (mt.), N.S. Wales 97/A1
Sturt (plain), North. Terr. 93/C4
Sturt (des.), Queensland 88/G5
Sturt (des.), Queensland 95/B3
Sturt (riv.), S. Australia 88/D8
Sturt (des.), S. Australia 94/G3
Sturt (riv.), S. Australia 94/B8
Sturt (creek), W. Australia 88/D3
Sturt (creek), W. Australia 92/D2
Sturtevant, Wis. 317/M3
Stutsman (co.), N. Dak. 282/M5
Stutterheim, S. Africa 118/D6
Stuttgart, Ark. 202/H4
Stuttgart, Kansas 232/C2
Stuttgart, Germany 7/E4
Stuttgart, Germany 22/C4
Styria (prov.), Austria 41/C3
Suai, Malaysia 85/E5
Suakin, Sudan 102/F3
Suakin, Sudan 59/C6
Suakin, Sudan 111/G4
Suakin (arch.), Sudan 111/G4
Suamico, Wis. 317/K6
Suao, China 77/K7
Suapi, Bolivia 136/B4
Suapure (riv.), Venezuela 124/E4
Suaqui, Mexico 150/E2
Suárez (riv.), Colombia 126/D4
Subang, Indonesia 85/H2
Subata, Latvia 53/D2
Subei, China 77/E4
Subeihi, Jordan 65/D3
Subh, Jebel (mt.), Saudi Arabia 59/C5
Subiaco, Ark. 202/C3
Subiaco, W. Australia 88/B2
Subi Besar (isl.), Indonesia 85/D5
Subic (bay), Philippines 82/C3
Sublett (mts.), Idaho 220/E7
Sublett, Ky. 237/P5
Sublette, Ill. 222/D2
Sublette, Kansas 232/B4
Sublette, Mo. 261/G2
Sublette (co.), Wyo. 319/C3
Subligna, Ga. 217/B1
Sublimity, Oreg. 291/E3
Subotica, Yugoslavia 7/F4
Subotica, Yugoslavia 45/D2
Subtle, Ky. 237/L7
Sucarnochee, Miss. 256/H5
Sucarnoochee (creek), Miss. 256/G5
Succasunna, N.J. 273/D2
Success, Ark. 202/J1
Success, Mo. 261/H8
Success, Sask. 181/D5
Succor (creek), Oreg. 291/K4
Suceava, Romania 45/G2
Suchedniów, Poland 47/E3
Suches, Bolivia 136/A4
Suches (riv.), Bolivia 136/A4
Suches, Ga. 217/E1
Suchitoto, El Salvador 154/C4
Süchow (Xuzhou), China 77/J5
Sucia (bay), P. Rico 161/A3
Sucia (isl.), Wash. 310/C2
Sucio (riv.), Colombia 126/B4
Suck (riv.), Ireland 17/E5
Sucre (cap.), Bolivia 2/F6
Sucre (cap.), Bolivia 120/C4
Sucre (cap.), Bolivia 136/C6
Sucre (dept.), Colombia 126/C3
Sucre, Bolívar, Colombia 126/C3
Sucre, Caquetá, Colombia 126/C7
Sucre, Ecuador 128/B3
Sucre (state), Venezuela 124/G2
Sucre, Venezuela 124/D3
Sucúa, Ecuador 128/C4
Sucuriju, Brazil 132/D2
Sud (dept.), Haiti 158/A6
Sud (chan.), Haiti 158/B6
Suda (riv.), Russia 52/E3
Sudak, Ukraine 52/E6
Sudan 2/L5
Sudan 102/E3
SUDAN 59/B6
SUDAN 111/E4
Sudan (reg.), Africa 102/D3
Sudan (reg.), Benin 106/E6
Sudan (reg.), Burkina Faso 106/D6
Sudan (reg.), Chad 111/C5
Sudan (reg.), Mali 106/D6
Sudan (reg.), Niger 106/F6
Sudan (reg.), Nigeria 106/F6
Sudan (reg.), Sudan 111/E5
Sudan, Texas 303/B3
Sudbury, England 10/G4
Sudbury, England 13/H5
Sudbury•, Mass. 249/A6
Sudbury (res.), Mass. 249/H3
Sudbury (riv.), Mass. 249/A6
Sudbury, Ontario 162/H6
Sudbury, Ontario 146/K5
Sudbury, Ontario 177/K5
Sudbury, Ontario 175/D3
Sudbury (reg. munic.), Ontario 175/D3
Sudbury (reg. munic.), Ontario 177/K6
Sudbury (terr. dist.), Ontario 175/D3
Sudbury (terr. dist.), Ontario 177/J5
Sudbury•, Vt. 268/A4
Sudd (swamp), Sudan 102/F4
Sudd (swamp), Sudan 111/F6
Suddie, Guyana 131/B2
Sudeten (mts.), Czech Rep. 41/C1
Sudeten (range), Poland 47/B3
Sudhuroy (isl.), Denmark 21/B3
Sudirman (range), Indonesia 85/K6
Sudith, Ky. 237/O4
Sudlersville, Md. 245/P4
Sue (riv.), Sudan 111/E6
Sueca, Spain 33/F3
Suemez (isl.), Alaska 196/M2
Suez (canal) 2/L4
Suez, Egypt 111/K3
Suez, Egypt 59/B4
Suez, Egypt 102/F2
Suez (canal), Egypt 102/F1
Suez (canal), Egypt 111/K3
Suez (canal), Egypt 59/B3
Suez (gulf), Egypt 111/F2
Suez (gulf), Egypt 59/B4
Suf, Jordan 65/D3
Sufeina, Saudi Arabia 59/D5
Sufers, Switzerland 39/H3
Suffern, N.Y. 276/J8
Suffield, Alberta 182/E4
Suffield, Conn. 210/E1
Suffield•, Conn. 210/E1
Suffield, Ohio 284/H3
Suffolk (co.), England 13/H5
Suffolk (co.), Mass. 249/K3
Suffolk, Mont. 262/G3
Suffolk (co.), N.Y. 276/P9
Suffolk (I.C.), Va. 307/P7
Sufian, Iran 66/E1
Sugar (creek), Ind. 227/B3
Sugar (creek), Ind. 227/F5
Sugar (creek), Ind. 227/C5
Sugar (isl.), Mich. 250/E2
Sugar (riv.), N.H. 268/C5
Sugar (creek), Pa. 294/J2
Sugar (riv.), Wis. 317/H10
Sugar Bush, Wis. 317/J7
Sugarbush Hill (mt.), Wis. 317/J4
Sugar City, Colo. 208/M6
Sugar City, Idaho 220/G6
Sugar Creek, Mo. 261/R5
Sugarcreek, Ohio 284/G5
Sugar Creek, Pa. 294/C3
Sugar Grove, Ark. 202/C3
Sugar Grove, Ill. 222/E2
Sugar Grove, Ohio 284/E6
Sugargrove, Pa. 294/D1
Sugar Grove, Va. 307/E7
Sugar Grove, W. Va. 312/H5
Sugar Hill, Ga. 217/E2
Sugar Hill•, N.H. 268/D3
Sugar Island, Mich. 250/E2
Sugar Land, Texas 303/J8
Sugarloaf (key), Fla. 212/E7
Sugarloaf (hill), Hawaii 218/C4
Sugarloaf (mt.), Ireland 17/B8
Sugarloaf (pt.), N. S. Wales 88/J6
Sugarloaf (pt.), N.S. Wales 97/J1
Sugarloaf (pt.), N.S. Wales 97/G3
Sugarloaf P.O. (Big Bear City), Calif. 204/J9
Sugar Notch, Pa. 294/E7
Sugartown, La. 238/D5
Sugar Tree, Tenn. 237/E9
Sugar Tree Ridge, Ohio 284/C7
Sugar Valley, Ga. 217/C1
Sugbai (passage), Philippines 82/C8
Sugden, Okla. 288/L6
Suggsville, Ala. 195/C7
Sühbaatar, Mongolia 77/H2
Sühbaatar (Sukhe Bator), Mongolia 77/G1
Sühbaatar, Mongolia 54/M5
Suheli Par (atoll), India 68/C6
Suhl, Germany 22/D3
Suhr, Switzerland 39/F2
Şuhut, Turkey 63/D3
Sui, Pakistan 68/B3
Suiattle (riv.), Wash. 310/D2
Suichang, China 77/J6
Suide, China 77/G4
Suifenhe, China 77/M3
Suihua, China 77/L2
Suijiang, China 77/F6
Suileng, China 77/L2
Suining, China 77/G5
Suipacha, Argentina 143/G7
Suipacha, Bolivia 136/C7
Suir (riv.), Ireland 10/C4
Suir (riv.), Ireland 17/G7
Suisun (bay), Calif. 204/K1
Suisun City, Calif. 204/K1
Suit, N.C. 281/A4
Suita, Japan 81/J7
Suitland-Silver Hill, Md. 245/F5
Sui Xian, China 77/H5
Suizhong, China 77/K3
Sukabumi, Indonesia 85/H2
Sukadana, Indonesia 85/E6
Sukagawa, Japan 81/K5
Sukhana, Russia 48/M3
Sukhinichi, Russia 52/E4
Sukhona (riv.), Russia 52/F2
Sukhothai, Thailand 72/D3
Sukhumi, Georgia 7/H4
Sukhumi, Georgia 48/D5
Sukhumi, Georgia 52/F6
Suki, Sudan 111/F5
Sukkertoppen (Maniitsoq), Greenl. 4/C12
Sukkur, Pakistan 54/H7
Sukkur, Pakistan 59/J4
Sukkur, Pakistan 68/B3
Süküsd, Hungary 41/E3
Sukumo, Japan 81/F7
Sul (chan.), Brazil 120/E2
Sul (chan.), Brazil 132/D2
Sula (isls.), Indonesia 54/O10
Sula (isls.), Indonesia 85/H6
Sula, Mont. 262/B5
Sulaco, Honduras 154/D3
Sulaco (riv.), Honduras 154/D3
Sulaiman (range), Pakistan 68/C3
Sulaimaniya (heads), Iraq 66/D3
Sulaimaniya, Iraq 59/E2
Sulaimaniya, Iraq 66/D3
Sulaiyil, Saudi Arabia 59/E5
Sulakyurt, Turkey 63/E2
Sulanheer, Mongolia 77/G3
Sulawesi (isl.), Indonesia 85/G6
Sulechów, Poland 47/B2
Sulęcin, Poland 47/B2
Sulgen, Switzerland 39/H1
Sulina, Romania 45/J3
Sulitelma (mt.), Sweden 18/K3
Sulitjelma, Norway 18/K3
Sulitjelma (mt.), Norway 18/J3
Sullana, Peru 128/B5
Sullana, Peru 120/A3
Sulligent, Ala. 195/B3
Sullivan (lake), Alberta 182/D3
Sullivan, Ill. 222/E4
Sullivan (co.), Ind. 227/C6
Sullivan, Ind. 227/C6
Sullivan, Ky. 237/E6
Sullivan, Maine 243/G6
Sullivan•, Maine 243/G6
Sullivan (co.), Mo. 261/F2
Sullivan, Mo. 261/K6
Sullivan (co.), N.H. 268/C5
Sullivan•, N.H. 268/C5
Sullivan (co.), N.Y. 276/L7
Sullivan, Ohio 284/F3
Sullivan (co.), Pa. 294/J3
Sullivan (co.), Tenn. 237/S7
Sullivan (lake), Wash. 310/H2
Sullivan, W. Va. 312/D7
Sullivan, Wis. 317/H1
Sullivan Gardens, Tenn. 237/R8
Sullivan Mines, Québec 174/B3
Sullivans Island, S.C. 296/H6
Sullom Voe, Scotland 15/G2
Sully, Iowa 229/H5
Sully, Québec 172/H2
Sully (co.), S. Dak. 298/J4
Sulmona, Italy 34/D3
Sulphide, Ontario 177/G3
Sulphur (riv.), Ark. 202/B7
Sulphur, Ind. 227/E8
Sulphur, Ky. 237/L4
Sulphur, La. 238/D6
Sulphur, Nev. 266/C2
Sulphur, Okla. 288/N5
Sulphur (creek), S. Dak. 298/D4
Sulphur (riv.), Texas 303/J4
Sulphur City, Ark. 202/B2
Sulphur Creek, Tasmania 99/C3
Sulphur Draw (dry riv.), Texas 303/B4
Sulphur Fork, Red (riv.), Tenn. 237/H8
Sulphur Rock, Ark. 202/H2
Sulphur Spring (valley), Ariz. 198/F6
Sulphur Spring (range), Nev. 266/E3
Sulphur Springs, Ala. 195/G1
Sulphur Springs, Ark. 202/B1
Sulphur Springs, Ind. 227/G4
Sulphur Springs, Iowa 229/C3
Sulphur Springs, Mo. 261/M6
Sulphur Springs, Ohio 284/E4
Sulphur Springs, Texas 303/J4
Sulphur Springs (creek), Texas 303/B4
Sulphur Well, Ky. 237/K6
Sultan, Ontario 175/D3
Sultan, Ontario 177/J5
Sultan (mts.), Turkey 63/D3
Sultan, Wash. 310/D3
Sultan (riv.), Wash. 310/D3
Sultanabad (Kashmar), Iran 66/L3
Sultandağı, Turkey 63/D3
Sultanhanı, Turkey 63/E3
Sultan Kudarat (prov.), Philippines 82/E7
Sulu (prov.), Philippines 82/C7
Sulu (arch.), Philippines 54/O9
Sulu (sea), Philippines 54/N9
Sulu (arch.), Philippines 82/B8
Sulu (arch.), Philippines 85/G4
Sulu (sea), Philippines 85/G4
Sulu (sea), Philippines 82/B6
Suluan (isl.), Philippines 82/F5
Suluova, Turkey 63/F2
Sulz, Switzerland 39/F1
Sulzbach, Germany 22/B4
Sulzbach-Rosenberg, Germany 22/D4
Sulzberger (bay), Ant. 5/B11
Sulzflüh (mt.), Switzerland 39/J2
Sumami Auma, Brazil 132/B4
Sumampa, Argentina 143/D2
Sumas, Wash. 310/C2
Sumatra, Fla. 212/B1
Sumatra (isl.), Indonesia 2/P6
Sumatra (isl.), Indonesia 54/L9
Sumatra (isl.), Indonesia 85/B5
Sumatra, Mont. 262/J4
Sumava Resorts, Ind. 227/C2
Sumba (isl.), Indonesia 54/N11
Sumba (isl.), Indonesia 85/F7
Sumba (str.), Indonesia 85/F7
Sumbawa (isl.), Indonesia 54/N11
Sumbawa (isl.), Indonesia 85/F7
Sumbawa Besar, Indonesia 85/F7
Sumbawanga, Tanzania 115/F5
Sumbay, Peru 128/G10
Sumbe, Angola 102/D6
Sumbe, Angola 115/B6
Sumbilca, Peru 128/D8
Sumbing (mt.), Indonesia 85/J2
Sumburgh (head), Scotland 15/G2
Sumedang, Indonesia 85/H2
Sümeg, Hungary 41/D3
Sumenep, Indonesia 85/L2
Sumgait, Azerbaijan 7/J4
Sumgait, Azerbaijan 52/G6
Sumidero, Cuba 158/A2
Sumiswald, Switzerland 39/E2
Sumiton, Ala. 195/D3
Summan (plat.), Saudi Arabia 59/E4
Summer (isl.), Mich. 250/C3
Summer (lake), Oreg. 188/C2
Summer (lake), Oreg. 291/G5
Summerberry, Sask. 181/J5
Summerdale, Ala. 195/C10
Summerfield, Ala. 195/E5
Summerfield, Fla. 212/D2
Summerfield, Ill. 222/D5
Summerfield, Kansas 232/F2
Summerfield, La. 238/E1
Summerfield, Mo. 261/J6
Summerfield, N.C. 281/K2
Summerfield, Ohio 284/H6
Summerfield, Okla. 288/S5
Summerfield, Texas 303/B3
Summerford, Newf. 166/C4
Summerford, Ohio 284/D6
Summer Hill, Ill. 222/C4
Summerhill, Pa. 294/E5
Summer Isles (isls.), Scotland 15/C2
Summer Lake, Oreg. 291/G5
Summerland, Br. Col. 184/G5
Summerland, Calif. 204/F9
Summerland, Miss. 256/F7
Summerland Key, Fla. 212/E7
Summers, Ark. 202/A2
Summers (co.), W. Va. 312/E7
Summerset, Iowa 229/F6
Summer Shade, Ky. 237/K7
Summerside, Pr. Edward I. 168/E2
Summersville, Ky. 237/K6
Summersville, Mo. 261/J8
Summersville, Ohio 284/D5
Summersville, W. Va. 312/E6
Summersville (lake), W. Va. 312/E6
Summerton, S.C. 296/G4
Summertown, Ga. 217/H5
Summertown, Tenn. 237/G10
Summerville, Ga. 217/B2
Summerville, La. 238/F3
Summerville, Newf. 166/D2
Summerville, Oreg. 291/K2
Summerville, Pa. 294/D3
Summerville, S.C. 296/G5
Summerville Centre, Nova Scotia 168/D5

Szczecin (prov.), Poland 47/B2
Szczecin, Poland 7/F3
Szczecin, Poland 47/B2
Szczecinek, Poland 47/C2
Szczytno, Poland 47/E2
Szechwan (Sichuan) (prov.), China 77/F5
Szécsény, Hungary 41/E2
Szeged, Hungary 41/E3
Szeged, Hungary 7/F4
Szeghalom, Hungary 41/F3
Szegvár, Hungary 41/F3
Székesfehérvár, Hungary 41/E3
Szekszárd, Hungary 41/E3
Szendrö, Hungary 41/F2
Szentendre, Hungary 41/E3
Szentendreisziget (isl.), Hungary 41/E3
Szentes, Hungary 41/F3
Szentgotthárd, Hungary 41/D3
Szentlőrinc, Hungary 41/E3
Szeping (Siping), China 77/K3
Szerencs, Hungary 41/F2
Szigetvár, Hungary 41/D3
Szikszó, Hungary 41/F2
Szil, Hungary 41/D3
Szirák, Hungary 41/E3
Szolnok (co.), Hungary 41/F3
Szolnok, Hungary 41/F3
Szombathely, Hungary 41/D3
Szprotawa, Poland 47/B3
Sztum, Poland 47/D2
Szubin, Poland 47/C2
Szydłowiec, Poland 47/E3

T

Taal (lake), Philippines 82/C4
Tab, Hungary 41/E3
Tab, Ind. 227/C4
Taba, Bir, Egypt 59/B4
Tabacal (pt.), Cuba 158/H4
Tabacundo, Ecuador 128/C2
Tabaquite, Trin. & Tob. 161/B11
Tabar (isls.), Papua N.G. 86/C1
Tabarka, Tunisia 106/F1
Tabas, Iran 59/G3
Tabas, Iran 66/L4
Tabas, Iran 66/K4
Tabasará (mts.), Panama 154/G6
Tabasco (state), Mexico 150/N7
Tabasco, Mexico 150/H6
Tabask, Kuh-e (mt.), Iran 66/G6
Tabas-Masina (Tabas), Iran 59/H3
Tabb, Va. 307/R6
Tabelbala, Algeria 106/D3
Taber, Alberta 182/E5
Taberg, N.Y. 276/J4
Tabernacle, St. Kitts & Nevis 161/C10
Tabernash, Colo. 208/H3
Tabernes de Valldigna, Spain 33/G3
Taberville, Mo. 261/E6
Tabiang, Kiribati 87/G6
Tabiona, Utah 304/D3
Tabiteuea (atoll), Kiribati 87/H6
Tablas (cape), Chile 138/A9
Tablas (isl.), Philippines 82/D4
Tablas (str.), Philippines 82/C4
Table (mt.), Nev. 266/C3
Table (bay), Newf. 166/C3
Table (bay), S. Africa 118/E6
Table (mt.), S. Africa 118/E6
Table (peak), Wyo. 319/B2
Table Grove, Ill. 222/C3
Tableland, Trin. & Tob. 161/B11
Tableland Station, W. Australia 92/D2
Tabler, Okla. 288/L4
Table Rock (riv.), Ark. 202/D1
Table Rock (res.), Mo. 261/E9
Table Rock, Nebr. 264/H4
Tablers Station, W. Va. 312/K4
Taboada, Spain 33/C1
Taboga (isl.), Panama 154/H6
Tábor, Czech Rep. 41/C2
Tabor, Iowa 229/B7
Tabor (mt.), Israel 65/C2
Tabor, Minn. 255/B2
Tabor, S. Dak. 298/O8
Tabor (mt.), Vt. 268/B5
Tabora (reg.), Tanzania 115/F5
Tabora, Tanzania 115/F5
Tabora, Tanzania 102/F5
Tabor City, N.C. 281/M6
Tabou, Ivory Coast 106/C8
Tabriz, Iran 54/F6
Tabriz, Iran 66/D2
Tabriz, Iran 59/E2
Tabuaeran (isl.), Kiribati 87/L5
Tabuk, Philippines 82/C2
Tabusintac, New Bruns. 170/E1
Tabusintac (gully), New Bruns. 170/F1
Tabusintac (riv.), New Bruns. 170/E1
Täby, Sweden 18/H1
Tacajó, Cuba 158/J3
Tacámbaro de Codallos, Mexico 150/J7
Tacaná, Guatemala 154/A3
Tacaná (vol.), Guatemala 154/A3
Tacarigua, Trin. & Tob. 161/B10
Taché (lake), Québec 172/J1
Tachen (Taizhou) (isls.), China 77/K6
Tacheng, China 77/B2
Tachikawa, Japan 81/O2
Tachina, Ecuador 128/C2
Táchira (state), Venezuela 124/C4
Tachov, Czech Rep. 41/B2
Tacloban, Philippines 82/E5
Tacloban, Philippines 85/H3
Tacna, Ariz. 198/B6
Tacna (dept.), Peru 128/G11
Tacna, Peru 128/G11
Tacna, Peru 120/B4
Tacobamba, Bolivia 136/C6
Tacoma, Va. 307/C7
Tacoma, Wash. 146/F5
Tacoma, Wash. 188/B1
Tacoma, Wash. 310/C3
Tacoma Park, S. Dak. 298/N2
Taconic, Conn. 210/B1
Taconic (mts.), Mass. 249/A2
Taconite, Minn. 255/E3
Taconite Harbor, Minn. 255/H3
Tacopaya, Bolivia 136/B5
Tacora (vol.), Chile 138/B1
Tacotalpa, Mexico 150/N8
Tacuaras, Paraguay 144/C5
Tacuarembó (dept.), Uruguay 145/D3
Tacuarembó, Uruguay 145/D2
Tacuarembó (riv.), Uruguay 145/D2
Tacuarí (riv.), Uruguay 145/E3
Tacuatí, Paraguay 144/D3
Tacutu (riv.), Brazil 132/B2
Tadcaster, England 13/K1
Tademaït (plat.), Algeria 102/C2
Tademaït, Plateau du (plat.), Algeria 106/E3
Tadine, New Caled. 86/H4
Tadjnout Hagguerete (well), Mali 106/D4
Tadjoura, Djibouti 111/H5
Tadley, England 13/F6
Tadmor (Palmyra) (ruin), Syria 59/C3
Tadmore, Sask. 181/J4
Tadmur, Syria 59/C3
Tadmur, Syria 63/H5
Tadó, Colombia 126/B5
Tadoule (lake), Manitoba 179/J2
Tadoussac, Que. 162/J6
Tadoussac, Québec 174/C3
Tadoussac, Québec 172/H1
TAJIKISTAN 48/H6
Tajikistan 54/H6
Taebaek (mt.), S. Korea 81/D5
Taedong (riv.), N. Korea 81/C4
Taegu, S. Korea 54/O6
Taegu, S. Korea 81/D6
Taejŏn, S. Korea 54/O6
Taejŏn, S. Korea 81/C5
Tafalla, Spain 33/F1
Tafassasset, Wadi (dry riv.), Algeria 106/F4
Tafassasset, Wadi (dry riv.), Niger 106/F4
Tafers, Switzerland 39/D3
Taff (riv.), Wales 13/B7
Tafí Viejo, Argentina 120/C5
Tafí Viejo, Argentina 143/C2
Taft, Calif. 204/F8
Taft, Fla. 212/E3
Taft, Iran 66/J5
Taft, La. 238/N4
Taft, Okla. 288/R3
Taft, Philippines 82/E5
Taft, Tenn. 237/H10
Taft, Texas 303/G9
Taftan, Kuh-e (mt.), Iran 66/M6
Taftan, Kuh-e (mt.), Iran 59/H4
Taftsville, Vt. 268/C4
Taftville, Conn. 210/G2
Tagab, Afghanistan 59/J3
Tagab, Afghanistan 68/B2
Taga Dzong, Bhutan 68/G3
Taganrog, Russia 7/H4
Taganrog, Russia 48/D5
Taganrog, Russia 52/E5
Tagant (reg.), Mauritania 106/B5
Tagapula (isl.), Philippines 82/E4
Tagawa, Japan 81/E7
Tagaytay, Philippines 82/C3
Tagbilaran, Philippines 82/E6
Taghit, Algeria 106/D2
Taghmon, Ireland 17/H7
Tagish (lake), Br. Col. 184/J1
Tagish, Yukon 187/E3
Tagliamento (riv.), Italy 34/D1
Tagolo (pt.), Philippines 82/D6
Tagolo (pt.), Philippines 85/G4
Tagoloan, Philippines 82/E6
Tagomago (isl.), Spain 33/G3
Tagounite, Morocco 106/C3
Tagua, Bolivia 136/B6
Taguatinga, Brazil 120/E4
Taguatinga, Goiás, Brazil 132/E6
Taguatinga, Fed. Dist., Brazil 132/D6
Tague (bay), Virgin Is. (U.S.) 161/G4
Tagula (isl.), Papua N.G. 85/C8
Tagum, Philippines 82/E7
Tagus (riv.) 7/D5
Tagus, N. Dak. 282/G3
Tagus (riv.), Portugal 33/B3
Tagus (riv.), Spain 33/D3
Tahaa (isl.), Fr. Poly. 87/L7
Tahakopa, N. Zealand 100/B7
Tahan, Gunong (mt.), Malaysia 72/D6
Tahat (mt.), Algeria 102/C2
Tahat (mt.), Algeria 106/F4
Tahawus, N.Y. 276/M2
Tahiryuak (lake), N.W.T. 187/G2
Tahiti (isl.), Fr. Polynesia 2/B6
TAHITI, Fr. Poly. 86/S13
Tahiti (isl.), Fr. Poly. 87/L7
Tahiti (isl.), Fr. Poly. 86/S13
Tahlequah, Okla. 288/R3
Tahma (riv.), Turkey 63/G3
Tahoe (lake) 188/C3
Tahoe (lake), Calif. 204/F4
Tahoe (lake), Nev. 266/B3
Tahoe City, Calif. 204/E4
Tahoka, Texas 303/C4
Taholah, Wash. 310/A3
Tahoma, Calif. 204/E4
Tahoua, Niger 102/C3
Tahoua, Niger 106/F6
Tahquamenon (falls), Mich. 250/D2
Tahquamenon (riv.), Mich. 250/D2
Tahsis, Br. Col. 184/D5
Tahta, Egypt 59/B4
Tahta, Egypt 111/F2
Tahtsa (lake), Br. Col. 184/D3
Tahua, Bolivia 136/B3
Tahuamanu (riv.), Bolivia 136/A2
Tahuamanu, Peru 128/H8
Tahuamanu (riv.), Peru 128/H8
Tahulandang (isl.), Indonesia 85/H5
Tahuna, Indonesia 85/G5
Tahuya, Wash. 310/B3
Tai'an, China 77/J4
Taiarapu (pen.), Fr. Poly. 86/T13
Taiban, N. Mex. 274/F4
Taibus, China 77/J3
Taichow (Taizhou), China 77/K5
Taichung, China 77/K7
Taichung, Taiwan 54/O7
Taieri (riv.), N. Zealand 100/C7
Taif, Saudi Arabia 54/F7
Taif, Saudi Arabia 59/D5
Taigu, China 77/H4
Taihape, N. Zealand 100/E3
Taihe, China 77/J6
Tai Hu (lake), China 77/J5
Tailem Bend, S. Australia 88/F7
Tailem Bend, S. Australia 94/F6
Taima, Saudi Arabia 59/C4
Tain, Scotland 15/D3
Tain, Scotland 10/D2
Tainan, China 77/J7
Taínaron (cape), Greece 7/G5
Taínaron (cape), Greece 45/F7
Taintor, Iowa 229/H6
Taipei, China 77/K7
Taipei (cap.), Taiwan 54/O7
Taipei (cap.), Taiwan 2/R4
Taiping, Malaysia 72/D6
Taitao (pen.), Chile 120/B7
Taitao (cape), Chile 138/D6
Taitao (pen.), Chile 138/D6
Taits Gap, Ala. 195/F3
Taitung, China 77/K7
Taivalkoski, Finland 18/P4
Taiwan 54/N7
Taiwan 2/R4
Taiwan (str.) 54/N7
Taiwan (isl.) 54/N7
TAIWAN, CHINA 77/K7
Taiwan, China 77/K7
Taiwan (Formosa) (isl.), China 77/K7
Taiwan (Formosa) (str.), China 77/J7
Taiyuan, China 77/H4
Taiyuan, China 54/N6
Taizhou (Taichow), China 77/K5
Taizhou (Tachen) (isls.), China 77/K6
Ta'izz, Yemen 54/F8
Ta'izz, Yemen 59/D7
Tajimi, Japan 81/H6
Tajique, N. Mex. 274/C4
Tajo (Tagus) (riv.), Spain 33/D3
Tajrish, Iran 66/G3
Tajumulco (vol.), Guatemala 154/B3
Tak, Thailand 72/C3
Takaishi, Japan 81/H8
Takaka, N. Zealand 100/D4
Takalar, Indonesia 85/F7
Takama, Guyana 131/C3
Takamatsu, Japan 81/F6
Takaoka, Japan 81/H5
Takapau, N. Zealand 100/F4
Takapuna, N. Zealand 100/B1
Takarazuka, Japan 81/H7
Takaroa (atoll), Fr. Poly. 87/M7
Takasaki, Japan 81/J5
Takatsuki, Japan 81/J7
Takayama, Japan 81/H5
Takefu, Japan 81/G6
Takeshima (isls.), Japan 81/F5
Takestan, Iran 66/F2
Takev, Cambodia 72/E5
Takhiatash, Turkmenistan 48/F5
Takhta-Bazar, Turkmenistan 48/G6
Takijuq (lake), N.W.T. 186/G3
Takikawa, Japan 81/K2
Takingeun, Indonesia 85/B5
Takitimu (mts.), N. Zealand 100/A6
Takkaze (riv.), Ethiopia 111/G5
Takla (lake), Br. Col. 184/D2
Takla Makan (des.), China 54/K6
Takla Makan (Taklimakan Shamo) (des.), China 77/B4
Taklimakan Shamo (des.), China 77/B4
Tako, Sask. 181/B3
Takoma Park, Md. 245/F4
Takoradi, Ghana 106/D8
Takoradi-Sekondi, Ghana 102/B4
Taksimo, Russia 48/M4
Taku (glac.), Alaska 196/N1
Taku (riv.), Alaska 196/N1
Taku (riv.), Br. Col. 184/J2
Takua Pa, Thailand 72/C5
Takutu (riv.), Guyana 131/B4
Tala, Mexico 150/H6
Tala, Uruguay 145/D5
Talab (riv.), Iran 59/H4
Talab (riv.), Iran 66/N6
Talab (riv.), Pakistan 68/A3
Talagante, Chile 138/G4
Talai (Da'an, Dalai), China 77/K2
Talak (reg.), Niger 106/E5
Talala, Okla. 288/P1
Talamanca (range), C. Rica 154/F6
Talangbetutu, Indonesia 85/C6
Talara, Peru 128/B5
Talara, Peru 120/A3
Talaud (isls.), Indonesia 54/O9
Talaud (isls.), Indonesia 85/H5
Talavera de la Reina, Spain 33/D2
Talawe (mt.), Papua N.G. 86/B2
Talbert, Ky. 237/P6
Talbingo, N.S. Wales 97/E4
Talbot, Alberta 182/E3
Talbot (isl.), Fla. 212/E1
Talbot (co.), Ga. 217/C5
Talbot, Ind. 227/C3
Talbot (co.), Md. 245/O5
Talbot (inlet), N.W.T. 187/L2
Talbot (cape), W. Australia 88/D2
Talbot (cape), W. Australia 92/D1
Talbott, Tenn. 237/P8
Talbotton, Ga. 217/C5
Talca, Chile 138/A11
Talca, Chile 120/B6
Talca (pt.), Chile 138/E3
Talcahuano, Chile 138/D1
Talcahuano, Chile 120/B6
Talcán (isl.), Chile 138/D4
Talco, Texas 303/K4
Talcott (range), Conn. 210/D1
Talcott, W. Va. 312/E7
Talcottville, Conn. 210/F1
Taldy-Kurgan, Kazakhstan 48/H5
Taldy-Kurgan, Kazakhstan 54/J5
Taleh, Somalia 115/J2
Talent, Oreg. 291/E5
Talgar, Kazakhstan 48/H5
Talgarth, Wales 13/D5
Tali (Dali), China 77/E6
Taliabu (isl.), Indonesia 85/G6
Taliaferro (co.), Ga. 217/G3
Talibon, Philippines 82/E5
Talihina, Okla. 288/S5
Talina, Bolivia 136/B7
Tali Post, Sudan 111/F6
Talisayan, Philippines 82/E6
Talisheek, La. 238/L5
Talita, Uruguay 145/D4
Tal Kaif, Iraq 66/C2
Talkeetna, Alaska 196/B1
Talkeetna (mts.), Alaska 196/J2
Talkheh (riv.), Iran 66/E1
Talking Rock, Ga. 217/D1
Tallaboa, P. Rico 161/B3
Talladega (co.), Ala. 195/F4
Talladega, Ala. 195/F4
Talladega Springs, Ala. 195/F4
Tallaght, Ireland 17/J5
Tallahaga (creek), Miss. 256/F4
Tallahala (creek), Miss. 256/F7
Tallahassee (cap.), Fla. 146/K6
Tallahassee (cap.), Fla. 188/K4
Tallahassee (cap.), Fla. 212/B1
Tallahatchie (co.), Miss. 256/D3
Tallahatchie (riv.), Miss. 256/D3
Tallahatta Springs, Ala. 195/C7
Tallangatta, Victoria 97/D5
Tallant, Okla. 288/O1
Tallapoosa (co.), Ala. 195/G5
Tallapoosa (riv.), Ala. 195/G4
Tallapoosa, Ga. 217/B3
Tallapoosa, Mo. 261/N9
Tallassee, Ala. 195/G5
Tallinn (cap.), Estonia 7/G3
Tallinn (cap.), Estonia 48/C4
Tallinn (cap.), Estonia 52/B3
Tallinn (cap.), Estonia 53/C1
Tallmadge, Ohio 284/H3
Tallman, N.Y. 276/J8
Tallman, Sask. 181/E3
Tallmansville, W. Va. 312/F5
Tallow, Ireland 17/F7
Tallula, Ill. 222/D4
Tallulah, La. 238/H2
Tallulah Falls, Ga. 217/F1
Talma, Ind. 227/E2
Talmage, Kansas 232/E2
Talmage, Nebr. 264/H4
Talmage, Sask. 181/H6
Talmage, Utah 304/D3
Talmo, Ga. 217/E2
Talmo, Kansas 232/E2
Talmoon, Minn. 255/E3
Talodi, Sudan 111/F5
Talofofo (bay), Guam 86/K7
Taloga, Okla. 288/J2
Talon (lake), Ontario 177/E1
Taloqan, Afghanistan 68/B1
Taloqan, Afghanistan 59/J2
Talpa, Texas 303/E6
Talpa de Allende, Mexico 150/G6
Talparo, Trin. & Tob. 161/B10
Talquin (lake), Fla. 212/B1
Talsi, Latvia 53/B2
Taltal, Chile 138/A5
Taltal, Chile 120/B5
Taltal, Quebrada de (riv.), Chile 138/B5
Taltson (riv.), N.W.T. 187/G3
Talvik, Norway 18/N2
Talyawalka (creek), N.S. Wales 97/B2
Talyawalka Ana Branch, Darling (riv.), N.S. Wales 97/B3
Tama (co.), Iowa 229/H4
Tama, Iowa 229/H5
Tama (riv.), Japan 81/O2
Tamaha, Okla. 288/S4
Tamaki (str.), N. Zealand 100/C1
Tamale, Ghana 102/B4
Tamale, Ghana 106/D7
Tamalpais (mt.), Calif. 204/H1
Tamana (mt.), Trin. & Tob. 161/B10
Tamanrasset, Algeria 106/F4
Tamanrasset, Algeria 102/C2
Tamanrasset, Wadi (dry riv.), Algeria 106/E4
Tamaqua, Pa. 294/L4
Tamar (riv.), England 13/C7
Tamar (riv.), England 10/D5
Tamar (riv.), Tasmania 99/D3
Támara, Colombia 126/D5
Tamarac, Fla. 212/B3
Tamarac (riv.), Minn. 255/A2
Tamarack, Idaho 220/B5
Tamarack (isl.), Manitoba 179/F3
Tamarack, Minn. 255/E4
Tamarack (riv.), Minn. 255/D2
Tamarack, Pa. 294/G3
Tamarite de Litera, Spain 33/G2
Tamaro (mt.), Switzerland 39/G4
Tamaroa, Ill. 222/D5
Tamarugal, Pampa del (plain), Chile 138/B3
Tamási, Hungary 41/E3
Tamassee, S.C. 296/A2
Tamatama, Venezuela 124/F6
Tamatave (Toamasina), Madagascar 118/H3
Tamaulipas (state), Mexico 150/K4
Tamaya, Chile 138/A8
Tamayo, Dom. Rep. 158/D6
Tamazula, Mexico 150/F4
Tamazulapan del Progreso, Mexico 150/L8
Tamazunchale, Mexico 150/K6
Tambacounda, Senegal 106/B6
Tambar Springs, N.S. Wales 97/E2
Tambelan (isls.), Indonesia 85/D5
Tamberías, Argentina 143/C3
Tambey, Russia 48/G2
Tambo (riv.), Peru 128/G11
Tambo, Queensland 88/H4
Tambo, Queensland 95/C5
Tambo de Mora, Peru 128/D9
Tambo Grande, Peru 128/B5
Tambohorano, Madagascar 118/G3
Tambopata (riv.), Peru 128/H9
Tambores, Uruguay 145/C2
Tamboril, Dom. Rep. 158/D5
Tamboritha (mt.), Victoria 97/D5
Tambov, Russia 7/J3
Tambov, Russia 48/E4
Tambov, Russia 52/F4
Tambura, Sudan 111/E6
Tamchakett, Mauritania 106/B5
Tame, Colombia 126/E4
Tame (riv.), England 10/G3
Tâmega (riv.), Portugal 33/C2
Tamentit, Algeria 106/D3
Tamiahua, Mexico 150/L6
Tamiami (canal), Fla. 212/E6
Tamil Nadu (state), India 68/D6
Tamin (gov.), Iraq 66/D3
Tamina (riv.), Switzerland 39/H3
Tamins, Switzerland 39/H3
Tamise (Temse), Belgium 27/E6
Tam Ky, Vietnam 72/F4
Tammisaari (Ekenäs), Finland 18/N6
Tamms, Ill. 222/D6
Tammun, West Bank 65/C3
Tamo, Ark. 202/G5
Tamora, Nebr. 264/G4
Tampa, Fla. 188/K5
Tampa, Fla. 146/K7
Tampa, Fla. 212/C2
Tampa (bay), Fla. 188/K5
Tampa (bay), Fla. 212/D4
Tampa, Kansas 232/E3
Tampere, Finland 7/G2
Tampere, Finland 18/N6
Tampico, Ill. 222/D2
Tampico, Ind. 227/F7
Tampico, Mexico 146/J7
Tampico, Mexico 150/L5
Tampico, Mont. 262/K2
Tampico, Wash. 310/E4
Tampoc (riv.), Fr. Guiana 131/E4
Tam Quan, Vietnam 72/F4
Tamra, Saudi Arabia 59/E5
Tams, W. Va. 312/D7
Tamsagbulag, Mongolia 77/J2
Tamsagout, Mauritania 106/C4
Tamshiyacu, Peru 128/F5
Tamsweg, Austria 41/B3
Tamuín, Mexico 150/K6
Tamuning, Guam 86/K7
Tamworth, Australia 87/E9
Tamworth, England 13/F5
Tamworth, England 10/G3
Tamworth•, N.H. 268/E4
Tamworth, N.S. Wales 88/J6
Tamworth, N.S. Wales 97/F2
Tamworth, Ontario 177/H3
Tamyang, S. Korea 81/C6
Tana (lake), Ethiopia 102/F3
Tana (lake), Ethiopia 111/G5
Tana (riv.), Finland 18/P2
Tana (riv.), Kenya 102/G5
Tana (riv.), Kenya 115/G4
Tana, Norway 18/Q1
Tana (riv.), Norway 18/P1
Tanabe, Kyoto, Japan 81/J7
Tanabe, Wakayama, Japan 81/G7
Tanacross, Alaska 196/K2
Tanafjord (fjord), Norway 18/Q1
Tanaga (isl.), Alaska 196/K4
Tanaga (vol.), Alaska 196/K4
Tanahgrogot, Indonesia 85/F6
Tanahmerah, Indonesia 85/K7
Tanah Merah, Malaysia 72/D6
Tanamá (riv.), P. Rico 161/B1
Tanami (des.), North. Terr. 88/E3
Tanami, North. Terr. 93/A5
Tanami (des.), North. Terr. 93/C5
Tánamo, Cuba 158/J3
Tan An, Vietnam 72/E5
Tanana, Alaska 188/D5
Tanana, Alaska 196/H1
Tanana (riv.), Alaska 146/D3
Tanana (riv.), Alaska 188/D5
Tanana (riv.), Alaska 196/J2
Tananarive (Antananarivo) (cap.), Madagascar 118/H3
Tanaro (riv.), Italy 34/B2
Tanch'ŏn, N. Korea 81/D3
Tancook Island, Nova Scotia 168/D4
Tanda, India 68/E3
Tandag, Philippines 82/F6
Tandil, Argentina 143/E4
Tandil, Argentina 120/D6
Tando Adam, Pakistan 68/B3
Tando Allahyar, Pakistan 68/B3
Tandou (lake), N.S. Wales 97/A3
Tandragee, N. Ireland 17/J3
Tanega (isl.), Japan 81/E8
Taney (co.), Mo. 261/F9
Taneycomo (lake), Mo. 261/F9
Taneytown, Md. 245/K2
Taneyville, Mo. 261/F9
Tanezrouft (des.), Algeria 102/C2
Tanezrouft (des.), Algeria 106/E4
Tang, Kas (isl.), Cambodia 72/D5
Tanga (isls.), Papua N.G. 86/C1
Tanga (reg.), Tanzania 115/G5
Tanga, Tanzania 115/G4
Tanga, Tanzania 102/G5
Tangainony, Madagascar 118/H4
Tangalla, Sri Lanka 68/E7
Tanganyika (lake) 102/F5
Tanganyika (lake), Burundi 115/E5
Tanganyika (lake), Tanzania 115/E5
Tanganyika (lake), D.R. Congo 115/E5
Tanganyika (lake), Zambia 115/E5
Tangent (pt.), Alaska 196/H1
Tangent, Alberta 182/B2
Tangent, Oreg. 291/D3
Tangerang, Indonesia 85/G1
Tangermünde, Germany 22/D2
Tanggula Shan (range), China 77/D5
Tangier, Ind. 227/C5
Tangier (sound), Md. 245/P8
Tangier (Tanger), Morocco 106/C1
Tangier, Morocco 102/B1
Tangier, Nova Scotia 168/F4
Tangier (riv.), Nova Scotia 168/F4
Tangier, Okla. 288/G2
Tangier, Va. 307/R5
Tangier (isl.), Va. 307/R5
Tangier (sound), Va. 307/S5
Tangipahoa (par.), La. 238/K5
Tangipahoa, La. 238/J5
Tangipahoa (riv.), La. 238/N1
Tangra Yumco (lake), China 77/C5
Tangshan, China 77/J4
Tangshan, China 54/N5
Tangub, Philippines 82/D6
Tangyanika (lake) 2/L6
Tangyuan, China 77/L2
Tanimbar (isls.), Indonesia 54/P10
Tanimbar (isls.), Indonesia 85/J7
Tanjay, Philippines 82/D6
Tanjore (Thanjovur), India 68/D6
Tanjungbalai, Indonesia 85/C5
Tanjungkarang, Indonesia 54/M10
Tanjungkarang, Indonesia 85/C7
Tanjungpandan, Indonesia 85/D6
Tanjungpinang, Indonesia 85/C5
Tanjungpriok, Indonesia 85/H1
Tanjungpura, Indonesia 85/B5
Tanjungredeb, Indonesia 85/F5
Tanjungselor, Indonesia 85/F5
Tanna (isl.), Vanuatu 87/H7
Tanner, Ala. 195/E1
Tanner, W. Va. 312/E5
Tannersville, N.Y. 276/M6
Tannersville, Pa. 294/M3
Tannis (bay), Denmark 21/D2
Tannu-Ola (range), Mongolia 77/D1
Tannu-Ola (range), Russia 48/K5
Tanon (str.), Philippines 82/D6
Tanout, Niger 106/F6
Tanque Verde, Ariz. 198/E6
Tanta, Egypt 111/J3
Tanta, Egypt 59/B3
Tantallon, Sask. 181/K5
Tantalus (mt.), Hawaii 218/D4
Tan-Tan, Morocco 106/B3
Tantoyuca, Mexico 150/L6
Tantung (Dandong), China 77/K3
Tanumshede, Sweden 18/G7
Tanunda, S. Australia 94/C6
Tanzania 2/L6
Tanzania 102/F5
TANZANIA 115/F5
Tao, Ko (isl.), Thailand 72/C5
Tao'an, China 77/K2
Taole, China 77/G4
Taongi (atoll), Marshall Is. 87/G4
Taopi, Minn. 255/F7
Taormina, Italy 34/E6
Taos, Mo. 261/H5
Taos (co.), N. Mex. 274/D2
Taos, N. Mex. 274/D2
Taos Pueblo, N. Mex. 274/D2
Taoudenni, Mali 106/D4
Taoudenni, Mali 102/B2
Taourirt, Algeria 106/E3
Taourirt, Morocco 106/D2
Taouz, Morocco 106/D2
Taoyuan, China 77/K6
Tapa, Estonia 53/C1
Tapacarí, Bolivia 136/B5
Tapachula, Mexico 150/N9
Tapajós (riv.), Brazil 2/G6
Tapajós (riv.), Brazil 120/D3
Tapajós (riv.), Brazil 132/B4
Tapaktuan, Indonesia 85/B5
Tapalquén, Argentina 143/E4
Tapanahoni (riv.), Suriname 131/D4
Tapani (lake), Québec 172/B3
Tapanui, N. Zealand 100/B6
Tapaz, Philippines 82/D5
Tapera do Jeronimo, Brazil 132/C2
Tapeta, Liberia 106/C7
Tapi, Mae Nam (riv.), Thailand 72/C5
Tapiantana Group (isls.), Philippines 82/D7
Tapiche (riv.), Peru 128/E6
Taping (riv.), Burma 72/C1
Tápiószele, Hungary 41/E3
Tapirapecó, Sierra (mts.), Venezuela 124/F7
Tapiutan (isl.), Philippines 82/B5
Tapoco, N.C. 281/A4
Tapolca, Hungary 41/D3
Tappahannock, Va. 307/O5
Tappan (lake), N.J. 273/C1
Tappan, N.Y. 276/K8
Tappan (lake), Ohio 284/H5
Tappen, N. Dak. 282/L6
Tappi (cape), Japan 81/K3
Tapti (riv.), India 68/D4
Tapul (isl.), Philippines 82/C8
Tapul Group (isls.), Philippines 85/G4
Tapul Group (isls.), Philippines 82/C8
Taputapu (cape), Amer. Samoa 86/N9
Taquari (riv.), Brazil 132/C7
Taquaritinga, Brazil 132/D8
Taquaritinga, Brazil 135/B2
Tar (riv.), N.C. 281/O3
Tara (riv.), Bos. 45/D4
Tara (hill), Ireland 17/H4
Tara, Ontario 177/C3
Tara (isl.), Philippines 82/C4
Tara, Queensland 95/D5
Tara, Queensland 88/J5

456 Tara

Tara, Russia 48/H4
Tarabuco, Bolivia 136/C6
Tarabulus, Lebanon 63/F5
Tarabulus, Lebanon 59/C3
Taradale, N. Zealand 100/F3
Taraíra (riv.), Colombia 126/F8
Tarairí, Bolivia 136/D7
Tarakan, Indonesia 54/N9
Tarakan, Indonesia 85/F5
Taralga, N.S. Wales 97/E4
Tarama (isl.), Japan 81/L7
Tarancón, Spain 33/E3
Tarangire Nat'l Park, Tanzania 115/G4
Taranna, Tasmania 99/D5
Taransay (isl.), Scotland 15/A3
Taranto (prov.), Italy 34/F4
Taranto, Italy 34/F4
Taranto, Italy 7/F4
Taranto (gulf), Italy 7/F5
Taranto (gulf), Italy 34/F5
Tarapacá (reg.), Chile 138/B2
Tarapacá, Chile 138/B2
Tarapacá, Colombia 126/F9
Tarapaya, Bolivia 136/B6
Tarapoto, Peru 120/B3
Tarapoto, Peru 128/D6
Tarare, France 28/F5
Tararua (range), N. Zealand 100/E4
Tarascon, France 28/F6
Tarasp, Switzerland 39/K3
Tarata, Bolivia 136/C5
Tarata, Peru 128/H11
Tarauacá, Brazil 132/G10
Tarauaca, Brazil 120/C3
Taravao (bay), Fr. Poly. 86/T13
Taravao (isth.), Fr. Poly. 86/T13
Tarawa (cap.), Kiribati 87/H5
Tarazona, Spain 33/E2
Tarazona de la Mancha, Spain 33/F3
Tarbat Ness (prom.), Scotland 15/E3
Tarbert, Ireland 17/C6
Tarbert, Strathclyde, Scotland 15/C5
Tarbert, W. Isles, Scotland 15/B3
Tarbert, East Loch (inlet), Scotland 15/B3
Tarbert, Loch (inlet), Scotland 15/B5
Tarbert, West Loch (inlet), Scotland 15/C5
Tarbert, West Loch (inlet), Scotland 15/A3
Tarbes, France 7/E4
Tarbes, France 28/D6
Tarbolton, Scotland 15/D5
Tarboro, Ga. 217/J8
Tarboro, N.C. 281/O3
Tarbot, Nova Scotia 168/H2
Tarcoola, S. Australia 88/E6
Tarcoola, S. Australia 94/D4
Tarcutta, N.S. Wales 97/D4
Tardienta, Spain 33/F2
Tardošked, Slovakia 41/E2
Taree, N. S. Wales 88/J6
Taree, N.S. Wales 97/G2
Tärendö, Sweden 18/N3
Tarentum, Pa. 294/C4
Tarfaya, Morocco 106/B3
Tarfaya, Morocco 102/A2
Tar Heel, N.C. 281/M5
Tarhuna, Libya 102/D1
Tarhuna, Libya 111/B1
Tariana, Colombia 126/F7
Táriba, Venezuela 124/B4
Tarifa, Spain 33/D4
Tariff, W. Va. 312/D5
Tariffville, Conn. 210/D1
Tarija (riv.), Argentina 143/D1
Tarija (dept.), Bolivia 136/D7
Tarija, Bolivia 120/C5
Tarija, Bolivia 136/C7
Tarija, Rio Grande de (riv.), Bolivia 136/C8
Tariku (riv.), Indonesia 85/K6
Tarim (riv.), China 54/K5
Tarim, Yemen 59/E6
Tarim He (riv.), China 77/B3
Tarim Pendi (basin), China 77/B4
Tar Island, Alberta 182/E1
Taritatu (riv.), Indonesia 85/K6
Tarkio, Mo. 261/B2
Tarkio, Mont. 262/B4
Tarko-Sale, Russia 48/H3
Tarkwa, Ghana 106/D7
Tarlac (prov.), Philippines 82/C3
Tarlac, Philippines 82/C3
Tarlac, Philippines 85/G2
Tarland, Scotland 15/F3
Tarleton (lake), N.H. 268/D4
Tarlton, Ohio 284/E6
Tarlton, Tenn. 237/K9
Tarlton Downs, North. Terr. 93/E7
Tarm, Denmark 21/B6
Tarma, Peru 128/E8
Tarn (dept.), France 28/E6
Tarn (riv.), France 28/E6
Tarna (riv.), Hungary 41/F3
Tärnaby, Sweden 18/J4
Tarnak (riv.), Afghanistan 68/B2
Tårnby, Denmark 21/F6
Tarn-et-Garonne (dept.), France 28/D5
Tarnobrzeg (prov.), Poland 47/E3
Tarnobrzeg, Poland 47/E3
Tarnopol, Sask. 181/F3
Tarnov, Nebr. 264/G3
Tarnów (prov.), Poland 47/E4
Tarnów, Poland 7/G3
Tarnów, Poland 47/E4
Tarnowskie Góry, Poland 47/A3
Tarom, Iran 66/J6
Tarom, Iran 59/G4
Taroom, Queensland 95/D5
Tarouca, Portugal 33/C2
Taroudannt, Morocco 106/C2
Taroudannt, Morocco 102/A2
Tarpa, Hungary 41/G2
Tarpon Springs, Fla. 212/D3
Tarqui, Peru 128/E3
Tarquinia, Italy 34/C3
Tarqumiya, West Bank 65/C4
Tarragona (prov.), Spain 33/G2
Tarragona, Spain 33/G2
Tarragona, Spain 7/E4
Tarraleah, Tasmania 99/C4
Tarrant (co.), Texas 303/G5
Tarrant, Ala. 195/E3
Tarrants, Mo. 261/K4
Tarrasa, Spain 33/G2
Tárrega, Spain 33/G2
Tarryall (creek), Colo. 208/H4
Tarrytown, Ga. 217/H6
Tarrytown, N.Y. 276/O6
Tarsney Lakes, Mo. 261/R6
Tarsus, Turkey 59/C2
Tarsus, Turkey 63/F4
Tart, China 77/D4
Tartagal, Argentina 143/D1
Tartagal, Argentina 120/C5
Tartas, France 28/C6
Tartu, Estonia 7/G3
Tartu, Estonia 48/C4
Tartu, Estonia 52/C3
Tartu, Estonia 53/D1
Tartus (prov.), Syria 63/G5
Tartus, Syria 63/F5
Tarutung, Indonesia 85/B5
Tarver, Ga. 217/G9
Tarzan, Texas 303/B5
Tarzana, Calif. 204/B10
Täsch, Switzerland 39/E4
Tasco, Kansas 232/B2
Tashauz, Turkmenistan 48/F5
Tashk (lake), Iran 59/F4
Tashk (lake), Iran 66/J6
Tashkent (cap.), Uzbekistan 2/N3
Tashkent (cap.), Uzbekistan 48/G5
Tashkent (cap.), Uzbekistan 54/H5
Tasikmalaya, Indonesia 85/H2
Tasisuak (lake), Newf. 166/B2
Taşkent, Turkey 63/E4
Taşköprü, Turkey 63/F2
Taşlıçay, Turkey 63/K3
Tasman (sea) 2/S7
Tasman (sea) 87/G9
Tasman (sea) 88/J7
Tasman (sea), N.S. Wales 97/F5
Tasman (bay), N. Zealand 100/D4
Tasman (mt.), N. Zealand 100/C5
Tasman (mts.), N. Zealand 100/D4
Tasman (sea), N. Zealand 100/B4
Tasman (head), Tasmania 99/D5
Tasman (pen.), Tasmania 88/H8
Tasman (pen.), Tasmania 99/E5
Tasman (sea), Tasmania 99/E4
Tasman (sea), Victoria 97/F5
TASMANIA 99
Tasmania, Australia 87/H8
Tasmania (state), Australia 87/E10
Tasmania (isl.), Australia 2/S8
Tăşnad, Romania 45/F2
Taşova, Turkey 63/F4
Tassili N'Ahaggar (plat.), Algeria 106/E4
Tassili N'Ajjer (plat.), Algeria 106/F3
Tåstrup, Denmark 21/F6
Tasu, Br. Col. 184/A4
Taşucu (gulf), Turkey 63/E4
Taswell, Ind. 227/D8
Tata, Hungary 41/E3
Tataa (pt.), Fr. Poly. 86/S13
Tatabánya, Hungary 41/E3
Tatahouine, Tunisia 106/G2
Tatalrose, Br. Col. 184/D3
Tatamagouche, Nova Scotia 168/E3
Tatamba, Solomon Is. 86/D3
Tatamy, Pa. 294/M4
Tatar (str.), Russia 48/P4
Tatar (str.), Russia 54/R5
Tatar Aut. Rep., Russia 52/G3
Tatar Aut. Rep., Russia 48/F4
Tatarsk, Russia 48/H4
Tate, Ga. 217/D2
Tate (co.), Miss. 256/E1
Tate, Sask. 181/G4
Tateville, Ky. 237/M7
Tateyama, Japan 81/K6
Tathlina (lake), N.W.T. 187/G3
Tathlith, Saudi Arabia 59/D6
Tathra, N.S. Wales 97/F5
Tati (riv.), Botswana 118/D4
Tatitlek, Alaska 196/D1
Tatla Lake, Br. Col. 184/E4
Tatlatui (lake), Br. Col. 184/D2
Tatlayoko (lake), Br. Col. 184/E4
Tatnam (cape), Manitoba 179/K2
Tatnum (cape), Man. 162/G4
Tatoosh (isl.), Wash. 310/A2
Tatra, High (mts.), Slovakia 41/E2
Tatra, High (range), Poland 47/D4
Tatta, Pakistan 59/J5
Tatta, Pakistan 68/B4
Tattnall (co.), Ga. 217/J6
Tatuí, Brazil 135/C3
Tatum, N. Mex. 274/F5
Tatum, S.C. 296/H2
Tatum, Texas 303/K5
Tatums, Okla. 288/M6
Tatung (Datong), China 77/H3
Tatura, Victoria 97/C5
Tatvan, Turkey 63/K3
Taubaté, Brazil 132/E8
Taubaté, Brazil 135/D3
Tauber (riv.), Germany 22/C4
Täuffelen, Switzerland 39/D2
Taumarunui, N. Zealand 100/E3
Taum Sauk (mt.), Mo. 261/L7
Taung, S. Africa 118/C5
Taungdwingyi, Burma 72/C2
Taunggyi, Burma 72/C2
Taungthonton (mt.), Burma 72/B1
Taungup, Burma 72/B3
Taunton, England 13/D6
Taunton, England 10/E5
Taunton, Mass. 249/K5
Taunton (riv.), Mass. 249/K5
Taunton, Minn. 255/B6
Taunus (range), Germany 22/C3
Taupo, N. Zealand 100/F3
Taupo (lake), N. Zealand 100/F3
Tauq, Iraq 66/D3
Tauragė, Lithuania 52/B3
Tauragė, Lithuania 53/B3
Tauranga, N. Zealand 100/F2
Taureau (res.), Québec 172/D3
Taurianova, Italy 34/E5
Tauroa (pt.), N. Zealand 100/D1
Taurus (mts.), Turkey 59/B2
Taurus (mts.), Turkey 63/D4
Tauste, Spain 33/F2
Tautira, Fr. Poly. 86/T13
Tautira (pt.), Fr. Poly. 86/T13
Tauu (isls.), Papua N.G. 86/D2
Tavai, Paraguay 144/E5
Tavan Bogd Uul (mt.), Mongolia 77/C2
Tavannes, Switzerland 39/D2
Tavaputs (plat.), Utah 304/D4
Tavares, Fla. 212/E3
Tavas, Turkey 63/C4
Tavda, Russia 48/G4
Tavernier, Fla. 212/F6
Taveta, Kenya 115/G4
Tavetsch, Switzerland 39/G3
Taveuni (isl.), Fiji 87/H7
Taveuni (isl.), Fiji 86/R10
Tavignano (riv.), France 28/B6
Tavira, Portugal 33/C4
Tavistock (rock), England 10/D5
Tavistock, England 13/C7
Tavistock, N.J. 273/B3
Tavistock, Ontario 177/D4
Tavoy, Burma 54/L8
Tavoy, Burma 72/C4
Tavoy (pt.), Burma 72/C4
Tavrichanka, Russia 48/O5
Tavşanlı, Turkey 63/C3
Taw (riv.), England 13/D7
Taw (riv.), England 10/D5
Tawa, N. Zealand 100/B2
Tawas (lake), Mich. 250/F4
Tawas (pt.), Mich. 250/F4
Tawas City, Mich. 250/F4
Tawatinaw, Alberta 182/D2
Tawau, Malaysia 85/F5
Tawin (isl.), Ireland 17/C5
Tawi-Tawi (prov.), Philippines 82/B8
Tawi-Tawi (isl.), Philippines 82/B8
Tawitawi Group (isls.), Philippines 85/G4
Taxco de Alarcón, Mexico 150/K7
Taxila (ruins), Pakistan 68/C2
Taxis River, New Bruns. 170/D2
Taxkorgan, China 77/A4
Tay (firth), Scotland 15/F4
Tay (firth), Scotland 10/E2
Tay, Loch (lake), Scotland 10/D2
Tay, Loch (lake), Scotland 15/D4
Tay (riv.), Scotland 10/E2
Tay (riv.), Scotland 15/E4
Tay (lake), W. Australia 88/C6
Tayabamba, Peru 128/D7
Tayabas (bay), Philippines 82/C4
Tayasan, Philippines 82/D6
Taycheedah, Wis. 317/K8
Tay Creek, New Bruns. 170/D2
Tayibe, Israel 65/C3
Tayinloan, Scotland 15/C5
Taylor, Ala. 195/H8
Taylor (mts.), Alaska 196/G2
Taylor, Ariz. 198/E4
Taylor, Ark. 202/D7
Taylor, Br. Col. 184/G2
Taylor (peak), Colo. 208/F5
Taylor (riv.), Colo. 208/F5
Taylor (co.), Fla. 212/C1
Taylor (co.), Ga. 217/D5
Taylor (mt.), Idaho 220/D5
Taylor (co.), Iowa 229/D7
Taylor (co.), Ky. 237/L6
Taylor, La. 238/D1
Taylor, Mich. 250/B7
Taylor, Miss. 256/E2
Taylor, Mo. 261/J3
Taylor, Nebr. 264/E3
Taylor (mt.), N. Mex. 274/B3
Taylor, N. Dak. 282/F6
Taylor (head), Nova Scotia 168/F4
Taylor, Pa. 294/F7
Taylor (co.), Texas 303/E5
Taylor, Texas 303/G7
Taylor, Texas 188/G4
Taylor (co.), W. Va. 312/F4
Taylor (co.), Wis. 317/E5
Taylor, Wis. 317/E7
Taylor Lake Village, Texas 303/K2
Taylor Mill, Ky. 237/S2
Taylor Park (res.), Colo. 208/F5
Taylors, S.C. 296/C2
Taylor's Arm, N.S. Wales 97/G2
Taylors Falls, Minn. 255/F5
Taylors Island, Md. 245/N7
Taylorsport, Ky. 237/R2
Taylor Springs, Ill. 222/D4
Taylorstown, Pa. 294/A5
Taylorsville, Calif. 204/E3
Taylorsville, Ga. 217/C2
Taylorsville, Ind. 227/F6
Taylorsville, Ky. 237/L4
Taylorsville, Md. 245/K3
Taylorsville, Miss. 256/F7
Taylorsville, N.C. 281/G3
Taylorsville (Philo), Ohio 284/G6
Taylorsville, Utah 304/B3
Taylortown, La. 238/C2
Taylorville, Ill. 222/D4
Taymouth, New Bruns. 170/D2
Taymyr (lake), Russia 4/B5
Taymyr (lake), Russia 48/K2
Taymyr (lake), Russia 54/M2
Taymyr (pen.), Russia 4/B4
Taymyr (pen.), Russia 48/L2
Taymyr (pen.), Russia 54/L2
Taymyr (riv.), Russia 48/K2
Taymyr Aut. Okr., Russia 48/K2
Tay Ninh, Vietnam 72/E5
Tayoltita, Mexico 150/G4
Tayport, Scotland 10/E2
Tayport, Scotland 15/F4
Tayshet, Russia 48/K4
Tayside (reg.), Scotland 15/E4
Taytay, Philippines 85/F3
Taytay, Philippines 82/B5
Taytay (bay), Philippines 82/B5
Tayyebat, Iran 66/M3
Taz (riv.), Russia 4/C5
Taz (riv.), Russia 48/J3
Taz (riv.), Russia 54/K3
Taza, Morocco 106/D2
Tazadit, Mauritania 106/B4
Taza Khurmatu, Iraq 66/D3
Tazawa (lake), Japan 81/K4
Tazerbo (oasis), Libya 111/D2
Tazewell, Ga. 217/D6
Tazewell (co.), Ill. 222/D3
Tazewell, Tenn. 237/O8
Tazewell (co.), Va. 307/E6
Tazewell, Va. 307/E6
Tazin (lake), Sask. 181/L2
Tazlina (lake), Alaska 196/D1
Tazlina (riv.), Alaska 196/D1
Tazlina Glacier Lodge, Alaska 196/C1
Tazovskiy, Russia 48/J3
Tbilisi (cap.), Georgia 7/J4
Tbilisi (cap.), Georgia 2/M3
Tbilisi (cap.), Georgia 48/E5
Tbilisi (cap.), Georgia 52/F6
Tchentlo (lake), Br. Col. 184/E2
Tchibanga, Gabon 115/B4
Tchollíré, Cameroon 115/B2
Tchula, Miss. 256/D4
Tchula (lake), Miss. 256/D4
Tczew, Poland 47/D1
Tea, S. Dak. 298/R7
Teacapán (inlet), Mexico 150/F5
Teachey, N.C. 281/N5
Teague, Texas 303/H6
Te Anau, N. Zealand 100/A6
Te Anau (lake), N. Zealand 100/A6
Teaneck•, N.J. 273/B2
Teapa, Mexico 150/N8
Teapot Dome (mt.), Wyo. 319/F2
Te Araroa, N. Zealand 100/G2
Te Aroha, N. Zealand 100/E2
Teasdale, Utah 304/C5
Te Atatu, N. Zealand 100/B1
Teaticket, Mass. 249/M6
Tea Tree Gully, S. Australia 88/E7
Tea Tree Gully, S. Australia 94/B7
Tea Tree Well, North. Terr. 93/C7
Te Awamutu, N. Zealand 100/E3
Teays, W. Va. 312/B6
Tebenkof (bay), Alaska 196/M2
Tébessa, Algeria 102/C1
Tébessa, Algeria 106/F1
Tebicuary (riv.), Paraguay 144/C5
Tebicuary Mí, Paraguay 144/B5
Tebicuary Mí (riv.), Paraguay 144/C5
Tebingtinggi, Indonesia 85/B5
Tebuk (Tabuk), Saudi Arabia 59/C4
Tecamachalco, Mexico 150/O2
Tecate, Mexico 150/A1
Tecer (mts.), Turkey 63/G3
Techirghiol, Romania 45/J3
Tecka, Argentina 143/B5
Tecolote (creek), N. Mex. 274/D3
Tecomán, Mexico 150/H7
Tecopa, Calif. 204/J8
Tecpan de Galeana, Mexico 150/J8
Tecuala, Mexico 150/G5
Tecuci, Romania 45/H3
Tecumseh, Kansas 232/G2
Tecumseh, Mich. 250/E7
Tecumseh, Mo. 261/H9
Tecumseh, Nebr. 264/H4
Tecumseh (mt.), N.H. 268/D4
Tecumseh, Okla. 288/N4
Tecumseh, Ontario 177/B5
Tedrow, Ohio 284/B2
Teduzara, Bolivia 136/B2
Tedzhen, Turkmenistan 48/F6
Teec Nos Pos, Ariz. 198/F2
Teeds Grove, Iowa 229/N4
Teegarden, Ind. 227/E2
Teepee Creek, Alberta 182/A2
Tees, Alberta 182/D3
Tees (riv.), England 10/F3
Tees (riv.), England 13/F3
Teeswater, Ontario 177/C3
Teeterville, Ontario 177/D5
Tefé, Brazil 132/G9
Tefé, Brazil 120/C3
Tefé (riv.), Brazil 132/G9
Tefenni, Turkey 63/C4
Tefft, Ind. 227/D2
Tegal, Indonesia 85/J2
Tegel, Germany 22/E3
Tegelen, Netherlands 27/J6
Tegernsee (lake), Germany 22/D5
Tegucigalpa (cap.), Hond. 146/K8
Tegucigalpa (cap.), Honduras 154/D3
Tehachapi, Calif. 204/G8
Tehachapi (mts.), Calif. 204/G9
Tehama (co.), Calif. 204/C3
Tehama, Calif. 204/C3
Tehchow (Dezhou), China 77/J4
Tehek (lake), N.W.T. 187/J3
Tehkummah, Ontario 177/B2
Tehran (cap.), Iran 2/M4
Tehran (cap.), Iran 66/G3
Tehran (cap.), Iran 59/F2
Tehran (cap.), Iran 54/G6
Tehri, India 68/D2
Tehuacán, Mexico 150/L7
Tehuantepec, Mexico 146/J8
Tehuantepec, Mexico 150/M8
Tehuantepec (gulf), Mexico 150/M9
Tehuantepec (isth.), Mexico 150/M8
Tehuipango, Mexico 150/P2
Teide, Pico de (peak), Spain 33/B5
Teifi (riv.), Wales 13/C5
Teifi (riv.), Wales 10/D4
Teigen, Mont. 262/H3
Teignmouth, England 10/E5
Teignmouth, England 13/D7
Teith (riv.), Scotland 15/D4
Tejerri, Libya 111/B3
Tejerri, Libya 102/D2
Tejo (Tagus) (riv.), Portugal 33/B3
Tejutla, Guatemala 154/B3
Tekamah, Nebr. 264/H3
Te Kao, N. Zealand 100/D1
Tekapo (lake), N. Zealand 100/C5
Te Karaka, N. Zealand 100/F3
Te Kauwhata, N. Zealand 100/E2
Tekax de álaro Obregón, Mexico 150/P6
Tekeli, Kazakhstan 48/H5
Tekes, China 77/B3
Tekirdağ (prov.), Turkey 63/B2
Tekirdağ, Turkey 59/A1
Tekirdağ, Turkey 63/B2
Tekman, Turkey 63/J3
Teknaf, Bangladesh 68/G4
Tekoa, Wash. 310/H3
Tekong Besar, Pulau (isl.), Singapore 72/F6
Tekonsha, Mich. 250/E6
Te Kopuru, N. Zealand 100/D2
Te Kuiti, N. Zealand 100/E3
Tel (riv.), India 68/E4
Tela, Honduras 154/D3
Telanaipura, Indonesia 54/M10
Telavi, Georgia 52/G6
Tel Aviv (dist.), Israel 65/B3
Tel Aviv, Israel 59/B3
Tel Aviv, Israel 65/B3
Tel Aviv, Israel 54/E6
Telč, Czech Rep. 41/C2
Telde, Spain 33/B5
Telefomin, Papua N.G. 85/B7
Telegraph, Texas 303/E7
Telegraph Creek, Br. Col. 184/K2
Telemark (co.), Norway 18/F7
Telephone, Texas 303/J4
Telescope (peak), Calif. 204/H7
Telescope (pt.), Grenada 161/D8
Teles Pires (riv.), Brazil 120/D3
Teles Pires (riv.), Brazil 132/B5
Telfair (co.), Ga. 217/G7
Telford, England 13/E5
Telford, Pa. 294/M5
Telford, Tenn. 237/S8
Telfordville, Alberta 182/C3
Telfs, Austria 41/A3
Telgte, Germany 22/B3
Télimélé, Guinea 106/B6
Telkalakh, Syria 63/F5
Tel Kotchek, Syria 59/D2
Tel Kotchek, Syria 63/K4
Telkwa, Br. Col. 184/D3
Tell, Ga. 217/J2
Tell, Texas 303/D3
Tell 'Asur (mt.), Jordan 65/C4
Tell City, Ind. 227/D9
Teller, Alaska 196/E1
Teller (co.), Colo. 208/J5
Tellicherry, India 68/C6
Tellico (riv.), Tenn. 237/N10
Tellico Plains, Tenn. 237/N10
Tellin, Belgium 27/G8
Telluride, Colo. 208/D7
Telma, Wash. 310/E3
Telocaset, Oreg. 291/K2
Telogia, Fla. 212/B1
Teloloapan, Mexico 150/J7
Telpaneca, Nicaragua 154/D4
Tel'pos-Iz (mt.), Russia 52/K2
Telsen, Argentina 143/C5
Telšiai, Lithuania 52/B3
Telšiai, Lithuania 53/B2
Teltow, Germany 22/E4
Teltown, Ireland 17/H4
Telukbayur, Indonesia 85/C6
Teluk Intan, Malaysia 72/D6
Tema, Ghana 106/E7
Tema, Ghana 102/C4
Temacine, Algeria 106/F2
Temae (lake), Fr. Poly. 86/S12
Temagami, Ontario 177/K5
Temagami, Ontario 175/E3
Temagami (lake), Ontario 177/K5
Temagami (lake), Ontario 175/D3
Temanggung, Indonesia 85/J2
Temascalapa, Mexico 150/M1
Tematangi (isl.), Fr. Poly. 87/M8
Temax, Mexico 150/P6
Tembisa, S. Africa 118/H6
Temblador, Venezuela 124/G3
Tembuè, Mozambique 118/E2
Temecula, Calif. 204/H10
Temerloh, Malaysia 72/D7
Temiang, Bukit (mt.), Malaysia 72/D6
Temirtau, Kazakhstan 54/J4
Temirtau, Kazakhstan 48/H4
Témiscaming, Québec 174/B3
Témiscamingue (county), Québec 174/B3
Témiscouata (co.), Québec 172/J2
Témiscouata (lake), Québec 172/H2
Temma, Tasmania 99/A3
Temora, N. S. Wales 88/H6
Temora, N.S. Wales 97/D4
Temoris, Mexico 150/E3
Temósachic, Mexico 150/E2
Tempe, Ariz. 198/D5
Tempe Downs, North. Terr. 93/C8
Tempelhof, Germany 22/F4
Temperance, Mich. 250/F7
Temperance Hall, Tenn. 237/K8
Temperance Vale, New Bruns. 170/C2
Temperanceville, Va. 307/T5
Tempio Pausania, Italy 34/B4
Temple (mt.), Alberta 182/B4
Temple, Ga. 217/B3
Temple, La. 238/E4
Temple•, Maine 243/C6
Temple, Mich. 250/E4
Temple•, N.H. 268/D6
Temple, Okla. 288/K6
Temple, Pa. 294/L5
Temple, Texas 303/G6
Temple, Texas 188/G4
Temple Bar, Ariz. 198/A2
Temple City, Calif. 204/D10
Templemore, Ireland 10/C4
Templemore, Ireland 17/F6
Templestowe and Doncaster, Victoria 97/J5
Temple Terrace, Fla. 212/C2
Templeton, Calif. 204/E8
Templeton, Ind. 227/C3
Templeton, Iowa 229/D5
Templeton•, Mass. 249/F2
Templeton, Pa. 294/C4
Templeton, Québec 172/B4
Templetuohy, Ireland 17/F6
Templeville, Md. 245/P4
Templin, Germany 22/E2
Tempo, N. Ireland 17/G3
Temryuk, Russia 52/E5
Temse, Belgium 27/E6
Temuco, Chile 120/B6
Temuco, Chile 138/E2
Temuka, N. Zealand 100/C6
Temvik, N. Dak. 282/K7
Ten, Colombia 126/D5
Tena, Ecuador 128/D3
Tenabo, Mexico 150/P6
Tenafly, N.J. 273/C1
Tenaha, Texas 303/K6
Tenakee Springs, Alaska 196/M1
Tenali, India 68/E5
Tenancingo de Degollado, Mexico 150/K7
Tenango de Río Blanco, Mexico 150/O2
Tenants Harbor, Maine 243/E8
Tenares, Dom. Rep. 158/E5
Tenasserim (div.), Burma 72/C4
Tenasserim, Burma 72/C5
Tenasserim (isl.), Burma 72/C4
Tenbury, England 13/E5
Tenby, Manitoba 179/C4
Tenby, Wales 10/D5
Tenby, Wales 13/C6
Tendal, La. 238/H2
Ten Degree (chan.), India 68/G7
Tendelti, Sudan 111/F5
Tendelti, Sudan 102/F3
Tendo, Japan 81/K4
Tendoy, Idaho 220/E5
Tendrara, Morocco 106/D2
Tendre (peak), Switzerland 39/B3
Tenecape, Nova Scotia 168/E3
Ténenkou, Mali 106/C6
Ténéré (des.), Niger 106/G5
Tenerife (isl.), Spain 102/A2
Tenerife (isl.), Spain 106/A3
Tenerife (isl.), Spain 33/B5
Ténès, Algeria 106/E1
Teng, Nam (riv.), Burma 72/C2
Tengchong, China 77/E6
Tenggarong, Indonesia 85/F6
Tenggol, Pulau (isl.), Malaysia 72/D6
Tengiz (lake), Kazakhstan 48/G4
Teng Xian, China 77/H7
Tenigerbad, Switzerland 39/G3
Tenino, Wash. 310/C4
Tenke, D.R. Congo 115/E6
Tenkiller Ferry (lake), Okla. 288/S3
Tenkodogo, Burkina Faso 106/E6
Tenleytown, D.C. 245/E4
Ten Mile (lake), Newf. 166/C3
Tenmile, Oreg. 291/D4
Tenmile (creek), Oreg. 291/K5
Ten Mile, Tenn. 237/M9
Tenmile (creek), Texas 303/G3
Tennant, Calif. 204/C2
Tennant, Iowa 229/C5
Tennant Creek, Australia 87/D7
Tennant Creek, North. Terr. 88/E3
Tennant Creek, North. Terr. 93/C5
Tennent, N.J. 273/E3
Tennessee 188/J3
TENNESSEE 237
Tennessee (riv.) 188/J3
Tennessee (riv.), Ala. 195/C1
Tennessee, Ill. 222/C3
Tennessee (riv.), Ky. 237/D6
Tennessee (riv.), Tenn. 237/E10
Tennessee (state), U.S. 146/K6
Tennessee City, Tenn. 237/F8
Tennessee Pass, Colo. 208/G4
Tennessee Ridge, Tenn. 237/F8
Tennessee-Tombigbee Waterway, Ala. 195/B4
Tennessee-Tombigbee Waterway, Miss. 256/H2
Tenneville, Belgium 27/H8
Tenney, Minn. 255/B4
Tennga, Ga. 217/C1
Tennille, Ala. 195/G7
Tennille, Ga. 217/G5
Tennyson, Ind. 227/C8
Tennyson, Texas 303/D6
Tennyson, Wis. 317/E10
Teno, Chile 138/A10
Tenosique de Pino Suárez, Mexico 150/O8
Tenquehuen (isl.), Chile 138/D6
Tenri, Japan 81/J8
Tensas (par.), La. 238/H2
Tensas (riv.), La. 238/G3
Tensaw, Ala. 195/C8
Tensaw (riv.), Ala. 195/C9
Tensed, Idaho 220/B2
Ten Sleep, Wyo. 319/E1
Tenstrike, Minn. 255/D3
Tenterden, England 13/H6
Tenterfield, N. S. Wales 88/J5
Tenterfield, N.S. Wales 97/G1
Ten Thousand (isls.), Fla. 188/K5
Ten Thousand (isls.), Fla. 212/E6
Ten Thousand Smokes (valley), Alaska 196/G3
Teocaltiche, Mexico 150/H6
Teocelo, Mexico 150/P1
Teófilo Otoni, Brazil 120/E4
Teófilo Otoni, Brazil 132/F7
Te One, N. Zealand 100/D7
Teotihuacán (ruin), Mexico 150/M1

Ticehurst 457

Teotihuacán de Arista, Mexico 150/L1
Teotitlán del Camino, Mexico 150/L8
Tepa, Indonesia 85/H7
Tepache, Mexico 150/E2
Tepalcingo, Mexico 150/M2
Tepatitlán de Morelos, Mexico 150/H6
Tepeaca, Mexico 150/N2
Tepeapulco, Mexico 150/M1
Tepehuanes, Mexico 150/G4
Tepeji del Río, Mexico 150/L1
Tepelenë, Albania 45/D5
Tepetlán, Mexico 150/P1
Tepexi de Rodríguez, Mexico 150/N2
Tepeyahualco, Mexico 150/O1
Tepic, Mexico 150/G6
Teplá u Toužimě, Czech Rep. 41/B1
Teplice, Czech Rep. 41/B1
Tepoztlán, Mexico 150/L1
Te Puke, N. Zealand 100/F2
Tequeje (riv.), Bolivia 136/B3
Tequendama (falls), Colombia 126/C5
Tequesquite (creek), N. Mex. 274/E2
Tequesta, Fla. 212/F5
Tequixquitla, Mexico 150/O1
Ter (riv.), Spain 33/H1
Téra, Niger 106/E6
Teraina (isl.), Kiribati 87/L5
Teramo (prov.), Italy 34/D3
Teramo, Italy 34/D3
Terán, Mexico 150/N8
Terang, Victoria 97/B6
Ter Apel, Netherlands 27/L3
Terawhiti (cape), N. Zealand 100/A3
Tercan, Turkey 63/J3
Terceira (isl.), Portugal 33/C1
Tercero (riv.), Argentina 143/D3
Terchová, Slovakia 41/E2
Terempa, Indonesia 85/D5
Terence Bay, Nova Scotia 168/E4
Terengganu (state), Malaysia 72/D6
Teresina, Brazil 120/E3
Teresina, Brazil 132/F4
Teresita, Mo. 261/J9
Teresópolis, Brazil 135/E3
Terespol, Poland 47/F2
Teressa (isl.), India 68/G7
Terevinto, Bolivia 136/D5
Terhazza (ruins), Mali 106/C4
Terhune, Ind. 227/E4
Teriberka, Russia 52/E1
Terlingua, Texas 303/D12
Terlingua (creek), Texas 303/D12
Terlton, Okla. 288/O2
Termas de Cauquenes, Chile 138/B10
Terme, Turkey 63/G2
Termez, Uzbekistan 48/G6
Termini Imerese, Italy 34/D6
Términos (lag.), Mexico 150/O7
Termo, Calif. 204/E3
Termoli, Italy 34/E3
Termonde (Dendermonde), Belgium 27/E6
Termonfeckin, Ireland 17/J4
Termunten, Netherlands 27/K2
Ternate, Indonesia 54/O9
Ternate, Indonesia 85/H5
Terneuzen, Netherlands 27/D6
Terni (prov.), Italy 34/D3
Terni, Italy 34/D3
Terni, Italy 7/F4
Ternitz, Austria 41/D3
Ternopol', Ukraine 48/C5
Ternopol', Ukraine 52/C5
Te Roto, N. Zealand 100/D7
Terowie, S. Australia 94/F5
Terpeniye (cape), Russia 48/P5
Terra Alta, W. Va. 312/H4
Terra Bella, Calif. 204/G8
Terrabona, Nicaragua 154/E4
Terrace, Br. Col. 162/D5
Terrace, Br. Col. 184/C3
Terrace, Br. Col. 184/C3
Terrace, Minn. 255/C5
Terrace Bay, Ontario 177/H5
Terrace Bay, Ontario 175/C3
Terrace Heights, Wash. 310/E4
Terra Ceia, Fla. 212/D4
Terrace Park, Ohio 284/D9
Terracina, Italy 34/D4
Terra Corra, Neth. Ant. 161/E8
Terråk, Norway 18/H4
Terral, Okla. 288/L7
Terralba, Italy 34/B5
Terra Nova, Newf. 166/C2
Terra Nova (riv.), Newf. 166/C2
Terra Nova Nat'l Park, Newf. 166/D2
Terrebonne (par.), La. 238/J8
Terrebonne (bay), La. 238/J8
Terrebonne, Minn. 255/B3
Terrebonne, Oreg. 291/F3
Terrebonne (co.), Québec 172/H4
Terrebonne, Québec 172/H4
Terre-de-Bas (isl.), Guadeloupe 161/A7
Terre-de-Haut (isl.), Guadeloupe 161/A7
Terre Haute, Ill. 222/C3
Terre Haute, Ind. 188/J3
Terre Haute, Ind. 227/C6
Terre Hill, Pa. 294/L5
Terrell (co.), Ga. 217/D7
Terrell, N.C. 281/G3
Terrell (co.), Texas 303/B7
Terrell, Texas 188/G4
Terrell, Texas 303/H5
Terrell Hills, Texas 303/K11
Terrenate, Mexico 150/N1
Terrenceville, Newf. 166/D4
Terre Neuve, Haiti 158/B5
Terreton, Idaho 220/F6
Terrey Hills, N. S. Wales 88/L3
Terrey Hills, N.S. Wales 97/J3
Terri (mt.), Switzerland 39/D2
Terri (peak), Switzerland 39/H3
Terrigal-Wamberal, N.S. Wales 97/F3
Terril, Iowa 229/C2
Terrill (mt.), Utah 304/C5
Territok (cape), Newf. 166/B2
Terry, La. 238/H1
Terry, Miss. 256/D6
Terry, Mont. 262/L4
Terry (co.), Texas 303/B4
Terry Town, La. 238/O4
Terrytown, Nebr. 264/A3
Terryville, Conn. 210/C2
Terschelling (isl.), Netherlands 27/G2
Teruel (prov.), Spain 33/F2
Teruel, Spain 33/F2
Terutao, Ko (isl.), Thailand 72/C6
Tervola, Finland 18/O3
Tesawa, Libya 111/B2
Tescott, Kansas 232/E2
Teshekpuk (lake), Alaska 196/H1
Teshio, Japan 81/K1
Teshio (mt.), Japan 81/L1
Teshio (riv.), Japan 81/L1
Tesla, W. Va. 312/E5
Teslić, Bos. 45/C3
Teslin (lake) 162/C3
Teslin (lake), Br. Col. 184/K1
Teslin, Yukon 187/E3
Teslin (lake), Yukon 187/E4
Teslin (riv.), Yukon 187/E3
Tessalit, Mali 106/E4
Tessaoua, Niger 106/F6
Tessenderlo, Belgium 27/G6
Tessenei, Eritrea 59/C6
Tessenei, Eritrea 111/G4
Tessier, Sask. 181/D4
Test (riv.), England 13/F6
Testa (cape), Italy 34/B4
Testa del Gargano (cape), Italy 34/F4
Tesuque, N. Mex. 274/C3
Tét, Hungary 41/D3
Tetachuck (lake), Br. Col. 184/E3
Tetagouche (riv.), New Bruns. 170/D1
Tetas (pt.), Chile 138/A4
Tete (prov.), Mozambique 118/E3
Tete, Mozambique 102/F6
Tete, Mozambique 118/E3
Tête-à-la-Baleine, Québec 174/E2
Tete Jaune Cache, Br. Col. 184/H4
Te Teko, N. Zealand 100/F3
Teterboro, N.J. 273/B2
Teterow, Germany 22/E2
Teterton, W. Va. 312/H5
Teteven, Bulgaria 45/G4
Tetiaroa (atoll), Fr. Poly. 87/M7
Tetlin, Alaska 196/K2
Teton (co.), Idaho 220/G6
Teton, Idaho 220/G6
Teton (riv.), Idaho 220/G6
Teton (co.), Mont. 262/D3
Teton (riv.), Mont. 262/E3
Teton (co.), Wyo. 319/B2
Teton (range), Wyo. 319/B2
Tetonia, Idaho 220/G6
Teton Village, Wyo. 319/B2
Tetotum, Va. 307/P4
Tétouan, Morocco 106/C1
Tétouan, Morocco 102/B1
Tetovo, Macedonia 45/E5
Teuco (riv.), Argentina 143/D1
Teufen, Switzerland 39/H2
Teulada (cape), Italy 7/E5
Teulada (cape), Italy 34/B5
Teulon, Manitoba 179/E4
Teupasenti, Honduras 154/D3
Teustepe, Nicaragua 154/E4
Teutoburger Wald (for.), Germany 22/C2
Teutopolis, Ill. 222/E4
Teuva, Finland 18/M5
Teviot (riv.), Scotland 15/F5
Teviot (riv.), Scotland 10/E3
Te Waewae (bay), N. Zealand 100/A7
Tewantin-Noosa, Queensland 95/E5
Te Whanga (mts.), N. Zealand 100/E7
Tewkesbury, England 10/F5
Tewkesbury, England 13/E6
Tewksbury, Mass. 249/K2
Texa (isl.), Scotland 15/B5
Texada (isl.), Br. Col. 184/J2
Texarkana, Ark. 188/H4
Texarkana, Ark. 202/C7
Texarkana, Texas 188/H4
Texarkana, Texas 146/J6
Texarkana, Texas 303/L4
Texas 188/G4
TEXAS 303
Texas, Ga. 217/B4
Texas, Ky. 237/L5
Texas, Md. 245/M3
Texas (co.), Mo. 261/J8
Texas (co.), Okla. 288/C1
Texas (state), U.S. 146/J6
Texas City, Texas 303/K3
Texas Creek, Colo. 208/H6
Texcoco de Mora, Mexico 150/M1
Texel (isl.), Netherlands 27/F2
Texhoma, Okla. 288/C1
Texhoma, Texas 303/C1
Texico, N. Mex. 274/F4
Texistepeque, El Salvador 154/C3
Texline, Texas 303/B1
Texola, Okla. 288/G4
Texoma (lake) 188/G4
Texoma (lake), Okla. 288/N7
Texoma (lake), Texas 303/H3
Texon, Texas 303/C6
Teykovo, Russia 52/E3
Teyvareh, Afghanistan 68/A2
Teyvareh, Afghanistan 59/H3
Teziutlán, Mexico 150/O1
Tezonapa, Mexico 150/P2
Tezontepec, Mexico 150/M1
Tezpur, India 68/G3
Tezu, India 68/H3
Tezzeron (lake), Br. Col. 184/E3
Tha, Nam (riv.), Laos 72/D2
Tha-anne (riv.), N.W.T. 187/J3
Thabazimbi, S. Africa 118/D4
Thacher (isl.), Mass. 249/M2
Tha Chin, Mae Nam (riv.), Thailand 72/C4
Thacker, W. Va. 312/B7
Thackeray, Ill. 222/E5
Thackeray, Ohio 284/C5
Thackerville, Okla. 288/M7
Thai Binh, Vietnam 72/E2
Thailand 2/Q5
Thailand 54/M8
THAILAND (SIAM) 72
Thailand (gulf) 2/Q5
Thailand (gulf) 54/M9
Thailand (gulf), Cambodia 72/D5
Thailand (gulf), Thailand 72/D5
Thai Nguyen (cliff), Vietnam 72/E2
Thakhek (Muang Khammouan), Laos 72/E3
Thal, Pakistan 59/K3
Thal, Switzerland 39/J2
Thalberg, Manitoba 179/F4
Thale, Germany 22/D3
Thale Luang (lag.), Thailand 72/D6
Thalia, Texas 303/E4
Thalmann, Ga. 217/J8
Thalu, Ko (isls.), Thailand 72/C5
Thalwil, Switzerland 39/G2
Thame, England 13/G6
Thame (riv.), England 13/G7
Thames (riv.), Conn. 210/G3
Thames (riv.), England 10/F5
Thames (riv.), England 13/H6
Thames, N. Zealand 100/E2
Thames (firth), N. Zealand 100/E2
Thames (riv.), Ontario 177/B5
Thamesford, Ontario 177/C4
Thamesville, Conn. 210/G2
Thamesville, Ontario 177/C5
Thana, India 68/B6
Thana (creek), India 68/B7
Thane, Alaska 196/N1
Thangool, Queensland 95/D5
Thanh Hoa, Vietnam 72/E3
Thanh Tri, Vietnam 72/E5
Thanjavur, India 68/D6
Thann, France 28/G4
Thar (des.), Pakistan 68/C3
Thargomindah, Queensland 88/G5
Thargomindah, Queensland 95/C5
Tharrawaddy, Burma 72/C3
Tharthar, Wadi (dry riv.), Iraq 66/C3
Tharthar (res.), Iraq 66/C3
Thásos, Greece 45/G5
Thásos (isl.), Greece 45/G5
Thatch (cay), Virgin Is. (U.S.) 161/B4
Thatcham, England 13/F6
Thatcher, Ariz. 198/F6
Thatcher, Colo. 208/L7
Thatcher, Idaho 220/G7
That Khe, Vietnam 72/E2
Thaton, Burma 72/C3
Thau (mts.), France 28/F6
Thaungdut, Burma 72/B1
Thawville, Ill. 222/E3
Thaxton, Miss. 256/F2
Thaxton, Va. 307/K6
Thaya (riv.), Austria 41/C2
Thayawthadangyi Kyun (isl.), Burma 72/C4
Thayer, Ill. 222/D4
Thayer, Ind. 227/C2
Thayer, Iowa 229/E6
Thayer, Kansas 232/G4
Thayer, Mo. 261/J9
Thayer (co.), Nebr. 264/G4
Thayer, Nebr. 264/G4
Thayer, W. Va. 312/E7
Thayer Junction, Wyo. 319/D4
Thayetmyo, Burma 72/B3
Thayne, Wyo. 319/A3
Thayngen, Switzerland 39/G1
Thazi, Burma 72/C2
The Alberga (riv.), S. Australia 94/D2
Thealka, Ky. 237/R5
Theano (pt.), Ontario 177/J5
THE ANTILLES 156
Thebarton, S. Australia 88/D8
Thebarton, S. Australia 94/A7
The Battlefords Prov. Park, Sask. 181/C2
Thebes, Ill. 222/D6
The Colony, Texas 303/G1
The Coorong (lag.), S. Australia 94/F6
The Dalles, Oreg. 188/B1
The Dalles, Oreg. 291/F2
The Dalles (dam), Oreg. 291/F2
The Dalles (dam), Wash. 310/D5
Thedford, Nebr. 264/D3
Thedford, Ontario 177/C4
The Entrance, N.S. Wales 88/J6
The Entrance, N.S. Wales 97/F3
The Gap, N.S. Wales 97/A2
The Gap, Queensland 88/J2
The Glen, N.Y. 276/N3
The Granites, North. Terr. 93/B6
The Hamilton (riv.), S. Australia 94/D2
The Hawk, Nova Scotia 168/C5
The Heads (prom.), Oreg. 291/C5
The Hermitage, N. Zealand 100/C5
Theilman, Minn. 255/F6
Thelon (riv.), N.W.T. 146/H3
Thelon (riv.), N.W.T. 162/F3
Thelon (riv.), N.W.T. 187/H3
Them, Denmark 21/C5
The Macumba (riv.), S. Australia 94/E2
The Narrows (str.), N.J. 273/E2
Thendara, N.Y. 276/K3
The Neales (riv.), S. Australia 94/E3
Theodore, Ala. 195/B9
Theodore, Queensland 95/D5
Theodore, Sask. 181/J4
Theodore Roosevelt (dam), Ariz. 198/D5
Theodore Roosevelt (lake), Ariz. 198/D5
Theodore Roosevelt Nat'l Mem. Park, N. Dak. 282/D4
Theodore Roosevelt Nat'l Mem. Park, N. Dak. 282/C5
Theodore Roosevelt Nat'l Mem. Park, N. Dak. 282/D6
Theodosia, Mo. 261/G9
The Pas, Man. 162/F5
The Pas, Manitoba 179/H3
The Plains, Ohio 284/F7
The Plains, Va. 307/N3
The Range, New Bruns. 170/E2
Theresa, N.Y. 276/J2
Theresa, Wis. 317/K8
Therien, Alberta 182/E2
Theriot, La. 238/J8
Thermaic (gulf), Greece 45/F6
Thermal, Calif. 204/J10
Thermalito, Calif. 204/D4
Thermopolis, Wyo. 319/D2
The Rock, Ga. 217/D5
The Rock, N.S. Wales 97/D4
The Round (mt.), N.S. Wales 97/G2
Therwil, Switzerland 39/E1
The Salt (lake), N.S. Wales 97/B2
Thesiger (bay), N.W.T. 187/F2
The Skaw (Skagens Odde) (cape), Denmark 21/D2
Thessalon, Ont. 162/H6
Thessalon, Ontario 177/J5
Thessalon, Ontario 175/D3
Thessaloníki, Greece 7/G4
Thessaloníki, Greece 45/F5
Thessaly (reg.), Greece 45/F6
The Stevenson (riv.), S. Australia 94/D2
Thetford, England 13/H5
Thetford, England 10/G4
Thetford•, Vt. 268/C4
Thetford Center, Vt. 268/C4
Thetford Mines, Québec 172/F3
Thetis Island, Br. Col. 184/J3
The Twins (mt.), Alberta 182/B3
Theux, Belgium 27/H8
The Village, Okla. 288/L3
The Warburton (riv.), S. Australia 94/F2
Thibault, New Bruns. 170/C1
Thibodaux, La. 238/J7
Thicket Portage, Manitoba 179/J3
Thickwood (hills), Alberta 182/D1
Thickwood (hills), Sask. 181/D2
Thida, Ark. 202/H2
Thief (lake), Minn. 255/C2
Thief (riv.), Minn. 255/B2
Thief River Falls, Minn. 255/B2
Thielsen (mt.), Oreg. 291/F4
Thiensville, Wis. 317/L1
Thiers, France 28/E5
Thiès, Senegal 106/A5
Thiès, Senegal 102/A3
Thika, Kenya 102/F5
Thika, Kenya 115/G4
Thimphu (cap.), Bhutan 54/L7
Thimphu (cap.), Bhutan 68/G3
Thio, Eritrea 111/H5
Thio, New Caled. 86/H4
Thionville, France 28/G3
Thíra, Greece 45/G7
Thíra (isl.), Greece 45/G7
Third (lake), Maine 243/H5
Third (lake), N.H. 268/E1
Third Cataract, Sudan 111/E4
Third Cataract (dam), Sudan 102/E3
Third Cataract, Sudan 59/B6
Third Lake, Ill. 222/B4
Thirsk, England 13/F3
Thirty Mile (creek), N. Dak. 282/F6
Thirtymile (creek), Oreg. 291/G2
Thisted, Denmark 21/B4
Thisted, Denmark 18/F8
Thistle (isl.), S. Australia 94/E6
Thistle, Utah 304/C4
Thithia (isl.), Fiji 86/R10
Thívai, Greece 45/F6
Thiviers, France 28/D5
Thjórsá (riv.), Iceland 21/C1
Thlewiaza (riv.), N.W.T. 187/J3
Thoa (riv.), N.W.T. 187/H3
Tho Chau, Hon (isl.), Vietnam 72/D5
Thoen, Thailand 72/C3
Thohoyandou, S. Africa 118/E4
Thohoyandou (cap.), Venda, S. Africa 102/F7
Tholen, Netherlands 27/E5
Thomas (co.), Ga. 217/E9
Thomas (co.), Kansas 232/A2
Thomas, Md. 245/N6
Thomas (co.), Nebr. 264/D3
Thomas, Okla. 288/J3
Thomas (creek), Oreg. 291/G5
Thomas, S. Dak. 298/P4
Thomas (lake), Texas 303/C5
Thomas (range), Utah 304/A4
Thomas, W. Va. 312/H4
Thomasboro, Ill. 222/E3
Thomas Stone Nat'l Hist. Site, Md. 245/K6
Thomaston, Ala. 195/C6
Thomaston•, Conn. 210/C2
Thomaston (res.), Conn. 210/C2
Thomaston, Ga. 217/D5
Thomaston, Maine 243/E7
Thomaston•, Maine 243/E7
Thomaston, N.Y. 276/P7
Thomastown, Ireland 10/C4
Thomastown, Ireland 17/G7
Thomastown, La. 238/H2
Thomastown, Miss. 256/E5
Thomastown, Victoria 97/J4
Thomasville, Ala. 195/C7
Thomasville, Ga. 188/K4
Thomasville, Ga. 217/E9
Thomasville, Miss. 256/E6
Thomasville, Mo. 261/J9
Thomasville, N.C. 281/J3
Thomasville, Pa. 294/J6
Thomonde, Haiti 158/C6
Thompson, Ala. 195/G6
Thompson (riv.), Br. Col. 184/G5
Thompson•, Conn. 210/H1
Thompson (peak), Idaho 220/C5
Thompson, Iowa 229/F2
Thompson (riv.), Iowa 229/E7
Thompson, Man. 162/G4
Thompson, Man. 146/J4
Thompson, Manitoba 179/J2
Thompson (isl.), Mass. 249/D7
Thompson, Mich. 250/C3
Thompson (creek), Miss. 256/G8
Thompson, Mo. 261/J4
Thompson (peak), N. Mex. 274/D3
Thompson, N. Dak. 282/R4
Thompson, Ohio 284/H2
Thompson, Pa. 294/L2
Thompson (riv.), Queensland 95/B5
Thompson (lake), S. Dak. 298/O5
Thompson (mt.), Wyo. 319/B3
Thompson Falls, Mont. 262/A3
Thompsons (creek), S.C. 296/G2
Thompson Springs, Utah 304/E5
Thompsons Station, Tenn. 237/H9
Thompsontown, Pa. 294/H4
Thompson Valley (res.), Oreg. 291/F5
Thompsonville, Conn. 210/E1
Thompsonville, Ill. 222/E6
Thompsonville, Mich. 250/C4
Thomsen (riv.), N.W.T. 187/G2
Thomson, Ga. 217/H4
Thomson, Ill. 222/C2
Thomson, Minn. 255/F4
Thomson (riv.), Queensland 88/G4
Thomson's Falls, Kenya 115/G3
Thon Buri, Thailand 72/D4
Thongwa, Burma 72/C3
Thonon-les-Bains, France 28/G4
Thonotosassa, Fla. 212/D3
Thor, Iowa 229/E3
Thorburn, Nova Scotia 168/F3
Thoreau, N. Mex. 274/A3
Thoresby (mt.), Newf. 166/B2
Thorhild, Alberta 182/D2
Thorn, Miss. 256/F3
Thornaby-on-Tees (hill), England 10/F3
Thornaby-on-Tees, England 13/F3
Thornburg, Iowa 229/J6
Thornburg, Va. 307/N4
Thornbury, England 13/E6
Thornbury, Ontario 177/D3
Thorndale, Ontario 177/C4
Thorndale, Texas 303/G7
Thorndike•, Maine 243/E6
Thorndike, Mass. 249/E4
Thorne, England 13/F4
Thorne, N. Dak. 282/L2
Thorne, Ontario 175/E3
Thorne Bay, Alaska 196/M2
Thornfield, Mo. 261/G9
Thornhill, Br. Col. 184/C3
Thornhill, Ky. 237/K1
Thornhill, Manitoba 179/D5
Thornhill, Central, Scotland 15/D4
Thornhill, Dumf. & Gall., Scotland 15/E5
Thorn Hill, Tenn. 237/P8
Thornhurst, Pa. 294/L3
Thornley, England 13/J4
Thornloe, Ontario 175/E3
Thornloe, Ontario 177/K5
Thornton, Ark. 202/F6
Thornton, Calif. 204/B9
Thornton, Colo. 208/K3
Thornton, Idaho 220/G6
Thornton, Ill. 222/C6
Thornton, Iowa 229/G3
Thornton, Miss. 256/D4
Thornton•, N.H. 268/D4
Thornton, Ontario 177/E3
Thornton, Texas 303/H6
Thornton, Wash. 310/H3
Thornton, W. Va. 312/G4
Thornton Cleveleys, England 13/G1
Thornton Cleveleys, England 10/F1
Thorntown, Ind. 227/D4
Thornville, Ohio 284/F6
Thornwell, La. 238/E6
Thornwood, W. Va. 312/G5
Thorofare, N.J. 273/B4
Thorold, Ontario 177/E4
Thorp, Wash. 310/E3
Thorp, Wis. 317/E6
Thorpe (lake), N.C. 281/C4
Thorpe, W. Va. 312/D8
Thorp Spring, Texas 303/F5
Thorsby, Ala. 195/E5
Thorsby, Alberta 182/C3
Thouars, France 28/C4
Thouin (pt.), W. Australia 88/B4
Thouin (pt.), W. Australia 92/B3
Thousand (isls.), N.Y. 276/H2
Thousand (isls.), Ontario 177/H3
Thousand Island Park, N.Y. 276/J2
Thousand Lake (mt.), Utah 304/C5
Thousand Oaks, Calif. 204/G9
Thousand Palms, Calif. 204/J10
Thousand Spring (creek), Nev. 266/G1
Thousand Springs, Nev. 266/G1
Thrace (reg.), Greece 45/G5
Thrall, Kansas 232/F3
Thrasher, Miss. 256/G1
Three (isls.), New Bruns. 170/D4
Three Bridges, N.J. 273/D2
Three Churches, W. Va. 312/J4
Three Creek, Idaho 220/C7
Three Creeks, Alberta 182/B1
Three Creeks, Ark. 202/E7
Three Forks, Mont. 262/E5
Three Guardsmen (mt.), Br. Col. 184/H1
Three Hills, Alberta 182/D4
Three Hummock (isl.), Tasmania 99/B2
Three Kings (isls.), N. Zealand 100/D1
Three Lakes, Wis. 317/H4
Three Mile Bay, N.Y. 276/H2
Three Mile Plains, Nova Scotia 168/D4
Three Notch, Ala. 195/G6
Three Oaks, Mich. 250/C7
Three Pagodas (pass), Burma 72/C4
Three Pagodas (pass), Thailand 72/C4
Three Points (cape), Ghana 106/D8
Three Rivers, Mass. 249/E4
Three Rivers, Mich. 250/D7
Three Rivers, N. Mex. 274/C5
Three Rivers (Trois-Rivières), Québec 172/E3
Three Rivers, Texas 303/F9
Three Rivers, W. Australia 92/B4
Three Sisters (mt.), Oreg. 291/F3
Three Springs, Pa. 294/G5
Three Springs, W. Australia 88/B5
Three Springs, W. Australia 92/A5
Throckmorton (co.), Texas 303/E4
Throckmorton, Texas 303/F4
Throne, Alberta 182/E3
Throop, Pa. 294/F7
Thrums, Br. Col. 184/J5
Thrumster, Scotland 15/E2
Thuin, Belgium 27/E8
Thule Air Base, Greenland 2/F2
Thule Air Base, Greenland 4/B13
Thule Air Base, Greenland 146/M2
Thumail, Iraq 66/C4
Thun, Switzerland 39/E3
Thunder (bay), Mich. 250/F4
Thunder (hills), Sask. 181/L4
Thunder (creek), S. Dak. 298/N4
Thunder (creek), S. Dak. 298/K6
Thunder (lake), Wis. 317/H4
Thunder Bay (riv.), Mich. 250/F3
Thunder Bay, Ont. 162/H6
Thunder Bay, Ont. 146/K5
Thunder Bay (terr. dist.), Ontario 175/C3
Thunder Bay (terr. dist.), Ontario 177/H5
Thunder Bay, Ontario 175/C3
Thunder Bay, Ontario 177/H5
Thunderbird (lake), Okla. 288/M4
Thunderbolt, Ga. 217/K6
Thunder Butte (creek), S. Dak. 298/E3
Thunder Hawk, S. Dak. 298/F2
Thunder Lake, Alberta 182/C2
Thunersee (lake), Switzerland 39/E3
Thunstetten, Switzerland 39/E2
Thur (riv.), Switzerland 39/G1
Thurgau (canton), Switzerland 39/H1
Thüringer Wald (for.), Germany 22/D3
Thuringia (state), Germany 22/D3
Thurles, Ireland 10/B4
Thurles, Ireland 17/F6
Thurloo Downs, N.S. Wales 97/B1
Thurlow (dam), Ala. 195/G6
Thurlow, Mont. 262/K4
Thurman, Iowa 229/B7
Thurman, N.Y. 276/M3
Thurman, Ohio 284/F8
Thurmond, W. Va. 312/D7
Thurmont, Md. 245/J2
Thurrock, England 13/J8
Thurrock, England 10/C5
Thursday Island, Queensland 88/G2
Thursday Island, Queensland 95/B1
Thurso, Québec 172/B4
Thurso, Scotland 10/E1
Thurso, Scotland 15/E2
Thurso (riv.), Scotland 15/E2
Thurston (isl.) 5/C14
Thurston (co.), Nebr. 264/H2
Thurston, Nebr. 264/H2
Thurston, Ohio 284/E6
Thurston (co.), Wash. 310/C4
Thusis, Switzerland 39/H3
Thutade (lake), Br. Col. 184/D2
Thyatira, Miss. 256/E1
Thyborøn, Denmark 21/A4
Thyolo, Malawi 115/F7
Thyregod, Denmark 21/C6
Tia, N.S. Wales 97/F2
Tiahuanacu, Bolivia 136/A5
Tia Juana, Venezuela 124/C2
Tiandong, China 77/G7
Tianjin, China 2/Q4
Tianjin, China 54/N6
Tianjin (Tientsin), China 77/J4
Tianjun, China 77/E4
Tianlin, China 77/G7
Tian Shan (range), China 77/C3
Tianshui, China 77/F5
Tianzhu, China 77/F4
Tiaret, Algeria 106/E1
Tiatucurá, Uruguay 145/C3
Tiavea, Samoa 86/M8
Tiawah, Okla. 288/P2
Tib, Ras el (Bon) (cape), Tunisia 106/G1
Tibagi, Brazil 135/A4
Tibagi (riv.), Brazil 135/A4
Tibaná, Colombia 126/D5
Tibati, Cameroon 115/B2
Tibbie, Ala. 195/B8
Tibbita, N.S. Wales 97/C4
Tiber (riv.), Italy 7/F4
Tiber (riv.), Italy 34/D3
Tiberias, Israel 65/C2
Tiberias (lake), Israel 65/D2
Tibesti (mts.) 102/D2
Tibesti, Serir (des.), Chad 111/C3
Tibesti (mts.), Chad 111/C3
Tibesti, Serir (des.), Libya 111/C3
Tibet (reg.), China 2/P4
Tibet (reg.), China 54/K6
Tibet (reg.), China 77/B5
Tibet Aut. Reg. (Xizang), China 77/B5
Tibooburra, N.S. Wales 88/G5
Tibooburra, N.S. Wales 97/B1
Tibro, Sweden 18/J7
Tibugá (gulf), Colombia 126/B5
Tiburon, Calif. 204/J2
Tiburon, Haiti 158/A6
Tiburon (cape), Haiti 156/C3
Tiburon (cape), Haiti 158/A6
Tiburón (isl.), Mexico 150/C2
Tiburón (pt.), Panama 154/J6
Ticaco, Peru 128/H11
Ticao (isl.), Philippines 82/D4
Tice, Fla. 212/E5
Ticehurst, England 13/H6

Três Marias 459

Tomasaki (mt.), Utah 304/E5
Tomás Barrón, Bolivia 136/B5
Tomás Gomensoro, Uruguay 145/B1
Tomaszów Lubelski, Poland 47/F3
Tomaszów Mazowiecki, Poland 47/E3
Tomatin, Scotland 15/D3
Tomatlán, Mexico 150/G6
Tomave, Bolivia 136/B7
Tombador, Serra do (range), Brazil 132/B6
Tomball, Texas 303/J7
Tombe, Sudan 111/F6
Tombigbee (riv.) 188/J4
Tombigbee (riv.), Ala. 195/B7
Tombigbee (riv.), Miss. 256/H4
Tombstone, Ariz. 198/F7
Tombua, Angola 115/B7
Tomé, Chile 138/D1
Tome, N. Mex. 274/C4
Tomelilla, Sweden 18/J9
Tomelloso, Spain 33/E3
Tom Green (co.), Texas 303/D6
Tomhannock (res.), N.Y. 276/O5
Tomichi (creek), Colo. 208/F5
Tomifobia, Québec 172/E4
Tomina, Bolivia 136/C6
Tomingley, N.S. Wales 97/E3
Tomini (gulf), Indonesia 54/O10
Tomini (gulf), Indonesia 85/G6
Tomintoul, Scotland 15/E3
Tomiyama, Japan 81/O3
Tomkinson (ranges), W. Australia 92/E4
Tommerup, Denmark 21/D7
Tommot, Russia 48/N4
Tomnolen, Miss. 256/F4
Tomo (riv.), Colombia 126/F5
To Mo, Thailand 72/D6
Tompa, Hungary 41/E3
Tompkins (co.), N.Y. 276/H6
Tompkins, Sask. 181/C5
Tompkinsville, Ky. 237/K7
Tompkinsville, Md. 245/L7
Tom Price, W. Australia 88/B4
Tom Price, W. Australia 92/B3
Toms (riv.), N.J. 273/E3
Toms Brook, Va. 307/L3
Toms Creek, Va. 307/D7
Tomsk, Russia 54/K4
Tomsk, Russia 48/J4
Tomslake, Br. Col. 184/H2
Toms River, N.J. 273/E4
Tom Steed (res.), Okla. 288/J5
Tümük, Turkey 63/F4
Tonalá, Mexico 150/N8
Tonalea, Ariz. 198/E2
Tonasket, Wash. 310/F2
Tonate, Fr. Guiana 131/E3
Tonawanda, N.Y. 276/B4
Tonawanda Ind. Res., N.Y. 276/D4
Tonbridge, England 13/H8
Tonckens (falls), Suriname 131/C3
Tondabayashi, Japan 81/J8
Tondano, Indonesia 85/H5
Tønder, Denmark 21/B8
Tønder, Denmark 18/F9
Tone (riv.), Japan 81/K6
Tonegrama, Peru 128/D4
Tonekabon, Iran 59/F2
Tonekabon, Iran 66/G2
Toney, Ala. 195/E1
Toney River, Nova Scotia 168/F3
Tonga 2/A6
Tonga 87/J8
Tonga, Sudan 111/F6
Tongala, Victoria 97/C5
Tonganoxie, Kansas 232/G2
Tongareva (atoll), Cook Is. 87/L6
Tongatapu (isls.), Tonga 87/J8
Tongcheng, China 77/J5
T'ongch'ŏn, N. Korea 81/D4
Tongchuan (Tungchwan), China 77/G5
Tongde, China 77/F4
Tongeren, Belgium 27/G7
Tonghai, China 77/F7
Tonghe, China 77/L2
Tonghua (Tunghwa), China 77/L3
Tongjiang (Tungkiang), China 77/M2
Tongliao, China 77/K3
Tongling, China 77/J5
Tongo, N.S. Wales 97/B2
Tongo (lake), N.S. Wales 97/B2
Tongoy, Chile 138/A8
Tongoy (bay), Chile 138/A8
Tongquil (isl.), Philippines 82/D8
Tongren, Qinghai, China 77/F4
Tongren, Guizhou, China 77/G6
Tongres (Tongeren), Belgium 27/G7
Tongs, Ky. 237/R3
Tongsa Dzong, Bhutan 68/G3
Tongtian He (Zhi Qu) (riv.), China 77/E5
Tongue (riv.), Mont. 262/K5
Tongue (pt.), N. Zealand 100/A3
Tongue (riv.), N. Dak. 282/P2
Tongue, Scotland 15/D2
Tongue (riv.), Wyo. 319/E1
Tongue of the Ocean (chan.), Bahamas 156/C1
Tongxin, China 77/G4
Tongyu, China 77/K3
Tongzi, China 77/G6
Tonica, Ill. 222/E2
Tonj, Sudan 111/E6
Tonk, India 68/D3
Tonka Bay, Minn. 255/F5
Tonkawa, Okla. 288/M1
Tonkin (gulf) 54/M8
Tonkin (gulf), China 77/G7
Tonkin, Sask. 181/J4
Tonkin (gulf), Vietnam 72/E3
Tonle Sap (lake), Cambodia 72/D4
Ton Mhor (pt.), Scotland 15/B5
Tonneins, France 28/D5
Tonnerre, France 28/E4
Tünning, Germany 22/C1
Tonopah, Ariz. 198/B5
Tonopah, Nev. 188/C3
Tonopah, Nev. 266/D4
Tonosí, Panama 154/G7
Tonota, Botswana 118/D4
Tonota, Botswana 102/E7
Tønsberg, Norway 18/D4
Tonsina, Alaska 196/J2
Tontitown, Ark. 202/B1
Tonto (basin), Ariz. 198/D4
Tonto (creek), Ariz. 198/D4
Tonto Basin, Ariz. 198/D5
Tontogany, Ohio 284/C3
Tonto Nat'l Mon., Ariz. 198/D5
Tony, Wis. 317/E5
Tonya, Turkey 63/H2
Toodyay, W. Australia 88/B2
Toodyay, W. Australia 92/B1
Tooele (co.), Utah 304/A3
Tooele, Utah 304/B3
Tooele, Utah 188/D2
Tooele Army Depot, Utah 304/B3
Toole (co.), Mont. 262/E2
Tooleybuc, N.S. Wales 97/B4
Toombs (co.), Ga. 217/H6
Toomevara, Ireland 17/E6
Tooms (lake), Tasmania 99/D4
Toomsboro, Ga. 217/F5
Toomsuba, Miss. 256/G6
Toone, Tenn. 237/D10
Tooraweenah, N.S. Wales 97/E2
Toowoomba, Australia 87/F8
Toowoomba, Queensland 88/J5
Toowoomba, Queensland 95/D5
Top (lake), Russia 52/D1
Topador, Uruguay 145/C1
Topanga, Calif. 204/B10
Topanga Beach, Calif. 204/B10
Topawa, Ariz. 198/D7
Topaz (lake), Nev. 266/B4
Topeka, Ill. 222/D3
Topeka, Ind. 227/F1
Topeka (cap.), Kans. 188/G3
Topeka (cap.), Kansas 146/J6
Topeka (cap.), Kansas 232/G2
Topia, Mexico 150/F4
Topinabee, Mich. 250/E3
Topl'a (riv.), Slovakia 41/F2
Topley, Br. Col. 184/D3
Toplița, Romania 45/G2
Topocalma (pt.), Chile 138/A10
Topock, Ariz. 198/A4
Top Of The World Prov. Park, Br. Col. 184/K5
Topographic Center, Md. 245/E4
Topoľčany, Slovakia 41/D2
Topolobampo, Mexico 150/E4
Topolovgrad, Bulgaria 45/H4
Toponas, Colo. 208/F2
Toppenish, Wash. 310/E4
Toppenish (creek), Wash. 310/E4
Topsail Beach, N.C. 281/O6
Topsfield•, Maine 243/H5
Topsfield, Mass. 249/L2
Topsfield•, Mass. 249/L2
Topsham, Maine 243/D8
Topsham•, Maine 243/D8
Topsham•, Vt. 268/C3
Top Springs, North. Terr. 93/C4
Topton, N.C. 281/B4
Topton, Pa. 294/L5
Toquepala, Peru 128/G11
Toquerville, Utah 304/A6
Toquima (range), Nev. 266/E4
Tor (bay), Nova Scotia 168/G3
Torata, Peru 128/G11
Torawitan (cape), Indonesia 85/G5
Torbalı, Turkey 63/B3
Torbat-e-Heydariyeh, Iran 66/L3
Torbat-e Heydariyeh, Iran 59/G2
Torbat-e Jam, Iran 66/M3
Torbat-e Jam, Iran 59/H2
Torbay, England 10/E5
Torbay, England 13/D7
Torbay, Newf. 166/D2
Torbay (pt.), Newf. 166/D2
Torbeck, Haiti 158/A6
Torch (key), Fla. 212/E7
Torch (lake), Mich. 250/D3
Torch, Ohio 284/G7
Torch (riv.), Sask. 181/H2
Torch River, Sask. 181/G2
Tordesillas, Spain 33/D2
Torgau, Germany 22/E3
Torgelow, Germany 22/F2
Torhout, Belgium 27/C6
Tori, Ethiopia 111/F6
Torino (Turin), Italy 34/A2
Torit, Sudan 111/F7
Torne (riv.) 7/G2
Torneälv (riv.), Sweden 18/M3
Tor Ness (prom.), Scotland 15/E2
Torneträsk (lake), Sweden 18/L2
Torngat (mts.), Newf. 166/B2
Tornillo, Texas 303/A10
Tornio, Finland 18/O4
Tornionjoki (riv.), Finland 18/O3
Tornquist, Argentina 143/D4
Toro, Cerro del (mt.), Argentina 143/B2
Toro (lake), Chile 138/D9
Toro, Cerro del (mt.), Chile 138/B7
Toro (pt.), Chile 138/A10
Toro, La. 238/C4
Toro, El (mt.), P. Rico 161/F2
Toro, Spain 33/D2
Türükszentmiklós, Hungary 41/F3
Toronaic (gulf), Greece 45/F5
Toronto, Canada 2/F3
Toronto, Iowa 229/M5
Toronto, Kansas 232/G4
Toronto (lake), Kansas 232/F4
Toronto (res.), N.Y. 276/L7
Toronto, Ohio 284/J5
Toronto (cap.), Ont. 146/K5
Toronto (cap.), Ont. 162/H7
Toronto (metro. munic.), Ontario 177/K4
Toronto (cap.), Ontario 177/K4
Toronto, S. Dak. 298/R4
Toropalca, Bolivia 136/B7
Toropets, Russia 52/D3
Tororo, Uganda 115/F3
Torote (riv.), Spain 33/G4
Torotoro, Bolivia 136/C6
Torpedo, Pa. 294/D2
Torphins, Scotland 15/F3
Torpoint, England 13/C7
Torquay, Sask. 181/H6
Torquemada, Spain 33/D1
Torr (head), N. Ireland 17/K1
Torrance, Calif. 188/C4
Torrance, Calif. 204/C11
Torrance (co.), N. Mex. 274/D4
Torrance, Ontario 177/E3
Torrance, Pa. 294/D5
Torre, Cerro de la (mt.), Chile 138/E4
Torre Annunziata, Italy 34/E4
Torreblanca, Spain 33/G2
Torrecilla (lag.), P. Rico 161/E1
Torre del Greco, Italy 34/E4
Torre de Moncorvo, Portugal 33/C2
Torredonjimeno, Spain 33/D4
Torre Gaia, Italy 34/F6
Torrejón (res.), Spain 33/D3
Torrejoncillo, Spain 33/C3
Torrejón de Ardoz, Spain 33/G4
Torrelaguna, Spain 33/E2
Torrelavega, Spain 33/D1
Torremaggiore, Italy 34/E4
Torremolinos, Spain 33/D4
Torrens (riv.) 88/E7
Torrens (lake), Australia 87/D9
Torrens (isl.), S. Australia 88/D7
Torrens (lake), S. Australia 88/F6
Torrens (lake), S. Australia 94/E4
Torrens (riv.), S. Australia 94/C7
Torrente, Spain 33/F3
Torreón, Mexico 146/H7
Torreón, Mexico 150/H4
Torreon, N. Mex. 274/C4
Torre-Pacheco, Spain 33/F4
Torres (strait) 87/E7
Torres (str.), Papua N.G. 85/A7
Torres (str.), Queensland 88/G2
Torres (str.), Queensland 95/B1
Torres (isls.), Vanuatu 87/G7
Torres Martinez Ind. Res., Calif. 204/J10
Torres Novas, Portugal 33/B3
Torres Vedras, Portugal 33/B3
Torrevieja, Spain 33/F4
Torrey, Utah 304/C5
Torridge (riv.), England 13/C7
Torridon, Loch (inlet), Scotland 15/C3
Torriente, Cuba 158/D1
Torrijos, Philippines 82/D4
Torrijos, Spain 33/D2
Tørring, Denmark 21/C6
Torringford, Conn. 210/C1
Torrington, Alberta 182/D4
Torrington, Conn. 210/C1
Torrington, Wyo. 319/H3
Torroella de Montgrí, Spain 33/H1
Torrowangee, N.S. Wales 97/A2
Torrox, Spain 33/E4
Torsby, Sweden 18/H6
Tors Cove, Newf. 166/D2
Torshälla, Sweden 18/K7
Tórshavn, Denmark 7/D2
Tórshavn (cap.), Faroe Is., Denmark 21/A3
Tortilla Flat, Ariz. 198/D5
Tortola (isl.), Virgin Is. (U.K.) 161/D3
Tortola (isl.), Virgin Is. (U.K.) 156/H1
Tórtolas, Cerro de las (mt.), Chile 138/B8
Tortona, Italy 34/B2
Tortorici, Italy 34/E6
Tortosa, Spain 33/G2
Tortosa (cape), Spain 33/G2
Tortue (chan.), Haiti 158/C5
Tortue (Tortuga) (isl.), Haiti 156/D2
Tortue (Tortuga) (isl.), Haiti 158/C4
Tortuga (isl.), Haiti 158/C4
Tortuga (isl.), Haiti 156/D2
Tortugas (gulf), Colombia 126/B6
Tortuguero (lag.), P. Rico 161/D1
Tortuguilla (pt.), Cuba 158/K4
Tortum, Turkey 63/J2
Torud, Iran 59/F2
Torud, Iran 66/J3
Torul, Turkey 63/H2
Toruń (prov.), Poland 47/D2
Toruń, Poland 7/F3
Toruń, Poland 47/D2
Torunos, Venezuela 124/C3
Tõrva, Estonia 53/C1
Tory (isl.), Ireland 17/E1
Tory (isl.), Ireland 10/B3
Tory (sound), Ireland 17/E1
Torysa (riv.), Slovakia 41/F2
Torzhok, Russia 52/D3
Tosa, Japan 81/F7
Tosa (bay), Japan 81/F7
Tosashimizu, Japan 81/F7
Toson Hu (lake), China 77/E4
Tüss (riv.), Switzerland 39/G1
Tostado, Argentina 143/D2
Toston, Mont. 262/E4
Tosu, Japan 81/E7
Tosya, Turkey 63/F2
Tota, Laguna de (lake), Colombia 126/D5
Totana, Spain 33/F4
Tótkomlós, Hungary 41/F3
Tot'ma, Russia 48/E4
Tot'ma, Russia 52/F3
Totnes, England 13/D7
Totnes, England 10/E5
Totnes, Sask. 181/C4
Totness, Suriname 131/C3
Toto, Ind. 227/D2
Totoket, Conn. 210/D3
Totonicapán, Guatemala 154/B3
Totora, Cochabamba, Bolivia 136/C5
Totora, Oruro, Bolivia 136/A5
Totoral, Chile 138/A6
Totoral, Quebrada (riv.), Chile 138/A6
Totoral, Uruguay 145/C3
Totowa, N.J. 273/B1
Totoya (isl.), Fiji 86/R11
Tottenham, N.S. Wales 97/D3
Tottenham, Ontario 177/E3
Tottori (pref.), Japan 81/G6
Tottori, Japan 81/G6
Touat (oasis), Algeria 106/E3
Touba, Ivory Coast 106/C7
Touba, Senegal 106/A6
Toubkal, Jebel (mt.), Morocco 102/B1
Toubkal, Jebel (mt.), Morocco 106/C2
Touchet, Wash. 310/G4
Touchet (riv.), Wash. 310/G4
Touchwood (lake), Alberta 182/E2
Touchwood (hills), Sask. 181/G4
Toufourine (well), Mali 106/C4
Tougaloo, Miss. 256/D6
Tougan, Burkina Faso 106/D6
Touggourt, Algeria 106/F2
Touggourt, Algeria 102/C1
Toughkenamon, Pa. 294/L6
Tougué, Guinea 106/B6
Touila (well), Algeria 106/C3
Touila (well), Mauritania 106/C3
Toukoto, Mali 106/C6
Toul, France 28/F3
Touladi, Grand Lac (lake), Québec 172/J1
Toulnustouc (riv.), Québec 174/D2
Toulon, France 7/E4
Toulon, France 28/F6
Toulon, Ill. 222/D2
Toulouse, France 7/E4
Toulouse, France 28/D6
Toumodi, Ivory Coast 106/D7
Toungo, Nigeria 106/G7
Toungoo, Burma 72/C3
Touraine (trad. prov.), France 29
Tourakom, Laos 72/D3
Tourbis (lake), Québec 172/C2
Tourcoing, France 28/E2
Tour d'Ai (mt.), Switzerland 39/C4
Tourelle, Québec 172/C1
Tournai, Belgium 27/C7
Tournavista, Peru 128/E7
Tournon, France 28/F5
Tournus, France 28/F4
Touros, Brazil 132/H4
Touro Synagogue Nat'l Hist. Site, R.I. 249/J7
Tours, France 28/D4
Tours, France 7/E4
Tourville, Québec 172/H2
Toutes Aides, Manitoba 179/C3
Toutle, Wash. 310/C4
Toutle, South Fork (riv.), Wash. 310/C4
Toutle, North Fork (riv.), Wash. 310/C4
Toužim, Czech Rep. 41/B1
Tüv, Mongolia 77/G2
Tovar, Venezuela 124/C3
Tovey, Ill. 222/D4
Towaco, N.J. 273/E2
Towada, Japan 81/K3
Towada (lake), Japan 81/K3
Towada-Hachimantai National Park, Japan 81/K3
Towakaima, Guyana 131/B2
Towanda, Ill. 222/E3
Towanda, Kansas 232/E4
Towanda, Pa. 294/J2
Towanda (creek), Pa. 294/J2
Towaoc, Colo. 208/B8
Towcester, England 13/F5
Tower, Mich. 250/E3
Tower, Minn. 255/F3
Tower, Wyo. 319/B1
Tower City, N. Dak. 282/P6
Tower City, Pa. 294/J4
Tower Hamlets, England 13/H8
Tower Hill, Ill. 222/E4
Tower Lakes, Ill. 222/A4
Towers of Silence, India 68/B7
Tow Law, England 13/H4
Town (creek), Ala. 195/C1
Town (creek), Md. 245/E2
Town and Country, Mo. 261/O3
Town and Country, Wash. 310/H3
Town Creek, Ala. 195/D1
Towner, Colo. 208/P6
Towner (co.), N. Dak. 282/M2
Towner, N. Dak. 282/K3
Townley, Ala. 195/D3
Town 'n Country, Fla. 212/C2
Town of Pines, Ind. 227/D1
Town Point, Md. 245/P3
Towns (co.), Ga. 217/E1
Towns, Ga. 217/G7
Townsend, Del. 245/R3
Townsend, Ga. 217/J7
Townsend, Mass. 249/H2
Townsend•, Mass. 249/H2
Townsend, Mont. 262/E4
Townsend (inlet), N.J. 273/D5
Townsend, Tenn. 237/O9
Townsend, Va. 307/R6
Townsend, Wis. 317/K5
Townsend Harbor, Mass. 249/G2
Townsends Inlet, N.J. 273/D5
Townshend•, Vt. 268/B5
Townsville, Australia 2/S6
Townsville, Australia 87/E7
Townsville, N.C. 281/N1
Townsville, Queensland 88/H3
Townsville, Queensland 95/C3
Townville, Pa. 294/C2
Townville, S.C. 296/B2
Towot, Sudan 111/F6
Towraghondi, Afghanistan 68/A1
Towson, Md. 245/M3
Towuti (lake), Indonesia 85/G6
Towy (riv.), Wales 13/D6
Towy (riv.), Wales 10/E5
Toxey, Ala. 195/B7
Toya (lake), Japan 81/K2
Toyah, Texas 303/D11
Toyah (creek), Texas 303/D11
Toyah (lake), Texas 303/A6
Toyahvale, Texas 303/D11
Toyama (pref.), Japan 81/H5
Toyama, Japan 81/H5
Toyama (bay), Japan 81/H5
Toyohashi, Japan 81/H6
Toyonaka, Japan 81/J7
Toyooka, Japan 81/G6
Toyota, Japan 81/H6
Tozeur, Tunisia 106/F2
Trabzon (prov.), Turkey 63/H2
Trabzon, Turkey 54/E5
Trabzon, Turkey 63/H2
Trabzon, Turkey 59/C1
Tracadie, New Bruns. 170/F1
Tracadie, Nova Scotia 168/G3
Tracadie (bay), Pr. Edward I. 168/F2
Trachselwald, Switzerland 39/E2
Tracy, Calif. 204/D6
Tracy, Conn. 210/D2
Tracy, Iowa 229/H6
Tracy, Ky. 237/K7
Tracy, Minn. 255/C6
Tracy, Mo. 261/C4
Tracy, New Bruns. 170/D3
Tracy, Québec 172/D3
Tracy Arm (inlet), Alaska 196/N1
Tracy City, Tenn. 237/K10
Tracyton, Wash. 310/A2
Trade, Tenn. 237/T8
Trade Lake, Wis. 317/A4
Tradespark, Scotland 15/E3
Tradesville, S.C. 296/F2
Tradewater (riv.), Ky. 237/F6
Trading (bay), Alaska 196/B1
Trading Post, Kansas 232/H3
Traer, Iowa 229/J4
Traer, Kansas 232/B2
Trafalgar, Ind. 227/E6
Trafalgar, Nova Scotia 168/F3
Trafalgar (cape), Spain 33/C4
Trafaria, Portugal 33/A1
Trafford, Ala. 195/E3
Trafford, Pa. 294/C5
Traghen, Libya 111/B2
Traiguén, Chile 138/D2
Traiguén (isl.), Chile 138/D6
Trail, Br. Col. 162/E6
Trail, Br. Col. 184/G4
Trail, Br. Col. 184/J6
Trail, Minn. 255/C3
Trail, Oreg. 291/E5
Trail City, S. Dak. 298/H3
Trail Creek, Ind. 227/D1
Traill (isl.), Greenl. 4/B10
Traill (co.), N. Dak. 282/R5
Traîne (lake), Québec 172/D2
Trainer, Pa. 294/L7
Traiskirchen, Austria 41/D2
Trakai, Lithuania 53/C3
Tralake, Miss. 256/C4
Tralee, Ireland 10/B4
Tralee, Ireland 17/B7
Tralee (bay), Ireland 17/B7
Tramán-tepuí (mt.), Venezuela 124/G5
Tramelan, Switzerland 39/D2
Trammel, Va. 307/D6
Tramore, Ireland 10/C4
Tramore, Ireland 17/G7
Tramore (bay), Ireland 17/G7
Trampas, N. Mex. 274/D2
Tramperos (creek), N. Mex. 274/F2
Tramping (lake), Sask. 181/C3
Tramping Lake, Sask. 181/B3
Tranås, Sweden 18/J7
Trancoso, Portugal 33/C2
Tranebjerg, Denmark 21/D6
Tranebjerg (mt.), Denmark 21/C6
Tranent, Scotland 15/F5
Trang, Thailand 72/C6
Trangan (isl.), Indonesia 85/J7
Trangie, N.S. Wales 97/D3
Trani, Italy 34/F4
Tranquebar, India 68/E6
Tranqueras, Uruguay 145/D2
Tranqui (isl.), Chile 138/D4
Tranquility, N.J. 273/D2
Tranquillity, Calif. 204/E7
Transantarctic (mts.) 5/B17
Trans-Carpathian Oblast, Ukraine 52/B5
Transfer, Pa. 294/A3
Transquaking (riv.), Md. 245/P7
Transylvania, La. 238/H1
Transylvania (co.), N.C. 281/D4
Transylvanian Alps (mts.), Romania 45/G3
Trapani (prov.), Italy 34/D5
Trapani, Italy 7/F5
Trapani, Italy 34/D5
Trap Falls (res.), Conn. 210/C3
Traphill, N.C. 281/H2
Trappe, Md. 245/O6
Trappers (lake), Colo. 208/E3
Traralgon, Victoria 97/D6
Traralgon, Victoria 88/H7
Trarza (reg.), Mauritania 106/A5
Trasimeno (lake), Italy 34/D3
Traskwood, Ark. 202/E5
Trat, Thailand 72/D4
Traun, Austria 41/C2
Traun (riv.), Austria 41/C2
Traun See (lake), Austria 41/B3
Traunstein, Germany 22/E5
Travancore (reg.), India 68/D7
Travelers Rest, S.C. 296/C2
Travellers (lake), N.S. Wales 97/B3
Travellers Rest, Ky. 237/O6
Travemünde, Germany 22/D2
Travers, Alberta 182/D4
Travers (res.), Alberta 182/D4
Traverse (bay), Manitoba 179/F4
Traverse (isl.), Mich. 250/A1
Traverse (pt.), Mich. 250/A1
Traverse (co.), Minn. 255/B5
Traverse, Minn. 255/D6
Traverse (lake), Minn. 255/B5
Traverse (lake), S. Dak. 298/R2
Traverse City, Mich. 188/K2
Traverse City, Mich. 250/D4
Tra Vinh (Phu Vinh), Vietnam 72/E5
Travis (co.), Texas 303/G7
Travis (lake), Texas 303/G7
Travis A.F.B., Calif. 204/L1
Travnik, Bos. 45/C3
Trawbreaga (bay), Ireland 17/F1
Traynor, Sask. 181/C3
Traytown, Newf. 166/D1
Trbovlje, Slovenia 45/B2
Treadway, Tenn. 237/P8
Treasure (isl.), Fla. 212/B3
Treasure (co.), Mont. 262/J4
Treasure Island, Fla. 212/B3
Treasury (isls.), Solomon Is. 86/C2
Treaty, Ind. 227/F3
Trebbia (riv.), Italy 34/B2
Třebíč, Czech Rep. 41/C2
Trebinje, Bos. 45/D4
Trebišov, Slovakia 41/F2
Trebizond (Trabzon), Turkey 63/H2
Trebloc, Miss. 256/G3
Třeboň, Czech Rep. 41/C2
Trece Martires, Philippines 82/C3
Tredegar, Wales 13/B6
Treece, Kansas 232/H4
Treelon, Sask. 181/C6
Trees, La. 238/B1
Treesbank, Manitoba 179/C5
Tregaron, Wales 13/D5
Tregaron, Wales 10/E4
Tregarva, Sask. 181/G5
Trego (co.), Kansas 232/C3
Trego, Mont. 262/B2
Trego, Wis. 317/C4
Treherne, Manitoba 179/D5
Treig, Loch (lake), Scotland 15/D4
Treinta y Tres (dept.), Uruguay 145/E4
Treinta y Tres, Uruguay 145/E4
Trelew, Argentina 143/C5
Trelleborg, Sweden 18/H9
Tremadoc (bay), Wales 10/D4
Tremadoc (prom.), Wales 13/C5
Tremblant (lake), Québec 172/C3
Trembleur (lake), Br. Col. 184/E3
Trementina, N. Mex. 274/E3
Tremiti (isls.), Italy 34/E3
Tremont, Ill. 222/D3
Tremont, Maine 243/G7
Tremont•, Maine 243/G7
Tremont, Miss. 256/H2
Tremont, Pa. 294/K4
Tremont City, Ohio 284/C5
Tremonton, Utah 304/B2
Tremp, Spain 33/G1
Trempealeau (co.), Wis. 317/D7
Trempealeau, Wis. 317/C8
Trempealeau (riv.), Wis. 317/C7
Trenary, Mich. 250/C2
Trenčín, Slovakia 41/E2
Trenel, Argentina 143/D4
Trenggalek, Indonesia 85/K2
Trenque Lauquen, Argentina 143/D4
Trent (riv.), England 13/G4
Trent (riv.), England 10/F4
Trent (riv.), N.C. 281/P4
Trent, Oreg. 291/E4
Trent, S. Dak. 298/R6
Trent, Texas 303/D5
Trente et un Milles (lake), Québec 172/B3
Trentham, Manitoba 179/F5
Trentham Cliffs, N.S. Wales 97/B4
Trentino-Alto Adige (reg.), Italy 34/C1
Trento (prov.), Italy 34/C1
Trento, Italy 34/C1
Trenton, Ala. 195/F1
Trenton, Ark. 202/J5
Trenton, Fla. 212/D2
Trenton, Ga. 217/A1
Trenton, Ill. 222/D5
Trenton, Iowa 229/K6
Trenton, Ky. 237/G7
Trenton, Maine 243/G7
Trenton•, Maine 243/G7
Trenton, Md. 245/L2
Trenton, Mich. 250/B7
Trenton, Miss. 256/E6
Trenton, Mo. 261/E2
Trenton, Nebr. 264/D4
Trenton (cap.), N.J. 146/L5
Trenton (cap.), N.J. 188/M2
Trenton (cap.), N.J. 273/D3
Trenton, N.C. 281/P4
Trenton, N. Dak. 282/C3
Trenton, Nova Scotia 168/F3
Trenton, Ohio 284/B7
Trenton, Ontario 177/G3
Trenton, S.C. 296/D4
Trenton, Tenn. 237/D9
Trenton, Texas 303/H4
Trenton, Utah 304/B2
Trent Woods, N.C. 281/P4
Trepassey, Newf. 166/D2
Treptow, Germany 22/F4
Tres Árboles, Uruguay 145/C3
Tres Arroyos, Argentina 143/D4
Tres Arroyos, Argentina 120/C6
Tres Bocas, Uruguay 145/B2
Tresckow, Pa. 294/K4
Tresco (isl.), England 13/A8
Três Corações, Brazil 132/E8
Três Corações, Brazil 135/D2
Tres Cruces, Nevada (mt.), Chile 138/B6
Tres Esquinas, Colombia 126/C7
Treshnish (isls.), Scotland 15/B4
Tres Islas, Uruguay 145/E3
Três Lagoas, Brazil 120/D5
Três Lagoas, Brazil 132/C8
Três Marias (res.), Brazil 120/E4

Union 461

Turen, Indonesia 85/K2
Turén, Venezuela 124/D3
Turfan (Turpan), China 77/C3
Turgay, Kazakhstan 48/G5
Tŭrgovishte, Bulgaria 45/H4
Turgutlu, Turkey 63/B3
Turhal, Turkey 63/F2
Türi, Estonia 53/C1
Turia (riv.), Spain 33/F3
Turiaçu, Brazil 132/E3
Turiaçu (riv.), Brazil 132/E3
Turiamo, Venezuela 124/E2
Turin, Alberta 182/D5
Turin, Ga. 217/C4
Turin, Iowa 229/B4
Turin (prov.), Italy 34/A2
Turin, Italy 34/A2
Turin, Italy 7/E4
Turin, N.Y. 276/K3
Turkana (lake), Ethiopia 111/G7
Turkana (lake), Kenya 102/F4
Turkana (lake), Kenya 115/G3
Türkeli, Turkey 63/F2
Turkestan, Kazakhstan 48/G5
Túrkeve, Hungary 41/F3
Turkey 2/L4
Turkey 7/H5
Turkey 54/E6
TURKEY 59/B2
TURKEY 63/D3
Turkey (riv.), Iowa 229/K2
Turkey, Ky. 237/P6
Turkey, N.C. 281/N4
Turkey (creek), Okla. 288/L2
Turkey (creek), S.C. 296/E2
Turkey, Texas 303/D3
Turkey Creek, La. 238/F5
Turkey Creek (lake), La. 238/G3
Turkey Creek, W. Australia 92/E2
Turkey Point, Ontario 177/D5
Türkmen Dağı (mt.), Turkey 63/D3
TURKMENISTAN 48/F6
Turkmenistan 54/G6
Türkoğlu, Turkey 63/G4
Turks (isls.), Turks & Caicos 156/D2
Turks and Caicos (isls.) 146/L7
TURKS AND CAICOS ISLANDS 156/D2
Turks Island (passage), Turks & Caicos 156/D2
Turku, Finland 7/G2
Turku, Finland 18/N6
Turku ja Pori (prov.), Finland 18/N6
Turlock, Calif. 204/E6
Turmero, Venezuela 124/E2
Turnagain (riv.), Br. Col. 184/K2
Turnagain (cape), N. Zealand 100/F4
Turnagain Arm (inlet), Alaska 196/B1
Turnavik (isls.), Newf. 166/C2
Turnberry, Scotland 15/D5
Turneffe (isls.), Belize 154/D2
Turnen (mt.), Switzerland 39/D3
Turner, Ark. 202/H5
Turner (co.), Ga. 217/E7
Turner, Maine 243/C7
Turner•, Maine 243/C7
Turner, Mich. 250/F4
Turner, Mont. 262/H2
Turner, Oreg. 291/E3
Turner (co.), S. Dak. 298/P7
Turner, Wash. 310/H4
Turner Center, Maine 243/C7
Turner Hole (bay), Virgin Is. (U.S.) 161/G4
Turners, Mo. 261/F8
Turnersburg, N.C. 281/H3
Turners Falls, Mass. 249/D2
Turners Station, Ky. 237/L3
Turnersville, N.J. 273/C4
Turnersville, Texas 303/G6
Turner Valley, Alberta 182/C4
Turnerville, Wyo. 319/A3
Turney, Mo. 261/D3
Turnhout, Belgium 27/F6
Turnor Lake, Sask. 181/L3
Turnov, Czech Rep. 41/C1
Turnu Măgurele, Romania 45/G4
Turon, Kansas 232/D4
Turpan (Turfan), China 77/C3
Turpan, China 54/L5
Turpin, Okla. 288/E1
Turquino (peak), Cuba 158/H4
Turrell, Ark. 202/K3
Turrialba, C. Rica 154/F6
Turriff, Scotland 10/E2
Turriff, Scotland 15/F3
Turtle (Penju) (isls.), Indonesia 85/H7
Turtle (mts.), Manitoba 179/B5
Turtle (riv.), Manitoba 179/C3
Turtle (lake), Mich. 250/F4
Turtle (lake), N. Dak. 282/H4
Turtle (mts.), N. Dak. 282/K2
Turtle (isls.), Philippines 82/B7
Turtle (lake), Sask. 181/C2
Turtle (creek), S. Dak. 298/M4
Turtle Creek, New Bruns. 170/F3
Turtle Creek, Pa. 294/C7
Turtle Creek, W. Va. 312/C6
Turtleford, Sask. 181/B2
Turtle Lake, N. Dak. 282/J4
Turtle Lake, Wis. 317/B5
Turtle Mountain Ind. Res., N. Dak. 282/L2
Turtle Mountain Prov. Park, Manitoba 179/B5
Turtlepoint, Pa. 294/F2
Turtle River, Minn. 255/D3
Turtletown, Tenn. 237/N10
Turtola, Finland 18/O3
Turton, England 13/H2
Turton, S. Dak. 298/N3
Turukhansk, Russia 48/J3
Turvo (riv.), Brazil 135/B2
Turzovka, Slovakia 41/E2
Tuscaloosa, Ala. 188/J4
Tuscaloosa (co.), Ala. 195/C4
Tuscaloosa, Ala. 195/C4
Tuscaloosa (lake), Ala. 195/D4
Tuscan (arch.), Italy 34/B3
Tuscany (reg.), Italy 34/C3
Tuscarawas (co.), Ohio 284/H5
Tuscarawas, Ohio 284/H5
Tuscarawas (riv.), Ohio 284/H5
Tuscarora, Nev. 266/E1
Tuscarora (mts.), Nev. 266/E1
Tuscarora (mt.), Pa. 294/G5
Tuscarora Ind. Res., N.Y. 276/B4
Tuscola, Ill. 222/E4
Tuscola (co.), Mich. 250/F5
Tuscola, Mich. 250/F5
Tuscola, Texas 303/E5
Tuscor, Mont. 262/A3
Tusculum, Ga. 217/K6
Tusculum, Tenn. 237/R8
Tuscumbia, Ala. 195/C1
Tuscumbia, Mo. 261/H6
Tushar (mts.), Utah 304/B5
Tushka, Okla. 288/O6
Tuskahoma, Okla. 288/R5
Tuskegee, Ala. 195/G6
Tuskegee Institute, Ala. 195/G6
Tuskegee Institute Nat'l Hist. Park, Ala. 195/G6
Tusket, Nova Scotia 168/C5
Tusket (isl.), Nova Scotia 168/B5
Tusket (riv.), Nova Scotia 168/C4
Tussy, Okla. 288/L6
Tustin, Calif. 204/D11
Tustin, Mich. 250/D4
Tustin, Wis. 317/J7
Tustumena (lake), Alaska 196/C1
Tutak, Turkey 63/K3
Tutamoe (range), N. Zealand 100/D1
Tutayev, Russia 52/E3
Tuthill, S. Dak. 298/G7
Tuticorin, India 68/D7
Tutóia, Brazil 132/F3
Tutrakan, Bulgaria 45/H4
Tuttle, Idaho 220/D7
Tuttle, N. Dak. 282/L5
Tuttle, Okla. 288/L4
Tuttle Creek (lake), Kansas 232/F2
Tuttlingen, Germany 22/C5
Tutuila (isl.), Amer. Samoa 87/J7
Tutuila (isl.), Amer. Samoa 86/N9
Tutwiler, Miss. 256/D2
Tuun (mt.), N. Korea 81/C3
Tuvalu 2/T6
Tuvalu 87/H6
Tuvinian Aut. Rep., Russia 48/K4
Tuwaiq, Jebel (range), Saudi Arabia 59/E5
Tuxedo, Md. 245/G5
Tuxedo Park, N.Y. 276/M8
Tuxford, Sask. 181/F5
Tuxpan, Nayarit, Mexico 150/G6
Tuxpan, Jalisco, Mexico 150/H7
Tuxpan de Rodríguez Cano, Mexico 150/L6
Tuxtepec, Mexico 150/L7
Tuxtla Gutiérrez, Mexico 146/J8
Tuxtla Gutiérrez, Mexico 150/N8
Túy, Spain 33/B1
Tuy (riv.), Venezuela 124/E2
Tuya (riv.), Br. Col. 184/K2
Tuyen Quang, Vietnam 72/E2
Tuy Hoa, Vietnam 72/F4
Tuymazy, Russia 52/H4
Tuysarkan, Iran 66/F3
Tuyün (Duyun), China 77/G6
Tuz (lake), Turkey 63/E3
Tuz (lake), Turkey 59/B2
Tuzigoot Nat'l Mon., Ariz. 198/D4
Tuz Khurmatu, Iraq 66/D3
Tuzla, Bos. 7/F4
Tuzla, Bos. 45/D3
Tuzluca, Turkey 63/K3
Tuzlukçu, Turkey 63/D3
Tvedestrand, Norway 18/F7
Tver', Russia 48/D4
Tver', Russia 52/E3
Tversted, Denmark 21/D2
Twain, Calif. 204/D4
Twain Harte, Calif. 204/E6
Tway, Sask. 181/F3
Tweed (riv.), England 13/E2
Tweed, Ontario 177/G3
Tweed (riv.), Scotland 15/F5
Tweed (riv.), Scotland 10/E3
Tweed Heads, N.S. Wales 97/G1
Tweedie, Alberta 182/E2
Tweedside, New Bruns. 170/C3
Tweedsmuir, Sask. 181/F2
Tweedsmuir, Scotland 15/E5
Tweedsmuir Prov. Park, Br. Col. 184/D3
Twello, Netherlands 27/J4
Twelve Mile, Ind. 227/E3
Twelvemile (lake), Sask. 181/E6
Twelve Mile (creek), Utah 304/C2
Twelve Pins (mt.), Ireland 17/B4
Twelvepole (creek), W. Va. 312/A6
Twentynine Palms, Calif. 204/K9
Twentynine Palms Marine Base, Calif. 204/J9
Twig, Minn. 255/F4
Twiggs (co.), Ga. 217/F5
Twila, Ky. 237/P7
Twillingate, Newf. 166/C4
Twin (lakes), Conn. 210/B1
Twin (falls), Idaho 220/D7
Twin (lakes), Maine 243/F4
Twin (lakes), Wash. 310/G2
Twin Bridges, Mont. 262/D5
Twin Brooks, S. Dak. 298/R3
Twin City, Ga. 217/H5
Twin Falls (co.), Idaho 220/D7
Twin Falls, Idaho 220/D7
Twin Falls, Idaho 188/C2
Twin Falls, Idaho 146/G5
Twin Falls, Newf. 166/B3
Twin Hills, Alaska 196/F3
Twining, Mich. 250/F4
Twin Lake, Mich. 250/C5
Twin Lakes, Calif. 204/K4
Twin Lakes, Colo. 208/G4
Twin Lakes (res.), Colo. 208/G4
Twin Lakes, Minn. 255/E7
Twin Lakes, Wis. 317/K11
Twin Mountain, N.H. 268/D3
Twin Oaks, Mo. 261/N3
Twin Peaks, Calif. 204/H9
Twin Peaks (mt.), Idaho 220/D5
Twin Rocks, Oreg. 291/C2
Twin Rocks, Pa. 294/E4
Twinsburg, Ohio 284/J10
Twin Sisters (mt.), Wash. 310/D2
Twin Valley, Minn. 255/B3
Twisp, Wash. 310/E2
Twisp (pass), Wash. 310/E2
Twisp (riv.), Wash. 310/E2
Twitchell (res.), Calif. 204/E9
Two Arm (bay), Alaska 196/C2
Two Butte (creek), Colo. 208/N7
Two Buttes, Colo. 208/O7
Two Buttes (res.), Colo. 208/O7
Twodot, Mont. 262/F4
Twofold (bay), N.S. Wales 97/F5
Two Harbors, Minn. 255/G3
Two Hearted (riv.), Mich. 250/D2
Two Hills, Alberta 182/E3
Two Rivers (riv.), Minn. 255/A1
Two Rivers (res.), N. Mex. 274/E5
Two Rivers, Wis. 317/M7
Two Water (creek), Utah 304/E4
Twynholm, Scotland 15/D6
Tyaskin, Md. 245/P7
Tybee Island, Ga. 217/L6
Tybee Roads (chan.), S.C. 296/F7
Tychy, Poland 47/B4
Tye, Texas 303/E5
Tye River, Va. 307/L5
Tygart (lake), W. Va. 312/G4
Tygart Valley (riv.), W. Va. 312/F5
Tyger (riv.), S.C. 296/D2
Tygh Valley, Oreg. 291/F2
Tyler, Ala. 195/E6
Tyler (lake), Conn. 210/B1
Tyler, Minn. 255/B6
Tyler, Mo. 261/N10
Tyler, N. Dak. 282/S7
Tyler, Pa. 294/F3
Tyler (co.), Texas 303/K7
Tyler, Texas 188/H4
Tyler, Texas 303/J5
Tyler, Wash. 310/H3
Tyler (co.), W. Va. 312/E4
Tylersburg, Pa. 294/D3
Tylersville, Pa. 294/G4
Tylertown, Miss. 256/D8
Tylerville, Conn. 210/F3
Tym (riv.), Russia 48/J3
Tymovskoye, Russia 48/P4
Týn, Czech Rep. 41/C2
Tynagh, Ireland 17/E5
Tynan, Texas 303/G9
Tynda, Russia 48/N4
Tyndall, Manitoba 179/F4
Tyndall, S. Dak. 298/O8
Tyndall A.F.B., Fla. 212/C6
Tyndrum, Scotland 15/D4
Tyne (riv.), England 13/F3
Tyne (riv.), England 10/F3
Tyne (riv.), Scotland 15/F5
Tyne and Wear (co.), England 13/H3
Tynemouth, England 13/J3
Tynemouth, England 10/F3
Tyner, Ind. 227/E2
Tyner, Ky. 237/O6
Tyner, N.C. 281/R2
Tyner, Sask. 181/C4
Tyne Valley, Pr. Edward I. 168/E2
Tyngsboro•, Mass. 249/J2
Tynset, Norway 18/G5
Tyntynder South, Victoria 97/B4
Tyonek, Alaska 196/B1
Tyra (cays), Nicaragua 154/F4
Tyre (Sur), Lebanon 63/F6
Tyrifjord (lake), Norway 18/C3
Tyringham•, Mass. 249/A4
Tyrnyauz, Russia 52/F6
Tyro, Kansas 232/G4
Tyro, Miss. 256/E1
Tyro, Va. 307/K5
Tyrol (Tirol) (prov.), Austria 41/A3
Tyrone, Colo. 208/L8
Tyrone, Ga. 217/C4
Tyrone, Ky. 237/M4
Tyrone, Mo. 261/J8
Tyrone, N. Mex. 274/A6
Tyrone, Okla. 288/D1
Tyrone, Pa. 294/F4
Tyronza, Ark. 202/K3
Tyronza (riv.), Ark. 202/K2
Tyrrell (co.), N.C. 281/S3
Tyrrell (lake), Victoria 97/B4
Tyrrellspass, Ireland 17/G5
Tyrrhenian (sea) 7/F4
Tyrrhenian (sea), Italy 34/C4
Tysnes, Norway 18/D6
Tyson, Vt. 268/B5
Tyson Wash (dry riv.), Ariz. 198/A5
Ty Ty, Ga. 217/E8
Tyumen', Russia 54/H4
Tyumen', Russia 48/G4
Tyung (riv.), Russia 48/M3
Tyvan, Sask. 181/H5
Tywyn, Wales 13/C5
Tywyn, Wales 10/D4
Tzaneen, S. Africa 118/E4
Tzekung (Zigong), China 77/F6
Tzepo (Zibo), China 77/J4
Tzucabab, Mexico 150/P7

U

Uahuka, Fr. Poly. 87/N6
Uanda, Queensland 95/C4
Uanle Uen, Somalia 115/H3
Uanle Uen, Somalia 102/G4
Uapou (isl.), Fr. Poly. 87/M6
Uatumã (riv.), Brazil 132/B3
Uaupés (riv.), Brazil 132/G9
Ub, Yugoslavia 45/E3
Ubá, Brazil 135/E2
Ubá, Brazil 132/F8
Übach-Palenberg, Germany 22/B3
Ubaíra, Brazil 132/G6
Ubaitaba, Brazil 132/G6
Ubaiyidh, Wadi (dry riv.), Iraq 66/B5
Ubangi (riv.) 102/D4
Ubangi (riv.), Cent. Afr. Rep. 115/C3
Ubangi (riv.), Congo 115/C3
Ubangi (riv.), D.R. Congo 115/C3
Ubari, Libya 102/D2
Ubari, Libya 111/B2
Ubaté, Colombia 126/D5
Ubatuba, Brazil 135/D3
Ubay, Philippines 82/E5
Ube, Japan 81/E6
Úbeda, Spain 33/E3
Uberaba (lag.), Bolivia 136/G5
Uberaba, Brazil 120/E4
Uberaba, Brazil 132/D7
Uberaba, Brazil 135/C1
Uberlândia, Brazil 120/E4
Uberlândia, Brazil 132/E7
Überlingen, Germany 22/C5
Ubina, Bolivia 136/B7
Ubinas, Peru 128/G11
Ubly, Mich. 250/G5
Ubombo, S. Africa 118/E5
Ubon, Thailand 54/M8
Ubon, Thailand 72/E4
Ubrique, Spain 33/D4
Ubundu, D.R. Congo 115/E4
Ucayali (dept.), Peru 128/E6
Ucayali (riv.), Peru 2/F6
Ucayali (riv.), Peru 120/B3
Ucayali (riv.), Peru 128/F5
Uccle, Belgium 27/B9
Uch, Pakistan 68/B3
Uchaly, Russia 7/K3
Uchaly, Russia 52/J4
Ucharonidge, North. Terr. 93/D4
Uchee, Ala. 195/H6
Uchiura (bay), Japan 81/K2
Uchiza, Peru 128/D7
Uch Turfan (Wushi), China 77/A3
Uckange, France 28/G3
Ücker (riv.), Germany 22/E2
Uckfield (forests), England 10/G5
Uckfield, England 13/H7
Ucluelet, Br. Col. 184/E6
Ucon, Idaho 220/F6
Ucross, Wyo. 319/F1
Ucumasi, Bolivia 136/B6
Uda (riv.), Russia 48/O4
Udaipur, India 68/C4
Udall, Kansas 232/E4
Udaypur, India 54/J7
Uddevalla, Sweden 18/G7
Uddingston, Scotland 15/B2
Uddjaur (lake), Sweden 18/L4
Udell, Iowa 229/H7
Uden, Netherlands 27/H5
Udhampur, India 68/D2
Udine (prov.), Italy 34/D1
Udine, Italy 34/D2
Udine, Italy 7/F4
Udipi, India 68/C6
Udmurt Aut. Rep., Russia 48/F4
Udmurt Aut. Rep., Russia 52/H3
Udon Thani, Thailand 54/M8
Udon Thani, Thailand 72/D3
Udora, Ontario 177/E3
Ueckermünde, Germany 22/F2
Ueda, Japan 81/J5
Uehling, Nebr. 264/H3
Uele (riv.) 102/E4
Uele (riv.), D.R. Congo 115/E3
Uelen, Russia 4/C18
Uelen, Russia 48/T3
Uelen, Russia 54/V3
Uelzen, Germany 22/D2
Uen (isl.), New Caled. 86/H5
Uetendorf, Switzerland 39/E3
Uetersen, Germany 22/C2
Ufa, Russia 2/M3
Ufa, Russia 7/K3
Ufa, Russia 48/F4
Ufa, Russia 52/J4
Ufa (riv.), Russia 52/J3
Ugab (riv.), Namibia 118/A4
Uganda 2/L5
Uganda 102/F4
UGANDA 115/F3
Ugashik, Alaska 196/G3
Ugashik (lakes), Alaska 196/G3
Ugie (riv.), Scotland 15/G3
Ugíjar, Spain 33/E4
Ugjoktok (bay), Newf. 166/B2
Uglegorsk, Russia 48/P5
Uglich, Russia 52/E3
Ugo, Japan 81/K4
Ugod, Hungary 41/D3
Uherské Hradiště, Czech Rep. 41/D2
Uherský Brod, Czech Rep. 41/D2
Uhlava (riv.), Czech Rep. 41/B2
Uhlířské Janovice, Czech Rep. 41/C2
Uhrichsville, Ohio 284/H5
Uig, Scotland 10/C2
Uig, Highland, Scotland 15/B3
Uig, W. Isles, Scotland 15/A2
Uige (prov.), Angola 115/B5
Uige, Angola 115/C5
Üiju, N. Korea 81/B3
Uinkaret (plat.), Ariz. 198/B2
Uinta (mts.), Utah 304/D3
Uinta (riv.), Utah 304/D3
Uinta (co.), Wyo. 319/B4
Uintah (co.), Utah 304/E3
Uintah, Utah 304/C2
Uintah and Ouray Ind. Res., Utah 304/D3
Üisŏng, S. Korea 81/D5
Uitenhage, S. Africa 102/E8
Uitenhage, S. Africa 118/C6
Uithoorn, Netherlands 27/F4
Uithuizen, Netherlands 27/K2
Uitkijk, Suriname 131/D3
Uivak (cape), Newf. 166/B2
Ujelang (atoll), Marshall Is. 87/F5
Újfehértó, Hungary 41/F3
Uji, Honduras 154/F3
Uji, Japan 81/J7
Ujjain, India 68/D4
Ujiji (Kigoma-Ujiji), Tanzania 115/E4
Újpest, Hungary 41/E3
Újszász, Hungary 41/F2
Ujung Pandang, Indonesia 54/N10
Ujung Pandang, Indonesia 85/F7
Ukasiksalik (isl.), Newf. 166/B2
Ukhta, Russia 48/F3
Ukiah, Calif. 204/B4
Ukiah, Oreg. 291/J2
Ukkel (Uccle), Belgium 27/B9
Ukmergė, Lithuania 52/C3
Ukmergė, Lithuania 53/C3
Ukraine 7/G4
Ukraine 48/C5
UKRAINE 52/D5
Uku, Angola 115/B6
Ula, Turkey 63/C4
Ulaanbaatar (Ulan Bator) (cap.), Mongolia 77/G2
Ulaanbaatar (cap.), Mongolia 54/M5
Ulaanbaatar (cap.), Mongolia 2/Q3
Ulaangom (Ulangom), Mongolia 77/D2
Ulaangom, Mongolia 54/L5
Ulah, N.C. 281/K3
Ulak (isl.), Alaska 196/K4
Ulan, China 77/E4
Ulanhot (Horquin Youyi Qianqi), China 77/K2
Ulan-Ude, Russia 2/Q3
Ulan-Ude, Russia 48/L4
Ulan-Ude, Russia 54/M4
Ulapes, Argentina 143/C3
Ulaş, Turkey 63/G3
Ulchin, S. Korea 81/D5
Ulcinj, Yugoslavia 45/D5
Uldum, Denmark 21/C6
Ulegei (Ulgiy), Mongolia 77/C2
Ulen, Ind. 227/E4
Ulen, Minn. 255/B3
Uler, W. Va. 312/D5
Ulfborg, Denmark 21/B5
Ulhasnagar, India 68/C5
Uliastay (Jibhalanta), Mongolia 77/E2
Uliastay, Mongolia 54/L5
Ulindi (riv.), D.R. Congo 115/E4
Ulithi (atoll), Micronesia 87/D4
Ulla (riv.), Spain 33/B1
Ulladulla, N.S. Wales 97/F4
Ullapool, Scotland 10/D2
Ullapool, Scotland 15/C3
Ulla Ulla, Bolivia 136/A4
Ulldecona, Spain 33/G2
Ullensvang, Norway 18/E6
Ullin, Ill. 222/D6
Ulloma, Bolivia 136/A5
Ullŭng (isl.), S. Korea 81/E5
Ulm, Ark. 202/H4
Ulm, Mont. 262/E3
Ulm, Germany 22/C4
Ulm, Wyo. 319/F1
Ulman, Mo. 261/H6
Ulmarra, N.S. Wales 97/G1
Ulmer, Iowa 229/D4
Ulmer, S.C. 296/E5
Ulongue, Mozambique 118/E2
Ulricehamn, Sweden 18/H8
Ulrichen, Switzerland 39/F3
Ulriksfors, Sweden 18/K5
Ulrum, Netherlands 27/J2
Ulsan, S. Korea 81/D6
Ulster (part) (trad. prov.), Ireland 17/G2
Ulster (co.), N.Y. 276/M7
Ulster (part) (trad. prov.), N. Ireland 17/G2
Ulster, Pa. 294/J2
Ulster Spring, Jamaica 158/H6
Última Esperanza (sound), Chile 138/E9
Ulúa (riv.), Honduras 154/D3
Ulubat (lake), Turkey 63/C2
Ulubey, Turkey 63/C3
Uluborlu, Turkey 63/D3
Uludağ (mt.), Turkey 63/C3
Uludere, Turkey 63/K4
Ulugan (bay), Philippines 82/B5
Ulughchat (Wuqia), China 77/A4
Ulukışla, Turkey 63/F4
Ulumalu, Hawaii 218/K2
Ulu Muztag (mt.), China 77/C4
Ulungur He (riv.), China 77/C2
Ulungur Hu (lake), China 77/C2
Ulupalakua, Hawaii 218/J2
Uluru (Ayers Rock) (mt.), North. Terr. 88/E5
Uluru Nat'l Park, North. Terr. 88/E5
Uluru Nat'l Park, North. Terr. 93/B8
Ulus, Turkey 63/E2
Ulutau (mts.), Kazakhstan 48/G5
Ulu Tiram, Malaysia 72/F5
Ulva (isl.), Scotland 15/B4
Ulverston, England 13/D3
Ulverston, England 10/E3
Ulverstone, Tasmania 99/C3
Ulvik, Norway 18/E6
Ulvila, Finland 18/N6
Ul'yanovsk, Russia 7/J3
Ul'yanovsk, Russia 48/E4
Ul'yanovsk, Russia 52/G4
Ulysses, Kansas 232/A4
Ulysses, Ky. 237/R5
Ulysses, Nebr. 264/G3
Ulysses, Pa. 294/G2
Umag, Croatia 45/A3
Umala, Bolivia 136/B5
Umán, Mexico 150/P6
Uman', Ukraine 52/D5
Umanun (pt.), Philippines 82/F6
Umapine, Oreg. 291/J2
Umarkot, Pakistan 59/J4
Umatilla, Fla. 212/E3
Umatilla (co.), Oreg. 291/J2
Umatilla, Oreg. 291/H2
Umatilla (lake), Oreg. 291/G2
Umatilla (riv.), Oreg. 291/H2
Umatilla (lake), Wash. 310/E5
Umatilla Army Depot, Oreg. 291/H2
Umatilla Ind. Res., Oreg. 291/J2
Umba, Russia 52/D1
Umbagog (lake), Maine 243/A6
Umbagog (lake), N.H. 268/E2
Umbakumba, North. Terr. 93/E3
Umbarger, Texas 303/B3
Umbeara, North. Terr. 93/C8
Umbertide, Italy 34/D3
Umboi (isl.), Papua N.G. 86/A2
Umbrail (peak), Switzerland 39/K3
Umbría, Colombia 126/B7
Umbria (reg.), Italy 34/D3
Umcalcus (lake), Maine 243/G3
Ume (riv.), Sweden 7/F2
Umeå, Sweden 7/F2
Umeå, Sweden 18/M5
Umeälv (riv.), Sweden 18/L4
Umiakovik (lake), Newf. 166/B2
Umiat, Alaska 196/H1
Umikoa, Hawaii 218/H4
Umingmatok, N.W.T. 187/H3
Um Jauza, Jordan 65/D3
Umm al Qaiwain, U.A.E. 59/G4
Umm el Abid, Libya 111/C2
Umm el Fahm, Israel 65/C2
Umm Hajar, Eritrea 111/G5
Umm Keddada, Sudan 111/E5
Umm Lajj, Saudi Arabia 59/C4
Umm Qasr, Iraq 66/E5
Umm Ruwaba, Sudan 111/F5
Umm Ruwaba, Sudan 102/F3
Umm Ruwaba, Sudan 59/B7
Umm Sa'id, Qatar 59/F5
Umnak (isl.), Alaska 196/E4
Umnak (passage), Alaska 196/E4
Umnak (isl.), U.S. 4/D18
Umpire, Ark. 202/B5
Umpqua, Oreg. 291/D4
Umpqua (riv.), Oreg. 291/D4
Umrer, India 68/D4
Umsaskis (lake), Maine 243/E2
Umtata, S. Africa 118/D6
Umtata (cap.), Transkei, S. Africa 102/E8
Umurbey, Turkey 63/C6
Umvukwe (range), Zimbabwe 118/E3
Umzimbuvu, S. Africa 118/D6
Umzinto, S. Africa 118/E6
Una (riv.), Bos. 45/C3
Una (mt.), N. Zealand 100/D5
Unadilla, Ga. 217/E6
Unadilla, Nebr. 264/H4
Unadilla, N.Y. 276/K6
Unadilla (riv.), N.Y. 276/K5
Unaí, Brazil 132/E7
Unaka, N.C. 281/A4
Unaka (mts.), N.C. 281/E2
Unaka (mts.), Tenn. 237/S8
Unalakleet, Alaska 196/G2
Unalakleet, Alaska 188/C5
Unalaska, Alaska 188/C6
Unalaska, Alaska 196/E4
Unalaska (isl.), Alaska 196/E4
Unalaska (isl.), U.S. 4/D18
Unare (riv.), Venezuela 124/F3
Un Azaou (well), Niger 106/F4
Uncastillo, Spain 33/F1
Uncasville, Conn. 210/G3
Uncertain, Texas 303/K5
Uncía, Bolivia 136/B6
Uncompahgre (peak), Colo. 208/E6
Uncompahgre (plat.), Colo. 208/B5
Uncompahgre (riv.), Colo. 208/D5
Underbool, Victoria 97/A4
Underhill, Manitoba 179/B5
Underhill•, Vt. 268/B2
Underhill, Wis. 317/K6
Underhill Center, Vt. 268/B2
Underwood, Ind. 227/F7
Underwood, Iowa 229/B6
Underwood, Minn. 255/C4
Underwood, N. Dak. 282/H5
Underwood, Ontario 177/C3
Underwood, Wash. 310/D5
Undu (pt.), Fiji 86/R10
Undzha (riv.), Russia 52/F3
Unecha, Russia 52/D4
Uneeda, W. Va. 312/C6
Unga (isl.), Alaska 196/F3
Ungalik, Alaska 196/F2
Ungarie, N.S. Wales 97/D3
Ungava (bay), Canada 146/M4
Ungava (bay), N.W.T. 162/K4
Ungava (bay), N.W.T. 187/M4
Ungava (bay), Québec 174/F1
Ungava (pen.), Que. 146/L3
Ungava (pen.), Que. 162/J3
Ungava (pen.), Que. 174/E1
Ungeny, Moldova 52/C5
Unger, W. Va. 312/K4
Unggi, N. Korea 81/E2
União, Brazil 132/F4
União da Vitória, Brazil 132/D9
União dos Palmares, Brazil 132/H5
Unicoi (mts.), N.C. 281/A4
Unicoi (co.), Tenn. 237/S8
Unicoi, Tenn. 237/S8
Unicoi (mts.), Tenn. 237/N10
Uničov, Czech Rep. 41/D2
Unimak (bight), Alaska 196/F4
Unimak (isl.), Alaska 188/C6
Unimak (isl.), Alaska 196/E4
Unimak (passage), Alaska 196/F4
Unimak (isl.), U.S. 4/D18
Unini, Peru 128/F8
Union, Ala. 195/C5
Union (mt.), Ariz. 198/C4
Union (co.), Ark. 202/E7
Union, Ark. 202/G1
Union•, Conn. 210/G1

V

Verona 463

Valga, Estonia 53/D2
Valhalla, Alberta 182/A2
Valhalla, N.Y. 276/P6
Valhalla Centre, Alberta 182/A2
Valhermoso Springs, Ala. 195/E2
Valiente (pen.), Panama 154/G6
Valier, Ill. 222/D5
Valier, Mont. 262/D2
Valier, Pa. 294/D4
Valjean, Sask. 181/E5
Valjevo, Yugoslavia 45/D3
Valka, Latvia 53/C2
Valkeakoski, Finland 18/N6
Valkenswaard, Netherlands 27/H6
Valladolid, Mexico 146/K7
Valladolid, Mexico 150/P6
Valladolid (prov.), Spain 33/D2
Valladolid, Spain 33/D2
Valladolid, Spain 7/E4
Vallay (isl.), Scotland 15/A3
Vall de Uxó, Spain 33/F3
Valle, Norway 18/E7
Valle Alegre, Chile 138/F2
Vallecas, Spain 33/G4
Vallecito (res.), Colo. 208/D8
Vallecitos, N. Mex. 274/C2
Valle de Allende, Mexico 150/G3
Valle de Bravo, Mexico 150/J7
Valle de Guanape, Venezuela 124/F3
Valle de la Pascua, Venezuela 124/F3
Valle del Cauca (dept.), Colombia 126/B6
Valledupar, Colombia 120/B1
Valledupar, Colombia 126/D2
Vallée-Jonction, Québec 172/G3
Vallegrande, Bolivia 120/C4
Vallegrande, Bolivia 136/C6
Valle Hermoso, Mexico 150/L4
Vallehermoso, Spain 33/A5
Vallejo, Calif. 188/B3
Vallejo, Calif. 204/J1
Valle Mí, Paraguay 144/D3
Vallenar, Chile 138/A7
Vallentuna, Sweden 18/H1
Valle San Telmo, Mexico 150/A1
Valles Mines, Mo. 261/L6
Valletta (cap.), Malta 7/F5
Valletta (cap.), Malta 34/E7
Valley, Ala. 195/H5
Valley (co.), Idaho 220/C5
Valley (riv.), Manitoba 179/B3
Valley (co.), Mont. 262/K2
Valley (co.), Nebr. 264/E3
Valley, Nebr. 264/H3
Valley, Nova Scotia 168/E3
Valley, Wash. 310/H2
Valley, Wis. 317/F8
Valley, Wyo. 319/C1
Valley Bend, W. Va. 312/F5
Valley Brook, Okla. 288/M4
Valley Center, Kansas 232/E4
Valley Centre, Sask. 181/D4
Valley City, Ill. 222/C4
Valley City, N. Dak. 282/P6
Valley City, Ohio 284/G3
Valley Cottage, N.Y. 276/K8
Valley East, Ontario 177/J5
Valley East, Ontario 175/D3
Valley Falls, Kansas 232/G2
Valley Falls, N.Y. 276/N5
Valley Falls, Oreg. 291/G5
Valley Falls, R.I. 249/J5
Valley Farms, Ariz. 198/D6
Valleyfield, Québec 172/C4
Valleyford, Wash. 310/H3
Valley Forge, Pa. 294/L5
Valley Grove, W. Va. 312/E2
Valley Head, Ala. 195/G1
Valley Head, W. Va. 312/G5
Valley Hi, Ohio 284/C5
Valley Lee, Md. 245/M8
Valley Mills, Texas 303/G6
Valley Park, Miss. 256/C5
Valley Park, Mo. 261/O3
Valley Point, W. Va. 312/G3
Valley River, Manitoba 179/B3
Valley Spring, Texas 303/F7
Valley Springs, Ark. 202/D1
Valley Springs, Calif. 204/C9
Valley Springs, S. Dak. 298/S6
Valley Station, Ky. 237/K4
Valley Stream, N.Y. 276/P7
Valleyview, Alberta 182/B2
Valley View, Ky. 237/N5
Valley View, Ohio 284/D6
Valley View, Ohio 284/H9
Valley View, Pa. 294/J4
Valley View, Texas 303/H4
Vallgrund (isl.), Finland 18/M5
Valliant, Okla. 288/R6
Vallières, Haiti 158/C5
Vallimanca (riv.), Argentina 143/F7
Vallonia, Ind. 227/E7
Vallon-Pont-d'Arc, France 28/F5
Vallorbe, Switzerland 39/B3
Valls, Spain 33/G2
Val Marie, Sask. 181/D6
Valmeyer, Ill. 222/C5
Valmiera, Latvia 52/C3
Valmiera, Latvia 53/C2
Valmont, Québec 172/E3
Valmontone, Italy 34/F7
Valmora, N. Mex. 274/D3
Valmy, Nev. 266/D2
Valmy, Wis. 317/M6
Valognes, France 28/C3
Valona, Ga. 217/K8
Valor, Sask. 181/E6
Valpaços, Portugal 33/C2
Valparaíso (reg.), Chile 138/A9
Valparaíso, Chile 2/F7
Valparaíso, Chile 120/B6
Valparaíso, Chile 138/E2
Valparaiso, Fla. 212/C6
Valparaiso, Ind. 227/C2
Valparaiso, Nebr. 264/H3
Valparaiso, Sask. 181/G3
Val-Racine, Québec 172/G4
Vals (cape), Indonesia 85/K7
Vals, Switzerland 39/H3
Valsad, India 68/C4
Valsequillo (res.), Mexico 150/N2
Valserrhein (riv.), Switzerland 39/H3
Valsetz, Oreg. 291/D3
Value, Miss. 256/D6
Valuyki, Russia 52/E4
Valverda, La. 238/G5
Valverde (prov.), Dom. Rep. 158/D5
Valverde, Dom. Rep. 158/D5
Val Verde (co.), Texas 303/C8
Valverde del Camino, Spain 33/C4
Vamdrup, Denmark 21/C7
Vammala, Finland 18/N6
Vámos, Greece 45/F8
Vámospércs, Hungary 41/F3
Van, Ky. 237/R6
Van (lake), N. Dak. 282/L5
Van, Oreg. 291/J4
Van, Pa. 294/C3
Van, Texas 303/J5
Van (prov.), Turkey 63/K3
Van, Turkey 59/D2
Van, Turkey 63/K3
Van (lake), Turkey 54/F6
Van (lake), Turkey 59/D2
Van (lake), Turkey 63/K3
Van, W. Va. 312/C7
Vanadium, N. Mex. 274/A6
Van Alstyne, Texas 303/H4
Vananda, Br. Col. 184/E5
Vananda, Mont. 262/K4
Vanatta, Ohio 284/E5
Vanavara, Russia 48/L3
Van Blommenstein (lake), Suriname 120/D2
Van Blommenstein (lake), Suriname 131/D3
Van Bruyssel, Québec 172/E2
Van Buren (co.), Ark. 202/E2
Van Buren, Ark. 202/B3
Van Buren, Ind. 227/F3
Van Buren (co.), Iowa 229/K7
Van Buren, Maine 243/G1
Van Buren•, Maine 243/G1
Van Buren (co.), Mich. 250/C6
Van Buren, Mo. 261/L8
Van Buren, Ohio 284/C3
Van Buren (co.), Tenn. 237/L9
Vance, Ala. 195/D4
Vance, Miss. 256/D2
Vance (co.), N.C. 281/N2
Vance, S.C. 296/G5
Vance A.F.B., Okla. 288/K2
Vanceboro•, Maine 243/J4
Vanceboro, N.C. 281/P4
Vanceburg, Ky. 237/P3
Vancleave, Miss. 256/G9
Van Cleve, Iowa 229/G5
Vancourt, Texas 303/D6
Vancouver (mt.), Alaska 196/L2
Vancouver, Br. Col. 146/F4
Vancouver, Br. Col. 162/D6
Vancouver (Greater), Br. Col. 184/K3
Vancouver (isl.), Br. Col. 146/F5
Vancouver (isl.), Br. Col. 162/D6
Vancouver, Br. Col. 184/K3
Vancouver (isl.), Br. Col. 184/D5
Vancouver, Canada 2/C3
Vancouver (isl.), Canada 2/C3
Vancouver, Wash. 188/B1
Vancouver, Wash. 310/C5
Vancouver (lake), Wash. 310/C5
Vandalia, Ill. 222/D5
Vandalia, Mich. 250/D7
Vandalia, Mo. 261/J4
Vandalia, Mont. 262/J2
Vandalia, Ohio 284/B6
Vandalia, W. Va. 312/F5
Vandemere, N.C. 281/R4
Vandenberg A.F.B., Calif. 204/E9
Vanderbijl Park, S. Africa 118/D5
Vanderbilt, Mich. 250/E3
Vanderbilt, Pa. 294/C5
Vanderbilt, Texas 303/H9
Vanderburgh (co.), Ind. 227/B8
Vandergrift, Pa. 294/D4
Vanderhoof, Br. Col. 162/D5
Vanderhoof, Br. Col. 184/E3
Vanderlin (isl.), North. Terr. 88/F3
Vanderlin (isl.), North. Terr. 93/E3
Vanderpool, Texas 303/E8
Vanderpool, Va. 307/J4
Vandervoort, Ark. 202/B5
Van Diemen (cape), North. Terr 88/D2
Van Diemen (cape), North. Terr 93/A1
Van Diemen (gulf), North. Terr 88/E2
Van Diemen (gulf), North. Terr 93/B1
Vandiver, Ala. 195/F4
Vandiver, Mo. 261/J4
Vandling, Pa. 294/M2
Vändra, Estonia 53/C1
Vandura, Sask. 181/K5
Vanduser, Mo. 261/N9
Vanegas, Mexico 150/J5
Vänern (lake), Sweden 7/F3
Vänern (lake), Sweden 18/H7
Vänersborg, Sweden 18/G7
Van Etten, N.Y. 276/G6
Vanga, Kenya 115/G4
Vangaindrano, Madagascar 118/H4
Vanguard, Sask. 181/D6
Vangunu (isl.), Solomon Is. 86/D3
Van Hoa, Vietnam 72/E2
Van Horn, Texas 303/C11
Van Horne, Iowa 229/J4
Van Hornesville, N.Y. 276/L5
Vanier, Ontario 177/J2
Vanier, Québec 172/J3
Vanikoro (isl.), Solomon Is. 87/G7
Vanil Noir (mt.), Switzerland 39/D3
Vanimo, Papua N.G. 87/E6
Vanimo, Papua N.G. 85/B6
Vanino, Russia 48/P5
Vaniyambadi, India 68/D6
Vankleek Hill, Ontario 177/K2
Van Lear, Ky. 237/R5
Vanleer, Tenn. 237/G8
Vanlue, Ohio 284/C4
Van Meter, Iowa 229/E5
Vanna, Ga. 217/F2
Vännäs, Sweden 18/L5
Vanndale, Ark. 202/J3
Vannes, France 28/B4
Van Ninh, Vietnam 72/F4
Vannøy (isl.), Norway 18/L1
Van Nuys, Calif. 204/B10
Van Orin, Ill. 222/D2
Vanoss, Okla. 288/N5
Vanrhynsdorp, S. Africa 118/B6
Van Rook, Queensland 95/B3
Vansant, Va. 307/D6
Vansbro, Sweden 18/H6
Vanscoy, Sask. 181/D4
Vansittart (isl.), N.W.T. 187/K3
Vansittart (isl.), Tasmania 99/E2
Vantaa, Finland 18/O6
Vantage, Sask. 181/F6
Vantage, Wash. 310/E4
Van Tassell, Wyo. 319/H3
Vanua Levu (isl.), Fiji 87/H7
Vanua Levu (isl.), Fiji 86/Q10
Vanuatu 2/T6
Vanuatu 87/G7
VANUATU 87/G7
Van Vleet, Miss. 256/G3
Vanvoorhis, W. Va. 312/G3
Van Wert, Ga. 217/B3
Van Wert, Iowa 229/F7
Van Wert (co.), Ohio 284/A4
Van Wert, Ohio 284/A4
Van Wyck, S.C. 296/F2
Van Yen, Vietnam 72/E2
Vanylven, Norway 18/E5
Van Zandt (co.), Texas 303/J5
Van Zandt, Wash. 310/C2
Vanzant, Mo. 261/H9
Var (dept.), France 28/G6
Vara, Sweden 18/H7
Vara de María, Venezuela 124/C4
Varadero, Cuba 158/D1
Varakļāni, Latvia 53/D2
Varallo Pombia, Italy 34/B2
Varamin, Iran 66/G3
Varanasi, India 54/K7
Varanasi, India 68/E3
Varangerfjord (fjord), Norway 18/Q2
Varangerfjorden (fjord), Norway 7/H1
Varangerhalvøya (pen.), Norway 18/Q1
Varano (lake), Italy 34/F3
Varaždin, Croatia 45/B2
Varazze, Italy 34/B2
Varberg, Sweden 18/G8
Vardaman, Miss. 256/F3
Vardar (riv.), Greece 45/E5
Vardar (riv.), Macedonia 45/E5
Varde, Denmark 18/F9
Varde, Denmark 21/B6
Varde (riv.), Denmark 21/B6
Vardø, Norway 18/R1
Varel, Germany 22/C2
Varella, Mui (cape), Vietnam 72/F4
Varėna, Russia 53/C3
Varennes, Québec 172/J4
Vareš, Bos. 45/D3
Varese (prov.), Italy 34/B2
Varese, Italy 34/B2
Vargem Bonita, Brazil 135/E3
Varginha, Brazil 135/D2
Varginha, Brazil 132/E8
Varina, Iowa 229/D3
Varkaus, Finland 18/Q5
Värmland (co.), Sweden 18/H7
Varna, Bulgaria 7/G4
Varna, Bulgaria 45/J4
Varna, Ill. 222/D2
Varnado, La. 238/L5
Värnamo, Sweden 18/J8
Varnek, Russia 52/J1
Varnell, Ga. 217/C1
Varner, Kansas 232/D4
Varney, Ontario 177/D3
Varney, W. Va. 312/B7
Varnsdorf, Czech Rep. 41/C1
Varnville, S.C. 296/E6
Várpalota, Hungary 41/E3
Vars, Ontario 177/J2
Vartholomión, Greece 45/E7
Varto, Turkey 63/J3
Varysburg, N.Y. 276/D5
Varzarin, Kuh-e (mt.), Iran 59/E3
Varzarin, Kuh-e (mt.), Iran 66/E4
Vas (co.), Hungary 41/D3
Vasa (Vaasa), Finland 18/M5
Vasa, Minn. 255/F6
Vasa Barris (riv.), Brazil 132/G5
Vásárosnamény, Hungary 41/G2
Vascongadas (reg.), Spain 33/E1
Vashi, India 68/B7
Vashka (riv.), Russia 52/G2
Vashon, Wash. 310/A2
Vasile Roaită, Romania 45/J3
Vasil'kov, Ukraine 52/D4
Vaslui, Romania 45/H2
Vass, N.C. 281/L4
Vassalboro, Maine 243/D7
Vassalboro•, Maine 243/D7
Vassar, Kansas 232/G3
Vassar, Manitoba 179/G5
Vassar, Mich. 250/F5
Vassouras, Brazil 135/E3
Vastenjaure (lake), Sweden 18/K3
Västerås, Sweden 7/F3
Västerås, Sweden 18/K7
Västerbotten (co.), Sweden 18/K4
Västerdalälven (riv.), Sweden 18/H6
Västerhaninge, Sweden 18/H1
Västernorrland (co.), Sweden 18/K5
Västervik, Sweden 18/K8
Västmanland (co.), Sweden 18/K7
Vasto, Italy 34/E3
Vasvár, Hungary 41/D3
Vaternish (dist.), Scotland 15/B3
Vaternish (pt.), Scotland 15/B3
Vatersay (isl.), Scotland 15/A4
Vathí, Greece 45/H7
Vatican City 7/F4
VATICAN CITY 34
Vatican City, Vatican City 34/B6
Vaticano (cape), Italy 34/E5
Vatnajökull (glac.), Iceland 21/C1
Vatomandry, Madagascar 118/H3
Vatra Dornei, Romania 45/G2
Vättern (lake), Sweden 7/F3
Vättern (lake), Sweden 18/J7
Vatukoula, Fiji 86/P10
Vatulele (isl.), Fiji 86/P11
Vauclin (mt.), Martinique 161/D6
Vaucluse (dept.), France 28/F6
Vaucluse, S.C. 296/D7
Vaud (canton), Switzerland 39/B3
Vaudreuil (co.), Québec 172/C4
Vaudreuil, Québec 172/C4
Vaughan, Miss. 256/D5
Vaughan, N.C. 281/N2
Vaughan, Ontario 177/J4
Vaughan, W. Va. 312/D6
Vaughn, Mont. 262/E3
Vaughn, N. Mex. 274/D4
Vaughn, Wash. 310/C3
Vaughnsville, Ohio 284/B4
Vaupés (comm.), Colombia 126/E7
Vaupés (riv.), Colombia 120/B2
Vaupés (riv.), Colombia 126/E7
Vauxhall, Alberta 182/D4
Vauxhall, N.J. 273/A2
Vaux-sur-Sûre, Belgium 27/H9
Vava'u Group (isls.), Tonga 87/J7
Vavenby, Br. Col. 184/H4
Vavuniya, Sri Lanka 68/E7
Vawn, Sask. 181/C2
Vaxholm, Sweden 18/J1
Växjö, Sweden 7/F3
Växjö, Sweden 18/J8
Vaygach (isl.), Russia 4/C6
Vaygach (isl.), Russia 52/K1
Vayland, S. Dak. 298/M5
Važec, Slovakia 41/E2
Vazhgort, Russia 52/G2
Vaz-Obervaz, Switzerland 39/J3
Vázquez, Cuba 158/H3
Veagh (lake), Ireland 17/F1
Vealmoor, Texas 303/C5
Veazie•, Maine 243/F6
Veblen, S. Dak. 298/P2
Vechigen, Switzerland 39/E3
Vecht (riv.), Netherlands 27/F4
Vechta, Germany 22/C2
Vechte (riv.), Germany 22/B2
Vechte (riv.), Netherlands 27/J3
Vecsés, Hungary 41/E3
Vedaranniyam, India 68/E6
Vedia, Argentina 143/F7
Veedersburg, Ind. 227/C4
Veendam, Netherlands 27/K2
Veenendaal, Netherlands 27/G4
Veenhuizen, Netherlands 27/J2
Veere, Netherlands 27/D5
Veersche Meer (lake), Netherlands 27/D5
Vega (pt.), Alaska 196/J4
Vega, Alberta 182/C2
Vega (isl.), Norway 18/G4
Vega, Texas 303/B2
Vega Alta, P. Rico 161/D1
Vega Baja, P. Rico 161/D1
Vegafjorden (fjord), Norway 18/G4
Vegas Creek, Nev. 266/G6
Veghel, Netherlands 27/H5
Vegreville, Alberta 182/E3
Vègreville, Alta. 162/E5
Veguita, N. Mex. 274/C4
Vehar (lake), India 68/B7
Veinticinco de Agosto, Uruguay 145/A6
Veinticinco de Diciembre, Paraguay 144/D4
Veinticinco de Mayo, Argentina 143/F7
Veinticinco de Mayo, Ecuador 128/C4
Veinticinco de Mayo, Uruguay 145/C5
Veintiocho de Noviembre, Argentina 143/B7
Vejen, Denmark 21/C7
Vejer de la Frontera, Spain 33/C4
Vejle (co.), Denmark 21/C6
Vejle, Denmark 18/F9
Vejle, Denmark 21/C6
Vejle (fjord), Denmark 21/C6
Vejprty, Czech Rep. 41/B1
Vela, La (cape), Colombia 126/D1
Vela, Roca que (cay), Colombia 126/B8
Vélan (mt.), Switzerland 39/D5
Velarde, N. Mex. 274/C2
Velas (cape), C. Rica 154/D5
Velasco, Ciego de Ávila, Cuba 158/G2
Velasco, Holguín, Cuba 158/H3
Velázquez, Uruguay 145/E5
Velda, Mo. 261/P2
Velden am Würthersee, Austria 41/C3
Veldhoven, Netherlands 27/G6
Veldrif, S. Africa 118/B6
Velence, Hungary 41/E3
Velenje, Slovenia 45/B2
Vélez, Colombia 126/D4
Vélez-Blanco, Spain 33/E4
Vélez-Málaga, Spain 33/E4
Vélez-Rubio, Spain 33/E4
Velhas (riv.), Brazil 132/E7
Velika Plana, Yugoslavia 45/E3
Velikaya (riv.), Russia 48/S3
Velikaya (riv.), Russia 52/C3
Veliki Bečkerek (Zrenjanin), Yugoslavia 45/E3
Velikiye Luki, Russia 7/H3
Velikiye Luki, Russia 52/D3
Velikiye Luki, Russia 48/D4
Velikiy Ustyug, Russia 7/J2
Velikiy Ustyug, Russia 48/E3
Velikiy Ustyug, Russia 52/F2
Veliko Tŭrnovo, Bulgaria 45/G4
Velikovisochnoye, Russia 52/H1
Velizh, Russia 52/D3
Velká Bíteš, Czech Rep. 41/D2
Velká Bystřice, Czech Rep. 41/D2
Vel'ké Kapušany, Slovakia 41/G2
Velké Meziříčí, Czech Rep. 41/D2
Vel'ké Rovné, Slovakia 41/E2
Vella Lavella (isl.), Solomon Is. 86/D2
Velletri, Italy 34/F7
Vellore, India 68/D6
Velluda, Sierra (mt.), Chile 138/E1
Velma, Okla. 288/L6
Velp, Netherlands 27/J5
Velpen, Ind. 227/C8
Velsen, Netherlands 27/F4
Vel'sk, Russia 48/E3
Vel'sk, Russia 52/F2
Velten, Germany 22/E2
Veluwe (reg.), Netherlands 27/H4
Velva, N. Dak. 282/J3
Velvendós, Greece 45/F5
Vemb, Denmark 21/B5
Véménd, Hungary 41/E3
Venadillo, Colombia 126/C5
Venado, Mexico 150/J5
Venado Tuerto, Argentina 143/D3
Venafro, Italy 34/E4
Venaissin (trad. prov.), France 29
Venamo (mt.), Guyana 131/A3
Venamo, Cerro (mt.), Venezuela 124/H4
Venamo (riv.), Venezuela 124/H4
Venango, Nebr. 264/C4
Venango (co.), Pa. 294/C3
Venango, Pa. 294/B2
Vena Park, Queensland 95/B3
Vence, France 28/G6
Vendas Novas, Portugal 33/B3
Vendée (dept.), France 28/C4
Vendôme, France 28/D4
Vendrell, Spain 33/G2
Venedocia, Ohio 284/B4
Venedy, Ill. 222/D5
Veneta, Oreg. 291/D3
Venetie, Alaska 196/J1
Veneto (reg.), Italy 34/D3
Venezia (Venice), Italy 34/D2
Venezuela 2/F5
Venezuela 120/C2
VENEZUELA 124
Venezuela, Cuba 158/F2
Venezuela (gulf), Venezuela 120/B1
Venezuela (gulf), Venezuela 124/C2
Vengurla, India 68/C5
Veniaminof (crater), Alaska 196/F3
Venice, Alberta 182/E2
Venice, Calif. 204/B11
Venice, Fla. 212/D4
Venice, Ill. 222/A2
Venice (prov.), Italy 34/D2
Venice, Italy 7/F4
Venice, Italy 34/D2
Venice (gulf), Italy 34/D2
Venice, La. 238/M8
Venice, Utah 304/C5
Vénissieux, France 28/F5
Venkatagiri, India 68/D6
Venlo, Netherlands 27/J6
Venn, Sask. 181/F4
Venosa, Italy 34/E4
Venraij, Netherlands 27/H6
Venta (riv.), Latvia 53/B2
Venta (riv.), Lithuania 53/B2
Venterspos, S. Africa 118/G6
Ventimiglia, Italy 34/A3
Ventnor, England 10/F5
Ventnor, England 13/F7
Ventnor City, N.J. 273/E5
Ventotene (isl.), Italy 34/D4
Ventspils, Estonia 48/B4
Ventspils, Estonia 52/B3
Ventspils, Estonia 53/A2
Ventuari (riv.), Venezuela 124/E5
Ventura (co.), Calif. 204/F9
Ventura, Calif. 204/F9
Ventura, Iowa 229/F2
Venturia, N. Dak. 282/L7
Venus, Fla. 212/E4
Venus (pt.), Fr. Poly. 86/T12
Venus, Pa. 294/C3
Venus (bay), Victoria 97/C6
Venustiano Carranza, Mexico 150/N8
Venustiano Carranza (res.), Mexico 150/J3
Ver (riv.), England 13/H7
Vera, Argentina 143/F5
Vera, Ill. 222/D4
Vera, Okla. 288/P2
Vera (lag.), Paraguay 144/D5
Vera, Spain 33/F4
Vera, Texas 303/E4
Vera, Va. 307/L6
Vera Cruz, Brazil 135/B3
Vera Cruz, Ind. 227/G3
Veracruz (state), Mexico 150/L7
Veracruz, Mexico 150/Q1
Veracruz, Mexico 2/E5
Veracruz, Mexico 146/J8
Veradale, Wash. 310/H3
Veragua Abajo, Dom. Rep. 158/E5
Veras, Uruguay 145/C2
Veraval, India 68/C4
Verbania, Italy 34/B2
Verbena, Ala. 195/E5
Verboort, Oreg. 291/A2
Vercelli (prov.), Italy 34/B2
Vercelli, Italy 34/B2
Verchères (co.), Québec 172/J4
Verchères, Québec 172/J4
Verçinin Tepesi (mt.), Turkey 63/J2
Verda, Ky. 237/P7
Verda, La. 238/E3
Verde (riv.), Ariz. 188/D4
Verde (riv.), Ariz. 198/D5
Verde (cay), Bahamas 156/C2
Verde (riv.), Brazil 132/C7
Verde (riv.), Mexico 150/F3
Verde (riv.), Mexico 150/L8
Verde (riv.), Paraguay 144/C3
Verde (cape), Senegal 102/A3
Verde (cape), Senegal 106/A6
Verde Island (passage), Philippines 82/C4
Verdel, Nebr. 264/F2
Verden, Okla. 288/K4
Verden, Germany 22/C2
Verdery, S.C. 296/C3
Verdi, Minn. 255/B6
Verdi, Nev. 266/B3
Verdigre, Nebr. 264/F2
Verdigris (riv.), Kansas 232/G5
Verdigris, Okla. 288/P2
Verdigris (riv.), Okla. 288/P2
Verdinho (riv.), Brazil 132/D7
Verdon, Nebr. 264/J4
Verdon, S. Dak. 298/N3
Verdun, Québec 172/H4
Verdún, Uruguay 145/D5
Verdun-sur-Meuse, France 28/F3
Verdunville, W. Va. 312/B7
Vereeniging, S. Africa 102/E7
Vereeniging, S. Africa 118/D5
Veregin, Sask. 181/K4
Verendrye, N. Dak. 282/J3
Vereshchagino, Russia 52/H3
Verga (cape), Guinea 106/B6
Vergara, Argentina 143/H7
Vergara, Spain 33/E1
Vergara, Uruguay 145/E3
Vergas, Minn. 255/C4
Vergeletto, Switzerland 39/G4
Vergennes, Ill. 222/D6
Vergennes, Vt. 268/A3
Veribest, Texas 303/D6
Verín, Spain 33/C2
Veríssimo, Brazil 135/B1
Verkhnevilyuysk, Russia 48/N3
Verkhnyaya Toyma, Russia 52/G2
Verkhoyansk, Russia 2/R2
Verkhoyansk, Russia 4/C3
Verkhoyansk, Russia 48/N3
Verkhoyansk, Russia 54/P3
Verkhoyansk (range), Russia 4/C3
Verkhoyansk (range), Russia 48/N3
Verkhoyansk (range), Russia 54/O3
Verkniy At-Uryakh, Russia 48/Q3
Verlo, Sask. 181/C5
Vermejo (riv.), N. Mex. 274/E2
Vermejo Park, N. Mex. 274/D2
Vermilion, Alberta 182/E3
Vermilion (riv.), Alberta 182/E3
Vermilion (cliffs), Ariz. 198/D2
Vermilion (co.), Ill. 222/F3
Vermilion, Ill. 222/F4
Vermilion (riv.), Ind. 227/B4
Vermilion (par.), La. 238/F7
Vermilion (bay), La. 238/F7
Vermilion (lake), Minn. 188/H1
Vermilion (lake), Minn. 255/F3
Vermilion (range), Minn. 255/F3
Vermilion (riv.), Minn. 255/F2
Vermilion, Ohio 284/F3
Vermilion (riv.), Ohio 284/F3
Vermilion (hills), Sask. 181/E5
Vermilion (cliffs), Utah 304/B6
Vermilion Bay, Ontario 177/G4
Vermilion Bay, Ontario 175/B3
Vermilion Grove, Ill. 222/F4
Vermillion (co.), Ind. 227/C5
Vermillion, Kansas 232/F2
Vermillion, Minn. 255/F6
Vermillion, S. Dak. 298/R8
Vermillion (riv.), S. Dak. 298/P6
Vermillion (riv.), Québec 172/D2
Vermont 188/M2
VERMONT 268
Vermont, Ill. 222/C3
Vermont (state), U.S. 146/L5
Vermontville, Mich. 250/E6
Vernal, Utah 304/E3
Vernayaz, Switzerland 39/D4
Verndale, Minn. 255/C4
Verndon, Minn. 255/E4
Verner, Ontario 177/D1
Verneuil-sur-Avre, France 28/D3
Vernon, Ala. 195/B3
Vernon, Ariz. 198/F4
Vernon, Br. Col. 162/E5
Vernon, Br. Col. 184/H5
Vernon, Colo. 208/P3
Vernon•, Conn. 210/F1
Vernon, Fla. 212/C6
Vernon, France 28/D3
Vernon, Ill. 222/D5
Vernon, Ind. 227/F7
Vernon, Ky. 237/L7
Vernon (par.), La. 238/D4
Vernon, La. 238/E2
Vernon (lake), La. 238/D4
Vernon, Mich. 250/F6
Vernon (co.), Mo. 261/D7
Vernon, N.J. 273/E1
Vernon, Okla. 288/P4
Vernon, Ontario 177/J2
Vernon (lake), Ontario 177/E2
Vernon, Pr. Edward I. 168/E2
Vernon, Texas 303/E3
Vernon, Utah 304/B3
Vernon•, Vt. 268/B6
Vernon (co.), Wis. 317/E8
Vernonburg, Ga. 217/K7
Vernon Center, Conn. 210/F1
Vernon Center, Minn. 255/D7
Vernon Fork (creek), Ind. 227/F7
Vernon Hill, Va. 307/K7
Vernon Hills, Ill. 222/B4
Vernonia, Oreg. 291/D2
Vero Beach, Fla. 212/F4
Veroli, Italy 34/D4
Verona, Ill. 222/E2
Verona (prov.), Italy 34/C2
Verona, Italy 34/C2
Verona, Italy 7/F4
Verona, Ky. 237/M3
Verona, Miss. 256/G2
Verona, Mo. 261/E9
Verona, N.J. 273/B2
Verona, N. Dak. 282/O7

West Alexandria 467

Waterloo, Belgium 27/E7
Waterloo, Ill. 222/C5
Waterloo, Ind. 227/G2
Waterloo, Iowa 188/H2
Waterloo, Iowa 146/J5
Waterloo, Iowa 229/J4
Waterloo, Kansas 232/E4
Waterloo, Mont. 262/D5
Waterloo, Nebr. 264/H3
Waterloo, N.Y. 276/G5
Waterloo, North. Terr. 93/A4
Waterloo, Ohio 284/F8
Waterloo (reg. munic.), Ontario 177/D4
Waterloo, Ontario 177/D4
Waterloo, Oreg. 291/E3
Waterloo, Québec 172/E4
Waterloo, S.C. 296/C3
Waterloo, Trin. & Tob. 161/A10
Waterloo, Wis. 317/J9
Watermaal-Bosvoorde (Watermael Boitsfort), Belgium 27/C9
Watermael-Boitsfort, Belgium 27/C9
Waterman, Ill. 222/E2
Waterman, Ind. 227/C5
Waterpocket Fold (cliffs), Utah 304/D6
Waterport, N.Y. 276/D4
Waterproof, La. 238/H3
Waters, Mich. 250/E4
Watersmeet, Mich. 250/G2
Waterton-Glacier Int'l Peace Park, Alberta 182/C5
Waterton-Glacier International Peace Park, Alta. 162/E6
Waterton-Glacier Int'l Peace Park, Mont. 262/C2
Waterton Lakes Nat'l Park, Alberta 182/C5
Waterton Park, Alberta 182/D5
Watertown•, Conn. 210/C2
Watertown, Fla. 212/D1
Watertown•, Mass. 249/C6
Watertown, Minn. 255/E6
Watertown, N.Y. 188/M2
Watertown, N.Y. 276/J3
Watertown, Ohio 284/G7
Watertown, S. Dak. 188/G1
Watertown, S. Dak. 298/P4
Watertown, Tenn. 237/J8
Watertown, Wis. 317/J9
Water Valley, Ala. 195/B7
Water Valley, Alberta 182/C4
Water Valley, Ky. 237/D7
Water Valley, Miss. 256/E2
Water Valley, Texas 303/C6
Waterview, Ky. 237/L7
Waterview, Md. 245/P8
Water View, Va. 307/P5
Waterville, Iowa 229/L2
Waterville, Ireland 17/A8
Waterville, Kansas 232/F2
Waterville, Maine 188/N2
Waterville, Maine 243/D6
Waterville, Mass. 249/F2
Waterville, Minn. 255/E6
Waterville, New Bruns. 170/C2
Waterville, N.Y. 276/K5
Waterville, Nova Scotia 168/D3
Waterville, Ohio 284/C3
Waterville, Québec 172/F4
Waterville•, Vt. 268/B2
Waterville, Wash. 310/E3
Waterville Valley•, N.H. 268/D4
Watervliet, Mich. 250/C6
Watervliet, N.Y. 276/N5
Waterways, Alberta 182/E1
Watford, England 10/B5
Watford, England 13/H7
Watford, Ontario 177/C5
Watford City, N. Dak. 282/D4
Watha, N.C. 281/O5
Wathaman (riv.), Sask. 181/M3
Wathena, Kansas 232/H2
Watheroo, W. Australia 92/A5
Watino, Alberta 182/B2
Watkins, Iowa 229/J5
Watkins, Minn. 255/D5
Watkins Glen, N.Y. 276/G6
Watkinsville, Ga. 217/E3
Watling (San Salvador) (isl.), Bahamas 156/C1
Watonga, Okla. 288/K3
Watonwan (co.), Minn. 255/D7
Watova, Okla. 288/P1
Watrous, N. Mex. 274/D3
Watrous, Sask. 162/F5
Watrous, Sask. 181/F4
Watsa, D.R. Congo 115/E3
Watseka, Ill. 222/F3
Watson, Ark. 202/H6
Watson, Ill. 222/E4
Watson, Ind. 227/F8
Watson, La. 238/L1
Watson, Minn. 255/C5
Watson, Mo. 261/A1
Watson, Okla. 288/S6
Watson, Sask. 181/G3
Watson (mt.), Utah 304/C3
Watson Lake, Yukon 187/F3
Watson Lake, Yukon 162/D3
Watsontown, Pa. 294/J3
Watsonville, Calif. 204/D7
Watten, Scotland 15/E2
Watten, Loch (lake), Scotland 15/E2
Wattensaw (bayou), Ark. 202/G4
Watton, England 13/H5
Watton, Mich. 250/G2
Watts, Okla. 288/S2
Watts Bar (dam), Tenn. 237/M9
Watts Bar (lake), Tenn. 237/M9
Watts Bar Dam, Tenn. 237/M9
Wattsburg, Pa. 294/C1
Watt Section Sheet Harbour, Nova Scotia 168/F4
Watts Mills, S.C. 296/D2
Wattsview, Manitoba 179/A4
Wattsville, Ala. 195/F3
Wattwil, Switzerland 39/H2
Watubela (isls.), Indonesia 85/J6
Watuppa (pond), Mass. 249/K6
Watzmann (mt.), Germany 22/E5
Wau, Papua N.G. 85/B7
Wau, Papua N.G. 87/E6
Wau, Sudan 111/E6
Wau, Sudan 102/E4
Waubamik, Ontario 177/E2
Waubaushene, Ontario 177/E3
Waubay, S. Dak. 298/P3
Waubay (lake), S. Dak. 298/O3
Waubeek, Iowa 229/K4
Waubeka, Wis. 317/L9
Waubun, Minn. 255/C3
Waucedah, Mich. 250/B3
Wauchope, N.S. Wales 97/G2
Wauchope, Sask. 181/K6
Wauchula, Fla. 212/E4
Waucoma, Iowa 229/J2
Wauconda, Ill. 222/A4
Wauconda, Wash. 310/F2
Wau el Kebir, Libya 111/C2
Waugh, Ala. 195/F6
Waugh (mt.), Idaho 220/D4
Waugh, Manitoba 179/G5
Waukarlyearly (lake), W. Australia 88/C4
Waukee, Iowa 229/F5
Waukeenah, Fla. 212/C1
Waukegan, Ill. 222/B4
Waukesha (co.), Wis. 317/K9
Waukesha, Wis. 317/K1
Waukomis, Okla. 288/K2
Waukon, Iowa 229/L2
Waukon, Wash. 310/H3
Waukon Junction, Iowa 229/L2
Waumandee, Wis. 317/C7
Waumbek (mt.), N.H. 268/E3
Wauna, Oreg. 291/D1
Wauna, Wash. 310/C3
Waunakee, Wis. 317/G9
Wauneta, Kansas 232/F4
Wauneta, Nebr. 264/C4
Waupaca (co.), Wis. 317/J6
Waupaca, Wis. 317/H7
Waupun, Wis. 317/J8
Wauregan, Conn. 210/H2
Waurika, Okla. 288/L6
Waurika (lake), Okla. 288/K6
Wausa, Nebr. 264/G2
Wausau, Fla. 212/D6
Wausau, Wis. 188/J2
Wausau, Wis. 317/G6
Wausau•, Wis. 317/80
Wausaukee, Wis. 317/K5
Wauseon, Ohio 284/B2
Waushara (co.), Wis. 317/H7
Wautoma, Wis. 317/H7
Wauwatosa, Wis. 317/L1
Wauzeka, Wis. 317/E9
Wave Hill, North. Terr. 88/E3
Wave Hill, North. Terr. 93/B4
Waveland, Ark. 202/C3
Waveland, Ind. 227/D5
Waveland, Miss. 256/F10
Waver (Wavre), Belgium 27/F7
Waverley, Mass. 249/B6
Waverley, N.S. Wales 88/L4
Waverley, N.S. Wales 97/K3
Waverley, N. Zealand 100/E3
Waverley, Nova Scotia 168/E4
Waverley, Ontario 177/E3
Waverley, Victoria 97/J5
Waverley, Victoria 88/L7
Waverley Downs, N.S. Wales 97/B1
Waverly, Ala. 195/G5
Waverly, Fla. 212/E4
Waverly, Ga. 217/J8
Waverly, Ill. 222/D4
Waverly, Iowa 229/J3
Waverly, Kansas 232/G3
Waverly, Ky. 237/F5
Waverly, La. 238/H2
Waverly, Minn. 255/E5
Waverly, Mo. 261/E4
Waverly, Nebr. 264/H4
Waverly, N.Y. 276/G7
Waverly, Ohio 284/D7
Waverly, S. Dak. 298/R3
Waverly, Tenn. 237/F8
Waverly, Va. 307/O6
Waverly, Wash. 310/H3
Waverly, W. Va. 312/D4
Waverly Hall, Ga. 217/C5
Waves, N.C. 281/U3
Wavre, Belgium 27/F7
Wawa (riv.), Nicaragua 154/E3
Wawa, Ontario 175/C3
Wawa, Ontario 177/J5
Wawaka, Ind. 227/F2
Wawanesa, Manitoba 179/C5
Wawasee, Ind. 227/F2
Wawasee (lake), Ind. 227/F2
Wawayanda (lake), N.J. 273/E1
Waweig, New Bruns. 170/C3
Wawina, Minn. 255/E3
Wawota, Sask. 181/J6
Wawpecong, Ind. 227/F3
Wax, Ky. 237/J6
Waxahachie, Texas 303/H5
Waxhaw, N.C. 281/H5
Way, Miss. 256/E5
Way (lake), W. Australia 88/C5
Way (lake), W. Australia 92/C4
Wayagamac (lake), Québec 172/E2
Wayan, Idaho 220/G7
Wayatinah, Tasmania 99/C4
Waycross, Ga. 188/K4
Waycross, Ga. 217/H8
Wayerton, New Bruns. 170/E1
Wayland, Iowa 229/K6
Wayland, Ky. 237/R6
Wayland•, Mass. 249/A7
Wayland, Mich. 250/D6
Wayland, Mo. 261/J2
Wayland, N.Y. 276/E5
Wayland, Ohio 284/H3
Waymansville, Ind. 227/E6
Waymart, Pa. 294/M2
Wayne, Ala. 195/C6
Wayne, Alberta 182/D4
Wayne (co.), Ga. 217/J7
Wayne (co.), Ill. 222/E5
Wayne, Ill. 222/E2
Wayne (co.), Ind. 227/G5
Wayne (co.), Iowa 229/G7
Wayne, Kansas 232/E2
Wayne (co.), Ky. 237/M7
Wayne, Maine 243/D7
Wayne•, Maine 243/D7
Wayne (co.), Mich. 250/F6
Wayne, Mich. 250/F6
Wayne (co.), Miss. 256/G7
Wayne (co.), Mo. 261/L8
Wayne (co.), Nebr. 264/G2
Wayne, Nebr. 264/G2
Wayne•, N.J. 273/A1
Wayne (co.), N.Y. 276/F4
Wayne, N.Y. 276/F6
Wayne (co.), N.C. 281/N4
Wayne (co.), Ohio 284/G4
Wayne, Ohio 284/C3
Wayne, Okla. 288/M5
Wayne (co.), Pa. 294/M2
Wayne, Pa. 294/M6
Wayne (co.), Tenn. 237/F10
Wayne (co.), Utah 304/C5
Wayne (co.), W. Va. 312/B6
Wayne, W. Va. 312/B6
Wayne City, Ill. 222/E5
Waynesboro, Ga. 217/J4
Waynesboro, Miss. 256/G7
Waynesboro, Pa. 294/G6
Waynesboro, Tenn. 237/F10
Waynesboro (I.C.), Va. 307/K4
Waynesburg, Ky. 237/M6
Waynesburg, Ohio 284/H4
Waynesburg, Pa. 294/B6
Waynesfield, Ohio 284/C4
Waynesville, Ga. 217/J8
Waynesville, Ill. 222/D3
Waynesville, Ind. 227/F6
Waynesville, Mo. 261/H7
Waynesville, N.C. 281/D4
Waynesville, Ohio 284/B6
Waynetown, Ind. 227/C4
Waynoka, Okla. 288/J1
Wayside, Ga. 217/E4
Wayside, Kansas 232/G4
Wayside, Miss. 256/C4
Wayside, Texas 303/C3
Wayside, Wis. 317/L7
Wayzata, Minn. 255/G5
Wazirabad, Pakistan 59/K3
We (isl.), Indonesia 85/B4
Wé, New Caled. 86/H4
Weagamow Lake, Ontario 175/B2
Weakley (co.), Tenn. 237/D8
Weald, The (reg.), England 13/H6
Wear (riv.), England 13/F3
Wear (riv.), England 10/F3
Weare•, N.H. 268/D5
Weare P.O. (North Weare), N.H. 268/D5
Weatherby, Mo. 261/D3
Weatherby Lake, Mo. 261/O5
Weatherford, Okla. 288/J4
Weatherford, Texas 303/G5
Weatherly, Pa. 294/L4
Weathers, Okla. 288/P5
Weathersby, Miss. 256/E7
Weatogue, Conn. 210/D1
Weaubleau, Mo. 261/F7
Weaver, Ala. 195/G3
Weaver (riv.), England 13/G2
Weaver (lake), Manitoba 179/F2
Weaver, Minn. 255/G6
Weaver, New Bruns. 170/E2
Weaver, N. Dak. 282/N2
Weaverville, Calif. 204/B3
Weaverville, N.C. 281/D3
Webb, Ala. 195/H8
Webb, Iowa 229/D3
Webb (lake), Maine 243/C6
Webb, Miss. 256/D3
Webb (bay), Newf. 166/B2
Webb, Sask. 181/C5
Webb (co.), Texas 303/E10
Webb, Texas 303/F3
Webb City, Ark. 202/C3
Webb City, Mo. 261/C8
Webb City, Okla. 288/N1
Webber, Kansas 232/D2
Webbers Falls, Okla. 288/R3
Webbers Falls (res.), Okla. 288/R3
Webberville, Mich. 250/E6
Webb Lake, Wis. 317/B3
Webbs Cross Roads, Ky. 237/L6
Webbville, Ky. 237/R4
Webbwood, Ontario 177/C1
Webequie, Ontario 175/C2
Weber (co.), Utah 304/B2
Weber (riv.), Utah 304/C3
Weber City, Va. 307/C7
Webi Shabelle (riv.), Somalia 115/H3
Webster, Fla. 212/D3
Webster (co.), Ga. 217/C6
Webster, Ind. 227/H5
Webster (co.), Iowa 229/E4
Webster, Iowa 229/J6
Webster (res.), Kansas 232/C2
Webster (co.), Ky. 237/F5
Webster, Ky. 237/J5
Webster (par.), La. 238/D1
Webster (brook), Maine 243/E3
Webster, Mass. 249/G4
Webster•, Mass. 249/G4
Webster (lake), Mass. 249/G4
Webster, Minn. 255/E6
Webster (co.), Miss. 256/F3
Webster (co.), Mo. 261/G8
Webster (co.), Nebr. 264/F4
Webster•, N.H. 268/D5
Webster, N.Y. 276/F4
Webster, N.C. 281/C4
Webster, N. Dak. 282/N3
Webster, Pa. 294/C5
Webster, S. Dak. 298/P3
Webster, Texas 303/K2
Webster (co.), W. Va. 312/F6
Webster, Wis. 317/B4
Webster City, Iowa 229/F4
Webster Groves, Mo. 261/P3
Webster Mills, Pa. 294/F6
Webster Springs, W. Va. 312/F6
Websterville, Vt. 268/B3
Wecota, S. Dak. 298/L3
Weda, Indonesia 85/H5
Wedau, Papua N.G. 85/C7
Weddel (isl.) 143/D7
Weddell (sea), Ant. 2/H10
Weddell (sea), Ant. 5/C16
Wedderburn, Oreg. 291/C5
Wedderburn, Victoria 97/B5
Weddington, Ark. 202/B1
Wedel, Germany 22/C2
Wedgefield, S.C. 296/F4
Wedgeport, Nova Scotia 168/C5
Wedgeworth, Ala. 195/C5
Wedowee, Ala. 195/H4
Weed, Calif. 204/C2
Weed, N. Mex. 274/D6
Weed (hills), Sask. 181/J5
Weed Heights, Nev. 266/B4
Weedon-Centre, Québec 172/F4
Weedsport, N.Y. 276/G4
Weedville, Pa. 294/F3
Weehawken•, N.J. 273/C2
Week (isls.), Chile 138/D10
Weekapaug, R.I. 249/G7
Weekes, Sask. 181/J3
Weeki Wachee, Fla. 212/D3
Weeks, La. 238/G7
Weeks, Nev. 266/B3
Weeks (isl.), N. Zealand 100/B1
Weeksbury, Ky. 237/R6
Weeks Mills, Maine 243/E7
Weeksville, N.C. 281/S2
Weems, Va. 307/P5
Weeping Water, Nebr. 264/J4
Weert, Netherlands 27/H6
Weesatche, Texas 303/G9
Weesen, Switzerland 39/H2
Weesp, Netherlands 27/C5
Weethalle, N.S. Wales 97/D3
Wee Waa, N.S. Wales 97/E2
Wegdahl, Minn. 255/C6
Weggis, Switzerland 39/F2
Węgorzewo, Poland 47/E1
Wegra-Flat Creek, Ala. 195/D3
Węgrów, Poland 47/E2
Weichang, China 77/J3
Weida, Germany 22/D3
Weiden in der Oberpfalz, Germany 22/D4
Weidman, Mich. 250/D5
Weifang, China 77/J4
Weihai (Weihaiwei), China 77/K4
Wei He (riv.), China 77/G5
Weilburg, Germany 22/C3
Weilheim im Oberbayern, Germany 22/D5
Weimar, Germany 22/D3
Weimar, Texas 303/H8
Weinan, China 77/H5
Weiner, Ark. 202/J2
Weinert, Texas 303/E4
Weinfelden, Switzerland 39/H1
Weingarten, Germany 22/C5
Weinheim, Germany 22/C4
Weining, China 77/F6
Weinsberg, Germany 22/C4
Weipa, Queensland 88/G1
Weipa, Queensland 95/B2
Weippe, Idaho 220/C3
Weir (lake), Fla. 212/E2
Weir, Kansas 232/H4
Weir, Miss. 256/F4
Weirdale, Sask. 181/F2
Weirgor, Wis. 317/D4
Weir River, Manitoba 179/J2
Weirsdale, Fla. 212/D3
Weirton, W. Va. 312/E2
Weirwood, Va. 307/S6
Weisburg, Ind. 227/H6
Weiser, Idaho 220/B5
Weiser (riv.), Idaho 220/B5
Weishan, China 77/F6
Weismes (Waimes), Belgium 27/J8
Weiss (lake), Ala. 195/G2
Weiss (lake), Ga. 217/A2
Weissenburg im Bayern, Germany 22/D4
Weissenfels, Germany 22/D3
Weissensee, Germany 22/F3
Weissenstein (mts.), Switzerland 39/D2
Weisserstein (mt.), Belgium 27/J8
Weissert, Nebr. 264/E3
Weisshorn (mt.), Switzerland 39/J3
Weisshorn (mt.), Switzerland 39/E4
Weissmies (mt.), Switzerland 39/F4
Weisswasser, Germany 22/F3
Weitchpec, Calif. 204/B2
Weitensfeld-Flattnitz, Austria 41/B3
Weitra, Austria 41/C2
Weixi, China 77/E6
Weixin, China 77/F6
Weiz, Austria 41/C3
Wejh, Saudi Arabia 59/C4
Wejh, Saudi Arabia 54/E7
Wejherowo, Poland 47/D1
Welaka, Fla. 212/E2
Welbekend, S. Africa 118/J6
Welch, Okla. 288/R1
Welch, Texas 303/B5
Welch, W. Va. 312/C8
Welches, Oreg. 291/E2
Welchman Hall, Barbados 161/B8
Welchville, Maine 243/C7
Welcome, La. 238/L3
Welcome, Md. 245/K7
Welcome, Minn. 255/D7
Welcome, N.C. 281/J3
Welcome, Ontario 177/F4
Welcome All, Ga. 217/J2
Weld (co.), Colo. 208/L1
Weld•, Maine 243/C6
Weld (range), W. Australia 92/B4
Welda, Kansas 232/G3
Weldon, Ark. 202/H3
Weldon, Calif. 204/G8
Weldon, Ill. 222/E3
Weldon, Iowa 229/F7
Weldon, New Bruns. 170/F3
Weldon, N.C. 281/O2
Weldon, Sask. 181/F2
Weldon, Texas 303/J6
Weldona, Colo. 208/M2
Weldon Spring Heights, Mo. 261/M2
Weleetka, Okla. 288/O4
Welford, Queensland 95/C5
Welkom, S. Africa 102/E7
Welkom, S. Africa 118/D5
Welland (riv.), England 13/G5
Welland (riv.), England 10/F4
Welland, Ontario 177/E5
Welland (canal), Ontario 177/E5
Wellandport, Ontario 177/E4
Wellborn, Fla. 212/D1
Wellersburg, Pa. 294/E6
Wellesley (isls.), Australia 87/D7
Wellesley•, Mass. 249/B7
Wellesley, Ontario 177/D4
Wellesley (isls.), Queensland 88/F3
Wellesley (isls.), Queensland 95/A3
Wellesley Hills, Mass. 249/B7
Wellfleet•, Mass. 249/O5
Wellfleet (harb.), Mass. 249/O5
Wellfleet, Nebr. 264/D4
Wellford, S.C. 296/C2
Wellin, Belgium 27/G8
Welling, Alberta 182/D5
Welling, Okla. 288/S3
Wellingborough, England 13/G5
Wellingborough, England 10/F4
Wellington, Ala. 195/G3
Wellington (isl.), Chile 120/B7
Wellington (isl.), Chile 138/D8
Wellington, Colo. 208/K1
Wellington, England 13/D7
Wellington, England 10/E5
Wellington, Ill. 222/F3
Wellington, Kansas 232/E4
Wellington, Ky. 237/K2
Wellington, Ky. 237/O5
Wellington•, Maine 243/D5
Wellington, Mo. 261/E4
Wellington, Nev. 266/B4
Wellington, N.S. Wales 97/E3
Wellington (cap.), N. Zealand 2/T8
Wellington (cap.), N. Zealand 100/A3
Wellington (bay), N.W.T. 187/H3
Wellington (chan.), N.W.T. 162/G1
Wellington (chan.), N.W.T. 187/J2
Wellington, Nova Scotia 168/E4
Wellington, Ohio 284/F3
Wellington (co.), Ontario 177/D4
Wellington, Ontario 177/G4
Wellington, Pr. Edward I. 168/D2
Wellington, S. Africa 118/B6
Wellington, Texas 303/D3
Wellington, Utah 304/D4
Wellington (lake), Victoria 97/D6
Wellington, Va. 307/T3
Wellman, Iowa 229/K6
Wellman (lake), Manitoba 179/B3
Wellman, Texas 303/B5
Wellpinit, Wash. 310/G3
Wells, Br. Col. 184/G3
Wells, England 13/E6
Wells, England 10/E5
Wells (co.), Ind. 227/G3
Wells, Kansas 232/E2
Wells, Maine 243/B9
Wells•, Maine 243/B9
Wells, Mich. 250/B3
Wells, Minn. 255/E7
Wells, Nev. 266/G1
Wells, N.Y. 276/M4
Wells (co.), N. Dak. 282/L4
Wells, Texas 303/J6
Wells•, Vt. 268/A5
Wells (riv.), Vt. 268/C3
Wells (lake), W. Australia 88/C5
Wells (dam), Wash. 310/F3
Wells (lake), W. Australia 92/C4
Wells Beach, Maine 243/B9
Wellsboro, Ind. 227/D1
Wellsboro, Pa. 294/H2
Wells Bridge, N.Y. 276/K6
Wellsburg, Iowa 229/H4
Wellsburg, N.Y. 276/G6
Wellsburg, N. Dak. 282/L4
Wellsburg, W. Va. 312/E2
Wellsford, N. Zealand 100/E2
Wells Gray Prov. Park, Br. Col. 184/H4
Wells-next-the-Sea, England 13/H5
Wells-next-the-Sea, England 10/G4
Wells River, Vt. 268/C3
Wellston, Mich. 250/D4
Wellston, Mo. 261/R2
Wellston, Ohio 284/F7
Wellston, Okla. 288/M3
Wellsville, Kansas 232/G3
Wellsville, Mo. 261/K4
Wellsville, N.Y. 276/E6
Wellsville, Ohio 284/J4
Wellsville, Pa. 294/J5
Wellsville, Utah 304/C2
Wellton, Ariz. 198/A6
Wellwood, Manitoba 179/C4
Wels, Austria 41/C2
Welsford, New Bruns. 170/D3
Welsford, Nova Scotia 168/E3
Welsh, La. 238/E6
Welshfield, Ohio 284/H3
Welshpool, New Bruns. 170/D4
Welshpool, Wales 10/E4
Welshpool, Wales 13/D5
Welton, Iowa 229/M5
Welty, Okla. 288/O3
Welwyn, England 13/H7
Welwyn, England 10/F5
Welwyn, Sask. 181/K5
Wem, England 13/E5
Wembere (riv.), Tanzania 115/F4
Wembley, Alberta 182/A2
Wemindji, Québec 174/B2
Wemmel, Belgium 27/B9
Wemyss Bay, Scotland 15/A2
Wenamu (riv.), Guyana 131/A2
Wenas (creek), Wash. 310/E4
Wenasoga, Miss. 256/G1
Wenatchee, Wash. 188/B1
Wenatchee, Wash. 310/E3
Wenatchee (lake), Wash. 310/E3
Wenatchee (mts.), Wash. 310/E3
Wenatchee (riv.), Wash. 310/E3
Wenchi, Ghana 106/D7
Wenchow (Wenzhou), China 77/J6
Wendel, Calif. 204/E3
Wendel, W. Va. 312/F4
Wendell, Idaho 220/D7
Wendell•, Mass. 249/E2
Wendell, Minn. 255/B4
Wendell, N.H. 268/C5
Wendell, N.C. 281/N3
Wendell Depot, Mass. 249/E2
Wenden, Ariz. 198/B5
Wendeng, China 77/K4
Wendover, England 13/G7
Wendover, Ontario 177/J2
Wendover, Utah 304/A3
Wendover, Wyo. 319/H3
Wendron, England 13/B7
Wendte, S. Dak. 298/H5
Wenham•, Mass. 249/L2
Wenling, China 77/K6
Wenlock (riv.), Queensland 88/G2
Wenman (isl.), Ecuador 128/B8
Wenona, Ga. 217/E7
Wenona, Ill. 222/E2
Wenona, Md. 245/P8
Wenona, N.C. 281/R3
Wenonah, Ill. 222/D4
Wenonah, N.J. 273/C4
Wenquan, Qinghai, China 77/D5
Wenquan, Xinjiang Uygur, China 77/B3
Wenshan, China 77/F7
Wensu, China 77/B3
Wensum (riv.), England 13/J5
Wentworth, Mo. 261/D8
Wentworth•, N.H. 268/D4
Wentworth (lake), N.H. 268/E4
Wentworth, N.S. Wales 97/B4
Wentworth, N.C. 281/K2
Wentworth, Nova Scotia 168/E3
Wentworth, S. Dak. 298/R6
Wentworth, Wis. 317/C2
Wentworths Location•, N.H. 268/E2
Wentzville, Mo. 261/L5
Wen Xian, China 77/G5
Wenzhou (Wenchow), China 77/J6
Wenzhou, China 54/N7
Weogufka, Ala. 195/F4
Weohyakapka (lake), Fla. 212/E4
Weott, Calif. 204/A3
Wepawaug (riv.), Conn. 210/C3
Wequetequock, Conn. 210/H3
Werdau, Germany 22/E3
Werder, Germany 22/E2
Werner Lake, Ontario 175/A2
Wernersville, Pa. 294/K5
Wernigerode, Germany 22/D3
Werra (riv.), Germany 22/D3
Werra (riv.), Germany 22/D3
Werribee, Victoria 88/G7
Werrimull, Victoria 97/A4
Werris Creek, N.S. Wales 97/F2
Wertheim, Germany 22/C4
Wervik, Belgium 27/B7
Wesco, Mo. 261/K7
Wesel, Germany 22/B3
Weser (riv.), Germany 7/E3
Weser (riv.), Germany 22/C2
Weskan, Kansas 232/A3
Weslaco, Texas 303/F11
Weslemkoon (lake), Ontario 177/G2
Wesley, Ark. 202/C1
Wesley, Dominica 161/F5
Wesley, Ga. 217/H6
Wesley, Iowa 229/E2
Wesley, Maine 243/H6
Wesley•, Maine 243/H6
Wesley Vale, Tasmania 99/C3
Wesleyville, Newf. 166/D4
Wesleyville, Pa. 294/C1
Wes-Rand, S. Africa 118/G6
Wessel (isls.), Australia 87/D7
Wessel (cape), North. Terr. 88/F2
Wessel (cape), North. Terr. 93/E1
Wessel (isls.), North. Terr. 88/F2
Wessel (isls.), North. Terr. 93/E1
Wessington, S. Dak. 298/M5
Wessington Springs, S. Dak. 298/M5
Wesson, Ark. 202/E7
Wesson, Miss. 256/D7
West (riv.), Conn. 210/D3
West (riv.), Conn. 210/E3
West, Iowa 229/J5
West (bay), La. 238/M8
West (isl.), Mass. 249/L6
West (riv.), Mass. 249/H4
West, Miss. 256/E4
West (isls.), New Bruns. 170/D4
West (cape), N. Zealand 100/A6
West (bay), Nova Scotia 168/G3
West (pt.), Nova Scotia 168/H5
West (riv.), Nova Scotia 168/F3
West (pt.), Pr. Edward I. 168/D2
West (pt.), Tasmania 99/A2
West, Texas 303/G6
West (bay), Texas 303/K3
West (riv.), Vt. 268/B5
West Acton, Mass. 249/H3
West Alexander, Pa. 294/B5
West Alexandria, Ohio 284/A6

GEOGRAPHICAL TERMS

A. = Arabic Burm. = Burmese Camb. = Cambodian Ch. = Chinese Czech. = Czechoslovakian Dan. = Danish Du. = Dutch Finn. = Finnish Fr. = French Ger. = German Ice. = Icelandic

It. = Italian Jap. = Japanese Mong. = Mongol Nor. = Norwegian Per. = Persian Port. = Portuguese Russ. = Russian Sp. = Spanish Sw. = Swedish Turk. = Turkish

Term	Language	Meaning
A	Nor., Sw	Stream
Aas	Dan., Nor	Hills
Abajo	Sp	Lower
Ada, Adasi	Turk	Island
Altipiano	It	Plateau
Altiplano	Sp	Plateau
Alv, Alf, Elf	Sw	River
Arrecife	Sp	Reef
Asa	Nor., Sw	Hill
Asaga	Turk	Lower
Austral	Sp	Southern
Baai	Du	Bay
Bab	Arabic	Gate or Strait
Bahia	Sp	Bay
Bahr	Arabic	Marsh, Lake, Sea, River
Baia	Port	Bay
Baie	Fr	Bay, Gulf
Baizo	Port	Low
Bakke	Dan	Hill
Bana	Jap	Cape
Bañados	Sp	Marshes
Band	Per	Mt. Range
Bandao	Ch	Peninsula
Bandar	Per	Harbor
Barra	Sp	Reef
Bel	Turk	Pass
Belt	Ger	Strait
Ben	Gaelic	Mountain
Bera	Du	Mountain
Berg	Ger., Du	Mountain
Bir	Arabic	Well
Boca	Sp	Gulf, Inlet
Boğhaz	Turk	Strait
Bolshoi, Bolshaya	Russ	Big
Bolson	Sp	Depression
Bong	Korean	Mountain
Boreal	Sp	Northern
Breen	Nor	Glacier
Bro	Dan., Nor., Sw	Bridge
Bucht	Ger	Bay
Bugt	Dan	Bay
Bukhta	Russ	Bay
Bukit	Malay	Hill, Mountain
Bukt	Nor., Sw	Bay, Gulf
Burnu, Burun	Turk	Cape, Point
By	Dan., Nor., Sw	Town
Cabo	Port., Sp	Cape
Campos	Port	Plains
Canal	Port., Sp	Channel
Cap, Capo	Fr., It	Cape
Cataratas	Sp	Falls
Catena	It	Mt. Range
Catingas	Port	Open Woodlands
Cayos	Sp	Islands
Central, Centrale	Fr., It	Middle
Cerrito, Cerro	Sp	Hill
Cerros	Sp	Hills, Mountains
Chai	Turk	River
Chott	Arabic	Salt Lake
Ciénaga	Sp	Swamp
Ciudad	Sp	City
Col	Fr	Pass
Cordillera	Sp	Mt. Range, Mts.
Côte	Fr	Coast
Csatoria	Magyar	Canal
Cuchilla	Sp	Mt. Range
Curiche	Sp	Swamp
Dağ, Daği	Turk	Mountain, Peak
Dağlari	Turk	Mt. Range
Dal	Nor., Sw	Valley
Dar	Arabic	Land
Dar'ya	Russ	River
Daryacheh	Per	Marshy Lake
Dasht	Per	Desert, Plain
Deniz, Denizi	Turk	Sea, Lake
Desierto	Sp	Desert
Détroit	Fr	Strait
Djeziret	Arabic, Turk	Island
Do	Korean	Island
Doi	Thai	Mountain
Eiland	Du	Island
Elv	Dan., Nor	River
Embalse	Sp	Reservoir
Emi	Berber	Mountain
Erg	Arabic	Dune, Desert
Eski	Turk	Old
Est, Este	Fr., Port., Sp	East
Estero	Sp	Estuary, Creek
Estrecho, Estreito	Sp., Port	Strait
Etang	Fr	Pond, Lagoon, Lake
Feng	Ch	Mountain
Fiume	It	River
Fjäll	Sw	Mountain
Fjeld, Fjell	Nor	Hills, Mountain
Fjord	Dan., Nor., Sw	Fiord
Fleuve	Fr	River
Fljót	Ice	Stream
Fluss	Ger	River
Fors	Sw	Waterfall
Fos, Foss	Dan., Nor	Waterfall
Gamla	Nor	Old
Gamle	Dan	Old
Gata	Jap	Lake
Gawa	Jap	River
Gebel	Arabic	Mountain
Gebergte	Du	Mt. Range
Gebirge	Ger	Mt. Range
Gobi	Mongol	Desert
Goe	Jap	Pass
Gol	Mongol, Turk	Lake, Stream
Golf	Ger., Du	Gulf
Golfe	Fr	Gulf
Golfo	Sp., It., Port	Gulf
Gölü	Turk	Lake
Gora	Russ	Mountain
Grand, Grande	Fr., Sp	Big
Groot	Du	Big
Gross	Ger	Big
Grosso	It., Port	Big
Guba	Russ	Bay, Gulf
Gunto	Jap	Archipelago
Gunung	Malay	Mountain
Hai	Ch	Sea
Haixia	Ch	Strait
Halbinsel	Ger	Peninsula
Hamáda, Hammada	Arabic	Rocky Plateau
Hamn	Sw	Harbor
Hamún	Per	Marsh
Hanto	Jap	Peninsula
Has, Hassi	Arabic	Well
Hav	Dan., Nor., Sw	Sea, Ocean
Havet	Nor	Bay
Havn	Dan., Nor	Harbor
Havre	Fr	Harbor
He	Ch	River, Stream
Higashi, Higasi	Jap	East
Hochebene	Ger	Plateau
Hoek	Du	Cape
Hoku	Jap	North
Holm	Dan., Nor., Sw	Island
Hory	Czech	Mountains
Hoved	Dan., Nor	Cape, Promontory
Hu	Ch	Lake
Huang	Ch	Yellow
Huk	Dan., Nor., Sw	Point
Hus, Huus	Dan., Nor., Sw	House
Idehan	Arabic	Desert
Ile	Fr	Island
Ilet	Fr	Islet
Ilot	Fr	Islet
Indre	Dan., Nor	Inner
Inferieur, Inferiore	Fr., It	Lower
Inner, Inre	Sw	Inner
Insel	Ger	Island
Irmak	Turk	River
Isla	Sp	Island
Isola	It	Island
Jabal, Jebel	Arabic	Mountains
Järvi	Finn	Lake
Jaure	Sw	Lake
Jiang	Ch	River, Stream
Jima	Jap	Island
Joki	Finn	River
Kaap	Du	Cape
Kabir, Kebir	Arabic	Big
Kai	Jap	Sea
Kaikyo	Jap	Strait
Kami	Turk	Upper
Kanaal	Du	Canal
Kanal	Russ., Ger	Canal, Channel
Kao	Thai	Mountain
Kap, Kapp	Nor., Sw., Ice	Cape
Kaupunki	Finn	Town
Kawa	Jap	River
Khao	Thai	Mountain
Khrebet	Russ	Mt. Range
Kita	Jap	North
Klein	Du., Ger	Small
Klint	Dan	Promontory
Kô	Jap	Lake
Ko	Thai	Island
Koh	Camb., Khmer	Island
Kop	Du	Peak, Head
Köping	Sw	Market, Borough
Körfez, Körfezi	Turk	Gulf
Kosa	Russ	Spit
Kosui	Jap	Lake
Kraal	Du	Native Village
Kuchuk	Turk	Small
Kuh, Kuhha	Per	Mt. Range, Mts.
Kul	Sinkiang Turki	Lake
Kum	Turk	Desert
Kuro	Jap	Black
Laag	Du	Low
Lac	Fr	Lake
Lago	Port., Sp., It	Lake
Lagoa	Port	Lagoon
Laguna	Sp	Lagoon
Laguna	Sp	Lagoon
Lahti	Finn	Bay, Bight
Län	Sw	County
Liedao	Ch	Islands, Archipelago
Lilla	Sw	Small
Lille	Dan., Nor	Small
Ling	Ch	Mountain
Llanos	Sp	Plains
Mae Nam	Thai	River
Mali, Malaya	Russ	Small
Man	Korean	Bay
Mar	Sp., Port	Sea
Mare	It	Sea
Medio	Sp	Middle
Meer	Du	Lake
Meer	Ger	Sea
Mer	Fr	Sea
Meridionale	It	Southern
Meseta	Sp	Plateau
Middelst, Midden	Du	Middle
Minami	Jap	Southern
Mis	Russ	Cape
Misaki	Jap	Cape
Mittel	Ger	Middle
Mont	Fr	Mountain
Montagne	Fr	Mountain
Montaña	Sp	Mountains
Monte	Sp., It., Port	Mountain
More	Russ	Sea
Mörön	Mong	Stream
Morro	Port., Sp	Mountain, Promontory
Morue	Fr	Hill
Moyen	Fr	Middle
Muang	Siamese	Town
Mui	Vietnamese	Cape, Point
Mys	Russ	Cape
Nada	Jap	Sea
Naka	Jap	Middle
Nam	Burm., Lao	River
Namakzar	Per	Salt Waste
Nan	Ch	South
Nes	Nor	Cape, Point
Nevado	Sp	Snow-covered Peak
Nieder	Ger	Lower
Nishi, Nisi	Jap	West
Nizhni, Nizhnyaya	Russ	Lower
Njarga	Finn	Peninsula, Promontory
Nong	Thai	Lake
Noord	Du	North
Nord	Fr., Ger	North
Norte	Sp., It., Port	North
Nos	Russ	Cape
Novi, Novaya	Russ	New
Nur, Nuur	Ch., Mong	Lake
Nuruu	Mong	Mountains
Nusa	Malay	Island
Ny, Nya	Nor., Sw	New
O	Jap	Big
Ö	Nor., Sw	Island
Ober	Ger	Upper
Occidental, Occidentale	Sp., It	Western
Odde	Dan	Point
Oeste	Port	West
Ooster	Du	Eastern
Opper, Over	Du	Upper
Oriental	Sp., Fr	Eastern
Orientale	It	Eastern
Orta	Turk	Middle
Ost	Ger	East
Ostrov	Russ	Island
Ouest	Fr	West
Öy	Nor	Island
Ozero	Russ	Lake
Pampa	Sp	Plain
Pas	Fr	Channel, Strait
Paso	Sp	Pass
Passo	It., Port	Pass
Peña	Sp	Rock, Mountain
Pendi	Ch	Basin
Penisola	It	Peninsula
Pequeño	Sp	Small
Pereval	Russ	Pass
Peski	Russ	Desert
Petit, Petite	Fr	Small
Phu	Lao, Annamese	Mtn.
Pic	Fr	Mountain
Piccolo	It	Small
Pico	Port., Sp	Mountain, Peak
Pik	Russ	Mountain, Peak
Piton	Fr	Mountain, Peak
Planalto	Port	Plateau
Plato	Russ	Plateau
Pointe	Fr	Point
Poluostrov	Russ	Peninsula
Ponta	Port	Point
Presa	Sp	Reservoir
Presqu'île	Fr	Peninsula
Proliv	Russ	Strait
Pulou, Pulo	Malay	Island
Punt	Du	Point
Punta	Sp., It., Port	Point
Qiryat	Hebrew	City, Settlement
Qum	Turk	Desert
Qundao	Ch	Islands
Rada	Sp	Inlet
Rade	Fr	Bay, Inlet
Ras	Arabic	Cape
Reka	Russ	River
Retto	Jap	Archipelago
Ria	Sp	Estuary
Rio	Sp	River
Rivier, Rivière	Du., Fr	River
Rud	Per	River
Sai	Jap	West
Saki	Jap	Cape
Salar, Salina	Sp., Port	Salt Deposit
Salto	Sp., Port	Falls
San	Jap., Korean	Hill
Sanmaek	Korean	Mt. Range
Schiereiland	Du	Peninsula
Se	Camb., Khmer	River
See	Ger	Sea, Lake
Selvas	Sp., Port	Woods, Forest
Seno	Sp	Bay, Gulf
Serra	Port	Mts.
Serranía	Sp	Mts.
Seto	Jap	Strait
Settentrionale	It	Northern
Severni, Severnaya	Russ	North
Shamo	Ch	Desert
Shan	Ch., Jap	Hill, Mts.
Shankou	Ch	Pass
Shatt	Arabic	River
Shima	Jap	Island
Shimo	Jap	Lower
Shin	Jap	Land
Shiro	Jap	White
Shoto	Jap	Islands
Si	Jap	West
Sierra	Sp	Mt. Range, Mts.
Sjö	Nor., Sw	Lake, Sea
Sok, Suk, Souk	Arabic	Market
Song	Annamese	River
Sopka	Russ	Volcano
Spitze	Ger	Mt. Peak
Sredni, Srednyaya	Russ	Middle
Stad	Dan., Nor., Sw	City
Stari, Staraya	Russ	Old
Step	Russ	Treeless Plain
Straat	Du	Strait
Strasse	Ger	Strait
Stretto	It	Strait
Ström	Dan., Nor., Sw	Sound
Stung	Camb., Khmer	River
Su	Turk	River
Sud, Süd	Sp., Fr., Ger	South
Suido	Jap	Strait, Channel
Sul	Port	South
Sund	Dan., Nor., Sw	Sound
Sungei	Malay	River
Supérieur	Fr	Upper
Superior, Superiore	Sp., It	Upper
Sur	Sp	South
Suyu	Turk	River
Ta	Ch	Big
Tafelland	Du	Plateau
Tagh	Turk	Mt. Range
Take	Jap	Peak, Ridge
Takht	Arabic	Lower
Tal	Ger	Valley
Tanjung	Malay	Cape, Point
Tell	Arabic	Hill
Thale	Thai	Sea, Lake
Tind	Nor	Peak
Tö	Jap	East
To	Jap	Island
Toge	Jap	Pass
Trask	Finn	Lake
Tugh	Somali	Dry River
Ujung	Malay	Point
Umi	Jap	Bay
Unter	Ger	Lower
Ura	Jap	Inlet
Uul	Mong	Mountain
Val	Fr	Valley
Vatn	Nor	Lake
Vecchio	It	Old
Veld	Du	Plain, Field
Velho	Port	Old
Verkhni	Russ	Upper
Vesi	Finn	Lake
Viejo	Sp	Old
Vik	Nor., Sw	Bay
Vishni, Vishnyaya	Russ	High
Vodokhranilishche	Russ	Reservoir
Volcán	Sp	Volcano
Vostochni, Vostochnaya	Russ	East, Eastern
Wadi	Arabic	Dry River
Wald	Ger	Forest
Wan	Jap	Bay
Westersch	Du	Western
Wüste	Ger	Desert
Yama	Jap	Mountain
Yug, Yuzhni, Yuzhnaya	Russ	South, Southern
Zaki	Jap	Cape
Zaliv	Russ	Bay, Gulf
Zangbo	Tibetan	River, Stream
Zapadni, Zapadnaya	Russ	Western
Zee	Du	Sea
Zemlya	Russ	Land
Zizhiqu	Ch	Autonomous Region
Zuid	Du	South

MAP PROJECTIONS

by Erwin Raisz

Our earth is rotating around its *axis* once a day. The two end points of its axis are the *poles;* the line circling the earth midway between the poles is the *equator.* The arc from either of the poles to the equator is divided into 90 *degrees.* The distance, expressed in degrees, from the equator to any point is its *latitude* and circles of equal latitude are the *parallels.* On maps it is customary to show parallels of evenly-spaced degrees such as every fifth or every tenth.

The equator is divided into 360 degrees. Lines circling from pole to pole through the degree points on the equator are called *meridians.* They are all equal in length but by international agreement the meridian passing through the Greenwich Observatory in London has been chosen as *prime meridian.* The distance, expressed in degrees, from the prime meridian to any point is its *longitude.* While meridians are all equal in length, parallels become shorter and shorter as they approach the poles. Whereas one degree of latitude represents everywhere approximately 69 miles, one degree of longitude varies from 69 miles at the equator to nothing at the poles.

Each degree is divided into 60 minutes and each minute into 60 seconds. One minute of latitude equals a nautical mile.

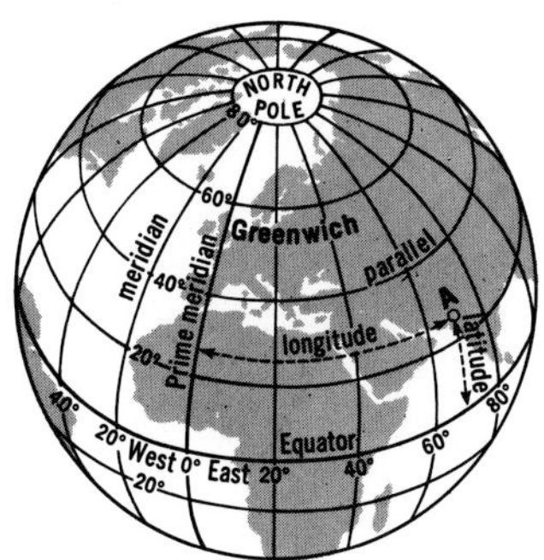

The map is flat but the earth is nearly spherical. Neither a rubber ball nor any part of a rubber ball may be flattened without stretching or tearing unless the part is very small. To present the curved surface of the earth on a flat map is not difficult as long as the areas under consideration are small, but the mapping of countries, continents, or the whole earth requires some kind of *projection.* Any regular set of parallels and meridians upon which a map can be drawn makes a map projection. Many systems are used.

In any projection only the parallels or the meridians or some other set of lines can be *true* (the same length as on the globe of corresponding scale); all other lines are too long or too short. Only on a globe is it possible to have both the parallels and the meridians true. The scale given on a flat map cannot be true everywhere. The construction of the various projections begins usually with laying out the parallels or meridians which have true lengths.

RECTANGULAR PROJECTION — This is a set of evenly-placed meridians and horizontal parallels. The central or *standard parallel* and all meridians are true. All other parallels are either too long or too short. The projection is used for simple maps of small areas, as city plans, etc.

Rectangular Projection

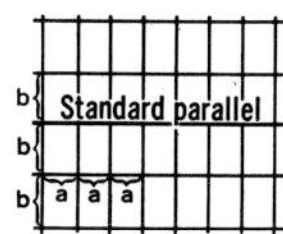

MERCATOR PROJECTION — In this projection the meridians are evenly-spaced vertical lines. The parallels are horizontal, spaced so that their length has the same relation to the meridians as on a globe. As the meridians converge at higher latitudes on the globe, while on the map they do not, the parallels have to be drawn also farther and farther apart to maintain the correct relationship. When every very small area has the same shape as on a globe we call the projection *conformal.* The most interesting quality of this projection is that all *compass directions* appear as straight lines. For this reason it is generally used for marine charts. It is also frequently used for world maps in spite of the fact that the high latitudes are very much exaggerated in size. Only the equator is true to scale; all other parallels and meridians are too long. The Mercator projection did *not* derive from projecting a globe upon a cylinder.

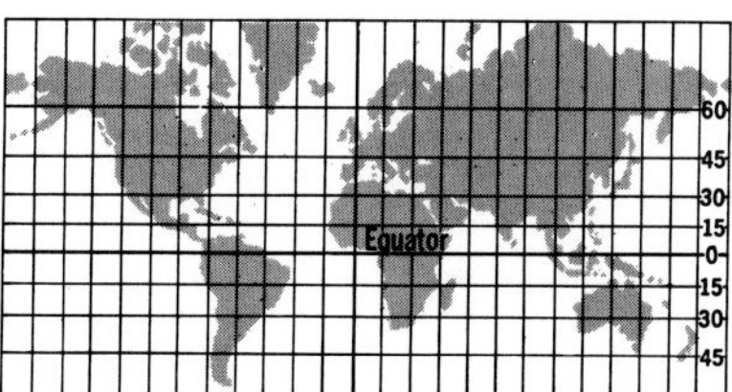

Mercator Projection

SINUSOIDAL PROJECTION — The parallels are truly-spaced horizontal lines. They are divided truly and the connecting curves make the meridians. It does not make a good world map because the outer regions are distorted, but the

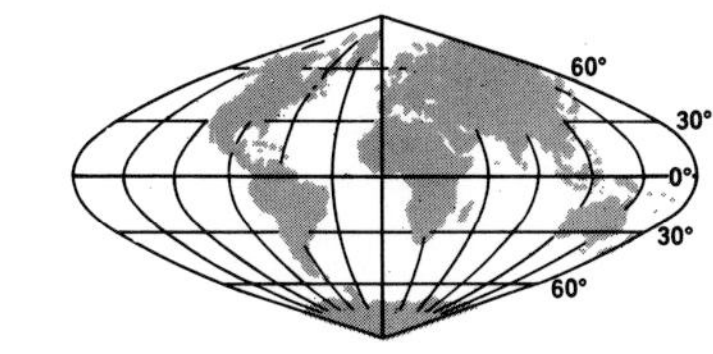

Sinusoidal Projection

central portion is good and this part is often used for maps of Africa and South America. Every part of the map has the same area as the corresponding area on the globe. It is an *equal-area* projection.

MOLLWEIDE PROJECTION — The meridians are equally-spaced ellipses; the parallels are horizontal lines spaced so that every belt of latitude should have the same area as on a globe. This projection is popular for world maps, especially in European atlases.

GOODE'S INTERRUPTED PROJECTIONS—Only the good central part of the Mollweide or sinusoidal (or both) projection is used and the oceans are cut. This makes an equal-area map with little distortion of shape. It is commonly used for world maps.

ECKERT PROJECTIONS — These are similar to the sinusoidal or the Mollweide projections, but the poles are shown as lines half the length of the equator. There are several variants; the meridians are either sine curves or ellipses; the parallels are horizontal and spaced either evenly or so as to make the projection equal area. Their use for world maps is increasing. The figure shows the elliptical equal-area variant.

CONIC PROJECTION — The original idea of the conic projection is that of capping the globe by a cone upon which both the parallels and meridians are projected from the center of the globe. The cone is then cut open and laid flat. A cone can be made tangent to any chosen *standard parallel*.

The actually-used conic projection is a modification of this idea. The radius of the standard parallel is obtained as above. The meridians are straight radiating lines spaced truly on the standard parallel. The parallels are concentric circles spaced at true distances. All parallels except the standard are too long. The projection is used for maps of countries in middle latitudes, as it presents good shapes with small scale error.

There are several variants: The use of *two standard parallels*, one near the top, the other near the bottom of the map, reduces the scale error. In the *Albers projection* the parallels are spaced unevenly, to make the projection equal-area. This is a good projection for the United States. In the *Lambert conformal conic projection* the parallels are spaced so that any small quadrangle of the grid should have the same shape as on the globe. This is the best projection for air-navigation charts as it has relatively straight azimuths.

An *azimuth* is a great-circle direction reckoned clockwise from north. A *great-circle direction* points to a place along the shortest line on the earth's surface. This is not the same as compass direction. The center of a great circle is the center of the globe.

BONNE PROJECTION — The parallels are laid out exactly as in the conic projection. All parallels are divided truly and the connecting curves make the meridians. It is an equal-area projection. It is used for maps of the northern continents, as Asia, Europe, and North America.

POLYCONIC PROJECTION — The central meridian is divided truly. The parallels are non-concentric circles, the radii of which are obtained by drawing tangents to the globe as though the globe were covered by several cones rather than by only one. Each parallel is divided truly and the connecting curves make the meridians. All meridians except the central one are too long. This projection is used for large-scale topographic sheets — less often for countries or continents.

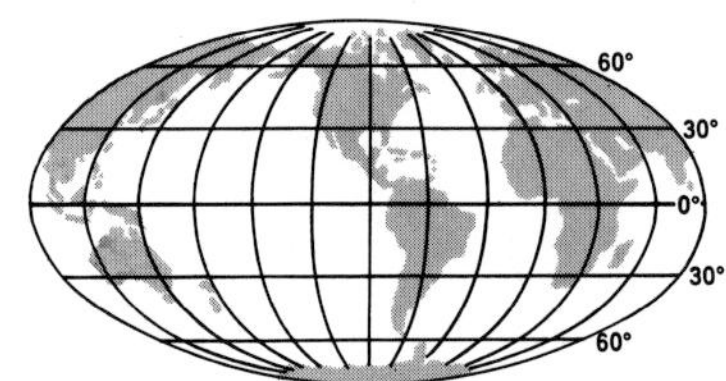

Mollweide Projection

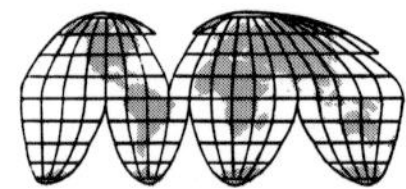

Goode's Interrupted Projection

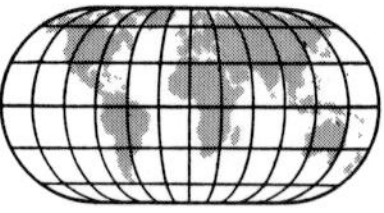

Eckert Projection

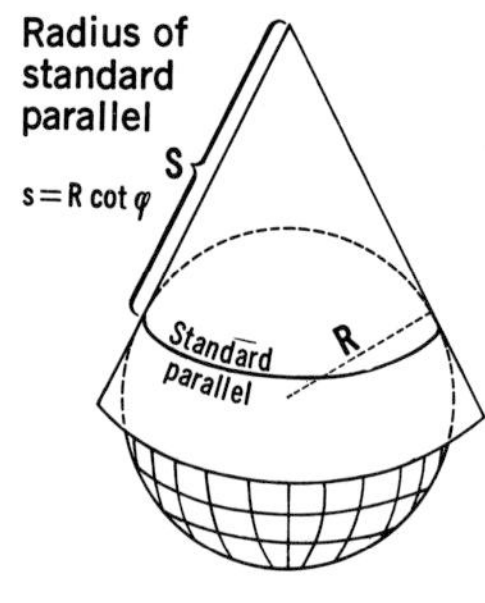

Conic Projection

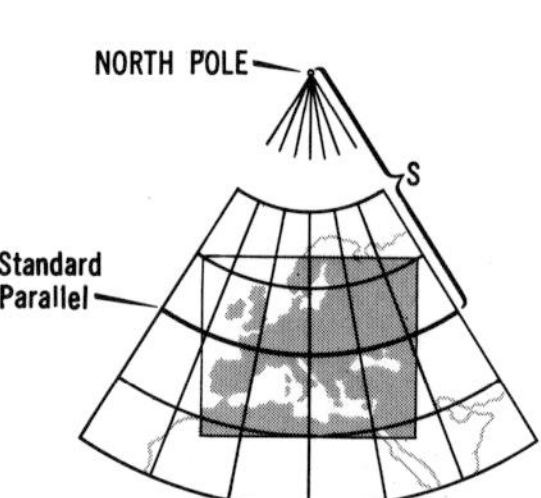

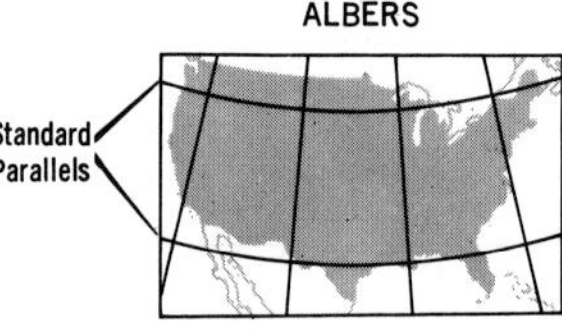

ALBERS

Albers Projection

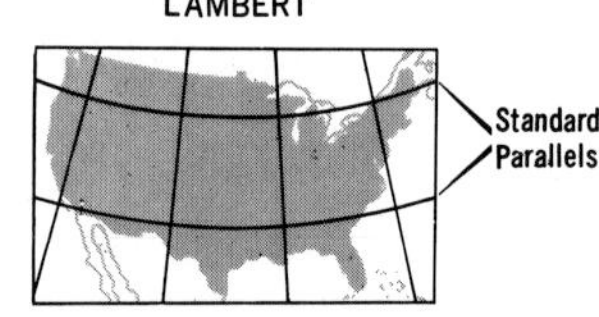

LAMBERT

Lambert Conformal Conic Projection

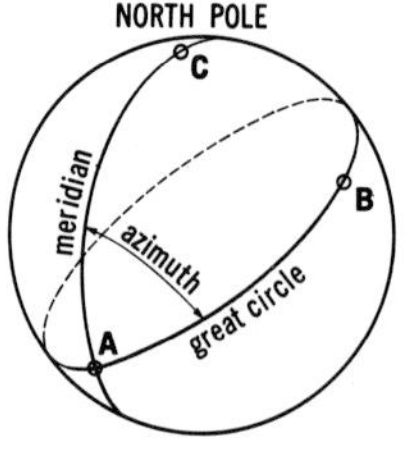

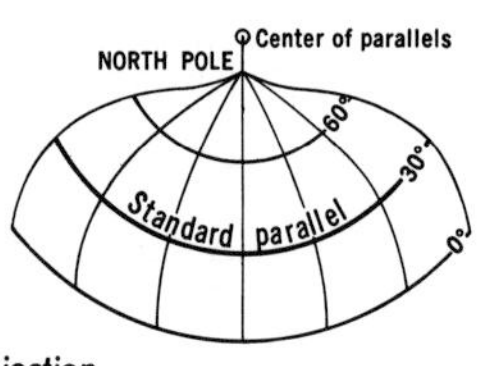

Bonne Projection

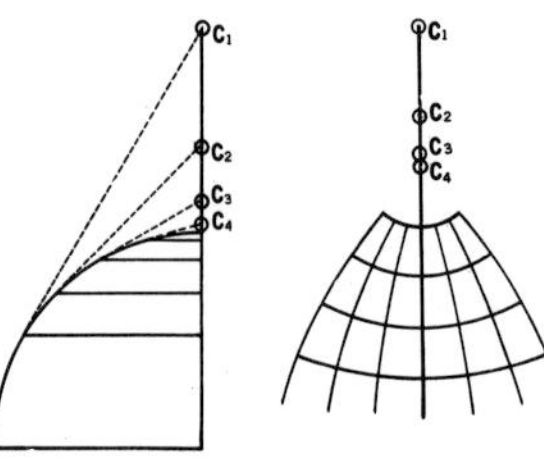

Polyconic Projection

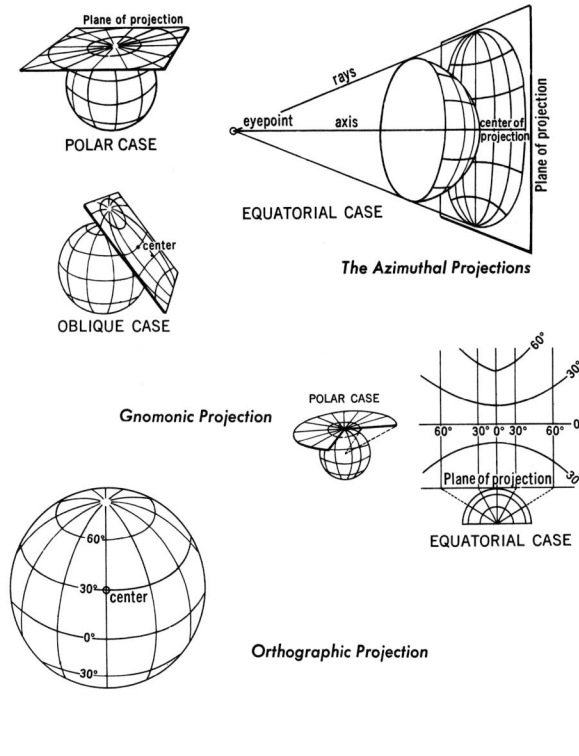

The Azimuthal Projections

Gnomonic Projection

Orthographic Projection

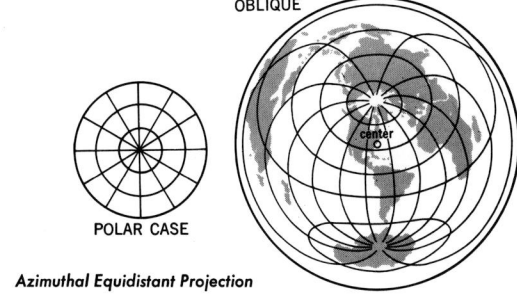

Azimuthal Equidistant Projection

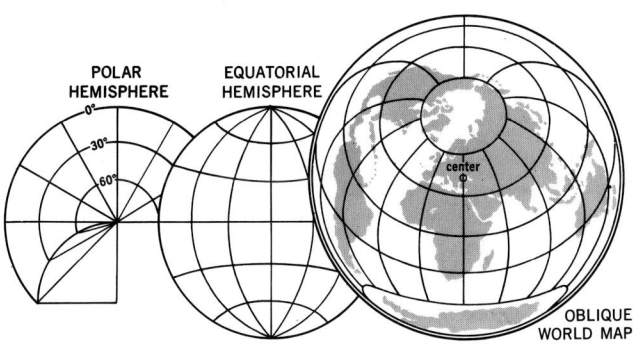

Lambert Azimuthal Equal-Area Projection

THE AZIMUTHAL PROJECTIONS — In this group a part of the globe is projected from an eyepoint onto a plane. The eyepoint can be at different distances, making different projections. The plane of projection can be tangent at the equator, at a pole, or at any other point on which we want to focus attention. The most important quality of all azimuthal projections is that they show every point at its true direction (azimuth) from the center point, and all points equally distant from the center point will be equally distant on the map also.

GNOMONIC PROJECTION — This projection has the eyepoint at the center of the globe Only the central part is good; the outer regions are badly distorted. Yet the projection has one important quality, all great circles being shown as straight lines. For this reason it is used for laying out the routes for long range flying or trans-oceanic navigation.

ORTHOGRAPHIC PROJECTION — This projection has the eyepoint at infinite distance and the projecting rays are parallel. The polar or equatorial varieties are rare but the oblique case became very popular on account of its visual quality. It looks like a picture of a globe. Although the distortion on the peripheries is extreme, we see it correctly because the eye perceives it not as a map but as a picture of a three-dimensional globe. Obviously only a hemisphere (half globe) can be shown.

Some azimuthal projections do not derive from the actual process of projecting from an eyepoint, but are arrived at by other means:

AZIMUTHAL EQUIDISTANT PROJECTION — This is the only projection in which every point is shown both at true great-circle direction and at true distance from the center point, but all other directions and distances are distorted. The principle of the projection can best be understood from the polar case. Most polar maps are in this projection. The oblique case is used for radio direction finding, for earthquake research, and in long-distance flying. A separate map has to be constructed for each central point selected.

LAMBERT AZIMUTHAL EQUAL-AREA PROJECTION—The construction of this projection can best be understood from the polar case. All three cases are widely used. It makes a good polar map and it is often extended to include the southern continents. It is the most common projection used for maps of the Eastern and Western Hemispheres, and it is a good projection for continents as it shows correct areas with relatively little distortion of shape. Most of the continent maps in this atlas are in this projection.

IN THIS ATLAS, on almost all maps, parallels and meridians have been marked because they are useful for the following:

(a) They show the north-south and east-west directions which appear on many maps at oblique angles especially near the margins.

(b) With the help of parallels and meridians every place can be exactly located; for instance, New York City is at 41° N and 74° W on any map.

(c) They help to measure distances even in the distorted parts of the map. The scale given on each map is true only along certain lines which are specified in the foregoing discussion for each projection. One degree of latitude equals nearly 69 statute miles or 60 nautical miles. The length of one degree of longitude varies (1° long. = 1° lat. × cos lat.).

WORLD STATISTICS

Elements of the Solar System

	Mean Distance from Sun: in Miles	in Kilometers	Period of Revolution around Sun	Period of Rotation on Axis	Equatorial Diameter in Miles	in Kilometers	Surface Gravity (Earth = 1)	Mass (Earth = 1)	Mean Density (Water = 1)	Number of Satellites
Mercury	35,990,000	57,900,000	87.97 days	58.7 days	3,032	4,880	0.38	0.055	5.4	0
Venus	67,240,000	108,200,000	224.70 days	243.7 days†	7,521	12,104	0.91	0.815	5.2	0
Earth	93,000,000	149,700,000	365.26 days	23h 56m	7,926	12,755	1.00	1.00	5.5	1
Mars	141,610,000	227,900,000	686.98 days	24h 37m	4,221	6,794	0.38	0.107	3.9	2
Jupiter	483,675,000	778,400,000	11.86 years	9h 55m	88,846	142,984	2.36	317.8	1.3	16
Saturn	886,572,000	1,426,800,000	29.46 years	10h 30m	74,898	120,536	0.92	95.2	0.7	18
Uranus	1,783,957,000	2,871,000,000	84.01 years	17h 14m†	31,763	51,118	0.89	14.5	1.3	15
Neptune	2,795,114,000	4,498,300,000	164.79 years	16h 6m	30,778	49,532	1.13	17.1	1.6	8
Pluto	3,670,000,000	5,906,400,000	247.70 years	6.4 days†	1,413	2,274	0.07	0.002	2.1	1

† Retrograde motion

Source: NASA, National Space Science Data Center

Dimensions of the Earth

	Area in: Sq. Miles	Sq. Kilometers
Superficial area	196,939,000	510,072,000
Land surface	57,506,000	148,940,000
Water surface	139,433,000	361,132,000

	Distance in: Miles	Kilometers
Equatorial circumference	24,902	40,075
Polar circumference	24,860	40,007
Equatorial diameter	7,926.4	12,756.4
Polar diameter	7,899.8	12,713.6
Equatorial radius	3,963.2	6,378.2
Polar radius	3,949.9	6,356.8

Volume of the Earth	2.6×10^{11} cubic miles	10.84×10^{11} cubic kilometers
Mass or weight	6.6×10^{21} short tons	6.0×10^{21} metric tons
Maximum distance from Sun	94,600,000 miles	152,000,000 kilometers
Minimum distance from Sun	91,300,000 miles	147,000,000 kilometers

Oceans and Major Seas

	Area in: Sq. Miles	Sq. Kms.	Greatest Depth in: Feet	Meters
Pacific Ocean	63,855,000	166,241,000	36,198	11,033
Atlantic Ocean	31,744,000	82,217,000	28,374	8,648
Indian Ocean	28,417,000	73,600,000	25,344	7,725
Arctic Ocean	5,427,000	14,056,000	17,880	5,450
Caribbean Sea	970,000	2,512,300	24,720	7,535
Mediterranean Sea	969,000	2,509,700	16,896	5,150
South China Sea	895,000	2,318,000	15,000	4,600
Bering Sea	875,000	2,266,250	15,800	4,800
Gulf of Mexico	600,000	1,554,000	12,300	3,750
Sea of Okhotsk	590,000	1,528,100	11,070	3,370
East China Sea	482,000	1,248,400	9,500	2,900
Yellow Sea	480,000	1,243,200	350	107
Sea of Japan	389,000	1,007,500	12,280	3,740
Hudson Bay	317,500	822,300	846	258
North Sea	222,000	575,000	2,200	670
Black Sea	185,000	479,150	7,365	2,245
Red Sea	169,000	437,700	7,200	2,195
Baltic Sea	163,000	422,170	1,506	459

The Continents

	Area in: Sq. Miles	Sq. Kms.	Percent of World's Land
Asia	17,128,500	44,362,815	29.5
Africa	11,707,000	30,321,130	20.2
North America	9,363,000	24,250,170	16.2
South America	6,879,725	17,818,505	11.9
Antarctica	5,405,000	14,000,000	9.4
Europe	4,057,000	10,507,630	7.0
Australia	2,967,893	7,686,850	5.1

Major Ship Canals

	Length in: Miles	Kms.	Minimum Depth in: Feet	Meters
Volga-Baltic, Russia	225	362	–	–
Baltic-White Sea, Russia	140	225	16	5
Suez, Egypt	100.76	162	42	13
Albert, Belgium	80	129	16.5	5
Moscow-Volga, Russia	80	129	18	6
Volga-Don, Russia	62	100	–	–
Göta, Sweden	54	87	10	3
Kiel (Nord-Ostsee), Germany	53.2	86	38	12
Panama Canal, Panama	50.72	82	41.6	13
Houston Ship, U.S.A.	50	81	36	11

Largest Islands

	Area in: Sq. Miles	Sq. Kms.
Greenland	840,000	2,175,600
New Guinea	305,000	789,950
Borneo	286,000	740,740
Madagascar	226,656	587,040
Baffin, Canada	195,928	507,454
Sumatra, Indonesia	164,000	424,760
Honshu, Japan	88,000	227,920
Great Britain	84,400	218,896
Victoria, Canada	83,896	217,290
Ellesmere, Canada	75,767	196,236
Celebes, Indonesia	72,986	189,034
South I., New Zealand	58,393	151,238
Java, Indonesia	48,842	126,501
North I., New Zealand	44,187	114,444
Cuba	42,803	110,860
Newfoundland, Canada	42,031	108,860
Luzon, Philippines	40,420	104,688
Iceland	39,768	103,000
Mindanao, Philippines	36,537	94,631
Ireland	32,589	84,406
Hokkaido, Japan	30,436	75,066
Sakhalin, Russia	29,500	76,405

	Area in: Sq. Miles	Sq. Kms.
Hispaniola, Haiti & Dom. Rep.	29,399	76,143
Banks, Canada	27,038	70,028
Ceylon, Sri Lanka	25,332	65,610
Tasmania, Australia	24,600	63,710
Svalbard, Norway	23,957	62,049
Devon, Canada	21,331	55,247
Novaya Zemlya (north isl.), Russia	18,600	48,200
Marajó, Brazil	17,991	46,597
Tierra del Fuego, Chile & Argentina	17,900	46,360
Alexander, Antarctica	16,700	43,250
Axel Heiberg, Canada	16,671	43,178
Melville, Canada	16,274	42,150
Southhampton, Canada	15,913	41,215
New Britain, Papua New Guinea	14,100	36,519
Taiwan, China	13,836	35,835
Kyushu, Japan	13,770	35,664
Hainan, China	13,127	33,999
Prince of Wales, Canada	12,872	33,338
Spitsbergen, Norway	12,355	31,999
Vancouver, Canada	12,079	31,285
Timor, Indonesia	11,527	29,855
Sicily, Italy	9,926	25,708

	Area in: Sq. Miles	Sq. Kms.
Somerset, Canada	9,570	24,786
Sardinia, Italy	9,301	24,090
Shikoku, Japan	6,860	17,767
New Caledonia, France	6,530	16,913
Nordaustlandet, Norway	6,409	16,599
Samar, Philippines	5,050	13,080
Negros, Philippines	4,906	12,707
Palawan, Philippines	4,550	11,785
Panay, Philippines	4,446	11,515
Jamaica	4,232	10,961
Hawaii, United States	4,038	10,458
Viti Levu, Fiji	4,010	10,386
Cape Breton, Canada	3,981	10,311
Mindoro, Philippines	3,759	9,736
Kodiak, Alaska, U.S.A.	3,670	9,505
Cyprus	3,572	9,251
Puerto Rico, U.S.A.	3,435	8,897
Corsica, France	3,352	8,682
New Ireland, Papua New Guinea	3,340	8,651
Crete, Greece	3,218	8,335
Anticosti, Canada	3,066	7,941
Wrangel, Russia	2,819	7,301